THE PHILOSOPHER'S INDEX

1985 CUMULATIVE EDITION

Special Editions

The Philosopher's Index: A Retrospective Index to U.S. Publications from 1940 includes approximately 15,000 articles from U.S. journals published during the 27-year period, 1940-1966, and approximately 5,000 books published during the 37-year period, 1940-1976. Supported by NEH Grant RT-23984-76-375.

Published in April 1978. 1619 pages. Hardbound in three volumes. $195 (Individuals: $130). ISBN 0-912632-09-7

The Philosopher's Index: A Retrospective Index to Non-U.S. English Language Publications from 1940 includes approximately 12,000 articles published during 1940-1966 and approximately 5,000 philosophy books published during 1940-1978. Supported by NEH Grant RT-27265-77-1360.

Published in April 1980. 1265 pages. Hardbound in three volumes. $180 (Individuals: $120). ISBN 0-912632-12-7

THE PHILOSOPHER'S INDEX

An International Index
To Philosophical Periodicals And Books

1985 CUMULATIVE EDITION

VOLUME XIX

Published by

PHILOSOPHY DOCUMENTATION CENTER
BOWLING GREEN STATE UNIVERSITY
BOWLING GREEN, OHIO 43403-0189 U.S.A.

Distributed outside the United States
of America and Canada by

D. REIDEL PUBLISHING COMPANY, P.O. BOX 17
3300 AA DORDRECHT, HOLLAND

PHILOSOPHY DOCUMENTATION CENTER

The Philosophy Documentation Center at Bowling Green State University is an organization for the collection, storage, and dissemination of bibliographic and other types of information in philosophy.

The Philosopher's Index

The Philosopher's Index, a publication of the Philosophy Documentation Center, is a subject and author index with abstracts. All major philosophy journals in English, French, German, Spanish, and Italian are indexed, along with selected journals in other languages and related interdisciplinary publications. All English language books and some books in other languages are also indexed. This periodical is published quarterly as a service to the philosophic community. Suggestions for improving this service are solicited and should be sent to the Editor.

Policies: Each number of the *Index* indexes the articles of journals and the books that are received in the months prior to its publication. For example, Number One, which is published in May, includes journals and books received during January, February, and March. The dates on the journals indexed vary due to dissimilar publishing schedules and to delays encountered in overseas mailing.

The following factors are weighed in selecting journals to be indexed: 1) the purpose of the journal, 2) its circulation and 3) recommendations from members of the philosophic community. Articles in interdisciplinary journals are indexed only if they are related to philosophy.

Most of the journal articles and books cited in *The Philosopher's Index* can be obtained from the Bowling Green State University library, through the Inter-Library Loan Department. The library, though, requests that you first try to locate the articles and books through your local or regional library facilities.

Subscriptions from the United States and Canada should be mailed to *The Philosopher's Index*, Bowling Green State University, Bowling Green, Ohio 43403-0189. The annual subscription price (4 numbers) is $89 (Individuals $30). The price of single numbers, including back issues, is $25 (Individuals $9). An annual Cumulative Edition of *The Philosopher's Index* is published in the spring following the volume year.

THE PHILOSOPHER'S INDEX

Richard H. Lineback, Editor
Bowling Green State University

Gerald E. Slivka, Business Manager
Bowling Green State University

Editorial Staff

Thomas Attig, Assistant Editor
Bowling Green State University

Ermanno Bencivenga, Assistant Editor
University of California, Irvine

Douglas D. Daye, Assitant Editor
Bowling Green State University

Antón Donoso, Assistant Editor
University of Detroit

Allan Gotthelf, Assistant Editor
Trenton State College

Brenda Jubin, Assistant Editor
Yale University

Fred Miller, Jr., Assistant Editor
Bowling Green State University

René Ruiz, Assistant Editor
Bowling Green State University

Robert Wolf, Assistant Editor
Southern Illinois University

Table of Contents

Abbreviations of Periodicals Indexed

Acta Phil Fennica	Acta Philosophica Fennica
Agora	Agora
Agr Human Values	Agriculture and Human Values
Aitia	Aitia
Ajatus	Ajatus
Aletheia	Aletheia
Alg Log	Algebra and Logic
Alg Ned Tijdschr Wijs	Algemeen Nederlands Tijdschrift voor Wijsbegeerte
Amer J Philo	American Journal of Philology
Amer J Theol Phil	American Journal of Theology & Philosophy
Amer Phil Quart	American Philosophical Quarterly
An Cated Suarez	Anales de la Catedra Francisco Suarez
Analysis	Analysis
Ancient Phil	Ancient Philosophy
Annals Pure Applied Log	Annals of Pure and Applied Logic (formerly Annals of Mathematical Logic)
Ann Esth	Annales D'Esthétique
Ann Fac Lett Filosof	Annali della Facolta di Lettere e Filosofia
An Seminar Metaf	Annales del Seminario de Metafisica
Annals Math Log	Annals of Mathematical Logic
Antioch Rev	Antioch Review
Anu Filosof	Anuario Filosofico
Apeiron	Apeiron
Aquinas	Aquinas
Arch Begriff	Archiv fur Begriffsgeschichte
Arch Filosof	Archivio di Filosofia
Arch Gesch Phil	Archiv fur Geschichte der Philosophie
Arch Math Log	Archiv fur Mathematische Logik und Grundlagen Forschung
Arch Phil	Archives de Philosophie
Arch Rechts Soz	Archiv fur Rechts und Sozialphilosophie
Aris Soc	The Aristotelian Society: Supplementary Volume
Augustin Stud	Augustinian Studies
Augustinus	Augustinus
Auslegung	Auslegung
Austl J Phil	The Australasian Journal of Philosophy
Behaviorism	Behaviorism
Berkeley News	Berkeley Newsletter
Between Species	Between the Species: A Journal of Ethics
Bigaku	Bigaku
Bioethics Quart	Bioethics Quarterly
Boll Centro Stud Vichiani	Bollettino del Centro di Studi Vichiani
Boston Col Stud Phil	Boston College Studies in Philosophy
Brahmavadin	Brahmavadin
Brit J Aes	British Journal of Aesthetics
Brit J Phil Sci	British Journal for the Philosophy of Science
Bull Hegel Soc Bt Brit	Bulletin of the Hegel Society of Great Britain
Bull Sect Log	Bulletin of the Section of Logic
Bull Soc Fr Phil	Bulletin de la Société Française de Philosophie
Bus Prof Ethics J	Business & Professional Ethics Journal
Can J Phil	Canadian Journal of Philosophy
Can Phil Rev	Canadian Philosophical Reviews
Chin Stud Phil	Chinese Studies in Philosophy
Cl Quart	The Classical Quarterly
Clio	Clio
Cogito	Cogito
Cognition	Cognition, International Journal of Cognitive Psychology
Commun Cog	Communication & Cognition
Conceptus	Conceptus
Convivium	Convivium
Crim Just Ethics	Criminal Justice Ethics
Crítica	Crítica
Cuad Filosof	Cuadernos de Filosofia
Dan Yrbk Phil	Danish Yearbook of Philosophy

Indian Phil Quart	Indian Philosophical Quarterly
Inform Log	Informal Logic
Inquiry	Inquiry
Interchange	Interchange
Int Dialog Z	Internationale Dialog Zeitschrift
Int J Applied Phil	International Journal of Applied Philosophy (formerly Applied Philosophy)
Int J Phil Relig	International Journal for Philosophy of Religion
Int Log Rev	International Logic Review
Int Phil Quart	International Philosophical Quarterly
Int Stud Phil	International Studies in Philosophy
Interpretation	Interpretation
Irish Phil J	Irish Philosophical Journal
Iyyun	Iyyun
J Aes Art Crit	The Journal of Aesthetics and Art Criticism
J Aes Educ	Journal of Aesthetic Education
J Applied Phil	Journal of Applied Philosophy
J Brit Soc Phenomenol	The Journal of the British Society for Phenomenology
J Bus Ethics	Journal of Business Ethics
J Chin Phil	Journal of Chinese Philosophy
J Crit Anal	Journal of Critical Analysis
J Dharma	Journal of Dharma
J Hellen Stud	The Journal of Hellenic Studies
J Hist Ideas	Journal of the History of Ideas
J Hist Phil	Journal of the History of Philosophy
J Indian Counc Phil Res	Journal of Indian Council of Philosophical Research
J Indian Phil	Journal of Indian Philosophy
J Liber Stud	The Journal of Libertarian Studies
J Med Ethics	Journal of Medical Ethics
J Med Phil	Journal of Medicine and Philosophy
J Mind Behav	The Journal of Mind and Behavior
J Moral Educ	Journal of Moral Education
J Phil	The Journal of Philosophy
J Phil Educ	Journal of Philosophy of Education
J Phil Log	Journal of Philosophical Logic
J Phil Sport	Journal of the Philosophy of Sport
J Prag	Journal of Pragmatics
J Relig Ethics	Journal of Religious Ethics
J Soc Phil	Journal of Social Philosophy
J Sym Log	Journal of Symbolic Logic
J Theor Crit Vis Arts	The Journal of the Theory and Criticism of the Visual Arts
J Theor Soc Behav	Journal for the Theory of Social Behaviour
J Thought	Journal of Thought
J Value Inq	The Journal of Value Inquiry
J W Vir Phil Soc	Journal of the West Virginia Philosophical Society
Kantstudien	Kant-Studien
Kennis Methode	Kennis en Methode
Kinesis	Kinesis
Kodikas/Code	Kodikas/Code: An International Journal of Semiotics
Koelner Z Soz	Koelner Zeitschrift fur Soziologie und Sozial-Psychologie
Kursbuch	Kursbuch
Laval Theol Phil	Laval Théologique et Philosophique
Law Phil	Law and Philosophy
Ling Phil	Linguistics and Philosophy
Listening	Listening
Locke News	Locke Newsletter
Log Anal	Logique et Analyse
Logos (Italy)	Logos (Italy)
Logos (Mexico)	Logos (Mexico)
Logos (USA)	Logos (USA)
Magyar Filozof Szemle	Magyar Filozofiai Szemle
Man World	Man and World
Med Stud	Mediaeval Studies
Merkur	Merkur
Metaphilosophy	Metaphilosophy
Method	Method: Journal of Lonergan Studies

Polit Theory	Political Theory
Poznán Stud	Poznán Studies
Prag Micro	Pragmatics Microfiche
Praxis	Praxis
Praxis Int	Praxis International
Problemos	Problemos
Proc Amer Phil Ass	Proceedings and Addresses of the American Philosophical Association
Proc Aris Soc	Proceedings of the Aristotelian Society
Proc Cath Phil Ass	Proceedings of the American Catholic Philosophical Association
Proc Phil Educ	Philosophy of Education: Proceedings
Proc Phil Educ Soc Austrl	Proceedings of the Philosophy of Education Society of Australasia
Process Stud	Process Studies
Rad Phil News	Radical Philosopher's Newsjournal
Ratio	Ratio
Reason Papers	Reason Papers
Rechtstheor	Rechtstheorie
Relev Log News	Relevance Logic Newsletter
Relig Hum	Religious Humanism
Relig Stud	Religious Studies
Rep Math Log	Reports on Mathematical Logic
Rep Phil	Reports on Philosophy
Res Phenomenol	Research in Phenomenology
Rev Esth	Revue d'Esthétique
Rev Etud Augustin	Revue des Etudes Augustiniennes
Rev Exist Psych Psychiat	Review of Existential Psychology & Psychiatry
Rev Filosof (Argentina)	Revista de Filosofía (Argentina)
Rev Filosof (Costa Rica)	Revista de Filosofía de la Universidad de Costa Rica
Rev Filosof (Mexico)	Revista de Filosofía (Mexico)
Rev Filosof (Spain)	Revista de Filosofía (Spain)
Rev Filosof	Revista de Filosofie (Romania)
Rev Int Phil	Revue Internationale de Philosophie
Rev J Phil Soc Sci	Review Journal of Philosophy and Social Science
Rev Latin de Filosof	Revista Latinoamericana de Filosofía
Rev Metaph	Review of Metaphysics
Rev Metaph Morale	Revue de Métaphysique et de Morale
Rev Phil Fr	Revue Philosophique de la France et de l'Etranger
Rev Phil Louvain	Revue Philosophique de Louvain
Rev Port Filosof	Revista Portuguesa de Filosofia
Rev Sci Phil Theol	Revue des Sciences Philosophiques et Theologiques
Rev Teilhard de Chardin	Revue Teilhard de Chardin
Rev Theol Phil	Revue de Théologie et de Philosophie
Rev Thomiste	Revue Thomiste
Rev Univ Ottawa	Revue de l'Université d'Ottawa
Rev Ven Filosof	Revista Venezolana de Filosofía
Riv Filosof	Rivista di Filosofia
Riv Filosof Neo-Scolas	Rivista di Filosofia Neo-Scolastica
Riv Int Filosof Diritto	Rivista Internazionale di Filosofia del Diritto
Riv Stud Croce	Rivista di Studi Crociani
Russell	Russell
Salzburger Jrbh Phil	Salzburger Jahrbuch fur Philosophie
Sapientia	Sapientia
Sapienza	Sapienza
Schopenhauer Jahr	Schopenhauer-Jahrbuch
Sci Tech Human Values	Science, Technology, and Human Values
Scientia	Scientia
Second Order	Second Order
S Afr J Phil	South African Journal of Philosophy
S J Phil	Southern Journal of Philosophy
Soc Indic Res	Social Indicators Research
Soc Phil Pol	Social Philosophy and Policy
Soc Prax	Social Praxis: International and Interdisciplinary Journal of Social Thought
Soc Theor Pract	Social Theory and Practice
Sophia (Australia)	Sophia (Australia)
Soviet Stud Phil	Soviet Studies in Philosophy
Sowjet Ges Beitr	Sowjetwissenschaft Gesellschaftswissenschaftliche Beitraege

Key to Abbreviations

List of Periodicals Indexed

Acta Philosophica Fennica. Single volume varies from $9 to $25. (2 to 3 times a year) North-Holland Publishing Company, P.O. 211, Amsterdam, The Netherlands

Agora. $4. (semi-ann) Martin A. Bertman, *Editor,* Department of Philosophy, SUNY, Potsdam, NY 13676

Agriculture and Human Values. $10; foreign $15 (Institutions: $25; foreign $30) (q) Managing Editor, 243 ASB, University of Florida, Gainesville, FL 32611

Aitia: Philosophy-Humanities Magazine. $8 for 2 yrs; $11 for 3 yrs (Institutions $10 for 2 yrs; $14 for 3 yrs). (3 times a yr) *Aita* /Friel, Knapp Hall 22, SUNY, Farmingdale, NY 11735

Ajatus. $5. (ann) Akateeminen Kirjakauppa, 00100 Helsinki 10, Finland

Aletheia. $15; foreign $15. (Institutions $15). Single copies $15.00. (ann) *Aletheia,* P.O. 477, University of Dallas Station, Irving, TX 75061

Algebra and Logic. $120. (6 times a yr) Consultants Bureau, Plenum Publishing Corporation, 227 West 17th Street, New York, NY 10011

Algemeen Nederlands Tijdschrift voor Wijsbegeerte. $24; foreign $24. (Institutions $29). (q) Van Gorcum Publ. Cy., Postbus 43, 9400 AA Assen, The Netherlands

American Journal of Philology. $8.50 (Institutions $15). (q) The Johns Hopkins Press, Journals Department, Baltimore, MD 21218

American Journal of Theology & Philosophy. $9; foreign $15. (3 times a year) W. Creighton Peden, *Editor, American Journal of Theology & Philosophy,* Dept. of Philosophy, Augusta College, Augusta, GA 30910

American Philosophical Quarterly. $25 (Institutions $80; Single copies $25). (q) Philosophy Documentation Center, Bowling Green State University, Bowling Green, OH 43403-0189

Anales de la Catedra Francisco Suarez. $6. (semi-ann) Departamento de Filosofía del Derecho, Universidad de Granada, Facultad de Derecho, Granada, Spain

Anales del Seminario de Metafísica. $2 or $120 pts. (ann) Catedra de Metafísica (Crítica), Facultad de Filosofía y Letras, Universidad Complutense, Madrid, Spain

Analysis. $21 (Institutions $33; Single copies $10.50). (q) Basil Blackwell, 108 Cowley Road, Oxford OX4 1JF, England

Ancient Philosophy. $9; foreign $12. (Institutions $12; foreign $12). Students $7. (bi-ann) Prof. Ronald Polansky, *Ancient Philosophy*, Duquesne University, Pittsburgh, PA 15282

Annales d'Esthétique. $4 (Institutions $7). (ann) The Hellenic Society for Aesthetics, 79 Vasilissis Sophias, Athens, 140, Greece

Annali della Facolta di Lettere e Filosofia. (ann) Publicazioni Dell'Universita de Bari, Bari, Italy

Annals of Pure and Applied Logic (Formerly: *Annals of Mathematical Logic*) North-Holland Publishing Company, P.O. Box 211, Amsterdam, The Netherlands

Antioch Review. $18. (Institutions $25; Foreign $30; Single copies: $4.75) (q) *Antioch Review,* Antioch College, Yellow Springs, OH 45387

Anuario Filosófico. 200 pts. or $5. Ediciones Universidad de Navarra, SA, Pamplona (Navarra), Spain

Apeiron: A Journal for Ancient Philosophy and Science. $15.50 (Institutions $21; Students $14; Single copies $10.50). (semi-ann) The Accountant, Department of Classical Studies, Monash University, Clayton, Victoria 3168, Australia

Aquinas. $8. (3 times a yr) Direzione "Aquinas," Pontificia Universita Lateranense, Piazza S. Giovanni in Laterano, 4, 00184 Roma, Italy

Archiv fur Begriffsgeschichte. 40 DM. (semi-ann) H. Bouvier Verlag H. Grundmann, 53 Bonn 1, Germany

Archiv fur Geschichte der Philosophie. $17.80. (3 times a yr) Walter de Gruyter, Inc., 162 Fifth Avenue, 5th Floor, New York, NY 10010

Archiv fur Mathematische Logik und Grundlagenforschung. 60 DM. (semi-ann) Verlag W. Kohlhammer GmbH, 7 Stuttgart, Postfach 747, West Germany

Archiv fur Rechts und Sozialphilosophie. 64 DM. (q) Franz Steiner Verlag GmbH, D-62 Wiesbaden Bahnhofstr 39, West Germany

Archives de Philosophie. 182 French francs (foreign 250 French francs). 72, rue des Saints-Peres, 75007, Paris, France

Archivio di Filosofia. 12,000 Lire. (3 times a yr) Editrice CEDAM, Via Jappelli 5, 35100 Padova, Itlay

Aristotelian Society: Supplementary Volume. $15 (Institutions $24). (ann) The Aristotelian Society, 31 West Heath Drive, London NW11, England

Augustinian Studies. $10 (Institutions $9). (ann) Augustinian Institute, Department F-1, Villanova University, Villanova, PA 19085

Augustinus. $8. (q) P. José Oroz Reta, General Davila 5, Madrid 28003, Spain

Auslegung: A Graduate Journal of Philosophy. $6 (Institutions $10; Students $4; Single copies $2.50). (3 times a yr) *Editors, Auslegung,* Department of Philosophy, University of Kansas, Lawrence, KS 66044

Australasian Journal of Philosophy. $18 (Institutions $36; Single copies $10). (q) *Australasian Journal of Philosophy,* Department of Philosophy, La Trobe University, Bundoora, Victoria, 3083, Australia

Behaviorism: A Forum for Critical Discussion. $13 (Institutions $20; Foreign add $5 beginning with Volume X; Students $10). (semi-ann) Department of Philosophy, University of Alabama at Birmingham, Birmingham, AL 35294

Berkeley Newsletter. Free. (ann) The Editors, Philosophy Department Trinity College, Dublin 2, Ireland

Between the Species: A Journal of Ethics. $12; foreign $12 (Institutions $20; foreign $20) (q) Schweitzer Center, San Francisco Bay Institute, P.O. Box 254, Berkeley, CA 94701

Bigaku (The Japanese Journal of Aesthetics). $4. (q) The Japanese Society for Aesthetics, c/o Faculty of Letters, University of Tokyo, Bunkyo-Ku, Tokyo, Japan

Bioethics Quarterly. $20; foreign $24 (Institutions $40; foreign $44). (q) Human Sciences Press, 72 Fifth Avenue, New York, NY 10011

Bollettino del Centro di Studi Vichiani. $4.50. (ann) S.R.L. GUIDA, via Port'Alba 19, 1 80134, Napoli, Italy

Boston College Studies in Philosophy. $7.50. (ann) Martinus Nijhoff, Lange Voorhout 9-11, The Hague, The Netherlands

Brahmavadin. $4. (q) Brahmavadin Prakatana Samithi, Basavangudi, Bangalore 4, India

The British Journal of Aesthetics. $28; foreign £13 (Institutions $28; foreign £13; To UK addresses £11) (q) Journals Department, Oxford University Press, Press Road, London NW10 ODD, England

British Journal for the Philosophy of Science. £14; foreign £17). (q) Aberdeen University Press, Farmers Hall, Aberdeen, Scotland AB9 2XT

Bulletin de la Société Française de Philosophie. 35 French francs (foreign 40 French francs). (q) Librairie Armand Colin, 103 B. Saint-Michel, 75240 Paris Cedex 5, France

Bulletin of the Hegel Society of Great Britain. $9 (Free to Society members) (bi-ann) David Lamb, Secretary, Department of Philosophy, The University, Manchester M13 9PL, England

Bulletin of the Section of Logic. (q) Managing editor, Szewsja 36, 50-139 Wroclaw, Poland

Business and Professional Ethics Journal. $15 (Institutions $30). (q) Subscription Office, Human Dimensions Center, Rensselaer Polytechnic Institute, Troy, NY 12181

Canadian Journal of Philosophy. $33; non-Canadian $23 (Institutions [non-Canadian $32; Canadian $36]) Students $13; Single copies $8. (q) Brenda Baker, *Mg Editor,* Department of Philosophy, University of Calgary, Alberta, Canada T2N 1N4

Canadian Philosophical Reviews. $20 (Institutions $40; Single copies $7) Students $11. (six times a year) Ruth Richardson, Academic Printing and Publishing, Box 4834, South Edmonton, Alta., Canada T6E 5G7

Chinese Studies in Philosophy. $44 (Institutions $170). (q) M. E. Sharpe, Inc., 80 Business Park Dr., Armonk, NY 10504

The Classical Quarterly. £9.00; US $22.(semi-ann) Oxford University Press, Subscriptions Department, Press Road, Neasden, London NW10 ODD, England

Clio. $6 (Institutions $15). (3 times a yr) Indiana University-Purdue University, Fort Wayne, IN 46805

Cogito. $25; foreign $25 (Institutions $45; foreign $45). (q) The Journal Secretary, *Cogito,* University of the Philippines, UPPO Box 206, Diliman, Quezon City 3004, Philippines

Cognition, International Journal of Cognitive Psychology. 60 SFrs or $36 (Institutions 100 SFrs or $60.50). (q) *Cognition,* Elsevier Sequoia SA, P.O. Box 851, CH-1001 Lausanne 1, Switzerland

Communication & Cognition. 400 BFrs plus 100 BFrs mailing costs. (q) Blandijnberg 2, B G000, Ghent, Belgium

Conceptus: Zeitschrift fur Philosophie. $1.50. (5 times a yr) Redaktion Conceptus Hoettingerg, 26, A-6020, Innsbruch, Austria

Convivium. $4. (3 times a yr) Facultad de Filosofía y Letras, Universidad de Barcelona, Barcelona, Spain

Criminal Justice Ethics. $10 (Institutions $20). (semi-ann) The Institute for Criminal Justice Ethics, 444 West 56th Street, New York, NY 10019

Crítica: Revista Hispanoamericana de Filosofía. $8 (Institutions $8; Students $8; Single copies $3). (3 times a yr) Revista *Crítica,* Apartado Postal 70-447, Mexico 20, DF, Mexico

Cuadernos de Filosofía. $15. (semi-ann) Instituto de Filosofía, 25 de Mayo 217 (2 piso), Buenos Aires, Argentina

Danish Yearbook of Philosophy. $6 or 40 Dkr. (ann) Munksgaard, 35 Norre Sogade, 1370 Copenhagen, Denmark

Darshana International. 30 Rs. or $10. (q) Professor J.P. Atreya, *Managing Editor, Darshana International,* Moradabad, India

De Philosophia. Editor, Department of Philosophy, University of Ottawa, Ottawa, Canada, K1N 6N5

Deutsche Vierteljahrsschrift fur Literaturwissenschaft und Geistesgeschichte. 70 DM. (q) J.B. Metzlersche Verlagsbuchhandlung, 7 Stuttgart 1, Postfach 529, West Germany

Deutsche Zeitschrift fur Philosophie. (m) VEB Deutscher Verlag der Wissenschafter, 108 Berlin, DDR, Germany

Dialectica: Revue Internationale de Philosophie de la Connaissance. 70 Swiss francs. (q) Postal Account, Dialectica Lausanne 10-5708, Case Postale 1081, 2501 Bienne, Switzerland

Dialectics and Humanism. $10. (q) Libreria Commissionaria Sansoni LICOSA, 45, via Lamarmora, Casella, Postale 552, 50121 Firenze, Italy

Diálogos. $4. (semi-ann) *Diálogos,* Box 21572, UPR Station, Río Piedras, Puerto Rico 00931

Dialogue: Canadian Philosophical Review—Revue Canadienne de Philosophie. $24 (Institutions $32; Students $8; Single copies $8). (q) Michael McDonald, The Canadian Philosophical Association, University of Waterloo, Waterloo, Ontario N2L 3G1

Dialogue (Phi Sigma Tau). $5 (Single copies $3). (semi-ann) Phi Sigma Tau, Department of Philosophy, Marquette University, Milwaukee, Wisconsin 53233

Dialoog. 350 Belgian francs. (q) S.V. Ontvikkeling, 2000 Antwerpen, Belgium

Dianoia. (ann) Instituto de Investigaciones Filosóficas, Dirección del Anuario de Filosofía, Torres de Humanidades, 4 piso, Ciudad Universitaria, Mexico 20 DF, Mexico

Diogenes. $20 (Single copies $6). (q) International Council for Philosophy and Humanistic Studies, 9, Place de Fontenoy, Paris 7e, France

Dionysius. $8; foreign $8. (ann) *Dionysius,* Department of Classics, Dalhousie University, Halifax, Nova Scotia, Canada B3H 3J5

Diotima. $10. (ann) Hellenic Society for Philosophical Studies, 40, Hypsilantou Street, Athens, 140, Greece

Discurso. (semi-ann) The journal is available only on an exchange basis. Professor Gilda de Mello e Souza, *Editor,* Faculdade de Filosofia, Letras, e Ciencias Humanas, Universidade de São Paulo, Caiza Postal 8105, São Paulo, Brazil

Doctor Communis. 16,000 Lire ($16). (3 times a year) *Revista Doctor Communis,* Palazzo Canonici, 00120 del Vaticano, The Vatican

Economics and Philosophy. $25; foreign £12 (Institutions: $45; foreign £22) Cambridge University Press, 32 East 57th Street, New York, NY 10022 (or Cambridge University Press, The Edinburgh Building, Shaftesbury Road, Cambridge CB2 2RU, England

Educational Philosophy and Theory. $10. (semi-ann) *Editor,* School of Education, University of New South Wales, P.O. Box 1, Kensington, NSW 2033, Australia

Educational Studies. $12 (Institutions $21). (q) Wayne J. Urban, *Editor, Educational Studies,* Box 655, Georgia Street, University Plaza, Atlanta, Georgia

Educational Theory. $12 (Institutions $12; Students $12; Single copies $5). (q) Education Building, University of Illinois, Urbana, IL 61801

Eidos: The Canadian Graduate Journal of Philosophy. $12 (Institutions: $20; Students: $6) (semi-ann) Editors, EIDOS, Department of Philosophy, University of Waterloo, Waterloo, Ontario, N2L 3G1 Canada

Ensayos y Estudios: Revista de Filosofía y Cultura. (q) Jorge Estrella, Director, Aberdi 340, San Miguel de Tucumán, Argentina

Environmental Ethics: An Interdisciplinary Journal Dedicated to the Philosophical Aspects of Environmental Problems. $18 (Institutions $24). Single copies $6. (q) *Environmental Ethics,* Department of Philosophy and Religion, The University of Georgia, Athens, GA 30602

Erkenntnis: An International Journal of Analytic Philosophy. D. Reidel Publishing Company, P.O. Box 17, 3300 AA Dordrecht,

Holland, or 190 Old Derby Street, Hingham, MA 02043

Espíritu. 90 pts.; foreign 110 pts. (semi-ann) Durán Y Bas Nr 9, Apartado 1382, Barcelona-2, Spain

Estetika. 46Dfl (q) John Benjamins, B.V. Amsteldijk 44, Amsterdam (Z), Holland

Estudios Filosóficos. $5. (q) Apartado 586, Valladolid, Spain

Ethics: An International Journal of Social, Political, and Legal Philosophy. $10.50 (Institutions $14). (q) University of Chicago Press, 5801 Ellis Avenue, Chicago, IL 60637

Etudes. 225 francs; foreign 280 francs. (m) Paul Valadier, *Rédacteur,* 14-14 bis, rue d'Assas, 75006 Paris, France

Les Etudes Philosophiques. 40 francs. (q) Presses Universitaires de France, Départmente des Periodiques, 12, rue Jean-de-Beauvais, Paris 5e France

Etyka. (semi-ann) Zaklad Etyki, Instytut Filozofii UW, Krakowskie Przedmiescie 3, 00-326, Warszawa, Poland

Exercices de la Patience. $80; Outside of France $100. (three times a year) *Exercices de la Patience,* Association Loi 1901, 50 rue des Abbesses, 75018 Paris, France

Faith and Philosophy. $15 (Institutions $25; Single copies: $5). (q) Michael Peterson, *Managing Editor,* Asbury College, Wilmore, KY 40390

Feminist Studies. $8 (Institutions $12). (semi-ann) Claire G. Moses, Women's Studies Program, University of Maryland, College Park, Maryland 20742

Filosofia. $15. (q) *Filosofia,* Piazzo Statuto 26, 10144 Torino, Italy

Filozoficky Casopis CSAV. $9. (6 times a yr) PNS Ustredni expedice tisku, odd vyvoz tisku Jinkrisska 14, Praha 1, Czechoslovakia

Franciscan Studies. $7. (ann) *Franciscan Studies,* St. Bonaventure University, St. Bonaventure, NY 14778

Free Inquiry. $12; foreign $14 (Institutions $12; foreign $14). (q) *Free Inquiry,* Box 5, Central Park Station, Buffalo, NY 14215

Freiburger Zeitschrift fur Philosophie und Theologie. 25 Swiss francs. (q) Albertinum Place G Python 1, CH-1700 Freiburg, Switzerland

Futurum: Zeitschrift fur Zukunftsforschung. Carl Hanser Verlag, Kolbergerstrasse 22, D 8000, Munich 80, West Germany

Giornale Critico della Filosofia Italiana. 3,500 Lire; foreign 10,000 Lire. (q) Ll.CO.SA, Sip A, 50121 Firenze, via Lamarmora 45, Italy 343509

Giornale de Metafisica. $7. (6 times a yr) Maria A. Raschini, via Assarotti 36-7, 16122 Genova, Italy

Gnosis: A Journal of Philosophic Interest. Free. (irr) The Editors of *Gnosis,* Philosophy Department, Concordia University, Philosophy Department, 1455 de Maisonneuve Blvd. West, Montreal, Quebec, Canada H3G 1M8

Graduate Faculty Philosophy Journal. $9.50 (Institutions $12.50). (semi-ann) *Editor,* Department of Philosophy, New School for Social Research, 65 Fifth Avenue, New York, NY 10003

Grazer Philosophische Studien. $16 for Vol. I; $17 for Vol. II (ann) Humanities Press Inc., Atlantic Highlands, NJ 07716

Gregorianum. $20. (q) *Gregorianum,* 4 Piazza della Pilotta, 1-00187, Roma, Italy

Hastings Center Report. $33 (Institutions $45; Students $28). (6 times a yr) Institute of Society, Ethics and the Life Sciences, The Hastings Center, 360 Broadway, Hastings-on-Hudson, NY 10706

Hegel-Jahrbuch. 39.50 DM. (ann) Verlag Anton Hain K.G., 6554 Meisenheim am Glan, Postfach, 180 West Germany

Hermathena: A Dublin University Review. $7.50. (semi-ann) *The Editor, Hermathena,* Trinity College, Dublin 2, Ireland

The Heythrop Journal. £8.50 or $11 (Single copies £2.50 or $27). (q) The Manager, 114 Mount Street, London W1Y/6AH, England

History of European Ideas. $20; foreign £18.18 (Institutions $40; Students $10). (q) *History of European Ideas,* Pergamon Press Ltd., Headington Hill Hall, Oxford OX3 0BW, England

History and Philosophy of Logic. (Institutions $71; foreign £18) (semi-ann) Editor, Taylor & Francis Ltd., 4 John Street, London WC1N 2ET, England

History of Philosophy Quarterly. $24 (Institutions $75; Single copies $25). (q) Philosophy Documentation Center, Bowling Green State University, Bowling Green, OH 43403-0189

History of Political Thought. £11.50; out of UK £12.50 (Institutions £22.43; out of UK £27.60) (3 times a yr) Imprint Academic, 61 Howell Road, Exeter, EX4 4EY, England

History and Theory: Studies in the Philosophy of History. $15; foreign $17 (Institutions $25; foreign $27) (q) Wesleyan University Press, Wesleyan Station, Middletown, CT 06457

Human Studies: A Journal for Philosophy and the Social Sciences. $15; foreign $19.50. (Institutions $45; Students $19.50; Single copies $5). (q) Subscription Department, Ablex Publishing Corporation, 355 Chestnut Street, Norwood, New Jersey 07648

The Humanist. $10 (Single copies $2.50). (6 times a yr) Lloyd L. Morain, *Editor,* American Humanist Association, 7 Harwood Dr., P.O. Box 146, Amherst, NY 14226-0146

Humanitas. $10.50; foreign $11.50. (3 times a yr) Publication Manager, Center for the Study of Human Development, Institute of Formative Spirituality, Duquesne University, Pittsburgh, PA 15219

Humanities in Society. $12; foreign $15.50 (Institutions $20; foreign $23.50). (q) *Editor, Humanities in Society,* Center for the Humanities, DML 303, University of Southern California, Los Angeles, CA 90007

Hume Studies. Free to Hume Scholars (Institutions $5.50). (semi-ann) *Editor*, Department of Philosophy, University of Western Ontario, London, Ontario, Canada N6A 3K7

Husserl Studies. $28; foreign Dfl 70 (Institutions $58; foreign Dfl 145). (q) Kluwer Adacemic Publishers, P.O. Box 322, 3300 AA Dordrecht, Holland (or Kluwer Academic Publishers, 190 Old Derby Street, Hingham, MA 02043

Hypatia: A Journal of Feminist Philosophy. $20; foreign $25 (Institutions $40; foreign $45) (semi-ann in 1986, then 3 times a year) Editor, Department of Philosophical Studies, Box 1437, Southern Illinois University at Edwardsville, Edwardsville, IL 62026-1001

Idealistic Studies: An International Philosophical Journal. $10 (Institutions $20; Students $10; Single copies $4). (3 times a yr) Walter Wright, *Editor, Idealistic Studies,* Department of Philosophy, Clark University, Worcester, MA 01610

The Independent Journal of Philosophy. $12 (Institutions $18; Students $8.50). (ann) George Elliott Tucker, *General Editor, The Independent Journal of Philosophy,* 38, rue St.-Louis-en-l'Ile, F-75004 Paris, France

Indian Philosophical Quarterly. 15 Rs., $6, or £2.00 (Institutions 25 Rs., $8, or £2.50). *The Editor,* University of Poona, Poona-7, India

Indian Philosophy and Culture. 15 Rs. or $5. (q) Institute of Oriental Philosophy, Vrindaban, U.P., India

Informal Logic. $10; foreign $14 (Institutions $15, foreign $19). (3 times a yr) *Managing Editor, Informal Logic,* Dept of Philosophy, University of Windsor, Windsor, Ontario, Canada N9B 3P4

Inquiry: An Interdisciplinary Journal of Philosophy. 140 Nkr. or $23 (Institutions 270 Nkr. or $45). (q) *Inquiry,* Universitetsforlaget, P.O. Box 2959, Tøyen, 0608 Oslo 6, Norway

Interchange. $5. (semi-ann) *Interchange,* Australian Fellowship of Evangelical Students, 405-411 Sussex Street, Sydney, 2000 Australia

International Journal of Applied Philosophy. (formerly *Applied Philosophy*) $5 (Institutions $7; Students $5). (bi-ann) Indian River Community College, Fort Pierce, FL 33454

International Journal for Philosophy of Religion. $28 plus postage (Institutions $56 plus postage). (q) Kluwer Academic Publishers Group, Distribution Centre, P.O.Box 322, 3300 AH Dordrecht, The Netherlands

International Logic Review. $2.25 (Institutions $5.50). (semi-ann) *Editor,* Via Belmeloro 3, 40126 Bologna, Italy

International Philosophical Quarterly. $15 (Institutions $20; Students $8; Single copies $5). (q) Vincent Potter, S.J., *International Philosophical Quarterly,* Fordham University, Bronx, NY 10458

International Studies in Philosophy. $15. (semi-ann) Department of Philosophy, SUNY at Binghamton, Binghamton, NY 13901

Internationale Dialog Zeitschrift. 38 DM. (q) Verlag Herder, D-78 Freiburg/Br., Hermann-Herder-Str 4, West Germany

Interpretation: A Journal of Political Philosophy. $13 (Institutions $16). (3 times a yr) Hilail Gildin, *Editor-in-Chief, Interpretation,* Building B 205, Queens College, Flushing, NY 11367

Irish Philosophical Journal. £2.50 (Institutions: £5) (semi-ann) Dr. Bernard Cullen, *Editor,* Department of Scholastic Philosophy, Queen's University, Belfast BT7 1NN, North Ireland

Iyyun: A Hebrew Philosophical Quarterly. $8 (Institutions $10; Students $6; Single copies $3). Back issues available. (q) Manager, *Iyyun,* The S.H. Bergman Centre for Philosophical Studies, The Hebrew University of Jerusalem, Jerusalem, Israel

The Journal of Aesthetics and Art Criticism. $20 (Institutions $25; Students $8; Single copies $7.25). (q) John Fisher, *Editor,* Department of Philosophy, Temple University, Philadelphia, PA 19122

The Journal of Aesthetic Education. $7.50. (q) University of Illinois Press, Urbana, IL 61801

Journal of Applied Philosophy. $40 (Institutions $80). (bi-ann) Carfax Publishing Company, Hopkinton Office and Research Park, 35 South Street, Hopkinton, MA 01748

The Journal of the British Society for Phenomenology. £15 or $33 (Single copies £5 or $11). (3 times a year) Haigh & Hochland Ltd., (JBSP Dept), Precinct Centre, Manchester M13 9QA, England

Journal of Business Ethics. D. Reidel Publishing Company, P.O. Box 17, 3300 AA, Dordrecht, Holland, or 190 Old Derby Street, Hingham, MA 02043

Journal of Chinese Philosophy. $39 (Institutions $95; Single copy $24). (q) Dialogue Publishing Company, P.O. Box 11071, Honolulu, HI 96828

The Journal of Critical Analysis. $10 (Institutions $12). (q) The National Council for Critical Analysis, Shirley Schievella, P.O. Box 137, Port Jefferson, NY 11777

Journal of Dharma. $3 (Institutions $8). (q) *Journal of Dharma,* Center for the Study of World Religions, Dharmaram College, Bangalore 560029 India

The Journal of Hellenic Studies. $11. (ann) The Secretary, The Hellenic Society, 31-34 Gordon Square, London WC1H 0PP England

Journal of the History of Ideas. $15 a year, $27/two years, $40/three years (Institutions $25 a year, $45/two years, $65/three years) Add $3 outside US. (q) *Journal of the History of Ideas,* Philip P. Wiener, *Executive Editor,* 748-750 Humanities Building, Temple University, Philadelphia, PA 19122

Journal of the History of Philosophy. $12 (Institutions $20). (q) *Journal of the History of Philosophy,* Harper Hall, Claremont Graduate School, 900 N. College Avenue, Claremont, CA 91711

Journal of Indian Council of Philosophical Research. $12; foreign Rs.40 (Institutions: $15; foreign Rs.60; Students: $8 or Rs.20) (semi-ann) Subscription Department, Motilal Banarsidass, Bungalow Road, Jawahar Nagar, Delhi - 110 007, India

Journal of Indian Philosophy. D. Reidel Publishing Company, P.O. Box 17, 3300 AA Dordrecht, Holland, or 190 Old Derby Street, Hingham, MA 02043

The Journal of Libertarian Studies. $20 if library also subscribes. (Institutions $44; Student $10). (q) Center for Libertarian Studies, P.O. Box 4091, Burlingame, CA 94011

Journal of Medical Ethics: The Journal of the Society for the Study of Medical Ethics. $56. (q) The Subscription Manager, Tavistock House East, Tavistock Square, London WC1H 9JR England, or Professional and Scientific Publications, 1172 Commonwealth Avenue, Boston, MA 02134

The Journal of Medicine and Philosophy. D. Reidel Publishing Company, P.O. Box 17, 3300 AA Dordrecht, Holland, or 190 Old Derby Street, Hingham, MA 02043

The Journal of Mind and Behavior. $25; foriegn $41 [air] $28 [surface] (Institutions $45; foreign $61 [air] $48 [surface]; students $20). (q) Circulation Department, P.O. Box 522, Village Station, New York City, NY 10014

Journal of Moral Education. £18.50 or $50 (Single copies $18.50). (3 times a yr) Carfax Publishing Co., P.O. Box 25, Abingdon, Oxon, OX14 1RL England

Journal of Philosophical Logic. D. Reidel Publishing Company, P.O. Box 17, 3300 AA Dordrecht, Holland, or 190 Old Derby Street, Hingham, MA 02043

The Journal of Philosophy. $15 (Institutions $20; Students $12; Single copies $2). Special issues $3 plus $.25 postage. (m) *The Journal of Philosophy,* 720 Philosophy Hall, Columbia University, New York, NY 10027

Journal of Philosophy of Education. $64 (Institutions $128; Single copies $70.50). (semi-ann) Carfax Publishing Company, Haddon House, Dorchester-on-Thames, Oxford OX9 8JZ England

The Journal of the Philosophy of Sport. $8 (Institutions $8; Students $5 (members in P.S.S.S.); Single copies $8). (ann) *The Journal of the Philosophy of Sport,* Indiana University-Purdue University at Fort Wayne, 2101 Coliseum Blvd. E., Fort Wayne, IN 46805

Journal of Pragmatics. $29 or Dfl. 65; foreign same (Institutions $66.75 or Dfl. 150; foreign same). (bi-monthly) Elsevier/ North-Holland Inc., 52 Vanderbilt Avenue, New York, NY 10017 (Foreign: North-Holland Publishing Company, P.O. Box 211, Amsterdam, The Netherlands)

The Journal of Religious Ethics. $8 (Institutions $10). (bi-ann) Department of Religious Studies, University of Tennessee, Knoxville, TN 37916

Journal of Social Philosophy. $8 (Institutions $12). (3 times a yr) Dr. W. Creighton Peden, *Editor, Journal of Social Philosophy,* Augusta College, Augusta, GA 30904

The Journal of Symbolic Logic. $40 (Association members $15). Association for Symbolic Logic, P.O. Box 1571, Annex Station, Providence, RI 02901

The Journal of the Theory and Criticism of the Visual Arts. $7 (Institutions: $7) (ann) Joseph E. Young and Robert E. Barela, Editors, School of Art, Arizona State University, Tempe, AZ 85287

Journal for the Theory of Social Behavior. $35.95 (Institutions $74). (3 times a year) Basil Blackwell, 108 Cowley Road, Oxford, England

Journal of Thought. $12; foreign $15 (Institutions $12; foreign $15) (q) *Journal of Thought,* College of Education, 820 Van Vleet Oval, University of Oklahoma, Norman OK 73019

The Journal of Value Inquiry. Dfl 55 (Institutions Dfl 95). (q) Martinus Nijhoff, 9-11 Lange Voorhout, P.O. Box 269, The Hague, The Netherlands

The Journal of the West Virginia Philosophical Society. $1.50 (Institutions $3). Gratis to members of the Society. (semi-ann) *Editor,* West Liberty State College, West Liberty, WV 26074

Kant-Studien: Philosophische Zeitschrift der Kant-Gesellschaft. 68 DM. (q) Walter de Gruyter, Genthiner Str 13, 1 Berlin 30, West Germany

Kennis en Methode - Tijdschrift voor Wetenschapsfilosofie en Methodologie. $30 (q) Boompers, Postbus 58, Meppel,The Netherlands

Kinesis: Graduate Journal in Philosophy. $5.00 (Institutions $7.50). (semi-ann) Department of Philosophy, Southern Illinois University, Carbondale, IL 62901

Kodikas/Code: An International Journal of Semiotics. 48 DM; foreign 48 DM (Institutions 56 DM; foreign 56 DM). (q) Gunter Narr Verlag, P.O. Box 2567, D-7400 Tubingen 1, West Germany

Koelner Zeitschrift fur Soziologie und Sozial-Psychologie. 72 DM. (q) Westdeutscher Verlag, 567 Opladen, Ophovener Str 1-3, West Germany

Kursbuch. 20 DM. (irr, at least q) Insel-Syhrkamp Verlag, 6 Frankfort M., Lindenstr 29-35, West Germany

Laval Théologique et Philosophique. $10 (Institutions $20; Students $6; Single copies $15.25). (3 times a yr) Service des Revues, Les Presses de l'Université Laval, C.P. 2447, Quebec, G1K 7R4, Canada

Law and Philosophy: An International Journal for Jurisprudence and Legal Philosophy. D. Reidel Publishing Company, P.O. Box 17, 3300 AA, Dordrecht, Holland, or 190 Old Derby Street, Hingham, MA 02043

Linguistics and Philosophy. D. Reidel Publishing Company, P.O. Box 17, 3300 AA Dordrecht, Holland, or 190 Old Derby Street, Hingham, MA 02043

Listening. $7; foreign $11.50 (Institutions $9.50; foreign $11.50). (3 times a yr) Victor S. LaMotte, *Editor,* 3642 Lindell Blvd., St. Louis, MO 63108

The Locke Newsletter. £4. (ann) Roland Hall, Department of Philosophy, University of York, Heslington, York, England

Logique et Analyse. 600 Belgian francs or $15. (q) Editions E. Nauwelaerts, Munstraat 10, B-3000, Leuven, Belgium

Logos: Philosophic Issues in Christian Perspective. $7. (ann) Libreria Scientifica Editrice, Corso Umberto 1, 40, 80138, Napoli, Italy

Logos. 1000 Pesos; foreign $15 (3 times a yr) Apartado 18-907, Col. Tacubaya, Delegacion Miguel Hidalgo, C.P. 11870, Mexico, D.F.

Logos. $7. (ann) *Logos,* Department of Philosophy, University of Santa Clara, Santa Clara, CA 95053

Magyar Filozofiai Szemle. $5. (six times a year) Kultura, POB 149, Budapest 62, Hungary

Man and World: An International Philosophical Review. $21 (Institutions $38). *Man and World,* Martinus Nijhoff, Lange Voorhout 9-11, P.O. Box 269, The Hague, The Netherlands

Mediaeval Studies. $14. (ann) Walter M. Hayes, S.J., Director of Publications, 59 Queen's Park Crescent East, Toronto, Ontario, Canada M5S 2C4

Merkur. 44 DM. (m) Ernst Klett Verlag, 7 Stuttgart 1, Postfach 809, West Germany

Metaphilosophy. $38.30 (Institutions $65). (q) Basil Blackwell, 5 Alfred Street, Oxford, England OX1 4HB

Method: Journal of Lonergan Studies. $12; foreign $12 (Institutions $20; foreign $40). (bi-ann) Manager, Department of Philosophy, Loyola Marymount University, Loyola Blvd. at W. 80th Street, Los Angeles, CA 90045

Methodology and Science. 60.00 Hfl. (q) Dr. P. H. Esser, *Secretary and Editor,* Beelslaan 20, Haarlem, The Netherlands

Midwest Studies in Philosophy. $8.50 (Institutions $12.50). *Editor, Midwest Studies in Philosophy,* University of Minnesota Press, 2037 University Avenue S.E., Minneapolis, MN 55455

Midwestern Journal of Philosophy. $3 (Institutions $8). (ann) Dr. Wayne Sheeks, *Editor,* Box 733 University Sta., Murray State University, Murray, KY 42071

The Mill News Letter. No charge. (semi-ann) *Editors, Mill News Letter,* Department of English, Victoria College, University of Toronto, Toronto, Ontario, Canada M5S 1K7

Mind: A Quarterly Review of Psychology and Philosophy. $22.50 (Institutions $32.50). (q) Basil Blackwell & Mott Ltd, 108 Cowley Road, Oxford OX4 1JF England

The Modern Schoolman. $24 (Single copies $24). (q) John L. Treloar, S.J., 3700 West Pine Blvd., St. Louis, Missouri

The Monist. $15 (Institutions $24). (q) *The Monist,* P.O. Box 599, Lasalle, IL 61301

Music and Man. $12 (Institutions $28). (q) Gordon and Breach, 1 Park Avenue, New York, NY 10016, or 41-42 William IV Street, London WC2 England

National Forum: Phi Kappa Phi Journal. $10; foreign same. (Institutions $12.50; foreign same). (q) *Managing Editor, National Forum,* Box 19420A, East Tennessee State University, Johnson City, TN 37601

Neue Hefte fur Philosophie. 59.40 DM for 3 issues. (Irr; at least 2 times a year) Vandenhoeck & Ruprecht, Postfach 77, D-3400 Gottingen, Federal Republic of Germany

The New Scholasticism. $12 (Institutions $12; Students $12; Single copies $3.25). (q) Treasurer, The American Catholic Philosophical Association, Catholic University of America, Washington, DC 20064

New Vico Studies. $12.50; foreign $12.50 (add $1 for postage; overseas $3). (ann) *New Vico Studies,* 69 Fifth Ave. Suite 17A, New York, NY 10003

Notre Dame Journal of Formal Logic. $20 (Institutions $35). (q) Business Manager, *Notre Dame Journal of Formal Logic,* Box 5, Notre Dame, IN 46556

Noûs. $16 (Institutions $32; Students $13; Single copies $8). (q) Department of Philosophy, 126 Sycamore Hall, Indiana University, Bloomington, IN 47401

Organon. $10. (ann) Foreign Trade Enterprise, "ARS POLONA-RUCH" 7 Krakowskie Przedmiescie, 00-0068 Warsaw, Poland

The Owl of Minerva. $10 (Institutions $16). (semi-ann) Department of Philosophy, Villanova University, Villanova, PA 19085

Pacific Philosophical Quarterly (formerly *The Personalist*). $16 (Institutions $30; Single copies $7.50). (q) *Managing Editor, Pacific Philosophical Quarterly,* School of Philosophy, University of Southern California, Los Angeles, CA 90007

The Pakistan Philosophical Journal. 10 Rs., £1.50, or $4 (semi-ann) M. Saeed Sheikh, *Managing Editor,* Pakistan Philosophical Congress, Narsingda Garden Villa Club Road, Lahore-3, Pakistan

Pensamiento. $9. (q) *Pensamiento* (Administracion) Pablo Aranda, 3, Madrid 6, Spain

Perspekitiven der Philosophie. 48 Hfl. (Institutions 80 Hfl.). (ann) Editions Rodopi N.V., Keizersgracht 302-304, Amsterdam, The Netherlands, or Humanities Press, Atlantic Highlands, NJ 07716

La Petite Revue de Philosophie. $7 (Institutions $12). (bi-ann) Service de l'edition, Collège Edouard-Montpetit, 945, chemin Chambly, Longueuil, QC, Canada J4H 3M6

Philosophia. $14 (Institutions $18; Students $14). (ann) Editorial Office-Distribution, Research Center for Greek Philosophy at the Academy of Athens, 14 Anagnostopoulou Street, Athens, 136, Greece

Philosophia: Philosophical Quarterly of Israel. $7 (Institutions $10). (q) Bar-Ilan University, *Philosophia,* Subscriptions, Department of Philosophy, Ramat-Gan, Israel

Philosophia Mathematica. $8. (semi-ann) J. Fang, Department of Philosophy, Old Dominion University, Norfolk, VA 23508

Philosophia Naturalis. $11. (q) Verlag Anton Hain KG, 6554 Meisenhelm am Glan, Postfach 180, West Germany

Philosophia Reformata. 50 Dutch guilders. (q) Centrum voor Reformatorische wijsbegeerte, Postbus 149, 3600 AC, Maarssen, Pauwenkamp 115, Maarssenbroek, The Netherlands

Philosophic Exchange: Annual Proceedings. $3.50 (Institutions $5.50; Students $3). (ann) The Center for Philosophic Exchange, State University College at Brockport, Brockport, NY 14420

Philosophica. 400 Belgian francs (Institutions 500 Belgian francs (members); Students 250 Belgian francs; Single copies 250 Belgian francs). (semi-ann) *Philosophica,* Blandijnberg 2, B-9000 Gent, Belgium

Philosophical Books. $28 (Institutions $55.50; Single copies $8). (q) Basil Blackwell, Ltd., 108 Cowley Road, Oxford OX4 4JF, England

The Philosophical Forum. $10 (Institutions $25; Students $10; Single copies $3). (q) Marx Wartofsky, *Editor, The Philosophical Forum,* Box 239, Baruch College of CUNY, 17 Lexington Avenue, New York, New York

Philosophical Investigations. $30.35 (Institutions $65.55). (q) Basil Blackwell Publisher Ltd., 108 Crowley Rd., Oxford OX4 1JF, England; D. Z. Phillips, Editor, University College of Swansea SA2 8PP, Wales, UK

Philosophical Inquiry: An International Philosophical Quarterly. $18 (Institutions $22) (q) Professor D. Z. Andriopoulos, *Editor,* Department of Philosophy, Adelphi University, Garden City, L.I., NY 11530

Philosophical Linguistics. $3.50 (ann) Great Expectations Bookstore, 909 Foster Street, Evanston, IL 60201

Philosophical Papers. $12, R20 (Institutions: $30 or R40; Students $8 or R12). (3 times a year) Secretary, *Philosophical Papers,* Rhodes University, P.O. Box 94, Grahamstown 6140, Republic of South Africa

Philosophical Quarterly. $25 (Institutions $50). (q) Journals Department, Basil Blackwell Pub. Ltd., 108 Cowley Rd., Oxford, England.

The Philosophical Review. $18 (Institutions $30; Single copies $9). (q) *The Philosophical Review,* 218 Goldwin Smith Hall, Cornell University, Ithaca, NY 14853

Philosophical Review (Taiwan). Free. (semi-ann) *Editor-in-Chief, Philosophical Review,* Department of Philosophy, National Taiwan University, Taipei 107, Taiwan, Republic of China

Philosophical Studies: An International Journal for Philosophy in the Analytic Tradition. D. Reidel Publishing Company, P.O. Box 17, 3300 AA Dordrecht, Holland, or 190 Old Derby Street, Hingham, MA 02043

Philosophical Studies (Ireland). $18.50 (Institutions $57). (8 times a year) The Secretary, *Philosophical Studies,* The National University of Ireland, 57 Trimleston Gardens, Boostertown, Dublin, Ireland

Philosophical Studies in Education: Proceedings of the Annual Meeting of the Ohio Valley Philosophy of Education Society. $2.50; foreign $3 (Institutions $5; foreign $5.50). (ann) Dennis Senchuk, *Editor,* Department of History & Philosophy of Education, Indiana University, Bloomington, IN 47401

Philosophical Topics (formerly *Southwestern Journal of Philosophy*). $15. (Institutions $20; Student $10) (3 times a yr) Robert Shahan, *Editor,* Office of the Chancellor, 1100 14th Street/UCD, Denver, CO 80202

Philosophie et Logique. $8. (q) Editura Academiei Republicii Socialiste Romania, Str. Gutenberg 3 bis, Sector 6, Bucuresti, Romania

Philosophiques. $14 (Institutions $17; Students $9; Single copies $9). (semi-ann) *Philosophiques,* Les Editions, Bellarmin, 8100, Boulevard Saint-Laurent, Montreal, P.Q., Canada H2P 2L9

Philosophische Perspektiven. 38.50 DM. (ann) Verlag Vittorio Klostermann, 6 Frankfurt/Main, Frauenlobstr 22, West Germany

Philosophische Rundschau: Zeitschrift fur Philosophische Kritik. 36 DM. (q) J. C. B. Mohr (Paul Siebeck), 7400 Tubingen, Postfach 2040, West Germany

Philosophisches Jahrbuch. 42 DM. (semi-ann) Verlag Karl Alber, Hermann-Herder-Str-4, 78 Freiburg 1 Br., West Germany

Philosophy. £6.50 or $19.50 (Free to members of Royal Institute of Philosophy). (q) Cambridge University Press, P.O. Box 92, London NW1 2DB England, or Cambridge University Press, 32 East 57th Street, New York, NY 10022

Philosophy in Context. $3. (semi-ann) *Philosophy in Context,* Department of Philosophy, Cleveland State University, Cleveland, OH 44115

Philosophy East and West. $10. (q) *Philosophy East and West,* 2424 Maile Way, Porteus Hall 713, Honolulu, HI 96822

Philosophy of Education: Proceedings. $10.50. (ann) Proceedings: Studies in Philosophy and Education, Dr. Francis T. Villemain, School of Education, San Jose State University, San Jose, CA 95192

The Philosophy Forum. $43 per volume. (semi-ann) Gordon & Breach Science Publishers, Ltd, 42 William IV Street, London WC2 England

Philosophy and Literature. $12 (Institutions $21; Single copies $7). (semi-ann) *Philosophy and Literature,* University of Michigan at Dearborn, Dearborn, MI 48128

Philosophy and Phenomenological Research. $12; foreign $13 (Institutions $15; foreign $18). (q) *Philosophy and Phenomenological Research,* Brown University, Box 1947, Providence, RI 02912

Philosophy and Public Affairs. $14.50 (Institutions $22.50; Students $9; Single copies $5; foreign add $3.75 postage). (q) *Philosophy and Public Affairs,* Princeton University Press, P.O. Box 231, Princeton, NJ 08540

Philosophy Research Archives. $16.50 (Institutions $33). Add $2 for postage outside the United States. (ann) Philosophy Documentation Center, Bowling Green State University, Bowling Green, OH 43403-0189 [For additional information on the *Archives,* including the ordering of page prints of articles, please see the section on the *Archives* in the back of this issue.]

Philosophy and Rhetoric. $16.50 (Institutions $22.50; Single copies $7.50). (q) *Philosophy and Rhetoric,* Department of Philosophy, Emory University, Atlanta, GA 30322

Philosophy in Science. $38; foreign $38 (Institutions $38; foreign $38). (ann) Pachart Publishing House, 1130 San Lucas Circle, Tucson, AZ 85704

Philosophy of Science. $17.50. (q) *Managing Editor, Philosophy of Science,* Department of Philosophy, 18 Morrill Hall, Michigan State University, East Lansing, MI 48823

Philosophy and Social Action. $15; foreign £5.50. (Institutions $25; foreign £9.50). (q) Business manager, *Philosophy & Social Action,* M-120 Greater Kailash-I, New Delhi 110048, India

Philosophy and Social Criticism. $16 (Institutions $42; Students $12; Single copies $3.50). (q) *Editor,* Department of Philosophy, Boston College, Chestnut Hill, MA 02167

Philosophy of the Social Sciences. $15. (q) Wilfrid Laurier University Press, Wilfrid Laurier University, Waterloo, Ontario, Canada N2L 3C5

Philosophy Today. $12 (Single copies $3.50) (q) *Philosophy Today,* Carthagena Station, Celina, OH 45822

Phoenix. $10. (q) Professor H. J. Mason, Treasurer, University College, Toronto, Ontario, Canada M5S 1A1

Phronesis: A Journal for Ancient Philosophy. 77.50 DG (Institutions 77.50 DG; Students 77.50 DG; Single copies 29.00 DG). (3 times a year) Royal Van Gorcum Ltd, P.O. Box 43, 9400AA Assen, The Netherlands

Political Theory. $13.50 (Institutions $22.50). (q) Sage Publications Ltd, 275 South Beverly Drive, Beverly Hills, CA 90212

Poznán Studies in the Philosophy of the Sciences and the Humanities. $29 (Institutions $36). (q) B. R. Gruner Publishing Company, P.O. Box 70020, Amsterdam, The Netherlands

Pragmatics Microfiche. $10 (Institutions $20). (3 times a yr) *Editor, Pragmatics Microfiche,* Department of Linguistics, University of Cambridge, Sidgwick Avenue, Cambridge, England

Praxis. $7. (q)*Praxis,* Filozofski Facultet Zagreb, Dure Salaja bb, Yugoslavia

Praxis International. $33.50 (Institutions $85). Basil Blackwell Publishers, Journals Department, 108 Cowley Road, Oxford OX4 1JF, England

Problemos. (q) Lietuvos TSR, Vilnius, Valstybinis V. Kapusko Universitetas G3, Lithuania

Proceedings and Addresses of the American Philosophical Association. $5. (ann) The American Philosophical Association, University of Delaware, Newark, DE 19711

Proceedings of the American Catholic Philosophical Association. $8. (ann) Treasurer, The American Catholic Philosophical Association, Catholic University of America, Washington, DC 20017

Proceedings of the Aristotelian Society. $8.35. (ann) The Aristotelian Society, 31 West Heath Drive, London NW11 England

Proceedings of the Far Western Philosophy of Education Society. Dr. Earl L. Grossen, College of Education, Brigham Young University, Box 65, McKay, Provo, UT 84602

Proceedings of the Philosophy of Education Society. $1.50; foreign $2.20. (ann) The Philosophy of Education Society of Australasia, Treasurer of the Society, School of Education, University of New South Wales, P.O. Box 1, Kensington, 2033, Australia

Process Studies. $8 (Institutions $10). (q)*Process Studies,* 1325 North College Avenue, Claremont, CA 91711

Radical Philosophers' Newsjournal. $4 (Institutions $8). (2-3 times a yr) 12 Dartmouth Street, Somerville, MA 02145

Ratio. $42 (Institutions $59.55). (semi-ann) Basil Blackwell & Mott Ltd, 108 Cowley Rd., Oxford, England

Reason Papers: A Journal of Interdisciplinary Normative Studies. $4; foreign $4 (Institutions $4; foreign $4). (ann)*Reason Papers,* The Reason Foundation, 1129 State Street, No. 4, Santa Barbara, CA 73101

Rechtstheorie. (semi-ann) Bucker and Humboldt, West Berlin, West Germany

Relevance Logic Newsletter. $5. (3 times a yr) Robert G. Wolf, *Editor,* Department of Philosophical Studies, Southern Illinois University, Edwardsville, IL 62026

Religious Humanism. $8. (q) Fellowship of Religious Humanism, 105 West North College Street, Yellow Springs, OH 45387

Religious Studies. £8.50 or $24.50 (Institutions £10.50 or $32). (q) Cambridge University Press, Bentley House, 200 Euston Road, London NW1 2DB England, or (U.S. and Canada) Cambridge University Press, 32 East 57th Street, New York, NY 10022

Reports on Mathematical Logic. (semi-ann) Centrala Handlu Zagranicznego "Ars Polona," ul. Krakowskie Przedmiescie 7, 00-068, Warszawa, Poland

Reports on Philosophy. Dr. Zbigniew Kuderowicz, *Editor-in-Chief,* Instytut Filozofii, ul. Grodzka 52, 31-044 Krakow, Poland

Research in Phenomenology. $7.50 (Institutions $10; Students $7.50). (ann) Humanities Press, Inc., 450 Park Avenue South, New York, NY 10016

Review of Existential Psychology & Psychiatry. $20; (Institutions $40; Students $16; Single copies $10) (3 times a year) Keith Hoeller, *Editor*, Box 23220, Seattle, WA 98102

Philosophy and Social Science, Dr. Michael V. Belok, Secondary Education, Arizona State University, Tempe, AZ 85281

The Review of Metaphysics. $12 (Institutions $18; Students $8). (q) *The Review of Metaphysics,* The Catholic University of America, Washington, DC 20064

Revista de Filosofía. Instituto de Filosofía, Universidad Nacional de La Plata, Argentina

Revista de Filosofía. $5. (3 times a yr) Revista de Filosofía Universidad Iberoamericana, Av. Cerro de las Torres No. 395, Mexico 21, DF, Mexico

Revista de Filosofía. 100 Pts. (q) *Revista de Filosofía,* Serrano 127, Madrid 6 Spain

Revista de Filosofía de la Universidad de Costa Rica. $5. (semi-ann) Oficina de Coordinación Editorial y Difusión Científica, Universidad de Costa Rica, San José, Costa Rica

Revista de Filosofie. $18. (m) Rompresfilatelia, Calea Grivitei 64-66, P.O. Box 2001, Bucharest, Romania

Revista Internazionale di Folosofia del Diritto. 10,000 Lire. (q) Casa Editrice Dott. A. Giuffre, Via Statuto, 2-20121 Milano, Italy

Revista Latinoamericana de Filosofía. $11 (Institutions $15). (3 times a yr) *Revista Latinoamericana de Filosofía,* Box 1192, Birmingham, AL 35201 or Casilla de Correo 5379, Correo Central, 1000 Capital Federal, Agentina

Revista Portuguesa de Filosofia. $30. (Single copies $8) (q) Faculdade de Filosofia, UCP, 4719 BRAGA CODEX, Portugal or Oficinias Graficas da Livraria Cruz & Cª, L.ᵈᵃ—, Braga, Portugal

Revista Venezolana de Filosofía. $4 (Institutions $3). (semi-ann) Dr. Angel Cappelletti, Apartado 5354, Caracas, Venezuela

Revue d'Esthétique. 40 French francs. Librairie C. Klincksieck C.C.P., Paris 734-94, France

Revue de l'Université d'Ottawa. $10. (q) Editions de l'Université d'Ottawa, 65, Avenue Hastey, Ottawa, Ontario, Canada K1N 6N5

Revue de Métaphysique et de Morale. 86 francs; foreign 42 francs. (q) Librairie Armand Colin, 102, Boulevard Saint-Michel, 75240 Paris CEDEX 5, France

Revue de Théologie et de Philosophie. 3 Swiss francs. (6 times a yr) *Revue de Théologie et de Philosophie,* Imprimérie la Concorde, rue des Terreaux 29, 1003 Lausanne, Switzerland

Revue des Etudes Augustinienne. 56 francs. (q) Etudes Augustinienne, 8 rue François-ler, Paris 8e, France

Revue des Sciences Philosophiques et Théologiques. 95 francs; foreign 112 francs. (q) Librairie J. Vrin, 6, Place de la Sorbonne, 75005 Paris, France

Revue Internationale de Philosophie. 1.660 Belgian francs; foreign 1.800 Beligan francs or $14. (q) *Revue Internationale de Philosophie,* Imprimérie Universa, rue Hoender, 24, B-9200, Wetteren, Belgium

Revue Philosophique de la France et de l'Etranger. 200 francs. (q) Redaction de la Revue Philosophique, 12, rue Jean-de-Beauvais, 75005 Paris, France

Revue Philosophique de Louvain. 1,250 Belgian francs or $36. (q) *Revue Philosophique de Louvain,* Editions Peeters, B.P. 41, B-3000 Louvain, Belgium

Revue Teilhard de Chardin. $5 (Institutions $4). (q) Société Teilhard de Chardin, 99, rue Souveraine, Brussels 5, Belgium

Revue Thomiste: Revue doctrinale de Théologie et de Philosophie. 120 French francs or 1600 Belgian francs. (q) Ecole de Théologie, Avenue Lacordaire, 31078-Toulouse, CEDEX, France

Rivista di Filosofia. 7,500 Lire. (q) Casa Editrice Taylor, *Rivista di Filosofia,* Corso Stati Uniti, 53 C.C. Postale 2/2322, Italy

Rivista di Filosofia Neo-Scolastica. 10,000 Lire. (6 times a yr) Pubblicazioni dell'Universita Cattolica del Sacro Cuore, Largo A. Gemelli, 20123 Milano Italy

Rivista di Studi Crociani. 6,000 Lire; foreign 7,000 Lire. (q) *Revista di Studi Crociani,* Presso la Societa di Storia Partia, Piazza Municipio, Maschio Angiolino, 80133 Napoli, Italy

Russell: Journal of the Bertrand Russell Archives. $3 (Institutions $4). (q) McMaster University Library Press, McMaster University, Hamilton, Ontario, Canada

Salzburger Jahrbuch fur Philosophie. 50 DM. (ann) Universitaetsverlag Angon Pustet, Salzburg/Sigmund-Haffner-Gasse 18, West Germany

Sapientia. $5. (q) Revista Sapientia, Calle 24, entre 65 y 66, La Plata Argentina

Sapienza. $7.50. (q) Vicoletto S. Pietro a Maiella, 4-80134 Napoli, Italy

Schopenhauer-Jahrbuch. 25 DM. (ann) Verlag Waldemar Kramer, 6 Frankfurt/Main, West Germany

Science, Technology, and Human Values. $12; foreign $12 (Institutions $22). (q) MIT Press Journals, 28 Carleton Street, Cambridge, MA 02142

Scientia: An International Review of Scientific Synthesis. $60. (3 times a yr) *Scientia,* Via Guastalla 9, 20122 Milano, Italy

Second Order: An African Journal of Philosophy. $11; foreign £4 (Institutions $16; foreign £6.75) (semi-ann) The Executive Editor, Periodicals Department, University of Ife Press, University of Ife, Ife, Nigeria

Social Indicators Research: An International and Interdisciplinary Journal for Quality-of-Life Measurement. D. Reidel Publishing Company, P.O. Box 17, 3300 AA Dordrecht, Holland, or 190 Old Derby Street, Hingham, MA 02043

Social Philosophy and Policy. $14.50; foreign £10.50 (Institutions $40; foreign £24.50) (Canada $17.75; institutions $49).

(bi-ann) Journals Dept, Basil Blackwell Publishers Ltd, 108 Cowley Road, Oxford OX4 19F, England

Social Praxis: International and Interdisciplinary Journal of Social Thought. $8 (Institutions $19). (q) Mouton and Company, P.O. Box 1132, The Hague, The Netherlands

Social Theory and Practice. $12; Single copies $4 (Institutions $27; Single copies $9). (3 times a year) *Social Theory and Practice,* Department of Philosophy, The Florida State University, Tallahassee, FL 32306

Sophia. $3.50. (3 times a yr) *Sophia,* Department of Philosophy, University of Melbourne, Parkville 3052, Australia

South African Journal of Philosophy. R20-00 (Institutions R20-00). (q) Bureau for Scientific Publications, P.O. Box 1758, Pretoria, 0001 South Africa

The Southern Journal of Philosophy. $10 (Institutions $14; Students $5). (q) *Editor, The Southern Journal of Philosophy,* Department of Philosophy, Memphis State University, Memphis, TN 38152

Southwest Philosophical Studies. $16 (Institutions $30). (3 times a year) Alvin E. Keaton, *Editor,* Department of Philosophy, New Mexico State University, Las Cruces, NM 88003

Southwestern Journal of Philosophy. (see *Philosophical Topics*)

Soviet Studies in Philosophy. $44 (Institutions $170). (q) *Soviet Studies in Philosophy IASP,* M. E. Sharpe Publisher, 80 Business Park Dr., Armonk, NY 10504

Sowjetwissenschaft Gesellschaftswissenschaftliche Beitraege. 72.80 DM. (m) Verlag Kultur und Fortschritt, 108 Berlin-Pst, Glinkastr 13/15, East Germany

Soziale Welt. (q) Otto Schwartz and Company, Goettingen, West Germany

Sprache im Technischen Zeitalter. 20 DM. (q) Verlag W. Kohlhammer GmbH, 7 Stuttgart 1, Postfach 747, West Germany

Stromata. $8. (q) *Stromata,* Facultades de la Filosofía y Teología, Universidad del Salvador, San Miguel, Argentina

Studia Leibnitiana. 72 DM. (q) Franz Steiner Verlag GmbH, Wiesbaden, West Germany

Studia Logica. Dfl. 190 or $72 (q) D. Reidel Publishing Company, P.O. Box 17, 3300AA Dordrecht, Holland, or 190 Old Derby Street, Hingham, MA 02043, USA.

Studia Philosophiae Christiane. 80 Zl.; foreign $3.25. (semi-ann) Jozef Iwanicki, Warszawa 43, VI Gwiazdzista 81, Poland

Studia Philosophica. (ann) Daniel Christoff and Hans Kunz, *Editors,* Verlag Paul Haupt, Falkenplatz 14, CH-3001, Berne, Switzerland

Studies in History and Philosophy of Science $15 (Institutions $80). (q) Pergamon Press, Inc., Maxwell House, Fairview Park, Elmsford, NY 10523

Studies in Philosophy and Education. $8(Institutions $9). (q) *Studies in Philosophy and Education,* Dr. Francis T. Villemain, Dean, School of Education, San Jose State University, San Jose, CA 95192

Studies in Philosophy and the History of Philosophy. $12.95. (bi-ann) The Catholic University of America Press, 620 Michigan Avenue N.E., Washington DC 20017

Studies in Soviet Thought. D. Reidel Publishing Company, P.O. Box 17, 3300AA Dordrecht, Holland, or 190 Old Derby Street, Hingham, MA 02043

Synthese: An International Journal for Epistemology, Methodology, and Philosophy of Science. D. Reidel Publishing Company, P.O. Box 17, 3300AA Dordrecht, Holland, or 190 Old Derby Street, Hingham, MA 02043

Teaching Philosophy. $16 (Institutions $32; Single copies $9). (q) Philosophy Documentation Center, Bowling Green State University, Bowling Green, OH 43403-0189. Add $2 postage outside the United States.

Telos. $8 (Institutions $10). *Telos,* Department of Sociology, Washington University, St. Louis, MO 63130

Teorema. 500 Pts.; foreign $10. (q) *Teorema,* Apartado 1, 107, Valencia, Spain

Teoresi. 4,000 Lire; foreign 6,000 Lire. (semi-ann) Direzione di Teoresi - Faculte Lettere e Filosofia, Universita de Catani, Catania, Italy

Theologie und Philosophie. 72 DM. (q) Herder Verlag, D-78 Freiburg/Br., Hermann-Herder Str. 4, West Germany

Theoretical Medicine: An International Journal for the Philosophy and Methodology of Medical Research and Practice (formerly *Metamedicine*). D. Reidel Publishing Company, P.O. Box 17, 3300AA Dordrecht, Holland, or 190 Old Derby Street, Hingham, MA 02043

Theoria: A Swedish Journal of Philosophy. SKr. 35 (Institutions SKr. 70). (3 times a yr) Liber Laromedel, Box 1250, 221 05 Lund 1, Sweden

Theoria to Theory. $17.50 (Institutions $36) (q) Gordon and Breach Science Publishers Ltd., 42 William IV Street, London WC2 England

Theory and Decision: An International Journal for Philosophy and Methodology of the Social Sciences. D. Reidel Publishing Company, P.O. Box 17, 3300AA Dordrecht, Holland, or 190 Old Derby Street, Hingham, MA 02043

Thinking: The Journal of Philosophy for Children. $12; Single copies $5 (Institutions $20 [Single copies $5]; Students $8 [Single copies $2]) (q) The Institute for the Advancement of Philosophy for Children, Montclair State College, Upper Montclair, NJ 07043

The Thomist. $7. (q) The Thomist Press, 487 Michigan Avenue N.E., Washington, DC 20017

Thought: A Review of Culture and Idea. $15. (q) *Thought,* Fordham University Press, Fordham University, Bronx, NY 10458

Tijdschrift voor Filosofie. 1900 BF / 125 guilders; foreign & USA $78. (q) Kardinaal Mercierplein 2, B-3000 Leuven, Belgium

Topoi. D. Reidel Publishing Company, P.O. Box 17, 3300AA Dordrecht, Holland, or 190 Old Derby Street, Hingham, MA 02043

Trans/Form/Acao. $10 (Institutions $10; All other $10) (ann) Biblioteca Central da UNESP, Av. Vicente Ferreira, 1278, Caixa Postal 420, 17.5000 - Marilia - SP - Brazil

Transactions of the Charles S. Peirce Society: A Journal in American Philosophy. $18 (Institutions $27; Students $18; Single copies $4.50). (q) *Editor*, Philosophy Department, Baldy Hall, SUNY at Buffalo, Buffalo, NY 14260

Tribuene: Zeitschrift Zum Verstaendnis des Judentums. (q) Tribuene-Verlag, Frankfurt/Main, Habsburger Allee 72, West Germany

Tulane Studies in Philosophy. $3 to $4.50. (ann) Department of Philosophy, Tulane University, New Orleans, LA 70118

Ultimate Reality and Meaning: Interdisciplinary Studies in the Philosophy of Understanding. $22 (Institutions $40). (q) University of Toronto Press, Journals Department, 5201 Dufferin Street, Downsview, Ontario, Canada M3H 5T8

Universal Human Rights: A Comparative and International Journal of the Social Sciences, Philosophy and Law. $19.50 (Institutions $39.50; Students $19.50; Single copies $12.50). (q) Earl M. Coleman Enterprises, Inc., P.O. Box 143, Pine Plains, NY 12567 (or: Sweet and Maxwell, 11 New Fetter Lane, London EC4P 4EE England)

Universitas. 48 DM. (m) Wissenschftliche Verlagsgesellschft BmbH, 7 Stuttgart, Postfach 40, West Germany

Vivarium: A Journal for Mediaeval Philosophy and the Intellectual Life of the Middle Ages. 25 Fl. (semi-ann) Royal Van Gorcum Ltd, Assen, The Netherlands

Wissenschaft und Weisheit. 25 DM. (3 times a yr) Postfach 6213, 4000 Dusseldorf 1, Germany

Wissenschaft und Weltbild. 16.50 DM. (q) Europa Verlags-A.G., Altmannsdorfer, Strass 154-156, A-1232 Wein, Austria

Zeitschrift fur Allgemeine Wissenschaftstheorie. 56 DM. (semi-ann) Franz Steiner Verlag GmbH, 62 Wiesbaden postfach 472, West Germany

Zeitschrift fur Mathematische Logik und Grundlagen der Mathematik. $24.50 (q) Deutscher Buch-Export und Import GmbH, DDR-701, Leipzig, P.O. Box 160, German Democratic Rupublic

Zeitschrift fur Philosophische Forschung. $16.50. (q) Verlag Anton Hain KF, 6554 Meisenheim am Glan, Postfach 180, West Germany

Zeitschrift fur Religions-und Geistesgeschichte. 30 DM. E.J. Brill-Verlag GmbH, 5 Koeln, Haus am Friesenplatz, West Germany

Zygon: Journal of Religion and Science. $17 (Institutions $22). (q) Karl E. Peters, *Editor*, Rollins College, Winter Park, FL 32789

Guidance on the Use of the Subject Index

The Subject Index lists in alphabetical order the significant subject descriptors and proper names that describe the content of the articles and books indexed. Since titles are frequently misleading, the editors read each article and study each book to determine which subject headings accurately describe it. Each entry under a subject heading includes the complete title and the author's name.

Subject entries fall into the following classes:

1) proper names, such as Quine, Kant, and Hegel;
2) nationalities, such as American and Soviet
3) historical periods, which are: ancient, medieval, renaissance, modern, nineteenth-century, and twentieth-century;
4) major fields of philosophy, which are: aesthetics, axiology, education, epistemology, ethics, history, language, logic, metaphysics, philosophical anthropology, philosophy, political philosophy, religion, science, and social philosophy;
5) subdivisions of the major fields of philosophy, such as: utilitarianism, induction, realism, and nominalism;
6) other specific topics, such as grue, pain, paradox, and Turing-machine;
7) bibliographies, which are listed under "bibliographies," the person or subject, and the appropriate historical period.

The Subject Index is used like the index found in the back of a textbook. Scan the alphabetical listing of significant words until the desired subject is found. If the title confirms your interest, then locate the author's name, which occurs after the title, in the section entitled "Author Index with Abstracts." The title, in addition to suggesting the content of the article or book provides additional information. The language in which the article of book is written is indicated by the title.

Although every effort was made to standardize subject headings, complete uniformity was impossible. Hence, check for various spellings of subject headings, particularly of proper names. Due consideration should be given to subject headings that sometimes are written with a space, a hyphen, or an umlaut. The following example illustrates some possibilities and the order in which they would be sorted by the computer:

DE MORGAN
DE-MORGAN
DEMORGAN

Not only does the computer treat the above subject headings as different, but it may interfile other subject headings between them.

Generally, only the last names of famous philosophers are used as subject headings. Last names and first initials usually are used for other philosophers. The following list indicates who of two or more philosophers with the same last name is designated by last name only:

Alexander (Samuel)	James (William)
Austin (J L)	Jung (Carl G)
Bacon (Francis)	Lewis (C I)
Bradley (Francis H)	Mill (John Stuart)
Brown (Thomas)	Moore (G E)
Butler (Joseph)	Niebuhr (Reinhold)
Collins (Anthony)	Paul (Saint)
Darwin (Charles)	Price (Richard)
Eckhart (Meister)	Russell (Bertrand)
Edwards (Jonathan)	Schiller (Friedrich)
Green (Thomas H)	Toynbee (Arnold)
Hartmann (Edward von)	Wolff (Christian)
Huxley (T H)	

ALGEBRA

Aldo.

Consequence Operations Defined By Partial Matrices. Marek, Iwona.

Considérations Algébriques Sur La Théorie De La Démonstration. Both, Nicolas.

DFC–Algorithms For Suszko, Logic SCI And One–to–one Gentzen Type Formalizations. Wasilewska, Anita.

Decidable Regularly Closed Fields Of Algebraic Numbers. Van Den Dries, Lou and Smith, Rick L.

Filter Distributive Logics. Czelakowski, Janusz.

On The Degree Of Complexity Of Sentential Logics; An Example Of The Logic With Semi–negation. Hawranek, Jacek and Zygmunt, Jan.

On The Period Of Sequences $(A^n(p))$ In Intuitionistic Propositional Calculus. Ruitenburg, Wim.

On Three–Valued Moisil Algebras. Monteiro, Luiz and Abad, M.

Paraconsistent Algebras. Carnielli, Walter A and De Alcantara, Luiz P.

Pavelka's Fuzzy Logic And Free L–Subsemigroups. Gerla, Giangiacomo.

Recursive Properties Of Euclidean Domains. Schrieber, Leonard.

Some Investigations Of Varieties Of N–Lattices. Sendlewski, Andrzej.

Some Undecidability Results In Strong Algebraic Languages. Kalfa, Cornelia.

The Generalised RK–Order, Orthogonality And Regular Types For Modules. Prest, Mike.

The Real–Algebraic Structure Of Scott's Model Of Intuitionistic Analysis. Scowcroft, Philip.

Topological Duality For Nelson Algebras And Its Applications. Sendlewski, Andrzej.

Ultrafilters And Types On Models Of Arithmetic. Kirby, L A S.

Untersuchungen Zur Algebraischen Theorie Der Partiellen Mengen. Kuhnrich, Martin.

Zum Aufbau Einer Mehrsortigen Elementaren Logik. Kaphengst, Heinz.

3088 Varieties: A Solution To The Ackermann Constant Problem. Slaney, John K.

ALGEBRAIC LOGIC

Topoi: The Categorial Analysis Of Logic. Goldblatt, R and Suppes, P (ed) and Troelstra, A S (ed).

ALGORITHM(S)

DFC–Algorithms For Suszko, Logic SCI And One–to–one Gentzen Type Formalizations. Wasilewska, Anita.

Some Remarks On A Theorem Of Iraj Kalantari Concerning Convexity And Recursion Theory. Downey, Rod.

ALIENATION

Foundations Of Humanism. Van Praag, J P.

Home From Exile: An Approach To Post–Existentialist Philosophizing. Hickey, Denis.

"Marcuse And The Meaning Of Radical Philosophy" in *Continuity And Change In Marxism*, Fischer, Norman And Others (ed), 114–130. Perrin, Ronald.

"Marx And Kierkegaard On Alienation" in *International Kierkegaard Commentary*, Perkins, Robert L (ed), 155–174. Marsh, James L.

"Sartre And Alienation" in *Continuity And Change In Marxism*, Fischer, Norman And Others (ed), 144–169. Georgopoulos, N.

"The Alienation And Liberation Of Nature" in *On Nature*, Rouner, Leroy S (ed), 133–144. Moltmann, Jürgen.

A Brief Discussion Of Marx's Theory Of Alienation. Tianyu, Cao.

Alienation And Aesthetics In Marx And Tolstoy: A Comparative Analysis. Kiros, Teodros.

Alvin Gouldner: Vervreemding, Reflexiviteit, En De Naderende Crisis Van De Sociologie. Disco, Cornelis.

Das Eigentum Als Eschatologische Potenz: Zur Eigentumskonzeption Von Karl Marx. Künzli, Arnold.

Dialectical Phenomenology As Critical Social Theory. Marsh, James L.

Discussing The Problem Of Alienation. Ruoshui, Wang.

Limitations Of The Theory Of Alienation Propounded By Marx In His Youth. Wandan, Xin.

Marx On The Return Of Man To Himself. Gongcai, Fan.

On The Concept Of "Alienation" From Hegel To Marx. Ruoshui, Wang.

Sartre O Las Dificultades De Escribir Una Moral. Fornet– Betancourt, Raul.

Several Issues Concerning The Theory Of Human Beings. Tongsen, Huang.

Should Marxists Be Interested In Exploitation? Roemer, John E.

The Alienation Of Revolution Or The Criticism Of Real Socialism In The Conception Of A Schaff (in Czechoslovakian). Hrzal, Ladislav and Kuzminski, V.

The Inalienability Of Autonomy. Kuflik, Arthur.

The Power Of Ideas: China's Campaign Against Ideological Pollution. Yudkin, Marcia.

Welfare State Versus Welfare Society? Skillen, Anthony.

ALLAIS, M

A Mistaken Argument Against The Expected Utility Theory Of Rationality. Broome, John.

The St Petersburg Gamble And Risk. Weirich, Paul.

ALLEGORY(–RIES)

"L'allégorie De La Caverne": République En Petit. Gendron, Edmond.

"Simbolizzazione E Temporalizzazione, Differenza Di Simbolo E Allegoria" in *Il Tempo Dell'Arte*, Papi, Fulvio and others (ed), 92–101. Raio, Giulio.

"The Structure Of Allegory" in *Existential Coordinates Of Human Condition*, Tymieniecka, A (ed), 505–520. Gellrich, Jesse.

ALLISON, H

Incongruence And The Unity Of Transcendental Idealism: Reply To Henry E Allison. Buroker, Jill Vance.

ALLOCATION

Good Approximations To Maximin Allocations. Grout, Paul.

ALMEDER, R

On Basic Knowledge Without Justification. Moser, Paul K.

ALTHUSSER, L

The Rise And Fall Of Structural Marxism: Althusser And His Influence. Benton, Ted.

Althusser On Overdetermination And Structural Causation. Emerson, Michael.

Empiricism And Speculation In *the German Ideology.* Taminiaux, Jacques.

The Anatomy Of Knowledge: Althusser's Epistemology And Its Consequences. Atkinson, D.

ALTMAN, I

A Critical Evaluation Of Altman's Definition Of Privacy As A Dialectic Process. Foddy, W H.

ALTRUISM

"Out With The "Old" And In With The "New"" in *Ethical Questions In Brain And Behavior*, Pfaff, Donald W (ed), 91–110. Caplan, Arthur L.

Group Selection And Methodological Individualism. Glaser, Gerald.

Non–Patient Decision–Making In Medicine: The Eclipse Of Altruism. Battin, Margaret P.

Professions As The Conscience Of Society. Sieghart, Paul.

The Calculus Of Moral Obligation. Mc Guire, Martin C.

The Concept Of Altruism. Clark, Ralph W.

The Martyr's Dilemma. Moore, F C T.

The Theory Of Reciprocal Altruism. Lipkin, Robert J.

Three Approaches Toward An Understanding Of Sportsmanship. Arnold, Peter J.

Unsolicited Medical Opinion. Ratzan, Richard.

AMBIGUITY

Analysis And Dialectic: Studies In The Logic Of Foundation Problems. Russell, Joseph J.

"Dem Dichten Vor–Denken": Aspekte Von Heideggers "Zwiesprache" Mit Hölderlin Im Kontext Seiner Kunstphilosophie. Jamme, Christoph.

A Problem About Ambiguity In Truth–!Theoretical Semantics. Cohen, L Jonathan.

Ambiguity Vs Generality: Removal Of A Logical Confusion. Roberts, Lawrence.

Commentary On "A Response To 'Is Business Bluffing Ethical'". Powell, Donald C.

Grammatical Non–Specification: The Mistaken Disjunction 'Theory'. Atlas, Jay David.

Typical Ambiguity And The Axiom Of Choice. Crabbe, Marcel.

AMERICAN

see also Latin American

Creativity In American Philosophy. Hartshorne, Charles.

Cuban And North American Marxism. D' Angelo, Edward (ed).

The Naturalists And The Supernatural: Studies In Horizon And An American Philosophy Of Religion. Shea, William M.

"Anarchism And American Traditions" in *Freedom, Feminism, And The State*, Mc Elroy, Wendy (ed), 35–48. De Cleyre, Voltairine.

"Confronting 'The Russian Question': The Ideological Journey Of A Generation" in *On Freedom*, Howard, John A (ed), 133–154. Lasky, Melvin J.

"New Hymns For The Republic: The Religious Right And America's Moral Purpose" in *On Freedom*, Howard, John A (ed), 112–132. Neuhaus, Richard John.

"Recent Soviet Evaluations Of American Philosophy" in *Contemporary Marxism*, O' Rourke, James J (ed), 215–220. Blakeley, Thomas J.

"The Way To S0mewhere: Ethics In American Archaeology" in *Ethics And Values In Archaeology*, Green, Ernestene L (ed), 36–50. Winter, Joseph C.

Classical American Philosophy: A Reflective Bequest To The Twenty–First Century. Mc Dermott, John J.

Ethical Considerations For Planned Social Change In The Education Of American Indian People. Thomas, Linda Sue.

Europa Und Die Vereinigten Staaten Von Amerika Philosophiegeschichtlich Betrachtet. Moser, Simon.

Individual And Community: An American View. Kegley, Jacquelyn A K.

La Recepción Argentina Del Pensamiento Norteamericano. Biagini, Hugo E.

More's *Utopia* And The New World Utopias: Is The Good Life An Easy Life? Dooley, Patrick K.

Politologie Und Political Science In Den USA. Lowe, Bernd P.

AMERICAN DREAM

"For Your Freedom, And Ours" in *On Freedom*, Howard, John A (ed), 3–6. Tyrmand, Leopold.

ANALOGICAL ARGUMENT(S)

"The Second Analogy" in *Kant On Causality, Freedom, And Objectivity*, Harper, William A (ed), 58–64. Dryer, D P.

Analogical Inference In Hume's Philosophy Of Religion. Jacquette, Dale.

Classical Utilitarianism And The Analogy Argument. Mc Gray, James.

ANALOGY(–GIES)

Portraying Analogy. Ross, J F.

Kant, Analogy, And Natural Theology. Gill, Jerry H.

Le Caractère Mythique De L'Analogie Du Bien Dans *République VI*. Couloubaritsis, Lambros.

Metaphor, Analogy, And System: A Reply To Burbidge "Professor Burbidge Responds". Vaught, Carl G.

On Theoretical Terms. Dilworth, Craig.

Problemática De La Analogía. Giralt, Edualdo Forment.

Sissela Bok On The Analogy Of Deception And Violence. Betz, Joseph.

The Role Of The Visual Arts In Plato's Ideal State. Belfiore, Elizabeth.

ANALYSIS

see also Linguistic–analysis

Análisis Propositional Y Ontologia. Sanchez, Juan Carlos.

Analysis And Dialectic: Studies In The Logic Of Foundation Problems. Russell, Joseph

ANIMAL RIGHTS
Rights, Inherent Values, And 'Deep Ecology'. Partridge, Ernest.

ANIMISM
Awareness Of The Unseen: The Indian's Contract With Life. Bunge, Robert.

ANNIHILATION
The Origin Of Extermination In The Imagination. Gass, William H.

ANONYMITY
Anonymity In The Academy: The Case Of Faculty Evaluation. Riegle, Rodney P and Rhodes, Dent M.

ANSCOMBE, E
The Refutation Of Determinism. Shutte, Augustine.

ANSCOMBE, G
Without Proof Or Evidence: Essays Of O K Bouwsma. Craft, J L (ed) and Hustwit, Ronald E (ed).
Anscombe, Davidson And Lehrer On A Point About Freedom. Harrison, Jonathan.

ANSELM
Without Proof Or Evidence: Essays Of O K Bouwsma. Craft, J L (ed) and Hustwit, Ronald E (ed).
A No Nonsense Approach To St Anselm. Malcolm, John F.
Charles Hartshorne And The Ontological Argument. Peters, Eugene H.
Existential Import In Anselm's Ontological Argument. Bäck, Allan.
The Aseity Of God In St Anselm. Morreall, John.
The Ontological Argument. Russell, Bruce.
Where Does The Ontological Argument Go Wrong? Mc Grath, Patrick J.

ANSERMET, E
The Tonal And The Foundational: Ansermet On Stravinsky. Krausz, Michael.

ANSWER(S)
Logic, Philosophy, And History: A Study In The Philosophy Of History Based On The Work Of R G Collingwood. Russell, Anthony F.

ANTHROPOCENTRISM
A Note On Deep Ecology. Watson, Richard A.
Color And The Anthropocentric Problem. Averill, Edward Wilson.
Gustafson's God: Who; What; Where? Mc Cormick, Richard A.
In Praise Of Anthropomorphism. Ferré, Frederick.
Non–Anthropocentric Value Theory And Environmental Ethics. Callicott, J Baird.
The Critique Of Natural Rights And The Search For A Non–Anthropocentric Basis For Moral Behavior. Zimmerman, Michael F.

ANTHROPOLOGY
A Dialogue With Barth And Farrer On Theological Method. Buckley, James J and Wilson, William Mcf.
Anthropological Definitions Of Religion. Segal, Robert A.
Anthropological Concepts: Some Notes On Their Epistemological Status. Pinxten, Rik.
Antropologische Geneeskunde In Discussie. Verwey, G.
Carlos Monge: Ideas Filosófico–Antropológicas. Soto, José Alberto.
Dieter Wyss Y La Medicina Antropológica. Csef, Herbert.
Emotions Across Cultures: Objectivity And Cultural Divergence. Heelas, Paul.
German Philosophy And The Rise Of Modern Clinical Medicine. Tsouyopoulos, Nelly.
Human Sociobiology: A Philosophical Perspective. Ruse, Michael.
John Paul The Second Anthropology Of Concrete Totality. Min, Anselm K.
L' "Oratio Ad Divinam Sapientiam" Del Vichiano Lorenzo Boturini–Beneduci. Ghelardi, Maurizio.
L'anthropologie Dans Le Contexte De La Culture. Milcu, Stefan.
L'anthropologie Ches Les Pères Orientaux. Khalife– Hachem, Elie.
La Teologia Come Antropologia In Heinrich Fries. Belletti, Brunpo.
Law And Social Order: On Leopold Pospisil's Anthropology Of Law. Opoku, Kwame.
Le Matérialisme Biologique De Lévi–Strauss. Steinmetz, Rudy.
Marx—Anthropology And Praxis. Panasiuk, Ryszard.
Modelos Hermenéuticos Y Mitológicos. Ortiz– Osés, Andrés.
Norm Und Recht In Niklas Luhmanns Rechtssoziologie: Kritische Anmerkungen Aus Der Sicht Der Rechtsethnologie. Von Benda– Beckmann, Franz.
Objectivity And Social Anthropology. Beattie, J H M.
On The Indeterminacy Of Action. Soles, Deborah Hansen.
Personalisme Et Anthropologie Chrétienne. Walgrave, Jan H.
Plädoyer Für Eine Ökonomische Anthropologie Auf Der Grundlage Von Interessen. Koubek, Norbert.
Semantical Anthropology. Almog, Joseph.
The Anthropological Approach To Theology. Macquarrie, John and Rahner, Karl.
The Paradoxes Are Numerous. Wax, Murray L.
What Is Explained By AI Models? Kobsa, Alfred.

ANTHROPOMORPHISM
Eliminating "God" And Gathering The Real Gods. Hayes, Victor C.
In Praise Of Anthropomorphism. Ferré, Frederick.
Kant, Analogy, And Natural Theology. Gill, Jerry H.

ANTI–ART
Antiaesthetics: An Appreciation Of The Cow With The Subtile Nose. Ziff, Paul.

ANTI–INTELLECTUALISM
The Young Mao—A Soviet Portrait. Krancberg, Sigmund.

ANTI–SEMITISM
A Political Theorist From Eastern Europe. Tar, Zoltán.
Christianity And The Final Solution. Reese, William L.
How To Make Hitler's Ideas Clear? Roth, John K.

ANTINOMY(–MIES)
The Transcendental Turn: The Foundations Of Kant's Idealism. Gram, Moltke.
Kant's Practical Antinomy. Wike, Victoria S.
Kants Antinomien Und Die Logik Der Erkenntnis. Narski, I S.
L'ombre De La Raison. Trotignon, Pierre.
The Thesis Of The Second Antinomy. De Paul, Michael R.

ANTIPOSITIVISM
The Tendency Of Tendermindedness In Educational Research, Or, The New Anti–Formalism. Phillips, D C.

ANTISEMITISM
Radical Humanism. Améry, Jean and Rosenfeld, Sidney (ed) and Rosenfeld, Stella (ed).

ANTISERI, D
Metafisica, Scienza E Fede: Una Discusione Con Dario Antiseri. Messinese, Leonardo.

ANTONI, C
Carlo Antoni E Lo Storicismo Crociano (Continua). Fantini, Stefano.

ANXIETY
The New Image Of The Person: The Theory And Practice Of Clinical Philosophy. Koestenbaum, Peter.
Zu Möglichkeiten Und Grezen Der Überwindung Der Angst Vor Dem Sterben Und Dem Frühen Tod. Volland, Hannelore.

APA
see American Philosophical Association

APE(S)
Over De Menselijkheid Van Vroege Hominidae. Corbey, R.

APEL, K
Die Funktion Der Hermeneutik In Den Positiven Wissenschaften. Kimmerle, Heinz.
Hermeneutik—Theorie Einer Praxis? Kamper, Dietmar.
K O Apel Over "Erklären" En "Verstehen". Strasser, St.
Wittgenstein's Solution Of The 'Hermeneutic Problem'. Shanker, Stuart G.
Zur Ortsbestimmung Der Historischen Wissenschaften. Kramer, Hans.

APHORISM(S)
Nietzschean Aphorism As Art And Act. Shapiro, Gary.

APOCALYPSE
Deux Visions De La Fin Du Monde: Le Dernier Jugement, De Jean–Baptiste Chassignet Et Le Jugement D'Agrippa D'Aué. Miernowski, Jan.

APOLLONIAN
I Of The Cyclops: The Herdsman–Poet. Foster, Donald W.

APOSTOL, P
Comment On Pavel Apostol's Paper. Bunge, Mario.

APPEARANCE(S)
Berkeley: Inconsistencies And Common Sense. Lascola, Russell A.
Identity, Appearances, And Things In Themselves. Bencivenga, Ermanno.
Sextus Empiricus: Skepticism As A Therapy. Cohen, Avner.

APPETITION
Spinoza's Account Of Sexuality. Rice, Lee.

APPLICATION(S)
'Elegance' In Science And Mathematics: A Discussion. Macnamara, Michael and Kistner, Wietske and Wilkinson, Jennifer.
Approaches To Applied Anthropology. Cohen, Ronald.
Probability And Laws. Constantini, D.

APPLIED ETHICS
Teaching As A Moral Craft. Tom, Alan R.
Bribery. D' Andrade Jr, Kendall.
Ethical Theory In The Twenty–First Century. Bayles, Michael D.
Normative Contexts And Moral Decision. Philips, Michael.
Regulation, Deregulation, Self–Regulation: The Case Of Engineers In Ontario. Stevenson, J T.
Situating The Employee Rights Debate. Kirby, Donald.
The Case Method: A Perspective. Gini, A R.

APPLIED PHILOSOPHY
A Reply To "On Reading Environmental Ethics". Lemons, John.
Applied Philosophy In Health Care Outside The Medical Ethics Arena. Butler, Nance Cunningham.
Applying Philosophy. Wilson, John and Cowell, Barbara.
Normative Contexts And Moral Decision. Philips, Michael.
Philosophy And A Career In Law. Perkins, Jeffrey J.
Philosophy In The Legislative Process. Hare, John E.
Philosophy's Relevance To Technical Writing. Girill, T R.
The Case Method: A Perspective. Gini, A R.
The Philosopher In The Workplace. Elliston, Frederick.

APPRECIATION
Antiaesthetics: An Appreciation Of The Cow With The Subtile Nose. Ziff, Paul.
Bosanquet's Concept Of Difficult Beauty. Jacquette, Dale.
Is There A Correct Aesthetic Appreciation Of Nature? Saito, Yuriko.
Medicine And The Arts. Stone, John.
Music Education As Aesthetic Education: Concepts And Skills For The Appreciation Of Music. Goolsby, Thomas W.

APPREHENSION
On The Visual Constitution Of Society: The Contributions Of Georg Simmel And Jean–Paul Sartre To A Sociology Of The Senses. Weinstein, Deena and Weinstein, Michael.

AUGUSTINE

Vita. De Capitani, Franco.
Presencia De San Agustín En Suárez. Reta, Jose Oroz.
Saint Augustine On The Road To Damascus. Ferrari, Leo C.
Sissela Bok On The Analogy Of Deception And Violence. Betz, Joseph.
St Augustine's Quest For The Truth: The Adequacy Of A Christian Philosophy. Kuntz, Paul G.
The *Uti/Frui* Distinction In Augustine's Ethics. O' Connor, William Riordan.
The Concept Of The Person In St Augustine's *De Trinitate*. O' Connor, William R.
The Phases Of Light In Augustine (in Japanese). Hikasa, Katsushi.
The Priority Of Reason Over Faith In Augustine. Ramirez, J Roland.
The Problem Of Evil: Augustine And Ricoeur. Stark, Judith C.
The Problem Of The Common Good In Saint Augustine's *Civitas Terrena*. Lavere, George J.
The World–Soul And Time In St Augustine. Teske, Roland J.
To Kill Or Let Live: Augustine On Killing The Innocent. Burt, Donald X.
Twelfth–Century Concepts Of Time: Three Reinterpretations Of Augustine's Doctrine Of Creation *Simul*. Gross, Charlotte.
Two Classical Western Theologians: Augustine And Newman. Penaskovic, Richard.
Wordsworth's "Real Language Of Men" And Augustine's Theory Of Language. Chivers, Frances J.

AUGUSTINISM

Influencia Del Pensamiento De San Agustín En La Filosofía Catalana Actual. Rovira Martínez, José.

AUREOLI

Walter Chatton *Vs* Aureoli And Ockham Regarding The Universal Concept. Kelley, Francis E.

AUROBINDO GHOSE

Mystical Consciousness In A Process Perspective. Simmons, Ernest L.
The Central Argument Of Aurobindo's *The Life Divine*. Phillips, Stephen H.

AUSTIN

"Meaning, Force And Explicit Performatives" in *Philosophical Analysis In Latin America*, Gracia, Jorge J E and others (eds), 141–164. Rabossi, Eduardo.
Sanction And Obligation. Hardin, Russell.
Speech And The Social Contract. Turner, Roy.
The Constitutive Force Of Language. Harris, James F.
What We Do And Say In Saying And Doing Something. Gandhi, Ramchandra.

AUSTRALIAN

Prospects For Regional Philosophies In Australia. Sylvan, Richard.

AUSTRIAN

Philosophy Of Medicine In Austria. Kenner, Thomas.

AUTHENTICITY

Anachronistic Inauthenticity In Art. Bertman, Martin A.
Bultmann's Criticisms Of Heidegger. Chryssides, George D.
Dasein As Self: Some Implications Of Heideggerian Ontology. Anderson, Scott William.
Heidegger's "Existentialism" Revisited. Zimmerman, Michael E.
Ortega E Gasset: Perfil Ético De Uma Filosofia. Araújo, Luís De.
The Assignation. Lingis, Alphonso.
The Authentic And The Aesthetic. Currie, Gregory.

AUTHORITY(–TIES)

Locke's Education For Liberty. Tarcov, Nathan.
Progress And Chaos: Modernization And Rediscovery Of Religion And Authority. Groth, Alexander J.
Authority And Justification. Raz, Joseph.
Authority And Persuasion In Philosophy. Jordan, Mark D.
Authority, Law And Morality. Raz, Joseph.
Children In Care: Are Social Workers Abusing Their Authority? Benians, R C.
Coercion, Deterrence, And Authority. Airaksinen, Timo.
Critical Thinking And Obedience To Authority. Sabini, John and Silver, Maury.
Frege's Justificationism: Truth And The Recognition Of Authority. Notturno, M A.
Philosophy And The Mirror Of Rorty. Munz, Peter.
Respect For Autonomy And Medical Paternalism Reconsidered. Wear, Stephen and Mc Cullough, L B.
Response To "Children In Care: Are Social Workers Abusing Their Authority". Foster, Judy.
Sartre's Dialectical Anarchism: Institution, Sovereignty, And The State. Barker, Jeffrey H.
The Authority Of The Moral Agent. Johnson, Conrad D.

AUTOBIOGRAPHY

"D M Armstrong—Self Profile" in *D M Armstrong*, Bogdan, Radu J (ed), 3–54. Armstrong, D M.
Augustine, Memory, And The Development Of Autobiography. Archambault, Paul J.
In Response To Miller's "Meland: Worship And His Recent Thought". Meland, Bernard E.
In Response To Suchocki's "The Appeal To Ultimacy In Meland's Thought". Meland, Bernard E.
In Response To Inbody's "Bernard Meland: A Rebel Among Process Theologians". Meland, Bernard E.
Two Pathographies: A Study In Illness And Literature. Hawkins, Anne.

AUTOMATA

Zur Raumkompliziertheit Mehrdimensionaler Turing–Automaten. Hemmerling, Armin and Murawski, Gerd.

AUTOMATION

The Ancient Concept Of Casus And Its Early Medieval Interpretations. Frakes, Jerold C.

AUTOMORPHISM(S)

Automorphisms Of Supermaximal Subspaces. Downey, R G and Hird, G R.
Variations On Promptly Simple Sets. Maas, Wolfgang.

AUTONOMY

The Silent World Of Doctor And Patient. Katz, Jay.
The Will At The Crossroads: A Reconstruction Of Kant's Moral Philosophy. Cox, J Gray.
"Patient Autonomy And The Refusal Of Psychotropic Medications" in *Difficult Decisions In Medical Ethics*, Ganos, Doreen L (ed), 13–30. Baumgarten, Elias.
"Patient Autonomy In Intensive Care" in *Difficult Decisions In Medical Ethics*, Ganos, Doreen L (ed), 111–124. Miller, Bruce.
"The Right To Refuse Psychotropic Medications" in *Difficult Decisions In Medical Ethics*, Ganos, Doreen L (ed), 31–38. Gallant, Donald M and Irwin, Martin.
"Treatment Refusals" in *Ethical Questions In Brain And Behavior*, Pfaff, Donald W (ed), 41–56. Macklin, Ruth.
Autonomy And Benevolent Lies. Hill Jr, Thomas E.
Autonomy And Utility. Haworth, Lawrence.
Autonomy And Human Rights Claims. Gough, Jim.
Autonomy's Temporary Triumph. Veatch, Robert M and Callahan, Daniel.
Care Of The Dying: Withholding Nutrition. Capron, Alexander M and Cassell, Eric J.
Commentary On "Kicking Against The Pricks: Two Patients Wish To End Essential Insulin Treatment". Parsons, Victor.
Commentary On "Kicking Against The Pricks: Two Patients Wish To End Essential Insulin Treatment". Marsden, David.
Commentary On "Kicking Against The Pricks: Two Patients Wish To End Essential Insulin Treatments". Gillon, Raanan.
Commentary On "Kicking Against The Pricks: Two Patients Wish To End Essential Insulin Treatments". Kennedy, Ian.
Divine Omniscience And Human Privacy. Lackey, Douglas P.
Engineering Human Reproduction: A Challenge To Public Policy. Gorovitz, Samuel.
Exemplarische Bronnen Van Het Westers Autonomie–Begrip. Nauta, L W.
Freedom And The Development Of Autonomy: A Reply To Victor Quinn. Dearden, R F.
Freedom Of Expression In Commerce. Machina, Kenton F.
Historical Roots Of The Concept Of Autonomy In Western Philosophy. Nauta, Lolle.
Informed Consent, Autonomy, And The Law. Annis, David B.
Non–Patient Decision–Making In Medicine: The Eclipse Of Altruism. Battin, Margaret P.
On Removing Food & Water: Against The Stream. Meilaender, Gilbert.
Paternalism And Partial Autonomy. O' Neill, Onora.
Prisoner In The ICU: The Tragedy Of William Bartling. Annas, George J.
Promoting The Autonomy Of Another Person: The Difficult Case Of The High School Dropout. Hedman, Carl G.
Respect For Autonomy And Medical Paternalism Reconsidered. Wear, Stephen and Mc Cullough, L B.
Roles And Responsibilities: Theoretical Issues In The Definition Of Consultation Liaison Psychiatry. Agich, George J.
Théorie Et Vérité: La Réflexion Contemporaine Face À Ses Origines Grecques Et Idéalistes. Grondin, Jean.
The 'Right' Not To Know. Ost, David E.
The Autonomy Of The Mentally Ill: A Case Study In Individualistic Ethics. Laor, Nathaniel.
The Biological Limits On Autonomy. Morison, Robert S.
The Inalienability Of Autonomy. Kuflik, Arthur.
The Objection Of Circularity In Groundwork III. Mc Carthy, Michael H.
Through The Doors Of Reason: Dissolving Four Paradoxes Of Education. Oliver, R Graham.
To Develop Autonomy: A Critique Of R F Dearden And Two Proposals. Quinn, Victor.
Towards A Concept Of Shared Autonomy. Bergsma, Jurrit.
When Meeting Needs Becomes A Threat To Autonomy. Summers, Jim.
When The Doctor And The Minister Disagree (Case Study With Commentaries). Weikart, Robert and Klar, Howard.
Why You Don't Owe It To Yourself To Seek Health. Gorovitz, Samuel.

AVANT GARDE

Myth, Philosophy, Avant–Gardism. Davydov, Yuri.

AVERROES

Algunos Aspectos De La Doctrina Tomista Del Entendimiento Posible. De Stier, Maria L.
Galileo's Lunar Observations In The Context Of Medieval Lunar Theory. Ariew, Roger.

AVERSION(S)

On The Risk–Aversion Comparability Of State–Dependent Utility Functions. Nordquist, Gerald L.

AVICENNA

"L'épître Sur La Connaissance De L'âme Rationnelle Et De Ses États" Attribuée À Avicenne. Michot, Jean.
Razón Y Revelación En El Islam. Guzmán, Roberto M.

AWARENESS

see also Consciousness
John Dewey's Theory Of Consciousness. Smith, Barry D.
On Russell's Rejection Of Akoluthic Sensations. Roberts, Joy H.
Overcoming Ethnocentrism In The Philosophy Classroom. Schutte, Ofelia.
Tsung–Mi And The Single Word "Awareness" (*chih*). Gregory, Peter N.

BEHAVIORISM

Language And Experience: Descriptions Of Living Language In Husserl And Wittgenstein. Reeder, Harry P.
"Drive": In Defense Of A Concept. Smith, Kendon.
A Widely Accepted But Nonetheless Astonishingly Flimsy Argument Against Analytical Behaviorism. Boyer, David L.
Action, Causality, And Teleological Explanation. Collins, Arthur.
Against Holism. Weir, Alan.
Background And Change In B F Skinner's Metatheory From 1930 To 1938. Coleman, S R.
Clark Hull, Robert Cummins, And Functional Analysis. Amundson, Ron and Smith, Laurence.
De Incommensurabiliteit Van Aanleg En Omgeving. Smit, Harry.
Emergent Behaviorism. Killeen, Peter R.
Gustav Bergmann's Psychophysiological Parallelism. Natsoulas, Thomas.
Is Consciousness Important? Wilkes, Kathleen V.
Logical Learning Theory: Kuhnian Anomaly Or Medievalism Revisited? Rychlak, Joseph R.
Man And Machine. Bandyopadhyay, Tirhanath.
On The Persistence Of Cognitive Explanation: Implications For Behavior Analysis. Pierce, W David and Epling, W Frank.
Psychology And Philosophical Anthropology: The Problem Of Their Interaction. Kozulin, Alex.
Simulation Research In The Analysis Of Behavior. Epstein, Robert.
Skinner On The "Mental And The "Physical". Schnaitter, Roger.
The Behaviorism Of A Phenomenologist: The Structure Of Behavior And The Concept Of Mind. Glenn, John D.
The Behaviourists' Struggle With Introspection. Lyons, William.
The Failure Of An *A Priori* Argument For Realism. Brueckner, Anthony L.

BEING

see also Dasein, Existence, Ontology
An Interpretation Of The Logic Of Hegel. Harris, Errol E.
Hegel's Logic. Hibben, John Grier.
Hegel's Logic: An Essay In Interpretation. Hibben, John G and Harris, H S (ed).
On The Essence Of Finite Being As Such, On The Existence Of That Essence And Their Distinction. Suárez, Francis.
On The Truth Of Being: Reflections On Heidegger's Later Philosophy. Kockelmans, Joseph J.
Phenomenology And Existentialism: An Introduction. Grossman, Reinhardt.
Principles Of Interpretation: Series In Continental Thought, V5. Ballard, Edward G.
The Metaphysical Foundations Of Logic, Michael Heim (trans). Heidegger, Martin.
The Multiple States Of Being. Guénon, René.
The New Image Of The Person: The Theory And Practice Of Clinical Philosophy. Koestenbaum, Peter.
The Question Of Play. Hyland, Drew A.
The Rhythm Of Being: A Study Of Temporality. Trivers, Howard.
Über Das Verhältnis Von Werner Marx Zu Martin Heidegger. Schoeller– Von Haslingen, Karin.
"Act, The Self–Revelation Of Being In St Thomas" in *History Of Philosophy In Making,* Thro, Linus J (ed), 63–80. Clarke, W Norris.
"Poetic Thinking To Be" in *Existential Coordinates Of Human Condition,* Tymieniecka, A (ed), 99–118. Adamczewski, Z.
"The Continuity Of Being: Chinese Visions Of Nature" in *On Nature,* Rouner, Leroy S (ed), 113–132. Wei– Ming, Tu.
"Why Be A Poet" in *Existential Coordinates Of Human Condition,* Tymieniecka, A (ed), 37–46. Bertelloni, Maria– Teresa.
Anatomia Del Potere: Dalla Logica Dell'Avere Alla Logica Dell'Essere. Nicolosi, Salavatore.
Aristotle On The Extension Of Non–Contradiction. Halper, Edward.
Art, Poetry, And The Sense Of Prevalence: Some Implications Of Buchler's Theory Of Poetry. Singer, Beth J.
Compagni Di Cammino: Heidegger E San Giovanni Della Croce. Pax, Clyde.
Concepto Communísimo Del Ente Y Nombres Divinos, Por José Hellín. Hellin, Jose.
Del Ente Participado Al Ser Imparticipado. Derisi, Octavio N.
Die Cartesianische Onto–Theo–Logie. Marion, Jean–Luc.
Die Seins– Und Erkenntnisfrage In Der Philosophie Brentanos. Melle, U.
Eine Betrachtung Über Das Problem Des Seins Und Der Schönheit In Der Philosophie Des Aristoteles (in Japanese). Fujita, Kazuyoshi.
El Concepto En La Fenomenología Del Espíritu. Vásquez, Eduardo.
El Ser En Domingo Báez, Por Eudaldo Forment Giralt. Giralt, Eudaldo F.
El Ser En El "Sistema De Identidad" Según Gustav Siewerth (Segunda Parte). Corona, Nester A.
Hölderlin E La *Vereinigungsphilosophie.* Gargano, Antonio.
Hedonic Pluralism. Goldstein, Irwin.
Heidegger's Overcoming Of Metaphysics: A Critique. Marsh, James L.
Homonimia Y Géneros Del Ser En Plotino. Santa Cruz, María I.
Il Problema Critico Della Conoscenza. Blandino, Giovanni.
Il Problema Critico. Iammarone, Luigi.
Is Aristotle A Metaphysician? Brogan, Walter.
Is There A Measure On Earth: A Discussion Of Werner Marx's 'Nonmetaphysiccl Ethics'. Krell, David Farrell.
Kosmische Technik Als Zuspruch Des Seins: Bemerkungen Zu W Schirmachers Weiterdenken Nach Heidegger. Rapp, Friedrich.
Las Tesis De C Fabro. Mendez, Julio Raul.
On Aristotle's Mind And Being. Broniak, Christopher.
On Confucian Jen And Heideggerian Being (II) (in Chinese). Chern, Jiunn–Huei.

Parmenides And Ultimate Reality. Austin, Scott.
St Thomas And The Integration Of Knowledge Into Being. Dewan, Lawrence.
The Number Of Being. Flower, Robert J.
Thomas Aquinas On The Distinction And Derivation Of The Many From The One: A Dialectic Between Being And Nonbeing. Wippel, John F.
Weiss On Adumbration. Wood, Robert.
Zum Problem Der Kehre Im Denken Heideggers. Rosales, Alberto.

BEING–IN–ITSELF

Being–In–Itself Revisited. Holmes, Richard.
Ser–En–sí Y Ser–Para–Otro. Walton, Roberto J.

BEING–IN–THE–WORLD

"Act Of Writing" in *Existential Coordinates Of Human Condition,* Tymieniecka, A (ed), 451–478. Garelli, Jacques.

BEITZ, C

Ideal And Non–Ideal Theory: How Should We Approach Questions Of Globel Justice. Nielsen, Kai.

BELIEF(S)

see also Faith
A Dissertation On Miracles. Campbell, George.
De Re Senses. Mc Dowell, John.
Inquiries Into Truth And Interpretation. Davidson, Donald.
Inquiry. Stalnaker, Robert C.
Methphysics: Its Structure And Function. Korner, Stephan.
On Certainty And Religious Belief. Martin, Dean.
Postures Of The Mind: Essays On Mind And Morals. Baier, Annette.
Rational Decision And Causality. Eells, Ellery.
William James On The Courage To Believe. O' Connell, Robert J.
"Armstrong On Belief" in *D M Armstrong,* Bogdan, Radu J (ed), 121–138. Stich, Stephen P.
"Theoretical Preliminaries To The Study Of Action" in *The Analysis Of Action,* Von Cranach, Mario (ed), 5–34. Harré, Rom.
A Critique Of Holyer's Volitionalism. Pojman, Louis P.
Ackerman On Propositional Identity. Bertolet, Rod.
An Argument That The Language Of Belief Is Not English. Hall, Richard J.
Augustine's *Confessions* As A Circular Journey. Leigh, David J.
Belief And Possibility. Altrichter, Ferenc.
Beliefs Essential In The Struggle For Peace And Development. Parsons, Howard L.
Beliefs, Dispositions And Demonstratives. Kraemer, Eric Russert.
Believing And Willing. Pojman, Louis P.
Can There Be An Infinite Regress Of Justified Beliefs? Harker, Jay E.
Cognition And Epistemic Closure. Bogdan, Radu J.
Contra Reliabilism. Ginet, Carl.
Creating Facts And Values. Putnam, Ruth Anna.
Croyances, Dispositions Et Probabilliés (Peirce Et Ramsey). Engel, Pascal.
Davidson's Theism? Foley, Richard and Fumerton, Richard.
Demonstratives And Belief States. Chien, A J.
Dissolving Kripke's Puzzle About Belief. Pettit, Philip.
Does Belief In God Need Proof? Robbins, J Wesley.
Epistemic Dependence. Hardwig, John.
Epistemic Supervenience And The Rule Of Belief. Van Cleve, James.
Ethical Realism Defended. Werner, Richard.
Evidentialism. Feldman, Richard and Conee, Earl.
Finocchiaro On Rational Explanation. Doppelt, Gerald.
Goede Redenen Om Iets Te Geloven. Derksen, A A.
Inaccessible Routes To The Problem Of Privileged Access. Schlesinger, George N.
Instinctive Beliefs. Davis, William H.
Interpreting Peirce. Grossman, Morris.
Is A Logic For Belief Sentences Possible? Green, Karen.
Is Knowledge Information–Produced Belief? Doyle, Anthony.
It's Not What You Know That Counts. Kaplan, Mark.
Justification And Truth. Cohen, Stewart.
Knowledge As Tracking? Schmitt, Frederick F.
Must The Description Of A Religion Be Acceptable To A Believer? Burke, T Patrick.
O'Hear On An Argument Of Popper's. Glassen, Peter.
On Explaining Beliefs. Koertge, Noretta.
Pierre And The New World Makers. Hall, Richard J.
Popper En Question. Reichberg, G.
Propositional Logic Based On The Dynamics Of Belief. Gardenfors, Peter.
Rationality And Psychological Explanation. Heil, John.
Refutation Of Dogmatism: Putnam's Brains In Vats. Feldman, Susan.
Reply To Peter Glassen's "O'Hear On An Argument Of Popper's". O' Hear, Anthony.
Representation And Explanation. Papineau, David.
Reviving The Isolation Argument. Rosenbaum, Stephen E.
Self–Control, Action, And Belief. Mele, Alfred R.
Speaking Of Belief. Zemach, Eddy M.
Swain On The Basing Relation. Kvanvig, Jonathan L.
The Availability Of Evidence In Support Of Religious Belief. Schlesinger, George N.
The Basis Of Belief: Philosophy, Science And Religion In Seventeenth–Century England. Rogers, G A J.
The Concept Of Rational Belief. Brandt, R B.
The Mapping Argument And Descartes' Deceitful Demon. Shirley, Edward S.
The Object Of Belief. Lepage, Francois.
The Reasonableness Of Agnosticism. Brinton, Alan.
The Umpire's Dilemma. Radford, Colin.
The Virtues Of Inconsistency. Klein, Peter.
Three Realist Claims. Ward, Andrew.

BELIEF(S)

Tractatus Sociologico–Philosophicus. Gellner, Ernest.

Traditional Epistemology And Naturalistic Replies To Its Skeptical Critics. Bogen, James.

Translucent Belief. Elgin, Catherine Z.

Unconscious Belief And Natural Theology. Holyer, Robert.

Voluntary Belief. Naylor, Margery Bedford.

What Is Virtuous About Faith? Muyskens, James.

What's In A Belief? Biro, J I.

What's The Matter With *The Matter Of Chance*? Burnor, Richard N.

Wilfred Cantwell Smith On Faith And Belief. Wainwright, William J.

Wittgenstein On The Phenomena Of Belief. Churchill, John.

BELIEVING

Chisholm, Deliberation, And The Free Acquisition Of Belief. Knaster, Stephen M.

How And Why Seeing Is Not Believing. Nelson, John O.

More On Self–Deception: Reply To Hellman. Bach, Kent.

True Believers And Radical Sceptics. Gallois, André.

BELINSKI

Gogol' In The Context Of Aesthetic Controversies (V G Belinskii's Polemic With Konstantin Aksakov). Mann, Iu V.

BELL'S THEOREM

Sailing Into The Charybdis: Van Fraassen On Bell's Theorem. Stairs, Allen.

BENACERRAF, P

Hypertasks. Clark, Peter and Read, Stephen.

McGinn On Benacerraf. Spinks, Graham.

The Philosopher Behind The Last Logicist. Weiner, Joan.

BENEFICIAL

Commentary On "Kicking Against The Pricks: Two Patients Wish To End Essential Insulin Treatments". Gillon, Raanan.

BENEFIT(S)

Benefit Rights In Education: An Entitlement View. Beversluis, Eric H.

BENJAMIN, W

Adorno. Jay, Martin.

"Immagine Mitica E Immagine Dialettica: Note Sul "Passagenwerk"" in *Il Tempo Dell'Arte*, Papi, Fulvio and others (ed), 127–138. Pezzella, Mario.

Messianic Time And Materialistic Progress. Hering, Christoph.

The Place Of The Work Of Art In The Age Of Technology. Wright, Kathleen.

BENN, S

Benn, Mackie And Basic Rights. Holborow, Les C.

The Informative And Persuasive Functions Of Advertising: A Moral Appraisal—A Comment. Emamalizadeh, Hossein.

BENTHAM

The Contemporary Significance Of Bentham's Anarchical Fallacies: A Reply To William Twining. Dalgarno, Melvin T.

The Contemporary Significance Of Bentham's Anarchical Fallacies. Twining, William.

Welfare State Versus Welfare Society? Skillen, Anthony.

BENTHAMISM

Imprisonment. O' Hear, Anthony.

BERGMANN, G

Gustav Bergmann's Psychophysiological Parallelism. Natsoulas, Thomas.

BERGSON

Creativity In American Philosophy. Hartshorne, Charles.

From Aristotle To Darwin And Back Again: A Journey In Final Causality, Species, And Evolution. Gilson, Etienne.

A Bergsonian View Of Agent–Causation. Sarnoff, Sigrid.

Bergson: Metafísica Del Arte. Carranza, Cristián Golcher.

Bergson's Philosophy Of Language (in Hebrew). Idan, Asher.

Habitual Body And Memory In Merleau–Ponty. Casey, Edward S.

Il Tempo Nel Pensiero Di Gaston Bachelard. Ventura, Antonino.

Origen Común Y Desarrollo Divergente En Bergson Y Ortega. Venegas, Juana Sanchez.

Why Is There Something Rather Than Nothing? Smith, Joseph Wayne.

William James And The Epochal Theory Of Time. Field, Richard W.

BERKA, K

Formal Axiomatic Systems And Dialectic And Materialist Way Of Thought (in Czechoslovakian). Kofátko, P.

Opposites And Time In The Logic Of Aristotle's Philosophy (in Czechoslovakian). Mráz, M.

Remarks Concerning The Problems Of Dialectical Logic (in Czechoslovakian). Zeman, J.

BERKELEY

Berkeley. Pitcher, George and Honderich, Ted (ed).

The Georgetown Symposium On Ethics. Porreco, Rocco (ed).

"An Idea Can Be Like Nothing But An Idea". Dicker, Georges.

"Berkeley And Hume: A Question Of Influence" in *Philosophy In History*, Rorty, Richard and others (ed), 303–328. Ayers, Michael.

"Our Non–Ethical Educational Ethos" in *The Georgetown Symposium On Ethics*, Porreco, Rocco (ed), 269–278. Young, Theodore A.

"Seven Thinkers And How They Grew" in *Philosophy In History*, Rorty, Richard and others (ed), 125–140. Kuklick, Bruce.

Adhering To Inherence: A New Look At The Old Steps In Berkeley's March To Idealism. Hausman, Alan.

Berkeley And Nieuwentijt On Infinitesimals. Vermeulen, Ben.

Berkeley On Volition, Power, And The Complexity Of Causation. Winkler, Kenneth P.

Berkeley, Epistemology, And Science. Steinkraus, Warren E.

Berkeley, Scientific Realism And Creation. Byrne, P A.

Berkeley: Inconsistencies And Common Sense. Lascola, Russell A.

Berkeley's Notions. Flage, Daniel E.

Dating Berkeley's Notebook B. Belfrage, Bertil.

Facts And Reasons Concerning Berkeley's Reprinted *Works*. Park, Désirée.

Facts Concerning Berkeley's Notebooks. Belfrage, Bertil.

Hume On The 'Distinction Of Reason'. Bracken, Harry M.

Kant On Space, Empirical Realism And The Foundations Of Geometry. Harper, William.

La Realidad En Kant Y Berkeley. Montero, Bernal Herrera.

Science, Design And The Science Of Signs. Terrell, Burnham.

The Authorship Of *Guardian* 69. Winkler, Kenneth P.

The Ideology Of Jacobitism On The Eve Of The Rising Of 1745—Part I. Mc Lynn, F J.

The Primary/Secondary Quality Distinction: Berkeley, Locke, And The Foundations Of Corpuscularian Science. Davidson, Arnold I and Hornstein, Norbert.

The Tree In The Quad. Fleming, Noel.

BERLIN, I

Berlin On Vico. Zagorin, Perez.

BERNAT

Thanatos And Euthanatos: Persons And Practical Policies. Smith, James Leroy.

BERNSTEIN, B

Soziolinguistische Codes Und Kategorischer Imperativ. Werner, H –J.

BETH, E

Intuitionistic Truth. Rabinowicz, Wlodzimierz.

BETTY, L

How Not To Criticize Nāgārjuna: A Response To L Stafford Betty. Loy, David.

BHAGAVAD GITA

Bhagavad–Gita: An Exegetical Commentary. Minor, Robert N.

Hindu Ethics. Singh, Balbir.

BHATTACHARYA, K

Svaraj In Ideas: Some Reflections. Goel, Dharmendra.

The Indian Tradition And Our Intellectual Task. Shah, K J.

BIAS(ES)

Ideology And Partiality In David Hume's "History Of England". Okie, Laird.

Prospects For Regional Philosophies In Australia. Sylvan, Richard.

BIBLE

A Book Of Jewish Ethical Concepts: Biblical And Postbiblical. Bloch, Abraham P.

Biathanatos, Ernest W Sullivan (ed). Donne, John.

Christian Biblical Ethics: From Biblical Revelation To Contemporary Christian Praxis: Method And Content. Daly, Robert J (ed).

"Buber And Modern Biblical Scholarship" in *Martin Buber*, Gordon, Haim (ed), 163–214. Uffenheimer, Benyamin.

"Cardinal Gibbons's Ignorance" in *Freedom, Feminism, And The State*, Mc Elroy, Wendy (ed), 305–310. Dietrick, Ellen Battelle.

"Hobbes And Skepticism" in *History Of Philosophy In Making*, Thro, Linus J (ed), 133–148. Popkin, Richard H.

"The Myth Of Man In The Hebraic Epic" in *Existential Coordinates Of Human Condition*, Tymieniecka, A (ed), 175–184. Famras– Rauch, Gila.

Biblia Y Vida Monástica En San Agustín. Veissmann, F.

Biblical Doctrine On The Rights And Duties Of Man. Ahern, Barnabas M.

Filone Di Alessandria Nella Interpretazione Di V Nikiprowetzky E Della Sua Scuola. Radice, Roberto.

Philosophy, Language And The Reform Of Public Worship. Warner, Martin.

Taxation In Biblical Israel. Oden Jr, Robert A.

BIBLIOGRAPHY

Bio–Bibliografia De La Filosofia En Chile Desde El Siglo XVI Hasta 1980. Pizarro, Fernando A (ed).

Catalogo Del Fondo Haller. Monti, Maria Teresa.

Edmund Burke: A Bibliography Of Secondary Studies To 1982. Gandy, Clara I and Stanlis, Peter J.

Ethics In Nursing: An Annotated Bibliography. Pence, Terry.

Gli Instituti Filosofici In Italia (1970–1980). Pasqualotto, Giangiorgio.

"Bibliography" in *History Of Philosophy In The Making*, Thro, Linus J (ed), 313–320. Rice, Lee C and others.

Bibliography Of Works In Philosophy Of History 1978–1982. David, Zdenek V and Strassfeld, Robert.

Contemporary British Philosophy: A Survey Of Developments Over The Last Three Decades. Hall, Roland.

Die Situation Der Philosophie In Brasilien. Martins, Estevão De Rezende.

El *Protréptico* De Aristóteles: Interpretación, Desarrollo Y Bibliografía. Buela, Alberto.

Italian Literature On Thomas Hobbes After The Second World War: Part I; 1946–1955. Felice, Domenico.

Le Lettere Di Croce A Gentile. Coli, Daniela.

Origine E Diffusione Del Calcolo Differenziale In Italia: Con Un'Appendice Di Lettere Inedite. Palladino, Franco.

Some Sources For A History Of English Socinianism; A Bibliography Of 17th Century English Socinian Writings. Bianchi, Daniela.

The Hume Literature Of The 1970's. Capaldi, Nicholas and King, James and Livingston, Donald.

BIBO, I

A Political Theorist From Eastern Europe. Tar, Zoltán.

BINSWANGER, L

Absent At The Creation: The Existential Psychiatry Of Ludwig Binswanger. Seidman, Bradley.

BUCHANAN, A
Fair Equality Of Opportunity And Decent Minimums: A Reply To Buchanan. Daniels, Norman.
BUCHANAN, J
Unanimity, Agreement, And Liberalism: A Critique Of James Buchanan's Social Philosophy. Barry, Norman P.
BUCHLER, J
Art, Poetry, And The Sense Of Prevalence: Some Implications Of Buchler's Theory Of Poetry. Singer, Beth J.
BUCKNER, D
Buckner Quoting Goldstein And Davidson On Quotation. Van Brackel, J.
BUDDHISM
Buddhist And Western Psychology. Katz, Nathan (ed).
Discipline: The Canonical Buddhism Of The Vinayapitaka. Holt, John C.
Human Rights In Religious Traditions. Swidler, Arlene (ed).
Oriental Philosophies. Koller, John M.
Studies In Indian Thought. Coward, Harold (ed).
Studies In Ch'an And Huy-Yen. Gimello, Robert M (ed) and Gregory, Peter N (ed).
"Buddhist Views Of Nature: Variations On The Theme Of Mother–Father Harmony" in *On Nature*, Rouner, Leroy S (ed), 96–112. Thurman, Robert A F.
A Critical Account Of Yang Kuei–Shan's Philosophical Thought (in Chinese). Chang, Jun–Chun.
Action And Suffering In The Theravadin Tradition. Smart, Ninian.
Beyond Process Theology? Sontag, Frederick.
Buddhism In Huxley's Evolution And Ethics. Rajapakse, Vijitha.
Chinese Buddhist Responses To Contemporary Problems. Yü, Chun–Fang.
Dharmakīrti On The Existence Of Other Minds. Sharma, Ramesh Kumar.
Dharmakīrti On Trairupya And Trirupa Linga. Bapat, Lata.
Entity And Antinomy In Tibetan Bsdus Grwa Logic (Part 1). Goldberg, Margaret.
Hedonism And Nirvana: Paradoxes, Dilemmas And Solutions. Herman, Arthur L.
How Not To Criticize Nāgārjuna: A Response To L Stafford Betty. Loy, David.
Hui–Neng And The Transcendental Standpoint. Laycock, Steven W.
Karma And Personal Identity: A Response To Professor White. Griffiths, Paul.
Nāgārjuna And The Naiyāyikas. Bronkhorst, Johannes.
Nāgārjuna's Catustava. Tola, Fernando.
Nāgārjuna And Zeno On Motion. Mabbett, I W.
Some Significant Contributions Of Buddhist Logicians In The Development Of Indian Philosophy. Gupta, Rita.
The Concept Of Language And The Use Of Paradox In Buddhism And Taoism. Ch'ien, Edward T.
Tsung–Mi And The Single Word "Awareness" (*chih*). Gregory, Peter N.
Two Strains In Buddhist Causality. Inada, Kenneth K.
Two Tibetan Texts On The "Neither One Nor Many" Argument For *Śūnyatā*. Tillemans, Tom J F.
Word Meaning, Sentence Menaing And Apoha. Siderits, Mark.
BULL, G
Some Sources For A History Of English Socinianism; A Bibliography Of 17th Century English Socinian Writings. Bianchi, Daniela.
BULLOUGH, E
A Note On Audience Participation And Psychical Distance. Lewis, Peter.
BULTMANN
Bultmann On The New Testament And Mythology. Smith, Joseph Wayne and Ward, Sharyn.
Bultmann's Criticisms Of Heidegger. Chryssides, George D.
New Testament Miracle Stories And Hellenistic Culture Of Late Antiquity. Lattke, Michael.
BUNDLE THEORY
Three Versions Of The Budles Theory. Van Cleve, James.
BUNGE, M
About Mario Bunge's 'A Critical Examination Of Dialectics'. Apostol, Pavel.
Normative Wissenschaft Mit Normen—Ohne Werte. Knapp, Hans Georg.
On Relevance Of M Bunge's Concept Of Difference In Meaning, Two Studies Of Inter–Theory Relations. Grobler, Adam.
The Middle Term Between Science And Scientific Metaphysics. Latuch, David Paul.
BURBIDGE, J
Metaphor, Analogy, And System: A Reply To Burbidge "Professor Burbidge Responds". Vaught, Carl G.
BUREAUCRACY(–CIES)
"Antigone's Daughters" in *Freedom, Feminism, And The State*, Mc Elroy, Wendy (ed), 61–76. Elshtain, Jean Bethke.
Presidential Address: For And Against Bureaucracy. Luebke, Neil.
BURGE, T
Fregean Thoughts. Noonan, Harold.
BURIDAN
John Buridan On Self–Reference: Chapter Eight Of Buridan's 'Sophismata'. Hughes, G E.
"Buridan's Ontology" in *How Things Are*, Bogen, James (ed), 189–204. Normore, Calvin.
Buridan On Interval Semantics For Temporal Logic. Ohrstrom, Peter.
BURKE
Edmund Burke: A Bibliography Of Secondary Studies To 1982. Gandy, Clara I and Stanlis, Peter J.
Edmund Burke Et Joseph De Maistre. Fuchs, Michel.
Le "Reflections On The Revolution In France": Categorie Dell'Agire Politico E Filosofia Della Storia In Edmund Burke. Panella, Giuseppe.

BURLEIGH, W
Supposition–Theory And The Problem Of Universals. Wagner, Michael F.
BURLEY, W
The Logic Of Disputation In Walter Burley's Treatise On Obligations. Stump, Eleonore.
BURY, A
Some Sources For A History Of English Socinianism; A Bibliography Of 17th Century English Socinian Writings. Bianchi, Daniela.
BUSINESS
"I Don't Have No Education" And Other Reflections. Chamberlin, Gordon J.
"The Profits Of Freedom: Investing In The Defense Of Business" in *On Freedom*, Howard, John A (ed), 59–78. Shenfield, Arthur.
Biotechnology And The Social Reconstruction Of Molecular Biology. Markle, Gerald E and Robin, Stanley S.
Commentary On "A Response To 'Is Business Bluffing Ethical'". Langley, Van E.
Corporate Control Through The Criminal System. Lansing, Paul and Hatfield, Donald. Okosophie. Kilga, Bernhard.
Public And Firm Interests In Public Service Diversifications. Fannin, William R and Gilmore, Carol B.
BUSINESS ETHICS
Collective And Corporate Responsibility. French, Peter A.
A Business Model Of Enlightenment. Barnett, John H.
A Quick Justification For Business Ethics. Lombardi, Louis G.
A Response To "Is Business Bluffing Ethical". Sullivan, Roger J.
A Suggested Approach To Linking Decision Styles With Business Ethics. Fleming, John E.
An Ethical Analysis Of Deception In Advertising. Carson, Thomas L and Wokutch, Richard E and Cox, James E.
Are Business Ethics And Engineering Ethics Members Of The Same Family? Bowie, Norman E.
Bluffing: Its Demise As A Subject Unto Itself. Beach, John.
Bribery. D' Andrade Jr, Kendall.
Business Ethics: Micro And Macro. Brummer, James.
Business Ethics, Interdisciplinarity And Higher Education. Madsen, Peter.
Business Ethics, Ideology, And The Naturalistic Fallacy. Goodpaster, Kenneth E.
Cognitive Development And Teaching Business Ethics. Cooper, David E.
Commentary On B Lichter And M Hodges' "Perceptions Of The Engineers' 'Professionalism' In The Chemical Industry". Gross, Milton S.
Commentary On "A Response To 'Is Business Bluffing Ethical'". Powell, Donald C.
Commentary On Danley's "Toward A Theory Of Bribery". D' Andrade, Kendall.
Commentary On K Alpern's "Moral Responsibility For Engineers". Oldenquist, Andrew.
Commentary On Daley's "Toward A Theory Of Bribery". Turow, Scott.
Commentary On K Alpern's "Moral Responsibility For Engineers". Florman, Samuel C.
Commentary On B Lichter And M Hodges' "Perceptions Of The Engineers' 'Professionalism' In The Chemical Industry". Nixon, Alan C.
Commentary On J Pichler's "The Liberty Principle: A Basis For Management Ethics". Mack, Eric.
Commentary On L Jung's "Commercialization And The Professions". Machan, Tibor R.
Commentary On J Pichler's "The Liberty Principle: A Basis For Management Ethics". Lehman, Elliot.
Commentary Upon 'Should Collective Bargaining And Labor Relations Be Less Advesarial'? Koehn, Donald R.
Commercialization And The Professions. Jung, L Shannon.
Conflict In The Workplace, And Its Resolution. Campbell, Keith.
Corporate Social Responsibility And Public Accountability. Filios, Vassilios P.
Correlates Of Salespeople's Ethical Conflict: An Exploratory Investigation. Dubinsky, Alan J and Ingram, Thomas N.
Defining 'Business Ethics': Like Nailing Jello To A Wall. Lewis, Phillip V.
Displaced Workers: America's Unpaid Debt. Byrne, Edmund F.
Do Corporations Have Moral Rights? Ozar, David T.
Enhancing Perceptions Of Auditor Independence. Pearson, Michael A.
Ethical Behavior In Business: A Hierarchical Approach From The Talmud. Friedman, Hershey H.
Ethical Dilemmas In Performance Appraisal. Banner, David K and Cooke, Robert Allan.
Ethics As An Integrating Force In Management. Pastin, Mark.
Ethics In Business Education: Working Toward A Meaningful Reciprocity. Hoffman, W Michael.
Laborem Exercens: A Theological And Philosophical Foundation For Business Ethics. Sullivan, Brian G.
Management And Ethical Decision–Making. Robinson, Wade L.
Management Priorities And Management Ethics. Longenecker, Justin G.
Management–Think. Pastin, Mark.
Managerial Ethics And Microeconomic Theory. Hosmer, Larue Tone.
Moral Fictions And Scientific Management. Santilli, Paul.
Moral Rules And Moral Ideals: A Useful Distinction In Business And Professional Practice. Hennessey, John W and Gert, Bernard.
Multinational Decision–Making: Reconciling International Norms. Donaldson, Thomas.
Organizational Dissidence: The Case Of Whistle–Blowing. Near, Janet P and Miceli, Marcia P.
Pluralism In The Mass Media: Can Management Help? Nielsen, Richard P.
Professionalism: Foundation For Business Ethics. Schaefer, Thomas E.
ROBOTS, RIFs, And Rights. Arthur, Alcott.
Situating The Employee Rights Debate. Kirby, Donald.

BUSINESS ETHICS

Social Systems Analytics And Ethics. Mulcahy, John W and Natale, Samuel M.

Team—Teaching With The Corporate Executive. Hiley, David and Layton, William.

The Contributions Of Religious Traditions To Business Ethics. Mc Mahon, Thomas F.

The Corporation And Individual Moral Agency. Camenisch, Paul F.

The Corporation, Its Members, And Moral Accountability. Meyers, Christopher.

The Employer—Employee Relationship And The Right To Know. Superson, Anita M.

The Future Of Business Ethics. Cooke, Robert Allan.

The Informative And Persuasive Functions Of Advertising: A Moral Appraisal—A Comment. Emamalizadeh, Hossein.

The International Infant Formula Controversy: A Dilemma In Corporate Social Responsibility. Baker, James C.

The Liberty Principle: A Basis For Management Ethics. Pichler, Joseph A.

The Other 338: Why A Majority Of Our Schools Of Business Administration Do Not Offer A Course In Business Ethics. Hosmer, Larue T.

Thomas Mann And The Business Ethic. Brennan Joseph G.

Thoughts On 'Management—Think'. Brenkert, George G.

Toward An Integrated Approach To Business Ethics. Goodpaster, Kenneth E.

Two Views Of Business Ethics: A Popular Philosophical Approach And A Value Based Interdisciplinary One. Klein, Sherwin.

What's Wrong With Bribery? Turow, Scott.

BUTCHVAROV, P

Material Identity And Sameness. Swindler, J K.

BUTLER

"The Collapse Of American Evangelical Academia" in *Faith And Rationality*, Plantinga, Alvin (ed), 219—264. Marsden, George.

BUYTENDIJK, F

Merleau—Ponty En Buytendijk: Relaas Van Een Relatie. Boudier, C E M Struyker.

BYZANTINE

Relativism And Pictorial Realism. Grigg, Robert.

CALCULUS

"Consistency Tests In Estimating The Completeness Of The Fossil Record" in *Testing Scientific Theories*, Earman, John (ed), 413—476. Meehl, Paul E.

Berkeley And Nieuwentijt On Infinitesimals. Vermeulen, Ben.

La Manière Exacte Dont Leibniz A Inventé L'intégration Par Sommation. Violette, R.

On The Consistency Of A Three—Valued Logical Calculus. Bochvar, D A.

Origine E Diffusione Del Calcolo Differenziale In Italia: Con Un'Appendice Di Lettere Inedite. Palladino, Franco.

The Calculus Of Moral Obligation. Mc Guire, Martin C.

Zur Entstehung Und Begründung Des Newtonschen Calculus Fluxionum Und Des Leibnizschen Calculus Differentialis. Stiegler, Karl D.

CALHOUN, J

Taylor, Calhoun, And The Decline Of A Theory Of Political Disharmony. Harp, Gillis J.

CALLIGRAPHY

Theories Of The Arts In China. Bush, Susan (ed) and Murck, Christian (ed).

CALMAN, K

Quality Of Life—A Response To K C Calman. Cribb, Alan.

CALVIN

Taxation In The History Of Protestant Ethics. Shriver, Donald W and Knox, E Richard.

CALVINISM

The Catholic And The Calvinist: A Dialogue On Faith And Reason. Gutting, Gary.

CAMBRIDGE PLATONISTS

Platonism's Inference From Logic To God. Peikoff, Leonard.

CAMPBELL, D

The Relation Between Epistemology And Psychology. Goldman, Alvin I.

CAMPBELL, G

Campbell, Vico, And The Rhetorical Science Of Human Nature. Bevilacqua, Vincent M.

CAMUS

Langage Du Pouvoir, Pouvoir Du Langage, Ou La Narration À La Première Personne Dans *La Chute* D'Albert Camus. Cliche, Elaine.

Play And The Absurd. Feezell, Randolph.

CAN

'Ought To Have' And 'Could Have'. Sinnott— Armstrong, Walter.

Cans, Advantages, And Possible Worlds. Walton, Douglas N.

CANADIAN

The Contemporary Status Of Continental Philosophy In Canada: A Narrative. Madison, Gary B.

CANCER

Cancer And The Development Of Will. Rijke, R P C.

Quality Of Life In Cancer Patients—A Hypothesis. Calman, K C.

CANETTI

"Canetti E La Metafisica Involontaria" in *Il Tempo Dell'Arte*, Papi, Fulvio and others (ed), 139—155. Papi, Fulvio.

CANON(S)

Bergson's Philosophy Of Language (in Hebrew). Idan, Asher.

CANON LAW

The Western Case Against Usury. Gottfried, Paul E.

CANTOR

Cantorian Set Theory And Limitation Of Size. Hallett, Michael.

Beyond First—order Logic: The Historical Interplay Between Mathematical Logic And Axiomatic Set Theory. Moore, Gregory H.

Georg Cantor's Influence On Bertrand Russell. Grattan— Guiness, I.

Set Theories: Their Philosophic Issues And Foundations (in Chinese). Hung, Cheng—Uan and Liu, Fu—tseng.

There Is No Set Of All Truths. Grim, Patrick.

CAPEK, J

The Painter Otakar Marvánek As Art Critic (in Czechoslovakian). Ondracka, Pavel.

CAPITAL

Max, The Cynic (in Portuguese). Moraes, Reginaldo C C.

CAPITALISM

Arguing For Socialism: Theoretical Considerations. Levine, Andrew.

Contradictions Of The Welfare State, John Keane (ed). Offe, Claus.

John Locke And Agrarian Capitalism. Wood, Neal.

Marx's Economics. Junankar, P N.

"Are Feminist Businesses Capitalistic" in *Freedom, Feminism, And The State*, Mc Elroy, Wendy (ed), 207—212. Nichols, Rosalie.

"Catharsis Or Kitsch" in *Continental Philosophy And The Arts*, Winters, Laurence E and others (ed), 193—218. Hermann, Istvan.

Bedingungen Und Merkmale Des Klassenkampfes In Den Kapitalistischen Ländern Europas. Beyer, Hans.

Capitalism At Risk: The Political Economy Of The Educational Reports Of 1983. Shapiro, H Svi.

Capitalists And The Ethics Of Contribution. Arnold, N Scott.

Das Eigentum Als Eschatologische Potenz: Zur Eigentumskonzeption Von Karl Marx. Künzli, Arnold.

Democratic Capitalism: Developing A Conscience For The Corporation. Grcic, Joseph M.

Die Reaktionäre Marxkritik Nach Dem Gothaer Programm Der Deutschen Sozialdemokratie. Kopf, Eike.

Doing Marx Justice. Young, Gary.

Eigentum Und Macht In Der Modernen Industriegesellschaft. Levy, René.

Eigentum Und Verfügungsmacht: Zum Korporativen Eigentum. Bornschier, Volker.

Exemplarische Bronnen Van Het Westers Autonomie—Begrip. Nauta, L W.

Global Justice, Capitalism And The Third World. Nielsen, Kai.

Human Rights And International Finance: A Synthetical Overview. Khoshkish, A.

Ideology, Class, And The Autonomy Of The Capitalist State: The Petit—Bourgeois' World View And Schooling. Shapiro, H Svi.

Keynes Versus Hayek: Interne En Externe Factoren In Een Controverse In De Economie. Birner, Jack.

Marx And Engels On The Distributive Justice Of Capitalism. Allen, Derek P H.

Marx's Critique Of Capitalist Technology: Form And Content. Rehg, William R.

Marxism And The Transition Problem. Ross, Howard.

Marxism, Morality And Ideology. Kellner, Douglas M.

On DiQuattro, "Rawls And Left Criticism". Connin, Lawrence J.

The Controversy About Marx And Justice. Geras, Norman.

The French Revolution And Capitalism: An Explanatory Schema. Wallerstein, Immanuel.

The Marxian Ideal Of Freedom And The Problem Of Justice. Van Der Veen, Robert J.

The Marxian Critique Of Justice And Rights. Buchanan, Allen E.

Values And Socialism: An Axiological Approach To Marx's Socialism. Siewierski, Jacenty.

Whitehead And Marx: Toward A Political Metaphysics. Marsh, James L and Hamrick, William S.

CARDINALITY

A New Proof For Craig's Theorem. Bellot, P.

CARDINALS

Progress In Utility And Risk Theory. Hagen, Ole (ed) and Wenstop, Fred (ed).

"Precipitousness Of Ideal Of Thin Sets On Measurable Cardinal" in *Lecture Notes In Mathematics*, Muller, G H And Others (ed), 49—56. Kakuda, Yuzuru.

An AD—like Model. Apter, Arthur W.

Cancellation Laws For Surjective Cardinals. Truss, J K.

Co—Critical Points Of Elementary Embeddings. Sheard, Michael.

Complexity Of κ—Ultrafilters And Inner Models With Measurable Cardinals. Sureson, Claude.

Diamonds, Uniformization. Shelah, Saharon.

Forcing The Failure Of CH By Adding A Real. Shelah, Saharon and Woodin, Hugh.

Georg Cantor's Influence On Bertrand Russell. Grattan— Guiness, I.

Non—closure Of The Image Model And Absence Of Fixed Points. Sureson, Claude.

On The Ultrafilters And Ultrapowers Of Strong Partition Cardinals. Henle, J M and Kleinberg, E M and Watro, R J.

On Violating The GCH Below The Least Measurable Cardinal. Pelletier, D H.

P—Points And Q—Points Over A Measurable Cardinal. Sureson, C.

Strongly Compact Cardinals, Elementary Embeddings And Fixed Points. Abe, Yoshihiro.

The Cardinality Of The Set Of Dedekind Finite Cardinals In Fraenkel—Mostowski Models. Rubin, Arthur L and Rubin, Jean E.

The Consistency Strength Of The Free—Subset Property Of Ω_ω. Koepke, Peter.

The Consistency Of The Axiom Of Universality For The Ordering Of Cardinalities. Forti, Marco and Honsell, Furio.

The First—Order Theory Of The c—Degrees. Farrington, Paddy.

Vopenka's Principle And Compact Logics. Makowsky, J A.

Weakly Compact Cardinals In Models Of Set Theory. Enayat, Ali.

CARE

Care: The Essence Of Nursing And Health. Leininger, Madeleine M.

In Pursuit Of Wholeness: Moral Development, The Ethics Of Care And The Virtue Of *Philia*. Prakash, Madhu Suri.

On Removing Food & Water: Against The Stream. Meilaender, Gilbert.

CLASSIFICATION
Case For Common Sense. Atran, Scott.
Primitive Classification And The Sociology Of Knowledge: A Response To Bloor. Smith, Joseph Wayne.

CLAUDEL, P
"The Birth Of Tragedy Out Of The Spirit Of Music" in *Existential Coordinates Of Human Condition*, Tymieniecka, A (ed), 273–294. Kronegger, Marlies.

CLEITOPHON
The Riddle Of The *Cleitophon*. Roochnik, David L.

CLIENT(S)
Lawyer–Client Confidences Under The A B A Model Rules: Ethical Rules Without Ethical Reason. Freedman, Monroe H.

CLINICAL PSYCHOLOGY
The New Image Of The Person: The Theory And Practice Of Clinical Philosophy. Koestenbaum, Peter.

CLOSURE
"Kant, Closure, And Causality" in *Kant On Causality, Freedom, And Objectivity*, Harper, William A (ed), 66–82. Brittan Jr, Gordon G.
A Conjunction In Closure Spaces. Jankowski, Andrzej W.
Abstraction And Definability In Semantically Closed Structures. Mc Carthy, Timothy.
Non–closure Of The Image Model And Absence Of Fixed Points. Sureson, Claude.
Polysemantic Structure And Semantic Closedness Of Natural Languages. Djankov, Bogdan.
Semantic Closure. Priest, Graham.

COALITION(S)
Solzhenitsyn And Yanov. Boldyrev, Peter and Vertlieb, E.
The Stability Of Bargains Behind The Veil Of Ignorance. Gaa, James C.

COBB, J
Beyond Process Theology? Sontag, Frederick.

CODE(S)
"Approaches To Ethical Problems By Archaeological Organizations" in *Ethics And Values In Archaeology*, Green, Ernestene L (ed), 13–21. Davis, Hester A.
Commentary On "Advertising Professional Success Rates". Clancy, Katherine L.
Soziolinguistische Codes Und Kategorischer Imperativ. Werner, H–J.

CODE OF CONDUCT
A Duty To Warn, An Uncertain Danger. Reamer, Frederic G and Schaffer, Sylvan J.
Are Business Ethics And Engineering Ethics Members Of The Same Family? Bowie, Norman E.

COERCION
Coercion, Deterrence, And Authority. Airaksinen, Timo.

COEXISTENCE
Friedenskampf Und Philosophie. Buhr, Manfred.
Peaceful Coexistence As The Nuclear Traumatization Of Humanity. Butler, Clark.

COGITO
'Si Fallor, Sum' Revisited. Coughlan, M J.
Cogito, Ergo Sum: Inference And Performance. Reeder, Harry.
Descartes' *Cogito*. Flage, Daniel E.
Descartes' 'Demonstrations' Of His Existence. Tweyman, Stanley.
Genealogisches Zum Cogito: Über Ein Motiv Des Cartesischen Denkens. Dörr, Hartmut.
Kant's Cogito. Patten, St C.
La Pensée De Gabriel Marcel. Ricoeur, M Paul.

COGNITION
see also Knowing, Thinking
Logic And The Objectivity Of Knowledge: Studies In Husserl's Early Philosophy. Willard, Dallas.
Methphysics: Its Structure And Function. Korner, Stephan.
Morality In The Making. Weinreich Haste, Helen (ed) and Locke, Don (ed).
Mutual Knowledge. Smith, N V (ed).
Piaget's Logic: A Critique Of Genetic Epistemology. Seltman, Muriel and Seltman, Peter.
Sense And Content: Experience, Thought, And Their Relations. Peacocke, Christopher.
Talking Minds: The Study Of Language In The Cognitive Sciences. Bever, Thomas G (ed) and Carroll, John M (ed) and Miller, Lance A (ed).
The Limits Of Scientific Reasoning. Faust, David.
The Limits Of Science. Rescher, Nicholas.
Treatise On Basic Philosophy, V5. Bunge, Mario.
"Cognitive Change In Technology And Science" in *Technological Knowledge*, Laudan, Rachel (ed), 83–104. Laudan, Rachel.
"Duns Scotus On Intuition, Memory And Knowledge Of Individuals" in *History Of Philosophy In Making*, Thro, Linus J (ed), 81–104. Wolter, Allan B.
About Being A Bat. Maloney, J Christopher.
Artificial Intelligence And The Problem Solving Theory (in Portuguese). Teixiera, João De F.
Cognition And Epistemic Closure. Bogdan, Radu J.
Cognitive Intuition Of Singulars Revisited (Matthew Of Aquaparta Versus B J F Lonergan). Payne, Gordon R.
Conceptual Progress And Word/World Relations: In Search Of The Essence Of Natural Kinds. Churchland, Paul M.
Culture, Cognition And Communication. Yoshikawa, M J.
Descartes' *Cogito*. Flage, Daniel E.
Descartes' Proto–Critique. Glouberman, M.
Descartes's Meditations As Cognitive Exercises. Hatfield, Gary.
Engels' "Dialektik Der Natur" Und Die Einheit Der Naturwissenschaftlichen Erkenntnis.

Korch, Helmut and Ennuschat, W.
Erkenntnis Und Bewusste Gestaltung Sozialer Prozesse. Winzer, Rosemarie.
Evolutionary Epistemology And Ontological Realism. Clark, A J.
Hume And The Missing Shade Of Blue. Fogelin, Robert J.
Intuitive Cognition And The Philosophy Of God (in Polish). Kowalczyk, Stanislaw.
Mending Wall: Response To David Ericson's "Emotion And Action In Cognitive Psychology". De Nicola, Daniel R.
Philosophy's Relevance To Technical Writing. Girill, T R.
Simulation Research In The Analysis Of Behavior. Epstein, Robert.
The Cognition Of Indivisibles And The Argument Of De Anima. Pritzl, Kurt.
The Sources Of Intuitive Cognition In William Of Ockham. Wengert, Robert G.
Wittgenstein's Language–Games And The Call To Cognition. Deizt, Samuel M and Arrington, Robert L.

COGNITIVE
Dialogues With Children. Matthews, Gareth B.
"Decidability In Carnap" in *Philosophical Analysis In Latin America*, Gracia, Jorge J E and others (eds), 313–338. Loparić, Zeljko.
"Metaphor As Synergy" in *Metaphor*, Miall, David S (ed), 55–70. Apter, Michael.
Coercion And The Authority Of Reason. Churchill, John.
Hume And Cognitive Science. Biro, J I.
Representation And Explanation. Papineau, David.

COGNITIVISM
A Comment On Ken Westphal's "Nietzsche's Sting And The Possibility Of Good Philology". Zimmerman, R I.
Nietzsche's Sting And The Possibility Of Good Philology. Westphal, Kenneth.
On The Persistence Of Cognitive Explanation: Implications For Behavior Analysis. Pierce, W David and Epling, W Frank.
The Cognitive Status Of Religious Belief. Wiebe, Donald.
The Methodological Imperative In Psychology. Danziger, Kurt.
Was Nietzsche A Cognitivist? Westphal, Kenneth.
Wittgenstein's Rejection Of Scientific Psychology. Williams, Meredith.

COHEN, G
Cohen On Proletarian Unfreedom. Brenkert, George G.
Forces Of Production And Social Primacy. Gottlieb, Roger S.

COHEN, L
Could Man Be An Irrational Animal: Some Notes On The Epistemology Of Rationality. Stich, Stephen P.

COHERENCE
Epistemic Analysis: A Coherence Theory Of Knowledge. Ziff, Paul.
A Metacompleteness Theorem For Contraction–Free Relevant Logics. Slaney, John K.
Brains In Vats And The Internalist Perspective. Stephens, James and Russow, Lilly-marlene.
Calibration, Coherence, And Scoring Rules. Seidenfeld, Teddy.
Links, Loops, And The Global Structure Of Science. Moulines, C Ulises.
Nicholas Rescher On Hypothetical Reasoning And The Coherence Of Systems Of Knowledge. Moutafakis, Nicholas J.
On Coherence Theories Of Justification: Can An Empiricist Be A Coherentist? Dancy, Jonathan.
Prolegomena To Discourse–Pragmatics. Givón, T.
Reviving The Isolation Argument. Rosenbaum, Stephen E.
The Coherence Of Virtue And The Virtue Of Coherence: Justification In Epistemology. Sosa, Ernest.
The Preservation Of Coherence. Jennings, R E and Schotch, P K.
The Role Of Coherence In Legal Reasoning. Levenbook, Barbara Baum.
Truth As Ideal Coherence. Rescher, Nicholas.

COHESION
Public Education And Social Harmony: The Roots Of An American Dream. Mc Clellan, B Edward.

COIMBRA, L
Notas Históricas E Filosóficas Sobre O Conhecimento. De Soveral, Eduardo Abranches.

COLBECK, J
Sameness And Equality: A Rejoinder To John Colbeck's Response To "Procrustes And Private Schooling". Shaw, Beverley.

COLBY, A
Current Research In Moral Development As A Decision Support System. Penn, William Y and Collier, Boyd D.

COLD WAR
The Representation And Resolution Of The Nuclear Conflict. Anderson, Lyle V.

COLEMAN, J
Law, Economics, And Philosophy. Kuperberg, Mark (ed) and Beitz, Charles (ed).
Negative Positivism And The Hard Facts Of Life. Silver, Charles.

COLERIDGE
Coleridge's Philosophical And Theological Thinking And Its Significance For Today. Roberts, Martin.

COLLECTION(S)
That Most Subtle Question (Quaestio Subtilissima). Henry, Desmond Paul.
Collections And Collectors. Ergmann, Raoul.

COLLECTIVE(S)
A Theory Of Social Action. Tuomela, Raimo.
Collective And Corporate Responsibility. French, Peter A.
What Collectives Are: Agency, Individualism And Legal Theory. Copp, David.

COLLECTIVE BARGAINING
Commentary Upon 'Should Collective Bargaining And Labor Relations Be Less Adversarial'? Koehn, Donald R.

COLLECTIVE BARGAINING

Should Collective Bargaining And Labor Relations Be Less Adversarial? Bowie, Norman E.

Situating The Employee Rights Debate. Kirby, Donald.

COLLECTIVE CONSCIOUSNESS

"Toward A Pedagogy Of The Useful Past For Teacher Preparation": A Reaction. Gutek, Gerald L.

COLLECTIVISM

Die Kategorie Der Sache. Nef, Robert.

Genossenschaftsbauern Und Dorf Improzek Der Sozialistischen Intensivierung. Krambach, K.

Kollektive Meinung Und Individuelles Leistungsverhalten Im Socialismus. Dresler, Peter.

COLLIER, J

Discussion: What Would Happen If Everyone Did It? Sober, Elliott.

COLLINGWOOD

Logic, Philosophy, And History: A Study In The Philosophy Of History Based On The Work Of R G Collingwood. Russell, Anthony F.

The Magdalen Metaphysicals: Idealism And Orthodoxy At Oxford, 1901–1945. Patrick, James.

Art And Goodness: Collingwood's Aesthetics And Moore's Ethics Compared. Diffey, T J.

Gadamer's Criticisms Of Collingwood. Bertoldi, E F.

History And Reality: R G Collingwood's Theory Of Absolute Presuppositions. Trainor, Paul J.

How To Be An Idealist (II). Mc Fee, Graham.

Vico And Collingwood On 'The Conceit Of Scholars'. Todd, Joan and Cono, Joseph.

COLLINS, J

History Of Philosophy In The Making. Thro, Linus J (ed).

"Bibliography" in *History Of Philosophy In The Making*, Thro, Linus J (ed), 313–320. Rice, Lee C and others.

"Collins And Gadamer On Interpretation" in *History Of Philosophy In The Making*, Thro, Linus J (ed), 231–246. Marsh, James L.

"Introductory: James Collins—The Man, The Scholar, The Teacher" in *History Of Philosophy In Making*, Thro, Linus J (ed), 1–18. Murray, John Patrick and others and Dahlstrom, Daniel O.

"Religion Within The Scope Of Philosophy" in *History Of Philosophy In The Making*, Thro, Linus J (ed), 247–254. Smith, John E.

COLOR

Are 'Scientific' Objects Coloured? Hardin, C L.

Color And The Anthropocentric Problem. Averill, Edward Wilson.

The Complexity Of Quality. Westphal, Jonathan.

The Resemblances Of Colors. Hardin, C L.

COMBINATORICS

"Boolean Valued Combinatorics" in *Lecture Notes In Mathematics*, Muller, G H And Others (ed), 117–154. Namba, Kanji.

Almost Disjoint Families Of Representing Sets. Balanda, Kevin P.

An Undecidable Problem In Finite Combinatorics. Compton, Kevin J.

Sets Derived By Deterministic Systems With Axiom. Hughes, Charles E.

Simplified Morasses With Linear Limits. Velleman, Dan.

COMBINATORY LOGIC

A New Proof For Craig's Theorem. Bellot, P.

Conjunction Without Conditions In Illative Combinatory Logic. Bunder, M W.

COMEDY

"Tragical, Comical, Historical" in *Existential Coordinates Of Human Condition*, Tymieniecka, A (ed), 379–400. Platt, Michael.

Descartes's Comedy. Rée, Jonathan.

Getting To Know You. Shiner, Roger A.

Recherches Et Réflexions Sur Le Rire Le Risible, Le Comique Et L'humour. Fourastié, M Jean and others.

The Idea Of The Comic. Armstrong, A M.

COMIC

Giulio Augusto Levi E La "Scienza Del Comico". Cavaglion, Alberto.

COMMAND(S)

Clark On God's Law And Morality. Chandler, John.

Gedankliche Systeme Mit Aufforderungscharakter. Heitsch, Wolfram.

COMMENSURABILITY

Psychology And Philosophical Anthropology: The Problem Of Their Interaction. Kozulin, Alex.

COMMENTARY(–RIES)

Parmenides Of Elea: Fragments. Gallop, David.

COMMERCE

A Pamphlet Attributed To John Toland And An Unpublished Reply By Archbishop William King. Kelly, Patrick.

Commercialization And The Professions. Jung, L Shannon.

Freedom Of Expression In Commerce. Machina, Kenton F.

COMMITMENT(S)

Thoughts On The Moral Relationship Of Intent And Training In Sport. Thomas, Carolyn E.

COMMON GOOD

Elementos De Filosofia Politica No Concilio Vaticano II. Borges, J F Pereira.

The Problem Of The Common Good In Saint Augustine's *Civitas Terrena*. Lavere, George J.

COMMON SENSE

La Gnoseologia Di George E Moore. Borioni, Marco.

"Natural Conjectures" in *Philosophical Analysis In Latin America*, Gracia, Jorge J E and others (eds), 339–364. Monteiro, Joao Paulo.

"Philosophy, Common Sense, And Science" in *Philosophical Analysis In Latin America*, Gracia, Jorge J E and others (eds), 285–312. Dascal, Marcelo.

Berkeley: Inconsistencies And Common Sense. Lascola, Russell A.

Common Sense: Who Can Deny It? Govier, Trudy.

Einige Bemerkungen Zur Struktur Des Alltagsdenkens. Trader, Wilfried.

One World Or Many: Popper's Three World Theory And The Problem Of Scientific Determinism. Baigrie, Brian.

Science And Common Sense. Jason, Gary J.

Sir William Hamilton, Critical Philosophy, And The Commonsense Tradition. Madden, Edward H.

Towards An Exact Philosophy Of Action. Segerberg, Krister.

COMMUNICATION

Boston Studies In The Philosophy Of Science: Dialectical Theory Of Meaning, R S Cohen And M W Wartofsky (eds) V81. Markovic, Mihailo.

Inquiries Into Truth And Interpretation. Davidson, Donald.

The Theory Of Communicative Action: Reason And The Rationalization Of Society, V1. Habermas, Jurgen and Mc Carthy, Thomas (trans).

Treatise On Basic Philosophy, V5. Bunge, Mario.

'Communicative Competence' And The Skeptic. Beatty, Joseph.

"Communicative Acts And Extralinguistic Knowledge" in *The Analysis Of Action*, Von Cranach, Mario (ed), 267–308. Kreckel, Marga.

"Habermas, Eurocommunism, & Theory Of Communication" in *Continuity And Change In Marxism*, Fischer, Norman And Others (ed), 131–143. Flay, Joseph C.

A Comment On Performative, Subject, And Proposition In Habermas's Theory Of Communication. Skjei, Erling.

Communicative Reference: An Inferential Model. Harnish, Robert M.

Creating A Candid Corporate Culture. Serpa, Roy.

Critical Thinking In The Electronic Era. Postman, Neil.

Culture, Cognition And Communication. Yoshikawa, M J.

Dialectical Fields And Transformations: Brouwer–Fields, Beth–Fields, And Naess–Transformations. Barth, E M.

El Cuerpo Como Lenguaje, Expresion Y Comunicacion. Rovaletti, Maria L.

Karl Rahner's Conception Of God's Self–Communication To Man. Cawte, John.

Kierkegaard, Indirect Communication, And Religious Truth. Kellenberger, J.

New Directions In The Logic Of Dialogue. Walton, Douglas N.

On Defining Information. Szaniawski, Klemens.

On The Principle Of Information Retention. Hilpinen, Risto.

Reply To Skjei's "A Comment On Performative, Subject, And Proposition In Habermas's Theory Of Communication". Habermas, Jurgen.

Saying And Conveying. Sainsbury, Mark.

Theory Dynamics And Knowledge Representation From An Information–Theoretical Point Of View. Hauffe, Heinz.

Towards One Type Of Non–Artistic Expression And Communication (in Czechoslovakian). Pospisil, Zdenek.

Zwischen Einsamkeit Und Wechselrede: Zur Kommunikation Und Ihrer Konstitution Bei Edmund Husserl. Knoblauch, Hubert.

COMMUNISM

see also Historical Materialism, Leninism, Marxism

How Democracies Perish. Revel, Jean–François.

Red Emma Speaks: An Emma Goldman Reader. Shulman, Alix Kates (ed).

'Romania's Marx' And The National Question: Constantin Dobrogeanu–Gherea. Shafir, Michael.

"Gramsci And Eurocommunism" in *Continuity And Change In Marxism*, Fischer, Norman And Others (ed), 189–210. Boggs, Carl.

A Political Theorist From Eastern Europe. Tar, Zoltán.

Das Ökonomische Grundgesetz Der Kommunistischen Gesellschaftsformation Und Einige Philosophische Probleme. Leisering, Heinz.

Der Atheistische Charakter Der Marxistisch–Leninistischen Philosophie Und Weltanschauung. Klohr, Olof and Handel, G.

Der Kampf Der KPD Gegen Die Ideologie Des Hitlerfaschismus. Ullrich, Horst.

Die Reaktionäre Marxkritik Nach Dem Gothaer Programm Der Deutschen Sozialdemokratie. Kopf, Eike.

Die Sowjetische Hilfe Für Die Entwicklung Der Marxistisch–Leninistischen Philosophie An Den Universitäten (1945–1949). Handel, Gottfried.

Die Weltgeschichtliche Bedeutung Des Sieges Der Sowjetunion Im Grossen Vaterländischen Krieg Im Lichte Des Leninismus. Uhlig, Dieter.

Erfahrungen Aus Der Arbeit Am Lehrbuch "Wissenschaftlicher Kommunismus". Grosser, Gunther.

Kommunisten Und Christen Gemeinsam Im Kampf Um Den Frieden. Kliem, Wolfgang.

Leninism And The Enlightenment. Moran, Philip.

More's *Utopia* And The New World Utopias: Is The Good Life An Easy Life? Dooley, Patrick K.

Owen's Communism And The Neo–Left–Wing Reconstruction Of History; War And Peace In The Ideological Confrontation (in German). Jauch, Liane.

Politologie Und Political Science In Den USA. Lowe, Bernd P.

Several Issues Concerning The Theory Of Human Beings. Tongsen, Huang.

The Dialectics Of Subjectivity. Ochocki, Aleksander.

The Nature Of Liberal Civilization. Hook, Sidney and Russell, Bertrand.

The Relation Of Theory And Practice In The Process Of Formation And Action Of Laws Of Communist Socio–Economic Formation (in Czechoslovakian). Kroh, Michael.

The Young Mao—A Soviet Portrait. Krancberg, Sigmund.

COMMUNISM

Weltanschauung Und Klassenbewusstsein In Marx' Kritik Am Gothaer Programm. Finger, Otto.

Zum Platz Der "Randglossen" In Der Geschichte Der Theorie Des Wissenschaftlichen Kommunismus. Fieber, Hans–Joachim and Schneider, W.

COMMUNITARIANISM

Relation—The Ultimate Reality And Human Praxis Of Togetherness: On The Meaning Of The Kibbutz, The Israeli Co–Relational Community. Barzel, Alexander.

COMMUNITY(–TIES)

Community As A Social Ideal. Kamenka, Eugene (ed).

"Communities And Hierarchies: Structure In The Practice Of Science And Technology" in *Technological Knowledge*, Laudan, Rachel (ed), 27–46. Constant, Edward W.

"Political Community And Individual Freedom In Hegel's Philosophy" in *The State And Civil Society*, Pelczynski, Z A (ed), 55–76. Pelczynski, Z A.

A Note On Motivation And Future Generations. Mackenzie, Michael.

Comments On A S Cua's "Confucian Vision And Human Community". Smith, John.

Confucian Vision And Human Community. Cua, Antonio S.

Ethical Theory In The Twenty–First Century. Bayles, Michael D.

Heidegger's Contribution To Modern Political Thought. Dauenhauer, Bernard P.

Individual And Community: An American View. Kegley, Jacquelyn A K.

On Professor Kegley's "Individual And Community". Cheng, Chung–Ying.

Organism, Community, And The "Substitution Problem". Katz, Eric.

The Elements Of Character. Bondi, Richard.

The Great Republic. Heller, Agnes.

The Learning Community: A Response. Giarelli, James M.

The Learning Community. Benne, Kenneth D.

COMMUNITY LIVING

Relation—The Ultimate Reality And Human Praxis Of Togetherness: On The Meaning Of The Kibbutz, The Israeli Co–Relational Community. Barzel, Alexander.

COMMUTATIVE JUSTICE

Social Justice And Legal Justice. Sadurski, Wojciech.

COMPACTNESS

A Note On The Compactness Theorem. Gill, R R Rockingham.

Carnapian Extensions Of S5. Hendry, Herbert E and Pokriefka, M L.

Compactness And Recursive Enumerability In Intensional Logic. Stephan, Bernd J.

Vopenka's Principle And Compact Logics. Makowsky, J A.

Weakly Compact Cardinals In Models Of Set Theory. Enayat, Ali.

COMPARATIVE(S)

Alienation And Aesthetics In Marx And Tolstoy: A Comparative Analysis. Kiros, Teodros.

COMPARATIVE PHILOSOPHY

Critique Of Scope And Method Of The Northropian Philosophical Anthropology And The Projection Of A Hope For A Meeting Of East And West. Lee, Kuang–Sae.

India And The Comparative Method. Halbfass, Wilhelm.

COMPARATIVE RELIGION

Human Rights In Religious Traditions. Swidler, Arlene (ed).

Mysticism And Religious Traditions. Katz, Steven (ed).

Religion As Critique. Ackerman, Robert John.

"Martin Buber's Approach To Comparative Religion" in *Martin Buber*, Gordon, Haim (ed), 367–384. Friedman, Maurice.

Wilfred Cantwell Smith On Faith And Belief. Wainwright, William J.

World Problems And The Emergence Of A New Interreligious Perspective. Chethimattam, John B.

COMPARISON(S)

Degrees Of Comparison. Clark, Michael.

Formal Justice, Moral Commitment, And Judicial Precedent. Lyons, David.

Interpersonal Level Comparability Implies Comparability Of Utility Differences. Ng, Yew–Kwang.

COMPASSION

Thailand: Buddhism Meets The Western Model. Lindbeck, Violette.

COMPATIBILISM

Compatibilism And The Consequence Argument. Horgan, Terence.

Davidson's Compatibilism. Fales, Evan.

On Two Arguments For Compatibilism. Van Inwagen, Peter.

COMPATIBILITY

Issues Of Computer Compatibility. Roemer, Robert E.

COMPENSATION

Affirmative Action: A Philosophical Critique. Capaldi, Nicholas.

Displaced Workers: America's Unpaid Debt. Byrne, Edmund F.

COMPETENCE

"Illness And Incompetence" in *Contemporary Issues In Health Care*, Schnall, David J (ed), 112–128. Szasz, Thomas.

"Problems Of Informed Consent With Cognitively Impaired" in *Ethical Questions In Brain And Behavior*, Pfaff, Donald W (ed), 23–40. Macklin, Ruth.

"Treatment Refusals" in *Ethical Questions In Brain And Behavior*, Pfaff, Donald W (ed), 41–56. Macklin, Ruth.

Competencies As Powers. Norris, Stephen P.

Reflexive Reflections. Putnam, Hilary.

Response To Rebecca Dresser's 'Involuntary Confinement: Legal And Psychiatric Perspectives'. Callahan, Joan C.

The Power Of A Realist Interpretation Of Competency. Weinberg, Lois A.

COMPETITION

Sports And Social Values. Simon, Robert L.

Advertising Professional Success Rates. Gorovitz, Samuel.

Commentary On "Advertising Professional Success Rates". De George, Richard T.

Commentary On "Professional Advertising: Price Fixing And Professional Dignity Versus The Public's Right To A Free Market". Doughton, James E.

Competition And Moral Development. Stengel, Barbara S.

Competition In Consumption As Viewed By Jewish Law. Liebermann, Yehoshua.

Forms Of Competition And Sociological Knowledge In Organized American Sociology. Stehr, Nico and Avison, William.

Good Competition And Drug–Enhanced Performance. Simon, Robert L.

Opponents, Contestants, And Competitors: The Dialectic Of Sport. Hyland, Drew A.

Sport And Hegemony: On The Construction Of The Dominant Culture. Whitson, David.

COMPLACENCY

Relativism And Moral Complacency. Unwin, Nicholas.

COMPLEMENTARITY

A Note On Quantum Theory, Complementarity, And Uncertainity. Busch, Paul and Lahti, Pekka J.

COMPLETENESS

see also Incompleteness

The Limits Of Science. Rescher, Nicholas.

A Completeness Result For Fixed–Point Algebras. Montagna, Franco.

A Natural Extension Of Natural Deduction. Schroeder– Heister, Peter.

A Note On *xy* Languages. Sadock, J M and Zwicky, Arnold M.

A Property Of 2–Sorted Peano Models And Program Verification. Paris, J B and Csirmaz, L.

An Elementary Method Of Determining The Degree Of Completeness On N–Valued Lukasiewicz Propositional Calculus. Suchoń, Wojciech.

Beyond Legal Gaps. Broekman, Jan M.

Carnapian Extensions Of S5. Hendry, Herbert E and Pokriefka, M L.

Consistency, Completeness And Decidability With Respect To The Logic Of Law And The Provability Of Juristic Arguments. Brkić, Jovan.

Diamonds, Uniformization. Shelah, Saharon.

Leibniz Und Die Boolesche Algebra. Lenzen, Wolfgang.

Paraconsistent Logic And Model Theory. Alves, Elias H.

Strong Completeness Of A Pure Free Logic. Bencivenga, Ermanno.

The Completeness Of Monotonic Modal Logics. Chellas, Brian F and Mc Kinney, Audrey.

The Strong Amalgamation Property For Complete Boolean Algebras. Monro, G P.

Weak Completeness And Abelian Semigroups. Wesselkamper, T C.

COMPLEXITY

Complexity And Intersubjectivity: Towards The Theory Of Niklas Luhmann. Bednarz Jr, John.

Complexity Of κ–Ultrafilters And Inner Models With Measurable Cardinals. Sureson, Claude.

Niklas Luhmann And His View Of The Social Function Of Law. Murphy, John W.

On Speedability Of Recursively Enumerable Sets. Marques, Ivan.

On The Degree Of Complexity Of Sentential Logics; An Example Of The Logic With Semi–negation. Hawranek, Jacek and Zygmunt, Jan.

Proof Theory And Complexity. Cellucci, Carlo.

Simple Wholes And Complex Parts: Limited Principles In Spinoza. Sacksteder, William.

Tautologies With A Unique Craig Interpolant, Uniform *Vs* Nonuniform Complexity. Mundici, Daniele.

Zur Raumkompliziertheit Mehrdimensionaler Turing–Automaten. Hemmerling, Armin and Murawski, Gerd.

COMPLIANCE

Dr Krankheit And The Concept Of Compliance. Schwartz, Thomas.

Volitional Disability And Physician Attitudes Toward Noncompliance. Ferrell, Richard B and others.

COMPOSITION

On Musical Improvisation. Alperson, Philip.

COMPREHENSION

The Principle Of Comprehension As A Present–Day Contribution To Mathesis Universalis. Marciszewski, Witold.

COMPULSION

Commentary: Compulsory Health And Safety In A Free Society. Downie, R S.

COMPUTABILITY

Computable Explanations. Howard, J V.

Foundational Problems From Computation Theory. Lolli, Gabriele.

On A Simple Definition Of Computable Function Of A Real Variable––With Applications To Functions Of A Complex Variable. Caldwell, Jerome and Pour– El, Marion Boykan.

On The Notion Of Effectiveness. Shapiro, Stewart.

Reflexive Reflections. Putnam, Hilary.

COMPUTATIONAL COMPLEXITY

Über Die Erfüllung Gewisser Erhaltungssätze Durch Kompliziertheitsmasse. Lischke, Gerhard.

"Representation For Spector Second Order Classes Computation Theory" in *Lecture Notes In Mathematics*, Muller, G H And Others (ed), 31–48. Hirose, Ken and Nakayasu, Fujio.

A Characterization Of Complexity Sequences. Schnorr, C P and Stumpf, G.

Abstrakte Tempomasse Und Speed–Up–Theoreme Für Enumerationen Rekursiv–Aufzählbarer Mengen. Hecker, Hans–Dietrich.

Complete Second Order Spectra. Scarpellini, Bruno.

Computational Complexity And The Universal Acceptance Of Logic. Cherniak, Christopher.

COMPUTATIONAL COMPLEXITY

Das Kompressionstheorem Für Tempomasse. Hecker, Hans–Dietrich.

Definability Of Recursively Enumerable Sets In Abstract Computational Complexity Theory. Byerly, Robert E.

Narrow Taxonomy And Wide Functionalism. Kitcher, Patricia.

Towards A Computational Phenomenology (1). Harlan, Robert M.

COMPUTER(S)

Cognitive Science And The Semantics Of Natural Language. Skidmore, Arthur.

Computer Power And Intellectual Failure In Education: The Significance Of Joseph Weizenbaum's Criticism. Raitz, Keith L.

Computermusik Und Die Identität Des Musikwerks. Simons, Peter M.

Issues Of Computer Compatibility. Roemer, Robert E.

Lucas, Gödel And Astaire: A Rejoinder To David Boyer. Lucas, J R.

Some Bits And Bytes: A Response To Raitz's "The Computer Revolution, The Technological Fallacy, And Education". Skovira, Robert J.

The Computer Revolution, The Technological Fallacy, And Education. Raitz, Keith L.

COMPUTER SCIENCE

"Dynamic Logic" in *Handbook Of Philosophical Logic*, Gabbay, Dov (ed), 497–604. Harel, David.

Foundational Problems From Computation Theory. Lolli, Gabriele.

Modal Logics In The Theory Of Information Systems. Orlowska, Ewa.

COMTE

Auguste Comte And Positivism: The Essential Writings. Lenzer, Gertrud (ed).

The Nature Of Social Laws: Machiavelli To Mill. Brown, Robert.

Auguste Comte And The Withering–Away Of The State. Vernon, Richard.

Hypotheses And Historical Analysis In Durkheim's Sociological Methodology: A Comtean Tradition. Schmaus, Warren.

The Revelation Of Humanity. Munson, Thomas N.

CONCATENATION

Abstract Measurement Theory. Narens, Louis.

Zur Benutzung Der Verkettung Als Basis Für Die Arithmetik. Deutsch, Michael.

CONCEPT(S)

see also Idea(s)

A Theory Of Social Action. Tuomela, Raimo.

An Interpretation Of The Logic Of Hegel. Harris, Errol E.

Analysis And Dialectic: Studies In The Logic Of Foundation Problems. Russell, Joseph J.

Bruno. Schelling, F W J and Vater, Michael G (ed).

Epicurus' Scientific Method. Asmis, Elizabeth.

Hegel's Logic: An Essay In Interpretation. Hibben, John G and Harris, H S (ed).

Hegel's Logic. Hibben, John Grier.

Methphysics: Its Structure And Function. Korner, Stephan.

Sense And Content: Experience, Thought, And Their Relations. Peacocke, Christopher.

What Is Living And What Is Dead In The Philosophy Of Hegel? Croce, Benedetto.

'Elegance' In Science And Mathematics: A Discussion. Macnamara, Michael and Kistner, Wietske and Wilkinson, Jennifer.

"Precritical Fragments On Art" in *Continental Philosophy And The Arts*, Winters, Laurence E and others (ed), 63–86. Scalia, Gianni.

"Unbestimmte Begriffe" Bei Leibniz. Lenzen, Wolfgang.

A Semiotic–Pragmatic Theory Of Concepts. Lee, Harold N.

Aether/Or: The Creation Of Scientific Concepts. Nersessian, Nancy J.

Anthropological Concepts: Some Notes On Their Epistemological Status. Pinxten, Rik.

Begriffsbildung In Der Psychologie: Zur Logik Des Begriffes "Intelligenz". Perner, Josef.

Concept–Formation And Value Education. Haldane, John J.

Correcting Concepts. Tiles, Mary.

Die Natur In Marx' Begriffssystem. Ghideanu, Tudor.

Die Wahrheit Des 'Impliziten Denkers': Zur Logikbegründungsproblematik In Hegels "Wissenschaft Der Logik". Zimmerli, Walter.

Einfuhrung In Die Philosophie Der Gegenwart: Dargestellt In Einem Handbuch Philosophischer Grundbegriffe. Steinbeck, W.

El Concepto En La Fenomenología Del Espíritu. Vásquez, Eduardo.

Fichtes Gottesbegriff. Schulte, G.

Formation And Development Of Scientific Concepts. Pedersen, Stig Andur.

Frege's Metaphysical Argument. Currie, Gregory.

Leibniz And The Doctrine Of Inter–World Identity. Mondadori, Fabrizio.

Misdescribing A Cow: The Question Of Conceptual Correctness. Barrow, Robin.

Remarks On The Ontology Of "Right" And "Left". Spaemann, Robert.

The Inevitability Of Certain Concepts (Including Education): A Reply To Robin Barrow. Wilson, John.

Topology Of Internal And External Factors In The Development Of Knowledge. Lelas, Srdan.

CONCEPTION

Treatise On Basic Philosophy, V5. Bunge, Mario.

Two Conceptions Of The Self. Piper, Adrian M S.

CONCEPTUAL ANALYSIS

Internal Problems Of The "State–Nation" Conception In The Last Third Of The 19th Century And At The Turn Of The Century (in Hungarian). Diószegi, István.

Philosophy In The Legislative Process. Hare, John E.

Reflections On Perspectivism In Nietzsche. Strong, Tracy B.

The Incoherence Of Intergenerational Justice. Ball, Terence.

The Philosopher In The Workplace. Elliston, Frederick.

CONCEPTUALISM

The Principle Of 'Maximum Inheritance' And The Growth Of Scientific Knowledge. Mamchur, Elena.

CONCEPTUALIZATION

Conceptualization And Measurement In The Social Sciences. Blalock Jr, Hubert M.

A Semiotic–Pragmatic Theory Of Consciousness. Lee, Harold N.

Theoretical Terms And The Causal View Of Reference. Kroon, Frederick W.

CONCRESCENCE

Whitehead Ou Le Cosmos Torrentiel. Dumoncel, Jean–Claude.

CONCRETE

Das Aufsteigen Der Erkenntnis Vom Abstrakten Zum Konkreten. Pröhl, Joachim.

Konkrete Utopie: Zukunft Als Bewusstsein Und Handlung. Czuma, Hans.

CONCRETENESS

Art, Philosophy And Concreteness In Hegel. Desmond, William.

Philosophical Ideas Of Tadeusz Kotarbiński. Szaniawski, Klemens.

CONDILLAC

Condillac Und Delisle De Sales: Ein Neuer Brief. Kreimendahl, Lothar.

La Statue De Condillac, Image Du Réel Ou Fiction Logique? Baertschi, Bernard.

CONDITION(S)

Epistemic Analysis: A Coherence Theory Of Knowledge. Ziff, Paul.

Conditions Versus Transference: A Reply To Ehring. Aronson, Jerrold.

Philosophical Conditions Of Scientific Development. Bunge, Mario.

CONDITIONAL(S)

see also Implication

Inquiry. Stalnaker, Robert C.

Pragmatics And Empiricism. Skyrms, Brian.

"Conditional Logic" in *Handbook Of Philosophical Logic*, Gabbay, Dov (ed), 387–440. Nute, Donald.

"If A And B, Then A". Lowe, E J.

"Three Ways To Give A Probability Assignment A Memory" in *Testing Scientific Theories*, Earman, John (ed), 157–162. Skyrms, Brian.

A Couple Of Novelties In The Propositional Calculus. Hoare, C A R.

A Syntactically Motivated Theory Of Conditionals. Lycan, William G.

Addis On Analysing Disposition Concepts. Wilson, Fred.

Generalising The Probabilistic Semantics Of Conditionals. Appiah, Anthony.

I Will, If You Will. Radford, Colin.

Jonathan Bennett On 'Even If'. Cross, Charles B.

Maximum Entropy Inference As A Special Case Of Conditionalization. Skyrms, Brian.

Nicholas Rescher On Hypothetical Reasoning And The Coherence Of Systems Of Knowledge. Moutafakis, Nicholas J.

On Indicative Conditionals With Contrary Consequents. Jackson, Frank.

On What Is Strictly Speaking True. Travis, Charles.

Parsing 'If'–Sentences. Dudman, V H.

Permission. Nute, Donald.

Prior Probabilities. Skilling, John.

Probability Logic With Conditional Expectation. Fajardo, Sergio.

Probability, Kinematics, Conditionals, And Entropy Principles. Domotor, Zoltan.

Some Random Observations. Jaynes, E T.

The Conditional Analysis. Heller, Mark.

The Status Of The Principle Of Maximum Entropy. Shimony, Abner.

Weak Conditional Comparative Probability As A Formal Semantic Theory. Morgan, Charles G.

Wright *Versus* Lewis On The Transitivity Of Counterfactuals. Lowe, E J.

CONDITIONALISM

Analytical Approaches To Determinism. Odegard, Douglas.

CONDITIONING

Purpose And Conditioning: A Reply To Waller. Mills, John A.

CONDORCET

Condorcet Studies 1. Rosenfield, Leonora C and Popkin, Richard H (ed).

CONDUCT

Evaluations And Norms Of Conduct In Leon Petrazycki's Psychologistic Concept Of Law And Morality (in Polish). Smoczynski, P J.

What Is So Special About (Free) Speech? Husak, Douglas N.

CONFESSION(S)

Augustine, Memory, And The Development Of Autobiography. Archambault, Paul J.

CONFIDENTIALITY

Groping For Ethics In Journalism. Goodwin, H Eugene.

"Confidentiality And The Obligation To Report Child Abuse" in *Difficult Decisions In Medical Ethics*, Ganos, Doreen L (ed), 63–74. Adelson, Edna.

"Should We Be Discussing This". Hart, Richard E and Bowie, Norman.

"The Necessity For Reporting Child Abuse" in *Difficult Decisions In Medical Ethics*, Ganos, Doreen and others (eds), 49–62. Heins, Marilyn.

A Duty To Warn, An Uncertain Danger. Reamer, Frederic G and Schaffer, Sylvan J.

A Father Says 'Don't Tell My Son The Truth'. Higgs, Roger and others.

Confidentiality In The Teaching Of Medical Ethics: A Case Report. Ellin, Joseph.

Confidentiality, Rules, And Codes Of Ethics. Goldman, Alan H.

Iconoclastic Ethics. Black, Douglas.

Lawyer–Client Confidences Under The A B A Model Rules: Ethical Rules Without Ethical Reason. Freedman, Monroe H.

Medical Confidence. Havard, John.

Mum's The Word: Confidentiality And Incest. Higgs, Roger and others.

Trust. Cooper, David E.

CONFIRMABILITY

"Idealizations And Testing Of Theories" in *Observation, Experiment, Hypothesis In Modern Physical Science*, Achinstein, Peter (ed), 147–174. Laymon, Ronald.

CONFIRMATION
see also Verification
Probability And Evidence. Horwich, Paul.
The Concept Of Evidence. Achinstein, Peter (ed).
A Historical Comment Concerning Novel Confirmation. Good, I J.
Another Look At The Predictivist Thesis. Jones, William B.
Confirmation, Paradoxes, And Possible Worlds. Stillwell, Shelley.
Goede Redenen Om Iets Te Geloven. Derksen, A A.
Inductive Inference In The Limit. Glymour, Clark.
The Confirmation Of Quantitative Laws. Kyburg, Henry E.
Theoretical Functions, Theory And Evidence. Forge, John.

CONFLICT(S)
Love And Conflict: A Covenantal Model Of Christian Ethics. Allen, Joseph L.
"Archaeology And The Native American: A Case At Hopi" in *Ethics And Values In Archaeology*, Green, Ernestene L (ed), 236–242. Adams, E Charles.
"Archaeology: Science Or Sacrilege" in *Ethics And Values In Archaeology*, Green, Ernestene L (ed), 208–223. Meighan, Clement W.
"Value Conflicts In Osteo–Archaeology" in *Ethics And Values In Archaeology*, Green, Ernestene L (ed), 194–207. Cheek, Annetta L and Keel, Bennie C.
"When Human Rights Conflict: Two Persons, One Body" in *Defining Human Life*, Shaw, Margery W (ed), 225–239. Macklin, Ruth.
Aeschylus And Practical Conflict. Nussbaum, Martha.
Christian Resources For Peace Making In A World Of Conflict. Courtney, Charles.
Conflict In The Workplace, And Its Resolution. Campbell, Keith.
Eine Analyse Und Kritische Bewertung Der Methode Und Des Prinzips Der Praktischen Argumentation Oswald Schwemmers. Asouzu, Innocent.
Equal Treatment And Equal Chances. Kamm, Frances Myrna.
Hare On Moral Conflicts. Primorac, Igor.
Hobbes's State Of War. Hampton, Jean.
Moral Conflict And Moral Realism. Tännsjö, Torbjörn.
Moral Conflict In Agriculture: Conquest Or Moral Coevolution? Shepard, Philip T.
Persons And Values: Reasons In Conflict And Moral Disagreement. Benn, S I.

CONFLICT OF INTEREST
Ethics–In–Government Laws: Are They Too "ethical"? Neely, Alfred S.
Problems In Legal Ethics. Schwartz, Mortimer D and Wydick, Richard C.

CONFUCIANISM
Ethical Argumentation: A Study In Hsun Tzu's Moral Epistemology. Cua, A S.
Mysticism And Religious Traditions. Katz, Steven (ed).
Commemoration And Perdurance In The Analects, Books 1 And 2. Casey, Edward S.
Comments On A S Cua's "Confucian Vision And Human Community". Smith, John.
Confucian Spirituality. Ching, Julia.
Confucian Vision And Human Community. Cua, Antonio S.
Confucianism And Zen (Ch'an) Philosophy Of Education. Cheng, Hsueh–li.
Einig Grundlinien Der Chinesischen Philosophie. Brock, Erich.
Ethical Uses Of The Past In Early Confucianism: The Case Of Hsün Tzu. Cua, A S.
On Confucian Jen And Heideggerian Being (II) (in Chinese). Chern, Jiunn–Huei.
On The Contingency Of Confucius' Emergent *Tao*. Ames, Roger T.
Pain And Suffering In Confucian Self–Cultivation. Wei– Ming, Tu.
Philosophical Hermeneutics And The Analects: The Paradigm Of "Tradition". Chan, Alan.
The Concept Of Mind In Chu Hsi's Ethics. Jiang, Paul Yun–Ming.

CONFUCIUS
Leibniz: De Cultu Confucii Civili: Introduction, Édition Du Texte Et Traduction. Klutstein– Rojtman, Ilana and Werblowsky, R J Zwi.
On The Contingency Of Confucius' Emergent *Tao*. Ames, Roger T.
Rectification: An Ancient Solution To A Modern Problem. Cummins, Robert E.
Two Models Of Spiritual Journey: Yoga And Confucius. Podgorski, Frang.

CONGAR, Y
Soteriology In The Nuclear Age. Hellwig, Monika K.
The Essence Of Catholicism: Protestant And Catholic Perspectives. Dulles, Avery.

CONJECTURING
Conjectures And Rational Preferences. Levy, Robert J.
Il *De Coniecturis* Nell'Epistemologia Di Nicolò Cusano. Nardelli, Domenica.

CONJUNCTION(S)
A Conjunction In Closure Spaces. Jankowski, Andrzej W.
Conjunction Without Conditions In Illative Combinatory Logic. Bunder, M W.
Conjunctive Properties Revisited. Casullo, Albert.
I Will, If You Will. Radford, Colin.

CONNECTION(S)
Concepts Of Supervenience. Kim, Jaegwon.
Hume Was Right, Almost; And Where He Wasn't, Kant Was. Shwayder, D S.

CONNECTIVE(S)
A Couple Of Novelties In The Propositional Calculus. Hoare, C A R.
A Syntactic Characterization Of Kleene's Strong Connectives With Two Designated Values. Martin, John N.

CONNEXIVE LOGIC
Aristotle's Thesis In Consistent And Inconsistent Logics. Mortensen, Chris.

CONNOLLY, B
Connolly, Coucault, And Truth. Taylor, Charles.

CONSCIENCE
Conscientization And Creativity. Schipani, Daniel S.
"A Scale Of Values For A Changing World" in *The Good Life And Its Pursuit*, Dougherty, Jude P (ed), 186–195. Basile, Joseph.
Democratic Capitalism: Developing A Conscience For The Corporation. Grcic, Joseph M.

Practical Reasoning And Moral Judgment. Boyle, Joseph M.

CONSCIENTIOUS OBJECTION
Can Modern War Be Just? Johnson, James T.
Civil Disobedience, Conscientious Objection, And Evasive Noncompliance: Analysis And Assessment Of Illegal Actions In Health Care. Childress, James F.

CONSCIOUSNESS
Action (1893): Essay On A Critique Of Life And A Science Of Practice. Blanchette, Oliva (trans) and Blondel, Maurice.
Consciousness: Natural And Artificial. Culbertson, James T.
Language, Thought, And Other Biological Categories: New Foundations For Realism. Millikan, Ruth Garret.
Mahler: Consciousness And Temporality. Greene, David B.
Science And Consciousness: Two Views Of The Universe. Cazenave, Michel (ed).
The Multiple States Of Being. Guénon, René.
The New Image Of The Person: The Theory And Practice Of Clinical Philosophy. Koestenbaum, Peter.
"Ethical Considerations In Care Of Unconscious Patients" in *Ethical Questions In Brain And Behavior*, Pfaff, Donald W (ed), 57–72. Levy, David E.
A Semiotic–Pragmatic Theory Of Consciousness. Lee, Harold N.
About Being A Bat. Maloney, J Christopher.
An Infinite Time Of One's Own. Lingis, Alphonso F.
Can My Survival Be Subrogated? Cherry, Christopher.
Changed Concepts Of Brain And Consciousness: Some Value Implications. Sperry, Roger.
Consciousness And Dennett's Intentionalist Net. Bricke, John.
Consciousness And Content–Formation. Cam, Philip.
El Cuerpo Como Lenguaje, Expresion Y Comunicacion. Rovaletti, Maria L.
George Herbert Mead's Conception Of Consciousness. Natsoulas, Thomas.
In Search Of A Whole–System Ethic. Holler, Linda D.
Is Consciousness Important? Wilkes, Kathleen V.
John Dewey's Theory Of Consciousness. Smith, Barry D.
Karol Cardinal Wojtyla And Jean–Paul Sartre On The Intentionality Of Consciousness. Pappin, Joseph.
Locke On Consciousness And Reflection. Kulstad, Mark A.
On The Concept Of Unity Of Consciousness. Schleichert, Hubert.
Person–Stages And Unity Of Consciousness. Mc Inerney, Peter K.
Reconsidering The Ethics Of Infanticide. Warren, Mary Anne.
Sperry's Concept Of Consciousness. Ripley, Charles.
Spinoza, Bennett, And Teleology. Rice, Lee C.
Subjektiver Faktor Und Massenbewusstsein. Müller, Werner.
The Anthropogenetic Meaning Of The Growth Of The Human Hand. Cackowski, Zdzislaw.
The Life Of Consciousness And The World Come Alive. Lauer, Quentin S J.
The Significance And Dignity Of Labor: A Keyword In Marxian Anthropology. Ehlen, Peter.
The World According To Husserl. Holmes, Richard.

CONSENSUS
Consensus And The Ideal Observer. Lehrer, Keith.
Consensus As Shared Agreement And Outcome Of Inquiry. Levi, Isaac.
Consensus, Respect, And Weighted Averaging. Schmitt, Frederick F.
Destroying The Consensus. Loewer, Barry and Laddaga, Robert.
Lehrer–Wagner Consensual Probabilities Do Not Adequately Summarize The Available Information. Baird, Davis.
On The Formal Properties Of Weighted Averaging As A Method Of Aggregation. Wagner, Carl.
Some Properties Of The Lehrer–Wagner Method For Reaching Rational Consensus. Nurmi, Hannu.
The Lehrer–Wagner Theory Of Consensus And The Zero Weight Problem. Forrest, Peter.

CONSENT
"87–100" in *Freedom, Feminism, And The State*, Mc Elroy, Wendy (ed), 87–100. Harman, Lillian.
A Definition For Paternalism. Hershey, Paul Turner.
A Duty To Warn, An Uncertain Danger. Reamer, Frederic G and Schaffer, Sylvan J.
Baby Fae: The "Anything Goes School Of Human Experimentation". Annas, George J.
Manufacture Of Consent In Democracy. Chomsky, Noam.
Parental Discretion And Children's Rights: Background And Implications For Medical Decision–Making. Schoeman, Ferdinand.
Paternalism And Sovereignty In Athletics: Limits And Justifications Of The Coach's Exercise Of Authority Over The Adult Athlete. Ravizza, Kenneth and Daruty, Kathy.
Socialism, Democracy And Marxism: The Need For Dialogue. Benn, Tony.

CONSEQUENCE(S)
A Sufficient And Necessary Condition For Tarski's Property In Lindenbaum's Extensions. Stepień, Teodor.
Act Utilitarianism And The Moral Fanaticism Argument. Timmons, Mark.
Compatibilism And The Consequence Argument. Horgan, Terence.
Consequence Operations Defined By Partial Matrices. Marek, Iwona.
Filter Distributive Logics. Czelakowski, Janusz.
Invariant Matrix Consequences. Dzik, Wojciech and Tokarz, Marek.
On Hilbert's Operation On Logical Rules, II. Pogorzelski, Witold A.
Remarks On Some Approaches To The Concept Of Logical Consequence. Prawitz, Dag.
The Logical Consequence Relation Of Propositional Trense Logic. Thomason, S K.
Variations Of Core Semantic Techniques And Their Methodological Import. Vakarelov, Krista.

CONTINUUM

Het Continuum–Debat Bij Gregorius Van Rimini. Thijssen, J.
The Limits Of Change. Mortensen, Chris.

CONTINUUM HYPOTHESIS

Forcing The Failure Of CH By Adding A Real. Shelah, Saharon and Woodin, Hugh.
On Violating The GCH Below The Least Measurable Cardinal. Pelletier, D H.

CONTRACEPTION

Contraception, Copulation Domination, And The Theoretical Barrenness Of Sex Education Literature. Diorio, Joseph A.
Mending Mother Nature: Alpha, Beta And Omega Pills. Fleck, Leonard M.

CONTRACT(S)

"Achieving Professionalism Through Ethical Fragmentation" in *Ethics And Values In Archaeology*, Green, Ernestene L (ed), 51–61. Raab, L Mark.
"Ethics In Contract Archaeology" in *Ethics And Values In Archaeology*, Green, Ernestene L (ed), 108–116. Fowler, Don D.
"Hegel's Radical Idealism: Family And State As Ethical Communities" in *The State And Civil Society*, Pelczynski, Z A (ed), 77–92. Westphal, Merold.
"Marriage Contract" in *Freedom, Feminism, And The State*, Mc Elroy, Wendy (ed), 119–120. Stone, Lucy and Blackwell, Henry.
"Obligation, Contract And Exchange: On Hegel's Abstract Right" in *The State And Civil Society*, Pelczynski, Z A (ed), 159–177. Benhabib, Seyla.
A Defense Of Employee Rights. Des Jardins, Joseph R and Mc Call, John J.
Contracts To Bear Children. Davies, Iwan.
Distributive Justice, Contract, And Equality. Macleod, Alistair M.
Enforcing Slavery Contracts: A Liberal View. Callahan, Joan C.
Lay Obligations In Professional Relations. Benjamin, Martin.
Natural Advantages And Contractual Justice. Alexander, Larry and Wang, William.
ROBOTS, RIFs, And Rights. Arthur, Alcott.

CONTRACTUALISM

Market Contractarianism And The Unanimity Rule. Coleman, Jules L.
The Matrix Of Contractarian Justice. Buchanan, James M and Lomasky, Loren E.

CONTRADICTION

Über Die Widersprüche Der Sozialistischen Gesellschaft. Kosing, Alfred.
Aristotle On The Extension Of Non–Contradiction. Halper, Edward.
Arten Des Herangehens An Dialektische Widersprüche Besonders In Der Technischen Entwicklung. Thiel, Rainer.
Augusto Guzzo E Il Pensiero Metafisico: L'Avvistamento E La Distanza. Ferrari, Piermario.
Commentary: Unearthing Contradictions: An Essay Inspired By Women And Male Violence. Fine, Michelle.
Contradiction In The Will. Doore, Gary.
Contradictional Logic—Its Limits And The Significance Of A Reformatory Programme. Ioan, Petru.
Dissolving Kripke's Puzzle About Belief. Pettit, Philip.
Gesellschaftliche Widersprüche In Der Volksrepublik China. Moritz, Rolf.
Hyper–Contradictions. Priest, Graham.
Kritisches Zur Widerspruchsdebatte. Eichhorn, Wolfgang.
Lässt Sich Eine Kernlogik Konstituieren: Ein Versuch Dazu Vom Standpunkt Des Pankritischen Rationalismus Aus. Klowski, Joachim.
Methodological Approaches To The Utilization Of Science And Technology In Practice. Boucek, Karel.
N A Vasil'év: A Forerunner Of Paraconsistent Logic. Arruda, Ayda I.
Objective And Subjective–Objective Aspects Of Contradictions Under Socialism (in Czechoslovakian). Flek, Antonín.
On The Position Of The Category Of Transformation In Dialectics. Baimao, Yao.
Ontological And Epistemological Aspect Of Contradictions: Importance For Analysis Of Development Of Society (in Czechoslovakian). Zeman, Jirí.
Schelling–Konferenz In Jena. Biedermann, Georg and Lindner, F.
The Dialectic Of The Contradictions Of Real Socialism (in Czechoslovakian). Houska, Jirí.
The Distinctiveness Of The Process Of Solving Social Contradictions (in German). Schwarz, Eckart.
The Economic Contradictions And The Function Of Managing Workers (in Czechoslovakian). Hlavatý, Karel.
Theoretical–Methodological And Practical Importance Of The Category Of Dialectical Contradiction (in Czechoslovakian). Vook, Jozef.
Truthfulness And Non–trivial Contradictions. Smolenov, Hristo.

CONTRADICTORIES

Contraries And Contradictories: Reasoning In Schelling's Late Philosophy. Burbidge, John.
Popper And Metaphysical Skepticism. Waterhouse, Joseph.

CONTRARIES

Contraries And Contradictories: Reasoning In Schelling's Late Philosophy. Burbidge, John.
On Indicative Conditionals With Contrary Consequents. Jackson, Frank.

CONTROL THEORY(–RIES)

On Recent Analyses Of The Semantics Of Control. Dowty, David R.

CONTROLS

Elbow Room: The Varieties Of Free Will Worth Wanting. Dennett, Daniel C.
"Controlling The Uncontrollable" in *Feeling Good And Doing Better*, Murray, Thomas H (ed), 49–64. Conrad, John P.
"Implications Of Constitutional Right Of Privacy For Control Of Drugs" in *Feeling Good And Doing Better*, Murray, Thomas H (ed), 129–156. Schwartz, Robert L.
"The Social Dilemma Of The Development Of A Policy On Intoxicant Use" in *Feeling Good And Doing Better*, Murray, Thomas H (ed), 27–48. Zinberg, Norman E.

"The State's Intervention In Individuals' Drug Use: A Normative Account" in *Feeling Good And Doing Better*, Murray, Thomas H (ed), 65–82. Neville, Robert.
Pluralism In The Mass Media: Can Management Help? Nielsen, Richard P.

CONVENTION(S)

Assertion And Convention. Miller, S R.
L'Apport De La Convention En Litterature. Marchand, Alain Bernard and Rochon, Claire.
Negative Positivism And The Hard Facts Of Life. Silver, Charles.
Social Habits And Enlightened Cooperation: Do Humans Measure Up To Lewis Conventions? Von Savigny, Eike.

CONVENTIONALISM

Carnap's Early Conventionalism: An Inquiry Into The Historical Background Of The Vienna Circle. Runggaldier, Edmund.
"On Popper's Conventionalism" in *Methodology, Metaphysics And The History Of Science*, Cohen, Robert S (ed), 263–282. Ströker, Elisabeth.
Der Erste Wiener Kreis. Haller, Rudolf.
Geochronometrie Und Geometrodynamik: Zum Problem Des Konventionalismus. Kanitscheider, Bernulf.
In Difesa Della Filosofia: Enriques E Poincaré. Centi, Beatrice.
Moral Conventionalism. Kekes, John.
Realism And Conventionalism In Einstein's Philosophy Of Science: The Einstein–Schlick Correspondence. Howard, Don.
Zum Problem Der Diskutierbarkeit Von Normensystemen. Weinke, Kurt.

CONVERGENCE

Filterkonvergenz In Der Nichtstandard–Analysis Bei Nichtelementaren Funktionen. Döpp, Klemens.

CONVERSION

"The Stranger" in *Faith And Rationality*, Plantinga, Alvin (ed), 94–102. Mavrodes, George I.
A Recovery Of Innocence: The Dynamics Of Sartrean Radical Conversion. Walters, Kerry S.
Saint Augustine On The Road To Damascus. Ferrari, Leo C.

CONWAY, D

Miracfles And Rival Systems Of Religion. Langtry, Bruce.

COOPERATION

Ideology As Brain Disease. Tiger, Lionel.
Social Habits And Enlightened Cooperation: Do Humans Measure Up To Lewis Conventions? Von Savigny, Eike.

COPERNICUS

On Argument *Ex Suppositione Falsa*. Wisan, Winifred Lovell.
The Dissolution Of The Solid Celestial Spheres. Rosen, Edward.

COPP, D

Democratic Capitalism: Developing A Conscience For The Corporation. Grcic, Joseph M.

CORNEILLE, P

"Du Désordre Àl'ordre" in *Existential Coordinates Of Human Condition*, Tymieniecka, A (ed), 435–450. Murphy, B L.
"Tragic Closure And The Cornelian Wager" in *Existential Coordinates Of Human Condition*, Tymieniecka, A (ed), 409–416. Lyons, John.

CORPORATION(S)

Collective And Corporate Responsibility. French, Peter A.
A Defense Of Utilitarian Policy Processes In Corporate And Public Management. Brady, F Neil.
Corporate Culture And The Common Good: The Need For Thick Description And Critical Interpretation. Sturm, Douglas.
Democratic Capitalism: Developing A Conscience For The Corporation. Grcic, Joseph M.
Displaced Workers: America's Unpaid Debt. Byrne, Edmund F.
Do Corporations Have Moral Rights? Ozar, David T.
Eigentum Und Verfügungsmacht: Zum Korporativen Eigentum. Bornschier, Volker.
The Corporation And Individual Moral Agency. Camenisch, Paul F.
The Corporation, Its Members, And Moral Accountability. Meyers, Christopher.
The International Infant Formula Controversy: A Dilemma In Corporate Social Responsibility. Baker, James C.

CORPOREITY

"Personal Identity And Imagination": One Objection. Flew, Antony.
Teleologie Und Leiblichkeit Beim Späten Kant. Duque, Felix.

CORPUSCLE(S)

The Primary/Secondary Quality Distinction: Berkeley, Locke, And The Foundations Of Corpuscularian Science. Davidson, Arnold I and Hornstein, Norbert.

CORRECTNESS

"Dynamic Logic" in *Handbook Of Philosophical Logic*, Gabbay, Dov (ed), 497–604. Harel, David.

CORRELATION(S)

Kairos And Logos: Studies In The Roots And Implications Of Tillich's Theology. Carey, John J (ed).
Compensatory Neoplasia: Chronic Erythrocytosis And Neuroblastic Tumors. De La Monte, Suzanne M and Hutchins, Grover M and Moore, G William.
Frege's Double Correlation Thesis And Quine's Set Theories NF And ML. Cocchiarella, Nino B.

CORRESPONDENCE

"Correspondence Theory" in *Handbook Of Philosophical Logic*, Gabbay, Dov (ed), 167–248. Van Benthem, Johan.
Approximative Explanation Is Deductive Nomological. Pearce, David and Rantala, Veikko.

CREDULITY
Credulism. Kvanvig, Jonathan L.

CREED(S)
Creeds, Society, And Human Rights: A Study In Three Cultures. Stackhouse, Max L.

CREEL, R
Reflections On The Value Of Knowledge: A Reply To Creel. Keller, James.

CRENSHAW, J
Philosophy, Religion And Theodicy. Moulder, James.

CRIME(S)
Biology, Crime And Ethics: A Study Of Biological Explanations For Criminal Behavior. Marsh, Frank H (ed) and Katz, Janet (ed).
"Mental Illness And Crime" in *Biomedical Ethics Reviews*, Humber, James M (ed), 149–162. Arrington, Robert L.
Corporate Control Through The Criminal System. Lansing, Paul and Hatfield, Donald.
Der 'Labeling Approach'—Ein Paradigmawechsel In Der Modernen Kriminalsoziologie. Kunz, Karl–Ludwig.
Intolerable Wrong And Punishment. Wolgast, Elizabeth H.

CRIMINAL(S)
Electronic Monitoring Of Felons By Computer: Threat Or Boon To Civil Liberties? Alexander, Elaine and Alexander, Larry.
The Courageous Villain: A Needless Paradox. Cunningham, Stanley B.
The Criminal And The Artist: Violence And Neurosis. Donnell– Kotrozo, Carol.
The Serpent Beguiled Me And I Did Eat: Entrapment And The Creation Of Crime. Dworkin, Gerald.

CRIMINAL JUSTICE
Collective And Corporate Responsibility. French, Peter A.
"The Processes Of Adjudication And Regulation, A Comparison" in *Rights And Regulation*, Machan, Tibor (ed), 71–98. Smith, J C.
Discretionary Waiver Of Juvenile Court Jurisdiction: An Invitation To Procedural Arbitrariness. Wizner, Stephen.
Electronic Monitoring Of Felons By Computer: Threat Or Boon To Civil Liberties? Alexander, Elaine and Alexander, Larry.
Insanity And Criminality. Simon, Michael A.
Marxism And The Criminal Question. Ferrajoli, Luigi and Zolo, Danilo.
The Decision To Seek Criminal Charges: Just Deserts And The Waiver Decision. Feld, Barry C.

CRIMINAL LAWS
"Limits Of The Enforcement Of Morality" in *Philosophical Analysis In Latin America*, Gracia, Jorge J E and others (eds), 93–114. Nino, Carlos Santiago.

CRIMINOLOGY
Punishment And Restitution: A Restitutionary Approach To Crime And The Criminal. Abel, Charles F and Marsh, Frank H.
The Sign Of Three. Sebok, Thomas A (ed) and Eco, Umberto (ed).
Der 'Labeling Approach'—Ein Paradigmawechsel In Der Modernen Kriminalsoziologie. Kunz, Karl–Ludwig.
Formal Justice And Township Justice. Hund, John.
Kants Straftheorie In Ihrer Bedeutung Für Die Entwicklung Einer Theorie Der Straffälligenpädagogik. Eberle, Hans–Jurgen.

CRISIS(ES)
Crise De Civilisation Et Université: Enseigner Aujourd'hui. Vachet, André.
The Concept Of Crisis And The Unity Of Husserl's Position. Rockmore, Tom.

CRITERIA
A Consistent Alternative View Within The Just War Family. Yoder, John H.
Criteria And Circumstances. Caraway, Carol.
Some Introductory Criteria Of Contemporary Art Creation (in Czechoslovakian). Simunek, Eugen.
The Origins And Functions Of Evaluative Criteria. Sadler, Royce D.

CRITIC(S)
Museums And Their Enemies. Haskell, Francis.

CRITICAL RATIONALISM
Der Kritische Rationalismus Und Kant. Richter, Gundrun.

CRITICAL THEORY
Polis And Praxis. Dallmayr, Fred R.
A Case Of Creative Misreading: Habermas's Evolution Of Gadamer's Hermeneutics. How, Alan R.
Dialectical Phenomenology As Critical Social Theory. Marsh, James L.
From The Contemplative Materialism To The Materialism Of Praxis: On The Evolution Of Bukharin's Philosophy (in Hungarian). Szabo, Tibor.
Habermas On Rationality. Roderick, Rick.
Habermas's Contribution To Hermeneutic Theory. Davey, Nicholas.
Human Agency Between Life–world And System: Habermas's Latest Version Of Critical Theory. Hartmann, Klaus.
Modern Movements In European Philosophy: Some Introductory Remarks. Kearney, Richard.
Moksa And Critical Theory. Klostermaier, Klaus.
The Marxian Method Of Critique: Normative Presuppositions. Benhabib, Seyla.
Theory And Practice From The Point Of View Of Materialism (in Hungarian). Buharin, N I.
Towards A Critical Theory Of Value. Luntley, Michael.

CRITICAL THINKING
Beyond Feelings: A Guide To Critical Thinking, Second Edition. Ruggiero, Vincent Ryan.
Critical For Survival. Scriven, Michael.
Critical Reflection: Reply To Oscanyan. Moore, Brooke.
Critical Thinking: Response To Moore. Oscanyan, Frederick.

Critical Thinking In The Electronic Era. Postman, Neil.
Critical Thinking And Obedience To Authority. Sabini, John and Silver, Maury.
Critical Thinking And The Curriculum. Ennis, Robert H.
Educating For Responsible Citizenship In A Democracy. Glaser, Edward M.
Il Problema Critico Della Conoscenza. Blandino, Giovanni.
Il Problema Critico. Iammarone, Luigi.
Informal Logic: The Past Five Years 1978–1983. Johnson, Ralph H and Blair, J Anthony.
Philosophy For Children And Critical Thinking: With Examples Of Critical Thinking Skills. Lipman, Matthew.
The Critical–Thinking Movement. Paul, Richard W.
The Evaluation Of Critical Thinking Programs: Dangers And Dogmas. Mc Peck, John E.
The Nature Of Critical Thinking. Reeder, Harry P.

CRITICISM
see also Literary Criticism, Textual Criticism
Aesthetics: Problems In The Philosophy Of Criticism. Beardsley, Monroe C.
Continental Philosophy And The Arts. Winters, Laurence E and others (ed).
The Politics Of Interpretation. Mitchell, W J T.
The Retreat To Commitment. Bartley, W W.
"Criticism, Philosophy, Phenomenology" in *Continental Philosophy And The Arts*, Winters, Laurence E and others (ed), 243–264. Anceschi, Luciano.
A Problem With Johnstone's Self. Mader, Thomas F.
Aesthetic Censorship: Censoring Art For Art's Sake. Shusterman, Richard.
Afterwords "The Aesthetic Attitude" In The Rise Of Modern Aesthetics–Again. Stolnitz, Jerome.
Critical For Survival. Scriven, Michael.
Marx's Contributions To Social Science And His Errors. Horvat, Branko.
Max Weber's Defense Of Historical Inquiry. Mc Lemore, Lelan.
Mystery And Mumbo–Jumbo. Graham, Gordon.
Philosophy And The Mirror Of Rorty. Munz, Peter.
Prospects Regarding The Science Of Criticism. Margolis, Joseph.
The Painter Otakar Marvánek As Art Critic (in Czechoslovakian). Ondracka, Pavel.
Theory And Practice: From Ideally Separated To Pragmatically Joined. Rosmarin, Adena.
Validity In Interpretation And The Literary Institution. Newton, K M.

CROCE
Antonio Gramsci's Reformulation Of Benedetto Croce's Speculative Idealism. Kahn, Beverly L.
Benedetto Croce, Philosopher, Ethics And Politics (in Hungarian). Bausola, Adriano.
Carlo Antoni E Lo Storicismo Crociano (Continua). Fantini, Stefano.
Croce, Gentile And Hegel And The Doctrine Of The Ethical State (Continuazione E Fine). Bellamy, Richard.
Getting Croce Straight. Paton, Margaret.
Giulio Augusto Levi E La "Scienza Del Comico". Cavaglion, Alberto.
Le Lettere Di Croce A Gentile. Coli, Daniela.

CRONBACH, L
Psychological Terms, Logical Positivism, And Realism: Issues Related To Construct Validation. Ellett Jr, Frederick S.

CUA, A
Comments On A S Cua's "Confucian Vision And Human Community". Smith, John.

CUBAN
Cuban And North American Marxism. D' Angelo, Edward (ed).
José Marfí: Mentor Of The Cuban Nation. Kirk, John M.
Russell And The Cuban Missile Crisis. Seckel, Al.

CULPABILITY
Rights And Excuses. Fletcher, George P.
Sentiments De Culpabilité Et Signification Du Péché: Approche Psychanalytique. De Saussure, Thierry.

CULTURAL ANTHROPOLOGY
"Beyond Cultural Relativism" in *Popper And The Human Sciences*, Currie, Gregory (ed), 121–132. Koertge, Noretta.
An African Concept Of Human Personality: The Yoruba Example. Makinde, M Akin.
Conceptual Relativism And Europocentrism: The Reply Of A Philosopher To An Anthropologist. Perkins, Robert L.
Dagara Traditional Cultic Sacrifice As A Thematization Of Ultimate Reality And Meaning. Yangyuoro, Yvon.
Destiny, Personality And The Ultimate Reality Of Human Existence: A Yoruba Perspective. Gbadegesin, Olusegun.
The Asantes: Ancestors And The Social Meaning Of Life. Twumasi, Patrick A.
The Ontology Of The Body: A Study In Philosophical And Cultural Anthropology. Krawczyk, Zbigniew.
Visión Filosófica De La Cultura Desde La Perspectiva Actual. Alonso, Luz García.
Where Are The Barbarians: Ethnocentrism Versus The Illusion Of Cultural Universalism: The Answer Of An Anthropologist To A Philosopher. Kronenberg, Andreas.
Wittgenstein's Anthropology. Bell, Richard.

CULTURAL PLURALISM
Ethical Considerations For Planned Social Change In The Education Of American Indian People. Thomas, Linda Sue.

CULTURAL RELATIVISM
Ethical Relativism. Ladd, John (ed).
Rationality And Relativism: In Search Of A Philosophy And History Of Anthropology. Jarvie, I C.
"Beyond Cultural Relativism" in *Popper And The Human Sciences*, Currie, Gregory (ed), 121–132. Koertge, Noretta.

DARWINISM

Darwinism And Determinism: The Role Of Direction In Evolution. Ruffa, Anthony R.

Evolution, The History Of An Idea. Bowler, Peter J.

"Darwinism And Ethics: A Response To Antony Flew" in *Darwin, Marx And Freud*, Caplan, Arthur L (ed), 47–72. Kass, Leon R.

Darwinism And The Modern Scientific Revolution—175 Years From C Darwin's Birth. Ghiţa, Simion.

Evolution And The Fundamentalist Critique: Contributions To Educational Philosophy. Vold, David J.

The Religion Of Humanity. Chandler, Daniel Ross.

DASEIN

Bultmann's Criticisms Of Heidegger. Chryssides, George D.

Dasein As Self: Some Implications Of Heideggerian Ontology. Anderson, Scott William.

Diagrammatic Approach To Heidegger's Schematism Of Existence. Kisiel, Theodore.

DATA

Some Methodological Problems In Data Gathering For Discourse Analysis. Orletti, Franca.

DATABASE(S)

A Meditation On Critical Mass In The Philosophy Of Sport. Meier, Klaus V.

DAUBERT, J

Against Idealism: Johannes Daubert Vs Husserl's *Ideas* I. Schuhmann, Karl and Smith, Barry.

DAVIDSON, D

Against Holism. Weir, Alan.

Anscombe, Davidson And Lehrer On A Point About Freedom. Harrison, Jonathan.

Buckner Quoting Goldstein And Davidson On Quotation. Van Brackel, J.

Davidson And Indeterminacy Of Translation. Kirk, Robert E.

Davidson's Compatibilism. Fales, Evan.

Davidson's Theism? Foley, Richard and Fumerton, Richard.

Davidson's Theory Of Meaning: Some Questions. Taylor, Kenneth A.

La Sémantique De L'action De D Davidson. Petit, Jean–Luc.

Pears On *Akrasia*, And Defeated Intentions. Mele, Alfred R.

The Trouble With Extensional Semantics. Asher, Nicholas.

DAVIS, W

A Reply To Wayne A Davis' "Miller On Wanting, Intending, And Being Willing". Miller, Arthur.

DAWKINS, R

Mutual Aid And Selfish Genes. Thompson, Janna L.

DE BEAUVOIR

Beauvoir And Satre: The Forms Of Farewell. Barnes, Hazel E.

Gender–Specific Values. Seigfried, Charlene H.

Lordship, Bondage, And The Dialectic Of Work In Traditional Male/Female Relationships. Bell, Linda A and Alcoff, Linda.

Simone De Beauvoir Et La Femme. Zephyr, Jacques J.

DE CHARDIN, PIERRE TEILHARD

see Teilhard

DE COUBERTIN, P

Social Essence And Value Of The Olympic Idea. Stolarov, Vladislav I.

DE FINETTI, B

"Probability And Art Of Judgment" in *Observation, Experiment, And Hypothesis In Modern Physical Science*, Achinstein, Peter (ed), 95–126. Jeffrey, R C.

DE LA CRUZ, S

Logos Y Eros En San Juan De La Cruz Y Platón. Herrera, Bernal.

DE MAN, P

The Intersection Of Theory Of Science And Theory Of Literature. Margolis, Joseph.

DE ROJAS, F

"Myth & Tragic Action In La Celestina And Romeo And Juliet" in *Existential Coordinates Of Human Condition*, Tymieniecka, A (ed), 425–435. Stewart, Marilyn.

DE SADE

On The Discourse Of Pornography. Paden, Roger.

DE SOTO, D

El Problema De Los Universales En Domingo De Soto Y Alonso De La Veracruz. Beuchot, Mauricio.

DE VRIES, B

Om De Feiten Te Laten Spreken: Een Repliek. Hofstee, Willem K B.

DEAD

Do Not Disturb: Archaeology And The Rights Of The Dead. Bahn, Paul.

DEAN, T

On Primordialism Versus Postmodernism: A Response To Thomas Dean. Olson, Alan M.

Response To Thomas Dean's Review Of *Knowledge And The Sacred*. Nasr, Seyyed Hossein.

DEARDEN, R

To Develop Autonomy: A Critique Of R F Dearden And Two Proposals. Quinn, Victor.

DEATH

Buddhist And Western Psychology. Katz, Nathan (ed).

God, Guilt, And Death: An Existential Phenomenology Of Religion. Westphal, Merold.

I–Man: An Outline Of Philosophical Anthropology. Krąpiec, Mieczylaw A and Lescoe, Marie (trans) and Woznicki, Theresa (trans).

Medical Nemesis: The Expropiation Of Health. Illich, Ivan.

The "Phaedo": A Platonic Labyrinth. Burger, Ronna.

"Can Art Die" in *Continental Philosophy And The Arts*, Winters, Laurence E and others (ed), 239–242. Pentzoupoulou– Valais, Teresa.

"Definitions Of Life And Death: Should There Be Consistency" in *Defining Human Life*, Shaw, Margery W (ed), 99–113. Veatch, Robert M.

A Phenomenology Of Nuclear Weapons. Weinberger, David.

Can My Survival Be Subrogated? Cherry, Christopher.

L'Attitude Intérieure Envers La Mort. Krüger, Gerhard.

Mourir—Une Fois De Plus. Morin, Michel.

Nascere E Morire Come Estremi Dell'Io. Vigna, Carmelo.

Omega: Some Reflections On The Meaning Of Death And Afterlife. Cain, Clifford C.

On Surrender, Death, And The Sociology Of Knowledge. Feher, Judith.

Self, Near–Death And Death. Cherry, Christopher.

Suffer The Little Children: Death, Autonomy, And Responsibility For A Changing "Low Technology" Environment. Belote, Linda and Belote, James.

The Assignation. Lingis, Alphonso.

The Mistreatment Of Dead Bodies. Feinberg, Joel.

Thinking About The Body. Kass, Leon R.

Tolstoy, Death And The Meaning Of Life. Perrett, Roy W.

Who Counts? Smith, David H.

Zu Möglichkeiten Und Grezen Der Überwindung Der Angst Vor Dem Sterben Und Dem Frühen Tod. Volland, Hannelore.

DEATH PENALTY

Does It Matter If The Death Penalty Is Arbitrarily Administered? Nathanson, Stephen.

Is The Death Penalty Irrevocable? Davis, Michael.

Justice, Civilization, And The Death Penalty: Answering Van Den Haag. Reiman, Jeffrey H.

Refuting Reiman And Nathanson. Van Den Haag, Ernest.

The Death Penalty And The U S Supreme Court. Bruening, William H.

DEATH WISH

Wickedness: A Philosophical Essay. Midgley, Mary.

DEBATE(S)

Entity And Antinomy In Tibetan Bsdus Grwa Logic (Part 1). Goldberg, Margaret.

László Rudas And The Lukács Debate In The Twenties (in Hungarian). Mesterházi, Miklós.

DECENTRALIZATION

Auguste Comte And The Withering–Away Of The State. Vernon, Richard.

DECEPTION

"Deception In The Teaching Hospital" in *Difficult Decisions In Medical Ethics*, Ganos, Doreen L (ed), 87–94. Liepman, Marcia K.

An Ethical Analysis Of Deception In Advertising. Carson, Thomas L and Wokutch, Richard E and Cox, James E.

Bluffing: Its Demise As A Subject Unto Itself. Beach, John.

Distrust, Secrecy, And The Arms Race. Bok, Sissela.

Self–Plagiarism. Goldblatt, David A.

The Case For Deception In Medical Experimentation. Newell, J David.

DECIDABILITY

"Decidability In Carnap" in *Philosophical Analysis In Latin America*, Gracia, Jorge J E and others (eds), 313–338. Loparić, Zelijko.

A Decidable Subclass Of The Minimal Gödel Class With Identity. Goldfarb, Warren D and Gurevich, Yuri and Shelah, Saharon.

Consistency, Completeness And Decidability With Respect To The Logic Of Law And The Provability Of Juristic Arguments. Brkić, Jovan.

Decidability And The Number Of Countable Models. Millar, Terrence.

Decidability Of Some Problems Pertaining To Base 2 Exponential Diophantine Equations. Levitz, Hilbert.

Decidable Properties Of Finite Sets Of Equations In Trivial Languages. Kalfa, Cornelia.

Decidable Regularly Closed Fields Of Algebraic Numbers. Van Den Dries, Lou and Smith, Rick L.

Decidable Subspaces And Recursively Enumerable Subspaces. Downey, R G and Ash, C J.

Entscheidbarkeit Der Arithmetik Mit Addition Und Ordnung In Logiken Mit Verallgemeinerten Quantoren. Wolter, Helmut.

Entscheidbarkeit Von Theorien In Logiken Mit Verallgemeinerten Quantoren. Wolter, Helmut and Herre, Heinrich.

Register Machine Proof Of The Theorem On Exponential Diophantine Representation Of Enumerable Sets. Jones, J P and Matijasevic, Y V.

TW+ And RW+ Are Decidable. Giambrone, Steve.

The Decidable Normal Modal Logics Are Not Recursively Enumerable. Cresswell, M J.

DECIDING

Ethics As An Integrating Force In Management. Pastin, Mark.

Management And Ethical Decision–Making. Robinson, Wade L.

DECISION(S)

Institutional Ethics Committees And Health Care Decision Making. Cranford, Ronald E (ed) and Doudera, A Edward (ed).

Rational Decision And Causality. Eells, Ellery.

The Social Sciences: Their Nature And Uses. Kruskal, William H (ed).

"Decision Review: A Problematic Task" in *Ethics Committees And Health Care Decisions*, Cranford, Ronald (ed), 174–185. Capron, Alexander M.

"Ethical Decision Making In The Politics Of Archaeology" in *Ethics And Values In Archaeology*, Green, Ernestene L (ed), 243–263. Knudson, Ruthann.

"From Then To Now: Perinatal Intensive Care" in *Bioethical Frontiers In Perinatal Intensive Care*, Snowden, Fraser (ed), 19–38. Francoeur, Robert T.

"Guidelines For Decision Making" in *Ethics Committees And Health Care Decisions*,

DENNETT, D

Could Man Be An Irrational Animal: Some Notes On The Epistemology Of Rationality. Stich, Stephen P.

Daniel Dennett On Responsibility. Waller, Bruce N.

De Angst Van De Homunculus Voor Hetscheermes. Draaisma, Douwe.

Dennett On Intelligent Storage. Cam, Philip.

Dennett, Mental Images, And Images In Context. Russow, Lilly–Marlene.

Epistemic Value. Lycan, William G.

Is The Concept Of Pain Incoherent? Kaufman, Rick.

Panglossian Functionalism And The Philosophy Of Mind. Sober, Elliott.

The Experience Of Dreaming. Horne, James.

DENOTATION

"General Intensional Logic" in *Handbook Of Philosophical Logic*, Gabbay, Dov (ed), 355–386. Anderson, C Anthony.

Denotación Y Referencia. Fernandez, Wenceslao J G.

Substitutional Quantification And Existence. Copeland, B J.

The Concept Of Truth In Frege's Program. Burge, Tyler.

DEONTIC LOGIC

Practical Reason. Von Wright, G H.

"Deontic Logic" in *Handbook Of Philosophical Logic*, Gabbay, Dov (ed), 605–714. Aqvist, Lennart.

A Solution To Forrester's Paradox Of Gentle Murder. Sinnott– Armstrong, Walter.

Deontic Alternative Worlds And The Truth–Value Of 'OA'. Solt, Kornél.

Die Relevanz Der Deontischen Logik Für Die Ethik. Frey, Gerhard.

Filling A Gap In Professor Von Kutschera's Decision Procedure For Deontic Logic. Speller, J.

Gedankliche Systeme Mit Aufforderungscharakter. Heitsch, Wolfram.

Moral Dilemmas, Deliberation, And Choice. Anderson, Lyle V.

Permission. Nute, Donald.

Quelques Foncteurs Faussement Primitifs En Logique Déontique (Trivalence Et Action). Bailhache, P.

Reasons, Dilemmas And The Logic Of 'Ought'. Swank, Casey.

The Central Principle Of Deontic Logic. Schlesinger, George N.

The Deontic Calculus D_{krz}. Suchoń, Wojciech.

Un Logicien Déontique Avant La Lettre: Gottfried Wilhelm Leibniz. Kalinowski, Georges and Garoddies, Jean–louis.

DEONTOLOGICAL ETHICS

"Deontologism, Negative Causation, And The Duty Of Rescue" in *Gewirth's Ethical Rationalism*, Regis Jr, Edward (ed), 147–166. Mack, Eric.

Are Business Ethics And Engineering Ethics Members Of The Same Family? Bowie, Norman E.

Disarming Nuclear Apologists. Goodin, Robert E.

Lying And The "Methods Of Ethics". Primoratz, Igor.

DEONTOLOGY

Deontology: Together With A Table Of The Springs Of Action And Article On Utilitarianism. Goldworth, Amnon (ed).

Deterrence And Deontology. Mc Mahan, Jeff.

Nuclear Intentions. Dworkin, Gerald.

Right And Good: False Dichotomy? Maclean, Anne.

The *Uti/Frui* Distinction In Augustine's Ethics. O' Connor, William Riordan.

DEPENDENCY

Dependence, Reliance And Abortion. Strasser, Mark.

Epistemic Dependence. Dauer, Francis W.

DEPTH

Quelques Précisions Sur La DOP Et La Profondeur D'une Théorie. Lascar, D.

DERIVATION

On Reduction Of Theories. Kamlah, Andreas.

DERRIDA, J

Taking Chances: Derrida, Psychoanalysis, And Literature. Kerrigan, William (ed) and Smith, Joseph H (ed).

Death And The Machine: From Jules Verne To Derrida And Beyond. Kemp, Peter.

Et Pourtant: Puissance De La Bonne Volonté (Une Réplique À Jacques Derrida). Gadamer, Hans–Georg.

Heidegger/Derrida—Presence. Sallis, John.

Jacques Derrida: A Rhetoric That Deconstructs Common Sense. Murphy, John W.

La Loi Du Langage Et L'anarchie Du Sens: A Propos Du Débat Searle–Derrida. Frank, Manfred.

Origin(S) In (Of) Heidegger/Derrida. Casey, Edward S.

Pierre Bourdieu En De Filosofische Esthetica. Groot, Ger and Crego, Charo.

Redoubled: The Bridging Of Derrida And Heidegger. Pressler, Charles A.

Representation And The Image: Between Heidegger, Derrida, And Plato. Fóti, Véronique M.

Speech And The Social Contract. Turner, Roy.

The Eclipse Of Being: Heidegger And Derrida. Chang, Briankle G.

The Limits Of Logocentrism (On The Way To Grammatology). Silverman, Hugh J.

Writing Philosophy And Literature: Apology For Narcissism In Merleau–Ponty. Cook, Deborah.

DESCARTES

Peirce: Textes Anticartésiens. Chenu, Joseph.

Phenomenology And Existentialism: An Introduction. Grossman, Reinhardt.

The Man Of Reason: "Male" And "Female" In Western Philosophy. Lloyd, Genevieve.

The Significance Of Philosophical Scepticism. Stroud, Barry.

Über Einige Erkenntnistheoretische Schwierigkeiten Des Klassischen Rationalismus. Pacho, Julian.

" interesting Questions' In The History Of Philosophy Elsewhere" in *Philosophy In History*, Rorty, Richard and others (ed), 141–172. Lepenies, Wolf.

"Probability And Art Of Judgment" in *Observation, Experiment, And Hypothesis In Modern Physical Science*, Achinstein, Peter (ed), 95–126. Jeffrey, R C.

"Reflections On Descartes' Methods Of Analysis And Synthesis" in *History Of Philosophy In Making*, Thro, Linus J (ed), 119–132. Blackwell, Richard J.

"Seven Thinkers And How They Grew" in *Philosophy In History*, Rorty, Richard and others (ed), 125–140. Kuklick, Bruce.

A Defense Of Kant's Refutation Of Descartes. Shirley, Edward S.

Can There Be A Method Of Doubt? Hanfling, Oswald.

Cartesio E Kant Nella "Terminologia Filosofica" Di Adorno. Galeazzi, Umberto.

Cogito, Ergo Sum: Inference And Performance. Reeder, Harry.

Descarte's *Cogito*. Flage, Daniel E.

Descartes Face À Leibniz Sur La Question De La Substance. Ayoub, J Boulad.

Descartes Knows Nothing. Watson, Richard A.

Descartes Onmyth And Ingenuity/Ingenium. Daniel, Stephen H.

Descartes On God's Ability To Do The Logically Impossible. La Croix, Richard R.

Descartes: Methodological Ideal And Actual Procedure. Shea, William R.

Descartes' 'Demonstrations' Of His Existence. Tweyman, Stanley.

Descartes' First Meditation: Something Old, Something New, Something Borrowed. Groarke, Leo.

Descartes' Proto–Critique. Glouberman, M.

Descartes's Meditations As Cognitive Exercises. Hatfield, Gary.

Descarte's Comedy. Rée, Jonathan.

Die Cartesianische Onto–Theo–Logie. Marion, Jean–Luc.

Einige Methodische Regeln Descartes' Und Das Erfindende Denken. Hammacher, Klaus.

Epistemic Value. Lycan, William G.

Eternal Truths And The Laws Of Nature: The Theological Foundations Of Descartes' Philosophy Of Nature. Osler, Margaret.

Ever Since Descartes. Kornblith, Hilary.

Film, Fantasy, And The Extension Of Reality. Linden, George W.

Finocchiaro On Rational Explanation. Doppelt, Gerald.

Formal Traces In Cartesian Functional Explanation. Rorty, Amelie Oksenberg.

Foundationalism And Permanence In Descartes' Epistemology. Cling, Andrew D.

Frankfurt On Descartes' Dream Argument. Stuart, James D.

From Cartesian Epistemology To Cartesian Metaphysics. Markie, Peter J.

Genealogisches Zum Cogito: Über Ein Motiv Des Cartesischen Denkens. Dörr, Hartmut.

Hume On The Cartesian Theory Of Substance. Glass, Ronald J and Flage, Daniel E.

Il Pensiero Storico–Filosofico Di Olgiati E L'Interpretazione Della Filosofia Cartesiana. Grosso, Giuseppe.

Is There A Problem Of Cartesian Interaction? Radner, Daisie.

Kant's Cogito. Patten, St C.

L'Evoluzione Del Problema Morale Nel Pensiero Di Cartesio. Cesareo, Rosa.

L'ordre Du Connaître Et L'ordre De L'être Ou L'ordre Des Choses Et Celui De La Pensée. Theau, Jean.

Levels Of Truth And Reality In The Philosophies Of Descartes And Samkara. Schroeder, Craig.

Locke And Descartes Through Victorian Eyes. Sell, Alan P F.

Mind And Body: Two Real Distinctions. Glouberman, Mark.

Note Sur Deux Antipathies Cartésiennes. De Buzon, Frederic.

Note Sur Le Mécanisme Ordonné Chez Descartes. Bernhardt, Jean.

On Macintyre, Rationality, And Dramatic Space. Monasterio, Xavier O.

Other Problems About The Self. Theron, Stephen.

Reason And Antecedent Doubt. Frankel, Lois.

Skepticism And The Cartesian Circle. Broughton, Janet.

Skepticism Without Indubitability. Wilson, Margaret D.

Subjectivity. Shalom, Albert.

The Coherence Of Virtue And The Virtue Of Coherence: Justification In Epistemology. Sosa, Ernest.

The Mapping Argument And Descartes' Deceitful Demon. Shirley, Edward S.

The Nature And Origin Of Ideas: The Controversy Over Innate Ideas Reconsidered. Simpson, Peter.

Traditional Epistemology And Naturalistic Replies To Its Skeptical Critics. Bogen, James.

Waarheid Als Effect; Richard Rorty En De Natuur Van De Spiegel. Kwaad, G C.

Widerlegt Descartes' Vierte Meditation Den Gottesbeweis Der Dritten: Zur Stellung Descartes' In Der Philosophiegeschichte. Engfer, Hans–Jurgen.

DESCRIBING

Descriptive Epistemology. Duran, Jane.

DESCRIPTION(S)

Análisis Propositional Y Ontologia. Sanchez, Juan Carlos.

Justifying Historical Descriptions. Mc Cullagh, C Behan.

Language, Thought, And Other Biological Categories: New Foundations For Realism. Millikan, Ruth Garret.

"Descriptions, Meaning And Presupposition" in *Philosophical Analysis In Latin America*, Gracia, Jorge J E and others (eds), 219–242. Rossi, Alejandro.

Acquaintance. Rosenkrantz, Gary.

Between The "Thoughts": Topics In Frege's "Logical Investigations" (in Hebrew). Kasher, Asa.

Descriptions In Mathematical Logic. Renardel De Lavalette, Gerard R.

Does The Description Theory Make Contingent Truths Necessary? Eudaly, Thomas D.

Indeterminate Descriptions. Fitch, G W.

Knowledge By Description. Wahl, Russell.

Misdescribing A Cow: The Question Of Conceptual Correctness. Barrow, Robin.

DEWEY

Genderism And The Reconstitution Of Philosophy Of Education. Sherman, Ann L.

John Dewey And Creative Dramatics. Schwartz, Philip J.

John Dewey's Theory Of Consciousness. Smith, Barry D.

Lifelong Education: A Deweyian Challenge. Wain, Kenneth.

Nature And Art. Levi, Albert W.

Rorty's Pragmatism: Afloat In Neurath's Boat, But Why Adrift? Sleeper, R W.

The Art Museum As An Agency Of Culture. Levi, Albert William.

The Democratic "Myth" And The Search For A Rational Concept Of Education. Maxcy, Spencer J.

The Ecological Perspective In John Dewey's Philosophy Of Education. Colwell, Tom.

The Place Of Foresight In Deliberation: An Interpretation Of Dewey's View. Pekarsky, Daniel.

DHARMAKIRTI

Dharmakīrti On The Existence Of Other Minds. Sharma, Ramesh Kumar.

Dharmakīrti On Trairupya And Trirupa Linga. Bapat, Lata.

DIAGNOSIS

Ethical Questions In Brain And Behavior. Pfaff, Donald W (ed).

"Ethical Considerations In Care Of Unconscious Patients" in *Ethical Questions In Brain And Behavior*, Pfaff, Donald W (ed), 57–72. Levy, David E.

"Ethical Issues In Prenatal Therapies" in *Biomedical Ethics Reviews*, Humber, James M (ed), 225–250. Hull, Richard T and Nelson, James A and Gartner, Lou Ann.

"Legal Aspects Of Ethics In Neural And Behavioral Sciences" in *Ethical Questions In Brain And Behavior*, Pfaff, Donald W (ed), 73–90. Beresford, H Richard.

"Making And Using Psychiatric Diagnoses: Ethical Issues" in *Ethical Questions In Brain And Behavior*, Pfaff, Donald W (ed), 11–22. Endicott, Jean.

Knowledge As Tracking? Schmitt, Frederick F.

Psychiatric Diagnosis As An Ethical Problem. Shackle, E M.

DIAGONALIZATION

Lower Bound Results On Lengths Of Second–order Formulas. Scarpellini, Bruno.

DIALECT(S)

On The Position Of The Category Of Transformation In Dialectics. Baimao, Yao.

DIALECTIC

An Interpretation Of The Logic Of Hegel. Harris, Errol E.

Analysis And Dialectic: Studies In The Logic Of Foundation Problems. Russell, Joseph J.

Boston Studies In The Philosophy Of Science: Dialectical Theory Of Meaning, R S Cohen And M W Wartofsky (eds) V81. Markovic, Mihailo.

Dialogue Within The Dialectic. Levine, Norman.

Hegel's Recollection: A Study Of Images In The Phenomenology Of Spirit. Verene, Donald P.

Hume's Philosophy Of Common Life. Livingston, Donald W.

In Search Of Deity: An Essay In Dialectical Theism. Macquarrie, John.

Logic, Philosophy, And History: A Study In The Philosophy Of History Based On The Work Of R G Collingwood. Russell, Anthony F.

Marx's Social Critique Of Culture. Dupré, Louis.

Non Pie Quaerunt: Rhetoric, Dialectic, And The Discovery Of The True In Augustine's Confessions. Di Lorenzo, Raymond D.

Plato's Defence Of Poetry. Elias, Julius A.

Principles Of Interpretation: Series In Continental Thought, V5. Ballard, Edward G.

The Dialogical And The Dialectical Nerveau De Rameau. Jauss, Hans Robert.

The Emergence Of Dialectical Theory: Philosophy And Political Inquiry. Warren, Scott.

The Epistemology Of Hans–Georg Gadamer. Schmidt, Lawrence K.

The Politics Of Salvation: The Hegelian Idea Of The State. Lakeland, Paul.

What Is Living And What Is Dead In The Philosophy Of Hegel? Croce, Benedetto.

'On The Terminology Of "Abstraction" In Aristotle'. Cleary, John.

"Le Neveu De Rameau": Dialogique Et Dialectique (Ou: Diderot Lecteur De Socrate Et Hegel Lecteur De Diderot). Jauss, Hans Robert.

"Marcuse And The Meaning Of Radical Philosophy" in *Continuity And Change In Marxism*, Fischer, Norman And Others (eds), 114–130. Perrin, Ronald.

"Plato's Dialectic Of The Sun" in *History Of Philosophy In Making*, Thro, Linus J (ed), 19–34. Eslick, Leonard J.

"The Dialectic Of Civil Society" in *The State And Civil Society*, Pelczynski, Z A (ed), 211–226. Ilting, K –H.

"The Dialectic In Hegel's Philosophy Of History, Joseph Flay (commentator)" in *History And System*, Perkins, Robert (ed), 149–172. Ahlers, Rolf.

"The Historical Dialectic Of Spirit" in *History And System*, Perkins, Robert (ed), 15–46. Walsh, David.

A Critical Evaluation Of Altman's Definition Of Privacy As A Dialectic Process. Foddy, W H.

About Mario Bunge's 'A Critical Examination Of Dialectics'. Apostol, Pavel.

Answer On The Impulses Of J Zelený Concerning The Character Of So–called Dialectical And Logical Deduction (in Czechoslovakian). Gorsky, D P.

Arbeiterklasse Und Intelligenz In Der Dialektik Von Wissenschaftlichtechnischem, Ökonomischem Und Sozialem Fortschritt. Lötsch, M.

Axiología De José Vasconcelos. Patiño, Joel Rodríguez.

Beyond Dialetical Thinking: Political Logics And The Construction Of Individuality. Boedi, Remo.

Can Rhetoric And Dialectic Serve The Purposes Of Logic? Harpine, William D.

Chemie Und Dialektik. Simon, Rudiger.

Comment On Pavel Apostol's Paper. Bunge, Mario.

Critical Examination Of Dialectics (in Hungarian). Bunge, Mario.

Croce's Interpretation Of Hegel. Bellamy, Richard.

Das Apriorische Moment Der Subjekt–Objekt–Dialektik In Der Transzendentalen Phänomenologie. Kochler, Hans.

Das Individuelle Bewusstsein Und Die Dialektik Von Objektiven Bedingungen Und Subjektivem Faktor. Hahn, Toni.

Deconstruction Is Not Enough: On Gianni Vattimo's Call For "Weak Thinking". Schürmann, Reiner.

Dialectic And Intersubjectivity. Westphal, Merold.

Dialectic And The Role Of The Phenomenologist (in Hebrew). Marx, Werner.

Dialectic In The Eleventh And Twelfth Centuries: Garlandus Compotista. Stump, Eleonore.

Dialectical Unity Of The Dynamic And The Statistical In Nature And Society And Prigogine's Universal Evolution Theory (in Czechoslovakian). Skramovska, Svatoslava and Celeda, J.

Dialectical Reason And Education: Sartre's Fused Group. Gordon, Haim.

Dialectics, Difference, And Weak Thought. Vattimo, Gianni.

Dialektik Von Individuum Und Gesellschaft Als Dialektik Von Persönlicher Und Sozialer Indentität. Wetzel, Manfred.

Dialektik—Logik—Wissenschaftsentwicklung. Erpenbeck, John.

Die Anwendung Der Marxschen Dialektik Beim Aufbau Des Kategoriensystems Des Historischen Materialismus. Stiehler, Gottfried.

Die Dialektik Von Nationalem Und Internationalem In Der Entwicklung Der Sozialistischen Gesellschaft. Wirt, Adam.

Engels' "Dialektik Der Natur" Und Die Einheit Der Naturwissenschaftlichen Erkenntnis. Korch, Helmut und Ennuschat, W.

Filosofie En Wetenschap In De Frankfurter Schule (1930–1950). Koenis, Sjaak.

Friedrich Engels' "Dialektik Der Natur". Bauer, Ileana.

Gaston Bachelard Et Ferdinand Gonseth, Philosophes De La Dialectique Scientifique. Lauener, Henri.

How Is Sport Possible? Lipiec, Józef.

Hume's "Dialectic". Coleman, Dorothy P.

Hypothetical Method And Rationality In Plato. Scolnicov, S.

Logik Und Dialektik Als Wissenschaftsmethoden. Tsouyopoulos, Nelly.

Merleau–Ponty: The Triumph Of Dialectics Over Structuralism. Edie, James M.

Must Time Have A Stop? O' Hagan, Timothy.

Noncumulative Dialectical Models And Formal Dialectics. Krabbe, Erik C W.

On Popper's Implicit Hegelianism. Yulina, N S.

On The Dialectic Of Modernism And Postmodernism. Wellmer, Albrecht.

On The Relation Of Dialectical And Mathematical Logic (in Czechoslovakian). Havas, K G.

Opponents, Contestants, And Competitors: The Dialectic Of Sport. Hyland, Drew A.

Pour Une Définition Claire Et Nette Du Lieu Dialectique. Pelletier, Yvan.

Prigogine's And Piaget's Theory Of Dynamic Equilibrium And Dialectical And Materialist Conception Of Human Evolution (in Czechoslovakian). Linhart, J.

Remarks Concerning The Problems Of Dialectical Logic (in Czechoslovakian). Zeman, J.

Rhetoric And Reality In Kierkegaard's *Postscript*. Dunning, Stephan N.

Rhetorical Polemics And The Dialectics Of *Kritik* In Hegel's Jena Essays. Smith, John H.

Schelling–Konferenz In Jena. Biedermann, Georg and Lindner, F.

Some Aspects Of The Investigation Of Dialectic Of The Spontaneous And The Conscious In Social Development (in Czechoslovakian). Nesvadba, Petr.

Some Remarks On A Theory Of Research In The Work Of Aristotle. Elzinga, Aant.

Some Theoretical Problems Of The Object–Subject Dialectics In The Development Of The Community Of Socialist States (in German). Rygol, Reiner.

The Dialectic Of Becoming In Hegel's Logic. Cave, George P.

The Dialectic Of The Contradictions Of Real Socialism (in Czechoslovakian). Houska, Jiří.

The Forming Of Social Consciousness As Dialectical Process Of Continuity And Discontinuity Of Its Development (in Czechoslovakian). Tomek, V.

The Nature Of Critical Thinking. Reeder, Harry P.

Thermodynamics Without Equilibrium, Totality, Dialectic (in Czechoslovakian). Rajchl, Jaroslav.

Two Problems Of Induction. Jason, Gary J.

Widerspiegelung Objektiver Naturdialektik In Mathematisierten Naturwissenschaftlichen Theorien. Roseberg, Ulrich.

Zeno's Paradoxes And Temporal Becoming In Dialectical Atomism. Smolenov, Hristo.

Zum Stand Der Entwicklungstheorie In Den Naturwissenschaften. Ley, Hermann.

Zur Dialektik Von Freiheit Und Sicherheit. Hagen, Johann J.

Zur Dialektik Des Vergesellschaftungsprozesses In Der Sozialistischen Industrie Der DDR. Braun, Hans–Joachim and Dorschel, E.

DIALECTICAL MATERIALISM

see also Historical Materialism

Dialogue Within The Dialectic. Levine, Norman.

Über Die Wahrheit Und Den Wahrheitsbegriff. Steussloff, Hans.

"Marxism As History—A Theory And Its Consequences" in *Contemporary Marxism*, O' Rourke, James J (ed), 39–54. Fleischer, Helmut.

An Investigation On The Philosophical Problem Of Identity On The Basis Of The Kantian And Hegelian Concept Of It (in Hungarian). Tagai, Imbre.

Arten Des Herangehens An Dialektische Widersprüche Besonders In Der Technischen Entwicklung. Thiel, Rainer.

Biologische Gesetze Und Dialektische Methode. Nowiński, Czesław.

Der Mechanismus Der Technikentwicklung. Banse, G.

Determiniertheit Und Entwicklung. Stieler, Gottfried.

Dialectical Logic And Social Practice (in Czechoslovakian). Valencik, R.

Dialektik—Logik—Wissenschaftsentwicklung. Erpenbeck, John.

Die Materialistische Dialektik—Antwort Auf Die Frage Nach Der Selbstbewegung Der Materie. Kummer, Wolf.

Formal Axiomatic Systems And Dialectic And Materialist Way Of Thought (in

DUTY(–TIES)

Baron, Marcia.
The Neonatologist's Duty To Patient And Parents. Strong, Carson.

DWORKIN, R

Law, Economics, And Philosophy. Kuperberg, Mark (ed) and Beitz, Charles (ed).
Dworkin Giusnaturalista? Pastore, Baldassare.
Ethics And Markets. Bennett, John G.
Hart, Dworkin, Judges, And New Law. Yanal, Robert J.
Legal Positivism, Natural Law, And The Hart/Dworkin Debate. Ball, Stephen W.
Liberal Egalitarianism. Wein, Sheldon.
Rights–Based Rights. Meyers, Diane T.
The Role Of Coherence In Legal Reasoning. Levenbook, Barbara Baum.

DYING

see also Death
Contemporary Issues In Health Care. Schnall, David J (ed) and Figliola, Carl L (ed).
"Ethics And The Dying" in *Contemporary Issues In Health Care*, Schnall, David J (ed), 89–111. Veatch, Robert.
Care Of The Dying: Withholding Nutrition. Capron, Alexander M and Cassell, Eric J.

DYNAMIC LOGIC

"Dynamic Logic" in *Handbook Of Philosophical Logic*, Gabbay, Dov (ed), 497–604. Harel, David.
Structured Nonstandard Dynamic Logic. Sain, Ildikó.

DYNAMICS

Dialectical Unity Of The Dynamic And The Statistical In Nature And Society And Prigogine's Universal Evolution Theory (in Czechoslovakian). Skramovska, Svatoslava and Celeda, J.
Propositional Logic Based On The Dynamics Of Belief. Gardenfors, Peter.

DYNAMISM

Pierre Rousselot And The Dynamism Of Human Spirit. Sheehan, Thomas.

DYSTOPIA

Castañeda's Dystopia. Kapitan, Tomis.

EARTH

On The Truth Of Being: Reflections On Heidegger's Later Philosophy. Kockelmans, Joseph J.
Do We Really Need Environmental Ethics? Spitler, Gene.

EAST EUROPEAN

"The Critique Of Marxist Philosophy: 1956–81" in *Contemporary Marxism: Essays In Honor Of J M Bocheński*, O' Rourke, James J (ed), 9–20. De George, Richard T.
Ehrenfels And Eastern Europe (in Hungarian). Nyiri, Kristóf.
László Rudas And The Lukács Debate In The Twenties (in Hungarian). Mesterházi, Miklós.

EASTERN PHILOSOPHY

see Oriental

EBNER, F

"Ferdinand Ebner As A Source Of Buber's Dialogic Thought In *I And Thou*" in *Martin Buber*, Gordon, Haim (ed), 121–138. Horwitz, Rivka.

ECO, U

De Literatuur Naar De Letter. Verbeeck, Louis.
Teken, Waarheid, Macht. Van Velthoven, Theo.

ECOLOGY

"An Ecological Argument For Vegetarianism". Wenz, Peter S.
"Gaia And Philosophy" in *On Nature*, Rouner, Leroy S (ed), 60–78. Sagan, Dorion and Margulis, Lynn.
A Note On Deep Ecology. Watson, Richard A.
Deeper Than Deep Ecology: The Eco–Feminist Connection. Salleh, Ariel Kay.
Die Beziehungen Des Menschen Zum Oikos: Ein Konstruktiver Rahmen Für Die Sinnfrage. Zelger, Josef.
Eigentum Und Lebenswelt: Zum Wandel Des Eigentumsverständnisses In Der Komplexen Gesellschaft. Wildermuth, Armin.
Engels Und Die Okologie. Paucke, H.
Fact And Value In Ecological Science. Sagoff, Mark.
Is Big Beautiful? Sagoff, Mark.
Is There A Correct Aesthetic Appreciation Of Nature? Saito, Yuriko.
La Philosophie Et L'écologie. Kainz, Howard P.
Okosophie. Kilga, Bernhard.
Stichwort Okologie. Vester, Frederic.
The Ecological Perspective In John Dewey's Philosophy Of Education. Colwell, Tom.
Theoretische Oberlegungen Zum Okoproblem. Bach, Hans.
Was Erwartet Uns Jenseits Der Wissenschaft: Ethno–Philosophie: Erfahrungen Und Möglichkeiten Im Umgang Mit Dem Irrationalen. Stuben, Peter E.
Zum Okologiegehalt Der Nationalökonomie. Nussbaumer, Josef and Holleis, Wilfried.

ECONOMETRICS

The Calibration Question. Lad, Frank.

ECONOMICS

An Inquiry Into The Nature And Causes Of The Wealth Of Nations, 2v. Smith, Adam.
Contemporary Issues In Health Care. Schnall, David J (ed) and Figliola, Carl L (ed).
Dialogue Within The Dialectic. Levine, Norman.
John Locke And Agrarian Capitalism. Wood, Neal.
Law, Economics, And Philosophy. Kuperberg, Mark (ed) and Beitz, Charles (ed).
Marx's Economics. Junankar, P N.
Marx's Social Critique Of Culture. Dupré, Louis.
Marxism: Last Refuge Of The Bourgeoisie? Mattick, Paul and Mattick Jr, Paul (ed).
On Freedom. Howard, John A (ed).
Political Economy And Freedom. Nutter, Warren G.

Rawls And Rights. Martin, Rex.
Rights And Regulation: Ethical, Political, And Economic Issues. Machan, Tibor R (ed) and Johnson, M Bruce (ed).
Science Policy, Ethics, And Economic Methodology. Shrader–Frechette, K S.
The Nature Of Social Laws: Machiavelli To Mill. Brown, Robert.
The Social Sciences: Their Nature And Uses. Kruskal, William H (ed).
Uncertainty Studies In Philosophy, Economics And Socio–Political Theory. Bonatti, Luigi.
Über Die Produktivkräfte Und Ihre Entwicklung. Ruben, Peter.
"Economics And Archaeology" in *Ethics And Values In Archaeology*, Green, Ernestene L (ed), 117–122. Fitting, James E.
"Hegel's Challenge To The Modern Economy" in *History And System*, Perkins, Robert (ed), 219–253. Winfield, Richard D.
"Karl Marx And Adam Smith: Remarks About The Critique Of Political Economy" in *Contemporary Marxism*, O' Rourke, James J (ed), 21–38. Ballestrem, Karl G.
"Movement In The Market: Mobility And Economics In The Free Society" in *On Freedom*, Howard, John A (ed), 39–58. Johnson, Paul.
"Popper's Critique Of Marx's Method" in *Popper And The Human Sciences*, Currie, Gregory (ed), 147–164. Suchting, W A.
"Romanticism & Modernity In Lukacsian & Althusserian Marxism" in *Continuity And Change In Marxism*, Fischer, Norman And Others (ed), 70–85. Goldstein, Philip.
"The Economic Position Of Women" in *Freedom, Feminism, And The State*, Mc Elroy, Wendy (ed), 213–236. La Follette, Suzanne.
A Remark On The Connexion Between Procedure And Value. Hederstierna, Anders.
Again On "The Crisis In Economic Theory": An Epistemological Approach. Munteanu, Costea.
Althusser On Overdetermination And Structural Causation. Emerson, Michael.
Bribery, Extortion, And "The Foreign Corrupt Practices Act". Carson, Thomas L.
Capitalists And The Ethics Of Contribution. Arnold, N Scott.
Comment On Pommerehne Et Al, "Concordia Discors: Or: What Do Economists Think". Meile, Richard and Shanks, Stephanie L.
Consistency In The Valuation Of Life: A Wild Goose Chase? Mishan, E J.
Cost Containment: Issues Of Moral Conflict And Justice For Physicians. Morreim, E Haavi.
Das Ökonomische Grundgesetz Der Kommunistischen Gesellschaftsformation Und Einige Philosophische Probleme. Leisering, Heinz.
David Hume And Eighteenth Century Monetary Thought: A Critical Comment On Recent Views. Rashid, Salim.
Defending Microeconomic Theory. Hausman, Daniel.
Die Einheit Von Wirtschafts—Und Sozialpolitik—Triebkraft Ökonomischen Und Sozialen Fortschritts. Winkler, G.
Discussion: What Economics Is Not: An Economist's Response To Rosenberg. Hands, Douglas W.
Dugald Stewart: "Baconian" Methodology And Political Economy. Rashid, Salim.
Entwicklung Und Nutzung Der Qualifikation Der Facharbeiter Als Faktor Ökonomischer Effektivität. Rudolph, W.
Equality Vs Liberty: Advantage, Liberty. Narveson, Jan.
Est–ce "L'Esprit", Est–ce "Le Capital"? Mercier– Josa, Solange.
Ethics And Taxation: The Perspective Of The Islamic Tradition. Nanji, Azim A.
Exemplarische Bronnen Van Het Westers Autonomie–Begrip. Nauta, L W.
Formal Properties Of Interpersonal Envy. Chaudhuri, Adhip.
Hegel's Early Thought. Lin, He.
Historical Materialism As The Philosophy Of Marxism (II). Siemek, Marek.
Hombre–Trabajo–Economiá: Aporte Al Tema A Partir De La Antropología Filosófica. Scannone, J C.
Just Taxation In The Roman Catholic Tradition. Curran, Charles E.
Justice–Constrained Libertarian Claims And Pareto Effiecient Collective Decisions. Gaertner, Wulf.
Keynes Versus Hayek: Interne En Externe Factoren In Een Controverse In De Economie. Birner, Jack.
Land–Use Planning: Implications Of The Economic Calculation Debate. Pasour Jr, E C.
Liberal Egalitarianism. Wein, Sheldon.
Lonergan's Economics. Mathews, William.
Management And Ethical Decision–Making. Robinson, Wade L.
Managerial Ethics And Microeconomic Theory. Hosmer, Larue Tone.
Marx' Kulturkonzeption In "Grundrisse Der Kritik Der Politischen Ökonomie": Zugleich Ein Programm Des Realen Humanismus. Kahle, Werner.
Medical Ethics: An Excuse For Inefficiency? Mooney, Gavin.
Nutzenkalkül Und Eigentumsrechte: Ein Ökonomischer Ansatz Zu Einer Positiven Theorie Des Eigentums. Janssen, Martin.
Okosophie. Kilga, Bernhard.
Plädoyer Für Eine Ökonomische Anthropologie Auf Der Grundlage Von Interessen. Koubek, Norbert.
Positional Goods. Hollis, Martin.
Postmortem On An Era: A Citizenly Perspective On The Economy. Scheuer, Irene C.
Prospects For The Elimination Of Tastes From Economics And Ethics. Rosenberg, Alexander.
Quattro Punti Da Rivedere Nel Gramsci Dei Quaderni. Mastroianni, Giovanni.
Rationality And Uncertainty. Sen, Amartya.
Recent Calls For Economic Democracy. Christie, Drew.
Should Marxists Be Interested In Exploitation? Roemer, John E.
Some Issues Surrounding The Reduction Of Macroeconomics To Microeconomics. Nelson, Alan.
Some Problems With Falsificationism In Economics. Caldwell, Bruce J.
Soziale Bedingungen Und Triebkräfte Hoher Arbeitsleistungen. Weidig, R.

ECONOMICS

Soziologische Probleme Des Nullwachstums. Meier, A.

Struktur Der Sozialistischen Produktionsverhältnisse Und Ökonomische Gesetze Des Sozialismus. Becher, Jurgen and Friedrich, P.

Taxation In The History Of Protestant Ethics. Shriver, Donald W and Knox, E Richard.

The Dialectics Of Subjectivity. Ochocki, Aleksander.

The Economic Contradictions And The Function Of Managing Workers (in Czechoslovakian). Hlavatý, Karel.

The Economy Of Tribal Societies (in Hungarian). Sárkány, Mihály.

The Methodological Function Of Political Economy In Materialist Explanation Of The Development Of Socialist Society (in Czechoslovakian). Valencik, Radim.

The Proper Reconstruction Of Exchange Economics. Balzer, W.

The Role Of Conservation Principles In Twentieth—Century Economic Theory. Mirowski, Philip.

The Role Of Economics And Ethical Principles In Determining U S Policies Toward Poor Nations. Piderit, John J.

The Science Of A Legislator In James Mackintosh's Moral Philosophy. Haakonssen, Knud.

Theories Of Justice And The United Nations Declaration On The Establishment Of A New International Economic Order. Boxill, Bernard.

Towards An Economic Theory Of Scientific Revolutions—A Cynical View. Wieland, Bernhard.

What's Morally Special About Free Exchange? Gibbard, Allan.

Zum Okologiegehalt Der Nationalökonomie. Nussbaumer, Josef and Holleis, Wilfried.

ECONOMY

Wealth And Virtue: The Shaping Of Political Economy In The Scottish Enlightenment. Hont, Istvan (ed) and Ignatieff, Michael (ed).

"Economy, Utility And Community In Hegel's Theory Of Civil Society" in *The State And Civil Society*, Pelczynski, Z A (ed), 244–261. Walton, A S.

"Is There A Bias Toward Overregulation" in *Rights And Regulation*, Machan, Tibor (ed), 99–126. Yeager, Leland B.

"Regulation And Justice: An Economist's Perspective" in *Rights And Regulation*, Machan, Tibor (ed), 127–136. Johnson, M Bruce.

Forces Of Production And Social Primacy. Gottlieb, Roger S.

Public Goods And Externalities: The Case Of Roads. Block, Walter.

The Life—World Roots Of Economy. Stikkers, Kenneth W.

ECOSYSTEM(S)

"An Ecological Argument For Vegetarianism". Wenz, Peter S.

National Park Management And Values. Bratton, Susan Power.

The Medical Treatment Of Wild Animals. Loftin, Robert W.

ECUMENISM

Perspectives On Political Ethics: An Ecumenical Enquiry. Srisang, Koson (ed).

The Slippery Slope Of Religious Relativism. Kellenberger, James.

EDEL, A

Comments On Sleeper And Edel. Rorty, Richard.

EDUCATION

see also Moral Education

"I Don't Have No Education" And Other Reflections. Chamberlin, Gordon J.

Beyond Domination: An Essay In The Political Philosophy Of Education. White, Patricia and Peters, R S (ed).

Condorcet Studies 1. Rosenfield, Leonora C and Popkin, Richard H (ed).

Conscientization And Creativity. Schipani, Daniel S.

Deeper Insights In Education: The Waldorf Approach. Steiner, Rudolf.

Enige Kernproblemen In Het Filosofie Onderwijs. Van Der Leeuw, Karel and Mostert, Pieter.

Happiness Through Tranquility: The School Of Epicurus. Hibler, Richard W.

Locke's Education For Liberty. Tarcov, Nathan.

Models Of Man: Explorations In The Western Educational Tradition. Nash, Paul.

Moral Principles In Education: A Reevaluation. Freiberg, Jo Ann.

Nietzsche As Educator. Murphy, Timothy F.

Professional Ethics In Education. Rich, John Martin.

Religious Education: Philosophical Perspectives. Sealey, John.

Teaching As A Moral Craft. Tom, Alan R.

Theory And Practice In Education. Dearden, R F.

Über Die Kategorien Inhalt Und Methode In Der Pädagogik. Naumann, Werner.

'Introduction To Philosophy' As A Large Class Tutorial. Reese, William.

"Discussion Upon Fundamental Principles Of Education" (1919). Whitehead, Alfred N and Brumbaugh, Robert S (ed).

"I'm The Teacher". Benjamin, Martin and Baum, Robert.

"Reopening The Books On Ethics: The Role Of Education In A Free Society" in *On Freedom*, Howard, John A (ed), 79–94. Howard, John A.

"Should We Be Discussing This". Hart, Richard E and Bowie, Norman.

"Symmetry, Independence, Continuity, Boundedness, And Additivity": The Game Of Education. Krolikowski, Walter P and Hablutzel, Nancy and Hoffman, Wilma.

"The Borrowed Syllabus". Wright, Richard A and Newton, Lisa.

"The Proof Of The Pudding Lies In The Eating" (in German). Loeser, Franz.

"Toward A Pedagogy Of The Useful Past For Teacher Preparation": A Reaction. Gutek, Gerald L.

A Process View Of Philosophy And Teaching Philosophy. Pecorino, Philip.

A Public Philosophical Perspective On Teacher Education Reform. Giarelli, James M.

A Rejoinder To Essiet's "Callan And Dewey's Conception Of Education As Growth". Callan, Eamonn.

A Reply To Callan's 'Moral Education In A Liberal Society'. Hooker, Brad.

A Reply To Kieran Egan's "Development In Education". Jones, Reynold.

A Response To Boyd And Bogdan On Values And Teaching. Mc Aninch, Amy Raths.

Academic Freedom: A Structural Approach. Aronowitz, Stanley.

After Art History, What? Mühlberger, Richard.

An Historicist View Of Teaching Philosophy. Portmess, Lisa.

Anonymity In The Academy: The Case Of Faculty Evaluation. Riegle, Rodney P and Rhodes, Dent M.

Are We Teaching Students That Patients Don't Matter? Robinson, Jean.

Art And Knowledge. Gingell, J.

Artistic Meaning And Aesthetic Education: A Formalist View. Miller, Bruce E.

Axiología De José Vasconcelos. Patiño, Joel Rodríguez.

Before Virtue: A Critique Of The New Essentialism In Ethics And Education. Collins, Clinton.

Benefit Rights In Education: An Entitlement View. Beversluis, Eric H.

Bringing Women Into Educational Thought. Martin, Jane R.

Britain: The Public Gets Involved. Gillon, Raanan.

Business Ethics, Interdisciplinarity And Higher Education. Madsen, Peter.

Callan And Dewey's Conception Of Education As Growth. Essiet, Fabian S.

Canada: The Mandarin Bureaucracy. Bayles, Michael D and Freedman, Benjamin.

Capitalism At Risk: The Political Economy Of The Educational Reports Of 1983. Shapiro, H Svi.

Choosing Between Love And Logic. Page, Ralph C.

Classical Living And Classical Learning: The Search For Equity And Excellence In Education. Smith, Philip L and Traver, Rob.

Classroom Logic Terminology: Response To Seech. Lugenbehl, Dale.

Competencies As Powers. Norris, Stephen P.

Competing Cultural Ideals For The School: Liberal Education And Multicultural Education. Reagan, Timothy.

Computer Power And Intellectual Failure In Education: The Significance Of Joseph Weizenbaum's Criticism. Raitz, Keith L.

Concept—Formation And Value Education. Haldane, John J.

Confucianism And Zen (Ch'an) Philosophy Of Education. Cheng, Hsueh–li.

Contraception, Copulation Domination, And The Theoretical Barrenness Of Sex Education Literature. Diorio, Joseph A.

Creativity And Quality. Bailin, Sharon.

Creativity, Progress, And Personality. Osborne, Harold.

Crise De Civilisation Et Université: Enseigner Aujourd'hui. Vachet, André.

Critical For Survival. Scriven, Michael.

Critical Reflection: Reply To Oscanyan. Moore, Brooke.

Critical Thinking And The Curriculum. Ennis, Robert H.

Critical Thinking In The Electronic Era. Postman, Neil.

Critical Thinking: Response To Moore. Oscanyan, Frederick.

Critical Thinking And Obedience To Authority. Sabini, John and Silver, Maury.

Crossword Puzzles For Introductory Courses In Philosophy. Jackson, Jerry.

Dance Education, Skill, And Behavioral Objectives. Carr, David.

Development Of Education. Egan, Kieran.

Dewey And Pekarsky On The Efficacy Of Intelligence And Foresight. Burnett, Joe R.

Dialectical Reason And Education: Sartre's Fused Group. Gordon, Haim.

Die Heranbildung Eines Der Arbeiterklasse Würdigen Nachwuchses. Meier, Artur.

Die Sowjetische Hilfe Für Die Entwicklung Der Marxistisch–Leninistischen Philosophie An Den Universitäten (1945–1949). Handel, Gottfried.

Educación Universitaria Para El Amor. Basave, Agustín.

Educating For Responsible Citizenship In A Democracy. Glaser, Edward M.

Education And Historical Materialism. Schrag, Francis.

Education And Essential Contestability Revisited. Naish, Michael.

Educational Excellence In Art Museums: An Agenda For Reform. Williams, Patterson B.

Emotions And Education. Griffiths, Morwenna.

Encouraging Positive Justice Reasoning And Perspective–Taking Skills: Two Educational Interventions. Krogh, Suzanne Lowell.

Equality, Excellence, Paideia, And The Good Old Days Before Adam And Eve And Social Science. Arnstine, Donald.

Erkenntnistheoretische Und Pädagogische Probleme Bei Der Verwendung Von Lehr– Und Lernmitteln In Der Ausbildung Von Philosophiestudenten. Kirchgässner, Werner and Sanger, H.

Ethical Concerns For The Modern University. Miles, Leland and others.

Ethical Considerations For Planned Social Change In The Education Of American Indian People. Thomas, Linda Sue.

Ethics In Business Education: Working Toward A Meaningful Reciprocity. Hoffman, W Michael.

Evolution And The Fundamentalist Critique: Contributions To Educational Philosophy. Vold, David J.

Exigencias Filosóficas Para Determinar "Lo Psicológico" En El Proceso De Aprendizaje. Daros, William R.

First Steps In Moral And Ethical Education. Wilson, John and Natale, Samuel M.

Formal The Teleological Elements In Hirst's Argument For A Liberal Curriculum. Scarlett, B F.

Fragen Der Philosophischen Lehre. Wittich, Dieter.

Freedom And The Development Of Autonomy: A Reply To Victor Quinn. Dearden, R F.

From Basics To Aesthetics In The Curriculum. Proctor, Nigel.

Genderism And The Reconstitution Of Philosophy Of Education. Sherman, Ann L.

Graduate Study In Continental Philosophy In The United States. Solomon, Robert.

Hermeneutics And The Teaching Of Philosophy. Walhout, Donald.

Ideology, Class, And The Autonomy Of The Capitalist State: The Petit–Bourgeois' World View And Schooling. Shapiro, H Svi.

In Pursuit Of Wholeness: Moral Development, The Ethics Of Care And The Virtue Of *Philia*. Prakash, Madhu Suri.

EDUCATION

Intentionality: A Reexamination Of Its Role In A Literary Education. Kasprisin, Lorraine.

Is Education Real—A Reply To Robin Barrow. Nordberg, Robert B.

Issues Of Computer Compatibility. Roemer, Robert E.

Jacques Maritain: La Educatión En Una Encrucijada. Radchik, Laura.

John Dewey And Creative Dramatics. Schwartz, Philip J.

John Dewey's Theory Of Consciousness. Smith, Barry D.

La Lecture Rationnelle—Nécessaire Et Facilement Assimilable (in German). Ziegler, Heinz.

Leadership, Administration, And The Educational Policy Operation. Maxcy, Spencer J.

Learning To Experience. Simons, Martin.

Lifelong Education: A Deweyian Challenge. Wain, Kenneth.

Logics And Languages Of Pedagogical Research. Soltis, Jonas F.

Love And Logic In 1984. Macmillan, C J B.

Maimonides' Life Of Learning. Finkel, Asher.

Making A Mess Of Marxism. Mc Clellan, James.

Marxism And Schooling: A Failed Or Limited Tradition: A Response To Henry Giroux. Liston, Daniel P.

Mass Haben Und Mass Sein. Buchheim, Thomas.

Meaning In The Experience Of Literature. Thompson, Audrey.

Misdescribing A Cow: The Question Of Conceptual Correctness. Barrow, Robin.

Moral And Religious Education For Nigeria. Woodhouse, Howard R.

Moral Education In A Liberal Society. Callan, Eamonn.

Moral Education Theory And Research. Brown, L M.

Moral Education In Holland. Van Der Plas, Paul L.

Moral Skepticism And Tolerance. Ihara, Craig K.

Museums And Their Enemies. Haskell, Francis.

O Pedagogismo Reformista De Frei Manuel Do Cenáulo. Ganho, Maria De Lourdes Sirgado.

On Children's Philosophical Style. Lipman, Matthew.

On Enriching The Content Of Art History Courses. Flint, Richard C.

On Teaching, Education, Theory And Practice—And The Usefulness Of Science (in Hungarian). Szabó, János.

On Total Cultural Relativism: A Rejoinder. White, F C.

Overcoming Ethnocentrism In The Philosophy Classroom. Schutte, Ofelia.

Painting And Painter In Aesthetic Education. Stolnitz, Jerome.

Parallels Between Moral And Aesthetic Judging, Moral And Aesthetic Education. Swanger, David.

Perception And The Mind—Body Problem. Heslep, Robert D.

Philosophy For Children And Critical Thinking: With Examples Of Critical Thinking Skills. Lipman, Matthew.

Philosophy In Teacher Education And Research. Nelson, Thomas W.

Plato's View On Teaching. Beck, Robert H.

Preparing For The Perils Of Practice. Gorovitz, Samuel.

Privacy And Public Moral Education: Aristotle's Critique Of The Family. Blits, Jan H.

Programmatic Aesthetic Education From The Point Of View Of Social Psychology (in Czechoslovakian). Macková– Holecková, Iva.

Promoting The Autonomy Of Another Person: The Difficult Case Of The High School Dropout. Hedman, Carl G.

Psychological Terms, Logical Positivism, And Realism: Issues Related To Construct Validation. Ellett Jr, Frederick S.

Public Education And Social Harmony: The Roots Of An American Dream. Mc Clellan, B Edward.

Quality And Creativity: A False Dichotomy? Ennis, Robert H.

Rectification: An Ancient Solution To A Modern Problem. Cummins, Robert E.

Reflections Of The Mutual Benefits Of Philosophical And Global Education. Silvers, Anita.

Response To Spencer Maxcy's "Leadership, Administration, And The Educational Policy Operation". Sokoloff, Harris J.

Response To Macmillan's "Love And Logic In 1984". Sherman, Ann L.

Response To Benne's "The Learning Community". Tozer, Steven.

Rethinking Power Relations. Pratte, Richard.

Rhetorical Realities: A Response To McAninch's Interpretation Of Values And Teaching. Boyd, Dwight and Bogdan, Deanne.

Sameness And Equality: A Rejoinder To John Colbeck's Response To "Procrustes And Private Schooling". Shaw, Beverley.

Self Help In Medical Ethics. Shotter, Edward.

Semiotics And Existential Concerns: Reforming An Old Versus. Denton, David E.

Sentiment And Structure: A Durkheimian Critique Of Kohlberg's Moral Theory. Wallwork, Ernest.

Sobre El Feminismo De Platón. Cappelletti, Angel J.

Sociobiology: The World As Given Or The World As Created. Pickens, Donald K.

Socrates On The Problem Of Political Science Education. Pangle, Thomas L.

Socrates, Meet The Buddha. Hoekema, David.

Soldiers For Christ In The Army Of God: The Christian School Movement In America. Reese, William J.

Some Bits And Bytes: A Response To Raitz's "The Computer Revolution, The Technological Fallacy, And Education". Skovira, Robert J.

Sport, Moral Education And The Development Of Character. Arnold, Peter.

Symposium: Knowledge And The Humanities–The Continuing Debate. Brinton, Crane and others.

Taking Dwight Boyd Seriously. Parsons, Michael.

Taking Teachers Seriously. Boyd, Dwight R.

Teacher Education And Research: The Place Of Philosophy. Barrow, Robin.

Teachers' Basic Philosophies And Curriculum. Törnvall, Anders.

Ten Years Of Gallery Education. Luckett, Helen.

The Art Museum As An Agency Of Culture. Levi, Albert William.

The Compulsory Curriculum And Beyond: A Consideration Of Some Aspects Of The Educational Philosophy Of J P White. Gardner, Peter.

The Computer Revolution, The Technological Fallacy, And Education. Raitz, Keith L.

The Critical–Thinking Movement. Paul, Richard W.

The Democratic "Myth" And The Search For A Rational Concept Of Education. Maxcy, Spencer J.

The Dominant Protection Association And Education. G0ldstone, Peter.

The Ecological Perspective In John Dewey's Philosophy Of Education. Colwell, Tom.

The Education Of The Emotions. White, John.

The Education Of The Emotions. Dunlop, Francis.

The Erotic Education Of The Slave. Nails, Debra.

The Erotic Education Of The Slave. Nails, Debra.

The Ethics Of Duty/Ethics Of Virtue Debate And Its Relevance To Educational Theory. Baron, Marcia.

The Fundamentalist Student And Introductory Philosophy. Mc Kenzie, David.

The Human Predicament: A Context For Rights And Learning About Rights. Edwards, Philip.

The Ideal Of The Educated Woman: Jane Roland Martin On Education And Gender. Walker, J C and O' Loughlin, M A.

The Inevitability Of Certain Concepts (Including Education): A Reply To Robin Barrow. Wilson, John.

The Learning Community: A Response. Giarelli, James M.

The Learning–Cell Technique For Teaching Philosophy. Langer, Monika.

The Learning Community. Benne, Kenneth D.

The Liberal Point Of View. Enslin, Penny.

The Logos And The Lotos. Stigliano, Tony.

The Materialist Dilemma: Education And The Changing Of Circumstances. Smith, Michael C.

The Mathematical Imagery Of Plato, *Republic* X. Brumbaugh, Robert S.

The Nature Of Aims And Ends In Education. Mellema, Gregory.

The Origin Of Life: Science Or Religion. Howick, William H.

The Origins And Functions Of Evaluative Criteria. Sadler, Royce D.

The Pedagogical Usefulness Of Speech Act Theory. Reagan, Gerald M.

The Philosopher As Teacher, Humor And Philosophy. Morreall, John.

The Philosophy Of Education Since Dewey. Hendley, Brian P.

The Place Of Foresight In Deliberation: An Interpretation Of Dewey's View. Pekarsky, Daniel.

The Power Of A Realist Interpretation Of Competency. Weinberg, Lois A.

The Principle Of Reason: The University In The Eyes Of Its Pupils. Derrida, Jacques.

The Public School Movement Vs The Libertarian Tradition. Spring, Joel.

The Public School's Search For A Public. Broudy, Harry S.

The Role Of Aesthetic Education In The Forming Of Socialist Consciousness (in Czechoslovakian). Hnizdova, Kvetoslava and Hnizdova, Vlastislav.

The Scientific Destruction Of Humanity And The Educational Project Of The Humanities. Lawler, Peter A.

The Self–Assertion Of The German University And The Rectorate 1933/34: Facts And Thoughts. Heidegger, Martin.

The Tendency Of Tendermindedness In Educational Research, Or, The New Anti–Formalism. Phillips, D C.

The Tension Between Intellectual And Moral Education In The Thought Of John Henry Newman. Tillman, Mary Katherine.

The Theory And Practice Of Just Community In Schools. Socoski, Patrick.

The Tuition Tax Credit Debate. Ackley, Timothy.

The Virtues Of *Philia* And Justice: Who Learns These In Our Society. Diller, Ann.

Through The Doors Of Reason: Dissolving Four Paradoxes Of Education. Oliver, R Graham.

To Develop Autonomy: A Critique Of R F Dearden And Two Proposals. Quinn, Victor.

Tolerance And Evil: Teaching The Holocaust. Lang, Berel.

Topics In Speech Act Theory And Pedagogy. Broidy, Steve.

Toward A Critical Theory Of Education: Beyond A Marxism With Guarantees—A Response To Daniel Liston. Giroux, Henry A.

Toward A Pedagogy Of The Useful Past For Teacher Preparation. Lucas, Christopher J.

Toward A Theory Of Power In Education. Burbules, Nicholas C.

Two Conceptions Of Philosophy. Lugenbehl, Dale.

Verbal Deficit And Educational Success. Winch, C A.

Weltanschaulich–Philosophische Bildung Und Erziehung Im Mathematisch–Naturwissenschaftlichen Unterricht. Viebahn, Ursula and Viebahn, W.

Whitehead's Educational Ontology. Spraggins, John R.

Who Decides The Worth Of Educational Research? Fenstermacher, Gary D.

Why Not Tuition–Tax Credit? Tannenbaum, Margaret D.

Writing To Learn In Philosophy. Berger, Jeffrey.

EDUCATIONAL THEORY(–RIES)

"The New Sophists: Emotivists As Teachers Of Ethics" in *The Georgetown Symposium On Ethics*, Porreco, Rocco (ed), 235–242. Duska, Ronald.

Los Valores Educativos. Dacal Alonso, José Antonio.

The Principle Of Reason: The University In The Eyes Of Its Pupils. Derrida, Jacques.

EDWARDS

Beauty: A Foundation For Environmental Ethics. Austin, Richard Cartwright.

Hume And Edwards On 'Why Is There Something Rather Than Nothing'? Burke, Michael B.

EFFECTIVENESS

Effective Topological Spaces I: A Definability Theory. Kalantari, Iraj and Weitkamp, G.

Effective Topological Spaces II: A Hierarchy. Weitkamp, Galen and Kalantari, I.

On The Notion Of Effectiveness. Shapiro, Stewart.

The Hereditary Partial Effective Functionals And Recursion Theory In Higher Types. Longo, G and Moggi, E.

EFFICACY

The Effectiveness Of Causes. Emmet, Dorothy.

The Public School's Search For A Public. Broudy, Harry S.

EFFICIENCY

Über Den Wirkungs– Und Ausnutzungsmechanismus Der Gesellschaftlichen Entwicklungsgetsetze. Drjachlow, N I and Tscherkassow, G K.

Entwicklung Und Nutzung Der Qualifikation Der Facharbeiter Als Faktor Ökonomischer Effektivität. Rudolph, W.

EGALITARIANISM

Rawls And Rights. Martin, Rex.

"Distributing Health Care: A Case Study" in *Biomedical Ethics Reviews*, Humber, James M (ed), 107–126. Fotion, Nicholas.

"On The Rationale Of Governmental Regulation" in *Rights And Regulation*, Machan, Tibor (ed), 249–258. Rescher, Nicholas.

A Contradiction In The Egalitarian Theory Of Justice. Howard, Michael W.

Egalitarianism. Mc Kerlie, Dennis.

Nozick On Explaining Nothing. Wedin, Michael V.

Two Interpretations Of The Difference Principle In Rawls's Theory Of Justice. Shenoy, Prakash P and Martin, Rex.

Zur Problematik Des Egalitarismus. Höppner, Joachim.

EGO

see also Self(–ves)

The Network Of Thought. Krishnamurti, J.

Fragmentation And Wholeness In Religion And In Science. Bohm, David.

Karol Cardinal Wojtyla And Jean–Paul Sartre On The Intentionality Of Consciousness. Pappin, Joseph.

Nascere E Morire Come Estremi Dell'Io. Vigna, Carmelo.

EGOISM

"Public Pursuit And Private Escape: The Persistence Of Egoism" in *Gewirth's Ethical Rationalism*, Regis Jr, Edward (ed), 128–146. Kalin, Jesse.

A Refutation Of Egoism. Vadas, Melinda.

Egoism, Desires, And Friendship. Chong, Kim–Chong.

High–Minded Egoism And The Problem Of Priggishness. Lemos, Noah M.

On Some So–called Refutations Of Ethical Egoism. Taiwo, Olufemi.

Purposes, Conditioning, And Skinner's Moral Theory: Comments On Mills' Observations. Waller, Bruce.

Spinoza's Ethical Doctrine And The Unity Of Human Nature. Steinberg, Diane.

The Voices Of Egoism. Nielsen, Kai.

EHRENFELS, C

Ehrenfels And Eastern Europe (in Hungarian). Nyiri, Kristóf.

EHRING, D

Conditions Versus Transference: A Reply To Ehring. Aronson, Jerrold.

EIDETIC REDUCTION

Diagrammatic Approach To Heidegger's Schematism Of Existence. Kisiel, Theodore.

The Roots Of The Existentialist Theory Of Freedom In *Ideas I*. Edie, James M.

Type And Eidos—Schutz And Husserl. Pritchard, Colin W.

EIGHTEENTH CENTURY

see Modern

EINSTEIN

Einstein And The Poet: In Search Of The Cosmic Man. Hermanns, William.

"Modestly Radical Empiricism" in *Observation, Experiment, And Hypothesis In Modern Physical Science*, Achinstein, Peter (ed), 1–20. Sklar, Lawrence.

Aether/Or: The Creation Of Scientific Concepts. Nersessian, Nancy J.

Albert Einstein—Versuch Einer Totalisierenden Würdigung. Zimmerman, Rainer E.

Einstein On Locality And Separability. Howard, Don.

Ernst Mach And The Theory Of Relativity. Wolters, Gereon.

Mental Activity And Physical Reality. Snyder, Douglas M.

Realism And Conventionalism In Einstein's Philosophy Of Science: The Einstein–Schlick Correspondence. Howard, Don.

The History Of Quantum Mechanics As A Decisive Argument Favoring Einstein Over Lorentz. Nugayev, R M.

What Is Einstein's Statistical Interpretation, Or, Is It Einstein For Whom Bell's Theorem Tolls. Fine, Arthur.

What Was Einstein's Principle Of Equivalence? Norton, John.

ELEATIC

Plato's *politicus*: An Eleatic Sophist On Politics. Tejera, V.

ELECTRON(S)

Experimentation And Scientific Realism. Hacking, Ian.

ELEMENT(S)

Anaxagoras' Cosmogony. Potts, Ronald.

ELEMENTARY SCHOOL(S)

Philosophy For Children And Critical Thinking: With Examples Of Critical Thinking Skills. Lipman, Matthew.

ELIADE, M

Mito E Verità In Mircea Eliade. Fiore, Crescenzo.

ELIMINATION

On The Elimination Of Singular Terms. Lambert, K.

ELIOT, T

The Hidden Advantage Of Tradition: On The Significance Of T S Eliot's Indic Studies. Perl, Jeffrey M and Tuck, Andrew.

ELITISM

An Egalitarian Epistemology: A Note On E P Thompson's Critique Of Althusser And Popper. Green, David G.

Le Rapport Masse–élite Comme Modèle Canonique De La Dialectique Sociale. Gohier, Christiane.

ELSE, G

Goethe Y La Kátharsis Trágica. Herrán, Carlos M.

ELSHTAIN, J

A Public Philosophical Perspective On Teacher Education Reform. Giarelli, James M.

Citizenship With A Feminist Face: The Problem With Maternal Thinking. Dietz, Mary G.

EMANCIPATION

Jews And German Philosophy: The Polemics Of Emancipation. Rotenstreich, Nathan.

Emancipation And Rationality: Foundational Problems In The Theories Of Marx And Habermas. Zimmermann, Rolf.

Marxism And Intellectual Emancipation. Ruoshui, Wang.

EMBRYOLOGY

Potentialités Morphogénétiques Et Auto–Organisation. Bernier, Réjane.

EMERGENCE

Prospects For Regional Philosophies In Australia. Sylvan, Richard.

EMERSON

Friendship. Armstrong, Robert L.

EMIGRATION

Solzhenitsyn And Yanov. Boldyrev, Peter and Vertlieb, E.

EMOTION(S)

see also Feeling(s)

$\Phi\theta o\nu o\varsigma$ And Its Related $\Pi\alpha\theta\eta$ In Plato And Aristotle. Mills, Michael J.

"Emotions And Choice" in *The Good Life And Its Pursuit*, Dougherty, Jude P (ed), 111–132. Solomon, Robert C.

A New View Of Emotion. Leighton, Stephen R.

Emotion And Action In Cognitive Psychology: Breaching A Fashionable Philosophical Fence. Ericson, David P.

Emotions Across Cultures: Objectivity And Cultural Divergence. Heelas, Paul.

Emotions And Education. Griffiths, Morwenna.

Enjoying Negative Emotions In Fiction. Morreall, John.

Expression Of Emotion In (Some Of) The Arts. Stecker, Robert.

Feelings And Emotion. Leighton, Stephen R.

Genderism And The Reconstitution Of Philosophy Of Education. Sherman, Ann L.

Hanfling And Radford On Art And Real Life. Mounce, H O.

Mending Wall: Response To David Ericson's "Emotion And Action In Cognitive Psychology". De Nicola, Daniel R.

On Being Moved By Fiction. Mannison, Don.

Prescription, Explication And The Social Construction Of Emotion. Armon– Jones, Claire.

Spinoza Und Die Reue. Birnbacher, Dieter.

The Education Of The Emotions. White, John.

The Education Of The Emotions. Dunlop, Francis.

EMOTIVISM

"The New Sophists: Emotivists As Teachers Of Ethics" in *The Georgetown Symposium On Ethics*, Porreco, Rocco (ed), 235–242. Duska, Ronald.

Moral Faith And Ethical Skepticism Reconsidered. Kurtz, Paul.

Moral Fictions And Scientific Management. Santilli, Paul.

The Modern Malaise: A Case History. Cleary, John.

EMPEDOCLES

El Sueño Y Los Sueños En La Filosofía Prearistotélica. Cappelletti, Angel J.

The Cosmological Theory Of Empedocles. Brown, Geoffrey.

EMPIRICAL

El Método Empírico–Reflexivo. Buela, Alberto E.

Empirische Wetten En Theorieën. En Kuipers, Theo and Zandvoort, Henk.

Poppers Zwei Definitionsvarianten Von 'Falsifizierbar': Eine Logische Notiz Zu Einer Klassischen Stelle Aus Der *Logik Der Forschung*. Dorn, Georg J W.

EMPIRICAL KNOWLEDGE

Kant On Space, Empirical Realism And The Foundations Of Geometry. Harper, William.

Morality And Human Nature. Lazari– Pawlowska, Ija.

Sellars On Kantian Intuitions. Woods, Michael.

EMPIRICAL SCIENCE(S)

Interrogatives, Problems And Scientific Inquiry. Kleiner, Scott A.

Nature And Nature's God. Toulmin, Stephen.

EMPIRICAL STATEMENT(S)

Acceptance Of Empirical Statements: A Bayesian Theory Without Cognitive Utilities. Harsanyi, John C.

EMPIRICISM

see also Pragmatism

A Sceptical Dialogue On Induction. Naess, Arne.

Anti–Skepticism. Lee, Henry and Schouls, Peter A (ed).

Berkeley. Pitcher, George and Honderich, Ted (ed).

Beyond Empiricism: Michael Polanyi Reconsidered. Kane, Jeffrey.

Faith And Rationality: Reason And Belief In God. Plantinga, Alvin (ed) and Wolterstorff, Nicholas (ed).

John Locke And Medicine: A New Key To Locke. Romanell, Patrick.

EMPIRICISM

Locke's Writings And Philosophy: Historically Considered. Tagart, Edward.
Methodology, Metaphysics And The History Of Science. Cohen, Robert S (ed) and Wartofsky, Marx W (ed).
Pragmatics And Empiricism. Skyrms, Brian.
The Life And Letters Of John Locke. King, Peter and Schouls, Peter A (ed).
The Worlds Of Hume And Kant. Wilbur, James B (ed) and Allen, H J (ed).
"Can Belief In God Be Rational If It Has No Foundations" in *Faith And Rationality*, Plantinga, Alvin (ed), 135–186. Wolterstorff, Nicholas.
"How To Be A Good Philosopher Of Science" in *Methodology, Metaphysics And The History Of Science*, Cohen, Robert S (ed), 33–42. Martin, Michael.
"Laws Of Nature: The Empiricist Challenge" in *D M Armstrong*, Bogdan, Radu J (ed), 191–224. Earman, John.
"Metaphysics And The History Of Philosophy: The Case Of Whitehead" in *History Of Philosophy In Making*, Thro, Linus J (ed), 213–230. Levi, Albert Williams.
"On The Concept Of Reason" in *Philosophical Analysis In Latin America*, Gracia, Jorge J E and others (eds), 397–412. Quesada, Francisco Miró.
"Reason And Belief In God" in *Faith And Rationality*, Plantinga, Alvin (ed), 16–93. Plantinga, Alvin.
"Reflections On Descartes' Methods Of Analysis And Synthesis" in *History Of Philosophy In Making*, Thro, Linus J (ed), 119–132. Blackwell, Richard J.
A New Field: Empirical Logic. Barth, E M.
Constructive Empiricism And The Problem Of Aboutness. Sober, Elliott.
Correcting Concepts. Tiles, Mary.
Deconstruction And Its Alternatives. Eldridge, Richard.
Discussion: Galileo And The Continuity Thesis. Wallace, William A.
Empiricism And The Theory Of Meaning. Cockburn, David.
How To Revive Empiricism. Brown, Harold I.
Hume's Missing Shade Of Blue, Interpreted As Involving Habitual Spectra. Johnson, David M.
In Response To Frankenberry's "Meland's Empirical Realism And The Appeal To Lived Experience". Meland, Bernard E.
J G H Feder—Beitrag Zu Einer Verhinderungsgeschichte Eines Deutschen Empirismus. Röttgers, Kurt.
Konstruktiver Empirismus. Kraft, Victor.
Lyons And Tigers. Simpson, Paul.
Meland's Empirical Realism And The Appeal To Lived Experience. Frankenberry, Nancy.
Moral Education Theory And Research. Brown, L M.
On Coherence Theories Of Justification: Can An Empiricist Be A Coherentist? Dancy, Jonathan.
Was Ist Inkommensurabilität? Blazer, W.
Why Constructive Empiricism Collapses Into Scientific Realism. Melchert, Norman.

EMPLOYEE(S)

Patent Rights And Better Mousetraps. Michael, Mark.
The Employer–Employee Relationship And The Right To Know. Superson, Anita M.

EMPLOYER(S)

The Employer–Employee Relationship And The Right To Know. Superson, Anita M.

EMPLOYER–EMPLOYEE RELATION(S)

"Government Regulation Of The Employment Relationship" in *Rights And Regulation*, Machan, Tibor (ed), 13–42. Haggard, Thomas R.

EMPTINESS

How Not To Criticize Nāgārjuna: A Response To L Stafford Betty. Loy, David.
Is Nāgārjuna A Philosopher: A Response To Professor Loy. Betty, L Stafford.
Nāgārjuna's Catustava. Tola, Fernando.
Two Tibetan Texts On The "Neither One Nor Many" Argument For *Śūnyatā*. Tillemans, Tom J F.

ENCYCLOPEDIA(S)

La Quadrature Du Cercle: Remarques Sur Diderot Et L'Encyclopédie. Lewinter, Roger.

END(S)

see also Teleology
Explaining Masochism. Warren, Virginia L.
In Defense Of Natural End Ethics: A Rejoinder To O'Neil And Osterfeld. Den Uyl, Douglas J and Rasmussen, Douglas B.
The Nature Of Aims And Ends In Education. Mellema, Gregory.

ENERGY

Energieproblem Und Wissenschaftlich–Technischer Fortschritt. Winckelmann, J.

ENFORCEMENT

Whether Professional Associations May Enforce Professional Codes. Snapper, John W.

ENGELS

Dialogue Within The Dialectic. Levine, Norman.
Marx & Engels: The Intellectual Relationship. Carver, Terrell.
Marxism And The Oppression Of Women: Toward A Unitary Theory. Vogel, Lise.
Methodology, Metaphysics And The History Of Science. Cohen, Robert S (ed) and Wartofsky, Marx W (ed).
"Toward The Vindication Of Friedrich Engels" in *Methodology, Metaphysics And The History Of Science*, Cohen, Robert S (ed), 331–358. Weiss, Donald D.
Engels Und Die Okologie. Paucke, H.
Engels' "Dialektik Der Natur" Und Die Einheit Der Naturwissenschaftlichen Erkenntnis. Korch, Helmut and Ennuschat, W.
Frederick Engels And Contemporary Problems Concerning The History Of Primitive Society. Bromlei, Iu V and Pershits, A I.
Friedrich Engels' "Dialektik Der Natur". Bauer, Ileana.
Gedanken Zum Begriff Und Zur Geschichte Des Humanismus. Seidel, Helmut.

Ideology And Truth. Oruka, H Odera.
Marx And Engels On The Distributive Justice Of Capitalism. Allen, Derek P H.
The Actuality Of Marx's And Engels' Conception Of The Relation Of Property And The Division Of Labour (in Czechoslovakian). Heller, J.
Zum Platz Der "Randglossen" In Der Geschichte Der Theorie Des Wissenschaftlichen Kommunismus. Fieber, Hans–Joachim and Schneider, W.
Zum Stand Der Entwicklungstheorie In Den Naturwissenschaften. Ley, Hermann.
Zum Verhältnis Von Sozialistischer Ideologie Und Subjektivem Faktor. Rauh, Hans–Christoph.

ENGINEERING

Commentary On B Lichter And M Hodges' "Perceptions Of The Engineers' 'Professionalism' In The Chemical Industry". Leckie, John D.
Commentary: Informed Consent In Engineering And Medicine. Martin, Mike W and Schinzinger, Roland.
Engineering And The Philosophy Of Science. Broome, Taft H.
Informed Consent And Engineering: An Essay Review. Long, Thomas A.
Perceptions Of The Engineers' "Professionalism" In The Chemical Industry. Lichter, Barry D and Hodges, Michael P.
Regulation, Deregulation, Self–Regulation: The Case Of Engineers In Ontario. Stevenson, J T.
Weltanschauliche Und Wissenschaftstheoretische Probleme Des Verhältnisses Von Natur– Und Technikwissenschaften. Jobst, Eberhard and Marmai, U.

ENGLAND, G

Work–Related Ethical Attitudes: Impact On Business Profitability. Dunfee, Thomas W and Robertson, Diana C.

ENGLISH

see also British
An Argument That The Language Of Belief Is Not English. Hall, Richard J.
Imagination In The Gothic Hierarchy Of *Scientia*—A Study On Medieval English Mysticism (in Japanese). Ebi, Hisato.
Semantic Closure. Priest, Graham.

ENJOYMENT

Experience And Value In Moritz Geiger's Aesthetics. Beardsley, Monroe C.

ENLIGHTENMENT

Benjamin Constant And The Making Of Modern Liberalism. Holmes, Stephen.
Hegel's Critique Of The Enlightenment. Hinchman, Lewis P.
Radical Humanism. Améry, Jean and Rosenfeld, Sidney (ed) and Rosenfeld, Stella (ed).
The Third Earl Of Shaftesbury 1671–1713. Voitle, Robert.
"From Epistemology To Romance Via Wisdom" in *Philosophy And Life: Essays On John Wisdom*, Dilman, Ilham (ed), 291–316. Shiner, Roger.
Alcune Riflessioni Sulla Cultura Illuministica Napoletana E L'eredità Di Galilei. Ferrone, Vincenzo.
Aufklärung Und Religionskritik Bei Kant. Liepert, Anita.
Feuerbach Y La Ilustración. Fernandez, Arsenio Ginzo.
Gefühl—Sinnlichkeit—Verstand. Gerlach, Hans–Martin.
Hegel Und Die Aufklärung: Oder: Vom Versuch, Den Verstand Zur Vernunft Zu Bringen. Hasler, Ludwig.
Ilustración Y Ciencia En España Y En La Nueva España. De Micheli, Alfredo.
Interpreting The Enlightenment: A Political Approach. Crocker, Lester G.
La Polémique Contre Les Lumières Et Contre Le Rationalisme Dans Un Journal Peu Connu De Gasparo Gozzi. Cataudella, Michele.
On Nature And Society: Rousseau Versus The Enlightenment. Luke, Timothy W.

ENQUIRY

see Inquiry

ENRIQUES, F

In Difesa Della Filosofia: Enriques E Poincaré. Centi, Beatrice.

ENTAILMENT

A Syntactic Characterization Of Kleene's Strong Connectives With Two Designated Values. Martin, John N.
Perfect Validity, Entailment And Paraconsistency. Tennant, Neil.
The Undecidability Of Entailment And Relevant Implication. Urquhart, Alasdair.
Two Variants Of The System Of Entailment. Imre, Ruzsa.

ENTELECHY

From Entelechy Of The "Feedback Systems Hypothesis". Postelnicu, Paul.

ENTITLEMENT

An Analysis Of Rights. Stoljar, Samuel.
Benefit Rights In Education: An Entitlement View. Beversluis, Eric H.
The Dominant Protection Association And Education. G0ldstone, Peter.

ENTITY(–TIES)

Experimentation And Scientific Realism. Hacking, Ian.
Realism And Anti–Realism About Mathematics. Field, Hartry.

ENTRAPMENT

The Serpent Beguiled Me And I Did Eat: Entrapment And The Creation Of Crime. Dworkin, Gerald.

ENTROPY

Epistemic Analysis: A Coherence Theory Of Knowledge. Ziff, Paul.
Order Out Of Chaos: Man's New Dialogue With Nature. Prigogine, Ilya and Stengers, Isabelle.
Entropy And Evil. Russell, Robert John.
God And Chaos: The Demiurge Versus The *Ungrund*. Hefner, Philip.
Irreversibility Of Time, Entropy And Stability (in Czechoslovakian). Marsík, Frantisek.
Maximum Entropy Inference As A Special Case Of Conditionalization. Skyrms, Brian.
Prior Probabilities. Skilling, John.
Probability, Kinematics, Conditionals, And Entropy Principles. Domotor, Zoltan.
Some Random Observations. Jaynes, E T.

ENTROPY

The Status Of The Principle Of Maximum Entropy. Shimony, Abner.
Thermodynamics And Life. Peacocke, Arthur.

ENUMERATION

A Solution To The Problem Of Induction. Pollock, John L.
Abstrakte Tempomasse Und Speed–Up–Theoreme Für Enumerationen Rekursiv–Aufzählbarer Mengen. Hecker, Hans–Dietrich.
Compactness And Recursive Enumerability In Intensional Logic. Stephan, Bernd J.
Das Kompressionstheorem Für Tempomasse. Hecker, Hans–Dietrich.

ENVIRONMENT(S)

Preparing For The Future: An Essay On The Rights Of Future Generations. Ahrens, John.
Technology And The Character Of Contemporary Life: A Philosophical Inquiry. Borgmann, Albert.
"Two Evolutions" in *On Nature*, Rouner, Leroy S (ed), 42–59. Smith, Huston.
Beauty: A Foundation For Environmental Ethics. Austin, Richard Cartwright.
The Ecological Perspective In John Dewey's Philosophy Of Education. Colwell, Tom.
The Ethics Of Earthworks. Humphrey, Peter.
The Schopenauerian Challenge In Environmental Ethics. Varner, G E.

ENVIRONMENTAL ETHICS

Bioethics: A Casebook. Coppenger, Mark.
A Reply To "On Reading Environmental Ethics". Lemons, John.
Comments On "The Unnatural Jew". Kay, Jeanne.
Die Beziehungen Des Menschen Zum Oikos: Ein Konstruktiver Rahmen Für Die Sinnfrage. Zelger, Josef.
Do We Really Need Environmental Ethics? Spitler, Gene.
Engels Und Die Okologie. Paucke, H.
Intrinsic Value, Quantum Theory, And Environmental Ethics. Callicott, J Baird.
Modern Pantheism As An Approach To Environmental Ethics. Wood Jr, Harold W.
No Tragedy Of The Commons. Cox, Susan Jane Buck.
Non–Anthropocentric Value Theory And Environmental Ethics. Callicott, J Baird.
Okosophie. Kilga, Bernhard.
On Heidegger And The Interpretation Of Environmental Crisis. Foltz, Bruce V.
Organism, Community, And The "Substitution Problem". Katz, Eric.
Stichwort Okologie. Vester, Frederic.
The Development Of Nature Resources And The Integrity Of Nature. Devall, Bill and Sessions, George.
The Liberation Of Nature: A Circular Affair. Kheel, Marti.
Theoretische Oberlegungen Zum Okoproblem. Bach, Hans.
Three Wrong Leads In A Search For An Environmental Ethic: Tom Regan On Animal Rights, Inherent Values, And 'Deep Ecology'. Partridge, Ernest.
What Philosophers Can Learn From Agriculture. Thompson, Paul.
Zum Okologiegehalt Der Nationalökonomie. Nussbaumer, Josef and Holleis, Wilfried.

ENVIRONMENTALISM

Deeper Than Deep Ecology: The Eco–Feminist Connection. Salleh, Ariel Kay.
Marx's Critique Of Capitalist Technology: Form And Content. Rehg, William R.
The Unnatural Jew. Schwarzschild, Steven S.

ENVY

Φθονος And Its Related Παθη In Plato And Aristotle. Mills, Michael J.
"Envy As Personal Phenomenon And As Politics" in *International Kierkegaard Commentary*, Perkins, Robert L (ed), 107–132. Perkins, Robert L.
Formal Properties Of Interpersonal Envy. Chaudhuri, Adhip.

EPIC

"On Medieval Interpretation And Mythology" in *Existential Coordinates Of Human Condition*, Tymieniecka, A (ed), 185–194. Gellrich, Jesse.
"The Epic Element In Japanese Literature" in *Existential Coordinates Of Human Condition*, Tymieniecka, A (ed), 195–208. Viglielmo, Valdo H.
"The Existential Sources Of Rhetoric" in *Existential Coordinates Of Human Condition*, Tymieniecka, A (ed), 227–240. Medina, Angel.
"The Myth Of Man In The Hebraic Epic" in *Existential Coordinates Of Human Condition*, Tymieniecka, A (ed), 175–184. Famras–Rauch, Gila.
"The Shield And The Horizon" in *Existential Coordinates Of Human Condition*, Tymieniecka, A (ed), 163–174. Findlay, L M.

EPICUREANISM

Zu Kants Unterscheidung Von Platonismus Und Epikureismus. Ley, Hermann.

EPICUREANS

Die Induktive Methode Und Das Induktionsproblem In Der Griechischen Philosophie. Tsouyopoulos, Nelly.

EPICURUS

Epicurus' Scientific Method. Asmis, Elizabeth.
Happiness Through Tranquility: The School Of Epicurus. Hibler, Richard W.
Epicurus And Lucretius On Sex, Love, And Marriage. Arkins, B.

EPIDEMIOLOGY

Epidemiology And Anthropology: Notes On Science And Scientism. Rubinstein, Robert A.

EPIPHENOMENALISM

Epiphenomenal And Supervenient Causation. Kim, Jaegwon.

EPISTEMIC

Legal Positivism And Natural Law Reconsidered. Brink, David O.
On The Notion Of Effectiveness. Shapiro, Stewart.

EPISTEMIC LOGIC

Epistemic And Alethic Iteration In Later Medieval Logic. Boh, Ivan.
Salvaging 'The F–er Is F': The Lesson Of Clark's Paradox. Landini, Gregory.
The Relation Between Epistemology And Psychology. Goldman, Alvin I.

EPISTEMOLOGY

see also Action(s), Empiricism, Idealism, Imagination, Knowledge, Memory, Perception, Rationalism, Realism, Truth(s)

A Celebration Of Subjective Thought. Diefenbeck, James A.
A Priori Knowledge For Fallibilists. Edidin, Aron.
A Sceptical Dialogue On Induction. Naess, Arne.
An American Urphilosophie. Bunge, Robert.
An Essay Concerning The Use Of Reason In Propositions: A Discourse Of Free Thinking. Collins, Anthony and Schouls, Peter A (ed).
An Outline Of The Idealistic Construction Of Experience. Baillie, J B.
Anti–Skepticism. Lee, Henry and Schouls, Peter A (ed).
Bachelard: Science And Objectivity. Tiles, Mary.
Beyond Empiricism: Michael Polanyi Reconsidered. Kane, Jeffrey.
Boston Studies In The Philosophy Of Science: Dialectical Theory Of Meaning, R S Cohen And M W Wartofsky (eds) V81. Markovic, Mihailo.
Buddhist And Western Psychology. Katz, Nathan (ed).
Carnap's Early Conventionalism: An Inquiry Into The Historical Background Of The Vienna Circle. Runggaldier, Edmund.
Conscientization And Creativity. Schipani, Daniel S.
Criticism And Objectivity. Selden, Raman.
D M Armstrong. Bogdan, Radu J (ed).
Epistemic Analysis: A Coherence Theory Of Knowledge. Ziff, Paul.
Essays In The Unknown Wittgenstein. Lazerowitz, Morris and Ambrose, Alice.
Ethical Argumentation: A Study In Hsun Tzu's Moral Epistemology. Cua, A S.
Faith And Rationality: Reason And Belief In God. Plantinga, Alvin (ed) and Wolterstorff, Nicholas (ed).
Hegel's Critique Of The Enlightenment. Hinchman, Lewis P.
Hermeneutics: A Sociology Of Misunderstanding. Flanagan, Kieran.
Ideology, Philosophy And Politics. Parel, Anthony (ed).
Imagination And Reflection: Intersubjectivity. Hohler, T P (ed).
Informatique Pour Les Sciences Del'homme. Borillo, Mario.
Inquiry. Stalnaker, Robert C.
Introducing Philosophy: A Text With Readings. Solomon, Robert C.
Jñāna And Pramā: The Logic Of Knowing—A Critical Appraisal. Bilimoria, Purusottama.
John Locke And English Literature Of The Eighteenth Century. Mac Lean, Kenneth and Schouls, Peter A (ed).
Kant's Critical Philosophy. Deleuw, Gilles.
Lehrbuch Der Philosophie. Wuchterl, Kurt.
Leibniz And Locke: A Study Of The "New Essays On Human Understanding". Jolley, Nicholas.
Leibniz. Brown, Stuart.
Locke's Writings And Philosophy: Historically Considered. Tagart, Edward.
Logic And The Objectivity Of Knowledge: Studies In Husserl's Early Philosophy. Willard, Dallas.
Logic, Philosophy, And History: A Study In The Philosophy Of History Based On The Work Of R G Collingwood. Russell, Anthony F.
Logick: Or, The Right Use Of Reason. Watts, Isaac and Schouls, Peter A (ed).
Methodology, Metaphysics And The History Of Science. Cohen, Robert S (ed) and Wartofsky, Marx W (ed).
Mutual Knowledge. Smith, N V (ed).
Non Pie Quaerunt: Rhetoric, Dialectic, And The Discovery Of The True In Augustine's Confessions. Di Lorenzo, Raymond D.
Peirce: Textes Anticartésiens. Chenu, Joseph.
Perennial Philosophical Issues. Grassian, Victor.
Persons And Their World: An Introduction To Philosophy. Olen, Jeffrey.
Philosophical Problems. Stumpf, Samuel Enoch.
Philosophy: An Introduction To The Central Issues. Landesman, Charles.
Popper Selections. Miller, David (ed).
Postures Of The Mind: Essays On Mind And Morals. Baier, Annette.
Pragmatics And Empiricism. Skyrms, Brian.
Principles Of Language And Mind: An Evolutionary Theory Of Meaning. Waldron, T P.
Probability And Evidence. Horwich, Paul.
Probability, Objectivity And Evidence. Benenson, F C.
Rational Decision And Causality. Eells, Ellery.
Realism And Truth. Devitt, Michael.
Realism And Reason: Philosophical Papers, V3. Putnam, Hillary.
Reason And The Search For Knowledge: Investigations In The Philosophy Of Science. Shapere, Dudley.
Sense And Content: Experience, Thought, And Their Relations. Peacocke, Christopher.
Subjecting And Objecting. Deutscher, Max.
The Central Problem Of David Hume's Philosophy. Salmon, C V.
The Concept Of Evidence. Achinstein, Peter (ed).
The Epistemology Of Hans–Georg Gadamer. Schmidt, Lawrence K.
The Essential Writings, Bruce W Wilshire (ed). James, William.
The Knower And The Known. Grene, Marjorie G.
The Limits Of Scientific Reasoning. Faust, David.
The Limits Of Science. Rescher, Nicholas.
The Man Of Reason: "Male" And "Female" In Western Philosophy. Lloyd, Genevieve.
The Nature Of Selection: Evolutionary Theory In Philosophical Focus. Sober, Elliott.
The New Scientific Spirit. Bachelard, Gaston and Goldhammer, Arthur (trans).
The Postmodern Condition: A Report On Knowledge. Lyotard, Jean François.
The Retreat To Commitment. Bartley, W W.
The Sign Of Three. Sebok, Thomas A (ed) and Eco, Umberto (ed).

EPISTEMOLOGY

EPISTEMOLOGY

Criteria And Circumstances. Caraway, Carol.

Critique Du Rationalisme Critique. Largeault, Jean.

Croyances, Dispositions Et Probabilities (Peirce Et Ramsey). Engel, Pascal.

Culture Et Vérité Chez Aristote. Cauchy, Venant.

Das Apriorische Moment Der Subjekt–Objekt–Dialektik In Der Transzendentalen Phänomenologie. Kochler, Hans.

Das Aufsteigen Der Erkenntnis Vom Abstrakten Zum Konkreten. Pröhl, Joachim.

Das Erkennen Als Ein Erkennen In Blosser Erscheinung: Zu Ingeborg Heidemanns Verständnis Der Kritik Der Reiner Vernuft. Kopper, J.

Das Individuelle Bewusstsein Und Die Dialektik Von Objektiven Bedingungen Und Subjektivem Faktor. Hahn, Toni.

Das Problem Der Rationalität. Agassi, Joseph.

Das Solipsistisch–Intuitionistische Konzept Der Vernunft Und Des Verstehens: Traditionskritische Bemerkungen. Böhler, Dietrich.

Das Verhältnis Der *Kritik Der Reinen Vernunft* Zu Den *Metaphysischen Anfangsgründen Der Naturwissenschaft*, Demonstr Am Substanzsatz. Gloy, Karen.

Davidson's Theism? Foley, Richard and Fumerton, Richard.

Davidson's Theory Of Meaning: Some Questions. Taylor, Kenneth A.

De l'illusion Transcendantale. Theis, Robert.

De La Physique À L'épistémologie B D'Espagnat Et I Prigogine. Gauthier, Yvon.

De La Sensibilité. Levinas, E.

Der Erkenntniswert Von Metaphorischen Aussagen. Brulisauer, Bruno.

Der Grundgedanke Des Tractatus Als Metamorphose Des Obersten Grundsatzes Der Kritik Der Reinen Vernunft. Ferber, Rafael.

Der Kritische Rationalismus Und Kant. Richter, Gundrun.

Derek Parfit And Greta Garbo. Madell, Geoffrey.

Descarte's *Cogito*. Flage, Daniel E.

Descartes Knows Nothing. Watson, Richard A.

Descartes' Proto–Critique. Glouberman, M.

Descriptive Epistemology. Duran, Jane.

Destroying The Consensus. Loewer, Barry and Laddaga, Robert.

Dewey's Theory Of Inquiry: Problems Of Foundations. Lakomski, Gabriele.

Dialectic And The Role Of The Phenomenologist (in Hebrew). Marx, Werner.

Die Bedeutung Der Methode Galileis Für Die Entwicklung Der Transzendentalphilosophie Kants. Holz, Fr.

Die Seins– Und Erkenntnisfrage In Der Philosophie Brentanos. Melle, U.

Difference And Dissonance In Ethnographic Data. Ward, Jeffrey J and Werner, O.

Dissolving Kripke's Puzzle About Belief. Pettit, Philip.

Does Indian Epistemology Concern Justified True Belief? Potter, K H.

Does The Description Theory Make Contingent Truths Necessary? Eudaly, Thomas D.

Does The Gettier Problem Rest On A Mistake? Kirkham, Richard L.

Editorial: Philosophy Of Medicine In The U S A. Thomasma, David C.

Educación Universitaria Para El Amor. Basave, Agustín.

Einige Methodische Regeln Descartes' Und Das Erfindende Denken. Hammacher, Klaus.

Einstein, Gibbins And The Unity Of Time. Lockwood, Michael.

El Método Empírico–Reflexivo. Buela, Alberto E.

El Triángulo Universal De Locke: Su Inmerecida Fama. Angelelli, Ignacio.

Emergent Behaviorism. Killeen, Peter R.

Emotions Across Cultures: Objectivity And Cultural Divergence. Heelas, Paul.

Empirical Psychology, Naturalized Epistemology, And First Philosophy. Siegel, Harvey.

Empiricism And The Theory Of Meaning. Cockburn, David.

En Marge De Quelques Textes Épistémologiques Récents. Robert, Jean–Dominique.

Enkele Opmerkingen Over Geldigheid En Gelding. Hage, J C.

Entity And Antinomy In Tibetan Bsdus Grwa Logic (Part 1). Goldberg, Margaret.

Epiphenomenal And Supervenient Causation. Kim, Jaegwon.

Epistemic Dependence. Dauer, Francis W.

Epistemic Dependence. Hardwig, John.

Epistemic Supervenience And The Rule Of Belief. Van Cleve, James.

Epistemic Universalizability Principles. Brueckner, Anthony.

Epistemic Value. Lycan, William G.

Epistemological Internalism. Montmarquet, James A.

Epistemology Must Not Lose Sight Of Man. Ruoshui, Wang.

Equality And Length. Steenburgh Van, E W.

Erkenntnistheoretische Und Pädagogische Probleme Bei Der Verwendung Von Lehr– Und Lernmitteln In Der Ausbildung Von Philosophiestudenten. Kirchgässner, Werner and Sanger, H.

Establishing Causal Connections: Meta–Analysis And Psychotherapy. Erwin, Edward.

Europa Und Die Vereinigten Staaten Von Amerika Philosophiegeschichtlich Betrachtet. Moser, Simon.

Ever Since Descartes. Kornblith, Hilary.

Evidentialism. Feldman, Richard and Conee, Earl.

Evolutionary Epistemology And Ontological Realism. Clark, A J.

Expected Utilities And Rational Actions And Choices. Sobel, Jordan Howard.

Explaining The Unpredictable. Suppes, Patrick.

Explaining The Actions Of The Explainers. Baier, Annette.

Extending The Darwinian Model: James's Struggle With Royce And Spencer. Seigfried, Charlene H.

Faces. Stroll, Avrum.

Faith As Kant's Key To The Justification Of Transcendental Reflection. Palmquist, Stephen.

Fenomenología De La Sensación. Chalmeta, Gabriel.

Fichte's Emendation Of Kant. Taber, John.

Fiction And Fabrication. Deutsch, Harry.

For A Syncretism Of The Faculties Of The Mind: Art As A Means Of Knowledge. Dehaye, Pierre.

Formal Traces In Cartesian Functional Explanation. Rorty, Amelie Oksenberg.

Foucault's Archaeological Method: A Response To Hacking And Rorty. Wartenberg, Thomas E.

Foundationalism And Permanence In Descartes' Epistemology. Cling, Andrew D.

Foundations For Direct Inference. Pollock, John L.

Frames, Knowledge, And Inference. Thagard, Paul.

Frammenti: Sulla Crisi Della Epistemologia. Centrone, Marino.

Frankfurt On Descartes' Dream Argument. Stuart, James D.

Freedom Defined As The Power To Decide. Mc Call, Storrs.

Frege's Justificationism: Truth And The Recognition Of Authority. Notturno, M A.

Frege's Paradox Of Reference And Castañeda's Guise Theory. Lee, Jig–Chuen.

Fregean Thoughts. Noonan, Harold.

From Cartesian Epistemology To Cartesian Metaphysics. Markie, Peter J.

Fugitive Truth. Earle, William James.

Gaston Bachelard Et Ferdinand Gonseth, Philosophes De La Dialectique Scientifique. Lauener, Henri.

Gaston Bachelard Ou "La Surveillance Intellectuelle De Soi". Desanti, Jean–Toussaint.

Gedanken Zur Lektüre Platonischer Dialoge. Dalfen, Joachim.

Gefühl—Sinnlichkeit—Verstand. Gerlach, Hans–Martin.

Genealogisches Zum Cogito: Über Ein Motiv Des Cartesischen Denkens. Dörr, Hartmut.

Genetic Epistemology And Philosophical Epistemology. Loptson, P J and Kelly, J W.

Genetic Epistemology And The Child's Understanding Of Logic. Smith, Leslie.

Goede Redenen Om Iets Te Geloven. Derksen, A A.

Good Transcendental Arguments. Genova, A C.

Hacking On Frege. Dummett, Michael.

Hamanns Kantkritik. Wohlfart, Cunter.

Hermeneutics As Practical Philosophy And Practical Wisdom (in Dutch). Van Der Walt, J W G.

History And The Brewmaster's Nose. Martin, Raymond.

Horwich's Justification Of Induction. Chihara, Charles S.

How And Why Seeing Is Not Believing. Nelson, John O.

How To Be An Idealist (II). Mc Fee, Graham.

How To Become A Moderate Skeptic: Hume's Way Out Of Pyrrhonism. Michaud, Yves.

How To Revive Empiricism. Brown, Harold I.

How Wrong Was Kant About Geometry? Barker, Stephen F.

Hume And The Missing Shade Of Blue. Fogelin, Robert J.

Hume On Causal Necessity: A Study From The Perspective Of Hume's Theory Of Passions. Enc, Berent.

Hume On The Perception Of Causality. Shanks, David R.

Hume's "Dialectic". Coleman, Dorothy P.

Hume's Criterion Of Significance. Williams, Michael.

Hume's Labyrinth. Behan, David P.

Hume's Missing Shade Of Blue, Interpreted As Involving Habitual Spectra. Johnson, David M.

Hume's Naturalism—'Proof' And Practice. Ferreira, M J.

Hutcheson's Moral Realism. Norton, David F.

Hypothetical Method And Rationality In Plato. Scolnicov, S.

I Am The Way: Michael Polanyi's Taoism. Stines, James W.

I Percorsi Multipli Dell'epistemologia Di G Bachelard: Il Rapporto Filosofia–Epistemologia: Problemi E Dinamiche. Arazzi, Graziella.

Idea, Esquema E Imaginación En Kant. Ferreres, Jose M Rubio.

Identity, Appearances, And Things In Themselves. Bencivenga, Ermanno.

Ignoring Available Evidence. Clarke, David S.

Ilustración Y Ciencia En España Y En La Nueva España. De Micheli, Alfredo.

Imagery: From Hume To Cognitive Science. Bower, Kenneth J.

In Defense Of A Nontraditional Theory Of Memory. Naylor, Andrew.

In Response To Suchocki's "The Appeal To Ultimacy In Meland's Thought". Meland, Bernard E.

Inaccessible Routes To The Problem Of Privileged Access. Schlesinger, George N.

Incongruence And The Unity Of Transcendental Idealism: Reply To Henry E Allison. Buroker, Jill Vance.

Indeterminate People. Chandler, Hugh S.

Indian Epistemology—A Synthetic Study. Basu, Shankar.

Inexhaustibility And Ontological Plurality. Ross, Stephen David.

Instinctive Beliefs. Davis, William H.

Intelligibilité Et Réalité Chez Hobbes Et Spinoza. Bernhardt, Jean.

Interpreting Peirce. Grossman, Morris.

Interrelations Between Subject And Object In Perception. Lijun, Song.

Intuition And Manifold In The Transcendental Deduction. Robinson, Hoke.

Investigating Lonergan's Inaccessibility. Walmsley, Gerard.

Is Hume A Sceptic With Regard To Reason? Wilson, Fred.

Is Knowledge Information–Produced Belief? Doyle, Anthony.

Is Object–Seeing Really Propositional Seeing? Nelson, John O.

Is Relativism Self–Refuting? Weckert, John.

Is The Causal Structure Of The Physical Itself Something Physical? Putnam, Hilary.

Is The Concept Of Pain Incoherent? Kaufman, Rick.

Is There An 'Us' In 'Justification'? Kvanvig, J L.

It's Not What You Know That Counts. Kaplan, Mark.

J G H Feder—Beitrag Zu Einer Verhinderungsgeschichte Eines Deutschen Empirismus. Röttgers, Kurt.

J S Beck And Husserl: The New Episteme In The Kantian Tradition. Wallner, Ingrid M.

EPISTEMOLOGY

EPISTEMOLOGY

The Origins Of Hume's Sceptical Argument Against Reason. Wilson, Fred.

The Origins And Issues Of Scepticism, East And West. Sprung, Mervyn.

The Passivity Assumption Of The Sensation–Perception Distinction. Ben–Zeev, Aaron.

The Path Of French Epistemology To The Concept Of Chaos (in Czechoslovakian). Marcelli, Miroslav.

The Phases Of Light In Augustine (in Japanese). Hikasa, Katsushi.

The Present Meaning Of The Idea Of Rationality. Kuderowicz, Zbigniew.

The Primary/Secondary Quality Distinction: Berkeley, Locke, And The Foundations Of Corpuscularian Science. Davidson, Arnold I and Hornstein, Norbert.

The Priority Of Reason Over Faith In Augustine. Ramirez, J Roland.

The Process Of Meaning–Creation: A Transcendental Argument. Falck, Colin.

The Projection Postulate: A New Perspective. Teller, Paul.

The Referential And The Attributive: A Distinction In Use? Yagisawa, Takashi.

The Relation Between Epistemology And Psychology. Goldman, Alvin I.

The Reliabilist Theory Of Rational Belief. Luper–Foy, Steven.

The Resemblances Of Colors. Hardin, C L.

The Role Of Problems And Problem Solving In Popper's Early Work On Psychology. Petersen, Arne Friemuth.

The Scientific And The Ethical. Williams, Bernard.

The Scope Of Reason: An Epistle To The Persians. Bambrough, Renford.

The Scope Of Knowledge In Republic V. White, F C.

The Second Edition Of The Critique: Toward An Understanding Of Its Nature And Genesis. Washburn, M C.

The Separation Of Ontological Idealism From Epistemological Idealism (in Hungarian). Petho, Bertalan.

The Transfer Principle. Suzuki, Yoshindo.

The Tree In The Quad. Fleming, Noel.

The Umpire's Dilemma. Radford, Colin.

The Virtues Of Inconsistency. Klein, Peter.

Theaetetus, Part II: A Dialogical Review. Goodman, William H.

Timing Contradictions In Von Neumann And Morgenstern's Axioms And In Savage's "Sure–Thing" Proof. Pope, Robin.

Tomberlin, Frege, And Guise Theory: A Note On The Methodology Of Dia–Philosophical Comparisons. Castaneda, Hector–Neri.

Towards A Computational Phenomenology (1). Harlan, Robert M.

Towards A Critical Theory Of Value. Luntley, Michael.

Traditional Epistemology And Naturalistic Replies To Its Skeptical Critics. Bogen, James.

Transference And The Direction Of Causation. Kline, A David.

Transmission For Knowledge Not Established. Brueckner, Anthony.

True Believers And Radical Sceptics. Gallois, André.

Truth And Best Explanation. Tuomela, Raimo.

Two Alternative Epistemological Frameworks In Psychology: The Typological And Variational Modes Of Thinking. Valsiner, Jaan.

Two Classical Western Theologians: Augustine And Newman. Penaskovic, Richard.

Two Notions Of Realism? Mc Ginn, Colin.

Un Nuevo Paraqdigma Para Las Ciencias Del Concocimiento. Gutiérrez, Claudio.

Understanding Art And Understanding Persons. Berenson, Frances.

Van Wezensschouw Naar Hermeneuse. De Boer, Th.

Veridicality: More On Searle. Millar, Alan.

Veritas Filia Temporis: Hume On Time And Causation. Lennon, Thomas M.

Visual Space From The Perspective Of Possible World Semantics II. Wiesenthal, L.

Voluntary Belief. Naylor, Margery Bedford.

Waarheid Als Effect; Richard Rorty En De Natuur Van De Spiegel. Kwaad, G C.

Was Nietzsche A Cognitivist? Westphal, Kenneth.

Was Wittgenstein A Sceptic? Hanfling, Oswald.

Welfare Functions And Group Decisions. Borch, Karl.

What Is Explained By AI Models? Kobsa, Alfred.

What Is The Difference That Makes A Difference: Gadamer, Habermas, And Rorty (in Hebrew). Bernstein, Richard G.

What Is Wrong With Verisimilitude? Smith, Joseph W.

What's Historical About Historical Materialism? Levine, Andrew and Sober, Elliott.

What's Wrong With Reliabilism? Foley, Richard.

Whither Infinite Regresses Of Justification. Moser, Paul D.

Wie Ist Sinn Des Sinnlosen Möglich? Kohler, Rudolf.

Wittgenstein's Solution Of The 'Hermeneutic Problem'. Shanker, Stuart G.

Wittgenstein's Language–Games And The Call To Cognition. Deitz, Samuel M and Arrington, Robert L.

Wittgenstein And Nāgārjuna's Paradox. Anderson, Tyson.

Wittgenstein On Sensation And 'Seeing–As'. Dunlop, Charles E M.

Zur Kritischen Analyse Des Induktionsproblems. Kronthaler, Engelbert.

Zur Sowjetphilosophischen Kritik Der "Idealistischen" Erkenntnistheorie. Weinzierl, Emil.

EQUAL OPPORTUNITY

Equal Opportunity. Nelson, William.

Fair Equality Of Opportunity And Decent Minimums: A Reply To Buchanan. Daniels, Norman.

Hiring By Competence. Werhane, Patricia H.

The Concept Of Equal Opportunity. Westen, Peter.

The Human Right To Be Treated As A Person. Khatchadourian, Haig.

EQUALITY

see also Egalitarianism

"Popper And Liberalism" in Popper And The Human Sciences, Currie, Gregory (ed), 89–104. Ryan, Alan.

A Normal Form Theorem For First Order Formulas And Its Application To Gaifman's Splitting Theorem. Motohashi, Nobuyoshi.

Distributive Justice, Contract, And Equality. Macleod, Alistair M.

Does Liberalism Rest On A Mistake? Rodewald, Richard.

Eigentum Und Ungleichheit: Rousseaus Eigentumslehre. Ryffel, Hans.

Equal Opportunity. Nelson, William.

Equality Vs Liberty: Advantage, Liberty. Narveson, Jan.

Equality And Length. Steenburgh Van, E W.

Equality, Excellence, Paideia, And The Good Old Days Before Adam And Eve And Social Science. Arnstine, Donald.

Ethics And Markets. Bennett, John G.

Fibered Categories And The Foundations Of Naive Category Theory. Benabou, Jean.

Gleichheit Und Eigentum: Metaethische Und Normative Bemerkungen Zum Verfassungsentwurf. Hügli, Anton.

Justifying Departures From Equal Treatment. Murphy, Jeffrie G.

Karl Marx On Democracy, Participation, Voting, And Equality. Springborg, Patricia.

Les Avatars De La Différence. Morosoli, Michele.

Liberty And Equality: How Politics Masquerades As Philosophy. Hare, R M.

Liberty, Equality, Honor. Kristol, William.

Note Sur La Syntaxe Et La Sémantique Du Concept D'égalité. Gauthier, Yvon.

Preferences Opposed To The Market. Braybrooke, David.

Rousseau On Equality. Cranston, Maurice.

Rule Utilitarianism, Equality, And Justice. Harsanyi, John C.

Sameness And Equality: A Rejoinder To John Colbeck's Response To "Procrustes And Private Schooling". Shaw, Beverley.

Sobre El Feminismo De Platón. Cappelletti, Angel J.

Some Thoughts On Liberty, Equality, And Tocqueville's democracy In America. Dannhauser, Werner J.

The Demands Of Justice. Benditt, Theodore M.

EQUATION(S)

Decidable Properties Of Finite Sets Of Equations In Trivial Languages. Kalfa, Cornelia.

Equality And Length. Steenburgh Van, E W.

Homogeneous Forms In Two Ordinal Variables. Hickman, John L.

EQUILIBRIUM

Thermodynamics Without Equilibrium, Totality, Dialectic (in Czechoslovakian). Rajchl, Jaroslav.

EQUITY

Classical Living And Classical Learning: The Search For Equity And Excellence In Education. Smith, Philip L and Traver, Rob.

Equal Treatment And Equal Chances. Kamm, Frances Myrna.

Yugoslavia: Equity And Imported Ethical Dilemmas. Lang, Slobodan and others.

EQUIVALENCE

Realism And Reason: Philosophical Papers, V3. Putnam, Hillary.

Accessible Sets And $(L_{\omega_1\omega})$–Equivalence For T_3 Spaces. Martínez, Juan Carlos.

Fuzzy Recursion, RET's, And Isols. Harkleroad, Leon.

On Σ^1_1 Equivalence Relations With Borel Classes Of Bounded Rank. Sami, Ramez L.

On Definitional Equivalence And Related Topics. Corcoran, John.

Six Problems In "Translational Equivalence". Pelletier, F J.

What Was Einstein's Principle Of Equivalence? Norton, John.

EQUIVOCATION

Roger Bacon On Equivocation. Maloney, Thomas S.

ERIKSON, E

Moral Development Foundations: Judeo–Christian Alternatives To Piaget/Kohlberg. Joy, Donald M (ed).

ERIUGENA

L'acte Libre Démission Ou Courage D'etre Devant Le Sensible Selon Jean Scot Érigène. Wohlman, Avital.

Sprache Und Sache: Reflexionen Zu Eriugenas Einschätzung Von Leistung Und Funktion Der Sprache. Beierwaltes, Werner.

EROS

Logos Y Eros En San Juan De La Cruz Y Platón. Herrera, Bernal.

The Erotic Education Of The Slave. Nails, Debra.

ERROR(S)

Theory And Measurement. Kyburg Jr, Henry E.

A Principle Of Responsive Adjustment. French, Peter A.

The Confirmation Of Quantitative Laws. Kyburg, Henry E.

ESCHATOLOGY

"L'épître Sur La Connaissance De L'âme Rationnelle Et De Ses États" Attribuée À Avicenne. Michot, Jean.

In Response To Suchocki's "The Appeal To Ultimacy In Meland's Thought". Meland, Bernard E.

Menschenwürde Und Menschenrechte Im Light Der "Offenbarung Jesu Christi". Schürmann, Heinz.

The Appeal To Ultimacy In Meland's Thought. Suchocki, Marjorie.

Theorieën Over Ethiek En Over De Levenspraktijk. Troost, A.

ESSENCE(S)

see also Form(s)

An Interpretation Of The Logic Of Hegel. Harris, Errol E.

Hegel's Logic. Hibben, John Grier.

Hegel's Logic: An Essay In Interpretation. Hibben, John G and Harris, H S (ed).

Leibniz And Locke: A Study Of The "New Essays On Human Understanding". Jolley, Nicholas.

"Armstrong On Determinable And Substantial Universals" in D M Armstrong, Bogdan,

ETHICS

Practical Reason. Von Wright, G H.

Problems And Materials On Professional Responsibility. Morgan, Thomas D and Rotunda, Ronald D.

Problems In Legal Ethics. Schwartz, Mortimer D and Wydick, Richard C.

Professional Ethics In Education. Rich, John Martin.

Psychiatry And Ethics. Edwards, Rem B (ed).

Rationality And Relativism: In Search Of A Philosophy And History Of Anthropology. Jarvie, I C.

Reason And Right. Hallett, Garth.

Renaissance Eloquence: Studies In The Theory And Practice Of Renaissance Rhetoric. Murphy, James J (ed).

Reproductive Ethics. Bayles, Michael D.

Research Ethics. Berg, Kare (ed) and Tranoy, Knut Erik (ed).

Right Actions In Sport: Ethics For Contestants. Fraleigh, Warren P.

Rights And Goods: Justifying Social Action. Held, Virginia.

Selected Standards On Professional Responsibility. Rotunda, Ronald D and Morgan, Thomas D.

Social And Political Ethics. Brodsky, Garry (ed) and Troyer, John (ed) and Vance, David (ed).

Sports And Social Values. Simon, Robert L.

Taking Care Of Strangers: The Rule Of Law In Doctor–Patient Relations. Burt, Robert A.

Technology And The Character Of Contemporary Life: A Philosophical Inquiry. Borgmann, Albert.

The Essential Writings, Bruce W Wilshire (ed). James, William.

The Freedom Of Morality. Yannaras, Christos.

The Georgetown Symposium On Ethics. Porreco, Rocco (ed).

The Good Life And Its Pursuit. Dougherty, Jude P (ed).

The Great Reversal: Ethics And The New Testament. Verhey, Allen.

The Islamic Conception Of Justice. Khadduri, Majid.

The Legal Profession: Responsibility And Regulation. Hazard, Geoffrey C and Rhode, Deborah L.

The Moral Psychology Of The Virtues. Dent, N J H.

The Nature Of Love: Plato To Luther, Second Edition. Singer, Irving.

The Security Gamble: Deterrence Dilemmas In The Nuclear Age. Mac Lean, Douglas (ed).

The Silent World Of Doctor And Patient. Katz, Jay.

The Theory And Practice Of Virtue. Meilaender, Gilbert C.

The Third Earl Of Shaftesbury 1671–1713. Voitle, Robert.

The Will At The Crossroads: A Reconstruction Of Kant's Moral Philosophy. Cox, J Gray.

Unacceptable Essays. Roe, M F H.

Vice And Virtue In Everyday Life: Introductory Readings In Ethics. Sommers, Christina Hoff.

War And Justice. Phillips, Robert L.

Wickedness: A Philosophical Essay. Midgley, Mary.

Φθονος And Its Related Παθη In Plato And Aristotle. Mills, Michael J.

'Communicative Competence' And The Skeptic. Beatty, Joseph.

'Constraints On Freedom' As A Descriptive Concept. Oppenheim, Felix.

'Doing Business With The Gods'. Burns, Steven A M.

'Ethics And Aesthetics Are One'. Collinson, Diané.

'Is' Presupposes 'Ought'. Hinman, Lawrence M.

'My Husband Won't Tell The Children!'. Dubler, Nancy Neveloff and Schneiderman, Lawrence J.

'Ought Implies Can' And Two Kinds Of Morality. Kekes, John.

'Ought To Have' And 'Could Have'. Sinnott– Armstrong, Walter.

"A Future Analysis Of Marxism And Ethics" in *Darwin, Marx And Freud*, Caplan, Arthur L (ed), 73–112. Harrington, Michael.

"An Ecological Argument For Vegetarianism". Wenz, Peter S.

"Darwinism And Ethics: A Response To Antony Flew" in *Darwin, Marx And Freud*, Caplan, Arthur L (ed), 47–72. Kass, Leon R.

"Drugs, Models, And Moral Principles" in *Feeling Good And Doing Better*, Murray, Thomas H (ed), 187–214. Macklin, Ruth.

"Drugs, Sports, And Ethics" in *Feeling Good And Doing Better*, Murray, Thomas H (ed), 107–128. Murray, Thomas H.

"El Justo Es Feliz Y El Injusto Desgraciado": Justicia Y Felicidad En La "República" De Platón. Perez Ruiz, Francisco.

"Ethics And Excuses: Ethical Implications Of Psychoanalysis" in *Darwin, Marx And Freud*, Caplan, Arthur L (ed), 201–208. Izenberg, Gerald N.

"Ethics And The Language Of Morality" in *Philosophical Analysis In Latin America*, Gracia, Jorge J E and others (eds), 243–254. Salmerón, Fernando.

"Ethics Of Institutional Ethics Committees" in *Ethics Committees And Health Care Decisions*, Cranford, Ronald (ed), 35–50. Veatch, Robert M.

"Evolution And Ethics" in *Darwin, Marx And Freud*, Caplan, Arthur L (ed), 35–46. Mayr, Ernst.

"Hegel, Plato And Greek 'Sittlichkeit'" in *The State And Civil Society*, Pelczynski, Z A (ed), 40–54. Inwood, M J.

"Marxism And Ethics Today" in *Darwin, Marx And Freud*, Caplan, Arthur L (ed), 113–130. Rapaport, Elizabeth.

"Medicolegal And Ethical Dilemmas In A Teaching Hospital" in *Ethics Committees And Health Care Decisions*, Cranford, Ronald (ed), 118–128. Grodin, Michael and Markley, William S and Mc Donald, Anne E.

"Our Non–Ethical Educational Ethos" in *The Georgetown Symposium On Ethics*, Porreco, Rocco (ed), 269–278. Young, Theodore A.

"Playing God": The Ethics Of Biotechnical Intervention. Varga, Andrew C.

"Reopening The Books On Ethics: The Role Of Education In A Free Society" in *On Freedom*, Howard, John A (ed), 79–94. Howard, John A.

"Some Paradoxical Goals Of Cells And Organisms" in *Ethical Questions In Brain And Behavior*, Pfaff, Donald W (ed), 111–124. Brown, Jerram L.

"The Divine Corporation And The History Of Ethics" in *Philosophy In History*, Rorty, Richard and others (ed), 173–192. Schneewind, J B.

"The Kantian Critique Of Aristotle's Moral Philosophy" in *The Good Life And Its Pursuit*, Dougherty, Jude P (ed), 77–110. Sullivan, Roger J.

"The Morality Of Killing Animals: Four Arguments". Young, Thomas.

"The Profits Of Freedom: Investing In The Defense Of Business" in *On Freedom*, Howard, John A (ed), 59–78. Shenfield, Arthur.

"The State's Intervention In Individuals' Drug Use: A Normative Account" in *Feeling Good And Doing Better*, Murray, Thomas H (ed), 65–82. Neville, Robert.

"Treatment Refusals" in *Ethical Questions In Brain And Behavior*, Pfaff, Donald W (ed), 41–56. Macklin, Ruth.

A Biological Interpretation Of Moral Systems. Alexander, Richard D.

A Business Model Of Enlightenment. Barnett, John H.

A Certain Just War, A Certain Pacifism. Conley, John J.

A Comment To J Gockowski's *Situational Tests Of A Scholar's Faithfullness To His Ethos* (in Polish). Jankowski, H.

A Contractarian Defense Of Nuclear Deterrence. Morris, Christopher W.

A Cotton Dust Study Unmasked. Levine, Carol.

A Critical Account Of Yang Kuei–Shan's Philosophical Thought (in Chinese). Chang, Jun–Chun.

A Defense Of Utilitarian Policy Processes In Corporate And Public Management. Brady, F Neil.

A Defense Of Employee Rights. Des Jardins, Joseph R and Mc Call, John J.

A Definition For Paternalism. Hershey, Paul Turner.

A Duty To Warn, An Uncertain Danger. Reamer, Frederic G and Schaffer, Sylvan J.

A Father Says 'Don't Tell My Son The Truth'. Higgs, Roger and others.

A Kantian Argument Against Abortion. Gensler, Harry J.

A Letter To James Gustafson. Ramsey, Paul.

A Model For Teaching Medical Ethics. Welbourn, R B.

A Non–Ethical Concept Of Ahimsa. Bhardwaja, V K.

A Note On Deep Ecology. Watson, Richard A.

A Pamphlet Attributed To John Toland And An Unpublished Reply By Archbishop William King. Kelly, Patrick.

A Principle Of Responsive Adjustment. French, Peter A.

A Public Policy Option On The Treatment Of Severly Handicapped Newborns. Walter, James J.

A Quick Justification For Business Ethics. Lombardi, Louis G.

A Recovery Of Innocence: The Dynamics Of Sartrean Radical Conversion. Walters, Kerry S.

A Refutation Of Egoism. Vadas, Melinda.

A Rejection Of Doctors As Moral Guides. Ackroyd, Elizabeth.

A Response To Preus' *Respect For The Dead And Dying*. Jones, Gary E.

A Response To "Is Business Bluffing Ethical". Sullivan, Roger J.

A Solution To Forrester's Paradox Of Gentle Murder. Sinnott– Armstrong, Walter.

A Suggested Approach To Linking Decision Styles With Business Ethics. Fleming, John E.

Abortion. Finger, Anne.

Abortion, Personhood And Vagueness. Levin, David S.

Acceptance And The Problem Of Slippery–Slope Insensitivity In Rule Utilitarianism. Whitt, L A.

Advertising Professional Success Rates. Gorovitz, Samuel.

Advertising And Program Content. Held, Virginia.

Advice On Good Practice From The Standards Committee. Happel, J S.

Aeschylus And Practical Conflict. Nussbaum, Martha.

Agricultural Ethics—The Setting. Kunkel, H O.

Algunas Preguntas Sobre Etica. Parent, Juan M.

An Analysis Of The Structure Of Justification Of Ethical Decisions In Medical Intervention. Self, Donnie J.

An Ethical Analysis Of Deception In Advertising. Carson, Thomas L and Wokutch, Richard E and Cox, James E.

An Examination Of Relationships Of Inherent, Intrinsic, Instrumental, And Contributive Values Of The Good Sports Contest. Fraleigh, Warren P.

An Open Question Argument In Cicero. Londey, David.

Another Look At Moral Blackmail. Alexander, Lawrence.

Another Look At Paternalism. Hobson, Peter.

Aquinas And Janssens On The Moral Meaning Of Human Acts. May, William E.

Are 'Killing' And 'Letting Die' Adequately Specified Moral Categories? Philips, Michael.

Are Business Ethics And Engineering Ethics Members Of The Same Family? Bowie, Norman E.

Are We Teaching Students That Patients Don't Matter? Robinson, Jean.

Ariston Of Chios And The Unity Of Virtue. Schofield, Malcolm.

Aristotle On The Goods Of Fortune. Cooper, John M.

Aristotle On Rawls: A Critique Of Quantitative Justice. Jackson, M W.

Arresting But Misleading Phrases. Harris, John.

Art And Goodness: Collingwood's Aesthetics And Moore's Ethics Compared. Diffey, T J.

Australia: In Vitro Fertilization And More. Thomson, Colin J H.

Authority, Law And Morality. Raz, Joseph.

Autoconocimiento Y Moral. Esquivel, Javier.

Autonomy And Utility. Haworth, Lawrence.

Autonomy's Temporary Triumph. Veatch, Robert M and Callahan, Daniel.

ETHICS

Autour D'Emmanuel Lévinas. Cornu, Michel.

Axiología De José Vasconcelos. Patiño, Joel Rodríguez.

Axiologische Cognities En Het Meta—Ethische Noncognivisme. Vos, H M.

Ayn Rand And The Is—Ought Problem. O' Neil, Patrick M.

Baby Fae: The "Anything Goes School Of Human Experimentation". Annas, George J.

Background And Work Experience Correlates Of The Ethics And Effect Of Organizational Politics. Zahra, Shaker A.

Beauty: A Foundation For Environmental Ethics. Austin, Richard Cartwright.

Before Virtue: A Critique Of The New Essentialism In Ethics And Education. Collins, Clinton.

Being A Person—Does It Matter? Lomasky, Loren E.

Benedetto Croce, Philosopher, Ethics And Politics (in Hungarian). Bausola, Adriano.

Benn, Mackie And Basic Rights. Holborow, Les C.

Between Assured Destruction And Nuclear Victory: The Case For The "Mad—Plus" Posture. Art, Robert J.

Bluffing: Its Demise As A Subject Unto Itself. Beach, John.

Bonnes Volontés De Puissance (Une Réponse À Hans—Georg Gadamer). Derrida, Jacques.

Brand Name Extortionists, Intellectual Prostitutes, And Generic Free Riders. Bayles, Michael D.

Breathing A Little Life Into A Distinction. Wreen, Michael.

Bribery. D' Andrade Jr, Kendall.

British Idealism: Its Political And Social Thought. Simchoni, Avital.

Broadcasting And The Moral Imperative: Patrolling The Perimeters. Wenham, Brian.

Broadcasting Ethics: Some Neglected Issues. Warnock, Mary.

Buddhism In Huxley's Evolution And Ethics. Rajapakse, Vijitha.

Business Ethics: Micro And Macro. Brummer, James.

Business Ethics, Ideology, And The Naturalistic Fallacy. Goodpaster, Kenneth E.

Can Evil Be Banal? Rotenstreich, Nathan.

Can Racial Discrimination Be Proved? Lesser, Harry.

Can There Be A Freedom Without Responsibility? Ghosh— Dastidar, Koyeli.

Care Of The Dying: Withholding Nutrition. Capron, Alexander M and Cassell, Eric J.

Castañeda's Dystopia. Kapitan, Tomis.

Child Abuse And Neglect: Ethical Issues. Harris, Jean.

Children As Consumers: An Ethical Evaluation Of Children's Advertising. Paine, Lynda Sharp.

Children In Care: Are Social Workers Abusing Their Authority? Benians, R C.

China: Diary Of A Barefoot Bioethicist. Fox, Steven.

Chronic Vegetative States: Intrinsic Value Of Biological Process. Freer, Jack P.

Cicero On The Moral Crisis Of The Late Republic. Mitchell, T N.

Civil Disobedience, Conscientious Objection, And Evasive Noncompliance: Analysis And Assessment Of Illegal Actions In Health Care. Childress, James F.

Classical Utilitarianism And The Analogy Argument. Mc Gray, James.

Cognitive Development And Teaching Business Ethics. Cooper, David E.

Commentary On "Striking Responsibilities". Cannell, Hugh.

Commentary On "Kicking Against The Pricks: Two Patients Wish To End Essential Insulin Treatment". Parsons, Victor.

Commentary On "Kicking Against The Pricks: Two Patients Wish To End Essential Insulin Treatments". Gillon, Raanan.

Commentary On L Jung's "Commercialization And The Professions". Machan, Tibor R.

Commentary On Gilligan's "In A Different Voice". Auerbach, Judy and others.

Commentary On "Advertising And Program Content". Christians, Clifford G.

Commentary On "Kicking Against The Pricks: Two Patients Wish To End Essential Insulin Treatment". Marsden, David.

Commentary On "Whether Professional Associations May Enforce Professional Codes". Ladd, John.

Commentary On "Kicking Against The Pricks: Two Patients Wish To End Essential Insulin Treatments". Kennedy, Ian.

Commentary On K Alpern's "Moral Responsibility For Engineers". Oldenquist, Andrew.

Commentary On "A Response To 'Is Business Bluffing Ethical'". Langley, Van E.

Commentary On "Advertising Professional Success Rates". Goldman, Alan H.

Commentary On L Jung's "Commercialization And The Professions". Marcus, Sanford A.

Commentary On B Lichter And M Hodges' "Perceptions Of The Engineers' 'Professionalism' In The Chemical Industry". Gross, Milton S.

Commentary On "Whether Professional Associations May Enforce Professional Codes". Lunch, Milton F.

Commentary On Daley's "Toward A Theory Of Bribery". Turow, Scott.

Commentary On K Alpern's "Moral Responsibility For Engineers". Florman, Samuel C.

Commentary On B Lichter And M Hodges' "Perceptions Of The Engineers' 'Professionalism' In The Chemical Industry". Nixon, Alan C.

Commentary On "A Response To 'Is Business Bluffing Ethical'". Powell, Donald C.

Commentary On "Children As Consumers". Brenkert, George G.

Commentary On J Pichler's "The Liberty Principle: A Basis For Management Ethics". Mack, Eric.

Commentary On J Pichler's "The Liberty Principle: A Basis For Management Ethics". Lehman, Elliot.

Commentary On "Work—Related Ethical Attitudes: Impact On Business Profitability". Braybrooke, David.

Commentary On Beauchamp's "Manipulative Advertising". Biederman, Barry.

Commentary On "Whether Professional Associations May Enforce Professional Codes". Wilson, Donald E.

Commentary On B Lichter And M Hodges' "Perceptions Of The Engineers' 'Professionalism' In The Chemical Industry". Leckie, John D.

Commentary On Beauchamp's "Manipulative Advertising". Hare, R M.

Commentary On Danley's "Toward A Theory Of Bribery". D' Andrade, Kendall.

Commentary On "Advertising Professional Success Rates". Clancy, Katherine L.

Commentary On "Professional Advertising: Price Fixing And Professional Dignity Versus The Public's Right To A Free Market". Doughton, James E.

Commentary On "Children As Consumers". Weisskoff, Rita.

Commentary On "Advertising And Program Content". Berman, Ronald.

Commentary On "Professional Advertising: Price Fixing And Professional Dignity Versus The Public's Right To A Free Market". Macklin, Ruth.

Commentary On "Children As Consumers". Kimmel, Lawrence D.

Commentary On "Advertising Professional Success Rates". De George, Richard T.

Commentary On "Advertising And Program Content". Bowie, Norman E.

Commentary Upon 'Should Collective Bargaining And Labor Relations Be Less Advesarial'? Koehn, Donald R.

Commentary: Compulsory Health And Safety In A Free Society. Downie, R S.

Commentary: Informed Consent In Engineering And Medicine. Martin, Mike W and Schinzinger, Roland.

Comments On "The Unnatural Jew". Kay, Jeanne.

Comments On Dan Brock And Terrence Reynolds. Donagan, Alan.

Commercialization And The Professions. Jung, L Shannon.

Competition And Moral Development. Stengel, Barbara S.

Competition In Consumption As Viewed By Jewish Law. Liebermann, Yehoshua.

Compulsory Health And Safety In A Free Society. Boughton, B J.

Confidentiality, Rules, And Codes Of Ethics. Goldman, Alan H.

Confidentiality In The Teaching Of Medical Ethics: A Case Report. Ellin, Joseph.

Consent In Time Of Affliction: The Ethics Of A Circumspect Theist. Cahill, Lisa Sowle.

Consequences, Desirability, And The Moral Fanaticism Argument. Singer, Marcus G.

Contemporary Moral Philosophy And Practical Reason. Sterba, James P.

Contracts To Bear Children. Davies, Iwan.

Contradiction In The Will. Doore, Gary.

Controlling Military Technology. Lautenschlager, Karl.

Corporate Control Through The Criminal System. Lansing, Paul and Hatfield, Donald.

Corporate Culture And The Common Good: The Need For Thick Description And Critical Interpretation. Sturm, Douglas.

Corporate Social Responsibility And Public Accountability. Filios, Vassilios P.

Correlates Of Salespeople's Ethical Conflict: An Exploratory Investigation. Dubinsky, Alan J and Ingram, Thomas N.

Cost Containment: Issues Of Moral Conflict And Justice For Physicians. Morreim, E Haavi.

Creating A Candid Corporate Culture. Serpa, Roy.

Current Arrangements For Teaching Medical Ethics To Undergraduate Medical Students. Bicknell, D J.

Current Research In Moral Development As A Decision Support System. Penn, William Y and Collier, Boyd D.

Daniel Dennett On Responsibility. Waller, Bruce N.

Das Diktat Des Besseren Arguments: Eine Entscheidungslogische Rekonstruktion Des Praktischen Diskurses. Kern, Lucian.

De Ondergang Van De Deugden En De Inconsequentie Van McIntyre. Kunneman, Harry.

Deeper Than Deep Ecology: The Eco—Feminist Connection. Salleh, Ariel Kay.

Defining 'Business Ethics': Like Nailing Jello To A Wall. Lewis, Phillip V.

Democratic Capitalism: Developing A Conscience For The Corporation. Grcic, Joseph M.

Democritus And The Origins Of Moral Psychology. Kahn, Charles H.

Denuclearizing International Politics. Ullman, Richard H.

Dependence, Reliance And Abortion. Strasser, Mark.

Derivability, Defensibility, And The Justification Of Judicial Decisions. Lyons, David.

Desert And The Moral Arbitrariness Of The Natural Lottery. Hill, Christopher.

Deterrence And Deontology. Mc Mahan, Jeff.

Die Ethischen Grenzen Der Klinischen Experimente (in Polish). Bogusz, Jozef.

Die Ethische Bedeutung Des Schoönen Bei Kant. Drescher, Wilhelmine.

Die Philosophische Tätigkeit Von Johannes Klein. Darowski, Roman.

Die Relevanz Der Deontischen Logik Für Die Ethik. Frey, Gerhard.

Dignity And Cost—Effectiveness: A Rejection Of The Utilitarian Approach To Death. Brooks, Simon A.

Dignity And Death: A Reply. Brooks, Simon A.

Dignity And Cost—Effectiveness: Analysing The Responsibility For Decisions In Medical Ethics. Robertson, George S.

Disarming Nuclear Apologists. Goodin, Robert E.

Discussion: On Seeking A Rationale. Conee, Earl.

Displaced Workers: America's Unpaid Debt. Byrne, Edmund F.

Distributive Justice In Aristotle's Ethics And Politics. Keyt, David.

Distrust, Secrecy, And The Arms Race. Bok, Sissela.

Divine Command Theories And The Appeal To Love. Chandler, John.

Do Corporations Have Moral Rights? Ozar, David T.

Do We Really Need Environmental Ethics? Spitler, Gene.

Doctors Helping Doctors. Morrow, Carol K.

Does Rightness Always Involve Wrongness? Bahm, Archie J.

Doing The World's Unhealthy Work: The Fiction Of Free Choice. Graebner, William.

Donagan's Critique Of *Sittlichkeit*. Westphal, Merold.

Editorial: Philosophy Of Medicine In The U S A. Thomasma, David C.

Egoism, Desires, And Friendship. Chong, Kim—Chong.

En Torno A La Eutanasia. Chaves, Rodolfo.

Enhancing Perceptions Of Auditor Independence. Pearson, Michael A.

Epicycles. Levi, Isaac.

ETHICS

Ethical Behavior In Business: A Hierarchical Approach From The Talmud. Friedman, Hershey H.

Ethical Concerns For The Modern University. Miles, Leland and others.

Ethical Considerations For Planned Social Change In The Education Of American Indian People. Thomas, Linda Sue.

Ethical Consistency Principles. Gensler, Harry J.

Ethical Dilemmas Of The Doctors' Strike In Israel. Grosskopf, I and Buckman, G and Garty, M.

Ethical Dilemmas In Performance Appraisal. Banner, David K and Cooke, Robert Allan.

Ethical Issues In Private And Public Ranch Land Management. Blatz, Charles V.

Ethical Issues In And Beyond Prospective Clinical Trials Of Human Gene Therapy. Fletcher, John C.

Ethical Perspectives On Health Policy For An Aging Society. Creedon, Michael A.

Ethical Problems In The Science Of Nutrition (in Polish). Kunachowicz, Hanna.

Ethical Problems In Arguments From Potentiality. Kottow, Michael.

Ethical Realism Defended. Werner, Richard.

Ethical Relativism (in Polish). Pawlowska, I–Lazari.

Ethical Theory In The Twenty–First Century. Bayles, Michael D.

Ethical Uses Of The Past In Early Confucianism: The Case Of Hsün Tzu. Cua, A S.

Ethics And Markets. Bennett, John G.

Ethics And Sport: An Overview. Kretchmar, R Scott.

Ethics And Taxation: The Perspective Of The Islamic Tradition. Nanji, Azim A.

Ethics And Taxation: A Theoretical Framework. Green, Ronald M.

Ethics And The Archangelic Prescriber. Harrison, Jonathan.

Ethics As An Integrating Force In Management. Pastin, Mark.

Ethics In Business Education: Working Toward A Meaningful Reciprocity. Hoffman, W Michael.

Ethics, Advertising And The Definition Of A Profession. Dyer, Allen R.

Etica E Narrazione In Novalis. Moretto, Giovanni.

Eticità E Logica Nella Crisi Jenense Del Pensiero Di Hegel. Pallavidini, Renato.

Eutanasia O Derecho A Morir? López, Antonio Marlasca.

Excuse Me, But You Have A Melanoma On Your Neck: Unsolicited Medical Opinions. Moseley, Ray.

Fact And Value In Ecological Science. Sagoff, Mark.

Feinberg On Moral Rights. Markie, Peter J.

Felix Adler: Artist Of The Ideal Good. Hemstreet, Robert M.

First Steps In Moral And Ethical Education. Wilson, John and Natale, Samuel M.

Forgiveness And Regret. Golding, Martin P.

France: A National Committee Debates The Issues. Ambroselli, Claire.

Francis Hutcheson: Morality And Nature. Kupperman, Joel J.

Frankfurt On The Principle Of Alternate Possibilities. Naylor, Margery B.

Freedom And Moral Therapy In Leibniz. Seidler, Michael J.

Freedom As A Condition For Truth: Jaspers On The Significance Of Temporality In Science. Koterski, Joseph W.

Friendship, Justice, And Superogation. Badhwar, Neera K.

From The Prudential To The Moral: Reply To Marcus Singer. Gewirth, Alan.

Full Humans And Empty Morality. Harris, John.

Games And The Action–Guiding Force Of Morality. Eggerman, Richard W.

Gehirnverpflanzung—Ethische Implikationen. Demmer, Klaus.

Getting On The Road To Peace: A Modest Proposal. Narveson, Jan.

Gibt Es Auf Erden Ein Mass? Gadamer, Hans–Georg.

Gillespie On Singer's Generalization Argument. Gordon, David.

Grete Henry–Hermann's Development Of Leonard Nelson's Ethics. Heckmann, Gustav.

Groups, Responsibility, And The Failure To Act. Mellema, Gregory.

Gustafson's God: Who; What; Where? Mc Cormick, Richard A.

Habermas' Communicative Ethics And The Development Of Moral Consciousness. White, Stephen K.

Happiness And Virtue In Socrates' Moral Theory. Vlastos, Gregory.

Hare On Moral Conflicts. Primorac, Igor.

Health Promotion—Caring Concern Or Slick Salesmanship? Williams, Gill.

Hegel's Evaluation And Analysis Of Socrates' Proposition "Virtue Is Knowledge". Xiuliang, Lan.

High–Minded Egoism And The Problem Of Priggishness. Lemos, Noah M.

Historical Materialism, Ideology And Ethics. Nielsen, Kai.

Hobbes As Moralist. Farrell, Daniel M.

Hobbes's State Of War. Hampton, Jean.

How Ethical Is Abraham's "Suspension Of The Ethical"? Magno, Joseph A.

How The Inadequate Models For Virtue In The *Protagoras* Illuminate Socrates' View Of The Unity Of The Virtues. Hartman, Margaret.

Human Nature And Morality: The Case Of The Ik. Sogolo, Godwin.

Human Nature And Moral Theories. Kekes, John.

Hume On Morality, Action, And Character. Davie, William.

Hume, Animals And The Objectivity Of Morals. Clark, Stephen.

Hume's Moral Enquiry: An Analysis Of Its Catalogue. Vodraska, Stanley L.

Hume's Second Enquiry: Ethics As Natural Science. Hughes, R I G.

Hutcheson, Hume And The Ontology Of Morals. Stafford, J Martin.

I Could Not Have Done Otherwise—So What? Dennett, Daniel C.

Iconoclastic Ethics. Black, Douglas.

Improving Applied Ethics: A Response To Reinsmith's Response To "Improving Applied Ethics". Bahm, Archie J.

Improving Applied Ethics: A Response To Bahm's "Improving Applied Ethics". Reinsmith, William A.

In Defence Of Situational Ethics, The NHS And The Permissive Society. Black, Douglas.

In Defense Of Natural End Ethics: A Rejoinder To O'Neil And Osterfeld. Den Uyl, Douglas J and Rasmussen, Douglas B.

In Defense Of Speciesism. Wreen, Michael.

In Defense Of The Dignity Of Being Human. Gaylin, Willard.

In Search Of A Whole–System Ethic. Holler, Linda D.

In The Interest Of Infants. Mahowald, Mary B.

Informatics And Society: Will There Be An 'Information Revolution'? Tepperman, Lorne.

Informed Consent, Autonomy, And The Law. Annis, David B.

Informed Consent: Patient's Right Or Patient's Duty? Hull, Richard T.

Informed Consent And Engineering: An Essay Review. Long, Thomas A.

Intended Goals And Appropriate Treatment: An Alternative To The Ordinary/Extraordinary Distinction. Meyers, Christopher.

Internal Conflicts In Desires And Morals. Jackson, Frank.

Intrinsic Value, Quantum Theory, And Environmental Ethics. Callicott, J Baird.

Intuitions In Ethics. Bayles, Michael D.

Is "Ethicist" Anything To Call A Philosopher? Zaner, Richard M.

Is Moral Relativism Consistent? Hugly, Philip and Sayward, Charles.

Is Socrates An Instrumentalist? Lesses, Glenn.

Is The Divine Command Theory Defensible? Chandler, J H.

Is To Will It As Bad As To Do It (The Fourteenth Century Debate)? Adams, Marilyn McCord and Wood, Rega.

Is–Ought: Prescribing And A Present Controversy. Schultz, Janice L.

Italian Literature On Thomas Hobbes After The Second World War: Part I; 1946–1955. Felice, Domenico.

Italy: Abortion And Nationalized Health Care. Mori, Maurizio.

J S Mill And Robert Veatch's Critique Of Utilitarianism. Edwards, Rem B.

Jewish Ethics After The Holocaust. Morgan, Michael L.

John T Noonan And Baby Jane Doe. Levin, David S.

Jucios Morales Y Verdad. De Gandolfi, Maria.

Just Taxation In The Roman Catholic Tradition. Curran, Charles E.

Kant And Foucault: On The Ends Of Man. Watson, Stephen.

Kant And The Moral Sense Theory (in Hebrew). Golomb, Jacob.

Kidney Pooling. Alexander, Larry.

Knowledge And Value. Cavell, Marcia.

Knowledge As Tracking? Schmitt, Frederick F.

L'Evoluzione Del Problema Morale Nel Pensiero Di Cartesio. Cesareo, Rosa.

L'Uomo Freud: Personalità Morale E Religiosa. Lambertino, Antonio.

L'acte Libre Démission Ou Courage D'etre Devant Le Sensible Selon Jean Scot Érigène. Wohlman, Avital.

La "Conferenza Sull'etica" Di L Wittgenstein. Marini, Sergio.

La Cancelación Hegeliana De La Ética: Origen Y Conscuencias. Guariglia, Osvaldo N.

La Morale Socialiste Et La Valeur De L'homme. Popescu, Vasile.

La Philosophie En Tant Qu'éthique. Danişor, Gheorghe.

La Question Des Actes Intrinsèquement Mauvais. Pinckaers, S.

La Renovición Kantiana Del Derecho Natural Y La Crítica De Hegel: Una Crítica A La Crítica. Guariglia, Osvaldo.

Laborem Exercens: A Theological And Philosophical Foundation For Business Ethics. Sullivan, Brian G.

Law And The Life Sciences. Annas, George J.

Lawyer–Client Confidences Under The A B A Model Rules: Ethical Rules Without Ethical Reason. Freedman, Monroe H.

Lay Medical Ethics. Veatch, Robert M.

Lay Obligations In Professional Relations. Benjamin, Martin.

Le Problème Moral Comme Totalisation Chez Sartre. Knee, Philip.

Le Théme De L'amitié Dans L'Éthique Á Nicomaque Et L'Éthique Á Eudéme. Proulx, Évelyne.

Levi's "The Wrong Box". Eells, Ellery.

Locke's Negative Hedonism. Kraus, Pamela.

Lying And The "Methods Of Ethics". Primoratz, Igor.

Madness. Quinton, Anthony.

Making Intelligent Choices, How Useful Is Decision Theory? Black, Max.

Management And Ethical Decision–Making. Robinson, Wade L.

Management Priorities And Management Ethics. Longenecker, Justin G.

Management–Think. Pastin, Mark.

Managerial Ethics And Microeconomic Theory. Hosmer, Larue Tone.

Marx And The Abolition Of Morality. Kain, Philip J.

Marx's Critique Of Utilitarianism. Brenkert, George G.

Marx's Social Ethics And Critique Of Traditional Morality. Mc Carthy, George.

Marxism And Moral Objectivity. Shaw, William H.

Maximin And Other Decision Principles. Ihara, Craig K.

Measuring Responsibility. Bar– On, A Zvie.

Medical Confidence. Havard, John.

Medical Ethics: An Excuse For Inefficiency? Mooney, Gavin.

Medical Ethics And Medical Practice: A Social Science View. Stacey, Margaret.

Medical Ethics And The Value Of Human Life. Khatchadourian, Haig.

Medical Ethics—A Christian View. Habgood, J S.

Medical Negligence: Who Sets The Standard? Norrie, Kenneth McK.

Mending Mother Nature: Alpha, Beta And Omega Pills. Fleck, Leonard M.

Methods Of Teaching Medical Ethics At The University Of Nottingham. Fentem, P H.

Modern Pantheism As An Approach To Environmental Ethics. Wood Jr, Harold W.

Moral Absolutism And Abortion: Alan Donagan On The Hysterectomy And Craniotomy Cases. Reynolds, Terrence.

Moral Community And Animal Rights. Sapontzis, Steve F.

ETHICS

Moral Conflict And Moral Realism. Tännsjö, Torbjörn.

Moral Conflict In Agriculture: Conquest Or Moral Coevolution? Shepard, Philip T.

Moral Dilemmas, Deliberation, And Choice. Anderson, Lyle V.

Moral Faith And Ethical Skepticism Reconsidered. Kurtz, Paul.

Moral Fictions And Scientific Management. Santilli, Paul.

Moral Integrity And The Deferential Wife. Friedman, Marylin A.

Moral Issues And Social Problems: The Moral Relevance Of Moral Philosophy. Singer, Marcus G.

Moral Objectivity. Lear, Jonathan.

Moral Objectivity. Benedict– Gill, Diane.

Moral Reasoning And Action In Young Children. Hannaford, Robert V.

Moral Reasoning In Adolescents: A Feature Of Intelligence Or Social Adjustment? Hanks, Richard.

Moral Responsibility For Engineers. Alpern, Kenneth D.

Moral Rules And Moral Ideals: A Useful Distinction In Business And Professional Practice. Hennessey, John W and Gert, Bernard.

Moral Scepticism And Moral Conduct. Mac Kenzie, J C.

Moral Skepticism And International Relations. Cohen, Marshall.

Moral Theories; Aristotle's Ethics. Price, A W.

Moral Theory And Educational Practice: A Reply To Ian Gregory. Straughan, Roger R.

Moral Y Politica En "Para La Paz Perpetua" De Kant. Amado, Maria Teresa and Lisboa, Joao Luis.

Morality And Deterrence. Tucker, Robert W.

Morality And The Market In Blood. Stewart, Robert M.

More's *Utopia* And The New World Utopias: Is The Good Life An Easy Life? Dooley, Patrick K.

Multinational Decision–Making: Reconciling International Norms. Donaldson, Thomas.

Mum's The Word: Confidentiality And Incest. Higgs, Roger and others.

Must The Bearer Of A Right Have The Concept Of That To Which He Has A Right? Stevens, John C.

Myths And Misconceptions About Drug Industry Ethics. Spilker, Bert.

Natural Law: Before And Beyond Bifurcation. Caspar, Ruth.

Nature And Nature's God. Toulmin, Stephen.

Negative Positivism And The Hard Facts Of Life. Silver, Charles.

Nietzsche Y El Intento De Ir Más Allá De Sócrates. Troncoso, Alfredo.

Nietzsche's Existential Ethic. Mc Bride, Joseph.

Non–Medical Burdens Of The Defective Infant. Jones, Gary E.

Non–Patient Decision–Making In Medicine: The Eclipse Of Altruism. Battin, Margaret P.

Nontreatment Decisions For Severely Compromised Newborns. Kipnis, Kenneth.

Normative Contexts And Moral Decision. Philips, Michael.

Normative Wissenschaft Mit Normen—Ohne Werte. Knapp, Hans Georg.

Notas Sobre La Fundamentación De La Ética Aristotélica. De Kirchner, Beatriz Bossi.

Note Sur La Syntaxe Et La Sémantique Du Concept D'égalité. Gauthier, Yvon.

Nuclear Deterrence And Self–Defense. Donaldson, Thomas.

Nuclear Deterrence: Moral Dilemmas And Risks. Volbrecht, Rose Mary.

Nuclear Disarmament As A Moral Certainty. Goodin, Robert E.

Nuclear Intentions. Dworkin, Gerald.

Nuclear Weapons, No First Use, And European Order. Joffe, Josef.

O Moralismo Escocês Do Séc XVIII E A Concepção De Liberdade No Kant Pré–Crítico. Martins, Estevao De Rezende.

Objections To Hospital Philosophers. Ruddick, William and Finn, William.

Objectivity And Moral Expertise. Mc Connell, Terrance C.

On Gewirth's Derivation Of The Principle Of Generic Consistency. Singer, Marcus G.

On Heidegger And The Interpretation Of Environmental Crisis. Foltz, Bruce V.

On Mill's Qualitative Distinction Of Pleasures. Nagaoka, Shigeo.

On Removing Food & Water: Against The Stream. Meilaender, Gilbert.

On Some So–called Refutations Of Ethical Egoism. Taiwo, Olufemi.

On Spinoza's Ideals Of Man And Morals (in Hungarian). Kalocsai, Dezsö.

On The Captivity Of The Will: Sympathy, Caring, And A Moral Sense Of The Human. Sabini, John and Silver, Maury.

On The Moral Agent And Object (in Hebrew). Ben– Zeev, Aaron.

On Two Arguments For Compatibilism. Van Inwagen, Peter.

On Two Meanings Of Good And The Foundations Of Ethics In Aristotle And St Thomas. Flippen, Douglas.

Ontologie Et Pathologie Du Symbole Chez L Tieck: Le Conte Du Tannenhäuser. Stanguennec, Andre.

Organ Donation: Is Voluntarism Still Valid? Sadler Jr, Alfred M and Sadler, Blair L and Caplan, Arthur L.

Organism, Community, And The "Substitution Problem". Katz, Eric.

Organizational Dissidence: The Case Of Whistle–Blowing. Near, Janet P and Miceli, Marcia P.

Ortega E Gasset: Perfil Ético De Uma Filosofia. Araújo, Luís De.

Parental Discretion And Children's Rights: Background And Implications For Medical Decision–Making. Schoeman, Ferdinand.

Parental Rights. Page, Edgar.

Patent Rights And Better Mousetraps. Michael, Mark.

Paternalism And Partial Autonomy. O' Neill, Onora.

Paternalism And The Regulation Of Drugs. Sagoff, Mark.

Patient Truthfulness: A Test Of Models Of The Physician–Patient Relationship. Vanderpool, Harold Y and Weiss, Gary B.

Patients With Reduced Agency: Conceptual, Empirical, And Ethical Considerations. Mc Cullough, Laurence B.

Patients' Ethical Obligation For Their Health. Sider, Roger C and Clements, Colleen D.

Perceptions Of The Engineers' "Professionalism" In The Chemical Industry. Lichter, Barry D and Hodges, Michael P.

Persons And The Measurement Of Illness. Bartlett, Edward T.

Persons And Values: Reasons In Conflict And Moral Disagreement. Benn, S I.

Pflichtethik Oder Wertethik: Zu Franz Von Kutscheras "Grundlagen Der Ethik". Rohs, Peter.

Philanthropia In The Poetics. Moles, John.

Philosophical Aspects Of Brain Death. Spicker, Stuart F.

Philosophy Of Medicine In The Netherlands. Have, Henk Ten and Van Der Arend, Arie.

Philosophy Of Medicine And Other Humanities: Toward A Wholistic View. Brody, Howard.

Philosophy Of Medicine In Austria. Kenner, Thomas.

Plato's *Lysis*: A Reconsideration. Tindale, Christopher W.

Plato's Moral Theory. Mackenzie, Mary Margaret.

Pluralism In The Mass Media: Can Management Help? Nielsen, Richard P.

Political Finance In The United States: A Survey Of Research. Beitz, Charles R.

Practical Reason, Hermeneutics, And Social Life. Risser, James.

Predation. Sapontzis, Steve F.

Principles And Virtues—Or—Principles Or Virtues. Coetzee, Pieter.

Principles For Individual Actions. Wilkins, Burleigh T and Zelikovitz, Kelly M.

Prisoner In The ICU: The Tragedy Of William Bartling. Annas, George J.

Problematic Of Kant's Determinants Of Practical Reason—il. O' Farrell, Francis.

Problematic Of Kant's Determinants Of Practical Reason—I. O' Farrell, Francis.

Professionalism: Foundation For Business Ethics. Schaefer, Thomas E.

Professional Advertising: Price Fixing And Professional Dignity Versus The Public's Right To A Free Market. Leiser, Burton M.

Professions As The Conscience Of Society. Sieghart, Paul.

Prospects For The Elimination Of Tastes From Economics And Ethics. Rosenberg, Alexander.

Protest Petitions. Margalit, Avishai and Ullmann– Margalit, Edna.

Psychiatric Diagnosis As An Ethical Problem. Shackle, E M.

Psychosurgery, The Brain And Violent Behavior. Wilkins, Burleigh T.

Public And Firm Interests In Public Service Diversifications. Fannin, William R and Gilmore, Carol B.

Pure Legal Advocates And Moral Agents: Two Concepts Of A Lawyer In An Adversary System. Cohen, Elliot D.

Purposes, Conditioning, And Skinner's Moral Theory: Comments On Mills' Observations. Waller, Bruce.

Pursuing The Good—Indirectly. Alexander, Larry.

Quality Of Life—A Response To K C Calman. Cribb, Alan.

Quality Of Life In Cancer Patients—A Hypothesis. Calman, K C.

ROBOTS, RIFs, And Rights. Arthur, Alcott.

Radical Freedom. Reinhardt, Lloyd.

Reason As Response To Nuclear Terror. Heim, Michael.

Rebuilding Rawls: An Alternative Theory Of Justice. Groarke, Leo.

Recent Studies In Animal Ethics. Nelson, James A.

Recent Work On Virtues. Pence, Gregory E.

Reconsidering The Ethics Of Infanticide. Warren, Mary Anne.

Reconstruction Of Schlick's Psycho–Sociological Ethics. Leinfellner, Werner.

Reflective Equilibrium And Justification. Little, Daniel.

Regulation, Deregulation, Self–Regulation: The Case Of Engineers In Ontario. Stevenson, J T.

Relative Virtue. Vorobej, Mark.

Relativism And Moral Complacency. Unwin, Nicholas.

Religious Justifications For Donating Body Parts. May, William F.

Remarks In Praise Of Guilt. Phillips, D L.

Remarks On Three Formulations Of Ethical Relativism. Peterson, Sandra.

Reply To J Narveson's Review Of *Reason And Value*. Bond, E J.

Reply To Oppenheim's "Constraints On Freedom". Miller, David.

Reporting The Case Of Baby Jane Doe. Kerr, Kathleen.

Respect For The Dead And Dying. Preus, Anthony.

Response To Mary Anne Warren's "Reconsidering The Ethics Of Infanticide". Tooley, Michael.

Response To Rebecca Dresser's 'Involuntary Confinement: Legal And Psychiatric Perspectives'. Callahan, Joan C.

Response To "Children In Care: Are Social Workers Abusing Their Authority". Foster, Judy.

Responsibility For Personal Health: A Historical Perspective. Reiser, Stanley J.

Retributive Punishment And Humbling The Will. Johnson, Oliver A.

Right And Good: False Dichotomy? Maclean, Anne.

Roles And Responsibilities: Theoretical Issues In The Definition Of Consultation Liaison Psychiatry. Agich, George J.

Royce's Revaluation Of Values. Hallman, Max O.

Rules And Relevance: The Au–Ru Equivalence Issue. Lennon, Thomas M.

Russell And The Attainability Of Happiness. Kohl, Marvin.

Sacrificing Persons For The General Welfare: A Comment Of Sayward. Wein, Sheldon.

Saints And Heroes: A Plea For The Supererogatory. Mc Goldrick, Patricia M.

Sandra Day O'Connor And The Justification Of Abortion. Werhane, Patricia.

Sartre O Las Dificultades De Escribir Una Moral. Fornet– Betancourt, Raul.

Sartre's Acceptance Of The Principle Of Universality. Lee, Sander H.

Scepticism And The Basis Of Morality. Mc Clintock, Thomas.

Scepticism, Narrative, And Holocaust Ethics. Hallie, Philip P.

ETHICS

Two Views Of Business Ethics: A Popular Philosophical Approach And A Value Based Interdisciplinary One. Klein, Sherwin.

Un Droit À L'enfant? Verspieren, Patrick.

Un Logicien Déontique Avant La Lettre: Gottfried Wilhelm Leibniz. Kalinowski, Georges and Garoddies, Jean–louis.

Une Douloureuse Théorie Du Plaisir. Thiriart, Philippe.

Unsolicited Medical Opinion. Ratzan, Richard.

Use Of Privileged Information For Attorney Self–Interest: A Moral Dilemma. Seigel, Michael.

Utilitarianism, Moral Dilemmas, And Moral Cost. Slote, Michael.

Utilitarianism And The Divine Command Theory. Wierenga, Edward.

Utilitarians And The Use Of Examples. Cox, J W Roxbee.

Utility And Rational Self–Interest. Mc Dermott, Michael.

Utility, Autonomy And Drug Regulation. Scriven, Tal.

Valor Y Valor Moral. Derisi, Octavio N.

Value And Human Condition. Sarin, Indu.

Value, Fact And Facing Fact. Graham, A C.

Valuing Wildlands. Rolston, Holmes.

Varieties Of Ethics Of Virtue. Baron, Marcia.

Von Den Voraussetzungen Einer Christlichen Ethik. Schwarz, P.

Wahrheit Und Moral. Loeser, Franz.

Walden Two And Skinner's Ideal Observer. Mc Gray, James W.

War, Nuclear War, And Nuclear Deterrence: Some Conceptual And Moral Issues. Wasserstrom, Richard.

Weakness And Dignity In Conrad's *Lord Jim*. Ross, Steven L.

Well–being, Agency And Freedom: The Dewey Lectures 1984. Sen, Amartya.

Werner's Ethical Realism. Postow, B C.

What Does Medicine Contribute To Ethics? Thomasma, David C.

What Is A Fundamental Ethical Disagreement? Wasserman, Wayne.

What Is Professional Ethics? James, David.

What Is Wrong With 'Wrongful Life' Cases? Bell, Nora K and Loewer, Barry M.

What Kind Of Good Is A Kind And Caring Heart. Lundberg, Randolph.

What's Wrong With Bribery? Turow, Scott.

When The Doctor And The Minister Disagree (Case Study With Commentaries). Weikart, Robert and Klar, Howard.

Whether Professional Associations May Enforce Professional Codes. Snapper, John W.

Which Clients Should A Sheltered Workshop Serve: Case Study. Mc Donald, Michael and Herr, Stanley S.

Who Benefits From The Artificial Heart? Preston, Thomas A.

Who Counts? Smith, David H.

Who Is A Refugee? Shacknove, Andrew E.

Who We Are: The Political Origins Of The Medical Humanities. Fox, Daniel M.

Why Be Ethical Amongst Villains? Bacard, Andre.

Why Be Just: Hume's Response In The *Inquiry*. Costa, Michael J.

Why There Are No Human Rights. Husak, Douglas N.

Why Tolerate The Statistical Victim? Trachtman, Leon E.

Why You Don't Owe It To Yourself To Seek Health. Gorovitz, Samuel.

Wickedness. Benn, S I.

Wie Erhalten Ethische Grundsaetze Relevanz Fuer Die Forschung (in Polish). Furger, Franz.

Wittgensteinian Moralism Ethnomethodology And Moral Ideology. Nielsen, Kai.

Words; Interests. Kuhse, Helga.

Work–Related Ethical Attitudes: Impact On Business Profitability. Dunfee, Thomas W and Robertson, Diana C.

Yugoslavia: Equity And Imported Ethical Dilemmas. Lang, Slobodan and others.

Zu Einigen Unterschieden Zwischen Moralischen Normen, Werturteilen Und Aussagen. Bönisch, Siegfried and Noack, Klaus–peter.

Zu Kants Unterscheidung Von Platonismus Und Epikureismus. Ley, Hermann.

Zu Möglichkeiten Und Grezen Der Überwindung Der Angst Vor Dem Sterben Und Dem Frühen Tod. Volland, Hannelore.

Zum Problem Der Diskutierbarkeit Von Normensystemen. Weinke, Kurt.

Zum Problem Der Willensschwäche. Wolf, Ursula.

ETHNOCENTRISM

Objectivity And Social Anthropology. Beattie, J H M.

Overcoming Ethnocentrism In The Philosophy Classroom. Schutte, Ofelia.

Where Are The Barbarians: Ethnocentrism Versus The Illusion Of Cultural Universalism: The Answer Of An Anthropologist To A Philosopher. Kronenberg, Andreas.

ETHNOGRAPHY

Difference And Dissonance In Ethnographic Data. Ward, Jeffrey J and Werner, O.

Oral History And Archival Data Combined: The Removal Of Saramakan Granman Kofi Bosuman As An Epistemological Problem. Hoogbergen, Wim and Hoeree, J.

ETHNOLOGY

Was Erwartet Uns Jenseits Der Wissenschaft: Ethno–Philosophie: Erfahrungen Und Möglichkeiten Im Umgang Mit Dem Irrationalen. Stuben, Peter E.

ETHNOMETHODOLOGY

Wittgensteinian Moralism Ethnomethodology And Moral Ideology. Nielsen, Kai.

ETHOS

Ethos Y Sociedad En América Latina: Perspectivas Sistemático–Pastorales. Scannone, J C.

EUCLID

Placing *Sectio Canonis* In Historical And Philosophical Contexts. Barbera, Andre.

EUDAIMONISM

Happiness And Virtue In Socrates' Moral Theory. Vlastos, Gregory.

The *Uti/Frui* Distinction In Augustine's Ethics. O' Connor, William Riordan.

EUGENICS

"Genetic Screening Of Prospective Parents And Of Workers" in *Biomedical Ethics Reviews*, Humber, James M (ed), 73–120. Hubbard, Ruth.

Ethical Issues In And Beyond Prospective Clinical Trials Of Human Gene Therapy. Fletcher, John C.

Eugenics And The Left. Paul, Diane B.

Human Gene Therapy: Scientific And Ethical Considerations. Anderson, W French.

EULER, L

Aktualität Und Historizität: Bemühungen Um Werk Und Wirken Leonhard Eulers. Hess, Heinz–Jürgen.

Berichte Und Diskussionen (in German). Fischer, Harald–Paul.

EURIPIDES

Language, Meaning And Reality In Euripides. Sansone, David.

EUROPEAN

"Gramsci And Eurocommunism" in *Continuity And Change In Marxism*, Fischer, Norman And Others (ed), 189–210. Boggs, Carl.

"The European Experience Of Nature" in *The Good Life And Its Pursuit*, Dougherty, Jude P (ed), 233–240. Crombie, Alistair.

A Sense Of *Rapprochement* Between Analytic And Continental Philosophy. Margolis, Joseph.

Bedingungen Und Merkmale Des Klassenkampfes In Den Kapitalistischen Ländern Europas. Beyer, Hans.

Europa Und Die Vereinigten Staaten Von Amerika Philosophiegeschichtlich Betrachtet. Moser, Simon.

Modern Movements In European Philosophy: Some Introductory Remarks. Kearney, Richard.

The Philosophy Of Medicine In Europe: Challenges For The Future. Thomasma, David C.

Theorie Zur Enstehung Der Europäischen Moderne. Hahn, Alois.

EUTHANASIA

Abortion And The Conscience Of The Nation. Reagan, Ronald.

Biomedical Ethics Reviews. Humber, James M (ed) and Almeder, Robert F (ed).

"Bioethical Challenges At The Dawn Of Life" in *Bioethical Frontiers In Perinatal Intensive Care*, Snowden, Fraser (ed), 1–18. Snowden, Fraser.

"On Euthanasia" in *Biomedical Ethics Reviews*, Humber, James M (ed), 5–28. Baker, Robert.

"The Decision To Withdraw Life–Sustaining Treatment" in *Ethics Committees And Health Care Decisions*, Cranford, Ronald (ed), 203–208. Paris, John J.

A Response To Preus' *Respect For The Dead And Dying*. Jones, Gary E.

Civil Disobedience, Conscientious Objection, And Evasive Noncompliance: Analysis And Assessment Of Illegal Actions In Health Care. Childress, James F.

Dignity And Cost–Effectiveness: Analysing The Responsibility For Decisions In Medical Ethics. Robertson, George S.

Dignity And Cost–Effectiveness: A Rejection Of The Utilitarian Approach To Death. Brooks, Simon A.

Dignity And Death: A Reply. Brooks, Simon A.

En Torno A La Eutanasia. Chaves, Rodolfo.

Eutanasia O Derecho A Morir? López, Antonio Marlasca.

Italy: Abortion And Nationalized Health Care. Mori, Maurizio.

Respect For The Dead And Dying. Preus, Anthony.

Thanatos And Euthanatos: Persons And Practical Policies. Smith, James Leroy.

The Duty Not To Kill Oneself. Linehan, Elizabeth A.

To Kill Or Let Live: Augustine On Killing The Innocent. Burt, Donald X.

EVALUATION(S)

Anonymity In The Academy: The Case Of Faculty Evaluation. Riegle, Rodney P and Rhodes, Dent M.

Ethical Dilemmas In Performance Appraisal. Banner, David K and Cooke, Robert Allan.

Medical Negligence: Who Sets The Standard? Norrie, Kenneth McK.

Quality Of Life—A Response To K C Calman. Cribb, Alan.

Some Problems Of The Formation Of Strategies And Evaluation In The Sphere Of Biotechnologies (in Czechoslovakian). Mrácek, F and Machleidt, P.

The Evaluation Of Critical Thinking Programs: Dangers And Dogmas. Mc Peck, John E.

EVANS, D

Developing Themes In Philosophy/La Philosophie En Cours. King– Farlow, John.

EVENT(S)

An Essay On Human Action. Zimmerman, Michael J.

On History And Other Essays. Oakeshott, Michael.

The Effectiveness Of Causes. Emmet, Dorothy.

The Logic Of Aspect: An Axiomatic Approach. Galton, Antony.

A Note On A Response Of Hornsby's. Lowe, E J.

Agency And Causation. Vendler, Zeno.

Causal Theories Of Knowledge. Dretske, Fred and Enc, Berent.

Lonergan's Metaphysics: Ontological Implications Of Insight–As–Event. Skrenes, Carol.

Mind–Body Identity And The Subjects Of Events. Mac Donald, Cynthia.

Situations And Events. Asher, Nicholas and Bonevac, Daniel.

Spatial Things And Kinematic Events. Stafleu, M D.

The French Revolution And Capitalism: An Explanatory Schema. Wallerstein, Immanuel.

EVIDENCE

Probability, Objectivity And Evidence. Benenson, F C.

EVIDENCE

Probability And Evidence. Horwich, Paul.

Testing Scientific Theories. Earman, John (ed).

The Concept Of Evidence. Achinstein, Peter (ed).

Without Proof Or Evidence: Essays Of O K Bouwsma. Craft, J L (ed) and Hustwit, Ronald E (ed).

"Explanations Of Irrelevance" in *Testing Scientific Theories*, Earman, John (ed), 55–66. Horwich, Paul.

"Glymour On Evidence And Explanation" in *Testing Scientific Theories*, Earman, John (ed), 165–176. Van Fraassen, Bas C.

"Old Evidence And Logical Omniscience In Bayesian Confirmation Theory" in *Testing Scientific Theories*, Earman, John (ed), 99–132. Garber, Daniel.

"On Testing And Evidence" in *Testing Scientific Theories*, Earman, John (ed), 3–26. Glymour, Clark.

"Theory Comparison And Relevant Evidence" in *Testing Scientific Theories*, Earman, John (ed), 27–42. Van Fraassen, Bas C.

"Why Glymour Is A Bayesian" in *Testing Scientific Theories*, Earman, John (ed), 69–98. Rosenkrantz, Roger.

Does The Evidence Confirm Theism More Than Naturalism? Martin, M.

Does The Gettier Problem Rest On A Mistake? Kirkham, Richard L.

Epistemic Dependence. Hardwig, John.

Evidentialism. Feldman, Richard and Conee, Earl.

Evil And The Theistic Hypothesis: A Response To S J Wykstra. Rowe, William L.

Horwich's Justification Of Induction. Chihara, Charles S.

Ignoring Available Evidence. Clarke, David S.

On Evidence According To Meinong And Chisholm. Schubert Kalsi, Marie–Luise.

Propositions And Empirical Evidence. O' Neil, Michael P.

The Availability Of Evidence In Support Of Religious Belief. Schlesinger, George N.

The Evidential Value Of Religious Experiences. Clark, R W.

The Humean Obstacle To Evidential Arguments From Suffering: On Avoiding The Evils Of "Appearance". Wykstra, Stephen J.

Theoretical Functions, Theory And Evidence. Forge, John.

True Believers And Radical Sceptics. Gallois, André.

EVIL

Augustine On Evil. Evans, G R.

Evil And The Process God. Whitney, Barry L.

God And Natural Evil. Jooharigian, Robert Badrik.

The Unknowable: An Ontological Introduction To The Philosophy Of Religion. Frank, S L.

Wickedness: A Philosophical Essay. Midgley, Mary.

A Jungian View Of Evil. Segal, Robert A.

A Response To The Problems Of Evil. Morris, Thomas V.

A Response To The Modal Problem Of Evil. Garcia, Laura L.

Aquinas And Janssens On The Moral Meaning Of Human Acts. May, William E.

Augustine On Evil: The Dilemma Of The Philosophers. Maker, William A.

Can Evil Be Banal? Rotenstreich, Nathan.

Consent In Time Of Affliction: The Ethics Of A Circumspect Theist. Cahill, Lisa Sowle.

Divine Sovereignty And The Free Will Defence. Flint, Thomas P.

Entropy And Evil. Russell, Robert John.

Evil And The Theistic Hypothesis: A Response To S J Wykstra. Rowe, William L.

God, Evil And Humanity. Campbell, Richmond.

God's Choice: Reflections On Evil In A Created World. Felt, James W.

Is Plantinga's God Omnipotent? Morriston, Wesley.

Is There A Problem With The Problem Of Evil? Springsted, Eric O.

Maimonides, Aquinas And Gersonides On Providence And Evil. Burrell, David.

Models For Understanding Evil In The *Guide For The Perplexed* (in Hebrew). Ben– Or, Ehud.

Morality And Deterrence. Tucker, Robert W.

Must God Do His Best? Hasker, W.

No Love For God? Lowe, Susan.

On Natural Evil's Being Necessary For Free Will. O' Connor, David.

The Central Argument Of Aurobindo's *The Life Divine*. Phillips, Stephen H.

The Dilemma Of Theodicy. Gordon, Jeffrey.

The Humean Obstacle To Evidential Arguments From Suffering: On Avoiding The Evils Of "Appearance". Wykstra, Stephen J.

The Problem Of Evil. Yandell, Keith E.

The Problem Of Evil: Augustine And Ricoeur. Stark, Judith C.

Tolerance And Evil: Teaching The Holocaust. Lang, Berel.

Why Me; Why Now? Phifer, Kenneth.

Wickedness. Benn, S I.

Worlds Without Evil. Mc Kim, Robert.

EVIL(S)

Diderot, Le Désordre, Le Mal. Leduc– Fayette, Denise.

La Question Des Actes Intrinsèquement Mauvais. Pinckaers, S.

EVOLUTION

see also Darwinism

Conceptual Issues In Evolutionary Biology. Sober, Elliott (ed).

Darwinism And Determinism: The Role Of Direction In Evolution. Ruffa, Anthony R.

Evolution, The History Of An Idea. Bowler, Peter J.

From Aristotle To Darwin And Back Again: A Journey In Final Causality, Species, And Evolution. Gilson, Etienne.

Genes, Organisms, Populations: Controversies Over The Units Of Selection. Brandon, Robert N (ed) and Burian, Richard M (ed).

Laws Of The Game: How The Principles Of Nature Govern Chance. Eigen, Manfred and Winkler, Ruthild.

Order Out Of Chaos: Man's New Dialogue With Nature. Prigogine, Ilya and Stengers, Isabelle.

Principles Of Language And Mind: An Evolutionary Theory Of Meaning. Waldron, T P.

Science, Reason & Religion. Stanesby, Derek.

The Nature Of Selection: Evolutionary Theory In Philosophical Focus. Sober, Elliott.

Zoological Philosophy: An Exposition In Regard To The Natural History Of Animals. Lamarck, J B.

Überlegungen Zur Gesetzesproblematik In Der Biologie. Skiebe, Kurt.

"Evolution And Ethics" in *Darwin, Marx And Freud*, Caplan, Arthur L (ed), 35–46. Mayr, Ernst.

"Progress And Evolution: A Reappraisal" in *The Good Life And Its Pursuit*, Dougherty, Jude P (ed), 163–174. Nasr, Seyyed Hossein.

"The Philosophical Implications Of Darwinism" in *Darwin, Marx And Freud*, Caplan, Arthur L (ed), 3–34. Flew, Antony G N.

"Two Evolutions" in *On Nature*, Rouner, Leroy S (ed), 42–59. Smith, Huston.

Are Punctuationists Wrong About The Modern Synthesis? Stidd, Benton M.

Biological Conception Of Evolution And The Problem Of Thermodynamics From The Standpoint Of The Work Of I Prigogine (in Czechoslovakian). Novák, Vladimir J A.

Biological Ideas And Their Cultural Uses. Benton, Ted.

Buddhism In Huxley's Evolution And Ethics. Rajapakse, Vijitha.

Dialectical Unity Of The Dynamic And The Statistical In Nature And Society And Prigogine's Universal Evolution Theory (in Czechoslovakian). Skramovska, Svatoslava and Celeda, J.

Die Entwicklung Der Paläoanthropologie Im Lichte Der Stammbäme Des Menschen. Halaczek, B.

Enkele Pogingen Tot Reconstructie Van De Evolutietheorie En De Populatiegenetica Als Wetenschappelijke Onderzoeks–Programma's. Van Balen, G A M.

Evolution And The Fundamentalist Critique: Contributions To Educational Philosophy. Vold, David J.

Evolution Und Revolution In Der Technischen Entwicklung Der Gegenwart. Wendt, H.

Evolutional Rheology And Mechanical Asymmetry (in Czechoslovakian). Sobotka, Zdenek.

Evolutionary Epistemology And Ontological Realism. Clark, A J.

Extending The Darwinian Model: James's Struggle With Royce And Spencer. Seigfried, Charlene H.

Freiheit Und Perfektion. Düll, Rupprecht.

Group Selection And Methodological Individualism. Glaser, Gerald.

Ist Die Evolutionstheorie Wissenschaftlich Begründet? Eisenstein, I.

Jan Christian Smuts And His Doctrine Of Holism. Brush, Francis W.

Kausalität, Teleologie Und Evolution: Methodologische Grundprobeme Der Moderne Biologie. Kotter, Rudolf.

Le Néo–Évolutionnisme Contemporain. Damian, Cornel.

Mutual Aid And Selfish Genes. Thompson, Janna L.

Nietzsche And Pragmatism. Hallman, Max O.

On Being Terrestrial. Midgley, Mary.

Over De Menselijkheid Van Vroege Hominidae. Corbey, R.

Prigogine's And Piaget's Theory Of Dynamic Equilibrium And Dialectical And Materialist Conception Of Human Evolution (in Czechoslovakian). Linhart, J.

Sexuality In Human Evolution: What Is "Natural" Sex? Caulfield, Mina Davis.

Sociobiology. Midgley, Mary.

The Cosmic Breath: Reflections On The Thermodynamics Of Creation. Wicken, Jeffrey S.

The Evolution Of Our Understanding Of The Cell: A Study In The Dynamics Of Scientific Progress. Bechtel, William P.

The Mystery Of Time: A New Sociological Approach. Gras, Alain.

Thermodynamics And Life. Peacocke, Arthur.

What's Historical About Historical Materialism? Levine, Andrew and Sober, Elliott.

Zur Dialektik In Der Biologischen Evolution. Beurton, Peter.

EVOLUTIONISM

Creation Science: Enough Is Enough Is Too Much. Ruse, Michael.

Panspermia And The Evolutionism—Creationism Controversies (in Polish). Slaga, Szczepan W.

The Origin Of Life: Science Or Religion. Howick, William H.

EXAMPLE(S)

Utilitarians And The Use Of Examples. Cox, J W Roxbee.

EXCELLENCE

Classical Living And Classical Learning: The Search For Equity And Excellence In Education. Smith, Philip L and Traver, Rob.

Equality, Excellence, Paideia, And The Good Old Days Before Adam And Eve And Social Science. Arnstine, Donald.

EXCHANGE(S)

"Obligation, Contract And Exchange: On Hegel's Abstract Right" in *The State And Civil Society*, Pelczynski, Z A (ed), 159–177. Benhabib, Seyla.

The Proper Reconstruction Of Exchange Economics. Balzer, W.

What (If Anything) Is Intrinsically Wrong With Capitalism? Van Parijs, Philippe.

What's Morally Special About Free Exchange? Gibbard, Allan.

EXCLUDED MIDDLE

Husserl And Realism In Logic And Mathematics. Tragesser, Robert S.

Das Prinzip Vom Nicht–Widerspruch Und Das Prinzip Vom Ausgeschlossenen Dritten. Welding, Streen O.

Jonathan Bennett On 'Even If'. Cross, Charles B.

Lässt Sich Eine Kernlogik Konstituieren: Ein Versuch Dazu Vom Standpunkt Des Pankritischen Rationalismus Aus. Klowski, Joachim.

EXCUSES

Rights And Excuses. Fletcher, George P.

EXEGESIS

Bhagavad—Gita: An Exegetical Commentary. Minor, Robert N.
John Toland: His Methods, Manners And Mind. Daniel, Stephen.
"Surrender—And—Catch And Hermeneutics". Wolff, Kurt H.

EXEMPLIFICATION

The Problem Of Divine Exemplarity In St Thomas. Farthing, John L.

EXISTENCE

see also Being, Dasein, Ontology, Reality
Das Existenzproblem Bei J G Fichte Und S Kierkegaard. Hochenbleicher— Schwarz, Anton.
Introduction To The Arguments For God. Caes, Charles J.
On The Essence Of Finite Being As Such, On The Existence Of That Essence And Their Distinction. Suárez, Francis.
'Can We Speak Literally Of God'? Levine, Michael P.
"A Long Day's Journey Into Night" in *Existential Coordinates Of Human Condition*, Tymieniecka, A (ed), 209–226. Schlack, Beverly A.
"The Suareziann Proof Of God's Existence" in *History Of Philosophy In Making*, Thro, Linus J (ed), 105–118. Doule, John P.
A Personalistic Philosophy Of History. Bartnik, Czeslaw Stanislaw.
Addendum To "Countable Algebra And Set Existence Axioms". Friedman, Harvey M and Simpson, S G and Smith, R L.
Are Synoptic Questions Illegitimate? Rescher, Nicholas.
As Provas Da Existência De Deus Na Filosofia Neo—Escolástica. Rüppel, Ernesto.
De Essentia Individua: In Defence Of Possible Worlds Existentialism. Miller, Barry.
Descartes' 'Demonstrations' Of His Existence. Tweyman, Stanley.
Descriptions In Mathematical Logic. Renardel De Lavalette, Gerard R.
Existence And Judgment. Connell, Desmond.
Existence, Eternality, And The Ontological Argument. Werhane, Patricia H.
Frankfurt On Descartes' Dream Argument. Stuart, James D.
Hume's Dialogue IX Defended. Stahl, Donald E.
Inconceivable? Gay, Robert.
La Eternidad Del Mundo: Un Capítulo De Filosofía Medieval. López, Antonio Marlasca.
La Originación Radical De Las Cosas Demostrada A Priori: Leibniz, Nozik, Rescher. Madanes, Leiser.
Loptson On Anselm And Davis. Davis, Stephen T.
On Macintyre, Rationality, And Dramatic Space. Monasterio, Xavier O.
On The Existence And Recursion Theoretic Properties Of Generic Sets Of Reals. Weitkamp, Galen.
Perishability, The Actual World, And The Non—Existence Of God. Chrzan, Keith.
Raum Und Zeit Als Existenzformen Der Materie. Gehlar, Fritz.
Religious Existence And The Philosophical Radicalization Of Phenomenological Theology. Bourgeois, Patrick L.
Reply To Professor Baker's "Religious Experience And The Possibility Of Divine Existence". Dore, Clement.
Stability Theory And Set Existence Axioms. Harnik, Victor.
Substitutional Quantification And Existence. Copeland, B J.
Supervaluations And Theories. Bencivenga, Ermanno.
The Dialectics Of "Essence" And "Existence". Zdanowicz, Piotr.
Thomas Aquinas On The Distinction And Derivation Of The Many From The One: A Dialectic Between Being And Nonbeing. Wippel, John F.
Which Set Existence Axioms Are Needed To Prove The Cauchy/Peano Theorem For Ordinary Differential Equations? Simpson, Stephen.
Why Is There Something Rather Than Nothing? Smith, Joseph Wayne.

EXISTENTIAL

Bounded Existential Induction. Wilmers, George.
The Trouble With Extensional Semantics. Asher, Nicholas.

EXISTENTIAL(S)

"Existential Quantifiers In Physical Theories" in *Philosophical Analysis In Latin America*, Gracia, Jorge J E and others (eds), 173–198. Moulines, C Ulises.

EXISTENTIAL IMPORT

Existential Import In Anselm's Ontological Argument. Bäck, Allan.
Systems Of Substitution Semantics. Bonevac, Daniel.

EXISTENTIALISM

see also Alienation, Being, Death, Essence(s), Existence, Nihilism
Absent At The Creation: The Existential Psychiatry Of Ludwig Binswanger. Seidman, Bradley.
Buddhist And Western Psychology. Katz, Nathan (ed).
Dimensions Of Moral Education. Carter, Robert E.
God, Guilt, And Death: An Existential Phenomenology Of Religion. Westphal, Merold.
Home From Exile: An Approach To Post—Existentialist Philosophizing. Hickey, Denis.
Human, All Too Human. Nietzsche, Fredrich and Faber, Marion (trans).
In Search Of Being: Man In Conflict With The Spectre Of Nothingness. De Carvalho, Manoel J.
Phenomenology And Existentialism: An Introduction. Grossman, Reinhardt.
The New Image Of The Person: The Theory And Practice Of Clinical Philosophy. Koestenbaum, Peter.
Vice And Virtue In Everyday Life: Introductory Readings In Ethics. Sommers, Christina Hoff.
"Existential Guilt And Buber's Social And Political Thought" in *Martin Buber*, Gordon, Haim (ed), 215–232. Gordon, Haim.
"Sartre And Alienation" in *Continuity And Change In Marxism*, Fischer, Norman And Others (eds), 144–169. Georgopoulos, N.
An Organism Of Words: Ruminations On The Philosophical—Poetics Of Merleau—Ponty. Walsh, Robert D.

Beauvoir And Satre: The Forms Of Farewell. Barnes, Hazel E.
Developing Themes In Philosophy: Modern Continental Philosophy. Nicholson, Graeme.
Diagrammatic Approach To Heidegger's Schematism Of Existence. Kisiel, Theodore.
Eternal Recurrence Again. Stack, George J.
Heidegger's "Existentialism" Revisited. Zimmerman, Michael E.
L'oggetto Primario Della Libertà Di Scelta. Szaszkiewicz, Jerzy.
Modern Movements In European Philosophy: Some Introductory Remarks. Kearney, Richard.
On Franz Rosenzweig's 'New Thinking'. Lichtigfeld, A.
Perspectivas Pedagógicas Da Filosofia Existencialista. Rocha, Filipe.
Semiotics And Existential Concerns: Reforming An Old Versus. Denton, David E.
The Central Role Of Universalization In Sartrean Ethics. Lee, Sander H.
The Contemporary Status Of Continental Philosophy In Canada: A Narrative. Madison, Gary B.
The Impasse Of *No Exit*. Kolenda, Konstantin.
The Logos And The Lotos. Stigliano, Tony.
The Religious Humanism Of The Future. Arisian, Khoren.
The Roots Of The Existentialist Theory Of Freedom In *Ideas I*. Edie, James M.
Welt Und Mythos: Das Mythische In Heideggers Seinsdenken. Villwock, Jörg.
Zur Sowjetphilosophischen Kritik Der "Idealistischen" Erkenntnistheorie. Weinzierl, Emil.

EXPECTATION(S)

Probability Logic With Conditional Expectation. Fajardo, Sergio.

EXPERIENCE(S)

see also Aesthetic Experience(s)
An Outline Of The Idealistic Construction Of Experience. Baillie, J B.
Consciousness: Natural And Artificial. Culbertson, James T.
Quine On Ontology, Necessity, And Experience: A Philosophical Critique. Dilman, Ilham.
Sense And Content: Experience, Thought, And Their Relations. Peacocke, Christopher.
The Knower And The Known. Grene, Marjorie G.
Über Einige Erkenntnistheoretische Schwierigkeiten Des Klassischen Rationalismus. Pacho, Julian.
"Metaphor & The Flux Of Human Experience" in *Existential Coordinates Of Human Condition*, Tymieniecka, A (ed), 241–248. Lawlor, Patricia M.
"Situational Art: Observations—Contemporary Art" in *Continental Philosophy/The Arts*, Winters, Laurence E and others (eds), 173–192. Biemel, Walter.
Comments On A Claim That Some Phenomenological Statements May Be *A Posteriori*. Van De Pitte, M M.
Empirical Realism And Creative Passage: Reflections On Meland's Theology. Axel, Larry E.
Grete Henry—Hermann's Development Of Leonard Nelson's Ethics. Heckmann, Gustav.
Hegel's *Phenomenology* As A Philosophy Of Culture. Levi, Albert William.
How Is Sport Possible? Lipiec, Józef.
John Dewey And Creative Dramatics. Schwartz, Philip J.
Kant Über Wahrnehmung Und Erfahrung. Bröcker, W.
Learning To Experience. Simons, Martin.
Meland: Worship And His Recent Thought. Miller, Randolph C.
On The Causal Self—Referentiality Of Perceptual Experiences And The Problem Of Concrete Perceptual Reference. Natsoulas, Thomas.
Professor Shoemaker And So—Called 'Qualia' Of Experience. White, Nicholas P.
Reply To Van De Pitte's "Comments On A Claim That Some Phenomenological Statements May Be *A Posteriori*". Schmitt, Richard.
Scepticism On Twin Earth. Hanfling, Oswald.
Subjectivity. Shalom, Albert.
The Concept Of Experimental Knowledge In The Thought Of Chang Tsai. Birdwhistell, Anne D.
The Evidential Value Of Religious Experiences. Clark, R W.
The Experience Of Dreaming. Horne, James.
The Experience Of Illness: Integrating Metaphors And The Transcendence Of Illness. Shelp, Earl E.
The Fake, The Non—Fake And The Genuine. Chakravarti, Mihir.
The Tree In The Quad. Fleming, Noel.
Thinking About The Body. Kass, Leon R.

EXPERIMENT(S)

Observation, Experiment, And Hypothesis In Modern Physical Science. Achinstein, Peter (ed) and Hannaway, Owen (ed).
"Bubble Chambers And Experiment" in *Observation, Experiment, And Hypothesis In Modern Physical Science*, Achinstein, Peter (ed), 309–374. Galison, Peter.
Die Ethischen Grenzen Der Klinischen Experimente (in Polish). Bogusz, Jozef.
Experiment—Modell—Theorie. Horz, Herbert.
Philosophers And Experimental Inquiry: A Reply To Milgram's "Reflections On Morelli's Dilemma Of Obedience". Morelli, Mario.
Randomization And The Design Of Experiments. Urbach, Peter.
The Use And Misuse Of Critical Gedankenexperimente. Krimsky, Sheldon.

EXPERIMENTAL

Commentary On Patrick A Heelan's "Hermeneutics Of Experimental Science In The Context Of The Life—World". Kisiel, Theodore.
Hermeneutics Of Experimental Science In The Context Of The Life—World. Heelan, Patrick A.

EXPERIMENTATION

The New Scientific Spirit. Bachelard, Gaston and Goldhammer, Arthur (trans).
"Playing God": The Ethics Of Biotechnical Intervention. Varga, Andrew C.

FLATHMAN, R

Peace, Human Rights, And Human Needs: A Comment On The Bay—Flathman Debate. Carens, Joseph H.

FLAUBERT

Flauberts Laughter. Caws, Peter.

FLEW, A

"Darwinism And Ethics: A Response To Antony Flew" in *Darwin, Marx And Freud*, Caplan, Arthur L (ed), 47—72. Kass, Leon R.

"Evolution And Ethics" in *Darwin, Marx And Freud*, Caplan, Arthur L (ed), 35—46. Mayr, Ernst.

FLIESS, W

"Subjectivity In Psychoanalytic Inference" in *Testing Scientific Theories*, Earman, John (ed), 349—412. Meehl, Paul E.

FODOR, J

De Angst Van De Homunculus Voor Hetscheermes. Draaisma, Douwe.

Fregean Thoughts. Noonan, Harold.

Panglossian Functionalism And The Philosophy Of Mind. Sober, Elliott.

Properties, Functionalism, And The Identity Theory. Adams, Frederick.

FOLKLORE

A Note On Mutual Belief Logic For Processing Definite Reference. Del Cerro, Fariñas.

FOLLESDAL, D

Perceptual Meaning And Husserl. Cunningham, Suzanne.

FOOD

"The Morality Of Killing Animals: Four Arguments". Young, Thomas.

FOOT, P

Games And The Action—Guiding Force Of Morality. Eggerman, Richard W.

Moral Scepticism And Moral Conduct. Mac Kenzie, J C.

Remarks On Three Formulations Of Ethical Relativism. Peterson, Sandra.

FORBES, G

Transmission For Knowledge Not Established. Brueckner, Anthony.

FORCE(S)

Über Die Produktivkräfte Und Ihre Entwicklung. Ruben, Peter.

Die Dynamische Naturvorstellung Als Naturphilosophische Grundlage Der Heutigen Physik. Adler, Norbert.

Eine Antwort Auf Kants Briefe Vom 23: August 1749. Fischer, Harald—Paul.

Entwicklung Und Effektive Nutzung Des Gesellschaft Arbeitsvermögens—Ausdruck Praktizierter Einheit Von Humanität Und Rationalität. Pietrzynski, Gerd.

Leibniz And The Cartesians On Motion And Force. Spector, Marshall.

Mental Activity And Physical Reality. Snyder, Douglas M.

Triebkräfte Des Sozialismus. Schonherr, L.

FORCING

Adjoining Dominating Functions. Baumgartner, James E and Dordal, Peter.

An AD—like Model. Apter, Arthur W.

C C C Forcing Without Combinatorics. Mekler, Alan H.

Cancellation Laws For Surjective Cardinals. Truss, J K.

Forcing The Failure Of CH By Adding A Real. Shelah, Saharon and Woodin, Hugh.

More On Proper Forcing. Shelah, Saharon.

More On The Weak Diamond. Shelah, Saharon.

On The Consistency Of Some Partition Theorems For Continuous Colorings, And The Structure Of Dense Real Order Types. Shelah, Saharon and Abraham, U and Rubin, M.

Reflection And Forcing In E—Recursion Theory. Slaman, Theodore A.

Simplified Morasses With Linear Limits. Velleman, Dan.

The Foreign Corrupt Practices Act And The Imposition Of Values. Brummer, James J.

The Strong Amalgamation Property For Complete Boolean Algebras. Monro, G P.

FOREIGN

"Archaeology Abroad" in *Ethics And Values In Archaeology*, Green, Ernestene L (ed), 123—132. Healy, Paul F.

FOREIGN POLICY

Moral Dimensions Of American Foreign Policy. Thompson, Kenneth W (ed).

"Foreign Aid: Justice For Whom" in *The Search For Justice*, Taitte, W Lawson (ed), 127—162. Rostow, W W.

Foreign Policy As A Goal Directed Activity. Anderson, Paul A.

Human Rights And U S Foreign Policy: Models And Options. Galloway, Jonathan F.

The Role Of Economics And Ethical Principles In Determining U S Policies Toward Poor Nations. Piderit, John J.

FOREKNOWLEDGE

Compatibilidad Entre La Presciencia Divina Y La Libertad De Los Actos Humanos. De Stier, María L Lukac.

Dewey And Pekarsky On The Efficacy Of Intelligence And Foresight. Burnett, Joe R.

Foreknowledge And Necessity. Hasker, William.

The Place Of Foresight In Deliberation: An Interpretation Of Dewey's View. Pekarsky, Daniel.

FORGERY(—RIES)

Historical Context And The Aesthetic Evaluation Of Forgeries. Clark, Roger.

FORGIVENESS

Forgiveness And Regret. Golding, Martin P.

FORM(S)

see also Essence(s), Idea(s)

Metaphysics Z 12 And H 6; The Unity Of Form And Composite. Halper, Edward.

Plato. Rowe, C J.

The Responsibility Of Forms: Critical Essays On Music, Art, And Representation. Barthes, Roland and Howard, Richard (trans).

'Form, Reproduction And Inherited Characteristics In Aristotle's GA'. Witt, Charlotte.

'Vlastos On Pauline Predication'. Malcolm, John F.

"Form And Predication In Aristotle's *Metaphysics*" in *How Things Are*, Bogen, James (ed), 59—84. Lewis, Frank A.

"Forms And Compounds" in *How Things Are*, Bogen, James (ed), 85—100. Modrak, D K.

Art And The Unsayable: Langer's Tractarian Aesthetics. Hagberg, Garry.

Art As Semblance. Morawski, Stefan.

Delimitating The Concept Of The Grotesque. Fingesten, Peter.

Die Lebensform In Wittgensteins *Philosophischen Untersuchungen*. Garver, Newton.

Die Platonischen Ideen Als Gegenstände Sprachlicher Referenz. Graeser, Andreas.

Homogeneous Forms In Two Ordinal Variables. Hickman, John L.

Hybrid Art Forms. Levinson, Jerrold.

Kant On Receptivity: Form And Content. Glouberman, M.

Lebensform Oder Lebensformen:—Eine Bemerkung Zu Newton Garvers Interpretation Von "Lebensform". Haller, Rudolf.

On R E Allen's *Plato's Parmenides*. Turnbull, Robert G.

The One, The Many, And The Forms: *Philebus* 15b1—8. Dancy, R M.

The Snub. Balme, D M.

The Uniqueness Proof For Forms In *Republic X*. Parry, Richard D.

FORMAL LANGUAGE(S)

A Note On *xy* Languages. Sadock, J M and Zwicky, Arnold M.

FORMAL LOGIC

Formal Logic: A Degenerating Research Programme In Crisis. Smith, Joseph Wayne.

How To Give It Up: A Survey Of Some Formal Aspects Of The Logic Of Theory Change. Makinson, David.

Schröder—Husserl—Scheler: Zur Formalen Logik. Willer, Jörg.

FORMAL STRUCTURE(S)

Logical Form And Natural Syntax. Englebretsen, George.

On A Formal Structure Of A Dialogue. Nowakowska, Maria.

FORMAL SYSTEM(S)

Lecture Notes In Mathematics. Muller, G H and others.

"On The Length Of Proofs In A Formal System Of Recursive Arithmetic" in *Lecture Notes In Mathematics*, Muller, G H And Others (ed), 81—108. Miyatake, Tohru.

Formal Systems Of Dialogue Rules. Krabbe, Erik C W.

FORMALISM

Criticism And Objectivity. Selden, Raman.

Der Formalismus Und Seine Grenzen: Untersuchungen Zur Neueren Philosophie Der Mathematik. Rheinwald, Rosemarie.

Formal Traces In Cartesian Functional Explanation. Rorty, Amelie Oksenberg.

Kant And Greenberg's Varieties Of Aesthetic Formalism. Crowther, Paul.

More Than 'Meets The Eye'. Devereaux, Mary.

Orígenes Y Proyecciones De La Lógica Cuántica. Lungarzo, Carlos.

Social Philosophy Of Sport: A Critical Interpretation. Morgan, William J.

The Tendency Of Tendermindedness In Educational Research, Or, The New Anti-Formalism. Phillips, D C.

FORMALIZATION

Informatique Pour Les Sciences Del'homme. Borillo, Mario.

Defining 'Business Ethics': Like Nailing Jello To A Wall. Lewis, Phillip V.

FORMATION

Aether/Or: The Creation Of Scientific Concepts. Nersessian, Nancy J.

Business Ethics: Micro And Macro. Brummer, James.

The Relation Of Theory And Practice In The Process Of Formation And Action Of Laws Of Communist Socio—Economic Formation (in Czechoslovakian). Kroh, Michael.

FORMULA(S)

"Homogeneous Formulas And Definability Theorems" in *Lecture Notes In Mathematics*, Muller, G H And Others (ed), 109—116. Motohashi, Nobuyoshi.

A Decidable Subclass Of The Minimal Gödel Class With Identity. Goldfarb, Warren D and Gurevich, Yuri and Shelah, Saharon.

A Remark On The Strict Order Property. Lachlan, A H.

An Application Of The Reiger—Nishimura Formulas To The Intuitionistic Modal Logics. Vakarelov, Dimiter.

Lower Bound Results On Lengths Of Second—order Formulas. Scarpellini, Bruno.

On Modal Logics Which Enrich First—Orders S5. Hodes, Harold.

Partial Isomorphism Extension Method And A Representation Theorem For Post-Language. Sette, Antonio M.

The Unsolvability Of The Gödel Class With Identity. Goldfarb, Warren D.

Truth Without Satisfaction. Fine, Kit and Mc Carthy, Timothy.

FORRESTER, J

A Solution To Forrester's Paradox Of Gentle Murder. Sinnott— Armstrong, Walter.

FORSTHOFF, E

Der Staat Der Industriegesellschaft: Zu Einer Publikation Von Ernst Forsthoff. Kodalle, Klaus—M.

FOUCAULT, M

Michel Foucault: Beyond Structuralism And Hermeneutics. Dreyfus, Hubert L and Rabinow, Paul.

Michel Foucault: An Introduction To The Study Of His Thought. Cooper, Barry.

Polis And Praxis. Dallmayr, Fred R.

"Beyond Hermeneutics" in *Hermeneutics*, Shapiro, Gary (ed), 66—83. Dreyfus, Hubert.

"Five Parables" in *Philosophy In History*, Rorty, Richard and others (ed), 103—124. Hacking, Ian.

Connolly, Coucault, And Truth. Taylor, Charles.

El Poder En Michel Foucault. Parent, Juan.

Foucault And The Question Of Enlightenment. Hiley, David R.

Foucault's Archaeological Method: A Response To Hacking And Rorty. Wartenberg,

FREEDOM

Howard, John A (ed), 95–111. Berman, Ronald.

"For Your Freedom, And Ours" in *On Freedom*, Howard, John A (ed), 3–6. Tyrmand, Leopold.

"Henry Veatch And The Problem Of A Noncognitivist Ethics" in *The Georgetown Symposium On Ethics*, Porreco, Rocco (ed), 159–170. Lee, Sander H.

"Kant On The Nondeterminate Character Of Human Actions" in *Kant On Causality, Freedom, And Objectivity*, Harper, William A (ed), 138–164. Meerbote, Ralf.

"Movement In The Market: Mobility And Economics In The Free Society" in *On Freedom*, Howard, John A (ed), 39–58. Johnson, Paul.

"New Hymns For The Republic: The Religious Right And America's Moral Purpose" in *On Freedom*, Howard, John A (ed), 112–132. Neuhaus, Richard John.

"Political Community And Individual Freedom In Hegel's Philosophy" in *The State And Civil Society*, Pelczynski, Z A (ed), 55–76. Pelczynski, Z A.

"Reopening The Books On Ethics: The Role Of Education In A Free Society" in *On Freedom*, Howard, John A (ed), 79–94. Howard, John A.

"The Profits Of Freedom: Investing In The Defense Of Business" in *On Freedom*, Howard, John A (ed), 59–78. Shenfield, Arthur.

"The Theory And Practice Of The History Of Freedom, Harry Brod (commentator)" in *History And System*, Perkins, Robert (ed), 123–148. Winfield, Richard D.

"Tragedy And The Completion Of Freedom" in *Existential Coordinates Of Human Condition*, Tymieniecka, A (ed), 295–306. Tymieniecka, A.

A Propósito De Un Libro. Radchick, Laura.

An Essay Towards Cultural Autonomy. Dasgupta, Probal.

Anmerkungen Zu Schelling. Schulz, Walter.

Anscombe, Davidson And Lehrer On A Point About Freedom. Harrison, Jonathan.

Bohm And Whitehead On Wholeness, Freedom, Causality, And Time. Griffin, David R.

Can There Be A Freedom Without Responsibility? Ghosh–Dastidar, Koyeli.

Carácter Racional De La Libertad. Derisi, Octavio N.

Commentary: Compulsory Health And Safety In A Free Society. Downie, R S.

Compatibilidad Entre La Presciencia Divina Y La Libertad De Los Actos Humanos. De Stier, María L Lukac.

Compulsory Health And Safety In A Free Society. Boughton, B J.

Davidson's Compatibilism. Fales, Evan.

Demystifying Doublethink: Self–Deception, Truth And Freedom In *1984*. Martin, Mike W.

Determining A Society's Freedom. Gould, James A.

Die Macht Zur Freiheit. Steussloff, Hans.

Divine Omniscience And Human Freedom: A 'Middle Knowledge' Perspective. Basinger, David.

Ethics And Taxation: A Theoretical Framework. Green, Ronald M.

Food And Freedom In *The Flounder*. Pitkin, Hanna F.

Foucault And The Question Of Enlightenment. Hiley, David R.

Freedom And Moral Therapy In Leibniz. Seidler, Michael J.

Freedom And Determinism In Spinoza. Russell, John M.

Freedom And Obedience. Wade, Francis C.

Freedom And Women. Gould, Carol C.

Freedom As A Condition For Truth: Jaspers On The Significance Of Temporality In Science. Koterski, Joseph W.

Freedom Defined As The Power To Decide. Mc Call, Storrs.

Freiheit Und Perfektion. Düll, Rupprecht.

Freiheit Und Eignetum. Ryffel, Hans.

Freirecht—Revisited, Emphasizing Its Property–Space. Schmidt, Joachim K H W.

Fundamentación Ontológica De La Libertad Psicológica. Bogliolo, Luis.

J Krishnamurti On Choiceless Awareness, Creative Emptiness And Ultimate Freedom. Mathur, Dinesh Chandra.

Jean–Paul Sartre And The Problem Of The Other. Andrews, Christine.

John Locke And The Antebellum Defense Of Slavery. Loewenberg, Robert J.

Kant's *Groundwork* Justification Of Freedom. Mc Carthy, Michael H.

Kritische Bemerkung Zu E Tielschs "Logik Des Freiheitsbegriffes". Schottlaender, Rudolf.

La Concezione Hegeliana Dello Stato Politico Come Sintesi Della Libertà. Torresetti, Giorgio.

La Critica De Cossio E La Escuela Del Derecho Libre. Chiappini, Julio O.

Lawless Freedom. Abelson, Raziel.

Leninism And The Enlightenment. Moran, Philip.

Libertad Política: Liberalismo Y Tomismo. Hernández, Héctor H.

Libertad–Necesidad En La *Quaestio Disputata De Malo, VI*. De Gandolfi, María C Donadío Maggi.

Libertarianism Versus Education For Freedom. Agassi, Joseph.

MacCallum And The Two Concepts Of Freedom. Baldwin, Tom.

Marx, Justice, Freedom: The Libertarian Prophet. Heller, Agnes.

Moksa And Critical Theory. Klostermaier, Klaus.

Natur Und Freiheit: Zwei Konkurrierende Traditionen. Krings, Hermann.

Negative Freedom: Constraints And Opportunities. Gould, James.

On Being Terrestrial. Midgley, Mary.

Politics, Nature And Freedom: On The Natural Foundation Of The Political Condition. Levy, David J.

Radical Freedom. Reinhardt, Lloyd.

Reply To Oppenheim's "Constraints On Freedom". Miller, David.

Rousseau On Equality. Cranston, Maurice.

Sartre O Las Dificultades De Escribir Una Moral. Fornet–Betancourt, Raul.

Svaraj, The Indian Ideal Of Freedom: A Political Or Religious Concept? Mac Kenzie Brown, C.

The Central Role Of Universalization In Sartrean Ethics. Lee, Sander H.

The Historical Evolution Of A Certain Concept Of Freedom (in Hebrew). Pines, Shlomo.

The Human Right To Be Treated As A Person. Khatchadourian, Haig.

The Marxian Ideal Of Freedom And The Problem Of Justice. Van Der Veen, Robert J.

The Objection Of Circularity In Groundwork III. Mc Carthy, Michael H.

The Practical And The Pathological. Mendus, Susan.

The Roots Of The Existentialist Theory Of Freedom In *Ideas I*. Edie, James M.

Toward A Critical Theory Of Education: Beyond A Marxism With Guarantees—A Response To Daniel Liston. Giroux, Henry A.

Trans–World Identity Of Future Contingents: Sartre On Leibnizian Freedom. Winant, Terry.

Value And Free Choice: Lavelle's Attempt At A Reconciliation. Hardy, Gilbert.

Well–being, Agency And Freedom: The Dewey Lectures 1984. Sen, Amartya.

What Spinoza's View Of Freedom Should Have Been. Lucash, Frank.

Zur Dialektik Von Freiheit Und Sicherheit. Hagen, Johann J.

Zur Philosophischen Leistung Friedrich Schillers. Lindner, Margit.

FREGE

De Re Senses. Mc Dowell, John.

Significato. Borutti, Silvana.

Überlegungen Zu Den Grundlegungsversuchen Der Mathematik Von Frege Und Hilbert Vom Standpunkt Der Transzendentalphilosophie Aus (II). Schuler, Wolfgang.

"Frege: The Early Years" in *Philosophy In History*, Rorty, Richard and others (ed), 329–356. Sluga, Hans.

Between The "Thoughts": Topics In Frege's "Logical Investigations" (in Hebrew). Kasher, Asa.

Dummett On Frege: A Review Discussion. Geach, Peter T.

Eternal Thoughts. Carruthers, Peter.

Frege And Abstraction. Angelelli, Ignacio.

Frege And Illogical Behaviour. Mackenzie, Jim.

Frege And The Slingshot Argument (in Hebrew). Margalit, Avishai.

Frege, Sommers, Singular Reference. Mc Culloch, Gregory.

Frege, The Proliferation Of Force, And Non–Cognitivism. Hurley, S L.

Frege's Double Correlation Thesis And Quine's Set Theories NF And ML. Cocchiarella, Nino B.

Frege's Early Conception Of Logic (in Hebrew). Bar–Elli, Gilead.

Frege's Justificationism: Truth And The Recognition Of Authority. Notturno, M A.

Frege's Metaphysical Argument. Currie, Gregory.

Frege's Paradox Of Reference And Castañeda's Guise Theory. Lee, Jig–Chuen.

Frege's Platonism. Hale, Bob.

Frege's Theory Of Number And The Distinction Between Function And Object. Kremer, Michael.

Fregean Connection: Bedeutung, Value And Truth–Value. Gabriel, Gottfried.

Fregean Thoughts. Noonan, Harold.

Freges Beitrag Zur Methodologie In "Die Grundlagen Der Arithmetik" Von 1884—Erbe Und Auftrag. Metzler, Helmut.

Hacking On Frege. Dummett, Michael.

In Search Of The Actual Historical Frege. Mohanty, J N.

Kant, Wittgenstein And The Limits Of Logic. Tiles, Mary.

Numbers As Qualities. Seidel, Asher.

Numbers. Zemach, E M.

Reference And Sense: An Epitome. Bell, David.

Sainsbury On Denying A Fregean Conclusion. Rasmussen, Stig Alstrup.

Some Problems About The Sense And Reference Of Proper Names. Geach, Peter.

The Concept Of Truth In Frege's Program. Burge, Tyler.

The Notion Of Aboutness In Frege (in Hebrew). Bar–Elli, Gilead.

The Philosopher Behind The Last Logicist. Weiner, Joan.

The Principle Of Comprehension As A Present–Day Contribution To Mathesis Universalis. Marciszewski, Witold.

The Sense And Reference Of Predicates: A Running Repair To Frege's Doctrine And A Plea For The Copula. Wiggins, David.

The Sense Of A Name. Luntley, Michael.

Tomberlin, Frege, And Guise Theory: A Note On The Methodology Of Dia–Philosophical Comparisons. Castaneda, Hector–Neri.

True, False, Etc. Herzberger, Hans G.

What Does A Concept Script Do? Diamond, Cora.

FREIRE, P

Conscientization And Creativity. Schipani, Daniel S.

FRENCH

Essays On French History And Historians. Mill, John Stuart and Robson, John M (ed).

"The Denial Of Tragedy" in *Existential Coordinates Of Human Condition*, Tymieniecka, A (ed), 401–408. Ravaux, Francoise.

"The French Nouveau Roman" in *Existential Coordinates Of Human Condition*, Tymieniecka, A (ed), 261–272. Carrabino, Victor.

The Path Of French Epistemology To The Concept Of Chaos (in Czechoslovakian). Marcelli, Miroslav.

FRENCH, P

The Random Collective As A Moral Agent. Manning, Rita.

FRENCH REVOLUTION

Community As A Social Ideal. Kamenka, Eugene (ed).

Conservatism Under Napoleon: The Political Writings Of Joseph Fiévée. Popkin, Jeremy D.

FREQUENCY

Discussion: What Would Happen If Everyone Did It? Sober, Elliott.

FREUD
Darwin, Marx, And Freud: Their Influence On Moral Theory. Caplan, Arthur L (ed) and Jennings, Bruce (ed).
Freud And The Mind. Dilman, Ilham.
Law, Psychiatry, And Morality. Stone, Alan R (ed).
Taking Chances: Derrida, Psychoanalysis, And Literature. Kerrigan, William (ed) and Smith, Joseph H (ed).
The Thread Of Life. Wollheim, Richard.
"Freud's Impact On Modern Morality And Our World View" in Darwin, Marx And Freud, Caplan, Arthur L (ed), 147–200. Holt, Robert R.
"Psychoanalysis, Pseudo–Science And Testability" in Popper And The Human Sciences, Currie, Gregory (ed), 13–44. Cioffi, Frank.
"Retrospective Vs Prospective Testing Of Aetiological Hypotheses" in Testing Scientific Theories, Earman, John (ed), 315–348. Grünbaum, Adolf.
A Propósito De Un Libro. Radchick, Laura.
Es El Psicoanálisis Una Pseudo–Ciencia? Rush, Alan A.
Freud, Adler, And Women: Powers Of The "Weak" And "Strong". De Vitis, Joseph L.
L'Uomo Freud: Personalità Morale E Religiosa. Lambertino, Antonio.
La Psychanalyse Sans L'inconscient? Knee, Philip.
On Strong's Psychoanalysis As A Vocation: Freud, Politics, And The Heroic. Odajnyk, V Walter.
On The Political Rhetoric Of Freud's Individual Psychology. Brunner, José.
Reading Habermas Reading Freud. Flynn, Bernard C.
The Logical Structure Of Freud's Idea Of The Unconscious: Toward A Psychology Of Ideas. Fisher, Harwood.
Wittgenstein On The 'Charm' Of Psychoanalysis. Geller, Jeffrey L.

FREUDIANISM
Wilhelm Reich: Culture As Power. Levine, Norman.

FREY, C
Theorieën Over Ethiek En Over De Levenspraktijk. Troost, A.

FRIED, C
Intentions, Rights And Wrongs: A Critique Of Fried. Fischer, Marilyn.
The Case For Deception In Medical Experimentation. Newell, J David.

FRIEDMAN, M
Defending Microeconomic Theory. Hausman, Daniel.

FRIEDRICH, C
1984—The Totalitarian Model Revisited. Krancberg, Sigmund.

FRIENDSHIP
Aristotle: Nicomachean Ethics. Irwin, Terence (trans).
Civility And Society. Kekes, John.
Egoism, Desires, And Friendship. Chong, Kim–Chong.
Friendship. Armstrong, Robert L.
Friendship, Justice, And Superogation. Badhwar, Neera K.
Il Primato Dell'Amicizia Nella Filosofia Antica. Piscione, Enrico.
Le Théme De L'amitié Dans L'Éthique Á Nicomaque Et L'Éthique Á Eudéme. Proulx, Évelyne.
Philosophical Ideas Of Tadeusz Kotarbiński. Szaniawski, Klemens.
Plato's Lysis: A Reconsideration. Tindale, Christopher W.
Strong Feelings. Kamler, Howard.
The Virtues Of Philia And Justice: Who Learns These In Our Society. Diller, Ann.

FRIES, H
La Teologia Come Antropologia In Heinrich Fries. Belletti, Brunpo.

FROMM
Personality: The Need For Liberty And Rights. Gotesky, Rubin.

FROTHINGHAM, O
The Religion Of Humanity. Chandler, Daniel Ross.

FULFILLMENT
"Feeling Unfree: Freedom And Fulfillment In Contemporary Culture" in On Freedom, Howard, John A (ed), 95–111. Berman, Ronald.
Problems In The Social Sciences: Prolegomena To A Study Of Cities. Jenner, Donald.

FUNCTION(S)
see also Recursive Function(s)
Conceptual Issues In Evolutionary Biology. Sober, Elliott (ed).
Über Die Erfüllung Gewisser Erhaltungssätze Durch Kompliziertheitsmasse. Lischke, Gerhard.
"Functions Of Institutional Ethics Committees" in (ethics Committees And Health Care Decisions, Cranford, Ronald (ed), 22–30. Lynn, Joanne.
A Conjunction In Closure Spaces. Jankowski, Andrzej W.
A Height Restricted Generation Of A Set Of Arithmetic Functions Of Order–type. Slessenger, Peter H.
A Second Normal Form For Functions Of The System EP. Mc Beth, Rod.
Adjoining Dominating Functions. Baumgartner, James E and Dordal, Peter.
Algebraische Charakterisierungen Präprimaler Algebren. Denecke, Klaus.
An Ordered Set Of Arithmetic Functions Representing The Least ϵ–number. Levitz, Hilbert.
Continuous Functions On Countable Ordinals. Heindorf, Lutz.
Decidability Of Some Problems Pertaining To Base 2 Exponential Diophantine Equations. Levitz, Hilbert.
Die Funktionale Vollstandigkeit Von Funktionenklassen Über Einer Familie Endlicher Mengen. Poschel, Reinhard.
Eine Neue Definition Berechenbarer Reeller Funktionen. Hauck, Jürgen.
Filterkonvergenz In Der Nichtstandard–Analysis Bei Nichtelementaren Funktionen. Döpp, Klemens.
Fragments Of Arithmetic. Sieg, Wilfried.
Frege's Metaphysical Argument. Currie, Gregory.

Frege's Theory Of Number And The Distinction Between Function And Object. Kremer, Michael.
Functors And Ordinal Notations. Vauzeilles, Jacqueline.
Global Quantification In Zermelo–Fraenkel Set Theory. Mayberry, John.
Mind, Structure, And Time. Addis, Laird.
On A Simple Definition Of Computable Function Of A Real Variable––With Applications To Functions Of A Complex Variable. Caldwell, Jerome and Pour– El, Marion Boykan.
On N–Place Strictly Monotonic Functions. Hickman, John.
On The "Problem Of The Last Root" For Exponential Terms. Wolter, Helmut.
On The Logic Of Theory Change: Partial Meet Contraction And Revision Functions. Alchourron, Carlos and Gardenfors, Peter and Makinson, David.
Ordered Fields With Several Exponential Functions. Dahn, Bernd I and Wolter, H.
Social Action–Functions. Tuomela, Raimo.
Sur Une Extension Simple Du Calcul Intuitionniste Des Prédicate Du Premier Ordre Appliquée À L'analyse. Margenstern, Maurice.
The Baire Category Of Sets Of Access. Humke, Paul D.
The Preservation Of Coherence. Jennings, R E and Schotch, P K.
Weak Completeness And Abelian Semigroups. Wesselkamper, T C.
Zur Wellengleichung Mit Konstruktiven Randbedingungen. Hauck, Jürgen.

FUNCTIONAL(S)
Axiomatic Recursion Theory And The Continuous Functionals. Thompson, Simon.
Gödelsche Funktionalinterpretation Für Eine Erweiterung Der Klassischen Analysis. Friedrich, Wolfgang.
Grace And Functionality. Cordner, C D.
Isomorphisms Between HEO And HRO, ECF And ICF. Bezem, Marc.
Non Recursive Functionals. Bird, Richard.
Reduction Of Higher Type Levels By Means Of An Ordinal Analysis Of Finite Terms. Terlouw, Jan.
The Hereditary Partial Effective Functionals And Recursion Theory In Higher Types. Longo, G and Moggi, E.

FUNCTIONAL ANALYSIS
Clark Hull, Robert Cummins, And Functional Analysis. Amundson, Ron and Smith, Laurence.
The Poverty Of Marx's Functional Explanation (in Hebrew). Margalit, Avishai.

FUNCTIONAL COMPLETENESS
Die Funktionale Vollstandigkeit Von Funktionenklassen Über Einer Familie Endlicher Mengen. Poschel, Reinhard.

FUNCTIONALISM
Language, Thought, And Other Biological Categories: New Foundations For Realism. Millikan, Ruth Garret.
The Theory Of Communicative Action: Reason And The Rationalization Of Society, V1. Habermas, Jurgen and Mc Carthy, Thomas (trans).
A Farewell To Functionalism. Baker, Rudder Lynne.
Against Neural Chauvinism. Cuda, Tom.
An Argument Against Anti–Realist Semantics. Appiah, Anthony.
Are Qualia A Pain In The Neck For Functionalists? Graham, George and Stephens, G Lynn.
Functional Method And Phenomenology: The View Of Niklas Luhmann. Bednarz Jr, John.
Functionalism And Theological Language. Alston, William P.
Functionalism And Psychologism. Mac Kenzie, J D.
Mind And Anti–Mind: Why Thinking Has No Functional Definition. Bealer, George.
Panglossian Functionalism And The Philosophy Of Mind. Sober, Elliott.
Professor Shoemaker And So–Called 'Qualia' Of Experience. White, Nicholas P.
Properties, Functionalism, And The Identity Theory. Adams, Frederick.
Representation And Explanation. Papineau, David.

FUNCTOR(S)
A Mathematical Characterization Of Interpretation Between Theories. Van Bentham, Johan and Pearce, David.
An Alternative Concept Of The Universal Decision Element In m–valued Logic. Loader, John.
Functors And Ordinal Notations I: A Functorial Construction Of The Veblen Hierarchy. Girard, Jean–Yves and Vauzeilles, Jacqueline.
Functors And Ordinal Notations: II, A Functorial Construction Of The Bachmann Hierarchy. Girard, Jean–Yves and Vauzeilles, Jacqueline.
On Propositional Calculus With A Variable Functor. Lesisz, Wlodzimierz.
Partial Isomorphism Extension Method And A Representation Theorem For Post–Language. Sette, Antonio M.
Quelques Foncteurs Faussement Primitifs En Logique Déontique (Trivalence Et Action). Bailhache, P.
Some Propositional Calculi With Constant And Variable Functors. Jones, John.

FUNDAMENTALISM
Art Natural Enemies. Carver, Ronald P.
Evolution And The Fundamentalist Critique: Contributions To Educational Philosophy. Vold, David J.
Soldiers For Christ In The Army Of God: The Christian School Movement In America. Reese, William J.
The Fundamentalist Student And Introductory Philosophy. Mc Kenzie, David.

FUNDING
Biotechnology And The Social Reconstruction Of Molecular Biology. Markle, Gerald E and Robin, Stanley S.
Pluralism And Responsibility In Post–Modern Science. Toulmin, Stephen E.
Toward An Epistemologically–Relevant Sociology Of Science. Campbell, Donald T.

FURER-HAIMENDORF, C

Culture And Morality. Mayer, Adrian C (ed).

FUTURE

A Dynamic Model Of Temporal Becoming. Mc Call, Storrs.

A Look At Fatalism. Sturgeon, Scott.

Carlyle's Past And Present, History, And A Question Of Hermeneutics. Childers, Joseph W.

Imaging The Future: New Visions And New Responsibilities. Cauthen, Kenneth.

Konkrete Utopie: Zukunft Als Bewusstsein Und Handlung. Czuma, Hans.

Modelling And Models In Future Research (in Hungarian). Nováky, Erzsébet and Hideg, Eva.

Nichilismo Attivo, Storicità, Futuro Nella Filosofia Di Pietro Piovani. Cacciatore, Giuseppe.

The Religious Humanism Of The Future. Arisian, Khoren.

Thinking Ahead. Kolenda, Konstantin.

FUTURE GENERATION(S)

Preparing For The Future: An Essay On The Rights Of Future Generations. Ahrens, John.

"Government Regulation And Intergenerational Justice" in *Rights And Regulation*, Machan, Tibor (ed), 177–202. Sartorius, Rolf.

"Reflections On The Rights Of Future Generations" in *Rights And Regulation*, Machan, Tibor (ed), 203–216. Dipert, Randall R.

A Note On Motivation And Future Generations. Mackenzie, Michael.

The Conception Of Possible People. Davies, Kim.

FUTUROLOGY

"History, Futurology And The Future Of Philosophy" in *History Of Philosophy In The Making*, Thro, Linus J (ed), 299–312. Bourke, Vernon J.

An Attempt At The Utilization Of Prigogine's Thermodynamics In American Futurology (in Czechoslovakian). Hohos, Ladislav.

Lebensansprüche Und Werte An Der Schwelle Zum 21, Jahrhundert. Luther, E.

FUZZY LOGIC

Intuitionistic Fuzzy Logic And Intuitionistic Fuzzy Set Theory. Takeuti, Gaisi and Titani, Satoko.

Pavelka's Fuzzy Logic And Free L–Subsemigroups. Gerla, Giangiacomo.

FUZZY SETS

Fuzzy Recursion, RET's, And Isols. Harkleroad, Leon.

Indeterminate People. Chandler, Hugh S.

Measurement Of Fuzziness: A General Approach. Chakravarty, Satya R and Roy, Tirthankar.

FYODOROV, N

Platonov And Fyodorov. Teskey, Ayleen.

GADAMER, H

The Epistemology Of Hans–Georg Gadamer. Schmidt, Lawrence K.

Über "Sinn" Und "Bedeutung" Bei Gadamer. Graeser, Andreas.

"Collins And Gadamer On Interpretation" in *History Of Philosophy In The Making*, Thro, Linus J (ed), 231–246. Marsh, James L.

"Surrender–And–Catch And Hermeneutics". Wolff, Kurt H.

"Zeit Und Musik" in *Asthetische Er Fahrung Und Das Wesen Der Kunst*, Holzhey, Helmut, 156–172. Ruck, C.

A Case Of Creative Misreading: Habermas's Evolution Of Gadamer's Hermeneutics. How, Alan R.

Action As A Text: Gadamer's Hermeneutics And The Social Scientific Analysis Of Action. Hekman, Susan.

Bonnes Volontés De Puissance (Une Réponse À Hans–Georg Gadamer). Derrida, Jacques.

Die Funktion Der Hermeneutik In Den Positiven Wissenschaften. Kimmerle, Heinz.

Gadamer, L'ermeneutica E—Les Bourgeois. Capanna, Francesco.

Gadamer's Criticisms Of Collingwood. Bertoldi, E F.

Herméneutique Philosophique Et Théologie. Petit, Jean–Claude.

Hermeneutics As Practical Philosophy And Practical Wisdom (in Dutch). Van Der Walt, J W G.

Hermeneutik—Theorie Einer Praxis? Kamper, Dietmar.

Language And The Transformation Of Philosophy. Derksen, L D.

Philosophical Hermeneutics And The Conflict Of Ontologies. Wallulis, Jerald.

Practical Reason, Hermeneutics, And Social Life. Risser, James.

The Conditions Of Dialogue: Approaches To The Habermas–Gadamer Debate. Hjort, Anne Meete.

What Is The Difference That Makes A Difference: Gadamer, Habermas, And Rorty (in Hebrew). Bernstein, Richard G.

Zur Ortsbestimmung Der Historischen Wissenschaften. Kramer, Hans.

GALEN

From Galen's Theory To William Harvey's Theory: A Case Study In The Rationality Of Scientific Theory Change. Mowry, Bryan.

GALILEO

Die Bedeutung Der Methode Galileis Für Die Entwicklung Der Transzendentalphilosophie Kants. Holz, Fr.

Discussion: Galileo And The Continuity Thesis. Wallace, William A.

Galilean Idealization. Mc Mullin, Ernan.

Galileo's Lunar Observations In The Context Of Medieval Lunar Theory. Ariew, Roger.

Galileo's Telescopic Observations Of Venus And Mars. Chalmers, Alan.

On Galileo's Writings On Mechanics: An Attempt At A Semantic Analysis Of Viviani's Scholium. Halbwachs, F.

The Phenomenology Of Trials: Text And Socio–Political Context. Gavin, William J and Conway, Jeremiah.

Three Explanatory Traditions In The Law Of Falling Bodies (in Portuguese). Nascimento, Carlos A R.

GALLIE, W

Education And Essential Contestability Revisited. Naish, Michael.

GALLINA, P

Gallina And Pitt: Similarities And Differences. Pitt, Jack.

GALTUNG, J

The Idea Of Violence. Coady, C A J.

GAMBLING

Progress In Utility And Risk Theory. Hagen, Ole (ed) and Wenstop, Fred (ed).

GAME(S)

see also Language Game(s)

Laws Of The Game: How The Principles Of Nature Govern Chance. Eigen, Manfred and Winkler, Ruthild.

A Question Of Borel Hyperdeterminacy. Cutland, Nigel J.

Determinacy Of Banach Games. Becker, Howard.

Dialogues, Strategies, And Intuitionistic Provability. Felscher, Walter.

Finite Level Borel Games And A Problem Concerning The Jump Hierarchy. Hodes, Harold T.

Games And The Action–Guiding Force Of Morality. Eggerman, Richard W.

Games, Graphs, And Circular Arguments. Walton, Douglas N and Batten, L M.

Insiders And Outsiders Models Of Deviance And Jurisprudence. Hund, John.

Monadic Generalized Spectra. Fagin, Ronald.

Noncumulative Dialectical Models And Formal Dialectics. Krabbe, Erik C W.

On Languages With Two Variables. Mortimer, Michael.

Simplified Morasses With Linear Limits. Velleman, Dan.

Theoretical And Practical Confusion In American Professional Sport. Rose, David A.

GAME THEORY

Game Theory: Concepts And Applications. Zagare, Frank C.

A Portfolio Of Risk Measures. Mac Crimmon, Kenneth R and Wehrung, Donald A.

A Response To "Is Business Bluffing Ethical". Sullivan, Roger J.

Commentary On "A Response To 'Is Business Bluffing Ethical'". Langley, Van E.

Games, Goals, And Bounded Rationality. Tesfatsion, Leigh.

Gideon's Paradox: A Paradox Of Rationality. Bar– Hillel, Maya and Margalit, Avishai.

Hobbes As Moralist. Farrell, Daniel M.

No Chain Store Paradox. Davis, Lawrence H.

Regret, Recrimination And Rationality. Sugden, Robert.

Risk Aversion In n–Person Bargaining. Peters, Hans and Tijs, Stef.

Rules Of Behavior And Expected Utility Theory: Compatibility Versus Dependence. Hagen, Ole.

The Impact Of Risk Attitude, Uncertainty And Disequilibria On Optimal Production And Inventory. Aiginger, Karl.

GANDHI

Gandhi's Religious Thought. Chatterjee, Margaret.

The Core Of Gandhi's Philosophy. Tahtinen, Unto.

GARDEN(S)

"The Wild And The Cultivated In Greek Religion" in *On Nature*, Rouner, Leroy S (ed), 79–95. Ruck, Carl.

Ut Hortus Poesis—Gardening And Her Sister Arts In Eighteenth–Century England. Ross, Stephanie A.

GARDNER, D

An Ethical Analysis Of Deception In Advertising. Carson, Thomas L and Wokutch, Richard E and Cox, James E.

GARDNER, J

A Word Of Order And Light: The Fiction Of John Gardner. Morris, Gregory L.

Seeking The Source: Cultural Relativism And The Arts. Anderson, Albert A.

GARLANDUS COMPOTISTA

Dialectic In The Eleventh And Twelfth Centuries: Garlandus Compotista. Stump, Eleonore.

GARNER, R

Ch'an And Taoist Mirrors: Reflections On Richard Garner's "Deconstruction Of The Mirror". Lusthaus, Dan.

GARVER, N

Lebensform Oder Lebensformen:—Eine Bemerkung Zu Newton Garvers Interpretation Von "Lebensform". Haller, Rudolf.

GAUTHIER, D

"Reason In Ethics—Or Reason Versus Ethics" in *Morality, Reason And Truth*, Copp, David (ed), 228–250. Narveson, Jan.

GAZE(S)

On The Visual Constitution Of Society: The Contributions Of Georg Simmel And Jean–Paul Sartre To A Sociology Of The Senses. Weinstein, Deena and Weinstein, Michael.

GEACH, P

Análisis Propositional Y Ontologia. Sanchez, Juan Carlos.

Defending Distribution. Englebretsen, George.

Some Radical Consequences Of Geach's Logical Theories. Cain, James.

GEHLEN, A

Politics, Nature And Freedom: On The Natural Foundation Of The Political Condition. Levy, David J.

GEIGER, M

"Aesthetic Enjoyment And Poetic Sense" in *Existential Coordinates Of Human Condition*, Tymieniecka, A (ed), 3–22. Tymieniecka, A.

Experience And Value In Moritz Geiger's Aesthetics. Beardsley, Monroe C.

GEIST
The Politics Of Salvation: The Hegelian Idea Of The State. Lakeland, Paul.
Croce's Interpretation Of Hegel. Bellamy, Richard.

GENDER
Beauty, Sport, And Gender. Boxill, J M.
Bringing Women Into Educational Thought. Martin, Jane R.
Genderism And The Reconstitution Of Philosophy Of Education. Sherman, Ann L.
Sport, Art, And Gender. Postow, B C.
The Epistemology Of Gender Identity: Implications For Social Policy. Ayim, Maryann and Houston, Barbara.
The Ideal Of The Educated Woman: Jane Roland Martin On Education And Gender. Walker, J C and O' Loughlin, M A.

GENE(S)
Genes, Organisms, Populations: Controversies Over The Units Of Selection. Brandon, Robert N (ed) and Burian, Richard M (ed).
The Nature Of Selection: Evolutionary Theory In Philosophical Focus. Sober, Elliott.

GENERAL WELFARE
Sacrificing Persons For The General Welfare: A Comment Of Sayward. Wein, Sheldon.

GENERAL WILL
Rousseau: Dreamer Of Democracy. Miller, James.
Rousseau On The General Will. Sparkes, A W.

GENERALITY
Ambiguity Vs Generality: Removal Of A Logical Confusion. Roberts, Lawrence.
The Rise Of General Theories In Contemporary Science. Laszlo, Ervin.

GENERALIZABILITY
On Gewirth's Derivation Of The Principle Of Generic Consistency. Singer, Marcus G.

GENERALIZATION(S)
see also Induction
Justifying Historical Descriptions. Mc Cullagh, C Behan.
"Gewirth's Ethical Monism" in *Gewirth's Ethical Rationalism*, Regis Jr, Edward (ed), 23–38. Singer, Marcus G.
Gillespie On Singer's Generalization Argument. Gordon, David.
Laws And Modal Realism. Pargetter, Robert.

GENERATIVE GRAMMAR(S)
Chomsky On Grammar And Mind: A Critique. Kuester, Harold H.
Some Issues Concerning The Interpretation Of Derived And Gerundive Nominals. Thomason, Richmond H.

GENETIC ENGINEERING
Ethical Issues In And Beyond Prospective Clinical Trials Of Human Gene Therapy. Fletcher, John C.
Human Gene Therapy: Scientific And Ethical Considerations. Anderson, W French.

GENETIC EPISTEMOLOGY
Piaget's Logic: A Critique Of Genetic Epistemology. Seltman, Muriel and Seltman, Peter.
The Practice Of Medical Ethics: A Structuralistic Approach. Ellos, William J.

GENETIC SCREENING
Biomedical Ethics Reviews. Humber, James M (ed) and Almeder, Robert T (ed).
"Current Issues In Genetic Screening" in *Biomedical Ethics Reviews*, Humber, James M (ed), 121–152. Capron, Alexander Morgan.
"Genetic Screening Of Prospective Parents And Of Workers" in *Biomedical Ethics Reviews*, Humber, James M (ed), 73–120. Hubbard, Ruth.
The New Technologies Of Genetic Screening. Lappé, Marc and Murray, Thomas H.

GENETICISM
Genetic Epistemology And Philosophical Epistemology. Loptson, P J and Kelly, J W.
Genetic Epistemology And The Child's Understanding Of Logic. Smith, Leslie.
Philosophy, Psychology, And Piaget: A Reply To Loptson And Kelly. Smith, Leslie.

GENETICS
A Genetic Counseling Casebook. Applebaum, Eleanor Gordon and Firestein, Stephen K.
Biology, Crime And Ethics: A Study Of Biological Explanations For Criminal Behavior. Marsh, Frank H (ed) and Katz, Janet (ed).
Conceptual Issues In Evolutionary Biology. Sober, Elliott (ed).
Evolution, The History Of An Idea. Bowler, Peter J.
"Contemporary Genetics: Some Ethical Considerations" in *The Good Life And Its Pursuit*, Dougherty, Jude P (ed), 175–185. Mascall, Eric L.
"Some Paradoxical Goals Of Cells And Organisms" in *Ethical Questions In Brain And Behavior*, Pfaff, Donald W (ed), 111–124. Brown, Jerram L.
Enkele Pogingen Tot Reconstructie Van De Evolutietheorie En De Populatiegenetica Als Wetenschappelijke Onderzoeks–Programma's. Van Balen, G A M.
Manipuler L'homme (in Polish). Boné, Edouard.
Significato E Attualità Dell'Epistemologia Genetica Di Jean Piaget. Simonetti, Iside.

GENETTE, G
"Literary Impressionism And Phenomenology" in *Existential Coordinates Of Human Condition*, Tymieniecka, A (ed), 521–534. Kronegger, Marlies.

GENIUS
"Discussion Upon Fundamental Principles Of Education" (1919). Whitehead, Alfred N and Brumbaugh, Robert S (ed).

GENOCIDE
Manufacture Of Consent In Democracy. Chomsky, Noam.
The Arms Race, Genocidal Intent And Individual Responsibility. Santoni, Ronald E.
The Concept Of Genocide. Lang, Berel.

GENTILE
Croce, Gentile And Hegel And The Doctrine Of The Ethical State (Continuazione E Fine). Bellamy, Richard.
Le Lettere Di Croce A Gentile. Coli, Daniela.

GENTZEN CALCULUS
DFC–Algorithms For Suszko, Logic SCI And One–to–one Gentzen Type Formalizations. Wasilewska, Anita.
Fragments Of Arithmetic. Sieg, Wilfried.
Well–Behaved Modal Logic. Hodes, Harold T.

GEOGRAPHY
Philosophy And Human Geography: An Introduction To Contemporary Approaches. Johnston, R J.

GEOLOGY
Karl Popper Et La Naissance De La Géologie. Gohau, Gabriel.

GEOMETRY
The New Scientific Spirit. Bachelard, Gaston and Goldhammer, Arthur (trans).
Albertus Magnus' View On The Angle With Special Emphasis On His Geometry And Metaphysics. Tummers, Paul M J E.
Francis Bacon Und Hobbes' Widmungsbrief Zu *De Cive*. Schuhmann, Karl.
Geochronometrie Und Geometrodynamik: Zum Problem Des Konventionalismus. Kanitscheider, Bernulf.
How Wrong Was Kant About Geometry? Barker, Stephen F.
Incongruence And The Unity Of Transcendental Idealism: Reply To Henry E Allison. Buroker, Jill Vance.
Is Nonstandard Analysis Relevant For The Philosophy Of Mathematics? Fenstad, Jens Erik.
Kant On Space, Empirical Realism And The Foundations Of Geometry. Harper, William.
Kant's Philosophy Of Mathematics. Miller, L W.
On The Fidelity Of Pictures: A Critique Of Goodman's Disjunction Of Perspective And Realism. Topper, David.
Synthetic Mechanics. Burgess, John P.
The Geometry Of A Form Of Intuition. Melnick, Arthur.
Unified Field Theory And The Conventionality Of Geometry. Pitowsky, Itamar.

GERIATRICS
Ethical Perspectives On Health Policy For An Aging Society. Creedon, Michael A.

GERMAN
Bithell Series Of Dissertations: Spinoza In Germany From 1670 To The Age Of Goethe, V7. Bell, David.
From Hegel To Nietzsche. Lowith, Karl.
Jews And German Philosophy: The Polemics Of Emancipation. Rotenstreich, Nathan.
"Literary Diary As A Witness Of Man's Historicity" in *Existential Coordinates Of Human Condition*, Tymieniecka, A (ed), 249–260. Eykman, Christoph.
"Popper And German Social Philosophy" in *Popper And The Human Sciences*, Currie, Gregory (ed), 165–184. Ackermann, Robert.
"Values And German Tragedy 1770–1840" in *Existential Coordinates Of Human Condition*, Tymieniecka, A (ed), 319–332. Wittkowski, W.
Bertrand Russell, Karl Marx, And *German Social Democracy* Revisited. Gallina, Paul.
Der Inhalt Des Begriffs "Nation" In Der Spätbürgerlichen Ideologie Der BRD. Lange, Gunter.
Der Kampf Der KPD Gegen Die Ideologie Des Hitlerfaschismus. Ullrich, Horst.
Did German Classical Philosophy Simply "End"? Ruoshui, Wang.
Die Aufgaben Der Marxistisch–Leninistischen Soziologischen Forschung In Der DDR. Weidig, Rudi.
Die Reaktionäre Marxkritik Nach Dem Gothaer Programm Der Deutschen Sozialdemokratie. Kopf, Eike.
Entwicklungstendenzen Nichtklassischer Logiken Und Probleme Ihrer Geschichtsschreibung. Kummer, Wolf.
Erfahrungen Aus Der Arbeit Am Lehrbuch "Wissenschaftlicher Kommunismus". Grosser, Gunther.
Ernst Cassirer's *Mythical Thought* In Weimar Culture. Strenski, Ivan T.
Feuerbach Y La Ilustración. Fernandez, Arsenio Ginzo.
Gallina And Pitt: Similarities And Differences. Pitt, Jack.
Gesellschaftliches Und Individuelles Bewusstein In Der Philosophischen Diskussion In Der DDR And UdSSR. Müller, W and Hirschmann, J.
Koschmieder On Speech Act Theory: A Historical Note. Kech, Gabriele and Stubbs, Michael.
Philosophy Of Medicine In The Federal Republic Of Germany (1945–1984). Kottow, Michael.
Rantzau And Welser: Aspects Of Later German Humanism. Evans, R J W.
Schellings Weltalter Und Die Ausstehende Vollendung Des Deutschen Idealismus. Oesterreich, Peter Lothar.
The German Philosophical Scene (2). Hartmann, Klaus.
The Self–Assertion Of The German University And The Rectorate 1933/34: Facts And Thoughts. Heidegger, Martin.
Theory Of History In Historical Lectures: The German Tradition Of *Historik*, 1750–1900. Blanke, Horst Walter and Fleischer, Dirk and Rusen, Jorn.
Weltanschauung Und Klassenbewusstsein In Marx' Kritik Am Gothaer Programm. Finger, Otto.
Wissenschaftstheorie Und Praxis: Zur Funktion Soziologischer Theorienbildung. Rust, Holger.
Zum Humanismus In Der Klassischen Deutschen Philosophie, Seinen Sozialhistorischen Und Theoretischen Voraussetzungen. Biedermann, Georg and Lange, E.
Zum Verhältnis Von Marxistisch–Leninistischer Philosophie Und Sozialistischer Politik In Der DDR. Heppener, Sieglinde.

GERSONIDES

Maimonides, Aquinas And Gersonides On Providence And Evil. Burrell, David.

GETTIER, E

It's Not What You Know That Counts. Kaplan, Mark.
Traditional Epistemology And Naturalistic Replies To Its Skeptical Critics. Bogen, James.

GETTIER CASES

Does The Gettier Problem Rest On A Mistake? Kirkham, Richard L.

GEWIRTH, A

Gewirth's Ethical Rationalism. Regis Jr, Edward (ed).
"Against Ethical Rationalism" in *Gewirth's Ethical Rationalism*, Regis Jr, Edward (ed), 59–83. Nielsen, Kai.
"Are Marginal Agents 'Our Recipients'" in *Gewirth's Ethical Rationalism*, Regis Jr, Edward (ed), 180–191. Hill, James F.
"Deontologism, Negative Causation, And The Duty Of Rescue" in *Gewirth's Ethical Rationalism*, Regis Jr, Edward (ed), 147–166. Mack, Eric.
"Do Agents Have To Be Moralists" in *Gewirth's Ethical Rationalism*, Regis Jr, Edward (ed), 52–58. Hare, R M.
"Gewirth And The Supportive State" in *Gewirth's Ethical Rationalism*, Regis Jr, Edward (ed), 167–179. Den Uyl, Douglas J and Machan, Tibor R.
"Gewirth's Ethical Monism" in *Gewirth's Ethical Rationalism*, Regis Jr, Edward (ed), 23–38. Singer, Marcus G.
"Negative And Positive Rights In Gewirth's 'Reason And Morality'" in *Gewirth's Ethical Rationalism*, Regis Jr, Edward (ed), 96–107. Narveson, Jan.
"Public Pursuit And Private Escape: The Persistence Of Egoism" in *Gewirth's Ethical Rationalism*, Regis Jr, Edward (ed), 128–146. Kalin, Jesse.
"Replies To My Critics" in *Gewirth's Ethical Rationalism*, Regis Jr, Edward (ed), 192–256. Gewirth, Alan.
"Rights And Conflicts" in *Gewirth's Ethical Rationalism*, Regis Jr, Edward (ed), 84–95. Raphael, D D.
"The 'Is–Ought' Problem Resolved" in *Gewirth's Ethical Rationalism*, Regis Jr, Edward (ed), 108–127. Hudson, W D.
"The Roots Of Moral Reason" in *Gewirth's Ethical Rationalism*, Regis Jr, Edward (ed), 39–51. Bambrough, Renford.
"The Subjective Normative Structure Of Agency" in *Gewirth's Ethical Rationalism*, Regis Jr, Edward (ed), 8–22. Adams, E M.
On Gewirth's Derivation Of The Principle Of Generic Consistency. Singer, Marcus G.
Skepticism And The Cartesian Circle. Broughton, Janet.
Why There Are No Human Rights. Husak, Douglas N.

GHAZALI

A Quest For The Values In Islam. Djaït, Hichem.

GIBBINS, P

The Not–So–Strange Modal Logic Of Indeterminacy. Pelletier, F J.

GIBBON, E

Incidence Sur Hegel De La Lecture De Gibbon. Muller, Philippe.

GIBSON, J

A Comparison Of Three Ways Of Knowing: Categorical, Structural, And Affirmative. Mc Cabe, Viki.

GIDDENS, A

Power, Structure And Agency. Layder, Derek.

GIERE, R

Discussion: What Would Happen If Everyone Did It? Sober, Elliott.

GILL, J

Mysticism Or Mediation: A Response To Gill. Perovich, Anthony.

GILLIGAN, C

Commentary On Gilligan's "In A Different Voice". Auerbach, Judy and others.
In Pursuit Of Wholeness: Moral Development, The Ethics Of Care And The Virtue Of *Philia*. Prakash, Madhu Suri.

GIROUX, H

Marxism And Schooling: A Failed Or Limited Tradition: A Response To Henry Giroux. Liston, Daniel P.

GIVEN

Other Problems About The Self. Theron, Stephen.

GLASER, D

"Bubble Chambers And Experiment" in *Observation, Experiment, And Hypothesis In Modern Physical Science*, Achinstein, Peter (ed), 309–374. Galison, Peter.

GLASSEN, P

Reply To Peter Glassen's "O'Hear On An Argument Of Popper's". O'Hear, Anthony.

GLEZERMAN, G

The Relation Of Theory And Practice In The Process Of Formation And Action Of Laws Of Communist Socio–Economic Formation (in Czechoslovakian). Kroh, Michael.

GLOVER, J

Utilitarians And The Use Of Examples. Cox, J W Roxbee.

GLUCKSMANN, A

A Critica Glucksmanniana Do Poder. Morais, Carlos.

GLYMOUR, C

"Bootstrapping Without Bootstraps" in *Testing Scientific Theories*, Earman, John (ed), 43–54. Edidin, Aron.
"Explanations Of Irrelevance" in *Testing Scientific Theories*, Earman, John (ed), 55–66. Horwich, Paul.
"Glymour On Evidence And Explanation" in *Testing Scientific Theories*, Earman, John (ed), 165–176. Van Fraassen, Bas C.
"Newton's Demonstration Of Universal Gravitation" in *Testing Scientific Theories*, Earman, John (ed), 179–200. Laymon, Ronald.
"Theory Comparison And Relevant Evidence" in *Testing Scientific Theories*, Earman, John (ed), 27–42. Van Fraassen, Bas C.
"Why Glymour Is A Bayesian" in *Testing Scientific Theories*, Earman, John (ed), 69–98. Rosenkrantz, Roger.
Theoretical Functions, Theory And Evidence. Forge, John.

GNOSEOLOGY

The Relation Of Ontology And Gnoseology As Seen From The Point Of View Of The Marxist Theory Of Literature (in Hungarian). Bécsi, Tamás.
Theorie Und Praxis In Technologischer Und Dialektischer Perspektive. Muller–Schmid, Peter P.

GNOSTICISM

Christianity And The Hellenistic World. Nash, Ronald H.
The New Gnosis. Avens, Robert.
Hegel And The Gnostic Tradition: I. Hanratty, Gerald.
Monachisme Et Gnose: Deuxième Partie: Contacts Littéraires Et Doctrinaux Entre Monachisme Et Gnose. Veilleux, Armand.
Mysticism And Gnosticism In Heidegger. Tyman, Stephen.
Wilhelm Reich: Culture As Power. Levine, Norman.

GOAL(S)

The Analysis Of Action. Von Cranach, Mario (ed) and Harre, Rom (ed).
"Feedback, Selection, And Function" in *Methodology, Metaphysics And The History Of Science*, Cohen, Robert S (ed), 43–136. Faber, Roger J.
"Psychological Study Of Goal–Directed Action" in *The Analysis Of Action*, Von Cranach, Mario (ed), 35–74. Von Cranach, Mario.
Ethics As An Integrating Force In Management. Pastin, Mark.
Foreign Policy As A Goal Directed Activity. Anderson, Paul A.
Negative Feedback And Goals. Ehring, Douglas.
The Defence Of The Ant—Work, Life And Utopia. Rives, Joel.

GOCKOWSKI, J

A Comment To J Gockowski's *Situational Tests Of A Scholar's Faithfullness To His Ethos* (in Polish). Jankowski, H.

GOD

see also Absolute, Atheism, Ontological Proof
A Demonstration Of The Divine Authority Of The Law Of Nature And Of The Christian Religion. Parker, Samuel.
C S Lewis And The Search For Rational Religion. Beversluis, John.
Creativity In American Philosophy. Hartshorne, Charles.
Divine Omniscience And Human Freedom. Moskop, John C.
Evil And The Process God. Whitney, Barry L.
Gandhi's Religious Thought. Chatterjee, Margaret.
God And Natural Evil. Jooharigian, Robert Badrik.
God, Guilt, And Death: An Existential Phenomenology Of Religion. Westphal, Merold.
God, The Center Of Value: Value Theory In The Theology Of H Richard Niebuhr. Grant, C David.
In Search Of Deity: An Essay In Dialectical Theism. Macquarrie, John.
Introduction To The Arguments For God. Caes, Charles J.
Moral Development Foundations: Judeo–Christian Alternatives To Piaget/Kohlberg. Joy, Donald M (ed).
Mystical And Ethical Experience. Heard, Gerry C.
Omnipotence And Other Theological Mistakes. Hartshorne, Charles.
The Emergence Of Whitehead's Metaphysics 1925–1929, R C Neville (ed). Ford, Lewis S.
The Islamic Conception Of Justice. Khadduri, Majid.
The Naturalists And The Supernatural: Studies In Horizon And An American Philosophy Of Religion. Shea, William M.
The New Scientific Case For God's Existence. Mahin, Mark.
The Unknowable: An Ontological Introduction To The Philosophy Of Religion. Frank, S L.
Without Proof Or Evidence: Essays Of O K Bouwsma. Craft, J L (ed) and Hustwit, Ronald E (ed).
'Can We Speak Literally Of God'? Levine, Michael P.
"God And The Meaning Of Life" in *On Nature*, Rouner, Leroy S (ed), 154–168. Hartshorne, Charles.
"The Finite Thou And The Eternal Thou In The Work Of Buber" in *Martin Buber*, Gordon, Haim (ed), 69–88. Amir, Yehoshua.
"The Suareziann Proof Of God's Existence" in *History Of Philosophy In Making*, Thro, Linus J (ed), 105–118. Doule, John P.
A Letter To James Gustafson. Ramsey, Paul.
A Response To The Problems Of Evil. Morris, Thomas V.
Another Note On The Ontological Argument. Beanblossom, Ronald.
Are Traditional Theists Pantheists? Downey, James Patrick.
As Provas Da Existência De Deus Na Filosofia Neo–Escolástica. Rüppel, Ernesto.
Augustine's Argument For God's Existence *De Libero Arbitrio*, Book II. Kondoleon, Theodore J.
Brahman, God, Substance And Nature: Samkara And Spinoza. Gupta, Bina.
Compatibilidad Entre La Presciencia Divina Y La Libertad De Los Actos Humanos. De Stier, María L Lukac.
Creativity, God, And Creation. Vitali, Theodore R.
Credulism. Kvanvig, Jonathan L.
De La "Mort De Dieu" Aux Noms Divins: L'itinéraire Théologique De La Métaphysique. Marion, Jean–Luc.
Del Ente Participado Al Ser Imparticipado. Derisi, Octavio N.
Descartes On God's Ability To Do The Logically Impossible. La Croix, Richard R.
Die Cartesianische Onto–Theo–Logie. Marion, Jean–Luc.

GOD

Divine Omnipotence And Impossible Tasks: An Intensional Analysis. Anderson, C A.
Divine Transcendence. Kvanvig, Jonathan L.
Divine–Human Dialogue And The Nature Of God. Alston, William P.
Does Belief In God Need Proof? Robbins, J Wesley.
Does Reason Demand That God Be Infinite? Pomerlau, Wayne P.
Een Eigen Gewaad Voor Een Oud En Steeds Actueel Probleem: Maurice Blondel Over Natuur En Genade, Rede En Geloof. Dengerink, J D.
El Ateismo Cotidiano: Ensayo De Comprension. Sansen, Raymond.
El Ser En El "Sistema De Identidad" Según Gustav Siewerth (Segunda Parte). Corona, Nester A.
Eliminating "God" And Gathering The Real Gods. Hayes, Victor C.
Eternal Truths And The Laws Of Nature: The Theological Foundations Of Descartes' Philosophy Of Nature. Osler, Margaret.
Ethics And The Archangelic Prescriber. Harrison, Jonathan.
Fichtes Gottesbegriff. Schulte, G.
Functionalism And Theological Language. Alston, William P.
Gebet Und Theologie: Skizzen Zur Neubesinnung Des Gebetes Im Kontext Der Systematisch–Theologischen Theoriebildung. Wriedt, Markus.
God And Chaos: The Demiurge Versus The *Ungrund*. Hefner, Philip.
God, Gods, And Moral Cosmos In Socrates' Apology. O' Connell, Robert J.
God's Eternity. Burrell, David B.
God's Omnipresent Agency. Van Den Brom, L J.
Harmonia Universalis. Schneiders, Werner.
Hoffman On Petitionary Prayer. Stump, Eleonore.
Hume, Language And God. Soles, Deborah Hansen.
Il Carattere Immediato Della Presenza Di Dio Nel Mondo Secondo Tommaso D'Aquino. Campodonico, Angelo.
Il Principio Del *Passo Indietro* Del Pensiero. Pellecchia, Pasquale.
Impeccability Revisited. Carter, W R.
In Response To Loomer's "Meland On God". Meland, Bernard E.
Inconceivable? Gay, Robert.
Intuitive Cognition And The Philosophy Of God (in Polish). Kowalczyk, Stanislaw.
Is God "Significantly Free"? Morriston, Wesley.
Is Plantinga's God Omnipotent? Morriston, Wesley.
John Reading On The Existence And Unicity Of God, Efficient And Final Causality (in Latin). Etzkorn, Girard J.
Kant's Transcendental Deduction Of God's Existence As A Postulate Of Pure Practical Reason. Kuehn, Manfred.
Kant's Transcendental Ideal—II. O' Farrell, Frank.
Karl Rahner's Conception Of God's Self–Communication To Man. Cawte, John.
L'acte Libre Démission Ou Courage D'etre Devant Le Sensible Selon Jean Scot Érigène. Wohlman, Avital.
L'homme Créé Par Dieu: Le Fondement De La Dignité De L'homme. Schönborn, Christoph.
La Théologie Modale De Leibniz: Réponse Á Georges Kalinowski. Dumoncel, Jean–Claude.
Levels Of Truth And Reality In The Philosophies Of Descartes And Samkara. Schroeder, Craig.
Lo Inteligible. De Paoli, Alejandro.
Lonergan's Metaphysics: Ontological Implications Of Insight–As–Event. Skrenes, Carol.
Loptson On Anselm And Davis. Davis, Stephen T.
Los Argumentos Teísticos De J B Manyà, Por Felipe Iriarte. Iriarte, Felipe.
Macht, Faktizität Und Die Frage Nach Dem Sinn. Kodalle, Klaus–M.
Maimonides And Aquinas On Man's Knowledge Of God: A Twentieth Century Perspective. Franck, Isaac.
Meland On God. Loomer, Bernard M.
Mirror And Enigma: The Meaning Of God On Earth. Dupré, Wilhelm.
Monade Und Welt: Ein Beitrag Zur Interpretation Der Monadologie. Hubner, Wulf.
Must God Do His Best? Hasker, W.
Must God Identify The Best? Gordon, David.
No Love For God? Lowe, Susan.
Omnipotence, Timelessness, And The Restoration Of Virgins. Brinton, Alan.
Omniscience And Deliberation. Reichenbach, B R.
On Petitionary Prayer. Hoffman, Joshua.
Other Problems About The Self. Theron, Stephen.
Perishability, The Actual World, And The Non–Existence Of God. Chrzan, Keith.
Philosophy And The Question Of God. Neville, Robert C.
Presencia De San Agustín En Suárez. Reta, Jose Oroz.
Process, Time, And God. Clarke, Bowman L.
Reply To Eleonore Stump's "Hoffman On Petitionary Prayer". Hoffman, Joshua.
Reply To Professor Baker's "Religious Experience And The Possibility Of Divine Existence". Dore, Clement.
Science, Design And The Science Of Signs. Terrell, Burnham.
Significación Actual Del Pensamiento Zubiriano. Quintás, Alfonso López.
Stump And Kretzmann On Time And Eternity. Fitzgerald, Paul.
Suicide And The Service Of God. Lombardi, Joseph J.
Sur l'argument Ontologique De Leibniz. Kalinowski, Georges.
The Aseity Of God In St Anselm. Morreall, John.
The Dilemma Of Theodicy. Gordon, Jeffrey.
The Evidential Value Of Religious Experiences. Clark, R W.
The God Of The Philosophers In The Jewish Tradition (in Hebrew). Hartman, David.
The Logically Possible, The Ontologically Possible And Ontological Proofs Of God's Existence. Paulsen, David L.
The Ontological Argument. Russell, Bruce.

The Ontological Argument. Robinson, William S.
The Personal God And A God Who Is A Person. Thatcher, Adrian.
The Possibility Of God. Dore, Clement.
The Problem Of Evil. Yandell, Keith E.
The Reasonableness Of Agnosticism. Brinton, Alan.
The Silence Of God. Roth, John K.
Theism And Pantheism Again. Oakes, Robert.
Time And History In Theological Ethics: The Work Of James Gustafson. Hauerwas, Stanley and Childress, James F.
Tolstoy's God Sees The Truth, But Waits: A Reflection. Archer, Dermot J.
Unamuno Ou Le Traité De L'amour De Dieu. Casañas, Mario.
Valor Y Valor Moral. Derisi, Octavio N.
Whitehead And Aquinas On The Eternity Of God. Baumer, Michael R.
Whitehead Ou Le Cosmos Torrentiel. Dumoncel, Jean–Claude.
Widerlegt Descartes' Vierte Meditation Den Gottesbeweis Der Dritten: Zur Stellung Descartes' In Der Philosophiegeschichte. Engfer, Hans–Jurgen.

GOD–TALK

In Search Of Deity: An Essay In Dialectical Theism. Macquarrie, John.
On Mucking Around About God: Some Methodological Animadversions. Nielsen, Kai.

GODEL

see Goedel

GODS

The Platonism Of Marsilio Ficino: A Study Of His Phaedrus Commentary, Its Sources And Genesis. Allen, Michael J B.
God, Gods, And Moral Cosmos In Socrates' Apology. O' Connell, Robert J.

GOEDEL

Beyond First–order Logic: The Historical Interplay Between Mathematical Logic And Axiomatic Set Theory. Moore, Gregory H.
Cataloging The Gödel "Nachlass". Dawson, John W.
Implicaciones Teórico–dfilosóficas Del Teorema De Gödel. Zúñiga, Angel Ruiz.
Kurt Gödel: Conviction And Caution. Feferman, Solomon.
Naturphilosophische Überlegungen Zum Leib–Seele–Problem. Buchel, W.

GOEDEL THEOREM(S)

"Modal Logic And Self–Reference" in *Handbook Of Philosophical Logic*, Gabbay, Dov (ed), 441–496. Smoryński, Craig.
Gödel's Theorem In Retrospect. Tabakov, Martin.

GOETHE

Chor Und Gesetz: Zur "Morphologischen Methode" Bei Goethe Und Wittgenstein. Schulte, Joachim.
Goethe Y La Kátharsis Trágica. Herrán, Carlos M.

GOFFMAN, E

System And Life World: Some Reflections On Goffman's Frame Analysis. Sundararajan, P T Saroja.

GOGOL, N

Gogol' In The Context Of Aesthetic Controversies (V G Belinskii's Polemic With Konstantin Aksakov). Mann, Iu V.

GOLDMAN, A

Justification, Reasons, And Reliability. Swain, Marshall.
Justification And Truth. Cohen, Stewart.
The Problem Of Writing, Enforcing, And Teaching Ethical Rules: A Reply To Goldman's "Confidentiality, Rules, And Codes Of Ethics". Freedman, Monroe H.

GOLDMAN, E

Red Emma Speaks. Shulman, Alix Kates (ed).

GOLDSTEIN, L

Goldstein On Quotation. Buckner, D K.

GONSETH, F

Gaston Bachelard Et Ferdinand Gonseth, Philosophes De La Dialectique Scientifique. Lauener, Henri.

GOOD

see also Evil(s), Virtue(s)

Non Pie Quaerunt: Rhetoric, Dialectic, And The Discovery Of The True In Augustine's *Confessions*. Di Lorenzo, Raymond D.
Plato. Rowe, C J.
Rights. White, Alan R.
Tractatus, Schön Und Gut. Siitonen, Arto.
"El Justo Es Feliz Y El Injusto Desgraciado": Justicia Y Felicidad En La "República" De Platón. Perez Ruiz, Francisco.
"Rationality, Reason, And The Good" in *Morality, Reason And Truth*, Copp, David (ed), 193–211. Baier, Kurt.
"The Metaphysics Of The Good" in *The Good Life And Its Pursuit*, Dougherty, Jude P (ed), 51–76. Leclerc, Ivor.
A Contradiction In The Egalitarian Theory Of Justice. Howard, Michael W.
A Proposito Del Trattato "De Bono Naturae" Nel "Tractatus De Natura Boni" Di Alberto Magno. Canavero, A Tarabochia.
Ethics And Sport: An Overview. Kretchmar, R Scott.
Le Caractère Mythique De L'Analogie Du Bien Dans *République VI*. Couloubaritsis, Lambros.
On Two Meanings Of Good And The Foundations Of Ethics In Aristotle And St Thomas. Flippen, Douglas.
Right And Good: False Dichotomy? Maclean, Anne.
The Importance And Function Of Kant's Highest Good. Friedman, R Z.
Valor Y Valor Moral. Derisi, Octavio N.

GOOD, I

A Historical Comment Concerning Novel Confirmation. Good, I J.

GOOD LIFE

Philosophical Questions: An Introductory Anthology. Purtill, Richard L and Macdonald, Michael H and Kreeft, Peter J.
The Good Life And Its Pursuit. Dougherty, Jude P (ed).
Aristotle On Rawls: A Critique Of Quantitative Justice. Jackson, M W.
Aristotle On The Goods Of Fortune. Cooper, John M.
Ethics And Sport: An Overview. Kretchmar, R Scott.
Words; Interests. Kuhse, Helga.

GOODMAN, N

Art In Realist Perspective. Wolterstorff, Nicholas.
Evaluating Art. Dickie, George T.
Goodman's Rigorous Relativism. Elgin, Catherine Z.
La Statue De Condillac, Image Du Réel Ou Fiction Logique? Baertschi, Bernard.
Nelson Goodman On Truth. Chokr, Nader.
On The Fidelity Of Pictures: A Critique Of Goodman's Disjunction Of Perspective And Realism. Topper, David.
Relativism, Realism, And Rightness: Notes On Goodmanian Worldmaking. Siegel, Harvey.
Seeking The Source: Cultural Relativism And The Arts. Anderson, Albert A.

GOODNESS

Art And Goodness: Collingwood's Aesthetics And Moore's Ethics Compared. Diffey, T J.

GOODPASTER, K

Normative Contexts And Moral Decision. Philips, Michael.

GOODS

Rights And Goods: Justifying Social Action. Held, Virginia.
"The State: Ethics And Economics" in *The Georgetown Symposium On Ethics*, Porreco, Rocco (ed), 195–204. Ver Eecke, Wilfried.
"The Subjective Normative Structure Of Agency" in *Gewirth's Ethical Rationalism*, Regis Jr, Edward (ed), 8–22. Adams, E M.
Aristotle On The Goods Of Fortune. Cooper, John M.
The Classification Of Goods In Plato's *Republic*. White, Nicholas.
The Moral Standing Of The Market. Sen, Amartya.

GOODWILL

Bonnes Volontés De Puissance (Une Réponse À Hans–Georg Gadamer). Derrida, Jacques.
Does Rightness Always Involve Wrongness? Bahm, Archie J.
Et Pourtant: Puissance De La Bonne Volonté (Une Réplique À Jacques Derrida). Gadamer, Hans–Georg.

GORDON, A

"Martin Buber And A D Gordon: A Comparison" in *Martin Buber*, Gordon, Haim (ed), 255–274. Schweid, Eliezer.

GORDON, D

Nozick And Knowledge—A Rejoinder. Garrett, B J.

GOROVITZ, S

Commentary On "Advertising Professional Success Rates". Clancy, Katherine L.
Commentary On "Advertising Professional Success Rates". De George, Richard T.
Commentary On "Advertising Professional Success Rates". Goldman, Alan H.

GOSPEL(S)

Regenerating Narrative: The Gospels As Fiction. Wright, T R.

GOTHIC

Imagination In The Gothic Hierarchy Of *Scientia*—A Study On Medieval English Mysticism (in Japanese). Ebi, Hisato.

GOULDNER, A

Alvin Gouldner: Vervreemding, Reflexiviteit, En De Naderende Crisis Van De Sociologie. Disco, Cornelis.

GOVERNMENT(S)

Ethics–In–Government Laws: Are They Too "ethical"? Neely, Alfred S.
"Archaeology Abroad" in *Ethics And Values In Archaeology*, Green, Ernestene L (ed), 123–132. Healy, Paul F.
"Ethical Dilemmas In Federal Cultural Resource Management" in *Ethics And Values In Archaeology*, Green, Ernestene L (ed), 97–107. Green, Dee F.
"State Aid To Science" in *Freedom, Feminism, And The State*, Mc Elroy, Wendy (ed), 275–284. Kelly, Gertrude.
A Cotton Dust Study Unmasked. Levine, Carol.
Brand Name Extortionists, Intellectual Prostitutes, And Generic Free Riders. Bayles, Michael D.
Issues In Agriculture. Hadwiger, Don F.
Paternalism And The Regulation Of Drugs. Sagoff, Mark.
The Commodity Form And Socialization In Locke's State Of Nature. Colella, E Paul.
The Intellectual Origins Of The American Constitution. Wood, Gordon S.
Utility, Autonomy And Drug Regulation. Scriven, Tal.

GOVERNMENT REGULATION(S)

"Government Regulation And Intergenerational Justice" in *Rights And Regulation*, Machan, Tibor (ed), 177–202. Sartorius, Rolf.
"Government Regulation Of The Employment Relationship" in *Rights And Regulation*, Machan, Tibor (ed), 13–42. Haggard, Thomas R.
"Is There A Bias Toward Overregulation" in *Rights And Regulation*, Machan, Tibor (ed), 99–126. Yeager, Leland B.
"On The Rationale Of Governmental Regulation" in *Rights And Regulation*, Machan, Tibor (ed), 249–258. Rescher, Nicholas.
"Regulation And Justice: An Economist's Perspective" in *Rights And Regulation*, Machan, Tibor (ed), 127–136. Johnson, M Bruce.
"Regulation And Paternalism" in *Rights And Regulation*, Machan, Tibor (ed), 217–248. Kelman, Steven.

"Some Questions About Government Regulation Of Behavior" in *Rights And Regulation*, Machan, Tibor (ed), 137–156. Thomson, Judith J.
"Substantive Due Process: A Doctrine For Regulatory Control" in *Rights And Regulation*, Machan, Tibor (ed), 43–70. Karlin, Norman.
"The Petty Tyranny Of Government Regulation" in *Rights And Regulation*, Machan, Tibor (ed), 259–288. Machan, Tibor R.

GOZZI, G

La Polémique Contre Les Lumières Et Contre Le Rationalisme Dans Un Journal Peu Connu De Gasparo Gozzi. Cataudella, Michele.

GRACE

Grace And Functionality. Cordner, C D.

GRADUATE

Graduate Study In Continental Philosophy In The United States. Solomon, Robert.

GRAMMAR(S)

La Naissance De La Grammaire Moderne. Dominicy, Marc and Mardaga, Pierre (ed).
That Most Subtle Question (Quaestio Subtilissima). Henry, Desmond Paul.
"An Outline Of Platonist Grammar" in *Talking Minds*, Bever, Thomas G (ed), 17–48. Katz, Jerrold J.
A Paradigm Of Art. Barela, Robert E.
Buckner Quoting Goldstein And Davidson On Quotation. Van Brackel, J.
Kritische Notities Bij Ferdinand De Saussure's. Bakker, D M.
LFG And Psychological Explanation. Steedman, Mark.
Once Upon A Tense. Verkuyl, H J and Le Loux–Schuringa, J A.
Quantifier Scope And The ECP. Cole, Peter.
Realism And Grammar. Screen, Donald P.
The Visual Arts As Language. Barela, Robert E.
Type Driven Translation. Klein, Ewan and Sag, Ivan A.
What Is Grammar? Tomkow, Terrance A.

GRAMSCI, A

"Gramsci And Eurocommunism" in *Continuity And Change In Marxism*, Fischer, Norman And Others (ed), 189–210. Boggs, Carl.
Antonio Gramsci's Reformulation Of Benedetto Croce's Speculative Idealism. Kahn, Beverly L.
Interpretative Sociology And The Philosophy Of Praxis: Comparing Max Weber And Antonio Gramsci. Shafir, Gershon.
Quattro Punti Da Rivedere Nel Gramsci Dei Quaderni. Mastroianni, Giovanni.

GRANT, G

George Grant And The Twilight Of Justice. O' Donovan, Joan E.

GRAPH(S)

A Note On Simple Graphic Algebras. Nieminen, Juhani.
Games, Graphs, And Circular Arguments. Walton, Douglas N and Batten, L M.

GRASS, G

Food And Freedom In *The Flounder*. Pitkin, Hanna F.

GRASSI, E

A Philosophy Of Comparison: Heidegger And Lao Tzu. Heim, Michael.

GRATITUDE

The Theory And Practice Of Virtue. Meilaender, Gilbert C.

GRAVITATION

Philosophical And Physical Arguments For The Existence Of The Gravitational Energy As Half Of The Whole Energy Of The Universe. Adamamuţi, I A.

GRAVITY

Unified Field Theory And The Conventionality Of Geometry. Pitowsky, Itamar.

GRAY, J

Pursuing The Good—Indirectly. Alexander, Larry.

GREEK

see also Ancient
"The Wild And The Cultivated In Greek Religion" in *On Nature*, Rouner, Leroy S (ed), 79–95. Ruck, Carl.
Aeschylus And Practical Conflict. Nussbaum, Martha.
Les Sources De L'Objectivité Hellénique. Gobry, Ivan.
Modelos Hermenéuticos Y Mitológicos. Ortiz– Osés, Andrés.
Orality And Literacy In The Origin Of Philosophy. Ferrari, Giovanni R F.
Prolégomènes À La Philosophie De La Culture Grecque. Moutsopoulos, Evanghleos.
Rousseau Et Les Législateurs Grecs. Goyard– Fabre, Simone.
The Case Of The Athenian Stranger: Philosophy And World Citzenship. Caws, Peter.
The Origins Of Early Greek Philosophy. Moulder, J.
Tragédie Grecque Et "Anti–Théâtre" En France Au Siècle Des Lumières. Christodoulou, Kyriaki.

GREEN

The Metaphysics Of T H Green. Hylton, Peter.

GREEN, L

Aspects Of Leon Green's Tort Theory: Causation And The Role Of The Judge. Winslade, William J.

GREENBERG, C

Kant And Greenberg's Varieties Of Aesthetic Formalism. Crowther, Paul.

GREGORY, I

Moral Theory And Educational Practice: A Reply To Ian Gregory. Straughan, Roger R.

GREGORY OF RIMINI

Het Continuum—Debat Bij Gregorius Van Rimini. Thijssen, J.
Mental Language And The Unity Of Propositions: A Semantic Problem Discussed By Early Sixteenth Century Logicians. Ashworth, E Jennifer.

GRICE, H

A Gricean Approach To Aesthetic Instrumentalism. Lord, Catherine.

HEGEL

HEMPEL

Observation, Experiment, And Hypothesis In Modern Physical Science. Achinstein, Peter (ed) and Hannaway, Owen (ed).

Another Look At The Predictivist Thesis. Jones, William B.

Confirmation, Paradoxes, And Possible Worlds. Stillwell, Shelley.

Explaining The Actions Of The Explainers. Baier, Annette.

Gesellschaftliche Bedingtheit Und Gesellschaftliche Relevanz Historishcer Aussagen. Mommsen, Wolfgang J.

Inductive Inference In The Limit. Glymour, Clark.

Probability And Laws. Constantini, D.

Theoretical Terms And Bridge Principles: A Critique Of Hempel's (Self–) Criticisms. Moulines, C Ulises.

Zur Verteidigung Einiger Hempelscher Thesen Gegen Kritiken Stegmüllers. Küttner, Michael.

HENKIN, L

Lectures On Propositional Calculi, R Ladniak (ed). Wojcicki, Ryszard.

An Abstract Setting For Henkin Proofs. Goldblatt, Robert.

HENRICH, D

The Dialectic Of Becoming In Hegel's Logic. Cave, George P.

HENRY OF HARCLAY

Henry Of Harclay On The Formal Distinction In The Trinity (in Latin). Henninger, Mark G.

HERACLES

El Sueño Y Los Sueños En La Filosofía Prearistotélica. Cappelletti, Angel J.

HERACLITUS

An Analysis And Assessment Of A Fragment From Jonathan Barnes's Reading Of Heraclitus. Marino, Gordon D.

HERBRAND'S THEOREM

A Proof Of Herbrand's Theorem. Wojtylak, Piotr.

HERCULANEUM

Les Papyrus D'Herculanum Aujourd'Hui. Gigante, M Marcello.

HERDER

Bithell Series Of Dissertations: Spinoza In Germany From 1670 To The Age Of Goethe, V7. Bell, David.

Herders Methode In Seiner Geschichtsphilosophie. Rathmann, Jnós.

Wirkung Und Anwendung Der Poesie—Untersuchungen Zur Ästhetik Herders (in Japanese). Otabe, Tanehisa.

HEREDITY

"Genetic Screening Of Prospective Parents And Of Workers" in *Biomedical Ethics Reviews*, Humber, James M (ed), 73–120. Hubbard, Ruth.

HERILLUS

'Lo Stoicismo Di Erillo'. Ioppolo, Anna Maria.

HERMANN, G

Grete Henry–Hermann's Development Of Leonard Nelson's Ethics. Heckmann, Gustav.

HERMENEUTICS

Dialogues With Contemporary Continental Thinkers. Kearney, Richard.

Erklaren Und Verstehen. Von Wright, Georg Henrik.

Hermeneutics: Questions And Prospects. Shapiro, Gary (ed) and Sica, Alan (ed).

Hermeneutics: A Sociology Of Misunderstanding. Flanagan, Kieran.

Relatedness: Essays In Metaphysics And Theology. Oliver, Harold H.

Seeing And Reading. Nicholson, Graeme.

The Dialogical And The Dialectical Nerveau De Rameau. Jauss, Hans Robert.

The Epistemology Of Hans–Georg Gadamer. Schmidt, Lawrence K.

Understanding And Explanation: A Transcendental–Pragmatic Perspective. Apel Otto, Karl and Warnke, Georgia (trans).

Wir Philologen: Überlegungen Zu Nietzsches Begriff Der Interpretation. Birus, Hendrik.

Über "Sinn" Und "Bedeutung" Bei Gadamer. Graeser, Andreas.

"Beyond Hermeneutics" in *Hermeneutics*, Shapiro, Gary (ed), 66–83. Dreyfus, Hubert.

"Epistemological Problem Of Understanding As Aspect Of General Problem Of Knowing" in *Hermeneutics*, Shapiro, Gary (ed), 25–53. Bettim Emilio.

"Literary Impressionism And Phenomenology" in *Existential Coordinates Of Human Condition*, Tymieniecka, A (ed), 521–534. Kronegger, Marlies.

"On Medieval Interpretation And Mythology" in *Existential Coordinates Of Human Condition*, Tymieniecka, A (ed), 185–194. Gellrich, Jesse.

"On The Transcendability Of Hermeneutics" in *Hermeneutics*, Shapiro, Gary (ed), 84–95. Palmer, Richard E.

"Phenomenality And Materiality In Kant" in *Hermeneutics*, Shapiro, Gary (ed), 121–144. De Man, Paul.

"Phenomenology And Literary Impressionism" in *Existential Coordinates Of Human Condition*, Tymieniecka, A (ed), 535–546. Stowell, Peter.

"Surrender–And–Catch And Hermeneutics". Wolff, Kurt H.

"The Denial Of Tragedy" in *Existential Coordinates Of Human Condition*, Tymieniecka, A (ed), 401–408. Ravaux, Francoise.

"The Hermeneutics Of Suspicion" in *Hermeneutics*, Shapiro, Gary (ed), 54–65. Gadamer, Hans– Georg.

"The Problem Of Reading, Phenomenologically Or Otherwise" in *Existential Coordinates Of Human Condition*, Tymieniecka, A (ed), 559–568. Margolis, Joseph.

"Toward A Theory Of Contemporary Tragedy" in *Existential Coordinates Of Human Condition*, Tymieniecka, A (ed), 341–362. Kaelin, Eugene.

"Tragical, Comical, Historical" in *Existential Coordinates Of Human Condition*, Tymieniecka, A (ed), 379–400. Platt, Michael.

"Transcendental Philosophy And The Hermeneutic Critique Of Consciousness" in

Hermeneutics, Shapiro, Gary (ed), 96–120. Mohanty, J N.

"Un Modèle D'analyse Dy Texte Dramatique" in *Existential Coordinates Of Human Condition*, Tymieniecka, A (ed), 547–558. Moussally, Adnan.

A Perennial Philosophy Perspective On Richard Rorty's Neo–Pragmatism. Isenberg, Sheldon R and Thursby, G R.

A Survey Of Recent Ricoeur–Literature. Sweeney, Robert.

Action As A Text: Gadamer's Hermeneutics And The Social Scientific Analysis Of Action. Hekman, Susan.

Aesthetics And The Sociology Of Art: A Critical Commentary On The Writings Of Janet Wolff. Hincks, Tony.

Algunas Consideraciones Acerca De La Hermeneutica En El Psicoanalisis Y La Historia. De La Garza, Teresa.

Boeckh And Dilthey: The Development Of Methodical Hermeneutics. Seebohm, Thomas M.

Can Heidegger Be Depicted As A Phenomenologist? Pavlich, G.

Carlyle's Past And Present, History, And A Question Of Hermeneutics. Childers, Joseph W.

Commentary On Patrick A Heelan's "Hermeneutics Of Experimental Science In The Context Of The Life–World". Kisiel, Theodore.

Comments Of Theodore Kisiel's Commentary On My Paper: Hermeneutics Of Experimental Science In The Context Of The Life–World. Heelan, Patrick A.

Der Mensch Und Seine Sprache. Hennigfeld, Jochem.

Dialectics, Difference, And Weak Thought. Vattimo, Gianni.

Die Funktion Der Hermeneutik In Den Positiven Wissenschaften. Kimmerle, Heinz.

Die Gegenwärtigkeit Des Mythos In Kants Mutmassungen Über Den Anfang Der Menschengeschichte. Gniffke, Franz.

Gadamer, L'ermeneutica E——Les Bourgeois. Capanna, Francesco.

Habermas's Contribution To Hermeneutic Theory. Davey, Nicholas.

Hegel's Dialectic Of Master And Slave As A Model For The Relation Between Artistic Creation And Aesthetic Appreciation. Klein, Itshaq and Gandelman, Claude.

Heidegger's Hermeneutical Grounding Of Science: A Phenomenological Critique Of Positivism. Bender, Frederic L.

Herméneutique Philosophique Et Théologie. Petit, Jean–Claude.

Herméneutique Et Fiction Chez M Foucault. Margot, Jean Paul.

Hermeneutic Hegelianism. Butler, Clark.

Hermeneutics And The Social Sciences: A Gadamerian Critique Of Rorty. Warnke, Georgia.

Hermeneutics And The Teaching Of Philosophy. Walhout, Donald.

Hermeneutics Of Experimental Science In The Context Of The Life–World. Heelan, Patrick A.

Hermeneutics And Intellectual History. Stern, Laurent.

Hermeneutics As Practical Philosophy And Practical Wisdom (in Dutch). Van Der Walt, J W G.

Hermeneutik Des Lebens Und Ästhetik Bei Wilhelm Dilthey (in Japanese). Omori, Atsushi.

Hermeneutik—Theorie Einer Praxis? Kamper, Dietmar.

How Not To Criticize Nāgārjuna: A Response To L Stafford Betty. Loy, David.

K O Apel Over "Erklären" En "Verstehen". Strasser, St.

Karl Adam's Christology: Towards A Post–Critical Method. Krieg, Robert A.

L'avenir Du Concept En Esthétique: L'actualité Herméneutique De Hegel. Grondin, Jean.

L'herméneutique De Schleiermacher: Relecture Autour Du Débat Herméneutique–Néostructuralisme. Frank, Manfred.

L'homme Qui Fait Une Narration (in Japanese). Kitamura, Kiyohiko.

Language And The Transformation Of Philosophy. Derksen, L D.

Le Défi Herméneutique. Gadamer, Hans–Georg.

Nietzschean Aphorism As Art And Act. Shapiro, Gary.

O *trabalho* Do Texto Filosófico E A Sua Interpretação. Sumares, Manuel.

On The Interpretation Of Pramānasamuccaya (Vrtti) I, 3d. Franco, Eli.

Paul Ricoeur's Philosophical Hermeneutics (in Hebrew). Levy, Zeev.

Philosophical Hermeneutics And The Conflict Of Ontologies. Wallulis, Jerald.

Philosophical Hermeneutics And The Analects: The Paradigm Of "Tradition". Chan, Alan.

Philosophie Et Religion Dans L'oeuvre De Paul Ricoeur. Lavaud, Claudie.

Philosophy Of Religion And The Mirror Of Nature: Rorty's Challenge To Analytic Philosophy Of Religion. Lauritzen, Paul.

Plurivocité Et Dis–Simultanéité: Questions Herméneutiques Pour Une Théorie Du Texte Littéraire. Frank, Manfred.

Practical Reason And Hermeneutics. Hollinger, Robert.

Practical Reason, Hermeneutics, And Social Life. Risser, James.

Questions And Counterquestions. Habermas, Jürgen.

Regenerating Narrative: The Gospels As Fiction. Wright, T R.

Sense, Hermeneutic Interpretations, Action. Di Bernardo, Giuliano.

Telos In Hegel's *Differenz Des Fichte'schen Und Schelling'schen Systems Der Philosophie.* Percesepe, Gary.

The Conditions Of Dialogue: Approaches To The Habermas–Gadamer Debate. Hjort, Anne Meete.

The Conflict Between Poetry And Literature. Murray, Michael.

The Contemporary Status Of Continental Philosophy In Canada: A Narrative. Madison, Gary B.

The Course And The Subtle: Contacting Direct Experience. Darroch Lozowski, Vivian.

The Hermeneutics Of Suspicion. Gadamer, Hans–Georg.

The Idea Of Language: Some Difficulties In Speaking About Language. Agamben, Giorgio.

The Rationality Debate And Gadamer's Hermeneutics: Reflections On Beyond Objectivism And Relativism. Sullivan, Robert.

HERMENEUTICS
Van Wezensschouw Naar Hermeneuse. De Boer, Th.
What Is The Difference That Makes A Difference: Gadamer, Habermas, And Rorty (in Hebrew). Bernstein, Richard G.
Why *Politikē Philosophia*? Umphrey, Stuart.
Wittgenstein's Solution Of The 'Hermeneutic Problem'. Shanker, Stuart G.
Zur Ortsbestimmung Der Historischen Wissenschaften. Kramer, Hans.

HERO(ES)
Theism, Morality And The 'Why Should I Be Moral' Question. Bishop, John.

HERZOG, I
Ethical Behavior In Business: A Hierarchical Approach From The Talmud. Friedman, Hershey H.

HETERODEXY
The Heterodox Interpretation Of Reference Talk. Hartman, Tom.

HICK, J
Kant, A Moral Criterion, And Religious Pluralism. Mc Kenzie, David E.
Karma And The Problem Of Suffering. Perrett, Roy W.
Philosophy, Religion And Theodicy. Moulder, James.

HIDDEN VARIABLE(S)
Einstein On Locality And Separability. Howard, Don.
Hidden Variables And The Implicate Order. Bohm, David.
L'inégalité De Bell: Démonstration Intuitive Et Commentaires (infrench). Bonsack, Francois.

HIERARCHY(—CHIES)
"Communities And Hierarchies: Structure In The Practice Of Science And Technology" in *Technological Knowledge*, Laudan, Rachel (ed), 27–46. Constant, Edward W.
A Cumulative Hierarchy Of Predicates. Friedman, Harvey.
A Hierarchy Of Families Of Recursively Enumerable Degrees. Welch, Lawrence V.
A Spectrum Hierarchy. Fagin, Ronald.
Effective Topological Spaces II: A Hierarchy. Weitkamp, Galen and Kalantari, I.
Ethical Behavior In Business: A Hierarchical Approach From The Talmud. Friedman, Hershey H.
Finite Level Borel Games And A Problem Concerning The Jump Hierarchy. Hodes, Harold T.
Functors And Ordinal Notations I: A Functorial Construction Of The Veblen Hierarchy. Girard, Jean–Yves and Vauzeilles, Jacqueline.
Pseudo–Jump Operators: II, Transfinite Iterations, Hierarchies And Minimal Covers. Jockusch Jr, Carl G and Shore, Richard A.
Two Episodes In The Unification Of Logic And Topology. Grosholz, E R.

HIGH SCHOOL(S)
Promoting The Autonomy Of Another Person: The Difficult Case Of The High School Dropout. Hedman, Carl G.

HIGHER EDUCATION
"Moral Formation And The Liberal Arts" in *The Georgetown Symposium On Ethics*, Porreco, Rocco (ed), 243–250. Mc Donnell, Kevin.
Business Ethics, Interdisciplinarity And Higher Education. Madsen, Peter.
Justifying A Curriculum And Justifying An Institution. Gray, W N and Wyatt, J F.

HIGHER ORDER LOGICS
Lower Bound Results On Lengths Of Second–order Formulas. Scarpellini, Bruno.
On Some Non–Classical Extensions Of Second–Order Intuitionistic Propositional Calculus. Scedrov, Andrej.
Reduction Of Second–Order Logic To Modal Logic. Thomason, S K.

HILBERT, D
Überlegungen Zu Den Grundlegungsversuchen Der Mathematik Von Frege Und Hilbert Vom Standpunkt Der Transzendentalphilosophie Aus (II). Schuler, Wolfgang.
Beyond First–order Logic: The Historical Interplay Between Mathematical Logic And Axiomatic Set Theory. Moore, Gregory H.
Foundations For Analysis And Proof Theory. Sieg, Wilfried.

HILLMAN, J
The New Gnosis. Avens, Robert.

HINDU
Bhagavad–Gita: An Exegetical Commentary. Minor, Robert N.
Hindu Ethics. Singh, Balbir.
Oriental Philosophies. Koller, John M.
Review Of *The Origin Of Subjectivity In Hindu Thought*. Bhattacharya, K C.
The 'Introduction' From Her *The Origin Of Subjectivity In Hindu Thought*. Kitch, Ethel May.

HINDUISM
Culture And Morality. Mayer, Adrian C (ed).
Gandhi's Religious Thought. Chatterjee, Margaret.
Harper's Dictionary Of Hinduism: Its Mythology, Folklore, Philosophy, Literature, And History. Stutley, James and Stutley, Margaret.
Human Rights In Religious Traditions. Swidler, Arlene (ed).
Mysticism And Religious Traditions. Katz, Steven (ed).
A Business Model Of Enlightenment. Barnett, John H.
Action And Suffering In The Bhagavad Gītā. Fingarette, Herbert.
Rammohun Roy And The Baptists Of Serampore: Moralism Vs Faith. Chatterjee, Shyamal K.
Religious Crisis, Hinduism And Common–ism. Nayak, G C.
The Hindu Vision And World Problems. Sivaraman, S K.

HINTIKKA, J
Cogito, Ergo Sum: Inference And Performance. Reeder, Harry.
Descartes, Russell, Hintikka And The Self. Imlay, Robert A.
Visual Space From The Perspective Of Possible World Semantics II. Wiesenthal, L.

HIPPOCRATES
El Sueño Y Los Sueños En La Filosofía Prearistotélica. Cappelletti, Angel J.

HIRSCH, E
Identity: Criteria Vs Necessary And Sufficient Conditions. Ward, David V.
On Justifying The Choice Of Interpretive Theories. Danneberg, Lutz and Muller, Hans–harald.

HIRST, P
A Revival Of The Propositional Theory Of Art? Goodrich, R A.
Art And Knowledge. Gingell, J.
Formal The Teleological Elements In Hirst's Argument For A Liberal Curriculum. Scarlett, B F.
The Philosophy Of Education Since Dewey. Hendley, Brian P.

HISTORIAN(S)
The History Of Ideas. King, Preston (ed).
K Marx's Historical Thinking: On 100th Anniversary Of His Death. Kuderowicz, Zbigniew.

HISTORICAL MATERIALISM
see also Dialectical Materialism
Marxism: Nomos XXVI. Pennock, J Roland (ed) and Chapman, John W (ed).
A Critique Of Marxist Legal Theoretical Constructs. Hyden, Timothy M.
Die Anwendung Der Marxschen Dialektik Beim Aufbau Des Kategoriensystems Des Historischen Materialismus. Stiehler, Gottfried.
Education And Historical Materialism. Schrag, Francis.
Forces Of Production And Social Primacy. Gottlieb, Roger S.
Frederick Engels And Contemporary Problems Concerning The History Of Primitive Society. Bromlei, Iu V and Pershits, A I.
Historical Materialism And Social Practice (in Czechoslovakian). Smirnov, G L.
Historical Materialism As The Philosophy Of Marxism (II). Siemek, Marek.
Historical Materialism And Some Actual Present Problems (in Czochoslovakian). Hohos, L.
Historical Materialism, Ideology And Ethics. Nielsen, Kai.
Making A Mess Of Marxism. Mc Clellan, James.
Marxistisch–Leninistische Philosophie In Indien. Litman, A D.
Messianic Time And Materialistic Progress. Hering, Christoph.
Objectless Activity: Marx's 'Theses On Feuerbach'. Giles– Peters, A.
Produktivität Und Individualität. Bauer, A.
The Natural, The Social, And Historical Materialism. Soble, Alan.
Theory And Practice In Marxism. Apostel, Leo.
What's Historical About Historical Materialism? Levine, Andrew and Sober, Elliott.
Zur Historisch–Materialistischen Auffassung Von Basis Und Überbau. Bauer, Adolf.

HISTORICAL REALISM
A Personalistic Philosophy Of History. Bartnik, Czeslaw Stanislaw.
Time And History In Theological Ethics: The Work Of James Gustafson. Hauerwas, Stanley and Childress, James F.

HISTORICISM
Relatedness: Essays In Metaphysics And Theology. Oliver, Harold H.
"Good And Bad Arguments Against Historicism" in *Popper And The Human Sciences*, Currie, Gregory (ed), 133–146. Urbach, Peter.
"Popper's Critique Of Marx's Method" in *Popper And The Human Sciences*, Currie, Gregory (ed), 147–164. Suchting, W A.
An Egalitarian Epistemology: A Note On E P Thompson's Critique Of Althusser And Popper. Green, David G.
An Historicist View Of Teaching Philosophy. Portmess, Lisa.
Carlo Antoni E Lo Storicismo Crociano (Continua). Fantini, Stefano.
Gesellschaftliche Bedingtheit Und Gesellschaftliche Relevanz Historishcer Aussagen. Mommsen, Wolfgang J.
Herders Methode In Seiner Geschichtsphilosophie. Rathmann, Jnos.
Human Nature And Moral Theories. Kekes, John.
Language And The Transformation Of Philosophy. Derksen, L D.
On The Change Of Social Laws. Sztompka, Piotr.
Person And Society: A View Of V P Tugarinov. Blakeley, Thomas J.
Prospects Regarding The Science Of Criticism. Margolis, Joseph.
Renaissance Historicism Reconsidered. Schiffman, Zachary S.
Sociobiology: The World As Given Or The World As Created. Pickens, Donald K.
Vico's View Of History. Henderson, R D.

HISTORICITY
Aktualität Und Historizität: Bemühungen Um Werk Und Wirken Leonhard Eulers. Hess, Heinz–Jürgen.
Concepto De Historicidad En "Ser Y Tiempo de Martin Heidegger. Andrade, Ciro Schmidt.
Does Historicity Require A Different Metaphysics? Burbidge, John W.
Heidegger's Contribution To Modern Political Thought. Dauenhauer, Bernard P.
Historicity, Narratives, And The Understanding Of Human Life. Johnson, Galen A.
L'Historicité Des Valeurs. Damnjanović, M.
On Representation And Essence: Barthes And Heidegger. Huckle, Nicholas.

HISTORIOGRAPHY
Philosophy In History. Rorty, Richard and others (ed).
"The Historiography Of Philosophy: Four Genres" in *Philosophy In History*, Rorty, Richard and others (ed), 49–76. Rorty, Richard.
Eric Voegelin: Politische Wissenschaft Und Geschichtsphilosophie. Baruzzi, Arno.
Gadamer's Criticisms Of Collingwood. Bertoldi, E F.
Georges Dumézil And The Trifunctional Approach To Roman Civilization. Momigliano, Arnaldo.
Gesellschaftliche Bedingtheit Und Gesellschaftliche Relevanz Historishcer Aussagen. Mommsen, Wolfgang J.

HISTORIOGRAPHY

In Search Of The Actual Historical Frege. Mohanty, J N.

Max Weber's Defense Of Historical Inquiry. Mc Lemore, Lelan.

Narrative Versus Analysis In History. Dray, W H.

The History Of Art: Its Methods And Their Limits. Von Haumeder, Ulrika.

Theory Of History In Historical Lectures: The German Tradition Of *Historik*, 1750–1900. Blanke, Horst Walter and Fleischer, Dirk and Rusen, Jorn.

HISTORY

'Hegel's Hellenic Ideal' AND 'The Mystical Element In Hegel's Early Writings'. Gray, Glenn J and Adams, George Plimpton.

A Guide To The Culture Of Science, Technology, And Medicine. Durbin, Paul T (ed).

After Virtue: Second Edition. Macintyre, Alasdair.

Against Fate: An Essay On Personal Dignity. Tinder, Glenn.

Criticism And Objectivity. Selden, Raman.

Erklaren Und Verstehen. Von Wright, Georg Henrik.

Essays On French History And Historians. Mill, John Stuart and Robson, John M (ed).

From Hegel To Nietzsche. Lowith, Karl.

George Grant And The Twilight Of Justice. O' Donovan, Joan E.

Historical Consciousness Or The Remembered Past. Lukacs, John.

History And System: Hegel's Philosophy Of History. Perkins, Robert L (ed).

Hume's Philosophy Of Common Life. Livingston, Donald W.

Ibn Khaldoun. Lacoste, Yves.

Justifying Historical Descriptions. Mc Cullagh, C Behan.

Logic, Philosophy, And History: A Study In The Philosophy Of History Based On The Work Of R G Collingwood. Russell, Anthony F.

Morality, Halakha And The Jewish Tradition. Spero, Shubert.

Nietzsche, Volume II: The External Recurrence Of The Same. Heidegger, Martin.

Observation, Experiment, And Hypothesis In Modern Physical Science. Achinstein, Peter (ed) and Hannaway, Owen (ed).

On History And Other Essays. Oakeshott, Michael.

Religious Inquiry—Participation And Detachment. Rolston, Holmes.

The Dark Abyss Of Time: The History Of The Earth And The History Of Nations From Hooke To Vico, Lydia G Cochrane (trans). Paolo, Rossi.

The Decline Of Juridical Reason: Doctrine And Theory In The Legal Order. Simmonds, N E.

The Emergence Of Dialectical Theory: Philosophy And Political Inquiry. Warren, Scott.

The History Of Ideas. King, Preston (ed).

The Intellectual And Social Organization Of The Sciences. Whitley, Richard.

The Philosophy Of F W J Schelling: History, System, And Freedom. Marx, Werner and Nenon, Thomas (trans).

The Politics Of Salvation: The Hegelian Idea Of The State. Lakeland, Paul.

The Rhythm Of Being: A Study Of Temporality. Trivers, Howard.

The Smiling Spleen: Paracelsianism In Storm And Stress. Pagel, Walter.

Time And Narrative, V1. Ricoeur, Paul and Mc Laughlin, Kathleen (trans) and Pellauer, David (trans).

Wahrheit Und Wahrheitsgrund. Fleischer, Margot.

What Is Living And What Is Dead In The Philosophy Of Hegel? Croce, Benedetto.

"Basic Modal Logic" in *Handbook Of Philosophical Logic*, Gabbay, Dov (ed), 1–88. Bull, Robert A and Segerberg, Krister.

"Between Aristotle And Anarchy: The Moral Challenge Of Freedom" in *On Freedom*, Howard, John A (ed), 7–26. Lobkowicz, Nikolaus.

"Hegel, Art, And History, Curtis Carter (commentator)" in *History And System*, Perkins, Robert (ed), 173–194. Desmond, William.

"Marxism As History—A Theory And Its Consequences" in *Contemporary Marxism*, O' Rourke, James J (ed), 39–54. Fleischer, Helmut.

"Marxism, Historicism, And Philosophy Of Art" in *Continuity And Change In Marxism*, Fischer, Norman And Others (ed), 24–38. Morawski, Stefan.

"Natural Justice And Natural Rights" in *The Search For Justice*, Taitte, W Lawson (ed), 43–82. Cecil, Andrew R.

"Philosophy And Ideology" in *Ideology, Philosophy And Politics*, Parel, Anthony (ed), 17–36. Copleston, Frederick C.

"Philosophy Of Science" in *The Culture Of Science, Technology, And Medicine*, Durbin, Paul T (ed), 197–281. Michalos, Alex C.

"Philosophy Of Technology" in *The Culture Of Science, Technology, And Medicine*, Durbin, Paul T (ed), 282–363. Mitcham, Carl.

"Philosophy Of Medicine" in *The Culture Of Science, Technology, And Medicine*, Durbin, Paul T (ed), 364–464. Engelhardt Jr, H Tristram and Erde, Edmund L.

"The Divine Corporation And The History Of Ethics" in *Philosophy In History*, Rorty, Richard and others (ed), 173–192. Schneewind, J B.

"The Sceptic In His Place And Time" in *Philosophy In History*, Rorty, Richard and others (ed), 225–254. Burnyeat, M F.

"The Shield And The Horizon" in *Existential Coordinates Of Human Condition*, Tymieniecka, A (ed), 163–174. Findlay, L M.

"Toward A Pedagogy Of The Useful Past For Teacher Preparation": A Reaction. Gutek, Gerald L.

"World History & The History Of The Absolute Spirit" in *History And System*, Perkins, Robert (ed), 101–122. Jaeschke, Walter.

A Personalistic Philosophy Of History. Bartnik, Czeslaw Stanislaw.

A Theory Of Historical Truth. Haecker, Dorothy.

Arnold J Toynbee: Das Höchste Gut Ist Der Frieden!. Schulze, Hans.

Arten Des Herangehens An Dialektische Widersprüche Besonders In Der Technischen Entwicklung. Thiel, Rainer.

Aspects Of The Logic Of History–Of–Science Explanation. Finocchiaro, Maurice A.

Assessing Relative Causal Importance In History. Pork, Andrus.

Benedetto Croce, Philosopher, Ethics And Politics (in Hungarian). Bausola, Adriano.

Berlin On Vico. Zagorin, Perez.

Bibliography Of Works In Philosophy Of History 1978–1982. David, Zdenek V and Strassfeld, Robert.

Carlo Antoni E Lo Storicismo Crociano (Continua). Fantini, Stefano.

Carlyle's Past And Present, History, And A Question Of Hermeneutics. Childers, Joseph W.

Collections And Collectors. Ergmann, Raoul.

Croce's Interpretation Of Hegel. Bellamy, Richard.

Cultural Epochs And Their Predominant Ideas (in Czechoslovakian). Steindl, Rudolf.

Der Kulturprozess Und Die Wachsende Rolle Des Subjektiven Faktors. Redeker, Horst.

Developing Themes In Philosophy/La Philosophie En Cours: The Hegel Renaissance In The Anglo–Saxon World Since 1945. Harris, H S.

Die Anwendung Der Marxschen Dialektik Beim Aufbau Des Kategoriensystems Des Historischen Materialismus. Stiehler, Gottfried.

Die Gegenwärtigkeit Des Mythos In Kants Mutmassungen Über Den Anfang Der Menschengeschichte. Gniffke, Franz.

Die Wachsende Rolle Des Subjektiven Faktors––Eine Gesetzmässigkeit Des Historischen Fortschritts. Lassow, Ekkhard.

Die Weltgeschichtliche Bedeutung Des Sieges Der Sowjetunion Im Grossen Vaterländischen Krieg Im Lichte Des Leninismus. Uhlig, Dieter.

Dimensions Du Penser Hégélien. Guibal, Francis.

Ehrenfels And Eastern Europe (in Hungarian). Nyiri, Kristóf.

El Progreso Según Juan Bautista Vico. Dondi, J.

Elements For A Theory Of Modernity. Secretan, Philibert.

Empiricism And Speculation In *the German Ideology*. Taminiaux, Jacques.

Eric Voegelin: Politische Wissenschaft Und Geschichtsphilosophie. Baruzzi, Arno.

Estructura De La Temporalidad Y Realidad Social. Ferreol, G.

Federalism And Socialism: A Reconsideration. Resnick, Philip.

Forty Years Of Socialist Cultural Evolution (in Czechoslovakian). Gawlik, Ladislav.

Frederick Engels And Contemporary Problems Concerning The History Of Primitive Society. Bromlei, Iu V and Pershits, A I.

From The Contemplative Materialism To The Materialism Of Praxis: On The Evolution Of Bukharin's Philosophy (in Hungarian). Szabo, Tibor.

Gadamer's Criticisms Of Collingwood. Bertoldi, E F.

Georges Dumézil And The Trifunctional Approach To Roman Civilization. Momigliano, Arnaldo.

Gesellschaftliche Bedingtheit Und Gesellschaftliche Relevanz Historishcer Aussagen. Mommsen, Wolfgang J.

Harrington's Elusive Balance. Reeve, Andrew.

Hegel, Jung, And The Spirit Of History. Kelly, Sean.

Herders Methode In Seiner Geschichtsphilosophie. Rathmann, Jňos.

Herméneutique Et Fiction Chez M Foucault. Margot, Jean Paul.

Historical Roots Of The Concept Of Autonomy In Western Philosophy. Nauta, Lolle.

History And The Brewmaster's Nose. Martin, Raymond.

History Of Philosophy In The Grand Manner: The Achievement Of H A Wolfson. Runia, D T.

Ideology And Truth. Oruka, H Odera.

Ideology And Social Psyche (in Hungarian). Stojchev, Todor.

Ideology And Partiality In David Hume's "History Of England". Okie, Laird.

Il Diluvio E L'Educazione. Guzzo, Augusto.

Incidence Sur Hegel De La Lecture De Gibbon. Muller, Philippe.

Internal Problems Of The "State–Nation" Conception In The Last Third Of The 19th Century And At The Turn Of The Century (in Hungarian). Diószegi, István.

Interpretative Sociology And The Philosophy Of Praxis: Comparing Max Weber And Antonio Gramsci. Shafir, Gershon.

Interpretation In History: Or What Historians Do And Philosophers Say. Levich, Marvin.

Interpreting The Enlightenment: A Political Approach. Crocker, Lester G.

K O Apel Over "Erklären" En "Verstehen". Strasser, St.

Kant And The History Of Philosophy (in Hebrew). Yovel, Yirmiyahu.

Knowing The Past. Cherry, Christopher.

László Rudas And The Lukács Debate In The Twenties (in Hungarian). Mesterházi, Miklós.

La Structure (Intériorité) Et La Formation (extériorité) De La Vie (Dilthey). Danek, Jaromir.

Land's End. Cocks, Edmond D.

Le "Reflections On The Revolution In France": Categorie Dell'Agire Politico E Filosofia Della Storia In Edmund Burke. Panella, Giuseppe.

Le Cours Manuscrit De Logique De Marcin Smiglecki SJ. Darowski, R.

Main Lines In The Hungarian Philosophy From The 1848/49 War Of Independence To The Compromise Of 1867 (in Hungarian). Kiss, Endre.

Marcuse On Hegel And Historicity. Pippin, Robert B.

Max Weber's Defense Of Historical Inquiry. Mc Lemore, Lelan.

Messianic Time And Materialistic Progress. Hering, Christoph.

Metafísica, Historia Y Antropología: Sobre El Fundamento De La Antropología *Filosófica*. Pintor– Ramos, Antonio.

Methodologies, History Of Science And Dialectical Materialism. Pala, Alberto.

Methodologie Und Geschichte: Ansätze Problemorienterter Gesellschaftsanalysen. Rust, Holger.

Modern Science And The Coexistence Of Rationalities. Salomon– Bayet, Claire.

Montaigne On War. Bonadeo, Alfredo.

More Than 'Meets The Eye'. Devereaux, Mary.

Narrative Versus Analysis In History. Dray, W H.

National Park Management And Values. Bratton, Susan Power.

Nichilismo Attivo, Storicità, Futuro Nella Filosofia Di Pietro Piovani. Cacciatore,

HISTORY

Giuseppe.

No Tragedy Of The Commons. Cox, Susan Jane Buck.

On The Dialectic Of Modernism And Postmodernism. Wellmer, Albrecht.

On The Experience Of Historical Objects. Harvey, Charles W.

Owen's Communism And The Neo–Left–Wing Reconstruction Of History; War And Peace In The Ideological Confrontation (in German). Jauch, Liane.

Per Una Storia Storica Delle Scienze. Roger, Jacques.

Philosophisch–Weltanschauliche Auseinandersetzungen Um Theoretische Positionen Zur Wissenschaftsgeschichte. Roseberg, Ulrich.

Political Thought As Traditionary Action: The Critical Response To Skinner And Pocock. Janssen, Peter L.

Prolégomènes À La Philosophie De La Culture Grecque. Moutsopoulos, Evanghleos.

Renaissance Historicism Reconsidered. Schiffman, Zachary S.

Riflessioni Sulla Storia Della Scienza. Boniolo, Giovanni.

Skepsis Ohne Selbstwiderspruch: Über O Marquards "Interimistischen Skeptizismus". Craemer, Heiner.

Some Recent Books On The Historical Status Of Women. Tormey, Judith.

Subjektiver Faktor Und Revolution. Stiehler, Gottfried.

System Of Literary History (in Czechoslovakian). Vasak, Pavel.

The Dialectics Of "Essence" And "Existence". Zdanowicz, Piotr.

The French Revolution And Capitalism: An Explanatory Schema. Wallerstein, Immanuel.

The Great Republic. Heller, Agnes.

The Hermeneutics Of Suspicion. Gadamer, Hans–Georg.

The History Of Art: Its Methods And Their Limits. Von Haumeder, Ulrika.

The Ideology Of Jacobitism On The Eve Of The Rising Of 1745—Part I. Mc Lynn, F J.

The Ideology Of Jacobitism—Part II. Mc Lynn, F J.

The Revelation Of Humanity. Munson, Thomas N.

The Rise Of Modern Bourgeois Ideology In The Baden Neokantianism (in Hungarian). Rozsnyai, Ervin.

The Role Of Aesthetic Education In The Forming Of Socialist Consciousness (in Czechoslovakian). Hnizdova, Kvetoslava and Hnizdova, Vlastislav.

The Structure Of Historical Knowledge And The Method Of Actualism (in Czechoslovakian). Cízek, F.

The Theological Significance Of Hegel's Four World–Historical Realms. Von Der Luft, Eric.

The Use And Abuse Of The Concept 'Weltanschauung'. Echeverria, Edward J.

Theorie Zur Enstehung Der Europäischen Moderne. Hahn, Alois.

Theory And Practice From The Point Of View Of Materialism (in Hungarian). Buharin, N I.

Theory Of History In Historical Lectures: The German Tradition Of *Historik*, 1750–1900. Blanke, Horst Walter and Fleischer, Dirk and Rusen, Jorn.

Toward A Pedagogy Of The Useful Past For Teacher Preparation. Lucas, Christopher J.

Two Ontologies Of Hegel, Marx, Lukács? Sleczka, Kazimierz.

Vico And Collingwood On 'The Conceit Of Scholars'. Todd, Joan and Cono, Joseph.

Vico's View Of History. Henderson, R D.

Who Is Fooled By The "Cunning Of Reason"? Drydyk, J J.

Zum Verhältnis Von Technikphilosophie Und Technikgeschichte. Bialas, Volker.

Zur Ortsbestimmung Der Historischen Wissenschaften. Kramer, Hans.

HISTORY OF IDEAS

Geschichte Der Ethik Im Überblick. Mac Intyre, Alasdair.

The History Of Ideas. King, Preston (ed).

Language, Meaning And Reality In Euripides. Sansone, David.

HISTORY OF PHILOSOPHY

History Of Philosophy In The Making. Thro, Linus J (ed).

Philosophy In History. Rorty, Richard and others (ed).

" interesting Questions' In The History Of Philosophy Elsewhere" in *Philosophy In History*, Rorty, Richard and others (ed), 141–172. Lepenies, Wolf.

"Five Parables" in *Philosophy In History*, Rorty, Richard and others (ed), 103–124. Hacking, Ian.

"Haecker, Kierkegaard, And The Early Brenner" in *International Kierkegaard Commentary*, Perkins, Robert L (ed), 189–222. Janik, Allan.

"History, Futurology And The Future Of Philosophy" in *History Of Philosophy In The Making*, Thro, Linus J (ed), 299–312. Bourke, Vernon J.

"Philosophy And Its History" in *Philosophy In History*, Rorty, Richard and others (ed), 17–30. Taylor, Charles.

"The Question Of Recurrent Problems In Philosophy" in *History Of Philosophy In Making*, Thro, Linus J (ed), 197–212. Coplestron, Frederick C.

"The Relationship Of Philosophy To Its Past" in *Philosophy In History*, Rorty, Richard and others (ed), 31–48. Macintyre, Alasdair.

"Why Do We Study The History Of Philosophy" in *Philosophy In History*, Rorty, Richard and others (ed), 77–102. Kruger, Lorenz.

Philosophy And The Mirror Of Rorty. Munz, Peter.

HITLER

How To Make Hitler's Ideas Clear? Roth, John K.

The Concept Of Genocide. Lang, Berel.

HOBBES

Locke's Education For Liberty. Tarcov, Nathan.

"Hobbes And Skepticism" in *History Of Philosophy In Making*, Thro, Linus J (ed), 133–148. Popkin, Richard H.

"The Reconciliation Project" in *Morality, Reason And Truth*, Copp, David (ed), 297–319. Kavka, Gregory S.

Commentary On "Whether Professional Associations May Enforce Professional Codes". Ladd, John.

El Racionalismo En El Inicio Del Inmanentismo Jurídico. Yacobucci, Guillermo J.

Francis Bacon Und Hobbes' Widmungsbrief Zu *De Cive*. Schuhmann, Karl.

Friends Of Leomofos. Collins, Aaron S.

Hobbes As Moralist. Farrell, Daniel M.

Hobbes, Spinoza, Rousseau Et La Formation De L'idée De Démocratie Comme Mesure De La Légitimité Du Pouvoir Politique. Tinland, Franck.

Hobbes's State Of War. Hampton, Jean.

Hume's *Treatise* And Hobbe's *The Elements Of Law*. Russell, Paul.

Intelligibilité Et Réalité Chez Hobbes Et Spinoza. Bernhardt, Jean.

Italian Literature On Thomas Hobbes After The Second World War: Part I; 1946–1955. Felice, Domenico.

La Conformación Del Estado Moderno En Relación A Textos Políticos. Durand, Graciela Alcocer.

La Dynamique De La Guerre Chez Hobbes. Abraham, Luc.

La Naissance Du Matérialisme Moderne Chez Hobbes Et Spinoza. Boscherini, Emilia G.

Le *Droit Du Plus Fort*: Hobbes Contre Spinoza. Matheron, Alexandre.

Les Mathématiques Chez Spinoza Et Hobbes. Medina, Jose.

Marx's Concept Of Justice And The Two Traditions In The European Political Thought. Commers, Ronald.

Moral Skepticism And International Relations. Cohen, Marshall.

Motion And Morality: Pierre Gassendi, Thomas Hobbes And The Mechanical World–View. Sarasohn, Lisa T.

Petty *Contra* Hobbes: A Previously Untranslated Manuscript. Amati, Frank and Aspromourgos, Tony.

Politiques Du Langage. Moreau, Pierre–Francois.

Renuncia Al Derecho Y Dominación En Los Pactos Fundamentales De Hobbes. Brandt, Reinhard.

The Hobbesian Conception Of Sovereignty And Aristotle's Politics. Johnson, Curtis.

The Natural Body And The Body Politic. Bertman, Martin A.

Thomas Hobbes And The Philosophy Of Punishment. Norrie, Alan.

Whether Professional Associations May Enforce Professional Codes. Snapper, John W.

Zum Recht Des Naturzustandes Und Seiner Dedeutung Für Die Stellung Der Staatsgewalt Bei Thomas Hobbes. Gehrmann, Siegfried.

HOELDERLIN

"Dem Dichten Vor–Denken": Aspekte Von Heideggers "Zwiesprache" Mit Hölderlin Im Kontext Seiner Kunstphilosophie. Jamme, Christoph.

Hölderlin E La *Vereinigungsphilosophie*. Gargano, Antonio.

HOFSTADTER, D

Elbow Room: The Varieties Of Free Will Worth Wanting. Dennett, Daniel C.

HOHFELD, W

An Analysis Of Rights. Stoljar, Samuel.

HOHLFELD, R

Biotechnology And The Social Reconstruction Of Molecular Biology. Markle, Gerald E and Robin, Stanley S.

HOLBACH

Diderot Et D'Holbach: Un Système Matérialiste De La Nature. Boulad– Ayoub, Josiane.

HOLECKOVA, I

Programmatic Aesthetic Education From The Point Of View Of Social Psychology (in Czechoslovakian). Macková– Holecková, Iva.

HOLISM

Deeper Insights In Education: The Waldorf Approach. Steiner, Rudolf.

Against Holism. Weir, Alan.

Antropologische Geneeskunde In Discussie. Verwey, G.

Intentionality, Causality And Holism. Mohanty, J N.

Jan Christian Smuts And His Doctrine Of Holism. Brush, Francis W.

Reference, Anti–Realism, And Holism. Farrell, Frank B.

The Liberation Of Nature: A Circular Affair. Kheel, Marti.

The Schopenhauerian Challenge In Environmental Ethics. Varner, G E.

Theoretische Oberlegungen Zum Okoproblem. Bach, Hans.

HOLMES, O

American Political Thought: The Philosophic Dimension Of American Statesmanship, Second Edition. Frisch, Morton J (ed) and Stevens, Richard G (ed).

HOLOCAUST

Radical Humanism. Améry, Jean and Rosenfeld, Sidney (ed) and Rosenfeld, Stella (ed).

Christianity And The Final Solution. Reese, William L.

Hannah Arendt's View Of Totalitarianism And The Holocaust. Ezorsky, Gertrude.

Jewish Ethics After The Holocaust. Morgan, Michael L.

Measuring Responsibility. Bar– On, A Zvie.

Scepticism, Narrative, And Holocaust Ethics. Hallie, Philip P.

The Silence Of God. Roth, John K.

The Theological Implications Of The Holocaust. Schlesinger, George.

Tolerance And Evil: Teaching The Holocaust. Lang, Berel.

HOLT, R

"Ethics And Excuses: Ethical Implications Of Psychoanalysis" in *Darwin, Marx And Freud*, Caplan, Arthur L (ed), 201–208. Izenberg, Gerald N.

HOLYER, R

A Critique Of Holyer's Volitionalism. Pojman, Louis P.

HOME

Heidegger And Jacob Grimm: On Dwelling And The Genesis Of Language. Stohrer, Walter J.

The Provisional Homecomer. Jones, Funmilayo M.

HOMER

A L'origine De La Notion D'amour En Occident. Fredette, Gatien.

Faut–Il Raconter Homère Aux Enfants: Ou: Des Valeurs Aux Anti–Valeurs. Joly, Henri.

HOMOGENEITY

The Uniqueness Of Envelopes In $\aleph_0$–Categorical, $\aleph_0$–Stable Structures. Loveys, James.

HOMOMORPHISM(S)

The Strong Amalgamation Property For Complete Boolean Algebras. Monro, G P.

HONESTY

Creating A Candid Corporate Culture. Serpa, Roy.

HONOR

Liberty, Equality, Honor. Kristol, William.

Montaigne On War. Bonadeo, Alfredo.

HOPE

A Matter Of Hope: A Theologian's Reflections On The Thought Of Karl Marx. Lash, Nicholas.

"Human Nature And The Human Hope" in On Nature, Rouner, Leroy S (ed), 169–184. Bennett, John C.

Hope And Its Ramifications For Politics. Dauenhauer, Bernard P.

HORIZON(S)

Zum Problem Der Kehre Im Denken Heideggers. Rosales, Alberto.

HORKHEIMER, M

Adorno. Jay, Martin.

Justifying A Curriculum And Justifying An Institution. Gray, W N and Wyatt, J F.

La Formación De La Teoría Crítica De Max Horkheimer. Estrada Juan A.

HORNSBY, J

A Note On A Response Of Hornsby's. Lowe, E J.

HORWICH, P

Horwich's Justification Of Induction. Chihara, Charles S.

HOSPERS, J

ROBOTS, RIFs, And Rights. Arthur, Alcott.

HOSPITAL(S)

"Childhood Death And Medical Ethics" in Difficult Decisions In Medical Ethics, Ganos, Doreen L (ed), 173–188. Pernick, Martin S.

"Contrasting Review Boards With Ethics Committees" in Ethics Committees And Health Care Decisions, Cranford, Ronald (ed), 129–137. Glantz, Leonard H.

"Deception In The Teaching Hospital" in Difficult Decisions In Medical Ethics, Ganos, Doreen and others (eds), 81–86. Brody, Howard.

"Ethical Decisions In The Intensive Care Unit" in Difficult Decisions In Medical Ethics, Ganos, Doreen L (ed), 125–134. Jackson, David.

"Ethical Issues In The Intensive Care Unit: Case For Discussion" in Difficult Decisions In Medical Ethics, Ganos, Doreen L (ed), 107–110. Miller, Bruce.

"Medicolegal And Ethical Dilemmas In A Teaching Hospital" in Ethics Committees And Health Care Decisions, Cranford, Ronald (ed), 118–128. Grodin, Michael and Markley, William S and Mc Donald, Anne E.

"Truth Telling In Pediatrics–In Degrees" in Difficult Decisions In Medical Ethics, Ganos, Doreen L (ed), 189–194. O Connor, Patricia A.

Objections To Hospital Philosophers. Ruddick, William and Finn, William.

HOTTOIS, G

L'essence Double Du Langage Selon Gilbert Hottois. Dumoncel, Jean–Claude.

HRDY, S

Gathering Stories For Hunting Human Nature. Zihlman, Adrienne L.

HSUN TZU

Ethical Argumentation: A Study In Hsun Tzu's Moral Epistemology. Cua, A S.

Ethical Uses Of The Past In Early Confucianism: The Case Of Hsün Tzu. Cua, A S.

HUGHEN, R

The Constancy Of Kantian Time: Reflections On Chronobiology. Gunter, Pete A Y.

HUI–NENG

Hui–Neng And The Transcendental Standpoint. Laycock, Steven W.

HUIZINGA, J

A General Theory Of Sport Reality. Urbankowski, Bohdan.

HULL, C

"Drive": In Defense Of A Concept. Smith, Kendon.

Clark Hull, Robert Cummins, And Functional Analysis. Amundson, Ron and Smith, Laurence.

HULL, D

Against The Monism Of The Moment: A Reply To Elliott Sober. Kitcher, Philip.

HUMAN(S)

see also Man, Person(s)

Abortion And The Conscience Of The Nation. Reagan, Ronald.

An Apology For The Value Of Human Life. Thomasma, David C.

Human, All Too Human. Nietzsche, Fredrich and Faber, Marion (trans).

I–Man: An Outline Of Philosophical Anthropology. Krąpiec, Mieczylaw A and Lescoe, Marie (trans) and Woznicki, Theresa (trans).

Images Of Man. Umen, Samuel.

In Search Of Being: Man In Conflict With The Spectre Of Nothingness. De Carvalho, Manoel J.

Models Of Man: Explorations In The Western Educational Tradition. Nash, Paul.

Philosophy And Human Geography: An Introduction To Contemporary Approaches. Johnston, R J.

The Analysis Of Action. Von Cranach, Mario (ed) and Harre, Rom (ed).

The Humanist Evangel. Saumur, Lucien.

"Human Nature And The Human Hope" in On Nature, Rouner, Leroy S (ed), 169–184. Bennett, John C.

Algunas Preguntas Sobre Etica. Parent, Juan M.

Baby Fae: The "Anything Goes School Of Human Experimentation". Annas, George J.

Concepto De Historicidad En "Ser Y Tiempo de Martin Heidegger. Andrade, Ciro Schmidt.

Der Mensch Und Seine Sprache. Hennigfeld, Jochem.

El Hombre Pecador. Pozo, Candido.

Four Teleological Orders Of Human Action. Smith, Quentin.

Human Diversity And Salvation In Christ. Jantzen, Grace M.

In Defense Of The Dignity Of Being Human. Gaylin, Willard.

Karma And The Problem Of Suffering. Perrett, Roy W.

L'homme Créé Par Dieu: Le Fondement De La Dignité De L'homme. Schönborn, Christoph.

La Creatividad Humana. Granja, Dulce M.

On Behalf Of Moderate Speciesism. Holland, Alan F.

On The Captivity Of The Will: Sympathy, Caring, And A Moral Sense Of The Human. Sabini, John and Silver, Maury.

Should The Nazi Research Data Be Cited? Moe, Kristine.

The Definition Of Person. Teichman, Jenny.

The Ecological Perspective In John Dewey's Philosophy Of Education. Colwell, Tom.

The Marxian Conception Of Man. Tuchanska, Barbara.

The Original Preface. Lonergan, Bernard.

The Thermodynamic And Phylogenetic Foundations Of Human Wickedness. Mansani, P R.

Theses De Dignitate Necnon De Iuribus Personae Humanae. Commissio Theologica Internationalis.

Towards The Aesthetic: A Journey With Friedrich Schiller. Schaper, Eva.

Valor Y Valor Moral. Derisi, Octavio N.

HUMAN CONDITION

On History And Other Essays. Oakeshott, Michael.

Imprisonment. O' Hear, Anthony.

On Reading And Mis–Reading Hannah Arendt. Bernauer, James.

Politics, Nature And Freedom: On The Natural Foundation Of The Political Condition. Levy, David J.

The Human Predicament: A Context For Rights And Learning About Rights. Edwards, Philip.

Value And Human Condition. Sarin, Indu.

HUMAN DEVELOPMENT

Deeper Insights In Education: The Waldorf Approach. Steiner, Rudolf.

The Supreme Doctrine: Psychological Encounters In Zen Thought. Benoit, Hubert.

"Legislating Morality: Should Life Be Defined" in Defining Human Life, Shaw, Margery W (ed), 335–340. Callahan, Daniel and others.

The Filial Art. Rosenthal, Abigail L.

HUMAN EXISTENCE

God, Guilt, And Death: An Existential Phenomenology Of Religion. Westphal, Merold.

Nietzsche As Educator. Murphy, Timothy F.

Armonía En El Devenir: La Espontaneidad De La Vida Y La Autoindividuación. Tymieniecka, Anna–Teresa.

Historicity, Narratives, And The Understanding Of Human Life. Johnson, Galen A.

La Cuestión Del Sentido Y El Sentido De La Cuestión. Alfaro, Juan.

On The Experience Of Historical Objects. Harvey, Charles W.

The Situation Of Humanity As An Ethical Problem. Apel, Karl–Otto.

HUMAN NATURE

On Nature. Rouner, Leroy S (ed).

"Human Nature And Absolute Values" in The Good Life And Its Pursuit, Dougherty, Jude P (ed), 133–144. Russell, John L.

"Sociobiology, Epistemology, And Human Nature" in Methodology, Metaphysics And The History Of Science, Cohen, Robert S (ed), 215–234. Leeds, Anthony.

Anthropologie In Metaphysik–Distanz: E Rothacker Zum 10: Todestag. Bucher, Alexius.

Emotions Across Cultures: Objectivity And Cultural Divergence. Heelas, Paul.

Human Nature And Moral Theories. Kekes, John.

Morality And Human Nature. Lazari– Pawlowska, Ija.

Mutual Aid And Selfish Genes. Thompson, Janna L.

Nuclear Deterrence And World Peace. Hampsch, George.

On The Experience Of Historical Objects. Harvey, Charles W.

On The Philosophical Foundations Of The Conception Of Human Rights. Rosenbaum, Alan S.

Radical Freedom. Reinhardt, Lloyd.

Several Issues Concerning The Theory Of Human Beings. Tongsen, Huang.

Spinoza's Ethical Doctrine And The Unity Of Human Nature. Steinberg, Diane.

The Concept Of Human Nature In The Huai Nan Tzu. Roth, H D.

The Natural, The Social, And Historical Materialism. Soble, Alan.

The Sociobiological View Of Man. Trigg, Roger.

HUMAN RELATIONS

On History And Other Essays. Oakeshott, Michael.

El Capítulo B De La Crítica De La Razón Dialéctica. Verstraeten, Pierre.

Organizational Dissidence: The Case Of Whistle–Blowing. Near, Janet P and Miceli, Marcia P.

Situating The Employee Rights Debate. Kirby, Donald.

HUMAN RIGHTS

Creeds, Society, And Human Rights: A Study In Three Cultures. Stackhouse, Max L.

Human Rights In Religious Traditions. Swidler, Arlene (ed).

"Human Rights Not Founded On Sex" in Freedom, Feminism, And The State, Mc Elroy, Wendy (ed), 29–34. Grimké, Angelina.

HUMAN RIGHTS

Autonomy And Human Rights Claims. Gough, Jim.

Conceptos Indeterminados, Derechos Humanos Y Seguridad Nacional. Haba, Enrique P.

Contemporary Reinterpretations Of The Concept Of Human Rights (in Hebrew) . Sidorsky, David.

De Dignitate Et Jure Hominis Status Quaestionis In "Tertio Mundo" (in English). Onaiyekan, John.

Human Rights And U S Foreign Policy: Models And Options. Galloway, Jonathan F.

Human Rights And International Finance: A Synthetical Overview. Khoshkish, A.

L'Église Et Les Droits De L'homme: Jalons D'histoire. Hamel, Edouard.

Menschenwürde Und Menschenrechte Im Light Der "Offenbarung Jesu Christi". Schürmann, Heinz.

Menschenwürde Und Menschenrechte Im Licht Der Reich–Gottes–Verkündigung Jesu. Schönborn, Christoph.

On The Philosophical Foundations Of The Conception Of Human Rights. Rosenbaum, Alan S.

Peace, Human Rights, And Human Needs: A Comment On The Bay–Flathman Debate. Carens, Joseph H.

Protection Of Human Rights And Public Interest In Nuclear Development. Menon, N R M.

The Concept Of Equal Opportunity. Westen, Peter.

The Dignity And Rights Of The Human Person As Saved, As Being Saved, As To Be Saved By Christ. Principe, Walter.

The Human Right To Be Treated As A Person. Khatchadourian, Haig.

The Human Rights Of Women In Islam. Talhami, Ghada.

The Right To Strike And The Right To Work. Smart, Brian.

Toward A Foundation For Human Rights. Khatchadourian, Haig.

Why There Are No Human Rights. Husak, Douglas N.

HUMAN SCIENCES

The Intellectual And Social Organization Of The Sciences. Whitley, Richard.

"Soviet Philosophical Anthropology And The Foundations Of Human Sciences" in *Contemporary Marxism*, O' Rourke, James J (ed), 167–174. O' Rourke, James J.

Human Sociobiology: A Philosophical Perspective. Ruse, Michael.

On The Origin Of 'Phenomenological' Sociology. Srubar, Ilja.

Questionnaire On Philosophy. Lonergan, Bernard.

HUMANISM

A Christian Humanism: Karol Wojtyla's Existential Personalism. Woznicki, Andrew N.

Esthetic Qualities And Values In Literature: A Humanistic And A Biometric Appraisal. Bresky, Dushan and Malik, Miroslav.

Foundations Of Humanism. Van Praag, J P.

Irving Babbitt: An Intellectual Study. Nevin, Thomas R.

Radical Humanism. Améry, Jean and Rosenfeld, Sidney (ed) and Rosenfeld, Stella (ed).

The Humanist Evangel. Saumur, Lucien.

The State And I: Hypotheses On Juridical And Technocratic Humanism. Lock, Grahame.

"Humanismus" Und "Tradition" Themen Der Gegenwärtigen Bürgerlichen Philosophie Im Subsaharischen Afrika. Hoffmann, G R.

"Humanistic Interpretation And Historical Materialism: (poznan School))" in *Contemporary Marxism*, O' Rourke, James J (ed), 97–108. Swiderski, Edward M.

A Defense Of Humanism. Ruoshui, Wang.

Deconstruction Is Not Enough: On Gianni Vattimo's Call For "Weak Thinking". Schürmann, Reiner.

Felix Adler: Artist Of The Ideal Good. Hemstreet, Robert M.

Gedanken Zum Sozialistischen Humanismus Als Anspruch An Individuum Und Gesellschaft. Erfurth, Andrea.

Gedanken Zum Begriff Und Zur Geschichte Des Humanismus. Seidel, Helmut.

Homo, Humanus, And The Meanings Of "Humanism". Giustiniani, Vito R.

Humanismo De Samuel Ramos. Posadas, Ofelia E.

Humanismus–Antihumanismus In Den Geistigen Auseinandersetzungen Unserer Zeit. Gerlach, H M.

Marx' Kulturkonzeption In "Grundrisse Der Kritik Der Politischen Ökonomie": Zugleich Ein Programm Des Realen Humanismus. Kahle, Werner.

Military Power And Human Values. Frank, Willard C.

Rantzau And Welser: Aspects Of Later German Humanism. Evans, R J W.

Scientific Socialism And The Question Of Socialist Values. Collier, Andrew.

Sozialismus–Humanismus–Toleranz. Wrona, Vera.

Sozialistischer Humanismus–Sozialistischer Realismus. John, Erhard.

Symposium On Humanism, Secularism, And Religion. Tonne, Herbert A and Eddy, Robert M and Wilson, Edwin H.

The Human Basis Of Laws And Ethics. Edwords, Frederick.

The Humanism Of Associated Work And The Problem Of The Technology Laws (in German). Jacobs, Hans–Jürgen and Herlitzius, Erwin.

The Religious Humanism Of The Future. Arisian, Khoren.

The Religious Humanism Of The Future. Arisian, Khoren.

To Be A Person. Kolenda, Konstantin.

Umanesimo E Teologia Nel Cusano "Disgiunzione" E "Metafora". Camporeale, Salvatore I.

Zum Humanismus In Der Klassischen Deutschen Philosophie, Seinen Sozialhistorischen Und Theoretischen Voraussetzungen. Biedermann, Georg and Lange, E.

HUMANITARIANISM

Gegen "Humanitarismus" Und "Illusionen Der Brüderlichkeit". Elm, Ludwig.

HUMANITIES

Symposium: Knowledge And The Humanities–The Continuing Debate. Brinton, Crane and others.

The Humanities In Medical Education: Entering The Post–Evangelical Era. Pellegrino, Edmund D.

The Scientific Destruction Of Humanity And The Educational Project Of The Humanities. Lawler, Peter A.

HUMANITY

The Moral Order: An Introduction To The Human Situation. Naroll, Raoul.

El Progreso Según Juan Bautista Vico. Dondi, J.

Human Embodiment: The Theme And The Encounter In Vedāntic Phenomenology. Sinha, Debabrata.

Man, Science, Morality. Anguelov, Stephan.

Marx–Anthropology And Praxis. Panasiuk, Ryszard.

Metaphysical Fall–Out From The Nuclear Predicament. Routley, Richard.

On Confucian Jen And Heideggerian Being (II) (in Chinese). Chern, Jiunn–Huei.

Over De Menselijkheid Van Vroege Hominidae. Corbey, R.

Peaceful Coexistence As The Nuclear Traumatization Of Humanity. Butler, Clark.

Thinking Ahead. Kolenda, Konstantin.

Umanità. Villa, Luigi.

HUMANIZATION

"From Then To Now: Perinatal Intensive Care" in *Bioethical Frontiers In Perinatal Intensive Care*, Snowden, Fraser (ed), 19–38. Francoeur, Robert T.

The Role Of Marxist–Leninist Philosophy In The Process Of The Humanisation Of Science (in Czechoslovakian). Machleidtova, S.

HUMANNESS

Man And Machine. Bandyopadhyay, Tirhanath.

Prudence And Folly. Rotenstreich, Nathan.

Who Counts? Smith, David H.

HUME

A Dissertation On Miracles. Campbell, George.

Beauty Restored. Mothersill, Mary.

Creativity In American Philosophy. Hartshorne, Charles.

God And Natural Evil. Jooharigian, Robert Badrik.

Hume's Philosophy Of Common Life. Livingston, Donald W.

The Central Problem Of David Hume's Philosophy. Salmon, C V.

The Moral Psychology Of The Virtues. Dent, N J H.

The Nature Of Social Laws: Machiavelli To Mill. Brown, Robert.

The Worlds Of Hume And Kant. Wilbur, James B (ed) and Allen, H J (ed).

Wealth And Virtue: The Shaping Of Political Economy In The Scottish Enlightenment. Hont, Istvan (ed) and Ignatieff, Michael (ed).

"Another Volley At Kant's Reply To Hume" in *Kant On Causality, Freedom, And Objectivity*, Harper, William A (ed), 42–57. Van Cleve, James.

"Berkeley And Hume: A Question Of Influence" in *Philosophy In History*, Rorty, Richard and others (ed), 303–328. Ayers, Michael.

"Observations, Explanatory Power, Simplicity" in *Observation, Experiment, Hypothesis In Physical Science*, Achinstein, Peter (ed), 45–94. Boyd, Richard N.

"Seven Thinkers And How They Grew" in *Philosophy In History*, Rorty, Richard and others (ed), 125–140. Kuklick, Bruce.

A Reasonable Reply To Hume's Scepticism. Schlagel, Richard H.

A Study In The Arguments From Theology With Reference To Hume And Samkara. Kar, Bijayananda.

Analogical Inference In Hume's Philosophy Of Religion. Jacquette, Dale.

Causation And Induction. Fales, Evan.

Causes, Causity, And Energy. Castañeda, Hector–Neri.

Civility And Society. Kekes, John.

Corrections Regarding "Hume's 'Two Definitions' Of Cause And The Ontology Of 'Double Existence'". Russell, Paul.

David Hume And Eighteenth Century Monetary Thought: A Critical Comment On Recent Views. Rashid, Salim.

De Wiskundige Rede (Summary: The Mathematical Reason). Klever, W N A.

Did Peirce Answer Hume On Necessary Connection? Roth, Robert J.

How To Become A Moderate Skeptic: Hume's Way Out Of Pyrrhonism. Michaud, Yves.

Hume And Cognitive Science. Biro, J I.

Hume And Edwards On 'Why Is There Something Rather Than Nothing'? Burke, Michael B.

Hume And The Missing Shade Of Blue. Fogelin, Robert J.

Hume And The Relation Of Science To Religion Among Certain Members Of The Royal Society. Force, James E.

Hume On Causal Necessity: A Study From The Perspective Of Hume's Theory Of Passions. Enc, Berent.

Hume On Finding An Impression Of The Self. Traiger, Saul.

Hume On Morality, Action, And Character. Davie, William.

Hume On Perceptions And Persons. Davie, William E.

Hume On The Cartesian Theory Of Substance. Glass, Ronald J and Flage, Daniel E.

Hume On The Perception Of Causality. Shanks, David R.

Hume On The 'Distinction Of Reason'. Bracken, Harry M.

Hume Was Right, Almost; And Where He Wasn't, Kant Was. Shwayder, D S.

Hume, Animals And The Objectivity Of Morals. Clark, Stephen.

Hume, Demonstratives, And Self–Ascriptions Of Identity. Ward, Andrew.

Hume, Language And God. Soles, Deborah Hansen.

Hume's *Treatise* And Hobbe's *The Elements Of Law*. Russell, Paul.

Hume's "Dialectic". Coleman, Dorothy P.

Hume's Bundle Theory Of The Mind. Brooks, D.

Hume's Criterion Of Significance. Williams, Michael.

Hume's Dialogue IX Defended. Stahl, Donald E.

Hume's Final Argument. Priest, Graham.

Hume's Labyrinth. Behan, David P.

Hume's Missing Shade Of Blue, Interpreted As Involving Habitual Spectra. Johnson,

HUME

David M.

Hume's Moral Enquiry: An Analysis Of Its Catalogue. Vodraska, Stanley L.

Hume's Natural History Of Religion: Positive Science Or Metaphysical Vision Of Religion. Badia Cabrera, Miguel A.

Hume's Naturalism—'Proof' And Practice. Ferreira, M J.

Hume's Second Enquiry: Ethics As Natural Science. Hughes, R I G.

Hume's Standard Of Taste. Carroll, Noel.

Hutcheson, Hume And The Ontology Of Morals. Stafford, J Martin.

Hutcheson's Alleged Realism. Winkler, Kenneth P.

Ideology And Partiality In David Hume's "History Of England". Okie, Laird.

In Praise Of Anthropomorphism. Ferré, Frederick.

Is Hume A Sceptic With Regard To Reason? Wilson, Fred.

Is The Causal Structure Of The Physical Itself Something Physical? Putnam, Hilary.

Le Problème De L'analyticité Et Le Statut Des Mathématiques Chez Hume. Spitz, Jean–Fabien.

Miracfles And Rival Systems Of Religion. Langtry, Bruce.

Moral Skepticism And International Relations. Cohen, Marshall.

Necessity In Kant: Subjective And Objective. Larson, David T.

On The Status Of Statistical Inferences. Pitowsky, Itamar.

On Two Meanings Of Good And The Foundations Of Ethics In Aristotle And St Thomas. Flippen, Douglas.

Other Problems About The Self. Theron, Stephen.

Paul Russell On Hume's 'Reconciling Project'. Flew, Anthony.

Philo's Reversal. Austin, William H.

The Complexity Of Quality. Westphal, Jonathan.

The Criteria Of Objectivity: Physical Science And The Challenge Of Phenomenology. Smitheram, Verner.

The Hume Literature Of The 1970's. Capaldi, Nicholas and King, James and Livingston, Donald.

The Humean Obstacle To Evidential Arguments From Suffering: On Avoiding The Evils Of "Appearance". Wykstra, Stephen J.

The Origins Of Hume's Sceptical Argument Against Reason. Wilson, Fred.

The Problem Of Induction. Czezowski, Tadeusz.

Theism And The Rationale Of Hume's Skepticism About Causation. Livingston, Donald.

Two Conceptions Of The Self. Piper, Adrian M S.

Verità Delle Azioni: Sul Fraintendimento Humiano Di W Wollaston. Paolinelli, Marco.

Veritas Filia Temporis: Hume On Time And Causation. Lennon, Thomas M.

Vindicating The "Principle Of Relative Likelihood". Chrzan, Keith.

Welfare State Versus Welfare Society? Skillen, Anthony.

Why Be Just: Hume's Response In The *Inquiry*. Costa, Michael J.

HUMOR

Recherches Et Réflexions Sur Le Rire Le Risible, Le Comique Et L'humour. Fourastié, M Jean and others.

The Philosopher As Teacher, Humor And Philosophy. Morreall, John.

HUNGARIAN

Main Lines In The Hungarian Philosophy From The 1848/49 War Of Independence To The Compromise Of 1867 (in Hungarian). Kiss, Endre.

The Possibility And Reality Of Self–Concious Work (in Hungarian). Szabó, Márton.

Two Experiments On The History Of Hungarian School Philosophy Between The Two World Wars (in Hungarian). Galicza, Peter.

HUNTER, D

Circumstances And Dominance In A Causal Decision Theory. Sobel, Jordan Howard.

HUSSERL

Husserl And Realism In Logic And Mathematics. Tragesser, Robert S.

Il Fenomeno Dell'essere: Fenomenologia E Ontologia In Heidegger. Esposito, Constantino.

Language And Experience: Descriptions Of Living Language In Husserl And Wittgenstein. Reeder, Harry P.

Logic And The Objectivity Of Knowledge: Studies In Husserl's Early Philosophy. Willard, Dallas.

Phenomenology And Existentialism: An Introduction. Grossman, Reinhardt.

The Search For An Alternative: Philosophical Perspectives Of Subjectivism And Marxism. Farber, Marvin.

" interesting Questions' In The History Of Philosophy Elsewhere" in *Philosophy In History*, Rorty, Richard and others (ed), 141–172. Lepenies, Wolf.

A Phenomenological Account Of The Linguistic Mediation Of The Public And The Private. Reeder, Harry P.

Acerca Del Programa De Fenomenologia. Presas, Mario A.

Against Idealism: Johannes Daubert Vs Husserl's *Ideas* I. Schuhmann, Karl and Smith, Barry.

An Analytic–Existential Solution To The 'Knowing That One Knows' Problem. Johnson, Steve A.

An Infinite Time Of One's Own. Lingis, Alphonso F.

Assertion And Predication In Husserl. Pietersma, H.

Being–In–Itself Revisited. Holmes, Richard.

Can Heidegger Be Depicted As A Phenomenologist? Pavlich, G.

De Filosofie Van Dooyeweerd. De Boer, Th.

De La Sensibilité. Levinas, E.

Fichte's Und Husserl's Critique Of Kant's Transcendental Deduction. Seebohm, Thomas M.

Functional Method And Phenomenology: The View Of Niklas Luhmann. Bednarz Jr, John.

Habitualität Als Potentialität: Zur Konkretisierung Des Ich Bei Husserl. Bergmann, Werner and Hoffmann, G.

Husserl And Hegel: A Historical And Religious Encounter. Kirkland, Frank M.

Husserl's Communal Spirit: A Phenomenological Study Of The Fundamental Structure Of Society. Allen, Jeffner.

Husserl's Concept Of World (in Chinese). Chan, Wing–Wah.

Husserl's Platonism And The Objective Truth (in Hungarian). Rozsnyai, Ervin.

Imagination Als Komplexakt (in Japanese). Kanata, Susumu.

J S Beck And Husserl: The New Episteme In The Kantian Tradition. Wallner, Ingrid M.

Le Problème De La Logique Pure: De Husserl À Une Nouvelle Position Phénoménologique. Richir, Mare.

On Macintyre, Rationality, And Dramatic Space. Monasterio, Xavier O.

On Marxian Epistemology And Phenomenology. Rockmore, Tom.

Perceptual Meaning And Husserl. Cunningham, Suzanne.

Perceptual Reference. Miller, Izchak.

Philosophical Anthropology: Revolt Against The Division Of Intellectual Labor. Wiggins, Osborne.

Schlick's Critique Of Phenomenological Propositions. Van De Pitte, M M.

Schröder–Husserl–Scheler: Zur Formalen Logik. Willer, Jörg.

Surrender–And–Catch And Phenomenology. Wolff, Kurt H.

The Apodicticity Of Recollection. Husserl, Edmund and Chaffin, D (trans).

The Concept Of Crisis And The Unity Of Husserl's Position. Rockmore, Tom.

The Criteria Of Objectivity: Physical Science And The Challenge Of Phenomenology. Smitheram, Verner.

The Hermeneutics Of Suspicion. Gadamer, Hans–Georg.

The Notion Of Mathematical Intuition And Husserl's Phenomenology. Tieszen, Richard.

The Roots Of The Existentialist Theory Of Freedom In *Ideas I*. Edie, James M.

The World According To Husserl. Holmes, Richard.

Towards A Computational Phenomenology (1). Harlan, Robert M.

Type And Eidos—Schutz And Husserl. Pritchard, Colin W.

Van Wezensschouw Naar Hermeneuse. De Boer, Th.

Zwischen Einsamkeit Und Wechselrede: Zur Kommunikation Und Ihrer Konstitution Bei Edmund Husserl. Knoblauch, Hubert.

HUTCHESON, F

Hutcheson, Hume And The Ontology Of Morals. Stafford, J Martin.

Hutcheson's Alleged Realism. Winkler, Kenneth P.

Hutcheson's Moral Realism. Norton, David F.

O Moralismo Escocês Do Séc XVIII E A Concepção De Liberdade No Kant Pré–Critíco. Martins, Estevao De Rezende.

HUXLEY

Buddhism In Huxley's Evolution And Ethics. Rajapakse, Vijitha.

HUYGHENS

Optique, Méchanique Et Calcul Des Chances Chez Huygens Et Spinoza (Sur Quelques Paradigmes Possibles Du Discours Philosophique). Parrochia, Daniel.

HYLAND, D

The Tyranny Of Scholarship. Levine, David L.

HYLOMORPHISM

Hilemorfismo Y Corporalidad. Bolzán, J E.

HYPOSTASES

Epistemic Analysis: A Coherence Theory Of Knowledge. Ziff, Paul.

HYPOTHESIS(–SES)

"Good And Bad Arguments Against Historicism" in *Popper And The Human Sciences*, Currie, Gregory (ed), 133–146. Urbach, Peter.

"Method Of Hypothesis" in *Observation, Experiment, And Hypothesis In Modern Physical Science*, Achinstein, Peter (ed), 127–146. Achinstein, Peter.

Free From Sin: On Living With Ad Hoc Hypotheses. Wettersten, John.

Hypotheses And Historical Analysis In Durkheim's Sociological Methodology: A Comtean Tradition. Schmaus, Warren.

Hypothetical Method And Rationality In Plato. Scolnicov, S.

Recollection And The Argument 'From A Hypothesis' In Plato's *Meno*. Bedu– Addo, J T.

HYPOTHETICAL(S)

Parsing 'If'–Sentences. Dudman, V H.

HYPOTHETICAL IMPERATIVE

The Hypothetical Imperative. Downie, R S.

HYPOTHETICO–DEDUCTIVE

Observation, Experiment, And Hypothesis In Modern Physical Science. Achinstein, Peter (ed) and Hannaway, Owen (ed).

"Logic And The Hypothetical–Deductive Method" in *Philosophical Analysis In Latin America*, Gracia, Jorge J E and others (eds), 73–92. Klimovsky, Gregorio.

Die Induktive Methode Und Das Induktionsproblem In Der Griechischen Philosophie. Tsouyopoulos, Nelly.

Justification As Discoverability II. Nickles, Thomas.

I

Philosophy In Process, V8. Weiss, Paul.

The Unknowable: An Ontological Introduction To The Philosophy Of Religion. Frank, S L.

A Comment On Performative, Subject, And Proposition In Habermas's Theory Of Communication. Skjei, Erling.

Habitualität Als Potentialität: Zur Konkretisierung Des Ich Bei Husserl. Bergmann, Werner and Hoffmann, G.

Other Problems About The Self. Theron, Stephen.

Reply To Skjei's "A Comment On Performative, Subject, And Proposition In Habermas's Theory Of Communication". Habermas, Jurgen.

I–THOU

Martin Buber: A Centenary Volume. Gordon, Haim (ed) and Bloch, Jochanan (ed).

I-THOU

Martin Buber's Life And Work: The Later Years, 1945–1965. Friedman, Maurice.

"A Critical Review Of Martin Buber's Epistemology Of I–Thou" in *Martin Buber*, Gordon, Haim (ed), 89–120. Katz, Steven.

"Ferdinand Ebner As A Source Of Buber's Dialogic Thought In *I And Thou*" in *Martin Buber*, Gordon, Haim (ed), 121–138. Horwitz, Rivka.

"Franz Rosenzweig's Criticism Of Buber's *I And Thou*" in *Martin Buber*, Gordon, Haim (ed), 139–162. Casper, Bernhard.

"Summary Of The Buber Centenary Conference At Ben–Gurion University In January 1978" in *Martin Buber*, Gordon, Haim (ed), 473–484. Rotenstreich, Nathan.

"The Finite Thou And The Eternal Thou In The Work Of Buber" in *Martin Buber*, Gordon, Haim (ed), 69–88. Amir, Yehoshua.

"The Justification And The Futility Of Dialogical Thinking" in *Martin Buber*, Gordon, Haim (ed), 43–68. Bloch, Yochanan.

The Premises Of Four Moral Conceptions: Classical, Modern, Totalitarian, And Utopian. Wilkie, Raymond.

IDEA(S)

see also Concept(s)

Hume's Philosophy Of Common Life. Livingston, Donald W.

Laws Of The Game: How The Principles Of Nature Govern Chance. Eigen, Manfred and Winkler, Ruthild.

Leibniz And Locke: A Study Of The "New Essays On Human Understanding". Jolley, Nicholas.

Logick: Or, The Right Use Of Reason. Watts, Isaac and Schouls, Peter A (ed).

The History Of Ideas. King, Preston (ed).

A Functionalist Interpretation Of Locke's Theory Of Simple Ideas. Vinci, Thomas.

Cultural Epochs And Their Predominant Ideas (in Czechoslovakian). Steindl, Rudolf.

El Triángulo Universal De Locke: Su Inmerecida Fama. Angelelli, Ignacio.

Hegel Und Die Aufklärung: Oder: Vom Versuch, Den Verstand Zur Vernunft Zu Bringen. Hasler, Ludwig

Hume And The Missing Shade Of Blue. Fogelin, Robert J.

Idea, Esquema E Imaginación En Kant. Ferreres, Jose M Rubio.

Locke's Empiricism And The Postulation Of Unobservables. Soles, David E.

Locke's Real Ideas, And Dr Woolhouse. Helm, Paul.

Svaraj In Ideas: Some Reflections. Goel, Dharmendra.

Svaraj Of India. Gandhi, Ramchandra.

The Indian Tradition And Our Intellectual Task. Shah, K J.

The Intelligibility Of The World And The Divine Ideas In Aquinas. Jordan, Mark D.

The Logical Structure Of Freud's Idea Of The Unconscious: Toward A Psychology Of Ideas. Fisher, Harwood.

The Problem Of Divine Exemplarity In St Thomas. Farthing, John L.

Wyclef's Philosophy And Platonic Ideas (in Czechoslovakian). Herold, Vilém.

IDEAL(S)

Ideal And Non–Ideal Theory: How Should We Approach Questions Of Global Justice. Nielsen, Kai.

Idempotent Ideals On Abelian Groups. Pelc, Andrzej.

Kant's Transcendental Ideal—II. O' Farrell, Frank.

La Idea Hegeliana De Materia Y El Tránsito De Lo Ideal A Lo Real. Albizu, Edgardo.

Moral Rules And Moral Ideals: A Useful Distinction In Business And Professional Practice. Hennessey, John W and Gert, Bernard.

Nicolai Hartmann's Doctrine Of Ideal Values: An Examination. Kraenzel, Frederick.

Regular Ideals And Boolean Pairs. Heindorf, Lutz.

Truth And Reflection. Yablo, Stephen.

IDEAL OBSERVER

Walden Two And Skinner's Ideal Observer. Mc Gray, James W.

IDEALISM

An Outline Of The Idealistic Construction Of Experience. Baillie, J B.

Berkeley. Pitcher, George and Honderich, Ted (ed).

From Hegel To Nietzsche. Lowith, Karl.

La Gnoseologia Di George E Moore. Borioni, Marco.

Studies In Hegelian Cosmology. Mc Taggart, John M and Harris, H S (ed).

The Magdalen Metaphysicals: Idealism And Orthodoxy At Oxford, 1901–1945. Patrick, James.

The Philosophy Of F W J Schelling: History, System, And Freedom. Marx, Werner and Nenon, Thomas (trans).

The Significance Of Philosophical Scepticism. Stroud, Barry.

"An Idea Can Be Like Nothing But An Idea". Dicker, Georges.

"Kant's Transcendental Idealism" in *Kant On Causality, Freedom, And Objectivity*, Harper, William A (ed), 83–96. Walsh, W H.

"Moore's Rejection Of Idealism" in *Philosophy In History*, Rorty, Richard and others (ed), 357–374. Baldwin, Thomas.

"The Nature Of The Proposition And The Revolt Against Idealism" in *Philosophy In History*, Rorty, Richard and others (ed), 375–398. Hylton, Peter.

"The Rational Idealism" Of Modern Times And The Idealistic Criticism Of Religion (in Czechoslovakian). Lesko, Vladimir.

"Wittgenstein And Philosophy Of Religion" in *History Of Philosophy In The Making*, Thro, Linus J (ed), 275–298. Punzo, Vincent C.

A Defense Of Kant's Refutation Of Descartes. Shirley, Edward S.

Adhering To Inherence: A New Look At The Old Steps In Berkeley's March To Idealism. Hausman, Alan.

Against Idealism: Johannes Daubert Vs Husserl's *Ideas* I. Schuhmann, Karl and Smith, Barry.

Antonio Gramsci's Reformulation Of Benedetto Croce's Speculative Idealism. Kahn, Beverly L.

British Idealism: Its Political And Social Thought. Simchoni, Avital.

Das Verhältnis Der *Kritik Der Reinen Vernunft* Zu Den *Metaphysischen Anfangsgründen Der Naturwissenschaft*, Demonstr Am Substanzsatz.* Gloy, Karen.

Die Bedeutung Der Freiheitsproblematik Für Kants Übergang Zum Transzendentalismus. Thom, Martina.

Fichte's Idealism In Theory And Practice. Mandt, A J.

German Idealism, Greek Materialism, And The Young Karl Marx. Baronovitch, Laurence.

Hegel And The Emerging World: The Jena Lectures On Naturphilosophie (1805–06). Rauch, Leo.

Hegel Oder Schelling Als Autor Eines Zwei–Seiten–Papiers? Beyer, Wilhelm.

Hegel's Critique Of Kant's Theoretical Philosophy. Ameriks, Karl.

Hermeneutic Hegelianism. Butler, Clark.

How To Be An Idealist (II). Mc Fee, Graham.

John Paul The Second Anthropology Of Concrete Totality. Min, Anselm K.

Marxian Epistemology And Two Kinds Of Pragmatism. Rockmore, Tom.

Non–Human Rights: An Idealist Perspective. Sprigge, T L S.

Objectless Activity: Marx's 'Theses On Feuerbach'. Giles–Peters, A.

Peirce's Doubts About Idealism. Meyers, Robert G.

Phenomenalism, Idealism And Mentalism: A Historical Note. Gupta, R K.

Rules And Relevance: The Au–Ru Equivalence Issue. Lennon, Thomas M.

Schelling Als Verfasser Der "Nachtwachen" Des Bonaventura. Gulyga, Arseni.

Schelling Und Hegel In Jena. Biedermann, Georg.

Schellings Weltalter Und Die Ausstehende Vollendung Des Deutschen Idealismus. Oesterreich, Peter Lothar.

Synthesis And Transcendental Idealism. Walker, Ralph S.

Théorie Et Vérité: La Réflexion Contemporaine Face À Ses Origines Grecques Et Idéalistes. Grondin, Jean.

The Metaphysics Of T H Green. Hylton, Peter.

The Place Of Process Cosmology In Absolute Idealism. Butler, Clark.

The Second Edition Of The Critique: Toward An Understanding Of Its Nature And Genesis. Washburn, M C.

The Separation Of Ontological Idealism From Epistemological Idealism (in Hungarian). Petho, Bertalan.

Transcendental Idealism In Wittgenstein And Theories Of Meaning. Moore, A W.

Zur Sowjetphilosophischen Kritik Der "Idealistischen" Erkenntnistheorie. Weinzierl, Emil.

IDEALIZATION

"Idealizations And Testing Of Theories" in *Observation, Experiment, Hypothesis In Modern Physical Science*, Achinstein, Peter (ed), 147–174. Laymon, Ronald.

Galilean Idealization. Mc Mullin, Ernan.

IDENTIFIABILITY

A Note On Referent Identifiability And Co–presence. Hawkins, John A.

IDENTIFICATION

The Origins And Functions Of Evaluative Criteria. Sadler, Royce D.

IDENTITY

see also Personal Identity

Bruno. Schelling, F W J and Vater, Michael G (ed).

Language, Thought, And Other Biological Categories: New Foundations For Realism. Millikan, Ruth Garret.

Leibniz And Locke: A Study Of The "New Essays On Human Understanding". Jolley, Nicholas.

"Hegel On Identity And Legitimation" in *The State And Civil Society*, Pelczynski, Z A (ed), 227–243. Plant, Raymond.

"Predication, Truth, And Transworld Identity In Leibniz" in *How Things Are*, Bogen, James (ed), 235–284. Adams, Robert M.

A Decidable Subclass Of The Minimal Gödel Class With Identity. Goldfarb, Warren D and Gurevich, Yuri and Shelah, Saharon.

A Note On Objective Identity And Diversity (Part III, Chapter I, Section VII). Cowan, Denis.

Ackerman On Propositional Identity. Bertolet, Rod.

An Investigation On The Philosophical Problem Of Identity On The Basis Of The Kantian And Hegelian Concept Of It (in Hungarian). Tagai, Imbre.

Brody's Essentialism. Griffin, Nicholas.

Can My Survival Be Subrogated? Cherry, Christopher.

Causation And Identity. Swoyer, Chris.

Child Adoption And Identity. Griffiths, A Phillips.

DFC–Algorithms For Suszko, Logic SCI And One–to–one Gentzen Type Formalizations. Wasilewska, Anita.

Der Grundgedanke Des Tractatus Als Metamorphose Des Obersten Grundsatzes Der Kritik Der Reinen Vernunft. Ferber, Rafael.

Derek Parfit And Greta Garbo. Madell, Geoffrey.

Dialektik Von Individuum Und Gesellschaft Als Dialektik Von Persönlicher Und Sozialer Indentität. Wetzel, Manfred.

El Ser En El "Sistema De Identidad" Según Gustav Siewerth (Segunda Parte). Corona, Nester A.

Explaining Masochism. Warren, Virginia L.

Identity And Immaterialism. Reid, G J.

Identity, Appearances, And Things In Themselves. Bencivenga, Ermanno.

Identity, Intensionality, And Intentionality. Toberlin, James.

Identity: Criteria Vs Necessary And Sufficient Conditions. Ward, David V.

Inquiry, Intrinsic Properties, And The Identity Of Indiscernibles. Hoy, Ronald C.

Jugend–Idole Und Identitätsbildung. Tafertshofer, Alois.

Kleist. Mondadori, Fabrizio.

Lässt Sich Eine Kernlogik Konstituieren: Ein Versuch Dazu Vom Standpunkt Des Pankritischen Rationalismus Aus. Klowski, Joachim.

Leibniz And The Doctrine Of Inter–World Identity. Mondadori, Fabrizio.

Material Identity And Sameness. Swindler, J K.

INDUSTRY

Myths And Misconceptions About Drug Industry Ethics. Spilker, Bert.

The New Technologies Of Genetic Screening. Lappé, Marc and Murray, Thomas H.

Zur Dialektik Des Vergesellschaftungsprozesses In Der Sozialistischen Industrie Der DDR. Braun, Hans–Joachim and Dorschel, E.

INEQUALITY

De La Société Civile À L'État: L'irruption De L'inégalité. Giroux, France.

Rousseau On The Fall Of Social Man. Skillen, Anthony.

What (If Anything) Is Intrinsically Wrong With Capitalism? Van Parijs, Philippe.

INEVITABILITY

Deliberating About The Inevitable. Waller, Bruce N.

INFALLIBILITY

Credulism. Kvanvig, Jonathan L.

Knowledge And Intellectual Virtue. Sosa, Ernest.

INFANT(S)

Bioethical Frontiers In Perinatal Intensive Care. Snowden, Fraser (ed) and Harris, Chandice C (ed).

Reproductive Ethics. Bayles, Michael D.

"A Transcultural Perspective On Perinatal Health Care" in *Bioethical Frontiers In Perinatal Intensive Care,* Snowden, Fraser (ed), 39–58. Clausen, Joy P.

A Public Policy Option On The Treatment Of Severly Handicapped Newborns. Walter, James J.

In The Interest Of Infants. Mahowald, Mary B.

John T Noonan And Baby Jane Doe. Levin, David S.

Non–Medical Burdens Of The Defective Infant. Jones, Gary E.

Some Moral Problems Of The Damaged Neonate. Hoaglund, John.

The Neonatologist's Duty To Patient And Parents. Strong, Carson.

INFANTICIDE

Reconsidering The Ethics Of Infanticide. Warren, Mary Anne.

Rosponse To Mary Anne Warren's "Reconsidering The Ethics Of Infanticide" Tooley, Michael.

INFERENCE(S)

Basic Reasoning. Mackinnon, Edward.

Epicurus' Scientific Method. Asmis, Elizabeth.

Logica Parva, Alan R Perreiah (trans). Venetus, Paulus.

Peirce: Textes Anticartésiens. Chenu, Joseph.

Treatise On Basic Philosophy, V5. Bunge, Mario.

"Subjectivity In Psychoanalytic Inference" in *Testing Scientific Theories,* Earman, John (ed), 349–412. Meehl, Paul E.

A Problem About Frequencies In Direct Inference. Leeds, Stephen.

Another Reply To Leeds: "A Problem About Frequencies In Direct Inference". Kyburg, Henry E.

Cogito, Ergo Sum: Inference And Performance. Reeder, Harry.

Communicative Reference: An Inferential Model. Harnish, Robert M.

Foundations For Direct Inference. Pollock, John L.

Frege's Early Conception Of Logic (in Hebrew). Bar– Elli, Gilead.

Goede Redenen Om Iets Te Geloven. Derksen, A A.

Nozick On Inferential Knowledge. Mazoué, James G.

On The Status Of Statistical Inferences. Pitowsky, Itamar.

Postscript To 'A Problem About Frequencies In Direct Inference'. Leeds, Stephen.

Probability, Symmetry And Frequency. Dawid, A P.

Reliability And Indirect Justification. Kapitan, Tomis.

Reply To Leeds: "A Problem About Frequencies In Direct Inference". Pollock, John L.

Respect For Autonomy And Medical Paternalism Reconsidered. Wear, Stephen and Mc Cullough, L B.

Response To Mazoué's "Nozick On Inferential Knowledge" And Brueckner's "Transmission For Knowledge Not Established". Forbes, Graeme.

The Logician's Dilemma: Deductive Logic, Inductive Inference And Logical Empiricism. Boyd, Richard N.

The Preservation Of Coherence. Jennings, R E and Schotch, P K.

When Explanation Leads To Inference. Cartwright, Nancy.

INFERENCE RULE(S)

A Natural Extension Of Natural Deduction. Schroeder– Heister, Peter.

Conjunction Without Conditions In Illative Combinatory Logic. Bunder, M W.

Could Man Be An Irrational Animal: Some Notes On The Epistemology Of Rationality. Stich, Stephen P.

Inductive Inference In The Limit. Glymour, Clark.

Logics Without The Contraction Rule. Ono, Hiroakira and Komori, Yuichi.

Multiple Forms Of Gentzen's Rules And Some Intermediate Forms. Sikic, Z.

Natural Deduction Systems For Some Quantified Relevant Logics. Brady, R T.

Noncumulative Dialectical Models And Formal Dialectics. Krabbe, Erik C W.

On Hilbert's Operation On Logical Rules, II. Pogorzelski, Witold A.

Sequent–Systems For Modal Logic. Dosen, Kosta.

Structural Completeness Of The First–Order Predicate Calculus. Pogorzelski, W A and Prucnal, T.

INFIDELITY

El Problema De La "Infidelidad" En Fray Alonso De La Veracruz. Cerezo– De Diego, Prometeo.

INFINITARY CONCEPT(S)

$\aleph_0$–Categorical, $\aleph_0$–Stable Structures. Cherlin, Gregory and Harrington, L and Lachlan, A H.

Deux Remarques À Propos De La Propriété De Recouvrement Fini. Poizat, Bruno.

Diamonds, Uniformization. Shelah, Saharon.

Kueker's Conjecture For Superstable Theories. Buechler, Steven.

Monotone Reducibility And The Family Of Infinite Sets. Cenzer, Douglas.

More On Proper Forcing. Shelah, Saharon.

Narrow Boolean Algebras. Shelah, Sharon and Bonnet, Robert.

On Pseudo–$\aleph_0$–Categorical Theories. Marcja, Annalisa and Toffalori, Carlo.

On The Consistency Of Some Partition Theorems For Continuous Colorings, And The Structure Of Dense Real Order Types. Shelah, Saharon and Abraham, U and Rubin, M.

On The Ultrafilters And Ultrapowers Of Strong Partition Cardinals. Henle, J M and Kleinberg, E M and Watro, R J.

P–Points And Q–Points Over A Measurable Cardinal. Sureson, C.

Pseudo–Jump Operators: II, Transfinite Iterations, Hierarchies And Minimal Covers. Jockusch Jr, Carl G and Shore, Richard A.

Strongly Compact Cardinals, Elementary Embeddings And Fixed Points. Abe, Yoshihiro.

INFINITARY LOGIC

Functors And Ordinal Notations I: A Functorial Construction Of The Veblen Hierarchy. Girard, Jean–Yves and Vauzeilles, Jacqueline.

Monadic Logic And Löwenheim Numbers. Shelah, Saharon.

Set Recursion And $\Pi 1/2$–Logic. Girard, Jean–Yves and Normann, D.

The Boolean Sentence Algebra Of The Theory Of Linear Ordering Is Atomic With Respect To Logics With A Malitz Quantifier. Goltz, Hans– Joachim.

The Ordered Field Of Real Numbers And Logics With Malitz Quantifiers. Rapp, Andreas.

Vopenka's Principle And Compact Logics. Makowsky, J A.

INFINITE

Is The Past Finite: On Craig's Kalām Argument. Shields, George W.

The Infinite Commitment Of Finite Minds. Williamson, Timothy.

INFINITE REGRESS

Whither Infinite Regresses Of Justification. Moser, Paul D.

INFINITESIMAL(S)

Berkeley And Nieuwentijt On Infinitesimals. Vermeulen, Ben.

Une Approche Naïve De L'analyse Non–Standard. Robert, A.

INFINITY

Aristotle's Physics. Hussey, Edward (trans) and Ackrill, J L (ed).

'It Would Have Happened Already': On One Argument For A First Cause. Conway, David A.

An Infinite Time Of One's Own. Lingis, Alphonso F.

Das Unedliche Urteil: Zur Interpretation Eines Kapitels Aus Hegels "Wissenschaft Der Logic". Wolfhart, Günter.

Does Reason Demand That God Be Infinite? Pomerlau, Wayne P.

Double Infinité Chez Pascal Et Monade. Naërt, Emilienne.

Formation And Development Of Scientific Concepts. Pedersen, Stig Andur.

Hypertasks. Clark, Peter and Read, Stephen.

Part And Whole In Aristotle's Concept Of Infinity. White, David A.

The Infinistic Thesis. Burke, Michael B.

Zeno's Paradoxes, Iteration, And Infinity. Seaton, Robert.

Zum Problem Der Unendlichkeit. Titze, H.

INFLUENCE(S)

"Gaia And Philosophy" in *On Nature,* Rouner, Leroy S (ed), 60–78. Sagan, Dorion and Margulis, Lynn.

INFORMAL LOGIC

A Concise Introduction To Logic. Hurley, Patrick J.

Informal Logic And The Theory Of Reasoning. Finocchiaro, Maurice A.

Informal Logic: The Past Five Years 1978–1983. Johnson, Ralph H and Blair, J Anthony.

Possible Worlds And Imagination In Informal Logic. Nolt, John Eric.

The Evaluation Of Critical Thinking Programs: Dangers And Dogmas. Mc Peck, John E.

The Nature Of Critical Thinking. Reeder, Harry P.

INFORMATION

Informatique Pour Les Sciences Del'homme. Borillo, Mario.

"Observation & Scientific Enterprise" in *Observation, Experiment, And Hypothesis In Modern Physical Science,* Achinstein, Peter (ed), 21–44. Shapere, Dudley.

Consensus, Respect, And Weighted Averaging. Schmitt, Frederick F.

Critical Thinking In The Electronic Era. Postman, Neil.

Dialectical Fields And Transformations: Brouwer–Fields, Beth–Fields, And Naess–Transformations. Barth, E M.

Informatics And Society: Will There Be An 'Information Revolution'? Tepperman, Lorne.

Is Knowledge Information–Produced Belief? Doyle, Anthony.

Lehrer–Wagner Consensual Probabilities Do Not Adequately Summarize The Available Information. Baird, Davis.

Modal Logics In The Theory Of Information Systems. Orlowska, Ewa.

On Defining Information. Szaniawski, Klemens.

On The Principle Of Information Retention. Hilpinen, Risto.

Shifting Situations And Shaken Attitudes: An Interview With Barwise And Perry. Perry, John and Barwise, Jon.

The Employer–Employee Relationship And The Right To Know. Superson, Anita M.

The Lehrer–Wagner Theory Of Consensus And The Zero Weight Problem. Forrest, Peter.

The Value Of Information In Newcomb's Problem And The Prisoners' Dilemma. Snow, Paul.

Theory Dynamics And Knowledge Representation From An Information–Theoretical Point Of View. Hauffe, Heinz.

INFORMATION THEORY

Informatique Et Philosophie: L'intervalle, La Distance, L'écart. Toros, Yvonne.

Philosophical Discussion Concerning The Issue Of Information (in German). Liebscher,

INFORMATION THEORY
Heinz.
Prolegomena To Discourse–Pragmatics. Givón, T.
Some Methodological Problems In Data Gathering For Discourse Analysis. Orletti, Franca.

INFORMED CONSENT
The Silent World Of Doctor And Patient. Katz, Jay.
"Problems Of Informed Consent With Cognitively Impaired" in *Ethical Questions In Brain And Behavior,* Pfaff, Donald W (ed), 23–40. Macklin, Ruth.
"The Family's Right To Decide For The Incompetent Patient" in *Ethics Committees And Health Care Decisions,* Cranford, Ronald (ed), 209–217. Buchanan, Allen.
China: Diary Of A Barefoot Bioethicist. Fox, Steven.
Commentary: Informed Consent In Engineering And Medicine. Martin, Mike W and Schinzinger, Roland.
Informed Consent: Patient's Right Or Patient's Duty? Hull, Richard T.
Informed Consent, Autonomy, And The Law. Annis, David B.
Informed Consent And Engineering: An Essay Review. Long, Thomas A.
Organ Donation: Is Voluntarism Still Valid? Sadler Jr, Alfred M and Sadler, Blair L and Caplan, Arthur L.
The 'Right' Not To Know. Ost, David E.
The New OSHA Rules And The Worker's Right To Know. Mc Garity, Thomas O.

INGARDEN, R
"Il Tempo Della Letteratura: Roman Ingarden" in *Il Tempo Dell'Arte,* Papi, Fulvio and others (ed), 40–59. Scaramuzza, Gabriele.
"Zeit Und Musik" in *Asthetische Er Fahrung Und Das Wesen Der Kunst,* Holzhey, Helmut, 156–172. Risch, C.
Phenomenology And Literature: Roman Ingarden And The 'Appropriate Aesthetic Attitude' To The Literary Work Of Art (in Hebrew). Brinker, Menahem.
Platonic Ideas In Ingarden's Phenomenological Aesthetics. Golaszewska, Maria.
Roman Ingarden's "The Literary Work Of Art": Exposition And Analyses. Mitscherling, Jeff.

INHERENCE
A Note On Inherence. Hetherington, Stephen C.
Adhering To Inherence: A New Look At The Old Steps In Berkeley's March To Idealism. Hausman, Alan.
Is Samavaya (Inherence) An Internal Relation? Mohanta, Dilip K.

INHERITANCE
Harrington's Elusive Balance. Reeve, Andrew.

INJUSTICE
"Injustice And Tragedy In Aristotle" in *The Georgetown Symposium On Ethics,* Porreco, Rocco (ed), 175–184. Forte, David F.
Le Raisonnement De L'injustice. Vitorino, Orlando.

INNATE IDEA(S)
The Nature And Origin Of Ideas: The Controversy Over Innate Ideas Reconsidered. Simpson, Peter.

INNATISM
Apriorismo Como Contenido Intelectual En Balmes, Reflejo De La "Memoria Dei" Agustiniana? Casado, Fidel.

INNOVATION(S)
Tradition And Innovation: The Idea Of Civilization As Culture And Its Significance. Wilson, H T.
"Innovation Und Kanonbildung Oder Das Ende Der Modernen Kunst" in *Asthetische Er Fahrung Und Das Wesen Der Kunst,* Holzhey, Helmut, 42–57. Simon–Schaeffer, R.

INQUIRY
Beyond Feelings: A Guide To Critical Thinking, Second Edition. Ruggiero, Vincent Ryan.
Epicurus' Scientific Method. Asmis, Elizabeth.
Inquiry. Stalnaker, Robert C.
The Retreat To Commitment. Bartley, W W.
A Common Sense Approach To Value Inquiry. Byrum, C Stephen.
Augustine's *Confessions* As A Circular Journey. Leigh, David J.
Critical For Survival. Scriven, Michael.
Dewey's Theory Of Inquiry: Problems Of Foundations. Lakomski, Gabriele.
Interrogatives, Problems And Scientific Inquiry. Kleiner, Scott A.
Meland's Empirical Realism And The Appeal To Lived Experience. Frankenberry, Nancy.
The Nature Of The Inquiry In The Philosophy Of Sport. Vander Zwaag, Harold J.

INSECURITY
Getting On The Road To Peace: A Modest Proposal. Narveson, Jan.

INSIGHT
Investigating Lonergan's Inaccessibility. Walmsley, Gerard.
Lonergan's Metaphysics: Ontological Implications Of Insight–As–Event. Skrenes, Carol.

INSOLVABILITY
Why Is There Something Rather Than Nothing? Smith, Joseph Wayne.

INSPIRATION
La Creatividad Humana. Granja, Dulce M.

INSTINCT(S)
De Incommensurabiliteit Van Aanleg En Omgeving. Smit, Harry.
Instinctive Beliefs. Davis, William H.

INSTITUTION(S)
Aristotle: The Politics. Lord, Carnes (trans).
A Critica Glucksmanniana Do Poder. Morais, Carlos.
Reporters And A Free Press. Funk, Nanette.

The Art Museum As An Agency Of Culture. Levi, Albert William.
Wollheim And The Institutional Theory Of Art. Mc Fee, Graham.

INSTITUTIONAL ETHICS COMMITTEE(S)
Institutional Ethics Committees And Health Care Decision Making. Cranford, Ronald E (ed) and Doudera, A Edward (ed).
"Consultative Roles And Responsibilities" in *Ethics Committees And Health Care Decisions,* Cranford, Ronald (ed), 157–168. Macklin, Ruth.
"Contrasting Review Boards With Ethics Committees" in *Ethics Committees And Health Care Decisions,* Cranford, Ronald (ed), 129–137. Glantz, Leonard H.
"Decision Review: A Problematic Task" in *Ethics Committees And Health Care Decisions,* Cranford, Ronald (ed), 174–185. Capron, Alexander M.
"Ethics Of Institutional Ethics Committees" in *Ethics Committees And Health Care Decisions,* Cranford, Ronald (ed), 35–50. Veatch, Robert M.
"Functions Of Institutional Ethics Committees" in (ethics Committees And Health Care Decisions, Cranford, Ronald (ed), 22–30. Lynn, Joanne.
"Guidelines For Decision Making" in *Ethics Committees And Health Care Decisions,* Cranford, Ronald (ed), 169–173. Rothenberg, Leslie Steven.
"Health Care Professionals And Ethical Relationships On IECs" in *Ethics Committees/ Health Care Decisions,* Cranford, Ronald (ed), 218–225. Aroskar, Mila Ann.
"Legal Aspects Of Ethics Committees" in *Ethics Committees And Health Care Decisions,* Cranford, Ronald (ed), 51–59. Annas, George J.
"The Decision To Withdraw Life–Sustaining Treatment" in *Ethics Committees And Health Care Decisions,* Cranford, Ronald (ed), 203–208. Paris, John J.

INSTRUMENT(S)
Knowledge As The Production Of Intellectual Instruments And Theoretical Constructions. Cekić, Miodrag.

INSTRUMENTAL VALUE(S)
Evaluating Art. Dickie, George T.

INSTRUMENTALISM
see also Pragmatism
Bachelard: Science And Objectivity. Tiles, Mary.
"Realism And Instrumentalism In Pre–Newtonian Astronomy" in *Testing Scientific Theories,* Earman, John (ed), 201–266. Gardner, Michael R.
A Gricean Approach To Aesthetic Instrumentalism. Lord, Catherine.
Is Socrates An Instrumentalist? Lesses, Glenn.

INTEGRITY
Fact And Value In Ecological Science. Sagoff, Mark.
Moral Integrity And The Deferential Wife. Friedman, Marylin A.
The Development Of Nature Resources And The Integrity Of Nature. Devall, Bill and Sessions, George.

INTELLECT
see also Reason
Carácter Racional De La Libertad. Derisi, Octavio N.
El Problema De Los Universales En Domingo De Soto Y Alonso De La Veracruz. Beuchot, Mauricio.
Gefühl—Sinnlichkeit—Verstand. Gerlach, Hans–Martin.
Intellectual And Sensuous Pleasure. Savedoff, Barbara E.
Knowledge As The Production Of Intellectual Instruments And Theoretical Constructions. Cekić, Miodrag.
La Abstracción En El Pensamiento Tomista. Alonso, Luz García.
On Two Meanings Of Good And The Foundations Of Ethics In Aristotle And St Thomas. Flippen, Douglas.
The Tension Between Intellectual And Moral Education In The Thought Of John Henry Newman. Tillman, Mary Katherine.

INTELLECTUAL HISTORY
"The Historiography Of Philosophy: Four Genres" in *Philosophy In History,* Rorty, Richard and others (ed), 49–76. Rorty, Richard.
Orwell And The Intellectuals. Israel, Joachim.

INTELLECTUAL VIRTUE(S)
Knowledge And Intellectual Virtue. Sosa, Ernest.

INTELLECTUALISM
"The Collapse Of American Evangelical Academia" in *Faith And Rationality,* Plantinga, Alvin (ed), 219–264. Marsden, George.
The Jewish Intellectual: Some Methodological Proposals (in Hebrew). Mendes– Flohr, Paul.
Theology And The Intellectual Endeavour Of Mankind. Hudson, W D.

INTELLECTUALS
Arbeiterklasse Und Intelligenz In Der Dialektik Von Wissenschaftlichtechnischem, Ökonomischem Und Sozialem Fortschritt. Lötsch, M.
L'intellectuel Américain. Emerson, Ralph Waldo.
The Changing Role Of Intellectuals In The Revolutionary Order. Gella, Aleksander.

INTELLIGENCE
About Being A Bat. Maloney, J Christopher.
Begriffsbildung In Der Psychologie: Zur Logik Des Begriffes "Intelligenz". Perner, Josef.
Dewey And Pekarsky On The Efficacy Of Intelligence And Foresight. Burnett, Joe R.
Extraterrestrial Science. Rescher, Nicholas.
Inaccessible Routes To The Problem Of Privileged Access. Schlesinger, George N.
Jacques Maritain, Filósofo Da Inteligência. Machado, Geraldo Pinheiro.

INTELLIGENTSIA
The Changing Role Of Intellectuals In The Revolutionary Order. Gella, Aleksander.

INTELLIGIBILITY
"Generality And The Importance Of The Particular Case" in *Philosophy And Life: Essays On John Wisdom,* Dilman, Ilham (ed), 241–270. Nammour, Jamil.
Intelligibilité Et Réalité Chez Hobbes Et Spinoza. Bernhardt, Jean.

INTELLIGIBILITY
Lo Inteligible. De Paoli, Alejandro.
Schmitz, Jordan And Wallace On Intelligibility. Lobkowicz, Nicholas.
The Intelligibility Of Nature: A Neo–Aristotelian View. Wallace, William A.
The Intelligibility Of The World And The Divine Ideas In Aquinas. Jordan, Mark D.

INTENDING
Armstrong's Intentions. Gustafson, Donald.

INTENSION
A Model For The Modern Malaise. Abraham, Adrian and Meyer, Robert K.
A Semiotic–Pragmatic Theory Of Concepts. Lee, Harold N.

INTENSIONAL LOGIC
Handbook Of Philosophical Logic: Extensions Of Classical Logic, V2. Gabbay, Dov M (ed) and Guenthner, Franz (ed).
"General Intensional Logic" in Handbook Of Philosophical Logic, Gabbay, Dov (ed), 355–386. Anderson, C Anthony.
"Quantification In Modal Logic" in Handbook Of Philosophical Logic, Gabbay, Dov (ed), 249–308. Garson, James W.
Compactness And Recursive Enumerability In Intensional Logic. Stephan, Bernd J.
Possible Worlds Semantics: A Research Program That Cannot Fail. Van Benthem, Johan.
Reference And Subordinating Descriptions. Dau, Paolo.

INTENSIONALISM
Deconstruction And Its Alternatives. Eldridge, Richard.

INTENSIONALITY
Identity, Intensionality, And Intentionality. Toberlin, James.
Intensionality In Mathematics. Feferman, Solomon.

INTENTION(S)
Action (1893): Essay On A Critique Of Life And A Science Of Practice. Blanchette, Oliva (trans) and Blondel, Maurice.
"Responses To The Paradox Of Deterrence" in The Security Gamble, Mac Lean, Douglas (ed), 155–162. Kavka, Gregory S and Gauthier, David.
"Theoretical Preliminaries To The Study Of Action" in The Analysis Of Action, Von Cranach, Mario (ed), 5–34. Harré, Rom.
A Reply To Wayne A Davis' "Miller On Wanting, Intending, And Being Willing". Miller, Arthur.
Anachronistic Inauthenticity In Art. Bertman, Martin A.
Armstrong's Intentions. Gustafson, Donald.
Art And Its Preservation. Carrier, David.
Causal Deviancy And Multiple Intentions: A Reply To James Montmarquet. Bishop, John.
Deviant Causal Chains And Non–Basic Action. Robins, Michael H.
Does Rightness Always Involve Wrongness? Bahm, Archie J.
Insanity And Criminality. Simon, Michael A.
Intentions, Rights And Wrongs: A Critique Of Fried. Fischer, Marilyn.
Le Rôle Du Concept D'intention Dans La Formation Du Jugement Esthétique: D'une Controverse Anglo–Saxonne Et De Son Précurseur Belge. Stern–Gillet, Suzanne.
Management–Think. Pastin, Mark.
Moral Reasoning And Action In Young Children. Hannaford, Robert V.
Pears On Akrasia, And Defeated Intentions. Mele, Alfred R.
Self–Consciousness And Agency. Richards, William M.
Self–Understanding And Rationalizing Explanations. Kim, Jaegwon.

INTENTIONAL
"Normal" Intentional Action. Ehrind, Douglas.

INTENTIONALISM
"Words Fail Me". Stern, Laurent.
Consciousness And Dennett's Intentionalist Net. Bricke, John.
On Justifying Interpretive Norms. Hirsch Jr, E D.
On Justifying The Choice Of Interpretive Theories. Danneberg, Lutz and Muller, Hans–harald.

INTENTIONALITY
An Essay On Human Action. Zimmerman, Michael J.
Erklaren Und Verstehen. Von Wright, Georg Henrik.
Inquiry. Stalnaker, Robert C.
Language, Thought, And Other Biological Categories: New Foundations For Realism. Millikan, Ruth Garret.
Wittgenstein: A Critique. Findlay, J N.
"Motives And Metaphors In Considerations Of Animal Nature" in Ethical Questions In Brain And Behavior, Pfaff, Donald W (ed), 125–140. Beer, Colin.
Content And Context Of Perception. Smith, David Woodruff.
Dennett, Mental Images, And Images In Context. Russow, Lilly–Marlene.
Deterrence And Deontology. Mc Mahan, Jeff.
Formal Traces In Cartesian Functional Explanation. Rorty, Amelie Oksenberg.
Identity, Intensionality, And Intentionality. Toberlin, James.
In Search Of A Whole–System Ethic. Holler, Linda D.
Intentionality And Its Place In Nature. Searle, John R.
Intentionality: A Reexamination Of Its Role In A Literary Education. Kasprisin, Lorraine.
Intentionality, Causality And Holism. Mohanty, J N.
Karol Cardinal Wojtyla And Jean–Paul Sartre On The Intentionality Of Consciousness. Pappin, Joseph.
Modes Of Intentionality (in Hebrew). Bar–On, A Z.
Naturalizing Intentions. Nelson, R J.
On Searle's "Solution" To The Mind–Body Problem. Lyons, William E.
Representation, Intentionality, And Quantifiers. Mc Carthy, Timothy.
Searle's Answer To 'Hume's Problem'. Double, Richard.

The Corporation, Its Members, And Moral Accountability. Meyers, Christopher.
The Primacy Of The Intentionality. Chisholm, Roderick M.
The Russell–Meinong Debate. Smith, Janet Farrell.
Veridicality: More On Searle. Millar, Alan.

INTERACTION(S)
"Notes Towards A Philosophy Of The Science/Technology Interaction" in Technological Knowledge, Laudan, Rachel (ed), 105–114. Price, Derek J De Solla.
Is There A Problem Of Cartesian Interaction? Radner, Daisie.
Persons And The Problem Of Interaction. Peterson, John.

INTERACTIONISM
Indéterminisme Et Interactionnisme Chez Popper. Quilliot, Roland.
Parallelism, Interactionism, And Causation. Addis, Laird.
Rejoinder To Richardson's And Loeb's: Replies To Radner's "Is There A Problem Of Cartesian Interaction"? Radner, Daisie.
Replies To Daisie Radner's "Is There A Problem Of Cartesian Interaction"? Richardson, Robert C and Loeb, Louis E.
Suggestions For A Symbolic Interactionist Conception Of Culture. Maines, David R.

INTERDISCIPLINARY
"Symmetry, Independence, Continuity, Boundedness, And Additivity": The Game Of Education. Krolikowski, Walter P and Hablutzel, Nancy and Hoffman, Wilma.
A Reply To "On Reading Environmental Ethics". Lemons, John.
Der Wissenschaftlich–Technische Fortschritt Und Die Interdisziplinäre Zusammenarbeit Von Philosophen Und Technikwissenschaftlern. Jobst, E.
Works Of Art As Cultural Probes. Gavin, William J and Conway, Jeremiah P.

INTEREST(S)
A Biological Interpretation Of Moral Systems. Alexander, Richard D.
Die Stellung Des Interesses In Der Ästhetik Kants (in Japanese). Kubo, Mitsushi.
Plädoyer Für Eine Ökonomische Anthropologie Auf Der Grundlage Von Interessen. Koubek, Norbert.
Russell And The Attainability Of Happiness. Kohl, Marvin.
The Role Of Interests In Science. Newton–Smith, W.
Words; Interests. Kuhse, Helga.

INTERFERENCE
"State Aid To Science" in Freedom, Feminism, And The State, Mc Elroy, Wendy (ed), 275–284. Kelly, Gertrude.

INTERMEDIATE LOGICS
Multiple Forms Of Gentzen's Rules And Some Intermediate Forms. Sikic, Z.

INTERNAL
Carnap's Internal—External Distinction. Wilson, Mark.

INTERNAL RELATION(S)
Marx And The Theory Of Internal Relations: A Critical Note On Ollman's Interpretation Of Marx. Hudelson, Richard.

INTERNALISM
A Rationale For Reliabilism. Bach, Kent.
Brains In Vats And The Internalist Perspective. Stephens, James and Russow, Lilly–marlene.
Epistemological Internalism. Montmarquet, James A.
The Coherence Of Virtue And The Virtue Of Coherence: Justification In Epistemology. Sosa, Ernest.
Wang Yang–Ming, Mencius And Internalism. Lee, Jig–Chuen.

INTERNALIZATION
"Observation & Scientific Enterprise" in Observation, Experiment, And Hypothesis In Modern Physical Science, Achinstein, Peter (ed), 21–44. Shapere, Dudley.

INTERNATIONAL
Die Dialektik Von Nationalem Und Internationalem In Der Entwicklung Der Sozialistischen Gesellschaft. Wirt, Adam.
Human Rights And International Finance: A Synthetical Overview. Khoshkish, A.
Some Theoretical Problems Of The Object–Subject Dialectics In The Development Of The Community Of Socialist States (in German). Rygol, Reiner.

INTERNATIONAL LAW
Can Modern War Be Just? Johnson, James T.

INTERNATIONAL RELATION(S)
Moral Dimensions Of American Foreign Policy. Thompson, Kenneth W (ed).
Political Economy And Freedom. Nutter, Warren G.
Global Justice, Capitalism And The Third World. Nielsen, Kai.
Moral Skepticism And International Relations. Cohen, Marshall.
Multinational Decision–Making: Reconciling International Norms. Donaldson, Thomas.
Strategists, Philosophers, And The Nuclear Question. Trachtenberg, Marc.

INTERPERSONAL
Interpersonal Utility In Principles Of Social Choice. Weirich, Paul.

INTERPERSONAL RELATION(S)
"Levels Of Interpersonal Relationships" in International Kierkegaard Commentary, Perkins, Robert L (ed), 73–86. Cutting, Patricia.
Applied Philosophy In Health Care Outside The Medical Ethics Arena. Butler, Nance Cunningham.
Formal Properties Of Interpersonal Envy. Chaudhuri, Adhip.
Interpersonal Level Comparability Implies Comparability Of Utility Differences. Ng, Yew–Kwang.

INTERPOLATION
A Recursive Theory For The {Upsidedown L, Λ, $\vee$, $\rightarrow$, o}: Fragment Of Intuitionistic Logic. Wojtylak, Piotr.
Tautologies With A Unique Craig Interpolant, Uniform Vs Nonuniform Complexity. Mundici, Daniele.

INTERPRETATION

History Of Philosophy In The Making. Thro, Linus J (ed).
Inquiries Into Truth And Interpretation. Davidson, Donald.
Justifying Historical Descriptions. Mc Cullagh, C Behan.
Knowledge Structure And Use: Implications For Synthesis And Interpretation, Linda J Reed (ed). Ward, Spencer (ed).
Max Weber And The Methodology Of The Social Sciences. Huff, Toby.
Principles Of Interpretation: Series In Continental Thought, V5. Ballard, Edward G.
Relatedness: Essays In Metaphysics And Theology. Oliver, Harold H.
Seeing And Reading. Nicholson, Graeme.
The Existential Coordinates Of The Human Condition: Poetic—Epic—Tragic. Tymienecka, Anna–Teresa (ed).
The Great Reversal: Ethics And The New Testament. Verhey, Allen.
The Politics Of Interpretation. Mitchell, W J T.
Wir Philologen: Überlegungen Zu Nietzsches Begriff Der Interpretation. Birus, Hendrik.
"Beyond Hermeneutics" in *Hermeneutics*, Shapiro, Gary (ed), 66–83. Dreyfus, Hubert.
"Buber And Modern Biblical Scholarship" in *Martin Buber*, Gordon, Haim (ed), 163–214. Uffenheimer, Benyamin.
"Interpretation Theory And Experiment" in *Observation, Experiment, Hypothesis In Modern Physical Science*, Achinstein, Peter (ed), 175–204. Joseph, Geoffrey.
"Literary Diary As A Witness Of Man's Historicity" in *Existential Coordinates Of Human Condition*, Tymienecka, A (ed), 249–260. Eykman, Christoph.
"Poetry As Essential Graphs" in *Existential Coordinates Of Human Condition*, Tymienecka, A (ed), 157–162. Gella, Teresa.
"The Hermeneutics Of Suspicion" in *Hermeneutics*, Shapiro, Gary (ed), 54–65. Gadamer, Hans– Georg.
"The Relationship Of Philosophy To Its Past" in *Philosophy In History*, Rorty, Richard and others (ed), 31–48. Macintyre, Alasdair.
"The Structure Of Allegory" in *Existential Coordinates Of Human Condition*, Tymienecka, A (ed), 505–520. Gellrich, Jesse.
"What Can The Poem Do Today" in *Existential Coordinates Of Human Condition*, Tymienecka, A (ed), 141–156. Eykman, Christoph.
A Mathematical Characterization Of Interpretation Between Theories. Van Bentham, Johan and Pearce, David.
A Note On Interpretations Of Many–sorted Theories. Hook, Julian L.
A Schutz And F Kaufmann: Sociology Between Science And Interpretation. Helling, Ingeborg K.
An Emergence View Of Linguistic Meaning. Von Savigny, Eike.
Assessing Relative Causal Importance In History. Pork, Andrus.
Cuts, Consistency Statements And Interpretations. Pudlak, Pavel.
Deconstruction And Its Alternatives. Eldridge, Richard.
Gödelsche Funktionalinterpretation Für Eine Erweiterung Der Klassischen Analysis. Friedrich, Wolfgang.
Hermeneutics And Intellectual History. Stern, Laurent.
Interpretation In History: Or What Historians Do And Philosophers Say. Levich, Marvin.
Knowledge And Value. Cavell, Marcia.
L'unité De L'oeuvre De Paul Ricoeur Saisie Selon La Perspective De Son Ouvrage Temps Et Récit I. Stevens, Bernard.
Legal Language And Legal Interpretation. Wroblewski, Jerzy.
Monadic Logic And Löwenheim Numbers. Shelah, Saharon.
More Than 'Meets The Eye'. Devereaux, Mary.
More's *Utopia*: An Interpretation Of Its Social Theory. Sargent, Lyman Tower.
Nietzsche On "The Subject Of Multiplicity". Booth, David.
On Definitional Equivalence And Related Topics. Corcoran, John.
On Justifying The Choice Of Interpretive Theories. Danneberg, Lutz and Muller, Hans–harald.
On Interpretive Norms. Hirsch Jr, E D.
Pierre Bourdieu En De Filosofische Esthetica. Groot, Ger and Crego, Charo.
Remarks On Leibniz's Conception Of Containment And Individual Substance. Schwerin, Alan.
Socratic Definition: Real Or Nominal? Gold, Jeffrey.
The Purposes Of Retribution. Manser, Anthony.
The Rhetoric Of Incommensurability. Kenshur, Oscar.
Truth And Reflection. Yablo, Stephen.
Waclaw Borowy's Views On Aesthetics. Wilkoszewska, Krystyna.
Wittgenstein's Solution Of The 'Hermeneutic Problem'. Shanker, Stuart G.

INTERROGATIVES

Interrogatives, Problems And Scientific Inquiry. Kleiner, Scott A.

INTERSUBJECTIVITY

Imagination And Reflection: Intersubjectivity. Hohler, T P (ed).
Complexity And Intersubjectivity: Towards The Theory Of Niklas Luhmann. Bednarz Jr, John.
Dialectic And Intersubjectivity. Westphal, Merold.
Husserl's Communal Spirit: A Phenomenological Study Of The Fundamental Structure Of Society. Allen, Jeffner.
Is There An 'Us' In 'Justification'? Kvanvig, J L.
Merleau–Ponty En Buytendijk: Relaas Van Een Relatie. Boudier, C E M Struyker.
Sentido E Intersubjectividade No Pensamento De E Levinas. Silva, M Augusto Ferreira Da.
Surrender–And–Catch And Phenomenology. Wolff, Kurt H.

INTERVAL(S)

A Short Proof Of A Well–Known Theorem Of Intuitionistic Analysis. Luckhardt, Horst.
Buridan On Interval Semantics For Temporal Logic. Ohrstrom, Peter.
Do We Need Interval Semantics? Tichý, Pavel.

On Three–Valued Moisil Algebras. Monteiro, Luiz and Abad, M.
The Elementary Theory Of Interval Reals Numbers. Comer, Stephen D.

INTERVENTION

An Analysis Of The Structure Of Justification Of Ethical Decisions In Medical Intervention. Self, Donnie J.

INTRINSIC

Inquiry, Intrinsic Properties, And The Identity Of Indiscernibles. Hoy, Ronald C.

INTRINSIC VALUE(S)

An Examination Of Relationships Of Inherent, Intrinsic, Instrumental, And Contributive Values Of The Good Sports Contest. Fraleigh, Warren P.
Hinlänglichkeit Und Notwendigheit Im Moralischen. Stuhlmann– Laeisz, Ranier.
Intrinsic Value, Quantum Theory, And Environmental Ethics. Callicott, J Baird.
Three Wrong Leads In A Search For An Environmental Ethic: Tom Regan On Animal Rights, Inherent Values, And 'Deep Ecology'. Partridge, Ernest.
What Kind Of Good Is A Kind And Caring Heart. Lundberg, Randolph.

INTROSPECTION

Disease And Social Theory: A Problem Of Conversation. Baross, Z.
Reduction, Qualia, And The Direct Introspection Of Brain States. Churchland, Paul M.
The Behaviourists' Struggle With Introspection. Lyons, William.

INTUITION

Husserl And Realism In Logic And Mathematics. Tragesser, Robert S.
"Duns Scotus On Intuition, Memory And Knowledge Of Individuals" in *History Of Philosophy In Making*, Thro, Linus J (ed), 81–104. Wolter, Allan B.
A Crack In The Foundations Of Descartes's Theory Of Knowledge. Hund, J.
Acerca Del Programa De Fenomenologia. Presas, Mario A.
Cognitive Intuition Of Singulars Revisited (Matthew Of Aquaparta Versus B J F Lonergan). Payne, Gordon R.
Descartes's Meditations As Cognitive Exercises. Hatfield, Gary.
Epistemological Internalism. Montmarquet, James A.
Intuition And Manifold In The Transcendental Deduction. Robinson, Hoke.
Intuitions In Ethics. Bayles, Michael D.
Intuitive Cognition And The Philosophy Of God (in Polish). Kowalczyk, Stanislaw.
Philosophy: Just Like Science Only Different. Edidin, Aron.
Sellars On Kantian Intuitions. Woods, Michael.
The Geometry Of A Form Of Intuition. Melnick, Arthur.
The Notion Of Mathematical Intuition And Husserl's Phenomenology. Tieszen, Richard.
The Sources Of Intuitive Cognition In William Of Ockham. Wengert, Robert G.

INTUITIONISM

A Defense Of Epistemic Intuitionism. Moser, Paul K.
A Short Proof Of A Well–Known Theorem Of Intuitionistic Analysis. Luckhardt, Horst.
An Analysis Of The Structure Of Justification Of Ethical Decisions In Medical Intervention. Self, Donnie J.
An Interpretation Of Martin–Löf's Type Theory In A Type–Free Theory Of Propositions. Smith, Jan.
Das Solipsistisch–Intuitionistische Konzept Der Vernunft Und Des Verstehens: Traditionskritische Bemerkungen. Böhler, Dietrich.
Dialectical Fields And Transformations: Brouwer–Fields, Beth–Fields, And Naess–Transformations. Barth, E M.
Dialogues, Strategies, And Intuitionistic Provability. Felscher, Walter.
Distributive Justice. Rollins, Mark.
Ethics And The Archangelic Prescriber. Harrison, Jonathan.
How To Glue Analysis Models. Van Dalen, D.
On Brouwer's Definition Of Unextendable Order. Posy, Carl J.
On Choice Sequences Determined By Spreads. Van Der Hoeven, Gerrit and Moerdijk, Ieke.
Principles For Individual Actions. Wilkins, Burleigh T and Zelikovitz, Kelly M.
Rebuilding Rawls: An Alternative Theory Of Justice. Groarke, Leo.
Replacement And Connection In Intuitionistic Set Theory. Goodman, Nicholas D.
Supuestos De La Metafísica. Giralt, Edualdo Forment.
The Real–Algebraic Structure Of Scott's Model Of Intuitionistic Analysis. Scowcroft, Philip.
The Umpire's Dilemma. Radford, Colin.
Topological Duality For Nelson Algebras And Its Applications. Sendlewski, Andrzej.

INTUITIONISTIC LOGIC

Lecture Notes In Mathematics. Muller, G H and others.
"Heyting Valued Universes Of Intuitionistic Set Theory" in *Lecture Notes In Mathematics*, Muller, G H And Others (ed), 189–306. Takeuti, Gaisi.
"Intuitionistic Theories And Toposes" in *Lecture Notes In Mathematics*, Muller, G H And Others (ed), 323–358. Uesu, Tadahiro.
"Kripke Semantics" = Algebra + Poetry. Fleischer, Isidore.
A Recursive Theory For The $\{$Upsidedown L, Λ, V, $\rightarrow$, $o\}$: Fragment Of Intuitionistic Logic. Wojtylak, Piotr.
An Application Of The Reiger–Nishimura Formulas To The Intuitionistic Modal Logics. Vakarelov, Dimiter.
Implication And Deduction In Some Intuitionistic Modal Logics. Font, Josep M.
Intuitionistic Fuzzy Logic And Intuitionistic Fuzzy Set Theory. Takeuti, Gaisi and Titani, Satoko.
Intuitionistic Truth. Rabinowicz, Wlodzimierz.
Models For Normal Intuitionistic Modal Logics. Bozic, Milan and Dosen, Kosta.
Noncumulative Dialectical Models And Formal Dialectics. Krabbe, Erik C W.
On Some Non–Classical Extensions Of Second–Order Intuitionistic Propositional Calculus. Scedrov, Andrej.
On The Period Of Sequences ($A^n(p)$) In Intuitionistic Propositional Calculus. Ruitenburg, Wim.
Realizability And Intuitionistic Logic. Diller, J and Troelstra, A S.

INTUITIONISTIC LOGIC
Some Investigations Of Varieties Of *N*–Lattices. Sendlewski, Andrzej.

Sur Une Extension Simple Du Calcul Intuitionniste Des Prédicate Du Premier Ordre Appliquée À L'analyse. Margenstern, Maurice.

INVARIANCE
Invarianzgesetze Und Zeitmetrik. Kamlah, Andreas.

INVOLUNTARY COMMITMENT(S)
"Involuntary Commitment & Treatment Of Persons Diagnosed As Mentally Ill" in *Biomedical Ethics Reviews*, Humber, James M (ed), 131–148. Hull, Richard T.

INVOLUNTARY CONFINEMENT
Involuntary Confinement: Legal And Psychiatric Perspectives. Dresser, Rebecca.

Liberty, Beneficence, And Involuntary Confinement. Callahan, Joan C.

IRONY
Irony And The Logic Of The Romantic Imagination. Alford, Steven E.

Art D'écrire Et Pratique Politique De Jean–Jacques Rousseau (II). Marshall, Terence.

Irony As A Post–Romantic Possibility For Art: Kierkegaard's Reply To Hegel. Crooks, James.

Melancholy, Irony, And Kierkegaard. Khan, Abrahim H.

Socrates And Post–Socratic Satire. Guilhamet, Leon.

Time And Stress: Alice In Wonderland. Petersen, Calvin R.

IRRATIONAL
L'ombre De La Raison. Trotignon, Pierre.

IRRATIONAL NUMBERS
Georg Cantor's Influence On Bertrand Russell. Grattan–Guiness, I.

IRRATIONALISM
Defensive Reactions Of Polish Professional Philosophy To Irrationalism In The Early 20th Century. Borzym, Stanislaw.

IRRATIONALITY
Could Man Be An Irrational Animal: Some Notes On The Epistemology Of Rationality. Stich, Stephen P.

Feyerabend's Irrational Science. Grünfeld, Joseph.

Was Erwartet Uns Jenseits Der Wissenschaft: Ethno–Philosophie: Erfahrungen Und Möglichkeiten Im Umgang Mit Dem Irrationalen. Stuben, Peter E.

IRREFUTABILITY
Popper Had A Brand New Bag. Brown, James M.

IRREVERSIBILITY
Order Out Of Chaos: Man's New Dialogue With Nature. Prigogine, Ilya and Stengers, Isabelle.

Is The Death Penalty Irrevocable? Davis, Michael.

IS
'Is' Presupposes 'Ought'. Hinman, Lawrence M.

Ayn Rand And The Is–Ought Problem. O' Neil, Patrick M.

Is–Ought: Prescribing And A Present Controversy. Schultz, Janice L.

La Renovición Kantiana Del Derecho Natural Y La Crítica De Hegel: Una Crítica A La Crítica. Guariglia, Osvaldo.

ISLAM
"La Destinée De La Tragédie Dans La Culture Islamique" in *Existential Coordinates Of Human Condition*, Tymieniecka, A (ed), 333–340. Chehida, A Ben.

A Quest For The Values In Islam. Djaït, Hichem.

Ethics And Taxation: The Perspective Of The Islamic Tradition. Nanji, Azim A.

Islam And The Loss Of Equilibrium. Chittick, William C.

La Teoria Islamica Dei Diritti Umani. Cordone, Claudio.

Razón Y Revelación En El Islam. Guzmán, Roberto M.

The Human Rights Of Women In Islam. Talhami, Ghada.

ISLAMIC
Human Rights In Religious Traditions. Swidler, Arlene (ed).

Mysticism And Religious Traditions. Katz, Steven (ed).

The Islamic Conception Of Justice. Khadduri, Majid.

ISOLATIONISM
Reflections Of The Mutual Benefits Of Philosophical And Global Education. Silvers, Anita.

ISOMORPHISM
Categoricity. Corcoran, John.

Hegemony And Sport. Parry, S J.

Isomorphisms Between HEO And HRO, ECF And ICF. Bezem, Marc.

The Number Of One–Generated Cylindric Set Algebras Of Dimension Greater Than Two. Larson, Jean A.

ISRAEL
Taxation In Biblical Israel. Oden Jr, Robert A.

ITALIAN
Gli Instituti Filosofici In Italia (1970–1980). Pasqualotto, Giangiorgio.

Prevention Of Admission And Continuity Of Care. Vanistendael, Clara.

The Difference Of The Italian Philosophical Culture. Perniola, Mario.

The Italian Difference And The Politics Of Culture. White, Hayden.

ITERATION
Pseudo–Jump Operators: II, Transfinite Iterations, Hierarchies And Minimal Covers. Jockusch Jr, Carl G and Shore, Richard A.

JACKSON, F
INUS Conditions. Dale, A J.

JACOBEAN
The Ideology Of Jacobitism On The Eve Of The Rising Of 1745—Part I. Mc Lynn, F J.

JACOBITISM
The Ideology Of Jacobitism—Part II. Mc Lynn, F J.

JACOBS, S
Periodization, Holism And Historicism: A Reply To Jacobs. Tilley, Nicholas.

JACQUES, F
De H P Grice À F Jacques: Remarques Sur La Maxime Pragmatique De Pertinence. Armengaud, Françoise.

JAGER, R
Russell's Scientific Mysticism. Nathanson, Stephen.

JAINISM
Syadvada Theory Of Jainism In Terms Of A Deviant Logic. Bharucha, Filita and Kamat, R V.

JAMES
Mysticism And Religious Traditions. Katz, Steven (ed).

The Emergence Of Whitehead's Metaphysics 1925–1929, R C Neville (ed). Ford, Lewis S.

The Essential Writings, Bruce W Wilshire (ed). James, William.

William James On The Courage To Believe. O' Connell, Robert J.

Classical American Philosophy: A Reflective Bequest To The Twenty–First Century. Mc Dermott, John J.

Europa Und Die Vereinigten Staaten Von Amerika Philosophiegeschichtlich Betrachtet. Moser, Simon.

John Dewey's Theory Of Consciousness. Smith, Barry D.

Moral Issues And Social Problems: The Moral Relevance Of Moral Philosophy. Singer, Marcus G.

Panthéisme Pluraliste Et Possibilité Actuelle: Réflexions Sur "A Pluralistic Universe" De William James. Gavin, William J.

Regional Ontologies, Types Of Meaning, And The Will To Believe In The Philosophy Of William James. Gavin, William J.

Some Marxist Interpretations Of James' Pragmatism: A Summary And Reply. Gavin, William J.

The 'Will To Believe' In Science And Religion. Gavin, William J.

Voluntary Belief. Naylor, Margery Bedford.

William James And The Epochal Theory Of Time. Field, Richard W.

JAMES, H
Extending The Darwinian Model: James's Struggle With Royce And Spencer. Seigfried, Charlene H.

JANKOWSKI, H
Rejoinder To Jankowski's "Comment To Goćkowski's *Situational Tests Of A Scholar's Faithfulness To His Ethos*". Gockowski, J.

JANSSENS, L
Aquinas And Janssens On The Moral Meaning Of Human Acts. May, William E.

JAPANESE
see also Buddhism

The Interior And Exterior In Zen Buddhism. Izutsu, Toshihiko.

Über Das Philosophische Leben In Japan. Iwasaki, Chikatsugu.

"Buber And Japanese Thought" in *Martin Buber*, Gordon, Haim (ed), 351–366. Hiraishi, Yoshimori.

"The Epic Element In Japanese Literature" in *Existential Coordinates Of Human Condition*, Tymieniecka, A (ed), 195–208. Viglielmo, Valdo H.

Japanese Spiritual Resources And Their Contemporary Relevance. Wei– Hsun Fu, Charles.

The Japanese Appreciation Of Nature. Saito, Yuriko.

JASPERS
Freedom As A Condition For Truth: Jaspers On The Significance Of Temporality In Science. Koterski, Joseph W.

Value And Human Condition. Sarin, Indu.

JAYNES, E
The Fallacy Of Intrinsic Distributions. Nathan, Amos.

The Status Of The Principle Of Maximum Entropy. Shimony, Abner.

JEFFERSON
American Political Thought: The Philosophic Dimension Of American Statesmanship, Second Edition. Frisch, Morton J (ed) and Stevens, Richard G (ed).

JEFFREY, R
Circumstances And Dominance In A Causal Decision Theory. Sobel, Jordan Howard.

Ratificationism Without Ratification: Jeffrey Meets Savage. Rabinowicz, Wlodzimierz.

JESUITS
Questionnaire On Philosophy. Lonergan, Bernard.

JESUS
see Christ

JEWISH
see also Judaism

A Book Of Jewish Ethical Concepts: Biblical And Postbiblical. Bloch, Abraham P.

Jewish Ethics And Halakhah For Our Time: Sources And Commentary. Herring, Basil F.

Jews And German Philosophy: The Polemics Of Emancipation. Rotenstreich, Nathan.

"Martin Buber And A D Gordon: A Comparison" in *Martin Buber*, Gordon, Haim (ed), 255–274. Schweid, Eliezer.

Liberalism And The Jewish Connection: A Study Of Spinoza And The Young Marx. Schwartz, Joel.

Maimonides' Life Of Learning. Finkel, Asher.

On Theology And On Jewish Concepts Of Ultimate Reality And Meaning In Modern Jewish Philosophy. Levy, Ze'ev.

Shakespeare And The Jewish Question. Arneson, Richard J.

JOACHIM, H
Dos Filósofos De La Universidad De Oxford Ante El Conocimiento Metafísico. Sacchi, Mario Enrique.

JOB(S)
Doing The World's Unhealthy Work: The Fiction Of Free Choice. Graebner, William.
Hiring By Competence. Werhane, Patricia H.

JOBE, E
Explanatory Asymmetries. Woodward, James.

JOHN OF THE CROSS
Compagni Di Cammino: Heidegger E San Giovanni Della Croce. Pax, Clyde.

JOHN PAUL II
John Paul The Second Anthropology Of Concrete Totality. Min, Anselm K.
Karol Cardinal Wojtyla And Jean–Paul Sartre On The Intentionality Of Consciousness. Pappin, Joseph.

JOHNSTONE, H
A Problem With Johnstone's Self. Mader, Thomas F.

JONAS, H
Politics, Nature And Freedom: On The Natural Foundation Of The Political Condition. Levy, David J.

JORDAN, M
Schmitz, Jordan And Wallace On Intelligibility. Lobkowicz, Nicholas.

JOURNAL(S)
A Meditation On Critical Mass In The Philosophy Of Sport. Meier, Klaus V.

JOURNALISM
Groping For Ethics In Journalism. Goodwin, H Eugene.
Reporting The Case Of Baby Jane Doe. Kerr, Kathleen.
The Philosophic Society For The Study Of Sport: 1972–1983. Fraleigh, Warren P.

JOYCE
The Aesthetics Of Dedalus And Bloom. Harkness, Marguerite.

JUDAISM
A Book Of Jewish Ethical Concepts: Biblical And Postbiblical. Bloch, Abraham P.
Human Rights In Religious Traditions. Swidler, Arlene (ed).
Martin Buber's Life And Work: The Later Years, 1945–1965. Friedman, Maurice.
Morality, Halakha And The Jewish Tradition. Spero, Shubert.
"Buber's Evaluation Of Christianity: A Jewish Perspective" in *Martin Buber*, Gordon, Haim (ed), 457–472. Wyschogrod, Michael.
"The Fossil And The Phoenix, Leo Rauch (commentator)" in *History And System*, Perkins, Robert (ed), 47–72. Avineri, Shlomo.
"'Jewish Religiousity' According To Buber" in *Martin Buber*, Gordon, Haim (ed), 419–436. Peli, Pinhas Ha–Cohen.
History Of Philosophy In The Grand Manner: The Achievement Of H A Wolfson. Runia, D T.
Jewish Ethics After The Holocaust. Morgan, Michael L.
Les Rasés Et Les Barbus: Diderot Et Le Judaïsme. Bourel, Dominique.
Mutual Responsibility Of The Jewish People And Self–Realization (in Hebrew). Schweid, Eliezer.
Some Thoughts On Nature And Judaism. Ehrenfeld, Joan G and Ehrenfeld, David.
Spiritual Resources: Contemporary Problems In Judaism. Pilchik, Ely E.
The God Of The Philosophers In The Jewish Tradition (in Hebrew). Hartman, David.
The Jewish Intellectual: Some Methodological Proposals (in Hebrew). Mendes– Flohr, Paul.
The Unnatural Jew. Schwarzschild, Steven S.
Un Autre Spinoza. Popkin, Richard H.

JUDEO–CHRISTIAN
The Tragic View Of Life. Beattie, Paul H.

JUDEO–CHRISTIAN TRADITION
Comments On "The Unnatural Jew". Kay, Jeanne.

JUDGE(S)
Selected Standards On Professional Responsibility. Rotunda, Ronald D and Morgan, Thomas D.
Aspects Of Leon Green's Tort Theory: Causation And The Role Of The Judge. Winslade, William J.

JUDGMENT(S)
see also Aesthetic Judgment, Moral Judgment(s)
Beauty Restored. Mothersill, Mary.
Kant's Critical Philosophy. Deleuw, Gilles.
Subjecting And Objecting. Deutscher, Max.
The Limits Of Scientific Reasoning. Faust, David.
"Judgment, Justice, And Mercy" in *The Search For Justice*, Taitte, W Lawson (ed), 83–100. Bailey, Barry.
"Probability And Art Of Judgment" in *Observation, Experiment, And Hypothesis In Modern Physical Science*, Achinstein, Peter (ed), 95–126. Jeffrey, R C.
A General Theorem And Eight Corollaries In Search Of Correct Decision. Nitzan, Shmuel and Paroush, Jacob.
A New View Of Emotion. Leighton, Stephen R.
Be Ye Therefore Perfect Or The Ineradicability Of Sin. Harrison, Jonathan.
Das Unedliche Urteil: Zur Interpretation Eines Kapitels Aus Hegels "Wissenschaft Der Logic". Wolfhart, Günter.
Egalitarianism. Mc Kerlie, Dennis.
Existence And Judgment. Connell, Desmond.
Feelings And Emotion. Leighton, Stephen R.
Judgment And Perception In *Theaetetus* 184–186. Shea, Joseph.
Kants Lehre Vom Urteil. Viertel, Wolfgang.
Pears On *Akrasia*, And Defeated Intentions. Mele, Alfred R.
Perceptual Meaning And Husserl. Cunningham, Suzanne.

Prudence And Folly. Rotenstreich, Nathan.
Reply To Schueler On Akrasia. Taylor, C C W.
Russell's Multiple Relation Theory Of Judgment. Griffin, Nicholas.
The Conclusion Of The Theaetetus. Wheeler, Samuel C.
The Foreign Corrupt Practices Act And The Imposition Of Values. Brummer, James J.
The Neo–Kantian Heritage And The Validity Of Aesthetic Judgments (in Hebrew). Levavi, Aryeh.
The Problem Of Art And Morality In The Context Of Kant's Aesthetics (in Dutch). Hattingh, J P.
Utility And Rational Self–Interest. Mc Dermott, Michael.

JUDICIAL PRECEDENT
Formal Justice, Moral Commitment, And Judicial Precedent. Lyons, David.

JUDICIARY
Derivability, Defensibility, And The Justification Of Judicial Decisions. Lyons, David.
Hart, Dworkin, Judges, And New Law. Yanal, Robert J.
The Ideological Role Of The Judiciary In South Africa. Suttner, Raymond.

JUNG
A Jungian View Of Evil. Segal, Robert A.
A Suggested Approach To Linking Decision Styles With Business Ethics. Fleming, John E.
Hegel, Jung, And The Spirit Of History. Kelly, Sean.
On Strong's *Psychoanalysis As A Vocation: Freud, Politics, And The Heroic.* Odajnyk, V Walter.

JURIDICAL
The State And I: Hypotheses On Juridical And Technocratic Humanism. Lock, Grahame.
Raisonnement Juridique Et Raisonnement Pratique. De Ruvo, Vincenzo.
Single– And Multiple–Rule Theories Of Judicial Reasoning. Gerber, David.

JURISPRUDENCE
see also Law
American Political Thought: The Philosophic Dimension Of American Statesmanship, Second Edition. Frisch, Morton J (ed) and Stevens, Richard G (ed).
Essays In Jurisprudence And Philosophy. Hart, H L A (ed).
The Decline Of Juridical Reason: Doctrine And Theory In The Legal Order. Simmonds, N E.
Wealth And Virtue: The Shaping Of Political Economy In The Scottish Enlightenment. Hont, Istvan (ed) and Ignatieff, Michael (ed).
Aufgaben Und Schwierigkeiten Der Analytischen Rechtstheorie. Weinberger, Ota.
Bedingungen Einer Rekonstruktion Rechtlichen Argumentierens: Zum Verhältnis Von Philosophie Und Rechtswissenschaft. Heyen, Erk Volkmar.
Beyond Legal Gaps. Broekman, Jan M.
Die Rechtstheorie In Polen Im XX. Jahrhundert. Opalek, Kazimierz.
Dishonesty And The Jury: A Case Study In The Moral Content Of Law. Tur, Richard.
Hart, Legal Rules And Palm Tree Justice. Waluchow, Wilfrid J.
Insiders And Outsiders Models Of Deviance And Jurisprudence. Hund, John.
Legal Justification And Control: Sociological Aspects Of Philosophy. Klami, Hanna T.
Legal Language And Legal Interpretation. Wroblewski, Jerzy.
Moral And Ontological Justification Of Legal Reasoning. Peczenik, Aleksander.
Norms And Logic: Kelsen And Weinberger On The Ontology Of Norms. Bulygin, Eugenio.
The Expressive Conception Of Norms—An Impasse For The Logic Of Norms. Weinberger, Ota.
The Rights Approach To Mental Illness. Campbell, Tom.
The Serpent Beguiled Me And I Did Eat: Entrapment And The Creation Of Crime. Dworkin, Gerald.
Trial By Charade. Mac' Kie, Pamela S.
What Is So Special About (Free) Speech? Husak, Douglas N.

JURY SYSTEM
Dishonesty And The Jury: A Case Study In The Moral Content Of Law. Tur, Richard.

JUST WAR
Can Modern War Be Just? Johnson, James T.
Moral Dimensions Of American Foreign Policy. Thompson, Kenneth W (ed).
War And Justice. Phillips, Robert L.
When War Is Unjust: Being Honest In Just–War Thinking. Yoder, John H.
When War Is Unjust: Being Honest In Just War Thinking. Yoder, John H.
A Certain Just War, A Certain Pacifism. Conley, John J.
A Consistent Alternative View Within The Just War Family. Yoder, John H.
Christianity And Pacifism. Mouw, Richard J.
Reflections On War And Political Discourse: Realism, Just War, And Feminism In A Nuclear Age. Elshtain, Jean Bethke.
Right Intention, Deterrence, And Nuclear Alternatives. Kunkel, Joseph C.
War, Nuclear War, And Nuclear Deterrence: Some Conceptual And Moral Issues. Wasserstrom, Richard.

JUSTICE
see also Distributive Justice
A Theory Of Law. Soper, Philip.
George Grant And The Twilight Of Justice. O' Donovan, Joan E.
Marxism: Nomos XXVI. Pennock, J Roland (ed) and Chapman, John W (ed).
Moral Development Foundations: Judeo–Christian Alternatives To Piaget/Kohlberg. Joy, Donald M (ed).
Private Justice: Towards Integrated Theorising In The Sociology Of Law. Henry, Stuart.
Rawls And Rights. Martin, Rex.
Rights And Goods: Justifying Social Action. Held, Virginia.
The Islamic Conception Of Justice. Khadduri, Majid.

JUSTICE

The Politics Of Moderation: An Interpretation Of Plato's "Republic". Wilson, John F.
The Search For Justice. Taitte, W Lawson (ed).
War And Justice. Phillips, Robert L.
"Eigentum Ist Nicht Eigentum", Zur Rechtfertigkeit Des Eigentums. Kohler, Georg.
"El Justo Es Feliz Y El Injusto Desgraciado": Justicia Y Felicidad En La "República" De Platón. Perez Ruiz, Francisco.
"Foreign Aid: Justice For Whom" in *The Search For Justice,* Taitte, W Lawson (ed), 127–162. Rostow, W W.
"Judgment, Justice, And Mercy" in *The Search For Justice,* Taitte, W Lawson (ed), 83–100. Bailey, Barry.
"Justice And Society: Beyond Individualism" in *The Search For Justice,* Taitte, W Lawson (ed), 101–126. Murphy, Ewell E.
"Justice As Social Choice" in *Morality, Reason And Truth,* Copp, David (ed), 251–269. Gauthier, David.
"Liberty And Justice For All: Keeping The Scales In Balance" in *The Search For Justice,* Taitte, W Lawson (ed), 25–42. Webster, William H.
"Symmetry, Independence, Continuity, Boundedness, And Additivity": The Game Of Education. Krolikowski, Walter P and Hablutzel, Nancy and Hoffman, Wilma.
"The Marxist Critique Of Rawls" in *Contemporary Marxism,* O' Rourke, James J (ed), 237–244. Küng, Guido.
"The Processes Of Adjudication And Regulation, A Comparison" in *Rights And Regulation,* Machan, Tibor (ed), 71–98. Smith, J C.
"The Search For Justice Introduction" in *The Search For Justice,* Taitte, W Lawson (ed), 11–24. Cecil, Andrew R.
"The Theory And Practice Of The History Of Freedom, Harry Brod (commentator)" in *History And System,* Perkins, Robert (ed), 123–148. Winfield, Richard D.
A Contradiction In The Egalitarian Theory Of Justice. Howard, Michael W.
Abusing The Unemployed: An Invisible Justice. Breakwell, Glynis M.
Aristotle On Rawls: A Critique Of Quantitative Justice. Jackson, M W.
Bargaining And Justice. Gauthier, David.
Die Lehre Vom Gerechten Krieg Bei Grotius Und Leibniz Und Ihre Bedeutung Für Die Gegenwart. Serra, Antonio Truyol.
Die Unmögliche Rechtsphilosophie: Zu Hans Ryffels Rechtsund Staatsphilosophie. Gil– Cremades, Juan-Jose.
Dilemmas Of Justness In Top Sport. Foldesi, Tamas and Foldesi, Gyongyi Szabo.
Distributive Justice In Aristotle's Ethics And Politics. Keyt, David.
Does It Matter If The Death Penalty Is Arbitrarily Administered? Nathanson, Stephen.
Does Liberalism Rest On A Mistake? Rodewald, Richard.
Does Marx Have A Concept Of Justice? Keyes, Thomas W.
Doing Marx Justice. Young, Gary.
Fair Equality Of Opportunity And Decent Minimums: A Reply To Buchanan. Daniels, Norman.
Faith And Justice: A New Synthesis—The Interface Of Process And Liberation Theologies. Bracken, Joseph A.
Formal Justice And Township Justice. Hund, John.
Friendship, Justice, And Superogation. Badhwar, Neera K.
Giustizia Rivoluzionaria E Violenza. Dal Brollo, Alessandro.
Global Justice, Capitalism And The Third World. Nielsen, Kai.
Hugo Grotius And The History Of Political Thought. Haakonssen, Knud.
In Pursuit Of Wholeness: Moral Development, The Ethics Of Care And The Virtue Of *Philia.* Prakash, Madhu Suri.
Introduzca Critica Alla Teoria Della Giustizia Di Rawls. Hoffe, Otfried.
Is Rawls' Theory Of Justice Really Kantian? Höffe, Otfried.
Just Taxation In The Roman Catholic Tradition. Curran, Charles E.
Justice And Class Interests. Wood, Allen W.
Justice Et Glorification: Double Préoccupation D'Ulrich Zwingli, Réformateur (1484–1531). Burki, Bruno.
Justice, Civilization, And The Death Penalty: Answering Van Den Haag. Reiman, Jeffrey H.
Justifying Departures From Equal Treatment. Murphy, Jeffrie G.
Le Raisonnement De L'injustice. Vitorino, Orlando.
Liberation Theology And Social Justice. Lamb, Matthew L.
Libertarians And Indians: Proprietary Justice And Aboriginal Land Rights. Watner, Carl.
Management And Ethical Decision–Making. Robinson, Wade L.
Marx's Concept Of Justice And The Two Traditions In The European Political Thought. Commers, Ronald.
Menschenwürde Und Menschenrechte Im Licht Der Reich–Gottes–Verkündigung Jesu. Schönborn, Christoph.
Nation, Justice And Liberty. Ki– Zerbo, Joseph.
On Retributivism And The Lex Talionis. Primorac, Igor.
Ontology And The Theory Of Justice. Grafstein, Robert.
Outlines Of A Marxist Conception Of Justice II (in Hungarian). Foldesi, Tamas.
Outlines Of A Possible Marxist Conception Of Justice I (in Hungarian). Földesi, Tamás.
Parenting As A Profession: Children's Rights And Parental Responsibility. Graybosch, Anthony.
Points Of Contact Between Process Theology And Liberation Theology In Matters Of Faith And Justice. Cobb, John B.
Preferences Opposed To The Market. Braybrooke, David.
Presidential Address: For And Against Bureaucracy. Luebke, Neil.
Principles For Individual Actions. Wilkins, Burleigh T and Zelikovitz, Kelly M.
Raisonnement Juridique Et Raisonnement Pratique. De Ruvo, Vincenzo.
Razionalismo Critico E Valutazione Del Diritto In Hans Albert. Giadrossi, Gianfranco.
Rebuilding Rawls: An Alternative Theory Of Justice. Groarke, Leo.

Refuting Reiman And Nathanson. Van Den Haag, Ernest.
Reiman's Libertarian Interpretation Of Rawls' Difference Principle. Alexander, Lawrence.
Rule Utilitarianism, Equality, And Justice. Harsanyi, John C.
Social Contract As A Basis Of Norms: A Critique. Machan, Tibor R.
Social Justice And Legal Justice. Sadurski, Wojciech.
Socrates On The Rule Of Law. Stephens, James.
Socratic Piety In The *Euthyphro.* Mc Pherran, Mark L.
Some Considerations About The Discovery Of Principles Of Justice. Suits, David B.
Strict Compliance And Rawls's Critique Of Utilitarianism. Carson, Thomas L.
The Classification Of Goods In Plato's *Republic.* White, Nicholas.
The Controversy About Marx And Justice. Geras, Norman.
The Demands Of Justice. Benditt, Theodore M.
The Ethics Of Anti–Moralism In Marx's Theory Of Communism: An Interpretation. Raes, Koen.
The Incoherence Of Intergenerational Justice. Ball, Terence.
The Indefeasibility Of Justice. Day, J P.
The Marxian Critique Of Justice And Rights. Buchanan, Allen E.
The Matrix Of Contractarian Justice. Buchanan, James M and Lomasky, Loren E.
The Maximin Rule Argument For Rawls's Principles Of Justice. Langtry, Bruce.
The Metaphysics Of Faith And Justice. Ogden, Schubert M.
The Paradox Of Eden. La Croix, Richard.
The Possibility Of A Marxian Theory Of Justice. Reiman, Jeffrey H.
The Riddle Of The *Cleitophon.* Roochnik, David L.
The Role Of The Laws Of Thought In The Administration Of Justice (in Hungarian). Lukács, Tibor.
The Virtues Of *Philia* And Justice: Who Learns These In Our Society. Diller, Ann.
Towards A Theory Of Taxation. Lucas, J R.
Two Interpretations Of The Difference Principle In Rawls's Theory Of Justice. Shenoy, Prakash P and Martin, Rex.
Welfare State Versus Welfare Society? Skillen, Anthony.
Why Be Just: Hume's Response In The *Inquiry.* Costa, Michael J.
Worker Control, Self–Respect, And Self–Esteem. Howard, Michael W.

JUSTIFIABILITY

A Situational Account Of Knowledge. Hanfling, Oswald.
An Indubitability Analysis Of Knowledge. Forrest, Peter.
In Defense Of A Nontraditional Theory Of Memory. Naylor, Andrew.
The Problem Of Induction: A New Approach. De Oliveira, Marcos Barbosa.

JUSTIFICATION

A Priori Knowledge For Fallibilists. Edidin, Aron.
Justifying Historical Descriptions. Mc Cullagh, C Behan.
A Defense Of Epistemic Intuitionism. Moser, Paul K.
A Quick Justification For Business Ethics. Lombardi, Louis G.
Another Look At Paternalism. Hobson, Peter.
Authority And Justification. Raz, Joseph.
Beyond Divorce: Current Status Of The Discovery Debate. Nickles, Thomas.
Can There Be An Infinite Regress Of Justified Beliefs? Harker, Jay E.
Concepts Of Epistemic Justification. Alston, William P.
Contemporary Moral Philosophy And Practical Reason. Sterba, James P.
Contra Reliabilism. Ginet, Carl.
Davidson's Theory Of Meaning: Some Questions. Taylor, Kenneth A.
Derivability, Defensibility, And The Justification Of Judicial Decisions. Lyons, David.
Descriptive Epistemology. Duran, Jane.
Dewey's Theory Of Inquiry: Problems Of Foundations. Lakomski, Gabriele.
Epistemic Universalizability Principles. Brueckner, Anthony.
Foundationalism And Permanence In Descartes' Epistemology. Cling, Andrew D.
Human Needs And The Justification Of Religious Belief. Holyer, Robert.
Intolerable Wrong And Punishment. Wolgast, Elizabeth H.
Is There An 'Us' In 'Justification'? Kvanvig, J L.
It's Not What You Know That Counts. Kaplan, Mark.
Justification, Reasons, And Reliability. Swain, Marshall.
Justification As Discoverability II. Nickles, Thomas.
Justification And Truth. Cohen, Stewart.
Legal Justification And Control: Sociological Aspects Of Philosophy. Klami, Hanna T.
Magical Aspects Of Political Terrorism. Miguens, José Enrique.
Moral And Ontological Justification Of Legal Reasoning. Peczenik, Aleksander.
Moritz Schlick On Self–Evidence. Von Kutschera, Franz.
Nozick And Knowledge—A Rejoinder. Garrett, B J.
On Basic Knowledge Without Justification. Moser, Paul K.
On The "Essential Contestedness" Of Political Concepts. Swanton, Christine.
On Ultimate Justification. Lubnicki, Narcyz.
Reflective Equilibrium And Justification. Little, Daniel.
Reliability And Epistemic Merit. Heil, John.
Reliability And Indirect Justification. Kapitan, Tomis.
Reliability And Justification. Feldman, Richard.
Reliability, Justification, And The Problem Of Induction. Van Cleve, James.
Scepticism Reconsidered. Meynell, Hugo.
The Coherence Of Virtue And The Virtue Of Coherence: Justification In Epistemology. Sosa, Ernest.
Theism And The Moral Point Of View. Hammond, John L.
Two Classical Western Theologians: Augustine And Newman. Penaskovic, Richard.
Violence And The Politics Of Explanation: Kampuchea Revisited. Hawkesworth, Mary E.
Whither Infinite Regresses Of Justification. Moser, Paul D.

JUSTIN MARTYR

Images Of Liberation: Justin, Jesus And The Jews. Root, Michael.

KIERKEGAARD

Commentary, Perkins, Robert L (ed), 87–106. Roberts, Robert C.

"Towards Apocalypse" in *International Kierkegaard Commentary*, Perkins, Robert L (ed), 19–52. Plekon, Michael.

"Two Ages: A Story Of Soren Kierkegaard And Isak Dinesen" in *International Kierkegaard Commentary*, Perkins, Robert L (ed), 175–188. Kleinman, Jackie.

Hamlet Without The Prince Of Denmark Revisited: Pörn On Kierkegaard And The Self. Hannay, Alastair.

Irony As A Post–Romantic Possibility For Art: Kierkegaard's Reply To Hegel. Crooks, James.

Kierkegaard, Indirect Communication, And Religious Truth. Kellenberger, J.

Le Carte Schleiermacheriane Di Kierkegaard. Spera, Salvatore.

Melancholy, Irony, And Kierkegaard. Khan, Abrahim H.

Rhetoric And Reality In Kierkegaard's *Postscript*. Dunning, Stephan N.

The Image Of The Father In Sartre's "L'universel Singulier" (in Hebrew). Neppi, Enzo.

The Rational Foundations Of Kierkegaard's Critique Of Reason. Marino, Gordon D.

KILLING

A Contractarian Defense Of Nuclear Deterrence. Morris, Christopher W.

Are 'Killing' And 'Letting Die' Adequately Specified Moral Categories? Philips, Michael.

Comments On Dan Brock And Terrence Reynolds. Donagan, Alan.

Moral Absolutism And Abortion: Alan Donagan On The Hysterectomy And Craniotomy Cases. Reynolds, Terrence.

Taking Human Life. Brock, Dan W.

KILVINGTON, R

Epistemic And Alethic Iteration In Later Medieval Logic. Boh, Ivan.

KIM, J

Folk Psychology Is Here To Stay. Horgan, Terence and Woodward, James.

KINEMATICS

Normative Kinematics (I): A Solution To A Problem About Permission. Belzer, Marvin.

Probability, Kinematics, Conditionals, And Entropy Principles. Domotor, Zoltan.

Spatial Things And Kinematic Events. Stafleu, M D.

KINESIS

The ΈΝΕΡΓΕΙΑ–ΚΙΝΗΣΙΣ Distinction And Aristotle's Conception Of ΠΡΑΞΙΣ. Hagen, Charles T.

KING–FARLOW, J

A Pointing Finger Kills "The Buddha": A Response To Chung–Ying Cheng And John King Farlow. Sellman, James.

An Anglo–Saxon Response To John King Farlow's Questions On Zen Language And Zen Paradoxes. Tucker, John.

KING, W

A Pamphlet Attributed To John Toland And An Unpublished Reply By Archbishop William King. Kelly, Patrick.

KIRK, R

USA: Conservatism Contra Liberalism (in Czechoslovakian). Krejcí, O.

KIRSCH, G

Observation, Experiment, And Hypothesis In Modern Physical Science. Achinstein, Peter (ed) and Hannaway, Owen (ed).

"Artificial Disintegration" in *Observation, Experiment, And Hypothesis In Modern Physical Science*, Achinstein, Peter (ed), 239–308. Stuewer, Roger H.

KISIEL, T

Comments Of Theodore Kisiel's Commentary On My Paper: Hermeneutics Of Experimental Science In The Context Of The Life–World. Heelan, Patrick A.

KLEIN, J

Die Philosophische Tätigkeit Von Johannes Klein. Darowski, Roman.

KLOSKOWSKA, A

The Ontology Of The Body: A Study In Philosophical And Cultural Anthropology. Krawczyk, Zbigniew.

KNAUER, P

La Question Des Actes Intrinsèquement Mauvais. Pinckaers, S.

KNOWING

Jñāna And Pramā: The Logic Of Knowing––A Critical Appraisal. Bilimoria, Purusottama.

'Knowing What It's Like' And The Essential Indexical. Mc Mullen, Carolyn.

"Armstrong's Theory Of Knowing" in *D M Armstrong*, Bogdan, Radu J (ed), 139–160. Lycan, William G.

De Opheffing Van De Religie In Het Absolute Weten Volgens Hegels Phänomenologie Des Geistes. Devos, R.

Knowability, Believability And Begging The Question: A Reply To David H Sanford. Biro, John I.

On Being Moved By Fiction. Mannison, Don.

St Thomas And The Integration Of Knowledge Into Being. Dewan, Lawrence.

The Paradox Of Eden. La Croix, Richard.

Two Alternative Epistemological Frameworks In Psychology: The Typological And Variational Modes Of Thinking. Valsiner, Jaan.

KNOWING HOW

Epistemic Analysis: A Coherence Theory Of Knowledge. Ziff, Paul.

KNOWLEDGE

see also Epistemology

A Priori Knowledge For Fallibilists. Edidin, Aron.

Action (1893): Essay On A Critique Of Life And A Science Of Practice. Blanchette, Oliva (trans) and Blondel, Maurice.

Beyond Empiricism: Michael Polanyi Reconsidered. Kane, Jeffrey.

Beyond Feelings: A Guide To Critical Thinking, Second Edition. Ruggiero, Vincent Ryan.

Epistemic Analysis: A Coherence Theory Of Knowledge. Ziff, Paul.

Freud And The Mind. Dilman, Ilham.

Historical Consciousness Or The Remembered Past. Lukacs, John.

I–Man: An Outline Of Philosophical Anthropology. Krąpiec, Mieczylaw A and Lescoe, Marie (trans) and Woznicki, Theresa (trans).

Jñāna And Pramā: The Logic Of Knowing––A Critical Appraisal. Bilimoria, Purusottama.

Knowledge Structure And Use: Implications For Synthesis And Interpretation, Linda J Reed (ed). Ward, Spencer (ed).

Leibniz And Locke: A Study Of The "New Essays On Human Understanding". Jolley, Nicholas.

Logic And The Objectivity Of Knowledge: Studies In Husserl's Early Philosophy. Willard, Dallas.

Logic, Philosophy, And History: A Study In The Philosophy Of History Based On The Work Of R G Collingwood. Russell, Anthony F.

Plato. Rowe, C J.

The Knower And The Known. Grene, Marjorie G.

The Nature Of Technological Knowledge: Are Models Of Scientific Change Relevant. Laudan, Rachel (ed).

The Postmodern Condition: A Report On Knowledge. Lyotard, Jean François.

The Significance Of Philosophical Scepticism. Stroud, Barry.

The State And I: Hypotheses On Juridical And Technocratic Humanism. Lock, Grahame.

Treatise On Basic Philosophy, V5. Bunge, Mario.

Über Die Wahrheit Und Den Wahrheitsbegriff. Steussloff, Hans.

"Can Philosophy Ever Be A Thing For Hoosiers" in *The Georgetown Symposium On Ethics*, Porreco, Rocco (ed), 1–18. Veatch, Henry B.

"Communicative Acts And Extralinguistic Knowledge" in *The Analysis Of Action*, Von Cranach, Mario (ed), 267–308. Kreckel, Marga.

"Discussion Upon Fundamental Principles Of Education" (1919). Whitehead, Alfred N and Brumbaugh, Robert S (ed).

"Plato's Dialectic Of The Sun" in *History Of Philosophy In Making*, Thro, Linus J (ed), 19–34. Eslick, Leonard J.

"Sticks And Stones; Or, The Ins And Outs Of Existence" in *On Nature*, Rouner, Leroy S (ed), 13–26. Quine, W V.

A Comparison Of Three Ways Of Knowing: Categorical, Structural, And Affirmative. Mc Cabe, Viki.

A Crack In The Foundations Of Descartes's Theory Of Knowledge. Hund, J.

A Problem About Frequencies In Direct Inference. Leeds, Stephen.

A Situational Account Of Knowledge. Hanfling, Oswald.

Absolutes Wesen/Absolutes Wissen. Horn, J C.

An Indubitability Analysis Of Knowledge. Forrest, Peter.

Approccio Fenomenologico Alla Conoscenza Metafisica. Lambertino, Antonio.

Apriorismo Como Contenido Intelectual En Balmes, Reflejo De La "Memoria Dei" Agustiniana? Casado, Fidel.

Aristotle On The Extension Of Non–Contradiction. Halper, Edward.

Art And Knowledge. Gingell, J.

Art And Knowledge. Reid, Louis Arnaud.

Berlin On Vico. Zagorin, Perez.

Beyond Being: Heidegger's Plato. Dostal, Robert.

Carta De San Agustín A Consencio: Sobre La Razón Y La Revelación. Moriones, Francisco.

Cassirer's Dialectic Of The Mythical Consciousness. Von Der Luft, Eric.

Causal Theories Of Knowledge. Dretske, Fred and Enc, Berent.

Cognition And Epistemic Closure. Bogdan, Radu J.

Commensurability, Incommensurability And Cumulativity In Scientific Knowledge. Agazzi, Evandro.

Connoisseurship. Meager, Ruby.

Correct Explanatory Arguments And Understanding–why An Approach To Scientific Understanding Based On Knowledge Dynamics. Schurz, Gerhard.

Das Aufsteigen Der Erkenntnis Vom Abstrakten Zum Konkreten. Pröhl, Joachim.

Das Erkennen Als Ein Erkennen In Blosser Erscheinung: Zu Ingeborg Heidemanns Verständnis Der Kritik Der Reiner Vernuft. Kopper, J.

Davidson's Theism? Foley, Richard and Fumerton, Richard.

Die Seins– Und Erkenntnisfrage In Der Philosophie Brentanos. Melle, U.

Does The Gettier Problem Rest On A Mistake? Kirkham, Richard L.

Epistemic Dependence. Hardwig, John.

Epistemic Dependence. Dauer, Francis W.

Erkenntnistheorie Ohne Erkenntnis. Hogrebe, Wolfram.

Eternal Truths And The Laws Of Nature: The Theological Foundations Of Descartes' Philosophy Of Nature. Osler, Margaret.

Fundamentación Ontológica De La Libertad Psicológica. Bogliolo, Luis.

Hegel's Evaluation And Analysis Of Socrates' Proposition "Virtue Is Knowledge". Xiuliang, Lan.

Investigating Lonergan's Inaccessibility. Walmsley, Gerard.

It's Not What You Know That Counts. Kaplan, Mark.

Kant And Foucault: On The Ends Of Man. Watson, Stephen.

Kant, Wittgenstein And The Limits Of Logic. Tiles, Mary.

Kants Antinomien Und Die Logik Der Erkenntnis. Narski, I S.

Knowledge And Certainty. Mclean, Don.

Knowledge As Tracking? Schmitt, Frederick F.

Knowledge As The Production Of Intellectual Instruments And Theoretical Constructions. Cekić, Miodrag.

Konstruktiver Empirismus. Kraft, Victor.

KNOWLEDGE

Kritik Und Bergründung In Transzendentaler Argumentation. Becker, Wolfgang.

La Réalité En Soi Et Connaissable Est-Elle Possible? Espinoza, Miguel.

Locke On Knowledge And Propositions. Soles, David E.

Maimonides And Aquinas On Man's Knowledge Of God: A Twentieth Century Perspective. Franck, Isaac.

Moritz Schlick On Self-Evidence. Von Kutschera, Franz.

Must Knowledge—Or 'Knowledge' Be Socially Constructed? Radford, Colin.

Must The Bearer Of A Right Have The Concept Of That To Which He Has A Right? Stevens, John C.

Nietzsche's Rereading Of Plato. Zuckert, Catherine.

Notas Históricas E Filosóficas Sobre O Conhecimento. De Soveral, Eduardo Abranches.

Nozick And Knowledge—A Rejoinder. Garrett, B J.

Nozick On Inferential Knowledge. Mazoué, James G.

On Vico. Berlin, Isaiah.

Ontological And Epistemological Aspect Of Contradictions: Importance For Analysis Of Development Of Society (in Czechoslovakian). Zeman, Jirí.

Philosophy And The Mirror Of Rorty. Munz, Peter.

Popper En Question. Reichberg, G.

Réflexions Sur Popper. Radnitzky, Gerard.

Recent Work On Epistemology. Harrison, Jonathan.

Reflections On The Value Of Knowledge: A Reply To Creel. Keller, James.

Response To Mazoué's "Nozick On Inferential Knowledge" And Brueckner's "Transmission For Knowledge Not Established". Forbes, Graeme.

Reversing Rorty. Meynell, Hugo.

Russell's *Theory Of Knowledge* And Wittgenstein's Earliest Writings. Iglesias, Teresa.

Scepticism Reconsidered. Meynell, Hugo.

Skepticism And The Possibility Of Knowledge. Stroud, Barry.

Socrates' Disavowal Of Knowledge. Vlastos, Gregory.

St Augustine's Quest For The Truth: The Adequacy Of A Christian Philosophy. Kuntz, Paul G.

Symposium: Knowledge And The Humanities—The Continuing Debate. Brinton, Crane and others.

The Affinities Of Literature. Boyd, John D.

The Concept Of Experimental Knowledge In The Thought Of Chang Tsai. Birdwhistell, Anne D.

The Concept Of Knowledge. Mc Ginn, Colin.

The Conclusion Of The Theaetetus. Wheeler, Samuel C.

The Meaning Of Proportionate Reason In Contemporary Moral Theology. Johnstone, Brian V.

The Particularity Of Moral Knowledge. Dinan, Stephen A.

The Problem Of The Integration Of Knowledge And Interdisciplinarity From The Viewpoint Of Biological Sciences (in Czechoslovakian). Zeman, J.

The Problem Of Divine Exemplarity In St Thomas. Farthing, John L.

The Scientific And The Ethical. Williams, Bernard.

The Scope Of Knowledge In Republic V. White, F C.

The Scope Of Reason: An Epistle To The Persians. Bambrough, Renford.

The Structure Of Historical Knowledge And The Method Of Actualism (in Czechoslovakian). Cízek, F.

Theory Dynamics And Knowledge Representation From An Information-Theoretical Point Of View. Hauffe, Heinz.

Topology Of Internal And External Factors In The Development Of Knowledge. Lelas, Srdan.

Toward A Social Theory Of Ignorance. Smithson, Michael.

Transmission For Knowledge Not Established. Brueckner, Anthony.

Un Nuevo Paraqdigma Para Las Ciencias Del Concocimiento. Gutiérrez, Claudio.

Unlicensed Brainwork: A Case Study In Suppressive Discourse From Above. Schäfer, Wolf.

Wahrheit Und Moral. Loeser, Franz.

Who Needs Paradigms? Roth, Paul A.

KNOX, T

T M Knox: His Life And Scholarship. Pelczynski, Zbigniew A.

T M Knox: His Life And Scholarship, Part II. Pelczynski, Zbigniew A.

KOBOZEV, N

The Problem Of The Integration Of Knowledge And Interdisciplinarity From The Viewpoint Of Biological Sciences (in Czechoslovakian). Zeman, J.

KOHLBERG, L

Dimensions Of Moral Education. Carter, Robert E.

Moral Development Foundations: Judeo-Christian Alternatives To Piaget/Kohlberg. Joy, Donald M (ed).

Morality In The Making. Weinreich Haste, Helen (ed) and Locke, Don (ed).

Current Research In Moral Development As A Decision Support System. Penn, William Y and Collier, Boyd D.

Habermas' Communicative Ethics And The Development Of Moral Consciousness. White, Stephen K.

Sentiment And Structure: A Durkheimian Critique Of Kohlberg's Moral Theory. Wallwork, Ernest.

KOLAKOWSKI, L

Kolakowski And Marković On Stalinism. Rockmore, Thomas.

Where Are The Barbarians: Ethnocentrism Versus The Illusion Of Cultural Universalism: The Answer Of An Anthropologist To A Philosopher. Kronenberg, Andreas.

KOLLEWIJN, R

Once Upon A Tense. Verkuyl, H J and Le Loux-Schuringa, J A.

KOOK

Perfection And Perfectibility In Rabbi Kook's Theology (in Hebrew). Ben-Shlomo, Joseph.

KOOTTE, A

A Critical Look At "A Critical Look": Castaneda Recrudescent. Paper, Jordan.

KORAN

"La Destinée De La Tragédie Dans La Culture Islamique" in *Existential Coordinates Of Human Condition*, Tymieniecka, A (ed), 333–340. Chehida, A Ben.

A Quest For The Values In Islam. Djaït, Hichem.

Ethics And Taxation: The Perspective Of The Islamic Tradition. Nanji, Azim A.

KORSCH, K

"Karl Korsch And Marxism" in *Continuity And Change In Marxism*, Fischer, Norman And Others (ed), 232–247. Kellner, Douglas.

KOTARBINSKI, T

Philosophical Ideas Of Tadeusz Kotarbiński. Szaniawski, Klemens.

KRAWCZYK, Z

The Ontology Of The Body: A Study In Philosophical And Cultural Anthropology. Krawczyk, Zbigniew.

The World Socio-Economic And Political Crisis Calls For Changes In The Position And Social Role Of Sports. Petrović, Kresimir.

KREIJCI, R

Is Wittgenstein Paradoxical? Sahu, Neelamani.

KRING, H

Einfuhrung In Die Philosophie Der Gegenwart: Dargestellt In Einem Handbuch Philosophischer Grundbegriffe. Steinbeck, W.

KRIPKE, S

Against Holism. Weir, Alan.

Belief And Possibility. Altrichter, Ferenc.

Conceptual Progress And Word/World Relations: In Search Of The Essence Of Natural Kinds. Churchland, Paul M.

Dissolving Kripke's Puzzle About Belief. Pettit, Philip.

Does The Description Theory Make Contingent Truths Necessary? Eudaly, Thomas D.

Intuitionistic Truth. Rabinowicz, Wlodzimierz.

Kripke And Wittgenstein: Intention Without Paradox. Moser, Paul K and Flannery, Kevin.

Kripke On Private Language. Hoffman, Paul.

Kripke's Account Of The Argument Against Private Language. Wright, Crispin.

Kritisches Zu Kripkes Theorie Der Eigennamen. Franzen, Winfried.

Le Sens D'un Nom Propre. Engel, Pascal.

Reference And Subordinating Descriptions. Dau, Paolo.

Remarks On The Semantics Of Non-Normal Modal Logics. Schotch, Peter K.

Rigid Designators And Disguised Descriptions. Cook, Monte.

Supervaluations Without Truth-Value Gaps. Herzberger, Hans G.

Visual Space From The Perspective Of Possible World Semantics II. Wiesenthal, L.

Was Wittgenstein A Sceptic? Hanfling, Oswald.

What's In A Belief? Biro, J I.

KRISHNAMURTI

J Krishnamurti On Choiceless Awareness, Creative Emptiness And Ultimate Freedom. Mathur, Dinesh Chandra.

Krishnamurti Zen. Bouchard, Roch.

KROCHMAL, N

"The Fossil And The Phoenix, Leo Rauch (commentator)" in *History And System*, Perkins, Robert (ed), 47–72. Avineri, Shlomo.

KRONMAN, A

Natural Advantages And Contractual Justice. Alexander, Larry and Wang, William.

KROPOTKIN, P

Mutual Aid And Selfish Genes. Thompson, Janna L.

KRUEGER, G

"Expérience Religieuse Et Expérience Profane Du Monde" Dans Les "aecrits Inédits De G Krüger. Schaeffler, Richard.

G Krüger: A La Recherche D'un Humanisme Religieux. Kluback, William.

KUCERA, J

Aesthetician Of Film And Television Jan Kucera (in Czechoslovakian). Svoboda, Jan.

KUHN, T

Is Science Progressive? Niiniluoto, Ilkka.

"Five Parables" in *Philosophy In History*, Rorty, Richard and others (ed), 103–124. Hacking, Ian.

"Observations, Explanatory Power, Simplicity" in *Observation, Experiment, Hypothesis In Physical Science*, Achinstein, Peter (ed), 45–94. Boyd, Richard N.

"Paradigms, Revolutions, And Technology" in *Technological Knowledge*, Laudan, Rachel (ed), 47–66. Gutting, Gary.

Aether/Or: The Creation Of Scientific Concepts. Nersessian, Nancy J.

Converging Reflections On The Philosophy Of Science. Newton Smith, W and Wilkes, K.

Das Problem Der Rationalität. Agassi, Joseph.

Knowledge And Certainty. Mclean, Don.

New Philosophies Of Science In The USA; A Selective Survey. Kisiel, Theodore and Johnson, Galen.

Popperian And Kuhnian Theories Of Truth And The Imputation Of Relativism. Edison, J.

Social Theory Without Wholes. Turner, Stephen P.

Some Epistemological Trends In Philosophy Of Science. Shekhawat, Virendra.

Testability, Flexibility: Kuhnian Values In Scientists' Discourse Concerning Theory Choice. Potter, Jonathan.

Toward An Epistemologically-Relevant Sociology Of Science. Campbell, Donald T.

LANGUAGE

LAWS

Commentary On Daley's "Toward A Theory Of Bribery". Turow, Scott.
Competition In Consumption As Viewed By Jewish Law. Liebermann, Yehoshua.
Derivability, Defensibility, And The Justification Of Judicial Decisions. Lyons, David.
Empirische Wetten En Theorieën. En Kuipers, Theo and Zandvoort, Henk.
Gesellschaftswissenschaftliche Methoden Auf Dem Wege Der Gesetzeserkenntnis. Zak, Christian.
Gesetzmässigkeiten Des Revolutionären Prozesses. Eichhorn, Wolfgang.
Hart, Dworkin, Judges, And New Law. Yanal, Robert J.
Incorrigible Laws: The State's Role In Resolving Intrafamily Conflict. Guggenheim, Martin.
Laws And Causal Relations. Tooley, Michael.
Laws Of Nature And Cosmic Coincidences. Smart, J J C.
Negative Positivism And The Hard Facts Of Life. Silver, Charles.
Nomische Notwendigkeit. Will, Ulrich.
On The Change Of Social Laws. Sztompka, Piotr.
Probability And Laws. Constantini, D.
The Confirmation Of Quantitative Laws. Kyburg, Henry E.
The Human Basis Of Laws And Ethics. Edwards, Frederick.
The Justification Of Legal Moralism. Kultgen, John.

LAWYER(S)

Problems And Materials On Professional Responsibility. Morgan, Thomas D and Rotunda, Ronald D.
Problems In Legal Ethics. Schwartz, Mortimer D and Wydick, Richard C.
Selected Standards On Professional Responsibility. Rotunda, Ronald D and Morgan, Thomas D.
The Legal Profession: Responsibility And Regulation. Hazard, Geoffrey C and Rhode, Deborah L.
Lawyer–Client Confidences Under The A B A Model Rules: Ethical Rules Without Ethical Reason. Freedman, Monroe H.
Pure Legal Advocates And Moral Agents: Two Concepts Of A Lawyer In An Adversary System. Cohen, Elliot D.
Use Of Privileged Information For Attorney Self–Interest: A Moral Dilemma. Seigel, Michael.

LAYMON, R

"Idealizations And Testing Of Theories" in *Observation, Experiment, Hypothesis In Modern Physical Science*, Achinstein, Peter (ed), 147–174. Laymon, Ronald.

LE CLERC, J

Con Jean Le Clerc Alla Scuola Cartesiana. Sina, Mario.

LEADERSHIP

The Philosophy Of Leadership. Hodgkinson, Christopher.
Leadership, Administration, And The Educational Policy Operation. Maxcy, Spencer J.
Response To Spencer Maxcy's "Leadership, Administration, And The Educational Policy Operation". Sokoloff, Harris J.

LEAKEY, L

Die Entwicklung Der Paläoanthropologie Im Lichte Der Stammbäme Des Menschen. Halaczek, B.

LEARNING

Theory And Practice In Education. Dearden, R F.
A Reply To Kieran Egan's "Development In Education". Jones, Reynold.
Classical Living And Classical Learning: The Search For Equity And Excellence In Education. Smith, Philip L and Traver, Rob.
Computer Power And Intellectual Failure In Education: The Significance Of Joseph Weizenbaum's Criticism. Raitz, Keith L.
Development Of Education. Egan, Kieran.
Exigencias Filosóficas Para Determinar "Lo Psicológico" En El Proceso De Aprendizaje. Daros, William R.
Learning To Experience. Simons, Martin.
Logical Learning Theory: Kuhnian Anomaly Or Medievalism Revisited? Rychlak, Joseph R.
The Critical–Thinking Movement. Paul, Richard W.
The Human Predicament: A Context For Rights And Learning About Rights. Edwards, Philip.
The Learning Community: A Response. Giarelli, James M.
The Learning Community. Benne, Kenneth D.
Writing To Learn In Philosophy. Berger, Jeffrey.

LEARNING THEORY

Negative Feedback And Goals. Ehring, Douglas.
The Learning–Cell Technique For Teaching Philosophy. Langer, Monika.

LEBENSWELT

Explorations Of The *Lebenswelt*: Reflections On Schutz And Habermas. Rasmussen, David M.
J S Beck And Husserl: The New Episteme In The Kantian Tradition. Wallner, Ingrid M.

LEEDS, S

Another Reply To Leeds: "A Problem About Frequencies In Direct Inference". Kyburg, Henry E.
Reply To Leeds: "A Problem About Frequencies In Direct Inference". Pollock, John L.

LEFEBVRE, H

Elements For A Theory Of Modernity. Secretan, Philibert.

LEGAL

Bedingungen Einer Rekonstruktion Rechtlichen Argumentierens: Zum Verhältnis Von Philosophie Und Rechtswissenschaft. Heyen, Erk Volkmar.
What Is Wrong With 'Wrongful Life' Cases? Bell, Nora K and Loewer, Barry M.

LEGAL POSITIVISM

A Theory Of Law. Soper, Philip.
The Unity Of Law And Morality: A Refutation Of Legal Positivism. Detmold, M J.
"Legal Principles And Legal Positivism" in *Philosophical Analysis In Latin America*, Gracia, Jorge J E and others (eds), 47–72. Carrió, Genaro.
Legal Positivism And The African Legal Tradition. Taiwo, Olufemi.
Legal Positivism, Natural Law, And The Hart/Dworkin Debate. Ball, Stephen W.
Legal Positivism And Natural Law Reconsidered. Brink, David O.
Negative Positivism And The Hard Facts Of Life. Silver, Charles.

LEGAL REASONING

Law, Economics, And Philosophy. Kuperberg, Mark (ed) and Beitz, Charles (ed).
The Decline Of Juridical Reason: Doctrine And Theory In The Legal Order. Simmonds, N E.
Beyond Legal Gaps. Broekman, Jan M.
Legal Justification And Control: Sociological Aspects Of Philosophy. Klami, Hanna T.
Legal Language And Legal Interpretation. Wroblewski, Jerzy.
Moral And Ontological Justification Of Legal Reasoning. Peczenik, Aleksander.
On The Construction Of A Legal Logic In Retrospect And In Prospect. Tammelo, Ilmar.
Prisoner In The ICU: The Tragedy Of William Bartling. Annas, George J.
The Role Of Coherence In Legal Reasoning. Levenbook, Barbara Baum.

LEGAL RIGHT(S)

Defining Human Life: Medical, Legal, And Ethical Implications. Shaw, Margery W (ed) and Doudera, A Edward (ed).
A Pamphlet Attributed To John Toland And An Unpublished Reply By Archbishop William King. Kelly, Patrick.
Child Abuse And Neglect: Ethical Issues. Harris, Jean.
Professions As The Conscience Of Society. Sieghart, Paul.

LEGAL SYSTEM(S)

The State And I: Hypotheses On Juridical And Technocratic Humanism. Lock, Grahame.

LEGALITY

"Legal Aspects Of Ethics In Neural And Behavioral Sciences" in *Ethical Questions In Brain And Behavior*, Pfaff, Donald W (ed), 73–90. Beresford, H Richard.

LEGISLATION

"Legislating Morality: Should Life Be Defined" in *Defining Human Life*, Shaw, Margery W (ed), 335–340. Callahan, Daniel and others.
"Role Of Science In Moral And Societal Decision Making" in *Defining Human Life*, Shaw, Margery W (ed), 314–325. Callahan, Daniel.
Fact And Value In Ecological Science. Sagoff, Mark.

LEGISLATOR(S)

Rousseau Et Les Législateurs Grecs. Goyard– Fabre, Simone.

LEGISLATURE

Philosophy In The Legislative Process. Hare, John E.

LEGITIMACY

The Place Of Ideology In Political Life. Manning, D J and Robinson, T J.
"Some Problems Of Social Freedom" in *Freedom, Feminism, And The State*, Mc Elroy, Wendy (ed), 193–206. Harman, Lillian.
Auf Der Suche Nach Der Verlorenen Glaubwürdigkeit: Verfassungsrevision Und Helvetisches Malaise. Hoby, Jean–Pierre.

LEGITIMATION

The Postmodern Condition: A Report On Knowledge. Lyotard, Jean François.
"Hegel On Identity And Legitimation" in *The State And Civil Society*, Pelczynski, Z A (ed), 227–243. Plant, Raymond.
Dharmakirti On Trairupya And Trirupa Linga. Bapat, Lata.

LEHRER, K

Anscombe, Davidson And Lehrer On A Point About Freedom. Harrison, Jonathan.
Consensus, Respect, And Weighted Averaging. Schmitt, Frederick F.
Destroying The Consensus. Loewer, Barry and Laddaga, Robert.
Is There An 'Us' In 'Justification'? Kvanvig, J L.
Lehrer–Wagner Consensual Probabilities Do Not Adequately Summarize The Available Information. Baird, Davis.
On The Formal Properties Of Weighted Averaging As A Method Of Aggregation. Wagner, Carl.
Some Properties Of The Lehrer–Wagner Method For Reaching Rational Consensus. Nurmi, Hannu.
The Lehrer–Wagner Theory Of Consensus And The Zero Weight Problem. Forrest, Peter.

LEIBNIZ

Contemporary German Philosophy, V4. Christensen, Darrel and other (eds).
Creativity In American Philosophy. Hartshorne, Charles.
Leibniz And Locke: A Study Of The "New Essays On Human Understanding". Jolley, Nicholas.
Leibniz. Brown, Stuart.
The Metaphysical Foundations Of Logic, Michael Heim (trans). Heidegger, Martin.
"Phenomenalism, Relations, And Monadic Representation" in *How Things Are*, Bogen, James (ed), 205–234. Mc Guire, James E.
"Predication, Truth, And Transworld Identity In Leibniz" in *How Things Are*, Bogen, James (ed), 235–284. Adams, Robert M.
"Seven Thinkers And How They Grew" in *Philosophy In History*, Rorty, Richard and others (ed), 125–140. Kuklick, Bruce.
"Unbestimmte Begriffe" Bei Leibniz. Lenzen, Wolfgang.
Being Able To Do Otherwise: Leibniz On Freedom And Contingency. Frankel, Lois.
Casula On Baumgarten's Metaphysics. Tonelli, G.
Descartes Face À Leibniz Sur La Question De La Substance. Ayoub, J Boulad.
Die Lehre Vom Gerechten Krieg Bei Grotius Und Leibniz Und Ihre Bedeutung Für Die

LEIBNIZ

Gegenwart. Serra, Antonio Truyol.

Eine Antwort Auf Kants Briefe Vom 23: August 1749. Fischer, Harald–Paul.

Freedom And Moral Therapy In Leibniz. Seidler, Michael J.

Harmonia Universalis. Schneiders, Werner.

Korrespondenten Von G W Leibniz. Orzschig, Johannes and Jurgens, Madeleine.

La Manière Exacte Dont Leibniz A Inventé L'intégration Par Sommation. Violette, R.

La Originación Radical De Las Cosas Demostrada A Priori: Leibniz, Nozik, Rescher. Madanes, Leiser.

La Théologie Modale De Leibniz: Réponse Á Georges Kalinowski. Dumoncel, Jean–Claude.

Leibniz And The Doctrine Of Inter–World Identity. Mondadori, Fabrizio.

Leibniz And Atomism. Bregman, Robert.

Leibniz And The Cartesians On Motion And Force. Spector, Marshall.

Leibniz Devant Le Labyrinthe De La Liberté. Moreau, Joseph.

Leibniz On Contingency And Infinite Analysis. Blumenfeld, David.

Leibniz Und Der Materialismus (1881): Aud Dem Nachlass Herausgegeben Von Helmut Holzhey (zürich). Natorp, Paul.

Leibniz Und Die Boolesche Algebra. Lenzen, Wolfgang.

Leibniz Y El Escepticismo. De Olaso, Ezequiel.

Leibniz, Materialism, And The Relational Account Of Space And Time. Sayre– Mc Cord, Geoffrey.

Leibniz, Ou L'origine De L'esthétique Descendante. Lenain, Thierry.

Leibniz: De Cultu Confucii Civili: Introduction, Édition Du Texte Et Traduction. Klutstein– Rojtman, Ilana and Werblowsky, R J Zwi.

Leibniz' Gebrochenes Verhältnis Zur Erkenntnismetaphysik Der Scholastik. Hübener, Wolfgang.

Leibniz's Theory Of Personal Identity In The *New Essays*. Vailati, Ezio.

Monade Und Welt: Ein Beitrag Zur Interpretation Der Monadologie. Hubner, Wulf.

Plato, Leibniz, And The Furnished Soul. Hunter, Graeme and Inwood, Brad.

Platonian Rationalism As Expressed In Leibniz's Program For Science. Marciszewski, Witold.

Platonism's Inference From Logic To God. Peikoff, Leonard.

Predication. Abraham, William E.

Remarks On Leibniz's Conception Of Containment And Individual Substance. Schwerin, Alan.

Replies To Daisie Radner's "Is There A Problem Of Cartesian Interaction"? Richardson, Robert C and Loeb, Louis E.

Schulenburg's Leibniz Als Sprachforscher, With Some Observations On Leibniz And The Study Of Language. Aarsleff, Hans.

Sozietätspläne Und Sozialutopie Bei Leibniz. Schneiders, Werner.

Sur L'argument Ontologique De Leibniz. Kalinowski, Georges.

The Principle Of Comprehension As A Present–Day Contribution To Mathesis Universalis. Marciszewski, Witold.

Trans–World Identity Of Future Contingents: Sartre On Leibnizian Freedom. Winant, Terry.

Truth In A Contingent World. Campbell, R.

Un Logicien Déontique Avant La Lettre: Gottfried Wilhelm Leibniz. Kalinowski, Georges and Garoddies, Jean–louis.

Was Leibniz Entitled To Possible Worlds? Baker, Lynne Rudder.

Zur Entstehung Und Begründung Des Newtonschen Calculus Fluxionum Und Des Leibnizschen Calculus Differentialis. Stiegler, Karl D.

Zur Logik Und Semiotik Bei Leibniz. Schulthess, Peter.

LEISER, B

Commentary On "Professional Advertising: Price Fixing And Professional Dignity Versus The Public's Right To A Free Market". Macklin, Ruth.

Commentary On "Professional Advertising: Price Fixing And Professional Dignity Versus The Public's Right To A Free Market". Doughton, James E.

LEMMON, E

Lemmon On Logical Relations. Kennedy, Ralph.

LENIN

Dialogue Within The Dialectic. Levine, Norman.

Über Den Wirkungs– Und Ausnutzungsmechanismus Der Gesellschaftlichen Entwicklungsgetsetze. Drjachlow, N I and Tscherkassow, G K.

"Gramsci And Eurocommunism" in *Continuity And Change In Marxism*, Fischer, Norman And Others (ed), 189–210. Boggs, Carl.

"Lenin–Engineer Of Revolution" in *Continuity And Change In Marxism*, Fischer, Norman And Others (ed), 170–188. Masloff, Clement.

"Zur Kritik Der Bürgerlichen Ideologie". Lowe, Bernd P.

Chemie Und Dialektik. Simon, Rudiger.

Das Einfachste Und Grundlegendste Verhältnis Der Sozialistischen Gesellschaft. Hellborn, Rudolf.

Der Atheistische Charakter Der Marxistisch–Leninistischen Philosophie Und Weltanschauung. Klohr, Olof and Handel, G.

Der Kulturprozess Und Die Wachsende Rolle Des Subjektiven Faktors. Redeker, Horst.

Der Prinzipienbegriff In Der Marxistisch–Leninistischen Philosophie. Kirchhöfer, Dieter.

Die Wachsende Rolle Des Subjektiven Faktors––Eine Gesetzmässigkeit Des Historischen Fortschritts. Lassow, Ekkhard.

Einen Neuen Schwerpunkt In Der Zusammenarbeit Mit Naturwissenschaftlern–– Brauchen Wir Ihn Wirklich? Liebscher, Heinz and Simon, R.

Gedanken Zum Schicht–Begriff Der Marxistisch–Leninistischen Theorie Der Klassen Und Des Klassenkampfes. Lange, Arno.

Ideological Problems Of The Development Of Needs (in German). Döbler, Martin and others.

Kritisches Zur Widerspruchsdebatte. Eichhorn, Wolfgang.

Lenin's Utopianism. Levine, Norman.

Leninism And The Enlightenment. Moran, Philip.

Marxist Dialectics And Social Life. Fedoseev, P N.

Marxistisch–Leninistische Philosophie In Indien. Litman, A D.

On Revolutionary Democracy––Its State And Political System. Ul'ianovskii, R A.

Persönlichkeit Als Subjekt Des Gesellschaftlichen Fortschritts. Gutsche, Gunter.

Remarks Concerning The Problems Of Dialectical Logic (in Czechoslovakian). Zeman, J.

Subjektiver Faktor Und Revolution. Stiehler, Gottfried.

The Character Of The Interaction Of Working And Political Activity Of Personality (in Czechoslovakian). Rjadová, Vera and Rjadovoj, Alexandr.

The Counter–Revolution As Antipode Of Revolution (in Czechoslovakian). Khokhlyuk, G S.

The Distinctiveness Of The Process Of Solving Social Contradictions (in German). Schwarz, Eckart.

The Relation Of Theory And Practice In The Process Of Formation And Action Of Laws Of Communist Socio–Economic Formation (in Czechoslovakian). Kroh, Michael.

The Struggle Against The Revisionism For Creative Development Of Marxism– Leninism (in Czechoslovakian). Hrzal, L.

Zu Den Funktionen Der Marxistisch–Leninistischen Philosophie In Bezug Auf Die Einzelwissenschaften. Hager, Nina.

Zum Platz Der "Randglossen" In Der Geschichte Der Theorie Des Wissenschaftlichen Kommunismus. Fieber, Hans–Joachim and Schneider, W.

Zum Verhältnis Von Marxistisch–Leninistischer Philosophie Und Sozialistischer Politik In Der DDR. Heppener, Sieglinde.

Zur Historisch–Materialistischen Auffassung Von Basis Und Überbau. Bauer, Adolf.

Zur Problematik Des Egalitarismus. Höppner, Joachim.

Zur Realisierung Des Verhältnisses Von Philosophie Und Einzelwissenschaften Im Marxistisch–Leninistischen Grundstudium. Bernhardt, Herbert and Richter, F.

LENINISM

"Midwives, Vanguards, And Class Consciousness" in *Continuity And Change In Marxism*, Fischer, Norman And Others (ed), 97–113. Grytting, Wayne.

Anti–Leninist Essence Of The Conception Of "New Philosophers" On Social Revolution (in Czechoslovakian). Jurukova, M M.

Die Aufgaben Der Marxistisch–Leninistischen Soziologischen Forschung In Der DDR. Weidig, Rudi.

El Papel Del Leninismo En "Historia Y Conciencia De Clase". Giglioli, Giovanna.

Inhaltliche Fragen Der Ausarbeitung Eines Lehrbuches Der Marxistisch–Leninistischen Soziologie. Assmann, Georg and Stollberg, R.

La Philosophie Marxiste–Léniniste––Base Théorique Pour La Solution Des Problèmes De Notre Époque (in German). Rupprecht, Frank.

Remarks Concerning The Ontological Prerequisites Of Marxist–Leninist Theory Of Values (in Czechoslovakian). Baran, P.

Soviet–Marxist Philosophy Of Technology. Rapp, Friedrich.

The Role Of Marxist–Leninist Philosophy In The Process Of The Humanisation Of Science (in Czechoslovakian). Machleidtova, S.

The Struggle Against The Revisionism For Creative Development Of Marxism– Leninism (in Czechoslovakian). Hrzal, L.

To Some Questions Of Art Theory And Marxist–Leninist Aesthetics (in Czechoslovakian). Kovar, Miloslav.

LENTRICCHIA, F

The Poetry Of Theory: Reflections On *After The New Criticism*. Sircello, Guy.

LESNIEWSKI, S

A Brentanian Basis For Leśniewskian Logic. Simons, Peter M.

LETTER(S)

Hegel: The Letters. Butler, Clark (trans) and Seiler, Christiane (trans).

LETTING DIE

Are 'Killing' And 'Letting Die' Adequately Specified Moral Categories? Philips, Michael.

LEVI–STRAUSS, C

Le Matérialisme Biologique De Lévi–Strauss. Steinmetz, Rudy.

Man And Metaphor: An Exploration In Entropy And Coherence. Prattis, J I.

Philosophical Anthropology: Revolt Against The Division Of Intellectual Labor. Wiggins, Osborne.

LEVI, A

Giulio Augusto Levi E La "Scienza Del Comico". Cavaglion, Alberto.

LEVI, I

Levi's "The Wrong Box". Eells, Ellery.

LEVINAS, E

Autour D'Emmanuel Lévinas. Cornu, Michel.

Scepticisme Et Raison. De Greef, Jan.

Sentido E Intersubjectividade No Pensamento De E Levinas. Silva, M Augusto Ferreira Da.

LEVINE, M

Theism And Pantheism Again. Oakes, Robert.

LEWIS

"Forms And Compounds" in *How Things Are*, Bogen, James (ed), 85–100. Modrak, D K.

C I Lewis And The Pragmatic Focus On Action: Some Systematic Implications. Rosenthal, Sandra B.

Merleau–Ponty, Lewis And Ontological Presence. Rosenthal, Sandra and Bourgeois, Patrick.

LEWIS, C

C S Lewis And The Search For Rational Religion. Beversluis, John.

LITERATURE

The Logic Of Tragedy: Morals And Integrity In Aeschylus' Oresteia. Vellacott, Philip.

The Responsibility Of Forms: Critical Essays On Music, Art, And Representation. Barthes, Roland and Howard, Richard (trans).

The Sign Of Three. Sebok, Thomas A (ed) and Eco, Umberto (ed).

"Act Of Writing" in *Existential Coordinates Of Human Condition,* Tymieniecka, A (ed), 451–478. Garelli, Jacques.

"Die Ästhetisch-Semiotische Relation Und Das Problem" in *Asthetische Er Fahrung Und Das Wesen Der Kunst,* Holzhey, Helmut, 173–189. Zimmerli, W Ch.

"Fiction & Transposition Of Presence" in *Existential Coordinates Of Human Condition,* Tymieniecka, A (ed), 495–504. Martinez– Bonati, Felix.

"From Helikon To Aetna" in *Existential Coordinates Of Human Condition,* Tymieniecka, A (ed), 119–140. Findlay, L M.

"Il Tempo Della Letteratura: Roman Ingarden" in *Il Tempo Dell'Arte,* Papi, Fulvio and others (ed), 40–59. Scaramuzza, Gabriele.

"John Wisdom And The Breadth Of Philosophy" in *Philosophy And Life: Essays On John Wisdom,* Dilman, Ilham (ed), 1–26. Dilman, Ilham.

"Literary Diary As A Witness Of Man's Historicity" in *Existential Coordinates Of Human Condition,* Tymieniecka, A (ed), 249–260. Eykman, Christoph.

"Literary Impressionism And Phenomenology" in *Existential Coordinates Of Human Condition,* Tymieniecka, A (ed), 521–534. Kronegger, Marlies.

"Nel Regno Della Metamorfosi, La Figura Nelle "Elegie Duinesi" Di R M Rilke" in *Il Tempo Dell'Arte,* Papi, Fulvio and others (ed), 29–39. Rella, Franco.

"Phenomenology And Literary Impressionism" in *Existential Coordinates Of Human Condition,* Tymieniecka, A (ed), 535–546. Stowell, Peter.

"The Art Of Saying What Can Be Imagined" in *Philosophy And Life: Essays On John Wisdom,* Dilman, Ilham (ed), 123–144. Lewis, Meirlys.

"The Epic Element In Japanese Literature" in *Existential Coordinates Of Human Condition,* Tymieniecka, A (ed), 195–208. Viglielmo, Valdo H.

"The French Nouveau Roman" in *Existential Coordinates Of Human Condition,* Tymieniecka, A (ed), 261–272. Carrabino, Victor.

"The Re–emergence Of Tragedy In Late Medieval England" in *Existential Coordinates Of Human Condition,* Tymieniecka, A (ed), 363–378. Kennedy, Beverly.

"The Truth Of The Body" in *Existential Coordinates Of Human Condition,* Tymieniecka, A (ed), 479–494. Riley, Michael.

"Toward A Theory Of Contemporary Tragedy" in *Existential Coordinates Of Human Condition,* Tymieniecka, A (ed), 341–362. Kaelin, Eugene.

"Two Ages: A Story Of Soren Kierkegaard And Isak Dinesen" in *International Kierkegaard Commentary,* Perkins, Robert L (ed), 175–188. Kleinman, Jackie.

"Un Modèle D'analyse Dy Texte Dramatique" in *Existential Coordinates Of Human Condition,* Tymieniecka, A (ed), 547–558. Moussally, Adnan.

"What Is There In Horse Racing" in *Philosophy And Life: Essays On John Wisdom,* Dilman, Ilham (ed), 27–34. Wisdom, John.

"You Can't Separate The Work Of Art From The Artist". Stolnitz, Jerome.

A Note On Audience Participation And Psychical Distance. Lewis, Peter.

Bias In Stories For Children: Black Marks For Authors. Hare, William.

Big Brother In America. Beauchamp, Gorman.

Contraception, Copulation Domination, And The Theoretical Barrenness Of Sex Education Literature. Diorio, Joseph A.

De Literatuur Naar De Letter. Verbeeck, Louis.

Descartes's Comedy. Rée, Jonathan.

Enjoying Negative Emotions In Fiction. Morreall, John.

Explaining The Unity Of The Platonic Dialogue. Hathaway, Ronald.

General And Individual Style In Literature. Robinson, Jenefer.

Getting Croce Straight. Paton, Margaret.

Hegel's *Phenomenology*: Facing The Preface. Adelman, Howard.

I Of The Cyclops: The Herdsman–Poet. Foster, Donald W.

Intentionality: A Reexamination Of Its Role In A Literary Education. Kasprisin, Lorraine.

Karl Marx And Literature. Markiewicz, Henryk.

L'Apport De La Convention En Litterature. Marchand, Alain Bernard and Rochon, Claire.

Meaning In The Experience Of Literature. Thompson, Audrey.

Morality And The Self In Robert Musil's *The Perfecting Of A Love.* Wilson, Catherine.

Nineteen Eighty–Four: Should Political Theory Care? Shklar, Judith N.

On Being Moved By Fiction. Mannison, Don.

Phenomenology And Literature: Roman Ingarden And The 'Appropriate Aesthetic Attitude' To The Literary Work Of Art (in Hebrew). Brinker, Menahem.

Plurivocité Et Dis–Simultanéité: Questions Herméneutiques Pour Une Théorie Du Texte Littéraire. Frank, Manfred.

Prospects Regarding The Science Of Criticism. Margolis, Joseph.

Reader–Response And Implication–Realization. Hoyt, Reed J.

Schelling Alas Verfasser Der Nachtwachen Des Bonaventura: Eine Replik Eine Replik. Dietzsch, St.

Socratic Philosophy And The Dialogue Form. Seeskin, Kenneth.

Soziologische Und Sozialpsychologische Probleme Der Wissenschaft Im Spiegel Sowjetischer Literatur (Literaturbericht). Winkler, Rose–Luise.

Style And Personality In The Literary Work. Robinson, Jenefer.

Teken, Waarheid, Macht. Van Velthoven, Theo.

The Authentic And The Aesthetic. Currie, Gregory.

The Conflict Between Poetry And Literature. Murray, Michael.

The Great Guide Of Human Life. Kekes, John.

The Hidden Advantage Of Tradition: On The Significance Of T S Eliot's Indic Studies. Perl, Jeffrey M and Tuck, Andrew.

The Idea Of The Comic. Armstrong, A M.

The Impasse Of *No Exit.* Kolenda, Konstantin.

The Intersection Of Theory Of Science And Theory Of Literature. Margolis, Joseph.

The Japanese Appreciation Of Nature. Saito, Yuriko.

The Potency Of Imagery—The Impotence Of Rational Language: Ernesto Grassi's Contribution To Modern Epistemology. Veit, Walter.

Validity In Interpretation And The Literary Institution. Newton, K M.

Writing Philosophy And Literature: Apology For Narcissism In Merleau–Ponty. Cook, Deborah.

LITURGY

Sociology And Liturgical Renewal. Flanagan, Kieran.

LOAR, B

Anti–Reductionist Materialism. Lennon, Kathleen.

LOCHAK, G

La Non–Séparabilité (Response À G Lochak). D' Espagnat, Bernard.

LOCKE

An Essay Concerning The Use Of Reason In Propositions: A Discourse Of Free Thinking. Collins, Anthony and Schouls, Peter A (ed).

Anti–Skepticism. Lee, Henry and Schouls, Peter A (ed).

Ideology, Philosophy And Politics. Parel, Anthony (ed).

John Locke And Agrarian Capitalism. Wood, Neal.

John Locke (1632–1704), Physician And Philosopher. Dewhurst, Kenneth.

John Locke And Medicine: A New Key To Locke. Romanell, Patrick.

John Locke And English Literature Of The Eighteenth Century. Mac Lean, Kenneth and Schouls, Peter A (ed).

Leibniz And Locke: A Study Of The "New Essays On Human Understanding". Jolley, Nicholas.

Locke's Education For Liberty. Tarcov, Nathan.

Locke's Travels In France 1675–1679. Lough, John.

Locke's Writings And Philosophy: Historically Considered. Tagart, Edward.

Logick: Or, The Right Use Of Reason. Watts, Isaac and Schouls, Peter A (ed).

Some Thoughts Concerning The Several Causes And Occasions Of Atheism Socinianism Unmask'd. Edwards, John.

The Georgetown Symposium On Ethics. Porreco, Rocco (ed).

The Life And Letters Of John Locke. King, Peter and Schouls, Peter A (ed).

The Nature Of Social Laws: Machiavelli To Mill. Brown, Robert.

The Third Earl Of Shaftesbury 1671–1713. Voitle, Robert.

"Bacon And Locke: Or Ideology As Mental Hygiene" in *Ideology, Philosophy And Politics,* Parel, Anthony (ed), 179–198. Minogue, Kenneth.

"Can Belief In God Be Rational If It Has No Foundations" in *Faith And Rationality,* Plantinga, Alvin (ed), 135–186. Wolterstorff, Nicholas.

"Conceptions Of The Common Good And The Natural Right To Liberty" in *The Georgetown Symposium On Ethics,* Porreco, Rocco (ed), 185–194. Rasmussen, Douglas B.

"Seven Thinkers And How They Grew" in *Philosophy In History,* Rorty, Richard and others (ed), 125–140. Kuklick, Bruce.

"The Concept Of 'trust' In The Politics Of John Locke" in *Philosophy In History,* Rorty, Richard and others (ed), 279–302. Dunn, John.

A Functionalist Interpretation Of Locke's Theory Of Simple Ideas. Vinci, Thomas.

Considerazioni Su Power E Liberty Nel "Saggio Sull'Intelletto Umano" Secondo Un Manoscritto Di Coste. Simonutti, Luisa.

El Triángulo Universal De Locke: Su Inmerecida Fama. Angelelli, Ignacio.

Friendly Persuasion: Quakers, Liberal Toleration, And The Birth Of The Prison. Dumm, Thomas L.

John Locke And The Antebellum Defense Of Slavery. Loewenberg, Robert J.

Knowledge Of Substance And Knowledge Of Science In Locke's Essay. Atherton, Margaret.

La Conformación Del Estado Moderno En Relación A Textos Políticos. Durand, Graciela Alcocer.

Les Fondements Personnalistes De La Propriété. Cottier, Georges.

Libertad Política: Liberalismo Y Tomismo. Hernández, Héctor H.

Locke And Descartes Through Victorian Eyes. Sell, Alan P F.

Locke On Consciousness And Reflection. Kulstad, Mark A.

Locke On Knowledge And Propositions. Soles, David E.

Locke's Empiricism And The Postulation Of Unobservables. Soles, David E.

Locke's Negative Hedonism. Kraus, Pamela.

Locke's Real Ideas, And Dr Woolhouse. Helm, Paul.

Locke's Theory Of Property: A Re–Examination. Cvek, Peter Paul.

Lockean Provisos And State Of Nature Theories. Bogart, J H.

Lockes Begründung Des Privateigentums In Der Arbeit. Holzhey, Helmut.

Lockes Perspektiventheorie Der Persönlichen Identität. Kienzle, Bertram.

Logical Problems For Lockean Persons. Welker, David.

Natural Rights In Locke. Mautner, Thomas.

Particles And Ideas In Locke's Theory Of Meaning. Berman, David.

Some Sources For A History Of English Socinianism; A Bibliography Of 17th Century English Socinian Writings. Bianchi, Daniela.

The Commodity Form And Socialization In Locke's State Of Nature. Colella, E Paul.

The Complexity Of Quality. Westphal, Jonathan.

The Ideology Of Jacobitism On The Eve Of The Rising Of 1745—Part I. Mc Lynn, F J.

The Inalienability Of Autonomy. Kuflik, Arthur.

The Inessentiality Of Lockean Essences. Atherton, Margaret.

The Liberal Point Of View. Enslin, Penny.

The Nature And Origin Of Ideas: The Controversy Over Innate Ideas Reconsidered. Simpson, Peter.

The Primary/Secondary Quality Distinction: Berkeley, Locke, And The Foundations Of Corpuscularian Science. Davidson, Arnold I and Hornstein, Norbert.

The Scholastic Background To Locke's Thought. Milton, J.

LOCUTIONARY ACT(S)

Beyond The Literal Meaning. Charlton, William.

LOEB, R

Rejoinder To Richardson's And Loeb's: Replies To Radner's "Is There A Problem Of Cartesian Interaction"? Radner, Daisie.

LOGIC

see also Deontic Logic, Infinitary Logic, Intuitionistic Logic, Many–valued Logics, Modal Logic, Propositional Logic, Relevant Logics, Tense Logic

A Concise Introduction To Logic. Hurley, Patrick J.

Abstract Measurement Theory. Narens, Louis.

An Interpretation Of The Logic Of Hegel. Harris, Errol E.

Análisis Propositional Y Ontologia. Sanchez, Juan Carlos.

Analysis And Dialectic: Studies In The Logic Of Foundation Problems. Russell, Joseph J.

Averroes' Middle Commentaries On Aristotle's "Categories" And "De Interpretatione". Butterworth, Charles E.

Basic Reasoning. Mackinnon, Edward.

Beyond Feelings: A Guide To Critical Thinking, Second Edition. Ruggiero, Vincent Ryan.

Cantorian Set Theory And Limitation Of Size. Hallett, Michael.

D M Armstrong. Bogdan, Radu J (ed).

Der Formalismus Und Seine Grenzen: Untersuchungen Zur Neueren Philosophie Der Mathematik. Rheinwald, Rosemarie.

Handbook Of Philosophical Logic: Extensions Of Classical Logic, V2. Gabbay, Dov M (ed) and Guenthner, Franz (ed).

Hegel's Logic: An Essay In Interpretation. Hibben, John G and Harris, H S (ed).

Hegel's Logic. Hibben, John Grier.

Heidegger: Perspektiven Zur Deutung Seines Werkes. Pöggeler, Otto (ed).

Husserl And Realism In Logic And Mathematics. Tragesser, Robert S.

Introduction To The Problem Of Individuation In The Early Middle Ages. Gracia, Jorge J E.

Introduction To Logic: Propositional Logic. Pospesel, Howard.

Introduction To Logic. Copi, Irving M.

John Buridan On Self–Reference: Chapter Eight Of Buridan's 'Sophismata'. Hughes, G E.

Kant Im Original: Band II. Kant, Immanuel.

La Naissance De La Grammaire Moderne. Dominicy, Marc and Mardaga, Pierre (ed).

Lecture Notes In Mathematics. Muller, G H and others.

Lectures On Propositional Calculi, R Ladniak (ed). Wójcicki, Ryszard.

Logic And The Objectivity Of Knowledge: Studies In Husserl's Early Philosophy. Willard, Dallas.

Logic Made Simple. Rubin, Ronald.

Logic, Philosophy, And History: A Study In The Philosophy Of History Based On The Work Of R G Collingwood. Russell, Anthony F.

Logic, Semantics, Meta–Mathematics. Tarski, Alfred and Woodger, J H (trans).

Logic, Third Edition. Salmon, Wesley C.

Logica Parva, Alan R Perreiah (trans). Venetus, Paulus.

Logical Form In Natural Language. Lycan, William G.

Marsilius Of Inghen: Treatises On The Properties Of Terms. Bos, Egbert P.

Modern Logic And Quantum Mechanics. Garden, Rachel Wallace.

N–ary Almost Recursive Functions. Berry, John W.

Philosophy And Life: Essays On John Wisdom. Dilman, Ilham (ed).

Piaget's Logic: A Critique Of Genetic Epistemology. Seltman, Muriel and Seltman, Peter.

Practical Reason. Von Wright, G H.

Principles Of Language And Mind: An Evolutionary Theory Of Meaning. Waldron, T P.

Probability, Objectivity And Evidence. Benenson, F C.

Progress In Utility And Risk Theory. Hagen, Ole (ed) and Wenstop, Fred (ed).

Quine On Ontology, Necessity, And Experience: A Philosophical Critique. Dilman, Ilham.

Realism And Reason: Philosophical Papers, V3. Putnam, Hillary.

Set Theory: An Introduction To Independence Proofs, J Barwise and others (eds). Kunen, Kenneth.

That Most Subtle Question (Quaestio Subtilissima). Henry, Desmond Paul.

The Logic Of Aspect: An Axiomatic Approach. Galton, Antony.

The Metaphysical Foundations Of Logic, Michael Heim (trans). Heidegger, Martin.

Topoi: The Categorial Analysis Of Logic. Goldblatt, R and Suppes, P (ed) and Troelstra, A S (ed).

Wittgenstein Regole E Sistema. Frongia, Guido.

Wittgenstein: A Critique. Findlay, J N.

Über Des Problem Von Nichtstandardgrössen (in Polish). Lubanski, Mieczyslaw.

Über Die Erfüllung Gewisser Erhaltungssätze Durch Kompliziertheitsmasse. Lischke, Gerhard.

'It Would Have Happened Already': On One Argument For A First Cause. Conway, David A.

"Frege: The Early Years" in *Philosophy In History,* Rorty, Richard and others (ed), 329–356. Sluga, Hans.

"John Wisdom And The Breadth Of Philosophy" in *Philosophy And Life: Essays On John Wisdom,* Dilman, Ilham (ed), 1–26. Dilman, Ilham.

"Kripke Semantics" = Algebra + Poetry. Fleischer, Isidore.

"Logic And The Hypothetical–Deductive Method" in *Philosophical Analysis In Latin America,* Gracia, Jorge J E and others (eds), 73–92. Klimovsky, Gregorio.

"On The Concept Of Reason" in *Philosophical Analysis In Latin America,* Gracia, Jorge J E and others (eds), 397–412. Quesada, Francisco Miró.

"Sobre Las Oraciones Modales" Por Fray Alonso De La Veracruz. Redmond, Walter.

"Substance And Its Logical Significance" in *Methodology, Metaphysics And The History Of Science,* Cohen, Robert S (ed), 235–246. Panova, Elena.

"Testing Theoretical Hypotheses" in *Testing Scientific Theories,* Earman, John (ed), 269–298. Giere, Ronald N.

"The Scope Of Reason: Wisdom, Kuhn And James" in *Philosophy And Life: Essays On John Wisdom,* Dilman, Ilham (ed), 219–240. Newell, R W.

"Unbestimmte Begriffe" Bei Leibniz. Lenzen, Wolfgang.

$\aleph_0$–Categorical, $\aleph_0$–Stable Structures. Cherlin, Gregory and Harrington, L and Lachlan, A H.

A Brentanian Basis For Leśniewskian Logic. Simons, Peter M.

A Characterization Of Complexity Sequences. Schnorr, C P and Stumpf, G.

A Classical Rhetoric Of Modern Science. Schollmeier, Paul.

A Comparison Of Logical Form In Russell And Wittgenstein. May, Philip.

A Completeness Result For Fixed–Point Algebras. Montagna, Franco.

A Conjunction In Closure Spaces. Jankowski, Andrzej W.

A Consistent Propositional Logic Without Any Finite Models. Mc Kay, C G.

A Couple Of Novelties In The Propositional Calculus. Hoare, C A R.

A Cumulative Hierarchy Of Predicates. Friedman, Harvey.

A Decidable Subclass Of The Minimal Gödel Class With Identity. Goldfarb, Warren D and Gurevich, Yuri and Shelah, Saharon.

A Direct Proof Of The Finite Developments Theorem. De Vrijer, Roel.

A Height Restricted Generation Of A Set Of Arithmetic Functions Of Order–type. Slessenger, Peter H.

A Hierarchy Of Families Of Recursively Enumerable Degrees. Welch, Lawrence V.

A Mathematical Characterization Of Interpretation Between Theories. Van Bentham, Johan and Pearce, David.

A Metacompleteness Theorem For Contraction–Free Relevant Logics. Slaney, John K.

A Modal Approach To Sneed's "Theoretical Functions". Miroiu, Adrian.

A Model For The Modern Malaise. Abraham, Adrian and Meyer, Robert K.

A Natural Extension Of Natural Deduction. Schroeder– Heister, Peter.

A New Proof For Craig's Theorem. Bellot, P.

A New Semantics For First–Order Logic, Multivalent And Mostly Intensional. Le Blanc, Hugues.

A No Nonsense Approach To St Anselm. Malcolm, John F.

A Nonconservativity Result On Global Choice. Kaufman, Matt and Shelah, S.

A Normal Form Theorem For First Order Formulas And Its Application To Gaifman's Splitting Theorem. Motohashi, Nobuyoshi.

A Note Concerning The V* Relation On GAMMA–sur–R. Mc Laughlin, T G.

A Note On Decompositions Of Recursively Enumerable Subspaces. Downey, R G.

A Note On Interpretations Of Many–sorted Theories. Hook, Julian L.

A Note On Simple Graphic Algebras. Nieminen, Juhani.

A Note On The Compactness Theorem. Gill, R R Rockingham.

A Note On The Existence Of Tautologies Without Constants. Rose, Alan.

A Portfolio Of Risk Measures. Mac Crimmon, Kenneth R and Wehrung, Donald A.

A Proof Of Herbrand's Theorem. Wojtylak, Piotr.

A Property Of 2–Sorted Peano Models And Program Verification. Paris, J B and Csirmaz, L.

A Question Of Borel Hyperdeterminacy. Cutland, Nigel J.

A Recursive Theory For The $\{$Upsidedown L, Λ, V, $\rightarrow$, $o\}$: Fragment Of Intuitionistic Logic. Wojtylak, Piotr.

A Recursive Model For Arithmetic With Weak Induction. Adamowicz, Zofia and Morales– Luna, Guillermo.

A Remark On The Strict Order Property. Lachlan, A H.

A Rhetorical View Of The *Ad Hominem.* Brinton, Alan.

A Second Normal Form For Functions Of The System EP. Mc Beth, Rod.

A Short Proof Of A Well–Known Theorem Of Intuitionistic Analysis. Luckhardt, Horst.

A Simple Solution To Mortensen And Priest's Truth Teller Paradox. Wayne Smith, Joseph.

A Solution To The Problem Of Induction. Pollock, John L.

A Spectrum Hierarchy. Fagin, Ronald.

A Sufficient And Necessary Condition For Tarski's Property In Lindenbaum's Extensions. Stępień, Teodor.

A Syntactic Characterization Of Kleene's Strong Connectives With Two Designated Values. Martin, John N.

A Syntactically Motivated Theory Of Conditionals. Lycan, William G.

A Test To Determine Distinct Modalities In The Extensions Of S4. Bellissima, Fabio.

A Topological Logic Of Action. Segerberg, Krister.

A Topology For Logical Space. Wolniewicz, Boguslaw.

A Two–Cardinal Characterization Of Double Spectra. Fagin, Ronald.

Abstraction And Definability In Semantically Closed Structures. Mc Carthy, Timothy.

Abstrakte Tempomasse Und Speed–Up–Theoreme Für Enumerationen Rekursiv– Aufzählbarer Mengen. Hecker, Hans–Dietrich.

Accessible Sets And $(L_{\omega_1\omega})$–Equivalence For T_3 Spaces. Martínez, Juan Carlos.

Addendum To "Countable Algebra And Set Existence Axioms". Friedman, Harvey M and Simpson, S G and Smith, R L.

Addis On Analysing Disposition Concepts. Wilson, Fred.

Adjoining Dominating Functions. Baumgartner, James E and Dordal, Peter.

Affine Ebenen Mit Orthogonalitätsrelation. Struve, Horst.

Almost Disjoint Families Of Representing Sets. Balanda, Kevin P.

An AD–like Model. Apter, Arthur W.

An Abstract Setting For Henkin Proofs. Goldblatt, Robert.

An Alternative Concept Of The Universal Decision Element In *m*–valued Logic. Loader, John.

An Application Of The Reiger–Nishimura Formulas To The Intuitionistic Modal Logics. Vakarelov, Dimiter.

An Elementary Method Of Determining The Degree Of Completeness On N–Valued

LOGIC

LOGIC

Frege, The Proliferation Of Force, And Non—Cognitivism. Hurley, S L.

Frege's Double Correlation Thesis And Quine's Set Theories NF And ML. Cocchiarella, Nino B.

Frege's Early Conception Of Logic (in Hebrew). Bar— Elli, Gilead.

Freges Beitrag Zur Methodologie In "Die Grundlagen Der Arithmetik" Von 1884— Erbe Und Auftrag. Metzler, Helmut.

Functionalism And Psychologism. Mac Kenzie, J D.

Functors And Ordinal Notations: II, A Functorial Construction Of The Bachmann Hierarchy. Girard, Jean—Yves and Vauzeilles, Jacqueline.

Functors And Ordinal Notations. Vauzeilles, Jacqueline.

Functors And Ordinal Notations I: A Functorial Construction Of The Veblen Hierarchy. Girard, Jean—Yves and Vauzeilles, Jacqueline.

Fuzzy Recursion, RET's, And Isols. Harkleroad, Leon.

Gödel's Theorem In Retrospect. Tabakov, Martin.

Gödelsche Funktionalinterpretation Für Eine Erweiterung Der Klassischen Analysis. Friedrich, Wolfgang.

Games, Graphs, And Circular Arguments. Walton, Douglas N and Batten, L M.

Gedankliche Systeme Mit Aufforderungscharakter. Heitsch, Wolfram.

Generalising The Probabilistic Semantics Of Conditionals. Appiah, Anthony.

Genetic Epistemology And The Child's Understanding Of Logic. Smith, Leslie.

Georg Cantor's Influence On Bertrand Russell. Grattan— Guiness, I.

Global Quantification In Zermelo—Fraenkel Set Theory. Mayberry, John.

Hairier Than Putnam Thought. Read, Stephen and Wright, Crispin.

Homogeneous Forms In Two Ordinal Variables. Hickman, John L.

How To Give It Up: A Survey Of Some Formal Aspects Of The Logic Of Theory Change. Makinson, David.

How To Glue Analysis Models. Van Dalen, D.

Hyper—Contradictions. Priest, Graham.

Hypertasks. Clark, Peter and Read, Stephen.

I Will, If You Will. Radford, Colin.

INUS Conditions. Dale, A J.

Idempotent Ideals On Abelian Groups. Pelc, Andrzej.

Il Problema Della Certezza E La Spiritualità Dell'uomo: Psicologia, Logica E Teoria Della Scienza Nel Pensiero Di Désiré Mercier. Mangiagalli, Maurizio.

Implication And Deduction In Some Intuitionistic Modal Logics. Font, Josep M.

Inconsistent Models For Relevant Arithmetics. Meyer, Robert K and Mortensen, Chris.

Individuating Propositional Attitudes. Brownstein, Donald.

Informal Logic: The Past Five Years 1978–1983. Johnson, Ralph H and Blair, J Anthony.

Informal Logic And The Theory Of Reasoning. Finocchiaro, Maurice A.

Intensionality In Mathematics. Feferman, Solomon.

Introduction To 2 1/2 Logic. Girard, Jean—Yves.

Intuitionistic Fuzzy Logic And Intuitionistic Fuzzy Set Theory. Takeuti, Gaisi and Titani, Satoko.

Intuitionistic Truth. Rabinowicz, Wlodzimierz.

Invariant Matrix Consequences. Dzik, Wojciech and Tokarz, Marek.

Is A Logic For Belief Sentences Possible? Green, Karen.

Is Nonstandard Analysis Relevant For The Philosophy Of Mathematics? Fenstad, Jens Erik.

Is Supervenience Just Undisguised Reduction? Teller, Paul.

Isomorphisms Between HEO And HRO, ECF And ICF. Bezem, Marc.

Jankov—Theorems For Some Implicational Calculi. Pahi, Biswambham.

Kant, Wittgenstein And The Limits Of Logic. Tiles, Mary.

Kants Antinomien Und Die Logik Der Erkenntnis. Narski, I S.

Kueker's Conjecture For Superstable Theories. Buechler, Steven.

Lógica Formal, Lógica Trascendental Y Verdad En La Primera "Crítica". Dotti, Jorge E.

Lässt Sich Eine Kernlogik Konstituieren: Ein Versuch Dazu Vom Standpunkt Des Pankritischen Rationalismus Aus. Klowski, Joachim.

L'unité Du Monde Selon Guillaume D'Ockham (Ou La Logique De La Cosmologie Ockhamiste). Biard, Joel.

La Crítica De Herbert Marcuse A La Racionalidad Instrumentalista Y Su Receptción Por Corrientes Izquierdistas. Mansilla, H C F.

La Multiplicidad De Axiomáticas Conjuntistas Y Su Incidencia En La Lógica Cuántica. Lungarzo, Carlos.

La Naissance De La Théorie Des Types. Lepage, Francois.

La Teoría De Conjuntos En Sentido Colectivo. Freund, Max.

La Teoria De La Argumentacion En Aristoteles. Beuchot, Mauricio.

Lattice—Points In Metric Spaces. Brunner, Norbert.

Le Cours Manuscrit De Logique De Marcin Smiglecki SJ. Darowski, R.

Le Problème De La Logique Pure: De Husserl À Une Nouvelle Position Phénoménologique. Richir, Mare.

Legal Justification And Control: Sociological Aspects Of Philosophy. Klami, Hanna T.

Legal Language And Legal Interpretation. Wroblewski, Jerzy.

Leibniz Und Die Boolesche Algebra. Lenzen, Wolfgang.

Linear Reasoning In Modal Logic. Fitting, Melvin.

Logic And Contingent Existence. Lopston, Peter.

Logic: Normative Or Descriptive; The Ethics Of Belief Or A Branch Of Psychology? Resnik, Michael D.

Logico—Semantic Aspects Of Truthfulness. Yanuva, Jana.

Logics Without The Contraction Rule. Ono, Hiroakira and Komori, Yuichi.

Logik Und Dialektik Als Wissenschaftsmethoden. Tsouyopoulos, Nelly.

Logistik: Eine Renaissance Der Scholastischen Spitzfindigkeiten? Schulthess, Peter.

Lower Bound Results On Lengths Of Second—order Formulas. Scarpellini, Bruno.

Lucas Against Mechanism II: A Rejoinder. Lucas, J R.

Mathematical Logic: Tool And Object Lesson For Science. Kreisel, Goerg.

McGinn On Benacerraf. Spinks, Graham.

Meaning—Yet Another Approach. Mikhailova, Th.

Minimale Gruppen. Reineke, Joachim.

Modal Logic And Model Theory. Gerla, Giangiacomo and Vaccaro, Virginia.

Modal Logics In The Theory Of Information Systems. Orlowska, Ewa.

Modality As Many Metalinguistic Predicates. Hazen, Allen.

Models For Normal Intuitionistic Modal Logics. Bozic, Milan and Dosen, Kosta.

Modifications Of Logical And Ontological Foundations Of Physics Of The 20th Century (in Czechoslovakian). Ulehla, Ivan.

Monadic Generalized Spectra. Fagin, Ronald.

Monadic Logic And Löwenheim Numbers. Shelah, Saharon.

Monotone Reducibility And The Family Of Infinite Sets. Cenzer, Douglas.

Moore's Paradox And Epistemic Justification. Hambourger, Robert.

More On Proper Forcing. Shelah, Saharon.

More On The Weak Diamond. Shelah, Saharon.

Multiple Forms Of Gentzen's Rules And Some Intermediate Forms. Sikic, Z.

Mythe Et Réalité De La Formule De Barcan. Stahl, Gérold.

N A Vasil'év: A Forerunner Of Paraconsistent Logic. Arruda, Ayda I.

Narrow Boolean Algebras. Shelah, Sharon and Bonnet, Robert.

Natural Deduction And Arbitrary Objects. Fine, Kit.

Natural Deduction Systems For Some Quantified Relevant Logics. Brady, R T.

No Minimal Transitive Model Of Z—. Marek, W and Srebrny, M.

Nomic Probability. Pollock, John L.

Non Recursive Functionals. Bird, Richard.

Non—closure Of The Image Model And Absence Of Fixed Points. Sureson, Claude.

Noncumulative Dialectical Models And Formal Dialectics. Krabbe, Erik C W.

Normative Kinematics (I): A Solution To A Problem About Permission. Belzer, Marvin.

Norms And Logic: Kelsen And Weinberger On The Ontology Of Norms. Bulygin, Eugenio.

Numbers. Zemach, E M.

On Σ_1^1 Equivalence Relations With Borel Classes Of Bounded Rank. Sami, Ramez L.

On A Modal—Type Language For The Predicate Calculus. Skordev, Dimiter.

On A Simple Definition Of Computable Function Of A Real Variable—With Applications To Functions Of A Complex Variable. Caldwell, Jerome and Pour— El, Marion Boykan.

On Automorphisms Of Resplendent Models Of Arithmetic. Seremet, Zofia.

On Brouwer's Definition Of Unextendable Order. Posy, Carl J.

On Characterizing Unary Probability Functions And Truth—Value Functions. Leblanc, Hugues.

On Choice Sequences Determined By Spreads. Van Der Hoeven, Gerrit and Moerdijk, Ieke.

On Complementedly Normal Lattices II: Extensions. Kaiser, Klaus.

On Conservativeness And Incompleteness. Field, Hartry.

On Definitional Equivalence And Related Topics. Corcoran, John.

On Hilbert's Operation On Logical Rules, II. Pogorzelski, Witold A.

On Indicative Conditionals With Contrary Consequents. Jackson, Frank.

On Languages With Two Variables. Mortimer, Michael.

On Modal Logics Which Enrich First—Orders S5. Hodes, Harold.

On Modal Systems Having Arithmetical Interpretations. Avron, Arnon.

On N—Place Strictly Monotonic Functions. Hickman, John.

On Propositional Calculus With A Variable Functor. Lesisz, Wlodzimierz.

On Pseudo—$\aleph_0$—Categorical Theories. Marcja, Annalisa and Toffalori, Carlo.

On Skala's Set Theory. Manakos, Jannis.

On Some Non—Classical Extensions Of Second—Order Intuitionistic Propositional Calculus. Scedrov, Andrej.

On Speedability Of Recursively Enumerable Sets. Marques, Ivan.

On Supervaluations In Free Logic. Woodruff, Peter W.

On The "Problem Of The Last Root" For Exponential Terms. Wolter, Helmut.

On The Consistency Of Some Partition Theorems For Continuous Colorings, And The Structure Of Dense Real Order Types. Shelah, Saharon and Abraham, U and Rubin, M.

On The Consistency Of A Three—Valued Logical Calculus. Bochvar, D A.

On The Construction Of A Legal Logic In Retrospect And In Prospect. Tammelo, Ilmar.

On The Definition Of Ordered n—Tupels. Neumann, Olaf.

On The Degree Of Complexity Of Sentential Logics; An Example Of The Logic With Semi—negation. Hawranek, Jacek and Zygmunt, Jan.

On The Elimination Of Singular Terms. Lambert, K.

On The Existence And Recursion Theoretic Properties Of Generic Sets Of Reals. Weitkamp, Galen.

On The Independence Of The Kinna Wagner Principle. Pincus, David.

On The Logic Of Theory Change: Partial Meet Contraction And Revision Functions. Alchourron, Carlos and Gardenfors, Peter and Makinson, David.

On The Logical Structure Of Political Doctrines (Pragmatical Aspects). Solcan, Mihail—Radu.

On The Logic And Criteriology Of Causality. Leman, Marc.

On The Notion Of Effectiveness. Shapiro, Stewart.

On The Period Of Sequences $(A^n(p))$ In Intuitionistic Propositional Calculus. Ruitenburg, Wim.

On The Reality Of Existence And Identity. Hazen, Allen.

On The Relation Of Dialectical And Mathematical Logic (in Czechoslovakian). Havas, K G.

On The Relation Between Science And Logic. Otakpor, Nkeonye.

On The Relevant Systems **p** And **p*** And Some Related Systems. Arruda, Ayda I and Da Costa, Newton C A.

On The Role Of The Baire Category Theorem And Dependent Choice In The Foundations Of Logic. Goldblatt, Robert.

LOGIC

LOGIC

Mason, Ian.

The Modal Theory Of Pure Identity And Some Related Decision Problems. Hodes, Harold T.

The Model Theory Of Finitely Generated Finite–By–Abelian Groups. Oger, Francis.

The Model–Theoretic Structure Of Abelian Group Rings. Pappas, Peter C.

The Nature Of Critical Thinking. Reeder, Harry P.

The Not–So–Strange Modal Logic Of Indeterminacy. Pelletier, F J.

The Notion Of Mathematical Intuition And Husserl's Phenomenology. Tieszen, Richard.

The Number Of One–Generated Cylindric Set Algebras Of Dimension Greater Than Two. Larson, Jean A.

The Object Of Belief. Lepage, Francois.

The Ordered Field Of Real Numbers And Logics With Malitz Quantifiers. Rapp, Andreas.

The Philosopher Behind The Last Logicist. Weiner, Joan.

The Preservation Of Coherence. Jennings, R E and Schotch, P K.

The Principle Of Comprehension As A Present–Day Contribution To Mathesis Universalis. Marciszewski, Witold.

The Principle Of Contra–Action. Fox, Douglas A.

The Problem Of Induction. Czezowski, Tadeusz.

The Process Of Discovery. Lugg, Andrew.

The Real–Algebraic Structure Of Scott's Model Of Intuitionistic Analysis. Scowcroft, Philip.

The Sorites Paradox. Thorpe, Dale A.

The Status Of The Debate On Rights In The USSR. Lee, Sander H.

The Strength Of Nonstandard Methods In Arithmetic. Henson, C Ward and Kaufmann, Matt and Keisler, H Jerome.

The Strength Of Admissibility Without Foundation. Jager, Gerhard.

The Strong Amalgamation Property For Complete Boolean Algebras. Monro, G P.

The Success Of Mathematics. Magari, Roberto.

The Undecidability Of Entailment And Relevant Implication. Urquhart, Alasdair.

The Uniqueness Of Envelopes In $\aleph_0$–Categorical, $\aleph_0$–Stable Structures. Loveys, James.

The Unity And Employments Of The Understanding: The Relationship Between Kant's Logics (in Hebrew). Gilead, Amihud.

The Universal Complementation Property. Downey, R G and Remmel, J B.

The Unsolvability Of The Gödel Class With Identity. Goldfarb, Warren D.

There Is No Set Of All Truths. Grim, Patrick.

Topological Duality For Nelson Algebras And Its Applications. Sendlewski, Andrzej.

Toposes In Logic And Logic In Toposes. Bunge, Marta.

Trace Expansions Of Initial Segments. Murawski, Roman.

Triadic Partial Implicational Propositional Calculi. Hughes, Charles E and Singletary, W E.

Truth And Reflection. Yablo, Stephen.

Truth In All Of Certain Well–Founded Countable Models Arising In Set Theory. Rosenthal, John W.

Truth Without Satisfaction. Fine, Kit and Mc Carthy, Timothy.

Truthfulness And Non–trivial Contradictions. Smolenov, Hristo.

Two Episodes In The Unification Of Logic And Topology. Grosholz, E R.

Two Problems Of Induction. Jason, Gary J.

Two Solutions To Chisholm's Paradox. Forbes, Graeme.

Two Variants Of The System Of Entailment. Imre, Ruzsa.

Typical Ambiguity And The Axiom Of Choice. Crabbe, Marcel.

Ultrafilters And Types On Models Of Arithmetic. Kirby, L A S.

Unbekannte Manuskripte Aus Der Jenaer Und Nürnberger Zeit Im Berliner Hegel–Nachlass. Ziesche, Eva.

Universal Recursion Theoretic Properties Of R E Preordered Structures. Montagna, Franco and Sorbi, Andrea.

Untersuchungen Zur Algebraischen Theorie Der Partiellen Mengen. Kuhnrich, Martin.

Utility Theory And Preference Logic. Trapp, Rainer W.

Variable Truth. Szabo, Manfred Egon.

Variations On Promptly Simple Sets. Maas, Wolfgang.

Variations Of Core Semantic Techniques And Their Methodological Import. Vakarelov, Krista.

Vindicating Strawson. Hutcheson, Peter.

Vopenka's Principle And Compact Logics. Makowsky, J A.

Weak Completeness And Abelian Semigroups. Wesselkamper, T C.

Weak Conditional Comparative Probability As A Formal Semantic Theory. Morgan, Charles G.

Weakly Compact Cardinals In Models Of Set Theory. Enayat, Ali.

Welfare Functions And Group Decisions. Borch, Karl.

Well–Behaved Modal Logic. Hodes, Harold T.

What Is Einstein's Statistical Interpretation, Or, Is It Einstein For Whom Bell's Theorem Tolls. Fine, Arthur.

What's In A Belief? Biro, J I.

Where Gamma Fails. Meyer, Robert K and Giambrone, Steve and Brady, Ross T.

Which Set Existence Axioms Are Needed To Prove The Cauchy/Peano Theorem For Ordinary Differential Equations? Simpson, Stephen.

Why Hegel At All? Bole, Thomas and Stevens, John Mark.

Working Foundations. Feferman, Solomon.

Wright *Versus* Lewis On The Transitivity Of Counterfactuals. Lowe, E J.

Zeno's Paradoxes And Temporal Becoming In Dialectical Atomism. Smolenov, Hristo.

Zeno's Paradoxes, Iteration, And Infinity. Seaton, Robert.

Zum Aufbau Einer Mehrsortigen Elementaren Logik. Kaphengst, Heinz.

Zur Benutzung Der Verkettung Als Basis Für Die Arithmetik. Deutsch, Michael.

Zur Frage Der IV: Syllogistischen Figur In Der "Dissertatio De Arte Commbinatoria", Eine Jugendsünde Leibnizens? Moriconi, Enrico and Offenberger, Niels.

Zur Logik Und Semiotik Bei Leibniz. Schulthess, Peter.

Zur Raumkompliziertheit Mehrdimensionaler Turing–Automaten. Hemmerling, Armin and Murawski, Gerd.

Zur Wellengleichung Mit Konstruktiven Randbedingungen. Hauck, Jürgen.

3088 Varieties: A Solution To The Ackermann Constant Problem. Slaney, John K.

LOGICAL ANALYSIS

Gremlins Revenged: Gremlins Repulsed. Grim, Patrick and Brecher, Robert.

Theology And The Intellectual Endeavour Of Mankind. Hudson, W D.

Where Does The Ontological Argument Go Wrong? Mc Grath, Patrick J.

LOGICAL EMPIRICISM

see also Logical Positivism

L'Empirismo Logico E Il Problema Dei Valori. Petruzzellis, Nicola.

New Philosophies Of Science In The USA; A Selective Survey. Kisiel, Theodore and Johnson, Galen.

The Logician's Dilemma: Deductive Logic, Inductive Inference And Logical Empiricism. Boyd, Richard N.

LOGICAL FORM

"On The Origins Of Some Aristotelian Theses About Predication" in *How Things Are*, Bogen, James (ed), 323–326. Code, Alan.

A Comparison Of Logical Form In Russell And Wittgenstein. May, Philip.

What Is Grammar? Tomkow, Terrance A.

LOGICAL IMPOSSIBILITY

Descartes On God's Ability To Do The Logically Impossible. La Croix, Richard R.

LOGICAL NECESSITY

Universals And Laws Of Nature. Tweedale, Martin.

LOGICAL POSITIVISM

Philosophy Of Science And Sociology: From The Methodological Doctrine To Research Practice. Mokrzycki, Edmund.

Clark Hull, Robert Cummins, And Functional Analysis. Amundson, Ron and Smith, Laurence.

Psychological Terms, Logical Positivism, And Realism: Issues Related To Construct Validation. Ellett Jr, Frederick S.

LOGICAL POSSIBILITY

How Nominalist Is Hartry Field's Nominalism? Resnik, Michael D.

LOGICAL THEORY

"If A And B, Then A". Lowe, E J.

"Theory Comparison And Relevant Evidence" in *Testing Scientific Theories*, Earman, John (ed), 27–42. Van Fraassen, Bas C.

A Logic Of Message And Reply. Harrah, David.

A New Field: Empirical Logic. Barth, E M.

Formal Logic: A Degenerating Research Programme In Crisis. Smith, Joseph Wayne.

Formal Systems Of Dialogue Rules. Krabbe, Erik C W.

Lemmon On Logical Relations. Kennedy, Ralph.

New Directions In The Logic Of Dialogue. Walton, Douglas N.

No Logic Before Friday. Mackenzie, Jim.

On A Formal Structure Of A Dialogue. Nowakowska, Maria.

Rejoinder To Tenant's "Were Those Disproofs I Saw Before Me"? Weir, Alan.

Some Radical Consequences Of Geach's Logical Theories. Cain, James.

The Logic Of Disputation In Walter Burley's Treatise On Obligations. Stump, Eleonore.

LOGICAL TRUTH(S)

see also Analytic

Logique Et Ontologie. Kalinowski, Georges.

LOGICISM

An Analytic–Existential Solution To The 'Knowing That One Knows' Problem. Johnson, Steve A.

LOGOS

The "Phaedo": A Platonic Labyrinth. Burger, Ronna.

An Analysis And Assessment Of A Fragment From Jonathan Barnes's Reading Of Heraclitus. Marino, Gordon D.

History Of Philosophy In The Grand Manner: The Achievement Of H A Wolfson. Runia, D T.

Logos Y Eros En San Juan De La Cruz Y Platón. Herrera, Bernal.

The Limits Of Logocentrism (On The Way To Grammatology). Silverman, Hugh J.

LONERGAN, B

A Note On The Prefaces Of Insight. Crowe, F E.

Investigating Lonergan's Inaccessibility. Walmsley, Gerard.

Lonergan's Economics. Mathews, William.

Lonergan's Metaphysics: Ontological Implications Of Insight–As–Event. Skrenes, Carol.

The Mind Of Christ In Transcendental Theology: Rahner, Lonergan And Crowe. Moloney, Raymond.

LONGINO, H

Pornography: Defamation And The Endorsement Of Degradation. Soble, Alan.

LOOMER, B

In Response To Loomer's "Meland On God". Meland, Bernard E.

LOOS, A

Die Utopie Künstlerischer Wahrheit In Der Ästhetik Von Adolf Loos Und Arnold Schönberg. Waibl, Elmar.

LOPTSON, P

Loptson On Anselm And Davis. Davis, Stephen T.

Philosophy, Psychology, And Piaget: A Reply To Loptson And Kelly. Smith, Leslie.

LORENTZ
Aether/Or: The Creation Of Scientific Concepts. Nersessian, Nancy J.
The History Of Quantum Mechanics As A Decisive Argument Favoring Einstein Over Lorentz. Nugayev, R M.

LOSEV, A
"A F Losev And The Rebirth Of Soviet Aesthetics After Stalin" in *Contemporary Marxism*, O' Rourke, James J (ed), 221–236. Scanlan, James P.

LOVE
see also Eros
Having Love Affairs. Taylor, Richard.
Love And Conflict: A Covenantal Model Of Christian Ethics. Allen, Joseph L.
The Nature Of Love: Courtly And Romantic. Singer, Irving.
The Nature Of Love: Plato To Luther, Second Edition. Singer, Irving.
A Comparison Of Three Ways Of Knowing: Categorical, Structural, And Affirmative. Mc Cabe, Viki.
A L'origine De La Notion D'amour En Occident. Fredette, Gatien.
Chaucer And Augustine: Human Love And The Doctrine Of "Use". Clasby, E.
Choosing Between Love And Logic. Page, Ralph C.
Divine Command Theories And The Appeal To Love. Chandler, John.
Educación Universitaria Para El Amor. Basave, Agustín.
Epicurus And Lucretius On Sex, Love, And Marriage. Arkins, B.
Love, Rhetoric, And The Aristocratic Way Of Life. Levi, Albert William.
Love: Augustine And Chaucer. Thundy, Zacharias P.
Personalisme Et Anthropologie Chrétienne. Walgrave, Jan H.
Plato's *Lysis*: A Reconsideration. Tindale, Christopher W.
Rousseau On The Fall Of Social Man. Skillen, Anthony.
Spinoza's Account Of Sexuality. Rice, Lee.
The *Uti/Frui* Distinction In Augustine's Ethics. O' Connor, William Riordan.

LOVEJOY, A
Kant On Reality. Mijuskovic, Ben.

LOVEJOY, O
Gathering Stories For Hunting Human Nature. Zihlman, Adrienne L.

LOWE, E
Comment On Lowe's "Wright *Versus* Lewis On The Transitivity Of Counterfactuals". Wright, Crispin.

LOY, D
Is Nāgārjuna A Philosopher: A Response To Professor Loy. Betty, L Stafford.

LOY, J
Theoretical And Practical Confusion In American Professional Sport. Rose, David A.

LUCAS, C
"Toward A Pedagogy Of The Useful Past For Teacher Preparation": A Reaction. Gutek, Gerald L.

LUCK
The Calibration Question. Lad, Frank.

LUCRETIUS
Epicurus And Lucretius On Sex, Love, And Marriage. Arkins, B.

LUHMANN, N
Complexity And Intersubjectivity: Towards The Theory Of Niklas Luhmann. Bednarz Jr, John.
Das Schwierige Recht Der Systemtheoretischen Soziologie: Zur Rechtssoziologie Von Niklas Luhmann. Folkers, Horst.
Functional Method And Phenomenology: The View Of Niklas Luhmann. Bednarz Jr, John.
Niklas Luhmann And His View Of The Social Function Of Law. Murphy, John W.
Norm Und Recht In Niklas Luhmanns Rechtssoziologie: Kritische Anmerkungen Aus Der Sicht Der Rechtsethnologie. Von Benda– Beckmann, Franz.

LUKACS, G
"Lukács, Class Consciousness, And Rationality" in *Continuity And Change In Marxism*, Fischer, Norman And Others (ed), 86–96. Wenger, Morton G.
El Papel Del Leninismo En "Historia Y Conciencia De Clase". Giglioli, Giovanna.
Georg Lukács Und Die Frage Nach Der Spezifik Des Asthetischen. Sailer, J.
Two Ontologies Of Hegel, Marx, Lukács? Sleczka, Kazimierz.
Vernunft Contra Unvernunft Zu Georg Lukács' Faschismus–Kritik. Wrona, V.

LUKES, S
Power, Structure And Agency. Layder, Derek.

LUPASCO, S
Contradictional Logic—Its Limits And The Significance Of A Reformatory Programme. Ioan, Petru.

LUTHER
The Theory And Practice Of Virtue. Meilaender, Gilbert C.
Luther's Word On Man's Will: A Case Study In Comparative Intellectual History. Migotti, Mark.
Taxation In The History Of Protestant Ethics. Shriver, Donald W and Knox, E Richard.

LYING
Lying And The "Methods Of Ethics". Primoratz, Igor.
Sissela Bok On The Analogy Of Deception And Violence. Betz, Joseph.

LYONS, W
Feelings And Emotion. Leighton, Stephen R.
Lyons And Tigers. Simpson, Paul.

LYOTARD, J
Jürgen Habermas And Jean–François Lyotard: Post Modernism And The Crisis Of Rationality. Watson, Stephen.

LYRIC
The Question Of Value In Nietzsche And Heidegger. Hans, James S.

MACCALLUM, G
MacCallum And The Two Concepts Of Freedom. Baldwin, Tom.

MACDONALD, M
Über Drei Methoden Der Sprachanalytischen Ästhetik. Strube, Werner.

MACFARLANE, L
The Right To Strike And The Right To Work. Smart, Brian.

MACH
Ernst Mach And The Theory Of Relativity. Wolters, Gereon.
The Influence Of Mach's Thought On Science. Hiebert, Erwin N.

MACHIAVELLI
La Conformación Del Estado Moderno En Relación A Textos Políticos. Durand, Graciela Alcocer.
Machiavelli On Social Class And Class Conflict. Brudney, Kent M.
Perennidad De Maquiavelo. Formoso, Manuel.
Public Versus Private Claims: Machiavellianism From Another Perspective. Leonard, John.
The Picaresque Prince: Reflections On Machiavelli And Moral Change. Ball, Terence.

MACHINE(S)
Lower Bound Results On Lengths Of Second–order Formulas. Scarpellini, Bruno.
Man And Machine. Bandyopadhyay, Tirhanath.

MACINTOSH, J
The Science Of A Legislator In James Mackintosh's Moral Philosophy. Haakonssen, Knud.

MACINTYRE, A
The Georgetown Symposium On Ethics. Porreco, Rocco (ed).
"Veatch And MacIntyre On The Virtues" in *The Georgetown Symposium On Ethics*, Porreco, Rocco (ed), 117–130. Robins, Michael H.
Before Virtue: A Critique Of The New Essentialism In Ethics And Education. Collins, Clinton.
De Ondergang Van De Deugden En De Inconsequentie Van McIntyre. Kunneman, Harry.
Gibt Es Auf Erden Ein Mass? Gadamer, Hans–Georg.
Moral Fictions And Scientific Management. Santilli, Paul.
Moral Objectivity. Benedict– Gill, Diane.
On Macintyre, Rationality, And Dramatic Space. Monasterio, Xavier O.
Principles And Virtues—Or—Principles Or Virtues. Coetzee, Pieter.
Recent Reconstructions Of Political Philosophy. Doody, John A.
Recent Work On Virtues. Pence, Gregory E.
The Critique Of Natural Rights And The Search For A Non–Anthropocentric Basis For Moral Behavior. Zimmerman, Michael F.
The Modern Malaise: A Case History. Cleary, John.
The Premises Of Four Moral Conceptions: Classical, Modern, Totalitarian, And Utopian. Wilkie, Raymond.

MACKIE, J
Benn, Mackie And Basic Rights. Holborow, Les C.
INUS Conditions. Dale, A J.
Mackie And Shoemaker On Dispositions And Properties. Rosenberg, Alexander.
On The Logic And Criteriology Of Causality. Leman, Marc.
Professor Mackie And The Kalam Cosmological Argument. Craig, William Lane.
The Direction Of Causation And The Direction Of Time. Sanford, David H.

MADHYAMIKA
Studies In Ch'an And Huy–Yen. Gimello, Robert M (ed) and Gregory, Peter N (ed).
The Paradox Of Causality In Madhyamika. Loy, David.
The Yogācāra And Mādhyamika Interpretations Of The Buddha–Nature Concept In Chinese Buddhism. Liu, Ming–wood.

MADNESS
Madness. Quinton, Anthony.

MAEZTU, R
Maxima Aportacion Del Pensamiento Hispanico A La Cultura: El "Sentido Universalista". Rivera, Enrique.

MAGIC
Magical Aspects Of Political Terrorism. Miguens, José Enrique.

MAGNETISM
"Birth Of Magnetic–Resonance" in *Observation, Experiment, And Hypothesis In Modern Physical Science*, Achinstein, Peter (ed), 205–238. Rigden, John S.
Aether/Or: The Creation Of Scientific Concepts. Nersessian, Nancy J.

MAHARSI, R
Predetermination And Free Will In The Teaching Of Ramana Maharisi (1879–1950). Sharma, Arvind.

MAHAYANA
Studies In Ch'an And Huy–Yen. Gimello, Robert M (ed) and Gregory, Peter N (ed).

MAHLER, G
Mahler: Consciousness And Temporality. Greene, David B.

MAIMON, S
Solomon Maimon's Interpretation Of Kant's Copernican Revolution. Katzoff, Ch.

MAIMONIDES
Maimonides And Aquinas On Man's Knowledge Of God: A Twentieth Century Perspective. Franck, Isaac.
Maimonides, Aquinas And Gersonides On Providence And Evil. Burrell, David.
Maimonides' Life Of Learning. Finkel, Asher.

MAISTRE, J
Edmund Burke Et Joseph De Maistre. Fuchs, Michel.

MAJORITY RULE
Community As A Social Ideal. Kamenka, Eugene (ed).

MALEBRANCHE
Replies To Daisie Radner's "Is There A Problem Of Cartesian Interaction"? Richardson, Robert C and Loeb, Louis E.
The Linking Of Spinoza To Chinese Thought By Bayle And Male-branche. Lai, Yuen-Ting.

MALENESS
The Man Of Reason: "Male" And "Female" In Western Philosophy. Lloyd, Genevieve.

MALORY, T
"The Re-emergence Of Tragedy In Late Medieval England" in *Existential Coordinates Of Human Condition*, Tymieniecka, A (ed), 363-378. Kennedy, Beverly.

MALPRACTICE
China: Diary Of A Barefoot Bioethicist. Fox, Steven.

MALTHUS
"An Ecological Argument For Vegetarianism". Wenz, Peter S.
Population And Ideology. Feldman, Jan.

MAN
see also Human(s), Individual(s), Person(s), Philosophical Anthropology
Concepts Of Man In The Náhuatlan Culture (in Polish). Curylo-Gonzales, I.
Das Von Der Naturwissenschaft Gepraegte Menschenbild (in Polish). Luyten, Norbert A.
Der Mensch Als Biopsychosoziale Einheit. Freye, Ha and others.
God, The World And Man As A Social Being In Marcus Aurelius' Stoicism. Dragona-Monachou, M.
Hombre-Trabajo-Economía: Aporte Al Tema A Partir De La Antropología Filosófica. Scannone, J C.
Il Principio Del *Passo Indietro* Del Pensiero. Pellecchia, Pasquale.
L'America Primitiva E L'Europa Cristiana. Petyx, Vincenza.
La Morale Socialiste Et La Valeur De L'homme. Popescu, Vasile.
La Société Comme Intermédiaire Entre L'Homme Individuel Et L'Absolu Chez Platon Et Chez Plotin. Hager, F P.
Man As APXH. Strózewski, Wladyslaw.
Manipuler L'homme (in Polish). Boné, Edouard.
Post-Classical Philosophers' Concept Of Man As A Social Animal. Chronis, Nicholas.
The Anthropogenetic Meaning Of The Growth Of The Human Hand. Cackowski, Zdzislaw.
Thermodynamics, Man, Universe (in Czechoslovakian). Andrle, Pavel.
Une Altenative À L'exclusion: La Dialogie. Roumanes, Jacques-Bernard.

MANAGEMENT
Private Justice: Towards Integrated Theorising In The Sociology Of Law. Henry, Stuart.
"Ethical Dilemmas In Federal Cultural Resource Management" in *Ethics And Values In Archaeology*, Green, Ernestene L (ed), 97-107. Green, Dee F.
A Suggested Approach To Linking Decision Styles With Business Ethics. Fleming, John E.
Creating A Candid Corporate Culture. Serpa, Roy.
Ethical Issues In Private And Public Ranch Land Management. Blatz, Charles V.
Ethics As An Integrating Force In Management. Pastin, Mark.
Fact And Value In Ecological Science. Sagoff, Mark.
Management And Ethical Decision-Making. Robinson, Wade L.
Management Priorities And Management Ethics. Longenecker, Justin G.
Management-Think. Pastin, Mark.
Moral Fictions And Scientific Management. Santilli, Paul.
Morality, Reason, And Management Science: The Rationale Of Cost-Benefit Analysis. Copp, David.
National Park Management And Values. Bratton, Susan Power.
Pluralism In The Mass Media: Can Management Help? Nielsen, Richard P.
The Economic Contradictions And The Function Of Managing Workers (in Czechoslovakian). Hlavatý, Karel.
Valuing Wildlands. Rolston, Holmes.

MANDELBROT, B
Toward An Integrated Approach To Business Ethics. Goodpaster, Kenneth E.

MANICHEISM
Augustine On Evil. Evans, G R.
Augustine And Theological Falsification. Collinge, William.

MANIFOLD(S)
Intuition And Manifold In The Transcendental Deduction. Robinson, Hoke.

MANIPULATION
Commentary On Beauchamp's "Manipulative Advertising". Biederman, Barry.
Manipulative Advertising. Beauchamp, Tom L.

MANN, T
Thomas Mann And The Business Ethic. Brennan Joseph G.

MANNHEIM, K
"Ideology And Utopia: Looking Backward At Karl Mannheim" in *Ideology, Philosophy And Politics*, Parel, Anthony (ed), 210-224. Sargent, Lyman T.
Faces Of Truth And The Sociology Of Knowledge: John Stuart Mill And Karl Mannheim. Laffey, John F.
Forms Of Competition And Sociological Knowledge In Organized American Sociology. Stehr, Nico and Avison, William.

MANUSCRIPT(S)
Unbekeannte Manuskripte Aus Der Jenaer Und Nürnberger Zeit Im Berliner Hegel-Nachlass. Ziesche, Eva.

MANY
see also Pluralism

MANY-SORTED LOGIC(S)
A Note On Interpretations Of Many-sorted Theories. Hook, Julian L.
Zum Aufbau Einer Mehrsortigen Elementaren Logik. Kaphengst, Heinz.

MANY-VALUED LOGICS
A Syntactic Characterization Of Kleene's Strong Connectives With Two Designated Values. Martin, John N.
Algebraische Charakterisierungen Präprimaler Algebren. Denecke, Klaus.
An Alternative Concept Of The Universal Decision Element In *m*-valued Logic. Loader, John.
An Elementary Method Of Determining The Degree Of Completeness On N-Valued Lukasiewicz Propositional Calculus. Suchoń, Wojciech.
Characterization Of Three-Valued Lukasiewicz Algebras. Abad, Manuel and Figallo, Aldo.
Das Prinzip Vom Nicht-Widerspruch Und Das Prinzip Vom Ausgeschlossenen Dritten. Welding, Streen O.
N A Vasil'év: A Forerunner Of Paraconsistent Logic. Arruda, Ayda I.
On Three-Valued Moisil Algebras. Monteiro, Luiz and Abad, M.
Quelques Foncteurs Faussement Primitifs En Logique Déontique (Trivalence Et Action). Bailhache, P.
Simplified Axiom Schemes For Implication And Iterated Implication. Jones, John.
Some Propositional Calculi With Constant And Variable Functors. Jones, John.
Untersuchungen Zur Algebraischen Theorie Der Partiellen Mengen. Kuhnrich, Martin.
Where Gamma Fails. Meyer, Robert K and Giambrone, Steve and Brady, Ross T.

MANYA, J
Los Argumentos Teísticos De J B Manyà, Por Felipe Iriarte. Iriarte, Felipe.

MAO
Dialogue Within The Dialectic. Levine, Norman.
"Mao Zedong: The Long Road Of Revolution To Communism" in *Continuity And Change In Marxism*, Fischer, Norman And Others (ed), 211-231. Patsouras, Louis.
The Young Mao - A Soviet Portrait. Krancberg, Sigmund.

MAOISM
A Defense Of Humanism. Ruoshui, Wang.
Did German Classical Philosophy Simply "End"? Ruoshui, Wang.
Discussing The Problem Of Alienation. Ruoshui, Wang.
Preface To *On The Philosophy Front*. Ruoshui, Wang.
The Criterion Of Truth And Theoretical Research. Ruoshui, Wang.

MAP(S)
Monotone Reducibility And The Family Of Infinite Sets. Cenzer, Douglas.

MAPPING
The Mapping Argument And Descartes' Deceitful Demon. Shirley, Edward S.

MARCEL
"Martin Buber, Gabriel Marcel, And Philosophy" in *Martin Buber*, Gordon, Haim (ed), 305-324. Levinas, Emanuel.
Gabriel Marcel's Pensée Pensante As The Ultimate Reality And Meaning Of Human Existence. Peccorini, Francisco L.
La Pensée De Gabriel Marcel. Ricoeur, M Paul.
Redeeming The Earth: Tragic Wisdom And The Plains Indians. Hamrick, William S.

MARCUS, R
Belief And Possibility. Altrichter, Ferenc.
Moral Dilemmas, Deliberation, And Choice. Anderson, Lyle V.
Substitutional Quantification And Existence. Copeland, B J.

MARCUS AURELIUS
God, The World And Man As A Social Being In Marcus Aurelius' Stoicism. Dragona-Monachou, M.

MARCUSE, H
"Marcuse And The Meaning Of Radical Philosophy" in *Continuity And Change In Marxism*, Fischer, Norman And Others (ed), 114-130. Perrin, Ronald.
La Crítica De Herbert Marcuse A La Racionalidad Instrumentalista Y Su Receptción Por Corrientes Izquierdistas. Mansilla, H C F.
Marcuse On Hegel And Historicity. Pippin, Robert B.

MARGALIT, A
Grammatical Non-Specification: The Mistaken Disjunction 'Theory'. Atlas, Jay David.

MARITAIN
"Wittgenstein And Philosophy Of Religion" in *History Of Philosophy In The Making*, Thro, Linus J (ed), 275-298. Punzo, Vincent C.
Jacques Maritain, Filósofo Da Inteligência. Machado, Geraldo Pinheiro.
Jacques Maritain: La Educatión En Una Encrucijada. Radchik, Laura.
Le Philosophie Dans La Cité. Floucat, Y.

MARKET(S)
"The Petty Tyranny Of Government Regulation" in *Rights And Regulation*, Machan, Tibor (ed), 259-288. Machan, Tibor R.
Ethics And Markets. Bennett, John G.
Formal Properties Of Interpersonal Envy. Chaudhuri, Adhip.
Market Contractarianism And The Unanimity Rule. Coleman, Jules L.
Morality And The Market In Blood. Stewart, Robert M.
Preferences Opposed To The Market. Braybrooke, David.

MARKETING
"The International Traffic In Antiquities" in *Ethics And Values In Archaeology*, Green, Ernestene L (ed), 143-155. Vitelli, Karen D.
Correlates Of Salespeople's Ethical Conflict: An Exploratory Investigation. Dubinsky, Alan J and Ingram, Thomas N.

MARKOVIC, M
Kolakowski And Marković On Stalinism. Rockmore, Thomas.

MARQUARD, O

Hermeneutics As Practical Philosophy And Practical Wisdom (in Dutch). Van Der Walt, J W G.

Skepsis Ohne Selbstwiderspruch: Über O Marquards "Interimistischen Skeptizismus". Craemer, Heiner.

MARRIAGE

"Cupid's Yokes" in *Freedom, Feminism, And The State*, Mc Elroy, Wendy (ed), 129–142. Heywood, Ezra H.

"Irrelevancies" in *Freedom, Feminism, And The State*, Mc Elroy, Wendy (ed), 101–110. Marvin, Bertha.

"Love, Marriage And Divorce" in *Freedom, Feminism, And The State*, Mc Elroy, Wendy (ed), 143–154. Andrews, Stephen Pearl.

"Marriage Contract" in *Freedom, Feminism, And The State*, Mc Elroy, Wendy (ed), 119–120. Stone, Lucy and Blackwell, Henry.

Epicurus And Lucretius On Sex, Love, And Marriage. Arkins, B.

Getting To Know You. Shiner, Roger A.

MARSHALL, J

American Political Thought: The Philosophic Dimension Of American Statesmanship, Second Edition. Frisch, Morton J (ed) and Stevens, Richard G (ed).

MARSILUS OF INGHEN

Marsilius Of Inghen: Treatises On The Properties Of Terms. Bos, Egbert P.

MARTI, J

José Marfí: Mentor Of The Cuban Nation. Kirk, John M.

MARTIN, J

The Ideal Of The Educated Woman: Jane Roland Martin On Education And Gender. Walker, J C and O' Loughlin, M A.

MARTYRDOM

The Martyr's Dilemma. Moore, F C T.

MARVANEK, O

The Painter Otakar Marvánek As Art Critic (in Czechoslovakian). Ondracka, Pavel.

MARX

A Matter Of Hope: A Theologian's Reflections On The Thought Of Karl Marx. Lash, Nicholas.

Darwin, Marx, And Freud: Their Influence On Moral Theory. Caplan, Arthur L (ed) and Jennings, Bruce (ed).

Dialogue Within The Dialectic. Levine, Norman.

Ideology, Philosophy And Politics. Parel, Anthony (ed).

Marx & Engels: The Intellectual Relationship. Carver, Terrell.

Marx's Economics. Junankar, P N.

Marx's Social Critique Of Culture. Dupré, Louis.

Marxism And The Oppression Of Women: Toward A Unitary Theory. Vogel, Lise.

Marxism: Nomos XXVI. Pennock, J Roland (ed) and Chapman, John W (ed).

Myth, Philosophy, Avant-Gardism. Davydov, Yuri.

Ragione–Libertà–Scienza In Kant–Hegel–Marx. Sena, Michelantonio.

The Search For An Alternative: Philosophical Perspectives Of Subjectivism And Marxism. Farber, Marvin.

Über Den Wirkungs– Und Ausnutzungsmechanismus Der Gesellschaftlichen Entwicklungsgetsetze. Drjachlow, N I and Tscherkassow, G K.

Über Die Kategorien Inhalt Und Methode In Der Pädagogik. Naumann, Werner.

Über Die Wahrheit Und Den Wahrheitsbegriff. Steussloff, Hans.

"A Marxist Conception Of Ideology" in *Ideology, Philosophy And Politics*, Parel, Anthony (ed), 139–162. Nielsen, Kai.

"Gramsci And Eurocommunism" in *Continuity And Change In Marxism*, Fischer, Norman And Others (ed), 189–210. Boggs, Carl.

"Hegel's Concept Of The State And Marx's Early Critique" in *The State And Civil Society*, Pelczynski, Z A (ed), 93–113. Ilting, K –H.

"Karl Marx And Adam Smith: Remarks About The Critique Of Political Economy" in *Contemporary Marxism*, O' Rourke, James J (ed), 21–38. Ballestrem, Karl G.

"Marcuse And The Meaning Of Radical Philosophy" in *Continuity And Change In Marxism*, Fischer, Norman And Others (ed), 114–130. Perrin, Ronald.

"Marx And Kierkegaard On Alienation" in *International Kierkegaard Commentary*, Perkins, Robert L (ed), 155–174. Marsh, James L.

"Marx's Three Worlds And Their Interrelation" in *Continuity And Change In Marxism*, Fischer, Norman And Others (ed), 1–23. Rader, Melvin.

"Philosophy And Ideology" in *Ideology, Philosophy And Politics*, Parel, Anthony (ed), 17–36. Copleston, Frederick C.

"Philosophy And Ideology In Rousseau" in *Ideology, Philosophy And Politics*, Parel, Anthony (ed), 199–210. Lange, Lynda.

"Popper's Critique Of Marx's Method" in *Popper And The Human Sciences*, Currie, Gregory (ed), 147–164. Suchting, W A.

"Sartre And Alienation" in *Continuity And Change In Marxism*, Fischer, Norman And Others (ed), 144–169. Georgopoulos, N.

"The Alienation And Liberation Of Nature" in *On Nature*, Rouner, Leroy S (ed), 133–144. Moltmann, Jürgen.

"Theses On Marx" in *Continuity And Change In Marxism*, Fischer, Norman And Others (ed), 66–69. Axelos, Kostas.

"Toward The Vindication Of Friedrich Engels" in *Methodology, Metaphysics And The History Of Science*, Cohen, Robert S (ed), 331–358. Weiss, Donald D.

"Use And Abuse Of Theory" in *Ideology, Philosophy And Politics*, Parel, Anthony (ed), 37–60. Taylor, Charles.

"Zur Kritik Der Bürgerlichen Ideologie". Lowe, Bernd P.

A Brief Discussion Of Marx's Theory Of Alienation. Tianyu, Cao.

A Defense Of Humanism. Ruoshui, Wang.

Alienation And Aesthetics In Marx And Tolstoy: A Comparative Analysis. Kiros, Teodros.

Alltag Und Alltagsbewuktsein. Luutz, W.

Althusser On Overdetermination And Structural Causation. Emerson, Michael.

An Investigation On The Philosophical Problem Of Identity On The Basis Of The Kantian And Hegelian Concept Of It (in Hungarian). Tagai, Imbre.

Bedürfnisse Und Produktion. Rohrberg, Peter.

Bertrand Russell, Karl Marx, And *German Social Democracy* Revisited. Gallina, Paul.

Beyond Dialetical Thinking: Political Logics And The Construction Of Individuality. Boedi, Nicholas.

Chemie Und Dialektik. Simon, Rudiger.

Class In Social Stratification And Marxist Theories. Levin, David S.

Das Ökonomische Grundgesetz Der Kommunistischen Gesellschaftsformation Und Einige Philosophische Probleme. Leisering, Heinz.

Das Eigentum Als Eschatologische Potenz: Zur Eigentumskonzeption Von Karl Marx. Künzli, Arnold.

Das Einfachste Und Grundlegendste Verhältnis Der Sozialistischen Gesellschaft. Hellborn, Rudolf.

Das Individuelle Bewusstsein Und Die Dialektik Von Objektiven Bedingungen Und Subjektivem Faktor. Hahn, Toni.

Der Atheistische Charakter Der Marxistisch–Leninistischen Philosophie Und Weltanschauung. Klohr, Olof and Handel, G.

Der Kulturprozess Und Die Wachsende Rolle Des Subjektiven Faktors. Redeker, Horst.

Determiniertheit Und Entwicklung. Stieler, Gottfried.

Did German Classical Philosophy Simply "End"? Ruoshui, Wang.

Die Anwendung Der Marxschen Dialektik Beim Aufbau Des Kategoriensystems Des Historischen Materialismus. Stiehler, Gottfried.

Die Bedeutung Der Freiheitsproblematik Für Kants Übergang Zum Transzendentalismus. Thom, Martina.

Die Macht Zur Freiheit. Steussloff, Hans.

Die Natur In Marx' Begriffssystem. Ghideanu, Tudor.

Die Reaktionäre Marxkritik Nach Dem Gothaer Programm Der Deutschen Sozialdemokratie. Kopf, Eike.

Does Marx Have A Concept Of Justice? Keyes, Thomas W.

Doing Marx Justice. Young, Gary.

Education And Historical Materialism. Schrag, Francis.

Emancipation And Rationality: Foundational Problems In The Theories Of Marx And Habermas. Zimmermann, Rolf.

Empiricism And Speculation In *the German Ideology*. Taminiaux, Jacques.

Est–ce "L'Esprit", Est–ce "Le Capital"? Mercier– Josa, Solange.

Feuerbach Y La Ilustración. Fernandez, Arsenio Ginzo.

Forces Of Production And Social Primacy. Gottlieb, Roger S.

Gallina And Pitt: Similarities And Differences. Pitt, Jack.

Gedanken Zum Begriff Und Zur Geschichte Des Humanismus. Seidel, Helmut.

Gedanken Zum Schicht–Begriff Der Marxistisch–Leninistischen Theorie Der Klassen Und Des Klassenkampfes. Lange, Arno.

German Idealism, Greek Materialism, And The Young Karl Marx. Baronovitch, Laurence.

Gesetzmaässigkeiten Des Revolutionären Prozesses. Eichhorn, Wolfgang.

Hegel, Marx And Wittgenstein. Cook, Daniel.

Hegemony And Sport. Parry, S J.

Hermeneutic Hegelianism. Butler, Clark.

Historical Materialism, Ideology And Ethics. Nielsen, Kai.

Human Nature And Morality: The Case Of The Ik. Sogolo, Godwin.

Ideological Problems Of The Development Of Needs (in German). Döbler, Martin and others.

Ideology And Truth. Oruka, H Odera.

Ideology, Class, And The Autonomy Of The Capitalist State: The Petit–Bourgeois' World View And Schooling. Shapiro, H Svi.

Is There A Marxist Personal Morality? Mc Murtry, John.

Justice And Class Interests. Wood, Allen W.

K Marx's Historical Thinking: On 100th Anniversary Of His Death. Kuderowicz, Zbigniew.

Kant Und Das Grundproblem Der Klassischen Bürgerlichen Philosophie. Buhr, Manfred.

Karl Marx And Literature. Markiewicz, Henryk.

Karl Marx On Democracy, Participation, Voting, And Equality. Springborg, Patricia.

Karl Marx—A Great Friend Of Poland. Zuraw, Jozef.

Kritisches Zur Widerspruchsdebatte. Eichhorn, Wolfgang.

La Concepción Hegeliana Del Estado Y Su Crítica Por El Joven Marx. Jiménez, Carlos Molina.

La Philosophie En Tant Qu'éthique. Danişor, Gheorghe.

Les Fondements Personnalistes De La Propriété. Cottier, Georges.

Liberalism And The Jewish Connection: A Study Of Spinoza And The Young Marx. Schwartz, Joel.

Limitations Of The Theory Of Alienation Propounded By Marx In His Youth. Wandan, Xin.

Logik Und Dialektik Als Wissenschaftsmethoden. Tsouyopoulos, Nelly.

Marx And Aristotle. Miller, Richard W.

Marx And Engels On The Distributive Justice Of Capitalism. Allen, Derek P H.

Marx And The Theory Of Internal Relations: A Critical Note On Ollman's Interpretation Of Marx. Hudelson, Richard.

Marx And The Abolition Of Morality. Kain, Philip J.

Marx On The Return Of Man To Himself. Gongcai, Fan.

Marx Or Weber: A Genuine Of Or An Imaginary Dilemma. Markiewicz, Wladyslaw.

Marx—Anthropology And Praxis. Panasiuk, Ryszard.

Marx, Justice, Freedom: The Libertarian Prophet. Heller, Agnes.

MEDICAL ETHICS

see also Abortion, Bioethics, Euthanasia

A Genetic Counseling Casebook. Applebaum, Eleanor Gordon and Firestein, Stephen K.

Bioethics: A Casebook. Coppenger, Mark.

Care: The Essence Of Nursing And Health. Leininger, Madeleine M.

Defining Human Life: Medical, Legal, And Ethical Implications. Shaw, Margery W (ed) and Doudera, A Edward (ed).

Difficult Decisions In Medical Ethics, V4. Ganos, Doreen L and others (ed).

Ethics In The Practice Of Psychology. Carroll, Mary Ann and Schneider, Henry G and Wesley, George R.

Health Care Ethics: A Theological Analysis. Ashley, Benedict M and O' Rourke, Kevin D.

Medical Ethics: The Moral Responsibilities Of Physicians. Beauchamp, Tom L and Mc Cullough, Laurence B.

Psychiatry And Ethics. Edwards, Rem B (ed).

Reproductive Ethics. Bayles, Michael D.

Taking Care Of Strangers: The Rule Of Law In Doctor–Patient Relations. Burt, Robert A.

The Silent World Of Doctor And Patient. Katz, Jay.

"Contemporary Genetics: Some Ethical Considerations" in The Good Life And Its Pursuit, Dougherty, Jude P (ed), 175–185. Mascall, Eric L.

"Ethical Issues In The Intensive Care Unit: Case For Discussion" in Difficult Decisions In Medical Ethics, Ganos, Doreen L (ed), 107–110. Miller, Bruce.

"Freud's Influence On The Moral Aspects Of The Physician–Patient Relationship" in Darwin, Marx And Freud, Caplan, Arthur L (ed), 209–220. Brody, Eugene B.

"When Pharmacist And Physician Disagree" in Difficult Decisions In Medical Ethics, Ganos, Doreen L (ed), 203–210. Shea, Michael.

"When Pharmacist And Physician Disagree" in Difficult Decisions In Medical Ethics, Ganos, Doreen L (ed), 211–222. Lacina, Norman.

A Definition For Paternalism. Hershey, Paul Turner.

A Father Says 'Don't Tell My Son The Truth'. Higgs, Roger and others.

A Model For Teaching Medical Ethics. Welbourn, R B.

A Public Policy Option On The Treatment Of Severly Handicapped Newborns. Walter, James J.

A Rejection Of Doctors As Moral Guides. Ackroyd, Elizabeth.

Advice On Good Practice From The Standards Committee. Happel, J S.

An Analysis Of The Structure Of Justification Of Ethical Decisions In Medical Intervention. Self, Donnie J.

Arresting But Misleading Phrases. Harris, John.

Autonomy's Temporary Triumph. Veatch, Robert M and Callahan, Daniel.

Britain: The Public Gets Involved. Gillon, Raanan.

Commentary On "Striking Responsibilities". Cannell, Hugh.

Commentary On "Kicking Against The Pricks: Two Patients Wish To End Essential Insulin Treatment". Parsons, Victor.

Confidentiality In The Teaching Of Medical Ethics: A Case Report. Ellin, Joseph.

Contracts To Bear Children. Davies, Iwan.

Current Arrangements For Teaching Medical Ethics To Undergraduate Medical Students. Bicknell, D J.

Dignity And Death: A Reply. Brooks, Simon A.

Ethical Dilemmas Of The Doctors' Strike In Israel. Grosskopf, I and Buckman, G and Garty, M.

Ethics, Advertising And The Definition Of A Profession. Dyer, Allen R.

Excuse Me, But You Have A Melanoma On Your Neck: Unsolicited Medical Opinions. Moseley, Ray.

Health Promotion—Caring Concern. Tannahill, Andrew.

Iconoclastic Ethics. Black, Douglas.

In Defence Of Situational Ethics, The NHS And The Permissive Society. Black, Douglas.

In The Interest Of Infants. Mahowald, Mary B.

Informed Consent: Patient's Right Or Patient's Duty? Hull, Richard T.

Is "Ethicist" Anything To Call A Philosopher? Zaner, Richard M.

John T Noonan And Baby Jane Doe. Levin, David S.

Lay Medical Ethics. Veatch, Robert M.

Madness. Quinton, Anthony.

Medical Confidence. Havard, John.

Medical Ethics: An Excuse For Inefficiency? Mooney, Gavin.

Medical Ethics—A Christian View. Habgood, J S.

Medical Ethics And The Value Of Human Life. Khatchadourian, Haig.

Medical Ethics And Medical Practice: A Social Science View. Stacey, Margaret.

Methods Of Teaching Medical Ethics At The University Of Nottingham. Fentem, P H.

Moral Theories; Aristotle's Ethics. Price, A W.

Mum's The Word: Confidentiality And Incest. Higgs, Roger and others.

Non–Medical Burdens Of The Defective Infant. Jones, Gary E.

Objections To Hospital Philosophers. Ruddick, William and Finn, William.

Patient Truthfulness: A Test Of Models Of The Physician–Patient Relationship. Vanderpool, Harold Y and Weiss, Gary B.

Patients With Reduced Agency: Conceptual, Empirical, And Ethical Considerations. Mc Cullough, Laurence B.

Persons And The Measurement Of Illness. Bartlett, Edward T.

Psychiatric Diagnosis As An Ethical Problem. Shackle, E M.

Quality Of Life—A Response To K C Calman. Cribb, Alan.

Roles And Responsibilities: Theoretical Issues In The Definition Of Consultation Liaison Psychiatry. Agich, George J.

Self Help In Medical Ethics. Shotter, Edward.

Some Moral Problems Of The Damaged Neonate. Hoaglund, John.

Sperm And Ova As Property. Jansen, Robert P S.

Striking Responsibilities. Brecher, R.

Taking Blood From Children Causes No More Than Minimal Harm. Smith, Marjorie.

Teaching Medical Ethics In Other Countries. Wolstenholme, Gordon.

The 'Right' Not To Know. Ost, David E.

The Case For Deception In Medical Experimentation. Newell, J David.

The Conception Of Possible People. Davies, Kim.

The Humanities In Medical Education: Entering The Post–Evangelical Era. Pellegrino, Edmund D.

The Moral Significance Of Spontaneous Abortion. Murphy, Timothy F.

The Philosophy Of Medicine In Europe: Challenges For The Future. Thomasma, David C.

The Positive Aspects Of Medical Ethics Today. Boyd, Kenneth.

The Restoration Of Medical Ethics. Rogers, Adrian.

The Subject Of Baby Fae. Capron, Alexander M and others.

The Teaching Of Medical Ethics. Smith, Andrew.

The Teaching Of Medical Ethics From A Junior Doctor's Viewpoint. Law, Susan A T.

Trust. Cooper, David E.

Un Droit A L'enfant? Verspieren, Patrick.

Were You A Zygote? Anscombe, G E M.

Who Benefits From The Artificial Heart? Preston, Thomas A.

Who Counts? Smith, David H.

Yugoslavia: Equity And Imported Ethical Dilemmas. Lang, Slobodan and others.

MEDICAL SCHOOL(S)

Difficult Decisions In Medical Ethics, V4. Ganos, Doreen L and others (ed).

"Deception In The Teaching Hospital" in Difficult Decisions In Medical Ethics, Ganos, Doreen L (ed), 87–94. Liepman, Marcia K.

Preparing For The Perils Of Practice. Gorovitz, Samuel.

MEDICINE

A Guide To The Culture Of Science, Technology, And Medicine. Durbin, Paul T (ed).

Difficult Decisions In Medical Ethics, V4. Ganos, Doreen L and others (ed).

Feeling Good And Doing Better; Ethics And Nontherapeutic Drug Use. Murray, Thomas H (ed) and Gaylin, Willard (ed) and Macklin, Ruth (ed).

John Locke And Medicine: A New Key To Locke. Romanell, Patrick.

John Locke (1632–1704), Physician And Philosopher. Dewhurst, Kenneth.

Letter To The Editors: A Response To Abrams. Raymond, Janice G.

Medical Nemesis: The Expropiation Of Health. Illich, Ivan.

Paracelsus: An Introduction To Philosophical Medicine In The Era Of The Renaissance. Pagel, Walter.

The Smiling Spleen: Paracelsianism In Storm And Stress. Pagel, Walter.

"Philosophy Of Medicine" in The Culture Of Science, Technology, And Medicine, Durbin, Paul T (ed), 364–464. Engelhardt Jr, H Tristram and Erde, Edmund L.

"Scarcity And Basic Medical Care" in Biomedical Ethics Reviews, Humber, James M (ed), 95–106. Almeder, Robert.

"Women And The Rise Of The American Medical Profession" in Freedom, Feminism, And The State, Mc Elroy, Wendy (ed), 285–304. Ehrenreich, Barbara and English, Deirdre.

Ancient Psychotherapy. Gill, Christopher.

Antropologische Geneeskunde In Discussie. Verwey, G.

Australia: In Vitro Fertilization And More. Thomson, Colin J H.

China: Diary Of A Barefoot Bioethicist. Fox, Steven.

Commentary: Informed Consent In Engineering And Medicine. Martin, Mike W and Schinzinger, Roland.

Cost Containment: Issues Of Moral Conflict And Justice For Physicians. Morreim, E Haavi.

France: A National Committee Debates The Issues. Ambroselli, Claire.

German Philosophy And The Rise Of Modern Clinical Medicine. Tsouyopoulos, Nelly.

Kant Für Mediziner? Funke, G.

Medical Ethics And Medical Practice: A Social Science View. Stacey, Margaret.

Medical Negligence: Who Sets The Standard? Norrie, Kenneth McK.

Medicine And The Arts. Stone, John.

Non–Patient Decision–Making In Medicine: The Eclipse Of Altruism. Battin, Margaret P.

Philosophy Of Medicine In The Netherlands. Have, Henk Ten and Van Der Arend, Arie.

Philosophy Of Medicine In The Federal Republic Of Germany (1945–1984). Kottow, Michael.

Philosophy Of Medicine In Scandinavia. Lindahl, B Ingemar B.

Philosophy Of Medicine In Austria. Kenner, Thomas.

Prevention Of Admission And Continuity Of Care. Vanistendael, Clara.

Rejoinder To 'Medicine As Patriarchal Religion'. Abrams, Frederick R.

Response To Professor Rawlinson's Article "Women, Medicine, And Religion". Abrams, Frederick R.

Social Ethics, The Philosophy Of Medicine, And Professional Responsibility. Ozar, David T.

Thailand: Buddhism Meets The Western Model. Lindbeck, Violette.

The Medical Treatment Of Wild Animals. Loftin, Robert W.

The Philosophy Of Medicine In Europe: Challenges For The Future. Thomasma, David C.

Towards A Concept Of Shared Autonomy. Bergsma, Jurrit.

Two Pathographies: A Study In Illness And Literature. Hawkins, Anne.

Volitional Disability And Physician Attitudes Toward Noncompliance. Ferrell, Richard B and others.

What Does Medicine Contribute To Ethics? Thomasma, David C.

MEDICINE

Who We Are: The Political Origins Of The Medical Humanities. Fox, Daniel M.

Women, Medicine, And Religion: A Response To Raymond And Abrams. Rawlinson, Mary C.

MEDIEVAL

A Cultural Introduction To Philosophy: From Antiquity To Descartes. Mc Dermott, John J (ed).

Ibn Khaldoun. Lacoste, Yves.

Introduction To The Problem Of Individuation In The Early Middle Ages. Gracia, Jorge J E.

Logica Parva, Alan R Perreiah (trans). Venetus, Paulus.

Models Of Man: Explorations In The Western Educational Tradition. Nash, Paul.

Origen; Spirit And Fire: A Thematic Anthology Of His Writings. Daly, Robert (trans) and Von Balthasar, Hans Urs.

That Most Subtle Question (Quaestio Subtilissima). Henry, Desmond Paul.

The Nature Of Love: Plato To Luther, Second Edition. Singer, Irving.

Über Die Ästhetischen Grundsätze Der Musik Bei H G Nägeli (in Japanese). Nishihara, Minoru.

A No Nonsense Approach To St Anselm. Malcolm, John F.

A Proposito Del Trattato "De Bono Naturae" Nel "Tractatus De Natura Boni" Di Alberto Magno. Canavero, A Tarabochia.

Augustine, Memory, And The Development Of Autobiography. Archambault, Paul J.

Buridan On Interval Semantics For Temporal Logic. Ohrstrom, Peter.

Cognitive Intuition Of Singulars Revisited (Matthew Of Aquaparta Versus B J F Lonergan). Payne, Gordon R.

Connotative Terms In Ockham. Boler, John F.

Dialectic In The Eleventh And Twelfth Centuries: Garlandus Compotista. Stump, Eleonore.

Heidegger, 1916–1921: Hegelianismo Y Filosofía Medieval En Los Orígenes Del Pensamiento Heideggeriano. Bertelloni, C Francisco.

Henry Of Harclay On The Formal Distinction In The Trinity (in Latin). Henninger, Mark G.

Il "De Institutione Arithmetica" Di Severino Boezio. Di Mieri, Fernando.

Is To Will It As Bad As To Do It (The Fourteenth Century Debate)? Adams, Marilyn McCord and Wood, Rega.

John Reading On The Existence And Unicity Of God, Efficient And Final Causality (in Latin). Etzkorn, Girard J.

Mental Language And The Unity Of Propositions: A Semantic Problem Discussed By Early Sixteenth Century Logicians. Ashworth, E Jennifer.

Roger Bacon On Equivocation. Maloney, Thomas S.

Supposition–Theory And The Problem Of Universals. Wagner, Michael F.

The Sources Of Intuitive Cognition In William Of Ockham. Wengert, Robert G.

Walter Chatton *Vs* Aureoli And Ockham Regarding The Universal Concept. Kelley, Francis E.

MEDITATION

A Non–Ethical Concept Of Ahimsa. Bhardwaja, V K.

Descartes's Meditations As Cognitive Exercises. Hatfield, Gary.

Greenham: A Concrete Reality. Seller, Anne.

Mysticism Or Mediation: A Response To Gill. Perovich, Anthony.

Response To Perovich. Gill, Jerry H.

Thomas Traherne And The Art Of Meditation. Jordan, Richard D.

MEDIUM(S)

Hybrid Art Forms. Levinson, Jerrold.

MEILAND, J

Coercion And The Authority Of Reason. Churchill, John.

MEINONG

"On The Inconsistency Of Meinong's Ontology" in *Philosophical Analysis In Latin America*, Gracia, Jorge J E and others (eds), 115–140. Orayen, Raul.

Nonexistent Objects Versus Definite Descriptions. Grossmann, Reinhardt.

On Evidence According To Meinong And Chisholm. Schubert Kalsi, Marie–Luise.

The Russell–Meinong Debate. Smith, Janet Farrell.

MELANCHOLY

Melancholy, Irony, And Kierkegaard. Khan, Abrahim H.

MELAND, B

Bernard Meland: "A Rebel Among Process Theologians". Inbody, Tyron.

Empirical Realism And Creative Passage: Reflections On Meland's Theology. Axel, Larry E.

In Response To Frankenberry's "Meland's Empirical Realism And The Appeal To Lived Experience". Meland, Bernard E.

In Response To Suchocki's "The Appeal To Ultimacy In Meland's Thought". Meland, Bernard E.

In Response To Loomer's "Meland On God". Meland, Bernard E.

In Response To Inbody's "Bernard Meland: A Rebel Among Process Theologians". Meland, Bernard E.

Meland On God. Loomer, Bernard M.

Meland: Worship And His Recent Thought. Miller, Randolph C.

Meland's Empirical Realism And The Appeal To Lived Experience. Frankenberry, Nancy.

The Appeal To Ultimacy In Meland's Thought. Suchocki, Marjorie.

MELDEN, A

Natural Rights In Locke. Mautner, Thomas.

MELLEN, S

Gathering Stories For Hunting Human Nature. Zihlman, Adrienne L.

MELLOR, D

Towards Putting Real Tense Back Into The World: A Reply To D H Mellor's Reconstruction Of The McTaggart Argument. Smith, Joseph Wayne.

What's The Matter With *The Matter Of Chance*? Burnor, Richard N.

MELODY

Aristoxenus' Theorems And The Foundations Of Harmonic Science. Barker, Andrew.

MELOE, J

The Agent In A Northern Landscape. Londey, David.

MEMORY

The Thread Of Life. Wollheim, Richard.

Habitual Body And Memory In Merleau–Ponty. Casey, Edward S.

Imagery: From Hume To Cognitive Science. Bower, Kenneth J.

In Defense Of A Nontraditional Theory Of Memory. Naylor, Andrew.

Matière Et Mémoire Dans L'oeuvre De Diderot. Chouillet, Jacques.

The Experience Of Dreaming. Horne, James.

MEN

Philosophy In Process, V8. Weiss, Paul.

Ensayo Didáctico: Una Pieza Teatral Para La Enseñanza De Antropología Filosófica. Alonso, Luz Garcia.

La Teoria Islamica Dei Diritti Umani. Cordone, Claudio.

MENCIUS

Wang Yang–Ming, Mencius And Internalism. Lee, Jig–Chuen.

MENTAL

Mental Activity And Physical Reality. Snyder, Douglas M.

Mental Language And The Unity Of Propositions: A Semantic Problem Discussed By Early Sixteenth Century Logicians. Ashworth, E Jennifer.

Skinner On The "Mental And The "Physical". Schnaitter, Roger.

MENTAL ACT(S)

Against Holism. Weir, Alan.

Tomberlin, Frege, And Guise Theory: A Note On The Methodology Of Dia– Philosophical Comparisons. Castaneda, Hector–Neri.

MENTAL EVENT(S)

Are Mental Events In Space–Time? Gibbins, P F.

MENTAL HEALTH

Difficult Decisions In Medical Ethics, V4. Ganos, Doreen L and others (ed).

Psychiatry And Ethics. Edwards, Rem B (ed).

Can We Think Of Salvation As A Return To Mental Health? Sontag, Frederick.

Epidemiology And Anthropology: Notes On Science And Scientism. Rubinstein, Robert A.

Madness. Quinton, Anthony.

MENTAL ILLNESS

Biomedical Ethics Reviews. Humber, James M (ed) and Almeder, Robert F (ed).

Difficult Decisions In Medical Ethics, V4. Ganos, Doreen L and others (ed).

"Illness And Incompetence" in *Contemporary Issues In Health Care*, Schnall, David J (ed), 112–128. Szasz, Thomas.

"Mental Illness And Crime" in *Biomedical Ethics Reviews*, Humber, James M (ed), 149–162. Arrington, Robert L.

Insanity And Criminality. Simon, Michael A.

Involuntary Confinement: Legal And Psychiatric Perspectives. Dresser, Rebecca.

Psychiatric Diagnosis As An Ethical Problem. Shackle, E M.

The Autonomy Of The Mentally Ill: A Case Study In Individualistic Ethics. Laor, Nathaniel.

The Rights Approach To Mental Illness. Campbell, Tom.

MENTAL IMAGE(S)

Consciousness: Natural And Artificial. Culbertson, James T.

'There Is In Wittgenstein's Work No Argument And No Conclusion'. Malone, Michael E.

Dennett, Mental Images, And Images In Context. Russow, Lilly–Marlene.

Imagery: From Hume To Cognitive Science. Bower, Kenneth J.

The Debate About Mental Imagery. Tye, Michael.

MENTAL STATES

The Thread Of Life. Wollheim, Richard.

A Farewell To Functionalism. Baker, Rudder Lynne.

Against Neural Chauvinism. Cuda, Tom.

Eliminativism, Meaning, And Qualitative States. Jacoby, Henry.

Hume's Bundle Theory Of The Mind. Brooks, D.

Lawless Freedom. Abelson, Raziel.

Methodological Solipsism: A Reply To Morris. Noonan, Harold W.

Narrow Taxonomy And Wide Functionalism. Kitcher, Patricia.

On Searle's "Solution" To The Mind–Body Problem. Lyons, William E.

Professor Putnam On Brains In Vats. Harrison, J.

Thought. Swinburne, Richard.

Toward A Theory Of Moods. Lormand, Eric.

MENTALISM

Emergent Behaviorism. Killeen, Peter R.

Phenomenalism, Idealism And Mentalism: A Historical Note. Gupta, R K.

Remembering. Cascardi, Anthony J.

Where's The Use In Meaning? Millar, Alan.

MENTALLY RETARDED

Which Clients Should A Sheltered Workshop Serve: Case Study. Mc Donald, Michael and Herr, Stanley S.

MERCIER, D

Il Problema Della Certezza E La Spiritualità Dell'uomo: Psicologia, Logica E Teoria Della Scienza Nel Pensiero Di Désiré Mercier. Mangiagalli, Maurizio.

MERCY

"Judgment, Justice, And Mercy" in *The Search For Justice*, Taitte, W Lawson (ed), 83–100. Bailey, Barry.

MEREOLOGY

La Teoría De Conjuntos En Sentido Colectivo. Freund, Max.

MERIT

"The State: Ethics And Economics" in *The Georgetown Symposium On Ethics*, Porreco, Rocco (ed), 195–204. Ver Eecke, Wilfried.

Hiring By Competence. Werhane, Patricia H.

MERLEAU-PONTY

"Literary Impressionism And Phenomenology" in *Existential Coordinates Of Human Condition*, Tymieniecka, A (ed), 521–534. Kronegger, Marlies.

"The Truth Of The Body" in *Existential Coordinates Of Human Condition*, Tymieniecka, A (ed), 479–494. Riley, Michael.

An Organism Of Words: Ruminations On The Philosophical–Poetics Of Merleau–Ponty. Walsh, Robert D.

De La Sensibilité. Levinas, E.

Habitual Body And Memory In Merleau–Ponty. Casey, Edward S.

Merleau–Ponty En Buytendijk: Relaas Van Een Relatie. Boudier, C E M Struyker.

Merleau–Ponty, Lewis And Ontological Presence. Rosenthal, Sandra and Bourgeois, Patrick.

Merleau–Ponty, The Flesh And Foucault. Cohen, Richard.

Merleau–Ponty: The Triumph Of Dialectics Over Structuralism. Edie, James M.

Metaphysics And The 'Eye And Mind'. Bertoldi, Eugene F.

Methodologie Und Geschichte: Ansätze Problemorientierter Gesellschaftsanalysen. Rust, Holger.

The Behaviorism Of A Phenomenologist: The Structure Of Behavior And The Concept Of Mind. Glenn, John D.

Writing Philosophy And Literature: Apology For Narcissism In Merleau–Ponty. Cook, Deborah.

MERSENNE, M

Spazi Del Moto In Divina Proporzione. Nardi, Antonio.

MERTON, R

Corruption In Science: The Chinese Case. Suttmeier, Richard P.

Toward An Epistemologically–Relevant Sociology Of Science. Campbell, Donald T.

MERTZ, D

On Argument *Ex Suppositione Falsa*. Wisan, Winifred Lovell.

MESSAGE(S)

A Logic Of Message And Reply. Harrah, David.

METACRITICISM

Methodology, Metaphysics And The History Of Science. Cohen, Robert S (ed) and Wartofsky, Marx W (ed).

"On Popper's Conventionalism" in *Methodology, Metaphysics And The History Of Science*, Cohen, Robert S (ed), 263–282. Ströker, Elisabeth.

METAETHICS

Contemporary German Philosophy, V4. Christensen, Darrel and other (eds).

Ethics, Persuasion And Truth. Smart, J J C.

God, The Center Of Value: Value Theory In The Theology Of H Richard Niebuhr. Grant, C David.

"Making Sense Of Critical Dualism" in *Popper And The Human Sciences*, Currie, Gregory (ed), 105–120. Waldron, Jeremy.

Autonomy And Human Rights Claims. Gough, Jim.

Axiologische Cognities En Het Meta–Ethische Noncognivisme. Vos, H M.

Human Nature And Morality: The Case Of The Ik. Sogolo, Godwin.

Rebuilding Rawls: An Alternative Theory Of Justice. Groarke, Leo.

The Schopenhauerian Challenge In Environmental Ethics. Varner, G E.

METAMATHEMATICS

Logic, Semantics, Meta–Mathematics. Tarski, Alfred and Woodger, J H (trans).

METAPHILOSOPHY

A Process View Of Philosophy And Teaching Philosophy. Pecorino, Philip.

Engineering And The Philosophy Of Science. Broome, Taft H.

Fragmentos De Filosofía. Pegueroles, Juan.

Is Philosophical Anthropology Possible. Rickman, H P.

Metamorfosis Interna De Los Conceptos: Entre Filosofía Y Ciencia. Lara, Luis.

On Finding One's Feet In Philosophy: From Wittgenstein To Marx. Nielsen, Kai.

On The Possibility Of Continuing The Conversation Of Mankind. Conway, Jeremiah and Conway, Gertrude.

Philosophers And Experimental Inquiry: A Reply To Milgram's "Reflections On Morelli's Dilemma Of Obedience". Morelli, Mario.

Sentence Meaning And Speech Acts. Edwards, Michael and Katz, Jerrold J.

Subjectivism And The Question Of Social Criticism. Weston, Anthony.

The Generalized Argument From Verification: Work Towards The Metaepistemology Of Perception. Roberts, Scott P.

METAPHOR(S)

Inquiries Into Truth And Interpretation. Davidson, Donald.

Intimations Of Reality: Critical Realism In Science And Religion. Peacocke, Arthur.

Metaphor: Problems And Perspectives. Miall, David S (ed).

Portraying Analogy. Ross, J F.

"Are Scientific Analogies Metaphors" in *Metaphor*, Miall, David S (ed), 106–132. Gentner, Dedre.

"Friedrich Nietzsche: The Use And Abuse Of Metaphor" in *Metaphor*, Miall, David S (ed), 71–88. Cantor, Paul.

"Metaphor & The Flux Of Human Experience" in *Existential Coordinates Of Human Condition*, Tymieniecka, A (ed), 241–248. Lawlor, Patricia M.

"Metaphor And Cognitive Structure" in *Metaphor*, Miall, David S (ed), 14–35.

Tourangeau, Roger.

"Metaphor As Synergy" in *Metaphor*, Miall, David S (ed), 55–70. Apter, Michael.

"Metaphor In Science" in *Metaphor*, Miall, David S (ed), 89–105. Martin, J and Harre, R.

"Motives And Metaphors In Considerations Of Animal Nature" in *Ethical Questions In Brain And Behavior*, Pfaff, Donald W (ed), 125–140. Beer, Colin.

"On Taking Metaphor Literally" in *Metaphor*, Miall, David S (ed), 1–13. Moore, F C T.

"The Metaphorical Plot" in *Metaphor*, Miall, David S (ed), 133–158. Parker, Patricia.

"Understanding Literary Metaphors" in *Metaphor*, Miall, David S (ed), 36–54. Olsen, Stein Haugom.

A Survey Of Recent Ricoeur–Literature. Sweeney, Robert.

Campbell, Vico, And The Rhetorical Science Of Human Nature. Bevilacqua, Vincent M.

Der Erkenntniswert Von Metaphorischen Aussagen. Brulisauer, Bruno.

Images Of Liberation: Justin, Jesus And The Jews. Root, Michael.

La Métaphore De La Sensation (in Japanese). Higuchi Keiko.

Language, Metaphor, Rhetoric: Nietzsche's Deconstruction Of Epistemology. Schrift, Alan D.

Medicine And The Arts. Stone, John.

Metaphor, Analogy, And System: A Reply To Burbidge "Professor Burbidge Responds". Vaught, Carl G.

Metaphors We Live By. Cooper, David E.

On The Political Rhetoric Of Freud's Individual Psychology. Brunner, José.

Peirce And Metaphor. Anderson, Douglas.

Philosophical Creativity And Metaphorical Philosophy. Hausman, Carl R.

Relational Model Systems: The Craft Of Logic. Stern, Raphael.

The Experience Of Illness: Integrating Metaphors And The Transcendence Of Illness. Shelp, Earl E.

The Metaphorical Character Of Science. Bradie, M.

The Semantics Of Metaphor And The Structure Of Science. Rothbart, Daniel.

Two Pathographies: A Study In Illness And Literature. Hawkins, Anne.

METAPHYSICS

see also Being, Causation, Change, Determinism, Essence(s), Existence, Existentialism, Idealism, Materialism, Naturalism, Ontology, Philosophical Anthropology, Pluralism, Religion, Substance(s)

Absent At The Creation: The Existential Psychiatry Of Ludwig Binswanger. Seidman, Bradley.

Action (1893): Essay On A Critique Of Life And A Science Of Practice. Blanchette, Oliva (trans) and Blondel, Maurice.

An American Urphilosophie. Bunge, Robert.

An Essay On Human Action. Zimmerman, Michael J.

Análisis Propositional Y Ontologia. Sanchez, Juan Carlos.

Aristotle Metaphysics: Books Zeta, Eta, Theta, Iota. Furth, Montgomery (trans).

Augustine On Evil. Evans, G R.

Bodily Reflective Modes: A Phenomenological Method For Psychology. Shapiro, Kenneth Joel.

Bruno. Schelling, F W J and Vater, Michael G (ed).

Buddhist And Western Psychology. Katz, Nathan (ed).

Consciousness: Natural And Artificial. Culbertson, James T.

Contemporary German Philosophy, V4. Christensen, Darrel and other (eds).

Cosmological Biology. Lovenal, M.

Creativity In American Philosophy. Hartshorne, Charles.

Das Existenzproblem Bei J G Fichte Und S Kierkegaard. Hochenbleicher– Schwarz, Anton.

Elbow Room: The Varieties Of Free Will Worth Wanting. Dennett, Daniel C.

Erklaren Und Verstehen. Von Wright, Georg Henrik.

Freud And The Mind. Dilman, Ilham.

Hegel's Critique Of The Enlightenment. Hinchman, Lewis P.

Heidegger: Perspektiven Zur Deutung Seines Werkes. Pöggeler, Otto (ed).

Human, All Too Human. Nietzsche, Fredrich and Faber, Marion (trans).

Il Fenomeno Dell'essere: Fenomenologia E Ontologia In Heidegger. Esposito, Constantino.

Image And Reality In Plato's Metaphysics. Patterson, Richard.

Images Of Man. Umen, Samuel.

In Search Of Being: Man In Conflict With The Spectre Of Nothingness. De Carvalho, Manoel J.

Intimations Of Reality: Critical Realism In Science And Religion. Peacocke, Arthur.

Introducing Philosophy: A Text With Readings. Solomon, Robert C.

Introduction To The Problem Of Individuation In The Early Middle Ages. Gracia, Jorge J E.

Jean–Paul Sartre (in Hungarian). István, Fehér M.

Kant Im Original: BandII. Kant, Immanuel.

Kant On Causality, Freedom, And Objectivity. Harper, William A (ed) and Meerbote, Ralf (ed).

L'architecture De L'univers Intelligible Dans La Philosophie De Plotin. Armstrong, A H.

La Gnoseologia Di George E Moore. Borioni, Marco.

Lehrbuch Der Philosophie. Wuchterl, Kurt.

Leibniz And Locke: A Study Of The "New Essays On Human Understanding". Jolley, Nicholas.

Leibniz. Brown, Stuart.

Logic, Philosophy, And History: A Study In The Philosophy Of History Based On The Work Of R G Collingwood. Russell, Anthony F.

Martin Heidegger (in Hungarian). István, Fehér M.

Metaphysics Z 12 And H 6; The Unity Of Form And Composite. Halper, Edward.

Methodology, Metaphysics And The History Of Science. Cohen, Robert S (ed) and Wartofsky, Marx W (ed).

METAPHYSICS

Methphysics: Its Structure And Function. Korner, Stephan.

Michel Foucault: Beyond Structuralism And Hermeneutics. Dreyfus, Hubert L and Rabinow, Paul.

On The Essence Of Finite Being As Such, On The Existence Of That Essence And Their Distinction. Suárez, Francis.

On The Truth Of Being: Reflections On Heidegger's Later Philosophy. Kockelmans, Joseph J.

Ontologie Und Relationen. Horstmann, Rolf–Peter.

Order & Organism: Steps To A Whiteheadian Philosophy Of Mathematics & The Natural Sciences. Murray, Code.

Orme Ed Enigmi Nella Filosofia Di Plotino. Bonanate, Ugo.

Parmenides Of Elea: Fragments. Gallop, David.

Persons And Their World: An Introduction To Philosophy. Olen, Jeffrey.

Phenomenology And Existentialism: An Introduction. Grossman, Reinhardt.

Philosophical Problems. Stumpf, Samuel Enoch.

Philosophy In Process, V8. Weiss, Paul.

Philosophy Of Man And The Universe. Loeschmann, Fred.

Philosophy: An Introduction To The Central Issues. Landesman, Charles.

Popper Selections. Miller, David (ed).

Postures Of The Mind: Essays On Mind And Morals. Baier, Annette.

Principles Of Interpretation: Series In Continental Thought, V5. Ballard, Edward G.

Questions On The Soul, James H Robb (trans). Aquinas, Thomas.

Ragione–Libertà–Scienza In Kant–Hegel–Marx. Sena, Michelantonio.

Realism And Truth. Devitt, Michael.

Reflection And Action. Rotenstreich, Nathan.

Relatedness: Essays In Metaphysics And Theology. Oliver, Harold H.

Sartre After Sartre. Jameson, Fredric (ed).

Science And Consciousness: Two Views Of The Universe. Cazenave, Michel (ed).

Seeing And Reading. Nicholson, Graeme.

Studies In Hegelian Cosmology. Mc Taggart, John M and Harris, H S (ed).

Temporal Relations And Temporal Becoming: A Defense Of A Russellian Theory Of Time. Oaklander, L Nathan.

That Most Subtle Question (Quaestio Subtilissima). Henry, Desmond Paul.

The "Phaedo": A Platonic Labyrinth. Burger, Ronna.

The Accidental Universe. Davies, P C W.

The Arguments From The Sciences In Aristotle's Peri Ideon'. Frank, Daniel H.

The Dialogical And The Dialectical Nerveau De Rameau. Jauss, Hans Robert.

The Effectiveness Of Causes. Emmet, Dorothy.

The Emergence Of Whitehead's Metaphysics 1925–1929, R C Neville (ed). Ford, Lewis S.

The Essential Writings, Bruce W Wilshire (ed). James, William.

The Existential Coordinates Of The Human Condition: Poetic—Epic—Tragic. Tymieniecka, Anna–Teresa (ed).

The Limits Of Science. Medawar, P B.

The Magdalen Metaphysicals: Idealism And Orthodoxy At Oxford, 1901–1945. Patrick, James.

The Metaphysical Foundations Of Logic, Michael Heim (trans). Heidegger, Martin.

The Multiple States Of Being. Guénon, René.

The Nature Of Love: Plato To Luther, Second Edition. Singer, Irving.

The Nature Of Love: Courtly And Romantic. Singer, Irving.

The Network Of Thought. Krishnamurti, J.

The New Image Of The Person: The Theory And Practice Of Clinical Philosophy. Koestenbaum, Peter.

The New Story Of Science. Augros, Robert and Stanciu, George N.

The Platonism Of Marsilio Ficino: A Study Of His Phaedrus Commentary, Its Sources And Genesis. Allen, Michael J B.

The Problem Of Social Reality: Collected Papers 1. Schutz, Alfred.

The Rhythm Of Being: A Study Of Temporality. Trivers, Howard.

The Supreme Doctrine: Psychological Encounters In Zen Thought. Benoit, Hubert.

The Thread Of Life. Wollheim, Richard.

Theory And Practice: An Introduction To Philosophy. Runkle, Gerald.

Unacceptable Essays. Roe, M F H.

Unreality And Time. Brumbaugh, Robert S.

What Is Thought? Stirling, James Hutchison.

(Reflections On) The Dialectical Relationship Between Technique And (The Problem Of) Liberation. Griffith, William T.

Über Das Verhältnis Von Werner Marx Zu Martin Heidegger. Schoeller– Von Haslingen, Karin.

Über Die Rolle Von Substanzbegriffen Beim Zeigen Und Zählen Von Gegenständen. Hoche, Hans–Ulrich.

'Form, Reproduction And Inherited Characteristics In Aristotle's GA'. Witt, Charlotte.

'Metaphysics Is Not Your Strong Point': Orwell And Those Who Speak For Civilization. Strug, Cordell.

'Rosicrucianism Or Cross–rosism' In Hegel's Phenomenology. Roberts, Marie.

'Vlastos On Pauline Predication'. Malcolm, John F.

"Beyond Empiricism: The Need For A Metaphysical Foundation For Freedom" in On Freedom, Howard, John A (ed), 27–38. Kolakowski, Leszek.

"Canetti E La Metafisica Involontaria" in Il Tempo Dell'Arte, Papi, Fulvio and others (ed), 139–155. Papi, Fulvio.

"Comment Le Monde Vrai Devint, Pour Finir, Une Fable" in Asthetische Er Fahrung Und Das Wesen Der Kunst, Holzhey, Helmut, 9–22. Schüssler, I.

"Drive": In Defense Of A Concept. Smith, Kendon.

"Introductory: James Collins—The Man, The Scholar, The Teacher" in History Of Philosophy In Making, Thro, Linus J (ed), 1–18. Murray, John Patrick and others and Dahlstrom, Daniel O.

"Kierkegaard's Two Ages And Heidegger's Critique Of Modernity" in International Kierkegaard Commentary, Perkins, Robert L (ed), 223–258. Hoberman, John M.

"L'épître Sur La Connaissance De L'âme Rationnelle Et De Ses États" Attribuée À Avicenne. Michot, Jean.

"L'allégorie De La Caverne": République En Petit. Gendron, Edmond.

"Metaphysics And Poetry" in Continental Philosophy And The Arts, Winters, Laurence E and others (ed), 219–224. Bachelard, Gaston.

"Normal" Intentional Action. Ehrind, Douglas.

"Personal Identity And Imagination": One Objection. Flew, Antony.

"Surrender–And–Catch And Hermeneutics". Wolff, Kurt H.

"The Deutsche Metaphysik Of Christian Wolff: Text And Transitions" in History Of Philosophy In Making, Thro, Linus J (ed), 149–164. Corr, Charles A.

"The Metaphysics Of The Good" in The Good Life And Its Pursuit, Dougherty, Jude P (ed), 51–76. Leclerc, Ivor.

"The Order And Connection Of Things"—Are They Constructed Mathematically— Deductively According To Spinoza? Gilead, Amihud.

A Case Of Creative Misreading: Habermas's Evolution Of Gadamer's Hermeneutics. How, Alan R.

A Commentary On 'Two Pathographies: A Study In Illness And Literature'. Jones, Anne H.

A Conceptual Analysis Of Self–Disclosure. Fisher, D V.

A Consideration Of Hilary Putnam. Norton Smith, Thomas Michael.

A Critical Account Of Yang Kuei–Shan's Philosophical Thought (in Chinese). Chang, Jun–Chun.

A Critical Evaluation Of Altman's Definition Of Privacy As A Dialectic Process. Foddy, W H.

A Defence Of Sellars. Wright, Edmond L.

A Defense Of Pain. Conee, Earl.

A Farewell To Functionalism. Baker, Rudder Lynne.

A Jungian View Of Evil. Segal, Robert A.

A Missing Chapter: A Marginal Note Concerning The Second Volume Of Schutz/ Luckmann: Strukturen Der Lebenswelt. Wagner, Helmut R.

A Mistaken Argument Against The Expected Utility Theory Of Rationality. Broome, John.

A Note On A Response Of Hornsby's. Lowe, E J.

A Note On Inherence. Hetherington, Stephen C.

A Note On Objective Identity And Diversity (Part III, Chapter I, Section VII). Cowan, Denis.

A Paradoxical Train Of Thought. Hollis, Martin.

A Philosophy Of Comparison: Heidegger And Lao Tzu. Heim, Michael.

A Reply To Schlesinger's "How To Navigate The River Of Time". Oaklander, L Nathan.

A Reply To Wayne A Davis' "Miller On Wanting, Intending, And Being Willing". Miller, Arthur.

A Schutz And F Kaufmann: Sociology Between Science And Interpretation. Helling, Ingeborg K.

A Semiotic–Pragmatic Theory Of Consciousness. Lee, Harold N.

A Travers La Definition Artistotelicienne De L'Ame. Laflamme, Simon.

About Being A Bat. Maloney, J Christopher.

About Mario Bunge's 'A Critical Examination Of Dialectics'. Apostol, Pavel.

Acerca Del Programa De Fenomenologia. Presas, Mario A.

Action As A Text: Gadamer's Hermeneutics And The Social Scientific Analysis Of Action. Hekman, Susan.

Action, Causality, And Teleological Explanation. Collins, Arthur.

Adam Wodeham's Anti–Aristotelian Anti–Atomism. Kretzmann, Norman.

Adhering To Inherence: A New Look At The Old Steps In Berkeley's March To Idealism. Hausman, Alan.

Affective And Non–Affective Desire. Vadas, Melinda.

Against Idealism: Johannes Daubert Vs Husserl's Ideas I. Schuhmann, Karl and Smith, Barry.

Agency And Causation. Vendler, Zeno.

Albertus Magnus' View On The Angle With Special Emphasis On His Geometry And Metaphysics. Tummers, Paul M J E.

An African Concept Of Human Personality: The Yoruba Example. Makinde, M Akin.

An Analysis And Assessment Of A Fragment From Jonathan Barnes's Reading Of Heraclitus. Marino, Gordon D.

An Analysis And Critique Of Wang Fu–Chih's Theory Of "Tao Ta Shan Hsiao, Shan Ta Hsing Hsiao" (in Chinese). Huang, Yih–Mei.

An Infinite Time Of One's Own. Lingis, Alphonso F.

An Investigation On The Philosophical Problem Of Identity On The Basis Of The Kantian And Hegelian Concept Of It (in Hungarian). Tagai, Imbre.

Analytical Approaches To Determinism. Odegard, Douglas.

Anatomia Del Potere: Dalla Logica Dell'Avere Alla Logica Dell'Essere. Nicolosi, Salavotore.

Anaxagoras' Cosmogony. Potts, Ronald.

Anmerkungen Zu Schelling. Schulz, Walter.

Anscombe, Davidson And Lehrer On A Point About Freedom. Harrison, Jonathan.

Anthropologie In Metaphysik–Distanz: E Rothacker Zum 10: Todestag. Bucher, Alexius.

Anti–Realism And Recognitional Capacities. Clark, A J.

Anti–Reductionism And The Mind–Body Problem. Murphy, Claudia M.

Approccio Fenomenologico Alla Conoscenza Metafisica. Lambertino, Antonio.

Aquinas On Individuals And Their Essences. Edwards, Sandra.

Are 'Scientific' Objects Coloured? Hardin, C L.

Are Qualia A Pain In The Neck For Functionalists? Graham, George and Stephens, G Lynn.

METAPHYSICS

METAPHYSICS

George Herbert Mead's Conception Of Consciousness. Natsoulas, Thomas.

German Idealism, Greek Materialism, And The Young Karl Marx. Baronovitch, Laurence.

God And Chaos: The Demiurge Versus The *Ungrund*. Hefner, Philip.

Goodman's Rigorous Relativism. Elgin, Catherine Z.

Griffin And Pike On Divine Power: Some Clarifications. Basinger, David.

Gustav Bergmann's Psychophysiological Parallelism. Natsoulas, Thomas.

Hölderlin E La *Vereinigungsphilosophie*. Gargano, Antonio.

Habermas's Contribution To Hermeneutic Theory. Davey, Nicholas.

Habitual Body And Memory In Merleau–Ponty. Casey, Edward S.

Habitualität Als Potentialität: Zur Konkretisierung Des Ich Bei Husserl. Bergmann, Werner and Hoffmann, G.

Hamlet Without The Prince Of Denmark Revisited: Pörn On Kierkegaard And The Self. Hannay, Alastair.

Harmless Actualism. White, Michael J.

Harmonia Universalis. Schneiders, Werner.

Hedonic Pluralism. Goldstein, Irwin.

Hegel And The Emerging World: The Jena Lectures On Naturphilosophie (1805–06). Rauch, Leo.

Hegel And The Deformation Of Symbols. Walsh, David.

Hegel, Marx And Wittgenstein. Cook, Daniel.

Hegels 'Naturphilosophie' Und Platons 'Timaios'—Ein Strukturvergleich. Hosle, Vittorio.

Heidegger And The Deconstruction Of Foundations. Tyman, Stephen.

Heidegger/Derrida—Presence. Sallis, John.

Heidegger, Taoism And The Question Of Metaphysics. Stambough, Joan.

Heidegger: Remembrance And Metaphysics. Foti, Veronique M.

Heidegger's Overcoming Of Metaphysics: A Critique. Marsh, James L.

Heidegger's "Existentialism" Revisited. Zimmerman, Michael E.

Hermeneutics And Intellectual History. Stern, Laurent.

Hilemorfismo Y Corporalidad. Bolzán, J E.

Historicity, Narratives, And The Understanding Of Human Life. Johnson, Galen A.

History And Reality: R G Collingwood's Theory Of Absolute Presuppositions. Trainor, Paul J.

Homonimia Y Géneros Del Ser En Plotino. Santa Cruz, María I.

How Nominalist Is Hartry Field's Nominalism? Resnik, Michael D.

How To Navigate The River Of Time. Schlesinger, George N.

Human Agency Between Life–world And System: Habermas's Latest Version Of Critical Theory. Hartmann, Klaus.

Human Embodiment: The Theme And The Encounter In Vedāntic Phenomenology. Sinha, Debabrata.

Hume And Edwards On 'Why Is There Something Rather Than Nothing'? Burke, Michael B.

Hume On Finding An Impression Of The Self. Traiger, Saul.

Hume On Perceptions And Persons. Davie, William E.

Hume On The Cartesian Theory Of Substance. Glass, Ronald J and Flage, Daniel E.

Hume Was Right, Almost; And Where He Wasn't, Kant Was. Shwayder, D S.

Hume, Demonstratives, And Self–Ascriptions Of Identity. Ward, Andrew.

Hume, Language And God. Soles, Deborah Hansen.

Hume's Bundle Theory Of The Mind. Brooks, D.

Hume's Dialogue IX Defended. Stahl, Donald E.

Hume's Natural History Of Religion: Positive Science Or Metaphysical Vision Of Religion. Badia Cabrera, Miguel A.

Husserl And Hegel: A Historical And Religious Encounter. Kirkland, Frank M.

Husserl's Concept Of World (in Chinese). Chan, Wing–Wah.

Husserl's Platonism And The Objective Truth (in Hungarian). Rozsnyai, Ervin.

Hutcheson's Alleged Realism. Winkler, Kenneth P.

Identity And Immaterialism. Reid, G J.

Identity, Intensionality, And Intentionality. Toberlin, James.

Identity: Criteria Vs Necessary And Sufficient Conditions. Ward, David V.

Il Carattere Immediato Della Presenza Di Dio Nel Mondo Secondo Tommaso D'Aquino. Campodonico, Angelo.

Il Pensiero Storico–Filosofico Di Olgiati E L'Interpretazione Della Filosofia Cartesiana. Grosso, Giuseppe.

Il Principio Del *Passo Indietro* Nel Pensiero. Pellecchia, Pasquale.

Il Problema Critico. Iammarone, Luigi.

Il Problema Critico Della Conoscenza. Blandino, Giovanni.

Il Tempo Nel Pensiero Di Gaston Bachelard. Ventura, Antonino.

Impeccability Revisited. Carter, W R.

Implicaciones Teórico–dfilosóficas Del Teorema De Gödel. Zúñiga, Angel Ruiz.

Inconceivable? Gay, Robert.

Indéterminisme Et Interactionnisme Chez Popper. Quilliot, Roland.

Indeterministic Freedom As Universal Principle. Hartshorne, Charles.

Inexhaustibility And Ontological Plurality. Ross, Stephen David.

Inquiry, Intrinsic Properties, And The Identity Of Indiscernibles. Hoy, Ronald C.

Intentionality And Its Place In Nature. Searle, John R.

Intentionality, Causality And Holism. Mohanty, J N.

Interrelations Between Subject And Object In Perception. Lijun, Song.

Intimations Of Taoist Themes In Early Heidegger. Parks, Graham.

Irony As A Post–Romantic Possibility For Art: Kierkegaard's Reply To Hegel. Crooks, James.

Is Aristotle A Metaphysician? Brogan, Walter.

Is Everyone A *Mentalité* Case: Transference And The "Culture" Concept. La Capra, Dominick.

Is Samavaya (Inherence) An Internal Relation? Mohanta, Dilip K.

Is The Causal Structure Of The Physical Itself Something Physical? Putnam, Hilary.

Is The Past Finite: On Craig's Kalām Argument. Shields, George W.

Is There A Measure On Earth: A Discussion Of Werner Marx's 'Nonmetaphysiccl Ethics'. Krell, David Farrell.

Is There A Problem Of Cartesian Interaction? Radner, Daisie.

Is There Just One Possible World? Cushing, James T.

J Krishnamurti On Choiceless Awareness, Creative Emptiness And Ultimate Freedom. Mathur, Dinesh Chandra.

J S Beck And Husserl: The New Episteme In The Kantian Tradition. Wallner, Ingrid M.

Jacques Maritain, Filósofo Da Inteligência. Machado, Geraldo Pinheiro.

Jan Christian Smuts And His Doctrine Of Holism. Brush, Francis W.

Janus Bifrons. Granger, Gilles–Gaston.

Jean–Paul Sartre And The Problem Of The Other. Andrews, Christine.

John Paul The Second Anthropology Of Concrete Totality. Min, Anselm K.

Kant And The Problem Of The General. Thakar, Archana.

Kant On Reality. Mijuskovic, Ben.

Kant's Transcendental Schematism. Woods, Michael.

Karol Cardinal Wojtyla And Jean–Paul Sartre On The Intentionality Of Consciousness. Pappin, Joseph.

Kosmische Technik Als Zuspruch Des Seins: Bemerkungen Zu W Schirmachers Weiterdenken Nach Heidegger. Rapp, Friedrich.

Krishnamurti Zen. Bouchard, Roch.

L'Evoluzione Del Problema Morale Nel Pensiero Di Cartesio. Cesareo, Rosa.

L'absolu Et La Philosophie De Schelling. Tilliette, Xavier.

L'ordre Du Connaître Et L'ordre De L'être Ou L'ordre Des Choses Et Celui De La Pensée. Theau, Jean.

La Cuestión Del Sentido Y El Sentido De La Cuestión. Alfaro, Juan.

La Estructura De La Ciudad Ideal. Paris, Elisa R.

La Eternidad Del Mundo: Un Capítulo De Filosofía Medieval. López, Antonio Marlasca.

La Idea Hegeliana De Materia Y El Tránsito De Lo Ideal A Lo Real. Albizu, Edgardo.

La Monadologie De Diderot. Marquet, Jean–François.

La Naissance Du Matérialisme Moderne Chez Hobbes Et Spinoza. Boscherini, Emilia G.

La Non–Séparabilité (Response À G Lochak). D' Espagnat, Bernard.

La Originación Radical De Las Cosas Demostrada A Priori: Leibniz, Nozik, Rescher. Madanes, Leiser.

La Pseudo–Métaphysique Du Signe. Bouchard, Guy.

La Récessivité Comme Structure Du Monde. Florian, Mircea.

La Realidad En Kant Y Berkeley. Montero, Bernal Herrera.

La Systématicité Et Le Cercle Hégélien. Rockmore, Tom.

La Teologia Come Antropologia In Heinrich Fries. Belletti, Brunpo.

Language And Reality In Martin Heidegger. Nwodo, C S.

Lao Tzu And Nietzsche: Wanderer And Superman. Park, Ynhui.

Las Tesis De C Fabro. Mendez, Julio Raul.

Lawless Freedom. Abelson, Raziel.

Laws And Causal Relations. Tooley, Michael.

Laws And Modal Realism. Pargetter, Robert.

Laws Of Nature As Relations Between Universals And As Universals. Armstrong, D M.

Le Caractère Mythique De L'Analogie Du Bien Dans *République VI*. Couloubaritsis, Lambros.

Le Problème De L'unité. Dagognet, François.

Le Sens De La Métaphysique Dans La Critique De La Raison Pure. Theis, Robert.

Le Temps Raconté. Ricoeur, Paul.

Legislation–Transgression: Strategies And Counter–Strategies In The Transcendental Justification Of Norms. Schürmann, Reiner.

Leibniz And The Doctrine Of Inter–World Identity. Mondadori, Fabrizio.

Leibniz And Atomism. Bregman, Robert.

Leibniz Devant Le Labyrinthe De La Liberté. Moreau, Joseph.

Leibniz Und Der Materialismus (1881): Aud Dem Nachlass Herausgegeben Von Helmut Holzhey (zürich). Natorp, Paul.

Leibniz, Materialism, And The Relational Account Of Space And Time. Sayre– Mc Cord, Geoffrey.

Leibniz, Ou L'origine De L'esthétique Descendante. Lenain, Thierry.

Leibniz' Gebrochenes Verhältnis Zur Erkenntnismetaphysik Der Scholastik. Hübener, Wolfgang.

Leibniz's Theory Of Personal Identity In The *New Essays*. Vailati, Ezio.

Les Sources De L'Objectivité Hellénique. Gobry, Ivan.

Levels Of Truth And Reality In The Philosophies Of Descartes And Samkara. Schroeder, Craig.

Libertad–Necesidad En La *Quaestio Disputata De Malo, VI*. De Gandolfi, María C Donadío Maggi.

Life After Death In Whitehead's Metaphysics. Broniak, Christopher J.

Lo Inteligible. De Paoli, Alejandro.

Lockes Perspektiventheorie Der Persönlichen Identität. Kienzle, Bertram.

Logical Problems For Lockean Persons. Welker, David.

Lonergan's Metaphysics: Ontological Implications Of Insight–As–Event. Skrenes, Carol.

Los Niveles Temporales Según J T Fraser Y El Orden Subyacente Según D Bohm. Delacre, Georges.

Los Problemas Filosóficos De La Individualidad. Gracia, Jorge J E.

Love, Rhetoric, And The Aristocratic Way Of Life. Levi, Albert William.

Love: Augustine And Chaucer. Thundy, Zacharias P.

Lucas, Gödel And Astaire: A Rejoinder To David Boyer. Lucas, J R.

Mackie And Shoemaker On Dispositions And Properties. Rosenberg, Alexander.

Maimonides And Aquinas On Man's Knowledge Of God: A Twentieth Century

METAPHYSICS

METAPHYSICS

Towards Putting Real Tense Back Into The World: A Reply To D H Mellor's Reconstruction Of The McTaggart Argument. Smith, Joseph Wayne.

Trans–World Identity Of Future Contingents: Sartre On Leibnizian Freedom. Winant, Terry.

Transcendental Idealism In Wittgenstein And Theories Of Meaning. Moore, A W.

Translucent Belief. Elgin, Catherine Z.

Transmission, Inheritance, And Efficient Causation. Field, Richard W.

Triálogo Sobre El Fin Del Principio Del Mundo. Labson, S.

Troubles With Token Identity. Leder, Drew.

Truth As Ideal Coherence. Rescher, Nicholas.

Truth In A Contingent World. Campbell, R.

Two Conceptions Of The Self. Piper, Adrian M S.

Two Strains In Buddhist Causality. Inada, Kenneth K.

Two Tibetan Texts On The "Neither One Nor Many" Argument For Śūnyatā. Tillemans, Tom J F.

Type And Eidos—Schutz And Husserl. Pritchard, Colin W.

Umanità. Villa, Luigi.

Unbekeannte Manuskripte Aus Der Jenaer Und Nürnberger Zeit Im Berliner Hegel–Nachlass. Ziesche, Eva.

Universals And Laws Of Nature. Tweedale, Martin.

Validity And Applicability Of Thermodynamics Out Of The Framework Of Physical Systems (in Czechoslovakian). Marvan, Milan.

Value And Free Choice: Lavelle's Attempt At A Reconciliation. Hardy, Gilbert.

Value And Human Condition. Sarin, Indu.

Volitional Disability And Physician Attitudes Toward Noncompliance. Ferrell, Richard B and others.

Wang Yang–Ming, Mencius And Internalism. Lee, Jig–Chuen.

Was Leibniz Entitled To Possible Worlds? Baker, Lynne Rudder.

Watsonian Freedom And Freedom Of The Will. Hill, Christopher S.

Wei–Wu–Wei: Nondual Action. Loy, David.

Weiss On Adumbration. Wood, Robert.

Weltvernunft Und Sinnlichkeit: Hegel Und Feuerbach In Bamberg. Beck, Heinrich.

What Ontology Can Be About: A Spacetime Example. Nerlich, Graham and Westwell Roper, Andrew.

What's The Matter With The Matter Of Chance? Burnor, Richard N.

Where Are The Barbarians: Ethnocentrism Versus The Illusion Of Cultural Universalism: The Answer Of An Anthropologist To A Philosopher. Kronenberg, Andreas.

Whitehead And Aquinas On The Eternity Of God. Baumer, Michael R.

Whitehead And Marx: Toward A Political Metaphysics. Marsh, James L and Hamrick, William S.

Whitehead Ou Le Cosmos Torrentiel. Dumoncel, Jean–Claude.

Whitehead Ou Le Cosmos Torrentiel. Dumoncel, Jean–Claude.

Whitehead's "Prehension" And Hegel's "Mediation". Christensen, Darrel E.

Whitehead's Epochal Theory Of Time. Hughen, Richard.

Whitehead's Double Debt To The Greeks. Bargeliotes, Leonidas C.

Why Fire Goes Up: An Elementary Problem In Aristotle's Physics. Lang, Helen S.

Why Hegel At All? Bole, Thomas and Stevens, John Mark.

Why Is There Something Rather Than Nothing? Smith, Joseph Wayne.

Why Kant Couldn't Be An Anti–Realist. Clark, A J.

Wiggins, Artefact Identity And 'Best Candidate' Theories. Noonan, Harold W.

Will And Reason: A Critical Analysis Of Kant's Concepts. Rotenstreich, Nathan.

William James And The Epochal Theory Of Time. Field, Richard W.

Wittgenstein's Rejection Of Scientific Psychology. Williams, Meredith.

Wittgenstein On The 'Charm' Of Psychoanalysis. Geller, Jeffrey L.

Wittgenstein's Anthropology. Bell, Richard.

Would It Have Been Me (Against The Necessity Of Origin). Elliot, Robert and Gallois, Andre.

Wyclef's Philosophy And Platonic Ideas (in Czechoslovakian). Herold, Vilém.

Yates On Feyerabend's Democratic Relativism. Alford, C Fred.

Yu Guang–Yuan's Two Categories Of Matter. Pfeifer, Karl.

Zum Problem Der Kehre Im Denken Heideggers. Rosales, Alberto.

Zur Diskussion Des Leib–Seele–Problems. Del– Negro, Walter V.

Zur Philosophischen Leistung Friedrich Schillers. Lindner, Margit.

Zwischen Einsamkeit Und Wechselrede: Zur Kommunikation Und Ihrer Konstitution Bei Edmund Husserl. Knoblauch, Hubert.

METASCIENCE

"Comment's On Jost Halfmann's Article" in Methodology, Metaphysics And The History Of Science, Cohen, Robert S (ed), 173–182. Janik, Allan.

"The Dethroning Of The Philosophy Of Science" in Methodology, Metaphysics And The History Of Science, Cohen, Robert S (ed), 149–172. Halfmann, Jost.

The New Metascientific Paradigm And The Linguistic Turn. Iliescu, Adrian–Paul.

METATHEORY

"Ideology And Political Culture" in Ideology, Philosophy And Politics, Parel, Anthony (ed), 111–138. Mullins, Willard A.

"Use And Abuse Of Theory" in Ideology, Philosophy And Politics, Parel, Anthony (ed), 37–60. Taylor, Charles.

The Metatheory Of The Classical Propositional Calculus Is Not Axiomatizable. Mason, Ian.

The Proper Reconstruction Of Exchange Economics. Balzer, W.

METHOD(S)

see also Scientific Method

Analysis And Dialectic: Studies In The Logic Of Foundation Problems. Russell, Joseph J.

Wittgenstein's Conception Of Philosophy. Fann, K T.

'There Is In Wittgenstein's Work No Argument And No Conclusion'. Malone, Michael E.

"Logic And The Hypothetical–Deductive Method" in Philosophical Analysis In Latin America, Gracia, Jorge J E and others (eds), 73–92. Klimovsky, Gregorio.

A Case Of Creative Misreading: Habermas's Evolution Of Gadamer's Hermeneutics. How, Alan R.

Approaches To Applied Anthropology. Cohen, Ronald.

Berlin On Vico. Zagorin, Perez.

Boeckh And Dilthey: The Development Of Methodical Hermeneutics. Seebohm, Thomas M.

Hermeneutic Hegelianism. Butler, Clark.

On Argument Ex Suppositione Falsa. Wisan, Winifred Lovell.

On Vico. Berlin, Isaiah.

Philosophers And Experimental Inquiry: A Reply To Milgram's "Reflections On Morelli's Dilemma Of Obedience". Morelli, Mario.

Popper's Piecemeal Engineering: What Is Good For Science Is Not Always Good For Society. Irzik, Gürol.

Questionnaire On Philosophy. Lonergan, Bernard.

Remarks On Bouwsma's Method Of Failure. Craft, J L.

Sense And Sensibility. Kimmel, Lawrence.

Suggestions For A Symbolic Interactionist Conception Of Culture. Maines, David R.

METHODOLOGICAL INDIVIDUALISM

Group Selection And Methodological Individualism. Glaser, Gerald.

Individualism And Global Supervenience. Currie, Gregory.

METHODOLOGY

History Of Philosophy In The Making. Thro, Linus J (ed).

John Locke And Agrarian Capitalism. Wood, Neal.

Max Weber And The Methodology Of The Social Sciences. Huff, Toby.

Methodology, Metaphysics And The History Of Science. Cohen, Robert S (ed) and Wartofsky, Marx W (ed).

Philosophy Of Science And Sociology: From The Methodological Doctrine To Research Practice. Mokrzycki, Edmund.

Probability And Evidence. Horwich, Paul.

Reason And The Search For Knowledge: Investigations In The Philosophy Of Science. Shapere, Dudley.

Science Policy, Ethics, And Economic Methodology. Shrader– Frechette, K S.

The History Of Ideas. King, Preston (ed).

The Problem Of Social Reality: Collected Papers 1. Schutz, Alfred.

Unacceptable Essays. Roe, M F H.

"Collins And Gadamer On Interpretation" in History Of Philosophy In The Making, Thro, Linus J (ed), 231–246. Marsh, James L.

"How To Be A Good Philosopher Of Science" in Methodology, Metaphysics And The History Of Science, Cohen, Robert S (ed), 33–42. Martin, Michael.

"Is The Planning Of Science Possible" in Contemporary Marxism, O' Rourke, James J (ed), 109–146. Sarlemijn, Andries.

"Out With The "Old" And In With The "New"" in Ethical Questions In Brain And Behavior, Pfaff, Donald W (ed), 91–110. Caplan, Arthur L.

"Scientific Realism And Incommensurability" in Methodology, Metaphysics And The History Of Science, Cohen, Robert S (ed), 1–32. Burian, Richard M.

"Wittgenstein And Philosophy Of Religion" in History Of Philosophy In The Making, Thro, Linus J (ed), 247–254. Carlson, John W.

Action As A Text: Gadamer's Hermeneutics And The Social Scientific Analysis Of Action. Hekman, Susan.

Beyond Divorce: Current Status Of The Discovery Debate. Nickles, Thomas.

Comment On Pommerehne Et Al, "Concordia Discors: Or: What Do Economists Think". Meile, Richard and Shanks, Stephanie L.

Comparative Narratives: Some Rules For The Study Of Action. Abell, Peter.

Consent In Time Of Affliction: The Ethics Of A Circumspect Theist. Cahill, Lisa Sowle.

Demarkation Und Rationale Rekonstruktion Bei Imre Lakatos. Schramm, Alfred.

Descartes: Methodological Ideal And Actual Procedure. Shea, William R.

Discussion: Galileo And The Continuity Thesis. Wallace, William A.

Discussion: Are We Only Five Minutes Old: Acock On The Age Of The Universe. Smith, Joseph W and Ward, Sharyn.

Discussion: What Economics Is Not: An Economist's Response To Rosenberg. Hands, Douglas W.

Explanatory Asymmetries. Woodward, James.

Feyerabend's Irrational Science. Grünfeld, Joseph.

Gesellschaftswissenschaftliche Methoden Auf Dem Wege Der Gesetzeserkenntnis. Zak, Christian.

Hermeneutics And The Social Sciences: A Gadamerian Critique Of Rorty. Warnke, Georgia.

Hypotheses And Historical Analysis In Durkheim's Sociological Methodology: A Comtean Tradition. Schmaus, Warren.

K Marx's Historical Thinking: On 100th Anniversary Of His Death. Kuderowicz, Zbigniew.

Methodological Problems In Psychology (in Dutch). Mauer, K F and Retief, A I.

Methodological Approaches To The Utilization Of Science And Technology In Practice. Boucek, Karel.

Methodological Starting Points Of The Investigation Of The Way Of Life (in Czechoslovakian). Velek, J.

Methodologie Und Geschichte: Ansätze Problemorientierter Gesellschaftsanalysen. Rust, Holger.

Methodologies, History Of Science And Dialectical Materialism. Pala, Alberto.

Metodologias E Historia De Las Ciencias. Marqués, Gustavo.

Philosophy And Policy. Thompson, Dennis.

Philosophy Of Medicine In The Federal Republic Of Germany (1945–1984). Kottow,

MIRACLE(S)

Vindicating The "Principle Of Relative Likelihood". Chrzan, Keith.

MITROFF, I

A Suggested Approach To Linking Decision Styles With Business Ethics. Fleming, John E.

MITTELMAN, W

Comments On Mittelman's "Perspectivism, Becoming, And Truth In Nietzsche". Hinman, Lawrence M.

MOBILITY

Art And Media On The Road To Abdera? Berger, René.

MODAL LOGIC

"Basic Modal Logic" in *Handbook Of Philosophical Logic*, Gabbay, Dov (ed), 1–88. Bull, Robert A and Segerberg, Krister.

"Combinations Of Tense And Modality" in *Handbook Of Philosophical Logic*, Gabbay, Dov (ed), 135–166. Thomason, Richmond H.

"Kripke Semantics" = Algebra + Poetry. Fleischer, Isidore.

"Modal Logic And Self–Reference" in *Handbook Of Philosophical Logic*, Gabbay, Dov (ed), 441–496. Smoryński, Craig.

"Quantification In Modal Logic" in *Handbook Of Philosophical Logic*, Gabbay, Dov (ed), 249–308. Garson, James W.

"Quantification In Tense And Modal Logic" in *Handbook Of Philosophical Logic*, Gabbay, Dov (ed), 309–354. Cocchiarella, Nino B.

"Sobre Las Oraciones Modales" Por Fray Alonso De La Veracruz. Redmond, Walter.

A Consistent Propositional Logic Without Any Finite Models. Mc Kay, C G.

A Modal Approach To Sneed's "Theoretical Functions". Miroiu, Adrian.

A Test To Determine Distinct Modalities In The Extensions Of S4. Bellissima, Fabio.

An Application Of The Reiger–Nishimura Formulas To The Intuitionistic Modal Logics. Vakarelov, Dimiter.

Answer To A Question Suggested By Schumm. Ulrich, Dolph E.

Atoms In Modal Algebras. Bellissima, Fabio.

Cans, Advantages, And Possible Worlds. Walton, Douglas N.

Carnapian Extensions Of S5. Hendry, Herbert E and Pokriefka, M L.

Compactness And Recursive Enumerability In Intensional Logic. Stephan, Bernd J.

Disjunctive Extensions Of S4 And A Conjecture Of Goldblatt's. Schumm, George F.

Epistemic And Alethic Iteration In Later Medieval Logic. Boh, Ivan.

Harmless Actualism. White, Michael J.

Implication And Deduction In Some Intuitionistic Modal Logics. Font, Josep M.

Jankov–Theorems For Some Implicational Calculi. Pahi, Biswambham.

La Théologie Modale De Leibniz: Réponse Á Georges Kalinowski. Dumoncel, Jean–Claude.

Linear Reasoning In Modal Logic. Fitting, Melvin.

Logic And Contingent Existence. Lopston, Peter.

Modal Logic And Model Theory. Gerla, Giangiacomo and Vaccaro, Virginia.

Modal Logics In The Theory Of Information Systems. Orlowska, Ewa.

Models For Normal Intuitionistic Modal Logics. Bozic, Milan and Dosen, Kosta.

Mythe Et Réalité De La Formule De Barcan. Stahl, Gérold.

Necessary Agnosticism? Mc Laughlin, Robert.

On A Modal–Type Language For The Predicate Calculus. Skordev, Dimiter.

On Modal Logics Which Enrich First–Orders S5. Hodes, Harold.

On Modal Systems Having Arithmetical Interpretations. Avron, Arnon.

Possible Worlds Semantics: A Research Program That Cannot Fail. Van Benthem, Johan.

Reduction Of Second–Order Logic To Modal Logic. Thomason, S K.

Remarks On The Semantics Of Non–Normal Modal Logics. Schotch, Peter K.

Sequent–Systems For Modal Logic. Dosen, Kosta.

Six Problems In "Translational Equivalence". Pelletier, F J.

Some Paraconsistent Sentential Calculi. Blaszczuk, Jerzy.

Supervenience, Realism, Necessity. Mc Fetridge, I G.

Syadvada Theory Of Jainism In Terms Of A Deviant Logic. Bharucha, Filita and Kamat, R V.

The Completeness Of Monotonic Modal Logics. Chellas, Brian F and Mc Kinney, Audrey.

The Decidable Normal Modal Logics Are Not Recursively Enumerable. Cresswell, M J.

The Extensions Of The Modal Logic *K5*. Nagle, Michael C and Thomason, S K.

The Modal Theory Of Pure Identity And Some Related Decision Problems. Hodes, Harold T.

The Not–So–Strange Modal Logic Of Indeterminacy. Pelletier, F J.

The Preservation Of Coherence. Jennings, R E and Schotch, P K.

Un Logicien Déontique Avant La Lettre: Gottfried Wilhelm Leibniz. Kalinowski, Georges and Garoddies, Jean–louis.

Well–Behaved Modal Logic. Hodes, Harold T.

Zeno's Paradoxes And Temporal Becoming In Dialectical Atomism. Smolenov, Hristo.

MODAL THEORY

Der Formalismus Und Seine Grenzen: Untersuchungen Zur Neueren Philosophie Der Mathematik. Rheinwald, Rosemarie.

Defending Microeconomic Theory. Hausman, Daniel.

Laws And Modal Realism. Pargetter, Robert.

Modality As Many Metalinguistic Predicates. Hazen, Allen.

Two Solutions To Chisholm's Paradox. Forbes, Graeme.

MODALITY

"Correspondence Theory" in *Handbook Of Philosophical Logic*, Gabbay, Dov (ed), 167–248. Van Benthem, Johan.

A Test To Determine Distinct Modalities In The Extensions Of S4. Bellissima, Fabio.

Davidson's Theory Of Meaning: Some Questions. Taylor, Kenneth A.

Mysticism, Veridicality, And Modality. Oakes, Robert.

The De Re Modality And Essentialism. Sanyal, Indrani.

MODE(S)

Insiders And Outsiders Models Of Deviance And Jurisprudence. Hund, John.

MODEL(S)

"Bootstrapping Without Bootstraps" in *Testing Scientific Theories*, Earman, John (ed), 43–54. Edidin, Aron.

"Drugs, Models, And Moral Principles" in *Feeling Good And Doing Better*, Murray, Thomas H (ed), 187–214. Macklin, Ruth.

"Metaphor In Science" in *Metaphor*, Miall, David S (ed), 89–105. Martin, J and Harre, R.

"On Testing And Evidence" in *Testing Scientific Theories*, Earman, John (ed), 3–26. Glymour, Clark.

"Testing Theoretical Hypotheses" in *Testing Scientific Theories*, Earman, John (ed), 269–298. Giere, Ronald N.

"The Deductive Model: Does It Have Instances" in *Testing Scientific Theories*, Earman, John (ed), 299–312. Kyburg, Henry.

A Consistent Propositional Logic Without Any Finite Models. Mc Kay, C G.

A Mathematical Characterization Of Interpretation Between Theories. Van Bentham, Johan and Pearce, David.

A Property Of 2–Sorted Peano Models And Program Verification. Paris, J B and Csirmaz, L.

A Recursive Model For Arithmetic With Weak Induction. Adamowicz, Zofia and Morales– Luna, Guillermo.

A Spectrum Hierarchy. Fagin, Ronald.

A Test To Determine Distinct Modalities In The Extensions Of S4. Bellissima, Fabio.

A Two–Cardinal Characterization Of Double Spectra. Fagin, Ronald.

Adjoining Dominating Functions. Baumgartner, James E and Dordal, Peter.

An AD–like Model. Apter, Arthur W.

Analysis Of Quantum Probability Theory I. Van Aken, James.

Aristotle's Thesis In Consistent And Inconsistent Logics. Mortensen, Chris.

Cancellation Laws For Surjective Cardinals. Truss, J K.

Co–Critical Points Of Elementary Embeddings. Sheard, Michael.

Concerning The Axioms Of Ackermann's Set Theory. Buszkowski, Wojciech.

Converging Reflections On The Philosophy Of Science. Newton Smith, W and Wilkes, K.

Correcting Concepts. Tiles, Mary.

Decidability And The Number Of Countable Models. Millar, Terrence.

Deux Remarques À Propos De La Propriété De Recouvrement Fini. Poizat, Bruno.

Disturbing Arithmetic. Grilliot, Thomas J.

Eastern Model–Theory For Boolean–Valued Theories. Georgescu, George and Voiculescu, Ioana.

Experiment—Modell—Theorie. Horz, Herbert.

Gödelsche Funktionalinterpretation Für Eine Erweiterung Der Klassischen Analysis. Friedrich, Wolfgang.

How To Glue Analysis Models. Van Dalen, D.

Inconsistent Models For Relevant Arithmetics. Meyer, Robert K and Mortensen, Chris.

Jankov–Theorems For Some Implicational Calculi. Pahi, Biswambhram.

Kueker's Conjecture For Superstable Theories. Buechler, Steven.

Modelling And Models In Future Research (in Hungarian). Nováky, Erzsébet and Hideg, Eva.

Models For Normal Intuitionistic Modal Logics. Bozic, Milan and Dosen, Kosta.

Monadic Generalized Spectra. Fagin, Ronald.

More On Proper Forcing. Shelah, Saharon.

Non–closure Of The Image Model And Absence Of Fixed Points. Sureson, Claude.

Noncumulative Dialectical Models And Formal Dialectics. Krabbe, Erik C W.

On Σ^1_1 Equivalence Relations With Borel Classes Of Bounded Rank. Sami, Ramez L.

On Automorphisms Of Resplendent Models Of Arithmetic. Seremet, Zofia.

On Choice Sequences Determined By Spreads. Van Der Hoeven, Gerrit and Moerdijk, Ieke.

On Languages With Two Variables. Mortimer, Michael.

On The Concept Of Reconstruction. Mittelstrass, Jurgen.

On The Independence Of The Kinna Wagner Principle. Pincus, David.

On The Standard–Model Hypothesis Of ZF. Abian, Alexander.

Partial Aleph–1–homogeniety Of The Countable Saturated Model Of An Aleph–sub–1–categorical Theory. Rosenthal, John W.

Possible Worlds Semantics: A Research Program That Cannot Fail. Van Benthem, Johan.

Propositional Logic Based On The Dynamics Of Belief. Gardenfors, Peter.

Regular Ideals And Boolean Pairs. Heindorf, Lutz.

Regular Types In Nonmultidimensional ω–Stable Theories. Pillay, Anand.

Saturation And Simple Extensions Of Models Of Peano Arithmetic. Kaufmann, Matt and Schmerl, James H.

Should Philosophers Of Science Consider Scientific Discovery? Pietruska– Madej, Elzbieta.

Some Remarks On Initial Segments In Models Of Peano Arithmetic. Kotlarski, Henryk.

Strong Completeness Of A Pure Free Logic. Bencivenga, Ermanno.

The Cardinality Of The Set Of Dedekind Finite Cardinals In Fraenkel–Mostowski Models. Rubin, Arthur L and Rubin, Jean E.

The Consistency Of The Axiom Of Universality For The Ordering Of Cardinalities. Forti, Marco and Honsell, Furio.

The Consistency Of Some 4–stratified Subsystem Of NF Including NF3. Boffa, Maurice and Casalegno, Paolo.

The Elementary Theory Of Interval Reals Numbers. Comer, Stephen D.

The Generalised RK–Order, Orthogonality And Regular Types For Modules. Prest, Mike.

The Metaphorical Character Of Science. Bradie, M.

MODEL(S)

The Metatheory Of The Classical Propositional Calculus Is Not Axiomatizable. Mason, Ian.

The Not–So–Strange Modal Logic Of Indeterminacy. Pelletier, F J.

The Principle Of 'Maximum Inheritance' And The Growth Of Scientific Knowledge. Mamchur, Elena.

The Real–Algebraic Structure Of Scott's Model Of Intuitionistic Analysis. Scowcroft, Philip.

Truth In All Of Certain Well–Founded Countable Models Arising In Set Theory. Rosenthal, John W.

Ultrafilters And Types On Models Of Arithmetic. Kirby, L A S.

Weakly Compact Cardinals In Models Of Set Theory. Enayat, Ali.

Well–Behaved Modal Logic. Hodes, Harold T.

Zum Aufbau Einer Mehrsortigen Elementaren Logik. Kaphengst, Heinz.

3088 Varieties: A Solution To The Ackermann Constant Problem. Slaney, John K.

MODEL THEORY

Allgemeine Modelltheorie. Reitzer, Alfons.

Characterising The Largest, Countable Partial Ordering. Lake, John.

Modal Logic And Model Theory. Gerla, Giangiacomo and Vaccaro, Virginia.

Paraconsistent Logic And Model Theory. Alves, Elias H.

Putnam's Paradox. Lewis, David.

Relational Model Systems: The Craft Of Logic. Stern, Raphael.

Structured Nonstandard Dynamic Logic. Sain, Ildikó.

The Logical Consequence Relation Of Propositional Trense Logic. Thomason, S K.

The Model Theory Of Finitely Generated Finite–By–Abelian Groups. Oger, Francis.

The Model–Theoretic Structure Of Abelian Group Rings. Pappas, Peter C.

Vopenka's Principle And Compact Logics. Makowsky, J A.

MODELING

Formalism And Application Of Catastrophe Theory. Poole Jr, Charles P.

MODERATION

The Politics Of Moderation: An Interpretation Of Plato's "Republic". Wilson, John F.

MODERN

A Cultural Introduction To Philosophy: From Antiquity To Descartes. Mc Dermott, John J (ed).

Berkeley. Pitcher, George and Honderich, Ted (ed).

Bithell Series Of Dissertations: Spinoza In Germany From 1670 To The Age Of Goethe, V7. Bell, David.

Catalogo Del Fondo Haller. Monti, Maria Teresa.

Edmund Burke: A Bibliography Of Secondary Studies To 1982. Gandy, Clara I and Stanlis, Peter J.

Hume's Philosophy Of Common Life. Livingston, Donald W.

John Locke (1632–1704), Physician And Philosopher. Dewhurst, Kenneth.

John Locke And Medicine: A New Key To Locke. Romanell, Patrick.

John Locke And English Literature Of The Eighteenth Century. Mac Lean, Kenneth and Schouls, Peter A (ed).

John Locke And Agrarian Capitalism. Wood, Neal.

John Toland: His Methods, Manners And Mind. Daniel, Stephen.

Kant's Critical Philosophy. Deleuw, Gilles.

Leibniz. Brown, Stuart.

Locke's Travels In France 1675–1679. Lough, John.

Locke's Writings And Philosophy: Historically Considered. Tagart, Edward.

Models Of Man: Explorations In The Western Educational Tradition. Nash, Paul.

Pantheisticon. Toland, John.

Rousseau: Dreamer Of Democracy. Miller, James.

The Life And Letters Of John Locke. King, Peter and Schouls, Peter A (ed).

The Nature Of Love: Courtly And Romantic. Singer, Irving.

The Third Earl Of Shaftesbury 1671–1713. Voitle, Robert.

The Transcendental Turn: The Foundations Of Kant's Idealism. Gram, Moltke.

The Worlds Of Hume And Kant. Wilbur, James B (ed) and Allen, H J (ed).

Wahrheit Und Wahrheitsgrund. Fleischer, Margot.

"Berkeley And Hume: A Question Of Influence" in Philosophy In History, Rorty, Richard and others (ed), 303–328. Ayers, Michael.

"Seven Thinkers And How They Grew" in Philosophy In History, Rorty, Richard and others (ed), 125–140. Kuklick, Bruce.

Ancient Features Of The Modern State. Sternberger, Dolf.

Berkeley On Volition, Power, And The Complexity Of Causation. Winkler, Kenneth P.

Breve Historia De La Fortuna Literaria Y De La Crítica De J J Rousseau. Hernandez, Jose Lopez.

Con Jean Le Clerc Alla Scuola Cartesiana. Sina, Mario.

Considerazioni Su Power E Liberty Nel "Saggio Sull'Intelletto Umano" Secondo Un Manoscritto Di Coste. Simonutti, Luisa.

Dating Berkeley's Notebook B. Belfrage, Bertil.

David Hume And Eighteenth Century Monetary Thought: A Critical Comment On Recent Views. Rashid, Salim.

Descartes' First Meditation: Something Old, Something New, Something Borrowed. Groarke, Leo.

Facts And Reasons Concerning Berkeley's Reprinted Works. Park, Désirée.

Facts Concerning Berkeley's Notebooks. Belfrage, Bertil.

Homo, Humanus, And The Meanings Of "Humanism". Giustiniani, Vito R.

Hume On The 'Distinction Of Reason'. Bracken, Harry M.

Kant's Politics As An Expression Of The Need For His Aesthetics. De Lue, Steven M.

Korrespondenten Von G W Leibniz. Orzschig, Johannes and Jurgens, Madeleine.

L' "Oratio Ad Divinam Sapientiam" Del Vichiano Lorenzo Boturini–Beneduci. Ghelardi, Maurizio.

L'America Primitiva E L'Europa Cristiana. Petyx, Vincenza.

L'Evoluzione Del Problema Morale Nel Pensiero Di Cartesio. Cesareo, Rosa.

La Quadrature Du Cercle: Remarques Sur Diderot Et L'Encyclopédie. Lewinter, Roger.

Replies To Daisie Radner's "Is There A Problem Of Cartesian Interaction"? Richardson, Robert C and Loeb, Louis E.

Rhetorical Polemics And The Dialectics Of Kritik In Hegel's Jena Essays. Smith, John H.

Skepticism And Kant's B Deduction. Mc Cann, Edwin.

Taylor, Calhoun, And The Decline Of A Theory Of Political Disharmony. Harp, Gillis J.

The Authorship Of Guardian 69. Winkler, Kenneth P.

The Basis Of Belief: Philosophy, Science And Religion In Seventeenth–Century England. Rogers, G A J.

The Hume Literature Of The 1970's. Capaldi, Nicholas and King, James and Livingston, Donald.

The Legacy Of Voltaire (Part 1). Edwards, Paul.

The Linking Of Spinoza To Chinese Thought By Bayle And Male–branche. Lai, Yuen–Ting.

The Origin Of Property And The Development Of Scottish Historical Science. Bowles, Paul.

The Scholastic Background To Locke's Thought. Milton, J.

The Science Of A Legislator In James Mackintosh's Moral Philosophy. Haakonssen, Knud.

Un Autre Spinoza. Popkin, Richard H.

Voltaire Versus Needham: Atheism, Materialism, And The Generation Of Life. Roe, Shirley A.

MODERN ART

Herbert Read: Formlessness And Form. Thistlewood, David.

"Innovation Und Kanonbildung Oder Das Ende Der Modernen Kunst" in Asthetische Er Fahrung Und Das Wesen Der Kunst, Holzhey, Helmut, 42–57. Simon– Schaeffer, R.

"The Problem Of Objectivity In Modern Art" in Continental Philosophy And The Arts, Winters, Laurence E and others (ed), 87–108. Bandemann, Gunter.

Das Ästhetische Vor–Urteil. Neumaier, Otto.

Die Utopie Künstlerischer Wahrheit In Der Ästhetik Von Adolf Loos Und Arnold Schönberg. Waibl, Elmar.

MODERNISM

On Primordialism Versus Postmodernism: A Response To Thomas Dean. Olson, Alan M.

The Politics Of Interpretation. Mitchell, W J T.

The Postmodern Condition: A Report On Knowledge. Lyotard, Jean François.

Jürgen Habermas And Jean–François Lyotard: Post Modernism And The Crisis Of Rationality. Watson, Stephen.

On The Dialectic Of Modernism And Postmodernism. Wellmer, Albrecht.

Response To Thomas Dean's Review Of Knowledge And The Sacred. Nasr, Seyyed Hossein.

The Essence Of Catholicism: Protestant And Catholic Perspectives. Dulles, Avery.

The Modern Malaise: A Case History. Cleary, John.

The Original Preface. Lonergan, Bernard.

MODERNITY

The Theory Of Communicative Action: Reason And The Rationalization Of Society, V1. Habermas, Jurgen and Mc Carthy, Thomas (trans).

Theonomy And Autonomy: Studies In Paul Tillich's Engagement With Modern Culture. Carey, John J (ed).

"Kierkegaard's Two Ages And Heidegger's Critique Of Modernity" in International Kierkegaard Commentary, Perkins, Robert L (ed), 223–258. Hoberman, John M.

Cultural Frames For Social Intervention: A Personal Credo. Nandy, Ashis.

Elements For A Theory Of Modernity. Secretan, Philibert.

Theorie Zur Enstehung Der Europäischen Moderne. Hahn, Alois.

MODERNIZATION

Theorie Zur Enstehung Der Europäischen Moderne. Hahn, Alois.

MODIFIER(S)

Modifiers And Quantifiers In Natural Language. Parsons, Terence.

MODULE(S)

The Generalised RK–Order, Orthogonality And Regular Types For Modules. Prest, Mike.

MODUS PONENS

Frege, The Proliferation Of Force, And Non–Cognitivism. Hurley, S L.

MOKSHA

Can There Be A Freedom Without Responsibility? Ghosh– Dastidar, Koyeli.

Moksa And Critical Theory. Klostermaier, Klaus.

Vidyaranya On Method, Object And Limit Of Philosophical Investigation. Mishra, Ganeswar.

MONADOLOGY

Double Infinité Chez Pascal Et Monade. Naërt, Emilienne.

Monade Und Welt: Ein Beitrag Zur Interpretation Der Monadologie. Hubner, Wulf.

MONADS

Leibniz. Brown, Stuart.

La Monadologie De Diderot. Marquet, Jean–François.

MONARCHY

Petty Contra Hobbes: A Previously Untranslated Manuscript. Amati, Frank and Aspromourgos, Tony.

MONASTICISM

Discipline: The Canonical Buddhism Of The Vinayapitaka. Holt, John C.

Biblia Y Vida Monástica En San Agustín. Veissmann, F.

MONEY

Das Eigentum Als Eschatologische Potenz: Zur Eigentumskonzeption Von Karl Marx. Künzli, Arnold.

MORAL JUDGMENT(S)

"Two Approaches To Theory Acceptance In Ethics" in *Morality, Reason And Truth*, Copp, David (ed), 120–140. Daniels, Norman.

Aquinas And Janssens On The Moral Meaning Of Human Acts. May, William E.

Being A Person—Does It Matter? Lomasky, Loren E.

Broadcasting And The Moral Imperative: Patrolling The Perimeters. Wenham, Brian.

Deterrence And Deontology. Mc Mahan, Jeff.

Internal Conflicts In Desires And Morals. Jackson, Frank.

Jucios Morales Y Verdad. De Gandolfi, Maria.

Some Reasoning About Preferences: A Response To Essays By Person, Feldman, And Schueler. Hare, R M.

Some Reasoning About Preferences. Schueler, G F.

Supervenience, Realism, Necessity. Mc Fetridge, I G.

The Practice Of Moral Judgment. Hermann, Barbara.

MORAL LAWS

Hume, Animals And The Objectivity Of Morals. Clark, Stephen.

Moral Conflict And Moral Realism. Tännsjö, Torbjörn.

On The Moral Agent And Object (in Hebrew). Ben–Zeev, Aaron.

The Practice Of Moral Judgment. Hermann, Barbara.

MORAL POINT OF VIEW

Postures Of The Mind: Essays On Mind And Morals. Baier, Annette.

Moral And Aesthetic Values. Osborne, Harold.

MORAL PRINCIPLE(S)

Moral Principles In Education: A Reevaluation. Freiberg, Jo Ann.

The Good Life And Its Pursuit. Dougherty, Jude P (ed).

"The Roots Of Moral Reason" in *Gewirth's Ethical Rationalism*, Regis Jr, Edward (ed), 39–51. Bambrough, Renford.

A Biological Interpretation Of Moral Systems. Alexander, Richard D.

A Definition For Paternalism. Hershey, Paul Turner.

A Refutation Of Egoism. Vadas, Melinda.

Bribery, Extortion, And "The Foreign Corrupt Practices Act". Carson, Thomas L.

Formal Justice, Moral Commitment, And Judicial Precedent. Lyons, David.

Human Nature And Moral Theories. Kekes, John.

Kant, A Moral Criterion, And Religious Pluralism. Mc Kenzie, David E.

Moral Responsibility For Engineers. Alpern, Kenneth D.

Principles And Virtues—Or—Principles Or Virtues. Coetzee, Pieter.

The Role Of Economics And Ethical Principles In Determining U S Policies Toward Poor Nations. Piderit, John J.

MORAL PROOF

Moral Conflict And Moral Realism. Tännsjö, Torbjörn.

Nature And Nature's God. Toulmin, Stephen.

MORAL PSYCHOLOGY

The Moral Psychology Of The Virtues. Dent, N J H.

MORAL REASONING

Ethical Argumentation: A Study In Hsun Tzu's Moral Epistemology. Cua, A S.

Ethics: Approaching Moral Decisions. Holmes, Arthur F.

Gewirth's Ethical Rationalism. Regis Jr, Edward (ed).

Morality, Reason And Truth: New Essays On The Foundations Of Ethics. Copp, David (ed) and Zimmerman, David (ed).

"Against Ethical Rationalism" in *Gewirth's Ethical Rationalism*, Regis Jr, Edward (ed), 59–83. Nielsen, Kai.

"Public Pursuit And Private Escape: The Persistence Of Egoism" in *Gewirth's Ethical Rationalism*, Regis Jr, Edward (ed), 128–146. Kalin, Jesse.

"Replies To My Critics" in *Gewirth's Ethical Rationalism*, Regis Jr, Edward (ed), 192–256. Gewirth, Alan.

Hutcheson, Hume And The Ontology Of Morals. Stafford, J Martin.

Moral Dilemmas, Deliberation, And Choice. Anderson, Lyle V.

Moral Education In A Liberal Society. Callan, Eamonn.

Moral Reasoning In Adolescents: A Feature Of Intelligence Or Social Adjustment? Hanks, Richard.

Non–Medical Burdens Of The Defective Infant. Jones, Gary E.

Reflective Equilibrium And Justification. Little, Daniel.

The Central Principle Of Deontic Logic. Schlesinger, George N.

The Meaning Of Proportionate Reason In Contemporary Moral Theology. Johnstone, Brian V.

MORAL SENSE

Commentary On Gilligan's "In A Different Voice". Auerbach, Judy and others.

Kant And The Moral Sense Theory (in Hebrew). Golomb, Jacob.

Liberty And Equality: How Politics Masquerades As Philosophy. Hare, R M.

MORAL SENTIMENT(S)

Philanthropia In The Poetics. Moles, John.

MORAL SITUATION(S)

"I'm The Teacher". Benjamin, Martin and Baum, Robert.

The Random Collective As A Moral Agent. Manning, Rita.

MORAL WEAKNESS

"Aristotle On Practical Knowledge And Moral Weakness" in *The Georgetown Symposium On Ethics*, Porreco, Rocco (ed), 131–144. Miller Jr, Fred D.

Cicero On The Moral Crisis Of The Late Republic. Mitchell, T N.

Zum Problem Der Willensschwäche. Wolf, Ursula.

MORALISM

The Ethics Of Anti–Moralism In Marx's Theory Of Communism: An Interpretation. Raes, Koen.

The Justification Of Legal Moralism. Kultgen, John.

MORALITY

"I Don't Have No Education" And Other Reflections. Chamberlin, Gordon J.

A Book Of Jewish Ethical Concepts: Biblical And Postbiblical. Bloch, Abraham P.

A Word Of Order And Light: The Fiction Of John Gardner. Morris, Gregory L.

Aristotle: Nicomachean Ethics. Irwin, Terence (trans).

Culture And Morality. Mayer, Adrian C (ed).

Exuberance: An Affirmative Philosophy Of Life. Kurtz, Paul.

Having Love Affairs. Taylor, Richard.

Human, All Too Human. Nietzsche, Fredrich and Faber, Marion (trans).

Law, Psychiatry, And Morality. Stone, Alan R (ed).

Marxism: Nomos XXVI. Pennock, J Roland (ed) and Chapman, John W (ed).

Morality And The Perfect Life. James, Henry.

Morality In The Making. Weinreich Haste, Helen (ed) and Locke, Don (ed).

Morality, Halakha And The Jewish Tradition. Spero, Shubert.

Social And Political Morality. Lovett, William and Leventhal, F M (ed).

The Core Of Gandhi's Philosophy. Tahtinen, Unto.

The Freedom Of Morality. Yannaras, Christos.

The Georgetown Symposium On Ethics. Porreco, Rocco (ed).

The Magisterium And Morality. Curran, Charles E (ed) and Mc Cormick, Richard A (ed).

The Myth Of Natural Rights. Rollins, L A.

The Unity Of Law And Morality: A Refutation Of Legal Positivism. Detmold, M J.

Three Essays, 1793–1795, Peter Fuss And John Dobbins (eds). Hegel, G W F.

"Ethics And The Language Of Morality" in *Philosophical Analysis In Latin America*, Gracia, Jorge J E and others (eds), 243–254. Salmerón, Fernando.

"Freud's Impact On Modern Morality And Our World View" in *Darwin, Marx And Freud*, Caplan, Arthur L (ed), 147–200. Holt, Robert R.

"Injustice And Tragedy In Aristotle" in *The Georgetown Symposium On Ethics*, Porreco, Rocco (ed), 175–184. Forte, David F.

"Limits Of The Enforcement Of Morality" in *Philosophical Analysis In Latin America*, Gracia, Jorge J E and others (eds), 93–114. Nino, Carlos Santiago.

"Marx And Morality" in *Darwin, Marx And Freud*, Caplan, Arthur L (ed), 131–146. Wood, Allon W.

"Metaphysics And Poetry" in *Continental Philosophy And The Arts*, Winters, Laurence E and others (ed), 219–224. Bachelard, Gaston.

"Natural Law, Human Action, And Morality" in *The Georgetown Symposium On Ethics*, Porreco, Rocco (ed), 67–90. Gewirth, Alan.

"Neurobiological Origins Of Human Values" in *Ethical Questions In Brain And Behavior*, Pfaff, Donald W (ed), 141–152. Pfaff, Donald W.

"Reason In Ethics—Or Reason Versus Ethics" in *Morality, Reason And Truth*, Copp, David (ed), 228–250. Narveson, Jan.

"Saints And Supererogation" in *Philosophy And Life: Essays On John Wisdom*, Dilman, Ilham (ed), 61–82. Melden, A I.

"The Morality Of Checks And Balances" in *The Search For Justice*, Taitte, W Lawson (ed), 163–191. Thompson, Kenneth W.

A Comment On Dr John J Haldane's Article, "The Morality Of Deterrence". Thomas, Janice.

An Essay Towards Cultural Autonomy. Dasgupta, Probal.

Authority And Justification. Raz, Joseph.

Authority, Law And Morality. Raz, Joseph.

Autoconocimiento Y Moral. Esquivel, Javier.

Clark On God's Law And Morality. Chandler, John.

Contemporary Moral Philosophy And Practical Reason. Sterba, James P.

De Ondergang Van De Deugden En De Inconsequentie Van McIntyre. Kunneman, Harry.

Eigentum—Moralität. Schmidig, Dominik.

Encouraging Positive Justice Reasoning And Perspective–Taking Skills: Two Educational Interventions. Krogh, Suzanne Lowell.

Francis Hutcheson: Morality And Nature. Kupperman, Joel J.

Games And The Action–Guiding Force Of Morality. Eggerman, Richard W.

Hutcheson's Moral Realism. Norton, David F.

La Cancelación Hegeliana De La Ética: Origen Y Conscuencias. Guariglia, Osvaldo N.

Le *natura* Norma Di Moralitá? Valori, Paolo.

Mackie On The Objectivity Of Values. Wreen, Michael.

Man, Science, Morality. Anguelov, Stephan.

Marx's Moral Skepticism. Panichas, George E.

Marx's Social Ethics And Critique Of Traditional Morality. Mc Carthy, George.

Marxism, Morality And Ideology. Kellner, Douglas M.

Moral And Religious Education For Nigeria. Woodhouse, Howard R.

Moral Education In Holland. Van Der Plas, Paul L.

Moral Faith And Ethical Skepticism Reconsidered. Kurtz, Paul.

Moral Objectivity. Lear, Jonathan.

Moral Reasoning And Action In Young Children. Hannaford, Robert V.

Moral Values And The Assimilation Of Social Necessity. Stroe, Constantin.

Morality And The Marxist Concept Of Ideology. Peffer, Rodney G.

Morality And Religion. Wine, Sherwin P.

Morality And The Self In Robert Musil's *The Perfecting Of A Love*. Wilson, Catherine.

Morality And Human Nature. Lazari–Pawlowska, Ija.

Morality, Reason, And Management Science: The Rationale Of Cost–Benefit Analysis. Copp, David.

Morality, Survival And Nuclear War. Zaw, Susan Khin.

On Some So–called Refutations Of Ethical Egoism. Taiwo, Olufemi.

On The Discourse Of Pornography. Paden, Roger.

On The Morality Of Nuclear Deterrence. Shaw, William H.

Philosophy And The Nuclear Debate. Gay, William C.

Philosophy Of Medicine And Other Humanities: Toward A Wholistic View. Brody, Howard.

MORALITY

Practical Reasoning And Moral Judgment. Boyle, Joseph M.

Presidential Address: Practical Reasoning And Christian Faith. Grisez, Germain.

Prudential Insight And Moral Reasoning. Caputo, John D.

Pure Legal Advocates And Moral Agents: Two Concepts Of A Lawyer In An Adversary System. Cohen, Elliot D.

Rammonhun Roy And The Baptists Of Serampore: Moralism Vs Faith. Chatterjee, Shyamal K.

Remarks In Praise Of Guilt. Phillips, D L.

Right, Morality, And Religion (in Hebrew). Perelman, Haim.

Rights And Virtues. Gewirth, Alan.

Sartre O Las Dificultades De Escribir Una Moral. Fornet– Betancourt, Raul.

Sharing Responsibility. Zimmerman, Michael J.

The Basic Question Of Moral Philosophy. Heller, Agnes.

The Critique Of Natural Rights And The Search For A Non–Anthropocentric Basis For Moral Behavior. Zimmerman, Michael F.

The Duty Not To Kill Oneself. Linehan, Elizabeth A.

The Force Of Irony: On The Morality Of Affirmative Action And *United Steelworkers* Versus *Weber*. Lempert, Richard.

The Great Guide Of Human Life. Kekes, John.

The Human Basis Of Laws And Ethics. Edwords, Frederick.

The Morality Of Deterrence. Haldane, John J.

The Particularity Of Moral Knowledge. Dinan, Stephen A.

The Picaresque Prince: Reflections On Machiavelli And Moral Change. Ball, Terence.

The Problem Of Art And Morality In The Context Of Kant's Aesthetics (in Dutch). Hattingh, J P.

Theism And The Moral Point Of View. Hammond, John L.

Theism, Morality And The 'Why Should I Be Moral' Question. Bishop, John.

To Kill Or Let Live: Augustine On Killing The Innocent. Burt, Donald X.

Towards The Relation Of Art And Morality (in Czechoslovakian). John, Erhard.

Two Views Of Business Ethics: A Popular Philosophical Approach And A Value Based Interdisciplinary One. Klein, Sherwin.

Utilitarianism, Moral Dilemmas, And Moral Cost. Slote, Michael.

Utopianism And Nuclear Deterrence. Howard, Michael W.

Weakness And Dignity In Conrad's *Lord Jim*. Ross, Steven L.

What Is So Special About (Free) Speech? Husak, Douglas N.

What Philosophers Talk About When They Talk About Sex. Earle, William J.

What's Morally Special About Free Exchange? Gibbard, Allan.

Workers' Interest And The Proletarian Ethic: Conflicting Strains In Marxian Anti–Moralism. Skillen, Anthony.

MORASS(ES)

Simplified Morasses With Linear Limits. Velleman, Dan.

MORE, T

L'*Utopie* De Thomas More Ou Le Penseur, Le Pouvoir Et L'engagement. Allard, Gerald.

More's *Utopia*: An Interpretation Of Its Social Theory. Sargent, Lyman Tower.

More's *Utopia* And The New World Utopias: Is The Good Life An Easy Life? Dooley, Patrick K.

MORGENSTERN, O

Assessment Response Surface: Investigating Utility Dependence On Probability. Mc Cord, Mark R and De Neufville, Richard.

Timing Contradictions In Von Neumann And Morgenstern's Axioms And In Savage's "Sure–Thing" Proof. Pope, Robin.

MORPHOLOGY

Chor Und Gesetz: Zur "Morphologischen Methode" Bei Goethe Und Wittgenstein. Schulte, Joachim.

MORRIS, C

Simple Réaction À Un Double Commentaire. Lagueux, Maurice.

MORRIS, K

Methodological Solipsism: A Reply To Morris. Noonan, Harold W.

MORRIS, T

Impeccability Revisited. Carter, W R.

MORTENSEN, C

A Simple Solution To Mortensen And Priest's Truth Teller Paradox. Wayne Smith, Joseph.

MOSKOWITZ, M

Work–Related Ethical Attitudes: Impact On Business Profitability. Dunfee, Thomas W and Robertson, Diana C.

MOTHERHOOD

"On Surrogate Mothers" in *Difficult Decisions In Medical Ethics*, Ganos, Doreen L (ed), 145–154. Gorovitz, Samuel.

"Some Problems Of Social Freedom" in *Freedom, Feminism, And The State*, Mc Elroy, Wendy (ed), 193–206. Harman, Lillian.

"Surrogate Motherhood: The Ethical Implications" in *Biomedical Ethics Reviews*, Humber, James M (ed), 69–90. Newton, Lisa H.

"Surrogate Motherhood: Past, Present, And Future" in *Difficult Decisions In Medical Ethics*, Ganos, Doreen L (ed), 155–164. Keane, Noel P and others.

MOTION(S)

Aristotle's Distinction Between Motion And Activity. Stone, Mark A.

Is Motion Change Of Location? Forrest, Peter.

Leibniz And The Cartesians On Motion And Force. Spector, Marshall.

Nāgārjuna And Zeno On Motion. Mabbett, I W.

Part And Whole In Aristotle's Concept Of Infinity. White, David A.

The Idea Of Motion. Shamsi, F A.

The Limits Of Change. Mortensen, Chris.

Three Explanatory Traditions In The Law Of Falling Bodies (in Portuguese). Nascimento, Carlos A R.

Wholes, Parts, And Laws Of Motion. Hassing, R F.

Why Fire Goes Up: An Elementary Problem In Aristotle's *Physics*. Lang, Helen S.

MOTIVATION(S)

"Drive": In Defense Of A Concept. Smith, Kendon.

La Teoría Relacional De La Personalidad Según J Nuttin. Darós, William R.

Moral Objectivity. Lear, Jonathan.

Moral Scepticism And Moral Conduct. Mac Kenzie, J C.

On Being Terrestrial. Midgley, Mary.

MOTIVE(S)

Wickedness: A Philosophical Essay. Midgley, Mary.

MOVEMENT(S)

Aristotle Metaphysics: Books Zeta, Eta, Theta, Iota. Furth, Montgomery (trans).

"Movement In German Poems" in *Existential Coordinates Of Human Condition*, Tymieniecka, A (ed), 23–36. Wittkowski, W.

Die Materialistische Dialektik—Antwort Auf Die Frage Nach Der Selbstbewegung Der Materie. Kummer, Wolf.

MUCCIOLO, L

Properties, Functionalism, And The Identity Theory. Adams, Frederick.

MUEHLFELD, C

Ideologie Und Ideologiekritik: Bemerkungen Zu Einem Aufsatz Von Claus Mühlfeld. Schmid, Michael.

MUIR, J

The Development Of Nature Resources And The Integrity Of Nature. Devall, Bill and Sessions, George.

MULTIPLICITY

Causal Dependence And Multiplicity. Sanford, David H.

Nietzsche On "The Subject Of Multiplicity". Booth, David.

MURE, G

Striking 'Commensurate' From The Oxford Translation. Jones, Joe E.

MUSEUM(S)

"Ethics And The Museum Archaeologist" in *Ethics And Values In Archaeology*, Green, Ernestene L (ed), 133–142. Ford, Richard I.

Educational Excellence In Art Museums: An Agenda For Reform. Williams, Patterson B.

Museums And Their Enemies. Haskell, Francis.

Museums And Their Functions. Osborne, Harold.

Showing And Saying, Looking And Learning: An Outsider's View Of Art Museums. Sparshott, Francis.

Ten Years Of Gallery Education. Luckett, Helen.

The Art Museum As An Agency Of Culture. Levi, Albert William.

The End Of The Museum? Goodman, Nelson.

The Museum In The City. Lilla, Mark.

MUSIC

Aesthetics: Problems In The Philosophy Of Criticism. Beardsley, Monroe C.

Antiaesthetics: An Appreciation Of The Cow With The Subtile Nose. Ziff, Paul.

Mahler: Consciousness And Temporality. Greene, David B.

The Responsibility Of Forms: Critical Essays On Music, Art, And Representation. Barthes, Roland and Howard, Richard (trans).

"Ästhetik Und Musiktheorie Um 1750" in *Asthetische Er Fahrung Und Das Wesen Der Kunst*, Holzhey, Helmut, 143–155. Benary, P.

"Zeit Und Musik" in *Asthetische Er Fahrung Und Das Wesen Der Kunst*, Holzhey, Helmut, 156–172. Risch, C.

Aristoxenus' Theorems And The Foundations Of Harmonic Science. Barker, Andrew.

Computermusik Und Die Identität Des Musikwerks. Simons, Peter M.

Expression Of Emotion In (Some Of) The Arts. Stecker, Robert.

Musical Kinds. Anderson, James C.

On Musical Improvisation. Alperson, Philip.

Philosophy Of Music And Artistic Performance (in Hungarian). Ramisvili, G Z.

Placing *Sectio Canonis* In Historical And Philosophical Contexts. Barbera, Andre.

Reader–Response And Implication–Realization. Hoyt, Reed J.

Soothing The Savage Beast: A Note On Animals And Music. Hicks, Michael.

The Expression Of Emotion In Music. Mew, Peter.

MUSIC EDUCATION

Music Education As Aesthetic Education: Concepts And Skills For The Appreciation Of Music. Goolsby, Thomas W.

MUSICOLOGY

Theories Of The Arts In China. Bush, Susan (ed) and Murck, Christian (ed).

MUSIL, R

Morality And The Self In Robert Musil's *The Perfecting Of A Love*. Wilson, Catherine.

MYSTERY(–RIES)

Christianity And The Hellenistic World. Nash, Ronald H.

Mystery And Mumbo–Jumbo. Graham, Gordon.

The Mystery Of Faith In The Theology Of Karl Rahner. O' Donnell, John.

The Mystery Of Christ: Clue To Paul's Thinking On Wisdom. Hill, Robert.

MYSTICAL EXPERIENCE(S)

Mystical And Ethical Experience. Heard, Gerry C.

Mystical Consciousness In A Process Perspective. Simmons, Ernest L.

Mysticism, Identity And Realism: A Debate Reviewed. Byrne, Peter.

The Christian Character Of Christian Mystical Experiences. Payne, Steven.

MYSTICISM

Evanescence. Earle, William.

Mysticism And Religious Traditions. Katz, Steven (ed).

NATURAL LANGUAGE(S)

The Study Of Language. Aarsleff, Hans.

The Complexity Of The Vocabulary Of Bambara. Culy, Christopher.

NATURAL LAW(S)

A Demonstration Of The Divine Authority Of The Law Of Nature And Of The Christian Religion. Parker, Samuel.

A Theory Of Law. Soper, Philip.

The Georgetown Symposium On Ethics. Porreco, Rocco (ed).

The Nature Of Social Laws: Machiavelli To Mill. Brown, Robert.

"Foundations, Objective And Objections" in *The Georgetown Symposium On Ethics*, Porreco, Rocco (ed), 109–116. Russman, Thomas.

Freirecht—Revisited, Emphasizing Its Property–Space. Schmidt, Joachim K H W.

Hobbes's State Of War. Hampton, Jean.

Hugo Grotius And The History Of Political Thought. Haakonssen, Knud.

La Renovición Kantiana Del Derecho Natural Y La Crítica De Hegel: Una Crítica A La Crítica. Guariglia, Osvaldo.

Laws Of Nature As Relations Between Universals And As Universals. Armstrong, D M.

Legal Positivism And Natural Law Reconsidered. Brink, David O.

Legal Positivism, Natural Law, And The Hart/Dworkin Debate. Ball, Stephen W.

Natural Law: Before And Beyond Bifurcation. Caspar, Ruth.

Rechtsbeginselen: Tussen Natuurrecht En Rechtspositivisme. Cliteur, P B.

The Contemporary Significance Of Bentham's Anarchical Fallacies: A Reply To William Twining. Dalgarno, Melvin T.

The Contemporary Significance Of Bentham's Anarchical Fallacies. Twining, William.

The Western Case Against Usury. Gottfried, Paul E.

Universals And Laws Of Nature. Tweedale, Martin.

Ursprung Und Entwicklung Der Menschenrechte In Geschichte Und Gegenwart. Ernst, Wilhelm.

NATURAL PHILOSOPHY

Epicurus' Scientific Method. Asmis, Elizabeth.

Die Dynamische Naturvorstellung Als Naturphilosophische Grundlage Der Heutigen Physik. Adler, Norbert.

Hegels 'Naturphilosophie' Und Platons 'Timaios'—Ein Strukturvergleich. Hosle, Vittorio.

Naturphilosophische Überlegungen Zum Leib–Seele–Problem. Buchel, W.

NATURAL RESOURCES

The Development Of Nature Resources And The Integrity Of Nature. Devall, Bill and Sessions, George.

NATURAL RIGHT(S)

The Myth Of Natural Rights. Rollins, L A.

"Conceptions Of The Common Good And The Natural Right To Liberty" in *The Georgetown Symposium On Ethics*, Porreco, Rocco (ed), 185–194. Rasmussen, Douglas B.

"Natural Justice And Natural Rights" in *The Search For Justice*, Taitte, W Lawson (ed), 43–82. Cecil, Andrew R.

"Reflections On The Rights Of Future Generations" in *Rights And Regulation*, Machan, Tibor (ed), 203–216. Dipert, Randall R.

Dworkin Giusnaturalista? Pastore, Baldassare.

Gibt Es Auf Erden Ein Mass? Gadamer, Hans–Georg.

Hugo Grotius And The History Of Political Thought. Haakonssen, Knud.

Il Diritto Naturale Fondamento E Criterio Di Giustizia Del Diritto Positivo E Della Sua Obbligatorietà. Pizzorni, Reginaldo M.

Labour—Natural, Property—Artificial: The Radical Insights Of Gerrard Winstanley. Kenyon, Timothy.

Maxima Aportacion Del Pensamiento Hispanico A La Cultura: El "Sentido Universalista". Rivera, Enrique.

Natural Rights In Locke. Mautner, Thomas.

Rechtsbeginselen: Tussen Natuurrecht En Rechtspositivisme. Cliteur, P B.

Renuncia Al Derecho Y Dominación En Los Pactos Fundamentales De Hobbes. Brandt, Reinhard.

The Contemporary Significance Of Bentham's Anarchical Fallacies: A Reply To William Twining. Dalgarno, Melvin T.

The Contemporary Significance Of Bentham's Anarchical Fallacies. Twining, William.

The Critique Of Natural Rights And The Search For A Non–Anthropocentric Basis For Moral Behavior. Zimmerman, Michael F.

The Natural Rights Debate: A Comment On A Reply. Osterfeld, David.

Two Domains Of Rights. Perry, Thomas D.

Zum Recht Des Naturzustandes Und Seiner Dedeutung Für Die Stellung Der Staatsgewalt Bei Thomas Hobbes. Gehrmann, Siegfried.

NATURAL SCIENCES

Order & Organism: Steps To A Whiteheadian Philosophy Of Mathematics & The Natural Sciences. Murray, Code.

The Limits Of Science. Rescher, Nicholas.

Das Verhältnis Der *Kritik Der Reinen Vernunft Zu Den Metaphysischen Anfangsgründen Der Naturwissenschaft*, Demonstr Am Substanzsatz. Gloy, Karen.

Einen Neuen Schwerpunkt In Der Zusammenarbeit Mit Naturwissenschaftlern— Brauchen Wir Ihn Wirklich? Liebscher, Heinz and Simon, R.

Two Ideals Of Explanation In Natural Science. Mc Mullin, Ernan.

Weltanschauliche Und Wissenschaftstheoretische Probleme Des Verhältnisses Von Natur– Und Technikwissenschaften. Jobst, Eberhard and Marmai, U.

Zu Den Funktionen Der Marxistisch–Leninistischen Philosophie In Bezug Auf Die Einzelwissenschaften. Hager, Nina.

Zum Stand Der Entwicklungstheorie In Den Naturwissenschaften. Ley, Hermann.

Zur Theorien– Und Methodenentwicklung In Den Naturwissenschaften. Kannegiesser, Karlheinz and Uebeschar, K.

NATURAL SELECTION

Conceptual Issues In Evolutionary Biology. Sober, Elliott (ed).

Darwinism And Determinism: The Role Of Direction In Evolution. Ruffa, Anthony R.

Genes, Organisms, Populations: Controversies Over The Units Of Selection. Brandon, Robert N (ed) and Burian, Richard M (ed).

The Accidental Universe. Davies, P C W.

The Nature Of Selection: Evolutionary Theory In Philosophical Focus. Sober, Elliott.

NATURAL THEOLOGY

A Demonstration Of The Divine Authority Of The Law Of Nature And Of The Christian Religion. Parker, Samuel.

On Natural Evil's Being Necessary For Free Will. O' Connor, David.

Unconscious Belief And Natural Theology. Holyer, Robert.

NATURALISM

Realism And Truth. Devitt, Michael.

The Aesthetics Of Dedalus And Bloom. Harkness, Marguerite.

The Naturalists And The Supernatural: Studies In Horizon And An American Philosophy Of Religion. Shea, William M.

"Arguments From Nature" in *Morality, Reason And Truth*, Copp, David (ed), 169–192. De Sousa, Ronald.

"Is There A Single True Morality" in *Morality, Reason And Truth*, Copp, David (ed), 27–48. Harman, Gilbert.

"Sociobiology And The Possibility Of Ethical Naturalism" in *Morality, Reason And Truth*, Copp, David (ed), 270–296. Campbell, Richmond.

Does The Evidence Confirm Theism More Than Naturalism? Martin, M.

Epistemic Value. Lycan, William G.

Ever Since Descartes. Kornblith, Hilary.

Human Nature And Moral Theories. Kekes, John.

Hume's Criterion Of Significance. Williams, Michael.

Hume's Naturalism—'Proof' And Practice. Ferreira, M J.

Naturalism And The Resurrection: A Reply To Habermas. Davis, Stephen T.

Naturalism, Measure And The Ontological Difference. Corrington, Robert S.

Naturalism, Epistemological Individualism And "The Strong Programme" In Sociology Of Knowledge. Manicas, Peter T and Rosenberg, Alan.

Naturalized Epistemology And Metaphysical Realism: A Response To Rorty And Putnam. Stabler, Edward.

Naturalizing Intentions. Nelson, R J.

Nature And Art. Levi, Albert W.

Panglossian Functionalism And The Philosophy Of Mind. Sober, Elliott.

Quine's Epistemological Naturalism. O' Gorman, Paschal.

Relativism And Pictorial Realism. Grigg, Robert.

The Modern Evasion Of Creation. Henry, Carl F H.

The Quaker Background Of William Bartram's View Of Nature. Clarke, Larry R.

Traditional Epistemology And Naturalistic Replies To Its Skeptical Critics. Bogen, James.

Visual Space From The Perspective Of Possible World Semantics II. Wiesenthal, L.

NATURALISTIC FALLACY

Ethics, Persuasion And Truth. Smart, J J C.

Gewirth's Ethical Rationalism. Regis Jr, Edward (ed).

"The 'Is–Ought' Problem Resolved" in *Gewirth's Ethical Rationalism*, Regis Jr, Edward (ed), 108–127. Hudson, W D.

"The Philosophical Implications Of Darwinism" in *Darwin, Marx And Freud*, Caplan, Arthur L (ed), 3–34. Flew, Antony G N.

An Open Question Argument In Cicero. Londey, David.

Business Ethics, Ideology, And The Naturalistic Fallacy. Goodpaster, Kenneth E.

NATURE

Against Fate: An Essay On Personal Dignity. Tinder, Glenn.

Laws Of The Game: How The Principles Of Nature Govern Chance. Eigen, Manfred and Winkler, Ruthild.

Marx's Social Critique Of Culture. Dupré, Louis.

On Nature. Rouner, Leroy S (ed).

Order Out Of Chaos: Man's New Dialogue With Nature. Prigogine, Ilya and Stengers, Isabelle.

"Buddhist Views Of Nature: Variations On The Theme Of Mother–Father Harmony" in *On Nature*, Rouner, Leroy S (ed), 96–112. Thurman, Robert A F.

"Die Bedeutung Von Naturkonzeptionen In Und Für Die Kulturwissenschaften". Dolling, Evelyn.

"Laws Of Nature: The Empiricist Challenge" in *D M Armstrong*, Bogdan, Radu J (ed), 191–224. Earman, John.

"Nature On Trial" in *Methodology, Metaphysics And The History Of Science*, Cohen, Robert S (ed), 295–322. Walter, E V.

"On The Impotence Of Spirit, Thomas Wartenberg (commentator)" in *History And System*, Perkins, Robert (ed), 195–218. Di Giovanni, George.

"Reflections On 'Nature On Trial'" in *Methodology, Metaphysics And The History Of Science*, Cohen, Robert S (ed), 323–330. Sivin, Nathan.

"The Alienation And Liberation Of Nature" in *On Nature*, Rouner, Leroy S (ed), 133–144. Moltmann, Jürgen.

"The Continuity Of Being: Chinese Visions Of Nature" in *On Nature*, Rouner, Leroy S (ed), 113–132. Wei– Ming, Tu.

"The European Experience Of Nature" in *The Good Life And Its Pursuit*, Dougherty, Jude P (ed), 233–240. Crombie, Alistair.

A Proposito Del Trattato "De Bono Naturae" Nel "Tractatus De Natura Boni" Di Alberto Magno. Canavero, A Tarabochia.

Ars Et Natura Dans La Pensée De Nicolas De Cues (in Japanese). Sakai, Noriyuki.

Brahman, God, Substance And Nature: Samkara And Spinoza. Gupta, Bina.

Condillac Und Delisle De Sales: Ein Neuer Brief. Kreimendahl, Lothar.

Desert And The Moral Arbitrariness Of The Natural Lottery. Hill, Christopher.

NOMINALISM

How Nominalist Is Hartry Field's Nominalism? Resnik, Michael D.

Leibniz' Gebrochenes Verhältnis Zur Erkenntnismetaphysik Der Scholastik. Hübener, Wolfgang.

Nominalism And Abstract Entities. Hazen, Allen.

Numbers. Zemach, E M.

On Conservativeness And Incompleteness. Field, Hartry.

Supposition—Theory And The Problem Of Universals. Wagner, Michael F.

NOMINALIZATION

Science Nominalized. Horgan, Terence.

NOMOLOGICAL

Ansätze Zur Semiotischen Analyse Der Gesetze Der Wissenschaft. Leiţoiu, Rodica.

NONBEING

Thomas Aquinas On The Distinction And Derivation Of The Many From The One: A Dialectic Between Being And Nonbeing. Wippel, John F.

NONCOGNITIVISM

Axiologische Cognities En Het Meta—Ethische Noncognivisme. Vos, H M.

Frege, The Proliferation Of Force, And Non—Cognitivism. Hurley, S L.

The Ontological Power Of Speech. Deutsch, Eliot.

NONCONTRADICTION

Das Prinzip Vom Nicht—Widerspruch Und Das Prinzip Vom Ausgeschlossenen Dritten. Welding, Streen O.

NONEXISTENCE

Did The Greeks Really Worship Zeus? Wettstein, Howard.

Nonexistent Objects Versus Definite Descriptions. Grossmann, Reinhardt.

Reference, Fiction, And Fictions. Bertolet, Rod.

The Russell—Meinong Debate. Smith, Janet Farrell.

NONSTANDARD ANALYSIS

Filterkonvergenz In Der Nichtstandard—Analysis Bei Nichtelementaren Funktionen. Döpp, Klemens.

Is Nonstandard Analysis Relevant For The Philosophy Of Mathematics? Fenstad, Jens Erik.

On The Plausibility Of Nonstandard Proofs In Analysis. Farkas, E J and Szabo, M E.

The Strength Of Nonstandard Methods In Arithmetic. Henson, C Ward and Kaufmann, Matt and Keisler, H Jerome.

Une Approche Naïve De L'analyse Non—Standard. Robert, A.

NONSTANDARD MODELS

Trace Expansions Of Initial Segments. Murawski, Roman.

Variable Truth. Szabo, Manfred Egon.

NONSTANDARD SYSTEMS

"Axiom Systems Of Nonstandard Set Theory" in *Lecture Notes In Mathematics*, Muller, G H And Others (ed), 57—66. Kawai, Toru.

NOONAN, J

John T Noonan And Baby Jane Doe. Levin, David S.

NORM(S)

Michel Foucault: An Introduction To The Study Of His Thought. Cooper, Barry.

Practical Reason. Von Wright, G H.

Right Actions In Sport: Ethics For Contestants. Fraleigh, Warren P.

The Moral Order: An Introduction To The Human Situation. Naroll, Raoul.

"How Flexible Is Aristotelian "Right Reason"" in *The Georgetown Symposium On Ethics*, Porreco, Rocco (ed), 49—66. Owens, Joseph.

Aufgaben Und Schwierigkeiten Der Analytischen Rechtstheorie. Weinberger, Ota.

Corruption In Science: The Chinese Case. Suttmeier, Richard P.

Eine Analyse Und Kritische Bewertung Der Methode Und Des Prinzips Der Praktischen Argumentation Oswald Schwemmers. Asouzu, Innocent.

Legal Justification And Control: Sociological Aspects Of Philosophy. Klami, Hanna T.

Legislation—Transgression: Strategies And Counter—Strategies In The Transcendental Justification Of Norms. Schürmann, Reiner.

Musical Kinds. Anderson, James C.

Norm Und Recht In Niklas Luhmanns Rechtssoziologie: Kritische Anmerkungen Aus Der Sicht Der Rechtsethnologie. Von Benda— Beckmann, Franz.

Normative Wissenschaft Mit Normen—Ohne Werte. Knapp, Hans Georg.

Norms And Logic: Kelsen And Weinberger On The Ontology Of Norms. Bulygin, Eugenio.

On Justifying Interpretive Norms. Hirsch Jr, E D.

Potentielles Und Positives Recht. Lachmayer, Friedrich and Reisinger, Leo.

Practical Reasoning And Moral Judgment. Boyle, Joseph M.

The Expressive Conception Of Norms—An Impasse For The Logic Of Norms. Weinberger, Ota.

The Particularity Of Moral Knowledge. Dinan, Stephen A.

Un Logicien Déontique Avant La Lettre: Gottfried Wilhelm Leibniz. Kalinowski, Georges and Garoddies, Jean–louis.

Zum Problem Der Diskutierbarkeit Von Normensystemen. Weinke, Kurt.

NORMAL

Carnapian Extensions Of S5. Hendry, Herbert E and Pokriefka, M L.

Le Normal Et Le Pathologique En Politique. Mineau, André.

NORMAL FORMS

Game Theory: Concepts And Applications. Zagare, Frank C.

A Normal Form Theorem For First Order Formulas And Its Application To Gaifman's Splitting Theorem. Motohashi, Nobuyoshi.

A Second Normal Form For Functions Of The System EP. Mc Beth, Rod.

On A Modal—Type Language For The Predicate Calculus. Skordev, Dimiter.

Zur Benutzung Der Verkettung Als Basis Für Die Arithmetik. Deutsch, Michael.

NORMALIZATION

Which Clients Should A Sheltered Workshop Serve: Case Study. Mc Donald, Michael and Herr, Stanley S.

NORMATIVE

Between The "Thoughts": Topics In Frege's "Logical Investigations" (in Hebrew). Kasher, Asa.

Castañeda's Dystopia. Kapitan, Tomis.

Descriptive Epistemology. Duran, Jane.

Epistemic Value. Lycan, William G.

Habermas On Rationality. Roderick, Rick.

Logic: Normative Or Descriptive; The Ethics Of Belief Or A Branch Of Psychology? Resnik, Michael D.

The Relation Between Epistemology And Psychology. Goldman, Alvin I.

NORMATIVE DISCOURSE

"Deontic Logic" in *Handbook Of Philosophical Logic*, Gabbay, Dov (ed), 605–714. Aqvist, Lennart.

NORMATIVE ETHICS

Contemporary Moral Problems. White, James E.

Axiologische Cognities En Het Meta—Ethische Noncognivisme. Vos, H M.

NORMATIVE JUDGMENT(S)

Practical Reason. Von Wright, G H.

"Normative Knowledge And Truth" in *Philosophical Analysis In Latin America*, Gracia, Jorge J E and others (eds), 25–46. Alchourron, Carlos and Bulygin, Eugenio.

Finocchiaro On Rational Explanation. Doppelt, Gerald.

Marxism And Moral Objectivity. Shaw, William H.

NORMATIVE SCIENCE(S)

Game Theory: Concepts And Applications. Zagare, Frank C.

Progress In Utility And Risk Theory. Hagen, Ole (ed) and Wenstop, Fred (ed).

Normative Wissenschaft Mit Normen—Ohne Werte. Knapp, Hans Georg.

NORTHROP, F

Critique Of Scope And Method Of The Northropian Philosophical Anthropology And The Projection Of A Hope For A Meeting Of East And West. Lee, Kuang—Sae.

NOTATION(S)

Functors And Ordinal Notations: II, A Functorial Construction Of The Bachmann Hierarchy. Girard, Jean—Yves and Vauzeilles, Jacqueline.

Functors And Ordinal Notations. Vauzeilles, Jacqueline.

Functors And Ordinal Notations I: A Functorial Construction Of The Veblen Hierarchy. Girard, Jean—Yves and Vauzeilles, Jacqueline.

NOTHING

Hume And Edwards On 'Why Is There Something Rather Than Nothing'? Burke, Michael B.

Nozick On Explaining Nothing. Wedin, Michael V.

NOTHINGNESS

In Search Of Being: Man In Conflict With The Spectre Of Nothingness. De Carvalho, Manoel J.

Über Das Verhältnis Von Werner Marx Zu Martin Heidegger. Schoeller— Von Haslingen, Karin.

The Problem Of Evil: Augustine And Ricoeur. Stark, Judith C.

NOTION(S)

Berkeley's Notions. Flage, Daniel E.

NOUMENA

Saving The Noumena. Sklar, Lawrence.

The Practical And The Pathological. Mendus, Susan.

NOVALIS

Etica E Narrazione In Novalis. Moretto, Giovanni.

NOVEL

Mikhail Bakhtin: The Dialogical Principle, Wlad Godzich (trans). Todorov, Tzvetan.

Death And The Machine: From Jules Verne To Derrida And Beyond. Kemp, Peter.

Etica E Narrazione In Novalis. Moretto, Giovanni.

NOVELTY

Bayesianism And Support By Novel Facts. Howson, Colin.

Originality And Value. Sibley, F N.

NOZICK, R

"Utility, Natural Rights, And The Right To Health Care" in *Biomedical Ethics Reviews*, Humber, James M (ed), 23–46. Arras, John D.

Autonomy And Human Rights Claims. Gough, Jim.

Benefit Rights In Education: An Entitlement View. Beversluis, Eric H.

Coercion, Deterrence, And Authority. Airaksinen, Timo.

Distributive Justice. Rollins, Mark.

Justifying Law: An Explanation Of The Deep Structure Of American Law. Gibbons, Hugh.

Knowledge As Tracking? Schmitt, Frederick F.

La Originación Radical De Las Cosas Demostrada A Priori: Leibniz, Nozik, Rescher. Madanes, Leiser.

Losing Track Of The Sceptic. Brueckner, Anthony L.

Minimalstaat Oder Sozialrechte—Eine Philosophische Problemskizze. Hoffe, Otfried.

Nozick And Knowledge—A Rejoinder. Garrett, B J.

Nozick On Explaining Nothing. Wedin, Michael V.

Nozick On Inferential Knowledge. Mazoué, James G.

Response To Mazoué's "Nozick On Inferential Knowledge" And Brueckner's "Transmission For Knowledge Not Established". Forbes, Graeme.

Self—Consciousness And Agency. Richards, William M.

The Closest Continuer Theory Of Identity. Noonan, Harold W.

The Concept Of Knowledge. Mc Ginn, Colin.

The Dominant Protection Association And Education. G0ldstone, Peter.

OBJECTIVISM

Boston Studies In The Philosophy Of Science: Dialectical Theory Of Meaning, R S Cohen And M W Wartofsky (eds) V81. Markovic, Mihailo.

"Foundations, Objective And Objections" in *The Georgetown Symposium On Ethics*, Porreco, Rocco (ed), 109–116. Russman, Thomas.

A Refutation Of Egoism. Vadas, Melinda.

Are 'Scientific' Objects Coloured? Hardin, C L.

Ayn Rand And The Is–Ought Problem. O' Neil, Patrick M.

Hume's Standard Of Taste. Carroll, Noel.

In Defense Of Objectivist Art Criticism. Lichtenbert, Robert H.

The Devil's Disguises: Philosophy Of Religion, 'Objectivity' And 'Cultural Divergence'. Phillips, D Z.

The Rationality Debate And Gadamer's Hermeneutics: Reflections On Beyond Objectivism And Relativism. Sullivan, Robert.

The Relativity Of Refutations. Tormey, Alan.

The Scientific And The Ethical. Williams, Bernard.

OBJECTIVITY

A Celebration Of Subjective Thought. Diefenbeck, James A.

Bachelard: Science And Objectivity. Tiles, Mary.

Continental Philosophy And The Arts. Winters, Laurence E and others (ed).

Criticism And Objectivity. Selden, Raman.

Kant On Causality, Freedom, And Objectivity. Harper, William A (ed) and Meerbote, Ralf (ed).

Practical Reason, Aristotle, And Weakness Of The Will. Dahl, Norman O.

Probability, Objectivity And Evidence. Benenson, F C.

Subjecting And Objecting. Deutscher, Max.

The Contemplation Of Otherness: The Critical Vision Of Religion. Wentz, Richard.

"The Problem Of Objectivity In Modern Art" in *Continental Philosophy And The Arts*, Winters, Laurence E and others (ed), 87–108. Bandemann, Gunter.

A Sociological Theory Of Objectivity. Bloor, David.

Hacking On Frege. Dummett, Michael.

Heidegger's Later Philosophy Of Science. Rouse, Joseph T.

Hume, Animals And The Objectivity Of Morals. Clark, Stephen.

L'objectivité Dans Les Théories Logiques De La Signification. Leblanc, Suzanne.

Les Sources De L'Objectivité Hellénique. Gobry, Ivan.

Marxism And Moral Objectivity. Shaw, William H.

Moral Objectivity. Lear, Jonathan.

Moral Objectivity. Benedict– Gill, Diane.

Objectivity And Social Anthropology. Beattie, J H M.

Objectivity And Moral Expertise. Mc Connell, Terrance C.

The Criteria Of Objectivity: Physical Science And The Challenge Of Phenomenology. Smitheram, Verner.

The Objectivity Of Mystical Truth Claims. Price, James Robertson.

The Rational Foundations Of Kierkegaard's Critique Of Reason. Marino, Gordon D.

Towards A Critical Theory Of Value. Luntley, Michael.

OBLIGATION(S)

see also Duty(–ties)

A Theory Of Law. Soper, Philip.

Rights. White, Alan R.

Social And Political Morality. Lovett, William and Leventhal, F M (ed).

"Henry Veatch And The Problem Of A Noncognitivist Ethics" in *The Georgetown Symposium On Ethics*, Porreco, Rocco (ed), 159–170. Lee, Sander H.

"Obligation, Contract And Exchange: On Hegel's Abstract Right" in *The State And Civil Society*, Pelczynski, Z A (ed), 159–177. Benhabib, Seyla.

"Saints And Supererogation" in *Philosophy And Life: Essays On John Wisdom*, Dilman, Ilham (ed), 61–82. Melden, A I.

A Rejection Of Doctors As Moral Guides. Ackroyd, Elizabeth.

Act Utilitarianism And The Moral Fanaticism Argument. Timmons, Mark.

Concepts Of Epistemic Justification. Alston, William P.

Consequences, Desirability, And The Moral Fanaticism Argument. Singer, Marcus G.

Excuse Me, But You Have A Melanoma On Your Neck: Unsolicited Medical Opinions. Moseley, Ray.

Hugo Grotius And The History Of Political Thought. Haakonssen, Knud.

J S Mill And Robert Veatch's Critique Of Utilitarianism. Edwards, Rem B.

La Renovición Kantiana Del Derecho Natural Y La Crítica De Hegel: Una Crítica A La Crítica. Guariglia, Osvaldo.

Moral And Aesthetic Values. Osborne, Harold.

Patients' Ethical Obligation For Their Health. Sider, Roger C and Clements, Colleen D.

Protest Petitions. Margalit, Avishai and Ullmann– Margalit, Edna.

Rule Utilitarianism, Rational Decision And Obligations. Sowden, Lanning.

Sanction And Obligation. Hardin, Russell.

Supererogation And Obligation. Kamm, Frances Myrna.

The 'Right' Not To Know. Ost, David E.

The Calculus Of Moral Obligation. Mc Guire, Martin C.

The Logic Of Disputation In Walter Burley's Treatise On Obligations. Stump, Eleonore.

The Random Collective As A Moral Agent. Manning, Rita.

Three Accounts Of Promising. Downie, R S.

Why You Don't Owe It To Yourself To Seek Health. Gorovitz, Samuel.

OBSCENITY

"The Persecution Of Moses Harman" in *Freedom, Feminism, And The State*, Mc Elroy, Wendy (ed), 159–168. Day, Stanley.

OBSERVABILITY

The Everett Interpretation. Geroch, Robert.

OBSERVABLES

"Progress And The Limits Of Science" in *The Good Life And Its Pursuit*, Dougherty, Jude P (ed), 268–282. Shapere, Dudley.

OBSERVATION(S)

Epicurus' Scientific Method. Asmis, Elizabeth.

Observation, Experiment, And Hypothesis In Modern Physical Science. Achinstein, Peter (ed) and Hannaway, Owen (ed).

Reason And The Search For Knowledge: Investigations In The Philosophy Of Science. Shapere, Dudley.

"Bootstrapping Without Bootstraps" in *Testing Scientific Theories*, Earman, John (ed), 43–54. Edidin, Aron.

Explaining The Success Of Science. Brown, James Robert.

Galileo's Telescopic Observations Of Venus And Mars. Chalmers, Alan.

Gaston Bachelard Ou "La Surveillance Intellectuelle De Soi". Desanti, Jean– Toussaint.

Semantic Holism And Observation Statements. Schwerin, Alan.

The Everett Interpretation Of Quantum Mechanics: Many Worlds Or None? Stein, Howard.

Theory, Observation And Inductive Learning. Lane, N R.

Von Neumann And The Anti–Realists. Brown, James R.

Werner's Ethical Realism. Postow, B C.

OCCIDENTAL

"Happiness And The Idea Of Happiness" in *The Good Life And Its Pursuit*, Dougherty, Jude P (ed), 45–50. Matsushita, Masatoshi.

The Origins And Issues Of Scepticism, East And West. Sprung, Mervyn.

OCCURRENCE(S)

In Defense Of A Nontraditional Theory Of Memory. Naylor, Andrew.

OCHS, W

Note On An Argument Of W Ochs Against The Ignorance Interpretation Of State In Quantum Mechanics. Redei, Miklos.

OCKHAM

"Buridan's Ontology" in *How Things Are*, Bogen, James (ed), 189–204. Normore, Calvin.

"Things Versus 'Hows', Or Ockham On Predication And Ontology" in *How Things Are*, Bogen, James (ed), 175–188. Adams, Marilyn McCord.

Connotative Terms In Ockham. Boler, John F.

Is To Will It As Bad As To Do It (The Fourteenth Century Debate)? Adams, Marilyn McCord and Wood, Rega.

L'unité Du Monde Selon Guillaume D'Ockham (Ou La Logique De La Cosmologie Ockhamiste). Biard, Joel.

Supposition–Theory And The Problem Of Universals. Wagner, Michael F.

The Sources Of Intuitive Cognition In William Of Ockham. Wengert, Robert G.

Walter Chatton *Vs* Aureoli And Ockham Regarding The Universal Concept. Kelley, Francis E.

OCKHAM'S RAZOR

Necessary Agnosticism? Mc Laughlin, Robert.

OCKHAMISM

Leibniz' Gebrochenes Verhältnis Zur Erkenntnismetaphysik Der Scholastik. Hübener, Wolfgang.

OEDIPUS COMPLEX

Oedipus Rex: The Oedipus Rule And Its Subversion. Lingis, Alphonso.

OESTERLE, J

Medalist's Address: The Importance Of Philosophy And Of This Association. Oesterle, Jean T.

OFFENSIVENESS

Offensiveness In The Williams Report. Smart, Brian.

OLDENBURG, H

Baruch Spinoza, A Critic Of Robert Boyle: On Matter. Lewis, Christopher E.

OLGIATI, F

Il Pensiero Storico–Filosofico Di Olgiati E L'Interpretazione Della Filosofia Cartesiana. Grosso, Giuseppe.

OLIN, D

Olin, Quine, And The Surprise Examination. Chihara, Charles S.

OLIVECRONA, K

Law As Fact. Mac Cormack, Geoffrey.

OLLMAN, B

Marx And The Theory Of Internal Relations: A Critical Note On Ollman's Interpretation Of Marx. Hudelson, Richard.

OMISSION(S)

An Essay On Human Action. Zimmerman, Michael J.

Milanich And The Structure Of Omissions. Lemos, Noah M.

OMNIPOTENCE

Omnipotence And Other Theological Mistakes. Hartshorne, Charles.

Divine Omnipotence And Impossible Tasks: An Intensional Analysis. Anderson, C A.

Impeccability Revisited. Carter, W R.

Omnipotence, Timelessness, And The Restoration Of Virgins. Brinton, Alan.

Swinburne On Omnipotence. Hoffman, Joshua.

OMNIPRESENCE

God's Omnipresent Agency. Van Den Brom, L J.

OMNISCIENCE

Divine Omniscience And Human Freedom. Moskop, John C.

Divine Omniscience And Human Freedom: A 'Middle Knowledge' Perspective. Basinger, David.

Divine Omniscience And Human Privacy. Lackey, Douglas P.

PARADOX(ES)
Edward T.
The Direction Of Causation And The Newcomb Paradox (in Hebrew). Aharoni, Ron.
The Non–logical Character Of Zen. Nakamura, Hajime.
The Paradox Of The Liar—A Case Of Mistaken Identity. Goldstein, Laurence.
The Principle Of 'Maximum Inheritance' And The Growth Of Scientific Knowledge. Mamchur, Elena.
The Sorites Paradox. Thorpe, Dale A.
Through The Doors Of Reason: Dissolving Four Paradoxes Of Education. Oliver, R Graham.
Two Paradoxes Of Rational Acceptance. Moser, Paul K and Tlumak, Jeffrey.
Wittgenstein And Nāgārjuna's Paradox. Anderson, Tyson.

PARALLELISM
Gustav Bergmann's Psychophysiological Parallelism. Natsoulas, Thomas.
On Enriching The Content Of Art History Courses. Flint, Richard C.
Parallelism, Interactionism, And Causation. Addis, Laird.

PARAPSYCHOLOGY
Science, Religion And The Paranormal. Beloff, John.

PARENT(S)
The Neonatologist's Duty To Patient And Parents. Strong, Carson.

PARENT'S RIGHTS
Parental Rights. Page, Edgar.

PARENTHOOD
Parenting As A Profession: Children's Rights And Parental Responsibility. Graybosch, Anthony.
Would It Have Been Me (Against The Necessity Of Origin). Elliot, Robert and Gallois, Andre.

PARETO
Risk Aversion In n–Person Bargaining. Peters, Hans and Tijs, Stef.
Unanimity, Agreement, And Liberalism: A Critique Of James Buchanan's Social Philosophy. Barry, Norman P.
Welfare Functions And Group Decisions. Borch, Karl.

PARFIT, D
Derek Parfit And Greta Garbo. Madell, Geoffrey.
The Conception Of Possible People. Davies, Kim.

PARK(S)
National Park Management And Values. Bratton, Susan Power.

PARMENIDES
Parmenides Of Elea: Fragments. Gallop, David.
Man As APXH. Strózewski, Wladyslaw.
Parmenides And Ultimate Reality. Austin, Scott.
Plato's *Parmenides*: Prolegomena To A Reinterpretation (in Hebrew). Scolnicov, Samuel.

PARODY
Comments: Parody And The Eternal Recurrence In Nietzsche's Project Of Transvaluation. Schrift, Alan D.
Metaphysics And Metalepsis In *Thus Spoke Zarathustra*. Williams, R J.

PARONYMY
Portraying Analogy. Ross, J F.

PARRY, W
Logic And Contingent Existence. Lopston, Peter.

PARSONS, T
Are There Nonexistent Objects: Why Not: But Where Are They? Hintikka, Jaakko.
Did The Greeks Really Worship Zeus? Wettstein, Howard.
Parsons And Possible Objects. Hetherington, Stephen.

PART(S)
Othmar Spanns Ganzheitslehre In Neuer Interpretation. Pittioni, Veit.
Part And Whole In Aristotle's Concept Of Infinity. White, David A.
Simple Wholes And Complex Parts: Limited Principles In Spinoza. Sacksteder, William.
Temporal Parts Of Four Dimensional Objects. Heller, Mark.

PARTICIPATION
Religious Inquiry—Participation And Detachment. Rolston, Holmes.
Del Ente Participado Al Ser Imparticipado. Derisi, Octavio N.
El "Haber" Categorial En La Ontologia Clasica. Cruz, Juan C.
Karl Marx On Democracy, Participation, Voting, And Equality. Springborg, Patricia.
On R E Allen's *Plato's Parmenides*. Turnbull, Robert G.

PARTICLE(S)
Particles And Ideas In Locke's Theory Of Meaning. Berman, David.

PARTICULARS
"Armstrong On Universals And Particulars" in *D M Armstrong*, Bogdan, Radu J (ed), 161–170. Aune, Bruce.
"Generality And The Importance Of The Particular Case" in *Philosophy And Life: Essays On John Wisdom*, Dilman, Ilham (ed), 241–270. Nammour, Jamil.
Bradley And Realism About Universals. Forrest, Peter.
L'articulation Du Général Et Du Particulier: Une Approche Méthodologique Dans Le Champ Des Sciences Sociales. Miguelez, Roberto.
Realism, Resemblances, And Russell's Regress. Lehman, Craig K.
Spatial, Temporal And Cosmic Parts. Schlesinger, George N.
The Contingent Identity Of Particulars And Universals. Casullo, Albert.
The Extreme Realism Of Roger Bacon. Maloney, Thomas S.
The Resemblances Of Colors. Hardin, C L.
The Scope Of Knowledge In Republic V. White, F C.
The Uniqueness Of Particulars. Scaltsas, Theodore.

PARTITION(S)
Circumstances And Dominance In A Causal Decision Theory. Sobel, Jordan Howard.
On The Consistency Of Some Partition Theorems For Continuous Colorings, And The Structure Of Dense Real Order Types. Shelah, Saharon and Abraham, U and Rubin, M.

PARTNERSHIP(S)
Against Couples. Gregory, Paul.

PASCAL
Nietzsche And Pascal On Christianity. Natoli, Charles M.
Three Outsiders. Allen, Diogenes.
A Defence Of Pascal's Wager. Brown, Geoffrey.
Double Infinité Chez Pascal Et Monade. Naërt, Emilienne.

PASSION(S)
Postures Of The Mind: Essays On Mind And Morals. Baier, Annette.
The Moral Psychology Of The Virtues. Dent, N J H.
"Passion, Reflection, And Particularity In Two Ages" in *International Kierkegaard Commentary*, Perkins, Robert L (ed), 1–18. Elrod, John W.
"Some Remarks On The Concept Of Passion" in *International Kierkegaard Commentary*, Perkins, Robert L (ed), 87–106. Roberts, Robert C.
L'Evoluzione Del Problema Morale Nel Pensiero Di Cartesio. Cesareo, Rosa.
Spinoza Und Die Reue. Birnbacher, Dieter.

PASSIVE EUTHANASIA
Breathing A Little Life Into A Distinction. Wreen, Michael.

PASSIVITY
The Passivity Assumption Of The Sensation–Perception Distinction. Ben– Zeev, Aaron.

PAST
Historical Consciousness Or The Remembered Past. Lukacs, John.
On History And Other Essays. Oakeshott, Michael.
Ethical Uses Of The Past In Early Confucianism: The Case Of Hsün Tzu. Cua, A S.
Is The Past Finite: On Craig's Kalām Argument. Shields, George W.
Knowing The Past. Cherry, Christopher.
Praying About The Past. Brown, Geoffrey.
The Philosophy And Physics Of Affecting The Past. Price, Huw.

PASTIN, M
Thoughts On 'Management–Think'. Brenkert, George G.

PASTORAL
"Moral Issues In Deterrence Policy" in *The Security Gamble*, Mac Lean, Douglas (ed), 53–71. Hehir, J Bryan.

PATENT(S)
"Ethical Issues Raised By The Patenting Of New Forms Of Life" in *Biomedical Ethics Reviews*, Humber, James M (ed), 187–200. Muyskens, James.
"Patenting New Forms Of Life: Are There Any Ethical Issues" in *Biomedical Ethics Reviews*, Humber, James M (ed), 165–186. Cebik, L B.
Brand Name Extortionists, Intellectual Prostitutes, And Generic Free Riders. Bayles, Michael D.
Patent Rights And Better Mousetraps. Michael, Mark.

PATERNALISM
The Silent World Of Doctor And Patient. Katz, Jay.
"Paternalism" And Social Policy. Sankowski, Edward.
"Regulation And Paternalism" in *Rights And Regulation*, Machan, Tibor (ed), 217–248. Kelman, Steven.
"Treatment Refusals" in *Ethical Questions In Brain And Behavior*, Pfaff, Donald W (ed), 41–56. Macklin, Ruth.
A Definition For Paternalism. Hershey, Paul Turner.
Another Look At Paternalism. Hobson, Peter.
Autonomy's Temporary Triumph. Veatch, Robert M and Callahan, Daniel.
Commentary On "Kicking Against The Pricks: Two Patients Wish To End Essential Insulin Treatments". Gillon, Raanan.
Commentary On "Kicking Against The Pricks: Two Patients Wish To End Essential Insulin Treatment". Parsons, Victor.
Commentary On "Kicking Against The Pricks: Two Patients Wish To End Essential Insulin Treatments". Kennedy, Ian.
Commentary On "Kicking Against The Pricks: Two Patients Wish To End Essential Insulin Treatment". Marsden, David.
Compulsory Health And Safety In A Free Society. Boughton, B J.
Doctors Helping Doctors. Morrow, Carol K.
Involuntary Confinement: Legal And Psychiatric Perspectives. Dresser, Rebecca.
Law And The Life Sciences. Annas, George J.
Liberty, Beneficence, And Involuntary Confinement. Callahan, Joan C.
Parental Discretion And Children's Rights: Background And Implications For Medical Decision–Making. Schoeman, Ferdinand.
Paternalism And The Regulation Of Drugs. Sagoff, Mark.
Paternalism And Partial Autonomy. O' Neill, Onora.
Paternalism And Sovereignty In Athletics: Limits And Justifications Of The Coach's Exercise Of Authority Over The Adult Athlete. Ravizza, Kenneth and Daruty, Kathy.
Paternalism, Drugs, And The Nature Of Sports. Brown, W M.
Patient Truthfulness: A Test Of Models Of The Physician–Patient Relationship. Vanderpool, Harold Y and Weiss, Gary B.
Response To Rebecca Dresser's 'Involuntary Confinement: Legal And Psychiatric Perspectives'. Callahan, Joan C.
When The Doctor And The Minister Disagree (Case Study With Commentaries). Weikart, Robert and Klar, Howard.

PATHOLOGY

The New Image Of The Person: The Theory And Practice Of Clinical Philosophy. Koestenbaum, Peter.

Le Normal Et Le Pathologique En Politique. Mineau, André.

PATIENT(S)

Taking Care Of Strangers: The Rule Of Law In Doctor–Patient Relations. Burt, Robert A.

The Silent World Of Doctor And Patient. Katz, Jay.

"Ethical Decisions In The Intensive Care Unit" in *Difficult Decisions In Medical Ethics*, Ganos, Doreen L (ed), 125–134. Jackson, David.

"Patient Autonomy In Intensive Care" in *Difficult Decisions In Medical Ethics*, Ganos, Doreen L (ed), 111–124. Miller, Bruce.

"The Family's Right To Decide For The Incompetent Patient" in *Ethics Committees And Health Care Decisions*, Cranford, Ronald (ed), 209–217. Buchanan, Allen.

A Commentary On 'Two Pathographies: A Study In Illness And Literature'. Jones, Anne H.

Are We Teaching Students That Patients Don't Matter? Robinson, Jean.

Lay Obligations In Professional Relations. Benjamin, Martin.

On Removing Food & Water: Against The Stream. Meilaender, Gilbert.

Patients With Reduced Agency: Conceptual, Empirical, And Ethical Considerations. Mc Cullough, Laurence B.

Patients' Ethical Obligation For Their Health. Sider, Roger C and Clements, Colleen D.

Setting Boundaries For Artificial Feeding. Green, Willard.

Two Pathographies: A Study In Illness And Literature. Hawkins, Anne.

Unsolicited Medical Opinion. Ratzan, Richard.

Why You Don't Owe It To Yourself To Seek Health. Gorovitz, Samuel.

Wittgenstein On The 'Charm' Of Psychoanalysis. Geller, Jeffrey L.

PATON, H

Kant On Reality. Mijuskovic, Ben.

PATRIARCHY

Letter To The Editors: A Response To Abrams. Raymond, Janice G.

Science And Gender: A Critique Of Biology And Its Theories On Women. Bleier, Ruth.

Rejoinder To 'Medicine As Patriarchal Religion'. Abrams, Frederick R.

Response To Professor Rawlinson's Article "Women, Medicine, And Religion". Abrams, Frederick R.

Women, Medicine, And Religion: A Response To Raymond And Abrams. Rawlinson, Mary C.

PATRIOTISM

"Patriotism: A Menace To Liberty" in *Freedom, Feminism, And The State*, Mc Elroy, Wendy (ed), 337–350. Goldman, Emma.

Die Bedeutung Des Vaterlandsbegriffes Für Die Erziehung Zum Sozialistischen Patriotismus. Abelmann, Xenia.

PAUL

The Georgetown Symposium On Ethics. Porreco, Rocco (ed).

"Religion, Grace, And The Law On The Heart" in *The Georgetown Symposium On Ethics*, Porreco, Rocco (ed), 213–218. Dreisbach, Donald F.

Saint Augustine On The Road To Damascus. Ferrari, Leo C.

Taxes In The New Testament. Perkins, Pheme.

The Mystery Of Christ: Clue To Paul's Thinking On Wisdom. Hill, Robert.

PAVELKA, J

Pavelka's Fuzzy Logic And Free L–Subsemigroups. Gerla, Giangiacomo.

PEACE

When War Is Unjust: Being Honest In Just War Thinking. Yoder, John H.

"Moral Issues In Deterrence Policy" in *The Security Gamble*, Mac Lean, Douglas (ed), 53–71. Hehir, J Bryan.

Arnold J Toynbee: Das Höchste Gut Ist Der Frieden!. Schulze, Hans.

Beliefs Essential In The Struggle For Peace And Development. Parsons, Howard L.

Dialogue On "The Meaning Of History And Peace". Borgosz, Józef.

Die Einheit Von Sozialismus Und Frieden. Hocke, Erich.

Die Frage Von Krieg Und Frieden In Der Weltanschaulichen Auseinandersetzung. Hahn, Erich.

Die Macht Zur Freiheit. Steussloff, Hans.

For The Sake Of Humanity. Georgiadis, Constantine.

Friedenskampf Und Philosophie. Buhr, Manfred.

Global Philosophy As A Foundation Of Global Peace. Skolimowski, Henryk.

Hobbes's State Of War. Hampton, Jean.

Kommunisten Und Christen Gemeinsam Im Kampf Um Den Frieden. Kliem, Wolfgang.

Moral Y Politica En "Para La Paz Perpetua" De Kant. Amado, Maria Teresa and Lisboa, Joao Luis.

National Self–Determination: Peace Beyond Detente. Cunningham, Frank.

Nuclear Deterrence And World Peace. Hampsch, George.

Peace And The Role Of The Philosopher. Grassi, Joseph G.

Peace, Human Rights, And Human Needs: A Comment On The Bay–Flathman Debate. Carens, Joseph H.

Peaceful Coexistence As The Nuclear Traumatization Of Humanity. Butler, Clark.

Philosophy And Practice: Some Issues About War And Peace. Hare, R M.

Philosophy And The Pursuit Of World Peace. Madison, Gary B.

Philosophy And The Nuclear Debate. Gay, William C.

Philosophy And Peace Today. Szmyd, Jan.

Philosophy Of Relations Between Sports And Peace. Güldenpfennig, Sven.

Strategic Defense, Deterrence, And The Prospects For Peace. Gray, Colin.

The First And The Second Day Of War. Hubert, Jerry Z.

The Victory Over Fascism A Historic Chance For Peace And Progress (in German). Löwe, Bernd P.

Thoughts And Suggestions Concerning An International Society For Philosophers Concerned With Peace. Cox, John Gray.

PEARS, D

Existence And Judgment. Connell, Desmond.

Pears On *Akrasia*, And Defeated Intentions. Mele, Alfred R.

PEDAGOGY

Über Die Kategorien Inhalt Und Methode In Der Pädagogik. Naumann, Werner.

"The Proof Of The Pudding Lies In The Eating" (in German). Loeser, Franz.

"Toward A Pedagogy Of The Useful Past For Teacher Preparation": A Reaction. Gutek, Gerald L.

Erkenntnistheoretische Und Pädagogische Probleme Bei Der Verwendung Von Lehr– Und Lernmitteln In Der Ausbildung Von Philosophiestudenten. Kirchgässner, Werner and Sanger, H.

Fragen Der Philosophischen Lehre. Wittich, Dieter.

Kants Straftheorie In Ihrer Bedeutung Für Die Entwicklung Einer Theorie Der Straffälligenpädagogik. Eberle, Hans–Jurgen.

La Lecture Rationnelle—Nécessaire Et Facilement Assimilable (in German). Ziegler, Heinz.

Logics And Languages Of Pedagogical Research. Soltis, Jonas F.

Perspectivas Pedagógicas Da Filosofia Existencialista. Rocha, Filipe.

The Pedagogical Usefulness Of Speech Act Theory. Reagan, Gerald M.

Topics In Speech Act Theory And Pedagogy. Broidy, Steve.

Toward A Pedagogy Of The Useful Past For Teacher Preparation. Lucas, Christopher J.

PEIRCE

Is Science Progressive? Niiniluoto, Ilkka.

The Sign Of Three. Sebok, Thomas A (ed) and Eco, Umberto (ed).

"Peirce And The Conditions Of Possibility Of Science" in *History Of Philosophy In Making*, Thro, Linus J (ed), 177–196. Delaney, C F.

Croyances, Dispositions Et Probabiliies (Peirce Et Ramsey). Engel, Pascal.

Did Peirce Answer Hume On Necessary Connection? Roth, Robert J.

Essentialism And Santayana's Realm Of Essence. Kerr– Lawson, Angus.

Interpreting Peirce. Grossman, Morris.

Noumenal Qualia: C S Peirce On Our Epistemic Access To Feelings. Stephens, G Lynn.

On The Principle Of Information Retention. Hilpinen, Risto.

Peirce And Metaphor. Anderson, Douglas.

Peirce's Alpha Graphs: The Completeness Of Propositional Logic And The Fast Simplification Of Truth Functions. White, Richard B.

Peirce's Doubts About Idealism. Meyers, Robert G.

Peirce's Examination Of Mill's Philosophy. Smyth, Richard.

Peirce's Thirteen Theories Of Truth. Almeder, Robert.

Peircean Semiotics And Poetic Production (in Portuguese). Silveira, Lauro F B.

Que Signifie: Voir Rouge—La Sensation Et La Couleur Selon C S Peirce. Engel– Tiercelin, Claudine.

Semiotic Idealism. Mc Carthy, Jeremiah E.

Temporality, Perceptual Experience And Peirce's "Proofs" Of Realism. Rosenthal, Sandra B.

What Are Representamens? Benedict, George A.

PENALTY(–TIES)

Insanity And Criminality. Simon, Michael A.

PENOLOGY

Punishment And Restitution: A Restitutionary Approach To Crime And The Criminal. Abel, Charles F and Marsh, Frank H.

PERCEIVING

Treatise On Basic Philosophy, V5. Bunge, Mario.

Berkeley, Epistemology, And Science. Steinkraus, Warren E.

How And Why Seeing Is Not Believing. Nelson, John O.

PERCEPTION

see also Sense Data

Berkeley. Pitcher, George and Honderich, Ted (ed).

Logick: Or, The Right Use Of Reason. Watts, Isaac and Schouls, Peter A (ed).

Seeing And Reading. Nicholson, Graeme.

Subjecting And Objecting. Deutscher, Max.

The Central Problem Of David Hume's Philosophy. Salmon, C V.

Toward A Structural Theory Of Action: Network Models Of Social Structure, Perception, And Action. Burt, Ronald S.

"Armstrong's Theory Of Perception" in *D M Armstrong*, Bogdan, Radu J (ed), 55–78. Sanford, David H.

"The Truth Of The Body" in *Existential Coordinates Of Human Condition*, Tymieniecka, A (ed), 479–494. Riley, Michael.

A Defence Of Sellars. Wright, Edmond L.

A Semiotic–Pragmatic Theory Of Consciousness. Lee, Harold N.

A Transparent Case For Subjectivism. Hardin, C L.

Aristotelian Perception And The Hellenistic Problem Of Representation. Glidden, David.

Aristotle On Perceptual Truth And Falsity. Ben– Zeev, Aaron.

Berkeley's Notions. Flage, Daniel E.

Brains In Vats And The Internalist Perspective. Stephens, James and Russow, Lilly– marlene.

Brody's Essentialism. Griffin, Nicholas.

Can Indirect Realism Be Demonstrated In The Psychological Laboratory? Wilcox, Stephen and Katz, Stuart.

Cause In Perception: A Note On Searle's *Intentionality*. Mc Culloch, Gregory.

Content And Context Of Perception. Smith, David Woodruff.

Faces. Stroll, Avrum.

PERCEPTION
Foundationalism And Permanence In Descartes' Epistemology. Cling, Andrew D.
Gefühl—Sinnlichkeit—Verstand. Gerlach, Hans–Martin.
How Extensional Is Extensional Perception? Asher, Nicholas M and Bonevac, Daniel.
Hume And The Missing Shade Of Blue. Fogelin, Robert J.
Hume On The Perception Of Causality. Shanks, David R.
Hume's Labyrinth. Behan, David P.
Hutcheson's Moral Realism. Norton, David F.
Interrelations Between Subject And Object In Perception. Lijun, Song.
Is Object–Seeing Really Propositional Seeing? Nelson, John O.
Is The Concept Of Pain Incoherent? Kaufman, Rick.
Judgment And Perception In *Theaetetus* 184–186. Shea, Joseph.
Kant Über Wahrnehmung Und Erfahrung. Bröcker, W.
Knowledge And Value. Cavell, Marcia.
Locke On Consciousness And Reflection. Kulstad, Mark A.
Locke's Empiricism And The Postulation Of Unobservables. Soles, David E.
Metaphysics And The 'Eye And Mind'. Bertoldi, Eugene F.
Monade Und Welt: Ein Beitrag Zur Interpretation Der Monadologie. Hubner, Wulf.
Nietzsche And Pragmatism. Hallman, Max O.
On Representation And Essence: Barthes And Heidegger. Huckle, Nicholas.
On The Causal Self–Referentiality Of Perceptual Experiences And The Problem Of Concrete Perceptual Reference. Natsoulas, Thomas.
Perceived Worlds, Inferred Worlds, *The* World. Sklar, Lawrence.
Perception And The Mind–Body Problem. Heslep, Robert D.
Perception, Relativism, And Truth: Reflections On Plato's Theaetetus 152–160. Matthen, Mohan.
Perception, Causation, And Supervenience. Mc Laughlin, Brian P.
Perceptual Meaning And Husserl. Cunningham, Suzanne.
Perceptual Reference. Miller, Izchak.
Phenomenal Realism. Persson, Ingmar.
Russell's Later Theory Of Perception. Wilson, Thomas A.
Skepticism And The Possibility Of Knowledge. Stroud, Barry.
Skepticism Without Indubitability. Wilson, Margaret D.
Stolnitz's Attitude: Taste And Perception. Dickie, George.
Technics And The Bias Of Perception. Innis, Robert E.
Temporality, Perceptual Experience And Peirce's "Proofs" Of Realism. Rosenthal, Sandra B.
The Debate About Mental Imagery. Tye, Michael.
The Diversity Of Perception. Nelson, Jack.
The Generalized Argument From Verification: Work Towards The Metaepistemology Of Perception. Roberts, Scott P.
The Passivity Assumption Of The Sensation–Perception Distinction. Ben– Zeev, Aaron.
The Process Of Meaning–Creation: A Transcendental Argument. Falck, Colin.
Three Realist Claims. Ward, Andrew.

PERELMAN, C
La Philosophie Du Raisonnable De Chaïm Perelman. Cote, Marcel.

PERFECTIBILITY
Perfection And Perfectibility In Rabbi Kook's Theology (in Hebrew). Ben– Shlomo, Joseph.

PERFECTION
Freiheit Und Perfektion. Düll, Rupprecht.

PERFECTIONISM
Be Ye Therefore Perfect Or The Ineradicability Of Sin. Harrison, Jonathan.

PERFORMANCE(S)
A Commentary On Jan Boxill's "Beauty, Sport, And Gender". Kupfer, Joseph.
Cogito, Ergo Sum: Inference And Performance. Reeder, Harry.
Ethical Dilemmas In Performance Appraisal. Banner, David K and Cooke, Robert Allan.
Kunst Als Dasein Und Ereignis: Zum Ontologischen Und Performativen Kunstbegriff. Frey, Gerhard.
On Musical Improvisation. Alperson, Philip.
Sport, Art, And Gender. Postow, B C.
The Aesthetics Of Sport. Saraf, Mikhail Y.

PERFORMATIVES
"Meaning, Force And Explicit Performatives" in *Philosophical Analysis In Latin America*, Gracia, Jorge J E and others (eds), 141–164. Rabossi, Eduardo.
The Constitutive Force Of Language. Harris, James F.

PERFORMING ART(S)
A Response To Best On Art And Sport. Wertz, S K.
Philosophy Of Music And Artistic Performance (in Hungarian). Ramisvili, G Z.

PERIODICITY
On The Period Of Sequences (*A*ⁿ(*p*)) In Intuitionistic Propositional Calculus. Ruitenburg, Wim.

PERIODIZATION
Periodization, Holism And Historicism: A Reply To Jacobs. Tilley, Nicholas.

PERMISSION(S)
An Analysis Of Rights. Stoljar, Samuel.
Normative Kinematics (I): A Solution To A Problem About Permission. Belzer, Marvin.
Permission. Nute, Donald.

PERMISSIVENESS
The Restoration Of Medical Ethics. Rogers, Adrian.

PERMUTATION(S)
An Undecidable Problem In Finite Combinatorics. Compton, Kevin J.

PEROVICH, A
Response To Perovich. Gill, Jerry H.

PERRY, J
'Knowing What It's Like' And The Essential Indexical. Mc Mullen, Carolyn.
Data Semantics For Attitude Reports. Landman, Fred.
Demonstratives And Belief States. Chien, A J.
Fregean Thoughts. Noonan, Harold.

PERSON(S)
see also Human(s), Individual(s)
A Christian Humanism: Karol Wojtyla's Existential Personalism. Woznicki, Andrew N.
Collective And Corporate Responsibility. French, Peter A.
Contours Of A World View. Holmes, Arthur F.
Defining Human Life: Medical, Legal, And Ethical Implications. Shaw, Margery W (ed) and Doudera, A Edward (ed).
Research Ethics. Berg, Kare (ed) and Tranoy, Knut Erik (ed).
The Freedom Of Morality. Yannaras, Christos.
The New Image Of The Person: The Theory And Practice Of Clinical Philosophy. Koestenbaum, Peter.
The Thread Of Life. Wollheim, Richard.
"Concepts Of Personhood: A Philosophical Perspective" in *Defining Human Life*, Shaw, Margery W (ed), 12–23. Wikler, Daniel.
"Marx's Three Worlds And Their Interrelation" in *Continuity And Change In Marxism*, Fischer, Norman And Others (ed), 1–23. Rader, Melvin.
"Our Knowledge Of Other People" in *Philosophy And Life: Essays On John Wisdom*, Dilman, Ilham (ed), 145–178. Dilman, Ilham.
A Personalistic Philosophy Of History. Bartnik, Czeslaw Stanislaw.
Abortion, Personhood And Vagueness. Levin, David S.
Being A Person—Does It Matter? Lomasky, Loren E.
Das Verhältnis Von "Person" Und "Eigentum" In Hegels Philosophie Des Rechts. Meyer, Rudolf W.
Edith Stein Et Karol Wojtyla Sur La Personne. Kalinowski, Georges.
Elementos De Filosofia Politica No Concilio Vaticano II. Borges, J F Pereira.
Full Humans And Empty Morality. Harris, John.
Indeterminate People. Chandler, Hugh S.
Life After Death In Whitehead's Metaphysics. Broniak, Christopher J.
Logical Problems For Lockean Persons. Welker, David.
Los Problemas Filosóficos De La Individualidad. Gracia, Jorge J E.
On The Philosophical Foundations Of The Conception Of Human Rights. Rosenbaum, Alan S.
Ontology And The Theory Of Justice. Grafstein, Robert.
Person And Law In Kant And Hegel. Siep, Ludwig.
Personhood And Human Embryos And Fetuses. Tauer, Carol A.
Personhood, Covenant, And Abortion. Reiley Maguire, Marjorie.
Persons And The Measurement Of Illness. Bartlett, Edward T.
Persons And The Problem Of Interaction. Peterson, John.
Philosophy And Culture (in Dutch). De Beer, C S.
Sacrificing Persons For The General Welfare: A Comment Of Sayward. Wein, Sheldon.
Significación Actual Del Pensamiento Zubiriano. Quintás, Alfonso López.
Strawson And Lonergan On 'Person'. Fitzpatrick, Joseph.
Thanatos And Euthanatos: Persons And Practical Policies. Smith, James Leroy.
The Concept Of The Person In St Augustine's *De Trinitate*. O' Connor, William R.
The Definition Of Person. Teichman, Jenny.
The Human Right To Be Treated As A Person. Khatchadourian, Haig.
The Role Of Reflection In The Structure Of The Human Person. Chudy, W.
Who Counts? Smith, David H.

PERSONAL IDENTITY
see also Identity
"From Then To Now: Perinatal Intensive Care" in *Bioethical Frontiers In Perinatal Intensive Care*, Snowden, Fraser (ed), 19–38. Francoeur, Robert T.
"Personal Identity And Imagination": One Objection. Flew, Antony.
Beyond Dialetical Thinking: Political Logics And The Construction Of Individuality. Boedi, Remo.
Gehirnverpflanzung—Ethische Implikationen. Demmer, Klaus.
Hume On Finding An Impression Of The Self. Traiger, Saul.
Hume On Perceptions And Persons. Davie, William E.
Hume, Demonstratives, And Self–Ascriptions Of Identity. Ward, Andrew.
Hume's Bundle Theory Of The Mind. Brooks, D.
Karma And Personal Identity: A Response To Professor White. Griffiths, Paul.
Leibniz's Theory Of Personal Identity In The *New Essays*. Vailati, Ezio.
Lockes Perspektiventheorie Der Persönlichen Identität. Kienzle, Bertram.
Logical Problems For Lockean Persons. Welker, David.
Person–Stages And Unity Of Consciousness. Mc Inerney, Peter K.
Three Versions Of The Budles Theory. Van Cleve, James.

PERSONALISM
Laborem Exercens: A Theological And Philosophical Foundation For Business Ethics. Sullivan, Brian G.
Personalisme Et Anthropologie Chrétienne. Walgrave, Jan H.

PERSONALITY
Personality: The Need For Liberty And Rights. Gotesky, Rubin.
"Bayesianism With A Human Face" in *Testing Scientific Theories*, Earman, John (ed), 133–156. Jeffrey, Richard.
An African Concept Of Human Personality: The Yoruba Example. Makinde, M Akin.
Creativity, Progress, And Personality. Osborne, Harold.
Kant Für Mediziner? Funke, G.
La Teoría Relacional De La Personalidad Según J Nuttin. Darós, William R.

PERSONALITY

Logical Learning Theory: Kuhnian Anomaly Or Medievalism Revisited? Rychlak, Joseph R.

Persönlichkeit Als Subjekt Des Gesellschaftlichen Fortschritts. Gutsche, Gunter.

Sozialistische Persönlichkeit Und Intensiv Erweiterte Reproduktion. Kretzschmar, A.

Sozialistische Persönlichkeitsentwicklung Und Soziologische Forschung. Adler, Frank and Kretzschmar, A.

Style And Personality In The Literary Work. Robinson, Jenefer.

The Character Of The Interaction Of Working And Political Activity Of Personality (in Czechoslovakian). Rjadová, Vera and Rjadovoj, Alexandr.

The Concept Of Personal Pattern As An Axiological Structure. Śpiewak, Anna.

Umanità. Villa, Luigi.

PERSONALITY THEORY

Melancholy, Irony, And Kierkegaard. Khan, Abrahim H.

PERSONIFICATION

The Personal God And A God Who Is A Person. Thatcher, Adrian.

PERSPECTIVE(S)

Global Perspectives: Spiritualities In Interaction. Panikkar, Raimundo.

On The Fidelity Of Pictures: A Critique Of Goodman's Disjunction Of Perspective And Realism. Topper, David.

Russell's Construction Of Space From Perspectives. Irvine, William B.

PERSPECTIVISM

Comments On Mittelman's "Perspectivism, Becoming, And Truth In Nietzsche". Hinman, Lawrence M.

Nietzsche's Sting And The Possibility Of Good Philology. Westphal, Kenneth.

Perspectivism, Becoming, And Truth In Nietzsche. Mittelman, Willard.

Reflections On Perspectivism In Nietzsche. Strong, Tracy B.

PERSUASION

Authority And Persuasion In Philosophy. Jordan, Mark D.

Commentary On Beauchamp's "Manipulative Advertising". Hare, R M.

Manipulative Advertising. Beauchamp, Tom L.

PETERS, R

Emotion And Action In Cognitive Psychology: Breaching A Fashionable Philosophical Fence. Ericson, David P.

Genderism And The Reconstitution Of Philosophy Of Education. Sherman, Ann L.

The Nature Of Aims And Ends In Education. Mellema, Gregory.

The Philosophy Of Education Since Dewey. Hendley, Brian P.

PETRAZYCKI, L

Evaluations And Norms Of Conduct In Leon Petrazycki's Psychologistic Concept Of Law And Morality (in Polish). Smoczynski, P J.

PETROVIC, K

The World Socio–Economic And Political Crisis Calls For Changes In The Position And Social Role Of Sports. Petrović, Kresimir.

PETTERSSON, H

"Artificial Disintegration" in *Observation, Experiment, And Hypothesis In Modern Physical Science*, Achinstein, Peter (ed), 239–308. Stuewer, Roger H.

PETTY, W

Petty *Contra* Hobbes: A Previously Untranslated Manuscript. Amati, Frank and Aspromourgos, Tony.

PFEIFER, K

Laughter, Suddenness, And Pleasure. Morreall, John.

PHAEDO

The *"Phaedo": A Platonic Labyrinth*. Burger, Ronna.

PHARMACOLOGY

Brand Name Extortionists, Intellectual Prostitutes, And Generic Free Riders. Bayles, Michael D.

PHENOMENA

"Phenomenality And Materiality In Kant" in *Hermeneutics*, Shapiro, Gary (ed), 121–144. De Man, Paul.

Must Knowledge—Or 'Knowledge' Be Socially Constructed? Radford, Colin.

On Macintyre, Rationality, And Dramatic Space. Monasterio, Xavier O.

Phenomenal Properties. Double, Richard.

Physicalism And Phenomenal Qualities. Conee, Earl.

PHENOMENALISM

Necessity And Irreversibility In The Second Analogy. Aquila, Richard E.

Phenomenal Realism. Persson, Ingmar.

Phenomenalism, Idealism And Mentalism: A Historical Note. Gupta, R K.

Russell's Later Theory Of Perception. Wilson, Thomas A.

The Failure Of An *A Priori* Argument For Realism. Brueckner, Anthony L.

PHENOMENOLOGY

Bodily Reflective Modes: A Phenomenological Method For Psychology. Shapiro, Kenneth Joel.

Buddhist And Western Psychology. Katz, Nathan (ed).

Continental Philosophy And The Arts. Winters, Laurence E and others (ed).

Dialogues With Contemporary Continental Thinkers. Kearney, Richard.

God, Guilt, And Death: An Existential Phenomenology Of Religion. Westphal, Merold.

Heidegger: Perspektiven Zur Deutung Seines Werkes. Pöggeler, Otto (ed).

Husserl And Realism In Logic And Mathematics. Tragesser, Robert S.

Il Fenomeno Dell'essere: Fenomenologia E Ontologia In Heidegger. Esposito, Constantino.

Language And Experience: Descriptions Of Living Language In Husserl And Wittgenstein. Reeder, Harry P.

Logic And The Objectivity Of Knowledge: Studies In Husserl's Early Philosophy.

Willard, Dallas.

Martin Heidegger (in Hungarian). István, Fehér M.

Phenomenology And Psychiatry. Jenner, F A (ed) and De Koning, A J J (ed).

Phenomenology And Existentialism: An Introduction. Grossman, Reinhardt.

Reflection And Action. Rotenstreich, Nathan.

The New Image Of The Person: The Theory And Practice Of Clinical Philosophy. Koestenbaum, Peter.

The Problem Of Social Reality: Collected Papers 1. Schutz, Alfred.

The Search For An Alternative: Philosophical Perspectives Of Subjectivism And Marxism. Farber, Marvin.

Time And Narrative, V1. Ricoeur, Paul and Mc Laughlin, Kathleen (trans) and Pellauer, David (trans).

Wittgenstein: A Critique. Findlay, J N.

"Criticism, Philosophy, Phenomenology" in *Continental Philosophy And The Arts*, Winters, Laurence E and others (ed), 243–264. Anceschi, Luciano.

"Fiction & Transposition Of Presence" in *Existential Coordinates Of Human Condition*, Tymieniecka, A (ed), 495–504. Martinez–Bonati, Felix.

"Limits To A Phenomenology Of Art" in *Continental Philosophy And The Arts*, Winters, Laurence E and others (ed), 3–14. Kelly, Eugene.

"Nature, Feeling, & Disclosure In Poetry Of Wallace Stevens" in *Existential Coordinates Of Human Condition*, Tymieniecka, A (ed), 75–90. Ruppert, Jeanne.

"Normal" Intentional Action. Ehrind, Douglas.

"Phenomenology And Aesthetics" in *Continental Philosophy And The Arts*, Winters, Laurence E and others (ed), 163–172. Neri, Guido D.

"Phenomenology And Literary Criticism" in *Continental Philosophy And The Arts*, Winters, Laurence E and others (ed), 123–138. Dufrenne, Mikel.

"The Hermeneutics Of Suspicion" in *Hermeneutics*, Shapiro, Gary (ed), 54–65. Gadamer, Hans–Georg.

"The Poet In The Poem" in *Existential Coordinates Of Human Condition*, Tymieniecka, A (ed), 61–74. Miller, Cynthia A.

"The Problem Of Reading, Phenomenologically Or Otherwise" in *Existential Coordinates Of Human Condition*, Tymieniecka, A (ed), 559–568. Margolis, Joseph.

"Towards A Phenomenology Of Bad Taste" in *Continental Philosophy And The Arts*, Winters, Laurence E and others (ed), 109–122. Dorfles, Gillo.

A Defence Of Sellars. Wright, Edmond L.

A Missing Chapter: A Marginal Note Concerning The Second Volume Of Schutz/Luckmann: Strukturen Der Lebenswelt. Wagner, Helmut R.

A Phenomenological Account Of The Linguistic Mediation Of The Public And The Private. Reeder, Harry P.

A Phenomenology For Christian Ethics. Prust, Richard C.

A Survey Of Recent Ricoeur–Literature. Sweeney, Robert.

Acerca Del Programa De Fenomenologia. Presas, Mario A.

Affective And Non–Affective Desire. Vadas, Melinda.

Against Idealism: Johannes Daubert Vs Husserl's *Ideas* I. Schuhmann, Karl and Smith, Barry.

Approccio Fenomenologico Alla Conoscenza Metafisica. Lambertino, Antonio.

Are Qualia A Pain In The Neck For Functionalists? Graham, George and Stephens, G Lynn.

Assertion And Predication In Husserl. Pietersma, H.

Can Heidegger Be Depicted As A Phenomenologist? Pavlich, G.

Comments On A Claim That Some Phenomenological Statements May Be *A Posteriori*. Van De Pitte, M M.

Complexity And Intersubjectivity: Towards The Theory Of Niklas Luhmann. Bednarz Jr, John.

Das Apriorische Moment Der Subjekt–Objekt–Dialektik In Der Transzendentalen Phänomenologie. Kochler, Hans.

De La Sensibilité. Levinas, E.

Der Mensch Und Seine Sprache. Hennigfeld, Jochem.

Developing Themes In Philosophy: Modern Continental Philosophy. Nicholson, Graeme.

Dialectic And The Role Of The Phenomenologist (in Hebrew). Marx, Werner.

Discussion Of Wagner, Imber, And Rasmussen. Wolff, Kurt H.

Experience And Value In Moritz Geiger's Aesthetics. Beardsley, Monroe C.

Explorations Of The *Lebenswelt*: Reflections On Schutz And Habermas. Rasmussen, David M.

Fichte's Und Husserl's Critique Of Kant's Transcendental Deduction. Seebohm, Thomas M.

Hegel's Critique Of Kant's Theoretical Philosophy. Ameriks, Karl.

Heidegger And The Deconstruction Of Foundations. Tyman, Stephen.

Heidegger's Overcoming Of Metaphysics: A Critique. Marsh, James L.

Heidegger's Hermeneutical Grounding Of Science: A Phenomenological Critique Of Positivism. Bender, Frederic L.

Husserl And Hegel: A Historical And Religious Encounter. Kirkland, Frank M.

Husserl's Communal Spirit: A Phenomenological Study Of The Fundamental Structure Of Society. Allen, Jeffner.

Imagination Als Komplexakt (in Japanese). Kanata, Susumu.

Janus Bifrons. Granger, Gilles–Gaston.

L'unité De L'oeuvre De Paul Ricoeur Saisie Selon La Perspective De Son Ouvrage Temps Et Récit I. Stevens, Bernard.

Le Problème De La Logique Pure: De Husserl À Une Nouvelle Position Phénoménologique. Richir, Mare.

Leiblicher Raum Und Räumlichkeit Der Gefühle. Hoppe, Hansgeorg.

Marx's Critique Of Capitalist Technology: Form And Content. Rehg, William R.

Merleau–Ponty, Lewis And Ontological Presence. Rosenthal, Sandra and Bourgeois, Patrick.

PHILOSOPHY

PHILOSOPHY

The Status Of The Debate On Rights In The USSR. Lee, Sander H.

The Tragic View Of Life. Beattie, Paul H.

The Tyranny Of Scholarship. Levine, David L.

Thinking Ahead. Kolenda, Konstantin.

Thoughts And Suggestions Concerning An International Society For Philosophers Concerned With Peace. Cox, John Gray.

Two Conceptions Of Philosophy. Lugenbehl, Dale.

Understanding Happiness. Hagberg, G.

Vidyaranya On Method, Object And Limit Of Philosophical Investigation. Mishra, Ganeswar.

Was Wittgenstein Influenced By Hegel? Cook, Daniel J.

What Philosophers Can Learn From Agriculture. Thompson, Paul.

World Congresses Of Philosophy. Cauchy, Venant and Kuczynski, Janusz.

Writing Philosophy And Literature: Apology For Narcissism In Merleau–Ponty. Cook, Deborah.

Writing To Learn In Philosophy. Berger, Jeffrey.

Zur Realisierung Des Verhältnisses Von Philosophie Und Einzelwissenschaften Im Marxistisch–Leninistischen Grundstudium. Bernhardt, Herbert and Richter, F.

PHILOSOPHY OF EDUCATION

see Education

PHILOSOPHY OF HISTORY

see History

PHILOSOPHY OF LANGUAGE

see Language

PHILOSOPHY OF LAW

see Law

PHILOSOPHY OF MIND

see Mind

PHILOSOPHY OF RELIGION

see Religion

PHILOSOPHY OF SCIENCE

see Science

PHONOLOGY

What Is Grammar? Tomkow, Terrance A.

PHOTOGRAPHY

Roland Barthes On The Aesthetics Of Photography. Jacquette, Dale.

PHOTON(S)

Gentle Quantum Events As The Source Of Explicate Order. Chew, Geoffrey F.

PHYLOGENY

Die Entwicklung Der Paläoanthropologie Im Lichte Der Stammbäme Des Menschen. Halaczek, B.

PHYSICAL

Skinner On The "Mental And The "Physical". Schnaitter, Roger.

Sport, Moral Education And The Development Of Character. Arnold, Peter.

What Is Explained By AI Models? Kobsa, Alfred.

PHYSICAL OBJECT(S)

Causation And Identity. Swoyer, Chris.

On Determining Dispositions. Essler, W K.

PHYSICAL REALITY

An Exchange On Local Beables. Bell, J S and others.

Hume And Edwards On 'Why Is There Something Rather Than Nothing'? Burke, Michael B.

Mental Activity And Physical Reality. Snyder, Douglas M.

PHYSICAL SCIENCES

Causes, Causity, And Energy. Castañeda, Hector–Neri.

Mathematical Beauty And Physical Science. Osborne, Harold.

Minimizing Arbitrariness: Toward A Metaphysics Of Infinitely Many Isolated Concrete Worlds. Unger, Peter.

The Role Of Interests In Science. Newton– Smith, W.

PHYSICAL THEORY(–RIES)

Realism And Truth. Devitt, Michael.

"Existential Quantifiers In Physical Theories" in *Philosophical Analysis In Latin America*, Gracia, Jorge J E and others (eds), 173–198. Moulines, C Ulises.

Explanation In Physical Cosmology: Essay In Honor Of C G Hempel's Eightieth Birthday. Kanitscheider, Bernule.

PHYSICALISM

Reductionism And Cultural Being. Smith, Joseph W.

Mind And Matter: A Problem That Refuses Dissolution. Skillen, Anthony.

On Physicalism. Melzer, Heinrich and Schachter, Josef.

Physicalism And Phenomenal Qualities. Conee, Earl.

Thalberg On Immateriality. Glassen, Peter.

PHYSICIAN(S)

Medical Ethics: The Moral Responsibilities Of Physicians. Beauchamp, Tom L and Mc Cullough, Laurence B.

Medical Nemesis: The Expropiation Of Health. Illich, Ivan.

Taking Care Of Strangers: The Rule Of Law In Doctor–Patient Relations. Burt, Robert A.

The Silent World Of Doctor And Patient. Katz, Jay.

"Doctors, Drugs Used For Pleasure And Performance, And Medical Model" in *Feeling Good And Doing Better*, Murray, Thomas H (ed), 175–186. Michels, Robert.

"Health Care Professionals And Ethical Relationships On IECs" in *Ethics Committees/ Health Care Decisions*, Cranford, Ronald (ed), 218–225. Aroskar, Mila Ann.

"When Pharmacist And Physician Disagree" in *Difficult Decisions In Medical Ethics*, Ganos, Doreen L (ed), 203–210. Shea, Michael.

"When Pharmacist And Physician Disagree" in *Difficult Decisions In Medical Ethics*, Ganos, Doreen L (ed), 211–222. Lacina, Norman.

Ethical Dilemmas Of The Doctors' Strike In Israel. Grosskopf, I and Buckman, G and Garty, M.

Excuse Me, But You Have A Melanoma On Your Neck: Unsolicited Medical Opinions. Moseley, Ray.

Rejoinder To 'Medicine As Patriarchal Religion'. Abrams, Frederick R.

The Netherlands: Tolerance And Teaching. Terborgh– Dupuis, Heleen.

Unsolicited Medical Opinion. Ratzan, Richard.

Volitional Disability And Physician Attitudes Toward Noncompliance. Ferrell, Richard B and others.

PHYSICS

Modern Logic And Quantum Mechanics. Garden, Rachel Wallace.

Order Out Of Chaos: Man's New Dialogue With Nature. Prigogine, Ilya and Stengers, Isabelle.

The Accidental Universe. Davies, P C W.

The New Scientific Spirit. Bachelard, Gaston and Goldhammer, Arthur (trans).

Albert Einstein—Versuch Einer Totalisierenden Würdigung. Zimmerman, Rainer E.

De La Physique À L'épistémologie B D'Espagnat Et I Prigogine. Gauthier, Yvon.

Die Dynamische Naturvorstellung Als Naturphilosophische Grundlage Der Heutigen Physik. Adler, Norbert.

EPR: Lessons For Metaphysics. Skyrms, Brian.

Evolutional Rheology And Mechanical Asymmetry (in Czechoslovakian). Sobotka, Zdenek.

Geochronometrie Und Geometrodynamik: Zum Problem Des Konventionalismus. Kanitscheider, Bernulf.

Invarianzgesetze Und Zeitmetrik. Kamlah, Andreas.

Is There Just One Possible World? Cushing, James T.

La Palingénesie De La Théorie Scientifique. Zaharia, D N.

La Thermodynamique Sera–T–Elle Intégrée Dans La Physique Théorique? Haas, André.

Laws Of Nature And Cosmic Coincidences. Smart, J J C.

Mesure De Spin Et Paradoxe E P R. Canals– Frau, D.

Mesure Et Théorie En Physique. Fevrier, Paulette.

Models Of Rationality In Physics. Such, Jan.

Modifications Of Logical And Ontological Foundations Of Physics Of The 20th Century (in Czechoslovakian). Ulehla, Ivan.

On A Paradox In Quantum Mechanics. Ginsberg, Allen.

Science Nominalized. Horgan, Terence.

Shimony, The Dilemma Of Quantum Mechanics, And The History Of Philosophy. Sanchez, Halley D.

Some Foundational Problems In Mathematics Suggested By Physics. Chiara, Maria Luisa Dalla.

The Influence Of Mach's Thought On Science. Hiebert, Erwin N.

The Later Work Of E Schödinger. Bertotti, Bruno.

The Philosophy And Physics Of Affecting The Past. Price, Huw.

The Physics Of David Bohm And Its Relevance To Philosophy And Theology. Russell, Robert J.

The Silence Of Physics. Meurers, Joseph.

The Use And Misuse Of Critical Gedankenexperimente. Krimsky, Sheldon.

Validity And Applicability Of Thermodynamics Out Of The Framework Of Physical Systems (in Czechoslovakian). Marvan, Milan.

Why Fire Goes Up: An Elementary Problem In Aristotle's *Physics*. Lang, Helen S.

Zum Problem Der Unendlichkeit. Titze, H.

PHYSIOLOGY

Moral Theories; Aristotle's Ethics. Price, A W.

Motion And Morality: Pierre Gassendi, Thomas Hobbes And The Mechanical World–View. Sarasohn, Lisa T.

PIAGET

Moral Development Foundations: Judeo–Christian Alternatives To Piaget/Kohlberg. Joy, Donald M (ed).

Piaget's Logic: A Critique Of Genetic Epistemology. Seltman, Muriel and Seltman, Peter.

Competition And Moral Development. Stengel, Barbara S.

Genetic Epistemology And Philosophical Epistemology. Loptson, P J and Kelly, J W.

Genetic Epistemology And The Child's Understanding Of Logic. Smith, Leslie.

Jean Piaget Y La Estructuración Genética Del Lenguaje. Beuchot, Mauricio.

Moral Reasoning And Action In Young Children. Hannaford, Robert V.

Philosophy, Psychology, And Piaget: A Reply To Loptson And Kelly. Smith, Leslie.

Prigogine's And Piaget's Theory Of Dynamic Equilibrium And Dialectical And Materialist Conception Of Human Evolution (in Czechoslovakian). Linhart, J.

Significato E Attualità Dell'Epistemologia Genetica Di Jean Piaget. Simonetti, Iside.

The Knowing Subject. Code, Lorraine B.

The Relation Between Epistemology And Psychology. Goldman, Alvin I.

PICASSO

Developmental Psychology And The Problem Of Artistic Change. Bornstein, Marc.

PICO

Des *Conclusiones* Aux *Disputationes*: Numérologie Et Mathématiques Chez Jean Pic De La Mirandole. Valcke, Louis.

PICTORIALISM

The Debate About Mental Imagery. Tye, Michael.

PICTURE(S)

On The Fidelity Of Pictures: A Critique Of Goodman's Disjunction Of Perspective And Realism. Topper, David.

Pictorial Assertion. Korsmeyer, Carolyn.

POLISH

Die Rechtstheorie In Polen Im XX: Jahrhundert. Opalek, Kazimierz.

Karl Marx—A Great Friend Of Poland. Zuraw, Jozef.

The History Of Marxist Ideology In Poland. Dziamski, Seweryn.

The Idea Of Socialism In Polish Social Thought At The Turn Of The 19th Century. Wojnar–Sujecka, Janina.

The Marxist Trend In Polish Socialism. Mackiewicz, Witold.

POLITICAL ACTION(S)

Christian Ethics And Political Action. Messer, Donald E.

Reflection And Action. Rotenstreich, Nathan.

Beyond Process Theology? Sontag, Frederick.

Political Thought As Traditionary Action: The Critical Response To Skinner And Pocock. Janssen, Peter L.

The Character Of The Interaction Of Working And Political Activity Of Personality (in Czechoslovakian). Rjadová, Vera and Rjadovoj, Alexandr.

POLITICAL PHIL

see also Authority(–ties), Communism, Democracy, Ethics, Freedom, Liberalism, Right(s), Social Phil, Society(–ties), State(s), Utopia

A Theory Of Law. Soper, Philip.

Against Fate: An Essay On Personal Dignity. Tinder, Glenn.

American Political Thought: The Philosophic Dimension Of American Statesmanship, Second Edition. Frisch, Morton J (ed) and Stevens, Richard G (ed).

Aristotle: The Politics. Lord, Carnes (trans).

Between Tradition And Revolution: The Hegelian Transformation Of Political Philosophy. Riedel, Manfred.

Beyond Domination: An Essay In The Political Philosophy Of Education. White, Patricia and Peters, R S (ed).

Cuban And North American Marxism. D' Angelo, Edward (ed).

Essays In Jurisprudence And Philosophy. Hart, H L A (ed).

Ideology, Philosophy And Politics. Parel, Anthony (ed).

Law, Economics, And Philosophy. Kuperberg, Mark (ed) and Beitz, Charles (ed).

Perspectives On Political Ethics: An Ecumenical Enquiry. Srisang, Koson (ed).

Political Writings. Hegel, Georg Wilhelm.

Reinhold Niebuhr: His Religious, Social And Political Thought. Kegley, Charles W (ed).

Social And Political Ethics. Brodsky, Garry (ed) and Troyer, John (ed) and Vance, David (ed).

The Decline Of Juridical Reason: Doctrine And Theory In The Legal Order. Simmonds, N E.

The Emergence Of Dialectical Theory: Philosophy And Political Inquiry. Warren, Scott.

The Place Of Ideology In Political Life. Manning, D J and Robinson, T J.

The Politics Of Salvation: The Hegelian Idea Of The State. Lakeland, Paul.

The Politics Of Heaven & Hell: Christian Themes From Classical, Medieval And Modern Political Philosophy. Schall, James V.

The Politics Of Moderation: An Interpretation Of Plato's "Republic". Wilson, John F.

The Recovery Of Political Theory: Limits And Possibilities. Havard, William C.

The Two Cities Of Otto, Bishop Of Freising: A Study In Neo–Augustinian Political Theory. Lavers, George J.

The Unity Of Law And Morality: A Refutation Of Legal Positivism. Detmold, M J.

Über Den Inhalt Sozial–Politischer Gesetze. Huar, Ulrich.

'Romania's Marx' And The National Question: Constantin Dobrogeanu–Gherea. Shafir, Michael.

"Eigentum Ist Nicht Eigentum", Zur Rechtfertigbarkeit Des Eigentums. Kohler, Georg.

"Kierkegaard, Abraham And The Modern State" in *History Of Philosophy In Making*, Thro, Linus J (ed), 165–176. Elrod, John W.

A Brief Discussion Of Marx's Theory Of Alienation. Tianyu, Cao.

A Critica Glucksmanniana Do Poder. Morais, Carlos.

A Critique Of Marxist Legal Theoretical Constructs. Hyden, Timothy M.

A Defense Of Humanism. Ruoshui, Wang.

A Little Platonic Heresy For The Eighties. Nails, Debra.

A Pamphlet Attributed To John Toland And An Unpublished Reply By Archbishop William King. Kelly, Patrick.

A Political Theorist From Eastern Europe. Tar, Zoltán.

African Socialism And Nyerere. Okolo, Chukwudum Barnabas.

Ancient Features Of The Modern State. Sternberger, Dolf.

Art D'écrire Et Pratique Politique De Jean–Jacques Rousseau (I). Marshall, Terence.

Art D'écrire Et Pratique Politique De Jean–Jacques Rousseau (II). Marshall, Terence.

Aspects Of Leon Green's Tort Theory: Causation And The Role Of The Judge. Winslade, William J.

Aufgaben Und Schwierigkeiten Der Analytischen Rechtstheorie. Weinberger, Ota.

Auguste Comte And The Withering–Away Of The State. Vernon, Richard.

Authority And Justification. Raz, Joseph.

Bürgerliche Konzeptionen Über Die Gesellschaftliche Entwicklung/Revolutionären Prozess–Lateinamerikas. Reuter, Walter.

Bedingungen Einer Rekonstruktion Rechtlichen Argumentierens: Zum Verhältnis Von Philosophie Und Rechtswissenschaft. Heyen, Erk Volkmar.

Begriff Und Logik Des "Öffentlichen Interesses". Fach, Wolfgang.

Bertrand Russell, Karl Marx, And *German Social Democracy* Revisited. Gallina, Paul.

Bribery, Extortion, And "The Foreign Corrupt Practices Act". Carson, Thomas L.

Cicero's Paradoxes And His Idea Of Utility. Nicgorski, Walter.

Citizenship With A Feminist Face: The Problem With Maternal Thinking. Dietz, Mary G.

Comments On A S Cua's "Confucian Vision And Human Community". Smith, John.

Confucian Vision And Human Community. Cua, Antonio S.

Connolly, Coucault, And Truth. Taylor, Charles.

Conservatism Under Napoleon: The Political Writings Of Joseph Fiévée. Popkin, Jeremy D.

Consistency, Completeness And Decidability With Respect To The Logic Of Law And The Provability Of Juristic Arguments. Brkić, Jovan.

Constitutional System And Social Change: Concerning A Publication By Frank Rotter. Souto, Cláudio.

Das Eigentum Als Eschatologische Potenz: Zur Eigentumskonzeption Von Karl Marx. Künzli, Arnold.

Das Schwierige Recht Der Systemtheoretischen Soziologie: Zur Rechtssoziologie Von Niklas Luhmann. Folkers, Horst.

Das Verhältnis Von "Person" Und "Eigentum" In Hegels Philosophie Des Rechts. Meyer, Rudolf W.

Der 'Labeling Approach'—Ein Paradigmawechsel In Der Modernen Kriminalsoziologie. Kunz, Karl–Ludwig.

Der Inhalt Des Begriffs "Nation" In Der Spätbürgerlichen Ideologie Der BRD. Lange, Gunter.

Der Kampf Der KPD Gegen Die Ideologie Des Hitlerfaschismus. Ullrich, Horst.

Der Rassenwahn Als Feind Des Menschilichen Fortschritts. Lukács, G.

Der Streit Um Die Eigentumsordnung Des Verfassungsentwurfes 1977. Müller, Georg.

Did German Classical Philosophy Simply "End"? Ruoshui, Wang.

Did The Greeks Invent Democracy? Veyne, Paul.

Die Bedeutung Des Vaterlandsbegriffes Für Die Erziehung Zum Sozialistischen Patriotismus. Abelmann, Xenia.

Die Frage Von Krieg Und Frieden In Der Weltanschaulichen Auseinandersetzung. Hahn, Erich.

Die Kategorie Der Sache. Nef, Robert.

Die Lehre Vom Gerechten Krieg Bei Grotius Und Leibniz Und Ihre Bedeutung Für Die Gegenwart. Serra, Antonio Truyol.

Die Reaktionäre Marxkritik Nach Dem Gothaer Programm Der Deutschen Sozialdemokratie. Kopf, Eike.

Die Rechtstheorie In Polen Im XX: Jahrhundert. Opalek, Kazimierz.

Die Sozialpflichtigkeit Des Eigentums: Gesichtspunkte Der Christlichen Sozialethik. Furger, Franz.

Die Unmögliche Rechtsphilosophie: Zu Hans Ryffels Rechtsund Staatsphilosophie. Gil– Cremades, Juan–Jose.

Discretionary Waiver Of Juvenile Court Jurisdiction: An Invitation To Procedural Arbitrariness. Wizner, Stephen.

Discussing The Problem Of Alienation. Ruoshui, Wang.

Distributive Justice In Aristotle's Ethics And Politics. Keyt, David.

Edmund Burke Et Joseph De Maistre. Fuchs, Michel.

Eigentum Und Teilungsvertrag: Zu Kants Begründung Des Eigentumsrechts. Schmidlin, Bruno.

Eigentum Und Verfügungsmacht: Zum Korporativen Eigentum. Bornschier, Volker.

Eigentum Und Macht In Der Modernen Industriegesellschaft. Levy, René.

Eigentum Und Lebenswelt: Zum Wandel Des Eigentumsverständnisses In Der Komplexen Gesellschaft. Wildermuth, Armin.

Eigentum Und Ungleichheit: Rousseaus Eigentumslehre. Ryffel, Hans.

Eigentum—Moralität. Schmidig, Dominik.

El Papel Del Leninismo En "Historia Y Conciencia De Clase". Giglioli, Giovanna.

El Poder En Michel Foucault. Parent, Juan.

El Poder En Aristoteles Y Romano Guardini. Rodriguez, Virgilio R.

Epistemology Must Not Lose Sight Of Man. Ruoshui, Wang.

Erfahrungen Aus Der Arbeit Am Lehrbuch "Wissenschaftlicher Kommunismus". Grosser, Gunther.

Families In Need Of Supervision. Leddy, Daniel D .

Finitud, Poder, Ternura. Betancourt, Raul Fornet.

Food And Freedom In *The Flounder*. Pitkin, Hanna F.

Formal Justice And Township Justice. Hund, John.

Formal Justice, Moral Commitment, And Judicial Precedent. Lyons, David.

Francis Bacon Und Hobbes' Widmungsbrief Zu *De Cive*. Schuhmann, Karl.

Freiheit Und Eignetum. Ryffel, Hans.

Freirecht—Revisited, Emphasizing Its Property–Space. Schmidt, Joachim K H W.

Friedenskampf Und Philosophie. Buhr, Manfred.

Friends Of Leomofos. Collins, Aaron S.

Gallina And Pitt: Similarities And Differences. Pitt, Jack.

Gesetzgeberrecht Vs Richterrecht In Der Eigentumskonzeption Des Verfassungsentwurfs. Brühlmeier, Daniel.

Gesetzmässigkeiten Des Revolutionären Prozesses. Eichhorn, Wolfgang.

Gleichheit Und Eigentum: Metaethische Und Normative Bemerkungen Zum Verfassungsentwurf. Hügli, Anton.

Harrington's Elusive Balance. Reeve, Andrew.

Hart, Legal Rules And Palm Tree Justice. Waluchow, Wilfrid J.

Hegel And Roman Liberalism. Cristi, F R.

Hobbes, Spinoza, Rousseau Et La Formation De L'idée De Démocratie Comme Mesure De La Légitimité Du Pouvoir Politique. Tinland, Franck.

Hobbes's State Of War. Hampton, Jean.

Hope And Its Ramifications For Politics. Dauenhauer, Bernard P.

Hugo Grotius And The History Of Political Thought. Haakonssen, Knud.

Ideology And Social Goals. Mohapatra, P K.

Incorrigibility Laws: The State's Role In Resolving Intrafamily Conflict. Guggenheim, Martin.

Insiders And Outsiders Models Of Deviance And Jurisprudence. Hund, John.

John Locke And The Antebellum Defense Of Slavery. Loewenberg, Robert J.

Justifying Departures From Equal Treatment. Murphy, Jeffrie G.

Justifying Law: An Explanation Of The Deep Structure Of American Law. Gibbons, Hugh.

POLITICAL THEORY

On The "Essential Contestedness" Of Political Concepts. Swanton, Christine.
On The Political Rhetoric Of Freud's Individual Psychology. Brunner, José.
Ontological Grounding Of A Political Ethics: On The Metaphysics Of Commitment To The Future Of Man. Jonas, Hans.
Philosophy And Policy. Thompson, Dennis.
Political Theory And Politics: The Case Of Leo Strauss. Gunnell, John G.
Provisionality In Plato's Ideal State. Klosko, George.
Remarks On The Ontology Of "Right" And "Left". Spaemann, Robert.
Socrates On The Problem Of Political Science Education. Pangle, Thomas L.
The Esoteric Philosophy Of Leo Strauss. Drury, S B.
W E B Du Bois: A Perspective On The Bases Of His Political Thought. Reed, Adolph L.
Yates On Feyerabend's Democratic Relativism. Alford, C Fred.

POLITICS

Christian Ethics And Political Action. Messer, Donald E.
Heidegger: Perspektiven Zur Deutung Seines Werkes. Pöggeler, Otto (ed).
How Democracies Perish. Revel, Jean–François.
Polis And Praxis. Dallmayr, Fred R.
Progress And Chaos: Modernization And Rediscovery Of Religion And Authority. Groth, Alexander J.
Renaissance Eloquence: Studies In The Theory And Practice Of Renaissance Rhetoric. Murphy, James J (ed).
The Politics Of Interpretation. Mitchell, W J T.
Wealth And Virtue: The Shaping Of Political Economy In The Scottish Enlightenment. Hont, Istvan (ed) and Ignatieff, Michael (ed).
Über Den Inhalt Sozial–Politischer Gesetze. Huar, Ulrich.
"Envy As Personal Phenomenon And As Politics" in *International Kierkegaard Commentary*, Perkins, Robert L (ed), 107–132. Perkins, Robert L.
"Ethical Decision Making In The Politics Of Archaeology" in *Ethics And Values In Archaeology*, Green, Ernestene L (ed), 243–263. Knudson, Ruthann.
"Foreign Aid: Justice For Whom" in *The Search For Justice*, Taitte, W Lawson (ed), 127–162. Rostow, W W.
"Ideology And Technology, Truth And Power" in *Ideology, Philosophy And Politics*, Parel, Anthony (ed), 93–110. Cooper, Barry.
"Ideology And The Epistemology Of Politics" in *Ideology, Philosophy And Politics*, Parel, Anthony (ed), 77–92. Meynell, Hugo.
"Ideology And Political Culture" in *Ideology, Philosophy And Politics*, Parel, Anthony (ed), 111–138. Mullins, Willard A.
"L'allégorie De La Caverne": République En Petit. Gendron, Edmond.
"The Concept Of 'trust' In The Politics Of John Locke" in *Philosophy In History*, Rorty, Richard and others (ed), 279–302. Dunn, John.
"What Do Religion, Politics, And Science Each Contribute To Society" in *The Good Life And Its Pursuit*, Dougherty, Jude P (ed), 209–232. Richardson, Herbert.
Academic Freedom: A Structural Approach. Aronowitz, Stanley.
Algunas Preguntas Sobre Etica. Parent, Juan M.
Background And Work Experience Correlates Of The Ethics And Effect Of Organizational Politics. Zahra, Shaker A.
Bannisterless Politics: Hannah Arendt And Her Children. Mc Kenna, George.
Benedetto Croce, Philosopher, Ethics And Politics (in Hungarian). Bausola, Adriano.
Between Assured Destruction And Nuclear Victory: The Case For The "Mad–Plus" Posture. Art, Robert J.
Dewey's Method Of Social Reconstruction. Campbell, James.
El Pensamiento Filosofico–Religioso De Manuel Demetrio Pizarro. Caturelli, Alberto.
Elementos De Filosofia Politica No Concilio Vaticano II. Borges, J F Pereira.
Hegel's Early Thought. Lin, He.
Interpreting The Enlightenment: A Political Approach. Crocker, Lester G.
Kant's System And (Its) Politics. Howard, Dick.
La Società Aperta Nel Pensiero Politico Del '900 (Bergson, Popper, Maritain). Possenti, Vittorio.
Land's End. Cocks, Edmond D.
Le "Reflections On The Revolution In France": Categorie Dell'Agire Politico E Filosofia Della Storia In Edmund Burke. Panella, Giuseppe.
Political Finance In The United States: A Survey Of Research. Beitz, Charles R.
Political Technics/Technological Politics: MIRVS Dangerous Agenda. Kilbourne, Lawrence.
Politics Or Nothing: Nazism's Origin In Scientific Contempt For Politics. Neumann, Harry.
Politiques Du Langage. Moreau, Pierre–Francois.
Science, Technology, And Political Decision. Radnitzky, Gerard.
The Compatibility Of Richard Price's Politics And His Ethics. Peterson, Susan Rae.
The Difference Of The Italian Philosophical Culture. Perniola, Mario.
The Idea Of Socialism In Polish Social Thought At The Turn Of The 19th Century. Wojnar– Sujecka, Janina.
The Italian Difference And The Politics Of Culture. White, Hayden.
The Science Of A Legislator In James Mackintosh's Moral Philosophy. Haakonssen, Knud.
The World Socio–Economic And Political Crisis Calls For Changes In The Position And Social Role Of Sports. Petrović, Kresimir.
Who Is Fooled By The "Cunning Of Reason"? Drydyk, J J.
Zur Aktualität Der Politischen Theologie Ulrich Zwinglis. Winzeler, Peter.

POLLOCK, J

In Defense Of A Nontraditional Theory Of Memory. Naylor, Andrew.

POLYNOMIALS

Complete Second Order Spectra. Scarpellini, Bruno.
Formalism And Application Of Catastrophe Theory. Poole Jr, Charles P.
Homogeneous Forms In Two Ordinal Variables. Hickman, John L.

POOR

"The Poor Have A Claim Found In The Law Of Nature": William Paley And The Rights Of The Poor. Horne, Thomas A.
The Role Of Economics And Ethical Principles In Determining U S Policies Toward Poor Nations. Piderit, John J.

POP ART

The Visual Arts As Language. Barela, Robert E.

POPPER

Observation, Experiment, And Hypothesis In Modern Physical Science. Achinstein, Peter (ed) and Hannaway, Owen (ed).
Popper And The Human Sciences. Currie, Gregory (ed) and Musgrave, Alan (ed).
Science, Reason & Religion. Stanesby, Derek.
The Sign Of Three. Sebok, Thomas A (ed) and Eco, Umberto (ed).
"Methodological Individualism" in *Popper And The Human Sciences*, Currie, Gregory (ed), 57–72. Chalmers, A F.
"On Popper's Conventionalism" in *Methodology, Metaphysics And The History Of Science*, Cohen, Robert S (ed), 263–282. Ströker, Elisabeth.
"Popper And The Mind–Body Problem" in *Popper And The Human Sciences*, Currie, Gregory (ed), 45–56. Puccetti, Roland.
"Popper And Liberalism" in *Popper And The Human Sciences*, Currie, Gregory (ed), 89–104. Ryan, Alan.
"Popper And German Social Philosophy" in *Popper And The Human Sciences*, Currie, Gregory (ed), 165–184. Ackermann, Robert.
"Popper's Solution To The Problem Of Induction" in *Philosophical Analysis In Latin America*, Gracia, Jorge J E and others (eds), 381–396. Lluberes, Pedro.
"Retrospective *Vs* Prospective Testing Of Aetiological Hypotheses" in *Testing Scientific Theories*, Earman, John (ed), 315–348. Grünbaum, Adolf.
"Third World Epistemology" in *Popper And The Human Sciences*, Currie, Gregory (ed), 1–12. Cohen, L J.
A Note On Popper, Propensities, And The Two–Slit Experiment. Milne, Peter.
A Sociological Theory Of Objectivity. Bloor, David.
An Egalitarian Epistemology: A Note On E P Thompson's Critique Of Althusser And Popper. Green, David G.
Bemerkungen Zu Roehles Arbeit Und Zur Axiomatik. Popper, Karl.
Conjectures And Rational Preferences. Levy, Robert J.
Critique Du Rationalisme Critique. Largeault, Jean.
Das Problem Der Rationalität. Agassi, Joseph.
Der Kritische Rationalismus Und Kant. Richter, Gundrun.
Empiricus Mogelijkheden; Sleutelbegrip Van De Wetenschapsfilosofie. Kuipers, Theo A F.
Es El Psicoanálisis Una Pseudo–Ciencia? Rush, Alan A.
Indéterminisme Et Interactionnisme Chez Popper. Quilliot, Roland.
Karl Popper Et La Naissance De La Géologie. Gohau, Gabriel.
Knowledge And Certainty. Mclean, Don.
Konventionalistische Argumente In Poppers Wissenschaftsphilosophie. Ströker, Elisabeth.
Logik Und Dialektik Als Wissenschaftsmethoden. Tsouyopoulos, Nelly.
Metodologias E Historia De Las Ciencias. Marqués, Gustavo.
O'Hear On An Argument Of Popper's. Glassen, Peter.
On Characterizing Unary Probability Functions And Truth–Value Functions. Leblanc, Hugues.
On Popper's Use Of Tarski's Theory Of Truth. Grattan– Guinness, I.
On Popper's Implicit Hegelianism. Yulina, N S.
On The Impossibility Of Inductive Probability. Redhead, Michael.
On The Status Of Statistical Inferences. Pitowsky, Itamar.
On Theoretical Terms. Dilworth, Craig.
One World Or Many: Popper's Three World Theory And The Problem Of Scientific Determinism. Baigrie, Brian.
Periodization, Holism And Historicism: A Reply To Jacobs. Tilley, Nicholas.
Popper And Metaphysical Skepticism. Waterhouse, Joseph.
Popper En Question. Reichberg, G.
Popper Had A Brand New Bag. Brown, James M.
Popper's 'World 3' And The Problem Of The Printed Line. Church, Rolin.
Popper's Piecemeal Engineering: What Is Good For Science Is Not Always Good For Society. Irzik, Gürol.
Popperian And Kuhnian Theories Of Truth And The Imputation Of Relativism. Edison, J.
Poppers Zwei Definitionsvarianten Von 'Falsifizierbar': Eine Logische Notiz Zu Einer Klassischen Stelle Aus Der *Logik Der Forschung*. Dorn, Georg J W.
Probabilities, Propensities, And Chances. Howson, Colin.
Probability, Symmetry And Frequency. Dawid, A P.
Réflexions Sur Popper. Radnitzky, Gerard.
Reply To Peter Glassen's "O'Hear On An Argument Of Popper's". O' Hear, Anthony.
Science And Pseudoscience. Lakatos, Imre.
Should Philosophers Of Science Consider Scientific Discovery? Pietruska– Madej, Elzbieta.
Some Epistemological Trends In Philosophy Of Science. Shekhawat, Virendra.
Some Problems With Falsificationism In Economics. Caldwell, Bruce J.
The Criteria Of Objectivity: Physical Science And The Challenge Of Phenomenology. Smitheram, Verner.
The Role Of Problems And Problem Solving In Popper's Early Work On Psychology. Petersen, Arne Friemuth.
The Use And Misuse Of Critical Gedankenexperimente. Krimsky, Sheldon.
What Is Wrong With Verisimilitude? Smith, Joseph W.
Zur Sowjetphilosophischen Kritik Der "Idealistischen" Erkenntnistheorie. Weinzierl, Emil.

PREDICATION

Análisis Propositional Y Ontologia. Sanchez, Juan Carlos.

How Things Are: Studies In Predication And The History Of Philosophy And Science. Bogen, James (ed) and Mc Guire, James E (ed).

'Vlastos On Pauline Predication'. Malcolm, John F.

"Form And Predication In Aristotle's *Metaphysics*" in *How Things Are*, Bogen, James (ed), 59–84. Lewis, Frank A.

"Forms And Compounds" in *How Things Are*, Bogen, James (ed), 85–100. Modrak, D K.

"On The Origins Of Some Aristotelian Theses About Predication" in *How Things Are*, Bogen, James (ed), 101–132. Code, Alan.

"Phenomenalism, Relations, And Monadic Representation" in *How Things Are*, Bogen, James (ed), 205–234. Mc Guire, James E.

"Prediction, Truth, And Transworld Identity In Leibniz" in *How Things Are*, Bogen, James (ed), 235–284. Adams, Robert M.

"Things Versus 'Hows', Or Ockham On Predication And Ontology" in *How Things Are*, Bogen, James (ed), 175–188. Adams, Marilyn McCord.

"Towards A Theory Of Predication" in *How Things Are*, Bogen, James (ed), 285–322. Sellars, Wilfrid.

"Zeno's Stricture And Predication In Plato, Aristotle, And Plotinus" in *How Things Are*, Bogen, James (ed), 21–58. Turnbull, Robert G.

A Note On Inherence. Hetherington, Stephen C.

Addis On Analysing Disposition Concepts. Wilson, Fred.

Assertion And Predication In Husserl. Pietersma, H.

Bezeichnen Und Behaupten. Nuchelmans, Gabriel.

Die Platonischen Ideen Als Gegenstände Sprachlicher Referenz. Graeser, Andreas.

Frege And Abstraction. Angelelli, Ignacio.

Predication. Abraham, William E.

Prolegomena To A Study Of Extrinsic Denomination In The Work Of Francis Suarez, S J. Doyle, John P.

The Proof Of Pauline Self–Predication In The *Phaedo*. Morris, T F.

Zur Frage Der IV: Syllogistischen Figur In Der "Dissertatio De Arte Commbinatoria", Eine Jugendsünde Leibnizens? Moriconi, Enrico and Offenberger, Niels.

PREDICTION

Probability And Evidence. Horwich, Paul.

Progress In Utility And Risk Theory. Hagen, Ole (ed) and Wenstop, Fred (ed).

Another Look At The Predictivist Thesis. Jones, William B.

Science And Pseudoscience. Lakatos, Imre.

The Direction Of Causation And The Newcomb Paradox (in Hebrew). Aharoni, Ron.

PREDISPOSITION(S)

The New Technologies Of Genetic Screening. Lappé, Marc and Murray, Thomas H.

PREFERENCE(S)

A Remark On The Connexion Between Procedure And Value. Hederstierna, Anders.

Measurement Of Preference And Utility. Händler, Ernst W.

Some Reasoning About Preferences. Schueler, G F.

Some Reasoning About Preferences: A Response To Essays By Person, Feldman, And Schueler. Hare, R M.

The Ordinal Utility Under Uncertainty And The Measure Of Risk Aversion In Terms Of Preferences. Montesano, Aldo.

PREFERENCE LOGIC

Utility Theory And Preference Logic. Trapp, Rainer W.

PREJUDICE(S)

Vico And Collingwood On 'The Conceit Of Scholars'. Todd, Joan and Cono, Joseph.

PREPARATION

Thoughts On The Moral Relationship Of Intent And Training In Sport. Thomas, Carolyn E.

PRESCRIPTION

"The Incoherence Of Universal Prescriptivism" in *The Georgetown Symposium On Ethics*, Porreco, Rocco (ed), 145–158. Beatty, Joseph.

Is–Ought: Prescribing And A Present Controversy. Schultz, Janice L.

Prescription, Explication And The Social Construction Of Emotion. Armon– Jones, Claire.

The Origins And Functions Of Evaluative Criteria. Sadler, Royce D.

PRESCRIPTIVISM

Moral Scepticism And Moral Conduct. Mac Kenzie, J C.

PRESENCE

Heidegger/Derrida—Presence. Sallis, John.

PRESENT

Rasgos Y Ambigüedades Del Venir A La Presencia De Lo Presente. Walton, Roberto J.

PRESENTATION

When A Poem Refers. Martland, T R.

PRESOCRATICS

Ancient Greek Philosophy: Sourcebook And Perspective. Yartz, Frank J.

The Presocratic Philosophers. Kirk, G S and Raven, J E and Schofield, M.

Situación Actual De Los Estudios En Torno A La Filosofía Presocrática: Filósofos O Filólogos? Muñoz, Alfredo Troncoso.

PRESTES, L

Vargas And Prestes: A Comparison Between The Labourism And Communism In Brazil (in Portuguese). Piozzi, Patrizia.

PRESUPPOSITION(S)

"Descriptions, Meaning And Presupposition" in *Philosophical Analysis In Latin America*, Gracia, Jorge J E and others (eds), 219–242. Rossi, Alejandro.

History And Reality: R G Collingwood's Theory Of Absolute Presuppositions. Trainor, Paul J.

Practice As Presupposition Of Science (in Czechoslovakian). Znoj, M.

PRICE

The Compatibility Of Richard Price's Politics And His Ethics. Peterson, Susan Rae.

PRICE(S)

Professional Advertising: Price Fixing And Professional Dignity Versus The Public's Right To A Free Market. Leiser, Burton M.

PRIEST, G

A Simple Solution To Mortensen And Priest's Truth Teller Paradox. Wayne Smith, Joseph.

PRIGOGINE, I

An Attempt At The Utilization Of Prigogine's Thermodynamics In American Futurology (in Czechoslovakian). Hohos, Ladislav.

Biological Conception Of Evolution And The Problem Of Thermodynamics From The Standpoint Of The Work Of I Prigogine (in Czechoslovakian). Novák, Vladimir J A.

De La Physique À L'épistémologie B D'Espagnat Et I Prigogine. Gauthier, Yvon.

Dialectical Unity Of The Dynamic And The Statistical In Nature And Society And Prigogine's Universal Evolution Theory (in Czechoslovakian). Skramovska, Svatoslava and Celeda, J.

Prigogine's And Piaget's Theory Of Dynamic Equilibrium And Dialectical And Materialist Conception Of Human Evolution (in Czechoslovakian). Linhart, J.

Prigogine's Situationism (in Czechoslovakian). Jirásek, Jaroslav.

Prigogine's Characteristics Of The Results Of Ancient Philosophy (in Czechslovakian). Mráz, Milan.

The Vital Attitude Of Man From The Standpoint Of Prigogine's Thermodynamics (in Czechoslovakian). Stoll, Ivan.

PRIMARY QUALITY(–TIES)

A Functionalist Interpretation Of Locke's Theory Of Simple Ideas. Vinci, Thomas.

PRIMITIVE

Frederick Engels And Contemporary Problems Concerning The History Of Primitive Society. Bromlei, Iu V and Pershits, A I.

PRINCIPLE(S)

"Existential Quantifiers In Physical Theories" in *Philosophical Analysis In Latin America*, Gracia, Jorge J E and others (eds), 173–198. Moulines, C Ulises.

Der Prinzipienbegriff In Der Marxistisch–Leninistischen Philosophie. Kirchhöfer, Dieter.

Epistemic Universalizability Principles. Brueckner, Anthony.

Informal Logic And The Theory Of Reasoning. Finocchiaro, Maurice A.

PRIOR, A

Logic And Contingent Existence. Lopston, Peter.

Once Upon A Tense. Verkuyl, H J and Le Loux– Schuringa, J A.

PRIORITY

The Priority Of Needs. Goodin, Robert E.

PRISON(S)

Friendly Persuasion: Quakers, Liberal Toleration, And The Birth Of The Prison. Dumm, Thomas L.

Imprisonment. O' Hear, Anthony.

PRISONER'S DILEMMA

Hobbes As Moralist. Farrell, Daniel M.

Market Contractarianism And The Unanimity Rule. Coleman, Jules L.

Rationality, Group Choice And Expected Utility. Richter, Reed.

The Iterated Versions Of Newcomb's Problem And The Prisoner's Dilemma. Sorensen, Roy A.

The Martyr's Dilemma. Moore, F C T.

The Value Of Information In Newcomb's Problem And The Prisoners' Dilemma. Snow, Paul.

PRIVACY

Emily Dickinson And The Problem Of Others. Benfey, Christopher E G.

Groping For Ethics In Journalism. Goodwin, H Eugene.

Philosophy In Process, V8. Weiss, Paul.

'My Husband Won't Tell The Children!'. Dubler, Nancy Neveloff and Schneiderman, Lawrence J.

"Implications Of Constitutional Right Of Privacy For Control Of Drugs" in *Feeling Good And Doing Better*, Murray, Thomas H (ed), 129–156. Schwartz, Robert L.

A Critical Evaluation Of Altman's Definition Of Privacy As A Dialectic Process. Foddy, W H.

A Phenomenological Account Of The Linguistic Mediation Of The Public And The Private. Reeder, Harry P.

Divine Omniscience And Human Privacy. Lackey, Douglas P.

Excuse Me, But You Have A Melanoma On Your Neck: Unsolicited Medical Opinions. Moseley, Ray.

Privacy And Public Moral Education: Aristotle's Critique Of The Family. Blits, Jan H.

Unsolicited Medical Opinion. Ratzan, Richard.

PRIVATE

"The Private Language Argument" in *Philosophical Analysis In Latin America*, Gracia, Jorge J E and others (eds), 255–276. Villanueva, Enrique.

PRIVATE LANGUAGE(S)

Kripke On Private Language. Hoffman, Paul.

Kripke's Account Of The Argument Against Private Language. Wright, Crispin.

L'argument Du Langage Privé. Sauve, Denis.

What Does The Private Language Argument Prove? Hanfling, Oswald.

PRIVILEGE(S)

Rights. White, Alan R.

Use Of Privileged Information For Attorney Self–Interest: A Moral Dilemma. Seigel, Michael.

PROBABILISM

Are Probabilism And Special Relativity Incompatible? Maxwell, Nicholas.

Conflicting Intuitions About Causation. Suppes, Patrick.

PROBABILISM

Probabilistic Causality And Simpson's Paradox. Otte, Richard.

PROBABILITY

Modern Logic And Quantum Mechanics. Garden, Rachel Wallace.

Probability And Evidence. Horwich, Paul.

Probability, Objectivity And Evidence. Benenson, F C.

Rational Decision And Causality. Eells, Ellery.

Theory And Measurement. Kyburg Jr, Henry E.

"Bayesianism With A Human Face" in *Testing Scientific Theories*, Earman, John (ed), 133–156. Jeffrey, Richard.

"Bootstrapping Without Bootstraps" in *Testing Scientific Theories*, Earman, John (ed), 43–54. Edidin, Aron.

"Consistency Tests In Estimating The Completeness Of The Fossil Record" in *Testing Scientific Theories*, Earman, John (ed), 413–476. Meehl, Paul E.

"Explanations Of Irrelevance" in *Testing Scientific Theories*, Earman, John (ed), 55–66. Horwich, Paul.

"Interpretation Theory And Experiment" in *Observation, Experiment, Hypothesis In Modern Physical Science*, Achinstein, Peter (ed), 175–204. Joseph, Geoffrey.

"Newton's Demonstration Of Universal Gravitation" in *Testing Scientific Theories*, Earman, John (ed), 179–200. Laymon, Ronald.

"Old Evidence And Logical Omniscience In Bayesian Confirmation Theory" in *Testing Scientific Theories*, Earman, John (ed), 99–132. Garber, Daniel.

"On Testing And Evidence" in *Testing Scientific Theories*, Earman, John (ed), 3–26. Glymour, Clark.

"Probability And Art Of Judgment" in *Observation, Experiment, And Hypothesis In Modern Physical Science*, Achinstein, Peter (ed), 95–126. Jeffrey, R C.

"Testing Theoretical Hypotheses" in *Testing Scientific Theories*, Earman, John (ed), 269–298. Giere, Ronald N.

"The Deductive Model: Does It Have Instances" in *Testing Scientific Theories*, Earman, John (ed), 299–312. Kyburg, Henry.

"Theory Comparison And Relevant Evidence" in *Testing Scientific Theories*, Earman, John (ed), 27–42. Van Fraassen, Bas C.

"Three Ways To Give A Probability Assignment A Memory" in *Testing Scientific Theories*, Earman, John (ed), 157–162. Skyrms, Brian.

"Why Glymour Is A Bayesian" in *Testing Scientific Theories*, Earman, John (ed), 69–98. Rosenkrantz, Roger.

A Historical Comment Concerning Novel Confirmation. Good, I J.

A New Basis For Decision Theory. Davidson, Donald.

A Note On Popper, Propensities, And The Two–Slit Experiment. Milne, Peter.

A Problem About Frequencies In Direct Inference. Leeds, Stephen.

An Approximation Of Carnap's Optimum Estimation Method. Kuipers, Theo A F.

An Undecidable Problem In Finite Combinatorics. Compton, Kevin J.

Analysis Of Quantum Probability Theory I. Van Aken, James.

Another Reply To Leeds: "A Problem About Frequencies In Direct Inference". Kyburg, Henry E.

Bayesianism And Support By Novel Facts. Howson, Colin.

Calibration, Coherence, And Scoring Rules. Seidenfeld, Teddy.

Croyances, Dispositions Et Probabilités (Peirce Et Ramsey). Engel, Pascal.

Ethical Problems In Arguments From Potentiality. Kottow, Michael.

Foundations For Direct Inference. Pollock, John L.

Generalising The Probabilistic Semantics Of Conditionals. Appiah, Anthony.

Horwich's Justification Of Induction. Chihara, Charles S.

Maximum Entropy Inference As A Special Case Of Conditionalization. Skyrms, Brian.

Nomic Probability. Pollock, John L.

On Characterizing Unary Probability Functions And Truth–Value Functions. Leblanc, Hugues.

On Defining Information. Szaniawski, Klemens.

On Inductive Support And Some Recent Tricks. Gaifman, Haim.

On The Impossibility Of Inductive Probability. Redhead, Michael.

On The Status Of Statistical Inferences. Pitowsky, Itamar.

Optique, Méchanique Et Calcul Des Chances Chez Huygens Et Spinoza (Sur Quelques Paradigmes Possibles Du Discours Philosophique). Parrochia, Daniel.

Postscript To 'A Problem About Frequencies In Direct Inference'. Leeds, Stephen.

Prior Probabilities. Skilling, John.

Probabilistic Causality Emancipated. Dupré, John.

Probabilities, Propensities, And Chances. Howson, Colin.

Probabilities And Causes. Papineau, David.

Probability Logic With Conditional Expectation. Fajardo, Sergio.

Probability And Laws. Constantini, D.

Probability, Kinematics, Conditionals, And Entropy Principles. Domotor, Zoltan.

Probability, Symmetry And Frequency. Dawid, A P.

Provability And Mathematical Truth. Fair, David.

Regret, Recrimination And Rationality. Sugden, Robert.

Reply To Leeds: "A Problem About Frequencies In Direct Inference". Pollock, John L.

Richard Von Mises: L'échec D'une Axiomatique. Szafarz, Ariane.

Some Random Observations. Jaynes, E T.

The Calibration Question. Lad, Frank.

The Fallacy Of Intrinsic Distributions. Nathan, Amos.

The Origins Of Hume's Sceptical Argument Against Reason. Wilson, Fred.

The Status Of The Principle Of Maximum Entropy. Shimony, Abner.

Weak Conditional Comparative Probability As A Formal Semantic Theory. Morgan, Charles G.

Zur Kritischen Analyse Des Induktionsproblems. Kronthaler, Engelbert.

PROBLEM(S)

Demarcation Of Science From The Point Of View Of Problems And Problem–Stating. Siitonen, Arto.

Karma And The Problem Of Suffering. Perrett, Roy W.

Models For Understanding Evil In The *Guide For The Perplexed* (in Hebrew). Ben– Or, Ehud.

Must God Do His Best? Hasker, W.

Outlines Of A Mathematical Theory Of General Problems. Veloso, Paulo A S.

Problems Surrounding The Solution Of Mathematical Problems (in Hungarian). Dobó, Andor.

PROBLEM SOLVING

Artificial Intelligence And The Problem Solving Theory (in Portuguese). Teixiera, João De F.

Demarcation Of Science From The Point Of View Of Problems And Problem–Stating. Siitonen, Arto.

Kekes On Problem–Solving And Rationality. Hauptli, Bruce.

Outlines Of A Mathematical Theory Of General Problems. Veloso, Paulo A S.

Scientific Change, Continuity, And Problem Solving. Pearce, David and Rantala, V.

The Role Of Problems And Problem Solving In Popper's Early Work On Psychology. Petersen, Arne Friemuth.

PROCEDURE(S)

A Guide To The Culture Of Science, Technology, And Medicine. Durbin, Paul T (ed).

A Remark On The Connexion Between Procedure And Value. Hederstierna, Anders.

PROCESS(ES)

Unreality And Time. Brumbaugh, Robert S.

Competing Cultural Ideals For The School: Liberal Education And Multicultural Education. Reagan, Timothy.

Erkenntnis Und Bewusste Gestaltung Sozialer Prozesse. Winzer, Rosemarie.

Sozialstrukturforschung Und Leitung Sozialer Prozesse. Lötsch, Manfred and Meyer, H.

Text And Process In Poetry And Philosophy. Sparshott, Francis.

PROCESS PHILOSOPHY

A Note On Objective Identity And Diversity (Part III, Chapter I, Section VII). Cowan, Denis.

A Process View Of Philosophy And Teaching Philosophy. Pecorino, Philip.

Bernard Meland: "A Rebel Among Process Theologians". Inbody, Tyron.

Creativity, God, And Creation. Vitali, Theodore R.

In Response To Inbody's "Bernard Meland: A Rebel Among Process Theologians". Meland, Bernard E.

Liberation Theology And Social Justice. Lamb, Matthew L.

Mystical Consciousness In A Process Perspective. Simmons, Ernest L.

Outside The Camp: Recent Work On Whitehead's Philosophy, Part I. Lucas Jr, George R.

The Mind/Body Function: Not One, Not Two, But A Process. Conway, Patrick.

The Place Of Process Cosmology In Absolute Idealism. Butler, Clark.

Transmission, Inheritance, And Efficient Causation. Field, Richard W.

Whitehead And Marx: Toward A Political Metaphysics. Marsh, James L and Hamrick, William S.

PROCESS THEOLOGY

Evil And The Process God. Whitney, Barry L.

The Emergence Of Whitehead's Metaphysics 1925–1929, R C Neville (ed). Ford, Lewis S.

Bernard Meland: "A Rebel Among Process Theologians". Inbody, Tyron.

Beyond Process Theology? Sontag, Frederick.

In Response To Inbody's "Bernard Meland: A Rebel Among Process Theologians". Meland, Bernard E.

Points Of Contact Between Process Theology And Liberation Theology In Matters Of Faith And Justice. Cobb, John B.

The Metaphysics Of Faith And Justice. Ogden, Schubert M.

Weaving The World. Suchocki, Marjorie.

PROCREATION

"Surrogate Gestation, Law, And Morality" in *Biomedical Ethics Reviews*, Humber, James M (ed), 47–68. Benditt, Theodore M.

PRODUCT(S)

Competing Cultural Ideals For The School: Liberal Education And Multicultural Education. Reagan, Timothy.

PRODUCTION

Über Die Produktivkräfte Und Ihre Entwicklung. Ruben, Peter.

Bedürfnisse Und Produktion. Rohrberg, Peter.

Empiricism And Speculation In *the German Ideology*. Taminiaux, Jacques.

Kollektive Meinung Und Individuelles Leistungsverhalten Im Sozialismus. Dresler, Peter.

Lonergan's Economics. Mathews, William.

Probleme Der Gesellschaftlichen Aktivität Der Arbeiterklasse In Der Materiellen Produktion. Jetzschmann, Horst.

Produktivität Und Individualität. Bauer, A.

Sozialistische Persönlichkeit Und Intensiv Erweiterte Reproduktion. Kretzschmar, A.

Sport As A Contemporary Form Of Cultural Motor Activity. Wohl, Andrzej.

Struktur Der Sozialistischen Produktionsverhältnisse Und Ökonomische Gesetze Des Sozialismus. Becher, Jurgen and Friedrich, P.

The Impact Of Risk Attitude, Uncertainty And Disequilibria On Optimal Production And Inventory. Aiginger, Karl.

The Perspectives Of The Distinction Between *Agere* And *Facere*. Garcia– Alonso, Luz.

PROFANE

The Sacred And The Profane In Arts. Golaszewska, Maria.

PROFESSION(S)

Ethics, Advertising And The Definition Of A Profession. Dyer, Allen R.

PROFESSION(S)

What Is Professional Ethics? James, David.

PROFESSIONAL(S)

Problems And Materials On Professional Responsibility. Morgan, Thomas D and Rotunda, Ronald D.

The Legal Profession: Responsibility And Regulation. Hazard, Geoffrey C and Rhode, Deborah L.

"The Borrowed Syllabus". Wright, Richard A and Newton, Lisa.

Lay Medical Ethics. Veatch, Robert M.

Lay Obligations In Professional Relations. Benjamin, Martin.

Responsibility For Personal Health: A Historical Perspective. Reiser, Stanley J.

Theoretical And Practical Confusion In American Professional Sport. Rose, David A.

PROFESSIONAL CODE(S)

Problems In Legal Ethics. Schwartz, Mortimer D and Wydick, Richard C.

Professional Ethics In Education. Rich, John Martin.

Selected Standards On Professional Responsibility. Rotunda, Ronald D and Morgan, Thomas D.

Commentary On "Whether Professional Associations May Enforce Professional Codes". Wilson, Donald E.

Commentary On B Lichter And M Hodges' "Perceptions Of The Engineers' 'Professionalism' In The Chemical Industry". Nixon, Alan C.

Commentary On "Whether Professional Associations May Enforce Professional Codes". Lunch, Milton F.

Commentary On L Jung's "Commercialization And The Professions". Marcus, Sanford A.

Commentary On B Lichter And M Hodges' "Perceptions Of The Engineers' 'Professionalism' In The Chemical Industry". Gross, Milton S.

Commentary On K Alpern's "Moral Responsibility For Engineers". Florman, Samuel C.

Commentary On "Whether Professional Associations May Enforce Professional Codes". Ladd, John.

Commentary On B Lichter And M Hodges' "Perceptions Of The Engineers' 'Professionalism' In The Chemical Industry". Leckie, John D.

Lawyer–Client Confidences Under The A B A Model Rules: Ethical Rules Without Ethical Reason. Freedman, Monroe H.

Medical Negligence: Who Sets The Standard? Norrie, Kenneth McK.

Perceptions Of The Engineers' "Professionalism" In The Chemical Industry. Lichter, Barry D and Hodges, Michael P.

Professions As The Conscience Of Society. Sieghart, Paul.

Pure Legal Advocates And Moral Agents: Two Concepts Of A Lawyer In An Adversary System. Cohen, Elliot D.

Regulation, Deregulation, Self–Regulation: The Case Of Engineers In Ontario. Stevenson, J T.

The Problem Of Writing, Enforcing, And Teaching Ethical Rules: A Reply To Goldman's "Confidentiality, Rules, And Codes Of Ethics". Freedman, Monroe H.

The Specificity Of Rules Of Professional Conduct: A Rejoinder To Freedman's "the Problem Of Writing, Enforcing, And Teaching Ethical Rules". Goldman, Alan H.

Whether Professional Associations May Enforce Professional Codes. Snapper, John W.

PROFESSIONALISM

"Achieving Professionalism Through Ethical Fragmentation" in *Ethics And Values In Archaeology*, Green, Ernestene L (ed), 51–61. Raab, L Mark.

"Archaeological Ethics In A Resource Program At The Pueblo Of Zuni" in *Ethics And Values In Archaeology*, Green, Ernestene L (ed), 224–235. Ferguson, T J.

Child Abuse And Neglect: Ethical Issues. Harris, Jean.

Commentary On L Jung's "Commercialization And The Professions". Machan, Tibor R.

Commentary On B Lichter And M Hodges' "Perceptions Of The Engineers' 'Professionalism' In The Chemical Industry". Leckie, John D.

Commentary On L Jung's "Commercialization And The Professions". Marcus, Sanford A.

Commercialization And The Professions. Jung, L Shannon.

Enhancing Perceptions Of Auditor Independence. Pearson, Michael A.

Perceptions Of The Engineers' "Professionalism" In The Chemical Industry. Lichter, Barry D and Hodges, Michael P.

Professionalism: Foundation For Business Ethics. Schaefer, Thomas E.

Situational Tests Of A Scholar's Faithfulness To His Ethos (in Polish). Gockowski, J.

PROFESSOR(S)

"I'm The Teacher". Benjamin, Martin and Baum, Robert.

PROFIT(S)

Work–Related Ethical Attitudes: Impact On Business Profitability. Dunfee, Thomas W and Robertson, Diana C.

PROGRAM(S)

A Property Of 2–Sorted Peano Models And Program Verification. Paris, J B and Csirmaz, L.

Programmatic Aesthetic Education From The Point Of View Of Social Psychology (in Czechoslovakian). Macková– Holecková, Iva.

Structured Nonstandard Dynamic Logic. Sain, Ildikó.

PROGRESS

Benjamin Constant And The Making Of Modern Liberalism. Holmes, Stephen.

Is Science Progressive? Niiniluoto, Ilkka.

The Limits Of Science. Rescher, Nicholas.

"Progress And Evolution: A Reappraisal" in *The Good Life And Its Pursuit*, Dougherty, Jude P (ed), 163–174. Nasr, Seyyed Hossein.

Arbeiterklasse Und Intelligenz In Der Dialektik Von Wissenschaftlichtechnischem, Ökonomischem Und Sozialem Fortschritt. Lötsch, M.

Der Wissenschaftlich–Technische Fortschritt Und Die Interdisziplinäre

Zusammenarbeit Von Philosophen Und Technikwissenschaftlern. Jobst, E.

Die Einheit Von Wirtschafts—Und Sozialpolitik—Triebkraft Ökonomischen Und Sozialen Fortschritts. Winkler, G.

Die Wachsende Rolle Des Subjektiven Faktors—Eine Gesetzmässigkeit Des Historischen Fortschritts. Lassow, Ekkhard.

El Progreso Según Juan Bautista Vico. Dondi, J.

Elements For A Theory Of Modernity. Secretan, Philibert.

Energieproblem Und Wissenschaftlich–Technischer Fortschritt. Winckelmann, J.

Heidegger's Later Philosophy Of Science. Rouse, Joseph T.

History And Reality: R G Collingwood's Theory Of Absolute Presuppositions. Trainor, Paul J.

The Evolution Of Our Understanding Of The Cell: A Study In The Dynamics Of Scientific Progress. Bechtel, William P.

The Victory Over Fascism A Historic Chance For Peace And Progress (in German). Löwe, Bernd P.

Who Is Fooled By The "Cunning Of Reason"? Drydyk, J J.

PROJECTIBILITY

Response To "Referential Inscrutability". Meyer, Michael.

PROLETARIAT

Cohen On Proletarian Unfreedom. Brenkert, George G.

Probleme Der Gesellschaftlichen Aktivität Der Arbeiterklasse In Der Materiellen Produktion. Jetzschmann, Horst.

Rationality, Democracy, And Freedom In Marxist Critiques Of Hegel's Philosophy Of Right. Campbell, David.

Who Speaks For The Workers? Legters, Lyman H.

Workers' Interest And The Proletarian Ethic: Conflicting Strains In Marxian Anti–Moralism. Skillen, Anthony.

Zur Entwicklung Kultureller Bedürfnisse In Der Arbeiterklasse. Staufenbiel, Fred.

PROMISE(S)

Postures Of The Mind: Essays On Mind And Morals. Baier, Annette.

Practical Reason. Von Wright, G H.

PROMISING

The Promising Game (in Polish). Hare, R M.

Three Accounts Of Promising. Downie, R S.

PROOF(S)

Introduction To Logic: Propositional Logic. Pospesel, Howard.

Introduction To The Arguments For God. Caes, Charles J.

Lecture Notes In Mathematics. Muller, G H and others.

Set Theory: An Introduction To Independence Proofs, J Barwise and others (eds). Kunen, Kenneth.

The New Scientific Case For God's Existence. Mahin, Mark.

'Can We Speak Literally Of God'? Levine, Michael P.

"On The Length Of Proofs In A Formal System Of Recursive Arithmetic" in *Lecture Notes In Mathematics,* Muller, G H And Others (ed), 81–108. Miyatake, Tohru.

"Semi–formal Finitist Proof Of Transfinite Induction" in *Lecture Notes In Mathematics,* Muller, G H And Others (ed), 67–80. Maehara, Shoji.

A Defence Of Pascal's Wager. Brown, Geoffrey.

An Abstract Setting For Henkin Proofs. Goldblatt, Robert.

Augustine's Argument For God's Existence *De Libero Arbitrio*, Book II. Kondoleon, Theodore J.

Bouwsma On Moore's Proof. Carney, James D.

Can Racial Discrimination Be Proved? Lesser, Harry.

DFC–Algorithms For Suszko, Logic SCI And One–to–one Gentzen Type Formalizations. Wasilewska, Anita.

Does Belief In God Need Proof? Robbins, J Wesley.

Eliminating "God" And Gathering The Real Gods. Hayes, Victor C.

Linear Reasoning In Modal Logic. Fitting, Melvin.

Remarks On Some Approaches To The Concept Of Logical Consequence. Prawitz, Dag.

The Evaluation Of Critical Thinking Programs: Dangers And Dogmas. Mc Peck, John E.

PROOF THEORY

Aristotle As Proof Theorist. Smith, Robin.

Foundations For Analysis And Proof Theory. Sieg, Wilfried.

Introduction To 2 1/2 Logic. Girard, Jean–Yves.

Proof Theory And Set Theory. Takeuti, Gaisi.

Proof Theory And Complexity. Cellucci, Carlo.

PROPAGANDA

"Propaganda And Analysis: Hegel's Article On The English Reform Bill" in *The State And Civil Society*, Pelczynski, Z A (ed), 137–158. Petry, M J.

PROPENSITY(–TIES)

A Note On Popper, Propensities, And The Two–Slit Experiment. Milne, Peter.

Probabilities, Propensities, And Chances. Howson, Colin.

PROPER NAME(S)

Kritisches Zu Kripkes Theorie Der Eigennamen. Franzen, Winfried.

Le Sens D'un Nom Propre. Engel, Pascal.

Rigid Designators And Disguised Descriptions. Cook, Monte.

Some Problems About The Sense And Reference Of Proper Names. Geach, Peter.

The Semantics And The Causal Roles Of Proper Names. Castaneda, Hector–Neri.

PROPERTY(–TIES)

How Things Are: Studies In Predication And The History Of Philosophy And Science. Bogen, James (ed) and Mc Guire, James E (ed).

John Locke And Agrarian Capitalism. Wood, Neal.

Law, Economics, And Philosophy. Kuperberg, Mark (ed) and Beitz, Charles (ed).

Lectures And Miscellanies. James, Henry.

Marsilius Of Inghen: Treatises On The Properties Of Terms. Bos, Egbert P.

PROPERTY(–TIES)

Wealth And Virtue: The Shaping Of Political Economy In The Scottish Enlightenment. Hont, Istvan (ed) and Ignatieff, Michael (ed).

"Eigentum Ist Nicht Eigentum", Zur Rechtfertigbarkeit Des Eigentums. Kohler, Georg.

"The Poor Have A Claim Found In The Law Of Nature": William Paley And The Rights Of The Poor. Horne, Thomas A.

"Universals: Logic And Metaphor" in *Philosophy And Life: Essays On John Wisdom*, Dilman, Ilham (ed), 271–290. Long, Peter.

Concepts Of Supervenience. Kim, Jaegwon.

Conjunctive Properties Revisited. Casullo, Albert.

Das Eigentum Als Eschatologische Potenz: Zur Eigentumskonzeption Von Karl Marx. Künzli, Arnold.

Das Verhältnis Von "Person" Und "Eigentum" In Hegels Philosophie Des Rechts. Meyer, Rudolf W.

Der Streit Um Die Eigentumsordnung Des Verfassungsentwurfes 1977. Müller, Georg.

Die Kategorie Der Sache. Nef, Robert.

Die Sozialpflichtigkeit Des Eigentums: Gesichtspunkte Der Christlichen Sozialethik. Furger, Franz.

Eigentum Und Ungleichheit: Rousseaus Eigentumslehre. Ryffel, Hans.

Eigentum Und Seine Grenzen. Fleiner– Gerster, Thomas.

Eigentum Und Macht In Der Modernen Industriegesellschaft. Levy, René.

Eigentum Und Lebenswelt: Zum Wandel Des Eigentumsverständnisses In Der Komplexen Gesellschaft. Wildermuth, Armin.

Eigentum Und Teilungsvertrag: Zu Kants Begründung Des Eigentumsrechts. Schmidlin, Bruno.

Eigentum—Moralität. Schmidig, Dominik.

Freiheit Und Eignetum. Ryffel, Hans.

Gesetzgeberrecht Vs Richterrecht In Der Eigentumskonzeption Des Verfassungsentwurfs. Brühlmeier, Daniel.

Gleichheit Und Eigentum: Metaethische Und Normative Bemerkungen Zum Verfassungsentwurf. Hügli, Anton.

Inquiry, Intrinsic Properties, And The Identity Of Indiscernibles. Hoy, Ronald C.

La Propriété Et Ses Limites. Schmidlin, Bruno.

Labour—Natural, Property—Artificial: The Radical Insights Of Gerrard Winstanley. Kenyon, Timothy.

Les Fondements Personnalistes De La Propriété. Cottier, Georges.

Locke's Theory Of Property: A Re–Examination. Cvek, Peter Paul.

Lockean Provisos And State Of Nature Theories. Bogart, J H.

Lockes Begründung Des Privateigentums In Der Arbeit. Holzhey, Helmut.

Mackie And Shoemaker On Dispositions And Properties. Rosenberg, Alexander.

Nutzenkalkül Und Eigentumsrechte: Ein Ökonomischer Ansatz Zu Einer Positiven Theorie Des Eigentums. Janssen, Martin.

Parental Rights. Page, Edgar.

Parsons And Possible Objects. Hetherington, Stephen.

Phenomenal Properties. Double, Richard.

Properties, Functionalism, And The Identity Theory. Adams, Frederick.

Property Rights, Liberty And Redistribution. Nelson, William N.

Sperm And Ova As Property. Jansen, Robert P S.

The Actuality Of Marx's And Engels' Conception Of The Relation Of Property And The Division Of Labour (in Czechoslovakian). Heller, J.

The Commodity Form And Socialization In Locke's State Of Nature. Colella, E Paul.

The Origin Of Property And The Development Of Scottish Historical Science. Bowles, Paul.

PROPORTION

La Question Des Actes Intrinsèquement Mauvais. Pinckaers, S.

PROPORTIONALITY

Husserl's Communal Spirit: A Phenomenological Study Of The Fundamental Structure Of Society. Allen, Jeffner.

The Meaning Of Proportionate Reason In Contemporary Moral Theology. Johnstone, Brian V.

What (If Anything) Is Intrinsically Wrong With Capitalism? Van Parijs, Philippe.

PROPOSITION(S)

see also Sentence(s), Statement(s)

An Essay Concerning The Use Of Reason In Propositions: A Discourse Of Free Thinking. Collins, Anthony and Schouls, Peter A (ed).

Averroes' Middle Commentaries On Aristotle's "Categories" And "De Interpretatione". Butterworth, Charles E.

Inquiry. Stalnaker, Robert C.

La Naissance De La Grammaire Moderne. Dominicy, Marc and Mardaga, Pierre (ed).

Logica Parva, Alan R Perreiah (trans). Venetus, Paulus.

"The Nature Of The Proposition And The Revolt Against Idealism" in *Philosophy In History*, Rorty, Richard and others (ed), 375–398. Hylton, Peter.

A Brentanian Basis For Leśniewskian Logic. Simons, Peter M.

A Revival Of The Propositional Theory Of Art? Goodrich, R A.

Ackerman On Propositional Identity. Bertolet, Rod.

An Interpretation Of Martin–Löf's Type Theory In A Type–Free Theory Of Propositions. Smith, Jan.

Art And Knowledge. Reid, Louis Arnaud.

Elementary Propositions In Wittgenstein's *Tractatus* (in Chinese). Liu, Fu–Tseng.

Is Object–Seeing Really Propositional Seeing? Nelson, John O.

Locke On Knowledge And Propositions. Soles, David E.

On Evidence According To Meinong And Chisholm. Schubert Kalsi, Marie–Luise.

On The Proper Treatment Of Negative Names. Englebretsen, George.

Propositions For Semantics And Propositions For Epistemology. Wilson, N L.

Propositions And Empirical Evidence. O' Neil, Michael P.

Russell's Theory Of Identity Of Propositions. Church, Alonzo.

Tenselessness And The Absolute Present. Plecha, James L.

PROPOSITIONAL ATTITUDES

Individuating Propositional Attitudes. Brownstein, Donald.

PROPOSITIONAL LOGIC

A Concise Introduction To Logic. Hurley, Patrick J.

Análisis Propositional Y Ontologia. Sanchez, Juan Carlos.

Introduction To Logic: Propositional Logic. Pospesel, Howard.

Introduction To Logic. Copi, Irving M.

Lectures On Propositional Calculi, R Ladniak (ed). Wojcicki, Ryszard.

Logic Made Simple. Rubin, Ronald.

A Couple Of Novelties In The Propositional Calculus. Hoare, C A R.

A Note On The Existence Of Tautologies Without Constants. Rose, Alan.

A Sufficient And Necessary Condition For Tarski's Property In Lindenbaum's Extensions. Stepień, Teodor.

On Propositional Calculus With A Variable Functor. Lesisz, Wlodzimierz.

Peirce's Alpha Graphs: The Completeness Of Propositional Logic And The Fast Simplification Of Truth Functions. White, Richard B.

Propositional Logic Based On The Dynamics Of Belief. Gardenfors, Peter.

Russell's Theory Of Identity Of Propositions. Church, Alonzo.

Some Paraconsistent Sentential Calculi. Blaszczuk, Jerzy.

Some Propositional Calculi With Constant And Variable Functors. Jones, John.

Tautologies With A Unique Craig Interpolant, Uniform *Vs* Nonuniform Complexity. Mundici, Daniele.

The Logical Consequence Relation Of Propositional Trense Logic. Thomason, S K.

The Metatheory Of The Classical Propositional Calculus Is Not Axiomatizable. Mason, Ian.

Triadic Partial Implicational Propositional Calculi. Hughes, Charles E and Singletary, W E.

Two Variants Of The System Of Entailment. Imre, Ruzsa.

PROSE

Art, Religion And Musement. Raposa, Michael L.

Prose Rhythm: An Analysis For Instruction. O' Callaghan, Timothy M B.

PROSODY

Modifying Illocutionary Force. Holmes, Janet.

PROSTITUTION

"Prostitution" in *Freedom, Feminism, And The State*, Mc Elroy, Wendy (ed), 111–118. Danielle.

PROTAGORAS

Man As APXH. Strózewski, Wladyslaw.

Mass Haben Und Mass Sein. Buchheim, Thomas.

Perception, Relativism, And Truth: Reflections On Plato's Theaetetus 152–160. Matthen, Mohan.

PROTECTION

"If You Liked Gun Control, You'll Love The Antiabortion Amendment" in *Freedom, Feminism, And The State*, Mc Elroy, Wendy (ed), 169–178. Combs, Beverly J.

Fact And Value In Ecological Science. Sagoff, Mark.

PROTEST(S)

Greenham: A Concrete Reality. Seller, Anne.

On The Nature Of Protest Petitions (in Hebrew). Margalit, Avishai and Ullmann– Margalit, Edna.

Protest Petitions. Margalit, Avishai and Ullmann– Margalit, Edna.

PROTESTANT

"The Significance Of Martin Buber For Protestant Theology" in *Martin Buber*, Gordon, Haim (ed), 385–418. Gollwitzer, Helmut.

PROTESTANT ETHICS

Taxation In The History Of Protestant Ethics. Shriver, Donald W and Knox, E Richard.

PROTESTANTISM

Human Rights In Religious Traditions. Swidler, Arlene (ed).

The Retreat To Commitment. Bartley, W W.

A Sociological Account Of Liberal Protestantism. Bruce, S.

Justice Et Glorification: Double Préoccupation D'Ulrich Zwingli, Réformateur (1484– 1531). Burki, Bruno.

The Essence Of Catholicism: Protestant And Catholic Perspectives. Dulles, Avery.

Zur Aktualität Der Politischen Theologie Ulrich Zwinglis. Winzeler, Peter.

PROTOTYPE(S)

Two Alternative Epistemological Frameworks In Psychology: The Typological And Variational Modes Of Thinking. Valsiner, Jaan.

PROUST

The Thread Of Life. Wollheim, Richard.

PROVABILITY

Dialogues, Strategies, And Intuitionistic Provability. Felscher, Walter.

Explicit Henkin Sentences. Solovay, Robert M.

PROVIDENCE

Maimonides, Aquinas And Gersonides On Providence And Evil. Burrell, David.

PSYCHE

Ideology And Social Psyche (in Hungarian). Stojchev, Todor.

On The Political Rhetoric Of Freud's Individual Psychology. Brunner, José.

PSYCHIATRY

Absent At The Creation: The Existential Psychiatry Of Ludwig Binswanger. Seidman, Bradley.

Law, Psychiatry, And Morality. Stone, Alan R (ed).

Phenomenology And Psychiatry. Jenner, F A (ed) and De Koning, A J J (ed).

Psychiatry And Ethics. Edwards, Rem B (ed).

"Making And Using Psychiatric Diagnoses: Ethical Issues" in *Ethical Questions In Brain*

PSYCHIATRY

And Behavior, Pfaff, Donald W (ed), 11–22. Endicott, Jean.

Children In Care: Are Social Workers Abusing Their Authority? Benians, R C.

Involuntary Confinement: Legal And Psychiatric Perspectives. Dresser, Rebecca.

Philosophy Of Medicine In Scandinavia. Lindahl, B Ingemar B.

Prevention Of Admission And Continuity Of Care. Vanistendael, Clara.

Psychiatric Diagnosis As An Ethical Problem. Shackle, E M.

Response To "Children In Care: Are Social Workers Abusing Their Authority". Foster, Judy.

Roles And Responsibilities: Theoretical Issues In The Definition Of Consultation Liaison Psychiatry. Agich, George J.

PSYCHICAL DISTANCE

A Note On Audience Participation And Psychical Distance. Lewis, Peter.

PSYCHOANALYSIS

Taking Chances: Derrida, Psychoanalysis, And Literature. Kerrigan, William (ed) and Smith, Joseph H (ed).

"Ethics And Excuses: Ethical Implications Of Psychoanalysis" in *Darwin, Marx And Freud*, Caplan, Arthur L (ed), 201–208. Izenberg, Gerald N.

"Freud's Influence On The Moral Aspects Of The Physician–Patient Relationship" in *Darwin, Marx And Freud*, Caplan, Arthur L (ed), 209–220. Brody, Eugene B.

"Psycho–Analysis And Philosophy" in *Philosophy And Life: Essays On John Wisdom*, Dilman, Ilham (ed), 179–200. Brearley, Mike.

"Psychoanalysis, Pseudo–Science And Testability" in *Popper And The Human Sciences*, Currie, Gregory (ed), 13–44. Cioffi, Frank.

"Subjectivity In Psychoanalytic Inference" in *Testing Scientific Theories*, Earman, John (ed), 349–412. Meehl, Paul E.

Es El Psicoanálisis Una Pseudo–Ciencia? Rush, Alan A.

Janus Bifrons. Granger, Gilles–Gaston.

La Psychanalyse Sans L'inconscient? Knee, Philip.

Oedipus Rex: The Oedipus Rule And Its Subversion. Lingis, Alphonso.

On Strong's *Psychoanalysis As A Vocation: Freud, Politics, And The Heroic*. Odajnyk, V Walter.

Reading Habermas Reading Freud. Flynn, Bernard C.

Rechtssoziologie Und Psychoanalyse: Neun Thesen In Rechtspolitischer Absicht. Rotter, Frank.

Sentiments De Culpabilité Et Signification Du Péché: Approche Psychanalytique. De Saussure, Thierry.

The Criminal And The Artist: Violence And Neurosis. Donnell– Kotrozo, Carol.

Wittgenstein On The 'Charm' Of Psychoanalysis. Geller, Jeffrey L.

PSYCHOLINGUISTICS

Jean Piaget Y La Estructuración Genética Del Lenguaje. Beuchot, Mauricio.

PSYCHOLOGICAL EGOISM

Human Nature And Morality: The Case Of The Ik. Sogolo, Godwin.

The Concept Of Altruism. Clark, Ralph W.

PSYCHOLOGISM

"Methodological Individualism" in *Popper And The Human Sciences*, Currie, Gregory (ed), 57–72. Chalmers, A F.

Boole And Mill: Differing Perspectives On Logical Psychologism. Richards, John.

Evaluations And Norms Of Conduct In Leon Petrazycki's Psychologistic Concept Of Law And Morality (in Polish). Smoczynski, P J.

Frege's Justificationism: Truth And The Recognition Of Authority. Notturno, M A.

Functionalism And Psychologism. Mac Kenzie, J D.

Naturalized Epistemology And Metaphysical Realism: A Response To Rorty And Putnam. Stabler, Edward.

PSYCHOLOGY

see also Behaviorism, Psychiatry, Psychoanalysis

Bodily Reflective Modes: A Phenomenological Method For Psychology. Shapiro, Kenneth Joel.

Buddhist And Western Psychology. Katz, Nathan (ed).

Ethics In The Practice Of Psychology. Carroll, Mary Ann and Schneider, Henry G and Wesley, George R.

Imagination Is Reality. Avens, Robert.

Logical Form In Natural Language. Lycan, William G.

Moral Development Foundations: Judeo–Christian Alternatives To Piaget/Kohlberg. Joy, Donald M (ed).

Morality In The Making. Weinreich Haste, Helen (ed) and Locke, Don (ed).

Phenomenology And Psychiatry. Jenner, F A (ed) and De Koning, A J J (ed).

Piaget's Logic: A Critique Of Genetic Epistemology. Seltman, Muriel and Seltman, Peter.

Principles Of Language And Mind: An Evolutionary Theory Of Meaning. Waldron, T P.

The Limits Of Scientific Reasoning. Faust, David.

The Supreme Doctrine: Psychological Encounters In Zen Thought. Benoit, Hubert.

"Concepts Of Personhood: A Philosophical Perspective" in *Defining Human Life*, Shaw, Margery W (ed), 12–23. Wikler, Daniel.

"Psychological Study Of Goal–Directed Action" in *The Analysis Of Action*, Von Cranach, Mario (ed), 35–74. Von Cranach, Mario.

"Sense And Reference In A Psychologically Based Semantics" in *Talking Minds*, Bever, Thomas G (ed), 49–72. Jackendoff, Ray.

"Social Facts And Psychological Facts" in *Popper And The Human Sciences*, Currie, Gregory (ed), 57–72. Papineau, David.

"Using And Refusing Psychotropic Drugs" in *Feeling Good And Doing Better*, Murray, Thomas H (ed), 157–174. Rhoden, Nancy K.

A Jungian View Of Evil. Segal, Robert A.

Begriffsbildung In Der Psychologie: Zur Logik Des Begriffes "Intelligenz". Perner, Josef.

Can Indirect Realism Be Demonstrated In The Psychological Laboratory? Wilcox, Stephen and Katz, Stuart.

Clark Hull, Robert Cummins, And Functional Analysis. Amundson, Ron and Smith, Laurence.

De Angst Van De Homunculus Voor Hetscheermes. Draaisma, Douwe.

De Incommensurabiliteit Van Aanleg En Omgeving. Smit, Harry.

Democritus And The Origins Of Moral Psychology. Kahn, Charles H.

Dennett, Mental Images, And Images In Context. Russow, Lilly–Marlene.

Developmental Psychology And The Problem Of Artistic Change. Bornstein, Marc.

Die Seins– Und Erkenntnisfrage In Der Philosophie Brentanos. Melle, U.

Emotion And Action In Cognitive Psychology: Breaching A Fashionable Philosophical Fence. Ericson, David P.

Emotions And Education. Griffiths, Morwenna.

Empirical Psychology, Naturalized Epistemology, And First Philosophy. Siegel, Harvey.

Exigencias Filosóficas Para Determinar "Lo Psicológico" En El Proceso De Aprendizaje. Daros, William R.

Folk Psychology Is Here To Stay. Horgan, Terence and Woodward, James.

Hume's Labyrinth. Behan, David P.

Il Problema Della Certezza E La Spiritualità Dell'uomo: Psicologia, Logica E Teoria Della Scienza Nel Pensiero Di Désiré Mercier. Mangiagalli, Maurizio.

Is Consciousness Important? Wilkes, Kathleen V.

LFG And Psychological Explanation. Steedman, Mark.

La Teoría Relacional De La Personalidad Según J Nuttin. Darós, William R.

Logic: Normative Or Descriptive; The Ethics Of Belief Or A Branch Of Psychology? Resnik, Michael D.

Logical Learning Theory: Kuhnian Anomaly Or Medievalism Revisited? Rychlak, Joseph R.

Methodological Problems In Psychology (in Dutch). Mauer, K F and Retief, A I.

Narrow Taxonomy And Wide Functionalism. Kitcher, Patricia.

On Galileo's Writings On Mechanics: An Attempt At A Semantic Analysis Of Viviani's Scholium. Halbwachs, F.

On The Political Rhetoric Of Freud's Individual Psychology. Brunner, José.

On The Psychological Reality Of Pragmatics. Kasher, Asa.

Philosophical Anthropology: Revolt Against The Division Of Intellectual Labor. Wiggins, Osborne.

Psychology And Philosophical Anthropology: The Problem Of Their Interaction. Kozulin, Alex.

Reconstruction Of Schlick's Psycho–Sociological Ethics. Leinfellner, Werner.

The Churchlands On Methodological Solipsism And Computational Psychology. Marras, Ausonio.

The Computer Revolution, The Technological Fallacy, And Education. Raitz, Keith L.

The Logical Structure Of Freud's Idea Of The Unconscious: Toward A Psychology Of Ideas. Fisher, Harwood.

The Methodological Imperative In Psychology. Danziger, Kurt.

The Relation Between Epistemology And Psychology. Goldman, Alvin I.

The Role Of Problems And Problem Solving In Popper's Early Work On Psychology. Petersen, Arne Friemuth.

Toward Eliminating Churchland's Eliminationism. Robinson, William S.

Towards A Concept Of Shared Autonomy. Bergsma, Jurrit.

Towards A Computational Phenomenology (1). Harlan, Robert M.

Two Alternative Epistemological Frameworks In Psychology: The Typological And Variational Modes Of Thinking. Valsiner, Jaan.

Wissenschaft Als Gegenstand Der Wissenschaft Vom Menschlichen Erleben Und Verhalten. Brandtstädter, Jochen and Reinert, Gunther.

Wittgenstein's Rejection Of Scientific Psychology. Williams, Meredith.

PSYCHOPATHY

The Psychopath As Moral. Smith, Robert J.

PSYCHOSURGERY

Psychosurgery, The Brain And Violent Behavior. Wilkins, Burleigh T.

PSYCHOTHERAPY

Ancient Psychotherapy. Gill, Christopher.

Antropologische Geneeskunde In Discussie. Verwey, G.

Computer Power And Intellectual Failure In Education: The Significance Of Joseph Weizenbaum's Criticism. Raitz, Keith L.

Establishing Causal Connections: Meta–Analysis And Psychotherapy. Erwin, Edward.

PUBLIC

Ethical Issues In Private And Public Ranch Land Management. Blatz, Charles V.

Public And Firm Interests In Public Service Diversifications. Fannin, William R and Gilmore, Carol B.

PUBLIC GOOD

A Note On The Relationship Of Interdependent Action To The Optimality Of Certain Voting Decisions. Putterman, Louis.

Public Goods And Externalities: The Case Of Roads. Block, Walter.

The Value Of Life For Decision Making In The Public Sector. Usher, Dan.

Who Benefits From The Artificial Heart? Preston, Thomas A.

PUBLIC INTEREST(S)

"Archaeology And The Wider Audience" in *Ethics And Values In Archaeology*, Green, Ernestene L (ed), 175–183. Fagan, Brian M.

"Archaeological Ethics In A Resource Program At The Pueblo Of Zuni" in *Ethics And Values In Archaeology*, Green, Ernestene L (ed), 224–235. Ferguson, T J.

Begriff Und Logik Des "Öffentlichen Interesses". Fach, Wolfgang.

Protection Of Human Rights And Public Interest In Nuclear Development. Menon, N R M.

Towards A Theory Of Taxation. Lucas, J R.

PUBLIC OPINION

"The People Versus The Experts" in *The Security Gamble*, Mac Lean, Douglas (ed), 89–99. Greider, William.

PUBLIC POLICY(–CIES)

Rights And Regulation: Ethical, Political, And Economic Issues. Machan, Tibor R (ed) and Johnson, M Bruce (ed).

"Government Regulation Of The Employment Relationship" in *Rights And Regulation*, Machan, Tibor (ed), 13–42. Haggard, Thomas R.

"Public Policy And Human Research" in *Biomedical Ethics Reviews*, Humber, James M (ed), 3–22. Jonsen, Albert R.

"The Processes Of Adjudication And Regulation, A Comparison" in *Rights And Regulation*, Machan, Tibor (ed), 71–98. Smith, J C.

Die Einheit Von Wirtschafts—Und Sozialpolitik—Triebkraft Ökonomischen Und Sozialen Fortschritts. Winkler, G.

Engineering Human Reproduction: A Challenge To Public Policy. Gorovitz, Samuel.

Philosophy And Policy. Thompson, Dennis.

PUBLICATION(S)

Should The Nazi Research Data Be Cited? Moe, Kristine.

PUCCIARELLI, E

E Pucciarelli: La Filosofía Como Deslinde. Carpio, Adolfo P.

PUNCTUATION

Are Punctuationists Wrong About The Modern Synthesis? Stidd, Benton M.

PUNISHMENT

Punishment And Restitution: A Restitutionary Approach To Crime And The Criminal. Abel, Charles F and Marsh, Frank H.

Corporate Control Through The Criminal System. Lansing, Paul and Hatfield, Donald.

Does It Matter If The Death Penalty Is Arbitrarily Administered? Nathanson, Stephen.

Intolerable Wrong And Punishment. Wolgast, Elizabeth H.

Justice, Civilization, And The Death Penalty: Answering Van Den Haag. Reiman, Jeffrey H.

Kants Straftheorie In Ihrer Bedeutung Für Die Entwicklung Einer Theorie Der Straffälligenpädagogik. Eberle, Hans–Jurgen.

Marxism And The Criminal Question. Ferrajoli, Luigi and Zolo, Danilo.

Punishment, The New Retributivism, And Political Philosophy. Honderich, Ted.

Refuting Reiman And Nathanson. Van Den Haag, Ernest.

Retributive Punishment And Humbling The Will. Johnson, Oliver A.

Retributivism, Moral Education, And The Liberal State. Murphy, Jeffrie G.

The Death Penalty And The U S Supreme Court. Bruening, William H.

The Legalist Paradigm And MAD. Myers, David B.

The Morality Of Nuclear Deterrence: Hostage Holding And Consequences. Lee, Steven.

Thomas Hobbes And The Philosophy Of Punishment. Norrie, Alan.

PURPOSE(S)

After Art History, What? Mühlberger, Richard.

La Fin De L'homme Et Le Destin De La Pensée: La Mutation Anthropologique De La Philosophie M Heidegger Et M Foucault. Kelkel, Arion L.

Museums And Their Functions. Osborne, Harold.

Purpose And Conditioning: A Reply To Waller. Mills, John A.

Purposes, Conditioning, And Skinner's Moral Theory: Comments On Mills' Observations. Waller, Bruce.

Showing And Saying, Looking And Learning: An Outsider's View Of Art Museums. Sparshott, Francis.

The End Of The Museum? Goodman, Nelson.

The Museum In The City. Lilla, Mark.

PURPOSIVENESS

A Theory Of Social Action. Tuomela, Raimo.

PUTNAM, H

A Consideration Of Hilary Putnam. Norton Smith, Thomas Michael.

Analyticity And Apriority: The Qine–Putnam Dispute. Yu, Paul.

Brains In Vats And The Internalist Perspective. Stephens, James and Russow, Lilly–marlene.

Conceptual Progress And Word/World Relations: In Search Of The Essence Of Natural Kinds. Churchland, Paul M.

Hairier Than Putnam Thought. Read, Stephen and Wright, Crispin.

Methodological Solipsism: A Reply To Morris. Noonan, Harold W.

Naturalized Epistemology And Metaphysical Realism: A Response To Rorty And Putnam. Stabler, Edward.

Professor Putnam On Brains In Vats. Harrison, J.

Properties, Functionalism, And The Identity Theory. Adams, Frederick.

Putnam's Paradox. Lewis, David.

Realism And Reference. Brooks, D H M.

Refutation Of Dogmatism: Putnam's Brains In Vats. Feldman, Susan.

The Intersection Of Theory Of Science And Theory Of Literature. Margolis, Joseph.

The Rejection Of Truth–Conditional Semantics By Putnam And Dummett. Demopoulos, William.

Von Neumann And The Anti–Realists. Brown, James R.

Why Kant Couldn't Be An Anti–Realist. Clark, A J.

PUZZLE(S)

Crossword Puzzles For Introductory Courses In Philosophy. Jackson, Jerry.

Dissolving Kripke's Puzzle About Belief. Pettit, Philip.

PYRRHONISM

How To Become A Moderate Skeptic: Hume's Way Out Of Pyrrhonism. Michaud, Yves.

Is Hume A Sceptic With Regard To Reason? Wilson, Fred.

Montaigne And The Rise Of Skepticism In Early Modern Europe: A Reappraisal.

Schiffman, Zachary S.

PYTHAGORAS

Placing *Sectio Canonis* In Historical And Philosophical Contexts. Barbera, Andre.

PYTHAGOREANS

De Wiskundige Rede (Summary: The Mathematical Reason). Klever, W N A.

QUAKERS

Friendly Persuasion: Quakers, Liberal Toleration, And The Birth Of The Prison. Dumm, Thomas L.

QUALITATIVE

Eliminativism, Meaning, And Qualitative States. Jacoby, Henry.

On Mill's Qualitative Distinction Of Pleasures. Nagaoka, Shigeo.

QUALITY(–TIES)

"(Simple) Qualities And Resemblance" in *Philosophical Analysis In Latin America*, Gracia, Jorge J E and others (eds), 199–218. Robles, Jose A.

A Functionalist Interpretation Of Locke's Theory Of Simple Ideas. Vinci, Thomas.

An Analysis And Critique Of Wang Fu–Chih's Theory Of "*Tao Ta Shan Hsiao, Shan Ta Hsing Hsiao*" (in Chinese). Huang, Yih–Mei.

Creativity And Quality. Bailin, Sharon.

Fundamental Features Of The Transition From The Old To The New Quality Under Socialism (in Czechoslovakian). Pospíchalová, Milena.

Numbers As Qualities. Seidel, Asher.

Qualité—Une Notion (in German). Fritzsche, Lothar.

Quality And Creativity: A False Dichotomy? Ennis, Robert H.

The Meaning Of Life: A Qualitative Perspective. Bennett, James O.

QUALITY OF LIFE

Conditions Of Happiness. Veenhoven, Ruut.

Quality Of Life In Cancer Patients—A Hypothesis. Calman, K C.

Quality Of Life—A Response To K C Calman. Cribb, Alan.

QUANTIFICATION

Introduction To Logic. Copi, Irving M.

"Quantification In Modal Logic" in *Handbook Of Philosophical Logic*, Gabbay, Dov (ed), 249–308. Garson, James W.

"Quantification In Tense And Modal Logic" in *Handbook Of Philosophical Logic*, Gabbay, Dov (ed), 309–354. Cocchiarella, Nino B.

A Model For The Modern Malaise. Abraham, Adrian and Meyer, Robert K.

Global Quantification In Zermelo–Fraenkel Set Theory. Mayberry, John.

Rejoinder To Tenant's "Were Those Disproofs I Saw Before Me"? Weir, Alan.

Substitutional Quantification And Existence. Copeland, B J.

QUANTIFIER(S)

"Unbestimmte Begriffe" Bei Leibniz. Lenzen, Wolfgang.

A Proof Of Herbrand's Theorem. Wojtylak, Piotr.

Deux Remarques À Propos De La Propriété De Recouvrement Fini. Poizat, Bruno.

Entscheidbarkeit Von Theorien In Logiken Mit Verallgemeinerten Quantoren. Wolter, Helmut and Herre, Heinrich.

Entscheidbarkeit Der Arithmetik Mit Addition Und Ordnung In Logiken Mit Verallgemeinerten Quantoren. Wolter, Helmut.

Finite QE Rings In Characteristic p^2. Saracino, Dan and Wood, Carol.

Modifiers And Quantifiers In Natural Language. Parsons, Terence.

Mythe Et Réalité De La Formule De Barcan. Stahl, Gérold.

Natural Deduction Systems For Some Quantified Relevant Logics. Brady, R T.

Quantifier Scope And The ECP. Cole, Peter.

Referential And Nonreferential Substitutional Quantifiers. Orenstein, Alex.

Representation, Intentionality, And Quantifiers. Mc Carthy, Timothy.

Set Recursion And $\Pi 1/2$–Logic. Girard, Jean–Yves and Normann, D.

The Boolean Sentence Algebra Of The Theory Of Linear Ordering Is Atomic With Respect To Logics With A Malitz Quantifier. Goltz, Hans–Joachim.

QUANTITY(–TIES)

Abstract Measurement Theory. Narens, Louis.

QUANTUM LOGIC

Modern Logic And Quantum Mechanics. Garden, Rachel Wallace.

La Multiplicidad De Axiomáticas Conjuntistas Y Su Incidencia En La Lógica Cuántica. Lungarzo, Carlos.

Orígenes Y Proyecciones De La Lógica Cuántica. Lungarzo, Carlos.

Proof Tableau Formulations Of Some First–Order Relevant Ortho–Logics. Mc Robbie, Michael and Belnap, Nuel D.

QUANTUM MECHANICS

Modern Logic And Quantum Mechanics. Garden, Rachel Wallace.

"Interpretation Theory And Experiment" in *Observation, Experiment, Hypothesis In Modern Physical Science*, Achinstein, Peter (ed), 175–204. Joseph, Geoffrey.

"Unification And Fractionation In Science" in *The Good Life And Its Pursuit*, Dougherty, Jude P (ed), 251–266. Shapere, Dudley.

An Exchange On Local Beables. Bell, J S and others.

Chance, Realism, Quantum Mechanics. Leeds, Stephen.

Das Verhältnis Der *Kritik Der Reinen Vernunft* Zu Den *Metaphysischen Anfangsgründen Der Naturwissenschaft*, Demonstr Am Substanzsatz. Gloy, Karen.

De La Physique À L'épistémologie B D'Espagnat Et I Prigogine. Gauthier, Yvon.

Discussion: Quantum Mechanics And Value Definiteness. Pitowsky, Itamar.

EPR Resuscitated: A Reply To Halpin's 'EPR Resuscitated: A Reply To Wessels'. Wessels, Linda.

EPR: Lessons For Metaphysics. Skyrms, Brian.

Einstein On Locality And Separability. Howard, Don.

Gentle Quantum Events As The Source Of Explicate Order. Chew, Geoffrey F.

L'inégalité De Bell: Démonstration Intuitive Et Commentaires (infrench). Bonsack, Francois.

Note On An Argument Of W Ochs Against The Ignorance Interpretation Of State In

RAWLS, J

Justifying Law: An Explanation Of The Deep Structure Of American Law. Gibbons, Hugh.

Maximin And Other Decision Principles. Ihara, Craig K.

Moral Reasoning And Action In Young Children. Hannaford, Robert V.

On DiQuattro, "Rawls And Left Criticism". Connin, Lawrence J.

Presidential Address: For And Against Bureaucracy. Luebke, Neil.

Principles For Individual Actions. Wilkins, Burleigh T and Zelikovitz, Kelly M.

Rawls' Difference Principle, Marxian Alienation And The Japanese Economy: Bringing Justice To The Least Advantaged. Grcic, Joseph M.

Rebuilding Rawls: An Alternative Theory Of Justice. Groarke, Leo.

Reflective Equilibrium And Justification. Little, Daniel.

Reiman's Libertarian Interpretation Of Rawls' Difference Principle. Alexander, Lawrence.

Social Contract As A Basis Of Norms: A Critique. Machan, Tibor R.

Some Considerations About The Discovery Of Principles Of Justice. Suits, David B.

Strict Compliance And Rawls's Critique Of Utilitarianism. Carson, Thomas L.

The Authority Of The Moral Agent. Johnson, Conrad D.

The Matrix Of Contractarian Justice. Buchanan, James M and Lomasky, Loren E.

The Maximin Rule Argument For Rawls's Principles Of Justice. Langtry, Bruce.

The Possibility Of A Marxian Theory Of Justice. Reiman, Jeffrey H.

The Stability Of Bargains Behind The Veil Of Ignorance. Gaa, James C.

Theories Of Justice And The United Nations Declaration On The Establishment Of A New International Economic Order. Boxill, Bernard.

Two Interpretations Of The Difference Principle In Rawls's Theory Of Justice. Shenoy, Prakash P and Martin, Rex.

READ, H

Herbert Read: Formlessness And Form. Thistlewood, David.

READING

Seeing And Reading. Nicholson, Graeme.

"The Problem Of Reading, Phenomenologically Or Otherwise" in *Existential Coordinates Of Human Condition*, Tymieniecka, A (ed), 559–568. Margolis, Joseph.

"The Proof Of The Pudding Lies In The Eating" (in German). Loeser, Franz.

La Lecture Rationnelle—Nécessaire Et Facilement Assimilable (in German). Ziegler, Heinz.

On Reading And Mis–Reading Hannah Arendt. Bernauer, James.

READING, J

John Reading On The Existence And Unicity Of God, Efficient And Final Causality (in Latin). Etzkorn, Girard J.

REAL

Eine Neue Definition Berechenbarer Reeller Funktionen. Hauck, Jürgen.

La Idea Hegeliana De Materia Y El Tránsito De Lo Ideal A Lo Real. Albizu, Edgardo.

On A Simple Definition Of Computable Function Of A Real Variable—With Applications To Functions Of A Complex Variable. Caldwell, Jerome and Pour– El, Marion Boykan.

On The Consistency Of Some Partition Theorems For Continuous Colorings, And The Structure Of Dense Real Order Types. Shelah, Saharon and Abraham, U and Rubin, M.

On The Existence And Recursion Theoretic Properties Of Generic Sets Of Reals. Weitkamp, Galen.

The Fake, The Non–Fake And The Genuine. Chakravarti, Mihir.

The Ordered Field Of Real Numbers And Logics With Malitz Quantifiers. Rapp, Andreas.

REAL NUMBER(S)

Is Nonstandard Analysis Relevant For The Philosophy Of Mathematics? Fenstad, Jens Erik.

The Elementary Theory Of Interval Reals Numbers. Comer, Stephen D.

The First–Order Theory Of The c–Degrees. Farrington, Paddy.

REALISM

Bachelard: Science And Objectivity. Tiles, Mary.

Husserl And Realism In Logic And Mathematics. Tragesser, Robert S.

Inquiry. Stalnaker, Robert C.

Is Science Progressive? Niiniluoto, Ilkka.

Probability And Evidence. Horwich, Paul.

Realism And Truth. Devitt, Michael.

Realism And Reason: Philosophical Papers, V3. Putnam, Hillary.

The Interior And Exterior In Zen Buddhism. Izutsu, Toshihiko.

The New Scientific Spirit. Bachelard, Gaston and Goldhammer, Arthur (trans).

The Significance Of Philosophical Scepticism. Stroud, Barry.

"Kant's Empirical Realism" in *Kant On Causality, Freedom, And Objectivity*, Harper, William A (ed), 108–147. Harper, William L.

"Moral Realism And Explanatory Necessity" in *Morality, Reason And Truth*, Copp, David (ed), 79–103. Zimmerman, David.

"Realism And Instrumentalism In Pre–Newtonian Astronomy" in *Testing Scientific Theories*, Earman, John (ed), 201–266. Gardner, Michael R.

"Scientific Realism And Incommensurability" in *Methodology, Metaphysics And The History Of Science*, Cohen, Robert S (ed), 1–32. Burian, Richard M.

A Consideration Of Hilary Putnam. Norton Smith, Thomas Michael.

An Argument Against Anti–Realist Semantics. Appiah, Anthony.

Anti–Realism And Recognitional Capacities. Clark, A J.

Approaching The Truth With The Rule Of Success. Kuipers, Theo A F.

Art In Realist Perspective. Wolterstorff, Nicholas.

Berkeley, Scientific Realism And Creation. Byrne, P A.

Bradley And Realism About Universals. Forrest, Peter.

Chance, Realism, Quantum Mechanics. Leeds, Stephen.

Ethical Realism Defended. Werner, Richard.

Evolutionary Epistemology And Ontological Realism. Clark, A J.

Experimentation And Scientific Realism. Hacking, Ian.

Explaining The Success Of Science. Brown, James Robert.

Goodman's Rigorous Relativism. Elgin, Catherine Z.

Hutcheson, Hume And The Ontology Of Morals. Stafford, J Martin.

Hutcheson's Alleged Realism. Winkler, Kenneth P.

In Response To Frankenberry's "Meland's Empirical Realism And The Appeal To Lived Experience". Meland, Bernard E.

Information Is In The Mind Of The Beholder. Jackendoff, Ray.

Is The Causal Structure Of The Physical Itself Something Physical? Putnam, Hilary.

Kant On Space, Empirical Realism And The Foundations Of Geometry. Harper, William.

La Réalité En Soi Et Connaissable Est–Elle Possible? Espinoza, Miguel.

Laws And Modal Realism. Pargetter, Robert.

Laws Of Nature As Relations Between Universals And As Universals. Armstrong, D M.

Meland's Empirical Realism And The Appeal To Lived Experience. Frankenberry, Nancy.

Moral Skepticism And International Relations. Cohen, Marshall.

Naturalized Epistemology And Metaphysical Realism: A Response To Rorty And Putnam. Stabler, Edward.

On The Fidelity Of Pictures: A Critique Of Goodman's Disjunction Of Perspective And Realism. Topper, David.

One World Or Many: Popper's Three World Theory And The Problem Of Scientific Determinism. Baigrie, Brian.

Phenomenal Realism. Persson, Ingmar.

Psychological Terms, Logical Positivism, And Realism: Issues Related To Construct Validation. Ellett Jr, Frederick S.

Putnam's Paradox. Lewis, David.

Quasi–Realism And Mind–Dependence. Rasmussen, Stig Alstrup.

Realism And Reference. Brooks, D H M.

Realism And Conventionalism In Einstein's Philosophy Of Science: The Einstein– Schlick Correspondence. Howard, Don.

Realism And Anti–Realism About Mathematics. Field, Hartry.

Realism And Grammar. Screen, Donald P.

Reference, Anti–Realism, And Holism. Farrell, Frank B.

Reflections On War And Political Discourse: Realism, Just War, And Feminism In A Nuclear Age. Elshtain, Jean Bethke.

Relativism, Realism, And Rightness: Notes On Goodmanian Worldmaking. Siegel, Harvey.

Sailing Into The Charybdis: Van Fraassen On Bell's Theorem. Stairs, Allen.

Saving The Noumena. Sklar, Lawrence.

Shifting Situations And Shaken Attitudes: An Interview With Barwise And Perry. Perry, John and Barwise, Jon.

Significación Actual Del Pensamiento Zubiriano. Quintás, Alfonso López.

Skepticism And Realism In The *Chuang Tzu*. Goodman, Russell B.

Smart, Salmon, And Scientific Realism. Creath, Richard.

Sozialistischer Humanismus—Sozialistischer Realismus. John, Erhard.

Taking Theories Seriously. Creath, Richard.

Temporality, Perceptual Experience And Peirce's "Proofs" Of Realism. Rosenthal, Sandra B.

The Affinities Of Literature. Boyd, John D.

The Equation Of Information And Meaning From The Perspectives Of Situation Semantics And Gibson's Ecological Realism. Turvey, M T and Carello, Claudia.

The Extreme Realism Of Roger Bacon. Maloney, Thomas S.

The Failure Of An *A Priori* Argument For Realism. Brueckner, Anthony L.

The Generalized Argument From Verification: Work Towards The Metaepistemology Of Perception. Roberts, Scott P.

The Inessentiality Of Lockean Essences. Atherton, Margaret.

The Natural Shiftiness Of Natural Kinds. De Sousa, Ronald.

The Realist Theory Of Meaning. Landman, Fred.

The Rejection Of Truth–Conditional Semantics By Putnam And Dummett. Demopoulos, William.

Three Realist Claims. Ward, Andrew.

Two Notions Of Realism? Mc Ginn, Colin.

Underdetermination And Realism. Bergström, Lars.

Von Neumann And The Anti–Realists. Brown, James R.

Werner's Ethical Realism. Postow, B C.

What Does A Concept Script Do? Diamond, Cora.

When Explanation Leads To Inference. Cartwright, Nancy.

Why Constructive Empiricism Collapses Into Scientific Realism. Melchert, Norman.

Why Kant Couldn't Be An Anti–Realist. Clark, A J.

REALITY

see also Being, Existence, Ontology

Image And Reality In Plato's Metaphysics. Patterson, Richard.

Intimations Of Reality: Critical Realism In Science And Religion. Peacocke, Arthur.

Methphysics: Its Structure And Function. Korner, Stephan.

Order & Organism: Steps To A Whiteheadian Philosophy Of Mathematics & The Natural Sciences. Murray, Code.

Orme Ed Enigmi Nella Filosofia Di Plotino. Bonanate, Ugo.

The Metaphysical Foundations Of Logic, Michael Heim (trans). Heidegger, Martin.

The Unknowable: An Ontological Introduction To The Philosophy Of Religion. Frank, S L.

Thought And Reality In Hegel's System. Cunningham, G W.

"Happiness And The Good Life" in *The Good Life And Its Pursuit*, Dougherty, Jude P (ed), 19–34. Lieb, Irwin C.

REFLECTION

Imagination And Reflection: Intersubjectivity. Hohler, T P (ed).
Reflection And Action. Rotenstreich, Nathan.
"Fallings From Us, Vanishings" in *Existential Coordinates Of Human Condition*, Tymieniecka, A (ed), 91–98. Alexander, Meena.
"Some Remarks On The Concept Of Passion" in *International Kierkegaard Commentary*, Perkins, Robert L (ed), 87–106. Roberts, Robert C.
A Recovery Of Innocence: The Dynamics Of Sartrean Radical Conversion. Walters, Kerry S.
El Método Empírico–Reflexivo. Buela, Alberto E.
Hui–Neng And The Transcendental Standpoint. Laycock, Steven W.
Locke On Consciousness And Reflection. Kulstad, Mark A.
Reflection And Forcing In E–Recursion Theory. Slaman, Theodore A.
Reflexive Reflections. Putnam, Hilary.
The Role Of Reflection In The Structure Of The Human Person. Chudy, W.
Truth And Reflection. Yablo, Stephen.

REFLEX(ES)

Background And Change In B F Skinner's Metatheory From 1930 To 1938. Coleman, S R.

REFLEXIVITY

Alvin Gouldner: Vervreemding, Reflexiviteit, En De Naderende Crisis Van De Sociologie. Disco, Cornelis.

REFORM(S)

Auf Der Suche Nach Der Verlorenen Glaubwürdigkeit: Verfassungsrevision Und Helvetisches Malaise. Hoby, Jean–Pierre.
Educational Excellence In Art Museums: An Agenda For Reform. Williams, Patterson B.
Neukantianismus Und Sozialreformismus. Richter, Friedrich and Wrona, V.
Philosophy And A Career In Law. Perkins, Jeffrey J.

REFORMATION

"Hegel And The Reformation, David Duquette (commentator)" in *History And System*, Perkins, Robert (ed), 73–100. Westphal, Merold.
Taxation In The History Of Protestant Ethics. Shriver, Donald W and Knox, E Richard.

REFUGEE(S)

Who Is A Refugee? Shacknove, Andrew E.

REGAN, T

Three Wrong Leads In A Search For An Environmental Ethic: Tom Regan On Animal Rights, Inherent Values, And 'Deep Ecology'. Partridge, Ernest.

REGIONALISM

Prospects For Regional Philosophies In Australia. Sylvan, Richard.

REGRESS

On Basic Knowledge Without Justification. Moser, Paul K.

REGRETS

Forgiveness And Regret. Golding, Martin P.
Spinoza Und Die Reue. Birnbacher, Dieter.

REGULARITY(–TIES)

Laws Of Nature As Relations Between Universals And As Universals. Armstrong, D M.
On Inductive Support And Some Recent Tricks. Gaifman, Haim.
Possible Worlds Counterfactuals. Adler, Richard.
Regularities, Rules And Strategies. Parret, Herman.

REGULATION(S)

Rights And Regulation: Ethical, Political, And Economic Issues. Machan, Tibor R (ed) and Johnson, M Bruce (ed).
The Legal Profession: Responsibility And Regulation. Hazard, Geoffrey C and Rhode, Deborah L.
"Paternalism" And Social Policy. Sankowski, Edward.
Advertising Professional Success Rates. Gorovitz, Samuel.
Brand Name Extortionists, Intellectual Prostitutes, And Generic Free Riders. Bayles, Michael D.
Commentary On "Advertising Professional Success Rates". Goldman, Alan H.
Paternalism And The Regulation Of Drugs. Sagoff, Mark.
Theoretical And Practical Confusion In American Professional Sport. Rose, David A.
Utility, Autonomy And Drug Regulation. Scriven, Tal.

REICH, W

Wilhelm Reich: Culture As Power. Levine, Norman.

REICHENBACH

Once Upon A Tense. Verkuyl, H J and Le Loux– Schuringa, J A.
The Hans Reichenbach Correspondence—An Overview. Traiger, Saul.
The Problem Of Induction: A New Approach. De Oliveira, Marcos Barbosa.

REID

"Can Belief In God Be Rational If It Has No Foundations" in *Faith And Rationality*, Plantinga, Alvin (ed), 135–186. Wolterstorff, Nicholas.
"The Collapse Of American Evangelical Academia" in *Faith And Rationality*, Plantinga, Alvin (ed), 219–264. Marsden, George.

REIMAN, J

Refuting Reiman And Nathanson. Van Den Haag, Ernest.
Reiman's Libertarian Interpretation Of Rawls' Difference Principle. Alexander, Lawrence.

REINSMITH, W

Improving Applied Ethics: A Response To Reinsmith's Response To "Improving Applied Ethics". Bahm, Archie J.

REJECTION

The Filial Art. Rosenthal, Abigail L.

RELATION(S)

see also International Relation(s)
Ontologie Und Relationen. Horstmann, Rolf–Peter.
Probability, Objectivity And Evidence. Benenson, F C.
Relatedness: Essays In Metaphysics And Theology. Oliver, Harold H.
"Marx's Three Worlds And Their Interrelation" in *Continuity And Change In Marxism*, Fischer, Norman And Others (ed), 1–23. Rader, Melvin.
A Note Concerning The V* Relation On GAMMA–sur–R. Mc Laughlin, T G.
Affine Ebenen Mit Orthogonalitätsrelation. Struve, Horst.
Berkeley's Notions. Flage, Daniel E.
Bradley's Paradox And Russell's Theory Of Relations. Parker, Richard.
Converse Relations. Williamson, Timothy.
Die Funktionale Vollstandigkeit Von Funktionenklassen Über Einer Familie Endlicher Mengen. Poschel, Reinhard.
Is Samavaya (Inherence) An Internal Relation? Mohanta, Dilip K.
Laws And Causal Relations. Tooley, Michael.
Laws Of Nature As Relations Between Universals And As Universals. Armstrong, D M.
Lemmon On Logical Relations. Kennedy, Ralph.
Locke's Empiricism And The Postulation Of Unobservables. Soles, David E.
Moral Community And Animal Rights. Sapontzis, Steve F.
On Σ^1_1 Equivalence Relations With Borel Classes Of Bounded Rank. Sami, Ramez L.
On Relevance Of M Bunge's Concept Of Difference In Meaning, Two Studies Of Inter–Theory Relations. Grobler, Adam.
On The Notion Of Effectiveness. Shapiro, Stewart.
Prolegomena To A Study Of Extrinsic Denomination In The Work Of Francis Suarez, S J. Doyle, John P.
Reduction Of Higher Type Levels By Means Of An Ordinal Analysis Of Finite Terms. Terlouw, Jan.
Register Machine Proof Of The Theorem On Exponential Diophantine Representation Of Enumerable Sets. Jones, J P and Matijasevic, Y V.
Russell's Multiple Relation Theory Of Judgment. Griffin, Nicholas.
The Correlation Of Science And Art (in Czechoslovakian). Pinkava, Jindrich.
Towards The Relation Of Art And Morality (in Czechoslovakian). John, Erhard.
Universals And Laws Of Nature. Tweedale, Martin.

RELATIONSHIP(S)

On Heidegger And The Interpretation Of Environmental Crisis. Foltz, Bruce V.

RELATIVISM

see also Cultural Relativism, Ethical Relativism
After Virtue: Second Edition. Macintyre, Alasdair.
Dimensions Of Moral Education. Carter, Robert E.
The Man Of Reason: "Male" And "Female" In Western Philosophy. Lloyd, Genevieve.
"Is There A Single True Morality" in *Morality, Reason And Truth*, Copp, David (ed), 27–48. Harman, Gilbert.
A Perennial Philosophy Perspective On Richard Rorty's Neo–Pragmatism. Isenberg, Sheldon R and Thursby, G R.
Coercion And The Authority Of Reason. Churchill, John.
Goodman's Rigorous Relativism. Elgin, Catherine Z.
Husserl's Platonism And The Objective Truth (in Hungarian). Rozsnyai, Ervin.
Is Moral Relativism Consistent? Hugly, Philip and Sayward, Charles.
Is Relativism Self–Refuting? Weckert, John.
Perception, Relativism, And Truth: Reflections On Plato's Theaetetus 152–160. Matthen, Mohan.
Popperian And Kuhnian Theories Of Truth And The Imputation Of Relativism. Edison, J.
Rechtstheorie Heute: Kritische Anmerkungen Zu Drei Sammelbänden. Wielinger, Gerhart.
Relative Virtue. Vorobej, Mark.
Relativism And Moral Complacency. Unwin, Nicholas.
Relativism, Realism, And Rightness: Notes On Goodmanian Worldmaking. Siegel, Harvey.
Remarks In Praise Of Guilt. Phillips, D L.
Social Time And Place. Airaksinen, Timo.
Tarski A Relativist? Siegel, Harvey.
The Foreign Corrupt Practices Act And The Imposition Of Values. Brummer, James J.
The Rationality Debate And Gadamer's Hermeneutics: Reflections On Beyond Objectivism And Relativism. Sullivan, Robert.
The Relativity Of Refutations. Tormey, Alan.
The Riddle Of The *Cleitophon*. Roochnik, David L.
The Slippery Slope Of Religious Relativism. Kellenberger, James.
Theaetetus, Part II: A Dialogical Review. Goodman, William H.
Tractatus Sociologico–Philosophicus. Gellner, Ernest.
What Is A Fundamental Ethical Disagreement? Wasserman, Wayne.
Yates On Feyerabend's Democratic Relativism. Alford, C Fred.
Zum Problem Der Diskutierbarkeit Von Normensystemen. Weinke, Kurt.

RELATIVITY

Albert Einstein—Versuch Einer Totalisierenden Würdigung. Zimmerman, Rainer E.
Einstein, Gibbins And The Unity Of Time. Lockwood, Michael.
Ernst Mach And The Theory Of Relativity. Wolters, Gereon.
Néo–Kantisme Et Relativité. Seidengart, Jean.
Set Theory, Skolem's Paradox And The *Tractatus*. Moore, A W.
What Was Einstein's Principle Of Equivalence? Norton, John.

RELEVANCE

A Reply To "On Reading Environmental Ethics". Lemons, John.
Applying Philosophy. Wilson, John and Cowell, Barbara.
De H P Grice À F Jacques: Remarques Sur La Maxime Pragmatique De Pertinence. Armengaud, Françoise.

REPRODUCTION(S)

Sperm And Ova As Property. Jansen, Robert P S.

The Restoration And Reproduction Of Works Of Art. Wreen, Michael.

REPUBLIC(S)

Cicero On The Moral Crisis Of The Late Republic. Mitchell, T N.

The Great Republic. Heller, Agnes.

REPUBLICANISM

The Intellectual Origins Of The American Constitution. Wood, Gordon S.

REPUTATION

The Intellectual And Social Organization Of The Sciences. Whitley, Richard.

RESCHER, N

Conjectures And Rational Preferences. Levy, Robert J.

La Originación Radical De Las Cosas Demostrada A Priori: Leibniz, Nozik, Rescher. Madanes, Leiser.

Nicholas Rescher On Hypothetical Reasoning And The Coherence Of Systems Of Knowledge. Moutafakis, Nicholas J.

On The Relation Of Dialectical And Mathematical Logic (in Czechoslovakian). Havas, K G.

The Illogic Of Inconsistency. Dale, A J.

Why Is There Something Rather Than Nothing? Smith, Joseph Wayne.

RESEARCH

Professional Ethics In Education. Rich, John Martin.

Research Ethics. Berg, Kare (ed) and Tranoy, Knut Erik (ed).

The Social Sciences: Their Nature And Uses. Kruskal, William H (ed).

"Ethics And Values Of Research Design In Archaeology" in *Ethics And Values In Archaeology*, Green, Ernestene L (ed), 75–88. Raab, L Mark.

"Public Policy And Human Research" in *Biomedical Ethics Reviews*, Humber, James M (ed), 3–22. Jonsen, Albert R.

Demarcation Of Science From The Point Of View Of Problems And Problem–Stating. Siitonen, Arto.

Logics And Languages Of Pedagogical Research. Soltis, Jonas F.

Modelling And Models In Future Research (in Hungarian). Nováky, Erzsébet and Hideg, Eva.

On The Strategy Of Scientific Research In Connection With The Coming Into Being Of Television 1839–1934 (in Hungarian). Balázs, Tibor.

Philosophy In Teacher Education And Research. Nelson, Thomas W.

Political Finance In The United States: A Survey Of Research. Beitz, Charles R.

Science, Technology, And Political Decision: From The Creation Of A Theory To The Evaluation Of The Consequences Of Its Application. Radnitzky, Gerard.

Science, Technology, And Political Decision. Radnitzky, Gerard.

Some Remarks On A Theory Of Research In The Work Of Aristotle. Elzinga, Aant.

Taking Blood From Children Causes No More Than Minimal Harm. Smith, Marjorie.

Teacher Education And Research: The Place Of Philosophy. Barrow, Robin.

The Subject Of Baby Fae. Capron, Alexander M and others.

The Tendency Of Tendermindedness In Educational Research, Or, The New Anti–Formalism. Phillips, D C.

The University And Research Ethics. Steneck, Nicholas H.

What Philosophers Can Learn From Agriculture. Thompson, Paul.

Who Decides The Worth Of Educational Research? Fenstermacher, Gary D.

RESEMBLANCE(S)

"(Simple) Qualities And Resemblance" in *Philosophical Analysis In Latin America*, Gracia, Jorge J E and others (eds), 199–218. Robles, Jose A.

RESOURCE(S)

Preparing For The Future: An Essay On The Rights Of Future Generations. Ahrens, John.

"The Ethics Of Archaeological Significance Decisions" in *Ethics And Values In Archaeology*, Green, Ernestene L (ed), 62–74. Dunnell, Robert C.

Allocation Of Resources: The Artificial Heart. Green, Harold P and Gorovitz, Samuel.

Christian Resources For Peace Making In A World Of Conflict. Courtney, Charles.

Japanese Spiritual Resources And Their Contemporary Relevance. Wei– Hsun Fu, Charles.

Kidney Pooling. Alexander, Larry.

Spiritual Resources: Contemporary Problems In Judaism. Pilchik, Ely E.

RESPECT

Consensus, Respect, And Weighted Averaging. Schmitt, Frederick F.

Words; Interests. Kuhse, Helga.

RESPONSIBILITY(–TIES)

Elbow Room: The Varieties Of Free Will Worth Wanting. Dennett, Daniel C.

Medical Ethics: The Moral Responsibilities Of Physicians. Beauchamp, Tom L and Mc Cullough, Laurence B.

Problems And Materials On Professional Responsibility. Morgan, Thomas D and Rotunda, Ronald D.

Research Ethics. Berg, Kare (ed) and Tranoy, Knut Erik (ed).

"I'm The Teacher". Benjamin, Martin and Baum, Robert.

"Individual Responsibility In Advanced Societies" in *The Good Life And Its Pursuit*, Dougherty, Jude P (ed), 145–162. Peperzak, Adrian.

"Rights To Health Care In A Democratic Society" in *Biomedical Ethics Reviews*, Humber, James M (ed), 47–72. Childress, James F.

"The Borrowed Syllabus". Wright, Richard A and Newton, Lisa.

A Cotton Dust Study Unmasked. Levine, Carol.

A Principle Of Responsive Adjustment. French, Peter A.

Can There Be A Freedom Without Responsibility? Ghosh– Dastidar, Koyeli.

Compulsory Health And Safety In A Free Society. Boughton, B J.

Daniel Dennett On Responsibility. Waller, Bruce N.

Food And Freedom In *The Flounder*. Pitkin, Hanna F.

Frankfurt On The Principle Of Alternate Possibilities. Naylor, Margery B.

Groups, Responsibility, And The Failure To Act. Mellema, Gregory.

Hume On Morality, Action, And Character. Davie, William.

I Could Not Have Done Otherwise—So What? Dennett, Daniel C.

Ideal And Non–Ideal Theory: How Should We Approach Questions Of Global Justice. Nielsen, Kai.

Law And The Life Sciences. Annas, George J.

Measuring Responsibility. Bar– On, A Zvie.

Moral Responsibility For Engineers. Alpern, Kenneth D.

Mutual Responsibility Of The Jewish People And Self–Realization (in Hebrew). Schweid, Eliezer.

Nontreatment Decisions For Severely Compromised Newborns. Kipnis, Kenneth.

Pluralism And Responsibility In Post–Modern Science. Toulmin, Stephen E.

Remarks In Praise Of Guilt. Phillips, D L.

Responsibility For Personal Health: A Historical Perspective. Reiser, Stanley J.

Shared Responsibility And Ethical Dilutionism. Mellema, Gregory.

Sharing Responsibility. Zimmerman, Michael J.

Social Ethics, The Philosophy Of Medicine, And Professional Responsibility. Ozar, David T.

Sorabji And The Dilemma Of Determinism. Russell, Paul.

The Arms Race, Genocidal Intent And Individual Responsibility. Santoni, Ronald E.

The International Infant Formula Controversy: A Dilemma In Corporate Social Responsibility. Baker, James C.

The Psychopath As Moral. Smith, Robert J.

Watsonian Freedom And Freedom Of The Will. Hill, Christopher S.

Wissenschaftlich–Technische Revolution—Schöpfertum—Verantwortung. Banse, Gerhard and Horz, H.

REST, J

Current Research In Moral Development As A Decision Support System. Penn, William Y and Collier, Boyd D.

RESTITUTION

Punishment And Restitution: A Restitutionary Approach To Crime And The Criminal. Abel, Charles F and Marsh, Frank H.

RESTORATION

Art And Its Preservation. Carrier, David.

The Restoration And Reproduction Of Works Of Art. Wreen, Michael.

RESTRAINT(S)

Between Assured Destruction And Nuclear Victory: The Case For The "Mad–Plus" Posture. Art, Robert J.

RESTRICTION(S)

The Ethics Of Immigration Restriction. Hudson, James L.

RESURRECTION

Knowing That Jesus' Resurrection Occurred: A Response To Davis. Habermas, Gary R.

Naturalism And The Resurrection: A Reply To Habermas. Davis, Stephen T.

Paul Ricoeur: The Resurrection As Hope And Freedom. Barral, Mary Rose.

RETALIATION

"Deterrence, Maximization, And Rationality" in *The Security Gamble*, Mac Lean, Douglas (ed), 100–122. Gauthier, David.

"Responses To The Paradox Of Deterrence" in *The Security Gamble*, Mac Lean, Douglas (ed), 155–162. Kavka, Gregory S and Gauthier, David.

RETRIBUTION

The Purposes Of Retribution. Manser, Anthony.

Thomas Hobbes And The Philosophy Of Punishment. Norrie, Alan.

RETRIBUTIVE JUSTICE

Retributive Punishment And Humbling The Will. Johnson, Oliver A.

RETRIBUTIVISM

On Retributivism And The Lex Talionis. Primorac, Igor.

Punishment, The New Retributivism, And Political Philosophy. Honderich, Ted.

Retributivism, Moral Education, And The Liberal State. Murphy, Jeffrie G.

RETRODUCTION

Two Ideals Of Explanation In Natural Science. Mc Mullin, Ernan.

REVEALING

The Battle Between Art And Truth. Brogan, Walter.

REVELATION

Christian Biblical Ethics: From Biblical Revelation To Contemporary Christian Praxis: Method And Content. Daly, Robert J (ed).

The Reconstruction Of The Christian Revelation Claim. Hackett, Stuart.

"Christian Experience And Christian Belief" in *Faith And Rationality*, Plantinga, Alvin (ed), 103–134. Alston, William P.

Carta De San Agustín A Consencio: Sobre La Razón Y La Revelación. Moriones, Francisco.

Gustafson's God: Who; What; Where? Mc Cormick, Richard A.

Razón Y Revelación En El Islam. Guzmán, Roberto M.

The Revelation Of Humanity. Munson, Thomas N.

REVERENCE

Svaraj, Reverence, And Creativity. Prasad, Rajendra.

REVERSAL

Merleau–Ponty, The Flesh And Foucault. Cohen, Richard.

REVISION(S)

Der Sinn Der BV–Revision Und Das "(Helvetische) Malaise". Kohler, Georg.

Eigentum Und Seine Grenzen. Fleiner– Gerster, Thomas.

On The Logic Of Theory Change: Partial Meet Contraction And Revision Functions. Alchourron, Carlos and Gardenfors, Peter and Makinson, David.

RIGHT(S)

From The Prudential To The Moral: Reply To Marcus Singer. Gewirth, Alan.
Incorrigibility Laws: The State's Role In Resolving Intrafamily Conflict. Guggenheim, Martin.
Informed Consent: Patient's Right Or Patient's Duty? Hull, Richard T.
Intentions, Rights And Wrongs: A Critique Of Fried. Fischer, Marilyn.
La Teoria Islamica Dei Diritti Umani. Cordone, Claudio.
Law As Fact. Mac Cormack, Geoffrey.
Le *Droit Du Plus Fort*: Hobbes Contre Spinoza. Matheron, Alexandre.
Locke's Theory Of Property: A Re–Examination. Cvek, Peter Paul.
Lockean Provisos And State Of Nature Theories. Bogart, J H.
Moral Y Politica En "Para La Paz Perpetua" De Kant. Amado, Maria Teresa and Lisboa, Joao Luis.
Must The Bearer Of A Right Have The Concept Of That To Which He Has A Right? Stevens, John C.
Negative Liberty. Levin, Michael.
Non–Human Rights: An Idealist Perspective. Sprigge, T L S.
On Gewirth's Derivation Of The Principle Of Generic Consistency. Singer, Marcus G.
Parental Discretion And Children's Rights: Background And Implications For Medical Decision–Making. Schoeman, Ferdinand.
Patent Rights And Better Mousetraps. Michael, Mark.
Problems In The Interpretation Of Hegel's *Philosophy Of Right* (in Hebrew). Avineri, Shlomo.
Property Rights, Liberty And Redistribution. Nelson, William N.
ROBOTS, RIFs, And Rights. Arthur, Alcott.
Right, Morality, And Religion (in Hebrew). Perelman, Haim.
Rights And Excuses. Fletcher, George P.
Rights And Virtues. Gewirth, Alan.
Rights–Based Rights. Meyers, Diane T.
Some Thoughts On The Value Of Saving Lives. Bloom, Gerald.
The Demands Of Justice. Benditt, Theodore M.
The Dominant Protection Association And Education. G0ldstone, Peter.
The Employer–Employee Relationship And The Right To Know. Superson, Anita M.
The Force Of Rights: Parent On 'Moral Specification'. Donnelly, Jack.
The Human Predicament: A Context For Rights And Learning About Rights. Edwards, Philip.
The Marxian Critique Of Justice And Rights. Buchanan, Allen E.
The New OSHA Rules And The Worker's Right To Know. Mc Garity, Thomas O.
The Rights Approach To Mental Illness. Campbell, Tom.
The Status Of The Debate On Rights In The USSR. Lee, Sander H.
Utilitarianism, Rights, And Duties To Self. Sartorius, Rolf.
What's So Special About Rights? Buchanan, Allen.
Why There Are No Human Rights. Husak, Douglas N.

RIGHT TO LIFE

In Defense Of Speciesism. Wreen, Michael.
In The Interest Of Infants. Mahowald, Mary B.
Reporting The Case Of Baby Jane Doe. Kerr, Kathleen.
Thomson And The Current State Of The The Abortion Controversy. Levin, David S.

RIGHTEOUSNESS

The Basic Question Of Moral Philosophy. Heller, Agnes.

RIGHTNESS

Does Rightness Always Involve Wrongness? Bahm, Archie J.

RILKE

"Nel Regno Della Metamorfosi, La Figura Nelle "Elegie Duinesi" Di R M Rilke" in *Il Tempo Dell'Arte*, Papi, Fulvio and others (ed), 29–39. Rella, Franco.

RING(S)

Finite QE Rings In Characteristic p^2. Saracino, Dan and Wood, Carol.
The Model–Theoretic Structure Of Abelian Group Rings. Pappas, Peter C.

RISK(S)

Progress In Utility And Risk Theory. Hagen, Ole (ed) and Wenstop, Fred (ed).
Research Ethics. Berg, Kare (ed) and Tranoy, Knut Erik (ed).
"The US Bishops' Position On Nuclear Deterrence: A Moral Assessment" in *The Security Gamble*, Mac Lean, Douglas (ed), 72–81. Sher, George.
A Portfolio Of Risk Measures. Mac Crimmon, Kenneth R and Wehrung, Donald A.
Nuclear Deterrence: Moral Dilemmas And Risks. Volbrecht, Rose Mary.
On The Risk–Aversion Comparability Of State–Dependent Utility Functions. Nordquist, Gerald L.
The Ordinal Utility Under Uncertainty And The Measure Of Risk Aversion In Terms Of Preferences. Montesano, Aldo.
The St Petersburg Gamble And Risk. Weirich, Paul.

RISK–BENEFIT ANALYSIS

A Cotton Dust Study Unmasked. Levine, Carol.

RITE(S)

Awareness Of The Unseen: The Indian's Contract With Life. Bunge, Robert.

ROBBE–GRILLET, A

"The Denial Of Tragedy" in *Existential Coordinates Of Human Condition*, Tymieniecka, A (ed), 401–408. Ravaux, Francoise.

ROBERTSON, D

Commentary On "Work–Related Ethical Attitudes: Impact On Business Profitability". Braybrooke, David.

ROEHLE, F

Bemerkungen Zu Roehles Arbeit Und Zur Axiomatik. Popper, Karl.

ROGERS, H

Locke And Descartes Through Victorian Eyes. Sell, Alan P F.

ROKEACH, M

Work–Related Ethical Attitudes: Impact On Business Profitability. Dunfee, Thomas W and Robertson, Diana C.

ROLE(S)

Beneath Role Theory: Reformulating A Theory With Nietzsche's Philosophy. Kaplan, Charles D and Weiglus, Karl.
Lordship, Bondage, And The Dialectic Of Work In Traditional Male/Female Relationships. Bell, Linda A and Alcoff, Linda.
Some Recent Books On The Historical Status Of Women. Tormey, Judith.

ROLE PLAYING

Encouraging Positive Justice Reasoning And Perspective–Taking Skills: Two Educational Interventions. Krogh, Suzanne Lowell.

ROMAN

Familia, Domus, And The Roman Conception Of The Family. Saller, Richard P.
Georges Dumézil And The Trifunctional Approach To Roman Civilization. Momigliano, Arnaldo.
Hegel And Roman Liberalism. Cristi, F R.

ROMANIAN

'Romania's Marx' And The National Question: Constantin Dobrogeanu–Gherea. Shafir, Michael.

ROMANTICISM

Benjamin Constant And The Making Of Modern Liberalism. Holmes, Stephen.
Irony And The Logic Of The Romantic Imagination. Alford, Steven E.
Between Enlightenment And Romanticism: Rosenzweig And Hegel (in Hebrew). Pöggeler, Otto.
German Philosophy And The Rise Of Modern Clinical Medicine. Tsouyopoulos, Nelly.
The Romanticism Of Tradition And The Romanticism Of Charisma. Walicki, Andrzej.

ROME

Cicero On The Moral Crisis Of The Late Republic. Mitchell, T N.

ROOSEVELT, F

American Political Thought: The Philosophic Dimension Of American Statesmanship, Second Edition. Frisch, Morton J (ed) and Stevens, Richard G (ed).

RORTY, R

A Missing Dimension In Rorty's Use Of Pragmatism. Edel, Abraham.
A Perennial Philosophy Perspective On Richard Rorty's Neo–Pragmatism. Isenberg, Sheldon R and Thursby, G R.
An Historicist View Of Teaching Philosophy. Portmess, Lisa.
Ch'an And Taoist Mirrors: Reflections On Richard Garner's "Deconstruction Of The Mirror". Lusthaus, Dan.
Foucault's Archaeological Method: A Response To Hacking And Rorty. Wartenberg, Thomas E.
Hermeneutics And The Social Sciences: A Gadamerian Critique Of Rorty. Warnke, Georgia.
Hermeneutics And The Teaching Of Philosophy. Walhout, Donald.
Naturalized Epistemology And Metaphysical Realism: A Response To Rorty And Putnam. Stabler, Edward.
On The Possibility Of Continuing The Conversation Of Mankind. Conway, Jeremiah and Conway, Gertrude.
Philosophy And The Mirror Of Rorty. Munz, Peter.
Philosophy Of Religion And The Mirror Of Nature: Rorty's Challenge To Analytic Philosophy Of Religion. Lauritzen, Paul.
Pragmatism And The Fate Of Philosophy. Young, James O.
Questions And Counterquestions. Habermas, Jürgen.
Reference And Rorty's Veil. Losonsky, Michael.
Reversing Rorty. Meynell, Hugo.
Rorty's Antipodeans: An Impossible Illustration? Gallagher, Kenneth T.
Rorty's Pragmatism: Afloat In Neurath's Boat, But Why Adrift? Sleeper, R W.
The Deconstruction Of The Mirror And Other Heresies: Ch'an And Taoism As Abnormal Discourse. Garner, Richard T.
The Need For Truth. Prado, C G.
Theaetetus, Part II: A Dialogical Review. Goodman, William H.
Waarheid Als Effect; Richard Rorty En De Natuur Van De Spiegel. Kwaad, G C.
What Is The Difference That Makes A Difference: Gadamer, Habermas, And Rorty (in Hebrew). Bernstein, Richard G.

ROSENBERG, A

Defending Microeconomic Theory. Hausman, Daniel.
Discussion: What Economics Is Not: An Economist's Response To Rosenberg. Hands, Douglas W.

ROSENZWEIG, F

"Franz Rosenzweig's Criticism Of Buber's *I And Thou*" in *Martin Buber*, Gordon, Haim (ed), 139–162. Casper, Bernhard.
Between Enlightenment And Romanticism: Rosenzweig And Hegel (in Hebrew). Pöggeler, Otto.
On Franz Rosenzweig's 'New Thinking'. Lichtigfeld, A.
Rosenzweig's Hegel (in Hebrew). Bienenstock, Myriam.

ROSICRUCIAN

'Rosicrucianism Or Cross–rosism' In Hegel's *Phenomenology*. Roberts, Marie.

ROSS, W

Lying And The "Methods Of Ethics". Primoratz, Igor.
On Aristotle's Mind And Being. Broniak, Christopher.

ROTH, P

Empirical Psychology, Naturalized Epistemology, And First Philosophy. Siegel, Harvey.

SALVATION

Equivalencia Y Subordinación, Según San Agustín: Naturaleza Y Papel De La Mujer. Borresen, Kari E.

Human Diversity And Salvation In Christ. Jantzen, Grace M.

Libération Et Salut D'aprés Ernst Bloch (II). Pelletier, Lucien.

Libération Et Salut D'aprés Ernst Bloch (I). Pelletier, Lucien.

The Dignity And Rights Of The Human Person As Saved, As Being Saved, As To Be Saved By Christ. Principe, Walter.

SAMENESS

Material Identity And Sameness. Swindler, J K.

SAMKARA

A Study In The Arguments From Theology With Reference To Hume And Samkara. Kar, Bijayananda.

SAMKYHA

see Sankyha

SAMUELSON, P

ROBOTS, RIFs, And Rights. Arthur, Alcott.

The Role Of Conservation Principles In Twentieth–Century Economic Theory. Mirowski, Philip.

SANCHEZ VILLASENOR, J

La Filosofia Del Dr Jose Sanchez Villasenor. Uribe, Héctor G.

SANCTION(S)

Sanction And Obligation. Hardin, Russell.

The Foreign Corrupt Practices Act And The Imposition Of Values. Brummer, James J.

SANCTITY OF LIFE

"Religious Traditions In Bioethical Decision Making" in *Bioethical Frontiers In Perinatal Intensive Care*, Snowden, Fraser (ed), 77–88. Paris, John J.

"The Sanctity Of Life" in *Biomedical Ethics Reviews*, Humber, James M (ed), 29–42. Rachels, James.

SANFORD, D

Knowability, Believability And Begging The Question: A Reply To David H Sanford. Biro, John I.

SANKARA

Brahman, God, Substance And Nature: Samkara And Spinoza. Gupta, Bina.

Human Embodiment: The Theme And The Encounter In Vedāntic Phenomenology. Sinha, Debabrata.

Levels Of Truth And Reality In The Philosophies Of Descartes And Samkara. Schroeder, Craig.

SANSKRIT

Bhagavad–Gita: An Exegetical Commentary. Minor, Robert N.

Harper's Dictionary Of Hinduism: Its Mythology, Folklore, Philosophy, Literature, And History. Stutley, James and Stutley, Margaret.

Philosophy East And West: Two Fundamentally Different Approaches To Philosophizing. Kanti Sarkar, Tushar.

SANTAYANA

The Naturalists And The Supernatural: Studies In Horizon And An American Philosophy Of Religion. Shea, William M.

Essentialism And Santayana's Realm Of Essence. Kerr–Lawson, Angus.

Nature And Art. Levi, Albert W.

SANTILLI, P

The Informative And Persuasive Functions Of Advertising: A Moral Appraisal—A Comment. Emamalizadeh, Hossein.

SARTORIUS, R

The Role Of Coherence In Legal Reasoning. Levenbook, Barbara Baum.

SARTRE

Jean–Paul Sartre (in Hungarian). István, Fehér M.

Phenomenology And Existentialism: An Introduction. Grossman, Reinhardt.

Radical Humanism. Améry, Jean and Rosenfeld, Sidney (ed) and Rosenfeld, Stella (ed).

Sartre After Sartre. Jameson, Fredric (ed).

The Georgetown Symposium On Ethics. Porreco, Rocco (ed).

"Henry Veatch And The Problem Of A Noncognitivist Ethics" in *The Georgetown Symposium On Ethics*, Porreco, Rocco (ed), 159–170. Lee, Sander H.

"Out From Under The Railroad Bridge: Sartre And The Soviets" in *Contemporary Marxism*, O' Rourke, James J (ed), 245–254. Blakeley, Thomas J.

"Sartre And Alienation" in *Continuity And Change In Marxism*, Fischer, Norman And Others (ed), 144–169. Georgopoulos, N.

A Recovery Of Innocence: The Dynamics Of Sartrean Radical Conversion. Walters, Kerry S.

An Analytic–Existential Solution To The 'Knowing That One Knows' Problem. Johnson, Steve A.

Bad Faith: A Dilemma. Gordon, Jeffrey.

Beauvoir And Satre: The Forms Of Farewell. Barnes, Hazel E.

Being–In–Itself Revisited. Holmes, Richard.

Bonne Et Mauvaise Foi, Notions Faible Et Forte. Catalano, Joseph S.

Dialectical Reason And Education: Sartre's Fused Group. Gordon, Haim.

Flauberts Laughter. Caws, Peter.

Improving Applied Ethics: A Response To Bahm's "Improving Applied Ethics". Reinsmith, William A.

Jean–Paul Sartre And The Problem Of The Other. Andrews, Christine.

Karol Cardinal Wojtyla And Jean–Paul Sartre On The Intentionality Of Consciousness. Pappin, Joseph.

La Psychanalyse Sans L'inconscient? Knee, Philip.

Le Problème Moral Comme Totalisation Chez Sartre. Knee, Philip.

Le Souverain Dans La "Critique De La Raison Dialectique". Saint–Sernin, Bertrand.

On The Visual Constitution Of Society: The Contributions Of Georg Simmel And

Jean–Paul Sartre To A Sociology Of The Senses. Weinstein, Deena and Weinstein, Michael.

Play As Negation And Creation Of The World. Kuczyński, Janusz.

Sartre O Las Dificultades De Escribir Una Moral. Fornet–Betancourt, Raul.

Sartre's Acceptance Of The Principle Of Universality. Lee, Sander H.

Sartre's Dialectical Anarchism: Institution, Sovereignty, And The State. Barker, Jeffrey H.

The Central Role Of Universalization In Sartrean Ethics. Lee, Sander H.

The Image Of The Father In Sartre's "L'universel Singulier" (in Hebrew). Neppi, Enzo.

The Impasse Of *No Exit*. Kolenda, Konstantin.

The Revelation Of Humanity. Munson, Thomas N.

The Role Of Rules In Ethical Decision Making. Hargrove, Eugene C.

The Roots Of The Existentialist Theory Of Freedom In *Ideas I*. Edie, James M.

Trans–World Identity Of Future Contingents: Sartre On Leibnizian Freedom. Winant, Terry.

SATAN

Milton, Duns Scotus, And The Fall Of Satan. Rumrich, John Peter.

SATIRE

Socrates And Post–Socratic Satire. Guilhamet, Leon.

SATISFACTION

Truth Without Satisfaction. Fine, Kit and Mc Carthy, Timothy.

SAUSSURE, F

Kritische Notities Bij Ferdinand De Saussure's. Bakker, D M.

Reflexiones Filosóficas Sobre La Lingüística Estructuralista De Ferdinand De Saussure. Beuchot, Mauricio.

SAVAGE(S)

L'America Primitiva E L'Europa Cristiana. Petyx, Vincenza.

SAVAGE, L

Timing Contradictions In Von Neumann And Morgenstern's Axioms And In Savage's "Sure–Thing" Proof. Pope, Robin.

SAYING

Saying And Conveying. Sainsbury, Mark.

What We Do And Say In Saying And Doing Something. Gandhi, Ramchandra.

SAYWARD, C

Sacrificing Persons For The General Welfare: A Comment Of Sayward. Wein, Sheldon.

SCANDINAVIAN

Philosophy Of Medicine In Scandinavia. Lindahl, B Ingemar B.

SCARCE MEDICAL RESOURCE(S)

The Medical Treatment Of Wild Animals. Loftin, Robert W.

SCARCITY

"Scarcity And Basic Medical Care" in *Biomedical Ethics Reviews*, Humber, James M (ed), 95–106. Almeder, Robert.

SCEPTICISM

A Sceptical Dialogue On Induction. Naess, Arne.

Anti–Skepticism. Lee, Henry and Schouls, Peter A (ed).

Beyond Good And Evil: Nietzsche's "Free Spirit" Mask. Lampert, Laurence.

Epistemic Analysis: A Coherence Theory Of Knowledge. Ziff, Paul.

The Central Problem Of David Hume's Philosophy. Salmon, C V.

The Significance Of Philosophical Scepticism. Stroud, Barry.

'Communicative Competence' And The Skeptic. Beatty, Joseph.

"Hobbes And Skepticism" in *History Of Philosophy In Making*, Thro, Linus J (ed), 133–148. Popkin, Richard H.

"Philosophy And Scepticism" in *Philosophy And Life: Essays On John Wisdom*, Dilman, Ilham (ed), 317–345. Dilman, Ilham.

"Sceptic's Two Kinds Of Assent & Question Of Possibility Of Knowledge" in *Philosophy In History*, Rorty, Richard and others (ed), 255–278. Frede, Michael.

"The Sceptic In His Place And Time" in *Philosophy In History*, Rorty, Richard and others (ed), 225–254. Burnyeat, M F.

A Reasonable Reply To Hume's Scepticism. Schlagel, Richard H.

Common Sense: Who Can Deny It? Govier, Trudy.

Descartes Knows Nothing. Watson, Richard A.

Descartes' First Meditation: Something Old, Something New, Something Borrowed. Groarke, Leo.

How To Become A Moderate Skeptic: Hume's Way Out Of Pyrrhonism. Michaud, Yves.

Hume And The Relation Of Science To Religion Among Certain Members Of The Royal Society. Force, James E.

Hume's "Dialectic". Coleman, Dorothy P.

Hume's Criterion Of Significance. Williams, Michael.

Hume's Naturalism—'Proof' And Practice. Ferreira, M J.

Is Hume A Sceptic With Regard To Reason? Wilson, Fred.

Is There A Language–Game That Even The Deconstructionist Can Play? Fuller, Steven.

Leibniz Y El Escepticismo. De Olaso, Ezequiel.

Losing Track Of The Sceptic. Brueckner, Anthony L.

Marx's Moral Skepticism. Panichas, George E.

Montaigne And The Rise Of Skepticism In Early Modern Europe: A Reappraisal. Schiffman, Zachary S.

Moral Faith And Ethical Skepticism Reconsidered. Kurtz, Paul.

Moral Skepticism And Tolerance. Ihara, Craig K.

Nietzsche's Speech Of Indirection: Commentary On Laurence Lampert's *"Beyond Good And Evil*: Nietzsche's 'Free Spirit' Mask". Zanardi, William J.

Nozick On Inferential Knowledge. Mazoué, James G.

Popper And Metaphysical Skepticism. Waterhouse, Joseph.

Reason And Antecedent Doubt. Frankel, Lois.

SCIENCE

A Note On Quantum Theory, Complementarity, And Uncertainity. Busch, Paul and Lahti, Pekka J.

A Propósito De Un Libro. Radchick, Laura.

A Restrictive Interpretation Of Lakatos' Rationality Theory. Kalfas, Vassilis.

A Schutz And F Kaufmann: Sociology Between Science And Interpretation. Helling, Ingeborg K.

A Study Of Theory Unification. Nugayev, Renat.

A Type Of Non–Causal Explanation. Achinstein, Peter.

A Widely Accepted But Nonetheless Astonishingly Flimsy Argument Against Analytical Behaviorism. Boyer, David L.

Accelerated Twins. Keswani, G H.

Acceptance Of Empirical Statements: A Bayesian Theory Without Cognitive Utilities. Harsanyi, John C.

Adams On Theoretical Reduction. Day, Michael A.

Aether/Or: The Creation Of Scientific Concepts. Nersessian, Nancy J.

Against The Monism Of The Moment: A Reply To Elliott Sober. Kitcher, Philip.

Aktualität Und Historizität: Bemühungen Um Werk Und Wirken Leonhard Eulers. Hess, Heinz–Jürgen.

Aktuelle Probleme Der Wissenschaftlich–Technischen Revolution In Der Sowjetischen Philosophie. Thiele, Gabriele.

Albert Einstein—Versuch Einer Totalisierenden Würdigung. Zimmerman, Rainer E.

Alcune Riflessioni Sulla Cultura Illuministica Napoletana E L'eredità Di Galilei. Ferrone, Vincenzo.

Algunas Preguntas Sobre Etica. Parent, Juan M.

Allgemeine Modelltheorie. Reitzer, Alfons.

Alvin Gouldner: Vervreemding, Reflexiviteit, En De Naderende Crisis Van De Sociologie. Disco, Cornelis.

An Attempt At The Utilization Of Prigogine's Thermodynamics In American Futurology (in Czechoslovakian). Hohos, Ladislav.

An Exchange On Local Beables. Bell, J S and others.

An Interview With E O Wilson On Sociobiology And Religion. Saver, Jeffrey.

Another Look At The Predictivist Thesis. Jones, William R.

Anthropological Definitions Of Religion. Segal, Robert A.

Approaching The Truth With The Rule Of Success. Kuipers, Theo A F.

Approximative Explanation Is Deductive Nomological. Pearce, David and Rantala, Veikko.

Are 'Scientific' Objects Coloured? Hardin, C L.

Are Probabilism And Special Relativity Incompatible? Maxwell, Nicholas.

Are Punctuationists Wrong About The Modern Synthesis? Stidd, Benton M.

Aristoteles Como Cientifico. Serrano, Jorge A.

Aristotle As Proof Theorist. Smith, Robin.

Art Natural Enemies. Carver, Ronald P.

Aspects Of The Logic Of History–Of–Science Explanation. Finocchiaro, Maurice A.

Background And Change In B F Skinner's Metatheory From 1930 To 1938. Coleman, S R.

Bayesianism And Support By Novel Facts. Howson, Colin.

Begriffsbildung In Der Psychologie: Zur Logik Des Begriffes "Intelligenz". Perner, Josef.

Bemerkungen Aur Pragmatisch–epistemischen Wende In Der Wissenschaftstheoretische Analyse Der Ereigniserklärungen. Lenk, Hans.

Berichte Und Diskussionen (in German). Fischer, Harald–Paul.

Berkeley, Epistemology, And Science. Steinkraus, Warren E.

Beyond Divorce: Current Status Of The Discovery Debate. Nickles, Thomas.

Biological Conception Of Evolution And The Problem Of Thermodynamics From The Standpoint Of The Work Of I Prigogine (in Czechoslovakian). Novák, Vladimir J A.

Biologische Gesetze Und Dialektische Methode. Nowiński, Czeslaw.

Biology And Ideology: The Interpenetration Of Science And Values. Richardson, Robert C.

Biotechnology And The Social Reconstruction Of Molecular Biology. Markle, Gerald E and Robin, Stanley S.

Calibration, Coherence, And Scoring Rules. Seidenfeld, Teddy.

Changed Concepts Of Brain And Consciousness: Some Value Implications. Sperry, Roger.

Chemie Und Dialektik. Simon, Rudiger.

Commensurability, Incommensurability And Cumulativity In Scientific Knowledge. Agazzi, Evandro.

Comment On Pommerehne Et Al, "Concordia Discors: Or: What Do Economists Think". Meile, Richard and Shanks, Stephanie L.

Commentary On Patrick A Heelan's "Hermeneutics Of Experimental Science In The Context Of The Life–World". Kisiel, Theodore.

Comments Of Theodore Kisiel's Commentary On My Paper: Hermeneutics Of Experimental Science In The Context Of The Life–World. Heelan, Patrick A.

Compensatory Neoplasia: Chronic Erythrocytosis And Neuroblastic Tumors. De La Monte, Suzanne M and Hutchins, Grover M and Moore, G William.

Conditions Versus Transference: A Reply To Ehring. Aronson, Jerrold.

Contemporary Biotechnologies And The Concept Of Material Production (in Czechoslovakia. Kolársky, R.

Converging Reflections On The Philosophy Of Science. Newton Smith, W and Wilkes, K.

Correct Explanatory Arguments And Understanding–why An Approach To Scientific Understanding Based On Knowledge Dynamics. Schurz, Gerhard.

Correcting Concepts. Tiles, Mary.

Corruption In Science: The Chinese Case. Suttmeier, Richard P.

Creation Science: Enough Is Enough Is Too Much. Ruse, Michael.

Critique Du Rationalisme Critique. Largeault, Jean.

Darwinism And The Modern Scientific Revolution—175 Years From C Darwin's Birth. Ghiţa, Simion.

Das Von Der Naturwissenchaft Gepraegte Menschenbild (in Polish). Luyten, Norbert A.

De Ethogene Methode Van Sociaal–Wetenschappelijk Onderzoek Van Rom Harré. Van Der Veen, Romke.

De Incommensurabiliteit Van Aanleg En Omgeving. Smit, Harry.

De La Ideología A La Ciencia. Rodríguez, José M.

De La Physique À L'épistémologie B D'Espagnat Et I Prigogine. Gauthier, Yvon.

De Wiskundige Rede (Summary: The Mathematical Reason). Klever, W N A.

Demarcation Of Science From The Point Of View Of Problems And Problem–Stating. Siitonen, Arto.

Demarkation Und Rationale Rekonstruktion Bei Imre Lakatos. Schramm, Alfred.

Der Erste Wiener Kreis. Haller, Rudolf.

Der Wissenschaftlich–Technische Fortschritt Und Die Interdisziplinäre Zusammenarbeit Von Philosophen Und Technikwissenschaftlern. Jobst, E.

Descartes: Methodological Ideal And Actual Procedure. Shea, William R.

Descartes' Proto–Critique. Glouberman, M.

Development And Continuity In Schlick's Thought. Geymonat, Ludovico.

Dialectical Fields And Transformations: Brouwer–Fields, Beth–Fields, And Naess–Transformations. Barth, E M.

Dialektik—Logik—Wissenschaftsentwicklung. Erpenbeck, John.

Die Dynamische Naturvorstellung Als Naturphilosophische Grundlage Der Heutigen Physik. Adler, Norbert.

Die Entwicklung Der Paläoanthropologie Im Lichte Der Stammbäme Des Menschen. Halaczek, B.

Die Funktion Der Hermeneutik In Den Positiven Wissenschaften. Kimmerle, Heinz.

Die Induktive Methode Und Das Induktionsproblem In Der Griechischen Philosophie. Tsouyopoulos, Nelly.

Die Sozialökonomische Determiniertheit Wissenschaftlichen Schöpfertums. Steiner, Helmut.

Discussion: What Would Happen If Everyone Did It? Sober, Elliott.

Discussion: Galileo And The Continuity Thesis. Wallace, William A.

Discussion: What Economics Is Not: An Economist's Response To Rosenberg. Hands, Douglas W.

Discussion: Quantum Mechanics And Value Definiteness. Pitowsky, Itamar.

Discussion: A Note On Tense And Subjunctive Conditionals. Thomason, Richard.

Discussion: Woodfield's Analysis Of Teleology. Nissen, Lowell.

Discussion: Are We Only Five Minutes Old: Acock On The Age Of The Universe. Smith, Joseph W and Ward, Sharyn.

E Pucciarelli: La Filosofía Como Deslinde. Carpio, Adolfo P.

EPR Resuscitated: A Reply To Halpin's 'EPR Resuscitated: A Reply To Wessels'. Wessels, Linda.

Eine Analyse Und Kritische Bewertung Der Methode Und Des Prinzips Der Praktischen Argumentation Oswald Schwemmers. Asouzu, Innocent.

Einen Neuen Schwerpunkt In Der Zusammenarbeit Mit Naturwissenschaftlern—Brauchen Wir Ihn Wirklich? Liebscher, Heinz and Simon, R.

Einstein On Locality And Separability. Howard, Don.

Elementos De Continuidad Y Discontinuidad Entre La Ciencia Medieval Y La Primera Revolución Científica. Ramirez, Edgar R.

Emotion And Action In Cognitive Psychology: Breaching A Fashionable Philosophical Fence. Ericson, David P.

Empirische Mogelijkheden; Sleutelbegrip Van De Wetenschapsfilosofie. Kuipers, Theo A F.

Empirische Wetten En Theorieën. En Kuipers, Theo and Zandvoort, Henk.

Engels' "Dialektik Der Natur" Und Die Einheit Der Naturwissenschaftlichen Erkenntnis. Korch, Helmut and Ennuschat, W.

Engineering Human Reproduction: A Challenge To Public Policy. Gorovitz, Samuel.

Engineering And The Philosophy Of Science. Broome, Taft H.

Enkele Pogingen Tot Reconstructie Van De Evolutietheorie En De Populatiegenetica Als Wetenschappelijke Onderzoeks–Programma's. Van Balen, G A M.

Ernst Mach And The Theory Of Relativity. Wolters, Gereon.

Es El Psicoanálisis Una Pseudo–Ciencia? Rush, Alan A.

Evaluations And Norms Of Conduct In Leon Petrazycki's Psychologistic Concept Of Law And Morality (in Polish). Smoczynski, P J.

Events And Causality (in Hebrew). Steiner, Mark.

Evolution And The Fundamentalist Critique: Contributions To Educational Philosophy. Vold, David J.

Evolutional Rheology And Mechanical Asymmetry (in Czechoslovakian). Sobotka, Zdenek.

Experiment—Modell—Theorie. Horz, Herbert.

Experimentation And Scientific Realism. Hacking, Ian.

Explaining The Success Of Science. Brown, James Robert.

Explanation In Physical Cosmology: Essay In Honor Of C G Hempel's Eightieth Birthday. Kanitscheider, Bernule.

Explanatory Asymmetries. Woodward, James.

Extraterrestrial Science. Rescher, Nicholas.

Feyerabend's Irrational Science. Grünfeld, Joseph.

Filosofie En Wetenschap In De Frankfurter Schule (1930–1950). Koenis, Sjaak.

Finocchiaro On Rational Explanation. Doppelt, Gerald.

Formal Systems Of Dialogue Rules. Krabbe, Erik C W.

Formation And Development Of Scientific Concepts. Pedersen, Stig Andur.

Foucault's Archaeological Method: A Response To Hacking And Rorty. Wartenberg, Thomas E.

Fragmentation And Wholeness In Religion And In Science. Bohm, David.

Freiheit Und Perfektion. Düll, Rupprecht.

SCIENCE

The Use Of Interval Estimators As A Basis For Decision–Making In Medicine. Lie, Reidar K.

The Vital Attitude Of Man From The Standpoint Of Prigogine's Thermodynamics (in Czechoslovakian). Stoll, Ivan.

Theoretical Terms And Bridge Principles: A Critique Of Hempel's (Self–) Criticisms. Moulines, C Ulises.

Theoretical Functions, Theory And Evidence. Forge, John.

Theorieën Over Ethiek En Over De Levenspraktijk. Troost, A.

Theory Dynamics And Knowledge Representation From An Information–Theoretical Point Of View. Hauffe, Heinz.

Theory Testing In Science—The Case Of Solar Neutrinos. Pinch, Trevor.

Theory, Observation And Inductive Learning. Lane, N R.

Thermodynamics And Life. Peacocke, Arthur.

Thermodynamics Without Equilibrium, Totality, Dialectic (in Czechoslovakian). Rajchl, Jaroslav.

Three Explanatory Traditions In The Law Of Falling Bodies (in Portuguese). Nascimento, Carlos A R.

Time And Stress: Alice In Wonderland. Petersen, Calvin R.

Topology Of Internal And External Factors In The Development Of Knowledge. Lelas, Srdan.

Toward An Epistemologically–Relevant Sociology Of Science. Campbell, Donald T.

Towards An Economic Theory Of Scientific Revolutions—A Cynical View. Wieland, Bernhard.

Truth, Rationality And The Sociology Of Science. Jennings, Richard C.

Two Ideals Of Explanation In Natural Science. Mc Mullin, Ernan.

Two Pathographies: A Study In Illness And Literature. Hawkins, Anne.

Un Atelier Sur Les Concepts Fondamentaux Relatifs À La Mesure. Gonella, L.

Underdetermination And Realism. Bergström, Lars.

Understanding Peter Winch. Sharrock, W W and Anderson, R J.

Une Approche Naïve De L'analyse Non–Standard. Robert, A.

Unified Field Theory And The Conventionality Of Geometry. Pitowsky, Itamar.

Validity And Applicability Of Thermodynamics Out Of The Framework Of Physical Systems (in Czechoslovakian). Marvan, Milan.

Von Neumann And The Anti–Realists. Brown, James R.

Was Erwartet Uns Jenseits Der Wissenschaft: Ethno–Philosophie: Erfahrungen Und Möglichkeiten Im Umgang Mit Dem Irrationalen. Stuben, Peter E.

Was Ist Inkommensurabilität? Blazer, W.

Weltanschaulich–Philosophische Bildung Und Erziehung Im Mathematisch–Naturwissenschaftlichen Unterricht. Viebahn, Ursula and Viebahn, W.

Weltanschauliche Und Wissenschaftstheoretische Probleme Des Verhältnisses Von Natur– Und Technikwissenschaften. Jobst, Eberhard and Marmai, U.

Were You A Zygote? Anscombe, G E M.

What Was Einstein's Principle Of Equivalence? Norton, John.

When Explanation Leads To Inference. Cartwright, Nancy.

Whewell's Consilience Of Inductions—An Evaluation. Fisch, Menachem.

Whitehead, Special Relativity, And Simultaneity. White, Villard Alan.

Whitehead's "Prehension" And Hegel's "Mediation". Christensen, Darrel E.

Who Needs Paradigms? Roth, Paul A.

Wholes, Parts, And Laws Of Motion. Hassing, R F.

Why Constructive Empiricism Collapses Into Scientific Realism. Melchert, Norman.

Widerspiegelung Objektiver Naturdialektik In Mathematisierten Naturwissenschaftlichen Theorien. Roseberg, Ulrich.

Wissenschaftlich–Technische Revolution—Schöpfertum—Verantwortung. Banse, Gerhard and Horz, H.

Wissenschaftstheorie Und Praxis: Zur Funktion Soziologischer Theorienbildung. Rust, Holger.

Wissenschaft Als Gegenstand Der Wissenschaft Vom Menschlichen Erleben Und Verhalten. Brandtstädter, Jochen and Reinert, Gunther.

Zu Den Funktionen Der Marxistisch–Leninistischen Philosophie In Bezug Auf Die Einzelwissenschaften. Hager, Nina.

Zu Einigen Aktuellen Zügen Bürgerlicher Wissenschafts– Und Technikkritik. Kaizik, Peter.

Zum Platz Der "Randglossen" In Der Geschichte Der Theorie Des Wissenschaftlichen Kommunismus. Fieber, Hans–Joachim and Schneider, W.

Zum Problem Der Unendlichkeit. Titze, H.

Zum Stand Der Entwicklungstheorie In Den Naturwissenschaften. Ley, Hermann.

Zur Dialektik In Der Biologischen Evolution. Beurton, Peter.

Zur Entstehung Und Begründung Des Newtonschen Calculus Fluxionum Und Des Leibnizschen Calculus Differentialis. Stiegler, Karl D.

Zur Ortsbestimmung Der Historischen Wissenschaften. Kramer, Hans.

Zur Realisierung Des Verhältnisses Von Philosophie Und Einzelwissenschaften Im Marxistisch–Leninistischen Grundstudium. Bernhardt, Herbert and Richter, F.

Zur Rolle Des Subjektiven Faktors In Der Wissenschaftsentwicklung. Ludwig, Gerd and Brau, Richard and Rosenthal, Erwin.

Zur Theorien– Und Methodenentwicklung In Den Naturwissenschaften. Kannegiesser, Karlheinz and Uebeschar, K.

Zur Verteidigung Einiger Hempelscher Thesen Gegen Kritiken Stegmüllers. Küttner, Michael.

SCIENTIFIC

Habermas On Rationality. Roderick, Rick.

One World Or Many: Popper's Three World Theory And The Problem Of Scientific Determinism. Baigrie, Brian.

Ontological And Epistemological Aspect Of Contradictions: Importance For Analysis Of Development Of Society (in Czechoslovakian). Zeman, Jirí.

Philosophische Fragen Der Wissenschaftsentwicklung. Arnold, Alfred.

Popper's Piecemeal Engineering: What Is Good For Science Is Not Always Good For Society. Irzik, Gürol.

Theory And Practice In Marxism. Apostel, Leo.

SCIENTIFIC LANGUAGE

"Metaphor In Science" in *Metaphor*, Miall, David S (ed), 89–105. Martin, J and Harre, R.

On The Typology Of The Scientific Languages. Ginev, Dimiter.

Science And Common Sense. Jason, Gary J.

SCIENTIFIC METHOD

Theory And Measurement. Kyburg Jr, Henry E.

"Method Of Hypothesis" in *Observation, Experiment, And Hypothesis In Modern Physical Science*, Achinstein, Peter (ed), 127–146. Achinstein, Peter.

"Peirce And The Conditions Of Possibility Of Science" in *History Of Philosophy In Making*, Thro, Linus J (ed), 177–196. Delaney, C F.

Corruption In Science: The Chinese Case. Suttmeier, Richard P.

Philosophy: Just Like Science Only Different. Edidin, Aron.

SCIENTIFIC PHILOSOPHY

"Philosophical Element In Social Theory And Practice" in *Ideology, Philosophy And Politics*, Parel, Anthony (ed), 61–76. Plamenatz, John.

Russell's Scientific Mysticism. Nathanson, Stephen.

SCIENTIFIC REVOLUTION

Darwinism And The Modern Scientific Revolution—175 Years From C Darwin's Birth. Ghița, Simion.

Elementos De Continuidad Y Discontinuidad Entre La Ciencia Medieval Y La Primera Revolución Científica. Ramirez, Edgar R.

New Philosophies Of Science In The USA; A Selective Survey. Kisiel, Theodore and Johnson, Galen.

Philosophisch–Weltanschauliche Auseinandersetzungen Um Theoretische Positionen Zur Wissenschaftsgeschichte. Roseberg, Ulrich.

Scientific Change, Continuity, And Problem Solving. Pearce, David and Rantala, V.

Wissenschaftlich–Technische Revolution—Schöpfertum—Verantwortung. Banse, Gerhard and Horz, H.

SCIENTIFIC THEORY(–RIES)

Bachelard: Science And Objectivity. Tiles, Mary.

Testing Scientific Theories. Earman, John (ed).

"Newton's Demonstration Of Universal Gravitation" in *Testing Scientific Theories*, Earman, John (ed), 179–200. Laymon, Ronald.

Formal Truth And Objective Truth. Stefanov, Anguel S.

Taking Theories Seriously. Creath, Richard.

SCIENTIST(S)

The Intellectual And Social Organization Of The Sciences. Whitley, Richard.

SCOTISM

Leibniz' Gebrochenes Verhältnis Zur Erkenntnismetaphysik Der Scholastik. Hübener, Wolfgang.

SCOTT, D

Are Contexts Semantic Determinants? Hanson, Philip P.

SCOTTISH

The Origin Of Property And The Development Of Scottish Historical Science. Bowles, Paul.

SCRIPTURE(S)

The Disciple And The Master. Doyle, Eric (trans & Ed).

The Reconstruction Of The Christian Revelation Claim. Hackett, Stuart.

Ciceronianism And Augustine's Conception Of Philosophy. Di Lorenzo, Raymond D.

Karl Adam's Christology: Towards A Post–Critical Method. Krieg, Robert A.

SCRUTON, R

Intellectual And Sensuous Pleasure. Savedoff, Barbara E.

SCULPTURE

"Le Forme Dell'Antico: Immagini Della Scultura Classica In Winckelmann" in *Il Tempo Dell'Arte*, Papi, Fulvio and others (ed), 102–126. Bonesio, Luisa.

SEARLE, J

'Is' Presupposes 'Ought'. Hinman, Lawrence M.

Against Neural Chauvinism. Cuda, Tom.

Assertion And Convention. Miller, S R.

Cause In Perception: A Note On Searle's *Intentionality*. Mc Culloch, Gregory.

Kritisches Zu Kripkes Theorie Der Eigennamen. Franzen, Winfried.

La Loi Du Langage Et L'anarchie Du Sens: A Propos Du Débat Searle–Derrida. Frank, Manfred.

On Searle's "Solution" To The Mind–Body Problem. Lyons, William E.

On The Causal Self–Referentiality Of Perceptual Experiences And The Problem Of Concrete Perceptual Reference. Natsoulas, Thomas.

Searle's Answer To 'Hume's Problem'. Double, Richard.

Veridicality: More On Searle. Millar, Alan.

SEBALD, M

Logic Is Not Occultism. Kootte, Anton E.

SECONDARY QUALITY(–TIES)

A Functionalist Interpretation Of Locke's Theory Of Simple Ideas. Vinci, Thomas.

SECTS

Science, Sect, And Uncertainty In Voltaire's "dictionaire Philosophique". Shoaf, Richard.

SECULAR

Theorieën Over Ethiek En Over De Levenspraktijk. Troost, A.

SECULARISM

Positivism And Tradition In An Islamic Perspective: Kemalism. Arkoun, Mohammed.

Symposium On Humanism, Secularism, And Religion. Tonne, Herbert A and Eddy,

SET THEORY

On The Definition Of Ordered *n*–Tupels. Neumann, Olaf.

On The Independence Of The Kinna Wagner Principle. Pincus, David.

On The Role Of The Baire Category Theorem And Dependent Choice In The Foundations Of Logic. Goldblatt, Robert.

On The Standard–Model Hypothesis Of ZF. Abian, Alexander.

On The Structure Of Ext(A, z) In ZFC+. Sageev, G and Shelah, S.

On The Ultrafilters And Ultrapowers Of Strong Partition Cardinals. Henle, J M and Kleinberg, E M and Watro, R J.

On Violating The GCH Below The Least Measurable Cardinal. Pelletier, D H.

Proof Theory And Set Theory. Takeuti, Gaisi.

Replacement And Connection In Intuitionistic Set Theory. Goodman, Nicholas D.

Set Theories: Their Philosophic Issues And Foundations (in Chinese). Hung, Cheng–Uan and Liu, Fu–tseng.

Simplified Morasses With Linear Limits. Velleman, Dan.

Subgroups Of A Free Group And The Axiom Of Choice. Howard, Paul E.

The Cardinality Of The Set Of Dedekind Finite Cardinals In Fraenkel–Mostowski Models. Rubin, Arthur L and Rubin, Jean E.

The Consistency Of The Axiom Of Universality For The Ordering Of Cardinalities. Forti, Marco and Honsell, Furio.

The Consistency Of Some 4–stratified Subsystem Of NF Including NF3. Boffa, Maurice and Casalegno, Paolo.

The Illogic Of Inconsistency. Dale, A J.

Toposes In Logic And Logic In Toposes. Bunge, Marta.

Truth In All Of Certain Well–Founded Countable Models Arising In Set Theory. Rosenthal, John W.

Une Approche Naïve De L'analyse Non–Standard. Robert, A.

Weakly Compact Cardinals In Models Of Set Theory. Enayat, Ali.

Which Set Existence Axioms Are Needed To Prove The Cauchy/Peano Theorem For Ordinary Differential Equations? Simpson, Stephen.

SEVENTEENTH CENTURY

see Modern

SEVERINO, E

Necessità Del Significato E Destino Del Linguaggio In E Severino. Scilironi, Carlo.

SEX

Reproductive Ethics. Bayles, Michael D.

Science And Gender: A Critique Of Biology And Its Theories On Women. Bleier, Ruth.

"Cupid's Yokes" in *Freedom, Feminism, And The State*, Mc Elroy, Wendy (ed), 129–142. Heywood, Ezra H.

"Human Rights Not Founded On Sex" in *Freedom, Feminism, And The State*, Mc Elroy, Wendy (ed), 29–34. Grimké, Angelina.

"Irrelevancies" in *Freedom, Feminism, And The State*, Mc Elroy, Wendy (ed), 101–110. Marvin, Bertha.

Against Couples. Gregory, Paul.

Commentary On Gilligan's "In A Different Voice". Auerbach, Judy and others.

Epicurus And Lucretius On Sex, Love, And Marriage. Arkins, B.

Human Sexuality And Marriage. York, Ann.

L'Uomo Freud: Personalità Morale E Religiosa. Lambertino, Antonio.

The Vatican's View Of Sex: The Inaccurate Conception. Francoeur, Robert T.

SEXISM

Letter To The Editors: A Response To Abrams. Raymond, Janice G.

Lordship, Bondage, And The Dialectic Of Work In Traditional Male/Female Relationships. Bell, Linda A and Alcoff, Linda.

Pornography: Defamation And The Endorsement Of Degradation. Soble, Alan.

SEXTON, A

"The Poet In The Poem" in *Existential Coordinates Of Human Condition*, Tymieniecka, A (ed), 61–74. Miller, Cynthia A.

SEXTUS EMPIRICUS

Dos Problemas Concernientes S La Clasificacion Estoica De Falacias. Ruiz, Edgar Gonzalez.

Leibniz Y El Escepticismo. De Olaso, Ezequiel.

Sextus Empiricus: Skepticism As A Therapy. Cohen, Avner.

SEXUAL INTERCOURSE

"87–100" in *Freedom, Feminism, And The State*, Mc Elroy, Wendy (ed), 87–100. Harman, Lillian.

Contraception, Copulation Domination, And The Theoretical Barrenness Of Sex Education Literature. Diorio, Joseph A.

Sperm And Ova As Property. Jansen, Robert P S.

SEXUALITY

Women, Sex, And The Law. Tong, Rosemarie.

Sexual Arousal. Scruton, Roger.

Sexuality In Human Evolution: What Is "Natural" Sex? Caulfield, Mina Davis.

Spinoza's Account Of Sexuality. Rice, Lee.

What Philosophers Talk About When They Talk About Sex. Earle, William J.

Wilhelm Reich: Culture As Power. Levine, Norman.

SHAFTESBURY

The Third Earl Of Shaftesbury 1671–1713. Voitle, Robert.

SHAKESPEARE

"Myth & Tragic Action In La Celestina And Romeo And Juliet" in *Existential Coordinates Of Human Condition*, Tymieniecka, A (ed), 425–435. Stewart, Marilyn.

Shakespeare And The Jewish Question. Arneson, Richard J.

SHAPIRO, S

On Conservativeness And Incompleteness. Field, Hartry.

SHARING

Groups, Responsibility, And The Failure To Act. Mellema, Gregory.

Shared Responsibility And Ethical Dilutionism. Mellema, Gregory.

SHEAF(–VES)

On Choice Sequences Determined By Spreads. Van Der Hoeven, Gerrit and Moerdijk, Ieke.

SHELLEY, P

Cinq Images De Shelley Qui Ont Fasciné Bachelard. Clark, John G.

SHIMONY, A

Shimony, The Dilemma Of Quantum Mechanics, And The History Of Philosophy. Sanchez, Halley D.

SHOEMAKER, S

Mackie And Shoemaker On Dispositions And Properties. Rosenberg, Alexander.

Professor Shoemaker And So–Called 'Qualia' Of Experience. White, Nicholas P.

SHORT, T

Short On Teleology. Olding, A.

SHOSTAKOVICH, D

Official Culture And Cultural Repression: The Case Of Dmitri Shostakovich. Mulcahy, Kevin V.

SHUE, H

Ideal And Non–Ideal Theory: How Should We Approach Questions Of Globel Justice. Nielsen, Kai.

SIDGWICK

Lying And The "Methods Of Ethics". Primoratz, Igor.

SIEGEL, H

Goodman's Rigorous Relativism. Elgin, Catherine Z.

SIEWERTH, G

El Ser En El "Sistema De Identidad" Según Gustav Siewerth (Segunda Parte). Corona, Nester A.

SIGN(S)

see also Symbol(s)

Epicurus' Scientific Method. Asmis, Elizabeth.

La Naissance De La Grammaire Moderne. Dominicy, Marc and Mardaga, Pierre (ed).

J F L Schröder—Aanhanger En Tegenstander Van Kant. Wielema, M R.

La Pseudo–Métaphysique Du Signe. Bouchard, Guy.

Latratus Canis. Umberto, Eco.

Peircean Semiotics And Poetic Production (in Portuguese). Silveira, Lauro F B.

Science, Design And The Science Of Signs. Terrell, Burnham.

Teken, Waarheid, Macht. Van Velthoven, Theo.

What Are Representamens? Benedict, George A.

SIGNIFICANCE

Fregean Connection: Bedeutung, Value And Truth–Value. Gabriel, Gottfried.

Interpretation In History: Or What Historians Do And Philosophers Say. Levich, Marvin.

SIGNIFICATION

A No Nonsense Approach To St Anselm. Malcolm, John F.

Disclosedness And Signification: A Study Of The Conception Of Language Presented In Being And Time. Mitscherling, Jeff.

L'objectivité Dans Les Théories Logiques De La Signification. Leblanc, Suzanne.

Roger Bacon On Equivocation. Maloney, Thomas S.

SILENCE

The Silent World Of Doctor And Patient. Katz, Jay.

The Silence Of God. Roth, John K.

The Silence Of Physics. Meurers, Joseph.

SIMILARITY

Mysticism, Identity And Realism: A Debate Reviewed. Byrne, Peter.

On The Logic And Criteriology Of Causality. Leman, Marc.

SIMMEL, G

On The Visual Constitution Of Society: The Contributions Of Georg Simmel And Jean–Paul Sartre To A Sociology Of The Senses. Weinstein, Deena and Weinstein, Michael.

SIMON, R

Comments On Simon And Fraleigh. Brown, W M.

SIMPLICITY

"(Simple) Qualities And Resemblance" in *Philosophical Analysis In Latin America*, Gracia, Jorge J E and others (eds), 199–218. Robles, Jose A.

"Observations, Explanatory Power, Simplicity" in *Observation, Experiment, Hypothesis In Physical Science*, Achinstein, Peter (ed), 45–94. Boyd, Richard N.

"Peirce And The Conditions Of Possibility Of Science" in *History Of Philosophy In Making*, Thro, Linus J (ed), 177–196. Delaney, C F.

Simple Wholes And Complex Parts: Limited Principles In Spinoza. Sacksteder, William.

The Complexity Of Quality. Westphal, Jonathan.

SIMULATION

Simulation Research In The Analysis Of Behavior. Epstein, Robert.

SIMULTANEITY

Whitehead, Special Relativity, And Simultaneity. White, Villard Alan.

SIN(S)

Be Ye Therefore Perfect Or The Ineradicability Of Sin. Harrison, Jonathan.

El Hombre Pecador. Pozo, Candido.

Impeccability Revisited. Carter, W R.

Luther's Word On Man's Will: A Case Study In Comparative Intellectual History. Migotti, Mark.

Moral And Religious Appraisals. Wallace, Gerry.

SIN(S)

Sentiments De Culpabilité Et Signification Du Péché: Approche Psychanalytique. De Saussure, Thierry.

SINGER, M

From The Prudential To The Moral: Reply To Marcus Singer. Gewirth, Alan.

Gillespie On Singer's Generalization Argument. Gordon, David.

Singer, Moore, And The Metaphysics Of Morals. Temkin, Jack.

SINGER, P

"The Morality Of Killing Animals: Four Arguments". Young, Thomas.

In Defense Of Speciesism. Wreen, Michael.

Morality And The Market In Blood. Stewart, Robert M.

The Random Collective As A Moral Agent. Manning, Rita.

SINGULAR TERM(S)

Frege, Sommers, Singular Reference. Mc Culloch, Gregory.

On The Elimination Of Singular Terms. Lambert, K.

SINGULARITY

A Theory Of Singular Causal Explanation. Woodward, James.

SINGULARS

Cognitive Intuition Of Singulars Revisited (Matthew Of Aquaparta Versus B J F Lonergan). Payne, Gordon R.

Laws And Causal Relations. Tooley, Michael.

SIOUX

An American Urphilosophie. Bunge, Robert.

SITUATION(S)

A Situational Account Of Knowledge. Hanfling, Oswald.

Information Is In The Mind Of The Beholder. Jackendoff, Ray.

Lost Innocence. Soames, Scott.

Moving The Semantic Fulcrum. Winograd, Terry.

Prigogine's Situationism (in Czechoslovakian). Jirásek, Jaroslav.

R Suszko's Situational Semantics. Wojcicki, Ryszard.

Shifting Situations And Shaken Attitudes: An Interview With Barwise And Perry. Perry, John and Barwise, Jon.

Situations And Events. Asher, Nicholas and Bonevac, Daniel.

Situations And Inference. Van Bentham, Johan.

Situations And Representations. Fodor, Janet Dean.

Situations, Worlds And Contexts. Partee, Barbera H.

Some Issues Concerning The Interpretation Of Derived And Gerundive Nominals. Thomason, Richmond H.

The Equation Of Information And Meaning From The Perspectives Of Situation Semantics And Gibson's Ecological Realism. Turvey, M T and Carello, Claudia.

SITUATIONAL ETHICS

Christian Ethics For Today. Barclay, William.

Iconoclastic Ethics. Black, Douglas.

In Defence Of Situational Ethics, The NHS And The Permissive Society. Black, Douglas.

The Positive Aspects Of Medical Ethics Today. Boyd, Kenneth.

SITUATIONAL LOGIC

The Role Of Problems And Problem Solving In Popper's Early Work On Psychology. Petersen, Arne Friemuth.

SKALA, H

On Skala's Set Theory. Manakos, Jannis.

SKILL(S)

"What Beginner Skiers Can Teach Us About Actions" in *The Analysis Of Action*, Von Cranach, Mario (ed), 99–114. Kaminski, G.

Applied Philosophy In Health Care Outside The Medical Ethics Arena. Butler, Nance Cunningham.

Beauty, Sport, And Gender. Boxill, J M.

Dance Education, Skill, And Behavioral Objectives. Carr, David.

Philosophy And A Career In Law. Perkins, Jeffrey J.

SKINNER, B

Background And Change In B F Skinner's Metatheory From 1930 To 1938. Coleman, S R.

Emergent Behaviorism. Killeen, Peter R.

On The Persistence Of Cognitive Explanation: Implications For Behavior Analysis. Pierce, W David and Epling, W Frank.

Purpose And Conditioning: A Reply To Waller. Mills, John A.

Purposes, Conditioning, And Skinner's Moral Theory: Comments On Mills' Observations. Waller, Bruce.

Skinner On The "Mental And The "Physical". Schnaitter, Roger.

Some Notes On The Subject Matter Of Skinner's *Verbal Behavior*. Lee, Vicki L.

Walden Two And Skinner's Ideal Observer. Mc Gray, James W.

SKINNER, Q

Political Thought As Traditionary Action: The Critical Response To Skinner And Pocock. Janssen, Peter L.

SKJEI, E

Reply To Skjei's "A Comment On Performative, Subject, And Proposition In Habermas's Theory Of Communication". Habermas, Jurgen.

SKOLEM, T

Beyond First–order Logic: The Historical Interplay Between Mathematical Logic And Axiomatic Set Theory. Moore, Gregory H.

Set Theory, Skolem's Paradox And The *Tractatus*. Moore, A W.

SLAVERY

Enforcing Slavery Contracts: A Liberal View. Callahan, Joan C.

John Locke And The Antebellum Defense Of Slavery. Loewenberg, Robert J.

Slaves And Citizens. Clark, Stephen R L.

SLEEPER, R

Comments On Sleeper And Edel. Rorty, Richard.

SLEINIS, E

The Uses And Abuses Of Utility: A Reply To Sleinis. Farr, Richard.

SLOTE, M

Relative Virtue. Vorobej, Mark.

SLOVAK

The Revolutionary Heritage Of Slovak National Uprising (in Czechoslovakian). Netopilík, J.

SMART, J

A Dynamic Model Of Temporal Becoming. Mc Call, Storrs.

Color And The Anthropocentric Problem. Averill, Edward Wilson.

Smart, Salmon, And Scientific Realism. Creath, Richard.

SMITH

Wealth And Virtue: The Shaping Of Political Economy In The Scottish Enlightenment. Hont, Istvan (ed) and Ignatieff, Michael (ed).

"Karl Marx And Adam Smith: Remarks About The Critique Of Political Economy" in *Contemporary Marxism*, O' Rourke, James J (ed), 21–38. Ballestrem, Karl G.

The Origin Of Property And The Development Of Scottish Historical Science. Bowles, Paul.

Two Concepts Of Morality: A Distinction Of Adam Smith's Ethics And Its Stoic Origin. Waszek, Norbert.

SMITH, J

Reply To J W Smith's "Primitive Classification And The Sociology Of Knowledge". Bloor, David.

SMITH, L

Genetic Epistemology And Philosophical Epistemology. Loptson, P J and Kelly, J W.

SMITH, W

Wilfred Cantwell Smith On Faith And Belief. Wainwright, William J.

SMORODINSKY, J

A Study Of Theory Unification. Nugayev, Renat.

SMUTS, J

Jan Christian Smuts And His Doctrine Of Holism. Brush, Francis W.

SNAPPER, J

Commentary On "Whether Professional Associations May Enforce Professional Codes". Lunch, Milton F.

Commentary On "Whether Professional Associations May Enforce Professional Codes". Ladd, John.

Commentary On "Whether Professional Associations May Enforce Professional Codes". Wilson, Donald E.

SNEED, J

Is Science Progressive? Niiniluoto, Ilkka.

A Modal Approach To Sneed's "Theoretical Functions". Miroiu, Adrian.

SOBEL, H

Rationality, Group Choice And Expected Utility. Richter, Reed.

SOBEL, L

Theoretical And Practical Confusion In American Professional Sport. Rose, David A.

SOBER, E

Against The Monism Of The Moment: A Reply To Elliott Sober. Kitcher, Philip.

SOCIAL

Über Den Inhalt Sozial–Politischer Gesetze. Huar, Ulrich.

Bertrand Russell, Karl Marx, And *German Social Democracy* Revisited. Gallina, Paul.

Encouraging Positive Justice Reasoning And Perspective–Taking Skills: Two Educational Interventions. Krogh, Suzanne Lowell.

Erkenntnis Und Bewusste Gestaltung Sozialer Prozesse. Winzer, Rosemarie.

Gallina And Pitt: Similarities And Differences. Pitt, Jack.

Gesellschaftliche Widersprüche In Der Volksrepublik China. Moritz, Rolf.

Sozialstrukturforschung Und Leitung Sozialer Prozesse. Lötsch, Manfred and Meyer, H.

The Ecological Perspective In John Dewey's Philosophy Of Education. Colwell, Tom.

SOCIAL CHANGE

Moral Dimensions Of American Foreign Policy. Thompson, Kenneth W (ed).

Rights And Goods: Justifying Social Action. Held, Virginia.

"A Scale Of Values For A Changing World" in *The Good Life And Its Pursuit*, Dougherty, Jude P (ed), 186–195. Basile, Joseph.

"'All Powers To The Walking People' Feuerbach As A Fourth–World Marxist" in *Contemporary Marxism*, O' Rourke, James J (ed), 55–78. Gagern, Michael.

Academic Freedom: A Structural Approach. Aronowitz, Stanley.

Constitutional System And Social Change: Concerning A Publication By Frank Rotter. Souto, Cláudio.

Cultural Frames For Social Intervention: A Personal Credo. Nandy, Ashis.

Das Ökonomische Grundgesetz Der Kommunistischen Gesellschaftsformation Und Einige Philosophische Probleme. Leisering, Heinz.

Functional Method And Phenomenology: The View Of Niklas Luhmann. Bednarz Jr, John.

Rechtssoziologie Und Sozialer Wandel: Zum Dritten Band Des Jahrbuchs Für Rechtssoziologioe Und Rechtstheorie. Hagen, Johann J.

Security Crisis And Institutionalized Militarism. Tapia– Valdés, Jorge A.

Social Theory Without Wholes. Turner, Stephen P.

The Well–Informed Citizen: Alfred Schutz And Applied Theory. Imber, Jonathan B.

Who Speaks For The Workers? Legters, Lyman H.

SOCIAL CLASS(ES)

Machiavelli On Social Class And Class Conflict. Brudney, Kent M.

SOCIAL CONSCIOUSNESS

Gesellschaftliches Und Individuelles Bewusstein In Der Philosophischen Diskussion In Der DDR And UdSSR. Müller, W and Hirschmann, J.

SOCIAL CONTRACT

Rousseau: Dreamer Of Democracy. Miller, James.
Rousseau On The General Will. Sparkes, A W.
Social Contract As A Basis Of Norms: A Critique. Machan, Tibor R.
Speech And The Social Contract. Turner, Roy.

SOCIAL CRITICISM

Religion As Critique. Ackerman, Robert John.
"Towards Apocalypse" in *International Kierkegaard Commentary*, Perkins, Robert L (ed), 19–52. Plekon, Michael.
Subjectivism And The Question Of Social Criticism. Weston, Anthony.

SOCIAL DARWINISM

Biology And Ideology: The Interpenetration Of Science And Values. Richardson, Robert C.

SOCIAL ETHICS

Animals And Why They Matter. Midgley, Mary.
Christian Faith And Public Choices: The Social Ethics Of Barth, Brunner And Bonhoeffer. Lovin, Robin W.
Critical Concerns In Moral Theology. Curran, Charles E.
Philosophy Born Of Struggle: Anthology Of Afro–American Philosophy From 1917. Harris, Leonard (ed).
Social And Political Morality. Lovett, William and Leventhal, F M (ed).
"Current Issues In Genetic Screening" in *Biomedical Ethics Reviews*, Humber, James M (ed), 121–152. Capron, Alexander Morgan.
"Ethical Issues In Occupational Health In Biomedical Ethics Reviews" in *Biomedical Ethics Reviews*, Humber, James M (ed), 153–174. Murray, Thomas H and Bayer, Ronald.
"Making And Using Psychiatric Diagnoses: Ethical Issues" in *Ethical Questions In Brain And Behavior*, Pfaff, Donald W (ed), 11–22. Endicott, Jean.
"Perspective On Ethical Issues In Occupational Health" in *Biomedical Ethics Reviews*, Humber, James M (ed), 175–204. Hunt, Vilma R.
Die Sozialpflichtigkeit Des Eigentums: Gesichtspunkte Der Christlichen Sozialethik. Furger, Franz.
Ideal And Non–Ideal Theory: How Should We Approach Questions Of Globel Justice. Nielsen, Kai.
Positional Goods. Hollis, Martin.
Social Ethics, The Philosophy Of Medicine, And Professional Responsibility. Ozar, David T.
The Right To Strike. Locke, Don.

SOCIAL FORCE(S)

The Anthropogenetic Meaning Of The Growth Of The Human Hand. Cackowski, Zdzislaw.

SOCIAL INSTITUTION(S)

A Sociological Account Of Liberal Protestantism. Bruce, S.
Editorial: Philosophy Of Medicine In The U S A. Thomasma, David C.
Foucault's Archaeological Method: A Response To Hacking And Rorty. Wartenberg, Thomas E.
More's Utopia: An Interpretation Of Its Social Theory. Sargent, Lyman Tower.

SOCIAL ORDER

Comment: Response To A Arato And J Cohen, "Social Movements, Civil Society And The Problem Of Sovereignty". Thompson, E P.
Law And Social Order: On Leopold Pospisil's Anthropology Of Law. Opoku, Kwame.
Niklas Luhmann And His View Of The Social Function Of Law. Murphy, John W.
Rawls' Difference Principle, Marxian Alienation And The Japanese Economy: Bringing Justice To The Least Advantaged. Grcic, Joseph M.

SOCIAL PHIL

see also Authority(–ties), Communism, Conservatism, Equality, Ethics, Freedom, Political Phil, Progress, Punishment, Society(–ties), Utopia
A Book Of Jewish Ethical Concepts: Biblical And Postbiblical. Bloch, Abraham P.
A Critical Edition Of Mary Wollstonecraft's A Vindication Of The Rights Of Woman: With Strictures On Political And Moral Subjects. Hardt, Ulrich H.
A Matter Of Hope: A Theologian's Reflections On The Thought Of Karl Marx. Lash, Nicholas.
A Philosophy Of Individual Freedom: The Political Thought Of F A Hayek. Hoy, Calvin M.
A Theory Of Social Action. Tuomela, Raimo.
An Apology For The Value Of Human Life. Thomasma, David C.
An Inquiry Into The Nature And Causes Of The Wealth Of Nations, 2v. Smith, Adam.
Arguing For Socialism: Theoretical Considerations. Levine, Andrew.
Benjamin Constant And The Making Of Modern Liberalism. Holmes, Stephen.
Between Tradition And Revolution: The Hegelian Transformation Of Political Philosophy. Riedel, Manfred.
Beyond Domination: An Essay In The Political Philosophy Of Education. White, Patricia and Peters, R S (ed).
Biology, Crime And Ethics: A Study Of Biological Explanations For Criminal Behavior. Marsh, Frank H (ed) and Katz, Janet (ed).
Christian Ethics And Political Action. Messer, Donald E.
Collective And Corporate Responsibility. French, Peter A.
Community As A Social Ideal. Kamenka, Eugene (ed).
Condorcet Studies 1. Rosenfield, Leonora C and Popkin, Richard H (ed).
Contemporary Marxism: Essays In Honor Of J M Bocheński. O' Rourke, James J (ed) and Blakeley, Thomas J (ed) and Rapp, Friedrich J (ed).
Contemporary Moral Problems. White, James E.

Continuity And Change In Marxism. Fischer, Norman And Others (ed).
Contours Of A World View. Holmes, Arthur F.
Contradictions Of The Welfare State, John Keane (ed). Offe, Claus.
Creeds, Society, And Human Rights: A Study In Three Cultures. Stackhouse, Max L.
Culture And Morality. Mayer, Adrian C (ed).
Darwin, Marx, And Freud: Their Influence On Moral Theory. Caplan, Arthur L (ed) and Jennings, Bruce (ed).
Dialogue Within The Dialectic. Levine, Norman.
Edmund Burke: A Bibliography Of Secondary Studies To 1982. Gandy, Clara I and Stanlis, Peter J.
Einstein And The Poet: In Search Of The Cosmic Man. Hermanns, William.
Essays On French History And Historians. Mill, John Stuart and Robson, John M (ed).
Ethics–In–Government Laws: Are They Too "ethical"? Neely, Alfred S.
Foundations Of Humanism. Van Praag, J P.
Freedom, Feminism, And The State. Mc Elroy, Wendy (ed).
Game Theory: Concepts And Applications. Zagare, Frank C.
George Grant And The Twilight Of Justice. O' Donovan, Joan E.
Having Love Affairs. Taylor, Richard.
How Democracies Perish. Revel, Jean–François.
Human Rights In Religious Traditions. Swidler, Arlene (ed).
Jewish Ethics And Halakhah For Our Time: Sources And Commentary. Herring, Basil F.
John Locke And Agrarian Capitalism. Wood, Neal.
Knowledge Structure And Use: Implications For Synthesis And Interpretation, Linda J Reed (ed). Ward, Spencer (ed).
Letter To The Editors: A Response To Abrams. Raymond, Janice G.
Locke's Education For Liberty. Tarcov, Nathan.
Machina Ex Dea: Feminist Perspectives On Technology. Rothschild, Joan (ed).
Major Ideologies: An Interpretative Survey Of Democracy, Socialism And Nationalism. Groth, Alexander.
Martin Buber: A Centenary Volume. Gordon, Haim (ed) and Bloch, Jochanan (ed).
Marx & Engels: The Intellectual Relationship. Carver, Terrell.
Marx's Economics. Junankar, P N.
Marx's Social Critique Of Culture. Dupré, Louis.
Marxism And The Oppression Of Women: Toward A Unitary Theory. Vogel, Lise.
Marxism: Last Refuge Of The Bourgeoisie? Mattick, Paul and Mattick Jr, Paul (ed).
Marxism: Nomos XXVI. Pennock, J Roland (ed) and Chapman, John W (ed).
Max Weber And The Methodology Of The Social Sciences. Huff, Toby.
Medical Nemesis: The Expropiation Of Health. Illich, Ivan.
Michel Foucault: An Introduction To The Study Of His Thought. Cooper, Barry.
Moral Dimensions Of American Foreign Policy. Thompson, Kenneth W (ed).
Moral Principles And Nuclear Weapons. Lackey, Douglas P.
Morality In The Making. Weinreich Haste, Helen (ed) and Locke, Don (ed).
On Freedom. Howard, John A (ed).
Out Of Order: Affirmative Action And The Crisis Of Doctrinaire Liberalism. Capaldi, Nicholas.
Perennial Philosophical Issues. Grassian, Victor.
Personality: The Need For Liberty And Rights. Gotesky, Rubin.
Persons And Their World: An Introduction To Philosophy. Olen, Jeffrey.
Perspectives On Political Ethics: An Ecumenical Enquiry. Srisang, Koson (ed).
Philosophical Problems. Stumpf, Samuel Enoch.
Philosophy Born Of Struggle: Anthology Of Afro–American Philosophy From 1917. Harris, Leonard (ed).
Philosophy: An Introduction To The Central Issues. Landesman, Charles.
Plato And Aristophanes: Plato's Euthyphro, Apology, And Crito And Aristophanes' Clouds. West, Thomas G (trans) and West, Grace Starry (trans).
Polis And Praxis. Dallmayr, Fred R.
Political Economy And Freedom. Nutter, Warren G.
Political Writings. Hegel, Georg Wilhelm.
Popper And The Human Sciences. Currie, Gregory (ed) and Musgrave, Alan (ed).
Popper Selections. Miller, David (ed).
Preparing For The Future: An Essay On The Rights Of Future Generations. Ahrens, John.
Private Justice: Towards Integrated Theorising In The Sociology Of Law. Henry, Stuart.
Progress And Chaos: Modernization And Rediscovery Of Religion And Authority. Groth, Alexander J.
Progress In Utility And Risk Theory. Hagen, Ole (ed) and Wenstop, Fred (ed).
Punishment And Restitution: A Restitutionary Approach To Crime And The Criminal. Abel, Charles F and Marsh, Frank H.
Radical Humanism. Améry, Jean and Rosenfeld, Sidney (ed) and Rosenfeld, Stella (ed).
Rawls And Rights. Martin, Rex.
Red Emma Speaks. Shulman, Alix Kates (ed).
Red Emma Speaks: An Emma Goldman Reader. Shulman, Alix Kates (ed).
Reinhold Niebuhr: His Religious, Social And Political Thought. Kegley, Charles W (ed).
Religion As Critique. Ackerman, Robert John.
Rights And Goods: Justifying Social Action. Held, Virginia.
Rights And Regulation: Ethical, Political, And Economic Issues. Machan, Tibor R (ed) and Johnson, M Bruce (ed).
Rights. White, Alan R.
Sartre After Sartre. Jameson, Fredric (ed).
Science And Gender: A Critique Of Biology And Its Theories On Women. Bleier, Ruth.
Science Policy, Ethics, And Economic Methodology. Shrader– Frechette, K S.
Searching For Cultural Foundations. Mc Shane, Philip (ed).
Social And Political Ethics. Brodsky, Garry (ed) and Troyer, John (ed) and Vance,

SOCIAL PHIL

SOCIAL PHIL

Theory And Practice In Marxism. Apostel, Leo.
Thomson And The Current State Of The The Abortion Controversy. Levin, David S.
Three Approaches Toward An Understanding Of Sportsmanship. Arnold, Peter J.
Toward A Foundation For Human Rights. Khatchadourian, Haig.
Toward A Social Theory Of Ignorance. Smithson, Michael.
Towards A Concept Of Shared Autonomy. Bergsma, Jurrit.
Towards A Theory Of Taxation. Lucas, J R.
Towards An Ontological Foundation Of Law (in Hungarian). Varga, Csaba.
Towards The Aesthetic: A Journey With Friedrich Schiller. Schaper, Eva.
Triebkräfte Des Sozialismus. Schonherr, L.
Two Domains Of Rights. Perry, Thomas D.
Two Interpretations Of The Difference Principle In Rawls's Theory Of Justice. Shenoy, Prakash P and Martin, Rex.
Two Ontologies Of Hegel, Marx, Lukács? Sleczka, Kazimierz.
USA: Conservatism Contra Liberalism (in Czechoslovakian). Krejcí, O.
Une Altenative À L'exclusion: La Dialogie. Roumanes, Jacques–Bernard.
Une Approche Philosophique De La Culture. Godin, Guy.
Unlicensed Brainwork: A Case Study In Suppressive Discourse From Above. Schäfer, Wolf.
Utilitarianism, Rights, And Duties To Self. Sartorius, Rolf.
Utopianism And Nuclear Deterrence. Howard, Michael W.
Vain Hopes And A Fool's Fancy: Understanding US Nuclear Strategy. Beres, Louis René.
Value Conflicts In Agriculture. Aiken, William.
Values And Socialism: An Axiological Approach To Marx's Socialism. Siewierski, Jacenty.
Vargas And Prestes: A Comparison Between The Labourism And Communism In Brazil (in Portuguese). Piozzi, Patrizia.
Verbal Deficit And Educational Success. Winch, C A.
Vernunft Contra Unvernunft Zu Georg Lukács' Faschismus–Kritik. Wrona, V.
Violence And The Politics Of Explanation: Kampuchea Revisited. Hawkesworth, Mary E.
Weber And The Socialism (in Hungarian). Szabó, Máté.
Wei–Wu–Wei: Nondual Action. Loy, David.
Welfare State Versus Welfare Society? Skillen, Anthony.
Weltanschauliche Fragen Des Sozialistischen Wettbewerbs. Felgentreu, Herbert and Petruschka, G.
What (If Anything) Is Intrinsically Wrong With Capitalism? Van Parijs, Philippe.
What Collectives Are: Agency, Individualism And Legal Theory. Copp, David.
What Philosophers Talk About When They Talk About Sex. Earle, William J.
What Spinoza's View Of Freedom Should Have Been. Lucash, Frank.
What's Morally Special About Free Exchange? Gibbard, Allan.
What's So Special About Rights? Buchanan, Allen.
When Meeting Needs Becomes A Threat To Autonmy. Summers, Jim.
Who Speaks For The Workers? Legters, Lyman H.
Who We Are: The Political Origins Of The Medical Humanities. Fox, Daniel M.
Wilderness And Heritage Values. Hammond, John L.
Wilhelm Reich: Culture As Power. Levine, Norman.
Wissenschaftlich–Technischer Fortschritt Und Sozialistisches Verhältnis Zur Arbeit. Stollberg, R.
Woman As Truth In Nietzsche's Writing. Oliver, Kelly A.
Women, Medicine, And Religion: A Response To Raymond And Abrams. Rawlinson, Mary C.
Worker Control, Self–Respect, And Self–Esteem. Howard, Michael W.
Workers' Interest And The Proletarian Ethic: Conflicting Strains In Marxian Anti–Moralism. Skillen, Anthony.
Zu Einer Vermeintlichen Textlücke In Spinozas "Ethica Ordine Geometrico Demonstrata". Goldenbaum, Ursula.
Zu Einigen Aktuellen Zügen Bürgerlicher Wissenschafts– Und Technikkritik. Kaizik, Peter.
Zu Einigen Fragen Der, Sozialstruktur Und Der Sozialen Triebkräfte. Ernst, K.
Zum Humanismus In Der Klassischen Deutschen Philosophie, Seinen Sozialhistorischen Und Theoretischen Voraussetzungen. Biedermann, Georg and Lange, E.
Zum Platz Des Pluralismus In Der Gegenwärtigen Bürgerlichen Ideologie. Fromm, Eberhard and Sokolowski, K.
Zum Verhältnis Von Marxistisch–Leninistischer Philosophie Und Sozialistischer Politik In Der DDR. Heppener, Sieglinde.
Zum Verhältnis Von Sozialistischer Ideologie Und Subjektivem Faktor. Rauh, Hans–Christoph.
Zur Dialektik Des Vergesellschaftungsprozesses In Der Sozialistischen Industrie Der DDR. Braun, Hans–Joachim and Dorschel, E.
Zur Dialektik Von Freiheit Und Sicherheit. Hagen, Johann J.
Zur Entwicklung Kultureller Bedürfnisse In Der Arbeiterklasse. Staufenbiel, Fred.
Zur Entwicklung Und Befriedigung Kultureller Bedürfnisse. Bisky, L.
Zur Historisch–Materialistischen Auffassung Von Basis Und Überbau. Bauer, Adolf.
Zur Problematik Des Egalitarismus. Höppner, Joachim.
1984—The Totalitarian Model Revisited. Krancberg, Sigmund.

SOCIAL POLICY(–CIES)

Popper And The Human Sciences. Currie, Gregory (ed) and Musgrave, Alan (ed).
"Paternalism" And Social Policy. Sankowski, Edward.
Ethical Perspectives On Health Policy For An Aging Society. Creedon, Michael A.
Is Fairness Good: A Critique Of Varian's Theory Of Fairness. Sugden, Robert.
Positional Goods. Hollis, Martin.
The Epistemology Of Gender Identity: Implications For Social Policy. Ayim, Maryann and Houston, Barbara.

Why Tolerate The Statistical Victim? Trachtman, Leon E.
Wilderness And Heritage Values. Hammond, John L.

SOCIAL PROBLEMS

Chinese Buddhist Responses To Contemporary Problems. Yü, Chun–Fang.
La Philosophie Marxiste–Léniniste—Base Théorique Pour La Solution Des Problèmes De Notre Époque (in German). Rupprecht, Frank.
Moral Issues And Social Problems: The Moral Relevance Of Moral Philosophy. Singer, Marcus G.
Soziale Probleme, Soziologische Theorie Und Gesellschaftsplanung. Hondrich, Karl Otto.
The Hindu Vision And World Problems. Sivaraman, S K.
World Problems And The Emergence Of A New Interreligious Perspective. Chethimattam, John B.

SOCIAL PROGRESS

Progress And Chaos: Modernization And Rediscovery Of Religion And Authority. Groth, Alexander J.
Über Den Wirkungs– Und Ausnutzungsmechanismus Der Gesellschaftlichen Entwicklungsgetsetze. Drjachlow, N I and Tscherkassow, G K.
Persönlichkeit Als Subjekt Des Gesellschaftlichen Fortschritts. Gutsche, Gunter.
Social Movements, Civil Society, And The Problem Of Sovereignty. Arato, Andrew and Cohen, Jean.

SOCIAL PSYCHOLOGY

Popper And The Human Sciences. Currie, Gregory (ed) and Musgrave, Alan (ed).
Programmatic Aesthetic Education From The Point Of View Of Social Psychology (in Czechoslovakian). Macková– Holecková, Iva.

SOCIAL RELATIONS

A Conceptual Analysis Of Self–Disclosure. Fisher, D V.
Sport As A Contemporary Form Of Cultural Motor Activity. Wohl, Andrzej.
The Contributions Of Religious Traditions To Business Ethics. Mc Mahon, Thomas F.

SOCIAL ROLE(S)

Corporate Social Responsibility And Public Accountability. Filios, Vassilios P.
Role And Rational Action. Coyne, Margaret U.
Roles And Responsibilities: Theoretical Issues In The Definition Of Consultation Liaison Psychiatry. Agich, George J.
Social Action–Functions. Tuomela, Raimo.

SOCIAL SCIENCES

see also Economics, History, Law, Political Science
A Guide To The Culture Of Science, Technology, And Medicine. Durbin, Paul T (ed).
Auguste Comte And Positivism: The Essential Writings. Lenzer, Gertrud (ed).
Conceptualization And Measurement In The Social Sciences. Blalock Jr, Hubert M.
Condorcet Studies 1. Rosenfield, Leonora C and Popkin, Richard H (ed).
Erklaren Und Verstehen. Von Wright, Georg Henrik.
Hermeneutics: Questions And Prospects. Shapiro, Gary (ed) and Sica, Alan (ed).
Justifying Historical Descriptions. Mc Cullagh, C Behan.
Max Weber And The Methodology Of The Social Sciences. Huff, Toby.
Philosophy Of Science And Sociology: From The Methodological Doctrine To Research Practice. Mokrzycki, Edmund.
The Intellectual And Social Organization Of The Sciences. Whitley, Richard.
The Problem Of Social Reality: Collected Papers 1. Schutz, Alfred.
The Social Sciences: Their Nature And Uses. Kruskal, William H (ed).
Understanding And Explanation: A Transcendental–Pragmatic Perspective. Apel Otto, Karl and Warnke, Georgia (trans).
"Philosophical Element In Social Theory And Practice" in *Ideology, Philosophy And Politics*, Parel, Anthony (ed), 61–76. Plamenatz, John.
Acceptance Of Empirical Statements: A Bayesian Theory Without Cognitive Utilities. Harsanyi, John C.
Action As A Text: Gadamer's Hermeneutics And The Social Scientific Analysis Of Action. Hekman, Susan.
Biological Ideas And Their Cultural Uses. Benton, Ted.
De Ethogene Methode Van Sociaal–Wetenschappelijk Onderzoek Van Rom Harré. Van Der Veen, Romke.
Gesellschaftswissenschaftliche Methoden Auf Dem Wege Der Gesetzeserkenntnis. Zak, Christian.
Hermeneutics And The Social Sciences: A Gadamerian Critique Of Rorty. Warnke, Georgia.
L'articulation Du Général Et Du Particulier: Une Approche Méthodologique Dans Le Champ Des Sciences Sociales. Miguelez, Roberto.
Medical Ethics And Medical Practice: A Social Science View. Stacey, Margaret.
Must Knowledge—Or 'Knowledge' Be Socially Constructed? Radford, Colin.
Philosophical Anthropology: Revolt Against The Division Of Intellectual Labor. Wiggins, Osborne.
Postmortem On An Era: A Citizenly Perspective On The Economy. Scheuer, Irene C.
Problems In The Social Sciences: Prolegomena To A Study Of Cities. Jenner, Donald.
Sociobiology. Midgley, Mary.
The Concept Of Personal Pattern As An Axiological Structure. Śpiewak, Anna.
The Sociobiological View Of Man. Trigg, Roger.
Understanding Peter Winch. Sharrock, W W and Anderson, R J.
Who Needs Paradigms? Roth, Paul A.

SOCIAL STRUCTURE(S)

A Theory Of Social Action. Tuomela, Raimo.
The Intellectual And Social Organization Of The Sciences. Whitley, Richard.
Toward A Structural Theory Of Action: Network Models Of Social Structure, Perception, And Action. Burt, Ronald S.
Bannisterless Politics: Hannah Arendt And Her Children. Mc Kenna, George.
The Asantes: Ancestors And The Social Meaning Of Life. Twumasi, Patrick A.
Three Approaches Toward An Understanding Of Sportsmanship. Arnold, Peter J.

SOCIAL SYSTEM(S)

'Communicative Competence' And The Skeptic. Beatty, Joseph.

"Socrates And Democracy" in *Popper And The Human Sciences*, Currie, Gregory (ed), 185–204. Kraut, Richard.

A Little Platonic Heresy For The Eighties. Nails, Debra.

Complexity And Intersubjectivity: Towards The Theory Of Niklas Luhmann. Bednarz Jr, John.

On The Change Of Social Laws. Sztompka, Piotr.

Social Systems Analytics And Ethics. Mulcahy, John W and Natale, Samuel M.

SOCIAL THEORY(–RIES)

Adorno. Jay, Martin.

The Rise And Fall Of Structural Marxism: Althusser And His Influence. Benton, Ted.

The Theory Of Communicative Action: Reason And The Rationalization Of Society, V1. Habermas, Jurgen and Mc Carthy, Thomas (trans).

"Philosophical Element In Social Theory And Practice" in *Ideology, Philosophy And Politics*, Parel, Anthony (ed), 61–76. Plamenatz, John.

"Philosophy Of Science" in *The Culture Of Science, Technology, And Medicine*, Durbin, Paul T (ed), 197–281. Michalos, Alex C.

Biotechnology And The Social Reconstruction Of Molecular Biology. Markle, Gerald E and Robin, Stanley S.

British Idealism: Its Political And Social Thought. Simchoni, Avital.

Construction Of Illness: Deconstructing The Social. Karatheodoris, S G.

Dialectical Phenomenology As Critical Social Theory. Marsh, James L.

Ideal And Non–Ideal Theory: How Should We Approach Questions Of Global Justice. Nielsen, Kai.

Ideology And Social Psyche (in Hungarian). Stojchev, Todor.

Interpersonal Utility In Principles Of Social Choice. Weirich, Paul.

Logics And Languages Of Pedagogical Research. Soltis, Jonas F.

Marxism And The Criminal Question. Ferrajoli, Luigi and Zolo, Danilo.

What Is A Dictator? Green, Leslie.

SOCIAL WELFARE

Child Adoption And Identity. Griffiths, A Phillips.

SOCIAL WORK

Children In Care: Are Social Workers Abusing Their Authority? Benians, R C.

Response to "Children In Care: Are Social Workers Abusing Their Authority". Foster, Judy.

SOCIALISM

Arguing For Socialism: Theoretical Considerations. Levine, Andrew.

Contradictions Of The Welfare State, John Keane (ed). Offe, Claus.

Major Ideologies: An Interpretative Survey Of Democracy, Socialism And Nationalism. Groth, Alexander.

Marxism And The Oppression Of Women: Toward A Unitary Theory. Vogel, Lise.

Über Die Kategorien Inhalt Und Methode In Der Pädagogik. Naumann, Werner.

Über Die Widersprüche Der Sozialistischen Gesellschaft. Kosing, Alfred.

"Economic Value, Ethics, And Transition To Socialism" in *Continuity And Change In Marxism*, Fischer, Norman And Others (ed), 39–65. Fischer, Norman.

"Give Me Liberty" in *Freedom, Feminism, And The State*, Mc Elroy, Wendy (ed), 49–60. Lane, Rose Wilder.

"Romanticism & Modernity In Lukacsian & Althusserian Marxism" in *Continuity And Change In Marxism*, Fischer, Norman And Others (ed), 70–85. Goldstein, Philip.

"Theses On Marx" in *Continuity And Change In Marxism*, Fischer, Norman And Others (ed), 66–69. Axelos, Kostas.

A Defense Of Humanism. Ruoshui, Wang.

African Socialism And Nyerere. Okolo, Chukwudum Barnabas.

Bedürfnisse Und Produktion. Rohrberg, Peter.

Capitalists And The Ethics Of Contribution. Arnold, N Scott.

Comparative Social Philosophies: Individualism, Socialism, Solidarism. Mueller, Franz H.

Das Einfachste Und Grundlegendste Verhältnis Der Sozialistischen Gesellschaft. Hellborn, Rudolf.

Die Bedeutung Des Vaterlandsbegriffes Für Die Erziehung Zum Sozialistischen Patriotismus. Abelmann, Xenia.

Die Dialektik Von Nationalem Und Internationalem In Der Entwicklung Der Sozialistischen Gesellschaft. Wirt, Adam.

Die Einheit Von Sozialismus Und Frieden. Hocke, Erich.

Die Heranbildung Eines Der Arbeiterklasse Würdigen Nachwuchses. Meier, Artur.

Die Klasse Der Genossenschaftsbauern Im Prozess Der Gestaltung Der Entwickelten Sozialistischen Gesellschaft. Krambach, Kurt.

Die Macht Zur Freiheit. Steussloff, Hans.

Einige Bemerkungen Zur Struktur Des Alltagsdenkens. Trader, Wilfried.

Federalism And Socialism: A Reconsideration. Resnick, Philip.

Fundamental Characteristics Of Socialist National Relations (in Czechoslovakian). Pomaizl, K.

Fundamental Features Of The Transition From The Old To The New Quality Under Socialism (in Czechoslovakian). Pospíchalová, Milena.

Gedanken Zum Sozialistischen Humanismus Als Anspruch An Individuum Und Gesellschaft. Erfurth, Andrea.

Genossenschaftsbauern Und Dorf Improzek Der Sozialistischen Intensivierung. Krambach, K.

Gesetzmässigkeiten Des Revolutionären Prozesses. Eichhorn, Wolfgang.

Human Rights And International Finance: A Synthetical Overview. Khoshkish, A.

IV Philosophiekongress Der DDR. Blumenthal, Wolfgang and Rupprecht, F.

Inhaltliche Fragen Der Ausarbeitung Eines Lehrbuches Der Marxistisch–Leninistischen Soziologie. Assmann, Georg and Stollberg, R.

Introduction À La Lecture De George Orwell. Ruelland, Jacques G.

Kollektive Meinung Und Individuelles Leistungsverhalten Im Socialismus. Dresler, Peter.

Kritisches Zur Widerspruchsdebatte. Eichhorn, Wolfgang.

La Morale Socialiste Et La Valeur De L'homme. Popescu, Vasile.

La Philosophie Marxiste–Léniniste—Base Théorique Pour La Solution Des Problèmes De Notre Époque (in German). Rupprecht, Frank.

Logical Fallacies Or Ideological Justifications: Schaff's Arguments On The Socialistic Character Of "Really Existing Socialism". Golubović, Zagorka.

Marxist Dialectics And Social Life. Fedoseev, P N.

Minimalstaat Oder Sozialrechte—Eine Philosophische Problemskizze. Hoffe, Otfried.

Mit Lesern Und Autoren Im Gespräch. Teichmann, Werner.

Objective And Subjective–Objective Aspects Of Contradictions Under Socialism (in Czechoslovakian). Flek, Antonín.

Owen's Communism And The Neo–Left–Wing Reconstruction Of History; War And Peace In The Ideological Confrontation (in German). Jauch, Liane.

Revolutionäre Epoche Und Klassische Revolution. Baumgart, Joachim.

SPD And The Achievement Of The Discussion On Identity (in Czechoslovakian). Sevcik, Oldrich.

Scientific Socialism And The Question Of Socialist Values. Collier, Andrew.

Socialism, Democracy And Marxism: The Need For Dialogue. Benn, Tony.

Some Theoretical Problems Of The Object–Subject Dialectics In The Development Of The Community Of Socialist States (in German). Rygol, Reiner.

Sozialismus—Humanismus—Toleranz. Wrona, Vera.

Sozialistische Persönlichkeit Und Intensiv Erweiterte Reproduktion. Kretzschmar, A.

Sozialistischer Humanismus—Sozialistischer Realismus. John, Erhard.

Sozialistische Persönlichkeitsentwicklung Und Soziologische Forschung. Adler, Frank and Kretzschmar, A.

Struktur Der Sozialistischen Produktionsverhältnisse Und Ökonomische Gesetze Des Sozialismus. Becher, Jurgen and Friedrich, P.

The Alienation Of Revolution Or The Criticism Of Real Socialism In The Conception Of A Schaff (in Czechoslovakian). Hrzal, Ladislav and Kuzminski, V.

The Dialectic Of The Contradictions Of Real Socialism (in Czechoslovakian). Houska, Jirí.

The Marxist Trend In Polish Socialism. Mackiewicz, Witold.

The Methodological Function Of Political Economy In Materialist Explanation Of The Development Of Socialist Society (in Czechoslovakian). Valencik, Radim.

Triebkräfte Des Sozialismus. Schonherr, L.

Values And Socialism: An Axiological Approach To Marx's Socialism. Siewierski, Jacenty.

Vargas And Prestes: A Comparison Between The Labourism And Communism In Brazil (in Portuguese). Piozzi, Patrizia.

W E B Du Bois: A Perspective On The Bases Of His Political Thought. Reed, Adolph L.

Weber And The Socialism (in Hungarian). Szabó, Máté.

Weltanschauliche Fragen Des Sozialistischen Wettbewerbs. Felgentreu, Herbert and Petruschka, G.

Wissenschaftlich–Technischer Fortschritt Und Sozialistisches Verhältnis Zur Arbeit. Stollberg, R.

Zu Einigen Fragen Der, Sozialstruktur Und Der Sozialen Triebkräfte. Ernst, K.

Zum Verhältnis Von Sozialistischer Ideologie Und Subjektivem Faktor. Rauh, Hans–Christoph.

Zum Verhältnis Von Marxistisch–Leninistischer Philosophie Und Sozialistischer Politik In Der DDR. Heppener, Sieglinde.

Zur Dialektik Des Vergesellschaftungsprozesses In Der Sozialistischen Industrie Der DDR. Braun, Hans–Joachim and Dorschel, E.

Zur Problematik Der Sozialistischen Nationalität. Schiller, Klaus J.

Zur Problematik Des Egalitarismus. Höppner, Joachim.

SOCIALIST REALISM

Forty Years Of Socialist Cultural Evolution (in Czechoslovakian). Gawlik, Ladislav.

Philosophical Thinking And Art Creation (in Czechoslovakian). Zis, A J.

The Role Of Aesthetic Education In The Forming Of Socialist Consciousness (in Czechoslovakian). Hnizdova, Kvetoslava and Hnizdova, Vlastislav.

SOCIALIZATION

(Reflections On) The Dialectical Relationship Between Technique And (The Problem Of) Liberation. Griffith, William T.

Jugend—Idole Und Identitätsbildung. Tafertshofer, Alois.

Oedipus Rex: The Oedipus Rule And Its Subversion. Lingis, Alphonso.

Sport And Hegemony: On The Construction Of The Dominant Culture. Whitson, David.

SOCIETY(–TIES)

A Theory Of Social Action. Tuomela, Raimo.

An Inquiry Into The Nature And Causes Of The Wealth Of Nations, 2v. Smith, Adam.

Auguste Comte And Positivism: The Essential Writings. Lenzer, Gertrud (ed).

Conditions Of Happiness. Veenhoven, Ruut.

Feeling Good And Doing Better; Ethics And Nontherapeutic Drug Use. Murray, Thomas H (ed) and Gaylin, Willard (ed) and Macklin, Ruth (ed).

Foundations Of Humanism. Van Praag, J P.

I–Man: An Outline Of Philosophical Anthropology. Krąpiec, Mieczylaw A and Lescoe, Marie (trans) and Woznicki, Theresa (trans).

Michel Foucault: Beyond Structuralism And Hermeneutics. Dreyfus, Hubert L and Rabinow, Paul.

Michel Foucault: An Introduction To The Study Of His Thought. Cooper, Barry.

Technology And The Character Of Contemporary Life: A Philosophical Inquiry. Borgmann, Albert.

The Problem Of Social Reality: Collected Papers 1. Schutz, Alfred.

The Question Of Play. Hyland, Drew A.

"Actors' Powers" in *The Analysis Of Action*, Von Cranach, Mario (ed), 213–230. Brenner, Michael.

SOCIETY(-TIES)

"Hegel's Challenge To The Modern Economy" in *History And System*, Perkins, Robert (ed), 219–253. Winfield, Richard D.

"Individual Responsibility In Advanced Societies" in *The Good Life And Its Pursuit*, Dougherty, Jude P (ed), 145–162. Peperzak, Adrian.

"Individual Action And Social Knowledge" in *The Analysis Of Action*, Von Cranach, Mario (ed), 247–266. Luckmann, Thomas.

"Justice And Society: Beyond Individualism" in *The Search For Justice*, Taitte, W Lawson (ed), 101–126. Murphy, Ewell E.

"The Search For Justice Introduction" in *The Search For Justice*, Taitte, W Lawson (ed), 11–24. Cecil, Andrew R.

A Biological Interpretation Of Moral Systems. Alexander, Richard D.

Comment: Response To A Arato And J Cohen, "Social Movements, Civil Society And The Problem Of Sovereignty". Thompson, E P.

Création Et Phénomène Social. Mineau, André.

Das Einfachste Und Grundlegendste Verhältnis Der Sozialistischen Gesellschaft. Hellborn, Rudolf.

Dialektik Von Individuum Und Gesellschaft Als Dialektik Von Persönlicher Und Sozialer Indentität. Wetzel, Manfred.

El Progreso Según Juan Bautista Vico. Dondi, J.

Elementos De Filosofia Politica No Concilio Vaticano II. Borges, J F Pereira.

George Herbert Mead's Conception Of Consciousness. Natsoulas, Thomas.

God, The World And Man As A Social Being In Marcus Aurelius' Stoicism. Dragona–Monachou, M.

Jacques Maritain, Filósofo Da Inteligência. Machado, Geraldo Pinheiro.

La Société Comme Intermédiaire Entre L'Homme Individuel Et L'Absolu Chez Platon Et Chez Plotin. Hager, F P.

La Società Aperta Nel Pensiero Politico Del '900 (Bergson, Popper, Maritain). Possenti, Vittorio.

La Thématisation Hégélienne De La Société Civile Bourgeoise. Larouche–Tanguay, Camillia.

Logical Fallacies Or Ideological Justifications: Schaff's Arguments On The Socialistic Character Of "Really Existing Socialism". Golubović, Zagorka.

Max, The Cynic (in Portuguese). Moraes, Reginaldo C C.

On Nature And Society: Rousseau Versus The Enlightenment. Luke, Timothy W.

One Marx, And The Centrality Of The Historical Actor(s). Brosio, Richard A.

Post–Classical Philosophers' Concept Of Man As A Social Animal. Chronis, Nicholas.

Response To Benne's "The Learning Community". Tozer, Steven.

Rousseau On The Fall Of Social Man. Skillen, Anthony.

Scepticism And Public Health: On The Problem Of Disease For The Collective. Colfer, P.

Sobre El Feminismo De Platón. Cappelletti, Angel J.

Social Essence And Value Of The Olympic Idea. Stolarov, Vladislav I.

Subjektiver Faktor Und Zusammenhang Von Gesellschaft Und Natur. Müller, Klaus.

Substance–Society–Natural Systems: A Creative Rethinking Of Whitehead's Cosmology. Bracken, Joseph A.

The Great Republic. Heller, Agnes.

The Methodological Function Of Political Economy In Materialist Explanation Of The Development Of Socialist Society (in Czechoslovakian). Valencik, Radim.

The Philosophic Society For The Study Of Sport: 1972–1983. Fraleigh, Warren P.

The Virtues Of *Philia* And Justice: Who Learns These In Our Society. Diller, Ann.

Theoretical–Methodological And Practical Importance Of The Category Of Dialectical Contradiction (in Czechoslovakian). Vook, Jozef.

Thoughts And Suggestions Concerning An International Society For Philosophers Concerned With Peace. Cox, John Gray.

Welfare State Versus Welfare Society? Skillen, Anthony.

Wissenschaft Als Gegenstand Der Wissenschaft Vom Menschlichen Erleben Und Verhalten. Brandtstädter, Jochen and Reinert, Gunther.

SOCIOBIOLOGY

Ethical Questions In Brain And Behavior. Pfaff, Donald W (ed).

Methodology, Metaphysics And The History Of Science. Cohen, Robert S (ed) and Wartofsky, Marx W (ed).

Reductionism And Cultural Being. Smith, Joseph W.

Science And Gender: A Critique Of Biology And Its Theories On Women. Bleier, Ruth.

"Motives And Metaphors In Considerations Of Animal Nature" in *Ethical Questions In Brain And Behavior*, Pfaff, Donald W (ed), 125–140. Beer, Colin.

"Out With The "Old" And In With The "New"" in *Ethical Questions In Brain And Behavior*, Pfaff, Donald W (ed), 91–110. Caplan, Arthur L.

"Sociobiology And The Possibility Of Ethical Naturalism" in *Morality, Reason And Truth*, Copp, David (ed), 270–296. Campbell, Richmond.

"Sociobiology, Epistemology, And Human Nature" in *Methodology, Metaphysics And The History Of Science*, Cohen, Robert S (ed), 215–234. Leeds, Anthony.

An Interview With E O Wilson On Sociobiology And Religion. Saver, Jeffrey.

Biology And Ideology: The Interpenetration Of Science And Values. Richardson, Robert C.

Sexuality In Human Evolution: What Is "Natural" Sex? Caulfield, Mina Davis.

Sociobiology: The World As Given Or The World As Created. Pickens, Donald K.

Sociobiology. Midgley, Mary.

The Sociobiological View Of Man. Trigg, Roger.

SOCIOLINGUISTICS

Soziolinguistische Codes Und Kategorischer Imperativ. Werner, H –J.

SOCIOLOGY

A Guide To The Culture Of Science, Technology, And Medicine. Durbin, Paul T (ed).

Knowledge Structure And Use: Implications For Synthesis And Interpretation, Linda J

Reed (ed). Ward, Spencer (ed).

Philosophy Of Science And Sociology: From The Methodological Doctrine To Research Practice. Mokrzycki, Edmund.

Reductionism And Cultural Being. Smith, Joseph W.

The Nature Of Technological Knowledge: Are Models Of Scientific Change Relevant. Laudan, Rachel (ed).

The Social Sciences: Their Nature And Uses. Kruskal, William H (ed).

The Theory Of Communicative Action: Reason And The Rationalization Of Society, V1. Habermas, Jurgen and Mc Carthy, Thomas (trans).

"Kierkegaard's Sociology" in *International Kierkegaard Commentary*, Perkins, Robert L (ed), 133–154. Westphal, Merold.

"The Structure Of Technological Change: A Sociological Analysis Of Technology" in *Technological Knowledge*, Laudan, Rachel (ed), 115–142. Weingart, Peter.

A Political Theorist From Eastern Europe. Tar, Zoltán.

A Schutz And F Kaufmann: Sociology Between Science And Interpretation. Helling, Ingeborg K.

Aesthetics And The Sociology Of Art: A Critical Commentary On The Writings Of Janet Wolff. Hincks, Tony.

Alvin Gouldner: Vervreemding, Reflexiviteit, En De Naderende Crisis Van De Sociologie. Disco, Cornelis.

Beneath Role Theory: Reformulating A Theory With Nietzsche's Philosophy. Kaplan, Charles D and Weiglus, Karl.

Das Schwierige Recht Der Systemtheoretischen Soziologie: Zur Rechtssoziologie Von Niklas Luhmann. Folkers, Horst.

Der 'Labeling Approach'—Ein Paradigmawechsel In Der Modernen Kriminalsoziologie. Kunz, Karl—Ludwig.

Die Aufgaben Der Marxistisch–Leninistischen Soziologischen Forschung In Der DDR. Weidig, Rudi.

Forms Of Competition And Sociological Knowledge In Organized American Sociology. Stehr, Nico and Avison, William.

Gesellschaftliche Verflechtung Und Soziale Kontrolle. Prisching, Manfred.

Human Sociobiology: A Philosophical Perspective. Ruse, Michael.

Inhaltliche Fragen Der Ausarbeitung Eines Lehrbuches Der Marxistisch–Leninistischen Soziologie. Assmann, Georg and Stollberg, R.

Methodologie Und Geschichte: Ansätze Problemorientierter Gesellschaftsanalysen. Rust, Holger.

Norm Und Recht In Niklas Luhmanns Rechtssoziologie: Kritische Anmerkungen Aus Der Sicht Der Rechtsethnologie. Von Benda–Beckmann, Franz.

On The Visual Constitution Of Society: The Contributions Of Georg Simmel And Jean—Paul Sartre To A Sociology Of The Senses. Weinstein, Deena and Weinstein, Michael.

Rechtssoziologie Und Psychoanalyse: Neun Thesen In Rechtspolitischer Absicht. Rotter, Frank.

Rechtssoziologie Und Sozialer Wandel: Zum Dritten Band Des Jahrbuchs Für Rechtssoziologioe Und Rechtstheorie. Hagen, Johann J.

Reconstruction Of Schlick's Psycho–Sociological Ethics. Leinfellner, Werner.

Sociology And Liturgical Renewal. Flanagan, Kieran.

Soziale Probleme, Soziologische Theorie Und Gesellschaftsplanung. Hondrich, Karl Otto.

Sozialistische Persönlichkeitsentwicklung Und Soziologische Forschung. Adler, Frank and Kretzschmar, A.

Soziologische Probleme Des Nullwachstums. Meier, A.

Soziologische Forschung Zum Wohen Und Arbeiten In Der Stadt. Kahl, A.

The Axial Age (in Hebrew). Eisenstadt, S N.

The Laws Of Social Development According To Karl Marx And Oskar Lange. Kozyr–Kowalski, Stanislaw.

Toward An Epistemologically–Relevant Sociology Of Science. Campbell, Donald T.

Truth, Rationality And The Sociology Of Science. Jennings, Richard C.

Wissenschaftstheorie Und Praxis: Zur Funktion Soziologischer Theorienbildung. Rust, Holger.

SOCIOLOGY OF KNOWLEDGE

A Sociological Theory Of Objectivity. Bloor, David.

Faces Of Truth And The Sociology Of Knowledge: John Stuart Mill And Karl Mannheim. Laffey, John F.

Interpretative Sociology And The Philosophy Of Praxis: Comparing Max Weber And Antonio Gramsci. Shafir, Gershon.

Naturalism, Epistemological Individualism And "The Strong Programme" In Sociology Of Knowledge. Manicas, Peter T and Rosenberg, Alan.

On Surrender, Death, And The Sociology Of Knowledge. Feher, Judith.

Primitive Classification And The Sociology Of Knowledge: A Response To Bloor. Smith, Joseph Wayne.

Reasons, Causes, And The 'Strong Programme' In The Sociology Of Knowledge. Schmaus, Warren.

Reply To J W Smith's "Primitive Classification And The Sociology Of Knowledge". Bloor, David.

Reply To Steven Yearley's "The Relationship Between Epistemological And Sociological Cognitive Interests". Mackenzie, Donald.

Surrender–And–Catch And Phenomenology. Wolff, Kurt H.

System And Life World: Some Reflections On Goffman's Frame Analysis. Sundararajan, P T Saroja.

The Mystery Of Time: A New Sociological Approach. Gras, Alain.

The Well–Informed Citizen: Alfred Schutz And Applied Theory. Imber, Jonathan B.

SOCRATES

Ancient Greek Philosophy: Sourcebook And Perspective. Yartz, Frank J.

Plato And Aristophanes: Plato's Euthyphro, Apology, And Crito And Aristophanes' Clouds. West, Thomas G (trans) and West, Grace Starry (trans).

STRUCTURE(S)
H.
The Consistency Strength Of The Free–Subset Property Of Ω_ω. Koepke, Peter.
The Model–Theoretic Structure Of Abelian Group Rings. Pappas, Peter C.
The Role Of Reflection In The Structure Of The Human Person. Chudy, W.
The Uniqueness Of Envelopes In $\aleph_0$–Categorical, $\aleph_0$–Stable Structures. Loveys, James.
Universal Recursion Theoretic Properties Of R E Preordered Structures. Montagna, Franco and Sorbi, Andrea.
Vopenka's Principle And Compact Logics. Makowsky, J A.
What Ontology Can Be About: A Spacetime Example. Nerlich, Graham and Westwell Roper, Andrew.

STYLE
Anachronistic Inauthenticity In Art. Bertman, Martin A.
General And Individual Style In Literature. Robinson, Jenefer.
Political Theory And Politics: The Case Of Leo Strauss. Gunnell, John G.
Self–Plagiarism. Goldblatt, David A.
Style And Personality In The Literary Work. Robinson, Jenefer.
The Esoteric Philosophy Of Leo Strauss. Drury, S B.

SUAREZ
"The Suareziann Proof Of God's Existence" in *History Of Philosophy In Making*, Thro, Linus J (ed), 105–118. Doule, John P.
Presencia De San Agustín En Suárez. Reta, Jose Oroz.
Prolegomena To A Study Of Extrinsic Denomination In The Work Of Francis Suarez, S J. Doyle, John P.

SUBJECT(S)
Critical Thinking And The Curriculum. Ennis, Robert H.
Delimitating The Concept Of The Grotesque. Fingesten, Peter.
Interrelations Between Subject And Object In Perception. Lijun, Song.
La Teoría Relacional De La Personalidad Según J Nuttin. Darós, William R.
On Subject And Object. Gangjian, Luo.
Predication. Abraham, William E.
The Knowing Subject. Code, Lorraine B.
Une Définition Juridique Du Concept De L'Art. Pedersen, Ove K.

SUBJECTIVE
Das Individuelle Bewusstsein Und Die Dialektik Von Objektiven Bedingungen Und Subjektivem Faktor. Hahn, Toni.
Der Kulturprozess Und Die Wachsende Rolle Des Subjektiven Faktors. Redeker, Horst.
Die Wachsende Rolle Des Subjektiven Faktors––Eine Gesetzmässigkeit Des Historischen Fortschritts. Lassow, Ekkhard.
Mackie On The Objectivity Of Values. Wreen, Michael.
Objective And Subjective–Objective Aspects Of Contradictions Under Socialism (in Czechoslovakian). Flek, Antonín.
Rolle Des Subjektiven Faktors. Weidler, J.
Subjektiver Faktor Und Zusammenhang Von Gesellschaft Und Natur. Müller, Klaus.
Subjektiver Faktor Und Massenbewusstsein. Müller, Werner.
Subjektiver Faktor Und Revolution. Stiehler, Gottfried.
Zum Verhältnis Von Sozialistischer Ideologie Und Subjektivem Faktor. Rauh, Hans–Christoph.

SUBJECTIVISM
Probability And Evidence. Horwich, Paul.
Subjecting And Objecting. Deutscher, Max.
The Search For An Alternative: Philosophical Perspectives Of Subjectivism And Marxism. Farber, Marvin.
"Faith, Reason, And The Resurrection" in *Faith And Rationality*, Plantinga, Alvin (ed), 265–316. Holwerda, D.
A Transparent Case For Subjectivism. Hardin, C L.
Calibration, Coherence, And Scoring Rules. Seidenfeld, Teddy.
Human Nature And Morality: The Case Of The Ik. Sogolo, Godwin.
In Defense Of Objectivist Art Criticism. Lichtenbert, Robert H.
Solomon Maimon's Interpretation Of Kant's Copernican Revolution. Katzoff, Ch.
Subjectivism And The Question Of Social Criticism. Weston, Anthony.

SUBJECTIVITY
A Celebration Of Subjective Thought. Diefenbeck, James A.
Boston Studies In The Philosophy Of Science: Dialectical Theory Of Meaning, R S Cohen And M W Wartofsky (eds) V81. Markovic, Mihailo.
Ontologie Und Relationen. Horstmann, Rolf–Peter.
"Subjectivity And Civil Society" in *The State And Civil Society*, Pelczynski, Z A (ed), 197–210. Kortian, Garbis.
How Is Sport Possible? Lipiec, Józef.
Response To Comments On His "Twilight Of Subjectivity". Dallmayr, Fred R.
Review Of *The Origin Of Subjectivity In Hindu Thought*. Bhattacharya, K C.
Subjectivity. Shalom, Albert.
The 'Introduction' From Her *The Origin Of Subjectivity In Hindu Thought*. Kitch, Ethel May.
Zur Rolle Des Subjektiven Faktors In Der Wissenschaftsentwicklung. Ludwig, Gerd and Brau, Richard and Rosenthal, Erwin.

SUBJUNCTIVE(S)
A Syntactically Motivated Theory Of Conditionals. Lycan, William G.
Discussion: A Note On Tense And Subjunctive Conditionals. Thomason, Richard.

SUBLIME
Beauty Restored. Mothersill, Mary.

SUBSTANCE(S)
see also Attribute(s), Matter

Análisis Proposicional Y Ontologia. Sanchez, Juan Carlos.
Aristotle Metaphysics: Books Zeta, Eta, Theta, Iota. Furth, Montgomery (trans).
Introduction To The Problem Of Individuation In The Early Middle Ages. Gracia, Jorge J E.
Leibniz And Locke: A Study Of The "New Essays On Human Understanding". Jolley, Nicholas.
Leibniz. Brown, Stuart.
Über Die Rolle Von Substanzbegriffen Beim Zeigen Und Zählen Von Gegenständen. Hoche, Hans–Ulrich.
"Personal Identity And Imagination": One Objection. Flew, Antony.
"Substance And Causality" in *Kant On Causality, Freedom, And Objectivity*, Harper, William A (ed), 97–107. Nagel, Gordon.
"Substance And Its Logical Significance" in *Methodology, Metaphysics And The History Of Science*, Cohen, Robert S (ed), 235–246. Panova, Elena.
Berkeley, Epistemology, And Science. Steinkraus, Warren E.
Brahman, God, Substance And Nature: Samkara And Spinoza. Gupta, Bina.
Das Verhältnis Der *Kritik Der Reinen Vernunft* Zu Den *Metaphysischen Anfangsgründen Der Naturwissenschaft*, Demonstr Am Substanzsatz. Gloy, Karen.
Descartes Face À Leibniz Sur La Question De La Substance. Ayoub, J Boulad.
Hume On The Cartesian Theory Of Substance. Glass, Ronald J and Flage, Daniel E.
Knowledge Of Substance And Knowledge Of Science In Locke's Essay. Atherton, Margaret.
Leibniz Und Der Materialismus (1881): Aud Dem Nachlass Herausgegeben Von Helmut Holzhey (zürich). Natorp, Paul.
Remarks On Leibniz's Conception Of Containment And Individual Substance. Schwerin, Alan.
St Thomas And The Integration Of Knowledge Into Being. Dewan, Lawrence.
Substance–Society–Natural Systems: A Creative Rethinking Of Whitehead's Cosmology. Bracken, Joseph A.
Substitution In Aristotelian Technical Contexts. Peterson, Sandra.
The Thesis Of The Second Antinomy. De Paul, Michael R.

SUBSTITUTION
Organism, Community, And The "Substitution Problem". Katz, Eric.
Referential And Nonreferential Substitutional Quantifiers. Orenstein, Alex.
Substitution In Aristotelian Technical Contexts. Peterson, Sandra.
Systems Of Substitution Semantics. Bonevac, Daniel.

SUBSUMPTION
Rules And Subsumption: Mutative Aspects Of Logical Processes. Will, Frederick L.

SUCCESS
Approaching The Truth With The Rule Of Success. Kuipers, Theo A F.

SUCCESSION
"Kant's Empirical Realism" in *Kant On Causality, Freedom, And Objectivity*, Harper, William A (ed), 108–147. Harper, William L.

SUFFERING
Action And Suffering In The Bhagavad Gītā. Fingarette, Herbert.
Action And Suffering In The Theravadin Tradition. Smart, Ninian.
Commemoration And Perdurance In The Analects, Books 1 And 2. Casey, Edward S.
Karma And The Problem Of Suffering. Perrett, Roy W.
Pain And Suffering In Confucian Self–Cultivation. Wei– Ming, Tu.
Predation. Sapontzis, Steve F.
Reflections On The Centenary Of Marx's Death. Synowiecki, Adam.
Reply To J Narveson's Review Of *Reason And Value*. Bond, E J.
Some Doubts About Animal Rights. Machan, Tibor R.
The Collective Representation Of Affliction: Some Reflections On Disability And Disease As Social Facts. Blum, A.
Tolstoy's God Sees The Truth, But Waits: A Reflection. Archer, Dermot J.
Why Me; Why Now? Phifer, Kenneth.

SUFFICIENT
Happiness And Virtue In Socrates' Moral Theory. Vlastos, Gregory.

SUFFRAGE
"A Right To Make Laws" in *Freedom, Feminism, And The State*, Mc Elroy, Wendy (ed), 327–330. Spooner, Lysander.
"Perpetual Vassalage" in *Freedom, Feminism, And The State*, Mc Elroy, Wendy (ed), 331–336. Heywood, Ezra H.

SUFISM
Mysticism And Religious Traditions. Katz, Steven (ed).

SUICIDE
Biathanatos, Ernest W Sullivan (ed). Donne, John.
Preparing For The Perils Of Practice. Gorovitz, Samuel.
Prisoner In The ICU: The Tragedy Of William Bartling. Annas, George J.
Suicide And The Service Of God. Lombardi, Joseph J.
The Duty Not To Kill Oneself. Linehan, Elizabeth A.

SULLIVAN, R
Commentary On "A Response To 'Is Business Bluffing Ethical'". Powell, Donald C.
Commentary On "A Response To 'Is Business Bluffing Ethical'". Langley, Van E.

SUN
Le Caractère Mythique De L'Analogie Du Bien Dans *République VI*. Couloubaritsis, Lambros.

SUPEREROGATION
Friendship, Justice, And Superogation. Badhwar, Neera K.
Saints And Heroes: A Plea For The Supererogatory. Mc Goldrick, Patricia M.
Supererogation And Obligation. Kamm, Frances Myrna.

SUPERNATURAL
The Evidential Value Of Religious Experiences. Clark, R W.

TECHNOLOGY

Technological Knowledge, Laudan, Rachel (ed), 115–142. Weingart, Peter.

Aktuelle Probleme Der Wissenschaftlich–Technischen Revolution In Der Sowjetischen Philosophie. Thiele, Gabriele.

Algunas Preguntas Sobre Etica. Parent, Juan M.

Art And Media On The Road To Abdera? Berger, René.

Arten Des Herangehens An Dialektische Widersprüche Besonders In Der Technischen Entwicklung. Thiel, Rainer.

Biotechnology And The Social Reconstruction Of Molecular Biology. Markle, Gerald E and Robin, Stanley S.

Comment On Pavel Apostol's Paper. Bunge, Mario.

Contemporary Biotechnologies And The Concept Of Material Production (in Czechoslovakia. Kolársky, R.

Death And The Machine: From Jules Verne To Derrida And Beyond. Kemp, Peter.

Der Mechanismus Der Technikentwicklung. Banse, G.

Der Wissenschaftlich–Technische Fortschritt Und Die Interdisziplinäre Zusammenarbeit Von Philosophen Und Technikwissenschaftlern. Jobst, E.

Energieproblem Und Wissenschaftlich–Technischer Fortschritt. Winckelmann, J.

Engineering And The Philosophy Of Science. Broome, Taft H.

Evolution Und Revolution In Der Technischen Entwicklung Der Gegenwart. Wendt, H.

Extraterrestrial Science. Rescher, Nicholas.

France: A National Committee Debates The Issues. Ambroselli, Claire.

Heidegger's Later Philosophy Of Science. Rouse, Joseph T.

Is Big Beautiful? Sagoff, Mark.

Issues Of Computer Compatibility. Roemer, Robert E.

Man, Science, Morality. Anguelov, Stephan.

Marx's Critique Of Capitalist Technology: Form And Content. Rehg, William R.

Methodological Approaches To The Utilization Of Science And Technology In Practice. Boucek, Karel.

Philosophical Discussion Concerning The Issue Of Information (in German). Liebscher, Heinz.

Political Technics/Technological Politics: MIRVS Dangerous Agenda. Kilbourne, Lawrence.

Processed World: Technology And Culture In The Thought Of Marshall McLuhan. Kroker, Arthur.

Science, Technology, And Political Decision: From The Creation Of A Theory To The Evaluation Of The Consequences Of Its Application. Radnitzky, Gerard.

Science, Technology, And Political Decision. Radnitzky, Gerard.

Some Philosophical Aspects Of Modern Biotechnologies (in Czechoslovakian). Stachová, J.

Some Problems Of The Formation Of Strategies And Evaluation In The Sphere Of Biotechnologies (in Czechoslovakian). Mrácek, F and Machleidt, P.

Soviet–Marxist Philosophy Of Technology. Rapp, Friedrich.

Technics And The Bias Of Perception. Innis, Robert E.

Thailand: Buddhism Meets The Western Model. Lindbeck, Violette.

The Humanism Of Associated Work And The Problem Of The Technology Laws (in German). Jacobs, Hans–Jürgen and Herlitzius, Erwin.

The Importance Of The Changing Of Technological Ways Of Production In Marx's Conception Of Scientific Foreseeing (in Czechoslovakian). Jirasek, J.

The Place Of The Work Of Art In The Age Of Technology. Wright, Kathleen.

Theorie Und Praxis In Technologischer Und Dialektischer Perspektive. Muller–Schmid, Peter P.

Wissenschaftlich–Technischer Fortschritt Und Sozialistisches Verhältnis Zur Arbeit. Stollberg, R.

Zu Einigen Aktuellen Zügen Bürgerlicher Wissenschafts– Und Technikkritik. Kaizik, Peter.

Zum Verhältnis Von Technikphilosophie Und Technikgeschichte. Bialas, Volker.

TEILHARD

Immanence Et Transcendance Chez Teilhard De Chardin. Bonnet, Nicole.

TELEOLOGICAL ETHICS

"Kierkegaard's Teleological Suspension Of The Ethical" in *The Georgetown Symposium On Ethics*, Porreco, Rocco (ed), 19–48. Vogel, Manfred.

TELEOLOGICAL EXPLANATION

Formal The Teleological Elements In Hirst's Argument For A Liberal Curriculum. Scarlett, B F.

Michel Foucault: An Exchange: Taylor, Foucault, And Otherness. Connolly, William E.

Spinoza, Bennett, And Teleology. Rice, Lee C.

TELEOLOGY

Erklaren Und Verstehen. Von Wright, Georg Henrik.

From Aristotle To Darwin And Back Again: A Journey In Final Causality, Species, And Evolution. Gilson, Etienne.

The Georgetown Symposium On Ethics. Porreco, Rocco (ed).

"Conceptions Of The Common Good And The Natural Right To Liberty" in *The Georgetown Symposium On Ethics*, Porreco, Rocco (ed), 185–194. Rasmussen, Douglas B.

"Is Philosophy In Aristotle And Ideology:" in *Ideology, Philosophy And Politics*, Parel, Anthony (ed), 163–178. Owens, Joseph.

"Teleology And Consistency In Theories Of Morality As Natural Law" in *The Georgetown Symposium On Ethics*, Porreco, Rocco (ed), 91–108. Donagan, Alan.

"The Divine Command Theory And Objective Good" in *The Georgetown Symposium On Ethics*, Porreco, Rocco (ed), 219–234. Reichenbach, Bruce R.

Action, Causality, And Teleological Explanation. Collins, Arthur.

Causalité Et Finalité (in German). Pfeiffer, Alfred.

Discussion: Woodfield's Analysis Of Teleology. Nissen, Lowell.

Dispositions, Teleology And Reductionism. Roque, Alicia Juarrero.

Four Teleological Orders Of Human Action. Smith, Quentin.

Herders Methode In Seiner Geschichtsphilosophie. Rathmann, Jnos.

Human Goods And Practical Reasoning. Finnis, John.

Ist Die Evolutionstheorie Wissenschaftlich Begründet? Eisenstein, I.

Kausalität, Teleologie Und Evolution: Methodologische Grundprobeme Der Moderne Biologie. Kotter, Rudolf.

Principles And Virtues—Or—Principles Or Virtues. Coetzee, Pieter.

Right And Good: False Dichotomy? Maclean, Anne.

Short On Teleology. Olding, A.

Teleological Time: A Variation On A Kantian Theme. Gilead, Amihud.

Teleologie Und Leiblichkeit Beim Späten Kant. Duque, Felix.

Teleology And The Great Shift. De Sousa, Ronald B.

The *Uti/Frui* Distinction In Augustine's Ethics. O' Connor, William Riordan.

The Cosmic Breath: Reflections On The Thermodynamics Of Creation. Wicken, Jeffrey S.

The Place In Nature In Aristotle's Teleology. Boylan, Michael.

The Practice Of Medical Ethics: A Structuralistic Approach. Ellos, William J.

The Role Of Conservation Principles In Twentieth–Century Economic Theory. Mirowski, Philip.

The System–Property Theory Of Goal–Directed Processes. Ehring, Douglas.

TELEVISION

Aesthetician Of Film And Television Jan Kucera (in Czechoslovakia). Svoboda, Jan.

Broadcasting Ethics: Some Neglected Issues. Warnock, Mary.

Broadcasting And The Moral Imperative: Patrolling The Perimeters. Wenham, Brian.

Children As Consumers: An Ethical Evaluation Of Children's Advertising. Paine, Lynda Sharp.

On The Strategy Of Scientific Research In Connection With The Coming Into Being Of Television 1839–1934 (in Hungarian). Balázs, Tibor.

TELOH, H

The Erotic Education Of The Slave. Nails, Debra.

TEMPORAL LOGIC

Buridan On Interval Semantics For Temporal Logic. Ohrstrom, Peter.

TEMPORALITY

Mahler: Consciousness And Temporality. Greene, David B.

Temporal Relations And Temporal Becoming: A Defense Of A Russellian Theory Of Time. Oaklander, L Nathan.

The Rhythm Of Being: A Study Of Temporality. Trivers, Howard.

"Basic Tense Logic" in *Handbook Of Philosophical Logic*, Gabbay, Dov (ed), 89–134. Burgess, John P.

Aristotle's Distinction Between Motion And Activity. Stone, Mark A.

Estructura De La Temporalidad Y Realidad Social. Ferreol, G.

Eternal Thoughts. Carruthers, Peter.

On The Experience Of Historical Objects. Harvey, Charles W.

Temporal Parts Of Four Dimensional Objects. Heller, Mark.

Temporality, Perceptual Experience And Peirce's "Proofs" Of Realism. Rosenthal, Sandra B.

The Idea Of Motion. Shamsi, F A.

The Mind–Independence Of Temporal Becoming. Smith, Quentin.

Zeno's Paradoxes And Temporal Becoming In Dialectical Atomism. Smolenov, Hristo.

TENANT, N

Rejoinder To Tenant's "Were Those Disproofs I Saw Before Me"? Weir, Alan.

TENNANT, F

An Understanding Of Original Sin—Through The Interpretations Of Tennant, Rahner, And Ricoeur. Fu, Pei–Jung.

TENSE(S)

Discussion: A Note On Tense And Subjunctive Conditionals. Thomason, Richard.

Do We Need Interval Semantics? Tichý, Pavel.

Modifiers And Quantifiers In Natural Language. Parsons, Terence.

Towards Putting Real Tense Back Into The World: A Reply To D H Mellor's Reconstruction Of The McTaggart Argument. Smith, Joseph Wayne.

TENSE LOGIC

The Logic Of Aspect: An Axiomatic Approach. Galton, Antony.

"Basic Tense Logic" in *Handbook Of Philosophical Logic*, Gabbay, Dov (ed), 89–134. Burgess, John P.

"Combinations Of Tense And Modality" in *Handbook Of Philosophical Logic*, Gabbay, Dov (ed), 135–166. Thomason, Richmond H.

"Quantification In Tense And Modal Logic" in *Handbook Of Philosophical Logic*, Gabbay, Dov (ed), 309–354. Cocchiarella, Nino B.

Once Upon A Tense. Verkuyl, H J and Le Loux— Schuringa, J A.

Structured Nonstandard Dynamic Logic. Sain, Ildikó.

The Logical Consequence Relation Of Propositional Trense Logic. Thomason, S K.

The Reality Of Time. Shorter, J M.

TERM(S)

Logica Parva, Alan R Perreiah (trans). Venetus, Paulus.

Marsilius Of Inghen: Treatises On The Properties Of Terms. Bos, Egbert P.

On Theoretical Terms. Dilworth, Craig.

Reduction Of Higher Type Levels By Means Of An Ordinal Analysis Of Finite Terms. Terlouw, Jan.

Zum Aufbau Einer Mehrsortigen Elementaren Logik. Kaphengst, Heinz.

TERMINISM

Epiphenomenal And Supervenient Causation. Kim, Jaegwon.

TERMINOLOGY

Classroom Logic Terminology: Response To Seech. Lugenbehl, Dale.

TERRORISM

Magical Aspects Of Political Terrorism. Miguens, José Enrique.

The Morality Of Terrorism. Coady, C A J.

THEOLOGY

Modern Pantheism As An Approach To Environmental Ethics. Wood Jr, Harold W.

Nature And Nature's God. Toulmin, Stephen.

On Theology And On Jewish Concepts Of Ultimate Reality And Meaning In Modern Jewish Philosophy. Levy, Ze'ev.

Plato's Theology Reconsidered: What The Demiurge Does. Mohr, Richard D.

Presidential Address: Practical Reasoning And Christian Faith. Grisez, Germain.

Rationalistic Theology And Some Principles Of Explanation. Rowe, William L.

Religious Existence And The Philosophical Radicalization Of Phenomenological Theology. Bourgeois, Patrick L.

Some Sources For A History Of English Socinianism; A Bibliography Of 17th Century English Socinian Writings. Bianchi, Daniela.

The Anthropological Approach To Theology. Macquarrie, John and Rahner, Karl.

The Concept Of The Person In St Augustine's *De Trinitate*. O' Connor, William R.

The Contemplation Of Otherness. Wentz, Richard E.

The Meaning Of Proportionate Reason In Contemporary Moral Theology. Johnstone, Brian V.

The Mind Of Christ In Transcendental Theology: Rahner, Lonergan And Crowe. Moloney, Raymond.

The Original Preface. Lonergan, Bernard.

The Physics Of David Bohm And Its Relevance To Philosophy And Theology. Russell, Robert J.

The Problem Of Divine Exemplarity In St Thomas. Farthing, John L.

The Quaker Background Of William Bartram's View Of Nature. Clarke, Larry R.

The Slippery Slope Of Religious Relativism. Kellenberger, James.

The Theological Significance Of Hegel's Four World–Historical Realms. Von Der Luft, Eric.

Theology And The Intellectual Endeavour Of Mankind. Hudson, W D.

To Kill Or Let Live: Augustine On Killing The Innocent. Burt, Donald X.

Two Classical Western Theologians: Augustine And Newman. Penaskovic, Richard.

Umanesimo E Teologia Nel Cusano "Disgiunzione" E "Metafora". Camporeale, Salvatore I.

Zur Aktualität Der Politischen Theologie Ulrich Zwinglis. Winzeler, Peter.

THEOREM(S)

"Homogeneous Formulas And Definability Theorems" in *Lecture Notes In Mathematics*, Muller, G H And Others (ed), 109–116. Motohashi, Nobuyoshi.

"The Hahn—Branch Theorem And A Restricted Inductive Definition" in *Lecture Notes In Mathematics*, Muller, G H And Others (ed), 359–394. Yasugi, Mariko.

An Abstract Setting For Henkin Proofs. Goldblatt, Robert.

DFC–Algorithms For Suszko, Logic SCI And One-to-one Gentzen Type Formalizations. Wasilewska, Anita.

Toposes In Logic And Logic In Toposes. Bunge, Marta.

THEORETICAL CONCEPTS

An Occurrent Theory Of Practical And Theoretical Reasoning. Walker, Arthur F.

Knowledge As The Production Of Intellectual Instruments And Theoretical Constructions. Cekić, Miodrag.

Metapreferences And The Reasons For Stability In Social Choice: Thoughts On Broadening And Clarifying The Debate. Grofman, Bernard and Uhlaner, Carole.

THEORETICAL ENTITY(–TIES)

Are Probabilism And Special Relativity Incompatible? Maxwell, Nicholas.

THEORETICAL REASON

Faith And Rationality: Reason And Belief In God. Plantinga, Alvin (ed) and Wolterstorff, Nicholas (ed).

THEORETICAL TERM(S)

On A New Definition Of Theoreticity. Balzer, W.

Propositions And Empirical Evidence. O' Neil, Michael P.

Theoretical Terms And The Causal View Of Reference. Kroon, Frederick W.

Theoretical Terms And Bridge Principles: A Critique Of Hempel's (Self–) Criticisms. Moulines, C Ulises.

THEORY(–RIES)

see also Educational Theory(–ries), Ethical Theory(–ries), Political Theory, Recursion Theory, Set Theory

Marx's Social Critique Of Culture. Dupré, Louis.

Observation, Experiment, And Hypothesis In Modern Physical Science. Achinstein, Peter (ed) and Hannaway, Owen (ed).

Reason And The Search For Knowledge: Investigations In The Philosophy Of Science. Shapere, Dudley.

Treatise On Basic Philosophy, V5. Bunge, Mario.

A Formal Approach To The Theory–Dependence Of Measurement. Gahde, Ulrich.

A Mathematical Characterization Of Interpretation Between Theories. Van Bentham, Johan and Pearce, David.

A Modal Approach To Sneed's "Theoretical Functions". Miroiu, Adrian.

A Normal Form Theorem For First Order Formulas And Its Application To Gaifman's Splitting Theorem. Motohashi, Nobuyoshi.

A Note On Interpretations Of Many–sorted Theories. Hook, Julian L.

A Remark On The Strict Order Property. Lachlan, A H.

A Study Of Theory Unification. Nugayev, Renat.

Adams On Theoretical Reduction. Day, Michael A.

Again On "The Crisis In Economic Theory": An Epistemological Approach. Munteanu, Costea.

Approaching The Truth With The Rule Of Success. Kuipers, Theo A F.

Approximative Explanation Is Deductive Nomological. Pearce, David and Rantala, Veikko.

Categoricity And Ranks. Saffe, Jürgen.

Closed Sets And Chain Conditions In Stable Theories. Pillay, Anand and Srour, Gabriel.

Cuts, Consistency Statements And Interpretations. Pudlak, Pavel.

Decidability And The Number Of Countable Models. Millar, Terrence.

Eastern Model–Theory For Boolean–Valued Theories. Georgescu, George and Voiculescu, Ioana.

Empirische Wetten En Theorieën. En Kuipers, Theo and Zandvoort, Henk.

Entscheidbarkeit Von Theorien In Logiken Mit Verallgemeinerten Quantoren. Wolter, Helmut and Herre, Heinrich.

Experiment—Modell—Theorie. Horz, Herbert.

Explaining The Success Of Science. Brown, James Robert.

Explanatory Asymmetries. Woodward, James.

Free From Sin: On Living With Ad Hoc Hypotheses. Wettersten, John.

From Galen's Theory To William Harvey's Theory: A Case Study In The Rationality Of Scientific Theory Change. Mowry, Bryan.

How To Give It Up: A Survey Of Some Formal Aspects Of The Logic Of Theory Change. Makinson, David.

Inductive Inference In The Limit. Glymour, Clark.

Kueker's Conjecture For Superstable Theories. Buechler, Steven.

Mesure Et Théorie En Physique. Fevrier, Paulette.

On Pseudo–$\aleph_0$–Categorical Theories. Marcja, Annalisa and Toffalori, Carlo.

On Reduction Of Theories. Kamlah, Andreas.

On Relevance Of M Bunge's Concept Of Difference In Meaning, Two Studies Of Inter–Theory Relations. Grobler, Adam.

On The Logic Of Theory Change: Partial Meet Contraction And Revision Functions. Alchourron, Carlos and Gardenfors, Peter and Makinson, David.

On The Status Of Statistical Inferences. Pitowsky, Itamar.

Partial Aleph–1–homogeniety Of The Countable Saturated Model Of An Aleph–sub–1–categorical Theory. Rosenthal, John W.

Poppers Zwei Definitionsvarianten Von 'Falsifizierbar': Eine Logische Notiz Zu Einer Klassischen Stelle Aus Der *Logik Der Forschung*. Dorn, Georg J W.

Pragmatics In Science And Theory In Common Sense. Wilkes, K V.

Quelques Précisions Sur La DOP Et La Profondeur D'une Théorie. Lascar, D.

Regular Types In Nonmultidimensional ω–Stable Theories. Pillay, Anand.

Science, Technology, And Political Decision. Radnitzky, Gerard.

Scientific Change, Continuity, And Problem Solving. Pearce, David and Rantala, V.

Should Philosophers Of Science Consider Scientific Discovery? Pietruska– Madej, Elzbieta.

Social Theory Without Wholes. Turner, Stephen P.

Supervaluations And Theories. Bencivenga, Ermanno.

Testability, Flexibility: Kuhnian Values In Scientists' Discourse Concerning Theory Choice. Potter, Jonathan.

The First–Order Theory Of The c–Degrees. Farrington, Paddy.

The Incoherence Of Intergenerational Justice. Ball, Terence.

The Metaphorical Character Of Science. Bradie, M.

The Relation Of Theory And Practice In The Process Of Formation And Action Of Laws Of Communist Socio–Economic Formation (in Czechoslovakian). Kroh, Michael.

The Rise Of General Theories In Contemporary Science. Laszlo, Ervin.

The Strength Of Admissibility Without Foundation. Jager, Gerhard.

The Success Of Mathematics. Magari, Roberto.

The Use And Misuse Of Critical Gedankenexperimente. Krimsky, Sheldon.

Theoretical Functions, Theory And Evidence. Forge, John.

Theory Dynamics And Knowledge Representation From An Information–Theoretical Point Of View. Hauffe, Heinz.

Theory Testing In Science—The Case Of Solar Neutrinos. Pinch, Trevor.

Theory, Observation And Inductive Learning. Lane, N R.

Towards An Economic Theory Of Scientific Revolutions—A Cynical View. Wieland, Bernhard.

Truth And Best Explanation. Tuomela, Raimo.

Truth Without Satisfaction. Fine, Kit and Mc Carthy, Timothy.

Underdetermination And Realism. Bergström, Lars.

What Was Einstein's Principle Of Equivalence? Norton, John.

Why Constructive Empiricism Collapses Into Scientific Realism. Melchert, Norman.

Wissenschaftstheorie Und Praxis: Zur Funktion Soziologischer Theorienbildung. Rust, Holger.

Zur Theorien– Und Methodenentwicklung In Den Naturwissenschaften. Kannegiesser, Karlheinz and Uebeschar, K.

THEORY OF TYPES

La Naissance De La Théorie Des Types. Lepage, Francois.

Realizability And Intuitionistic Logic. Diller, J and Troelstra, A S.

THERAPEUTIC ABORTION

"Ethical Issues In Prenatal Therapies" in *Biomedical Ethics Reviews*, Humber, James M (ed), 225–250. Hull, Richard T and Nelson, James A and Gartner, Lou Ann.

"The Ethics Of Fetal Therapy" in *Biomedical Ethics Reviews*, Humber, James M (ed), 205–224. Macklin, Ruth.

THERAPY

see also Psychotherapy

Ethics In The Practice Of Psychology. Carroll, Mary Ann and Schneider, Henry G and Wesley, George R.

Psychiatry And Ethics. Edwards, Rem B (ed).

"The Ethics Of Fetal Therapy" in *Biomedical Ethics Reviews*, Humber, James M (ed), 205–224. Macklin, Ruth.

Freedom And Moral Therapy In Leibniz. Seidler, Michael J.

Is "Ethicist" Anything To Call A Philosopher? Zaner, Richard M.

THERAVADA

Discipline: The Canonical Buddhism Of The Vinayapitaka. Holt, John C.

TRAGEDY

"La Destinée De La Tragédie Dans La Culture Islamique" in *Existential Coordinates Of Human Condition*, Tymieniecka, A (ed), 333–340. Chehida, A Ben.

"Myth & Tragic Action In La Celestina And Romeo And Juliet" in *Existential Coordinates Of Human Condition*, Tymieniecka, A (ed), 425–435. Stewart, Marilyn.

"The Birth Of Tragedy Out Of The Spirit Of Music" in *Existential Coordinates Of Human Condition*, Tymieniecka, A (ed), 273–294. Kronegger, Marlies.

"The Denial Of Tragedy" in *Existential Coordinates Of Human Condition*, Tymieniecka, A (ed), 401–408. Ravaux, Francoise.

"The Re–emergence Of Tragedy In Late Medieval England" in *Existential Coordinates Of Human Condition*, Tymieniecka, A (ed), 363–378. Kennedy, Beverly.

"Toward A Theory Of Contemporary Tragedy" in *Existential Coordinates Of Human Condition*, Tymieniecka, A (ed), 341–362. Kaelin, Eugene.

"Tragedy And The Completion Of Freedom" in *Existential Coordinates Of Human Condition*, Tymieniecka, A (ed), 295–306. Tymieniecka, A.

"Tragic Closure And The Cornelian Wager" in *Existential Coordinates Of Human Condition*, Tymieniecka, A (ed), 409–416. Lyons, John.

"Tragical, Comical, Historical" in *Existential Coordinates Of Human Condition*, Tymieniecka, A (ed), 379–400. Platt, Michael.

"Values And German Tragedy 1770–1840" in *Existential Coordinates Of Human Condition*, Tymieniecka, A (ed), 319–332. Wittkowski, W.

Aeschylus And Practical Conflict. Nussbaum, Martha.

Enjoying Negative Emotions In Fiction. Morreall, John.

Le Paysage Arcadien De Nietzsche: Reflets D'Engadine. Berlinger, Rudolph.

Nietzsche Y El Intento De Ir Más Allá De Sócrates. Troncoso, Alfredo.

Philanthropia In The Poetics. Moles, John.

The Tragic View Of Life. Beattie, Paul H.

The Tragic View Of Life. Beattie, Paul H.

Tragédie Grecque Et "Anti–Théâtre" En France Au Siècle Des Lumières. Christodoulou, Kyriaki.

TRAHERNE, T

Thomas Traherne And The Art Of Meditation. Jordan, Richard D.

TRAINING

Thoughts On The Moral Relationship Of Intent And Training In Sport. Thomas, Carolyn E.

TRANSCENDENCE

Methpysics: Its Structure And Function. Korner, Stephan.

The Metaphysical Foundations Of Logic, Michael Heim (trans). Heidegger, Martin.

Divine Transcendence. Kvanvig, Jonathan L.

Gender–Specific Values. Seigfried, Charlene H.

History And Reality: R G Collingwood's Theory Of Absolute Presuppositions. Trainor, Paul J.

Immanence Et Transcendance Chez Teilhard De Chardin. Bonnet, Nicole.

TRANSCENDENTAL

Kant's Critical Philosophy. Deleuw, Gilles.

The Philosophy Of F W J Schelling: History, System, And Freedom. Marx, Werner and Nenon, Thomas (trans).

The Transcendental Turn: The Foundations Of Kant's Idealism. Gram, Moltke.

"Kant's Transcendental Idealism" in *Kant On Causality, Freedom, And Objectivity*, Harper, William A (ed), 83–96. Walsh, W H.

"Transcendental Philosophy And The Hermeneutic Critique Of Consciousness" in *Hermeneutics*, Shapiro, Gary (ed), 96–120. Mohanty, J N.

Auflösung Eines Einwandes Gegen Kants Transzendentale Ästhetik. Rohs, P.

Beyond Hegel's Ontological Claim. Allen, Robert Van Roden.

Das Apriorische Moment Der Subjekt–Objekt–Dialektik In Der Transzendentalen Phänomenologie. Kochler, Hans.

De l'illusion Transcendantale. Theis, Robert.

Der Grundgedanke Des Tractatus Als Metamorphose Des Obersten Grundsatzes Der Kritik Der Reinen Vernunft. Ferber, Rafael.

Die Bedeutung Der Methode Galileis Für Die Entwicklung Der Transzendentalphilosophie Kants. Holz, Fr.

Fundamental Ontology And Transcendent Beauty: An Approach To Kant's Aesthetics. Crowther, Paul.

Hui–Neng And The Transcendental Standpoint. Laycock, Steven W.

Kant's Transcendental Ideal—II. O' Farrell, Frank.

Legislation–Transgression: Strategies And Counter–Strategies In The Transcendental Justification Of Norms. Schürmann, Reiner.

Synthesis And Transcendental Idealism. Walker, Ralph S.

The Mind Of Christ In Transcendental Theology: Rahner, Lonergan And Crowe. Moloney, Raymond.

Transcendental Idealism In Wittgenstein And Theories Of Meaning. Moore, A W.

TRANSCENDENTAL ARGUMENT(S)

Faith As Kant's Key To The Justification Of Transcendental Reflection. Palmquist, Stephen.

Good Transcendental Arguments. Genova, A C.

Kritik Und Bergründung In Transzendentaler Argumentation. Becker, Wolfgang.

Wie Ist Sinn Des Sinnlosen Möglich? Kohler, Rudolf.

TRANSCENDENTAL DEDUCTION

Das Erkennen Als Ein Erkennen In Blosser Erscheinung: Zu Ingeborg Heidemanns Verständnis Der Kritik Der Reiner Vernuft. Kopper, J.

Good Transcendental Arguments. Genova, A C.

Hegel's Critique Of Kant's Theoretical Philosophy. Ameriks, Karl.

Kant's Transcendental Deduction Of God's Existence As A Postulate Of Pure Practical Reason. Kuehn, Manfred.

Kants Lehre Vom Urteil. Viertel, Wolfgang.

TRANSCENDENTAL EGO

The Roots Of The Existentialist Theory Of Freedom In *Ideas I*. Edie, James M.

TRANSCENDENTAL METHOD

Kant's Transcendental Method And His Theory Of Mathematics. Hintikka, Jaakko.

TRANSCENDENTALISM

Überlegungen Zu Den Grundlegungsversuchen Der Mathematik Von Frege Und Hilbert Vom Standpunkt Der Transzendentalphilosophie Aus (II). Schuler, Wolfgang.

"Transcendental Idealism And Causality" in *Kant On Causality, Freedom, And Objectivity*, Harper, William A (ed), 20–41. Posy, Carl J.

Die Bedeutung Der Freiheitsproblematik Für Kants Übergang Zum Transzendentalismus. Thom, Martina.

Kant's Transcendental Schematism. Woods, Michael.

The Process Of Meaning–Creation: A Transcendental Argument. Falck, Colin.

The Religion Of Humanity. Chandler, Daniel Ross.

TRANSFERENCE

Conditions Versus Transference: A Reply To Ehring. Aronson, Jerrold.

Is Everyone A *Mentalité* Case: Transference And The "Culture" Concept. La Capra, Dominick.

Transference And The Direction Of Causation. Kline, A David.

TRANSFORMATION

Creation As Transformation. Lath, Mukund.

Language And The Transformation Of Philosophy. Derksen, L D.

On The Position Of The Category Of Transformation In Dialectics. Baimao, Yao.

TRANSFORMATIONAL GRAMMAR(S)

Chomsky On Grammar And Mind: A Critique. Kuester, Harold H.

TRANSFORMATIONAL RULES

La Lingüística Generativo–Transformacional De Noam Chomsky. Beuchot, Mauricio.

TRANSITIVITY

Merleau–Ponty, The Flesh And Foucault. Cohen, Richard.

No Minimal Transitive Model Of Z–. Marek, W and Srebrny, M.

Wright *Versus* Lewis On The Transitivity Of Counterfactuals. Lowe, E J.

TRANSLATION

Davidson And Indeterminacy Of Translation. Kirk, Robert E.

On The Indeterminacy Of Action. Soles, Deborah Hansen.

Six Problems In "Translational Equivalence". Pelletier, F J.

Striking 'Commensurate' From The Oxford Translation. Jones, Joe E.

T M Knox: His Life And Scholarship. Pelczynski, Zbigniew A.

Translation, Indeterminacy And Triviality. Hanna, Patricia.

Type Driven Translation. Klein, Ewan and Sag, Ivan A.

TRANSMISSION

Transmission, Inheritance, And Efficient Causation. Field, Richard W.

TRANSPLANTATION

Baby Fae: The "Anything Goes School Of Human Experimentation". Annas, George J.

Religious Justifications For Donating Body Parts. May, William F.

The Subject Of Baby Fae. Capron, Alexander M and others.

TRAVEL

The Provisional Homecomer. Jones, Funmilayo M.

TREATMENT(S)

Nontreatment Decisions For Severely Compromised Newborns. Kipnis, Kenneth.

TREE(S)

Logic Made Simple. Rubin, Ronald.

"Various Kinds Of Aronszajn Tree With No Subtree Of Different Kind" in *Lecture Notes In Mathematics*, Muller, G H And Others (ed), 1–22. Hanazawa, Masazumi.

Don't Eliminate Cut. Boolos, George.

TRIAL(S)

The Phenomenology Of Trials: Text And Socio–Political Context. Gavin, William J and Conway, Jeremiah.

Trial By Charade. Mac' Kie, Pamela S.

TRIANOSKY, G

Acceptance And The Problem Of Slippery–Slope Insensitivity In Rule Utilitarianism. Whitt, L A.

TRIBALISM

The Economy Of Tribal Societies (in Hungarian). Sárkány, Mihály.

TRINITY

Henry Of Harclay On The Formal Distinction In The Trinity (in Latin). Henninger, Mark G.

Some Sources For A History Of English Socinianism; A Bibliography Of 17th Century English Socinian Writings. Bianchi, Daniela.

The Personal God And A God Who Is A Person. Thatcher, Adrian.

TRUST

The Silent World Of Doctor And Patient. Katz, Jay.

"The Concept Of 'trust' In The Politics Of John Locke" in *Philosophy In History*, Rorty, Richard and others (ed), 279–302. Dunn, John.

Distrust, Secrecy, And The Arms Race. Bok, Sissela.

Speech And The Social Contract. Turner, Roy.

The Cybernetic Analysis Of Distrust (in Hungarian). Tóth, János.

Trust. Cooper, David E.

TRUTH(S)

Der Formalismus Und Seine Grenzen: Untersuchungen Zur Neueren Philosophie Der Mathematik. Rheinwald, Rosemarie.

Ethics, Persuasion And Truth. Smart, J J C.

Heidegger: Perspektiven Zur Deutung Seines Werkes. Pöggeler, Otto (ed).

TRUTH(S)

Inquiries Into Truth And Interpretation. Davidson, Donald.

Is Science Progressive? Niiniluoto, Ilkka.

Justifying Historical Descriptions. Mc Cullagh, C Behan.

Laws Of The Game: How The Principles Of Nature Govern Chance. Eigen, Manfred and Winkler, Ruthild.

Logical Form In Natural Language. Lycan, William G.

Morality, Reason And Truth: New Essays On The Foundations Of Ethics. Copp, David (ed) and Zimmerman, David (ed).

Non Pie Quaerunt: Rhetoric, Dialectic, And The Discovery Of The True In Augustine's Confessions. Di Lorenzo, Raymond D.

On The Truth Of Being: Reflections On Heidegger's Later Philosophy. Kockelmans, Joseph J.

Practical Reason. Von Wright, G H.

Realism And Truth. Devitt, Michael.

Realism And Reason: Philosophical Papers, V3. Putnam, Hillary.

The Epistemology Of Hans–Georg Gadamer. Schmidt, Lawrence K.

The Metaphysical Foundations Of Logic, Michael Heim (trans). Heidegger, Martin.

Wahrheit Und Wahrheitsgrund. Fleischer, Margot.

Über Die Wahrheit Und Den Wahrheitsbegriff. Steussloff, Hans.

"Normative Knowledge And Truth" in *Philosophical Analysis In Latin America*, Gracia, Jorge J E and others (eds), 25–46. Alchourron, Carlos and Bulygin, Eugenio.

"Predication, Truth, And Transworld Identity In Leibniz" in *How Things Are*, Bogen, James (ed), 235–284. Adams, Robert M.

"Wahrheit Und Schönheit" in *Asthetische Er Fahrung Und Das Wesen Der Kunst*, Holzhey, Helmut, 107–122. Mercier, A.

A Case Of Creative Misreading: Habermas's Evolution Of Gadamer's Hermeneutics. How, Alan R.

A Comment On Ken Westphal's "Nietzsche's Sting And The Possibility Of Good Philology". Zimmerman, R I.

A Dynamic Model Of Temporal Becoming. Mc Call, Storrs.

A New Basis For Decision Theory. Davidson, Donald.

A Priori Truth. Horowitz, Tamara.

A Problem About Ambiguity In Truth–!Theoretical Semantics. Cohen, L Jonathan.

A Simple Solution To Mortensen And Priest's Truth Teller Paradox. Wayne Smith, Joseph.

A Theory Of Historical Truth. Haecker, Dorothy.

Acceptance Of Empirical Statements: A Bayesian Theory Without Cognitive Utilities. Harsanyi, John C.

Approaching The Truth With The Rule Of Success. Kuipers, Theo A F.

Aristotle On Perceptual Truth And Falsity. Ben–Zeev, Aaron.

Cause In Perception: A Note On Searle's *Intentionality*. Mc Culloch, Gregory.

Commensurability, Incommensurability And Cumulativity In Scientific Knowledge. Agazzi, Evandro.

Comments On Mittelman's "Perspectivism, Becoming, And Truth In Nietzsche". Hinman, Lawrence M.

Comments: Aims And Forms Of Discourse Regarding Nietzsche's Truth–Telling. Zanardi, William J.

Connolly, Coucault, And Truth. Taylor, Charles.

Culture Et Vérité Chez Aristote. Cauchy, Venant.

Demystifying Doublethink: Self–Deception, Truth And Freedom In *1984*. Martin, Mike W.

Die Utopie Künstlerischer Wahrheit In Der Ästhetik Von Adolf Loos Und Arnold Schönberg. Waibl, Elmar.

Does The Description Theory Make Contingent Truths Necessary? Eudaly, Thomas D.

Empirische Mogelijkheden; Sleutelbegrip Van De Wetenschapsfilosofie. Kuipers, Theo A F.

En Marge De Quelques Textes Épistémologiques Récents. Robert, Jean–Dominique.

Epistemic And Alethic Iteration In Later Medieval Logic. Boh, Ivan.

Eternal Thoughts. Carruthers, Peter.

Fenomenología De La Sensación. Chalmeta, Gabriel.

For A Syncretism Of The Faculties Of The Mind: Art As A Means Of Knowledge. Dehaye, Pierre.

Formal Truth And Objective Truth. Stefanov, Anguel S.

Foucault And The Question Of Enlightenment. Hiley, David R.

Freedom As A Condition For Truth: Jaspers On The Significance Of Temporality In Science. Koterski, Joseph W.

Fugitive Truth. Earle, William James.

Husserl's Platonism And The Objective Truth (in Hungarian). Rozsnyai, Ervin.

Ideology And Truth. Oruka, H Odera.

Intuitionistic Truth. Rabinowicz, Wlodzimierz.

Jucios Morales Y Verdad. De Gandolfi, Maria.

Justification And Truth. Cohen, Stewart.

Kants Auffassung Von Der Wissenschaftlichkeit Der Philosophie: Die Sinnwahrheit. Kaulbach, Friedrich.

Kierkegaard, Indirect Communication, And Religious Truth. Kellenberger, J.

Konstruktiver Empirismus. Kraft, Victor.

Kurt Gödel: Conviction And Caution. Feferman, Solomon.

Lógica Formal, Lógica Trascendental Y Verdad En La Primera "Crítica". Dotti, Jorge E.

La Verdad En La Inteligencia Humana. Derisi, Octavio N.

Lo Inteligible. De Paoli, Alejandro.

Logico–Semantic Aspects Of Truthfulness. Yanuva, Jana.

Meinungsstreit Zu Fragen Der Marxistischen Wahrheitstheorie. Kaiser, Eckhard and Poldrack, H.

Mito E Verità In Mircea Eliade. Fiore, Crescenzo.

Nelson Goodman On Truth. Chokr, Nader.

Nietzsche's Sting And The Possibility Of Good Philology. Westphal, Kenneth.

Nietzsche's Rereading Of Plato. Zuckert, Catherine.

O'Hear On An Argument Of Popper's. Glassen, Peter.

On "Truth And Lie In The Extra–Moral Sense". Clark, Maudemarie.

On Popper's Use Of Tarski's Theory Of Truth. Grattan–Guinness, I.

Peirce's Doubts About Idealism. Meyers, Robert G.

Peirce's Thirteen Theories Of Truth. Almeder, Robert.

Perception, Relativism, And Truth: Reflections On Plato's Theaetetus 152–160. Matthen, Mohan.

Perspectivism, Becoming, And Truth In Nietzsche. Mittelman, Willard.

Provability And Mathematical Truth. Fair, David.

Realism And Anti–Realism About Mathematics. Field, Hartry.

Reply To Peter Glassen's "O'Hear On An Argument Of Popper's". O'Hear, Anthony.

Self–Referential Incoherence. Mavrodes, George I.

Semiotic Idealism. Mc Carthy, Jeremiah E.

Some Remarks On Indian Theories Of Truth. Chakrabarti, Kisor Kumar.

St Augustine's Quest For The Truth: The Adequacy Of A Christian Philosophy. Kuntz, Paul G.

Tarski A Relativist? Siegel, Harvey.

Teken, Waarheid, Macht. Van Velthoven, Theo.

The Battle Between Art And Truth. Brogan, Walter.

The Concept Of Truth In Frege's Program. Burge, Tyler.

The Concept Of Knowledge. Mc Ginn, Colin.

The Objectivity Of Mystical Truth Claims. Price, James Robertson.

The Phases Of Light In Augustine (in Japanese). Hikasa, Katsushi.

The Problem Of Circularity In Wollaston's Moral Philosophy. Joynton, Olin.

The Truth Imperative. Lingis, Alphonso F.

There Is No Set Of All Truths. Grim, Patrick.

Towards A Critical Theory Of Value. Luntley, Michael.

Truth And Best Explanation. Tuomela, Raimo.

Truth And Reflection. Yablo, Stephen.

Truth As Ideal Coherence. Rescher, Nicholas.

Truth In A Contingent World. Campbell, R.

Truth In All Of Certain Well–Founded Countable Models Arising In Set Theory. Rosenthal, John W.

Truth Without Satisfaction. Fine, Kit and Mc Carthy, Timothy.

Truth, Rationality And The Sociology Of Science. Jennings, Richard C.

Truthfulness And Non–trivial Contradictions. Smolenov, Hristo.

Two Notions Of Realism? Mc Ginn, Colin.

Variable Truth. Szabo, Manfred Egon.

Waarheid Als Effect; Richard Rorty En De Natuur Van De Spiegel. Kwaad, G C.

Wahrheit Und Moral. Loeser, Franz.

Woman As Truth In Nietzsche's Writing. Oliver, Kelly A.

Zum Problem Der Kehre Im Denken Heideggers. Rosales, Alberto.

TRUTH CONDITION(S)

Are Contexts Semantic Determinants? Hanson, Philip P.

The Rejection Of Truth–Conditional Semantics By Putnam And Dummett. Demopoulos, William.

TRUTH FUNCTION(S)

Elementary Propositions In Wittgenstein's *Tractatus* (in Chinese). Liu, Fu–Tseng.

Peirce's Alpha Graphs: The Completeness Of Propositional Logic And The Fast Simplification Of Truth Functions. White, Richard B.

TRUTH TABLE(S)

Introduction To Logic: Propositional Logic. Pospesel, Howard.

TRUTH VALUE(S)

Frege And The Slingshot Argument (in Hebrew). Margalit, Avishai.

Fregean Connection: Bedeutung, Value And Truth–Value. Gabriel, Gottfried.

Pictorial Assertion. Korsmeyer, Carolyn.

Supervaluations Without Truth–Value Gaps. Herzberger, Hans G.

The Potency Of Imagery—The Impotence Of Rational Language: Ernesto Grassi's Contribution To Modern Epistemology. Veit, Walter.

True, False, Etc. Herzberger, Hans G.

TRUTHFULNESS

"Childhood Death And Medical Ethics" in *Difficult Decisions In Medical Ethics*, Ganos, Doreen L (ed), 173–188. Pernick, Martin S.

"Deception In The Teaching Hospital" in *Difficult Decisions In Medical Ethics*, Ganos, Doreen and others (eds), 81–86. Brody, Howard.

"Truth Telling In Pediatrics–In Degrees" in *Difficult Decisions In Medical Ethics*, Ganos, Doreen L (ed), 189–194. O Connor, Patricia A.

TSUNG–MI

Tsung–Mi And The Single Word "Awareness" (*chih*). Gregory, Peter N.

TUGARINOV, V

Person And Society: A View Of V P Tugarinov. Blakeley, Thomas J.

The Value Theory Of V P Tugarinov. O'Rourke, James J.

TUGENDHAT, E

Gibt Es Auf Erden Ein Mass? Gadamer, Hans–Georg.

TURING MACHINES

A Characterization Of Complexity Sequences. Schnorr, C P and Stumpf, G.

Complete Second Order Spectra. Scarpellini, Bruno.

Spectra And Halting Problems. Hay, Louise.

Zur Raumkompliziertheit Mehrdimensionaler Turing–Automaten. Hemmerling, Armin and Murawski, Gerd.

TWENTIETH

Adorno. Jay, Martin.

Contemporary German Philosophy, V4. Christensen, Darrel and other (eds).

TWENTIETH

Dialogues With Contemporary Continental Thinkers. Kearney, Richard.
Einstein And The Poet: In Search Of The Cosmic Man. Hermanns, William.
Essays In The Unknown Wittgenstein. Lazerowitz, Morris and Ambrose, Alice.
Gli Instituti Filosofici In Italia (1970–1980). Pasqualotto, Giangiorgio.
Martin Buber's Life And Work: The Later Years, 1945–1965. Friedman, Maurice.
Philosophical Analysis In Latin America. Gracia, Jorge J E and others (eds).
Philosophy Born Of Struggle: Anthology Of Afro–American Philosophy From 1917. Harris, Leonard (ed).
Popper Selections. Miller, David (ed).
Theonomy And Autonomy: Studies In Paul Tillich's Engagement With Modern Culture. Carey, John J (ed).
A Note On The Prefaces Of Insight. Crowe, F E.
Amleto E Il Tragico: A Proposito Di Un Saggio Di Carl Schmitt. Amato Mangiameli, Agata C.
Bachelard À Sa Table D'écriture. Ramnoux, Clervence.
Beauvoir And Satre: The Forms Of Farewell. Barnes, Hazel E.
Bibliography Of Works In Philosophy Of History 1978–1982. David, Zdenek V and Strassfeld, Robert.
Classical American Philosophy: A Reflective Bequest To The Twenty–First Century. Mc Dermott, John J.
Contemporary British Philosophy: A Survey Of Developments Over The Last Three Decades. Hall, Roland.
De Bar–Sur–Aube À Jérusalem: La Correspondance Entre Gaston Bachelard Et Martin Buber. Bourel, Dominique.
Defensive Reactions Of Polish Professional Philosophy To Irrationalism In The Early 20th Century. Borzym, Stanislaw.
Developing Themes In Philosophy: Modern Continental Philosophy. Nicholson, Graeme.
Die Situation Der Philosophie In Brasilien. Martins, Estevão De Rezende.
Ernst Cassirer's *Mythical Thought* In Weimar Culture. Strenski, Ivan T.
Giulio Augusto Levi E La "Scienza Del Comico". Cavaglion, Alberto.
Heidegger, 1916–1921: Hegelianismo Y Filosofía Medieval En Los Orígenes Del Pensamiento Heideggeriano. Bertelloni, C Francisco.
Homo, Humanus, And The Meanings Of "Humanism". Giustiniani, Vito R.
How To Make Hitler's Ideas Clear? Roth, John K.
László Rudas And The Lukács Debate In The Twenties (in Hungarian). Mesterházi, Miklós.
La Double Légitimité. Starobinski, Jean.
La Filosofia Del Dr Jose Sanchez Villasenor. Uribe, Héctor G.
Le Lettere Di Croce A Gentile. Coli, Daniela.
Orwell And The Intellectuals. Israel, Joachim.
Recent Developments In The Study Of Philosophy In The PRC. Tang, Yi–Jie.
Schutz's Life Story And The Understanding Of His Work. Wagner, Helmut R.
T M Knox: His Life And Scholarship, Part II. Pelczynski, Zbigniew A.
The *Vienna Circle Archive* And The Literary Remains Of Moritz Schlick And Otto Neurath. Mulder, Henk.
The Compositional History Of Whitehead's Writings. Lucas Jr, George R.
The Physics Of David Bohm And Its Relevance To Philosophy And Theology. Russell, Robert J.
The Rise And Fall Of Vito Volterra's World. Goodstein, Judith E.
Two Experiments On The History Of Hungarian School Philosophy Between The Two World Wars (in Hungarian). Galicza, Peter.
Wittgenstein And The Vienna Circle. Mc Guinnes, Brian.

TWINING, W

The Contemporary Significance Of Bentham's Anarchical Fallacies: A Reply To William Twining. Dalgarno, Melvin T.

TYPE(S)

"Towards A Theory Of Predication" in *How Things Are*, Bogen, James (ed), 285–322. Sellars, Wilfrid.
A Height Restricted Generation Of A Set Of Arithmetic Functions Of Order–type. Slessenger, Peter H.
Die Elementare Theorie Der Gruppe Vom Typ p–super–infinity–mit Untergruppen. Baudisch, Andreas.
Effective Discontinuity And A Characterisation Of The Superjump. Hartley, John P.
Fuzzy Recursion, RET's, And Isols. Harkleroad, Leon.
Gödelsche Funktionalinterpretation Für Eine Erweiterung Der Klassischen Analysis. Friedrich, Wolfgang.
Global Quantification In Zermelo–Fraenkel Set Theory. Mayberry, John.
Kant, Wittgenstein And The Limits Of Logic. Tiles, Mary.
On The Consistency Of Some Partition Theorems For Continuous Colorings, And The Structure Of Dense Real Order Types. Shelah, Saharon and Abraham, U and Rubin, M.
Reduction Of Higher Type Levels By Means Of An Ordinal Analysis Of Finite Terms. Terlouw, Jan.
Regular Types In Nonmultidimensional ω–Stable Theories. Pillay, Anand.
Saturation And Simple Extensions Of Models Of Peano Arithmetic. Kaufmann, Matt and Schmerl, James H.
Self–Reference With Negative Types. Hiller, A P and Zimbarg, J.
The Generalised RK–Order, Orthogonality And Regular Types For Modules. Prest, Mike.
The Hereditary Partial Effective Functionals And Recursion Theory In Higher Types. Longo, G and Moggi, E.
The Uniqueness Of Envelopes In $\aleph_0$–Categorical, $\aleph_0$–Stable Structures. Loveys, James.
Type And Eidos—Schutz And Husserl. Pritchard, Colin W.

Ultrafilters And Types On Models Of Arithmetic. Kirby, L A S.

TYPE THEORY

An Interpretation Of Martin–Löf's Type Theory In A Type–Free Theory Of Propositions. Smith, Jan.
Comparing Type Theory And Set Theory. Lake, John.

TYPOLOGY

On The Typology Of The Scientific Languages. Ginev, Dimiter.

TYRANNY

Benjamin Constant And The Making Of Modern Liberalism. Holmes, Stephen.
"The Petty Tyranny Of Government Regulation" in *Rights And Regulation*, Machan, Tibor (ed), 259–288. Machan, Tibor R.
Hope And Its Ramifications For Politics. Dauenhauer, Bernard P.

UGLINESS

Bosanquet's Concept Of Difficult Beauty. Jacquette, Dale.

ULTIMACY

The Appeal To Ultimacy In Meland's Thought. Suchocki, Marjorie.

ULTIMATE

Gabriel Marcel's Pensée Pensante As The Ultimate Reality And Meaning Of Human Existence. Peccorini, Francisco L.
The Upanisads And The Ultimate Real One. Dange, Sadashiv A.

ULTRAFILTERS

Complexity Of κ–Ultrafilters And Inner Models With Measurable Cardinals. Sureson, Claude.
Contributions To The Theory Of Semisets ∨, On Axiom Of General Collapse. Vopenka, Peter and Sochor, Antonin.
On The Ultrafilters And Ultrapowers Of Strong Partition Cardinals. Henle, J M and Kleinberg, E M and Watro, R J.
Strongly Compact Cardinals, Elementary Embeddings And Fixed Points. Abe, Yoshihiro.
Ultrafilters And Types On Models Of Arithmetic. Kirby, L A S.

ULTRAPOWERS

Double Enlargements Of Topological Spaces. Goodyear, Paul.
Non–closure Of The Image Model And Absence Of Fixed Points. Sureson, Claude.
On The Ultrafilters And Ultrapowers Of Strong Partition Cardinals. Henle, J M and Kleinberg, E M and Watro, R J.

ULTRAPRODUCTS

A Note On The Compactness Theorem. Gill, R R Rockingham.

UNAMUNO

Unamuno Ou Le Traité De L'amour De Dieu. Casañas, Mario.

UNANIMITY

Begriff Und Logik Des "Öffentlichen Interesses". Fach, Wolfgang.
Market Contractarianism And The Unanimity Rule. Coleman, Jules L.

UNCERTAINTY

The Intellectual And Social Organization Of The Sciences. Whitley, Richard.
Uncertainty Studies In Philosophy, Economics And Socio–Political Theory. Bonatti, Luigi.
A Note On Quantum Theory, Complementarity, And Uncertainty. Busch, Paul and Lahti, Pekka J.
The Silence Of Physics. Meurers, Joseph.

UNCERTAINTY PRINCIPLE

The New Scientific Spirit. Bachelard, Gaston and Goldhammer, Arthur (trans).

UNCONSCIOUS

Freud And The Mind. Dilman, Ilham.
Chronic Vegetative States: Intrinsic Value Of Biological Process. Freer, Jack P.
La Psychanalyse Sans L'inconscient? Knee, Philip.
Speech And The Unspeakable In The "Place" Of The Unconscious. Scott, Charles E.
Unconscious Belief And Natural Theology. Holyer, Robert.

UNDECIDABILITY

"Undecidability Of Extensions Of Monadic First–order Theory" in *Lecture Notes In Mathematics*, Muller, G H And Others (ed), 155–174. Ono, Hiroakira.
An Undecidable Problem In Finite Combinatorics. Compton, Kevin J.
Ordered Fields With Several Exponential Functions. Dahn, Bernd I and Wolter, H.
Some Undecidability Results In Strong Algebraic Languages. Kalfa, Cornelia.
The Undecidability Of Entailment And Relevant Implication. Urquhart, Alasdair.

UNDERDETERMINATION

Semantic Indeterminacy And Scientific Underdetermination. Peterson, Philip L.
The Duhem Thesis. Ariew, Roger.
Underdetermination And Realism. Bergström, Lars.

UNDERSTANDING

An Interpretation Of The Logic Of Hegel. Harris, Errol E.
Erklaren Und Verstehen. Von Wright, Georg Henrik.
Time And Narrative, V1. Ricoeur, Paul and Mc Laughlin, Kathleen (trans) and Pellauer, David (trans).
Understanding And Explanation: A Transcendental–Pragmatic Perspective. Apel Otto, Karl and Warnke, Georgia (trans).
"Epistemological Problem Of Understanding As Aspect Of General Problem Of Knowing" in *Hermeneutics*, Shapiro, Gary (ed), 25–53. Bettim Emilio.
Algunos Aspectos De La Doctrina Tomista Del Entendimiento Posible. De Stier, Maria L.
Correct Explanatory Arguments And Understanding–why An Approach To Scientific Understanding Based On Knowledge Dynamics. Schurz, Gerhard.
El Método Empírico–Reflexivo. Buela, Alberto E.
Expliquer Les Causes Et/Ou Comprendre Les Raisons: Note À Propos De *Meaning And Understanding*. Chiesa, Curzio.

UNDERSTANDING

History And The Brewmaster's Nose. Martin, Raymond.
J Krishnamurti On Choiceless Awareness, Creative Emptiness And Ultimate Freedom. Mathur, Dinesh Chandra.
K O Apel Over "Erklären" En "Verstehen". Strasser, St.
On Reading And Mis—Reading Hannah Arendt. Bernauer, James.
Saying And Conveying. Sainsbury, Mark.
Understanding Art And Understanding Persons. Berenson, Frances.
Unlocking The Chinese Room. Russow, Lilly—Marlene.
Wittgenstein's Anthropology. Bell, Richard.
Works Of Art As Cultural Probes. Gavin, William J and Conway, Jeremiah P.

UNEMPLOYMENT

Abusing The Unemployed: An Invisible Justice. Breakwell, Glynis M.

UNESCO

World Congresses Of Philosophy. Cauchy, Venant and Kuczynski, Janusz.

UNFREEDOM

Are Workers Forced To Sell Their Labor Power? Cohen, G A.
Cohen On Proletarian Unfreedom. Brenkert, George G.

UNGER, P

Taking Sorites Arguments Seriously: Some Hidden Costs. Grim, Patrick.
True Believers And Radical Sceptics. Gallois, André.

UNIFICATION

A Study Of Theory Unification. Nugayev, Renat.
Hölderlin E La *Vereinigungsphilosophie*. Gargano, Antonio.

UNIFORMITY

The Complexity Of Quality. Westphal, Jonathan.

UNION(S)

"Trade Unionism And Women's Work" in *Freedom, Feminism, And The State*, Mc Elroy, Wendy (ed), 237–266. Anthony, Susan.
A Defense Of Employee Rights. Des Jardins, Joseph R and Mc Call, John J.
Displaced Workers: America's Unpaid Debt. Byrne, Edmund F.

UNIQUENESS

The Uniqueness Of Particulars. Scaltsas, Theodore.
The Uniqueness Proof For Forms In *Republic X*. Parry, Richard D.

UNITARIANISM

Some Sources For A History Of English Socinianism; A Bibliography Of 17th Century English Socinian Writings. Bianchi, Daniela.

UNITED STATES

Moral Dimensions Of American Foreign Policy. Thompson, Kenneth W (ed).
"Latin Americans Residing In US And Canada" in *Philosophical Analysis In Latin America*, Gracia, Jorge J E and others (eds), 413–416. Gracia, Jorge.
Political Finance In The United States: A Survey Of Research. Beitz, Charles R.
The Representation And Resolution Of The Nuclear Conflict. Anderson, Lyle V.
Vain Hopes And A Fool's Fancy: Understanding US Nuclear Strategy. Beres, Louis René.

UNITY

Metaphysics Z 12 And H 6; The Unity Of Form And Composite. Halper, Edward.
Der Mensch Als Biopsychosoziale Einheit. Freye, Ha and others.
Explaining The Unity Of The Platonic Dialogue. Hathaway, Ronald.
Le Problème De L'unité. Dagognet, François.
On R E Allen's *Plato's Parmenides*. Turnbull, Robert G.
On The Concept Of Unity Of Consciousness. Schleichert, Hubert.
Person—Stages And Unity Of Consciousness. Mc Inerney, Peter K.
Schelling's Aphorisms Of 1805. Marti, Fritz.
Sympathy In Plotinus. Gurtler, Gary M.
The One, The Many, And The Forms: *Philebus* 15b1–8. Dancy, R M.

UNIVERSAL(S)

An Interpretation Of The Logic Of Hegel. Harris, Errol E.
Aristotle Metaphysics: Books Zeta, Eta, Theta, Iota. Furth, Montgomery (trans).
The Arguments From The Sciences In Aristotle's Peri Ideon'. Frank, Daniel H.
'Form, Reproduction And Inherited Characteristics In Aristotle's GA'. Witt, Charlotte.
'On The Terminology Of "Abstraction" In Aristotle'. Cleary, John.
"Armstrong On Determinable And Substantial Universals" in *D M Armstrong*, Bogdan, Radu J (ed), 171–190. Tweedale, Martin M.
"Armstrong On Universals And Particulars" in *D M Armstrong*, Bogdan, Radu J (ed), 161–170. Aune, Bruce.
"Replies" in *D M Armstrong*, Bogdan, Radu J (ed), 225–269. Armstrong, D M.
"Universals: Logic And Metaphor" in *Philosophy And Life: Essays On John Wisdom*, Dilman, Ilham (ed), 271–290. Long, Peter.
Bezeichnen Und Behaupten. Nuchelmans, Gabriel.
Bradley And Realism About Universals. Forrest, Peter.
El Problema De Los Universales En Domingo De Soto Y Alonso De La Veracruz. Beuchot, Mauricio.
El Triángulo Universal De Locke: Su Inmerecida Fama. Angelelli, Ignacio.
General And Individual Style In Literature. Robinson, Jenefer.
Improving Applied Ethics: A Response To Reinsmith's Response To "Improving Applied Ethics". Bahm, Archie J.
L'articulation Du Général Et Du Particulier: Une Approche Méthodologique Dans Le Champ Des Sciences Sociales. Miguelez, Roberto.
Laws Of Nature As Relations Between Universals And As Universals. Armstrong, D M.
Materia Universalis. Scheyer, Amram.
Modern Science And The Coexistence Of Rationalities. Salomon— Bayet, Claire.
Realism, Resemblances, And Russell's Regress. Lehman, Craig K.
Striking 'Commensurate' From The Oxford Translation. Jones, Joe E.
Supposition—Theory And The Problem Of Universals. Wagner, Michael F.

The Contingent Identity Of Particulars And Universals. Casullo, Albert.
The Extreme Realism Of Roger Bacon. Maloney, Thomas S.
Universals And Laws Of Nature. Tweedale, Martin.
Walter Chatton *Vs* Aureoli And Ockham Regarding The Universal Concept. Kelley, Francis E.

UNIVERSALISM

Dimensions Of Moral Education. Carter, Robert E.
"Collins And Gadamer On Interpretation" in *History Of Philosophy In The Making*, Thro, Linus J (ed), 231–246. Marsh, James L.

UNIVERSALITY

The Man Of Reason: "Male" And "Female" In Western Philosophy. Lloyd, Genevieve.
Comparison Of The Axioms Of Local And Global Universality. Forti, Marco and Honsell, Furio.

UNIVERSALIZABILITY

"The Incoherence Of Universal Prescriptivism" in *The Georgetown Symposium On Ethics*, Porreco, Rocco (ed), 145–158. Beatty, Joseph.
Contradiction In The Will. Doore, Gary.
Epistemic Universalizability Principles. Brueckner, Anthony.
Sartre's Acceptance Of The Principle Of Universality. Lee, Sander H.

UNIVERSALIZATION

The Central Role Of Universalization In Sartrean Ethics. Lee, Sander H.

UNIVERSE

Thermodynamics, Man, Universe (in Czechoslovakian). Andrle, Pavel.

UNIVERSITY(–TIES)

Crise De Civilisation Et Université: Enseigner Aujourd'hui. Vachet, André.
Die Sowjetische Hilfe Für Die Entwicklung Der Marxistisch—Leninistischen Philosophie An Den Universitäten (1945–1949). Handel, Gottfried.
Ethical Concerns For The Modern University. Miles, Leland and others.
Graduate Study In Continental Philosophy In The United States. Solomon, Robert.
The Other 338: Why A Majority Of Our Schools Of Business Administration Do Not Offer A Course In Business Ethics. Hosmer, Larue T.
The Principle Of Reason: The University In The Eyes Of Its Pupils. Derrida, Jacques.
The Self—Assertion Of The German University And The Rectorate 1933/34: Facts And Thoughts. Heidegger, Martin.

UNPREDICTABILITY

Explaining The Unpredictable. Suppes, Patrick.

UNREALITY

Unreality And Time. Brumbaugh, Robert S.

UNSOLVABILITY

The Unsolvability Of The Gödel Class With Identity. Goldfarb, Warren D.

UPANISHADS

Hindu Ethics. Singh, Balbir.
The Upanisads And The Ultimate Real One. Dange, Sadashiv A.

URMSON, J

Saints And Heroes: A Plea For The Supererogatory. Mc Goldrick, Patricia M.

USAGE

"On Taking Metaphor Literally" in *Metaphor*, Miall, David S (ed), 1–13. Moore, F C T.
Kripke And Wittgenstein: Intention Without Paradox. Moser, Paul K and Flannery, Kevin.

USEFUL

"Feeling Good And Doing Better" in *Feeling Good And Doing Better*, Murray, Thomas H (ed), 1–12. Gaylin, Willard.

USURY

The Western Case Against Usury. Gottfried, Paul E.

UTILITARIANISM

Deontology: Together With A Table Of The Springs Of Action And Article On Utilitarianism. Goldworth, Amnon (ed).
"What Is Happiness" in *The Good Life And Its Pursuit*, Dougherty, Jude P (ed), 35–44. Smart, Ninian.
A Contractarian Defense Of Nuclear Deterrence. Morris, Christopher W.
A Defense Of Utilitarian Policy Processes In Corporate And Public Management. Brady, F Neil.
Are Business Ethics And Engineering Ethics Members Of The Same Family? Bowie, Norman E.
Arresting But Misleading Phrases. Harris, John.
Classical Utilitarianism And The Analogy Argument. Mc Gray, James.
Consequences, Desirability, And The Moral Fanaticism Argument. Singer, Marcus G.
Dignity And Cost—Effectiveness: A Rejection Of The Utilitarian Approach To Death. Brooks, Simon A.
Dignity And Death: A Reply. Brooks, Simon A.
Dignity And Cost—Effectiveness: Analysing The Responsibility For Decisions In Medical Ethics. Robertson, George S.
Distributive Justice. Rollins, Mark.
Dr Krankheit And The Concept Of Compliance. Schwartz, Thomas.
Egalitarianism. Mc Kerlie, Dennis.
Equality *Vs* Liberty: Advantage, Liberty. Narveson, Jan.
Ethics And The Archangelic Prescriber. Harrison, Jonathan.
Introduzic Critica Alla Teoria Della Giustizia Di Rawls. Hoffe, Otfried.
Lying And The "Methods Of Ethics". Primoratz, Igor.
Marx's Critique Of Utilitarianism. Brenkert, George G.
Nathan On Projectivist Utilitarianism. Gordon, David.
On Mill's Qualitative Distinction Of Pleasures. Nagaoka, Shigeo.
Predation. Sapontzis, Steve F.
Pursuing The Good—Indirectly. Alexander, Larry.
Rules And Relevance: The Au–Ru Equivalence Issue. Lennon, Thomas M.

VALUE(S)

Rhetorical Realities: A Response To McAninch's Interpretation Of Values And Teaching. Boyd, Dwight and Bogdan, Deanne.

Royce's Revaluation Of Values. Hallman, Max O.

Scientific Socialism And The Question Of Socialist Values. Collier, Andrew.

The Foreign Corrupt Practices Act And The Imposition Of Values. Brummer, James J.

The Meaning Of Life: A Qualitative Perspective. Bennett, James O.

The Psychopath As Moral. Smith, Robert J.

The Right To Strike And The Right To Work. Smart, Brian.

The Scientific Character Of Marxism And Its Viewpoint Of Value. Zhiming, Yuan and Dezhen, Xue.

The Value Of Information In Newcomb's Problem And The Prisoners' Dilemma. Snow, Paul.

Thomas Mann And The Business Ethic. Brennan Joseph G.

To Be A Person. Kolenda, Konstantin.

Utility And Rational Self–Interest. Mc Dermott, Michael.

Valor Y Valor Moral. Derisi, Octavio N.

Value And Free Choice: Lavelle's Attempt At A Reconciliation. Hardy, Gilbert.

Value And Human Condition. Sarin, Indu.

Value Conflicts In Agriculture. Aiken, William.

Value, Fact And Facing Fact. Graham, A C.

Values And Socialism: An Axiological Approach To Marx's Socialism. Siewierski, Jacenty.

Valuing Wildlands. Rolston, Holmes.

Wilderness And Heritage Values. Hammond, John L.

VALUE FREE

Reply To Oppenheim's "Constraints On Freedom". Miller, David.

VALUE JUDGMENT(S)

Grete Henry–Hermann's Development Of Leonard Nelson's Ethics. Heckmann, Gustav.

Improving Applied Ethics: A Response To Reinsmith's Response To "Improving Applied Ethics". Bahm, Archie J.

Zu Einigen Unterschieden Zwischen Moralischen Normen, Werturteilen Und Aussagen. Bönisch, Siegfried and Noack, Klaus–peter.

VALUE THEORY

God, The Center Of Value: Value Theory In The Theology Of H Richard Niebuhr. Grant, C David.

"Economic Value, Ethics, And Transition To Socialism" in Continuity And Change In Marxism, Fischer, Norman And Others (ed), 39–65. Fischer, Norman.

Gender–Specific Values. Seigfried, Charlene H.

Philosophical Method And The Rise Of Social Philosophy. Mc Murtry, John.

The Problem Of Relativization Of Life As Value (in Czechoslovakian). Baran, P.

The Value Theory Of V P Tugarinov. O' Rourke, James J.

Towards A Critical Theory Of Value. Luntley, Michael.

VALUES CLARIFICATION

"The Poverty Of Moral Education" in The Georgetown Symposium On Ethics, Porreco, Rocco (ed), 251–260. Casement, William.

The Philosopher In The Workplace. Elliston, Frederick.

VALUING

Improving Applied Ethics: A Response To Reinsmith's Response To "Improving Applied Ethics". Bahm, Archie J.

VAN DE PITTE, M

Reply To Van De Pitte's "Comments On A Claim That Some Phenomenological Statements May Be A Posteriori". Schmitt, Richard.

VAN DEN HAAG

Does It Matter If The Death Penalty Is Arbitrarily Administered? Nathanson, Stephen.

Justice, Civilization, And The Death Penalty: Answering Van Den Haag. Reiman, Jeffrey H.

VAN FRAASSEN, B

Constructive Empiricism And The Problem Of Aboutness. Sober, Elliott.

Sailing Into The Charybdis: Van Fraassen On Bell's Theorem. Stairs, Allen.

Taking Theories Seriously. Creath, Richard.

When Explanation Leads To Inference. Cartwright, Nancy.

Why Constructive Empiricism Collapses Into Scientific Realism. Melchert, Norman.

VAN INWAGEN, P

Compatibilism And The Consequence Argument. Horgan, Terence.

Deliberating About The Inevitable. Waller, Bruce N.

VANCE, C

Human Rights And U S Foreign Policy: Models And Options. Galloway, Jonathan F.

VARGAS, G

Vargas And Prestes: A Comparison Between The Labourism And Communism In Brazil (in Portuguese). Piozzi, Patrizia.

VARIABLE(S)

On A Simple Definition Of Computable Function Of A Real Variable––With Applications To Functions Of A Complex Variable. Caldwell, Jerome and Pour– El, Marion Boykan.

On Languages With Two Variables. Mortimer, Michael.

On Propositional Calculus With A Variable Functor. Lesisz, Wlodzimierz.

Some Propositional Calculi With Constant And Variable Functors. Jones, John.

VARIAN, H

Is Fairness Good: A Critique Of Varian's Theory Of Fairness. Sugden, Robert.

VARIETY

Two Alternative Epistemological Frameworks In Psychology: The Typological And Variational Modes Of Thinking. Valsiner, Jaan.

VASARI, G

Collections And Collectors. Ergmann, Raoul.

The History Of Art: Its Methods And Their Limits. Von Haumeder, Ulrika.

VASCONCELOS, J

Axiología De José Vasconcelos. Patiño, Joel Rodríguez.

VASIL'EV, N

N A Vasil'év: A Forerunner Of Paraconsistent Logic. Arruda, Ayda I.

VATTIMO, G

Deconstruction Is Not Enough: On Gianni Vattimo's Call For "Weak Thinking". Schürmann, Reiner.

VAUGHT, C

Metaphor, Analogy, And System: A Reply To Burbidge "Professor Burbidge Responds". Vaught, Carl G.

VEATCH, H

The Georgetown Symposium On Ethics. Porreco, Rocco (ed).

"Contemplation In Aristotelian Ethics" in The Georgetown Symposium On Ethics, Porreco, Rocco (ed), 205–212. Parker, Francis H.

"Henry Veatch And The Problem Of A Noncognitivist Ethics" in The Georgetown Symposium On Ethics, Porreco, Rocco (ed), 159–170. Lee, Sander H.

"Moral Formation And The Liberal Arts" in The Georgetown Symposium On Ethics, Porreco, Rocco (ed), 243–250. Mc Donnell, Kevin.

"The State: Ethics And Economics" in The Georgetown Symposium On Ethics, Porreco, Rocco (ed), 195–204. Ver Eecke, Wilfried.

"Veatch And MacIntyre On The Virtues" in The Georgetown Symposium On Ethics, Porreco, Rocco (ed), 117–130. Robins, Michael H.

VEATCH, R

Editorial: Philosophy Of Medicine In The U S A. Thomasma, David C.

J S Mill And Robert Veatch's Critique Of Utilitarianism. Edwards, Rem B.

VEBLEN, T

The Role Of Conservation Principles In Twentieth–Century Economic Theory. Mirowski, Philip.

VECTOR(S)

A Note On Decompositions Of Recursively Enumberable Subspaces. Downey, R G.

Bases Of Supermaximal Subspaces And Steinitz Systems. Downey, Rod.

Decidable Subspaces And Recursively Enumerable Subspaces. Downey, R G and Ash, C J.

Some Remarks On A Theorem Of Iraj Kalantari Concerning Convexity And Recursion Theory. Downey, Rod.

The Universal Complementation Property. Downey, R G and Remmel, J B.

VEDANTA

Human Embodiment: The Theme And The Encounter In Vedāntic Phenomenology. Sinha, Debabrata.

Mystical Consciousness In A Process Perspective. Simmons, Ernest L.

The Upanisads And The Ultimate Real One. Dange, Sadashiv A.

What We Do And Say In Saying And Doing Something. Gandhi, Ramchandra.

VEDAS

Hindu Ethics. Singh, Balbir.

VEGETARIANISM

"An Ecological Argument For Vegetarianism". Wenz, Peter S.

"The Morality Of Killing Animals: Four Arguments". Young, Thomas.

VEIL OF IGNORANCE

The Stability Of Bargains Behind The Veil Of Ignorance. Gaa, James C.

VERACRUZ, A

Alonso De La Veracruz, Testigo De Su Tiempo. Ibargüengoitia, Antonio.

El Conocimiento En Fray Alonso De La Veracruz. Sanabria, José Rubén.

El Problema De La "Infidelidad" En Fray Alonso De La Veracruz. Cerezo– De Diego, Prometeo.

El Problema De Los Universales En Domingo De Soto Y Alonso De La Veracruz. Beuchot, Mauricio.

Fray Alonso De La Veracruz, Iniciador Del Derecho Agrario En Mexico. Zavala, Silvio.

Fray Alonso De La Veracruz, Misionero De La Filosofia. Navarro, Bernabé.

VERB(S)

Semantic, Pragmatic And Syntactic Correlates: An Analysis Of Performative Verbs Based On English Data. Partridge, John Geoffrey.

VERBALIZATION

Bergson's Philosophy Of Language (in Hebrew). Idan, Asher.

Some Notes On The Subject Matter Of Skinner's Verbal Behavior. Lee, Vicki L.

Translation, Indeterminacy And Triviality. Hanna, Patricia.

VERDICTIVE(S)

Mysticism, Veridicality, And Modality. Oakes, Robert.

VERIFIABILITY

Intuitionistic Truth. Rabinowicz, Wlodzimierz.

Singer, Moore, And The Metaphysics Of Morals. Temkin, Jack.

VERIFICATION

Der Formalismus Und Seine Grenzen: Untersuchungen Zur Neueren Philosophie Der Mathematik. Rheinwald, Rosemarie.

A Property Of 2–Sorted Peano Models And Program Verification. Paris, J B and Csirmaz, L.

Empirische Mogelijkheden; Sleutelbegrip Van De Wetenschapsfilosofie. Kuipers, Theo A F.

The Generalized Argument From Verification: Work Towards The Metaepistemology Of Perception. Roberts, Scott P.

Wittgenstein And The Vienna Circle. Mc Guinnes, Brian.

VERIFICATIONISM
Frammenti: Sulla Crisi Della Epistemologia. Centrone, Marino.
Good Transcendental Arguments. Genova, A C.

VERISIMILITUDE
What Is Wrong With Verisimilitude? Smith, Joseph W.

VERZCRUZ, A
"Sobre Las Oraciones Modales" Por Fray Alonso De La Veracruz. Redmond, Walter.

VICE(S)
Hume's Moral Enquiry: An Analysis Of Its Catalogue. Vodraska, Stanley L.

VICO
Ragione–Libertà–Scienza In Kant–Hegel–Marx. Sena, Michelantonio.
Berlin On Vico. Zagorin, Perez.
Campbell, Vico, And The Rhetorical Science Of Human Nature. Bevilacqua, Vincent M.
El Progreso Según Juan Bautista Vico. Dondi, J.
On Vico. Berlin, Isaiah.
Vico And Collingwood On 'The Conceit Of Scholars'. Todd, Joan and Cono, Joseph.
Vico's View Of History. Henderson, R D.

VICTIM(S)
Abortion And Victimisability. Winkler, Earl R.
Why Tolerate The Statistical Victim? Trachtman, Leon E.

VICTORIAN
Semiotics And Oscar Wilde's Accounts Of Art. Small, Ian C.

VIDYARANYA
Vidyaranya On Method, Object And Limit Of Philosophical Investigation. Mishra, Ganeswar.

VIENNA CIRCLE
Der Erste Wiener Kreis. Haller, Rudolf.
The Vienna Circle Archive And The Literary Remains Of Moritz Schlick And Otto Neurath. Mulder, Henk.
Wittgenstein And The Vienna Circle. Mc Guinnes, Brian.

VIOLENCE
Ethics & Politics: Cases And Comments. Gutman, Amy (ed) and Thompson, Dennis (ed).
"Du Désordre Al'ordre" in Existential Coordinates Of Human Condition, Tymieniecka, A (ed), 435–450. Murphy, B L.
Giustizia Rivoluzionaria E Violenza. Dal Brollo, Alessandro.
Psychosurgery, The Brain And Violent Behavior. Wilkins, Burleigh T.
The Idea Of Violence. Coady, C A J.
The Morality Of Terrorism. Coady, C A J.
The Random Collective As A Moral Agent. Manning, Rita.
Violence And The Politics Of Explanation: Kampuchea Revisited. Hawkesworth, Mary E.

VIRTUE(S)
After Virtue: Second Edition. Macintyre, Alasdair.
Deontology: Together With A Table Of The Springs Of Action And Article On Utilitarianism. Goldworth, Amnon (ed).
Locke's Education For Liberty. Tarcov, Nathan.
Practical Reason, Aristotle, And Weakness Of The Will. Dahl, Norman O.
The Moral Psychology Of The Virtues. Dent, N J H.
The Theory And Practice Of Virtue. Meilaender, Gilbert C.
Vice And Virtue In Everyday Life: Introductory Readings In Ethics. Sommers, Christina Hoff.
Wealth And Virtue: The Shaping Of Political Economy In The Scottish Enlightenment. Hont, Istvan (ed) and Ignatieff, Michael (ed).
Φθονος And Its Related Παθη In Plato And Aristotle. Mills, Michael J.
"The Proper Context Of Moral Education" in The Georgetown Symposium On Ethics, Porreco, Rocco (ed), 261–268. Mann, Jesse A.
"Veatch And MacIntyre On The Virtues" in The Georgetown Symposium On Ethics, Porreco, Rocco (ed), 117–130. Robins, Michael H.
Ariston Of Chios And The Unity Of Virtue. Schofield, Malcolm.
De Ondergang Van De Deugden En De Inconsequentie Van McIntyre. Kunneman, Harry.
Happiness And Virtue In Socrates' Moral Theory. Vlastos, Gregory.
Hegel's Evaluation And Analysis Of Socrates' Proposition "Virtue Is Knowledge". Xiuliang, Lan.
High–Minded Egoism And The Problem Of Priggishness. Lemos, Noah M.
How The Inadequate Models For Virtue In The Protagoras Illuminate Socrates' View Of The Unity Of The Virtues. Hartman, Margaret.
Hume's Moral Enquiry: An Analysis Of Its Catalogue. Vodraska, Stanley L.
Is Socrates An Instrumentalist? Lesses, Glenn.
Machiavelli On Social Class And Class Conflict. Brudney, Kent M.
Montaigne On War. Bonadeo, Alfredo.
Principles And Virtues—Or—Principles Or Virtues. Coetzee, Pieter.
Public Versus Private Claims: Machiavellianism From Another Perspective. Leonard, John.
Recent Work On Virtues. Pence, Gregory E.
Relative Virtue. Vorobej, Mark.
The Ethics Of Duty/Ethics Of Virtue Debate And Its Relevance To Educational Theory. Baron, Marcia.
The Place Of Virtue In Happiness. Jacobs, Jonathan.
The Premises Of Four Moral Conceptions: Classical, Modern, Totalitarian, And Utopian. Wilkie, Raymond.
The Structure Of Kant's Metaphysics Of Morals. Donagan, Alan.
The Tension Between Intellectual And Moral Education In The Thought Of John Henry Newman. Tillman, Mary Katherine.

Thoughts On The Virtues. Heil, John.
Varieties Of Ethics Of Virtue. Baron, Marcia.
What Is Professional Ethics? James, David.
What Is Virtuous About Faith? Muyskens, James.

VISION
The Battle Between Art And Truth. Brogan, Walter.

VISUAL ART(S)
Aesthetics: Problems In The Philosophy Of Criticism. Beardsley, Monroe C.
"Essai Sur L'auto–référence Dans Les Arts Visuels" in Asthetische Er Fahrung Und Das Wesen Der Kunst, Holzhey, Helmut, 123–142. Pinkas, D.
Delimitating The Concept Of The Grotesque. Fingesten, Peter.
The Authentic And The Aesthetic. Currie, Gregory.
The Visual Arts As Language. Barela, Robert E.

VLASTOS, G
'Vlastos On Pauline Predication'. Malcolm, John F.

VOCABULARY(–RIES)
The Complexity Of The Vocabulary Of Bambara. Culy, Christopher.

VOEGELIN, E
Eric Voegelin: Politische Wissenschaft Und Geschichtsphilosophie. Baruzzi, Arno.

VOID
Aristotle's Physics. Hussey, Edward (trans) and Ackrill, J L (ed).
Adam Wodeham's Anti–Aristotelian Anti–Atomism. Kretzmann, Norman.

VOLITION(S)
An Essay On Human Action. Zimmerman, Michael J.
A Critique Of Holyer's Volitionalism. Pojman, Louis P.
Believing And Willing. Pojman, Louis P.
Berkeley On Volition, Power, And The Complexity Of Causation. Winkler, Kenneth P.
Is To Will It As Bad As To Do It (The Fourteenth Century Debate)? Adams, Marilyn McCord and Wood, Rega.
Sitting On Ryle's Dilemma. Weir, George R S.
Volitional Disability And Physician Attitudes Toward Noncompliance. Ferrell, Richard B and others.

VOLTAIRE
Science, Sect, And Uncertainty In Voltaire's "dictionnaire Philosophique". Shoaf, Richard.
The Legacy Of Voltaire (Part 1). Edwards, Paul.
Voltaire Versus Needham: Atheism, Materialism, And The Generation Of Life. Roe, Shirley A.

VOLTERRA, V
The Rise And Fall Of Vito Volterra's World. Goodstein, Judith E.

VOLUNTARINESS
Saints And Heroes: A Plea For The Supererogatory. Mc Goldrick, Patricia M.
Voluntary Belief. Naylor, Margery Bedford.

VOLUNTARISM
Organ Donation: Is Voluntarism Still Valid? Sadler Jr, Alfred M and Sadler, Blair L and Caplan, Arthur L.

VON BERTALANFFY, L
The Systems Approach. Bello, Rafael E.

VON KUTSCHERA, F
Filling A Gap In Professor Von Kutschera's Decision Procedure For Deontic Logic. Speller, J.

VON MISES, R
Richard Von Mises: L'échec D'une Axiomatique. Szafarz, Ariane.

VON NEUMANN, J
Cantorian Set Theory And Limitation Of Size. Hallett, Michael.
Assessment Response Surface: Investigating Utility Dependence On Probability. Mc Cord, Mark R and De Neufville, Richard.
Beyond First–order Logic: The Historical Interplay Between Mathematical Logic And Axiomatic Set Theory. Moore, Gregory H.
Timing Contradictions In Von Neumann And Morgenstern's Axioms And In Savage's "Sure–Thing" Proof. Pope, Robin.
Von Neumann And The Anti–Realists. Brown, James R.

VON WRIGHT, G
Understanding And Explanation: A Transcendental–Pragmatic Perspective. Apel Otto, Karl and Warnke, Georgia (trans).
Formal Axiomatic Systems And Dialectic And Materialist Way Of Thought (in Czechoslovakian). Kofátko, P.
On The Logic And Criteriology Of Causality. Leman, Marc.

VOTING
Karl Marx On Democracy, Participation, Voting, And Equality. Springborg, Patricia.
Sophisticated Voting Under The Plurality Procedure: A Test Of A New Definition. Niemi, Richard G and Frank, Arthur Q.

WAGNER, C
Consensus, Respect, And Weighted Averaging. Schmitt, Frederick F.
Destroying The Consensus. Loewer, Barry and Laddaga, Robert.
Lehrer–Wagner Consensual Probabilities Do Not Adequately Summarize The Available Information. Baird, Davis.
Some Properties Of The Lehrer–Wagner Method For Reaching Rational Consensus. Nurmi, Hannu.
The Lehrer–Wagner Theory Of Consensus And The Zero Weight Problem. Forrest, Peter.

WAGNER, H
Discussion Of Wagner, Imber, And Rasmussen. Wolff, Kurt H.

WAINWRIGHT, W
The Ontological Argument. Russell, Bruce.

WALLACE, J
The Courageous Villain: A Needless Paradox. Cunningham, Stanley B.

WALLACE, W
Schmitz, Jordan And Wallace On Intelligibility. Lobkowicz, Nicholas.

WALLER, B
Purpose And Conditioning: A Reply To Waller. Mills, John A.

WALLERSTEIN, I
Marxism And The Transition Problem. Ross, Howard.

WALPOLE, H
Ut Hortus Poesis—Gardening And Her Sister Arts In Eighteenth-Century England. Ross, Stephanie A.

WALZER, M
Can Modern War Be Just? Johnson, James T.
The Legalist Paradigm And MAD. Myers, David B.

WANG, F
An Analysis And Critique Of Wang Fu-Chih's Theory Of "Tao Ta Shan Hsiao, Shan Ta Hsing Hsiao" (in Chinese). Huang, Yih-Mei.

WANG, Y
Wang Yang-Ming, Mencius And Internalism. Lee, Jig-Chuen.

WANT(S)
Understanding Happiness. Hagberg, G.

WANTING
A Reply To Wayne A Davis' "Miller On Wanting, Intending, And Being Willing". Miller, Arthur.

WAR(S)
see also Nuclear War
Can Modern War Be Just? Johnson, James T.
Moral Dimensions Of American Foreign Policy. Thompson, Kenneth W (ed).
War And Justice. Phillips, Robert L.
When War Is Unjust: Being Honest In Just War Thinking. Yoder, John H.
"Patriotism: A Menace To Liberty" in Freedom, Feminism, And The State, Mc Elroy, Wendy (ed), 337–350. Goldman, Emma.
Arnold J Toynbee: Das Höchste Gut Ist Der Frieden!. Schulze, Hans.
Die Frage Von Krieg Und Frieden In Der Weltanschaulichen Auseinandersetzung. Hahn, Erich.
Die Lehre Vom Gerechten Krieg Bei Grotius Und Leibniz Und Ihre Bedeutung Für Die Gegenwart. Serra, Antonio Truyol.
Die Weltgeschichtliche Bedeutung Des Sieges Der Sowjetunion Im Grossen Vaterländischen Krieg Im Lichte Des Leninismus. Uhlig, Dieter.
Friedenskampf Und Philosophie. Buhr, Manfred.
La Dynamique De La Guerre Chez Hobbes. Abraham, Luc.
Montaigne On War. Bonadeo, Alfredo.
Philosophy And Practice: Some Issues About War And Peace. Hare, R M.
Philosophy Of Relations Between Sports And Peace. Güldenpfennig, Sven.
Postmortem On An Era: A Citizenly Perspective On The Economy. Scheuer, Irene C.
The First And The Second Day Of War. Hubert, Jerry Z.

WARD, K
Theistic Arguments And Rational Theism. Surin, Kenneth.

WARFARE
When War Is Unjust: Being Honest In Just-War Thinking. Yoder, John H.

WARRANT(S)
Inaccessible Routes To The Problem Of Privileged Access. Schlesinger, George N.
Rules And Subsumption: Mutative Aspects Of Logical Processes. Will, Frederick L.

WARREN, M
Response To Mary Anne Warren's "Reconsidering The Ethics Of Infanticide". Tooley, Michael.

WATSON, G
Watsonian Freedom And Freedom Of The Will. Hill, Christopher S.

WATTS, A
Alan Watts. Stuart, David.

WEAKNESS(ES)
Weakness And Dignity In Conrad's Lord Jim. Ross, Steven L.

WEALTH
An Inquiry Into The Nature And Causes Of The Wealth Of Nations, 2v. Smith, Adam.
Wealth And Virtue: The Shaping Of Political Economy In The Scottish Enlightenment. Hont, Istvan (ed) and Ignatieff, Michael (ed).

WEAPON(S)
Can Modern War Be Just? Johnson, James T.

WEBER, M
Max Weber And The Methodology Of The Social Sciences. Huff, Toby.
Uncertainty Studies In Philosophy, Economics And Socio-Political Theory. Bonatti, Luigi.
Explorations Of The Lebenswelt: Reflections On Schutz And Habermas. Rasmussen, David M.
Interpretative Sociology And The Philosophy Of Praxis: Comparing Max Weber And Antonio Gramsci. Shafir, Gershon.
Karma And The Problem Of Suffering. Perrett, Roy W.
Marx Or Weber: A Genuine Of Or An Imaginary Dilemma. Markiewicz, Wladyslaw.
Max Weber's Defense Of Historical Inquiry. Mc Lemore, Lelan.
Methodologie Und Geschichte: Ansätze Problemorientierter Gesellschaftsanalysen. Rust, Holger.
Weber And The Socialism (in Hungarian). Szabó, Máté.

WEIL, S
Radical Humanism. Améry, Jean and Rosenfeld, Sidney (ed) and Rosenfeld, Stella (ed).
Three Outsiders. Allen, Diogenes.

WEINBERGER, O
Legal Justification And Control: Sociological Aspects Of Philosophy. Klami, Hanna T.
Norms And Logic: Kelsen And Weinberger On The Ontology Of Norms. Bulygin, Eugenio.

WEISS, P
Weiss On Adumbration. Wood, Robert.

WEITZ, M
Philosophie Analytique Et Définition De L'art. Lories, Danielle.

WEIZENBAUM, J
Computer Power And Intellectual Failure In Education: The Significance Of Joseph Weizenbaum's Criticism. Raitz, Keith L.

WELCH, J
Response To "Referential Inscrutability". Meyer, Michael.

WELFARE
An Analysis Of Rights. Stoljar, Samuel.
Good Approximations To Maximin Allocations. Grout, Paul.
Liberal Egalitarianism. Wein, Sheldon.
The Demands Of Justice. Benditt, Theodore M.
The Dimensions Of Poverty. Ellis, G F R.

WELFARE STATE
Contradictions Of The Welfare State, John Keane (ed). Offe, Claus.
Welfare State Versus Welfare Society? Skillen, Anthony.

WELL-BEING
Well-being, Agency And Freedom: The Dewey Lectures 1984. Sen, Amartya.

WELSER, M
Rantzau And Welser: Aspects Of Later German Humanism. Evans, R J W.

WERNER, R
Werner's Ethical Realism. Postow, B C.

WESLEY, J
Taxation In The History Of Protestant Ethics. Shriver, Donald W and Knox, E Richard.

WESTERN PHILOSOPHY
see Occidental

WESTPHAL, K
A Comment On Ken Westphal's "Nietzsche's Sting And The Possibility Of Good Philology". Zimmerman, R I.

WEYL, H
Beyond First-order Logic: The Historical Interplay Between Mathematical Logic And Axiomatic Set Theory. Moore, Gregory H.

WHEWELL, W
Whewell's Consilience Of Inductions—An Evaluation. Fisch, Menachem.

WHIG
The Ideology Of Jacobitism On The Eve Of The Rising Of 1745—Part I. Mc Lynn, F J.

WHITE, A
Discussion: White On Rights And Claims. Stoljar, Samuel.

WHITE, D
Methodological Problems In Psychology (in Dutch). Mauer, K F and Retief, A I.

WHITE, J
The Compulsory Curriculum And Beyond: A Consideration Of Some Aspects Of The Educational Philosophy Of J P White. Gardner, Peter.
The Education Of The Emotions. Dunlop, Francis.

WHITEHEAD
Order & Organism: Steps To A Whiteheadian Philosophy Of Mathematics & The Natural Sciences. Murray, Code.
The Emergence Of Whitehead's Metaphysics 1925–1929, R C Neville (ed). Ford, Lewis S.
Unreality And Time. Brumbaugh, Robert S.
"Metaphysics And The History Of Philosophy: The Case Of Whitehead" in History Of Philosophy In Making, Thro, Linus J (ed), 213–230. Levi, Albert Williams.
A Reply To Kieran Egan's "Development In Education". Jones, Reynold.
Atom, Duration, Form: Difficulties With Process Philosophy. Pannenberg, Wolfhart.
Bernard Meland: "A Rebel Among Process Theologians". Inbody, Tyron.
Bohm And Whitehead On Wholeness, Freedom, Causality, And Time. Griffin, David R.
Development Of Education. Egan, Kieran.
In Response To Inbody's "Bernard Meland: A Rebel Among Process Theologians". Meland, Bernard E.
Life After Death In Whitehead's Metaphysics. Broniak, Christopher J.
Outside The Camp: Recent Work On Whitehead's Philosophy, Part I. Lucas Jr, George R.
Process, Time, And God. Clarke, Bowman L.
Substance-Society-Natural Systems: A Creative Rethinking Of Whitehead's Cosmology. Bracken, Joseph A.
The Compositional History Of Whitehead's Writings. Lucas Jr, George R.
The Place Of Process Cosmology In Absolute Idealism. Butler, Clark.
Whitehead And Marx: Toward A Political Metaphysics. Marsh, James L and Hamrick, William S.
Whitehead And Aquinas On The Eternity Of God. Baumer, Michael R.
Whitehead Ou Le Cosmos Torrentiel. Dumoncel, Jean-Claude.
Whitehead Ou Le Cosmos Torrentiel. Dumoncel, Jean-Claude.
Whitehead, Special Relativity, And Simultaneity. White, Villard Alan.
Whitehead's "Prehension" And Hegel's "Mediation". Christensen, Darrel E.

WITTGENSTEIN

Interpretation Von "Lebensform". Haller, Rudolf.
Love And Logic In 1984. Macmillan, C J B.
Moore's Paradox And Epistemic Justification. Hambourger, Robert.
Moral Objectivity. Lear, Jonathan.
On Finding One's Feet In Philosophy: From Wittgenstein To Marx. Nielsen, Kai.
On Mucking Around About God: Some Methodological Animadversions. Nielsen, Kai.
On The Possibility Of Continuing The Conversation Of Mankind. Conway, Jeremiah and Conway, Gertrude.
Programmatische Oberlegungen Formal–Strukturaler Natur Zur "suche Nach Einer Verlorene Ästhetik". Born, Rainer P.
Realism And Grammar. Screen, Donald P.
Remembering. Cascardi, Anthony J.
Russell's *Theory Of Knowledge* And Wittgenstein's Earliest Writings. Iglesias, Teresa.
Russell's Multiple Relation Theory Of Judgment. Griffin, Nicholas.
Schlick Before Wittgenstein. Quinton, Anthony.
Sense And Sensibility. Kimmel, Lawrence.
Set Theory, Skolem's Paradox And The *Tractatus*. Moore, A W.
The Evidential Value Of Religious Experiences. Clark, R W.
The Metaphysics Of Wittgenstein's On Certainty. Cook, John W.
The Silence Of Physics. Meurers, Joseph.
Transcendental Idealism In Wittgenstein And Theories Of Meaning. Moore, A W.
Visual Space From The Perspective Of Possible World Semantics II. Wiesenthal, L.
Was Wittgenstein Influenced By Hegel? Cook, Daniel J.
Was Wittgenstein A Sceptic? Hanfling, Oswald.
What Does A Concept Script Do? Diamond, Cora.
What Does The Private Language Argument Prove? Hanfling, Oswald.
Wittgenstein's Language–Games And The Call To Cognition. Deizt, Samuel M and Arrington, Robert L.
Wittgenstein On The 'Charm' Of Psychoanalysis. Geller, Jeffrey L.
Wittgenstein And Nāgārjuna's Paradox. Anderson, Tyson.
Wittgensteinian Moralism Ethnomethodology And Moral Ideology. Nielsen, Kai.
Wittgenstein's Anthropology. Bell, Richard.
Wittgenstein On Sensation And 'Seeing–As'. Dunlop, Charles E M.
Wittgenstein's Solution Of The 'Hermeneutic Problem'. Shanker, Stuart G.
Wittgenstein On The Phenomena Of Belief. Churchill, John.
Wittgenstein's Rejection Of Scientific Psychology. Williams, Meredith.
Wittgenstein On Ostensive Definition. Prasad, Brij Kishore.
Wittgenstein And The Vienna Circle. Mc Guinnes, Brian.

WODEHAM, A

Adam Wodeham's Anti–Aristotelian Anti–Atomism. Kretzmann, Norman.

WOJTYLA, K

A Christian Humanism: Karol Wojtyla's Existential Personalism. Woznicki, Andrew N.
Edith Stein Et Karol Wojtyla Sur La Personne. Kalinowski, Georges.

WOKUTCH, R

Bluffing: Its Demise As A Subject Unto Itself. Beach, John.

WOLFF

"The Deutsche Metaphysik Of Christian Wolff: Text And Transitions" in *History Of Philosophy In Making*, Thro, Linus J (ed), 149–164. Corr, Charles A.
Casula On Baumgarten's Metaphysics. Tonelli, G.

WOLFF, J

Aesthetics And The Sociology Of Art: A Critical Commentary On The Writings Of Janet Wolff. Hincks, Tony.

WOLFF, R

On Robert Paul Wolff's Transcendental Interpretation Of Marx's Labor Theory Of Value. Schweickart, David.
The Idea Of Violence. Coady, C A J.

WOLFSON, H

History Of Philosophy In The Grand Manner: The Achievement Of H A Wolfson. Runia, D T.

WOLLASTON, W

The Problem Of Circularity In Wollaston's Moral Philosophy. Joynton, Olin.
Verità Delle Azioni: Sul Fraintendimento Humiano Di W Wollaston. Paolinelli, Marco.

WOLLHEIM, R

Wollheim And The Institutional Theory Of Art. Mc Fee, Graham.

WOLLSTONECRAFT, M

A Critical Edition Of Mary Wollstonecraft's A Vindication Of The Rights Of Woman: With Strictures On Political And Moral Subjects. Hardt, Ulrich H.

WOLTERSTORFF, N

Musical Kinds. Anderson, James C.

WOMAN

see also Feminism
A Critical Edition Of Mary Wollstonecraft's A Vindication Of The Rights Of Woman: With Strictures On Political And Moral Subjects. Hardt, Ulrich H.
Machina Ex Dea: Feminist Perspectives On Technology. Rothschild, Joan (ed).
Women, Sex, And The Law. Tong, Rosemarie.
"Cardinal Gibbons's Ignorance" in *Freedom, Feminism, And The State*, Mc Elroy, Wendy (ed), 305–310. Dietrick, Ellen Battelle.
"Irrelevancies" in *Freedom, Feminism, And The State*, Mc Elroy, Wendy (ed), 101–110. Marvin, Bertha.
"Protective Labor Legislation" in *Freedom, Feminism, And The State*, Mc Elroy, Wendy (ed), 267–274. Taylor, Joan Kennedy.
"Trade Unionism And Women's Work" in *Freedom, Feminism, And The State*, Mc Elroy, Wendy (ed), 237–266. Anthony, Susan.

"Women And The Rise Of The American Medical Profession" in *Freedom, Feminism, And The State*, Mc Elroy, Wendy (ed), 285–304. Ehrenreich, Barbara and English, Deirdre.
"87–100" in *Freedom, Feminism, And The State*, Mc Elroy, Wendy (ed), 87–100. Harman, Lillian.
Equivalencia Y Subordinación, Según San Agustín: Naturaleza Y Papel De La Mujer. Borresen, Kari E.
Freud, Adler, And Women: Powers Of The "Weak" And "Strong". De Vitis, Joseph L.
Les Avatars De La Différence. Morosoli, Michele.
Mujer, Biología O Historia Y Poder. Polimeni, Dante and Rojas, Oscar.
Nietzsche Et Les Femmes. Joós, Ernest.
Power, Oppression And Gender. Andre, Judith.
Some Recent Books On The Historical Status Of Women. Tormey, Judith.
The Human Rights Of Women In Islam. Talhami, Ghada.
Une Altenative À L'exclusion: La Dialogie. Roumanes, Jacques–Bernard.
Woman As Truth In Nietzsche's Writing. Oliver, Kelly A.
Women, Medicine, And Religion: A Response To Raymond And Abrams. Rawlinson, Mary C.

WOMEN'S LIBERATION

"Anarchism And American Traditions" in *Freedom, Feminism, And The State*, Mc Elroy, Wendy (ed), 35–48. De Cleyre, Voltairine.
"Legal Disabilities Of Women" in *Freedom, Feminism, And The State*, Mc Elroy, Wendy (ed), 121–128. Grimké, Sarah.
"The Economic Position Of Women" in *Freedom, Feminism, And The State*, Mc Elroy, Wendy (ed), 213–236. La Follette, Suzanne.
Freedom And Women. Gould, Carol C.
Lordship, Bondage, And The Dialectic Of Work In Traditional Male/Female Relationships. Bell, Linda A and Alcoff, Linda.

WONDER

Art, Poetry, And The Sense Of Prevalence: Some Implications Of Buchler's Theory Of Poetry. Singer, Beth J.

WOODFIELD, A

Discussion: Woodfield's Analysis Of Teleology. Nissen, Lowell.

WOOLBRIDGE, F

The Naturalists And The Supernatural: Studies In Horizon And An American Philosophy Of Religion. Shea, William M.

WOOLF, V

"A Long Day's Journey Into Night" in *Existential Coordinates Of Human Condition*, Tymieniecka, A (ed), 209–226. Schlack, Beverly A.

WOOLHOUSE, R

Locke's Real Ideas, And Dr Woolhouse. Helm, Paul.

WOOZLEY, A

The Indefeasibility Of Justice. Day, J P.

WORD(S)

Palabra Y Deseo. Neri, Miguel A Z.
Word Meaning, Sentence Menaing And Apoha. Siderits, Mark.

WORDSWORTH

Wordsworth's "Real Language Of Men" And Augustine's Theory Of Language. Chivers, Frances J.

WORK

"Hegel On Work, Ownership And Citizenship" in *The State And Civil Society*, Pelczynski, Z A (ed), 178–196. Ryan, Alan.
Alltag Und Alltagsbewuktsein. Luutz, W.
Concept Du Travail Et Travail Du Concept Chez Hegel. Jarczyk, Gwendoline.
Content And Dimension Of Aesthetic Valuation Of Working Environment (in Czechoslovakian). Klivar, Miroslav.
Entwicklung Und Effektive Nutzung Des Gesellschaft Arbeitsvermögens—Ausdruck Praktizierter Einheit Von Humanität Und Rationalität. Pietrzynski, Gerd.
Hombre–Trabajo–Economiá: Aporte Al Tema A Partir De La Antropología Filosófica. Scannone, J C.
Laborem Exercens: A Theological And Philosophical Foundation For Business Ethics. Sullivan, Brian G.
Max, The Cynic (in Portuguese). Moraes, Reginaldo C C.
More's *Utopia* And The New World Utopias: Is The Good Life An Easy Life? Dooley, Patrick K.
Soziale Bedingungen Und Triebkräfte Hoher Arbeitsleistungen. Weidig, R.
Soziologische Forschung Zum Wohen Und Arbeiten In Der Stadt. Kahl, A.
The Character Of The Interaction Of Working And Political Activity Of Personality (in Czechoslovakian). Rjadová, Vera and Rjadovoj, Alexandr.
The Defence Of The Ant—Work, Life And Utopia. Rives, Joel.
The Humanism Of Associated Work And The Problem Of The Technology Laws (in German). Jacobs, Hans–Jürgen and Herlitzius, Erwin.
The Possibility And Reality Of Self–Concious Work (in Hungarian). Szabó, Márton.
The Right To Strike And The Right To Work. Smart, Brian.
Trabajo, Cultura Y Evangelización: Creatividad E Identidad De La Enseñanza Social De La Iglesia. Scannone, J C.
Wissenschaftlich–Technischer Fortschritt Und Sozialistisches Verhältnis Zur Arbeit. Stollberg, R.
Work–Related Ethical Attitudes: Impact On Business Profitability. Dunfee, Thomas W and Robertson, Diana C.

WORK OF ART

The Restoration And Reproduction Of Works Of Art. Wreen, Michael.

WORKER(S)

A Cotton Dust Study Unmasked. Levine, Carol.
A Defense Of Employee Rights. Des Jardins, Joseph R and Mc Call, John J.

WORKER(S)

Conflict In The Workplace, And Its Resolution. Campbell, Keith.

Entwicklung Und Nutzung Der Qualifikation Der Facharbeiter Als Faktor Ökonomischer Effektivität. Rudolph, W.

ROBOTS, RIFs, And Rights. Arthur, Alcott.

The New OSHA Rules And The Worker's Right To Know. Mc Garity, Thomas O.

Vargas And Prestes: A Comparison Between The Labourism And Communism In Brazil (in Portuguese). Piozzi, Patrizia.

Who Speaks For The Workers? Legters, Lyman H.

Worker Control, Self–Respect, And Self–Esteem. Howard, Michael W.

WORKING CLASS

Activité Sociale Et Besoins Culturels De La Classe Ouvrière (in German). Geidel, Werner.

Arbeiterklasse Und Intelligenz In Der Dialektik Von Wissenschaftlichtechnischem, Ökonomischem Und Sozialem Fortschritt. Lötsch, M.

Die Heranbildung Eines Der Arbeiterklasse Würdigen Nachwuchses. Meier, Artur.

Probleme Der Führenden Rolle Der Arbeiterklasse Im Sozialismus. Friedrich, Gert and Kastner, H and Possneck, E.

Probleme Der Gesellschaftlichen Aktivität Der Arbeiterklasse In Der Materiellen Produktion. Jetzschmann, Horst.

Zur Entwicklung Kultureller Bedürfnisse In Der Arbeiterklasse. Staufenbiel, Fred.

WORKS

Dating Berkeley's Notebook B. Belfrage, Bertil.

Facts And Reasons Concerning Berkeley's Reprinted *Works*. Park, Désirée.

Facts Concerning Berkeley's Notebooks. Belfrage, Bertil.

On Missing Neurath's Boat: Some Reflections On Recent Quine Literature. Roth, Paul A.

The Authorship Of *Guardian* 69. Winkler, Kenneth P.

The Compositional History Of Whitehead's Writings. Lucas Jr, George R.

The Hegel Archive And The Hegel Edition. Rameil, Udo.

Three Notes On Seneca *De Providentia*. Grant, John N.

WORLD(S)

see also Possible World(s)

Searching For Cultural Foundations. Mc Shane, Philip (ed).

A Phenomenology Of Nuclear Weapons. Weinberger, David.

Das Von Der Naturwissenschaft Gepraegte Menschenbild (in Polish). Luyten, Norbert A.

How Many Worlds? Healey, Richard A.

Il Carattere Immediato Della Presenza Di Dio Nel Mondo Secondo Tommaso D'Aquino. Campodonico, Angelo.

La Eternidad Del Mundo: Un Capítulo De Filosofía Medieval. López, Antonio Marlasca.

La Récessivité Comme Structure Du Monde. Florian, Mircea.

La Teoría Relacional De La Personalidad Según J Nuttin. Darós, William R.

Mesure Et Objectivité Dans L'investigation Du Monde Sensible. Fevrier, Paulette.

Metaphysical Fall–Out From The Nuclear Predicament. Routley, Richard.

Minimizing Arbitrariness: Toward A Metaphysics Of Infinitely Many Isolated Concrete Worlds. Unger, Peter.

Perceived Worlds, Inferred Worlds, *The* World. Sklar, Lawrence.

Perishability, The Actual World, And The Non–Existence Of God. Chrzan, Keith.

The Significance And Dignity Of Labor: A Keyword In Marxian Anthropology. Ehlen, Peter.

The World–Soul And Time In St Augustine. Teske, Roland J.

Triálogo Sobre El Fin Del Principio Del Mundo. Labson, S.

WORLD CONGRESS(ES)

World Congresses Of Philosophy. Cauchy, Venant and Kuczynski, Janusz.

WORLD COUNCIL OF CHURCHES

Perspectives On Political Ethics: An Ecumenical Enquiry. Srisang, Koson (ed).

WORLD VIEW(S)

Contours Of A World View. Holmes, Arthur F.

Philosophy Of Man And The Universe. Loeschmann, Fred.

Reductionism And Cultural Being. Smith, Joseph W.

Global Perspectives: Spiritualities In Interaction. Panikkar, Raimundo.

Los Niveles Temporales Según J T Fraser Y El Orden Subyacente Según D Bohm. Delacre, Georges.

Overcoming Ethnocentrism In The Philosophy Classroom. Schutte, Ofelia.

Reflections Of The Mutual Benefits Of Philosophical And Global Education. Silvers, Anita.

Science—Ideology—*Weltanschauung*. Dobrosielski, Marian.

Socrates, Meet The Buddha. Hoekema, David.

The Case Of The Athenian Stranger: Philosophy And World Citzenship. Caws, Peter.

The Use And Abuse Of The Concept 'Weltanschauung'. Echeverria, Edward J.

The World According To Husserl. Holmes, Richard.

Theism And Monism—Reconciled In Absolutistic World View. Jhingran, Saral.

WORRINGER, W

"Bathos", Immagini Del Tempo Alla Fine Del Tempo" in *Il Tempo Dell'Arte*, Papi, Fulvio and others (ed), 60–91. Franck, Giorgio.

WORSHIP

In Response To Miller's "Meland: Worship And His Recent Thought". Meland, Bernard E.

Meland: Worship And His Recent Thought. Miller, Randolph C.

WORTH

Distributive Justice In Aristotle's Ethics And Politics. Keyt, David.

WRIGHT, C

McGinn's Reply To Wright's Reply To Benacerraf. Hazen, Allen.

Wright *Versus* Lewis On The Transitivity Of Counterfactuals. Lowe, E J.

WRIGHT, L

Dispositions, Teleology And Reductionism. Roque, Alicia Juarrero.

WRITER(S)

The Western Intellectual Heritage And The Soviet Dissent. Milikotin, Anthony.

WRITING

Art D'écrire Et Pratique Politique De Jean–Jacques Rousseau (I). Marshall, Terence.

Moral Theory And Educational Practice: A Reply To Ian Gregory. Straughan, Roger R.

Philosophy's Relevance To Technical Writing. Girill, T R.

Writing To Learn In Philosophy. Berger, Jeffrey.

WRONGFUL LIFE

What Is Wrong With 'Wrongful Life' Cases? Bell, Nora K and Loewer, Barry M.

WRONGNESS

Does Rightness Always Involve Wrongness? Bahm, Archie J.

WRONGS

Intentions, Rights And Wrongs: A Critique Of Fried. Fischer, Marilyn.

WYCLYF

Wyclef's Philosophy And Platonic Ideas (in Czechoslovakian). Herold, Vilém.

WYKSTRA, S

Evil And The Theistic Hypothesis: A Response To S J Wykstra. Rowe, William L.

WYSS, D

Dieter Wyss Y La Medicina Antropológica. Csef, Herbert.

YANG, K

A Critical Account Of Yang Kuei–Shan's Philosophical Thought (in Chinese). Chang, Jun–Chun.

YANG, X

Did German Classical Philosophy Simply "End"? Ruoshui, Wang.

YANOV

Solzhenitsyn And Yanov. Boldyrev, Peter and Vertlieb, E.

YATES, S

Yates On Feyerabend's Democratic Relativism. Alford, C Fred.

YEARLEY, S

Reply To Steven Yearley's "The Relationship Between Epistemological And Sociological Cognitive Interests". Mackenzie, Donald.

YOGA

A Non–Ethical Concept Of Ahimsa. Bhardwaja, V K.

Two Models Of Spiritual Journey: Yoga And Confucius. Podgorski, Frang.

YOGACARA

The Yogācāra And Mādhyamika Interpretations Of The Buddha–Nature Concept In Chinese Buddhism. Liu, Ming–wood.

YOUNG, J

The Need For Truth. Prado, C G.

Toward An Epistemologically–Relevant Sociology Of Science. Campbell, Donald T.

YOUTH

"Buber's Address "Herut" And Its Influence On The Jewish Youth Movement In Germany" in *Martin Buber*, Gordon, Haim (ed), 233–254. Dorman, Menahem.

Abusing The Unemployed: An Invisible Justice. Breakwell, Glynis M.

YOXEN, E

Biotechnology And The Social Reconstruction Of Molecular Biology. Markle, Gerald E and Robin, Stanley S.

YU, G

Yu Guang–Yuan's Two Categories Of Matter. Pfeifer, Karl.

ZAGLADIN, V

The Struggle Against The Revisionism For Creative Development Of Marxism–Leninism (in Czechoslovakian). Hrzal, L.

ZANER, R

Operative Dimensions Of Zaner's Context Of Self. Schenck, David.

ZELENY, J

Answer On The Impulses Of J Zelený Concerning The Character Of So–called Dialectical And Logical Deduction (in Czechoslovakian). Gorsky, D P.

Methodological Starting Points Of The Investigation Of The Way Of Life (in Czechoslovakian). Velek, J.

Practice And Rationality (in Czechoslovakian). Tabachkovsky, V G.

Practice As Presupposition Of Science (in Czechoslovakian). Znoj, M.

ZEMACH, E

The Diversity Of Perception. Nelson, Jack.

ZEN BUDDHISM

Studies In Ch'an And Huy–Yen. Gimello, Robert M (ed) and Gregory, Peter N (ed).

The Interior And Exterior In Zen Buddhism. Izutsu, Toshihiko.

The Supreme Doctrine: Psychological Encounters In Zen Thought. Benoit, Hubert.

A Pointing Finger Kills "The Buddha": A Response To Chung–Ying Cheng And John King Farlow. Sellman, James.

An Anglo–Saxon Response To John King Farlow's Questions On Zen Language And Zen Paradoxes. Tucker, John.

Ch'an And Taoist Mirrors: Reflections On Richard Garner's "Deconstruction Of The Mirror". Lusthaus, Dan.

Confucianism And Zen (Ch'an) Philosophy Of Education. Cheng, Hsueh–li.

Einig Grundlien Der Chinesischen Philosophie. Brock, Erich.

Krishnamurti Zen. Bouchard, Roch.

On Chinese Ch'an In Relation To Taoism. Yi, Wu.

The Bodymind Experience In Dōgen's *Shōbōgenzō*: A Phenomenological Perspective. Shaner, David E.

ZEN BUDDHISM

The Deconstruction Of The Mirror And Other Heresies: Ch'an And Taoism As Abnormal Discourse. Garner, Richard T.

The Non—logical Character Of Zen. Nakamura, Hajime.

ZENO

'Lo Stoicismo Di Erillo'. Ioppolo, Anna Maria.

"Zeno's Stricture And Predication In Plato, Aristotle, And Plotinus" in *How Things Are*, Bogen, James (ed), 21—58. Turnbull, Robert G.

Nāgārjuna And Zeno On Motion. Mabbett, I W.

ZENO'S PARADOX(ES)

The Infinistic Thesis. Burke, Michael B.

Zeno's Paradoxes, Iteration, And Infinity. Seaton, Robert.

Zeno's Paradoxes And Temporal Becoming In Dialectical Atomism. Smolenov, Hristo.

ZERMELO

Cantorian Set Theory And Limitation Of Size. Hallett, Michael.

Beyond First—order Logic: The Historical Interplay Between Mathematical Logic And Axiomatic Set Theory. Moore, Gregory H.

ZEUTHEN, F

Bargaining And Justice. Gauthier, David.

ZIFF, P

Context And What Is Said. Bertolet, Rod.

ZINOV'EV, A

Logique Et Ontologie. Kalinowski, Georges.

ZIONISM

"Buber's Address "Herut" And Its Influence On The Jewish Youth Movement In Germany" in *Martin Buber*, Gordon, Haim (ed), 233—254. Dorman, Menahem.

ZOOLOGY

Zoological Philosophy: An Exposition In Regard To The Natural History Of Animals. Lamarck, J B.

ZUBIRI, X

Significación Actual Del Pensamiento Zubiriano. Quintás, Alfonso López.

ZWART, P

The Constancy Of Kantian Time: Reflections On Chronobiology. Gunter, Pete A Y.

ZWINGLI, U

Justice Et Glorification: Double Préoccupation D'Ulrich Zwingli, Réformateur (1484—1531). Burki, Bruno.

Zur Aktualität Der Politischen Theologie Ulrich Zwinglis. Winzeler, Peter.

Guidance on the Use of the Author Index With Abstracts

Each entry in this section begins with the author's name and contains the complete title of the article or book, other bibliographic information, and an abstract if available. The list is arranged in alphabetical order with the author's last name first. Articles by multiple authors are listed under each author's name. Names preceded by the articles De, La, Le, etc. or the prepositions Da, De, Van, Von, etc. are treated as if the article or presposition were a part of the last name.

The vast majority of abstracts are provided by the authors of the articles and books; where an abstract does not appear, it was not received from the author prior to the publication of this edition. The staff of the *Index* prepares some abstracts. These abstracts are followed by "(staff)".

In order to locate all the articles and books written by a given author, various spellings of the author's name should be checked. This publication uses the form of the author's name given in the articles and books. Because some authors have changed the form of their name that they attach to articles and because some editors took liberties with the proper name submitted, variations of an author's name may occur in this index. Particular care should be given to names that have a space, a dash, or an apostrophe in their surnames. Because the computer sorts on each character, the names of other authors may be "filed" between different spellings of a given author's name.

AARSLEFF, Hans. Schulenburg's Leibniz Als Sprachforscher, With Some Observations On Leibniz And The Study Of Language. *Stud Leibniz* 7,122–134 1975.

This book is the best and most comprehensive treatment we have of Leibniz' study of natural languages. With its rich detail and source references, it is indispensable both to Leibniz scholars and to students of the history of the study of language. The editor's indices make it possible to use the book also as a work of reference. The reviewer shows that the chief impulse to Leibniz' study of languages was the need to disprove the Swedish thesis of the northern origin of the Germanic languages. (edited)

ABAD, M and Monteiro, Luiz. On Three–Valued Moisil Algebras. *Log Anal* 27,407–414 D 84.

In this paper we investigate the properties of the family I(A) of all intervals of the form [x, x] with x less than or equal to x, in a De Morgan algebra A, and we obtain a necessary and sufficient condition for a complete De Morgan algebra A to be a Kleene algebra in terms of I(A). We prove that I(A) is a complete Boolean algebra if A is a complete Moisil algebra.

ABAD, Manuel and Figallo, Aldo. Characterization Of Three–Valued Lukasiewicz Algebras. *Rep Math Log* 18,47–60 1984.

In this paper we give a characterization of three–valued Lukasiewicz algebras by means of weak implication, infimum and strong negation. This problem has been earlier solved by using Zermelo's theorem and representation theorem of three–valued Lukasiewicz algebras by means of a subalgebra of a direct product of simple three–valued Lukasiewicz algebras. In this work we obtain these results but we make no use of Zermelo's theorem and representation theorem.

ABDOO, Sherlyn. "Hardy's Jude" in *Existential Coordinates Of Human Condition*, Tymieniecka, A (ed), 307–318. Boston Reidel 1984.

ABE, Yoshihiro. Strongly Compact Cardinals, Elementary Embeddings And Fixed Points. *J Sym Log* 49,808–812 S 84.

Let j be the cannonical embedding induced by a fine ultrafilter. We characterize the class of cardinals which are fixed by j. This is the same thing that J B Barbanel did in the case that the ultrafilter is normal.

ABEL, Charles F and Marsh, Frank H. *Punishment And Restitution: A Restitutionary Approach To Crime And The Criminal*. Westport Greenwood Pr 1984.

ABELL, Peter. Comparative Narratives: Some Rules For The Study Of Action. *J Theor Soc Behav* 14,309–332 O 84.

The paper explores the concept of a Narrative which is defined as a connected structure on a set of constrained actions and forbearances. Explanation via Narratives is compared with explanation through variable centered methodology and an interpretation of correlations in terms of Narratives is also outlined.

ABELMANN, Xenia. Die Bedeutung Des Vaterlandsbegriffes Für Die Erziehung Zum Sozialistischen Patriotismus. *Deut Z Phil* 23,731–736 1975.

ABELSON, Raziel. Lawless Freedom. *J Soc Phil* 15,35–45 Fall 84.

I contend that the mind–body problem and the free will problem must be solved together or not at all. Reductive materialists succeed in explaining mind–body interaction at the exorbitant price of eliminating the distinctive features of mind, thus leaving us with a mindless body problem. Functional accounts of mind like those of Dennett and Davidson seem to avoid this result, but when probed, their views collapse into reductionism. The reason for this collapse is traced to their assumption that psychological causality is as law–like as physical causality. Once this assumption is abandoned, a functional account of mind can be stated in a non–reductionist form, and the causal interaction between mental and physical processes can be described in a way consistent with genuine free will.

ABIAN, Alexander. On The Standard–Model Hypothesis Of ZF. *Z Math Log* 21,87–88 1975.

ABOUSENNA, Mona. Metaphysics Of The Absolute In Aristotle's *Poetics*. *Diotima* 12,29–32 1984.

According to Aristotle art is imitation. Imitation is contemplation of Being. Thus, it does not involve any element of changing reality. Aristotle conceives of poetry as universal, and the universal is absolute. Accordingly, catharsis is the release of emotions in order to give to logos which is necessary for grasping the absolute. And as Being is absolute, so Aristotle establishes an organic relation between metaphysics and poetry. In this sense, Aristotle stagnates the status quo.

ABRAHAM, Adrian and Meyer, Robert K. A Model For The Modern Malaise. *Philosophia (Israel)* 14,25–40 Ag 84.

ABRAHAM, Luc. La Dynamique De La Guerre Chez Hobbes. *Petit Rev Phil* 6,109–122 Autumn 84.

Quels rôles jouent la gloire, la crainte, et le désir dans le phénomène querre? Nous avons analysé la dialectique de la guerre en regard de la théorie de la connaissance chez Hobbes, c'est–à–dire, la guerre comme connaissance prenant sa forme dans le monde de l'empirisme et du sensualisme: tout savoir dérive de l'expérience et cell–ci s'alimente à un *premier moteur*, la sensation. Enfin, l'expérience de la guerre est–elle nécessaire pour le "Savoir" et le progrès de l'humanité? Pouvons–nous penser à un adieu aux armes?

ABRAHAM, U and Rubin, M and Shelah, Saharon. On The Consistency Of Some Partition Theorems For Continuous Colorings, And The Structure Of Dense Real Order Types. *Annals Pure Applied Log* 29,123–206 S 85.

ABRAHAM, William E. Predication. *Stud Leibniz* 7,1–21 1975.

Paralogismen betreffs der Leibnizschen Präkikatlehre werden aufgezeigt und widerlegt. Enthaltensein heisst die Inverse von Ableitung; den zwei Arten von Ableitung, die Leibniz kennt, entsprechen zwei Arten von Enthaltensein. Die beiden Arten von Enthaltensein bieten Leibniz di Möglichkeit zu der logischen und irreduziblen Unterscheidung zwischen notwendigen und bedingten Wahrheiten.

ABRAMS, Frederick R. Rejoinder To 'Medicine As Patriarchal Religion'. *J Med Phil* 9,313–318 Ag 84.

The article rebuts the concept that medicine continues to be a patriarchal religion exploiting females. The Raymond article subjectively defined the goals and purposes of medicine, then with excellent vocabulary, lively imagination, and prejudicial selectivity, the author created a paper tiger to be sacrificed on the altar of outraged feminism. Inflammatory scenarios which the author invented are questioned, and incorrect medical presumptions are refuted.

ABRAMS, Frederick R. Response To Professor Rawlinson's Article "Women, Medicine, And Religion". *J Med Phil* 9,325–326 Ag 84.

Dr. rawlinson critiqued the rejoinder by pointing out many abuses by practitioners of medicine historically. This response acknowledged past abuses, as did the original rejoinder, but objected to the thrust of the original Raymond article by concluding "To treat the historical evolution in the present tense, as if it were immutable, universal, and unchallenged from within the profession, is to wave a red flag at those physicians who are appalled at the plethora of genuine abuses and are working to correct them."

ACHINSTEIN, Peter (ed). *The Concept Of Evidence*. Oxford Oxford Univ Pr 1983.

ACHINSTEIN, Peter (ed) and Hannaway, Owen (ed). *Observation, Experiment, And Hypothesis In Modern Physical Science*. Cambridge MIT Pr 1985.

ACHINSTEIN, Peter. "Method Of Hypothesis" in *Observation, Experiment, And Hypothesis In Modern Physical Science*, Achinstein, Peter (ed), 127–146. Cambridge MIT Pr 1985.

ACHINSTEIN, Peter. A Type Of Non–Causal Explanation. *Midwest Stud Phil* 9,221–244 1984.

ACKERMAN, Robert John. *Religion As Critique*. Amherst Univ Of Mass Pr 1985.

ACKERMANN, Robert. "Popper And German Social Philosophy" in *Popper And The Human Sciences*, Currie, Gregory (ed), 165–184. Boston Nijhoff 1985.

ACKLEY, Timothy. The Tuition Tax Credit Debate. *Proc Phil Educ* 40,225–234 1984.

ACKRILL, J L (ed) and Hussey, Edward (trans). *Aristotle's Physics*. NY Clarendon Pr 1983.

ACKROYD, Elizabeth. A Rejection Of Doctors As Moral Guides. *J Med Ethics* 10,147 S 84.

Rejecting the claim that patients have a moral obligation to themselves to preserve their own health and thus a moral obligaton to follow their doctor's medical advice, the Chairman of the Patients Association suggests that a more equal partnership between doctor and patient, based on better communication, plus reasonable concern for their own health on the part of all are the objectives justifiably pursued in the common interest.

ADAMAMUŢI, I A. Philosophical And Physical Arguments For The Existence Of The Gravitational Energy As Half Of The Whole Energy Of The Universe. *Phil Log* 27,340–347 O–D 83.

ADAMCZEWSKI, Z. "Poetic Thinking To Be" in *Existential Coordinates Of Human Condition*, Tymieniecka, A (ed), 99–118. Boston Reidel 1984.

ADAMOWICZ, Zofia and Morales– Luna, Guillermo. A Recursive Model For Arithmetic With Weak Induction. *J Sym Log* 50,49–54 Mr 85.

ADAMS, E Charles. "Archaeology And The Native American: A Case At Hopi" in *Ethics And Values In Archaeology*, Green, Ernestene L (ed), 236–242. NY Free Pr 1984.

ADAMS, E M. "The Subjective Normative Structure Of Agency" in *Gewirth's Ethical Rationalism*, Regis Jr, Edward (ed), 8–22. Chicago Univ Of Chicago Pr 1984.

ADAMS, Frederick. Properties, Functionalism, And The Identity Theory. *Eidos* 1,153–179 D 79.

When functionalism burst on the scene in the philosophy of mind it quickly became clear that the difference between it and type–identity theory would turn on the nature of properties. If mental properties are multiply instantiable in diverse physical systems (as are functional properties), then no smooth reduction of the mental to the physical will be possible. However, little attention was paid to functional properties themselves. I argue that the received views about them are false.

ADAMS, George Plimpton and Gray, Glenn J. *'Hegel's Hellenic Ideal' AND 'The Mystical Element In Hegel's Early Writings'*. NY Garland 1984.

ADAMS, Marilyn McCord. "Things Versus 'Hows', Or Ockham On Predication And Ontology" in *How Things Are*, Bogen, James (ed), 175–188. Boston Reidel 1985.

ADAMS, Marilyn McCord and Wood, Rega. Is To Will It As Bad As To Do It (The Fourteenth Century Debate)? *Fran Stud* 41,5–60 1981.

ADAMS, Robert M. "Predication, Truth, And Transworld Identity In Leibniz" in *How Things Are*, Bogen, James (ed), 235–284. Boston Reidel 1985.

ADDIS, Laird. Mind, Structure, And Time. *Phil Topics* 12,39–52 Wint 81.

Following an explication of the distinction between structure and function is appied to the mind, it is argued that the mind has no structure but that this does not imply, as some have supposed, the impossibility of scientific explanation of mental life. It is further argued that the absence of structure does imply the impossibility of a mind in a timeless world.

ADDIS, Laird. Parallelism, Interactionism, And Causation. *Midwest Stud Phil* 9,329–344 1984.

Assuming that a dualism of properties is true, parallelism and interactionism are the only plausible candidates for the nature of the lawful relations between the two kinds of properties. (the third abstract possibility, fatalism, is phenomenologically absurd in denying any such lawful connections). While the standard objections to parallelism concerning mental efficacy can be answered, interactionism faces the insuperable objection that if it were true, no one could ever know what another person is thinking.

ADELMAN, Howard. Hegel's *Phenomenology*: Facing The Preface. *Ideal Stud* 14,159–170 My 84.

ADELSON, Edna. "Confidentiality And The Obligation To Report Child Abuse" in *Difficult Decisions In Medical Ethics*, Ganos, Doreen L (ed), 63–74. NY Liss 1983.

ADLER, Frank and Kretzschmar, A. Sozialistische Persönlichkeitsentwicklung Und Soziologische Forschung. *Deut Z Phil* 22,154–166 1974.

Das Werden sozialistischer Persönlichkeiten ist seinem grundlegenden sozialen Inhalt nach identisch mit der Aneignung des sozialen Wesens der herrschenden Arbeiterklasse. Deshalb ist ein nur normatives Herangehn an die Persönlichkeit nicht geeignet, ihre Entwicklung soziologisch zu erklären. Zentrale Bedeutung für die soziologische Persönlichkeitsforschung hat die Analyse des sozialen Wesens Arbeiterklasse, der Vermittlungen zwischen Arbeiterklasse und Klassenindividuum und der personalen Besonderheiten.

ADLER, Norbert. Die Dynamische Naturvorstellung Als Naturphilosophische Grundlage Der Heutigen Physik. *Phil Natur* 21,101–125 1984.

Newton's mechanics traces all changes in nature back to movements of unchangeable particles. Atoms, subparticles and light show particle–wave–dualism. Quantum theory reduces dualism to a theory of measuring process. Here, in this article, light and subparticles are regarded as simple changeable corpuscles appearing once as particles, another time as waves caused by different intensities of their inner force. This dynamical conception is related to transcendentalism, monadology and to equations of quantum theory and theory of relativity.

ADLER, Richard. Possible Worlds Counterfactuals. *Can J Phil* 6,119–138 80 Supp.

It is argued that counterfactual theories of causation give rise to problems directly analogous to those facing standard Humean regularity accounts. David Lewis' possible worlds counterfactual theory is analyzed in detail. Objections are raised against his account of natural laws and his theory's inability to reflect causal environments. Finally, Lewis' primitive relation of similarity is shown to be parasitically dependent on the Humean constant conjunction analysis of causation.

AGAMBEN, Giorgio. The Idea Of Language: Some Difficulties In Speaking About Language. *Grad Fac Phil J* 10,141–150 Spr 84.

AGASSI, Joseph. Das Problem Der Rationalität. *Conceptus* 18,101–105 1984.

Classical skepticism disproves classical rationalism which identifies rationality with proof. Classical skepticism itself is a poor alternative, as is classical fideism. The Popperian theory of rationality as openness to criticism reopened the problem of rationalitiy to new theoretical ventures.

AGASSI, Joseph. Libertarianism Versus Education For Freedom. *Phil Forum (Boston)* 15,471–473 Sum 84.

Classical liberalism assumed that individuals are naturally autonomous. Contemporary libertarians tacitly omit this assumption, thus allowing individuals to sell their freedom. This permission must be restricted, as tacitly conceded by Milton Friedman when he endorsed some form of compulsory education. Consequently, contemporary libertarianism is a vague doctrine in need of careful restatement.

AGAZZI, Evandro. Commensurability, Incommensurability And Cumulativity In Scientific Knowledge. *Erkenntnis* 22,51–78 Ja 85.

Through a suitable characterization of the notion of scientific object, the paper shows that, in spite of all concepts in a scientific theory being context–dependent, some of them contain a "referential component" of operational character which is not such. This fact allows a comparison between theories speaking about the same objects, accounts for incommensurability in terms of difference of objects, and makes both compatible with different forms of cumulative scientific progress.

AGICH, George J. Roles And Responsibilities: Theoretical Issues In The Definition Of Consultation Liaison Psychiatry. *J Med Phil* 10,105–126 My 85.

Central to much medical ethical analysis is the concept of the role of the physician. While this concept plays an important role in medical ethics, its function is largely tacit. The present paper attempts to bring the concept of a social role to prominence by focusing on a historically recent and rather richly contextured role, namely, that of consultation liaison psychiatry. Since my intention is primarily theoretical, I largely ignore the empirical studies which purport to develop the detailed functioning of the role. My limited intent is to draw attention to the theoretical complexity of the consultation liaison role as an example of the general relevance of role concepts to medical ethics. For this reason, consultation liaison psychiatry will function as an illustration of fundamental concepts of medical ethics rather than as a subject of analysis in its own right. Similarly, the concept of the social role will be developed only as is necessary to explore the general relationship between the consultation liaison role and ethical analysis.

AHARONI, Ron. The Direction Of Causation And The Newcomb Paradox (in Hebrew). *Iyyun* 33,505–511 O 84.

The paper discusses the origin of our deep–rooted belief that we cannot determine by our actions past events. The analysis of this belief sheds light on the so–called Newcomb Paradox. In this paradox a situation is presented in which a link exists between a possible action and an event preceding it via a prediction of that action. A solution is offered which explains why such a link cannot be used for determining the event.

AHERN, Barnabas M. Biblical Doctrine On The Rights And Duties Of Man. *Gregorianum* 65,301–317 1984.

This article was intended to provide the biblical doctrine for the document of the International Theological Commision on Human Dignity and Human Rights. The biblical teaching of the Old Testament had to deal with humanity in its gradual maturing from historical beginnings blighted by ignorance and limitation. Biblical teaching in the New Testament treats of human dignity, rights and duties within a context to be progressively illumined by the growing light of Christ.

AHLERS, Rolf. "The Dialectic In Hegel's Philosophy Of History, Joseph Flay (commentator)" in *History And System*, Perkins, Robert (ed), 149–172. Albany SUNY Pr 1984.

AHRENS, John. *Preparing For The Future: An Essay On The Rights Of Future Generations*. Bowling Green Social Phil Ctr 1983.

AIGINGER, Karl. The Impact Of Risk Attitude, Uncertainty And Disequilibria On Optimal Production And Inventory. *Theor Decis* 19,51–75 Jl 85.

The paper derives four alternative sufficient conditions under which economic agents will behave different under uncertainty as compared to certainty. In contrast to the literature we shift importance from risk attitude to technological factors, from equilibrium to disequilibrium and from a mathematical concept of Rational Expectation to economically rational expectation. Empirical data on the risk attitude, on the importance of disequilibria and on asymmetric losses for optimistic respectively pessimistic forecasts are supplied.

AIKEN, William. Value Conflicts In Agriculture. *Agr Human Values* 1,24–27 Wint 84.

A brief exposition of two types of value conflicts which surface in controversies surrounding American agriculture. The first concerns responsibility agriculturalists have toward other people (consumers, future generations, and peoples in other lands); the second concerns their responsibility toward non–human Nature. Since many debates on agricultural policy hinge upon value assumptions in these two areas, an appeal is made to disputants to examine their value differences with an open mind.

AIRAKSINEN, Timo. Coercion, Deterrence, And Authority. *Theor Decis* 17,105–118 S 84.

Coercion and authority are two different forms of social power. Deterrence is a subtype of coercion. Coercion should be analyzed in terms of threats. A definition of authority is given. Authority is a social consensus notion. Unlike coercion, the object of authority–claims can always reject these claims. This does not mean that authority collapses but it makes authority motivationally void. Coercion is never motivationally void.

AIRAKSINEN, Timo. Social Time And Place. *Man World* 18,99–106 1985.

This paper discusses the historical and geographical roots of ethical relativism. Some illustrations are taken from Hegel's philosophy of history. His attitude towards the life and conditions in Black Africa is described. McTaggart's theory of time is used as a methodological tool. His A and B series are used to explicate the construction of the historical distance in time. Relativism entails an interplay between the understanding of distant times and places.

AJKUKIEWICZ, Kazimierz. On Definitions. *Dialec Hum* 11,235–256 Spr/Sum 84.

ALBIZU, Edgardo. La Idea Hegeliana De Materia Y El Tránsito De Lo Ideal A Lo Real. *Dialogos* 20,51–70 Ap 85.

ALBIZU, E. Tiempo Y Lenguaje. *Stromata* 41,63–85 Ja–Je 85.

The author presents an auto–critical extension of Heidegger's thinking. He interprets the idea of *Ereignis* (e–vent) in so far as it leads to the subject of the word (*das Wort*), which gives being and time. Both ideas are studied until one arrives at their confluence with Heidegger's latter thinking, whose consummation lies, beyond metaphysics, in the opening of time. The speciality of Heidegger's thinking is found, then, in the nexus time–language.

ALCHOURRON, Carlos and Bulygin, Eugenio. "Normative Knowledge And Truth" in *Philosophical Analysis In Latin America*, Gracia, Jorge J E and others (eds), 25–46. Boston Reidel 1984.

ALCHOURRON, Carlos and Gardenfors, Peter and Makinson, David. On The Logic Of Theory Change: Partial Meet Contraction And Revision Functions. *J Sym Log* 50,510–530 Je 85.

This paper extends earlier work by its authors on formal aspects of the processes of contracting a theory to eliminate a proposition and revising a theory to introduce a proposition. In the course of the earlier work, Gärdenfors developed general postulates of a more or less equational nature for such processes, whilst Alchourrón and Makinson studied the particular case of contraction functions that are maximal, in the sense of yielding a maximal subset of the theory (or alternatively, of one of its axiomatic bases), that fails to imply the proposition being eliminated. In the present paper, the authors study a broader class, including contraction functions that may be less than maximal. Specifically, they investigate "partial meet contraction functions," which are defined to yield the intersection of some nonempty family of maximal subsets of the theory that fail to imply the proposition being eliminated. (edited)

ALCOFF, Linda and Bell, Linda A. Lordship, Bondage, And The Dialectic Of Work In Traditional Male/Female Relationships. *Cogito* 2,79–94 S 84.

In each of four traditional relationships between women and men—the gallant man and the pedestal woman, the lustful man and the female prostitute, the business man and the female secretary–typist, and the working man and the housewife–mother—there is some recognized subordination of one to the other. Hegel's notions of idle consumption, work, and recognition to help us understand the relative stability of these relationships compared to that of Hegel's lord and bondsman.

ALEXANDER, Elaine and Alexander, Larry. Electronic Monitoring Of Felons By Computer: Threat Or Boon To Civil Liberties? *Soc Theor Pract* 11,89–96 Spr 85.

In this article we examine possible objections, related to bodily integrity and privacy concerns, to computer tracking of convicted felons. We conclude that, with or without the felon's consent, such a practice, appropriately designed, would not contravene any moral or constitutional principles and would undoubtedly be a major deterrent to most crimes.

ALEXANDER, Larry and Alexander, Elaine. Electronic Monitoring Of Felons By Computer: Threat Or Boon To Civil Liberties? *Soc Theor Pract* 11,89–96 Spr 85.

In this article we examine possible objections, related to bodily integrity and privacy concerns, to computer tracking of convicted felons. We conclude that, with or without the felon's consent, such a practice, appropriately designed, would not contravene any moral or constitutional principles and would undoubtedly be a major deterrent to most crimes.

ALEXANDER, Larry and Wang, William. Natural Advantages And Contractual Justice. *Law Phil* 3,281–297 Ag 84.

Anthony Kronman has argued that libertarians cannot distinguish non–arbitrarily between legitimate and illegitimate advantage–taking in contractual relations except by reference to a liberal, wealth–redistributive standard Kronman calls "paretianism." We argue to the contrary that libertarians need not concede that any advantage–taking in contracts is legitimate and thus need not be liberal "paretians" with respect to advantage–taking.

ALEXANDER, Larry. Kidney Pooling. *Cogito* 2,15–20 D 84.

In this article I test the commitment of welfare–state liberals to the imposition of affirmative obligations to aid the less fortunate by examining one such obligation: the obligation to submit to a system that treats healthy kidneys as part of a common pool.

ALEXANDER, Larry. Pursuing The Good—Indirectly. *Ethics* 95,315–332 Ja 85.

In this article, I analyze the practical paradox that attends the pursuit of the Good through the promulgation of rules and the acquisition of dispositions, rules and dispositions that due to their specificity will conflict with achievement of the Good in particular cases. In those cases the indirect pursuit of the Good is inferior to the direct pursuit of the Good, though is superior as an overall strategy. The result, I contend, is a practical paradox that can only be resolved by abandoning the constraint of publicity.

ALEXANDER, Lawrence. Another Look At Moral Blackmail. *Phil Res Arch* 10,189–196 1984.

In this paper I describe cases of moral blackmail as cases where A is told by B that if A does not commit an otherwise immoral act, B will commit an immoral act of equal or greater gravity. I describe cases of moral dilemma as cases where A must commit an otherwise immoral act to avert a natural disaster of equal or greater gravity. I then argue that cases of moral blackmail are structurally identical to cases of moral dilemma in all respects but one: In cases of moral blackmail, A is predicting the free actions of a moral agent (B), whereas in cases of moral dilemma, A is predicting natural events. I conclude that cases of moral blackmail are more problematic than otherwise similar cases of moral dilemma for this reason alone.

ALEXANDER, Lawrence. Reiman's Libertarian Interpretation Of Rawls' Difference Principle. *Phil Res Arch* 10,13–18 1984.

John Rawls' Difference Principle, which requires that primary goods—income, wealth, and opportunities—be distributed so as to maximize the primary goods of the least advantaged class, has both a libertarian and a welfarist interpretation. The welfarist interpretation, which fits somewhat more easily with Rawls' method for deriving principles of justice—rational contractors choosing principles behind the veil of ignorance—and with Rawls' contention that there is a natural affirmative duty to aid others and to help establish and maintain just institutions, is the orthodox interpretation. But there is a scattered, fragmentary evidence for the libertarian interpretation as well. In this article I examine a recent version of the libertarian interpretation put forward by Jeffrey Reiman and discuss the implications as a standard for justice in cooperative arrangements.

ALEXANDER, Meena. "Fallings From Us, Vanishings" in *Existential Coordinates Of Human Condition*, Tymieniecka, A (ed), 91–98. Boston Reidel 1984.

ALEXANDER, Richard D. A Biological Interpretation Of Moral Systems. *Zygon* 20,3–20 Mr 85.

Moral systems are described as systems of indirect reciprocity, existing because of histories of conflicts of interest and arising as outcomes of the complexity of social interactions in groups of long–lived individuals with varying conflicts and confluences of interest and indefinitely iterated social interactions. Although morality is commonly defined as involving justice for all people, or consistency in the social treatment of all humans, it may have arisen for immoral reasons, as a force leading to cohesiveness within human groups but specifically excluding and directed against other human groups with different interests.

ALFARO, Juan. La Cuestión Del Sentido Y El Sentido De La Cuestión. *Gregorianum* 66,387–403 1985.

L–article veut poser de facon radical la question du sens de l'existence humaine. La question provient de la structure auto–reflexive de l'homme; elle surgit de l'expérience de l'existence, qui se révèle comme temporellement limitée à son début comme à sa fin. Une telle expérience manifeste la structure ontologique qui constitue l'homme comme radicalement mis en question.

ALFORD, C Fred. Yates On Feyerabend's Democratic Relativism. *Inquiry* 28,113–118 Mr 85.

Stephen Yates's objections to Feyerabend's political theory (*Inquiry* 27 (1984), pp. 137–142) are presented in a way that makes them unnecessarily vulnerable to a rhetorical strategy often employed by Feyerbend. Like many other critics, Yates seems to assume that it is the implausibility of Feyerbend's claims that opens them to refutation, whereas it is really this that makes them such slippery targets of criticism. Rather than claim that Feyerbend's ideal would be virtually impossible to realize, I argue that Feyerbend does not demonstrate why 'democratic relativism' is at all desirable.

ALFORD, Steven E. *Irony And The Logic Of The Romantic Imagination.* NY Lang 1984.

ALISJAHBANA, S Takdir. The Emerging World And The Task Of Philosophy. *Dialec Hum* 11,431–434 Spr/Sum 84.

The increase of the speed of transportation and communication has suddenly made the world a unity with political, economic and religious conflicts. People are still living with ideas and ideals of the time of the steamship when in reality they already live in the time of the airplane and electronic communication. The whole of mankind shares

the same threat of annihilation. In our age of global amalgamasium in a shrinking planet, greater and more courageous philosophers and religious builders have to arise to bring the existing conflicting structures to new syntheses and creativities. (edited)

ALLARD, Gerald. L'Utopie De Thomas More Ou Le Penseur, Le Pouvoir Et L'engagement. *Laval Theol Phil* 40,309–334 O 84.

ALLEGRETTI, Joseph and Dougherty, Charles. Teaching Ethics In Law School. *Teach Phil* 8,13–26 Ja 85.

The challenge of teaching ethics in law school is described, citing: a training which discourages consideration of ethical dimensions of issues when thinking "like a lawyer," the existence of a professional responsibility code which many take to be exhaustive of the moral responsibilities of attorneys, and the peculiar character of the Angl0–American adversary system of litigation. An ethics course addressing these difficulties is then described. The course is taught by a philosopher and a lawyer, is problem–oriented and discussion–based.

ALLEN, Derek P H. Marx And Engels On The Distributive Justice Of Capitalism. *Can J Phil* Supp 7,221–250 1981.

ALLEN, Diogenes. *Three Outsiders.* Cambridge Cowley 1983.

A study of the "hiddeness of God" in Pascal, Kierkegaard, and Simone Weil. In Pascal the focus is on his analysis of the human condition and human nature, showing thereby the credibility of Christianity. In Kierkegaard the focus is on love of neighbor, as found in his *Works of Love*; in Weil the focus is on love for God, especially as it relates to suffering and natural evil.

ALLEN, H J (ed) and Wilbur, James B (ed). *The Worlds Of Hume And Kant.* Buffalo Prometheus Books 1982.

ALLEN, Jeffner. Husserl's Communal Spirit: A Phenomenological Study Of The Fundamental Structure Of Society. *Phil Soc Crit* 5,67–82 Ja 78.

The paper develops a new direction for Husserl studies on intersubjectivity through examination of issues of intersubjectivity on a societal, rather than the customary individual, level. Central to the research are Husserl's previously unpublished manuscripts on intersubjectivity.

ALLEN, Joseph L. *Love And Conflict: A Covenantal Model Of Christian Ethics.* Nashville Abingdon Pr 1984.

This work offers a convenantal interpretation of human life, reflected in "the inclusive covenant" between God and all persons and in various special covenants. It portrays "covenant love" as the basic standard of Christian ethics. This convenantal view is related to several conflicts of moral claims: between self and others, claims of various covenants, claims to justice, and wrongdoers and the wronged. Finally three special relationships—marriage, political community, and the church—are interpreted covenantally.

ALLEN, Michael J B. *The Platonism Of Marsilio Ficino: A Study Of His Phaedrus Commentary, Its Sources And Genesis.* Berkeley Univ Of Calif Pr 1984.

ALLEN, R E (trans). *The Dialogues Of Plato.* New Haven Yale Univ Pr 1985.

ALLEN, Robert Van Roden. Beyond Hegel's Ontological Claim. *Dialogue (Canada)* 23,305–314 Je 84.

Allen discusses what he terms the ontological claim in Hegel's *Logic*. Through an initial discussion of Charles Taylor's approach to Hegel and through an historical contrast of Hegel's ontological claim with the intent of the Kantian categories, Allen moves directly to consider Hegel's *Logic* as a development of the *Phenomenology*. In this context, he then explores the primacy of the ontological claim for Hegel's work, the possibility of nihilism consequent upon its collapse, and an access to a post–Hegelian and post–nihilistic future for human thought and activity.

ALMEDER, Robert F (ed) and Humber, James M (ed). *Biomedical Ethics Reviews.* Clifton Humana Pr 1983.

biomedical Ethics Reviews: 1983 is the first volume in a series of texts designed to review and update the literature on issues of centra importance in bioethics today. Five topics are discussed in the present volume: "Euthanasia", "Surrogate Gestation", "The Distribution of Health Care", "The Involuntary Commitment and Treatment of Mentally Ill Persons", and "Patenting New Life Forms". Two articles deal with each topic; all essays are previously unpublished.

ALMEDER, Robert T (ed) and Humber, James M (ed). *Biomedical Ethics Reviews.* Clifton Humana Pr 1984.

ALMEDER, Robert. "Scarcity And Basic Medical Care" in *Biomedical Ethics Reviews*, Humber, James M (ed), 95–106. Clifton Humana Pr 1983.

ALMEDER, Robert. Peirce's Thirteen Theories Of Truth. *Trans Peirce Soc* 21,77–94 Wint 85.

In this paper I show that no fewer than thirteen distinct interpretations of Peirce's views on truth exist in the literature, that most are the product of sloppy scholarship, that the standard view is wrong, and that the only two plausible views are offered by N Rescher and David Savan respectively. Whether the correct view of what Peirce argued is defensible is not examined.

ALMOG, Joseph. Semantical Anthropology. *Midwest Stud Phil* 9,479–490 1984.

ALONSO, Dra Luz García. Constitutivo Interno, Finalidad Y Génesis Del Artefacto Bello. *Logos (Mexico)* 13,109–118 Ja–Ap 85.

ALONSO, Luz Garcia. Ensayo Didáctico: Una Pieza Teatral Para La Enseñanza De Antropología Filosófica. *Logos (Mexico)* 8,91–104 My–Ag 85.

Esta pieza teatral se intitula "Las fuerzas del hombre". Los personales son las facultades y la naturaleza humanas. Cada una explica sus funciones y sus relaciones con los demas.

ALONSO, Luz Garcia. La Abstracción En El Pensamiento Tomista. *Logos (Mexico)* 12,103–115 My–Ag 84.

ALONSO, Luz García. Visión Filosófica De La Cultura Desde La Perspectiva Actual. *Logos (Mexico)* 12,121–127 S–D 84.

Modern man ignores the true nature, and the ends of culture, and that is why he also ignores his role in regard to it. The complexity of contemporary culture includes intuition, thus difficulting its intelligibility making a paradox. The solution to this paradox consists in achieving the excellence of man, which will enable him to understand that which is too obscure because it is so bright.

ALPERN, Kenneth D. Moral Responsibility For Engineers. *Bus Prof Ethics J* 2,39–48 Wint 83.

This paper argues that ordinary moral principles create a high degree of moral responsibility for engineers practicing in large organizations. The merits of several commonly heard excuses for questionable activities are considered. These excuses, colloquially put, are: "I'd lose my job if I didn't;" "If I don't, someone else will;" "It's not my job;" and "There's no alternative."

ALPERSON, Philip. On Musical Improvisation. *J Aes Art Crit* 43,17–30 Fall 84.

The nature and significance of improvisation in music are not much discussed by philosophers. In this paper, I examine certain assumptions which I believe to underlie our familiar ways of thinking about musical improvisation, and I advance an analysis which I hope will lead to a philosophical understanding of improvisation in music, indicating the essential aesthetic value of this activity in the context of more general questions of aesthetic theory and artistic practice.

ALSTON, William P. "Christian Experience And Christian Belief" in *Faith And Rationality*, Plantinga, Alvin (ed), 103–134. Notre Dame Univ Notre Dame Pr 1983.

ALSTON, William P. Concepts Of Epistemic Justification. *Monist* 62,57–89 Ja 85.

Different understandings of what we are saying of a belief when we say that it is justified are distinguished and interrelated. On "deontological" conceptions, to be justified in believing that *p* is to be free of blame (for violation of intellectual obligations) in believing that *p*. On "evaluative" conceptions it is rather a matter of one's believing that *p*, as one does, being a good thing from the epistemic point of view. Reasons are given for rejecting deontological conceptions and for preferring a form of evaluative conception according to which justification is a matter of being based on an adequate ground.

ALSTON, William P. Divine–Human Dialogue And The Nature Of God. *Faith Phil* 2,5–20 Ja 85.

What must be true of God and God's relation to the world is genuine divine–human dialogue is to be possible? This paper considers certain facets of this problem. It is argued that (1) such dialogue is not possible if God determines every detail of His creation, (2) such dialogue is compatible with divine omniscience only if God is timeless, and (3) contrary to what might be supposed, genuine dialogue with a timeless God is possible.

ALSTON, William P. Functionalism And Theological Language. *Amer Phil Quart* 22,221–230 Jl 85.

This paper uses a functionalist account of psychological concepts to show that the radical "otherness" of God is compatible with a degree of univocity in the application of psychological concepts to human beings and to God. The basic idea is that on a functionalist theory the concept of a psychological state or activity is a concept of a functional role in the operation of the psyche; the same concept of a belief or a desire can be applied to beings that are radically different in nature and in which this function is carried out in radically different ways. Thus the radical difference between God and us does not of itself prevent the application of the same functional concepts. Upon further consideration it turns out that although human psychological concepts cannot be applied to God in just the same form, we can specify more abstract functional concepts that can plausible be claimed to have a common application.

ALTRICHTER, Ferenc. Belief And Possibility. *J Phil* 82,364–381 Jl 85.

ALVES, Elias H. Paraconsistent Logic And Model Theory. *Stud Log* 43,17–32 1984.

The object of this paper is to show how one is able to construct a paraconsistent theory of models that reflects much of the classical one. In other words, the aim is to demonstrate that there is a very smooth and natural transition from the model theory of classical logic to that of certain categories of paraconsistent logic. (edited)

AMADO, Maria Teresa and Lisboa, Joao Luis. Moral Y Politica En "Para La Paz Perpetua" De Kant. *Pensamiento* 40,431–458 O–D 84.

To Kant peace is a categorical imperative. It is the realization of the reign of reason and freedom of the will. It corresponds to the maximum of humanization permitting the insertion of the individual in the Human Community. The kantian idea that the world is a rational construction therefore acquires ontological value. Kant bases theoretically the action on constructing politics in the moral theories, thus ruling the basic moral principle. The rational law will be the ground of this action.

AMAGASAKI, Kikuko. Problem Of Rhetoric In Plato's *Phaedrus* (in Japanese). *Bigaku* 35,25–36 S 84.

The apparent elusiveness or inconsistency of Plato's view of rhetoric has engendered a vast accumulation of commentary, and the only uniformity of commentators is, according to Edwin Black, the judgement that Plato was rhetoric's most effective historical opponent. But we don't agree to it. Plato differentiated so–called rhetoric and true one in the *Phaedrus*, the constructive complement of the *Gorgias*. In both dialogues, at least, there cannot be found out any general condemnation of rhetoric.

AMATI, Frank and Aspromourgos, Tony. Petty *Contra* Hobbes: A Previously Untranslated Manuscript. *J Hist Ideas* 46,127–132 Ja–Mr 85.

AMATO MANGIAMELI, Agata C. Amleto E Il Tragico: A Proposito Di Un Saggio Di Carl Schmitt. *Riv Int Filosof Diritto* 61,324–336 Ap–Je 84.

AMBROSE, Alice and Lazerowitz, Morris. *Essays In The Unknown Wittgenstein.* Buffalo Prometheus Books 1984.

This book makes application to a number of philosophical problems, certain statements which Wittgenstein made about their nature. For the most part they are inconoclastic statements which have received little attention, but which promise an understanding of the inconclusiveness of philosophical views. Views chosen for illustration are: *a priori* necessity, the infinite, mathematical proof, abstract entities, empiricism, solipsism.

AMBROSELLI, Claire. France: A National Committee Debates The Issues. *Hastings Center Rep* 14,20–21 D 84.

AMBROSETTI, Giovanni. Il Diritto Come Valore: Osservazioni Sulla Filosofia Del Diritto Di Enrico Opocher. *Riv Int Filosof Diritto* 61,569–577 O–D 84.

AMENGUAL, Gabriel. L Feuerbach En La Crítica Marxista: Hacia Una Reconsideración De Su Lugar En La Discusión Marxista Actual. *Pensamiento* 41,201–216 Ap–Je 85.

Se expone la aportación propia de L Feuerbach: superación de toda escisión (identidad) y toda mediación (inmediatez). Esta identidad en inmediatez es presentada a base de dos conceptos fundamentales. (complementarios entre sí): sensibilidad y naturaleza (pp 207–211). Propuesta de relectura postmariana de L Feuerbach dentro de la discusión marxista, valorando su aportación, puesta de relieve por la Escuela de Frankfurt, el problema ecológico.

AMERIKS, Karl. Hegel's Critique Of Kant's Theoretical Philosophy. *Phil Phenomenol Res* 46,1–36 S 85.

This paper analyzes Hegel's critique of Kant's theoretical philosophy in terms of three specific objections to Kant's transcendental deduction (concerning the representation of the I, the necessity of the categories, and the problem of a preliminary epistemology) and three specific objections to Kant's transcendental idealism (concerning the thing in itself, the Antinomies, and other specific problems of the Transcendental Dialectic).

AMÉRY, Jean and Rosenfeld, Sidney (ed) and Rosenfeld, Stella (ed). *Radical Humanism*. Bloomington Indiana Univ Pr 1984.

AMES, Roger T. On The Contingency Of Confucius' Emergent *Tao*. *Phil Rev (Taiwan)* 7,117–140 Ja 84.

AMIR, Yehoshua. "The Finite Thou And The Eternal Thou In The Work Of Buber" in *Martin Buber*, Gordon, Haim (ed), 69–88. Beersheva Ktav 1984.

AMUNDSON, Ron and Smith, Laurence. Clark Hull, Robert Cummins, And Functional Analysis. *Phil Sci* 51,657–666 D 84.

Robert Cummins has recently used the program of Clark Hull to illustrate the effects of logical positivist epistemology upon psychological theory. On Cummins' account, Hull's theory is best understood as a functional analysis, rather than a nomological subsumption. Hull's commitment to the logical positivist view of explanation is said to have blinded him to this aspect of his theory, and thus restricted its scope. We will argue this interpretation of Hull's epistemology, though common, is mistaken. Hull's epistemological views were developed independently of, and in considerable contrast to, the principles of logical positivism.

ANCESCHI, Luciano. "Criticism, Philosophy, Phenomenology" in *Continental Philosophy And The Arts*, Winters, Laurence E and others (ed), 243–264. Lanham Univ Pr Of America 1984.

ANDERSON, Albert A. Seeking The Source: Cultural Relativism And The Arts. *Ideal Stud* 15,101–120 My 85.

The problem of cultural relativism is posed through comparing two literary texts, John Gardner's *Grendel* and the eighth–century version of that story. Solving this problem requires ontological analysis. Plato's *Sophist* provides an ontology which helps in this task, but only after the dualistic ontology frequently attributed to Plato is discarded through arguments presented in Plato's *Parmenides*. A contemporary response to the problem of relativism is developed around the concept of the manifestation of ideas.

ANDERSON, C A. Divine Omnipotence And Impossible Tasks: An Intensional Analysis. *Int J Phil Relig* 15,109–124 1984.

Atheists argue that omnipotence is an inconsistent concept because it requires, for example, the ability to create unliftable stones. The standard reply, that omnipotence entails only the ability to perform possible tasks, is here defended against critics. A formalization, in an intensional logic, of the Paradox of the Stone is given which seems to show that alternative solutions fail. A definition of omnipotence compatible with the standard solution is suggested.

ANDERSON, C Anthony. "General Intensional Logic" in *Handbook Of Philosophical Logic*, Gabbay, Dov (ed), 355–386. Boston Reidel 1984.

ANDERSON, Douglas. Peirce And Metaphor. *Trans Peirce Soc* 20,453–468 Fall 84.

This article examines Peirce's technical use of metaphor. In doing so it looks at certain aspects of his semiotics and, in particular, his division of signs into icons, indexes, and symbols. The upshot is that, for peirce, metaphor plays a central role in artistic thought while analogy is central to scientific thought.

ANDERSON, James C. Musical Kinds. *Brit J Aes* 25,43–49 Wint 85.

The paper attempts to provide an ontology of musical works that accounts for two intuitions which seem to be in conflict: i. That musical works are abstract entities not to be identified with their various scores and performances; and ii. That musical works are created. It is argued that musical works are norm–kinds but, contrary to Wolterstorff, some norm–kinds, among them musical works, are brought into existence by way of human creative activity.

ANDERSON, Lyle V. Moral Dilemmas, Deliberation, And Choice. *J Phil* 82,139–161 Mr 85.

ANDERSON, Lyle V. The Representation And Resolution Of The Nuclear Conflict. *Phil Soc Crit* 10,67–80 Wint 84.

ANDERSON, Paul A. Foreign Policy As A Goal Directed Activity. *Phil Soc Sci* 14,159–182 Je 84.

Although definitions of 'foreign policy' invariably make reference to action directed at achieving some end, it is not at all clear whether any collective can act in a goal directed manner. This paper develops an account of goal directedness which does not presume a controlling mind and identifies four properties which any system must satisfy if it is to be capable of goal directed behavior. Thus, whether foreign policy is goal directed depends upon whether our theories of governments imply the truth of the four necessary properties. The paper concludes with a discussion of the implications of the analysis for the study of foreign policy.

ANDERSON, R J and Sharrock, W W. Understanding Peter Winch. *Inquiry* 28,119–122 Mr 85.

Peter Winch's *The Idea of Social Science* has been the subject of repeated misunderstanding. This discussion takes one recent example and shows how Winch's argument is gravely distorted. What is at issue is not, as is usually supposed, whether we can accept or endorse another society's explanations of its activities, but whether we *have* to look for an explanatory connection between concepts and action. winch's argument is that before we can try to explain actions, we have to identify them correctly. This can only be done by seeing how they, and the concepts they are associated with, fit within a way of life. Grasping its rule–following character is understanding action. Once the difficulties in making such identifications are appreciated, we will be less inclined to accept facile explanations why people in other societies do the things they do.

ANDERSON, Scott William. Dasein As Self: Some Implications Of Heideggerian Ontology. *Kinesis* 14,106–129 Spr 85.

ANDERSON, Tyson. Wittgenstein And Nāgārjuna's Paradox. *Phil East West* 35,157–170 Ap 85.

It is argued against certain authors that Nagarjuna's work is more comparible to Wittgenstein's *Tractatus* than to the *Philosophical Investigations*. Nagarjuna's pithy and oracular pronouncements on behalf of "emptiness" paradoxically resulted historically in more words rather than silence, thus suggesting that further reflections on language and reality are needed.

ANDERSON, W French. Human Gene Therapy: Scientific And Ethical Considerations. *J Med Phil* 10,275–292 Ag 85.

The term 'gene therapy' encompasses at least four types of application of genetic engineering for the insertion of genes into humans. The scientific requirements of the ethical issues associated with each type are discussed. Somatic cell gene therapy is technically the simplest and ethically the least controversial. The first clinical trials will probably be undertaken within the next year. Germ line gene therapy will require major advances in our present knowledge and it raises ethical issues that are now being debated. In order to provide guidelines for determining when germ line gene therapy would be ethical, the author presents three criteria which should be satisfied prior to the time that a clinical protocol is attempted in humans. Enhancement genetic engineering presents significant, and troubling, ethical concerns. Except where this type of engineering can be justified on the grounds of preventive medicine, enhancement engineering should not be performed. The fourth type, eugenic genetic engineering, is impossible at present and will probably remain so for the foreseeable future, despite the widespread media attention it has received.

ANDRADE, Ciro Schmidt. Concepto De Historicidad En "Ser Y Tiempo de Martin Heidegger. *Pensamiento* 40,459–488 O–D 84.

The purpose of this work is to reflect on the historicity of Heidegger's thought, through a vision of chapter V and II of "Sein und Zeit", relating it to his whole problematic. It's attempted to show the historicity concept, it's only understood from an ontologic comprehension, being the horizon in which Truth and Being are revealed. The essence of the history lies in the Being, and Man (Dasein) is his humble and vigilant shepherd.

ANDRE, Judith. Power, Oppression And Gender. *Soc Theor Pract* 11,107–121 Spr 85.

Traditional relationships between middle–class men and women reveal that the oppressed may have power and yet remain oppressed: first, because undue attention paid to that power may signal and partially constitute oppression; secondly because the need to use morally próscribed forms of power—such as manipulation—may also manifest and partially constitute oppression (manipulation: the deliberate but concealed attempt to influence someone's attitudes and actions); finally, because it is authority, not power alone, which confers status.

ANDREWS, Christine. Jean–Paul Sartre And The Problem Of The Other. *Dialogue (PST)* 27,23–28 O 84.

ANDREWS, Stephen Pearl. "Love, Marriage And Divorce" in *Freedom, Feminism, And The State*, Mc Elroy, Wendy (ed), 143–154. Cato Institute Washington 1982.

ANDRLE, Pavel. Thermodynamics, Man, Universe (in Czechoslovakian). *Filozof Cas* 32,901–903 1984.

ANDRZEJEWSKI, Boleslaw. Der Pragmatismus Und Praktizismus In Polen. *Z Phil Forsch* 29,453–461 Jl–S 75.

ANGELELLI, Ignacio. El Triángulo Universal De Locke: Su Inmerecida Fama. *Rev Latin De Filosof* 11,47–54 Mr 85.

Main target of the paper is the famous Lockian phrase about the general triangle, which is "neither oblique nor rectangle, but all and none of these at once". It is shown how in the scholastic tradition this issue had been treated in a much more refined way.

ANGELELLI, Ignacio. Frege And Abstraction. *Phil Natur* 21,453–471 1984.

The main goal of the essay is to examine all Frege's texts on the concept of *abstraction*. The content of these passages is then classified and analyzed. Frege refers to an "ordinary abstraction", to a "magical abstraction" and, very incidentally, to "definitions by abstraction". Frege, however, is not interested in abstraction: he thinks this notion belongs in psychology. The article refers also to "modern

abstraction" (P Lorenzen), a view of abstraction unknown to frege.

ANGUELOV, Stephan. Man, Science, Morality. *Stud Soviet Tho* 29,65–70 Ja 85.

ANNAS, George J. "Legal Aspects Of Ethics Committees" in *Ethics Committees And Health Care Decisions*, Cranford, Ronald (ed), 51–59. Ann Arbor Health Admin Pr 1984.

ANNAS, George J. Baby Fae: The "Anything Goes School Of Human Experimentation". *Hastings Center Rep* 15,15–16 F 85.

ANNAS, George J. Law And The Life Sciences. *Hastings Center Rep* 14,23–25 Ag 84.

ANNAS, George J. Prisoner In The ICU: The Tragedy Of William Bartling. *Hastings Center Rep* 14,28–29 D 84.

ANNIS, David B. Informed Consent, Autonomy, And The Law. *Phil Res Arch* 10,249–260 1984.

Informed consent to therapy is the legal doctrine which imposes on a physician the duty to explain the nature and risks of a proposed treatment so the patient can make an informed decision whether to undergo the treatment. The doctrine has spawned tremendous controversy in the legal and medical professions. In this paper I examine the doctrine of informed consent as developed by the courts. The thrust of my criticism is that as the doctrine has been developed, it significantly undercuts individual autonomy. Several modifications are suggested which would provide more support for autonomy interests.

ANSCOMBE, G E M. Were You A Zygote? *Philosophy* 18,111–116 84 Supp.

Identical twins raise a problem whether the zygoto is a human who splits or from which another sprouts or is already two humans or is not yet a human, but with organization and differentiation of cells becomes one or more humans.

ANTHONY, Susan. "Trade Unionism And Women's Work" in *Freedom, Feminism, And The State*, Mc Elroy, Wendy (ed), 237–266. Cato Institute Washington 1982.

APEL OTTO, Karl and Warnke, Georgia (trans). *Understanding And Explanation: A Transcendental–Pragmatic Perspective*. Cambridge MIT Pr 1985.

APEL, Karl–Otto. The Situation Of Humanity As An Ethical Problem. *Praxis Int* 4,250–265 O 84.

APOSTEL, Leo. Theory And Practice In Marxism. *Philosophica* 34,3–22 1984.

The author compares three answers to the question "Why should a Marxist be a socialist?" (the purely factual answer of Kautsky–Plechanov, the Kantian answers of Austro Marxism, and the epistemological and activist answers of Lucacz and Korsch. He criticizes all three and tries to formulate in six points the elements of an answer taking into account recent philosophical and scientific research. The socialism defended is self–governing socialism.

APOSTOL, Pavel. About Mario Bunge's 'A Critical Examination Of Dialectics'. *Stud Soviet Tho* 29,89–136 F 85.

APPIAH, Anthony. An Argument Against Anti–Realist Semantics. *Mind* 93,559–565 O 84.

In this paper I argue that no theory of meaning given purely in terms of assertibility conditions can work. The basic argument is due to Demmett, but was developed by Brandom in his J. phil. Paper "Truth and Assertibility." Essentially the argument is that assertibility conditions of compound sentences are not a function of those of their component sentences, while meanings of compound sentences *are* functions of the meanings of components. I develop this insight by showing why this is.

APPIAH, Anthony. Generalising The Probabilistic Semantics Of Conditionals. *J Phil Log* 13,351–372 N 84.

Adams has offered an account of the indicative conditionals as assertible if the probability of the consequent given the antecedent is high. I argue that, since "probable" means "probably true", this account only works where antecedent and consequent have truth conditions; and I defend a more general view, which has his treatment as a special case. I test the general theory out on some conditional with the modal "may" in their consequents.

APPLEBAUM, Eleanor Gordon and Firestein, Stephen K. *A Genetic Counseling Casebook.* NY Free Pr 1983.

APTER, Arthur W. An AD–like Model. *J Sym Log* 50,531–543 Je 85.

APTER, Michael. "Metaphor As Synergy" in *Metaphor*, Miall, David S (ed), 55–70. Atlantic Highlands Humanities Pr 1982.

AQUILA, Richard E. Necessity And Irreversibility In The Second Analogy. *Hist Phil Quart* 2,203–216 Ap 85.

AQUINAS, Thomas. *Questions On The Soul*, James H Robb (trans). Milwaukee Marquette Univ Pr 1984.

AQVIST, Lennart. "Deontic Logic" in *Handbook Of Philosophical Logic*, Gabbay, Dov (ed), 605–714. Boston Reidel 1984.

ARATO, Andrew and Cohen, Jean. Social Movements, Civil Society, And The Problem Of Sovereignty. *Praxis Int* 4,266–283 O 84.

ARAÚJO, Luís De. Ortega E Gasset: Perfil Ético De Uma Filosofia. *Rev Port Filosof* 40,248–263 Jl–S 84.

ARAZZI, Graziella. I Percorsi Multipli Dell'epistemologia Di G Bachelard: Il Rapporto Filosofia–Epistemologia: Problemi E Dinamiche. *Sapienza* 37,149–177 Ap–Je 84.

The purpose of this work is of demonstrating the Bachelard's epistemology to oppose to the Kant's criticism. It is based on two orders of grounds: (a) the Kant's system stand for a closed reason not suitable the complexity of the scientific facts to recorder; (b) the synthesis of the epistemology makes against to Kant's system a dialectic between the reality and the thought that produces the ontological dynamics of the rectification of the concepts and notions.

ARCHAMBAULT, Paul J. Augustine, Memory, And The Development Of Autobiography. *Augustin Stud* 13,23–30 1982.

ARCHER, Dermot J. Tolstoy's God Sees The Truth, But Waits: A Reflection. *Relig Stud* 21,75–90 Mr 85.

ARIEW, Roger. Galileo's Lunar Observations In The Context Of Medieval Lunar Theory. *Stud Hist Phil Sci* 15,213–226 S 84.

I argue that since the medieval theory of lunar light (Averroes' elaboration of Aristotle's theory) is not that light is reflected off the surface of the moon, but that the moon receives sunlight in proportion to its density, Galileo's observations of "mountains on the moon," which assume that sunlight is reflected off the moon, cannot succeed in demolishing Aristotelian cosmology by destroying the distinction between the sublunar and celestial substances, as it is often claimed.

ARIEW, Roger. The Duhem Thesis. *Brit J Phil Sci* 35,313–325 D 84.

Close reading of Duhem's text and its variations reveals the many limitations that Duhem imposed upon his own thesis. Based on that reading, I argue that (i) Duhem's thesis is not the same as the Duhem–Quine thesis and cannot be faulted by the criticism that would be proper against the Duhem–Quine thesis, and that (ii) Duhem's primary thesis is the separability thesis and that he regards the falsifiability thesis to be a consequence of the separability thesis.

ARISIAN, Khoren. The Religious Humanism Of The Future. *Relig Hum* 19,62–68 Spr 85.

ARISIAN, Khoren. The Religious Humanism Of The Future. *Relig Hum* 19,23–31 Wint 85.

ARISIAN, Khoren. The Religious Humanism Of The Future. *Relig Hum* 19,122–131 Sum 85.

ARKINS, B. Epicurus And Lucretius On Sex, Love, And Marriage. *Apeiron* 18,141–143 1984.

The purpose of this note is to argue (1) that Epicurus condoned casual sexual intercourse, condemned sexual love, and approved of marriage under certain circumstances, and (2) that Epicurus' Roman disciple, Lucretius, adheres strictly to the doctrines of his philosophical mentor in these matters.

ARKOUN, Mohammed. Positivism And Tradition In An Islamic Perspective: Kemalism. *Diogenes* 127,82–100 Fall 84.

How Kemal Atatürk perceived Islamic tradition through his positivist ideology and his will to create a secularist nation according to the European model of 19th Century.

ARMENGAUD, Françoise. De H P Grice À F Jacques: Remarques Sur La Maxime Pragmatique De Pertinence. *Rev Metaph Morale* 89,389–404 Jl–S 84.

A context–sensitive and pragmatic definition of relevance is looked for. Knowledge about relevance is different from knowledge as such. From a transcendental point of view it has to do with categorial conditions of knowledge. Grice's maxim is estimated not sufficiently explained. The characterization of communicative relevance by Francis Jacques in *Dialogiques* (Paris 1979) is made explicit.

ARMON– JONES, Claire. Prescription, Explication And The Social Construction Of Emotion. *J Theor Soc Behav* 15,1–22 Mr 85.

The aim of the paper is to examine the claim that emotions are socioculturally constructed phenomena. Two theses concerning the ontological and semantic status of 'emotion feeling' are proposed which permit the extension of the role of prescription to emotion acquisition. I conclude that emotion experience and behavior can be regarded as responses prescribed for appropriate contexts, and as having a special function in maintaining the sociocultural beliefs and values embedded in such prescriptions.

ARMSTRONG, A H. *L'architecture De L'univers Intelligible Dans La Philosophie De Plotin.* Ottawa Univ D'Ottawa 1984.

French translation of a work published in 1940 and re–published in 1967, by now fairly well known to Plotinus specialists. It has a new preface by the author with some versions and corrections of his earlier views.

ARMSTRONG, A M. The Idea Of The Comic. *Brit J Aes* 25,232–238 Sum 85.

Theories setting forth what renders something comic are all inadequate, since there is no such ground. It would be hopeless to try generalizing from instances of the comic, but if we ask what we are getting up to when we are being intentionally comic, the answer is that we are engaging in levity, foolery and trifling. The essence of the unintentionally comic then proves to gravity–removal.

ARMSTRONG, D M. "D M Armstrong—Self Profile" in *D M Armstrong*, Bogdan, Radu J (ed), 3–54. Boston Reidel 1984.

ARMSTRONG, D M. "Replies" in *D M Armstrong*, Bogdan, Radu J (ed), 225–269. Boston Reidel 1984.

ARMSTRONG, D M. Laws Of Nature As Relations Between Universals And As Universals. *Phil Topics* 13,7–24 Spr 82.

It is argued that laws of nature are objective, contingent, relations between universals. They issue in, but are more than, mere regularities. These relationships are themselves universals, so that the instantiation of a law is a special case of the instantiation of a universal.

ARMSTRONG, Robert L. Friendship. *J Value Inq* 19,211–216 1985.

The purpose of this paper is to formulate a more precise and comprehensive definition of friendship than the several dictionary definitions that are presented. The observations, theories and opinions of Ralph Waldo Emerson and C S Lewis are examined at some length. Reference is also made to Aristotle and others. The new definition (Friendship is a non–sexual relationship of two people, based upon shared experience and characterized by mutual personal regard, understanding, and loyalty) is examined and compared to the dictionary definitions. The intrinsic worth of friendship is emphasized and friendly acts are explained in terms of their source rather than their purpose.

ARNESON, Richard J. Shakespeare And The Jewish Question. *Polit Theory* 13,85–111 F 85.

Should persons be free to contract with any persons whatsoever on mutually

agreeable terms and be bound to those terms? In my view Shakespeare's *The Merchant of Venice* answers "No" for interesting reasons that amount to a criticism of the young Marx's treatment of the same theme.

ARNOLD, Alfred. Philosophische Fragen Der Wissenschaftsentwicklung. *Deut Z Phil* 22,749–752 1974.

ARNOLD, N Scott. Capitalists And The Ethics Of Contribution. *Can J Phil* 15,87–102 Mr 85.

The author reconstructs and criticizes a common socialist argument that the capitalist, *qua* capitalist, is a "parasite" who makes no productive contribution. The time preference theory of interest developed by economists such as Fetter and Rothbard is used to explain why capitalists do receive a return on their investments. In effect, the capitalist contributes time by exchanging present goods, (capital, money) for future goods (principle plus interest). A final section discusses some ambiguities in the concept of contribution.

ARNOLD, Peter J. Three Approaches Toward An Understanding Of Sportsmanship. *J Phil Sport* 10,61–70 1983.

ARNOLD, Peter. Sport, Moral Education And The Development Of Character. *J Phil Educ* 18,275–280 1984.

ARNSTINE, Donald. Equality, Excellence, Paideia, And The Good Old Days Before Adam And Eve And Social Science. *Proc Phil Educ* 40,309–312 1984.

Neither equity nor excellence can serve as educational objectives because they refer to the *manner*, not the *matter* of teaching. Thus to conduct schooling equitably and excellently gives us no clue about what (e.G., math, music, backpacking) should appear in the curriculum. Heedless of this, Mortimer Adler (*The Paideia Proposal*) dictates a universal curriculum and, likening children's intelligence to different–sizd containers, thinks equity consists in pouring this same curriculum into each container until all are filled to the brim.

ARONOWITZ, Stanley. Academic Freedom: A Structural Approach. *Educ Theor* 35,1–14 Wint 85.

The purpose of this article is to show that issues of the organization of American academic life, the credentialling process and teacher tenure are structurally linked to academic freedom. Further, it argues that scientific criteria for evaluating research are elements of political and ideological constraints of the professoriate. Further, that the current cutbacks in university funding are policies inimical to the general social interest.

ARONSON, Jerrold. Conditions Versus Transference: A Reply To Ehring. *Synthese* 63,249–256 My 85.

The transference model of causation is compared to the more traditional conditions analysis and it is defended against a series of objections to it presented by Douglas Ehring in "The Transference View of Causation".

AROSKAR, Mila Ann. "Health Care Professionals And Ethical Relationships On IECs" in *Ethics Committees/Health Care Decisions*, Cranford, Ronald (ed), 218–225. Ann Arbor Health Admin Pr 1984.

ARRAS, John D. "Utility, Natural Rights, And The Right To Health Care" in *Biomedical Ethics Reviews*, Humber, James M (ed), 23–46. Clifton Humana Pr 1984.

ARRINGTON, Robert L. "Mental Illness And Crime" in *Biomedical Ethics Reviews*, Humber, James M (ed), 149–162. Clifton Humana Pr 1983.

ARRINGTON, Robert L and Deitz, Samuel M. Wittgenstein's Language–Games And The Call To Cognition. *Behaviorism* 12,1–14 Fall 84.

The transition toward cognitive issues in radical behaviorism is examined. The article shows how the conceptual analysis provided by Wittgenstein in his descriptions of language–games can assist behaviorists in evaluating that transition. Various philosophical theories of meaning are discussed as are four components of language–games. It is concluded that Wittgenstein's analysis allows behaviorists to use cognitive terms within a behavioristic system; with such a system, sharper distinctions among types of behavior are possible.

ARRUDA, Ayda I and Da Costa, Newton C A. On The Relevant Systems **p** And **p*** And Some Related Systems. *Stud Log* 43,33–50 1984.

In this paper we study the systems **P** and **P***(see Arruda and da Costa, *O paradoxo de Curry–Moh Shaw–Kwei*, Boletim da Sociedade Matemática de São Paulo 18 (1966)) and some related systems. In the last section, we prove that certain set theories having **P** and **P***as their underlying logics are non–trivial.

ARRUDA, Ayda I. N A Vasil'év: A Forerunner Of Paraconsistent Logic. *Phil Natur* 21,472–491 1984.

ART, Robert J. Between Assured Destruction And Nuclear Victory: The Case For The "Mad–Plus" Posture. *Ethics* 95,497–516 Ap 85.

The purpose of the article is to argue that neither a finite deterrent nor a war–winning posture for nuclear forces is sensible. The "MAD–plus" position argues that nuclear weapons deter a whole range of political actions and that for esculation control some limited counterforce options are required.

ARTAMENDI, P. Acción Y Contemplación: Una Carta De San Agustín A Los Monjes De La Isla De Cabrera. *Augustinus* 25,23–28 Ja–D 80.

ARTHUR, Alcott. ROBOTS, RIFs, And Rights. *J Bus Ethics* 4,197–204 Je 85.

The increasing use of technological advances in business operations very often leads to the displacement of the employee whose skills become obsolete in light of such advances. There is no doubt that the interests of both company and employee are significantly affected by the implementation of labor–saving devices. Given that those interests are pursued in an environment which is usually, if not essentially, competitive, then there arises the serious question of what rights should be accorded the employee and the company in the event that the employee is likely to be displaced by technological innovation. I argue that, given the constraints of a competitive environment, certain rights must be justified through a very limited application of the highly morally intuitive principles of utility, respect for persons, fairness, and the honoring of contracts.

ASH, C J and Downey, R G. Decidable Subspaces And Recursively Enumerable Subspaces. *J Sym Log* 49,1137–1145 D 84.

ASHER, Nicholas M and Bonevac, Daniel. How Extensional Is Extensional Perception? *Ling Phil* 8,203–228 My 85.

ASHER, Nicholas and Bonevac, Daniel. Situations And Events. *Phil Stud* 47,57–78 Ja 85.

ASHER, Nicholas. The Trouble With Extensional Semantics. *Phil Stud* 47,1–14 Ja 85.

ASHLEY, Benedict M and O' Rourke, Kevin D. *Health Care Ethics: A Theological Analysis.* St Louis Cath Health Assoc 1982.

A comprehensive treatment of bioethics from a Roman Catholic, but ecumenical, perspective. Patients' rights, professional ethics, confidentiality, the social organization of health care, scarce resources, reproduction, transplantation, experimentation, genetic reconstruction, behavior control, dying and pastoral care are treated in detail. Chapters seven and eight provide a systematic discussion of the methodology and guiding principles of medical–ethical decision. Extensive bibliography and index.

ASHWORTH, E Jennifer. Mental Language And The Unity Of Propositions: A Semantic Problem Discussed By Early Sixteenth Century Logicians. *Fran Stud* 41,61–96 1981.

In the 14th century Gregory of Rimini argued that (1) there is a mental language separate from spoken language and (2) mental propositions are unified wholes with no discernible parts. This article examines the reactions of later logicians, showing that they accepted the doctrine of mental language; but argued that mental propositions must have a discernible structure, which involves parts.

ASMIS, Elizabeth. *Epicurus' Scientific Method.* Ithaca Cornell Univ Pr 1984.

This is a study of Epicurus's method of scientific inquiry. It deals both with the theory (the "canonic") and its application in Epicurus's physics. The author concludes that Epicurus proposed a single, unified, empirical method which consists in drawing conclusions from the phenomena, understood as the immediate data of sensory perception. It is argued that Epicurus derived this method, known to Aristotle as the method of "signs," from the early atomists.

ASOUZU, Innocent. Eine Analyse Und Kritische Bewertung Der Methode Und Des Prinzips Der Praktischen Argumentation Oswald Schwemmers. *Conceptus* 18,85–103 1984.

This essay aims at a critical presentation and evaluation of one of the mostly discussed aspects of Constructive Theory of Science. The aspect in question is concerned with the Method and the Principle of practical arguments over norms and the goals of human action. This theory was first systematised by Paul Lorenzen and later elaborated by Oswald Schwemmer. The first part of the essay discusses mainly Oswald Schwemmer's contributions to the subject. The second part of the essay is seen mainly as a critical evaluation of the subject matter, whereby ample suggestions are made for the principle guiding the regulation of human action in situations of conflict.

ASPROMOURGOS, Tony and Amati, Frank. Petty *Contra* Hobbes: A Previously Untranslated Manuscript. *J Hist Ideas* 46,127–132 Ja–Mr 85.

ASSMANN, Georg and Stollberg, R. Inhaltliche Fragen Der Ausarbeitung Eines Lehrbuches Der Marxistisch–Leninistischen Soziologie. *Deut Z Phil* 22,228–235 1974.

ATHERTON, Margaret. Knowledge Of Substance And Knowledge Of Science In Locke's Essay. *Hist Phil Quart* 1,413–428 O 84.

Locke says our idea of substance is limited, but why? This problem is rendered acute when we realize Locke says we know a lot about corporeal particles, and yet we know little about corporeal substance. I reject the view Locke regards 'substance' as a stand–in for knowledge we will gain about particles, and argue it represents knowledge we are not equipped to have, a grasp of that from which all other qualities necessarily flow.

ATHERTON, Margaret. The Inessentiality Of Lockean Essences. *Can J Phil* 14,277–294 Je 84.

Locke, in his discussion of essences, makes extensive use of a distinction between nominal and real essences. Interpretations of Locke's point in making such a distinction have varied sharply, depending upon whether the importance of the real or the nominal essence is stressed. I propose that Locke is not, in fact, in his discussion of essences, endorsing an essentialism of any kind, but instead, introduced the distinction to downplay the notion of an essence.

ATKINSON, D. The Anatomy Of Knowledge: Althusser's Epistemology And Its Consequences. *Phil Papers* 13,1–18 O 84.

Althusser's philosophical system contains a tension between its epistemology and structuralist ontology. His epistemology tends towards idealism, because it rejects the real as the basis for theory. This throws doubt on the absolute existence of structures. The article pleads for a far–reaching revision of his epistemology, so that his ontology can be retained.

ATLAS, Jay David. Comparative Adjectives And Adverbials Of Degree: An Introduction To Radically Radical Pragmatics. *Ling Phil* 7,347–378 N 84.

I show that the standard linguistic and philosophical applications of H Paul Grice's Maxims of Conversation (William James Lectures, Harvard University, 1967) are inaccurate, inadequate, and logically incoherent. See J D Atlas & S C Levinson, "It–Clefts, Informativeness, and Logical Form," *Radical Pragmatics*, edition P Cole, New York: Academic Press, 1981, pages 1–61, for preliminary discussion from which the present essay departs.

ATLAS, Jay David. Grammatical Non–Specification: The Mistaken Disjunction 'Theory'. *Ling Phil* 7,433–444 N 84.

Philosophers are ignorant of the difference between "sense" non–specification and ambiguity; they also confuse "sense" non–specification with "reference" non–

specification. In this essay I repair the ignorance to be found in The Journal of Philosophy and elsewhere.

ATRAN, Scott. Pre–Theoretical Aspects Of Aristotelian Definition And Classification Of Animals: The Case For Common Sense. *Stud Hist Phil Sci* 16,113–164 Je 85.

Treated are the folktaxonomic origins of Aristotelian biology, particularly, and the anthropological foundations of science, generally. Animal classifications, cross–culturally, manifest two ranks, correlating with "nondimensional" species and zoological classes. The universal presumption that each taxon's organisms have a nature in kind underpins taxonomic stability of ordinary phenomenal types despite obvious token variation. Aristotelian "essentialism" would connect these underlying natures into an integrated understanding of Nature, by systematically deriving taxa of the first rank from the second.

AUERBACH, Judy and others. Commentary On Gilligan's "In A Different Voice". *Fem Stud* 11,149–162 Spr 85.

Gilligan is praised for revealing the sexist bias in the popular literature of life cycle and moral development. Yet her own work poses several theoretical and methodological problems which force us to caution against uncritical acceptance of her book. Specifically, the lack of a clear foundation for perceived gender differences in moral development, the dichotomization of male and female moral sensibilities—with its inherent valorization of female's—and the choice of study samples, all yield ambiguities that allow this book to be appropriated by feminists and non–feminists alike.

AUGROS, Robert and Stanciu, George N. *The New Story Of Science.* Lake Bluff Regnery 1984.

The New Story of Science synthesizes the new world view emerging from contemporary physics, neuroscience, and humanistic psychology. Through ample testimony of eminent scientists, and with reasons and examples, the authors argue that science itself is transcending the narrow materialism of the 19th century. The role of beauty in physics, the place of God in the new cosmology of astrophysicists, and the origins of modern philosophy in Renaissance science are lucidly debated and thoroughly documented.

AUNE, Bruce. "Armstrong On Universals And Particulars" in *D M Armstrong*, Bogdan, Radu J (ed), 161–170. Boston Reidel 1984.

AUSTIN, Richard Cartwright. Beauty: A Foundation For Environmental Ethics. *Environ Ethics* 7,197–208 Fall 85.

Human awareness of natural beauty stimulates the formation of environmental ethics. I build from the insights of Jonathan Edwards, the American Puritan theologian. The experience of beauty creates and sustains relationships. Natural beauty is an aspect of that which holds together, supporting life and individuation. Beauty joins experience to ethics. We experience beauty intuitively; it is an affecting experience which motivates thought and action. The experience of beauty gives us a stake in the existence of the beautiful. Ecology can explore the relationships of natural beauty scientifically; it may be a science of the beauty of the Earth. They beauty of the world is necessary to its survival. Beauty is manifest in the interplay of interdependence with individuality, yielding diversity. The most beautiful relationships are those which recognize diversity, support individuality, and empathetically span the distinctions between beings. The sense of beauty is not a luxury, but a distinctive human vocation.

AUSTIN, Scott. Parmenides And Ultimate Reality. *Ultim Real Mean* 7,220–232 S 84.

This article attempts to introduce a reader to the poem of Parmenides and to current scholarly controversies, to propose a new interpretation, and to sketch Parmenides' influence on subsequent philosophy. The existential reading (Taran, Barnes), The Owen–Furth–Nussbaum interpretation, and the view of Mourelatos are criticized. I claim that Parmenides tolerated some assertoric negative language not involving directly and unambiguously negated copulas. Thus the poem does not violate its own strictures against negative language.

AUSTIN, William H. Philo's Reversal. *Phil Topics* 13,103–112 Spr 85.

An interpretation of the structure of Hume's *Dialogues* is suggested within which Philo's apparent endorsement of the design argument in Part XII is taken to be a tactical concession (nearly emptied by qualifications, at that) meant to gain a hearing for his attack on popular religion. That religion should never be taken as a source of *distinctive* guidance for conduct is the point Hume most wanted to drive home.

AVENS, Robert. *Imagination Is Reality.* Dallas Spring 1980.

Imagination Reality places Jung and archetypal psychology within the tradition of mythical thinking and Eastern spirituality. Imagination in the sense of active or "true imagination" (Corbin, Jung, Paracelsus) is seen as providing access to the Kantian noumenon and thus abolishing the customary dualisms between spiritual and material, divine and human, reason and faith, etc. Ultimately, imaginative seeing and living results in a process of re–solving the world.

AVENS, Robert. *The New Gnosis.* Dallas Spring 1984.

Gnosis as the middle term between the categories of 'belief' and 'reason' connotes inner vision, active imagination; it is redemptive knowledge having to do with the cultivation of the soul. The author sees gnosis going on today in the poetical thought of Martin Heidegger and archetypal psychology of James Hillman.

AVERILL, Edward Wilson. Color And The Anthropocentric Problem. *J Phil* 82,281–303 Je 85.

All accounts of color face a trilemma, which most solve by making an anthropocentric assumption of this form; two objects have the same color if they would appear to be exactly the same color to normal observers under such–and–such conditions. Smart's physicalist anthropocentric account of color is criticized, as well as some other accounts. The best solution to the trilemma is a physicalist account where "yellow," but not "color," is an anthropocentric concept.

AVINERI, Shlomo. "The Fossil And The Phoenix, Leo Rauch (commentator)" in *History And System*, Perkins, Robert (ed), 47–72. Albany SUNY Pr 1984.

Author Index with Abstracts 239 Bailhache, P

AVINERI, Shlomo. Problems In The Interpretation Of Hegel's *Philosophy Of Right* (in Hebrew). *Iyyun* 33,30–43 Ja–Ap 84.

AVISON, William and Stehr, Nico. Forms Of Competition And Sociological Knowledge In Organized American Sociology. *Arch Rechts Soz* 60,213–230 1974.

Utilizing Mannheim's paradigm of competition in the intellectual realm, it is suggested that the degree of socio–structural homogeneity within organized American sociology finds its expression in the form and content of sociological knowledge. Changes over time in the concentration of control of professional certification sustain a trend toward theoretical pluralism in American sociology as opposed to the previous hegemony of functionalism.

AVRON, Arnon. On Modal Systems Having Arithmetical Interpretations. *J Sym Log* 49,935–942 S 84.

In the first part of this paper sequential calculi for the arithmetically–important modal systems GL and Grz are introduced and cut elimination for both is proved. We show that this theorem fails for QGL (the extensions of GL to first order language) but this extension still has some of GL's interesting properties, like the disjunction property. Using fixed–point techniques we prove that the natural arithmetical interpretation of QGL has similar properties.

AXEL, Larry E. Empirical Realism And Creative Passage: Reflections On Meland's Theology. *Amer J Theol Phil* 5,37–41 My & S 84.

This essay is an introduction to and summary of the issues treated in the Purdue Conference, "Bernard Meland and the Future of Theology," October, 1982. Often associated with process theology, Meland incorporates and extends the legacies of William James and Alfred North Whitehead in forging an "empirical realism" in theological inquiry. The essay introduces treatments of Meland's criticism of process rationalism, his notion of "ultimacy," the relation of his early work to his current efforts, the internal logic of his epistemology, and his notion of God.

AXELOS, Kostas. "Theses On Marx" in *Continuity And Change In Marxism*, Fischer, Norman And Others (ed), 66–69. Atlantic Highlands Humanities Pr 1982.

AYERS, Michael. "Berkeley And Hume: A Question Of Influence" in *Philosophy In History*, Rorty, Richard and others (ed), 303–328. NY Cambridge Univ Pr 1984.

AYIM, Maryann and Houston, Barbara. The Epistemology Of Gender Identity: Implications For Social Policy. *Soc Theor Pract* 11,25–59 Spr 85.

The article's purpose is to examine the epistemological status of claims regarding one's core gender identity. We assess the implications of considering such claims as analytic statements, as inductive summaries of experience, and as expressions of preference. We examine the claims in the literature about when the core gender identity is established, its connection with language acquisition, and its supposed permanence. In the final part of the paper, we draw out important implications for social policy.

AYOUB, J Boulad. Descartes Face À Leibniz Sur La Question De La Substance. *Philosophiques* 11,225–250 O 84.

We will first examine the manner in which Descartes and Leibniz each defines the notion of substance; then the meaning that each of these authors attributes to this notion; finally, we shall analyze the relations between substances in their respective systems. This comparison should serve to throw light on the ontological determinations of this notion as it appears in the respective systems of Descartes and Leibniz as well as to differentiate between the rationalism of each of them.

BACARD, Andre. Why Be Ethical Amongst Villains? *Humanist* 45,32–33 Ja–F 85.

This article's purpose is to resolve the conflict between two opposing themes, "Honesty is the best policy" and "Nice persons finish last". In conclusion, an ethical life is shown to affirm good health, success, meaning, and progress.

BACH, Hans. Theoretische Oberlegungen Zum Okoproblem. *Conceptus* 18,23–32 1984.

The present ecological crisis is both a threat to our existence and a challenge. Although this task can be achieved by political means a theoretical discussion of and reflection on the origins of the crisis and the goals of an eco–symbiosis is required. Most emphasis is placed on the relationship between man and nature and man's understanding of nature, which determines his attitude and behavior towards nature. A "change of attitude and change of course" (Vester) in regard to nature is necessary, and a possible source of this change is to be found in an organic and holistic view of nature—as opposed to the traditional, mechanistic one. There are a number of holistic approaches to theories of nature and in this context the holistic ones of Othmar Spann and Walter Heinrich are to be considered seminal.

BACH, Kent. A Rationale For Reliabilism. *Monist* 68,246–263 Ap 85.

Properly formulated, reliabilism can avoid counterexamples and meet the objection that it ignores epistemic rationality and responsibility. The latter requires distinguishing between a belief being justified and a person being justified in holding it. This distinction also helps do justice to the fact that most justified beliefs are not formed deliberately but result from default reasoning. I argue that even though we generally jump to conclusions, our beliefs are justified to the extent that we know when to think twice. I formulate a version of reliabilism that adverts to counterfactual as well as actual cognitive processes.

BACH, Kent. More On Self–Deception: Reply To Hellman. *Phil Phenomenol Res* 45,611–614 Je 85.

This is a reply to Nathan Hellman's two objections, in "Bach on Self–Deception" (PPR 44, september, 1983), to "An Analysis of Self–Deception" (PPR 41, march, 1981). For me self–deception is not a matter of getting oneself to believe the opposite of a proposition *p* one believes (or has patently strong evidence for) but is something weaker than that: avoiding the thought that *p*, at least on a sustained or recurrent basis. Hellman finds it "puzzling that one could think that not–*p* on a sustained, recurrent basis" if one possessed considerable evidence for *p*. His puzzle suffers from a misplaced "not": my analysis requires not that the self–deceiver think that not–*p* but that he not think that *p* on a sustained, recurrent basis. Hellman's second objection is also answered.

BACHELARD, Gaston. "Metaphysics And Poetry" in *Continental Philosophy And The Arts*, Winters, Laurence E and others (ed), 219–224. *Lanham* Univ Pr Of America 1984.

BACHELARD, Gaston and Goldhammer, Arthur (trans). *The New Scientific Spirit.* Boston Beacon Pr 1985.

BÄCK, Allan. Existential Import In Anselm's Ontological Argument. *Fran Stud* 41,97–109 1981.

BADHWAR, Neera K. Friendship, Justice, And Superogation. *Amer Phil Quart* 22,123–132 Ap 85.

Philosophical discussions emphasize supererogation in friendship, and ignore justice. But greater attention to justice in its fundamental sense of fairness in our judgments of others, and the rejection of Kant's unjustified reason–inclination dichotomy, show that justice and supererogation are mutually supportive, hence equally important in friendship. They also show how nonforgiveness can be wrong, even though forgiveness is beyond justice; and how friendship *increases* the demands of justice, even though justice is "universal" and "impersonal".

BADIA CABRERA, Miguel A. Hume's Natural History Of Religion: Positive Science Or Metaphysical Vision Of Religion. *Dialogos* 20,71–78 Ap 85.

Although the *Natural History of Religion* historically paves the way for scientific studies of religion, its theoretical importance lies in being a philosophical reflection of the religious life of humanity, which assess its ultimate significance for a existence viewed within the framework of the whole of reality of Nature. Bereft from this metaphysical basis, Hume's account of religion seems to commit the genetic fallacy, when it is but a logical outcome of the former.

BAERTSCHI, Bernard. La Statue De Condillac, Image Du Réel Ou Fiction Logique? *Rev Phil Louvain* 82,335–364 Ag 84.

BAHM, Archie J. Does Rightness Always Involve Wrongness? *Cogito* 2,123–138 D 84.

Since some ignorance of consequences conditions most intentions to act, rightness (i.E., intending to produce the best results) usually involves some wrongness (i.E., intending to produce less than the best results), because lack of clarity does not deter choosing and acting. Persons aware of such usual wrongness may intend to minimize it by (1) recognizing that such permissive intention is actually the only, and thus best way to intend, or (2) by intending to revise intentions as new evidence appears to be responsible for remedying any bad results that one can.

BAHM, Archie J. Improving Applied Ethics: A Response To Reinsmith's Response To "Improving Applied Ethics". *Int J Applied Phil* 2,85–88 Spr 85.

Replying to William Reinsmith's criticisms of my "Improving Applied Ethics," I reject four claims: (1) One cannot decide between equal values. When equal, no ought. (2) "Better" has many meanings. All are specifics of a general. (3) "actually better" is better than "apparently better". But the actual can be known only by appearing. (4) He claims confusedly both a sound theory should hold for all and relativism is unavoidable. My distinction between actual (situational, relative) and conditional (universal, other things being equal) oughts accounts for both.

BAHN, Paul. Do Not Disturb: Archaeology And The Rights Of The Dead. *J Applied Phil* 1,213–226 O 84.

The ethics of the archaeological disturbance of the dead rarely attract much discussion. This paper, a preliminary essay on the topic, attempts to open the debate as to whether science can justifiably override the wishes of the dead. It finds that there are no simple conclusions to be drawn, and the advice of clergy or of moral philosophers will be needed.

BAIER, Annette. *Postures Of The Mind: Essays On Mind And Morals.* Minneapolis Univ Minnesota Pr 1985.

BAIER, Annette. Explaining The Actions Of The Explainers. *Erkenntnis* 22,155–174 Ja 85.

Hempel's version of how we explain human actions is examined, and questions are raised about the relation of our capacity to explain to our other distinctively human doings, including changing our goals and norms. It is suggested that Hempelian explanations fail to explain the actions of those whose goals and norms are in the process of intentional change. Neither general laws, nor the postulated end of utility maximization, seem to help us get such understanding of these changes as we think we have. Our higher–order disposition to turn norms on norms, and criticisms on criticisms, may be involved, but that seems to work in unpredictable ways.

BAIER, Kurt. "Rationality, Reason, And The Good" in *Morality, Reason And Truth*, Copp, David (ed), 193–211. Totowa Rowman & Allanheld 1984.

BAIGRIE, Brian. One World Or Many: Popper's Three World Theory And The Problem Of Scientific Determinism. *Eidos* 3,26–45 Je 84.

This paper analyzes the relationship between Karl Popper's three world theory and his contributions to quantum mechanics. Its thesis is that Popper's propensity interpretation of probability furnishes the grounds for the indeterminism of his mature metaphysics. A further consideration of the present debate in microphysics shows that Popper's theory does not overcome the challenge presented by scientific determinism. Whether there is one world or many remains an open question, Popper's views notwithstanding.

BAILEY, Barry. "Judgment, Justice, And Mercy" in *The Search For Justice*, Taitte, W Lawson (ed), 83–100. Austin Univ Of Texas Pr 1983.

BAILHACHE, P. Quelques Foncteurs Faussement Primitifs En Logique Déontique (Trivalence Et Action). *Log Anal* 27,393–406 D 84.

Some concepts created by logicians the mere bivalent propositional calculus are erroneously primitive. First, it is proved that "is better than" is not more primitive than "it is obligatory that" (Åquvist 1962). Further, a similar criticism is made towards several formalisms of action (von Wright).

BAILIN, Sharon. Creativity And Quality. *Proc Phil Educ* 40,313–322 1984.

The current educational view of creativity suggests that creativity must sometimes be purchased at the expense of the quality of the work produced. It is maintained here that this dichotomy between creativity and quality is a false one, based on an erroneous theory of creative process. It is argued that the notions of creativity and quality are intimately connected and that, thus, the question of the choices between the two does not really arise.

BAILLIE, J B. An Outline Of The Idealistic Construction Of Experience. NY Garland 1984.

BAIMAO, Yao. On The Position Of The Category Of Transformation In Dialectics. *Chin Stud Phil* 16,62–77 Fall 84.

BAIRD, Davis. Lehrer–Wagner Consensual Probabilities Do Not Adequately Summarize The Available Information. *Synthese* 62,47–62 Ja 85.

I show that Lerher and Wagner's method for combining divergent opinions to produce the "rational consensus" destroys important information. I consider augmenting their "rational consensus" with a measure of the original divergence of opinion, and with information about the participants mutual respect for each other. Important information is still lost. I conclude that it is rational to appreciate sincere differences of opinion and irrational to hide them behind a "rational consensus".

BAKALAR, James B and Grinspoon, Lester. "Drug Abuse Policies And Social Attitudes To Risk Taking" in *Feeling Good And Doing Better*, Murray, Thomas H (ed), 13–26. Clifton Humana Pr 1984.

BAKER, James C. The International Infant Formula Controversy: A Dilemma In Corporate Social Responsibility. *J Bus Ethics* 4,181–190 Je 85.

One of the most controversial issues to face any industry has been the infant formula problem, especially in the less–developed countries (LCDs). Producers of infant formula were confronted with a boycott which evolved from a grass–roots level to one which involved many nations, international and national public agencies, non–profit organizations, scientific research institutions, large church denominations, and every company in the industry. An international boycott was aimed at Neestlé, one of the largest producers of infant formula. The aim of this paper is (1) to examine both sides of the controversy, and (2) to analyze the results of the boycott, specifically the introduction of product codes and changes in industry and company strategies. In both areas ethical implications were involved.

BAKER, Lynne Rudder. Was Leibniz Entitled To Possible Worlds? *Can J Phil* 15,57–74 Mr 85.

Leibniz is well–known for his thought about possible worlds. I argue that on Leibniz's account of contingency, as reconstructed by Robert C Sleigh, Jr, possible worlds may be invoked only on pain of inconsistency; for Leibnizian contingency in terms of infinite analysis precludes propositions with different truth–values in different possible worlds. After considering a couple of interpretations of infinite analysis, I modify the account in terms of counterpart theory and show that it fares no better.

BAKER, Robert. "On Euthanasia" in *Biomedical Ethics Reviews*, Humber, James M (ed), 5–28. Clifton Humana Pr 1983.

BAKER, Rudder Lynne. A Farewell To Functionalism. *Phil Stud* 48,1–14 Jl 85.

A dilemma concerning the individuation of psychological states that explain behavior is posed for classical functionalism. Does individuation in terms of 'that'–clauses coincide with individuation by functional state? An affirmative answer leads to an inconsistent triad; a negative answer leads to a denial that beliefs are functional states. Either way, beliefs cannot be construed as classical functional states, on pain of contradiction.

BAKKER, D M. Kritische Notities Bij Ferdinand De Saussure's. *Phil Reform* 49,1–34 1984.

De Saussure's sign concept fails to account for such achievements of language use as translation and description of reality, and for the phenomenon of language change. These shortcomings appear to result from the false assumption that individual signs exist merely by virtue of their systematic position (valuer), whereas in fact this very position presupposes a difference among signs founded *outside* the sign system, which accounts for the phenomena that De Saussure's sign concept cannot logically explain.

BALANDA, Kevin P. Almost Disjoint Families Of Representing Sets. *Z Math Log* 31,71–77 1985.

Suppose GCH holds; s, k are infinite cardinals with equal confinalities and A is an almost disjoint decomposition of s consisting of $s+$ sets of size k. Let rsA be the largest cardinal c so that A possesses an almost disjoint family of c representing sets of size s. We show there is a family A with rsA equal to c if and only if c is less than or equal to $k+$ or c equals $s+$.

BALÁZS, Tibor. On The Strategy Of Scientific Research In Connection With The Coming Into Being Of Television 1839–1934 (in Hungarian). *Magyar Filozof Szemle* 4,608–625 1983.

The human being can secure his existence if he follows the laws of nature and as far as the nature of things demands it, he obeys and adapts to them. This substantiates the freedom and power of human being, namely, according to which, not simply his desires, passions, but the necessities guided by reason determine him to act. In so far as the human beings secure their existence by the guiding of reason, they will be not only free, but they eliminate the particularities separating them and together they seek for their common good. At the same time the fulfillment of this rational command becomes the basis of virtue and happiness. On the basis of all these, for Spinoza, the egoism formed on the basis of cooperation, which enriches the rational cognition and friendship, becomes virtue and morals. (edited)

BALDWIN, Thomas. "Moore's Rejection Of Idealism" in *Philosophy In History*, Rorty, Richard and others (ed), 357–374. NY Cambridge Univ Pr 1984.

BALDWIN, Tom. MacCallum And The Two Concepts Of Freedom. *Ratio* 26,125–142 D 84.

MacCallum suggested that the traditional distinction between negative and positive freedom was founded upon a confused distinction between freedom from and freedom to. It is shown that this criticism of the traditional distinction is incorrect; and the hypothesis is then proposed that the traditional distinction does embody two coherent, but distinct, conceptions of freedom.

BALL, Stephen W. Legal Positivism, Natural Law, And The Hart/Dworkin Debate. *Crim Just Ethics* 3,68–85 Sum/Fall 84.

This essay is an analysis of the main issues and arguments in the debate over the conceptual relation between law and morality. An initial examination of the problem indicates that there is no single criterion for evaluating the competing definitions of law. The elements of Hart's positivist theory are then sketched, and Fuller's natural–law arguments against Hart—with emphasis on applications to the criminal law, Nazi Germany and the Nuremberg trials—are critically surveyed and found inadequate. dworkin's theory of judicial decision making is analyzed into a sequence of logically connected steps, and a final section focuses on the current points of contention between Hart and Dworkin. This essay is written in a bibliographical format with twenty–one sources.

BALL, Terence. The Incoherence Of Intergenerational Justice. *Inquiry* 28,321–338 S 85.

Contemporary theories of justice fail to recognize that the concepts constitutive of our political practices—including 'justice' itself—have historically mutable meanings. To recognize the fact of conceptual change entails an alteration in our understanding of justice between generations. Because there can be no transhistorical theory of justice, there can be no valid theory of intergenerational justice either—especially where the generations in question are distant ones having very different understandings of justice. The upshot is that an earlier generation cannot aspire to act justly toward a later distant generation whose members' understanding of justice differs radically from theirs. Conceptual change and incommensurability render the very idea of intergenerational justice coherent. Even so, such radical relativism need not entail moral nihilism.

BALL, Terence. The Picaresque Prince: Reflections On Machiavelli And Moral Change. *Polit Theory* 12,521–536 N 84.

Machiavelli's central concept of *virtú* differs from Ciceronian–humanist understandings of *virtus* and the Christian 'virtue'. My argument is that Machiavellian *virtú* shares certain crucial conceptual affinities with the archaic Homeric conception of 'virtue' (*areté*) as role–related specific excellence. Instead of creating a new moral framework, Machiavelli in effect attempted to resurrect an older one. In this respect he resembles Don Quixote, who also attempted to revive an archaic code of conduct.

BALLARD, Edward G. Principles Of Interpretation: Series In Continental Thought, V5. Athens Ohio Univ Pr 1983.

BALLESTREM, Karl G. "Karl Marx And Adam Smith: Remarks About The Critique Of Political Economy" in *Contemporary Marxism*, O' Rourke, James J (ed), 21–38. Boston Reidel 1984.

BALME, D M. The Snub. *Ancient Phil* 4,1–8 Spr 84.

Aristotle uses the snub nose paradox in Metaphysics Z to show that matter must be brought into the definition. The solution offered briefly in Metaphysics H, that at any given instant an object's form and matter are one, is exemplified by his theory of animal generation.

BALZER, W. On A New Definition Of Theoreticity. *Dialectica* 39,127–145 1985.

A simple and precise definition is offered of "term t of theory being T–theoretical" which can be applied to any formalized theory. The definition is in line with and emends traditional accounts of theoreticity. Its adequacy is demonstrated by application to three examples: exchange economics, classical mechanics and collision mechanics.

BALZER, W. The Proper Reconstruction Of Exchange Economics. *Erkenntnis* 23,185–200 Ag 85.

The paper contains a reply to criticism of the author's earlier reconstruction of exchange economics put forward by F Haslinger in Erkenntnis 20 (1983). Three main criticisms are dealt with: choice of primitives, problems with the concept of equilibrium, and the status of utility as a theoretical concept. Whereas the first two criticisms are rejected, the third is acknowledged.

BAMBROUGH, Renford. "Discipline And Discipleship" in *Philosophy And Life: Essays On John Wisdom*, Dilman, Ilham (ed), 201–218. Boston Nijhoff 1984.

BAMBROUGH, Renford. "The Roots Of Moral Reason" in *Gewirth's Ethical Rationalism*, Regis Jr, Edward (ed), 39–51. Chicago Univ Of Chicago Pr 1984.

BAMBROUGH, Renford. The Scope Of Reason: An Epistle To The Persians. *Philosophy* 17,195–208 84 Supp.

BANDEMANN, Gunter. "The Problem Of Objectivity In Modern Art" in *Continental Philosophy And The Arts*, Winters, Laurence E and others (ed), 87–108. Lanham Univ Pr Of America 1984.

BANDYOPADHYAY, Tirhanath. Man And Machine. *Indian Phil Quart* 12,37–66 Ja–Mr 85.

The purpose of the essay is to show the limitation of the mechanical model of the human mind. In the first place it is difficult to deny the element of *being conscious* of man. On the other hand it is difficult to ascribe any c – predicate (consciousness – implying predicate) to a machine. Some further essential differences between man and machine are noted. Behaviorism is shown to be inadequate, identity – thesis untenable. The conclusion is that man *is* not a machine.

BANNER, David K and Cooke, Robert Allan. Ethical Dilemmas In Performance Appraisal. *J Bus Ethics* 3,327–334 N 84.

This paper is an examination of performance appraisal (PA). We examine some of the main conceptual issues in PA, and we sketch some key, practical dilemmas that may arise in the use of PA. We conclude that one can morally justify the use of PA under certain conditions, and we suggest possible solutions to key ethical dilemmas that are faced by the manager and the employee. (edited)

BANSE, G. Der Mechanismus Der Technikentwicklung. *Deut Z Phil* 33,339–347 1985.

BANSE, Gerhard and Horz, H. Wissenschaftlich–Technische Revolution—Schöpfertum—Verantwortung. *Deut Z Phil* 32,785–795 1984.

BAPAT, Lata. Dharmakirti On Trairupya And Trirupa Linga. *Indian Phil Quart* 11,7–17 Jl 84.

Distinguishing between *Trirūpa Linga* and *Trairūpya Lings*, Dharmakīrti demarcates conditions determinative of validity of an argument and those of obtainability or non–obtainability of the object of the conclusion. To him, *Trairūpya Linga* (three characteristics of *Hetu*), *Paksa sattva*, *Sapaksa sattva* and *Vipaksa Asattva* conjointly make an argument valid, while *Trirūpa Linga* (three kinds of *Linga*) *Svabhīva*, *Kārya* and *Anupalabdhi*, determine obtainability of non–obtainability of the object. Among these, third kind of *Hetus* gives valid argument while first two give valid as well as sound argument.

BAR– ELLI, Gilead. Frege's Early Conception Of Logic (in Hebrew). *Iyyun* 33,403–413 Jl 84.

Following scattered remarks in Frege's early writings the content and force of his conception of logic as *lingua characterica* (in distinction to a mere *calculus ratiocinator*) is presented as comprising a conception according to which logic is a *homogeneous* and *explanatory* system which unifies in a natural and integrated way the main notions operative in a theory of inference, a theory of definition (or concept formation), and a theory of meaning (or reference).

BAR– ELLI, Gilead. The Notion Of Aboutness In Frege (in Hebrew). *Iyyun* 33,434–453 Jl 84.

The paper presents an analysis of the *role* the notion of aboutness plays in Frege's theory of meaning. (edited)

BAR– HILLEL, Maya and Margalit, Avishai. Gideon's Paradox: A Paradox Of Rationality. *Synthese* 63,139–156 My 85.

A decision maker who is about to choose between two options such that A > B, is promised a prize—which (s)he prefers to either option—for "choosing irrationally". The dilemma into which this promise plunges the decision maker constitutes Gideon's Paradox. The paper draws parallels between this paradox and several other well–known paradoxes, offers a "solution" to the various possible interpretations of the paradox, and discusses its implications for the concept of rationality.

BAR– ON, A Z. Modes Of Intentionality (in Hebrew). *Iyyun* 33,124–136 Ja–Ap 84.

The article attempts to explicate the concept of a cognitive propositional attitude as a half–way house to an analysis of the concept of knowledge. The Brentano–Husserl controversy about the nature of intentionality is re–examined, as is Husserl's ground–breaking distinction between the matter and the quality of an intentional experience. An illustration of the general features of what may be called "the cognitive intending of an object" follows.

BAR– ON, A Zvie. Measuring Responsibility. *Phil Forum (Boston)* 16,95–109 Fall–Wint 84.

The responsibility for the Holocaust is estimated by dialectically confronting the responses of three Germans: Adolf Eichmann, Günter Grass and Karl Jaspers. Eichmann's argument is shown to be totally invalid, Grass' position—in need of correction. Jasper's analysis, according to which the whole German nation is responsible in at least one important sense, is found basically acceptable. Consequences regarding the concept of collective guilt are drawn from this last position.

BARAN, P. Remarks Concerning The Ontological Prerequisites Of Marxist–Leninist Theory Of Values (in Czechoslovakian). *Filozof Cas* 33,352–363 1985.

BARAN, P. The Problem Of Relativization Of Life As Value (in Czechoslovakian). *Filozof Cas* 33,394–396 1985.

BARBERA, Andre. Placing *Sectio Canonis* In Historical And Philosophical Contexts. *J Hellen Stud* 104,157–160 1984.

Comparison of the three versions of *Sectio canonis*—the long version ascribed to Euclid, the version by Porphyry, and the Latin version by Boethius—prevents us from singling out one version as the model for the other two. The comparison indicates that the composition of the *Sectio*, possibly protracted over several centuries, was a product of the living Pythagorean tradition. Ancient authors consulted: Archytas, Aristotle, Aristoxenus, Boethius, Euclid, Marinus, Nicomachus, Plato, Plutarch, Porphyry, Proclus, Ptolemy, Theon of Smyrna.

BARCLAY, William. *Christian Ethics For Today*. Cambridge Harper & Row 1971.

The purpose of this book is to determine the nature of true Christian ethics and to show how they can be applied to our contemporary situation. This goal is accomplished through examination of the OLD TESTAMENT, of situational ethics, and finally of specific day–to–day subjects. The conclusion reached is that people should develop a 'person–to–person ethic' in which privilege is united with responsibility. (staff)

BARELA, Robert E. A Paradigm Of Art. *J Theor Crit Vis Arts* 1,7–19 1981.

BARELA, Robert E. The Visual Arts As Language. *J Theor Crit Vis Arts* 1,149–164 1982.

BARGELIOTES, Leonidas C. Whitehead's Double Debt To The Greeks. *Diotima* 12,33–40 1984.

Plato is commonly considered as the protagonist of Whitehead's *Process and Reality*. This should be extended in order to include Aristotle as a symprotagonist of *Process and Reality*. This means that Whitehead's debt to the Greeks is double: to Plato and to Aristotle. This is shown by Whitehead's two fundamental types of entities, "eternal objects" and "actual entities". For the former type of entity Whitehead relies heavily

on the "Platonic Forms" and for the latter on the Aristotelian principle, that is, on Aristotle's concept of *ousia–energeia*.

BARKER, Andrew. Aristoxenus' Theorems And The Foundations Of Harmonic Science. *Ancient Phil* 4,23–64 Spr 84.

BARKER, Jeffrey H. Sartre's Dialectical Anarchism: Institution, Sovereignty, And The State. *Cogito* 2,93–116 Je 84.

This article examines Sartre's view of the dialectical relationship between political institutions and material forces, one that stresses the constitutive role of the freedom of individual *praxis*. The particular focus of the article is Sartre's description of the development of sovereignty and the state as a response to the threat of individual *praxis*. The article concludes that Sartre's *Critique* provides a sophisticated social anarchism rather than a more radical Marxism.

BARKER, Stephen F. How Wrong Was Kant About Geometry? *Topoi* 3,133–142 D 84.

BARNES, Hazel E. Beauvoir And Satre: The Forms Of Farewell. *Phil Lit* 19,21–40 Ap 85.

Simone de Beauvoir's *Ceremonie des adieux* and her 1974 interviews with Sartre shed new light on their relations with one another. The chronicle of their last decade together has implications beyond those grasped by Beauvoir herself. It shows Sartre deliberately trying to assume a passive role basically alien to him. The narrative displays striking similarities to Beauvoir's fictional account of an aging couple in her earlier novella, *The Age of Discretion*.

BARNETT, John H. A Business Model Of Enlightenment. *J Bus Ethics* 4,57–64 F 85.

BARON, Marcia. The Ethics Of Duty/Ethics Of Virtue Debate And Its Relevance To Educational Theory. *Educ Theor* 35,135–150 Spr 85.

This paper disentangles three strains of the ethics of duty/ethics of virtue debate which are usually conflated and tries to say what is at issue in each case and how the issues bear on educational theory. I argue that the most important version of the debate is the debate over the value of a sense of duty, and that the issue is best understood in terms of moral education, I also briefly defend an ethics of duty position.

BARON, Marcia. Varieties Of Ethics Of Virtue. *Amer Phil Quart* 22,47–54 Ja 85.

This paper distinguishes and evaluates five types of ethics of virtue, taking the mark of an ethics of virtue to be the denial that it is a necessary condition of perfectly moral personhood that one be governed by a sense of what one morally ought to do. Appealing to Charles Taylor's notion of strong evaluation, I argue that all such ethics of virtue are inadequate because they fail to leave room for a distinction between valuing and desiring.

BARONOVITCH, Laurence. German Idealism, Greek Materialism, And The Young Karl Marx. *Int Phil Quart* 24,245–266 S 84.

BAROSS, Z. Disease And Social Theory: A Problem Of Conversation. *Theor Med* 6,189–204 Je 85.

The paper offers a critical examination of 'introspection' and 'stoicism' as two apparently opposing responses to pain, and examines their adequacy as theoretical postures vis–a–vis the life–world. Following Wittgenstein, who suggest that introspection is fundamentally at fault, the paper moves to consider the 'theoretic' stoicism of Durkheim as a possible alternative for inquiry. It comes to the conclusion, however, that stoicism, just as introspection fails to develop a strong theoretical interest in pain when it refuses to make the problem pain poses for discourse conversational.

BARRAL, Mary Rose. Paul Ricoeur: The Resurrection As Hope And Freedom. *Phil Today* 29,72–82 Spr 85.

The relation of faith and reason or whether there can be a Christian philosophy, rather then simply philosophers who are Christians, is reconsidered in the light of Ricoeur's thought. The focus, few specific points dealing with the Christian faith, centers on the notion of hope in the light of freedom. An inquiry is made into the possibility of a person's passage from sin to grace by the fulfillment of the promise in the Resurrection. Can Ricoeur's reflections (though buttressed by Kant) be universalized and be philosophically valid even to non–believers? It seems doubtful.

BARRETT, Lee. "Kierkegaard's Two Ages: Immediate Stage On Way To Religious Life" in *International Kierkegaard Commentary*, Perkins, Robert L (ed), 53–72. Macon Mercer Univ Pr 1984.

BARROW, Robin. Misdescribing A Cow: The Question Of Conceptual Correctness. *Educ Theor* 35,205–208 Spr 85.

It is argued that it does not make sense to describe someone's conception of anything as incorrect. We may make verbal errors (calling a cow a horse), perceptual errors (seeing a cow as a horse), and we are to some extent constrained by material reality and logic. But whether a new product of selective breeding should or should not count as a cow (a true conceptual question) has no correct answer.

BARROW, Robin. Teacher Education And Research: The Place Of Philosophy. *Proc Phil Educ* 40,183–192 1984.

I wish to pinpoint certain specific weaknesses in empirical research in education. Then, by focusing on the reasons that lie behind the weaknesses, I shall argue that teacher education needs to be reorganized in a manner that makes better use of philosophy than is at present made. Although most of my paper concentrated on criticism of empirical work, it will become clear that philosophy of education is also to be criticized for failing to play the important role that it could in relation to both research into education and the education of teachers.

BARRY, Norman P. Unanimity, Agreement, And Liberalism: A Critique Of James Buchanan's Social Philosophy. *Polit Theory* 12,579–596 N 84.

This critique of James Buchanan's social philosophy centers on the impossibility of deriving the normative political philosophy of classical liberal philosophy from a subjectivist meta–ethics. U–shows that the Pareto criterion for welfare improvement is inadequate unless it is supplemented by a theory of property rights. Buchanan's

Hobbesion derivation of property rights is not necessarily consistent with liberalism. The unanimity requirement for permissible change is demonstrated to be internally ambiguous.

BARTH, E M. A New Field: Empirical Logic. *Synthese* 63,375–388 Je 85.

New sub–disciplines of logic as an academic discipline are needed: a technical normative logic, for clinical use in society, based on a theoretical logic that is systematically related to the results of an *empirical logic*. (E W Beth was a forerunner here). In addition to theoretical logic(s) there are, empirically, lodgins and logoles (cf pigeons and creoles). These are of the utmost importance in politics and culture. A list of the components of a complete description or a lodgin or of a logole is given. Empirical methods are discussed. It is recommended to see logics, too, as institutions, and to bring the institutional features of systems of logic and of semantics to the fore.

BARTH, E M. Dialectical Fields And Transformations: Brouwer–Fields, Beth–Fields, And Naess–Transformations. *Phil Natur* 21,425–434 1984.

The concept of a dialectical field is presented as a contribution to *logic*. A dialectical field is not the same as the rational field assumed in the rationalist philosophical tradition (discussed elsewhere). An individual who is introduced into a dialectical field is subjected to semiotical field forces that either invite or disencourage active discussion. For these semiotical/dialectical fields reality is claimed. On the basis of the writings of the mathematician L E J Brouwer and the philosopher logician E W Beth, Brouwer fields and Beth fields are distinguished and compared. In the interest of the cultural discussion Brouwer fields ought to be eradicated. This can be done through careful pragmatization of theories in philosophy and science. Examples of pragmatizing (Naess) transformations are given, taken from logic, semanitcs, and the exact sciences. The bibliography to the paper has dropped out and is available from the author.

BARTHES, Roland and Howard, Richard (trans). *The Responsibility Of Forms: Critical Essays On Music, Art, And Representation.* NY Hill And Wang 1985.

BARTLETT, Edward T. Persons And The Measurement Of Illness. *Phil Context* 14,60–69 1984.

The article asserts the need to treat the patient as a person because of the logical connection that exists between the concept of disease and the idea of the experience of feeling ill. Accounts of disease that exclude this subjective element are criticized.

BARTLEY, W W. *The Retreat To Commitment.* LaSalle Open Court 1984.

BARTNIK, Czeslaw Stanislaw. A Personalistic Philosophy Of History. *Dialec Hum* 11,193–200 Wint 84.

BARTSCH, Renate. Norms, Tolerance, Lexical Change, And Context–Dependence Of Meaning. *J Prag* 8,367–394 Je 84.

In this paper, context dependence of meaning, vagueness, and semantic change are investigated in interdependence. This interdependence is created by the fact that lexical meanings are the contents of semantic norms, and tolerance with respect to those norms is required. In this relationship between different levels of norms lies the pragmatic aspect of this paper. (edited)

BARUZZI, Arno. Eric Voegelin: Politische Wissenschaft Und Geschichtsphilosophie. *Phil Rundsch* 31,216–235 1984.

Historiogenetic an ecumenic intentions are both ancient and modern patterns of political order. Marxism, for example, gives an historiogenetic and ecumenic speculation and pragmatic politics. Here is the most important problem: conquest and exodus. Voegelin reflects this order and leads us from political science to philosophy of history.

BARWISE, Jon and Perry, John. Shifting Situations And Shaken Attitudes: An Interview With Barwise And Perry. *Ling Phil* 8,105–161 F 85.

In this essay, the authors respond to the questions of an anonymous, and quite possibly mythical, interviewer concerning the basic ideas of their book "Situations and Attitudes" and their reactions to the criticisms of it made by authors of earlier essays in the same journal. A number of changes in situation theory are explained.

BARZEL, Alexander. Relation––The Ultimate Reality And Human Praxis Of Togetherness: On The Meaning Of The Kibbutz, The Israeli Co–Relational Community. *Ultim Real Mean* 8,123–133 Je 85.

Ultimate reality––the construction of being and the feature of understanding and acting in the work––is *relation*. The Western culture moved on the paths of an atomistic ontology and epistemology toward crisis; the latent 'war of everyone against everyone' of the Hobbesian attitude is immanent in the human situation. The purpose is to show, that the understanding of being as *relatedness* may change the attitude. The We–consciousness should be the foundation of togetherness. A new dominant universal culture, the techno–logical one rises. Its assignments for forms of reasoning and forms of social existence correspond to the *relational* ontology and epistemology. The co–relational community has the highest 'index of compatibility'. The Israeli Kibbutz is presented as proof for the possibility of a radical transformation of society.

BASAVE, Agustín. Educación Universitaria Para El Amor. *Logos (Mexico)* 13,93–108 Ja–Ap 85.

BASILE, Joseph. "A Scale Of Values For A Changing World" in *The Good Life And Its Pursuit,* Dougherty, Jude P (ed), 186–195. NY Paragon House 1984.

BASINGER, David. Divine Omniscience And Human Freedom: A 'Middle Knowledge' Perspective. *Faith Phil* 1,291–302 Jl 84.

Human freedom is only compatible with divine omniscience, some have argued, if what God knows about our future actions is contingent upon what we will in fact do. But such contingency, they claim, is only possible if we can in some sense by our present actions determine beliefs held by God in the past and this is impossible. Thus if God is omniscient, they conclude, humans cannot be considered free. I argue that if God possesses middle knowledge, this criticism fails.

BASINGER, David. Griffin And Pike On Divine Power: Some Clarifications. *Phil Res Arch* 10,347–352 1984.

David Griffin and Nelson Pike recently had a spirited discussion on divine power. The essence of the discussion centered around what was labelled Premise X: "It is possible for one actual being's condition to be completely determined by a being or beings other than itself". Pike maintains that 'traditional' theists have affirmed Premise X but denies that this entails that God has all the power there is and thus denies that Premise X can be considered incoherent for this reason. griffin maintains that traditional theists have as a matter of fact affirmed that God has all the power there is and then argues that, given standard Process metaphysical assumptions, to say that God has all the power there is is coherent. Griffin succeeds in demonstrating that, given Process assumptions, God cannot determine all of the activities of any human–– i.E., all of an individual's desires, choices and actions. But Pike is primarily interested in whether God could determine all of the bodily behaviors of any given human. And to this question Griffin gives no response.

BASTOW, David. The Possibility Of Religious Symbolism. *Relig Stud* 20,559–578 D 84.

Some symbols rest not just on mere coincidence of properties, but on the assumption of some real metaphysical relationship. This may be that the symbolizandum creates the symbol–which, to be comprehensible to man, must be worldly. The relation is less direct when the worldliness of the symbol distances it from the religious Focus; in Mahayana Buddhism, the very fact that worldly things can only be provisional symbols indicates the emptiness of the highest truth.

BASU, Shankar. Indian Epistemology—A Synthetic Study. *Philosophica (India)* 10,46–47 Ja–D 81.

Indian Epistemology is a 'development', not a history. The study of this epistemology should be a comparative one of its concepts and also of different phases of the development of Indian epistemology. This requires an analysis of the nature of knowledge along with conceptions of the nature of truth and error from the Indian point of view. And a study by Indian thinkers, of the problem of how a knowledge of the meaning of words arises, trails the development of the theory of meaning.

BATTEN, L M and Walton, Douglas N. Games, Graphs, And Circular Arguments. *Log Anal* 27,133–164 Je 84.

This paper uses the theory of directed graphs as a way of modelling arguments. In particular, the fallacy of *petitio principii* is given an analysis in the theory.

BATTIN, Margaret P. Non–Patient Decision–Making In Medicine: The Eclipse Of Altruism. *J Med Phil* 10,19–44 F 85.

Despite its virtues, lay decision–making in medicine shares with professional decision–making a disturbing common feature, reflected both in formal policies prohibiting high–risk research and in informal policies favoring treatment decisions made when a crisis or change of status occurs, often late in a downhill course. By discouraging patient decision–making but requiring dedication to the patient's interests by those who make decisions on the patient's behalf, such practices tend to prelude altruistic choice on the part of the patient. This eclipse is to be regretted not just because widescale altruism has the capacity to provide important social goods and correct injustices in distribution, but for intrinsic reasons as well. It is argued that preserving the possibility of altruism obliges patients––and future patients––to make decisions about dying and other medical matters in advance, thus avoiding that displacement of decision–making onto lay and professional second parties which results in altruism's eclipse.

BAUDISCH, Andreas. Die Elementare Theorie Der Gruppe Vom Typ p–super–infinity–mit Untergruppen. *Z Math Log* 21,347–352 1975.

BAUER, Adolf. Zur Historisch–Materialistischen Auffassung Von Basis Und Überbau. *Deut Z Phil* 22,669–680 1974.

Die gesetzmässigen Beziehungen der Basis–Überbau–Dialektik tragen den Charakter von entwicklungsgesetzmässigkeiten, da sie erstens die Entwicklung des Überbaus auf der Grundlage der Basisveränderungen bestimmen und die rückwirkende Einflufsnahme des Überbaus auf die Basisentwicklung regulieren. Zweitens geht aus ihnen hervor, welchen Anteil Basis und Überbau an der Entwicklung der gesamten ökonomischen Gesellschaftsformation haben. Der Klassenkampf bezieht sich stets sowohl auf die Basis als auch auf den Überbau. Seinem inhalt nach ist er materielle gesellshaftliche Tätigkeit, seine Austragungsformen sine Überbaubeziehungen.

BAUER, A. Produktivität Und Individualität. *Deut Z Phil* 33,193–201 1985.

BAUER, Ileana. Friedrich Engels' "Dialektik Der Natur". *Deut Z Phil* 23,955–964 1975.

BAUM, Robert and Benjamin, Martin. "I'm The Teacher". *Teach Phil* 8,151–156 Ap 85.

BAUMER, Michael R. Whitehead And Aquinas On The Eternity Of God. *Mod Sch* 62,27–42 N 84.

BAUMGART, Joachim. Revolutionäre Epoche Und Klassische Revolution. *Deut Z Phil* 33,491–499 1985.

BAUMGARTEN, Elias. "Patient Autonomy And The Refusal Of Psychotropic Medications" in *Difficult Decisions In Medical Ethics,* Ganos, Doreen L (ed), 13–30. NY Liss 1983.

BAUMGARTNER, James E and Dordal, Peter. Adjoining Dominating Functions. *J Sym Log* 50,94–101 Mr 85.

If dominating functions in $^\omega\omega$ are adjoined repeatedly over a model of GCH via a finite–support c.C.C. Iteration, then in the resulting generic extension there are no long towers, every well–ordered unbounded family of increasing functions is a scale, and the splitting numbers s(and hence the distributivity number h) remains ω_1.

BAUSOLA, Adriano. Benedetto Croce, Philosopher, Ethics And Politics (in Hungarian). *Magyar Filozof Szemle* 1–2,219–231 1984.

BAY, Christian. Limits To Liberty In A Shrinking World. *J Soc Phil* 15,12–19 Fall 84.

BAYER, Ronald and Murray, Thomas H. "Ethical Issues In Occupational Health In Biomedical Ethics Reviews" in *Biomedical Ethics Reviews*, Humber, James M (ed), 153–174. Clifton Humana Pr 1984.

BAYER, Samuel and Horn, Laurence R. Short–Circuited Implicature: A Negative Contribution. *Ling Phil* 7,397–414 N 84.

BAYLES, Michael D. *Reproductive Ethics.* Englewood Cliffs Prentice–Hall 1984.

Ethical issues pertaining to human reproduction are analyzed. The topics considered include AIDS, surrogate motherhood, *in vitro* fertilization, sex pre–selection, genetic screening, abortion, homebirths, defective newborns, *in utero* treatment, and futuristic issues of cloning, genetic engineering, and ectogenesis. Each topic is analyzed in terms of personal values, ethical considerations, and social policy. The general conclusion is that most of the valuable reproductive techniques have been developed and that most others are not worth developing.

BAYLES, Michael D and Freedman, Benjamin. Canada: The Mandarin Bureaucracy. *Hastings Center Rep* 14,17–18 D 84.

BAYLES, Michael D. Brand Name Extortionists, Intellectual Prostitutes, And Generic Free Riders. *Int J Applied Phil* 2,13–26 Fall 84.

This paper explores patent law as it affects ethical conduct in the pharmaceutical industry. After formulating policy aims and exploring alternative policies, I conclude that the best policy provides patents to companies that develop drugs but allows the government to authorize others to manufacture and sell them if a fair royalty is paid.

BAYLES, Michael D. Ethical Theory In The Twenty–First Century. *S J Phil* 22,439–451 Wint 84.

This paper examines nine assumptions often made in developing normative ethical theories. It argues that recent work in applied ethics show that none of them are legitimate. Future normative theories must defend any of these claims and will therefore be more difficult to justify.

BAYLES, Michael D. Intuitions In Ethics. *Dialogue (Canada)* 23,439–456 S 84.

This paper examines and rejects appeals to intuitions of substantive moral claims as in (1) W D Ross's work and (2) reflective equilibrium. I conclude that intuitions have only a heuristic role in ethics.

BEACH, John. Bluffing: Its Demise As A Subject Unto Itself. *J Bus Ethics* 4,191–196 Je 85.

'business bluffing' as a subject has been mentioned in various journals for at least the past 16 years. Its treatment has become one of apparent serious intent to identify it as a subject matter unto itself. Definitionally and theoretically, its essence has been specified but seemingly without due regard to its true nature. Business bluffing is an act of puffing at best and misrepresentation or fraud at worst. In either case, its legality and morality are already well defined and discussions of the subject should be directed along these established pathes.

BEALER, George. Mind And Anti–Mind: Why Thinking Has No Functional Definition. *Midwest Stud Phil* 9,283–328 1984.

BEANBLOSSOM, Ronald. Another Note On The Ontological Argument. *Faith Phil* 2,175–178 Ap 85.

I have argued that Anselm's second formulation of the ontological argument, like the previous formulation, begs the question. Moreover, I show that Malcolm's defense of the ontological argument fails; there is an appropriate use of 'possible' such that it is not self–contradictory to claim "God necessarily exists but it is possible God does not exist."

BEARDSLEY, Monroe C. *Aesthetics: Problems In The Philosophy Of Criticism.* Indianapolis Hackett 1981.

BEARDSLEY, Monroe C. Experience And Value In Moritz Geiger's Aesthetics. *J Brit Soc Phenomenol* 16,6–19 Ja 85.

BEATTIE, J H M. Objectivity And Social Anthropology. *Philosophy* 17,1–20 84 Supp.

Socio–cultural "facts" are different from other kinds of facts, and as such need different methods of inquiry. These methods will vary according to whether the emphasis is on institutionalized patterns of social behavior (social action), or on the conceptual systems through which people make their words intelligible to themselves (modes of thought). In both cases ethnocentricity (or socio–centricity) may stand in the way of objectivity, but the difficulties involved in this state of affairs are not altogether insuperable.

BEATTIE, Paul H. The Tragic View Of Life. *Relig Hum* 19,111–121 Sum 85.

BEATTIE, Paul H. The Tragic View Of Life. *Relig Hum* 19,54–61 Spr 85.

This is the first of a three–part article (two parts to be published in succeeding quarterly issues) which attempts to show the radical incongruity between the Judeo–Christian and the Greco–Roman traditions. Christianity was not a blend of Greek and Hebrew ideas, it was a blend of decadent Hellenism with Hebraism. The concept of tragedy is a touchstone for understanding the difference between the two traditions. Prometheus is contrasted with Job, and Socrates is contrasted with Jesus. Job and Jesus develop out of a tradition promising salvation or "cosmic guarantees" for human endeavors, whereas Prometheus and Socrates represent the tragic view of life.

BEATTY, Joseph. 'Communicative Competence' And The Skeptic. *Phil Soc Crit* 6,267–288 Fall 79.

I reconstruct the "communicative competence" argument of Jürgen Habermas and show how it is successful against some of the strongest relativist and skeptical challenges. The key to the strength of the Habermasian argument, I hold, is its ability to show the inescapability of certain sorts of claims in *any* society or language. The rational justification of such claims, in turn, presupposes certain fundamental moral principles.

BEATTY, Joseph. "The Incoherence Of Universal Prescriptivism" in *The Georgetown Symposium On Ethics*, Porreco, Rocco (ed), 145–158. Lanham Univ Pr Of America 1984.

BEAUCHAMP, Gorman. Big Brother In America. *Soc Theor Pract* 10,247–260 Fall 84.

BEAUCHAMP, Tom L and Mc Cullough, Laurence B. *Medical Ethics: The Moral Responsibilities Of Physicians.* Englewoods Cliffs Prentice–Hall 1984.

BEAUCHAMP, Tom L. Manipulative Advertising. *Bus Prof Ethics J* 3,1–22 Spr/Sum 84.

"this essay presents a theory of influence broad enough to include education, persuasion, manipulation, and coercion. Manipulation is then defined so as to exclude both persuasion and coercion, but not so as to entail a moral wrong or harm. How contemporary advertising is manipulative under the definition is then discussed, and some examples of manipulative advertising taken from bank advertisements are presented."

BEAUSOLEIL, Claude. Duras, L'amant, Le Public. *Petite Rev Phil* 6,135–149 Spr 85.

BECHER, Jurgen and Friedrich, P. Struktur Der Sozialistischen Produktionsverhältnisse Und Ökonomische Gesetze Des Sozialismus. *Deut Z Phil* 23,1013–1024 1975.

Ausgangspunkt der sozialistischen Produktionsweise ist die Nationalisierung der grundlegenden Produktionsmittel durch die Dikatur des Proletariats. Die Nationalisierung (Konfiskation) darf nicht mit der sozialistischen Vergesellschaftung gleichgestzt werden. Das Ausgangsproduktionsverhältnis der sozialistischen Produktionsverhältnisse stellt die unmittelbare Vergesellschaftung der Produktion und der Arbeit dar. Das grundlegende Produktionsverhältnis im Sozialismus ist das gesellschaftliche Eigentum an Produktionsmitteln.

BECHTEL, William P. The Evolution Of Our Understanding Of The Cell: A Study In The Dynamics Of Scientific Progress. *Stud Hist Phil Sci* 15,309–356 D 84.

BECK, Heinrich. Weltvernunft Und Sinnlichkeit: Hegel Und Feuerbach In Bamberg. *Z Phil Forsch* 29,409–424 Jl–S 75.

BECK, Robert H. Plato's View On Teaching. *Educ Theor* 35,119–134 Spr 85.

The chief purpose of the essay is to suggest that the *Theaetetus*, not the *Meno*, is to be read for an idea of Plato's theory of education. It is a theory that likens educating and learning to philosophize. The teacher both is a midwife and a lover while instructing in how to reach the maturity of the dialectician. The youth granting that she/he be able, can learn to make distinctions, to formulate study assumptions and advance substantial analysis. At no time is the teaching a matter of recalling what the student what was shown in a previous life.

BECKER, Howard. Determinacy Of Banach Games. *J Sym Log* 50,110–122 Mr 85.

BECKER, Wolfgang. Das Selbstverhältnis Des Sprachlich Handelnden: Sprachpragmatische Überlegungen Zum Handlungsbegriff Bei Fichte. *Z Phil Forsch* 39,35–59 Ja–Mr 85.

Fichte's notions of action and reflection and his term "Setzen" are considered in view of a pragmatic theory of language. They are understood as referring to necessary conditions of the meaningfulness of acts of assertion. According to Fichte's theory of interpersonality the use of language is a form of interaction which presupposes both a common knowledge of the actors and a reflective relation of an actor to his own action.

BECKER, Wolfgang. Kritik Und Bergründung In Transzendentaler Argumentation. *Kantstudien* 76,170–195 1985.

In the use of transcendental arguments and the method of critique, Kant is concerned with the justification of knowledge claims. Transcendental principles can be understood as conditions that are necessary for the redeemableness of claims to empirical truth. Because, on the other hand, objects must be given in intuition to redeem such claims, transcendental proofs are successful in showing the validity of transcendental principles only, if they relate transcendental knowledge indirectly to possible intuitions and hence to possible experience.

BÉCSI, Tamás. The Relation Of Ontology And Gnoseology As Seen From The Point Of View Of The Marxist Theory Of Literature (in Hungarian). *Magyar Filozof Szemle* 4,651–676 1983.

BEDNARZ JR, John. Complexity And Intersubjectivity: Towards The Theory Of Niklas Luhmann. *Human Stud* 7,55–70 1984.

BEDNARZ JR, John. Functional Method And Phenomenology: The View Of Niklas Luhmann. *Human Stud* 7,343–362 1984.

BEDU– ADDO, J T. Recollection And The Argument 'From A Hypothesis' In Plato's *Meno*. *J Hellen Stud* 104,1–14 1984.

BEER, Colin. "Motives And Metaphors In Considerations Of Animal Nature" in *Ethical Questions In Brain And Behavior*, Pfaff, Donald W (ed), 125–140. NY Springer 1983.

BEHAN, David P. Hume's Labyrinth. *Hist Phil Quart* 2,309–322 Jl 85.

Hume's difficulties with his account of personal identity (*Treatise* I.4.6 and Appendix) extend beyond Book I to Books II and III of the *Treatise*. His theory of personal identity is in irreconcilable conflict with his moral and political philosophy.

BEIERWALTES, Werner. Sprache Und Sache: Reflexionen Zu Eriugenas Einschätzung Von Leistung Und Funktion Der Sprache. *Z Phil Forsch* 38,523–544 N–D 84.

BEITZ, Charles (ed) and Kuperberg, Mark (ed). *Law, Economics, And Philosophy.* Totowa Rowman & Allanheld 1983.

BEITZ, Charles R. Political Finance In The United States: A Survey Of Research. *Ethics* 95,129–148 O 84.

BELFIORE, Elizabeth. The Role Of The Visual Arts In Plato's Ideal State. *J Theor Crit Vis Arts* 1,115–127 1981.

The analogy between painting and poetry in Plato's *Republic* Book 10, is not as strict as is often thought. Painting is not blamed on moral grounds, as poetry is, and only an inferior kind of painting is attacked on aesthetic grounds. In Plato's ideal state there is

Belfrage, Bertil 244 **Author Index with Abstracts**

room for genuine crafts of painting and sculpture that create likenesses of true beauty.

BELFRAGE, Bertil. Dating Berkeley's Notebook B. *Berkeley News* 7,7–13 1984.

BELFRAGE, Bertil. Facts Concerning Berkeley's Notebooks. *Berkeley News* 7,17–22 1984.

BELL, David. *Bithell Series Of Dissertations: Spinoza In Germany From 1670 To The Age Of Goethe*, V7. Atlantic Highlands Humanities Pr 1984.

BELL, David. Reference And Sense: An Epitome. *Phil Quart* 34,369–371 Jl 84.

BELL, J S and others. An Exchange On Local Beables. *Dialectica* 39,85–110 1985.

Bell tries to formulate more explicitly a notion of "local causality": correlations between physical events in different space–time regions should be explicable in terms of physical events in the overlap of the backward light cones. It is shown that ordinary relativistic quantum field theory is not locally causal in this sense, and cannot be embedded in a locally causal theory. In response to criticism by Shimony, Horne, and Clauser, Bell tries to clarify the argument of "The theory of local beables", and to defend as permissible the hypothesis of free variables. (edited)

BELL, Linda A and Alcoff, Linda. Lordship, Bondage, And The Dialectic Of Work In Traditional Male/Female Relationships. *Cogito* 2,79–94 S 84.

In each of four traditional relationships between women and men—the gallant man and the pedestal woman, the lustful man and the female prostitute, the business man and the female secretary–typist, and the working man and the housewife–mother—there is some recognized subordination of one to the other. Hegel's notions of idle consumption, work, and recognition to help us understand the relative stability of these relationships compared to that of Hegel's lord and bondsman.

BELL, Nora K and Loewer, Barry M. What Is Wrong With 'Wrongful Life' Cases? *J Med Phil* 10,127–146 My 85.

'wrongful life' torts raise a number of interesting and perplexing philosophical issues. In a suit for 'wrongful life', the plaintiff (usually an infant) brings an action (usually against a physician) claiming that some negligent action has caused the plaintiff's life, say by not informing the parents of the likely prospect that their child would be born with severe defects. The most perplexing feature of this is that the plaintiff is claiming the he would have been better off if he had never been born. A number of arguments have appeared with purport to show that 'wrongful life' claims should not be allowed, either because it is senseless to claim that one would be better off if one had not existed or that it is impossible to assess the extent to which someone has been damaged by being brought into existence. In our paper we rebut these arguments and suggest a procedure for determining damages in 'wrongful life cases'.

BELL, Richard. Wittgenstein's Anthropology. *Phil Invest* 7,295–312 O 84.

A discussion of the complimentary views on understanding culture of Wittgenstein and Geertz. The discussion tackles the question: How can we contemplate the depth of certain practices in the lives of persons who hold beliefs and customs different from our own? Following Wittgenstein and Geertz this can be done by careful ethnographic description of the beliefs and practices of the alien culture, and self–reflection to identify both personal biases and analogous practices within one's own culture.

BELLAMY, Richard. Croce, Gentile And Hegel And The Doctrine Of The Ethical State (Continuazione E Fine). *Riv Stud Croce* 21,67–73 Ja–Mr 84.

This article compares the different uses and analyses of Hegel's theory of the state made by Croce and Gentile. It criticized both the immanentist liberal interpretation of Croce and the transcendental fascist view of Gentile, setting the discussion in the context of debates of the time. The second part of the article restates the ethical conception of the state and argues for its superiority to the liberal individualist view of politics, while rejecting any implication of its inherently totalitarian nature.

BELLAMY, Richard. Croce's Interpretation Of Hegel. *Bull Hegel Soc Gt Brit* 9,5–14 Spr/Sum 84.

Croce, although usually regarded as a Hegelian, was as ambivalent about Hegel's philosophy as the title of his famous study, *What is Living and What is Dead in the Philosophy of Hegel* (1906), suggests. Croce's main criticism was that Hegel imposed an *a priori* scheme on reality. For Croce, history was rather a never ending immanent process which was inherently rational, but in a manner we could never fully know but only accept on faith. Croce's interpretation has been very influential, but far from giving us the "life" of the Hegelian system leaves us with just the "dead wood" of uninterpreted history.

BELLETTI, Brunpo. La Teologia Come Antropologia In Heinrich Fries. *Sapienza* 37,203–216 Ap–Je 84.

BELLISSIMA, Fabio. A Test To Determine Distinct Modalities In The Extensions Of S4. *Z Math Log* 31,57–62 1985.

The main result of the paper is the following: given an extension L of the Lewis's modal system S4, it is possible to define Kripke–model M, which contains less then 8 points, such that, for each pair A, a' of modalities, L A A' if and only if M A A'. Furthermore, it is shown that only 6 among all the possible charts of modalities are satisfied by at least an extension of S4.

BELLISSIMA, Fabio. Atoms In Modal Algebras. *Z Math Log* 30,303–312 1984.

Let $V_k$be the equational class of modal algebras; then there is a 1–1 correspondence between normal modal logics and equational subclasses of V_k. We show that if V is $V_k$or an equational subclass of $V_k$satisfying the further identity of Lx LLx, then each finitely generated free algebra over K is atomic, and the set of atoms is inductively determined. We show moreover some negative results concerning equational subclasses of $V_k$whose finitely generated free algebras are, for some n, either not atomic or atomless.

BELLO, Angela Ales. Libro E Immagine. *Aquinas* 27,335–342 My–Ag 84.

Painting and writing are two different ways of expressing human mind and feelings, one more immediate and intuitive, the other one reflexive and mediate. The essay analyzes Volume XIII of *Memorie Domenicane* (Pistoia, Italy 1982) in which there is an example of "theological iconography" (a description of a fresco in the Church of S Domenico at Pistoia) and a census of ancient manuscripts of the library of S Maria Novella in Florence.

BELLO, Rafael E. The Systems Approach. *Stud Soviet Tho* 30,131–148 Ag 85.

We undertake the comparison between Ledwid von Bertalanffy's General Systems Theory and Alexandr Bogdanov's Tektology as two theories proposing a holist interpretation of reality and claiming to solve problems which are insolveable via conventional philosophic and scientific theories and methodologies. Basic misunderstandings by some soviet authors regarding the nature of these theories is pointed out. The comparison is made in what concerns the general origins and purposes of the theories, their approaches to the problem of organization, their treatment of mathematics and their understanding of the cybernetic concept of regulation. We contend that Tektology contains all the basic concepts which will be later developed by GST. Tektology is the ultimate expansion of any theory of systems. We finally contend that Tektology and GST are a sign of the times. A holistic secular monism is an alternative to the failure of contemporary science and philosophy in guiding the life of men, in providing a raison d'etre for human existence. However, we do not explore into the soundness of this alternative.

BELLOT, P. A New Proof For Craig's Theorem. *J Sym Log* 50,395–396 Je 85.

This paper describes a short and elegant proof for the well–known theorem of Craig. The preceding proof was long and unsound. This theorem establishes that a basis for Combinatory Logic contains at least two combinators. It is related to Logic and to Computation theory.

BELNAP, Nuel D and Mc Robbie, Michael. Proof Tableau Formulations Of Some First–Order Relevant Ortho–Logics. *Bull Sect Log* 13,233–240 D 84.

In this paper proof tableau formulations are given for the first–order relevant logics (called OEQ, ORQ, and ORMQ) obtained by dropping the (zero–order) axiom of distribution and the (first–order) axiom of confinement from the well–known first–order relevant logics EQ, RQ, and RMQ. This paper extends the results presented in the author's previous paper "Relevant Analytic Tableaux", *Studia Logica*, 38 (1979), 1870200.

BELOFF, John. Science, Religion And The Paranormal. *Free Inq* 5,36–41 Spr 85.

In the absence of paranormal phenomena the physicalist interpretation of science would be difficult to challenge and hence a religious option would be difficult to defend. Here a number of historical miracles involving levitation or healing are examined which no parapsychologist can afford to ignore because they stand comparison with some of the best spontaneous cases in the literature of physical research.

BELOTE, James and Belote, Linda. Suffer The Little Children: Death, Autonomy, And Responsibility For A Changing "Low Technology" Environment. *Sci Tech Human Values* 9,35–48 Fall 84.

Between the 1960s and 1980s the Saraguros of the Ecuadorian Andes experienced a changing technological context that involved declining childhood mortality; increasing educational/occupational opportunity and diversity; expanding engagement with hierarchical structures; growing separation between adult and childhood domains; and increasing exposure to many dangerous and fragile products of modern technology. The potential consequences of this changing context—on what had been culturally well–integrated Saraguro approaches to childhood death, autonomy and responsibility—are examined.

BELOTE, Linda and Belote, James. Suffer The Little Children: Death, Autonomy, And Responsibility For A Changing "Low Technology" Environment. *Sci Tech Human Values* 9,35–48 Fall 84.

Between the 1960s and 1980s the Saraguros of the Ecuadorian Andes experienced a changing technological context that involved declining childhood mortality; increasing educational/occupational opportunity and diversity; expanding engagement with hierarchical structures; growing separation between adult and childhood domains; and increasing exposure to many dangerous and fragile products of modern technology. The potential consequences of this changing context—on what had been culturally well–integrated Saraguro approaches to childhood death, autonomy and responsibility—are examined.

BELZER, Marvin. Normative Kinematics (I): A Solution To A Problem About Permission. *Law Phil* 4,257–288 Ag 85.

This paper contains a solution to David Lewis' "problem about permission" which exists in some situations in which it is not clear how a normative system should evolve when something that had been permitted becomes forbidden. Lewis formulates the problem in terms of a language game for imperative and permission sentences. The game rules are revised to handle "contrary–to–duty" conditionals, secondly to define relationships between imperatives of relative weight and relative defeasibility, and finally to provide and defend a solution to the problem about permission.

BEN– OR, Ehud. Models For Understanding Evil In The *Guide For The Perplexed* (in Hebrew). *Iyyun* 34,3–33 Ja–Ap 85.

Maimonides' statements regarding the problem of evil are usually interpreted, along the lines of classical Theodicy, as reducing evil to privation. On the basis of Maimonides' anthropology that contrasts rational and imaginative modes of thought this essay suggests that the problem of evil was not, for him, a theoretical problem. The discussion of evil in *Guide* III is interpreted accordingly as analyzing the sources of judgements that something is evil. Such judgements are shown to be recognitions of a lack of correspondence between fact and expectation. This is further analyzed to be a disparity between the way things are and the way we wish them to be; the latter being a projection of desires. Having discovered the epistemological foundation of the problem of evil the philosopher can assume the therapist's role. Maimonides rejects several theories of Providence as inadequate models for understanding evil. On the basis of a theory of religious language as imaginative approximation to metaphysical truth through gradual reinterpretation, he suggests a model of divine justice as a model for understanding evil that "solves" the problem and gradually transcends it.

BEN– SHLOMO, Joseph. Perfection And Perfectibility In Rabbi Kook's Theology (in Hebrew). *Iyyun* 33,289–309 Ja–Ap 84.

BEN– ZEEV, Aaron. Aristotle On Perceptual Truth And Falsity. *Apeiron* 18,118–125 1984.

The article argues that Aristotle's criterion for perceptual truth and falsity is perceiving under normal conditions. After describing the criterion, it is applied to the three Aristotelian objects of perception (special, common and incidental objects), to the connection between falsity and synthesis, and to the classical problem of seeing the sun's size as being only a foot across. The suggested criterion is indeed compatible with Aristotle's stands in these issues.

BEN– ZEEV, Aaron. On The Moral Agent And Object (in Hebrew). *Iyyun* 33,480–497 O 84.

Moral rules consist of at least two factors: the moral agent who performs the moral act and the moral object at which the moral behavior is directed. In this paper I describe the features of these factors. Contrary to many traditional views, I argue that a suitable category for describing the moral agent and object is not a binary category but a prototypical category. The former is an 'all or nothing' category. Its boundaries are well defined and all its members have an equal degree of membership. In a prototypical category the members are centered around a typical member; there are neither clear boundaries nor an equal degree of membership. The degree of membership is determined by the similarity to the prototype. I show that in our everyday moral behavior our categories of moral agent and object are prototypical categories. Thus there are no clear boundaries which indicate the point at which a child becomes a moral agent. Similarly, we do not consider all moral objects as having the same moral rights. Therefore, the moral attitudes toward mice are not the same as those toward children. (edited)

BEN– ZEEV, Aaron. The Passivity Assumption Of The Sensation–Perception Distinction. *Brit J Phil Sci* 35,327–343 D 84.

The sensation–perception distinction has gained wide acceptance since its emergence in the seventeenth century. A basic assumption underlying the distinction is the passivity assumption, i.e., the postulation of a pure sensory stage—viz. Sensation—devoid of active influence of the agent's cognitive, emotional and evaluative features. The article describes the assumption, the reasons for its emergence, and some empirical and theoretical considerations indicating its flaws.

BENABOU, Jean. Fibered Categories And The Foundations Of Naive Category Theory. *J Sym Log* 50,10–37 Mr 85.

All the foundations of category–theory are based on sets, hence suppose some distinctions between big and small sets (classes, universes, etc.). We propose a "set–free" foundation which avoids such distinctions. It generalizes the ideas of Lawvere about the relation between set–theory and elementary toposes. Apart from its interest for foundations, our approach provides both a better understanding and a mathematical tool for the study of categories based on an elementary topos.

BENARY, P. "Ästhetik Und Musiktheorie Um 1750" in *Asthetische Er Fahrung Und Das Wesen Der Kunst*, Holzhey, Helmut, 143–155. Bern Haupt 1984.

BENCIVENGA, Ermanno. Identity, Appearances, And Things In Themselves. *Dialogue (Canada)* 23,421–438 S 84.

A classical problem of Kantian scholarship is that of understanding whether things in themselves are numerically the same as or distinct from appearances. This paper's proposal is that appearances and things in themselves be regarded as (numerically) the same objects in different possible worlds.

BENCIVENGA, Ermanno. Strong Completeness Of A Pure Free Logic. *Z Math Log* 31,35–38 1985.

A pure free logic is a free quantification theory without identity and without the special existence symbol E! The semantic completeness of a pure free logic QC* was proved by Leblanc and Meyer in 1970, but theirs was a *weak* completeness proof, that is, a proof that all logically true sentences are provable in QC*. In this paper, I give a *strong* completeness proof for QC*, that is I prove that all semantic consequences of a set *K* of sentences are deductive consequences of *K* in QC*.

BENCIVENGA, Ermanno. Supervaluations And Theories. *Grazer Phil Stud* 21,89–98 1984.

BENDER, Frederic L. Heidegger's Hermeneutical Grounding Of Science: A Phenomenological Critique Of Positivism. *Phil Res Arch* 10,203–238 1984.

It is argued that, despite the neglect which Heidegger's writings on science have generally received, the "fundamental ontology" of *Being and Time* reveals certain structures of experience crucial for our understanding of science; and that, as these insights cast considerable doubt upon the validity of the empiricist/positivist conception of science, Heidegger deserves considerably better treatment as an incipient philosopher of science than has been the case thus far. His arguments for the distortive effects of the alleged "change over" from *praxis* to *theoria*, for the circularity of all human understanding (including scientific understanding), for the necessity of interpreting scientific method in terms of the hermeneutic circle, and for viewing scientific "crises" in ontological terms, are examined and evaluated. The article concludes with some reflections on the later Heidegger's views on the limits of his earlier idea of science.

BENDITT, Theodore M. "Surrogate Gestation, Law, And Morality" in *Biomedical Ethics Reviews*, Humber, James M (ed), 47–68. Clifton Humana Pr 1983.

BENDITT, Theodore M. The Demands Of Justice. *Ethics* 95,224–232 Ja 85.

Some elements of justice are morally required and others are desirable but not required. Rights of justice pertain only to: (1) certain elements of welfare—where deficiencies are attributable to one's being a victim of the economic life of the collective; (2) conditional equality—one has a right to equal treatment when social policies affect distribution; and (3) reciprocity—in exchanges one has a right to a balance

between the value of what he gives and of what he gets.

BENEDICT– GILL, Diane. Moral Objectivity. *Proc Phil Educ* 40,219–224 1984.

BENEDICT, George A. What Are Representamens? *Trans Peirce Soc* 21,240–270 Spr 85.

BENENSON, F C. *Probability, Objectivity And Evidence.* Boston Routledge & K Paul 1984.

BENFEY, Christopher E G. *Emily Dickinson And The Problem Of Others.* Amherst Univ Of Mass Pr 1984.

BENHABIB, Seyla. "Obligation, Contract And Exchange: On Hegel's Abstract Right" in *The State And Civil Society*, Pelczynski, Z A (ed), 159–177. Cambridge Cambridge Univ Pr 1984.

BENHABIB, Seyla. The Marxian Method Of Critique: Normative Presuppositions. *Praxis Int* 4,284–298 O 84.

This essay examines the normative presuppositions of the Marxian method of critique by focusing on Marx's *Capital*. I suggest that throughout his writings Marx remains faithful to the vision of an active humanity, reappropriating the essential human wealth which it has alienated in the course of history. This view is named the "philosophy of the subject", and the difficulties of the Marxian concept of "class", as historical and moral agent, are discussed in light of it.

BENIANS, R C. Children In Care: Are Social Workers Abusing Their Authority? *J Med Ethics* 10,133–135 S 84.

This paper is a plea, from a child psychiatrist, for greater consultation between professionals who have skills in promoting the welfare of children, namely social workers, teachers and doctors. Three much shortened case histories are presented where insufficient consultation between social workers and child psychiatrists led, in the author's opinion, to abuse of social work authority and therefore to unnecessary professional and legal conflict. (edited)

BENJAMIN, Martin and Baum, Robert. "I'm The Teacher". *Teach Phil* 8,151–156 Ap 85.

BENJAMIN, Martin. Lay Obligations In Professional Relations. *J Med Phil* 10,85–103 F 85.

Little has been written recently about the obligation of lay people in professional relationships. Yet the Code of Medical Ethics adopted by the American Medical Association in 1847 included an extensive statement on Obligations of patients to their physicians'. After critically examining the philosophical foundations of this statement, I provide an alternative account of lay obligations in professional relationships. Based on a hypothetical social contract and included in full specifiaction of professional as well as lay obligations, this account requires lay people to honor commitments and disclose relevant information. Ethically, the account assumes that all parties in layprofessional relationships should be given equal consideration and respect in determing rights and obligations. Factually, it assumes that the treatment of many illnesses and injuries requires collaboration and cooperation among lay persons and health professionals, that medical resources and personnel are limited, and that medicine, nursing, and related health professions are, in MacIntyre's sense, practices.

BENN, S I. Persons And Values: Reasons In Conflict And Moral Disagreement. *Ethics* 95,20–37 O 84.

Reasons for action are of diverse types, value–centered, person–centered, symbolic, etc. These reasons are explained. The debate on paternalism illustrates the conflict between such reasoned commitments. Hare's rationalized preferentialism, though seemingly centered on persons, is shown to be value–maximizing morality. The fragmentation of moral culture (MacIntyre) is due to the acceleration of social change so that priority principles for resolving conflicts do not emerge. Consequently, in the modern consciousness, the burden of rational moral decision rests on the individual judgment, unsupported by social consensus. This does not entail either that rational agreement is ultimately unattainable, nor that individual moral judgments cannot claim to be rational, irrespective of consensus.

BENN, S I. Wickedness. *Ethics* 95,795–810 Jl 85.

The subject is forms of wickedness, their relation to other evils in human beings, and to freedom of choice and motivation to evil. Self–centered wickedness, which includes selfishness and psychopathy, and conscientious wickedness, which may be autonomous or heteronomous, are distinguished from malignity, which *pace* Socrates consists in knowingly acting on evil maxims for the sake of their being evil. Consideration is given to the way in which ignorance, error, and incapacity modify judgments of wickedness.

BENN, Tony. Socialism, Democracy And Marxism: The Need For Dialogue. *Phil Soc Act* 11,5–20 Ja–Mr 85.

BENNE, Kenneth D. The Learning Community. *Proc Phil Educ* 40,27–52 1984.

BENNETT, James O. The Meaning Of Life: A Qualitative Perspective. *Can J Phil* 14,581–592 D 84.

I argue that meaningfulness can be analyzed in terms of the experience of intrinsic value, which—like experience in general—is a product of the interaction of organism and environment. I attempt to indicate the importance of "the qualitative dimension" of value experience, which is the range of what individuals can "get out of" any given situation, as determined by the intellectual, emotional, and volitional resources that they bring into that situation.

BENNETT, James R. Oceania And The United States In *1984*: The Selling Of The Soviet Threat. *Soc Theor Pract* 10,301–318 Fall 84.

George Orwell's *1984* describes the machinery of totalitarian repression and provides an index for judging how far democratic societies have fallen into authoritarian practices. By projecting an ever–threatening, diabolical Enemy through constant "Two Minutes Hate" and recurrent "Hate Weeks", the United States imitates Oceania.

BENNETT, John C. "Human Nature And The Human Hope" in *On Nature*, Rouner, Leroy S (ed), 169–184. Notre Dame Univ Notre Dame Pr 1984.

BENNETT, John G. Ethics And Markets. *Phil Pub Affairs* 14,195–204 Spr 85.

This article argues that Ronald Dworkin is wrong to claim (in *Philosophy & Public Affairs* 10:4, Fall 1984) that markets are required for equality and also mistaken in claiming that markets ensure that what you get depends on how important what you want is to others. The argument is based on simple facts about the preferences we express by market choices which show these cannot plausibly be a measure of what is important to us.

BENOIT, Hubert. *The Supreme Doctrine: Psychological Encounters In Zen Thought.* NY Inner Traditions 1984.

BENTON, Ted. *The Rise And Fall Of Structural Marxism: Althusser And His Influence.* NY St Martin's Pr 1984.

A wide–ranging and ambitious interpretation and evaluation of the work of French Marxist Philosopher, Louis Althusser, and his most influential associates and followers. The book sets Althusser's work in the context of the post–war French intellectual and political life, and critically engages with structural Marxist work in philosophy, anthropology, state–theory, class–analysis and feminism. Two chapters examine critiques of a structural Marxism by post–structuralists, sociologists and historians.

BENTON, Ted. Biological Ideas And Their Cultural Uses. *Philosophy* 17,111–134 84 Supp.

BERENSON, Frances. Understanding Art And Understanding Persons. *Philosophy* 17,43–60 84 Supp.

Relativism questions the possibility of cross–cultural understanding in general; the Institutional Theory of Art raises similar difficulties for Aesthetics. Nevertheless, the impulse to create and express are exclusively human and universal; art has universal appeal. It follows that difficulties in understanding are universal, not specifically cultural, as alleged, in some mysterious way. I indicate some directions in identifying *the nature* of difficulties arising and suggest that we stop adding gratuitous mysteries to this undeniably complex field.

BERES, Louis René. Vain Hopes And A Fool's Fancy: Understanding US Nuclear Strategy. *Phil Soc Crit* 10,35–52 Wint 84.

BERESFORD, H Richard. "Legal Aspects Of Ethics In Neural And Behavioral Sciences" in *Ethical Questions In Brain And Behavior*, Pfaff, Donald W (ed), 73–90. NY Springer 1983.

BERG, Kare (ed) and Tranoy, Knut Erik (ed). *Research Ethics.* NY Liss 1983.

BERGER, Jeffrey. Writing To Learn In Philosophy. *Teach Phil* 7,217–222 Jl 84.

Be redesigning assignments to include an audience and purpose, by the use of one paragraph assignments, and by building faculty supervised revision into the writing process, philosophy teachers can increase not only the writing, but the conceptual level in student papers. Various strategies for accomplishing this are discussed.

BERGER, René. Art And Media On The Road To Abdera? *Diogenes* 128,1–16 Wint 84.

Today the term *art* includes, beside the Fine Arts, the public or mass arts, the new technological arts, all related to the development of the media. The media (information, transportation, computing) are made up of *configuring structures* which impregnate the audience with *configured structures*, process that I call *topic*. Reaching a new turning point we are giving up Plato to rediscover the model of the sophists, Democritus being the first epistemologist of our information society.

BERGMANN, Werner and Hoffmann, G. Habitualität Als Potentialität: Zur Konkretisierung Des Ich Bei Husserl. *Husserl Stud* 1,281–306 1984.

BERGSMA, Jurrit. Towards A Concept Of Shared Autonomy. *Theor Med* 5,325–332 O 84.

The theoretical analysis shows that patient's autonomy only can exist in a relation with an autonomous physician. Patients urging their physician to autonomous behavior chain both partners to each other so autonomy cannot be developed. The semi-solution is found in continuing new appointments. (edited)

BERGSTRÖM, Lars. Underdetermination And Realism. *Erkenntnis* 21,349–365 N 84.

This paper criticizes Newton–Smith's arguments for the theses that scientific theories can be underdetermined by all possible data and that underdetermined theories are neither true nor false. Several distinct notions of underdetermination are distinguished. Some of Quine's views on the subject are defended; others are criticized. Underdetermination is held to be compatible with theoretical realism.

BERLIN, Isaiah. On Vico. *Phil Quart* 35,281–289 Jl 85.

The article is a response to Professor Zagorin's essay on Vico in a previous number of the Phil Quart. My principle theses were (1) that there is no evidence in Locke's writings for Professor Zagorin's assertion that Locke was one of the anticipators of Vico's views that man understands only what he makes and that therefore moral and political principles and values are no objective. (2) That Vico drew a sharp distinction between the methods of the natural sciences and those of the humanities, and that Professor Zagorin's view that for Vico his 'new science' was a science in the sense of the natural sciences of Vico's time is mistaken, since the central thesis of Vico's entire work rests on the distinction between our knowledge of the external world and that of human thought, feeling and activity.

BERLINGER, Rudolph. Le Paysage Arcadien De Nietzsche: Reflets D'Engadine. *Rev Metaph Morale* 89,490–504 O–D 84.

BERMAN, David. Particles And Ideas In Locke's Theory Of Meaning. *Locke News* 15,15–24 1984.

It used to be thought that Locke enthusiastically accepted the thesis that all significant words stand for ideas. Recent commentators, however, such as R I Aaron, C B Martin, D J O'Connor, J G Clapp, J Jenkins, have contested this older view, adducing *Essay* 111 vii, "of Particles", as plain evidence that Locke's semantic theory is not

unrestrictive. In this paper I argue that the recent view is mistaken: particles, according to Locke, are meaningfully used only when they stand for ideas.

BERMAN, Ronald. "Feeling Unfree: Freedom And Fulfillment In Contemporary Culture" in *On Freedom*, Howard, John A (ed), 95–111. Greenwich Devin–Adair 1984.

BERMAN, Ronald. Commentary On "Advertising And Program Content". *Bus Prof Ethics J* 3,81–86 Spr/Sum 84.

BERNARDO, J M and Ferrandiz, J R and Smith, A F M. The Foundations Of Decision Theory: An Intuitive, Operational Approach With Mathematical Extensions. *Theor Decis* 19,127–150 S 85.

A new axiomatic basis for the foundations of decision theory is introduced and its mathematical development outlined. The system combines direct intuitive operational appeal with considerable structural flexibility in the resulting mathematical framework.

BERNAUER, James. On Reading And Mis–Reading Hannah Arendt. *Phil Soc Crit* 11,1–34 Sum 85.

This essay examines the published literature on Hannah Arendt as well as recent dissertations devoted to her in addition to her own writings and unpublished papers. It attempts to account for the surge of interest in her work and the major reasons for mis–reading it, namely, the failure to appreciate her thought as a radical form of anti-modernism and the lack of attention to the influence of her earliest theological studies.

BERNHARDT, Herbert and Richter, F. Zur Realisierung Des Verhältnisses Von Philosophie Und Einzelwissenschaften Im Marxistisch–Leninistischen Grundstudium. *Deut Z Phil* 32,1017–1020 1984.

In the work is proved a position to the discussion in Deut Z Phil if there is today a changed situation concerning the connection of philosophy with science in the GDR, related to the time 20 years ago. In fact there is a problem shifting from philosophical problems of science to such of social sciences. We can see this if we teach philosophy for non–philosophy students at a technical university.

BERNHARDT, Jean. Intelligibilité Et Réalité Chez Hobbes Et Spinoza. *Rev Phil Fr* 175,115–133 Ap–Je 85.

This text is but a reprint of *Dialogue* 1981 december, pp. 716–723 (by permission from Fi Duchesneau, Montrél, as part of the set of texts issued from a meeting on Hobbet and Spinoza, Paris, 1977). This article is devoted to a study of the probable influence of Hobbes and Spinoza through a gift by Olenburg (July 1661)—the point of view is general theory of science, not specifically politics.

BERNHARDT, Jean. Note Sur Le Mécanisme Ordonné Chez Descartes. *Rev Phil Fr* 174,219–220 Ap–Je 84.

BERNIER, Réjane. Potentialités Morphogénétiques Et Auto–Organisation. *Arch Phil* 47,529–556 O–D 84.

The author focuses her study of the organization of the living on the phenomena of embryonic morphogenesis. The first part aims at showing the ontological implications in the notion of morphogenetic potentiality as used by embryologists. The second part will show the self–organizing role of the morphogenetic function. The immanence of the principle of organization in the living distinguishes organic from inorganic morphogenesis. (edited)

BERNSTEIN, J M. "From Self–Consciousness To Community" in *The State And Civil Society*, Pelczynski, Z A (ed), 14–39. Cambridge Cambridge Univ Pr 1984.

BERNSTEIN, Richard G. What Is The Difference That Makes A Difference: Gadamer, Habermas, And Rorty (in Hebrew). *Iyyun* 33,96–123 Ja–Ap 84.

BERRY, John W. N–ary Almost Recursive Functions. *Z Math Log* 20,551–559 1974.

BERTELLONI, C Francisco. Heidegger, 1916–1921: Hegelianismo Y Filosofía Medieval En Los Orígenes Del Pensamiento Heideggeriano. *Cuad Filosof* 19,135–154 Ja–D 83.

BERTELLONI, Maria–Teresa. "Why Be A Poet" in *Existential Coordinates Of Human Condition*, Tymieniecka, A (ed), 37–46. Boston Reidel 1984.

BERTMAN, Martin A. Anachronistic Inauthenticity In Art. *J Aes Educ* 18,115–118 Fall 84.

This is a brief discussion of the meaning of imitating a particular art style that is not of one's own time (or culture). It brings to the forefront the point that such an imitation must use techniques, themes, and an involvement with the problems that are either alien to one's own time or which have already been solved, thus it is a suppression of knowledge which is considered a inauthentic.

BERTMAN, Martin A. Augustine: History And Wholeness. *Cogito* 2,69–78 S 84.

BERTMAN, Martin A. The Natural Body And The Body Politic. *Phil Soc Crit* 5,17–34 Ja 78.

This paper discusses the relationship of Hobbes' understanding of the human body in his attempt to relate it to human psychology and with that to show the material and physiological/psychological foundation of his theory of politics.

BERTOLDI, E F. Gadamer's Criticisms Of Collingwood. *Ideal Stud* 14,213–228 S 84.

BERTOLDI, Eugene F. Metaphysics And The 'Eye And Mind'. *S J Phil* 23,1–18 Spr 85.

BERTOLET, Rod. Ackerman On Propositional Identity. *Phil Quart* 34,499–504 O 84.

Diana Ackerman is perhaps the most recent philosopher to deploy one of the principles often entitled "Leibniz's Law" to argue that at least some propositions containing different but coreferential singular terms must be distinct. I attempt to show that her argument (and by implication its predecessors) fails because the attempt to appeal to the allegedly Leibnizian principle is illegitimate: either the principle is unacceptable, or else its use in the argument is question–begging.

BERTOLET, Rod. Context And What Is Said. *Can J Phil* 6,97–110 80 Supp.

A popular answer to the question of what, in addition to what a sentence means, determines what a speaker who utters that sentence says, is the context in which it is uttered. While this answer is often not developed in any detail, Paul Ziff in "What is Said" attempts to specify just what contextual features are relevant and how they operate. This paper argues that the factors Ziff offers are in fact irrelevant to the determination of what is said. The general outline of an alternative approach is briefly sketched.

BERTOLET, Rod. Reference, Fiction, And Fictions. *Synthese* 60,413–438 S 84.

This paper develops a theory of what is said by speakers who use sentences containing empty names such as 'Pegasus' and other non–denoting noun phrases. The view allows us to say that speakers who use the sentence 'Pegasus has wings' say something true, without postulating a nonexistent object which is named 'Pegasus', but also without claiming that the sentence 'Pegasus has wings' is itself true, obviating the need to explain how that sentence can be true if there is not some nonexistent Pegasus. Applications beyond such stock examples are detailed.

BERTOTTI, Bruno. The Later Work Of E Schödinger. *Stud Hist Phil Sci* 16,83–100 Je 85.

Schrödinger's later work is characterized by a research committment on Unified Field Theory, an attempt to unify outside quantum theory forces occurring in nature. This work was conducted in almost isolation and did not lead to the expected results. The connection of this committment with his opposition to conventional quantum theory and with his general philosophical outlook is discussed. His "view of the world" is summarized and described as "rational mysticism."

BERTRAND, Pierre. Pour Un Pacifisme Viscéral. *Petit Rev Phil* 6,123–128 Autumn 84.

The figure of Big Brother has become an extra–literary cultural symbol of all that we fear about Big Government. The shadowy symbol serves as a rhetorical device, invoked by both Left and Right to arouse fear of policies they oppose: the argumentum–ad–Orwell. Frequently the rhetorical invocations have little or no relation to the situations of Orwell's novel: but—like Frankenstein's monster—Big Brother has assumed a life of his own.

BETANCOURT, Raul Fornet. Finitud, Poder, Ternura. *Logos (Mexico)* 8,57–74 My–Ag 85.

The intention of this essay is to contribute to philosophical anthropology by analyzing the dimensions of finiteness, power and tenderness and thus opening a possibility for the adequate understanding of human existence. Finiteness is explained as the fundamental experience which makes man aware of his commitment. The experience of finiteness leads to revolt of man. He relies on power in order to secure his existence. But power is self–deception. The only response to finiteness is tenderness.

BETTIM EMILIO. "Epistemological Problem Of Understanding As Aspect Of General Problem Of Knowing" in *Hermeneutics*, Shapiro, Gary (ed), 25–53. Amherst Univ Of Mass Pr 1984.

BETTY, L Stafford. Is Nāgārjuna A Philosopher: A Response To Professor Loy. *Phil East West* 34,447–450 O 84.

BETZ, Joseph. Sissela Bok On The Analogy Of Deception And Violence. *J Value Inq* 19,217–224 1985.

Is it morally right to save the life of an innocent person by telling a lie to the pursuing murderer? Sissela Bok, in her book, *Lying*, says yes and supports this conclusion, in large part, by her analogy of deception and violence. This involves an *a fortiori* argument which I find faulty and which I correct by constructing a valid analogy which implies a definition of lying which Bok had rejected.

BEUCHOT, Mauricio. El Problema De Los Universales En Domingo De Soto Y Alonso De La Veracruz. *Rev Filosof (Mexico)* 17,249–274 My–Jl 84.

BEUCHOT, Mauricio. Jean Piaget Y La Estructuración Genética Del Lenguaje. *Logos (Mexico)* 13,55–68 Ja–Ap 85.

BEUCHOT, Mauricio. La Lingüística Generativo–Transformacional De Noam Chomsky. *Logos (Mexico)* 12,11–40 My–Ag 84.

BEUCHOT, Mauricio. La Teoria De La Argumentacion En Aristoteles. *Rev Filosof (Mexico)* 18,79–88 Ja–Ap 85.

BEUCHOT, Mauricio. Reflexiones Filosóficas Sobre La Lingüística Estructuralista De Ferdinand De Saussure. *Logos (Mexico)* 12,57–92 S–D 84.

BEURTON, Peter. Zur Dialektik In Der Biologischen Evolution. *Deut Z Phil* 23,913–925 1975.

Der Autor umreifsst die s E wichtigsten philosophischen Probleme der heutigen Evolutionsbiologie. Nach seiner Meinung mufss die moderne Evolutionsbiologie über Darwin hinausgehen, da von der Evolutionsbiologie in ihrer Geschichte die dialektische Sprünge in der theoretischen Erfassung der Evolution nicht bewältigt wurden. Es wird ferner die Frage der Höherentwicklung und ihrer Kriterien diskutiert. Den der Höherentwicklung zugrunde liegenden allgemeingültigen Zusammenhang sieht der Autor in der Negation der Negation.

BEVER, Thomas G (ed) and Carroll, John M (ed) and Miller, Lance A (ed). *Talking Minds: The Study Of Language In The Cognitive Sciences*. Cambridge MIT Pr 1984.

BEVERSLUIS, Eric H. Benefit Rights In Education: An Entitlement View. *Proc Phil Educ* 40,381–390 1984.

Do people have *benefit rights* (enforceable claims to receive certain economic goods) or merely *liberty rights* (rights to choose freely what to do)? Nozick's historical– entitlement view of economic justice implies that people do no have benefit rights to educational resources. Yet a newborn child has a right to nurture (and, a fortiori, a benefit right). The essay modifies Nozick's notion of entitlement and fits it with a correct understanding of people's liberty rights.

BEVERSLUIS, John. *C S Lewis And The Search For Rational Religion*. Grand Rapids Eerdmans 1985.

This book is the first *critical* study of Lewis's apologetic writings. In it I argue that the evidence, as presented by Lewis, does not support belief in God and that his "case for Christianity" therefore fails. In addition to discussing Lewis's arguments for the existence of God and his answer to the problem of evil, I assess his apologetic method in light of the debate among contemporary Anglo–American philosophers of religion.

BEVILACQUA, Vincent M. Campbell, Vico, And The Rhetorical Science Of Human Nature. *Phil Rhet* 18,23–30 1985.

BEYER, Hans. Bedingungen Und Merkmale Des Klassenkampfes In Den Kapitalistischen Ländern Europas. *Deut Z Phil* 23,1025–1035 1975.

Die veränderten Bedingunger des Klassenkampfes führten zu einem Aufschwung der Kämpfe. Die Streiks haben zugenommen, die Auseinandersetzungen nehmen an Härte zu. Die neuen Bedingungen haben neue gesellschaftliche Bedürfnisse der Massen erzeugt, diese haben ihrerseits neue Forderungen auf sozialer und politischer Ebene hervorgebracht. Die ökonomischen Kämpfe verschmelzen immer häufiger mit politischen Aktionen. ausdruck für den Aufschwung des Klassenkampfes ist z. B die Zunahme von Massenstreiks und von Aktionen mit nationalem Ausmafss.

BEYER, Wilhelm R. Gegendarstellung. *Z Phil Forsch* 29,462 Jl–S 75.

BEYER, Wilhelm. Hegel Oder Schelling Als Autor Eines Zwei–Seiten–Papiers? *Deut Z Phil* 23,744–747 1975.

BEZEM, Marc. Isomorphisms Between HEO And HRO, ECF And ICF. *J Sym Log* 50,359–371 Je 85.

In this paper it will be shown that HEO and HRO^E are isomorphic with respect to extensional equality. This answers a question of Troelstra [T, 2.4.12, p 128]. The main problem is to extend effective operations to a larger domain. This will be achieved by a modification of the proof of the continuity of effective operations. Following a suggestion of A S Troelstra, similar results were obtained for ECF(U) and $ICF^E(U)$, where U is any universe of functions closed under "recursive in."

BHARDWAJA, V K. A Non–Ethical Concept Of Ahimsa. *Indian Phil Quart* 11,171–180 Ap 84.

ahimsa in Yoga–sutra is a causal, not moral or social concept. It constitutes a behavioral condition which produces certain other conditions of *yogic* growth. In this causal chain, there is no scope for moral judgment of conduct; for, causality only and no responsibility is involved. Also, this nonethical concept is differentiated from Gandhi's concept of *ahimsa*, and it is observed that for a Gandhi *ahimsa* is a tool of prudent political policy and action.

BHARUCHA, Filita and Kamat, R V. Syadvada Theory Of Jainism In Terms Of A Deviant Logic. *Indian Phil Quart* 11,181–188 Ap 84.

This paper seeks to investigate whether a 3–valued deviant (extended) logic can represent the Syādvāda Theory (the doctrine of 'may be' or the relativity of judgements) of Jainism. The Syādvāda Theory describing an object of the phenomenal world subject to factors of space, time, mode and substance, is presented as seven logical propositional statements. Two types of conjunctions (simultaneous and nonsimultaneous) are introduced. The paper ends with a suggestion that a Pramāna (complete judgement) can be interpreted as a tautology.

BHATTACHARYA, K C. Review Of *The Origin Of Subjectivity In Hindu Thought*. *Indian Phil Quart* 11,401–410 O–D 84.

BIAGINI, Hugo E. La Recepción Argentina Del Pensamiento Norteamericano. *Cuad Filosof* 19,167–192 Ja–D 83.

BIALAS, Volker. Zum Verhältnis Von Technikphilosophie Und Technikgeschichte. *Deut Z Phil* 32,943–948 1984.

BIALAS, Wolfgang. Hegel's Religion Philosophy In The Context Of His Theory Of Bourgeois Society (in German). *Deut Z Phil* 33,425–434 1985.

BIANCHI, Daniela. Some Sources For A History Of English Socinianism; A Bibliography Of 17th Century English Socinian Writings. *Topoi* 4,91–120 Mr 85.

BIARD, Joel. L'unité Du Monde Selon Guillaume D'Ockham (Ou La Logique De La Cosmologie Ockhamiste). *Vivarium* 22,63–83 My 84.

BICKNELL, D J. Current Arrangements For Teaching Medical Ethics To Undergraduate Medical Students. *J Med Ethics* 11,25–26 Mr 85.

Those teachers in contact with medical students from pre–clinical days onwards will impart their ethical views by example and by precept, but such learning by 'osmosis' is insufficient. There is a knowledge base to be imparted which will enrich the understanding of ethical judgements on clinical problems seen during the undergraduate years. However, the learning process continues after qualification and in particular the doctor's capacity to make ethical clinical judgements will evolve with maturity and experience. It is essential therefore that students see their teachers willing and able to debate ethical issues at the postgraduate level.

BIEDERMAN, Barry. Commentary On Beauchamp's "Manipulative Advertising". *Bus Prof Ethics J* 3,29–30 Spr/Sum 84.

BIEDERMANN, Georg and Lange, E. Zum Humanismus In Der Klassischen Deutschen Philosophie, Seinen Sozialhistorischen Und Theoretischen Voraussetzungen. *Deut Z Phil* 32,805–818 1984.

BIEDERMANN, Georg and Lindner, F. Schelling–Konferenz In Jena. *Deut Z Phil* 23,1072–1075 1975.

BIEDERMANN, Georg. Schelling Und Hegel In Jena. *Deut Z Phil* 23,737–744 1975.

BIEMEL, Walter. "Situational Art: Observations—Contemporary Art" in *Continental Philosophy/The Arts*, Winters, Laurence E and others (ed), 173–192. Lanham Univ Pr Of America 1984.

BIENENSTOCK, Myriam. Rosenzweig's Hegel (in Hebrew). *Iyyun* 33,91–95 Ja–Ap 84.

Bilimoria, Purusottama 248 **Author Index with Abstracts**

BILIMORIA, Purusottama. *Jñāna* And *Pramā*: The Logic Of Knowing—A Critical Appraisal. *J Indian Phil* 13,73–102 Mr 85.

The thrust of this paper is to investigate the relative difference between *jñāna* and *pramā*, two crucial concepts in Indian epistemology, since more recent treatment of them would seem to be confused. Utilizing the framework developed by Nyāya and Advaita, it is argued that the former describes a wide range of cognitive processes, such as 'cognition', 'judgment', 'remembering', 'doubting', etc., while the latter defines the bounds of cognition in respect of its truth–value. A theory of knowledge is developed that accounts for the rise of 'true' knowledge in terms of the 'psyche–activity' involved and the set of criteria (*pramanya*) that renders a *jnana* as a *prama*. The intensional structure of such a judgment, it is argued, involves a complex qualified–qualifier relation in conformity with the property–content relation of the objective correlate.

BIRD, Richard. Non Recursive Functionals. *Z Math Log* 21,41–46 1975.

BIRDWHISTELL, Anne D. The Concept Of Experimental Knowledge In The Thought Of Chang Tsai. *Phil East West* 35,39–60 Ja 85.

This article examines Chang Tsai's conception of experiential knowledge. Not an object of philosophical concern in its own right, experiential knowledge was discussed in relationship to moral knowledge, with which it was paired, inappropriately, on the model of yin and yang. Experiential knowledge was subjected to the standards of moral knowledge and judged inferior. Nonetheless, it was important because it emphasized the empirical grounding of Neo–Confucian thought as opposed to Buddhist idealism.

BIRNBACHER, Dieter. Spinoza Und Die Reue. *Z Phil Forsch* 38,219–240 Ap–Je 84.

Spinoza's psychology as developed in his *Ethics* anticipates a lot of modern psychological theory. The article shows that this is particularly true of Spinoza's treatment of *repentance*. It is argued that Spinoza's (together with Nietzsche's and Walter Kaufmann's) rejection of the justifiability of guilt, repentance, etc., has excellent reasons on its side and is not jeopardized by the attacks launched on it by Max Scheler and (indirectly) P F Strawson.

BIRNER, Jack. Keynes Versus Hayek: Interne En Externe Factoren In Een Controverse In De Economie. *Kennis Methode* 9,26–48 1985.

BIRO, J I. Hume And Cognitive Science. *Hist Phil Quart* 2,257–274 Jl 85.

In this paper I explore some similarities and some differences between Hume's science of man and contemporary cognitivism. After discussing some matters of general approach and methodology, I examine three questions of particular interest in the philosophy of cognitive science: the problem of the content of mental states, the problem of qualia, and the problem of so–called exempt agent. I argue that all three matters Hume had something of interest to say, indeed, that there are some lessons in his treatment of them the cognitivist would do well to take to heart.

BIRO, J I. What's In A Belief? *Log Anal* 27,267–282 S 84.

I attempt to show that there is no real puzzle of the sort Kripke worries about in "A Puzzle about Belief". The key to seeing this is appreciating that the unrestricted use of the principle of disquotation that generates the apparent puzzle is not well motivated. Certain natural restrictions on the principle, consistent with our actual practices of belief attribution, are discussed and applied to Kripke's story about Pierre.

BIRO, John I. Knowability, Believability And Begging The Question: A Reply To David H Sanford. *Metaphilosophy* 15,239–247 Jl–O 84.

I attempt to reply to some criticisms of David Sanford of an account I offered earlier of the fallacy of begging the question. (Biro, *Metaphilosophy* 1977; Sanford, *Metaphilosophy* 1981). In that account, I advocated the notion of epistemic seriousness as a criterion for non–question–begging arguments. An epistemically serious argument was said to be on whose premises were knowable independently of its conclusion. Such a criterion could yield an account of the fallacy that was neither purely formal nor purely psychological. Here I try to show that Sanford's alternative account of the fallacy in terms of the arguer's beliefs fails, as do all psychological accounts, to do justice to the normative dimension of the notion, unless we take seriously his occasional talk of *reasonable* belief. But then there is no real difference between our accounts: what propositions an arguer reasonably believes and what propositions are knowable for him come, for the present purpose, to much the same thing.

BIRUS, Hendrik. *Wir Philologen*: Überlegungen Zu Nietzsches Begriff Der Interpretation. *Rev Int Phil* 38,373–395 1984.

BISHOP, John. Causal Deviancy And Multiple Intentions: A Reply To James Montmarquet. *Analysis* 45,163–168 Je 85.

How can a causal theory of action deal with deviant cases involving causal chains passing through the intentional action of a second agent? Montmarquet defends an augmented version of Peacocke's "differential explanation" version of the causal theory (*Analysis*, 42 (1982) 106–110). I argue that this account mistakenly rules out *a priori* the possibility that a second agent should be part of a prosthetic aid to basic action, but this does *not* entail that Peacocke's unaugmented theory was correct. The crucial distinction required is that between a pre–emptive and a non–pre–emptive intervention by a second agent; and this cannot be analyzed as a matter of the "sensitivity" of the relevant causal chain.

BISHOP, John. Theism, Morality And The 'Why Should I Be Moral' Question. *Int J Phil Relig* 17,3–22 1985.

It is argued that only a theistic metaphysic can provide a rational justification for the individual's acceptance of the unconditional claim of an objective morality which bans exploiting others for self–gain. The theist's rational grounding of morality is defended against the common charge that it undermines morality by providing a self–interested ground for moral conformity. (Ethical egoism is unattractive only given the assumption that individual interests conflict: but theism, counter–evidentially, denies this assumption.)

BISKY, L. Zur Entwicklung Und Befriedigung Kultureller Bedürfnisse. *Deut Z Phil* 33,63–72 1985.

BLACK, Douglas. Iconoclastic Ethics. *J Med Ethics* 10,179–182 D 84.

Arguments are advanced, on a pragmatic basis, for preferring a 'situational' approach to medical ethical problems, rather than an approach based on any one of the dogmatic formulations on offer. The consequences of such a preference are exemplified in relation to confidentiality; and in relation to the ethical dilemmas which surround the beginning and the end of terrestrial life.

BLACK, Douglas. In Defence Of Situational Ethics, The NHS And The Permissive Society. *J Med Ethics* 10,121 S 84.

Dr Adrian Rogers delivers a three–pronged assault on the concepts of 'situational ethics'; the eleemosynary principles underlying the National Health Service, and the permissiveness of modern society. I hold strong, and largely opposite, views on each of these matters, which are outlined in this paper.

BLACK, Max. Making Intelligent Choices, How Useful Is Decision Theory? *Dialectica* 39,19–34 1985.

A critical outline, primarily for non–professionals, of some leading ideas and normative implications of "Bayesian Decision Theory". Violations of the postulated transitivity of the chooser's preference relation are not necessarily symptoms of irrationality. Indeed, the overall normative constraint of "consistency" is too restrictive a guide for many real–life choices. Rational choice might perhaps be more usefully conceived as an informal *art*, rather than as the pursuit, in Bayesian style, of maximal expected utility.

BLACKWELL, Henry and Stone, Lucy. "Marriage Contract" in *Freedom, Feminism, And The State*, Mc Elroy, Wendy (ed), 119–120. Washington Cato Institute 1982.

BLACKWELL, Kenneth. Part I Of *The Principles Of Mathematics*. *Russell* 4,271–288 Wint 84.

BLACKWELL, Richard J. "Reflections On Descartes' Methods Of Analysis And Synthesis" in *History Of Philosophy In Making*, Thro, Linus J (ed), 119–132. Washington Univ Pr Of America 1982.

BLAIR, J Anthony and Johnson, Ralph H. Informal Logic: The Past Five Years 1978–1983. *Amer Phil Quart* 22,181–196 Jl 85.

This article surveys developments in informal logic during the period from 1978–1983. It is a review of the monograph, journal article and textbook literature. A 90–item bibliography of works cited is appended. The authors detail developments in the theory of argument, the theory of criticism (including fallacy theory), testing and teaching. They conclude that informal logic has achieved a certain definition in a relatively short time, and recommend that future work include closer investigation of related problems of philosophy and of related work being done in cognate fields.

BLAKELEY, Thomas J (ed) and Rapp, Friedrich J (ed) and O' Rourke, James J (ed). *Contemporary Marxism: Essays In Honor Of J M Bocheński*. Boston Reidel 1984.

BLAKELEY, Thomas J. "Out From Under The Railroad Bridge: Sartre And The Soviets" in *Contemporary Marxism*, O' Rourke, James J (ed), 245–254. Boston Reidel 1984.

BLAKELEY, Thomas J. "Recent Soviet Evaluations Of American Philosophy" in *Contemporary Marxism*, O' Rourke, James J (ed), 215–220. Boston Reidel 1984.

BLAKELEY, Thomas J. Person And Society: A View Of V P Tugarinov. *Stud Soviet Tho* 28,101–106 Ag 84.

Of all the contemporary Soviet philosophers working in social theory, V P Tugarinov comes closest to successfully using Aristotelian categories in historical materialism. But, does this have any relevance to Marx?

BLAKEMORE, Steven. Language And Ideology In Orwell's *1984*. *Soc Theor Pract* 10,349–356 Fall 84.

BLALOCK JR, Hubert M. *Conceptualization And Measurement In The Social Sciences*. Beverly Hills Sage 1982.

The focus is on a number of implications of the fact that, in the social sciences, measurement is often both indirect and requires complex casual assumptions involving multiple sources of measurement error. Implications are especially serious as we wish to assess measurement comparability across diverse settings, and whenever measurement–error models are imperfectly specified or whenever important variables are omitted from the model. Implications for moving between micro and macro levels are also discussed.

BLANCHETTE, Oliva (trans) and Blondel, Maurice. *Action (1893): Essay On A Critique Of Life And A Science Of Practice*. Notre Dame Univ Notre Dame Pr 1984.

BLANDINO, Giovanni. Il Problema Critico Della Conoscenza. *Aquinas* 27,405–424 My–Ag 84.

For the solution of the critical problem of knowledge the A distinguishes two phases: 1) the cognition of myself and my subjective world; 2) the cognition of the realities distinct from myself. The objects of the first phase are known by *direct cognition*. The objects of the second phase are known by *indirect cognition*, and precisely by *induction* (conceived as a hypothetical–deductive–verificative procedure). For example i know that, with extremely probability, the hypothesis of the existence of material bodies is true because my sensorial data are and behave exactly *as if* they were caused by material bodies. This fact should be extremely improbable if that hypothesis were not true.

BLANKE, Horst Walter and Fleischer, Dirk and Rusen, Jorn. Theory Of History In Historical Lectures: The German Tradition Of *Historik*, 1750–1900. *Hist Theor* 23,331–356 O 84.

The essay examines the German tradition of a particular type of lectures and literature on the theory of history; it is based on the analysis of the lectures held at 60 German–speaking universities during 1750–1900. Four traditions reflecting on history by ideal types are to be distinguished: humanistic–rhetorical, auxiliary–encyclopedic, historicophilosophical, and epistomological or historicological. These types are related in complex ways; in different theories of history ("Histöriken") they form different functional/causal patterns and syntheses.

BLASZCZUK, Jerzy. Some Paraconsistent Sentential Calculi. *Stud Log* 43,51–62 1984.

Jáskowski defined by means of an appropriate interpretation a paraconsistent calculus D_2. J Kotas showed that D_2 is equivalent to the calculus $M(S5)$ those theses are exactly all formulas a such that Ma is a thesis of $S5$. Other papers showed that interesting paraconsistent calculi could be obtained using modal systems other than $S5$ and modalities other than M. This paper generalizes the above work. (edited)

BLATZ, Charles V. Ethical Issues In Private And Public Ranch Land Management. *Agr Human Values* 1,3–16 Fall 84.

BLAU, Ulrich. Die Logik Der Unbestimmtheiten Und Paradoxien. *Erkenntnis* 22,369–460 Ja 85.

A 6-valued logic LR with infinitely many levels of reflection is presented. LR contains its metatheoretical concepts: true, false, undetermined, unfounded, paradox, satisfaction, denotation, quotation. Problems of vagueness, category-mistakes, presupposition and all semantic paradoxes are solved by analyzing the semantic process of reflection, which ascribes oscillating truth-values to unfounded sentences. A similar process, yielding stronger and stronger systems, solves the set-paradoxes: Each class from inside is a set from outside—inside the next universal class.

BLAZER, W. Was Ist Inkommensurabilität? *Kantstudien* 76,196–213 1985.

A new precise notion of incommensurability as "meaning invariance in the light of strong indicators of identity in other respects" is developed in a non-technical way. Standard examples are briefly considered. The notion can be made formally precise.

BLEIER, Ruth. *Science And Gender: A Critique Of Biology And Its Theories On Women.* NY Pergamon 1984.

This book is concerned with the role of science in the creation of theories of women's biological inferiority as explanation for the subordinate position in western cultures. It critically examines theories and methodologies used by scientists to measure and explain how the sexes are different and to establish biological bases for differences in social, economic, and political positions. Specific areas examined include sociobiology, evolution, anthropology, and research on the effects of hormones on the brain and behaviors.

BLITS, Jan H. Privacy And Public Moral Education: Aristotle's Critique Of The Family. *Educ Theor* 35,225–238 Sum 85.

This article examines Aristotle's critique of the family and shows that the family's greatest strengths in moral education prove to contain its essential limitations. The family, the most private of associations, is indispensible to moral education; but what makes it indispensible—namely, the natural recalcitrance of passion to reason and the natural love of one's own—also, paradoxically, renders it insufficient to the task and in need of support from public institutions, including good laws.

BLOCH, Abraham P. *A Book Of Jewish Ethical Concepts: Biblical And Postbiblical.* NY KTAV 1984.

The author draws upon biblical and talmudic sources to establish Jewish ethical standards. He considers 58 topics, including: charity, justice, friendship, labor, and promises. (staff)

BLOCH, Jochanan (ed) and Gordon, Haim (ed). *Martin Buber: A Centenary Volume.* Beersheva Ktav 1984.

The book contains the lectures and discussions of the Buber Centenary Conference held at Ben Gurion University of the Negev in Beersheva in January 1978. Buber scholars from Europe, North America, Japan, and Israel convened and evaluated the significance of Buber's thought, criticized many of his tenets, and discussed his profound originality and broad influence.

BLOCH, Yochanan. "The Justification And The Futility Of Dialogical Thinking" in *Martin Buber*, Gordon, Haim (ed), 43–68. Beersheva Ktav 1984.

BLOCK, Walter. Public Goods And Externalities: The Case Of Roads. *J Liber Stud* 7,1–34 Spr 83.

BLONDEL, Maurice and Blanchette, Oliva (trans). *Action (1893): Essay On A Critique Of Life And A Science Of Practice.* Notre Dame Univ Notre Dame Pr 1984.

BLOOM, Gerald. Some Thoughts On The Value Of Saving Lives. *Theor Med* 5,241–252 O 84.

The increasing willingness of people to agree that societies currently spend too much on health care is noted. It is argued that this is more an expression of financial pressures on the state than a reflection of new technological possibilities. The meaning of such statements is questioned in the context of demonstrated social underutilization of skilled personnel and wasteful expenditure. The discussion then focusses on approaches to defining *medical need* in clinical situations. It is pointed out that this issue has risen to prominence with the establishment of a *right to care* and the subsequent attempt to define limits to this right. (edited)

BLOOR, David. A Sociological Theory Of Objectivity. *Philosophy* 17,229–246 84 Supp.

The aim is to explain and defend the slogan that 'objectivity is social'. The sense of external reference of our common sense classifications and our moral and scientific beliefs derives from their having the character of social institutions. This claim provides a fruitful way of interpreting Popper's doctrine of the 'third world' of objective knowledge. The implications of the sociological approach are explored with material drawn from the history of science and religion.

BLOOR, David. Reply To J W Smith's "Primitive Classification And The Sociology Of Knowledge". *Stud Hist Phil Sci* 15,245–250 S 84.

BLUM, A. The Collective Representation Of Affliction: Some Reflections On Disability And Disease As Social Facts. *Theor Med* 6,221–232 Je 85.

A perspective is developed for approaching affliction as a social fact. Disability and disease are considered as two ways in which we suffer a disjunction which arises form the need to take initiative with respect to the inexorable, whether that means the mark

of disabiltiy or the unconquerability of disease. The story of affliction always raises and masks in certain respects the problem of suffering as the collective representation of our experience of subjectivity where that experience passes through the separateness of being marked to the singularity of being without hope.

BLUMENFELD, David. Leibniz On Contingency And Infinite Analysis. *Phil Phenomenol Res* 45,483–514 Je 85.

BLUMENTHAL, Wolfgang and Rupprecht, F. IV Philosophiekongress Der DDR. *Deut Z Phil* 23,714–726 1975.

BOCHVAR, D A. On The Consistency Of A Three-Valued Logical Calculus. *Topoi* 3,3–12 Je 84.

The present paper contains an investigation of a three-valued logical calculus (the Σ system) previously described by the author. A constructive consistence proof is given for a part of this calculus rendering the results previously published concerning the Russell paradox. A method for a non-constructive completeness proof for the complete calculus is briefly indicated. (edited)

BOEDI, Remo. Beyond Dialetical Thinking: Political Logics And The Construction Of Individuality. *Grad Fac Phil J* 10,123–140 Spr 84.

BOFFA, Maurice and Casalegno, Paolo. The Consistency Of Some 4-stratified Subsystem Of NF Including NF3. *J Sym Log* 50,407–411 Je 85.

The system NF_3 is formed by those axioms of NF (Quine's set theory) which are 3-stratified (i.E., using only 3 consecutive types). It is not known whether NF is consistent, but NF_3 has been proved consistent (Grishin). The authors show that NF_3 remains consistent after adding the (4-stratified) axiom which asserts the existence of the set of natural numbers.

BOGART, J H. Lockean Provisos And State Of Nature Theories. *Ethics* 95,828–836 Jl 85.

This article argues for two related claims: (1) Lockean provisos are inherently powerful pattern principles of justice. Therefore no state of nature theory which includes such a proviso may provide a purely historical theory of justice. (2) The motivation for Lockean provisos lies it the effect of changes of circumstances on theories of justice. I conclude that the assumption of invariance of principles of justice across changes of circumstance is unwarranted.

BOGDAN, Deanne and Boyd, Dwight. Rhetorical Realities: A Response To McAninch's Interpretation Of Values And Teaching. *Educ Theor* 35,327–330 Sum 85.

BOGDAN, Radu J (ed). *D M Armstrong.* Boston Reidel 1984.

The volume surveys and critically examines David Armstrong's philosophical work on perception, belief, knowledge, mind, universals and laws of nature. The volume opens with Armstrong's Self-Profile, which is an autobiographical survey of his intellectual life and work. Then D Sanford, D Rosenthal, S Stich, W Lycan, B Aune, M Tweedale, and J Earman examine and evaluate Armstrong's views on the above mentioned topics. The volume concludes with Armstrong's replies on up-to-date, definitive bibliography of Armstrong's works. The most important of these works have been summarized by their author.

BOGDAN, Radu J. Cognition And Epistemic Closure. *Amer Phil Quart* 22,55–64 Ja 85.

The paper criticizes the standard notion that belief, justification and knowledge are closed under known implication. The argument is based on aspects of cognition which have epistemological import. In particular, it is shown that we believe under specific mental categories, some (concepts) more optimal than others (ideas). The cognitive type identiy of a belief therefore depends on its categorial profile. This being the case, it is possible to show that an inference which enables one to see that a belief implies another may fail to transfer and preserve the categorial profile of the beliefs involved. Since the categorial profile of a belief affects its epistemic worth, we may thus have cases in which the epistemic worth of a belief is not transferred to another, although one implies the other and the implication is known to the believer.

BOGEN, James (ed) and Mc Guire, James E (ed). *How Things Are: Studies In Predication And The History Of Philosophy And Science.* Boston Reidel 1985.

A collection of commentaries and historical studies on crucial writings on the nature of properties and how things have properties. The authors include R G Turnbull, Alan Code, Frank Lewis, and D K Modrak (on Ancient Greek theories); Calvin Mormore and Marilyn Adams (Ockham and Buridan); J E McGuire and Robert M Adams (Leibniz) and Wilfrid Sellars (on Wilfrid Sellars). There is an introductory essay by James Bogen.

BOGEN, James. Traditional Epistemology And Naturalistic Replies To Its Skeptical Critics. *Synthese* 64,195–224 Ag 85.

Traditional epistemology says well justified beliefs are the best guides to action because they tend to correspond well to the world. I argue that skeptical objections to this arising from Descartes and Gettier can be refuted without question begging by appeal to empirically confirmable scientific theories (e.G., of perception). Carnapian accounts of existence are considered, as is a Humean skeptical position which seems immune to naturalized refutation.

BOGGS, Carl. "Gramsci And Eurocommunism" in *Continuity And Change In Marxism*, Fischer, Norman And Others (ed), 189–210. Atlantic Highlands Humanities Pr 1982.

BOGLIOLO, Luis. Fundamentación Ontológica De La Libertad Psicológica. *Sapientia* 39,249–256 O–D 84.

BOGUSZ, Jozef. Die Ethischen Grenzen Der Klinischen Experimente (in Polish). *Stud Phil Christ* 20,165–178 1984.

BOH, Ivan. Epistemic And Alethic Iteration In Later Medieval Logic. *Phil Natur* 21,492–506 1984.

The article attempts to show that in the late Middle Ages lively discussions of problems in both the alethic and the epistemic modal logic took place in England (William Heytesbury, Ralph Strode) and, subsequently, in northern Italian universities. Among the theses discussed, the following two are most interesting: (i) 'If *a* knows that *p*, then *a* knows that he knows that *p*', and (ii) 'If it is necessary that *p*, then it is necessarily necessary that *p*'.

BÖHLER, Dietrich. Das Solipsistisch–Intuitionistische Konzept Der Vernunft Und Des Verstehens: Traditionskritische Bemerkungen. *Z Phil Forsch* 38,263–277 Ap–Je 84.

BOHM, David. Fragmentation And Wholeness In Religion And In Science. *Zygon* 20,125–134 Je 85.

This paper starts with a discussion of the nature of religion and of science, viewing them both as embodying a search for wholeness, although each does so in its own way. Attention is called to the fact that science and religion have both become fragmented and that this fragmentation has a deeper origin in the structure of the ego itself. The source of fragmentation in the ego is discussed. Finally, a possible way for the religious attitude and the scientific attitude to work together is proposed, which involves a common approach to ordering the fragmentary divisive structure and activity of the ego.

BOHM, David. Hidden Variables And The Implicate Order. *Zygon* 20,111–124 Je 85.

This paper explains how my ideas of hidden variables tie up to those in the implicate order, and how all these notions are related to my views on religion. Beginning with my work on the quantum theory, it traces how I was led to question the usual interpretation, and goes on to show how both the notion of hidden variables and that of the implicate order were implicit in my thought more than thirty years ago. The further development through quantum field theory brings all the various threads together. Finally, the general world view that comes our of this development is seen to be compatible with a religious approach to life.

BOK, Sissela. Distrust, Secrecy, And The Arms Race. *Ethics* 95,712–727 Ap 85.

BOLDYREV, Peter and Vertlieb, E. Solzhenitsyn And Yanov. *Stud Soviet Tho* 29,11–16 Ja 85.

This article addresses the traditional conflict between conservative and liberal Russian historical thought reproduced once more in contemporary emigre literature. The main project of the article is to analyze and evaluate two sharply different approaches to Russian history, one offering a moral–religious judgment (Solzhemitsyn), and the other evaluating it politically (Yanov). Correspondingly, two different ways of opposing communism are recommended. The article concludes that both approaches are too one–sided and should supplement each other.

BOLE, Thomas and Stevens, John Mark. Why Hegel At All? *Phil Topics* 13,113–122 Spr 85.

We propose that Hegel's system is serious philosophy, if his dialectic is interpreted logically. We make this interpretation by showing how to take the *logic's* dialectic as an explanation of thought in its function as explanatory, and of being as thought's most general *explanadum*. We then indicate cosequences for what is indispensable, reviseable, and untenable in Hegel's *Realphilosophie*, and for Hegel's remarks about contradiction within the *Logic*.

BOLER, John F. Connotative Terms In Ockham. *Hist Phil Quart* 2,21–38 Ja 85.

The distinction of absolute and connotative terms in Ockham creates semantical complexities that have too often been ignored. His account of connotativity, it is argued, suggests that the role of categorematic extremes in "S is P" form propositions is not basic and, therefore, that Ockham's primitive notion of significance is vague. Connotative terms are a function on absolute terms; the need for an account of such functions is developed.

BOLZÁN, J E. Hilemorfismo Y Corporalidad. *Sapientia* 40,25–32 Ja–Mr 85.

Se desecha el hilemorfismo de Arstóteles y especialmente la "materia prima", recurriéndose a la mixis o "combinación entre substancias" (Gen Corr, I, 10) para explicar la corporalidad del hombre; el alma aparece aquí como la causa radical estructurante de un cuerpo preexistente sólo como posibilidad de ser en las diversas substancias cósmicas capaces de ser asimiladas por la actividad megemónica del alma.

BONADEO, Alfredo. Montaigne On War. *J Hist Ideas* 46,417–426 Jl–S 85.

The work studies the *Essays* to conclude that Montaigne opposes war.

BONANATE, Ugo. *Orme Ed Enigmi Nella Filosofia Di Plotino*. Milano Angeli 1985.

The book aims at showing that the philosophy of Plotinus, even in its most metaphysical parts, may be read as the outcome of his polemics with the magical and gnostic world–view widely diffused in the IIIrd century A D. The image of the philosopher Plotinus draws is the result of his role of interpreter of platonic thought, founded on his power of solving the platonic enigmas.

BONATTI, Luigi. *Uncertainty Studies In Philosophy, Economics And Socio–Political Theory*. Amsterdam Gruner 1984.

BOND, E J. Reply To J Narveson's Review Of *Reason And Value*. *Dialogue (Canada)* 23,337–340 Je 84.

Contra Narveson, it is easy to see why understanding that something is worth having, getting, or doing, creates a desire for that thing. If this is neither empirical nor analytic, that is just one more reason for abandoning that outworn distinction. Nor is the attribution of any supposed property of goodness (beyond a thing's being worth having, etc.) involved. Contra Narveson, if feeling good were something enjoyed (a pleasure), then one *could* find it unpleasant, which is absurd. narveson reaffirms his hedonism but his anti–hedonistic arguments of *Reason and Value* remain, as far as I can see untouched.

BONDI, Richard. The Elements Of Character. *J Relig Ethics* 12,201–218 Fall 84.

Legitimate confusion over the use of the language of character arises over the topic of that language and its relation to the concepts of story and community often associated with it. This essay argues that the proper topic of the language of character is the self in relation, and that a phenomenology of the self in relation is the first step in ethics of character. Four elements of character are thus described, and a consideration of the role of story and community in the formation of character over

time points the way to the use of the language of character in practical moral reflection.

BONÉ, Edouard. Manipuler L'homme (in Polish). *Stud Phil Christ* 20,149–152 1984.

BONESIO, Luisa. "Le Forme Dell'Antico: Immagini Della Scultura Classica In Winckelmann" in *Il Tempo Dell'Arte*, Papi, Fulvio and others (ed), 102–126. Milano Franco Angeli 1984.

BONEVAC, Daniel and Asher, Nicholas M. How Extensional Is Extensional Perception? *Ling Phil* 8,203–228 My 85.

BONEVAC, Daniel and Asher, Nicholas. Situations And Events. *Phil Stud* 47,57–78 Ja 85.

BONEVAC, Daniel. Systems Of Substitution Semantics. *Phil Sci* 51,631–656 D 84.

I investigate substitutional interpretations of quantifiers that count existential sentences true just in case they have true instances in a parametric extension of the language. I devise a semantics meeting four criteria: (1) it accounts adequately for natural language quantification; (2) it provides an account of justification in abstract sciences; (3) it constitutes a continuous semantics for natural and formal language; and (4) it is purely substitutional, containing no appeal to referential interpretations. The prospects for a purely substitutional theory of quantification are thus no worse than for a referential account.

BONIOLO, Giovanni. Riflessioni Sulla Storia Della Scienza. *Sapienza* 37,217–223 Ap–Je 84.

In out essay we have tried to demonstrate: a) the historical fact is a pluri–perspective fact. In a critical approach to a historical work we havae to recognize the perspective of the historian, and understand if his explication is scientific or ideologic; b) the division between internal and external science (cf. kuhn, Lakatos, Feyerabend) is fictitious; c) we have to discover the methodology of the scientists through a particular historical hypothesis (see), not through the epistemologies of the philosophers.

BÖNISCH, Siegfried and Noack, Klaus–peter. Zu Einigen Unterschieden Zwischen Moralischen Normen, Werturteilen Und Aussagen. *Deut Z Phil* 23,818–829 1975.

BONNET, Nicole. Immanence Et Transcendance Chez Teilhard De Chardin. *Arch Phil* 47,591–612 O–D 84.

The theme "immanence and transcendence" which has been the guiding line throughout the reading of Teilhard's works and turned out to apply to the different levels of his research: (phenomenological—scientifical—philosophical and religious) has enabled to grasp its deeply existential aspect and profound unity. Indeed the philosophy of union is gradually coming out as the term of an intelligence of life and the thresholds of its emergence—but also, as union can only be personalizing and "amorisante"—as the criterion of socialization and the touchstone of religions.

BONNET, Robert and Shelah, Sharon. Narrow Boolean Algebras. *Annals Pure Applied Log* 28,1–12 Ja 85.

BONSACK, Francois. L'inégalité De Bell: Démonstration Intuitive Et Commentaires (infrench). *Dialectica* 39,111–125 1985.

An elementary and intuitive demonstration of Bell's inequality is given that should be accessible to non–specialists, including philosophers. This inequality, the premises of which are made prominent, holds for all theories with local hidden variables. It does not hold for quantum mechanics, however, and the possible consequences of this are considered.

BOOLOS, George. Don't Eliminate Cut. *J Phil Log* 13,373–378 N 84.

There is a simple inference that can be shown valid by means of a deduction in a standard system of natural deduction containing c. 3000 symbols, but for which the smallest tree proof contains more symbols than there are nanoseconds between Big Bangs. If this is a defect of the method of trees, then it can be remedied by supplementing the method with a suitable formation of the rule *cut*, i.E., *modus ponens*.

BOOTH, David. Nietzsche On "The Subject Of Multiplicity". *Man World* 18,121–146 1985.

This article explores relations between Nietzsche's critique of the "subject–atom" and his hortatory and metaphysical pronouncements. Does the "deconstruction" of subject undermine the ideals of the noble or the Overman? Do Nietzsche's claims about the figural character of language undermine his own language in asserting Will to Power? The critique of subjectivity is considered in its polemical context. Ultimately the "subject as multiplicity" and a responsible public subject qualify, but do not cancel each other.

BORCH, Karl. Welfare Functions And Group Decisions. *Theor Decis* 17,207–210 N 84.

The paper shows that Pareto optimal sharing rules imply that group decisions will be made unanimously. An example is given.

BORGEANU, Constantin. L'idée D'absolu Face Au Spiritualisme Religieux Contemporain. *Phil Log* 28,103–108 Ap–Je 84.

BORGES, J F Pereira. Elementos De Filosofia Politica No Concilio Vaticano II. *Rev Port Filosof* 40,274–290 Jl–S 84.

BORGMANN, Albert. *Technology And The Character Of Contemporary Life: A Philosophical Inquiry*. Chicago Univ Of Chicago Pr 1984.

Modern technology can be understood as the characteristic way in which we today take up with the world. The character of technology, spelled out paradigmatically, illuminates the concrete objects and social structures of contemporary life and reveals a tendency towards disengagement and distraction. This tendency can be countered through the engagement in things and practices that center our lives provided those focal concerns are given a central place privately and publicly.

BORGOSZ, Józef. Dialogue On "The Meaning Of History And Peace". *Dialec Hum* 11,471–480 Spr/Sum 84.

BORILLO, Mario. *Informatique Pour Les Sciences Del'homme.* Bruxelles Mardaga 1984.

This text addresses the question 'What is thought in regard to information systems and the human sciences: semiotics, linguistics, artificial language theory'. The author analyzes the way information is disseminated through formal linguistic systems and how information of a culture, through archeological investigation can be stored by contemporary data gathering systems, such as computers. Borillo's analysis intends to describe a synthesis of the acquisition of information by historical–archeological methodology and computer data interpretation.

BORIONI, Marco. *La Gnoseologia Di George E Moore.* Roma Dell'Ateneo 1984.

BORN, Rainer P. Programmatische Oberlegungen Formal–Strukturaler Natur Zur "suche Nach Einer Verlorene Ästhetik". *Conceptus* 19,29–38 1985.

The aim of this paper is to give a formal and structural reconstruction of the main ideas contained in "Das ästhetische Vor–Urteil" by O Neumaier (this volume). Especially the parallels between this approach of philosophical aesthetics and wittgenstein's philosophy of language will be clarified. Finally the prospects of a "logic of aesthetics" will be discussed.

BORNSCHIER, Volker. Eigentum Und Verfügungsmacht: Zum Korporativen Eigentum. *Stud Phil (Switzerland)* Supp 12,161–198 1983.

The paper deals with the nature and institutionalization of property rights in Western society. It is argued that the emergence of large scale formal organization in the economy has split property rights in important respects. The partial disjunction of property and control, elements that originally formed a tight unity, may pose problems of legitimacy of modern Western society in various areas. The study relies on evidence from various previous studies on industrial organization.

BORNSTEIN, Marc. Developmental Psychology And The Problem Of Artistic Change. *J Aes Art Crit* 43,131–146 Wint 84.

This paper explores whether and how principles of behavioral change as promulgated by the discipline of developmental psychology help to explain how and why artists change styles over their life–cycle. Developmental psychology proposes that human individuals change over the course of the life span on account of maturation, equilibration, contingent reinforcement, imitation, and adaptation. Each of these mechanisms is examined in relation to changes in the artistic styles of different artists. In particular, the early artistic life of Pablo Picasso (1900–1930) is used as a principal illustration.

BORRESEN, Kari E. Equivalencia Y Subordinación, Según San Agustín: Naturaleza Y Papel De La Mujer. *Augustinus* 30,97–107 Ja–Je 85.

The order of creation establishes the subordination of woman to man as well as the unique character of the conjugal relationship. The fecundity of the order of creation was contaminated by concuspiscense, while the spiritual fecundity of the virgin in connection with the order of salvation escapes the punishment of sin. Woman, by virtue of virginity, will not be dominated by man as consequence of original sin. Therefore, chastity in temporal existence will produce equivalence between woman and man as in the order of salvation.

BORUTTI, Silvana. *Significato.* Bologna Zanichelli 1983.

Against the background of a survey of the main philosophical theories of meaning in the nineteenth century—in paricular the models suggested by Frege, Wittgenstein and logical positivism—the author's chief concern is to show that these theories are dominated by a notion of meaning as object. In alternative to this referentialistic approach, the author, starting from the Wittgensteinian notion of linguistic game and a pragmatically oriented notion of utterance, sets up a concept of meaning closely connected with the process of socialization.

BORUTTI, Silvana. Pragmatics And Its Discontents. *J Prag* 8,437–448 Ag 84.

This paper deals with a number of epistemological amgiguities in pragmatic theories. In particular, stress will be placed on the fact that a great amount of idealization is still presupposed by pragmatics. The author claims that is necessary to develop alternative theoretical models in which the *hic et nunc* uses of language (here referred to as 'discourses') are the places where subjects are constituted with their social features. This viewpoint entails a notion of 'ideology' not as 'superstructure', but as a level of reality offering patterns of identity to subjects.

BORZYM, Stanislaw. Defensive Reactions Of Polish Professional Philosophy To Irrationalism In The Early 20th Century. *Dialec Hum* 11,365–372 Spr/Sum 84.

BOS, Egbert P. *Marsilius Of Inghen: Treatises On The Properties Of Terms.* Dordrecht Reidel 1983.

BOSCHERINI, Emilia G. La Naissance Du Matérialisme Moderne Chez Hobbes Et Spinoza. *Rev Phil Fr* 175,135–148 Ap–Je 85.

The author's aim is to demonstrate that Hobbes and Spinoza belong to the rising phase of modern materialism. The problems dealt with are: in Hobbes, the function of sensation in the elaboration of science or philosophy, the object and the end of philosophy, the ontological level of knowledge; in Spinoza the significance of the concept of extension or matter as an attribute of God and the realistic outcome of the theory of knowledge. The ontological character of Hobbesian materialism and the elements of continuity with modern materialism of Spinozism are stressed.

BOTH, Nicolas. Considérations Algébriques Sur La Théorie De La Démonstration. *Z Math Log* 20,529–536 1974.

BOUCEK, Karel. Methodological Approaches To The Utilization Of Science And Technology In Practice. *Filozof Cas* 32,521–533 1984.

BOUCHARD, Guy. La Pseudo–Métaphysique Du Signe. *Dialogue (Canada)* 23,597–618 D 84.

Many scholars argue that the sign is a two–sided, part sensible and part intelligible, entity. According to Jacques Derrida, this means that the sign belongs to the phonocentric and logocentric occidental metaphysics. In order to evaluate this claim, I examine five outstanding notions of the sign and I show that, strictly speaking, none of them amounts to a simple dyadic relation between a sensible half and an intelligible half. Hence, there is no such thing as *the* metaphysics of *the* sign.

BOUCHARD, Roch. Krishnamurti Zen. *Rev Univ Ottawa* 54,91–100 O–D 84.

BOUDIER, C E M Struyker. Merleau–Ponty En Buytendijk: Relaas Van Een Relatie. *Alg Ned Tijdschr Wijs* 76,228–246 O 84.

The correspondence between Maurice Merleau–Ponty and Frederik Buytendijk and the passages in their works where they refer to each other are analyzed is order to throw light on their phenomenological view on man and nature. This view can afford basis for theory about the relations between intercorporeity, intersubjectivity, and intertextuality.

BOUGHTON, B J. Compulsory Health And Safety In A Free Society. *J Med Ethics* 10,186–188 D 84.

The ageing population and new technology are both increasing the cost of our free health service, and there are sound economic reasons for extending measures which reduce the diseases common to our society. But if education fails to change public attitudes towards habits such as tobacco smoking and poor diet, to what extent is the State justified in compelling us to be healthy? This issue touches on the sensitive areas of personal freedom and responsibility and involves complex cultural, historical, and economic considerations. Both governments and individuals can be criticized for the way this issue has been handled in the past, and it is hoped that the examples discussed in this paper will stimulate further debate.

BOULAD– AYOUB, Josiane. Diderot Et D'Holbach: Un Système Matérialiste De La Nature. *Dialogue (Canada)* 24,59–90 Spr 85.

This is an analysis of one aspect of French 18th century materialism, i.E., the positions on Nature of Diderot in *L'interprétation de la Nature* and *Le Rêve de d'Alembert*, and of d'Holbach in *Le Système de la Nature*, bringing forward the ideological determinations of their concepts of Nature and the ontological determinations of their representations of Nature, thus underlining the originality of their theoretical and methodological intuitions particularly in respect to the notion of System.

BOULDING, Elise. New Frames Of Reference For A Peaceful International Order. *Dialec Hum* 11,449–458 Spr/Sum 84.

BOUREL, Dominique. De Bar–Sur–Aube À Jérusalem: La Correspondance Entre Gaston Bachelard Et Martin Buber. *Rev Int Phil* 38,201–216 1984.

BOUREL, Dominique. Les Rasés Et Les Barbus: Diderot Et Le Judaïsme. *Rev Phil Fr* 174,275–285 Jl–S 84.

This article wanted to reopen the dossier of the relationship between Diderot and the Jews, the Judaism and the Hebrew culture. The article shows that he was not an antisemite at all as the previous research assumed. He was relatively well informed and a neutral, or semineutral observer of the Jewish culture of his time.

BOURGEOIS, Patrick L. Religious Existence And The Philosophical Radicalization Of Phenomenological Theology. *Proc Cath Phil Ass* 58,165–172 1984.

It is the thesis of this study that to radicalize philosophy the phenomenological analysis of existence within theological reflection, the radical, structured level of existence as the ultimate presuppositional base must at some point be attained through reflection. Such a fundamental, philosophical project requires a focus on existence as the presuppositional context and substrate of the commitments from which reflection emerges. A phenomenological analysis, delving into the fundamental level of existence, as the root and foundation of religious experience and below the subjecct and other disjunction, shows the fundamental openness at the heart of human existence as the foundation of all experience, even religious experience. However, it becomes clear that, for such a phenomenological reflection on this foundational level, the structures of existence are neutral to God–belief or God non–belief. (edited)

BOURGEOIS, Patrick and Rosenthal, Sandra. Merleau–Ponty, Lewis And Ontological Presence. *Phil Topics* 13,239–246 Spr 85.

Although phenomenology and pragmatism have emerged as almost entirely independent traditions, they manifest striking similarities in basic stances toward certain issues. This essay focuses on the way mutual rejection of the Kantian distinction between noumena and phenomena influences the positions of Merleau–Ponty and Lewis in a way in which manifests important common elements between them.

BOURKE, Vernon J. "History, Futurology And The Future Of Philosophy" in *History Of Philosophy In The Making*, Thro, Linus J (ed), 299–312. Washington Univ Pr Of America 1982.

BOUVERESSE, Jacques. La Philosophie Peut–Elle Être Systématique? *Stud Phil (Switzerland)* 41,9–39 1982.

BOWER, Kenneth J. Imagery: From Hume To Cognitive Science. *Can J Phil* 14,217–234 Je 84.

BOWIE, Norman E. Are Business Ethics And Engineering Ethics Members Of The Same Family? *J Bus Ethics* 4,43–52 F 85.

BOWIE, Norman E. Commentary On "Advertising And Program Content". *Bus Prof Ethics J* 3,87–92 Spr/Sum 84.

I argue that Professor Held is more concerned with the liberation of culture than with deceptive or offensive advertising. I then argue that providing a general right to free expression will not increase intellectual honesty or creativity. Indeed if the right to free expression were implemented in certain specified ways, intellectual honesty and creativity might be inhibited.

BOWIE, Norman E. Should Collective Bargaining And Labor Relations Be Less Adversarial? *J Bus Ethics* 4,283–291 Ag 85.

In this paper I argue that the poker analogy is unsuitable as a model for collective bargaining negotiations. Using the poker game analogy is imprudent, its use undermines trust and ignores the cooperative features of business, and its use fails to take into account the values of dignity and fairness which should characterize labor–management negotiation. I propose and defend a model of ideal family decision–making as a superior model to the poker game.

BOWIE, Norman and Hart, Richard E. "Should We Be Discussing This". *Teach Phil* 7,230–234 Jl 84.

My commentary poses two fundamental and interrelated questions: Does the principle of confidentiality apply to the relationship between student and teacher on matters such as grades? Moreover, are there specific contexts in which faculty discussion of grades and records is morally unacceptable, or, conversely, contexts in which, because of overriding educational or social objectives, such discussion is morally appropriate, perhaps even obligatory? I conclude that clearly articulated reasons or objectives are crucial to moral evaluation of such actions.

BOWLER, Peter J. *Evolution, The History Of An Idea*. Berkeley Univ Of Calif Pr 1984.

BOWLES, Paul. The Origin Of Property And The Development Of Scottish Historical Science. *J Hist Ideas* 46,197–210 Ap–Je 85.

The discussion of the origin of property in the works of Hutcheson, Smith and Millar reveals interesting shifts of emphasis in the writings of the Scottish Enlightenment period. Specifically, the discussion reveals a shift from a concern with the moral justification for private property to a concern with its historical origin and evolution. Smith is a pivotal figure discussing both the moral and, with the aid of the four–stages theory of social development, historical aspects.

BOXILL, Bernard. Theories Of Justice And The United Nations Declaration On The Establishment Of A New International Economic Order. *Teach Phil* 8,129–136 Ap 85.

BOXILL, J M. Beauty, Sport, And Gender. *J Phil Sport* 11,36–47 1984.

BOYD, Dwight R. Taking Teachers Seriously. *Proc Phil Educ* 40,131–144 1984.

BOYD, Dwight and Bogdan, Deanne. Rhetorical Realities: A Response To McAninch's Interpretation Of Values And Teaching. *Educ Theor* 35,327–330 Sum 85.

BOYD, John D. The Affinities Of Literature. *Thought* 60,335–352 S 85.

This article aims at showing the necessary intrinsic analogy that exists between literature and life, a notion not congenial to much contemporary literary theory. It derives from a new and major interpretation of the concept of literature as mimetic at an epistemological level, for which see John D Boyd, S J, "A New Mimesis," *Renascence* (Marquette University, 37, Spring, 1985). This in turn depends upon Transcendental Realism (Thomistic) and the ontological principle of participation.

BOYD, Kenneth. The Positive Aspects Of Medical Ethics Today. *J Med Ethics* 10,122–123 S 84.

The author of this comment suggests that some of the important points made by Dr Adrian Rogers are vitiated by a tendency to contrast the worst of modern medical practice with an over–idealized view of the past. The state of medical ethics today, the author suggests, is more hopeful than Dr Rogers allows.

BOYD, Richard N. "Observations, Explanatory Power, Simplicity" in *Observation, Experiment, Hypothesis In Physical Science*, Achinstein, Peter (ed), 45–94. Cambridge MIT Pr 1985.

BOYD, Richard N. The Logician's Dilemma: Deductive Logic, Inductive Inference And Logical Empiricism. *Erkenntnis* 22,197–252 Ja 85.

BOYER, David L. A Widely Accepted But Nonetheless Astonishingly Flimsy Argument Against Analytical Behaviorism. *Philosophia (Israel)* 14,153–172 Ag 84.

I refute the argument against behaviorism which asserts that no particular behavior "fits" any particular belief. The refutation is interesting because, first, that argument would work as well against any theory which entails that there is any "fit" at all between belief and behavior, excluding only some radical skeptics; second, the refutation suggests properties of a behavioral correlate of belief; and third, it defuses the notion that belief and desire can at most be interdefined.

BOYLAN, Michael. The Place In Nature In Aristotle's Teleology. *Apeiron* 18,126–140 1984.

This article examines the place of *phusis* (nature) in Aristotle's biological science. It is the contention of this essay that there are several senses of *phusis* including one that regulates the *eidos* of a species. This essay follows more specific studies I have published in the *Journal of the History of Biology* in the past few years.

BOYLE, Joseph M. Practical Reasoning And Moral Judgment. *Proc Cath Phil Ass* 58,37–49 1984.

BOZIC, Milan and Dosen, Kosta. Models For Normal Intuitionistic Modal Logics. *Stud Log* 43,217–246 1984.

Kripke–style models with two accessibility relations, on intuitionistic and the other modal, are given for analogues of the modal system *K* based on Heyting's propositional logic. It is shown that these two relations can combine with each other in various ways. Soundness and completeness are proved for systems with only the necessity operator, or only the possibility operator, or both. Embeddings in modal systems with several modal operators, based on classical propositional logic, are also considered. This paper lays the ground for an investigation of intuitionistic analogues of systems stronger than *K*. A brief survey is given of the existing literature on intuitionistic modal logic.

BRACKEN, Harry M. Hume On The 'Distinction Of Reason'. *Hume Stud* 10,1–108 N 84.

The Locke–Berkeley–Hume 'partnership' doctrine is discussed. On several topics Hume seems not to follow Berkeley; rather, he appears ignorant of Berkeley's positions, e.G., on *minima sensibilia* (and anti–abstractionism). Hume's own analysis of this takes one to his account of the 'distinction of reason'. George E Davie's significant contribution to making sense of Hume's doctrine, building on the work of Christopher Salmon (1929), is discussed.

BRACKEN, Joseph A. Faith And Justice: A New Synthesis—The Interface Of Process And Liberation Theologies. *Process Stud* 14,73–75 Sum 85.

In this introductory essay to a series of papers delivered at a conference on the Interface between Process and Liberation Theologies (October 20–22, 1983, Xavier University, Cincinnati, Ohio), the author notes the underlying complementarity of the two theologies with respect to a common task: namely, the creative transformation of the existing social order. The praxis–orientation of liberation theologians needs the speculative framework provided by process thinkers, and vice–versa.

BRACKEN, Joseph A. Substance–Society–Natural Systems: A Creative Rethinking Of Whitehead's Cosmology. *Int Phil Quart* 25,3–14 Mr 85.

The article compares the key concepts of three process–oriented philosophers: the concept of substance for Ivor Leclerc, of society for Alfred North Whitehead, and of natural system for Ervin Laszlo. The author concludes that Whitehead's notion of society is best equipped to serve as the foundational concept for a contemporary cosmology. It is more comprehensive than the notion of substance and it better specifies the ultimate constituents of natural systems.

BRADIE, M. The Metaphorical Character Of Science. *Phil Natur* 21,229–243 1984.

The "semantic" analysis of theories has gained prominence in recent years. Semantic analyses construe scientific theories as abstract model–structures with empirical applications. In this paper, I sketch a version of this position which derives from work by Ron Giere, illustrated by examples from biology. Interpretation, I suggest, is accomplished by means of metaphors. I outline an analysis of the role of metaphor in scientific theory and discuss some of the implications of this approach.

BRADY, F Neil. A Defense Of Utilitarian Policy Processes In Corporate And Public Management. *J Bus Ethics* 4,23–30 F 85.

BRADY, R T. Natural Deduction Systems For Some Quantified Relevant Logics. *Log Anal* 27,355–378 D 84.

The purpose of the paper is to provide Fitch–style natural deduction systems for a large range of quantified relevant logics that have appeared or are appearing in the literature in the form of Hilbert–style axiomatizations. That the natural deduction systems have the same theorems are their corresponding axiomatizations is proved in all cases by an extension of the Anderson technique which he developed for the relevant logics of E and EQ.

BRADY, Ross T and Meyer, Robert K and Giambrone, Steve. Where Gamma Fails. *Stud Log* 43,247–256 1984.

A major question for the relevant logics has been, "Under what conditions is Ackermann's rule γ, from—A V B and A to infer B, admissible for one of these logics?" For a large number of logics and theories, the question has led to an affirmative answer to the γ problem itself, so that such an answer has almost come to be expected for relevant logics worth taking seriously. We exhibit here, however, another large and interesting class of logics—roughly, the Boolean extensions of the **W**—free relevant logics (and, precisely, the well–behaved subsystems of the four–valued logic **BN4**)—for which γ fails.

BRADY, Ross T. Depth Relevance Of Some Paraconsistent Logics. *Stud Log* 43,63–74 1984.

The paper essentially shows that the paraconsistent logic **DR** satisfies the depth relevance condition. The system **DR** is an extension of the system **DK** and the non–triviality of a dialectical set theory based on **DR** has been shown. (edited)

BRANDON, Robert N (ed) and Burian, Richard M (ed). *Genes, Organisms, Populations: Controversies Over The Units Of Selection*. Cambridge MIT Pr 1984.

BRANDT, R B. The Concept Of Rational Belief. *Monist* 62,3–23 Ja 85.

Is argued that aceptic who offers reasons must admit the reliability of some introspection, some memory, and simple entailments. But if a science is to be possible, there must be sensory inputs, a fairly reliable recording device, and some lawlike regularities. Therefore it is rational for a person who wants knowledge to accept beliefs based on these assumptions. The concept of "rational belief" should be framed accordingly.

BRANDT, Reinhard. Renuncia Al Derecho Y Dominación En Los Pactos Fundamentales De Hobbes. *Rev Ven Filosof* 12,7–30 1980.

BRANDT, Richard B. "The Explanation Of Moral Language" in *Morality, Reason And Truth*, Copp, David (ed), 104–119. Totowa Rowman & Allanheld 1984.

BRANDTSTÄDTER, Jochen and Reinert, Gunther. Wissenschaft Als Gegenstand Der Wissenschaft Vom Menschlichen Erleben Und Verhalten. *Z Allg Wiss* 4,368–401 1973.

Science is considered as an open system that constitutes a sub–entity of the total system "society" and whose functions include the production, systematization, communication and application of knowledge. Since this system is made up of individuals and groups, its functions are dependent on psychological factors. This fact serves as a starting point for a psychology of science, which can contribute to optimizing scientific practice by treating the heuristic, organizational, technological, and normative aspects of scientific activity.

BRATTON, Susan Power. National Park Management And Values. *Environ Ethics* 7,117–134 Sum 85.

Throughout the history of the U S national park system, park advocates and managers have changed both acquisition priorities and internal management policies. The park movement began with the establishment of large, spectacular natural areas, primarily in the West. As the movement developed there was more emphasis on the biological, on recreation, and on parks near population centers. Gradually, scenic wonders and uniqueness have become less necessary to designation and the types of sites eligible have diversified. Early managers treated the parks as relatively unchanging, threatened by little other than human vandalism. Initially managers removed "bad" animals, such as wolves, and suppressed disturbances, such as fire. Modern management values processes as well as objects and recognizes change and disturbance as integral to park maintanence. A conversion to an ecosystem mode of management does not answer all questions concerning values, however, and may present some disadvantages, such as a tendency to treat nature as a series of functions and energy equations, thus weakening aesthetic values.

BRÄU, Richard and Rosenthal, Erwin and Ludwig, Gerd. Zur Rolle Des Subjektiven Faktors In Der Wissenschaftsentwicklung. *Deut Z Phil* 33,459–462 1985.

BRAUN, Hans–Joachim and Dorschel, E. Zur Dialektik Des Vergesellschaftungsprozesses In Der Sozialistischen Industrie Der DDR. *Deut Z Phil* 32,737–747 1984.

BRAYBROOKE, David. Commentary On "Work–Related Ethical Attitudes: Impact On Business Profitability". *Bus Prof Ethics J* 3,41–42 Wint 84.

BRAYBROOKE, David. Preferences Opposed To The Market. *Soc Phil Pol* 2,101–114 Autumn 84.

Contractarian theory should take into account not only Ants–enthusiasts for market activity–but contracting agents, Grasshoppers, who prefer on a variety of grounds to engage in as little market activity as possible. To work through a contract reconciling the preferences of Ants and Grasshoppers is to arrive at a welfare state and mixed economy on a route different from the usual one through current needs that the market fails to meet.

BREAKWELL, Glynis M. Abusing The Unemployed: An Invisible Justice. *J Moral Educ* 14,56–62 Ja 85.

The study reported examined how young people respond to abuse directed at them purely because they are unemployed. Since young unemployed are known to blame themselves for their failure to gain a job, it was predicted they would not regard the abuse as unjust and would be unable to defend themselves adequately. This was found to be the case: young people sought to justify themselves by pleas of helplessness or totally failed to evolve any argument in self–defense. Alternatively, the attacker's empathy was sought by offering to swap places. It is suggested that the unemployed can be taught coping strategies based upon a reconceptualization of the causes of unemployment and a re–evaluation of the moral standing of those who offer abuse.

BREARLEY, Mike. "Psycho–Analysis And Philosophy" in *Philosophy And Life: Essays On John Wisdom*, Dilman, Ilham (ed), 179–200. Boston Nijhoff 1984.

BRECHER, Robert and Grim, Patrick. Gremlins Revenged: Gremlins Repulsed. *Phil Stud (Ireland)* 30,165–176 Spr 84.

My contributions to this discussion are an attempt to construct and defend parodies of the ontological argument in the tradition of Gaunilo. I first did this in "Plantinga's God and Other Monstrosities" (*Religious Studies*, 15 (1979), 91–97), to which Robert Brecher replied in "Gremlins and Parodies," *Philosophical Studies* (Eire), XXIX (1983), 48–54. Here I attempt to counter Brecher's criticisms, which I consider closely akin to earlier criticisms of Gaunilo by Plantinga and Hartshorne, by constructing a range of Gauniloesque parodies which do not rely on dubiously necessary beings or on dubiously intrinsic maxima. Neither necessity nor intrinsic maximality, I maintain, are essential to the logical structure of the ontological argument or its parodies. This piece in its entirety is in effect a debate. My impression is that I win hands down.

BRECHER, R. Striking Responsibilities. *J Med Ethics* 11,66–69 Je 85.

It is commonly held that National Health Service (NHS) workers are under a moral obligation not to go on strike, because doing so might result in people's dying. Unless sainthood is demanded, however, this position is untenable: indeed, those most vociferously pursuing it are often those who bear the greatest responsiblity, on their own grounds, for needless death and suffering.

BREGMAN, Robert. Leibniz And Atomism. *Nature Syst* 6,237–248 D 84.

BRENKERT, George G. Cohen On Proletarian Unfreedom. *Phil Pub Affairs* 14,91–98 Wint 85.

BRENKERT, George G. Commentary On "Children As Consumers". *Bus Prof Ethics J* 3,147–154 Spr/Sum 84.

BRENKERT, George G. Marx's Critique Of Utilitarianism. *Can J Phil* Supp 7,193–220 1981.

BRENKERT, George G. Thoughts On 'Management–Think'. *J Bus Ethics* 4,309–312 Ag 85.

In this paper I briefly summarize Pastin's views on the problem of good business thinking (GBT) and the solution (Perspectival Analysis) which he offers. In discussing Pastin's solution I offer a number of criticisms which call for further elucidation on Pastin's part. Specifically, I challenge his vagueness on which perspectives a manager must consider, the manner in which the moral components of these perspectives are to be evaluated, and whether Pastin in not the end committed simply to an economic account of GBT. Finally, I contend that Pastin's account of GBT errors in being too intellectualistic and too individualistic.

BRENNAN JOSEPH G. Thomas Mann And The Business Ethic. *J Bus Ethics* 4,401–407 O 85.

Son of a North German businessman, Thomas Mann chose as a theme for his early narrative work the conflict between the standards and values of business and those of the artist–writer. *buddenbrooks* and *Tonio Kröger* exhibit the tension of values in opposite ways. In *The Magic Mountain*, Mann expands his canvas to include military as well as business values in their relation to the creative potential in a young engineer who exiles himself to an Alpine tuberculosis sanatorium to enjoy a unique educational experience. Mann believed that the businessman, like the artist, had a light and dark side, committed by the Protestant ethic, yet bound on entrepreneurial standards of utility and profit. On that account, the businessman, like the creative artist, may experience a certain alienation from 'Life'.

BRENNER, Michael. "Actors' Powers" in *The Analysis Of Action*, Von Cranach, Mario (ed), 213–230. Cambridge Cambridge Univ Pr 1982.

BRESKY, Dushan and Malik, Miroslav. *Esthetic Qualities And Values In Literature: A Humanistic And A Biometric Appraisal*. NY Lang 1984.

First volume of *Literary Practice*, trilogy, written by critic Bresky and biocybernetist Makik, develops two seminal methods of literary evaluation. Bresky estimates density and intensity of esthetic stimuli in microcontext. His synthesis corroborates subsequent

empirical macrocontextual assessment. Malik outlines pertinent neurological research, records physiological changes occurring during Bresky's perception of text and compiles biometric sentic profile paralleling Bresky's resume of stimuli. *literary Practice II – Esthetics of Style* and III – *Literay Subjects* will soon appear.

BRICKE, John. Consciousness And Dennett's Intentionalist Net. *Phil Stud* 48,249–256 S 85.

Dennett develops two theories of consciousness: a personal–level intentionalist theory that provides its analysis; a sub–personal cognitivist theory whose task is to explain it. The austere intentionalist theory analyzes consciousness in terms of behavior–control and of introspective and retrospective linguistic capacities and proclivities. Close scrutiny reveals that Dennett's intentionalist theory does not enable his to capture the phenomena of consciousness "in the net of intentional systems".

BRIGHT, Michael. The Poetry Of Art. *J Hist Ideas* 46,259–278 Ap–Je 85.

Modern critics believe that "poetry" in its abstract sense (e.G., the poetry of architecture) has no more precise definition in the nineteenth century than "essence" or "spirit". But the fact is that when most writers of the last century used "poetry" in this way, they were rather specific, at least insofar as an abstraction permits, and from specificity proceeded variation, so that there are differences in meaning, some subtle and some pronounced.

BRINGSJORD, Selmer. Are There Set Theoretic Possible Worlds? *Analysis* 45,64 Ja 85.

One conception of (possible) worlds is that they are maximal and consistent sets of states of affairs or propositions. This article is a proof that, with the help of Cantor's Theorem, shows such a conception to be formally incoherent.

BRINK, David O. Legal Positivism And Natural Law Reconsidered. *Monist* 68,364–387 Jl 85.

BRINKER, Menahem. Phenomenology And Literature: Roman Ingarden And The 'Appropriate Aesthetic Attitude' To The Literary Work Of Art (in Hebrew). *Iyyun* 33,137–155 Ja–Ap 84.

The concept of an "appropriate" attitude towards the Literary Work of art reveals the dependence of Ingarden's phenomenology on various traditional assumptions characteristic of Classical Aesthetics. Their true origin is in his general phenomenology of the aesthetic object. It is possible to imagine an alternative phenomenology of Literature that will do justice to the indirect referential powers of the fictional work.

BRINTON, Alan. A Rhetorical View Of The *Ad Hominem*. *Austl J Phil* 63,50–63 Mr 85.

It is suggested that classical rhetorical theory provides the c0ntext for a more adequate understanding of the so–called "informal fallacies" which is characteristic of contemporary treatments. An analysis and justification of the *ad hominem* as a form of argument is developed in terms of the notion of rhetorical *ethos*.

BRINTON, Alan. Omnipotence, Timelessness, And The Restoration Of Virgins. *Dialogos* 20,149–156 Ap 85.

BRINTON, Alan. The Reasonableness Of Agnosticism. *Relig Stud* 20,627–630 D 84.

This essay is a critique of Clement Dore's claim (in *Religious Studies*, 18 (1983)) that the onus of proof is on the religious skeptic for the following principle: that "there is the same—or almost the same—amount of evidence" in favor of both belief and disbelief.

BRINTON, Crane and others. Symposium: Knowledge And The Humanities—The Continuing Debate. *J Aes Educ* 18,77–94 Wint 84.

BRITTAN JR, Gordon G. "Kant, Closure, And Causality" in *Kant On Causality, Freedom, And Objectivity*, Harper, William A (ed), 66–82. Minneapolis Univ Minnesota Pr 1984.

BRITTON, Karl. "Wonders" in *Philosophy And Life: Essays On John Wisdom*, Dilman, Ilham (ed), 49–60. Boston Nijhoff 1984.

BRKIĆ, Jovan. Consistency, Completeness And Decidability With Respect To The Logic Of Law And The Provability Of Juristic Arguments. *Arch Rechts Soz* 59,473–498 1973.

The first section of the article presents a general position of the author with respect to the metalogic of law and then focuses on the basic metalogical properties of consistency, completeness and decidability. The second section presents the formulation of the fundamental thesis of philosophical logic together with a demonstration of it. The final section of the article presents the proofs of paradigmatic examples of *argumentum a contrario, argumentum a maiore ad minus*, and *argumentum a minore ad maius*.

BROCK, Dan W. "The Use Of Drugs For Pleasure: Some Philosophical Issues" in *Feeling Good And Doing Better*, Murray, Thomas H (ed), 83–106. Clifton Humana Pr 1984.

BROCK, Dan W. Taking Human Life. *Ethics* 95,851–865 Jl 85.

BROCK, Erich. Einig Grundlinien Der Chinesischen Philosophie. *Z Phil Forsch* 29,241–256 Ap–Je 75.

BRÖCKER, W. Kant Über Wahrnehmung Und Erfahrung. *Kantstudien* 66,309–312 1975.

BRODSKY, Garry (ed) and Troyer, John (ed) and Vance, David (ed). *Social And Political Ethics*. Buffalo Prometheus 1985.

BRODY, Eugene B. "Freud's Influence On The Moral Aspects Of The Physician–Patient Relationship" in *Darwin, Marx And Freud*, Caplan, Arthur L (ed), 209–220. NY Plenum Pr 1984.

BRODY, Howard. "Deception In The Teaching Hospital" in *Difficult Decisions In Medical Ethics*, Ganos, Doreen and others (eds), 81–86. NY Liss 1983.

BRODY, Howard. Philosophy Of Medicine And Other Humanities: Toward A Wholistic View. *Theor Med* 6,243–256 O 85.

A less analytic and more wholistic approach to philosophy, described as 'best overall fit' or 'seeing how things all hang together,' is defended in recent works by John Rawls and Richard Rorty and can usefully be applied to problems in philosophy of medicine. Looking at sickness and its impact upon the person as a central problem for philosophy of medicine, this approach discourages a search for necessary and sufficient conditions for being sick, and instead encourages a listing of "true and interesting observations" about sickness which reflect the convergence of a number of different viewpoints. Among the relevant viewpoints are other humanities disciplines besides philosophy and the social sciences. Literature, in particular, provides insights into the meaning and the uniqueness of episodes of sickness in a way that philosophers may otherwise fail to grasp.

BROEKMAN, Jan M. Beyond Legal Gaps. *Law Phil* 4,217–238 Ag 85.

Legal gaps are elements of the strategies of the legal discourse itself. They are, like cases, determined by the requirements of consistency, coherence and consequence. Neither are they reified objects nor defects of the legal system. Gaps express the need to project an image of the legal discourse as a discourse aiming at the maintenance of our society at a society *with* law.

BROGAN, Walter. Is Aristotle A Metaphysician? *J Brit Soc Phenomenol* 15,249–261 O 84.

In the context of Martin Heidegger's interpretation, the article challenges the traditional understanding of Aristotle's philosophy. It shows that (1) the categories are not the original level at which Being is understood, (2) movement is not excluded from Aristotle's notion of Being, (3) the meaning of the eternity, necessity and simplicity of Being is misunderstood. The article reconsiders such terms as universal, induction, principle, cause, substratum and substance. A coherent but controversial picture of Aristotle's philosophy emerges.

BROGAN, Walter. The Battle Between Art And Truth. *Phil Today* 28,349–357 Wint 84.

In Heidegger's philosophy, art and truth converge in an originary unity of disclosure. The thesis of this paper is that Heidegger's uncovering of the primordial unity of art and truth rests on his insight into the necessity of the opposition between art and truth that is at play throughout the metaphysical tradition. The paper demonstrates that what is at issue for Plato in his confrontation with the artist is the relation between Being and non–being.

BROIDY, Steve. Topics In Speech Act Theory And Pedagogy. *Proc Phil Educ* 40,97–110 1984.

In this paper I intend to apply some results of philosophical inquiry in the area of speech–act theory to some particular problems of pedagogy. There are a variety of rather frustrating problems involving classroom talk that have bedeviled teachers, teacher educators, and educational researchers; problems which, I think, some attention to speech act theory may help to resolve. This paper will serve both as a means to address a selection of these problems, and as an occasion to demonstrate the general usefulness of speech act theory in practical educational matters.

BROMLEI, Iu V and Pershits, A I. Frederick Engels And Contemporary Problems Concerning The History Of Primitive Society. *Soviet Stud Phil* 23,17–49 Wint 84–85.

BRONIAK, Christopher J. Life After Death In Whitehead's Metaphysics. *Auslegung* 11,514–527 Sum 85.

The article asks what, in Whitehead's metaphysics, makes personal immortality possible. The value that fulfills and completes a temporal occasion makes immortality possible, since that value is important to God in God's nontemporality. This possibility needs a Whiteheadian conception of time–as–future and a sense of how this kind of time operates with respect to God's consequent nature. The article concludes that subjective immortality is a synthesis of subjective immediacy and objective immortality, constituting the "stubborn value" of the universe.

BRONIAK, Christopher. On Aristotle's Mind And Being. *Dialogue (PST)* 27,54–60 Ap 85.

BRONKHORST, Johannes. Nāgārjuna And The Naiyāyikas. *J Indian Phil* 13,107–132 Je 85.

BROOKS, D H M. Realism And Reference. *Phil Papers* 14,36–42 My 85.

Putnam in his book *Reason, Truth and History* puts forward two arguments against realism based on theories about how words refer. I argue against the first argument about brains in a vat that some words can pick out objects even though their user has had no causal commerce with those objects and against his second argument that the reference of terms is determined by more than the truth values of sentences containing them.

BROOKS, D. Hume's Bundle Theory Of The Mind. *S Afr J Phil* 4,75–84 Ag 85.

BROOKS, Simon A. Dignity And Cost–Effectiveness: A Rejection Of The Utilitarian Approach To Death. *J Med Ethics* 10,148–151 S 84.

Utilitarianism is commonly assumed to be the most appropriate sub–structure for medical ethics. This view is challenged. It is suggested that the utilitarian approach to euthanasia works against the patient's individual advantage and is a corrupting influence in the relationship between the physician and society. Dignity for the individual patient is not easily achieved by assessing that person's worth against the yardstick of others' needs and wishes.

BROOKS, Simon A. Dignity And Death: A Reply. *J Med Ethics* 11,84–87 Je 85.

Some form of utilitarian approach can be discerned as underlying much current medical ethical decision–making. Criticisms of the practical effects of such an approach are not parried by asserting the fundamental strengths of utilitarianism as theory.

BROOME, John. A Mistaken Argument Against The Expected Utility Theory Of Rationality. *Theor Decis* 18,313–319 My 85.

Maurice Allais has persistently directed a number of arguments against expected utility theory, considered as a theory of rationality. This paper exposes a mathematical error that vitiates one of these arguments.

BROOME, John. Selecting People Randomly. *Ethics* 95,38–55 O 84.

When there are several candidates to receive a good, and there is not enough to go round them all, it sometimes seems fair to choose between them randomly. This paper considers in what circumstances (if any) fairness does indeed require random selection. It argues that a utilitarian approach to this question is inadequate, and it uses the problem of random selection to throw some light on the notion of fairness in general.

BROOME, Taft H. Engineering And The Philosophy Of Science. *Metaphilosophy* 16,47–56 Ja 85.

The purpose of this work is to present a correct conception of engineering. The main argument is that, whereas science is a theory for obtaining knowledge about the physical world, engineering is a theory for constructing new physical worlds. Conclusions drawn from this argument are (1) engineering is not an applied science and is separate from technology; and (2) the present structure of philosophy cannot accommodate discusions about engineering—thus, a new structure should be considered.

BROSIO, Richard A. One Marx, And The Centrality Of The Historical Actor(s). *Educ Theor* 35,73–84 Wint 85.

There is a continuing thread throughout Marx's work. Without the early philosophic assumptions, Marx's later work in s makes little sense. The young Marx of the 1844 *Manuscripts* presented man as being capable of human agency, not as being determined by iron–clad economic laws. Because there is only one Marx, it is possible to evaluate his work as being championed the historical actor(s), not as a spokesman for determinism.

BROUDY, Harry S. The Public School's Search For A Public. *Phil Stud Educ* No Vol,24–33 1983.

A public school without a public is at best an oddity, at worst an absurdity, yet in many communities in the U S schools can no longer identify their public. The school is no longer a surrogate of the family, the community or a common set of values. If the public school is to have a public, it will have to find it in the class of educated minds: minds that construe experience with the concepts and images validated by the consensus of the learned arts and sciences.

BROUGHTON, Janet. Skepticism And The Cartesian Circle. *Can J Phil* 14,593–616 D 84.

I argue that Descartes thinks he can be metaphysically certain about each premise in the argument for God's existence, even before he draws the argument's final conclusion that all his distinct ideas are metaphysically certain. The certainty of the personal premises is secured in the Second Meditation. The certainty of the causal premises, I argue, arises from their central role in generating reasons for doubt of the kind that interest Descartes.

BROWN, Geoffrey. A Defence Of Pascal's Wager. *Relig Stud* 20,465–480 S 84.

The object of the paper is to offer an analysis of the Wager argument and an assessment of its value. The role of the will in belief is discussed, and Pascal's argument is defended against some criticisms, including those of Swinburne and Flew. Following a direct treatment of the argument's logic, it is maintained that certain conclusions about the nature of the God we are to believe in follow from the Wager argument itself.

BROWN, Geoffrey. Praying About The Past. *Phil Quart* 35,83–86 Ja 85.

The subject of this paper is C S Lewis's argument that it makes sense for a religious believer to pray concerning events now in the past but the (past) outcomes of which are unknown. This argument is defended against the criticisms of Peter Geach whose critique, it is maintained, embodies a misunderstanding of Lewis's philosophy.

BROWN, Geoffrey. The Cosmological Theory Of Empedocles. *Apeiron* 18,97–101 1984.

It is argued that Jonathan Barnes's treatment of Empedocles is incoherent, since the reasons given by Barnes for thinking that Empedoclean cosmology could support eternal recurrence are incompatible with his traditional interpretation of directionality in the Empedoclean cosmic cycle. The relationship between cosmology and personal immortality is further discussed. A less orthodox interpretation of Empedocles is defended.

BROWN, Harold I. How To Revive Empiricism. *Diogenes* 126,52–70 Sum 84.

Empiricism holds that claims about the world must be justified by observation. Familiar analyses of observation in terms of awareness of sensory qualia have failed to provide an adequate epistemology, but I argue that empiricism can be revived by recognizing that observation aims at the acquisition of information about entities that exist independently of our sensations, and that sensory experience, enhanced by instrumentation, provides an indirect means of access to this information.

BROWN, James M. Popper Had A Brand New Bag. *Philosophy* 59,512–515 O 84.

D C Stove's article 'How Popper's Philosophy Began' (*Philosophy* 57, No. 221, July 1982) presents the thesis that Popper's philosophy of science grew from a dictum of Popper's, "Irrefutability is not a virtue of a theory (as people often think) but a vice," and that this dictum arose from an equivocation on the word 'irrefutable'. But there seems to be no good reason for thinking that such an equivocation occurred, that such an equivocation was needed to make the dictum appear significant or that Popper's philosophy of science grew out of the dictum.

BROWN, James Robert. Explaining The Success Of Science. *Ratio* 27,49–66 Je 85.

A common realist argument says *truth* explains the *success* of a theory. Problems with this argument are discussed. Problems with anti—realist explanations of success are also pointed out. A different *style* of realist explanation is proposed.

BROWN, James R. Von Neumann And The Anti—Realists. *Erkenntnis* 23,149–160 Ag 85.

A discussion of some of the problems facing realists and anti—realists in their attempts to interpret quantum mechanics. The views of von Neumann, Wigner, and Putnam, and the problem of superluminal connections are given particular attention.

BROWN, Jerram L. "Some Paradoxical Goals Of Cells And Organisms" in *Ethical Questions In Brain And Behavior*, Pfaff, Donald W (ed), 111–124. NY Springer 1983.

BROWN, L M. Moral Education Theory And Research. *Educ Phil Theor* 16,10–21 O 84.

The purpose is to show that rationalist traditions have misdirected moral education theory by ignoring the central place—along with reason—of attitudes and values, and that researchers have similarly been misdirected in their interpretations by rationalist influences. A secondary purpose is to show that educational research (including moral education research) should not be merely imitative of models, such as from the philosophy of science.

BROWN, Robert. *The Nature Of Social Laws: Machiavelli To Mill.* Cambridge Cambridge Univ Pr 1984.

This is a history of the idea that human social behavior is governed by laws comparable to those of natural science. The account begins with the medieval belief in the Divine Legislator and then concentrates on the arguments put forward from the sixteenth to the nineteenth centuries about the nature and possibility of social laws. The author concludes that there are, and can be, no social laws comparable to the natural laws of Newtonian mechanics.

BROWN, Stuart. *Leibniz.* Minneapolis Univ Minnesota Pr 1985.

BROWN, W M. Comments On Simon And Fraleigh. *J Phil Sport* 11,33–35 1984.

This article is a reply to criticism of "Paternalism, Drugs, and the Nature of Sports," *The Journal of the Philosophy of Sport* 11, 14–22, 1984.

BROWN, W M. Paternalism, Drugs, And The Nature Of Sports. *J Phil Sport* 11,14–22 1984.

This essay examines paternalistic arguments used to justify prohibition of performance enhancing drugs by adult athletes. While acknowledging that paternalistic prohibition is justified for children and young people, the article concludes that such arguments do not hold for adults, nor are they strengthened by efforts to define 'sport' in such a way that their prohibition is thereby required.

BROWNSTEIN, Donald. Individuating Propositional Attitudes. *Phil Topics* 13,205–212 Spr 85.

Some of the problems surrounding the propositional attitudes involve questions of their identities. I consider views like Hartry Field's about mental representations with regard to whether they generate difficulties in individuating particular cases of propositional attitudes (e.G., Jones believing that Fritz is a cat). I conclude that serious questions exist about how such cases are to be individuated.

BRUCE, S. A Sociological Account Of Liberal Protestantism. *Relig Stud* 20,401–416 S 84.

This sociological explanation of the rise and fall of liberal Protestantism (LP) sees it as a response to modernity; initially tactical but then as valuable in its own the fall was an inevitable result of a lack of cohesion, the erosion of shared beliefs, the inability to maintain boundaries between believers and nonbelievers, leading to greater heterogeneity in each generation of liberal. The parasitic dependence of LP on previous periods of orthodoxy is illustrated from Presbyterian church history and biography.

BRUDNEY, Kent M. Machiavelli On Social Class And Class Conflict. *Polit Theory* 12,507–520 N 84.

BRUECKNER, Anthony L. Losing Track Of The Sceptic. *Analysis* 45,103–104 Mr 85.

This paper is an examination of the claim that Cartesian sceptical arguments require an epistemic Universalizability Principle which is sufficient to generate scepticism and independent of the thesis that knowledge is closed under known entailment. The paper's conclusion is that the Principle is false and not independent of closure.

BRUECKNER, Anthony L. The Failure Of An *A Priori* Argument For Realism. *Phil Quart* 34,491–498 O 84.

Colin McGinn (in "An A Priori Argument for Realism", J Phil 76 (1979)) attempts to refute phenomenalism and behaviorism, thereby establishing a thorough—going realism about mental states and physical objects. I show that McGinn's argument fails.

BRUECKNER, Anthony. Epistemic Universalizability Principles. *Phil Stud* 46,297–306 N 84.

BRUECKNER, Anthony. Transmission For Knowledge Not Established. *Phil Quart* 35,193–195 Ap 85.

A controversial principle allegedly required by Cartesian skeptical arguments is that if one knows that ϕ and that ϕ entails ψ, then one knows that ψ. In this paper, an argument by Graeme Forbes meant to establish the foregoing principle is criticized.

BRUENING, William H. The Death Penalty And The U S Supreme Court. *Arch Rechts Soz* 61,387–412 1975.

Le 29 Juin 1972 la Cour Suprême des Etats—Unis a prononcé la décision que voici: "La Cour maintient que l'imposition et l'exécution de la peine de mort dans ces cas constituent un châtiment cruel et insolite qui enfreint les 8°et 14°amendments (de la Constitution)." Ce jugement a été cause de beaucoup de controverses et a mené a plusieurs fausses interprétations de conclusions exactes de la Cour. La thèse ici présentée examine plusieurs opinions, touten soulignant maintes critiques, surtout celles des opinions dissidentes.

BRÜHLMEIER, Daniel. Gesetzgeberrecht Vs Richterrecht In Der Eigentumskonzeption Des Verfassungsentwurfs. *Stud Phil (Switzerland)* Supp 12,267–276 1983.

The purpose of this article is to analyze the proposed property clause in the project of a new Swiss Federal Constitution in the light of the dichotomy between a legislative monopoly and a more judge—made law oriented legal philosophy. In conclusion, it advocates, in particular in the perspective of the human rights, a restricted use of legislative instruments.

BRULISAUER, Bruno. Der Erkenntniswert Von Metaphorischen Aussagen. *Stud Phil (Switzerland)* 41,177–200 1982.

Es werden mehrere Typen von Metaphern unterschieden: 1) Stilistische Metaphern; 2) Metaphern durch Kategorien Vertauschung; 3) metaphern durch Dehnung. Die Ausgangsfragen, ob metaphorische Aussagen einen spezifischen, d.H. Einen auf nicht—metaphorische Aussagen nicht reduzierbaren Erkenntniswert haben, wird am Ende verneint. Einen "indirekten" Erkennisbeitrag wird jedoch ausgeführt—leisten allerdings jene Metaphern, die implizite Regel vorschläge darstellen und dadurch Initiativen zur Erweiterung und Differenzierung unseres Vokabulars sein können.

BRUMBAUGH, Robert S (ed) and Whitehead, Alfred N. "Discussion Upon Fundamental Principles Of Education" (1919). *Process Stud* 14,41–43 Spr 84.

An abstract of a speech on education by Whitehead in 1919 is reprinted here to make it more readily available. Attention is drawn to the relevance of several key ideas to Whitehead's other writings on educational theory. In addition, it is noted that the date and theme add evidence that Whitehead's interest in education continued unabated through the period of composition of his most technical work in the philosophy of science.

BRUMBAUGH, Robert S. *Unreality And Time.* Albany SUNY Pr 1984.

This book questions the tacit assumption that time is enough like either a substance or a quality to be subject to the law of contradiction. This helps explain how there can be, and are, four different accounts of time, internally consistent but mutually incompatible. It also follows that we can select, or mis—select, the kind of time appropriate to particular purposes at hand.

BRUMBAUGH, Robert S. The Mathematical Imagery Of Plato, *Republic* X. *Teach Phil* 7,223–228 Jl 84.

This article suggests that the details of the cosmic model in *Republic* 10 are the fourth in a set of mathematical images that Plato designed to illustrate the argument of the *Republic*. (The Dividend Line in Bk 6, the "Nuptial Number" in Bk 8, the Tyrant's Number in Bk 9, and the present passage in Bk 10). Later readers seem to have soon lost the sensitivity to a Pythagorean symbolism, attributing balance and weight to numbers, which this passage presupposes.

BRUMMER, James J. The Foreign Corrupt Practices Act And The Imposition Of Values. *Int J Applied Phil* 2,1–18 Spr 85.

The article seeks do to three things. (1) Clarify the concept of value imposition. (2) Apply this analysis to the criticism raised of the FCPA which alleges that it entails value imposition. It suggests that either the bill does not involve such imposition, or where it does, this imposition is neither necessarily unjustified nor unique to the bill. It is merely an attempt to protect values already exported to other countries. (3) Show that the bill does not represent an ethnocentric attitude toward the values and practices of other countries or cultures.

BRUMMER, James. Business Ethics: Micro And Macro. *J Bus Ethics* 4,81–92 Ap 85.

BRUNNER, José. On The Political Rhetoric Of Freud's Individual Psychology. *Hist Polit Thought* 5,315–332 Sum 84.

Freud's theory of mind is articulated in political, social, and military metaphors. It represents the psyche as a sociomorphic hierarchy of agencies in conflict with one another and suggests that the individual's autonomy can only be guaranteed by reason's benevolent authoritarian rule over the mind's other parts. Freud's model reaches beyond the liberal idea of freedom and eschews categorization into Isaiah Berlin's dichotomous scheme of positive and negative freedom, combining internal authoritarianism with external freedom in a way that avoids the danger of liberty's travesty into depotism.

BRUNNER, Norbert. Lattice—Points In Metric Spaces. *Rep Math Log* 18,45–46 1984.

If X is a metric space with a distant function *dist*, then a subset L of X is a nontrivial ϵ—lattice ($\epsilon > 0$ and $\epsilon <$ maximum of dist) if L≠X, L has at least three elements and L is maximal with respect to the property X≠Y => *dist* (X, Y) => ϵ. The existence of nontrivial lattices (for some ϵ) is equivalent to the axiom of choice.

BRUNTON, Paul. *The Notebooks Of Paul Brunton.* Burdett Larson 1984.

BRUSH, Francis W. Jan Christian Smuts And His Doctrine Of Holism. *Ultim Real Mean* 7,288–297 D 84.

BUCHANAN, Allen E. The Marxian Critique Of Justice And Rights. *Can J Phil* Supp 7,269–306 1981.

BUCHANAN, Allen. "The Family's Right To Decide For The Incompetent Patient" in *Ethics Committees And Health Care Decisions*, Cranford, Ronald (ed), 209–217. Ann Arbor Health Admin Pr 1984.

BUCHANAN, Allen. What's So Special About Rights? *Soc Phil Pol* 2,61–83 Autumn 84.

BUCHANAN, James M and Lomasky, Loren E. The Matrix Of Contractarian Justice. *Soc Phil Pol* 2,12–32 Autumn 84.

We examine two traditions of contractarianism, "Hobbesian" contract made in full knowledge of individuating circumstances and "Rawlsian" contract behind a veil of ignorance, and we consider how each can justify the assignment of equal liberties to all parties. Then, concentrating on Rawlsian contract, we set out presuppositions to justify the priority of liberty over economic goods and reasons why equal liberty is a stipulation of justice while economic equality is not.

BUCHEL, W. Naturphilosophische Überlegungen Zum Leib–Seele–Problem. *Phil Natur* 15,308–343 1975.

BUCHER, Alexius. Anthropologie In Metaphysik–Distanz: E Rothacker Zum 10: Todestag. *Z Phil Forsch* 29,349–360 Jl–S 75.

BUCHHEIM, Thomas. Mass Haben Und Mass Sein. *Z Phil Forsch* 38,629–637 N–D 84.

The chief argument is that the hedonistic passage in Plato's Protagoras is in fact a paradigm of Socratic rational teaching (having a metron) in contrast to the Protagorean method of conditioning disciples through the influence of phenomena (being a metron). This interpretation offers i) a consistent understanding of the whole dialogue ii) the connection to Plato's Theaetetus iii) an explanation for the change of opinion at the end and, iv) shows the importance of the homo–mensura–sentence for this dialogue.

BUCKLEY, James J and Wilson, William Mcf. A Dialogue With Barth And Farrer On Theological Method. *Heythrop J* 26,274–293 Jl 85.

BUCKMAN, G and Garty, M and Grosskopf, I. Ethical Dilemmas Of The Doctors' Strike In Israel. *J Med Ethics* 11,70–71 Je 85.

The authors discuss some of the moral dilemmas confronting Israeli doctors in the context of their strike in 1983. Concern for their patients militated against a strike. On the other hand their salaries were far below the mean standard of the country. To earn as much as nurses and radiographers doctors were forced to work 65–70 hours a week. The authors argue that if a doctor is underpaid and forced to work excessively the quality of medical care and ability to act in their best interests of patients is adversely affected. To avoid 'the necessity to strike' doctors' salaries and working conditions should be set by independent bodies in those countries where doctors are paid by the State.

BUCKNER, D K. Goldstein On Quotation. *Analysis* 44,189–190 O 84.

The article discusses the contention of Davidson (*Theory and Decision* 11, pp 27–40) and Goldstein (*Analysis* 44.1, p 1) that (eg) the sentence '"man" has three letters' can be equated with 'This word: man: has three letters'. But (I argue) there is no exact equation, since 'man' is read as a part of the first sentence, but is not read as a part of the second.

BUECHLER, Steven. Kueker's Conjecture For Superstable Theories. *J Sym Log* 49,930–934 S 84.

BUELA, Alberto E. El Método Empírico–Reflexivo. *Sapientia* 40,67–72 Ja–Mr 85.

BUELA, Alberto. El Protréptico De Aristóteles: Interpretación, Desarrollo Y Bibliografía. *Sapientia* 39,231–234 Jl–S 84.

BUHARIN, N I. Theory And Practice From The Point Of View Of Materialism (in Hungarian). *Magyar Filozof Szemle* 6,880–897 1983.

BUHR, Manfred. Friedenskampf Und Philosophie. *Deut Z Phil* 32,961–971 1984.

BUHR, Manfred. Kant Und Das Grundproblem Der Klassischen Bürgerlichen Philosophie. *Deut Z Phil* 22,261–268 1974.

Kant bringt als erster die philosophische Problematik der rationalen Herrschaft des Menschen über Natur und Gesellschaft umfassend zur Sprache. Mit ihm beginnt damit die klassische bürgerliche deutsche Philosophie; in ihr ist das historisch–gesellschaftliche Grundproblem der Epoche theoretisch fixiert. Kants Lösungsversuch des Grundproblems der klassischen bürgerlichen Philosophie erscheint als das Bemühen um wirklich gesicherte wissenschaftliche Erkenntnis und als Suchen nach wirklich sicheren wissenschaftlichen Kriterien für die ethischen Werte.

BULL, Robert A and Segerberg, Krister. "Basic Modal Logic" in *Handbook Of Philosophical Logic*, Gabbay, Dov (ed), 1–88. Boston Reidel 1984.

BULYGIN, Eugenio and Alchourron, Carlos. "Normative Knowledge And Truth" in *Philosophical Analysis In Latin America*, Gracia, Jorge J E and others (eds), 25–46. Boston Reidel 1984.

BULYGIN, Eugenio. Norms And Logic: Kelsen And Weinberger On The Ontology Of Norms. *Law Phil* 4,145–164 Ag 85.

BUNDER, M W. Conjunction Without Conditions In Illative Combinatory Logic. *Bull Sect Log* 13,207–214 D 84.

This paper introduces a new definition of conjunction in terms of combinators, restricted generality and the class of all propositions. The standard rules for conjunction are proved to hold for arbitrary terms, previous definitions, required restrictions. Also probable is that the conjunction of two propositions is a proposition. Proofs are carried out in logic that allows generalization over the class of theorems, the class of propositions, and the class of binary connectives.

BUNDER, M W. Some Definitions Of Negation Leading To Paraconsistent Logics. *Stud Log* 43,75–78 1984.

In positive logic the negation of a proposition A is defined by $A \supset X$ where X is some fixed proposition. A number of standard properties of negation, including *reductio ad absurdum*, can then be proved, but not the law of noncontradiction so that this forms a paraconsistent logic. Various stronger paraconsistent logics are then generated by putting in particular propositions for X. These propositions range from true through contingent to false.

BUNGE, Mario. *Treatise On Basic Philosophy*, V5. Dordrecht Reidel 1983.

The first part of a systematic treatment of descriptive and normative epistemology—the second being Volume 6 of the same treatise. The approach is basically biopsychological and sociological rather than historical. Main subjects treated: cognition (as brain process), knowledge, communication, perception, concept formation, inference, problem, conjecture, and systematization (in particular theorizing).

BUNGE, Mario. Comment On Pavel Apostol's Paper. *Stud Soviet Tho* 29,137–138 F 85.

BUNGE, Mario. Critical Examination Of Dialectics (in Hungarian). *Magyar Filozof Szemle* 4,566–578 1983.

This is a translation of a paper originally included in Ch Perelman, Ed., *Dialectics/Dialectique* (The Hague: Martinus Nijhoff, 1975). A revised version of this paper is included in the author's *Scientific Materialism* (Dordrecht–Boston: Reidel, 1981). The main criticisms leveled against dialectics as an ontology is that (a) it is vague and largely metaphorical to the point of being incapable of being formalized, (b) most of its alleged laws have counterexamples as well as instances, and (c) the plausible kernel of dialectics is common to a number of dynamicist ontologies.

BUNGE, Mario. Philosophical Conditions Of Scientific Development. *Phil Soc Act* 10,9–26 Ja–Je 84.

"science" is defined as a system that includes ontological, epistemological and ethical components—namely an ontology of changing things, a realistic epistemology, and the ethics of the free search for truth. When the dominant ideology does not tolerate such philosophical principles, scientific research is jeopardized.

BUNGE, Marta. Toposes In Logic And Logic In Toposes. *Topoi* 3,13–22 Je 84.

The purpose of this paper is to justify the claim that Topos theory and Logic (the latter interpreted in a wide enough sense to include Model theory and Set theory) may interact to the advantage of both fields. (edited)

BUNGE, Robert. *An American Urphilosophie*. Lanham Univ Pr Of America 1984.

This is the first book, to the author's knowledge, which treats the philosophic assumptions of the Teton Sioux apart from the religious trappings in which these assumptions are wrapped. The unspoken, often unconscious, implicit assumptions undergirding Sioux life are made explicit. The last chapter of the work illustrates the degree to which the grid of language forces thought into certain patterns and how language accounts for what we see as well as what we do not see.

BUNGE, Robert. Awareness Of The Unseen: The Indian's Contract With Life. *Listening* 19,181–191 Fall 84.

The interaction of the spheres Seen and Unseen are discussed and ontological suppositions such as the harmony of the universe and the "relatedness of all that is," along with complexual vs. Analytic thought and the "reciprocal appropriation" of objective nature is plains aboriginal thought. The Native American psychophysical world which forms one indivisible whole and the moral person–ality or personhood of all that is. Also discussed is the metaphysical question of what it means "to be" in traditional Native American thought.

BUNZL, Martin. Causal Factuals. *Erkenntnis* 21,367–384 N 84.

Recent work on causation has concentrated on the notion of counterfactuals which are grounded in a possible worlds analysis. This paper criticizes such approaches. An analysis of causation based directly on possible worlds analysis is proposed as a substitute.

BURBIDGE, John W. Does Historicity Require A Different Metaphysics? *Man World* 18,39–54 1985.

Since historicity affirms that singular events are decisive, it contrasts sharply with traditional metaphysics, which explores the universal principles underlying all reality. This means that historicity involves a distinctive logic of identity, contradiction and generalization. In addition, ontology is replaced by a pluralistic philosophy of traditions, and faithfulness replaces normative law as the foundation of ethics. It is suggested in conclusion that some intellectual traditions do embody the patterns of historicity.

BURBIDGE, John. Contraries And Contradictories: Reasoning In Schelling's Late Philosophy. *Owl Minerva* 16,55–68 Fall 84.

In his lectures after Hegel's death, Schelling accused Hegel of not recognizing the limits of reason. This paper explores the role of reason in those lectures, first, as articulating the possibilities that lie behind the world, and second as proposing the alternatives that will may actualize. Schelling is shown to take less account of contingency than Hegel.

BURBULES, Nicholas C. Toward A Theory Of Power In Education. *Proc Phil Educ* 40,79–90 1984.

This essay offers a review and critique of the arguments in David Nyberg's book, *Power Over Power*. It continues with a discussion of some of the issues a theory of social and political power should address.

BURGE, Tyler. The Concept Of Truth In Frege's Program. *Phil Natur* 21,507–512 1984.

The paper is abstracted from a longer treatment of the subject, 'Frege on Truth'. Two issues are discussed. One is the significant set of differences between Frege's argument that every true statement denotes the same thing—truth—and the argument by Church and Godel that was inspired by Frege and that is often mistakenly attributed to him. The second issue is the reasons Frege had for identifying a particular extension as the object, truth, that is denoted by true sentences.

BURGER, Ronna. *The "Phaedo": A Platonic Labyrinth*. New Haven Yale Univ Pr 1984.

The *Phaedo* has long been considered the source of the "twin pillars of Platonism," the theory of ideas and the immortality of the soul. The present interpretation examines the arguments in light of the structural division of the dialogue in two. In the turn from the first to the second half, the understanding of knowledge, the ideas, the soul, death, and immortality is radically transformed; with the "second sailing," the "Platonism" presented in the first half of the dialogue emerges as a target of critique.

BURGESS, John P. "Basic Tense Logic" in *Handbook Of Philosophical Logic*, Gabbay, Dov (ed), 89–134. Boston Reidel 1984.

BURGESS, John P. Synthetic Mechanics. *J Phil Log* 13,379–396 N 84.

BURHOE, Ralph W. Religion's Importance As Seen In Natural History. *Relig Hum* 18,178–185 Autumn 84.

Seeks to account for religion in the light of advanced evolutionary theory that embraces astrophysical, genetic, and psycho–socio–cultural studies. This illuminates the functioning of the brain, feelings, cognition, and religious experience and history. Finds religion is created and selected by the universal laws that account for human revolution, is the key to the evolution of altruism and humanity in *Homo*, is still essential for the human future, but its interpretation is temporarily unadapted to its necessary role in the new, scientific, world community.

BURIAN, Richard M (ed) and Brandon, Robert N (ed). *Genes, Organisms, Populations: Controversies Over The Units Of Selection*. Cambridge MIT Pr 1984.

BURIAN, Richard M. "Scientific Realism And Incommensurability" in *Methodology, Metaphysics And The History Of Science*, Cohen, Robert S (ed), 1–32. Boston Reidel 1984.

BURKE, Michael B. Hume And Edwards On 'Why Is There Something Rather Than Nothing'? *Austl J Phil* 62,355–362 D 84.

There is no known proof that the physical universe had a beginning. For this reason, if no other, proponents of the Cosmological Argument are barred from asking, 'What caused the physical universe to begin to exist?' What they can do instead to make the unfavorable assumption that the physical universe always has existed and then ask, 'Why is it that instead of never having existed, the physical universe always has existed'?

BURKE, Michael B. Spatial Analogues Of 'Annihilation And Re–Creation'. *Analysis* 45,24–29 Ja 85.

In *Metaphysics* (1983), as in his much discussed 1955 article on analogies between space and time, Richard Taylor gives as the spatial analogue of "annihilation and re–creation" something I call "multiple location". I show that annihilation and re–creation comes in two varieties, that multiple location is the analogue of one (much the more problematic one), and that what I call "discontinuous extension" is the analogue of the other. I also argue that none of the four concepts, properly understood, is trivially self–contradictory.

BURKE, Michael B. The Infinistic Thesis. *S J Phil* 22,295–306 Fall 84.

The paper aims to demonstrate the failure of two arguments by James Thompson against what Thompson has called 'the infinitistic thesis': "...An w–sequence of tasks can be completed if and only if any finite segment of them can be completed." The arguments were advanced when Thompson had already acknowledged the failure of his better known "lamp argument." (It is also explained why the thesis is unchallenged by the writings of Grünbaum).

BURKE, T Patrick. Must The Description Of A Religion Be Acceptable To A Believer? *Relig Stud* 20,631–636 D 84.

BURKI, Bruno. Justice Et Glorification: Double Préoccupation D'Ulrich Zwingli, Réformateur (1484–1531). *Frei Z Phil Theol* 31,411–420 1984.

Debating with the revolted farmers at the 16th Century, Ulrich Zwingli published a treaty about the divine justice and the human justice. His social judgment is judicious, but Christian life is finally turned toward's God's glorification. Praises liturgy socially engaged is suggested to the Zürich's Church in "action or use of the Holy Communion, Christ's memorial or eucharisty". Zwingli knew how to unit those two worries; justice and glorification.

BURNETT, Joe R. Dewey And Pekarsky On The Efficacy Of Intelligence And Foresight. *Proc Phil Educ* 40,205–208 1984.

BURNOR, Richard N. What's The Matter With *The Matter Of Chance*? *Phil Stud* 46,349–366 N 84.

This paper considers Mellor's "propensity" interpretation, which purports to provide an analysis of objective chance based upon a personalist framework. The most serious difficulty with this approach is that the dispositional (propensity) basis is an *ad hoc* addendum to what turns out to be merely a personalist theory. I further consider alterations to Mellor's approach, but conclude that no such personalist–based approach is viable as an analysis of objective probability.

BURNS, Steven A M. 'Doing Business With The Gods'. *Can J Phil* 15,311–326 Je 85.

Plato's *Euthyphro* is here interpreted (contrary to R E Allen and others) as offering, in each of its attempted definitions, positive teachings about the nature of piety. The cumulative account of piety as the part of justice marked by self–denying reverence for the divine is defended as consistent with the character exemplified by Socrates.

BURNYEAT, M F. "The Sceptic In His Place And Time" in *Philosophy In History*, Rorty, Richard and others (ed), 225–254. NY Cambridge Univ Pr 1984.

BUROKER, Jill Vance. Incongruence And The Unity Of Transcendental Idealism: Reply To Henry E Allison. *Topoi* 3,177–180 D 84.

This article responds to Henry Allison's criticisms of the author's claim that Kant's incongruent counterparts argument suppOrts his Critical conclusions that things in themselves must be both non–spatial and unknowable. The first part of the article treats four objections Allison raises. The second part discusses differences between Allison's and the author's readings of Kant's claims about things in themselves.

BURRELL, David B. God's Eternity. *Faith Phil* 1,389–406 O 84.

The essay first distinguishes God's eternity from *atemporal ity*, showing how eternity functions as a "formal feature" of divinity. To the more difficult task of properly conceiving such eternity, Kretzmann and Stump's recent proposals are adopted in a critical fashion, while the positive notion of eternity attained there is linked with creation, as in Aquinas' account of that action. The need for appropriate images is explored and some suggestions made.

BURRELL, David. Maimonides, Aquinas And Gersonides On Providence And Evil. *Relig Stud* 20,335–352 S 84.

This essay shows how interfaith and intercultural was the treatment of issues in medieval times, as two Jewish and one Christian thinker's commentaries on Job are compared to determine the parameters for the "problem of evil" and to set the stage for an analysis of Aquinas' treatment. One reading of Aquinas (Peter Geach) is considered, and a constructive alternative offered which keeps God's knowledge rigorously in the practical mode.

BURT, Donald X. To Kill Or Let Live: Augustine On Killing The Innocent. *Proc Cath Phil Ass* 58,112–119 1984.

This paper presents Augustine's answer to the question: "is it ever morally justified to directly intend the killing of an innocent human being?" Augustine claims that homicide is moraly evil if it is done without proper authority. Thus, killing the innocent is forbidden if it is authorized by God. Implications for modern cases of conflict of life between innocents are then explored.

BURT, Robert A. *Taking Care Of Strangers: The Rule Of Law In Doctor–Patient Relations*. NY Free Pr 1979.

The author disputes both traditional claims for physicians' prerogatives to administer life–prolonging treatment and newer assertions of patients' legal rights, including the "right to die." Using detailed examination of several cases, he identifies psychological forces unleashed by life–threatening illnesses that confound conventional distinctions between "self" and whether patient, physician or judge. The author argues that courts should not place exclusive power to make death–dispensing decisions in patients, their families or physicians but that legal rules should ensure that all parties remain uncertain of their ultimate authority or power to coerce one another.

BURT, Ronald S. *Toward A Structural Theory Of Action: Network Models Of Social Structure, Perception, And Action*. Orlando Academic Pr 1982.

BUSCH, Lawrence and Lacy, William B. Agricultural Policy: Issues For The 80s And Beyond. *Agr Human Values* 1,5–9 Wint 84.

The United States is currently rethinking its agricultural policies. This paper examines those policies in light of ethical and value decisions that face American agriculture.

BUSCH, Paul and Lahti, Pekka J. A Note On Quantum Theory, Complementarity, And Uncertainity. *Phil Sci* 52,64–77 Mr 85.

Uncertainty relations and complementarity of canonically conjugate position and momentum observables in quantum theory are discussed with respect to some general coupling properties of a function and its Fourier transform. The question of joint localization of a particle on bounded position and momentum value sets and the relevance of this question is the interpretation of position–momentum uncertainty relations is surveyed. In particular, it is argued that the Heisenberg interpretation of the uncertainty relations can consistently be carried through in a natural extension of the usual Hilbert space frame of the quantum theory.

BUSH, Susan (ed) and Murck, Christian (ed). *Theories Of The Arts In China*. Princeton Princeton Univ Pr 1983.

This symposium volume contains sixteen essays first produced for a 1979 conference sponsored by the American Council of Learned Societies to promote studies of Chinese aesthetics. Papers and introduction trace the evolution of terminology dealing with aesthetic appreciation in the context of China's holistic culture. Early Chinese concepts of moral philosophy, medicine, and cosmology, along with pre–modern theories of music, poetry, calligraphy, and painting, are discussed in comparison with each other and with Western developments.

BUSZKOWSKI, Wojciech. Concerning The Axioms Of Ackermann's Set Theory. *Z Math Log* 31,63–70 1985.

The paper shows that Ackermann's set theory (W Ackermann 1956) can be interpreted in its subtheory that results from dropping the axioms of extensionality and heredity. This is impossible if one drops any other axiom (axiom–schema). There are proposed some alternative systems (with a strengthened set–existence schema), being offered as to be more compatible with philosophical motivations of the theory (in particular the principle of transition from potential to actual infinity is considered). Some systems of that kind are proved to be equivalent to Zermelo and Zermelo–Fraenkel set–theories.

BUTLER, Clark (trans) and Seiler, Christiane (trans). *Hegel: The Letters*. Bloomington Indiana Univ Pr 1984.

This volume is a complete edition of available letters by Hegel. The letters are organized into chapters, where they are introduced by and alternate with commentary. The book thus approaches a "life in letters". The interpretive thesis, which is grounded in the letters as well as Hegel's published works, is that Hegelianism should be placed in the German hermeneutic tradition since Herder, and should not be understood as a form of Neoplatonism or panlogism.

BUTLER, Clark. Hermeneutic Hegelianism. *Ideal Stud* 15,121–136 My 85.

Three Hegel interpretations are distinguished: panlogist interpretations (e.G., Gilson) of the system as an original self–construction of divine thought; Neoplatonic interpretations (e.G., Findlay) of it as an imperfect approach to a timeless divine vision; and the *hermeneutic* interpretation of it as an empathetic reconstruction of an historical dialectic of cosmic self–consciousness. The third interpretation is defended, related to Hegel's major works, contrasted to Herder, Marxist method, and Rawl's/Nozick's argument from a *hypothetical* original position.

BUTLER, Clark. Peaceful Coexistence As The Nuclear Traumatization Of Humanity. *Phil Soc Crit* 10,81–94 Wint 84.

BUTLER, Clark. The Place Of Process Cosmology In Absolute Idealism. *Owl Minerva* 16,161–174 Spr 85.

Hegel's theology deciphers cosmic purpose by a single category defining the Absolute, but it did not develop the event cosmology it required: a Whiteheadian process cosmology without a transcendent God—with a list of *many* cosmic constants or categories. This cosmology bars all but momentary events from ontological status. Hegel himself denies an *existing* God beyond events in the life of Spirit. God (Spirit), like a nation, is not an entity, but is eliminably posited to simplify conceiving a process of events actualizing a common purpose.

BUTLER, Nance Cunningham. Applied Philosophy In Health Care Outside The Medical Ethics Arena. *Int J Applied Phil* 2,75–80 Spr 85.

Butler describes what she does as a strategic analyst for a consulting firm which develops strategic marketing plans for hospitals. To show how an applied philosopher might define him or herself in terms of certain skills and attitudes, rather in terms of knowledge of a particular kind, Butler lists her duties, gives examples of her written work, talks about relationships with her non–philosopher colleagues and makes suggestions about the appropriate character of a graduate degree in applied philosophy.

BUTTERFIELD, J. Spatial And Temporal Parts. *Phil Quart* 35,32–44 Ja 85.

Authors who believe the present is an epistemological notion reflecting our limited access to a temporally extended reality have traditionally held that objects have temporal as well as spatial parts; e.G., Russell, Quine, Smart. I argue that we can agree with this view of the present, but reject temporal parts. The argument also reveals some disanalogies between spatial and temporal parts; and enables us to explain a time–space disanalogy described by Dummett.

BUTTERWORTH, Charles E. *Averroes' Middle Commentaries On Aristotle's "Categories" And "De Interpretatione".* Princeton Princeton Univ Pr 1983.

BYERLY, Robert E. Definability Of Recursively Enumberable Sets In Abstract Computational Complexity Theory. *Z Math Log* 30,499–503 1984.

We consider recursively enumerable sets definable in a language devised by Blum and Gill which contains as non–logical primitives only universal functions for a gödel numbering of the partial recursive functions and a computational complexity measure. We examine how the class of definable recursively enumberable sets depends on the complexity measure. In particular, it is shown that for a suitable complexity measure, only trivial and one–complete sets are definable.

BYRNE, Edmund F. Displaced Workers: America's Unpaid Debt. *J Bus Ethics* 4,31–42 F 85.

BYRNE, P A. Berkeley, Scientific Realism And Creation. *Relig Stud* 20,453–464 S 84.

berkeley's arguments for immaterialism from the premise of God's creation are examined and defended in the paper. They are shown to be crucial to his system and valid if his account of creation is accepted. The possibility of consistently believing in creation and in a realist account of objects is explored.

BYRNE, Peter. Mysticism, Identity And Realism: A Debate Reviewed. *Int J Phil Relig* 16,237–244 1984.

The subject of this paper is S T Katz's arguments on the nature of mystical experience in his *Mysticism and Philosophical Analysis*, and the debate they have provoked. It aims to show that if we distinguish between modes of identity and between purposes in classifying mystical experiences, there may be an acceptable sense in which all mysticism is the same despite the differences Katz notes. Not all versions of the identity thesis Katz attacks need to depend on a false distinction between experience and its interpretation.

BYRUM, C Stephen. A Common Sense Approach To Value Inquiry. *J Value Inq* 18,307–318 1984.

Value questions often get lost in vagueness and abstraction. The attempt of this discussion is to bridge some of that vagueness by speaking about value inquiry in concrete, common sense terms that could have a high level of understanding in the marketplace. The basic principles of Robert S Hartman are relied upon throughout. The idea is ultimately advanced that value inquiry has more to do with the MODE of inquiry itself rather than some particular content, object, or ideology.

CABRERA, Julio. Posibilidad Del Lenguaje Metafísico. *Rev Latin De Filosof* 11,27–46 Mr 85.

Metaphysical objects were usually identified as: a) being fundamental or "basic", b) never being done in any possible experience. In Physics and in Religion as well, the need of ultratheoretical elements having a) and b) and making (physical, religious, etc) experience possible, can be proved. Although analytical philosophers have always been extremely cautious concerning Kantian concepts as "things–in–themselves", "transcendental idealism", etc, this paper shows that a Kantian apparatus can be (and have already been) adopted by an analytic paradigm, if if interpreted in a functional and pluralistic way.

CACCIATORE, Giuseppe. Nichilismo Attivo, Storicità, Futuro Nella Filosofia Di Pietro Piovani. *G Crit Filosof Ital* 63,217–259 My–Ag 84.

CACKOWSKI, Zdzislaw. The Anthropogenetic Meaning Of The Growth Of The Human Hand. *Dialec Hum* 11,201–212 Wint 84.

CADY, Duane L. Backing Into Pacifism. *Phil Soc Crit* 10,173–180 Wint 84.

The stereotypic conception of pacifism and its automatic dismissal are exposed as superficial and confused. The position is developed that pacifism is a range of views united in regarding war as morally wrong by its nature yet consisting in stages along a continuum. The conclusion is drawn that individuals committed to reversing the arms race and reducing the likelihood of nuclear war are backing into pacifism if their commitments are based on moral grounds.

CAES, Charles J. *Introduction To The Arguments For God.* Roslyn Heights Libra 1983.

This book presents the ontological, cosmological, teleological, and moral arguments for God's existence as put forth and criticized by various philosophers. (staff)

CAFFI, Claudia. Some Remarks On Illocution And Metacommunication. *J Prag* 8,449–468 Ag 84.

This paper raises a number of questions dealing with potential relationships between (some aspects of) illocution and (some aspects of) metacommunication which give rise to theoretical problems. In particular the problem of a metacommunicative re–interpretation of illocutionary markers and the problem of 'metacommunicative speech acts' will be discussed. From this discussion it becomes clear that 'metacommunicative speech acts' may function as a meeting point between the general questions, related to discourse sequencing and others, related to discourse hierarchy.

CAHILL, Lisa Sowle. Consent In Time Of Affliction: The Ethics Of A Circumspect Theist. *J Relig Ethics* 13,22–36 Spr 85.

ethics from a Theocentric Perspective develops a position which begins from *experience*, which asks whether traditional Christian symbols and theology are credible in the light of experience, and which insists that any adequate theology must take into account the findings of the natural sciences as important descriptions of human experience. This essay argues that the *problem of evil* is an important point of departure for Gustafson's position, and that it has significant consequences both for his theological "method" and for his "doctrine" of God.

CAIMI, Mario P M. La Sensación En La "Crítica" De La Razón Pura. *Cuad Filosof* 19,109–120 Ja–D 83.

CAIN, Clifford C. Omega: Some Reflections On The Meaning Of Death And Afterlife. *Faith Phil* 1,327–336 Jl 84.

This article addresses the phenomenon of death from a religious perspective in order to make death a theological topic again. An attempt is made to join existentialism's emphasis on the present ("authentic existence") and religion's assertion about future life ("death is not the final curtain"). The "eternal return," a seminal idea from the philosophy of A N Whitehead, is introduced to facilitate the attempt. In the course of the discussion, several traditional Christian terms are re–interpreted.

CAIN, James. Some Radical Consequences Of Geach's Logical Theories. *Analysis* 45,83–88 Mr 85.

For every form of general categorical syllogism normally accepted as valid there exists a corresponding argument that is invalid given Geach's theory of relative identity and his account of restricted quantification worked out in *Reference and Generality*, third edition (Cornell University Press; these results do not hold when quantifiers are construed according to the "Lewis Carroll" method of the appendix).

CALDWELL, Bruce J. Some Problems With Falsificationism In Economics. *Phil Soc Sci* 14,489–496 D 84.

It is argued that falsificationism, though dominant in the methodological literature, is little practiced by economists. Five obstacles to the successful practice of falsificationism in economics are discussed: initial conditions are numerous, some critical conditions are not independently testable, falsifiable general laws are absent, tests are of models rather than of theories, and empirical data do not accurately represent theoretical constructs.

CALDWELL, Jerome and Pour– El, Marion Boykan. On A Simple Definition Of Computable Function Of A Real Variable—With Applications To Functions Of A Complex Variable. *Z Math Log* 21,1–19 1975.

CALLAHAN, Daniel and others. "Legislating Morality: Should Life Be Defined" in *Defining Human Life*, Shaw, Margery W (ed), 335–340. Ann Arbor Aupha Pr 1983.

CALLAHAN, Daniel. "Role Of Science In Moral And Societal Decision Making" in *Defining Human Life*, Shaw, Margery W (ed), 314–325. Ann Arbor Aupha Pr 1983.

CALLAHAN, Daniel and Veatch, Robert M. Autonomy's Temporary Triumph. *Hastings Center Rep* 14,38–40 O 84.

In the medical ethical debates of the 1970s the focus was on the individual patient. The consequentialistic Hippocratic principle of patient benefit was in tension with the deontological principle of autonomy. Autonomy won a clear, but temporary victory. In the 1980s, social resource allocation questions became critical. Two social ethical principles are now in conflict: one focusing on social consequences and the other on deontologically just patterns of distribution. Just as the deontological principle of autonomy won out, so the principle of justice should.

CALLAHAN, Joan C. Enforcing Slavery Contracts: A Liberal View. *Phil Forum* 16,223–236 Spr 85.

This paper examines the case for a blanket refusal by the state to enforce voluntary slavery contracts. Although it is argued that none of the existing arguments against recognizing slavery contracts justifies a blanket refusal to recognize such contracts, it is argued that such refusal is justified in societies relevantly like our own. It is also argued, however, that in societies existing under conditions of extreme scarcity, fairness may require the recognition of dissoluble contracts for slavery.

CALLAHAN, Joan C. Liberty, Beneficence, And Involuntary Confinement. *J Med Phil* 9,261–294 Ag 84.

My purpose in this paper is to show that current legal criteria for paternalistic involuntary psychiatric confinement of the mentally ill are both too narrow and too broad. After offering an analysis of current legal criteria for involuntary confinement, I argue that an acceptable theory of paternalistic interference reveals that those criteria (1) exclude some cases where confinement would be morally permissible, and (2) allow paternalistic confinement of many whose detention is not morally justifiable. (edited)

CALLAHAN, Joan C. Response To Rebecca Dresser's 'Involuntary Confinement: Legal And Psychiatric Perspectives'. *J Med Phil* 10,199–202 My 85.

CALLAN, Eamonn. A Rejoinder To Essiet's "Callan And Dewey's Conception Of Education As Growth". *Educ Theor* 35,199–200 Spr 85.

CALLAN, Eamonn. Moral Education In A Liberal Society. *J Moral Educ* 14,9–22 Ja 85.

The perpetuation of a liberal society depends upon the perpetuation of a strong and widespread allegiance to the contestable values which shape societies of this kind. How can the goal of socialization in a liberal society be achieved while maintaining a thorough respect for the individual learner's potential for rationality and independence of mind? A fashionable answer to this question has been derived from theories of moral reasoning such as R M Hare's. In this paper the author argues that the fashionable answer is inadequate and puts forward some positive suggestions about the true nature of a liberal moral education. (edited)

CALLICOTT, J Baird. Intrinsic Value, Quantum Theory, And Environmental Ethics. *Environ Ethics* 7,257–276 Fall 85.

The central and most recalcitrant problem for environmental ethics is the problem of constructing an adequate theory of intrinsic value for nonhuman natural entities and for nature as a whole. In part one, I retrospectively survey the problem, review certain classical approaches to it, and recommend one as an adequate, albeit only partial, solution. In part two, I show that the classical theory of inherent value for nonhuman entities and nature as a whole outlined in part one is inconsistent with a contemporary scientific world view because it assumes the validity of the classical Cartesian partition between subject and object which has been overturned by quantum theory. Based upon the minimalistic Copenhagen Interpretation quantum theory, I then develop a theory of inherent value which does not repose upon the obsolete subject/object and ancillary fact/value dichotomies. In part three, I suggest that a more speculative metaphysical interpretation of quantum theory—one involving the notion of real internal relations and a holistic picture of nature—permits a principle of "axiological complementary," a theory of "intrinsic"—as opposed to "inherent"—value in nature as a simple extension of ego.

CALLICOTT, J Baird. Non–Anthropocentric Value Theory And Environmental Ethics. *Amer Phil Quart* 21,299–310 O 84.

Theoretical environmental ethics is distinguished from applied. The central problem for theoretical environmental ethics is the development of a non–anthropocentric axiology. A Humean sentimentalism evolutionarily stabilized by Darwin and ecologically informed by Leopold is recommended as the best available axiology for theoretical environmental ethics. (edited)

CALMAN, K C. Quality Of Life In Cancer Patients—A Hypothesis. *J Med Ethics* 10,124–127 S 84.

Quality of life is a difficult concept to define and to measure. An hypothesis is proposed which suggest that the quality of life measures the difference, or the gap, at a particular period of time between the hopes and expectations of the individual and that individual's present experience. Quality of life can only be described by the individual, and must take into account many aspects of life. The approach is goal–orientated, and one of task analysis. The hypothesis is developed in a diagramatic way, and several methods of testing the hypothesis suggested.

CAM, Philip. Consciousness And Content–Formation. *Inquiry* 27,381–398 D 84.

How can materialists begin to do justice to the experiencing subject? Some materialists, whom I call 'structuralists', believe that the brain sciences offer at least the distant prospect of a materialist psychology with an experiencing subject. Others, and notably those materialists who are functionalists, believe that this faith is misplaced, and offer us instead a functional psychology. I argue, briefly, that functionalism cannot deliver the goods, and go on to elaborate and defend the structuralist claim that consciousness or experience is the formation of content conceived as that laying down of traces commonly assumed to be involved in perception and cognition.

CAM, Philip. Dennett On Intelligent Storage. *Phil Phenomenol Res* 45,247–262 D 84.

According to Dennett, there are only two sorts of answers to the question how the brain stores and uses information in satisfying the organism's needs. First, there are functional accounts of the kind sketched by Dennett in *Content and Consciousness* and, secondly, there is the "brain–writing" hypothesis that the brain employs its own language. I attempt both to bring out the inadequacy of Dennett's approach and to show that the "brain–writing" hypothesis is not undermined by his criticisms. If, as Dennett says, this hypothesis forms the only alternative to his own account, then the fact that Dennett's story must be rejected shows that some such alternative is correct.

CAM, Philip. Phenomenology And Speech Dispositions. *Phil Stud* 47,357–368 My 85.

According to D C dennett our phenomenology is entirely propositional and is exhausted by the access that each of us has to our own speech dispositions. I attempt to show that this thesis is implausible through an analysis of the phenomenon of blindsight.

CAMACHO, Luis A. Desarrollo Y Cultura: Enfoques Y Desenfoques. *Rev Filosof (Costa Rica)* 22,31–38 D 84.

La revista *Desarrollo*, publicada por el Capítulo Español de la Sociedad Internacional para el Desarrollo, dedica el número 1 de año 1982 al tema "La cultura, dimensión olvidada del desarrollo". Las numerosas colaboraciones se agrupan en cuatro partes: "El problema", "Las victimas", "El reto a los instrumentos de análisis e intervención", "La búsqueda de nuevas respuestas". Diferentes nociones tanto de cultura como de desarrollo aparecen en los distintos artículos; algo semejante ocurre con la forma como se concibe la relación entre ambos. Intentamos sistematizar estos puntos de vista, y mostrar serias objeciones a la mayoría de ellos. En general creemos que la noción de desarrollo debe ser tomada más en serio y que la relación entre éste y la cultura debe ser analizada con más detalle.

CAMENISCH, Paul F. The Corporation And Individual Moral Agency. *Listening* 20,106–117 Spr 85.

This article explores possible conflicts confronting the conscientious moral agent in corporations on two major levels: the level of moral agency includes the question of the possibility of effective individual moral agency within complex corporate structures; the level of moral commitments focuses on substantive conflict between the individual's and the corporation's moral values and commitments. Factors affecting the level of conflict and the possibility of resolution are noted.

CAMPBELL, David. Rationality, Democracy, And Freedom In Marxist Critiques Of Hegel's Philosophy Of Right. *Inquiry* 28,55–74 Mr 85.

The most valuable political theoretical contribution made by Marx's idea of socialism is towards the resolution of the seeming opposition of mass democracy and rational government. Marx follows Hegel's redefinition of political rationalization as the actualization of the nascent self–consciousness of the existing ethical world when he uses socialism as a statement of those tendencies of *bourgeois* society that will create the perspectives of social awareness that allow mass democracy. This thesis is made against aspects of the interpretation of Marx's relation to Hegel in Bolshevik political theory. I claim that the Bolshevik idea of socialism as the militant political intervention of the dictatorship of the proletariat develops, through Engels, a position taken with respect to Hegel's philosophy of right in Marx's *Rhenish Journal* articles. This idea is, however, pre–Hegelian in the sense that it is open to a democratic criticism based on the philosophy of right understood in an alternative fashion. (edited)

CAMPBELL, Donald T. Toward An Epistemologically–Relevant Sociology Of Science. *Sci Tech Human Values* 10,38–48 Wint 85.

CAMPBELL, George. *A Dissertation On Miracles*. NY Garland 1983.

CAMPBELL, James. Dewey's Method Of Social Reconstruction. *Trans Peirce Soc* 20,363–393 Fall 84.

This paper sets out to clarify some fundamental aspects of Dewey's social thought—particularly those aspects related to his emphasis upon programmatic and methodical change. It does so through an examination of Dewey's two–level method of social reconstruction, exploring both intellectual and institutional reconstruction and considering some of the implications of this method for democratic change.

CAMPBELL, Keith. Conflict In The Workplace, And Its Resolution. *J Applied Phil* 1,239–252 O 84.

This paper identifies four areas of conflict which arise in contemporary workplaces, conflict between management and workforce over initiative, especially with respect to decisions over choice of product and methods of production, over productivity and the response to declining demand, over innovation and technological redundancy, and over division of the company's income. (edited)

CAMPBELL, Richmond. "Sociobiology And The Possibility Of Ethical Naturalism" in *Morality, Reason And Truth*, Copp, David (ed), 270–296. Totowa Rowman & Allanheld 1984.

CAMPBELL, Richmond. God, Evil And Humanity. *Sophia (Australia)* 23,21–35 Jl 84.

Recent objections to the premises of the classical problem of evil are reviewed. It is then argued: first, that there is no satisfactory way to modify these premises to circumvent these objections; but, second, that the existence of evil can be viewed as an obstacle to reconciling one's humanity to a belief in God and hence to making sense of salvation; and, third, that the aforementioned objections do not apply to this form of problem.

CAMPBELL, R. Truth In A Contingent World. *Phil Papers* 14,20–35 My 85.

This paper explores difficulties in Leibniz's attempt to maintain the contingency of truths about this world while holding that they are rationally explicable. It considers his account of truth as analytic, of existence as extrinsic and his doctrine of relations. Could God have created another possible world? For Leibniz, God must create the best world and which is best is determined logically. But Leibniz can hold all this consistently, since the most rational *action* is not *logically* necessary.

CAMPBELL, Tom. The Rights Approach To Mental Illness. *Philosophy* 18,221–254 84 Supp.

The 'will' or 'power' theory of rights militates against the ascription of rights to the mentally ill. The 'interest' theory of rights, which is in any case preferrable on philosophical grounds, opens the way for a possible right to compulsory treatment in the case of certain types of mental illness.

CAMPODONICO, Angelo. Il Carattere Immediato Della Presenza Di Dio Nel Mondo Secondo Tommaso D'Aquino. *Riv Filosof Neo–Scolas* 76,245–268 Ap–Je 84.

This article is concerned with the immediateness of God's imminence in the world and in the human being. According to Aquinas, God's imminence permanently pervades the universe because He is both "Esse", i.E., the Cause of created beings, and Spirit. The difference that exists in creatures between "esse" and "essentia" and the hyerarchical participation (Proclus, Dyonisius) are also required. The author shows that God's immediate imminence is the basis of entities' value and complementarity.

CAMPOREALE, Salvatore I. Umanesimo E Teologia Nel Cusano "Disgiunzione" E "Metafora". *Sapienza* 37,301–312 Jl–S 84.

CANALS– FRAU, D. Mesure De Spin Et Paradoxe E P R. *Rev Metaph Morale* 89,405–409 Jl–S 84.

CANAVERO, A Tarabochia. A Proposito Del Trattato "De Bono Naturae" Nel "Tractatus De Natura Boni" Di Alberto Magno. *Riv Filosof Neo–Scolas* 76,353–373 Jl–S 84.

This article analyzes the first part of Albert the Great's *Tractatus de natura boni* (1236–1237). Albert defines the Good of nature and divides it according to the Augustinian tripartition (modus, species, ordo), linked to the triad of the Wisdom (Wisdom, XI, 21: mensura, numerus, pondus). In those years, other authors examined in various books (such as William of Auxerre's *Summa aurea*, the anonymous *Summa duacensis*, and Philip the Chanchellor's *Summa de bono*) the question of dividing the Good of nature and of its lowering owing to the sin. Albert didn't take part in this controversy with *Tractatus*, but only later, with *De bono* (about 1246) and *Commentary to Sentences* (1244–1249).

CANNELL, Hugh. Commentary On "Striking Responsibilities". *J Med Ethics* 11,69 Je 85.

The moral status of those who voluntarily undertake certain supererogatory commitments in their work, is relatively greater than those who do not. Such status accrues to volunteer unpaid life–boat men (in the U K) and to many paid health care workers (e.G., paramedics). Acceptance of this "moral relativism" implies that there is a duty to honor the obligations of the job. This may include not withdrawing labor even when wages are too low.

CANTOR, Paul. "Friedrich Nietzsche: The Use And Abuse Of Metaphor" in *Metaphor*, Miall, David S (ed), 71–88. Atlantic Highlands Humanities Pr 1982.

CAPALDI, Nicholas. *Out Of Order: Affirmative Action And The Crisis Of Doctrinaire Liberalism.* Buffalo Prometheus Books 1985.

This article is a sustained and comprehensive examination of the historical, legal, political, sociological, economic, and moral dimensions of the issue. It documents how the definition of the problem of discrimination was shifted from equality of opportunity to equality of result. Affirmative action (with intellectual roots of liberalism, the entrenched ideology of academic social science) is a logically incoherent policy which undermines democracy and supplants it with fascism. It very nearly destroyed the American university.

CAPALDI, Nicholas. Affirmative Action: A Philosophical Critique. *Cogito* 2,61–92 Je 84.

CAPALDI, Nicholas and King, James and Livingston, Donald. The Hume Literature Of The 1970's. *Phil Topics* 12,167–192 Wint 81.

CAPANNA, Francesco. Gadamer, L'ermeneutica E——Les Bourgeois. *Riv Stud Croce* 21,13–30 Ja–Mr 84.

Dal confronto delle impostazioni e soluzioni date ad alcuni problemi fondamentali (l'ermeneutica, lo storicismo, la morte, la vertà) dal Croce e dal Gadamer, risulta che il successo di quest'ultimo non è dovuto ad un suo valore di filosofo *genuino* ma ad un "modsa" favorita dall superficialità d'un pubblicco che si lascia incantare da chi sa sfruttare i massmedia, permettendo d'esser presentato come autore di dottrine "nuove", non solo invece già not ai competenti, ma ora impoverite o addirittura mistificate rispetto alla loro origine nel Croce.

CAPLAN, Arthur L (ed) and Jennings, Bruce (ed). *Darwin, Marx, And Freud: Their Influence On Moral Theory.* NY Plenum Pr 1984.

While many philosophers and theologians have attempted to give Marxist, Freudian, or Darwinian interpretations of morality, little inquiry has been devoted to the views about morality held by these three thinkers. None of them can be said to have held explicit normative theories of ethics, but all of them advanced claims about the objectivity and testability of moral claims. The essays in this book attempt to examine both the views of these three thinkers regarding ethics as well as their influence on contemporary moral thought.

CAPLAN, Arthur L. "Out With The "Old" And In With The "New"" in *Ethical Questions In Brain And Behavior*, Pfaff, Donald W (ed), 91–110. NY Springer 1983.

CAPLAN, Arthur L and Sadler Jr, Alfred M and Sadler, Blair L. Organ Donation: Is Voluntarism Still Valid? *Hastings Center Rep* 14,6–12 O 84.

CAPPELLETTI, Angel J. El Sueño Y Los Sueños En La Filosofía Prearistotélica. *Rev Filosof (Costa Rica)* 23,71–81 Je 85.

We deal here with Pre–Socratic psycho–physiological theories on the nature of dreams, as well as with their epistemological, anthropological and metaphysical implications. Alcmaeon of Croton, Heraclitus, Empedocles, Democritus and other philosophers are considered. The Platonic conception of dreams is exposed in the *Dialogues* is analyzed, with special emphasis on the anticipations of Freudian notions (such as repression). Finally, Hippocrate's medico–philosophical theories are taken into account, in particular his conception of dreams as messengers of the body.

CAPPELLETTI, Angel J. Sobre El Feminismo De Platón. *Rev Ven Filosof* 12,87–96 1980.

Platón defiende en la "República" la tesis de que hombres y mujeres deben recibir igual educación. Ello no arquye, sin embargo, que defienda la igualdad de los sexos. Bien por el contrario, Platón considera que la mujer debe estar jurídica y moral mente sometida al rarón porque, enconjunto, es decir, como gropo, es más débil. La igualdad se da sólo en el plano de la defensa militar del Estado.

CAPRON, Alexander M and others. The Subject Of Baby Fae. *Hastings Center Rep* 15,8–13 F 85.

"the Subject is Baby Fae." *The Hastings Center Report* 15 (February 1985), 8–13 [The Hastings Center, 360 Broadway, Hastings-on-Hudson, NY 10706]. Six commentators (Alexander M Capron, Tom Regan, Keith Reemtsma, Richard Sheldon, Richard A McCormick, and Albert Gore) discuss the October 1984 xenograft performed on Baby Fae at Loma Linda University Medical Center. They consider the tension between science and medicine vis–a–vis society and the public interest; the role of the media and the public's right to know; animal rights; and the need of the IRB for anonymity and protection from the press.

CAPRON, Alexander M. "Decision Review: A Problematic Task" in *Ethics Committees And Health Care Decisions*, Cranford, Ronald (ed), 174–185. Ann Arbor Health Admin Pr 1984.

CAPRON, Alexander M and Cassell, Eric J. Care Of The Dying: Withholding Nutrition. *Hastings Center Rep* 14,32–37 O 84.

The article examines three basic ethical themes—autonomy, paternalism, and community—in the context of artificial feeding (by nasogastric or gastrostomy tubes) of gravely ill patients. It argues that the issue of the limits of care has not been well resolved by the law (through court cases) or by medicine. Three recent cases—Barber & Nejdl (Calif), *Conroy* (N J) and *Hier* (Mass)—are analyzed. Despite its heavy symbolic component, artificial feeding should be regarded as any other treatment and analyzed in terms of the proportionality of its burdens and benefits. If the patient can be made comfortable and the feeding provides an opportunity to treat the underlying illness, such measures are usually appropriate. Conversely, life–sustaining food and water may be withdrawn upon the instruction of the patient and is not mandatory for incompetent patients if such treatment is painful (particularly when it renders the patient unable to communicate), the underlying condition is irreversible, and death is imminent.

CAPRON, Alexander Morgan. "Current Issues In Genetic Screening" in *Biomedical Ethics Reviews*, Humber, James M (ed), 121–152. Clifton Humana Pr 1984.

CAPUTO, John D. Prudential Insight And Moral Reasoning. *Proc Cath Phil Ass* 58,50–55 1984.

Following the lead of Gadamer and of Robert Henle, I argue for the limitations of moral reasoning and for the necessity of prudential insight into concrete moral situations, an insight which both generate moral "laws" to begin with and also adapts them to changing circumstances. Moral rules are schemas needing practical application, not theoretical principles from which one simply deduces consequences.

CARAWAY, Carol. Criteria And Circumstances. *S J Phil* 22,307–316 Fall 84.

Traditional formulations of Wittgenstein's criterial relationship ignore the different roles that different types of circumstances play in criterial relations. General circumstances provide the necessary background for the significant functioning of criterial rules; particular circumstances determine both whether a person's behavior (B) is functioning as a criterion for a particular psychological state (S) and whether a person's doing B shows us (or justifies our assertion or claim to know) that the person is in S.

CARELLO, Claudia and Turvey, M T. The Equation Of Information And Meaning From The Perspectives Of Situation Semantics And Gibson's Ecological Realism. *Ling Phil* 8,81–90 F 85.

CARENS, Joseph H. Peace, Human Rights, And Human Needs: A Comment On The Bay–Flathman Debate. *J Soc Phil* 16,25–32 Wint 85.

CAREY, John J (ed). *Kairos And Logos: Studies In The Roots And Implications Of Tillich's Theology.* Macon Mercer Univ Pr 1984.

CAREY, John J (ed). *Theonomy And Autonomy: Studies In Paul Tillich's Engagement With Modern Culture.* Macon Mercer Univ Pr 1984.

CARLSON, Allen. On Appreciating Agricultural Landscapes. *J Aes Art Crit* 34,301–312 Spr 85.

This discussion addresses the difficulties involved in the aesthetic appreciation of the landscapes produced by agriculture, in particular the new agriculture landscapes of modern large scale farming. It is argued that although these new landscapes may seem bland and featureless in comparison with more traditional rural landscapes, they yet offer much of aesthetic interest and value when appreciated in light of their functional nature and in terms of appropriate appreciative models.

CARLSON, John W. "Wittgenstein And Philosophy Of Religion" in *History Of Philosophy In The Making*, Thro, Linus J (ed), 247–254. Washington Univ Pr Of America 1982.

CARNEY, James D. Bouwsma On Moore's Proof. *Phil Invest* 8,189–198 Jl 85.

CARNIELLI, Walter A and De Alcantara, Luiz P. Paraconsistent Algebras. *Stud Log* 43,79–88 1984.

The concept of da Costa algebra, which reflects most of the logical properties of C_n, as well as the concept of paraconsistent closure system, are introduced in this paper. We show that every de Costa algebra is isomorphic with a paraconsistent algebra of sets, and that the closure system of all filters of a da Costa algebra is paraconsistent. (edited)

CARPIO, Adolfo P. E Pucciarelli: La Filosofía Como Deslinde. *Cuad Filosof* 19,19–23 Ja–D 83.

CARR, David. Dance Education, Skill, And Behavioral Objectives. *J Aes Educ* 18,67–76 Wint 84.

From the viewpoint of educational philosophy, the author sets out to examine some common unsatisfactory approaches to dance teaching apparent among student teachers from education colleges. It is argued that the main reason for the widespread misunderstanding of the educational significance of both creative and ethnic dance may be traced to the influence of certain mechanistic models of skill acquisition taught as part of educational psychology in very many colleges.

CARRABINO, Victor. "The French Nouveau Roman" in *Existential Coordinates Of Human Condition*, Tymieniecka, A (ed), 261–272. Boston Reidel 1984.

CARRANZA, Cristián Golcher. Bergson: Metafísica Del Arte. *Rev Filosof (Costa Rica)* 23,83–89 Je 85.

CARRIER, David. Art And Its Preservation. *J Aes Art Crit* 34,291–300 Spr 85.

CARRIÓ, Genaro. "Legal Principles And Legal Positivism" in *Philosophical Analysis In Latin America*, Gracia, Jorge J E and others (eds), 47–72. Boston Reidel 1984.

CARROLL, John M (ed) and Miller, Lance A (ed) and Bever, Thomas G (ed). *Talking Minds: The Study Of Language In The Cognitive Sciences.* Cambridge MIT Pr 1984.

CARROLL, Mary Ann and Schneider, Henry G and Wesley, George R. *Ethics In The Practice Of Psychology.* Englewood Cliffs Prentice–Hall 1985.

This book will acquaint not only philosophers and psychologists with ethical issues arising in psychology but also anyone interested in the profession. Hence, no background knowledge of philosophy or psychology is presupposed. Some of the areas covered are therapeutic techniques, research, special populations, testing, and consulting. Attention is given to consent, confidentiality and competence. Chapters contain case studies for discussion. The *Ethical Principles of Psychologists* as formulated by The American Psychological Association are included.

CARROLL, Noel. Hume's Standard Of Taste. *J Aes Art Crit* 43,181–194 Wint 84.

CARRUTHERS, Peter. Eternal Thoughts. *Phil Quart* 34,186–204 Jl 84.

The paper considers Frege's arguments for the eternal existence of thoughts (senses of context–free sentences). These are the arguments from communication, from the omnitemporality of truth, from the objectivity of truth, and from the omnitemporality of analytic truth. Since all four arguments fail, I conclude that we have no good reason to believe that thoughts and propositions exist independently of the human mind.

CARSON, Thomas L and Wokutch, Richard E and Cox, James E. An Ethical Analysis Of Deception In Advertising. *J Bus Ethics* 4,93–104 Ap 85.

CARSON, Thomas L. Bribery, Extortion, And "The Foreign Corrupt Practices Act". *Phil Pub Affairs* 14,66–90 Wint 85.

CARSON, Thomas L. Strict Compliance And Rawls's Critique Of Utilitarianism. *Theoria* 49,142–158 1983.

CARTER, Robert E. *Dimensions Of Moral Education.* Toronto Univ Of Toronto Pr 1984.

This inquiry into the philosophy of moral education attempts to steer a course between moral relativism and moral absolutism. It is rooted in the Socratic method of teaching and learning, emphasizing the virtues of intellectual myopia (partial knowing) as against blindness (hopeless ignorance) or perfect vision (arrogance). Applying the 'critical method' to contemporary moral education, the author examines values clarification, Kohlberg's developmental thesis, and Existentialism. The notions of the person, choice, responsibility and commitment are explored, and an analysis of valuation is offered.

CARTER, W R. Impeccability Revisited. *Analysis* 45,52–55 Ja 85.

Some theorists argue that it is possible that (i) God is omnipotent and (ii) God is essentially "impeccable" or sinless. I argue that this view is mistaken. If God cannot sin, there are things we (humans) can do which God cannot do. If that is so, God cannot be omnipotent, on any plausible analysis of omnipotence.

CARTWRIGHT, Nancy. When Explanation Leads To Inference. *Phil Topics* 13,111–122 Spr 82.

CARVER, Ronald P. Art Natural Enemies. *Relig Hum* 19,138–144 Sum 85.

CARVER, Terrell. *Marx & Engels: The Intellectual Relationship.* Bloomington Indiana Univ Pr 1984.

The young Engels was accomplished in historical, political, economic and sociological analysis. His influence on the early Marx and his contributions to his collaborative works have been underrated. After 1859 Engels popularized Marx's work as a philosophical system. In doing so he implicitly redefined Marx's project and superimposed his own notions of materialism, dialectic, determinism, method and science. Claims that Marx approved of this do not stand up to scrutiny.

CASADO, Fidel. Apriorismo Como Contenido Intelectual En Balmes, Reflejo De La "Memoria Dei" Agustiniana? *Augustinus* 25,353–362 Ja–D 80.

CASALEGNO, Paolo and Boffa, Maurice. The Consistency Of Some 4–stratified Subsystem Of NF Including NF3. *J Sym Log* 50,407–411 Je 85.

The system NF_3 is formed by those axioms of NF (Quine's set theory) which are 3–stratified (i.E., using only 3 consecutive types). It is not known whether NF is consistent, but NF_3 has been proved consistent (Grishin). The authors show that NF_3 remains consistent after adding the (4–stratified) axiom which asserts the existence of the set of natural numbers.

CASAÑAS, Mario. Unamuno Ou Le Traité De L'amour De Dieu. *Rev Phil Louvain* 82,523–544 N 84.

Setting out from Unamuno's project, which he left incomplete, of writing a Treatise on the love of God, the A proposes to show, contrary to other interpretations, how in this Spanish author a spiritual, Christian and mystical experience is to be found, which in the midst of the profound disarray struggles to remain open to hope. In this way of the paradoxes in the thought of Unamuno are taken seriously as a means of acceding to an apophatic experience, beyond rationality. This study also attempts to situate Unamuno within religious philosophy of Biblical inspiration which seeks to be a free thought rooted in the sacred, as an experience of Justice, and hence a reply to the present future of modernity and to the oncome of subsequent nihilism.

CASARI, Ettore. Remarks On The Foundational Inquiry. *Synthese* 62,125–138 F 85.

CASCARDI, A J. On Heidegger And The Recourse To Poetic Language. *Thomist* 49,99–115 Ja 85.

CASCARDI, Anthony J. Remembering. *Rev Metaph* 38,275–302 D 84.

This essay offers a critique of "mentalist" models of memory such as are found in Augustine, Descartes, and Locke. Beginning from the concepts of "following a rule" and "going on" in Wittgenstein's *Philosophical Investigations*, I propose a model of memory as a practice, and distinguish this also from contemporary psychological models of memory (e.G., in Piaget) and from information–storage models. Throughout the essay, I discuss the relationship between following rules and the problems, associated with modernist aesthetics and philosophy, of fraudulence and authenticity; and I explain the relationship between memory and determinism. Literary and historical examples from Cervantes to Foucault conclude the essay.

CASEMENT, William. "The Poverty Of Moral Education" in *The Georgetown Symposium On Ethics*, Porreco, Rocco (ed), 251–260. Lanham Univ Pr Of America 1984.

CASEY, Edward S. Commemoration And Perdurance In The Analects, Books 1 And 2. *Phil East West* 34,389–400 O 84.

CASEY, Edward S. Habitual Body And Memory In Merleau–Ponty. *Man World* 17,279–298 1984.

CASEY, Edward S. Origin(S) In (Of) Heidegger/Derrida. *J Phil* 81,601–610 O 84.

CASPAR, Ruth. Natural Law: Before And Beyond Bifurcation. *Thought* 60,58–72 Mr 85.

I argue that presentations of ethical theory in bioethical literature rarely provide adequate treatment of the natural law tradition. I suggest that the reason for this failure is the uncritical acceptance of the deontological/teleological distinction. When ethical theories are so classified, there is no way to do justice to natural law, which is both more ancient than this dichotomy (a legacy of analytic philosophy) and an ever–renewing system of thought that deserves to be presented on its own terms.

CASPER, Bernhard. "Franz Rosenzweig's Criticism Of Buber's *I And Thou*" in *Martin Buber*, Gordon, Haim (ed), 139–162. Beersheva Ktav 1984.

CASSELL, Eric J and Capron, Alexander M. Care Of The Dying: Withholding Nutrition. *Hastings Center Rep* 14,32–37 O 84.

The article examines three basic ethical themes—autonomy, paternalism, and

community—in the context of artificial feeding (by nasogastric or gastrostomy tubes) of gravely ill patients. It argues that the issue of the limits of care has not been well resolved by the law (through court cases) or by medicine. Three recent cases—Barber & Nejdl (Calif), *Conroy* (N J) and *Hier* (Mass)—are analyzed. Despite its heavy symbolic component, artificial feeding should be regarded as any other treatment and analyzed in terms of the proportionality of its burdens and benefits. If the patient can be made comfortable and the feeding provides an opportunity to treat the underlying illness, such measures are usually appropriate. Conversely, life–sustaining food and water may be withdrawn upon the instruction of the patient and is not mandatory for incompetent patients if such treatment is painful (particularly when it renders the patient unable to communicate), the underlying condition is irreversible, and death is imminent.

CASTAÑEDA, Hector–Neri. Causes, Causity, And Energy. *Midwest Stud Phil* 9,17–28 1984.

CASTANEDA, Hector–Neri. The Semantics And The Causal Roles Of Proper Names. *Phil Phenomenol Res* 46,91–114 S 85.

Here is a somewhat comprehensive account of proper names as they function in ordinary experience. It is the *Restricted–Variable/Retrieval View of Proper Names*. Since the way any standard piece of language functions in experience hinges on the meaning of that piece of language, we are here concerned both with the main pragmatic roles of proper names and with their fundamental semantic properties. Because we aim at comprehensiveness, as well as correctness, we collect rich and diversified data, capable of exhibiting some important conceptual and psychological patterns of our uses of proper names; we also collect rich and careful exegesis so as to distill criteria of adequacy that can guide us in developing a good account of such patterns.

CASTANEDA, Hector–Neri. Tomberlin, Frege, And Guise Theory: A Note On The Methodology Of Dia–Philosophical Comparisons. *Synthese* 61,135–148 N 84.

The Paradox of Reference may be solved in many different ways. E.G., (A)Frege's Sense/Referent solution at the level of individuals by means of a two–dimensional semantics; (B) Guise Theory's solution at the level of prediction, distinguishing between semantic and doxastic reference; (C) Tomberlin's Quinean DeDicto/DeRe promise of a one–dimensional unified ontology and semantics, by breaking the mind into two separate compartments: one opening to and one hermetically sealed from the world. tomberlin deals ingeniously with intentional action. However, (C) is still to be underdeveloped for a fruitful dia–philosophical comparison with (A) and (B).

CASULLO, Albert. Conjunctive Properties Revisited. *Austl J Phil* 62,289–291 S 84.

D M Armstrong maintains that there are conjunctive properties. His supporting argument is based on the intriguing possibility that properties are all infinitely complex; that is, the possibility that there are no simple properties. The primary purpose of this paper is to argue that even if all properties are infinitely complex, one need not admit the existence of conjunctive properties.

CASULLO, Albert. The Contingent Identity Of Particulars And Universals. *Mind* 93,527–541 O 84.

The primary purpose of this paper is to argue that particulars in the actual world are nothing but complexes of universals. I begin by briefly presenting Bertrand Russell's version of this view and exposing its primary difficulty. I then examine the key assumption which leads Russell to difficulty and show that it is mistaken. The rejection of this assumption forms the basis of an alternative version of the view which is articulated and defended.

CATALANO, Joseph S. Bonne Et Mauvaise Foi, Notions Faible Et Forte. *Petit Rev Phil* 6,37–60 Autumn 84.

This is a translation of an article, with minor revisions, that appeared in "Review of Existential Psychology & Psychiatry" volume XVII, No 1. In this article, I distinguish two notions of good and bad faiths, weak and strong. My thesis is that *Being and Nothingness* provides the context for elucidating a viable notion of "good faith", in the strong sense of that term.

CATAUDELLA, Michele. La Polémique Contre Les Lumières Et Contre Le Rationalisme Dans Un Journal Peu Connu De Gasparo Gozzi. *Rev Univ Ottawa* 54,17–26 Jl–S 84.

The "Songnatore italiano" a newspaper written by Gasparo Gozzi and published in Venice in 1768, contains a strong attack on rationalist philosophy in general and on Rousseau's two principal arguments in particular, the concept of the origin of inequality and the return to nature. Gozzi opposes what he calls philosophical abstraction with common sense and detail; in other words a sense of history and tradition.

CATURELLI, Alberto. El Pensamiento Filosofico–Religioso De Manuel Demetrio Pizarro. *Sapientia* 39,283–308 O–D 84.

CATURELLI, Alberto. En El X Aniversario Del "Conjunto De Pesquisa Filosófica". *Sapientia* 39,309–311 O–D 84.

CAUCHY, Venant and Kuczynski, Janusz. World Congresses Of Philosophy. *Phil Today* 29,28–37 Spr 85.

CAUCHY, Venant. Culture And Human Deviancy. *Dialec Hum* 11,225–234 Spr/Sum 84.

CAUCHY, Venant. Culture Et Vérité Chez Aristote. *Diotima* 12,41–47 1984.

CAUCHY, Venant. The Role Of Chinese Philosophy Within The Thought Of The World. *J Chin Phil* 11,199–202 S 84.

CAULFIELD, Mina Davis. Sexuality In Human Evolution: What Is "Natural" Sex? *Fem Stud* 11,343–364 Sum 85.

This paper deals with the evolutionary change in human female anatomy referred to as the loss of the estrous cycle. Theoretical formulations by sociobiologists that interpret the loss of estrus as indicating biologically determined male dominance, pair bonding, or other specific forms of human sexuality, are critiqued. Drawing on the work of feminist anthropologists, the author suggests that the loss of estrus signals the change to a form a sexual behavior that is completely socially constructed; symbolic meanings rather than the biological cues of the estrous cycle have come to govern sexual arousal in our species.

CAUTHEN, Kenneth. Imaging The Future: New Visions And New Responsibilities. *Zygon* 20,321–339 S 85.

History may be pregnant with a new paradigm centering around the organic features of systems in four areas: the global–ecological, the national–social, the organizational–institutional, and the individual–psychological. Key terms are holistic, synergy, harmony, interdependence, and synthesis. A transition is occuring in each of these realms that has great potential for human fulfillment, if the shift can be successfully managed. Movements in theology can be similarly illuminated by this analysis at three points: the global conversation between liberation and establishment theologies, the renewed discussion among Christian theologians regarding other world religions, and the current influence of process theology.

CAVAGLION, Alberto. Giulio Augusto Levi E La "Scienza Del Comico". *G Crit Filosof Ital* 63,444–454 S–D 84.

CAVE, George P. The Dialectic Of Becoming In Hegel's Logic. *Owl Minerva* 16,147–160 Spr 85.

CAVELL, Marcia. Knowledge And Value. *J Value Inq* 19,111–118 1985.

The author takes issue with 'subjectivism' in ethics. It is argued that holding on object to be intrinsically valuable is one form of acknowledging it as an object, something that exists and has many of the characteristics it does independently of its capacities to please, gratify, or frustrate. This acknowledgment is developmentally located in the child's capacity for gratitude and mourning.

CAWS, Peter. Flauberts Laughter. *Phil Lit* 8,167–180 O 84.

In *L'Idiot de la famille* Sartre develops a theory of laughter, whose point of departure is in the idea of the comic exemplified in the life and writings of Flaubert, and which, it is argued, is superior to the theories of Schopenhauer, Bergson, and Freud. He suggests that laughter protects the seriousness of those who laugh, that is a conservative. The question is raised as to whether that makes it incompatible with revolution.

CAWS, Peter. The Case Of The Athenian Stranger: Philosophy And World Citzenship. *Teach Phil* 8,103–110 Ap 85.

CAWTE, John. Karl Rahner's Conception To God's Self–Communication To Man. *Heythrop J* 25,260–271 Jl 84.

CAZENAVE, Michel (ed). *Science And Consciousness: Two Views Of The Universe.* NY Pergamon Pr 1984.

CEBIK, L B. "Patenting New Forms Of Life: Are There Any Ethical Issues" in *Biomedical Ethics Reviews*, Humber, James M (ed), 165–186. Clifton Humana Pr 1983.

CECIL, Andrew R. "Natural Justice And Natural Rights" in *The Search For Justice*, Taitte, W Lawson (ed), 43–82. Austin Univ Of Texas Pr 1983.

CECIL, Andrew R. "The Search For Justice Introduction" in *The Search For Justice*, Taitte, W Lawson (ed), 11–24. Austin Univ Of Texas Pr 1983.

CEKIĆ, Miodrag. Knowledge As The Production Of Intellectual Instruments And Theoretical Constructions. *Man World* 18,185–202 1985.

CELEDA, J and Skramovska, Svatoslava. Dialectical Unity Of The Dynamic And The Statistical In Nature And Society And Prigogine's Universal Evolution Theory (in Czechoslovakian). *Filozof Cas* 32,856–875 1984.

Prigogines' theory of fortuitous formation of highly organized systems inside assemblies of micro–particles far from theromodynamical equilibrium is analyzed. The authors' attempt to generalize this mechanism to all other evolutional levels of matter is submitted to criticism, especially if extended to socio–economical systems in human society, created by man as macroscopical "Maxwellian thermodynamical demon" (whose individual knowledge, observation, evaluation, social communication, education—by former generation through tradition, literature etc.) are not determined by thermodynamical axiomatism.

CELLUCCI, Carlo. Proof Theory And Complexity. *Synthese* 62,173–190 F 85.

CENTI, Beatrice. In Difesa Della Filosofia: Enriques E Poincaré. *G Crit Filosof Ital* 63,420–443 S–D 84.

CENTRONE, Marino. Frammenti: Sulla Crisi Della Epistemologia. *Ann Fac Lett Filosof* 25 & 26,519–552 1982–83.

The subject of this essay it is to analyze the crisis of the contemporary epistemology relatively to the definition of a theoretical status. The evolution from the Inductivism of the Verificationistic perspective to the Popperian school has produced an intrinsic formalistic regression of the epistemological discussion, partially preserved for the postulation of the Tarskian concept of truth. The central topic of the essay is that only a diachronic interpretation can be, today conceived to the analysis of the epistemology.

CENZER, Douglas. Monotone Reducibility And The Family Of Infinite Sets. *J Sym Log* 49,774–782 S 84.

CEREZO– DE DIEGO, Prometeo. El Problema De La "Infidelidad" En Fray Alonso De La Veracruz. *Rev Filosof (Mexico)* 17,291–310 My–Jl 84.

The problem of the "infidelity" of the American Indians is studied by Fr Alonso de la Veracruz in his treatise *De dominio infidelium et iusto bello*. Starting from the known classification of unbelievers by Cardinal Caietanus, he works out a very complete new classification of unbelievers and he concludes that no power, neither spiritual (the Roman Pontiff) nor political (the Emperor), may justly wage war against unbelievers to deprive them of their rights because of their unbelief.

CERVERA C, Carmen. Análisis Filosófico De La Cultura En Su Perspectiva Tridimensional. *Logos (Mexico)* 8,83–90 My–Ag 85.

CESAREO, Rosa. L'Evoluzione Del Problema Morale Nel Pensiero Di Cartesio. *Filosofia* 36,79–108 Ja–Mr 85.

CH'IEN, Edward T. The Concept Of Language And The Use Of Paradox In Buddhism And Taoism. *J Chin Phil* 11,375–400 D 84.

CHAFFIN, D (trans) and Husserl, Edmund. The Apodicticity Of Recollection. *Husserl Stud* 2,3–32 1985.

CHAKRABARTI, Kisor Kumar. Some Remarks On Indian Theories Of Truth. *J Indian Phil* 12,339–356 D 84.

Some of the points sought to be established are (1) an overly pragmatic reading of the concept of truth in Indian philosophy should be avoided; (2) notions similar to that of knowledge as justified true belief and to the distinction between analytic and synthetic truths are found in Indian philosophy; (3) confirmation of truth through an inferential process, when properly analyzed, does not lead to an infinite regress and that (4) in some cases truth is known immediately.

CHAKRAVARTI, Mihir. The Fake, The Non–Fake And The Genuine. *Indian Phil Quart* 12,1–8 Ja–Mr 85.

The paper is an attempt at understanding the distinction between the notion of *fake* and that of *genuine* in theoretical terms. For this purpose, a comparison has been undertaken between the application of these two concepts in the context of art and in the context of those things which are not works of art. The concept of *non–fake* has been introduced to cover certain borderline cases, that is, those which cannot be characterized either as *fake* or as *genuine*.

CHAKRAVARTY, Satya R and Roy, Tirthankar. Measurement Of Fuzziness: A General Approach. *Theor Decis* 19,163–169 S 85.

A new general index for the measurement of fuzziness has been suggested in this paper. It has been shown that a continuous S–concave function of the fuzzy membership values will suffice for constructing an index of fuzziness. The general index satisfies all the postulates for an index of fuzziness proposed by De Luca and Termini (1972).

CHALMERS, A F. "Methodological Individualism" in *Popper And The Human Sciences*, Currie, Gregory (ed), 57–72. Boston Nijhoff 1985.

CHALMERS, Alan. Galileo's Telescopic Observations Of Venus And Mars. *Brit J Phil Sci* 36,175–184 Je 85.

Paul Feyerabend's claim that Galilee's defense of the Copernican theory by appeal to telescopic evidence was ad hoc is contested. It is argued, nevertheless, that Galilee's use of the telescope constituted a change in method and epistemological standards.

CHALMETA, Gabriel. Fenomenología De La Sensación. *Sapientia* 40,33–48 Ja–Mr 85.

CHAMBERLIN, Gordon J. "I Don't Have No Education" And Other Reflections. Greensboro Education Pr 1984.

"*I Don't Have No Education*" and other reflections puts together nine papers which I presented on a variety of different occasions. The papers are reflections on personal experiences which illuminated some of the less frequently considered aspects of the educating process. Following an introduction on "Reflecting" they are grouped under four headings: On Education, On Being an Educator, On Teaching Teachers and On Academia. Each paper illustrates how understanding is an a posteriori interpretive activity.

CHAN, Alan. Philosophical Hermeneutics And The Analects: The Paradigm Of "Tradition". *Phil East West* 34,421–436 O 84.

Gadamer's understanding of "tradition" and of hermeneutics as a "practical philosophy" serves as the starting point of this comparative study. Using this Gadamerian framework, the controversial question of the place of "tradition" in the thought of Confucius is then explored. The paradigm of tradition that emerges is primarily a dialectical one, and it is suggested that this paradigm should prove useful as an initial focus for an East–West philosophical dialogue.

CHAN, Wing–Wah. Husserl's Concept Of World (in Chinese). *Phil Rev (Taiwan)* 7,199–224 Ja 84.

CHANDLER, Daniel Ross. The Religion Of Humanity. *Relig Hum* 19,102–110 Sum 85.

CHANDLER, Hugh S. Indeterminate People. *Analysis* 45,141–145 Je 85.

It is physically possible that there be creatures such that it is intrinsically indeterminate whether or not they are *people* or have *minds* at all. Such creatures show that these classes are unnecessarily fuzzy and open to refinement. Their language shows that sometimes we must be non–realists about meanings.

CHANDLER, J H. Is The Divine Command Theory Defensible? *Relig Stud* 20,443–452 S 84.

This paper argues that Philip Quinn's recent defense of the divine command theory (in his book *Divine Commandments and Moral Requirements*) fails to rebut several standard objections to the theory. In particular, he fails to show that a supporter of the theory can consistently judge God to be good in a significant sense. It is also argued that a full–blooded divine command theory such as Quinn's is incompatible with moral autonomy.

CHANDLER, John. Clark On God's Law And Morality. *Phil Quart* 35,87–90 Ja 85.

This paper criticizes Stephen Clark 'God's Law and Morality', *Philosophical Quarterly*, Volume 32, 1982. I seek to show that Clark has failed to show that a Divine Command Theory, whether in definist or non–definist forms, allows the possibility of significant praise of God as good.

CHANDLER, John. Divine Command Theories And The Appeal To Love. *Amer Phil Quart* 22,231–239 Jl 85.

Several recent writers, among them R M Adams, E Wierenga and R Burch, have sought to modify the Divine Command Theory in order to overcome well–known defects in its simple form. An emphasis on God's nature as loving, in addition to the role of His will in determining rightness, overcomes these problems. It is argued however that the modified theory is not a genuine divine command theory. In order for love to perform the tasks required, there must be co—extensiveness between the properties of being a loving act, or being the act a loving being would perform, and being morally required. But, it is argued, if this is the case, God's will becomes redundant to morality. In fact, it is argued that it is doubtful whether co—extensiveness obtains.

CHANG, Briankle G. The Eclipse Of Being: Heidegger And Derrida. *Int Phil Quart* 25,113–138 Je 85.

This paper compares and contrasts Heidegger's "destruction" with Derrida's "deconstruction" by first examining the former's discussion of the "ontological difference." The paper then advances a reading of "deconstruction" as a "textual practice" that works on its object by way of 1) a strategic seduction/seductive strategy, and 2) a double science/overturning. By applying the deconstructive analysis developed above to some of Heidegger's texts, the paper concludes by arguing that Heidegger's discourse on Being can never be totally free from metaphorical displacements, that *Seinsfrage* is as "textually" determined as any linguistic question.

CHANG, Jun—Chun. A Critical Account Of Yang Kuei—Shan's Philosophical Thought (in Chinese). *Phil Rev (Taiwan)* 7,163–198 Ja 84.

This paper is a tentative evaluation of Yang Kuei—shan's philosophy of principle (*li—hsueh*) and its historical position in the development of Sung Neo—Confucianism as a whole. It seems (1) to demonstrate that Yang Kuei—shan's thought served as an important bridge between the two Cheng Brothers and Chu Hsi, and (2) to explain the actual content of Yang's philosophy as a process of synthesis drawing from Confucianism, Taoism and Buddhism. The approach of the argument, therefore, can be divided in the following four categories: (1) Historical: the original source of his philosophy; (2) Ontological: the principle of *ying* and *yang*, the transformation of material force (*ch'i*) and the Way of Heaven (*t'ien*) and its mandate; (3) Epistemological: the investigation of things in the extension of knowledge, and the principal of one—in—all; (4) Ethical: the concept of self—cultivation and the contemplation of equilibrium (*chung*). In the analysis of Yang's philosophy, this paper also attempts to deal with his sivotal methodology of "directness" (*chih*) in an effort to explicate his doctrines of loyalty and altruism. (edited)

CHAPMAN, John W (ed) and Pennock, J Roland (ed). *Marxism: Nomos XXVI.* NY Columbia Univ Pr 1983.

These essays on Marxism deal especially with the moral, political, and legal aspects of Marx's theories. They are written by philosophers, political theorists and lawmen, and feature cross—disciplinary commentary. An extensive bibliography on Marx and Marxisms is included.

CHARLTON, William. Beyond The Literal Meaning. *Brit J Aes* 25,220–231 Sum 85.

CHATTERJEE, Margaret. *Gandhi's Religious Thought.* Notre Dame Notre Dame Pr 1984.

Gandhi's religious thought is explored in the context of Indian religious traditions, his life—work as a politician and reformer. The theme is related to contemporary theological concerns, inter—religious dialogue, the possibility of non—violent social change. Gandhi's religious life was non—meditative. He did not isolate the "spiritual" from the rest of life. His "experiments with Truth" are a challenging alternative to theologising.

CHATTERJEE, Shyamal K. Rammonhun Roy And The Baptists Of Serampore: Moralism Vs Faith. *Relig Stud* 20,669–680 D 84.

This is about the historic encounter between Rammonhun Roy (Unitarian) and the "Particular" Baptists (Calvinist) of Serampore (India). Rejecting Trinitarianism and "justification *by faith only*," Roy avowed his faith in Jesus as moral teacher. Man had been endowed with "reason" to discriminate between moral good and evil. Roy rejected "fallibilism"— the corruptibility of the will since the Fall. All this was anathema to the Baptists, but had affinities with the ameliorism of the Enlightenment.

CHAUDHURI, Adhip. Formal Properties Of Interpersonal Envy. *Theor Decis* 18,301–312 My 85.

CHAVES, Rodolfo. En Torno A La Eutanasia. *Rev Filosof (Costa Rica)* 23,227–231 D 85.

Throughout the history of man a series of sacrifices has been practiced which have been considered to be mercy killing practices. Today this problem is presented in the light of the decisions that can be made in borderline cases in which the respect of the human being's dignity, his self—determination and the doctor's verdict may generate a moral dilemma which is difficult to solve. This essay is an attempt at presenting the christian point of view concerning this problem.

CHEEK, Annetta L and Keel, Bennie C. "Value Conflicts In Osteo—Archaeology" in *Ethics And Values In Archaeology*, Green, Ernestene L (ed), 194–207. NY Free Pr 1984.

CHEHIDA, A Ben. "La Destinée De La Tragédie Dans La Culture Islamique" in *Existential Coordinates Of Human Condition*, Tymieniecka, A (ed), 333–340. Boston Reidel 1984.

CHELLAS, Brian F and Mc Kinney, Audrey. The Completeness Of Monotonic Modal Logics. *Z Math Log* 21,379–383 1975.

CHENG, Chung—Ying. On Professor Kegley's "Individual And Community". *J Chin Phil* 11,217–226 S 84.

The purpose of this work is to further develop the concepts of individual and community and their relationship. Specific attention is called to the dialectic of relationship between the concept of individual and various concepts of community.

CHENG, Hsueh—li. Confucianism And Zen (Ch'an) Philosophy Of Education. *J Chin Phil* 12,197–216 Je 85.

The purpose of this paper is to investigate the theoretical foundation of Zen education. When contemporary scholars talk about how Confucianism and Zen might have influenced each other, usually they refer only to the fact that Zen led Confucianism to develop Neo—Confucianism. And when they discuss the relationship

between Zen Buddhism and Chinese traditional philosophy, they mention only the great impact of Taoist philosophy upon Zen. This paper seeks to show that Confucianism has provided an important philosophical foundation for the formation of Zen instruction. The basis, nature, methods, and goal of Zen education will be expounded.

CHENU, Joseph. *Peirce: Textes Anticartésiens.* Paris Aubier 1984.

CHERLIN, Gregory and Harrington, L and Lachlan, A H. $\aleph_0$–Categorical, $\aleph_0$–Stable Structures. *Annals Pure Applied Log* 28,103–136 Mr 85.

We give a Coordinatization Theorem and related results which facilitate the systematic analysis of $\aleph_0$–categorical $\aleph_0$–stable structures. We combine a number of Zil'ber's ideas with the recent classification of the finite permutation groups called Jordan groups. The use of group theory can be avoided (Zil'ber, D Evans), but it plays an essential role in related work on stable structures homogeneous for a finite relational language. Applications include finiteness of the Morley rank of such structures, refinements of Zil'ber's results on the finite submodel property, and more technical results.

CHERN, Jiunn—Huei. On Confucian Jen And Heideggerian Being (II) (in Chinese). *Phil Rev (Taiwan)* 7,235–248 Ja 85.

In this paper, I continue my comparative analysis of the Confucian concept Jen and Heideggerian Being. I trace the origins and attempt to reconstruct the essential meaning of Confucian Jen and Heideggerian Being. Then, from the respective of their basic presuppositions, I try to compare these two concepts, identifying and expanding upon points of apparent similarity. Finally, I suggest the possibility of utilizing their complementarity as an aid to expressing more fully their respective ontologies. In conclusion, I explore ways in which this methodology might contribute to the reconstruction of Chinese Philosophy.

CHERNIAK, Christopher. Computational Complexity And The Universal Acceptance Of Logic. *J Phil* 81,739–758 D 84.

(1) Acceptance of a deductive logic is not required for an agent's rationality. (2) Using a sound or complete logic may even be inadvisable. (3) Use of such logic seems sometimes entirely incompatible with rationality, because of computational complexity constraints; it entails intractable processes, hence computational paralysis. The discussion identifies relationships between more realistic rationality models in philosophy, computational complexity theory, and recent psychological studies of the formal incorrectness of everyday "quick but dirty" reasoning heuristics.

CHERRY, Christopher. Can My Survival Be Subrogated? *Philosophy* 59,443–456 O 84.

If the desire to survive death is the desire to persist as a self—conscious being it is radically unclear that anything could count as a substitute, and that any candidate substitute could approximate any more or less closely than any other to the real thing. However, once it is acknowledged that indefinite personal survival is impossible the original want may become, very differently, that after death there should continue, perhaps indefinitely, self—conscious subjects of experience. Although *not* a surrogate—want (for there can be no such), this want connects in importantly complex ways with the original. (edited)

CHERRY, Christopher. Knowing The Past. *Phil Invest* 7,265–280 O 84.

There are two broad kinds of interests in the past: accidental and historical. Wittgenstein's, in "Remarks on Frege's *Golden Bough*" (and elsewhere) is *essential* in nature. He is concerned with the *continuity* of certain ideas and forms of behavior. In general, it is necessary to explain *how* and *why* such ideas and forms are constantly reaffirmed by new generations. (edited)

CHERRY, Christopher. Meaning And The Idol Of Origins. *Phil Quart* 35,58–69 Ja 85.

It is always possible to inquire into the origins and development of practices. In many cases, however, decisions about where to start looking for origins turn upon prior ones about identity. Where it is available and significant, the distinction between antecedents and first stages is commonly overlooked and different varieties of genetic and reductionist fallacy, and of theories of meaning, result, as instanced by Frazer and Wittgenstein's discussion of his work.

CHERRY, Christopher. Self, Near—Death And Death. *Int J Phil Relig* 16,3–12 1984.

Much recent philosophical writing about death makes sense only on certain more or less covert egoistic presuppositions. Thus, it is assumed (1) that the living cannot interest themselves in what will happen after their deaths; and (2) that fear of death is typically and primarily egoistic *and*, as such, confused. (2) is false on both counts. It is perfectly possible to make sense of such fear, as is revealed by proper philosophical understanding of the phenomenon of near—death experiences.

CHETHIMATTAM, John B. World Problems And The Emergence Of A New Interreligious Perspective. *J Dharma* 10,90–101 Ja—Mr 85.

CHEW, Geoffrey F. Gentle Quantum Events As The Source Of Explicate Order. *Zygon* 20,159–164 Je 85.

It is proposed that multiple emission and absorption of soft photons in a discrete quantum world (implicate order) generates the continuous Cartesian—Newtonian—Einsteinian space—time world of localizable objects and conscious observers with measuring rods and clocks (explicate order).

CHIAPPINI, Julio O. La Critica De Cossio E La Escuela Del Derecho Libre. *Riv Int Filosof Diritto* 61,195–204 Ap—Je 84.

La Escuela del Derecho Libre nació como una reacción al positivismo jurídico del siglo XIX. Delega la interpretación de las normas al albedrío de los jueces: quienes, en el caso concreto, pueden incluso fallar contra legem. Así, el programa de Kantorowicz entroniza las expectaciones de la jurisprudencia, lo cual le acarreó le crítica del argentino Carlos Cossio (Escuela Egológica); quien, en sus observaciones, señala fundamentalmente el carácter voluntarista, acientífico y emocional del fries recht.

CHIARA, Maria Luisa Dalla. Some Foundational Problems In Mathematics Suggested By Physics. *Synthese* 62,303–315 F 85.

The paper discusses in what sense contemporary physics provides some arguments, which might have a bearing in the foudational studies about mathematics. A) The metalogical properties of *Quantum Logic* suggest a significant dividing line in the universe of weak logics. B) The physical properties of the particles governed by the Bose–Einstein statistics, seem to put in question some fundamental logical and mathematical concepts, regarding the notions of *individual*, *identity*, *cardinal*, and *ordinal* number.

CHIEN, A J. Demonstratives And Belief States. *Phil Stud* 47,271–290 Mr 85.

A partial examination of Perry's notion of a belief state. It is shown that there may be a problem with the individuation of belief states by sentences containing demonstrative terms. A number of solutions are proposed and assessed.

CHIESA, Curzio. Expliquer Les Causes Et/Ou Comprendre Les Raisons: Note À Propos De *Meaning And Understanding*. *Stud Phil (Switzerland)* 41,221–230 1982.

CHIHARA, Charles S. Horwich's Justification Of Induction. *Phil Stud* 48,107–110 Jl 85.

CHIHARA, Charles S. Olin, Quine, And The Surprise Examination. *Phil Stud* 47,191–200 Mr 85.

CHILDERS, Joseph W. Carlyle's Past And Present, History, And A Question Of Hermeneutics. *Clio* 13,247–258 Spr 84.

CHILDRESS, James F. "Rights To Health Care In A Democratic Society" in *Biomedical Ethics Reviews*, Humber, James M (ed), 47–72. Clifton Humana Pr 1984.

CHILDRESS, James F and Hauerwas, Stanley. Time And History In Theological Ethics: The Work Of James Gustafson. *J Relig Ethics* 13,3–21 Spr 85.

This essay traces Gustafson's understanding of the methodological significance of history and time for theological ethics. I argue that Gustafson qualifies his original thoroughgoing historicist perspective in the interest of developing a natural theology and ethics. His continuing emphasis on a historical perspective, I suggest, is best understood by attending to his recommendation that the theologian's task is best captured by the image of the "participant".

CHILDRESS, James F and Siegler, Mark. Should Age Be A Criterion In Health Care? *Hastings Center Rep* 14,24–31 O 84.

CHILDRESS, James F. Civil Disobedience, Conscientious Objection, And Evasive Noncompliance: Analysis And Assessment Of Illegal Actions In Health Care. *J Med Phil* 10,63–84 F 85.

This essay explores some of the conceptual and moral issues raised by illegal actions in health care. The author first identifies several types of illegal action, concentrating on civil disobedience, conscientious objection or refusal, and evasive noncompliance. Then he sketches a framework for the moral justification of these types of illegal action. Finally, he applies the conceptual and normative frameworks to several major cases of illegal action in health care, such as "mercy killing" and some decisions not to treat incompetent patients.

CHING, Julia. Confucian Spirituality. *J Dharma* 10,75–81 Ja–Mr 85.

CHISHOLM, Roderick M. The Primacy Of The Intentionality. *Synthese* 61,89–110 O 84.

CHITTICK, William C. Islam And The Loss Of Equilibrium. *J Dharma* 10,42–59 Ja–Mr 85.

The Koran and Muhammad self–consciously established Islam as an equilibrium between God and the world in three dimensions of human existence: legal/social, intellectual/rational, and moral/spiritual. After explaining the theological basis for this complex equilibrium, the article demonstrates how it gradually came to be upset through the course of Islamic history and concludes by alluding to its final destruction by contemporary fundamentalism.

CHIVERS, Frances J. Wordsworth's "Real Language Of Men" And Augustine's Theory Of Language. *Augustin Stud* 14,11–24 1983.

CHOKR, Nader. Nelson Goodman On Truth. *Kinesis* 14,42–56 Fall 84.

This paper offers an original interpretation of Goodman's theory of truth. Though limited and partial, its goal is to bring together some of the themes of the latest work of a centrally important contemporary American philosopher. These are to be found namely in his discussions of literal and metaphorical truth, linguistic and non–linguistic world versions, rightness—instead of truth—as criterion for the evaluation and constructions of versions, and the continuity between art, perception, and science. Though not everything that he has investigated is beyond doubt and totally to our satisfaction, it is undeniable that he raises some fundamental issues and points in directions that are worth exploring. A more critical analysis of these issues and directions shall be taken up in a later paper. Until then, let us consider the approach adopted herein as just an attempt to exemplify the effort to understand what is said before turning to a criticism of it.

CHOKR, Nader. The French Epistemological Tradition And The "Analytic" Tradition In Philosophy Of Science. *Dialogos* 20,93–112 Ap 85.

The purpose of this paper is to suggest that our understanding of certain fundamental issues in epistemology, philosophy and history of sciences can be improved considerably by learning how to bridge the longstanding divide between the continental (e.G., the French) and English language philosophical traditions, show that the French epist tradition, as it is exhibited in the works of Bachelard, Canguilhem, and Foucault, can be easily coupled, compared, and contrasted with the work of (Anglo–Saxon) critics of the "received view on theories," (e.G., Popper, Kuhn, Feyerabend, Lakatos, Toulmin, Shapere, suppe).

CHOMSKY, Noam. Manufacture Of Consent In Democracy. *Phil Soc Act* 11,21–40 Ja–Mr 85.

CHONG, Kim–Chong. Egoism, Desires, And Friendship. *Amer Phil Quart* 21,349–358 O 84.

Given two views of rational action, (1) only a person's own wants and desires provide him with reasons for acting, (2) the rational act is that which maximizes the agent's utility, an egoist can claim close personal relationships which evince genuine concern. The author argues, that (1) rests on a confusion between being motivated and having a reason to act while (2) rests on a distorted account of concern for another as desire–satisfaction. This leads to a discussion of friendship which is contrasted critically with the conception of friendship embedded within the egoistic position. (edited)

CHOUILLET, Jacques. Matière Et Mémoire Dans L'oeuvre De Diderot. *Rev Metaph Morale* 89,214–225 Ap–Je 84.

CHRISTENSEN, Darrel and other (eds). *Contemporary German Philosophy*, V4. University Park Penn State Univ Pr 1984.

contemporary German Philosophy is devoted principally to making available in English contributions to philosophical comprehension originating in German. cGP is open to the full range of philosophical interests and orientations to which such philosophy in the German language reflects cognizance of its historical roots importantly contributes. It is open as well to items of content which consider the bearings of insights within such allied fields as mathematics, political science, historiography, and linguistics upon philosophical issues. The term "contemporary" is intended to refer to philosophical literature of recent origin.

CHRISTENSEN, Darrel E. Can Hegel's Concept Of Self–Evidence Be Salvaged? *Ideal Stud* 14,93–108 My 84.

Hegel's thought is appropriated within the context of a "critical process philosophy," since accorded further development by the author in a succession of other essays, listed in an appendix. Locating Hegel within "the critical tradition that had its inception in Kant," exposition is accorded to his concept of self–evidence—the author's rendition of Hegel's "self–certainty of reason," negatively understood as presuppositionlessness. After subjecting the concept to criticism, a strategy is proposed for salvaging it.

CHRISTENSEN, Darrel E. Whitehead's "Prehension" And Hegel's "Mediation". *Rev Metaph* 38,341–374 D 84.

CHRISTIANS, Clifford G. Commentary On "Advertising And Program Content". *Bus Prof Ethics J* 3,77–80 Spr/Sum 84.

CHRISTIE, Drew. Recent Calls For Economic Democracy. *Ethics* 95,112–128 O 84.

The article examines and defends the claim of a number of contemporary authors to find in "economic democracy" (also "self–management" and "worker control") a desirable alternative to both libertarian and liberal visions of society. Inspired in part by Yugoslavian market socialism, the Mondragon experiment in Spain, and worker cooperatives throughout the world, the ideal includes employee control of the means of production, a market in goods and services, civil liberties, and democratic control of investment funds.

CHRISTODOULOU, Kyriaki. Tragédie Grecque Et "Anti–Théâtre" En France Au Siècle Des Lumières. *Diotima* 12,48–56 1984.

The author investigates the evolution of the neoclassic tragedy during the 18th century in France, which is inspired by classical Greek models. The reasons of the decline of Neoclassic tragedy are related to historical and social factors and the esthetic needs as well, which led to new conceptions about theatre during the century of the French Enlightenment.

CHRONIS, Nicholas. Post–Classical Philosophers' Concept Of Man As A Social Animal. *Diotima* 12,57–70 1984.

To the question why post–classical philosophers call man a social animal, my answer is as follows: Once the city was abolished, the Aristotelian proposition "man is by nature a political animal" was rendered void. It was then substituted by another, analogous to the new course of events. By calling man a social animal, philosophers point out man's communion with logos, nature and the whole universe, and demonstrate the bond of one man to another.

CHRYSSIDES, George D. Bultmann's Criticisms Of Heidegger. *Sophia (Australia)* 24,28–35 Jl 85.

Three of Bultmann's criticisms of Heidegger are assessed: that achievement of authenticity is merely correct understanding of man's true nature, that existentialist philosophy cannot enable authenticity to be attained, and that man is incapable of attaining it, requiring an act of diving grace in Jesus Christ. It is argued that there is nothing in Bultmann's theology which is genuinely incompatible with Heidegger's philosophy and that Bultmann's criticisms demonstrate misunderstanding of Heidegger's position.

CHRZAN, Keith. Perishability, The Actual World, And The Non–Existence Of God. *Sophia (Australia)* 24,45–49 Jl 85.

CHRZAN, Keith. Vindicating The "Principle Of Relative Likelihood". *Int J Phil Relig* 16,13–18 1984.

CHUDY, W. The Role Of Reflection In The Structure Of The Human Person. *Stud Phil Christ* 20,7–30 1984.

CHURCH, Alonzo. Russell's Theory Of Identity Of Propositions. *Phil Natur* 21,513–522 1984.

Bertrand Russell's theory of identity of propositions, as it appears in *The principles of Mathematics*, is explained and a system of axioms is proposed which might be taken as underlying it. Russell's antinomy about propositions, in section 500 of *The Principles*, is resolved by ramified theory.

CHURCH, Rolin. Popper's 'World 3' And The Problem Of The Printed Line. *Austl J Phil* 62,378–392 D 84.

Sir Karl Popper's Three World epistemology is intended, in part, to explain how human beings gain intersubjective access to one another's ideas—and so become capable of exchanging information, criticizing each other's theories, and offering new theories for public discussion. popper's solution is to posit a class of non–mental and non–physical *propositions* to serve as possible "objects" of human thoughts. This "third world" of publicly accessible propositions includes the information inscribed in books and computer memories, as well as the (potentially publishable) informational contents of human thoughts. This paper attempts to show (1) that Popper's account of third–world propositions, and their relationship to their physical inscriptions, is empirically false; and (2) that assuming such a Third World exists, it could not, on Popper's account, solve the original problem: namely, to explain how it is possible for us to have public access to encoded information.

CHURCHILL, John. Coercion And The Authority Of Reason. *Metaphilosophy* 15,172–184 Jl–O 84.

The authority of reason, as emplotted against Thrasymachus in Plato's *Republic*, and as construed in modern attempts to refute skepticism, is implicitly coercive, aiming toward a conclusive confrontation with reality, a confrontation designed by the rationalist to end the conversation of reasons and arguments. An alternative employment of reason, eschewing the foundationalist strategy, portrays its authority not as coercive but as conductive to the continuity of a philosophical conversation that forgoes metaphysical or epistemological guarantees.

CHURCHILL, John. Wittgenstein On The Phenomena Of Belief. *Int J Phil Relig* 16,139–152 1984.

Wittgenstein's account of the nature of believing shapes the relevance of his later work to philosophy of religion. His analysis of the language of sensation and of the grammar of verbs such as "believe" and "understand" make it clear that believing is not an action or a state of consciousness. Believing is, rather, a dispositional "state of mind", a state not reducible to introspectible events. This conclusion undercuts a crucial presupposition involved in the distinction between cognitive and non–cognitive interpretations of religious belief.

CHURCHLAND, Paul M. Conceptual Progress And Word/World Relations: In Search Of The Essence Of Natural Kinds. *Can J Phil* 15,1–18 Mr 85.

I here criticize the idea, associated with Putnam and Kripke, that there is a theory–neutral or intension–independent relation that connects natural–kind terms to unique natural sections of the world. Further, I pursue an analysis of the notion of a natural kind, and reach the sceptical conclusion that there is no objective distinction between genuinely natural kinds and those merely practical kinds we invent for our predictive and manipulative convenience.

CHURCHLAND, Paul M. Reduction, Qualia, And The Direct Introspection Of Brain States. *J Phil* 82,8–28 Ja 85.

My aim is to defeat some standard anti–reductionist arguments concerning sensory qualia. I begin by establishing the conditions of intertheoretic reduction in general. The standard arguments are then shown to presuppose a false conception of what reduction requires; or to commit a familiar intensional fallacy; or to be unsound; or to equivocate on crucial terms. I conclude with an exploration of our making direct introspective contact with our neurophysiological states.

CIOFFI, Frank. "Psychoanalysis, Pseudo–Science And Testability" in *Popper And The Human Sciences*, Currie, Gregory (ed), 13–44. Boston Nijhoff 1985.

CÍZEK, F. The Structure Of Historical Knowledge And The Method Of Actualism (in Czechoslovakian). *Filozof Cas* 33,364–377 1985.

CLANCY, Katherine L. Commentary On "Advertising Professional Success Rates". *Bus Prof Ethics J* 3,53–56 Spr/Sum 84.

After expressing agreement with many points Gorovitz made in his paper brief comment is made on three items: (1) profit–making hospitals; (2) misleading advertising and problems of substantiation; and (3) differences in the advertising of goods and services.

CLANCY, Katherine. Human Nutrition, Agriculture, And Human Value. *Agr Human Values* 1,10–15 Wint 84.

A review of government policies regarding food, health, nutrition and agriculture identifies many issues and concerns. Among the problems mentioned are domestic malnutrition and hunger, dairy surpluses, food advertising and vitamin supplementation. Contradictions in U S food policy are described and ethical questions raised with regard to some of these issues.

CLARK, A J. Anti–Realism And Recognitional Capacities. *Phil Quart* 35,171–178 Ap 85.

The semantic anti–realist argues that we can make no sense of notion of verification–transcendent truth. Yet he believes also that grasp of meaning may sometimes require the exercise of a direct recognitional capacity. I argue that the possibility of alternative direct recognitional capacities establishes the possibility of a range of statements, intelligible in an alien language, whose truth–conditions are entirely verification–transcendent to speakers of the home language.

CLARK, A J. Evolutionary Epistemology And Ontological Realism. *Phil Quart* 34,482–490 0 84.

The paper charts the ontological commitments of an evolutionary epistemology and asks whether these commitments are fully intelligible in the light of an anti–realist analysis of meaning. The evolutionary theorists claims are shown to be intelligible only when they are presented in negated universal form.

CLARK, A J. Why Kant Couldn't Be An Anti–Realist. *Analysis* 45,61–63 Ja 85.

The paper outlines a problem facing any interpretation of Kant as a semantic anti–realist. It argues that such an interpretation deprives Kant of any convincing defense against the accusation that his contentions about the Thing–in–itself are strictly meaningless. The coherence of such contentions depends on his distinction between the real and the mere possibility of a concept. This distinction is shown to be unintelligible to the anti–realist.

CLARK, John G. Cinq Images De Shelley Qui Ont Fasciné Bachelard. *Rev Int Phil* 38,287–314 1984.

CLARK, Maudemarie. On "Truth And Lie In The Extra–Moral Sense". *Int Stud Phil* 16,57–66 1984.

CLARK, Michael. Degrees Of Comparison. *Analysis* 44,178–180 O 84.

CLARK, Peter and Read, Stephen. Hypertasks. *Synthese* 61,387–390 D 84.

CLARK, R W. The Evidential Value Of Religious Experiences. *Int J Phil Relig* 16,189–202 1984.

CLARK, Ralph W. The Concept Of Altruism. *Faith Phil* 2,158–167 Ap 85.

CLARK, Roger. Historical Context And The Aesthetic Evaluation Of Forgeries. *S J Phil* 22,317–322 Fall 84.

The article attempts refute recent arguments that the historical context in which an artwork is produced is relevant to its aesthetic value. These arguments claim that forgeries are intrinsically less aesthetically valuable than originals because forgeries lack the appropriate relation to the past. These arguments fail because demanding an "appropriate" historical context of a work for it to be aesthetically respectable confuses aesthetic merit with artistic merit, a work's significance within its culture and the history of art.

CLARK, Stephen R L. Slaves And Citizens. *Philosophy* 60,27–46 Ja 85.

CLARK, Stephen. Hume, Animals And The Objectivity Of Morals. *Phil Quart* 35,117–133 Ap 85.

Hume argues that moral distinctions are not matters of fact because, e.G., dogs do no wrong in committing incest. Three different answers to this atrocious argument are considered, and the framework of a sound, objective morality (transcending egoism, naturalism, and rationalism) laid down.

CLARKE, Bowman L. Process, Time, And God. *Process Stud* 13,245–259 Wint 83.

The purpose of this essay is to explicate the two forms of process in *Process and Reality*, the temporal process of transition, ordered in terms of before and after, and the genetic process, the process of becoming, the stages of which are not temporally ordered. Since God has no before or after, God does not participate in the temporal process. God only becomes, which is not a temporal process. God is one non–temporal actual entity with one everlasting present.

CLARKE, David D. "The Sequential Analysis Of Action Structure" in *The Analysis Of Action*, Von Cranach, Mario (ed), 191–212. Cambridge Cambridge Univ Pr 1982.

CLARKE, David S. Ignoring Available Evidence. *S J Phil* 22,452–468 Wint 84.

Acceptance of a proposition is based usually on evidence which is only a partial subset of that which is available. The central problem of this paper is to determine the conditions under which acceptance is justified when available evidence is ignored. Rejected are attempts to state purely epistemic conditions which mention only the reliability of the methods used in inferring a proposition from evidence. Instead, it is argued that a pragmatic condition requiring the weighing of costs of a mistake against costs of acquiring evidence must also be imposed.

CLARKE, Larry R. The Quaker Background Of William Bartram's View Of Nature. *J Hist Ideas* 46,435–448 Jl–S 85.

CLARKE, W Norris. "Act, The Self–Revelation Of Being In St Thomas" in *History Of Philosophy In Making*, Thro, Linus J (ed), 63–80. Washington Univ Pr Of America 1982.

CLASBY, E. Chaucer And Augustine: Human Love And The Doctrine Of "Use". *Augustin Stud* 13,81–86 1982.

CLAUSEN, Joy P. "A Transcultural Perspective On Perinatal Health Care" in *Bioethical Frontiers In Perinatal Intensive Care*, Snowden, Fraser (ed), 39–58. Natchitoches Northwestern Pr 1985.

CLEARY, John. 'On The Terminology Of "Abstraction" In Aristotle'. *Phronesis* 30,13–45 1985.

By taking a fresh look at Aristotle's use of 'abstraction' terminology, this paper challenges the traditional assumption that he propounded a general epistemological theory of abstraction. It shows that such terminology must be understood as referring to a logical method of subtraction that is used to isolate the primary subject of per se attributes. If one adopts this new perspective, one can explain many puzzling uses of this terminology even in epistemological contexts.

CLEARY, John. The Modern Malaise: A Case History. *Phil Soc Crit* 10,97–110 Fall 84.

In *After Virtue*, Alasdair MacIntyre claims that ethical dilemmas are symptoms of moral disease in modern pluralist societies. By discussing this claim through an analogy with clinical practice, this paper argues that his proposed "cure" in terms of the narrative unity of human life based in history is also plagued by cultural relativism. Finally, it is suggested that to escape from relativism he needs a trans–cultural notion of rationality grounded in a normative concept of human nature.

CLEMENTS, Colleen D and Sider, Roger C. Patients' Ethical Obligation For Their Health. *J Med Ethics* 10,138–142 S 84.

A naturalistic model for medical ethics is proposed which builds upon biological and medical values. This perspective clarifies ethical obligations to ourselves and to others for life and health. It provides a normative framework for the doctor–patient relationship within which to formulate medical advice and by which to evaluate patient choice. (edited)

CLICHE, Élaine. Langage Du Pouvoir, Pouvoir Du Langage, Ou La Narration À La Première Personne Dans *La Chute* D'Albert Camus. *Rev Univ Ottawa* 54,15–24 O–D 84.

CLING, Andrew D. Foundationalism And Permanence In Descartes' Epistemology. *S J Phil* 23,145–156 Sum 85.

Descartes' goal of providing a "firm and permanent structure in the sciences" can be achieved only by securing the basic descriptive and explanatory concepts needed by science. Descartes' doctrine of "simple natures" attempts to provide such a guarantee. I argue that a foundationalist epistemology cannot by itself satisfy a significant motive for foundationalism because it cannot guarantee the adequacy of the concepts we use in representing the world even at the level of "immediate data."

CLITEUR, P B. Rechtsbeginselen: Tussen Natuurrecht En Rechtspositivisme. *Phil Reform* 49,57–70 1984.

This article is about the philosophy of law developed by the Dutch philosopher Dooyeweerd. Dooyeweerd and his pupil Van Eikema Hommes advocated the view that all positive law results from juridical form–giving to material–legal principles. Both legal positivism and the doctrine of natural law emphasized a partial truth. The first stressed the importance of juridicial form–giving, the second the normative basis of law. The author of this article defends this theory of legal principles against criticism made by J J M van der Ven.

COADY, C A J. The Idea Of Violence. *Phil Papers* 14,1–19 My 85.

This paper examines some fashionable approaches to the concept of violence and argues against "wide" definitions, particularly "structuralist" accounts such as Johan Galtung's. A critique is also given of "legitimist" definitions which incorporate some strong notion of illegitimacy into the very meaning of violence. A defense of a more restricted definition is presented. The paper concludes with some remarks about the point of having a concept of violence of the type delineated.

COADY, C A J. The Morality Of Terrorism. *Philosophy* 60,47–70 Ja 85.

It is argued that terrorism is a tactic not an ideology and is most illuminatingly defined as involving the intentional killing or other severe harming of non–combatants. Some consequences of the full definition are discussed and it is argued that, although terrorism is immoral (on "just war" grounds) its condemnation requires adopting a moral stance which many anti–terrorists refuse to adopt consistently when their own governments or its allies engage in terrorism.

COBB, John B. Points Of Contact Between Process Theology And Liberation Theology In Matters Of Faith And Justice. *Process Stud* 14,124–141 Sum 85.

Process theology can learn from Latin American liberation theology to be self–critical with regard to its social location, the importance of praxis, the urgency of justice, and social analysis in terms of class interests. It may contribute to liberation theology from its attention to cultural and religious perspectives, the value and nature of dialogue, and the ecological context of all human life. The most fruitful relation of these traditions will be mutual transformation.

COCCHIARELLA, Nino B. "Quantification In Tense And Modal Logic" in *Handbook Of Philosophical Logic*, Gabbay, Dov (ed), 309–354. Boston Reidel 1984.

COCCHIARELLA, Nino B. Frege's Double Correlation Thesis And Quine's Set Theories NF And ML. *J Phil Log* 14,1–40 F 85.

Frege's form of logicism (where classes have their being in the concepts whose extensions they are rather than in the objects that belong to them) is defended and reconstructed as a second order logic with nominalized predicates (as singular terms). Two consistent reconstructions are given; one by modifying Frege's correlation of first level concept and relations with second level concepts and relations (by dropping unequal leveled relations); the other by modifying the correlation of extensions (as the referents of nominalized predicates) with first level concepts. The two reconstructions are shown to be similar to Quine's set theories NF and ML when the latter are modified to include urelements (as non–sets).

COCKBURN, David. Empiricism And The Theory Of Meaning. *Phil Invest* 8,17–50 Ja 85.

A widespread conception of the task facing a theory of meaning rests on empiricist presuppositions. It involves an indefensible understanding of what is 'given' in experience and leaves no room for a satisfactory account of the notion of a situation providing a reason for action. wittgenstein's suggestion that it is our reactions to the world which are basic undercuts the dispute between realism and anti–realism as it is widely understood.

COCKS, Edmond D. Land's End. *Hist Euro Ideas* 6,129–152 1985.

The European economics of scarcity was challenged in America as inapplicable to republican institutions. Although still rich in resources, many worried that the explosive growth of population would in time produce social misery. Communally organized industrialization was promoted as a means of avoiding this crisis. Wealth was increased but also social disparity, communal breakdown and the rate of resource exploitation. The growing demand for foreign markets and resources ended the idylic isolation from world conflicts.

CODE, Alan. "On The Origins Of Some Aristotelian Theses About Predication" in *How Things Are*, Bogen, James (ed), 323–326. Boston Reidel 1985.

CODE, Alan. "On The Origins Of Some Aristotelian Theses About Predication" in *How Things Are*, Bogen, James (ed), 101–132. Boston Reidel 1985.

CODE, Lorraine B. The Knowing Subject. *Ideal Stud* 14,109–126 My 84.

The Kantian characterization of cognitive activity as a *creative synthesis* of the *imagination* is revolutionary in the history of epistemology, but it falls short of providing an account of the activity of individual knowers in creating the products we call knowledge. Jean Piaget's Kantian–oriented genetic epistemology adds importantly to the account of the role of persons (rather than abstract individuals) as knowing subjects. And Thomas Kuhn's assertion of the importance of community in the growth of knowledge helps to fill out the picture.

COETZEE, Pieter. Principles And Virtues—Or—Principles Or Virtues. *S Afr J Phil* 4,25–28 F 85.

This article attempts to show that MacIntyre's socially teleological model of moral life is defective in that it does not offer his moral agent the means to evaluate the ends that he must pursue. MacIntyre simply presupposes that his agent will be willing to accept certain socially given ends. The argument maintained in this article shows that MacIntyre's notion of *telos* will not help him to account for his willingness to live his life in a self–contained community. The problem arises from MacIntyre's treatment of the relationship between the virtues and moral principles. His *telos* operates with a virtue–centered ethic in which the role of moral rules is reduced to secondary importance. They have the negative function of prohibiting undesirable practices. But moral principles do not even have a peripheral role. Their definitive function in connection with the virtues, understood as dispositions to act in certain ways, is altogether eshewed. Yet recourse to principles is what his agent needs for his rationality. Without such recourse the notion of *telos* becomes a limiting factor in his agent's moral life.

COHEN, Avner. Sextus Empiricus: Skepticism As A Therapy. *Phil Forum (Boston)* 15,405–424 Sum 84.

COHEN, Elliot D. Pure Legal Advocates And Moral Agents: Two Concepts Of A Lawyer In An Adversary System. *Crim Just Ethics* 4,38–59 Wint/Spr 85.

This paper distinguishes two concepts of "lawyer"—the pure legal advocate and moral agent concepts—and shows how pure legal advocate practitioners, unlike moral agents, tend to develop and/or reinforce morally undesirable personality traits. It then shows how the moral agent concept can be used as a basis for revising the ABA's *Code* and *Model Rules*; and it answers certain objections to applying this concept.

COHEN, G A. Are Workers Forced To Sell Their Labor Power? *Phil Pub Affairs* 14,99–105 Wint 85.

The article is a reply to George Brenkert's "Cohen on Proletarian Unfreedom", which criticizes my "Structure of Proletarian Unfreedom". Brenkert challenges my argument that, since there are more routes out of the proletariat that there are workers trying to escape it, each worker is free to leave the proletariat. The argument is reiterated and defended in the present article.

COHEN, Jean and Arato, Andrew. Social Movements, Civil Society, And The Problem Of Sovereignty. *Praxis Int* 4,266–283 O 84.

COHEN, L J. "Third World Epistemology" in *Popper And The Human Sciences*, Currie, Gregory (ed), 1–12. Boston Nijhoff 1985.

COHEN, L Jonathan. A Problem About Ambiguity In Truth–!Theoretical Semantics. *Analysis* 45,129–134 Je 85.

Davidson's T–sentences cannot handle verbal ambiguity in the same way as vagueness. Nor can they handle it in any paraticular case via a finite disjunction of context–relative truth–conditions, because, though homonyms are rare, most words in natural language are polysemes, and some are infinitely ambiguous. So the Tarskian paradigm is less closely applicable to natural language than Davidson suggests.

COHEN, Marshall. Moral Skepticism And International Relations. *Phil Pub Affairs* 13,299–346 Fall 84.

Moral scepticism about international relations is rejected. It is argued that the scepticism of the American realists presupposes an inadequate view of morality. It is then argued that even in a Hobbesian state of nature moral obligations would obtain. Finally, a milder, Humean skepticism is examined. But the view that although morality applies in the international realm it applies there with reduced force is rejected.

COHEN, Richard. Merleau–Ponty, The Flesh And Foucault. *Phil Today* 28,329–338 Wint 84.

The article has two related purposes: (1) To clarify the central notion of Merleau–Ponty's late thought, the flesh; (2) To correct Foucault's misunderstanding expressed in *The Order of Things*, of Merleau–Ponty. Merleau–Ponty's notion of the flesh is shown to be compatible with Foucalt's post–anthropological thought.

COHEN, Robert S (ed) and Wartofsky, Marx W (ed). *Methodology, Metaphysics And The History Of Science*. Boston Reidel 1984.

COHEN, Ronald. Approaches To Applied Anthropology. *Commun Cog* 17,135–162 1984.

COHEN, Stewart. Justification And Truth. *Phil Stud* 46,279–296 N 84.

COLE, Peter. Quantifier Scope And The ECP. *Ling Phil* 8,283–289 My 85.

COLELLA, E Paul. The Commodity Form And Socialization In Locke's State Of Nature. *Int Stud Phil* 16,1–14 1984.

This article explores the structural affinities which connect Locke's political ideas with bourgeois social relations. Marx's analysis of the commodity–form is employed as an interpretive instrument on Locke's notions of the State of Nature and the Law of Nature. While the predominance of the category of use forces social fragmentation onto the State of Nature, the Law of Nature provides the social bond as does the activity of exchange upon which it is based.

COLEMAN, Dorothy P. Hume's "Dialectic". *Hume Stud* 10,139–155 N 84.

Hume's treatment of contradiction in his discussion of external existence has generally been taken to resemble the Pyrrhonian model of dialectic; consequently Hume has been viewed as a sceptic. The author argues Hume's treatment of contradiction differs significantly from Pyrrhonian dialectic but strongly resembles the Kantian model of dialectic. The parallels between Hume's treatment of contradiction and Kant's dialectic show that Hume's "dialectic", like Kant's, is a method for resolving, rather than generating, scepticism.

COLEMAN, Jules L. Market Contractarianism And The Unanimity Rule. *Soc Phil Pol* 2,69–114 Spr 85.

COLEMAN, S R. Background And Change In B F Skinner's Metatheory From 1930 To 1938. *J Mind Behavior* 5,471–500 Autumn 84.

From 1930 to 1938, B F Skinner developed, and then altered in several ways, a scientific methatheory or philosophy of science. In the present article, the reflexological background of his hearly methatheory is described, and the problems it created for him are discussed. Difficulties in his early methatheory and discoveries in his rat research brought metatheoretical changes that were announced in his publications of 1935, 1937, and 1938. The present article suggests several themes to characterize his metatheoretical development between 1930 and 1938.

COLFER, P. Scepticism And Public Health: On The Problem Of Disease For The Collective. *Theor Med* 6,143–152 Je 85.

This paper argues that modern society does not meet the problems posed by the experience of disease in a satisfactory way. It attempts to show this by examining the distinction between disease and plague. Disease is formulated as necessarily involving the self in unforeseeable ways with what is other to itself: the challenge of disease is treated as the challenge of involvement. On the other hand, plague as an abstract threat is that towards which the collective shows principled indifference. The strength and limits of this indifference are explored. Subsequent upon this, the paper examines the consequences of the loss of the distinction between disease and plague, particularly with respect to the implications of that loss for the treatment, management, and control of disease in modern society.

COLI, Daniela. Le Lettere Di Croce A Gentile. *G Crit Filosof Ital* 63,268–273 My–Ag 84.

COLLIER, Andrew. Scientific Socialism And The Question Of Socialist Values. *Can J Phil* Supp 7,121–154 1981.

COLLIER, Boyd D and Penn, William Y. Current Research In Moral Development As A Decision Support System. *J Bus Ethics* 4,131–136 Ap 85.

COLLINGE, William. Augustine And Theological Falsification. *Augustin Stud* 13,43–54 1982.

In the context of the debate, touched off by Antony Flew, on the falsifiability of religious beliefs, this paper considers Augustine's loss of faith in Manichaeism as a case study illustrating the logic of religious falsification. It concludes that some religious beliefs are empirically falsifiable, but the bearing of their falsification on the reasonableness of a religious commitment depends on their place in a larger system comprising both theoretical and existential factors.

COLLINS, Aaron S. Friends Of Leomofos. *Cogito* 3,25–54 Mr 85.

COLLINS, Anthony and Schouls, Peter A (ed). *An Essay Concerning The Use Of Reason In Propositions: A Discourse Of Free Thinking.* NY Garland 1984.

COLLINS, Arthur. Action, Causality, And Teleological Explanation. *Midwest Stud Phil* 9,345–370 1984.

COLLINS, Clinton. Before Virtue: A Critique Of The New Essentialism In Ethics And Education. *Proc Phil Educ* 40,209–218 1984.

COLLINS, James D. "Response: "Conspectus" in *History Of Philosophy In The Making*, Thro, Linus J (ed), 321–326. Washington Univ Pr Of America 1982.

COLLINSON, Diané. 'Ethics And Aesthetics Are One'. *Brit J Aes* 25,266–272 Sum 85.

What did Wittgenstein mean when he said that 'Ethics and aesthetics are one', since these are generally contrasted than amalgamated? His *1914–1916 Notebooks*, the *Tractatus*, and the *Lecture on Ethics*, show that he regarded them as one because they shared a *sub specie aeternitatis* attitude. Study of his remarks reveals the implications of his account and shows that Wittgenstein, in this phase of development, belonged in the mainstream of ethical and aesthetic philosophy.

COLWELL, Tom. The Ecological Perspective In John Dewey's Philosophy Of Education. *Educ Theor* 35,255–266 Sum 85.

Dewey has long been viewed as a social philosopher of education, but when his naturalistic metaphysics is interpreted ecologically involving a unitary conception of nature and inclusive of organism and environment, human and non–human interrelationships, Dewey provides a new biocentric framework for education based on the unity of social and natural educational experience in place of the prevailing dualism between culture and nature.

COMBS, Beverly J. "If You Liked Gun Control, You'll Love The Antiabortion Amendment" in *Freedom, Feminism, And The State*, Mc Elroy, Wendy (ed), 169–178. Cato Institute Washington 1982.

COMER, Stephen D. The Elementary Theory Of Interval Reals Numbers. *Z Math Log* 31,89–95 1985.

The set of all compact intervals of real numbers, with suitable operations, forms a "real numbers" model $g(R)$ that is used in numerical analysis studies. The main results show that the first–order theory of $g(R)$ is axiomatizable, decidable, and model–complete.

COMMERS, Ronald. Marx's Concept Of Justice And The Two Traditions In The European Political Thought. *Philosophica* 33,107–130 1984.

COMMISSIO THEOLOGICA INTERNATIONALIS. Theses De Dignitate Necnon De Iuribus Personae Humanae. *Gregorianum* 66,5–23 1985.

The ICTh publishes the text of the "relations" (proceedings) presented by 10 members during the ordinary session of 1983 about some modern aspects of christian anthropology and ethics. Special points of view are: teaching of the Pope, philosophy of personalism, history of salvation theology, differences between the free worlds, human rights (USA; Europe).

COMPTON, Kevin J. An Undecidable Problem In Finite Combinatorics. *J Sym Log* 49,842–850 S 84.

CONEE, Earl. A Defense Of Pain. *Phil Stud* 46,239–248 S 84.

In the paper, 'Why You Can't Make a Computer That Feels Pain', Daniel Dennett argues against the coherence of the concept of pain. The present paper argues for the coherence of the concept. It also argues that there are no individual pains. It concludes with a discussion of how to find out whether computers can feel pain.

CONEE, Earl and Feldman, Richard. Evidentialism. *Phil Stud* 48,15–34 Jl 85.

In this paper we defend evidentialism, the view that the epistemic justification of a belief is determined entirely by the believer's evidence for the belief. A defense of this seems appropriate now because theses incompatible with evidentialism have been prominent in recent literature of epistemology. The conflicting theses imply that the epistemic justification of a belief depends upon cognitive capacities, or the cognitive or information–gathering processes that led to the belief. We find no adequate grounds for accepting these theses and argue that evidentialism remains the best view of epistemic justification.

CONEE, Earl. Discussion: On Seeking A Rationale. *Phil Phenomenol Res* 45,601–610 Je 85.

In Samuel Scheffler's book, *The Rejection of Consequentialism*, a certain sort of defense—a "rationale"—is sought on behalf of various moral theses. The present paper argues against the philosophical value of this project.

CONEE, Earl. Physicalism And Phenomenal Qualities. *Phil Quart* 35,296–302 Jl 85.

Frank Jackson has offered an epistemic argument against physicalism construed as the thesis that all correct information is physical information. Jackson describes a sort of case where, he argues, someone who already knows all of the physical information learns something new. In this paper I attempt to refute objections to Jackson's argument by David Lewis, Lawrence Nimerow, and Terence Horgan. Then I offer what I take to be a successful objection. Finally, I use the version of physicalism that underlies this objection in an attempt to render physicalism more attractive, especially to those who feel the force of Jackson's argument.

CONLEY, John J. A Certain Just War, A Certain Pacifism. *Thought* 60,242–257 Je 85.

CONNELL, Desmond. Existence And Judgment. *Phil Stud (Ireland)* 30,127–143 Spr 84.

The purpose of this article is to defend the value of the judgment of existence against the objections contained in C J F Williams, *What is Existence?* And in D F Pears "Is Existence a Predicate?" Williams' view unjustifiably reduces metaphysics to logic and disregards the occurence of existence as a first–level predicate. Pears' view that the judgment of existence is a referential tautology is mistaken. A positive account of the judgment of existence is attempted.

CONNIN, Lawrence J. On DiQuattro, "Rawls And Left Criticism". *Polit Theory* 13,138–141 F 85.

CONNOLLY, William E. Michel Foucault: An Exchange: Taylor, Foucault, And Otherness. *Polit Theory* 13,365–376 Ag 85.

CONO, Joseph and Todd, Joan. Vico And Collingwood On 'The Conceit Of Scholars'. *Hist Euro Ideas* 6,59–70 1985.

The purpose of the paper is to show some sources of error arising out of human conceit and the possible valid methods for self–correction. For Vico and Collingwood nationalistic and individualistic conceits are part of the major sources of human error. With the awareness of conceits emerges historical consciousness of a finite existence and it is this recognition which demands interdisciplinary analyses in order to validate epistemological answers.

CONRAD, John P. "Controlling The Uncontrollable" in *Feeling Good And Doing Better*, Murray, Thomas H (ed), 49–64. Clifton Humana Pr 1984.

CONSTANT, Edward W. "Communities And Hierarchies: Structure In The Practice Of Science And Technology" in *Technological Knowledge*, Laudan, Rachel (ed), 27–46. Boston Reidel 1984.

CONSTANTINI, D. Probability And Laws. *Erkenntnis* 22,33–50 Ja 85.

CONWAY, David A. 'It Would Have Happened Already': On One Argument For A First Cause. *Analysis* 44,159–166 O 84.

CONWAY, Gertrude and Conway, Jeremiah. On The Possibility Of Continuing The Conversation Of Mankind. *Cogito* 2,1–25 Je 84.

CONWAY, Jeremiah P and Gavin, William J. Works Of Art As Cultural Probes. *J Theor Crit Vis Arts* 1,115–132 1982.

Outstanding works of art may be regarded as "probes" into the thought or general attitudes of the cultures that produced them. In addition, a perennial pedagogic problem facing interdisciplinary courses consists in finding an appropriate story line which is broad enough to encompass a variety of disciplines; yet concrete enough to hold student attention. In this article we argue that the medium of trials fulfills this dual need. We begin with an analysis of the educational potential of the trial situation by revealing the trial text as a wedge or lens into its interdisciplinary subtextual or contextual framework. In the course from which this article stems, we focus on three trials: the trial of Socrates; the trial of Galileo; and the trial of Joseph K in Kafka's novel, *The Trial*. In each of these instances, we are presented with a text which if taken literally, i.e., on the surface level, makes no sense. What appears as absurd on a surface level becomes somewhat understandable when the trial text is viewed in a wider interdisciplinary context. As one illustration of this use of trial texts, the present article concentrates on the trial of Joseph K in Kafka's novel *The Trial*.

CONWAY, Jeremiah and Conway, Gertrude. On The Possibility Of Continuing The Conversation Of Mankind. *Cogito* 2,1–25 Je 84.

CONWAY, Jeremiah and Gavin, William J. The Phenomenology Of Trials: Text And Socio–Political Context. *Cogito* 3,1–24 Mr 85.

A perennial pedagogic problem facing interdisciplinary courses consists in finding an appropriate story line which is broad enough to encompass a variety of disciplines, yet concrete enough to hold student attention. In this article we argue that the medium of trials fulfills this dual need, when utilized in a critically philosophical manner. We begin with an analysis of the educational potential of the trial situation by revealing the trial text as a wedge or lens into its interdisciplinary subtextual or contextual framework. In the course from which this article stems, we focus on three trials; the trial of Socrates; the trial of Galileo; and the trial of Joseph K in Kafka's novel, *The Trial*. In each of these instances, we are presented with a text which is taken literally, i.e., on the surface level, makes no sense. What appears as absurd on a surface level becomes somewhat understandable when the trial text is viewed in a wider interdisciplinary context.

CONWAY, Patrick. The Mind/Body Function: Not One, Not Two, But A Process. *J Thought* 19,90–104 Wint 84.

COOK, Daniel J. Was Wittgenstein Influenced By Hegel? *Owl Minerva* 16,102–107 Fall 84.

Whatever affinities one finds between the Hegelian tradition and Wittgenstein's thought, there is no substance to the suggestions that Wittgenstein's philosophy (especially in its later forms) may have been influenced by Hegel. There is no evidence—either biographical or textual—that Wittgenstein ever read Hegel. Furthermore, there is little to sustain the claim that he may have indirectly known Hegel's philosophy through contact with European Hegelians, British neo–Hegelians or his reading of Kierkegaard and Marx.

COOK, Daniel. Hegel, Marx And Wittgenstein. *Phil Soc Crit* 10,49–74 Fall 84.

Several writers have recently claimed that there are definite affinities between Wittgenstein's (later) thought and that of Hegel and Marx, especially in their respective conceptions of dialectic, language and *praxis*. I show that these purported areas of agreement between the Hegelian tradition and Wittgenstein are neither substantive nor illuminating.

COOK, Deborah. Writing Philosophy And Literature: Apology For Narcissism In Merleau–Ponty. *Eidos* 4,1–9 Je 85.

The paper attempts to show just what Merleau–Ponty thought about philosophy and literature and the relation between them. In it, philosophy and literature are discussed as intentional activities which share a number of things in common including the search for truth, newly defined. This search for a newly defined truth has led to a heightened self–reflexivity on the part of both activities. The value of self–reflexivity is assessed at the end of the paper.

COOK, John W. The Metaphysics Of Wittgenstein's On Certainty. *Phil Invest* 8,81–119 Ap 85.

The essay argues that Wittgensteins's problems and solutions in *On Certainty* are those of a phenomenalist.

COOK, Monte. Names And Possible Objects. *Phil Quart* 35,303–309 Jl 85.

COOK, Monte. Rigid Designators And Disguised Descriptions. *Can J Phil* 6,111–118 80 Supp.

In "Naming and Necessity" Saul Kripke repeatedly uses modal arguments to show that proper names are not abbreviated or disguised descriptions. I defend these modal arguments against the frequent criticism that they rest on an ambiguous premise.

COOKE, Robert Allan and Banner, David K. Ethical Dilemmas In Performance Appraisal. *J Bus Ethics* 3,327–334 N 84.

This paper is an examination of performance appraisal (PA). We examine some of the main conceptual issues in PA, and we sketch some key, practical dilemmas that may arise in the use of PA. We conclude that one can morally justify the use of PA under certain conditions, and we suggest possible solutions to key ethical dilemmas that are faced by the manager and the employee. (edited)

COOKE, Robert Allan. The Future Of Business Ethics. *Listening* 20,147–153 Spr 85.

COOMARASWAMY, Radhika (ed) and Gunatilleke, Godfrey (ed) and Tiruchelvam, Neelan (ed). *Ethical Dilemmas Of Development In Asia*. Lexington Heath 1983.

The study analyses the social, political, and economic consequences of current development strategies in terms of their human costs, with detailed case studies. These strategies will always be constrained by imperfect choices. The system making a choice must be aware of its imperfection, have a sustained concern for what is lost in human terms through its choice and possess built–in motivations to restore what is lost through constant assessment and participation of all the social groups affected by the gains and losses.

COOPER, Barry. *Michel Foucault: An Introduction To The Study Of His Thought*. NY Mellen Pr 1981.

COOPER, Barry. "Ideology And Technology, Truth And Power" in *Ideology, Philosophy And Politics*, Parel, Anthony (ed), 93–110. Waterloo Laurier Univ Pr 1983.

COOPER, David E. Cognitive Development And Teaching Business Ethics. *J Bus Ethics* 4,313–329 Ag 85.

This paper discusses how to use cognitive developmental psychology to create a business ethics course that has philosophical integrity. It begins with the pedagogical problem to be overcome when students are not philosophy majors. To provide a context for the practical recommendations, Kohlberg's cognitive developmental theory is summarized and then the relationship between Kohlberg's theory, normative philosophy, and teaching is analyzed. The conclusion recommends strategies that should help overcome some of the vexing pedagogical problems mentioned in the first section. In particular, the approach is designed to teach an appreciation for the practical necessity of philosophy in a pluralistic society.

COOPER, David E. Metaphors We Live By. *Philosophy* 18,43–58 84 Supp.

COOPER, David E. Trust. *J Med Ethics* 11,92–93 Je 85.

COOPER, John M. Aristotle On The Goods Of Fortune. *Phil Rev* 94,173–196 Ap 85.

COPELAND, B J. Substitutional Quantification And Existence. *Analysis* 45,1–4 Ja 85.

A substitutional semantics for the quantifiers assigns determinate meaning to the quantifiers only once an interpretation is given to the formal notion of a substitution class. The meaning assigned depends on the interpretations given. On some interpretations it is true, but on others false, that substantional quantifiers have no ontic import. Van Inwagen's charge that substitutional quantification is unintelligible is countered, as is Marcus' claim that the Barcan formula is problematic only on 'existence readings' of the quantifiers.

COPI, Irving M. *Introduction To Logic*. NY Macmillan 1982.

COPLESTON, Frederick C. "Philosophy And Ideology" in *Ideology, Philosophy And Politics*, Parel, Anthony (ed), 17–36. Waterloo Laurier Univ Pr 1983.

COPLESTRON, Frederick C. "The Question Of Recurrent Problems In Philosophy" in *History Of Philosophy In Making*, Thro, Linus J (ed), 197–212. Washington Univ Pr Of America 1982.

COPP, David (ed) and Zimmerman, David (ed). *Morality, Reason And Truth: New Essays On The Foundations Of Ethics*. Totowa Rowman & Allanheld 1984.

A collection of mainly previously unpublished essays on the foundations of morality. The issues which are emphasized are the relation between moral justification and the theory of practical reason, and the place of morality in a scientific view of the world. Contents: Introduction by David Copp. Essays by Gilbert Harman, Nicholas Sturgeon, David Zimmerman, Richard Brandt, Norman Daniels, Copp, Ronald deSousa, Kurt Baier, Kai Nielsen, Jan Narveson, David Gauthier, Richmond Campbell, Gregory Kavka.

COPP, David. "Considered Judgments And Moral Justification: Conservatism In Moral Theory" in *Morality, Reason And Truth*, Copp, David (ed), 141–168. Totowa Rowman & Allanheld 1984.

COPP, David. Morality, Reason, And Management Science: The Rationale Of Cost–Benefit Analysis. *Soc Phil Pol* 2,128–151 Spr 85.

If cost–benefit analysis is defensible, it must be possible to state on what basis it can be recommended for use in public policy decision making. This essay discusses and rejects three proposals: "management science accounts," "moralist accounts," and "rationalist accounts" according to which CB analysis contributes to public policy which is rational "from the point of view of society." The essay argues that none of these proposed rationales is satisfactory.

COPP, David. What Collectives Are: Agency, Individualism And Legal Theory. *Dialogue (Canada)* 23,249–270 Je 84.

An account of the ontology of collectives, such as mobs and states, must meet three constraints: (1) It must be compatible with the claim that collectives perform actions. (2) It must explain our idea that collectives are merely collections of persons. (3) It must imply a plausible account of the legal system. The account proposed is claimed to meet these constraints. There are implications for action theory, social philosophy, philosophy of law, and philosophy of social science.

COPPENGER, Mark. *Bioethics: A Casebook*. Englewood Cliffs Prentice–Hall 1985.

CORBEY, R. Over De Menselijkheid Van Vroege Hominidae. *Alg Ned Tijdschr Wijs* 77,64–78 Ap 85.

Which early Hominids can be qualified as *human*, and why? In paleoanthropological and archeological literature of the last decennia tool manufacture is seen as a decisive indicator of human status, betraying an underlying naturalistic view of man as *homo faber*. An alternative approach to the problem is developed, departing from Max Scheler's phenomenological crtiticism of naturalism: the difficult but promising analysis of cognitive processes, especially anticipatory ones, underlying the archeologically reconstructed behavior of early Hominids.

CORCORAN, John. Categoricity. *Hist Phil Log* 1,187–208 1980.

After a short preface, the first of the three sections of this paper is devoted to historical and philosophic aspects of categoricity. The second section is a self–contained exposition, including detailed definitions, of a proof that every mathematical system whose domain is the closure of its set of distinguished individuals under its distinguished functions is categorically characterized by its induction principle together with its true atoms (atomic sentences and negations of atomic sentences). The third section deals with applications especially those involving the distinction between characterizing a system and axiomatizing the truths of a system.

CORCORAN, John. On Definitional Equivalence And Related Topics. *Hist Phil Log* 1,231–234 1980.

The purpose of this department is to facilitate the communication of research topics in the history and philosophy of logic. Contributions should be written up in a coherent form (rather that as rough notes, say) and with detailed references, in order to facilitate their appraisal. Especially welcome are answers or addenda to material already published in the department. Requests to publish contributions in the form submitted will be honored as far as possible, but rewriting may be needed (in light of other contributions which overlap, for example, and in conformity with house style). The proposed published version of a contribution will be sent to its author before publication, where his work will be acknowledged. Contributions should be sent to the editor of the department: J Corcoran, Department of Philosophy, State University of New York at Buffalo, Buffalo, New York 14260, U S A, who has prepared all the material for the edition.

CORDNER, C D. Grace And Functionality. *Brit J Aes* 24,301–313 Autumn 84.

CORDONE, Claudio. La Teoria Islamica Dei Diritti Umani. *Riv Int Filosof Diritto* 61,578–602 O–D 84.

Proponents of the Islamic theory of human rights usually present it as universal. However, comparison with a theory hinged on the modern Western concept of human rights—rights of human beings as such—shows that the Islamic theory does not meet fundamental requirements of universality. This theory is therefore insufficient to justify the value of human dignity, although possibilities of development in that direction should be considered.

CORNU, Michel. Autour D'Emmanuel Lévinas. *Rev Theol Phil* 116,241–246 1984.

CORONA, Nester A. El Ser En El "Sistema De Identidad" Según Gustav Siewerth (Segunda Parte). *Stromata* 40,299–319 Jl–D 84.

CORONADO, Luis Guillermo. Consideraciones Acerca De La Teoría Platónica De Los Cuatro Elementos: Su Status Epistemológico. *Rev Filosof (Costa Rica)* 23,143–150 D 85.

The principle aim of this paper will be an appraisal of Plato's explanation of the so–called mathematical structure of the 'four elements' in order to show his conception of the epistemological and ontological status of physical theories. To carry out this task, I will need to examine Plato's views about knowledge, especially the simile of the

'Line' in *Republic* VI, and the Prelude of Timaeus' discourse. After that, I will deal with Plato's proper theory about mathematical structures and the 'four' elements. Finally, I will consider and reject a widely held interpretation of Plato's thought, the atomism of discrete surfaces, and other misunderstandings of his natural philosophy.

CORR, Charles A. "The Deutsche Metaphysik Of Christian Wolff: Text And Transitions" in *History Of Philosophy In Making*, Thro, Linus J (ed), 149–164. Washington Univ Pr Of America 1982.

CORRIGAN, Kevin. The Irreducible Opposition Between The Platonic And Aristotelian Conceptions Of Soul And Body In Some Ancient And Mediaeval Thinkers. *Laval Theol Phil* 41,391–401 O 85.

This article attempts to show that the Aristotelian view of soul was not absolutely limited to the entelechy theory. It further suggests that the irreducible opposition between the extreme formulations of the Platonic and Aristotelian positions was clearly recognized before Aquinas (in particular by Plotinus) and that an attempt was then made to "reconcile" the two theories.

CORRINGTON, Robert S. Naturalism, Measure And The Ontological Difference. *S J Phil* 23,19–32 Spr 85.

This essay shows the main traits of American Naturalism as it has evolved through Dewey to Justus Buchler. Buchler's principle of ordinality clarifies fundamental problems in the notion of measure which was utilized in a partial and inadequate way by Heidegger. The ontological difference is regrounded in the ordinal perspective to show previously undisclosed dimensions of difference. Ordinality is shown to receive its own measure in the Encompassing which measures all complexes, including the Divine.

CORTÉS, Eugenio S. Palabra Socrática. *Rev Filosof (Costa Rica)* 22,151–156 D 84.

A menudo entre nosotros, Sócrates es propuesto como modelo de maestro y filósofo. Sin embargo, textos antiguos muestran abundantemente más bien su desprecio para la filosofía no solo porque se rehusara a escribir, sino sobre todo por plantear de entrada que él no aportado nada pues en su compañia el mismo discípulo se percataba de lo único que se puede obtener: la conciencia de la propia ignorancia. (edited)

COSTA, Michael J. Why Be Just: Hume's Response In The *Inquiry*. *S J Phil* 22,469–480 Wint 84.

The author attempts to reconstruct in some detail the answer given by Hume in the *Inquiry* to the question of why one should value a concern for justice. Hume says that a person with such a concern: (1) will be less likely to make errors in deciding how to act, and (2) will be likely to experience greater and special quality satisfactions throughout life. hume's answer, thus construed, is defended against several objections.

COTE, Marcel. La Philosophie Du Raisonnable De Chaïm Perelman. *Laval Theol Phil* 41,195–204 Je 85.

La conception de discours philosophique de Chaïm Perelman est mal connue. Si ell est certes tributaire de ses rescherches sur la rhétorique argumentative, elle veut aussi répondre aux interrogations contemporaines sur la nature de ce discours. Il s'agit ici d'indiquer en quoi consiste la "philosophie du raisonnable" (conception qui est disséminée dans toute l'oeuvre de Perelman) et de discuter les principaux axes de cette démarche.

COTTIER, Georges. Les Fondements Personnalistes De La Propriété. *Stud Phil (Switzerland)* Supp 12,313–330 1983.

COUGHLAN, M J. 'Si Fallor, Sum' Revisited. *Augustin Stud* 13,145–150 1982.

Attempts to tease a demonstrative argument for the knowledge, or even certainty, or one's own existence from the 'Si fallor, sum' passage in Augustine's *City of God*, invariably found both on philosophical difficulties and on lack of textual support. 'si fallor, sum' is a grammatical observation, not an elliptical demonstration.

COULOUBARITSIS, Lambros. Le Caractère Mythique De L'Analogie Du Bien Dans *République VI. Diotima* 12,71–80 1984.

COURTNEY, Charles. Christian Resources For Peace Making In A World Of Conflict. *J Dharma* 10,25–33 Ja–Mr 85.

COWAN, Denis. A Note On Objective Identity And Diversity (Part III, Chapter I, Section VII). *Process Stud* 14,46–48 Spr 84.

This note resolves doubts, regarding the ordering of paragraphs in Section 7, Chapter 1, Part III of *Process and Reality* by Whitehead. The original ordering is shown to adhere firmly to the distinction drawn between objective identity and objective diversity: The idea of "oneness" is clearly developed first, transcending any contributing elements as such; and only then is the antithetical idea of "complexity" developed, requiring a complementary status beyond "sham diversity" and "mere multiplicity".

COWARD, Harold (ed). *Studies In Indian Thought.* Columbia South Asia 1983.

The aim was to publish key articles of Professor T R V Murti that still have relevance for ongoing philosophic discussion. Especially useful to today's students are the six essays on Advaita Vedanta, the seven essays on Buddhism and the essay on "The Philosophy of Language in the Indian Context." An academic biography of Professor Murti is included along with a complete listing of his writings. The majority of these essays were first published in obscure Indian journals, now defunct, and thus outside this volume are not easily available.

COWELL, Barbara and Wilson, John. Applying Philosophy. *J Applied Phil* 2,127–132 Mr 85.

COX, J Gray. *The Will At The Crossroads: A Reconstruction Of Kant's Moral Philosophy.* NY Univ Pr Of America 1984.

Argues that (often in spite of themselves) most readings of Kant's ethics presuppose at least one of three claims that are mutually implying: 1) the moral agent has a will of *pure* practical reason 2) which applies the moral law wholly *a priori* 3) in the realm of the *noumenal*. Argues all such readings are incoherent. Develops in detail and

defends a reading in which the moral agent has a will of empirical practical reason which applies the moral law *a posteriori* in a non–noumenal, non–phenomenal realm of a temporal subject who experiences respect as a formal, non–sensuous feeling.

COX, J W Roxbee. Utilitarians And The Use Of Examples. *Ethics* 95,268–273 Ja 85.

Utilitarians sometimes decide between competing versions of utilitarianism by appealing to the judgment we would make about a certain action, and showing that one such judgment will favor a particular version. Such a procedure presupposes the possession of some non–utilitarian standard of right or of good. A utilitarian cannot use the procedure without inconsistency. The criticism is applied to the problem of whether utilitarians should accept the 'person–affecting restriction'.

COX, James E and Carson, Thomas L and Wokutch, Richard E. An Ethical Analysis Of Deception In Advertising. *J Bus Ethics* 4,93–104 Ap 85.

COX, John Gray. Thoughts And Suggestions Concerning An International Society For Philosophers Concerned With Peace. *Dialec Hum* 11,429–430 Spr/Sum 84.

In light of dialogues held at the 1983 World Congress in Montreal, a format for cooperative international philosophical research on peace issues is discussed and some specific proposals are offered.

COX, Susan Jane Buck. No Tragedy Of The Commons. *Environ Ethics* 7,49–62 Spr 85.

The historical antecedents of Garrett Hardin's "tradegy of the commons" are generally understood to lie in the common grazing lands of medieval and post-medieval England. The concept of the commons current in medieval England is significantly different from the modern concept; the English common was not available to the general public but rather only to certain individuals who inherited or were granted the right to use it, and use of the common even by these people was not unregulated. Thus, the traditional commons system is not an example of an inherently flawed land–use policy, as is widely supposed, but of a policy which succeeded admirably in its time. (edited)

COYNE, Margaret U. Role And Rational Action. *J Theor Soc Behav* 14,259–276 O 84.

This philosophical analysis of the concept role discusses six typical features of role-structured behavior. Four categories of role (situational, micro–social, macro–social, institutional) are distinguished. Examination of the possible motivational structures of role suggests that role–behavior is often *non–rational action*, in a sense defined: this accounts for a common suspicion that roles stand in need of moral scrutiny. In conclusion, the example of sex roles is used to illustrate why all types macro–social roles are most questionable morally.

CRABBE, Marcel. Typical Ambiguity And The Axiom Of Choice. *J Sym Log* 49,1074–1078 D 84.

We prove that the axiom of choice is refuted in type theory with two axioms of ambiguity added. This is done by translating Specker's disproof of AC for Quine's New Foundations in type theory. On the other hand, we show that each single ambiguity axiom is consistent with the axiom of choice. For this we use a forcing construction. This last result answers affirmatively a conjecture of E Specker.

CRAEMER, Heiner. Skepsis Ohne Selbstwiderspruch: Über O Marquards "Interimistischen Skeptizismus". *Z Phil Forsch* 29,382–403 Jl–S 75.

CRAFT, J L (ed) and Hustwit, Ronald E (ed). *Without Proof Or Evidence: Essays Of O K Bouwsma.* Lincoln Univ Nebraska Pr 1984.

This collection of O K Bouwsma's essays addresses the central topics of Western religion: the rationality of religious belief, the nature of Christianity, the promise of eternal life, the definition of faith, and proofs of the existence of God. Analyzing the concepts Descartes, Moore, Wittgenstein, Anselm, Nietzsche, and Kierkegaard. Bouwsma focuses on the remark ableness of a book which God has sent to mankind.

CRAFT, J L. Remarks On Bouwsma's Method Of Failure. *Phil Invest* 8,161–173 Jl 85.

CRAIG, William Lane. Professor Mackie And The Kalam Cosmological Argument. *Relig Stud* 20,367–376 S 84.

Mackie's objections to the first cause cosmological argument as enunciated in his *Miracle of Theism* are examined and found to be superficial.

CRANFORD, Ronald E (ed) and Doudera, A Edward (ed). *Institutional Ethics Committees And Health Care Decision Making.* Ann Arbor Health Admin Pr 1984.

CRANSTON, Maurice. Rousseau On Equality. *Soc Phil Pol* 2,115–124 Autumn 84.

CREATH, Richard. Smart, Salmon, And Scientific Realism. *Austl J Phil* 62,404–409 D 84.

¡ J C Smart has argued for a long time that not being a scientific realist commits one to the occurrence of what he calls "cosmic coincidences", and Wesley Salmon has recently advanced a sophisticated version of this argument. In this paper I examine and assess the arguments of Smart and Salmon. Two separate questions are important for scientific realism, and properly construed the Smart–Salmon argument is a forceful and intuitively sound answer to the first, but not the second, of these questions. Their argument is therefore incomplete, and in particular it fails to confute the anti–realism currently being developed by Bas van Fraassen.

CREATH, Richard. Taking Theories Seriously. *Synthese* 62,317–346 Mr 85.

This paper defends scientific realism, the doctrine that we should interpret theories as being just as ontologically committing as beliefs at the observational level. I examine the character of observation to show that the difference in interpretation suggested by anti–realists is unwarranted. Second, I discuss Wilfrid Sellars' approach to the issue. Finally, I provide a detailed study of recent work by Bas van Fraassen. While van Fraassen's work is the focus of the paper, the conclusions are far broader: That a wide family of anti–realist views (of which van Fraassen's is only one) is problematic and unmotivated and hence to be rejected.

CREEDON, Michael A. Ethical Perspectives On Health Policy For An Aging Society. *Thought* 60,196–204 Je 85.

CREGO, Charo and Groot, Ger. Pierre Bourdieu En De Filosofische Esthetica. *Alg Ned Tijdschr Wijs* 77,21–35 Ja 85.

The authors fight the conclusions of Bourdieu in postscript to *La distinction* reducing philosophical aesthetics to the social background of the thinkers who conceived them. They show how Bourdieu's interpretation has been biassed by his intention to disqualify philosophical aesthetics and how he develops a highly disputable reading of Kant's philosophy of art, of which they present a more faithful reading. Finally, they defend the view that both approaches (the philosophical and the sociological) have their own rights of existence.

CRESSWELL, M J. The Decidable Normal Modal Logics Are Not Recursively Enumerable. *J Phil Log* 14,231–234 Ag 85.

In this paper it is proved that there is no effective enumeration of algorithms which includes one for every decidable normal modal logic and not others. The proof uses a way of coding sets of natural numbers by modal systems which was invented by Alasdair Urquhart.

CRIBB, Alan. Quality Of Life—A Response To K C Calman. *J Med Ethics* 11,142–145 S 85.

There is no technical language with which to speak of patients' quality of life, there are no standard measures and no authority to validate criteria of measurement. It is well known that 'professionals' tend, often for institutional reasons, to play down or undervalue factors which are not defined by their particular expertise. It is fortunate that, despite this tendency, there is a growing interest in broadening the evaluation of medical care, but there is still a need to clarify what is at issue in considerations of quality of life. This article examines the strengths and weaknesses of one approach of assessing quality of life, and sketches out the implications for anyone concerned to establish a framework within which both medical and non–medical objectives of care can be taken into account.

CRISTI, F R. Hegel And Roman Liberalism. *Hist Polit Thought* 5,281–294 Sum 84.

Hegel interprets the development of Roman attitudes and institutions by means of categories abstracted from modern liberal society. Liberalism in its classical formulation assumes the separation of state and civil society, a separation defined and protected by a constitution. In Hegel's interpretation, the Roman constitution eventually required the protection of an extra–constitutional force: Caesar's sovereign dictatorship. Thus, Roman liberalism ultimately entails authoritarianism. This serves, I submit, as an indictment of classical liberalism.

CROCE, Benedetto. *What Is Living And What Is Dead In The Philosophy Of Hegel?* NY Garland 1984.

CROCKER, Lester G. Interpreting The Enlightenment: A Political Approach. *J Hist Ideas* 46,211–230 Ap–Je 85.

My purpose is to interpret the interpretations of the Enlightenment. The approach to eighteenth–century political theory and ideas for reform taken by twentieth–century historians and philosophers is shown to be a clue to their "preconceptions" and conclusions. The basic disagreements among them are analyzed, and their strengths and weaknesses evaluated. Remarks on the notion of "Enlightenments" and the problem of interpreting it conclude the essay.

CROMBIE, Alistair. "The European Experience Of Nature" in *The Good Life And Its Pursuit*, Dougherty, Jude P (ed), 233–240. NY Paragon House 1984.

CROOKS, James. Irony As A Post–Romantic Possibility For Art: Kierkegaard's Reply To Hegel. *Eidos* 3,118–134 D 84.

CROSS, Charles B. Jonathan Bennett On 'Even If'. *Ling Phil* 8,353–358 Ag 85.

I show that giveP Jonathan Bennett's theory of 'evin if,' the following statement is logically true iff the principle of conditional excluded is valid: (SE) If Q and P wouldn't rule out Q, then Q even if P. Hence whatever intuitions support the validity of (SE) support the validity of conditional excluded middle, too. Finally I show that Bennett's objection to John Bigelow's theory of the conditional can be turned into a (perhaps) more telling one, viz. That on Bigelow's theory 'if P then Q' and 'if P then Q then R' do not jointly entail 'if P then R'.

CROWE, F E. A Note On The Prefaces Of Insight. *Method* 3,1–2 Mr 85.

Bernard Lonergan's *Insight* has a seven page Preface explaining what the book is about. But this is not the original Preface; it is a new one Lonergan wrote at the suggestion of his publisher. My note gives the history of the two Prefaces, and introduces the original one, now published for the first time.

CROWTHER, Paul. Fundamental Ontology And Transcendent Beauty: An Approach To Kant's Aesthetics. *Kantstudien* 76,55–71 1985.

In Part One of this paper, it is argued that Heidegger's attempt to link fundamental ontology with Kant's doctrines of transcendental imagination and free beauty, is unsuccessful. In Part Two, following a clue from Schiller, a gap in Kant's aesthetics is traced which points in the direction of a 'transcendent beauty' grounded in fundamental ontology. In Part Three, it is argued that this sense of beauty is anticipated in Kant's notion of the 'aesthetic idea'.

CROWTHER, Paul. Kant And Greenberg's Varieties Of Aesthetic Formalism. *J Aes Art Crit* 42,442–445 Sum 84.

CRUZ, Juan C. El "Haber" Categorial En La Ontologia Clasica. *Rev Filosof (Mexico)* 17,505–530 S–D 84.

CRUZ, Juan Cruz. El "Haber" Categorial En La Ontologia Clasica (Continuacion). *Rev Filosof (Mexico)* 18,3–18 Ja–Ap 85.

CSEF, Herbert. Dieter Wyss Y La Medicina Antropológica. *Rev Filosof (Costa Rica)* 23,3–14 Je 85.

This text is a diachronical revision of Dieter Wyss' intellectual path as a contemporary psychiatrist, heterodox psychoanalist, philosopher and writer, beginning with his introduction of subjectivity in medical anthropology until his most recent work, 1982, devoted to the anthropological treatment of the patient.

CSIRMAZ, L and Paris, J B. A Property Of 2–Sorted Peano Models And Program Verification. *Z Math Log* 30,325–334 1984.

Using properties of non–standard models of arithmetic a completeness theorem is established for the Floyd–Hoare program verification method in the case where non–standard runs are allowed and the time is measured in a non–standard model of arithmetic.

CUA, A S. *Ethical Argumentation: A Study In Hsun Tzu's Moral Epistemology.* Honolulu Univ Of Hawaii Pr 1985.

This study is a philosophical reconstruction of a central aspect of the ethical theory of Hsun Tzu (fl. 298–238 B C). The principal aim is to offer a Confucian conception of ethical argumentation, consisting of style of performance, standards of competence, and phases of discourse. Attention is given especially to the problems of justification, the uses of ethical definitions, and diagnosis of erroneous beliefs as exemplified in different types of conceptual confusions.

CUA, A S. Ethical Uses Of The Past In Early Confucianism: The Case Of Hsün Tzu. *Phil East West* 35,133–156 Ap 85.

This paper characterizes four different uses of history in the *Works of Hsün Tzu*: the pedagogical, rhetorical, explanatory, and evaluative uses. It is argued that the use of historical personages and events in classical Confucian ethics can only be properly assessed in terms of these various uses, particularly in light of their roles in ethical argumentation. The paper is an application of some of the main themes in the writer's Ethical Argumentation: A Study in Hsün Tzu's *Moral Epistemology* (Honolulu: University of Hawaii Press, 1985).

CUA, Antonio S. Confucian Vision And Human Community. *J Chin Phil* 11,227–238 S 84.

This essay inquires into the Confucian conception of the harmony of man and nature and its implication for human community as a community of personal relationships. Special attention is given to the possibility of realizing of *jen* (humanity) as an ideal of extensive concern in terms of the guide of loyalty (*chung*) and other–regarding attitude (*shu*).

CUDA, Tom. Against Neural Chauvinism. *Phil Stud* 48,111–128 Jl 85.

I argue that the thesis that something could have the same functional organization as a human being, at a certain specified level, yet lack qualia or intentional states, is false, by arguing that the thesis entails a proposition that we have good inductive (as well as other grounds) for believing false. The conclusion is that one cannot criticize functionalism by thought experiments involving descriptions of creatures functionally equivalent to humans, yet supposedly lacking conscious states.

CULBERTSON, James T. *Consciousness: Natural And Artificial.* Roslyn Heights Libra 1982.

This book concerns the ontological status of sensations, percepts and mental images. It is a materialism but not a Central State Materialism. It claims that sensations, percepts, and mental images consist of sets of particles at the perceived and remembered objects. These sets appear red, blue, hard, soft, noisy, etc., because of the way they are interconnected by the world–lines extending from them into the brain—i.E., interconnected by stimuli and ensuing neuron impulse world–lines.

CULY, Christopher. The Complexity Of The Vocabulary Of Bambara. *Ling Phil* 8,345–352 Ag 85.

CUMMINS, Robert E. Rectification: An Ancient Solution To A Modern Problem. *J Thought* 19,86–89 Wint 84.

The article intended to demonstrate the value of the analysis of terms in weighing educational issues. It focuses on clarifying the concept, teaching. It analyzes three sets of items: behavior–action–conduct; work–labor–action; power–influence–authority. It concludes that teaching is conduct which relies primarily on influence to achieve its objectives. When influence fails, it must fall back on authority.

CUNNINGHAM, Frank. National Self–Determination: Peace Beyond Detente. *Dialec Hum* 11,459–462 Spr/Sum 84.

Contrary to those approaches that see nationalism as a threat to peace, this discussion note sketches an argument that secure peace and the self–determination of the world's nations are complementary goals. The argument links democracy and national self–determination, and defends a comment of Engels that a nation ('people') that oppresses another nation cannot itself be free.

CUNNINGHAM, G W. *Thought And Reality In Hegel's System.* NY Garland 1984.

CUNNINGHAM, Stanley B. The Courageous Villain: A Needless Paradox. *Mod Sch* 62,97–110 Ja 85.

Courage is generally regarded as a paradigm of moral excellence. Recently, however, the paradoxical suggestion has been made that courageous action can just as easily be allied to villainous intent and social abuse as it can to noble motives. This claim is shown to be unconvincing. An amendment is added to James D Wallace's definition of courage to help restore focus to the concept of fortitude as an indefectible virtue.

CUNNINGHAM, Suzanne. Perceptual Meaning And Husserl. *Phil Phenomenol Res* 45,553–566 Je 85.

This paper takes issue with two of the more recent interpretations of Husserl's notion of *noema* (roughly, 'meaning'). The first, by Dagfinn Follesdal, argues that the *noema* should be understood on analogy with Fregean *Sinn* as an abstract, timeless entity. The second, by Robert Solomon, argues that this is not adequate for *noemata*/ meanings in perception; they must be perceived. I argue against both that perceptual meaning is neither an abstract entity or a perceived entity. It is a highly particularized, time–bound entity uncovered only in reflection on perceptual experience.

CURRAN, Charles E and Mc Cormick, Richard A (ed). *The Magisterium And Morality.* Ramsey Paulist Pr 1982.

CURRAN, Charles E. *Critical Concerns In Moral Theology.* Notre Dame Notre Dame Univ Pr 1984.

CURRAN, Charles E. Just Taxation In The Roman Catholic Tradition. *J Relig Ethics* 13,113–133 Spr 85.

There is general agreement about the very broad outlines of a just tax structure in the Roman Catholic tradition, and these are sketched in part 1. There has been, however, no sustained, systematic, in–depth treatment of the question. Part II develops those aspects of the Roman Catholic ethical tradition which ground a just tax structure–the role of the state in working for the common good, distributive justice with its proportional equality, the universal destiny of the goods of creation to serve the needs of all. In addition, some attention is given to the historical practice of tithing, the state's obligation to care for the poor, and the moral obligation to pay just taxes. Part III proposes the goals which should govern a just tax structure in the Roman Catholic perspective and defends these goals against other possible interpretations.

CURRIE, Gregory (ed) and Musgrave, Alan (ed). *Popper And The Human Sciences.* Boston Nijhoff 1985.

CURRIE, Gregory. Frege's Metaphysical Argument. *Phil Quart* 34,329–342 Jl 84.

Frege's views on functions, concepts, and objects are explained in terms of his committment to a metaphysical theory that is traditional and non linguistic. The linguistic construal of Frege's theory fails to account for major features of the doctrine. The metaphysical theory was officially rejected by Frege when he was made the distinction between sense and reference, but continued to influence Frege's thought in unacknowledged ways. In this way certain passages where Frege appears to confuse sense and reference are explained.

CURRIE, Gregory. Individualism And Global Supervenience. *Brit J Phil Sci* 35,345–358 D 84.

A supervenience thesis is presented as containing the rational core of 'methodological individualism'. Local and global formulations are distinguished; a global formulation is chosen as appropriate for the case under consideration. It is shown that the thesis provides an individualistic solution to Tyler Burge's problem of the social determination of belief. It is argued that the thesis of supervenience is compatible with the ontological irreducibility of social objects.

CURRIE, Gregory. The Authentic And The Aesthetic. *Amer Phil Quart* 22,153–160 Ap 85.

Painting and literature are thought to differ in this: that full aesthetic appreciation of the literary work may be had by reading any correctly transcribed copy, but no copy of the painting, however it resembles the original, has the aesthetic value of the original. I argue, to the contrary, that transferability of aesthetic value from original to copy is possible in painting as in literature.

CURYLO– GONZALES, I. Concepts Of Man In The Náhuatlan Culture (in Polish). *Etyka* 21,131–150 1985.

CUSHING, James T. Is There Just One Possible World? *Stud Hist Phil Sci* 16,31–48 Mr 85.

As an example of what might be considered a candidate for an interesting and significant development in the methodology of recent science, I examine some of the epistemological and ontological commitments of the bootstrap conjecture of high energy theoretical physics. This conjecture holds that a well defined but infinite set of self–consistency conditions determines *uniquely* the entities of particles which can exist. That is, once we are given any partial information about the actually existing world, nothing else about that world is contingent or arbitrarily adjustable. This almost Leibnizian idea is implemented in S–matrix theory through a unitarity equation, which is a statement of conservation of probability. The S–matrix program is contrasted with quantum field theory which does have arbitrarily assignable quantities. In spite of the highly constrained structure of S–matrix theory, that theory makes far fewer ontological and epistemological assumptions than does quantum field theory.

CUTLAND, Nigel J. A Question Of Borel Hyperdeterminacy. *Z Math Log* 30,313–316 1984.

CUTTING, Patricia. "Levels Of Interpersonal Relationships" in *International Kierkegaard Commentary*, Perkins, Robert L (ed), 73–86. Macon Mercer Univ Pr 1984.

CVEK, Peter Paul. Locke's Theory Of Property: A Re–Examination. *Auslegung* 11,390–411 Fall 84.

The paper re–examines John Locke's theory of property in light of the recent interpretations presented by C B Macpherson, Leo Strauss, and especially James Tully. It is argued that Locke did propound a conception of property rights which remained rooted in the tradition of natural law theory, but that he modified this theory in order to accommodate a natural, not conventional, right in private property.

CZELAKOWSKI, Janusz. Filter Distributive Logics. *Stud Log* 43,353–378 1984.

The present paper is thought as a formal study of distributive closure systems which arise in the domain of sentential logics. Special stress is laid on the notion of a C–filter, playing the role analogous to that of a congruence in universal algebra. A sentential logic C is called filter distributive if the lattice of C–filters in every algebra similar to the language of C is distributive. Theorem IV.2 in Section IV gives a method of axiomatization of those filter distributive logics for which the class Matr(C) prime of C–prime matrices (models) is axiomatizable. In Section V, the attention is focused on axiomatic strengthenings of filter distributive logics. The theorems placed there may be regarded, to some extent, as the matrix counterparts of Baker's well–known theorem from universal algebra [9, section 62, Theorem 2].

CZEZOWSKI, Tadeusz. The Problem Of Induction. *Dialec Hum* 11,257–264 Spr/Sum 84.

CZUMA, Hans. Konkrete Utopie: Zukunft Als Bewusstsein Und Handlung. *Conceptus* 18,60–73 1984.

Ich stelle die Bewegung dar, die von einem utopischen Grundsatz (als Gedanken im Kopf) zum Plan der Handlung führt, die den Grundsatz verwirklichen soll. Der ausformulierte Handlungsplan, dessen Veröffentlichung der erste Akt der Handlung

ist, macht es möglich zu überprüfen, auf welche Weise der utopische Gedanke in ihm konkretisiert worden ist.

D' AGOSTINO, Fred. Ontology And Explanation In Historical Linguistics. *Phil Soc Sci* 15,147–166 Je 85.

How is language change to be explained? Three basic answers to this question are examined and their relevance to the question of the nature of social explanation examined. An account of language change which conforms to the structures of methodological individualism is found to be preferable on general methodological grounds to competing, non–individualistic accounts.

D' ANDRADE JR, Kendall. Bribery. *J Bus Ethics* 4,239–248 Ag 85.

Bribery has previously been viewed as a two–party transaction between the bribe–offerer and the bribe–taker. But there is a third party; the one who has a prior claim on the bribe–taker's loyalty. Breaking the first contract in response to the offer of a bribe is *alienation of agency* (a category that strictly includes bribes): alienation of agency is the additional immorality of bribery beyond any immorality of the act solicited by the bribe.

D' ANDRADE, Kendall. Commentary On Danley's "Toward A Theory Of Bribery". *Bus Prof Ethics J* 3,80–83 Fall 83.

D' ANGELO, Edward (ed). *Cuban And North American Marxism.* Atlantic Highlands Humanities Pr 1984.

The first organized encounter and dialogue between Cuban and North American Marxist philosophers. Cuban philosophers probe into dialectics of the Cuban revolution, José Martí's ideas, bourgeois ideology, science and value, the Cuban economy, education, culture, and socio–political life. The North American philosophers examine such diverse topics as the absence of socialism in the United States, ideological struggle and détente, education and revolutionary change, and Marxist ethics.

D' ESPAGNAT, Bernard. La Non–Séparabilité (Response À G Lochak). *Rev Metaph Morale* 89,381–388 Jl–S 84.

This article is a reply to some criticism published in the same review by G Lochak with respect to the content of one of the author's books, entitled *In Search of Reality* (English translation, Springer N. y. 1983). It is shown that these criticism are based on erroneous conceptions and that in fact they are unfounded.

DA COSTA, N C and Loparic, A. Paraconsistency, Paracompleteness, And Valuations. *Log Anal* 27,119–132 Je 84.

DA COSTA, Newton C A and Arruda, Ayda I. On The Relevant Systems *p*And *p** And Some Related Systems. *Stud Log* 43,33–50 1984.

In this paper we study the systems *P*and *P**(see Arruda and da Costa, *O paradoxo de Curry–Moh Shaw–Kwei,* Boletim da Sociedade Matemática de São Paulo 18 (1966)) and some related systems. In the last section, we prove that certain set theories having *P*and *P**as their underlying logics are non–trivial.

DACAL ALONSO, José Antonio. Los Valores Educativos. *Logos (Mexico)* 13,9–54 Ja–Ap 85.

El objectivo de este artículo es analizar los valores educativos y no los valores que transmite la educacion. Son distintos unos y otros por cuanto a su ser y realidad y eso lo intentado en el trabajo. Los veintisiete valores estudiados se describen y señalan las actitudes extremas o equivocadas. Los veintisiete valores estudiados se describen y se muestran los extremos en que se incurre en su realización práctica. Gracias a un principio de síntesis que explica la naturaleza de cado valor.

DAGOGNET, François. Le Problème De L'unité. *Rev Int Phil* 38,245–256 1984.

DAHL, Norman O. *Practical Reason, Aristotle, And Weakness Of The Will.* Minneapolis Univ Minnesota Pr 1984.

This book argues that, despite opinion to the contrary, Aristotle held a position on practical reason that provides an objective basis for ethics and satisfies an important criterion of adequacy—that it acknowledge genuine cases of weakness of the will. Included are a contrast of Aristotle's position on practical reason with that of David Hume, and a comparison of Aristotle's attempt to base ethics on practical reason with those of Kant, Nagel, and Rawls.

DAHLSTROM, Daniel O and Murray, John Patrick and others. "Introductory: James Collins—The Man, The Scholar, The Teacher" in *History Of Philosophy In Making*, Thro, Linus J (ed), 1–18. Washington Univ Pr Of America 1982.

DAHM, Helmut. "The Present State Of The Marxist–Leninist Core Belief In Revolution" in *Contemporary Marxism*, O' Rourke, James J (ed), 147–166. Boston Reidel 1984.

DAHN, Bernd I and Wolter, H. Ordered Fields With Several Exponential Functions. *Z Math Log* 30,341–348 1984.

DAL BROLLO, Alessandro. Giustizia Rivoluzionaria E Violenza. *Riv Int Filosof Diritto* 61,205–290 Ap–Je 84.

DALE, A J. INUS Conditions. *Analysis* 44,186–188 O 84.

DALE, A J. The Illogic Of Inconsistency. *Phil Stud* 46,417–425 N 84.

This is a critical discussion of the views expressed in Rercher's *The Logic of Inconsistency* regarding the net–theoretical paradoxes. I conclude that the views there elaborated are without theoretical justification and useless in practice.

DALFEN, Joachim. Gedanken Zur Lektüre Platonischer Dialoge. *Z Phil Forsch* 29,169–194 Ap–Je 75.

DALGARNO, Melvin T. The Contemporary Significance Of Bentham's Anarchical Fallacies: A Reply To William Twining. *Arch Rechts Soz* 61,357–368 1975.

Documents which seek to protect and provide for human freedoms and needs differ considerably. Some may be exposed to criticisms Bentham directs at the French Declaration while others are not. The arguments of this paper is that the contemporary draftsmen of such documents should attend to all the leading arguments of Bentham's *Anarchical Fallacies*. But it is argued that Bentham is not committed to opposing Bills of Rights, the European Convention, or even the U. n.

declaration of Human Rights conceived as a declaration of moral principles.

DALLMAYR, Fred R. *Polis And Praxis*. Cambridge MIT Pr 1985.

The study pursues a question raised earlier in *Twilight of Subjectivity* (1981), namely: What happens if the human "subject" is dislodged as linchpin of theoretical inquiriy, without being entirely abolished (as in versions of anti-humanism)? In a series of exploratory "exercises", the study probes the implications of this change for our understanding of political life, focusing on such topics as the relation between poitical *praxis* and "experience", an ontological construal of "freedom" (Heidegger), a non-intentional conception of "power" (Foucault), and the merits and disadvantages of Habermasian critical theory. In the end the study encourages a polyphonic political "conversation" transcending rationalist discourse as well as liberal-pragmatic pluralism.

DALLMAYR, Fred R. Response To Comments On His "Twilight Of Subjectivity". *Phil Soc Crit* 10,121–130 Fall 84.

The paper responds to a number of critical queries concerning *Twilight of Subjectivity*: especially Rasmussen's doubts regarding the status of Heidegger's *Mitsein* (co-being), regarding the linkage of Heidegger and Adorno, and regarding a certain retrospective or "nostalgic" quality of the book; also McCarthy's critical observations regarding a bent toward "counterenlightenment" (or non-rationalism), regarding a miscontrual of Habermas' perspective (especially his "dialect of subjectivity and intersubjectivity"), and regarding the status of the proposed "recollective ethics.

DALY, Robert (trans) and Von Balthasar, Hans Urs. *Origen; Spirit And Fire: A Thematic Anthology Of His Writings*. Washington Cath Univ Amer Pr 1984.

DALY, Robert J (ed). *Christian Biblical Ethics: From Biblical Revelation To Contemporary Christian Praxis: Method And Content*. NY Paulist Pr 1984.

DAMIAN, Cornel. Le Néo-Évolutionnisme Contemporain. *Phil Log* 28,130–136 Ap–Je 84.

DAMNJANOVIĆ, M. L'Historicité Des Valeurs. *Diotima* 12,81–85 1984.

In the beginning of the modern epoch the separation of "facts and values" (D Hume) as the effect of modern science destroyed the unity of the Christian Weltanschauung; in the end of that epoch, after the "break with tradition", after Marx and Nietzsche was formal in question the Christian-antic suprahistorical system of values. The philosophical axiologic problem became historicism of values faced with nihilistic consequences. The creation of new values is possible.

DANCY, Jonathan. On Coherence Theories Of Justification: Can An Empiricist Be A Coherentist? *Amer Phil Quart* 21,359–366 O 84.

A standard objection to a coherentist account of justification is that the only way to avoid an unwelcome profusion of coherent and so justified sets of beliefs is to require some kind of empirical grounding as a condition for justification. This paper considers this empiricist demand and asks what sorts of strategy are available to the coherentist to answer it. Contrasting the work of Quine and Bradley, it offers a way in which a pure Coherentism can ascribe a certain degree of 'antecedent security' to sensory beliefs, and hence give its own expression to the empiricist's asymmetric reliance upon empirical data.

DANCY, R M. The One, The Many, And The Forms: *Philebus* 15b1–8. *Ancient Phil* 4,160–193 Fall 84.

DANEK, Jaromir. La Structure (Intériorité) Et La Formation (extériorité) De La Vie (Dilthey). *Laval Theol Phil* 41,69–78 F 85.

La conception métaphysique "la plus totale" de la subjectivité et de son vécu est articulée en ces points thématiques: Critique de la Raison historique et critique historique de la Raison. —Structure comme indice d'immanence; structure de la vie et de l'histoire. —La concrétude catégoriale et l'immanence télélogique ouvrant sur l'histoire; l'horizon de l'historicité et la finitude.

DANGE, Sadashiv A. The Upanisads And The Ultimate Real One. *Ultim Real Mean* 7,252–269 D 84.

The work deals with the Upanisadic thinkers ideas about the Ultimate principle behind the Universe, and creation. There is apparently no unanimous opinion, some thinkers taking Water as the Ultimate, others ether, and yet others Fire. However, the sum total of the ideas is that all these elements are manifestations of the Self, which is the Ultimate. This is the Soul of the Universe, and it is viewed both at microcosmic as well as the macrocosmic level. This idea is symbolized by two birds on a tree, which is the cosmic tree. The goal of a human's life is to realize the oneness of the two aspects.

DANIEL, Stephen H. Descartes Onmyth And Ingenuity/Ingenium. *S J Phil* 23,157–170 Sum 85.

Many of Descartes' writings, especially his early ones, reveal his fascination with the philosophic function of dreams, myth, fable and poetic inspiration. Not only does Descartes repeatedly refer to his physical description of the world as a myth or fable; he also points out that philosophic ingenuity (ingenium), by its very nature, embodies the imaginative character of mythopoesis. For Descartes myth codifies the sensible and provides the activity of figuration of sensible instantiation upon which rational thought is based.

DANIEL, Stephen. *John Toland: His Methods, Manners And Mind*. Buffalo McGill-queen's 1984.

A sympathetic philosophical treatment of the complete works of John Toland (1670–1722), this study presents Toland as a champion of religious toleration and civil liberty. It brings together themes and controversies relating the mystification of religion, biography, biblical exegesis, polemical and esoteric methodologies, and philosophical materialism within pantheistic metaphysics. In addition, the work indicates Toland's connections with Locke, Swift, Bayle, Leibniz, Shaftesbury, Bruno, Milton, Harrington, Eugene of Savoy, Sophie Charlotte of Prussia, Freemasonry, Robert Harley, and English diplomatic and political history.

DANIELLE. "Prostitution" in *Freedom, Feminism, And The State*, Mc Elroy, Wendy (ed), 111–118. Cato Institute Washington 1982.

DANIELS, Norman. "Two Approaches To Theory Acceptance In Ethics" in *Morality, Reason And Truth*, Copp, David (ed), 120–140. Totowa Rowman & Allanheld 1984.

DANIELS, Norman. Fair Equality Of Opportunity And Decent Minimums: A Reply To Buchanan. *Phil Pub Affairs* 14,106–110 Wint 85.

The view that health care is of 'special' moral importance because of its effects on individual opportunity is defended against several criticisms made by Allan Buchanan. Specifically, because equal opportunity is defined relative to individual variation in talents and skills, health care is not required to be a 'leveling' principle, removing all differences among persons. Also, though the 'normal opportunity range' is defined in a socially relative way, there is no damaging circularity in the account because health care services in general affect the distribution of opportunity in a society, not the normal opportunity range.

DANIŞOR, Gheorghe. La Philosophie En Tant Qu'éthique. *Phil Log* 27,307–310 O–D 83.

DANNEBERG, Lutz and Muller, Hans-harald. On Justifying The Choice Of Interpretive Theories. *J Aes Art Crit* 43,7–16 Fall 84.

The essay examines E D Hirsch's 'ethical' argumentation in respect of the choice of theories of interpretation. Looking firstly at the premises of Hirsch's theory, we analyze the general structure of his argument. Subsequently, we discuss the individual stages in Hirsch's attempt to ground the choice of an interpretative theory, which we show to be inadequate. Finally we outline an alternative framework for grounding interpretive theories which are, however, weaker than the theory proposed by Hirsch.

DANNHAUSER, Werner J. Some Thoughts On Liberty, Equality, And Tocqueville's *democracy In America*. *Soc Phil Pol* 2,141–160 Autumn 84.

This article provides a summary of Tocqueville's views on the intertwined relationship and tension between equality and liberty. It seeks to apply Tocqueville's insights to the relation between equality and liberty in today's United States, exploring the affinity of both concepts to justice.

DANTO, Arthur C. Mind As Feeling, Form As Presence. *J Phil* 81,641–646 N 84.

DANZIGER, Kurt. The Methodological Imperative In Psychology. *Phil Soc Sci* 15,1–14 Mr 85.

It has come to be widely believed that the only valid way to test theoretical claims in Psychology is by the use of statistical inference. However, these techniques are not theory neutral instruments but involve very definite assumptions about the nature of the material to which they are applied. Only certain kinds of theoretical statements can be tested by means of statistical inference and classical psychological theory generally did not yield statements of this type. Statistical tests therefore do not test the original theory but some derivation from it which may owe little to the theory and everything to the methodology.

DAROS, William R. Exigencias Filosóficas Para Determinar "Lo Psicológico" En El Proceso De Aprendizaje. *Sapientia* 39,193–216 Jl–S 84.

DARÓS, William R. La Teoría Relacional De La Personalidad Según J Nuttin. *Sapientia* 40,49–66 Ja–Mr 85.

DAROWSKI, R. Le Cours Manuscrit De Logique De Marcin Smiglecki SJ. *Stud Phil Christ* 20,31–54 1984.

śmiglecki (1563–1618), célebre par sa "Logica" (Ingolstadt 1618, Oxford 1634, 1638, 1658), est aussi l'auteur d'un cours manuscrit de logique provenant de la période où il l'enseignait à Wilno. Le manuscrit constitue un çommentaire de l'Organon d'Aristote et présente les conceptions "du jeune Śmiglecki". Bien gu'Aristote soit son principal maître, on trouve dans la doctrine proposée par Śmiglecki des influences postérieures (St Thomas d'Aquin, Duns Scot, Suárez, F Tolet, G Vázquez). il admet p ex les modes (modi) de l'être (haecceitas, existentia etc).

DAROWSKI, Roman. Die Philosophische Tätigkeit Von Johannes Klein. *Gregorianum* 66,315–331 1985.

L'article constitue une brève monographie de Klein en tant que philosophie. Klein enseigna la philosophie au Collège des Jésuites a Poznan en Pologne de 1587 à 1590. Un cours manuscrit qui contient des commentaires aux 4 traités d'Aristote provient de la péridoe de son enseignement. La philosophie y contenue se base sur Aristote, mais dénote plusieures modifications postérieures. Klein affirme p ex qu'il y a 7 modes de prédication (praedicabilia): la transcendance et le mode intérieur (modus intrinsecus) étant le sixième et le septième mode. Il admet aussi des modes ontiques (modi entis).

DARROCH LOZOWSKI, Vivian. The Course And The Subtle: Contacting Direct Experience. *Human Stud* 8,77–84 1985.

This essay is a theoretical one which demonstrates language is dependent upon itself following and articulating what the physical body comes to know. It discusses the importance of expressing the subliminal in speech and of bringing the physical into consciousness. The thesis of the essay is that only as the body moves forward, so does the subtlety of our reflection.

DARUTY, Kathy and Ravizza, Kenneth. Paternalism And Soverignty In Athletics: Limits And Justifications Of The Coach's Exercise Of Authority Over The Adult Athlete. *J Phil Sport* 11,71–82 1984.

DAS GUPTA, Amitabha. An Ambiguity In The Paradigm: A Critique Of Cartesian Linguistics. *Phil Soc Sci* 14,351–366 S 84.

DASCAL, Marcelo. "Philosophical Analysis In Brazil" in *Philosophical Analysis In Latin America*, Gracia, Jorge J E and others (eds), 277–284. Boston Reidel 1984.

DASCAL, Marcelo. "Philosophy, Common Sense, And Science" in *Philosophical Analysis In Latin America*, Gracia, Jorge J E and others (eds), 285–312. Boston Reidel 1984.

DASGUPTA, Probal. An Essay Towards Cultural Autonomy. *Indian Phil Quart* 11,437–460 O–D 84.

In the tradition of the Indian style of schematization, this paper offers a schematic history of the philosophy of mathematical and scientific inquiry in terms of four stages that focus on Deduction, Induction, Conjecture, Programmes; suggests a parallel view of moral thought and links the fourth stage of this to modern Indian thought, especially Gandhi and Tagore; and speculates about a fifth, universalizing stage that will thematize Parity and Rhythm.

DAU, Paolo. Reference And Subordinating Descriptions. *S J Phil* 23,171–180 Sum 85.

DAUENHAUER, Bernard P. Heidegger's Contribution To Modern Political Thought. *S J Phil* 22,481–496 Wint 84.

DAUENHAUER, Bernard P. Hope And Its Ramifications For Politics. *Man World* 17,453–476 1984.

This paper first delineates a precise sense of the concept of hope. It then shows some of the ways in which hope is ingredient in and makes possible a non–tyrannical politics. Hope is incompatible with tyranny. As such, hope is a sufficient condition for non–tyrannical politics. Whether hope is also a necessary condition for such politics is not fully shown here, though evidence suggests that it is.

DAUER, Francis W. Epistemic Dependence. *Phil Topics* 12,53–58 Wint 81.

Difficulties in solving the Gettier problem are argued to be difficulties in analyzing the notion of one's knowledge or justification depending on something. The intractability of this epistemic dependence is compared to the intractability of semantic dependence (on observations as envisioned by positivists) and causal dependence (of one event on another), and it is suggested that the notion of dependence is in general intractable.

DAVEY, Nicholas. Habermas's Contribution To Hermeneutic Theory. *J Brit Soc Phenomenol* 16,109–131 My 85.

The article examines habermas's hermeneutic theory in the light of the major presuppositions of both traditional hermeneutic theory (Dilthey, Heidegger, Gadamer) and the critical school of hermeneutics (Adorno, Marcuse *et al*), and suggests that both schools lack a genuine historical reflexivity. The article closes with some speculations as to how an adequately 'reflexive' hermeneutic theory might be constructed.

DAVID, Zdenek V and Strassfeld, Robert. Bibliography Of Works In Philosophy Of History 1978–1982. *Hist Theor* 73,1–107 D 84.

DAVIDSON, Arnold I and Hornstein, Norbert. The Primary/Secondary Quality Distinction: Berkeley, Locke, And The Foundations Of Corpuscularian Science. *Dialogue (Canada)* 23,281–304 Je 84.

Some advocates of determinism defend the theory by reconciling it with common beliefs. Critics generally respond by looking for genuine friction. The opposing sides thus generate two sets of analyses of the key statements, one compatibilistic, the other not. These analytic disputes often end in stalemate, and two debates concerning the possibility of alternative actions are offered as illustrations. The general moral is that something in addition to pure analysis is needed to achieve real progress on determinism.

DAVIDSON, Clara Dixon. "Relations Between Parents And Children" in *Freedom, Feminism, And The State*, Mc Elroy, Wendy (ed), 179–188. Cato Institute Washington 1982.

DAVIDSON, Donald. *Inquiries Into Truth And Interpretation*. NY Oxford Univ Pr 1984.

This is a collection of 18 closely interrelated essays in which it is argued that formal theories of truth can serve as theories of meaning for natural languages, the theories being fitted to linguistic behavior by a process of radical interpretation. The constraints imposed by this method preclude making sense of conceptual relativism or of reference as usually understood. There are discussions of indirect discourse, metaphor, grammatical mood, and the role, if any, of convention in the understanding of speech.

DAVIDSON, Donald. A New Basis For Decision Theory. *Theor Decis* 18,87–98 Ja 85.

A new way of determining the subjective probabilities and desirabilities of options to an agent is described. The approach drops the usual assumption that the propositional contents of the options is known in advance to an interpreter or experimenter. The data are preferences that one sentence rather than another be true. Assuming that the agent rational in a defined sense, the method determines the subjective probability, desirability, and semantic interpretation of each sentence.

DAVIE, William E. Hume On Perceptions And Persons. *Hume Stud* 10,125–138 N 84.

Hume's account of personal identity, though defective by his own lights as an answer to the questions he frames, is not wildly unacceptable as many readers have supposed. Many have missed the fact that Hume can cite any bit of date which *we* could in the course of trying to ascertain the identity of a person. In particular, it is evident that facts about the body of a person are relevent to a determination of identity or "oneness". It is argued that such facts are fully available to the would–be Knower within Hume's perspective.

DAVIE, William. Hume On Morality, Action, And Character. *Hist Phil Quart* 2,337–348 Jl 85.

How could a philosopher endorse the Utilitarian picture of morality and nature, yet reject the idea that morality focuses essentially upon actions? Hume does so; in two separate passages he pronounces that moral appraisal must focus upon something other than actions. What is his reasoning on this matter? The author concludes: What is wonderful about Hume is that he can remain stubbornly faithful to the facts about moral life even where his own theory of knowledge gets in the way.

DAVIES, Iwan. Contracts To Bear Children. *J Med Ethics* 11,61–64 Je 85.

In the surrogate mother procreation can be divorced both from sex as well as any anticipation of child rearing. Often the risks of surrogate motherhood are presented in terms of alternative family structures and economic exploitation of women. Such possibilities must invite critical reflection in order for there to be legal reform. Of paramount importance is the child's best interest and until the full psychological

ramifications for the child, adoptive parents and natural mother are determined then the law's role must be ambivalent. In this impasse the minority view of the Warnock Report has much to commend itself.

DAVIES, Kim. The Conception Of Possible People. *Cogito* 2,53–60 S 84.

DAVIES, P C W. *The Accidental Universe*. Cambridge Cambridge Univ Pr 1982.

This non–specialist book examines the mysterious coincidences underlying the structure of the universe, and asks: Is our universe an accident? The apparently contrived nature of the laws of physics and of the organization of the cosmos is reviewed, and the so–called 'anthropic principle' is discussed which postulates that 'miraculous coincidences' are inevitable in any universe containing conscious observers.

DAVIS, Hester A. "Approaches To Ethical Problems By Archaeological Organizations" in *Ethics And Values In Archaeology*, Green, Ernestene L (ed), 13–21. NY Free Pr 1984.

DAVIS, Lawrence H. No Chain Store Paradox. *Theor Decis* 18,139–144 Mr 85.

Two simple facts show there is no "chain store paradox" as described by Reinhard Selten (*Theory and Decision* 9 (1978) , 127–159), and support my analysis of Prisoner's Dilemma. (1) What it is rational to do is relative to the information you have. (2) Assuming someone is rational and assumes you are rational is not the same as assuming he assumes that you assume he is rational.

DAVIS, Michael. Is The Death Penalty Irrevocable? *Soc Theor Pract* 10,143–156 Sum 84.

It is sometimes argued that we should abolish the death penalty (in part at least) because the death penalty is *irrevocable* in a way imprisonment is not. Human beings are (it is said) fallible and fallible beings should not use a penalty that in effect assumes their infallibility. This is the "argument from irrevocability." We may, I note, distinguish various senses of "irrevocabiity," for example, whatever distinctions we make, there is no nontrivial form of the argument that will distinguish the death penalty from imprisonment. The argument from irrevocability seems to be a dramatic but unsound formulation of a much more modest claim about how much we can do to correct error given one sentence rather than another, a claim about the relative advantages of various modes of compensation.

DAVIS, Stephen T. Loptson On Anselm And Davis. *Int J Phil Relig* 16,245–250 1984.

DAVIS, Stephen T. Naturalism And The Resurrection: A Reply To Habermas. *Faith Phil* 2,303–308 Jl 85.

DAVIS, Stephen. Speech Acts And Action Theory. *J Prag* 8,469–488 Ag 84.

There are two basic approaches to human action, the multiplier theory and the unifier theory. In this paper the author offers a revised version of The Multiplier Theory of A I Goldman and J Kim and then applies it to illocutionary and perlocutionary acts. The author's goal is to show on a given occasion when a speaker performs an utterance act, an illocutionary act and a perlocutionary act, how these acts are related.

DAVIS, William H. Instinctive Beliefs. *J Thought* 19,76–85 Wint 84.

All human cognitive operations appear to be molded and guided by the nature of the brain. Pierce refers to these biases as "instinctive beliefs". But if our cognitive activity is thus molded, our ability freely and objectively to seek truth seems seriously compromised.

DAVYDOV, Yuri. *Myth, Philosophy, Avant–Gardism*. Moscow Raduga 1983.

This recent translation is an analysis of the contemporary avant garde in Western literature and arts. Emphasized the philosophical influences on television, film, plays, and the novel.

DAWID, A P. Probability, Symmetry And Frequency. *Brit J Phil Sci* 36,107–128 Je 85.

This paper examines the meaning to be ascribed to the probability assignments and the parameters of a parametric statistical model. Traditional frequentist understandings are reviewed and rejected. It is argued that many statistical models, both simple and complex, can be interpreted as the concrete expressions of underlying symmetry judgements. The underlying mathematical theory, which extends de Finetti's theory of exchangeability, is described mainly by example.

DAWSON, John W. Cataloging The Gödel "Nachlass". *Phil Natur* 21,538–545 1984.

This article is the text of a lecture delivered at the Seventh International Congress of Logic, Methodology, and Philosophy of Science in Salzburg, Austria, July 1984. It surveys the contents of the papers of Kurt Gödel (now available to scholars at Princeton University Library) and discusses problems encountered in cataloguing them.

DAY, J P. The Indefeasibility Of Justice. *Cogito* 3,55–90 Mr 85.

DAY, Michael A. Adams On Theoretical Reduction. *Erkenntnis* 23,161–184 Ag 85.

The work of E W Adams on theoretical reduction is critically reviewed. Adams' account of reduction is found to be open to some serious criticisms. Certain modifications and extensions of his account are developed which makes it more acceptable. His account is also compared to other accounts of reduction. An argument is presented for the mutual reduction of rigid body mechanics to particle mechanics.

DAY, Stanley. "The Persecution Of Moses Harman" in *Freedom, Feminism, And The State*, Mc Elroy, Wendy (ed), 159–168. Cato Institute Washington 1982.

DE ALCANTARA, Luiz P and Carnielli, Walter A. Paraconsistent Algebras. *Stud Log* 43,79–88 1984.

The concept of da Costa algebra, which reflects most of the logical properties of C_n, as well as the concept of paraconsistent closure system, are introduced in this paper. We show that every de Costa algebra is isomorphic with a paraconsistent algebra of sets, and that the closure system of all filters of a da Costa algebra is paraconsistent. (edited)

DE BEER, C S. Philosophy And Culture (in Dutch). *S Afr J Phil* 4,85–92 Ag 85.

The relevance of the theme 'Philosophy and culture' stands to reason. Discussions on this theme takes place in three sections: the philosophical determination of the phenomenon of culture; persons and cultures in the contemporary world; and perspectives for the future. The determination of the nature of culture comprises a fundamental reflection on the underlying principles of a civilization and a way of life, which includes matters such as the origin and destination of culture, wisdom and culture, the multiplicity of cultural expressions, culture and nature, culture and tradition, culture and values, etc. While focusing on the dialectic between persons and cultures strong emphasis is laid on various perspectives concerning the relationship between the individual and society, especially in view of the impact of scientific universality on a world of various particular cultures. By this the existence of different cultures is endorsed, the possibility of dialogue as well as conflict between cultures is accepted, the problem of the interpretation of cultures is elicited, and the threat of suspicion owing to cultural imperialism is highlighted. (edited)

DE BOER, Th. De Filosofie Van Dooyeweerd. *Alg Ned Tijdschr Wijs* 76,247–261 O 84.

The article offers an analysis of the religious basic motives, the transcendental critique of philosophical thought, and the theory of modalities is the philosophy of Herman Dooyeweerd. It is argued that the transcendental critique is intrinsically antinomic and not radical insofar as the subject of the critique itself is not criticized. To avoid the difficulties of Dooyeweerd's thought it is necessary that the theory is abandoned that philosophical thinking has the structure of an antithetical theoretical relation.

DE BOER, Th. Van Wezensschouw Naar Hermeneuse. *Alg Ned Tijdschr Wijs* 77,36–59 Ja 85.

The article contains an interpretation and reinterpretation of Husserl's doctrine of intuition of essences. The first part refutes to the misunderstanding that it deals about universals and discusses the problems of ontological status and absolute evidence. In the second part it is argued that these problems can be solved when this doctrine is interpreted not as dealing with ideal objects but as a reflection of constitutive rules which open up domains of reality.

DE BUZON, Frederic. Note Sur Deux Antipathies Cartésiennes. *Rev Phil Fr* 175,27–28 Ja–Mr 85.

Comparaison de l'explication de deux faits surnaturels (*mirabiles antipathiae*) rapportés par Descates dans le *Compendium musicae* et les *Principes de la philosophie* (traduction francaise).

DE CAPITANI, Franco. Platone, Plotino, Porfirio E Sant'Agostino Sull'Immortalità Dell'Anima Intesa Come Vita. *Riv Filosof Neo–Scolas* 76,230–244 Ap–Je 84.

DE CARVALHO, Manoel J. In Search Of Being: Man In Conflict With The Spectre Of Nothingness. NY Philosophical Lib 1985.

DE CLEYRE, Voltairine. "Anarchism And American Traditions" in *Freedom, Feminism, And The State*, Mc Elroy, Wendy (ed), 35–48. Cato Institute Washington 1982.

DE CLEYRE, Voltairine. "The Economic Tendency Of Freethought" in *Freedom, Feminism, And The State*, Mc Elroy, Wendy (ed), 311–326. Cato Institute Washington 1982.

DE GANDOLFI, María C Donadío Maggi. Libertad–Necesidad En La *Quaestio Disputata De Malo, VI. Sapientia* 39,257–266 O–D 84.

DE GANDOLFI, Maria. Jucios Morales Y Verdad. *Sapientia* 40,97–108 Ap–Je 85.

DE GEORGE, Richard T. "The Critique Of Marxist Philosophy: 1956–81" in *Contemporary Marxism: Essays In Honor Of J M Bocheński*, O'Rourke, James J (ed), 9–20. Boston Reidel 1984.

DE GEORGE, Richard T. Commentary On "Advertising Professional Success Rates". *Bus Prof Ethics J* 3,47–52 Spr/Sum 84.

In professional advertising the major problem is not immoral advertising but lack of informative advertising. The issue is not how to keep hospitals from misusing success rates but how to get them to reveal such rates. Advertising that is in bad taste is not necessarily immoral, and provides those with better taste information about the advertiser. Expanding governmental regulation to police advertising in bad taste would produce more harm than good.

DE GOURMONT, Robert. *Les Estudes En Philosophie.* Paris Trimestre 1982.

This text is a manual for the study of philosophy for the use of examinations and for the grounding of the proper writing of a philosophical dissertation. The first part presents the rudiments of philosophical study techniques, including an exposition of classical philosophical problems. The second part involves rules of dissertation research and composition. The final section has rules of documentation and an index of important terms for consideration in the research. (staff)

DE GREEF, Jan. Scepticisme Et Raison. *Rev Phil Louvain* 82,365–384 Ag 84.

DE KIRCHNER, Beatriz Bossi. Notas Sobre La Fundamentación De La Ética Aristotélica. *Sapientia* 40,89–96 Ap–Je 85.

DE KONING, A J J (ed) and Jenner, F A (ed). *Phenomenology And Psychiatry.* London Academic Pr 1982.

This book attempts to present facets of the Phenomenological Movement to the English–speaking world of Psychiatry and Clinical Psychology. In particular it includes translations from French, German, Spanish, dutch, and Japanese writers, each influenced by Husserl, Heidegger, Jaspers, Merleau–Ponty and/or Sartre, and attempting to establish their relevance in Clinical Psychiatry.

DE LA GARZA, Teresa. Algunas Consideraciones Acerca De La Hermeneutica En El Psicoanalisis Y La Historia. *Rev Filosof (Mexico)* 18,149–164 Ja–Ap 85.

DE LA MONTE, Suzanne M and Hutchins, Grover M and Moore, G William. Compensatory Neoplasia: Chronic Erythrocytosis And Neuroblastic Tumors. *Theor Med* 5,279–292 O 84.

In a recent study, we observed a strong association between chronic hypoxic states and the occurrence of peripheral neuroblastic tumors, a relatively uncommon group of neural neoplasms. In this report we review those findings and formulate an hypothesis to explain why conditions which lead to chronic erythrocytosis may also cause compensatory neoplasia of neural tissues. (edited)

DE LUE, Steven M. Kant's Politics As An Expression Of The Need For His Aesthetics. *Polit Theory* 13,409–430 Ag 85.

Kant's ethics is useful to his politics if the lessons of the Third Critique are taken as the basis for his political theory. Central to the emergence of Kant's politics is the need for persons to learn to make judgments about issues in a manner that incorporated enlarged thinking. As persons maintain that demeanor necessary for enlarged thought, they manifest a tendency respectful of the moral law that politics should embody.

DE MAN, Paul. "Phenomenality And Materiality In Kant" in *Hermeneutics*, Shapiro, Gary (ed), 121–144. Amherst Univ Of Mass Pr 1984.

DE MICHELI, Alfredo. Ilustracion Y Ciencia En España Y En La Nueva España. *Logos (Mexico)* 8,47–56 My–Ag 85.

The purpose of this work is to outline the influence of Feijoo and his pupils on the enlightened scientific movement in Spain and New Spain during the second half of the XVIII century. In New Spain, among many distinguished figures, Doctor Bartolache was outstanding. Following the ideas of Boerhaave and Piquer, he established the basis of the Mexican scientific revolution of the XIX century. Bartolache's philosophical–scientific contribution supports the non–materialist character of Latin Enlightenment.

DE NEUFVILLE, Richard and Mc Cord, Mark R. Assessment Response Surface: Investigating Utility Dependence On Probability. *Theor Decis* 18,263–285 My 85.

We design a three–dimensional response surface to investigate utility dependence on probability. The surface portrays basic utility assessment data as a function of the necessary assessment parameters. We construct surfaces for a group of individuals exhibiting utility dependence on probability. Analysis indicates that the dependence is related to an overvaluing of certain outcomes. This indication is supported by theoretical arguments and a specially designed subsequent study.

DE NICOLA, Daniel R. Mending Wall: Response To David Ericson's "Emotion And Action In Cognitive Psychology". *Proc Phil Educ* 40,163–166 1984.

DE OLASO, Ezequiel. Leibniz Y El Escepticismo. *Rev Latin De Filosof* 10,197–230 N 84.

This is a study in the history of Modern Philosophy. Its purpose is twofold: I do not only seek to show that no history of Modern Skepticism would be correct or complete if Leibniz' reactions to the Skeptic challenge were not recognized, but also to affirm that an interest in Skepticism played a neglected and extremely important part in the development of Leibniz' own philosophy.

DE OLIVEIRA, Marcos Barbosa. The Problem Of Induction: A New Approach. *Brit J Phil Sci* 36,129–145 Je 85.

DE PAOLI, Alejandro. Lo Inteligible. *Sapientia* 39,217–230 Jl–S 84.

DE PAUL, Michael R. The Thesis Of The Second Antinomy. *Hist Phil Quart* 1,445–452 O 84.

My primary aim is to show invalid Kant's argument for the thesis of the second antinomy. I first explicate the thesis, i.e., that composite substances must be composed of simple substances, and then reconstruct the argument. This reconstruction is invalid if it is possible for there to be a certain type of simple substance which I precisely describe. I then describe a different, but related, type of simple substance which also provides a counterexample to the argument. But which one might more plausibly hold to exist than the first.

DE RIVERA, Javier S D. Michel Foucault Y La Microfisica Del Poder. *Rev Filosof (Mexico)* 18,109–126 Ja–Ap 85.

DE RUVO, Vincenzo. Raisonnement Juridique Et Raisonnement Pratique. *Arch Rechts Soz* 59,465–472 1973.

Philosophical research envisaging legal argumentation stresses the aspect of history which is the basis of theoretical inferences. Concerning the notion of Justice it is possible to extract a fundamental and eternal principle: Justice means the respect of reciprocity. Practical Reasoning can be considered in two ways which are diverse but not necessarily detachable: the first joining the exigencies of Justice, the second pointing to human life in its concrete development.

DE SAUSSURE, Thierry. Sentiments De Culpabilité Et Signification Du Péché: Approche Psychanalytique. *Rev Theol Phil* 116,201–216 1984.

A psycho–analytical study about the feeling of guiltiness on the psyche's different levels can lead to an interesting convergence of the unconscious roots of shame and guiltiness in their manifest and usual expressions and of the Judeo–christian concept of sin. This essay, in common language, is based on the Freudian psycho–analysis and on the reformed theology and is referred to Biblical texts (Luke 15 : 11–32 et Gen 2 : 25 á 3 : 13).

DE SOUSA, Ronald B. Teleology And The Great Shift. *J Phil* 81,647–653 N 84.

Seven considerations are listed, which motivate the philosophical search for Natural Kinds, including the hope of finding ontological categories that are independent of our interests. But no non–trivial set of purported natural kinds satisfies all these motivations at once, and no such categories are to be found. The device of referring to natural kinds by rigid designators does not help. Any kind can be termed 'natural' relative to some set of interests and epistemic priorities.

DE SOUSA, Ronald. "Arguments From Nature" in *Morality, Reason And Truth*, Copp, David (ed), 169–192. Totowa Rowman & Allanheld 1984.

Author Index with Abstracts 275 **Denton, David E**

DE SOUSA, Ronald. The Natural Shiftiness Of Natural Kinds. *Can J Phil* 14,561–580 D 84.

Seven features are generally held to be characteristic of Natural Kinds; most importantly, that they be ontological categories independent of our interests. But no natural kinds meeting these requirements are to be found. The claim that natural kinds are identified by science and referred to by rigid designators depends on a false analogy with individuals, virtually any kind, even artifacts, can be viewed as 'natural' relative to some set of interests and epistemic priorities.

DE SOVERAL, Eduardo Abranches. Notas Históricas E Filosóficas Sobre O Conhecimento. *Rev Port Filosof* 41,23–49 Ja–Mr 85.

DE STIER, María L Lukac. Compatibilidad Entre La Presciencia Divina Y La Libertad De Los Actos Humanos. *Sapientia* 39,267–276 O–D 84.

This paper intends to refute Anthony Kenny's objections to Thomas Aquinas' arguments proving the compatibility between God's foreknowledge and the freedom of human actions, which the former exposes in his paper "Divine foreknowledge and human freedom" published in *Aquinas: A Collection of Critical Essays*. The main critique consists in an erroneus interpretation of Aquinas' divine knowledge and his fundamental notion of future as "presentialiter" known. Besides, methodologically Kenny omits not only other very important Aquinas' texts but even the "corpus" of the article he analyzes.

DE STIER, Maria L. Algunos Aspectos De La Doctrina Tomista Del Entendimiento Posible. *Sapientia* 40,109–120 Ap–Je 85.

DE VITIS, Joseph L. Freud, Adler, And Women: Powers Of The "Weak" And "Strong". *Educ Theor* 35,151–160 Spr 85.

Adler's analysis is seen as contrasting with Freud's more internal, self–contained individualistic ideal. Adler's central concepts of "social interest" and "masculine protest" offer a larger external lens to focus women's lives in a wider context of social relationship. Adler's work thus serves to foreshadow recent pioneering studies by Carol Gilligan in psychological theory and women's development. Reacquaintance with his work may well extend the social parameters of such important contemporary research.

DE VOS, L. Systeem En Vrijheid In Hegels Logica. *Tijdschr Filosof* 46,498–503 S 84.

My critical review of G Jarczyk's *Système et Liberté dans la Logique de Hegel* points out the value of this commentary to some chapters of Hegel's *Wissenschaft der Logik*. Critical remarks are given about Jarczyk's interpretation of the relation between logic and system: the true meaning of the logic can be found only within the logical movement itself.

DE VRIJER, Roel. A Direct Proof Of The Finite Developments Theorem. *J Sym Log* 50,339–343 Je 85.

DE WACHTER, Frans. The Symbolism Of The Healthy Body: A Philosophical Analysis Of The Sportive Imagery Of Health. *J Phil Sport* 11,56–62 1984.

In our civilization bodily health is often represented by the athletic body. This imagery is not self–evident but reveals how health is conceived as a symbol of dynamic freedom and of social election. The final conclusion is that somatic culture tries to transcend the naturality of the body by the symbolic creation of a bodily world of freedom and differentiation. Of this world the athletic body is the perfect image.

DEARDEN, R F. *Theory And Practice In Education.* Boston Routledge & K Paul 1984.

This book is a collection of 13 papers in philosophy of education published in various journals during the period of 1974–82. The first three concern the relation of theory to practice in education and more particularly the changing conceptions of philosophy of education itself. Further articles concern education and politics, general education, controversial issues and the curriculum, the ethics of belief, autonomy and intellectual education, assessment of learning, behaviour modification and primary education.

DEARDEN, R F. Freedom And The Development Of Autonomy: A Reply To Victor Quinn. *J Phil Educ* 18,271–273 1984.

I disagree with Quinn's assumption that the main question concerning autonomy is whether freedom is a necessary condition of its development. I argue that its nature, value and direction of development are of prior importance. I also defend the contention, which Quinn has criticized, that freedom is not a necessary condition for the development of autonomy. However, the reasons for making that point relate to certain recent practical trends within education.

DEFOIS, Gérard. Se Défendre Aujourd'hui. *Etudes* 362,777–789 Je 85.

DEGROOT, Morris H. Changes In Utility As Information. *Theor Decis* 17,287–304 N 84.

The central topic of this paper is the measurement of the amount of information about some parameter θ that is present in a set of data X. Various methods that have been proposed for defining this information and the expected information to be gained from observing X are reviewed. Measures of information based on a decision maker's utility function and subjective probability distribution for θ are emphasized. A new concept of retrospective information is introduced.

DEHAYE, Pierre. For A Syncretism Of The Faculties Of The Mind: Art As A Means Of Knowledge. *Diogenes* 128,42–53 Wint 84.

Ce texte vise, d'une part, à la réhabilitation des facultés de la sensibilité, ainsi que des intuitions poétiques, amoureuses ou spirituelles, objectivement méprisées par rapport aux facultés purement rationnelles; d'autre part, à l'intégration d'une formation artistique dans toute éducation générale. Une analyse des différents niveaux de conscience montre qu'une connaissance approfondie des réalités—toute vraie culture—exige la mise jeu de l'ensemble des facultés de l'esprit.

DEIZT, Samuel M and Arrington, Robert L. Wittgenstein's Language–Games And The Call To Cognition. *Behaviorism* 12,1–14 Fall 84.

The transition toward cognitive issues in radical behaviorism is examined. The article shows how the conceptual analysis provided by Wittgenstein in his descriptions of language–games can assist behaviorists in evaluating that transition. Various philosophical theories of meaning are discussed as are four components of language–games. It is concluded that Wittgenstein's analysis allows behaviorists to use cognitive terms within a behavioristic system; with such a system, sharper distinctions among types of behavior are possible.

DEL CERRO, Fariñas. A Note On Mutual Belief Logic For Processing Definite Reference. *Commun Cog* 17,43–48 1984.

DEL– NEGRO, Walter V. Zur Diskussion Des Leib–Seele–Problems. *Z Phil Forsch* 29,425–429 Jl–S 75.

DELACRE, Georges. Los Niveles Temporales Según J T Fraser Y El Orden Subyacente Según D Bohm. *Rev Latin De Filosof* 11,99–113 Jl 85.

Both J T fraser and D Bohm search for a new view of the world capable of restoring the lost unity of physics in particular and science in general. Fraser's theory of time, briefly described in this paper, purports to do just that, and it is claimed that Bohm's ideas, although quite different are compatible with and in part support Fraser's principle of temporal levels as characteristic of reality's evolving nature. Such a view, however unorthodox it may seem at first, is a likely candidate to help overcome some current ontological difficulties.

DELANEY, C F. "Peirce And The Conditions Of Possibility Of Science" in *History Of Philosophy In Making*, Thro, Linus J (ed), 177–196. Washington Univ Pr Of America 1982.

DELEUW, Gilles. *Kant's Critical Philosophy.* Minneapolis Univ Minnesota Pr 1985.

DEMMER, Klaus. Gehirnverpflanzung—Ethische Implikationen. *Gregorianum* 65,695–717 1984.

The possibility of what has been called a brain transplant marks a new stage in the field of medical technology. This advance necessitates that the moral theologian come to a more appropriate understanding of traditional paradigms concerning the transplant issue. Since the crucial problem consists in the preservation of the recipient's personal identity, the basic elements of the hylomorphic theory with regard to the soul–body relationship have to be taken into account. Particular emphasis is to be put on the role of the brain in guaranteeing the conscious functioning of personal identity, for it is the role of memory to safeguard one's historical continuity. (edited)

DEMOPOULOS, William. The Rejection Of Truth–Conditional Semantics By Putnam And Dummett. *Phil Topics* 13,135–154 Spr 82.

The aim of this paper is the modest one of reviewing some of the recent work of Putnam and Dummett on realism. I have attempted to clarify what this work takes the issues surrounding realism to be, and I've tried to clarify and evaluate some of the arguments against various forms of realism each has given.

DEN UYL, Douglas J and Machan, Tibor R. "Gewirth And The Supportive State" in *Gewirth's Ethical Rationalism*, Regis Jr, Edward (ed), 167–179. Chicago Univ Of Chicago Pr 1984.

DEN UYL, Douglas J and Rasmussen, Douglas B. In Defense Of Natural End Ethics: A Rejoinder To O'Neil And Osterfeld. *J Liber Stud* 7,115–126 Spr 83.

DENECKE, Klaus. Algebraische Charakterisierungen Präprimaler Algebren. *Z Math Log* 30,455–464 1984.

DENGERINK, J D. Een Eigen Gewaad Voor Een Oud En Steeds Actueel Probleem: Maurice Blondel Over Natuur En Genade, Rede En Geloof. *Phil Reform* 50,21–46 1985.

DENNETT, Daniel C. *Elbow Room: The Varieties Of Free Will Worth Wanting.* Cambridge MIT Pr 1984.

The traditional philosophical problems of free will have been generated by a family of anxieties revealed in a host of standard thought experiments or intuition pumps. These have misled us, and once they are examined carefully, the problems of free will dissolve, and a detailed naturalism is developed, with accounts of rationality, control, selfhood, responsibility, possibility, and other central concepts.

DENNETT, Daniel C. I Could Not Have Done Otherwise—So What? *J Phil* 81,553–565 O 84.

The traditional assumption that one is responsible for an act only if one could have done otherwise is shown to be unsupported by argument, challenged by many familiar facts, unmotivated, and probably descended illegitimately from concerns that do matter, but that are entirely neutral with regard to determinism and indeterminism.

DENT, N J H. *The Moral Psychology Of The Virtues.* NY Cambridge Univ Pr 1984.

The components and structure of virtuous dispositions are examined. It is argued that there are three sources of activity in men, sense–desire, emotion, and rational desire, by the differing inter–relations and dependencies of which different virtues are constituted. In central cases, virtuous dispositions comprise not merely acting on desire, nor acting on the belief that something is right alone, but comprise a complex structure in which desire is informed and ordered by right practical reason and action expresses both the assent of the 'heart' and of the 'mind' to what is proposed.

DENTON, David E. Semiotics And Existential Concerns: Reforming An Old Versus. *Proc Phil Educ* 40,343–352 1984.

This is an exercise in hermeneutics, which is to say that I am interpreting a text, with 'text' being understood in the enlarged sense of Wilhelm Dilthey. In this case, the text is that longstanding debate in education between the toughminded and the tenderminded, to use the categories in William James. Others have called the two sides the scientific and the existential; others, the behaviorist and the humanist; and so on. However characterized, it is a debate which spreads through many areas of education, especially philosophy of education. In the language of Jacques Derrida, this exercise may be seen as a process of de–sedimentation. In any debate, the points of view become frozen or ossified at various moments. One may say that debates consist of nodules of sediment (which is not the language of Derrida!). To dissolve those nodules, one must bracket the immediate contexts of the debates, that is, the particular historical and logical contingencies of those moments, and locate the contours of the debate in the context of the larger issue. This process of de-sedimentation, of interpretation, requires not the introduction of new thinkers and concepts, but a fresh viewing of the old. (edited)

DERISI, Octavio N. Carácter Racional De La Libertad. *Sapientia* 40,9–12 Ja–Mr 85.

La libertad de la voluntad se funda en el juicio de indiferencia de la inteligencia frente a un determinado bien. La decisión libre es la conjunción de un acto de la voluntad como fuerza o causa eficiente y de un acto de inteligencia como causa formal: la elección es un acto de la voluntad informada por un juicio práctico de la inteligencia. El último fin el hombre, que es Dios o el Bien infinito está siempre presente en cualquier acto libre, ya que el bien apetecido por éste, es por participación de aquél.

DERISI, Octavio N. Del Ente Participado Al Ser Imparticipado. *Sapientia* 39,169–180 Jl–S 84.

DERISI, Octavio N. La Verdad En La Inteligencia Humana. *Sapientia* 40,83–88 Ap–Je 85.

DERISI, Octavio N. Valor Y Valor Moral. *Sapientia* 39,277–282 O–D 84.

DERKSEN, A A. Goede Redenen Om Iets Te Geloven. *Alg Ned Tijdschr Wijs* 77,79–108 Ap 85.

I argue that, though applicable, the frequency principle is acceptable for direct inference, and that, though acceptable, the chance principle is not applicable. The some chance principle turns out to be both acceptable and applicable.

DERKSEN, L D. Language And The Transformation Of Philosophy. *Phil Reform* 49,134–149 1984.

The question is discussed of how Gadamer's turn to language can provide an alternative to the dilemma of either totally accepting or rejecting the tradition of metaphysics. This thesis is illustrated by a discussion of three characteristics of language: as finite but directed to an infinity of meaning; as medium of interpretation and that in which truth is revealed; as contingent conversation and that in which the absolute reveals itself immediately.

DERRIDA, Jacques. Bonnes Volontés De Puissance (Une Réponse À Hans–Georg Gadamer). *Rev Int Phil* 38,341–343 1984.

DERRIDA, Jacques. The Principle Of Reason: The University In The Eyes Of Its Pupils. *Grad Fac Phil J* 10,5–45 Spr 84.

DES JARDINS, Joseph R and Mc Call, John J. A Defense Of Employee Rights. *J Bus Ethics* 4,367–376 O 85.

Recent business trends in business ethics along with growing attacks upon unions, suggest that employee rights will be a major social concern for business managers during the next decade. However, in most of the discussions of employee rights to date, the very meaning and legitimacy of such rights are often uncritically taken for granted. In this paper, we develop an account of employee rights and defend this conception against what we take to be the strongest in–principle objections to it.

DESANTI, Jean–Toussaint. Gaston Bachelard Ou "La Surveillance Intellectuelle De Soi". *Rev Int Phil* 38,272–286 1984.

DESMOND, William. "Hegel, Art, And History, Curtis Carter (commentator)" in *History And System*, Perkins, Robert (ed), 173–194. Albany SUNY Pr 1984.

DESMOND, William. Art, Philosophy And Concreteness In Hegel. *Owl Minerva* 16,131–146 Spr 85.

DESMOND, William. Hegel And The Problem Of Religious Representation. *Phil Stud (Ireland)* 30,9–22 Spr 84.

This explores the relations of reason and religious representation, particularly in the complex dialectical view of Hegel. It finds in Hegel's view an ambiguity or "doubleness" that can be exploited for onesidedly negative ends by Left Hegelians, despite Hegel's own affirmative intentions. It considers whether religion, through its own inherent resources, can deal with its own ambiguity, or whether ultimately only philosophical reason can do so, as Hegel seems to suggest.

DESTOUCHES, Jean–Louis. Tendances Nouvelles Dans L'expression Des Résultats De Mesure. *Rev Phil Fr* 174,173–181 Ap–Je 84.

DETMOLD, M J. *The Unity Of Law And Morality: A Refutation Of Legal Positivism*. London Routledge & K Paul 1984.

The book argues for the rejection of any significant distinction between legal and moral principles. Legal judgment is shown to entail a claim to its corresponding moral truth. A new theory of rules is put forward, and beyond rules a theory of moral/legal judgment is developed based upon particulars rather than universals. Moral judgment consists in a passionate response to the particulars of the world; and the twin problems for such a theory—moral freedom and objectivity—are faced and answered.

DEUTSCH, Eliot. The Ontological Power Of Speech. *J Chin Phil* 12,117–130 Je 85.

DEUTSCH, Harry. Fiction And Fabrication. *Phil Stud* 47,201–213 Mr 85.

DEUTSCH, Michael. Zur Benutzung Der Verkettung Als Basis Für Die Arithmetik. *Z Math Log* 21,145–158 1975.

DEUTSCHER, Max. *Subjecting And Objecting*. NY Blackwell 1985.

How is objectivity possible, though we can attain only a limited detachment? Objectivity is "a characteristic of one's approach or attitude, in which understanding is worked out in interchange with its objects". As a concept of 'tact', objectivity involves balances between liberality and commitment, confidence and doubt, and privacy and public dealing. Moral dimensions of objectivity, and the way perception interconnects with our forms of life, are considered. Relativism and idealism are rejected.

DEVALL, Bill and Sessions, George. The Development Of Nature Resources And The Integrity Of Nature. *Environ Ethics* 6,293–322 Wint 84.

During the twentieth century, John Muir's ideas of "righteous management" were eclipsed by Gifford Pinchot's anthropocentric scientific management ideas concerning the conversation and development of Nature as a human resource. Ecology as a subversive science, however, has now undercut the foundations of this resource conservation and development ideology. Using the philosophical principles of deep ecology, we explore a contemporary version of Muir's "righteous management" by developing the ideas of holistic management and ecosystem rehabilitation.

DEVEREAUX, Mary. More Than 'Meets The Eye'. *J Aes Art Crit* 43,159–170 Wint 84.

DEVITT, Michael. *Realism And Truth*. Princeton Princeton Univ Pr 1984.

The metaphysical issue of realism about the external world is commonly conflated with a semantic issue about truth. The work sharply distinguishes these issues and argues, from a naturalistic perspective, that the metaphysical one is prior. It argues for a thoroughgoing realism about the physical world and for a correspondence notion of truth, explained in terms of reference, in turn explained by a causal theory. The views of Kuhn, Davidson, Putnam, Dummett, and others, are criticized.

DEVITT, Michael. Thoughts And Their Ascription. *Midwest Stud Phil* 9,385–420 1984.

The theory of thoughts should be prior to the theory of their ascription. For the former the paper urges a functionalist theory including a "language of thought". For the latter it urges a theory involving two distinctions: transparent/opaque and designational/attributive. Both theories draw on a casual theory of reference. The theories are applied to various problems: the classification of thoughts; "de se" and identity thoughts and their ascription; Kripke's "puzzle". The paper rejects popular talk of propositions and *de dicto/dere*.

DEVOS, R. De Opheffing Van De Religie In Het Absolute Weten Volgens Hegels Phänomenologie Des Geistes. *Tijdschr Filosof* 46,585–610 D 84.

Throughout the *Phänomenologie des Geistes* we watch a gradual victory over the alienation that weighs over the object of consciousness. In the manifest religion consciousness becomes reconciled with the selfconsciousness: the life of community realizes the movement through which the divine being externalizes into individuals and through which the singularity negates itself in the generality. Still the religious reconciliation remains insufficient: it does not leave the form of representation. The absolute knowing unifies the content of religion and the form of selfconsciousness, which came about at the end of the section *der Geist*.

DEWAN, Lawrence. St Albert, Creation, And The Philosophers. *Laval Theol Phil* 40,295–308 O 84.

DEWAN, Lawrence. St Thomas And The Integration Of Knowledge Into Being. *Int Phil Quart* 24,383–394 D 84.

The paper aims to show the role of the distinction between substance and accident, in Saint Thomas' view of the relation between the knower and the act of knowing. It presents first the nature of the distinction between the act of being and the act of knowing. It secondly presents the productive causal relation between the knower and its knowing power. It concludes with a view of the immaterial nature of the knowing substance.

DEWHURST, Kenneth. John Locke (1632–1704), Physician And Philosopher. NY Garland 1984.

DEZHEN, Xue and Zhiming, Yuan. The Scientific Character Of Marxism And Its Viewpoint Of Value. *Chin Stud Phil* 16,65–82 Wint 84–85.

DI BERNARDO, Giuliano. Sense, Hermeneutic Interpretations, Action. *Nous* 18,479–504 S 84.

The Author's fundamental assumption is that sense equals conformity to a rule or a complex of rules. Every kind of rule has some relationship to the constitution of the topic of sense. The rules that constitute the sense of a context include both the constitutive rules and the prescriptive rules. The contexts of sense considered are limited to particular domain of reality: the physical context, the formal context, the ludic context, the practical–social context, etc. The Author suggests that it make sense to speak both of a context of sense referred to the whole totality (the hermeneutic context of reality), and of its interpretation. This hermenuetic context may be connected to actions and therefore to the fundamental axiom of action. This axiom is the fundamental law that explains the action of a given subject in a given situation.

DI GIOVANNI, George. "On The Impotence Of Spirit, Thomas Wartenberg (commentator)" in *History And System*, Perkins, Robert (ed), 195–218. Albany SUNY Pr 1984.

DI LORENZO, Raymond D. *Non Pie Quaerunt*: Rhetoric, Dialectic, And The Discovery Of The True In Augustine's *Confessions*. *Augustin Stud* 14,117–128 1983. .

DI LORENZO, Raymond D. Ciceronianism And Augustine's Conception Of Philosophy. *Augustin Stud* 13,171–176 1982.

DI MIERI, Fernando. Il "De Institutione Arithmetica" Di Severino Boezio. *Sapienza* 37,179–202 Ap–Je 84.

The main objective of this work is to show the possible symbolical valencies that, perhaps beyond the intentions of Boethius himself, are present in the "De Institutione Arithmetica" and justify the religious–mystical interpretation of Middle Age and Renaissance. It considers arithmetic in the frame of the general organization of knowledge in the classical tradition and Boethius, then analyzes the boethian text; lastly delineates the symbological characteristics of some particularly significative numbers.

DIAMOND, Cora. What Does A Concept Script Do? *Phil Quart* 34,343–368 Jl 84.

In Wittgenstein, the development of a concept script is connected with the disappearance of philosophy as it has been practiced. This paper examines the question whether there are any such links implicit in Frege's thought. I also describe a kind of realist view to which Frege's thought is opposed.

DICKER, Georges. "An Idea Can Be Like Nothing But An Idea". *Hist Phil Quart* 2,39–52 Ja 85.

After criticizing Pitcher's critique and Phillip Cummins' explication of Berkeley's "Likeness Principle" that "an idea can be like nothing but an idea," I give my own reconstruction and assessment of Berkeley's case for this Principle. The Principle is shown to follow from plausible premisses about resemblance, conjoined with Berkeley's doctrine that we perceive only ideas. i argue that by distinguishing clearly between perception and immediate perception, a representationalist can undercut the argumentative support that the Principle requires.

DICKIE, George T. Evaluating Art. *Brit J Aes* 25,3–16 Wint 85.

DICKIE, George. Stolnitz's Attitude: Taste And Perception. *J Aes Art Crit* 43,195–204 Wint 84.

DIEFENBECK, James A. *A Celebration Of Subjective Thought.* Carbondale S Illinois Univ Pr 1984.

DIETRICK, Ellen Battelle. "Cardinal Gibbons's Ignorance" in *Freedom, Feminism, And The State*, Mc Elroy, Wendy (ed), 305–310. Cato Institute Washington 1982.

DIETZ, Mary G. Citizenship With A Feminist Face: The Problem With Maternal Thinking. *Polit Theory* 13,19–38 F 85.

DIETZSCH, St. Schelling Alas Verfasser Der Nachtwachen Des Bonaventura: Eine Replik Eine Replik. *Deut Z Phil* 33,352–355 1985.

DIFFEY, T J. Art And Goodness: Collingwood's Aesthetics And Moore's Ethics Compared. *Brit J Aes* 25,185–198 Spr 85.

Comparing Moore's *Principia Ethica* with Collingwood's *Principles of Art* seems pointless. Moore, a realist, writes on ethics and Collingwood, an anti–realist, on aesthetics. However, the principle of identity is important in both books: in Moore's it distinguishes goodness from things confused with goodness such as pleasure; in Collingwood's it distinguishes art from, say, representation. The comparison reveals interesting differences in their theories of meaning. Moore's non–natural properties offer a model of some contemporary art.

DILLER, Ann. The Virtues Of *Philia* And Justice: Who Learns These In Our Society. *Proc Phil Educ* 40,75–78 1984.

DILLER, J and Troelstra, A S. Realizability And Intuitionistic Logic. *Synthese* 60,253–282 Ag 84.

DILMAN, Ilham (ed). *Philosophy And Life: Essays On John Wisdom.* Boston Nijhoff 1984.

DILMAN, Ilham. *Freud And The Mind.* NY Blackwell 1984.

The book discusses the concept of the unconscious, the prominence which Freud gave to fantasy and the emotions of human life, and the way he conceived of the relation between reason and the emotions. It then considers Freud's ideas on repression and the division of the personality into id, ego, and super–ego, his conception of self–knowledge, and his views on free will and determinism.

DILMAN, Ilham. *Quine On Ontology, Necessity, And Experience: A Philosophical Critique.* NY SUNY Pr 1984.

The book argues, first, that Quine's whole notion of ontology is riddled with confusion and tries to single out for discussion some of these confusions. It argues, secondly, that Quine's rejection of the distinction between necessary and contingent truths is unwarranted, and that the notion of analyticity in terms of which he conducts this discussion is a red herring. It argues, thirdly, that the notion of experience and the subordinate notion of the senses in terms of which Quine discusses the confirmation of propositions and expands his brand of empiricism are crude.

DILMAN, Ilham. "John Wisdom And The Breadth Of Philosophy" in *Philosophy And Life: Essays On John Wisdom*, Dilman, Ilham (ed), 1–26. Boston Nijhoff 1984.

DILMAN, Ilham. "Our Knowledge Of Other People" in *Philosophy And Life: Essays On John Wisdom*, Dilman, Ilham (ed), 145–178. Boston Nijhoff 1984.

DILMAN, Ilham. "Philosophy And Scepticism" in *Philosophy And Life: Essays On John Wisdom*, Dilman, Ilham (ed), 317–345. Boston Nijhoff 1984.

DILWORTH, Craig. On Theoretical Terms. *Erkenntnis* 21,405–422 N 84.

The nature of theoretical terms is clarified in an overview which includes both the theoretical and empirical aspects of science. Where the empirical aspect is seen to include experimental laws and be based on measurement, the theoretical aspect consists of idealized models capable of explaining the relations posited by the experimental laws. In this way, theoretical terms may be understood as terms used in referring to the entities depicted as existing in such idealized models.

DINAN, Stephen A. The Particularity Of Moral Knowledge. *Proc Cath Phil Ass* 58,65–72 1984.

This paper considers the relationship between universal and particular moral knowledge. It argues that particular moral judgments are neither derived from, nor adequately summarized in universal moral standards, but require creative moral insight into particular situations. This insight provides normative content to universal moral standard, which have no meaning or normative content apart from particular situations. Moral universals are thus analogous universals, whose meaning changes in different situations as they morally shed light on those situations.

DIORIO, Joseph A. Contraception, Copulation Domination, And The Theoretical Barrenness Of Sex Education Literature. *Educ Theor* 35,239–254 Sum 85.

The paper argues against an instrumentalist approach to sex education, and shows that such approaches place unwarranted epistemological constraints on freedom of inquiry within any educational field. The conception of sexuality prevailing within sex education literature is focused on heterosexual copulatory intercourse because of the interest of sex educators in the problem of unwanted pregnancies. This leads sex education programs to overlook regarding controversies regarding the nature of sexuality.

DIÓSZEGI, István. Internal Problems Of The "State–Nation" Conception In The Last Third Of The 19th Century And At The Turn Of The Century (in Hungarian). *Magyar Filozof Szemle* 1–2,1–25 1984.

Der Autor untersucht die innere Problematik der Staatsnation–Konzeption im Zusammenhang mit der Mationalitätenpolitik. Im ersten Teil des Aufsatzes setzt er sich mit den verschiedenen konkreten Ausserungen der Nationalitätenpolitik auseinander. Im zweiten Teil des Aufsatzes berührt der Autor publizistische und historiographische Beziehungen der Nationalitätenpolitik, und stellt fest, dass für dies im allgemeinen die undifferenzierte Anschauung charakteristisch war. Der letzte Teil des Aufsatzes legt zuerst die Motive der Nationalitätenpolitik dar. (edited)

DIPERT, Randall R. "Reflections On The Rights Of Future Generations" in *Rights And Regulation*, Machan, Tibor (ed), 203–216. Cambridge Ballinger 1983.

DISCO, Cornelis. Alvin Gouldner: Vervreemding, Reflexiviteit, En De Naderende Crisis Van De Sociologie. *Kennis Methode* 8,328–347 1984.

Alvin Gouldner's identification of a crisis in sociology is seen as moral indignation giving rise to "ethical marginality" and consequent reflexivity. A new crisis is identified, using Dutch sociology as an example, which arises out of funding cutbacks and state–bureaucratization of the field. These two trends are seen to produce a generation of "structurally marginal" sociologists who are identified as the bearers of a new radical reflexivity and as the source of sociological innovation.

DJAÏT, Hichem. A Quest For The Values In Islam. *Diogenes* 124,90–106 Wint 83.

DJANKOV, Bogdan. Polysemantic Structure And Semantic Closedness Of Natural Languages. *Bull Sect Log* 13,188–198 O 84.

DÖBLER, Martin and others. Ideological Problems Of The Development Of Needs (in German). *Deut Z Phil* 22,5–22 1974.

Der wissenschaftlich begründete Nachweis der Abhängigkeit der Berdürfnisse von der Entwicklung der Produkition bildet die Grundlage für die Abestimmung des gesellschaftlichen Charakters der Bedürnfnisse im historischen Materialismus. Das Bedürfnis verkörpert die Einheit von Objektivem und Subjektivem. zugleich ist es Einheit von Aktivem und Passivem in der Tätigkeit des Subjekts. Die Bedürfnisse richten sich auf die Schaffung und Aneignung von materiellen und geistigen Gütern oder Werten, auf die Entwicklung von gesellschaftlichen Verhältnissen und auf die Herausbildung von Fähigkeiten.

DOBÓ, Andor. Problems Surrounding The Solution Of Mathematical Problems (in Hungarian). *Magyar Filozof Szemle* 5,832–841 1983.

DOBROSIELSKI, Marian. Science—Ideology—Weltanschauung. *Dialec Hum* 10,45–56 Sum 83.

The author attempts to explain the manifold interrelations between science, ideology, and a comprehensive world–outlook from a modern Marxist point of view. He tries to define the above mentioned notions, to show that they are interdependent and mutually complementary, but emphasizes their distinctness. He considers the identification by some Marxist's of ideology as science erroneous and leading to socially dammaging consequences. Weltanschauung is for him a creative synthesis of science and ideology which again cannot be reduced to science alone.

DOLLING, Evelyn. "Die Bedeutung Von Naturkonzeptionen In Und Für Die Kulturwissenschaften". *Deut Z Phil* 33,454–457 1985.

DOMBROWSKI, Daniel A. Kazantzakis' Dipolar Theism. *Sophia (Australia)* 24,4–17 Jl 85.

Everyone who has studied Kazantzakis' thought on God admits that his theism differs from the traditional conception of God in Christianity; but scholars often go too far in emphasizing the differences between Kazantzakis' theism and classical theism. My thesis is that progress can be made by looking at him as a dipolar theist: the text I examine is *The Saviours of God: Spiritual Exercises*.

DOMINICY, Marc and Mardaga, Pierre (ed). *La Naissance De La Grammaire Moderne.* La Province Mardaga 1984.

This book provides a formal reconstruction of the linguistic theory outlined by the Port–Royal logicians and grammarians. Evidence is adduced in favour of three theses: the logical and semiotic foundations of Port–Royal linguistics are to be found in Descartes's philosophy; the theory has a pragmatical component, whose importance was enhanced by controversies within the Jansenist movement; the Port–Royalist's views on the proposition and the complex term follow from a synthesis of the logico–semiotic and pragmatical components.

DOMOTOR, Zoltan. Probability, Kinematics, Conditionals, And Entropy Principles. *Synthese* 63,75–114 Ap 85.

In this paper the author argues (with the aid of some formal machinery) that *generalized* Bayesian conditionalization includes all (irreversible) probability kinematics, including kinematics arising from the maximum entropy and the minimum relative information principles. Gibbs kinematics, Jeffrey kinematics and measurement kinematics are used as illustrative examples.

DONAGAN, Alan. "Teleology And Consistency In Theories Of Morality As Natural Law" in *The Georgetown Symposium On Ethics*, Porreco, Rocco (ed), 91–108. Lanham Univ Pr Of America 1984.

DONAGAN, Alan. Comments On Dan Brock And Terrence Reynolds. *Ethics* 95,874–886 Jl 85.

Brock's use of the Rachels–Tooley argument against the Kantian principle of respect for persons both begs the question and ignores the reason given for that principle; and Reynolds fails to take account of the implications of the distinction between material and formal lack of innocence.

DONAGAN, Alan. The Structure Of Kant's Metaphysics Of Morals. *Topoi* 4,61–72 Mr 85.

An analysis of the structure of Kant's metaphysics of morals based on the *Meaphysik der Sitten* itself, rather than the *Grundlegung*. The *Rechtslehre* is given more weight than is usual.

DONALDSON, Thomas. Multinational Decision–Making: Reconciling International Norms. *J Bus Ethics* 4,357–366 Ag 85.

How should highly–placed multinational managers, typically schooled in home country moral traditions, reconcile conflicts between those traditions and ones of the host country? When host country standards for pollution, discrimination, and salary schedules appear substandard from the prespective of the home country, should the manager take the high road and implement home country standards? Or does the high road imply a failure to respect cultural diversity and national integrity? In this paper, I construct and defend and ethical algorithm for multinational managers to use in reconciling such international normative conflicts.

DONALDSON, Thomas. Nuclear Deterrence And Self–Defense. *Ethics* 95,537–548 Ap 85.

The paper argues that a policy of nuclear deterrence fails to meet key enabling conditions upon a nation's exercise of its right to self–defense, especially when the right to national self–defense is inferred from the right to individual self–defense on the basis of what Michael Walzer calls the "domestic analogy." After showing how the concept of self–defense is needed to buttress consequential considerations in arguments defending nuclear deterrence, the paper proceeds to establish hypothetical analogues to national policies of nuclear deterrence on the level of individual moral life. When viewed in the light of common moral intuition, these analogues reveal that a national policy of nuclear deterrence cannot be justified by appeal to a right of individual self–defense.

DONDI, J. El Progreso Según Juan Bautista Vico. *Stromata* 40,341–361 Jl–D 84.

Does the Vico's history ages succession determine a gradual transformation in direction to a superior state of culture? Is there an internal principle that can justify the historical development? According to Vico, the history is a mind progress from the sensitive bestial form until pure reason. Having got to this state the rational mind can degenerate back and find itself as sense, for a "better" analogous history course.

DONNE, John. *Biathanatos*, Ernest W Sullivan (ed). Cranbury Univ Delaware Pr 1984.

DONNELL– KOTROZO, Carol. The Criminal And The Artist: Violence And Neurosis. *J Theor Crit Vis Arts* 1,63–73 1981.

DONNELLY, Jack. The Force Of Rights: Parent On 'Moral Specification'. *Phil Stud* 47,131–140 Ja 85.

How can we account for the fact that valid rights may fail to establish the proper course of action, all things considered? Parent, in criticizing Thomson's work on rights, argues that every right includes an implicit qualifier such as "in so far as in accord with the demands of justice". I argue, however, that instead of the range of rights being implicitly limited in this fashion, there are limits on the force of any right; rights are only one of many potentially relevant considerations. Therefore, rights may be overridden, by other rights, and in extreme cases even by certain non–rights demands.

DOODY, John A. Recent Reconstructions Of Political Philosophy. *Phil Today* 28,215–228 Fall 84.

DOOLEY, Patrick K. More's *Utopia* And The New World Utopias: Is The Good Life An Easy Life? *Thought* 60,31–48 Mr 85.

St Thomas More's *Utopia* is compared with the New World, "real" utopias which flourished in America between 1800 and 1900. The successes and failures of the widespread and respected American communitarian reform movement constitute an experimental test of "the best order of a commonwealth" depicted in *Utopia*. In particular, More's views on economic communism and work–leisure arrangements are measured against actual practices in the New World counterparts. I conclude that in the successful real utopias "the hard life (not an easy one) was the good life".

DOORE, Gary. Contradiction In The Will. *Kantstudien* 76,138–151 1985.

The purpose of this article is to show the practical application of Kant's categorical imperative in the moral decision–making process. Secondarily, it shows how a type of utilitarian principle is derivable from the categorical imperative, suggesting that Kant's ethical theory and utilitarianism are not necessarily incompatible.

DÖPP, Klemens. Filterkonvergenz In Der Nichtstandard–Analysis Bei Nichtelementaren Funktionen. *Z Math Log* 30,353–384 1984.

DOPPELT, Gerald. Finocchiaro On Rational Explanation. *Synthese* 62,455–458 Mr 85.

DORDAL, Peter and Baumgartner, James E. Adjoining Dominating Functions. *J Sym Log* 50,94–101 Mr 85.

If dominating functions in $^\omega\omega$ are adjoined repeatedly over a model of GCH via a finite–support c.c.C. Iteration, then in the resulting generic extension there are no long towers, every well–ordered unbounded family of increasing functions is a scale, and the splitting numbers s (and hence the distributivity number h) remains ω_1.

DORE, Clement. Reply To Professor Baker's "Religious Experience And The Possibility Of Divine Existence". *Int J Phil Relig* 16,251–256 1984.

DORE, Clement. Reply To Professor Brinton. *Relig Stud* 21,91–92 Mr 85.

DORE, Clement. The Possibility Of God. *Faith Phil* 1,303–315 Jl 84.

I argue that the logical possibility of God can be derived just from the concept of God. If I am right, then those modal arguments for God's *existence* which require the premise that God is a logically possible being can be buttressed by the envisaged argument.

DORFLES, Gillo. "Towards A Phenomenology Of Bad Taste" in *Continental Philosophy And The Arts*, Winters, Laurence E and others (ed), 109–122. Lanham Univ Pr Of America 1984.

DORMAN, Menahem. "Buber's Address "Herut" And Its Influence On The Jewish Youth Movement In Germany" in *Martin Buber*, Gordon, Haim (ed), 233–254. Beersheva Ktav 1984.

DORN, Georg J W. Poppers Zwei Definitionsvarianten Von 'Falsifizierbar': Eine Logische Notiz Zu Einer Klassischen Stelle Aus Der *Logik Der Forschung*. *Conceptus* 18,42–49 1984.

In paragraph 21 of his *Logic of Scientific Discovery*, Popper characterizes with the help of two seemingly synonymous definitions for the falsifiability of a theory as a logical relation between the theory itself and its basic statements. It is shown that his definitions lead to contradictions, and this result is applied to the problem of the falsifiability of contradictions, to the difference between falsifiable and empirical statements, and to the demarcation criterion.

DÖRR, Hartmut. Genealogisches Zum Cogito: Über Ein Motiv Des Cartesischen Denkens. *Conceptus* 18,104–115 1984.

The philosophy of Descartes is sustained by the claim to have realized an entirely new beginning in science, which claim is made primarily in reference to the 'Cogito'—the self–certainty of thinking—as a scientific foundation in absolute undubitableness. Descartes represents the discovery of the 'Cogito' as the result of an attempt to overcome his disappointment at the capacity of traditonal sciences. By reading this representation as a literary revision of his real disillusionment with his own previous work on a mathematically based method—caused by the condemnation of Galilei in 1633—it can be seen that Descartes' decisively new contribution to science is to define science as a special kind of human 'Praxis' which requires to be bound. The 'Cogito' does bind: it binds scientific conduct to reasonable thinking.

DÖRSCHEL, E and Braun, Hans–Joachim. Zur Dialektik Des Vergesellschaftungsprozesses In Der Sozialistischen Industrie Der DDR. *Deut Z Phil* 32,737–747 1984.

DORVAL– GUAY, Georgette. Document—Sur Le Sens Du Terme "Placet" Dans La Définition Thomiste Du Beau. *Laval Theol Phil* 41,443–447 O 85.

DOSEN, Kosta and Bozic, Milan. Models For Normal Intuitionistic Modal Logics. *Stud Log* 43,217–246 1984.

Kripke–style models with two accessibility relations, on intuitionistic and the other modal, are given for analogues of the modal system *K* based on Heyting's propositional logic. It is shown that these two relations can combine with each other in various ways. Soundness and completeness are proved for systems with only the necessity operator, or only the possibility operator, or both. Embeddings in modal systems with several modal operators, based on classical propositional logic, are also considered. This paper lays the ground for an investigation of intuitionistic analogues of systems stronger than *K*. A brief survey is given of the existing literature on intuitionistic modal logic.

DOSEN, Kosta. Sequent–Systems For Modal Logic. *J Sym Log* 50,149–168 Mr 85.

The purpose of this work is to present Gentzen–style of formulations of *S5* and *S4* based on sequents of higher levels. Sequents of level 1 are like ordinary sequents, sequents of level 2 have collections of sequents of level 1 on the left and right of the turnstile, etc. Rules for modal constants involve sequents of level 2, whereas rules for customary logical constants of first–order logic with identity involve only sequents of level 1. A restriction on *Thinning* on the right of level 2, which when applied to *Thinning* on the right of level 1 produces intuitionistic out of classical logic (without changing anything else), produces *S4* out of *S5* (without changing anything else). (edited)

DOSTAL, Robert. Beyond Being: Heidegger's Plato. *J Hist Phil* 23,71–98 Ja 85.

A consideration of Heidegger's critique of Plato in the context of Heidegger's early project of *Being and Time* and the subsequent development of his thought. He would escape the dilemma of the transcendental vs. The transcendental (idealism/realism) but he allows Plato to be confounded by this same dilemma. Heidegger accepts the critique of Platonism as "other–wordly" but makes fundamental to the development of his own early position the question of transcendence to which he often refers as the "epekeina." He allows Natorp to set the framework for the interpretation of Plato.

DOTTI, Jorge E. Lógica Formal, Lógica Trascendental Y Verdad En La Primera "Crítica". *Cuad Filosof* 19,121–134 Ja–D 83.

DOUBLE, Richard. Phenomenal Properties. *Phil Phenomenol Res* 45,383–392 Mr 85.

Many friends and foes of materialism believe that phenomenal properties (phenomenological properties, qualia, the subjective features of experience) pose severe difficulties for materialism and require materialists to deny the existence of such properties. This paper argues that this belief is unwarranted because: (1) there is no ontological ground between materialism and substance dualism, and (2) phenomenal properties provide no reasonable grounds for substance dualism. Materialists should acknowledge the existence of the phenomenal (something many do not), while anti–materialists cannot use the phenomenal character of the mental to discredit materialism.

DOUBLE, Richard. Searle's Answer To 'Hume's Problem'. *S J Phil* 22,435–438 Fall 84.

John Searle has recently claimed to have dissolved what Daniel Dennett calls 'Hume's problem'—the question whether the explanation of behavior by appeal to mental representations can be done without circularity or infinite regress. Searle argues that a careful analysis of the concept of an intentional state shows that mental representations do not require intentional "homunculi" to explain how intentional states have their contents, and, hence Dennett's worry is groundless. I argue that Searle's conceptual analysis of intentional states, even if correct, provides no clue of an answer to the worry underlying Hume's problem.

DOUDERA, A Edward (ed) and Cranford, Ronald E (ed). *Institutional Ethics Committees And Health Care Decision Making*. Ann Arbor Health Admin Pr 1984.

DOUDERA, A Edward (ed) and Shaw, Margery W (ed). *Defining Human Life: Medical, Legal, And Ethical Implications*. Ann Arbor Aupha Pr 1983.

DOUGHERTY, Charles and Allegretti, Joseph. Teaching Ethics In Law School. *Teach Phil* 8,13–26 Ja 85.

The challenge of teaching ethics in law school is described, citing: a training which discourages consideration of ethical dimensions of issues when thinking "like a lawyer," the existence of a professional responsibility code which many take to be exhaustive of the moral responsibilities of attorneys, and the peculiar character of the Angl0–American adversary system of litigation. An ethics course addressing these difficulties is then described. The course is taught by a philosopher and a lawyer, is problem–oriented and discussion–based.

DOUGHERTY, Jude P (ed). *The Good Life And Its Pursuit.* NY Paragon House 1984.

A collection of essays by a group of prominent scholars who explore the metaphysical grounding of moral philosophy, and the methods by which it proceeds to rationally supported conclusions. The volume includes essays by Irwin Lieb, Ivor LeClerc, Ninian Smart, John Findlay, and Erich Mascall. The editor's introductory essay gives its title to the book.

DOUGHTON, James E. Commentary On "Professional Advertising: Price Fixing And Professional Dignity Versus The Public's Right To A Free Market". *Bus Prof Ethics J* 3,109–110 Spr/Sum 84.

DOULE, John P. "The Suareziann Proof Of God's Existence" in *History Of Philosophy In Making*, Thro, Linus J (ed), 105–118. Washington Univ Pr Of America 1982.

DOWNEY, James Patrick. Are Traditional Theists Pantheists? *S J Phil* 23,127–136 Spr 85.

Robert Oakes (*APQ*, volume 20, number 1, January 1983) believes the mind–experience relationship is a paradigm of the God–world conservation relationship of traditional theism. He concludes it is reasonable that traditionalists believe it follows that we are ontological aspects of God. I reply that Oakes fails to adequately characterize the conservation relationship, does not prove the mind–experience relationship is such a paradigm (I suggest it is not), nor proves it reasonable that traditionalists believe experiences are aspects of minds.

DOWNEY, R G. A Note On Decompositions Of Recursively Enumberable Subspaces. *Z Math Log* 30,465–470 1984.

It is proved that every nondecidable recursively enumberable subspace can be split into the direct sum of a pair of recursively enumberable subspaces no recursively enumberable basis of either being fully extendible. The argument mixes with various others in the literature. For example, we may ensure that each subspace is nowhere simple, or, similarly, mix various degree c0ntrolling arguments.

DOWNEY, R G and Ash, C J. Decidable Subspaces And Recursively Enumerable Subspaces. *J Sym Log* 49,1137–1145 D 84.

DOWNEY, R G and Hird, G R. Automorphisms Of Supermaximal Subspaces. *J Sym Log* 50,1–9 Mr 85.

In this paper several extensions of the notion of supermaximality are introduced. The key on is that an r e V is strongly supermaximal if dim (V_∞ mod V) = ∞ are given any r e independent set I with I ∩ V = q, dim ((V ∪ I) *mod V) is finite. Every strongly supermaximal subspace is nonrecursive and supermaximal. There exist supermaximal subspaces with the same "degree structure" one which is strongly supermaximal, one which is not. In view of Guichard's work, this means that such spaces are not in the same orbit in the group of automorphisms of L(V_∞). Several extensions are discussed.

DOWNEY, R G and Remmel, J B. The Universal Complementation Property. *J Sym Log* 49,1125–1136 D 84.

There are very few lattice theoretic restrictions on the r e complement of a fully co–r e subspace. This paper analyzes the degree–theoretic ones. Thus a fully co–r e subspace C has the universal complementation property if C has r e complements in each degree below that of C. For example, it is shown that the degrees containing fully co–r e subspaces without the universal complementation property are dense. Some results are obtained connecting splittings and complementation.

DOWNEY, Rod. Bases Of Supermaximal Subspaces And Steinitz Systems. *J Sym Log* 49,1146–1159 D 84.

The paper begins an analysis of the question of whether any pair of supermaximal subspaces are elementarily equivalent. The paper concentrates on the question: let B be an r e basis of a supermaximal subspace. If we remove an element from B does the result generate a supermaximal subspace? This leads naturally to the concepts of superfluous and essential bases. The techniques have found applications in other settings.

DOWNEY, Rod. Some Remarks On A Theorem Of Iraj Kalantari Concerning Convexity And Recursion Theory. *Z Math Log* 30,295–302 1984.

Kalantari investigated the effective content of Stone's separation theorem. The paper extends Kalantari's results in both lattice theoretic and degree theoretic ways, by further analyzing the structure of the lattice of r.E. Convex subspaces.

DOWNIE, R S. Commentary: Compulsory Health And Safety In A Free Society. *J Med Ethics* 10,189–190 D 84.

Within liberalism the only justification for compulsion in health care is that one's activities are harming others, although granted the way diseases are transmitted J S Mill's 'harm principle' can justify extensive compulsion. Against this there is the issue of the procedures for enforcing compulsion. Collective socialism offers a different justification since it draws a different distinction between self and others. The Welfare State is a theoretically inconsistent mixture of individualism and socialism.

DOWNIE, R S. The Hypothetical Imperative. *Mind* 93,481–490 O 84.

There is a well–established distinction between hypothetical or non–moral uses of 'ought' and categorical or moral uses. The central thesis of this paper is that this distinction must be rejected in its usual form, for insofar as a so–called hypothetical imperative expresses an 'ought' of practical agency it is really a special type of categorical or moral imperative. Various non–moral uses of 'ought' are discussed and

the specifically hypothetical imperative is distinguished from them. It is then argued that this use of 'ought' signals the moral requirement of practical consistency, which is itself a form of the moral 'ought' of rationality. Various factors which lead us to overlook the moral force of the hypothetical 'ought' are discussed.

DOWNIE, R S. Three Accounts Of Promising. *Phil Quart* 35,259–271 Jl 85.

DOWTY, David R. On Recent Analyses Of The Semantics Of Control. *Ling Phil* 8,291–332 Ag 85.

DOYLE, Anthony. Is Knowledge Information–Produced Belief? *S J Phil* 23,33–46 Spr 85.

In this paper, I begin by placing Fred Dretske's *Knowledge and the Flow of Information* in its naturalistic, post–Gettier context. Next, I review the notion of information as Dretske appropriates it from communication theory. The main part of my paper consists of a defense of Dretske against counterexamples offered by C Ginet, K Lehrer and S Cohen, G Harman, and myself. I close with some remarks on the belief–causing efficacy of information.

DOYLE, Eric (trans & Ed). *The Disciple And The Master.* Chicago Franciscan Her Pr 1983.

DOYLE, John P. Prolegomena To A Study Of Extrinsic Denomination In The Work Of Francis Suarez, S J. *Vivarium* 22,121–146 N 84.

At times, extrinsic denomination for Suarez seems close to, if not synonymous with, a mere naming from the outside. But at other times, it is regarded as a feature of things themselves. In this article, there is some description and some examples of extrinsic denomination according to Suarez. Following this, are some of his reasons for and sources of such denomination. Special attention is paid to his use of extrinsic denomination in connection with the properties and categories of being. Finally, there are listed conventions and other items observed in Suarez's use of extrinsic denomination.

DRAAISMA, Douwe. De Angst Van De Homunculus Voor Hetscheermes. *Kennis Methode* 8,225–239 1984.

In psychology the homunculus duplicates the problem, instead of solving it, therefore homuncular theories lack economy. The author discusses some instances of (alleged) regressions. Next he outlines Dennett's 'homuncular functionalism', the attempt to reduce homunculi (psychological functions) to 'armies of idiots' (material mechanisms). It is shown how Kosslyn et al. Apply Dennett's analysis to 'mental imagery'. Finally it is argued that the functionalistic analysis of—say—a chess computer proves that an army of idiots can play chess, but that we still lack knowledge as to how a human chess player thinks. We know *what* the homunculus does, not *how* he does it.

DRAGONA– MONACHOU, M. God, The World And Man As A Social Being In Marcus Aurelius' Stoicism. *Diotima* 12,86–96 1984.

The Stoic idea of the connection between God, the world, and man has been fervently defended by Marcus Aurelius with the emphasis on sociability. This is shown from a survey of the frequency of the term "society" and its derivatives in the *Meditations* in reference to man and God as the authority of the rational community. Individual and common good coincide.

DRAY, W H. Narrative Versus Analysis In History. *Phil Soc Sci* 15,125–146 Je 85.

DREISBACH, Donald F. "Religion, Grace, And The Law On The Heart" in *The Georgetown Symposium On Ethics*, Porreco, Rocco (ed), 213–218. Lanham Univ Pr Of America 1984.

DRESCHER, Wilhelmine. Die Ethische Bedeutung Des Schoönen Bei Kant. *Z Phil Forsch* 29,445–449 Jl–S 75.

DRESLER, Peter. Kollektive Meinung Und Individuelles Leistungsverhalten Im Socialismus. *Deut Z Phil* 33,532–535 1985.

DRESSER, Rebecca. Involuntary Confinement: Legal And Psychiatric Perspectives. *J Med Phil* 9,295–300 Ag 84.

This article comments on "Liberty, Beneficence, and Involuntary Confinement," by Joan Callahan, same issue. The commentary notes that civil commitment criteria similar to those Callahan proposes already exist in some civil commitment and legal incompetency and guardianship legislation. In addition, psychiatrists have formulated commitment standards similar to those Callahan endorses. Finally, these proposed standards fail to demonstrate that they escape many of the difficulties present in other civil commitment criteria.

DRETSKE, Fred and Enc, Berent. Causal Theories Of Knowledge. *Midwest Stud Phil* 9,517–528 1984.

The prospects for a casual theory of knowledge are explored. A variety of cases are examined in which there is no casual connection, either direct or indirect, between the condition known to obtain and the knower's belief that it obtains. Evolutionary considerations are introduced to suggest that something resembling a casual theory may be salvaged if one looks at the development of those cognitive mechanisms (rather than merely the present use of those mechanisms) required to service an organism's needs.

DRETSKE, Frederick I. Constraints And Meaning. *Ling Phil* 8,9–12 F 85.

Barwise and Perry propose to understand the meaning of a linguistic utterance in terms of the information it carries, and this, in turn, by means of the constraints holding between situation types. There is, however, a tension between their notion of a constraint and something that will allow for false statements, i.E., the occasional, perhaps even frequent, breakdown in the "constraints" holding between situations. In what sense is anything constrained? (Barwise and Perry, *Situations and Attitudes*).

DREYFUS, Hubert L and Rabinow, Paul. *Michel Foucault: Beyond Structuralism And Hermeneutics.* Chicago Univ Of Chicago Pr 1983.

This text is a study of the major work of Michel Foucault, completed before his death in 1984. The text is described by its author as an interpretation of problems encountered by Foucault, using his method of investigation to derive meaning in the light of post–structuralist controversy. The book gives an interpretation of this contemporary French thinker on human discourse in relation to history and the various disciplines which attempt to elucidate it. foucault is a philosopher who reassesses history through radical interpretation of the texts which describe history. (staff)

DREYFUS, Hubert. "Beyond Hermeneutics" in *Hermeneutics*, Shapiro, Gary (ed), 66–83. Amherst Univ Of Mass Pr 1984.

DRJACHLOW, N I and Tscherkassow, G K. Über Den Wirkungs– Und Ausnutzungsmechanismus Der Gesellschaftlichen Entwicklungsgetsetze. *Deut Z Phil* 22,629–638 1974.

DROSTE, F G. Causaliteit En Syntaxis: Enkele Linguïstische Kanttekeningen. *Tijdschr Filosof* 46,444–465 S 84.

The phenomenon of causality is traditionally explained either as a natural connection, i.E., a relation active in reality, or as a mental operation upon that reality, i.E., a cognitive law. In this paper a third solution is proposed. (edited)

DRURY, S B. The Esoteric Philosophy Of Leo Strauss. *Polit Theory* 13,315–338 Ag 85.

Strauss is a man with a unique and disturbing set of ideas that he hides behind a veil of scholarship because he believes the truth is dangerous to political society. It undermines the belief in God and in morality. The purpose of this paper is to expose the fact that Strauss' own political ideas are closer to Machiavelli's and Nietzsche's than to Plato's. As a political philosopher, Strauss is a creator of the myths necessary for the survival of the herd, but he is not duped by them himself.

DRYDYK, J J. Who Is Fooled By The "Cunning Of Reason"? *Hist Theor* 24,147–169 My 85.

Hegel's 'cunning of reason' can be defended against charges that it is incoherent. But there are deeper problems. The young Hegel *sought* historical evidence that humans are capable of progress (vis–à–vis freedom). The *Phenomenology* was to demonstrate these capacities *without relying on* historical evidence. The 'cunning of reason' adds: These claims about possible progress *cannot be refuted* by historical evidence. Thus Hegel's view of history did indeed become increasingly dogmatic.

DRYER, D P. "The Second Analogy" in *Kant On Causality, Freedom, And Objectivity*, Harper, William A (ed), 58–64. Minneapolis Univ Minnesota Pr 1984.

DUBIED, Pierre–Luigi. La Théologie Pratique En Tant Que Théorie. *Rev Theol Phil* 116,189–200 1984.

This article intends to focus the task of practical Theology on the articulation between life as it occurs and the reality concerned with the contradiction brought in by life as it occurs. Thereon practical Theology tests its fellow disciplines on the questions of Truth, Justice, and Liberty. The hypothesis of conversation allows to account for the reality to which practical Theology belongs as a Theory and as a Practice.

DUBINSKY, Alan J and Ingram, Thomas N. Correlates Of Salespeople's Ethical Conflict: An Exploratory Investigation. *J Bus Ethics* 3,343–353 N 84.

Much have been written about marketing ethics. Virtually no published research, however, has examined what factors are related to the ethical conflict of salespeople. Such research is important because it could have direct implications for the management of sales personnel. This paper presents the results of an exploratory study that examined selected correlates of salespeoples's ethical conflict. Implications for practitioners and academics are also provided.

DUBLER, Nancy Neveloff and Schneiderman, Lawrence J. 'My Husband Won't Tell The Children!'. *Hastings Center Rep* 14,26–27 Ag 84.

DUDMAN, V H. Parsing 'If'–Sentences. *Analysis* 44,145–153 O 84.

Three ways are distinguished in which 'if'—sentences are generated from the messages they encode. The three different kinds of message thus encoded are described and compared. Finally, 'contraposition' is reconsidered in the light of the trichotomy.

DUFRENNE, Mikel. "Phenomenology And Literary Criticism" in *Continental Philosophy And The Arts*, Winters, Laurence E and others (ed), 123–138. *Lanham* Univ Pr Of America 1984.

DÜLL, Rupprecht. Freiheit Und Perfektion. *Conceptus* 18,62–84 1984.

In this paper the fundamental strategies of evolution, viz., self–preservation and variation, will be reduced to the basic principle of self–regulation. First, the functioning of self–regulating mechanisms will be discussed. Then, the evolutionary strategies will be defined within a model as degree of order and of liberty of open systems respectively, the functions of which will be discussed too. The different possibilities how open systems can react admit the following ways of development: (1) When positive feedback predominates, dissolving tendencies of the system will increase, with the consequence of instability and regression to lower stages of development. (2) When negative feedback predominates, stability of the system will increase, but may lead to stiffness and, therefore, to regression, too. (3) Only when the antagonistic strategies are balanced, the system will develop to higher stages. It will be argued that in the human world there is currently a growing tendency of perfection. The features of this perfection and possibilities of overcoming it will be discussed at the end.

DULLES, Avery. The Essence Of Catholicism: Protestant And Catholic Perspectives. *Thomist* 48,607–633 O 84.

Many efforts have been made to identify the "essence" or "idea" of Catholicism, usually in opposition to Protestantism. Protestants from Hegel to Tillich have tended to regard Catholicism as the religion of institutionalism, law, and dogma. Catholics from Moehler to von Balthasar have viewed Catholicism as the religion of Incarnation and sacramentality. At Vatican Council II (1962–1965) the Catholic Church emphasized personal freedom, appropriation, and participation, thus incorporating certain "Protestant" features into the self–understanding of Catholicism.

DUMM, Thomas L. Friendly Persuasion: Quakers, Liberal Toleration, And The Birth Of The Prison. *Polit Theory* 13,387–408 Ag 85.

DUMMETT, Michael. Hacking On Frege. *Phil Quart* 35,310 Jl 85.

DUMONCEL, Jean–Claude. L'essence Double Du Langage Selon Gilbert Hottois. *Rev Phil Louvain* 83,262–266 My 85.

DUMONCEL, Jean–Claude. La Théologie Modale De Leibniz: Réponse Á Georges Kalinowski. *Stud Leibniz* 17,98–104 1985.

DUMONCEL, Jean–Claude. Whitehead Ou Le Cosmos Torrentiel. *Arch Phil* 47,569–590 O–D 84.

The well–known eclectism of Whitehead is here intended as a ground of comparative philosophy. A reconstruction of the system is offered from three main lines of approach: (1) The affinities of Whitehead with Leibniz and Bergson; (2) His puzzling encounter of Analytical Philosophy, at least in the person of Bertrand Russell; (3) His familiarity with Mathematics and his concern with contemporary Physics.

DUMONCEL, Jean–Claude. Whitehead Ou Le Cosmos Torrentiel. *Arch Phil* 48,59–78 Ja–Mr 85.

DUNFEE, Thomas W and Robertson, Diana C. Work–Related Ethical Attitudes: Impact On Business Profitability. *Bus Prof Ethics J* 3,25–40 Wint 84.

Work–related attitudes (WREAs) are workforce ethical attitudes that affect business operations. WREAs are assumed to be situation–specific, changeable and predictive behavior. WREAs identified as critical to the profitability of a business firm are 1) honesty–related, 2) loyalty–related and 3) responsibility–related. Suggestions for measuring WREAs are presented. Arguments supporting both a positive and negative correlation between WREAs and profitability are discussed; the authors predict a positive correlation between WREAs and business profitability.

DUNLOP, Charles E M. Wittgenstein On Sensation And 'Seeing–As'. *Synthese* 60,349–368 S 84.

This essay begins by providing a new account of Wittgenstein's Private Language Argument. wittgenstein's rejection of a "cartesian" account of mind is examined, and it is argued that this rejection carries no commitment to Behaviorism, or to the view that sensation terms have public meanings and private references. Part II of the essay attempts to forge a link between the two parts of the *Philosophical Investigations*, by arguing that Wittgenstein's discussion of "seeing–as" reinforces and illuminates his account of how sensation language is mastered.

DUNLOP, Francis. The Education Of The Emotions. *J Phil Educ* 18,245–255 1984.

The paper defends the view that thought and will are developments of feeling and draws certain educational consequences. It also analyses inauthenticity and apathy, and the most important aspects of feeling in general, arguing that the various departments of reality are given to us through feeling. Education must therefore be broad in scope, balance the individual and the social, the Higher and the Lower, mastery and receptiveness, and encourage an atmosphere favorable to emotional development.

DUNN, John. "The Concept Of 'trust' In The Politics Of John Locke" in *Philosophy In History*, Rorty, Richard and others (ed), 279–302. NY Cambridge Univ Pr 1984.

DUNNELL, Robert C. "The Ethics Of Archaeological Significance Decisions" in *Ethics And Values In Archaeology*, Green, Ernestene L (ed), 62–74. NY Free Pr 1984.

DUNNING, Stephan N. Rhetoric And Reality In Kierkegaard's *Postscript*. *Int J Phil Relig* 15,125–138 1984.

DUPRÉ, John. Probabilistic Causality Emancipated. *Midwest Stud Phil* 9,169–176 1984.

DUPRÉ, Louis. *Marx's Social Critique Of Culture*. New Haven Yale Univ Pr 1983.

The lasting significance of Marx's theoretical achievement lies in his critique of society, a critique that extended beyond a concern with nineteenth century capitalism to the foundations of modern culture as a whole. Marx rejected the prevailing conception of culture as a quasi–religious, independent structure unrelated to man's "basic" activity. He shifted the focus on inquiry from the purely theoretical to all–encompassing, production–based social praxis. In doing so he attempted to reunite nature and culture as they had been in the Greek civilization. Unfortunately, the primacy granted to social–economic production relations unduly narrows the scope of the new "naturalism" that reflects the very onesidedness of the capitalist ideologies it combats.

DUPRÉ, Louis. The Despair Of Religion. *Owl Minerva* 16,21–30 Fall 84.

Four times in Hegel's *Phenomenology* religion "despairs": 1) in the "longing" of the unhappy consciousness for an ever escaping absolute. 2) in the "faith" that in order to live in unity with the infinite is forced to withdraw from the finite. 3) in the selfconsciousness of "comedy" which terminated the immediate experience of the sacred characteristic of ancient religion. 4) in the reconciliation of the finite with the infinite in Christian religion which despairs of all hope for a natural union with God.

DUPRÉ, Wilhelm. Mirror And Enigma: The Meaning Of God On Earth. *Listening* 20,65–83 Wint 85.

DUQUE, Felix. Teleologie Und Leiblichkeit Beim Späten Kant. *Kantstudien* 75,381–397 1984.

DURAN, Jane. Descriptive Epistemology. *Metaphilosophy* 15,185–195 Jl–O 84.

Adducing two major lines or argument, the paper concludes that a descriptive overview of the process of epistemic justification—based at least partially on work in psychology and cognitive science— is not irrelevant to normative epistemic justification theory. The first line of argument asks us to consider the problematic areas of certain contemporary theories of epistemic justification from a purely normative point of view. The second line reminds us that the extent theories cry out for some small descriptive adequacy.

DURAND, Graciela Alcocer. La Conformación Del Estado Moderno En Relación A Textos Políticos. *Logos (Mexico)* 8,21–46 My–Ag 85.

DURBIN, Paul T (ed). *A Guide To The Culture Of Science, Technology, And Medicine*. NY Free Pr 1984.

This is a paperback reissue, with expanded bibliography, of the edition which appeared in 1980. The volume is a survey, with extensive bibliographies of nine humanistic and social science fields which take as their scholarly focus science, technology, and medicine. An effort was made by the authors of the surveys to relate the fields by considering value issues they treat, as well as the value of science, technology, and medicine in contemporary society.

DUSKA, Ronald. "The New Sophists: Emotivists As Teachers Of Ethics" in *The Georgetown Symposium On Ethics*, Porreco, Rocco (ed), 235–242. Lanham Univ Pr Of America 1984.

DWORKIN, Gerald. Nuclear Intentions. *Ethics* 95,445–460 Ap 85.

This essay discusses the morality of nuclear deterrence. In particular I deal with the relationship between the morality of the use of nuclear weapons and the intention to use them in certain conditions. I argue for the moral wrongness of the conditional intention to use such weapons.

DWORKIN, Gerald. The Serpent Beguiled Me And I Did Eat: Entrapment And The Creation Of Crime. *Law Phil* 4,17–40 Ap 85.

This paper examines the legitimacy of pro–active law enforcement techniques, i.e., the use of deception to produce the performance of a criminal act in circumstances where it can be observed by law enforcement officials. It argues that law enforcement officials should only be allowed to create the intent to commit a crime in individuals who they have probable cause to suppose are already engaged or intending to engage in criminal activity of similar nature.

DYER, Allen R. Ethics, Advertising And The Definition Of A Profession. *J Med Ethics* 11,72–78 Je 85.

In the climate of concern about high medical costs, the relationship between the trade and professional aspects of medical practice is receiving close scrutiny. In the United Kingdom there is talk of increasing privatisation of health services, and in the United States the Federal Trade Commission (FTC) has attempted to define medicine as a trade for the purposes of commercial regulation. The Supreme Court recently upheld the FTC charge that the American Medical Association (AMA) has been in restraint of trade because of ethical structures against advertising. The concept of profession, as it has been analyzed in sociological, legal, philosophical, and historical perspectives, reveals the importance of an ethic of service as well as technical expertise as defining characteristics of professions. It is suggested that the medical profession should pay more attention to its service ideal at this time when doctors are widely perceived to be technically preoccupied.

DZIAMSKI, Seweryn. The History Of Marxist Ideology In Poland. *Dialec Hum* 10,193–208 Sum 83.

DZIK, Wojciech and Tokarz, Marek. Invariant Matrix Consequences. *Rep Math Log* 18,37–44 1984.

EARLE, William James. Fugitive Truth. *Phil Stud* 47,325–338 My 85.

Paper discusses John McDowell's "On 'The Reality of the Past'" focussing on the problem of our grasp of the meaning of past–tense statements, approached from the perspective of Dummett's antirealism. How we might learn to use, e.G., "It *was* raining," is considered in connection with: (i) Reliance on traces; (ii) Reliance on memories, (iii) reliance on truth–value links.

EARLE, William J. What Philosophers Talk About When They Talk About Sex. *Phil Forum* 16,157–179 Spr 85.

Paper attempts to loosen the connection between biological facts of gender/reproduction and "sexuality" as a distinctively human "disease." Instead sexuality is defined in terms of the purely, or almost purely, formal characteristic of pre–emptivity. Roughly, this means that a desire is sexual (whatever its object) if it destabilizes in–place projects, schemes, activities.

EARLE, William. *Evanescence*. Chicago Gateway 1984.

evanescence looks into some shadows of thought which, while having their own sense, tend to disappear in the light of full rational investigation. God, the World and the Soul are the central but not exclusive themes. From this point of view, we hover between what is eternally clear and what, in principle, is not. It concludes with a probe into the glories beyond the grave.

EARMAN, John (ed). *Testing Scientific Theories*. Minneapolis Univ Minnesota Pr 1983.

Topics covered include a discussion of Glymour's bootstrapping theory of confirmation, the Bayesian perspective and the problems of old evidence, evidence and explanation, historical case studies, alternative views on testing theories, and testing particular theories, including psychoanalytic hypotheses and hypotheses about the completeness of the fossil record. (edited)

EARMAN, John. "Laws Of Nature: The Empiricist Challenge" in *D M Armstrong*, Bogdan, Radu J (ed), 191–224. Boston Reidel 1984.

EBELING, Hans. Kant Oder Nietzsche: Folgelasten. *Phil Rundsch* 32,111–117 1985.

EBERLE, Hans–Jurgen. Kants Straftheorie In Ihrer Bedeutung Für Die Entwicklung Einer Theorie Der Straffälligenpädagogik. *Kantstudien* 76,90–106 1985.

In the 19th century many theorists of criminal law denied the state's claim on educating prisoners. They misunderstood Kant in founding this position on him. Contrasting these classical "absolute" theories (Feuerbach, Hegel) and the later so called "relative" (Kraepelin) theories of criminal law with Kant's theory, the author tries to evaluate Kant's contribution to a theoretical and ethical legitimate concept of education for the correctional system. In a second step the basic theoretical concept of such an education for criminals are pointed out.

EBI, Hisato. Imagination In The Gothic Hierarchy Of *Scientia*—A Study On Medieval English Mysticism (in Japanese). *Bigaku* 35,39–51 Mr 85.

Viollet–le–Duc defines the *esprit des moeurs* of medieval Gothic: "Le raisonnement remplace l'immagination, la logique tue la poésie." In medieval Christian mysticism there is found the idea that imagination is located above the senses and below reason. This idea is based on the structural system of human *scientia* or knowing. I call the system the "Gothic Hierarchy of *Scientia*" on the presumption that the *scientia* is analogous to Gothic architecture in structure. (edited)

ECHEVERRIA, Edward J. The Use And Abuse Of The Concept 'Weltanschauung'. *Heythrop J* 26,249–273 Jl 85.

ECKHARDT, Caroline D. A Commensensical Protest Against Deconstruction, Or, How The Real World At Last Became A Fable. *Thought* 60,310–321 S 85.

Recent literary criticism using a deconstructionist approach is reviewed. Its validity is questioned on a number of grounds. If language communicates only the impossibility of communication, how can we understand the deconstructionists themselves? Furthermore, a self–debating text is not necessarily a self–denying text. The major literary traditions of the past have assumed that literature is a reality and can indeed communicate; to break continuity with those traditions is a loss, not a gain, as well as a violation of common sense.

ECO, Umberto (ed) and Sebok, Thomas A (ed). *The Sign Of Three*. Bloomington Indiana Univ Pr 1983.

EDDY, Robert M and Wilson, Edwin H and Tonne, Herbert A. Symposium On Humanism, Secularism, And Religion. *Relig Hum* 19,32–39 Wint 85.

EDEL, Abraham. A Missing Dimension In Rorty's Use Of Pragmatism. *Trans Peirce Soc* 21,21–38 Wint 85.

The neglected dimension is the accumulation of knowledge and its impact on philosophy. This is illustrated particularly by changes in Dewey's conception of method and ethical theory in response to growing psychological and anthropological knowledge. With this dimension restored, Dewey need not be seen as overcoming the philosophical tradition (even metaphysics) but rather as reconstructing and correcting it. Admitted continuities between science and literature need not therefore weaken knowledge into self–formation and learning into edification.

EDELMANN, Eva. Internationale Sommerschule Für Grundlagenforschung. *Z Phil Forsch* 29,450–452 Jl–S 75.

EDIDIN, Aron. *A Priori* Knowledge For Fallibilists. *Phil Stud* 46,189–198 S 84.

EDIDIN, Aron. "Bootstrapping Without Bootstraps" in *Testing Scientific Theories*, Earman, John (ed), 43–54. Minneapolis Univ Minnesota Pr 1983.

EDIDIN, Aron. Philosophy: Just Like Science Only Different. *Phil Phenomenol Res* 45,537–552 Je 85.

A view of the nature of philosophical inquiry is developed which holds that it is like empirical science in the relationship between its theories and the data which can support them, but unlike science in the nature of the data. An account of philosophical intuition as the source of data for philosophical theory is proposed. Some objections to the view are considered and judged indecisive, but no final verdict on the view's adequacy is proposed.

EDIE, James M. Merleau–Ponty: The Triumph Of Dialectics Over Structuralism. *Man World* 17,299–312 1984.

EDIE, James M. The Roots Of The Existentialist Theory Of Freedom In *Ideas I*. *Husserl Stud* 1,243–261 1984.

EDISON, J. Popperian And Kuhnian Theories Of Truth And The Imputation Of Relativism. *Indian Phil Quart* 12,9–22 Ja–Mr 85.

EDWARDS, John. *Some Thoughts Concerning The Several Causes And Occasions Of Atheism Socinianism Unmask'd*. NY Garland 1984.

EDWARDS, Michael and Katz, Jerrold J. Sentence Meaning And Speech Acts. *Metaphilosophy* 16,12–20 Ja 85.

Kent Bach and Robert Harnish, in trying to show how performative utterances receive a meaning in speech contexts on the basis of the language user's knowledge of the meanings of constative sentences, defend a compromise position between the reductionism of use theorists and the use–independent semantics of their opponents. We argue that their proposed compromise is an attempt to reconcile irreconcilables.

EDWARDS, Paul. The Legacy Of Voltaire (Part 1). *Free Inq* 5,42–49 Spr 85.

EDWARDS, Philip. The Human Predicament: A Context For Rights And Learning About Rights. *Educ Phil Theor* 17,38–46 My 85.

In this paper I argue, contrary to utilitarians, that rights are morally substantive and important. A location for them in the deontological context is suggested on the basis of needs and interests in a world of limited sympathies (the human predicament). Relations between liberty, protected, special relationship and welfare rights are then explored. Given that rights help ameliorate the human predicament, it is concluded that they have a place in education.

EDWARDS, Rem B (ed). *Psychiatry And Ethics*. Buffalo Prometheus Books 1982.

This is a collection of readings by contemporary authors on value problems in the practice of psychiatry and clinical psychology. Chapters are devoted to such topics as: value dimensions of "mental health and illness," the ethico–medical model, therapist–patient relations and rights, voluntary informed consent and competency to consent, involuntary hospitalization and treatment, the right to refuse treatment, controversial behavior control therapies, responsibility and the insanity defense, and deprivation and coercion in custodial care and deinstitutionalization.

EDWARDS, Rem B. J S Mill And Robert Veatch's Critique Of Utilitarianism. *S J Phil* 23,181–200 Sum 85.

Mill did not regard all acts maximizing the "greatest happiness" as morally obligatory. He recognized only minimal moral duties to avoid harm, promote rights, and be minimally charitable. Only such minimal obligations are in accord with rules that are worth the price of social enforcement by the sanctions of law, public opinion, conscience, etc. Mill's Minimizing Utilitarianism, thus understood, is defended against five objections to Mill raised by Robert M Veatch, i.E., that his Utilitarianism (1) allows no place for supererogation, (2) moralizes the whole of life, even prudence, and cannot account adequately for (3) promise keeping, (4) penal justice, or (5) distributive justice.

EDWARDS, Sandra. Aquinas On Individuals And Their Essences. *Phil Topics* 13,155–164 Spr 85.

Occasionally philosophers like Henry Veatch have argued that Aquinas did not believe in individual essences, i.E., essences unique to the individuals which have them as opposed to the essences of kinds of things. I argue that there is much evidence to support the claim that Aquinas did accept individual essences; a close look at individuation and identity through time indicates that the individual essences of material objects consist largely in the way the individual's matter is composed.

EDWORDS, Frederick. The Human Basis Of Laws And Ethics. *Humanist* 45,9–13 My–Je 85.

Theology in not only unnecessary as a basis for a valid ethical and legal system, it is at best useless and at worst counter–productive. Theology is unnecessary because there exist objective points of reference upon which a non–theological moral system can be built. Theology is useless because it does not solve the problem of nihilism that it purports to solve—it simply passes the nihilism on to God. Theology is counter–productive when theological morals enjoin us to act counter to human need and interest.

EELLS, Ellery. *Rational Decision And Causality*. NY Cambridge Univ Pr 1982.

In the first three chapters, the principles of Bayesianism and Bayesian decision and confirmation theory are discussed, and several approaches along these lines compared. Chapter four discusses "Newcomb type" *prima facie* counter examples to "evidential" Bayesian decision theory, and chapter five assesses the "casual" decision theories that have recently emerged. In chapter six, seven, and eight, the evidential theory is defended, by examining the casual relation between states of the world, beliefs and desires, and actions.

EELLS, Ellery. Levi's "The Wrong Box". *J Phil* 82,91–103 F 85.

In Isaac Levi's "The Wrong Box" (*Journal of Philosophy*, 1983), Levi argues that "causal decision theory" is, in a sense, inconsistent. I support David Lewis' arguments (*Journal of Philosophy*, 1983) that Levi's arguments don't succeed. I also allude to arguments in support of "evidential decision theory".

EGAN, Kieran. Development Of Education. *J Phil Educ* 18,187–193 1984.

'development' has been used rather loosely in education, but, with the influence of Piaget, has come to refer primarily to natural processes with which educational activities should be coordinated. The influence of psychological developmental categories—such as Piaget's "operations"—in education have largely displaced other kinds of developmental schemes which use quite different kinds of categories for characterizing educational development. The article discussed Plato's *eikasia*, *pistis*, *dianoia*, and *moesis* categories, and, in more detail, Whitehead's and Elton's use of "romance", arguing for their greater appropriateness to education.

EGGERMAN, Richard W. Games And The Action–Guiding Force Of Morality. *Phil Topics* 13,31–36 Spr 85.

Contrary to Philippa Foot and others who hold that a person lacking the appropriate feelings has no reason to be moral, I argue by analogy that such a person does have a reason for being moral. The analogy compares reasons for being moral with reasons for observing rules in games. Finally, I suggest the underlying principle accounting for the action–guiding force of rules both in games and in morality.

EHERING, Douglas. Simultaneous Causation And Causal Chains. *Analysis* 45,98–102 Mr 85.

A standard objection to the thesis that all causation is simultaneous causation is that this claim rules out temporally extended causal chains. Defenders of universal simultaneous causation have suggested two replies: deny the supposed incompatibility between simultaneous causation and causal chains or deny the existense of causal chains. In this paper, I argue that neither type of defense of universal causation against this objection is plausible.

EHLEN, Peter. The Significance And Dignity Of Labor: A Keyword In Marxian Anthropology. *Stud Soviet Tho* 29,33–46 Ja 85.

To regain for labor the status and dignity of human vocation: this statement from the Paris Manuscrips can be seen as quintessential expression of Marx' writings. Ehlen describes labor as an essential keyword in Marx' anthropology and examines Marx' concept of "dignity".

EHLICH, K. The Language Of Pain. *Theor Med* 6,177–188 Je 85.

The expression 'pain' refers to a phenomenon intrinsic to individuals. The object of the language of pain is restricted to an individual experience which excludes any form of direct access by others. Speaking about pain is thus one of the most difficult forms of linguistic activities, as has been repeatedly pointed out by Wittgenstein. The difficulties involved in this type of communication are not only dependent upon individual linguistic ability but are also clearly reflected in the state and structure of the linguistic means which are at the disposal of the speakers of a language. Linguistic means vary in status and complexity with repect to the ends for which they can be used for. In this paper, I discuss two aspects of communicating pain: types of expression which are involved in speaking about pain, and linguistic activities which are carried out when speaking about pain. The two aspects are interrelated. My analysis makes use of categories belonging to the theory of linguistic activity and to the extended field theory of language (an expansion of Bühler's concept of symbolic and deictic field analysis of language).

EHRENFELD, David and Ehrenfeld, Joan G. Some Thoughts On Nature And Judaism. *Environ Ethics* 7,93–95 Spr 85.

EHRENFELD, Joan G and Ehrenfeld, David. Some Thoughts On Nature And Judaism. *Environ Ethics* 7,93–95 Spr 85.

EHRENREICH, Barbara and English, Deirdre. "Women And The Rise Of The American Medical Profession" in *Freedom, Feminism, And The State*, Mc Elroy, Wendy (ed), 285–304. Cato Institute Washington 1982.

EHRIND, Douglas. "Normal" Intentional Action. *Phil Phenomenol Res* 46,155–158 S 85.

Causal accounts of intentional action hold that S does B intentionally if and only if S desires G, S believes that B will contribute to the production of G, and this desire–belief complex causes B. Counterexamples involving unusual causal routes from complex to action have shown this account not to provide a sufficient condition. On a modified version of this view, restriction is made to "normal" causal paths. I argue that this modified account is unsatisfactory.

EHRING, Douglas. Negative Feedback And Goals. *Nature Syst* 6,217–220 D 84.

The negative feedback account of goal–directed activity has recently gained in philosophical popularity. A number of philosophers have argued that earlier criticisms are well taken only if a "naive behaviorist" understanding of negative feedback mechanisms is assumed. In this paper I argue that even with a more sophisticated picture of such mechanisms, it can be shown that control by a negative feedback mechanism is not necessary for goal–directed activity and that this account does not provide an adequate basis for goal specification.

EHRING, Douglas. The System–Property Theory Of Goal–Directed Processes. *Phil Soc Sci* 14,497–504 D 84.

Ernest Nagel in *Teleology Revisited* (New York: Columbia University Press, 1979), defends a "system–property" theory of goal–directed processes. In this paper, I argue that Nagel's account cannot handle the full range of goal–directed activities, especially those involving "non–contingent" goals or systematically missed targets. I further claim that Nagel's view has the unacceptable implication of treating unremarkable cases of causal preemption as goal–directed.

EICHHORN, Wolfgang. Gesetzmaässigkeiten Des Revolutionären Prozesses. *Deut Z Phil* 33,481–490 1985.

EICHHORN, Wolfgang. Kritisches Zur Widerspruchsdebatte. *Deut Z Phil* 32,1010–1016 1984.

EIGEN, Manfred and Winkler, Ruthild. *Laws Of The Game: How The Principles Of Nature Govern Chance*. NY Harper & Row 1983.

EISENSTADT, S N. The Axial Age (in Hebrew). *Iyyun* 33,172–194 Ja–Ap 84.

EISENSTEIN, I. Ist Die Evolutionstheorie Wissenschaftlich Begründet? *Phil Natur* 15,241–292 1975.

ELDRIDGE, Richard. Deconstruction And Its Alternatives. *Man World* 18,147–170 1985.

There is a puzzle about literary interpretation. We call particular interpretations justified; we believe justifications can be expressed in sound arguments; and we suppose the correct theory of interpretation is not yet known. Yet these three assumptions (more carefully formulated) are inconsistent. New critics, intentionalists, structuralists, and essentialists each reject one of these assumptions. Their positions are surveyed, and essentialism about literary interpretation is upheld as the stance that best suits our interests in interpreting.

ELGIN, Catherine Z. Goodman's Rigorous Relativism. *J Thought* 19,36–45 Wint 84.

This reply to Harvey Siegel's 'Relativism, Realism, and Rightness' identifies some of the rigorous restraints on Nelson Goodman's relativism. I show that Goodman's position is not, as Siegel contends, self–defeating. For the view that more than one world version is right, and more than one criterion of rightness acceptable, does not commit one to the view that every version is right or every criterion acceptable. I show why Goodman's relativism is more reasonable than absolutism.

ELGIN, Catherine Z. Translucent Belief. *J Phil* 82,74–90 F 85.

I suggest that the interpretation of belief ascriptions depends on both truth conditions and classification of content. The former determine what it takes for a belief to be true; the latter fix the limits on permissible paraphrase. Classification is sensitive to context; no general rule settles every case. Translucence, moreover, admits of degrees; for classification conditions differ in scope. I discuss incompatibilities among beliefs and explain why they are often unnoticed. Kripke's puzzle dissolves.

ELIAS, Julius A. *Plato's Defence Of Poetry*. Albany SUNY Pr 1984.

ELLETT JR, Frederick S. Psychological Terms, Logical Positivism, And Realism: Issues Related To Construct Validation. *Educ Theor* 35,273–284 Sum 85.

ELLIN, Joseph. Confidentiality In The Teaching Of Medical Ethics: A Case Report. *Teach Phil* 8,1–12 Ja 85.

Philosophers teaching medical ethics deal with confidentiality in medical practice, but rarely consider problems of confidentiality arising in the classroom. I describe an incident in which two nurses in my medical ethics class were told by their hospital that presentation of a medical ethics class would violate hospital's confidentiality policy and subject them to termination. I examine the principles of confidentiality in the classroom and offer some suggestions for coping with hectoring officials.

ELLIOT, Robert and Gallois, Andre. Would It Have Been Me (Against The Necessity Of Origin). *Austl J Phil* 62,292–293 S 84.

ELLIS, G F R. The Dimensions Of Poverty. *Soc Indic Res* 15,229–254 O 84.

The nature of 'poverty' is examined in relation to a model of causes affecting the welfare of a community. It is suggested that one can operationally distinguish four major dimensions of poverty, namely economic, social, political and legal poverty; and that one might in addition be able to characterize three further aspects, namely psychological, ideological and conceptual poverty. It is proposed that at least the first four aspects should be distinguished and explicitly named, thereby specifically characterizing these different dimensions of 'poverty'; and that this would serve a useful purpose in clarifying the nature of the problems faced by the community considered.

ELLISTON, Frederick. The Philosopher In The Workplace. *J Bus Ethics* 4,331–339 Ag 85.

This paper offers a series of reflections on the movement of philosophy beyond its traditional locus in colleges and universities into business settings. This movement is characterized as a variation on a persistent theme in the western tradition beginning with Socrates and running throughout modern (Spinoza, Hume, Locke, and Berkeley) and recent philosophers (Kierkegaard, Marx, Nietzsche, Sartre and Russell) who held no full time academic appointment. Increasingly philosophers are addressing the concerns of scientists, lawyers, and engineers on the job rather than in the classroom.

To what end? As one of the liberal arts, philosophy expands our horizons by locating immediate concerns within a broader historical cultural context and provides conceptual tools and techniques for analyzing problems. Teaching ethics in a board room rather than a graduate seminar can still serve to raise students' consciousness, clarify conflicting values, sharpen moral reasoning and help identify moral truths. (edited)

ELLOS, William J. The Practice Of Medical Ethics: A Structuralistic Approach. *Theor Med* 5,333–344 O 84.

Rule utilitarianism and rule deontology are correlated to psychological thought factors and phenotypical biological factors. Act utilitarianism and act deontology are correlated to emotive psychological factors and genotypical biological factors. A teleology links all six factors. While the roots of this teleology are Aristotelian, use of the techniques of the linguistic of genetic epistemology provides a working model not only to show the interplay of the six elements but also to provide a pragmatic approach to the practice of medical ethics. Three cases are discusssed and the structuralist methodology applied.

ELM, Ludwig. Gegen "Humanitarismus" Und "Illusionen Der Brüderlichkeit". *Deut Z Phil* 32,819–827 1984.

Conservatism in the Federal Republic of Germany includes an elitistly deformed understanding of humanism. The main functions are a way of dealing with the crisis which is hostile to people and progress, apology for social inequality and injustice, militarization, and intolerance towards revolutionary ideas and movements Polemics against "humanitarianism" alleges an illusory humanism to democratic and liberal forces. A militant concept of antagonists and the encouragement of right extremism are fatal consequences of contemporary conservative antihumanism.

ELROD, John W. "Kierkegaard, Abraham And The Modern State" in *History Of Philosophy In Making*, Thro, Linus J (ed), 165–176. Washington Univ Pr Of America 1982.

ELROD, John W. "Passion, Reflection, And Particularity In Two Ages" in *International Kierkegaard Commentary*, Perkins, Robert L (ed), 1–18. Macon Mercer Univ Pr 1984.

ELSHTAIN, Jean Bethke. "Antigone's Daughters" in *Freedom, Feminism, And The State*, Mc Elroy, Wendy (ed), 61–76. Cato Institute Washington 1982.

ELSHTAIN, Jean Bethke. Reflections On War And Political Discourse: Realism, Just War, And Feminism In A Nuclear Age. *Polit Theory* 13,39–57 F 85.

The author explores the tradition of 'realism' that dominates thinking about international relations in light of several feminist questions. She then assays just war theory with similar concerns in mind. As the arguments unfold, feminism as a critical lever gives way to contemporary feminisms as articulated positions and the ways in which feminist thinking on war and politics often gets stuck within received discursive forms is noted. Finally, the author concludes with an interpretation of Hannah Arendt's *On Violence*, a text that suggests an alternative discourse.

ELZINGA, Aant. Some Remarks On A Theory Of Research In The Work Of Aristotle. *Z Allg Wiss* 5,9–38 1974.

It appears Aristotle had a dialectical method with two main phases: a) doxographic induction—a form of re-collecting ideas of previous generations; it is related to Plato's *anamnesis*; b) organization of knowledge by classification (taxonomy); it is natural in view of Aristotle's organismic outlook. It is proposed that theory of science and classical scholarship must sometimes call on each other, just like theory of science and history of science. (edited)

EMAMALIZADEH, Hossein. The Informative And Persuasive Functions Of Advertising: A Moral Appraisal—A Comment. *J Bus Ethics* 4,151–153 Ap 85.

EMERSON, Michael. Althusser On Overdetermination And Structural Causation. *Phil Today* 28,203–214 Fall 84.

EMERSON, Ralph Waldo. L'intellectuel Américain. *Petite Rev Phil* 6,1–38 Spr 85.

"l'intellectuel américain" is the first translation of "The American Scholar" (1837), by Emerson, to appear in French (or, if such a translation already exists, it cannot be found). It is followed by a bibliographical and biographical note intended for French-speaking readers. In a short introduction, Marc Chabot identifies the kind of texts (mostly by Europeans and men) that seem to be studied in Quebec colleges and asks questions about the alleged "pluralism" of philosophy professors.

EMMET, Dorothy. *The Effectiveness Of Causes*. Albany SUNY Pr 1985.

This book attacks views of event causation where events succeed one another but do not move or change. This is called a Zeno universe after Zeno's arrow. Causes are participants in events having effects and not only successors. Sequences in transeunt causation depend on immanent causation, internal activities in the participants which are continuants. Persistence and internal change in these calls for such causation.

EN KUIPERS, Theo and Zandvoort, Henk. Empirische Wetten En Theorieën. *Kennis Methode* 9,49–63 1985.

ENAYAT, Ali. Weakly Compact Cardinals In Models Of Set Theory. *J Sym Log* 50,476–486 Je 85.

This work continues the project initiated by the author in an earlier paper of isolating, or proving the absence of, first order syntactic equivalents of semantic properties of set theories. A somewhat philosophical lesson learned is that, in spite of the "Löwenheim–Skolem" phenomena, in some cases it may be necessary to study the behavior of *uncountable* models of a given theory in order to learn something first order about it.

ENÇ, Berent and Dretske, Fred. Causal Theories Of Knowledge. *Midwest Stud Phil* 9,517–528 1984.

The prospects for a casual theory of knowledge are explored. A variety of cases are examined in which there is no casual connection, either direct or indirect, between the condition known to obtain and the knower's belief that it obtains. Evolutionary considerations are introduced to suggest that something resembling a casual theory may be salvaged if one looks at the development of those cognitive mechanisms (rather than merely the present use of those mechanisms) required to service an organism's needs.

ENC, Berent. Hume On Causal Necessity: A Study From The Perspective Of Hume's Theory Of Passions. *Hist Phil Quart* 2,235–256 Jl 85.

ENDICOTT, Jean. "Making And Using Psychiatric Diagnoses: Ethical Issues" in *Ethical Questions In Brain And Behavior*, Pfaff, Donald W (ed), 11–22. NY Springer 1983.

ENGEL- TIERCELIN, Claudine. Que Signifie: Voir Rouge—La Sensation Et La Couleur Selon C S Peirce. *Arch Phil* 47,409–430 Jl–S 84.

As soon as 1868, within the general context of the critique, Peirce elaborates against "the spirit of cartesianism" and the psychology of Common Sense. He offers a logical interpretation of sensation: sensation is neither an immediate or simple intuition, nor an image; it is an inference. However, by being more precise about the components of sensation, Peirce stresses the irreducible vagueness of sensation more and more, thus reminding of the difficulties that are met by any reductionism, be it physiological or psychological, or mental phenomena.

ENGEL, Pascal. Croyances, Dispositions Et Probabilitiés (Peirce Et Ramsey). *Rev Phil Fr* 174,401–426 O–D 84.

There are two versions of the "pragmatic" theory of belief as a disposition to act: Peirce's theory is associated with an "objectivistic" view of the theory of probability as a measure of degrees of belief, while Ramsey's theory is associated with the "subjectivist" and bayesian concept of probability. In this paper it is argued that both theories share a functionalist account of belief, as dependent on desire and action, and that the normative character of bayesian decision theory is the best approach for a theory of belief as a disposition to action.

ENGEL, Pascal. Le Sens D'un Nom Propre. *Arch Phil* 47,431–448 Jl–S 84.

Kripke's arguments for a theory of direct reference of proper names are not sufficient to establish the claim that proper names lack sense, and that Russell's theory of descriptions is false. When applied to belief contexts this theory fails as well, and the notion of belief *de re* is confused. Proper names have a minimal descriptive sense: they indicate that the individual designated is the bearer of the name.

ENGELHARDT JR, H Tristram and Erde, Edmund L. "Philosophy Of Medicine" in *The Culture Of Science, Technology, And Medicine*, Durbin, Paul T (ed), 364–464. NY Free Pr 1984.

ENGFER, Hans-Jurgen. Widerlegt Descartes' Vierte Meditation Den Gottesbeweis Der Dritten: Zur Stellung Descartes' In Der Philosophiegeschichte. *Stud Leibniz* 16,73–92 1984.

This paper deals with the question of whether the arguments Descartes put forward in his fourth Meditation can be used to refute the proof of the existence of God given in the third one. For in the third Meditation the core of the proof consists in saying that I myself, as a limited and finite being, cannot be the source of the infinite idea of God. (edited)

ENGLEBRETSEN, George. Defending Distribution. *Dialogos* 20,157–160 Ap 85.

At least one recent defender of the doctrine of distribution has conceded too much to the opposition. Friends of distribution must recognize the crucial distinction between denotation, a semantic feature of all terms, and reference, a semantic feature of quantified expressions. They must also be prepared to apply their doctrine to every kind of term—including relationals.

ENGLEBRETSEN, George. Logical Form And Natural Syntax. *Indian Phil Quart* 11,229–254 Ap 84.

Fred Sommers' recent work on logic has succeeded in the construction of a 'new syllogistic', comparable in expressive and inference powers to the standard predicate calculus. Modern logicians committed to the standard system have begun to counsel grammarians concerning the logical syntax of natural language. A quite different view of this syntax, one requiring far fewer concessions from grammarians, is provided by a phrase structure grammar based on Sommers' logic.

ENGLEBRETSEN, George. On The Proper Treatment Of Negative Names. *J Crit Anal* 8,109–116 1985.

The asymmetry thesis rests on the alleged failure of singular terms to be negatable. It is argued here that (1) singular terms (names) can be negated, (2) there is subject/predicate asymmetry, and (3) this is not due to singular/general asymmetry. The standard Fregean logician takes all referring phrases to be singular. But the feared senselessness or impossibility of a singular referent for a subject such as 'nonSocrates' is avoided by recognizing that such an expression is not singular.

ENGLEBRETSEN, George. Quadratum Auctum. *Log Anal* 27,309–326 S 84.

Drawing on ideas presented recently by F Sommers a variety of distinctions are made between different kinds of logical opposition. The principles governing these logical distinctions can be used to augment those governing a traditional square of opposition. The result is an augmented square of opposition useful for the analysis of not only normal categorical sentences, but vacuous sentences, singular sentences, and even compound sentences.

ENGLISH, Deirdre and Ehrenreich, Barbara. "Women And The Rise Of The American Medical Profession" in *Freedom, Feminism, And The State*, Mc Elroy, Wendy (ed), 285–304. Cato Institute Washington 1982.

ENNIS, Robert H. Critical Thinking And The Curriculum. *Nat Forum* 65,28–30 Wint 85.

ENNIS, Robert H. Quality And Creativity: A False Dichotomy? *Proc Phil Educ* 40,323–328 1984.

ENNUSCHAT, W and Korch, Helmut. Engels' "Dialektik Der Natur" Und Die Einheit Der Naturwissenschaftlichen Erkenntnis. *Deut Z Phil* 23,869–882 1975.

Die Engelssche Auffassung, dafss die Gesamtheit der Naturvorgänge in einem systematischen Zusammenhang steht und die Wissenschaft gesetzmäfssig dahin strebt, ihn in einem einheitlichen theoretischen System widerzuspiegeln, besitzt grofsse Aktualität. Eine besondere Rolle spielen in der modernen Wissenschaft die

Entstehung fundamentaler Begriffe und Abstraktionen und der Aufbau grundlegender Theorien, die das Wissen verschiedener Gebiete synthetisieren. Die fortschreitende Vereinheitlichung der naturwissenschaftlichen Erkenntnis ist weiterhin mit einer zunehmenden "Vereinfachung" wissenschaftlicher Systeme verbunden.

ENSLIN, Penny. The Liberal Point Of View. *Educ Phil Theor* 16,1–9 O 84.

EPLING, W Frank and Pierce, W David. On The Persistence Of Cognitive Explanation: Implications For Behavior Analysis. *Behaviorism* 12,15–28 Spr 84.

Skinner has assigned the persistence of cognitive explanations to the literature of freedom and dignity. This view is challenged especially as it applies to behavioral scientists. It is argued that cognitive explanations persist (a) because current behaviorism does not challenge cognitive epistemology; (b) because behavior analysts have failed to provide research evidence at the level of human behavior, and finally (c) because a science of behavior based solely on operant principles is necessarily incomplete. The implications of these problems for behavior analysis are addressed.

EPSTEIN, Robert. Simulation Research In The Analysis Of Behavior. *Behaviorism* 12,41–60 Fall 84.

ERDE, Edmund L and Engelhardt Jr, H Tristram. "Philosophy Of Medicine" in *The Culture Of Science, Technology, And Medicine*, Durbin, Paul T (ed), 364–464. NY Free Pr 1984.

ERFURTH, Andrea. Gedanken Zum Sozialistischen Humanismus Als Anspruch An Individuum Und Gesellschaft. *Deut Z Phil* 33,528–531 1985.

ERGMANN, Raoul. Collections And Collectors. *Diogenes* 128,54–76 Wint 84.

ERICSON, David P. Emotion And Action In Cognitive Psychology: Breaching A Fashionable Philosophical Fence. *Proc Phil Educ* 40,151–162 1984.

In a number of articles, philosopher R S Peters argues that emotions in principle have no explanatory role concerning actions. By examining psychologist Bernard Weiner's attributional theory of emotion, I argue that certain emotions are both conceptually connected with and causally explain certain actions. As opposed to Peters, all emotions are not necessarily connected with passive phenomena. And, as opposed to Weiner, not all emotions can explain actions.

ERNST, K. Zu Einigen Fragen Der, Sozialstruktur Und Der Sozialen Triebkräfte. *Deut Z Phil* 33,86–90 1985.

ERNST, Wilhelm. Ursprung Und Entwicklung Der Menschenrechte In Geschichte Und Gegenwart. *Gregorianum* 65,231–270 1984.

ERPENBECK, John. Dialektik—Logik—Wissenschaftsentwicklung. *Deut Z Phil* 22,753–757 1974.

ERWIN, Edward. Establishing Causal Connections: Meta–Analysis And Psychotherapy. *Midwest Stud Phil* 9,421–436 1984.

Meta–Analysis is a new statistical technique for integrating diverse empirical data and inferring casual connections. I discuss difficulties in its most widely known application: in establishing a casual connection between psychotherapy and beneficial outcomes. I also discuss the epistemological problem that motivates the use of the technique: the integration problem.

ESLICK, Leonard J. "Plato's Dialectic Of The Sun" in *History Of Philosophy In Making*, Thro, Linus J (ed), 19–34. Washington Univ Pr Of America 1982.

ESPINOZA, Miguel. La Réalité En Soi Et Connaissable Est–Elle Possible? *Arch Phil* 48,143–157 Ja–Mr 85.

Contemporary theories of knowledge have been conditioned by the idea that we cannot know the object–in–itself. The title of this essay will certainly appear to be a pseudoquestion. I disagree. I argue for a species of scientific realism. Knowledge is a natural and vital process; it results from a cooperation between an intelligent organism and an intelligible nature. Science becomes thus an interesting activity. Otherwise, we rest the prisoners of the webs of language or lost in the labyrinth of nonscientific metaphysics.

ESPOSITO, Constantino. Il Fenomeno Dell'essere: Fenomenologia E Ontologia In Heidegger. Bari Dedalo 1984.

The work reconstructs Heidegger's research between 1923 and 1928, using some "Marburger Vorlesungen", recently published, as a reinterpretation of the problematical framework of "Sein und Zeit" in the light of the intrinsic connection between phenomenology and ontology. Heidegger's philosophy is considered – through the relation and the separation from Husserl's teaching – as a ontological–hermeneutical radicalization of the phenomenological method, and, on the other side, as a original, phenomenological understanding of the philosophical "thing": the sense (as phenomenon) of being.

ESQUIVEL, Javier. Autoconocimiento Y Moral. *Rev Filosof (Mexico)* 17,423–440 S–D 84.

ESSIET, Fabian S. Callan And Dewey's Conception Of Education As Growth. *Educ Theor* 35,195–198 Spr 85.

The article is a rejoinder to Callan's article "Dewey's Conception of Education As Growth" (Educational Theory, 32, 1:19–27, Winter 1982). Generally, it attempts to show that Dewey's concept of growth can be best understood in terms of freedom which constitutes Dewey's democratic ideal. This is done in three steps: showing that freedom constitutes Dewey's democratic ideal, indicating Dewey's emphasis on freedom as the goal of the schools or of education, and delineating some advantages of understanding growth as freedom.

ESSLER, W K. On Determining Dispositions. *Erkenntnis* 22,365–368 Ja 85.

ESTRADA JUAN A. La Formación De La Teoría Crítica De Max Horkheimer. *Pensamiento* 41,159–178 Ap–Je 85.

ETZKORN, Girard J. John Reading On The Existence And Unicity Of God, Efficient And Final Causality (in Latin). *Fran Stud* 41,110–221 1981.

Essentially, this is a critical edition of John Reading's *Ordinatio in I Sent., d 2, qq 2–3.* The introduction to the article treats the medieval notion of causality, as being: (1)

founded directly in experience and (2) 'vertical' and hence traceable to a First source of all causality. Since Reading was a disciple of Scotus, there is a prefatory discussion of *per se* and *per accidens* causality, of univocal and equivocal causes and of accidentally and essentially ordered causes. Finally, the contribution of John Reading and codex Flor Nat D 4.95 are put in their historical context.

EUDALY, Thomas D. Does The Description Theory Make Contingent Truths Necessary? *Dialogue (PST)* 27,29–35 O 84.

Given that the set of descriptions logically equivalent lent to the name of an individual includes both ascriptions of world–indexed properties and introductory (archaic) descriptions, the description theory may be acquitted of the charge of making contingent truths necessary.

EVANGELIOU, Christos. Aristotle's Doctrine Of Predicables And Porphyry's *Isagoge. J Hist Phil* 23,15–34 Ja 85.

Porphyry has recently been criticized for "muddling" Aristotle's doctrine of predicables by adding species to the list. I argue that a careful comparison of the two lists shows that they differ more profoundly than Porphyry's critics suspect, and that these modern critics, unlike the ancient commentators, have been mislead by the title of *Isagoge* which they interpret as "introduction" to *Topics* or *Categories* exclusively. It is shown that this is not the case.

EVANS, G R. Augustine On Evil. Cambridge Cambridge Univ Pr 1982.

EVANS, R J W. Rantzau And Welser: Aspects Of Later German Humanism. *Hist Euro Ideas* 5,257–272 1984.

EYKMAN, Christoph. "Literary Diary As A Witness Of Man's Historicity" in *Existential Coordinates Of Human Condition*, Tymieniecka, A (ed), 249–260. Boston Reidel 1984.

EYKMAN, Christoph. "What Can The Poem Do Today" in *Existential Coordinates Of Human Condition*, Tymieniecka, A (ed), 141–156. Boston Reidel 1984.

EZORSKY, Gertrude. Hannah Arendt's View Of Totalitarianism And The Holocaust. *Phil Forum (Boston)* 16,63–81 Fall–Wint 84.

I suggest that Arendt's view is derived from her theory of totalitarianism and imposed against the facts, in her book *Eichmann in Jerusalem.*

FABER, Marion (trans) and Nietzsche, Fredrich. *Human, All Too Human.* Lincoln Univ Nebraska Pr 1984.

FABER, Roger J. "Feedback, Selection, And Function" in *Methodology, Metaphysics And The History Of Science*, Cohen, Robert S (ed), 43–136. Boston Reidel 1984.

FACH, Wolfgang. Begriff Und Logik Des "Öffentlichen Interesses". *Arch Rechts Soz* 60,231–264 1974.

In this essay, the concept of "public interest" is subjected to a dimensional analysis based on studies by Barry, Benn, Cassinelli, Flathman, Harmon, and Held. In a first step the various ways of its application are described, subsequently, the different dimensions of this notion are analyzed. The most important—though very abstract—result is the following: A conclusive concept of public interest has necessarily a *formal* character. It must be constructed on an *objective* basis and has to imply the *principle of unanimity.* (edited)

FAGAN, Brian M. "Archaeology And The Wider Audience" in *Ethics And Values In Archaeology*, Green, Ernestene L (ed), 175–183. NY Free Pr 1984.

FAGIN, Ronald. A Spectrum Hierarchy. *Z Math Log* 21,123–134 1975.

FAGIN, Ronald. A Two–Cardinal Characterization Of Double Spectra. *Z Math Log* 21,121–122 1975.

FAGIN, Ronald. Monadic Generalized Spectra. *Z Math Log* 21,89–96 1975.

FAIR, David. Provability And Mathematical Truth. *Synthese* 61,363–386 D 84.

An insight, central to platonism, that the objects of pure mathematics exist "in some sense" is probably essential to any adequate account of mathematical truth, mathematical language, and the objectivity of the mathematical enterprise. Yet a platonistic ontology makes how we can come to know anything about mathematical objects and how we use them a dark mystery. In this paper I propose a framework for reconciling a representation–relative provability theory of mathematical truth with platonism's valid insights. Besides helping to clarify the ontology of pure mathematics, I think this approach suggests a novel philosophical interpretation of some central results of modern mathematics, including Gödel's Incompleteness Theorems and the independence theorems for the Continuum Hypothesis.

FAJARDO, Sergio. Probability Logic With Conditional Expectation. *Annals Pure Applied Log* 28,137–162 Mr 85.

FALCK, Colin. The Process Of Meaning–Creation: A Transcendental Argument. *Rev Metaph* 38,503–528 Mr 85.

Transcentdental argument can show that before knowledge or logic, in the kierarchy of our awareness (*pace* Kant in his *Critique of Pure Reason*), there must be the response of life to life. The notion of the *emergence* of meaning is almost unmarked in our philosophical thinking. As an ideal to be pursued, the process of meaning–creation is perhaps the spirit behing the *aretē, dharma,* or *tao,* of pre–Socratic and non–Western philosophies.

FALES, Evan. Causation And Induction. *Midwest Stud Phil* 9,113–134 1984.

Hume was right in seeing that his analysis of causation undermines the possibility of justifying induction. Reinforcing Hume's insight, this paper explores the extent to which necessitarian view of causation improves the prospects of solving the problem. I briefly argue that a necessitarian analysis is supported by what is given in experience, then show how invoking casual mechanisms as explanatory hypotheses enables one to finitize the number of initial hypotheses. This provides the Bayesian with non–zero priors.

FALES, Evan. Davidson's Compatibilism. *Phil Phenomenol Res* 45,227–246 D 84.

Donald Davidson advocates a version of compatibilism motivated by his non–reductive materialism. While this position has a number of advantages over more classical forms of compatibilism, an examination of Davidson's views on causation and event–identity (upon which the argument depends) reveals a characterization of the former which renders the latter unintelligible. Finally a libertarian view is sketched which is grounded in a distinction between causal relations and the connection between reasons and actions.

FALK, Hans–Peter. Neuere Analytische Literatur Zur Theorie Des Selbstbewusstseins. *Phil Rundsch* 32,117–134 1985.

FAMRAS– RAUCH, Gila. "The Myth Of Man In The Hebraic Epic" in *Existential Coordinates Of Human Condition*, Tymieniecka, A (ed), 175–184. Boston Reidel 1984.

FANN, K T. *Wittgenstein's Conception Of Philosophy*. Berkeley Univ Of Calif Pr 1971.

FANNIN, William R and Gilmore, Carol B. Public And Firm Interests In Public Service Diversifications. *J Bus Ethics* 4,415–418 O 85.

Public service organization's increasingly are considering diversification into new "for–profit" or "high–profit" enterprises. Such undertakings offer a number of potential benefits to both the organization and the public. They also have potential problems. This article examines some of the major types of benefits and problems in hopes that both public service managers and public policy makers will give a balanced consideration to these diversification efforts.

FANTINI, Stefano. Carlo Antoni E Lo Storicismo Crociano (Continua). *Riv Stud Croce* 21,84–93 Ja–Mr 84.

FARBER, Marvin. *The Search For An Alternative: Philosophical Perspectives Of Subjectivism And Marxism*. Philadelphia Univ Of Penn Pr 1984.

The author is concerned with various meta–philosophical issues and with the analysis of contemporary phenomenology and Marxism. The author argues for a science–oriented materialistic philosophy which includes on it a type of phenomenology. The author characterizes phenomenology as a form of subjectivism, and Marxism as a form of naturalism. (staff)

FARKAS, E J and Szabo, M E. On The Plausibility Of Nonstandard Proofs In Analysis. *Dialectica* 38,297–310 1984.

We present a systematic discussion of the structural and conceptual simplifications of proofs of standard theorems afforded by nonstandard methods and examine to what extent the resulting nonstandard proofs satisfy the informal criterion of "plausibility". We introduce the concept of a "standard detour" and show that all nonstandard proofs considered avoid such detours. Among the proofs examined are proofs of the Intermediate Value Theorem, the Riemann Integration Theorem, the Spectral Theorem for compact Hermitian operators, and the Arzelà–Ascoli Theorem.

FARR, Richard. The Uses And Abuses Of Utility: A Reply To Sleinis. *J Value Inq* 19,153–154 1985.

FARRELL, Daniel M. Hobbes As Moralist. *Phil Stud* 48,257–284 S 85.

FARRELL, Frank B. Reference, Anti–Realism, And Holism. *S J Phil* 23,47–64 Spr 85.

Hilary Putnam's writing employs causal theories of reference in what is, if some recent commentaries on semantics are correct, an atypical fashion. Putnam inserts these causal theories in a framework that has strong anti–realist elements, whereas a more typical alliance is between causal theories of reference and realism. I intend to support the linkage of causal theories and anti–realist sentiments. That such a linkage is unexpected becomes clear if we look at some contemporary debates.

FARRINGTON, Paddy. The First–Order Theory Of The c–Degrees. *Z Math Log* 30,437–446 1984.

FARTHING, John L. The Problem Of Divine Exemplarity In St Thomas. *Thomist* 49,183–222 Ap 85.

Drawing on a variety of Biblical and Platonic resources (especially Philo and Augustine), Aquinas views Ideas as implied in the evident orderliness and rationality of the world but insists (against Plato) that they exist not subsistently but only in the mind of God. The plurality of Ideas is logical rather than ontological: thus the simplicity of the divine essence is preserved. Ideas are principles of both the intelligibility and the producibility of things (*rationes* and *exemplares*, respectively). The "blueprint" of the cosmos is its Idea, which is the divine essence itself. This doctrine is the basis of the possibility of a natural theology.

FAUST, David. *The Limits Of Scientific Reasoning*. Minneapolis Univ Minnesota Pr 1984.

Recent research on human judgment is applied to the conduct of science. It is argued that scientists have a surprisingly restricted capacity to manage or interpret complex information and do not perform many judgment tasks nearly as well as is assumed. Implications for science are discussed, including the need to revise many descriptions of scientific activity and to alter the content and thrust of many prescriptive programs for science.

FEAGIN, Susan L. Some Pleasures Of Imagination. *J Aes Art Crit* 43,41–56 Fall 84.

I focus on how sensory imagining provides pleasure in the appreciation of fiction. Pleasures in imaging don't necessarily reflect desires for what is imaged. Sensations interact differently with the text than imagings with respect to command on our attention. Imaging can also have greater effects than sensing, as a response to suggestiveness and subtlety, in understanding tropes such as metaphor and aposiopesis, and in its flexibility of temporal extent.

FEDOSEEV, P N. Marxist Dialectics And Social Life. *Soviet Stud Phil* 23,3–134 Fall 84.

FEEZELL, Randolph. Play And The Absurd. *Phil Today* 28,319–328 Wint 84.

In this article an understanding of human play is offered by interpreting it in relation to Camus' image of Sisyphus and Thomas Nagel's analysis of the absurd. It is argued that Nagel's analysis does disclose the essential nature of play, insofar as play involves the absurd discrepancy between a seriousness of attitude and a perspective from which the player understands that his activity doesn't really matter. Finally, the playful, ironic attitude is significant for life.

FEFERMAN, Solomon. Intensionality In Mathematics. *J Phil Log* 14,41–56 F 85.

FEFERMAN, Solomon. Kurt Gödel: Conviction And Caution. *Phil Natur* 21,546–562 1984.

FEFERMAN, Solomon. Working Foundations. *Synthese* 62,229–254 F 85.

FEHER, Judith. On Surrender, Death, And The Sociology Of Knowledge. *Human Stud* 7,211–226 1984.

FEIBLEMAN, James K. Presidential Address: The Third Sophistic. *Phil Topics* 13,7–18 Spr 85.

FEINBERG, Joel. The Mistreatment Of Dead Bodies. *Hastings Center Rep* 15,31–37 F 85.

This article has been extracted from my book *Offense to Others* (New York: Oxford University Press, 1985). An earlier version served as my A P A Pacific Division Presidential Address (1982). The essay considers, generally unsympathetically, arguments for the criminalization of certain ways of using dead bodies when they produce a natural repugnance in those who contemplate them.

FELD, Barry C. The Decision To Seek Criminal Charges: Just Deserts And The Waiver Decision. *Crim Just Ethics* 3,27–41 Sum/Fall 84.

FELDMAN, Jan. Population And Ideology. *Hist Polit Thought* 5,361–376 Sum 84.

"population and Ideology" traces the population debate and the rift that developed between socialists and neo–Malthusians when loyalty to their respective ideologies undermined commitment to dispassionate truth–seeking. The charge that birth control was a capitalist ploy stemmed from the gradual absorption of meanings: birth control shaded into population control and it became official policy in the USA and Britian to promote racial purity and preserve capitalism. Ideology continues to contaminate demography even today.

FELDMAN, Richard and Conee, Earl. Evidentialism. *Phil Stud* 48,15–34 Jl 85.

In this paper we defend evidentialism, the view that the epistemic justification of a belief is determined entirely by the believer's evidence for the belief. A defense of this seems appropriate now because theses incompatible with evidentialism have been prominent in recent literature of epistemology. The conflicting theses imply that the epistemic justification of a belief depends upon cognitive capacities, or the cognitive or information–gathering processes that led to the belief. We find no adequate grounds for accepting these theses and argue that evidentialism remains the best view of epistemic justification.

FELDMAN, Richard. Reliability And Justification. *Monist* 68,159–174 Ap 85.

This reliability theory of epistemic justification is the view that a belief is epistemically justified if and only if the process leading to that belief is reliable. This view may seem attractive as a vague and general statement about justification, but I argue that it is implausible when made precise. An important difficulty for the theory is "The Problem of Generality." This is the problem of finding a suitable way to identify the types of belief–forming processes used in determining the consequences of the theory. I argue that the proposals found in or suggested by the literature are all unsatisfactory and that no resolution of the problem seems to be forthcoming.

FELDMAN, Susan. Refutation Of Dogmatism: Putnam's Brains In Vats. *S J Phil* 22,323–330 Fall 84.

Putnam's argument against Cartesian skepticism about the external world, in Reason Truth and History, fails. The skeptical hypothesis can still be introduced even within the confines of Putnam's structures of reference.

FELGENTREU, Herbert and Petruschka, G. Weltanschauliche Fragen Des Sozialistischen Wettbewerbs. *Deut Z Phil* 22,745–749 1974.

FELICE, Domenico. Italian Literature On Thomas Hobbes After The Second World War: Part I; 1946–1955. *Topoi* 4,121–128 Mr 85.

FELSCHER, Walter. Dialogues, Strategies, And Intuitionistic Provability. *Annals Pure Applied Log* 28,217–254 My 85.

For any first order formula A, a proof of A in one of the familiar calculi of intuitionistic logic, can be transformed, by purely syntactical methods, into a winning strategy for A w.R.T., a system of dialogue rules, and vice versa. The idea of dialogue rules, and the statement of such a theorem, is due to Paul Lorenzen, but earlier attempts to prove it failed. The present, apparently first correct proof, may require mathematical thinking; philosophers, however, may appreciate the precise definitions.

FELT, James W. God's Choice: Reflections On Evil In A Created World. *Faith Phil* 1,370–377 O 84.

To ask why God created a world with evil in it makes sense only if God is either a playwright assuming total responsibility for all acts, or if, 'antecedent' to creating, God knows what *would* happen if he *should* create. This essay argues that no such knowledge is available, even to God, so that God's choice was not among pre–envisioned possible worlds, but whether or not to create a world with free agents.

FEMIA, Joseph V. Marxism And Radical Democracy. *Inquiry* 28,293–320 S 85.

Whether or not Marxism leads straight to authoritarianism and the destruction of individual liberty is a question which has long exercised both theorists and politicians. This paper deals with a narrower, though related issue: Is Marxism actually reconcilable with *radical* democracy, the type of democracy advocated by those, including Marxists, who berate the iniquities and hypocrisy of parliamentary liberalism? The answer, according to my paper, is no. The Marxist tradition contains four characteristic features which tend to contradict the participatory procedures most Marxists profess to desire. These features are: (1) the view of Marxism as a science, yielding objective solutions to social and political dilemmas; (2) the messianic aspiration for a society of perfect unity; (3) the belief that human rights are not independent moral norms but so much *bourgeois* 'ideological nonsense' (Marx), expressing the antagonistic relationships of the capitalist regime; and (4) hostility to the market mechanism, which results in a preference for a totally planned economy. (edited)

FENSTAD, Jens Erik. Is Nonstandard Analysis Relevant For The Philosophy Of Mathematics? *Synthese* 62,289–302 F 85.

Nonstandard analysis suggests a different view of the geometric continuum, viz., that the continuum is not a pointset, but acts as a support (ambient space) for pointsets, different from and even richer than the standard reals. This gives a richer frame for discussing phenomena occurring on different, even infinitesimal, scales and phenomena too singular to fit into the standard frame. This is illustrated by discussing a hyperfinite model for quantum fields.

FENSTERMACHER, Gary D. Who Decides The Worth Of Educational Research? *Proc Phil Educ* 40,295–298 1984.

FENTEM, P H. Methods Of Teaching Medical Ethics At The University Of Nottingham. *J Med Ethics* 11,27–28 Mr 85.

Medical ethics has been described as a thread woven into the fabric of the Nottingham curriculum. There exists a wide variety of relevant learning experiences, occurring at intervals throughout each of the five years of the course. The introduction of the students to clinical method from the start creates the need for early consideration of ethical aspects of professional behaviour and this in turn stimulates spontaneous discussion and inquiry amongst the students. The school has chosen to rely on having a sufficient number of medical teachers from various disciplines willing to discuss in all the necessary detail their own clinical decisions.

FERBER, Rafael. Der Grundgedanke Des Tractatus Als Metamorphose Des Obersten Grundsatzes Der Kritik Der Reinen Vernunft. *Kantstudien* 75,460–468 1984.

The *fundamental thought* of the *Tractatus* (4.0312) is a metamorphosis of the *Highest Principle of all Synthetic Judgments a priori* of the *Critique of Pure Reason* (A158/B197). Both state an identity. Cf. For further information: Rafael Ferber, *Platos Idee des Guten* (Hans Richarz—publisher), D–5205 Sankt Augustin 1 1984 (west Germany).

FERGUSON, T J. "Archaeological Ethics In A Resource Program At The Pueblo Of Zuni" in *Ethics And Values In Archaeology*, Green, Ernestene L (ed), 224–235. NY Free Pr 1984.

FERNANDEZ, Arsenio Ginzo. Feuerbach Y La Ilustración. *Pensamiento* 40,385–430 O–D 84.

The article studies, in the first place, and in a general way, the relation of authors such as Strauss, B Bauer, Stirner, and Marx with the tradition of enlightenment. Secondly, it looks more closely at the figure of Feuerbach, with the intention of demonstrating that his line of thought is an attempt at a mediation between the Hegelian heritage and a continuing of the philosophy of the enlightenment.

FERNANDEZ, Wensceslao J G. Denotación Y Referencia. *Pensamiento* 41,129–158 Ap–Je 85.

FERRAJOLI, Luigi and Zolo, Danilo. Marxism And The Criminal Question. *Law Phil* 4,71–100 Ap 85.

The question considered is whether it is possible to trace a theoretical strategy for a criminal policy on the basis of Marx's work. The answer offered is that Marxian political and economic analysis does not supply any "general theory" of criminality and that any attempt to formulate such a theory (as in Lenin, Pasukanis or Gramsci) necessarily leads to authoritarian and regressive conceptions of crime and punishment. Nevertheless the authors maintain that it is possible to trace three theoretical suggestions within Marxian thought which allow of a fruitful approach to the criminal question. The first suggestion relates to the economic roots of many aspects of modern criminality; the second regards the Christian and bourgeois "superstition" or moral liberty and individual culpability; the third suggestion deals with the lack of a guaranteed "social space" as the prime root of crime. These theoretical suggestions permit clarification of the social character of penal responsibility and this character points to the need for socialization (but not deregulation) of criminal treatment.

FERRAND, Dominique J. Problématique Des Méthodes De La Rationalisation Dans Les Organisations. *Phil Soc Sci* 14,289–302 S 84.

The specialized literature contains numerous descriptions of failures in implementation, or of the inability to install a new rationalization in organizations. This established fact leads to the questioning of the objectivist basis of current methods and to the proposal that new methods be formulated, founded on other presuppositions. This article identifies the dominant principles capable of directing a method of organizational rationalization conceived on a subjectivist basis.

FERRANDIZ, J R and Smith, A F M and Bernardo, J M. The Foundations Of Decision Theory: An Intuitive, Operational Approach With Mathematical Extensions. *Theor Decis* 19,127–150 S 85.

A new axiomatic basis for the foundations of decision theory is introduced and its mathematical development outlined. The system combines direct intuitive operational appeal with considerable structural flexibility in the resulting mathematical framework.

FERRARI, Giovanni R F. Orality And Literacy In The Origin Of Philosophy. *Ancient Phil* 4,194–205 Fall 84.

The thesis that the promulgation of literacy at the expense of orality was the decisive causal factor in the development of Greek culture and philosophy has found its most ardent defender in Eric Havelock; but his account of how literacy affects thought is not sufficiently rich, nor sufficiently developmental, and often consists in a description of thought under the rubric of description of language rather than directly addressing the effects of language and thought.

FERRARI, Leo C. Saint Augustine On The Road To Damascus. *Augustin Stud* 13,151–170 1982.

Tell-tale details in both descriptions indicate that Augustine's conversion (*Confessions* 8, 12) is based on that of saint Paul (Acts 9, 1–19, *etc.*). Also, analysis of biblical references in other firmly dated works of Augustine betray a unique period of preoccupation with the conversion of Paul precisely during the 397–401 period of

composing the *Confessions*. See also the author's "Paul at the Conversion of Augustine" *Augustine Stud.* 11, 5–20, 1980.

FERRARI, Piermario. Augusto Guzzo E Il Pensiero Metafisico: L'Avvisamento E La Distanza. *Riv Filosof Neo–Scolas* 76,385–408 Jl–S 84.

FERRÉ, Frederick. In Praise Of Anthropomorphism. *Int J Phil Relig* 16,203–212 1984.

Anthropomorphic language about the ultimate is rejected in strands of Judaism, Islam, and Christianity. Revulsion from describing God with words drawn from the vulgar human domain is valuationally understandable. As logical doctrine, however, negative theology, from Avicenna and Maimonides through Kant and Kierkegaard, proves theoretically and religiously self–defeating. Religious prohibitions against anthropomorphic speech should themselves not be taken literally. Clues to appropriate use of anthropomorphism are found in Midgley's treatment of talk about animals.

FERREIRA, M J. Hume's Naturalism—'Proof' And Practice. *Phil Quart* 35,45–57 Ja 85.

This article examines Hume's notion of "proof" as an argument from experience which leaves "no room for doubt" and yields "certainty". It considers other elements in Hume's thought which might be used to support a reading of "proof" as having philosophical import concerning the legitimacy of such assurance, rather than simply a description of assurance.

FERRELL, Richard B and others. Volitional Disability And Physician Attitudes Toward Noncompliance. *J Med Phil* 9,333–352 N 84.

We develop the concept of a volitional disability as an aid in understanding those patients who behave in ways that are harmful to themselves in spite of their desire to do otherwise. Using this concept enables us to describe their behavior as intentional but 'unvoluntary'. We demonstrate the clinical reality of such behavior by giving clinical examples of the behavior of those with phobic, compulsive, and addictive disorders. We then attempt to show how some kinds of self–harming behavior of noncompliant patients are similar to phobic and compulsive behavior. We propose use of the concept of volitional disability to make it easier for physicians to work with these noncompliant patients and thus to improve their ability to provide better care for them.

FERREOL, G. Estructura De La Temporalidad Y Realidad Social. *Stromata* 41,49–62 Ja–Je 85.

FERRERES, Jose M Rubio. Idea, Esquema E Imaginación En Kant. *Pensamiento* 40,297–316 Jl–S 84.

FERRONE, Vincenzo. Alcune Riflessioni Sulla Cultura Illuministica Napoletana E L'eredità Di Galilei. *G Crit Filosof Ital* 63,315–333 S–D 84.

FEVRIER, Paulette. Mesure Et Objectivité Dans L'investigation Du Monde Sensible. *Rev Phil Fr* 174,183–187 Ap–Je 84.

FEVRIER, Paulette. Mesure Et Théorie En Physique. *Rev Phil Fr* 174,149–151 Ap–Je 84.

The characteristics of the classical notion of measurement are not fulfilled by modern physical measurements, whose results can be described by a mathematical model and expressed by means of fuzzy subsets. Their new characteristics lead to a classification of systems playing a role when seeking a solution of the *Einstein–Podolsky–Rosen* paradox.

FEYERABEND, Paul K. "Philosophy Of Science 2001" in *Methodology, Metaphysics And The History Of Science*, Cohen, Robert S (ed), 137–148. Boston Reidel 1984.

FIEBER, Hans–Joachim and Schneider, W. Zum Platz Der "Randglossen" In Der Geschichte Der Theorie Des Wissenschaftlichen Kommunismus. *Deut Z Phil* 23,696–705 1975.

FIELD, Hartry. On Conservativeness And Incompleteness. *J Phil* 82,239–259 My 85.

This article is a reply to a line of objection that both Stewart Shapiro and Saul Kripke have put forward against the nominalist program in Field, *Science Without Numbers*.

FIELD, Hartry. Realism And Anti–Realism About Mathematics. *Phil Topics* 13,45–70 Spr 82.

FIELD, Richard W. Transmission, Inheritance, And Efficient Causation. *Process Stud* 14,44–45 Spr 84.

The main argument of this article is that the transmission theory of causation, which takes the quality of character of an effect to be numerically identical to that of its cause, is inadequate both as a theory of causation in general, and for the theory of inheritance, proposed by A N Whitehead in particular.

FIELD, Richard W. William James And The Epochal Theory Of Time. *Process Stud* 13,260–274 Wint 83.

William James, in his later works, developed a theory of time that closely resembles the epochal theory of time offered by A N Whitehead in *Process and Reality*. In this article the development of James's theory is traced through his works, and it is compared to the 'intuitive' theory of time offered by Bergson.

FIGALLO, Aldo and Abad, Manuel. Characterization Of Three–Valued Lukasiewicz Algebras. *Rep Math Log* 18,47–60 1984.

In this paper we give a characterization of three–valued Lukasiewicz algebras by means of weak implication, infimum and strong negation. This problem has been earlier solved by using Zermelo's theorem and representation theorem of three–valued Lukasiewicz algebras by means of a subalgebra of a direct product of simple three–valued Lukasiewicz algebras. In this work we obtain these results but we make no use of Zermelo's theorem and representation theorem.

FIGLIOLA, Carl L (ed) and Schnall, David J (ed). *Contemporary Issues In Health Care.* NY Praeger 1984.

FILICE, Carlo. Persons, Motivation, And Acts. *S J Phil* 23,201–216 Sum 85.

FILIOS, Vassilios P. Corporate Social Responsibility And Public Accountability. *J Bus Ethics* 3,305–314 N 84.

In this paper the following specific implications for accounting are examined: Should accountants get involved in social auditing and are they the 'core' persons in corporate social accounting systems? Should corporate social performance measurement and reporting become obligatory and to what extent? A general framework for the implementation of corporate social accounting systems is suggested and guidelines for its auditing are proposed. A tentative set of social auditing standard is outlined together with its methodological accompaniments. (edited)

FILLMORE, Charles J. "Some Thoughts On The Boundaries And Components Of Linguistics" in *Talking Minds*, Bever, Thomas G (ed), 73–110. Cambridge MIT Pr 1984.

FINDLAY, J N. *Wittgenstein: A Critique*. Boston Routledge & K Paul 1984.

This book is an appreciative but critical survey of the works of Wittgenstein. Wittgenstein, it holds, differed from his predecessors in treating language as autonomous and not as reflecting categorical differences in Being or in the conscious acts of subjects. Its standards of correctness lay in the agreements of speakers alone. The book argues that Wittgenstein's concept of use is wholly obscure, and demands a return to the ontological and phenomenological approaches of Frege, Russell, Husserl, Külpe, etc, and to views of meaning which allow it to sum up detail without spelling it out according to rules which are themselves experienced.

FINDLAY, J N. "Systematic Interrelations Of Different Types Of Value" in *The Good Life And Its Pursuit*, Dougherty, Jude P (ed), 196–208. NY Paragon House 1984.

FINDLAY, J N. "They Think Not, Neither Do They Care—The Place Of Matter In Reality" in *On Nature*, Rouner, Leroy S (ed), 145–153. Notre Dame Univ Notre Dame Pr 1984.

FINDLAY, L M. "From Helikon To Aetna" in *Existential Coordinates Of Human Condition*, Tymieniecka, A (ed), 119–140. Boston Reidel 1984.

FINDLAY, L M. "The Shield And The Horizon" in *Existential Coordinates Of Human Condition*, Tymieniecka, A (ed), 163–174. Boston Reidel 1984.

FINE, Arthur. What Is Einstein's Statistical Interpretation, Or, Is It Einstein For Whom Bell's Theorem Tolls. *Topoi* 3,23–36 Je 84.

In principle, the standard account of Einstein's statistical interpretation of the state functions of quantum theory is inconsistent with the quantum theory for coupled systems (Bell's Theorem). I show that the standard account is also inconsistent with the text provided by Einstein that describes his interpretation. I offer a different account of Einstein's interpretation, one that avoids Bell's Theorem, is consistent with quantum theory and that seems to fit Einstein's text exactly. I relate these issues to the program of hidden variables, where I try to explain Einstein's conception of that program, and *his* ideas on the right way to "complete" the quantum theory. (edited)

FINE, Kit and Mc Carthy, Timothy. Truth Without Satisfaction. *J Phil Log* 13,397–422 N 84.

Tarski defined truth in terms of satisfaction. But is this necessary? We give some answers to this question and thereby solve a problem of Kripke's and of Tharp's.

FINE, Kit. Natural Deduction And Arbitrary Objects. *J Phil Log* 14,57–107 F 85.

I sketch a theory of arbitrary or variable objects and then use it in interpreting systems of natural deduction that contain a rule of existential instantiation. Such an interpretation is able to motivate the restrictions on the rules and to provide simple and natural proofs of soundness. It also seems to correspond quite well to our actual understanding of quantificational reasoning.

FINE, Michelle. Commentary: Unearthing Contradictions: An Essay Inspired By Women And Male Violence. *Fem Stud* 11,391–408 Sum 85.

This essay reviews Susan Schechter's, *Women and Male Violence*, through an analysis of the contradictions introduced with state funding for feminist programs, and the contradictions inherent in the imposition of "feminist hegemony." As the state imposes one set of policies and practices on shelters, so too have white, middle class feminists imposed one set of politics and praxis on women who have been battered. This analysis of movement contradictions is located within the context of Reaganomics, cutbacks and New Right backlash.

FINGARETTE, Herbert. Action And Suffering In The Bhagavad Gītā. *Phil East West* 34,357–370 O 84.

An explanation and defense of the theme of "action in inaction" and "inaction in action" in the *Bhagavad Gita*. The account is presented by means of both phenomenological and conceptual analyses.

FINGER, Anne. Abortion. *Fem Stud* 11,409–423 Sum 85.

FINGER, Otto. Weltanschauung Und Klassenbewusstsein In Marx' Kritik Am Gothaer Programm. *Deut Z Phil* 23,682–695 1975.

Der Beitrag verdeutlicht den tiefen weltanschaulichen Gehalt der Marxschen Kritik am Gothaer Programm. Es wird dargelgt, wie Marx in ihr auf dem Boden der materialistischen Gesellschaftsanalyse die gesetmäfssige Entwicklung der kommunistischen Gesellschaftsformation und die Notwendigkeit der Dikatur des Proletariats begründet. Die hohe ideologische Aktualität der Programmkritik wird auch an Marx' Stellungnahme zu solchen fundamentalen Begriffen des weltanschaulichen Parteienkampfes wie Arbeit, Persönlichkeit, Staat, Nation, Freiheit, Gerechtigkeit, Kommunismus demonstriert.

FINGESTEN, Peter. Delimitating The Concept Of The Grotesque. *J Aes Art Crit* 42,419–426 Sum 84.

FINKEL, Asher. Maimonides' Life Of Learning. *J Dharma* 9,389–405 O–d 84.

FINN, William and Ruddick, William. Objections To Hospital Philosophers. *J Med Ethics* 11,42–46 Mr 85.

Like morally sensitive hospital staff, philosophers resist routine simplification of morally complex cases. Like hospital clergy, they favor reflective and principled decision–making. Like hospital lawyers, they refine and extend the language we use to formulate and defend our complex decisions. But hospital philosophers are not redundant: they have a wider range of self–serving presuppositions and implicit contradictions within our practices. As semi–outsiders, they are often best able to take an 'external point of view', unburdened by routine, details, and departmental loyalties. Their clarifications can temporarily disrupt routine, but can eventually improve staff morale, hence team practice and patient welfare.

FINNIS, John. Human Goods And Practical Reasoning. *Proc Cath Phil Ass* 58,23–36 1984.

FINOCCHIARO, Maurice A. Aspects Of The Logic Of History–Of–Science Explanation. *Synthese* 62,429–454 Mr 85.

The topic of history–of–science explanation is first briefly introduced as a generally important one for the light it may shed on action theory, on the logic of discovery, and on philosophy's relations with historiography of science, intellectual history, and the sociology of knowledge. Then some problems and some conclusions are formulated by reference to some recent relevant literature: a critical analysis of Laudan's views on the role of normative evaluations in rational explanations occasions the result that one must make a *conceptual* distinction between evaluations and explanations of belief, and that there are at least three subclasses of the latter, rational, critical, and theoretical; I then discuss the problem of whether explanations of discoveries are self–evidencing and predictive by focusing on views of Hempel and Nickles, and I attempt a formalization of some aspects of the problem. Finally, a more systematic and concrete analysis is undertaken by using as an example the explanation of Galileo's rejection of space–proportionality, and it is argued that the historical explanation of scientific beliefs is a type of logical analysis.

FINOCCHIARO, Maurice A. Informal Logic And The Theory Of Reasoning. *Inform Log* 6,3–8 Jl 84.

This is an attempt to delineate informal logic as an autonomous branch of philosophical inquiry. I do it by exploring the relationship between informal logic, the philosophical study of reasoning, and the psychology of reasoning. Informal logic is also defended from a number of recent criticisms.

FIORE, Crescenzo. Mito E Verità In Mircea Eliade. *Sapienza* 37,433–450 O–D 84.

Truth can be changed into an ideological machine that produces power. Holy appears as the depositary place of truth. For Mircea Eliade myth is holy history opposite profane history. The Eliade's hermeneutic proposal is to show the time's of myth holy character. So it runs the risk that the scientific knowledge changes into holy knowledge, and the scholar gives the place for the Master of truth.

FIRESTEIN, Stephen K and Applebaum, Eleanor Gordon. *A Genetic Counseling Casebook*. NY Free Pr 1983.

FISCH, Menachem. Whewell's Consilience Of Inductions—An Evaluation. *Phil Sci* 52,239–255 Je 85.

The paper attempts to elucidate and evaluate William Whewell's notion of a "consilience of inductions." In section I Whewellian consilience is defined and shown to differ considerably from what latter–day writers talk about when they use the term. In section II a primary analysis of consilience is shown to yield two types of consilient processes, one in which one of the lower–level laws undergoes a conceptual change (the case aptly discussed in Butts [1977]), and one in which the explanatory theory undergoes conceptual "stretching." In section III both consilient cases are compared to the non–consilient case in reference to L J Cohen's method of relevant variables. In section IV we examine the test procedures of the theory in all three cases, and it is shown that in the event of genuine consilience (consilience of the second type) a theory acquires extraordinarily high support. In the final section something is said the shortcomings of standard Bayesian confirmation theories that are highlighted by Whewellian consilience.

FISCHER, Harald–Paul. Berichte Und Diskussionen (in German). *Kantstudien* 76,214–216 1985.

FISCHER, Harald–Paul. Eine Antwort Auf Kants Briefe Vom 23: August 1749. *Kantstudien* 76,79–89 1985.

The addressee of Kant's letter from August 23, 1749 couldn't be Albrecht von Haller. The plain form of the address and of compliments signifies an addressee who wasn't celebrated, graduated or noble. In the "Frankfurtische Gelehrte Anzeigen" November 1749 there appeared an anonymous review of Kant's "Gedanken." Parts of this article agree word for word with the letter of Kant. Therefore the reviewer owned Kant's letter. It seems the author was a study colleague of Kant, perhaps Friedrich Wilhelm Mühlmann who was born in Frankfurt and began his studies of medicine in Königsberg in 1740.

FISCHER, Marilyn. Intentions, Rights And Wrongs: A Critique Of Fried. *Phil Res Arch* 10,239–248 1984.

In this paper I argue against Fried's thesis that a wrong must be intended by the violator in order for a person's negative rights to be violated. With Fried's requirement these rights become in a sense derivative from wrongs. This makes the relation between one's negative rights and one's moral integrity, upon which Fried wants to base rights, indirect and inappropriately weak. If rights are based on one's status as a freely choosing, rational, moral personality, then whether one's rights are violated should be determined by inspecting one's own loss of integrity or function, not by examining the assailant's intentions.

FISCHER, Norman And Others (ed). *Continuity And Change In Marxism*. Atlantic Highlands Humanities Pr 1982.

Continuity and Change in Marxism is primarily oriented to sketching how Marxism has remained a basic unifying force of the revolutionary and workers' movement, at the same time that it has developed in very different philosophical directions. The essays in the anthology, written from various points of view, all reflect the point of view that Marxism is a unique way of approaching social theory, but that philosophical interpretations of that social theory can and should be pluralistic.

FISCHER, Norman. "Economic Value, Ethics, And Transition To Socialism" in *Continuity And Change In Marxism*, Fischer, Norman And Others (ed), 39–65. Atlantic Highlands Humanities Pr 1982.

FISHER, D V. A Conceptual Analysis Of Self–Disclosure. *J Theor Soc Behav* 14,277–296 O 84.

A conceptual definition of self–disclosure is proposed in order to discriminate this type of self–referent speech behaviors as self–presentation and lying about oneself. The attributes of truth, sincerity, intentionality, novelty and "privacy" are proposed as a basis for discriminating different types of self–referent speech, including self–disclosure. Discriminating between types of self–referent behavior is necessary because their conditions of occurence and the social and psychological variables and effects associated with each type differ. Research design and theorizing needs to take these differences into account.

FISHER, Harwood. The Logical Structure Of Freud's Idea Of The Unconscious: Toward A Psychology Of Ideas. *J Brit Soc Phenomenol* 16,20–35 Ja 85.

The purpose of this paper is to specify the logical structure of an idea. To reveal aspects of the structure, issues concerning psychological defenses are reviewed. Taking as an example of an idea, Freud's own notion of the Unconscious, the relation of defense and idea is analyzed. A defense is a resolution to contradiction, and its logical dimensions expressed by negation transformations. An idea has a propositional structure relating at least three terms.

FITCH, G W. Indeterminate Descriptions. *Can J Phil* 14,257–276 Je 84.

FITTING, James E. "Economics And Archaeology" in *Ethics And Values In Archaeology*, Green, Ernestene L (ed), 117–122. NY Free Pr 1984.

FITTING, Melvin. Linear Reasoning In Modal Logic. *J Sym Log* 49,1363–1378 D 84.

A linear reasoning proof of an implication is a sequence of formulas, beginning with the antecedent, ending with the consequent, in which each formula implies the next. We present linear reasoning systems for the modal logics K, T, K4, S4, D, D4, in propositional and first order versions, without the Barcan formula, and for propositional GL. Completeness and correctness proofs are sketched. We also provide a simple, constructive proof of the Craig–Lyndon interpolation theorem for these logics.

FITZGERALD, Paul. Stump And Kretzmann On Time And Eternity. *J Phil* 82,260–268 My 85.

Kretzmann and Stump claim to explicate a traditional doctrine that God is eternal in a way that is different both from being everlasting in time and from being simply atemporal. The doctrine they set forth turns out to be self–contradictory, I argue. But some of the apparatus which they develop to span the gap between the temporal and the eternal is like what is needed by any dualist who holds that mental particulars are not in physical space.

FITZPATRICK, Joseph. Strawson And Lonergan On 'Person'. *Method* 2,36–41 O 84.

FLAGE, Daniel E and Glass, Ronald J. Hume On The Cartesian Theory Of Substance. *S J Phil* 22,497–508 Wint 84.

While most of Hume's criticisms of the doctrine of substance are epistemological and theory–independent, we show that in *Treatise* I.iv.5, Hume develops a metaphysical criticism of the Cartesian theory of substance. Using three of Pierre Bayle's arguments of his own ends, he argues that on an empiricist theory of meaning, the Cartesian theory of substance is reduced to absurdity.

FLAGE, Daniel E. Berkeley's Notions. *Phil Phenomenol Res* 45,407–426 Mr 85.

The paper examines the epistemic function of Berkeleian notions. Beginning with an elucidation of Berkeley's distinction between positive and relative notions, it is argued that relative notions function in the cognitive realm in a manner analogous to definite descriptions. It is shown that this model of relative notions is consistent with Berkeley's accounts of one's notions of substance and of relations among ideas, provided one allows that one has positive notions of the relations of perception and causation.

FLAGE, Daniel E. Descarte's *Cogito*. *Hist Phil Quart* 2,163–178 Ap 85.

It is argued that Descartes drew a methodological distinction between the order in which one entertains propositions and the order of epistemic primacy. Recognizing this reconciles any *prima facie* inconsistencies among the *Cogito* passages, most notably, those between the *Cogito* passages in the *Principles of Philosophy* and the *Second Replies*.

FLANAGAN, Kieran. Hermeneutics: A Sociology Of Misunderstanding. *Phil Stud (Ireland)* 30,270–281 Spr 84.

FLANAGAN, Kieran. Sociology And Liturgical Renewal. *Phil Stud (Ireland)* 30,182–204 Spr 84.

Pluralism of forms of rite, cultural engagement and intelligibility in performance are theological principles of efficacy in renewed Catholic liturgy that conflict with sociological assumptions for its characterization as ritual. Liturgical renewal has generated a hidden sociological agenda theologians have failed to confront. Older rubrics guiding liturgical performance are far more sociologically comprehensible than the newer rules of rite, which fail to cope with details in enactment. An element of mystery needs to be added to the social in rite to preserve its sacred cast as liturgy.

FLANNERY, Kevin and Moser, Paul K. Kripke And Wittgenstein: Intention Without Paradox. *Heythrop J* 26,310–318 Jl 85.

This paper discusses Wittgenstein's claim that: 'This was our paradox: no course of action could be determined by a rule, because every course of action, can be made out to accord with the rule'. First, the paper raises a dilemma facing Kripke's reconstruction of the paradox in question. Secondly, the paper sets forth Wittgenstein's way out of the paradox. And finally, the paper identifies a

questionable nominalist assumption in Kripke's construal of Wittgenstein.

FLAY, Joseph C. "Habermas, Eurocommunism, & Theory Of Communication" in *Continuity And Change In Marxism*, Fischer, Norman And Others (ed), 131–143. Atlantic Highlands Humanities Pr 1982.

FLECK, Leonard M. Mending Mother Nature: Alpha, Beta And Omega Pills. *Phil Stud* 46,381–394 N 84.

In "Abortion, Deformed Fetuses, and the Omega Pill" [*Philosophical Studies*, 1979] I noted 78 percent of conceptions are spontaneously aborted, primarily because of fetal deformity. If an Omega Pill suppressed this intra–uterine rejection mechanism, the abortion conservative would be philosophically committed to women being *morally obligated* to take the Omega Pill, despite absurd results. James Montmarquet argues in "Messing with Mother Nature" [1982] that *Nature* is responsible for these spontaneous abortions. Consequently, the conservative is not morally obligated to take the Omega Pill. In this paper I deploy five counter–arguments that sustain my original position.

FLEINER– GERSTER, Thomas. Eigentum Und Seine Grenzen. *Stud Phil (Switzerland)* 41,77–90 1982.

FLEISCHER, Dirk and Rusen, Jorn and Blanke, Horst Walter. Theory Of History In Historical Lectures: The German Tradition Of *Historik*, 1750–1900. *Hist Theor* 23,331–356 O 84.

The essay examines the German tradition of a particular type of lectures and literature on the theory of history; it is based on the analysis of the lectures held at 60 German–speaking universities during 1750–1900. Four traditions reflecting on history by ideal types are to be distinguished: humanistic–rhetorical, auxiliary–encyclopedic, historicophilosophical, and epistomological or historicological. These types are related in complex ways; in different theories of history ("Historiken") they form different functional/causal patterns and syntheses.

FLEISCHER, Helmut. "Marxism As History—A Theory And Its Consequences" in *Contemporary Marxism*, O' Rourke, James J (ed), 39–54. Boston Reidel 1984.

FLEISCHER, Isidore. "Kripke Semantics" = Algebra + Poetry. *Log Anal* 27,283–296 S 84.

L'équivalence (bien connue) entre la sémantique des calculs propositionnels non–classiques qui est basée sur des interprétations philosophiques et celle, plus sobre et plus ancienne, qui ne fait intervenir que les structures algébriques sous–jacentes, est explicitée et expliquée par la spécification d'une application démunissante qui réduit tout "modèle de Kripke" à un sous–modèle du "modèle" des filtres premiers de l'algèbre (pseudo–) Booléenne des classes de formules interdéductibles.

FLEISCHER, Margot. *Wahrheit Und Wahrheitsgrund*. NY De Gruyter 1984.

FLEK, Antonín. Objective And Subjective–Objective Aspects Of Contradictions Under Socialism (in Czechoslovakian). *Filozof Cas* 32,441–467 1984.

FLEMING, John E. A Suggested Approach To Linking Decision Styles With Business Ethics. *J Bus Ethics* 4,137–144 Ap 85.

FLEMING, Noel. The Tree In The Quad. *Amer Phil Quart* 22,25–36 Ja 85.

FLETCHER, George P. Rights And Excuses. *Crim Just Ethics* 3,17–27 Sum/Fall 84.

The purpose of this article is to explore the conceptual connection between rights and excusing conditions. The basic question is whether claiming a valid excuse implies a right to engage in the excused conduct. The view emerges that so far as a right exists, it is a right not to engage in the conduct but to be acquitted for conduct already committed.

FLETCHER, John C. Ethical Issues In And Beyond Prospective Clinical Trials Of Human Gene Therapy. *J Med Phil* 10,293–307 Ag 85.

As the potential for the first human trials of somatic cell gene therapy nears, two ethical issues are examined: (1) problems of moral choice for members of institutional review boards who consider the first protocols, for parents, and for the clinical researchers, and the special protections that may be required for the infants and children to be involved, and (2) ethical objections to somatic cell therapy made by those concerned about a putative inevitable progression of genetic knowledge from therapy to mass genetic engineering in human reproduction. The author' viewpoint is that a consensus exists on the required moral approach to somatic cell therapy, but that no moral approach yet exists for experiments beyond this level, especially in the germline cells of human beings.

FLEW, Anthony. Paul Russell On Hume's 'Reconciling Project'. *Mind* 93,587–588 O 84.

This response insists simply that discussion cannot be advanced until Paul Russell recognizes and comes to terms with the fact that it was Hume not Flew who insisted—mistakenly in Flew's view—that Hume's contribution showed "that the whole controversy has hitherto turned merely upon words."

FLEW, Antony G N. "The Philosophical Implications Of Darwinism" in *Darwin, Marx And Freud*, Caplan, Arthur L (ed), 3–34. NY Plenum Pr 1984.

FLEW, Antony. "Personal Identity And Imagination": One Objection. *Philosophy* 60,123–126 Ja 85.

P T Mackenzie's paper assumes that "I can conceive waking up and finding myself in a bodiless state". He altogether ignores the radical criticism deployed against this Cartesian assumption, that people are incorporeal. Flew therefore reiterates that criticism, citing various previous publications. The crux is that all person words, including the personal pronouns are, and have to be taught as, words for members of that special sort of creatures of flesh and blood which we are.

FLINT, Richard C. On Enriching The Content Of Art History Courses. *J Aes Educ* 18,118–122 Wint 84.

The essay considers three methods by which to infuse art history courses with meaningful ideas that go beyond the ostensible parameters of a syllabus. The broad spectrum of artistic endeavor is inextricably linked to an even more variegated spectrum of human thought. Accordingly, there is an omnipresent springboard from which to initiate both relevant and stimulating discussion. The enterprising instructor need only take the plunge.

FLINT, Thomas P. Divine Sovereignty And The Free Will Defence. *Sophia (Australia)* 23,41–52 Jl 84.

This article responds to David Basinger's charge that the Free Will Defense is incompatible with the degree of divine sovereignty assigned to God by orthodox Christianity. I contend that Basinger's argument relies upon a significant and widespread misunderstanding of the Free Will Defense; *pace* Basinger *et al*, that Defense need *not* assume that God must create the best world he can. Once this misunderstanding is dispelled, Basinger's argument collapses.

FLIPPEN, Douglas. On Two Meanings Of Good And The Foundations Of Ethics In Aristotle And St Thomas. *Proc Cath Phil Ass* 58,56–64 1984.

There are two definitions of good in Aristotle and St Thomas: 1) the naturally desirable, 2) the smooth functioning of a thing. Hume takes the first definition and makes ethics non–cognitive. Grisez avoids Hume by grounding ethics on practical reason. Aristotle and Thomas agree with Hume against Grisez on practical reason, and with Grisez against Hume on the intellectual basis of ethics. To understand them we must understand the systematic ambiguity of "ought" and "good".

FLORIAN, Mircea. La Récessivité Comme Structure Du Monde. *Phil Log* 28,155–166 Ap–Je 84.

FLORMAN, Samuel C. Commentary On K Alpern's "Moral Responsibility For Engineers". *Bus Prof Ethics J* 2,53–56 Wint 83.

FLOUCAT, Y. Le Philosophie Dans La Cité. *Rev Thomiste* 85,87–100 Ja–Mr 85.

FLOWER, Robert J. The Number Of Being. *Mod Sch* 62,1–26 N 84.

This is a comment on Plato's understanding of the proper uses of the verb 'to be'. By way of an argument by analogy, the paper demonstrates that Plato's theory of being is purely relational; i.E., that being is not a single–placed predicate. The analogy is drawn between the verb 'to be' and the mathematical concept of incommensurable powers. Textual evidence mainly from the *Sophist*.

FLYNN, Bernard C. Reading Habermas Reading Freud. *Human Stud* 8,57–76 1985.

FODDY, W H. A Critical Evaluation Of Altman's Definition Of Privacy As A Dialectic Process. *J Theor Soc Behav* 14,297–308 O 84.

Elements of Altman's definition of privacy are listed and analyzed. It is argued that: (1) core ideas such as control over access to the self and control over interaction with others are not clearly explicated, (2) these elements are not ground within an appropriate theoretical framework so that further explication is not possible, and, (3) the utility of viewing privacy as a dialectic process has not been demonstrated. Finally, it is suggested that these problems can be avoided by employing the symbolic interactionist perspective.

FODOR, Janet Dean. Situations And Representations. *Ling Phil* 8,13–22 F 85.

FOGELIN, Robert J. Hume And The Missing Shade Of Blue. *Phil Phenomenol Res* 45,263–272 D 84.

This essay addresses two questions: (i) Why did Hume think the imagination could supply the missing shade of blue? And (ii) Why was he undisturbed by this counter–example to his position? In answering the first question I argue that Hume held that colors form a highly structured internally related field. This structure provides the background for supplying the missing shade. I answer the second question by noting that no such corresponding background fields exist for the concepts Hume investigates.

FÖLDESI, Gyöngyi Szabó and Foldesi, Tamas. Dilemmas Of Justness In Top Sport. *Dialec Hum* 11,21–32 Wint 84.

FOLDESI, Tamas and Foldesi, Gyongyi Szabo. Dilemmas Of Justness In Top Sport. *Dialec Hum* 11,21–32 Wint 84.

FOLDESI, Tamas. Outlines Of A Marxist Conception Of Justice II (in Hungarian). *Magyar Filozof Szemle* 6,847–871 1983.

FÖLDESI, Tamás. Outlines Of A Possible Marxist Conception Of Justice I (in Hungarian). *Magyar Filozof Szemle* 5,687–711 1983.

FOLEY, Richard and Fumerton, Richard. Davidson's Theism? *Phil Stud* 48,83–90 Jl 85.

The authors examine and criticize a recent anti–skeptical argument forwarded by Donald Davidson, an argument that depends on the possibility of there being an omniscient interpreter of our beliefs who uses Davidson's recommended method of interpretation.

FOLEY, Richard. What's Wrong With Reliabilism? *Monist* 68,188–202 Ap 85.

It is argued that although reliability in some form may well be a crucial part of some set of conditions *sufficient* for knowledge, reliability is not in any interesting (i.E., non–trivial) sense a necessary condition of either knowledge or rational belief.

FOLKERS, Horst. Das Schwierige Recht Der Systemtheoretischen Soziologie: Zur Rechtssoziologie Von Niklas Luhmann. *Arch Rechts Soz* 60,413–420 1974.

FOLTZ, Bruce V. On Heidegger And The Interpretation Of Environmental Crisis. *Environ Ethics* 6,323–338 Wint 84.

Through an examination of the thought of Martin Heidegger, I argue that the relation between human beings and the natural environment can be more radically comprehended by critically examining the character of the relation itself with regard to how it has been shaped and articulated by the tradition of Western metaphysics, particularly in light of the manner in which this tradition contains the central presuppositions of both modern natural science as well as contemporary technology. I conclude with an examination of a "deconstructive analysis" of the concept of nature that has dominated Western philosophy; with a delineation of an alternative understanding of the environment, that is nevertheless deeply rooted in the Western tradition; and with a proposal that the present "environmental crisis" ultimately derives not from certain Judeo–Christian "values", as it is commonly claimed, but from the initial metaphysical orientation of early Greek philosophy.

FONT, Josep M. Implication And Deduction In Some Intuitionistic Modal Logics. *Rep Math Log* 17,27–38 1984.

We study the deductive properties of the system IM4 of intuitionistic modal logic, paying special attention to the implicative ones. This system is the intuitionistic counterpart of Lewis' S4 and its models are the topological pseudo–Boolean algebras. Its abstract deductive structure is analogous to that of pseud0–Boolean algebras but here with respect to new implicative operations. These satisfy the Deduction Theorem and allow us to find implicative characterizations of several types of deductive systems (such as irreducible, maximal, prime) and some related concepts from universal algebra (simplicity, semisimplicity, radical). (edited)

FORBES, Graeme. Response To Mazoué's "Nozick On Inferential Knowledge" And Brueckner's "Transmission For Knowledge Not Established". *Phil Quart* 35,196–198 Ap 85.

I defend the Transmission Principle, that knowledge is closed under knowing inference from known premises, against objections raised by Mazoue and Brueckner to my earlier defense of Transmission (Phil Quart 34, pages 43–52.

FORBES, Graeme. Two Solutions To Chisholm's Paradox. *Phil Stud* 46,171–188 S 84.

Chisholm's Paradox is that one plausible modal principle implies that certain changes in an artifact yield a different artifact, but another equally plausible principle says the changes preserve identity. Such paradoxes may be assimilated to classical Sorites paradoxes, and a resolution transported from the classical to the modal case by introducing either a many–valued accessibility relation or a many–valued counterpart relation. The paper argues against the former solution, and for the latter.

FORCE, James E. Hume And The Relation Of Science To Religion Among Certain Members Of The Royal Society. *J Hist Ideas* 45,517–536 O–D 84.

In this essay, I show first how both God's General and Special Providence are illustrated in the scientific apologetics of many of the founders of the Royal Society and their Newtonian successors. Then, I show how David Hume mounts a careful critical attack upon all the separate elements of this Royal Society synthesis of General and Special Divine Providence.

FORD, Lewis S. *The Emergence Of Whitehead's Metaphysics 1925–1929*, R C Neville (ed). Albany SUNY Pr 1984.

This study displays the growth of Whitehead's metaphysics in terms of some sixteen revisions made in constant self–criticism of his own theory. The first theory in terms of eternal and enduring objects, events, and prehensive unification was transformed even during the composition of *Science and the Modern World*, which introduced "transcendent" eternal objects and God. *process and Reality* reveals some thirteen layers of composition as Whitehead was steadily perfecting his theory, introducing quite late the categorial obligations, subjective aim, and God's consequent nature.

FORD, Richard I. "Ethics And The Museum Archaeologist" in *Ethics And Values In Archaeology*, Green, Ernestene L (ed), 133–142. NY Free Pr 1984.

FORGE, John. Theoretical Functions, Theory And Evidence. *Phil Sci* 51,443–463 S 84.

Glymour's account of confirmation is seen to have paradoxical consequences when applied to the confirmation of theories containing theoretical functions. An alternative conception of instances derived from Sneed's reconstruction of physical theories is conjoined with the instance view of confirmation to produce an account of confirmation that avoids these problems. The topic of selective confirmation is discussed, and it is argued that theories containing theoretical functions are not selectively confirmable.

FORMAGGIO, Dino. "Corpo–Tempo–Arte" in *Il Tempo Dell'Arte*, Papi, Fulvio and others (ed), 7–28. Milano Franco Angeli 1984.

FORMOSO, Manuel. Perennidad De Maquiavelo. *Rev Filosof (Costa Rica)* 23,161–168 D 85.

In 1513 Niccolo Michiavelli sent a small volume to Lorenzo de Medici, containing his political opinions obtained through the study of history and a long practice. Since that time The Prince has acquired a great celebrity opening an unfinished debate. To be efficient politics must be unmoral, otherwise we condemn ourselves to the failure, bound by current moral. The existence of a double moral pattern applied by Machiavelli shows the beginning of the State's reason and possibly the cause of his perennity.

FORNET– BETANCOURT, Raul. Sartre O Las Dificultades De Escribir Una Moral. *Dialogos* 20,113–148 Ap 85.

The essay explains and interprets the posthumous work of Jean–Paul Sartre "Cahiers pour une morale". Its central intent is therefore to describe Sartre's concept of moral. This is done in four steps which also form the four parts of the essay: 1) Pointing out the theoretical nexus between "Cahiers pour une morale" and "L'être et le néant," 2) The basic idea of Sartre's moral, 3) The fundamental problems of moral according to Sartre, and 4) Possibilities to promote Sartre's moral concept in our time.

FORREST, Peter. An Indubitability Analysis Of Knowledge. *Monist* 62,24–39 Ja 85.

In this paper I distinguish *perfect* from *approximate* knowledge. Perfect knowledge is analyzed as belief for which there are no objective grounds for any degree of doubt. Replacing 'any' by 'significant' I obtain an analysis of approximate knowledge. I argue that this analysis of knowledge satisfies our firm intuitions, and is illuminating. Finally I compare it with species–of–justified–true–belief analysis.

FORREST, Peter. Bradley And Realism About Universals. *Ideal Stud* 14,200–212 S 84.

In this paper I adapt Bradley's argument of chapter two of *Appearance and Reality*, in order to establish a presumption against what I call Hard Realism about Universals. By that I mean the treatment of universals as sufficiently like particulars to be called *things*, without hesitation. I leave open the possibility of overcoming this presumption.

FORREST, Peter. Is Motion Change Of Location? *Analysis* 44,177–178 O 84.

I argue, by means of counter–examples, that the analysis of motion as change of location either needs substantial modification or it should be rejected.

FORREST, Peter. The Lehrer–Wagner Theory Of Consensus And The Zero Weight Problem. *Synthese* 62,75–78 Ja 85.

Given the Lehrer/Wagner theory of consensus [Keith Lehrer and Carl Wagner *Rational Consensus* in Science and Society, Reidel, 1981], we need to know when to assign someone non–zero weight as an authority. Lehrer [page 20] proposes that if we prefer the person's guidance to a random device then we should assign him or her non–zero weight. In this note, I argue that that condition is not strict enough, unless we introduce infinitesimal weights.

FORTE, David F. "Injustice And Tragedy In Aristotle" in *The Georgetown Symposium On Ethics*, Porreco, Rocco (ed), 175–184. Lanham Univ Pr Of America 1984.

FORTI, Marco and Honsell, Furio. Comparison Of The Axioms Of Local And Global Universality. *Z Math Log* 30,193–196 1984.

FORTI, Marco and Honsell, Furio. The Consistency Of The Axiom Of Universality For The Ordering Of Cardinalities. *J Sym Log* 50,502–509 Je 85.

FOSTER, Donald W. I Of The Cyclops: The Herdsman–Poet. *Phil Lit* 8,250–260 O 84.

If Greek tragedy may be viewed as a Dionysian chorus discharging itself in an Apollonian world of images, pastoral may be viewed as a world of mere appearance which exists to preserve separation of self through an illusory and purely Apollonian image of the Dionysian, as the *Idylls* of Theocritus, wherein Homer's lawless Polyphemos is transfigured as the archetypal hardsman–poet. In the pastoral cosmos we behold a vision of natural man participating in a dreamlike bacchanal which obviates passion and suffering. The Idylls are nevertheless preserved from sentimentality by the poet's ironic stance toward the artifice of his pastoral vision.

FOSTER, Judy. Response To "Children In Care: Are Social Workers Abusing Their Authority". *J Med Ethics* 10,136–137 S 84.

In reply to Dr Benians' article which suggests that social workers at times abuse their authority, three areas can be considered: the broader context of the social work task, the legal process itself, and the contribution made by child psychiatrists.

FOSTER, Michael. *The Political Philosophies Of Plato And Hegel*. NY Garland 1984.

The author contrasts the political philosophies of Plato and Hegel by first distinguishing between the ancient Greek conception of "polis" and the modern conception of "state". After presenting the notions of justice and freedom in Plato's philosophy, the author discusses Hegel's criticism of Plato. Finally, Hegel's political philosophy is explicated, especially in terms of freedom, the state, and the sovereign.

FOTI, Veronique M. Heidegger: Remembrance And Metaphysics. *J Brit Soc Phenomenol* 15,243–248 O 84.

FÓTI, Véronique M. Representation And The Image: Between Heidegger, Derrida, And Plato. *Man World* 18,65–78 1985.

This essay addresses Derrida's critique of Heidegger's understanding of Greek thought as non–representational but as initiating the destiny of representation. The critique charges that Heidegger remains bound to a representational schema. However, in Heidegger's texts *two* senses of the image (*Bild*) are to be found which are problematically related to the Greek *eidos*. Only one of these is representational. The essay examines these two senses of the image and their unthematized tension over against the problematic of representation.

FOTION, Nicholas. "Distributing Health Care: A Case Study" in *Biomedical Ethics Reviews*, Humber, James M (ed), 107–126. Clifton Humana Pr 1983.

FOURASTIÉ, M Jean and others. Recherches Et Réflexions Sur Le Rire Le Risible, Le Comique Et L'humour. *Bull Soc Fr Phil* 78,5–126 Jl–S 84.

FOWLER, Don D. "Ethics In Contract Archaeology" in *Ethics And Values In Archaeology*, Green, Ernestene L (ed), 108–116. NY Free Pr 1984.

FOX, Daniel M. Who We Are: The Political Origins Of The Medical Humanities. *Theor Med* 6,327–342 O 85.

The medical humanities were organized, beginning in the late 1960s, by a small group of people who share a critique of medical education and a commitment to vigorous action to change it. They proposed to create several demonstration programs in humanities education at American schools. Although the group began with a religious orientation, it soon acquired a broader, more secular mission. As a result of shrewd political organizing, the group attracted members from within medicine, and was awarded a grant to promote the medical humanities. This paper describes these events and sets them in the context of the social and medical history of the 1960s and early 1970s.

FOX, Douglas A. The Principle Of Contra–Action. *Faith Phil* 2,168–174 Ap 85.

"contra–action" is a species of contradictions and is summarized in the formula: "That speech is invalid which denies the possibility or efective reality of action." It is argued that since speech is a form of action an absurdity is committed by speech that denies the possibility of action. Thus, certain traditional assertions, such as the Vedantic "That Thou Art," as well as other expression of non–dualism are shown to be fallacious.

FOX, Steven. China: Diary Of A Barefoot Bioethicist. *Hastings Center Rep* 14,18–20 D 84.

FRAKES, Jerold C. The Ancient Concept Of Casus And Its Early Medieval Interpretations. *Vivarium* 22,1–34 My 84.

The article analyses the late antique and medieval reception of the Aristotelian concept of 'chance', based on the works of Boethius and his early medieval translators and commentators (Alfred the Great, Notker Labeo, Remigius of Auxerre, the Anonymous of St Gall). The essential elements of the Aristotelian definition are preserved, although in different form and with different purposes.

FRALEIGH, Warren P. *Right Actions In Sport: Ethics For Contestants*. Champaign Human Kinetics 1984.

This book describes what a good sports contest is from the dual viewpoint of the nature of contests and the moral view. This description is a basis for stating guides for morally right actions for sports contestants. The ends pursued, winning–losing and quality of play, rules, relationships of opponents, and values are the categories of description while guides are organized as primary, supererogatory and secondary.

FRALEIGH, Warren P. An Examination Of Relationships Of Inherent, Intrinsic, Instrumental, And Contributive Values Of The Good Sports Contest. *J Phil Sport* 10,52–60 1983.

Taylor's description (*Normative Discourse*) of inherent, intrinsic, instrumental and contributive values is applied to sports contests. It is concluded that the inherent value of sports contests is knowledge of participant's relative ability to move mass in space and time in ways prescribed for particular sports. All sports contests provide this value, good sports contests give complete and accurate knowledge. Such knowledge is the capacity for sports contests to provide intrinsic satisfaction.

FRALEIGH, Warren P. Performance–Enhancing Drugs In Sport: The Ethical Issue. *J Phil Sport* 11,23–29 1984.

A reaction to Robert Simon and Miller Brown. The author agrees with these two in stating the moral issue: Is it morally right, for reasons of harm, coercion and/or fairness to restrict the informed choice of consenting adult athletes in taking harmful drugs for the purpose of enhancing sports performance? Fraleigh concludes that paternalistic restriction is justified because use of harmgul drugs by some forces other athletes to do likewise to remain competitive.

FRALEIGH, Warren P. The Philosophic Society For The Study Of Sport: 1972–1983. *J Phil Sport* 10,3–7 1983.

FRANCK, Giorgio. "Bathos", Immagini Del Tempo Alla Fine Del Tempo" in *Il Tempo Dell'Arte*, Papi, Fulvio and others (ed), 60–91. Milano Franco Angeli 1984.

FRANCK, Isaac. Maimonides And Aquinas On Man's Knowledge Of God: A Twentieth Century Perspective. *Rev Metaph* 38,591–616 Mr 85.

FRANCO, Eli. On The Interpretation Of Pramānasamuccaya (Vrtti) I, 3d. *J Indian Phil* 12,389–400 D 84.

The purpose of the paper is to point out that some Buddhist logicians considered substances, quantities, universals, etc., as real entities. Ironically enough, what led these logicians to give up some of the basic principles consecrated by Buddhism almost from its very beginning was a simple confusion between attribute and predicate in PSV I, 3d. The paper also explains an extremely difficult passage in the Tattvasaṅgraha and Pañjikā which defied the understanding of modern scholars. The discussion is quite technical in nature, and the details cannot be followed without some knowledge of Sanskrit.

FRANCOEUR, Robert T. "From Then To Now: Perinatal Intensive Care" in *Bioethical Frontiers In Perinatal Intensive Care*, Snowden, Fraser (ed), 19–38. Natchitoches Northwestern Pr 1985.

FRANCOEUR, Robert T. The Vatican's View Of Sex: The Inaccurate Conception. *Free Inq* 5,11–14 Spr 85.

FRANK, Arthur Q and Niemi, Richard G. Sophisticated Voting Under The Plurality Procedure: A Test Of A New Definition. *Theor Decis* 19,151–162 S 85.

A test of the Niemi–Frank definition of sophisticated voting under the plurality procedure. The simulation, using randomly–sized blocs of voters, is limited to three alternatives. The Niemi–Frank and the Farquharson definitions yield identical outcomes whenever both are determinate; both pick a high proportion of Condorcet winners. The Niemi–Frank definition is determinate 80 percent of the time; Farquharson less than 50 percent. Strategic behavior yields the Condorcet winner more often than sincere voting.

FRANK, Daniel H. *The Arguments From The Sciences In Aristotle's Peri Ideon'*. NY Lang 1984.

The "Peri Ideon" is Aristotle's first and most sustained critique of Platonic metaphysics. Arguments for the existence of Forms are presented; then Aristotle develops critical objections. This study is concerned with the first set of arguments in the "Peri Ideon," the so–called arguments 'from the sciences'.

FRANK, Manfred. L'herméneutique De Schleiermacher: Relecture Autour Du Débat Herméneutique–Néostructuralisme. *Rev Int Phil* 38,348–372 1984.

FRANK, Manfred. La Loi Du Langage Et L'anarchie Du Sens: A Propos Du Débat Searle–Derrida. *Rev Int Phil* 38,396–421 1984.

FRANK, Manfred. Plurivocité Et Dis–Simultanéité: Questions Herméneutiques Pour Une Théorie Du Texte Littéraire. *Rev Int Phil* 38,422–443 1984.

FRANK, S L. *The Unknowable: An Ontological Introduction To The Philosophy Of Religion*. Athens Ohio Univ Pr 1983.

FRANK, Willard C. Military Power And Human Values. *Relig Hum* 18,168–177 Autumn 84.

History shows that power counts in the world. War has been integral to the human experiment. There is no natural harmony. The values of civilization are fragile and can be destroyed. Government exists to protect these values, if necessary by armed force. Yet military action is destructive of the very values governments seek to defend. The human dilemma is whether to risk the destruction of one's values by utilizing or refraining from utilizing military force.

FRANKEL, Lois. Being Able To Do Otherwise: Leibniz On Freedom And Contingency. *Stud Leibniz* 16,45–59 1984.

Dieser Aufsatz möchte zeigen, dass Leibniz Freiheit nur in dem Sinne Kontingenz voraussetzt, dass andere Handlungsweisen als absolut möglich denkbar dein Müssen. Freiheit besteht nicht in der blossen Illusion, dass unsere Handlungen nicht durch unseren vollständingen Begriff verursacht und bestimmt sind, sondern in der epistemischen Möglichkeit des Handelnden, anders zu handeln. Für endliche Wesen impliziert diese epistemische Möglichkeit die Unkenntnis des göttlichen Plans. (edited)

FRANKEL, Lois. Reason And Antecedent Doubt. *S J Phil* 22,331–346 Fall 84.

This paper defends the following claims: (1) Descartes advocates general antecedent doubt, that is, doubt entertained in advance of skeptical arguments. (2) Such doubt is appropriate to his project. (3) In the context of general antecedent doubt, the skeptical arguments serve a less purely epistemic, more pedagogical purpose than is commonly allowed. (4) Reason neither is, nor ought to be included in general antecedent doubt.

FRANKENBERRY, Nancy. Meland's Empirical Realism And The Appeal To Lived Experience. *Amer J Theol Phil* 5,117–129 My & S 84.

FRANZEN, Winfried. Kritisches Zu Kripkes Theorie Der Eigennamen. *Conceptus* 18,3–19 1984.

It is argued that there is no real contrast between the 'causal' and the 'descriptive' theory of proper names. Especially, Kripke's criticism of the theory of proper names, as suggested by Searle and Strawson, is itself criticized. Kripke's counter–examples have only a certain surface plausibility, but do not prove anything. This is due (among other things) to his neglect of the fact that the 'backing of descriptions' which according to Strawson and Searle is a necessary condition for the use of proper names is itself embedded in something which could be dubbed 'backing of interests'. If, e.G., Aristotle had done nothing of what we think he has done, the question whether 'Aristotle' is still used as a name for Aristotle does not arise, because there wouldn't have been, since a long time, any use of the name, 'Aristotle' at all: nobody would be interested in Aristotle, and hence nobody would need refer to him.

FREDE, Michael. "Sceptic's Two Kinds Of Assent & Question Of Possibility Of Knowledge" in *Philosophy In History*, Rorty, Richard and others (ed), 255–278. NY Cambridge Univ Pr 1984.

FREDETTE, Gatien. A L'origine De La Notion D'amour En Occident. *Petit Rev Phil* 6,91–108 Autumn 84.

FREEDMAN, Benjamin and Bayles, Michael D. Canada: The Mandarin Bureaucracy. *Hastings Center Rep* 14,17–18 D 84.

FREEDMAN, Monroe H. Lawyer–Client Confidences Under The A B A Model Rules: Ethical Rules Without Ethical Reason. *Crim Just Ethics* 3,3–8 Sum/Fall 84.

FREEDMAN, Monroe H. The Problem Of Writing, Enforcing, And Teaching Ethical Rules: A Reply To Goldman's "Confidentiality, Rules, And Codes Of Ethics". *Crim Just Ethics* 3,14–16 Sum/Fall 84.

FREER, Jack P. Chronic Vegetative States: Intrinsic Value Of Biological Process. *J Med Phil* 9,395–408 N 84.

A 'naturalistic principle' has been put forth by Rolston, which leads to respect for the irreversibly comatose by virtue of the residual biological (objective) life. By comparing objective and subjective life, he develops a naturalistic principle which he contrasts with the humanistic norm of contemporary medical ethics. He claims there are clinical applications which would necessarily follow. A critique of this viewpoint is presented here, which begins with an analysis of what might be of value in spontaneous objective life. A measure of the moral worth of simple objective life is attempted by means of comparison with our attitudes toward animals. Finally, some of the clinical applications suggested by Rolston are reviewed. Except for euthanasia, there appears to be few clinical situations where the naturalistic principle helps in problem solving.

FREIBERG, Jo Ann. *Moral Principles In Education*: A Reevaluation. *Phil Stud Educ* No Vol,43–51 1983.

FRENCH, Peter A. *Collective And Corporate Responsibility*. NY Columbia Univ Pr 1984.

French develops, defends, and applies a metaphysical theory of corporate personhood. He draws deep distinctions between collective and corporate responsibility, and provides a concept of the moral states of corporations that has profound ethical, social, and legal consequences. Instead of trying to apply traditional moral theories to evaluate corporate managers, the book contends, those principles should be innovatively applied to the corporations itself, as a full–fledged person. (edited)

FRENCH, Peter A. A Principle Of Responsive Adjustment. *Philosophy* 59,491–504 O 84.

The standard principle accountability insists that for anyone to be held morally responsible for an event that event must have been the result of the intentional actions of the person in question. In effect, we can be held responsible only for our intentional actions. This principle, however, does not satisfy strong intuitions in a significant number of cases. In that class of cases are to be found some of the most important in contemporary life, including many corporate cases. Using a particularly dramatic event, the crash of a jetliner, I develop and defend a principle of accountability that allows attributions of responsibility retrospectively without insisting that the description of the untoward event be changed to make it intentional when it clearly was not intentional.

FREUND, Max. La Teoría De Conjuntos En Sentido Colectivo. *Rev Filosof (Costa Rica)* 22,73–80 D 84.

Este artículo constituye una introducción muy general y con el menor tecnicismo posible a una de las llamadas "teorías lógicas de Lesniewski", a saber: la Meriología. La Meriología es una teoría de conjuntos, pero conjunto tomado en sentido colectivo. A lo largo del artículo se describen varias axiomatizaciones de esta teoría y se mencionan algunos resultados metateóricos tales como la consistencia y la relación que tiene con el álgebra booleana.

FREY, Dagobert. "The Problem Of Time In The Plastic Arts" in *Continental Philosophy And The Arts*, Winters, Laurence E and others (ed), 139–162. Lanham Univ Pr Of America 1984.

FREY, Gerhard. Die Relevanz Der Deontischen Logik Für Die Ethik. *Z Allg Wiss* 4,345–355 1973.

Deontisch logische Systeme im engeren Sinne sind axiologisch. Um aber auch axiologisch relevante Rahmen–Normen aufstellen und angeben zu können, kommt es wesentlich auf die Art der verwendeten Formalismen an. Wie ein Beispiel zeigt, geht dies bis in die Boraussetzungen des zugrundegelegten Logikkalküls.

FREY, Gerhard. Kunst Als Dasein Und Ereignis: Zum Ontologischen Und Performativen Kunstbegriff. *Conceptus* 19,53–68 1985.

Aesthetic Platonism is the view that a work of art has an unchangeable, so to speak external existence, as contrasted with the view that many works of art appear only as representations, i.E., as unique events. The relation of the ontological to the performative aspect varies not only in regard to different kinds of art, but has also been different at different times. We explore the relation between reproductions and repetitions of a work with the so–called original, and with the creative process. Since every process of perception and reception presupposes a creative act it is natural to consider information and redundancy in relation to the concept of the work of art, the process of creation, and perception. If the creative process is itself understood as a work of art, it is purely performative. Insofar as the creative occurrence leaves relics, these can be declared as works in their own right with a permanent raison d'être. Contemporary art seems to be on the way to according ever increasing importance to the performative artistic interpretation.

FREYE, Ha and others. Der Mensch Als Biopsychosoziale Einheit. *Deut Z Phil* 33,134–160 1985.

FRIEDMAN, Harvey M and Simpson, S G and Smith, R L. Addendum To "Countable Algebra And Set Existence Axioms". *Annals Pure Applied Log* 28,319–320 My 85.

FRIEDMAN, Harvey. A Cumulative Hierarchy Of Predicates. *Z Math Log* 21,309–314 1975.

FRIEDMAN, Hershey H. Ethical Behavior In Business: A Hierarchical Approach From The Talmud. *J Bus Ethics* 4,117–130 Ap 85.

FRIEDMAN, Marylin A. Moral Integrity And The Deferential Wife. *Phil Stud* 47,141–150 Ja 85.

Thomas Hill Jr has attributed moral defectiveness to the "deferential wife": in his view, she fails either to understand or acknowledge her own moral rights and she thereby loses self–respect. I reject Hill's analysis and provide my own. I distinguish among different sorts of deference, identify one as morally problematic, and interpret the problem not in terms of rights but rather in terms of a (nonblameworthy) lack of moral integrity, or whole moral personhood.

FRIEDMAN, Maurice. *Martin Buber's Life And Work: The Later Years, 1945–1965.* NY Dutton 1983.

This third and last volume of Friedman's Buber biography portrays Buber's activities on behalf of Jewish–Arab rapprochement, including a large chapter on "Buber versus Ben–Gurion," his dialogue with Dag Hammarskjold, his encounters with psychotherapy, his confrontations with Carl Jung, Martin Heidegger, and Gershom Scholem, the former on "the eclipse of God," the latter on interpreting Hasidism. It also discusses in depth Buber's philosophical anthropology (*The Knowledge of Man*), his interpretation of Hasidism, *Two Types of Faith, Eclipse of God, Moses,* and his *Tales of the Hasidim.*

FRIEDMAN, Maurice. "Martin Buber's Approach To Comparative Religion" in *Martin Buber*, Gordon, Haim (ed), 367–384. Beersheva Ktav 1984.

FRIEDMAN, R Z. The Importance And Function Of Kant's Highest Good. *J Hist Phil* 22,325–342 Jl 84.

FRIEDRICH, Gert and Kastner, H and Possneck, E. Probleme Der Führenden Rolle Der Arbeiterklasse Im Sozialismus. *Deut Z Phil* 22,739–745 1974.

FRIEDRICH, P and Becher, Jurgen. Struktur Der Sozialistischen Produktionsverhältnisse Und Ökonomische Gesetze Des Sozialismus. *Deut Z Phil* 23,1013–1024 1975.

Ausgangspunkt der sozialistischen Produktionsweise ist die Nationalisierung der grundlegenden Produktionsmittel durch die Dikatur des Proletariats. Die Narionalisierung (Konfiskation) darf nicht mit der sozialistischen Vergesellschaftung gleichgestzt werden. Das Ausgangsproduktionsverhältnis der sozialistischen Produktionsverhältnisse stellt die unmittelbare Vergesellschaftung der Produktion und der Arbeit dar. Das grundlegende Produktionsverhältnis im Sozialismus ist das gesellschaftliche Eigentum an Produktionsmitteln.

FRIEDRICH, Wolfgang. Gödelsche Funktionalinterpretation Für Eine Erweiterung Der Klassischen Analysis. *Z Math Log* 31,3–29 1985.

The functional interpretation of Gödel, which has been shown to be app.licable to full classical analysis by Spector, is extended to capture a game quantifier predicate over continuous functionals of type 2. In "Spielquantorinterpretation unstetiger Funktionale der höheren Analysis" (Arch math Logic 24 (1984), pp 73–99) an interpretation of functional analytical comprehension in all types by means of this game quantifier has been given. So altogether we have a constructive interpretation of full classical analysis plus analytical comprehension.

FRISCH, Morton J (ed) and Stevens, Richard G (ed). *American Political Thought: The Philosophic Dimension Of American Statesmanship*, Second Edition. Itasca Peacock 1983.

FRISON, George C. "Avocational Archaeology: Its Past, Present, And Future" in *Ethics And Values In Archaeology*, Green, Ernestene L (ed), 184–193. NY Free Pr 1984.

FRITZSCHE, Lothar. Qualité—Une Notion (in German). *Deut Z Phil* 22,75–82 1974.

FROMM, Eberhard and Sokolowski, K. Zum Platz Des Pluralismus In Der Gegenwärtigen Bürgerlichen Ideologie. *Deut Z Phil* 23,1036–1046 1975.

Der Pluralismus ist eine Richtung innerhalb der idealistischen Philosophie der Genenwart, die vor allem in neopositivistischen Strömungen vorherrscht. Der "theoretische" Pluralismus ist erklärter Gegner jeglichen Monismus. Von der "philosophish–pluralistischen" Interpretation der Welt als Vielfalt voneinander unabhängiger Wirkungen wird auf das "politisch–pluralistische" Modell der

Gesellschaft geschlossen. Es geht den Pluralismustheoretikern um den "nachweis", dafss Sozailismus und Demokratie unvereinbar seien. In antikommunistischer Konfrontation zum realen Sozialismus verwirklicht der politische Pluralismus seine systemstabilisierende Funktion.

FRONGIA, Guido. *Wittgenstein Regole E Sistema.* Milano F Angeli 1983.

FU, Pei–Jung. An Understanding Of Original Sin—Through The Interpretations Of Tennant, Rahner, And Ricoeur. *Phil Rev (Taiwan)* 7,141–162 Ja 84.

FUCHS, Michel. Edmund Burke Et Joseph De Maistre. *Rev Univ Ottawa* 54,49–58 Jl–S 84.

The purpose of this paper is to reexamine Maistre's debt to Burke. Although they were both in the anti–revolutionary camp, they disagreed on everything else, including the causes of the French Revolution and the ends they tried to achieve. This disagreement is traced back to Burke's ambiguous political philosophy—his acceptance of possessive individualism bolstered up by feudal concepts—reduced by Maistre to a massive belief in providentialism, itself fraught with insoluble contradictions.

FUJITA, Kazuyoshi. Eine Betrachtung Über Das Problem Des Seins Und Der Schönheit In Der Philosophie Des Aristoteles (in Japanese). *Bigaku* 35,1–13 Mr 85.

Aristoteles redet von den zwei natürlichen Ursprüngen der Poiēsis in *Arspoetica* 1448b4–9. Nämlich: 1) Manthanein ist eigentlich Mimeisthai, 2) Die richtigkeit der Mimēsis gibt eine grosse Freude. [edited]

FULLER, Steven. Is There A Language–Game That Even The Deconstructionist Can Play? *Phil Lit* 19,104–109 Ap 85.

A J Cascardi has recently argued that deconstruction is a form of nihilism that rejects the epistemological enterprise of which foundationalism and skepticism are the two poles. I counter this claim by arguing that Cascardi's construal of skepticism relies too heavily on Descartes to illuminate the deconstructionist project. Deconstruction really aims to revive classical Pyrrhenian skepticism, which by no means entails nihilism.

FUMERTON, Richard and Foley, Richard. Davidson's Theism? *Phil Stud* 48,83–90 Jl 85.

The authors examine and criticize a recent anti–skeptical argument forwarded by Donald Davidson, an argument that depends on the possibility of there being an omniscient interpreter of our beliefs who uses Davidson's recommended method of interpretation.

FUNK, Nanette. Mill And Censorship. *Hist Phil Quart* 1,453–463 O 84.

FUNK, Nanette. Reporters And A Free Press. *J Applied Phil* 2,85–98 Mr 85.

A necessary condition for news to be produced under conditions of 'negative' freedom is for newspapers to become 'reporter codetermined newspapers', where reporters, along with editors and publishers, have a collective 'positive' freedom to vote on news–policy, select editors and hire reporters. 'publisher–controlled' newspapers systematically prevent reporters from reporting some news–stories and coerce and manipulate reporters into reporting others. It is argued here that all newspapers should be legally required to become reporter codetermined newspapers. This change is also required by Rawl' and Mill's arguments for freedom of the press. On the basis of empirical data it is unlikely that the demands of freedom or justice can be met within existing institutional structures.

FUNKE, G. Kant Für Mediziner? *Phil Natur* 15,293–307 1975.

FURGER, Franz. Die Sozialpflichtigkeit Des Eigentums: Gesichtspunkte Der Christlichen Sozialethik. *Stud Phil (Switzerland)* Supp 12,129–144 1983.

The article deals with the specific view points of christian social ethics and specially with the Catholic Social Doctrine. It understands, therefore, private property as a personal human right standing under social duty. The individual aspects prevailed in the classical concepts. But since the moralists become more aware of the worldwide connections of economics, the social dimension gets (specially since the Vatican II council and according to the view of the Bible) an ever major importance.

FURGER, Franz. Wie Erhalten Ethische Grundsaetze Relevanz Fuer Die Forschung (in Polish). *Stud Phil Christ* 20,142–148 1984.

FURTH, Montgomery (trans). *Aristotle Metaphysics: Books Zeta, Eta, Theta, Iota.* Indianapolis Hackett 1985.

An English translation of the seventh through tenth books of Aristotle's *Metaphysics*, aiming at the maximum possible literalness. Because the Greek original is exceedingly terse, some interpolation is always required to put it into intelligible English. In this version, everything not corresponding to something in the original is in square brackets [ ]. There are some interpretive notes.

GAA, James C. The Stability Of Bargains Behind The Veil Of Ignorance. *Theor Decis* 17,119–134 S 84.

Although analyses about what representative individuals would choose behind the veil of ignorance have been regarded as *n*–person non–zero–sum cooperative games, none of the apparatus of game theory beyond 2–person non–zero–sum non–cooperative games has actually been used. This paper investigates the consequences of extending the original position to allow three persons the possibility of forming binding coalitions behind the veil of ignorance. The analysis shows yet another way in which original position arguments are sensitive to assumptions about information and criteria of rational decision behind the veil of ignorance. [edited]

GABBAY, Dov M (ed) and Guenthner, Franz (ed). *Handbook Of Philosophical Logic: Extensions Of Classical Logic,* V2. Boston Reidel 1984.

GABRIEL, Gottfried. Fregean Connection: Bedeutung, Value And Truth–Value. *Phil Quart* 34,372–376 Jl 84.

It is shown how Frege's problematic connection between truth–value and *Bedeutung* (of a sentence) becomes more plausible when set against the background of German language and philosophy, especially by comparing Frege's position with the value–theoretical school of Neo–Kantianism (W Windelband).

GADAMER, Hans– Georg. "The Hermeneutics Of Suspicion" in *Hermeneutics,* Shapiro, Gary (ed), 54–65. Amherst Univ Of Mass Pr 1984.

GADAMER, Hans–Georg. Et Pourtant: Puissance De La Bonne Volonté (Une Réplique À Jacques Derrida). *Rev Int Phil* 38,344–347 1984.

GADAMER, Hans–Georg. Gibt Es Auf Erden Ein Mass? *Phil Rundsch* 32,1–25 1985.

GADAMER, Hans–Georg. Le Défi Herméneutique. *Rev Int Phil* 38,333–340 1984.

GADAMER, Hans–Georg. The Hermeneutics Of Suspicion. *Man World* 17,313–324 1984.

GAERTNER, Wulf. Justice–Constrained Libertarian Claims And Pareto Effiecient Collective Decisions. *Erkenntnis* 23,1–18 My 85.

This paper discusses justice–constrained libertarian claims that were proposed as a way to circumvent the impossibility of the Paretian liberal. Since most of the results are negative in character, we suggest an alternative route: A requirement on the structure of individual orderings should be combined with the idea that under particular circumstances individual decisiveness should be controlled by higher–order principles.

GAGERN, Michael. "'All Powers To The Walking People' Feuerbach As A Fourth–World Marxist" in *Contemporary Marxism,* O' Rourke, James J (ed), 55–78. Boston Reidel 1984.

GAHDE, Ulrich. A Formal Approach To The Theory–Dependence Of Measurement. *Phil Natur* 21,266–272 1984.

The paper shows how, in a precise technical framework, the theory–dependence of certain types of measurement can be analyzed. For that purpose, the semi–formal apparatus supplied by the structuralist metatheoretic approach is slightly modified and enlarged. The discussion focuses on relatively simple procedures of measurement, in which only one theory is involved. The main emphasis is put on the question in what way the theory–dependence of these procedures is related to the initial experimental setting.

GAIFMAN, Haim. On Inductive Support And Some Recent Tricks. *Erkenntnis* 22,5–22 Ja 85.

GALEAZZI, Umberto. Cartesio E Kant Nella "Terminologia Filosofica" Di Adorno. *Riv Filosof Neo–Scolas* 76,292–316 Ap–Je 84.

GALICZA, Peter. Two Experiments On The History Of Hungarian School Philosophy Between The Two World Wars (in Hungarian). *Magyar Filozof Szemle* 4,529–542 1983.

L'article est consacré à deux figures de la génération de philosophes d'après la République Hongroise des Conseils, Lajos Prohászka et Gyula Moór. L'auteur expose les causes principales de leur rapport conflictueux aux traditions théorétiques du début de siècle hongrois. En s'occupant de deux grandes figures de la vie philosophique de l'époque, Akos Pauler et Gyula Kornis, l'auteur cherche à démontrer que l'anti–psychologisme platonicien, influant essentiellement les idées de Pauler, était une base théorétique importante pour la vie philosophique en pleine consolidation. Il fait ressortir que l'intérêt public et l'irrationalisme de Kornis ainsi que la largeur de son horizon étaient aptes à synthétiser les différentes conceptions; ses jugements administratifs pouvaient refléter une exigence scientifique. [edited]

GALISON, Peter. "Bubble Chambers And Experiment" in *Observation, Experiment, And Hypothesis In Modern Physical Science,* Achinstein, Peter (ed), 309–374. Cambridge MIT Pr 1985.

GALLAGHER, Kenneth T. Rorty's Antipodeans: An Impossible Illustration? *Phil Phenomenol Res* 45,449–456 Mr 85.

Richard Rorty in *Philosophy and the Mirror of Nature* attempts to show that our use of mentalist predicates is not indispensable by imagining a race of people (Antipodeans) who get along perfectly well without them. This paper attempts to show that his illustration is internally inconsistent and hence that it cannot provide support for his materialist thesis. [Rorty bases the non–mentalist language of these beings on their advanced "science," but neither in respect to "pain" nor "thought," the two areas of his concern, could their purported ability be acquired as he suggests.

GALLANT, Donald M and Irwin, Martin. "The Right To Refuse Psychotropic Medications" in *Difficult Decisions In Medical Ethics,* Ganos, Doreen L (ed), 31–38. NY Liss 1983.

GALLINA, Paul. Bertrand Russell, Karl Marx, And *German Social Democracy* Revisited. *Russell* 4,302–310 Wint 84.

Section 1 discusses Russell's views on Marx (and Pitt's assessment) as they are presented in the first chapter of *German Social Democracy* entitled "Marx and the Theoretical Basis of Social Democracy". It suggests that the form of Russell's criticism is by no means original, and in matters of content he shares a great deal of similarity with Jevons. russell's treatment of historical materialism is cursory and simplistic. Section 2 discusses Marx and Russell on labor and religion.

GALLOIS, Andre and Elliot, Robert. Would It Have Been Me (Against The Necessity Of Origin). *Austl J Phil* 62,292–293 S 84.

GALLOIS, André. True Believers And Radical Sceptics. *Philosophia (Israel)* 14,349–368 D 84.

GALLOP, David. *Parmenides Of Elea: Fragments.* Toronto Univ Of Toronto Pr 1984.

GALLOWAY, Jonathan F. Human Rights And U S Foreign Policy: Models And Options. *J Soc Phil* 16,8–13 Wint 85.

Three models are used to explain or interpret foreign policy choices—a human rights perspective, one based on economic imperatives and one founded on the realities of balance of power politics. How can the advocates of power politics or economic efficiency models say that policy should be x when the assumptions in the models predict that behavior will tend toward x? Only the proponent of a human rights perspective avoids this problem.

GALTON, Antony. *The Logic Of Aspect: An Axiomatic Approach.* Oxford Clarendon Pr 1984.

GANDELMAN, Claude and Klein, Itshaq. Hegel's Dialectic Of Master And Slave As A Model For The Relation Between Artistic Creation And Aesthetic Appreciation. *Phil Soc Crit* 5,35–46 Ja 78.

GANDHI, Ramchandra. Svaraj Of India. *Indian Phil Quart* 11,461–472 O–D 84.

GANDHI, Ramchandra. What We Do And Say In Saying And Doing Something. *Indian Phil Quart* 11,145–160 Ap 84.

GANDY, Clara I and Stanlis, Peter J. *Edmund Burke: A Bibliography Of Secondary Studies To 1982.* NY Garland 1983.

GANGAL, Vaijayanti. Raja Rammohan Roy. *Indian Phil Quart* 12,13–18 Ja–Mr 85 Supp.

GANGAVANE, Diptee. Purity And Power: A Study In Two Renaissance Profiles. *Indian Phil Quart* 12,1–12 Ja–Mr 85 Supp.

GANGJIAN, Luo. On Subject And Object. *Chin Stud Phil* 16,33–47 Fall 84.

GANHO, Maria De Lourdes Sirgado. O Pedagogismo Reformista De Frei Manuel Do Cenáulo. *Rev Port Filosof* 40,419–440 O–D 84.

GANOS, Doreen L and others (ed). *Difficult Decisions In Medical Ethics*, V4. NY Liss 1983.

GARBER, Daniel. "Old Evidence And Logical Omniscience In Bayesian Confirmation Theory" in *Testing Scientific Theories*, Earman, John (ed), 99–132. Minneapolis Univ Minnesota Pr 1983.

GARCIA– ALONSO, Luz. The Perspectives Of The Distinction Between *Agere* And *Facere*. *Diotima* 12,97–103 1984.

GARCIA, Laura L. A Response To The Modal Problem Of Evil. *Faith Phil* 1,378–388 O 84.

The modal problem of evil is this: if God is a necessary being and has omnipotence, omniscience and moral perfection essentially, then worlds which it would be immoral for God to create are logically impossible; but morally degraded worlds seem perfectly possible since we can consistently describe such worlds. I conclude the modal argument fails because it does not distinguish between intrinsic or *prima facie* possibility and possibility *simpliciter*.

GARDEN, Rachel Wallace. *Modern Logic And Quantum Mechanics.* Bristol Hilger 1984.

Peculiarities of quantum mechanics are features of our own description rather than features of the microscopic world. This general view is not new but is supported here by a new and rigorous analysis of logic, logical foundations of probabilities in both classical and Quantum mechanics. It is in the search of a new bivalent description of subatomic systems that advance in the subject lies. (staff)

GARDENFORS, Peter and Makinson, David and Alchourron, Carlos. On The Logic Of Theory Change: Partial Meet Contraction And Revision Functions. *J Sym Log* 50,510–530 Je 85.

This paper extends earlier work by its authors on formal aspects of the processes of contracting a theory to eliminate a proposition and revising a theory to introduce a proposition. In the course of the earlier work, Gärdenfors developed general postulates of a more or less equational nature for such processes, whilst Alchourrón and Makinson studied the particular case of contraction functions that are maximal, in the sense of yielding a maximal subset of the theory (or alternatively, of one of its axiomatic bases), that fails to imply the proposition being eliminated. In the present paper, the authors study a broader class, including contraction functions that may be less than maximal. Specifically, they investigate "partial meet contraction functions," which are defined to yield the intersection of some nonempty family of maximal subsets of the theory that fail to imply the proposition being eliminated. (edited)

GARDENFORS, Peter. Propositional Logic Based On The Dynamics Of Belief. *J Sym Log* 50,390–394 Je 85.

The key idea is to identify propositions with a certain kind of changes of belief. The interpretation is that a proposition is characterized by the change it would induce if added to a state of belief. Propositions are thus defined as functions from states of belief to states of belief. A set of postulates concerning the properties and existence of propositions are formulated. A proposition is said to be a tautology if it is the identity function on states of belief. The main result is that the logic determined by the postulates is intuitionistic propositional logic.

GARDNER, Michael R. "Realism And Instrumentalism In Pre–Newtonian Astronomy" in *Testing Scientific Theories*, Earman, John (ed), 201–266. Minneapolis Univ Minnesota Pr 1983.

GARDNER, Peter. The Compulsory Curriculum And Beyond: A Consideration Of Some Aspects Of The Educational Philosophy Of J P White. *J Phil Educ* 18,167–185 1984.

This is a critical inquiry which explores some of the main ideas advanced in J P White's book *Towards a Compulsory Curriculum* and which considers these ideas in the light of views advanced in White's later book *The Aims of Education Restated*. In particular attention is paid to White's justifications for restricting pupils' freedom, his accounts of what is good for people, his curricular recommendations and his view of personal autonomy.

GARELLI, Jacques. "Act Of Writing" in *Existential Coordinates Of Human Condition*, Tymieniecka, A (ed), 451–478. Boston Reidel 1984.

GAREWICZ, J. Pilate And Parsifal: Two Culprits Judged From Schopenhauer's Vantage Point (in Polish). *Etyka* 21,25–40 1985.

The article is composed of three parts. In the first the author discusses Schopenhauer's concept of "unearned guilt". Guilt rests not with action but with being, and thus everybody bears guilt by the mere fact of existing in an objective world. All man can do is recognize this guilt and assume responsibility for it; if he shirks it, unprovoked guilt becomes his own guilt.

GARGANO, Antonio. Hölderlin E La *Vereinigungsphilosophie. Filosofia* 35,199–216 Jl–O 84.

GARNER, Richard T. The Deconstruction Of The Mirror And Other Heresies: Ch'an And Taoism As Abnormal Discourse. *J Chin Phil* 12,155–168 Je 85.

There is an innocent sense in which knowledge is a matter of accurate representations. But to take the metaphor of the mind as a mirror too literally is to become enmeshed in epistemology, engaged with skepticism, and alienated from the world as experienced. I discuss Rorty's attempt to dissolve epistemology by freeing us from the metaphor of a "Mirror of Nature." This modern pragmatism, the work of the later Wittgenstein, Hui Neng's anti–metaphysical criticism of the gradualism of the Northern School of Zen Buddhism, and the Daoist's "edifying" rejection of Confucianism, are instances of "abnormal discourse," designed to free us from the mirror metaphor and from resulting transcendent aspirations.

GARODDIES, Jean–Louis and Kalinowski, Georges. Un Logicien Déontique Avant La Lettre: Gottfried Wilhelm Leibniz. *Arch Rechts Soz* 60,79–112 1974.

In their introduction the authors sketch the story of R Blanché's rediscovery of Leibniz' texts containing his logic of norms. Then G Kalinowski analyses the *Theoremata qvibus combinantur Iuris Modalia inter se* (he draws from them Leibniz' theory of opposition of deontic statements, based on the analogy between these statements and the modal ones) and J –L Gardies studies the *Theoremata qvibus combinantur Iuris Modalibus Logicis*.

GARRETT, B J. Nozick And Knowledge—A Rejoinder. *Analysis* 44,194–196 O 84.

GARSON, James W. "Quantification In Modal Logic" in *Handbook Of Philosophical Logic*, Gabbay, Dov (ed), 249–308. Boston Reidel 1984.

GARTNER, Lou Ann and Hull, Richard T and Nelson, James A. "Ethical Issues In Prenatal Therapies" in *Biomedical Ethics Reviews*, Humber, James M (ed), 225–250. Clifton Humana Pr 1984.

GARTY, M and Grosskopf, I and Buckman, G. Ethical Dilemmas Of The Doctors' Strike In Israel. *J Med Ethics* 11,70–71 Je 85.

The authors discuss some of the moral dilemmas confronting Israeli doctors in the context of their strike in 1983. Concern for their patients militated against a strike. On the other hand their salaries were far below the mean standard of the country. To earn as much as nurses and radiographers doctors were forced to work 65–70 hours a week. The authors argue that if a doctor is underpaid and forced to work excessively the quality of medical care and ability to act in their best interests of patients is adversely affected. To avoid 'the necessity to strike' doctors' salaries and working conditions should be set by independent bodies in those countries where doctors are paid by the State.

GARVER, Newton. Die Lebensform In Wittgensteins *Philosophischen Untersuchungen. Grazer Phil Stud* 21,33–54 1984.

GASS, William H. The Origin Of Extermination In The Imagination. *Phil Forum (Boston)* 16,19–32 Fall–Wint 84.

GASSER, Johannes. The Mask As The Throughway To The Beyond: A Philosophical Analysis Of A Basic Way Of Thinking. *Ultim Real Mean* 8,24–39 Mr 85.

GAUTHIER, David. "Deterrence, Maximization, And Rationality" in *The Security Gamble*, Mac Lean, Douglas (ed), 100–122. Totowa Rowman & Allanheld 1984.

GAUTHIER, David. "Justice As Social Choice" in *Morality, Reason And Truth*, Copp, David (ed), 251–269. Totowa Rowman & Allanheld 1984.

GAUTHIER, David and Kavka, Gregory S. "Responses To The Paradox Of Deterrence" in *The Security Gamble*, Mac Lean, Douglas (ed), 155–162. Totowa Rowman & Allanheld 1984.

GAUTHIER, David. Bargaining And Justice. *Soc Phil Pol* 2,29–47 Spr 85.

GAUTHIER, Yvon. De La Physique À L'épistémologie B D'Espagnat Et I Prigogine. *Log Anal* 27,327–342 S 84.

L'épistémologie française de la physique a été une épistémologie historique jusqu'à Bachelard. Récemment elle a pris un tournant qui l'écarte de l'histoire régressive pour la rapprocher davantage des débats actuels de la physique: j'en veux pour exemples les discussions que suscitent l'inégalité (ou les inégalités) de Bell ou la théorie des variables cachées et les débats qui gravitent autour de la notion de désordre, surtout dans la perspective de la nouvelle thermodynamique proposée par I. Prigogine. Ces débats nontrent une vigueur nouvelle et s'ils ne sont pas toujours éclairants, il faut se réjouir de leur pertinence et de leur actualité. Dans ce article, je voudrais faire l'état de la question et essayer d'être le plus près possible de la rigueur sans pour autant faire un étalage impudique de formalisme; je ferai aussi référence, sans fausse humilité, à quelques travaux parus ailleurs et susceptibles de mieux suturer la problématique. Je ferai porter ma critique sur le réalisme en science.

GAUTHIER, Yvon. Note Sur La Syntaxe Et La Sémantique Du Concept D'égalité. *Philosophiques* 11,349–352 O 84.

In this note, we examine the logical structure of the notion of equality. After having introduced the various concepts which are traditionally linked with the notion of equality, extensional and intensional equality, we suggest that the notion of homotopic versus heterotopic properties constitute the logicosemantical basis for a theory of equality beyond the mere syntactical analysis of the relevant concepts.

GAUTHIER, Yvon. Répliques: Les Vices Cachés Ou Les Dessous De La Vertu. *Dialogue (Canada)* 24,131–136 Spr 85.

The author replies to two critical notices by Francois Lepage and Robert Nadeau on the author's book *Théoretiques. pour une philosophie constructiviste des sciences* (Le Préambule: Longueuil, 1982). It is mostly on misconceptions and mistakes in the interpretation of his work that the author insists. In particular, he shows that both critics have missed some important points of his contributions to Quantum Mechanics and the notion of the local observer. He also points out misinterpretations of his notion of proof in mathematical physics.

Gavin, William J 294 **Author Index with Abstracts**

GAVIN, William J and Conway, Jeremiah P. Works Of Art As Cultural Probes. *J Theor Crit Vis Arts* 1,115–132 1982.

Outstanding works of art may be regarded as "probes" into the thought or general attitudes of the cultures that produced them. In addition, a perennial pedagogic problem facing interdisciplinary courses consists in finding an appropriate story line which is broad enough to encompass a variety of disciplines; yet concrete enough to hold student attention. In this article we argue that the medium of trials fulfills this dual need. We begin with an analysis of the educational potential of the trial situation by revealing the trial text as a wedge or lens into its interdisciplinary subtextual or contextual framework. In the course from which this article stems, we focus on three trials: the trial of Socrates; the trial of Galileo; and the trial of Joseph K in Kafka's novel, *The Trial*. In each of these instances, we are presented with a text which if taken literally, i.E., on the surface level, makes no sense. What appears as absurd on a surface level becomes somewhat understandable when the trial text is viewed in a wider interdisciplinary context. As one illustration of this use of trial texts, the present article concentrates on the trial of Joseph K in Kafka's novel *The Trial*.

GAVIN, William J and Conway, Jeremiah. The Phenomenology Of Trials: Text And Socio–Political Context. *Cogito* 3,1–24 Mr 85.

A perennial pedagogic problem facing interdisciplinary courses consists in finding an appropriate story line which is broad enough to encompass a variety of disciplines, yet concrete enough to hold student attention. In this article we argue that the medium of trials fulfills this dual need, when utilized in a critically philosophical manner. We begin with an analysis of the educational potential of the trial situation by revealing the trial text as a wedge or lens into its interdisciplinary subtextual or contextual framework. In the course from which this article stems, we focus on three trials; the trial of Socrates; the trial of Galileo; and the trial of Joseph K in Kafka's novel, *The Trial*. In each of these instances, we are presented with a text which is taken literally, i.E., on the surface level, makes no sense. What appears as absurd on a surface level becomes somewhat understandable when the trial text is viewed in a wider interdisciplinary context.

GAVIN, William J. Panthéisme Pluraliste Et Possibilité Actuelle: Réflexions Sur "A Pluralistic Universe" De William James. *Arch Phil* 47,557–568 O–D 84.

In a Pluralistic Universe James' metaphysical position is not neutral or foundational, but rather is linked to a specific religious commitment entitled 'pluralistic pantheism'. Furthermore, James argues that, at a meta–theoretical level, any philosophic outlook is not self–sustaining, but rather involves existential choice, in terms of the 'faith ladder'. Such a position, I argue, ultimately leads James, acting as an empiricist, to defend actual possibility by way of adopting a metaphysical position where the 'really real' is broader not only than the known, but broader than the knowable, and essentially so.

GAVIN, William J. Regional Ontologies, Types Of Meaning, And The Will To Believe In The Philosophy Of William James. *J Brit Soc Phenomenol* 15,262–270 O 84.

There are at least two passages in the Jamesian corpus where he seems to establish a topology of "regional ontologies", or to set up multiple "language games". The first of these is *The Principles of Psychology* when he talks about "the many worlds", or "...Sub–universes commonly discriminated from each other...", the second is in *Pragmatism*, where he notes that there "are...At least three well–characterized levels, stages, or types of thought about the world we live in..." two questions immediately come to mind about these levels. First, is each of these areas of equal importance, epistemologically and ontologically speaking? Second, how, if at all, are these regional areas related to each other? Each of these questions has a seemingly obvious answer. To wit, the world of perception is more important than any of the other areas; and second, the regional areas are related in terms of the disjunctive and conjunctive transitions which James so strenuously upholds, resulting in an overall "concatenated" picture. I argue that both of these responses are insufficient, and that the issue is more complicated than it first appears. (edited)

GAVIN, William J. Some Marxist Interpretations Of James' Pragmatism: A Summary And Reply. *Stud Soviet Tho* 29,279–294 My 85.

GAVIN, William J. The 'Will To Believe' In Science And Religion. *Int J Phil Relig* 15,139–148 1984.

James sometimes seems to divide areas where "the will to believe" applies in terms of content, e.G., science vs religion, and sometimes in terms of form, e.G., forced, living, and momentous hypotheses vs non–forced, non–living, etc. I suggest that the second approach is better, and that James realized this in *Pragmatism*, where he became suspicious of the perceptual world of common sense. Ultimately, the differences between scientific hypotheses and religious hypotheses are ones of degree rather than kind. This is shown, briefly, by looking at *The Varieties of Religious Experience*.

GAWLIK, Ladislav. Forty Years Of Socialist Cultural Evolution (in Czechoslovakian). *Estetika* 22,5–16 1985.

GAY, Robert. Inconceivable? *Philosophy* 60,247–254 Ap 85.

GAY, William C. Philosophy And The Nuclear Debate. *Phil Soc Crit* 10,1–8 Wint 84.

In this "Introduction" to the special, double–issue of the journal on "Philosophy and the Debate on Nuclear Weapons Systems and Policies," the editor groups under four headings the fourteen articles included: 1) the extinction thesis, 2) power and domination, 3) nuclear weapons, and 4) the morality of deterrence and the quest for peace. The central argument of each article is summarized and various relations among the articles are noted. The "Introduction" ends with information on the philosophical organizations which are primarily focused on the nuclear debate.

GAYLIN, Willard (ed) and Macklin, Ruth (ed) and Murray, Thomas H (ed). *Feeling Good And Doing Better; Ethics And Nontherapeutic Drug Use*. Clifton Humana Pr 1984.

This book is a collection of original articles developed by members of a Research Group over two years of discussion and debate on the ethics of drug use for enhancing pleasure or performance. Problems addressed include performance aids in sports, public policy towards nontherapeutic drug use, the "medical model," and the nature of pleasure; drug use and risk–taking; and legal and constitutional aspects of nontherapeutic drug use.

GAYLIN, Willard. "Feeling Good And Doing Better" in *Feeling Good And Doing Better*, Murray, Thomas H (ed), 1–12. Clifton Humana Pr 1984.

GAYLIN, Willard. In Defense Of The Dignity Of Being Human. *Hastings Center Rep* 14,18–22 Ag 84.

The term "human dignity" appears with greater and greater circulation in the world of law and ideas. Yet the concept of dignity has been little examined in modern times. Kant equated human dignity with human autonomy, and this conflated state persists into the present. Unfortunately, recent psychological theory has questioned the very nature of autonomy. Without approaching that question, I have attempted to ground the special worth or dignity of the human species in five other specific attributes that distinguish it from even closely related animal forms. The biological uniqueness of the human species is underappreciated in the philosophical and psychological world today, as it never was in biblical and classic times.

GBADEGESIN, Olusegun. Destiny, Personality And The Ultimate Reality Of Human Existence: A Yoruba Perspective. *Ultim Real Mean* 7,173–188 S 84.

The paper examines the Yoruba perspective on ultimate reality and meaning by focussing on the concept of person as a combination of body, breathing spirit (emi) and destiny (ori). I argue that ori, conceived as man's meaning, introduces a factor in personhood unknown in Western philosophy. Underlying this conception, however, is a moral view according to which the ultimate meaning of human existence is the promotion of the good and service to community and humanity.

GEACH, Peter T. Dummett On Frege: A Review Discussion. *Thomist* 49,116–121 Ja 85.

GEACH, Peter. Some Problems About The Sense And Reference Of Proper Names. *Can J Phil* 6,83–96 80 Supp.

GEHLAR, Fritz. Raum Und Zeit Als Existenzformen Der Materie. *Deut Z Phil* 23,898–912 1975.

Es wird davon ausgegangen, dafss L Feuerbach und F Engels einen materialistischen, *philosophischen* Materiebegriff hatten und die Vorstellung von einer qualitativ einheitlichen Materie (Substanzauffassung) ablehnten. Es gibt keinen ausreichenden Grund für die Annahme, dafss von beiden das Verhältnis der Materie zu Raum und Zeit im Sinne einer Inhalt–Form–Relation interpretiert wurde. Auf der Grundlage der Charakerisierung der materiellen Erscheinungen als Komplexe von Eigenschaften, Beziehungen und Wechselwirkungen werden Raum und Zeit als wesentliche Bestandteile materieller Strukturen, als Aspekte des materiellen Beziehungsgefüges bestimmt.

GEHRMANN, Siegfried. Zum Recht Des Naturzustandes Und Seiner Dedeutung Für Die Stellung Der Staatsgewalt Bei Thomas Hobbes. *Z Phil Forsch* 29,195–205 Ap–Je 75.

GEIDEL, Werner. Activité Sociale Et Besoins Culturels De La Classe Ouvrière (in German). *Deut Z Phil* 22,71–74 1974.

GELLA, Aleksander. The Changing Role Of Intellectuals In The Revolutionary Order. *Stud Soviet Tho* 29,1–10 Ja 85.

Author tries to show the role of the intellectuals in there stages of revolutionary development. During the first stage they need to have "double personality"—that of intellectual and that of politician. During the second stage, revolutionary intellectuals must change into "men of action". After the revolution (3rd stage), they must be obedient servants of the state. Thus, the intellectuals in all stages of revolution cannot fulfill the essential role of men of thought without risking personal careers of lives.

GELLA, Teresa. "Poetry As Essential Graphs" in *Existential Coordinates Of Human Condition*, Tymieniecka, A (ed), 157–162. Boston Reidel 1984.

GELLER, Jeffrey L. Wittgenstein On The 'Charm' Of Psychoanalysis. *Phil Res Arch* 10,57–66 1984.

This paper presents Freud's argument that the clinical process of psychoanalysis must continually combat the patient's resistance to the analyst's interpretations. It also presents systematically Wittgenstein's counterargument. Wittgenstein contends that psychoanalytic interpretations are enormously attractive and that their "charm" predisposes the patient to accept them. He traces their charm to six sources, each of which is discussed.

GELLNER, Ernest. Tractatus Sociologico–Philosophicus. *Philosophy* 17,247–259 84 Supp.

GELLRICH, Jesse. "On Medieval Interpretation And Mythology" in *Existential Coordinates Of Human Condition*, Tymieniecka, A (ed), 185–194. Boston Reidel 1984.

GELLRICH, Jesse. "The Structure Of Allegory" in *Existential Coordinates Of Human Condition*, Tymieniecka, A (ed), 505–520. Boston Reidel 1984.

GENDRON, Edmond. "L'allégorie De La Caverne": République En Petit. *Laval Theol Phil* 41,329–343 O 85.

Cet article expose trois différentes facons dont l'allégorie de la caverne reprend en caractères plus petits la République entière. Ces trois regards sur la Réublique sont spécifieés par les qualificatifs suivants: a) politique ou métaphysique, b) structurel ou dramatique, c) philosophyique ou politique. L'auteur souligne quelques reflects éstranges, pour ne pas dire contradictoires, de ce petit texte placé au seuil du VII°livre de la République, qui, si on le prend au sérieux en tant qu'allégorie, non seulement éclaire la suite du dialogue, mais nous oblige à le reprendre tout entier sous un nouveau jour.

GENOVA, A C. Good Transcendental Arguments. *Kantstudien* 75,469–495 1984.

Do transcendental arguments exhibit a unique logical form? Does their validity require a verification principle? Recent views are examined and criticized. Transcendental arguments divide into hypothetical deductions, metaphysical deductions, transcendental deductions and transcendental refutations. A 'good' transcendental argument is always a transcendental deduction with straightforward deductive form, assumes no verification principle (contrary to recent detractors), and proves the so-called objectivity thesis with respect to a unique and necessary conceptual scheme (contrary to recent defenders).

GENSLER, Harry J. A Kantian Argument Against Abortion. *Phil Stud* 48,57–72 Jl 85.

I criticize various anti– and pro–abortion arguments. Then, using the principle that a consistent person who thinks it permissible to do A to another will also consent to the idea of someone doing A to him in similar circumstances, I argue that most people could not consistently hold that abortion is normally permissible. I discuss possible objections and distinguish my view from Hare's. (Pages 66 and 67 should have appeared between pages 69 and 70.)

GENSLER, Harry J. Ethical Consistency Principles. *Phil Quart* 35,156–170 Ap 85.

"always follow your conscience" seems important and obviously true—and yet it seems also to lead to absurdities ("If you conscience says commit mass murder, then commit mass murder!"). In this article I show that other prominent principles (the hypothetical imperative principle, the logicality principle, the golden rule, and the formula of universal law) lead to the same difficulty. And I try to resolve the difficulty by formulating these principles using the "Don't combine...With not..." Form instead of the "If...Then do..." Form.

GENTNER, Dedre. "Are Scientific Analogies Metaphors" in *Metaphor*, Miall, David S (ed), 106–132. Atlantic Highlands Humanities Pr 1982.

GEORGESCU, George and Voiculescu, Ioana. Eastern Model–Theory For Boolean–Valued Theories. *Z Math Log* 31,79–88 1985.

GEORGIADIS, Constantine. For The Sake Of Humanity. *Dialec Hum* 11,463–464 Spr/Sum 84.

GEORGOPOULOS, N. "Sartre And Alienation" in *Continuity And Change In Marxism*, Fischer, Norman And Others (ed), 144–169. Atlantic Highlands Humanities Pr 1982.

GERAETS, Theodore F. The Impossibility Of Philosophy And Its Realization. *Owl Minerva* 16,31–38 Fall 84.

In agreement with P J Labarrière's thesis that the *Phenomenology of Spirit* is the demonstration of the impossibility of "philosophy" as a positive doctrine, "localizing" the truth, the author explores Hegel's conception of philosophy as expressed in the section of the *Logic* on "the Absolute Idea" and in the final paragraphs of the *Encyclopedia*. The idea, or realized concept, of philosophy is a never–ending process of actualization: the only way to bring to a "close" a thinking that is irrovacably processual.

GERAS, Norman. The Controversy About Marx And Justice. *Philosophica* 33,33–86 1984.

The article summarizes in turn the case of those who deny and the case of those who affirm that Marx criticized capitalism for its injustice. It then argues that, despite some apparent textual evidence to the contrary, product of a confusion on Marx's own part, he did in effect consider capitalist society to be unjust, regarding exploitation as tantamount to theft and condemning the prevailing distribution of productive resources, freedoms and other benefits.

GERBER, David. Single– And Multiple–Rule Theories Of Judicial Reasoning. *Arch Rechts Soz* 60,53–78 1974.

Many writers have believed that there is exactly one rule for determining *rationes*, for interpreting statutes, or for making decisions. It is argued here that the evidence strongly disfavors such Single–Rule Theories in each of these areas. Certain Multiple–Rule Theories, which posit the existence of a plurality of rules in one or another area, are confirmed by the same evidence. (edited)

GERLA, Giangiacomo and Vaccaro, Virginia. Modal Logic And Model Theory. *Stud Log* 43,203–216 1984.

We propose a first order modal logic, the **QS4E**–logic, obtained by adding to the well–known first order modal **QS4** a *rigidity axiom schemas*: $A \rightarrow \Box A$, where A denotes a basic formula. In this logic, the *possibility* entails the possibility of extending a given classical first order model. This allows us to express some important concepts of classical model theory, such as existential completeness and the state of being infinitely generic, that are not expressible in classical first order logic. (edited)

GERLA, Giangiacomo. Pavelka's Fuzzy Logic And Free L–Subsemigroups. *Z Math Log* 31,123–129 1985.

In this paper one relates Fuzzy Logic to Fuzzy Algebras. Namely one proves that several classes of fuzzy subalgebras are axiomatizable in Pavelka's sense, and that the class of fuzzy filters defines a fuzzy logic.

GERLACH, H M. Humanismus–Antihumanismus In Den Geistigen Auseinandersetzungen Unserer Zeit. *Deut Z Phil* 33,216–222 1985.

Der Aufsatz beschäftigt sich mit dem Problem des Humanismus und Antihumanismus in unserer Zeit. Es werden zunächst die gesellschaftlichen Ursachen fur Humanismus und Antihumanismus heute aufgedeckt, die letztlich aus den sozialökonomischen Verhältnissen entspringen, Anschliessend werden Merkmale, die für antihumanes Denken und Handeln wesentlich sind, dargelegt (Zerstörung der Persönlichkeit, Leugnung der Perfektibilität und sozialen Gleichheit, Zerstörung der Vernunft, Irrationalismus, Pessimismus, Intoleranz). Die Krise des Humanismus offenbart sich im Zynismus, der Rationalität und Humanitat antinomisch gegenübertellt.

GERLACH, Hans–Martin. Gefühl—Sinnlichkeit—Verstand. *Deut Z Phil* 32,991–999 1984.

Der Aufsatz beschäftigt sich mit einem in der Geschichte der Erkenntnistheorie bisher wenig behandelten Problem. Er untersucht die Rolle, die das "Gefühl" in der Philosophie der Aufklärung spielte, vergleicht dabei den unterschiedlichen Stellenwert, den dieser Bereich der menschlichen Erkenntnis in der Phiosophie des 17 und 18. Jahrhunderts einnahm und gibt an ausgewählten Beispielen (französische Moralisten, Hume, Diderot, Tetens, Rousseau) einen Einblick in die Entwicklungsgeschichte de Gefühlsbegriffs in der duropäischen Aufklärung.

GEROCH, Robert. The Everett Interpretation. *Nous* 18,617–634 N 84.

GERT, Bernard and Hennessey, John W. Moral Rules And Moral Ideals: A Useful Distinction In Business And Professional Practice. *J Bus Ethics* 4,105–116 Ap 85.

GEWIRTH, Alan. "Natural Law, Human Action, And Morality" in *The Georgetown Symposium On Ethics*, Porreco, Rocco (ed), 67–90. Lanham Univ Pr Of America 1984.

GEWIRTH, Alan. "Replies To My Critics" in *Gewirth's Ethical Rationalism*, Regis Jr, Edward (ed), 192–256. Chicago Univ Of Chicago Pr 1984.

GEWIRTH, Alan. From The Prudential To The Moral: Reply To Marcus Singer. *Ethics* 95,302–304 Ja 85.

Prudential rights are claimed for the agents or the speaker's own interests; moral rights are claimed for the interests of other persons as well. Since each agent logically must accept that he has the rights of agency because he is a prospective agent (here the rights, so far are prudential), he also logically must accept that all prospective agents have the rights of agency (here the rights, as accepted by the original agent, are moral).

GEWIRTH, Alan. Rights And Virtues. *Rev Metaph* 38,739–762 Je 85.

After replying to A MacIntyre's criticisms of my argument for human rights, I show that his own doctrine of the virtues is unable to surmount the difficulty of moral indeterminancy, and that a chief reason for this is that he does not base his account of the virtues on human rights. My conclusion is that moral virtues must be based on human rights if the virtues are to have morally justified contents.

GEYMONAT, Ludovico. Development And Continuity In Schlick's Thought. *Synthese* 64,273–282 S 85.

GHELARDI, Maurizio. L' "Oratio Ad Divinam Sapientiam" Del Vichiano Lorenzo Boturini–Beneduci. *G Crit Filosof Ital* 63,406–419 S–D 84.

GHIDEANU, Tudor. Die Natur In Marx' Begriffssystem. *Phil Log* 28,119–124 Ap–Je 84.

The present work reconsiders the dignity of nature in the immanence of Marxist philosophy, against praxiologist one–sidedness, operated by A Gramsci, G Lukacs, L Goldmann, etc. Since the vainglorious neo–Freudian complementarity of the School of Frankfurt could be built on the idea of the absence of nature with Marx, our work proves the ontological importance of nature, beginning with Marx's and Engel's early works. The reasoning deals with the internal coherence of Marxist philosophy, the coherence between Marx and Engels, the unitary dialectics of nature and social.

GHIŢA, Simion. Darwinism And The Modern Scientific Revolution—175 Years From C Darwin's Birth. *Phil Log* 28,124–130 Ap–Je 84.

GHOSH– DASTIDAR, Koyeli. Can There Be A Freedom Without Responsibility? *Indian Phil Quart* 11,333–342 Jl 84.

This paper considers a certain charge often brought against the traditional Indian account of liberation (*moska*). A person, on the traditional Indian account, is not supposed to be free as long as he has responsibilities to undertake. He is supposed to be free when he attains *moska*, and when he attains *moska*, he has no responsibilities to undertake anymore. I consider this charge in the light of the different senses of in which the concept of responsibility has been used in the modern philosophical tradition of the West. I conclude that an individual *qua* individual (*qua* moral agent) cannot be free unless he is also responsible.

GIADROSSI, Gianfranco. Razionalismo Critico E Valutazione Del Diritto In Hans Albert. *Riv Int Filosof Diritto* 61,3–65 Ja–Mr 84.

The purpose of this article is to spell out the consequences of Albert's critical rationalism for the theory of justice. Special attention is given to the idea of non–justificational criticism, and to the forms it can assume in discussing the merits of alternatives legal arrangements. Albert's suggestions are not a refutation of skepticism; they show, however, how it is possible to exploit the critical potentialities of science in the choice among competing theories of justice.

GIAMBRONE, Steve and Brady, Ross T and Meyer, Robert K. Where Gamma Fails. *Stud Log* 43,247–256 1984.

A major question for the relevant logics has been, "Under what conditions is Ackermann's rule γ, from—A V B and A to infer B, admissible for one of these logics?" For a large number of logics and theories, the question has led to an affirmative answer to the γ problem itself, so that such an answer has almost come to be expected for relevant logics worth taking seriously. We exhibit here, however, another large and interesting class of logics—roughly, the Boolean extensions of the **W**—free relevant logics (and, precisely, the well–behaved subsystems of the four–valued logic **BN4**)—for which γ fails.

GIAMBRONE, Steve. TW+ And RW+ Are Decidable. *J Phil Log* 14,235–254 Ag 85.

This paper presents consecution calculi (Gentzen systems) for TW_+ and RW_+, being the positive fragments without the contraction axiom of the logics T of Ticket Entailment and R of Relevant Implication as presented in Anderson and Belnap's *Entailment*. Appropriate Cut Theorems and Equivalences are then proved. Finally, decision procedures are specified for the systems.

GIARELLI, James M. A Public Philosophical Perspective On Teacher Education Reform. *J Thought* 19,3–13 Wint 84.

A public philosophy is defined as a system of beliefs and communicative practices through which a society develops and expresses a shared sense of political meaning and commitment. This perspective is used to analyze historical and contemporary commentaries on teacher education reform. From this perspective, the purpose of public education is to form and re–form publics, the relationship between the state and the public is problematic, and the aim of teacher education is the preparation of public educators, rather than the training of state agents or technical experts.

GIARELLI, James M. The Learning Community: A Response. *Proc Phil Educ* 40,53–56 1984.

GIBBARD, Allan. What's Morally Special About Free Exchange? *Soc Phil Pol* 2,20–28 Spr 85.

GIBBINS, P F. Are Mental Events In Space–Time? *Analysis* 45,145–147 Je 85.

GIBBONS, Hugh. Justifying Law: An Explanation Of The Deep Structure Of American Law. *Law Phil* 3,165–279 Ag 84.

This paper advances the proposition that American law is based, implicitly, upon a single axiom and that a consistent body of legal principles, derivable from the axiom, undergird law. The axiom is explained and the layers of principle developed fully enough to connect with the major bodies of law and to provide a comprehensive test for the justification of particular laws.

GIBSON, Roger. On The Use Of The Name 'Logic'. *J Phil Educ* 18,199–211 1984.

What I call 'logic I' is, roughly, the classical modern calculi such as the propositional and first order predicate calculi: 'logic II' is 'the resolution and recomposition of predicates': 'logic III' studies ways of getting knowledge. There is a special prestige to the name: 'logic' which is exhibited by the austere certainties of logical, but not by findings of the other two. People make so free with the name 'logic' that it has become like a wild epistemic trump with which to bless any rationale, however haywire, with specious certitude. I cannot revise usages that have become established: but I call for an end to equivocation.

GIERE, Ronald N. "Testing Theoretical Hypotheses" in *Testing Scientific Theories*, Earman, John (ed), 269–298. Minneapolis Univ Minnesota Pr 1983.

GIGANTE, M Marcello. Les Papyrus D'Herculanum Aujourd'Hui. *Bull Soc Fr Phil* 78,1–30 Ja–Mr 84.

This work summarizes the present situation of Herculaneum Papyrology and shows how it has to proceed in the next future. It mentions the enterprises and studies which since 1969 (when the Centro Internazionale per lo Studio dei Papiri Ercolanesi was founded by M Gigante) contributed to give a new image of Herculaneum rolls and to document the great value of modern editions in reconstructing philosophy, poetry and ancient book.

GIGLIOLI, Giovanna. El Papel Del Leninismo En "Historia Y Conciencia De Clase". *Rev Filosof (Costa Rica)* 23,151–160 D 85.

This is the first of three articles destined to enlighten the role of Leninism in *History and class consciousness*. It suggests the hypothesis that the indisputable contrast between the writings of Lenist inspiration and adherence contained in Lukacs' work and the fundamental theoretica writings of Hegelean inspiration might be the result of a coherent project for rebuilding Marxist theoretical–revolutionary orthodoxy form the analysis and political demands of world–revolution Leninism, militantly assumed by the young Lukas during 1918–1922.

GIL– CREMADES, Juan–Jose. Die Unmögliche Rechtsphilosophie: Zu Hans Ryffels Rechtsund Staatsphilosophie. *Arch Rechts Soz* 60,421–428 1974.

GILBERT, Paul. La Christologie Sotériologique De Kant. *Gregorianum* 66,491–515 1985.

GILEAD, Amihud. "The Order And Connection Of Things"—Are They Constructed Mathematically—Deductively According To Spinoza? *Kantstudien* 76,72–78 1985.

"the order and connection of things–causes" do not consist in discrete, measurable mathematical units, e.G., numbers, which are not *entia realia* at all. These order and connection are not structured according to a foundational–deductive model. Spinoza's reality is not composed of geometrical figures, which are *entia rationis*, since the geometrical order, which is not based on the antecedence of the essences of things to their properties, cannot reflect the order of reality.

GILEAD, Amihud. Restless And Impelling Reason: On The Architectonic Of Human Reason According To Kant. *Ideal Stud* 15,137–150 My 85.

GILEAD, Amihud. Teleological Time: A Variation On A Kantian Theme. *Rev Metaph* 38,529–562 Mr 85.

GILEAD, Amihud. The Unity And Employments Of The Understanding: The Relationship Between Kant's Logics (in Hebrew). *Iyyun* 33,56–62 Ja–Ap 84.

GILES– PETERS, A. Objectless Activity: Marx's 'Theses On Feuerbach'. *Inquiry* 28,75–86 Mr 85.

According to Friedrich Engels (*Ludwig Feuerbach and the end of classical German philosophy*) the so–called 'Thesen über Feuerbach' are 'the brilliant germ of the new world conception'. For Karl Korsch ('Review of Vernon Venable', *Journal of Philosophy* 42 (1945), no 26) there are 'magnificently summed up' in them the 'texts of Marx and Engels's first (Hegelian and post–Hegelian) period'. Even given the important distinctions between the 'young' and the 'mature' Marx these two opinions are incompatible. The present paper's concern, however, is with the relationship of the 'Thesen' to the materialist conception of history. Once the 'Thesen' are read as a consistent whole it is clear that they are incompatible with any non–social (non–human) nature; hence with the ontological independence of nature from man; hence with any materialism, historical or otherwise. Furthermore, taken as a whole the 'Thesen' form an attempted solution to the problem of the justification of ideals, a solution both activist and dogmatist. (edited)

GILL, Christopher. Ancient Psychotherapy. *J Hist Ideas* 46,307–326 Jl–S 85.

This article examines the extent to which there existed in the Ancient World an equivalent for the modern technique of psychotherapy. Special attention is paid to the borders of religion and medicine, 'folk–psychotherapy' (as protrayed in Greek drama), and the borders of medicine and philosophy. It is concluded that, despite suggestive similarities between ancient practices and modern psychiatric techniques, psychotherapy involves methods and psychological assumptions not found in the Ancient World.

GILL, Jerry H. Kant, Analogy, And Natural Theology. *Int J Phil Relig* 16,19–28 1984.

The focus is on Kant's *Prolegomena* and the specific way he discusses the distinction between "the bounds" and "the limits" of pure reason as they pertain to what can be known and said about God. I am particularly interested in his discussion of the notion of analogy as a way of extracting Kant from his own epistemological dualism between the phenomenal and the noumenal.

GILL, Jerry H. Response To Perovich. *Faith Phil* 2,189–190 Ap 85.

GILL, Mary Louise. Aristotle On The Individuation Of Changes. *Ancient Phil* 4,9–22 Spr 84.

This paper defends an account of individual nonsubstances in the *Categories* and argues that in the *Physics* Aristotle rejects such an account for the special case of changes. In the *Physics* changes do not inhibit the categories of doing and suffering but are, I argue, composites. Individuation depends upon the specific identity of the range of properties lost and acquired, the numerical identity of the subject, and the continuity of the time which measures the motion.

GILL, R R Rockingham. A Note On The Compactness Theorem. *Z Math Log* 21,377–378 1975.

GILLON, Raanan. Britain: The Public Gets Involved. *Hastings Center Rep* 14,16–17 D 84.

A journalistic account of the medical ethics scene in Britain. Gillon discusses the medical profession's somewhat reluctant but increasing involvement in public discussion of medical ethics. Current topics of public interest are reported as: the British Abortion Act, which public and Parliament still seem to accept; in vito fertilization and the Warnock Commission's report; involvement of patients in drug trials without their consent. British medicine, reports Gillon, seems far less concerned with patient's autonomy and patient's rights than is American medicine.

GILLON, Raanan. Commentary On "Kicking Against The Pricks: Two Patients Wish To End Essential Insulin Treatments". *J Med Ethics* 10,204–206 D 84.

An ethics 'ground round' contribution, aimed at medical students and giving the sketchiest of thumbnail sketches of the principles of benefience and respect for autonomy in the context of two real cases of patients who had said they wished to die.

GILMAN, Robert H. Characteristically Simple $\aleph_0$–Categorical Groups. *J Sym Log* 49,900–907 S 84.

This paper investigates countable aleph–naught categorical groups which are characteristically simple and have proper subgroups of finite index. Such groups are determined up to isomorphism, and it is shown that their theories are finitely axiomatizable. There is considerable overlap with work of J S Wilson and his student A B Apps.

GILMORE, Carol B and Fannin, William R. Public And Firm Interests In Public Service Diversifications. *J Bus Ethics* 4,415–418 O 85.

Public service organization's increasingly are considering diversification into new "for–profit" or "high–profit" enterprises. Such undertakings offer a number of potential benefits to both the organization and the public. They also have potential problems. This article examines some of the major types of benefits and problems in hopes that both public service managers and public policy makers will give a balanced consideration to these diversification efforts.

GILSON, Etienne. *From Aristotle To Darwin And Back Again: A Journey In Final Causality, Species, And Evolution.* Notre Dame Notre Dame Pr 1984.

GIMELLO, Robert M (ed) and Gregory, Peter N (ed). *Studies In Ch'an And Huy–Yen.* Honolulu Univ Of Hawaii Pr 1984.

A collection of five original studies – based on recently discovered or previously neglected Chinese, Japanese, and Tibetan texts – of the history, thought and practice of the early Ch'an (Zen) and Hua–yen (Kegon) traditions of East Asian Buddhism. The purpose of the collection is to communicate – largely to other specialists – recent developments in Buddhist scholarship leading to a reassessment of these two schools.

GINET, Carl. Contra Reliabilism. *Monist* 68,175–187 Ap 85.

GINEV, Dimiter and Stefanov, Anguel. One Dimension Of The Scientific Type Of Rationality. *Stud Hist Phil Sci* 16,101–112 Je 85.

The paper contains the analysis of what is called "synchronic dimension" of scientific rationality. It is considered from the standpoint of the ideal for an optimum (best) scientific theory. H Sarkar's methodological approach of "group rationality" is critically analyzed and some new ideas are developed connected with the concept of ideal for an optimum theory and the non–formal synthesis of such ideals. A methodological criterion—interplay of ontologies—is proposed for the assessment of new theories.

GINEV, Dimiter. On The Typology Of The Scientific Languages. *Bull Sect Log* 13,165–172 O 84.

GINGELL, J. Art And Knowledge. *Educ Phil Theor* 17,10–21 My 85.

GINI, A R. The Case Method: A Perspective. *J Bus Ethics* 4,351–352 Ag 85.

The task of preparing a case is similar to writing a legal brief or an essay insofar as all three should contain a thesis or main point and argumentation or logically arranged facts and inferences. However, different from a brief or an essay, case studies should not contain a conclusion. A case should lead the reader through the facts, but it should not offer a firm or fixed resolution or moral judgment. Ideally it should leave the reader with the opportunity to create and insert their own conclusion. (edited)

GINSBERG, Allen. On A Paradox In Quantum Mechanics. *Synthese* 61,325–350 D 84.

I introduce a new paradox, the Paradox of Identical Particles (PIP)— a problem similar to Gibb's paradox—which seems to imply that Elementary Quantum Mechanics is committed to a paradoxical "mode of interaction" that I call "species sensitivity", a mode of interaction that things partake of *only because* they are of the same (or different) species. I discuss some unsuccessful attempts to solve PIP, mainly one which can be extrapolated from the work of Reichenbach, and then I show that Quantum Field Theory provides a simple and natural solution to the paradox.

GIRALT, Edualdo Forment. Problemática De La Analogía. *Espiritu* 33,147–158 Jl–D 84.

GIRALT, Edualdo Forment. Supuestos De La Metafísica. *Espiritu* 33,109–130 Jl–D 84.

GIRALT, Eudaldo F. El Ser En Domingo Báẽz, Por Eudaldo Forment Giralt. *Espiritu* 34,25–48 Ja–Je 85.

GIRARD, Jean–Yves and Normann, D. Set Recursion And $\Pi 1/2$–Logic. *Annals Pure Applied Log* 28,255–286 My 85.

Set recursion generalizes usual recursion by keeping the formal aspect, but forgetting effectivity. Dilators—functors from ordinals to ordinals preserving direct limits and pullbacks—enable us to deal with ordinals while keeping a finitary control. In this paper the authors reduce some uses of set–recursion (e.G., on a recursively inaccessible) to iteration along recursive dilators. The reduction is successful, but for the function enumerating the admissibles and their limits, which cannot, of course, be eliminated.

GIRARD, Jean–Yves and Vauzeilles, Jacqueline. Functors And Ordinal Notations: II, A Functorial Construction Of The Bachmann Hierarchy. *J Sym Log* 49,1079–1114 D 84.

The paper extends a previous work on the Veblen Hierarchy; the familiar Bachmann collections are replaced by "gardens". In a garden, fundamental sequences are given by means of functors, which are dilators, and furthermore, which is topologically continuous ("flowers"). A garden is something like a Bachmann collection of variable size; the work therefore shows the possibility of constructing the Bachmann hierarchy without fixing the size of the indexing collections; all this in a finitary way.

GIRARD, Jean–Yves and Vauzeilles, Jacqueline. Functors And Ordinal Notations I: A Functorial Construction Of The Veblen Hierarchy. *J Sym Log* 49,713–729 S 84.

Dilators are functors from Ordinals to Ordinals preserving direct limits and pullbacks. Since ordinals can be approximated by means of direct systems of integers, dilators are therefore a notion of ordinal function in the spirit of potential infinity. In this paper, the famous Veblen hierarchy of ordinal functions is shown to be a dilator in two variables (index, argument), so that this typical infinitary construction is indeed "finitary" in a very strong sense.

GIRARD, Jean–Yves. Introduction To 2 1/2 Logic. *Synthese* 62,191–216 F 85.

GIRILL, T R. Philosophy's Relevance To Technical Writing. *Int J Applied Phil* 2,89–96 Fall 84.

This paper shows how philosophical training promotes the cognitive maturity that is vital for effective technical writing. I inventory the skills needed for success as a technical writer and argue that while some are vocational, others are analytic. With specific examples, I then show the relevance of four mainstream philosophical skills (making distinctions, extracting the important for the trivial, detecting logical structure, assessing alternatives) to the problem of designing useful technical documents.

GIROUX, France. De La Société Civile À L'État: L'irruption De L'inégalité. *Philosophiques* 11,373–388 O 84.

The study of the transition from civil society to the state in the political hegelian philosophy reveals the irruption of two forms of inequality, one political (between the subjects and the rulers), the other social (between those who are included in the Universal Declaration of the Rights of Man and those who are excluded from it, i.E., in latter Marxian terminology, the working class.

GIROUX, Henry A. Toward A Critical Theory Of Education: Beyond A Marxism With Guarantees—A Response To Daniel Liston. *Educ Theor* 35,313–320 Sum 85.

This article argues that many radical educators who draw from a Marxian framework fail to identify the core assumptions of a Marxian problematic. As such, they have no theoretical tools to decipher when, through a method of modification or critique, they are no longer working within a Marxian position. Moreover, not being able to understand the notion of shifting problematics, they appear incapable of understanding that one can develop a radical form of social theory to inform an educational project while not situating one's work within a Marxist framework.

GIUSTINIANI, Vito R. Homo, Humanus, And The Meanings Of "Humanism". *J Hist Ideas* 46,167–196 Ap–Je 85.

The meanings of "Humanism" and its cognates in other languages are basically two: a literary one (revival of antiquity in the 15th Century), and a philosophical one (appreciation of man in his nature and natural needs). The literary one goes back to G Voigt (1859), the philosophical one is older (French Enlightenment, German Hegelianism, Marx), but underwent a modern resurgence (American Pragmatism, the 1933 Manifesto, Sartre, Heidegger, etc.). Although often attempted, no connection can be established between these variously shaped modern Humanisms and the way of thinking of the 15th Century Humanists.

GIVÓN, T. Prolegomena To Discourse–Pragmatics. *J Prag* 8,489–516 Ag 84.

The article covers basic notions of discourse–pragmatics, such as the relationship between multipropositional discourse and the notion of coherence; a pragmatic definition of 'information' in terms of relative compatibility with the knowledge and/or world–view of the hearer; thematic structure and multi–stranded coherence; foreground, background, and shared information; speech acts, propositional modalities, and the speaker–hearer communicative contract; focus and the scope of assertion; processing considerations in modeling discourse functions; the relationship between the generic knowledge pool and processing of new information.

GLANTZ, Leonard H. "Contrasting Review Boards With Ethics Committees" in *Ethics Committees And Health Care Decisions*, Cranford, Ronald (ed), 129–137. Ann Arbor Health Admin Pr 1984.

GLASER, Edward M. Educating For Responsible Citizenship In A Democracy. *Nat Forum* 65,24–27 Wint 85.

GLASER, Gerald. Group Selection And Methodological Individualism. *Eidos* 3,1–25 Je 84.

GLASS, Ronald J and Flage, Daniel E. Hume On The Cartesian Theory Of Substance. *S J Phil* 22,497–508 Wint 84.

While most of Hume's criticisms of the doctrine of substance are epistemological and theory–independent, we show that in *Treatise* I.Iv.5, Hume develops a metaphysical criticism of the Cartesian theory of substance. Using three of Pierre Bayle's arguments of his own ends, he argues that on an empiricist theory of meaning, the Cartesian theory of substance is reduced to absurdity.

GLASSEN, Peter. O'Hear On An Argument Of Popper's. *Brit J Phil Sci* 35,375–377 D 84.

Popper has argued that "there is something self–defeating about asserting that physical determinism is true"; against this, O'Hear has argued "that there is no reason why some people...Should not be determined in such a way as to accept", only sound arguments. I show that on O'Hear's view no one could ever tell whether any argument was sound or any proposition true, and that therefore his position leaves Popper's argument unscathed.

GLASSEN, Peter. Thalberg On Immateriality. *Mind* 93,566–569 O 84.

Thalberg doubts that the claim of dualists and the "friends of incorporeality" that the mental is immaterial is a meaningful claim because no one has ever been able to explain in positive terms what it means for something to be "immaterial," although in the case of all other terms with negative prefixes an account of their meaning in positive terms can be given. I argue that Thalberg displays both confusion and mistakes in his critique.

GLENN, John D. The Behaviorism Of A Phenomenologist: The Structure Of Behavior And The Concept Of Mind. *Phil Topics* 13,247–256 Spr 85.

Merleau–Ponty's critique, in *The Structure of Behavior*, of scientific behaviorism leads—strangely—to a position comparable to the "behaviorism" of Ryle's *The Concept of Mind*. I examine these positions. Merleau–Ponty argues that "the mental" can be defined as "structures of behavior"—comparable to Ryle's "dispositions". But where Ryle seems to reduce mind to body, Merleau–Ponty undermines abstract mind–body dichotomy. And, unlike Ryle, he raises the question of the subject *for whom* behavior is significant.

GLIDDEN, David. Aristotelian Perception And The Hellenistic Problem Of Representation. *Ancient Phil* 4,119–131 Fall 84.

An examination of a passage in Sextus (*Adversus Mathematicos* VII 219–222) regarding Aristotle's contribution to the history of epistemology suggests why Aristotle's theory of perception and cognition has been so variously misinterpreted by Hellenistic philosophers and moderns. It is unlikey Aristotle was worried whether thought or perception were representational in character. It is likely that Aristotle's interests were rather ontological, concerned with the different sorts of real things we perceive, remember, or think of.

GLOUBERMAN, Mark. Mind And Body: Two Real Distinctions. *S J Phil* 22,347–360 Fall 84.

Most commentators, though agreeing with Descartes that dualism isn't established in Meditation 1, fail to find any redeeming addition in the later Meditations. If, however, Descartes' distinction between the conception of body attacked in Meditation 1 and the Cartesian scientific conception of body is observed, many of the traditional problems vanish. Specifically, (a) the early argument, though insufficient, as Descartes asserts, doesn't fail due, as is usually alleged, to invalidity, and (b) a substantive contribution to the case *is* made after Meditation 1.

GLOUBERMAN, M. Descartes' Proto–Critique. *Hist Euro Ideas* 6,153–172 1985.

In the first *Critique* Kant treats the duality of sensibility and understanding as axiomatic. His practice must seem question–begging, since his concern is to overcome preceding views (e.G., the view of Leibniz) on which the duality isn't accepted as philosophically basic. Kant's procedure is explained, however, once it is recognized that his predecessors, in criticizing sense–involving cognition, acknowledge the duality; and the procedure is justified because of certain features of their acknowledgement. The thesis is developed with special reference to Descartes.

GLOUBERMAN, M. Kant On Receptivity: Form And Content. *Kantstudien* 66,313–330 1975.

GLOY, Karen. Aristoteles' Konzeption Der Seele In "Deanima". *Z Phil Forsch* 38,381–412 Je–D 84.

Aristotle's conception of "soul" occupies a position, which mediates between body and soul. To this end, the Aristotelian conception of "soul" is compared to the Cartesian conception of consciousness in chapter 2. In chapter 3 the individual possibilities of "soul" are explored. Chapter 4 assumes the task of grasping the unity of the individual possibilities of "soul", with the result, that these follow one another respectively are ordered by the teleological principles. The difficulty in bringing together the opposing spheres of body and soul arises as a result of the idealistic understanding of "soul", as chapter 5 illustrates. The solution on chapter 6, that the soul from the beginning relates to the body, does not resolve the difficulties of clarifying this relationship, as chapter 7 demonstrates.

GLOY, Karen. Das Verhältnis Der *Kritik Der Reinen Vernunft* Zu Den *Metaphysischen Anfangsgründen Der Naturwissenschaft*, Demonstr Am Substanzsatz. *Phil Natur* 21,32–63 1984.

The paper compares the "Critique of Pure Reason" with the "Metaphys Anf gr d Naturwiss" in respect of substance–category. In A 845ff B 873ff Kant differentiates between general and special metaphysics, the first of which deals with the object in general, the latter with the outer or inner object. In consequence the 1) Analogy, which belongs to the content of general metaphysic, treats the substance without differentiating between substance in inner or outer sense. The 1) Paralogism, which forms the content of pure psychology, treats the subject of inner sense and the 1) law of mechanic (pure physic) the substance in space, which is characterized by the predicate of motion. At the end there is a comparison with the concept of substance in modern physic.

GLYMOUR, Clark. "On Testing And Evidence" in *Testing Scientific Theories*, Earman, John (ed), 3–26. Minneapolis Univ Minnesota Pr 1983.

GLYMOUR, Clark. Inductive Inference In The Limit. *Erkenntnis* 22,23–32 Ja 85.

GNIFFKE, Franz. Die Gegenwärtigkeit Des Mythos In Kants Mutmassungen Über Den Anfang Der Menschengeschichte. *Z Phil Forsch* 38,593–607 N–D 84.

This article gives a detailed philosophical interpretation of Kant's dealing with the Fall of man in his essay on "MutmaBlicher Anfang der Menschengeschichte" (1786). The title formula mentioning the "presence of myth" in Kant's thinking marks a significant ambiguity as it refers to the different mythical motives that occur unthematically in Kant's explicitly discussing the myth of Adam. The "cycle of myths" (Paul Ricour) has to be passed in the explanation of this one, because Adam's sin is treated as the initial act necessary to invent *freedom* into the world: The myth of Adam is thus overlapped by a *prometheical* moment, and further on by the *cosmogonian* motive of mankind, once having fallen, developing up to the highest claim of nature herself. What had to be the *evil* in the story of Adam, by this inevitably loses its evil character.

GOBRY, Ivan. Les Sources De L'Objectivité Hellénique. *Diotima* 12,104–112 1984.

GOCKOWSKI, J. Rejoinder To Jankowski's "Comment To Goćkowski's *Situational Tests Of A Scholar's Faithfulness To His Ethos*". *Etyka* 21,171–176 1985.

GOCKOWSKI, J. Situational Tests Of A Scholar's Faithfulness To His Ethos (in Polish). *Etyka* 21,103–130 1985.

The article discusses the problem of a scholar's ethical integrity in his professional activity. Since a scholar's faithfulness toward the principles and injunctions of his professional, traditional and general axionormative orientation is a basic prerequisite for ethical steadfastness, the author considers the nature of the situation that test a scholar's ethical integrity. He focuses on one special category of such tests, namely on situations arranged with a view to getting a scholar to betray his faith by submitting him to temptation or pressure, or by manipulating information. The author considers sociotechnical measures aimed against research autonomy, or a scholar's independence in answering the questions of what is scientific knowledge, how to arrive at scientific knowledge, or who is a scholar. Situations and attitudes testifying to the choice of fundamental values are discussed. So is the question of ways and means of defense against moves intended to get a scholar to betray the principles and implications of his professional ethics. What is at stake is a scholar's dignity and freedom of scholarly inquiry.

GODDARD, Dorothy M and Mc Allister, Martin E and Wood, J Scott. "Cultural Resource Law Enforcement In The US" in *Ethics And Values In Archaeology*, Green, Ernestene L (ed), 156–170. NY Free Pr 1984.

GODIN, Guy. Une Approche Philosophique De La Culture. *Laval Theol Phil* 41,215–224 Je 85.

à titre de préliminaire à une approche philosophique de la culture, l'auteur propose un bref nettoyage de la situation verbale, dans le contexte d'enfermement dans le langage caractáerisant non seulement la philosophie contemporaine mais, plus globalement, la communication. 1) La nature de la culture comme cinquième critère d'humanité, en relation avec l'opposition nature/culture. 2) Le fondement de la culture dans la valeur, vu dans cette perspective de retour génétique àl'origine qui séduit la "sensibilité" intellectuelly contemporaine.

GOEL, Dharmendra. Svaraj In Ideas: Some Reflections. *Indian Phil Quart* 11,423–436 O–D 84.

My reflections estimate Bhattacharya's theme paper on Philosophy's cultural origins. Prima–facie, I endorse Indian Philosopher's call to autonomy to escape any colonised psyche. However, I dispute Bhattacharya's assumption of unity of Indian tradition. Any cultural predetermination of Philosophy seems problematic, while I argue notions of 'negation', 'identity', or 'meanings' and their analyses do stay culture–free. Lastly, I warn against reifying 'theoretical–constructs'–say 'class–consciousness' or 'Rule of Law' as Historical Agents.

GOHAU, Gabriel. Karl Popper Et La Naissance De La Géologie. *Rev Metaph Morale* 89,505–514 O–D 84.

Popper's idea of the falsification of theories can already be found in the works of several geologists as early as 1750. That of falsifiability has been suggested by Boué in 1830. Such statements were expressed at the same time as Hume's criticism of induction and the birth of geology. I suggest that this concept would draw a line between pre–scientific system and scientific theory since the concept of falsification has already appeared in the XVIIth century in the works of several physicists (Pascal, Hooke) with the birth of dynamics.

GOHIER, Christiane. Femme Et Philosophie Au Québec. *Petite Rev Phil* 6,83–94 Spr 85.

A historical statement can be made concerning women philosophers in Quebec. Until the 60's women philosophers went through a process of acculturation in the three spheres that define them, that is feminity, rationality and nationality. But the evolution of Western societies (in which Quebec is included) from patriarchal agriculture to industrial and post–industrial societies – the latter defined as programmed societies that are technologically based on computerized knowledge – has made clear that sexual division of labor is obsolete. women are then producers to the same extent as men. The cultural end result is a feminist revolution from which emerges the model of the "she–intellectual". In conclusion the author defines the conditions for a renewed formulation of the problem: what is the status of women in the theoretical field of philosophy.

GOHIER, Christiane. Le Rapport Masse–élite Comme Modèle Canonique De La Dialectique Sociale. *Philosophiques* 11,337–348 O 84.

The fact of an economic, social and political domination of a minority over the majority is an invariant of all societies of accumulation in the history of mankind. Whether it be the master and slave couple in the Greek City, the Lord and Serf duality in the Feudal society or the "dominant–dominé" division of the capitalist society, the relationship is built on the same pattern: only a few men have power over the mass. The postindustrial or "programmed" society duplicates the same pattern of the domination of an Elite of Intellectuals over an anonymous mass.

GOLASZEWSKA, Maria. Platonic Ideas In Ingarden's Phenomenological Aesthetics. *Diotima* 12,113–119 1984.

In Ingarden's conception of aesthetic values, we find echoes of the notion of beauty as an idea transcending the visible world /Plato/ as well as a proportions and numbers /Pythagoras/. It is not measure and number, however, that decide about the objective conditioning of the values, but the ontological laws of mutual co–occurence, mutual postulating and exclusion of aesthetically valuable qualities, necessary just as absolutely as the laws of mathematics.

GOLASZEWSKA, Maria. The Sacred And The Profane In Arts. *Rep Phil* 8,47–60 1984.

The chief thesis of the article is the following: aesthetic value is the necessary and sufficient condition for the given object to be a work of art, while the work of art, having achieved artistic and aesthetic fullness, may transcend towards values of other kinds: if the transcends is towards moral values, the work becomes a factor of ethos in social circulation, participates in building the ethos of human communities.

GOLD, Jeffrey. Socratic Definition: Real Or Nominal? *Phil Res Arch* 10,573–585 1985.

In Plato's early dialogues, Socrates frequently asks the questions of the form "What is X?" Seeking definitions of the substitution instances of X (e.G., Justice, Piety, and Courage). In attempting to elucidate Socratic definition, a number of interpreters have invoked a distinction between real and nominal definition (the distinction between the definition of a thing and the definition of a word. In using that distinction, several interpreters have pointed out that, when Socrates asked his "What is X question (e.G., "What is Justice?"), he was not seeking a nominal definition (a definition of the word 'διμαιοσυνη'), but rather a real definition (a definition of the thing, Justice). My purpose in this paper is to argue that the preceding interpretation of Socratic thought is mistaken, i.E., I shall argue that there is no real/nominal distinction to be found in the Socratic dialogues.

GOLDBERG, Margaret. Entity And Antinomy In Tibetan Bsdus Grwa Logic (Part 1). *J Indian Phil* 13,153–200 Je 85.

GOLDBLATT, David A. Self–Plagiarism. *J Aes Art Crit* 43,71–78 Fall 84.

"self–Plagiarism" deals with one aspect of the evaluation of artists as artists by employing an overtly contradictory concept, self–plagiarism, in order to call attention to misallocations of artistic credit. Self–plagiarism, in part, is analyzed by drawing an *analogy* between it and what we usually think of as plagiarism. Self–plagiarism occurs when the artist takes from the aesthetically significant features of his/her previous work and presents them under the false assumption that they are creatively original while the successful self–plagiarism is received by artworld members as if it were. The role style plays in allowing for successful self–plagiarisms, is examined. Hooking temporality to achievement, stress is placed upon *intra*–stylistic breaks in order to properly assign predicates to significantly similar works in a single artist's career.

GOLDBLATT, R and Suppes, P (ed) and Troelstra, A S (ed). *Topoi: The Categorial Analysis Of Logic*. NY North–Holland 1984.

GOLDBLATT, Robert. An Abstract Setting For Henkin Proofs. *Topoi* 3,37–42 Je 84.

A general result is proved about the existence of maximally consistent theories satisfying prescribed closure conditions. The principle is then used to give 'streamlined' proofs of completeness and omitting–types theorems, in which inductive Henkin–style constructions are replaced by a demonstration that a certain theory 'respects' a certain class of 'inference rules'.

GOLDBLATT, Robert. On The Role Of The Baire Category Theorem And Dependent Choice In The Foundations Of Logic. *J Sym Log* 50,412–422 Je 85.

The Principle of Dependent Choice is shown to be equivalent to: the Baire Category Theorem for Cech–complete spaces (or for complete metric spaces); the existence theorem for generic sets of forcing conditions; and a proof–theoretic principle that abstracts the "Henkin method" of proving deductive completeness of logical systems. The Rasiowa–Sikorski Lemma is shown to be equivalent to the conjunction of the Ultrafilter Theorem and the Baire Category Theorem for compact Hausdorff spaces.

GOLDENBAUM, Ursula. Zu Einer Vermeintlichen Textlücke In Spinozas "Ethica Ordine Geometrico Demonstrata". *Deut Z Phil* 32,1036–1040 1984.

The editors of German translation of Spinoza's "Ethics" suggest since about 80 years a gap between the first and the second part of chapter 28 in the Appendix of Part IV, because there was no connection between "help each other" in the first and "money" in the second part of the chapter. In this article we give a new German translation of the crucial point, where the connection becomes transparent. The decisive words sentence "traderent operas mutuas" doesn't mean in German just "gegenseitige Hilfe", but "gegenseitige Arbeiten übergeben", – by means of money.

GOLDFARB, Warren D and Gurevich, Yuri and Shelah, Saharon. A Decidable Subclass Of The Minimal Gödel Class With Identity. *J Sym Log* 49,1253–1261 D 84.

GOLDFARB, Warren D. The Unsolvability Of The Gödel Class With Identity. *J Sym Log* 49,1237–1252 D 84.

The problem of determining the satisfiability of prenex formulas of quantification theory whose prefixes have the form AAE and whose matrices contain the identity–sign is shown to be recursively unsolvable. This result refutes a claim made by Gödel in 1933. It and various corollaries settle the decision problem for all prefix–classes of quantification theory with identity.

GOLDHAMMER, Arthur (trans) and Bachelard, Gaston. *The New Scientific Spirit*. Boston Beacon Pr 1985.

GOLDING, Martin P. Forgiveness And Regret. *Phil Forum (Boston)* 16,121–137 Fall–Wint 84.

GOLDMAN, Alan H. Commentary On "Advertising Professional Success Rates". *Bus Prof Ethics J* 3,57–60 Spr/Sum 84.

GOLDMAN, Alan H. Confidentiality, Rules, And Codes Of Ethics. *Crim Just Ethics* 3,8–14 Sum/Fall 84.

GOLDMAN, Alan H. The Specificity Of Rules Of Professional Conduct: A Rejoinder To Freedman's "the Problem Of Writing, Enforcing, And Teaching Ethical Rules". *Crim Just Ethics* 3,16 Sum/Fall 84.

GOLDMAN, Alvin I. The Relation Between Epistemology And Psychology. *Synthese* 64,29–68 Jl 85.

Psychology has an important contribution to make to epistemology, even if the latter is viewed as a normative subject. The normative notion of epistemic justifiedness can be captured in terms of permissibility by right epistemic rules. Right epistemic rules should specify cognitive states and operations, and which cognitive states and operations are available can best be identified by empirical psychology. Examples of states and operations that psychology might identify are briefly canvassed.

GOLDMAN, Emma. "Patriotism: A Menace To Liberty" in *Freedom, Feminism, And The State*, Mc Elroy, Wendy (ed), 337–350. Cato Institute Washington 1982.

GOLDMAN, Michael. Some Reflections On The Concept Of Poverty. *Can J Phil* 14,401–420 S 84.

I offer an analysis of "poverty" as it is ascribed to a society. I demonstrate that the poverty line must rise over time even if poverty is defined in terms of "minimum survival needs," because these too must increase over time. Both "relative" and "absolute" definitions are seen to be partially correct. I also offer some suggestions for bringing my analysis to bear on the analysis of individual poverty, and consequently make some suggestions about the nature of distributive justice.

GOLDSTEIN, Irwin. Hedonic Pluralism. *Phil Stud* 48,49–56 Jl 85.

Many contemporary philosophers endorse hedonic pluralism, the view that 'pleasure' is not susceptible to a single all–embracing definition. The thesis has important implications for our understanding of 'pleasure' and for the most psychological and moral theories in which the term 'pleasure' is central. After noting important confusions in pluralist discussions, I show that the main argument which pluralists use to defend their view is a *non sequitur*. I outline a promising monist view of pleasure.

GOLDSTEIN, Laurence. The Paradox Of The Liar—A Case Of Mistaken Identity. *Analysis* 45,9–13 Ja 85.

A liar paradox arises by identifying a name 'k' with the quotation–name "'k is not true'". It is easy enough to show that such an identity is false, and that liar paradoxes, in common with many other paradoxes, rest on identifications that only a semantically incompetent person would seriously attempt to make.

GOLDSTEIN, Laurence. The Title Of This Paper Is 'Quotation'. *Analysis* 45,137–141 Je 85.

Any theory of quotation must handle both direct and indirect quotation, and must deal with examples such as 'The concept "horse" in not a horse', 'Baby don't say "don't"' and 'What he meant was "prick his boil"' where what is referred to by means of the quotation device is not a typographical or phonetic shape. Davidson's version of the demonstrative theory does not meet these requirements. My version of that theory does.

GOLDSTEIN, Philip. "Romanticism & Modernity In Lukacsian & Althusserian Marxism" in *Continuity And Change In Marxism*, Fischer, Norman And Others (ed), 70–85. Atlantic Highlands Humanities Pr 1982.

GOLDWORTH, Amnon (ed). *Deontology: Together With A Table Of The Springs Of Action And Article On Utilitarianism.* Oxford Clarendon Pr 1983.

This is a critical edition of three of Bentham's hitherto unpublished works. Together with Bentham's *An Introduction to the Principles of Morals and Legislation*, they provide a comprehensive picture of Bentham's psychological and ethical views. A full editorial introduction links these three works and provides a history of the manuscripts of each text. Each of the editorial works is accompanied by a full complement of critical and explanatory notes.

GOLLWITZER, Helmut. "The Significance Of Martin Buber For Protestant Theology" in *Martin Buber*, Gordon, Haim (ed), 385–418. Beersheva Ktav 1984.

GOLOMB, Jacob. Kant And The Moral Sense Theory (in Hebrew). *Iyyun* 33,44–55 Ja–Ap 84.

GOLTZ, Hans–Joachim. The Boolean Sentence Algebra Of The Theory Of Linear Ordering Is Atomic With Respect To Logics With A Malitz Quantifier. *Z Math Log* 31,131–162 1985.

GOLUBOVIĆ, Zagorka. Logical Fallacies Or Ideological Justifications: Schaff's Arguments On The Socialistic Character Of "Really Existing Socialism". *Praxis Int* 5,86–93 Ap 85.

GONELLA, L. La Notion De Mesure. *Rev Phil Fr* 174,157–171 Ap–Je 84.

GONELLA, L. Un Atelier Sur Les Concepts Fondamentaux Relatifs À La Mesure. *Rev Phil Fr* 174,153–156 Ap–Je 84.

GONGCAI, Fan. Marx On The Return Of Man To Himself. *Chin Stud Phil* 16,83–98 Wint 84–85.

GONZALEZ, Carlos Ignacio. Fausto Socino: La Salvación Del Hombre En Las Fuentes Del Racionalismo. *Gregorianum* 66,457–490 1985.

Socin's Doctrine springs from early Calvinism, and from the humanism, pietism and anti–rationalism of the Venetian anti–trinitarian radical Reformers. Sozzini (born in Siena) escaped Poland, where he united the antitrinitarian and anabaptist refugees, with a doctrine which eventually provided several important principles to the later deist and illuminist thinkers: he denied the possibility of knowing God in himself, original sin and Christ's redemption; and reduced religion to ethical life, and the Church to a school of morals.

GOOD, I J. A Historical Comment Concerning Novel Confirmation. *Brit J Phil Sci* 36,184–185 Je 85.

GOODIN, Robert E. Disarming Nuclear Apologists. *Inquiry* 28,153–176 Je 85.

Here I distinguish the four logically possible ways in which nuclear weapons might be used: in an all–out nuclear strike, either first or second; or in a limited strike, either first or second. I go on to show that neither of the two most basic moral perspectives, consequentialistic or deontological, would permit nuclear weapons to be used in any of those four ways; nor would they permit an empty threat to use them. Nuclear weapons are thus shown to be morally useless. Given the moral opportunity costs of maintaining this morally useless arsenal, nuclear weapons should therefore be abandoned, universally if possible and unilaterally if need be.

GOODIN, Robert E. Nuclear Disarmament As A Moral Certainty. *Ethics* 95,641–658 Ap 85.

The logic of nuclear deterrence is incorrigibly probabilistic, but probabilistic reasoning in this area is inappropriate. Instead we should seek moral certainties. That means not launching a nuclear attack upon the other superpower's homeland, since so doing would transform the possibility of an all–out nuclear war into a virtual certainty. It also suggests that each superpower should adopt, unilaterally if necessary, a policy of nuclear disarmament: that would make all–out nuclear war impossible. These modal changes carry special moral significance.

GOODIN, Robert E. The Priority Of Needs. *Phil Phenomenol Res* 45,615–626 Je 85.

Why give needs priority over mere desires? Some arguments assimilate meeting needs to avoiding harms, as opposed to merely providing (wanted) benefits. Others turn on the proposition that needs are, in some sense, less voluntary. Still others emphasize the relative urgency or primary–good nature of the needed resources. None of these arguments provide an ironclad case for the priority rule, however. At most, needs correlate in only a rough and ready way with various other factors which do deserve priority consideration.

GOODMAN, Nelson. Statements And Pictures. *Erkenntnis* 22,265–270 Ja 85.

GOODMAN, Nelson. The End Of The Museum? *J Aes Educ* 19,53–62 Sum 85.

GOODMAN, Nicholas D. Replacement And Connection In Intuitionistic Set Theory. *J Sym Log* 50,344–348 Je 85.

GOODMAN, Russel B. Cavell And The Problem Of Other Minds. *Phil Topics* 13,43–52 Spr 85.

Standard treatments of scepticism concerning other minds take it as parallel to, and an adjunct of, scepticism about the external world. In "Between Acknowledgment and Avoidance", Part IV of *The Claim of Reason*, Stanley Cavell challenges this received view by exploring assymetries between these two forms of scepticism, maintaining that the problem of other minds is "largely undiscovered for philosophy". I examine the main assymetries Cavell uncovers, and consider some criticisms of his position.

GOODMAN, Russell B. Skepticism And Realism In The *Chuang Tzu*. *Phil East West* 35,231–238 Jl 85.

Chuang Tzu knew how to play the sceptical game, but also how to dodge the philosophical entanglements and abstractions to which it may lead. Both a sceptic and a common–sense realist, Chuang Tzu uses humor—often in the form of a darting and acute playfulness—to cushion the impact of these traditionally opposed points of view. Rather than casting a pall of doubt over the world, his scepticism makes its pungency and freshness accessible.

GOODMAN, William H. Theaetetus, Part II: A Dialogical Review. *Antioch Rev* 42,393–408 Fall 84.

I aim to show that Richard Rorty's epistemological views in his *Philosophy and the Mirror of Nature* are effectively identical with those of the Greek Sophist Protagoras. Thus, Rorty's role in this dialogue, "Theaetetus, Part II," closely parallels Protagoras' role in Plato's "Theaetetus." Ultimately, both dialogues fail to "solve" the questions they raise about knowledge; so that, like Plato, in seeking to justify our continued *search* for knowledge, we turn to allegorical perspectives.

GOODPASTER, Kenneth E. Business Ethics, Ideology, And The Naturalistic Fallacy. *J Bus Ethics* 4,227–232 Ag 85.

GOODPASTER, Kenneth E. Toward An Integrated Approach To Business Ethics. *Thought* 60,161–180 Je 85.

This essay offers an interpretation of accountability in business ethics on three scales or levels of analysis–the person, the organization, and the economic system. Utilizing innovative work in mathematics on "fractals," the author suggests both descriptive and prescriptive implications of this conceptual model. Relationships of this account to recent literature in business ethics are indicated, as well as its classical roots. Theorists and practitioners alike are invited to expand and apply the ideas presented with a view toward future research.

GOODRICH, R A. A Revival Of The Propositional Theory Of Art? *Brit J Aes* 24,314–324 Autumn 84.

P H Hirst's influential advocacy in philosophy of education circles of the propositional theory of art is critically examined by way of the seemingly favorable case of representational painting. However, this article argues that the theory fails to account satisfactorily for significant difficulties arising from the problematical concepts of proposition and statement, resemblance, and representation. Nor does Hirst effectively counter alternatives to and omissions within the propositional theory.

GOODSTEIN, Judith E. The Rise And Fall Of Vito Volterra's World. *J Hist Ideas* 45,607–618 O–D 84.

Between 1900 and 1925, mathematics was Italy's premier scientific discipline. A close–knit circle of mathematicians, including Guido Castelnuovo, Federigo Enriques, Tullio Levi–Civita, and Vito Volterra dominated science in Italy. All were Jewish. Under Mussolini, the politics of the regime worked against the circle of mathematicians who, in effect, defined the old scientific order. Mussolini's new Academy of Italy discriminated against Jews from the very beginning. The fascist loyalty oath also took its toll.

GOODWIN, H Eugene. *Groping For Ethics In Journalism.* Ames Iowa St Univ Pr 1983.

This book assesses the state of ethics in American journalism. Making liberal use of case studies and drawing on interviews with about 150 journalists, the book describes and categorizes the main ethical problems in the field, such as freebies, conflicts of interest, reporter–source relationships, deception, fakery, dubious methods, shocking language and photos, invasion of privacy, and lack of compassion. It examines journalism as a business and a profession.

GOODYEAR, Paul. Double Enlargements Of Topological Spaces. *Z Math Log* 30,389–392 1984.

GOOLSBY, Thomas W. Music Education As Aesthetic Education: Concepts And Skills For The Appreciation Of Music. *J Aes Educ* 18,15–34 Wint 84.

GORDON, David. Gillespie On Singer's Generalization Argument. *Ethics* 95,75–77 O 84.

GORDON, David. Must God Identify The Best? *J Value Inq* 19,81–83 1985.

GORDON, David. Nathan On Projectivist Utilitarianism. *Erkenntnis* 23,201–202 Ag 85.

GORDON, Haim (ed) and Bloch, Jochanan (ed). *Martin Buber: A Centenary Volume.* Beersheva Ktav 1984.

The book contains the lectures and discussions of the Buber Centenary Conference held at Ben Gurion University of the Negev in Beersheva in January 1978. Buber scholars from Europe, North America, Japan, and Israel convened and evaluated the significance of Buber's thought, criticized many of his tenets, and discussed his profound originality and broad influence.

GORDON, Haim. "Existential Guilt And Buber's Social And Political Thought" in *Martin Buber*, Gordon, Haim (ed), 215–232. Beersheva Ktav 1984.

GORDON, Haim. "The Sheltered Aesthete: A New Apraisal Of Buber's Life" in *Martin Buber*, Gordon, Haim (ed), 25–42. Beersheva Ktav 1984.

GORDON, Haim. Dialectical Reason And Education: Sartre's Fused Group. *Educ Theor* 35,43–56 Wint 85.

The purpose of this work is to show a few of the insights that the philosopher of education and the educator can glean from Sartre's *Critique of Dialectical Reason.* In the process, the article shows the manners in which dialectical reason contribute to understand the developments in the field of education. Sartre's understanding of the third party and the fused group are discussed at length.

GORDON, Jeffrey. Bad Faith: A Dilemma. *Philosophy* 60,258–262 Ap 85.

In his contribution to the continuing debate in *Philosophy* on Sartre's concept of bad faith, Leslie Stevenson proposed that one is in bad faith when he denies reflectively what he pre–reflectively takes to be true. I argue that this proposal, promising though it may seem, is ensnared in inescapable dilemma.

GORDON, Jeffrey. The Dilemma Of Theodicy. *Sophia (Australia)* 23,22–34 O 84.

The theist must pay a high price for a successful resolution of the problem of evil; the price is the underminimg of the most fertile source of religious faith: the conviction that only God can console us for our sorrows. But failure to resolve the problem of evil extracts a higher price still. This is the dilemma of theodicy, and the burden of my paper is to explain its force.

GOROVITZ, Samuel. "On Surrogate Mothers" in *Difficult Decisions In Medical Ethics*, Ganos, Doreen L (ed), 145–154. NY Liss 1983.

GOROVITZ, Samuel. Advertising Professional Success Rates. *Bus Prof Ethics J* 3,31–45 Spr/Sum 84.

GOROVITZ, Samuel and Green, Harold P. Allocation Of Resources: The Artificial Heart. *Hastings Center Rep* 14,13–17 O 84.

GOROVITZ, Samuel. Engineering Human Reproduction: A Challenge To Public Policy. *J Med Phil* 10,267–274 Ag 85.

New prospects for technologically aided human reproduction require the development of a public policy concerning the setting of limits to reproductive autonomy and to research on human embryos. Previous American efforts to clarify policy on such matters have been ignored by the executive branch; there is a need for Congressional action to initiate the requisite processes of debate and policy formation.

GOROVITZ, Samuel. Preparing For The Perils Of Practice. *Hastings Center Rep* 14,38–41 D 84.

GOROVITZ, Samuel. Why You Don't Owe It To Yourself To Seek Health. *J Med Ethics* 10,143–146 S 84.

Sider and Clements provide a critical response to my view that there is no independent obligation to seek one's own health. They then argue that such an obligation exists. They are incorrect in their characterization of my view; their critical discussion of the view they erroneously attribute to me is unconvincing; the positive argument they offer for their own view is unsatisfactory; they misjudge the significance of what is at issue; and they conclude by affirming a position that lacks a due regard for the rights of patients.

GORSKY, D P. Answer On The Impulses Of J Zelený Concerning The Character Of So–called Dialectical And Logical Deduction (in Czechoslovakian). *Filozof Cas* 33,432–438 1985.

GOTESKY, Rubin. *Personality: The Need For Liberty And Rights.* NY Libra 1967.

The question asked in this little book is: Is the need for liberty biologically inborn or is it the product of social conditions? The answer is that this need is neither biologically inborn nor a psychological trait of the human personality. The need for liberty is a social product; it is a demand which may be peculiarly individual or widely socialized, i.E., a demand of a group, a social class. A generalized demand for liberty as such does not exist; it is legalized or customary. Frequently such demands form a cluster and are transformed into a system of social rights.

GOTTFRIED, Paul E. The Western Case Against Usury. *Thought* 60,89–98 Mr 85.

GOTTLIEB, Roger S. Forces Of Production And Social Primacy. *Soc Theor Pract* 11,1–24 Spr 85.

G A Cohen's *Karl Marx's Theory of History: A Defense* is in many ways a restatement of an older position: forces of production are primary in explaining historical change. Cohen's position is, I believe, essentially mistaken. Following a brief exposition of his views, I will express some doubts as to his interpretation of Marx and then raise both theoretical and historical criticisms of it as a theory in its own right.

GOUGH, Jim. Autonomy And Human Rights Claims. *Eidos* 2,110–138 D 81.

GOULD, Carol C. Freedom And Women. *J Soc Phil* 15,20–34 Fall 84.

GOULD, James A. Determining A Society's Freedom. *J Soc Phil* 15,46–54 Fall 84.

GOULD, James. Negative Freedom: Constraints And Opportunities. *J Value Inq* 19,67–72 1985.

GOVIER, Trudy. Common Sense: Who Can Deny It? *Eidos* 1,3–29 Jl 78.

GOYARD– FABRE, Simone. Diderot Et L'affaire De L'abbé De Prades. *Rev Phil Fr* 174,287–309 Jl–S 84.

Diderot, contempteur de la religion, a entretenu de troublants rapports avec les ministres de l'Eglise. L'affaire de l'abbé de Prades nous reporte aux heures héroïques des débuts de l'*Encyclopédie* puisque la thèse du jeune abbé – *La Jérusalem céleste* date de novembre 1751. Elle déclencha la tempête. Diderot, contre–attaquant les Jésuites, rédigea L'*Apologie de l'abbé de Prades* afin de montrer qu'il n'y avait pas trace d'irréligiosité dans les affirmations incriminées. Le débat opposa en fait des interlocuteurs irréductibles: d'un côté, la coterie religieuse enfermée dans un dogmatisme incurable; de l'autre, Diderot, entendant ne pas renoncer à l'esprit de libre examen. L' "insurrection philosophique" de Diderot, loin de vouloir détruire la religion, a pour but de servir la vérité et de faire croître l'arbre de la science.

GOYARD– FABRE, Simone. Rousseau Et Les Législateurs Grecs. *Diotima* 12,120–130 1984.

Rousseau n'a pas pour la Grèce antique le regard de l'historien Il lui prête le prestige éblouissant de l'*altérité*; elle le transporte, dit–il, "en un autre univers et parmi d'autres êtres". Il puise donc en elle l'exemple des *grands hommes et des héros* dont la silhouette se profile en ses écrits. Lacédémone en effet, à travers la légende de Lycurgue, lui révèle l'esprit du politique et l'importance normative de la loi civile. La prudence de Solon, qui sut adapter la léfislation de la Cité anthénienne à sa situation spécifique, symbolise à ses yeux le sens du relativisme politique. A la lumière de la figure paradigmatique des deux législateurs grecs, il comprend les raisons des mensonges de son temps et sa tristesse est infinie.

GRACIA, Jorge J E and others (eds). *Philosophical Analysis In Latin America.* Boston Reidel 1984.

The purpose of this anthology is to make available to the non–Spanish/ Portuguese speaking world a sample of the work of Latin American philosophers working in the tradition of philosophical analysis. In addition to seventeen articles on logical, metaphysical, epistemological and ethical issues, the book adds brief historical introductions to the four geographical areas (Argentina, Mexico, Brazil and other countries) into which the volume has been divided. These historical introductions are intended to place the papers in their appropriate historical milieu.

GRACIA, Jorge J E. *Introduction To The Problem Of Individuation In The Early Middle Ages.* Munchen Philosophia 1984.

This is a study of the problem of individuation in the early medieval period (500–1150). It argues, among other things, that the development of the problem divides into two traditions. One has primarily meta–physical character, develops a theory of individuation that became standard in the period and originates in Boethius' *On the Trinity.* The other is more logical, is less widespread and originates in Boethius' logical works. Main authors discussed: Boethius, Eriugena, Theirry, Gilbert, and Abailard.

GRACIA, Jorge J E. Los Problemas Filosóficos De La Individualidad. *Rev Latin De Filosof* 11,3–26 Mr 85.

The purpose of this article is two–fold. First, to clarify the general terminology of individuality current in the literature and, second, to distinguish six issues related to this notion. One of its theses is that both tasks are essential to maintain clarity in the investigation of individuality; another is that many difficulties surrounding individuality are the result of terminological confusions and/or of the confusion among logical, epistemic, ontological and semantic issues which should be kept separate.

GRACIA, Jorge. "Analysis In Other Latin American Countries" in *Philosophical Analysis In Latin America*, Gracia, Jorge J E and others (eds), 365–380. Boston Reidel 1984.

GRACIA, Jorge. "Introduction" in *Philosophical Analysis In Latin America*, Gracia, Jorge J E and others (eds), 1–16. Boston Reidel 1984.

GRACIA, Jorge. "Latin Americans Residing In US And Canada" in *Philosophical Analysis In Latin America*, Gracia, Jorge J E and others (eds), 413–416. Boston Reidel 1984.

GRAEBNER, William. Doing The World's Unhealthy Work: The Fiction Of Free Choice. *Hastings Center Rep* 14,28–37 Ag 84.

To ethically justify hazardous work, turn–of–the–century employers and "society" claimed that certain persons were adapted to such work, that hazardous labor was a social obligation, and that workers had the choice not to work in such industries. The essay concludes that these doctrines were part of a hegemonic system of social engineering, in which vocational guidance, children's literature, and industrial arts education created a working class "willing" to undertake dangerous tasks.

GRAESER, Andreas. Über "Sinn" Und "Bedeutung" Bei Gadamer. *Z Phil Forsch* 38,436–444 Je–D 84.

GRAESER, Andreas. Die Platonischen Ideen Als Gegenstände Sprachlicher Referenz. *Z Phil Forsch* 29,218–234 Ap–Je 75.

GRAFSTEIN, Robert. Ontology And The Theory Of Justice. *Phil Phenomenol Res* 46,115–138 S 85.

GRAHAM, A C. Value, Fact And Facing Fact. *J Value Inq* 19,35–42 1985.

GRAHAM, George and Stephens, G Lynn. Are Qualia A Pain In The Neck For Functionalists? *Amer Phil Quart* 22,73–80 Ja 85.

Pains and bodily sensations generally are allegedly resistent to functionalistic analysis, and this is supposed to undermine Functionalism as a general theory of mind. But it doesn't. We argue that pains are composite states, and that the component of pain which may be resistent to functionalistic analysis is not even psychological. This part is pain's qualitative component and is a sensible quality of human and animal bodies.

GRAHAM, Gordon. Mystery And Mumbo–Jumbo. *Phil Invest* 7,281–294 O 84.

This article argues that contradictions are endemic to religious thinking, but that this does not imply either that religious paradoxes are non–asserting or that we cannot exercise critical control over what is said or asserted in religion.

GRAM, Moltke. *The Transcendental Turn: The Foundations Of Kant's Idealism.* Gainesville Univ Pr Of Florida 1985.

The book is an assessment of the philosophical viability of the distinction between things in themselves and appearances, first, through a detailed examination of the notion of a thing in itself and its relation to the notion of transcendental ideality and, secondly, through the application of the results of that examination to conclusions that philosophical tradition has made about the nature of that relationship. These comparisons culminate in specific applications of those results to the Antinomies of the first *Kritik*.

GRANGER, Gilles–Gaston. Janus Bifrons. *Rev Int Phil* 38,257–271 1984.

Gaston Bachelard, as a philosopher, has played on a double keyboard. His evolution is interpreted as a progressive mastering of the deep complementarity uniting the diurnal *animus*, who creates scientific concepts, and the nocturnal *anima* who reigns over images. The phases of the philosopher's progress are described, and a sketch of Bachelard's philosophic style is proposed.

GRANJA, Dulce M. La Creatividad Humana. *Rev Filosof (Mexico)* 17,401–422 S–D 84.

GRANT, C David. *God, The Center Of Value: Value Theory In The Theology Of H Richard Niebuhr.* Fort Worth Tx Christ Univ Pr 1984.

This book examines the relational value theory of Christian ethicist and theologian H Richard Niebuhr with a view towards seeing how his theory relates to and grows out of his conception of God. Though it is intelligible as a philosophical theory, the author argues that its function within Niebuhr's work is primarily theological, in that it makes relative all finite values before God, for whom whatever is, is good.

GRANT, John N. Three Notes On Seneca *De Providentia. Phoenix* 38,171–174 Je 84.

GRAS, Alain. The Mystery Of Time: A New Sociological Approach. *Diogenes* 128,103–124 Wint 84.

Time is a naive dimension of social analysis. Few social scientists have concerned themselves with the basis of our modern representation of process ("le devenir") which are all cast in a common mold, that of oriented evolution and linear time. From our "cultural arbitrary" springs, for example, retrospective discourses on man such as history or cosmology. It is "time" to develop a sociology of forms in which the processes of social phenomena are conceived as autonomous and specific; the technical era in which we live having developed some forms as imaginary and provisory as others era. Some of these ideas have already been developed in "The time of evolution and spirit of times," Diogène, n. 108 pp 57–84.

GRASSI, Joseph G. Peace And The Role Of The Philosopher. *Dialec Hum* 11,427–428 Spr/Sum 84.

While peace is that which all men seek yet it is elusive. To attain this goal we must improve the quality of life, we must have faith without which the human mind and human society fail, and we must consider the sacredness of the human personality. In all of this, the role of the philosopher is to seek the truth as he sees it while at the same time carry on serious dialogue with his counterparts in various corners of the world. Their disagreements should not affect their faith in each other as a human being who, likewise, is a lover of truth.

GRASSIAN, Victor. *Perennial Philosophical Issues.* Englewood Cliffs Prentice–Hall 1984.

GRATTAN– GUINESS, I. Georg Cantor's Influence On Bertrand Russell. *Hist Phil Log* 1,61–94 1980.

This paper is concerned with the influence that the set theory of Georg Cantor (1845–1918) bore upon the mathematical logic of Bertrand Russell (1872–1970). In some respects the influence is positive, and stems directly from Cantor's writings or through intermediary figures such as Peano: but in various ways negative influence is evident, for Russell adopted alternative views about the form and foundations of set theory. After an opening biographical section, six sections compare and contrast their views on matters of common interest: irrational numbers, infinitesimals, cardinal and ordinal numbers, the axiom of infinity, the paradoxes, and the axioms of choice. Two further sections compare the two men over more general questions: the role of logic and the philosophy of mathematics. In a final section I draw some conclusions.

GRATTAN– GUINNESS, I. On Popper's Use Of Tarski's Theory Of Truth. *Philosophia (Israel)* 14,129–136 Ag 84.

Popper claims that Tarski's theory of truth founds the objectivist target of his fallibilistic epistemology; by contrast, Tarski regarded it as epistemologically neutral. These two positions are discussed here, with Tarski's position found to be the more intelligible; in addition, some related issues concerning the use of Tarski's theory in science are outlined.

GRAY, Colin. Strategic Defense, Deterrence, And The Prospects For Peace. *Ethics* 95,659–672 Ap 85.

GRAY, Glenn J and Adams, George Plimpton. 'Hegel's Hellenic Ideal' AND 'The Mystical Element In Hegel's Early Writings'. NY Garland 1984.

GRAY, W N and Wyatt, J F. Justifying A Curriculum And Justifying An Institution. *J Applied Phil* 2,63–68 Mr 85.

The recent revival of interest in theory leads the writers to examine a particular moment when a curriculum and the institution in which it occurred was explained and justified. Max Horkheimer's inaugural address to the Institute for Social Research in 1931 is summarized. The points made by the new Director of the Institute are examined in relation not only to his proposal for an inter–disciplinary curriculum, but also to the nature of the institution and to the general justification of higher education. The article concludes with a number of comments on the relevance of these proposals to some modern higher education issues.

GRAYBOSCH, Anthony. Parenting As A Profession: Children's Rights And Parental Responsibility. *Cogito* 2,95–110 S 84.

GRCIC, Joseph M. Democratic Capitalism: Developing A Conscience For The Corporation. *J Bus Ethics* 4,145–150 Ap 85.

GRCIC, Joseph M. Rawls' Difference Principle, Marxian Alienation And The Japanese Economy: Bringing Justice To The Least Advantaged. *Cogito* 2,45–60 Je 84.

I argue that Rawls' ideas of self–respect, and social union necessitates: 1) the restructuring of corporations towards a more democratic and worker participatory model, 2) that the Japanese model of the economy presents many useful features that should be emulated. I further suggest that the conditions for realizing Rawls' ideas of self–respect and social union correspond to the conditions necessary to actualize what Marx called species being or un–alienated authentic human existence.

GREEN, David G. An Egalitarian Epistemology: A Note On E P Thompson's Critique Of Althusser And Popper. *Phil Soc Sci* 14,183–190 Je 84.

GREEN, Dee F. "Ethical Dilemmas In Federal Cultural Resource Management" in *Ethics And Values In Archaeology,* Green, Ernestene L (ed), 97–107. NY Free Pr 1984.

GREEN, Ernestene L (ed). *Ethics And Values In Archaeology.* NY Free Pr 1984.

GREEN, Harold P and Gorovitz, Samuel. Allocation Of Resources: The Artificial Heart. *Hastings Center Rep* 14,13–17 O 84.

GREEN, Karen. Is A Logic For Belief Sentences Possible? *Phil Stud* 47,29–56 Ja 85.

GREEN, Leslie. What Is A Dictator? *Analysis* 45,124–127 Mr 85.

The Arrow Theorem depends on an assumption of "non–dictatorship", the formulation, justification, and status of which are here questioned. The author's earlier views about the relationship between economic rationality and non–dictatorship are clarified and defended.

GREEN, Ronald M. Ethics And Taxation: A Theoretical Framework. *J Relig Ethics* 12,146–161 Fall 84.

The issue of taxation raises essential moral questions about justice and fairness. Although the issue is an ancient one, systematic ethical reflection about taxation can be traced to the last few centuries. The author discusses five key values that have been identified as bearing on tax policy: freedom, material well–being and employment, health and welfare, equity, and distributive justice. He presents these values and their various interpretations as a conceptual framework for approaching the concrete teachings on taxation of the historical religious traditions surveyed in this Focus.

GREEN, Willard. Setting Boundaries For Artificial Feeding. *Hastings Center Rep* 14,8–10 D 84.

The paper reports on a Conference, sponsored by the Society for Health and Human Values, held to examine the medical, legal, and ethical ramifications of withholding and/or withdrawing food and water from a subset of persons who are terminally ill. The key questions addressed were: (a) Is nutrition and hydration a form of medical therapy; (b) Can limits be set for withholding/withdrawing that therapy; and (c) Who decided upon those limits?

GREENE, David B. *Mahler: Consciousness And Temporality.* NY Gordon & Breach 1984.

This book examines the temporal process that we ordinarily think structures our experience, as well as the connection between this concept and that of consciousness, and the confusions that characterize both concepts. It shows how Mahler's music (the Third, Fifth, Eighth, and Ninth Symphonies in particular) sometimes reflects these confusions about the nature of consciousness and temporality and sometimes tries to lead the listener into a new kind of temporality that would characterize a new kind of consciousness.

GREGORY, Paul. Against Couples. *J Applied Phil* 1,263–268 O 84.

The essay attacks the convention that a person should at any period in their life have not more than one sexual partner. The issues of the care of children and the desirability of a shared household are here bracketed out. The main argument proceeds by seeing conflicts between the requirement of exclusivity in sexual life, authenticity, and the principle that sexual communion should be an expression of love. (edited)

GREGORY, Peter N (ed) and Gimello, Robert M (ed). *Studies In Ch'an And Huy–Yen.* Honolulu Univ Of Hawaii Pr 1984.

A collection of five original studies – based on recently discovered or previously neglected Chinese, Japanese, and Tibetan texts – of the history, thought and practice of the early Ch'an (Zen) and Hua–yen (Kegon) traditions of East Asian Buddhism. The purpose of the collection is to communicate – largely to other specialists – recent developments in Buddhist scholarship leading to a reassessment of these two schools.

GREGORY, Peter N. Tsung–Mi And The Single Word "Awareness" (*chih*). *Phil East West* 35,249–270 Jl 85.

This article examines Tsung–mi's understanding of "awareness" (*chih*)—the central idea in his system of thought. It shows how awareness is integrally related to his vision of Ch'an history, his understanding of religious language, his sytematic classification of Buddhist teachings, and his emphasis on "nature origination." The article argues that Tsung–mi's theory of awareness must be understood within the historical context of his reaction to the more radical forms of Ch'an that were gaining momentum in the early ninth century.

GREIDER, William. "The People Versus The Experts" in *The Security Gamble*, Mac Lean, Douglas (ed), 89–99. Totowa Rowman & Allanheld 1984.

GREISCH, Jean. La Théologie Après Heidegger. *Etudes* 361,675–688 D 84.

GRENE, Marjorie G. *The Knower And The Known*. Lanham Univ Pr Of America 1974.

GREWENDORF, Gunther. On The Delimitation Of Semantics And Pragmatics: The Case Of Assertions. *J Prag* 8,517–538 Ag 84.

There are only two possible ways to answer the question of the delimitation of semantics and pragmatics. The first one refers to psychological criteria and can only be accomplished against the background of a modular cognitive theory of linguistic knowledge. The second one consists of a stipulation, i.E., a theoretical decision, which has to be based not only on empirical grounds, but also on considerations regarding purposes, simplicity, or fruitfulness of a certain division of labor among the various levels of linguistic theory. As long as we have not idea as to how the modular approach might accommodate the interplay of the various cognitive systems that together constitute pragmatic competence, we are forced to choose the second possibility. Focusing on pragmatics as a theory of linguistic action and semantics as a theory of truth–conditions, I want to illustrate in which respect various pragmatic factors determine the semantic evaluation of sentences, thereby showing why we are in fact forced to make a decision of the above mentioned kind, at which point it has to be made, what the respective alternatives consist of, and at what cost.

GRIER, Philip T. "O I Dzioev: A Soviet Critique Of Structuralist Social Theory" in *Contemporary Marxism*, O' Rourke, James J (ed), 183–198. Boston Reidel 1984.

GRIFFIN, David R. Bohm And Whitehead On Wholeness, Freedom, Causality, And Time. *Zygon* 20,165–192 Je 85.

David Bohm's developing postmodern thought (combining precision and wholeness) is seen to contain two tendencies. One is a vision of "underlying wholeness," in which all causation is vertical, and the implicate–explicate relation is ubiquitous. This provides a possible solution to certain problems, but creates many others involving freedom, causation, and time. Second, many of Bohm's statements suggest that his deepest intuitions could be formulated without those problems in terms of the distinctions developed in Alfred North Whitehead's philosophy of "prehensive wholeness," in which the ubiquity of creativity would require a more restricted use of the implicate–explicate relation.

GRIFFIN, Nicholas. Brody's Essentialism. *S J Phil* 23,273–278 Sum 85.

The paper criticizes Brody's recent attempt to characterize essential properties without appeal to trans–world identity. It is argued that all the alleged problems of trans–world identity return on Brody's account which requires identity across futures.

GRIFFIN, Nicholas. Russell's Multiple Relation Theory Of Judgment. *Phil Stud* 47,213–248 Mr 85.

The paper describes the evolution of Russell's theory of judgment between 1910 and 1913, with especial reference to his recently published *Theory of Knowledge* (1913). Russell abandoned the book and with it the theory of judgment as a result of Wittgenstein's criticisms. These criticisms are examined in detail and found to constitute a refutation of Russell's theory. Underlying differences between Wittgenstein's and Russell's views on logic are broached more sketchily.

GRIFFITH, William T. (Reflections On) The Dialectical Relationship Between Technique And (The Problem Of) Liberation. *Phil Soc Crit* 10,59–66 Sum 84.

GRIFFITHS, A Phillips. Child Adoption And Identity. *Philosophy* 18,275–286 84 Supp.

GRIFFITHS, Morwenna. Emotions And Education. *J Phil Educ* 18,223–231 1984.

The paper presents an account of emotion in terms of rationality and occurrent experience. It argues that emotions may be both rational or irrational. It criticizes both traditional and newer intentional accounts which underlie most discussions of emotion in education, arguing that they do not explain the influence of the whole curriculum on emotion and vice versa. Examples are pastoral care and girls science education.

GRIFFITHS, Paul. Karma And Personal Identity: A Response To Professor White. *Relig Stud* 20,481–486 S 84.

GRIGG, Robert. Relativism And Pictorial Realism. *J Aes Art Crit* 42,397–4o8 Sum 84.

Our appreciation of the "abstraction" of Byzantine art is based upon modern views about the value of realism in art and a faith in the rightness of cultural relativism. The relativism appealed to, however, is narrowly focused on the value of realism in art. Evidence of variability in the perception of pictorial realism is widely ignored. This leads scholars to dismiss Byzantine testimony characterizing their own art as realistic; but neither the analogy with the modern movements nor this dismissal appears sustainable.

GRILLIOT, Thomas J. Disturbing Arithmetic. *J Sym Log* 50,375–379 Je 85.

GRIM, Patrick and Brecher, Robert. Gremlins Revenged: Gremlins Repulsed. *Phil Stud (Ireland)* 30,165–176 Spr 84.

My contributions to this discussion are an attempt to construct and defend parodies of the ontological argument in the tradition of Gaunilo. I first did this in "Plantinga's God and Other Monstrosities" (*Religious Studies*, 15 (1979), 91–97), to which Robert Brecher replied in "Gremlins and Parodies," *Philosophical Studies* (Eire), XXIX (1983), 48–54. Here I attempt to counter Brecher's criticisms, which I consider closely akin to earlier criticisms of Gaunilo by Plantinga and Hartshorne, by constructing a range of Gauniloesque parodies which do not rely on dubiously necessary beings or on dubiously intrinsic maxima. Neither necessity nor intrinsic maximality, I maintain, are essential to the logical structure of the ontological argument or its parodies. This piece in its entirety is in effect a debate. My impression is that I win hands down.

GRIM, Patrick. Taking Sorites Arguments Seriously: Some Hidden Costs. *Philosophia (Israel)* 14,251–272 D 84.

For Peter Unger and W V O Quine, sorites arguments offer the following lesson: that our ordinary vague terms are in desperate need of precise replacement. I argue that the particular type of precise replacements proposed by Unger and Quine will not escape sorites arguments, and argue for a similar conclusion regarding a more sophisticated variant on this type of replacement. I also consider other strategies involving other types of replacement, and conclude that any attempt to avoid vagueness and escape sorites arguments by way of replacement, in whatever sense, is bound to exact quite considerable costs.

GRIM, Patrick. There Is No Set Of All Truths. *Analysis* 44,206–208 O 84.

An important philosophical consequence of Cantor's work has apparently been overlooked. There can be no set of all truths. I present the Cantorian argument against a set of all truths, and note one philosophical application, against a common approach to possible worlds. I conclude with brief comments on many–valued and alternative set theories and the merely apparent conflict with Lindenbaum's Lemma.

GRIMALDI, Nicolas. Quelques Paradoxes De L'esthétique De Diderot. *Rev Phil Fr* 174,311–336 Jl–S 84.

This study is trying to systematize Diderot's aesthetics by characterizing his apparent inconsistencies that turn in as many tensions. So (1) Art is an imitation of the reality, but all imitation of the reality is not art. (2) Representation of what is charming us in nature does not charm us in art. (3) Art must represent only what is true; there is nothing wronger than Christianity; but there is nothing more worthy of being represented. (4) Like Greuze is doing it, art has to be ethical, but there is nothing as beautiful as great crimes. (5) Aesthetics are subdued to logic, logic is subdued to empiricism, but nevertheless it is of a metaphysical idealism that art is taking its principles.

GRIMKÉ, Angelina. "Human Rights Not Founded On Sex" in *Freedom, Feminism, And The State*, Mc Elroy, Wendy (ed), 29–34. Cato Institute Washington 1982.

GRIMKÉ, Sarah. "Legal Disabilities Of Women" in *Freedom, Feminism, And The State*, Mc Elroy, Wendy (ed), 121–128. Cato Institute Washington 1982.

GRINSPOON, Lester and Bakalar, James B. "Drug Abuse Policies And Social Attitudes To Risk Taking" in *Feeling Good And Doing Better*, Murray, Thomas H (ed), 13–26. Clifton Humana Pr 1984.

GRISEZ, Germain. Presidential Address: Practical Reasoning And Christian Faith. *Proc Cath Phil Ass* 58,2–14 1984.

the thesis: Although there are no specifically Christian primary moral truths, there are specifically Christian moral norms. *the Argument:* The premises from which moral norms follow include not only primary moral truths but descriptions of acts whose choice or rejection will be guided by the norms. Since some (and perhaps all) of Christians' acts are intelligible only in terms of their faith and/or eligible only by believers, there are specifically Christian moral norms.

GROARKE, Leo. Descartes' First Meditation: Something Old, Something New, Something Borrowed. *J Hist Phil* 22,281–302 Jl 84.

According to most commentators, the evil demon Descartes presents in his first meditation is something new and original. I trace antecedents in the views of the academic sceptics, the tenth century Islamic philosopher al–Ghazālī, and the fourteenth century French philosopher Nicholas of Autrecourt. I argue that Descartes' argument is neither new nor original, and in all likelihood borrowed from Cicero's *Academica*.

GROARKE, Leo. Rebuilding Rawls: An Alternative Theory Of Justice. *Eidos* 2,93–109 D 81.

GROBLER, Adam. On Relevance Of M Bunge's Concept Of Difference In Meaning, Two Studies Of Inter–Theory Relations. *Rep Phil* 8,87–98 1984.

An analysis of some relations between geometrical theories in the light of M Bunge's theory of meaning reveals the context—dependence of the sense of inequality between the differences in meaning of geometrical concepts and theories. Hence, this theory of meaning misses one of its aims, i.E., the elucidation of the problem of incommensurability of scientific theories.

GRODIN, Michael and Markley, William S and Mc Donald, Anne E. "Medicolegal And Ethical Dilemmas In A Teaching Hospital" in *Ethics Committees And Health Care Decisions*, Cranford, Ronald (ed), 118–128. Ann Arbor Health Admin Pr 1984.

GROFMAN, Bernard and Uhlaner, Carole. Metapreferences And The Reasons For Stability In Social Choice: Thoughts On Broadening And Clarifying The Debate. *Theor Decis* 19,31–50 Jl 85.

The standard model of collective choice looks at aggression procedures which take individual preferences as existing for a specified set of alternatives. In this paper we propose that actors also have preferences for rules of choice or characteristics of choice processes (e.G., the perceived fairness of procedures or the popularity of outcomes) rather than simply for alternatives (outcomes) themselves. We argue that the positing of the existence of meta–preferences can illuminate a number of areas of choice theory. Here we focus on one such area: the problem of "too much" stability in majority rule decision making—a stability which belies the standard theoretical results on the generic instability of majority rule processes. We also show that discussion of the prevalence of stability in collective decision making needs to be clarified because there are at least six distinct types of stability which are sometimes confounded in the literature.

GRONDIN, Jean. L'avenir Du Concept En Esthétique: L'actualité Herméneutique De Hegel. *Laval Theol Phil* 40,335–338 O 84.

GRONDIN, Jean. Théorie Et Vérité: La Réflexion Contemporaine Face À Ses Origines Grecques Et Idéalistes. *Arch Phil* 47,613–624 O–D 84.

This paper aims at calling attention to a danger that lingers on the meta–theoretical trend of contemporary philosophy: the becoming autonomous and the closure of philosophical discourse. This auto–nomous reflexivity is then confronted with the transitivity of antique theoria as well as with the reflexive, albeit transitive conception of theory developed in German idealism. The impact of Kant's Critique of pure reason on idealist thinkers will appear as the birthplace of a radically meta–theoretical reflexion.

GROOT, Ger and Crego, Charo. Pierre Bourdieu En De Filosofische Esthetica. *Alg Ned Tijdschr Wijs* 77,21–35 Ja 85.

The authors fight the conclusions of Bourdieu in postscript to *La distinction* reducing philosophical aesthetics to the social background of the thinkers who conceived them. They show how Bourdieu's interpretation has been biassed by his intention to disqualify philosophical aesthetics and how he develops a highly disputable reading of Kant's philosophy of art, of which they present a more faithful reading. Finally, they defend the view that both approaches (the philosophical and the sociological) have their own rights of existence.

GROSHOLZ, E R. Two Episodes In The Unification Of Logic And Topology. *Brit J Phil Sci* 36,147–157 Je 85.

The partial reduction of logic and topology in the work of Tarski, Stone, Kleene, and McKinsey reveals much of interest about the status of logic as a mathematical discipline. It also exhibits how two distinct but related fields are unified by the hypothesis of a partial structural analogy, which allows for the combination of their resources in the solution and discovery of problem.

GROSS, Charlotte. Twelfth–Century Concepts Of Time: Three Reinterpretations Of Augustine's Doctrine Of Creation *Simul*. *J Hist Phil* 23,325–338 Jl 85.

According to Augustine, matter and form were co–created simultaneously and atemporally, as were all the works of the six days. In the twelfth century, Thierry of Chartres proposes a reading of Genesis "secundum phisicam," according to which the works of he six days are affected in time by the interaction of the four elements. Hugh of St Victor, overwhelmingly concerned with the historical and sacremental dimensions of creation, argues for an edifying progress from imperfection to perfection (i.E., a temporal creation). As Thierry describes matter as first creation as *informis*, so Hugh conceives first matter *in forma confusionis*, a break with Augustinian tradition even more radical than that suggested by Thierry. According to William of Conches' *Glosae Super Platonem*, matter and form are co–created *simul*, as are the works of the *creatio* (first three days of Genesis); the *ornatus* (latter three days), however, is affected in time by natural secondary causes. Each twelfth–century reinterpretation of Augustine's doctrine of creation *simul* reveals the distinct preoccupations of its author; all three reinterpretations suggest the emergence in the twelfth century of new concepts. (edited)

GROSS, Milton S. Commentary On B Lichter And M Hodges' "Perceptions Of The Engineers' 'Professionalism' In The Chemical Industry". *Bus Prof Ethics J* 2,11–14 Wint 83.

GROSSER, Gunther. Erfahrungen Aus Der Arbeit Am Lehrbuch "Wissenschaftlicher Kommunismus". *Deut Z Phil* 22,736–739 1974.

GROSSKOPF, I and Buckman, G and Garty, M. Ethical Dilemmas Of The Doctors' Strike In Israel. *J Med Ethics* 11,70–71 Je 85.

The authors discuss some of the moral dilemmas confronting Israeli doctors in the context of their strike in 1983. Concern for their patients militated against a strike. On the other hand their salaries were far below the mean standard of the country. To earn as much as nurses and radiographers doctors were forced to work 65–70 hours a week. The authors argue that if a doctor is underpaid and forced to work excessively the quality of medical care and ability to act in their best interests of patients is adversely affected. To avoid 'the necessity to strike' doctors' salaries and working conditions should be set by independent bodies in those countries where doctors are paid by the State.

GROSSMAN, Morris. Interpreting Peirce. *Trans Peirce Soc* 21,109–120 Wint 85.

This essay is an exploration of the bride simile at the end of Peirce's essay, "The Fixation of Belief". It presumes that the implications and reverberations of Peirce's literary figure are deeper and wider than might at first have been thought. Some of those implications and reverberations are explained and exhibited. Four interpretations of Peirce are proposed and one is selected.

GROSSMAN, Reinhardt. *Phenomenology And Existentialism: An Introduction*. Boston Routledge & K Paul 1984.

GROSSMANN, Reinhardt. Nonexistent Objects Versus Definite Descriptions. *Austl J Phil* 62,363–377 D 84.

The author defends his version of Russell's theory of definite descriptions against some recent objections, in particular against the objections raised in Routley's *Exploring Meinong's Jungle and Beyond*. Against Meinongians like Routley, he argues (a) that the golden mountain is not a constituent of any fact, and (b) that is has no such properties as being golden. The author's view can be summarized by means of the following nine theses: (1) the intentional nexus can connect existents with nonexistents; (2) the relation between the fact and its constituents is not "abnormal" like the intentional nexus; (3) a description expression must be distinguished both from what it represents (a description) and what it describes; (4) a description expression is not a *name* of what it describes; (5) while the golden mountain has no being, its description does; (6) while the golden mountain is not golden, its description contains the property of being golden; (7) an entity does not consist of its descriptions; (8) Leibniz's law holds for belief and modal contexts; and (9) there is only one kind of identity.

GROSSO, Giuseppe. Il Pensiero Storico–Filosofico Di Olgiati E L'Interpretazione Della Filosofia Cartesiana. *Ann Fac Lett Filosof* 25 & 26,503–518 1982–83.

The study regards the historical method practiced by Francesco Olgiati. In Olgiati's opinion we understand a philosophy understanding its conception of reality. An important example of this method is in the works about Descartes. Olgiati affirms the supremacy of metaphysics but we cannot affirm that the historical method by Olgiati is like the historical method by Giovanni Gentile.

GROTH, Alexander J. *Progress And Chaos: Modernization And Rediscovery Of Religion And Authority*. Malabar Krieger 1984.

This essay views the dominant spirit of modernity as secular rationalism which emphasizes effectiveness in goal attainment over the ends of human activity. Secular rationalism is infused with a mistaken underlying optimism about human nature; hence unwarranted hopes about linkage of material progress with general human well being. The essay argues that material progress has been accompanied by increasing chaos; attempts to reestablish religion and secular power as antidotes may be expected.

GROTH, Alexander. *Major Ideologies: An Interpretative Survey Of Democracy, Socialism And Nationalism*. Malabar Krieger 1983.

Democracy, socialism, and nationalism are analyzed in the context of historical changes occurring throughout the world with special emphasis on the phenomenon of "social mobilization." The "ideologies" are viewed not merely as systems of ideas but as social movements with distinctive institutional expressions. Social mobilization supported the diffusion of democracy, with socialism a response to both democracy and its attendant conditions, and nationalism a response to all these.

GROUT, Paul. Good Approximations To Maximin Allocations. *Theor Decis* 17,135–140 S 84.

The Rawlsian maximin welfare function differs from conventional welfare functions in two respects. Firstly it places a weight of one on the worst off individual in society. Secondly, as a direct consequence of this, the welfare function ignores almost everyone in society. This note considers the implications of rejecting the first but accepting the second property. It is shown that the fact that almost everyone receives no weight in the welfare function is the crucial element in determining the minimum utility level rather than the weight the worst off person receives.

GRÜNBAUM, Adolf. "Retrospective *Vs* Prospective Testing Of Aetiological Hypotheses" in *Testing Scientific Theories*, Earman, John (ed), 315–348. Minneapolis Univ Minnesota Pr 1983.

GRÜNFELD, Joseph. Feyerabend's Irrational Science. *Log Anal* 27,221–232 Je 84.

Feyerabend claims that tact and not logic determine the content of a concept and the permissible changes. Science has always been a matter of contextual plausibility, and not a context independent "organon of thought." But he nowhere explains what he means by "rational," he simply assumes that this is self evident and precise. He fails to provide criteria, let alone procedures, for the improvement of research programs and hence for progress in science. Renouncing "logic," a scientific language cannot even formulate problems that call for agreed upon solutions.

GRYTTING, Wayne. "Midwives, Vanguards, And Class Consciousness" in *Continuity And Change In Marxism*, Fischer, Norman And Others (ed), 97–113. Atlantic Highlands Humanities Pr 1982.

GUARIGLIA, Osvaldo N. La Cancelación Hegeliana De La Ética: Origen Y Conscuencias. *Rev Latin De Filosof* 10,231–254 N 84.

In section 1 of this paper the relationship between Hegel's terms, 'morality' and 'ethical life', and the traditional ethics terminology is shown. In section 2 I try to establish an independent criterion, in order to determine the central meaning of what is traditionally known as 'ethics'. In section 3 I prove, (i) that Hegel dissociates the core of classical ethics, namely the theory of virtue, from morals; (ii) that he reverses the relationship between philosophical ethics and habits; and lastly (iii) that he deprives morals of all its objective properties and restricts it merely to a subjective morality prone to relativism. In section 4 I conclude that the overcoming of subjective morality in an upper sphere, ethical life, is really the cancellation of any possible ethics and its substitution by the philosophy of history.

GUARIGLIA, Osvaldo. La Renovición Kantiana Del Derecho Natural Y La Crítica De Hegel: Una Crítica A La Crítica. *Dialogos* 20,7–50 Ap 85.

GUÉNON, René. *The Multiple States Of Being*. Burdett Larson 1984.

Guénon discusses the metaphysics of the absolute in order to come to grips with the individual. He focuses on the quest for permanent realization and inner spiritual freedom. (staff)

GUENTHNER, Franz (ed) and Gabbay, Dov M (ed). *Handbook Of Philosophical Logic: Extensions Of Classical Logic*, V2. Boston Reidel 1984.

GUGGENHEIM, Martin. Incorrigibility Laws: The State's Role In Resolving Intrafamily Conflict. *Crim Just Ethics* 4,11–18 Wint/Spr 85.

The article explores the state's role in resolving intra family conflict in light of recent decisions by the United States Supreme Court recognizing a constitutional right to privacy for adolescents in the area of sex related health care. It concludes that the state has no legitimate interest in judging for itself the proper resolution of an intra family dispute involving parents and their adolescent children.

GUIBAL, Francis. Dimensions Du Penser Hégélien. *Rev Metaph Morale* 89,465–489 O–D 84.

Centré sur l' oeuvre de la maturité cet article essaie de montrer comment le philosopher hégélien "relève" en lui, au présent de la pensée consciente de soi, les deux dimensions corrélatives de l'effectivité historique et de la profondeur religieuse. On formule, pour terminer, certaines interrogations qui invitent à recueillilr l'héritage de ce labeur raisonnable tout en gardant distance à l'égard de ses prétentions spéculatives.

GUILHAMET, Leon. Socrates And Post–Socratic Satire. *J Hist Ideas* 46,3–12 Ja–Mr 85.

GÜLDENPFENNIG, Sven. Philosophy Of Relations Between Sports And Peace. *Dialec Hum* 11,43–58 Wint 84.

GULYGA, Arseni. Schelling Als Verfasser Der "Nachtwachen" Des Bonaventura. *Deut Z Phil* 32,1027–1036 1984.

GUNATILLEKE, Godfrey (ed) and Tiruchelvam, Neelan (ed) and Coomaraswamy, Radhika (ed). *Ethical Dilemmas Of Development In Asia*. Lexington Heath 1983.

The study analyses the social, political, and economic consequences of current development strategies in terms of their human costs, with detailed case studies. These strategies will always be constrained by imperfect choices. The system making a choice must be aware of its imperfection, have a sustained concern for what is lost in human terms through its choice and possess built–in motivations to restore what is lost through constant assessment and participation of all the social groups affected by the gains and losses.

GUNNELL, John G. Political Theory And Politics: The Case Of Leo Strauss. *Polit Theory* 13,339–364 Ag 85.

Leo Strauss's arguments about the tradition of political theory reflect a deep concern about the relationship between academic political theory and politics. Despite his claims about natural law as accessible to reason, there are grounds for believing that Strauss realized that there was no philosophical answer to the problem of relativism but that it was the task of theory to keep the noble lie alive in order to sustain political society.

GUNTER, Pete A Y. The Constancy Of Kantian Time: Reflections On Chronobiology. *Phil Topics* 13,37–42 Spr 85.

This is a response to an article by Richard Hugen in a previous issue of *Philosophical Topics*. The author argues that it is a mistake to confuse psychological or physiological time with Kantian time. Kantian time is a necessary condition for the accurate application of Newtonian equations. It cannot, like physiological and psychological time, exhibit variable rates. Kantian time is not a subjective duration. It is subjective only in that it is applied by the knower. But it is applied by the knower to the objective world of Newtonian physics. Relatively physics, not chronobiology, is the falsification of Kantian time.

GUPTA, Bina. Brahman, God, Substance And Nature: Samkara And Spinoza. *Indian Phil Quart* 11,265–284 Jl 84.

GUPTA, R K. Phenomenalism, Idealism And Mentalism: A Historical Note. *Phil Natur* 21,157–160 1984.

There are different forms of Phenomenalism depending upon what one means by the term phenomenon. The form of Phenomenalism as found, say, in Hume is a form of Metaphysical Idealism, the view that the existence and nature of the world are dependent upon the mind. Metaphysical Idealism, just insofar as it makes the existence and nature of the world dependent upon the mind, manifestly turns out to be Mentalism.

GUPTA, Rita. Some Significant Contributions Of Buddhist Logicians In The Development Of Indian Philosophy. *Indian Phil Quart* 11,161–170 Ap 84.

GUREVICH, Yuri and Shelah, Saharon and Goldfarb, Warren D. A Decidable Subclass Of The Minimal Gödel Class With Identity. *J Sym Log* 49,1253–1261 D 84.

GURTLER, Gary M. Sympathy In Plotinus. *Int Phil Quart* 24,395–406 D 84.

A central problem in Plotinus is the reconciliation of unity and diversity, individuality and interdependence. His efforts to do this in the sense world have often been overlooked. The notion of sympathy thus provides a needed balance. It applies only to the sense world and illustrates the organic unity of the physical universe upon which are based sensation, the relation of body and soul, and the dynamic of human interaction.

GUSTAFSON, Donald. Armstrong's Intentions. *Philosophia (Israel)* 14,369–388 D 84.

GUTEK, Gerald L. "Toward A Pedagogy Of The Useful Past For Teacher Preparation": A Reaction. *J Thought* 20,34–38 Spr 85.

GUTIÉRREZ, Claudio. Un Nuevo Paraqdigma Para Las Ciencias Del Conocimiento. *Rev Filosof (Costa Rica)* 23,131–135 D 85.

The cognitive sciences (linguistics, cognitive psychology, neural science, epistemology...) developed independently of each other until the middle of this century. Something happened in the 40s that changed that: the formulation of Alan Turing of the universal machine and the invention of the general purpose digital computer. What is common to these two concepts is the capacity of a machine to imitate a machine of the same kind; everything points in the direction of the human mind having the same capacity, which we call knowledge. Thus the two events taken together constitute a paradigm which has unified and is making much more productive the cognitive sciences.

GUTMAN, Amy (ed) and Thompson, Dennis (ed). *Ethics & Politics: Cases And Comments*. Chicago Nelson 1984.

GUTSCHE, Gunter. Persönlichkeit Als Subjekt Des Gesellschaftlichen Fortschritts. *Deut Z Phil* 22,617–628 1974.

GUTTING, Gary. "Paradigms, Revolutions, And Technology" in *Technological Knowledge*, Laudan, Rachel (ed), 47–66. Boston Reidel 1984.

GUTTING, Gary. The Catholic And The Calvinist: A Dialogue On Faith And Reason. *Faith Phil* 2,236–256 Jl 85.

GUZMÁN, Roberto M. Razón Y Revelación En El Islam. *Rev Filosof (Costa Rica)* 22,133–150 D 84.

El presente ensayo analiza los conceptos de razón y revelación en el Islam, así como las más importantes controversias de parte de las distintas escuelas teológicas y las sectas islámicas. Con el propósito de lograr un acercamiento a Dios por medio de la

práctica mística, el sufismo centró su actividad en torno al conocimiento de Dios por el corazón (ma'rifa qalbiya) y destacó la importancia de la revelación sobre la razón. Las prácticas místicas de los sufis entraron en contradicción y recibieron la oposición de los 'ulama', juristas apegados al texto coránico y enemigos de cualquier experiencia u opinión que pudiera ser considerada bid'a (innovación). También se estudian en este trabajo las distintas visiones filosóficas de los más destacados filósofos musulmanes (al–Kindi, al–Farabi, Ibn Sina (Avicena), al–Ghazali y Averroes) y sus planteamientos con el propósito de conciliar razón con revelación. Asimismo, se presenta también la posición de algunos filósofos que dieron más importancia a la razón sobre la relavación. Tal fue el caso del persa Razi (Rhazes).

GUZZO, Augusto. Il Diluvio E L'Educazione. *Filosofia* 35,244–245 Jl–0 84.

GOLDSTONE, Peter. The Dominant Protection Association And Education. *Proc Phil Educ* 40,391–396 1984.

HAAKONSSEN, Knud. Hugo Grotius And The History Of Political Thought. *Polit Theory* 13,239–265 My 85.

Grotius's influence is divided into three problem areas, each of which is analyzed; the question of the nature of rights and their relationship to natural law; the question of the basis for, including the ground of obligation to, natural law; and the question of the scope and composition of natural law. The overall aim is to trace some broad lines of connection between modern natural law theory and Scottish eighteenth–century moral thought.

HAAKONSSEN, Knud. The Science Of A Legislator In James Mackintosh's Moral Philosophy. *Hist Polit Thought* 5,245–280 Sum 84.

The article relates Mackintosh to, on the one hand, Adam Smith's idea of "the science of a legislator" and, on the other, to the Common Sense moral philosophy of Dugald Stewart. In this way it becomes possible to trace the continuities between Mackintosh's early "radicalism" and his later 'Whiggism." At the same time, this is part of the story of how Smith's above–mentioned philosophical project was dissovled (cf. the author's *The Science of a Legislator. the Natural Jurisprudence of David Hume and Adam Smith, Cambridge, 1981*).

HAAS, André. La Thermodynamique Sera–T–Elle Intégrée Dans La Physique Théorique? *Rev Phil Fr* 174,188–200 Ap–Je 84.

The integration of thermodynamics is in retard by a century. Present physics was built on reversible principles borrowed from mechanics. Conditions of mechanical reversibility are insufficients. Reversible planet movements and e.M. Signals are thermodynamically irreversibles. Irreversibility is a general principle of nature. Among the far reaching consequences e.G. The flux of measurement information can not be described by reversible theories. The converse integration is therefore more likely.

HABA, Enrique P. Conceptos Indeterminados, Derechos Humanos Y Seguridad Nacional. *Rev Filosof (Costa Rica)* 22,3–30 D 84.

Este estudio subraya el peligro que, para el respeto de los derechos humanos fundamentales, representa el uso de ciertos conceptos indeterminados en el discurso politico jurídico. La primera mitad (Secciones I y li) contiene puntualizaciones sobre el papel general que allí desempeñan esos conceptos y también se señala cómo habilitan para afectar derechos humanos inclusive en el marco de Constituciones democrático–pluralistas. En la segunda mitad (Sección III) se examina en particular la Doctrina de la Seguridad Nacional, rúbrica dentro de la cual se distinguen como variantes cinco modelos ideológicos; se muestra que cada uno de estos conduce, llegado el caso, a justificar –en el nivel pragmático de dicho discurso– acciones estatales que a las autoridades les permiten promover "legítimamente" la violación de unos derechos humanos básicos.

HABERMAS, Gary R. Knowing That Jesus' Resurrection Occurred: A Response To Davis. *Faith Phil* 2,295–302 Jl 85.

HABERMAS, Jurgen and Mc Carthy, Thomas (trans). *The Theory Of Communicative Action: Reason And The Rationalization Of Society*, V1. Boston Beacon Pr 1981.

HABERMAS, Jürgen. Questions And Counterquestions. *Praxis Int* 4,229–249 O 84.

HABERMAS, Jurgen. Reply To Skjei's "A Comment On Performative, Subject, And Proposition In Habermas's Theory Of Communication". *Inquiry* 28,105–112 Mr 85.

Erling Skjei's criticisms (*Inquiry 28, this issue*) of my account of communicative action in *The Theory of Communicative Action* are based on a misunderstanding of the role of the analysis of speech acts at my work. I begin by restating the terms of my analysis, and after dealing with Skjei's objections to my claims for the explanatory power of illocutionary acts, draws attention to a problem with imperatives that I haven't yet done justice to.

HABGOOD, J S. Medical Ethics—A Christian View. *J Med Ethics* 11,12–13 Mr 85.

All ethics has a religious dimension. This paper considers how specific Christian insights concerning death, suffering, human nature and human creatureliness can help to expose more fully the moral issues at stake in some of the dilemmas faced by doctors. It ends up acknowledging the crushing burden of decision–making which rests on many in the medical profession, and indicates the importance of religious resources in dealing with this.

HABLUTZEL, Nancy and Hoffman, Wilma and Krolikowski, Walter P. "Symmetry, Independence, Continuity, Boundedness, And Additivity": The Game Of Education. *Educ Stud* 15,215–231 Fall 84.

A review of seven recent books on educational policy from the United States and Great Britain. The article touches on some of the new happenings in education, especially the situation in Yugoslavia, the influence of court cases on educational practice, and national plans of educational change. It points to a troubling but necessary double focus on minima and maxima, on laws and ideals, on policies and principles, and advocates looking past liberty and equality to fraternity.

HACKETT, Stuart. *The Reconstruction Of The Christian Revelation Claim*. Grand Rapids Baker 1984.

HACKING, Ian. "Five Parables" in *Philosophy In History*, Rorty, Richard and others (ed), 103–124. NY Cambridge Univ Pr 1984.

HACKING, Ian. Experimentation And Scientific Realism. *Phil Topics* 13,71–88 Spr 82.

Scientific realism can never be proven nor refuted at the level of theorizing. The only grounds for scientific realism are experimental. The best evidence for the reality of a hypothetical entity is that it can be used in order to investigate other bits of nature. A detailed example is given, namely a 1977 polarized electron gun used to show failure of parity conservation in weak neutral current interactions.

HADWIGER, Don F. Issues In Agriculture. *Agr Human Values* 1,16–19 Wint 84.

Agricultural subgovernments have generated an efficient agriculture in developed countries, checking the impulse of governments to ignore or abuse agriculture. This creative confrontation may be missing some less developed countries. It is because these subgovernments lack broad representation from the rural culture that they can freely prefer production goals over way–of–life, equity, or environmental goals. In the U S the subgovernment has generated the intellectual resources to planning one food economy. We should be careful not to let our subgovernments do all our thinking on agricultural development.

HAECKER, Dorothy. A Theory Of Historical Truth. *Phil Topics* 13,267–276 Spr 85.

A theory of historical truth must offer a mutually consistent and defensible account of historical meaningfulness, verification, and reference. The concepts of coherence and correspondence, in both their metaphysical and epistemological dimensions, are essential to this analysis. The concept of correspondence plays the major role in a proper understanding of historical reference; the concept of coherence is basic to the analysis of historical verification; both are necessary to make sense of historical meaningfulness.

HAGBERG, Garry. Art And The Unsayable: Langer's Tractarian Aesthetics. *Brit J Aes* 24,325–340 Autumn 84.

Suzanne Langer claims that "Art is the creation of forms symbolic of human feeling," and in developing that claim constructs a theory of artistic meaning modeled on the atomistic theory of linguistic meaning in Wittgenstein's *Tractatus Logico–Philosophicus*. In this paper an investigation is conducted into that assimilation of art to language, discussing specifically the outward representation in art of inner feeling through morphological correspondences between feeling and form and the actual significance of formal design in aesthetic experience.

HAGBERG, G. Understanding Happiness. *Mind* 93,589–591 O 84.

This paper is a critical discussion of a theory of happiness put forth in J Kekes, "Happiness", (*Mind*, 1982, volume XCI, pages 358–376), in which a distinction is developed between "episodic" and "attitudinal" forms of happiness. With the aid of a number of examples of the complex interactions between episodes and attitudes, it is suggested that the relationship is not direct in the way the theory implies, and moreover that the presumption of a unitary subject matter for a theory of happiness may be indefensible.

HAGE, J C. Enkele Opmerkingen Over Geldigheid En Gelding. *Alg Ned Tijdschr Wijs* 76,262–266 O 84.

The purpose of this paper is to distinguish two senses of "validity", senses which are rendered in Dutch as "geldigheid" and "gelding". Geldigheid is a property of things that are made according to rules, for example statutes and arguments. "Gelding" can be rendered as "has (the) meaning (of)". Rules have gelding, because they have meaning for human behavior. Sometimes geldigheid is a prerequisite of gelding, as with the geldigheid of a statute and the gelding of its rules.

HAGEN, Charles T. The 'ENEPΓEIA–KINHΣIΣ Distinction And Aristotle's Conception Of ΠΡΑΞΙΣ. *J Hist Phil* 22,263–280 Jl 84.

In *Metaphysics* 9.6, Aristotle classifies actions as either *energeiai* or *kineseis*. Recently Daniel Graham has argued that a correct understanding of the perfect–tensed verb forms in the so–called tense test in that passage shows that Aristotle's *energeiai* are states rather than activities. According to Graham, now joined by Michael White, Aristotle is pointing to states as the highest form of *praxis*. I argue that Graham's conclusions do not follow from Aristotle's use of the perfect tense here and that there is ample evidence elsewhere in the corpus to show that *energeiai* are not states. Developing Terry Penner's analysis of the *energeia–kinesis* distinction, I locate the basis of *energeia*–hood in Aristotle's teleology and connect that teleology with the Aristotelian conception of *praxis*.

HAGEN, Johann J. Rechtssoziologie Und Sozialer Wandel: Zum Dritten Band Des Jahrbuchs Für Rechtssoziologioe Und Rechtstheorie. *Arch Rechts Soz* 60,125–128 1974.

HAGEN, Johann J. Zur Dialektik Von Freiheit Und Sicherheit. *Arch Rechts Soz* 59,517–534 1973.

The general content of the notions Liberty and Security demands a theoretical treatment from a universal position, which can be reached by practical philosophy, by systems–theory or philosophical hermeneutic or by historical and dialectical materialism. The conclusion, that Liberty is in permanent connexion with social Security, as had to be proved through the various concepts of social theory, means, that the popular dichotomy is rooted in the structure of society and thereby becomes reality.

HAGEN, Michael. Der "Westliche" Marxismus—Eine Antikommunistische Variante Bürgerlicher Ideologie. *Deut Z Phil* 23,784–799 1975.

Seit den 50er Jahren wird durch Marxologen und Revisionisten verstärkt die Propagierung eines sogenannten westlichen Marxismus betrieben, die bewufsst gegen die philosophischen Grundlagen des Marxismus–Leninismus gerichtet ist. Der Autor untersucht die theoriegeschichtliche Begründung dieser Konzeption in den 1923 erschienenen Arbeiten "Geschichte und Klassenbewufsssein" von G Lukács und "Marxismus und Philosophie" von K Korsch. Er weist nach, dafss in diesen Arbeiten von Lukás und Korsch direkt Ergebnisse des damals in der bürgerlichen Philosophie in den Vordegrund tretenden Neuhegelianismus übernommen werden.

HAGEN, Ole (ed) and Wenstop, Fred (ed). *Progress In Utility And Risk Theory*. Boston Reidel 1983.

HAGEN, Ole. Rules Of Behavior And Expected Utility Theory: Compatibility Versus Dependence. *Theor Decis* 18,31–46 Ja 85.

Some rational rules of behavior are implied in expected utility theory (EUT) but not dependent of it, e.G., 1) order dominance and an expectation–variance preference function (when "rational"). On the other hand a recent example of "irrational" and "hon–EUT" preference ordering is neither. Some consequences of EUT are absurd and unrealistic. eUT is part redundant, part misleading, rightly named a "dogma" by Paul Sammuelson in 1983. The author's own alternative is consistent with 1) order dominance.

HAGER, F P. La Société Comme Intermédiaire Entre L'Homme Individuel Et L'Absolu Chez Platon Et Chez Plotin. *Diotima* 12,131–138 1984.

The article says that both Plato and Plotinus conceive reality in the form of a hierarchy of beings beginning with a supreme principle (the idea of the Good in Plato, the One–Good in Plotinus) and ending with the sensible world and matter, and that man has to find his way back to the ultimate metaphysical principles (the idea of the Good and the other ideas in Plato, the One–good and the Divine Intellect in Plotinus) in order to become really human. But whereas in Plato society (i.E., the ideal political community of his city–state) is a necessary intermediary between the single man and the Absolute in Plotinus there is no more such intermediary, but the single man has to find himself the way back to the Absolute.

HAGER, Nina. Zu Den Funktionen Der Marxistisch–Leninistischen Philosophie In Bezug Auf Die Einzelwissenschaften. *Deut Z Phil* 32,1098–1102 1984.

HAGGARD, Thomas R. "Government Regulation Of The Employment Relationship" in *Rights And Regulation*, Machan, Tibor (ed), 13–42. Cambridge Ballinger 1983.

HAHN, Alois. Theorie Zur Enstehung Der Europäischen Moderne. *Phil Rundsch* 31,178–202 1984.

The author compares theories of the origin of European modernity in order to show the hidden connection between the factors put forward in these theories. He investigates the role of growing functional differentiation (F H Tenbruck and N Luhmann), of the influence of the court with its impact on systematic emotional control (N Elias), of institutionalized surveillance and panoptism (M Foucault) and the famous theory of Max Weber of the relationship between the self–domestication of the capitalist entrepreneur and Puritanism. The author includes into this context his own researches on the history of the auricular confession and formulates a theory of the transformation of institutionalized forms of surveillance into systems of self–controlled behavior.

HAHN, Erich. Die Frage Von Krieg Und Frieden In Der Weltanschaulichen Auseinandersetzung. *Deut Z Phil* 32,1085–1097 1984.

HAHN, Toni. Das Individuelle Bewusstsein Und Die Dialektik Von Objektiven Bedingungen Und Subjektivem Faktor. *Deut Z Phil* 22,598–616 1974.

Um den Stellenwert des richtigen Bewufsstseins von gesetzmäfssigen gesellschaftlichen Zusammenhängen im subjektiven Faktor erfassen zu können, ist es erforderlich, den Begriff des gesellschaftlichen Bewufsstseins in seinen berschiedenen Aspekten klar zu fixieren und die Beziehungen zwischen gesellschaftlichem und individuellem Bewufsstsein zu bestimmen. Aufgabe soziologischer Bewufsseinsforschungen ist es, individuellers Bewufsstsein sowohl als eine der objektiven Bedingungen als auch als eine der subjektiven Voraussetzungen gesellschaftlicher Entwicklung zu untersuchen.

HALACZEK, B. Die Entwicklung Der Paläoanthropologie Im Lichte Der Stammbäme Des Menschen. *Stud Phil Christ* 20,55–96 1984.

HALBFASS, Wilhelm. India And The Comparative Method. *Phil East West* 35,3–16 Ja 85.

HALBWACHS, F. On Galileo's Writings On Mechanics: An Attempt At A Semantic Analysis Of Viviani's Scholium. *Synthese* 62,459–484 Mr 85.

In the third day of the Discorsi, Galileo presents a "demonstration" of the "principle of inclined plan". The cognitive basis of this principle can be shown to have its origin in the non–explicit handling of the conservation of Energy. In the demonstration given by Galileo, two terms, namely "Momento" and "Impeto", are used indifferently. A precise analysis shows that "Momento" has a static meaning and concerns the forces in equilibrium, while "Impeto" has a kinematic meaning and concerns the uniformly accelerated motion. The implicit identification of these two notions amounts to state the proportionality between them, what is Newton's second law.

HALDANE, John J. Concept–Formation And Value Education. *Educ Phil Theor* 16,22–28 O 84.

The natural supposition that our concepts are acquired through experience is challenged by a famous anti–abstractionist argument; yet the alternative appeal to innate ideas is also unsatisfactory. It is argued that the general objection to abstractionism is not conclusive. Concepts may be formed in the process of experience in which the subject seeks to discern a structure. Such attempts at discrimination involve valuation and the implicatons of these facts for education are explored.

HALDANE, John J. The Morality Of Deterrence. *Heythrop J* 26,41–46 Ja 85.

Defenders of Nuclear Deterrence have sought to rebut the charge that the policy involves murderous intentions and is therefore immoral. Here two such responses are examined and rejected. The first substitutes bluff for the intention to retaliate if attacked; the second argues that the intention to prevent war by intending to wage it does not entail the simple intention to retaliate. It is argued that both responses involve the maintenance or formation of murderous intentions.

HALDAR, Hiralal and Harris, H S (ed). *Neo–Hegelianism*. NY Garland 1984.

Hale, Bob 306 Author Index with Abstracts

HALE, Bob. Frege's Platonism. *Phil Quart* 34,225–241 Jl 84.

A line of argument which may be seen as underlying Frege's Platonism is set forth. This presupposes the availability of criteria of singular termhood of a certain kind. Such criteria are sketched. The central task of the paper is to defend the Fregean argument against various criticisms—in particular a charge of linguistic relativity to which it appears vulnerable.

HALFMANN, Jost. "The Dethroning Of The Philosophy Of Science" in *Methodology, Metaphysics And The History Of Science*, Cohen, Robert S (ed), 149–172. Boston Reidel 1984.

HALL, Richard J. An Argument That The Language Of Belief Is Not English. *Phil Stud* 48,235–240 S 85.

With 'say' we have both direct discourse, as in 'He said, "I like fish",' and indirect discourse, as in 'He said that he likes fish'. With 'believe' there is not direct discourse construction. Why? If we suppose there is a language of thought (or belief), the question is especially pressing. One possible answer is that the language of belief in not English. Arguments are given for this answer.

HALL, Richard J. Pierre And The New World Makers. *Austl J Phil* 62,283–288 S 84.

When Kripke left Pierre, he was in a puzzling doxastic state. We can view the puzzle as a puzzle about finding possible worlds to be compatible with Pierre's apparently logically impeccable beliefs. Worlds in which London is pretty, worlds in which London is not pretty, and of course worlds in which London is both or neither, seem to be ruled out. Stalnaker and Lewis have suggested new ways of world making which might alleviate the problem about Pierre. I show that if we give Pierre a few more beliefs—some beliefs about water—these new worlds won't solve the problem. Sets of possible worlds just don't seem to work as the objects of belief.

HALL, Roland. Contemporary British Philosophy: A Survey Of Developments Over The Last Three Decades. *Z Phil Forsch* 38,638–647 N–D 84.

HALLER, Rudolf. Der Erste Wiener Kreis. *Erkenntnis* 22,341–358 Ja 85.

The article stresses the new perspective on the Vienna Circle. It shows the role of Frank, Hahn, and Neurath in the formation of the Schlick–Circle and gives an outline of their philosophical positions between 1907 and 1917. Their neopragmisitic–conventionalistic point of view—nowadays discussed again as Duhem–Quine–theses—later on was dominated by Wittgenstein's influence within the Schlick–Circle, but clearly continued in Neurath's later work.

HALLER, Rudolf. Lebensform Oder Lebensformen:—Eine Bemerkung Zu Newton Garvers Interpretation Von "Lebensform". *Grazer Phil Stud* 21,55–64 1984.

HALLER, Rudolf. Problems Of Knowledge In Moritz Schlick. *Synthese* 64,283–296 S 85.

The aim of the paper is to throw fresh light on some problems of knowing empirical facts and to make more intelligible the presuppositions underlying the concept of protocol sentences.

HALLETT, Garth. *Reason And Right.* Notre Dame Notre Dame Univ Pr 1984.

This text reflects belief that an introduction to ethics should provide training in moral reasoning in addition to ethical theory and sample moral problems. The chapters of part one, on the nature, value, and validity of moral reasoning, prepare for the evaluation of varied moral arguments and issues, in part two, with the help of background theoretical essays. A teacher's guide is especially helpful for this second part.

HALLETT, Michael. *Cantorian Set Theory And Limitation Of Size.* Oxford Clarendon Pr 1984.

HALLIE, Philip P. Scepticism, Narrative, And Holocaust Ethics. *Phil Forum (Boston)* 16,33–49 Fall–Wint 84.

HALLMAN, Max O. Nietzsche And Pragmatism. *Kinesis* 14,63–78 Spr 85.

In this paper, I compare Nietzsche's epitemological views to the pragmatic theory of knowledge. After discussing important themes that are common to both, e.G., the denial of the possibility of absolute knowledge, and the rejection of both the spectator theory of knowledge and the correspondence theory of truth, I argue that for Nietzsche truth and knowledge, as well as the active structuring that makes knowledge possible, are pragmatic in nature.

HALLMAN, Max O. Royce's Revaluation Of Values. *S J Phil* 22,361–372 Fall 84.

In this paper, I reexamine the moral views of Josiah Royce, focusing specifically on the question of whether Royce's principle of loyalty necessitates a revaluation of traditional moral values. After preliminary analyses dealing with Royce's conception of traditional moral values and with his description of man's moral situation, I argue that the principle of loyalaty does require a revaluation of values. The paper ends with a brief comparison of Royce's revaluation with that of Nietzsche.

HALPER, Edward. *Metaphysics* Z 12 And H 6; The Unity Of Form And Composite. *Ancient Phil* 4,146–159 Fall 84.

This paper argues that, contrary to the usual view, Z 12 and H 6 address different problems and advance different solutions. Z 12 asks how form can be one if its definition consists of genus and *differentia*, and it invokes a doctrine of proper differentiation to argue that the definition need include only a single constituent, the ultimate *differentia*. H 6 also asks about the unity of definition, but its concern is how a composite of form and matter can be one. The paper explains how identifying form as actuality resolves this problem.

HALPER, Edward. Aristotle On The Extension Of Non–Contradiction. *Hist Phil Quart* 1,369–380 O 84.

While most discussions *Metaphysics* IV 4–8 have examined Aristotle's arguments for the principle of non–contradiction, this paper argues that Aristotle's chief concern in this section is not to establish the principle but to show its universal extension. Aristotle formulates the principle so that it can apply to things. He then makes it clear that in order for the principle to hold of something, that thing must have an essence. In removing reasons to doubt the universal extension of the principle, Aristotle is showing that all beings have essences.

HAMBOURGER, Robert. Moore's Paradox And Epistemic Justification. *Phil Res Arch* 10,1–12 1984.

The author discusses solutions to Moore's Paradox by Moore and Wittgenstein and then offers one of his own: 'I believe that P' and 'not–P' can both be true but nonetheless are not epistemically compatible; that is, it is logically impossible simultaneously to have sufficient evidence to justify assertions of each. The author then argues that similar transgressions are committed by other "paradoxical" utterances whose paradoxicality cannot be explained by the Moore or Wittgenstein solutions and also that this provides a technique that can be useful in studying the epistemic requirements for justified assertion.

HAMEL, Edouard. L'Église Et Les Droits De L'homme: Jalons D'histoire. *Gregorianum* 65,271–299 1984.

Human Rights in themselves belong to philosophy. They are a matter of concern for everyone, not only to Christians. They are founded on human dignity as on a common base valid for everybody. Philosophy studies Human Rights with its own light. But, Human Rights can be "Christianized," i.E., inserted in the horizon given by Revelation–Creation, Incarnation and Ecclesiology—where, without losing their "natural" meaning, they acquire a greater and fuller value.

HAMMACHER, Klaus. Einige Methodische Regeln Descartes' Und Das Erfindende Denken. *Z Allg Wiss* 4,203–223 1973.

Es soll die Aufgabe dieses Beitrages sein, die Verflechtungen, welche diese Regeln mit bestimmten Entscheidungen des Denkens haben, an Hand von Descartes' System aufzudecken und dabei so etwas wie eine philosophische Begründung dieses Denkstils in seiner noch aktuellen Funktion vorzuführen. Es soll damit zugleich die Situation erhellt werden, in der wir uns durch die wissenschaftliche Technik befinden, und schließlich soll angedeutet werden, welche Aufgaben für das Verhalten aus solchen Entscheidungen unserem Bewußtsein erwachsen sind.

HAMMOND, John L. Theism And The Moral Point Of View. *Int J Phil Relig* 17,23–28 1985.

This is a reply to a recent article in the same journal by A Steuer ("The Religious Justification of Morality", Int J Phil Relig, 13, 1982). Steuer argues that theism provides a logical justification for taking "the moral point of view". I contend that the premises of his argument are either false or doubtful. I also point to some larger implications of this discussion for other attempts to base ethics on theology, including the so–called "diving command theory".

HAMMOND, John L. Wilderness And Heritage Values. *Environ Ethics* 7,165–170 Sum 85.

Some proponents of the preservation of American wilderness—for example, Aldo Leopold—have argued in terms of the role of wilderness in forming and maintaining a set of distinctive national character traits. I examine and defend the value judgment implicit in Leopold's argument. The value of one's cultural heritage is, I contend, as important and valid as other familiar goods appealed to in defense of social policy.

HAMPLE, Dale. A Third Perspective On Argument. *Phil Rhet* 18,1–22 1985.

Argument_0, argument considered as cognition, is introduced and argued to be as legitimate a topic for argumentation scholars as argument_1, something a person makes, and argument_2, something people have. $\text{Argument}_0$is shown to be important to classical and contemporary treatments of argument. Strong and weak claims about $\text{argument}_0$are specified. The objections to this essay's viewpoint are considered and answered.

HAMPSCH, George. Nuclear Deterrence And World Peace. *Phil Soc Crit* 10,123–132 Wint 84.

This article addresses the problems of deterrence and peace from the three basic perspectives of human nature. It developes their implications in relation to the justifiability of nuclear deterrence and the possibilities of perpetual peace. Updating Kant, a specific suggestion is offered concerning nuclear weapons, as well as several others concerning international relations. The ethical need for alternate national security policies is emphasized.

HAMPTON, Jean. Hobbes's State Of War. *Topoi* 4,47–60 Mr 85.

This article attempts to explain the origins of warfare in Hobbes's state of nature. Two inconsistent accounts of its generation are found in *Leviathan*, both of which are shown to be inadequate. However, the author develops a third account from the text which succeeds in explaining the warfare consistent with Hobbes's psychological premisses and with the rest of the argument. It also explains how and why the laws of nature are "in foro interno" valid yet ineffective in the state of nature.

HAMRICK, William S and Marsh, James L. Whitehead And Marx: Toward A Political Metaphysics. *Phil Today* 28,191–202 Fall 84.

The essay demonstrates first, the affinities between Marx and Whitehead as philosophers of process; second the complementarity of Marx's critical social theory and Whitehead's metaphysics; and finally, the possibility of a political metaphysics at once speculative and practical, ontological and critical, reflective and committed.

HAMRICK, William S. Redeeming The Earth: Tragic Wisdom And The Plains Indians. *J Brit Soc Phenomenol* 16,36–54 Ja 85.

HANAZAWA, Masazumi. "Various Kinds Of Aronszajn Tree With No Subtree Of Different Kind" in *Lecture Notes In Mathematics*, Muller, G H And Others (ed), 1–22. NY Springer 1981.

HANDEL, G and Klohr, Olof. Der Atheistische Charakter Der Marxistisch–Leninistischen Philosophie Und Weltanschauung. *Deut Z Phil* 22,502–506 1974.

HANDEL, Gottfried. Die Sowjetische Hilfe Für Die Entwicklung Der Marxistisch–Leninistischen Philosophie An Den Universitäten (1945–1949). *Deut Z Phil* 23,644–661 1975.

Die sowjetische Hilfe umfatfsste zwei Hauptrichtungen: Kontrolle der Realisierung des Potsdamer Abkommens über die Entnazifizierung und Zusammenarbeit mit den antifachistischdemokratischen Kräften beim Aufbau von Hochschulen, an denen bis

1949 der marxistischleninistischen Philosophie Heimatrecht verschafft wurde. Die sowjetische Hilfe erfolgte hauptsächlich in drei Formen: durch Publikationen, Unterstützung bei der Grüng und dem Aufbau von philosophischen Einrichtungen und durch das Auftreten sowjetischer Wissenschaftler.

HÄNDLER, Ernst W. Measurement Of Preference And Utility. *Erkenntnis* 21,319–348 N 84.

The paper contains an analysis of actual measuring processes for preferences and utilities giving an axiomatization which renders possible a clear demarcation between different empirical applications and a precise formulation of the empirical claim involving a relationship to actually realized alternatives. The examples suggest a novel general explication of measuring processes accounting for partial measurement, constraints as an indispendable part of the measuring process, and for measurement depending on a predetermined value.

HANDS, Douglas W. Discussion: What Economics Is Not: An Economist's Response To Rosenberg. *Phil Sci* 51,495–503 S 84.

Alexander Rosenberg (1983) has argued, contrary to his previous work in the philosophy of economics, that economics *is not* science, and it *is* merely mathematics. This paper argues that Rosenberg fails to demonstrate either of these two claims. The questions of the predictive weakness of modern economics and the cognitive standing of abstract economic theory are discussed in detail.

HANFLING, Oswald. A Situational Account Of Knowledge. *Monist* 62,40–56 Ja 85.

HANFLING, Oswald. Can There Be A Method Of Doubt? *Philosophy* 59,505–511 O 84.

In Descartes' Meditations we find (1) reasons which seem to render his beliefs doubtful and (2) a *motive* for doubting (the "method of doubt"). But can doubting be done at will, as required by (2)? Descartes conflates doubting with various acts (supposing, etc.) that clearly *can* be done at will. But to *suppose* that p is false is not to make sceptical point at all. Descartes tries to soften the paradox of doubting at will by producing "powerful reasons" (dreams, the demon). But if these suppositions really rendered our beliefs doubtful, there would be no place for the will. Yet it is not clear that they do make them doubtful, or even that Descartes claimed this. Descartes' amalgam of reasons and will ("method") is untenable.

HANFLING, Oswald. Scepticism On Twin Earth. *Ratio* 26,195–198 D 84.

A capsule from "Twin Earth" contains an extract from a book on skepticism, closely resembling one published on earth, except for the transposition of "Cartesian demon" and "external world". There follows a Twin Earthian dialogue about these two ways of explaining "our sense experiences". It appears that the issue, whether posed on earth or Twin Earth, is meaningless.

HANFLING, Oswald. Was Wittgenstein A Sceptic? *Phil Invest* 8,1–16 Ja 85.

According to Kripke, Wittgenstein denied certain beliefs about meaning and other minds. But who holds these beliefs? We do *not* believe that "all future applications" of a word are "determined"; nor that "I give directions to myself"; nor that something has to "constitute" meaning. Such beliefs are distortions by realist philosophers; it needs no sceptic to deny them. Wittgenstein's "sympathy with the solipsist" is an illusion, due to misreadings (and mistranslations) of the text. Wittgenstein's position is clear and does not need Kripke's revision.

HANFLING, Oswald. What Does The Private Language Argument Prove? *Phil Quart* 34,468–481 0 84.

HANKS, Richard. Moral Reasoning In Adolescents: A Feature Of Intelligence Or Social Adjustment? *J Moral Educ* 14,43–55 Ja 85.

This paper summarizes certain aspects of an assessment of the level of the moral judgment of three groups of children: mildly educationally subnormal children, ESN (M), who are also maladjusted; stable ESN (M) children; and stable children of approximately average intelligence. A minimum age of twelve years was stipulated; all the children attended secondary school with the oldest in the total sample being 15 years 9 months. The assessment procedure which, although owing much if not all of its rationale to Piaget, is original in its mode of presentation and largely in its content, is described. The results of each of the three groups are compared. Also, the results are correlated with IQ. This enables a judgment to be arrived at as to the relative importance of (a) intelligence and (b) social adjustment in the making of mature moral decisions and choices.

HANNA, Patricia. Translation, Indeterminacy And Triviality. *Philosophia (Israel)* 14,341–348 D 84.

HANNAFORD, Robert V. Moral Reasoning And Action In Young Children. *J Value Inq* 19,85–98 1985.

I argue that moral reasoning and responsibility arises out of capacities found in infants. My argument is taken up in four parts: (I) I show how recent philosophical literature leads us to conlcude that concern for, and awareness of, others' intentions appear in very early childhood and that they are exercised in the reasoning and cooperating by which one can become a responsible person; (II) I point out the evidential and logical problem with two influential contrary accounts of the appearance of intention and concern—those of Piaget and Rawls; (III) I review empirical studies of psychological development which indicate the early presence of reciprocal awareness and concern; and (IV) I suppest the way moral reasoning develops from these.

HANNAWAY, Owen (ed) and Achinstein, Peter (ed). *Observation, Experiment, And Hypothesis In Modern Physical Science.* Cambridge MIT Pr 1985.

HANNAY, Alastair. Hamlet Without The Prince Of Denmark Revisited: Pörn On Kierkegaard And The Self. *Inquiry* 28,261–272 Je 85.

Ingmar Pörn (*Inquiry* 27 (1984), nos 2–3) claims the certain ideas of Kierkegaard's can illuminate a notion of the self articulated in action–theoretical terms. Through a reconstruction of Kierkegaard's concept of despair, couched in these terms, Pörn aims to show how these ideas can contribute to the study of the self. Because he misconstrues an important distinction in Kierkegaard's account of selfhood, Pörn fails to show this. It remains uncertain what use the study of the self would have for Kierkegaard's notion of selfhood, and whether an action–theoretical analysis is capable of bringing out whatever may be of interest in it.

HANRATTY, Gerald. Hegel And The Gnostic Tradition: I. *Phil Stud (Ireland)* 30,23–48 Spr 84.

HANS, James S. The Question Of Value In Nietzsche And Heidegger. *Phil Today* 28,283–299 Wint 84.

HANSON, Philip P. Are Contexts Semantic Determinants? *Can J Phil* 6,161–184 80 Supp.

HAPPEL, J S. Advice On Good Practice From The Standards Committee. *J Med Ethics* 11,39–41 Mr 85.

The role of the General Medical Council has changed over the last few years and this paper show how the GMC now gives advice on good practice, as well as a warning against bad practice.

HARDIN, C L. A Transparent Case For Subjectivism. *Analysis* 45,117–119 Mr 85.

Colin McGinn has argued that an explanation of the impossibility of a white transparency cannot be rendered in physicalistic terms alone, but instead requires an appeal to color experiences and their phenomenology. McGinn's argument proves to be of a white transparency which makes no essential reference to color sensations.

HARDIN, C L. Are 'Scientific' Objects Coloured? *Mind* 93,491–500 O 84.

Can objects characterizable entirely by what we take to be the laws of physics be colored? Those who answer in the affirmative are either *objectivists* or *subjectivists*. Objectivists identify colors with physical properties such as wavelengths, while subjectivists take colors to be the dispositions of things to generate color experiences in us. If we suppose colors to be qualities with which we are acquainted, it turns out that colors have necessary features which no physical complex exhibits, so objectivism is false. Subjectivism, on the other hand, requires a non–arbitrary specification of normal observers and standard conditions, and there are grave factual doubts about whether such a specification is possible.

HARDIN, C L. The Resemblances Of Colors. *Phil Stud* 48,35–48 Jl 85.

Because they have taken phenomenal hues to be paradigmatic of simple, unanalyzable qualities, many philosophers have despaired of giving a theoretical account of their resemblances to one another. In fact, phenomenal hues do display a structure, one which has been investigated in some detail by visual scientists, and this structure can be exploited to explain why, for example, orange and red resemble one another more than either resembles blue.

HARDIN, Russell. Sanction And Obligation. *Monist* 68,403–418 Jl 85.

HARDT, Ulrich H. *A Critical Edition Of Mary Wollstonecraft's A Vindication Of The Rights Of Woman: With Strictures On Political And Moral Subjects.* Troy Whitston 1982.

HARDWIG, John. Epistemic Dependence. *J Phil* 82,335–349 Jl 85.

Appeals to the epistemic authority of experts often ground rational belief and sometimes also justify claims to know. The epistemic dependence ingredient in such appeals undermines intellectual autonomy and challenges the individualism implicit in much epistemology. Consideration of expertise thus forces basic changes in our conception of rationality. Moreover, either one can know that p without possessing the evidence for the truth of p or there is knowledge which is known by a *community*, but not by any individual knower.

HARDY, Gilbert. Value And Free Choice: Lavelle's Attempt At A Reconciliation. *Phil Today* 28,308–318 Wint 84.

The article develops the interrelation of freedom and value in three steps: Analysis of the act of freedom; Value as a guide of freedom; Critical observations on Lavelle's existential axiology. The act of freedom is shown to be rooted in the "experience of being" and qualified by the objective nature of given possibilities. This objectivity establishes a preferential order; human freedom is an oscillation between the temporal order of choice and the transtemporal order of value. The article criticizes the interdependence of freedom and value in the same act of choice but acknowledges the merits of Lavelle's attempt to deal with this problem.

HARE, John E. Philosophy In The Legislative Process. *Int J Applied Phil* 2,81–88 Fall 84.

HARE, R M. "Do Agents Have To Be Moralists" in *Gewirth's Ethical Rationalism*, Regis Jr, Edward (ed), 52–58. Chicago Univ Of Chicago Pr 1984.

HARE, R M. Commentary On Beauchamp's "Manipulative Advertising". *Bus Prof Ethics J* 3,23–28 Spr/Sum 84.

Beauchamp writes as if advertising practices lay on a continuum from good to bad, their place depending on the amount of influence exerted. Yet influence, however strong, is not in itself bad, but only if wrongly exerted. There are a number of independent features that can make influence wrong (cf. hart on mens rea). A Kantian–utilitarian method is suggested for determining what these are. Advertising is permissible when beneficial, otherwise not.

HARE, R M. Liberty And Equality: How Politics Masquerades As Philosophy. *Soc Phil Pol* 2,1–11 Autumn 84.

Liberty and equality conflict both mutually and internally; but everyone agrees they are good things. Philosophers need to say why. Usually they appeal instead to intuitions, e.G., Rawls, Nozick. This is not philosophy but politics. In public discussions too, intuitions conflict, reflecting people's politics; rhetoric, not argument, results. Example of employment legislation. A Kantian–utilitarian way is suggested of determining by argument what kinds of liberty and equality are good things.

HARE, R M. Philosophy And Practice: Some Issues About War And Peace. *Philosophy* 18,1–16 84 Supp.

Pacifism and nationalism both result from one–level intuitive thinking, which pursues some single principle (non–violence; loyalty) and forgets others equally sound. Such conflicts demand critical thinking. It yields a kind of universalizable patriotism: peace is best preserved by allowing defense of one's own country but not aggression. In the case of nuclear arms the crucial question is: what policies are most likely to prevent nuclear war. It is doubtful whether the answer is 'unilateral disarmament'.

HARE, R M. Some Reasoning About Preferences: A Response To Essays By Person, Feldman, And Schueler. *Ethics* 95,81–85 O 84.

Misunderstandings of Hare, *Moral Thinking*, by Schueler (*Ethics* 95, 1984), Feldman (*Phil. studies* 45, 1984) and Persson (*Anal.* 43, 1983) cleared up. Although if A fully knows what B's situation is like for B, he must prefer *pro tanto* that were he in B's situation the preference that B now has should be satisfied, this preference may be outweighed by A's other preferences. Secondly, moral prescriptions have to cover hypothetical qualitatively identical cases as well as actual ones.

HARE, R M. The Promising Game (in Polish). *Etyka* 21,151–164 1985.

HARE, William. Bias In Stories For Children: Black Marks For Authors. *J Applied Phil* 2,99–108 Mr 85.

The Guidelines published in the United States by the Council on International Books for Children in 1980 appeal to such criteria as language, omission and caricature to support the view that certain popular children's books are racist. It is argued here, with reference to the books in question, that the guidelines blur the distinction betwen what is said and what sort of judgment it constitutes. Next it is shown that the interventionist, didactic role demanded of the writer ignores the complexities of literature. Finally, it is maintained that such factors as mood, tone and humor need to be weighed in assessing caricature. Such guidelines may foster a distorted view of literary criticism, and encourage a tendency to read in too much. The serious issue of racism is in danger of being trivialized, and moral education of turning into didacticism. The distinction between a guideline and a mechanical rule needs to be preserved, and more sophisticated guidelines required.

HAREL, David. "Dynamic Logic" in *Handbook Of Philosophical Logic*, Gabbay, Dov (ed), 497–604. Boston Reidel 1984.

HARGROVE, Eugene C. The Role Of Rules In Ethical Decision Making. *Inquiry* 28,3–42 Mr 85.

Using chess decision making as a model for ethical decision making, I show that ethical decisions rarely involve the conscious application of moral rules. I discuss the metaethical and normative implications of this aspect of ethical decision making in terms of the moral philosophies of Sartre, Hare, and Aristotle. I conclude with a discussion of the implications of the chess model in research and teaching in applied ethics.

HARKER, Jay E. Can There Be An Infinite Regress Of Justified Beliefs? *Austl J Phil* 62,255–264 S 84.

Most analytic epistemologists, foundationalists and coherentists alike, have rejected the possibility of an infinitely long, non–recurring regress of justified beliefs. It is instructive to inquire why this notion has received nearly universal condemnation. In a review of recent work six sorts of arguments against infinite justificatory chains are examined. It is concluded firstly that, while regresses in which each belief is justified solely via relations to further beliefs cannot exist, the impossiblity of other sorts of infinite justificatory chains has not been shown, and secondly that there may nevertheless be sound methodological reasons for provisionally rejecting the infinite regress possibility while more satisfactory alternatives are explored.

HARKLEROAD, Leon. Fuzzy Recursion, RET's, And Isols. *Z Math Log* 30,425–436 1984.

In this paper, many basic notions of recursion theory are generalized to the setting of fuzzy sets. Several of the classical properties hold in the fuzzy context, but some (such as the closure, under union, of the class of recursively enumerable sets) do not. This paper defines and investigates fuzzy versions of recursivity, recursive enumerability, isolic reducibility (and recursive equivalence types), and isolatedness.

HARKNESS, Marguerite. *The Aesthetics Of Dedalus And Bloom.* Lewisburg Bucknell Univ Pr 1984.

HARLAN, Robert M. Towards A Computational Phenomenology (1). *Man World* 17,261–278 1984.

HARMAN, Gilbert. "Is There A Single True Morality" in *Morality, Reason And Truth*, Copp, David (ed), 27–48. Totowa Rowman & Allanheld 1984.

HARMAN, Lillian. "Some Problems Of Social Freedom" in *Freedom, Feminism, And The State*, Mc Elroy, Wendy (ed), 193–206. Cato Institute Washington 1982.

HARMAN, Lillian. "87–100" in *Freedom, Feminism, And The State*, Mc Elroy, Wendy (ed), 87–100. Cato Institute Washington 1982.

HARNIK, Victor. Stability Theory And Set Existence Axioms. *J Sym Log* 50,123–137 Mr 85.

HARNISH, Robert M. Communicative Reference: An Inferential Model. *Conceptus* 18,20–41 1984.

This paper explores the nature of the inference principles required for reference to be communicated from speaker to hearer, within a general framework for successful communication (presented 1979 in *Linguistic Communication and Speech Acts* by K Bach and R M Harnish). The theory is worked out in some detail for indexicals and definite descriptions, and is integrated with a theory of gesturing. The theory is extended to nonliteral and indirect cases of reference, and connections with issues such as "referential and attributive", "proper names", and "Anaphora" are noted.

HARP, Gillis J. Taylor, Calhoun, And The Decline Of A Theory Of Political Disharmony. *J Hist Ideas* 46,107–120 Ja–Mr 85.

HARPER, William A (ed) and Meerbote, Ralf (ed). *Kant On Causality, Freedom, And Objectivity.* Minneapolis Univ Minnesota Pr 1984.

HARPER, William L. "Kant's Empirical Realism" in *Kant On Causality, Freedom, And Objectivity*, Harper, William A (ed), 108–147. Minneapolis Univ Minnesota Pr 1984.

HARPER, William L and Meerbote, Ralf. "Kant's Principle Of Causal Explanations" in *Kant On Causality, Freedom, And Objectivity*, Harper, William A (ed), 3–19. Minneapolis Univ Minnesota Pr 1984.

HARPER, William. Kant On Space, Empirical Realism And The Foundations Of Geometry. *Topoi* 3,143–162 D 84.

HARPINE, William D. Can Rhetoric And Dialectic Serve The Purposes Of Logic? *Phil Ret* 18,96–112 1985.

This paper asks if persuasive effectiveness in various contexts can be a criterion of logical soundness. After examining several recent attempts to derive communication–based criteria of logical excellence, the paper concludes that neither dialectic nor rhetoric is adequate to the tasks traditionally assigned to logic.

HARRAH, David. "The Logic Of Questions" in *Handbook Of Philosophical Logic*, Gabbay, Dov (ed), 715–764. Boston Reidel 1984.

HARRAH, David. A Logic Of Message And Reply. *Synthese* 63,275–294 Je 85.

In this paper we sketch a logic of message and reply. The logic is intended for application in a wide variety of situations, not restricted to the two–person, turn–taking situation. Each message has a body and a vector the vector specifies the "from," "to," and the like. To reply to a message, it suffices to give either (1) a complete reply to the body or (2) a corrective reply to at least one presumption derivable from the vector. We discuss the problems of achieving effectiveness and completeness with respect to certain aspects of communication. The results are mixed. In section 9 we argue semi–formally that, in a certain sense, dialogue is necessary. Finally we note that this logic is not a rival of other approaches but may be combinable with them.

HARRÉ, R and Martin, J. "Metaphor In Science" in *Metaphor*, Miall, David S (ed), 89–105. Atlantic Highlands Humanities Pr 1982.

HARRÉ, Rom (ed) and Von Cranach, Mario (ed). *The Analysis Of Action.* Cambridge Cambridge Univ Pr 1982.

HARRÉ, Rom. "Theoretical Preliminaries To The Study Of Action" in *The Analysis Of Action*, Von Cranach, Mario (ed), 5–34. Cambridge Cambridge Univ Pr 1982.

HARRINGTON, L and Lachlan, A H and Cherlin, Gregory. $\aleph_0$–Categorical, $\aleph_0$–Stable Structures. *Annals Pure Applied Log* 28,103–136 Mr 85.

We give a Coordinatization Theorem and related results which facilitate the systematic analysis of $\aleph_0$–categorical $\aleph_0$–stable structures. We combine a number of Zil'ber's ideas with the recent classification of the finite permutation groups called Jordan groups. The use of group theory can be avoided (Zil'ber, D Evans), but it plays an essential role in related work on stable structures homogeneous for a finite relational language. Applications include finiteness of the Morley rank of such structures, refinements of Zil'ber's results on the finite submodel property, and more technical results.

HARRINGTON, Michael. "A Future Analysis Of Marxism And Ethics" in *Darwin, Marx And Freud*, Caplan, Arthur L (ed), 73–112. NY Plenum Pr 1984.

HARRIS, Chandice C (ed) and Snowden, Fraser (ed). *Bioethical Frontiers In Perinatal Intensive Care.* Natchitoches Northwestern Pr 1985.

This book consists of papers by a philosopher, a bioethicist, a cultural anthropologist, an attorney, and a theologian on the broad bioethical issues raised by the birth of severely handicapped infants. A final paper, by a reproductive endocrinologist, reviews recent reproductive technologies and explores their value dimensions. The book attempts to demonstrate the importance of involving humanist scholars in the formulation of guidelines for handling Baby Doe–type cases.

HARRIS, Errol E. *An Interpretation Of The Logic Of Hegel.* Lanham Univ Pr Of America 1983.

Consists of an introduction to the encyclopedia logic followed by a detailed commentary on both logics section by section. Hegel's holism is emphasized and his realistic conception of nature, making his system as much absolute realism as absolute idealism.

HARRIS, H S (ed) and Haldar, Hiralal. *Neo–Hegelianism.* NY Garland 1984.

HARRIS, H S (ed) and Hibben, John G. *Hegel's Logic: An Essay In Interpretation.* NY Garland 1984.

HARRIS, H S (ed) and Mc Taggart, John M. *Studies In Hegelian Cosmology.* NY Garland 1984.

HARRIS, H S. Developing Themes In Philosophy/La Philosophie En Cours: The Hegel Renaissance In The Anglo–Saxon World Since 1945. *Eidos* 1,68–98 Jl 78.

HARRIS, Henry S. The Resurrection Of Art. *Owl Minerva* 16,5–20 Fall 84.

HARRIS, James F. The Constitutive Force Of Language. *Phil Invest* 8,51–65 Ja 85.

HARRIS, Jean. Child Abuse And Neglect: Ethical Issues. *J Med Ethics* 11,138–141 S 85.

Children may be abused physically, sexually, emotionally and by omission or commission in any permutation under these headings. This is discussed in terms of the separate overlapping responsibilities of parents, guardians, the community in which they live and the network of professional services developed to care for, protect and educate children. An attempt is made to place these issues within an ethical framework, with regard to the legislature of England and Wales.

HARRIS, John. Arresting But Misleading Phrases. *J Med Ethics* 10,155–157 S 84.

This paper discusses some common misconceptions of what a utilitarian approach to medical ethics is and of the conclusions it forces upon those disposed to accept such an approach. It suggests that broad and unargued characterizations of approaches to moral questions as 'utilitarian', 'Hippocratic' or whatever are likely to be misleading and counterproductive. What matters is not what to call the position that people feel inclined to accept but rather what arguments there are in its favor and what arguments there are against it.

HARRIS, John. Full Humans And Empty Morality. *Phil Quart* 35,70–72 Ja 85.

this paper argues that Mary Warnock's justification of the Warnock report and her defense of the philosophical basis of that report is totally inadequate. It shows in particular that the account of the moral status of the embryo is deficient and suggests a more successful account.

HARRIS, Leonard (ed). *Philosophy Born Of Struggle: Anthology Of Afro–American Philosophy From 1917.* Dubuque Kendall/Hunt 1983.

HARRISON, Jonathan. Anscombe, Davidson And Lehrer On A Point About Freedom. *Phil Stud* 46,259–262 S 84.

Professor Keith Lehrer has argued (roughly) that 'I can do A' cannot mean 'If I were to want to do A, I would' because this is compatible with my not wanting to do A *preventing* me from doing A. However, if I had a fairy godmother who prevented me from doing all and only the things I did not want to do, this would not mean that I *really* could not do these things.

HARRISON, Jonathan. Be Ye Therefore Perfect Or The Ineradicability Of Sin. *Relig Stud* 21,1–20 Mr 85.

Despite its appearing to be a tautology that one ought to do all the things one ought to do, the disposition to behave as one ought is not the only valuable characteristic there is. Possessing it is sometimes incompatible with possessing other valuable characteristics, which must sometimes be preferred to it. Virtue is subject to a law of diminishing value, can be taken too seriously by those who pursue it, and can be positively harmful if pursued to excess.

HARRISON, Jonathan. Ethics And The Archangelic Prescriber. *Cogito* 2,19–38 S 84.

The author puts forward and discusses sixteen objections, which are impossible to summarize, to the view, put forward by Professor R M Hare in 'Moral Thinking: its levels, Methods and Point', (O U P, 1981) that an archangel could arrive at a correct opinion of what ought to be done in any given situation simply from knowing all the relevant matters of fact about it.

HARRISON, Jonathan. Recent Work On Epistemology. *Phil Quart* 35,95–104 Ja 85.

Recent work in epistemology has many defects. It ignores the distinction, fatal to the standard view, between being justified in believing and being justified in being certain. It neglects the many contextual implications of knowledge statements. It forgets that there are many things one knows without having evidence. It does not do justice to the view that knowing implies (or contextually implies) the impossibility of one's being mistaken about what one claims to know.

HARRISON, J. Professor Putnam On Brains In Vats. *Erkenntnis* 23,55–58 My 85.

Since the proposition that we are asserting when we say that 'There are brains in vats' would be true, even though the proposition that brains in vats are asserting when they said 'There are brains in vats' (i.E., the proposition that there are image brains in image vats) was false, Putnam's *reductio ad absurdum* argument breaks down.

HARSANYI, John C. Acceptance Of Empirical Statements: A Bayesian Theory Without Cognitive Utilities. *Theor Decis* 18,1–30 Ja 85.

HARSANYI, John C. Rule Utilitarianism, Equality, And Justice. *Soc Phil Pol* 2,115–127 Spr 85.

Kant regarded morality as the *highest value*. But a utilitarian must treat morality as a *servant* of other values: its purpose is to help other people to obtain nonmoral values, such as economic welfare, friendship, knowledge, and whatever else they want. Of course, our moral duties always take precedence over other considerations. But in determing our social policies, moral values such as fairness and equality cannot always override other social interests; and strong moral fervor is not always an unmixed blessing for society.

HART, H L A (ed). *Essays In Jurisprudence And Philosophy.* NY Oxford Univ Pr 1984.

HART, Richard E and Bowie, Norman. "Should We Be Discussing This". *Teach Phil* 7,230–234 Jl 84.

My commentary poses two fundamental and interrelated questions: Does the principle of confidentiality apply to the relationship between student and teacher on matters such as grades? Moreover, are there specific contexts in which faculty discussion of grades and records is morally unacceptable, or, conversely, contexts in which, because of overriding educational or social objectives, such discussion is morally appropriate, perhaps even obligatory? I conclude that clearly articulated reasons or objectives are crucial to moral evaluation of such actions.

HARTLEY, John P. Effective Discontinuity And A Characterisation Of The Superjump. *J Sym Log* 50,349–358 Je 85.

By showing how to examine computation trees, an effective proof of the "only if" part of Grilliot's Theorem is given: the functional embodying number quantification, ^2E, is computable from a type–2 object F if and only if F has an effective discontinuity (Grilliot's proof was not constructive). The method is then applied to type–3 objects in which ^3E is computable (assuming AC and CH), and its application to the superjump is discussed.

HARTMAN, David. The God Of The Philosophers In The Jewish Tradition (in Hebrew). *Iyyun* 33,266–288 Ja–Ap 84.

HARTMAN, Hyman. "Philosophy Of Science And The Origin Of Life" in *Methodology, Metaphysics And The History Of Science*, Cohen, Robert S (ed), 183–214. Boston Reidel 1984.

HARTMAN, Margaret. How The Inadequate Models For Virtue In The *Protagoras* Illuminate Socrates' View Of The Unity Of The Virtues. *Apeiron* 18,110–117 1984.

Both models for the multiplicity of the virtues presented in the *Protagoras*, the face model and the gold model, are inadequate. Only when one combines the truths hinted at both models can one understand Socrates' own account of the unity of the virtues: the virtues are all one undifferentiated *dynamis*; their multiplicity is explained by the different spheres in which the *dynamis* operates.

HARTMAN, Tom. The Heterodox Interpretation Of Reference Talk. *Phil Stud* 46,145–170 S 84.

I argue, inspired by Wilfred Sellars, that reference statements are translation statements. Meaning statements tie mentioned phrases to mentioned phrases; reference statements tie mentioned phrases to phrases in use. The orthodox picture of reference as word–user–world relation is misbegotten. The connection of language to reality: words guide actions regarding things and things guide actions regarding words. Let ontologists turn from the siren of semantic language and get serious about Wittgensteinian language–game analysis.

HARTMANN, Klaus. "Towards A New Systematic Reading Of Hegel's Philosophy Of Right" in *The State And Civil Society*, Pelczynski, Z A (ed), 114–136. Cambridge Cambridge Univ Pr 1984.

HARTMANN, Klaus. Human Agency Between Life–world And System: Habermas's Latest Version Of Critical Theory. *J Brit Soc Phenomenol* 16,145–155 My 85.

By contrast with so-called Critical Theory, Habermas is credited with a positive move, affirming human interaction and communication in a life–world. However, it is argued that Habermas' distinction between social, or life–world, integration and system integration is ill–advised. The notion of system should not be construed as pinpointing a specific kind of alienation detrimental to communication since, as is clear from Parsons and Luhmann, it is designed to accommodate any type of social integration, including the life–world.

HARTMANN, Klaus. The German Philosophical Scene (2). *J Brit Soc Phenomenol* 15,301–306 O 84.

HARTSHORNE, Charles. *Creativity In American Philosophy.* Albany SUNY Pr 1984.

This book, like my *Insights and Oversights of Great Thinkers*, tries to interpret the history of philosophy (but with reference to American rather than European writers) as a partly successful struggle to overcome such sterile dilemmas as unembodied yet unfree minds, *or* lifeless, mindless, unfree bits of matter; also life and love without God, *or* God (so–called) without life or love; also political freedom without order *or* order without freedom.

HARTSHORNE, Charles. *Omnipotence And Other Theological Mistakes.* Albany SUNY Pr 1984.

In this book I argue that although it is possible give a good meaning to 'omnipotence', the meaning usually given is a mistake because it entails a lack of freedom in the creatures. I also argue that a number of other traditional religious terms, including perfect (therefore immutable), omniscient, revelation, immortality, can also be given good meanings but have usually been mistakenly interpreted. The book is less technical than most of my works.

HARTSHORNE, Charles. "God And The Meaning Of Life" in *On Nature*, Rouner, Leroy S (ed), 154–168. Notre Dame Univ Notre Dame Pr 1984.

HARTSHORNE, Charles. Indeterministic Freedom As Universal Principle. *J Soc Phil* 15,5–11 Fall 84.

A vigorous, partly historical criticism of unqualified determinism. In philosophy, theology, and natural science, there has been a movement away from an early deterministic phase to an irreduceably statistical phase allowing some freedom to all individuals, whether they be atoms or people. This universal freedom involves risk and a tragic aspect to life that is made worse than it need be by the refusal to recognize it.

HARVEY, Charles W. On The Experience Of Historical Objects. *Int J Applied Phil* 2,73–80 Fall 84.

This essay attempts to explain the *felt* experience that is often had when within the presence of historical objects. By substituting Heidegger's notion of a temporalized and involved care–structure for that of the "self", objects are described as extensions of this temporalized and concerned involvement. Consequently, even when spatially and temporally distant from the person that was involved with them, that person's presence is felt in the experience of their objects. It is this phenomenon that lies at the heart of the strange, felt experience of historical objects.

HASKELL, Francis. Museums And Their Enemies. *J Aes Educ* 19,13–22 Sum 85.

Already in the late eighteenth century it was held against museums that they distorted the significance of art by changing the original destination of paintings and sculpture. This article examines this and other objections, and also the defenses proposed of which the most necessary and important (based on the notion of moral improvement) is essentially mystical; and it suggests that by their contempt for the public and/or association with finance many contemporary directors are playing into the hands of their enemies.

HASKER, William. Foreknowledge And Necessity. *Faith Phil* 2,121–157 Ap 85.

I begin by setting out the argument for the incompatibility of free will and comprehensive divine foreknowledge, and I examine some obviously ineffective replies to this argument. I then examine the three major replies—the claim that truths about God's beliefs are "soft facts", claim that we have what may be termed "counterfactual power over the past" (Plantinga), and the claim that we have power to bring about and to prevent past events (Mavrodes). I conclude that none of these answers to the incompatibility argument is successful.

HASKER, W. Must God Do His Best? *Int J Phil Relig* 16,213–224 1984.

David Basinger has recently proposed as an ethical requirement on divine action that God must do his best to maximize the quality of life for all self–determing beings. I argue that this is an excessively strict requirement for theodicy, that it conflicts with the Judaeo–Christian belief that much of what God does for us is done gratuitously and exceeds all moral requirements, and that Basinger's case for his requirement is weak and unconvincing.

HASLER, Ludwig. Hegel Und Die Aufklärung: Oder: Vom Versuch, Den Verstand Zur Vernunft Zu Bringen. *Stud Phil (Switzerland)* 41,115–138 1982.

HASSING, R F. Wholes, Parts, And Laws Of Motion. *Nature Syst* 6,195–216 D 84.

There are deservedly well–known studies on the laws of motion in Newton and Descartes. The works of Boas, Jammer, Hall, Cohen, Koyre, Gabbey, and Westfall are among the most noteworthy. All have provided carefully crafted and highly instructive accounts of the structure and development of the physical thought of Newton and Descartes. Each has proceeded within, and contributed to, the history of science or the philosophy of science. Yet none has addressed the question of the relation of living beings to the laws of motion, a concern more characteristic of what could be called philosophy of nature. Now the meaning of 'living being' must involve at least this: a special relation of parts and whole, in which the former are what they are only in terms of, and are thus not neutral to, the latter. This of course appears to be fundamentally incompatible with the tradition of physics deriving from Newton. It is really incompatible? The present investigation seeks to clarify this issue by dispelling certain mistaken or incomplete conceptions of the philosophical implications of physics.

HATFIELD, Donald and Lansing, Paul. Corporate Control Through The Criminal System. *J Bus Ethics* 4,409–414 O 85.

Corporate violations of the law are occurring with increasing frequency and with increasing public attention. Solutions to date have proved ineffectual because of the problem of determining whom is to be punished for the offense of the corporation. Instead of individual jail terms or corporate fines, we propose that the dissolution of the corporation be considered as a more effectual means of conforming corporate behavior to the norms of the legal system.

HATFIELD, Gary. Descartes's Meditations As Cognitive Exercises. *Phil Lit* 19,41–58 Ap 85.

The aim of the article is to achieve greater philosophical understanding of the *Meditations* through investigation of its use of the meditative mode of writing. Parallels are drawn between spiritual exercises and Descartes' "cognitive exercises". The chief conclusions concern the use of meditation to direct the reader toward specific "cognitive experiences", which may be understood in connection with Descartes' conception of intellectual intuition, along with contemporary practices in mathematics and in devotional meditation.

HATHAWAY, Ronald. Explaining The Unity Of The Platonic Dialogue. *Phil Lit* 8,195–208 O 84.

I develop a form of explanation that justifies exegetic monism, viz., the view that the Platonic dialogue as work of philosophy and as artwork are in essence one. The explanation is developed in four stages: Plato's conception of products of image–craft, Plato's uses of models in philosophical inquiry, micro–dialogues within the finished macro–dialogues, and the emergence of the macro–dialogue itself as a model and a constraining frame. I further argue that no weaker explanation than the one offered could justify exegetic monism.

HATTINGH, J P. The Problem Of Art And Morality In The Context Of Kant's Aesthetics (in Dutch). *S Afr J Phil* 4,8–15 F 85.

In this article it is argued that Kant's view of the disinterestedness of aesthetic judgement does not give an adequate justification for the position that only artistic values are to be used in the judgement of works of art. This follows the fact that Kant's view of aesthetic judgement is in essence a theory about the judgement of beauty which provides far too narrow a framework for the judgement of works of art. Certain essential aspects important for the judgement of works of art are not taken into account in Kant's view of the aesthetic dimension. It is essential, therefore, to seek another approach—one that will escape the difficulties of Kant's narrow view and make it possible to obtain a meaningful answer to the question of the relationship between art and morality, specifically the question of the role of moral considerations in the judgement of artistic endeavours.

HAUCK, Jürgen. Eine Neue Definition Berechenbarer Reeller Funktionen. *Z Math Log* 30,259–268 1984.

HAUCK, Jürgen. Zur Wellengleichung Mit Konstruktiven Randbedingungen. *Z Math Log* 30,561–566 1984.

HAUERWAS, Stanley and Childress, James F. Time And History In Theological Ethics: The Work Of James Gustafson. *J Relig Ethics* 13,3–21 Spr 85.

This essay traces Gustafson's understanding of the methodological significance of history and time for theological ethics. I argue that Gustafson qualifies his original thoroughgoing historicist perspective in the interest of developing a natural theology and ethics. His continuing emphasis on a historical perspective, I suggest, is best understood by attending to his recommendation that the theologian's task is best captured by the image of the "participant".

HAUERWAS, Stanley. Pacifism: Some Philosophical Considerations. *Faith Phil* 2,99–104 Ap 85.

Rather than offering a philosophical defense of pacifism, this article claims that pacifism is unintelligible as a position apart from the theological convictions which form it. Pacifism is, however, a position which raises profound issues for philosophy. Given philosophers' general acceptance of violence as legitimate, pacifism challenges the philosophical understanding of the universality of moral rationality. Locating the universality is the *substance*, not the form, of convictions, pacifism itself becomes the *form* of moral rationality.

HAUFFE, Heinz. Theory Dynamics And Knowledge Representation From An Information–Theoretical Point Of View. *Phil Natur* 21,368–375 1984.

The higher the explanatory power of a scientific theory, the less is the capacity needed for the storage of the factual knowledge related to the theory. This result is drawn from an application of Shannon's information theory to a predicate calculus by which the system of all logically possible empirical statements is expressed. The more decisions are made by a theory within this system, the higher rises its redundancy and the less storage capacity is needed for its encoding.

HAUPTLI, Bruce. Kekes On Problem–Solving And Rationality. *Phil Soc Sci* 14,191–194 Je 84.

Skeptics challenge rationalists to show that their rationalism differs from the fideists' irrationalism. Rationalists' responses to this challenge generally beg the question or engender a fideism. John Kekes proposes a defense of rationality in terms of "problem–solving" which is to avoid these traps. I show that his justification does not meet the skeptics' challenge.

HAUSMAN, Alan. Adhering To Inherence: A New Look At The Old Steps In Berkeley's March To Idealism. *Can J Phil* 14,421–444 S 84.

The inherence account (IA) of Berkeley's idealism—that he arrives at *esse est perceipi* by "arguing" (or assuming) that perceived qualities, since they cannot be qualities of nonexistant physical substances, must be qualities of mental substances—suffers from its failure to account adequately for Berkeley's theory that perceived qualities are ideas. I show this theory complements the IA, contrary to beliefs of IA detractors. Further, I bolster old IA arguments, and review the current literature.

HAUSMAN, Carl R. Philosophical Creativity And Metaphorical Philosophy. *Phil Topics* 12,193–212 Wint 81.

HAUSMAN, Daniel. Defending Microeconomic Theory. *Phil Forum (Boston)* 15,392–404 Sum 84.

HAVARD, John. Medical Confidence. *J Med Ethics* 11,8–11 Mr 85.

If medical confidentiality is not observed patients may well be reluctant to disclose information to their doctors or even to seek medical advice. Therefore, argues the author, it is of the utmost importance that doctors strive to protect medical confidentiality, particularly now when it is under threat not only in this country but also overseas. The profession must cease to regard ethical issues to do with confidentiality, and indeed to do with all areas of medical practice, as abstract phenomena requiring no justification. If it does not then it will come under increasing and justified criticism from the community it serves.

HAVARD, William C. *The Recovery Of Political Theory: Limits And Possibilities.* Baton Rouge Louisiana Univ Pr 1984.

HAVAS, K G. On The Relation Of Dialectical And Mathematical Logic (in Czechoslovakian). *Filozof Cas* 33,460–466 1985.

HAVAS, Katalin G. The Results Of A Certain Ontological View (in Hungarian). *Magyar Filozof Szemle* 4,626–636 1983.

The object of this paper is utilizing an independent approach to the history of science, to reveal the vividly descriptive interconnection between science and techniques and the laws governing this complex interaction between these two spheres. Television merely serves as a case–study for this investigation. The notional system used in this paper corresponds to the objective sequence of research activities. The simultaneity of discoveries – a constant puzzle of history of science for centuries – shows that it occurs because scholars instinctly follow the strategy of research or, in other words, the objective process of cognition. Based on results, suggestions are made for research and guiding activities. The paper is completed with four models.

HAVE, Henk Ten and Van Der Arend, Arie. Philosophy Of Medicine In The Netherlands. *Theor Med* 6,1–42 F 85.

This report explores the relationship between philosophy and medicine in the Netherlands. In Section 1 we outline the ups and downs of medico–philosophical research in our country: pre–war flourishing, post–war decline, and modern renaissance. In Section 2 we review recent Dutch literature in the philosophy of medicine. The topics dealt with include methodology of medical science, alternative medicine, the basic concepts of medicine, anthropological medicine, medicalization, medicine and culture, and health care ethics.

HAWKESWORTH, Mary E. Violence And The Politics Of Explanation: Kampuchea Revisited. *J Applied Phil* 2,69–84 Mr 85.

The criteria for adequate exlplanation have been the subject of intense debate in the philosophy of social science. This paper examines a variety of explanations of a decade of violence in Kampuchea in order to clarify the dimensions of the Kampuchean tragedy and to challenge both the hypothetico–deductive and the Verstehen models of explanation central to contemporary debates in the philosophy of social science. Using the Kampuchean case as an example, I suggest that the analyst's propensity to assimilate new information into a tacit, pre–supposition–laden conceptual framework contributes to an oversimplification or caricature of the event to be explained. For this reason, no individual explanation of an event can be definitive. An adequate explanation can emerge only from the juxtaposition of and extrapolation from multiple, non–privileged interpretations representing different methodological and ideological perspectives on the socio–political event to be explained.

HAWKINS, Anne. Two Pathographies: A Study In Illness And Literature. *J Med Phil* 9,231–252 Ag 84.

This study compares two autobiographical descriptions of illness—the 17th–century John Donne's *Devotions Upon Emergent Occasions* and the 20th–century Cornelius and Kathryn Ryan's *A Private Battle*. I begin by identifying the basic structure in both narratives as parallel to that of the case history, and then show how each individual's experience is shaped by the conditions of illness appropriate to their respective cultures. Lastly, I discuss the way in which both authors understand and represent sickness, as well as their respective therapies, in terms of a particular metaphoric construct. (edited)

HAWKINS, John A. A Note On Referent Identifiability And Co–presence. *J Prag* 8,649–660 D84.

It is often suggested (most recently by Clark and Marshall (1981) that there are restrictive conditions on the appropriate use of definite descriptions, involving 'referent identifiability' or 'co–presence of the speaker, the hearer and the object referred to'. The purpose of this note is to argue that such conditions are neither necessary nor sufficient and miss a significant pragmatic generalization about appropriateness. A more abstract alternative is summarized in which the universe of discourse is structured on sets of objects defined pragmatically as well as logically. These pragmatic sets fix the boundaries relative to which the uniqueness of singular definite descriptions holds, and speakers exploit these sets when making their references unique and unambiguous for the hearer.

HAWORTH, Lawrence. Autonomy And Utility. *Ethics* 95,5–19 O 84.

Does the value of the good which utilitarians would maximize depend on the autonomy of those who experience it? I argue that a consistent utilitarian must maintain that it does. In particular, (1) Nonautonomous pleasures simply count for less than do autonomous pleasures; also, an action's effect of satisfying nonautonomous preferences contributes less to its rightness than does its effect of satisfying autonomous preferences. (2) Development of people's capacity for autonomy is (for the consistent utilitarian) an independent value which has a kind of priority to pursuit of happiness.

HAWRANEK, Jacek and Zygmunt, Jan. On The Degree Of Complexity Of Sentential Logics; An Example Of The Logic With Semi–negation. *Stud Log* 43,405–414 1984.

In this paper being a sequel to our [1] the logic with semi–negation is chosen as an example to elucidate some basic notions of the semantics for sentential calculi. E.G., there are shown some links between the Post number and the degree of complexity of a sentential logic, and it is proved that the degree of complexity of the sentential logic with semi–negation is $2\aleph_0 0$. This is the first known example of a logic with such a degree of complexity. The results of the final part of the paper cast a new light on the scope of the Kripke–style semantics in comparison to the matrix semantics.

HAY, Louise. Spectra And Halting Problems. *Z Math Log* 21,167–176 1975.

HAYASHI, Susumu. "On Set Theories In Toposes" in *Lecture Notes In Mathematics*, Muller, G H And Others (ed), 23–30. NY Springer 1981.

HAYES, Steven C. Making Sense Of Spirituality. *Behaviorism* 12,99–110 Fall 84.

In ordinary language a clear distinction is made between the world of matter and that of spirit. While dualism is typically thought to be incompatible with behaviorism, a behavioral analysis of self–awareness suggests that there are good reasons for dualistic talk. Reputed qualities of both the spiritual aspect of humans and of a metaphysical God seem to flow naturally from the analysis. The use of the spiritual facet of self in therapy is briefly discussed.

HAYES, Victor C. Eliminating "God" And Gathering The Real Gods. *Listening* 20,40–53 Wint 85.

The paper tries to show that "Philosophy of Religion" persists in operating, fruitlessly, as if it were one of the natural sciences (attempting to prove the existence of a god some philosophers call "God"). An entirely different agenda appears when a Philosophy of Religions models itself on the social sciences for whom the world's myriad gods and goddesses are real alright, but only within the lives of their devotees and faith communities.

HAZARD, Geoffrey C and Rhode, Deborah L. *The Legal Profession: Responsibility And Regulation.* Mineola Foundation Pr 1985.

A collection of edited essays. Subjects include the history, composition, functions, and the structure of the American legal profession, as these factors relate to the regulation of the profession and to the discharge of its ethical responsibilities.

HAZEN, Allen. McGinn's Reply To Wright's Reply To Benacerraf. *Analysis* 45,59–61 Ja 85.

Benacerraf claimed there was something funny about the notion of numbers being objects because of the problems of specifying just what objects they are. Wright argued that this was just a case of Quinean inscrutability and nothing special about NUMBERS. McGinn argued that it wasn't like Quinean inscrutability. I say yes it is. Stay tuned.

HAZEN, Allen. Modality As Many Metalinguistic Predicates. *Phil Stud* 46,271–277 S 84.

Analogies between metalinguistic treatments of modality and the theory of truth predicates are stressed. A speculative interpretative hypothesis about Carnap's *Logische Syntax* is suggested.

HAZEN, Allen. Nominalism And Abstract Entities. *Analysis* 45,65–68 Mr 85.

Whether or not Hartry Field's project of eliminating reference to mathematical abstract entities in physical theories succeeds, there are motives for quantifying over abstracta (laws, phenomena, properties) in the philosophy of science. I argue that the metascientific need for abstracts can be met by very weak theories (e.G., predicative ones), and is thus irrelevant to the problem of "platonism" we meet in the philosophy of mathematics.

HAZEN, Allen. On The Reality Of Existence And Identity. *Can J Phil* 15,25–36 Mr 85.

Ian Hacking having argued sloppily and asserted logical untruths in an earlier article of this title (*Can J Phil* 8 (1978)), I decided to respond to him. (edited)

HEALEY, Richard A. How Many Worlds? *Nous* 18,591–616 N 84.

HEALY, Paul F. "Archaeology Abroad" in *Ethics And Values In Archaeology*, Green, Ernestene L (ed), 123–132. NY Free Pr 1984.

HEARD, Gerry C. *Mystical And Ethical Experience.* Macon Mercer Univ Pr 1985.

This work explains the way that man experiences God. It claims that God is encountered both in a mystical and an ethical manner. The mystical is an intuitive and direct means of relating to the Divine, whereas in the ethical God is encountered through our interaction with other beings in the universe. Each of these experiences has the potential for inducing the occurrence of the other, and at times they may interact with each other.

HECKER, Hans–Dietrich. Abstrakte Tempomasse Und Speed–Up–Theoreme Für Enumerationen Rekursiv–Aufzählbarer Mengen. *Z Math Log* 30,269–281 1984.

The theory of enumerations—founded by P Young—is extended to a theory of

enumerations for so–called Lachlan–classes and for so–called abstract measures of time. Several speed–up–theorems are discussed. It is proved, that there is a set in every m–degree of recursive–enumerable sets, speedable only by changing the order of enumeration.

HECKER, Hans–Dietrich. Das Kompressionstheorem Für Tempomasse. *Z Math Log* 30,283–288 1984.

The compression–theorem of abstract complexity–theory is proved for so–called abstract measures of time for enumerations of recursive–enumerable sets. Several conclusions are discussed. It follows, that the results in the theory of complexity classes for enumerations are almost the same as in the abstract complexity theory of M Blum.

HECKMANN, Gustav. Grete Henry–Hermann's Development Of Leonard Nelson's Ethics. *Ratio* 26,97–102 D 84.

HEDERSTIERNA, Anders. A Remark On The Connexion Between Procedure And Value. *Theor Decis* 18,135–138 Mr 85.

The purpose of the paper is to question the common assumption that individual value and preference is ordered under rationality. It is shown that such an assumption must exclude the procedure for assessing value. Order can therefore be a part of rationality but not an implication of it. Implicitly, it has remarked that some results in collective choice theories, e.G., Arrows Impossibility Theorem, question the assumptions of individual rationality on which they rest themselves.

HEDMAN, Carl G. Promoting The Autonomy Of Another Person: The Difficult Case Of The High School Dropout. *Educ Theor* 34,355–366 Fall 84.

The educator who is committed to promoting the autonomy of dropouts faces a dilemma that arises whenever we commit ourselves to promoting the autonomy of another person who makes a decision we believe will thwart their autonomy in the long run. Drawing on the work of Jon Elster and Charles Taylor, it is argued that we cannot resolve such dilemmas either by "benign neglect" or by "benign compulsion." This general analysis is used to sketch a more acceptable strategy for meeting the needs of dropouts.

HEELAN, Patrick A. Comments Of Theodore Kisiel's Commentary On My Paper: Hermeneutics Of Experimental Science In The Context Of The Life–World. *Z Allg Wiss* 5,135–137 1974.

HEELAN, Patrick A. Hermeneutics Of Experimental Science In The Context Of The Life–World. *Z Allg Wiss* 5,123–124 1974.

HEELAS, Paul. Emotions Across Cultures: Objectivity And Cultural Divergence. *Philosophy* 17,21–42 84 Supp.

HEFNER, Philip. God And Chaos: The Demiurge Versus The *Ungrund*. *Zygon* 19,469–486 D 84.

The human quest for meaning is an attempt to bring experience into conjunction with illuminating concepts. The second law of thermodynamics is of wide human concern, because it touches experience which is existentially charged and therefore which humans must interpret in broad metaphysical terms. Five types of experience have been incorporated into the second law: running down, degeneracy, mixed–up–ness, irreversibility of time, and emergence of new possibilities. The dominant Western tradition (Plato) places these experiences within a metaphysical scheme that evaluates them negatively, whereas a minority tradition (Berdyaev) evaluates them positively. The former makes entropy anti–God; the latter places entropy within God.

HEGEL, G W F. *Three Essays, 1793–1795,* Peter Fuss And John Dobbins (eds). Notre Dame Univ Notre Dame Pr 1984.

HEGEL, Georg Wilhelm. *Political Writings.* NY Garland 1984.

HEHIR, J Bryan. "Moral Issues In Deterrence Policy" in *The Security Gamble*, Mac Lean, Douglas (ed), 53–71. Totowa Rowman & Allanheld 1984.

HEIDEGGER, Martin. *Nietzsche, Volume II: The External Recurrence Of The Same.* Cambridge Harper & Row 1984.

HEIDEGGER, Martin. *The Metaphysical Foundations Of Logic,* Michael Heim (trans). Bloomington Indiana Univ Pr 1984.

In *The Metaphysical Foundations of Logic*, Heidegger examines a theory of reality upon which modern logic is grounded. He begins with a critique of Leibniz and suggests that logic is rooted in a conception of Being. In the second half, Heidegger offers a theory of reasoning which is couched in concepts of freedom and transcendence.

HEIDEGGER, Martin. The Self–Assertion Of The German University And The Rectorate 1933/34: Facts And Thoughts. *Rev Metaph* 38,467–502 Mr 85.

HEIL, John. Rationality And Psychological Explanation. *Inquiry* 28,359–372 S 85.

Certain philosophical arguments apparently show that the having of beliefs is tied conceptually to rationality. Such a view, however, seems at odds both with the possibility of irrational belief and with recent empirical discoveries in the psychology of reasoning. The aim of this paper is to move toward a reconciliation of these apparently conflicting perspectives by distinguishing between *internalist* and *externalist* conceptions of rationality. It is argued that elements of each are required for a satisfactory theory, one that allows for the possibility of irrationality and makes sense of empirical findings without violating conditions on belief ascription. Normative theories, on this view, constrain the latter while remaining silent on the character of actual psychological mechanisms.

HEIL, John. Reliability And Epistemic Merit. *Austl J Phil* 62,327–338 D 84.

Roderick Firth, in his recent APA Presidential Address, has argued that reliabilist accounts of epistemic justification are both intuitively implausible and necessarily circular. I discuss these contentions and suggest that reliabilism, whatever its other faults, may not after all err in the ways charged by Firth.

HEIL, John. Thoughts On The Virtues. *J Value Inq* 19,27–34 1985.

A conception of the virtues and their place in the evaluation of actions is articulated and defended. A virtue is a disposition to act on a certain principle reflectively. An alternative, holistic account, recently advanced by John McDowell, is considered but rejected.

HEIM, Michael. A Philosophy Of Comparison: Heidegger And Lao Tzu. *J Chin Phil* 11,307–323 D 84.

This paper is an attempt to *generate* a philosophy of comparison, rather than assume what comparison means. From a planetary perspective, two new correlative categories emerge: the "unspeakable" (nuclear annihilation of life–forms), and the "unsayable" (non–rhetorical openness). The "unsayable" is developed from the language experiments of Heidegger and of Lao Tzu. In conclusion, some general theorems are stated regarding the use of "negative space" and indeterminacy in comparing divergent philosophies in an age of nuclear terror.

HEIM, Michael. Reason As Response To Nuclear Terror. *Phil Today* 28,300–307 Wint 84.

A current European response to nuclear terror is examined in its Kantian background. Hans Ebeling's philosophy of nuclear armaments is explicitly continuous with Idealist ethics, but his proposal for reviewing the problematic is also based on Heidegger's analysis of mortality, where being–towards–death is understood as species–ontological. A more adequate response to nuclear terror must be developed than the refurbishment of Enlightenment ideals of planetary reason. Dialogue with Eastern philosophy, as disciplined cultivation of the unsayable, is urged as necessary corrective to the out–worn rhetoric of "reason" in facing the terror of the unspeakable.

HEINAMAN, Robert. Aristotle On Accidents. *J Hist Phil* 23,311–324 Jl 85.

HEINAMAN, Robert. Aristotle On Housebuilding. *Hist Phil Quart* 2,145–162 Ap 85.

HEINAMAN, Robert. Emphasis, Causation And Extensionality. *Phil Stud* 46,367–380 N 84.

HEINDORF, Lutz. Continuous Functions On Countable Ordinals. *Z Math Log* 30,339–340 1984.

Answering two Questions of Henson, Jockusch, Rubel, and Takeuti (First order topology, Diss Math 143(1977)) two non–homeomorphic second countable Boolean spaces are constructed that have elementarily equivalent with respect to the language of ring theory rings of continuous real–valued functions. These spaces are countable ordinals with the order topology.

HEINDORF, Lutz. Regular Ideals And Boolean Pairs. *Z Math Log* 30,547–560 1984.

HEINS, Marilyn. "The Necessity For Reporting Child Abuse" in *Difficult Decisions In Medical Ethics*, Ganos, Doreen and others (eds), 49–62. NY Liss 1983.

HEINTZ, Lawrence L. The Occasional Rightness Of Not Following The Requirements Of Morality. *Phil Res Arch* 10,477–490 1985.

Laymen and philosophers alike find it counterintuitive to consent to the assertion that "it is sometimes right not to follow the requirements of morality". This may be because the conventions of ordinary language do much to encourage the view that "morally ought to do" functions as an equivalent for "what one ought to do all things considered". In this paper I will argue against such an equivalence and attempt to shake the holders of the prevailing view, that moral reasons are always overriding, from their dogmatism. The primary theses of this paper are (1) there is no acceptable ordering of reasons for acting—not between types of reasons nor withing the category of moral reasons, and (2) moral reasons are not unconditional or unexceptional. (edited)

HEITSCH, Wolfram. Gedankliche Systeme Mit Aufforderungscharakter. *Deut Z Phil* 22,760–762 1974.

HEKMAN, Susan. Action As A Text: Gadamer's Hermeneutics And The Social Scientific Analysis Of Action. *J Theor Soc Behav* 14,333–354 O 84.

This paper argues that Gadamer's hermeneutics offers a methodological perspective for social and political theory that overcomes the impasse created by the dichotomy between the positivist and humanist approaches to social action. Gadamer's approach, which is based on the hermeneutical method of textual interpretation, offers an alternative to both the positivist and humanist perspectives. Gadamer argues that understanding a text involves the fusing of the conceptual schemes of author and interpreter. Relying on Ricoeur's analysis of the parallels between actions and texts, it is argued that this understanding of the process of textual interpretation can be profitably applied to the analysis of social action. (edited)

HELD, Virginia. *Rights And Goods: Justifying Social Action.* NY Free Pr 1984.

HELD, Virginia. Advertising And Program Content. *Bus Prof Ethics J* 3,61–76 Spr/Sum 84.

HELD, Virginia. Philosophy And International Problems. *Teach Phil* 8,121–128 Ap 85.

HELLBORN, Rudolf. Das Einfachste Und Grundlegendste Verhältnis Der Sozialistischen Gesellschaft. *Deut Z Phil* 22,496–501 1974.

HELLER, Agnes. Marx, Justice, Freedom: The Libertarian Prophet. *Philosophica* 33,87–106 1984.

HELLER, Agnes. The Basic Question Of Moral Philosophy. *Phil Soc Crit* 11,35–62 Sum 85.

HELLER, Agnes. The Great Republic. *Praxis Int* 5,23–34 Ap 85.

HELLER, J. The Actuality Of Marx's And Engels' Conception Of The Relation Of Property And The Division Of Labour (in Czechoslovakian). *Filozof Cas* 33,313–336 1985.

HELLER, Mark. Temporal Parts Of Four Dimensional Objects. *Phil Stud* 46,323–334 N 84.

I offer a clear conception of a temporal part that does not make the existence of temporal parts implausible. This can be done if (and only if) we think of physical objects as four dimensional, the fourth dimension being time. Unless we are willing to

deny the existence of most spatial parts, or willing to accept the possibility of coincident entities, or accept something even more implausible, we should accept the existence of temporal parts.

HELLER, Mark. The Conditional Analysis. *Can J Phil* 15,75–86 Mr 85.

I argue, with examples and appeals to intuition, that the counterfactuals involved in the conditional analysis of ability statements must be non–backtracking. I also examine the backtracking/non–backtracking distinction, arguing that for a non–backtracking counterfactual closeness is a function of similarity of *time slices*. Thus, different–past/no–miracle worlds and miracle/similar–past worlds may be equally close. I also apply the distinction to counterfactuals whose antecedents entail their consequents.

HELLIN, Jose. Concepto Communísimo Del Ente Y Nombres Divinos, Por José Hellín. *Espiritu* 34,5–24 Ja–Je 85.

HELLING, Ingeborg K. A Schutz And F Kaufmann: Sociology Between Science And Interpretation. *Human Stud* 7,141–162 1984.

HELLWIG, Monika K. Soteriology In The Nuclear Age. *Thomist* 48,634–644 O 84.

This article traces the changing content and focus of Christian theological reflection on human destiny, as this reflection has developed in the twentieth century. The changes are related to world events, Church events and contemporary philosophies. The theological reflection is related to process philosophy, existentialist and phenomenological thought and to Marxist theory.

HELM, Paul. Locke's Real Ideas, And Dr Woolhouse. *Locke News* 15,35–42 1984.

HEMMERLING, Armin and Murawski, Gerd. Zur Raumkompliziertheit Mehrdimensionaler Turing–Automaten. *Z Math Log* 30,233–258 1984.

The paper deals with problems concerning the space–complexity of Turing automata with n–dimensional input tapes (n "less than or equal to" 2). Upper and lower bounds of the space–complexity of searching all finite n–dimensional patterns (arrays) are given. Furthermore, relationships between the recognition and decision of sets of patterns by deterministic and nondeterministic automata, respectively, are investigated (D–ND problems). Using a linearization method it is shown that, for certain space–bounds, these n–dimensional D–ND problems are logically equivalent to the analogous one–dimensional problems.

HEMSTREET, Robert M. Felix Adler: Artist Of The Ideal Good. *Relig Hum* 18,146–155 Autumn 84.

HENDERSON, R D. Vico's View Of History. *Phil Reform* 49,97–111 1984.

Can Vico rightly be considered the first historicist, 'historicism'' being the view that history is a continuous sequence of concrete events constituting social–cultural reality of such? Vico's view of history is considered in light of the problem of origins; and in view of his 1) platonistic ideas, 2) scholastic influences, 3) juridical orientation, 4) philological pre–occupation and his belief in divine providence. The conclusion being that Vico was not the first (fullfledged) historicist but he was the first clear forerunner of historicism.

HENDLEY, Brian P. The Philosophy Of Education Since Dewey. *Eidos* 3,191–215 D 84.

Since the death of John Dewey in 1952, the philosophy of education has undergone a rebirth. Led by thinkers such as Richard Peters, philosophers have attempted to clarify basic educational concepts. Unfortunately, this effort has turned into an inner–directed, abstract enterprise which has little to offer the educational practitioner. I argue for a return to the task of theory–building and increased communication with those in other disciplines who share a concern for education.

HENDRY, Herbert E and Pokriefka, M L. Carnapian Extensions Of S5. *J Phil Log* 14,111–128 My 85.

HENLE, J M and Kleinberg, E M and Watro, R J. On The Ultrafilters And Ultrapowers Of Strong Partition Cardinals. *J Sym Log* 49,1268–1272 D 84.

HENNESSEY, John W and Gert, Bernard. Moral Rules And Moral Ideals: A Useful Distinction In Business And Professional Practice. *J Bus Ethics* 4,105–116 Ap 85.

HENNIGFELD, Jochem. Der Mensch Und Seine Sprache. *Phil Rundsch* 32,104–111 1985.

HENNINGER, Mark G. Henry Of Harclay On The Formal Distinction In The Trinity (in Latin). *Fran Stud* 41,250–335 1981.

HENRY, Carl F H. The Modern Evasion Of Creation. *Nat Forum* 65,39–41 Wint 85.

Our century is the first aiming to establish Western culture on the premise of God's irrelevance. Credibility accrued to evolution when Darwin claimed empirical verifiability of its mechanism. Today its verificatory claims are highly disputed. Model cosmic models speak confusingly on ongoing "creation". If schoolrooms teach evolutionary metaphysics (theoretical cosmology), creationist metaphysics should also be taught. Naturalism cannot sustain permanent and universal human rights, nor are such rights self–evident. Even the charter American political documents connected them with a transcendent creator.

HENRY, Desmond Paul. *That Most Subtle Question (Quaestio Subtilissima).* Dover Manchester Univ Pr 1984.

Contemporary logical grammar, founded on appropriately flexible logical and ontological theory, is used for the analysis of medieval metaphysics. Non–nominalist and non–Platonic but realist construal of quidditative discourse, and hence of universals, matter, and form. Anselm, Abelard, Aquinas, Ockham, Boethius of Dacia, Roger Bacon, Giles of Rome, Garland the Computist and Patrick of Ireland are among medieval authors discussed.

HENRY, Stuart. *Private Justice: Towards Integrated Theorising In The Sociology Of Law.* Boston Routledge K & Paul 1983.

Private Justice is about the law and justice operative outside of the formal legal system in groups and organizations. The central argument is that formal law and private justice are integrally related, such that each is mutually dependent upon the other. To understand law in society we must understand this interdependence and the ideological process whereby it is obscured. The book draws extensive original research on discipline in industry to illustrate these arguments.

HENSON, C Ward and Kaufmann, Matt and Keisler, H Jerome. The Strength Of Nonstandard Methods In Arithmetic. *J Sym Log* 49,1039–1058 D 84.

We consider extensions of Peano arithmetic suitable for doing some of nonstandard analysis, in which there is a predicate N(x) for an elementary initial segment, along with axiom schemes approximating (1),—saturation. We prove that such systems have the same proof–theoretic strength as their natural analogues in second order arithmetic. We close by presenting an even stronger extension of Peano arithmetic, which is equivalent to ZF for arithmetic statements.

HEPPENER, Sieglinde. Zum Verhältnis Von Marxistisch–Leninistischer Philosophie Und Sozialistischer Politik In Der DDR. *Deut Z Phil* 32,713–726 1984.

HERING, Christoph. Messianic Time And Materialistic Progress. *J Brit Soc Phenomenol* 16,156–166 My 85.

Hering argues that to separate Historical Materialism from Messianic Theology in the late Benjamin's 'Theses on the Philosophy of History' would destroy the essence of his thinking. Both have to be understood as necessary critical complements to each other. While the messianic concept of time emancipates Historical Materialism from its growing ontological petrification, the materialistic concept of revolutionary praxis liberates Messianic Theology from its idealistic confinement.

HERLITZIUS, Erwin and Jacobs, Hans–Jürgen. The Humanism Of Associated Work And The Problem Of The Technology Laws (in German). *Deut Z Phil* 33,415–424 1985.

Laws of technology are concerned with dynamic systems depending on associated labor and human work design criteria. Descriptive and normative modes unite to integrating information technology to realize goals and effective means. Structural and functional equivalence is brought into focus. Any innovation proceeds from evolutionary potentials: qualitative redundancy, variability and flexibility. Reliability tends to informational certainty including control of embedded (still unexplained) interdependency. Hierarchical structures need complex timing in processing and prognostication of differently substituted equipment.

HERMAN, Arthur L. Hedonism And Nirvana: Paradoxes, Dilemmas And Solutions. *Philosophica (India)* 10,1–10 Ja–D 81.

The paradox of hedonism from Western moral philosophy bears a striking resemblance to the paradox of nirvana from Hindu and Buddhist philosophy. One of the more credible solutions to the former paradox, viz., that happiness to be got must be forgot, can also be used to solve the latter paradox, viz., that nirvana to be to get must be forgot. Following the solution of the latter paradox a number of other solutions to other philosophical problems, e.G., the dilemma of nirvana, now become possible.

HERMANN, Barbara. The Practice Of Moral Judgment. *J Phil* 82,414–435 Ag 85.

In a Kantian theory of moral judgment, agents must make use of moral concepts before they come to the Categorical Imperative procedure in order to identify occasions that are morally salient. This fact alters our understanding of conflicts of duty and the place of moral perception in Kantian theory. The connection of this moral knowledge to the Categorical Imperative, the possibility of moral change or progress, and the implications for moral relativism are discussed.

HERMANN, Istvan. "Catharsis Or Kitsch" in *Continental Philosophy And The Arts*, Winters, Laurence E and others (ed), 193–218. *Lanham* Univ Pr Of America 1984.

HERMANNS, William. *Einstein And The Poet: In Search Of The Cosmic Man.* Brookline Village Branden Pr 1983.

HERNÁNDEZ, Héctor H. Libertad Política: Liberalismo Y Tomismo. *Sapientia* 40,13–24 Ja–Mr 85.

HERNANDEZ, Jose Lopez. Breve Historia De La Fortuna Literaria Y De La Crítica De J J Rousseau. *Pensamiento* 41,179–200 Ap–Je 85.

HEROLD, Vilém. Wyclef's Philosophy And Platonic Ideas (in Czechoslovakian). *Filosof Cas* 33,47–96 1985.

HERR, Stanley S and Mc Donald, Michael. Which Clients Should A Sheltered Workshop Serve: Case Study. *Hastings Center Rep* 14,52–54 O 84.

Sheltered workshops provide the mentally retarded with training and work experience. Due to a lack of resources, workshops have hard choices to make in regard to clients and wages. While normalization is the goal, training and maintenance perspectives may conflict. McDonald explores a utilitarian approach to such tradeoffs, while Stanley Herr urges a more rights–centered approach.

HERRÁN, Carlos M. Goethe Y La Kátharsis Trágica. *Cuad Filosof* 19,37–56 Ja–D 83.

HERRE, Heinrich and Wolter, Helmut. Entscheidbarkeit Von Theorien In Logiken Mit Verallgemeinerten Quantoren. *Z Math Log* 21,229–246 1975.

HERRERA, Bernal. Logos Y Eros En San Juan De La Cruz Y Platón. *Rev Filosof (Costa Rica)* 22,119–132 D 84.

Se analizan las relaciones que hay entre el Eros y el Logos en San Juan y en Platón, y se comparan los puntos de vista de ambos autores, en especial con respecto a la teoría del conocimiento. En ambos casos el Eros constituye una fuerza única, susceptible de diversos usos, que aporta la energía necesaria para alcanzar el conocimiento. En Platón también el Logos presenta un carácter unitario, mientras que en San Juan no. Se llega a la conclusión de que si bien el Eros es igualmente importante para ambos, el Logos es mucho más importante en Platón.

HERRING, Basil F. *Jewish Ethics And Halakhah For Our Time: Sources And Commentary.* NY KTAV 1984.

HERRMANN, E. Definable Structures In The Lattice Of Recursively Enumerable Sets. *J Sym Log* 49,1190–1197 D 84.

It will be shown that in the lattice of recursively enumerable sets one can define elementarily with parameters a structure isomorphic to (σ^0_4, σ^0_3), i.e., isomorphic to the lattice of σ^0_4 together with a unary predicate selecting out exactly the σ^0_3 sets.

HERSHEY, Paul Turner. A Definition For Paternalism. *J Med Phil* 10,171–182 My 85.

Several definitions of paternalism from the contemporary literature are examined. These are all found to be more or less defective when tested against various counterexamples. An alternative definition is subsequently developed using two necessary conditions which taken together are considered sufficient to define paternalistic actions. Those conditions are (1) the paternalistic action is primarily intended to benefit the recipient, and (2) the recipient's consent or dissent is not relevant consideration for the initiator.

HERZBERGER, Hans G. Supervaluations Without Truth–Value Gaps. *Can J Phil* 6,15–28 80 Supp.

HERZBERGER, Hans G. True, False, Etc. *Can J Phil* 6,1–14 80 Supp.

HERZBRUN, Philip. "The Case For Esthetics And Ethical Values" in *The Georgetown Symposium On Ethics*, Porreco, Rocco (ed), 279–284. Lanham Univ Pr Of America 1984.

HESLEP, Robert D. Perception And The Mind–Body Problem. *Educ Theor* 34,367–372 Fall 84.

This essay seeks to give an account of perception that regards the sensation factor of any perception as being nonphysical, that recognizes that this factor relates to physical objects, and avoids the mind–body problem. It proposes that a perception, rather than being viewed as having sensory contact as a conceptual contact, be seen as having reference to a physical object as a conceptual criterion. Sensory contact is to be understood as an empirical condition of perception.

HESS, Heinz–Jürgen. Aktualität Und Historizität: Bemühungen Um Werk Und Wirken Leonhard Eulers. *Stud Leibniz* 17,87–93 1985.

Essay–review of two memorial–volumes on L. Euler and two volumes of Euler's Opera omnia. The editing and interpretating Euler's writings regarding their historical contexts on the one and modern mathematical developments on the other hand.

HETHERINGTON, Stephen C. A Note On Inherence. *Ancient Phil* 4,218–223 Fall 84.

Aristotle's *Categories* quarters the world via the interaction of two relations—the said–of relation and the inherence relation. Aristotle's definition of the latter is unperspicuous, and many scholars have attempted its clarification. The matter's still unresolved; for instance, Owen's important account is vague. I construct an Aristotelian account of conceptual inherence; I then make Owen's account precise. Plausibly, the result is that Aristotle's view of the world's structure is a little clearer.

HETHERINGTON, Stephen. Parsons And Possible Objects. *Austl J Phil* 62,246–254 S 84.

Meinongian theories of objects are again under investigation, and Terence Parsons' recent book, *Nonexistent Objects*, provides one such investigation. The author argues that theories of possible worlds and theories of possible objects face largely parallel theoretical demands—for instance, the demand for an adequate account of entailments between properties. Parsons' theory fails in this regard, and so must be either discarded or modified. The author suggests some modifications. (edited)

HEYEN, Erk Volkmar. Bedingungen Einer Rekonstruktion Rechtlichen Argumentierens: Zum Verhältnis Von Philosophie Und Rechtswissenschaft. *Arch Rechts Soz* 60,353–376 1974.

Starting from considerations of philosophical anthropology, the author tries to outline how the philosophy of legal science can be understood—within the frame of the dependency between theory and practice—as part of the practical (political) philosophy (I). Thereafter, selected opinions on the main problem of the justification of legal institutions are examined (II), and the possibility of such a justification is explained (III). Out of this the author draws some conclusions for the reconstruction of legal science (IV). (edited)

HEYWOOD, Angela. "Body Housekeeping" in *Freedom, Feminism, And The State*, Mc Elroy, Wendy (ed), 155–158. Cato Institute Washington 1982.

HEYWOOD, Ezra H. "Cupid's Yokes" in *Freedom, Feminism, And The State*, Mc Elroy, Wendy (ed), 129–142. Cato Institute Washington 1982.

HEYWOOD, Ezra H. "Perpetual Vassalage" in *Freedom, Feminism, And The State*, Mc Elroy, Wendy (ed), 331–336. Cato Institute Washington 1982.

HIBBEN, John G and Harris, H S (ed). *Hegel's Logic: An Essay In Interpretation.* NY Garland 1984.

HIBBEN, John Grier. *Hegel's Logic.* NY Garland 1984.

HIBLER, Richard W. *Happiness Through Tranquility: The School Of Epicurus.* Lanham Univ Pr Of America 1984.

The author contends that Epicurus' contributions to philosophy and education have been misunderstood, and that Epicurus should be recognized as one of history's great teachers. epicurus' Garden School advocated happiness through mental serenity in a program of anticipating modern social adjustment theories of education. The author suggests that the Garden School should rank with Plato's Academy and Aristotle's Lyceum in the influence of its educational philosophy.

HICKEY, Denis. *Home From Exile: An Approach To Post–Existentialist Philosophizing.* Lanham Univ Pr Of America 1982.

Philosophy should be written for each generation, and for each culture. Mostly, Americans seem content to use anthologies written by ancient Europeans—for Europeans. *Home From Exile* is one American's attempt to deal with a transcendental problem of our country and our age. THE PROBLEM is alienation, not being–at–home. The suggestion challenging the reader is this: We must each create our own home together—with—others in a human—made world.

HICKMAN, John L. Homogeneous Forms In Two Ordinal Variables. *Z Math Log* 30,505–508 1984.

HICKMAN, John. On N–Place Strictly Monotonic Functions. *Z Math Log* 31,169–171 1985.

HICKS, Michael. Soothing The Savage Beast: A Note On Animals And Music. *J Aes Educ* 18,47–56 Wint 84.

HIDEG, Éva and Nováky, Erzsébet. Modelling And Models In Future Research (in Hungarian). *Magyar Filozof Szemle* 5,712–728 1983.

The authors had a threefold objective: to give a general idea of a model—concept that will also include the models used in future research, to outline the role of the model—methods in the cognition of future, and to define the special characteristics of modelling in future research. In order to fulfill these goals, the authors first give a brief historic survey of modelling and their conclusions drawn from it, then they examine the main types of model—definition that can distinctly be separated from each other from the view—point whether they reflect and if they do so how, the epistemological and practical aspects and those of the methodology of epistemology. For the authors hold the opinion that these functions must be fulfilled by all models. (edited)

HIEBERT, Erwin N. The Influence Of Mach's Thought On Science. *Phil Natur* 21,598–615 1984.

This is an analysis of how Mach's diverse investigations into various sciences and their history are related to his philosophical reflections concerning the genesis, rationale, and meaning of methodologically significant scientific problems. The influence of Mach's thought on science was primarily as a scientist's philosopher, and not as a philosopher's philosophy—because the gulf that separates them is immense, especially when seen from Mach's point of view.

HIGGS, Roger and others. A Father Says 'Don't Tell My Son The Truth'. *J Med Ethics* 11,153–167 S 85.

HIGGS, Roger and others. Mum's The Word: Confidentiality And Incest. *J Med Ethics* 11,100–104 Je 85.

HIGUCHI KEIKO. La Métaphore De La Sensation (in Japanese). *Bigaku* 35,13–24 S 84.

La lecture de la métaphore est interprétée généralement comme opération de reduire l'écard à degré O; mais la métaphore qui exprime la sensation ne peut pas être analysée comme les autres, car il lui manque ce degré O. (edited)

HIKASA, Katsushi. The Phases Of Light In Augustine (in Japanese). *Bigaku* 35,15–27 Je 84.

The purpose of this paper is to clarify the signification of *inventio* (*vidi lucem*) in "the experience in Milan" in the Book VII of *Confessions. confessions*, as we understand, aims at the interpretation of *Scriptura*. And this *inventio* also consists in the orientation of interpretation. (edited)

HILEY, David R. Foucault And The Question Of Enlightenment. *Phil Soc Crit* 11,63–84 Sum 85.

I construct a confrontation between Foucault and his critics—especially Habermas and Taylor—over the Enlightenment commitment to the connection betwen rational critique, emancipation and autonomy. I consider Foucault's anti–humanism both in terms of his analysis of the human sciences and of modern forms of power, and I argue that *pace* Habermas and Taylor there is a sense of autonomy and emancipation in Foucault. I conclude, however, that it is deeply problematic for other reasons.

HILEY, David and Layton, William. Team–Teaching With The Corporate Executive. *Teach Phil* 8,27–32 Ja 85.

HILL JR, Thomas E. Autonomy And Benevolent Lies. *J Value Inq* 18,251–268 1984.

The paper distinguishes several conceptions of autonomy, with associated principles, and inquires how these might provide non–utilitarian arguments against benevolent lies. The conceptions include Kantian and Sartrean autonomy, psychological maturity, a right against manipulation, a capacity for distinctly human values, and rational control over one's life. The principles oppose benevolent lies in several ways to help to explain why some lies are worse than others; but they are not always decisive and sometimes even favor lying.

HILL, Christopher S. On Getting To Know Others. *Phil Topics* 13,257–266 Spr 85.

I defend common sense realism about other minds by constructing a new version of the Analogical Argument.

HILL, Christopher S. Watsonian Freedom And Freedom Of The Will. *Austl J Phil* 62,294–298 S 84.

In "Free Agency" (*The Journal of Philosophy* 82 (1974), pp 205–220), Gary Watson defines a state of rational agents that may be called *Watsonian Freedom*. I examine Watsonian Freedom and several related forms of freedom and argue that none of them can be identified with the form of freedom that is most intimately related to moral responsibility. Thus, for example, I describe individuals who lack Watsonian freedom but who are clearly responsible for their actions.

HILL, Christopher. Desert And The Moral Arbitrariness Of The Natural Lottery. *Phil Forum* 16,207–222 Spr 85.

According to several influential philosophers (e.G., John Rawls and Thomas Nagel), the following propositions can be used to show that a number of our ordinary views about desert are in need of revision: (i) what one comes to deserve in life depends to a large extent upon the package of assets and deficiencies that one receives in the natural lottery; and (ii) the natural lottery is morally arbitrary. I describe what I take to be the most important ways of defending this claim, and I try to show that these lines of defense are all incorribly defective.

HILL, James F. "Are Marginal Agents 'Our Recipients'" in *Gewirth's Ethical Rationalism*, Regis Jr, Edward (ed), 180–191. Chicago Univ Of Chicago Pr 1984.

HILL, Patricia. Religion And Myth In Orwell's *1984*. *Soc Theor Pract* 10,273–288 Fall 84.

HILL, Robert. The Mystery Of Christ: Clue To Paul's Thinking On Wisdom. *Heythrop J* 25,475–483 O 84.

Paul employs the term "the mystery (of Christ)", not to suggest some "secret" revelation only (despite some translators), but to denote the whole divine plan achieved "in Christ", in all its dimensions: personal, historical, ecclesial, and cosmic. The vastness of the notion suggests the sapiential view of God's designs already evident in OT Wisdom. There is, in fact, a close relationship between Paul's use of "wisdom" and his phrase "the mystery of Christ"; in the letters the terms illuminate each other.

HILLER, A P and Zimbarg, J. Self–Reference With Negative Types. *J Sym Log* 49,754–773 S 84.

HILPINEN, Risto. On The Principle Of Information Retention. *Phil Natur* 21,435–443 1984.

HINCHMAN, Lewis P. *Hegel's Critique Of The Enlightenment*. Gainesville Univ S Florida Pr 1984.

Hegel is the first modern philosopher (so the author argues) to appreciate and analyze the ambiguous nature of the Enlightenment, our "predecessor culture." He shows why its vaunted achievements—human rights, toleration, popular sovereignty, the idea of progess—have been accompanied by a darker side: "instrumental" reason, mechanistic determinism, hostility to religion and political "atomism." The author sees in Hegel's critique of the Enlightenment important (even unsurpassed) anticipations of modern debates about liberalism and social science.

HINCKS, Tony. Aesthetics And The Sociology Of Art: A Critical Commentary On The Writings Of Janet Wolff. *Brit J Aes* 24,341–354 Autumn 84.

HINMAN, Lawrence M. 'Is' Presupposes 'Ought'. *Phil Stud (Ireland)* 30,122–126 Spr 84.

HINMAN, Lawrence M. Comments On Mittelman's "Perspectivism, Becoming, And Truth In Nietzsche". *Int Stud Phil* 16,23–26 1984.

HINTIKKA, Jaakko. Are There Nonexistent Objects: Why Not: But Where Are They? *Synthese* 60,451–458 S 84.

HINTIKKA, Jaakko. Kant's Transcendental Method And His Theory Of Mathematics. *Topoi* 3,99–108 D 84.

Following his transcendental method, Kant tried to explain mathematical knowledge as reflecting the way we humans come to know particulars. This way Kant mistakenly identified with sense—perception, concluding that mathematical knowledge reflects the forms of our sense—perception. Here is the reason why things—considered—in—themselves are transcendent causes of perceptions. A true Kantian should identify it with the "language—games" of seeking and finding, which would lead him to my game—theoretical semantics.

HIRAISHI, Yoshimori. "Buber And Japanese Thought" in *Martin Buber*, Gordon, Haim (ed), 351–366. Beersheva Ktav 1984.

HIRD, G R and Downey, R G. Automorphisms Of Supermaximal Subspaces. *J Sym Log* 50,1–9 Mr 85.

In this paper several extensions of the notion of supermaximality are introduced. The key on is that an r e V is strongly supermaximal if dim (V_∞ mod V) = ∞ are given any r e independent set I with I ∩ V = q, dim ((V ∪ I) *mod V) is finite. Every strongly supermaximal subspace is nonrecursive and supermaximal. There exist supermaximal subspaces with the same "degree structure" one which is strongly supermaximal, one which is not. In view of Guichard's work, this means that such spaces are not in the same orbit in the group of automorphisms of L(V_∞). Several extensions are discussed.

HIROSE, Ken and Nakayasu, Fujio. "Representation For Spector Second Order Classes Computation Theory" in *Lecture Notes In Mathematics*, Muller, G H And Others (ed), 31–48. NY Springer 1981.

HIRSCH JR, E D. On Justifying Interpretive Norms. *J Aes Art Crit* 43,89–92 Fall 84.

HIRSCHMANN, J and Müller, W. Gesellschaftliches Und Individuelles Bewusstein In Der Philosophischen Diskussion In Der DDR And UdSSR. *Deut Z Phil* 33,168–170 1985.

HJORT, Anne Meete. The Conditions Of Dialogue: Approaches To The Habermas—Gadamer Debate. *Eidos* 4,11–37 Je 85.

HLAVATÝ, Karel. The Economic Contradictions And The Function Of Managing Workers (in Czechoslovakian). *Filozof Cas* 32,468–482 1984.

HNIZDOVA, Kvetoslava and Hnizdova, Vlastislav. The Role Of Aesthetic Education In The Forming Of Socialist Consciousness (in Czechoslovakian). *Estetika* 22,17–28 1985.

HNIZDOVA, Vlastislav and Hnizdova, Kvetoslava. The Role Of Aesthetic Education In The Forming Of Socialist Consciousness (in Czechoslovakian). *Estetika* 22,17–28 1985.

HOAGLUND, John. Some Moral Problems Of The Damaged Neonate. *Phil Context* 14,19–28 1984.

Should vigorous medical intervention be practiced on even the most severely damaged neonate? Should this decision be made by parents, physicians, courts, or the federal government? It is argued that preserving the life of the neonate is a prima facie duty, but that it can be overridden by poor prognosis, quality of life factors, or impact on the family. The decision should rest with parents consulting with physicians, and is at the aspirational standard where deciding to intervene merits praise but deciding against it censurable.

HOARE, C A R. A Couple Of Novelties In The Propositional Calculus. *Z Math Log* 31,173–178 1985.

It is often convenient to regard a dyadic operator as a 'curried' monadic operator, in order to facilitate expression of its algebraic properties. Similarly, a triadic operator can be curried to give a dyadic one; and when the resulting operator is expressed in infix form, its algebraic properties may be surprisingly elegant. This paper gives two amusing examples, a conditional and a majority logic operator, which were prompted by a study of the logical foundations of computer programming.

HOBERMAN, John M. "Kierkegaard's Two Ages And Heidegger's Critique Of Modernity" in *International Kierkegaard Commentary*, Perkins, Robert L (ed), 223–258. Macon Mercer Univ Pr 1984.

HOBSON, Marian. Pantomime, Spasme Et Parataxe: "Le Neveu De Rameau"k. *Rev Metaph Morale* 89,197–213 Ap–Je 84.

The article compares the relation between intention and involuntary action in eighteenth century medical theory and in Diderot's text. Contemporary nosology puts stress on the "spasm" as general symptom of nervous disease. rameau's nephew is taken over by a series of jerky gestures, frequently expressed in the text by parataxis; he presents a complex interplay of determined and voluntary gesture and actions and Diderot's text explores this both at the psychological and grammatical level.

HOBSON, Peter. Another Look At Paternalism. *J Applied Phil* 1,293–304 O 84.

This paper attempts to provide some new insights into the prpoblem of justifying paternalism. To begin with, there is a general analysis of the concept of paternalism which examines the conditions that must be present for it to occur. A distinction is then drawn between two contexts in which paternalism exists—first, where it applies to individuals or clearly specifiable groups and second, where it applies to society in general. Different approaches to justification are required in each case. (edited)

HOBY, Jean–Pierre. Auf Der Suche Nach Der Verlorenen Glaubwürdigkeit: Verfassungsrevision Und Helvetisches Malaise. *Stud Phil (Switzerland)* 41,49–62 1982.

HOCHE, Hans–Ulrich. Über Die Rolle Von Substanzbegriffen Beim Zeigen Und Zählen Von Gegenständen. *Z Phil Forsch* 29,337–348 Jl–S 75.

HOCHENBLEICHER– SCHWARZ, Anton. *Das Existenzproblem Bei J G Fichte Und S Kierkegaard.* Konigstein Athenaum 1984.

This book deals with Fichte's and Kierkegaard's treatment of the self as existing, becoming, and transcendental, as well as the problem of absolute knowledge and the possibility of a systematic treatment of Dasein. Also, Kierkegaard's analysis of the relation between existential subjectivity and faith in God is discussed. (staff)

HOCKE, Erich. Die Einheit Von Sozialismus Und Frieden. *Deut Z Phil* 33,385–394 1985.

HODES, Harold T. Finite Level Borel Games And A Problem Concerning The Jump Hierarchy. *J Sym Log* 49,1301–1318 D 84.

Suppose x is a countable non–admissible limit of admissible ordinals. This paper concerns the relationship between $0^{(x)}$ and the class of upper bounds on the set of $0^{(y)}$ for all y less than x. For certain x's, that relationship is linked to the least n such that sigma–n–0 games are determined in L_x.

HODES, Harold T. The Modal Theory Of Pure Identity And Some Related Decision Problems. *Z Math Log* 30,415–423 1984.

For a broad range of modal logics, the class of first–order modal formulae containing only '=' (or only a single one–place predicate) is undecidable; but when models are required to have expanding domains and the logic is K, K4, B, S4 or S5, the class of formulae containing only '=' is decidable.

HODES, Harold T. Well–Behaved Modal Logic. *J Sym Log* 49,1393–1402 D 84.

Roughly speaking, a modal logic L (identified with a class of frames) is well–behaved when a K–model can have its accessibility relation expanded to yield a L–model, preserving satisfaction of all formulas. Thus model–theoretic results about K transfer to L "automatically". The familiar quantified model logics T, K4, S4, B, and S5 are shown to be well–behaved.

HODES, Harold. On Modal Logics Which Enrich First–Orders S5. *J Phil Log* 13,423–454 N 84.

This paper studies the languages obtained from first–order modal languages (with actualistic quantifiers) by adding possibilistic quantifiers, an actuality operator, a world–travelling operator, quantification over individual essences, over essences, and over attributes; the expressive powers of these languages are compared; there is some discussion of Allen Hazen's claim about the pre–individuative nature of possible worlds and Alvin Plantinga's preference for individual essences over possible individuals.

HODGES, Michael P and Lichter, Barry D. Perceptions Of The Engineers' "Professionalism" In The Chemical Industry. *Bus Prof Ethics J* 2,1–8 Wint 83.

The purpose of this work is to clarify the nature of engineering professionalism by looking to the experience of practicing engineers. An analysis is presented based on the experiences of offering workshops to technical employees at plant sites in the chemical industry. The authors conclude that role proliferation discourages professional autonomy in a corporate setting and that we require a new concept of professionalism that accounts for the essential coupling of business and engineering.

HODGKINSON, Christopher. *The Philosophy Of Leadership.* NY St Martin's Pr 1983.

HOEKEMA, David. Socrates, Meet The Buddha. *Teach Phil* 8,145–150 Ap 85.

Reflecting on experiences teaching American students on a five–month program of study in Taiwan and Thailand, the author suggests that the opportunity to study philosophy in an unfamiliar cultural context alters students' perception of the world and of philosophy itself. Implications for three topics of philosophical importance—the concept of the self, political relationships, and the nature of education—are suggested. It is appropriate, the author concludes, to include options for overseas study in a philosophy curriculum and to include philosophy in oversees study

programs.

HOELLER, Keith. Is Heidegger Really A Poet? *Phil Topics* 12,121–138 Wint 81.

Although it has been generally accepted that Heidegger is a poet who has written and published numerous poems, the author of this paper thouroughly questions this view by examining Heidegger's thoughts on the precise relation between thinking and poetizing. The conclusion is that while Heidegger is not in fact of poet, he is nevertheless attempting to think in a poetic style that is proper to his subject matter. Nevertheless, this style always remains thinking, and not poetry.

HOEREE, J and Hoogbergen, Wim. Oral History And Archival Data Combined: The Removal Of Saramakan Granman Kofi Bosuman As An Epistemological Problem. *Commun Cog* 17,245–290 1984.

HOFFE, Otfried. Introduzione Critica Alla Teoria Della Giustizia Di Rawls. *Riv Int Filosof Diritto* 61,603–637 O–D 84.

Otfried Höffe scrutinizes Rawls' claim that his *Theory of Justice* is Kantian. After having precised the two possible interpretations, a weak and a strong one, he shows how irritating this claim is: 1) Rawls' first principles of Justice are Kantian but the second one, the difference principle is not. 2) As rational egoists people in the original position do not choose principles of Justice but the utilitarian ones. 3) Although Rawls takes moral persons to form the basis of his theory, he does not clearly stress the differences between ethical and juridical persons. 4) Finally his theory of the well–organized society amounts to an "invisible church" in Kantian terms.

HÖFFE, Otfried. Is Rawls' Theory Of Justice Really Kantian? *Ratio* 26,103–124 D 84.

HOFFE, Otfried. Minimalstaat Oder Sozialrechte–Eine Philosophische Problemskizze. *Stud Phil (Switzerland)* 41,91–114 1982.

In the first part the author expounds Nozicks philosophy of the Minimal State. Then he argues against Nozicks political theory in favour of the social responsibility of the State, which means a defense of a social welfare state functionally able to safeguard freedom but not for a "State caring for people." In the third part he finally discussed how the social responsibility of the state could be legally justified.

HOFFHEIMER, Michael H. The Influence Of Schiller's Theory Of Nature On Hegel's Philosophical Development. *J Hist Ideas* 46,231–244 Ap–Je 85.

HOFFMAN, Joshua. On Petitionary Prayer. *Faith Phil* 2,30–37 Ja 85.

HOFFMAN, Joshua. Reply To Eleonore Stump's "Hoffman On Petitionary Prayer". *Faith Phil* 2,38–42 Ja 85.

HOFFMAN, Joshua. Swinburne On Omnipotence. *Sophia (Australia)* 23,36–40 Jl 84.

HOFFMAN, Paul. Kripke On Private Language. *Phil Stud* 47,23–28 Ja 85.

HOFFMAN, W Michael. Ethics In Business Education: Working Toward A Meaningful Reciprocity. *J Bus Ethics* 3,259–268 N 84.

This paper outlines and argues against some criticisms of business ethics education. It maintains that these criticisms have been put forward due to a misunderstanding of the nature of business and/or ethics. (edited)

HOFFMAN, Wilma and Krolikowski, Walter P and Hablutzel, Nancy. "Symmetry, Independence, Continuity, Boundedness, And Additivity": The Game Of Education. *Educ Stud* 15,215–231 Fall 84.

A review of seven recent books on educational policy from the United States and Great Britain. The article touches on some of the new happenings in education, especially the situation in Yugoslavia, the influence of court cases on educational practice, and national plans of educational change. It points to a troubling but necessary double focus on minima and maxima, on laws and ideals, on policies and principles, and advocates looking past liberty and equality to fraternity.

HOFFMANN, G R. "Humanismus" Und "Tradition" Themen Der Gegenwärtigen Bürgerlichen Philosophie Im Subsaharischen Afrika. *Deut Z Phil* 33,97–104 1985.

HOFFMANN, G and Bergmann, Werner. Habitualität Als Potentialität: Zur Konkretisierung Des Ich Bei Husserl. *Husserl Stud* 1,281–306 1984.

HOFSTEE, Willem K B. Om De Feiten Te Laten Spreken: Een Repliek. *Kennis Methode* 8,316–327 1984.

Boon and De Vries (1984) have criticized the betting model of empirical research with arguments that do not stand up to closer analysis. Their alternative appears not to represent an improvement over the alledged anomalies of the betting model, but rather a restatement of an unsatisfactory mehtodological paradigm which inspired the launching of the betting model.

HOGREBE, Wolfram. Erkenntnistheorie Ohne Erkenntnis. *Z Phil Forsch* 38,545–560 N–D 84.

HOHLER, T P (ed). *Imagination And Reflection: Intersubjectivity.* Boston Nijhoff 1982.

The intention of his work is to ground Fichte's early work in a thesis. The thesis operates on a triparate synthesis of the concept of I. Starting with Kant's Transcendental Imagination, Hohlen attempts to adambrate Fichte's egology within the concepts of intersubjectivity, the form and content–matter of imagination, and the synthesis of intuition. (staff)

HOHOS, Ladislav. An Attempt At The Utilization Of Prigogine's Thermodynamics In American Futurology (in Czechoslovakian). *Filozof Cas* 32,821–824 1984.

The paper is a polemic with the reductionism in A Toffler's "The Third Wave" concerning his argumentation on Prigogine's idea of dissipative structures applied in social research. The term "feed–back" may be productive when qualitative particularly of the social form of matter is involved. If the methods of thermodynamics and synergetics are used there is the basic characteristic of social relations to be taken into account as a primary supposition.

HOHOS, L. Historical Materialism And Some Actual Present Problems (in Czechoslovakian). *Filozof Cas* 32,697–703 1984.

HOLBOROW, Les C. Benn, Mackie And Basic Rights. *Austl J Phil* 63,11–25 Mr 85.

The ethical theories of Stanley Benn and John Mackie both seek to give a central place to the notion of individual rights. This paper considers the arguments advanced in favour of this view and seeks to clarify the logical geography of the concepts involved. A critique of Benn's strong reliance on the basic deontological requirement that persons be respected leads to the consideration of Mackie's attempt to deploy arguments of a more teleological character. It is concluded that a position such as his, which argues for the priority of rights as providing the opportunities to achieve a worthwhile life and maintains that this provision rather than the achievement of any more aggregative goal is the basic moral requirement, is attractive and worthy of further development.

HOLLAND, Alan F. On Behalf Of Moderate Speciesism. *J Applied Phil* 1,281–292 O 84.

Because of the existence of severely defective humans it is commonly held that whatever consideration is due to all humans is also due to many other animals, and that therefore speciesism, or the readiness to prefer the interest of humans to those of other animals, is unjustified. After criticism of this reasoning a 'naturalised' speciesism, acknowledging, for example, the affinities between species, is articulated and defended. The conclusion is that more traditional vices than speciesism are chiefly to blame for the shabby treatment of animals by humans. (edited)

HOLLEIS, Wilfried and Nussbaumer, Josef. Zum Okologiegehalt Der Nationalökonomie. *Conceptus* 18,52–82 1984.

The essay deals with the question, how different historical schools of economic theory and the present (neoclassical) theory tackle the problem of ecology in their conceptions. Amongst the schools analyzed are Classical Economic Theory, Early–Marxian and Marxian Economics, the German Historical School, the Marginalists, and Institutionalism. After having examined the Neoclassical Paradigm and the so-called "Alternative Economics", the essay concludes with an outlook into the future concerning the possible development of economic theory under the impact of ecological problems.

HOLLER, Linda D. In Search Of A Whole–System Ethic. *J Relig Ethics* 12,219–239 Fall 84.

A "whole–system ethic" is an ethic which finds its theory of value and moral agency in the relational nature of reality. Such an ethic is necessarily ontological. It proposes a relational theory of value, based on the contextual existence of the agent as being–in–the–world. Also, because primary attention is given to the relational nature of reality, such an ethic is concerned to expose the illusion of the separate self and point out the dangers of action in accord with this illusion. Drawing on insights from H Richard Niebuhr, Edmund Husserl, and Alfred Schulz, this paper explores the experimental relations through which value occurs as meaning–event, as self–interested, and as moral. niebuhr's model of the responsible self and his proposed "ethics of the fitting" are reinterpreted using phenomenological categories, so as to provide a possible ground for a whole–system ethic.

HOLLINGER, Robert. Practical Reason And Hermeneutics. *Phil Ret* 18,113–122 1985.

This paper takes the recent works of writers such as Gadamer, Heidegger, and Rorty as background, and explores the implications of their critique of traditional ideals of truth knowledge and rationality for our notions of reasoning and argumentation. I then criticize some ideas of Habermas and MacIntyre, which seems to me incompatible with the thrust of the recent efforts to rethink the nature of reasoning and argumentation.

HOLLIS, Martin. A Paradoxical Train Of Thought. *Analysis* 44,205–206 O 84.

a and *B* each thinks of a number and whispers it to *C*, who says, 'The numbers are different. Neither of you can deduce whose is higher'. *a* reasons that what *C* has said is true, and yet true only if it is false.

HOLLIS, Martin. Positional Goods. *Philosophy* 18,97–110 84 Supp.

Positional goods are those which a person values only if others lack them. Some are necessarily positional (prizes, secrets), some contingently (motoring on uncongested roads). They set a problem for extracting a best social choice from individual preferences. The general good requires *x*% to ahve the positional good: individual justice has no automatic tendency *x*%. The problem is practical, when entitled demand exceeds supply, and also awkward for ethics of perfect compliance.

HOLMES, Arthur F. *Contours Of A World View.* Grand Rapids W B Eerdmans 1983.

Operating at the intersection between philosophy and theology, this work discusses the anatomy of world views, and contrasts "secular humanism" with the Christian intellectual tradition. The bulk of the work looks at central Christian themes as they both shaped and were shaped by the history of philosophy. In a final section, applications are suggested to human creativity, technology, work and play.

HOLMES, Arthur F. *Ethics: Approaching Moral Decisions.* Downers Grove InterVarsity Pr 1984.

This is an introduction to ethics for the beginning student, about half of it on ethical theory (relativism, emotivism, egoism, utilitarianism, etc.) and half on applied ethics (rights, punishment, law and morality, sex and marriage). At the same time it explores the contribution of Christian theology to the problem of moral knowledge, and the basis of moral obligation. The latter introduces divine command theories, the former opens into moral sense theories, Kant, and natural law. A mixed deontological–teleological view is proposed.

HOLMES, Janet. Modifying Illocutionary Force. *J Prag* 8,345–366 Je 84.

Mitigation is an interesting pragmatic concept which has attracted some attention. It can usefully be considered in relation to the more general communicative strategies for modifying the strength or force of speech acts, namely, attenuation and boosting. The effects of these strategies on positively affective and negatively affective speech acts are discussed and exemplified, and reasons for using them are considered. A range of linguistic devices which may be used to modify the illocutionary force of speech acts is described and illustrated.

HOLMES, Richard. Being–In–Itself Revisited. *Dialogue (Canada)* 23,397–406 S 84.

In the introduction to *Being and Nothingness,* Jean–Paul Sartre states that Edmund Husserl has misunderstood his own essential discovery of the intentionality of consciousness. In this work, I assess this claim as I explicate Sartre's concept of intentionality. In addition, I show how an understanding of Husserl and Sartre reveals a basic convergence. My primary purpose is to further develop the correct description of the objects of the world through an analysis of their accounts.

HOLMES, Richard. The World According To Husserl. *Eidos* 4,39–50 Je 85.

HOLMES, Stephen. *Benjamin Constant And The Making Of Modern Liberalism.* New Haven Yale Univ Pr 1984.

HOLT, John C. *Discipline: The Canonical Buddhism Of The Vinayapitaka.* Delhi Indological 1983.

An analytical, historical, and structural analysis of the principles of buddhist monasticism, the thesis of this book is that mental discipline depends upon the quality of intention. Vinaya (or discipline) is what defines a Buddhist monk and consists of the basis for collective identity. This is clearly expressed within the vicissitudes of the Sangha's cultic life. It is also the means by which spiritual progress toward the goal of Nirvàna is won.

HOLT, Robert R. "Freud's Impact On Modern Morality And Our World View" in *Darwin, Marx And Freud,* Caplan, Arthur L (ed), 147–200. NY Plenum Pr 1984.

HOLWERDA, D. "Faith, Reason, And The Resurrection" in *Faith And Rationality,* Plantinga, Alvin (ed), 265–316. Notre Dame Univ Notre Dame Pr 1983.

HOLYER, Robert. Human Needs And The Justification Of Religious Belief. *Int J Phil Relig* 17,29–40 1985.

I argue that the satisfaction of human needs afforded by believing in God is evidence that there is a God. I make my case, first, by a critical examination of two recent efforts (that of Diogenes Allen and William Lad Sessions) to construe it as affording only a utilitarian justification of belief, and second, by sketching three lines of argument that may be used in support of my claim that is provides evidential justification.

HOLYER, Robert. Unconscious Belief And Natural Theology. *Heythrop J* 25,423–441 O 84.

Drawing on an analysis of the different types of unconscious religious belief, the author argues for a revision of the sort of natural theology that claims a universal but unconscious knowledge of God.

HOLZ, Fr. Die Bedeutung Der Methode Galileis Für Die Entwicklung Der Transzendentalphilosophie Kants. *Phil Natur* 15,344–358 1975.

HOLZHEY, Helmut (ed) and Leyvraz, Jean– Pierre. *Ästhetische Erfahrung Und Das Wesen Der Kunst.* Bern Haupt 1984.

HOLZHEY, Helmut. Lockes Begründung Des Privateigentums In Der Arbeit. *Stud Phil (Switzerland)* Supp 12,19–34 1983.

Part I deals with Locke's conception of the state of nature and the development of private property through labor. Part II discusses the disappearance of limits on the acquisition of property as a result of the introduction of money. Part III critically examines Locke's theory. Since Locke provides a justification of unlimited acquisition of property, his thesis stands in conflict with present day conceptions of just, government implemented schemes to distribute property with a view to dealing with ecological problems.

HONDERICH, Ted (ed) and Pitcher, George. *Berkeley.* Boston Routledge & K Paul 1977.

HONDERICH, Ted. Punishment, The New Retributivism, And Political Philosophy. *Philosophy* 18,117–148 84 Supp.

HONDRICH, Karl Otto. Soziale Probleme, Soziologische Theorie Und Gesellschaftsplanung. *Arch Rechts Soz* 60,161–186 1974.

An attempt is made to look at problems from the point of view of systems theory, need–dispositions and interactionism. The difference between social, personal, and material problems is emphasized. A proposal is made to explain social problems in an evolutionary framework. (edited)

HONSELL, Furio and Forti, Marco. Comparison Of The Axioms Of Local And Global Universality. *Z Math Log* 30,193–196 1984.

HONSELL, Furio and Forti, Marco. The Consistency Of The Axiom Of Universality For The Ordering Of Cardinalities. *J Sym Log* 50,502–509 Je 85.

HONT, Istvan (ed) and Ignatieff, Michael (ed). *Wealth And Virtue: The Shaping Of Political Economy In The Scottish Enlightenment.* NY Cambridge Univ Pr 1983.

HOOGBERGEN, Wim and Hoeree, J. Oral History And Archival Data Combined: The Removal Of Saramakan Granman Kofi Bosuman As An Epistemological Problem. *Commun Cog* 17,245–290 1984.

HOOK, Julian L. A Note On Interpretations Of Many–sorted Theories. *J Sym Log* 50,372–374 Je 85.

It is well–known that every many–sorted theory T can be effectively replaced by an equally powerful one–sorted theory T*. In this paper it is shown that a theory U can be interpretable in T without U* being interpretable in T*. This observation is useful in giving finitary proofs of relative consistency.

HOOK, Sidney and Russell, Bertrand. The Nature Of Liberal Civilization. *Russell* 5,5–13 Sum 85.

The text of a discussion between Bertrand Russell and Sidney Hook conducted over the BBC in the Fall of 1953 on the nature of liberal civilization. The point of departure was Hook's proposal to define a liberal civilization as one in which there is a free market of ideas from which it followed that "our moral obligation is the toleration of dissent, no matter how heretical, not to the toleration of conspiracy, not matter how disguised. The practical problem is to fund ways of implementing that destruction."

HOOKER, Brad. A Reply To Callan's 'Moral Education In A Liberal Society'. *J Moral Educ* 14,23–32 Ja 85.

In the preceding paper Callan (1985) argues that liberalism is rejectable by reasonable people and that inculcating liberal beliefs in the minds of children is therefore inconsistent with liberalism. Callan attacks in particular R M Hare's defence of teaching liberal morality as being consistent with liberal morality itself. In this reply the author argues that making distinctions between different senses of 'reasonable' and of 'liberalism' helps undermine some of Callan's main arguments.

HOPPE, Hansgeorg. Leiblicher Raum Und Räumlichkeit Der Gefühle. *Z Phil Forsch* 29,292–304 Ap–Je 75.

HÖPPNER, Joachim. Zur Problematik Des Egalitarismus. *Deut Z Phil* 23,800–817 1975.

Unter Heranziehung von Resultaten der internationalen Historiographie wird die Bedeutung des von der Philosophie bislang wenig beachteten Egalitarismus herausgearbeitet. Die Untersuchung bezieht sich neben einzelnen Zeugnissen der Antike auf die hauptsächlichen Systeme des 18 Jh in Frankreich und England und ihre sozialphilosophischen, ökonomischen und politischen Anschauungen. dauüber hinaus wird auf egalitaristische Tendenzen im philosophischen Denken Deutschlands hingewiesen.

HORÁLEK, Karel. Semiology, Linguistics And Culturology (in Czechoslovakian). *Estetika* 21,133–137 1984.

HORGAN, Terence and Woodward, James. Folk Psychology Is Here To Stay. *Phil Rev* 94,197–226 Ap 85.

Paul Churchland and Stephan Stich recently have given distinct but related arguments for saying that "folk psychology" is radically false, i.E., that humans do not have beliefs, desires, or other propositional attitudes. We examine their arguments critically, and find them wanting. In particular, we argue that they each impose implausibly strong constraints upon the way that folk psychology must be related to lower–level theories in cognitive science or neuroscience in order to be compatible with them.

HORGAN, Terence. Compatibilism And The Consequence Argument. *Phil Stud* 47,339–356 My 85.

Peter van Inwagen, in an influential paper and again in a recent book, propounds an important argument (the "consequence argument") for the incompatibility of free will and determinism. While the book was at press, David Lewis published an important critique of the earlier paper. The book's elaboration of the consequence argument suggests response to Lewis's critique. I set forth that response, and I argue that it fails to evade Lewis's essential criticism.

HORGAN, Terence. Science Nominalized. *Phil Sci* 51,529–549 D 84.

I propose a way of formulating scientific laws and magnitude attributions which eliminates ontological commitment to mathematical entities. I argue that science only requires quantitative sentences as thus formulated, and hence that we ought to deny the existence of sets and numbers. I argue that my approach cannot plausibly be extended to the concrete "theoretical" entities of science.

HORÍNEK, Zdenek. Possibilities Of Theatrical Montage (in Czechoslovakian). *Estetika* 21,172–184 1984.

HORN, J C. Absolutes Wesen/Absolutes Wissen. *Kantstudien* 66,169–180 1975.

HORN, Laurence R and Bayer, Samuel. Short–Circuited Implicature: A Negative Contribution. *Ling Phil* 7,397–414 N 84.

HORNE, James. The Experience Of Dreaming. *Phil Forum (Boston)* 15,459–470 Sum 84.

Reports of dreams are peculiar because they can be confirmed only by the dreamer's memory of them. Therefore, D C Dennett argues that it is an open question whether dreams are experiences. This paper argues that they are, partly for the reasons that pain, love, and mystical illumination are, but primarily because they have psychological effects, which they indicate solutions to technical or personal problems.

HORNE, Thomas A. "The Poor Have A Claim Found In The Law Of Nature": William Paley And The Rights Of The Poor. *J Hist Phil* 23,51–70 Ja 85.

The Reverend William Paley's widely read textbook, *The Principles of Moral and Political Philosophy* (1785) played an important role in defending the right of the poor to government aid in the debates over the Poor Law in the early 19th century. His argument was that the poor's right to subsistence was based on natural law and that this right took precedence over the property rights of individuals, which were based only on the positive laws of a particular country.

HORNSTEIN, Norbert and Davidson, Arnold I. The Primary/Secondary Quality Distinction: Berkeley, Locke, And The Foundations Of Corpuscularian Science. *Dialogue (Canada)* 23,281–304 Je 84.

Some advocates of determinism defend the theory by reconciling it with common beliefs. Critics generally respond by looking for genuine friction. The opposing sides thus generate two sets of analyses of the key statements, one compatibilistic, the other not. These analytic disputes often end in stalemate, and two debates concerning the possibility of alternative actions are offered as illustrations. The general moral is that something in addition to pure analysis is needed to achieve real progress on determinism.

HOROWITZ, Tamara. A Priori Truth. *J Phil* 82,225–238 My 85.

HORSTMANN, Hubert. The Philosophy Of Life In Positivist Thought (in German). *Deut Z Phil* 33,435–443 1985.

Wittgenstein's "Tractatus" demonstrates, that Positivism and Philosophy of live reciprocal precondition and complement. Theme of the analyse is: 1) correlation between conceptions of structures of the thought and language and conceptions of unrational, unscientific character of the ethical and sense–problems (sense of live, sense of history, etc.); 2) cooperation between Positivism and Philosophy of live in the endeavor to confront as irreconcilable antagonism facts and values, knowledge

and interests, objectivity and judgments as to value.

HORSTMANN, Rolf–Peter. Ontologie Und Relationen. Konigstein Athenaum 1984.

The main purpose of the book is to find out what led to the confrontation between continental dialectical and Anglo–American analytical philosophy. The author shows that questions concerning alternatives in ontology (monism versus pluralism) played a major role in producing that confrontation. Especially the controversy over internal and external relations between Bradley and Russell is considered to be of central importance, and is discussed with respect to the ontological issue.

HORVAT, Branko. Marx's Contributions To Social Science And His Errors. *Praxis Int* 4,299–312 O 84.

HORWICH, Paul. Probability And Evidence. Cambridge Cambridge Univ Pr 1982.

HORWICH, Paul. "Explanations Of Irrelevance" in *Testing Scientific Theories*, Earman, John (ed), 55–66. Minneapolis Univ Minnesota Pr 1983.

HORWITZ, Rivka. "Ferdinand Ebner As A Source Of Buber's Dialogic Thought In *I And Thou*" in *Martin Buber*, Gordon, Haim (ed), 121–138. Beersheva Ktav 1984.

HÖRZ, H and Banse, Gerhard. Wissenschaftlich–Technische Revolution––Schöpfertum––Verantwortung. *Deut Z Phil* 32,785–795 1984.

HORZ, Herbert. Experiment—Modell—Theorie. *Deut Z Phil* 23,883–897 1975.

Die Stellung von Experiment, Modell und Theorie im Erkenntnisprozefss wird untersucht. Das Experiment ist seinem Wesen nach ein objektiver Analysator der Wirklichkeit. Es ist von der experimentellen Methode zu unterscheiden, die aus verschiedenen Schritten besteht. Die Theorie synthetisiert Momente des Wesens, die durch das Experiment analysiert werden. Durch die Theorie wird die empirische Erkenntnis auf die Ebene der systematischen Gesetzeserkenntnis gehoben. In ihr liegt das schöpferische Moment der Wissenschaftsentwicklung.

HOSLE, Vittorio. Hegels 'Naturphilosophie' Und Platons 'Timaios'—Ein Strukturvergleich. *Phil Natur* 21,64–100 1984.

In the systems of Plato and Hegel, nature occupies an analogous position; nevertheless, the former displays a more monistic structure, whereas Hegel designs a dialectical version of objective idealism. The author points out corresponding details in the tripartite organization of Plato's *Timaeus* and Hegel's *Philosophy of Nature*, in the respective concepts of the world's creation and its spatial form, the planetary movement, matter, organic life, sexuality and death. These similarities are shown to have historical and objective reasons.

HOSMER, Larue Tone. Managerial Ethics And Microeconomic Theory. *J Bus Ethics* 3,315–326 N 84.

The article examines the moral constructs in microeconomic theory and the ethical objections to that theory at both the pragmatic and theoretic levels, and concludes that inappropriate assumptions about the nature and worth of human beings in the economic paradigm require the use of moral standards for business decisions and actions. (edited)

HOSMER, Larue T. The Other 338: Why A Majority Of Our Schools Of Business Administration Do Not Offer A Course In Business Ethics. *J Bus Ethics* 4,17–22 F 85.

HOSPERS, John. Artistic Creativity. *J Aes Art Crit* 43,243–256 Spr 85.

Several views of what artistic creation is are first criticized: (1) creation as a making; (2) creation as requiring pre–existing materials; (3) creation as requiring uniqueness and novelty; (4) creation as causally inexplicable. Theories of the creative process (1) in relation to unconscious drives, (2) in relation to the classical expression theory, and (3) as a species of problem–solving activity, are described and evaluated. A conclusion reached is that there is no general theory of creative activity in the arts which both covers all examples and also only examples, of artistic creativity.

HOUSKA, Jiri. The Dialectic Of The Contradictions Of Real Socialism (in Czechoslovakian). *Filozof Cas* 32,505–520 1984.

HOUSTON, Barbara and Ayim, Maryann. The Epistemology Of Gender Identity: Implications For Social Policy. *Soc Theor Pract* 11,25–59 Spr 85.

The article's purpose is to examine the epistemological status of claims regarding one's core gender identity. We assess the implications of considering such claims as analytic statements, as inductive summaries of experience, and as expressions of preference. We examine the claims in the literature about when the core gender identity is established, its connection with language acquisition, and its supposed permanence. In the final part of the paper, we draw out important implications for social policy.

HOW, Alan R. A Case Of Creative Misreading: Habermas's Evolution Of Gadamer's Hermeneutics. *J Brit Soc Phenomenol* 16,132–144 My 85.

HOWARD, Dick. Kant's System And (Its) Politics. *Man World* 18,79–98 1985.

Kant's "perpetual Peace" is apparently contradictory or inconsequential, or simply the work of an old man. No, No, No! Looked at within the context of the entire *opus*, the essay is the recapitulation and completion of a system that Kant only hinted at—and that Hegel and Marx only dimly suspected. The essay builds on materials in the author's recently published *From Marx to Kant* (SUNY Press, 1985). The role of the third critique is both evaluated and devaluated.

HOWARD, Don. Einstein On Locality And Separability. *Stud Hist Phil Sci* 16,171–201 S 85.

Analysis of the Einstein–Schrödinger correspondence and later publications reveals that Einstein did not write the EPR paper, did not like the argument it contains, and developed his own argument for the incompleteness of quantum mechanics (QM). Einstein argues that the completeness of QM contradicts two independent assumptions: (a) separability, which asserts that spatio–temporally separated systems possess separate real states, and (b) locality, which asserts that no physical effects can be communicated between space–like separated systems.

HOWARD, Don. Realism And Conventionalism In Einstein's Philosophy Of Science: The Einstein–Schlick Correspondence. *Phil Natur* 21,616–629 1984.

Einstein's correspondence with Schlick, and other sources from 1915–30, show that Einstein's emerging philosophy of science combined conventionalism with realism; Einstein's conventionalism, like Schlick's rested on the denial that theories are uniquely determined, either by empirical evidence or by *a priori* categories. Schlick became Einstein's ally against neo–Kantian misinterpretations of relativity in the early 1920s. It is conjectured that Einstein's solution of the final problems holding up general relativity left him open to Schlick's influence.

HOWARD, J V. Computable Explanations. *Z Math Log* 21,215–224 1975.

HOWARD, John A (ed). On Freedom. Greenwich Devin–Adair 1984.

on Freedom is a collection of nine essays assessing the philosophical, religious, social, and economic meanings of Western freedom. Among the topics of analysis are the rise of the American religious right, the growing tensions between security and liberty, the spurious New Left equation of freedom and happiness, the need for a metaphysical definition of freedom, and the decline in ethical education in public schools. Contributors include Leszek Kolakowski, Nikolaus Lobkowicz, and Richard John Neuhaus.

HOWARD, John A. "Reopening The Books On Ethics: The Role Of Education In A Free Society" in *On Freedom*, Howard, John A (ed), 79–94. Greenwich Devin–Adair 1984.

HOWARD, Michael W. A Contradiction In The Egalitarian Theory Of Justice. *Phil Res Arch* 10,35–56 1984.

This paper sets out to account for conflicting interpretations of Rawls' theory of justice by Marxian critics, by uncovering an unresolved contradiction in the theory between individualist and communitarian values. The contradiction comes to light particularly in the more egalitarian interpretation of Rawls, and can only be overcome by incorporating a fuller theory of the good than that with which Rawls has provided us. It may not be possible to do this without giving up the claim that the theory of justice articulates the considered judgments of all thoughtful persons in our society, irrespective of class or ideology.

HOWARD, Michael W. Utopianism And Nuclear Deterrence. *Phil Soc Crit* 10,53–66 Wint 84.

This paper examines some unquestioned assumptions and limitations in the writings of critics of both the morality and the rationality of deterrence. Jonathan Schell's Hobbesian critique of deterrence assumes that nuclear weapons have been developed primarily to deter an attack by the Soviet Union against the U S and its allies, while aggressive threats to use nuclear weapons in the context of military interventions are ignored. Schell, the Catholic Bishops, and Michael Walzer discuss deterrence in abstraction from the actual history and the economic, political and ideological character of the states concerned, resulting in utopian analyses or equivocal moral stances.

HOWARD, Michael W. Worker Control, Self–Respect, And Self–Esteem. *Phil Res Arch* 10,455–472 1985.

In this paper it is argued that the predominant mode of organization of work in capitalist society undermines the conditions of self–respect and self–esteem. Although no society can guarantee that everyone have self–respect and self–esteem, it is a requirement of justice that a society provide conditions favorable to their development. Worker control is a form of society which can satisfy this requirement, in a manner that is compatible with political democracy and basic liberties, and thus, from the standpoint of justice, is to be preferred to capitalism.

HOWARD, Paul E. Subgroups Of A Free Group And The Axiom Of Choice. *J Sym Log* 50,458–467 Je 85.

It is shown that the subgroup theorem for free groups (a subgroup of a free group is free) implies the axiom of choice for sets of finite sets. A proof that a strengthened version of the subgroup theorem implies the full axiom of choice is also given.

HOWARD, Richard (trans) and Barthes, Roland. The Responsibility Of Forms: Critical Essays On Music, Art, And Representation. NY Hill And Wang 1985.

HOWICK, William H. The Origin Of Life: Science Or Religion. *J Thought* 20,60–66 Spr 85.

This work traces the history of the controversy from the publication of Darwin's *Origin of Species* through the Scopes Trial to the recent legislation of several states and the action of the courts to control the teaching of theories in the public schools. Sociological aspects which promoted the revival of the argument are described, and the contrast between the two sides is clearly stated. The move toward theistic evolution is offered some support as a mediating position. The purpose of the work has to "... Assess the battle and bring the record up to date", especially for the benefit of newer and younger scholars.

HOWSON, Colin. Bayesianism And Support By Novel Facts. *Brit J Phil Sci* 35,245–251 S 84.

This paper seeks to correct the elementary but common misapprehension that according to Bayesian kinematics hypotheses acquire zero support from known data. It is pointed out that for good reasons the probability function is relativised to background information omitting e when support by e is being assessed. The question of whether known facts ever support a hypothesis constructed using them is addressed, and it is shown that in certain circumstances they do.

HOWSON, Colin. Probabilities, Propensities, And Chances. *Erkenntnis* 21,279–294 N 84.

In this paper the frequency, propensity and chance theories of probability are shown to be inadequate. A new approach is suggested, in which the physical probability distribution of some stochastic set up reflects features of the physical structure of the set up and it gives a measure of the extent to which those features bias the set up towards delivering its various outcomes, the measure originally being calibrated in the interval [−1,1].

HOY, Calvin M. A Philosophy Of Individual Freedom: The Political Thought Of F A Hayek. Westport Greenwood Pr 1984.

HOY, Ronald C. Inquiry, Intrinsic Properties, And The Identity Of Indiscernibles. *Synthese* 61,275–298 D 84.

After reviewing arguments that the Principle of the Identity of Indiscernibles is not a logical truth, the suggestion that it is a methodological principle is defended. Alleged counterexamples to PII are shown to use concepts of properties that are in need of analysis. An analysis of intrinsic properties in terms of invariance is proposed which allows them to be relational and dependent. Leibniz and others may have worked with a controversial "phenomenal property paradigm" for intrinsic properties. Finally, it is suggested that "specific dispositional properties" can always be found to save PII from refutation.

HOYT, Reed J. Reader–Response And Implication–Realization. *J Aes Art Crit* 34,281–290 Spr 85.

Despite the differences between the definitions of meaning in music and literature, certain analogies in analytical methodology arise. The article stresses the similarities between Stanley Fish's reader–response method in literature and Eugene Narmour's implication–realization model in music. Both are essentially processive methods that account for both prospective (hypothesized) and retrospective structural meanings within their respective art–forms.

HRZAL, Ladislav and Kuzminski, V. The Alienation Of Revolution Or The Criticism Of Real Socialism In The Conception Of A Schaff (in Czechoslovakian). *Filosof Cas* 33,108–140 1985.

HRZAL, L. The Struggle Against The Revisionism For Creative Development Of Marxism–Leninism (in Czechoslovakian). *Filozof Cas* 33,282–293 1985.

HUANG, Yih–Mei. An Analysis And Critique Of Wang Fu–Chih's Theory Of "*Tao Ta Shan Hsiao, Shan Ta Hsing Hsiao*" (in Chinese). *Phil Rev (Taiwan)* 7,225–234 Ja 84.

HUAR, Ulrich. Über Den Inhalt Sozial–Politischer Gesetze. *Deut Z Phil* 22,681–693 1974.

Ausgangspunkt für Bestimmung des Inhalts sozial–politischer Gesetze ist die Klärung der Frage, was unter sozial–politischen Verhältnissen zu verstehen ist. So wie alle gesellschaftlichen Verhältnisse funktionieren und entwickeln sich diese auf der Grundlage objektiver Gesetze. Die sozial–politischen Gesetze tragen einen relativ eigenständigen Charakter. über die in den Gegenstandsbereich des wissenschaftlichen Kommunismus gehörenden Gesetze gibt es in der sowjetischen Literatur verschiedene Auffassungen. Sozial–politische Gesetze sind allgemeine, wesentliche, notwendige Zusammenhänge der sozialen und politischen Verhältnisse, die zugleich durch ökonomische Verhältnisse determiniert sind.

HUBBARD, Ruth. "Genetic Screening Of Prospective Parents And Of Workers" in *Biomedical Ethics Reviews*, Humber, James M (ed), 73–120. Clifton Humana Pr 1984.

HÜBENER, Wolfgang. Leibniz' Gebrochenes Verhältnis Zur Erkenntnismetaphysik Der Scholastik. *Stud Leibniz* 17,66–76 1985.

To explain the nature of scientific hypothesis Leibniz refers to the economical principle of nominalistic philosophy, well–known as Occam's razor. In his drafts of characterization Leibniz makes use of the scotistic concept of formalitas. But pertaining to the thing he neither continues the Occamistic methodology nor does he tie up to scotistic metaphysics of concept. Hence there is no passage in Leibniz's works that could definitely be incorporated into the tradition of nominalistic or formalistic thought.

HUBERT, Jerry Z. The First And The Second Day Of War. *Dialec Hum* 11,469–470 Spr/Sum 84.

HUBNER, Wulf. Monade Und Welt: Ein Beitrag Zur Interpretation Der Monadologie. *Stud Leibniz* 7,105–121 1975.

In this paper I put forward the thesis that relevant so–called ontological notions in the Monadology have to be reformulated as logical ones to understand them reasonably. (edited)

HUCKLE, Nicholas. On Representation And Essence: Barthes And Heidegger. *J Aes Art Crit* 34,275–280 Spr 85.

Some parallels and differences between the concepts of human essence found in Martin Heidegger's *The Origin of the Work of Art* and in Roland Barthes's *Camera Lucida* are explored. It is pointed out how the differing mediums and subjects discussed reflect fundamentally divergent attitudes.

HUCKLENBROICH, Peter. System And Disease: On The Fundamental Problem Of Theoretical Pathology. *Theor Med* 5,307–324 O 84.

The article gives a sketch of a systems view in Theoretical Pathology, i.E., the medical theory of organisms and their health diseases. Three main levels of systems are distinguished which are of relevance: objective systems, subjective systems, and reflexive systems. This distinction is illustrated by the possibilities of computer systems. Consequences for the conceptions of disease, etiology, pathogenesis, and their criteria are discussed.

HUDELSON, Richard. Marx And The Theory Of Internal Relations: A Critical Note On Ollman's Interpretation Of Marx. *Phil Soc Sci* 14,505–508 D 84.

Bertell Ollman has argued that the Marxism of Marx rests upon a theory of internal relations. I argue against this claim.

HUDSON, James L. The Ethics Of Immigration Restriction. *Soc Theor Pract* 10,201–240 Sum 84.

Governmental restrictions on immigration are commonly defended as being necessary to protect either (1) domestic wage–levels; (2) citizens' sensibilities, which would be irritated by contact with undesirable ethnic groups; (3) the institutions of the welfare state; or (4) domestic order and justice. The author considers each type of defense in turn, and finds wanting all except a heavily qualified version of (4). He concludes that immigration restrictions are very seldom morally justified.

HUDSON, W D. "The 'Is–Ought' Problem Resolved" in *Gewirth's Ethical Rationalism*, Regis Jr, Edward (ed), 108–127. Chicago Univ Of Chicago Pr 1984.

HUDSON, W D. Theology And The Intellectual Endeavour Of Mankind. *Relig Stud* 21,21–38 Mr 85.

The logical structure, which makes any discipline (e.G., science, morality, etc.) definable justifiably as an aspect of man's intellectual endeavour, is analyzed and outlined. Then Theology is considered. It is conformable to the given analysis: can it be justifiably defined *tout court* with the other disciplines as part of mankind's intellectual endeavor? The author argues that it can.

HUFF, Toby. *Max Weber And The Methodology Of The Social Sciences*. New Brunswick Transaction Books 1983.

An examination of Max Weber's early methodological writings finds Weber's position to be opposed to the epistemological assumptions of phenomenology; very close to the spirit of post–empiricist philosophy of science as refelcted in the work of N R Hanson, Popper, Kuhn, and others; and both foundational for and consistent with recent advances in the logic of social scientific explanation as found in the work of such philosophers as Hart and Honoré and Davidson.

HUGHEN, Richard. Whitehead's Epochal Theory Of Time. *Phil Topics* 13,95–102 Spr 85.

HUGHES, Charles E and Singletary, W E. Triadic Partial Implicational Propositional Calculi. *Z Math Log* 21,21–28 1975.

HUGHES, Charles E. Sets Derived By Deterministic Systems With Axiom. *Z Math Log* 21,71–80 1975.

HUGHES, G E. *John Buridan On Self–Reference: Chapter Eight Of Buridan's 'Sophismata'*. NY Cambridge Univ Pr 1982.

HUGHES, Justin. Group Speech Acts. *Ling Phil* 7,379–396 N 84.

This article argues that speech act theory to date has failed to account for utterances from groups of people: juries, judicial panels, summit meetings of heads of states, etc. The paper establishes the criteria for a "group speech act" from a relatively small group and discusses what ramifications the existence of group speech acts will have for speech act theory.

HUGHES, R I G. Hume's Second Enquiry: Ethics As Natural Science. *Hist Phil Quart* 2,291–308 Jl 85.

Hume announces in the Second Enquiry that he is going to apply "the experimental method" in his discussion of ethics. The paper shows how the Newtonian model Hume adopts determines the structure of the Enquiry as a whole, the modes of argument used within it, and, most importantly, the moral theory that he propounds.

HÜGLI, Anton. Gleichheit Und Eigentum: Metaethische Und Normative Bemerkungen Zum Verfassungsentwurf. *Stud Phil (Switzerland)* Supp 12,349–374 1983.

HUGLY, Philip and Sayward, Charles. Is Moral Relativism Consistent? *Analysis* 45,40–44 Ja 85.

The version of moral relativism we consider says that the correctness of moral judgments is code–relative. There is no moral analogue to truth. An objection to this view is that the fact that norms admit of logical relations shows that a code–independent notion of correctness is applicable to them. We show this objection is unsound.

HULL, Richard T. "Involuntary Commitment & Treatment Of Persons Diagnosed As Mentally Ill" in *Biomedical Ethics Reviews*, Humber, James M (ed), 131–148. Clifton Humana Pr 1983.

HULL, Richard T and Nelson, James A and Gartner, Lou Ann. "Ethical Issues In Prenatal Therapies" in *Biomedical Ethics Reviews*, Humber, James M (ed), 225–250. Clifton Humana Pr 1984.

HULL, Richard T. Informed Consent: Patient's Right Or Patient's Duty? *J Med Phil* 10,183–198 My 85.

The rule that a patient should give a free, fully–informed consent to any therapeutic intervention is traditionally thought to express merely a right of the patient against the physician, and a duty of the physician towards the patient. On this view, the patient may waive the right with impunity, a fact sometimes expressed in the notion of a right not to know. This paper argues that the rule also expresses a duty of the patient. The argument turns, first, on the truism that a physician has no obligation to commit a battery, or unauthorized touching, and, second, on the thesis that a patient necessarily cannot consent to something that is unknown to him. The conclusion is drawn that a patient is not free to receive treatment voluntarily without knowledgeably authorizing it.

HUMBER, James M (ed) and Almeder, Robert F (ed). *Biomedical Ethics Reviews*. Clifton Humana Pr 1983.

biomedical Ethics Reviews: 1983 is the first volume in a series of texts designed to review and update the literature on issues of centra importance in bioethics today. Five topics are discussed in the present volume: "Euthanasia", "Surrogate Gestation", "The Distribution of Health Care", "The Involuntary Commitment and Treatment of Mentally Ill Persons", and "Patenting New Life Forms". Two articles deal with each topic; all essays are previously unpublished.

HUMBER, James M (ed) and Almeder, Robert T (ed). *Biomedical Ethics Reviews*. Clifton Humana Pr 1984.

HUMKE, Paul D. The Baire Category Of Sets Of Access. *Z Math Log* 21,331–342 1975.

HUMMON, Norman P. "Organizational Aspects Of Technological Change" in *Technological Knowledge*, Laudan, Rachel (ed), 67–82. Boston Reidel 1984.

HUMPHREY, Peter. The Ethics Of Earthworks. *Environ Ethics* 7,5–22 Spr 85.

Use of the environment for industrial purposes has long been the object of moral criticism. What about use of the environment for the purpose of making art? Is this, too, open to ethical questioning? I show that earthworks, even though they are

artworks, are not free from such criticism. I then examine defenses of them which either have been offered by earthworks artists or are plausible claims. Problems with these defenses show that earthworks are at least not obviously ethical.

HUND, J. A Crack In The Foundations Of Descartes's Theory Of Knowledge. *S Afr J Phil* 3,125–129 N 84.

There is a deep ambivalence in Descartes' theory of knowledge. The author shows that, under Descartes' theory of intuition, the propositions of mathematics and pure physics are indubitable in the same way the *cogito* is indubitable and, notwithstanding Descartes disclaimer to the contrary, to the same degree. He then shows that, under Descartes' doctrine of simple natures, the *cogito* is not indubitable after all. The author suggests that Descartes introduced his doctrine of simple natures in order to salvage his metaphysical theology from his doctrine of human intuition, but that he did so at the expense of undermining the foundations of his Rationalist theory of knowledge.

HUND, John. Formal Justice And Township Justice. *Phil Papers* 13,50–58 O 84.

The paper conceptualizes and traces out the connections between the formal legal system as it exists in South Africa and informal pockets of justice that exist in townships and in other areas in the Republic of South Africa. The philosophical dimension of the paper lies in its discussion of the relationship between law and justice. The South African doctrine of legal positivism is discussed as an ideology preserving the formal legal system.

HUND, John. Insiders And Outsiders Models Of Deviance And Jurisprudence. *Phil Soc Sci* 15,35–44 Mr 85.

The statements "law is what the courts say it is" and "deviant behavior is behavior that people so label" both possess a spurious surface credibility that trades on certain ambiguities. These ambiguities are exposed and legal realism and the view that Pollner attributes to Becker are stripped of their specious surface tenability.

HUNG, Cheng–Uan and Liu, Fu–tseng. Set Theories: Their Philosophic Issues And Foundations (in Chinese). *Phil Rev (Taiwan)* 7,91–116 Ja 84.

This paper traces the main philosophic issues and the foundations of Cantorian set theory and the contemporary cumulative hierarchy theory (c h t). From a platonistic view point, we formulate two theories of c h t that is, stage theory and level theory. The latter is characteristically stronger than the former. Axioms of Zermelo Fraenkel set theory, ZF, that can be deduced within two theories, are explained and left as logical exercises. We believe that, for a deep understanding of model–theoretic results in axiomatic set theory, we must capture fully the philosophy (and the picture) of the cumulative hierarchy.

HUNG, Tscha. Remarks On Affirmations. *Synthese* 64,297–306 S 85.

In the last phase of the development of his thought, Schlick was subject to a strong Wittgensteinian influence. He used the verification principle as criterion of scientific meaning, abandoning his previous critical realism in favor of empirico–positivistic realism. Schlick was also using Wittgenstein's concept of showing, as well as his own individual conception of affirmation (Konstatierung) as standard of empirical reality, attempting to refute the Neurath–Carnap's conventionalist and Carnap–Hempel's "crude rationalism" and to replace them by what he called "consistent empiricism". Inspiring though Schlick's time exploration of the concept of an affirmanionis is, I am inclined to think that he not only had not success in this enterprise, but eventually came, instead a conventionalist or a "crude rationalist, a linguistic solipsist.

HUNT, Vilma R. "Perspective On Ethical Issues In Occupational Health" in *Biomedical Ethics Reviews*, Humber, James M (ed), 175–204. Clifton Humana Pr 1984.

HUNTER, Graeme and Inwood, Brad. Plato, Leibniz, And The Furnished Soul. *J Hist Phil* 22,423–434 O 84.

This paper is an examination and comparison of Plato's and Leibniz's views on innate knowledge. Examining first the theory of recollection in the *Meno* and the *Phaedo*, with emphasis on Plato's exploitation of the analogy with ordinary remembering and his consequent acceptance of the soul's pre–existence, we then consider Leibniz, with special regard to his *Discourse on Metaphysics* and *New Essays*. (edited)

HURLEY, Patrick J. *A Concise Introduction To Logic*. Belmont Wadsworth 1982.

HURLEY, S L. Frege, The Proliferation Of Force, And Non–Cognitivism. *Mind* 93,570–576 O 84.

HUSAK, Douglas N. What Is So Special About (Free) Speech? *Law Phil* 4,1–16 Ap 85.

Legal and political philosophers (e.G., Scanlon, Schauer, etc.) typically regard speech as *special* in the sense that conduct that causes harm should be less subject to regulation if it involves speech than if it does not. Though speech is special in legal analysis, I argue that it should not be given comparable status in moral theory. I maintain that most limitations on state authority enacted on behalf of a moral principle of freedom of speech can be retained without supposing that speech is entitled to a degree of protection not affordable to (most) other forms of conduct. My argument questions some standard assumptions made by philosophers about the relationship between moral and legal principles.

HUSAK, Douglas N. Why There Are No Human Rights. *Soc Theor Pract* 10,125–142 Sum 84.

I argue that the legitimate and noble aims of the human rights movement can be achieved without the highly problematic assumption that all members of the human species share moral rights.

HUSSERL, Edmund and Chaffin, D (trans). The Apodicticity Of Recollection. *Husserl Stud* 2,3–32 1985.

HUSSEY, Edward (trans) and Ackrill, J L (ed). *Aristotle's Physics*. NY Clarendon Pr 1983.

HUSTWIT, Ronald E (ed) and Craft, J L (ed). *Without Proof Or Evidence: Essays Of O K Bouwsma*. Lincoln Univ Nebraska Pr 1984.

This collection of O K Bouwsma's essays addresses the central topics of Western religion: the rationality of religious belief, the nature of Christianity, the promise of eternal life, the definition of faith, and proofs of the existence of God. Analyzing the concepts Descartes, Moore, Wittgenstein, Anselm, Nietzsche, and Kierkegaard. Bouwsma focuses on the remark ableness of a book which God has sent to mankind.

HUTCHESON, Peter. Vindicating Strawson. *Phil Topics* 13,175–184 Spr 85.

Wesley Salmon and others have argued that Strawson's arguments concerning the problem of induction (1) neglect questions about the rationale for the ordinary use of 'rational,' and (2) erroneously identify justification and validation. I argue that (1) is ill–founded because it is based on a failure to consider the arguments other than the "ordinary language" argument. I argue that (2) is inconclusive because, although Strawson does not use the word 'vindication,' the substance of one of his arguments addresses, if only incompletely, the problem of vindicating induction.

HUTCHINS, Grover M and Moore, G William and De La Monte, Suzanne M. Compensatory Neoplasia: Chronic Erythrocytosis And Neuroblastic Tumors. *Theor Med* 5,279–292 O 84.

In a recent study, we observed a strong association between chronic hypoxic states and the occurrence of peripheral neuroblastic tumors, a relatively uncommon group of neural neoplasms. In this report we review those findings and formulate an hypothesis to explain why conditions which lead to chronic erythrocytosis may also cause compensatory neoplasia of neural tissues. (edited)

HYDEN, Timothy M. A Critique Of Marxist Legal Theoretical Constructs. *Stud Soviet Tho* 28,345–355 N 84.

This article considers whether there exists a formal Marxist theory of law. Historical materialism and Marxs' theories regarding ideology are analyzed as theoretical foundations for such a theory. The logicality and cogency of a Marxist theory of law is analyzed within the context of syllogistic logic. The article concludes that even in a perfect communist society, there must exist some coercive order as a form of law, e.G., public pressure.

HYLAND, Drew A. *The Question Of Play.* Lanham Univ Pr Of America 1984.

After a critique of the sociological, psychological, and historical perspectives on play, I develop my own conception of the "stance of play" which I call "responsive openness". I then contrast my view to the treatment of play by thinkers in the continental tradition (Nietzsche, Heidegger, Gadamer, Fink, Foucault, Derrida) and conclude with a discussion of some of the implications of my view of play for philosophy.

HYLAND, Drew A. Opponents, Contestants, And Competitors: The Dialectic Of Sport. *J Phil Sport* 11,63–70 1984.

HYLTON, Peter. "The Nature Of The Proposition And The Revolt Against Idealism" in *Philosophy In History*, Rorty, Richard and others (ed), 375–398. NY Cambridge Univ Pr 1984.

HYLTON, Peter. The Metaphysics Of T H Green. *Hist Phil Quart* 2,91–110 Ja 85.

HYPPOLITE, Jean. "Philosophy And Painting" in *Continental Philosophy And The Arts*, Winters, Laurence E and others (ed), 225–238. *Lanham* Univ Pr Of America 1984.

IAMMARONE, Luigi. Il Problema Critico. *Aquinas* 27,373–404 My–Ag 84.

IANNONE, Carol. Feminist Mysticism. *Antioch Rev* 42,416–426 Fall 84.

Feminist scholars have reversed themselves, and have gone from denying sexual differences to emphasizing them. In doing so, they inadvertently glorify elements of "male chauvinist" myth. This new direction provided an exit for feminists from the impasse of egalitarian sameness. But to work in terms of "female culture" is to intensify the limitations of gender. Such mysticism constitutes a retreat from real life into an esoteric ideology that may seem comforting but is finally pernicious.

IBARGÜENGOITIA, Antonio. Alonso De La Veracruz, Testigo De Su Tiempo. *Rev Filosof(Mexico)* 17,275–290 My–Jl 84.

Exposición biobibliográfica de Alonso de la Veracruz, en la cual se describe su papel en la Orden Agustiniana, su labor como fundador de la primera biblioteca de América, su actuación como evangelizador de los ingígenas, tantao en América como en Filipinas, así como su obra escrita que lo señala como el protofilósofo del Nuevo Mundo.

IDAN, Asher. Bergson's Philosophy Of Language (in Hebrew). *Iyyun* 34,34–48 Ja–Ap 85.

The paper analyzes Bergson's philosophy of language according to four modern areas: (1) philosophical logic and analytical philosophy; (2) philosophy of action and natural language; (3) psycholinguistics and sociolinguistics; (4) biology and the evolution of language. My contention is that non–canonical Continental philosophy of language (like that of Hegel or Bergson) can throw light on many issues that the canonical philosophy of language (Russell, Wittgenstein, Carnap, Austin, Searle, etc.) deals with. I try to show that Bergson anticipated many recent insights concerning the primacy of action in linguistic affairs, the importance of social considerations in understanding verbal behavior, and the practical origins of semantical and logical paradoxes and antinomies.

IGLESIAS, Teresa. Russell's *Theory Of Knowledge* And Wittgenstein's Earliest Writings. *Synthese* 60,285–332 S 84.

Bertrand Russell's *Theory of Knowledge* (1913) marks a new stage of development in his theory of the proposition which deeply affected Wittgenstein's emerging views on the matter: both Russell and Wittgenstein maintained that "we understand a proposition when we understand its constituents and form". Later in *The Tractatus*, Wittgenstein holds that a proposition is understood by any one who understands its constituents, (4.024). The reasons for this movement from *'constituents and form'* to *'constituents'* only, in Wittgenstein's earliest writings, and for Russell's own position, are elucidated in detail.

IGNATIEFF, Michael (ed) and Hont, Istvan (ed). *Wealth And Virtue: The Shaping Of Political Economy In The Scottish Enlightenment.* NY Cambridge Univ Pr 1983.

IHARA, Craig K. Maximin And Other Decision Principles. *Phil Topics* 12,59–72 Wint 81.

Given the conditions set out in Rawls' original position, I argue that the two principles of justice are the rational choice according to several rational strategies, and not only according to maximin. One consequence is that much of the discussion of risk aversion and maximin in Rawls and many commentators has been misguided and unnecessary. Another is that the two principles also can be regarded as a utilitarian solution to the original position.

IHARA, Craig K. Moral Skepticism And Tolerance. *Teach Phil* 7,193–198 Jl 84.

Students frequently maintain that moral skepticism, defined as the view that "there are not rationally justified moral judgements", entails that one "ought to be tolerant". Philosophy instructors are quick to reply that believing "you ought to be tolerant" is itself a moral judgement and, as such, pragmatically inconsistent with belief in ethical skepticism. In defense of students, this paper constructs a valid argument that derives the claim "you ought to be tolerant" from moral skepticism.

ILIESCU, Adrian–Paul. The New Metascientific Paradigm And The Linguistic Turn. *Phil Log* 28,139–146 Ap–Je 84.

ILLICH, Ivan. *Medical Nemesis: The Expropiation Of Health.* NY Pantheon Books 1976.

The author argues that the medical establishment has become a major threat to our health. He presents an analysis of doctor caused illnesses and traces their effects on our social order, our concept of death, and on politics. (staff)

ILTING, K –H. "Hegel's Concept Of The State And Marx's Early Critique" in *The State And Civil Society*, Pelczynski, Z A (ed), 93–113. Cambridge Cambridge Univ Pr 1984.

ILTING, K –H. "The Dialectic Of Civil Society" in *The State And Civil Society*, Pelczynski, Z A (ed), 211–226. Cambridge Cambridge Univ Pr 1984.

IMBER, Jonathan B. The Well–Informed Citizen: Alfred Schutz And Applied Theory. *Human Stud* 7,117–126 1984.

This essay assesses Alfred Schutz's concepts of intrinsic and imposed relevances; his elaboration of the notions of socially approved and socially derived knowledge; and his implicit view of authority given these previous distinctions. The well–informed citizen, the expert and the man on the street are described. The relationships among these ideal–typical ways of knowing are addressed. In conclusion, Schutz's choice of public opinion as the main principle of authority in modern societies are discussed.

IMLAY, Robert A. Descartes, Russell, Hintikka And The Self. *Stud Leibniz* 17,77–86 1985.

This article is divided into three sections. In the first section we examine Descartes' contention that a mode of thought makes essential reference to a person along with Russell's contention that it does not. In the second section we try to show how Descartes might reply to the criticism that his contention renders his proof for his own existence question–begging. Finally, in the last section we examine his complex attitude towards the general principle "it is impossible for that which is thinking to be nonexistent".

IMRE, Ruzsa. Two Variants Of The System Of Entailment. *Z Math Log* 21,57–68 1975.

INADA, Kenneth K. Two Strains In Buddhist Causality. *J Chin Phil* 12,49–56 Mr 85.

Buddhist causality refers to the technical term, pratityasamutpada, variously translated as dependent origination or relational origination. It is the deepest metaphysical penetration into the nature of experience attributed to the historical Buddha. Problems in interpreting it stem largely from the inability to distinguish between the bounded and unbounded strains of the experiential process. The essay sets out to demonstrate such strains.

INBODY, Tyron. Bernard Meland: "A Rebel Among Process Theologians". *Amer J Theol Phil* 5,43–71 My & S 84.

Although Bernard Meland is a major representative of the basic insights and convictions of process theology, he is a "rebel" in at least four different ways from the direction recent process theology has gone. He differs over the nature and role of process philosophy in process theology; he stresses radical empiricism over rational empiricism; he emphasizes the "principle of limitation" within all human structures; and he balances a theme of dissonance as well as coherence in his view of experience.

INGRAM, Thomas N and Dubinsky, Alan J. Correlates Of Salespeople's Ethical Conflict: An Exploratory Investigation. *J Bus Ethics* 3,343–353 N 84.

Much have been written about marketing ethics. Virtually no published research, however, has examined what factors are related to the ethical conflict of salespeople. Such research is important because it could have direct implications for the management of sales personnel. This paper presents the results of an exploratory study that examined selected correlates of salespeoples's ethical conflict. Implications for practitioners and academics are also provided.

INNIS, Robert E. Technics And The Bias Of Perception. *Phil Soc Crit* 10,67–90 Sum 84.

What types of categories and methods and what types of paradigmatic examples enable us to thematize, radically and comprehensively, the transformations of perceptual structures attendant upon technics, understood as 'organ projection'? Materials from phenomenology, Dewey's aesthetics, and Polanyi's cognitional theory are applied to a wide range of historical examples to illustrate a method of analysis. The conclusion is: perceptual structures are a–critically transformed by our 'indwelling' in novel sets of subsidiarily intended particulars.

INWOOD, Brad and Hunter, Graeme. Plato, Leibniz, And The Furnished Soul. *J Hist Phil* 22,423–434 O 84.

This paper is an examination and comparison of Plato's and Leibniz's views on innate knowledge. Examining first the theory of recollection in the *Meno* and the *Phaedo*, with emphasis on Plato's exploitation of the analogy with ordinary remembering and his consequent acceptance of the soul's pre-existence, we then consider Leibniz, with special regard to his *Discourse on Metaphysics* and *New Essays*. (edited)

INWOOD, M J. "Hegel, Plato And Greek 'Sittlichkeit'" in *The State And Civil Society*, Pelczynski, Z A (ed), 40-54. Cambridge Cambridge Univ Pr 1984.

IOAN, Petru. Contradictional Logic--Its Limits And The Significance Of A Reformatory Programme. *Phil Log* 27,315-323 O-D 83.

IOPPOLO, Anna Maria. 'Lo Stoicismo Di Erillo'. *Phronesis* 30,58-78 1985.

Herillus of Calcedonias is considered by ancient sources a heterodox Stoic. The fact that he saw the end in science does not indicate a substantial deviation from the zenonian point of view, from which he retained the necessity of internal consistency of logos, but is determined by the need to defend the Stoic doctrine from the objection of Arcesilaus. If such little memory of Hercillus' philosophy is found in the sources this is due to the fact--as Cicero tells us--Chrysippus argued against him in such a way as to make his doctrine lack any interest for future philosophers.

IRIARTE, Felipe. Los Argumentos Teísticos De J B Manyà, Por Felipe Iriarte. *Espiritu* 34,49-76 Ja-Je 85.

IRVINE, William B. Russell's Construction Of Space From Perspectives. *Synthese* 60,333-348 S 84.

In *Our Knowledge of the External World* and other early works, Bertrand Russell describes a program to construct the external world from sensibilia. Central to this program is Russell's construction of space from perspectives. In my paper, I describe Russell's constructive method, I discuss Russell's notion of a perspective and his construction of space from perspectives, and I present reasons of a technical sort for thinking this construction to be a failure.

IRWIN, Martin and Gallant, Donald M. "The Right To Refuse Psychotropic Medications" in *Difficult Decisions In Medical Ethics*, Ganos, Doreen L (ed), 31-38. NY Liss 1983.

IRWIN, Terence (trans). *Aristotle: Nicomachean Ethics*. Indianapolis Hackett 1985.

IRZIK, Gürol. Popper's Piecemeal Engineering: What Is Good For Science Is Not Always Good For Society. *Brit J Phil Sci* 36,1-10 Mr 85.

ISENBERG, Sheldon R and Thursby, G R. A Perennial Philosophy Perspective On Richard Rorty's Neo-Pragmatism. *Int J Phil Relig* 17,41-66 1985.

The article examines the assumptive frameworks of critiques of modern philosophy underlying Richard Rorty's neo-pragmatism and Seyyed Hossein Nasr's "perennial philosophy". Although their evaluations of positivism and linguistic analysis are remarkably similar, each perspective is grounded in a vastly different philosophical anthropology. The difference is illustrated in their understanding of the function of philosophy: Rorty's neo-pragmatist "philosophy of vacuum" serves solely a deconstructive, critical function, while the perennialist "philosophy of plenum" is redemptive.

ISRAEL, Joachim. Orwell And The Intellectuals. *Praxis Int* 4,313-321 O 84.

ISTVÁN, Fehér M. *Jean-Paul Sartre (in Hungarian)*. Budapest Kossuth 1980.

ISTVÁN, Fehér M. *Martin Heidegger* (in Hungarian). Budapest Kossuth 1984.

IWASAKI, Chikatsugu. Über Das Philosophische Leben In Japan. *Deut Z Phil* 23,1076-1082 1975.

IZENBERG, Gerald N. "Ethics And Excuses: Ethical Implications Of Psychoanalysis" in *Darwin, Marx And Freud*, Caplan, Arthur L (ed), 201-208. NY Plenum Pr 1984.

IZUTSU, Toshihiko. *The Interior And Exterior In Zen Buddhism*. Dallas Spring 1975.

JACKENDOFF, Ray. "Sense And Reference In A Psychologically Based Semantics" in *Talking Minds*, Bever, Thomas G (ed), 49-72. Cambridge MIT Pr 1984.

JACKENDOFF, Ray. Information Is In The Mind Of The Beholder. *Ling Phil* 8,23-34 F 85.

The approach of Barwise and Perry's situation semantics (*Situations and Attitudes*, 1983) is compared with my representationalist mentalist position (*Semantics and Cognition*, 1983). It is shown that many aspects of language depend on speaker's construal of the external world, not on the "objective, Real" situation in the world. Such aspects include the use of pragmatic anaphora (deixis), the system of thematic relations, and the description of representational objects such as pictures, stories, and beliefs. It is concluded that semantic theory should not be concerned with relation between sentences and the world, but the relation between sentences and speaker's mental representations.

JACKSON, David. "Ethical Decisions In The Intensive Care Unit" in *Difficult Decisions In Medical Ethics*, Ganos, Doreen L (ed), 125-134. NY Liss 1983.

JACKSON, Frank. Internal Conflicts In Desires And Morals. *Amer Phil Quart* 22,105-114 Ap 85.

Some writers on moral dilemmas have argued that it may be the case that some agent ought to do A and ought to do B, even when A and B are mutually exclusive. Many writers on action have assumed that an agent may want to do A and want to do B, even when A and B are known to be mutually exclusive. This paper is a constructive attack on both positions, particularly focusing on the second.

JACKSON, Frank. On Indicative Conditionals With Contrary Consequents. *Phil Stud* 46,141-144 S 84.

I show how David Lewis's result that for some P, $P(A \rightarrow C) \neq P(C/A)$, together with Ernest Adam's widely accepted thesis that the assertibility of $(A \rightarrow C) = P(C/A)$, counts against the often expressed view that indicative conditionals with the same, possible antecedent and contrary consequents are themselves contraries.

JACKSON, Jerry. Crossword Puzzles For Introductory Courses In Philosophy. *Teach Phil* 8,47-53 Ja 85.

The purpose is to help students learn philosophical terminology through the use of four crossword puzzles, one each for ethics, metaphysics and epistemology, philosophy of religion, and social and political philosophy. Suggestions are also given for creating your own crossword puzzles for other topics.

JACKSON, M W. Aristotle On Rawls: A Critique Of Quantitative Justice. *J Value Inq* 19,99-110 1985.

Imagine that in Book II of *The Politics* Aristotle reviews John Rawls *A Theory of Justice*. In this review Aristotle finds Rawl's theory to be based upon quantitative justice, satisfied by equal shares of material goods. For Aristotle this material equality is neither a means to nor an end of justice. In response Aristotle advocates a complex theory of justice combining identity, excellence and capacity.

JACOBS, Hans-Jürgen and Herlitzius, Erwin. The Humanism Of Associated Work And The Problem Of The Technology Laws (in German). *Deut Z Phil* 33,415-424 1985.

Laws of technology are concerned with dynamic systems depending on associated labor and human work design criteria. Descriptive and normative modes unite to integrating information technology to realize goals and effective means. Structural and functional equivalence is brought into focus. Any innovation proceeds from evolutionary potentials: qualitative redundancy, variability and flexibility. Reliability tends to informational certainty including control of embedded (still unexplained) interdependency. Hierarchical structures need complex timing in processing and prognostication of differently substituted equipment.

JACOBS, Jonathan. The Place Of Virtue In Happiness. *J Value Inq* 19,171-182 1985.

Essential to happiness is the enjoyment of how one exercises their capacity of self-determination. The place of virtue in happiness is central because virtue is the maximal exercise of that capacity. It is the end over which an agent has maximal authority and responsibility, and it is desirable for its own sake and worthwhile to strive to realize it.

JACOBY, Henry. Eliminativism, Meaning, And Qualitative States. *Phil Stud* 47,257-270 Mr 85.

In this paper I argue that many of the arguments for eliminative materialism presuppose our acceptance of a certain theory of meaning for theoretical terms. I show that by adopting a version of Putnam's theory of meaning, we can undermine the eliminativists' arguments. This theory of meaning also provides us with the basis for a reply to an argument against a certain kind of functionalism, raised by Sydney Shoemaker.

JACQUETTE, Dale. Analogical Inference In Hume's Philosophy Of Religion. *Faith Phil* 2,287-294 Jl 85.

The problem of evil in Hume's philosophy of religion is supposed to establish a moral disanalogy between human and divine intelligence. But consistent application of the principles of analogical inference in Hume's discussion of the argument from design supports the contrary conclusion that if there is an intelligent designer of the universe, then most probably the designer is not amoral, but has good, evil, or some combination of good and evil human-like psychological qualities.

JACQUETTE, Dale. Bosanquet's Concept Of Difficult Beauty. *J Aes Art Crit* 43,79-88 Fall 84.

Bosanquet introduces the concept of difficult beauty to describe an aesthetic paradox about the nonexistence of true ugliness. The argument is undermined by another, structurally similar paradox to the effect that nothing has genuinely difficult beauty in Bosanquet's sense of the word. An alternative characterization is proposed, according to which an object is difficultly beautiful if unusual effort is required to appreciate its beauty.

JACQUETTE, Dale. Roland Barthes On The Aesthetics Of Photography. *J Theor Crit Vis Arts* 1,17-34 1982.

Roland Barthes' scientific semiology in *Image-Music-text* is contrasted with his nonscientific subjective phenomenology of photography in *Camera Lucida: Reflections on Photography*. The distinction between *studium* and *punctum*, and the intentionality of photographic images derived from Sartre's existential philosophical psychology are explained. Barthes' theory is criticized on a number of grounds as failing to provide a satisfactory definition of photography. Hypotheses linking Barthes' alternative approaches to the aesthetics of photography are offered.

JAESCHKE, Walter. "World History & The History Of The Absolute Spirit" in *History And System*, Perkins, Robert (ed), 101-122. Albany SUNY Pr 1984.

JAFFRAY, J Y. Interpersonal Level Comparability Does Not Imply Comparability Of Utility Differences—A Comment On Ng. *Theor Decis* 19,201-203 S 85.

A counter-example to NG's claim that interpersonal level comparability implies comparability of utility differences is provided and the real significance of NG's result is evaluated.

JAGER, Gerhard. The Strength Of Admissibility Without Foundation. *J Sym Log* 49,867-879 S 84.

JAMES, David. What Is Professional Ethics? *Phil Res Arch* 10,micro Supp 1985.

Both the writings of moral philosophers and of reflective professionals are employed to answer the title's question. A rule-utilitarian moral theory is defended and the alleged relativism of role-specific duties is argued to be a badly posed issue. Alternative theories of the foundations of professional ethics are criticized, and a sorting scheme is developed to clarify differences among types of moral rules. Finally, a theory of virtue is defended as a way of incorporating the most significant aspects of virtue ethics into an overall rule-utilitarian framework.

JAMES, Henry. *Lectures And Miscellanies*. NY AMS Pr 1983.

JAMES, Henry. *Morality And The Perfect Life*. NY AMS Pr 1983.

JAMES, William. *The Essential Writings*, Bruce W Wilshire (ed). Albany SUNY Pr 1984.

JAMESON, Fredric (ed). *Sartre After Sartre*. New Haven Yale Univ Pr 1985.

JAMME, Christoph. "Dem Dichten Vor–Denken": Aspekte Von Heideggers "Zwiesprache" Mit Hölderlin Im Kontext Seiner Kunstphilosophie. *Z Phil Forsch* 38,191–218 Ap–Je 84.

Nachdem mittlerweile alle drei Vorlesungen über Hölderlin von Heidegger im Druck vorliegen, versucht Verf, Heideggers Deutung dieses Dichters entwicklungsgeschichtlich zu untersuchen und in den Kontext seiner zweiphasigen Kunstphilosophie zu stellen. Gezeigt werden dabei weniger die philologischen Mängel der Deutung, als vielmehr ihre praktisch–politischen Implikationen, die sie mit der Kritischen Theorie verbinden.

JANIK, Allan. "Comment's On Jost Halfmann's Article" in *Methodology, Metaphysics And The History Of Science*, Cohen, Robert S (ed), 173–182. Boston Reidel 1984.

JANIK, Allan. "Haecker, Kierkegaard, And The Early Brenner" in *International Kierkegaard Commentary*, Perkins, Robert L (ed), 189–222. Macon Mercer Univ Pr 1984.

JANKOWSKI, Andrzej W. A Conjunction In Closure Spaces. *Stud Log* 43,341–352 1984.

This paper is closely related to investigations of abstract properties by basic logical notions expressible in terms of closure spaces as they were begun by A Tarski (see [6]). We shall prove many properties of ω–conjunctive closure spaces (X is ω–conjunctive provided that for every two elements of X their conjunction in X exists). For example we prove the following theorems: 1. for every closed and proper subset of an ω–conjunctive closure space its interior is empty (i.E., it is a boundary set). 2. if X is aω–conjunctive closure space which satisfies the ω–compactness theorem and $\hat{P}$ [X] is a meet–distributive semilattice (see [3]), then the lattice of all closed subsets in X is a Heyting lattice. 3. a closure space is linear iff it is an ω conjunctive and topological space. 4. every continuous function preserves all conjunctions.

JANKOWSKI, H. A Comment To J Gockowski's *Situational Tests Of A Scholar's Faithfullness To His Ethos* (in Polish). *Etyka* 21,165–170 1985.

JANSEN, Robert P S. Sperm And Ova As Property. *J Med Ethics* 11,123–126 S 85.

To whom do sperm and ova belong? Few tissues are produced by the human body with more waste than the germ cells. Yet dominion over the germ cells, and over the early embryo that results from their union in vitro, is behind much of the emotion that modern reproductive intervention can engender. The germ cells differ from other human tissues that can be donated or transplanted because they carry readily utilisable genetic information. Eventual expression of the germ cells' genetic potential is the legitimate concern and responsibility for their donors, although in the right circumstances the responsibility can by agreement be entrusted to institutions administering gamete or embryo donor programs; these institutions, in turn, may need to assume responsibility for decisions if, in the case of embryo storage, the wishes of the two donors confict. The fact of sperm and ovum ownership (and the genetic potential that goes with it) before individuals part with these tissues is beyond dispute. Some contentious issues may be clarified if this area of human dominion, namely control over genetic expression of offsring, is acknowledged to be legitimate persisting concern of those who have produced sperm and ova after storage.

JANSSEN, Martin. Nutzenkalkül Und Eigentumsrechte: Ein Ökonomischer Ansatz Zu Einer Positiven Theorie Des Eigentums. *Stud Phil (Switzerland)* Supp 12,331–348 1983.

JANSSEN, Peter L. Political Thought As Traditionary Action: The Critical Response To Skinner And Pocock. *Hist Theor* 24,115–146 My 85.

The methodological work of Quentin Skinner and J G A Pocock in the history of political thought has generated intense debate. Much of the response continues to be preoccupied with a number of familiar dichotomies—"history" vs "philosophy"; the autonomy of texts vs ideas as expressions of social relations; voluntarism vs determinism; language as either instrumental or restrictive—along with certain epistemological assumptions and a reified concept of tradition. A new approach to these issues, based upon Skinner's and Pocock's work, points towards a theory of traditionary action.

JANTZEN, Grace M. Human Diversity And Salvation In Christ. *Relig Stud* 20,579–592 D 84.

What sense can be made of a doctrine of salvation within Christianity when once it takes seriously the fact of human diversity? I argue that any adequate doctrine of salvation will need to indicate *from* what we are saved, *to* what we are saved, and what is the *means* of salvation. When these questions are examined in the light of cultural diversity, exclusivist answers of heaven and hell are seen to be inadequate, though I argue that it is still possible to find salvation in Christ as the manifestation of the law of God.

JARCZYK, Gwendoline. Concept Du Travail Et Travail Du Concept Chez Hegel. *Arch Phil* 48,21–36 Ja–Mr 85.

According to Hegel, work just as language, is an "exterioration" (Äusserung) of the spirit, making the world's immediacy into the middle term of "formation" or "culture" of man and of men. It is a syllogistical movement akin to reflexion, with its double movement of presupposition: work of the concept on itself which determines the content of work.

JARRETT, Jon P. On The Physical Significance Of The Locality Conditions In The Bell Arguments. *Nous* 18,569–590 N 84.

The "locality" condition employed in the derivation of generalized Bell–type inequalities is shown to be equivalent to the conjunction of two weaker conditions, one of which is the relativistic prohibition against superluminal signals and the other of which is a classically–plausible "completeness" constraint on state descriptions. Bell–type experiments provide good evidence that the quantum–mechanical violation of the completeness condition reflects a genuine feature of the world itself.

JARVIE, I C. *Rationality And Relativism: In Search Of A Philosophy And History Of Anthropology*. Boston Routledge & K Paul 1984.

It is argued that the doctrine of the rational unity of mankind is inconsistent with the forms of relativism usually adopted by anthropologists. The full ramifications of this doctrine of relativism in anthropological thought and practice are explored in order to understand its appeal. It is shown to offer no barrier to the morally repugnant ideas it sought to replace. A reaffirmation of the moral unity and rationality of mankind is suggested as a philosophy for anthropology, with its consequences of treating other peoples as responsible equals.

JASON, Gary J. Science And Common Sense. *J Crit Anal* 8,117–124 1985.

The issue of whether the epistemologist should focus upon ordinary contexts of knowledge or cases from the history of science is raised. The advantages of both approaches are explored, and a compromise approach (namely, the use of model research games) is suggested.

JASON, Gary J. Two Problems Of Induction. *Dialectica* 39,53–74 1985.

In this paper, two different theoretical problems of induction are delineated. The first problem is addressed; the second problem is deferred to the sequel of this paper. The first problem of induction is taken to be the seemingly unformalizable nature of traditional inductive arguments. It is shown that the problem does not arise out of some particularly dubious argument form (all inductive argument forms being interderivable), but rather from the presupposition that inductive "logic" is, like deductive logic, assertoric. Rather (it is argued), inductive logic is dialectical in nature.

JAUCH, Liane. Owen's Communism And The Neo–Left–Wing Reconstruction Of History; War And Peace In The Ideological Confrontation (in German). *Deut Z Phil* 32,1075–1084 1984.

JAUSS, Hans Robert. *The Dialogical And The Dialectical Nerveau De Rameau*. Berkeley Ctr For Herm Stud 1983.

JAUSS, Hans Robert. "Le Neveu De Rameau": Dialogique Et Dialectique (Ou: Diderot Lecteur De Socrate Et Hegel Lecteur De Diderot). *Rev Metaph Morale* 89,145–181 Ap–Je 84.

JAY, Martin. *Adorno*. Cambridge Harvard Univ Pr 1984.

JAYNES, E T. Some Random Observations. *Synthese* 63,115–138 Ap 85.

A summary of recent developments in the conceptual status and scientific use of probability theory. Attempts to clear up some widespread misconceptions about the nature and relation of Bayesian and Maximum Entropy principles, and to point out the dangers of careless use of infinite sets.

JEANNIÈRE, Abel. Dans Le Maquis Des Racismes. *Etudes* 361,293–307 O 84.

An attempt to classify the different types of racism with their psychological and social causes. Racism founded on biology, on cultural difference or disarray. Egalitariam also may be connected with racism by denying the differences.

JEFFREY, R C. "Probability And Art Of Judgment" in *Observation, Experiment, And Hypothesis In Modern Physical Science*, Achinstein, Peter (ed), 95–126. Cambridge MIT Pr 1985.

JEFFREY, Richard. "Bayesianism With A Human Face" in *Testing Scientific Theories*, Earman, John (ed), 133–156. Minneapolis Univ Minnesota Pr 1983.

JEHENSON, Roger. Effectiveness, Expertise And Excellence As Ideological Fictions: A Contribution To A Critical Phenomenology Of The Formal Organization. *Human Stud* 7,3–22 1984.

JENNER, Donald. Problems In The Social Sciences: Prolegomena To A Study Of Cities. *Cogito* 3,91–132 Mr 85.

The paper is a preliminary study for a book on the ontology of cities as specifically human enclaves. It has two intentions, to express (again) some of the problems which obtain in social–scientific accounts of things in general, and specifically, to focus on the problems of social–scientific accounts of cities. Taking a hint from Aristotle, it seems modern sciences, and social science especially, only afford what might be called "material" and "efficient" accounts of their objects. Cities, on the other hand, as specifically human, need "formal," and more especially, "final" accounts to make sense of them.

JENNER, F A (ed) and De Koning, A J J (ed). *Phenomenology And Psychiatry*. London Academic Pr 1982.

This book attempts to present facets of the Phenomenological Movement to the English–speaking world of Psychiatry and Clinical Psychology. In particular it includes translations from French, German, Spanish, dutch, and Japanese writers, each influenced by Husserl, Heidegger, Jaspers, Merleau–Ponty and/or Sartre, and attempting to establish their relevance in Clinical Psychiatry.

JENNINGS, Bruce (ed) and Caplan, Arthur L (ed). *Darwin, Marx, And Freud: Their Influence On Moral Theory*. NY Plenum Pr 1984.

While many philosophers and theologians have attempted to give Marxist, Freudian, or Darwinian interpretations of morality, little inquiry has been devoted to the views about morality held by these three thinkers. None of them can be said to have held explicit normative theories of ethics, but all of them advanced claims about the objectivity and testability of moral claims. The essays in this book attempt to examine both the views of these three thinkers regarding ethics as well as their influence on contemporary moral thought.

JENNINGS, R E and Schotch, P K. The Preservation Of Coherence. *Stud Log* 43,89–106 1984.

It is argued that the preservation of truth by an inference relation is of little interest when premiss sets are contradictory. The notion of a level of coherence is introduced and the utility of modal logics in the semantic representation of sets of higher coherence levels is noted. It is shown that this representative role cannot be transferred to first order logic via frame theory since the modal formula expressing coherence level restrictions are not first order definable. Finally, an inference relation, called *yielding*, is introduced which is intermediate between the coherence preserving *forcing* relation introduced elsewhere by the authors and the coherence destroying inference relation of classical logic.

JENNINGS, Richard C. Truth, Rationality And The Sociology Of Science. *Brit J Phil Sci* 35,201–211 S 84.

Some philosophers of science argue that sociology of science can only be concerned with scientific claims which are not rational (or 'not true'). Taking Larry Laudan's defense of his 'arationality assumption' as typical, I show that his arguments are not sound, that the arationality assumption has absurd consequences, and that the arationality assumption undermines the possibility of fruitful cooperation between philosophers and sociologists of science. I conclude that the arationality assumption should be rejected.

JETZSCHMANN, Horst. Probleme Der Gesellschaftlichen Aktivität Der Arbeiterklasse In Der Materiellen Produktion. *Deut Z Phil* 22,145–153 1974.

Der Begriff gesellschaftliche Aktivität bringt jene Eigenschaften zum Ausdruck, deren Grad der Entwicklung und qualitativen Ausprägung die Fähigkeit der Arbeiterklasse widerspiegelt, auf dem Wege zum entwickelten Sozialismus voranzuschreiten und alle progressiven Kräfte um sich zu vereinigen. Der Begriff orientiert darauf, nicht einseitig Kenntnisniveau und Meinungen über gesellschaftliche Vorgänge und ihre Gesetzmäßigkeiten zu erfassen, sondern ausgehend von den objektiven Erfordernissen das Subjekt der Geschichte in seiner Einheit von Bewußtsein und Handeln zu begreifen.

JHINGRAN, Saral. Theism And Monism—Reconciled In Absolutistic World View. *Indian Phil Quart* 11,217–228 Ap 84.

Theism emphasizes God's transcendence and otherness, pantheism denies them and monism affirms both transcendence and immanence. While personal God of theism seems limited by his creation, monistic Absolute is too abstract. A new version of absolutistic monism, as suggested by C Hartshorne and W L Reese, and anticipated by Upanisads, Ramanuja, Echhart, Ibnu'l Arabi, conceives Absolute as an all–inclusive reality which comprehends within It universal cause (creator God) and effects (creation) and is transcendent to and immanent in universe.

JIANG, Paul Yun–Ming. The Concept Of Mind In Chu Hsi's Ethics. *Phil Rev (Taiwan)* 7,27–54 Ja 84.

The purpose of the paper is to attempt to examine Chu Hsi's concept of mind in the context of his ethical system, as well as the ontological status of the mind and its relation with human nature, feelings and principle in particular, and in addition to make some reflections on his epistemology. It was because of his concerted effort that a rational and practical basis for Confucian philosophy was firmly established as the guiding principle for Chinese culture.

JIMÉNEZ, Carlos Molina. La Concepción Hegeliana Del Estado Y Su Crítica Por El Joven Marx. *Rev Filosof (Costa Rica)* 23,31–48 Je 85.

This essay studies, in the first place, the Hegelian concept of state. It explains how this idea was established along the development of Hegel thinking further on it stops to consider in detail the concept of state in Hegel's mature thinking. In this last step, it talks about the dialectics of the Objective Spirit, because it involves the knowledge that makes up the idea of state.

JIRÁSEK, Jaroslav. Prigogine's Situationism (in Czechoslovakian). *Filozof Cas* 32,825–830 1984.

Prigogine's discoveries implicate corrections not only of the body of natural science. He himself extended them to philosophy. Applying new knowledge to society he employs situational approach. Terms as "self–organizing memory", "successive instability", "organizing opportunity", "turbulence of life", etc., are definitely close to the pluralistic concept of western political life. His statememt "truth is in the situation" relativises studies of society. The author argues critical discord from the Marxist point of view.

JIRASEK, J. The Importance Of The Changing Of Technological Ways Of Production In Marx's Conception Of Scientific Foreseeing (in Czechoslovakian). *Filozof Cas* 32,683–696 1984.

JOBST, Eberhard and Marmai, U. Weltanschauliche Und Wissenschaftstheoretische Probleme Des Verhältnisses Von Natur– Und Technikwissenschaften. *Deut Z Phil* 23,757–766 1975.

Die Autoren behandeln die Notwendigkeit und Spezifik der technikwissenschaftlichen Umsetzung naturwissenschaftlicher Erkenntnisse. Die allgemeinen Merkmale des Wechselverhältnisses von Natur– und Technikwissenschaften werden am Beispiel der historischen und gegenwärtigen Entwicklung der thermodynamischen Theorian über die gemeinsame Wärmeund Stoffübertragung dargestellt. Ferner werden einige Momente der Beziehungen von Technik– und Gesellschaftswissenschaften im Sozialismus untersucht.

JOBST, E. Der Wissenschaftlich–Technische Fortschritt Und Die Interdisziplinäre Zusammenarbeit Von Philosophen Und Technikwissenschaftlern. *Deut Z Phil* 33,323–331 1985.

JOCKUSCH JR, Carl G and Shore, Richard A. Pseudo–Jump Operators: II, Transfinite Iterations, Hierarchies And Minimal Covers. *J Sym Log* 49,1205–1236 D 84.

JOFFE, Josef. Nuclear Weapons, No First Use, And European Order. *Ethics* 95,606–618 Ap 85.

The article defines the nature of Europe's postwar order and elucidates the prominent role of nuclear weapons have played in maintaining the stability of that order. It argues that a runciation of the current "no–first–use" posture, as contained in NATO's official "flexible response" doctrine, will diminish stability rather than enhance it as the proponents of "no–first–use" have argued.

JOHN, Erhard. Sozialistischer Humanismus—Sozialistischer Realismus. *Deut Z Phil* 32,908–915 1984.

JOHN, Erhard. Towards The Relation Of Art And Morality (in Czechoslovakian). *Estetika* 22,41–51 1985.

JOHNSON, Conrad D. The Authority Of The Moral Agent. *J Phil* 82,391–413 Ag 85.

The purpose of this article is to reconcile agent–constrraints of the deontological point of view with a broader consequentialism. It is proposed that a two–level model—a kind of rule consequentialism—can accomplish this. The proposal here is to use the notion of actual, rather than hypothetical rules (within limits) defining the morally right, and to use the notion of collective social authority external to the moral agent as the key to providing for stability of the two levels. The evaluation and revision of moral rules is thus taken to be an exercise of collective, rather than individual, authority.

JOHNSON, Curtis. The Hobbesian Conception Of Sovereignty And Aristotle's Politics. *J Hist Ideas* 46,327–348 Jl–S 85.

Hobbes criticized Aristotle's *Politics* sharply for its failure to locate sovereign authority in the laws of the state instead of in men wielding instruments of coersion. I argue here that Aristotle was not guilty of this defect charged by Hobbes. One finds in the *Politics* a theory of positive sovereign power much like Hobbes' own—one which located sovereignty in the coercive apparatus of the state, above the laws and giving them their force.

JOHNSON, David M. Hume's Missing Shade Of Blue, Interpreted As Involving Habitual Spectra. *Hume Stud* 10,109–124 N 84.

I deny Hume's claim that the case of the missing shade of blue is "singular", and therefore does not undermine his empiricism. Perhaps he meant one cannot generalize from it to (many) other cases because colors have no intrinsic, but only habitual relations. This is implausible for the reasons (1) It presupposes without proof that no child could imagine an unseen color. (2) It predicts that people from different 'habitual spectra' and thus have different abilities to imagine colors—which is empirically false. (3) It implies that we know with variable assurance that different pairs of colors exclude one another—which common sense shows is wrong.

JOHNSON, Galen A. Historicity, Narratives, And The Understanding Of Human Life. *J Brit Soc Phenomenol* 15,216–230 O 84.

JOHNSON, Galen and Kisiel, Theodore. New Philosophies Of Science In The USA; A Selective Survey. *Z Allg Wiss* 5,138–191 1974.

The following overview of the present situation and recent trends in the philosophy of science in the USA brings together bibliographical and institutional evidence to document the last stages of the suppression (Aufhebung) of logical positivism, the emergence of the historical school (Toulmin, Hanson, Kuhn, Feyerabend), its widespread influence upon other fields as well as within philosophy of science, and finally some of the reactions to it, many of which envision their endeavors as mediations between the historical school and the older logical approaches. (edited)

JOHNSON, James T. *Can Modern War Be Just?* New Haven Yale Univ Pr 1984.

JOHNSON, M Bruce (ed) and Machan, Tibor R (ed). *Rights And Regulation: Ethical, Political, And Economic Issues.* Cambridge Ballinger 1983.

This book examines the ethical/moral defenses and objections surrounding the institution of government regulation. Contributors include philosophers and economists, as well as legal theorists, who offer varied perspectives on the topic. A Foreward is offered by Aaron Wildowsky. The book has received awards for providing a unique approach to its subject matter, one not found in the economic or philosophical discussion of commerce.

JOHNSON, M Bruce. "Regulation And Justice: An Economist's Perspective" in *Rights And Regulation*, Machan, Tibor (ed), 127–136. Cambridge Ballinger 1983.

JOHNSON, Oliver A. Retributive Punishment And Humbling The Will. *J Value Inq* 19,155–162 1985.

The paper is an examination of Professor Herbert Fingarette's defense of retributive punishment, as it appears in his APA Presidential Address "Punishment and Suffering." According to that defense retributive punishment is a necessity internal to law. In other words, crime entails its rightful punishment. My paper maintains that there is a gap in the logic of this argument. Because crime does not entail punishment, a defense of retributivism based on such an assumtion breaks down.

JOHNSON, Paul. "Movement In The Market: Mobility And Economics In The Free Society" in *On Freedom*, Howard, John A (ed), 39–58. Greenwich Devin–Adair 1984.

JOHNSON, Ralph H and Blair, J Anthony. Informal Logic: The Past Five Years 1978–1983. *Amer Phil Quart* 22,181–196 Jl 85.

This article surveys developments in informal logic during the period from 1978–1983. It is a review of the monograph, journal article and textbook literature. A 90–item bibliography of works cited is appended. The authors detail developments in the theory of argument, the theory of criticism (including fallacy theory), testing and teaching. They conclude that informal logic has achieved a certain definition in a relatively short time, and recommend that future work include closer investigation of related problems of philosophy and of related work being done in cognate fields.

JOHNSON, Steve N. An Analytic–Existential Solution To The 'Knowing That One Knows' Problem. *Dialogue (PST)* 27,37–43 Ap 85.

JOHNSTON, R J. *Philosophy And Human Geography: An Introduction To Contemporary Approaches.* Baltimore Arnold 1983.

A brief, general introduction to the major philosophies employed by contemporary human geographers. Three sets of approaches are highlighted, with separate chapters on positivist, humanistic, and structuralist work; each chapter provides a brief outline of the relevant philosophies, and illustrates their use in human geography. A final chapter looks at the conflicts among the three and at arguments for their integration.

JOHNSTONE, Brian V. The Meaning Of Proportionate Reason In Contemporary Moral Theology. *Thomist* 49,223–247 Ap 85.

This article seeks to clarify the notion of proportionate reason as used by contemporary proponents of the method of moral analysis commonly called "proportionalism." Contemporary theories seek to determine the moral quality of acts by an assessment of the presence or absence of proportion. There are at least three distinct meanings and functions or proportions and five ways of calculating proportion. The notion is insufficiently clear to provide an instrument for moral analysis.

JOLLEY, Nicholas. *Leibniz And Locke: A Study Of The "New Essays On Human Understanding".* Oxford Clarendon Pr 1984.

The book aims to provide the first modern interpretation of Leibniz's *New Essays on Human Understanding.* It is argued that the work is no mere series of random criticisms of Locke's *Essay;* it is controlled throughout by the overriding purpose of refuting what Leibniz takes to be materialist tendency to Locke's philosophy. leibniz's views in the *New Essays* are also related to contemporary debates over such issues as innate ideas, personal identity, and natural kinds.

JOLY, H. "Faut-il Raconter Homère Aux Enfants" in *Asthetische Er Fahrung Und Das Wesen Der Kunst,* Holzhey, Helmut, 71-92. Bern Haupt 1984.

JOLY, Henri. Faut-Il Raconter Homère Aux Enfants: Ou: Des Valeurs Aux Anti-Valeurs. *Diotima* 12,139-157 1984.

JONAS, Hans. Ontological Grounding Of A Political Ethics: On The Metaphysics Of Commitment To The Future Of Man. *Grad Fac Phil J* 10,47-62 Spr 84.

JONES, Anne H. A Commentary On 'Two Pathographies: A Study In Illness And Literature'. *J Med Phil* 9,257-260 Ag 84.

JONES, Funmilayo M. The Provisional Homecomer. *Human Stud* 7,227-248 1984.

JONES, Gary E. A Response To Preus' *Respect For The Dead And Dying. J Med Phil* 9,417-418 N 84.

JONES, Gary E. Non-Medical Burdens Of The Defective Infant. *Phil Context* 14,29-34 1984.

JONES, J P and Matijasevic, Y V. Register Machine Proof Of The Theorem On Exponential Diophantine Representation Of Enumerable Sets. *J Sym Log* 49,818-829 S 84.

One of the historically important first steps in the eventual solution of Hilbert's tenth problem was the 1961 Theorem of Martin Davis, Hilary Putnam and Julia Robinson which states that every recursively enumerable set, *A* can be represented in exponential diophantine form. Recently a new very simple proof of this theorem was founded by James P Jones and Ju V Matijasevic. This new proof is based on register machines and uses only very elementary number theory, we need only the partial ordering less than or equal to defined by κ less than or equal to $\eta \leftrightarrow (\eta$ over $\kappa) \equiv 1$ (mod 2).

JONES, Joe E. Striking 'Commensurate' From The Oxford Translation. *Phil Res Arch* 10,197-202 1984.

This paper argues that G R G mure's use of "'commensurate universal' to translate 'katholou' is mistaken in An Post A24, and that throughout this chapter whenever the word 'katholou' appears it is to be translated 'universal' simpliciter. Establishing this requires a short commentary on Aristotle's use of the word 'katholou', which apparently he coined, and used none too carefully.

JONES, John. Simplified Axiom Schemes For Implication And Iterated Implication. *Z Math Log* 31,31-33 1985.

A general result (Jones, j Implication and iterated implication Z Math Log 29, pp 543-556 (1983)) giving complete formalizations of certain finite- and infinite- valued propositional calculi with variable functors taking values from a range of sets whose members are defined in terms of the primitive implication functor of Lukasiewicz is simplified for particular examples of sets in the finite-valued case.

JONES, John. Some Propositional Calculi With Constant And Variable Functors. *Z Math Log* 30,477-479 1984.

Existing formalizations of finite-and infinite-valued propositional calculi with variable functors taking values from sets whose members are defined in terms of Lukasiewiczs primitive implication functor are amended to give complete formalizations of the corresponding calculi having Lukasiewiczs primitve negation functor as an additional primitive constant.

JONES, Reynold. A Reply To Kieran Egan's "Development In Education". *J Phil Educ* 18,195-198 1984.

JONES, William B. Another Look At The Predictivist Thesis. *Phil Natur* 21,301-308 1984.

JONSEN, Albert R. "Public Policy And Human Research" in *Biomedical Ethics Reviews,* Humber, James M (ed), 3-22. Clifton Humana Pr 1984.

JOOHARIGIAN, Robert Badrik. *God And Natural Evil.* Bristol Wyndham Hall Pr 1985.

The author formulates an argument against religious belief based upon Hume's appeal to natural evil. He then responds to the argument by considering whether and to what extent a justification can be given for such evil in a world believed to be created by God. In his response, the author develops a cumulative theodicy of personality, communality, "theologicality," and of non-human creaturely life, in an effort to meet the objection posed by the Humean argument.

JOÓS, Ernest. Nietzsche Et Les Femmes. *Laval Theol Phil* 41,305-315 O 85.

L'auteur se propose de dissiper les malentendus les plus fréquents au sujet de l'interprétation du grand poète qu'est Nietzsche. Il étudie ensuite dans cet esprit les principaux textes nietzschéens sur les femmes.

JORDAN, Mark D. Authority And Persuasion In Philosophy. *Phil Ret* 18,67-85 1985.

JORDAN, Mark D. The Intelligibility Of The World And The Divine Ideas In Aquinas. *Rev Metaph* 38,17-32 S 84.

JORDAN, Richard D. Thomas Traherne And The Art Of Meditation. *J Hist Ideas* 46,381-404 Jl-S 85.

The writings of Thomas Traherne are set in the context of English devotional literature of the period 1650-1675. Works from the period are listed and described, with emphasis on the themes and techniques which they advocate for use in formal meditations. Traherne's own works are then shown to be similar in themes, techniques and in literary style to the works of their contemporary writers on meditation.

JOSEPH, Geoffrey. "Interpretation Theory And Experiment" in *Observation, Experiment, Hypothesis In Modern Physical Science,* Achinstein, Peter (ed), 175-204. Cambridge MIT Pr 1985.

JOY, Donald M (ed). *Moral Development Foundations: Judeo-Christian Alternatives To Piaget/Kohlberg.* Nashville Abington 1983.

The agnostic structural research/theory base of Jean Piaget and Lawrence Kohlberg is constructively critiqued and modified by nine of ten authors; one rejects. They identify both common ground and indicate corrections/adaptations they make in applying structural insights to their work in religious education. They speak from Jewish, Roman Catholic, Reformed, Lutheran, Baptist, Methodist, and Charismatic perspectives. Major emphases stress "community" versus privatism and individualism; blending of the noumenal with the phenomenal/empirical; interfacing the justice and love of Kohlberg and Gilligan with Bible concepts of righteousness, holiness, and love in the "image of God."

JOYNTON, Olin. The Problem Of Circularity In Wollaston's Moral Philosophy. *J Hist Phil* 22,435-444 O 84.

In *The Religion of Nature Delineated* (1722), William Wollaston argues that 1) some of our actions signify (or declare) propositions and 2) morally right actions declare true propositions, whereas wrong actions declare false ones. Hume, Price and Bentham charge circularity because of cases in which the proposition declared by the action involves prior moral valuations. This unjust charge of circularity confuses 1) what makes an action wrong and 2) what we use to identify wrongness. In fact, Wollaston's declarative action theory pertains only to the latter, not the former, and thus circularity of the kind alleged. (edited)

JUNANKAR, P N. *Marx's Economics.* Oxford Allan 1985.

The book provides an exposition, interpretation and evaluation of Marx's *economic* analysis: the labor theory of value and transformation problem, the dynamics of capital accumulation and its effects on the industrial reserve army and interaction with the falling rate of profit. Two chapters emphasize the role of money in a capitalist economy and its potential for crises. The penultimate chapter provides a consistent explanation of crises and the final chapter concludes with observations on Marx's contribution to Economics.

JUNG, L Shannon. Commercialization And The Professions. *Bus Prof Ethics J* 2,57-82 Wint 83.

Among the forces that motivate professional activity, the instrumental drive for personal rewards rather than public service is being bolstered by the social dynamic of commercialization. A survey of the literature (Magali Lawson, Eliot Freidson, Lieberman, Collins, Cullen) supporting this thesis precedes an examination of contemporary professions—particularly medicine, business, law, and education. The article concludes with a moral assessment of this development and suggestions for ameliorating the effects of commercialization.

JURGENS, Madeleine and Orzschig, Johannes. Korrespondenten Von G W Leibniz. *Stud Leibniz* 16,102-112 1984.

Brosseau, résident (1671-1717) of the Dukes of Hannover, got to know Leibniz in Paris. His correspondence and friendship with the philosopher helped to enlarge the république des lettres, "greatly animated by Leibniz" and "a consolation amidst the evils which ambition and politics are spreading over the earth" (Voltaire).

JUROS, Helmut. Remarques Sur L'éthique De La Science (in Polish). *Stud Phil Christ* 20,129-132 1984.

JURUKOVA, M M. Anti-Leninist Essence Of The Conception Of "New Philosophers" On Social Revolution (in Czechoslovakian). *Filozof Cas* 32,640-645 1984.

KAELIN, Eugene. "Toward A Theory Of Contemporary Tragedy" in *Existential Coordinates Of Human Condition,* Tymienecka, A (ed), 341-362. Boston Reidel 1984.

KAHL, A. Soziologische Forschung Zum Wohen Und Arbeiten In Der Stadt. *Deut Z Phil* 33,77-80 1985.

KAHLE, Werner. Marx' Kulturkonzeption In "Grundrisse Der Kritik Der Politischen Ökonomie": Zugleich Ein Programm Des Realen Humanismus. *Deut Z Phil* 32,899-907 1984.

KAHN, Beverly L. Antonio Gramsci's Reformulation Of Benedetto Croce's Speculative Idealism. *Ideal Stud* 15,18-40 Ja 85.

KAHN, Charles H. Democritus And The Origins Of Moral Psychology. *Amer J Philo* 106,1-31 Spr 85.

KAIN, Philip J. Marx And The Abolition Of Morality. *J Value Inq* 18,283-298 1984.

Marx's views on morality do not remain the same throughout all periods of his thought. This article examines his views only in the period of 1845-1857. It tries to show that especially in the *German Idealogy* Marx develops a doctrine of historical materialism according to which material conditions determine consciousness in such a strict way that moral obligation independent of those conditions is impossible. Morality, for Marx, is ideological illusion destined to disappear in communist society.

KAINZ, Howard P. La Philosophie Et L'écologie. *Laval Theol Phil* 41,433-435 O 85.

This article is concerned with the various theories of "stages of consciousness" in Hegel, Marx, Freud, Jung, Chardin and others, and the possible implications of these theories for ecology. Jl-S 85.

KAISER, Eckhard and Poldrack, H. Meinungsstreit Zu Fragen Der Marxistischen Wahrheitstheorie. *Deut Z Phil* 23,1067–1071 1975.

KAISER, Klaus. On Complementedly Normal Lattices II: Extensions. *Z Math Log* 30,567–573 1984.

KAIZIK, Peter. Zu Einigen Aktuellen Zügen Bürgerlicher Wissenschafts— Und Technikkritik. *Deut Z Phil* 33,544–547 1985.

KAKUDA, Yuzuru. "Precipitousness Of Ideal Of Thin Sets On Measurable Cardinal" in *Lecture Notes In Mathematics*, Muller, G H And Others (ed), 49–56. NY Springer 1981.

KALANTARI, I and Weitkamp, Galen. Effective Topological Spaces II: A Hierarchy. *Annals Pure Applied Log* 29,207–224 S 85.

KALANTARI, Iraj and Weitkamp, G. Effective Topological Spaces I: A Definability Theory. *Annals Pure Applied Log* 29,1–28 Jl 85.

KALFA, Cornelia. Decidable Properties Of Finite Sets Of Equations In Trivial Languages. *J Sym Log* 49,1333–1338 D 84.

Using Ehrenfeucht's theorem, that the theory generated by the logical axioms of trivial languages is decidable, I prove that in such languages the properties of finite sets σ of equations "the equational theory of σ is equationally complete," "the theory of the infinite models of σ is complete" and "σ has the joint embedding property" are decidable.

KALFA, Cornelia. Some Undecidability Results In Strong Algebraic Languages. *J Sym Log* 49,951–954 S 84.

It is proved that there is no algorithm for deciding whether a field is finite. This is used to prove that there are no algorithms for deciding whether a finite set Σ of equations of a strong algebraic with infinitely many operation symbols has the properties "the first–order theory of the non–trivial models of Σ is complete" and "the first–order theory of the non–trivial models of Σ is model complete."

KALFAS, Vassilis. A Restrictive Interpretation Of Lakatos' Rationality Theory. *Phil Natur* 21,376–381 1984.

A corroboration of Lakatos' theory of rationality requires the addition of three restrictive conditions: (a) that we concern ourselves only with the rigorously scientific rationality; (b) that our conclusions must be drawn and applied only the the mature sciences of the last 2 or 3 centuries; and (c) that we consider science as the collective product of scientific communities.

KALIN, Jesse. "Public Pursuit And Private Escape: The Persistence Of Egoism" in *Gewirth's Ethical Rationalism*, Regis Jr, Edward (ed), 128–146. Chicago Univ Of Chicago Pr 1984.

KALINOWSKI, Georges and Garoddies, Jean–louis. Un Logicien Déontique Avant La Lettre: Gottfried Wilhelm Leibniz. *Arch Rechts Soz* 60,79–112 1974.

In their introduction the authors sketch the story of R Blanché's rediscovery of Leibniz' texts containing his logic of norms. Then G Kalinowski analyses the *Theoremata qvibus combinantur Iuris Modalia inter se* (he draws from them Leibniz' theory of opposition of deontic statements, based on the analogy between these statements and the modal ones) and J –L Gardies studies the *Theoremata qvibus combinantur Iuris Modalibus Logicis*.

KALINOWSKI, Georges. Edith Stein Et Karol Wojtyla Sur La Personne. *Rev Phil Louvain* 82,545–561 N 84.

E Stein and K Wojtyla deserve comparison, although the thought of the latter was formed without the slightest influence of the former assistant E Husserl and even for that reason. The reason is because the phenomenologist, who came to initiate herself in the thought of St Thomas Aquinas, and the disciple of the Angelicum who was greatly influenced by Scheler both studied the human person in the light of the two philosophers synthesised by each of them. It is in fact interesting to observe that they characterize the human person in almost identical terms without attempting to prove in advance that man is in reality endowed with that which constitutes a person according to the view which they hold.

KALINOWSKI, Georges. Logique Et Ontologie. *Arch Phil* 47,625–640 O–D 84.

Two theses of Zinov'ev: (1) Logical laws owe nothing to the world (they speak only about expressions). (2) Truth depends on expressions and not on objects.

KALINOWSKI, Georges. Sur L'argument Ontologique De Leibniz. *Stud Leibniz* 17,94–97 1985.

J–Cl Dumoncel voit dans l'argument ontologique de Leibniz un simple illustration de l'un des théorèmes du S5. Or la phrase de Leibniz considérée par J–Cl D comme formule de son argument ontologique ne mérite d'être appelé "argument" ni au sens propre (elle est l'interprétation d'une loi logique et non une inférence) ni au sens métonymique (certes, elle fonde une règle on ne démontre pas la vérité (au sens fort) de "Dieu existe" sans admettre au préalable que Dieu existe).

KALOCSAI, Dezsö. On Spinoza's Ideals Of Man And Morals (in Hungarian). *Magyar Filozof Szemle* 4,585–607 1983.

KAMAT, R V and Bharucha, Filita. Syadvada Theory Of Jainism In Terms Of A Deviant Logic. *Indian Phil Quart* 11,181–188 Ap 84.

This paper seeks to investigate whether a 3–valued deviant (extended) logic can represent the Syādvāda Theory (the doctrine of 'may be' or the relativity of judgements) of Jainism. The Syādvāda Theory describing an object of the phenomenal world subject to factors of space, time, mode and substance, is presented as seven logical propositional statements. Two types of conjunctions (simultaneous and nonsimultaneous) are introduced. The paper ends with a suggestion that a Pramāna (complete judgement) can be interpreted as a tautology.

KAMENKA, Eugene (ed). *Community As A Social Ideal*. NY St Martin's Pr 1983.

In this volume Eugene Kamenka, George Mosse, and S I Benn examine the concept of community as a social ideal in socialism, in fascist and Nationalist thought and in relation to the moral principles of liberalism. r B Rose, Israel Getzler, Kamenka, Alice Erh–soon Tay and Erik Cohen then look at the historic fate of communitarian ideals in

the French Revolution, the Russian and Chinese Revolution and in the Israeli Kibbutz. Tony Honore brings the volume to a close by looking at the concept of a world community.

KAMINSKI, G. "What Beginner Skiers Can Teach Us About Actions" in *The Analysis Of Action*, Von Cranach, Mario (ed), 99–114. Cambridge Cambridge Univ Pr 1982.

KAMLAH, Andreas. Invarianzgesetze Und Zeitmetrik. *Z Allg Wiss* 4,224–260 1973.

In this paper we investigate as a simple example, how time independence or time translational invariance of natural laws determines the time scale. (edited)

KAMLAH, Andreas. On Reduction Of Theories. *Erkenntnis* 22,119–142 Ja 85.

Unlike the early analysis of Hempel and Nagel many present day explications of theory reduction do not start any more from concepts actually used by scientists. By avoiding this mistake one is lead to an explication which is essentially the logical deduction of the approximate validity of the secondary theory from that of the primary theory. This is tried in my paper using the theoretical formalism of J D Sneed.

KAMLER, Howard. Strong Feelings. *J Value Inq* 19,3–12 1985.

KAMM, Frances Myrna. Equal Treatment And Equal Chances. *Phil Pub Affairs* 14,177–194 Spr 85.

KAMM, Frances Myrna. Supererogation And Obligation. *J Phil* 82,118–138 Mr 85.

KAMPER, Dietmar. Hermeneutik—Theorie Einer Praxis? *Z Allg Wiss* 5,39–53 1974.

Der Aufsatz verfolgt eine doppelte Absicht: einerseits soll das Selbstverständnis der Hermeneutik gegen die verbreitete Miβverständnisse der wissenschaftstheoretischen Diskussion verteidigt, andrerseits soll es im Rahmen einer Methodologie der Gesellschaftsund Humanwissenschaften kritisiert werden. (edited)

KANATA, Susumu. Imagination Als Komplexakt (in Japanese). *Bigaku* 35,1–12 S 84.

E Husserl hat in der Imagination die Intentionalität, den allgemeinen Charakter des Bewusstseins gefunden. Das imaginative Gemeinte fasst man als unansetzbar bergegenständlichte Vorstellung auf. Noch dazu unterscheidet er zwischen der schlichten Imagination, der blossen Phantasie, und der abbildenden oder produktiven Imagination, die Husserl insbesondere "Bildbewusstsein" nennt. (edited)

KANE, Jeffrey. *Beyond Empiricism: Michael Polanyi Reconsidered*. NY Lang 1984.

Beyond empiricism: Michael Polanyi reconsidered systematically develops Polanyi's argument that despite all attempts to establish empirical parameters, modern science rests upon metaphysical bedrock. It establishes parallels between the referents of scientific theory and the scientist where the non–empirical elements of the former are reflected in the non–explicit elements of the latter. A variety of practical implications for the scientific and educational communities is offered.

KANITSCHEIDER, Bernule. Explanation In Physical Cosmology: Essay In Honor Of C G Hempel's Eightieth Birthday. *Erkenntnis* 22,253–264 Ja 85.

In this paper we focus our attention on the special problem whether it is possible to apply Hempel's classical analysis of causal explanation if the domain in question is the largest possible physical system, the universe. Furthermore we are concerned with the result of the customary analysis of scientific explanation, that there are no final and complete explanations, in opposition to the recent attempts of mathematical physics to build up so–called 'complete cosmological theories'.

KANITSCHEIDER, Bernulf. Geochronometrie Und Geometrodynamik: Zum Problem Des Konventionalismus. *Z Allg Wiss* 4,261–302 1973.

Die Frage, ob die Gültigkeit alternativer begrifflicher Strukturen empirisch entscheidbar oder eine Sache der willkürlichen Festsetzung ist, wird, eingeschränkt auf den Fall der physikalischen Geometrie, diskutiert. Die erkenntnistheoretischen Komponenten der empirischen Bestimmung von metrischen und topologischen Eigenschaften des physikalischen Raumes werden in der neueren Wissenschaftstheorie verfolgt. (edited)

KANNEGIESSER, Karlheinz and Uebeschar, K. Zur Theorien– Und Methodenentwicklung In Den Naturwissenschaften. *Deut Z Phil* 33,509–518 1985.

KANT, Immanuel. *Kant Im Original: Band III*. Erlangen Fischer 1984.

KANTI SARKAR, Tushar. Philosophy East And West: Two Fundamentally Different Approaches To Philosophizing. *Eidos* 1,139–152 D 79.

KAPHENGST, Heinz. Zum Aufbau Einer Mehrsortigen Elementaren Logik. *Z Math Log* 31,39–66 1985.

KAPITAN, Tomis. Castañeda's Dystopia. *Phil Stud* 46,263–270 S 84.

According to Castañeda's *Thinking and Doing*, the validity of a practical inference is based on the *legitimacy* values of practitions (imperatives, intentions, etc.), values determined by *ideal harmonizations* of agents' *de facto* ends and which, in turn, ground normative truths. A concealed normative ethic in this system sanctions an objectionable measure of conservativism: if everyone is satisfied with the *status quo*, no matter how unjust, it is wrong to do anything which would substantially alter it.

KAPITAN, Tomis. Reliability And Indirect Justification. *Monist* 68,277–287 Ap 85.

It is disputed whether a person who is *indirectly justified* in believing a proposition, i.E., justified by one or more *reasons* he has for it, must also be justified in believing that the reasons in some way support that proposition. Reliabilists have generally taken a negative stance. Here it is argued that the requirement is based upon powerful intuitions concerning reason–based belief, but that there is no inconsistency between it and the reliabilist program *per se*.

KAPLAN, Charles D and Weiglus, Karl. Beneath Role Theory: Reformulating A Theory With Nietzsche's Philosophy. *Phil Soc Crit* 6,289–308 Fall 79.

KAPLAN, Mark. It's Not What You Know That Counts. *J Phil* 82,350–363 Jl 85.

It has been a little over twenty years since the publication of Edmund Gettier's famous counterexamples to the claim that justified true belief is knowledge. Where the sheer volume of work published on a topic unequivocal evidence of its importance, then it would be clear that, in posing its problem for the analysis of propositional knowledge, Gettier's paper had uncovered a major problem for epistemology. But in fact, I contend, Gettier's paper did no such thing. I argue that the assumption lying behind the constructive responses to Gettier's paper—to the effect that Gettier's counterexamples show that an historically important definition of knowledge is in need of revision—is mistaken. My contention is that neither is the definition of knowledge Gettier showed defective of historical importance nor is its revision of contempory importance—that the moral to draw from Gettier's counterexamples is that what you know doesn't matter.

KAR, Bijayananda. A Study In The Arguments From Theology With Reference To Hume And Samkara. *Philosophica (India)* 10,18–22 Ja–D 81.

Hume and Samkara, though centuries apart, are found as critical about theological arguments. Hume's arguments against design are shown in the paper as being founded on extra–logical considerations. Those do not reveal the impossibility of speculating God on logical ground. But Samkara's arguments, it is noted, are advanced from the standpoint of logic. To him, inferential argument cannot be extended from empirical to transcendental and as such the creationist's claim is illogical.

KARATHEODORIS, S G. Construction Of Illness: Deconstructing The Social. *Theor Med* 6,205–220 Je 85.

This paper relates the discursive practices of teaching the concept of illness to some of the underlying metaphysical assumptions that secure an unproblematic sense of the subjective meaning of illness as a course of action. The paper explicates the normative character of the structures that form the subjectivity of theorist and patient by theorizing these statuses as qualitative relations to language.

KARLIN, Norman. "Substantive Due Process: A Doctrine For Regulatory Control" in *Rights And Regulation*, Machan, Tibor (ed), 43–70. Cambridge Ballinger 1983.

KASHER, Asa. Between The "Thoughts": Topics In Frege's "Logical Investigations" (in Hebrew). *Iyyun* 33,422–433 Jl 84.

Two topics are presently discussed. First, the distinction Frege draws between two kinds of laws, natural and normative. Secondly, we show how a remark made by Frege with respect to different notions of truth is related to the analysis of meaning by family resemblances, as stressed later by Wittgenstein. The historical dimension of family formation is discussed and references to 18th and 19th–century philosophers holding similar views are made. (edited)

KASHER, Asa. On The Psychological Reality Of Pragmatics. *J Prag* 8,539–558 Ag 84.

A major way of putting a theory of language use to a test is to see whether it is compatible with some background, relatively established psychological theory of language. In the present paper we investigate the compatibility of Fodor's framework, as presented in his 'The Modularity of Mind', with theories of deixis, presupposition, force, performatives, implicatures and politeness principles. Within each of these areas some insights are gained, by the study of compatibility, difficulties are discovered and suggestions are made for obviating them. Some light is shed on the very nature of pragmatics as a unified field of study.

KASPRISIN, Lorraine. Intentionality: A Reexamination Of Its Role In A Literary Education. *Proc Phil Educ* 40,361–372 1984.

Literary study in American secondary schools and colleges has been dominated by a set of practices aimed at removing literary studies from the context of intentional communication. Any appeal to the intention of the author was termed an "intentional fallacy." The purpose of this paper is to find a way to readmit the notion of intention into literary discussions that will not be open to the incisive critiques directed against intentionalist criticism. I attempt (1) to distinguish the different uses of intention, and (2) to propose a role for intention in the student's reading and understanding of a text by reexamining the question in light of recent philosophical inquiries into a communication intention, specifically, John Searle's theory of speech acts.

KASPRISIN, Lorraine. The Concept Of Distance: A Conceptual Problem In The Study Of Literature. *J Aes Educ* 18,55–68 Fall 84.

This paper examines the role of distance in a reader's encounter with a literary work. Three models are distinguished. In the Formal Model, the notion of distance presupposes a certain definition of literature; i.E., the definition of literature stands as a prior notion dictating this stance as a critical procedure. In the Psychological Model, the notion of distance is required prior to anything being called literature. In the Institutional Model, distance is part of the set of attitudes or expectations which make up the characteristic ways literature is taken by an interpretive community of readers. The concept of distance, in this account, is explicated by analyzing the structure of the institution in which it is embedded. Ways in which these conceptualizations illuminate or distort our understanding of the literary encounter is then examined.

KASS, Leon R. "Darwinism And Ethics: A Response To Antony Flew" in *Darwin, Marx And Freud*, Caplan, Arthur L (ed), 47–72. NY Plenum Pr 1984.

KASS, Leon R. Thinking About The Body. *Hastings Center Rep* 15,20–30 F 85.

KÄSTNER, H and Possneck, E and Friedrich, Gert. Probleme Der Führenden Rolle Der Arbeiterklasse Im Sozialismus. *Deut Z Phil* 22,739–745 1974.

KATZ, Eric. Organism, Community, And The "Substitution Problem". *Environ Ethics* 7,241–256 Fall 85.

Holistic accounts of the natural environment in environmental ethics fail to stress the distinction between the concepts of community and organism. Aldo Leopold's "Land Ethic" adds to this confusion, for it can be interpreted as promoting either a community or an organic model of nature. The difference between the two concepts lies in the degree of autonomy possessed by constituent entities within the holistic system. Members within a community are autonomous, while the parts of an organism are not. Different moral conclusions and environmental policies may result from this theoretical distinction. Treating natural entities as parts of an organism downgrades their intrinsic value as individual natural beings, since the only relevant moral criterion in an organic environmental ethic is the instrumental value that each natural entity has for the system. This ethic allows instances of the "substitution problem"—the replacement of one entity in an ecosystem by another provided that the overall functioning of the system is not harmed. (edited)

KATZ, Janet (ed) and Marsh, Frank H (ed). *Biology, Crime And Ethics: A Study Of Biological Explanations For Criminal Behavior*. Cincinnati Anderson 1985.

KATZ, Jay. *The Silent World Of Doctor And Patient*. NY Free Pr 1984.

KATZ, Jerrold J. "An Outline Of Platonist Grammar" in *Talking Minds*, Bever, Thomas G (ed), 17–48. Cambridge MIT Pr 1984.

KATZ, Jerrold J and Edwards, Michael. Sentence Meaning And Speech Acts. *Metaphilosophy* 16,12–20 Ja 85.

Kent Bach and Robert Harnish, in trying to show how performative utterances receive a meaning in speech contexts on the basis of the language user's knowledge of the meanings of constative sentences, defend a compromise position between the reductionism of use theorists and the use–independent semantics of their opponents. We argue that their proposed compromise is an attempt to reconcile irreconcilables.

KATZ, Michael. An Exact Philosophy Of Inexactness. *Topoi* 3,43–54 Je 84.

The paper summarizes and extends earlier works of the author on the "logic of approximation," a device enabling us to handle in an exact manner the problem of inexactness and approximation in science. This is a multi–valued logic with truth–values viewed as degrees of error and with deductions based on the idea that $\Gamma \vdash \Delta$ ("from Γ we can deduce Δ") if for every $\epsilon > o$ there is a $\vdash > o$ s.T. The error in Δ is smaller than ϵ whenever the error in Γ is smaller than δ. We axiomatize similarity (and other predicates) in this logic, obtaining metric structures with uniformly continuous interpretations of substitutability of similar elements. Then we show how this and other results can be applied to disciplines as divergent as quantum physics, utility theory and measurement in the behavioral sciences.

KATZ, Nathan (ed). *Buddhist And Western Psychology*. Boulder Prajna Pr 1983.

In this collection, fourteen scholars compare Buddhist and western psychological theories. Western psychologists considered include: Freud, Jung, Horney, Anna Freud, Medard Boss, the Stanford School and Pribram's holographic theories. These are compared with such Buddhist systems as: the Pali canon, the Mahayana schools of Madhyamaka, Yogacara and Zen, Nagarjuna, Dogen Zenji, tantric hagiographical texts and the Tibetan rdzogs–chen lineage.

KATZ, Steven (ed). *Mysticism And Religious Traditions*. NY Oxford Univ Pr 1983.

This collection of distinguished, original essays seeks to explore and analyze mysticism within its broader religious and socio–historic contexts. The main thesis of the volume is that mystics are not religious anarchists or spiritual 'lone–rangers' but part and parcel of given theological environments, exemplifying and 'experiencing' reality in light of specific preconditions and theological problematics.

KATZ, Steven. "A Critical Review Of Martin Buber's Epistemology Of I–Thou" in *Martin Buber*, Gordon, Haim (ed), 89–120. Beersheva Ktav 1984.

KATZ, Stuart and Wilcox, Stephen. Can Indirect Realism Be Demonstrated In The Psychological Laboratory? *Phil Soc Sci* 14,149–158 Je 84.

KATZOFF, Ch. Solomon Maimon's Interpretation Of Kant's Copernican Revolution. *Kantstudien* 66,342–356 1975.

KAUFMAN, Matt and Shelah, S. A Nonconservativity Result On Global Choice. *Annals Pure Applied Log* 27,209–214 N 84.

KAUFMAN, Rick. Is The Concept Of Pain Incoherent? *S J Phil* 23,279–284 Sum 85.

In *Brainstorms*, D C Dennett claims that 'pain' could not be a referring term because the very concept of pain is incoherent. To show that the concept is incoherent, Dennett argues that two necessary features of pain, incorrigibility and awfulness, cannot be true together. I argue that Dennett has not shown that these features are incompatible, and I go on to sketch a version of incorrigibility which avoids some of the problems raised by Dennett.

KAUFMANN, Matt and Keisler, H Jerome and Henson, C Ward. The Strength Of Nonstandard Methods In Arithmetic. *J Sym Log* 49,1039–1058 D 84.

We consider extensions of Peano arithmetic suitable for doing some of nonstandard analysis, in which there is a predicate N(x) for an elementary initial segment, along with axiom schemes approximating $(1)_1$—saturation. We prove that such systems have the same proof–theoretic strength as their natural analogues in second order arithmetic. We close by presenting an even stronger extension of Peano arithmetic, which is equivalent to ZF for arithmetic statements.

KAUFMANN, Matt and Schmerl, James H. Saturation And Simple Extensions Of Models Of Peano Arithmetic. *Annals Pure Applied Log* 27,109–136 O 84.

KAUFMANN, Walter. "Buber's Failures And Triumph" in *Martin Buber*, Gordon, Haim (ed), 3–24. Beersheva Ktav 1984.

KAULBACH, Friedrich. Kants Auffassung Von Der Wissenschaftlichkeit Der Philosophie: Die Sinnwahrheit. *Kantstudien* 76,1–13 1985.

Bei Kant findet sich folgende Aporie: einerseits will er die Philosophie (Metaphysik) zum Status der Wissenschaft erheben, andererseits zeigt er die Unfähigkeit der Wissenschaft, mit ihren Methoden des Begründens und Beweisens dem philosophischen Denken gerecht zu werden. Die Aporie ist dadurch zu überwinden, dass Kant jenseits des geläufigen Standards der Wissenschaftlichkeit für die Philosophie einen spezifischen Wissenscharakter postuliert: dieser hat die Züge juristischen Denkens und besteht in einer Selbstgesetzgebung de philosphischen Vernunft, durch welche der Gebrauch von Weltperspektiven, z B derjenigen der Naturnotwendigkeit oder der Freiheit normiert wird: eine von dieser Gesetzgebung legitimierte Perspektive heisst: "sinn–wahr".

KAVKA, Gregory S. "Nuclear Deterrence: Some Moral Perspectives" in *The Security Gamble*, Mac Lean, Douglas (ed), 123–140. Totowa Rowman & Allanheld 1984.

KAVKA, Gregory S. "The Reconciliation Project" in *Morality, Reason And Truth*, Copp, David (ed), 297–319. Totowa Rowman & Allanheld 1984.

KAVKA, Gregory S and Gauthier, David. "Responses To The Paradox Of Deterrence" in *The Security Gamble*, Mac Lean, Douglas (ed), 155–162. Totowa Rowman & Allanheld 1984.

KAVKA, Gregory S. Space War Ethics. *Ethics* 95,673–691 Ap 85.

The question of whether the USA should develop and deploy space–based weapons is examined from a consequentialist moral perspective. Three possible kinds of weapons are considered: space–based nuclear weapons, defenses against ballistic missiles (as in the planned Strategic Defense Initiative), and anti–satellite weapons. In each case, it is argued that mutual bans on such weapons by the USA and USSR would be preferable to the USA pursuing their deployment.

KAWAI, Toru. "Axiom Systems Of Nonstandard Set Theory" in *Lecture Notes In Mathematics*, Muller, G H And Others (ed), 57–66. NY Springer 1981.

KAY, Jeanne. Comments On "The Unnatural Jew". *Environ Ethics* 7,189–191 Sum 85.

The comments critique Steven S Schwarzschild's, "The Unnatural Jew", (Envir Ethics, 6, 1984). Schwarzschild's interpretation of Judaism is seen as too narrow to support his claim that Judaism has not appreciated nature. Much evidence supports Jewish love of nature, while pantheism and Christianity were not necessarily environmentally sound. To the extent that Jews have been divorced from nature, historical factors may be most important.

KEANE, Noel P and others. "Surrogate Motherhood: Past, Present, And Future" in *Difficult Decisions In Medical Ethics*, Ganos, Doreen L (ed), 155–164. NY Liss 1983.

KEARNEY, Richard. *Dialogues With Contemporary Continental Thinkers*. Dover Manchester Univ Pr 1984.

KEARNEY, Richard. Modern Movements In European Philosophy: Some Introductory Remarks. *Eidos* 4,51–61 Je 85.

This book provides an introductory account of three major movements in modern Continental philosophy—i) *Phenomenology* (Husserl, Heidegger, Sartre, Merleau–Ponty, Ricoeur, Derrida, (ii) *Critical Theory* (Lukács, Gramsci, Marcuse, Benjamin, Habemas, Bloch), (iii) *Structuralism* (Saussure, Lévi–Strauss, Lacan, Foucault, Althusser, Barthes). This work is primarily designed for undergraduate courses of contemporary European Philosophy (though it also contains a series of more specialized 'appendices' for the advanced student or scholar). It is published by Manchester University Press; and it serves as a follow up to Richard Kearney's interviews with Ricoeur, Levinas, Derrida, Marcuse and Breton entitled *Dialogues with Contemporary Continental Thinkers* (M U P, 1984).

KECH, Gabriele and Stubbs, Michael. Koschmieder On Speech Act Theory: A Historical Note. *J Prag* 8,305–310 Je 84.

The discovery of the characteristics of performative verbs, and other basic concepts of speech act theory, is usually attributed exclusively to John L Austin. However, many of the same concepts were discovered and discussed in detail, apparently independently and at about the same time or even earlier, by Erwin Koschmieder.

KEEL, Bennie C and Cheek, Annetta L. "Value Conflicts In Osteo–Archaeology" in *Ethics And Values In Archaeology*, Green, Ernestene L (ed), 194–207. NY Free Pr 1984.

KEGLEY, Charles W (ed). *Reinhold Niebuhr: His Religious, Social And Political Thought*. NY Pilgrim Pr 1984.

KEGLEY, Jacquelyn A K. Individual And Community: An American View. *J Chin Phil* 11,203–216 S 84.

The essay presents the main notions of individual and community and their relationship as found in American thought. The conclusion is that, for the American mind, individuality and community are inextricably bound together, arising out of their mutual interaction in a creative ongoing, infinite process. It is also argued that the creation of genuine individuality and community is difficult in America because of a sense of rootlessness, and a lack of social tradition and ritual.

KEISLER, H Jerome and Henson, C Ward and Kaufmann, Matt. The Strength Of Nonstandard Methods In Arithmetic. *J Sym Log* 49,1039–1058 D 84.

We consider extensions of Peano arithmetic suitable for doing some of nonstandard analysis, in which there is a predicate N(x) for an elementary initial segment, along with axiom schemes approximating $(1)_1$—saturation. We prove that such systems have the same proof–theoretic strength as their natural analogues in second order arithmetic. We close by presenting an even stronger extension of Peano arithmetic, which is equivalent to ZF for arithmetic statements.

KEKES, John. 'Ought Implies Can' And Two Kinds Of Morality. *Phil Quart* 34,460–467 O 84.

The principle, ought implies can, has two versions. The strong version expresses a necessary condition for the appropriateness of moral judgments; the weak version expresses a possible ground for excusing wrongdoing. The strong version is presupposed by choice–morality, while the weak one is presupposed by character–morality. It is argues that the strong version and choice–morality are mistaken and that the weak version and character–morality give a much more plausible account of our moral experience. The general conclusion is that choice is not necessary for the appropriateness of moral disapproval.

KEKES, John. Civility And Society. *Hist Phil Quart* 1,429–444 O 84.

Civility is a mixture of spontaneous good will, casual friendliness, and a spirit of mutual helpfulness. It is generally thought to be good, but unimportant. The thesis of this paper is that civility is important, because it is an essential ingredient of a good life, for it makes it possible to have harmonious relationships with fellow members of one's society. A way of understanding civility is proposed by considering three notions similar to it: Aristotle's civic friendship and Hume's sympathy and custom.

KEKES, John. Human Nature And Moral Theories. *Inquiry* 28,231–246 Je 85.

This paper defends a modest conception of human nature and argues that any adequate moral theory must incorporate this conception. Against the extreme historicist view it is argued that there are morally important necessary characteristics all human beings possess, and that many moral theories can be justified and criticized on the basis of these characteristics. Against the extreme naturalist view it is argued that the morally important and necessary characteristics give only a minimum content to moral theories and an adequate theory must both include and go beyond this minimum. In conclusion, it is claimed that it follows that purely formal, some relativistic, some élitist, and some natural law moral theories are mistaken.

KEKES, John. Moral Conventionalism. *Amer Phil Quart* 22,37–46 Ja 85.

Moral conventionalism is the combination of three theses: the existence of a conventional morality is necessary for the welfare of any society; everyone in a society has a prima facie obligation to conform to its conventional morality; and society is prima facie justified in upholding its conventional morality. Contemporary liberal opinion is largely opposed to moral conventionalism. I believe that this is a sign of misunderstanding rather than of genuine disagreement. Accordingly, my first task is to remove the misunderstanding by making moral conventionalism clear. This involves reminding readers of what they must know. The obvious, however, leads to the less than obvious conclusion that moral conventionalism is right. The conclusion is supported by arguments.

KEKES, John. The Great Guide Of Human Life. *Phil Lit* 8,236–249 O 84.

The great guide of life is custom. Decency is to conduct oneself in accordance with custom. Decency is a fundamentally important moral attitude, yet it is not generally recognized as such. My aim here is to make a case for its indispensability and to explain its neglect. I do so by reflecting on Edith Wharton's great novel, *The Age of Innocence*. She shows how decency is connected with two people's sense of identity, worth, and conception of the meaning of their lives. I argue that what is true in the case she presents is also true generally. This is why decency is important.

KELKEL, Arion L. La Fin De L'homme Et Le Destin De La Pensée: La Mutation Anthropologique De La Philosophie M Heidegger Et M Foucault. *Man World* 18,3–38 1985.

KELLENBERGER, James. The Slippery Slope Of Religious Relativism. *Relig Stud* 21,39–52 Mr 85.

This paper speaks to concerns raised by Roger Trigg (in "Religion and the Threat of Relativism," *Religious Studies*, 19, (1983)). Drawing upon Trigg's discussion, I identify seven steps down a slippery slope of religious relativism, beginning with the denial of literal truth in religion and ending with accepting the pointlessness of belief. It is argued that those who get onto the slippery slope, and John Hick in particular, can logically stop at one or another intermediate step before reaching the last nihilistic step and that, in any case, some of the steps can be understood in non–threatening ways.

KELLENBERGER, J. Kierkegaard, Indirect Communication, And Religious Truth. *Int J Phil Relig* 16,153–160 1984.

Kierkegaard's category of indirect communication, it is shown, relates to the subjectivity of appropriating the objective *what* of religious belief. For Kierkegaard in various works the *what* of religion cannot be directly communicated because it is contradictory. But, it is argued, the category of indirect communication itself does not necessitate such a role for contradiction and in other places Kierkegaard himself offers the ingredients of a different reason why the subjectively appropriated *what* of religious belief must be indirectly communicated.

KELLER, James. Reflections On The Value Of Knowledge: A Reply To Creel. *Faith Phil* 2,191–194 Ap 85.

Recently Richard E Creel argued that if confronted with a choice between a knowledge of the way reality is and an enduring faith in the God of traditional theism, one should choose the latter. This paper disputes his conclusion on the grounds (1) that his argument will work only if the faith is not misplaced and (2) that in determining whether or not it is misplaced, knowledge of the way reality is would be more useful than enduring faith.

KELLEY, Francis E. Walter Chatton *Vs* Aureoli And Ockham Regarding The Universal Concept. *Fran Stud* 41,222–249 1981.

Scholars are agreed that Walter Chatton very likely caused Ockham to modify his explanation of the universal concept. Here for the first time is published Chatton's *second* critique of Ockham's original position which is found in *cod Paris Nat lat 15886, f* 134ra–137va and *cod Florence Bibl Naz Conv Sopp t 5 357, f* 84vb–86vb. In this second critique, Chatton already knows about Ockham's revised account, but goes on to take him to task again anyway. He also considers and objects to Aureoli's doctrine.

KELLNER, Douglas M. Marxism, Morality And Ideology. *Can J Phil* Supp 7,93–120 1981.

Kellner argues that there is a moral dimension to Marx's critique of capitalism and his vision of socialism. The author claims that Marx uses moral language and makes moral claims in both his early writings and his later works like *Capital*. He examines the complex relations between Marxism, morality, and ideology and explicates a concept of moral critique which he finds operative in Marx's writings. Next, Kellner discusses what he sees as Marx's moral vision of socialism and implicit revolutionary morality.

KELLNER, Douglas. "Karl Korsch And Marxism" in *Continuity And Change In Marxism*, Fischer, Norman And Others (ed), 232–247. Atlantic Highlands Humanities Pr 1982.

KELLY, Eugene. "Limits To A Phenomenology Of Art" in *Continental Philosophy And The Arts*, Winters, Laurence E and others (ed), 3–14. *Lanham* Univ Pr Of America 1984.

KELLY, Gertrude. "State Aid To Science" in *Freedom, Feminism, And The State*, Mc Elroy, Wendy (ed), 275–284. Cato Institute Washington 1982.

KELLY, J W and Loptson, P J. Genetic Epistemology And Philosophical Epistemology. *Phil Soc Sci* 14,377–384 S 84.

KELLY, Patrick. A Pamphlet Attributed To John Toland And An Unpublished Reply By Archbishop William King. *Topoi* 4,81–90 Mr 85.

The paper prints *A Letter... In Reference to the Votes of the 14th Inst*, [1697], which William King claimed in a letter of january 6, 1698 (also printed here) was by Toland. The pamphlet attacks Irish trade and the existence of an Irish parliament, and very probably led William Molyneux to write *The Case of Ireland Stated*. As well as arguing for Toland's authorship, King's letter (which has signs of preparation for publication) mainly defends Irish trade.

KELLY, Sean. Hegel, Jung, And The Spirit Of History. *De Phil* 5,1–19 1984.

The paper begins by making a case for the compatibility of Jung's psychology with the "speculative" approach to universal history. This is followed by an outline of Hegel's schema of history, interwoven with a psychological commentary consisting of Jung's own reflections on the data in question along with the author's inferences from Jung's general psychological stance. The paper does not deal with the course of history after Hegel's death.

KELMAN, Steven. "Regulation And Paternalism" in *Rights And Regulation*, Machan, Tibor (ed), 217–248. Cambridge Ballinger 1983.

KEMP, Peter. Death And The Machine: From Jules Verne To Derrida And Beyond. *Phil Soc Crit* 10,75–96 Fall 84.

This critique of "Jules Vernian reason" commences with an analysis of Jules Verne's novel *Twenty Thousand Leagues under the Sea* and concentrates on the relation between Death and the Machine. The novel is interpreted from various philosophical positions: those of Hegel, Bataille and Derrida. Having subjected these positions to a critical test the author concludes that the death of the Other must be taken into consideration if the interpretation is to correspond with the view of technology expressed in the novel.

KENDRICK, Walter. Literary Criticism: The State Of The Art. *Thought* 59,514–526 D 84.

KENNEDY, Beverly. "The Re-emergence Of Tragedy In Late Medieval England" in *Existential Coordinates Of Human Condition*, Tymieniecka, A (ed), 363–378. Boston Reidel 1984.

KENNEDY, Ian. Commentary On "Kicking Against The Pricks: Two Patients Wish To End Essential Insulin Treatments". *J Med Ethics* 10,206–208 D 84.

KENNEDY, Ralph. Lemmon On Logical Relations. *Analysis* 45,89–93 Mr 85.

According to various writers in the "traditional" logic tradition there are just six "logical" relations among propositions: implication and its converse; equivalence; contrariety; sub-contrariety; contradiction. Lemmon (in *Beginning Logic*) argues that this list is incomplete. I argue for an interpretation of what the traditional logicians were trying to do given which the list is not obviously incomplete, since on my interpretation none of the additional relations proposed by Lemmon should be on the list.

KENNER, Thomas. Philosophy Of Medicine In Austria. *Theor Med* 6,85–92 F 85.

It seems impossible to completely cover the field indicated by the title of this report because of the many contributions of individual physicians and non-physicians to problems of the philosophy of medicine in Austria, and to their solution. The main trends are rooted in historic developments and in the current problems of medicine and health care, which are similar worldwide. In Austria famous names like empress Maria Theresia or the physician Ignaz Semmelweis have to be mentioned in connection with the development of the ideas of a philosophy of medicine. In recent times again influential and well-known persons in related fields of medicine and health care are Austrians. However, the main line of new developments goes mostly unseen by the public: activities in medical ethics with the goal to humanize health care, carried on by groups of young physicians, biomedical engineers, and students.

KENSHUR, Oscar. The Rhetoric Of Incommensurability. *J Aes Art Crit* 42,375–382 Sum 84.

Fish's account of literacy interpretation and Feyerabend's account of scientific interpretation both claim that facts are theory-laden and that so-called demonstration is really persuasion. For Feyerabend, however, persuasion is a function of textual facts. Since the existence of such facts is precisely what Fish denies, he tries to save his account by making "persuasion" identical to "interpretation", thus depriving persuasion of its explanatory function, and reducing his "theory" to a mere assertion--of philosophical idealism.

KENYON, Timothy. Labour—Natural, Property—Artificial: The Radical Insights Of Gerrard Winstanley. *Hist Euro Ideas* 6,105–128 1985.

KERN, Lucian. Das Diktat Des Besseren Arguments: Eine Entscheidungslogische Rekonstruktion Des Praktischen Diskurses. *Conceptus* 18,33–45 1984.

Die hier vorgelegte entscheidungslogische Rekonstruktion des praktischen Diskurses versucht zu zeigen, dass die Bedingungen, die Habermas an den Diskurs stellt, nur dann erfüllt sind, wenn der Diskurs dem gehorcht, was Habermas den "Zwang des besseren Arguments" nennt. Dieses "Diktat des besseren Arguments" sagt uns zwar, dass es im Diskurs stets ein Argument geben wird, das obsiegt, weil es das bessere Argument ist, nicht aber, welches Argument das sein wird. (edited)

KERR- LAWSON, Angus. Essentialism And Santayana's Realm Of Essence. *Trans Peirce Soc* 21,200–221 Spr 85.

KERR, Kathleen. Reporting The Case Of Baby Jane Doe. *Hastings Center Rep* 14,7–9 Ag 84.

KERRIGAN, William (ed) and Smith, Joseph H (ed). *Taking Chances: Derrida, Psychoanalysis, And Literature*. Baltimore Johns Hopkins Pr 1984.

KESWANI, G H. Accelerated Twins. *Brit J Phil Sci* 36,53–61 Mr 85.

Einstein derived a "peculiar (paradoxical) consequence" of Lorentz equations, viz., if one of two clocks or twins travels away, it/he/she will, on return, be found slower. Later, accelerations to which the traveler is subjected, was given as explanation. Paper shows that both can be given identical accelerations, between separation and reunion, differing only in constant-velocity phases. Inexorable time-difference attributable to uniform velocity alone then arises, violating relativity.

KEYES, Thomas W. Does Marx Have A Concept Of Justice? *Phil Topics* 13,277–286 Spr 85.

Given Marx's critique of capitalism, especially from alienation, exploitation and inequality, it has seemed obvious to many that Marx condemned capitalism from some nonpositivistic standard of justice. Recently, however, this seemingly unassailable position has been challenged by several Marxologists, namely, Robert Tucker and Allen Wood. In this paper I attempt to show that their challenge to the more traditional view has fallen short and should be rejected.

KEYT, David. Distributive Justice In Aristotle's Ethics And Politics. *Topoi* 4,23–46 Mr 85.

Aristotle's political philosophy is essentially a theory about the just distribution of political authority. The basic principle of this theory is introduced and given mathematical expression in *Nicomachean Ethics* V but only in the *Politics* is the theory fully developed and applied. This paper has two aims: first, to explain the middle course Aristotle tries to steer between Protagorean relativism and Platonic absolutism; and, secondly, to show how Aristotle uses his theory to justify three seemingly incompatible distributions of political authority.

KHADDURI, Majid. *The Islamic Conception Of Justice*. Baltimore Johns Hopkins Pr 1984.

KHALIFE- HACHEM, Elie. L'anthropologie Ches Les Pères Orientaux. *Gregorianum* 65,431–443 1984.

KHAN, Abrahim H. Melancholy, Irony, And Kierkegaard. *Int J Phil Relig* 17,67–86 1985.

This article aims to explain how Kierkegaard links melancholy and irony and what distinction he might have intended in his use of "*Melancholi*" and "*Tungsind*" in the *Concept of Irony*. The link is the notion of detachment associated with Greek scepticism. The discussion of the two terms shows that "*Melancholi*" is closely associated with irony as a personal standpoint, while "*Tungsind*" is a condition akin to Freud's melancholia and associated with imagination and desire.

KHATCHADOURIAN, Haig. Medical Ethics And The Value Of Human Life. *Phil Context* 14,42–50 1984.

KHATCHADOURIAN, Haig. The Human Right To Be Treated As A Person. *J Value Inq* 19,183–196 1985.

KHATCHADOURIAN, Haig. Toward A Foundation For Human Rights. *Man World* 18,219–238 1985.

I maintain that we have a human right to be treated as persons, and attempt to provide a more secure foundation for human rights, in man's nature, than has hitherto been done in recent writings. Specifically, I argue that we have an equal human right to be free to pursue our welfare as human beings and as individuals, to find meaning in our lives, to realize ourselves. I argue that the (full) satisfaction of our universal human needs—the need for love, achievement, recognition and belonging, and possibly meaningfulness—and the (full) recognition of our human and individual interests, require that we acknowledge the existence of such a right.

KHEEL, Marti. The Liberation Of Nature: A Circular Affair. *Environ Ethics* 7,135–150 Sum 85.

I show the relevance of feminist thought to some of the major debates within the field of environmental ethics. The feminist vision of a holistic universe is contrasted with the dualistic notions inherent in both the "individual rights" and traditionally defined "holist" camps. I criticize the attempt in environmental ethics to establish universal, hierarchical rules of conduct for our dealing with nature (an up-down dualism) as well as the attempt to derive an ethic from reason alone (the dualism of reason and emotion). I maintain that the division between the "holist" and "individual rights" camps is yet another form of dualist thinking, and propose in its stead a holistic vision that concerns itself *both* with the individual *and* with the whole of which the individual is part.

KHOKHLYUK, G S. The Counter-Revolution As Antipode Of Revolution (in Czechoslovakian). *Filozof Cas* 33,196–227 1985.

KHOSHKISH, A. Human Rights And International Finance: A Synthetical Overview. *J Soc Phil* 16,14–24 Wint 85.

International finance is functional and materialistic; its goal is profit. Human rights are affectional, their goal is human dignity. The relationship between international finance and human rights is dialectical. International finance hasn't got a soul. But, where workers become class conscious, churches preach social justice and governments promulgate social laws and claim national dignity; or where these agencies fail in their task and revolutionary movements emerge, international finance should strive for a synthesis and compromise—sooner, rather than later.

KI- ZERBO, Joseph. Nation, Justice And Liberty. *Diogenes* 124,68–77 Wint 83.

KIENZLE, Bertram. Lockes Perspektiventheorie Der Persönlichen Identität. *Stud Leibniz* 17,52–65 1985.

In this paper I argue that Locke's account of personal identity is a perspectival theory of how persons appear from different temporal and personal points of view. I sketch some principles governing the use of the phrase "I think" in order to show how "it is by the consciousness it [viz. The self] has of its present Thoughts and Actions that it is self to it self now, and so will be the same self as far as the same consciousness can extend to Actions past or to come". Locke's thesis that my own picture of my future identity depends upon my concern for happiness is shown to be insufficient. The discussion of how another persons identity appears from my point of view finally leads to the author's suggestion that it is our common will which is constitutive of how I conceive of the other's as well as my own future identity.

KILBOURNE, Lawrence. Political Technics/Technological Politics: MIRVS Dangerous Agenda. *Phil Soc Crit* 10,107–122 Wint 84.

This essay examines the influence of nuclear arms upon U S foreign policy, challenging traditional distinctions between political and technological activity. Through a study of Multiple Independently Targetable Reentry Vechiles (MIRVs), it shows how missiles function as political agents, and how politics becomes a technological enterprise. It concludes that MIRV may be the supreme expression of political technics, and the practical denouement of technologically conceived politics.

KILGA, Bernhard. Okosophie. *Conceptus* 18,33–51 1984.

These thoughts on ecological philosophy (ecosophy), which investigate the historical foundations, philosophical origins and the values or value–judgements of ecological thinking, derive from the idea of natural order and ordered subsystems. This approach leads to a number of problems and consequences. Some such subsystems in particular (agriculture, nutrition, medicine and the social system) are outlined, an environmentally compatible system of business and economy is discussed and environmentally emergency measures developed. Finally positions opposing ecological thinking are discussed.

KILLEEN, Peter R. Emergent Behaviorism. *Behaviorism* 12,25–40 Fall 84.

KIM, Jaegwon. Concepts Of Supervenience. *Phil Phenomenol Res* 45,153–176 D 84.

Two relations of supervenience, "weak" and "strong supervenience," are distinguished and their strengths compared. What supervenience between two families of properties entails about the existence of property–to–property connections between the families is considered in detail, and its philosophical implications discussed. It is shown that "global supervenience," i.E., the supervenience relation defined in terms of "possible worlds," is equivalent to "strong supervenience." Some applications of the supervenience concepts are considered.

KIM, Jaegwon. Epiphenomenal And Supervenient Causation. *Midwest Stud Phil* 9,257–270 1984.

Casual relations involving macro–events and processes can be understood as cases of "supervenient causation"—supervenient upon casual relations obtaining at the micro–level. It is argued that if the thesis of psychophysical supervenience is granted, casual relations involving mental events, too, can be understood on the model of supervenient causation, and that this resolves many of the puzzles surrounding psychophysical casual relations.

KIM, Jaegwon. Self–Understanding And Rationalizing Explanations. *Phil Natur* 21,309–320 1984.

KIMMEL, Lawrence D. Commentary On "Children As Consumers". *Bus Prof Ethics J* 3,159–169 Spr/Sum 84.

Paine argues that advertisement directed to children is morally objectionable in that it violates certain basic moral principles and runs counter to the principle of consumer sovereignty, the rule of moral justification in business. The logic of her attempt to give prima facie grounds for prohibiting childrens' advertising fails. Worse, it misses the developmental point of morality, favoring a protective moral posture that would keep children "children," and defenseless against projected ill, imagined and real.

KIMMEL, Lawrence. Sense And Sensibility. *Phil Invest* 8,199–207 Jl 85.

Has philosophy become a private matter among professional academics? Many philosophers believe with the public that philosophy is "merely about language." I review "ordinary language" philosophers Wittgenstein and Bouwsma to show how the concerns of ordinary men and the activities of the philosopher are brought together. I set out an oral tradition of philosophy whose task is the centering of sense, not the determination of truth. Philosophy investigates language as the shared domain of sensibility.

KIMMERLE, Heinz. Die Funktion Der Hermeneutik In Den Positiven Wissenschaften. *Z Allg Wiss* 5,54–73 1974.

Hermeneutik und Wissenschaftstheorie, die von unterschiedlichen Voraussetzungen ausgehen, konvergieren in ihrer Bemühung um die Sprache. Der universale Anspruch der Hermeneutik kann aber nicht sprachphilosophisch Begründet werden, sondern liegt auf der Ebene einer Metatheorie der wissenschaftlichen Arbeit überhaupt. (edited)

KING– FARLOW, John. Developing Themes In Philosophy/La Philosophie En Cours. *Eidos* 1,211–226 D 79.

KING, James and Livingston, Donald and Capaldi, Nicholas. The Hume Literature Of The 1970's. *Phil Topics* 12,167–192 Wint 81.

KING, Peter and Schouls, Peter A (ed). *The Life And Letters Of John Locke*. NY Garland 1984.

KING, Preston (ed). *The History Of Ideas*. Totowa Barnes & Noble 1983.

KINSKY, Lynn and Presley, Sharon. "Government Is Women's Enemy" in *Freedom, Feminism, And The State*, Mc Elroy, Wendy (ed), 77–86. Cato Institute Washington 1982.

KIPNIS, Kenneth. Nontreatment Decisions For Severely Compromised Newborns. *Ethics* 95,90–111 O 84.

Clinically, when are an infant's deficits large enough to justify withdrawing life-prolonging care? And, practically, who ought to have the right to decide? It is argued that (1) infants are not helped by burdensome care that cannot be expected to secure lives they will want to live and (2), parental prerogative is not broad enough to forbid others from assuming responsibilities for compromised infants when there is evidence they can be managed on the child's behalf.

KIRBY, Donald. Situating The Employee Rights Debate. *J Bus Ethics* 4,269–276 Ag 85.

Theological ethics provides a framework for at least adequately resolving the dilemma inherent in the issue of employee rights: the tension between individual rights and organizational authority. The central question is what constitutes the human dignity of the worker. The Roman Catholic theological tradition centers on the concept of human dignity and recognizes the causal relationship between how one's social conditions are divided and structured and the realization of one's human dignity. The author discussed why and how this tradition provides a useful methodology for resolving the employee rights debate.

KIRBY, L A S. Ultrafilters And Types On Models Of Arithmetic. *Annals Pure Applied Log* 27,215–252 N 84.

KIRCHGÄSSNER, Werner and Sanger, H. Erkenntnistheoretische Und Pädagogische Probleme Bei Der Verwendung Von Lehr– Und Lernmitteln In Der Ausbildung Von Philosophiestudenten. *Deut Z Phil* 23,1061–1067 1975.

KIRCHHÖFER, Dieter. Der Prinzipienbegriff In Der Marxistisch–Leninistischen Philosophie. *Deut Z Phil* 22,411–428 1974.

Unter den regulativen Mitteln (Werte, Normen, Aufforderungen) gewinnen Prinzipien zunehmend an Bedeutung. Die Tatsache dafss die konkreten Prinzipien der marxistisch–leninistischen Philosophie regulative Mittel eines wissenschaftlich begründeten Handelns im Interesse der Arbeiterklasse sind, hat bestimmte Forderungen an den Prinzipienbegriff zur Konsequenz, denen sein gegenwärtiger Gebrauch in der marxistisch–leninistischen Philosophie noch nicht genügt. Der Autor widmet sich daher Fragen, deren Klärung zu der notwendigen Präzisierung des Prinzipiengegriffs führen kann.

KIRK, G S and Raven, J E and Schofield, M. *The Presocratic Philosophers*. NY Cambridge Univ Pr 1984.

KIRK, John M. *José Marfi: Mentor Of The Cuban Nation*. Tampa Univ Pr Of Florida 1983.

An examination of Mati's political, social, economic, and educational ideas as they pertain to his quest for revolution and the establishment of a Cuban republic.

KIRK, Robert E. Davidson And Indeterminacy Of Translation. *Analysis* 45,20–24 Ja 85.

KIRKHAM, Richard L. Does The Gettier Problem Rest On A Mistake? *Mind* 93,501–513 O 84.

Attempts to resolve the Gettier Problem rest on the assumption that an analysis of knowledge can be found which is (a) generous enough to include as knowledge all, or most, of those beliefs we commonly regard as items of knowledge, and (b) rigorous enough to exclude from the class of knowledge any beliefs held in real or hypothetical cases which we would agree on reflection are situations where the epistemic agent does not know the belief in question. I show that no possible analysis, past, present, or future, could fulfill both condition (a) and condition (b). I also discuss the inadequacies of Robert Nozick's analysis of knowledge.

KIRKLAND, Frank M. Husserl And Hegel: A Historical And Religious Encounter. *J Brit Soc Phenomenol* 16,70–87 Ja 85.

KIROS, Teodros. Alienation And Aesthetics In Marx And Tolstoy: A Comparative Analysis. *Man World* 18,171–184 1985.

KIRSCHENMANN, Peter P. "Philosophical Evaluations Of Systems Theory" in *Contemporary Marxism*, O' Rourke, James J (ed), 79–96. Boston Reidel 1984.

KISIEL, Theodore and Johnson, Galen. New Philosophies Of Science In The USA; A Selective Survey. *Z Allg Wiss* 5,138–191 1974.

The following overview of the present situation and recent trends in the philosophy of science in the USA brings together bibliographical and institutional evidence to document the last stages of the suppression (Aufhebung) of logical positivism, the emergence of the historical school (Toulmin, Hanson, Kuhn, Feyerabend), its widespread influence upon other fields as well as within philosophy of science, and finally some of the reactions to it, many of which envision their endeavors as mediations between the historical school and the older logical approaches. (edited)

KISIEL, Theodore. Commentary On Patrick A Heelan's "Hermeneutics Of Experimental Science In The Context Of The Life–World". *Z Allg Wiss* 5,124–134 1974.

KISIEL, Theodore. Diagrammatic Approach To Heidegger's Schematism Of Existence. *Phil Today* 28,229–241 Fall 84.

KISS, Endre. Main Lines In The Hungarian Philosophy From The 1848/49 War Of Independence To The Compromise Of 1867 (in Hungarian). *Magyar Filozof Szemle* 1–2,26–69 1984.

Die analysierten fünf grossen Denkansätze sind von der allegemeinen, für den ganzen Kontinent charakteristischen philosophischen Atmosphäre der vereitelten Revolutionen sowie von den konkreten ungarischen Situation geprägt. Letztere enthält Eigentümlichkeiten, die darau resulttieren dass Ungarn nicht nur Schauplatz einer bürgerlichen Revolution, sondern auch der eines langen Freiheitskampfes war, der damals die Bewunderung des Kontinents auslöste. (edited)

KISTNER, Wietske and Wilkinson, Jennifer and Macnamara, Michael. 'Elegance' In Science And Mathematics: A Discussion. *S Afr J Phil* 4,95–99 Ag 85.

The authors discuss, along conceptual–analytical lines, the concept of elegance as it occurs in science and mathematics with reference to methods, solutions, proofs, and theories. Aspects considered include a comparison of the meanings of the term 'elegant' as it is applied in science, mathematics, and art, respectively; the intrinsic significance of elegance in a scientific theory; the significance of the relation between aesthetic criteria and truth; and the time–shift of criteria of elegance. Several possible lines for further inquiry are suggested, for example the question of whether it is elegant scientific theories that are the most fruitful ones.

KITAMURA, Kiyohiko. L'homme Qui Fait Une Narration (in Japanese). *Bigaku* 35,12–26 D 84.

KITCH, Ethel May. The 'Introduction' From Her *The Origin Of Subjectivity In Hindu Thought*. *Indian Phil Quart* 11,395–400 O–D 84.

KITCHER, Patricia. Narrow Taxonomy And Wide Functionalism. *Phil Sci* 52,78–97 Mr 85.

Three recent, influential critiques (Stich 1978; Fodor 1981c; Block 1980) have argued that various tasks of the agenda for computational psychology put conflicting pressures on its theoretical constructs. Unless something is done, the inevitable result will be confusion of outright incoherence. Stich, Fodor, and Block present different versions of this worry and each proposes a different remedy. Stich wants the central notion of belief to be jettisoned if it cannot be shown to be sound. Fodor tries to reduce confusion in computational psychology by dismissing some putative tasks as impossible. Block argues that the widespread faith in functionalism is just not warranted. I argue that all these critiques are misguided because they depend on holding cognitive psychology to taxonomic standards that other sciences routinely rise above.

KITCHER, Philip. Against The Monism Of The Moment: A Reply To Elliott Sober. *Phil Sci* 51,616–630 D 84.

In his "Discussion" (1984), Elliot Sober offers some criticisms of the view about species—*pluralistic realim*—advocated in my 1984. Sober's comments divide into three parts. He attempts to show that species are not sets; he responds to my critique of David Hull's thesis that species are individuals; and he offers some arguments for the claim that species are "chunks of the genealogical nexus". I consider each of these objections in turn, arguing that each of them fails. I attempt to use Sober's insightful critique to explain and defend pluralistic realism more fully.

KLAMI, Hanna T. Legal Justification And Control: Sociological Aspects Of Philosophy. *Law Phil* 4,199–216 Ag 85.

KLAR, Howard and Weikart, Robert. When The Doctor And The Minister Disagree (Case Study With Commentaries). *Hastings Center Rep* 14,30–31 D 84.

KLEIN, Ewan and Sag, Ivan A. Type Driven Translation. *Ling Phil* 8,163–202 My 85.

Assume that in a grammar–fragment for English, every syntactic rule which assigns constituent structure to a phrase is accompanied by a semantic rule which assigns it a compositional interpretation; and that every syntactic category of the grammar has an associated semantic type. We show that, given a syntactic rule plus the semantic types of the participating categories, there are a small number of general principles which derive the corresponding semantic rule.

KLEIN, Itshaq and Gandelman, Claude. Hegel's Dialectic Of Master And Slave As A Model For The Relation Between Artistic Creation And Aesthetic Appreciation. *Phil Soc Crit* 5,35–46 Ja 78.

KLEIN, Peter. The Virtues Of Inconsistency. *Monist* 62,105–135 Ja 85.

I *argue* that by knowingly accepting a set of propositions which is logically inconsistent, an epistemic agent need not violate any valid epistemic rule. Those types of logically inconsistent sets which it is permissible to accept are distinguished from those which may not be accepted. The results of the discussion are applied to the Lottery Paradox set of propositions and the Preface Paradox set. I also *suggest* that it may be an epistemic virtue to accept some inconsistent sets.

KLEIN, Sherwin. Two Views Of Business Ethics: A Popular Philosophical Approach And A Value Based Interdisciplinary One. *J Bus Ethics* 4,71–79 F 85.

KLEINBERG, E M and Watro, R J and Henle, J M. On The Ultrafilters And Ultrapowers Of Strong Partition Cardinals. *J Sym Log* 49,1268–1272 D 84.

KLEINER, Scott A. Interrogatives, Problems And Scientific Inquiry. *Synthese* 62,365–428 Mr 85.

KLEINMAN, Jackie. "Two Ages: A Story Of Soren Kierkegaard And Isak Dinesen" in *International Kierkegaard Commentary*, Perkins, Robert L (ed), 175–188. Macon Mercer Univ Pr 1984.

KLEVER, W N A. De Wiskundige Rede (Summary: The Mathematical Reason). *Tijdschr Filosof* 46,611–642 D 84.

In a plea for an intuitionistic or ontological interpretation of mathematics (against the view that math is only a language) the theory is developed that mathematics has to be conceived as the central and therefore normative part in the totality of our beliefs, as our logic of science 'par excellence'. Much attention is given to Wittgenstein's philosophy of mathematics (15 pages), to Hume's classification of sciences and to the not so curious antique Pythagorism.

KLIEM, Wolfgang. Kommunisten Und Christen Gemeinsam Im Kampf Um Den Frieden. *Deut Z Phil* 32,767–775 1984.

KLIMOVSKY, Gregorio. "Logic And The Hypothetical–Deductive Method" in *Philosophical Analysis In Latin America*, Gracia, Jorge J E and others (eds), 73–92. Boston Reidel 1984.

KLINE, A David. Transference And The Direction Of Causation. *Erkenntnis* 23,51–54 My 85.

KLIVAR, Miroslav. Aesthetics Of Non–Aesthetical In Czechoslovakia (in Czechoslovakian). *Estetika* 21,161–165 1984.

KLIVAR, Miroslav. Content And Dimension Of Aesthetic Valuation Of Working Environment (in Czechoslovakian). *Estetika* 21,100–112 1984.

KLOHR, Olof and Handel, G. Der Atheistische Charakter Der Marxistisch–Leninistischen Philosophie Und Weltanschauung. *Deut Z Phil* 22,502–506 1974.

KLOSKO, George. Provisionality In Plato's Ideal State. *Hist Polit Thought* 5,171–194 Sum 84.

It is commonly believed that, in the *Republic*, Plato deserts the commitment to rationality exhibited by Socrates in the early dialogues, while this view forms one part of the widespread allegation that the *Republic* presents an "authoritarian" state. This assessment of the *Republic* can be qualified by showing (a) the extent to which the work contains an element of discursive reason, and (b) the extent to which its

institutional structures are subject to criticism and change.

KLOSTERMAIER, Klaus. Moksa And Critical Theory. *Phil East West* 35,61–72 Ja 85.

The essay attempts to identify Jürgen Habermas' "emancipatory interest" and Samkara's "desire for liberation" is such a way as to provide a basis for comparison and critique. Both Critical Theory and Advaita Vedānta have a practical orientation insofar as they endeavour to help liberate the human person from ideological misidentifications of reality.

KLOWSKI, Joachim. Lässt Sich Eine Kernlogik Konstituieren: Ein Versuch Dazu Vom Standpunkt Des Pankritischen Rationalismus Aus. *Z Allg Wiss* 4,303–312 1973.

Bleibt der pankritische Rationalismus ohne logisch–methodisches Grundkonzept, so besteht entweder die Gefahr der Positionslosigkeit oder die des Neoirrationalismus. Andererseits könnte er durch ein solches Grundkonzept zu einem neuen Dogmatismus werden, der dort seine Grenzen hat, wo die Dialektik beginnt. Man glaubt nämlich irrtümlicherweise mit Popper, da β sich aus *einem* Widerspruch Beliebiges ableiten lasse. (edited)

KLUBACK, William. G Krüger: A La Recherche D'un Humanisme Religieux. *Arch Phil* 47,385–408 Jl–S 84.

This article attempts to show the life–long struggle of the philosopher, Gerhard Krüger, to clarify the close and intimate relationship and dependence of philosophical and religious speculation. He rejected the artificial separation that has developed in modern times between a "secular philosophy" and the cultural tradition that assumed the undeniable tie between philosophy and theology. Their mutual interdependence makes it possible to comprehend the spiritual heritage that lies in the values of philosophy and theology.

KLUTSTEIN– ROJTMAN, Ilana and Werblowsky, R J Zwi. Leibniz: De Cultu Confucii Civili: Introduction, Édition Du Texte Et Traduction. *Stud Leibniz* 16,93–101 1984.

KNAPP, Hans Georg. Normative Wissenschaft Mit Normen—Ohne Werte. *Conceptus* 8,57–62 1974.

Es wird gezeigt, da β das Problem der rationalen Begründung von Normen *nicht* durch eine Ersetzung der Norm durch eine bewertete Proposition gelöst werden kann: Die Konfrontation mit der genannten Arbeit *Bunge's* legt vielmehr die Deutung des 'Grundes einer Norm' als Ergebnis eines *Einigungsprozesses*, der Normbegründung, nahe. (edited)

KNASTER, Stephen M. Chisholm, Deliberation, And The Free Acquisition Of Belief. *Phil Stud* 46,307–322 N 84.

Is it possible for an agent to freely acquire beliefs? And can an agent acquire beliefs rationally as well as freely? My answer to both questions is a resounding 'yes', though I restrict my analysis to beliefs we acquire through deliberation, and use as my model of freedom Chisholm's theory of agency. I focus my argument by considering different ways in which an agent might deliberate about the morality of abortion.

KNEE, Philip. La Psychanalyse Sans L'inconscient? *Laval Theol Phil* 41,225–238 Je 85.

La publication de ce texte littéraire de Sartre su Freud, écrit il y a vingt–cinq ans, est l'occasion d'un nouveau regard sur long débat de Sartre avec la psychanalyse. Souvent négligé ou caricaturé, ce rapport n'en révèle pas moins avec force, à travers ses différentes figures et ses changements, l'irréducible "résistance" d'une pensée d'inspiration phénoménologique face à la notion d'inconscient.

KNEE, Philip. Le Problème Moral Comme Totalisation Chez Sartre. *Dialogue (Canada)* 23,379–396 S 84.

Some basic developments of Sartre's moral thought are described here, as it unfolds after *Being and Nothingness* through the central idea of his latter works, that of totalization. His critique of Marxism and his biographical method, as applied to Flaubert, express both a continuity and a fundamental shift with his earlier positions, particularly concerning the problem of a possible reciprocity in human relations.

KNOBLAUCH, Hubert. Zwischen Einsamkeit Und Wechselrede: Zur Kommunikation Und Ihrer Konstitution Bei Edmund Husserl. *Husserl Stud* 2,33–52 1985.

Husserl's notion of communication is analyzed systematically: starting by establishing the problems of this notion in his early work its foundations in intersubjectivity and the constitutional steps to communication are reconstructed. Husserl's notion of communication turns out to be twofold: phenomenologically purified as well as mundane. Whereas Husserl restricted himself to clarifying the first, the impact of the latter on modern social thinking is hinted at throughout the essay.

KNOX, E Richard and Shriver, Donald W. Taxation In The History Of Protestant Ethics. *J Relig Ethics* 13,134–160 Spr 85.

Taxation and government policy related to it have only episodic appearance in classical Protestant ethical sources. Of the early sixteenth century reformers, Luther gave most attention to the subject, justifying taxation in general as necessary for the just service of the government to the public good and calling the princes to spend tax monies for that good rather than their own luxury. Calvin made much the same claims but called more clearly for official church scrutiny of all government than did Luther. Two centuries later John Wesley criticized English tax policy, appealing to standards of economic efficiency and compassion for the poor with little reference overtly to theology. The churches of colonial and post–revolutionary America developed no systematic, theologically rooted rationale for taxation ethics, either; but official Protestant denominational concern for such ethics has grown measurably in the most recent fifteen years. After a survey of these recent national church statements, and on the basis of them and the slender Protestant heritage on this issue, we by posing four questions into which we see as worthy of much serious thinking by contemporary American Protestant ethicists.

KNUDSON, Ruthann. "Ethical Decision Making In The Politics Of Archaeology" in *Ethics And Values In Archaeology*, Green, Ernestene L (ed), 243–263. NY Free Pr 1984.

KOBSA, Alfred. What Is Explained By AI Models? *Commun Cog* 17,49–65 1984.

The paper investigates the claim that a successful artificial intelligence model can also be regarded as some kind of "explanation". It shows that this thesis holds true in a very weak interpretation only, and that, on the contrary, artificial intelligence models themselves ought to be subsumed under higher–level explanatory generalizations. Functional generalizations are shown to be promising candidates for this purpose. Key words: artificial intelligence, intelligence, theory, model, explanation.

KOCHLER, Hans. Das Apriorische Moment Der Subjekt–Objekt–Dialektik In Der Transzendentalen Phänomenologie. *Z Phil Forsch* 29,206–217 Ap–Je 75.

KOCKELMANS, Joseph J. *On The Truth Of Being: Reflections On Heidegger's Later Philosophy.* Bloomington Indiana Univ Pr 1984.

In this book the author has tried to present some basic themes of Heidegger's later philosophy in a systematic fashion. The following topics are discussed successively: truth, philosophical thinking, the meaning of Being, the relationship between time and Being, the ontological difference, Heidegger's concern with the earth, the place of God in Heidegger's thought, the essence of language, art and art works, thinking and poetizing, science and metaphysics in the modern era, the essence of technicity, and ethics and politics.

KODALLE, Klaus–M. Der Staat Der Industriegesellschaft: Zu Einer Publikation Von Ernst Forsthoff. *Arch Rechts Soz* 59,571–576 1973.

KODALLE, Klaus–M. Macht, Faktizität Und Die Frage Nach Dem Sinn. *Z Phil Forsch* 29,235–240 Ap–Je 75.

KOEHN, Donald R. Commentary Upon 'Should Collective Bargaining And Labor Relations Be Less Advesarial'? *J Bus Ethics* 4,293–295 Ag 85.

My commentary calls attention to what makes Mr Bowie's paper well worth intensive consideration. In my brief evaluation, however, I only lay out three incoherent elements of his proposed family model of labor–management relations. I argue that complete job security is not compatible with complete freedom to change firms; that, in practice, such security for all employees is not compatible with the shifting demand of our economic system, and the model includes two kinds of spouse relationships—one affectional and another competitive—that are incoherent with one another. My point is not that Mr Bowie's model is fatally flawed, but that it needs to be improved.

KOENIS, Sjaak. Filosofie En Wetenschap In De Frankfurter Schule (1930–1950). *Kennis Methode* 8,295–315 1984.

KOEPKE, Peter. The Consistency Strength Of The Free–Subset Property Of Ω_ω. *J Sym Log* 49,1198–1204 D 84.

The consistency–strength of the free–subset property for aleph–omega (every structure of cardinality aleph–omega has an infinite free subset) is shown to be equal to that of a measurable cardinal: Collapsing the elements of a Prikry–sequence yields the free–subset property. The converse uses the core model K of Dodd and Jensen.

KOERTGE, Noretta. "Beyond Cultural Relativism" in *Popper And The Human Sciences*, Currie, Gregory (ed), 121–132. Boston Nijhoff 1985.

KOERTGE, Noretta. On Explaining Beliefs. *Erkenntnis* 22,175–186 Ja 85.

Hempel's model has been used to explain actions. Can it also explain the formation of beliefs? I propose a pragmatic model of acceptance in which both evidence and the cost of error play a role. By distinguishing two types of error we can resolve certain puzzling features of most ideological and contextual accounts of beliefs.

KOESTENBAUM, Peter. *The New Image Of The Person: The Theory And Practice Of Clinical Philosophy.* Westport Greenwood Pr 1978.

KOFÁTKO, P. Formal Axiomatic Systems And Dialectic And Materialist Way Of Thought (in Czechoslovakian). *Filozof Cas* 33,228–247 1985.

KOHL, Marvin. Russell And The Attainability Of Happiness. *Int Stud Phil* 16,15–24 1984.

According to Russell, happiness depends upon having and appreciating reasonably continuous success at satisfying one's basic needs and correlate interests and, when understood in this way, is attainable for most ordinary men and women. After a discussion of the nature of meliorism, two objections are considered: first, that happiness is not attainable largely because of man's unavoidable fear of death and second, Russell's characterization is too rich, too loose, and that because of this, because the nature of the goal is unclear, happiness is generally less attainable.

KOHLER, G. "< ist Das Noch Kunst Oder" in *Asthetische Er Fahrung Und Das Wesen Der Kunst*, Holzhey, Helmut, 23–41. Bern Haupt 1984.

KOHLER, Georg. "Eigentum Ist Nicht Eigentum", Zur Rechtfertigbarkeit Des Eigentums. *Stud Phil (Switzerland)* Supp 12,277–298 1983.

KOHLER, Georg. Der Sinn Der BV–Revision Und Das "(Helvetische) Malaise". *Stud Phil (Switzerland)* 41,40–48 1982.

KOHLER, Rudolf. Wie Ist Sinn Des Sinnlosen Möglich? *Z Phil Forsch* 29,361–381 Jl–S 75.

KOLAKOWSKI, Leszek. "Beyond Empiricism: The Need For A Metaphysical Foundation For Freedom" in *On Freedom*, Howard, John A (ed), 27–38. Greenwich Devin–Adair 1984.

KOLÁRSKÝ, R. Contemporary Biotechnologies And The Concept Of Material Production (in Czechoslovakia. *Filozof Cas* 33,384–388 1985.

KOLENDA, Konstantin. The Impasse Of *No Exit*. *Phil Lit* 8,261–265 O 84.

Sartre makes a clear break with all attempts to represent human reality as conditioned on something non–human, be that something natural or divine. But when he portrays the relations among human beings in his fictional works, the story about freedom does not cohere with his philosophical theory. *no Exit* undermines that theory. As a dramatist, Sartre was closer to the truth than he was as a speculative philosopher.

KOLENDA, Konstantin. The Importance Of Character. *Humanist* 44,41–42 N–D 84.

In a person of character there is a coalescence of doing and being; a person is what he or she habitually and usually does. One reason why we look for a connection between action and character is that such a connection has obvious social utility—it brings into being loyalty to persons and projects. Besides being socially useful, the presence of character benefits its possessors. There is satisfaction in knowing one's mind and acting in the light of one's convictions.

KOLENDA, Konstantin. Thinking Ahead. *Humanist* 45,38 My–Je 85.

Current worries tend to absorb most of our attention. Anxious about tomorrow, we seldom detach ourselves sufficiently from the present to muse about the more distant future. And yet is has been said that where there is no vision the people perish. A visionless existence is a diminished existence. Concern about the future can tell us something about our present fears, expectations, and hopes.

KOLENDA, Konstantin. To Be A Person. *Humanist* 45,20–23 Ja–F 85.

To be a person is to be an active contributor to the meaning and value of the universe. States of affairs which generate intrinsically good states of mind can be proclaimed good, literally *bene–dicted*. Deep in our psyche there lies a conviction that it is wrong for something good to be wasted. We need not be ashamed of this yearning; it can only help us to become better than we are. In celebrating our own personhood, we are celebrating the personhood of others as well.

KOLLER, John M. *Oriental Philosophies.* NY Scribner's 1985.

oRIENTAL PHILOSOPHIES, second edition, (N Y: Scribner's, 1985) is a revised edition of a widely used text originally published in 1970. Divided into three parts, the Hindu system, Buddhist Philosophies and Chinese Philosophies, the book introduces students to the major philosophical traditions of Asia. Much of the text has been revised, with new chapters on the Vedas, Hindu Theism, the continuing Hindu tradition, and recent Chinese thought. The chapters on yoga and zen contain much new material. There are study questions and a brief annotated bibliography at the end of each of the 21 chapters. Available in paperback and hard cover.

KOMORI, Yuichi and Ono, Hiroakira. Logics Without The Contraction Rule. *J Sym Log* 50,169–201 Mr 85.

Propositional logics without structural rules are studied. Firstly, Gentzen–type formal systems for them are introduced, and then the semantics is defined by using partially ordered monoids. Completeness theorems are shown. Our approach will offer a common ground in the study of nonclassical logics, since it can cover a wide variety of logics, including the intuitionistic logic, Lukasiewicz's many–valued logics, relevant logics, non–monotonic logics and so on.

KONDOLEON, Theodore J. Augustine's Argument For God's Existence *De Libero Arbitrio*, Book II. *Augustin Stud* 14,105–116 1983.

This article attempts to show how Augustine's argument for God's existence in book II, De Libero Arbitrio is unsound. Its basic contention is that Augustine offers no proof for the existence of a truth superior to the truth in the human mind that could be properly equated with God. In this connection it claims that Augustine's argument entails the ontologistic view that the human mind, even in this life, can know God, of Truth Itself, directly. However, it also recognizes that Augustine's concept of God as the supreme being anticipates Anselm's view of God as that being than which no greater can be thought.

KOOTTE, Anton E. Logic Is Not Occultism. *J Mind Behavior* 5,505–508 Autumn 84.

Criticisms (DeMille, 1984; Paper, 1984; Sebald, 1984) of an earlier article by Kootte (1984) in which it was argued that DeMille has failed to prove Castaneda's work to be fiction are refuted. Simply dismissing anomalous phenomena and attempting to place the author in the untenable position of anti–science through the use of false assertion and ad hominem attack, my critics reveal their own biases and delusions.

KOPF, Eike. Die Reaktionäre Marxkritik Nach Dem Gothaer Programm Der Deutschen Sozialdemokratie. *Deut Z Phil* 23,706–713 1975.

KOPPER, J. Das Erkennen Als Ein Erkennen In Blosser Erscheinung: Zu Ingeborg Heidemanns Verständnis Der Kritik Der Reiner Vernuft. *Kantstudien* 66,220–230 1975.

KORCH, Helmut and Ennuschat, W. Engels' "Dialektik Der Natur" Und Die Einheit Der Naturwissenschaftlichen Erkenntnis. *Deut Z Phil* 23,869–882 1975.

Die Engelssche Auffassung, dafss die Gesamtheit der Naturvorgänge in einem systematischen Zusammenhang steht und die Wissenschaft gesetzmäfssig dahin strebt, ihn in einem einheitlichen theoretischen System widerzuspiegeln, besitzt grofsse Aktualität. Eine besondere Rolle spielen in der modernen Wissenschaft die Entstehung fundamentaler Begriffe und Abstraktionen und der Aufbau grundlegender Theorien, die das Wissen verschiedener Gebiete synthetisieren. Die fortschreitende Vereinheitlichung der naturwissenschaftlichen Erkenntnis ist weiterhin mit einer zunehmenden "Vereinfachung" wissenschaftlicher Systeme verbunden.

KORNBLITH, Hilary. Ever Since Descartes. *Monist* 68,264–276 Ap 85.

It is argued that four sets of epistemological questions which Descartes treated as interchangeable will have to be separated by naturalistically–minded epistemologists. In the course of evaluating these questions from a naturalistic point of view, light is shed on the relation between justification and reliability, internalist and externalist theories of justification, and the relation between ethics and epistemology.

KORNER, Stephan. *Methphysics: Its Structure And Function.* NY Cambridge Univ Pr 1984.

KORSMEYER, Carolyn. Pictorial Assertion. *J Aes Art Crit* 43,257–266 Spr 85.

This paper examines the claim that pictures can express propositions and thus may have truth value. Problems that arise with pictorial propositions are analyzed through consideration of Revere's "Boston Massacre." The paper concludes that while pictures unquestionably may convey ideas, specifying those ideas in a form that makes assignment of propositional truth or falsity to a picture possible is neither easy nor of pressing importance.

KORTIAN, Garbis. "Subjectivity And Civil Society" in *The State And Civil Society*, Pelczynski, Z A (ed), 197–210. Cambridge Cambridge Univ Pr 1984.

KOSIEWICZ, J. Physical Activity And Human Well–Being. *Dialec Hum* 11,175–178 Wint 84.

KOSING, Alfred. Über Die Widersprüche Der Sozialistischen Gesellschaft. *Deut Z Phil* 32,727–736 1984.

KOTERSKI, Joseph W. Freedom As A Condition For Truth: Jaspers On The Significance Of Temporality In Science. *Proc Cath Phil Ass* 58,93–103 1984.

Although truths in science are compellingly cogent for any mind sufficiently trained to appreciate the arguments and evidence, freedom is nonetheless a condition for the possibility of knowing these truths. The temporality of every aspect of science (the objects, the scientist, the community of inquirers, the theories, the standards and methods in use) is an indicator of the necessity of freedom in the knower of even the timeless truths.

KOTLARSKI, Henryk. Some Remarks On Initial Segments In Models Of Peano Arithmetic. *J Sym Log* 49,955–960 S 84.

KOTTER, Rudolf. Kausalität, Teleologie Und Evolution: Methodologische Grundprobeme Der Moderne Biologie. *Phil Natur* 21,3–31 1984.

The author discusses the significance of regulative ideas (Kant) for biology. He argues that the principles of teleology and of causality do not compete with each other, but are relevant for different regions of scientific research. A comparison of M Eigen's theory of self–organization with the traditional theory of evolution reveals that the fundamental assumptions of the latter should be understood at regulative ideas of the natural historiography of life, not as empirical claims.

KOTTOW, Michael. Ethical Problems In Arguments From Potentiality. *Theor Med* 5,293–306 O 84.

Potentiality can only be attributed to actual features of real entities. In medicine, potentiality arguments are most adequately exemplified in prognostication. It is wrongly employed in abortion debates (conservatives overextend human potentiality, liberals underrate it). Wrong attribution of potentiality occurs in argumentation from the potentially unexpected (unanticipated clinical course, therapeutic break–throughs, mollifying diagnostic mistakes), all of which are insufficiently substantiated by the actual clinical situation.

KOTTOW, Michael. Philosophy Of Medicine In The Federal Republic Of Germany (1945–1984). *Theor Med* 6,43–64 F 85.

The development of the philosophy of medicine in the Federal Republic of Germany since 1945 is presented in a thematic form. The first two decades were characterized by the evolution of an anthropological school of thought that aimed at relating physician and patient in a more personal and existential form than had hitherto been the case. In the last years, this tendency to demand deeper psychic and broader social involvement with medical problems has increased. Somatic disorders were considered to be fundamentally caused by socially induced mental stress. After a brief period during which the theme of organisms in general and phenomenologically grasped living–body of human beings in particular were discussed, there followed since the mid–seventies an essential preoccupation with the methodology and epistemology of medicine. According to this trend, medicine is to be analyzed in terms of theory of action, with its conceptual and strategic orientation towards practice and not, as generally believed, towards the standards of scientific truth. The concepts of disease, diagnosis, and therapy are therefore relative and their validity is dependent on time, persons, and circumstances involved.

KOUBEK, Norbert. Plädoyer Für Eine Ökonomische Anthropologie Auf Der Grundlage Von Interessen. *Arch Rechts Soz* 60,327–352 1974.

The economy in Western industrial societies will be discussed in a critical manner and concentrating upon the rationality of capital invested. This will be followed by an outline of aspects of an alternative labor–oriented form of economic action such outline to be based upon the rationality of labor invested. (edited)

KOVAR, Miloslav. To Some Questions Of Art Theory And Marxist–Leninist Aesthetics (in Czechoslovakian). *Estetika* 22,33–40 1985.

KOWALCZYK, Stanislaw. Intuitive Cognition And The Philosophy Of God (in Polish). *Stud Phil Christ* 20,7–52 1984.

KOZULIN, Alex. Psychology And Philosophical Anthropology: The Problem Of Their Interaction. *Phil Forum (Boston)* 15,443–458 Sum 84.

The changing subject matter and methodology of psychology and philosophical anthropology are discussed. The following problem seems to be central for both disciplines: By what means does the social–historical process converge upon the individual and how then it is further developed by his activity? The concept of the development of higher mental functions suggested by L Vygotsky serves as an example of such a theory which is insightful both for professional psychology and for philosophical anthropology.

KOZYR– KOWALSKI, Stanislaw. The Laws Of Social Development According To Karl Marx And Oskar Lange. *Dialec Hum* 10,217–220 Sum 83.

KRABBE, Erik C W. Formal Systems Of Dialogue Rules. *Synthese* 63,295–328 Je 85.

Section 1 contains a survey of options in constructing a formal system of dialogue rules. The distinction between *material* and *formal* systems is discussed (section 1.1). It is stressed that the material systems are, in several senses, formal as well. In section 1.2 variants as to language form (choices of logical constants and logical rules) are pointed out. Section 1.3 is concerned with options as to initial positions and the permissibility of attacks on elementary statements. The problem of ending a dialogue, and of infinite dialogues, is treated in section 1.4. Other options, e.G., as to the number of attacks allowed with respect to each statement, are listed in section 1.5. Section 1.6 explains the concept of a 'chain of arguments. From section 2 onward four types of dialectic systems are picked out for closer study: D, E, Di and Ei. After a preliminary section on dialogue sequents and winning strategies, the equivalence of derivability and intuitionistic logic and the existence of a winning strategy (for the Proponent) on the strength of Ei is shown to by simple inductive proofs. (edited)

KRABBE, Erik C W. Noncumulative Dialectical Models And Formal Dialectics. *J Phil Log* 14,129–168 My 85.

The paper investigates the effect of banning the Principle of Cumulation from Kripke semantics for intuitionistic logic and the dialectic systems (i.E., systems of rules for conducting critical discussions) that correspond to the resulting noncumulative logics. It contains an introduction to dialectic systems in general and goes on to discuss several implementations of a fundamental norm: a strict thesis is to be defended, ultimately, on the basis of strict concessions. Several completeness theorems are shown to hold.

KRAEMER, Eric Russert. Beliefs, Dispositions And Demonstratives. *Austl J Phil* 63,167–176 Je 85.

The analysis of belief is a troublesome problem, since both its dispositional and occurrent aspects need to be accounted for. Towards this end I propose modifying D M Armstrong's Ramsey–inspired account (1973). Armstrong analyzes general beliefs as dispositions to have singular beliefs. I show how singular beliefs might also be analyzed as dispositions to have demonstrative beliefs. Some likely objections are discussed and met, and some significant advantages of this proposed extension are explained.

KRAENZEL, Frederick. Nicolai Hartmann's Doctrine Of Ideal Values: An Examination. *J Value Inq* 18,299–306 1984.

This article evaluates Hartmann's claims that values are independent of our judgement of value, that they are independent of the real world, and that they are a multiplicity of ideal Forms. By examining our moral consciousness, the article concludes that some values have ideal necessity. However, it is only a conditioned, hypothetical necessity. And the number of different ideal values is very limited.

KRAFT, Victor. Konstruktiver Empirismus. *Z Allg Wiss* 4,313–322 1973.

In den apriorischen Formen und Begriffen des Verstandes wird das aufzudecken gesucht, was außer dem Erlebnisgegebenen in die Erkenntnis noch hinzutritt. Es sind in Wahrheit die Konstruktionen. Die Erfahrung, besser das Erlebnisgegebene, bildet die Grundlage für ihre Aufstellung und für die Begründung ihre Giltigkeit. Es ist der Empirismus, nicht der Sensualismus, aber ein konstruktiver Empirismus, der die Erkenntnis der Wirklichkeit ergibt.

KRAMBACH, K. Genossenschaftsbauern Und Dorf Improzek Der Sozialistischen Intensivierung. *Deut Z Phil* 33,42–52 1985.

KRAMBACH, Kurt. Die Klasse Der Genossenschaftsbauern Im Prozess Der Gestaltung Der Entwickelten Sozialistischen Gesellschaft. *Deut Z Phil* 22,179–189 1974.

Gesellschaftliche Stellung und Verantwortung der Klasse der Genossenschaftsbauern werden durch ihre Rolle im Bündnis mit der führenden Arbeiterklasse bestimmt, das die politische Grundlage der sozialistischen Gesellschaft bildet. In dem gemeinsam mit der Arbeiterklasse gestalteten %dubergang zu industriemäffsiger Produktion in der Landwirtschaft auf dem Wege der Kooperation entwickelt sich die Klasse der Genossenschaftsbauern und ihre soziale Struktur weiter. (edited)

KRAMER, Hans. Zur Ortsbestimmung Der Historischen Wissenschaften. *Z Allg Wiss* 5,74–93 1974.

Die Fragen nach der Funktion und der Effizienz der historischen Wissenschaften in ihrem Verhältnis zu en übrigen Wissenschaften und zur Gesamtheit menschlicher Lebensverhältnisse sind in der bisherigen Diskussion weitgehend hinter Methodenproblemen Zurückgetreten oder unscharf geblieben. (edited)

KRANCBERG, Sigmund. The Young Mao—A Soviet Portrait. *Stud Soviet Tho* 29,295–310 My 85.

The article examines Fyodor M Burlatsky's book *Mao Tse–tung—An Ideological and Psychological Portrait* (Moscow 1980) which, not surprisingly, is a strange mixture of censorious and biased analysis of Mao's political career assayed from the vantage point of Soviet perceptions of China and its late leader. With frequent and unscrupulous rewriting of history, Burlatsky's biography of Mao reflects Soviet unwillingness to identify as well as to acknowledge the historical symptoms of the no longer monolithic international Communist movement.

KRANCBERG, Sigmund. 1984—The Totalitarian Model Revisited. *Stud Soviet Tho* 29,71–78 Ja 85.

KRAPIEC, Mieczylaw A and Lescoe, Marie (trans) and Woznicki, Theresa (trans). *I–Man: An Outline Of Philosophical Anthropology.* New Britain Mariel 1983.

KRAUS, Pamela. Locke's Negative Hedonism. *Locke News* 15,43–63 1984.

KRAUSZ, Michael. The Tonal And The Foundational: Ansermet On Stravinsky. *J Aes Art Crit* 42,383–386 Sum 84.

In an attack on the atonal idiom of the later Stravinsky, Ansermet offers a characteristically foundational argument. This article analyzes such arguments, and suggests how they are inapplicable in the arts.

KRAUT, Richard. *Socrates And The State.* Princeton Princeton Univ Pr 1984.

This book analyzes the speech of the Laws in Plato's *Crito*, and discusses Socrates' general attitude towards politics. The speech balances the legitimate interests of city and citizen, and is consistent with the *Apology's* endorsement of disobedience. Its leniency emerges most clearly in the requirement that citizens obey *or persuade*. I also argue that Socrates' attitude towards democracy is ambivalent, and I relate this ambivalence to the unteachability of virtue and his unsuccessful search for definitions.

KRAUT, Richard. "Socrates And Democracy" in *Popper And The Human Sciences*, Currie, Gregory (ed), 185–204. Boston Nijhoff 1985.

KRAWCZYK, Zbigniew. The Ontology Of The Body: A Study In Philosophical And Cultural Anthropology. *Dialec Hum* 11,59–74 Wint 84.

KRECKEL, Marga. "Communicative Acts And Extralinguistic Knowledge" in *The Analysis Of Action*, Von Cranach, Mario (ed), 267–308. Cambridge Cambridge Univ Pr 1982.

KREEFT, Peter J and Purtill, Richard L and Macdonald, Michael H. *Philosophical Questions: An Introductory Anthology.* Englewood Cliffs Prentice–Hall 1985.

KREIMENDAHL, Lothar. Condillac Und Delisle De Sales: Ein Neuer Brief. *Z Phil Forsch* 39,122–123 Ja–Mr 85.

This article is a short commentary on a hitherto unknown letter from condillac to Delisle de Sales showing the widespread diffusion of Condillac's *Traité des Sensations* and the significance of the Pygmalion–motive in the French philosophy in the 18th century. (edited)

KREISEL, Goerg. Mathematical Logic: Tool And Object Lesson For Science. *Synthese* 62,139–152 F 85.

The object lesson concerns the passage *from* the foundational aims for which various branches of modern logic were originally developed to the discovery of areas and problems for which logical methods are effective tools. The main point stressed here is that this passage did not consist of successive refinements, a gradual evolution by adaptation as it were, but required radical changes of direction, to be compared to evolution by migration. These conflicts are illustrated by reference to set theory, model theory, recursion theory, and proof theory. At the end there is a brief autobiographical note, including the touchy point to what extent the original aims of *logical* foundations are adequate for the broad question of *heroic* tradition in the philosophy of mathematics concerned with the 'nature' of the latter or, in modern jargon, with the architecture of mathematics and our intuitive resonances to it.

KREJCI, O. American Neoconservatism (in Czechoslovakian). *Filozof Cas* 32,626–639 1984.

KREJCÍ, O. USA: Conservatism Contra Liberalism (in Czechoslovakian). *Filozof Cas* 33,337–351 1985.

KRELL, David Farrell. Is There A Measure On Earth: A Discussion Of Werner Marx's 'Nonmetaphysiccl Ethics'. *J Brit Soc Phenomenol* 16,196–201 My 85.

Werner Marx tries to "think further" Heidegger's ideas about mortality and death in order to elaborate a "nonmetaphysical ethics". I reply that no ethical discourse, especially not one involving "standards" and "measures", can achieve what Marx hopes to achieve by it. "Is there a measure on Earth? there is none".

KREMER, Michael. Frege's Theory Of Number And The Distinction Between Function And Object. *Phil Stud* 47,313–324 My 85.

The theory of number presented in Frege's *Grundlagen* rests on two principles: (i) numbers are objects, and (ii) a statement of number makes an assertion about a concept. When combined with his later views on concepts and objects, this theory leads to several puzzles. I argue that these difficulties can be resolved by abandoning Frege's ontological distinctions between function and object. This distinction should be reformulated as language–relative. The implications of this revision for Frege's philosophy of language are discussed.

KREMPASKÝ, J. Synergetics––An Integral Middle Level Theory (in Czechoslovakian). *Filozof Cas* 32,876–880 1984.

KRETCHMAR, R Scott. Ethics And Sport: An Overview. *J Phil Sport* 10,21–32 1983.

The purpose of the essay is to provide a critical assessment of the major portion of the English–language literature in the ethics of sport. It is argued that the relatively slow and sporadic progress made on understanding proper behavior in sport is due in large measure to repeated attempts to do ethics before paying sufficient attention to foundational metaphysical issues. Specifically, attempts are made to construct ethical standards in the absence of a clear understanding of the "inner workings" of sport, games and play and ways in which modifications of these structures affect people.

KRETZMANN, Norman. Adam Wodeham's Anti–Aristotelian Anti–Atomism. *Hist Phil Quart* 1,381–398 O 84.

A critical analysis of the approach taken by Adam Wodeham (1298–1358) in Question IV of his *De indivisibilibus* to Aristotelian anti–atomism, which may for these purposes be summed up as follows: Every quantitative or qualitative magnitude is an infinitely divisible continuum, the infinite divisibility of which is actualized in the occurrence of the uncompletable process of dividing it *ad infinitum*.

KRETZSCHMAR, A and Adler, Frank. Sozialistische Persönlichkeitsentwicklung Und Soziologische Forschung. *Deut Z Phil* 22,154–166 1974.

Das Werden sozialistischer Persönlichkeiten ist seinem grundlegenden sozialen Inhalt nach identisch mit der Aneignung des sozialen Wesens der herrschenden Arbeiterklasse. Deshalb ist ein nur normatives Herangehn an die Persönlichkeit nicht geeignet, ihre Entwicklung soziologisch zu erklären. Zentrale Bedeutung für die soziologische Persönlichkeitsforschung hat die Analyse des sozialen Wesens Arbeiterklasse, der Vermittlungen zwischen Arbeiterklasse und Klassenindividuum und der personalen Besonderheiten.

KRETZSCHMAR, A. Sozialistische Persönlichkeit Und Intensiv Erweiterte Reproduktion. *Deut Z Phil* 33,21–30 1985.

KRIEG, Robert A. Karl Adam's Christology: Towards A Post–Critical Method. *Heythrop J* 25,456–474 O 84.

This essay argues for the post–critical use of scripture in christology. It lays out the characteristics of pre–critical, critical, and post–critical hermeneutics. Then it shows how one theologian, K Adam (d 1966), sought to implement such a use of scripture prior to today's more sophisticated understanding of forms of language, especially of narrative.

KRIMSKY, Sheldon. The Use And Misuse Of Critical Gedankenexperimente. *Z Allg Wiss* 4,323–334 1973.

Three uses of critical thought experiments outlined in the paper are related to general questions of evaluation. A proposal offered by Karl Popper concerning the so–called "apologetic" use of *Gedankenexperimente* is critically assessed. It is argued that the rescuing of one theory from conceptual anomaly by appealing to another need not constitute a misuse of a critical thought experiment. (edited)

KRINGS, Hermann. Natur Und Freiheit: Zwei Konkurrierende Traditionen. *Z Phil Forsch* 39,3–20 Ja–Mr 85.

KRISHNAMURTI, J. *The Network Of Thought.* San Francisco Harper & Row 1982.

KRISHNAN, S Bala. Kant As A Philosopher Of Science. *Philosophica (India)* 10,36–39 Ja–D 81.

I interpret Kant as a philosopher of science more leaning towards science whose purpose in the *CPR* is to register that: (i) certainty of knowledge is possible only through scientific method, (ii) scientific research is a never ending process, (iii) science should be guarded against metaphysical trends. The impact of the then existing sciences on modern philosophical thought is shown. The transcendental aesthetic and analytic representing the language of science and the negative role of the dialectic are shown. It is concluded how Kant's two–fold aim is to save science from metaphysical misleadings and knowledge from crude scientific tests. (edited)

KRISTOL, William. Liberty, Equality, Honor. *Soc Phil Pol* 2,125–140 Autumn 84.

Is the regime of liberal democracy, based on the principles of liberty and equality, worthy of defense and even admiration? The answer is a qualified "yes;" and an understanding is sketched, based on the *Declaration of Independence*, *The Federalist*, and Tocqueville's *Democracy in America*, of how the regime dedicated to liberty and equality might be understood as honorable.

KROES, Peter. Objective Versus Minddependent Theories Of Time Flow. *Synthese* 61,423–447 D 84.

On the basis of modern physical theories a comparison is made between mind dependent and objective theories of time flow. A distinction is introduced between mechanical, evolutive, historical and individual time; physics cannot account for individual time. Reichenbach's and McCall's proposals for an objective theory of time flow and Grünbaum's defense of the mind dependency of time flow are analyzed. Finally, it is shown that the widespread idea that the theory of relativity leads to the conclusion that time flow is mind dependent (or an illusion) is based upon a misunderstanding of the geometrical role of time in relativity theory.

KROGH, Suzanne Lowell. Encouraging Positive Justice Reasoning And Perspective–Taking Skills: Two Educational Interventions. *J Moral Educ* 14,102–110 My 85.

There has been a need for developmentally appropriate methods of social/moral instruction in the primary grades, particularly methods that would require little teacher preparation or financial investment in materials. This study investigated the efficacy of two such methods: role–play and structured discussion. Subjects were 90 children from Grades One–Three who participated over an eight–week period. Interviews of positive justice reasoning and perspective–taking skills showed significant growth for both role–play and structured discussion subjects when compared to those in a control group.

KROH, Michael. The Relation Of Theory And Practice In The Process Of Formation And Action Of Laws Of Communist Socio–Economic Formation (in Czechoslovakian). *Filozof Cas* 33,161–182 1985.

KROKER, Arthur. Processed World: Technology And Culture In The Thought Of Marshall McLuhan. *Phil Soc Sci* 14,433–460 D 84.

KROLIKOWSKI, Walter P and Hablutzel, Nancy and Hoffman, Wilma. "Symmetry, Independence, Continuity, Boundedness, And Additivity": The Game Of Education. *Educ Stud* 15,215–231 Fall 84.

A review of seven recent books on educational policy from the United States and Great Britain. The article touches on some of the new happenings in education, especially the situation in Yugoslavia, the influence of court cases on educational practice, and national plans of educational change. It points to a troubling but necessary double focus on minima and maxima, on laws and ideals, on policies and principles, and advocates looking past liberty and equality to fraternity.

KRONEGGER, Marlies. "Literary Impressionism And Phenomenology" in *Existential Coordinates Of Human Condition*, Tymieniecka, A (ed), 521–534. Boston Reidel 1984.

KRONEGGER, Marlies. "The Birth Of Tragedy Out Of The Spirit Of Music" in *Existential Coordinates Of Human Condition*, Tymieniecka, A (ed), 273–294. Boston Reidel 1984.

KRONENBERG, Andreas. Where Are The Barbarians: Ethnocentrism Versus The Illusion Of Cultural Universalism: The Answer Of An Anthropologist To A Philosopher. *Ultim Real Mean* 7,233–236 S 84.

KRONTHALER, Engelbert. Zur Kritischen Analyse Des Induktionsproblems. *Z Phil Forsch* 38,278–291 Ap–Je 84.

The article resumes attempts to solve the 'problem of induction', discussing some of them in greater detail. It shows the intended foundation and justification of induction to be ultimately impossible and the whole discussion of the process of knowledge within the two–valued scheme of induction/deduction to be a fundamental limitation. Analyzing and rejecting attempts to mechanize induction it specifies the demand *not to MECHANIZE ORGANISMS* but––within a new conception of science––to *'ORGANIZE' MECHANISMS!*.

KROON, Frederick W. Theoretical Terms And The Causal View Of Reference. *Austl J Phil* 63,143–166 Je 85.

This paper asks what explains the apparent failure of the causal view of reference, so successful elsewhere, in the case of theoretical terms from the special sciences: why does theoretical description play such a large role in the referential mechanism of such terms? After investigating a number of answers to this question, the paper develops an alternative answer, formulated in broadly epistemic terms, and it shows how this answer also explains the apparent success of the causal view of reference in the case of standard names and natural kind terms.

KRÜGER, Gerhard. L'Attitude Intérieure Envers La Mort. *Arch Phil* 47,365–374 Jl–S 84.

If everything we are ends with our death, how could the very act of sacrificing one's life have any meaning? We feel we are responsible for what we freely do with our life, but to what or to whom are we responsible? It must be to an eternal authority from which we have our being. Therefore all human inquiry ends up with the question of God and fear of death becomes fear of God.

KRUGER, Lorenz. "Why Do We Study The History Of Philosophy" in *Philosophy In History*, Rorty, Richard and others (ed), 77–102. NY Cambridge Univ Pr 1984.

KRUSKAL, William H (ed). *The Social Sciences: Their Nature And Uses.* Chicago Univ Of Chicago Pr 1982.

These 12 essays celebrate the 50th anniversary of the Social Science Building at the University of Chicago, yet they celebrate—through examination and exemplification—the social sciences more widely. Most of the papers relate to the use of social science in the formation and execution of broad policy decisions. Other papers illustrate or explain basic social science research. The authors are Herbert A Simon, Paul E Peterson, Marshall Sahlins, James S coleman, Theodore W Schultz, Norman Bradburn, Mary Jean Converse, Lee J Cronbach, Philip E Converse, Barry D Karl, and Richard C Atkinson.

KUBO, Mitsushi. Die Stellung Des Interesses In Der Ästhetik Kants (in Japanese). *Bigaku* 35,1–11 D 84.

KUCZYNSKI, Janusz and Cauchy, Venant. World Congresses Of Philosophy. *Phil Today* 29,28–37 Spr 85.

KUCZYŃSKI, Janusz. Play As Negation And Creation Of The World. *Dialec Hum* 11,137–168 Wint 84.

KUDEROWICZ, Zbigniew. K Marx's Historical Thinking: On 100th Anniversary Of His Death. *Rep Phil* 8,15–24 1984.

One must stress Marx's methodological insight to take up the problems arising with the application of model thinking to historical cognition. The union of synchrony and diachrony is still a key problem. Marx was developing the vision of history as a process of changes which realizes universal values. According to consistent historism Marx's universal values are not brought into history from the outside, but their universality is gradually shaped in the course of historical experience.

KUDEROWICZ, Zbigniew. The Present Meaning Of The Idea Of Rationality. *Dialec Hum* 11,271–280 Spr/Sum 84.

The article is devoted to a description of the present meaning of the idea of rationality, which is understood as the defence of the promacy of values which have meaning for all of humanity. The idea of rationality consists of three aspects: 1/ the methodological model which defends the methodological autonomy of science and the servitude of science to all humanity; 2/ the axiological model; 3/ the ecological model which as a universal value recognizes ecological alienation and the assurance of homeostasis.

KUEHN, Manfred. Kant's Transcendental Deduction Of God's Existence As A Postulate Of Pure Practical Reason. *Kantstudien* 76,152–169 1985.

KUESTER, Harold H. Chomsky On Grammar And Mind: A Critique. *Int Phil Quart* 25,157–172 Je 85.

The paper questions the basic tenets of Chomsky's approach to linguistics and the supporting empirical evidence. In addition, an alternative, more adequate approach to linguistics is proposed.

KUFLIK, Arthur. The Inalienability Of Autonomy. *Phil Pub Affairs* 13,271–298 Fall 84.

KUHNRICH, Martin. Untersuchungen Zur Algebraischen Theorie Der Partiellen Mengen. *Z Math Log* 31,179–192 1985.

The main purpose of the paper is to get connections between partial Boolean algebras in the sense of KLAUA ("partielle Boolesche Algebren in der intervallmathematik", Mathematische Nachrichten 83 (1978), 311–336, and Mathematische Nachrichten 88 (1979), 141–173), MV–algebras, Post algebras, Heyting algebras, and Lukasiewicz algebras.

KUHSE, Helga. Words; Interests. *J Med Ethics* 11,146–149 S 85.

Who or what has "moral standing", that is, what kinds of entities have a claim to be included in the deliberations of rational moral agents? The while examines the view that only those beings who have interests can have moral rights or moral standing and then goes on to raise some unresolved difficulties with the interests approach.

KUIPERS, Theo A F. An Approximation Of Carnap's Optimum Estimation Method. *Synthese* 61,361–362 D 84.

Carnap's optimum estimation method is not applicable in a direct way for trivial reasons. In this article (originating from 1972), a limit procedure will be defined that leads to an approximation of this method and that is applicable in the inductive situation.

KUIPERS, Theo A F. Approaching The Truth With The Rule Of Success. *Phil Natur* 21,244–253 1984.

From a realist point of view a methodological rule, prescribing the choice between theories in the face of evidence, is only adequate if it serves the purpose of approaching the truth, i.E., the true theory about the subject matter in question. In this paper we argue that the instrumentalist rule of success, prescribing to choose the theory with the highest empirical success, serves this purpose. Of course, a number of explications and qualifications are required.

KUIPERS, Theo A F. Empirische Mogelijkheden; Sleutelbegrip Van De Wetenschapsfilosofie. *Kennis Methode* 8,240–263 1984.

The view that many important epistemological intuitions are not about statements describing some realized possibility, but directly about the unknown set of empirical possibilities within some specified set of conceptual possibilities, is illustrated by some key–concepts of Popper as empirical content, potential falsifiers and truthlikeness.

Moreover, it is illustrated by the methodological rules of descriptive and explanatory success, which, in combination, turn out to be functional, though not a guarantee, for approaching the truth.

KUKLICK, Bruce. "Seven Thinkers And How They Grew" in *Philosophy In History*, Rorty, Richard and others (ed), 125–140. NY Cambridge Univ Pr 1984.

KULSTAD, Mark A. Locke On Consciousness And Reflection. *Stud Leibniz* 16,143–167 1984.

Wie geartet ist das Verhältnis zwischen den zentralen Begriffen "bewusswein" und "Reflexion" in Lockes *Essay*? Sind diese begriffe für Locke identisch oder voneinander verschieden? Falls sie verschieden sind, wie ist der Unterschied genau zu bestimmen? Diese Arbeit untersucht die Fragen, unter Berücksichtigung der unterschiedlichen Deutungen in der Sekundärliteratur; sie sichtet und prüft den Test des *Essays* sorgfältig und breites Spektrum philosophischer Implikationen von Lockes Ausführungen über das Bewusssein und Reflexion aus. Der abschliessende Teil legt dar, dass Locke niemals eine feste Position gegenüber dem Verhältnis zwischen den beiden Begriffen eingenommen hat, sondern dass er zwischen verschiedenen Positionen schwankte—als Resultat der starken philosophischen Kräfte, die ihn bald in die eine, bald in die andere Richtung zogen.

KULTGEN, John. The Justification Of Legal Moralism. *Phil Topics* 13,123–132 Spr 85.

Legal moralism is generally contrasted to legal paternalism, but the motive for some forms of moralism is paternalism. Hence, principles for justifying or prohibiting paternalism apply to moralism.

KUMMER, Wolf. Die Materialistische Dialektik—Antwort Auf Die Frage Nach Der Selbstbewegung Der Materie. *Deut Z Phil* 32,916–920 1984.

KUMMER, Wolf. Entwicklungstendenzen Nichtklassischer Logiken Und Probleme Ihrer Geschichtsschreibung. *Deut Z Phil* 33,457–459 1985.

This paper gives report about a meeting of logicians in Halle (GDR). Contributions were held about the approach of historians of logic to modern logic, the development of intuitionistic logic, the subject of fuzzy logic, the logical analysis of adjectives, the development of inductive logic and the logic of probability, the classification of conditional propositions, the relations between traditional and non-classical logic, and time–logical research in history.

KUNACHOWICZ, Hanna. Ethical Problems In The Science Of Nutrition (in Polish). *Stud Phil Christ* 20,153–164 1984.

KUNEN, Kenneth. *Set Theory: An Introduction To Independence Proofs*, J Barwise and others (eds). NY North–Holland 1983.

KÜNG, Guido. "The Marxist Critique Of Rawls" in *Contemporary Marxism*, O' Rourke, James J (ed), 237–244. Boston Reidel 1984.

KUNICKI– GOLDFINGER, Wladyslaw J H. Is Biology A Rationalistic Science And Can It Be Wise? *Dialec Hum* 11,339–348 Spr/Sum 84.

Scientific and common sense rationalisms are confronted. Singularities of biology are discussed: general laws, complexity of phenomena, limits of predicability, and role of indeterminism principle. Historical aspects of life, notion of organization, role of value judgments and of teleonomy are considered. Distinction between knowledge and wisdom, and tasks and limitations of science in relation to current social crises are stressed. Abuses of some mythogenic generalizations in anthropology and ethology are then stressed.

KUNKEL, H O. Agricultural Ethics—The Setting. *Agr Human Values* 1,20–23 Wint 84.

Questions such as those related to undemonstrated risk, food safety, stewardship of resources, rights of nonhuman life forms and the methods coping with controversial issues must concern the agricultural establishment. The problem is that there has been inadequate normative knowledge about situations and consequences of issues coming out of technological advances in agriculture and institutional and societal changes. But values requiring recognition will likely be molded in realities of the setting: the structure of agriculture, a populace increasingly removed from the site of food production, and the societal meanings of agriculture.

KUNKEL, Joseph C. Right Intention, Deterrence, And Nuclear Alternatives. *Phil Soc Crit* 10,143–156 Wint 84.

This article postulates right intention as the neglected unifying concept of the just–war doctrine. Right intention orients just–war toward peacebuilding, not toward excusing reasons for war. In such light the war–justifying arguments of the Soviet Union and the United States are found morally inadequate. Deterrence too is evaluated as lacking intentional justification. Lastly the superpower nonpursuance of various feasible alternatives evidences a serious lack of right intention.

KUNNEMAN, Harry. De Ondergang Van De Deugden En De Inconsequentie Van McIntyre. *Kennis Methode* 8,348–357 1984.

KUNTZ, Paul G. St Augustine's Quest For The Truth: The Adequacy Of A Christian Philosophy. *Augustin Stud* 13,1–22 1982.

KUNZ, Karl–Ludwig. Der 'Labeling Approach'—Ein Paradigmawechsel In Der Modernen Kriminalsoziologie. *Arch Rechts Soz* 61,413–428 1975.

Opposing *labeling approach* to traditional ways of doing sociology of crime, the paradigmatic typicity of labeling theory is worked out and it is explained to what extent the latter is preferable, under the aspect of the theory of cognition, to traditional sociology of crime. According to the author, labeling approach does not cause obsolescence of traditional methods, but integrates them into a global theory of crime which is characterized by a primacy of the labeling approach arising from theory of science and the counterpart of the labeling perspective to traditional methods in practical research.

KÜNZLI, Arnold. Das Eigentum Als Eschatologische Potenz: Zur Eigentumskonzeption Von Karl Marx. *Stud Phil (Switzerland)* Supp 12,87–128 1983.

KUPERBERG, Mark (ed) and Beitz, Charles (ed). *Law, Economics, And Philosophy.* Totowa Rowman & Allanheld 1983.

KUPFER, Joseph. A Commentary On Jan Boxill's "Beauty, Sport, And Gender". *J Phil Sport* 11,48–51 1984.

Professor Boxill mistakenly thinks that sport must be an art for it to provide rich aesthetic experience. She ironically overlooks non–competitive sports (e.G., diving, gymnastics, skating) in which emphasis on form makes them most art–like. Nevertheless, competitive sports offer great dynamic value because of the human opposition. They parallel real life in terms of character, plot, climax, irony, and metaphor. Finally, Boxill reduces the aesthetic to the emotional, short–changing the role of intellect, desire, and imagination.

KUPPERMAN, Joel J. Francis Hutcheson: Morality And Nature. *Hist Phil Quart* 2,195–202 Ap 85.

The central argument is that Francis Hutcheson was misinterpreted by a number of commentators, from Frankena on, because of inadequate assumptions about ethical theory with which the commentators were armed.

KURTH, R. Die Topologische Struktur Der Zeit. *Phil Natur* 15,359–374 1975.

KURTZ, Paul. *Exuberance: An Affirmative Philosophy Of Life.* Buffalo Prometheus Books 1985.

KURTZ, Paul. Moral Faith And Ethical Skepticism Reconsidered. *J Value Inq* 19,55–66 1985.

KÜTTNER, Michael. Zur Verteidigung Einiger Hempelscher Thesen Gegen Kritiken Stegmüllers. *Erkenntnis* 22,475–484 Ja 85.

KUZMINSKI, V and Hrzal, Ladislav. The Alienation Of Revolution Or The Criticism Of Real Socialism In The Conception Of A Schaff (in Czechoslovakian). *Filosof Cas* 33,108–140 1985.

KVANVIG, J L. Is There An 'Us' In 'Justification'? *Synthese* 62,63–74 Ja 85.

Keith Lehrer has recently proposed a view of justification on which there are conditions under which a person cannot rationally violate rational consensus in his beliefs. This requirement is inadequate, though, for on its agreement can be imposed when it is rational to believe that one's epistemic situation is superior to those with whom one disagrees and when, though it is reasonable to believe that those with whom one disagrees are generally reliable, the evidence provided by this reliability is misleading in the present case.

KVANVIG, Jonathan L. Credulism. *Int J Phil Relig* 16,101–110 1984.

Credulism is the view that experiences by others are efficacious in conferring rationality on one's own beliefs. Two recent credulists, Rowe and Swinburne, have disagreed over the implications credulism has for belief in God. This paper defends two claims: (i) Rowe's revised credulity principle allows, contrary to what he claims, that the experiences of others make belief in God rational—unless Rowe affirms infallibilism; and (ii) more importantly, credulism itself is faulty in virtue of a hidden commitment to a form of infallibilism.

KVANVIG, Jonathan L. Divine Transcendence. *Relig Stud* 20,377–388 S 84.

KVANVIG, Jonathan L. Swain On The Basing Relation. *Analysis* 45,153–158 Je 85.

Swain's counterfactual causal theory of the basing relation is argued against by noting that counterfactual causes can be "buried" by only the actual cause, or by an indefinite number of counterfactual causes. This fact undermines the theory because the reasons are as good for thinking that belief can be based on evidence when the causal efficacy of the evidence is buried by other counterfactual causes as when buried only by the actual cause. It is then argued that a counterfactual theory cannot succeed because of complexities arising from sorting which "buried" causes will be allowed and which will not.

KVART, Igal. The Hesperus–Phosphorus Case. *Theoria* 50,1–35 1984.

KWAAD, G C. Waarheid Als Effect; Richard Rorty En De Natuur Van De Spiegel. *Kennis Methode* 8,209–224 1984.

Richard Rorty is "victim" of the very conception of truth he is repudiating: he presents truth as an *effect* of the—social instead of mental—process of knowing; he does so more easily because he unduly identifies "traditional philosophy" with its cartesian version; doing so he gets mixed up in an inconsistency, very wide–spread indeed in post–Kantian philosophy, but which deserves to be carefully identified rather than blindly reiterated once again.

KYBURG JR, Henry E. *Theory And Measurement.* NY Cambridge Univ Pr 1984.

This book develops the theory of measurement from a probabilistic epistemological point of view. The conception of probability used is that developed by the author in a number of other publications. Central to the treatment of measurement is the theme that statistical theories of error must be developed simultaneously with measurement. Both direct and indirect measurement are considered.

KYBURG, Henry E. Another Reply To Leeds: "A Problem About Frequencies In Direct Inference". *Phil Stud* 48,145–148 Jl 85.

KYBURG, Henry E. The Confirmation Of Quantitative Laws. *Phil Sci* 52,1–22 Mr 85.

Quantitative laws are more typical of science than are generalizations involving observational predicates, yet much discussion of scientific inference takes the confirmation of a universal generalization by its instances to be typical and paradigmatic. The important difference is that measurement necessarily involves *error*. It is argued that because of error laws can no more be refuted by observation than they can be verified by observation. Without much background knowledge, tests of a law may provide evidence for the distributions of errors of measurement of the quantities involved. With more background knowledge, the data may contribute either to our knowledge of the error distributions, or to the grounds we have for accepting or rejecting the law. With enough background knowledge, data may verify as well as refute laws.

KYBURG, Henry. "The Deductive Model: Does It Have Instances" in *Testing Scientific Theories*, Earman, John (ed), 299–312. Minneapolis Univ Minnesota Pr 1983.

LA CAPRA, Dominick. Is Everyone A *Mentalité* Case: Transference And The "Culture" Concept. *Hist Theor* 23,296–311 O 84.

LA CROIX, Richard R. Descartes On God's Ability To Do The Logically Impossible. *Can J Phil* 14,455–476 S 84.

With very few exceptions philosophers believe that no account of the doctrine of divine omnipotence is adequate if it entails that God can do what is logically impossible. Descartes is credited with believing otherwise. In his article "Descartes on the Creation of the Eternal Truths" Harry Frankfurt attributes to Descartes the belief that God is "a being for whom the logically impossible is possible." I argue that this interpretation of Descartes' view is wrong.

LA CROIX, Richard. The Paradox Of Eden. *Int J Phil Relig* 15,171–172 1984.

Before they ate the fruit of the tree of the knowledge of good and evil either Adam and Eve knew that obeying God is good and disobeying God is evil or they did not know this. I argue that if they did not know it then God was unjust and if they did know it then God was unjust. I conclude that since it is true that they either knew it or not, God was unjust and that being just is not a property God possesses necessarily or essentially.

LA FOLLETTE, Suzanne. "The Economic Position Of Women" in *Freedom, Feminism, And The State*, Mc Elroy, Wendy (ed), 213–236. Cato Institute Washington 1982.

LABOURDETTE, M Michel. Le Péché Originel Dans La Tradition Vívante De L'église. *Rev Thomiste* 84,358–398 Jl–S 84.

LABSON, S. Triálogo Sobre El Fin Del Principio Del Mundo. *Logos (Mexico)* 12,93–104 S–D 84.

The first law of thermodynamic coupled with pertinent facts drawn from quantum mechanics compels us to realize (a) that the universe has no beginning or end (b) that questions about the "origin" of physical processes are based on the incorrect supposition that space–time is a fundamental, as opposed to derived, property of existence. The arguments are developed through the medium of triloque with competing philosophical views.

LACHLAN, A H. A Remark On The Strict Order Property. *Z Math Log* 21,69–70 1975.

LACHLAN, A H and Cherlin, Gregory and Harrington, L. $\aleph_0$–Categorical, $\aleph_0$–Stable Structures. *Annals Pure Applied Log* 28,103–136 Mr 85.

We give a Coordinatization Theorem and related results which facilitate the systematic analysis of $\aleph_0$–categorical $\aleph_0$–stable structures. We combine a number of Zil'ber's ideas with the recent classification of the finite permutation groups called Jordan groups. The use of group theory can be avoided (Zil'ber, D Evans), but it plays an essential role in related work on stable structures homogeneous for a finite relational language. Applications include finiteness of the Morley rank of such structures, refinements of Zil'ber's results on the finite submodel property, and more technical results.

LACHMAYER, Friedrich and Reisinger, Leo. Potentielles Und Positives Recht. *Arch Rechts Soz* 60,25–52 1974.

It seems necessary to develop appropriate theoretical instruments, by which the set of potential norms can be determined. Starting from this methodological approach the present paper examines the following problems: a) the construction of normative chains, b) the problem of personal identities in norms, and c) the institutions of the transfer of goods. The analysis of these normative topics is to illustrate the thesis that the handling of problems by means of formal methods is not only aiding jurisdiction but also the structural analysis of legal theory. (edited)

LACINA, Norman. "When Pharmacist And Physician Disagree" in *Difficult Decisions In Medical Ethics*, Ganos, Doreen L (ed), 211–222. NY Liss 1983.

LACKEY, Douglas P. *Moral Principles And Nuclear Weapons.* Totowa Rowman & Allanheld 1984.

This book suppies a history of nuclear weapons, nuclear strategies, and nuclear diplomacy, and then proceeds to consider three basic nuclear weapons policies (non–possession, finite deterrence, and extended deterrence) from the standpoint of four different moral theories (utilitarianism, rights theory, the theory of justice, and the theory of just war). Certain "bridge principles" are suggested which transform the traditional moral analysis of acts done to a more pertinent analysis of acts threatened. The author concludes that nonpossession is the morally preferable option, and suggests various schemes for the reduction and internationalization of nuclear weapons.

LACKEY, Douglas P. Divine Omniscience And Human Privacy. *Phil Res Arch* 10,383–392 1984.

This paper argues that there is a conflict between divine omniscience and the human right to privacy. The right to privacy derives from the right to moral autonomy, which human persons possess even against a divine being. It follows that if God exists and persists in knowing all things, his knowledge is a non–justifiable violation of a human right. On the other hand, if God exists and restricts his knowing in deference to human privacy, it follows that he cannot fulfill the traditional function of being the perfect and final judge of all things.

LACKEY, Douglas P. Russell's Contribution To The Study Of Nuclear Weapons Policy. *Russell* 4,243–252 Wint 84.

Russell is to be credited with discovering that some confrontations between nuclear powers are game–theoretically identical with the game of Highway Chicken. His general contribution to the study of nuclear weapons policy is limited by his failure to consider that nuclear powers might develop mutual second–strike capacity.

LACKEY, Douglas P. The Moral Case For Unilateral Nuclear Disarmament. *Phil Soc Crit* 10,157–172 Wint 84.

LACOSTE, Yves. *Ibn Khaldoun.* London Verso 1984.

LACY, William B and Busch, Lawrence. Agricultural Policy: Issues For The 80s And Beyond. *Agr Human Values* 1,5–9 Wint 84.

The United States is currently rethinking its agricultural policies. This paper examines those policies in light of ethical and value decisions that face American agriculture.

LAD, Frank. The Calibration Question. *Brit J Phil Sci* 35,213–221 S 84.

LADD, John (ed). *Ethical Relativism.* NY Univ Pr Of America 1985.

LADD, John. Commentary On "Whether Professional Associations May Enforce Professional Codes". *Bus Prof Ethics J* 3,55–60 Wint 84.

LADDAGA, Robert and Loewer, Barry. Destroying The Consensus. *Synthese* 62,79–96 Ja 85.

LAFFEY, John F. Faces Of Truth And The Sociology Of Knowledge: John Stuart Mill And Karl Mannheim. *Mill News* 20,2–19 Wint 85.

LAFLAMME, Simon. A Travers La Definition Artistotelicienne De L'Ame. *De Phil* 5,42–49 1984.

The notion of form, as it can be constructed from *De Anima* is rich, not as much for its transparency or its strict references, but rather for its mystery and its multiple characteristics. Its role lies less in the designation of an object than in the consolidation of a vision of the world which is indefinite but forceful, and in preventing its being jeopardized.

LAGUEUX, Maurice. Simple Réaction À Un Double Commentaire. *Dialogue (Canada)* 23,493–502 S 84.

This is a single answer to both Morris and Panaccio reviews of the author's book *Le Marxisme des années soixante*. While praising both reviewers on different grounds, the author argues against objections raised by them. Being in no way a Marxist himself, he rejects as out of point of the correct allegation that no reasons were provided to adopt Marxism. Then he rectifies important misinterpretations of his arguments and compares his project with the standard positivistic approach.

LAHTI, Pekka J and Busch, Paul. A Note On Quantum Theory, Complementarity, And Uncertainity. *Phil Sci* 52,64–77 Mr 85.

Uncertainty relations and complementarity of canonically conjugate position and momentum observables in quantum theory are discussed with respect to some general coupling properties of a function and its Fourier transform. The question of joint localization of a particle on bounded position and momentum value sets and the relevance of this question is the interpretation of position–momentum uncertainty relations is surveyed. In particular, it is argued that the Heisenberg interpretation of the uncertainty relations can consistently be carried through in a natural extension of the usual Hilbert space frame of the quantum theory.

LAI, Yuen–Ting. The Linking Of Spinoza To Chinese Thought By Bayle And Malebranche. *J Hist Phil* 23,151–178 Ap 85.

Bayle and Malebranche feature in this study of the initial phase of the persistent linking of Spinoza's philosophy with Chinese thought. Seeing both as species of monistic rationalism and as sources of support for religious scepticism, they explored alternative possibilities of the rational outlook. This paper discusses the basis they provided for the linking, the various philosophical options open to them, and the moves they took.

LAITA, Luis M. Boolean Algebra And Its Extra–logical Sources: The Testimony Of Mary Everest Boole. *Hist Phil Log* 1,37–60 1980.

Mary Everest, Boole's wife, claimed after the death of her husband that his logic has a psychological, pedagogical, and religious origin and aim rather than the mathematico–logical ones assigned to it by critics and scientists. It is the purpose of this paper to examine the validity of such a claim. The first section consists of an exposition of the claim without discussing its truthfulness; the discussion is left for sections 2–4, in which some arguments provided by the examination of the inner consistency of Mary Everest's writings, Boole's own writings, and other sources, lead to the conclusion that there are sound reasons to accept Mary Everest's viewpoint.

LAKATOS, Imre. Science And Pseudoscience. *Conceptus* 8,5–9 1974.

The problem of demarcation is not simply a philosophical one: One can easily show that it has also grave ethical and political implications. Different solutions to the problem have been proposed so far, but they all turned out to be insufficient. The "Methodology of Scientific Research Programmes" solves some of the difficulties into which other methodologies have led.

LAKE, John. Characterising The Largest, Countable Partial Ordering. *Z Math Log* 21,353–354 1975.

LAKE, John. Comparing Type Theory And Set Theory. *Z Math Log* 21,355–356 1975.

LAKELAND, Paul. *The Politics Of Salvation: The Hegelian Idea Of The State.* Albany SUNY Pr 1984.

The book begins by examining the place of the state in Hegel's mature philosophical system. It goes on to argue that the relation between state and religion in Hegel's system makes the system a fruitful theoretical basis for a theology of liberation.

LAKOMSKI, Gabriele. Dewey's Theory Of Inquiry: Problems Of Foundations. *Phil Stud Educ* No Vol,72–81 1983.

LAMARCK, J B. *Zoological Philosophy: An Exposition In Regard To The Natural History Of Animals.* Chicago Univ Of Chicago Pr 1984.

LAMB, Matthew L. Liberation Theology And Social Justice. *Process Stud* 14,102–123 Sum 85.

LAMBERT, K. On The Elimination Of Singular Terms. *Log Anal* 27,379–392 D 84.

This essay explains, discusses the motivation behind the criticizes Quine's method for eliminating singular terms as outlined in his book *Word and Object*.

LAMBERTINO, Antonio. Approccio Fenomenologico Alla Conoscenza Metafisica. *Riv Filosof Neo–Scolas* 76,135–139 Ja–Mr 84.

An historical and intensional understanding of being through the phenomenology of being itself goes beyond a deductive metaphysical system which by its very nature is

dogmatic and abstract. This suggests the possibility of presenting a dialectic and problematic metaphysical system which comprehends the being through the experience of being obtained by inductive and deductive procedures. The being as such is not immediately perceived nor is it a pure logical concept; rather it constitutes an immanent horizon for everything that is and represents that which makes it possible to construct ontology and knowledge.

LAMBERTINO, Antonio. L'Uomo Freud: Personalità Morale E Religiosa. *Filosofia* 36,51–78 Ja–Mr 85.

LAMPERT, Laurence. Beyond Good And Evil: Nietzsche's "Free Spirit" Mask. *Int Stud Phil* 16,41–52 1984.

A commentary on *Beyond Good and Evil*, this essay explores the relationship between the book and *Thus Spoke Zarathustra*. It concludes that Nietzsche practices an art of writing which masks himself as a free spirit in order to prepare the most advanced among his contemporaries for the achievements of the philosopher chronicled in *Zarathustra*. Nietzsche unmasked is himself the philosopher of the future and *Zarathustra* records his education.

LANDESMAN, Charles. *Philosophy: An Introduction To The Central Issues.* NY Holt Reinhart Wins 1985.

LANDINI, Gregory. Salvaging 'The F–er Is F': The Lesson Of Clark's Paradox. *Phil Stud* 48,129–136 Jl 85.

Romain Clark discovered a Russellian paradox in the "two–modes–of–predication" reconstruction of Meinong's theory of objects. Hector–Neri Castaneda, espousing such a reconstruction, averts paradox claiming his "Guise–Theory" distinguishes two forms of negation. Nonetheless, 'The F–er is (internally) F', establishes a one–one correlation from properties to subsets of properties, each subset depicting a Meinongian object. This, with a standard comprehension axiom for attributes, generates paradox. Salvaging requires a restricted axiom. A restriction is proposed which implies two forms of negation.

LANDMAN, Fred. Data Semantics For Attitude Reports. *Log Anal* 27,165–192 Je 84.

The semantic analysis of perception verbs in Situation Semantics is based on the distinction between direct and indirect evidence. It is argued that this analysis leads to several problems, having to do with the fact that this contrast is gradual, and not a contrast in levels of awareness. Data Semantics, a theory of propositions as epistemic constructions out of possible facts is formally developed, and an analysis of perception verbs, based on the distinction between having a simple representation of the world, and having the capacity to construct complex information out of this, is presented.

LANDMAN, Fred. The Realist Theory Of Meaning. *Ling Phil* 8,35–52 F 85.

LANE, N R. Theory, Observation And Inductive Learning. *Ratio* 26,167–180 D 84.

Popper's logical argument against Hume's psychological theory of induction if valid would vindicate theory – determined observation. But it is valid only in the weak tautological sense in which theory (a point of view) determines similarity (1) It is not valid in either of the two strong senses in which theory could affect what we see (2) and (3). Concepts, Kantian categories, *gestalt* laws and mental sets are considered not to affect perception in the sense required to rule out the possibility of inductive learning (3) Popper's error arises because he fails to distinguish between different kinds of category or theory – ladenness.

LANE, Rose Wilder. "Give Me Liberty" in *Freedom, Feminism, And The State,* Mc Elroy, Wendy (ed), 49–60. Cato Institute Washington 1982.

LANG, Berel. The Concept Of Genocide. *Phil Forum (Boston)* 16,1–18 Fall–Wint 84.

The definition of genocide is considered in its historical origins, as first formulated by Lemkin (1943) and then incorporated into the 1948 U N Convention on Genocide. Specific issues concerning the nature of the "group" and of the act involved in genocide are related to the Nazi genocide against the Jews; genocide is claimed to be a distinctive moral transgression on the basis of its deliberate character.

LANG, Berel. Tolerance And Evil: Teaching The Holocaust. *Teach Phil* 7,199–204 Jl 84.

Tolerance and pluralism which are standard values presupposed in classroom discussions of ethics were severely tested—for this teacher— when in a discussion (through Arendt and Wiesenthal) of the phenomenon of evil–doing in the Holocaust, a persistent response was to exculpate the agent (and act) or to blame the victim. This response itself seemed a product of the values of tolerance and pluralism—and the question thus remains of how such values can be analyzed or questioned without presupposing them.

LANG, Helen S. Why Fire Goes Up: An Elementary Problem In Aristotle's *Physics*. *Rev Metaph* 38,69–106 S 84.

In *Physics* VIII, 1–2 Aristotle proves that motion must be eternal and resolves objections to his proof. *physics* VIII, 3–10 is generally read as proving a first mover but failing to demonstrate its causality. I argue that *Physics* VIII, 3–10 constitutes further proof of the eternity of motion, rather that a first mover. I show how an important problem, identifying a mover for the four elements, can be resolved on this reading and suggest pathologies for traditional readings.

LANG, Slobodan and others. Yugoslavia: Equity And Imported Ethical Dilemmas. *Hastings Center Rep* 14,26–27 D 84.

LANGE, Arno. Gedanken Zum Schicht–Begriff Der Marxistisch–Leninistischen Theorie Of Der Klassen Und Des Klassenkampfes. *Deut Z Phil* 23,829–839 1975.

LANGE, E and Biedermann, Georg. Zum Humanismus In Der Klassischen Deutschen Philosophie, Seinen Sozialhistorischen Und Theoretischen Voraussetzungen. *Deut Z Phil* 32,805–818 1984.

LANGE, Gunter. Der Inhalt Des Begriffs "Nation" In Der Spätbürgerlichen Ideologie Der BRD. *Deut Z Phil* 23,767–783 1975.

Die Mannigfaltigkeit der bürgerlichen Bestimmungen des Wesens der Nation is bedingt durch die Spontaneität der Ideologiebildung, aber auch durch wechselnde und sich widersprechende Interessen bestimmter Fraktionen der herrschenden Klasse. Bestimmend wurden in der BRD voluntaristisch–psychologische Deutungen der Nation. Parallel dazu verstärkte sich die Manipulation mit der Einstufung der Nationen als "Staats–" oder "Kulturnation". In jüngster Zeit sind Vorstellungen von den Nationen als "Kommunikations– und Handlungsstrukturen" verbreitet worden.

LANGE, Lynda. "Philosophy And Ideology In Rousseau" in *Ideology, Philosophy And Politics*, Parel, Anthony (ed), 199–210. Waterloo Laurier Univ Pr 1983.

LANGER, Monika. The Learning–Cell Technique For Teaching Philosophy. *Teach Phil* 8,41–46 Ja 85.

Increases in student enrollments coupled with a freeze or decrease in operating budgets, are creating a situation which is particularly disturbing for philosophy. The learning cell technique provides a solution to many of the present problems. The main features of this technique are described and its use in three of the author's courses explained. Problems are noted and solutions recommended. The advantages of using the learning cell technique and its particular suitability for the teaching of philosophy are considered.

LANGLEY, Van E. Commentary On "A Response To 'Is Business Bluffing Ethical'". *Bus Prof Ethics J* 3,19–22 Wint 84.

LANGTRY, Bruce. Miracfles And Rival Systems Of Religion. *Sophia (Australia)* 24,21–31 Ap 85.

David Hume, *Enquiry* Section X, claims that alleged miracles reported in connection with different religions undermine each others credibility. Commentators often ascribe to Hume's argument the suppressed premise that miracles occur only in connection with true religion. I reject this interpretation, and offer a different conjecture as to what Hume's intended argument is. I then attack both the argument and its conclusion.

LANGTRY, Bruce. The Maximin Rule Argument For Rawls's Principles Of Justice. *Austl J Phil* 63,64–77 Mr 85.

Firstly, I argue that Rawls has not provided a satisfactory account of the task of the parties in the original position. I offer three different interpretations of what Rawls says about that relation between the parties and the well–ordered society that they are partialy designing, each interpretation consistent with many of Rawls's remarks but none of them consistent with all of his remarks. Secondly, I argue that there is little reason to believe that the maximin rule, when applied to the task of the parties in the original position, enjoins the choice of Rawls's two principles in preference to the other listed principles. For there is little reason to believe that the choice of Rawls's two principles has the best worst outcome.

LANSING, Paul and Hatfield, Donald. Corporate Control Through The Criminal System. *J Bus Ethics* 4,409–414 O 85.

Corporate violations of the law are occurring with increasing frequency and with increasing public attention. Solutions to date have proved ineffectual because of the problem of determining whom is to be punished for the offense of the corporation. Instead of individual jail terms or corporate fines, we propose that the dissolution of the corporation be considered as a more effectual means of conforming corporate behavior to the norms of the legal system.

LAOR, Nathaniel. The Autonomy Of The Mentally Ill: A Case Study In Individualistic Ethics. *Phil Soc Sci* 14,331–350 S 84.

The present dispute regarding the autonomy of the mentally ill takes place within the fixed framework of individualistic ethics. Since this framework forces us into a paradox—the paradox of the autonomy of the individual in general and of the mentally ill in particular—it can justify contrary views. Therefore, at this point, I do not deem the continuation of the psychiatric debate within the classical ethical framework to be of value.

LAPPÉ, Marc and Murray, Thomas H. The New Technologies Of Genetic Screening. *Hastings Center Rep* 14,18–23 O 84.

LARA, Luis. Metamorfosis Interna De Los Conceptos: Entre Filosofía Y Ciencia. *Rev Filosof (Costa Rica)* 22,87–118 D 84.

Esta investigación consiste en un análisis sistemático de los principios gnoseológicos y metafísicos que están a la base originaria del saber. La metafísica como ciencia filosófica por antonomasia, la teoría del conocimiento, que es su fundamento subjetual, y la física teórica, microfísica, de nuestra época convergen en un mismo crisol de intuiciones originarias. Las últimas páginas ponen como ejemplo de esa convergencia un análisis metafísico de las geometrías no–euclídeas. El enlace intrínseco de los diversos cauces de la ciencia y de la filosofía se analiza también en el decurso histórico de algunas ideas primordiales que de una manera tácita o paladina han funcionado como eje de los principales sistemas filosóficos de la historia. Sustenta e impulsa a toda la investigación una preferencia de prindipio y de convicción por las intuiciones genéticas, esto es, aprioxísticas.

LARGEAULT, Jean. Critique Du Rationalisme Critique. *Arch Phil* 48,129–142 Ja–Mr 85.

LAROUCHE– TANGUAY, Camillia. La Thématisation Hégélienne De La Société Civile Bourgeoise. *Laval Theol Phil* 41,345–360 O 85.

À l'instar de Joachim Ritter et de Jean–Pierre Lefebvre, l'auteur soutient que Hegel fait subir un déplacement au concept de la société civile propose par les économistes. La société civile est pour Hegel un moment du développement de l'Idée de la liberté. Hegel s'opposerait ainsi aux théoriciens conservateurs qui refusaient cette nouvelle société et aux théoriciens libéraux qui y voyaient, a toutes fins utiles, l'%aetat dans sa forme achevée. En insistant sur le thème de la culture, l'auteur récuse toutefois le point de vue selon lequel la société civile serait "l'ensemble des conditions matérielles de la vie", d'où proviendraient par dérivation le juridiction, la police et la corporation.

LARSON, David T. Necessity In Kant: Subjective And Objective. *Auslegung* 11,481–492 Sum 85.

LARSON, Jean A. The Number Of One–Generated Cylindric Set Algebras Of Dimension Greater Than Two. *J Sym Log* 50,59–71 Mr 85.

S Ulam asked about the number of nonisomorphic projective algebras with *k* generators. This paper answers his question for projective algebras of finite dimension at least three and shows that there are the maximum possible number, continuum many, of nonisomorphic one–generated structures of finite dimension *n*, where *n* is at least three, of the following kinds: projective set algebras, projective algebras, diagonal–free cylindric set algebras, diagonal–free cylindric algebras, cylindric set algebras, and cylindric algebras. The results of this paper extend earlier results to the collection of cylindric set algebras and provide a uniform proof for all the results. (edited)

LASCAR, D. Quelques Précisions Sur La DOP Et La Profondeur D'une Théorie. *J Sym Log* 50,316–330 Je 85.

We give here alternative definitions for the notions that S Shelah has introduced in recent papers: the dimensional order property and the depth of a theory. We will also give a proof that the depth of a countable theory, when defined, is an ordinal recursive in T.

LASCOLA, Russell A. Berkeley: Inconsistencies And Common Sense. *Ideal Stud* 14,193–199 S 84.

LASH, Nicholas. *A Matter Of Hope: A Theologian's Reflections On The Thought Of Karl Marx.* Notre Dame Univ Notre Dame Pr 1984.

LASKY, Melvin J. "Confronting 'The Russian Question': The Ideological Journey Of A Generation" in *On Freedom*, Howard, John A (ed), 133–154. Greenwich Devin–Adair 1984.

LASSOW, Ekkhard. Die Wachsende Rolle Des Subjektiven Faktors––Eine Gesetzmässigkeit Des Historischen Fortschritts. *Deut Z Phil* 22,533–553 1974.

Unter den einen gegebenen sozialen Zustand oder Prozefss bestimmenden Faktoren diejenigen die vom Bewufsstsein und der physischen Existenz des Subjektes dieses Prozesses unabhängig sind und aufsserhalb von ihm existieren, die objektiven Bedingungen dieses Prozesses; diejenigen, welch in Existenz und Reifegrad seines Subjektes selbst bestehen, stellen die subjektiven Bedingungen (den subjektiven Faktor, die subjektiven Faktoren) dieses Prozesses dar. Die wachsende Rolle des subjektiven Factors kann nur auf der Grundlage des materialistischen Monismus erklärt werden.

LASZLO, Ervin. The Rise Of General Theories In Contemporary Science. *Z Allg Wiss* 4,335–344 1973.

The developmental trend in many fields of contemporary science is toward integrated general theories. These trends are viewed as essential components of the nature of science rather than expressions of arbitrary preferences of scientists. The law–like factors which lead science toward reliance on general theories include empirical as well as rational components. A model is proposed which exhibits the balance of the relevant factors as calling for increasing use of theories the primitive terms of which are progressively more abstract and general, though no less precise and empirically adequate.

LATH, Mukund. Creation As Transformation. *Diogenes* 127,42–62 Fall 84.

LATTKE, Michael. New Testament Miracle Stories And Hellenistic Culture Of Late Antiquity. *Listening* 20,54–64 Wint 85.

Before the different messages of the New Testament miracle stories can be translated into modern language, their phenomena and terminologies must be form–critically interpreted in their cultural context of meaning. It is possible, even probable that there is already a certain criticism of miracle(s) in the New Testament, especially in comparison with Hellenistic and non–canonical aretalogies. However, today the whole idea of miracles has to come under question.

LATUCH, David Paul. The Middle Term Between Science And Scientific Metaphysics. *Dialogue (PST)* 27,44–53 Ap 85.

LAUDAN, Rachel (ed). *The Nature Of Technological Knowledge: Are Models Of Scientific Change Relevant.* Boston Reidel 1984.

LAUDAN, Rachel. "Cognitive Change In Technology And Science" in *Technological Knowledge*, Laudan, Rachel (ed), 83–104. Boston Reidel 1984.

LAUDAN, Rachel. "The Nature Of Technological Knowledge: Introduction" in *Technological Knowledge*, Laudan, Rachel (ed), 1–26. Boston Reidel 1984.

LAUENER, Henri. Gaston Bachelard Et Ferdinand Gonseth, Philosophes De La Dialectique Scientifique. *Dialectica* 39,5–18 1985.

The author describes Gatson Bachelard's and Ferdinand Gonseth's dialectical method which is at the origin of their so–called open philosophy. When faced with the task of giving a name to a planned review, edited together with Paul Bernays, they settled their choice on *Dialectica* in order to announce the orientation of the future publications.

LAUER, Quentin S J. The Life Of Consciousness And The World Come Alive. *Owl Minerva* 16,183–198 Spr 85.

LAUER, Quentin. "Hegel As Poet" in *History And System*, Perkins, Robert (ed), 1–14. Albany SUNY Pr 1984.

LAURITZEN, Paul. Philosophy Of Religion And The Mirror Of Nature: Rorty's Challenge To Analytic Philosophy Of Religion. *Int J Phil Relig* 16,29–40 1984.

This paper examines the implications for analytic philosophy of religion of Richard Rorty's general critique of analytic philosophy. Rorty's attack on epistemologically centered philosophy is sketched, as is his pragmatist response to foundationalist philosophy. It is argued that Rorty's epistemological behaviorism, developed out of the work of Quine and Sellars, represents a challenge to analytic philosophy of religion. This thesis is tested by examining the work of one analytic philosopher of religion, Richard Swinburne.

LAUTENSCHLAGER, Karl. Controlling Military Technology. *Ethics* 95,692–711 Ap 85.

LAVAUD, Claudie. Philosophie Et Religion Dans L'oeuvre De Paul Ricoeur. *Etudes* 362,519–533 Ap 85.

LAVERE, George J. The Problem Of The Common Good In Saint Augustine's *Civitas Terrena. Augustin Stud* 14,1–10 1983.

Two irreconcilable loves have made two cities—the City of God and the City of Man—yet the citizens of both mystical cities dwell together within the confines of the earthly city, sharing common civic interests and depending upon the collective vitality of the body politic for their material survival. In view of this, how is a *common* good possible? augustine analyzes this issue in the context of Rome, the archetypical *civitas terrena*, and concludes that while a genuine common good cannot be realized, a common set of interests can suffice for the temporary survival of the earthly city.

LAVERS, George J. *The Two Cities* Of Otto, Bishop Of Freising: A Study In Neo–Augustinian Political Theory. *Augustin Stud* 13,55–66 1982.

the Chronicle of Universal History to the Year 1146 AD is a 12th Century account of how the political doctrine of Saint Augustine underwent a gradual transformation from the strict separation of the mystical cities of God and Man to one city—medieval Christendom. Otto of Freising was acutely aware of the paradox of neo–Augustinian political theory, claiming to derive from Saint Augustine's eternal separation of the two cities, yet whole–heartedly embracing the ideal of one society ruled by "two swords" under God.

LAW, Susan A T. The Teaching Of Medical Ethics From A Junior Doctor's Viewpoint. *J Med Ethics* 11,37–38 Mr 85.

This is a short paper covering my own views on the methods and reasons behind the teaching of medical ethics. All the whys and wherefores are discussed and some conclusions reached. This paper is given from a junior doctor's viewpoint but could equally apply to others.

LAWLER, Peter A. The Scientific Destruction Of Humanity And The Educational Project Of The Humanities. *J Thought* 19,105–116 Wint 84.

Those who defend the possibility of humanity in our time must oppose the apparently omnipresent Hegelianism, which, when articulated consistently, shows that history and hence humanity has come to an end. They must show a greater capacity for human choice than does the historicist, who contends that the possibilities for human experience are fundamentally limited by the constraints of time and place. It is so clear that the West is, of necessity dead? How to make the Western, or Socratic affirmation of the harmony of reason and courage, truth and nobility, and self–consciousness and happiness credible within the context of a science–dependent mass democracy is the educational challenge of the humanist.

LAWLOR, Patricia M. "Metaphor & The Flux Of Human Experience" in *Existential Coordinates Of Human Condition*, Tymieniecka, A (ed), 241–248. Boston Reidel 1984.

LAYCOCK, Steven W. Hui–Neng And The Transcendental Standpoint. *J Chin Phil* 12,179–196 Je 85.

This paper undertakes to demonstrate that the prevailing interpretation of Hui–neng as espousing the doctrine that "prereflective consciousness" is Supreme Wisdom is incorrect, and that enlightened consciousness, for Hui–neng, has far greater affinities with the transcendentally reflecting conscsciousness of Husserlian phenomenology. Unlike Sartre's existentially committed prereflective consciousness, Hui–neng's "original" consciousness rises "above affirmation and negation," yet (*contra* Husserl) without presupposing a substantial transcendental ego occupying the transcendental standpoint.

LAYDER, Derek. Power, Structure And Agency. *J Theor Soc Behav* 15,131–150 Jl 85.

This paper is an attempt to establish a properly structural conception of power as a complement to the notion of power as agency, in order that a correct and comprehensive theorization of the relations between power, structure, and agency can be accomplished. The argument proceeds via a critique of the work of Lukes and Giddens who both erroneously believe that power is indissolubly and exclusively linked to human agency.

LAYMON, Ronald. "Idealizations And Testing Of Theories" in *Observation, Experiment, Hypothesis In Modern Physical Science*, Achinstein, Peter (ed), 147–174. Cambridge MIT Pr 1985.

LAYMON, Ronald. "Newton's Demonstration Of Universal Gravitation" in *Testing Scientific Theories*, Earman, John (ed), 179–200. Minneapolis Univ Minnesota Pr 1983.

LAYTON, William and Hiley, David. Team–Teaching With The Corporate Executive. *Teach Phil* 8,27–32 Ja 85.

LAZARI– PAWLOWSKA, Ija. Morality And Human Nature. *Dialec Hum* 11,213–216 Wint 84.

The attempt to find good reasons for a moral program in nature, understood in one or another way, has been undertaken for centuries. In the paper the problem is discussed whether and how our knowledge of "human nature" can be useful for normative ethics, especially knowledge which we owe to the development of such empirical sciences as biology, psychology, sociology, and cultural anthropology. The paper is a summary of a longer article published in Polish.

LAZEROWITZ, Morris and Ambrose, Alice. *Essays In The Unknown Wittgenstein.* Buffalo Prometheus Books 1984.

This book makes application to a number of philosophical problems, certain statements which Wittgenstein made about their nature. For the most part they are inconoclastic statements which have received little attention, but which promise an understanding of the inconclusiveness of philosophical views. Views chosen for illustration are: *a priori* necessity, the infinite, mathematical proof, abstract entities, empiricism, solipsism.

LE BLANC, Hugues. A New Semantics For First–Order Logic, Multivalent And Mostly Intensional. *Topoi* 3,55–62 Je 84.

LE LOUX– SCHURINGA, J A and Verkuyl, H J. Once Upon A Tense. *Ling Phil* 8,237–262 My 85.

The tense–systems proposed by two Dutch grammarians, Te Winkel in 1866 and Kollewijn in 1892, are examined, and compared with the systems proposed by Reichenbach (1947) and Prior (1967). Goals: (1) to show that knowledge of recent theories and technical tools provides valuable insight into older theories; (2) to show where recent theories fail as compared with the older ones; (3) to contribute to the discussion about the relationship between language forms and non–linguistic categories.

LEAL, Fernando. Al Oído Del Dogma. *Rev Filosof (Costa Rica)* 23,137–142 D 85.

This deals with a literary–philosophical fiction in which features of historical events are mixed with imaginary ones; in this manner, an attempt is made to show, vividly, the excesses of dogmatism and fanatism, which aniquilate human dignity and produce suffering. The action takes place in the times of Spanish Inquisition and the scene is configurated according to the customs, beliefs and ideas of the period, all within the limitations and possibilities of what is plausible.

LEAR, Jonathan. Moral Objectivity. *Philosophy* 17,135–170 84 Supp.

A discussion of Hegel's criticism of Kantian morality, Bernard William's criticism of Thomas Nagel, of the limitations of Critical Theory and the possibility of applying an Aristotelian conception of *Eudaimonia* within the framework of modern political society.

LEBLANC, Hugues. On Characterizing Unary Probability Functions And Truth–Value Functions. *Can J Phil* 15,19–24 Mr 85.

LEBLANC, Suzanne. L'objectivité Dans Les Théories Logiques De La Signification. *Dialogue (Canada)* 23,407–420 S 84.

LECKIE, John D. Commentary On B Lichter And M Hodges' "Perceptions Of The Engineers' 'Professionalism' In The Chemical Industry". *Bus Prof Ethics J* 2,9–10 Wint 83.

LECLERC, Ivor. "The Metaphysics Of The Good" in *The Good Life And Its Pursuit*, Dougherty, Jude P (ed), 51–76. NY Paragon House 1984.

LEDDY, Daniel D . Families In Need Of Supervision. *Crim Just Ethics* 4,19–37 Wint/Spr 85.

LEDER, Drew. Troubles With Token Identity. *Phil Stud* 47,79–94 Ja 85.

The thesis of "token identity" or "token physicalism" advanced by Fodor and others attempts to reconcile materialism with a non–reductionist view of the special sciences. However, I argue that since the individual events or "tokens" of any science are only designated according to its general types, the former cannot be specified physicalistically while the latter are not. Though attempting to combat a positivistic view of the sciences, Fodor's thesis rests on a positivistic opposition of token and type.

LEDUC– FAYETTE, Denise. Diderot, Le Désordre, Le Mal. *Rev Phil Fr* 174,337–351 Jl–S 84.

LEE, Harold N. A Semiotic–Pragmatic Theory Of Concepts. *S J Phil* 22,509–522 Wint 84.

Concepts arise from the impulse to communicate. A vocable is attached to a referent by conditioned reflex thus becoming a sign. The referent is a generality itself represented by a sign. A concept is a semiotic relation in which both sign and referent are language–signs. The sign is the name and the referent is the intension of the concept. Concepts are empirical or abstract or normative. Normative concepts are limits not found in experience.

LEE, Harold N. A Semiotic–Pragmatic Theory Of Consciousness. *S J Phil* 23,217–228 Sum 85.

Basic consciousness is distinguished from self consciousness. Consciousness is not an attribute of a self. Rather, the self develops from consciousnes by the aid of language. Consciousness is not substantive but adverbial. Some responses are consciously performed. Others are not. Those consciously performed are semiotic. Semiosis is the necessary and sufficient condition of consciousnes thus defining it. Problems of memory and subjectivity are addressed.

LEE, Henry and Schouls, Peter A (ed). Anti–Skepticism. NY Garland 1984.

LEE, J Roger. "Choice And Harms" in *Rights And Regulation*, Machan, Tibor (ed), 157–176. Cambridge Ballinger 1983.

LEE, Jig–Chuen. Frege's Paradox Of Reference And Castañeda's Guise Theory. *Phil Stud* 46,403–416 N 84.

According to Castañeda's Guise Theory, "The previous king of Thebes is the same as Oedipus' father" means that the–previous–King–of–Thebes–guise is consubstantiated with Oedipus'–father–guise. Guises are consubstantiated with each other iff they co–exist as ontological aspects of an object. Castañeda claims that Frege's paradox of reference can be solved by construing sameness as consubstantiation. I disagree with him and provide two counterexamples to his solution.

LEE, Jig–Chuen. Wang Yang–Ming, Mencius And Internalism. *J Chin Phil* 12,63–74 Mr 85.

My paper takes issue with Nivison's suggestion that Wang differs from Mencius in being a strict internalist. Not being a strict internalist, Wang allows the possibility of action against knowledge. However, Wang holds the doctrine on the unity of knowledge and action. There seems to be a contradiction between the idea that action against knowledge is possible and the doctrine of the unity of knowledge and action. I argue that the contradiction is not genuine.

LEE, Kuang–Sae. Critique Of Scope And Method Of The Northropian Philosophical Anthropology And The Projection Of A Hope For A Meeting Of East And West. *J Chin Phil* 11,255–274 S 84.

LEE, Sander H. "Henry Veatch And The Problem Of A Noncognitivist Ethics" in *The Georgetown Symposium On Ethics*, Porreco, Rocco (ed), 159–170. Lanham Univ Pr Of America 1984.

LEE, Sander H. Sartre's Acceptance Of The Principle Of Universality. *Phil Res Arch* 10,473–476 1985.

It is claimed, in a recently published introductory text book on ethics, that Jean-Paul Sartre did not accept a principle of universalizability. In this paper, I will briefly demonstrate that Sartre did indeed accept such a principle, and I will support my claim to reference to Sartre's own words.

LEE, Sander H. The Central Role Of Universalization In Sartrean Ethics. *Phil Phenomenol Res* 46,59–72 S 85.

Various attempts have been made over the years to specifically spell out exactly how an ethical theory based on the writings of Sartre would look and operate. In this paper, I concentrate on the fundamentally important role of a principle of universalization in the development of Sartrean ethics which is consistent with his other writings. The notion of universalization is usually associated with formalistic ethical theories such as Kant's, yet any understanding of how Sartrean ethics would operate must explicate a kind of "non-cognitivist" notion of universalization if it is to succeed.

LEE, Sander H. The Status Of The Debate On Rights In The USSR. *Stud Soviet Tho* 30,149–164 Ag 85.

In this paper, I argue that perhaps the Soviets are not quite the dogmatic madmen that we sometimes perceive them to be. I will submit that there exists a greater degree of flexibility within the sphere of official Soviet thought than we usually perceive there to be. I will be this by first taking as an example a debate concerning the proper use of logic within Soviet thought. I will then show that there exist significant implications of this debate for another issue of much greater current interest to observers of the USSR in the West, namely the issue of human rights in the Soviet Union.

LEE, Steven. The Morality Of Nuclear Deterrence: Hostage Holding And Consequences. *Ethics* 95,549–566 Ap 85.

Nuclear deterrence is an institution of hostage holding, and as such is shown to be unacceptable from a nonconsequentialist moral perspective. The consequentialist moral advantage claimed for the policy, the avoidance of nuclear war, would be of overriding weight, but only if certain conditions are satisfied. These conditions entail that if any form of nuclear deterrence is morally acceptable, it is not present policy, but rather the policy known as minimum deterrence.

LEE, Vicki L. Some Notes On The Subject Matter Of Skinner's *Verbal Behavior*. *Behaviorism* 12,29–40 Spr 84.

This paper comments on the subject matter of Skinner's book *Verbal Behavior* (1957). It argues against the misconception that *Verbal Behavior* is about language, and it clarifies several other aspects of Skinner's concept of verbal behavior. The paper concludes that the significance of *Verbal Behavior* lies most centrally in giving psychologists a better way of talking about this subclass of operant behavior.

LEEDS, Anthony. "Sociobiology, Epistemology, And Human Nature" in *Methodology, Metaphysics And The History Of Science*, Cohen, Robert S (ed), 215–234. Boston Reidel 1984.

LEEDS, Stephen. A Problem About Frequencies In Direct Inference. *Phil Stud* 48,137–140 Jl 85.

LEEDS, Stephen. Chance, Realism, Quantum Mechanics. *J Phil* 81,567–578 O 84.

LEEDS, Stephen. Postscript To 'A Problem About Frequencies In Direct Inference'. *Phil Stud* 48,149–152 Jl 85.

LEGTERS, Lyman H. Who Speaks For The Workers? *Praxis Int* 4,438–445 Ja 85.

The article takes issue in part with the argument advanced by Wolf Schaefer in *Dialectical Anthropology* (1982, 6) that bourgeois intellectuals like Marx suppressed the authentic voice of the working class and widened the gap between mental and manual labor. The contemporary case of Solidarity in Poland illustrates both sides of the argument: that a genuine working class movement need not be expressly Marxist but also that it can and should be welcomed by Marxist intellectuals.

LEHMAN, Christopher M. "Avoiding Armageddon: Whose Responsibility" in *The Security Gamble*, Mac Lean, Douglas (ed), 82–88. Totowa Rowman & Allanheld 1984.

LEHMAN, Craig K. Realism, Resemblances, And Russell's Regress. *J Crit Anal* 8,99–108 1985.

Bertrand Russell presented a classic objection to nominalism: that the nominalist covertly assumes the existence of a universal or Resemblance in order to articulate the view that there are no universals. I argue that it is in fact Russell who begs the question by formulating the nominalist view in a vocabulary which is covertly realistic. Related views of H H Price, Herbert Hochberg, and David Armstrong are also critically discussed.

LEHMAN, Elliot. Commentary On J Pichler's "The Liberty Principle: A Basis For Management Ethics". *Bus Prof Ethics J* 2,31–34 Wint 83.

LEHRER, Keith. Consensus And The Ideal Observer. *Synthese* 62,109–120 Ja 85.

This is a defense of the theory of rational consensus articulated by K Lehrer and C Wagner; (1981, *Rational Consensus in Science and Society*, D Reidel, Dordrecht) based on iterated weighted averaging of utilities and probabilities against the criticisms of I Levi, F F Schmidt, D Baird, J L Kranuip, B Loewer and R Laddage. The defense is that the rational consensus in question would be accepted by an ideal observer.

LEIGH, David J. Augustine's *Confessions* As A Circular Journey. *Thought* 60,73–88 Mr 85.

Influenced by the symmetrical form tradition of classical epics and by the neoplatonic and Biblical patterns of emanation and return, Augustine structured his autobiography in *Confessions* I–IX as a circular journey of chiasmic form in which the persons, events, and phrases of Books I–IV parallel in inverse order those of Books VI–IX, with Book V providing the transition from Manicheanism to Christianity. book I's Birth to Restless Search parallels Book IX's Restful Death; Book II's Garden of Perversion becomes Book VIII's Garden of Conversion; Book III's Intellectual Birth into Manicheanism is corrected by VII's Rebirth through Neoplatonic; IV's Wanderings into Morality becomes VI's Search for Permance.

LEIGHTON, Stephen R. A New View Of Emotion. *Amer Phil Quart* 22,133–142 Ap 85.

The author notes the recent emergence of wholly cognitive analyses of emotion. The attractions of such views are appreciated. Nonetheless, the author argues that, whatever the details of the particular version of this new view, it is mistaken. By a series of overlapping arguments, the following arguments are reached: (1) emotion is not identical to cognition; (2) cognition is never a sufficient condition for emotion; (3) in certain examples, the cognitions deemed relevant are not necessary to emotion; (4) cognition cannot adequately demarcate the realm of emotion. The upshot is not that cognition is irrelevant to emotion, but that what role it takes, if any, is yet to be established.

LEIGHTON, Stephen R. Feelings And Emotion. *Rev Metaph* 38,303–320 D 84.

When feelings are a feature relevant to emotion what is their status with regard to the (other) features of emotion? The author shows that the modern tradition views feelings as dependent for their indentity upon features other than the feelings themselves, in particular judgments. It is argued that this view is mistaken: some feelings are independent; their identity is determined by the nature of the feelings themselves. Objections are anticipated and responded to.

LEINFELLNER, Werner. Reconstruction Of Schlick's Psycho-Sociological Ethics. *Synthese* 64,317–350 S 85.

LEININGER, Madeleine M. *Care: The Essence Of Nursing And Health*. Thorofare Slack 1981.

This book focuses on care as the heart of nursing and health. The author contends that care provides a distinct characteristic of the discipline and profession of nursing, and serves as its dominant unifying and central focus. Nurse philosophers, theorists, clinicians and researchers demonstrate the above themes and show the obscure nature to investigate care phenomenon. The book is designed to stimulate research regarding the universal and specific features of care through qualitative types of research.

LEISER, Burton M. Professional Advertising: Price Fixing And Professional Dignity Versus The Public's Right To A Free Market. *Bus Prof Ethics J* 3,93–108 Spr/Sum 84.

The prohibitions embodied in various professional codes of ethics against advertising have been breaking down recently due to certain important court decisions. This article examines the rationales favoring those prohibitions and argues that they don't stand up under critical analysis. Focusing particularly on legal advertising, the article concludes that it should be encouraged. It concludes, finally, that the distinctions drawn between advertising and solicitation are immaterial, and that solicitation, too, should be permitted, although some forms of solicitation (like some forms of advertisement) would be unethical.

LEISERING, Heinz. Das Ökonomische Grundgesetz Der Kommunistischen Gesellschaftsformation Und Einige Philosophische Probleme. *Deut Z Phil* 22,458–474 1974.

Das ökonomische Grundgesetz verwirklicht sich in jeder Entwicklungsphase des Kommunismus unter konkreten historischen, geselschaftlichen und ökonomischen Verhältnissen, die sich in veränderter Qualität miteinander verflechten und ständig neue und höhere Anforderungen an die bewufsste Durchsetzung des Gesetzes stellen. Der Sozialismus-Kommunismus ist eine hochorganisierte, reich gegliederte Gesellschaft und mufss durch die marxistisch-leninistische Partei, den Staat und die Werktätigen stets neu gemeistert werden, damit die materiellen und kultrellen Bedürfnisse immer besser befriedigt werden können.

LEIŢOIU, Rodica. Ansätze Zur Semiotischen Analyse Der Gesetze Der Wissenschaft. *Phil Log* 27,323–331 O–D 83.

LELAS, Srdan. Topology Of Internal And External Factors In The Development Of Knowledge. *Ratio* 27,67–82 Je 85.

The aim of the paper is to show that an intellectual system, like a scientific discipline, is not a homogeneous unit and such subjected to internal and/or external forces that cause changes. At least three layers: meta-theoretical, theoretical and empirical can be discerned, each one with different sensibility towards internal and external factor and therefore with different developmental dynamics. The relations between them are examined and the thesis is put forward that the deepest level is in the closest relation to the way of life of a culture or epoch.

LEMAN, Marc. On The Logic And Criteriology Of Causality. *Log Anal* 27,245–266 S 84.

The paper is divided in two parts: in the first part it is argued that the separation between the logical analysis and the epistemological foundation leads to an ambiguous conception about the relation of cause and effect. I argue in favor of a dynamical contructionistic logic, which I propose to be the basis for our reasonings about causal relations. This logic refers to epistemological considerations and the evaluation proceeds in terms of constructivism.

LEMONS, John. A Reply To "On Reading Environmental Ethics". *Environ Ethics* 7,185–188 Sum 85.

Several points are raised about the relevancy of papers published in *Environmental Ethics* to environmental affairs. These are: (1) nonphilosopher environmental professionals have different perspectives about relevancy than environmental philosophers: (2) authors with nonphilosophy disciplines are underrepresented as a group and for each nonphilosophy discipline, even for applied papers: and (3) most papers concern metaethics and normative ethics, but ignore questions of fact. These facts suggest that most papers are not "applied".

LEMOS, Noah M. High-Minded Egoism And The Problem Of Priggishness. *Mind* 93,542–558 O 84.

A C Ewing and John Dewey argue that while the high-minded egoist may conceive of acting virtuously and good character as part of his own good, these are not things he can achieve. The most he can achieve is "priggishness." I examine the claims of Ewing and Dewey and, in more detail, the nature of priggishness itself. I suggest that if the egoist is committed to certain views about value, then it is not clear that he can account for those features of acts of virtue which make them good for their own sakes.

LEMOS, Noah M. Milanich And The Structure Of Omissions. *Phil Stud* 47,305–312 Mr 85.

LEMPERT, Richard. The Force Of Irony: On The Morality Of Affirmative Action And *United Steelworkers* Versus *Weber*. *Ethics* 95,86–89 O 84.

This comment argues that the "reverse discrimination" that some see as implicit in programs of affirmative action is of a different order than discrimination against blacks. It would be ironic if such programs were disallowed as themselves racists when this objection draws its force from the black experience of discrimination, and such programs are designed to overcome the legacy of that experience.

LENAIN, Thierry. Leibniz, Ou L'origine De L'esthétique Descendante. *Stud Leibniz* 16,168–186 1984.

Die leibnizsche Metaphysik stellt die Frage nach dem Verhältnis der Welt zu der ihr zugrundeliegenden göttlichen Vorlage auf eine ganz neue Weise und weist somit die Arbeit des Bewussseins und dessen Ringen um den Sinn in eine Richtung, die neuzeitliches Denken in vielem vorwegnimmt. Es geht nicht mehr darum, sich vom Sinnlichen aus zum Gedanklichen emporzuarbeiten, sondern, ausgehend von den Frundsätzen, die die Wahrnehmung bestimmen, soll sich der Geist um eine eigentliche Talfahrt bemühen, einen Abstieg in die Tiefen des Sinnlichen. Erst eine solche Umkehrung machte die Herausbildung einer philosophischen Ästhetik positiver Art möglich, die auf der Anerkennung des eigenen Wertes des Sinnlichen und der Einbildungskraft beruht. Durch diese beiden Neuerungen bahnte Leibniz der westlichen Philosophie den Weg, den sie im 19. Jahrhundert gegangen ist, und brachte den Verwandlungsprozess des Wesens des Zeichens überhaupt in Gang, indem er zum erstenmal mit der herkömmlichen, aprioristischen Auffassung desselben als voraussetzungsloser Energeia bricht.

LENK, Hans. Bemerkungen Aur Pragmatisch–epistemischen Wende In Der Wissenschaftstheoretischen Analyse Der Ereigniserklärungen. *Erkenntnis* 22,461–474 Ja 85.

The so–called "pragmatic–epistemic turn" (Gärdenfors, Stegmüller) does not distinguish any longer between covering law explanations and subjective arguments supporting beliefs. This extreme reaction against the traditional neglection of pragmatic factors in explanation leads to some counter–intuitive and undesirable consequences as regards the above–mentioned difference. The pragmatic turn certainly reveals some plausibility with respect to everyday explanations, but does not in its totality apply to scientific law covering explanation. Some respective totally pragmatic arguments by Schurz (1983) and Stegmüller (1983) as regards pragmatization and the so–called "detachment theses ("Abkoppelungsthese") of causal explanation are criticized. Some difficulties as regards the formation of basic intuitions for predictions and the interplay with methodological considerations in the philosophy of science community also show that albeit the pragmatic embedding of methodological constructs is necessary, the total pragmatisation of everything would amount to counter–intuitive, one–sided (as regards approximation of deductive explanations to inductive probabilistic belief–argument) exaggeration.

LENNON, Kathleen. Anti–Reductionist Materialism. *Inquiry* 27,363–380 D 84.

This paper characterizes a form of materialism which is strongly anti–reductionist with regard to mental predicates. It argues against the functionalist views of writers such as Brian Loar on the basis that the counterfactual interdependencies of intentional states are governed by constraints of rationality embodied in semantic links which cannot be captured in non–intentional functionalist terms. However, contrary to what is commonly supposed, such anti–reductionism requires neither instrumentalism about the mental nor opposition to a casual explanatory view of intentional explanation. The paper therefore aims to show that a realist causal explanatory view of psychological states is compatible with a non–reductive materialism (a position excluded by Brian Loar in his recent book *Mind and Meaning*.

LENNON, Thomas M. Rules And Relevance: The Au–Ru Equivalence Issue. *Ideal Stud* 14,148–158 My 84.

The literature discussing the extensional equivalence of act and rule utilitarianism has contested the issue using a conception of an act which is inapplicable to rule utilitarian theories. With a more appropriate conception, rule utilitarianism emerges as inequivalent to act utilitarianism, for they are seen to be theories about different kinds of events. Though it appeals to the consequences of the universal practice of acts, rule utilitarianism is the deontological theory it was intended to be and its prescriptions are thus more practicable than those of act utilitarianism.

LENNON, Thomas M. Veritas Filia Temporis: Hume On Time And Causation. *Hist Phil Quart* 2,275–290 Jl 85.

Hume has three arguments concerning time that have no parallels in his treatment of space. The paper explicates these arguments in detail and relates them, historically and systematically, to a broad thesis concerning causation, explanation and existence.

LENNOX, James. Recent Philosophical Studies Of Aristotle's Biology. *Ancient Phil* 4,75–82 Spr 84.

The author critically reviews three recent books on themes relating Aristotle's biological works to various aspects of his philosophy: Pierre Pellegrin's *La Classification des Animaux chez Aristote* (Paris, 1982), Johannes Morsink's *Aristotle on the Generation of Animals* (Washington, DC, 1982), and Michael Boylan's *Method and Practice in Aristotle's Biology* (Washington, DC, 1983). Pellegrin's work is highly recommended by the reviewer for those wishing to understand Aristotle's philosophy of science and scientific practice. Morsink's study is argued to add little, on the whole, to previous work on its subject, and to be confused on certain key issues. Boylan's work is simply not up to professional standards—this fact is briefly noted, and the book is not reviewed.

LENZEN, Wolfgang. "Unbestimmte Begriffe" Bei Leibniz. *Stud Leibniz* 16,1–26 1984.

In many of his logical writings, G W Leibniz makes use of two kinds of symbols: while A, B, C,...Stand for certain determinate or definite concepts, X, Y, Z,...Are referred to as "indefinite concepts." We investigate the various roles played by these variables and show: i) that their most important function consists in serving as (hidden) quantifiers; ii) that Leibniz's elliptic representation of the quantifiers (both universal and existential) by means of two sorts of "indefinite concepts" leads to certain difficulties; iii) that despite these problems Leibniz anticipated the most fundamental logical principles for the quantifiers and may thus be viewed as a forerunner of modern predicate logic. (edited)

LENZEN, Wolfgang. Leibniz Und Die Boolesche Algebra. *Stud Leibniz* 16,187–203 1984.

It is well known that in his logical writings Leibniz typically disregarded the operation of (conceptual) disjunction, confining himself to the theory of conjunction and negation. Now, while this fact has been interpreted by Couturat and others as indicating a serious incompleteness of the Leibnizian calculus, it is shown in this paper that actually Leibniz's conjunction–negation logic, with 'est Ens', i.E., 'is possible' as an additional (although definable) logical operator, is provably equivalent (or isomorphic) to Boolean algebra. Moreover, already in the *Generales Inquisitiones* of 1686 Leibniz had established all basic principles that are necessary for a complete axiomatization of "Boolean" (or better: Leibnizian) algebra. In this sense Leibniz should be acknowledged as the true inventor of the algebra of sets.

LENZER, Gertrud (ed). *Auguste Comte And Positivism: The Essential Writings*. Chicago Univ Of Chicago Pr 1975.

LEONARD, John. Public Versus Private Claims: Machiavellianism From Another Perspective. *Polit Theory* 12,491–506 N 84.

LEPAGE, Francois. La Naissance De La Théorie Des Types. *Philosophiques* 11,277–298 O 84.

The theory of types that Bertrand Russell proposed in 1908 didn't present itself as an ad hoc solution to the problem of contradictions. Rather it pretended to be the natural solution, the one that everybody would recognize as the expected solution. In fact, it is a philosophical theory materializing an imposing project: to reduce mathematics to logic. This paper examines the Russellian theses and their evolution from 1903 to 1907, i.E., for the *Principles* to the birth of the theory of types.

LEPAGE, Francois. The Object Of Belief. *Log Anal* 27,193–210 Je 84.

The purpose of this paper is to develop a characterization of knowledge compatible with intensional logic and based on the following property: what is known cannot induce the knower into error. A recursive definition of the notion of a *good representation* satisfying this property is given. The notion of *cognitive implication* is introduced and applied to belief sentences.

LEPENIES, Wolf. " interesting Questions' In The History Of Philosophy Elsewhere" in *Philosophy In History*, Rorty, Richard and others (ed), 141–172. NY Cambridge Univ Pr 1984.

LESCOE, Francis J (ed) and Liptak, David Q (ed). *Pope John Paul II Lecture Series In Bioethics*. New Britain Mariel 1983.

LESCOE, Marie (trans) and Woznicki, Theresa (trans) and Krąpiec, Mieczylaw A. *I–Man: An Outline Of Philosophical Anthropology*. New Britain Mariel 1983.

LESISZ, Wlodzimierz. On Propositional Calculus With A Variable Functor. *Rep Math Log* 17,19–26 1984.

LESKO, Vladimír. "The Rational Idealism" Of Modern Times And The Idealistic Criticism Of Religion (in Czechoslovakian). *Filosof Cas* 33,36–46 1985.

LESSER, Harry. Can Racial Discrimination Be Proved? *J Applied Phil* 1,253–262 O 84.

This article discusses a particular problem with the race relations legislation: the fact that to show that discrimination has taken place one must prove not only that a person was unfavorably treated but that this was on the grounds of race. The article considers first whether grounds should be interpreted subjectively or objectively, and argues for an objective interpretation, partly to make proof easier, partly because no obvious injustice is done. Then it considers the kinds of evidence relevant to such a proof, and argues that in many cases, although not all, it is in fact available, at least for the level of moral proof on the balance of the probabilities, required for civil, as opposed to criminal, proceedings. It is concluded that difficult cases remain, but not as many, or as difficult, as might appear at first sight.

LESSES, Glenn. Is Socrates An Instrumentalist? *Phil Topics* 13,165–174 Spr 85.

In this paper, it is argued that in Plato's early dialogues Socrates does not hold that moral virtue is an instrumental good, valuable for the sake of something else distinct from it. Texts from the *Gorgias*, *Euthydemus*, and *Lysis* are examined.

LEVAVI, Aryeh. The Neo–Kantian Heritage And The Validity Of Aesthetic Judgments (in Hebrew). *Iyyun* 33,63–77 Ja–Ap 84.

LEVENBOOK, Barbara Baum. The Role Of Coherence In Legal Reasoning. *Law Phil* 3,355–374 D 84.

Many contemporary philosophers of law agree that a necessary condition for a decision to be legally justified, even in a hard case, is that it coheres with established law. Some, namely Satorius and Dworkin, have gone beyond that relatively uncontroversial claim and described that role of coherence in legal justification as analogous to its role in moral and scientific justification, on contemporary theories. In this, I argue, they are mistaken. Specifically, coherence in legal justification is sometimes specific to a branch of law, and there is nothing isomorphic to this in the models of moral and scientific justification. Although Dworkin and Sartorius rely on the concept of coherence, they do not explicate it. In the course of examining their views, this essay offers a partial analysis of coherence on their models. Finally, two canons of relevance, governing when global coherence considerations are appropriate to legal justification, are presented.

LEVENTHAL, F M (ed) and Lovett, William. *Social And Political Morality*. NY Garland 1984.

LEVI, Albert William. Hegel's *Phenomenology* As A Philosophy Of Culture. *J Hist Phil* 22,445–470 O 84.

LEVI, Albert William. Love, Rhetoric, And The Aristocratic Way Of Life. *Phil Rhet* 17,189–208 1984.

LEVI, Albert Williams. "Metaphysics And The History Of Philosophy: The Case Of Whitehead" in *History Of Philosophy In Making*, Thro, Linus J (ed), 213–230. Washington Univ Pr Of America 1982.

LEVI, Albert William. The Art Museum As An Agency Of Culture. *J Aes Educ* 19,23–40 Sum 85.

LEVI, Albert W. Nature And Art. *J Aes Educ* 18,5–22 Fall 84.

LEVI, Isaac. Consensus As Shared Agreement And Outcome Of Inquiry. *Synthese* 62,3–12 Ja 85.

LEVI, Isaac. Epicycles. *J Phil* 82,104–106 F 85.

LEVICH, Marvin. Interpretation In History: Or What Historians Do And Philosophers Say. *Hist Theor* 24,44–61 F 85.

LEVIN, David S. Abortion, Personhood And Vagueness. *J Value Inq* 19,197–210 1985.

LEVIN, David S. Class In Social Stratification And Marxist Theories. *Cogito* 2,117–132 Je 84.

LEVIN, David S. John T Noonan And Baby Jane Doe. *Phil Context* 14,35–41 1984.

LEVIN, David S. Thomson And The Current State Of The The Abortion Controversy. *J Applied Phil* 2,121–126 Mr 85.

Many philosophers who wish to defend abortion, but who have become frustrated by the resistance of the personhood question to yield to any nonarbitrary solution welcomed Judith Thomson's 'A defense of abortion'. Thomson argues that abortion is sometimes justifiable even if the fetus is a person. In this paper I argue that Thomson's argument is a defense of abortion, rather than merely extraction without death, only because of the current state of medical technology. Once the technology is in place to extract foetuses while preserving their lives and to allow them to develop to full term outside the uterus, Thomsom cannot defend the killing of the foetus. If she is right, however, a women will still have the right to have a foetus extracted from her body. Finally, it is pointed out that the source of the problem with Thomson's argument is the major premise in most arguments for the permissibility of abortion: a woman's right to control her own body. If the defense of abortion is to entail a defense of the termination of the foetus, then this premise, understood as the right to remove an unwanted entity from one's body or the right to alter one's body as one wishes, simply will not do the trick.

LEVIN, Michael. Negative Liberty. *Soc Phil Pol* 2,84–100 Autumn 84.

I argue that the only basic rights that can exist in a policy are negative rights to non–interference. Only these are compatible with Kantian constraints. I also argue that the Civil Rights Act and the 1982 Extension of the voting rights act rest on confusions about positive and negative liberty.

LEVINAS, E. De La Sensibilité. *Tijdschr Filosof* 46,409–417 S 84.

LEVINAS, Emanuel. "Martin Buber, Gabriel Marcel, And Philosophy" in *Martin Buber*, Gordon, Haim (ed), 305–324. Beersheva Ktav 1984.

LEVINE, Andrew. *Arguing For Socialism: Theoretical Considerations*. Boston Routledge & K Paul 1984.

An examination of arguments for and against socialism and capitalism in view of prevailing notions of freedom, welfare, justice, democracy and respect for rights; and a discussion of specifically Marxian contributions to this debate. It is argued that pro–socialist arguments generally fare better than pro–capitalist arguments. There is a good deal of discussion of the standards for assessment themselves; and also some discussion of the kinds of institutional arrangements through which socialist societies might, in practice, realize their theoretical advantages.

LEVINE, Andrew and Sober, Elliott. What's Historical About Historical Materialism? *J Phil* 82,304–326 Je 85.

This article explicates the theoretically distinctive sense in which Marx's theory of history, historical materialism, is a historical theory. A contrast is drawn with the Darwinian theory of evolution by natural selection, particularly with regard to the difference between macro and micro theories of change and the distinction between endogenous and exogenous causes.

LEVINE, Carol. A Cotton Dust Study Unmasked. *Hastings Center Rep* 14,17 Ag 84.

This article is a critique of a proposed Dan River Company study that would have exposed workers in one of its textile mills to cotton dust levels that exceed the federal safety limits. The study is criticized on the grounds of research design, risk–benefit ratio, and the ability of workers in this situation to give informed and voluntary consent. The study was withdrawn from consideration for funding by the Occupational Safety and Health Administration.

LEVINE, David L. The Tyranny Of Scholarship. *Ancient Phil* 4,65–74 Spr 84.

LEVINE, Michael P. 'Can We Speak Literally Of God'? *Relig Stud* 21,53–60 Mr 85.

I argue that the question "Can we speak literally of God?" Is fundamentally an epistemological question concerning whether or not we can know that God can exist. If and only if we can know that God can exist can we know the we can speak literally of God. Following William Alston, with qualifications, I explain why we can speak literally of God in the relevant sense of true literal predication "if and only if we can form [coherent] concepts of intrinsic divine properties." I then argue that the question (1) "Can we know that we can form coherent concepts of such properties?" Reduces

to (2) "Can we know that it is possible that such properties are exemplified by God?"

LEVINE, Michael P. Self–Authenticating Experiences Of God: A Reply To Robert Oakes. *Int J Phil Relig* 16,161–164 1984.

Robert Oakes has argued that if it is possible that there is an experience to which the property "being–a–verdical–experience–of–God" is essential, then there could conceivably be self–be self–authenticating experiences of God. I argue that what Oakes needs to do to defend his thesis is not to defend the view that the property of being verdical essentially entails the property of being self–authenticating. Rather, he needs to elucidate and defend a non–criterial account of knowledge and certainty that extends beyond first person statements about one's own current mental states to statements about religious experience of a certain type. Previous articles by both Oakes and myself are referred to.

LEVINE, Michael P. Why Traditional Theism Does Not Entail Pantheism. *Sophia (Australia)* 23,13–20 Jl 84.

In his essay "Does Traditional Theism Entail Pantheism?", American Philosophical Quarterly volume 20, 1983, Professor Oakes attempts to defend the following thesis: Objects, including persons, that depend necessarily for their perdurance (i.E., lasting existence) upon some rational entity are, ontologically speaking, necessarily such that they are aspects or modifications of the entity that is their conserving agent. This essay is an examination of the modal aspects of Oakes' thesis and a critique of his conclusion that there is a good reason to suppose that theism does entail pantheism.

LEVINE, Norman. *Dialogue Within The Dialectic*. Winchester Allen & Unwin 1984.

LEVINE, Norman. Lenin's Utopianism. *Stud Soviet Tho* 30,95–108 Ag 85.

LEVINE, Norman. Wilhelm Reich: Culture As Power. *Hist Euro Ideas* 5,273–292 1984.

LEVINSON, Jerrold. Hybrid Art Forms. *J Aes Educ* 18,5–14 Wint 84.

This paper examines the notion of a hybrid artform, finds that it is essentially a historical notion, sketches a rough typology of hybrid artforms, and concludes with some reflections on the characteristic effects of works in such artforms.

LEVITZ, Hilbert. An Ordered Set Of Arithmetic Functions Representing The Least ϵ–number. *Z Math Log* 21,115–120 1975.

LEVITZ, Hilbert. Decidability Of Some Problems Pertaining To Base 2 Exponential Diophantine Equations. *Z Math Log* 31,109–115 1985.

LEVY, David E. "Ethical Considerations In Care Of Unconscious Patients" in *Ethical Questions In Brain And Behavior*, Pfaff, Donald W (ed), 57–72. NY Springer 1983.

LEVY, David J. Politics, Nature And Freedom: On The Natural Foundation Of The Political Condition. *J Brit Soc Phenomenol* 15,286–300 O 84.

LEVY, René. Eigentum Und Macht In Der Modernen Industriegesellschaft. *Stud Phil (Switzerland)* Supp 12,145–160 1983.

This contribution to a debate about the constitutional right to property stresses the link between private property and social power. Legal codification of property is one form of stabilizing power differentials. The property–power–nexus is explicated theoretically and illustrated by anthropological findings. Considering that private property is a cultural construct, excludes the non–possessing, and is profitable indistinctly to natural and juristic persons, the problem cannot be discussed realistically if its ethical and political nature is not recognized.

LEVY, Robert J. Conjectures And Rational Preferences. *Phil Res Arch* 10,173–188 1984.

I survey the difficulties of several probabilistic views on non–deductive argument and of inductive probability and propose to explicate non–deductive reasoning in terms of rational preference. Following a critical examination of Popper's allegedly deductive theory of rational preference, I draw upon the work of Popper and Rescher to present my view which includes: (i) the conjecturing of a set of alternative answers to or theories of hypotheses about the questions prompting the inquiry and (ii) the "reduction" of this set via plausibilistic principles of rational preference.

LEVY, Ze'ev. On Theology And On Jewish Concepts Of Ultimate Reality And Meaning In Modern Jewish Philosophy. *Ultim Real Mean* 8,40–48 Mr 85.

The essay attempts to elucidate the meaning of the term "Jewish Theology", and its relation to philosophy in general and to the concept of Ultimate Reality in particular. The main difficulty consists in the crucial difference between *choosing* a philosophical view which leaves all the options open, or *accepting a–priori* a theological credo. The question whether human beings can *In potentia* conceive of Ultimate Reality or whether it transcends the scope of the human intellect, is essentially a matter of faith.

LEVY, Zeev. Paul Ricoeur's Philosophical Hermeneutics (in Hebrew). *Iyyun* 33,156–171 Ja–Ap 84.

LEWINTER, Roger. La Quadrature Du Cercle: Remarques Sur Diderot Et L'Encyclopédie. *Rev Metaph Morale* 89,226–231 Ap–Je 84.

LEWIS, Christopher. Baruch Spinoza, A Critic Of Robert Boyle: On Matter. *Dialogue (PST)* 27,11–22 O 84.

Spinoza and Boyle on how Nitre and Spirit of Nitre differ. From experiments Boyle concluded they differ qualitatively. spinoza disagreed. At stake is a deeper philosophical issue: is matter qualitative or quantitative? The controversy is introduced in its historical setting. Then Boyle's view is outlined. Finally, some of Spinoza's criticisms are given.

LEWIS, David. "Devil's Bargains And The Real World" in *The Security Gamble*, Mac Lean, Douglas (ed), 141–154. Totowa Rowman & Allanheld 1984.

LEWIS, David. Putnam's Paradox. *Austl J Phil* 62,221–236 S 84.

Putnam's "model–theoretic argument against metaphysical realism" is a correct refutation of a global description theory of reference. It demonstrates that if, as we usually suppose, we achieve more–or–less determinate reference, that must be so in virtue of constraints not established by our own stipulation—perhaps, as Merrill has suggested, constraints based on an objective discrimination between things and classes which are more and less eligible to serve as referents.

LEWIS, Frank A. "Form And Predication In Aristotle's *Metaphysics*" in *How Things Are*, Bogen, James (ed), 59–84. Boston Reidel 1985.

LEWIS, Frank A. "Plato's Third Man Argument And The 'Platonism' Of Aristotle" in *How Things Are*, Bogen, James (ed), 133–174. Boston Reidel 1985.

LEWIS, Meirlys. "The Art Of Saying What Can Be Imagined" in *Philosophy And Life: Essays On John Wisdom*, Dilman, Ilham (ed), 123–144. Boston Nijhoff 1984.

LEWIS, Peter. A Note On Audience Participation And Psychical Distance. *Brit J Aes* 25,273–277 Sum 85.

It is argued that, contrary to the view of Susanne Langer and George Dickie, audience participation in the theatre is compatible with the maintenance of Psychical Distance. Scrutiny of Bullough's work reveals that his account of the "twofold character of the aesthetic state in which we know a thing not to exist but accept its existence' is in harmony with a number of recent theories of fiction.

LEWIS, Phillip V. Defining 'Business Ethics': Like Nailing Jello To A Wall. *J Bus Ethics* 4,377–383 O 85.

Business ethics is a topic receiving much attention in the literature. However, the term 'business ethics' is not adequately defined. Typical definitions refer to the rightness or wrongness of behavior, but not everyone agrees on what is morally right or wrong, good or bad, ethical or unethical. To complicate the problem, nearly all available definitions exist at highly abstract levels. This article focuses on contemporary definitions of business ethics by business writers and professionals and on possible areas of agreement among the available definitions. Then a definition is synthesized that is broad enough to cover the field of management in a sense as full as most managers might conceive of it.

LEY, Hermann. Zu Kants Unterscheidung Von Platonismus Und Epikureismus. *Deut Z Phil* 22,308–320 1974.

LEY, Hermann. Zum Stand Der Entwicklungstheorie In Den Naturwissenschaften. *Deut Z Phil* 23,964–980 1975.

LEYVRAZ, Jean–Pierre and Holzhey, Helmut (ed). *Ästhetische Erfahrung Und Das Wesen Der Kunst.* Bern Haupt 1984.

LICHTENBERT, Robert H. In Defense Of Objectivist Art Criticism. *J Aes Educ* 18,108–113 Wint 84.

The major arguments for Subjectivist art criticism can be criticized as follows: art criticism is 1) variable (factual, not normative), 2) personal (extremely solipsistic and isolationist) and 3) emotional (implies anti–rationalism). I defend Objectivist art criticism by the following arguments: 1) the philosophy of the arts contains principles of art criticism, 2) art criticism arises from facts, although not absolutely, 3) logic is more relevant to art criticism than psychology and 4) evaluation differs from valuation.

LICHTER, Barry D and Hodges, Michael P. Perceptions Of The Engineers' "Professionalism" In The Chemical Industry. *Bus Prof Ethics J* 2,1–8 Wint 83.

The purpose of this work is to clarify the nature of engineering professionalism by looking to the experience of practicing engineers. An analysis is presented based on the experiences of offering workshops to technical employees at plant sites in the chemical industry. The authors conclude that role proliferation discourages professional autonomy in a corporate setting and that we require a new concept of professionalism that accounts for the essential coupling of business and engineering.

LICHTIGFELD, A. On Franz Rosenzweig's 'New Thinking'. *Tijdschr Filosof* 46,647–651 D 84.

Rosenzweig defines his 'New Thinking' as in opposition to Hegel's way of thinking of the Absolute coming to itself through finite spirit. As against Hegel's totalitarian view, Rosenzweig thought of Reality to be composed of a 'plenitude of visions' (God, World, and Man), their true nature being in their reciprocal interaction in terms of creation, revelation and redemption. In this context, author points to R Wiehl's attempt (in: Philos Jahrb 1982, 269 ff) to justify Rosenzweig's approach on philosophical grounds.

LIE, Reidar K. The Use Of Interval Estimators As A Basis For Decision–Making In Medicine. *Theor Med* 5,233–240 O 84.

Decision analysts sometimes use the results of clinical trials in order to evaluate treatment alternatives. I discuss some problems associated with this, and in particular I point out that it is not valid to use the estimates from clinical trials as the probabilities of events which are needed for decision analysis. I also attempt to show that an approach based on objective statistical theory may have advantages over commonly used methods based on decision theory. (edited)

LIEB, Irwin C. "Happiness And The Good Life" in *The Good Life And Its Pursuit*, Dougherty, Jude P (ed), 19–34. NY Paragon House 1984.

LIEBERMANN, Yehoshua. Competition In Consumption As Viewed By Jewish Law. *J Bus Ethics* 4,385–393 O 85.

Competition is the most basic force traditionally regarded by Western economists as governing both society's resources allocation and income distribution. No wonder, then, that many legal systems have been concerned with various aspects of competitive activity, and formulated laws and rulings to keep market behavior within limits of ethical conduct. Jewish law has not been an exception.

LIEBICH, Andre. "Straussianism And Ideology" in *Ideology, Philosophy And Politics*, Parel, Anthony (ed), 225–245. Waterloo Laurier Univ Pr 1983.

LIEBSCHER, Heinz and Simon, R. Einen Neuen Schwerpunkt In Der Zusammenarbeit Mit Naturwissenschaftlern—Brauchen Wir Ihn Wirklich? *Deut Z Phil* 32,1020–1022 1984.

LIEBSCHER, Heinz. Philosophical Discussion Concerning The Issue Of Information (in German). *Deut Z Phil* 32,1068–1074 1984.

LIEPERT, Anita. Aufklärung Und Religionskritik Bei Kant. *Deut Z Phil* 22,359–368 1974.

Kant nimmt mit seinem Aufklärungsbegriff und seiner Religionskritik aufklärerische

Prinzipien unmittelbar in seine Weltanschauung auf und entwickelt sie weiter. Erringung der "Mündigkeit" als Zeil und Inhalt des Prozesses der Aufklärung bedurfte nach Kant vor allem des Kampfes gegen die Theologie, wo sie die Vernunft erniedrigt, und gegen die Religion, soweit sie das gesellschaftliche Leben im Interesse der Feudalmacht reguliert. (edited)

LIEPMAN, Marcia K. "Deception In The Teaching Hospital" in *Difficult Decisions In Medical Ethics*, Ganos, Doreen L (ed), 87–94. NY Liss 1983.

LIJUN, Song. Interrelations Between Subject And Object In Perception. *Chin Stud Phil* 16,48–61 Fall 84.

LILLA, Mark. The Museum In The City. *J Aes Educ* 19,79–92 Sum 85.

Despite the growing popularity of museums among visitors and public officials, no one knows how to *think* about the museum today. They are simply treated as aesthetic institutions or public–welfare programs, although they were originally built as *civic* institutions with a deeply political purpose: the cultural enfranchisement of all Americans. The distinction between "public" and "civic" institutions is examined at length, and is found to reveal important principles for museum building, education, and acquisitions.

LIN, He. Hegel's Early Thought. *Chin Stud Phil* 16,3–21 Wint 84–85.

LINDAHL, B Ingemar B. Philosophy Of Medicine In Scandinavia. *Theor Med* 6,65–84 F 85.

This article presents a brief general view of the recent literature and the scholarly activity in the field of philosophy of medicine in Scandinavia. The focus of attention is not on medical ethics, but on studies on topics like decision theory, medical classification, causality, causal explanations, concept formation, and on analyses of different ideals of medical science and clinical practice. A few principal works on medical ethics are mentioned by way of introduction and a brief account of a highly topical debate on the legislation on artificial insemination in Sweden is given at the end.

LINDBECK, Violette. Thailand: Buddhism Meets The Western Model. *Hastings Center Rep* 14,24–26 D 84.

LINDEN, George W. Film, Fantasy, And The Extension Of Reality. *J Aes Educ* 18,37–54 Fall 84.

The essence of the surrealist aesthetic is defined. Specific surrealist techniques are discussed. The theory and practice of surrealism are then applied to film, differentiating surrealism from other movements such as neo–realism. It is concluded that Luis Bunuel was the only complete surrealist film maker for he alone retained surrealist techniques while at the same time understanding film form.

LINDNER, F and Biedermann, Georg. Schelling–Konferenz In Jena. *Deut Z Phil* 23,1072–1075 1975.

LINDNER, Margit. Zur Philosophischen Leistung Friedrich Schillers. *Deut Z Phil* 32,865–873 1984.

LINEHAN, Elizabeth A. The Duty Not To Kill Oneself. *Proc Cath Phil Ass* 58,104–111 1984.

Suicide and voluntary active euthanasia are nearly always wrong because: 1) It cannot be shown that death is ever good for the one who dies; and there is good reason for supposing that it is generally an evil, not simply neutral. 2) The application of a consent–as–waiving–the–right–to–life analysis to voluntary euthanasia and suicide is not coherent; the appropriate discussion is not one of rights but of duties. 3) Bringing about one's own death—directly or indirectly—violates a duty to oneself.

LINGIS, Alphonso F. An Infinite Time Of One's Own. *Eidos* 1,180–198 D 79.

LINGIS, Alphonso F. The Truth Imperative. *Auslegung* 11,317–339 Fall 84.

This article shows how the will to truthfulness, not a trait of human nature, in Kant devolves from the categorical imperative. The autonomous life is also a completely public life, each of its gestures a sign of the universal truth. In Nietzsche too masters involves veracity. The will to truthfulness derives from the imperative of mastery, which in turn derives from the most universal of nature—that of eternal recurrence.

LINGIS, Alphonso. Oedipus Rex: The Oedipus Rule And Its Subversion. *Human Stud* 7,91–100 1984.

Jacques Lacan has made of the Oedipus complex the process by which the libido is detached from immediate gratification and acquires symbolic, linguistic intentionality. This study criticizes this conception, drawing on some theses of Gilles Deleuze and Félix Guattari.

LINGIS, Alphonso. The Assignation. *Phil Context* 14,70–79 1984.

An essay on anonymity, authenticity, and death, on the occasion of some individual artists and men and women who take on political responsibility. How the anxious sense of one's own morality is the basis of the authentic sense of one's own existence. How this singular existence is contested by the morality of another.

LINHART, J. Prigogine's And Piaget's Theory Of Dynamic Equilibrium And Dialectical And Materialist Conception Of Human Evolution (in Czechoslovakian). *Filozof Cas* 32,845–855 1984.

LIPIEC, Józef. How Is Sport Possible? *Dialec Hum* 11,115–124 Wint 84.

LIPKIN, Robert J. The Theory Of Reciprocal Altruism. *Phil Stud (Ireland)* 30,108–121 Spr 84.

LIPMAN, Matthew. On Children's Philosophical Style. *Metaphilosophy* 15,318–330 Jl–O 84.

Children can vigorously pursue a line of inquiry when they can think and discuss collaboratively. They are very quick to note alternatives, but they tend to give individual reasons for opinions rather than construct elaborate arguments. Their formulations are simple but strong, rude but to the point; one might even call them Doric. The paper is concomitantly concerned with what it is to do philosophy, the difference between philosophical and non–philosophical discussions, and the dangers of the pseudophilosophical.

LIPMAN, Matthew. Philosophy For Children And Critical Thinking: With Examples Of Critical Thinking Skills. *Nat Forum* 65,18–23 Wint 85.

There is a stir of interest in educational circles, and in higher education as well, in "critical thinking" and in "education for thinking". This article examines the movement in the light of scepticism such as voiced by Ryle, and argues for philosophy, it its primary version that has been prepared for children, as the most suitable response to this need. An appendix demonstrates some elementary examples of reasoning skills applied to ethical questions.

LIPTAK, David Q (ed) and Lescoe, Francis J (ed). *Pope John Paul II Lecture Series In Bioethics*. New Britain Mariel 1983.

LISBOA, Joao Luis and Amado, Maria Teresa. Moral Y Politica En "Para La Paz Perpetua" De Kant. *Pensamiento* 40,431–458 O–D 84.

To Kant peace is a categorical imperative. It is the realization of the reign of reason and freedom of the will. It corresponds to the maximum of humanization permitting the insertion of the individual in the Human Community. The kantian idea that the world is a racional construction therefore acquires ontological value. Kant bases theoretically the action on constructing politics in the moral theories, thus ruling the basic moral principle. The rational law will be the ground of this action.

LISCHKE, Gerhard. Über Die Erfüllung Gewisser Erhaltungssätze Durch Kompliziertheitsmasse. *Z Math Log* 21,159–166 1975.

LISTON, Daniel P. Marxism And Schooling: A Failed Or Limited Tradition: A Response To Henry Giroux. *Educ Theor* 35,307–312 Sum 85.

In a previous article H Giroux argued that the Marxist tradition is irredeemably flawed and, therefore, should be abandoned by those engaged in studies of schooling. I argue that Giroux's assertions that Marxism devalues politics, ideology and culture, falls into a trap of scientism, and is locked into a two class mode of analysis are incorrect. His critique overlooks major segments within the Marxist tradition.

LITMAN, A D. Marxistisch–Leninistische Philosophie In Indien. *Deut Z Phil* 22,698–717 1974.

Seit ihrer Gründung im Jahre 1925 betreibt die Kommunistische Partei Indiens eine aktive Propaganda der marxistisch–leninistischen Philosophie unter den indischen Werktätigen. Den dialektischen und historischen Materialismus hat sie konsequent zur theoretischen und methodologischen Grundlage ihrer praktischen Tätigkeit und ihres ideologischen Kampfes gemacht. Dabei standen solche sozialpolitischen und ökonomischen Fragen im Vordergrund ihrer Aufmerksamkeit, die unmittelbar mit dem Kampf der Partei um die Verbesserung der Lage der Werktätigen, für Frieden, Demokratie und Sozialismus verbunden sind.

LITTLE, Daniel. Reflective Equilibrium And Justification. *S J Phil* 22,373–388 Fall 84.

This article assesses the epistemic force of Rawls's concept of reflective equilibrium. It considers the status of coherence arguments in Rawls's account; the effectiveness of Rawls's appeal to considered judgments (narrow reflective equilibrium); and the epistemic utility of Rawls's appeal to intertheoretical support from adjoining philosophical theories (wide reflective equilibrium). It is concluded that none of these forms of argument possesses enough justificatory force to constitute a strong form of moral justification.

LIU, Fu–Tseng and Hung, Cheng–Uan. Set Theories: Their Philosophic Issues And Foundations (in Chinese). *Phil Rev (Taiwan)* 7,91–116 Ja 84.

This paper traces the main philosophic issues and the foundations of Cantorian set theory and the contemporary cumulative hierarchy theory (c h t). From a platonistic view point, we formulate two theories of c h t that is, stage theory and level theory. The latter is characteristically stronger than the former. Axioms of Zermelo Fraenkel set theory, ZF, that can be deduced within two theories, are explained and left as logical exercises. We believe that, for a deep understanding of model–theoretic results in axiomatic set theory, we must capture fully the philosophy (and the picture) of the cumulative hierarchy.

LIU, Fu–Tseng. Elementary Propositions In Wittgenstein's *Tractatus* (in Chinese). *Phil Rev (Taiwan)* 7,55–90 Ja 84.

This is the fourth paper in my continuing research on Wittgenstein's *Tractatus*. The *Tractatus* theory of language has mainly two components: the "picture theory" and the "truth–function theory". Elementary propositions is one of the basic concepts essentially connected with these two theories. In this paper I attempt a thorough study of the concept of elementary propositions. I identify and articulate seven basic features of elementary propositions. In addition to examining the accounts of other researchers on these basic features, I contribute what I call the metaphysical language formulized in the philosophy of the *Tractatus*, and the coordinate diagram of elementary propositions, to account for elementary propositions.

LIU, Ming–wood. The Yogācāra And Mādhyamika Interpretations Of The Buddha–Nature Concept In Chinese Buddhism. *Phil East West* 35,171–194 Ap 85.

This is the fourth of a series of essays ("The Doctrine of Buddha–Nature in the Mahāyāna Mahāparinirvān–sūtra", *Journal of the International Association of Buddhist Studies*, 5 (1982), "The Problem of the *Icchantika in the Mahāyāna Mahāparinirvāna–sūtra*", *Journal of the International Association of Buddhist Studies*, 7 (1984), "The Early Development of the Buddha–Nature Doctrine in China", forthcoming in *Journal of Chinese Philosophy*), which attempt to trace the transformation of the Buddha–nature concept after its introduction into China. It examines and compares the Buddha–nature theories of Hui–yüan and Chi–tsang, representative figures of the Chinese Yogācāra and Mādhyamika traditions respectively.

LIVINGSTON, Donald W. *Hume's Philosophy Of Common Life*. Chicago Univ Of Chicago Pr 1984.

This is the first study to unite Hume's philosophical writings with his long–neglected historical works. Hume emerges from this comprehensive reading as a philosopher whose main doctrines of knowledge and existence are structured by *historical*, *narrative* categories making his empiricism unique. By reference to these categories, Hume's entire philosophical enterprise takes on new meaning and his conceptions of causality, perception, imagination, reason, utility, and skepticism appear in a different light.

LIVINGSTON, Donald and Capaldi, Nicholas and King, James. The Hume Literature Of The 1970's. *Phil Topics* 12,167–192 Wint 81.

LIVINGSTON, Donald. Theism And The Rationale Of Hume's Skepticism About Causation. *Ideal Stud* 15,151–164 My 85.

Hume's well–known skepticism about causal connections is possible only because a belief in the existence of ultimate causal powers. The universe is viewed as an ultimately intelligible system of causal powers with God being the ultimate cause of the system. Hume's thesis is not a guide of his psychological make–up but is internal to his philosophical system.

LLOYD, Genevieve. *The Man Of Reason: "Male" And "Female" In Western Philosophy*. Minneapolis Univ Minnesota Pr 1984.

This work examines points in the history of western philosophy the male–female distinction has been associated with distinctions between Reason and its opposites, and the role of these associations in the formation of sexual stereotypes. Authors examined include Plato, Augustine, Aquinas, Descartes, Hume, Rousseau, Kant, Hegel, sartre, and de Beauvoir. The book includes a bibliographical essay on philosophical work on gender and on feminist critiques of the philosophical tradition.

LLUBERES, Pedro. "Popper's Solution To The Problem Of Induction" in *Philosophical Analysis In Latin America*, Gracia, Jorge J E and others (eds), 381–396. Boston Reidel 1984.

LOADER, John. An Alternative Concept Of The Universal Decision Element In *m*–valued Logic. *Z Math Log* 21,369–375 1975.

LOBKOWICZ, Nicholas. Schmitz, Jordan And Wallace On Intelligibility. *Rev Metaph* 38,57–68 S 84.

The paper tries to tie together the three lectures commented upon and set them into a larger context. It contradicts Father Wallace's claim that modern science continues what Aristotle has conceived; Aristotle did not know the modern notion of theory.

LOBKOWICZ, Nikolaus. "Between Aristotle And Anarchy: The Moral Challenge Of Freedom" in *On Freedom*, Howard, John A (ed), 7–26. Greenwich Devin–Adair 1984.

LOBKOWICZ, Nikolaus. Wie Koennte Politische Philosophie Aussehen? *Phil Rundsch* 31,236–263 1984.

Reviewing several recently published books, the paper tries to show that political philosophy cannot be construed on ethical (Aristotle), contractual (Enlightenment) or holistic (Hegel) lines alone. A synthesis presupposing metaphysics is what is needed. Klaus Hartmann's *Politische Philosophie* is promising in this respect.

LOCK, Grahame. *The State And I: Hypotheses On Juridical And Technocratic Humanism*. Hague Nijhoff 1981.

This work argues that it is wrong to conceive of an adequate theory of ideology as a theory of erroneous thinking. For any theory of this latter kind would require a corresponding obverse theory of correct thinking–that is, a set of principles of adjudication of an authorative nature. But, no such authorative supreme court of science can exist. The notion that it could indeed exist is itself derived from legal ideology, the dominant mode of thought of the modern age. Legal ideology can in turn only be properly analyzed as a material instance of the State.

LOCKE, Don (ed) and Weinreich Haste, Helen (ed). *Morality In The Making*. NY Wiley 1983.

This book is in three parts; the first discusses issues about the development of moral reasoning, and in particular critically addresses Kohlberg's work on stages of moral thought. The second section is concerned with the relationship between judgement and action, in particular the issue of weakness of will. In the final section, the papers consider social factors of morality; the role of early family life, the group and identity. The key feature of the book in the integration of philosophical and psychological approaches, and the authors are drawn from both disciplines.

LOCKE, Don. The Right To Strike. *Philosophy* 18,173–202 84 Supp.

A strike is not only a refusal to work but a refusal to allow others to work in your place. A right to strike means that people ought to be allowed to (they should not be prevented from) doing this. Just cause and lesser evil justifications of this right are rejected. The justification seems to be that a strike is a Prisoners' Dilemma situation in which some individuals need to be coerced for the good of all.

LOCKWOOD, Michael. Einstein, Gibbins And The Unity Of Time. *Analysis* 45,148–150 Je 85.

LOEB, Louis E and Richardson, Robert C. Replies To Daisie Radner's "Is There A Problem Of Cartesian Interaction"? *J Hist Phil* 23,221–226 Ap 85.

LOESCHMANN, Fred. *Philosophy Of Man And The Universe*. Roslyn Heights Libra 1976.

This book examines the fragmented and artificial nature of human categories and language as applied to the universe. With an awareness of such limits, Loeschmann examines the traditional problems in ethics, political theory, metaphysics, epistemology, education, and aesthetics. (staff)

LOESER, Franz. "The Proof Of The Pudding Lies In The Eating" (in German). *Deut Z Phil* 22,86–90 1974.

LOESER, Franz. Wahrheit Und Moral. *Deut Z Phil* 22,492–495 1974.

LOEWENBERG, Robert J. John Locke And The Antebellum Defense Of Slavery. *Polit Theory* 13,266–291 My 85.

LOEWER, Barry M and Bell, Nora K. What Is Wrong With 'Wrongful Life' Cases? *J Med Phil* 10,127–146 My 85.

'wrongful life' torts raise a number of interesting and perplexing philosophical issues. In a suit for 'wrongful life', the plaintiff (usually an infant) brings an action (usually against a physician) claiming that some negligent action has caused the plaintiff's life, say by not informing the parents of the likely prospect that their child would be born with severe defects. The most perplexing feature of this is that the plaintiff is claiming the he would have been better off if he had never been born. A number of arguments have appeared with purport to show that 'wrongful life' claims should not be allowed, either because it is senseless to claim that one would be better off if one had not existed or that it is impossible to assess the extent to which someone has been damaged by being brought into existence. In our paper we rebut these arguments and suggest a procedure for determining damages in 'wrongful life cases'.

LOEWER, Barry and Laddaga, Robert. Destroying The Consensus. *Synthese* 62,79–96 Ja 85.

LOFTIN, Robert W. The Medical Treatment Of Wild Animals. *Environ Ethics* 7,231–240 Fall 85.

The medical treatment of wild animals is an accepted practice in our society. Those who take it upon themselves to treat wildlife are well–intentioned and genuinely concerned about their charges. However, the doctoring of sick animals is of extremely limited value and for the most part based on biological illiteracy. It wastes scarce resources and diverts attention from more worthwhile goals. While it is not wrong to minister to wildlife it is not right either. The person who refuses to do so has not violated any moral duty and is not necessarily morally callous. The treatment of wildlife is based on the mistaken belief that value lies in individual wild animals rather than the entire ecosystem. The genuine concern of those who doctor wild animals should be channeled into more constructive directions.

LOLLI, Gabriele. Foundational Problems From Computation Theory. *Synthese* 62,275–288 F 85.

LOMASKY, Loren E and Buchanan, James M. The Matrix Of Contractarian Justice. *Soc Phil Pol* 2,12–32 Autumn 84.

We examine two traditions of contractarianism, "Hobbesian" contract made in full knowledge of individuating circumstances and "Rawlsian" contract behind a veil of ignorance, and we consider how each can justify the assignment of equal liberties to all parties. Then, concentrating on Rawlsian contract, we set out presuppositions to justify the priority of liberty over economic goods and reasons why equal liberty is a stipulation of justice while economic equality is not.

LOMASKY, Loren E. Being A Person—Does It Matter? *Phil Topics* 12,139–152 Wint 81.

Persons are overwhelmingly the beings to whom moral considerations apply. It may therefore be supposed that being a person is itself a moral consideration. It has been claimed, for example, that the proper policy to adopt toward fetuses and the irreversibly comatose hinges on whether they are persons. In this paper I examine three types of construals of 'person' and argue that none provides a sense in which being a person is morally relevant property. I conclude that no moral debate is likely to be advanced by determining whether some affected party is or is not a person.

LOMBARDI, Joseph J. Suicide And The Service Of God. *Ethics* 95,56–67 O 84.

In two recent articles, Baruch Brody suggests that religious considerations, e.G., the existence of God and His creation of persons, make a difference in the moral evaluation of suicide. This article argues that the religious considerations Brody introduces, when placed in the context of other commonly accepted religious beliefs, e.G., that God is benevolent, will not suffice to justify this alleged difference in the moral evaluation of suicide.

LOMBARDI, Louis G. A Quick Justification For Business Ethics. *J Bus Ethics* 4,353–356 Ag 85.

The article examines the question of whether business ethics courses ought to have an impact. Despite the still common attitude among students and some business professionals that ethical considerations are less pressing in busines, I argue that moral obligations are just as important there as elsewhere. The emphasis on profits in business is related to other realms (e.G., hobbies and seeking education) in which, though private goals are dominant, moral limits remain in force. Business ethics courses can play a crucial role in emphasizing the necessity of ethical analysis in business.

LONDEY, David. An Open Question Argument In Cicero. *Apeiron* 18,144–147 1984.

Cicero's *De Finibus* II, xv maintains against Epicurus that moral integrity (*honestum*) can be identified neither with what wins public approval nor with pleasure (*voluptas*). The Ciceronian argument against the *honestum/voluptas* identification is examined, and is found to have the structure of an Open Question Argument (in Moore's sense). It remains open, however, whether Cicero was aware of the general power of such arguments against ethical naturalist positions.

LONDEY, David. The Agent In A Northern Landscape. *Inquiry* 27,425–438 D 84.

Most of the paper is devoted to examining and discussing a conceptual scheme devised by Jakob Meloe for the description of human action. The main focus is on that part of the scheme which Meloe has developed in detail in his 'Aktoren og hans verden', and which is a scheme for describing single practical operations by a single agent. These operations have the form 'x' operates on 'y'. I identify as central in this scheme the four concepts of *the operation's tautologous object, the operation's tautologous subject, the agent and the agent's tautologous body*. The common thematic concern of Meloe's work and this paper is the question of the extent to which the agent's *landscape* (in a fairly broad sense of the term) is a determinant of the identity of his action.

LONERGAN, Bernard. Questionnaire On Philosophy. *Method* 2,1–35 O 84.

LONERGAN, Bernard. The Original Preface. *Method* 3,3–8 Mr 85.

LONG, Peter. "Universals: Logic And Metaphor" in *Philosophy And Life: Essays On John Wisdom*, Dilman, Ilham (ed), 271–290. Boston Nijhoff 1984.

LONG, Thomas A. Informed Consent And Engineering: An Essay Review. *Bus Prof Ethics J* 3,59–66 Fall 83.

The suggestion that informed consent procedures be introduced into engineering because engineering involves *social experimentation* is examined and rejected as largely unsound. Medicine is taken as the model for understanding informed consent procedures and important disanalogies between medicine and engineering are explored. Proxy consent, in the forms of "best interests" decisions and "substituted judgment," is examined for applicability to typical engineering practice. The unworkability of proxy consent in engineering is shown via discussion of examples.

LONGENECKER, Justin G. Management Priorities And Management Ethics. *J Bus Ethics* 4,65–70 F 85.

LONGO, G and Moggi, E. The Hereditary Partial Effective Functionals And Recursion Theory In Higher Types. *J Sym Log* 49,1319–1332 D 84.

A type–structure of partial effective functionals over the natural numbers, based on a canonical enumeration of the partial recursive functions, is developed. These partial functionals, defined by a direct elementary technique, turn out to be the computable elements of the hereditary continuous partial objects; moreover, there is a commutative system of enumerations of any given type by any type below (relative numberings). By this and by results in [1] and [2], the Kleene–Kreisel countable functionals and the hereditary effective operations (HEO) are easily characterized.

LOOMER, Bernard M. Meland On God. *Amer J Theol Phil* 5,138–143 My & S 84.

LOPARIC, A and Da Costa, N C. Paraconsistency, Paracompleteness, And Valuations. *Log Anal* 27,119–132 Je 84.

LOPARIĆ, Zelijko. "Decidability In Carnap" in *Philosophical Analysis In Latin America*, Gracia, Jorge J E and others (eds), 313–338. Boston Reidel 1984.

LÓPEZ, Antonio Marlasca. Eutanasia O Derecho A Morir? *Rev Filosof (Costa Rica)* 23,215–225 D 85.

The author of this article critically attempts to elucidate and clarify the basic concepts about the right to die and euthanasia from a fundamentally ethical perspective. The specific concepts which are developed are the following: (1) Dying as a natural phenomenon; (2) Dying as a human right; (3) explanation and critique of traditional theories on euthanasia and its different forms. The concluding part exposes a panoramic view of what today is commonly accepted as indisputable about euthanasia as well as what is considered problematical. The difficult problem of active and voluntary euthanasia is analyzed, both from the believer's perspective and from a non–religious and secularized perspective.

LÓPEZ, Antonio Marlasca. La Eternidad Del Mundo: Un Capítulo De Filosofía Medieval. *Rev Filosof (Costa Rica)* 23,169–182 D 85.

We present here the old discussion of the eternal and temporal character of the world, beginning with St Augustine. Our exposition centers on the antagonical positions of Bonaventure and Aquinas. The former affirms that the beginning of the world can be rationally demonstrated. The latter holds exactly the opposite. In the final selection a critique is made of the theses of dialectical materialism, as well as of the "popular" interpretations of modern astrophysics concerning the eternity or non–eternity of the world. The author ends with an agnostic viewpoint: so far, it has not been demonstrated either the absolute beginning or the eternity of the world.

LOPSTON, Peter. Logic And Contingent Existence. *Hist Phil Log* 1,171–186 1980.

It is argued here that Prior's non–standard modal system Q, and the Parry–Dunn system of analytic implication, though entirely independent and independently motivated systems, together provide a rationale for explicating the concept of validity in a non–standard way; their implications are explored for the theory of natural deduction as well as for modal logic and the concept of entailment. I give an account of formal logic from this non–standard viewpoint, together with an informal presentation of the system that unites the insights of Prior (drawing on Russell) and, Parry (drawing on Kant), and the motivations for both in the concept of the contingent existence—as opposed to the contingent truth or falsehood—of a proposition.

LOPTSON, P J and Kelly, J W. Genetic Epistemology And Philosophical Epistemology. *Phil Soc Sci* 14,377–384 S 84.

LORD, Carnes (trans). *Aristotle: The Politics*. Chicago Univ Of Chicago Pr 1984.

LORD, Catherine. A Gricean Approach To Aesthetic Instrumentalism. *Brit J Aes* 25,66–70 Wint 85.

LORIES, Danielle. Philosophie Analytique Et Définition De L'art. *Rev Phil Louvain* 83,214–230 My 85.

By way of introduction to a problem little known to French–speakers in general, namely the analytical philosophy of art, this article sets out two diverging theses by analytical philosophers on the question of the definition of art. There then follows a critical examination of the first thesis (the impossibility of the definition) defended by Weitz, in the perspective of his use of the teaching of Wittgenstein. Finally, some questions are raised in regard to the second thesis, defended by Dickie, on the possible presuppositions (in the transcendental order) of a definition of art in terms of institution (the artworld) and of conventions.

LORMAND, Eric. Toward A Theory Of Moods. *Phil Stud* 47,385–408 My 85.

This article summarizes and criticizes theories of moods currently on offer in analytic and continental philosophy, and in psychology. A model is developed which accounts for the pervasiveness, non–intentionality, and non–rationality of moods, and which sharply distinguishes moods from emotions. The account is offered as a foundation for further cognitive–psychological study.

LOSONSKY, Michael. Reference And Rorty's Veil. *Phil Stud* 47,291–294 Mr 85.

LÖTSCH, Manfred and Meyer, H. Sozialstrukturforschung Und Leitung Sozialer Prozesse. *Deut Z Phil* 22,167–178 1974.

Die Gestaltung der entwickelten sozialistischen Gesellschaft ist mit tiefgreifenden Veränderungen der sozialen Struktur verbunden, deren Analyse in der Erforschung der Entwicklung der Arbeiterklasse als der führenden Kraft ihren Ausgangspunkt nehmen mufss. Es wird die Frage zu beantworten versucht, wie auf der Grundlage der Struktur und Differenziertheit der Arbeiterklasse alle ihre Teile und Gruppen in den Prozefss der Verwirklichung ihrer führenden Rolle einzubeziehen sind.

LÖTSCH, M. Arbeiterklasse Und Intelligenz In Der Dialektik Von Wissenschaftlichtechnischem, Ökonomischem Und Sozialem Fortschritt. *Deut Z Phil* 33,31–41 1985.

LOUGH, John. *Locke's Travels In France 1675–1679.* NY Garland 1984.

This is simply a reprint of the first edition (Cambridge University Press, 1953) with additions and corrections supplied by the editor of the previous edition.

LOVENAL, M. *Cosmological Biology.* NY Philosophical Lib 1985.

LOVETT, William and Leventhal, F M (ed). *Social And Political Morality.* NY Garland 1984.

LOVEYS, James. The Uniqueness Of Envelopes In $\aleph_0$–Categorical, $\aleph_0$–Stable Structures. *J Sym Log* 49,1171–1184 D 84.

If H is a strictly minimal set attached to M, an w–stable w–categorical structure, and A is a subset of M, an H–*envelope of* A is a maximal subset of M with the same algebraic closure in H. We prove these envelopes are as unique as possible; also such structures are weakly homogeneous over any subset.

LOVIN, Robin W. *Christian Faith And Public Choices: The Social Ethics Of Barth, Brunner And Bonhoeffer.* Philadelphia Fortress Pr 1984.

This book is a study of European Protestant social ethics during the first half of this century, especially the works of Karl Barth, Emil Brunner, and Dietrich Bonhoeffer. The study contrasts Barth's theological radicalism, which emphasizes the difference between Christian action and ordinary moral reflection, with the theological realism of Brunner and Bonhoeffer, who stress Christian participation in public life. A final chapter considers the implications of these two approaches for contemporary religious ethics.

LOWE, Bernd P. "Zur Kritik Der Bürgerlichen Ideologie". *Deut Z Phil* 22,506–510 1974.

LOWE, Bernd P. Politologie Und Political Science In Den USA. *Deut Z Phil* 22,718–735 1974.

Die sozialtheoretischen Konzeptionsbildungen in der amerikanischen political science widerspiegeln in verzerrter Weise die Krise in den Existenzbedingungen der Monopolbourgeoisie. Der Autor analysiert grundlegende Merkmale dieser Sozialtheorien und weist ihre Erkenntnis– und Idealogiefunktion sowie den Widerspruch zwischen ihnen nach. In besonderem Mafsse ist die aus der political science hervorgegangene Politologie zur theoretischen Grundlage der antikommunistischen Ideologic und Politik geworden.

LÖWE, Bernd P. The Victory Over Fascism A Historic Chance For Peace And Progress (in German). *Deut Z Phil* 33,395–404 1985.

Hume was concerned with why we consider a collection of perceptions to be a single thing. In the body of the *Treatise* he put forward an explanation. He later believed that this attempt was a failure and despaired of finding a solution. He denied that the self exists on the grounds that we have no impression of it. This was bad philosophy of science; we now accept that there are unperceived theoretical entities and that we are justified in believing in them. We accept the external world for the same reason, since it is the best explanation of the order of our experiences. The writer argues that the reasons Hume gives for believing in the unity of the mind, once the idea of unifying self is given up, do not work, given that all that exists is the stream of consciousness. The writer claims that to explain the unity of the mind we must go beyond the stream of consciousness. Certain conscious courses of experience can only be explained by positing inner mechanisms that are not conscious. The best explanation of the stream of consciousness requires us to posit both an external world outside it and an inner mechanism this side of it. (edited)

LOWE, E J. "If A And B, Then A". *Analysis* 45,93–98 Mr 85.

LOWE, E J. A Note On A Response Of Hornsby's. *Analysis* 44,196–197 O 84.

LOWE, E J. Wright *Versus* Lewis On The Transitivity Of Counterfactuals. *Analysis* 44,180–183 O 84.

LOWE, Susan. No Love For God? *Philosophy* 60,263–264 Ap 85.

In an article on the problem of evil in *Philosophy* (1983) Freya Mora argued that love was necessary for happiness, evil and love, and so the compatibilist position would seem to be tenable—only the *amount* of evil remaining a difficulty. I suggest another problem arises. She contended that to be lovable one must be perishable and susceptible to misfortunes. I maintain this implies God is not lovable—surely too high a price for the help she offers the compatibilist position.

LOWITH, Karl. *From Hegel To Nietzsche.* NY Garland 1984.

The author is concerned not so much with presenting a complete history of nineteenth century philosophy as he is with showing the important contributions of the German philosophers to nineteenth century thought. The focus of the book is primarily upon the works of Hegel and Nietzsche and their influence on their contemporaries. Subjects such as Christianity, work, society, and education are discussed in their nineteenth century formulations.

LOY, David. How Not To Criticize Nāgārjuna: A Response To L Stafford Betty. *Phil East West* 34,437–446 O 84.

In response to an article criticizing Nāgārjuna, his *Mūlamadhyamakakārikās* is defended. Nāgārjuna's subtle distinctions are not a "play on words," but reveal the inconsistencies in the hypostatizations of ordinary language. More fundamentally, the major Western interpretations of Nāgārjuna may be seen as one–sided because each emphasizes one of the two aspects of Madhyamika at the price of misunderstanding the other, thus missing the fundamental tension at the heart of Nāgārjuna's approach.

LOY, David. The Paradox Of Causality In Madhyamika. *Int Phil Quart* 25,63–72 Mr 85.

LOY, David. Wei–Wu–Wei: Nondual Action. *Phil East West* 35,73–86 Ja 85.

The Taoist paradox of "Wei–wu–wei" ("the action of nonaction") means, not doing nothing or yielding merely natural action, but nondual action in which there is no

duality between a self and its actions. The delusive sense of such a duality arises because of superimposing intentions; without intention I *become* the action and thus lose the awareness that there is an objective action. Contrary to first appearances, Hampshire's account of intentionality (in *Thought and Action*) is consistent with this.

LUBANSKI, Mieczyslaw. Über Des Problem Von Nichtstandardgrössen (in Polish). *Stud Phil Christ* 20,53–68 1984.

LUBNICKI, Narcyz. On Ultimate Justification. *Dialec Hum* 11,265–268 Spr/Sum 84.

In logical systems we do not find sentences ultimately justified. Neither axioms nor directives possess this character. Their proof revolves in a vicious circle: it presupposes validity of principles which previously have to be proven. The search of their basis leads us beyond the purely logical sphere: to *practice*. A practical justification consists in demonstrating the value of a certain ratiocination or action pointing to their hitherto established efficiency. Thus instead of absolute laws we proceed in science and philosophy with relative *postulates*.

LUCAS JR, George R. Outside The Camp: Recent Work On Whitehead's Philosophy, Part I. *Trans Peirce Soc* 21,49–76 Wint 85.

This is the first of a two–part, commissioned article evaluating the major developments in Whiteheadian "process" scholarship during the past two decades (Pt II forthcoming in *Transactions* 21 (Summer, 1985). The title suggests the isolated minority status of Whitehead studies, and attempts comparisons of work in this field with recent concerns in mainstream Anglo–American thought. Issues discussed include: freedom, determinism and theories of agency, types of causal explanation, the status of the past, and naturalism in metaphysics.

LUCAS JR, George R. The Compositional History Of Whitehead's Writings. *Int Phil Quart* 24,313–326 S 84.

Discusses recent efforts to apply methods of textual analysis to the major works of A N Whitehead. In the absence of the traditional primary *Nachlass* (most of which was apparently destroyed by Whitehead himself), such techniques can provide hypothetical reconstructions of the developing phases of Whitehead's mature thought, suggesting critical points at which now familiar doctrines originated as developing transitions from earlier (presumably deficient) views. Such reconstructions in turn prove surprisingly useful in re–evaluating a number of controversies in contemporary Whiteheadian scholarship.

LUCAS, Christopher J. Toward A Pedagogy Of The Useful Past For Teacher Preparation. *J Thought* 20,19–33 Spr 85.

The act of historical inquiry is never a literal and unmediated factual transmission. Rather, it is argued, historical data significance only as they are shaped and given a form intelligible to contemporary questions. Historical recreation in this sense serves as an accounting of collective experience, as a means of "liberation" from the past, and as an explanatory mode of contemporary consciousness. Pedagogical imperatives for the revitalization of history derrived from the analysis are briefly explored.

LUCAS, J R. Lucas Against Mechanism II: A Rejoinder. *Can J Phil* 14,189–192 Je 84.

LUCAS, J R. Lucas, Gödel And Astaire: A Rejoinder To David Boyer. *Phil Quart* 34,507–508 0 84.

LUCAS, J R. Towards A Theory Of Taxation. *Soc Phil Pol* 2,161–173 Autumn 84.

LUCASH, Frank S. The Mind's Body: The Body's Self–Awareness. *Dialogue (Canada)* 23,619–634 D 84.

In examing what Spinoza's critics say about his views on 1) the nature of mind, 2) its relation to the body, 3) its adequate/inadequate, true/false ideas, I argue that the problems they believe he gets into are not really problems at all or they can be resolved within his system.

LUCASH, Frank. What Spinoza's View Of Freedom Should Have Been. *Phil Res Arch* 10,491–500 1985.

I argue that Spinoza's view of freedom in Part 5 of the *Ethics* is not incompatible with his view of determinism in Part 1, as Kolakowski claims, nor is it compatible for the reasons Parkinson, Hampshire, and Naess offer. Spinoza did not work out a clear view of how freedom differs from determinism. Using various resources in Spinoza, I present a view of freedom which is different from both internal or atemporal determinism and external or temporal determinism. Freedom, in the sense of the temporal process by which passive ideas become active is compatible with both temporal and atemporal determinism.

LUCKETT, Helen. Ten Years Of Gallery Education. *J Aes Educ* 19,125–142 Sum 85.

LUCKHARDT, Horst. A Short Proof Of A Well–Known Theorem Of Intuitionistic Analysis. *Z Math Log* 21,185–186 1975.

LUCKMANN, Thomas. "Individual Action And Social Knowledge" in *The Analysis Of Action*, Von Cranach, Mario (ed), 247–266. Cambridge Cambridge Univ Pr 1982.

LUDWIG, Gerd and Brau, Richard and Rosenthal, Erwin. Zur Rolle Des Subjektiven Faktors In Der Wissenschaftsentwicklung. *Deut Z Phil* 33,459–462 1985.

LUEBKE, Neil. Presidential Address: For And Against Bureaucracy. *Phil Topics* 13,143–154 Spr 85.

This 1982 Presidential Address before the Southwestern Philosophical Society reviews the meaning and treatment of bureaucracy in Marxian and liberal social thought and briefly discusses the question of justice in formal organizations.

LUEGENBIEHL, Heinz C. *1984 And The Power Of Technology.* Soc Theor Pract 10,289–300 Fall 84.

The "1984" which has found its way into popular consciousness represents Oceania as a technological superstate. Although this cultural appropriation fails to do justice to the novel's contents, there are good reasons for holding that a highly technologized society is compatible with the dictatorial impulses warned against. This conclusion is based on consideration of Oceania's technologies, a comparison of these to technological capabilities in Orwell's and our own eras, and the theme of autonomous technology.

LUGENBEHL, Dale. Classroom Logic Terminology: Response To Seech. *Teach Phil* 8,157–160 Ap 85.

LUGENBEHL, Dale. Two Conceptions Of Philosophy. *Teach Phil* 7,289–302 O 84.

This article argues that there are two conceptions of philosophy: one generally held by professionals and the other by lay people. This discrepancy in approach to philosophy frequently causes a barrier to communication and learning for beginners. A specific analysis is given of how the lay person's conception is related to: 1) the prevalence of the relativistic theory of truth among beginners and 2) irrational behavior in philosophical discussions which include beginners.

LUGG, Andrew. The Process Of Discovery. *Phil Sci* 52,207–220 Je 85.

The main argument of this paper is that philosophical difficulties regarding scientific discovery arise mainly because philosophers base their arguments on a flawed picture of scientific research. Careful examination of N R Hanson's treatment of Kepler's discovery not only puts the rationality of this discovery beyond question, it also reveals what its rationality consists in. We can retrieve the point stressed by Hanson concerning the rational character of discoveries such as Kepler's even as we reject this type of "logical" analysis he proposes.

LUKÁCS, G. Der Rassenwahn Als Feind Des Menschilichen Fortschritts. *Deut Z Phil* 33,314–322 1985.

LUKACS, John. *Historical Consciousness Or The Remembered Past.* NY Schocken Books 1985.

historical Consciousness sets forth the principal arguments for the recognition of history as a form of thought. This, among other things, is the opposite of a philosophy of history. The important matter is the awareness of the historicity of our knowledge, not the knowledgeability of history. But this too is but part and parcel of the evolution of our consciousness which, according to the author, is the only evolution we ought to talk about.

LUKÁCS, Tibor. The Role Of The Laws Of Thought In The Administration Of Justice (in Hungarian). *Magyar Filozof Szemle* 4,543–565 1983.

The study deals with the rules of cogitation and attempts to prove the practical value of their knowledge in jurisdiction. In the first place it discusses the laws of identity whose formulation and interpretation have always been subject to heated debates in the history of formal logic. Following this the author touches on the categories of identity and diversity, as well as on the importance of operation with the concepts, of comparison and identification in the judicial activity. Examining the importance of the rules of cogitation in jurisdiction, the study does not aim at completeness. It makes only an attempt to demonstrate the significance of formal logic rules and underlines that judicature cannot stagnate at the rules of formal logic, however, it may transgress them by no means. (edited)

LUKE, Timothy W. On Nature And Society: Rousseau Versus The Enlightenment. *Hist Polit Thought* 5,211–244 Sum 84.

This paper investigates the bases of Rousseau's critique of modern society. It suggests there are many parallels between Rousseau's system of critical analysis and the approaches taken toward social criticism in Marxism and post–Marxist critical theory. Indeed, Rousseau's critique of modern science, technology, economics and politics anticipates many of the more radical dimensions of Marxian critiques.

LUMSDEN, David. Does Speaker's Reference Have Semantic Relevance? *Phil Stud* 47,15–22 Ja 85.

Do the conventions that determine the semantic referent of a singular term need to involve speaker's reference? One might say that semantic conventions, to be helpful to a hearer in determining the speaker's comminicative intentions, cannot involve those intentions. But there is a way to justify exceptions to that general rule. Still, it can be shown that the semantics of definite descriptions does not depend wholly on speaker's reference.

LUMSDEN, David. Reference And Communication *De Re*[1]. *Philosophia (Israel)* 14,65–82 Ag 84.

With Donnellan's 'referential' use of a definite description the speaker intends to communicate *de re* about something. So a 'referential' use in a sentence, S, can be linked to a *de re* form in a sentence about the speaker's communicative intentions in uttering S. A causal approach to both the topic of the 'referential' use and the topic of designators in *de re* position in intensional contexts is supported in light of that linkage.

LUNCH, Milton F. Commentary On "Whether Professional Associations May Enforce Professional Codes". *Bus Prof Ethics J* 3,61–64 Wint 84.

The author questions and challenges whether professional associations should be allowed to engage in self–regulation to any real degree. His concerns, if implemented, would effectively wipe out the purpose of professional associations and replace their functions with governmental controls. His fear of professional self–regulation is theoretical, at best, in the face of the overhanging application of antitrust laws to professional activities. The present Administration hails professional self–regulation in theory, but in practice does not really mean it through the "chilling" of self–regulation by threat of antitrust action under a "per se" rule.

LUNDBERG, Randolph. What Kind Of Good Is A Kind And Caring Heart. *J Value Inq* 19,119–132 1985.

The terms "intrinsic value" and "extrinsic value" are defined in several different ways in reputable philosophical literature. The differences are more significant than they appear. There is a kind of value that is both intrinsic and extrinsic under one set of definitions, neiter intrinsic nor extrinsic under another set, only extrinsic under a third set, and only intrinsic under a fourth. This pivotal value type is exemplified by a kind and caring heart.

LUNGARZO, Carlos. La Multiplicidad De Axiomáticas Conjuntistas Y Su Incidencia En La Lógica Cuántica. *Rev Latin De Filosof* 11,115–136 Jl 85.

The thesis that the use of axiomatic set theory in quantum logics can help clarify certain aspects hidden by usual formalizations is taken up. We rephrase the statement that a good concept of randomness cannot be defined within the minimal model of Zermelo–Fraenkel, and conclude that some logical and mathematical concepts are not theoretically absolute. Thus, many usual notions and problems can be tackled from different viewpoints according to the chosen formalism. We claim that quantum logic may perhaps be regarded as an adequate description of situations in quantum mechanics. In this case, classical logic would only be a good common sense approach. The plausibility of adopting divergent formalism not necessarily to the intuitive set theory is defined.

LUNGARZO, Carlos. Orígenes Y Proyecciones De La Lógica Cuántica. *Rev Latin De Filosof* 11,63–70 Mr 85.

We discuss the origins and order–theoretically quantum structures as stated by Birkhoff and Von Neumann, and examine the thesis by Piron that 'quantum' logic is not actual logic. We show recent results that falsify Piron's argument. We support the thesis that the more accurate formal approaching to specific modelizations in QM, is provided by QL, viewed as a non–classical calculus, although the metamathematics in which QL is developed should remain classic.

LUNTLEY, Michael. The Sense Of A Name. *Phil Quart* 34,265–282 Jl 84.

The author argues not only that names have sense but that they *must*. Possession of sense by names is a necessary condition for the intelligible ascription of sortal concepts. A Fregean theory of sense is defended: Knowledge constitutive of sense is a complex cognitive state characterized dispositionally. This avoids common objections to 'description theories' of names and gives a dispositional account of 'modes of presentation' in contrast to the occurent psychologistic account commonly assumed.

LUNTLEY, Michael. Towards A Critical Theory Of Value. *Praxis Int* 5,51–62 Ap 85.

LUPER– FOY, Steven. The Reliabilist Theory Of Rational Belief. *Monist* 68,203–225 Ap 85.

Niceties aside, Reliabilism is the claim that a belief is rational if and only if it has a reliable source. After sketching an account of the conditions under which a belief's source is reliable, I refute Reliabilism by rejecting one of its consequences, namely, that a belief arrived at by applying a given rule of inference is rational if and only if arriving at that belief by applying the rule is reliable. I also describe how facts about reliability enter into an account of rational belief, and how the latter are related to knowledge.

LUPESCU, Florin. Philosophie, Réalité Et Poésie. *Phil Log* 27,310–314 O–D 83.

LUSTHAUS, Dan. Ch'an And Taoist Mirrors: Reflections On Richard Garner's "Deconstruction Of The Mirror". *J Chin Phil* 12,169–178 Je 85.

LUTHER, E. Lebensansprüche Und Werte An Der Schwelle Zum 21, Jahrhundert. *Deut Z Phil* 33,202–206 1985.

LUUTZ, W. Alltag Und Alltagsbewuktsein. *Deut Z Phil* 33,348–351 1985.

LUYTEN, Norbert A. Das Von Der Naturwissenschaft Gepraegte Menschenbild (in Polish). *Stud Phil Christ* 20,133–141 1984.

LYCAN, William G. *Logical Form In Natural Language.* Cambridge MIT Pr 1985.

This book's purpose is to detail the anatomy of linguistic meaning, showing how the various elements of meaning fit together. Part 1 defends the truth–theoretic conception of semantics, taking the notion of a sentence's truth–condition as the core of meaning. Part 2 explores the complex interconnections between syntax, semantics and various pragmatic notions and attempts to reconcile the apparent differences between natural and formal language. Part 3 examines the relation between semantics and psychology.

LYCAN, William G. "Armstrong's Theory Of Knowing" in *D M Armstrong*, Bogdan, Radu J (ed), 139–160. Boston Reidel 1984.

LYCAN, William G. A Syntactically Motivated Theory Of Conditionals. *Midwest Stud Phil* 9,437–456 1984.

This paper proposes and defends a new semantic theory of indicative conditionals. However, the theory is motivated by some syntactic facts about "if", "only if", and "even if" that have been ignored by logicians. I maintain that indicative conditionals are neither strict nor "variably strict" in David Lewis' sense, but what I call "parametrically strict". The theory further explains some otherwise puzzling pragmatic facts about conditionals, and illuminates the indicative/subjunctive distinction.

LYCAN, William G. Epistemic Value. *Synthese* 64,137–164 Ag 85.

This paper attempts to naturalize the evaluative notion of "best explanation," which the aid of some concepts loosely borrowed from evolutionary biology. It also claims to establish the epistemological ground of explanatory inference, and it sets up and responds to some popular skeptical and/or "anti–realist" challenges to explanationism.

LYNN, Joanne. "Functions Of Institutional Ethics Committees" in (ethics Committees And Health Care Decisions, Cranford, Ronald (ed), 22–30. Ann Arbor Health Admin Pr 1984.

LYONS, David. Derivability, Defensibility, And The Justification Of Judicial Decisions. *Monist* 68,325–346 Jl 85.

The connection between a judicial decision's being required by law and its being justified is shown to be contingent and exaggerated. The distinction between hard and easy cases is clarified, the relevant concept of justification, defensibility, is shown at work in theories of adjudication for hard cases, and it is distinguished from derivability within a system of law. The judicial obligation of fidelity to law is shown to be incapable of bridging the gap.

LYONS, David. Formal Justice, Moral Commitment, And Judicial Precedent. *J Phil* 81,580–587 O 84.

This paper criticizes the suggestion that the judicial practice of following precedent is required by justice in the sense of treating like cases alike. This inference construes comparative justice as essentially conservative, requiring the repetition of mistakes. It is suggested, to the contrary, that the doctrine of precedent involves institutional, not individual, consistency, and that the relevant requirement rests, within limits, on a commitment to decide future cases similarly.

LYONS, John. "Tragic Closure And The Cornelian Wager" in *Existential Coordinates Of Human Condition*, Tymieniecka, A (ed), 409–416. Boston Reidel 1984.

LYONS, William E. On Searle's "Solution" To The Mind–Body Problem. *Phil Stud* 48,291–294 S 85.

The article is a critique of Searle's account of the mental in chapter 10 of his book *Intentionality*. In particular I discuss Searle's claim that mental properties are "surface properties" of the brain "at a higher level of description" than the neurophysiological.

LYONS, William. The Behaviourists' Struggle With Introspection. *Int Phil Quart* 25,139–156 Je 85.

In this essay the author gives an extended critique of the behaviourists' attempt to grapple with the phenomenon of introspection. He deals with both the psychological and philosophical behaviourists, especially Watson, Lashley, Ryle, and Skinner.

LYOTARD, Jean François. *The Postmodern Condition: A Report On Knowledge.* Minneapolis Univ Minnesota Pr 1984.

MAAS, Wolfgang. Variations On Promptly Simple Sets. *J Sym Log* 50,138–148 Mr 85.

MABBETT, I W. Nāgārjuna And Zeno On Motion. *Phil East West* 34,401–420 O 84.

There are at least superficial resemblances between the views of Nāgārjuna and Zeno on motion. Both seek to show that the concept of motion entails contradictions. This article, addressed chiefly to clarifying the argument of the second chapter of Nāgārjuna's *Mūlamadhyamakakārikās*, begins by setting out the lines of thought most plausibly attributable to Zeno, then discusses Nāgārjuna's arguments verse by verse in order to show the differences. Nāgārjuna's thought was in no way mathematical.

MAC CORMACK, Geoffrey. Law As Fact. *Arch Rechts Soz* 60,393–412 1974.

In the second edition of *Law as Fact*, Olivecrona offers an interesting analysis of legal rules and legal rights. He attempts to show that both rules and rights may be explained through a description of people's behavior and beliefs. It is argued in this paper that such an explanation is unsatisfactory because (i) it has to make use of non-factual elements, (ii) it does not exhaust the notion of a rule or of a right. Some remarks are offered on Olivecrona's discussion of performatives and of law in primitive societies.

MAC CRIMMON, Kenneth R and Wehrung, Donald A. A Portfolio Of Risk Measures. *Theor Decis* 19,1–29 Jl 85.

A comprehensive set of sixteen measures of willingness to take risks has been developed. This set includes measures from three categories: measures from the standardized risky situations having an underlying theory of risk, measures inferred from revealed choices in financial decisions, and measures derived from attitudes. A study of over 500 top-level business executives shows significant relationships within categories, but relatively little relationship across categories. Context differences, especially personal versus business situations and opportunities versus threats, underlie the responses.

MAC DONALD, Cynthia. Mind–Body Identity And The Subjects Of Events. *Phil Stud* 48,73–82 Jl 85.

Token event—identity theories of the mental and physical typically commit themselves to the view that events form a fundamental ontological category of particulars, and consequently to the existence of an adequate theory of events and event identity. But the theory of events to which they subscribe (the property–exemplification account) leaves them vulnerable to a version of the objection from location. The author outlines and defines a strategy for handling the objection within the confines of this theory.

MAC INTOSH, J J. Fitch's Factives. *Analysis* 44,153–158 O 84.

Fitch has an argument which shows that, for any factive D which distributes over conjunction, the initially plausible 'p→MDp' is unavailable. I consider possible interpretations of D ('created by God', 'caused', 'knows') and show why they are unacceptable. The attempt to weaken 'p→MDp' so as to allow such interpretations is shown to fail, and I conclude that—contrary to some recent suggestions in the literature—no philosophically interesting interpretation of D can be found.

MAC INTYRE, Alasdair. *Geschichte Der Ethik Im Überblick.* Konigstein Athenaum 1984.

MAC KENZIE BROWN, C. Svaraj, The Indian Ideal Of Freedom: A Political Or Religious Concept? *Relig Stud* 20,429–442 S 84.

MAC KENZIE, J C. Moral Scepticism And Moral Conduct. *Philosophy* 59,473–480 O 84.

MAC KENZIE, J D. Functionalism And Psychologism. *Dialogue (Canada)* 23,239–248 Je 84.

Remel T Nunn argued ("Psychologism, Functionalism, and the Modal Status of Logical Laws" *Inquiry* 22 (1976) 343–357) that the functionalist account of mind explains the inconceivability of alternative logical laws, and that the claim that "the only kind of change which is possible does not allow the present laws of logic to be false" is unfounded. In the present paper, it is argued that his first conclusion is confused, and his second too weak.

MAC LEAN, Douglas (ed). *The Security Gamble: Deterrence Dilemmas In The Nuclear Age.* Totowa Rowman & Allanheld 1984.

MAC LEAN, Kenneth and Schouls, Peter A (ed). *John Locke And English Literature Of The Eighteenth Century.* NY Garland 1984.

MAC MILLAN, Claude. Kant's Deduction Of Pure Aesthetic Judgments. *Kantstudien* 76,43–54 1985.

In this article I argue that Kant's deduction of pure aesthetic judgments ought to be seen as wholly contained between sections 30–38 of the *Critique of Judgment*. When the deduction is seen in this way, it contributes to the clarification of Kant's aesthetic theory. My view runs counter to those who interpret Kant's deduction as an attempt to establish the universality of a "common sense" (Paul Guyer) or as incomplete until the Dialectical portion of the *Critique* (Donald W Crawford).

MAC' KIE, Pamela S. Trial By Charade. *Bus Prof Ethics J* 3,25–32 Fall 83.

MACDONALD, Michael H and Kreeft, Peter J and Purtill, Richard L. *Philosophical Questions: An Introductory Anthology.* Englewood Cliffs Prentice–Hall 1985.

MACHADO, Geraldo Pinheiro. Jacques Maritain, Filósofo Da Inteligência. *Rev Port Filosof* 41,60–68 Ja–Mr 85.

MACHAN, Tibor R (ed) and Johnson, M Bruce (ed). *Rights And Regulation: Ethical, Political, And Economic Issues.* Cambridge Ballinger 1983.

This book examines the ethical/moral defenses and objections surrounding the institution of government regulation. Contributors include philosophers and economists, as well as legal theorists, who offer varied perspectives on the topic. A Foreward is offered by Aaron Wildowsky. The book has received awards for providing a unique approach to its subject matter, one not found in the economic or philosophical discussion of commerce.

MACHAN, Tibor R. "The Petty Tyranny Of Government Regulation" in *Rights And Regulation*, Machan, Tibor (ed), 259–288. Cambridge Ballinger 1983.

MACHAN, Tibor R and Den Uyl, Douglas J. "Gewirth And The Supportive State" in *Gewirth's Ethical Rationalism*, Regis Jr, Edward (ed), 167–179. Chicago Univ Of Chicago Pr 1984.

MACHAN, Tibor R. Commentary On L Jung's "Commercialization And The Professions". *Bus Prof Ethics J* 2,83–88 Wint 83.

This comment proposes that commercialization of professions (a) isn't bad, (b) when overdone it could be due to the eagerness of many to prosper (and the momentum this has created), (c) could be matched by other ways in which professions might go astray (when such changes of focus do lead them astray), e.G., trivialization, pedantry, pontification and indoctrination (in scholarship and education), etc., and (d) certain kinds of corruption can undermine philosophy, such as becoming too ideological, pedagogical, pompous, etc.

MACHAN, Tibor R. Social Contract As A Basis Of Norms: A Critique. *J Liber Stud* 7,141–146 Spr 83.

In this note it is argued that contractarian approaches to establishing principles of morality and politics are flawed. E.G., one may always ask, "Ought A to enter the contract which aims to establish such principles?" This implies that precontractual moral principles are required, as a matter of the universalizability criterion of morality. Furthermore, contractarians such as Kant and Rawls refer to non–contractarain principles, e.G., rationality, in spelling out the substance of the morality that emerges from the contract, showing that the contract itself may be superfluous.

MACHAN, Tibor R. Some Doubts About Animal Rights. *J Value Inq* 19,73–76 1985.

This piece argues that basing rights on the existence of interests is inadequate and since several defenses of animal rights do rest such rights on the fact that animals have interests, they fail. Other arguments might succeed, but for now the judgment must be "not proven."

MACHINA, Kenton F. Freedom Of Expression In Commerce. *Law Phil* 3,375–406 D 84.

Does commercial speech deserve the same freedom from governmental interference as do noncommercial forms of expression? Examination of this question forces a reappraisal of the grounds upon which freedom of expression rests. I urge an analysis of those grounds which founds freedom of speech upon the requirements of individual autonomy over against society. I then apply the autonomy analysis to commercial expression by examining the empirical features which distinguish commercial forms of expression. Some such features –e.G., "triviality"—have been cited by others as justification for limiting the freedom accorded commercial speech, but I reject the power of those features to limit the freedom of expression. Instead, I identify three features of commercial expression which are relevant to the task: resiliency (coupled with potential for abuse), action–orientation, and intimate connection with conventional commercial structures. I discuss the implications of these features for legitimizing governmental restriction of freedom in commercial expression, with the general conclusion that such restriction must be more severely limited than is commonly thought.

MACHLEIDT, P and Mrácek, F. Some Problems Of The Formation Of Strategies And Evaluation In The Sphere Of Biotechnologies (in Czechoslovakian). *Filozof Cas* 33,389–393 1985.

MACHLEIDTOVA, S. The Role Of Marxist–Leninist Philosophy In The Process Of The Humanisation Of Science (in Czechoslovakian). *Filozof Cas* 32,671–682 1984.

MACINTYRE, Alasdair. *After Virtue: Second Edition.* Notre Dame Notre Dame Pr 1984.

This edition corrects errors identified in the first edition. It also includes an additional chapter devoted to replying to some major criticisms by reviewers of the first edition. The relationship of philosophy to history and the question of whether the implications of the argument concerning the virtues are or are not relativistic are discussed.

MACINTYRE, Alasdair. "The Relationship Of Philosophy To Its Past" in *Philosophy In History*, Rorty, Richard and others (ed), 31–48. NY Cambridge Univ Pr 1984.

MACK, Eric. "Deontologism, Negative Causation, And The Duty Of Rescue" in *Gewirth's Ethical Rationalism*, Regis Jr, Edward (ed), 147–166. Chicago Univ Of Chicago Pr 1984.

MACK, Eric. Commentary On J Pichler's "The Liberty Principle: A Basis For Management Ethics". *Bus Prof Ethics J* 2,35–38 Wint 83.

This comment mainly disputes Pichler's claim that "the Liberty Principle" both is "the ethical basis for capitalism" and provides the basis for important managerial directives. The main point is that the Liberty Principle vindicates liberty and, therefore, discretion. Thus, it cannot provide directives for managerial decisions where directives are distinguished from side–constraints.

MACKENZIE, Donald. Reply To Steven Yearley's "The Relationship Between Epistemological And Sociological Cognitive Interests". *Stud Hist Phil Sci* 15,251–260 S 84.

In his recent discussion of 'interest theory', Steven Yearly singles out a paper by MacKenzie for special, critical attention. The more specific aspects of Yearley's criticism are examined and shown to be wholly without foundation.

MACKENZIE, Jim. Frege And Illogical Behaviour. *Amer Phil Quart* 21,339–348 O 84.

Frege argued that though it is logically possible for an illogical community to exist, it is not possible that it should be right. Neither the assertion of false statements nor the acceptance of invalid arguments suffices to render a community illogical. The kinds of behavior which would suffice prove, on examination, to be very rare, but to justify Frege's rather obscure remarks on illogicality and the universality of logical laws. The laws of logic are to be understood as constraints on the kinds of rules governing linguistic exchanges needed if the language is to accomodate attempts to prove. (edited)

MACKENZIE, Jim. No Logic Before Friday. *Synthese* 63,329–342 Je 85.

Logic is concerned with arguments, and though Crusoe may have constructed derivations he could not engage in argument until Friday joined him. In this paper a system of dialogue, designed to explain the fallaciousness of question–begging arguments, is presented.

MACKENZIE, Mary Margaret. Plato's Moral Theory. *J Med Ethics* 11,88–91 Je 85.

This paper introduces a new series on important theories in moral philosophy. The series is primarily aimed at non–philosophers with an interest in ethics.

MACKENZIE, Michael. A Note On Motivation And Future Generations. *Environ Ethics* 7,63–70 Spr 85.

I examine the motivation issue in our relationship to future generations in light of a specific set of technol0gical practices—those of Chinese hydraulic agriculture. I conclude that these practices appear to embody a "community–bonding" relationship between present and future generations and that such a relationship provides a fruitful perspective on policy.

MACKIEWICZ, Witold. The Marxist Trend In Polish Socialism. *Dialec Hum* 10,179–192 Sum 83.

The Author would like to present the beginnings of Marxist thought in Poland, the divergencies which appeared at that time and the reasons for attempts to question its theory and praxis already in its initial stages of development.

MACKINNON, Edward. Basic Reasoning. Englewood Cliffs Printice–Hall 1985.

basic Reasoning is an introductory textbook. It treats such standard issues as argument diagrams, elementary logic, deduction, induction and fallacies. Novel features include methods of construction and reconstruction, a detailed treatment of practical reasoning and decision making, three different types of exercises, and a supplemental test bank of over 400 multiple choice questions arranged by chapters.

MACKLIN, Ruth (ed) and Murray, Thomas H (ed) and Gaylin, Willard (ed). *Feeling Good And Doing Better; Ethics And Nontherapeutic Drug Use*. Clifton Humana Pr 1984.

This book is a collection of original articles developed by members of a Research Group over two years of discussion and debate on the ethics of drug use for enhancing pleasure or performance. Problems addressed include performance aids in sports, public policy towards nontherapeutic drug use, the "medical model," and the nature of pleasure; drug use and risk–taking; and legal and constitutional aspects of nontherapeutic drug use.

MACKLIN, Ruth. "Consultative Roles And Responsibilities" in *Ethics Committees And Health Care Decisions*, Cranford, Ronald (ed), 157–168. Ann Arbor Health Admin Pr 1984.

MACKLIN, Ruth. "Drugs, Models, And Moral Principles" in *Feeling Good And Doing Better*, Murray, Thomas H (ed), 187–214. Clifton Humana Pr 1984.

MACKLIN, Ruth. "Problems Of Informed Consent With Cognitively Impaired" in *Ethical Questions In Brain And Behavior*, Pfaff, Donald W (ed), 23–40. NY Springer 1983.

MACKLIN, Ruth. "The Ethics Of Fetal Therapy" in *Biomedical Ethics Reviews*, Humber, James M (ed), 205–224. Clifton Humana Pr 1984.

MACKLIN, Ruth. "Treatment Refusals" in *Ethical Questions In Brain And Behavior*, Pfaff, Donald W (ed), 41–56. NY Springer 1983.

MACKLIN, Ruth. "When Human Rights Conflict: Two Persons, One Body" in *Defining Human Life*, Shaw, Margery W (ed), 225–239. Ann Arbor Aupha Pr 1983.

MACKLIN, Ruth. Commentary On "Professional Advertising: Price Fixing And Professional Dignity Versus The Public's Right To A Free Market". *Bus Prof Ethics J* 3,111–118 Spr/Sum 84.

Arguments offered by Burton Leiser in defense of the ethics of advertising by professionals are critically assessed. Two justifications are explored: one based on the value of free–market competition among professionals; the other grounded in precepts of justice. Arguments based on the value of free–market competition are found to be in need of empirical support. The most powerful justification is based on fairness to consumers as well as providers of professional services.

MACKOVÁ– HOLECKOVÁ, Iva. Programmatic Aesthetic Education From The Point Of View Of Social Psychology (in Czechoslovakian). *Estetika* 21,166–171 1984.

MACLEAN, Anne. Right And Good: False Dichotomy? *Philosophy* 60,129–132 Ja 85.

It is argued against Pybus (*Philosophy* Vol 58, No 223) that there is a genuine dichotomy between teleological and deontological accounts of morality. It is conceded that teleologists must talk of an obligation to pursue certain ends, but maintained that this is non–controversial. It is denied however that theories of obligation can only relate moral action to a view of the good by specifying the *aim(s)* of such action.

MACLEOD, Alistair M. Distributive Justice, Contract, And Equality. *J Phil* 81,709–718 N 84.

MACMILLAN, C J B. Love And Logic In 1984. *Proc Phil Educ* 40,3–16 1984.

MACNAMARA, Michael and Kistner, Wietske and Wilkinson, Jennifer. 'Elegance' In Science And Mathematics: A Discussion. *S Afr J Phil* 4,95–99 Ag 85.

The authors discuss, along conceptual–analytical lines, the concept of elegance as it occurs in science and mathematics with reference to methods, solutions, proofs, and theories. Aspects considered include a comparison of the meanings of the term 'elegant' as it is applied in science, mathematics, and art, respectively; the intrinsic significance of elegance in a scientific theory; the significance of the relation between aesthetic criteria and truth; and the time–shift of criteria of elegance. Several possible lines for further inquiry are suggested, for example the question of whether it is elegant scientific theories that are the most fruitful ones.

MACQUARRIE, John. In Search Of Deity: An Essay In Dialectical Theism. NY Crossroad 1985.

This book contains the Gifford Lectures on Natural Theology given at St Andrews University in 1983. The first part of the book defends the possibility of natural theology, but also criticizes classical theism, mainly on the ground that it makes too sharp a separation between God and the world. The middle part of the book discusses a number of philosophers in whose work the concepts of "God" and "world" are brought into intimate relationship with each other (Plotinus, Hegel, Whitehead, Heidegger and others). In line with the historical tradition, the final chapters try to construct a "dialectical" theism.

MACQUARRIE, John and Rahner, Karl. The Anthropological Approach To Theology. *Heythrop J* 25,272–287 Jl 84.

The purpose of the article is to commend the study of the human reality as a fruitful way into theology and, incidentally, to draw attention to the use of this approach in the work of Karl Rahner. It is argued that this approach is an appropriate one in an age which is both secular and which paradoxically has reintroduced the idea of transcendence as a fundamental characteristic of the human being.

MADANES, Leiser. La Originación Radical De Las Cosas Demostrada A Priori: Leibniz, Nozik, Rescher. *Rev Latin De Filosof* 11,55–62 Mr 85.

Most answers to the question "Why is there something rather than nothing?" Resort to arguments that are tantamount to a priori proofs of God's existence. An analysis of Leibniz's *De rerum originatione radicali* and of two recent works by Nozick and Rescher is given in order to illustrate this thesis.

MADDEN, Edward H. Sir William Hamilton, Critical Philosophy, And The Commonsense Tradition. *Rev Metaph* 38,839–866 Je 85.

MADDY, Penelope. How The Causal Theorist Follows A Rule. *Midwest Stud Phil* 9,457–478 1984.

A Kripean version of Wittgenstein's rule–following argument is rehearsed, and it is suggested that a realist with a casual theory of reference has at least the beginning of a reply.

MADELL, Geoffrey. Derek Parfit And Greta Garbo. *Analysis* 45,105–109 Mr 85.

In *Reasons and Persons*, Parfit argues that the possibility of combining some of the physical and psychological features of two different persons in a composite person favors a reductionist view of personal identity. But (1) the suggested experiments may well be contrary to the laws of nature, (2) the result, assuming possibility, could well be two different persons in one skin, and (3) central difficulties about the first person perspective are overlooked.

MADER, Thomas F. A Problem With Johnstone's Self. *Phil Ret* 18,86–95 1985.

In *The Problem of the Self*, Henry W Johnstone, Jr defines the self as the "locus of a contradiction," and says that this definition has implications for the meaning of guilt, responsibility, communication, and rhetoric. The article attempts to show that a person's awareness of guilt of responsibility requires the individual to accept the burden of choice, rather than acknowledge a contradiction and that communication and rhetoric are meaningful insofar as the self chooses between incompatible, rather than contradictory, propositions.

MADISON, Gary B. Philosophy And The Pursuit Of World Peace. *Dialec Hum* 11,411–426 Spr/Sum 84.

This paper argues that in the present–day situation when an all–inclusive world civilization is coming into being, genuine world peace can be attained only if it is possible to arrive at a set of basic values which while being universal, would nevertheless allow for cultural pluralism. A post–metaphysical theory of rationality is outlined, which in turn serves to generate, in a non–foundationalist way, a set of such values.

MADISON, Gary B. The Contemporary Status Of Continental Philosophy In Canada: A Narrative. *Eidos* 4,63–81 Je 85.

Author Index with Abstracts 349 Mann, Iu V

MADSEN, Peter. Business Ethics, Interdisciplinarity And Higher Education. *Listening* 20,93–105 Spr 85.

This article challenges teachers of business ethics to rethink the way in which they teach courses in business ethics. It suggests a cross–disciplinary method which includes a cross–institutional component. Suggested course content and strategies of teaching business ethics are advanced and defined.

MAEHARA, Shoji. "Semi–formal Finitist Proof Of Transfinite Induction" in *Lecture Notes In Mathematics*, Muller, G H And Others (ed), 67–80. NY Springer 1981.

MAGARI, Roberto. The Success Of Mathematics. *Synthese* 62,265–274 F 85.

The Author discusses: 1) The status of metamathematics and proposes that metamathematics is a natural science, 2) Mathematics as a system of degree sigma 2, and 3) The role of mathematics in applications. This problem concerns many different sciences and the author proposes an evolutionistic explication. (edited)

MAGENTA, Muriel. Feminist Art Criticism: A Political Definition. *J Theor Crit Vis Arts* 1,89–98 1981.

MAGNO, Joseph A. How Ethical Is Abraham's "Suspension Of The Ethical"? *Faith Phil* 2,53–65 Ja 85.

In Problema I of *Fear and Trembling*, Kierkegaard inquiries concerning the ethicality of Abraham's faith–act. This paper argues, first (against a current leading interpretation), that Kierkegaard's *primary* intent in FT must be to determine Abraham's ethicality in relation to normative reason, and second, that, as such, FT warrants an irrationalistic interpretation—but with this major qualification: it is contradictory (as is typically claimed), but rather because the relationship as told in FT is ultimately meaningless.

MAHIN, Mark. *The New Scientific Case For God's Existence*. Boston Mindlifter Pr 1985.

This book introduces three new arguments for God's existence: the mundinitive argument, the suitable constants argument, and the chronotenic argument. The first two of these arguments are based on recent scientific discoveries, such as findings about the universe's explosive origin (which astronomers call "the big bang"). The chronotenic argument asserts that we must reject the atheist's belief that the universe has existed forever, because this belief leads to absurd conclusions, such as the conclusion that every event that had any chance of occurring on the earth has occurred on other planets an infinite number of times. This book also introduces two new theodicies, and a new philosophy called scientheism, which seems to harmonize religious thinking and scientific thinking.

MAHOWALD, Mary B. In The Interest Of Infants. *Phil Context* 14,9–18 1984.

Two recent cases involving critically ill and disabled infants raise the question of criteria for provision of life–prolonging treatment. The priority of the child's own interests, including quality of life considerations, required treatment in the first case but not in the second. Although a child's life can be prolonged in the interests of others rather than those of the child, it is as true for infants as for adults that the right to life includes the right to die.

MAINES, David R. Suggestions For A Symbolic Interactionist Conception Of Culture. *Commun Cog* 17,205–218 1984.

MAKER, William A. Augustine On Evil: The Dilemma Of The Philosophers. *Int J Phil Relig* 15,149–160 1984.

This essay argues that Augustine is as much of a philosopher as he is a Christian thinker. That is, that his concern with the philosophical and human inadequacies of the Platonic and Manichean treatments of the problem of evil lead him to develop a Christian philosophical cosmology in which the problem of the presence of evil is dealt with in a manner which is more rationally and humanly satisfying, despite its difficulties, than the Platonic and Manichean treatments.

MAKINDE, M Akin. An African Concept Of Human Personality: The Yoruba Example. *Ultim Real Mean* 7,189–200 S 84.

Apart from the philosophical division of a person into body and soul the Yoruba conceives of a third element known as *Ori* (inner head) whose function is to determine the human destiny. The three elements are discussed, with the conclusion that, although some light could be thrown on our conception of human personality through the Yoruba concept of *Ori*, the question of what constitutes a person remains unresolved as it has been in Western Philosophy.

MAKINSON, David and Alchourron, Carlos and Gardenfors, Peter. On The Logic Of Theory Change: Partial Meet Contraction And Revision Functions. *J Sym Log* 50,510–530 Je 85.

This paper extends earlier work by its authors on formal aspects of the processes of contracting a theory to eliminate a proposition and revising a theory to introduce a proposition. In the course of the earlier work, Gärdenfors developed general postulates of a more or less equational nature for such processes, whilst Alchourrón and Makinson studied the particular case of contraction functions that are maximal, in the sense of yielding a maximal subset of the theory (or alternatively, of one of its axiomatic bases), that fails to imply the proposition being eliminated. In the present paper, the authors study a broader class, including contraction functions that may be less than maximal. Specifically, they investigate "partial meet contraction functions," which are defined to yield the intersection of some nonempty family of maximal subsets of the theory that fail to imply the proposition being eliminated. (edited)

MAKINSON, David. How To Give It Up: A Survey Of Some Formal Aspects Of The Logic Of Theory Change. *Synthese* 62,347–364 Mr 85.

The paper surveys some recent work on formal aspects of the logic of theory change. It begins with a general discussion of the intuitive processes of contraction and revision of a theory, and of differing strategies for their formal study. Specific work is then described, notably Gärdenfors' postulates for contraction and revision, maxichoice contraction and revision functions and the condition of orderliness, partial meet contraction and revision functions and the condition of relationality, and finally the operations of safe contraction and revision. Verifications and proofs are omitted, with references given to the literature, but definitions and principal results are presented with rigour, along with discussion of their significance.

MAKOWSKY, J A. Vopenka's Principle And Compact Logics. *J Sym Log* 50,42–48 Mr 85.

We study the effects of Vopenka's principle on properties of model theoretic logics. We show that Vopenka's principle is equivalent to the assumption that every finitely generated logic has a compact cardinal. We show also that it is equivalent to the assumption that every such logic has a global Hanf number.

MALCOLM, John F. 'Vlastos On Pauline Predication'. *Phronesis* 30,79–91 1985.

MALCOLM, John F. A No Nonsense Approach To St Anselm. *Fran Stud* 41,336–345 1981.

MALIANDI, Ricardo. Jerarquía Y Conflictividad Axiológica En La Ética De Scheler. *Cuad Filosof* 19,95–108 Ja–D 83.

In Max Scheler's axiological ethics, the relations between higher and lower "non–moral" values enables us to explain how "moral" values are given. But the importance placed by Scheler on the unidimensional hierarchical table of values leads to difficulties in the explanation of conflictive axiological relations. This constitutes a difference between Scheler and N Hartmann's ethics in which antinomies play a preponderant role.

MALIK, Miroslav and Bresky, Dushan. *Esthetic Qualities And Values In Literature: A Humanistic And A Biometric Appraisal*. NY Lang 1984.

First volume of *Literary Practice*, trilogy, written by critic Bresky and biocybernetist Makik, develops two seminal methods of literary evaluation. Bresky estimates density and intensity of esthetic stimuli in microcontext. His synthesis corroborates subsequent empirical macrocontextual assessment. Malik outlines pertinent neurological research, records physiological changes occurring during Bresky's perception of text and compiles biometric sentic profile paralleling Bresky's resume of stimuli. *literary Practice II – Esthetics of Style* and III – *Literay Subjects* will soon appear.

MALONE, Michael E. 'There Is In Wittgenstein's Work No Argument And No Conclusion'. *Phil Invest* 8,174–188 Jl 85.

MALONEY, J Christopher. About Being A Bat. *Austl J Phil* 63,26–49 Mr 85.

MALONEY, Thomas S. Roger Bacon On Equivocation. *Vivarium* 22,85–112 N 84.

Roger Bacon broke with the tradition of describing equivocation (with Aristotle) in terms of three modes or types. While his *Sumule dialectices* of ca. 1252 reflects the tradition, his *Metaphysica*, *Communia naturalium*, and *De signis* reveal considerable originality in proposing a five–fold division of the topic. Finally, in 1292 he expands even this to six modes in his *Compendium studii theologiae*. This article is a study of the six modes.

MALONEY, Thomas S. The Extreme Realism Of Roger Bacon. *Rev Metaph* 38,807–838 Je 85.

J A Sheridan thought Bacon a moderate realist; Theodore Crowley considered him an extreme realist, at least by the writing of the *Communia naturalium*. The author examines the *Questiones supra libros prime philosophie Aristotelis*, *Questiones altere supre prime philosophie Aristotelis*, and the above text and concludes that Bacon began and ended as an extreme realist. Against Crowley, however, he argues that Bacon did not consider universals simply relations, even though Bacon describes them as a *conveniencia* among individuals.

MAMCHUR, Elena. The Principle Of 'Maximum Inheritance' And The Growth Of Scientific Knowledge. *Ratio* 27,37–48 Je 85.

MANAKOS, Jannis. On Skala's Set Theory. *Z Math Log* 30,541–545 1984.

A logical point of H L Skala is reaxiomatized formalizing the distinction between a narrow and a wide reference mode of any predicate. The formalism demands an extension of classical set theory by objects satisfying an internal relation of conditional membership (subsistence conditions, the logic of "no Northpole without a Southpole"). The theory thus contradicts ontological atomism by denying the general isolability of objects. It is further concurrent to fuzzy logic by rendering vagueness of notions non–metrically treatable.

MANDT, A J. Fichte's Idealism In Theory And Practice. *Ideal Stud* 14,127–147 My 84.

J G Fichte viewed himself as a Kantian "critical" philosopher. Disagreeing, most interpreters have characterized him as a subjective idealist, and criticized him on these grounds. I defend Fichte's self–interpretation by showing that his "deduction" of experience from the Absolute Self involves less than meets the eye. Fichte's metaphysical argument is a thought experiment entered into for practical–moral reasons. In fact, the tortuous course of Fichte's reasoning foreshadows later existentialist accounts of the human condition.

MANGIAGALLI, Maurizio. Il Problema Della Certezza E La Spiritualità Dell'uomo: Psicologia, Logica E Teoria Della Scienza Nel Pensiero Di Désiré Mercier. *Riv Filosof Neo–Scolas* 76,42–97 Ja–Mr 84.

MANICAS, Peter T and Rosenberg, Alan. Naturalism, Epistemological Individualism And "The Strong Programme" In Sociology Of Knowledge. *J Theor Soc Behav* 15,76–101 Mr 85.

The essay, an assessment of the work of Barry Barnes and David Bloor, argues that their "strong programme in the sociology of knowledge" offers a thoroughgoing naturalistic epistemology which overcomes the individualism of prior naturalized epistemologies, as e.G., in W V Quine. We hold that their view presupposes a form of ontological realism and a realist theory of science, facts overlooked by critics. Finally, we argue that the implications for psychology and the social sciences are enormous and have not yet been appreciated.

MANN, Iu V. Gogol' In The Context Of Aesthetic Controversies (V G Belinskii's Polemic With Konstantin Aksakov). *Soviet Stud Phil* 23,68–90 Wint 84–85.

The polemics reflected the problem of the content and form of art, humour, the presentation of "lou" material etc. For Belinsky the problem of Gogol was a part of the movement of artistic form /stages/–the concept which united Russia with Western Europa. Aksakov solved the problem of Gogol in a more static way and as an alternative to modern European culture. At the same time, he raised the problem of the world importance of Gogol's works.

MANN, Jesse A. "The Proper Context Of Moral Education" in *The Georgetown Symposium On Ethics*, Porreco, Rocco (ed), 261–268. Lanham Univ Pr Of America 1984.

MANNING, D J and Robinson, T J. *The Place Of Ideology In Political Life*. Dover Croom Helm 1985.

Ideology's place in political life is, we learn, 'to provide the vocabulary within which the commendation or denigration of political institutions can be undertaken'. It is thus an essential component of politics, and cannot be dismissed as 'false consciousness' (as by Marx), an abridgement of political wisdom (as by Oakeshott), or senseless talk (as by T D Weldon, who is accused of attempting to clamp philosophical censorship upon politics). A proposition like 'all history is the history of class struggle' supplies a vocabulary of allegiance that allows parties to form and people to discuss their positions, but it tells us nothing at all. Manning and Robinson insist, about the world. It is on this point of absolute scepticism that people otherwise sympathetic to the analysis advanced by the Durham school (an earlier argument, *The Form of Ideology*, was published in 1980) find a stumbling block. (edited)

MANNING, Rita. The Random Collective As A Moral Agent. *Soc Theor Pract* 11,97–106 Spr 85.

I argue that random collectives can have obligations and be at fault for failing to fulfill these obligations, though this assignment of obligation and fault is contingent on the possibility of the members of the random collective organizing into a more formal group (a "minimally organized collective"). I offer the following defense. First, the moral fault of a random collective is not identical to the sum of the moral fault of the members. Second, if we deny that random collectives can have obligations, then no obligation to rescue would exist in cases where group action would be required to effect a rescue. Third, we want an analysis which allows us to influence the behavior of such groups.

MANNISON, Don. On Being Moved By Fiction. *Philosophy* 60,71–87 Ja 85.

It is argued here that, contrary to Radford, our emotional responses to fiction are not irrational. The core of the argument is the contention that although our concern is not for fictional characters, it is for their "fates" or situations.

MANOR, Ruth. Dialogue Representation. *Topoi* 3,63–74 Je 84.

We consider question–answer dialogues between participants who may disagree with each other. The main problems are: (a) How different speech–acts affect the information in the dialogue; and (b) How to represent what was said in a dialogue, so that we can summarize it even when it involves disagreements (i.E., inconsistencies). (edited)

MANSANI, P R. The Thermodynamic And Phylogenetic Foundations Of Human Wickedness. *Zygon* 20,283–320 S 85.

The problem of evil is brought under the ambit of science by explicating the theological concept "sinful" in thermodynamic and phylogenetic terms, and the proposition. "homo sapiens is a sinful species" is established. By a like explication, the theological concept of the "Fall of man" is shown to be amalgam of two concepts, Fall I and Fall Ii, of thermodynamic and anthropogenetic origins, respectively. fall I affects all life; Fall II ("original sin") affects Homo sapiens and its immediate forebears alone.

MANSER, Anthony. The Purposes Of Retribution. *Philosophy* 60,255–257 Ap 85.

MANSILLA, H C F. La Crítica De Herbert Marcuse A La Racionalidad Instrumentalista Y Su Receptción Por Corrientes Izquierdistas. *Rev Filosof (Costa Rica)* 22,63–72 D 84.

La relevancia de Herbert Marcuse reside en su visión globalizante de los problemas contemporáneos, incluido uno crítica de la sociedad altamente industrializada y de los presupuestos científico y comportamiento social es uno de los pilares centrales del *corpus* teórico de Marcuse, en análisis a los países del bloque socialista lleva a Marcuse a concluir que su configuración no es cualitativamente diferente de la den mundo capitalista en Occidente. marcuse ha cuestionado igualmente la validez de progresos centrales como progreso histórico y desarrollo hacia la industrialización como meta normativa, lo que hace importante su crítica vista desde el Tercer Mundo. La crítica izquierdista a Marcuse tiende necesariamente a pasar por alto sus puntos más originales (como su debate con la racionalidad instrumental) y a insistir en que Marcuse se habría alejado del marxismo.

MANVILLE, A and Santamaria, Ulysses. Marx: Entre L'idéalisme Radical Et L'individualisme Anarchique. *Philosophiques* 11,299–336 O 84.

The road to Marx's thought supposes as its condition a movement of radical depositioning in relation to the classically established guidelines for journeying through his work. Marx's thought, in opposition to any interpretation which sees therein a reflection on the social sphere, defines a radical form of individualism which is intended as the absolute criticism of any desire to construct a new order, an individualism which allows absolutely nothing which might obstruct the value of the meaning of autonomy to prevail.

MARCELLI, Miroslav. The Path Of French Epistemology To The Concept Of Chaos (in Czechoslovakian). *Filozof Cas* 32,814–820 1984.

MARCH, Peter. Sorting Out Sorites. *Can J Phil* 14,445–454 S 84.

MARCHAND, Alain Bernard and Rochon, Claire. L'Apport De La Convention En Litterature. *De Phil* 5,20–28 1984.

MARCISZEWSKI, Witold. Platonian Rationalism As Expressed In Leibniz's Program For Science. *Dialec Hum* 11,349–358 Spr/Sum 84.

Platonian rationalism involves a program of mathematization of knowledge. Its precisation and partial accomplishment took place in the 17th century under the name of mathesis universalis, esp. In Leibniz. The paper offers two case studies: one concerning mathematization of the philosophical idea of attractive force, as approached from two different philosophical positions, that of Leibniz and that of Newton; the second one concerning a step towards the idea of a class as made by Leibniz in his logical calculi.

MARCISZEWSKI, Witold. The Principle Of Comprehension As A Present–Day Contribution To Mathesis Universalis. *Phil Natur* 21,523–537 1984.

Mathematical logic with set theory partly realizes the 17th program of mathesis universalis. Following a historical hypothesis stated by Frege, the paper shows how a part of this realization, viz. The axiom of comprehension as expressing the idea of class, was anticipated by Leibniz's logical calculi. These developments are to exemplify the historical continuity in coming to modern logic.

MARCJA, Annalisa and Toffalori, Carlo. On Pseudo–$\aleph_0$–Categorical Theories. *Z Math Log* 30,533–540 1984.

MARCUS, Sanford A. Commentary On L Jung's "Commercialization And The Professions". *Bus Prof Ethics J* 2,89–92 Wint 83.

MARDAGA, Pierre (ed) and Dominicy, Marc. *La Naissance De La Grammaire Moderne*. La Province Mardaga 1984.

This book provides a formal reconstruction of the linguistic theory outlined by the Port–Royal logicians and grammarians. Evidence is adduced in favour of three theses: the logical and semiotic foundations of Port–Royal linguistics are to be found in Descartes's philosophy; the theory has a pragmatical component, whose importance was enhanced by controversies within the Jansenist movement; the Port–Royalist's views on the proposition and the complex term follow from a synthesis of the logico–semiotic and pragmatical components.

MAREK, Iwona. Consequence Operations Defined By Partial Matrices. *Rep Math Log* 17,47–55 1984.

Following LO's, Suszko and Grätzer we examine structural consequence operations defined by partial logical matrices. It is proved that the set of all matrix consequences of this form is either the set of all matrix consequences or the set of all structural consequences, depending on the language.

MAREK, W and Srebrny, M. No Minimal Transitive Model Of Z–. *Z Math Log* 21,225–228 1975.

MARGALIT, Avishai and Bar– Hillel, Maya. Gideon's Paradox: A Paradox Of Rationality. *Synthese* 63,139–156 My 85.

A decision maker who is about to choose between two options such that $A > B$, is promised a prize—which (s)he prefers to either option—for "choosing irrationally". The dilemma into which this promise plunges the decision maker constitutes Gideon's Paradox. The paper draws parallels between this paradox and several other well–known paradoxes, offers a "solution" to the various possible interpretations of the paradox, and discusses its implications for the concept of rationality.

MARGALIT, Avishai and Ullmann– Margalit, Edna. On The Nature Of Protest Petitions (in Hebrew). *Iyyun* 33,239–246 Ja–Ap 84.

MARGALIT, Avishai and Ullmann– Margalit, Edna. Protest Petitions. *J Applied Phil* 1,205–212 O 84.

This paper is concerned with the question of whether an individual has a moral obligation to sign a protest petition which has been initiated on moral grounds. It is argued that there is such an obligation when the petition represents a viewpoint with which one broadly agrees. (edited)

MARGALIT, Avishai. Frege And The Slingshot Argument (in Hebrew). *Iyyun* 33,414–421 Jl 84.

The argument referred to as "The Slingshot Argument" originated with Frege. Its conclusion is Frege's famous doctrine that the reference of a sentence is its truth value. Recently Barwise and Perry charged that this argument is in fact circular. This paper tries to rebut their charge and also to amend the premises of Frege's original argument.

MARGALIT, Avishai. The Poverty Of Marx's Functional Explanation (in Hebrew). *Iyyun* 33,498–504 O 84.

In the last few years a major controversy over the status of Marx's functional explanations centered around Gerald Cohen and Jon Elster. elster's main claim is that functional explanations in Marx are vacuous but, then, they are unimportant to his main tenets. Gerald Cohen claims that functional explanations are vital for Marx's thought but, then, they are not vacuous. I try to resolve the issue between the two contenders by suggesting that we construe functional explanations in Marx as recognitional explanations, i.E., explanations in which the beneficial effects of an institute are recognized without the emergence of the institute having been planned.

MARGENSTERN, Maurice. Sur Une Extension Simple Du Calcul Intuitionniste Des Prédicate Du Premier Ordre Appliquée À L'analyse. *Z Math Log* 30,317–324 1984.

MARGOLIS, Joseph. "The Problem Of Reading, Phenomenologically Or Otherwise" in *Existential Coordinates Of Human Condition*, Tymieniecka, A (ed), 559–568. Boston Reidel 1984.

MARGOLIS, Joseph. A Sense Of *Rapprochement* Between Analytic And Continental Philosophy. *Hist Phil Quart* 2,217–231 Ap 85.

Quine and Heidegger are examined, against the setting of their respective philosophical traditions, as exemplars of salient analytic and Continental currents. They are shown to converge in a very strong sense; and each is shown to require the complementary emphases of the other's tradition. In effect, a vocabulary is suggested for disciplined comparison of this unlikely sort, that suggests as well the direction of newer philosophical tendencies that bridge the two traditions.

MARGOLIS, Joseph. Prospects Regarding The Science Of Criticism. *Brit J Aes* 25,125–136 Spr 85.

Harold Osborne's assessment of the poverty of criticism in the arts is reviewed in the light of the current problems regarding the theory and methodology of the sciences and the current retreat from foundationalism and essentialism. A fair number of salient figures, both in the philosophy of science and aesthetics, are canvassed in this regard;

and Osborne's assessment is adjusted accordingly.

MARGOLIS, Joseph. The Intersection Of Theory Of Science And Theory Of Literature. *Conceptus* 19,97–109 1985.

Theory of science and theory of literature intersect in an important way currently, in that both exhibit characteristic difficulties in accounting for reference—respectively, in theories of narrative—within the problematic context of realism. The issue is pursued primarily by comparing Putnam's account of reference to theoretical entities and de Man's account of literature. Feyerabend, Goodman, Ricoeur, and Hillis Miller are considered briefly.

MARGOT, Jean Paul. Herméneutique Et Fiction Chez M Foucault. *Dialogue (Canada)* 23,635–648 D 84.

MARGULIS, Lynn and Sagan, Dorion. "Gaia And Philosophy" in *On Nature*, Rouner, Leroy S (ed), 60–78. Notre Dame Univ Notre Dame Pr 1984.

MARINI, Sergio. La "Conferenza Sull'etica" Di L Wittgenstein. *Riv Filosof Neo-Scolas* 76,122–134 Ja–Mr 84.

MARINO, Gordon D. An Analysis And Assessment Of A Fragment From Jonathan Barnes's Reading Of Heraclitus. *Apeiron* 18,77–89 1984.

MARINO, Gordon D. The Rational Foundations Of Kierkegaard's Critique Of Reason. *Dialogue (PST)* 27,1–10 O 84.

MARION, Jean–Luc. De La "Mort De Dieu" Aux Noms Divins: L'itinéraire Théologique De La Métaphysique. *Laval Theol Phil* 41,25–42 F 85.

MARION, Jean–Luc. Die Cartesianische Onto–Theo–Logie. *Z Phil Forsch* 38,349–380 Je–D 84.

MARKIE, Peter J. Feinberg On Moral Rights. *Austl J Phil* 62,237–245 S 84.

MARKIE, Peter J. From Cartesian Epistemology To Cartesian Metaphysics. *Phil Topics* 13,195–204 Spr 85.

MARKIEWICZ, Henryk. Karl Marx And Literature. *Dialec Hum* 10,157–166 Sum 83.

MARKIEWICZ, Wladyslaw. Marx Or Weber: A Genuine Of Or An Imaginary Dilemma. *Dialec Hum* 10,5–22 Sum 83.

MARKLE, Gerald E and Robin, Stanley S. Biotechnology And The Social Reconstruction Of Molecular Biology. *Sci Tech Human Values* 10,70–79 Wint 85.

MARKLEY, William S and Mc Donald, Anne E and Grodin, Michael. "Medicolegal And Ethical Dilemmas In A Teaching Hospital" in *Ethics Committees And Health Care Decisions*, Cranford, Ronald (ed), 118–128. Ann Arbor Health Admin Pr 1984.

MARKOVIC, Mihailo. *Boston Studies In The Philosophy Of Science: Dialectical Theory Of Meaning*, R S Cohen And M W Wartofsky (eds) V81. Boston Reidel 1984.

MARMAI, U and Jobst, Eberhard. Weltanschauliche Und Wissenschaftstheoretische Probleme Des Verhältnisses Von Natur– Und Technikwissenschaften. *Deut Z Phil* 23,757–766 1975.

Die Autoren behandeln die Notwendigkeit und Spezifik der technikwissenschaftlichen Umsetzung naturwissenschaftlicher Erkenntnisse. Die allgemeinen Merkmale des Wechselverhältnisses von Natur– und Technikwissenschaften werden am Beispiel der historischen und gegenwärtigen Entwicklung der thermodynamischen Theorian über die gemeinsame Wärmeund Stoffübertragung dargestellt. Ferner werden einige Momente der Beziehungen von Technik– und Gesellschaftswissenschaften im Sozialismus untersucht.

MARQUÉS, Gustavo. Metodologias E Historia De Las Ciencias. *Rev Latin De Filosof* 11,157–162 Jl 85.

MARQUES, Ivan. On Speedability Of Recursively Enumerable Sets. *Z Math Log* 21,199–214 1975.

MARQUET, Jean–François. La Monadologie De Diderot. *Rev Phil Fr* 174,353–370 Jl–S 84.

MARRAS, Ausonio. The Churchlands On Methodological Solipsism And Computational Psychology. *Phil Sci* 52,295–309 Je 85.

This paper addresses a recent argument of the Churchlands against the "linguistic-rationalist" tradition exemplified by current cognitive–computational psychology. Because of its commitment to methodological solipsism—the argument goes—computational psychology cannot provide an account of how organisms are able to represent and "hook up" to the world. First I attempt to determine the exact nature of this charge and its relation to the Churchlands' long-standing polemic against 'folk psychology' and the linguistic–rationalist methodology. I then turn my attention to the Churchlands' account of what it is for computational psychology to be methodologically solipsistic. I argue that there is no reason to suppose that methodological solipsism commits one to a purely syntactic theory of mind (of the kind that Stephen Stich has recently advocated): the formality constraints that methodological solipsism imposes on psychological explanation do not exclude 'essential' reference to the representational context of mental states, as long as this content is construed in the 'narrow' sense. I conclude by raising a problem for computational psychology that may provide some real cause for concern.

MARSDEN, David. Commentary On "Kicking Against The Pricks: Two Patients Wish To End Essential Insulin Treatment". *J Med Ethics* 10,203–204 D 84.

MARSDEN, George. "The Collapse Of American Evangelical Academia" in *Faith And Rationality*, Plantinga, Alvin (ed), 219–264. Notre Dame Univ Notre Dame Pr 1983.

MARSH, Frank H (ed) and Katz, Janet (ed). *Biology, Crime And Ethics: A Study Of Biological Explanations For Criminal Behavior.* Cincinnati Anderson 1985.

MARSH, Frank H and Abel, Charles F. *Punishment And Restitution: A Restitutionary Approach To Crime And The Criminal.* Westport Greenwood Pr 1984.

MARSH, James L. "Collins And Gadamer On Interpretation" in *History Of Philosophy In The Making*, Thro, Linus J (ed), 231–246. Washington Univ Pr Of America 1982.

MARSH, James L. "Marx And Kierkegaard On Alienation" in *International Kierkegaard Commentary*, Perkins, Robert L (ed), 155–174. Macon Mercer Univ Pr 1984.

MARSH, James L and Hamrick, William S. Whitehead And Marx: Toward A Political Metaphysics. *Phil Today* 28,191–202 Fall 84.

The essay demonstrates first, the affinities between Marx and Whitehead as philosophers of process; second the complementarity of Marx's critical social theory and Whitehead's metaphysics; and finally, the possibility of a political metaphysics at once speculative and practical, ontological and critical, reflective and committed.

MARSH, James L. Dialectical Phenomenology As Critical Social Theory. *J Brit Soc Phenomenol* 16,177–193 My 85.

The purpose of the essay is to show, first, how eidetic phenomenology is an element in and foundation for ideology critique in evaluating individualism, reification, and scientism. The second part of the essay shows how ideology critique already is hermeneutical phenomenology in understanding and criticizing these phenomena. The true notion of phenomenology that emerges is dialectical phenomenology, a union of universal and particular, description and dialectic, patient elucidation of experience and interpretation of experience.

MARSH, James L. Heidegger's Overcoming Of Metaphysics: A Critique. *J Brit Soc Phenomenol* 16,55–69 Ja 85.

The article is divided into two parts, the first of which describes Heidegger's development from phenomenology of thought, in which he claims to overcome metaphysics, the second part of the essay criticizes this attempt as self-refuting in several ways, confusing phenomenologically at least eight kinds of objectivity, and engaged in a facile dichotomy of method and truth. The way to metaphysics remains open.

MARSHALL, Terence. Art D'écrire Et Pratique Politique De Jean–Jacques Rousseau (II). *Rev Metaph Morale* 89,322–347 Jl–S 84.

From the *Discourse on the Arts and Sciences* it is clear that Rousseau considered the act of publishing to be a public, or political, act. As such, his writings might themselves be construed according to the requirements of prudence that his criticism of the Enlightment is designed to reveal. Starting from Rousseau's remarks on esotericism in the *Letter to Stanislas* and in the *Second Letter to Bordes*, the present study, published in two parts, seeks to examine: 1) the evidence that Rousseau dissimulates his thought; 2) why he might do so on the basis of the problem of theory and practice in political writing; and 3) how such dissimulation is consistent with his device "Vitam Impendere Vero". Particular attention is given to the argument on lying in the Fourth Promenade of the *Reveries of the Solitary Walker* and to the consistency of this argument in earlier writings, including the two versions of the *Social Contract* and the *Emile*. In this way the essay seeks to discern the practical reason relating Rousseau's aesthetic and philosophic modes.

MARSHALL, Terence. Art D'écrire Et Pratique Politique De Jean–Jacques Rousseau (I). *Rev Metaph Morale* 89,232–261 Ap–Je 84.

MARSÍK, Frantisek. Irreversibility Of Time, Entropy And Stability (in Czechoslovakian). *Filozof Cas* 32,892–900 1984.

MARTI, Fritz. Schelling's Aphorisms Of 1805. *Ideal Stud* 14,237–258 S 84.

The insights of the post–Kantian speculation are indispensable for any philosopher unwilling to reject religious thoughts merely because they speak a language of their own. Those insights offer sober philosophical terms. More particularly, Schelling's Aphorisms of 1805 show how one should *not* talk, if one wants to take religious truths seriously, though not as a mere convert. This translation renders the first half of the Aphorisms in English.

MARTIN, Dean. On Certainty And Religious Belief. *Relig Stud* 20,593–614 D 84.

First, a summary is given of the dominant themes in Wittgenstein's On Certainty. Next, it is argued that many beliefs in Christianity share significant logical features with the fundamental propositions discussed by Wittgenstein in On Certainty. Not least is the fact that, like the latter but unlike scientific hypotheses, basic Christian beliefs are removed from the traffic of verification/falsification. The essay concludes by noting various dissimilarities between Christian beliefs and Wittgenstein's fundamental propositions. Those differences serve to further illumine the peculiarities of the tenets of religious faith.

MARTIN, J and Harre, R. "Metaphor In Science" in *Metaphor*, Miall, David S (ed), 89–105. Atlantic Highlands Humanities Pr 1982.

MARTIN, Jane R. Bringing Women Into Educational Thought. *Educ Theor* 34,341–354 Fall 84.

MARTIN, John N. A Syntactic Characterization Of Kleene's Strong Connectives With Two Designated Values. *Z Math Log* 21,181–184 1975.

MARTIN, M. Does The Evidence Confirm Theism More Than Naturalism? *Int J Phil Relig* 16,257–262 1984.

This paper is a critique of Schlesinger's argument in *Religion and Scientific Method* that theism is confirmed more by the evidence than naturalism. It is shown that Schlesinger neglects certain evidence that seems to tell against theism, that his account of theism is mistaken and that his definition of confirmation has serious problems.

MARTIN, Michael. "How To Be A Good Philosopher Of Science" in *Methodology, Metaphysics And The History Of Science*, Cohen, Robert S (ed), 33–42. Boston Reidel 1984.

MARTIN, Mike W and Schinzinger, Roland. Commentary: Informed Consent In Engineering And Medicine. *Bus Prof Ethics J* 3,67–78 Fall 83.

Informed consent is the keystone in the interaction between engineers and the lay public. Yet three major difficulties arise in securing it: identifying the decision maker, proxy decision making, and respecting the rights of dissident minorities where projects affect many people and not everyone's wishes can be satisfied. We respond to Thomas A Long's challenge that informed consent has little relevance to engineering, and we identify analogs to these three problems that arise in medicine.

MARTIN, Mike W. Demystifying Doublethink: Self–Deception, Truth And Freedom In 1984. *Soc Theor Pract* 10,319–331 Fall 84.

Orwell treated doublethink as the most fundamental tool for undermining freedom within totalitarian regimes. Drawing on Sartre's conception of bad faith, I interpret doublethink as a form of self–deception and unravel Orwell's paradoxical description of it. Then I trace the role of self–deception in the power–worshiping government he portrays. orwell's use of the concept of doublethink can ve viewed as reconciling Marxist and Freudian approaches to understanding political self–deception.

MARTIN, Raymond. History And The Brewmaster's Nose. *Can J Phil* 15,253–272 Je 85.

I argue that *Verstehen* is a legitimate technique of confirmation in historical studies, and that the degree to which it is used by historians marks an important methodological difference between historical studies and the natural sciences. It also explains why historical studies are intractably more subjective than the natural sciences. Special attention is paid to the debate among New Testament scholars over the so–called "Synoptic Problem".

MARTIN, Rex. *Rawls And Rights.* Lawrence Univ Pr Of Kansas 1985.

MARTIN, Rex and Shenoy, Prakash P. Two Interpretations Of The Difference Principle In Rawls's Theory Of Justice. *Theoria* 49,113–141 1983.

This paper examines in detail Rawls' difference principle. An alternative formulation of the difference principle in terms of pareto efficiency and egalitarianism, with the former having lexical priority over the latter, is provided. Egalitarianism is defined as minimizing the difference between the expectations of the most favored and the least advantaged representative persons. This restatement is formally shown to be equivalent to the Rawlsian maximin version. Arguments for and advantages of the reformulation are given.

MARTINEZ– BONATI, Felix. "Fiction & Transposition Of Presence" in *Existential Coordinates Of Human Condition*, Tymieniecka, A (ed), 495–504. Boston Reidel 1984.

MARTÍNEZ, Juan Carlos. Accessible Sets And $(L_{\omega_1\omega})_r$–Equivalence For T_3Spaces. *J Sym Log* 49,961–967 S 84.

Ziegler has studied the expressibility of the first order topological language for T_3topological spaces by means of the notion of the type of a point. By looking at the behavior of convergence we refine Ziegler's notion of type and in this way we characterize the equivalence in the most interesting infinitary topological language for a wide class of T_3spaces.

MARTINS, Estevão De Rezende. Die Situation Der Philosophie In Brasilien. *Z Phil Forsch* 38,648–657 N–D 84.

On the basis of an historical approach to the history of philosophy in Brazil, mainly in the 20th century, this report describes the main currents: philosophy of science, political and social philosophy, history of ideas, their research centers and publications, concluding that only since 1945–1950 Brazilian philosophers began an original and creative philosophical reflexion.

MARTINS, Estevao De Rezende. O Moralismo Escocês Do Séc XVIII E A Concepção De Liberdade No Kant Pré–Critíco. *Rev Port Filosof* 40,225–247 Jl–S 84.

Kant's itinerary for the idea of liberty has been completed on the late 760's. One of the greatest influences was Hutchenson's thought. With Hutchenson's theory of moral sense it was possible to Kant to criticize traditional rationalistic moral heteronomy as a Hume for the moral theory in Kant's view. Hutchenson made it possible that Kant chose the way to the autonomy without basing it on emotional judgments and consciousness.

MARTLAND, T R. When A Poem Refers. *J Aes Art Crit* 34,267–274 Spr 85.

By considering E E Cummings poem "l(a)", this essay argues that while imitation presents empirical referents and representation presents interpreted referents, they both effect new understandings. It also argues poor imitation is a manipulative rearrangement of an understanding already established, an academic art done in the manner of an already established style while poor representation is minor art, of consequence only for audiences identifying with its narrowly conceived referents. It is oblivious to the dominant styles of the future.

MARVAN, Milan. Validity And Applicability Of Thermodynamics Out Of The Framework Of Physical Systems (in Czechoslovakian). *Filozof Cas* 32,904–906 1984.

It is argued that thermodynamics laws are valid for some aspects of biological, economic—ecological systems. These laws can give some limits of structures and processes, but in any case, they cannot explain the specific properties of considered systems.

MARVIN, Bertha. "Irrelevancies" in *Freedom, Feminism, And The State*, Mc Elroy, Wendy (ed), 101–110. Cato Institute Washington 1982.

MARX, Werner and Nenon, Thomas (trans). *The Philosophy Of F W J Schelling: History, System, And Freedom.* Bloomington Indiana Univ Pr 1984.

This book assesses Schelling's unique thought and its relevance for present–day philosophical issues. The first of three essays draws a comparison between Schelling's conception of history and that of the contemporary social philosopher Jürgen Habermas. The second part compares Schelling's *System of Transcendental Idealism* and Hegel's *Phenomenology of Spirit.* In the third part, the author demonstrates that Schelling resolved the problem of the relation of freedom to necessity through a metaphysics of the absolute.

MARX, Werner. Dialectic And The Role Of The Phenomenologist (in Hebrew). *Iyyun* 33,5–11 Ja–Ap 84.

This essay investigates the role of the phenomenologist in Hegel's *Phenomenology of Spirit.* His role turns out to be the following: 1) The phenomenologist thematizes knowing as "phenomenal" and thus initiates its dialectical movement. 2) He

comprehends the dialectical character of this movement and, from his insight into the necessity of the steps involved, undertakes their presentation as a justification of the scientific standpoint. 3) He steers and guides the entire movement as a movement of the concept by means of his reflections on the categorial level.

MASCALL, Eric L. "Contemporary Genetics: Some Ethical Considerations" in *The Good Life And Its Pursuit*, Dougherty, Jude P (ed), 175–185. NY Paragon House 1984.

MASLOFF, Clement. "Lenin–Engineer Of Revolution" in *Continuity And Change In Marxism*, Fischer, Norman And Others (ed), 170–188. Atlantic Highlands Humanities Pr 1982.

MASON, Ian. The Metatheory Of The Classical Propositional Calculus Is Not Axiomatizable. *J Sym Log* 50,451–457 Je 85.

Folklore has it that the interpolation theorem was the final elementary property of first order logic to be discovered. ¡ F A K van Benthem suggested this be demonstrated by showing its fundamental role in an axiomatization of the metatheory of the logic, viewing it as a first order structure. In this paper it is shown that the structure in question is a complex as true number theory. Thus the logic is axiomatizable but its metatheory is not.

MASTROIANNI, Giovanni. Quattro Punti Da Rivedere Nel Gramsci Dei Quaderni. *G Crit Filosof Ital* 63,260–267 My–Ag 84.

MATHAUSER, Zdene. Calculators Of Philosophers And Calculators Of Poets (in Czechoslovakian). *Estetika* 21,138–141 1984.

MATHERON, Alexandre. Le *Droit Du Plus Fort*: Hobbes Contre Spinoza. *Rev Phil Fr* 175,149–176 Ap–Je 85.

MATHEWS, William. Lonergan's Economics. *Method* 3,9–30 Mr 85.

Lonergan's work is concerned with the method of explanation and scientific status of economics. The task is to discover the system of significant variables relating the productive, exchange, and financial sectors of the economy. Production is such that from time to time it can shift the standard of living, wave–like, from one level to another. The critical problem in economics is to adapt finance to such take off points.

MATHUR, Dinesh Chandra. J Krishnamurti On Choiceless Awareness, Creative Emptiness And Ultimate Freedom. *Diogenes* 126,91–103 Sum 84.

The intention of this paper is to analyze J Krishnamurti's concepts of self, action and freedom. It attempts to give a critical estimate of his doctrines of "choiceless awareness" and "creative emptiness" as solutions for overcoming the pervasive human condition of suffering. It brings out the one–sidedness of his emphasis on individual transformation through "choiceless awareness" to the neglect of simultaneous transformation of socio–economic conditions. However, the paper recognizes the element of truth in Krishnamurti's emphasis on "creative emptiness" for providing valuable relaxation and detachment as necessary conditions for creative action.

MATIJASEVIC, Y V and Jones, J P. Register Machine Proof Of The Theorem On Exponential Diophantine Representation Of Enumerable Sets. *J Sym Log* 49,818–829 S 84.

One of the historically important first steps in the eventual solution of Hilbert's tenth problem was the 1961 Theorem of Martin Davis, Hilary Putnam and Julia Robinson which states that every recursively enumerable set, A can be represented in exponential diophantine form. Recently a new very simple proof of this theorem was founded by James P Jones and Ju V Matijasevic. This new proof is based on register machines and uses only very elementary number theory, we need only the partial ordering less than or equal to defined by κless than or equal to $\eta \leftrightarrow (\eta$over $\kappa) \equiv 1$ (mod 2).

MATSUSHITA, Masatoshi. "Happiness And The Idea Of Happiness" in *The Good Life And Its Pursuit*, Dougherty, Jude P (ed), 45–50. NY Paragon House 1984.

MATSUZAKI, Toshiyuki. Über Die Phasen Des Ästhetischen Urteils—In Beziehung Auf Kants Urteilslehre (in Japanese). *Bigaku* 35,28–39 Ja 84.

Das ästhetische Urteil enthält ästhetisches Reflexionsurteil und ästhetisches Sinnesurteil ("Erste Einleitung VII"). Das erstere lässt sich im Satz "Dies ist schön" darstellen, und das letztere im Satz "Dies ist angenehm"; in diesen Sätzen zeigen beide Urteile keinen empirischen Begriff als Prädikat, sondern die *Indexe*, die jeweils de inneren Zustand des Subjekts feststellen. Deshalb fällt es schwer, den Unterschied zwischen den beiden Urteilen nur durch Vergleichung ihrer Sätze klarzumachen. Wir müssen nun die erkenntnistheoretischen Modelle von jedem Urteil deutlicher auffassen. (edited)

MATTHEN, Mohan. Perception, Relativism, And Truth: Reflections On Plato's Theaetetus 152–160. *Dialogue (Canada)* 24,33–58 Spr 85.

The standard interpretation of *Theaetetus* 152–160 has Plato attribute to Protagoras a relativistic theory of truth and existence. It is argued here that in fact the individuals of Protagorean worlds are inter–personal. (thus the Protagorean theory has public objects, private truth). Also, a new interpretation is offered of Plato's use of Heraclitean flux to model relativism. The philosophical and semantic consequences of the interpretation are explored.

MATTHEWS, Gareth B. *Dialogues With Children.* Cambridge Harvard Univ Pr 1984.

This book reports on a philosophy class the author conducted among 8 1/2 to 11 year olds in Edinburgh, Scotland. Topics discussed with the children include whether flowers can be happy, what words are, and whether time travel is possible. The book demonstrates that children of this age can be astute and imaginative philosophers. The implication of this finding for philosophy and for developmental psychology are explored briefly.

MATTICK JR, Paul (ed) and Mattick, Paul. *Marxism: Last Refuge Of The Bourgeoisie?* NY Sharpe 1983.

MATTICK, Paul and Mattick Jr, Paul (ed). *Marxism: Last Refuge Of The Bourgeoisie?* NY Sharpe 1983.

MAUER, K F and Retief, A I. Methodological Problems In Psychology (in Dutch). *S Afr J Phil* 4,19–24 F 85.

While it ought to be possible to identify a virtually endless list of methodological problems in psychology, the authors of this article concentrate on two issues which cause, or indeed ought to cause, a considerable amount of concern at present. First, a description is provided of the situation which arises when researchers, particularly those in the field of therapeutic psychology, conceptualize their research problems in terms of the precepts of general systems theory and in the absence of appropriate research methodologies. This results in a confusion between circular conceptualization and linear methods. The second problem relates to the complexities of cross–cultural research. This is particularly evident when attempts are made to measure dimensions of personality, attitude, and interest with instruments developed for cultural groups other than those which are being investigated. As a rule the metric qualities of the instruments suffer to such an extent that the measurements are largely useless. The authors contend that there is an urgent need for philosophical reflection, and that philosophers could make an important contribution at both theoretical and metatheoretical levels.

MAUTNER, Thomas. Natural Rights In Locke. *Phil Topics* 12,73–78 Wint 81.

There are, according to Locke, certain things which we have not only a right to do, but also a duty. But this is not to say that having the right implies having the duty. Nor does Locke say it. So it should not feature in an account of the difference between Locke's right–concept and older ones. The views of some writers (chiefly Medlan, but also MacFarlane and Sterba), who seem to have misread Locke on this point, are briefly discussed.

MAVRODES, George I. "Jerusalem And Athens Revisited" in *Faith And Rationality*, Plantinga, Alvin (ed), 192–218. Notre Dame Univ Notre Dame Pr 1983.

MAVRODES, George I. "The Stranger" in *Faith And Rationality*, Plantinga, Alvin (ed), 94–102. Notre Dame Univ Notre Dame Pr 1983.

MAVRODES, George I. "Turning" in *Faith And Rationality*, Plantinga, Alvin (ed), 187–191. Notre Dame Univ Notre Dame Pr 1983.

MAVRODES, George I. Necessity, Possibility, And The Stone Which Cannot Be Moved. *Faith Phil* 2,265–271 Jl 85.

MAVRODES, George I. Self–Referential Incoherence. *Amer Phil Quart* 22,65–72 Ja 85.

MAXCY, Spencer J. Leadership, Administration, And The Educational Policy Operation. *Proc Phil Educ* 40,329–338 1984.

What does the concept of 'leadership' mean for the educational policy operation? The argument is made here that 'leadership' as it is currently utilized in educational administration is wrong–headed. It is proposed that leadership is intimately related to plans and policies, and that where administrators in an educational setting exercise policy–making skills, they ought to pay attention to consequences and be evaluated in terms of them. 'leadership' is seen as a fruitful notion where a moral–ethical requirement is attached to evaluation of policy.

MAXCY, Spencer J. The Democratic "Myth" And The Search For A Rational Concept Of Education. *Educ Phil Theor* 17,22–37 My 85.

After critiquing efforts by Wilson & Cowell (1983) and Barrow (1981) to reduce democracy to an ideology and myth, and to replace it with totalitarianism as an equally appealing organizational mode for schools, the present essay argues that 1) democracy is more than a myth and not necessarily undesirable because it is ideological; 2) democracy and education are related notions; and 3) democracy and education, rather than being neglected by educational philosophers, has been subjected to rigorous analysis (particulary by John Dewey). It is proposed that the intellectual geography of democracy and education is still a vital ground upon which to work, and as such may yield a fuller understanding of the contexts wherein schooling operates.

MAXWELL, Nicholas. Are Probabilism And Special Relativity Incompatible? *Phil Sci* 52,23–43 Mr 85.

In this paper I expound an argument which seems to establish the probabilism and special relativity are incompatible. I examine the argument critically, and consider its implications for interpretative problems of quantum theory, and for theoretical physics as a whole.

MAY, Philip. A Comparison Of Logical Form In Russell And Wittgenstein. *Eidos* 2,14–27 Jl 80.

MAY, William E. Aquinas And Janssens On The Moral Meaning Of Human Acts. *Thomist* 48,566–606 O 84.

This essay challenges Janssens' interpretation of Thomistic texts on the moral meaning of human acts. Janssens claims that for Aquinas the agent's intention is so decisive that one can will to evil for the sake of a higher good. This claim is not, it is argued, supported by a close study of Aquinas, who taught that an act morally wicked by reason of its object and known to be such cannot be made good by any end.

MAY, William F. Religious Justifications For Donating Body Parts. *Hastings Center Rep* 15,38–42 F 85.

MAYBERRY, John. Global Quantification In Zermelo–Fraenkel Set Theory. *J Sym Log* 50,289–301 Je 85.

MAYER, Adrian C (ed). *Culture And Morality.* Bombay Oxford Univ Pr 1981.

MAYR, Ernst. "Evolution And Ethics" in *Darwin, Marx And Freud*, Caplan, Arthur L (ed), 35–46. NY Plenum Pr 1984.

MAZOUÉ, James G. Nozick On Inferential Knowledge. *Phil Quart* 35,191–193 Ap 85.

The claim that Nozick's vase–in–the–box example in *Philosophical Explanations* is to be construed as a case of inferential knowledge rests upon the false assumption that one cannot believe there is a vase in a box on the basis of what one sees is a particular vase. Neither does Nozick's rejection of sceptical arguments based on the Transmission Principle entail a wholesale rejection of epistemic closure.

MC ALLISTER, Martin E and Wood, J Scott and Goddard, Dorothy M. "Cultural Resource Law Enforcement In The US" in *Ethics And Values In Archaeology*, Green, Ernestene L (ed), 156–170. NY Free Pr 1984.

MC ANINCH, Amy Raths. A Response To Boyd And Bogdan On Values And Teaching. *Educ Theor* 35,321–326 Sum 85.

MC BETH, Rod. A Second Normal Form For Functions Of The System EP. *Z Math Log* 30,393–400 1984.

MC BRIDE, Joseph. Nietzsche's Existential Ethic. *Phil Stud (Ireland)* 30,73–82 Spr 84.

This article examines Nietzsche's attempt to construct an existential ethic on the basis of a 'death of God' position. It argues that this attempt is an unsuccessful one. For while Nietzsche's first account of the moral life makes the will to power, a psych–biological function, the criterion of morality, the second is vitiated by a failure to provide a moral code which might justifiably be regarded as superior to the ethic he rejects.

MC CABE, Viki. A Comparison Of Three Ways Of Knowing: Categorical, Structural, And Affirmative. *J Mind Behav* 5,433–448 Autumn 84.

This paper compares three ways of knowing: *categorical*, from a phenomenalist perspective involving abstraction of and classification by criterial attributes; *structural*, from J J Gibson's critical realist perspective involving the direct perception of reciprocal compatibilities (affordance structures); and *affirmative*, from Martin Buber's existential perspective involving the direct affirmation of unique existences (I–Thou relationships). The view expressed here is that knowledge is not acquired through categorical analysis, but rather through the unmediated affordance and affirmation relationships provided by structural and affirmative perspectives; categorical knowing, in contrast, may come after knowledge acquisition and modulate processes such as communication and analysis. A comparison is made between knowledge pertinent to the category of, the affordance structure for, and the affirmation of love.

MC CALL, John J and Des Jardins, Joseph R. A Defense Of Employee Rights. *J Bus Ethics* 4,367–376 O 85.

Recent business trends in business ethics along with growing attacks upon unions, suggest that employee rights will be a major social concern for business managers during the next decade. However, in most of the discussions of employee rights to date, the very meaning and legitimacy of such rights are often uncritically taken for granted. In this paper, we develop an account of employee rights and defend this conception against what we take to be the strongest in–principle objections to it.

MC CALL, Storrs. A Dynamic Model Of Temporal Becoming. *Analysis* 44,172–176 O 84.

Adolf Grunbaum's and j j c Smart's theory of temporal becoming implies that without consciousness there is no such thing. An alternative is a theory in which time flow is independent of the existence of conscious observers. This theory requires a dynamic picture of the universe as a tree–like manifold of branching four–dimensional continua, later trees being sub–trees of earlier ones. The picture is consistent with two–valued not three–valued logic if truth is regarded as "supervenient" upon events.

MC CALL, Storrs. Counterfactuals Based On Real Possible Worlds. *Nous* 18,463–478 S 84.

The aim of the paper is to provide truth–conditions for counterfactual conditionals based on a forward–branching model of possible worlds or world–histories. The semantics are analogous to those of Lewis and Stalnaker except that the inherently vague concept of possible world similarity is replaced by the notion of length of shared or common past. The paper concludes with a Lockian theory of individuals which ties them to their origins and prevents them, if taken out of their temporal context, from appearing in meaningful counterfactuals. (edited)

MC CALL, Storrs. Freedom Defined As The Power To Decide. *Amer Phil Quart* 21,329–338 O 84.

It is argued that the power to decide requires the mutual compossibility of at least two different courses of action. Four conditions are proposed which would be required for an agent to be said to be acting on the basis of a decision. It is argued that if it met these conditions, even a robot or automaton could be described as possessing free will. (edited)

MC CANN, Edwin. Skepticism And Kant's B Deduction. *Hist Phil Quart* 2,71–90 Ja 85.

MC CARTHY, George. Marx's Social Ethics And Critique Of Traditional Morality. *Stud Soviet Tho* 29,177–200 Ap 85.

This works starts with an analysis of the Tucker–Wood thesis that Karl Marx did not have a moral philosophy and that his utilitarian and materialist concepts of alienation and exploitation precluded such a philosophy. A different interpretation of Marx and moral philosophy comes from an understanding of how 18th and 19th century German social philosophy developed from morality to social ethics (Moralitaet to Sittlichkeit). With the development of Hegel's moral critique of Kant's *Critique of Practical Reason* and Marx's critique of Hegel's social theory, morality is joined to both social theory and political economy.

MC CARTHY, Jeremiah E. Semiotic Idealism. *Trans Peirce Soc* 20,394–434 Fall 84.

My purpose is to understand the relation between truth, reality, and the final opinion. Peirce's writings suggest two different positions about relation. I argue that there is only one: that what is real is a proposition believed in a final opinion. Thus reality is a symbol. To say how this could be, I explicate Peirce's idea of the world as a symbol with a detailed and extensive analysis of material from the fragment "Kaina Stoicheia".

MC CARTHY, Michael H. Kant's *Groundwork* Justification Of Freedom. *Dialogue (Canada)* 23,457–474 S 84.

In *Groundwork* III, Kant justifies freedom to justify morality. First, I argue that commentators look to the wrong text for his justification of freedom; it is not to be found in paragraphs 10–16. Second, I argue that to the extent that they look to the correct text, paragraph 4, they misinterpret Kant. Third, I set out, evaluate, and properly qualify the justification of freedom which Kant presents in paragraph 4.

MC CARTHY, Michael H. The Objection Of Circularity In Groundwork III. *Kantstudien* 76,28–42 1985.

Most Kant–scholars regard the objection of circularity as an indication of Kant's dissatisfaction with his par 4 argument for freedom. They regard him as providing a new argument for freedom in pars 10–16. By focussing on Kant's own statements and the concept of necessitation, I show the standard interpretation to be mistaken and provide a new interpretation of the objection of circularity as well as a new interpretation of the course of the argument in *Groundwork* III.

MC CARTHY, Thomas (trans) and Habermas, Jurgen. *The Theory Of Communicative Action: Reason And The Rationalization Of Society*, V1. Boston Beacon Pr 1981.

MC CARTHY, Timothy. Abstraction And Definability In Semantically Closed Structures. *J Phil Log* 14,255–266 Ag 85.

MC CARTHY, Timothy and Fine, Kit. Truth Without Satisfaction. *J Phil Log* 13,397–422 N 84.

Tarski defined truth in terms of satisfaction. But is this necessary? We give some answers to this question and thereby solve a problem of Kripke's and of Tharp's.

MC CARTHY, Timothy. Representation, Intentionality, And Quantifiers. *Synthese* 60,369–412 S 84.

MC CLELLAN, B Edward. Public Education And Social Harmony: The Roots Of An American Dream. *Educ Theor* 35,33–42 Wint 85.

MC CLELLAN, James. Making A Mess Of Marxism. *Proc Phil Educ* 40,265–272 1984.

Michael Smith is praised for contributions to Marxist scholarship. francis Schrag is criticized on many grounds, especially for endorsing G A Cohen's analysis of functional explanation. The latter is shown to depend on an unacknowledged agency neither ontologically nor politically consistent with Marxism. What is true of arguments *modus pollens* is defined as true of arguments *modus ponens* or (vel) arguments *modus tollens*.

MC CLINTOCK, Thomas. Scepticism And The Basis Of Morality. *Phil Res Arch* 10,micro Supp 1985.

Part 1, *Skepticism*, is devoted to an analysis of ethical skepticism and culminates in an account of what must be proved to refute it. Part 2, *The Basis of Morality*, develops the methodology for its refutation and then proceeds to its actual refutation, which consists fundamentally of the proof and elucidation of the rational basis of morality: the one and only true or correct supreme principle of morality. I have had to stike out entirely on my own in Part 1 and largely on my own in Part 2, though I learned a great deal that I draw upon, especially in Part 2, from the following moral philosophers whom I regard as the greatest in our tradition: Plato, Aristotle, Hobbes, Butler, Rousseau, Hume, Kant, Mill and Moore. I have sifted through their works—in comparitive fashion—saving, integrating and developing what I found to be methodologically or/and substantively sound and discarding what I found to be otherwise. The result is a moral philosophy whose principal strands, though they can be found, at least in embryo, in the works of predecessors, are woven into a tapestry that I think will be found to be substantially now and original—at least in overall design.

MC CONNELL, Terrance C. Objectivity And Moral Expertise. *Can J Phil* 14,193–216 Je 84.

This paper argues that though the objectivity of moral judgments does not require that there be moral experts, nevertheless the objectivist has reasons to be concerned if there are no moral experts. It is then argued that there are good reasons for holding that there are moral experts. This paper also explains what moral expertise means and what one should expect (and not expect) from moral experts.

MC CORD, Mark R and De Neufville, Richard. Assessment Response Surface: Investigating Utility Dependence On Probability. *Theor Decis* 18,263–285 My 85.

We design a three–dimensional response surface to investigate utility dependence on probability. The surface portrays basic utility assessment data as a function of the necessary assessment parameters. We construct surfaces for a group of individuals exhibiting utility dependence on probability. Analysis indicates that the dependence is related to an overvaluing of certain outcomes. This indication is supported by theoretical arguments and a specially designed subsequent study.

MC CORMICK, Richard A (ed) and Curran, Charles E (ed). *The Magisterium And Morality*. Ramsey Paulist Pr 1982.

MC CORMICK, Richard A. Gustafson's God: Who; What; Where? *J Relig Ethics* 13,53–70 Spr 85.

This essay approaches Gustafson's work through his two–volume *Ethics from a Theocentric Perspective*. It puts questions to Gustafson in four areas of concern in religious ethics: anthropocentrism, christology, revelation–inspiration, and practical ethics. The essay suggests that in Gustafson's *magnum opus*, both far more and far less is known about God than is warranted, and it concludes by questioning the truly Christian character of such theocentrism.

MC CULLAGH, C Behan. *Justifying Historical Descriptions*. NY Cambridge Univ Pr 1984.

This book attempts to establish the conditions which warrant belief in the truth of historical descriptions: singular descriptions, generalizations and causal statements. It analyzes a large range of historical examples, illustrating the variety of arguments which historians employ. The books argues that although one cannot prove historical descriptions true beyond all possibility of error, one is often justified in believing well–supported descriptions for practical purposes.

MC CULLOCH, Gregory. Cause In Perception: A Note On Searle's *Intentionality*. *Analysis* 44,203–205 O 84.

MC CULLOCH, Gregory. Frege, Sommers, Singular Reference. *Phil Quart* 34,295–310 Jl 84.

MC CULLOUGH, L B and Wear, Stephen. Respect For Autonomy And Medical Paternalism Reconsidered. *Theor Med* 6,295–308 O 85.

We offer a critique of one prominent understanding of the principle of respect for autonomy and of analyses of medical paternalism based on that understanding. Our main critique is that understanding respect for autonomy as respect for freedom from interference is mistaken because it is overly influenced by 'four–alarm' cases, because it fails to appreciate the full dimensions of legal self–discrimination (one of its main sources), because it conflates the research and therapeutic settings, and because it fails to appreciate themes of authority and power that have historically shaped the principle of respect for freedom from interference. We argue that respect for autonomy involves more than just freedom from interference and, on this basis, offer a critique of prevailing accounts of medical paternalism.

MC CULLOUGH, Laurence B and Beauchamp, Tom L. *Medical Ethics: The Moral Responsibilities Of Physicians*. Englewoods Cliffs Prentice–Hall 1984.

MC CULLOUGH, Laurence B. Patients With Reduced Agency: Conceptual, Empirical, And Ethical Considerations. *J Med Phil* 9,329–332 N 84.

The moral responsibilities of physicians caring for elderly patients of diminished or marginal competence are analyzed. In the context of two case studies, it is argued that these responsibilities are not grounded simply in the patient's best interests as the physician understands them. Instead, they should be grounded in the patient's past autonomy, that is, the values and beliefs that the patient held prior to the loss of competence. Family members have a key role to play in assisting the physician to construct this "value history". An important role for the patient's primary care physician is also identified, namely, developing the patient's history in advance with the patient while he or she is competent, and recording this history in the patient's chart.

MC DERMOTT, John J (ed). *A Cultural Introduction To Philosophy: From Antiquity To Descartes*. NY Texas A&M Univ 1985.

This book, the first of two volumes, is an attempt to present the classics of Western philosophy in their cultural setting. To this end, many illustrations, maps and a detailed time–line accompanies the selections. Many of the selections are complete, and they are varied such that one can concentrate on the development of metaphysics, epistemology or the philosophy of religion.

MC DERMOTT, John J. Classical American Philosophy: A Reflective Bequest To The Twenty–First Century. *J Phil* 81,663–675 N 84.

It would seem that attempts to affect significant progress in response to the problems facing us in the next century, will have to proceed from a more multiple set of sources and feature a basic change in attitude with regard to both possibilities and frustrations. This attitude will have to be more pluralistic, more tolerant and less committed to ideology, closure and imposed solutions. In my judgment, the speculative bedding for this change in attitude was begun in nineteenth century America by William James, continued in the *late* thought of Josiah Royce and brought to fruition by John Dewey.

MC DERMOTT, Michael. Utility And Rational Self–Interest. *Phil Stud* 46,199–214 S 84.

MC DONALD, Anne E and Grodin, Michael and Markley, William S. "Medicolegal And Ethical Dilemmas In A Teaching Hospital" in *Ethics Committees And Health Care Decisions*, Cranford, Ronald (ed), 118–128. Ann Arbor Health Admin Pr 1984.

MC DONALD, Michael and Herr, Stanley S. Which Clients Should A Sheltered Workshop Serve: Case Study. *Hastings Center Rep* 14,52–54 O 84.

Sheltered workshops provide the mentally retarded with training and work experience. Due to a lack of resources, workshops have hard choices to make in regard to clients and wages. While normalization is the goal, training and maintenance perspectives may conflict. McDonald explores a utilitarian approach to such tradeoffs, while Stanley Herr urges a more rights–centered approach.

MC DONNELL, Kevin. "Moral Formation And The Liberal Arts" in *The Georgetown Symposium On Ethics*, Porreco, Rocco (ed), 243–250. Lanham Univ Pr Of America 1984.

MC DOWELL, John. *De Re* Senses. *Phil Quart* 34,283–294 Jl 84.

MC ELROY, Wendy (ed). *Freedom, Feminism, And The State*. Cato Institute Washington 1982.

An anthology of individualistic and libertarian feminist writings from the nineteenth and twentieth centuries which discuss such issues as liberty, sex, marriage, birth control, work, voting, religion, and war. Also included is a examination of individualist feminism's relationship to contemporary socialist and Marxist feminism. (staff)

MC ELROY, Wendy. "The Roots Of Individualist Feminism In 19th–Century America" in *Freedom, Feminism, And The State*, Mc Elroy, Wendy (ed), 3–28. Cato Institute Washington 1982.

MC FEE, Graham. "Wisdom On Aesthetics: Superstructure And Substructure" in *Philosophy And Life: Essays On John Wisdom*, Dilman, Ilham (ed), 83–122. Boston Nijhoff 1984.

MC FEE, Graham. How To Be An Idealist (II). *Ideal Stud* 15,41–53 Ja 85.

It is urged that to be an idealist in the 1980s is to give up the *Realist Assumption*: that to be real is to be susceptible to point–of–view–independent description. Giving up this assumption leads to an historicism which, the paper argues, is profitably developed as a theory of understanding using a notion such as Collingwood's *absolute presupposition* (or Wittgenstein's *form of representation*). Some exposition of Collingwood's views occupies the second part of the paper.

MC FEE, Graham. Wollheim And The Institutional Theory Of Art. *Phil Quart* 35,179–184 Ap 85.

An apparently insoluble dilemma for institutional theories of art, proposed by Wollheim, is considered. Either art status is conferred for good reasons, but then the theory is not genuinely institutional; or for no good reason, yet then it is not genuinely theorising *art*. This dilemma employs a misconceived, inherently Realist, conception of the notion of reasons. Its rebuttal requires adoption of a revised view of reasons: one giving due weight to the *categorial* difference art–status implies.

MC FETRIDGE, I G. Supervenience, Realism, Necessity. *Phil Quart* 35,245–258 Jl 85.

The aim is to assess a difficulty raised by Blackburn for moral realism in J Casey (ed) *Morality and Moral Reasoning* (London, 1971)––that of explaining (S) the supervenience of moral on naturalistic properties compatibly with (L) the non–entailment of moral by naturalistic propositions. It is argued that in the sense the argument requires (L) is false: and that Blackburn's 'non–realist' explanation of (S) is compatible with *moral* realism––it requires only *modal* non–realism.

MC GARITY, Thomas O. The New OSHA Rules And The Worker's Right To Know. *Hastings Center Rep* 14,38–45 Ag 84.

MC GIMSEY, Charles R. "The Value Of Archaeology" in *Ethics And Values In Archaeology*, Green, Ernestene L (ed), 171–174. NY Free Pr 1984.

MC GINN, Colin. The Concept Of Knowledge. *Midwest Stud Phil* 9,529–554 1984.

MC GINN, Colin. Two Notions Of Realism? *Phil Topics* 13,123–134 Spr 82.

MC GOLDRICK, P M. Causes, Correlations And Mind–Brain Identity. *Phil Stud (Ireland)* 30,230–232 Spr 84.

In this paper I have suggested that the single most persuasive argument offered by mind–brain identity theorists, namely that neurophysiological events cause mental events, is in fact incoherent. Causal relationships are two place relationships, but identity relationships are one place. Thus the former preclude the latter. If neurophysiological events are causally responsible for mental events, then they must be distinct from them. Accordingly, if any monism is true, only anomalous monism is.

MC GOLDRICK, Patricia M. Saints And Heroes: A Plea For The Supererogatory. *Philosophy* 59,523–528 O 84.

It has been argued that moral praise logically entails the belief that we ought to aspire to the moral ideal praised, and that therefore, while actions identical to those performed by saints and heroes are not encumberant upon us as a duty, aspiration towards the ideals they embody is. I have argued that this begs the question in favor of a trichotomous classification of actions into the permissible, the obligatory and the forbidden, which is in fact what it proports to establish. And that good Kantian reasons can be evoked to preserve the additional category of the supererogatory— actions which we praise but do not feel the need to emulate. (edited)

MC GRATH, Patrick J. Where Does The Ontological Argument Go Wrong? *Phil Stud (Ireland)* 30,144–164 Spr 84.

MC GRAY, James W. Walden Two And Skinner's Ideal Observer. *Behaviorism* 12,15–24 Fall 84.

Skinner's official position on values and ethics is radical relativism. Nevertheless, he has continued to recommend a particular model of a flourishing culture. The puzzle comes in attempting to harmonize his official position with his specific recommendations. I argue that he makes implicit use of a variant of the Ideal Observer Theory to justify his recommendations.

MC GRAY, James. Classical Utilitarianism And The Analogy Argument. *S J Phil* 22,389–402 Fall 84.

The essential core of the argument from analogy is that just as it is rational from the perspective of individual persons to maximize their net level of satisfaction, so also it is rational from the perspective of everyone to maximize over the entire set of satisfactions. I argue that the objections of Rawls, Gauthier, and Nozick to this argument can be answered, and that this argument provides a foundation for classical utilitarianism.

MC GUINNES, Brian. Wittgenstein And The Vienna Circle. *Synthese* 64,351–358 S 85.

MC GUIRE, James E (ed) and Bogen, James (ed). *How Things Are: Studies In Predication And The History Of Philosophy And Science.* Boston Reidel 1985.

A collection of commentaries and historical studies on crucial writings on the nature of properties and how things have properties. The authors include R G Turnbull, Alan Code, Frank Lewis, and D K Modrak (on Ancient Greek theories); Calvin Mormore and Marilyn Adams (Ockham and Buridan); J E McGuire and Robert M Adams (Leibniz) and Wilfrid Sellars (on Wilfrid Sellars). There is an introductory essay by James Bogen.

MC GUIRE, James E. "Phenomenalism, Relations, And Monadic Representation" in *How Things Are*, Bogen, James (ed), 205–234. Boston Reidel 1985.

MC GUIRE, Martin C. The Calculus Of Moral Obligation. *Ethics* 95,199–223 Ja 85.

MC INERNEY, Peter K. Person–Stages And Unity Of Consciousness. *Amer Phil Quart* 22,197–209 Jl 85.

Contemporary discussions of personal identity have focussed upon the nature of the relationships between person–stages at different times which constitute them all as the stages of one person. I argue in this paper that the unity of one person–stage, what makes diverse psychological factors into one person–stage rather than many or none, is dependent upon the relations between person–stages that make them all into the stages of one person. Working from our commonsense notions of unity of consciousness, I first develop and defend several necessary conditions for a psychological factor to be part of a unitary consciousness, and then argue that these conditions depend upon forward relations between consciousness–stages. In the next section I examine the special type of unity of a person beyond that of a mere unitary consciousness and argue that this unity also depends upon relations between person–stages. The paper concludes with an application of these conditions for one consciousness and for one person to the real world problem cases of multiple personality humans and split–brain humans.

MC KAY, C G. A Consistent Propositional Logic Without Any Finite Models. *J Sym Log* 50,38–41 Mr 85.

MC KAY, Thomas J. Actions And De Re Beliefs. *Can J Phil* 14,631–636 D 84.

I present evidence that *de re* attributions of belief are important in the explanation of actions. I show that an explanatory schema offered by Ernest Sosa and Mark Pastin is inadequate unless it is amended to include *de re* belief attributions. *s's* acting on *x* can be explained in part by *S's* belief of *x* that *x* is *F*, but not by *x's* being *F* together with *S's de dicto* belief that he is acting on the *F*.

MC KENNA, George. Bannisterless Politics: Hannah Arendt And Her Children. *Hist Polit Thought* 5,333–360 Sum 84.

A central theme in Hannah Arendt's writings is the breakdown of tradition. In her early writings, she sees the breakdown as tragic, but in her later works she welcomes it as an opportunity for man to rediscover his political potential. The chief defect in her later writings is their failure to develop standards. The result is a politics of "action" without principle, power without purpose. It was the earlier, more rigorous Arendt who stands the better chance of being remembered.

MC KENZIE, David E. Kant, A Moral Criterion, And Religious Pluralism. *Amer J Theol Phil* 6,47–56 Ja 85.

The purpose of this article is to establish a moral criterion by which claims to revelation might be assessed. It argues that among several different approaches suggested Kant's *Religion*, a negative criterion, according to which any revelational claim which is not immoral is acceptable as possibly true, is the most feasible. Such a criterion clearly eliminates certain doctrines such as eternal punishment, but allows for a plurality of possibly true doctrines, and thus preserves the integrity of the different living religious traditions.

MC KENZIE, David. The Fundamentalist Student And Introductory Philosophy. *Teach Phil* 7,205–216 Jl 84.

The article is designed to be of assistance to philosophy professors who teach fundamentalist students. It argues for a moderate stance in which fundamentalism is seen as a significant threat to academic and especially philosophical integrity, but in which students who hold such a position are encouraged to participate in philosophical dialogue. A review of stock fundamentalist arguments and an assessment of the value of the Halverson and Christian introductory texts for this purpose of communication with fundamentalists are also included.

MC KERLIE, Dennis. Egalitarianism. *Dialogue (Canada)* 23,223–238 Je 84.

MC KIM, Robert. Worlds Without Evil. *Int J Phil Relig* 15,161–170 1984.

Steven Boër claims that Plantinga's Free Will Defense shows that God may not be able to create a world in which persons are free but never make morally wrong choices, but not that God may be unable to prevent the *consequences* of such choices. Some philosophers have thought that Boër is wrong. I examine his arguments and attempt to show that they are not telling.

MC KINNEY, Audrey and Chellas, Brian F. The Completeness Of Monotonic Modal Logics. *Z Math Log* 21,379–383 1975.

MC KINSEY, Michael. Causality And The Paradox Of Names. *Midwest Stud Phil* 9,491–516 1984.

MC LAUGHLIN, Brian P. Perception, Causation, And Supervenience. *Midwest Stud Phil* 9,569–592 1984.

While a necessary condition for perceiving a physical object is that the object cause the perceiver to undergo a sense experience, this condition is not sufficient. Causal theorists attempt to provide a sufficient condition by placing contraints on the way the object causes the perceiver's experience. I argue that this is not possible since the relationship between a perceiver's experience and an object in virtue of which the perceiver perceives the object does not supervene on any of the ways in which the object causes the perceiver's experience.

MC LAUGHLIN, Kathleen (trans) and Pellauer, David (trans) and Ricoeur, Paul. *Time And Narrative*, V1. Chicago Univ Of Chicago Pr 1984.

MC LAUGHLIN, Robert. Necessary Agnosticism? *Analysis* 44,198–202 O 84.

Some Friends of the Ontological Argument evidently regard *modal* (necessary or impossible) existence–claims as immune to Occam's Razor; whence they view agnosticism, not rejection, as the sole rational response to such a claim in a justificatory vacuum. Against this, I argue that the Razor does apply to modal existence–claims. Failure to justify 'God exists', even if this claim is modal, rationally compels atheism, not agnosticism.

MC LAUGHLIN, T G. A Note Concerning The V* Relation On GAMMA–sur–R. *Z Math Log* 21,177–179 1975.

MC LEMORE, Lelan. Max Weber's Defense Of Historical Inquiry. *Hist Theor* 23,277–295 O 84.

MC LYNN, F J. The Ideology Of Jacobitism On The Eve Of The Rising Of 1745— Part I. *Hist Euro Ideas* 6,1–18 1985.

MC LYNN, F J. The Ideology Of Jacobitism—Part II. *Hist Euro Ideas* 6,173–188 1985.

MC MAHAN, Jeff. Deterrence And Deontology. *Ethics* 95,517–536 Ap 85.

The paper examines and criticizes a common argument against nuclear deterrence based on the claim that it is wrong to intend, even conditionally, to do that which it would be wrong to do. I contend that, depending on how the argument is interpreted, it will either have unacceptable implications or be too weak to carry conviction. I conclude by sketching an alternative deontological argument against nuclear deterrence which seems considerably more powerful and is not vulnerable to the objections I have made to the standard deontological argument.

MC MAHON, Thomas F. The Contributions Of Religious Traditions To Business Ethics. *J Bus Ethics* 4,341–349 Ag 85.

Critics claim that business ethics is philosophical, not theological: it depends exclusively on reason. This article traces three concepts (living wage, stewardship and participation/subsidiarity) from their religious origins to contemporary business practice. The unique contributions of religious traditions may be found in such aspects as vocation and co-creation which provide a spiritual motive which broadens and strengthens the deeper aspirations of business professionals. Thus, the contribution of religion has been more positive than unique.

MC MULLEN, Carolyn. 'Knowing What It's Like' And The Essential Indexical. *Phil Stud* 48,211–234 S 85.

MC MULLIN, Ernan. Galilean Idealization. *Stud Hist Phil Sci* 16,247–273 S 85.

It is customary to note that idealization played an important part in the style of science often called "Galilean." The term is, however, ambiguous though it generally signifies the simplifying of something complicated with a view to achieving a partial understanding of that thing. It is helpful to distinguish between five very different ways in which the scientist "idealizes": mathematical idealization, construct idealization (both formal and material), causal idealization and subjunctive idealization. Each of these can be exemplified in Galileo's work.

MC MULLIN, Ernan. Two Ideals Of Explanation In Natural Science. *Midwest Stud Phil* 9,205–220 1984.

Nomothetic explanation situates the explanandum as an instance of an empirical regularity (law). Retroductive explanation derives the explanandum from a postulated structure (model) and its associated text (theory). Many philosophers from Hume onwards have taken nomothetic explanation to be the ideal that physical science ought to pursue. The DN account of explanation was the most recent attempt to validate this claim. I argue that nomothetic explanation is ordinarily only a preliminary to the more basic retroductive account, where the laws themselves are explained in terms of underlying structures. Implications for the theory–observation distinction, casual connection, and scientific realism are explored.

MC MURTRY, John. Is There A Marxist Personal Morality? *Can J Phil* Supp 7,171–192 1981.

The article considers the widely made claim that Marxism is an amoral doctrine, and identifies the important theoretical and practical costs of this claim to Marxian thought and action. It then outlines three major reasons internal to Marx's theory that appear to support this claim—its concerns with classes rather than individuals, its deterministic rather than voluntaristic explanation of actions, and its historically relative rather than universal judgments—and shows why none in fact rules out a Marxian morality. The article then states in systematic form Marx's underlying moral theory and shows how it "fits" with historical materialism as a whole.

MC MURTRY, John. Philosophical Method And The Rise Of Social Philosophy. *Eidos* 2,139–176 D 81.

MC PECK, John E. The Evaluation Of Critical Thinking Programs: Dangers And Dogmas. *Inform Log* 6,9–13 Jl 84.

This paper reviews the literature which attempts to empirically evaluate critical thinking programs with quantitative methods. It is pointed out that most evaluation schemes assume: (1) that critical thinking consists of certain discrete skills, and (2) that these skills are ameanable to quantitative measurement. It is argued that both of these assumptions are false, that the tests are crucially theory–laden, and that critical thinking is too diffuse and multi–faceted to be measured quantitatively.

MC PHERRAN, Mark L. Socratic Piety In The *Euthyphro*. *J Hist Phil* 23,283–310 Jl 85.

The majority of commentators on the *Euthyphro* have found it to be a source of positive Socratic doctrine on the nature of piety. A few prominent scholars have raised objections to this constructivist approach. The author of this paper contends that the anticonstructivists are wrong, and that the interpretations the constructivists have offered are variously flawed. The author then draws upon a variety of texts to argue for a cautiously constructive view of Socratic piety.

MC ROBBIE, Michael and Belnap, Nuel D. Proof Tableau Formulations Of Some First–Order Relevant Ortho–Logics. *Bull Sect Log* 13,233–240 D 84.

In this paper proof tableau formulations are given for the first–order relevant logics (called OEQ, ORQ, and ORMQ) obtained by dropping the (zero–order) axiom of distribution and the (first–order) axiom of confinement from the well–known first–order relevant logics EQ, RQ, and RMQ. This paper extends the results presented in the author's previous paper "Relevant Analytic Tableaux", *Studia Logica*, 38 (1979), 1870200.

MC SHANE, Philip (ed). Searching For Cultural Foundations. NY Univ Pr Of America 1984.

MC TAGGART, John M and Harris, H S (ed). Studies In Hegelian Cosmology. NY Garland 1984.

MC TIGHE, Thomas P. "Eternity And Time In Boethius" in *History Of Philosophy In Making*, Thro, Linus J (ed), 35–62. Washington Univ Pr Of America 1982.

MCLEAN, Don. Knowledge And Certainty. *Eidos* 3,163–190 D 84.

MEAGER, Ruby. Connoisseurship. *Brit J Aes* 25,137–152 Spr 85.

The knowledge–claim in "connoisseur" is assessed, using reflection on usage backed by quotation from Goethe's "The Collector and his Circle" (John Gage: *Goethe on Art*, 1980). Connoisseurs assume authority over works of art, but only of material art–forms, and within restricted fields, suggesting a form of "knowledge–by–acquaintance" like our knowledge of persons, peculiar in focussing on particular, and particularly sympathetic, embodied objects, and suffering, like all such "knowledge", from spotty scope, incommunicability, untestability, and therefore dubiety.

MEDAWAR, P B. The Limits Of Science. NY Harper & Row 1984.

Medawar addresses a variety of philosophical topics ranging from the nature of science to the existence of God. He argues that science is quite limited in its ability to provide answers for many important questions. (staff)

MEDINA, Angel. "The Existential Sources Of Rhetoric" in *Existential Coordinates Of Human Condition*, Tymieniecka, A (ed), 227–240. Boston Reidel 1984.

MEDINA, Jose. Les Mathématiques Chez Spinoza Et Hobbes. *Rev Phil Fr* 175,177–188 Ap–Je 85.

MEEHL, Paul E. "Consistency Tests In Estimating The Completeness Of The Fossil Record" in *Testing Scientific Theories*, Earman, John (ed), 413–476. Minneapolis Univ Minnesota Pr 1983.

MEEHL, Paul E. "Subjectivity In Psychoanalytic Inference" in *Testing Scientific Theories*, Earman, John (ed), 349–412. Minneapolis Univ Minnesota Pr 1983.

MEERBOTE, Ralf (ed) and Harper, William A (ed). Kant On Causality, Freedom, And Objectivity. Minneapolis Univ Minnesota Pr 1984.

MEERBOTE, Ralf. "Kant On The Nondeterminate Character Of Human Actions" in *Kant On Causality, Freedom, And Objectivity*, Harper, William A (ed), 138–164. Minneapolis Univ Minnesota Pr 1984.

MEERBOTE, Ralf and Harper, William L. "Kant's Principle Of Causal Explanations" in *Kant On Causality, Freedom, And Objectivity*, Harper, William A (ed), 3–19. Minneapolis Univ Minnesota Pr 1984.

MEIER, Artur. Die Heranbildung Eines Der Arbeiterklasse Würdigen Nachwuchses. *Deut Z Phil* 22,223–228 1974.

MEIER, A. Soziologische Probleme Des Nullwachstums. *Deut Z Phil* 33,81–85 1985.

MEIER, Klaus V. A Meditation On Critical Mass In The Philosophy Of Sport. *J Phil Sport* 10,8–20 1983.

This paper explores the contemporary state of the art of the philosophy of sport through the analysis of data reflecting the scope of the existent "critical mass"—both the body of literature and number of active researchers. Three facets are discussed: first, the emergence and development of scholarly writing in the area; second, the productivity of North American based philosophers; and third, an assessment of current problems of direction, structure, and content in the field.

MEIGHAN, Clement W. "Archaeology: Science Or Sacrilege" in *Ethics And Values In Archaeology*, Green, Ernestene L (ed), 208–223. NY Free Pr 1984.

MEILAENDER, Gilbert C. The Theory And Practice Of Virtue. Notre Dame Univ Notre Dame Pr 1984.

This book focuses on the renewed interest in virtues. Duties are not stressed, breaking from traditional ethical analysis. The moral life, according to Meilaender, is based on moral education. A theology of grace is also stressed. Chapters devoted to the vices of curiosity and the virtues of gratitude illustrate the books central concepts. (staff)

MEILAENDER, Gilbert. On Removing Food & Water: Against The Stream. *Hastings Center Rep* 14,11–13 D 84.

MEILE, Richard and Shanks, Stephanie L. Comment On Pommerehne Et Al, "Concordia Discors: Or: What Do Economists Think". *Theor Decis* 18,99–104 Ja 85.

In our paper, we raise theoretical and methodological questions concerning the research of Pommerehne et al., on the views of European and American economists. We conclude that a theoretical perspective which takes into account the cultural components of science will provide an explanation of the opinion and behavior of economists more in keeping with the empirical findings of Pommerehne and associates than their theory of self interest.

MEKLER, Alan H. C C C Forcing Without Combinatorics. *J Sym Log* 49,830–832 S 84.

MELAND, Bernard E. In Response To Frankenberry's "Meland's Empirical Realism And The Appeal To Lived Experience". *Amer J Theol Phil* 5,130–137 My & S 84.

MELAND, Bernard E. In Response To Inbody's "Bernard Meland: A Rebel Among Process Theologians". *Amer J Theol Phil* 5,72–79 My & S 84.

MELAND, Bernard E. In Response To Loomer's "Meland On God". *Amer J Theol Phil* 5,144–155 My & S 84.

MELAND, Bernard E. In Response To Miller's "Meland: Worship And His Recent Thought". *Amer J Theol Phil* 5,107–116 My & S 84.

MELAND, Bernard E. In Response To Suchocki's "The Appeal To Ultimacy In Meland's Thought". *Amer J Theol Phil* 5,89–95 My & S 84.

MELCHERT, Norman. Why Constructive Empiricism Collapses Into Scientific Realism. *Austl J Phil* 63,213–215 Je 85.

Bas van Fraassen's constructive empiricism opens up the prospect of accepting a scientific theory without believing that it is true. We need only believe that it is "empirically adequate". On this view, the very aim of science is restricted to providing empirically adequate theories. I argue that he has given us no way to make sense of the distinction between accepting and believing; nor can he, given his view of the meaning of theories.

MELDEN, A I. "Saints And Supererogation" in *Philosophy And Life: Essays On John Wisdom*, Dilman, Ilham (ed), 61–82. Boston Nijhoff 1984.

MELE, Alfred R. Pears On Akrasia, And Defeated Intentions. *Philosophia (Israel)* 14,145–152 Ag 84.

David Pears, in "How Easy is Akrasia?" (*Philosophia* II [1982]), refutes a Davidsonian argument for the impossibility of "last ditch" incontinent action. I construct and refute an even stronger Davidsonian argument for this conclusion. An agent can act incontinently even against an *intention* to do an A here and now—and without changing his mind about what it is best to do.

MELE, Alfred R. Self–Control, Action, And Belief. *Amer Phil Quart* 22,169–176 Ap 85.

Self–control is the capacity to master motivation that is contrary to one's better judgment. This is true only of self–control exhibited in actions upon the world, but also of self–control displayed in practical reasoning and in the formation and maintenance of non–evaluative beliefs. The better judgments served by self–control range from judgments about a particular action to be performed at once to personal commitments to general epistemic principles.

MELLE, U. Die Seins– Und Erkenntnisfrage In Der Philosophie Brentanos. *Tijdschr Filosof* 46,418–443 S 84.

MELLEMA, Gregory. Groups, Responsibility, And The Failure To Act. *Int J Applied Phil* 2,57–66 Spr 85.

The purpose of this essay is to distinguish several possible ways of thinking about the moral responsibility an agent bears for a state of affairs as the result of failing to act, where the responsibility for this state of affairs is shared with other moral agents.

MELLEMA, Gregory. Shared Responsibility And Ethical Dilutionism. *Austl J Phil* 63,177–187 Je 85.

There seems to be a widespread tendency to assume that the more people who share responsibility for what happens, the more thinly this responsibility is spread among the participants. I consider some refined versions of this view, which I call 'ethical dilutionism', and I subsequently defend an anti-dilutionist position, maintaining (in the spirit of Nuremburg) that the extent to which one incurs moral responsibility is not affected by the fact that others are likewise responsible.

MELLEMA, Gregory. The Nature Of Aims And Ends In Education. *Phil Res Arch* 10,321–336 1984.

In this paper it is argued that educational aims be approached as states of affairs susceptible of analysis in terms of means and ends. And educator's various aims, in this way, can be classified according to the means–end relationship they bear to one another. This approach, which stands squarely in the tradition of Aristotle and enjoys little support among contemporary educational theorists, is defended from objections by R S Peters, a popular and influential proponent of an alternative approach.

MELNICK, Arthur. The Geometry Of A Form Of Intuition. *Topoi* 3,163–168 D 84.

MELZER, Heinrich and Schachter, Josef. On Physicalism. *Synthese* 64,359–374 S 85.

MENDES– FLOHR, Paul. The Jewish Intellectual: Some Methodological Proposals (in Hebrew). *Iyyun* 33,310–326 Ja–Ap 84.

MENDEZ, Julio Raul. Las Tesis De C Fabro. *Sapientia* 39,181–192 Jl–S 84.

The 54 Thomistic hermeneutical theses of Fabro seem as a whole to be critically founded. The notions of *esse ut actus*, metaphysical participation, and the integrative function of the cognitive faculty are recovered authentically from St Thomas. The primacy of the will in the concrete decision of the ultimate end, however, represents an original contribution beyond what St Thomas says explicitly. It seems, nonetheless, a legitimate development consistent with his thought.

MENDUS, Susan. The Practical And The Pathological. *J Value Inq* 19,235–244 1985.

In this paper I assess Kant's account of emotional motivation and its role in moral evaluation. I argue that commentators exaggerate the extent to which the Kantian good man may be cold and unfeeling, but suggest also that in so far as Kant rejects emotion as important in moral evaluation, he is right to do so. His criticisms here are therefore both moderate and an important counterbalance to the sentimentality of the Romantics, whose theories he rightly rejects.

MENON, N R M. Protection Of Human Rights And Public Interest In Nuclear Development. *Phil Soc Act* 11,51–55 Ja–Je 85.

MERCIER– JOSA, Solange. Est–ce "L'Esprit", Est–ce "Le Capital"? *Rev Metaph Morale* 89,348–360 Jl–S 84.

MERCIER, A. "Wahrheit Und Schönheit" in *Asthetische Er Fahrung Und Das Wesen Der Kunst*, Holzhey, Helmut, 107–122. Bern Haupt 1984.

MERRIAM, Sharan. *Selected Writings On Philosophy And Adult Education*. Melbourne Krieger 1984.

This volume offers a sampling from a wide range of philosophical thought that has had an impact on education in general and adult education in particular. Selections are included by such thinkers as Ivan Illich, John Dewey, Eduard Lindeman, Paulo Friere, B F Skinner, R W K Paterson, and Herbert Spiegelberg, and are loosely representative of six philosophical categories: liberal adult education, humanistic adult education, behavioristic adult educaton, progressive adult education, radical adult education, and analytical philosophy of adult education.

MESSER, Donald E. *Christian Ethics And Political Action*. Valley Forge Judson Pr 1984.

This book develops a theory of Christian political action, in accord with Christian theology but appropriate to a pluralistic democracy. Critiquing attitudes of both apathy and authoritarianism, Christians are encouraged to be involved in politics as an obligation, not as an option. Related to the natural law tradition, reason, not revelation, bridges gaps between ethical norms and political reality. w D Ross' right–and–wrong–making characteristics are offered as a basis for Christian realism in politics.

MESSINESE, Leonardo. Metafisica, Scienza E Fede: Una Discusione Con Dario Antiseri. *Aquinas* 27,327–334 My–Ag 84.

MESTERHÁZI, Miklós. László Rudas And The Lukács Debate In The Twenties (in Hungarian). *Magyar Filozof Szemle* 1–2,93–118 1984.

Der ungarische Philosoph Ladislaus Rudas wurde nicht zuletzt durch die zwei Diskussionen allgemein bekannt, die 1924 und—in einem vollständig veränderten historischen Kontext—1949 gegen Lukács geführt wurde, und in denen L Rudas eine nicht unbedeutende Rolle spielte. (edited)

METZLER, Helmut. Freges Beitrag Zur Methodologie In "Die Grundlagen Der Arithmetik" Von 1884—Erbe Und Auftrag. *Deut Z Phil* 32,936–943 1984.

The paper appreciates Frege as a methodologist and gives an analysis of Frege's book as an explication of the concept of natural number: Frege begins with a philosophical discussion of the subject, followed by a conceptual derivation of objective concept of number. Frege also develops the new method "definition by abstraction". This is a special kind of proceeding from the abstract to the concrete in the sense of dialectical methodology.

MEUNIER, Jean–Guy. Syntaxe Formelle Et Tableau. *Dialogue (Canada)* 23,199–222 Je 84.

MEURERS, Joseph. The Silence Of Physics. *Phil Natur* 21,382–388 1984.

It is demonstrated, that L Wittgenstein's end–conclusion in his Tractatus logico–philosophicus: "Wovon man nicht sprechen kann, darüber muss man schweigen" ("Whereof one cannot speak, thereof one must be silent") characterizes the intellectual behavior of modern Physics and Astronomy. Examples are Heisenberg's Uncertainty–Relation, the unsolved problems of the so–called world models in the cosmology today or also the problems about the red–shift.

MEW, Peter. The Expression Of Emotion In Music. *Brit J Aes* 25,33–42 Wint 85.

MEYER, H and Lötsch, Manfred. Sozialstrukturforschung Und Leitung Sozialer Prozesse. *Deut Z Phil* 22,167–178 1974.

Die Gestaltung der entwickelten sozialistischen Gesellschaft ist mit tiefgreifenden Veränderungen der sozialen Struktur verbunden, deren Analyse in der Erforschung der Entwicklung der Arbeiterklasse als der führenden Kraft ihren Ausgangspunkt nehmen mufss. Es wird die Frage zu beantworten versucht, wie auf der Grundlage der Struktur und Differenziertheit der Arbeiterklasse alle ihre Teile und Gruppen in den Prozefss der Verwirklichung ihrer führenden Rolle einzubeziehen sind.

MEYER, Michael. Response To "Referential Inscrutability". *S J Phil* 23,137–142 Spr 85.

MEYER, Robert K and Abraham, Adrian. A Model For The Modern Malaise. *Philosophia (Israel)* 14,25–40 Ag 84.

MEYER, Robert K and Giambrone, Steve and Brady, Ross T. Where Gamma Fails. *Stud Log* 43,247–256 1984.

A major question for the relevant logics has been, "Under what conditions is Ackermann's rule γ, from—A V B and A to infer B, admissible for one of these logics?" For a large number of logics and theories, the question has led to an affirmative answer to the γ problem itself, so that such an answer has almost come to be expected for relevant logics worth taking seriously. We exhibit here, however, another large and interesting class of logics—roughly, the Boolean extensions of the **W**—free relevant logics (and, precisely, the well–behaved subsystems of the four–valued logic **BN4**)—for which γ fails.

MEYER, Robert K and Mortensen, Chris. Inconsistent Models For Relevant Arithmetics. *J Sym Log* 49,917–929 S 84.

A series of inconsistent models for relevant arithmetics (such as R #, RM #) is set out. The domains of these models are the integers mod n (for finite n). Their propositional structure is given by the well–known Sugihara matrices, especially the three–element one. It is shown that the existence of such models suffices for the non–triviality of arithmetic formulated relevantly, in a strictly finitary sense. Here, further properties of the models are developed, culminating in Mortensen's paraconsistent arithmetic RM–omega.

MEYER, Rudolf W. Das Verhältnis Von "Person" Und "Eigentum" In Hegels Philosophie Des Rechts. *Stud Phil (Switzerland)* Supp 12,69–86 1983.

MEYERS, Christopher. Intended Goals And Appropriate Treatment: An Alternative To The Ordinary/Extraordinary Distinction. *J Med Ethics* 10,128–132 S 84.

This article argues that the ordinary/extraordinary distinction has little or no moral value when preservation of life is not given a near absolute status. What is appealed to instead is a determination of both medical and moral duties, upon which appropriate treatment decisions should be based. Included is a partial delineation of those duties.

MEYERS, Christopher. The Corporation, Its Members, And Moral Accountability. *Bus Prof Ethics J* 3,33–44 Fall 83.

MEYERS, Diane T. Rights–Based Rights. *Law Phil* 3,407–422 D 84.

Ronald Dworkin maintains that particular rights, like the right to free speech and the right to own personal property, can be derived from a foundational right, the right to equal concern and respect. This paper questions the tenability of this program for rights–based rights. A right is an individuated moral or political guarantee which confers a specified benefit on each right–holder and which resists conduct that would derogate it. For there to be rights–based rights, both the foundational right and the rights it implies must satisfy this definition. It is doubtful, however, that the right to equal concern and respect should count as a right since the benefits it confers are at best highly controversial and may not be assignable to individuals. (edited)

MEYERS, Robert G. Peirce's Doubts About Idealism. *Trans Peirce Soc* 21,222–239 Spr 85.

MEYNELL, Hugo. "Ideology And The Epistemology Of Politics" in *Ideology, Philosophy And Politics*, Parel, Anthony (ed), 77–92. Waterloo Laurier Univ Pr 1983.

MEYNELL, Hugo. Reversing Rorty. *Method* 3,31–48 Mr 85.

Rorty is quite correct that most philosophy since Descartes has been concerned with finding and setting out the foundations of knowledge. It is argued in this article that his own great merit is to have taken the fashionable view, that knowledge has no foundations, to somewhere very near its absurd and terrifying conclusions. The reverse of Rorty's view is defended; that philosophy's primary concern is and ought to be with the theory of knowledge.

MEYNELL, Hugo. Scepticism Reconsidered. *Philosophy* 59,431–442 O 84.

There are two typical reactions to scepticism in philosophy, to attempt to refute it, and to show that its irrefutability does not matter. It is argued that the irrefutability of scepticism would matter a great deal, since force not reason would have to be ultimate arbiter in important controversial issues; but that it can be refuted. If justified true judgments are impossible, the sceptic can neither justify his sceptical position nor claim that it is true; if they are possible, 'knowledge', as consisting of propositions which are true and justified, is obtainable.

MIALL, David S (ed). *Metaphor: Problems And Perspectives*. Atlantic Highlands Humanities Pr 1982.

MICELI, Marcia P and Near, Janet P. Organizational Dissidence: The Case Of Whistle–Blowing. *J Bus Ethics* 4,1–16 F 85.

MICHAEL, Mark. Patent Rights And Better Mousetraps. *Bus Prof Ethics J* 3,13–24 Fall 83.

Many businesses currently require their employees to sign a statement in which they agree to turn over their right to patent any formula or product which they might develop to the company. This paper questions the legitimacy of such an open–ended agreement, based on the principle that it is wrong to ask for someone's property as a condition for hiring them. This leads to a discussion of property and the employment relationship in general.

MICHALOS, Alex C. "Philosophy Of Science" in *The Culture Of Science, Technology, And Medicine*, Durbin, Paul T (ed), 197–281. NY Free Pr 1984.

MICHAUD, Yves. How To Become A Moderate Skeptic: Hume's Way Out Of Pyrrhonism. *Hume Stud* 11,33–46 Ap 85.

MICHELS, Robert. "Doctors, Drugs Used For Pleasure And Performance, And Medical Model" in *Feeling Good And Doing Better*, Murray, Thomas H (ed), 175–186. Clifton Humana Pr 1984.

MICHOT, Jean. "L'épître Sur La Connaissance De L'âme Rationnelle Et De Ses États" Attribuée À Avicenne. *Rev Phil Louvain* 82,479–499 N 84.

Presentation and French translation of the *Treatise concerning the knowledge of the rational soul and its states* attributed to Avicenna. This is an eschatological work, a work concerning the "return" (al–ma'âd) as the philosopher conceives it. The topic fundamentally dealt with is human destiny. In the three main sections, it is examined from a psychological point of view and, in the epilogue, from a more metaphysical perspective. However Avicennian the character of this treatise may be, the feeling of the translator is that it was not actually written by Avicenna, a point which he intends to take up in a forthcoming article.

MIDGLEY, Mary. *Animals And Why They Matter*. Athens Univ Of Georgia Pr 1983.

A sense of unreality often blocks our attempts to understand our moral relations with animals. Human beings try to deny their kinship with other life–forms by posing as pure spirits, pure intellects or pure socially–contracting wills. This move, used to excuse their abuse of animals, causes endless trouble within the human scene itself. A more realistic approach, admitting honestly our continuity with other sentient and social creatures, would clear up many difficulties about our own emotional nature as well as removing inexcusable cruelties.

MIDGLEY, Mary. *Wickedness: A Philosophical Essay*. London Routledge & K Paul 1984.

This book examines the concept of wickedness or deliberate wrong–doing, attempting first to rescue it from the limbo into which it has fallen from being currently reduced to mental illness, social variation or mere superstition. It points out that penal wickedness, which has got the practice of moral judgment a bad name, is itself just one form of wickedness among others. It then examines the Socratic paradox that no one does wrong willingly, pointing to fascinating issues which lie behind it, and to resultant complications in the notion of personal identity.

MIDGLEY, Mary. On Being Terrestrial. *Philosophy* 17,79–82 84 Supp.

MIDGLEY, Mary. Sociobiology. *J Med Ethics* 10,158–160 S 84.

MIERNOWSKI, Jan. Deux Visions De La Fin Du Monde: Le *Dernier Jugement*, De Jean–Baptiste Chassignet Et Le *Jugement* D'Agrippa D'Aué. *Rev Univ Ottawa* 54,27–36 Ap–Je 84.

MIGOTTI, Mark. Luther's Word On Man's Will: A Case Study In Comparative Intellectual History. *Relig Stud* 20,657–668 D 84.

MIGUELEZ, Roberto. L'articulation Du Général Et Du Particulier: Une Approche Méthodologique Dans Le Champ Des Sciences Sociales. *Philosophiques* 11,251–276 O 84.

The articulation of the general and the particular is not a question merely of epistemology. It also comprises a relationship between theory and enlightened practice to the extent that processes and individualized phenomena always take place in practice. In this paper we examine critically three approaches to this question of articulation: that of traditional positivism, that based on the notion of "model" and that of Weberian "ideal types". We propose that this articulation is a particular relation between theoretical concepts relating to formal abstract objects or determinations and empirical concepts relating to particular determinations of concrete objects. We illustrate this methodological solution with the concept of "social formation" examining the sense in which it applies to the concrete case of Latin American societies.

MIGUENS, José Enrique. Magical Aspects Of Political Terrorism. *Diogenes* 126,104–122 Sum 84.

In order to study from the sociological standpoint state and private political terrorism that morally absolves itself, I take as unit of analysis those who kill and those who approve. Their normative orientations and cultural logic are analyzed showing their similarity with mythic–magic religious orientations and ways of thinking. This impels us to change the methods applied up to now for stopping the propagation of this plague.

MIJUSKOVIC, Ben. Kant On Reality. *Cogito* 2,61–68 S 84.

MIKHAILOVA, Th. Meaning—Yet Another Approach. *Bull Sect Log* 13,173–187 O 84.

MILCU, Stefan. L'anthropologie Dans Le Contexte De La Culture. *Phil Log* 28,136–139 Ap–Je 84.

MILES, Leland and others. Ethical Concerns For The Modern University. *Thought* 60,221–233 Je 85.

This article summarizes the areas of ethical conflicts within administration of a university. The article analyzes the university's ethical responsibility within the larger global and national as well as local community. The rift between classical and

vocational education is analyzed and these ethical dilemmas are analyzed within our national experience. The exploration of value–based education is evaluated and analyzed with a historical perspective. Attention is given to the significant roadblocks to reform which include the myth of "worldly education" "neutrality" and other pertinent myths.

MILIKOTIN, Anthony. The Western Intellectual Heritage And The Soviet Dissent. *Stud Soviet Tho* 29,17–32 Ja 85.

MILL, John Stuart and Robson, John M (ed). *Essays On French History And Historians*. Toronto Univ Of Toronto Pr 1985.

MILLAR, Alan. Veridicality: More On Searle. *Analysis* 45,120–124 Mr 85.

Searle thinks that the contents of visual experiences have a causal ingredient. Thus an experience of an F is veridical only if it is caused by there being an F before the subject. It is argued that there is no more reason to suppose that the contents of experiences have a causal ingredient than to suppose that the contents of beliefs have a causal ingredient. A simpler account of veridicality is suggested.

MILLAR, Alan. Where's The Use In Meaning? *Dialectica* 39,35–52 1985.

The article presents an analysis of Quine's critique of mentalism in semantics. Quine is right to demand that theories of meaning show how the meanings of linguistic expressions are grounded in verbal dispositions. His own account of verbal dispositions is inadequate to the task. It is argued that the dispositions in which meanings are grounded (i) are dispositions to accept and reject sentences, (ii) essentially involve beliefs, (iii) link sentences with one another, as well as with experience, and (iv) are conventional. The importance of the distinction between disposition–based relations between sentences and logical relations between sentences is stressed.

MILLAR, Terrence. Decidability And The Number Of Countable Models. *Annals Pure Applied Log* 27,137–154 O 84.

A natural question from recursive model theory is how recursive complexity can be reflected in first order theories. This paper demonstrates that it is possible to encode recursive complexity at the level of the type spectrum of an isomorphism type of the theory while keeping the number of countable isomorphism types countable. Specifically, there is a theory with only recursive complete types, countably many countable models, and whose countable saturated model is not decidable.

MILLER JR, Fred D. "Aristotle On Practical Knowledge And Moral Weakness" in *The Georgetown Symposium On Ethics*, Porreco, Rocco (ed), 131–144. Lanham Univ Pr Of America 1984.

MILLER, Arthur. A Reply To Wayne A Davis' "Miller On Wanting, Intending, And Being Willing". *Phil Phenomenol Res* 45,457–458 Mr 85.

This is a brief reply to Wayne A Davis' "Miller on Wanting, Intending, and Being Willing," which in turn is written in response to my earlier "Wanting, Intending, and Knowing What One Is Doing." The present defense emphasizes three things: (1) my analysis of the relationship between desiring and intending was restricted almost exclusively to the assessment of already completed actions (as opposed to future–looking intentions); (2) the distinction between '*A* intends/intended to *X*' (where the relevant intention commonly entails the corresponding desire), and '*A* did *X* and thereby caused *Y* (a "natural"—but unwanted—consequence of *X* foreseen by *A* herself); and (3) having two senses of "being willing", (viz. Acquiescing vs being willing to *do*), it does not follow that all instances of the action—relevant sense are necessarily intentional on the part of the agent.

MILLER, Barry. De Essentia Individua: In Defence Of Possible Worlds Existentialism. *Grazer Phil Stud* 21,99–114 1984.

MILLER, Bruce E. Artistic Meaning And Aesthetic Education: A Formalist View. *J Aes Educ* 18,85–100 Fall 84.

Distinguishing between subject matter (reference outward to the world) and content (dense inward specification), this article ascribes a preponderance of subject matter to discursive language and of content to artworks. Rather than convey messages about external reality, artworks mainly project patterns of sentience, mental processes in themselves. Effective teaching of artworks will emphasize their content over their subject matter.

MILLER, Bruce. "Ethical Issues In The Intensive Care Unit: Case For Discussion" in *Difficult Decisions In Medical Ethics*, Ganos, Doreen L (ed), 107–110. NY Liss 1983.

MILLER, Bruce. "Patient Autonomy In Intensive Care" in *Difficult Decisions In Medical Ethics*, Ganos, Doreen L (ed), 111–124. NY Liss 1983.

MILLER, Cynthia A. "The Poet In The Poem" in *Existential Coordinates Of Human Condition*, Tymieniecka, A (ed), 61–74. Boston Reidel 1984.

MILLER, David (ed). *Popper Selections*. Princeton Princeton Univ Pr 1985.

MILLER, David. Reply To Oppenheim's "Constraints On Freedom". *Ethics* 95,310–314 Ja 85.

MILLER, Izchak. Perceptual Reference. *Synthese* 61,35–60 O 84.

MILLER, James. *Rousseau: Dreamer Of Democracy*. New Haven Yale Univ Pr 1984.

Through a blend of biography, philosophy, and history, the author shows how Rousseau's thinking inspired a generation of radicals. The author explores the pivotal role played by imagination in Rousseau's thought, analyzes the argument of the *Social Contract*, and explains how Rousseau's treatment of democracy amounted to a bold break with traditional theories. (staff)

MILLER, L W. Kant's Philosophy Of Mathematics. *Kantstudien* 66,297–308 1975.

MILLER, Lance A (ed) and Bever, Thomas G (ed) and Carroll, John M (ed). *Talking Minds: The Study Of Language In The Cognitive Sciences*. Cambridge MIT Pr 1984.

MILLER, Randolph C. Meland: Worship And His Recent Thought. *Amer J Theol Phil* 5,96–106 My & S 84.

MILLER, Richard W. Marx And Aristotle. *Can J Phil* Supp 7,323–352 1981.

MILLER, S R. Assertion And Convention. *S Afr J Phil* 3,130–134 N 84.

Let us take H P Grice's well–known theory of speaker–meaning and transform it into a theory of assertion. Is assertion (on this theory of assertion) essentially conventional? It seems not. The Gricean mechanism itself, for example, is not conventional. Again the element of belief is not, it seems, irreducibly conventional; for arguable beliefs are not language dependent. (edited)

MILLIKAN, Ruth Garret. *Language, Thought, And Other Biological Categories: New Foundations For Realism.* Cambridge MIT Pr 1984.

Beginning with a general theory of function applied to body organs, behaviors, customs, and both inner and outer representations, this book covers such topics as three dimensions of meaning the functions of indexicals, descriptions, "is", "exists", "all", negation and intentional contexts the act of identifying the ontology of identity including identity over time and the significance of subject–predicate structure for construction of a nonholist realist epistemology.

MILLS, John A. Purpose And Conditioning: A Reply To Waller. *J Theor Soc Behav* 14,363–367 O 84.

Mills concentrates on one of Waller's objections (that he has improperly introduced purpose into Skinner's theory). He shows that recent evidence demonstrates that cognitions form a necessary part of the explanation of animal behavior, so that Skinner cannot extrapolate his theory of animal behavior to humans. Often, following moral principles entails behaving in ways for which one has received no prior reinforcement, so that Skinner's theory cannot be applied to such cases.

MILLS, Michael J. Φθονος And Its Related Παθη In Plato And Aristotle. *Phronesis* 30,1–12 1985.

The article traces the development of the treatment of *Phthonos* from the Philebus, through the Topics and the Rhetoric, to the Aristotelian Ethics. It shows how and why Aristotle succumbed to the temptation to treat *Nemesis* as a Mean between *Phthonos* and *Epichairekakia*. It concludes that, nonetheless, he understood well how these complex emotions are to be distinguished one from another, as well as how intimately they are interconnected.

MILNE, Peter. A Note On Popper, Propensities, And The Two–Slit Experiment. *Brit J Phil Sci* 36,66–70 Mr 85.

Popper has claimed that his propensity interpretation of probability sheds light on the two–slit experiment in quantum mechanics. I argue that in view of what Popper tells us is the essential characteristic of propensities, their dependence on the whole experimental set–up, his analysis of the two–slit experiment is invalid.

MILSTEIN, Bonnie. "The Law And Bioethics" in *Bioethical Frontiers In Perinatal Intensive Care*, Snowden, Fraser (ed), 59–76. Natchitoches Northwestern Pr 1985.

MILTON, J. The Scholastic Background To Locke's Thought. *Locke News* 15,25–34 1984.

The mentions of scholastic authors in Locke's own works and the evidence provided by his manuscripts in the Lovelace Collection show the Locke had little if any direct acquaintance with the writings of the medieval schoolmen, and derived his knowledge of scholastic logic and metaphysics from modern authors, mostly from England, Germany, and other parts of northern Europe.

MIN, Anselm K. John Paul The Second Anthropology Of Concrete Totality. *Proc Cath Phil Ass* 58,120–129 1984.

I present John Paul II's critique of both Aristotelian Thomism and Husserlian Idealism as abstract, partial visions of the reality of the person, and go on to discuss his alternative to both in terms of the human act (actus humanus), which he takes not as an ethical category (Aristotle) but as an ontological category which both discloses and actualizes the person precisely as a "concrete totality" of many distinct yet internally related dimensions of personal existence of which the act is a unifying principle.

MINEAU, André. Création Et Phénomène Social. *Laval Theol Phil* 41,65–68 F 85.

Deux champs théoriques principaux s'imposent à la pensée, à partir du moment où l'on s'interoge sur la signification du concept de création eu égard à la genèse des formes sociales humaines. Création de la société ell–même, sur la base de l'association des individus, et création à l'intérieur de la société déjà constituée apparaissent comme étant deux questions distinctes. Concernant la première de ces questions, une conclusion d'après moi s'impose: il n'est plus possible de parler de création de la société à la manière de Hobbes, et le concept de création doit être situé par rapport aux données sociobiologiques relatives á l'évolution de l'espèce humaine. Mais le phénomène social humain se manifeste à travers des formes ou structures particulières, qui constituent son intèrieur variable. Et à ce niveau, l'usage du concept de création semble aller de soi, dans la mesure où la société humaine, comme le dit W Buckley, ne réussit à se maintenir que par la créaton incessante de structures nouvelles.

MINEAU, André. Le Normal Et Le Pathologique En Politique. *Laval Theol Phil* 41,385–390 O 85.

Dès que l'on concoit la politique comme ayant une finalité qui lui serait inhérente, on pose de ce fait le problème de l'attitude et du comportement des entités politiques réelles eu égard à cette finalite. Ma thèse est la suivante: il y a bel et bien une finalité inhérente à l'essence de la politique, et dans la mesure ou les unités politiques particulières peuvent de fait s'en éloigner, il y a par conséquent une pathologie politique. À l'aide de quelques exemples, je propose une mainière d'appliquer ici les catégories du normal et du pathologique.

MINOGUE, Kenneth. "Bacon And Locke: Or Ideology As Mental Hygiene" in *Ideology, Philosophy And Politics*, Parel, Anthony (ed), 179–198. Waterloo Laurier Univ Pr 1983.

MINOR, Robert N. *Bhagavad–Gita: An Exegetical Commentary.* New Delhi Heritage 1982.

A sixty page introduction summarizes the history of *Gita* interpretation, and the evidence for its relationship to the *Mahabharata*, authorship and date. This is followed by a verse by verse historical–exegetical commentary on the Sanskrit text, which is best used with a translation such as Edgerton or Buitenen. The commentary discusses the variety of interpretations, the Sanskrit text, and the judgments of Minor as to the original author's intentions. Philosophical issues are discussed. A "Foreword" is written by Norvin Hein.

MIROIU, Adrian. A Modal Approach To Sneed's "Theoretical Functions". *Phil Natur* 21,273–286 1984.

It is argued that a modal *de re* version of a statement view of theories could capture some of Sneed's basic claims. First, theoretical concepts are reconstructed in a modal framework. Second, it is argued that claims about "constraints" (in Sneed's sense) have not a direct linguistic counterpart; rather they could be rendered in a holistic manner by use of "generalized" modal *de re* laws. Finally, the results are applied to the theoretization relation between theories.

MIROIU, Adrian. A Programme For Local Semantics. *Phil Log* 28,146–154 Ap–Je 84.

MIROWSKI, Philip. The Role Of Conservation Principles In Twentieth–Century Economic Theory. *Phil Soc Sci* 14,461–474 D 84.

This article calls attention to some parallels between the twentieth century neoclassical economics and nineteenth century physics. It suggests that, contrary to recent commentators such as Paul Samuelson, neoclassical models do possess analogues to mechanics and thermodynamics, particularly in the arena of conservation principles. The lack of realization of that fact is traced to the influence of mathematical exposition in recent economic discourse.

MISHAN, E J. Consistency In The Valuation Of Life: A Wild Goose Chase? *Soc Phil Pol* 2,152–167 Spr 85.

MISHRA, Ganeswar. Vidyaranya On Method, Object And Limit Of Philosophical Investigation. *Indian Phil Quart* 11,343–364 Jl 84.

Vidyaranya, is the first philosopher to recognize method and object of philosophical knowledge as logico–linguistic. Philosophy and science are autonomous. Philosophy analyzes the form of assertions. Negation contradicts the predicate alone and all predicates compete. This is necessary for correction and growth of knowledge. Identity of the subject is logical not empirical. Consciousness–existence–completeness are the end–points of the conceptual system. A substantially identical world not nihilism, is a necessary condition of knowledge. Philosophy reveals meaning–rules of depth grammar.

MITCHAM, Carl. "Philosophy Of Technology" in *The Culture Of Science, Technology, And Medicine*, Durbin, Paul T (ed), 282–363. NY Free Pr 1984.

MITCHELL, T N. Cicero On The Moral Crisis Of The Late Republic. *Hermathena* 136,21–41 Sum 84.

The article examines the general Roman view that the problems of the late Republic were principally due to a moral decline rooted in the affluence and luxury that followed Rome's conquests. It then considers Cicero's ideas. He broadly accepted the traditional view but saw its most disastrous manifestation in the character and aims of popular politicians. His solutions are indicated in his philosophical writings. They centered on education and on his concept of *humanitas*.

MITCHELL, W J T. *The Politics Of Interpretation.* Chicago Univ Of Chicago Pr 1983.

This is a collection of essays by several hands examining the relationship between politics and interpretation. It includes contributions from philosophy (Stanley Cavell, Stephen Toulmin), law (Ronald dworkin), history (Hayden White), political theory (Garry Wills), psychoanalysis (Julia Kristeva), art history (Michael Fried and T J Clark), Marxist criticism (Terry Eagleton, Gayatri Spivak), hermeneutics (Gerald Bruns, E D Hirsch, Stanley Fish), literary criticism (Gerald Graff, Walter Benn Michaels, Edward Said, Wayne Booth), and one poet–critic (Donald Davie).

MITSCHERLING, Jeff. Disclosedness And Signification: A Study Of The Conception Of Language Presented In Being And Time. *Eidos* 1,199–210 D 79.

MITSCHERLING, Jeff. Roman Ingarden's "The Literary Work Of Art": Exposition And Analyses. *Phil Phenomenol Res* 45,351–382 Mr 85.

In the first part of this paper I offer a partial exposition of Roman Ingarden's *The Literary Work of Art*. In the second part of the paper, I present two short analyses of particular works, in which I demonstrate how the theory worked out in *The Literary Work of Art* may be applied in the consideration of actual texts. I have chosen the opening sentences of Joyce's 'The Dead' and Poe's 'The Philosophy of Composition'.

MITTELMAN, Willard. Perspectivism, Becoming, And Truth In Nietzsche. *Int Stud Phil* 16,3–22 1984.

MITTELSTRASS, Jurgen. On The Concept Of Reconstruction. *Ratio* 27,83–96 Je 85.

The aim of this paper is to analyze the concept of (rational) reconstruction in contemporary philosophy of science (since Carnap) and to establish a new concept which not only aims at a formal description of theories but also at justified judgements about theories and theoretical developments. An example (Newton's methodology) is given in order to illustrate the applicability of the proposed concept, in addition to several remarks about the concept of (rational) reconstruction related, in general, to a theory of interpretation (hermeneutics) and, in particular, to problems of historical understanding.

MIYATAKE, Tohru. "On The Length Of Proofs In A Formal System Of Recursive Arithmetic" in *Lecture Notes In Mathematics*, Muller, G H And Others (ed), 81–108. NY Springer 1981.

MODRAK, D K. "Forms And Compounds" in *How Things Are*, Bogen, James (ed), 85–100. Boston Reidel 1985.

MOE, Kristine. Should The Nazi Research Data Be Cited? *Hastings Center Rep* 14,5–7 D 84.

This article describes some of the citations in post–World–War II medical journals to data from Nazi experiments on prisoners of concentration camps; the article also quotes various people on the ethical issues of using information from such a heinous source. The author is a newspaper reporter for The Journal—American in Bellevue, washington, who has independently identified 44 citations to the Nazi data. This article is a condensation of the newspaper series on this topic.

MOERDIJK, Ieke and Van Der Hoeven, Gerrit. On Choice Sequences Determined By Spreads. *J Sym Log* 49,908–916 S 84.

The paper provides a model for a theory of choice sequences satisfying the axiom of spread data. The axiom was proposed by Kreisel as a first formalization of one of the leading ideas in Brouwer's work on choice sequences. The model presented is an interpretation in sheaves over a monoid of continuous maps (so—called chr mappings) from baire space to baire space.

MOGGI, E and Longo, G. The Hereditary Partial Effective Functionals And Recursion Theory In Higher Types. *J Sym Log* 49,1319–1332 D 84.

A type—structure of partial effective functionals over the natural numbers, based on a canonical enumeration of the partial recursive functions, is developed. These partial functionals, defined by a direct elementary technique, turn out to be the computable elements of the hereditary continuous partial objects; moreover, there is a commutative system of enumerations of any given type by any type below (relative numberings). By this and by results in [1] and [2], the Kleene–Kreisel countable functionals and the hereditary effective operations (HEO) are easily characterized.

MOHANTA, Dilip K. Is Samavaya (Inherence) An Internal Relation? *Indian Phil Quart* 11,1–6 Jl 84.

MOHANTY, J N. "Transcendental Philosophy And The Hermeneutic Critique Of Consciousness" in *Hermeneutics*, Shapiro, Gary (ed), 96–120. Amherst Univ Of Mass Pr 1984.

MOHANTY, J N. In Search Of The Actual Historical Frege. *J Hist Phil* 23,237–248 Ap 85.

MOHANTY, J N. Intentionality, Causality And Holism. *Synthese* 61,17–34 O 84.

Recognition of the phenomenon of intentionality is threatened from two sides. From one side, Nature as an interconnected seamless order of causality leaves no room for intentionality. From another side, holisms of various kinds—the Helgelian absolute spirit as much as Richard Rorty's 'conversation of mankind', with many intermediate forms in between—present the same threat though with less abruptness and with more tolerance. The thrust of this paper is to argue that not only do the causal order of Nature and the various holistic systems fail to eliminate intentionality, but they in fact presuppose it. Whereas such a thesis is reputedly a form of transcendental philosophy, an exact and satisfactory formulation of the thesis is a matter of utmost difficulty. This is the task I have set for myself in this paper.

MOHANTY, J N. Prāmānya And Workability—Response To Potter. *J Indian Phil* 12,329–338 D 84.

MOHAPATRA, P K. Ideology And Social Goals. *Philosophica (India)* 10,23–27 Ja–D 81.

MOHR, Richard D. Plato's Theology Reconsidered: What The Demiurge Does. *Hist Phil Quart* 2,131–144 Ap 85.

This paper argues that the aims of Plato's craftsman god are primarily epistemological rather than moral and aesthetic. What the Demiurge does is to introduce into the phenomenal world standards which image to the degree possible both the content and the formal properties of Forms viewed as standards. The immanent standards serve as the objects of true opinion. For more discussion see chapters one and two of *The Platonic Cosmology* (Leiden: Brill, 1985).

MOKRZYCKI, Edmund. *Philosophy Of Science And Sociology: From The Methodological Doctrine To Research Practice.* Boston Routledge & K Paul 1983.

This is an examination of the impact of the neopositivistic philosophy of science on sociology over the past fifty years. It is argued that the standard methodology of sociological research is derived from an uncritical adaptation of logical positivism of the early, most radical, period. As a result, sociology has lost much of its humanistic nature without acquiring the character of a science. The argument is based on case studies of several major works in "scientific" sociology.

MOLES, John. Philanthropia In The Poetics. *Phoenix* 38,325–335 D84.

MOLINO, Jean. Esquisse D'Une Sémiologie De La Poésie. *Petit Rev Phil* 6,1–36 Autumn 84.

MOLONEY, Raymond. The Mind Of Christ In Transcendental Theology: Rahner, Lonergan And Crowe. *Heythrop J* 25,288–300 Jl 84.

Starting from a contrast with Rahner's position, this article outlines how Bernard Lonergan's philosophy leads to an independent approach to the problem of Christ's mind, an approach that is developed by his commentator, Frederick Crowe. One main difference between Rahner and Lonergan arises from their different notions of consciousness. Finally the article describes Lonergan's transposition of traditional Christology into terms of interiority and how this helps him deal with the question of Christ's developing subjectivity.

MOLTMANN, Jürgen. "The Alienation And Liberation Of Nature" in *On Nature*, Rouner, Leroy S (ed), 133–144. Notre Dame Univ Notre Dame Pr 1984.

MOMIGLIANO, Arnaldo. Georges Dumézil And The Trifunctional Approach To Roman Civilization. *Hist Theor* 23,312–330 O 84.

MOMMSEN, Wolfgang J. Gesellschaftliche Bedingtheit Und Gesellschaftliche Relevanz Historishcer Aussagen. *Conceptus* 8,17–29 1974.

The initial section of this essay the author dissociates himself from traditional historicism. He deals briefly with the varials suggestions of the analytical philosophy as to the nature of historical judgments, and arrives at the conclusion that while Hempel's thesis regarding the nomological character of historical judgments is on the whole correct it says little about the specific function of historical knowledge. In the main section the relevancy of historical judgments is derived from considerations regarding the 'transcendental' preconditions of historical knowledge. (edited)

MONASTERIO, Xavier O. On Macintyre, Rationality, And Dramatic Space. *Proc Cath Phil Ass* 58,151–164 1984.

The Platonic conception of rationality that has become paradigmatic presupposes that the subject is a pure mind which stands in a contemplative relationship to the world. Our actual relationship to the world, however, is that of vulnerable participants. This demands a different notion of rationality, if we are to make sense. On this basis, I suggest that MacIntyre's idea of the narrative structure of life is a step in the right direction.

MONDADORI, Fabrizio. Kleist. *Can J Phil* 6,185–223 80 Supp.

MONDADORI, Fabrizio. Leibniz And The Doctrine Of Inter–World Identity. *Stud Leibniz* 7,22–57 1975.

In this paper my objective is two–fold. First, I will try to provide further arguments in favor of the view defended in my earlier paper. Second, I will try to show that a suggestive way of saving contingency in the framework of Leibniz's theory of complete concepts is bound to fail: and the reasons for this failure will provide further evidence in favor of the view under present discussion. The remaining sections of the paper will be concerned with fixing and making precise some of the loose ends of the previous three sections. (edited)

MONRO, G P. The Strong Amalgamation Property For Complete Boolean Algebras. *Z Math Log* 20,499–502 1974.

MONTAGNA, Franco. A Completeness Result For Fixed–Point Algebras. *Z Math Log* 30,525–531 1984.

Fixed point algebras (shortly: FPA's) have been introduced by Smoryński and constitute an algebraic tool for the study of self–reference. The main example of FPA is the Lindenbaum sentence algebra L_{PA} of PA enriched with the set O_{PA} of all operators associated with extensional formulas—in this paper, it is shown that the countable freely generated FPA is a subalgebra of $L_{PA}; O_{PA}$. Therefore, PA has a countable set of generic extensional formulas.

MONTAGNA, Franco and Sorbi, Andrea. Universal Recursion Theoretic Properties Of R E Preordered Structures. *J Sym Log* 50,397–406 Je 85.

In this paper it is shown that the preordering less than or equal to PA induced by provable implication in Peano Arithmetic is recursively universal w.R. To the class of r.E. Preorderings. Less than or equal to PA can also be characterized as the (unique up to recursive isomorphism) lattice preordering which is recursively homogeneous universal with respect to the class of r.E. Lattice preorderings. A consequence of this fact is that, every r.E. Preordering is "representable" in PA as provable implication of $\Sigma 1$ formulas.

MONTEIRO, Joao Paulo. "Natural Conjectures" in *Philosophical Analysis In Latin America*, Gracia, Jorge J E and others (eds), 339–364. Boston Reidel 1984.

MONTEIRO, Luiz and Abad, M. On Three–Valued Moisil Algebras. *Log Anal* 27,407–414 D 84.

In this paper we investigate the properties of the family I(A) of all intervals of the form [x, x] with x less than or equal to x, in a De Morgan algebra A, and we obtain a necessary and sufficient condition for a complete De Morgan algebra A to be a Kleene algebra in terms of I(A). We prove that I(A) is a complete Boolean algebra if A is a complete Moisil algebra.

MONTERO, Bernal Herrera. La Realidad En Kant Y Berkeley. *Rev Filosof (Costa Rica)* 23,49–69 Je 85.

The reality concept that Kant and Berkeley formulate is expounded. Opposite to other interpretations, the hypotheses used here is that, while Berkeley postulates a total spiritualism, in Kant the "existence" of things in themselves is stated as necessary.

MONTESANO, Aldo. The Ordinal Utility Under Uncertainty And The Measure Of Risk Aversion In Terms Of Preferences. *Theor Decis* 18,73–86 Ja 85.

Two main, related questions are considered. First, ordinal utility is specified in the von Neumann–Morgenstern case. Second, a new index of risk aversion is proposed. It requires only the existence of a certainty equivalent for each action. This index turns out to be zero when the von Neumann–Morgenstern axioms hold and its derivative proportional to the Arrow–Pratt index. Its value can be positive when not all the von–Neumann–Morgenstern axioms hold.

MONTI, Maria Teresa. *Catalogo Del Fondo Haller.* Milano Angeli 1984.

MONTMARQUET, James A. Epistemological Internalism. *S J Phil* 23,229–240 Sum 85.

In this paper I distinguish three forms of internalism—based on notions of epistemological responsibility, defeasibility and coherentism—and a fourth view due to Alvin Goldman. I argue that, of these, only the coherentist view provides a plausible and comprehensive rival to the now influential externalist view.

MOONEY, Gavin. Medical Ethics: An Excuse For Inefficiency? *J Med Ethics* 10,183–185 D 84.

There is frequently an appearance of conflict between medicine and economics. This arises first because the nature of health and health care requires the doctor to make decisions on behalf of the patient and thus serves to explain why medical ethics exist. But secondly it is due to the relative lack of acceptance of the ethics of the common good within medical ethics. As a result while economics in the field of health has an objective the maximization of the health of the community, subject to resource contraints, medical ethics pushes individual doctors to try to maximize the health of their patients. There is no reason to believe that the latter will sum to the former. To make the maximization of health of the community the goal of the medical profession requires institutional changes, particularly with regard to budgeting, which will cajole and if necessary coerce doctors to adopt the good of the community as their objective.

MOORE, A W. Set Theory, Skolem's Paradox And The *Tractatus*. *Analysis* 45,13–20 Ja 85.

I argue that there are certain structural parallels between paradoxes found in the "Tractatus" and various set–theoretical paradoxes (including Skolem's Paradox). In the light of these parallels, I suggest that themain debate occasioned by Skolem's Paradox, that between the relativist and the non–relativist, is irresoluble: what the relativist means is correct, but it has to be shown and cannot be said.

MOORE, A W. Transcendental Idealism In Wittgenstein And Theories Of Meaning. *Phil Quart* 35,134–155 Ap 85.

In this paper I explore the repercussions of the view that there is, in Wittgenstein's later work, an element of transcendental idealism akin to that found in the "Tractatus". I argue that if this view is correct, then that later work is incompatible with a belief in the possibility of a philosophically substantial theory of meaning.

MOORE, Brooke. Critical Reflection: Reply To Oscanyan. *Teach Phil* 7,247 Jl 84.

MOORE, F C T. "On Taking Metaphor Literally" in *Metaphor*, Miall, David S (ed), 1–13. Atlantic Highlands Humanities Pr 1982.

MOORE, F C T. The Martyr's Dilemma. *Analysis* 45,29–33 Ja 85.

The common assumption that the Prisoner's Dilemma arises only for rationally self–interested behavior is disproved by giving an example in which the dilemma arises for altruistic agents.

MOORE, G William and De La Monte, Suzanne M and Hutchins, Grover M. Compensatory Neoplasia: Chronic Erythrocytosis And Neuroblastic Tumors. *Theor Med* 5,279–292 O 84.

In a recent study, we observed a strong association between chronic hypoxic states and the occurrence of peripheral neuroblastic tumors, a relatively uncommon group of neural neoplasms. In this report we review those findings and formulate an hypothesis to explain why conditions which lead to chronic erythrocytosis may also cause compensatory neoplasia of neural tissues. (edited)

MOORE, Gregory H. Beyond First–order Logic: The Historical Interplay Between Mathematical Logic And Axiomatic Set Theory. *Hist Phil Log* 1,95–138 1980.

What has been the historical relationship between set theory and logic? On the one hand, Zermelo and other mathematicians developed set theory as a Hilbert–style axiomatic system. On the other hand, set theory influenced logic by suggesting to Schröder, Löwenheim and others the use of infinitely long expressions. The question of which logic was appropriate for set theory—first–order logic, second–order logic, or an infinitary logic—culminated in a vigourous exchange between Zermelo and Göel around 1930.

MORA, Eric. Reconocer Lo Irrazonable: Posición Crítica Ante La Racionalidad Científica. *Rev Filosof (Costa Rica)* 22,39–50 D 84.

Actuar y pensar conforme a la razón, con apego exclusivo a ella, pareciera ser un presupuesto racional básico de le época actual; un presupuesto que se asume pere que no se discute. En este trabajo me propongo discutir el origen histórico concreto de la racionalidad vigente, para monstrar hast dónde esta especie de sacralización de la razón que vivimos hoy corresponde al desrrollo. (edited)

MORAES, Reginaldo C C. Max, The Cynic (in Portuguese). *Trans/Form/Acao* 6,37–44 1983.

We begin with an approximation between Hegel and Marx and then we discuss the idea of work's force reproduction understood as a part of the capital. The latter is viewed as a kind of social relationship. This approach is attempted on the basis of certain passages of Marx's The Capital and The Grundrisse as well. Finally, we interpret some nowdays developments under the point of view of this "cynical anatomy." (edited)

MORAIS, Carlos. A Critica Glucksmanniana Do Poder. *Rev Port Filosof* 41,69–94 Ja–Mr 85.

MORALES– LUNA, Guillermo and Adamowicz, Zofia. A Recursive Model For Arithmetic With Weak Induction. *J Sym Log* 50,49–54 Mr 85.

MORAN, Philip. Leninism And The Enlightenment. *Stud Soviet Tho* 30,109–130 Ag 85.

There are *continuities* and tensions between Leninist political philosophy and that of liberalism. For example, the Warren Court justifies restrictions on organizations (KKK) having a history of damaging the public interest (not unlike a Leninist approach to free speech). And liberals echo Lenin's critique of formal equality when Senator Humphrey said: "What good does it do a Negro to be able to eat in a fine restaurant if he cannot afford to pay the bill?"

MORAWIEC, Edmund. Some Ways Of Actualizing Classical Philosophy (in Polish). *Stud Phil Christ* 20,69–90 1984.

MORAWSKI, Stefan. "Marxism, Historicism, And Philosophy Of Art" in *Continuity And Change In Marxism*, Fischer, Norman And Others (ed), 24–38. Atlantic Highlands Humanities Pr 1982.

MORAWSKI, Stefan. Art As Semblance. *J Phil* 81,654–662 N 84.

MOREAU, Joseph. Leibniz Devant Le Labyrinthe De La Liberté. *Stud Leibniz* 16,217–229 1984.

Dieser Konflikt zwischen der Freiheit und der Vorherbestimmung kann bei Leibniz in der Betrachtung des unendlichen Fortschritts des Reiches der Geister seine Lösung finden. Als korrelative Entsprechung dieses Fortschritts kann die asymptotische Abnahme des Leidens der Verdammten betrachtet werden. (edited)

MOREAU, Pierre–Francois. Politiques Du Langage. *Rev Phil Fr* 175,189–194 Ap–Je 85.

Chez Hobbes, l'individu entretient un rapport originaire et immédiat avec le langage, source de l'engagement et du pacte social; chez Spinoza au contraire, le langage n'échappe pas à la nécessité; il dépend de l'imagination, dont la théorie donne le moyen de le régler; le pouvoir des mots suppose un processus de libération dont la liberté de penser est, dans la Cité, la condition.

MOREH, J. On Harrod's First Refining Principle. *Theor Decis* 19,103–125 S 85.

Harrod introduced a refinement to 'crude' Utilitarianism with the aim of reconciling it with common sense ethics. It is shown (a) that this refinement (later known as 'Rule Utilitarianism) does not maximize utility (b) the principle which truly maximizes utility,

marginal private benefit equals marginal social cost, requires a number of forbidden acts like lying to be performed. Hence Harrod's claim that his refined Utilitarianism is the foundation of moral institutions cannot be sustained. Some more modern forms of Utilitarianism are reinterpreted in this paper as utility maximizing decision rules. While they produce more utility than Harrod's rule, they require breaking the moral rules some of the time, just like the "marginal" rule mentioned above. However, Harrod's rule is useful in warning the members of a group, considered as a single moral agent, of the externalities that lie beyond the immediate consequences of the collective action.

MORELLI, Mario. Philosophers And Experimental Inquiry: A Reply To Milgram's "Reflections On Morelli's Dilemma Of Obedience". *Metaphilosophy* 16,66–69 Ja 85.

In this note I respond to several criticisms by Stanley Milgram of a paper I had written about his obedience experiments. While agreeing with Milgram's point that philosophers tend to rely on "argument and rational analysis" in contrast to experimental psychologists who seek "evidence and experimental inquiry," I claim that Milgram fails to appreciate the fact that philosophers (particularly moral philosophers) usually make normative claims that are not amenable to experimental testing. I also argue that Milgram misunderstands the point I make about the dilemma of obedience that is posed to subjects in his experiments.

MORETTO, Giovanni. Etica E Narrazione In Novalis. *Filosofia* 35,183–198 Jl–0 84.

MORGAN, Charles G. Weak Conditional Comparative Probability As A Formal Semantic Theory. *Z Math Log* 30,199–212 1984.

Classical probability theory is too determinate in detail to permit its plausible interpretation as idealized degrees of rational belief. We develop a very weak conditional comparative probability theory and prove soundness and completeness results for classical propositional and first–order logics. We also show that any conditional measure which yields soundness and completeness must satisfy the conditions of our weak theory.

MORGAN, Michael L. Jewish Ethics After The Holocaust. *J Relig Ethics* 12,256–277 Fall 84.

This paper attempts to develop the foundations of a contemporary Jewish moral theory. It treats the Jewish legal and moral tradition as the object of an act of interpretive recovery that is carried out by contemporary Jews who are sensitive to the demands of their historical situation, a situation defined by the Nazi destruction of European Jewry and by the reestablishment of the Jewish state. In the course of the paper I develop an approach to post–Holocaust Jewish experience that derives from the work of Emil Fackenheim and try to show how Jewish moral imperatives arise within Fackenheim's account of the Jewish situation. The Jew's understanding of the role of God in moral obligation, his appreciation of the demands of the historical moment, and his interpretive recovery of the Jewish moral tradition—all are shown to depend upon and emerge from a reflective examination of Jewish moral and legal resistance during the Holocaust.

MORGAN, Thomas D and Rotunda, Ronald D. *Problems And Materials On Professional Responsibility*. Mineola Foundation Pr 1984.

The book is for a law school course in legal ethics. It poses realistic hypothetical situations in which lawyers face ethical choices. Questions are posed to highlight the issues. Legal and non–legal material is suggested which may be helpful in deciding the best courses of action for lawyers to take.

MORGAN, Thomas D and Rotunda, Ronald D. *Selected Standards On Professional Responsibility*. Mineola Foundation Pr 1985.

MORGAN, William J. Social Philosophy Of Sport: A Critical Interpretation. *J Phil Sport* 10,33–51 1983.

MORI, Maurizio. Italy: Abortion And Nationalized Health Care. *Hastings Center Rep* 14,22–23 D 84.

MORICONI, Enrico and Offenberger, Niels. Zur Frage Der IV: Syllogistischen Figur In Der "Dissertatio De Arte Commbinatoria", Eine Jugendsünde Leibnizens? *Stud Leibniz* 16,212–216 1984.

This paper is a discussion of Leibniz's juvinile thesis according to which "quarta figura aequè bona est ac ipsa prima; imò si modo, non praedicationis, ut vulgò solent, sed subjectionis, ut Aristoteles, eam enunciemus, ex IV fiet I et contra" (DAC 25). The authors maintain that that thesis is syllogistically untendable, since the reduction device Leibniz suggested does not change the logical function of Termini, but introduces a difference only from a grammatical point of view.

MORIN, Michel. Mourir—Une Fois De Plus. *Petite Rev Phil* 6,39–62 Spr 85.

MORIONES, Francisco. Carta De San Agustín A Consencio: Sobre La Razón Y La Revelación. *Augustinus* 25,29–50 Ja–D 80.

MORISON, Robert S. The Biological Limits On Autonomy. *Hastings Center Rep* 14,43–50 O 84.

MORITZ, Rolf. Gesellschaftliche Widersprüche In Der Volksrepublik China. *Deut Z Phil* 23,1047–1060 1975.

In China war die Vorbereitung des übergangs von der Spontaneität gesellschaftlicher Widersprüche zu ihrer bewußtesten Gestaltung aufserodentlich kompliziert. Unter den gegenwärtigen Bedingungen wirken die objektiven gesellschaftlichen Gesetze des Sozialismus in China elementar. Aus ihrem Wirken erwachsen objektive Kräfte und Faktoren, die zu einer sich vertiefenden Krise der Grundlagen der maoistischen Politik führen.

MOROSOLI, Michele. Les Avatars De La Différence. *Philosophiques* 11,389–414 O 84.

Equality, when it is understood as equality for all, even thought it is judged favorably in general, is hardly realizable because of the structure of our thinking that organizes the differences in dichotomies and in hierarchial oppositions. When we examine the discourses written by women that tend to define a difference of the woman, we realize the difficulty to name this difference. When we compare a text written by E Harding, a jungian psychoanalyst and another written by M Montrelay, a lacanian psychoanalyst, we observe that despite their distant theorical and historical sources, the feminine is said in reference to the masculine. By our way of thinking (that converts all differences in hierarchical oppositions), the desire for a generalized equality becomes erratic. Only a fragmented discourse, that gives place to the differences could permit an equality in the mentalities.

MORPHIS, Maxine. Creativity And AI: The Creative Products Of Man And Machine. *Int J Applied Phil* 2,59–72 Fall 84.

What claims about creativity of programs can Artificial intelligence make? I argue first, the question "can a computer program *in principle* be creative?" Is conceptually ill–formed. Second, the focus of AI's claims for computer creativity should be on the creative product. The concept of the creative product is well established in the literature on creativity. Under the common application of this concept, the computer program *in principle* has the potential to produce a creative result.

MORREALL, John. Enjoying Negative Emotions In Fiction. *Phil Lit* 19,95–103 Ap 85.

I argue that the most basic pleasure we take in tragedy, horror stories, and the like, is the pleasure of feeling negative emotions. First I examine several situations in real life in which we enjoy fear, anger, sadness, and pity. The basic requirement here is that we retain overall control of our situation. Then I show how fiction is ideally suited to providing us control, and so to allowing us to enjoy negative emotions.

MORREALL, John. Laughter, Suddenness, And Pleasure. *Dialogue (Canada)* 23,689–694 D 84.

This article is a response to Karl Pfeifer's "Laughing Matters" (*Dialogue* 23 (1983), pp 695–697). Pfeifer objects to two elements in my formula that *Laughter results from a pleasant psychological shift* ("shift" is shorthand for "sudden change")—the claim that what causes laughter is a *sudden* change of psychological state, and the claim that that change is pleasant, I argue that Pfeifer's purported counter examples to these claims are not true counter examples.

MORREALL, John. The Aseity Of God In St Anselm. *Sophia (Australia)* 23,35–44 0 84.

St Anselm extended the traditional notion that God is *agenetos*, unoriginated, by claiming that God has self–existence or "aseity", that God is *a se* or *ex se*, from himself, and *per se*, through himself. I shoe the untenability of two positive ways in which St Anselm may have understood God's aseity, and conclude that we should understand aseity only in a negative way, as based on God's absolute simplicity and independence.

MORREALL, John. The Philosopher As Teacher, Humor And Philosophy. *Metaphilosophy* 15,305–317 Jl–O 84.

This paper is a defense of humor against several traditional philosophical attacks, and a discussion of the value of humor in teaching and in doing philosophy. My defense is based on the claims that amusement is often a kind of aesthetic experience, and that humor can be seen as our rationality operating in a play mode. The most important value I find in humor for teaching and doing philosophy is the mental flexibility which humor fosters.

MORREIM, E Haavi. Cost Containment: Issues Of Moral Conflict And Justice For Physicians. *Theor Med* 6,257–280 O 85.

In response to rapidly rising health care costs in the United States, federal and state governments and private industry are instituting numerous and diverse cost–containment plans. As devices for coping with a scarcity of resources, such plans present serious challenges to physicians' traditional single–minded devotion to patient welfare. Those which contain costs by directly limiting medical options or by controlling physicians' daily clinical decisions can threaten the quality of medical care by allowing economic authorities to make essentially medical judgments. In contrast, other plans coax compliance by arranging incentives, e.G., offering financial rewards for successful cost containment. While they allow for clinical freedom, these plans create conflicts between physicians' fiduciary obligations to their patients and the competing interests of the payers. Such conflicts arise as physicians try to work within governmental or corporated cost containment policies, and also as they attempt to "streamline" clinical efficiency. Throughout, issues of justice emerge as physicians seek to reconcile their own patients' claims upon limited common resources with others' equally legitimate claims.

MORRIS, Christopher W. A Contractarian Defense Of Nuclear Deterrence. *Ethics* 95,479–496 Ap 85.

While the direct killing of the innocent is ordinarily morally wrong, I argue that we are not morally prohibited from doing so (or from threatening to do so) in order to retaliate against (or to deter) an enemy nuclear attack. I sketch an account of the justification of the killing of the innocent and argue that in the event of a nuclear attack (almost) no retaliatory act is prohibited by justice given that such an attack effectively returns one to a Hobbesian state of nature.

MORRIS, Gregory L. A Word Of Order And Light: The Fiction Of John Gardner. Athens Univ Of Georgia Pr 1984.

MORRIS, T F. The Proof Of Pauline Self–Predication In The *Phaedo*. *Phil Res Arch* 10,139–152 1984.

This article shows that Plato is discussing Pauline predication and Pauline self–prediction in the *Phaedo*. The key in the recognition that the "something else" of *Phaedo* 103e2–5 cannot be a sensible object because any such object which participates in Form 'X' can sometimes appear not to be x. It is argued that Plato has not written in a straightforward manner, but rather has written in a series of riddles for the reader to solve. Thus this dialogue is an example of the playful use of the written word discussed at *Phaedrus* 275ff.

MORRIS, Thomas V. A Response To The Problems Of Evil. *Philosophia (Israel)* 14,173–186 Ag 84.

In this paper, I examine a novel and very interesting attempt made by George Schlesinger to block any argument from the existence of suffering to the non–existence of God. Attention is directed to different problems the reality of evil possess for the theist.

MORRISTON, Wesley. Is God "Significantly Free"? *Faith Phil* 2,257–264 Jl 85.

MORRISTON, Wesley. Is Plantinga's God Omnipotent? *Sophia (Australia)* 23,45–57 0 84.

MORROW, Carol K. Doctors Helping Doctors. *Hastings Center Rep* 14,32–38 D 84.

Organized medicine has recently linked "physician impairment" through addiction, alcoholism, and psychiatric disorders to substandard professional performance. Viewing professional deviance as a symptom or outcome of medical problems amenable to medical treatment leads to a distinctive self–regulatory system characterized by physician advocacy, nonjudgmental rehabilitation, paternalistic intervention in the name of health, and professional management of problem doctors. Social, ethical, and legal implications for problem doctors, the public, and professional self–governance are discussed.

MORTENSEN, Chris and Meyer, Robert K. Inconsistent Models For Relevant Arithmetics. *J Sym Log* 49,917–929 S 84.

A series of inconsistent models for relevant arithmetics (such as $R\#$, $RM\#$) is set out. The domains of these models are the integers mod n (for finite n). Their propositional structure is given by the well–known Sugihara matrices, especially the three–element one. It is known that the existence of such models suffices for the non–triviality of arithmetic formulated relevantly, in a strictly finitary sense. Here, further properties of the models are developed, culminating in Mortensen's paraconsistent arithmetic RM–omega.

MORTENSEN, Chris. Aristotle's Thesis In Consistent And Inconsistent Logics. *Stud Log* 43,107–116 1984.

One task of this paper is to give a more intuitive modelling for *A* in consistent logics. In addition, while inconsistent but nontrivial theories, and inconsistent nontrivial logics employing propositional constants (for which the rule of uniform substitution US fails), have both been studied extensively within the paraconsistent programme, inconsistent nontrivial logics (closed under US) do not seem to have been. This paper gives sufficient conditions for a logic containing *A* to be inconsistent, and then shows that there is a class of inconsistent nontrivial logics all containing *A*. A second semantical modelling for *A* in such logics is given. Finally, some informal remarks about the kind of modelling *A* seems to require are made. (edited)

MORTENSEN, Chris. The Limits Of Change. *Austl J Phil* 63,1–10 Mr 85.

MORTIMER, Michael. On Languages With Two Variables. *Z Math Log* 21,135–140 1975.

MOSELEY, Ray. Excuse Me, But You Have A Melanoma On Your Neck: Unsolicited Medical Opinions. *J Med Phil* 10,163–170 My 85.

MOSER, Paul D. Whither Infinite Regresses Of Justification. *S J Phil* 23,65–74 Spr 85.

The issue whether there are infinite regresses of epistemic justification is centrally important to proponents of an eliminative regress argument for epistemic foundationalism that first appears, if only in embryonic form, in Aristotle's *Posterior Analytics*. In what follows, I shall improve on the traditional eliminative argument for foundationalism by arguing that although one sort of infinite justificatory regress is possible, the sort of infinite justificatory regress relevant to foundationalist concerns is inadequate for epistemic justification.

MOSER, Paul K. A Defense Of Epistemic Intuitionism. *Metaphilosophy* 15,196–209 Jl–O 84.

This paper argues that to provide an acceptable analysis of epistemic empirical justification, we must rely on a version of epistemic intuitionism, the view that nonpropositional *de re* sensory intuitions are justifying conditions of at least some beliefs. Also, the paper constructs a dilemma that challenges the leading non–intuitionist accounts of epistemic justification.

MOSER, Paul K and Flannery, Kevin. Kripke And Wittgenstein: Intention Without Paradox. *Heythrop J* 26,310–318 Jl 85.

This paper discusses Wittgenstein's claim that: 'This was our paradox: no course of action could be determined by a rule, because every course of action, can be made out to accord with the rule'. First, the paper raises a dilemma facing Kripke's reconstruction of the paradox in question. Secondly, the paper sets forth Wittgenstein's way out of the paradox. And finally the paper identifies a questionable nominalist assumption in Kripke's construal of Wittgenstein.

MOSER, Paul K and Tlumak, Jeffrey. Two Paradoxes Of Rational Acceptance. *Erkenntnis* 23,127–142 Ag 85.

This article provides a straightforward diagnosis and resolution of the lottery paradox and the epistemic version of the paradox of the preface. In doing so, the article takes some steps in relating the notion of probability to the notion of epistemic justification.

MOSER, Paul K. On Basic Knowledge Without Justification. *Can J Phil* 15,305–310 Je 85.

Recently Robert Almeder has argued that Aristotle's celebrated regress argument shows that there is "basic knowledge" which does not require the satisfaction of any justification condition. This article outlines Almeder's argument, and shows that it ultimately fails.

MOSER, Simon. Europa Und Die Vereinigten Staaten Von Amerika Philosophiegeschichtlich Betrachtet. *Z Phil Forsch* 29,279–291 Ap–Je 75.

MOSES, Michael. Recursive Linear Orders With Recursive Successivities. *Annals Pure Applied Log* 27,253–264 N 84.

A *successivity* in a linear order is a pair of elements with no other elements between them. We characterize recursive linear orders with recursive successivities that are recursively categorical as precisely those that can be partitioned by a finite number of points into intervals each of which has order type from among $\{\omega,\omega,\omega+\omega\}\cup\{\kappa\cdot\nu:\kappa<\omega\}$.

MOSKOP, John C. *Divine Omniscience And Human Freedom*. Macon Mercer Univ Pr 1984.

MOSTERT, Pieter and Van Der Leeuw, Karel. *Enige Kernproblemen In Het Filosofie Onderwijs*. Rotterdam Onderwijs 1985.

This research report describes main problems in teaching and learning philosophy, and is based upon a detailed analysis of an introductory course in philosophy. The material is derived from classroom protocols. After a general introduction, the next chapters concentrate on reading philosophical texts, problem solving, and theory–learning in philosophy. In the final chapter a model for the construction of introductory courses in philosophy is introduced.

MOTHERSILL, Mary. *Beauty Restored*. Oxford Clarendon Pr 1984.

Current prejudice has it that a general aesthetic theory is neither desorable nor possible. I argue on the contrary that a theory is necessary and offer one in outline. I take as well established two claims: (1) There are neither laws nor principles of taste. (2) Some individual judgments of the form, "O is beautiful," are eligible to function in arguments etc. The task of a theory is to show in detail that (1) and (2) are not merely consistent but coherent.

MOTOHASHI, Nobuyoshi. "Homogeneous Formulas And Definability Theorems" in *Lecture Notes In Mathematics*, Muller, G H And Others (ed), 109–116. NY Springer 1981.

MOTOHASHI, Nobuyoshi. A Normal Form Theorem For First Order Formulas And Its Application To Gaifman's Splitting Theorem. *J Sym Log* 49,1262–1267 D 84.

MOULDER, James. Philosophy, Religion And Theodicy. *S Afr J Phil* 3,147–150 N 84.

MOULDER, J. The Origins Of Early Greek Philosophy. *S Afr J Phil* 4,29–33 F 85.

Every idea generates at least two questions: why did it arise? And, is it justified? The ideas which are preserved in the fragments of the early Greek philosophers are no exception. We would like to know what caused these people to have the ideas which they did have; why, for example, did Thales believe that everything was water? And we would like to know whether the ideas which they had are justified, either in the strong sense of being true or in the weaker sense of being reasonable; for example, is it reasonable to believe, as Heraclitus apparently did, that everything is always changing? Both kinds of questions are legitimate, and therefore they should neither be confused, for all the reasons which Hans Reichenbach (1938) and Karl Popper (1959) have given us, nor forbidden to influence each other, for all the reasons which Thomas Kuhn (1962) and Paul Feyerabend (1975) have given us. And because philosophical discussions of an idea tend to focus on whether or not it is justified, I want to change the perspective and emphasize what seven books on early Greek thought contribute to our understanding of why western philosophy began when and where it did.

MOULINES, C Ulises. "Existential Quantifiers In Physical Theories" in *Philosophical Analysis In Latin America*, Gracia, Jorge J E and others (eds), 173–198. Boston Reidel 1984.

MOULINES, C Ulises. Links, Loops, And The Global Structure Of Science. *Phil Natur* 21,254–265 1984.

MOULINES, C Ulises. Theoretical Terms And Bridge Principles: A Critique Of Hempel's (Self–) Criticisms. *Erkenntnis* 22,97–118 Ja 85.

By using the model–theoretically defined concept of an intertheoretic link, as introduced in the recent literature of the structuralist philosophy of science, a critical appraisal of Hempel's recent theses on the theoretical–observational dichotomy and on bridge principles is made. It is shown how the precisely defined links are to be distinguished from "normal" axioms and how they may be used to determine the non–theoretical terms of a theory.

MOULOUD, Noel. "The Sense And The Language Of The Work Of Art" in *Continental Philosophy And The Arts*, Winters, Laurence E and others (ed), 41–62. *Lanham* Univ Pr Of America 1984.

MOUNCE, H O. Hanfling And Radford On Art And Real Life. *Philosophy* 60,127–128 Ja 85.

MOUSSALLY, Adnan. "Un Modèle D'analyse Dy Texte Dramatique" in *Existential Coordinates Of Human Condition*, Tymieniecka, A (ed), 547–558. Boston Reidel 1984.

MOUTAFAKIS, Nicholas J. Nicholas Rescher On Hypothetical Reasoning And The Coherence Of Systems Of Knowledge. *Ideal Stud* 14,229–236 S 84.

The object of the inquiry is to illustrate how Rescher's general theory concerning the coherence of truth claims is not able to accommodate contrary to fact conditionals. It is argued that especially in the case of subjunctive conditionals, Rescher's position on the coherent character of truth claims disintegrates in view of the fact that the former demand the suspension of any neighboring truth claim.

MOUTSOPOULOS, Evanghleos. Prolégomènes À La Philosophie De La Culture Grecque. *Diotima* 12,17–28 1984.

Philosophy of Greek Culture is the denomination of a new philosophical discipline which, as the threshold of the 21st century is the only capable of uniting the actual presence of humanity to its past, considered under its most authentically experienced and conscious form. On the other hand, Philosophy of Greek Culture displays an extraordinary capacity of linking together, under a multiple problematic, the most diverse fields of culture understood as the universal form of the accomplishment of the human being. Finally, Philosophy of Greek Culture implies for itself the statute of a philosophy of the most subtle and valuable creation, that of the being which is conscious of its own creativity. This article reflects a programmatic diagram of the possible developments of the new discipline.

MOUW, Richard J. Christianity And Pacifism. *Faith Phil* 2,105–111 Ap 85.

MOWRY, Bryan. From Galen's Theory To William Harvey's Theory: A Case Study In The Rationality Of Scientific Theory Change. *Stud Hist Phil Sci* 16,49–82 Mr 85.

The history of science is that of older theories being challenged and eventually being superseded by newer theories. The rationality of this process of scientific theory change is a central issue in contemporary philosophy of science. This paper aims to elucidate this topic by examining an episode in the history of medical science, namely the change from Galen's theory of the movement of the heart and blood to Harvey's theory of the circulation of the blood. In part I the historical details include Galen's theory, the generation of Harvey's theory, Harvey's arguments for this theory, the reception of and arguments against Harvey's theory and the fate of Galen's theory. In part II to elucidate the topic, the change from Galen's theory to Harvey's theory is assumed to be rational, and the ideas of Imre Lakatos and Thomas Kuhn are examined in turn to see if they can account for this rationality. It is argued that they cannot. In part III a different conception, which does account for the rationality of this scientific theory change, is presented. (edited)

MRÁCEK, F and Machleidt, P. Some Problems Of The Formation Of Strategies And Evaluation In The Sphere Of Biotechnologies (in Czechoslovakian). *Filozof Cas* 33,389–393 1985.

MRÁZ, Milan. Prigogine's Characteristics Of The Results Of Ancient Philosophy (in Czechslovakian). *Filozof Cas* 32,808–813 1984.

MRÁZ, M. Opposites And Time In The Logic Of Aristotle's Philosophy (in Czechoslovakian). *Filozof Cas* 33,448–460 1985.

MUELLER, Franz H. Comparative Social Philosophies: Individualism, Socialism, Solidarism. *Thought* 60,297–309 S 85.

The author tries to show that economic systems are each based on a specific social philosophy which in turn is based on a philosophical anthropology. He avails himself of the theory of universals as a framework (*ante rem*: idealism/collectivism; *post rem*: nominalism/individualism; *in re*: moderate realism/solidarism). In connection with "solidarism" he presents a summary of the doctrine of subsidiarity. For heuristic, but especially didactic purposes, he encloses a table which demonstrates diagrammatically the association of the ideas presented.

MÜHLBERGER, Richard. After Art History, What? *J Aes Educ* 19,93–104 Sum 85.

MULCAHY, John W and Natale, Samuel M. Social Systems Analytics And Ethics. *Thought* 60,205–220 Je 85.

This article summarizes the conflicts which exist between the ideographic and nomothetic dimensions within any organization. The article analyzes the inherent conflict between values, attitudes, needs and expectations using the VANE model of analysis. Ethical conflicts are suggested and approaches recommended.

MULCAHY, Kevin V. Official Culture And Cultural Repression: The Case Of Dmitri Shostakovich. *J Aes Educ* 18,69–84 Fall 84.

Although much lionized by Soviet cultural authorities, Dimitri Shostakovich was, in fact, the victim of persistent official censure. Along with other artists, he was criticized for "formalism" among other "bourgeois deviations." By making periodic concessions to "socialist realism," Shostakovich escaped the worst of the cultural purges. He also began a remarkable body of chamber music as personal compensation for the censorship imposed on his large–scale symphonic works. Soviet music, in general, has been subject to politicization and stultification as a result of the Party's "cultural Lysenkoism."

MULDER, Henk. The *Vienna Circle Archive* And The Literary Remains Of Moritz Schlick And Otto Neurath. *Synthese* 64,375–388 S 85.

In his article 'The Vienna Circle Archive and the Literary Remains of Moritz Schlick and Otto Neurath, the author reports on his investigation from 1962–1967 into the scientific theory of the Vienna Circle. The aim of the investigation was especially the tracing of documents, such as letters, notices, and unpublished lectures, that would make possible a more detailed knowledge and description of the ideas and history of the Vienna Circle. After a disappointing start the author at last succeeded in laying hands on many interesting documents of the above–mentioned nature, of which the complete literary remains of Moritz Schlick and Otto Neurath form the most important element. All material is brought together in the Vienna Circle Archive, which is housed in the Royal Netherlands Academy of the Sciences and is administered by the Vienna Circle Foundation, of which the author is the chairman.

MULLER- SCHMID, Peter P. Theorie Und Praxis In Technologischer Und Dialektischer Perspektive. *Arch Rechts Soz* 60,187–212 1974.

The problem of the rational principles of the praxis is immediately followed by another: how to unite in the same norm the autonomy of the person and the common finality of the society in which the individual finds himself. Technology is able only to recognize the first principle, and marxism uniquely the second. According to the author there is a third possibility founded on an abstractive gnoseology. Due to this philosophy one can both distinguish and also unite the two principles, that is to say, to recognize on the one hand the autonomy, and on the other to look for its integration in the whole.

MULLER, Alfredo Gómez. Poder Y Contra–Poder. *Logos (Mexico)* 12,128–138 S–D 84.

Introduction to a criticism of power as a relationship of domination between human beings. Power is probably not an ontological structure of the human being, but rather a certain way of realizing existence, determined by a certain interpretation of being, endness and time. The philosophical criticism of power as alienated sociality and the historical possibility of constituting a counter–power necessitates a clear definition of the field of those phenomena which are essentially specific to power.

MULLER, G H and others. *Lecture Notes In Mathematics*. NY Springer 1981.

MÜLLER, Georg. Der Streit Um Die Eigentumsordnung Des Verfassungsentwurfes 1977. *Stud Phil (Switzerland)* Supp 12,249–266 1983.

MÜLLER, Hans–Harald and Danneberg, Lutz. On Justifying The Choice Of Interpretive Theories. *J Aes Art Crit* 43,7–16 Fall 84.

The essay examines E D Hirsch's 'ethical' argumentation in respect of the choice of theories of interpretation. Looking firstly at the premises of Hirsch's theory, we analyze the general structure of his argument. Subsequently, we discuss the individual stages in Hirsch's attempt to ground the choice of an interpretative theory, which we show to be inadequate. Finally we outline an alternative framework for grounding interpretive theories which are, however, weaker than the theory proposed by Hirsch.

MÜLLER, Klaus. Subjektiver Faktor Und Zusammenhang Von Gesellschaft Und Natur. *Deut Z Phil* 22,584–597 1974.

MULLER, Philippe. Incidence Sur Hegel De La Lecture De Gibbon. *Stud Phil (Switzerland)* 41,161–176 1982.

hEGEL left the Tübinger Stift as 'the man of LESSING' in the wake of the German Enlightenment. 'positivity' was then equaled with 'historic', superfluous', 'contrary to any sane reason'. Three years later, when he came to Frankfort, history for him begins to be the field where reason manifests itself, and 'positivity' must be seen as such as the transitory visage of reason. In between, HEGEL read GIBBON, and the thesis of this article claims that this reading was significant and determinant. As it is based on tentative reconstruction, it is formulated as a working hypothesis which deserves some attention.

MÜLLER, W and Hirschmann, J. Gesellschaftliches Und Individuelles Bewusstein In Der Philosophischen Diskussion In Der DDR And UdSSR. *Deut Z Phil* 33,168–170 1985.

MÜLLER, Werner. Subjektiver Faktor Und Massenbewusstsein. *Deut Z Phil* 32,796–804 1984.

MULLINS, Willard A. "Ideology And Political Culture" in *Ideology, Philosophy And Politics*, Parel, Anthony (ed), 111–138. Waterloo Laurier Univ Pr 1983.

MUNDICI, Daniele. Tautologies With A Unique Craig Interpolant, Uniform *Vs* Nonuniform Complexity. *Annals Pure Applied Log* 27,265–274 N 84.

Using Craig's interpolation theorem in sentential logic we relate, e.G., proof length and the complexity of decision procedures for theories in general formal systems. We also prove that if $P \neq NP \cap coNP$ then for every deterministic Turing machine M working in polynomial time there is in sentential logic a tautology D of the form A→B having a unique interpolant J (up to logical equivalence) such that M when placed over input D does not output J.

MUÑOZ, Alfredo Troncoso. Situación Actual De Los Estudios En Torno A La Filosofía Presocrática: Filósofos O Filólogos? *Logos (Mexico)* 8,9–20 My–Ag 85.

MUNSON, Thomas N. The Revelation Of Humanity. *Phil Today* 29,3–27 Spr 85.

This article argues that, even though the legacy of the Enlightenment has been a philosophy without religion, a renewed philosophico–religious dialogue is essential to a fuller understanding of our humanity. The author draws upon our history to show how freedom is jeopardized by either philosophical or religious dominance. Religion can save us from the tyranny of "absolute knowledge," just as philosophy unshackles us from an "impossible transcendence". An intergrated metaphysics of person needs both disciplines.

MUNTEANU, Costea. Again On "The Crisis In Economic Theory": An Epistemological Approach. *Phil Log* 28,109–117 Ap–Je 84.

MUNZ, Peter. Philosophy And The Mirror Of Rorty. *Phil Soc Sci* 14,195–238 Je 84.

R Rorty's argument in his *Philosophy and the Mirror of Nature* that philosophers know nothing special about knowledge but ought to follow the non–cognitive pragmatism of Heidegger and Wittgenstein, is fallacious because it does not consider the implications of evolution for the acquisition of knowledge. The biological dimensions of knowledge make Rorty's recourse to the epistemic authority of rule following communities superfluous and obviate his reliance on relativism and historicism.

MURAWSKI, Gerd and Hemmerling, Armin. Zur Raumkompliziertheit Mehrdimensionaler Turing–Automaten. *Z Math Log* 30,233–258 1984.

The paper deals with problems concerning the space–complexity of Turing automata with n–dimensional input tapes (n "less than or equal to" 2). Upper and lower bounds of the space–complexity of searching all finite n–dimensional patterns (arrays) are given. Furthermore, relationships between the recognition and decision of sets of patterns by deterministic and nondeterministic automata, respectively, are investigated (D–ND problems). Using a linearization method it is shown that, for certain space–bounds, these n–dimensional D–ND problems are logically equivalent to the analogous one–dimensional problems.

MURAWSKI, Roman. Trace Expansions Of Initial Segments. *Z Math Log* 30,471–476 1984.

The paper is devoted to a particular construction of definite A_2^-–expansions ($A_2^- =$ second order arithmetic) of initial segments of a given model of M of Peano arithmetic PA from a given A_2^-–expansion of M. We call expansions constructed in such a way trace–expansions. The technique of indicators is used. The properties of trace–expansion construction are studied.

MURCK, Christian (ed) and Bush, Susan (ed). *Theories Of The Arts In China*. Princeton Princeton Univ Pr 1983.

This symposium volume contains sixteen essays first produced for a 1979 conference sponsored by the American Council of Learned Societies to promote studies of Chinese aesthetics. Papers and introduction trace the evolution of terminology dealing with aesthetic appreciation in the context of China's holistic culture. Early Chinese concepts of moral philosophy, medicine, and cosmology, along with pre-modern theories of music, poetry, calligraphy, and painting, are discussed in comparison with each other and with Western developments.

MUREŞAN, Valentin. Der Praxiologische Wertbegriff. *Phil Log* 27,293–299 O–D 83.

MURPHY, B L. "Du Désordre Ál'ordre" in *Existential Coordinates Of Human Condition*, Tymieniecka, A (ed), 435–450. Boston Reidel 1984.

MURPHY, Claudia M. Anti–Reductionism And The Mind–Body Problem. *Phil Res Arch* 10,441–454 1984.

I argue that there are good reasons to deny both type–type and token–token mind–brain identity theories. Yet on the other hand there are compelling reasons for thinking that there is a causal basis for the mind. I argue that a path out of this impasse involves not only showing that criteria of individuation do not determine identity, but also that there are sound methodological reasons for thinking that the cause of intelligent behavior is a real natural kind. Finally, a commitment to this methodology suggests both that these familiar anti–reductionist arguments fail to establish that identity is impossible and at the same time suggest that the preferred alternative will be some version of neutral monism.

MURPHY, Ewell E. "Justice And Society: Beyond Individualism" in *The Search For Justice*, Taitte, W Lawson (ed), 101–126. Austin Univ Of Texas Pr 1983.

MURPHY, James J (ed). *Renaissance Eloquence: Studies In The Theory And Practice Of Renaissance Rhetoric*. Berkeley Univ Of Calif Pr 1983.

MURPHY, Jeffrie G. Justifying Departures From Equal Treatment. *J Phil* 81,587–593 O 84.

MURPHY, Jeffrie G. Retributivism, Moral Education, And The Liberal State. *Crim Just Ethics* 4,3–10 Wint/Spr 85.

Recent literature contains many attempts to justify punishment on retributive grounds or on the ground that punishment morally educates or improves the offender. These discussions tend to focus on the moral desirability of these goals and almost never raise the question of whether it is the *state's* legitimate business to pursue those goals. It is argued that the liberal theory of the state (captured in part in the constitutional doctrine of "compelling state interest") is inconsistent with these two justifications for punishment.

MURPHY, John W. Jacques Derrida: A Rhetoric That Deconstructs Common Sense. *Diogenes* 128,125–140 Wint 84.

Most often Derrida is understood to de–construct social life, thereby leaving behind only disorder. This portrayal of his work, however, is inaccurate. The rendition of order he advances is based on a version of rhetoric that has both an epistemological and ontological dimension. Accordingly, a communicative order is offered, which is normative without being representative.

MURPHY, John W. Niklas Luhmann And His View Of The Social Function Of Law. *Human Stud* 7,23–38 1984.

Luhmann argues that the traditional "centered" (realistic) image of social order is not appropriate for conceptualizing modern society. Social order must be based on direct discourse, or the recognition of differences, instead of the standard reality *sui generis*. Accordingly, Luhmann maintains that law should not be understood in terms of social ontological realism, as is typically the case. Law should be reflexive, thereby mediating the Self and Other and creating a society which encourages pluralism.

MURPHY, Timothy F. *Nietzsche As Educator*. Lanham Univ Pr Of America 1984.

This book attempts to establish that Nietzsche considered himself a philosopher not because he specifically engaged in metaphysics or epistemology, but because he attempted educating humanity about various patterns of living. Consequently he is to be taken seriously as a philosopher because he instructed in the art of human living. Various commentators (Heidegger, Kaufmann, and Dante among them) are investigated for the reasons they elevate Nietzsche to the rank of philosopher. (publisher)

MURPHY, Timothy F. The Moral Significance Of Spontaneous Abortion. *J Med Ethics* 11,79–83 Je 85.

Spontaneous abortion is rarely addressed in moral evaluations of abortion. Indeed, 'abortion' is virtually always taken to mean only induced abortion. After a brief review of medical aspects of spontaneous abortion, I attempt to articulate the moral implications of spontaneous abortion for the two poles of the abortion debate, the strong pro–abortion and the strong anti–abortion positions. I claim that spontaneous abortion has no moral relevance for strict pro–abortion positions but that the high incidence of spontaneous abortion is not (as some claim) eo ipso any sort of justification for voluntarily induced abortion. Secondly, I show that if the strict anti-abortionist position is to be taken seriously in its insistence that prenatal life has a right to be protected by virtue of its being conceived, then it seems necessary to take measures to prevent spontaneous abortion and its presumptive causes, and this as a matter of moral obligation.

MURRAY, Code. *Order & Organism: Steps To A Whiteheadian Philosophy Of Mathematics & The Natural Sciences*. Albany SUNY Pr 1985.

This work is an exploration of the relation between mathematics and the order of the world as this becomes manifest in science, especially in quantum physics. Recent advances indicate an urgent need for radical reinterpretation of fundamental notions, such as matter and natural law. It is maintained that the retroductive postulation of metaphysical schemes, such as that exemplified by A N Whitehead's theory of organism, is the most promising way to deal with this complex problem.

MURRAY, John Patrick and others and Dahlstrom, Daniel O. "Introductory: James Collins—The Man, The Scholar, The Teacher" in *History Of Philosophy In Making*, Thro, Linus J (ed), 1–18. Washington Univ Pr Of America 1982.

MURRAY, Kevin. Life As Fiction. *J Theor Soc Behav* 15,173–188 Jl 85.

The study of the everyday process of life construction may be aided by a marriage between the approaches of social science and literary criticism. The grounds for such a marriage can be found in the dramaturgical model, which uses the ways of the stage as a model of social behavior. The usefulness of this approach is demonstrated in the application of myth criticism to popular psychology and retirement.

MURRAY, Michael. The Conflict Between Poetry And Literature. *Phil Lit* 19,59–79 Ap 85.

MURRAY, Thomas H (ed) and Gaylin, Willard (ed) and Macklin, Ruth (ed). *Feeling Good And Doing Better; Ethics And Nontherapeutic Drug Use.* Clifton Humana Pr 1984.

This book is a collection of original articles developed by members of a Research Group over two years of discussion and debate on the ethics of drug use for enhancing pleasure or performance. Problems addressed include performance aids in sports, public policy towards nontherapeutic drug use, the "medical model," and the nature of pleasure; drug use and risk–taking; and legal and constitutional aspects of nontherapeutic drug use.

MURRAY, Thomas H. "Drugs, Sports, And Ethics" in *Feeling Good And Doing Better,* Murray, Thomas H (ed), 107–128. Clifton Humana Pr 1984.

MURRAY, Thomas H and Bayer, Ronald. "Ethical Issues In Occupational Health In Biomedical Ethics Reviews" in *Biomedical Ethics Reviews,* Humber, James M (ed), 153–174. Clifton Humana Pr 1984.

MURRAY, Thomas H and Lappé, Marc. The New Technologies Of Genetic Screening. *Hastings Center Rep* 14,18–23 O 84.

MUSGRAVE, Alan (ed) and Currie, Gregory (ed). *Popper And The Human Sciences.* Boston Nijhoff 1985.

MUSHKAT, Miron and Mushkat, Roda. The Legal Co–ordination Problem. *Riv Int Filosof Diritto* 61,638–646 O–D 84.

Jurists tend to perceive the application of the law by the courts as a mechanical process. The purpose of this article is to offer a more complex model of judicial decision–making. Specifically, the features of the law as a coordination mechanism are highlighted and the perceptual interdependence between judges and law subjects is underlined.

MUSHKAT, Roda and Mushkat, Miron. The Legal Co–ordination Problem. *Riv Int Filosof Diritto* 61,638–646 O–D 84.

Jurists tend to perceive the application of the law by the courts as a mechanical process. The purpose of this article is to offer a more complex model of judicial decision–making. Specifically, the features of the law as a coordination mechanism are highlighted and the perceptual interdependence between judges and law subjects is underlined.

MUYSKENS, James. "Ethical Issues Raised By The Patenting Of New Forms Of Life" in *Biomedical Ethics Reviews,* Humber, James M (ed), 187–200. Clifton Humana Pr 1983.

MUYSKENS, James. What Is Virtuous About Faith? *Faith Phil* 2,43–52 Ja 85.

The thesis of this essay is that fidelity rather than trust or belief is what makes faith a virtue. In opposition to Robert Adams, I argue that the trusting relationship that he discusses is faith's goal but not its virtue. Those who have attained the goal are not the sole possessors of the virtue of faith. It is present in doubtful as well as in trusting faith.

MYERS, David B. The Legalist Paradigm And MAD. *Int J Applied Phil* 2,19–32 Spr 85.

This paper is a critique of the claim that the nuclear strategy of mutual assured destruction is analogous to the penal theory of deterrence. I maintain that we are no longer talking about something significantly similar to domestic deterrence when we confront a doctrine which (1) conceives the *actual use* of the threatened punishment as an unmitigated disaster; (2) involves—if carried out—self destructive consequences such that the punisher is punished as severely as the offender; and (3) provides no agency of law enforcement.

NAERT, Emilienne. Double Infinité Chez Pascal Et Monade. *Stud Leibniz* 17,44–51 1985.

Um 1695 erläuterte Leibniz das Fragment von den "deux Infinis" (den beiden Unendlichkeiten) aus den *Pensées* von Pascal. In der umfassenden Darstellung der Monadenlehre—des Unendlichen, Unbegrenzten, das in jedem Endlichen, Begrenzten bereits impliziert ist—verändern sich der physische Punkt, welche das kleinste sichtbare Lebewesen bildet, und der mathematische Punkt, welcher die Mitte ist. Einerseits enthält jedes winzige Teilchen, jedes winzige Staubkorn eine Welt von unendlich vielen Lebewesen, "und die Mikroskope haben unseren Augen mehr als eine Million, levender Tierchen in einem Wassertröpfchen sichtbar gemacht". Dies ist die Theorie der Korpuskeln, wie sie sich im späteren Denken des Philsophen immer stärker abzeichnet und bestätigt: die Materie ist überall organisch. Andererseits ist die Mitte zwischen dem Nichts und dem All nicht mehr der Mensch, sondern die Monade, der einzige reale und exakte Punkt "das erste Fast–Nichts", "das letzte Fast Alles". Die Lektüre Pascals inspirierte Leibniz zu einem seiner grossartigsten Texte.

NAESS, Arne. *A Sceptical Dialogue On Induction.* Atlantic Highlands Humanities Pr 1984.

The so–called problem of inductive inference—what it is, its validity and scope—has not been decisively clarified or solved. In a friendly dialogue between and old Pyrrhonian Sceptic and representatives of contemporary philosophical schools, the former is the winner, if any.

NAGAOKA, Shigeo. On Mill's Qualitative Distinction Of Pleasures. *Mill News* 20,15–26 Sum 85.

NAGEL, Gordon. "Substance And Causality" in *Kant On Causality, Freedom, And Objectivity,* Harper, William A (ed), 97–107. Minneapolis Univ Minnesota Pr 1984.

NAGLE, Michael C and Thomason, S K. The Extensions Of The Modal Logic *K5*. *J Sym Log* 50,102–109 Mr 85.

NAILS, Debra. A Little Platonic Heresy For The Eighties. *Teach Phil* 8,33–40 Ja 85.

After a brief comparison of translations of Plato's *Republic,* three approaches to the structure of the Ideal City are illustrated. The first (Popperian) is medieval, including a dungeon of slaves, castes, and a philosopher–king; the second a hierarchy of classes led by a philosopher–ruler. The third depicts an equalitarian, horizontal

configuration: civil engineering, civil defense, and civil service, with a minister of education at the helm of society wherein intellect governs will and appetite in each individual.

NAILS, Debra. The Erotic Education Of The Slave. *S Afr J Phil* 4,1–7 F 85.

I maintain that Plato held *eros* to be the fundamental element of human psychology, and that his views about the erotic cannot be neglected in any fair formulation of his epistemology. Since the basic tenets of Plato's philosophy of education are constructed on epistemological—not political—principles, I conclude that Plato would favor an equalitarian state of educated individuals.

NAISH, Michael. Education And Essential Contestability Revisited. *J Phil Educ* 18,141–153 1984.

This article discusses the adequacy of W B Gallie's account of essential contestability. It argues that this account is seriously defective and offers a revision of it in terms of a distinction between concept and (competing) conceptions. This revised account is illustrated in a discussion of the concept of education. The article ends with some comments on the relationships between essential contestability, education, and political theory.

NAKAMURA, Hajime. The Non–logical Character Of Zen. *J Chin Phil* 12,105–116 Je 85.

NAKAYASU, Fujio and Hirose, Ken. "Representation For Spector Second Order Classes Computation Theory" in *Lecture Notes In Mathematics,* Muller, G H And Others (ed), 31–48. NY Springer 1981.

NAMBA, Kanji. "Boolean Valued Combinatorics" in *Lecture Notes In Mathematics,* Muller, G H And Others (ed), 117–154. NY Springer 1981.

NAMMOUR, Jamil. "Generality And The Importance Of The Particular Case" in *Philosophy And Life: Essays On John Wisdom,* Dilman, Ilham (ed), 241–270. Boston Nijhoff 1984.

NANDY, Ashis. Cultural Frames For Social Intervention: A Personal Credo. *Indian Phil Quart* 11,411–422 O–D 84.

Cultural traditions are a vital armory for the oppressed. What to the moderns look like a set of anachronisms, waiting to be museumised, hides a frame of reference shaping responses to violence, expropriation and ethnocide. The frame includes a native understanding of oppression and a native theory of survival and liberation. To establish a dialogue with this aspect of traditions, one must first learn to read the overtly irrational, ahistorical aspects of tradition as elements in a serious, alternative theory of our times.

NANJI, Azim A. Ethics And Taxation: The Perspective Of The Islamic Tradition. *J Relig Ethics* 13,161–178 Spr 85.

After tracing the foundational basis of taxation from the Qur'ān and early Islamic tradition, this paper studies the development and integration of tax policies within the moral framework of Islamic Law. It focuses on the role of jurists and scholars who sought to integrate and reconcile the Islamic values of taxation with changing economic and historical conditions and also touches upon attempts by modern Muslims to relate traditional values of taxation to contemporary economic life.

NAPOLI, Ernesto. Is Vagueness A Logical Enigma? *Erkenntnis* 23,115–122 Ag 85.

Vagueness has become a philosopher's nightmare. Philosophers have gone as far as saying that observational predicates infect language with inconsistency (Dummett) or other people and ordinary things do not exist (Unger). Some others, more on the positive side, have concerned themselves with infinitely many values, fuzzy sets, supervaluations. The purpose of the paper is to show that these are over–reactions since vaguenes and the sorites like paradoxes to which it supposedly leads do not pose any dramatic challenge either to our common sense beliefs or to classical logic.

NARDELLI, Domenica. Il De Coniecturis Nell'Epistemologia Di Nicolò Cusano. *Ann Fac Lett Filosof* 25 & 26,323–372 1982–83.

NARDI, Antonio. Spazi Del Moto In Divina Proporzione. *G Crit Filosof Ital* 63,334–376 S–D 84.

NARENS, Louis. *Abstract Measurement Theory.* Cambridge MIT Pr 1985.

NAROLL, Raoul. *The Moral Order: An Introduction To The Human Situation.* Beverly Hills Sage 1983.

The Moral *Order* looks at human social groups as having evolved through natural selection, and as governed most probably by cybernetic mechanisms which allow prediction and control—modeled by servomechanisms and positive feedback. The author's scope ranges from small–scale preliterate societies to modern nations sampled cross–culturally. Naroll applies socionomic standards to theory tests of universal social problems (mental illness, alcoholism, suicide, family problems, child abuse, youth stress, aging, sex roles, and the home). He finds that society is most damaged when the moralnet (the individual's social network, sustained by shared values) is weakened. He prescribes continued research into these profound problems, followed by corrective policy change.

NARSKI, I S. Kants Antinomien Und Die Logik Der Erkenntnis. *Deut Z Phil* 22,321–340 1984.

NARVESON, Jan. "Negative And Positive Rights In Gewirth's 'Reason And Morality'" in *Gewirth's Ethical Rationalism,* Regis Jr, Edward (ed), 96–107. Chicago Univ Of Chicago Pr 1984.

NARVESON, Jan. "Reason In Ethics—Or Reason Versus Ethics" in *Morality, Reason And Truth,* Copp, David (ed), 228–250. Totowa Rowman & Allanheld 1984.

NARVESON, Jan. Equality *Vs* Liberty: Advantage, Liberty. *Soc Phil Pol* 2,33–60 Autumn 84.

A number of arguments for economic equality as a right or major social goal are examined and found wanting. An attempt at a general characterization of the social ideal of liberty leads to the conclusion that only a private property conception of liberty is coherent. A contraction argument for a nearly–libertarian society concludes the essay.

NARVESON, Jan. Getting On The Road To Peace: A Modest Proposal. *Ethics* 95,589–605 Ap 85.

What is required if our intentions are strictly defensive, as we claim? First, that we must not adopt the most unfavorable hypothesis about enemy intentions, because to do so is to invite responses from him that will make matters worse. Second, that we should utilize the least threatening military establishment compatible with adequate defense, especially, ones that enable the enemy to reveal his non–threatening intentions if that's what he has. The proposed policy is a significant unilateral reduction in nuclear forces, to a level significantly less than the enemy's.

NASCIMENTO, Carlos A R. Three Explanatory Traditions In The Law Of Falling Bodies (in Portuguese). *Trans/Form/Acao* 6,5–12 1983.

This paper tries to show in the theoretical justification of the study of naturally accelerated motion in the *Discourses*, Galileo would have combined three not perfectly identical methodological attitudes. Those attitudes would be: the *ex-hypothesi* demonstration from the astronomical tradition, realistically interpreted; the necessary demonstration from the Aristotelian and Euclidean tradition; the typical demonstration of the "mixed sciences." Thus, even Galileo's last work would be far from unequivocal as it regards scientific methodology.

NASH, Paul. *Models Of Man: Explorations In The Western Educational Tradition.* Malabar Krieger 1983.

The motif of the book is the portrayal of a number of the most influential models of the educated person that have been created as part of the Western educational tradition. The purposes are to engender in the reader a broad knowledge of some of the dominant and persistent ideas and problems inherent in his/her own intellectual traditions; and to stimulate his/her to go further into the origins of this tradition in search of meanings and insights that are uniquely relevant to his/her own educational development.

NASH, Ronald H. *Christianity And The Hellenistic World.* Grand Rapids Zondervan 1984.

For at least a century, it has been fashionable in some circles to allege that first century Christianity borrowed essential beliefs and practices from the philosophical and religious systems of its time. This book examines such claims critically and finds the case for an early Christian syncretism unworthy of rational acceptance. Special attention is given to allegations of Christian dependence upon Platonism, Stoicism, Philo, the mystery religions, and Gnosticism.

NASR, S H. The Role Of The Traditional Sciences In The Encounter Of Religion And Science: An Oriental Perspective. *Relig Stud* 20,519–542 D 84.

NASR, Seyyed Hossein. "Progress And Evolution: A Reappraisal" in *The Good Life And Its Pursuit*, Dougherty, Jude P (ed), 163–174. NY Paragon House 1984.

NASR, Seyyed Hossein. Response To Thomas Dean's Review Of *Knowledge And The Sacred*. *Phil East West* 35,87–90 Ja 85.

NATALE, Samuel M and Mulcahy, John W. Social Systems Analytics And Ethics. *Thought* 60,205–220 Je 85.

This article summarizes the conflicts which exist between the ideographic and nomothetic dimensions within any organization. The article analyzes the inherent conflict between values, attitudes, needs and expectations using the VANE model of analysis. Ethical conflicts are suggested and approaches recommended.

NATALE, Samuel M and Wilson, John. First Steps In Moral And Ethical Education. *Thought* 60,119–140 Je 85.

The goal of this essay is to explore a new foundation for moral and ethical behaviors. The aim is to create empirical criteria which can be evaluated and assessed. A series of moral components are generated and methods of evaluation are explored. Emphasis is placed on implementing and operationalizing criteria which have been generally left untouched by most philosophers. The result is empirical research which touches on the problem of moral and ethical education.

NATHAN, Amos. The Fallacy Of Intrinsic Distributions. *Phil Sci* 51,677–684 D 84.

Jaynes contends that in many statistical problems a seemingly indeterminate probability distribution is made unique by the transformation group of necessarily implied invariance properties, thereby justifying the principle of indifference. To illustrate and substantiate his claims he considers Bertrand's Paradox. These assertions are here refuted and the traditional attitude is vindicated.

NATHANSON, Stephen. Does It Matter If The Death Penalty Is Arbitrarily Administered? *Phil Pub Affairs* 14,149–164 Spr 85.

Some argue that the death penalty ought to be abolished because it is imposed in an arbitrary and discriminatory manner. According to others, a punishment is just if the recipient deserves it; how other equally deserving people are treated is irrelevant. I try to show that arbitrariness and discrimination do matter and that it can be unjust to execute someone for murder even if he deserves to die.

NATHANSON, Stephen. Russell's Scientific Mysticism. *Russell* 5,14–25 Sum 85.

NATOLI, Charles M. *Nietzsche And Pascal On Christianity.* NY Lang 1985.

Although Pascal was one of the small group thinkers who influenced Nietzsche profoundly, he did not succeed in communicating to him his intense anxiety over the truth of Christian belief. Instead, Nietzsche chose to focus his trenchant anti–Christian polemics on the value of its effects on humankind. This study, one of very few on the Nietzsche/Pascal relationship, explores and appreciates the religious thought of each. It also assesses the nature and ground of their relationship and investigates the reasonableness of the Faith that divided them.

NATORP, Paul. Leibniz Und Der Materialismus (1881): Aud Dem Nachlass Herausgegeben Von Helmut Holzhey (zürich). *Stud Leibniz* 17,3–14 1985.

NATSOULAS, Thomas. George Herbert Mead's Conception Of Consciousness. *J Theor Soc Behav* 15,60–75 Mr 85.

NATSOULAS, Thomas. Gustav Bergmann's Psychophysiological Parallelism. *Behaviorism* 12,41–70 Spr 84.

NATSOULAS, Thomas. On The Causal Self–Referentiality Of Perceptual Experiences And The Problem Of Concrete Perceptual Reference. *Behaviorism* 12,61–80 Fall 84.

NAUMANN, Werner. Über Die Kategorien Inhalt Und Methode In Der Pädagogik. *Deut Z Phil* 22,443–457 1974.

NAUTA, L W. Exemplarische Bronnen Van Het Westers Autonomie–Begrip. *Kennis Methode* 8,190–208 1984.

NAUTA, Lolle. Historical Roots Of The Concept Of Autonomy In Western Philosophy. *Praxis Int* 4,363–377 Ja 85.

NAVARRO, Bernabé. Fray Alonso De La Veracruz, Misionero De La Filosofia. *Rev Filosof (Mexico)* 17,331–344 My–Jl 84.

NAWROCKA, Anna. Individual And State: The Consideration On Man's Dignity And Citizen's Duty In The Work *De Officiis* By M T Cicero (in Polish). *Stud Phil Christ* 20,91–110 1984.

NAYAK, G C. Religious Crisis, Hinduism And Common–ism. *Philosophica (India)* 10,28–35 Ja–D 81.

NAYLOR, Andrew. In Defense Of A Nontraditional Theory Of Memory. *Monist* 62,136–150 Ja 85.

A theory of occurrent factual memory knowledge is sketched out. The theory represents an alternative to John L Pollock's traditional theory in that it analyzes occurrently remembering that p without employing the notion of ostensible recollection that p. In defending his traditional theory against nontraditional alternatives, Pollock employs arguments that conflict with his own principle of implicit reasons. That principle, it is shown, sanctions cross–temporal justification of the sort presupposed by the alternative nontraditional theory.

NAYLOR, Margery Bedford. Voluntary Belief. *Phil Phenomenol Res* 45,427–436 Mr 85.

How is it possible for some person, S, to believe a given proposition, p, voluntarily— i.E., "at will," just because he has chosen to? I argue, first, that it is possible to induce, at will, the conviction that p is true. Then I argue that Alston's question 'Is S believing that p either (a) a "basic" act, or (b) a "necessary and immediate consequence" of a basic act'? Is irrelevant to the question, 'Does S believe that p voluntarily'? Finally, I formulate the necessary and sufficient conditions of voluntary belief in this way. s believes that p voluntarily if and only if (i) S chose to believe that p, and (ii) because he chose to believe that p, S himself brought it about, using means he himself chose to use, that he regards p as being conclusively evident or as being self–evident.

NAYLOR, Margery B. Frankfurt On The Principle Of Alternate Possibilities. *Phil Stud* 46,249–258 Mr 85.

Harry G Frankfurt gave what has been taken to be a counter–example to the principle that, "A person is morally responsible for what he has done only if he could have done otherwise." I argue that in his case the agent cannot be morally responsible for what he did, because it was not within his power not to be compelled to do it. So Frandfurt's case is not a counter–example to this principle.

NEAR, Janet P and Miceli, Marcia P. Organizational Dissidence: The Case Of Whistle–Blowing. *J Bus Ethics* 4,1–16 F 85.

NEELY, Alfred S. *Ethics–In–Government Laws: Are They Too "ethical"?* Washington AEI 1984.

This study addresses the question whether ethics–in–government laws create barriers to public service—Do they make entry and exit unnecessarily difficult, and can they discourage excellence? The author gives an overview of the existing law and analyzes their effects in a series of case studies. The direct costs of the present system are modest, according to the author, but the indirect costs may be much greater.

NEF, Robert. Die Kategorie Der Sache. *Stud Phil (Switzerland)* Supp 12,199–226 1983.

NELSON, Alan. Some Issues Surrounding The Reduction Of Macroeconomics To Microeconomics. *Phil Sci* 51,573–594 D 84.

This paper examines the relationship between modern theories of microeconomics and macroeconomics and, more generally, it evaluates the prospects of theoretically reducing macroeconomics to microeconomics. Many economists have shown strong interest in providing "microfoundations" for macroeconomics and much of their work is germane to the issue of theoretical reduction. Especially relevant is the work that has been done on what is called The Problem of Aggregation. On some accounts, The Problem of Aggregation just is the problem of reducing macroeconomics to microeconomics. I show how to separate these problems and then try to determine to what extent particular kinds of solutions to The Problem of Aggregation succeed in reducing macroeconomic to microeconomics as well. I argue that reduction is not possible by this means given the current state of microeconomics. I also describe how reduction may be possible by means of (dis)aggregation if microeconomics is supplemented in a certain way with the results of experimental research on individual economic agents.

NELSON, Jack. The Diversity Of Perception. *Synthese* 64,93–114 Jl 85.

NELSON, James A and Gartner, Lou Ann and Hull, Richard T. "Ethical Issues In Prenatal Therapies" in *Biomedical Ethics Reviews*, Humber, James M (ed), 225–250. Clifton Humana Pr 1984.

NELSON, James A. Recent Studies In Animal Ethics. *Amer Phil Quart* 22,13–24 Ja 85.

The last dozen years or so have seen a flurry of published work on the moral status of animals, and on the justifiability of their treatment at human hands. This article surveys that work, and also discusses some contributions to what might be called "philosophical ethology"—i.E., philosophical reflection on the nature of nonhuman animals.

NELSON, John O. How And Why Seeing Is Not Believing. *Phil Res Arch* 10,117–138 1984.

In this paper I attempt to show, first, that doxastic theories of seeing must be rejected on at least two counts: paradoxically, they commit us on the one hand to Pyrrhonic skepticism and on the other they fail to account for cases of defeasibility that a theory of perceiving ought to account for. So much for the "why". As for the "how" I attempt to show that a non–doxastic conception of seeing can be formulated, with the aid of theoretic interpretations of the perceiving of brute animals, which succeeds in overcoming the above two failings of doxastic theories.

NELSON, John O. Is Object–Seeing Really Propositional Seeing? *Phil Topics* 13,231–238 Spr 85.

The purpose of "Is Object–Seeing Really Propositional Seeing?" Is to show, in opposition to Hartnack and others, that the seeing of objects, construed as givens or presentations, is both logically and chronologically prior to propositional seeing, construed as the entertainment of propositions, as is beliefs. I present a variety of arguments to this effect, along with refutations of some main arguments appealed to by the propositionalist.

NELSON, R J. Naturalizing Intentions. *Synthese* 61,173–204 N 84.

This paper contrasts a number of attempts at naturalizing intentions including those of Quine, Searle, Hintikka, Smith, and McIntyre with my own approach in *The Logic of Mind*. I illustrate the latter with respect to the question of distinguishing between vague and precise perceptual expectations using a probabilistic automaton model. I conclude that satisfaction of the former is essentially unconscious, while that of the latter is a conscious *conceptual* activity.

NELSON, Thomas W. Philosophy In Teacher Education And Research. *Proc Phil Educ* 40,193–196 1984.

This is a response to Robin Barrow's "Teacher Education and Research: The Place of Philosophy." I support Barrow's critical comments in his Sections I and Ii and focus critically on Section Iii. I demonstrate that his three empirical generalizations about teacher education programs are faulty. His prescriptions for how our research in philosophy of education should be redirected lack explication of his main concepts, "central" and "problematic"; without such explication, these prescriptions give us little guidance.

NELSON, William N. Property Rights, Liberty And Redistribution. *Phil Topics* 13,133–140 Spr 85.

Defenders of liberty often view respect for property as a form of respect for liberty; but it is possible to argue for restrictions on property (e.G., redistributive taxation) just on the ground that property *restricts* liberty and that compensation is thus owed to those whose liberty is restricted. One argument of this form is examined and found wanting, but an alternative is developed and endorsed. In the process, it is argued that the relations between property and liberty are more complex than is often assumed by those on both sides.

NELSON, William. Equal Opportunity. *Soc Theor Pract* 10,157–184 Sum 84.

The question is whether there is an account of what equal opportunity requires under which it can *also* be given a plausible rationale. A number of analyses and possible rationales are considered and found wanting. The goal of equal opportunity for *specific* positions, it is argued, ought to be replaced by the goal of *universal* opportunity to live a *good* life.

NENON, Thomas (trans) and Marx, Werner. *The Philosophy Of F W J Schelling: History, System, And Freedom.* Bloomington Indiana Univ Pr 1984.

This book assesses Schelling's unique thought and its relevance for present–day philosophical issues. The first of three essays draws a comparison between Schelling's conception of history and that of the contemporary social philosopher Jürgen Habermas. The second part compares Schelling's *System of Transcendental Idealism* and Hegel's *Phenomenology of Spirit*. In the third part, the author demonstrates that Schelling resolved the problem of the relation of freedom to necessity through a metaphysics of the absolute.

NEPPI, Enzo. The Image Of The Father In Sartre's "L'universel Singulier" (in Hebrew). *Iyyun* 34,49–66 Ja–Ap 85.

The paper attempts to show that in "L'universel singulier"—written in 1966 on the relation between Hegel and Kierkegaard—an important shift takes place in Sartre's conception of fatherhood. The prevailing idea in Sartre's writing is that the paternal link is "rotten" (pourri). On the one hand, it is not possible to be a "father" without suppressing and silencing a child's desire for freedom. On the other hand, the only two possible responses left to the child are either violent revolt or servile submission and affective dependence. Most of Sartre's ideas about the Other, nothingness and freedom, bourgeois values, alienation and social conflicts may be traced back to this scheme. Kierkegaard's approach according to "L'universal singulier," is different. By his struggle against Hegelian science, by his refusal to be a "master thinker" and by his reluctance to propose any system or truth to his readers, Kierkegaard indirectly prompts future men to regard him as an anti–paternal model of freedom. In other words, if kierkegaard is a good, generous father figure, worthy of emulation, it is precisely because he rejects paternal values and refuses to play such a role. (edited)

NERI, Guido D. "Phenomenology And Aesthetics" in *Continental Philosophy And The Arts*, Winters, Laurence E and others (ed), 163–172. Lanham Univ Pr Of America 1984.

NERI, Miguel A Z. Palabra Y Deseo. *Rev Filosof (Mexico)* 18,89–98 Ja–Ap 85.

NERLICH, Graham and Westwell Roper, Andrew. What Ontology Can Be About: A Spacetime Example. *Austl J Phil* 63,127–142 Je 85.

Ontology can be about what structures, not merely about what objects, there are. A structural ontology of spacetime is about the relation of causal structures (for example) to topological on to metrical ones. To settle the questions which arise one needs to decide what is essential to the theory and what is contingent. This need gives rise to a distinction, which applies broadly, between a restrictive and a permissive core of a theory.

NERSESSIAN, Nancy J. Aether/Or: The Creation Of Scientific Concepts. *Stud Hist Phil Sci* 15,175–212 S 84.

This paper addresses the question of the nature of concept formation in science. A case study of some of the factors involved in the formation of the electromagnetic field concept is developed by considering the contributions of Faraday, Maxwell, Lorentz, and Einstein. It is argued that concept formation in science is a process in which we see commensurable, but not simply cumulative development. It is proposed that this process can be characterized as dividing into three stages: (a) 'heuristic guide', (b) 'elaborational' and (c) 'philosophical'.

NESVADBA, Petr. Some Aspects Of The Investigation Of Dialectic Of The Spontaneous And The Conscious In Social Development (in Czechoslovakian). *Filosof Cas* 33,12–21 1985.

NETOPILÍK, J. The Revolutionary Heritage Of Slovak National Uprising (in Czechoslovakian). *Filozof Cas* 32,577–595 1984.

NEUHAUS, Richard John. "New Hymns For The Republic: The Religious Right And America's Moral Purpose" in *On Freedom*, Howard, John A (ed), 112–132. Greenwich Devin–Adair 1984.

This is the second volume of *Biomedical Ethics Reviews*, an annually published series of texts designed to review and update the literature on issues of central importance in bioethics today. Nine articles address five topics: 1) Public Policy and Research with Human Subjects, 2) Genetic Screening, 3) Occupational Health, 4) The Right to Health Care in a Democratic Society, and 5) The Ethics of Fetal Research and Therapy.

NEUMAIER, Otto. Das Ästhetische Vor–Urteil. *Conceptus* 19,3–28 1985.

It is widely held within aesthetic theory that its subjects are "art and beauty." In this paper I shall argue that this is a prejudice causing a good deal of trouble for aesthetics. In particular, on this basis we are unable to account for the development of modern art. I first demonstrate the inadequacy of the traditional approach with an example. This inadequacy is then eliminated by adopting some of Aristotle's aesthetic categories. Finally some obstacles to understanding the new approach will be pointed out and discussed.

NEUMANN, Harry. Politics Or Nothing: Nazism's Origin In Scientific Contempt For Politics. *J Value Inq* 19,225–234 1985.

NEUMANN, Olaf. On The Definition Of Ordered *n*-Tupels. *Z Math Log* 30,197–198 1984.

NEVILLE, Michael. Nietzsche On Beauty And Taste: The Problem Of Aesthetic Evaluations. *Int Stud Phil* 16,103–120 1984.

Nietzsche offers a rather classical analysis of beauty but amends it in terms of his notion of strength. He also espouses a traditional view that only persons of "good taste" appreciate beauty. Yet he refrains from arguing for a set of criteria in light of which he could make universally valid aesthetic evaluations; mere agreement (consensus of aesthetic appreciations) is not of concern to him, and he would find no point in arguing for such criteria.

NEVILLE, Robert C. Philosophy And The Question Of God. *Int Phil Quart* 25,51–62 Mr 85.

The purpose here is to show the interesting compatibility of abstract metaphysics with heart religion, given a particular conception of God as creator of everything determinate. The dialectic sets this conception off from popular conceptions of God as finite.

NEVILLE, Robert. "The State's Intervention In Individuals' Drug Use: A Normative Account" in *Feeling Good And Doing Better*, Murray, Thomas H (ed), 65–82. Clifton Humana Pr 1984.

NEVIN, Thomas R. *Irving Babbitt: An Intellectual Study.* Chapel Hill Univ N Car Pr 1984.

This series of essays reviews Babbitt's application of European humanistic standards to problems which beset educational and political thought during America's Progressive Era. His prescription of a cultural decorum uniting Aristotelian tradition with Confucianism and Buddhism is also examined. This study concludes that while Babbitt's humanism was too aristocratic and exacting to secure general acceptance, its perspective on educational and political issues continues to impose a contemporary and critical relevance.

NEWELL, J David. The Case For Deception In Medical Experimentation. *Phil Context* 14,51–59 1984.

This essay argues that deception, when properly understood, can be justifiably used in research involving human subjects—even where informed consent is not obtained. An analysis of the concept of deception reveals the many and diverse forms deceptive practices take. It is argued that deception itself is a morally neutral strategy which can be justified in cases in which positive results are very likely and appropriate monitoring procedures are followed.

NEWELL, R W. "The Scope Of Reason: Wisdom, Kuhn And James" in *Philosophy And Life: Essays On John Wisdom*, Dilman, Ilham (ed), 219–240. Boston Nijhoff 1984.

NEWTON SMITH, W and Wilkes, K. Converging Reflections On The Philosophy Of Science. *Ratio* 27,1–6 Je 85.

This is the introduction to a selection of papers from the 1984 Dubrovnik Philosophy of Science seminar. It draws attention to a current convergence of interests on the part of philosophers of science in western and eastern bloc countries.

NEWTON– SMITH, W. The Role Of Interests In Science. *Philosophy* 18,59–74 84 Supp.

This paper considers the possibility that non–scientific interests might play a significant role in science. It is argued that such interests do not have any important effect in regard to theory choice in the physical sciences. It is further argued that on no viable thesis of the interest relative character of explanation do interest play a significant role in determining the content of science via determining what counts as a good explanation. However, it is suggested that interests may play a substantial role in determining the content of theories in the case of social sciences. The paper concludes with reflections on the role of interests in philosophy.

NEWTON, K M. Validity In Interpretation And The Literary Institution. *Brit J Aes* 25,207–219 Sum 85.

Although the dominant interpretative criterion within the literary institution is comprehensiveness of interpretation, in practice two logically contradictory perspectives operate: a text's interpetation (1) is determined by or (2) transcends its origins. The institution favors interpretations which hold these perspectives in balance, but this can only be partial criterion for validity, since several opposed interpretations could achieve this balance or interpretations which lack both balance and comprehensiveness could exert power within the institution for ideologica reasons.

NEWTON, Lisa H. "Surrogate Motherhood: The Ethical Implications" in *Biomedical Ethics Reviews*, Humber, James M (ed), 69–90. Clifton Humana Pr 1983.

NEWTON, Lisa and Wright, Richard A. "The Borrowed Syllabus". *Teach Phil* 7,235–240 Jl 84.

NG, Yew–Kwang. Interpersonal Level Comparability Implies Comparability Of Utility Differences. *Theor Decis* 17,141–148 S 84.

Contrary to the general view that no cardinal utility is involved in interpersonal comparisons of utility *levels*, it is shown that the general possibility of such comparisons really implies interpersonal comparison of utility *differences*. The sufficiency of ordinalism even just for level comparability is a mistaken belief.

NICGORSKI, Walter. Cicero's Paradoxes And His Idea Of Utility. *Polit Theory* 12,557–578 N 84.

Paradoxes involving Cicero's commitment both to the philosophic life and the political life and his skepticism and stoicism provides a sufficient basis for the strong tendency through the ages to question Cicero's integrity and importance as a philosopher, to regard him at worst as opportunistically eclectic or at best as hopelessly muddled. The paradoxes dissipate and a coherence and consistency is found in Cicero's teaching when the foundation of his philosophy is clearly understood. That foundation reveals the Socratic orientation of Cicero's thought and the idea of utility as Cicero's principle of coherence and consistency. That idea of utility is contrasted with the position of modern utilitarianism.

NICHOLLS, R P. The Meaning Of Chuang Tzu's Tao. *Eidos* 2,28–52 Jl 80.

NICHOLS, Rosalie. "Are Feminist Businesses Capitalistic" in *Freedom, Feminism, And The State*, Mc Elroy, Wendy (ed), 207–212. Cato Institute Washington 1982.

NICHOLS, Graeme. Seeing And Reading. New Jersey Humanities 1984.

NICHOLSON, Graeme. Developing Themes In Philosophy: Modern Continental Philosophy. *Eidos* 2,53–68 Jl 80.

NICKLES, Thomas. Beyond Divorce: Current Status Of The Discovery Debate. *Phil Sci* 52,177–206 Je 85.

Does the viability of the discovery program depend on showing either (1) that methods of generating new problem solutions, *per se*, have special probative weight (the *per se* thesis); or (2) that the original conception of an idea is logically continuous with its justification (anti–divorce thesis)? Many writers have identified these as the key issues of the discovery debate. McLaughlin, Pera, and others recently have defended the discovery program by attacking the divorce thesis, while Laudan has attacked the discovery program by rejecting the *per se* thesis. This disagreement over the central issue had led to communications breakdown. I contend that *both* friends and foes of discovery mistake the central issues. Recognizing a form of divorce helps rather than hurts the discovery program. However, the *per se* thesis is not essential to the program (nor is the related debate over novel prediction); hence the status of the *per se* thesis is a side issue. (edited)

NICKLES, Thomas. Justification As Discoverability II. *Phil Natur* 21,563–576 1984.

The viability of the "discovery program" depends on showing neither that: 1) methods of generating new problem solutions *per se* have special probative weight (the *per se* thesis) not that, 2) the original conception of an idea must be logically continuous with its justification (the anti–divorce thesis). Recognizing a form of divorce (between original discovery and discoverability—generative justification) helps rather than hurts the discovery program. Science needs and uses both generative and consequential justification.

NICOLOSI, Salavotore. Anatomia Del Potere: Dalla Logica Dell'Avere Alla Logica Dell'Essere. *Sapienza* 37,257–283 Jl–S 84.

NIELSEN, Kai. "A Marxist Conception Of Ideology" in *Ideology, Philosophy And Politics*, Parel, Anthony (ed), 139–162. Waterloo Laurier Univ Pr 1983.

NIELSEN, Kai. "Against Ethical Rationalism" in *Gewirth's Ethical Rationalism*, Regis Jr, Edward (ed), 59–83. Chicago Univ Of Chicago Pr 1984.

NIELSEN, Kai. "Must The Immoralist Act Contrary To Reason" in *Morality, Reason And Truth*, Copp, David (ed), 212–227. Totowa Rowman & Allanheld 1984.

NIELSEN, Kai. Global Justice, Capitalism And The Third World. *J Applied Phil* 1,175–186 O 84.

Reflecting on the North/South dialogue, I consider questions of global justice. I argue that questions of global justice are just as genuine as questions of domestic justice. I first set out concerning the situation in the North and the South and the relations between them coupled with some interpretive sociology. I then, while remaining mindful of the strains of commitment, argue that justice requires extensive redistribution between North and South but that this can be done without at all impoverishing the North, though to do so would indeed involve a radical re–ordering of the socio–economic system of the North. (edited)

NIELSEN, Kai. Historical Materialism, Ideology And Ethics. *Stud Soviet Tho* 29,47–64 Ja 85.

NIELSEN, Kai. Ideal And Non–Ideal Theory: How Should We Approach Questions Of Globel Justice. *Int J Applied Phil* 2,33–42 Spr 85.

NIELSEN, Kai. On Finding One's Feet In Philosophy: From Wittgenstein To Marx. *Metaphilosophy* 16,1–11 Ja 85.

NIELSEN, Kai. On Mucking Around About God: Some Methodological Animadversions. *Int J Phil Relig* 16,111–122 1984.

NIELSEN, Kai. The Role Of Radical Philosophers In Canada. *Eidos* 2,1–13 Jl 80.

NIELSEN, Kai. The Voices Of Egoism. *Phil Stud (Ireland)* 30,83–107 Spr 84.

NIELSEN, Kai. Wittgensteinian Moralism Ethnomethodology And Moral Ideology. *Indian Phil Quart* 11,189–200 Ap 84.

NIELSEN, Richard P. Pluralism In The Mass Media: Can Management Help? *J Bus Ethics* 3,335–342 N 84.

The potential danger to a democracy of a lack of plurality of media control is serious. There are opportunities for greater plurality and freedom of expression through professional employee decision making participation. There are practical precedents for professional employee management participation in the media. Therefore, professional media employee management participation deserves to be seriously considered. Limitations of the principle are also considered. (edited)

NIEMI, Richard G and Frank, Arthur Q. Sophisticated Voting Under The Plurality Procedure: A Test Of A New Definition. *Theor Decis* 19,151–162 S 85.

A test of the Niemi–Frank definition of sophisticated voting under the plurality procedure. The simulation, using randomly–sized blocs of voters, is limited to three alternatives. The Niemi–Frank and the Farquharson definitions yield identical outcomes whenever both are determinate; both pick a high proportion of Condorcet winners. The Niemi–Frank definition is determinate 80 percent of the time; Farquharson less than 50 percent. Strategic behavior yields the Condorcet winner more often than sincere voting.

NIEMINEN, Juhani. A Note On Simple Graphic Algebras. *Z Math Log* 21,365–367 1975.

NIETZSCHE, Fredrich and Faber, Marion (trans). *Human, All Too Human.* Lincoln Univ Nebraska Pr 1984.

NIEZNAŃSKI, E. Eine Klassische Ein—Und Mehr–Sortige Logik. *Stud Phil Christ* 20,97–112 1984.

NIINILUOTO, Ilkka. *Is Science Progressive?* Dordrecht Reidel 1984.

NINO, Carlos Santiago. "Limits Of The Enforcement Of Morality" in *Philosophical Analysis In Latin America*, Gracia, Jorge J E and others (eds), 93–114. Boston Reidel 1984.

NISHIHARA, Minoru. Über Die Ästhetischen Grundsätze Der Musik Bei H G Nägeli (in Japanese). *Bigaku* 35,51–61 S 84.

H G Nägeli (1773–1836), der Schweizer Musikpädagoge und Musikästhetiker war, ist bisher öfter im Zusammenhang mit Hanslick und Autonommusikästhetik diskutiert werden. Gebiss hat er vieles mit Hanslick gemein darin aussermusikalische Darstellung, die auf Literatur oder bildende Kunst beruht, zu verwefen und einen sogenannten "Inhalt" der Musik zu verneinen. (edited)

NISSEN, Lowell. Discussion: Woodfield's Analysis Of Teleology. *Phil Sci* 51,488–494 S 84.

Woodfield's analysis of teleology, though it has many virtues, nevertheless exhibits defects that are by no means peripheral. The acknowledged unity of teleological statements is removed because of the unnoticed difference between something being good and something appearing good. (edited)

NITZAN, Shmuel and Paroush, Jacob. A General Theorem And Eight Corollaries In Search Of Correct Decision. *Theor Decis* 17,211–220 N 84.

The main theorem established in this study and its corollaries summarize and generalize the existing results on optimal aggregation of experts judgments under uncertain pairwise choice situations. In particular, we explicate the link between the optimal decision procedure and the decision maker's preferences and biases and the judgmental competences of his consultants. The general theorem directly clarifies under what circumstances the optimal decision rule should be the democratic simple majority rule, the elitist rule, an intermediate weighted simple majority rule or a biased weighted or simple qualified majority rule.

NITZAN, Shmuel and Paroush, Jacob. Partial Information Of Decisional Competences And The Desirability Of The Expert Rule In Uncertain Dichotomous Choice Situations. *Theor Decis* 17,275–286 N 84.

The paper analyzes the expert resolution problem by employing extended versions of the uncertain dichotomous choice model. The main purpose of this study is to illustrate how the analysis of optimal decision rules can be carried out while dispensing with the common restrictive assumption of full information regarding individual decisional competences. In contrast to most previous studies in this field we here evaluate the expert rule under alternative assumptions regarding the available partial information on judgmental competences rather than compare it in an *ad hoc* manner to some common alternative rules, such as simple majority rule. A fuller optimality analysis allowing the evaluation of all relevant decision rules, and not merely the expert rule, is attempted for a five–member panel of experts assuming a uniform distribution of individual competences. For three–member groups the optimality issue is resolved by assuming no information on individual competences and interpreting the expert rule as an even–chance lottery on skills.

NIXON, Alan C. Commentary On B Lichter And M Hodges' "Perceptions Of The Engineers' 'Professionalism' In The Chemical Industry". *Bus Prof Ethics J* 2,15–18 Wint 83.

Licter and Hodges maintain that employed engineers cannot be truly professional because of the contra influence of their employers as demonstrated by workshops at Dupont and Tennessee Eastman. I challenged this on the basis of personal experience. The professional attitude can be fostered by professional societies if they operate independently of industry, otherwise professional unions are an alternative. Professional society employment guidelines are helpful but not legally enforceable. I advocated they be legalized.

NOACK, Klaus–Peter and Bönisch, Siegfried. Zu Einigen Unterschieden Zwischen Moralischen Normen, Werturteilen Und Aussagen. *Deut Z Phil* 23,818–829 1975.

NOLT, John Eric. Possible Worlds And Imagination In Informal Logic. *Inform Log* 6,14–16 Jl 84.

This article points out ways in which formal syntactic characterizations of validity and other logical concepts are inadequate in application to natural language reasoning and suggests an intuitive possible worlds semantics as a practical and pedagogically sound alternative framework for characterizing logical concepts applicable to natural languages.

NOMOTO, Hisao and Tugue, Tosiyuki. "Independence Of A Problem In Elementary Analysis From Set Theory" in *Lecture Notes In Mathematics*, Muller, G H And Others (ed), 307–322. NY Springer 1981.

NOONAN, H W. A Note On Temporal Parts. *Analysis* 45,151–152 Je 85.

NOONAN, H W. The Only x And y Principle. *Analysis* 45,79–83 Mr 85.

NOONAN, Harold W. Methodological Solipsism: A Reply To Morris. *Phil Stud* 48,285–290 S 85.

NOONAN, Harold W. The Closest Continuer Theory Of Identity. *Inquiry* 28,195–230 Je 85.

A plausible principle governing identity is that whether a later individual is identical with an earlier individual cannot ever merely depend on whether there are, at the later time, any *better candidates* for identity with the earlier individual around. This principle has been a bone of contention amongst philosophers interested in identity for many years. In his latest book *Philosophical Explanations* Robert Nozick presents what I believe to be the strongest case yet made out for the rejection of this principle. My aim in this paper is to argue, with reference in particular to personal and artifact identity, that Nozick's case can be met and that a theory of identity which entails the correctness of this principle is the equal, indeed the superior, in explanatory power of the theory Nozick develops on the basis of its rejection.

NOONAN, Harold W. Wiggins, Artefact Identity And 'Best Candidate' Theories. *Analysis* 45,4–8 Ja 85.

NOONAN, Harold. Fregean Thoughts. *Phil Quart* 34,205–224 Jl 84.

The aim of this paper is to defend the utility of Frege's notion of a thought against three sets of objections: those of the methodological solipsists, those of John Perry, and those of Tyler Burge. The discussion is concerned with indexicals, proper names and natural kind terms, the explanation of action and the analysis of belief sentences.

NORDBERG, Robert B. Is Education Real—A Reply To Robin Barrow. *Educ Theor* 35,201–202 Spr 85.

Robin Barrow had argued that "What is education?" Does not make sense if it implies an unalterable idea that will always answer to the name. This reply to Barrow argues that a real, as opposed to a nominal definition of education is possible, and defines education as "guided learning." As a logical universal, this idea is eternal. Hence, it is possible to say what education is in itself and unchangeably.

NORDQUIST, Gerald L. On The Risk–Aversion Comparability Of State–Dependent Utility Functions. *Theor Decis* 18,285–300 My 85.

We consider here the problem of how to measure risk aversion in the case of state–dependent utility. It is proved that two state–dependent utility functions are risk–aversion comparable (in the sense of Arrow–Pratt) on the set of sure (certain) wealth if the marginal rate of substitution of wealth across states is identical on the set. This extends and complements a similar result due to E Karni (*International Economic Review*, 24, October, 1983).

NORMANN, D and Girard, Jean–Yves. Set Recursion And $\Pi 1/2$–Logic. *Annals Pure Applied Log* 28,255–286 My 85.

Set recursion generalizes usual recursion by keeping the formal aspect, but forgetting effectivity. Dilators—functors from ordinals to ordinals preserving direct limits and pullbacks—enable us to deal with ordinals while keeping a finitary control. In this paper the authors reduce some uses of set–recursion (e.G., on a recursively inaccessible) to iteration along recursive dilators. The reduction is successful, but for the function enumerating the admissibles and their limits, which cannot, of course, be eliminated.

NORMORE, Calvin. "Buridan's Ontology" in *How Things Are*, Bogen, James (ed), 189–204. Boston Reidel 1985.

NORRIE, Alan. Thomas Hobbes And The Philosophy Of Punishment. *Law Phil* 3,299–320 Ag 84.

In this article I argue for a full appraisal of Hobbes' theory of punishment which takes account of its divergent and contradictory aspects. Examining his theory within the general context of his position in *Leviathan*, it is possible to see its centrality for the subsequent development of the modern philosophy of punishment. From this point of view, it is also possible to pinpoint the source of a central weakness in the retributive theory of punishment.

NORRIE, Kenneth McK. Medical Negligence: Who Sets The Standard? *J Med Ethics* 11,135–137 S 85.

'the law imposes the duty of care; but the standard of care is a matter of medical judgment'. So says Lord Scarman, outlining the hitherto accepted 'Bolam' standard, in his recent speech in the House of Lords decision of Sidaway v Bethlem Royal Hospital, reflecting earlier judicial dicta suggesting that it is for the medical profession rather than the courts to determine whether or not a medical practitioner has achieved the required standards of care. It is suggested here that this concept is bad in principle, and that the weight of judicial authority is against it.

NORRIS, Stephen P. Competencies As Powers. *Proc Phil Educ* 40,167–178 1984.

In this paper I have contrasted a strongly realist analysis of the nature of human

competencey with the positivistic conception often espoused in educational circles. I have contrasted the manner of establishing claims about people's competencies according to these two conceptions. The realist position I have outlined can lead to greater coherence in thinking and research about human abilities. I have indicated a few instances in which thinking of competencies as powers will provide insight into certain debates and long–standing problems concerning our knowledge of human abilities and our ways of measuring them. I hope to have provided reason to move away more forthrightly from positivistically–motivated research and conceptions of human competencies.

NORTON SMITH, Thomas Michael. A Consideration Of Hilary Putnam. *Auslegung* 11,493–504 Sum 85.

NORTON, David F. Hutcheson's Moral Realism. *J Hist Phil* 23,397–418 Jl 85.

In response to Kenneth Winkler's criticism of my suggestion (found in my *David Hume: Common Sense Moralist, Sceptical Metaphysician*) that Frances Hutcheson embraced an interesting form of moral realism. I show important differences between Hutcheson and Locke, amplify my previous account of Hutcheson's notion of concomitant ideas, and provide evidence that Hutcheson's contemporaries, including his student Adam Smith, believed him to have maintained "that there is a real and essential distinction between vice and virtue". (*Theory of Moral Sentiments*)

NORTON, John. What Was Einstein's Principle Of Equivalence? *Stud Hist Phil Sci* 16,203–246 S 85.

I examine what Einstein took his principle of equivalence to assert, how it figured in the historical development of general relativity and sketch out why Einstein believed his principle to extend the principle of relativity to acceleration. Einstein's principle was not the traditional infinitesimal principle, against which he raised a devastating objection. His principle was formulated in Minkowski spacetimes only and provided the crucial insight that gravitation could be accounted for by a spacetime metric.

NOTTURNO, M A. Frege's Justificationism: Truth And The Recognition Of Authority. *Metaphilosophy* 15,210–224 Jl–O 84.

NOVÁK, Vladimir J A. Biological Conception Of Evolution And The Problem Of Thermodynamics From The Standpoint Of The Work Of I Prigogine (in Czechoslovakian). *Filozof Cas* 32,839–844 1984.

The question is considered from the point of view of the work by Ilya Ptigogine. His conception of dissipative structures is stimulating as concerns the problem of origin of life but less so where applied to nervous activity and growth problems. Completely misleading are his conclusions against dialectical materialism, even if he seems to be more informed than J J Monod. His observations against subjectivity/relativity/ of time are positive and important.

NOVÁKY, Erzsébet and Hideg, Eva. Modelling And Models In Future Research (in Hungarian). *Magyar Filozof Szemle* 5,712–728 1983.

The authors had a threefold objective: to give a general idea of a model–concept that will also include the models used in future research, to outline the role of the model–methods in the cognition of future, and to define the special characteristics of modelling in future research. In order to fulfill these goals, the authors first give a brief historic survey of modelling and their conclusions drawn from it, then they examine the main types of model–definition that can distinctly be separated from each other from the view–point whether they reflect and if they do so, how, the epistemological and practical aspects and those of the methodology of epistemology. For the authors hold the opinion that these functions must be fulfilled by all models. (edited)

NOWAKOWSKA, Maria. On A Formal Structure Of A Dialogue. *Synthese* 63,343–354 Je 85.

NOWIŃSKI, Czeslaw. Biologische Gesetze Und Dialektische Methode. *Deut Z Phil* 23,926–937 1975.

NUCHELMANS, Gabriel. Bezeichnen Und Behaupten. *Conceptus* 8,45–52 1974.

On the level of the contents of such complete speech acts as asserting, asking, ordering, and wishing a problem arises which is very similar to the much discussed problem of universals. On the one hand, there seem to be good reasons to assume a peculiar kind of being for that which is asserted (asked, ordered, wished), a kind of being that is different from the way in which denoted things exist. On the other hand, the ontological unclarity of such states of affairs easily leads to theories which, in some way or other, try to replace the suspect notion of an asserted state of affairs by the less objectionable notion of a denoted thing. Already in ancient and medieval philosophy noteworthy arguments were abduced for each of these views.

NUGAYEV, R M. The History Of Quantum Mechanics As A Decisive Argument Favoring Einstein Over Lorentz. *Phil Sci* 52,44–63 Mr 85.

Einstein's papers on relativity, quantum theory, and statistical mechanics were all part of a single research program; the aim was to unify mechanics and electrodynamics. It was this broader program—which eventually split into relativistic physics and quantum mechanics—that superseded Lorentz's theory. The argument of this paper is partly historical and partly methodological. A notion of "crossbred objects"—theoretical objects with contradictory properties which are part of the domain of application of two different research programs—is developed that explains the dynamics of revolutionary theory change.

NUGAYEV, Renat. A Study Of Theory Unification. *Brit J Phil Sci* 36,159–173 Je 85.

NUNAN, Richard. Novel Facts, Bayesian Rationality, And The History Of Continental Drift. *Stud Hist Phil Sci* 15,267–308 D 84.

Lakatosian and Bayesian insights are treated as a complementary package rather that as rival models of rational theory choice. Imre Lakatos's conception of competing research programs is applied to the Bayesian problem of revising prior conditional probability estimates, and a new (Bayesian) account of novel facts is substituted for those proposed by Lakatos, Elie Zahar, and Henry Frankel. These suggestions are then employed to examine the initial rejection and subsequent acceptance of continental drift.

NURMI, Hannu. Some Properties Of The Lehrer–Wagner Method For Reaching Rational Consensus. *Synthese* 62,13–24 Ja 85.

The article describes Lehrer's and Wagner's procedure for finding a rational consensus in a group. Some well–known criteria of evaluating the social choice methods are then employed to evaluate the rational consensus procedure. The criteria used in the evaluation are i.E. Manipulability, consistency and Pareto criterion. In terms of these criteria, it turns out that the procedure leaves quite a few things to be desired.

NUSSBAUM, Martha. Aeschylus And Practical Conflict. *Ethics* 95,233–267 Ja 85.

NUSSBAUMER, Josef and Holleis, Wilfried. Zum Okologiegehalt Der Nationalökonomie. *Conceptus* 18,52–82 1984.

The essay deals with the question, how different historical schools of economic theory and the present (neoclassical) theory tackle the problem of ecology in their conceptions. Amongst the schools analyzed are Classical Economic Theory, Early–Marxian and Marxian Economics, the German Historical School, the Marginalists, and Institutionalism. After having examined the Neoclassical Paradigm and the so–called "Alternative Economics", the essay concludes with an outlook into the future concerning the possible development of economic theory under the impact of ecological problems.

NUTE, Donald. "Conditional Logic" in *Handbook Of Philosophical Logic*, Gabbay, Dov (ed), 387–440. Boston Reidel 1984.

NUTE, Donald. Permission. *J Phil Log* 14,169–190 My 85.

A semantics for permission is provided having features of both classical semantics for deontic logics and class selection function semantics for conditional logics. In this semantics, A is permitted if all the closest worlds where A is performed and where the agent does all he can, compatible with doing A, to fulfill all his obligations, are deontically accessible worlds. A solution to the problem of choice permissions is proposed.

NUTTER, Warren G. *Political Economy And Freedom.* Indianapolis Liberty Pr 1983.

NWODO, C S. Language And Reality In Martin Heidegger. *Indian Phil Quart* 12,23–36 Ja–Mr 85.

NYIRI, Kristóf. Ehrenfels And Eastern Europe (in Hungarian). *Magyar Filozof Szemle* 1–2,70–92 1984.

Christian von Ehrenfels ist als der Wegbereiter der *Gestalt–Theorie*, als der von Mach und Brentano inspirierte Entdecker der philosophischen Grundlagen der *Gestalt–Psychologie* berühmt geworden, aber auch seine Werttheorie, Sexualethik und *Kosmogonie* fand seinerzeit Widerhall, und erweckt heute wieder ein gewisses Interesse. (edited)

O CONNOR, Patricia A. "Truth Telling In Pediatrics–In Degrees" in *Difficult Decisions In Medical Ethics*, Ganos, Doreen L (ed), 189–194. NY Liss 1983.

O' CALLAGHAN, Timothy M B. Prose Rhythm: An Analysis For Instruction. *J Aes Educ* 18,101–110 Fall 84.

Prose rhythm is analyzed in a way that allows for the variability of readers. It is characterized as involving alternating units, the altercation being either smooth or staccato. Types of alternating units are examined along with criteria for evaluating them. A logical sequence for a course on the appreciation of prose rhythm is described.

O' CONNELL, Robert J. *William James On The Courage To Believe.* Bronx Fordham Univ Pr 1984.

This study views "The Will to Believe" in connection with James's other work, particularly his popular lectures, and against the background of his indebtedness to Renouvier and Pascal. In that light, James is successful in validating the will's intervention in the formation of our *weltanschaulich* "over–beliefs"; crucial to his argument, surprisingly, is the contention that our "passional nature" does and must legitimately intervene, not after, but before and throughout our intellectual weighing of the evidence.

O' CONNELL, Robert J. God, Gods, And Moral Cosmos In Socrates' Apology. *Int Phil Quart* 25,31–50 Mr 85.

In *Plato's Thought* (1935) G M A Grube contends that *theos* did not have an anthropopsychic (read: personal) meaning for Plato. That contention has influenced, among others, W K C Guthrie in *The Greek Philosophers* (1950). But it is based on a mistranslation *cum* misinterpretation of Wilamowitz–Moellendorf; Plato's faithfully Socratic notion of *theoi* as personal guardians of our "moral cosmos" is, paradoxically, more accurately fleshed out in Guthrie's *The Greeks and Their Gods* (1950).

O' CONNOR, David. On Natural Evil's Being Necessary For Free Will. *Sophia (Australia)* 24,36–44 Jl 85.

via consideration of what I maintain is a failed argument of Swinburne's, I argue for a solution to theism's problem of reconciling the existence of evil with the God of traditional theism. In particular, I argue for a way of seeing natural evil as logically necessary for freedom of choice.

O' CONNOR, William Riordan. The *Uti/Frui* Distinction In Augustine's Ethics. *Augustin Stud* 14,45–62 1983.

This paper studies the *uti/frui* distinction in Augustine's ethics—his notion that some things are to be enjoyed while others are merely to be used—in relation to two charges that have been brought against his ethics by Karl Holl and Anders Nygren. Holl and Nygren have claimed that Augustine's ethics is based on egoism and dictates an instrumental attitude towards others. A review of the key texts shows that Augustine's teleology allows him to transcend egoism and that the primary sense of "use" for him is non–instrumental. A final selection deals with the roles of eudaemonism and deontology in Christian ethics.

O' CONNOR, William R. The Concept Of The Person In St Augustine's *De Trinitate. Augustin Stud* 13,133–144 1982.

This paper examines Paul Henry's claim that Augustine broke with the traditional view of the human person as a substance and A C Lloyd's criticisms of that claim. An examination of the texts shows that while it cannot be said that Augustine developed a relational view of the human person, he did model the external relations of human persons on the internal relations of the persons of the Trinity and that this lays the foundation for a relational view of the human person.

O' DONNELL, John. The Mystery Of Faith In The Theology Of Karl Rahner. *Heythrop J* 25,301–318 Jl 84.

O' DONOVAN, Joan E. *George Grant And The Twilight Of Justice.* Toronto Univ Of Toronto Pr 1984.

O' FARRELL, Francis. Problematic Of Kant's Determinants Of Practical Reason—II. *Gregorianum* 66,517–537 1985.

This second part considers first the problems of practical reason's determinant to object: why it is required? Why it must be a practical concept of the category of freedom? Why it must determine both to the morally good and to the highest good. It then examines the problems of the determinant called incentive: What its difference from determining ground is? Why it is on it that the morality of the willed depends. It finds that the difference in the human will between the will as will and the will as subject to sensible influences is why there must be the determinant incentive.

O' FARRELL, Francis. Problematic Of Kant's Determinants Of Practical Reason—I. *Gregorianum* 66,269–293 1985.

The article considers that the notion of practical reason proper to Kant, i.E., the capacity of determining itself unconditionally is concentrated in the question of practical reason's determinants. This first part treats the determinant called determining ground. It first traces the development in Kant's writings of the notion of will and its identity with practical reason as hinging on the determining ground. It considers the function of determining ground and how it constitutes the subject of will and its relation to maxim.

O' FARRELL, Frank. Kant's Transcendental Ideal—II. *Gregorianum* 65,635–656 1984.

Dans cette seconde partie de l'article, l'auteur étudie comment la notion du possible, dans la forme qu'elle atteint finalement dans la pensée de Kant—ses stades de développement ont été retracés dans la première partie—requiert qu'il soit comme l'idéal transcendantal sous lequel Dieu doit être pensé dans la philosophie transcendantale. L'étude cherche à clarifier la complexité de cette notion et comment elle est seul concept que nous pouvons avoir d'un singulier. L'auteur discute ensuite la question de savoir l'idél transcendental est un objet ou purement une idée et donc la question de son caractère illusoire. Il traite de l'dèe, dialectiquement objectivisée sous l'idél transcendental,dans sa fonction subjective d'idée, l'inconditionnel de la troisième analogie de l'expérience et ainsi la forme de la sysématique de toutes les synthèses de l'entendement—la forme de raison correspondant á l'espace dans la sensibilité.

O' GORMAN, Paschal. Quine's Epistemological Naturalism. *Phil Stud (Ireland)* 30,205–219 Spr 84.

O' HAGAN, Timothy. Must Time Have A Stop? *J Brit Soc Phenomenol* 15,231–242 O 84.

Starting from Heidegger, Kojève, Sartre, and Derrida, the author investigates an unresolved tension within Hegel's conception(s) of time, a tension between: (a) historicism, according to which all Spirit's manifestations (cultural, political, theoretical) are embedded within an untranscendable historical context, within which alone they have meaning; (b) absolutism (millenarian in tone), according to which the day of (Hegelian) science is now dawning, when the normal criteria for application of temporal predicates no longer apply, in short "time must have a stop".

O' HEAR, Anthony. Imprisonment. *Philosophy* 18,203–220 84 Supp.

A Benthamite view of human nature forms the background to current systems of imprisonment. But these systems fail to reform, and are directed mainly against feeble and petty lower class offenders. In the absence of sound empirical knowledge of the deterrent effects of penal policy, bold experiments should be made in the handling of petty offenders, with the stress on separation for offenses, rather than deterrence or retribution, imprisonment to be reserved for the small minority of provenly dangerous criminals.

O' HEAR, Anthony. Reply To Peter Glassen's "O'Hear On An Argument Of Popper's". *Brit J Phil Sci* 35,377–380 D 84.

Against the arguments of Popper and Glassen that it cannot be rational to hold physical determinism (because if we are determined to accept a belief, then its truth or rationality cannot explain why we accept it), I argue that a belief might both be rational and determined in the believer without undermining the distinction between beliefs based on good grounds and those based on bad grounds. It would be intelligible for the determinist to regard his belief in determinism as brought about in him rationally (i.E., by truth–promoting methods).

O' LOUGHLIN, M A and Walker, J C. The Ideal Of The Educated Woman: Jane Roland Martin On Education And Gender. *Educ Theor* 34,327–340 Fall 84.

Contrary to the "maternalism" of Martin's version of "gender–sensitive" educational theory and practice, which implies a specifically feminine educational ideal, it is argued that the qualities historically associated with women's role in reproduction are neither a sufficient nor on their own a desirable source of political and educational objectives. A non–essentialist epistemology is advocated, as against Martin's epistemological "female essentialism" which further entrenches the epistemic inequality of women.

O' NEIL, Michael P. Propositions And Empirical Evidence. *Phil Topics* 13,213–222 Spr 85.

O' NEIL, Patrick M. Ayn Rand And The Is–Ought Problem. *J Liber Stud* 7,81–100 Spr 83.

This article demonstrates that Ayn Rand and her natural law reinterpreters failed to fulfill her claim to have bridged Hume's is/ought gap through her Objectivist ehtical philosophy. While exploring the nature of the is/ought problem, this piece shows the impossibility of solving the difficulty by positing life both as the *summum bonun* and as a *sine qua non* for the act of valuing.

O' NEILL, Louis. Le Développement: Utopie Et Projet. *Laval Theol Phil* 41,361–383 O 85.

Un impératif fait l'unanimité: se libérer du sous–développement et progresser vers le développement. Mais de celui–ci il n'est pas aisé de se faire une idée adéquate. Une facon de procéder apparaît fructueuse: dégager les composantes intégrales de développement que mettent en lumière les problématiques socio–économiques et politiques et, à partir de là, construire une définition opéarationnelle. Ainsi, rejoint–on l'idée que se fait du développement la pensée sociale chrétienne: utopie et projet, entreprise de dimension cosmique où doivent solidairement s'engager pays riches et nations en voie de développement.

O' NEILL, Onora. Paternalism And Partial Autonomy. *J Med Ethics* 10,173–178 D 84.

A contrast is often drawn between standard adult capacities for autonomy, which allow informed consent to be given or withheld, and patients' reduced capacities, which demand paternalistic treatment. But patients may not be radically different from the rest of us, in that all human capacities for autonomous action are limited. An adequate account of paternalism and the role that consent and respect for persons can play in medical and other practice has to be developed within an ethical theory that does not impose an idealised picture of unlimited autonomy but allows for the variable and partial character of actual human autonomy.

O' ROURKE, James J (ed) and Blakeley, Thomas J (ed) and Rapp, Friedrich J (ed). *Contemporary Marxism: Essays In Honor Of J M Bocheński.* Boston Reidel 1984.

O' ROURKE, James J. "Soviet Philosophical Anthropology And The Foundations Of Human Sciences" in *Contemporary Marxism*, O' Rourke, James J (ed), 167–174. Boston Reidel 1984.

O' ROURKE, James J. The Value Theory Of V P Tugarinov. *Stud Soviet Tho* 28,109–116 Ag 84.

O' ROURKE, Kevin D and Ashley, Benedict M. *Health Care Ethics: A Theological Analysis.* St Louis Cath Health Assoc 1982.

A comprehensive treatment of bioethics from a Roman Catholic, but ecumenical, perspective. Patients' rights, professional ethics, confidentiality, the social organization of health care, scarce resources, reproduction, transplantation, experimentation, genetic reconstruction, behavior control, dying and pastoral care are treated in detail. Chapters seven and eight provide a systematic discussion of the methodology and guiding principles of medical–ethical decision. Extensive bibliography and index.

OAKES, Robert. Mysticism, Veridicality, And Modality. *Faith Phil* 2,217–235 Jl 85.

OAKES, Robert. Theism And Pantheism Again. *Sophia (Australia)* 24,32–37 Ap 85.

OAKESHOTT, Michael. *On History And Other Essays.* Totowa Barnes & Noble 1983.

Three essays: first and longest is historigraphical: the identification of 'history' as an autonomous mode of enquiry and understanding. Historical enquiry is not designed to recover a past of actions and utterances modes as they were understood by their authors but to infer, from authenticated survivals. Second: the 'rule of law' considered as a mode of human relationship. Third: a modern version of the myths of the Tower of Babel.

OAKLANDER, L Nathan. *Temporal Relations And Temporal Becoming: A Defense Of A Russellian Theory Of Time.* Lanham Univ Pr Of America 1984.

The aim of this book is to defend the so–called B–theory of time according to which time consists solely of temporal relations between and among temporal objects. The strategy is to first consider and reject various passage (A–) theories and then state and defend the tenseless view against the numerous objections that have been raised against it. Particular attention is paid to the topic of translatability and fatalism.

OAKLANDER, L Nathan. A Reply To Schlesinger's "How To Navigate The River Of Time". *Phil Quart* 35,93–94 Ja 85.

In his reply to my paper, "McTaggart, Schlesinger, and the Two–Dimensional Time Hypothesis," Schlesinger claims to show that "there is no doubt that the transient theory of time is consistent and intelligible". In my reply I shall argue that the situation he describes is irrelevant to the task he wants to accomplish, and that, therefore, doubt does indeed arise concerning the coherence of the theory he propounds.

OCHOCKI, Aleksander. The Dialectics Of Subjectivity. *Dialec Hum* 10,81–98 Sum 83.

ODAJNYK, V Walter. On Strong's *Psychoanalysis As A Vocation: Freud, Politics, And The Heroic.* *Polit Theory* 12,601–604 N 84.

ODEGARD, Douglas. Analytical Approaches To Determinism. *Dialogue (Canada)* 23,271–280 Je 84.

ODEN JR, Robert A. Taxation In Biblical Israel. *J Relig Ethics* 12,162–181 Fall 84.

This essay represents an initial attempt to provide a comprehensive account of the systems of taxation described and/or mandated in the Hebrew Bible for various periods in ancient Israel. Beyond this preliminary descriptive task, a concentration here is upon the ethical evaluation of these taxation systems—evaluations both according to voices within the Hebrew Bible and according to the general criteria of freedom, equity, and distributive justice.

OESTERLE, Jean T. Medalist's Address: The Importance Of Philosophy And Of This Association. *Proc Cath Phil Ass* 58,17–22 1984.

OESTERREICH, Peter Lothar. Schellings Weltalter Und Die Ausstehende Vollendung Des Deutschen Idealismus. *Z Phil Forsch* 39,70–84 Ja–Mr 85.

The work tries to prove the superior importance of Schelling's *Weltalter* drafts (1811–1813). Their conception eventually led to a successful union of philosophy, myth, and *Lebenswelt* having been demanded before by the *Ältestes Systemfragment*. Based on the problem metaphor of "The Veiled image if isis" connected with a complex of ontobiologist, speculative evolutionary, and transcendental hermeneutical ideas a new paradigm is established: Schelling's panhistorical *Weltalter*–Idealism.

OFFE, Claus. *Contradictions Of The Welfare State*, John Keane (ed). Cambridge MIT Pr 1984.

ÖFFENBERGER, Niels and Moriconi, Enrico. Zur Frage Der IV: Syllogistischen Figur In Der "Dissertatio De Arte Commbinatoria", Eine Jugendsünde Leibnizens? *Stud Leibniz* 16,212–216 1984.

This paper is a discussion of Leibniz's juvinile thesis according to which "quarta figura aequè bona est ac ipsa prima; imò si modo, non praedicationis, ut vulgò solent, sed subjectionis, ut Aristoteles, eam enunciemus, ex IV fiet I et contra" (DAC 25). The authors maintain that that thesis is syllogistically untendable, since the reduction device Leibniz suggested does not change the logical function of Termini, but introduces a difference only from a grammatical point of view.

OGDEN, Schubert M. The Metaphysics Of Faith And Justice. *Process Stud* 14,87–101 Sum 85.

The relation between faith and justice has metaphysical as well as moral implications. Faith and justice are in principle different because faith is a matter of self–understanding while justice is a matter of human action. At the same time, faith and justice are in principle connected insofar as any self–understanding necessarily has implications for human action. But just as the moral implication of faith is the demand for justice, including political justice, so the justice that faith demands implies certain metaphysical positions, including "self" as duplex, "God" as dipolar, and "world" as attributively monistic but substantively pluralistic.

OGER, Francis. The Model Theory Of Finitely Generated Finite–By–Abelian Groups. *J Sym Log* 49,1115–1124 D 84.

In [o1], we gave algebraic characterizations of elementary equivalence for finitely generated finite–by–abelian groups, i.E., finitely generated FC–groups. We also provided several examples of finitely generated finite–by–abelian groups which are elementarily equivalent without being isomorphic. In this paper, we shall use our previous results to describe precisely the models of the theories of finitely generated finite–by–abelian groups and the elementary embeddings between these models.

OHRSTROM, Peter. Buridan On Interval Semantics For Temporal Logic. *Log Anal* 27,211–216 Je 84.

In this paper the basic ideas of Buridan regarding temporal logic are outlined. It is argued that Buridan's logic of time was a durational logic which involved two kinds of negation.

OKIE, Laird. Ideology And Partiality In David Hume's "History Of England". *Hume Stud* 11,1–32 Ap 85.

The article surveys critical reaction to Hume's *History of England* since its publication, focusing particularly on recent assessments. The author argues that recent commentators have exagerrated Hume's objectivity and critical acumen. Although Hume was not a Tory, he wrote his *History* to repudiate the Whig consensus. In the process he employed Royalist/Tory sources uncritically and reiterated untenable Tory positions.

OKOLO, Chukwudum Barnabas. African Socialism And Nyerere. *Phil Soc Act* 10,63–82 Ja–Je 84.

The article reviews the various meanings of "African Socialism" among contemporary African leaders and intellectuals, but focuses particulary on its meaning in Nyerere of Tanzania. His brand of "African Socialism" is called "Ujamaa Socialism". "ujamaa" (family–hood) becomes the basis of this socialism since it points to the social life of traditional extended African family.

OKOLO, Chukwudum Barnabas. Negritude: A Philosophy Of Social Action. *Int Phil Quart* 24,427–438 D 84.

One of the major historical factors which helped the contemporary black African in his self–understanding and knowledge of his world is the literal and cultural movement known as Negritude. It originated in Paris in the mid–thirties with three great names of Aime Cesaire, Leon Damas and Leopold Senghor. The article is a reflection on the meaning, root–causes and ultimate significance of this movement. Negritude, we concluded, was essentially a philosophy of social action.

OLDENQUIST, Andrew. Commentary On K Alpern's "Moral Responsibility For Engineers". *Bus Prof Ethics J* 2,49–52 Wint 83.

OLDING, A. Short On Teleology. *Analysis* 45,158–161 Je 85.

This article consists of a critical examination of T L Short's recent argument that teleological explanations of the Aristotelian sort are required in statistical mechanics and the Darwinian theory of evolution. The precise nature of Short's claim is looked at and it is argued that one cannot on the pain of contradiction, introduce the notion of final causes into these theories.

OLEN, Jeffrey. *Persons And Their World: An Introduction To Philosophy.* NY Random House 1983.

OLIVER, Harold H. *Relatedness: Essays In Metaphysics And Theology.* Macon Mercer Univ Pr 1984.

In this volume Oliver develops the theological and hermeneutical implications of the metaphysical theory set forth in his A Rational Metaphysics (1981, Nijhoff). The ten essays propose a major reinterpretation of religious discourse, of the ethical dimensions of religion, and of the nature of selfhood. A relational interpretation of the intentionality of myth is developed as an alternative to rationalism and historicism. Finally a relational view of selfhood is proposed as an alternative to the Western Augustinian view.

OLIVER, Kelly A. Woman As Truth In Nietzsche's Writing. *Soc Theor Pract* 10,185–200 Sum 84.

OLIVER, R Graham. Through The Doors Of Reason: Dissolving Four Paradoxes Of Education. *Educ Theor* 35,15–32 Wint 85.

OLSEN, Stein Haugom. "Understanding Literary Metaphors" in *Metaphor*, Miall, David S (ed), 36–54. Atlantic Highlands Humanities Pr 1982.

OLSON, Alan M. On Primordialism Versus Postmodernism: A Response To Thomas Dean. *Phil East West* 35,91–96 Ja 85.

A discussion of some of the issues in the foundationalist versus anti–foundationalist debate in hermeneutics and interpretation theory. This essay is a response to the position of Thomas Dean (in a previous issue of *Philosophy East and West*) that a post–modern hermeneutic is necessarily anti–primordialist. Olson takes the position that the choice between foundationalism and anti–foundationalism, primordialism and post–modernism is unnecessary and ill–founded when one attends to basic issues in epistemology and cognitional theory.

OMORI, Atsushi. Hermeneutik Des Lebens Und Ästhetik Bei Wilhelm Dilthey (in Japanese). *Bigaku* 35,14–25 Mr 85.

Als Dilthey seine philosophische Arbeit begann, war es für ihm schon unmöglich, zwischen Ich und Welt metaphysische oder transzendentale Bedingungen anzunehmen und damit die Erkenntnisse der Welt zu fundieren. Man kann in seinem philosophischen Standpunkt einen Wandel erkennen, den man für die Folge seiner ständigen Reflexionen über den Grund des Philosophierens halten darf. Wie schon öfter dargelegt, tritt dieser Wandel vom Psychologischen zum Hermeneutischen auch im Bereich der ästjhetischen Gedanken heraus. (edited)

ONAIYEKAN, John. De Dignitate Et Jure Hominis Status Quaestionis In "Tertio Mundo" (in English). *Gregorianum* 65,473–481 1984.

ONDRACKA, Pavel. The Painter Otakar Marvánek As Art Critic (in Czechoslovakian). *Estetika* 21,142–160 1984.

ONO, Hiroakira. "Undecidability Of Extensions Of Monadic First–order Theory" in *Lecture Notes In Mathematics*, Muller, G H And Others (ed), 155–174. NY Springer 1981.

ONO, Hiroakira and Komori, Yuichi. Logics Without The Contraction Rule. *J Sym Log* 50,169–201 Mr 85.

Propositional logics without structural rules are studied. Firstly, Gentzen–type formal systems for them are introduced, and then the semantics is defined by using partially ordered monoids. Completeness theorems are shown. Our approach will offer a common ground in the study of nonclassical logics, since it can cover a wide variety of logics, including the intuitionistic logic, Lukasiewicz's many–valued logics, relevant logics, non–monotonic logics and so on.

ONYEWUENYI, Innocent C. Traditional African Aesthetics: A Philosophical Perspective. *Int Phil Quart* 24,237–244 S 84.

The paper is an attempt to show the cultural difference between Western and African aesthetics. While the primary aim of Western art is to communicate personal experience and individualized intuition of the artist, African art has specific social function; it is community–oriented, depersonalized, contextualized and embedded. The philosophical basis of this difference rests on an understanding of Western metaphysics vis–a–vis African metaphysics. It is therefore erroneous to attach or impose descriptive terms deriving from Western art culture on African art.

OPALEK, Kazimierz. Die Rechtstheorie In Polen Im XX: Jahrhundert. *Arch Rechts Soz* 59,551–570 1973.

In legal theory of this period an integrative tendency (making use of results, methods and conceptual apparatus of other disciplines) as well as specialization (separation of sociology of law, logical–semantic analyses and legal cybernetics) has to be noted. (edited)

OPOKU, Kwame. Law And Social Order: On Leopold Pospisil's Anthropology Of Law. *Arch Rechts Soz* 60,265–274 1974.

OPPENHEIM, Felix. 'Constraints On Freedom' As A Descriptive Concept. *Ethics* 95,305–309 Ja 85.

OPPENHEIM, Lois. "The Field Of Poetic Constitution" in *Existential Coordinates Of Human Condition*, Tymieniecka, A (ed), 47–60. Boston Reidel 1984.

ORAYEN, Raul. "On The Inconsistency Of Meinong's Ontology" in *Philosophical Analysis In Latin America*, Gracia, Jorge J E and others (eds), 115–140. Boston Reidel 1984.

ORENSTEIN, Alex. Referential And Nonreferential Substitutional Quantifiers. *Synthese* 60,145–158 Ag 84.

It is common to find philosophers claiming that it is possible to free the quantifiers from question of ontology, by having recourse to what is now referred to as the substitutional interpretation of the quantifiers. Although there may be ontologically neutral uses of the substitutional interpretation, it is one of the goals of this paper to point out where this feature has been misconceived and to give equal due to uses of the substitutional account that have ontological import.

ORLETTI, Franca. Some Methodological Problems In Data Gathering For Discourse Analysis. *J Prag* 8,559–568 Ag 84.

What criteria do we need to build up a body of data and how can we identify the relevant phenomena in the analysis of natural communicative events? In this paper two methodological principles are compared: the linguistic principle and the microsociological one. When applied to the data, both principles reveal their limitations. The linguistic approach is too aprioristic, whereas the microsociological approach is overly dependent on the data analyzed. By suggesting a combination of the two approaches this paper stresses the function of metacommunicative practices, i.E., contextualization cues, as well as researcher intuitions, as heuristic devices.

ORLOWSKA, Ewa. Modal Logics In The Theory Of Information Systems. *Z Math Log* 30,213–222 1984.

ORTIZ– OSÉS, Andrés. Modelos Hermenéuticos Y Mitológicos. *Rev Port Filosof* 40,291–306 Jl–S 84.

En el artículo realizo un estudio del trasfondo mitológico que antecede a la Grecia clásica y a la Filosofía. Dicho trasfondo ofrece la materia prima de la posterior elaboración filosófica. Se estudia Creta, Eleusis, Delfos y Atenas, asi como el paso del sustrato matriarcal al patriarcal–racionalista.

ORUKA, H Odera. Ideology And Truth. *Praxis Int* 5,35–50 Ap 85.

A purpose of this article is to assess the extent to which *ideology* can be true or false. I explain two main elements in an ideology: belief and norm. The first makes ideology capable of truth–value, the second may not, but it is subservient to the former. The conclusion is that it is rationally possible to judge an ideological claim true or false and to make a cognitive choice between two rival ideological claims.

ORZSCHIG, Johannes and Jurgens, Madeleine. Korrespondenten Von G W Leibniz. *Stud Leibniz* 16,102–112 1984.

Brosseau, résident (1671–1717) of the Dukes of Hannover, got to know Leibniz in Paris. His correspondence and friendship with the philosopher helped to enlarge the république des lettres, "greatly animated by Leibniz" and "a consolation amidst the evils which ambition and politics are spreading over the earth" (Voltaire).

OSBORNE, Harold. Creativity, Progress, And Personality. *J Phil Educ* 18,213–221 1984.

The extraordinarily rapid progress of the human race has been achieved by means of social, not biological, evolution. This demands continual innovation to be perpetuated in tradition. Creative persons, who introduce valuable novelty, are probably few; those who perpetuate are many. Both are necessary if progress is to continue. We also speak of creativity in the sense of the integration of personality. Education is in a key position both for the perpetuation of tradition and for the cultivation of integrated personality.

OSBORNE, Harold. Mathematical Beauty And Physical Science. *Brit J Aes* 24,291–300 Autumn 84.

The purpose of the paper is to analyze the concept of intellectual beauty as it occurs in mathematics and scientific theory. The following qualities are most generally assumed to be constitutive of this beauty: coherence, rigour and lucidity of ideas; simplicity in the sense of economy of basic principles; elegance; predictive power and fertility in leading to new knowledge. The paper mentions the faith of many leading contemporary scientists that a mathematically beautiful theory will turn out to be in accordance with known facts and productive of new knowledge.

OSBORNE, Harold. Moral And Aesthetic Values. *Rep Phil* 8,41–46 1984.

The paper outlines the pervasiveness of aesthetic considerations in practical life outside the fine arts, including the "virtues" such as courage, loyalty, consideration for others, etc., which we approve but do not regard as moral duties. It then considers cases where aesthetic and moral values conflict. Moral duties cannot be justified by reason except by derivation from a higher moral principle. It is suggested that the recognition and justification of the ultimate moral principles is aesthetic in character.

OSBORNE, Harold. Museums And Their Functions. *J Aes Educ* 19,41–52 Sum 85.

After a short historical introduction the main thesis of the paper is to argue that a primary function of museums of art today should be to lead and guide public taste in the changing world of art production as was done in the past by wealthy patrons, etc.

OSCANYAN, Frederick. Critical Thinking: Response To Moore. *Teach Phil* 7,241–247 Jl 84.

Brooke Moore's argument in *Teaching Philosophy* (volume 6, 321–330, Oct 83), that the concept of critical thinking is hopelessly vague, is rejected. Citing texts used for teaching critical thinking, I argue that the concept specifically includes standards for evaluating mental acts and means for applying such criteria. A concept of reflective thinking is then introduced and shown better to meet a California state educational requirement than would elementary logic as Moore claims.

OSLER, Margaret. Eternal Truths And The Laws Of Nature: The Theological Foundations Of Descartes' Philosophy Of Nature. *J Hist Ideas* 46,349–362 Jl–S 85.

The purpose of this paper is to argue that Descartes' views on the status of eternal truths and the laws of nature derive from his views about the nature of God's relationship to the creation. Just as his theology is not strictly intellectualist, but contains some components of voluntarism, so his ontology is a mixture of realism and nominalism, and his epistemology of science is a mixture of rationalism and empiricism.

OST, David E. The 'Right' Not To Know. *J Med Phil* 9,301–312 Ag 84.

There is a common view in medical ethics that the patient's right to be informed entails, as well, a correlative right not to be informed, i.E., to waive one's right to information. This paper argues, from a consideration of the concept of autonomy as the foundation for rights, that there can be no such 'right' to refuse relevant information, and that the claims for such a right are inconsistent with both deontological and utilitarian ethics. Further, the right to be informed is shown to be a mandatory right (though not a welfare right); persons are thus seen to have both a right and a duty to be informed. Finally, the consequences of this view are addressed. (edited)

OSTERFELD, David. The Natural Rights Debate: A Comment On A Reply. *J Liber Stud* 7,101–114 Spr 83.

OTABE, Tanehisa. Wirkung Und Anwendung Der Poesie—Untersuchungen Zur Ästhetik Herders (in Japanese). *Bigaku* 35,26–38 Mr 85.

Die Ästhetik Herders hat noch den Charakter der aufklärerischen Wirkungsasthetik. Es stellt sich jedoch die Frage, in welchem Verhältnis dazu sein historishes Denken steht. Ist es richtig, dass zwischen beiden eine nicht augetragene Gegensatzspannung besteht (P Szondi)? überprüfen wir daraufhin besonders seine Theorie der Poesie. (edited)

OTAKPOR, Nkeonye. On The Relation Between Science And Logic. *Indian Phil Quart* 12,85–98 Ja–Mr 85.

OTTE, Richard. Probabilistic Causality And Simpson's Paradox. *Phil Sci* 52,110–125 Mr 85.

This paper discusses Simpson's paradox and the problem of positive relevance in probabilistic causality. It is argued that Cartwright's solution to Simpson's paradox fails because it ignores one crucial form of the paradox. After clarifying different forms of the paradox, it is shown that any adequate solution to the paradox must allow a cause to be both a negative cause and a positive cause of the same effect. A solution is then given that can handle the form of the paradox that Cartwright's solution ignored, and allows causes to be both a positive and a negative cause of an effect.

OVER, D E. Explaining Donnellan's Distinction—A Reply. *Analysis* 44,191–194 O 84.

OWENS, Joseph. "How Flexible Is Aristotelian "Right Reason"" in *The Georgetown Symposium On Ethics*, Porreco, Rocco (ed), 49–66. Lanham Univ Pr Of America 1984.

OWENS, Joseph. "Is Philosophy In Aristotle And Ideology:" in *Ideology, Philosophy And Politics*, Parel, Anthony (ed), 163–178. Waterloo Laurier Univ Pr 1983.

OZAR, David T. Do Corporations Have Moral Rights? *J Bus Ethics* 4,277–281 Ag 85.

My aim in this paper is to explore the notion that corporations have moral rights within the context of a constitutive rules model of corporate moral agency. The first part of the paper will briefly introduce the notion of moral rights, identifying the distinctive feature of moral rights, as contrasted with other moral categories, in Vlastos' terms of overridingness. The second part will briefly summarize the constitutive rules approach to the moral agency of corporations (à la French, Smith, Ozar) and pose the question of the paper. The third part will argue that, since the moral agency of corporations is dependent on the choices of those whose acceptance of the relevant rules constitutes the corporation as a moral agent, the rights of corporations are conventional, that is, they exist because they are so created. Thus, as a first answer, corporation do not have moral rights. (edited)

OZAR, David T. Social Ethics, The Philosophy Of Medicine, And Professional Responsibility. *Theor Med* 6,281–294 O 85.

The social ethics of medicine is the study and ethical analysis of social structures which impact on the provision of health care by physicians. There are many such social structures. Not all these structures are responsive to the influence of physicians as health professionals. But some social structures which impact on health care are prompted by or supported by important preconceptions of medical practice. In this article, three such elements of the philosophy of medicine are examined in terms of the negative impact on health care of the social structures to which they contribute. The responsibilities of the medical profession and of individual physicians to work to change these social structures are then examined in the light of a theory of profession.

PACHO, Julian. Über Einige Erkenntnistheoretische Schwierigkeiten Des Klassischen Rationalismus. *Z Phil Forsch* 38,561–581 N–D 84.

Starting from Descartes' Wax–Exempel, Pacho criticizes the idea of the classical rationalism, that pretends to cure the reason of its own excesses only with the means of the reason. It is shown that this rationalism does not have a theorie capable to justify the use of predicates dependent or independent from experience. Pacho concludes that this deficiency comes from a philosophical atavism consisting in believing in the absolute epistemological autarky of the pure reason.

PADEN, Roger. On The Discourse Of Pornography. *Phil Soc Crit* 10,17–38 Sum 84.

This article presents an analysis of the liberal and conservative arguments on the morality of pornography which shows that they both assume an unstated theory of sexuality and human nature. This theory, it is argued, also underlies pornography itself and is responsible for its erotic value. This theory is subjected to a philosophical analysis which shows it to be false, but self–fulfilling. The results of this analysis are then reapplied to the question of the morality of pornography.

PADEN, Roger. Surveillance And Torture: Foucault And Orwell On The Methods Of Discipline. *Soc Theor Pract* 10,261–272 Fall 84.

The use of torture in the modern world as a method of social control is compared to the regimes of punishment that Foucault describes in *Discipline and Punish*. It is found to be a unique social institution. The results of this comparitive analysis are used both to explain the current distribution of torture and to explain why both Orwell and the enlightened humanist have failed to accurately predict the future of torture.

PAGE, Edgar. Parental Rights. *J Applied Phil* 1,187–204 O 84.

This paper is concerned with the philosophical foundations of parental rights. Some commonly held accounts are rejected. The question of whether parental rights are property rights is examined. It is argued that there are useful analogies with property rights which help us to see that the ultimate justification of parental rights lies in the special value of parenthood in human life. It is further argued that the idea of generation is essential to our understanding of parenthood as having special value and that parental rights properly belong, in the first instance, to natural parents.

PAGE, Ralph C. Choosing Between Love And Logic. *Proc Phil Educ* 40,17–20 1984.

PAGEL, Walter. *Paracelsus: An Introduction To Philosophical Medicine In The Era Of The Renaissance.* NY Karger 1982.

PAGEL, Walter. *The Smiling Spleen: Paracelsianism In Storm And Stress.* NY Karger 1984.

PAHI, Biswambham. Jankov–Theorems For Some Implicational Calculi. *Z Math Log* 21,193–198 1975.

PAINE, Lynda Sharp. Children As Consumers: An Ethical Evaluation Of Children's Advertising. *Bus Prof Ethics J* 3,119–146 Spr/Sum 84.

The author argues that television advertising directed to young children does not fully satisfy the principle of consumer sovereignty. Since young children's conceptions of self, time, and money do not equip them to make responsible consumer decisions, their parents' role in these decisions must be taken into account. The author examines how children's advertising works and concludes that increased consumer satisfaction and increased sales do not correspond when the sales are achieved through child-oriented advertising.

PALA, Alberto. Methodologies, History Of Science And Dialectical Materialism. *Scientia* 118,627–658 1983.

Nell'articolo si presuppone che esista un'interazione fra l'"oggetto' scienza e la storia di esso. Per questa ragione le metodologie più frequentemente impiegate dagli odierni orici della scienza vengono esaminate per stabilire quanto rispettino quel presupposto o quanto se ne allontanino. Si comincia con Gentile e Preti per passare al più diffuso (almeno in Italia) metodo della storia delle idee. Viene osservato che pur avendo numerosi titoli di merito, la storia delle idee è viziata da unilateralità 'idealistica'; inoltre non riesce a spiegare il differente ritmo evolutivo della conoscenza scientifica e della conoscenza generale. (edited)

PALLADINO, Franco. Origine E Diffusione Del Calcolo Differenziale In Italia: Con Un'Appendice Di Lettere Inedite. *G Crit Filosof Ital* 63,377–405 S–D 84.

PALLAVIDINI, Renato. Eticità E Logica Nella Crisi Jenense Del Pensiero Di Hegel. *Filosofia* 35,217–243 Jl–O 84.

PALMER, Richard E. "On The Transcendability Of Hermeneutics" in *Hermeneutics*, Shapiro, Gary (ed), 84–95. Amherst Univ Of Mass Pr 1984.

PALMQUIST, Stephen. Faith As Kant's Key To The Justification Of Transcendental Reflection. *Heythrop J* 25,442–455 O 84.

Kant bases his Critical System on theoretical faith in the assumption of the thing in itself as the starting point of transcendental reflection. After this claim is clarified and defended, the inadequacy of any attempt to justify transcendental reflection with transcendental arguments is demonstrated. Finally, Kant's use of theoretical faith is contrasted with his use of moral faith, which is often mistakenly regarded as the only context in which he ever employs this key concept.

PANASIUK, Ryszard. From Absolute Reason To Finite Reason. *Dialec Hum* 11,359–364 Spr/Sum 84.

The author supposes various tendencies of the contemporary philosophy result from a disintegration of the classical German philosophy. It is particulary concerned with the concept of reason. Absolute reason of Schelling and Hegel has now become the finite reason of men. In this way man achieved an independent existence as a moral being, and the world lost rational absolute values.

PANASIUK, Ryszard. Marx—Anthropology And Praxis. *Dialec Hum* 10,141–156 Sum 83.

The author holds that in Marxian thought one can find an original concept of genesis and nature of human being. Man as a sensitive and rational being, existing in society and history, appeared and progressed by work, on the ground of productive activity. Act of work as purposeful activity, which satisfies the vital needs of man and is directed towards the transformation of the object—world constitutes the base and the very structure of all the various forms of the creative activities of man.

PANELLA, Giuseppe. Le "Reflections On The Revolution In France": Categorie Dell'Agire Politico E Filosofia Della Storia In Edmund Burke. *G Crit Filosof Ital* 63,200–216 My–Ag 84.

PANGLE, Thomas L. Socrates On The Problem Of Political Science Education. *Polit Theory* 13,112–137 F 85.

This article establishes the authenticity and provides a detailed interpretation of Plato's dialogue *Theages*. Socrates' elaboration of the chief meanings and goals of political science (*epistemē pliitilcē*), and the dangers to democracy of such a science, leads to a drama and a discussion that illuminates how Socrates himself, as a model teacher, carried on education in politics. The "demonic voice or sign" is in this dialogue fully explained, as a key to Socrates' teaching.

PANICHAS, George E. Marx's Moral Skepticism. *Can J Phil* Supp 7,45–66 1981.

This paper considers the theoretical and methodological origins of Marx's beliefs and attitudes towards classical moral theories so as to answer two questions: (1) In what sense, if at all, was Marx suspicious of classical moral views and theories?, and (2) What sort of moral position could a proponent of Marx's views support?

PANIKKAR, Raimundo. Global Perspectives: Spiritualities In Interaction. *J Dharma* 10,6–17 Ja–Mr 85.

The first way is to explode the "Global Village" syndrome, as if there were one single perspective to see the world, and thus denying a rightful pluralism. The awareness that there is a single issue is part of the problem itself. Second, to analyze secularity distinguishing it from secularization (an historical fact) and secularism (an ideology). Secularity does not necessarily exclude transcendence and can also be sacred. It is the conviction that the spatio–temporal and materials structures of the universe, and of Man especially, are not just passing phases, but that they belong to the warp and woop of reality.

PANNENBERG, Wolfhart. Atom, Duration, Form: Difficulties With Process Philosophy. *Process Stud* 14,21–30 Spr 84.

PANOVA, Elena. "Substance And Its Logical Significance" in *Methodology, Metaphysics And The History Of Science*, Cohen, Robert S (ed), 235–246. Boston Reidel 1984.

PAOLINELLI, Marco. Verità Delle Azioni: Sul Fraintendimento Humiano Di W Wollaston. *Riv Filosof Neo–Scolas* 76,185–229 Ap–Je 84.

PAOLO, Rossi. *The Dark Abyss Of Time: The History Of The Earth And The History Of Nations From Hooke To Vico*, Lydia G Cochrane (trans). Chicago Univ Of Chicago Pr 1985.

Fossilized seashells far from the sea, sacred writings older than the Bible: geological and anthropological discoveries such as these began a revolution that led to new scientific theories about the Earth and the origins of the Universe and to a new consideration of human history. The same philosophical problems were discussed by theologians and biologists, geologists and philologists. The book is concerned with great and obscure speakers in the debate from Lepeyrère to Vico's *Scienza Nuova*.

PAPER, Jordan. A Critical Look At "A Critical Look": Castaneda Recrudescent. *J Mind Behavior* 5,501–504 Autumn 84.

A recent article by Kootte (1984) criticized critics of Castaneda's writings for the temerity to question the veracity of Castaneda's "scientific" reports of shamanistic experience. A minimal familiarity with studies of shamanism of the last decade by historians of religions or of Mesoamerican cultures by anthropologists clearly indicates Castaneda's literary works are fictional. As fiction, his novels can be appreciated for their synthesis of concepts from many cultures. However, to consider these works a basic and unquestionable source of data for social scientists is to deny the foundation of social science—to give priority to faith over reason.

PAPI, Fulvio and others (ed). *Il Tempo Dell'Arte*. Milano Franco Angeli 1984.

PAPI, Fulvio. "Canetti E La Metafisica Involontaria" in *Il Tempo Dell'Arte*, Papi, Fulvio and others (ed), 139–155. Milano Franco Angeli 1984.

PAPINEAU, David. "Social Facts And Psychological Facts" in *Popper And The Human Sciences*, Currie, Gregory (ed), 57–72. Boston Nijhoff 1985.

PAPINEAU, David. Probabilities And Causes. *J Phil* 82,57–73 F 85.

The "standard view", according to which causes make their effects highly probable, and the "statistical-relevance view", according to which causes increase the probability of their effects, are contrasted with an "evidential approach", which takes probabilities to be indirect evidence for underlying causal connections, rather than the substance of such connections. It is argued that once the evidential approach is taken into account, the standard and statistical relevance views lose their attractions.

PAPINEAU, David. Representation And Explanation. *Phil Sci* 51,550–572 D 84.

Functionalism faces a problem in accounting for the semantic powers of beliefs and other mental states. Simple causal considerations will not solve this problem, nor will any appeal to the social utility of semantic interpretations. The correct analysis of semantic representation is a teleological one, in terms of the biological purposes of mental states; whereas functionalism focuses, so to speak, only on the *structure* of the cognitive mechanism, the semantic perspective requires in addition that we consider the *purposes* of the cognitive mechanism's parts.

PAPPAS, Peter C. The Model-Theoretic Structure Of Abelian Group Rings. *Annals Pure Applied Log* 28,163–202 Mr 85.

PAPPIN, Joseph. Karol Cardinal Wojtyla And Jean-Paul Sartre On The Intentionality Of Consciousness. *Proc Cath Phil Ass* 58,130–139 1984.

PAREL, Anthony (ed). *Ideology, Philosophy And Politics*. Waterloo Laurier Univ Pr 1983.

PARENT, Juan M. Algunas Preguntas Sobre Etica. *Logos (Mexico)* 12,41–62 My–Ag 84.

Some people think that philosophers carry out their social function as an internal activity. We think this is not so. Philosophy is a permanent reflection on ourselves and on our world. One of the most important impacts we suffer is the technology as a new life medium for the human kind. What are the questions philosophers do to the technicians? What are the questions the philosophers hope to answer to the technicians?

PARENT, Juan. El Poder En Michel Foucault. *Rev Filosof (Mexico)* 18,99–108 Ja–Ap 85.

PAREYSON, L. Minima Schellingiana. *Kantstudien* 66,231–241 1975.

PARGETTER, Robert. Laws And Modal Realism. *Phil Stud* 46,335–348 N 84.

PARIENTE, M Jean-Claude. Rationalisme Et Ontologie Chez Gaston Bachelard. *Bull Soc Fr Phil* 79,1–36 Ja–Mr 85.

PARIS, Elisa R. La Estructura De La Ciudad Ideal. *Cuad Filosof* 19,193–204 Ja–D 83.

PARIS, J B and Csirmaz, L. A Property Of 2-Sorted Peano Models And Program Verification. *Z Math Log* 30,325–334 1984.

Using properties of non-standard models of arithmetic a completeness theorem is established for the Floyd–Hoare program verification method in the case where non-standard runs are allowed and the time is measured in a non-standard model of arithmetic.

PARIS, John J. "Religious Traditions In Bioethical Decision Making" in *Bioethical Frontiers In Perinatal Intensive Care*, Snowden, Fraser (ed), 77–88. Natchitoches Northwestern Pr 1985.

PARIS, John J. "The Decision To Withdraw Life-Sustaining Treatment" in *Ethics Committees And Health Care Decisions*, Cranford, Ronald (ed), 203–208. Ann Arbor Health Admin Pr 1984.

PARK, Désirée. Facts And Reasons Concerning Berkeley's Reprinted *Works*. *Berkeley News* 7,14–16 1984.

PARK, Ynhui. Lao Tzu And Nietzsche: Wanderer And Superman. *J Chin Phil* 11,401–412 D 84.

The purpose of this paper is to show how difficult it is to transcend and overcome one's cultural tradition. Lao Tzu and Nietzsche are very similar in their view on the nature of reality and language, and on their attempt to make a radical criticism of their respective culture's ideology. However, they are completely apart in the proposal for a new ideology. Lao Tzu is still typically oriental and Nietzsche remains to be essentially occidental. The ideology of Lao Tzu is based on the universe or nature centered view of reality, whereas the ideology of Nietzsce derives from man-centered outlook of reality.

PARKER, Francis H. "Contemplation In Aristotelian Ethics" in *The Georgetown Symposium On Ethics*, Porreco, Rocco (ed), 205–212. Lanham Univ Pr Of America 1984.

PARKER, Patricia. "The Metaphorical Plot" in *Metaphor*, Miall, David S (ed), 133–158. Atlantic Highlands Humanities Pr 1982.

PARKER, Richard. Bradley's Paradox And Russell's Theory Of Relations. *Phil Res Arch* 10,261–274 1984.

A coherent theory of relations was a critical part of Russell's metaphysics. In *Appearance and Reality* Bradley posed a problem that sits squarely in the way of any doctrine of "external" relations. russell, determined to advance such a doctrine, tried several times to find a way around the paradox and apparently believed he had succeeded by making use of one of his inventions, the theory of logical types. Gilbert Ryle and Alan Donagan have advanced an argument that I read, over the objections of its authors, as a special case of Bradley's. In this paper I argue that the *ad hoc* solution suggested by Donagan to the special problem is one that Russell had already indicated a willingness to accept but that the general problem of the paradox remains. What finally prevents Russell from solving the paradox is a combination of his refusal to abandon the claim that relations are constituents of facts and the necessity of distinguishing a relational fact from its converse. Following some hints that Russell left, I do some reconstruction, showing how the theory of types would (and should) have been applied had Russell followed through on his own insights. (edited)

PARKER, Samuel. A Demonstration Of The Divine Authority Of The Law Of Nature And Of The Christian Religion. NY Garland 1984.

PARKES, Graham. Current Movements In Viewing Paintings: Reflections On Reflections. *J Aes Educ* 18,111–115 Fall 84.

Most of the literature on the aesthetic appreciation of paintings presupposes "ideal viewing conditions"—which rarely, if ever, obtain. This essay considers two kinds of circumstance that nowadays condition our viewing of "great" art—large crowds, and paintings' being displayed behind (plexi–) glass—and shows how both kinds of movement necessitated by the pressure of crowds and the reflections caused by glass can be engaged in such a way as to enhance our viewing experience.

PARKS, Graham. Intimations Of Taoist Themes In Early Heidegger. *J Chin Phil* 11,353–374 D 84.

An examination of the themes of nothingness, utility and possibility, and the emptiness of the self in Heidegger's earlier writings and in the *Lao Tzu* and *ChuangTzu* uncovers some remarkable similarities. The discovery of "Taoist" ideas in Heidegger's work prior to his contact with Chinese philosophy conduces to a greater sense of the unity of his thought, strengthens his claim to have overcome the Western metaphysical tradition, and sharpens our understanding of both philosophies.

PAROUSH, Jacob and Nitzan, Shmuel. A General Theorem And Eight Corollaries In Search Of Correct Decision. *Theor Decis* 17,211–220 N 84.

The main theorem established in this study and its corollaries summarize and generalize the existing results on optimal aggregation of experts judgments under uncertain pairwise choice situations. In particular, we explicate the link between the optimal decision procedure and the decision maker's preferences and biases and the judgmental competences of his consultants. The general theorem directly clarifies under what circumstances the optimal decision rule should be the democratic simple majority rule, the elitist rule, an intermediate weighted simple majority rule or a biased weighted or simple qualified majority rule.

PAROUSH, Jacob and Nitzan, Shmuel. Partial Information Of Decisional Competences And The Desirability Of The Expert Rule In Uncertain Dichotomous Choice Situations. *Theor Decis* 17,275–286 N 84.

The paper analyzes the expert resolution problem by employing extended versions of the uncertain dichotomous choice model. The main purpose of this study is to illustrate how the analysis of optimal decision rules can be carried out while dispensing with the common restrictive assumption of full information regarding individual decisional competences. In contrast to most previous studies in this field we here evaluate the expert rule under alternative assumptions regarding the available partial information on judgmental competences rather than compare it in an *ad hoc* manner to some common alternative rules, such as simple majority rule. A fuller optimality analysis allowing the evaluation of all relevant decision rules, and not merely the expert rule, is attempted for a five-member panel of experts assuming a uniform distribution of individual competences. For three-member groups the optimality issue is resolved by assuming no information on individual competences and interpreting the expert rule as an even–chance lottery on skills.

PARRET, Herman. Regularities, Rules And Strategies. *J Prag* 8,569–592 Ag 84.

Strategies are regularities externalized by a communicative competence—they are chains of reasons and thus based on processes of reasoning. Discourse, for the pragmatician, is a totality of regularities (recognizable because of their generality) expressing theoretical and practical reasoning. These strategies are inferential (not logical inferences, however, because they are realized in and by means of natural language use). Inferential activity here is, in fact, a procedure of transposition of meaning from one object-level to another paraphrastic level of discourse. Pragmatics manipulates a triangular model: reasoning is not determined by its relation to the real (whereby rationality would be reduced to a faculty of reconstructing the truth), but by the intermediation of the concept of a rational being or a reasoner. A pragmatic notion of rationality stresses the fact that one reasons—and one understands—within the generality of purposes which are common to the speaker and the understander. The paper intends not so much to be a criticism of the classical grammatical notion of 'rule', but rather to disentangle within the broad panorama of pragmatic theories. (edited)

PARROCHIA, Daniel. Optique, Méchanique Et Calcul Des Chances Chez Huygens Et Spinoza (Sur Quelques Paradigmes Possibles Du Discours Philosophique). *Dialectica* 38,319–346 1984.

The purpose of this article is to study some aspects of the relations between Huygens and Spinoza. After a short examination of the two authors' optics, we show that this science has been used as a "paradigm" for philosopher's metaphysics. We take account of the method (correction of aberrations) as well as the matter (Nature, like light, is an involving and expressive medium). But there are other paradigms: pendulum mechanics, for example, those contradictions with optics may be reduced, thanks to Huygens' geometry (theory of developed curves); or probability theory's beginning, with which we present a new explanation of the aims of *Ethics*.

PARRY, Richard D. The Uniqueness Proof For Forms In *Republic X*. *J Hist Phil* 23,133–150 Ap 85.

This article offers an interpretation of *Rep* X, 597cl–d3. This argument—the third bed argument—shows that the Form of bed is unique. This argument enunciates and applies a version of the one–over–many principle. The argument assumes two other principles. After adding these assumptions, one can see that neither explicit premisses nor assumptions imply an infinite regres, even if Forms are self–predicating. This result is compared to the first third–man argument of the *Parmenides* (132a1–b2).

PARRY, S J. Hegemony And Sport. *J Phil Sport* 10,71–83 1983.

PARSONS, Charles. Arithmetic And The Categories. *Topoi* 3,109–122 D 84.

PARSONS, Howard L. Beliefs Essential In The Struggle For Peace And Development. *Dialec Hum* 11,439–448 Spr/Sum 84.

Presupposed in the people's struggle for peace and development are certain beliefs: maintenance and development of human species is a basic value requiring peace; nuclear conflict and omnicide are made increasingly probable by the arms buildup and the US policy of Reagan to "prevail" over the USSR in a "winnable" nuclear conflict (in contrast to the Soviet position); the path to peace and development is reduction of the arms buildup, peaceful coexistence, and creative dialogue.

PARSONS, Michael. Taking Dwight Boyd Seriously. *Proc Phil Educ* 40,145–150 1984.

PARSONS, Terence. Modifiers And Quantifiers In Natural Language. *Can J Phil* 6,29–60 80 Supp.

PARSONS, Victor. Commentary On "Kicking Against The Pricks: Two Patients Wish To End Essential Insulin Treatment". *J Med Ethics* 10,201–203 D 84.

This clinical case commentary discusses the withdrawal of insulin therapy which has been requested by two patients while under treatment in hospital. The first case is of a patient who wishes to evade a criminal action in the courts against him; discussion revolves around the actions a physician might take to ensure the patient is kept alive to suffer sentence. The second case involves a lonely, elderly man with advanced gangrene of his leg who requests his insulin be withdrawn so that he dies peacefully of diabetic coma rather than painfully of gangrene. Discussion revolves around benevolence, autonomy, and the possibility of compulsory treatment under the Mental Health Act, on the argument that the patient is not sane in requesting the termination of his diabetic treatment.

PARTEE, Barbera H. Situations, Worlds And Contexts. *Ling Phil* 8,53–58 F 85.

PARTRIDGE, Ernest. Three Wrong Leads In A Search For An Environmental Ethic: Tom Regan On Animal Rights, Inherent Values, And 'Deep Ecology'. *Ethics Animals* 5,61–74 S 84.

The essay criticizes Tom Regan's attempt to articulate an environmental ethic upon a strongly individualistic foundation—namely, upon the concept of "rights of nature" which, in turn, he derives from a theory of inherent value." This approach, I argue, is incoherent, insensitive to unique human capacities, and in disregard of basic ecological principles. The paper closes with a sketch of a synthesis of individualism and holism in environmental ethics.

PARTRIDGE, John Geoffrey. *Semantic, Pragmatic And Syntactic Correlates: An Analysis Of Performative Verbs Based On English Data.* Germany Tubingen 1982.

PASOUR JR, E C. Land–Use Planning: Implications Of The Economic Calculation Debate. *J Liber Stud* 7,127–140 Spr 83.

Public planners have not adequately recognized the information and incentive problems inherent in central planning. Hayek and Mises emphasized the problem of rational planning without the use of decentralized market prices in the Economic Calculation Debate of the 1920s and the 1930s. This paper relates that Debate to land–use planning. The conclusion is that "market socialism" is not a realistic alternative to decentralized market prices in achieving efficient use of land resources.

PASQUALOTTO, Giangiorgio. *Gli Instituti Filosofici In Italia (1970–1980).* Padova Univ Di Padova 1983.

PASSANTI, Daniel. Cristianismo Y Libertad. *Sapientia* 40,143–152 Ap–Je 85.

PASTIN, Mark. Ethics As An Integrating Force In Management. *J Bus Ethics* 3,293–304 N 84.

This essay focuses on one ethical concept, *the good* or *the valuable*, and shows how to incorporate it in an ethically and economically effective decision process. We focus on this concept because it uncovers a key fault in strategic thinking and generates questions central to any complex decision. (edited)

PASTIN, Mark. Management–Think. *J Bus Ethics* 4,297–307 Ag 85.

This paper provides a comprehensive review of the philosophical foundations of business management. The need for such a review is established. Emphasis is placed upon the role of management ethos in such a philosophy. Philosophical concepts (such as the concept of an intention) which are widely applied in management, but not explored in the management literature, are examined. While the emphasis is on philosophy, the material presented is applicable in the practice of management.

PASTORE, Baldassare. Dworkin Giusnaturalista? *Riv Int Filosof Diritto* 61,66–82 Ja–Mr 84.

The author considers the Dworkin's thesis that principles are an essential part of the law. They are propositions that describe individual rights. The recognition of principles as binding legal standards eliminates discretion in the strong sense. The author argues that Dworkin's theory is not a natural law theory but it is a contribution to a correct analysis of the non–formal elements of legal system and of their role in judicial decision–making.

PATIÑO, Joel Rodríguez. Axiología De José Vasconcelos. *Logos (Mexico)* 12,87–102 My–Ag 84.

La investigación se propone hacer notar cómo el filósofo mexicano con su dialéctica de la síntesis metafísica de la realidad, que comprende todos los aspectos de la misma sin prescin dir de alguno, se orienta por la línea de Arquíloco de Paros, Pitágoras, Empédocles, Anaxágoras, etc; continuando por una axiología dentro del horizonte de los poetas, músicos y ar—quitectos griegos, debía llegar a una visión estructural de—los valores; pero no fue así, sino que jerarquiza los mismos y esto, a juicio del autor, carece de suficiente fundamento.

PATON, Margaret. Getting Croce Straight. *Brit J Aes* 25,252–265 Sum 85.

PATRICK, James. *The Magdalen Metaphysicals: Idealism And Orthodoxy At Oxford, 1901–1945.* Macon Mercer Univ Pr 1985.

PATSOURAS, Louis. "Mao Zedong: The Long Road Of Revolution To Communism" in *Continuity And Change In Marxism*, Fischer, Norman And Others (ed), 211–231. Atlantic Highlands Humanities Pr 1982.

PATTEN, St C. Kant's Cogito. *Kantstudien* 66,331–341 1975.

PATTERSON, Richard. *Image And Reality In Plato's Metaphysics.* Indianapolis Hackett 1985.

The purpose is to clarify and explain Plato's theory of the forms. Discussion on the theory: varieties of paradigmata, image and reality and predicates. The forms of paradigmata fill a wide range of philosophical roles. Forms should be spoken of as forms rather then as structures or patterns, sets or universals, Fregean concepts or eternal possibilities. (staff)

PAUCKE, H. Engels Und Die Okologie. *Deut Z Phil* 33,207–215 1985.

PAUL, Diane B. Eugenics And The Left. *J Hist Ideas* 45,567–590 O–D 84.

PAUL, Richard W. The Critical–Thinking Movement. *Nat Forum* 65,2–3 Wint 85.

PAULSEN, David L. The Logically Possible, The Ontologically Possible And Ontological Proofs Of God's Existence. *Int J Phil Relig* 16,41–50 1984.

The article attempts to show that all standard versions of the ontological argument for God's existence fail as proofs because they logically and/or epistemically depend on an implicit premise which cannot, without circular reasoning, be shown to be warranted. This premise is the assumption that for any proposition, p, affirming that some state of affairs, s, obtains, if p is logically possible, then s ontologically (or really) could obtain.

PAVLICH, G. Can Heidegger Be Depicted As A Phenomenologist? *S Afr J Phil* 3,135–138 N 84.

The author endeavors to situate Heidegger's hermeneutic phenomenology within the context of the phenomenological movement at large. To this end, a theoretical framework for the demarcation of phenomenologists from non–phenomenologists is enunciated. (edited)

PAWLOWSKA, I–Lazari. Ethical Relativism (in Polish). *Etyka* 21,7–24 1985.

Ethical relativism refers to different attitudes. The author discusses axiological, methodological, situational and cultural relativism, showing that a person may be a relativist in one sense but not in another and that one may accept one type of relativism in a moderate version while rejecting it in an extreme version.

PAX, Clyde. Compagni Di Cammino: Heidegger E San Giovanni Della Croce. *Aquinas* 27,243–260 My–Ag 84.

The article seeks to clarify several points of similarity, both onto logical and epistemological, between Heidegger and John of the Cross. Notable among the similarities discussed are a common insistence upon an experiential rather than conceptual beginning for thinking, a willingness to exploit the role of evidence beyond categorical evidence, and an emphasis upon language including the silence of language. The article concludes by suggesting several points left un–thought in the two writers.

PAYNE, Gordon R. Cognitive Intuition Of Singulars Revisited (Matthew Of Aquaparta Versus B J F Lonergan). *Fran Stud* 41,346–384 1981.

PAYNE, Steven. The Christian Character Of Christian Mystical Experiences. *Relig Stud* 20,417–428 S 84.

The author criticizes the claim that mysticism is "everywhere the same" and defends the view that at least some Christian mystical experiences may have what can be called a "phenomenally theistic" character. Focussing on Walter Stace's influential defense of the "common core" hypothesis in *Mysticism and Philosophy*, this article shows, among other things, that Stace's argument rests upon a serious misrepresentation of the teachings of Teresa of Avila and John of the Cross.

PEACOCKE, Arthur. *Intimations Of Reality: Critical Realism In Science And Religion.* Notre Dame Univ Notre Dame Pr 1984.

PEACOCKE, Arthur. Thermodynamics And Life. *Zygon* 19,395–432 D 84.

The basic features of thermodynamics as the "science of the possible" are outlined with a special emphasis on the role of the concept of entropy as a measure of irreversibility in natural processes and its relation to "order", precisely defined. Natural processes may lead to an increase in complexity, and this concept has a subtle relationship to those of order, organization, and information. These concepts are analyzed with respect to their relation to biological evolution, together with other ways of attempting to quantify it. Thermodynamic interpretations of evolution are described and critically compared, and the significance of dissipative structures, of "order through fluctuation", is emphasized in relation both to the evolutionary succession of temporarily stable forms and to kinetic mechanisms producing new patterns.

PEACOCKE, Christopher. *Sense And Content: Experience, Thought, And Their Relations*. Oxford Clarendon Pr 1983.

PEARCE, David and Rantala, Veikko. Approximative Explanation Is Deductive Nomological. *Phil Sci* 52,126–140 Mr 85.

We revive the idea that a deductive–nomological explanation of a scientific theory by its successor may be defensible, even in those common and troublesome cases where the theories concerned are mutually incompatible; and limiting, approximating and counterfactual assumptions may be required in order to define a logical relation between them. Our solution is based on a general characterization of limiting relations between physical theories using the method of nonstandard analysis.

PEARCE, David and Rantala, V. Scientific Change, Continuity, And Problem Solving. *Phil Natur* 21,389–399 1984.

PEARCE, David and Van Bentham, Johan. A Mathematical Characterization Of Interpretation Between Theories. *Stud Log* 43,295–304 1984.

Of the various notions of reduction in the logical literature, relative interpretability in the sense of Tarski and other [6] appears to be the central one. In the present note, this syntactic notion is characterized semantically, through the existence of a suitable reduction functor on models. The latter mathematical condition itself suggests a natural generalization, whose syntactic equivalent turns out to be a notion of interpretability quite close to that of Ershov [1], Szczerba [5] and Gaifman [2].

PEARSON, Michael A. Enhancing Perceptions Of Auditor Independence. *J Bus Ethics* 4,53–56 F 85.

PECCORINI, Francisco L. Gabriel Marcel's Pensée Pensante As The Ultimate Reality And Meaning Of Human Existence. *Ultim Real Mean* 8,4–23 Mr 85.

The author traces the premise (URAM) from which Marcel's philosophical issues flow––blind intuition, secondary reflection on the mysterious metaproblematic, the epistemological value of the nature of the will, the Light of Christ as the foundation of the community, love and absolute fidelity as well as the ontological affirmation as the source of Logic— to direct but "unverifiable" participation of the subject (or pensée pensante) in Being.

PECORINO, Philip. A Process View Of Philosophy And Teaching Philosophy. *Metaphilosophy* 16,80–91 Ja 85.

The article presents a view of philosophy which emphasizes its methodology over its content and then proceeds to indicate what the consequences of such a view would be for the way in which teachers of philosophy regard their students and the manner in which they might teach the subject in the contemporary electronic, non–literate culture.

PECZENIK, Aleksander. Moral And Ontological Justification Of Legal Reasoning. *Law Phil* 4,289–309 Ag 85.

PEDEN, Creighton W. Freeing Us From Ignorance And Superstition. *Dialec Hum* 11,435–438 Spr/Sum 84.

This paper examines the contention of Chauncey Wright if prescientific religions are going to contribute positively to the radical social process of our increasingly scientific culture, they are going to do so on the basis of adapting the scientific method to theological efforts.

PEDERSEN, Ove K. Une Définition Juridique Du Concept De L'Art. *Commun Cog* 17,405–412 1984.

The concept of creativity and its formal function in the droit d'auteur is discussed. The author argues that an element of creativity is the necessary condition of the distinction between a work of art and a common product of work. He also claims that this is so far for historical reasons. Under the present relations of production "the nature in its broadest sense" is already appropriated. The element of creativity is a condition of, that something already possessed can be over–appropriated and a product be accepted both as *a commodity* and as a work of art.

PEDERSEN, Stig Andur. Formation And Development Of Scientific Concepts. *Phil Natur* 21,287–300 1984.

A theory of scientific concepts is sketched and applied to a study of the dispute between the adherents of infinitesimals and their opponents in the late 19th century. It is argued that the two parties were talking at cross purposes because their mathematical concepts carried different sense.

PEFFER, Rodney G. Morality And The Marxist Concept Of Ideology. *Can J Phil* Supp 7,67–92 1981.

Eleven traditional criteria for something being ideological are examined. None—not even "defending the social status quo"—proves to be a defining characteristic of the Marxist concept of ideology. The "deep" criterion, it is argued, is that the view or theory in question militates against the improvement of the human condition. Though many moral views and theories meet this condition, some—including those of Marx––do not. Thus, morality as a whole is not ideological.

PEGUEROLES, Juan. Fragmentos De Filosofía. *Espíritu* 33,131–146 Jl–D 84.

Consideraciones breves sobre los siguientes temas: Dios rico, hombre pobre?; Platón, Buda, Nietzsche; Existe el mundo?; infinito e indefinido; infinito y/o finito; Totalidad y/o infinito; La paradoja del hombre; El espíritu y el tiempo; El tiempo factor de progreso?; Dios y el mundo en Sankara; La justicia no es un ideal; El amor precede al ser?; El falso infinito hegeliano; Verdadera y falsa transcendencia del amor; Determinatio negatio, determinatio affirmatio.

PEIKOFF, Leonard. Platonism's Inference From Logic To God. *Int Stud Phil* 16,25–34 1984.

I argue that according to the Platonic tradition—from Academics and Augustinians on through Cambridge Platonists and Continental Rationalists—the existence of God can be inferred from the view that the Law of Contradiction is an innately known truth. The article distinguishes three such lines of inference, and concludes that, in contrast

to the Aristotelian position, the laws of logic, for Platonism, are not primarily laws of or about the empirical world.

PEKÁREK, Ludek. Synergetics And Its Integrative Role In The Development Of Science (in Czechoslovakian). *Filozof Cas* 32,881–885 1984.

PEKARSKY, Daniel. The Place Of Foresight In Deliberation: An Interpretation Of Dewey's View. *Proc Phil Educ* 40,197–204 1984.

PELC, Andrzej. Idempotent Ideals On Abelian Groups. *J Sym Log* 49,812–817 S 84.

PELCZYNSKI, Z A (ed). *The State And Civil Society: Studies In Hegel's Political Philosophy*. Cambridge Cambridge Univ Pr 1984.

PELCZYNSKI, Z A. "Nation, Civil Society, State" in *The State And Civil Society*, Pelczynski, Z A (ed), 262–278. Cambridge Cambridge Univ Pr 1984.

PELCZYNSKI, Z A. "Political Community And Individual Freedom In Hegel's Philosophy" in *The State And Civil Society*, Pelczynski, Z A (ed), 55–76. Cambridge Cambridge Univ Pr 1984.

PELCZYNSKI, Z A. "The Significance Of Hegel's Separation Of The State And Civil Society" in *The State And Civil Society*, Pelczynski, Z A (ed), 1–13. Cambridge Cambridge Univ Pr 1984.

PELCZYNSKI, Zbigniew A. T M Knox: His Life And Scholarship. *Bull Hegel Soc Gt Brit* 3,2–16 Spr/Sum 81.

This second part of an appreciation of T M Knox deals with his work as translator and editor of several Hegel works (including the *Philosophy of Right*, the *Aesthetics* and the minor political writings). The principles of Knox's translation and his views on Hegel are noted, and it is suggested that through his translations Knox has made an important contribution to the contemporary revival of Hegel's ideas in the English–speaking countries.

PELCZYNSKI, Zbigniew A. T M Knox: His Life And Scholarship, Part II. *Bull Hegel Soc Gt Brit* 2,8–21 Autumn/Wint 80.

This first part of an appreciation of T M Knox deals with his family background, his education (which included study under R G R collinwood at Pembroke College, Oxford), and his academic career at Oxford and St Andrews University. The source and development of his interst in Hegel's philosophy up to the translation and publication of the *Philosophy of Right* are included.

PELI, Pinhas Ha–Cohen. "'Jewish Religiousity' According To Buber" in *Martin Buber*, Gordon, Haim (ed), 419–436. Beersheva Ktav 1984.

PELLAUER, David (trans) and Ricoeur, Paul and Mc Laughlin, Kathleen (trans). *Time And Narrative*, V1. Chicago Univ Of Chicago Pr 1984.

PELLECCHIA, Pasquale. Il Principio Del *Passo Indietro* Del Pensiero. *Aquinas* 27,343–372 My–Ag 84.

Heidegger sees in the oblivion of the Being the misfortune of our own time (age) that is dominated by the so–called technological advance and in the "Backward–step" of our thinking (he sees) the salvation. The essay shows that it was Descartes that first introduced the "Backward step" concept as method of thinking; however, this method not only does not drive to salvation but it really brings out a sense of desert (desolation) just as Heidegger points out (of which his own thought is an expression).

PELLEGRINO, Edmund D. The Humanities In Medical Education: Entering The Post–Evangelical Era. *Theor Med* 5,253–266 O 84.

In the last two decades, ethics, the humanities and human values have become , commonplace topics in the curricula of American medical schools. The reasons for teaching humanistic disciplines in medical schools, when, by whom, and in what manner, are reviewed together with their relevance to the arts of the clinician and patient care. The future viability of such teaching in the next decade is projected.

PELLETIER, D H. On Violating The GCH Below The Least Measurable Cardinal. *Z Math Log* 21,361–364 1975.

PELLETIER, F J. Six Problems In "Translational Equivalence". *Log Anal* 27,423–434 D 84.

Two logics are "translationally equivalent" if these are (syntactic) functions f and g which (a) map theorems of one logic into theorems of the other, (b) map rules of inference of one logic into admissible rules of the other, (c) have the properties that f (g(x)) is equivalent to X and g (f(x)) is equivalent to X (in the relevant logics). Various investigations are carried out in modal logics with the goal of showing when/if two modal systems are translationally equivalent. When two systems are translationally equivalent, the question arises of whether a Quinean radical translator can ever tell whether his informants are using one rather than the other logic. For example, a "logic for vagueness" is shown to be translationally equivalent to system T. Can our radical translator ever tell the informants are talking about vagueness or necessity?

PELLETIER, F J. The Not–So–Strange Modal Logic Of Indeterminacy. *Log Anal* 27,415–422 D 84.

p F Gibbins (Log Anal, No 100 1982) claims that a modal logic for an "indeterminacy" would be "strange" because it would presuppose classes of indeterminate worlds accessible to no worlds, not even to themselves. In this note, a class of modal logics is presented, no member of which has this feature, and all of which embody the basic institutions about indeterminacy. The Montague–Scott method is used to show their completeness. One of these logics is singled out as the most plausible modal of indeterminacy.

PELLETIER, Lucien. Libération Et Salut D'aprés Ernst Bloch (I). *Laval Theol Phil* 41,171–194 Je 85.

L'auteur tente d'indentifier une voie de cohésion qui permette d'établir des liens entre luttes de libération et le concept théologique du salut. De facon implicite, ce même problème se situe au coeur de la pensée d'Ernst Bloch. Après avoir établi des concepts préliminaires, la première partie de l'article examine de facon détaillée en quel sens Bloch intègre la religion (surtout le judéo–christianisme) à ses propres vues: en tant qu'elle est le lieu d'émergence des catégories les plus extrêmes du salut et de la visée eschatologique ultime, dont une herméneutique appropriée permet d'assumer l'héritage.

PELLETIER, Lucien. Libération Et Salut D'aprés Ernst Bloch (II). *Laval Theol Phil* 41,417–431 O 85.

Après avoir cerné dans la première partie de l'article la visée eschatologique du salut que Bloch hérite du judéo–christianisme, l'auteur montre comment cell–ci s'intègre à l'ensemble du système blochien: elly y ordonne tous les contensus à l'Ultimum, et se mue en problème du Tout à l'occasion du passage à la praxis de libération. Mais en même temps, ce passage révèle le caractère de postulat de la possibilité du salut. Cette découverte de la foi blichienne anène à considére la bilatéralité de la relation libération–salut. Enfin, une critique de Bloch est formulée, pour libérer un espace où la théologie puisse prendre pied.

PELLETIER, Yvan. Pour Une Définition Claire Et Nette Du Lieu Dialectique. *Laval Theol Phil* 41,403–415 O 85.

Tout au long de la tradition aristotélicienne, le lieu dialectique est défni assez confusément, et seulement dans la perspective de son utilité: c'est on nous le dit sur divers tons, un critère de sélection qui permet d'abonder en arguments. Cet article veut en proposer une définition plus intime et le présente comme une affinité d'attribution attachée aux corrélatifs d'une relation logique. Cette définition est expliquée, puis finalement confirmée par la lumiére qu'elle jette sur la distinction entre lieu commun et lieu propre, sur laquelle achoppent tant d'auteurs.

PENASKOVIC, Richard. Two Classical Western Theologians: Augustine And Newman. *Augustin Stud* 13,67–80 1982.

This essay compares the views of Augustine and John Henry Newman on justification, more specifically in regard to Augustine's treatise, *De Spiritu et Littera* and Newman's *Lectures on Justification*. Both thinkers use Scripture to understand justification and both had a polemical purpose in mind. Augustine wrote to counter Pelagianism, whereas Newman wrote against the Evangelicals. Finally, it is argued that both Augustine and Newman deserve to be called classic theologians.

PENCE, Gregory E. Recent Work On Virtues. *Amer Phil Quart* 21,281–298 O 84.

Philosophers interested in virtues over the last two decades have either been religiously–based such as Thomists or seeking an alternative to traditional deontology. In this latter group, Pritchard and Anscombe attacked contrasts between virtue (duty) and desire, and MacIntrye attacked deontological *virtue* as meaningless without God. Foot and Gauthier continued this attack on deontology. All of these writers would substitute *virtues* for virtue, basing the former on a naturalistic account of humans compatible with knowledge from the social sciences. This article reviews such attempts. (edited)

PENCE, Terry. *Ethics In Nursing: An Annotated Bibliography.* NY Ntl League Nursing 1983.

This bibliography contains nearly 800 entries covering the literature from 1901 to the present. Its exclusive focus is nursing ethics or biomedical ethics as discussed in nursing literature. The first part consists of 35 topical indexes. These mini–bibliographies contain only the author's name, title of work, and year of publication. The second part arranges the works according to the author's name. Here is the full citation as well as a short annotation are given.

PENN, William Y and Collier, Boyd D. Current Research In Moral Development As A Decision Support System. *J Bus Ethics* 4,131–136 Ap 85.

PENNOCK, J Roland (ed) and Chapman, John W (ed). *Marxism: Nomos XXVI.* NY Columbia Univ Pr 1983.

These essays on Marxism deal especially with the moral, political, and legal aspects of Marx's theories. They are written by philosophers, political theorists and lawmen, and feature cross–disciplinary commentary. An extensive bibliography on Marx and Marxisms is included.

PENTZOUPOULOU– VALAIS, Teresa. "Can Art Die" in *Continental Philosophy And The Arts*, Winters, Laurence E and others (ed), 239–242. *Lanham* Univ Pr Of America 1984.

PEPERZAK, Adrian. "Individual Responsibility In Advanced Societies" in *The Good Life And Its Pursuit*, Dougherty, Jude P (ed), 145–162. NY Paragon House 1984.

PERCESEPE, Gary. Telos In Hegel's *Differenz Des Fichte'schen Und Schelling'schen Systems Der Philosophie*. *Phil Res Arch* 10,393–440 1984.

The *Differenzschrift* in Hegel's first distinctively philosophical work. Traditionally, the chief significance of the work has been said to be its announcement of the breach between Fichte and Schelling. The purpose of the present paper is to move from this proximate perspective to a systematic–teleological perspective. Form the latter perspective we can see that it is the *Differenzschrift* that Hegel not only criticizes and comprehends the work of his immediate predecessors but also constructs the conceptual–hermeneutic frame which makes his critique possible. Essentially Hegel argues that philosophy–as–science advances by means of text and commentary, but its advance is not continuous. Its history is characterized by violent, epoch–making leaps, which must be viewed as necessary organic constituents of telic progress. The impulse of force behind this telic advance is the concrete historical situation, in Hegel's words, "the need of the times".

PERELMAN, Haim. Right, Morality, And Religion (in Hebrew). *Iyyun* 33,235–238 Ja–Ap 84.

PEREZ RUIZ, Francisco. "El Justo Es Feliz Y El Injusto Desgraciado": Justicia Y Felicidad En La "República" De Platón. *Pensamiento* 40,257–296 Jl–S 84.

Trato de ver cómo concibe Platón las relaciones entre justicia y felicidad y el profundo valor que tiene su modo de ver. Examino con atención el planteamiento del problema, el concepto platónico de justicia y la razón que tiene para verla ante todo en el interior del individuo, los frutos intrínsecos de la justicia y finalmente el problema de sus premios en esta vida y en la otra. Al mismo tiempo indico algunas consecuencias importantes sobre la estructura de la obra.

PERKINS, Jeffrey J. Philosophy And A Career In Law. *Int J Applied Phil* 2,67–74 Spr 85.

PERKINS, Pheme. Taxes In The New Testament. *J Relig Ethics* 12,182–200 Fall 84.

Early Christian thinking about taxation was shaped by an environment in which taxes were oppressive and rapaciously administered. New Testament passages dealing with taxation do not amount to a systematic ethic or philosophy of taxation but instead convey the basic Christian teachings of respect for government, "freedom in subordination", and love of neighbor. In Paul's effort on behalf of a collection for the Christian community at Jerusalem, however, there are suggestions of an emerging sense of responsibility to even the distant neighbor that is to be expressed through collective monetary contributions.

PERKINS, Robert L (ed). *History And System: Hegel's Philosophy Of History.* Albany SUNY Pr 1984.

This volume is proceedings of the biennial meeting of the Hegel Society of America at Clemson University in 1982 on the subject of Hegel's philosophy of history. The treatment is systematic rather than expository and demonstrates systematic, conceptual, and methodological unity of Hegel's thought.

PERKINS, Robert L (ed). *International Kierkegaard Commentary: Two Ages.* Macon Mercer Univ Pr 1984.

This collection of essays, the first ever assembled on this work, offers new insights into Kierkegaard's first published venture in social criticism. His individualism can be negotiated into a broad critique of modernity. Major essays by John W Elrod, Michael Plekon, Lee Barrett, Patricia Cutting, Robert C Roberts, Robert L Perkins, Merold Westphal, James L Marsh, Jackie Kleinman, Allen Janik, and John M Hoberman. This is the first of a projected twenty–four volume collaborative effort.

PERKINS, Robert L. "Buber And Kierkegaard: A Philosophic Encounter" in *Martin Buber*, Gordon, Haim (ed), 275–304. Beersheva Ktav 1984.

PERKINS, Robert L. "Envy As Personal Phenomenon And As Politics" in *International Kierkegaard Commentary*, Perkins, Robert L (ed), 107–132. Macon Mercer Univ Pr 1984.

PERKINS, Robert L. Conceptual Relativism And Europocentrism: The Reply Of A Philosopher To An Anthropologist. *Ultim Real Mean* 7,237–240 S 84.

This article is a criticism of a simple set of theses which were argued by Professor Kronenberg in a recent issue of *Ultimate Reality and Meaning*: (1) Professor Kolakowski's critique of cultural universalism is false; (2) That all cultures have the same value; (3) That anthropology is the source of modern "tolerance." Finally, Kronenberg's own brand of cultural relativism is Western. Is he biting the hand that supplied the very concepts he uses?

PERL, Jeffrey M and Tuck, Andrew. The Hidden Advantage Of Tradition: On The Significance Of T S Eliot's Indic Studies. *Phil East West* 35,115–132 Ap 85.

T S Eliot's graduate work at Harvard was in large part devoted to Asian philosophy and philology. His course notes and essays from that period are in restricted collections and are quoted here for the first time. His Indian studies influenced his philosophical, religious, and aesthetic positions far more deepley than has been previously understood. Further exploration of Eliot's "philosophical notebooks" appears in the Winter and Autumn, 1985, issues of *The Southern Review*.

PERNER, Josef. Begriffsbildung In Der Psychologie: Zur Logik Des Begriffes "Intelligenz". *Conceptus* 8,36–44 1974.

Following the chapter "Seinsweise" in E Roth, W D Oswald, and K Daumenlang's book *Intelligenz*, I want to show that a formal discussion of the matter renders the logical structure of the concept "intelligence" more transparence, than a merely verbal one. Many psychologists think of operationally defined concepts as the only admissable ones in an experimental science, but such thinking separates them from the phenomenological and intuitive tradition in psychology. It is more advisable to consider "intelligence" as a primitive theoretical term as it has been specified by Carnap, rather than to reduce it operationally to be observational concepts.

PERNICK, Martin S. "Childhood Death And Medical Ethics" in *Difficult Decisions In Medical Ethics*, Ganos, Doreen L (ed), 173–188. NY Liss 1983.

PERNIOLA, Mario. The Difference Of The Italian Philosophical Culture. *Grad Fac Phil J* 10,103–116 Spr 84.

PEROVICH, Anthony. Mysticism Or Mediation: A Response To Gill. *Faith Phil* 2,179–188 Ap 85.

PERRETT, Roy W. Karma And The Problem Of Suffering. *Sophia (Australia)* 24,4–10 Ap 85.

In his *Philosophy of Religion* John Hick disputes the common view that the doctrine of *karma* provides a solution to the (cognitive) problem of suffering. He claims that the theory involves an infinite regress of explanations that ultimately leaves the phenomenom unexplained. I argue that this charge is based upon a confusion about the nature of explanation and defend the adequacy of the *karma* theory as a theodicy.

PERRETT, Roy W. Tolstoy, Death And The Meaning Of Life. *Philosophy* 60,231–246 Ap 85.

Tolstoy's *A Confession* and *The death of Ivan Ilych* are examined in relation to philosophical questions about death and the meaning of life. I argue that understanding the meaning of life involves both knowledge–how and knowledge–that. Knowing how to live, how to integrate the subjective and objective significances of a life, includes the knowledge that we will all die and that it is irrational to build our lives on what can be destroyed by death.

PERRIN, Ronald. "Marcuse And The Meaning Of Radical Philosophy" in *Continuity And Change In Marxism*, Fischer, Norman And Others (ed), 114–130. Atlantic Highlands Humanities Pr 1982.

PERRY, John and Barwise, Jon. Shifting Situations And Shaken Attitudes: An Interview With Barwise And Perry. *Ling Phil* 8,105–161 F 85.

In this essay, the authors respond to the questions of an anonymous, and quite possibly mythical, interviewer concerning the basic ideas of their book "Situations and

Attitudes" and their reactions to the criticisms of it made by authors of earlier essays in the same journal. A number of changes in situation theory are explained.

PERRY, Thomas D. Two Domains Of Rights. *Phil Phenomenol Res* 45,567–580 Je 85.

PERSHITS, A I and Bromlei, Iu V. Frederick Engels And Contemporary Problems Concerning The History Of Primitive Society. *Soviet Stud Phil* 23,17–49 Wint 84–85.

PERSSON, Ingmar. Phenomenal Realism. *Erkenntnis* 23,59–78 My 85.

This paper sketches a new account of the relation between the objects of immediate perception and physical reality, an account which can be seen as a compromise between traditional realisms––direct realism and representationalism––and phenomenalism. The core of this theory––phenomenal realism––is that physical reality is something that enjoys an existence of being *causally* independent of immediate perception.

PETERS, Eugene H. Charles Hartshorne And The Ontological Argument. *Process Stud* 14,11–20 Spr 84.

PETERS, Hans and Tijs, Stef. Risk Aversion In n–Person Bargaining. *Theor Decis* 18,47–72 Ja 85.

PETERS, J U. Ruskin And The Language Of Art. *J Theor Crit Vis Arts* 1,35–48 1982.

PETERS, R S (ed) and White, Patricia. *Beyond Domination: An Essay In The Political Philosophy Of Education.* Boston Routledge K & Paul 1983.

Unashamedly radical in its approach, this philosophical critique of contemporary political and educational practice is based firmly in the liberal democratic tradition. It proposes curbing the power of teachers, includding headteachers, reducing parents' rights, and making political education the keystone of education. It considers educational strategies which would help to move a society towards greater democracy, including proposals for the democratic organization of political decision–making, and the development of democratic attitudes, notably fraternity.

PETERS, Ted. David Bohm, Postmodernism, And The Divine. *Zygon* 20,193–218 Je 85.

This is an exposition and critique of physicist David Bohm's theory of wholeness and the implicate order in light of the wider emerging postmodern consciousness. Postmodernity is defined primarily as advocacy for wholistic thinking over against the alleged fragmentation characteristic of the modern mind since René Descartes and Isaac Newton. When Bohm attempts to unite all things in the explicate order with his implicate "multi–dimensional ground," theological questions are raised and, in this article, addressed. The thesis is advanced that there is no whole which presently exists, meaning that the future is presently open, and that the unity of the cosmos awaits the eschatological act of God.

PETERSEN, Arne Friemuth. The Role Of Problems And Problem Solving In Popper's Early Work On Psychology. *Phil Soc Sci* 14,239–250 Je 84.

The ideas of problems and problem solving appear to have entered Popper's early works on psychology (1925–1933) from a reinterpretation of Kant's *Zweiweltenlehre*. It is shown how the method of trial–and–error elimination was seen by Popper to replace learning by association and other inductive procedures, and how the idea of problem solving later developed into a general characteristic of life. From this analysis situational logic emerges as a method suitable for studies of problem solving.

PETERSEN, Calvin R. Time And Stress: Alice In Wonderland. *J Hist Ideas* 46,427–434 Jl–S 85.

PETERSON, John. "The Interdependence Of Right And Good" in *The Georgetown Symposium On Ethics*, Porreco, Rocco (ed), 171–174. Lanham Univ Pr Of America 1984.

PETERSON, John. Persons And The Problem Of Interaction. *Mod Sch* 62,131–138 Ja 85.

It is argued that an identity materialist and/or an idealist on the body–mind issue cannot consistently deliberate about taking actions. But since as men they do and cannot help deliberating, their theories are inconsistent with their practice. But occasionalism, the pre–established harmony theory and epiphenomenalism are also untenable since they deny that what a person does is never the effect of what he or she believes. Cartesianism is not the answer since it raises the problem of interaction. For a solution that would avoid all three problems, persons are said to be instantiated human essences instead of being bodies, minds, or a composite of both substances.

PETERSON, Philip L. Semantic Indeterminacy And Scientific Underdetermination. *Phil Sci* 51,464–487 S 84.

The Quinean reply is that in scientific underdetermination cases there are facts of the matter making claims true or false (whether knowable or not), whereas in semantic indeterminacy cases there simply are not. The critics' rejoinder that there are such facts, studied in linguistics, is met by the final reply that linguistics either on the whole or in part is riddled with appeals to "meanings" and is, thereby, as suspect as analyticity and radical translation. I recommend "saving" linguistics by holding that it is permanently entangled in epistemology. Finally, the argument the critics should have made concerns paralleling semantic indeterminancy to indeterminacies in current quantum mechanics. (edited)

PETERSON, Sandra. Remarks On Three Formulations Of Ethical Relativism. *Ethics* 95,887–908 Jl 85.

PETERSON, Sandra. Substitution In Aristotelian Technical Contexts. *Phil Stud* 47,249–256 Mr 85.

This paper responds to "Accidental Sameness in Aristotle," by Frank Lewis, *Philosophical Studies* 42 (1982), which argues against the claim that various Aristotelian technical contexts, e.g., '—— is a primary substance' are referentially opaque. lewis's proposal about reference leaves an unappealing asymmetry between Aristotle's treatment of primary and secondary substance. Lewis's account also attributes to Aristotle an objectionable belief in many more *onta*, things which are, than an alternative account.

PETERSON, Susan Rae. The Compatibility Of Richard Price's Politics And His Ethics. *J Hist Ideas* 45,537–548 O–D 84.

PETHO, Bertalan. The Separation Of Ontological Idealism From Epistemological Idealism (in Hungarian). *Magyar Filozof Szemle* 5,788–816 1983.

PETIT, Jean–Claude. Herméneutique Philosophique Et Théologie. *Laval Theol Phil* 41,159–170 Je 85.

L'histoire de l'herméneutique est éstroitement liée à pratique même de la théologie. Alors qu'elle avait été jusque–là comprise comme une méthode d'interprétation, tributaire de la connaissance et de l'application de certaines rèles, l'merméneutique se voit ancrée par M Heidegger et H G Gadamer dans une compréhension de l'homme–dans–le–monde et déployée comme un mode d'être du dasein historique. Elle n'est plus alors un instrument au service d'une théologie mais inscrit celle–ci au coeur d'un véritable pluralisme comme elle inscrit le pluralisme en son centre, contribuant ainsi à modifier la compréhension que la théologie peut avoir d'elle–même.

PETIT, Jean–Luc. La Sémantique De L'action De D Davidson. *Arch Phil* 47,449–479 Jl–S 84.

Cleaving to elementary logic in the analysis of meaning in natural language is surely a major purpose of Davidson's semantics. Assuming as a general program the task of redistributing the expressions of discourse on these two hierarchical levels of language and metalanguage, the theory of meaning could do, to his mind, with the resources of elementary logic to account for our use of practical language in general communication. The first approach is limited to a synthetic exposition of Davidson's doctrine. (edited)

PETROVIĆ, Kresimir. The World Socio–Economic And Political Crisis Calls For Changes In The Position And Social Role Of Sports. *Dialec Hum* 11,97–104 Wint 84.

The world of socio–economic, political and also value crisis is more closely connected with the position and social role of sports and sport leaders are prepared to admit. The greater the moral crisis, higher are sport achievements because all otherwise present barriers no longer exist. This is an inescapable world of virtual endless violence, but it is nevertheless a world from which mankind must find a way out and in which sports play its part.

PETRUSCHKA, G and Felgentreu, Herbert. Weltanschauliche Fragen Des Sozialistischen Wettbewerbs. *Deut Z Phil* 22,745–749 1974.

PETRUZZELLIS, Nicola. L'Empirismo Logico E Il Problema Dei Valori. *Sapienza* 37,397–414 O–D 84.

From Carnap to Piaget, from Auer to Oppenheim, the judgment of values, opposed to the scientific thesis, is maintained to be an expression of emotions, of feelings, of wishes, of hopes, consequently, it is devoid of cognitive value, which cannot be considered "true" or "false." The one who is a failure, who thinks injustly of all the world, clearly gives vent to his frustration. But there are judgments of value, wholly impartial and disinterested which concern other people, never met, characters of a far off past, works of art, of thought, of scientific theories.

PETRUZZELLIS, Nicola. La Filosofia E L'arte Sacra: Il Beato Angelico. *Sapienza* 37,129–135 Ap–Je 84.

Genuine art implies the call to infinity, in the form of beauty, which cannot be reduced to separate elements (colors, volumes, sounds) where it fulfills itself. If the content is made up of a holy subject and if the artist lives it with religious inwardness, art is holy in a specific meaning. Beato Angelico lived what he painted.

PETRY, M J. "Propaganda And Analysis: Hegel's Article On The English Reform Bill" in *The State And Civil Society*, Pelczynski, Z A (ed), 137–158. Cambridge Cambridge Univ Pr 1984.

PETTERSSON, Anders. The Ontology Of Literary Works. *Theoria* 50,36–51 1984.

This paper describes the concept of literary work implicit in ordinary language, and argues (i) that this concept is inherently illogical, and (ii) that we do not need the concept of a literary work in theoretical contexts, since statements about a literary work can be rephrased as statements about the original and/or the text, the meaning, and the copies of that work. This analysis is contrasted with current theories about the ontology of literary works.

PETTIT, Philip. Dissolving Kripke's Puzzle About Belief. *Ratio* 26,181–194 D 84.

Saul Kripke has recently argued that we ought to countenance the possibility of the following phenomenon: that someone merits the attribution of two contradictory beliefs, the contradiction between which is indiscernible in principle to him. Kripke finds that phenomenon a puzzle, given his assumption that a person ought to be in a position to see any contradiction between his beliefs. I argue that the principles on which Kripke relies in arguing for the phenomenon and I show that they ought to prevent him from finding the phenomenon a puzzle: they are inconsistent with the assumption mentioned and they remove any reason for accepting it.

PETYX, Vincenza. L'America Primitiva E L'Europa Cristiana. *Filosofia* 36,3–50 Ja–Mr 85.

PEZZELLA, Mario. "Immagine Mitica E Immagine Dialettica: Note Sul "Passagenwerk"" in *Il Tempo Dell'Arte*, Papi, Fulvio and others (ed), 127–138. Milano Franco Angeli 1984.

PFAFF, Donald W (ed). *Ethical Questions In Brain And Behavior.* NY Springer 1983.

PFAFF, Donald W. "Neurobiological Origins Of Human Values" in *Ethical Questions In Brain And Behavior*, Pfaff, Donald W (ed), 141–152. NY Springer 1983.

PFEIFER, Karl. Yu Guang–Yuan's Two Categories Of Matter. *J Chin Phil* 12,57–62 Mr 85.

In "The Function of Consciousness on Matter", *Chinese Studies in Philosophy* 12 (1981) pages 38–54, Yu claims that in order to understand how consciousness can affect the physical world, two categories of matter must be distinguished. I argue that Yu's distinction has no explanatory force and, morever, is at odds with his materialist assumptions. I then suggest other strategies.

PFEIFFER, Alfred. Causalité Et Finalité (in German). *Deut Z Phil* 22,83–85 1974.

PHIFER, Kenneth. Why Me; Why Now? *Relig Hum* 19,40–45 Wint 85.

Santayana once wrote that "everything in nature is lyrical in its ideal essence, tragic in its fate, and comic in its existence." These words are a kind of lodestar for me in the struggle to answer the questions that accompany bad times, bad happenings: Why me? why now? how can I live with this? Our reliance must be on human experience, human sharing and caring, and the courage to forge meaning out of madness.

PHILIPS, Michael. Are 'Killing' And 'Letting Die' Adequately Specified Moral Categories? *Phil Stud* 47,151–158 Ja 85.

According to Rachels' "bare difference" argument there is no morally relevant difference between killing *per se* and letting die *per se*. But this position (and Rachels' argument for it) entails that the weights of the *prima facie* obligations not to kill and not to let die are constants. It is argued against this that the weights of these *prima facie* obligations vary from context to context.

PHILIPS, Michael. Normative Contexts And Moral Decision. *J Bus Ethics* 4,233–237 Ag 85.

This paper attempts to explain the significance of the 'ideologies'—or 'middle-level' normative discourse— described by Kenneth Goodpaster in his paper 'Business Ethics, Ideology, and the Naturalistic Fallacy'. It is argued that the propositions constitutive of this discourse are not invokable moral principles (i.E., principles which generate solutions to actual moral problems). Rather, they are characterizations of the normative contexts in which moral decisions are made. As such, they place limits on the ways in which the abstract moral principles of traditional moral theory may be applied or interpreted in making real-life moral decisions.

PHILLIPS, D C. The Tendency Of Tendermindedness In Educational Research, Or, The New Anti-Formalism. *Proc Phil Educ* 40,283–294 1984.

There is an ongoing debate in educational research and the applied social sciences between two groups reminiscent of James's "tenderminded" and "toughminded" thinkers. The tenderminded are anti-formalistic, and they misuse the ideas of Kuhn, Polanyi and Hanson to support various forms of relativism. Some examples are discussed.

PHILLIPS, D L. Remarks In Praise Of Guilt. *Theor Med* 6,165–176 Je 85.

This article is an elaboration and extension of an earlier article concerned with guilt and morality in the modern age. The focus is on two general issues arising from what was presented there. First, there is an attempt to explicate the conception of human agency underlying the emphasis on individual responsibility in the original essay. Second, there is a critical examination of the moral relativism position so common in the contemporary world. Both the shrinking conception of human agency and responsibilty and the growing acceptance of moral relativism are strongly criticized, and it is concluded that a rationally-based morality must be defended against those many persons today for whom 'anything goes' in the realm of human behavior.

PHILLIPS, D Z. The Devil's Disguises: Philosophy Of Religion, 'Objectivity' And 'Cultural Divergence'. *Philosophy* 17,61–78 84 Supp.

PHILLIPS, Robert L. *War And Justice*. Norman Univ Oklahoma Pr 1984.

This book is an interpretation and defense of the Just War tradition. The tradition deals with two questions: Under what circumstances is war justified and How may combat be limited? The work considers two modern challenges: Guerrilla war and nuclear deterrence. It is argued that the only grounds for objecting to these forms of violence is that the Just War Tradition itself. The work conclude that the Just War theory is the moral alternative to the extremes of pacifism and realism, and that it alone succesfully articulates the prudential concerns of modern states.

PHILLIPS, Stephen H. The Central Argument Of Aurobindo's *The Life Divine*. *Phil East West* 35,271–284 Jl 85.

Aurobindo argues that the Absolute's (or Brahmman's) nature as Sachchidananda necessitates further evolutionary advance. Otherwise our world with its evil could not exist since it would be incompatible with Brahmman (particularly in its aspect of Ananda or "Bliss"). The argument fails for reasons internal to Aurobindo's thought, but the theory of "divine life" is a remarkable Indian "theodicy" that would explain the significance of the cosmos both from Brahman's and human perspectives.

PICCIONE, Bruno L G. Nietzsche Y Heidegger: La Superación De La Metafísica Y El Pensar Futuro. *Cuad Filosof* 19,155–166 Ja–D 83.

The present work points out Heidegger's great contribution to the accurate revival of Nietzche's thought. It takes, though, a critical position in respect to his interpretation of Nietzsche and also in respect to the fact of having placed the latter as the last representative of Metaphysics of Subjectivity. Far from it, the work shows, through direct textual investigation and according to the main ideas in Nietzschean Philosophy, that Nietzsche is the forerunner of the surpassing of classical Metaphysics achieved by Heidegger. The work also asserts that the latter follows–genially–Nietzsche's steps along the path he has opened.

PICHLER, Joseph A. The Liberty Principle: A Basis For Management Ethics. *Bus Prof Ethics J* 2,19–30 Wint 83.

PICKENS, Donald K. Sociobiology: The World As Given Or The World As Created. *J Thought* 20,67–78 Spr 85.

This essay examines sociobiology's historical background, its prescription for the future, and the strong scholarly reaction to it. The current conflict between positivism (i.E., the contention that the cognitive aims of natural and social science are basically the same) and historicism (i.E., that human beings are creatures of experiences, free to shape their world in terms of increasing independence from biological necessity) has different implications for American social policies. The controversy over sociobiology also provides a useful method for teaching the history of ideas over the last two hundred years.

PIDERIT, John J. The Role Of Economics And Ethical Principles In Determining U S Policies Toward Poor Nations. *Thought* 60,353–369 S 85.

PIERCE, W David and Epling, W Frank. On The Persistence Of Cognitive Explanation: Implications For Behavior Analysis. *Behaviorism* 12,15–28 Spr 84.

Skinner has assigned the persistence of cognitive explanations to the literature of freedom and dignity. This view is challenged especially as it applies to behavioral scientists. It is argued that cognitive explanations persist (a) because current behaviorism does not challenge cognitive epistemology; (b) because behavior analysts have failed to provide research evidence at the level of human behavior, and finally (c) because a science of behavior based solely on operant principles is necessarily incomplete. The implications of these problems for behavior analysis are addressed.

PIETERSMA, H. Assertion And Predication In Husserl. *Husserl Stud* 2,75–96 1985.

Husserl's views add up to a very complex set of conceptual relationships, which I try to articulate in twelve theses. What I here call assertion—the author himself uses various terms—is the sort of propositional attitude Hume discussed as belief and Brentano as judgment, I show how he distinguishes it from such things as namings and predications, even from predications which assign existence, truth, or reality. I also deal with the neutral counterpart of assertion and its relation to the characteristically phenomenological attitude.

PIETRUSKA- MADEJ, Elzbieta. Should Philosophers Of Science Consider Scientific Discovery? *Ratio* 27,7–18 Je 85.

According to the view widely held in philosophy of science discovery is the proper subject for psychology alone. Against this the authoress asserts that the scientific discovery is, as such, something more than a psychological act of the individual's mind. It is a complex process which has an extrapsychological dimension. Philosophy of science then, applying its theoretical tools, should study the objective aspect of scientific discovery and reveal the typical characteristics of the objective discovery-generating situation.

PIETRZYNSKI, Gerd. Entwicklung Und Effektive Nutzung Des Gesellschaft Arbeitsvermögens—Ausdruck Praktizierter Einheit Von Humanität Und Rationalität. *Deut Z Phil* 32,894–898 1984.

Im Beitrag wird nachgewiesen, wie Grundwerte des Sozialismus, insbesondere die Einheit von ökonomischer Effektivität und sozialer Hummanität bei der Entwicklung und Nutzung des Arbeitsvermögens in der DDR verwirklicht werden. Das wird in folgenden Richtungen domonstriert: in gesicherter Vollbeschäftigung für alle Bürger bei ständiger Verbesserung ihrer Arbeits- und Lebensbedingungen; in der Erhöhung planmäβiger Disponibilität der Werktätigen in Übereinstimmung mit den Erfordernissen der wissenschaft-lich-technischen Revolution und persönlichen Interessen der Menschen; in der Ausschöpfung des hohen Bildungsniveaus der Bürger; in der Senkung des Krankenstandes und anderer Ausfallzeiten; in der umfassenden Teilnahme der Erktätigen an der Leitung und Planung der Volkswirtschaft, Kombinate und Betriebe.

PILCHIK, Ely E. Spiritual Resources: Contemporary Problems In Judaism. *J Dharma* 10,18–24 Ja–Mr 85.

PILLAY, Anand and Srour, Gabriel. Closed Sets And Chain Conditions In Stable Theories. *J Sym Log* 49,1350–1362 D 84.

Let T be a complete first order theory and M be a very saturated model of T. A definable set X of M is *closed* if the intersection of any collection of conjugates of X is equal to a finite subintersection. We call T equational if every definable set is a Boolean combination of closed sets and we show how for equational theories, the notions of stability theory, e.G. Forking have a simple and natural expression.

PILLAY, Anand. Regular Types In Nonmultidimensional ω-Stable Theories. *J Sym Log* 49,880–891 S 84.

A hierarchy is defined on the regular types of an omega-stable non-multidimensional theory, using generalized notions of algebraic and strongly minimal formulae. As an application, it is shown that any resplendent model of an omega-stable finite dimensional theory is saturated.

PINCH, Trevor. Theory Testing In Science—The Case Of Solar Neutrinos. *Phil Soc Sci* 15,167–188 Je 85.

The problem of logical-decision making during the crucial test of a theory by an experiment is considered. Popper's views are outlined and illustrated by reference to the experiment to detect solar neutrinos. It is shown that different views of the outcome of this test were held by different scientists. This presents difficulties for accounts of theory testing which give prominence to the place of logic. An alternative approach toward theory testing is suggested.

PINCKAERS, S. La Question Des Actes Intrinsèquement Mauvais. *Rev Thomiste* 84,618–624 O–D 84.

PINCUS, David. On The Independence Of The Kinna Wagner Principle. *Z Math Log* 20,503–516 1974.

PINES, Shlomo. The Historical Evolution Of A Certain Concept Of Freedom (in Hebrew). *Iyyun* 33,247–265 Ja–Ap 84.

PINKAS, D. "Essai Sur L'auto-référence Dans Les Arts Visuels" in *Asthetische Er Fahrung Und Das Wesen Der Kunst*, Holzhey, Helmut, 123–142. Bern Haupt 1984.

PINKAVA, Jindrich. The Correlation Of Science And Art (in Czechoslovakian). *Estetika* 22,52–66 1985.

PINTOR- RAMOS, Antonio. Metafísica, Historia Y Antropología: Sobre El Fundamento De La Antropología *Filosófica*. *Pensamiento* 41,3–36 Ja–Mr 85.

Estudio de las dificultades y fundamentos entre la doctrina *filosófica* del hombre. Se desarrolla desde una confrontación entre la teoría clásica y la historicista, mostrando en ambas supuestos problemáticos. Asumida la crítica de Heidegger, se postula una concepción más radical de la experiencia filosófica. Con el filósofo espanñol Zubiri, se propone un posible planteamiento neuvo para una doctrina filosófica del hombre.

PINXTEN, Rik. Anthropological Concepts: Some Notes On Their Epistemological Status. *Commun Cog* 17,291–314 1984.

PIOZZI, Patrizia. Vargas And Prestes: A Comparison Between The Labourism And Communism In Brazil (in Portuguese). *Trans/Form/Acao* 6,25–36 1983.

In this article, I show the impressive similarity between theoretical suppositions underlying a discourse that articulates a "bourgeois conception" of social relations, built for the control of the workers' class, and its supposed opponent, which intended to articulate a socialist conception and, explicitly, was developing the marxist point of view. I conclude this exposition with a brief reflection over the origin of these presuppositions in the womb of the international communist movement. (edited)

PIPER, Adrian M S. Two Conceptions Of The Self. *Phil Stud* 48,173–198 S 85.

The prevailing, Humean conception of the self consists in the desire model of motivation, and the model of reason as having a solely instrumental role in satisfying such desires. Harry Frankfurt has refined this conception to include second–order desires that evaluate the first–order desires on which we act. But this modification generates an infinite regress of orders of desires, and so makes self–evaluation impossible and moral paralysis probable. An alternative Kantian conception of the self, according to which we are overridingly motivated by a highest–order norm of theoretical rationality, solves both of these problems and better explains the psychological facts.

PIPPIN, Robert B. Marcuse On Hegel And Historicity. *Phil Forum* 16,180–206 Spr 85.

I propose here an interpretation of Marcuses's 1932 work, *Hegels Ontologie und die Grunlegung einer Theorie der Geschichlichkeit*. This work is shown to be a Heideggerean reconstruction of the early Hegel and, more importantly, to introduce a number of foundational theoretical issues that would appear again and again in Marcuse's own version of the critical theory project. Indeed, contrary to the view that this work, and its central, elusive issue, historicity, represents a dispensable piece of juvenelia, I argue that it can help illuminate a number of themes that remain unresolved in Marcuse, and to some extent, in Critical Theory itself.

PISCIONE, Enrico. Il Primato Dell'Amicizia Nella Filosofia Antica. *Sapienza* 37,377–396 O–D 84.

This work examines the theme of friendship in the most representative thinkers of ancient philosophy: Plato, Aristotle, Epicurus and Cicero. As far as Plato is concerned, the solipstic outcome of friendship and eros is emphasized. As for Aristotle, the almost scientific distinction of the various aspects of friendship is shown. As to Epicurus, the idea of friendship as a presage of happiness is stressed. As for Cicero, the doctrine of "disinterested friendship" is emphasized.

PITCHER, George and Honderich, Ted (ed). *Berkeley*. Boston Routledge & K Paul 1977.

PITKIN, Hanna F. Food And Freedom In *The Flounder*. *Polit Theory* 12,467–490 N 84.

Günter Grass's novel, *The Flounder*, illuminates the relationship between politics, action, and freedom, on the one hand, and economics, bodily needs, and historical necessity, on the other. These themes are also tied to relations between men and women. Grass asks who is responsible for history, and will it be different as women take it over, this essay both describes the novel's complex structure and explores its themes.

PITOWSKY, Itamar. Discussion: Quantum Mechanics And Value Definiteness. *Phil Sci* 52,154–156 Mr 85.

PITOWSKY, Itamar. On The Status Of Statistical Inferences. *Synthese* 63,233–248 My 85.

Can the axioms of probability theory and the classical patterns of statistical inference ever be falsified by observations? Various possible answers to this question are examined in a set theoretical context and in relation to the findings of microphysics.

PITOWSKY, Itamar. Unified Field Theory And The Conventionality Of Geometry. *Phil Sci* 51,685–689 D 84.

The existence of fields besides gravitation may provide us with a way to decide empirically whether spacetime is really a nonflat Riemannian manifold or a flat Minkowskian manifold that appears curved as a result of gravitational distortions. This idea is explained using a modification of Poincaré's famous 'diskworld'.

PITT, Jack. Gallina And Pitt: Similarities And Differences. *Russell* 4,311–312 Wint 84.

A reply to Gallina's response to my paper, "Russell and Marx: Similarities and Differences", Russell, pp. 37–40 (1980). I think Russell's *German Social Democracy* is a good book in spite of Gallina's harsh verdict on it, and I say why. We are in general accord with respect to Russell and Marx's views on religion and work.

PITTIONI, Veit. Othmar Spanns Ganzheitslehre In Neuer Interpretation. *Conceptus* 18,3–32 1984.

Die zu Unrecht heute fast vergessene Ganzheitlehre dient Othmar Spann als metaphysische Basis seines Systems. Anschliessend an deren Darstellung geben wir eine Spanns metaphysischen Ambitionen zuwiderlaufende Interpretation seiner Ganzheitslehre, die diese als eine geeignete Grundlage für eine Logik des sinnovollen Zusammenhanges erscheinen lässt.

PIZARRO, Fernando A (ed). *Bio–Bibliografia De La Filosofia En Chile Desde El Siglo XVI Hasta 1980*. Santiago Inst De Santiago 1982.

PIZZORNI, Reginaldo M. Il Diritto Naturale Fondamento E Criterio Di Giustizia Del Diritto Positivo E Della Sua Obbligatorietà. *Sapienza* 37,285–300 Jl–S 84.

Contro il positivismo e il neopoitivismo l'A riafferma che non si puō ammettere che la legalità si identifichi con la giustizia, e riconosce che sulla legge positiva, da chiunque essa venga, è sempre possibile, e anzi spesso doveroso, esprimere un *giudiio di valore*, cioè una *critica delle leggi*, per stabilire de esse siano giuste o ingiuste. E'lecita quindi la ricerca de *diritto del diritto positivo*, possible sole se si ammette l'invincibile ed eterna idea del *diritto naturale* fondato in ultima isstanza nell'Essere assoluto: Dio, per cui *"non auctoritas, sed veritas facit legem"*.

PLAMENATZ, John. "Philosophical Element In Social Theory And Practice" in *Ideology, Philosophy And Politics*, Parel, Anthony (ed), 61–76. Waterloo Laurier Univ Pr 1983.

PLANT, Raymond. "Hegel On Identity And Legitimation" in *The State And Civil Society*, Pelczynski, Z A (ed), 227–243. Cambridge Cambridge Univ Pr 1984.

PLANTINGA, Alvin (ed) and Wolterstorff, Nicholas (ed). *Faith And Rationality: Reason And Belief In God*. Notre Dame Univ Notre Dame Pr 1983.

This book contains four long essays in the epistemology of religious belief: "Reason and Belief in God" by Alvin Plantinga, "Christian Experience and Christian Belief" by William P Alston, "Can Belief in God be Rational If It Has No Foundations?" By Nicholas Wolterstorff and "Jerusalem and Athens Revisted" by George Mavrodes. It also contains an essay on the theology of W Pannenburg, "Faith, Reason and the Resurrection" by David Holwerda, an essay by George Marsden entitled "The Collapse of American Evangelical Academia, and two fables by George Mavrodes. Perhaps the unifying theme of the book is consideration and rejection of the evidentialist objection to theistic belief, the claim that theistic belief is rational or appropriate only if there is adequate evidence for it of the general sort provided by sound theistic arguments.

PLANTINGA, Alvin. "Reason And Belief In God" in *Faith And Rationality*, Plantinga, Alvin (ed), 16–93. Notre Dame Univ Notre Dame Pr 1983.

PLANTINGA, Alvin. Advice To Christian Philosophers. *Faith Phil* 1,253–271 Jl 84.

PLATT, David. The Seashore As Dwelling In The Fourfold: An Ontic Explication Of Heidegger. *Int Phil Quart* 25,173–184 Je 85.

The purpose of the article is to give an ontic explication of Heidegger's doctrine of the fourfold using a *specific* seashore location as illustration. A specific place is important because it is crucial to Heidegger's concept of "dwelling". The conclusion is that Heidegger's "dwelling" is a fruitful phenomenological concept which is more clearly understood when described in ontic terms applied to the fourfold.

PLATT, Michael. "Tragical, Comical, Historical" in *Existential Coordinates Of Human Condition*, Tymieniecka, A (ed), 379–400. Boston Reidel 1984.

PLECHA, James L. Tenselessness And The Absolute Present. *Philosophy* 59,529–534 O 84.

PLEKON, Michael. "Towards Apocalypse" in *International Kierkegaard Commentary*, Perkins, Robert L (ed), 19–52. Macon Mercer Univ Pr 1984.

PLOG, Fred. "The Ethics Of Excavation: Site Selection" in *Ethics And Values In Archaeology*, Green, Ernestene L (ed), 89–96. NY Free Pr 1984.

PODGORSKI, Frang. Two Models Of Spiritual Journey: Yoga And Confucius. *J Chin Phil* 12,23–48 Mr 85.

PÖGGELER, Otto (ed). *Heidegger: Perspektiven Zur Deutung Seines Werkes*. Konigstein Athenaum 1984.

PÖGGELER, Otto. Between Enlightenment And Romanticism: Rosenzweig And Hegel (in Hebrew). *Iyyun* 33,78–90 Ja–Ap 84.

POGGELER, Otto. Den Führer Führen: Heidegger Und Kein Ende. *Phil Rundsch* 32,26–67 1985.

POGORZELSKI, W A and Prucnal, T. Structural Completeness Of The First–Order Predicate Calculus. *Z Math Log* 21,315–320 1975.

POGORZELSKI, Witold A. On Hilbert's Operation On Logical Rules, II. *Rep Math Log* 17,3–12 1984.

The formalism used in this paper is presented in part I, Rep Math Log 12, 1981. The purpose of the part II is to introduce two notions: H–consistency, HCns, and H–completeness HCpl. These two notions are counterparts of the standard notions of consistency, Cns, and completeness, Cpl, post–completeness, of logical systems. The H–consistency of the system L is understood as the standard consistency of the system R–primeL, for all binary rules R–prime derivable in L and contained in R^+. Of course HCns⊂–underlinedCns but not conversely. The classical sentential system $L_2$is H–consistent. H–completeness of the consistent system L=/R,A/ consists in the inclusion of all permissible /in L/ rules in the set of all rules derivable in /R, 0. HCpl⊂–underlinedCpl but not conversely. The classical sentential systems are not H–complete, however there are some consistent strengthenings of the classical systems which are H–complete.

POIZAT, Bruno. Deux Remarques À Propos De La Propriété De Recouvrement Fini. *J Sym Log* 49,803–807 S 84.

A technical note on two questions in Model Theory.

POJMAN, Louis P. A Critique Of Holyer's Volitionalism. *Dialogue (Canada)* 23,695–700 D 84.

Robert Holyer in his article "Belief and Will Revisited" (DIALOGUE 22/2, 1983) defends a form of direct volitionalism, contending that arguments by Price, Williams, Classen, and myself focus too exclusively on one type of volitional belief acquisition. In this article I appraise Holyer's arguments and conclude that all of his points can either be shown to be dubious or be incorporated within an anti–volitional account of belief acquisition.

POJMAN, Louis P. Believing And Willing. *Can J Phil* 15,37–56 Mr 85.

It is a widely held belief that we can obtain beliefs and withhold believing directly upon performing an act of will. This thesis is sometimes identified with the view that acquiring a belief is sometimes a basic act, an act which is under our direct control. In this paper I examine this thesis and set forth two arguments to undermine it. The first argument is The Phenomenological Argument which proceeds on the basis of an introspective account of the nature of belief acquisition, indicating that, while there are anomolies, obtaining beliefs normally, if not always, occurs in a non–volitional manner. The second argument, The Logic of Belief Argument, shows that there is a conceptual connection between believing and non–volitional states so that even if someone came to believe directly by willing to believe, the person could not believe that the belief was solely based on an act of will and still hold the belief. I also deal with two possible objections to my account: the veto action of the will in belief formation and self–creative believings.

POKHARNA, S S. A New Investigation Into The Problem Of Perfect Determinism In Modern Science. *Indian Phil Quart* 12,67–84 Ja–Mr 85.

POKRIEFKA, M L and Hendry, Herbert E. Carnapian Extensions Of S5. *J Phil Log* 14,111–128 My 85.

POLDRACK, H and Kaiser, Eckhard. Meinungsstreit Zu Fragen Der Marxistischen Wahrheitstheorie. *Deut Z Phil* 23,1067–1071 1975.

POLIMENI, Dante and Rojas, Oscar. Mujer, Biología O Historia Y Poder. *Rev Filosof (Costa Rica)* 23,205–214 D 85.

The recent period in Costa Rica has meant an extensive discussion, in the public domain, about the problematic condition of woman in our times. The author attempts to make an examination of the doctrinary and social content of the sectors that are opposed in the formulated positions. In the analysis of the positions about the inevitability and therefore, universability and constant permanence of masculine influence, the plain biolocalization of these positions and their reactionary political content are declared. As it is propounded from Kosik and Foucault a globalizing perspective, the author presents the need for surpassing the positions of the sectors that are trying to get a place in the university and political domains, and proposes reflection about everyday life and the peasant's and the worker's situation.

POLLOCK, John L. A Solution To The Problem Of Induction. *Nous* 18,423–462 S 84.

It is shown that principles of enumerative and statistical induction can be derived from the probabilistic principles comprising the theory of "nomic probability." The parts of the theory employed in deriving principles of induction are an acceptance rule, a theory of direct inference, and several novel computational principles. This approach to induction differs markedly from more standard probabilistic approaches in that it is not assumed that degree of confirmation is a probabilistic notion satisfying the probability calculus (in fact, that is denied), and the principles of induction that are obtained are perfectly ordinary looking principles of the sort described in the philosophy of science outside probability theory. (edited)

POLLOCK, John L. Foundations For Direct Inference. *Theor Decis* 17,221–256 N 84.

It is shown that the theory of direct inference from nomic probability (developed in an earlier article) can be simplified by recognizing some general epistemological principles. Then it is shown that resulting theory is derivable from more basic parts of the theory of nomic probability. There is no need to posit primitive principles pertaining specifically to direct inference.

POLLOCK, John L. Nomic Probability. *Midwest Stud Phil* 9,177–204 1984.

Nomic probability is the kind of probability involved in statistical laws of nature. This paper sketches the general theory of nomic probability that i have been developing in a series of more technical articles and attempts to make the theory accessible to the general philosophical reader. The theory proceeds from a strengthened version of the probability calculus and an acceptance rule, deriving from these a theory of direct inference and a theory of statistical and enumerative induction.

POLLOCK, John L. Reply To Leeds: "A Problem About Frequencies In Direct Inference". *Phil Stud* 48,141–144 Jl 85.

POMAIZL, K. Fundamental Characteristics Of Socialist National Relations (in Czechoslovakian). *Filozof Cas* 32,611–625 1984.

POMEDLI, Michael. The Concept Of "Soul" In The Jesuit Relations: Were There Any Philosophers Among The North American Indians? *Laval Theol Phil* 41,57–64 F 85.

In this paper I try to recount, understand and become engaged in the philosophy of the North American Indians on the conception of the "soul" as found in The Jesuit Relations, 1610–1791.

POMERLAU, Wayne P. Does Reason Demand That God Be Infinite? *Sophia (Australia)* 24,18–27 Jl 85.

This paper considers six sorts of attempts at rationality justifying belief in divine infinity: (1) the ontological argument; (2) causal arguments; (3) arguments from miracles; (4) the moral argument; (5) arguments from tradition; and (6) arguments based on mystical experience. It contends that none of these approaches proves conclusively adequate and suggests that God's infinity is among what Aquinas calls "those truths that exceed natural knowledge."

POOLE JR, Charles P. Formalism And Application Of Catastrophe Theory. *Ultim Real Mean* 7,298–312 D 84.

POPE, Robin. Timing Contradictions In Von Neumann And Morgenstern's Axioms And In Savage's "Sure–Thing" Proof. *Theor Decis* 18,229–261 My 85.

At the point of choice, let N be the delay in learning the outcome. Then von Neumann and Morgenstern's postulates contradictorily imply that N = 0 and N > 0. As a consequence, Savage's 'sure–thing' proof, which has bestowed on expected utility theory most of its normative appeal, depends on inconsistent assumptions. Further, the validity of Savage's proof cannot be retrieved by minimizing N > 0, by making the delay a mere moment or so. The historical origins of these contradictions are traced to (i) von Neumann and Morgenstern inadvertently limiting their risk model to the certain period, that is the period after gamblers learn the outcome(s), and (ii) Savage's use of the sure–thing principle for analyzing "atemporally but also quite formally" compound gambles [Savage, 1954, p 23].

POPESCU, Vasile. La Morale Socialiste Et La Valeur De L'homme. *Phil Log* 27,279–285 O–D 83.

POPKIN, Jeremy D. Conservatism Under Napoleon: The Political Writings Of Joseph Fiévée. *Hist Euro Ideas* 5,385–400 1984.

POPKIN, Richard H (ed) and Rosenfield, Leonora C. *Condorcet Studies 1.* Atlantic Highlands Humanities Pr 1984.

This is the first American collection of scholarly studies of Condorcet, the last of the *philosophies*. He had wide-ranging reform ideas of secular liberalism, which are relevant to contemporary problems, and studied British philosophy and the

American Revolution. Lenora Cohen Rosenfield, the editor, writes a synoptic introduction. Four studies deal with Condorcet's views on rights and revolution, three on social sciences, three on the revolution in education, and two on the quest for justice.

POPKIN, Richard H. "Hobbes And Skepticism" in *History Of Philosophy In Making*, Thro, Linus J (ed), 133–148. Washington Univ Pr Of America 1982.

POPKIN, Richard H. Un Autre Spinoza. *Arch Phil* 48,37–58 Ja–Mr 85.

New researches concerning the young Spinoza and his intellectual milieu: discussion on Messianism and Millenarism which took place at Amsterdam between 1656 and 1666 throw some light on his discussions with the Quakers, Oldenbourg and Serrarius. Spinoza might be the heterodox Jew who agreed to translate the book of Margaret Fell on the Scripture, and, if so, it would be his first work, which has indeed some likeness with the Tractatus theologico–politicus.

POPPER, Karl. Bemerkungen Zu Roehles Arbeit Und Zur Axiomatik. *Conceptus* 8,53–56 1974.

Das zentrale Anliegen von *Roehles* Arbeit sieht Sir *Karl* in der Definition gewisser Begriffe, wie etwa des Geradenbegriffes. Die mit der transzendentalen Methode gewonnenen Definitionen und Resultate werden zwar grundsätzlich anerkannt, doch kritisiert *Popper*, daβ *Roehle* deren Adäquatheit nicht nachweist, und holt dies nach. (edited)

PORK, Andrus. Assessing Relative Causal Importance In History. *Hist Theor* 24,62–69 F 85.

The philosophical interpretation of how the historians show (or attempt to show) that one cause is more important than another is one of the most important tasks of the philosophy of history in the 1980s. A scheme that clarifies the intuitively acceptable sense of the statement 'A was a more important cause of P than was B' is proposed in the article. It is asserted that to analyze hypothetical counter–factual situations the historians try to find appropriate real situations.

PORRECO, Rocco (ed). *The Georgetown Symposium On Ethics.* Lanham Univ Pr Of America 1984.

A collection of essays presented at a two–day symposium on ethics sponsored by Georgetown University to honor Henry Babcock Veatch on the occassion of his retirement from active teaching. Represents bothea festschrfft for Veatch as well as a tribute to Georgetown University's specialization in ethics at the graduate level and moral education throughout all its curricula. Major papers were delivered by Alan Gerwith, Alan Donagan, Manfred Vogel and Joseph Owen.

PORTER, Lindsay. The Quirks And Turns In The Eighth Paragraph Of Kant's Chapter On The Ontological Argument. *Indian Phil Quart* 11,309–332 Jl 84.

Kemp Smith's translation obscures the fact that paragraph eight contains not one but two objections to the argument. *contra* Mr Ray Pinkerton, the second is that the conclusion is merely "God possibly exists", which Kant says is a miserable tautology. This objection involves a very whimsical application of the principle of charity. Kant should instead have objected that the conclusion "God exists" is putatively analytic, which presupposes that God is identical with the concept of him.

PORTMESS, Lisa. An Historicist View Of Teaching Philosophy. *Teach Phil* 7,313–324 O 84.

Traditional methods of teaching philosophy which assume the universality of philosophical problems and the intellectual autonomy of philosophers neglect the social and historical context of philosophical problems. They obscure what is distinctive in the way such problems are conceived and their solutions envisioned in different cultures and in different time periods. This article explores universalist and historicist assumptions in teaching and argues for the effectiveness of teaching introductory philosophy from an historicist perspective.

POSADAS, Ofelia E. Humanismo De Samuel Ramos. *Logos (Mexico)* 12,9–56 S–D 84.

POSCHEL, Reinhard. Die Funktionale Vollstandigkeit Von Funktionenklassen Über Einer Familie Endlicher Mengen. *Z Math Log* 20,537–550 1974.

POSPESEL, Howard. *Introduction To Logic: Propositional Logic.* Englewood Cliffs Prentice–Hall 1984.

POSPÍCHALOVÁ, Milena. Fundamental Features Of The Transition From The Old To The New Quality Under Socialism (in Czechoslovakian). *Filosof Cas* 33,22–35 1985.

POSPISIL, Zdenek. Towards One Type Of Non–Artistic Expression And Communication (in Czechoslovakian). *Estetika* 21,69–81 1984.

POSSENTI, Vittorio. La Società Aperta Nel Pensiero Politico Del '900 (Bergson, Popper, Maritain). *Riv Filosof Neo–Scolas* 76,269–291 Ap–Je 84.

PÖSSNECK, E and Friedrich, Gert and Kästner, H. Probleme Der Führenden Rolle Der Arbeiterklasse Im Sozialismus. *Deut Z Phil* 22,739–745 1974.

POSTELNICU, Paul. From Entelechy Of The "Feedback Systems Hypothesis". *Phil Log* 27,348–354 O–D 83.

POSTMAN, Neil. Critical Thinking In The Electronic Era. *Nat Forum* 65,4–8 Wint 85.

POSTOW, B C. Sport, Art, And Gender. *J Phil Sport* 11,52–55 1984.

Without committing myself to Boxill's thesis that sport is an art form, I defend that thesis against the objection that no participant in an athletic event is supposed to be concerned with the aesthetic quality of the performance as a whole. I also explore the implications of Boxill's thesis for the question of desirability of separate rules for women's and men's sports.

POSTOW, B C. Werner's Ethical Realism. *Ethics* 95,285–291 Ja 85.

On Werner's theory moral wrongs are objective facts which we observe as we observe trees; in both cases our concepts, prior experience, etc., play a part in our observations. I argue that a defender of the view that there are no objective moral facts could explain moral conversions better than Werner can. I also argue that

Werner fails to show that his theory is simpler than the view that there are no objective moral facts.

POSY, Carl J. "Transcendental Idealism And Causality" in *Kant On Causality, Freedom, And Objectivity*, Harper, William A (ed), 20–41. Minneapolis Univ Minnesota Pr 1984.

POSY, Carl J. On Brouwer's Definition Of Unextendable Order. *Hist Phil Log* 1,139–150 1980.

It is argued that the tensed theory of the creative subject provided a natural formulation of the logic underlying Brouwer's notion of unextendable order and explains the link between that notion and virtual order. The tensed theory of the creative subject is also shown to be a useful tool for interpreting recent evidence about the stages of Brouwer's thinking concerning these two notions of order.

POTTER, Jonathan. Testability, Flexibility: Kuhnian Values In Scientists' Discourse Concerning Theory Choice. *Phil Soc Sci* 14,303–330 S 84.

T S Kuhn argues that scientific theory choice is governed by values which provide a rational basis for theory selection. This claim is tested by examining the transcript of a scientific conference where the selection of theories is discussed. A detailed discourse analysis of this transcript reveals fundamental difficulties with the values–as–constraint model. It is suggested that values should be viewed as a flexible repertoire of interpretative resources with scientists' selcetively draw upon in warranting their own theory choices and undermining opponents.

POTTER, K H. Does Indian Epistemology Concern Justified True Belief? *J Indian Phil* 12,307–328 D 84.

I endeavor to show that J N Mohanty's claim of incommensurability among Indian epistemological theories is based on a justified true belief account of knowledge; that *prāmānya* doesn't mean truth but rather workability; that Indian theories of knowledge are not predicated on noncognitivism in values as Western ones are; that the claim incommensurability among Indian epistemological theories is a result of imposing on them shortcomings in contemporary Western ways of thinking.

POTTS, Ronald. Anaxagoras' Cosmogony. *Apeiron* 18,90–96 1984.

A brief description of Anaxagoras' system, which argues that: (1) He is describing the origin of our world and is not intent on analyzing it into ultimate constituents. (2) By 'seeds', he means seeds. (3) His grand generalization that all things are mixtures is indeed circular, regressive, non–reductive—yet a fair description of the way things are. (4) He sets the standard for scientific cosmogony (e.G., "big–bang" theory) by retrodicting origins from present–day appearances.

POUR- EL, Marion Boykan and Caldwell, Jerome. On A Simple Definition Of Computable Function Of A Real Variable—With Applications To Functions Of A Complex Variable. *Z Math Log* 21,1–19 1975.

POWELL, Donald C. Commentary On "A Response To 'Is Business Bluffing Ethical'". *Bus Prof Ethics J* 3,23–24 Wint 84.

POZO, Candido. El Hombre Pecador. *Gregorianum* 65,365–387 1984.

PRADO, C G. The Need For Truth. *Dialogue (Canada)* 23,687–688 D 84.

PRAKASH, Madhu Suri. In Pursuit Of Wholeness: Moral Development, The Ethics Of Care And The Virtue Of *Philia*. *Proc Phil Educ* 40,63–74 1984.

This paper explores the educational or developmental import of the virtue of philia, as well as the pedagogy appropriate for its nurture. This study of friendship directs attention to the contrasts drawn between the "ethic of care" and the "ethic of justice." How might these two ethics appropriately complement each other? This question, in turn, generates inquiry into the divisions drawn between our public and private selves, paralleling the distinction between public morals and private morality. Fresh re–approachments between these domains are entertained, suggested by compelling conceptions of civic friendship and holistic development.

PRASAD, Brij Kishore. Wittgenstein On Ostensive Definition. *Philosophica (India)* 10,40–45 Ja–D 81.

PRASAD, Rajendra. Svaraj, Reverence, And Creativity. *Indian Phil Quart* 11,485–512 O–D 84.

The paper, via criticizing K C Bhattacharya, shows that one's creativity is stifled by subjection to any culture, alien or indigenous, rather more by the latter. His reverence for it, aided by patriotism, deadens his reason's freedom and makes emancipation more difficult. To emancipate himself he needs some big jolt which an extremely sensitive person like Buddha may get from some external happenings. But an ordinary person can get it only from some deep personal crisis.

PRATTE, Richard. Rethinking Power Relations. *Proc Phil Educ* 40,91–96 1984.

PRATTIS, J I. Man And Metaphor: An Exploration In Entropy And Coherence. *Commun Cog* 17,187–204 1984.

The philosophical implications of Lévi–Strauss structuralism are examined in terms of treating structuralism as a myth that speaks to contradictions within Western civilization. The logic of structuralism is taken through myth, science, poetry, and cave art in order to return debate to a concern with theology. Analogies at the level of symbolic metaphor are made with the thought of Jung and Buddhist meditation practice. The question addressed is that of the structures necessary for man to retain a coherent sense of unity.

PRAWITZ, Dag. Remarks On Some Approaches To The Concept Of Logical Consequence. *Synthese* 62,153–172 F 85.

PRESAS, Mario A. Acerca Del Programa De Fenomenologia. *Rev Latin De Filosof* 10,255–268 N 84.

This paper describes: (1) the idea of philosophy as strict science, based on the phenomenological principle of intuition. This intuition is distinguished from an irrational and mystical interpretation of intuition, as in Heidegger. (2) the birth of the idea of philosophy in Greece and its teleological development in Descartes, Hume, Kant, and Husserl. (3) gives an outline of the program of phenomenology as a universal ontology.

PRESLEY, Sharon and Kinsky, Lynn. "Government Is Women's Enemy" in *Freedom, Feminism, And The State*, Mc Elroy, Wendy (ed), 77–86. Cato Institute Washington 1982.

PRESSLER, Charles A. Redoubled: The Bridging Of Derrida And Heidegger. *Human Stud* 7,325–342 1984.

A summary and criticism of Derrida's critique of Heidegger ("Ouisa and Gramme"). Derrida enters Heidegger's discourse through a footnote in *Being and Time* and , while deconstructing Heidegger's participation in the historical identification time as presence. Derrida replaces the concept of time itself with that of "difference." This replacement, however, is a synthetic maneuver that avoids the question.

PREST, Mike. The Generalised RK–Order, Orthogonality And Regular Types For Modules. *J Sym Log* 50,202–219 Mr 85.

PRESTON, Thomas A. Who Benefits From The Artificial Heart? *Hastings Center Rep* 15,5–7 F 85.

This article explores the non–biological elements behind the utilization of the artificial heart. A very few investigators and two "for–profit" companies have launched what amounts to a public policy, without representation of public interests. The policy is supported by claims of therapeutic efficacy which are unsubstantiated. The corporate backing of the program is primarily as a marketing strategy. There should be public participation in national health policy–making.

PREUS, Anthony. Respect For The Dead And Dying. *J Med Phil* 9,409–416 N 84.

Against the thesis that permanently unconscious persons cannot be harmed, and thus are not owed moral deference, it is argued that even the dead can be harmed and are owed moral respect, so a *fortiori* those dubiously or not quite dead deserve some moral deference.

PRICE, A W. Moral Theories; Aristotle's Ethics. *J Med Ethics* 11,150–152 S 85.

PRICE, Derek J De Solla. "Notes Towards A Philosophy Of The Science/ Technology Interaction" in *Technological Knowledge*, Laudan, Rachel (ed), 105–114. Boston Reidel 1984.

PRICE, Huw. The Philosophy And Physics Of Affecting The Past. *Synthese* 61,299–324 D 84.

Backward causation interpretations of quantum mechanics are usually regarded as conceptually untenable, even by the taxed standards of the discipline. I argue that this prejudice is illfounded. I present a philosophical case for the possibility of backwards influence, and discuss its application to quantum mechanics. I conclude that such interpretations have some clear advantages, and deserve more attention.

PRICE, James Robertson. The Objectivity Of Mystical Truth Claims. *Thomist* 49,81–98 Ja 85.

PRIEST, Graham. Hume's Final Argument. *Hist Phil Quart* 2,349–351 Jl 85.

The paper proposes a solution to the problems posed by Hume's apparent *volte face* of the Argument from Design in the last part of the *Dialogues Concerning Natural Religion*. It argues that the *volte face* is only apparent: this part of the *Dialogues* contains, in cloaked form, the final damning argument against the Argument.

PRIEST, Graham. Hyper–Contradictions. *Log Anal* 27,237–244 S 84.

The semantics of orthodox logic may be modified to allow sentences to take any *subset* of $\{0,1\}$ as a truth value. The paper shows how this construction can be repeated to allow sentences to take any subset of *these* truth values. The construction may be iterated into the transfinite. The main result of the paper is that the semantic consequence relation generated by this construction is identical with that produced by the original subset equation.

PRIEST, Graham. Semantic Closure. *Stud Log* 43,117–130 1984.

This paper argues for the claims that a) a natural language such as English is sematically closed b) semantic closure implies inconsistency. A corollary of these is that the semantics of English must be paraconsistent. The first part of the paper formulates a definition of semantic closure which applies to natural languages and shows that this implies inconsistency. The second section argues that English is semantically closed. The preceding discussion is predicated on the assumption that there are no truth value gaps. The next section of the paper considers whether the possibility of these makes any difference to the substantive conclusions of the previous sections, and argues that it does not. The crux of the preceding arguments is that none of the consistent semantical accounts have been offered for solving the semantical paradoxes is a semantic of *English*. The final section of the paper produces a general argument as to why this must always be the case.

PRIGOGINE, Ilya and Stengers, Isabelle. *Order Out Of Chaos: Man's New Dialogue With Nature*. NY Bantam Books 1984.

PRIGOGINE, Ilya. The Rediscovery Of Time. *Zygon* 19,433–448 D 84.

Central among problems in cosmology is the crucial question of the articulation of natural and historical time: how is human history related to natural processes described by science? A deterministic world view in which natural processes are reversible, as emphasized by classical Western science, is obviously not the answer. Recent research in fields such as far–from–equilibrium thermodynamics and statistical mechanics reveals irreversibility in natural processes and allows us to explore new forms of dialogue between science and the humanities.

PRIMORAC, Igor. Hare On Moral Conflicts. *Analysis* 45,171–175 Je 85.

In *Moral Thinking*, R M Hare rejects intuitionism for being indefinite and unhelpful with moral conflicts, and act–utilitarianism, partly because of its permissiveness regarding simple, everyday moral rules. His two–level theory is offered as a synthesis of utilitarianism and intuitionism which avoids both these faults. It is argued that the theory is vitiated by a combination of the very defects it is meant to avoid, and does not provide a plausible way of resolving moral conflicts.

PRIMORAC, Igor. On Retributivism And The Lex Talionis. *Riv Int Filosof Diritto* 61,83–94 Ja–Mr 84.

Response to criticism by Michael Mitias ('Is Retributivism Inconsistent Without *Lex*

Talionis?', *Riv Int Filosof Diritto*, 60, 211–230, Ap–Jn 83) of the author's defense of the principle of proportion between crime and punishment ('On Some Arguments against the Retributive Theory of Punishment', *ib.*, 56, 43–60, Ja–Mr 79). It is argued (1) that the principle is an integral part of any consistently retributive theory of punishment, (2) that it can be applied in practice, and (3) that the idea of combining this principle with utilitarian considerations when measuring out punishments, suggested by Mitias, is inconsistent and unworkable.

PRIMORATZ, Igor. Lying And The "Methods Of Ethics". *Int Stud Phil* 16,35–57 1984.

The author examines five ethical theories—act–utilitarianism, Kant's formalism, rule–utilitarianism, Ross's pluralism, and Hare's two–level utilitarianism—arguing that none of them provides an acceptable procedure for dealing with everyday moral choices involving lying, be it because of implausible implications,or indefiniteness, or both.

PRINCIPE, Walter. The Dignity And Rights Of The Human Person As Saved, As Being Saved, As To Be Saved By Christ. *Gregorianum* 65,389–430 1984.

This question is examined: Does Christ's saving work give new grounds for human dignity and human rights beyond their foundation in the philosophy of the human person and the doctrine of creation? The conclusion is that, in a Christian perspective, Christ's saving work, although founding no *new* human rights, does further enhance human dignity not only of Christians but of every man and woman individually and socially and thereby calls for deepest respect for every person's human rights.

PRISCHING, Manfred. Gesellschaftliche Verflechtung Und Soziale Kontrolle. *Conceptus* 18,83–93 1984.

Some theories of civilization maintain the erosion of normative orientations in hedonistic society, some point to the rise of a rational–bureaucratic apparatus with "machine–like" individuals; some prognoses warn of a break–down because of exogeneous (e.G., ecological) limits, some of endogenous self–destructing tendencies in the social order. In this paper a structural element – starting out from a paradigm of the civilizational process developed by sociologists such as Max Weber, Joseph Schumpeter, and Norbert Elias – is being provided to indicate the fact that the density of rules in modernizing societies increases in the course of the demands for differentiation and integration: that means growing outer and inner control mechanisms, which subdue the individuals to rising self–constraints as well as to extraneous forces. (edited)

PRITCHARD, Colin W. Type And Eidos—Schutz And Husserl. *J Brit Soc Phenomenol* 15,307–311 O 84.

PRITZL, Kurt. The Cognition Of Indivisibles And The Argument Of De Anima. *Proc Cath Phil Ass* 58,140–150 1984.

The role of *De Anima* 3.6 in the of the intellect (*De An* 3.4–8) has not been appreciated. Aristotle uses the principle of the convertibility of being and unity along with the notions of divisibility and indivisibility to extend the account of the intellect's objects from sensible and mathematical entities and their forms (*De An* 3.4.429b10–22) to genera, privations, and propositions. The nature of this extension is relevant to some fundamental Aristotelian positions on intellectual cognition.

PROCHAZKA, Miroslav. Two Theories Of Litterary History (in Czechoslovakian). *Estetika* 21,113–123 1984.

PROCTOR, Nigel. From Basics To Aesthetics In The Curriculum. *Brit J Aes* 25,57–65 Wint 85.

In the recent British debate on the school curriculum the Arts have been relatively neglected. This paper attempts to provide some justification for aesthetic education by classifying it into the five forms of communication (*Expressive* Arts) or languages of literacy, oracy, numeracy, graphicacy and physiognomy. These also represent the 'basics' of education (i.E. The basis of further learning) and comprises a curriculum framework which allows *all* children to develop their skills across the subjects.

PRÖHL, Joachim. Das Aufsteigen Der Erkenntnis Vom Abstrakten Zum Konkreten. *Deut Z Phil* 22,429–442 1974.

Eine materielle oder ideelle Totalität wissenschaftlich ze erkennen erfordert, durch Analyse und Abstraktion die ihr eigenen Abstrakta herauszusondern. Vom Ausgangsabstraktum, über das zuerst konkretes Wissen erwoben werden mufss, ist die Erkenntnis über jedes Abstraktum weiterzuführen; sie steigt mittels Synthese und Konkretion bis zum konkreten Erkennen des letzten Abstraktums auf, womit eine geistige Reproduktion des Konkreten und somit Wesenserkenntnis erreicht ist. So kommt es zur Herausbildung einer wissenschaftlichen Theorie.

PROIETTI, Omero. Distinzione Formale E Teoria Degli Attributi In Baruch Spinoza. *Riv Filosof Neo–Scolas* 76,374–384 Jl–S 84.

PROULX, Évelyne. Le Théme De L'amitié Dans L'Éthique Á Nicomaque Et L'Éthique Á Eudéme. *Laval Theol Phil* 41,317–328 O 85.

Une lecture de l'Éthique à Nicomaque et de l'Éthique à Eudème, affranchie momentanément des nombreux commentaires spécialisés, montre à quel point les idées contenues dans l'un et l'autre traité se recoupent et se complètent. L'étude du thème de l'amitié en rend fort bien compte. À partir de l'idée d'"habitat" suggérée par le mot $\eta\theta o\zeta$, l'auteur examine les différentes notions d'amitiévue comme un lien entre les cités, les citoyens, les familles et leurs membres, les individus, ou encore les tendances contraires que chacun doit concilier en soi–même, en insistant particulièrement sur l'amitié de soi, ainsi que sur l'ami percu en tant qu' "autre soi–même".

PRUCNAL, T and Pogorzelski, W A. Structural Completeness Of The First–Order Predicate Calculus. *Z Math Log* 21,315–320 1975.

PRUST, Richard C. A Phenomenology For Christian Ethics. *Faith Phil* 2,66–82 Ja 85.

The paper argues that the significance of an act has a different structure from the significance of an event or thing. A phenomenological description of its distinctiveness discloses not only a standard for value intrinsic to an act's significance but a basis for distinguishing absolute from relative value. These distinctions are then used to articulate what Christians claim about divine activity and to describe—on the basis of the relationship of divine to human acts—what it means to call an act moral or immoral.

PRZELECKI, Marian. Rationality In The Domain Of Valuation. *Dialec Hum* 11,281–288 Spr/Sum 84.

The paper discusses the problem of applicability of the notion of rationality to value judgments, which are considered to be an important element of philosophical thought. The content of this notion is said to depend on the way in which value judgments are interpreted from semantic and methodological point of view. The notions of "formal" and "material" rationality of valuation are distinguished and briefly analyzed.

PUCCETTI, Roland. "Popper And The Mind–Body Problem" in *Popper And The Human Sciences*, Currie, Gregory (ed), 45–56. Boston Nijhoff 1985.

PUDLAK, Pavel. Cuts, Consistency Statements And Interpretations. *J Sym Log* 50,423–441 Je 85.

The paper contains some strengthenings of the second Gödel incompleteness theorem. These results are used to characterize interpretability of theories and to derive some speed–up theorems of the lengths of proofs.

PUNZO, Vincent C. "Wittgenstein And Philosophy Of Religion" in *History Of Philosophy In The Making*, Thro, Linus J (ed), 275–298. Washington Univ Pr Of America 1982.

PURTILL, Richard L and Macdonald, Michael H and Kreeft, Peter J. *Philosophical Questions: An Introductory Anthology*. Englewood Cliffs Prentice–Hall 1985.

PUTNAM, Hilary. Is The Causal Structure Of The Physical Itself Something Physical? *Midwest Stud Phil* 9,3–16 1984.

PUTNAM, Hilary. Reflexive Reflections. *Erkenntnis* 22,143–154 Ja 85.

A description of the way human beings make inferences is called *prescriptive* if it describes the inferences we would be *warranted* in making (i.E., if it describes our idealized inductive and deductive competance). Using gödelian arguments, it is shown that human beings cannot, in principle, have well–confirmed knowledge of their own prescriptive competence description, if there is such a thing. The argument is related to the paradoxes of absolute provability.

PUTNAM, Hillary. *Realism And Reason: Philosophical Papers*, V3. NY Cambridge Univ Pr 1983.

This is a collection of papers written after 1975, and dealing with the realism issue in the philosophy of language. Five of the last six papers were written after *Reason, Truth, and History* and extend and further explain the argument against metaphysical realism in that book. Chapters 5, 6, and 7 deal with the question of a priori knowledge. The first four chapters provide an overview of current views in the philosophy of language.

PUTNAM, Ruth Anna. Creating Facts And Values. *Philosophy* 60,187–204 Ap 85.

Nature provides us neither with values nor with facts. Needing both, we make them, as we make artifacts and works of art. None of these are arbitrary, for we are constrained in the making of them by the needs which prompt us to make them. Our value making is constrained by the situation, the values already held, and the character of the chooser. Our fact making is constrained by our sensory inputs, our prior beliefs, and our need to be consistent.

PUTTERMAN, Louis. A Note On The Relationship Of Interdependent Action To The Optimality Of Certain Voting Decisions. *Theor Decis* 17,257–266 N 84.

While the theory of public goods points to socially suboptimal contributions by agents acting under Cournot assumptions, this externality can be rectified by the introduction of positive interdependence of actions to the idividual's choice calculus. This paper draws attention to the fact that the institution of democratic voting is itself a means of transforming the individual calculus in such a way that parameter changes are evaluated as simultaneous adjustments by the group, on the side of benefits, but by the individual only, on the side of costs, thus generating optimal parameter preference in the case of identical agents.

QINGLIN, Zheng. A Philosophic Inquiry Into The Issue Of Value. *Chin Stud Phil* 16,17–32 Fall 84.

QUESADA, Francisco Miró. "On The Concept Of Reason" in *Philosophical Analysis In Latin America*, Gracia, Jorge J E and others (eds), 397–412. Boston Reidel 1984.

QUESTER, George H. Substituting Conventional For Nuclear Weapons: Some Problems And Some Possibilities. *Ethics* 95,619–640 Ap 85.

The firebreak distinction between nuclear and "conventional" (non–nuclear) weapons has been very useful for keeping wars limited since 1945, but the logical and philosophical underpinnings for this distinction need further analysis. A greater reliance on conventional weapons, as advocated by Robert McNamara and others, has advantages and disadvantages. The extreme of such a substitution might involve using even intercontinental missiles with conventional warheads in some future war.

QUILLIOT, Roland. Indéterminisme Et Interactionnisme Chez Popper. *Arch Phil* 48,109–128 Ja–Mr 85.

Sir Karl Popper's last books show that his interest has moved progressively from methodology to cosmology. Of this cosmology, two aspects are here described: first indeterminism, as developed in the Open Universe, where new arguments are proposed against metaphysical and scientific determinism: secondly ontological pluralism, which entails, in The self and its brain, a rehabilitation of interactionnism. What appears is that this Popperian ontology, which, in the opposite of most contemporary scientific ontologies, is inspired by the spirit of metaphysical realism, tries fundamentally to understand the way in which the world must be built so that human knowledge can appear and grow in it.

QUINE, W V. "Sticks And Stones; Or, The Ins And Outs Of Existence" in *On Nature*, Rouner, Leroy S (ed), 13–26. Notre Dame Univ Notre Dame Pr 1984.

QUINE, W V. States Of Mind. *J Phil* 82,5–8 Ja 85.

QUINN, Victor. To Develop Autonomy: A Critique Of R F Dearden And Two Proposals. *J Phil Educ* 18,265–270 1984.

Dearden asks the educationally vital question, "Are any freedoms necessary to develop autonomy?", his answer is "No" is achieved, I argue, by his addressing five different questions, e.G., "Is freedom a sufficient condition?", "Is total freedom necessary?". I then argue that freedoms are necessary for autonomy, because of the skilled nature of autonomy, requiring freedom to practice choice, for the growth of foresight. The second positive proposal is an application to leisure, the autonomous use of which requires freedom to discover what is right for oneself.

QUINTÁS, Alfonso L. Art And Culture. *Int Phil Quart* 24,373–382 D 84.

Upon discovery of the "supra–objective," ludic nature of the realities of the human environment and the basic laws of development for human creative life, aesthetic experience enables us to understand the inner articulation of the different modes by which man binds himself culturally to reality. This free, creative bonding to entities which offer possibilities for play is the basic task of culture. Cultural activity should be based on a supra–objective–ludic concept of reality and, consequently, of truth, knowledge, and man. Human creativity is eminently promoted by aesthetic experience. Art, strictly speaking, shows itself to be a first–class cultural promoter.

QUINTÁS, Alfonso López. Significación Actual Del Pensamiento Zubiriano. *Rev Port Filosof* 41,3–22 Ja–Mr 85.

The Nietzsche's motto "fidelity to the earth" is fulfilled by the philosophical investigation of Zubiri. He understands the transcendent–religious reality not as something *external* to man but as *intim*, because it is the deepest ground of the personal existence of man.

QUINTON, Anthony. Madness. *Philosophy* 18,17–42 84 Supp.

QUINTON, Anthony. Schlick Before Wittgenstein. *Synthese* 64,389–410 S 85.

RAAB, L Mark. "Achieving Professionalism Through Ethical Fragmentation" in *Ethics And Values In Archaeology*, Green, Ernestene L (ed), 51–61. NY Free Pr 1984.

RAAB, L Mark. "Ethics And Values Of Research Design In Archaeology" in *Ethics And Values In Archaeology*, Green, Ernestene L (ed), 75–88. NY Free Pr 1984.

RABINOW, Paul and Dreyfus, Hubert L. *Michel Foucault: Beyond Structuralism And Hermeneutics*. Chicago Univ Of Chicago Pr 1983.

This text is a study of the major work of Michel Foucault, completed before his death in 1984. The text is described by its author as an interpretation of problems encountered by Foucault, using his method of investigation to derive meaning in the light of post–structuralist controversy. The book gives an interpretation of this contemporary French thinker on human discourse in relation to history and the various disciplines which attempt to elucidate it. foucault is a philosopher who reassesses history through radical interpretation of the texts which describe history. (staff)

RABINOWICZ, Wlodzimierz. Intuitionistic Truth. *J Phil Log* 14,191–228 My 85.

Intuitionistic truth is here analyzed as a *possibility* of verification (proof) on the basis of avail*able* information. Note that this analysis involves two distinct modal components. The proposed model–theoretical semantics is shown to differ from the ones constructed by Kripke and Beth. We also inquire what happens when the truth–operator is explicitly introduced into the intuitionistic object–language.

RABINOWICZ, Wlodzimierz. Ratificationism Without Ratification: Jeffrey Meets Savage. *Theor Decis* 19,171–200 S 85.

Richard jeffrey's maxim of ratifiability advises the agent to 'choose for the person he expects to be when he has chosen'. He should make his choice on the basis of his would–be *after–choice* probabilities, and not, as Savage would have it, on the basis of actual *pre–choice* probabilities. The two approaches conflict in some 'Newcomblike' cases (though not in Newcomb's Case itself). It is argued that, in such cases, Savage gives better advice.

RABOSSI, Eduardo. "Meaning, Force And Explicit Performatives" in *Philosophical Analysis In Latin America*, Gracia, Jorge J E and others (eds), 141–164. Boston Reidel 1984.

RABOSSI, Eduardo. "Philosophical Analysis In Argentina" in *Philosophical Analysis In Latin America*, Gracia, Jorge J E and others (eds), 17–24. Boston Reidel 1984.

RACHELS, James. "The Sanctity Of Life" in *Biomedical Ethics Reviews*, Humber, James M (ed), 29–42. Clifton Humana Pr 1983.

RADCHICK, Laura. A Propósito De Un Libro. *Logos (Mexico)* 13,119–127 Ja–Ap 85.

This work is based on a book written by Paul–Laurent Assoun in 1980. Its purpose is to show the links that exist between Nietzsche's Philosophy and Freud's Theory of Psychoanalysis. The themes that I analyze in this essay are: instinct and pulsion, life and death, love and sexuality, dream and symbolism, and art and culture. I come to the conclusion that both Nietzsche and Freud, by different ways, seek for the origin...That which propitiates man's behavior.

RADCHIK, Laura. Jacques Maritain: La Educatión En Una Encrucijada. *Logos (Mexico)* 8,75–82 My–Ag 85.

In a world in which technology takes the place of moral values, what's the purpose of education? Jacques Maritain intends to give a whole education for a whole man; education should establish a personalist civilization in which social and individual needs can be satisified—the goal: freedom.

RADER, Melvin. "Marx's Three Worlds And Their Interrelation" in *Continuity And Change In Marxism*, Fischer, Norman And Others (ed), 1–23. Atlantic Highlands Humanities Pr 1982.

RADFORD, Colin. I Will, If You Will. *Mind* 93,577–583 O 84.

RADFORD, Colin. Must Knowledge—Or 'Knowledge' Be Socially Constructed? *Phil Soc Sci* 15,15–34 Mr 85.

RADFORD, Colin. The Umpire's Dilemma. *Analysis* 45,109–111 Mr 85.

RADICE, Roberto. Filone Di Alessandria Nella Interpretazione Di V Nikiprowetzky E Della Sua Scuola. *Riv Filosof Neo–Scolas* 76,15–41 Ja–Mr 84.

RADIL, Tomás. Some Logical And Ontological Aspects Of Neurosciences. *Filozof Cas* 32,831–838 1984.

Analysis of some logical and ontological aspects of neurosciences is based upon ideas of Prigogine on "New alliance." Complexity of both elementary and global nervous processes, their unidirectionality in time, variability, diversity, as well as their inductive nature (as gnoseological aspects are concerned) are stressed. Progogine's general concepts on science and its social role are evaluated critically from the point of view of factography and conceptual framework of neurosciences.

RADNER, Daisie. Is There A Problem Of Cartesian Interaction? *J Hist Phil* 23,35–50 Ja 85.

The traditional view of the interaction problem is defended against recent claims that mind–body interaction poses no real problem for Descartes and that occasionalism and preestablished harmony are not responses to it. Descartes's general theory of causation involves three principles: (1) the communication principle, (2) the pre–existence principle, and (3) the "at least as much" principle. The second rules out mind–body interaction. The first, plus a further principle, rules out interaction between any two substances.

RADNER, Daisie. Rejoinder To Richardson's And Loeb's: Replies To Radner's "Is There A Problem Of Cartesian Interaction"? *J Hist Phil* 23,232–236 Ap 85.

RADNITZKY, Gerard. Réflexions Sur Popper. *Arch Phil* 48,79–108 Ja–Mr 85.

Popper's methodology does not entail any playing down of the various indispensible distinctions such as the distinction between knowing and guessing, the distinction between myth and science, the distinction between the observational and the theoretical, and between the vernacular and technical sublanguages or technical vocabulary. By avoiding both the totalization that led to the foundationalist position and the scepticist reactions to these frustrated foundationalist hopes, Popper's methodology makes it possible to combine fallibilism with a realist view of theories. It combines the perennial willingness to re–examine positions, statements, etc with the claim that a particular theory (as an item of knowledge in the objective sense) constitutes cognitive progress over its rivals. (edited)

RADNITZKY, Gerard. Science, Technology, And Political Decision. *Scientia* 118,583–594 1983.

The problem of rational science policy and technology policy as well as the question of the 'responsibility of the scientist' can only be answered by taking into account the development from theory to application. (edited)

RADNITZKY, Gerard. Science, Technology, And Political Decision: From The Creation Of A Theory To The Evaluation Of The Consequences Of Its Application. *Rev Port Filosof* 40,307–317 Jl–S 84.

RAES, Koen. The Ethics Of Anti–Moralism In Marx's Theory Of Communism: An Interpretation. *Philosophica* 34,23–84 1984.

The essay develops arguments in favor of an anti–moralistic interpretation of Marx's ethical viewpoints by arguing, (1) why and from what perspective it can be rational to take this position seriously, (2) against moralism because of its ineffectiveness, authoritarianism, alienating and counterfinal consequences, (3) about the specificity of the concept of morality and the implications of the distinction between moral and non–moral goods, within Marx's Aristotelian communist view.

RAFFEL, S. Health And Life. *Theor Med* 6,153–164 Je 85.

This paper considers some of the potential implications for an interest in health of the basic fact that to live is to have been given something in advance. It is suggested that various thinkers such as Alfred Adler, Sartre, and Heidegger are unable to develop a positive attitude toward this fact and therefore are not logically in a position to be committed to health. An alternative to all of these is found in Hannah and Arendt's notion that activity is an essential part of life. Following her lead, the paper moves on to consideration of various forms of human activity, labor, work, and finally action both in terms of how they constitute an advance over the givens of life and how they contribute to health.

RAHNER, Karl and Macquarrie, John. The Anthropological Approach To Theology. *Heythrop J* 25,272–287 Jl 84.

The purpose of the article is to commend the study of the human reality as a fruitful way into theology and, incidentally, to draw attention to the use of this approach in the work of Karl Rahner. It is argued that this approach is an appropriate one in an age which is both secular and which paradoxically has reintroduced the idea of transcendence as a fundamental characteristic of the human being.

RAIO, Giulio. "Simbolizzazione E Temporalizzazione, Differenza Di Simbolo E Allegoria" in *Il Tempo Dell'Arte*, Papi, Fulvio and others (ed), 92–101. Milano Franco Angeli 1984.

RAITZ, Keith L. Computer Power And Intellectual Failure In Education: The Significance Of Joseph Weizenbaum's Criticism. *Proc Phil Educ* 40,115–126 1984.

RAITZ, Keith L. The Computer Revolution, The Technological Fallacy, And Education. *Phil Stud Educ* No Vol,4–20 1983.

RAJAPAKSE, Vijitha. Buddhism In Huxley's Evolution And Ethics. *Phil East West* 35,295–304 Jl 85.

This article seeks to examine the excursus into Buddhist thought included in T H Huxley's Romanes Lecture of 1893, *Evolution and Ethics*. Notably appreciative in tone, the excursus is identified as a characteristically Victorian response to Buddhism which also highlights a striking East–West philosophic contact because of Huxley's pioneering attempt here to link certain Buddhist and Western philosophic positions. Buddhism's affinities to empiricism and science are also held to be underscored in the process.

RAJCHL, Jaroslav. Thermodynamics Without Equilibrium, Totality, Dialectic (in Czechoslovakian). *Filozof Cas* 32,886–891 1984.

RAMEIL, Udo. The Hegel Archive And The Hegel Edition. *Bull Hegel Soc Gt Brit* 2,22–27 Autumn/Wint 80.

RAMIREZ, Edgar R. Elementos De Continuidad Y Discontinuidad Entre La Ciencia Medieval Y La Primera Revolución Científica. *Rev Filosof (Costa Rica)* 22,81–86 D 84.

Además de la tendencia mecanicista que representa el elemento de discontinuidad, se muestra en este artículo la importancia decisiva que tuvo la labor de los traductores de los siglos XII y XIII. También se plantea como la tendencia realista y la tendencia "pitagórica" de matematización de los fenómenos, que luego ejercerían una gran influencia durante la primera revolución científica, tienen su despliegue conceptual durante la edad media. En suma, se trata de destacar los factores de continuidad que permiten valorar de una manera diferente la influencia de la edad media sobre la revolución científlica de siglo XVII.

RAMIREZ, J Roland. The Priority Of Reason Over Faith In Augustine. *Augustin Stud* 13,123–132 1982.

RAMISVILI, G Z. Philosophy Of Music And Artistic Performance (in Hungarian). *Magyar Filozof Szemle* 5,777–787 1983.

RAMNOUX, Clervence. Bachelard À Sa Table D'écriture. *Rev Int Phil* 38,217–230 1984.

RAMSEY, Paul. A Letter To James Gustafson. *J Relig Ethics* 13,71–100 Spr 85.

RANKIN, H D. *Sophists, Socratics And Cynics.* Totowa Barnes & Noble 1983.

The purpose of this book is to indicate and discuss the continuity of thought and method between the sophists of the Fifth Century BC and the Socrates and Cyrices of the Fourth Century BC and later. It points out the continuous use of arguments in natural language (dialektike) as the main investigative tool of these groups and considers the breakdown of this instrument as a credible guide to knowledge of reality.

RANTALA, V and Pearce, David. Scientific Change, Continuity, And Problem Solving. *Phil Natur* 21,389–399 1984.

RANTALA, Veikko and Pearce, David. Approximative Explanation Is Deductive Nomological. *Phil Sci* 52,126–140 Mr 85.

We revive the idea that a deductive–nomological explanation of a scientific theory by its successor may be defensible, even in those common and troublesome cases where the theories concerned are mutually incompatible; and limiting, approximating and counterfactual assumptions may be required in order to define a logical relation between them. Our solution is based on a general characterization of limiting relations between physical theories using the method of nonstandard analysis.

RAPAPORT, Elizabeth. "Marxism And Ethics Today" in *Darwin, Marx And Freud*, Caplan, Arthur L (ed), 113–130. NY Plenum Pr 1984.

RAPHAEL, D D. "Rights And Conflicts" in *Gewirth's Ethical Rationalism*, Regis Jr, Edward (ed), 84–95. Chicago Univ Of Chicago Pr 1984.

RAPOSA, Michael L. Art, Religion And Musement. *J Aes Art Crit* 42,427–438 Sum 84.

Barbara Herrnstein Smith's distinction between natural and fictive discourse and Charles Peirce's theory of abductive reasoning are utilized in an analysis of the religious significance of verbal artworks. It is argued that the playful quality of our typical responses to such artworks is the key to understanding their religious value.

RAPP, Andreas. The Ordered Field Of Real Numbers And Logics With Malitz Quantifiers. *J Sym Log* 50,380–389 Je 85.

Let $R = (R, +^R,...)$ be the ordered field of real numbers. It will be shown that the $L(Q_1^n)$ is greater than or equal to 1)–theory of R is decidable, where Q_1^n denotes the Malitz quantifier of order n in the $\aleph_1$–interpretation.

RAPP, Friedrich J (ed) and O' Rourke, James J (ed) and Blakeley, Thomas J (ed). *Contemporary Marxism: Essays In Honor Of J M Bocheński.* Boston Reidel 1984.

RAPP, Friedrich. "Technological Determinism And Revolutionary Class War In Marxist Thinking" in *Contemporary Marxism*, O' Rourke, James J (ed), 175–182. Boston Reidel 1984.

RAPP, Friedrich. Kosmische Technik Als Zuspruch Des Seins: Bemerkungen Zu W Schirmachers Weiterdenken Nach Heidegger. *Z Phil Forsch* 38,445–449 Je–D 84.

Schirmacher attempts to further develop Heidegger's philosophy of technology. He combines Heidegger's attitude of release with the performance of cosmic and bodily processes (which he takes to be of a technological nature), and he claims that this performance yields a model for a new and humane understanding of technology. This approach must fail, because it excludes by its very nature from normative issues, from historical development, and from social theory.

RAPP, Friedrich. Soviet–Marxist Philosophy Of Technology. *Stud Soviet Tho* 29,139–150 F 85.

Following historical materialism, Marxist–Leninist theoreticians regard technological innovation as a motive force for historical progress. There is an intensive discussion of philosophical problems of modern technology, concentrating more on solving practical problems (work efficiency) than on speculative issues. Usually technological determinism is taken for granted. The technological optimism of the 19th century is still prevailing. Yet, as in the West, there is a growing awareness of problems of ecology, natural resources, and life–style in the technological society.

RASHID, Salim. David Hume And Eighteenth Century Monetary Thought: A Critical Comment On Recent Views. *Hume Stud* 10,156–164 N 84.

RASHID, Salim. Dugald Stewart: "Baconian" Methodology And Political Economy. *J Hist Ideas* 46,245–258 Ap–Je 85.

RASMUSSEN, David M. Explorations Of The *Lebenswelt*: Reflections On Schutz And Habermas. *Human Stud* 7,127–132 1984.

RASMUSSEN, Douglas B. "Conceptions Of The Common Good And The Natural Right To Liberty" in *The Georgetown Symposium On Ethics*, Porreco, Rocco (ed), 185–194. Lanham Univ Pr Of America 1984.

RASMUSSEN, Douglas B and Den Uyl, Douglas J. In Defense Of Natural End Ethics: A Rejoinder To O'Neil And Osterfeld. *J Liber Stud* 7,115–126 Spr 83.

RASMUSSEN, Stig Alstrup. Quasi–Realism And Mind–Dependence. *Phil Quart* 35,185–190 Ap 85.

It is argued that, in *Spreading the Word* (Oxford 1984), Simon Blackburn fails to make good his claim that his 'quasi–realism' in respect of morals is compatible with endorsing mind–independence of moral truth. The quasi–realist account is thoroughly anti–realistic. In addition, Blackburn underestimates the extent to which his account involves moral relativism.

RASMUSSEN, Stig Alstrup. Sainsbury On Denying A Fregean Conclusion. *Analysis* 45,77–79 Mr 85.

This paper continues the discussion between M Sainsbury and the author initiated by the former in 'On a Fregean Argument for the Distinctness of Sense and Reference', *Analysis* 43.1, January 1983. It is argued that Sainsbury's rejoinder to a previous paper in criticism of the said article (*analysis* 43.3, June, 1984), leaves unaffected the Fregean's central contention that, in general, co–referentiality of names fails to ensure sameness of what it involves to know to what the names refer.

RATHMANN, Jnos. Herders Methode In Seiner Geschichtsphilosophie. *Deut Z Phil* 22,341–350 1974.

RATZAN, Richard. Unsolicited Medical Opinion. *J Med Phil* 10,147–162 My 85.

By virtue of their professional ethics as healers and because of their specialized technical knowledge and clinical experience in assessing and reacting to real and potential emergencies, physicians have an obligation to offer an unsolicited medical opinion when the following conditions are met: (1) physicians assess a high probability of potentially serious disease in a stranger because of information presented to them, either in the form of a communication or physical signs; (2) physicians judge this information to be latent (not readily interpretable as potentially dangerous by the stranger) and likely to remain latent prior to the onset of symptoms; (3) the physicians possess the medical knowledge appropriate to the professional interpretation of this information. Although not a morally risk–free endeavor (invasion of privacy and the potential creation of a 'sick role' whether or not the diagnosis is correct), offering an unsolicited medical opinion under the above conditions can prevent suffering and save lives in unsuspecting strangers.

RAUCH, Leo. Hegel And The Emerging World: The Jena Lectures On Naturphilosophie (1805–06). *Owl Minerva* 16,175–182 Spr 85.

In his 1805–6 lectures on *Realphilosophie*, Hegel responds to classic problems such as the dualism of matter and spirit, and their continuity by attempting to dissolve Cartesian dualism and to present a vision of coherent world–order.

RAUH, Hans–Christoph. Zum Verhältnis Von Sozialistischer Ideologie Und Subjektivem Faktor. *Deut Z Phil* 22,639–646 1974.

RAVAUX, Francoise. "The Denial Of Tragedy" in *Existential Coordinates Of Human Condition*, Tymieniecka, A (ed), 401–408. Boston Reidel 1984.

RAVEN, J E and Schofield, M and Kirk, G S. *The Presocratic Philosophers.* NY Cambridge Univ Pr 1984.

RAVIZZA, Kenneth and Daruty, Kathy. Paternalism And Sovereignty In Athletics: Limits And Justifications Of The Coach's Exercise Of Authority Over The Adult Athlete. *J Phil Sport* 11,71–82 1984.

RAWLINSON, Mary C. Women, Medicine, And Religion: A Response To Raymond And Abrams. *J Med Phil* 9,321–324 Ag 84.

RAYMOND, Francois. L'absence De Pensée Chez Nietzsche Et Castaneda. *Petite Rev Phil* 6,121–134 Spr 85.

RAYMOND, Janice G. *Letter To The Editors*: A Response To Abrams. *J Med Phil* 9,319–320 Ag 84.

RAZ, Joseph. Authority And Justification. *Phil Pub Affairs* 14,3–29 Wint 85.

This article defends a certain conception of the nature of practical authority, that is, with power to require action. The explanation proceeds through normative theses of three kinds. One concerns the type of argument required to justify a claim that certain authority is legitimate. The second states the general character of the considerations which should guide the actions of authorities. The last concerns the way the existence of a binding authoritative directive affects the reasoning of the subjects of authority. The explanation and defense of the three theses is preceded by an introductory section defending the general approach to the analysis of authority adopted here, and introducing some of the themes which are explored in greater detail later in the article.

RAZ, Joseph. Authority, Law And Morality. *Monist* 68,295–324 Jl 85.

The article argues that all law claims to be authoritatively binding. This is then used as a test of three theses about the nature of law: the sources thesis, which regards all questions concerning the identification of the law of a certain country as questions of social fact, the incorporation and the coherence theses, both of which regard them as mixed questions of fact and morality. It is argued that the authoritative nature of law is a reason for preferring the sources thesis over the others.

READ, Stephen and Clark, Peter. Hypertasks. *Synthese* 61,387–390 D 84.

READ, Stephen and Wright, Crispin. Hairier Than Putnam Thought. *Analysis* 45,56–58 Ja 85.

In *Realism and Reason* Hilary Putnam suggests a solution to the Sorites, or "bald man", paradox through intuitionistic logic, in which the denial of a sharp cutoff is not equivalent to the universal conditional apparently needed to derive contradiction. We show paradox still follows from other intuitionistic principles, and the nearest intuitionism comes to the correct logic of vagueness is in neither asserting nor denying statements whose contradictories must be denied.

REAGAN, Gerald M. The Pedagogical Usefulness Of Speech Act Theory. *Proc Phil Educ* 40,111–114 1984.

Reagan, Ronald 386 Author Index with Abstracts

REAGAN, Ronald. *Abortion And The Conscience Of The Nation.* Nashville Nelson 1984.

REAGAN, Timothy. Competing Cultural Ideals For The School: Liberal Education And Multicultural Education. *Phil Stud Educ* No Vol,63–71 1983.

REAMER, Frederic G and Schaffer, Sylvan J. A Duty To Warn, An Uncertain Danger. *Hastings Center Rep* 15,17–19 F 85.

REARDON, Bernard. Schelling's Critique Of Hegel. *Relig Stud* 20,543–558 D 84.

Schelling's later, 'positive' philosophy was seen by him not only as a necessary supplement to his early, 'negative' doctrine, but was intended as a criticism of his rival Hegel (motivated by dislike of the man, his system and his influence). It merits consideration because made within the same philosophical perspective and not from one of total opposition to idealism. But Schelling's philosophical ventures do not constitute a unified system, and his interest today lies mainly in his anticipations of existentialism.

REDEI, Miklos. Note On An Argument Of W Ochs Against The Ignorance Interpretation Of State In Quantum Mechanics. *Erkenntnis* 23,143–148 Ag 85.

According to the ignorance interpretation a quantum system is actually always in a pure state even if it is described by a mixed state. Och's argument against this interpretation is restricted to states represented by finite range density operators. By reformulating his argument in operator algebraic framework of quantum mechanics we generalize it to arbitrary states, thus the ignorance interpretation is shown not to be right for systems of infinitely many degrees of freedom either.

REDEKER, Horst. Der Kulturprozess Und Die Wachsende Rolle Des Subjektiven Faktors. *Deut Z Phil* 22,564–583 1974.

Die durch Arbeit menschlichen Bedürfnissen angepafsste Umwelt bildet die materielle Seite der Höherentwicklung des Menschen, einschliefsslich der Entwicklung seiner geistigen Fähigkeiten, seiner Sinne und Gefühle. Diese Beziehung von Industrie und Psychologie (Marx) ist in der Einheit von materieller und ideeller Seite, von Individual– und Gattungsentwicklung im marxistisch–leninistischen Kulturbegriff erfafsst. Im Kulturprozefss ist als eine wesentliche Seite der Wachstumsprozefss der Rolle des subjectiven Faktors enthalten. Die sozialistische Revolution ist die eigentliche Kulturrevolution in der Geschichte der Menschheit.

REDHEAD, Michael. On The Impossibility Of Inductive Probability. *Brit J Phil Sci* 36,185–191 Je 85.

REDMOND, Walter. "Sobre Las Oraciones Modales" Por Fray Alonso De La Veracruz. *Rev Filosof (Mexico)* 17,233–248 My–Jl 84.

RÉE, Jonathan. Descartes's Comedy. *Phil Lit* 8,151–166 O 84.

This essay examines the development of Descartes' literary aspirations, and the temporal and ironic structures of the *Discourse* and *Meditations.* Descartes emerges as an ingenious philosophical stylist, with complicated debts to Montaigne. His texts are shown to employ a 'rhetoric of edification', embodying the view that metaphysical wisdom can be achieved only through a lengthy apprenticeship to error.

REED, Adolph L. W E B Du Bois: A Perspective On The Bases Of His Political Thought. *Polit Theory* 13,431–456 Ag 85.

REEDER, Harry P. *Language And Experience: Descriptions Of Living Language In Husserl And Wittgenstein.* Lanham Univ Pr Of America 1984.

This work examines the philosophies of language of Edmund Husserl and Ludwig Wittgenstein in order to assess their overall purposes, structures, and methodologies. It is argued that these two approaches to language, being descriptive (with some limitations), can be combined to produce a fuller account of language than is available from either approach taken by itself. Thus, this work attempts to bridge the gap between phenomenology and the analytic philosophy of language.

REEDER, Harry P. A Phenomenological Account Of The Linguistic Mediation Of The Public And The Private. *Husserl Stud* 1,263–280 1984.

This essay shows the correlation between Edmund Husserl's phenomenological descriptions of language and analytic philosophy's discussions of "public" and "private" experiences, with special focus upon the topic of linguistic change. Husserl's account of the public and private features of language and their relation to the transcendental elements of experience is summarized. The essay ends with a brief discussion of the development of Husserl's thought and its relation to some other philosophies of language.

REEDER, Harry P. The Nature Of Critical Thinking. *Inform Log* 6,17–22 Jl 84.

This essay attempts to clarify the nature and pedagogy of the "new trend" in informal logic, called "critical thinking" (CT). CT is found to involve logical, rhetorical and philosophical skills, based in a (Socratic) dialectical approach to problems and arguments, and to involve social and ethical commitments, as well as commitment to reflection, reflexion, and interpretation of texts. The dialectical basis of CT is contrasted with the adversary approach to argumentation.

REEDER, Harry. Cogito, Ergo Sum: Inference And Performance. *Eidos* 1,30–49 Jl 78.

REESE, William J. Soldiers For Christ In The Army Of God: The Christian School Movement In America. *Educ Theor* 35,175–194 Spr 85.

This essay explores the history, characteristics, and public policy implications of the rise of fundamentalist Protestant schools in America between the 1960s and the present. It examines the philosophy of Christian education, the curriculum and social life of these private schools, and the political climate in which Christian day schools have been shaped. It concludes that these schools demonstrate the resilience of "traditional" and illiberal ideas in a "modern" society such as the United States and warns against the fragmentation of American education in the coming decade.

REESE, William L. Christianity And The Final Solution. *Phil Forum (Boston)* 16,138–147 Fall–Wint 84.

Christianity bears ultimate responsibility for the final solution because the Christian Gospels (and other portions of the New Testament) picture the Jewish people as the principle agents in Christ's crucifixion. This picture, and the consequences growing out of it on the part of believing Christians, placed an entire people in a suffering and vulnerable position. The final solution was but the final link in a long chain which practicing Christians had forged.

REESE, William. 'Introduction To Philosophy' As A Large Class Tutorial. *Teach Phil* 7,325–336 O 84.

The article describes a manner of teaching the large beginning class in philosophy as a tutorial where the student's attention is directed to the development of his or her own philosophy through concentration of unavoidable issues, the keeping of a journal in which these issues are explored, and use of the author's heavily cross referenced Dictionary of Philosophy and Religion as a student research tool, allowing alternative positions to be traced out on every issue.

REEVE, Andrew. Harrington's Elusive Balance. *Hist Euro Ideas* 5,401–426 1984.

James Harrington's Agrarian law is designed to maintain the political system of Oceana, his projected commonwealth. To understand the complexities of the Agrarian, we need to examine Harrington's method, his views on inheritance and the relative importance of different forms of property. This paper offers an interpretation of the difficulties in understanding the Agrarian in the light of these inquiries.

REGIS JR, Edward (ed). *Gewirth's Ethical Rationalism.* Chicago Univ Of Chicago Pr 1984.

This is a collection of twelve original, never–before published essays on various aspects of Alan Gewirth's book *Reason and Morality.* The authors focus on Gewirth's argument for rights, his claim to have derived on 'ought' from an 'is', his criticism of egoism, and the doctrine of a 'duty to rescue'. Authors include Marcus Singer, Renford Bambrough, Kai Nielsen, D D Rapheal, R M Hare, Jan Narveson, Jesse Kalin, W D, Hudson, and others. In addition, Professor Gewirth replies to all his critics.

REHG, William R. Marx's Critique Of Capitalist Technology: Form And Content. *Mod Sch* 62,111–130 Ja 85.

The aim of this article is to interpret the analysis of technology found in Karl Marx's *Grundrisse.* The interpretation attempt to show (1) how the methodology guiding Marx's analysis has both dialectical and phenomenological dimensions; (2) how this methodolgy affects the content of Marx's analysis.

REICHBERG, G. Popper En Question. *Rev Thomiste* 85,38–68 Ja–Mr 85.

REICHENBACH, B R. Omniscience And Deliberation. *Int J Phil Relig* 16,225–236 1984.

First I show that R Taylor's argument that, given God's omniscience, either there can be no human deliberation or God cannot foreknow any future actions which result from deliberation, is fallacious. Secondly, I argue that if deliberation be understood as a kind of inquiry about what are the best means to achieve the desired ends, deliberation is incompatible with foreknowledge of those means. However, this thesis cannot be used to show that God cannot act intentionally.

REICHENBACH, Bruce R. "The Divine Command Theory And Objective Good" in *The Georgetown Symposium On Ethics*, Porreco, Rocco (ed), 219–234. Lanham Univ Pr Of America 1984.

REID, G J. Identity And Immaterialism. *Amer Phil Quart* 21,367–370 O 84.

Three positive accounts of the immaterial are presented and related in terms of identity. First, whatever can be shared without diminishment is immaterial. Thus knowledge is immaterial, but cakes are not. Second, the intentional is immaterial. Intentionality involves both occurence identity and content identity. Third, immaterial items have clean cut classical identity features. The central objections to immaterial items, that they are non–empirical and that claims about them lack sufficient grounds, are discussed. (edited)

REID, Louis Arnaud. Art And Knowledge. *Brit J Aes* 25,115–124 Spr 85.

Art cannot be known in terms of justifiably evidenced propositional statements: only through direct holistic experiential awareness, cognitive, conative, affective. This entails a general non–propositional account of true knowledge: adequacy of personal grasp of meaning, whether artistic (as here) or factual. Truth is not, finally an adjectival relation between impersonal propositions and facts, fundamentally, adverbial, a quality of personal cognitive prehension of objects, artistic or factual. Justification is discussed.

REILEY MAGUIRE, Marjorie. Personhood, Covenant, And Abortion. *Amer J Theol Phil* 6,28–46 Ja 85.

REIMAN, Jeffrey H. Justice, Civilization, And The Death Penalty: Answering Van Den Haag. *Phil Pub Affairs* 14,115–148 Spr 85.

REIMAN, Jeffrey H. The Possibility Of A Marxian Theory Of Justice. *Can J Phil* Supp 7,307–322 1981.

REINEKE, Joachim. Minimale Gruppen. *Z Math Log* 21,357–359 1975.

REINERT, Günther and Brandtstädter, Jochen. Wissenschaft Als Gegenstand Der Wissenschaft Vom Menschlichen Erleben Und Verhalten. *Z Allg Wiss* 4,368–401 1973.

Science is considered as an open system that constitutes a sub–entity of the total system "society" and whose functions include the production, systematization, communication and application of knowledge. Since this system is made up of individuals and groups, its functions are dependent on psychological factors. This fact serves as a starting point for a psychology of science, which can contribute to optimizing scientific practice by treating the heuristic, organizational, technological, and normative aspects of scientific activity.

REINHARDT, Lloyd. Radical Freedom. *Philosophy* 60,88–104 Ja 85.

REINSMITH, William A. Improving Applied Ethics: A Response To Bahm's "Improving Applied Ethics". *Int J Applied Phil* 2,81–84 Spr 85.

"improving Applied Ethics: A Response" is a critique of Archie J Bahm's attempt ("improving Applied Ethics", J Applied Ethics, Fall, 1984) to provide a foundational theory that would serve as basis for all ethical decisions. Arguing that Bahm's principles still leave us in the state of relativism he seeks to avoid, the author says that seeking for such a broad theoretical foundation will always be unsuccessful, in that no one theory of ethics is free from serious objection. This is a situation we have to live with, and teachers of ethics should act as guides in helping students understand conflicting theories and their implications. Then responsible decisions can be made on how to live.

REISER, Stanley J. Responsibility For Personal Health: A Historical Perspective. *J Med Phil* 10,7–18 F 85.

Reflections about the role of human choice in determining personal health occur in writings of practitioners and laymen throughout history. The Greek and Roman writers emphasized the effect of life's activities. During the Middle Ages and Renaisance, disease continued to be seen as a consequence of disorder of the bodily humors, which were under the individual's control. The rise of the paternalistic national regimes in Europe produced the view that society had the responsibility to maintain health. Jacksonian egalitarianism led to a reaction against the aggressive therapies of established professional experts, a view furthered by the Thomsonian belief that people should wrest control of their health away from orhtodox physicians. Among the twentieth century reactions was the movement to urge people to have doctors evaluate laypersons' health. By the 1970s a movement emerged emphasizing again personal responsibility, which, in turn, produced a concern that this was merely "victim–blaming". Views on the role of lay people in determining personal health are heavily influenced by prevailing social, political, and moral climates.

REISINGER, Leo and Lachmayer, Friedrich. Potentielles Und Positives Recht. *Arch Rechts Soz* 60,25–52 1974.

It seems necessary to develop appropriate theoretical instruments, by which the set of potential norms can be determined. Starting from this methodological approach the present paper examines the following problems: a) the construction of normative chains, b) the problem of personal identities in norms, and c) the institutions of the transfer of goods. The analysis of these normative topics is to illustrate the thesis that the handling of problems by means of formal methods is not only aiding jurisdiction but also the structural analysis of legal theory. (edited)

REITZER, Alfons. Allgemeine Modelltheorie. *Z Phil Forsch* 29,257–269 Ap–Je 75.

RELLA, Franco. "Nel Regno Della Metamorfosi, La Figura Nelle "Elegie Duinesi" Di R M Rilke" in *Il Tempo Dell'Arte*, Papi, Fulvio and others (ed), 29–39. Milano Franco Angeli 1984.

REMMEL, J B and Downey, R G. The Universal Complementation Property. *J Sym Log* 49,1125–1136 D 84.

There are very few lattice theoretic restrictions on the r e complement of a fully co–r e subspace. This paper analyzes the degree–theoretic ones. Thus a fully co–r e subspace C has the universal complementation property if C has r e complements in each degree below that of C. For example, it is shown that the degrees containing fully co–r e subspaces without the universal complementation property are dense. Some results are obtained connecting splittings and complementation.

RENARDEL DE LAVALETTE, Gerard R. Descriptions In Mathematical Logic. *Stud Log* 43,281–294 1984.

We use (intuitionistic, classical or intermediate) logic with existence predicate, as introduced by D S Scott, to handle partial functions, and prove that adding function descriptors to a theory based on such a logic is conservative. (edited)

RESCHER, Nicholas. *The Limits Of Science*. Berkeley Univ Of Calif Pr 1984.

RESCHER, Nicholas. "On The Rationale Of Governmental Regulation" in *Rights And Regulation*, Machan, Tibor (ed), 249–258. Cambridge Ballinger 1983.

RESCHER, Nicholas. Are Synoptic Questions Illegitimate? *Erkenntnis* 22,359–364 Ja 85.

RESCHER, Nicholas. Extraterrestrial Science. *Phil Natur* 21,400–424 1984.

RESCHER, Nicholas. The Epistemology Of Pragmatic Beliefs. *Proc Cath Phil Ass* 58,173–187 1984.

RESCHER, Nicholas. Truth As Ideal Coherence. *Rev Metaph* 38,795–806 Je 85.

RESNICK, Philip. Federalism And Socialism: A Reconsideration. *Praxis Int* 4,400–420 Ja 85.

This article seeks to re–consider the relationship between socialist theory and federalism. It points to a historical bias on the left, stemming from the French Revolution, in favor of centralized government, and to the reasons which have led to 20th century socialists, at least in part, to re–assess their position. While reference is made to a wide number of cases, the article focuses more directly on Canada in the second part, concluding with a number of theoretical considerations.

RESNIK, Michael D. How Nominalist Is Hartry Field's Nominalism? *Phil Stud* 47,163–182 Mr 85.

I consider Hartry Field's use in his nominalist program of space–time points (or minimal regions) and the logical possibility of sets and strong systems of set theory. I argue that points are plagued with the same sort of epistemological problems that led Field to repudiate numbers and that a natural expansion of his epistemology for possibility is easily converted to an epistemology for numbers, sets and other mathematical objects, so long as these are conceived as positions in abstract structures.

RESNIK, Michael D. Logic: Normative Or Descriptive; The Ethics Of Belief Or A Branch Of Psychology? *Phil Sci* 52,221–238 Je 85.

By a logical theory I mean a formal system together with its semantics, metatheory, and rules for translating ordinary language into its notion. Logical theories can be used descriptively (for example, to represent particular arguments or to depict the logical form of certain sentences). Here the logician uses the usual methods of empirical science to assess the correctness of his descriptions. However, the most important applications of logical theories are normative, and here, I argue, the epistemology is that of wide reflective equilibrium. The result is that logic not only assesses our inferential practice but also changes it. I tie my discussion to Thagard's views concerning the relationship between psychology and logic, arguing against him that psychology has and should have only a peripheral role in normative (and most descriptive) applications of logic.

RETA, Jose Oroz. Presencia De San Agustín En Suárez. *Augustinus* 25,289–298 Ja–D 80.

RETIEF, A I and Mauer, K F. Methodological Problems In Psychology (in Dutch). *S Afr J Phil* 4,19–24 F 85.

While it ought to be possible to identify a virtually endless list of methodological problems in psychology, the authors of this article concentrate on two issues which cause, or indeed ought to cause, a considerable amount of concern at present. First, a description is provided of the situation which arises when researchers, particularly those in the field of therapeutic psychology, conceptualize their research problems in terms of the precepts of general systems theory and in the absence of appropriate research methodologies. This results in a confusion between circular conceptualization and linear methods. The second problem relates to the complexities of cross–cultural research. This is particularly evident when attempts are made to measure dimensions of personality, attitude, and interest with instruments developed for cultural groups other than those which are being investigated. As a rule the metric qualities of the instruments suffer to such an extent that the measurements are largely useless. The authors contend that there is an urgent need for philosophical reflection, and that philosophers could make an important contribution at both theoretical and metatheoretical levels.

REUTER, Walter. Bürgerliche Konzeptionen Über Die Gesellschaftliche Entwicklung/Revolutionären Prozess—Lateinamerikas. *Deut Z Phil* 33,450–453 1985.

REVEL, Jean–François. *How Democracies Perish*. Garden City Doubleday 1984.

The author argues that the Western democracies are becoming increasingly accepting of Soviet imperialism. These democracies, including the U S, are weakened by self–criticism, high moral standards, and a basic misunderstanding of the Soviets and their imperial intention. (staff)

REYNOLDS, Terrence. Moral Absolutism And Abortion: Alan Donagan On The Hysterectomy And Craniotomy Cases. *Ethics* 95,866–873 Jl 85.

RHEINWALD, Rosemarie. *Der Formalismus Und Seine Grenzen: Untersuchungen Zur Neueren Philosophie Der Mathematik*. Konigstein Hain 1984.

This book provides a study of recent versions of formalism and nominalism in the philosophy of mathematics. An attempt is made to clarify formalistic positions, to assess the advantages, and especially to determine the limits of formalism. It is argued that the price one has to pay for clarity of language, methodological reliability, and ontological parsimony is higher than might be expected. Formalism can't be reconciled with certain strong intuitions about the scope of mathematics.

RHODE, Deborah L and Hazard, Geoffrey C. *The Legal Profession: Responsibility And Regulation*. Mineola Foundation Pr 1985.

A collection of edited essays. Subjects include the history, composition, functions, and the structure of the American legal profession, as these factors relate to the regulation of the profession and to the discharge of its ethical responsibilities.

RHODEN, Nancy K. "Using And Refusing Psychotropic Drugs" in *Feeling Good And Doing Better*, Murray, Thomas H (ed), 157–174. Clifton Humana Pr 1984.

RHODES, Dent M and Riegle, Rodney P. Anonymity In The Academy: The Case Of Faculty Evaluation. *Educ Theor* 35,299–306 Sum 85.

In this article, the authors (1) outline the arguments and analogies most often used in support of anonymity, (2) identify a basic premise underlying these arguments, (3) examine the relationship between anonymity and the mission of the academy, (4) indicate why anonymity should be used only in exceptional cases rather than as a general rule, and (5) suggest the basis for an open method of evaluation faculty.

RICE, Lee C and others. "Bibliography" in *History Of Philosophy In The Making*, Thro, Linus J (ed), 313–320. Washington Univ Pr Of America 1982.

RICE, Lee C. Spinoza, Bennett, And Teleology. *S J Phil* 23,241–254 Sum 85.

I argue that Bennett's criticism of Spinoza's anti–teleological arguments misses the major thrust of Spinoza's argument due to a faulty understanding of the notion of 'conatus' on Bennett's part. While the alternative version of teleological argument which Bennett offers would also be unacceptable to Spinoza, much of Bennett's general interpretation of Spinoza is otherwise correct.

RICE, Lee. Spinoza's Account Of Sexuality. *Phil Res Arch* 10,19–34 1984.

I argue that Spinoza's account of appetition, and its application to human sexuality, is more original than many commentators suggest; and that it offers resolutions to several puzzles in the philosophy of sex. The paper first situates these puzzles in contemporary debates, offers a detailed analysis of Spinoza's remarks on love in general and sexual love in particular, and concludes with some of the normative consequences which Spinoza attempts to derive from these.

RICH, John Martin. *Professional Ethics In Education*. Springfield Thomas 1984.

The book's purpose is to survey and assess the principle problems and issues of professional ethics at all levels of education and to present a position on these issues whenever appropriate. The assessment focuses on the ethical ground for decision–making and the likely educational consequences. Topics presented include the study and function of professional ethics, characteristics of professional ethics codes, justification of professional ethics, academic freedom, testing, and the protection of student rights, ethics of research, faculty relations with colleagues and education officials, the educator in the community, disseminating, implementing, and enforcing ethical codes.

RICHARD, Jean. *L'évolution De Paul Tillich: Du Projet De 1913 Au Système Achevé*. *Laval Theol Phil* 40,339–362 O 84.

RICHARDS, John. Boole And Mill: Differing Perspectives On Logical Psychologism. *Hist Phil Log* 1,19–36 1980.

Logical psychologism is the position that logic is a special branch of psychology, that logical laws are descriptions of experience to be arrived at through observation, and are a *posteriori*. The accepted arguments against logical psychologism are effective only when directed against this extreme version. However, the clauses in the above characterization are independent and ambiguous, and may be considered separately. This separation permits a reconsideration of less extreme attempts to tie logic to psychology, such as those defended by Mill and Boole. It also provides the basis for a reexamination of the relationship between logic and psychology, and raises the possibility of a deeper investigation into the nature of logic itself.

RICHARDS, William M. Self–Consciousness And Agency. *Synthese* 61,149–172 N 84.

This paper sets forth a theory of self–consciousness which is responsive to the datum of 'self–certainty', i.E., the fact that in thinking thoughts of the form "I am F" the thinker invaribly knows that he or she is identical to the referent 'I'. It's principle contention is that the unique kind of self–reference involved is an act of self–awareness is not a *theoretical* attitude, i.E., an attitude directed upon a *propostion*; rather, self–reference is a *practical* attitude, i.E., an attitude directed upon a *practition*.

RICHARDSON, Herbert. "What Do Religion, Politics, And Science Each Contribute To Society" in *The Good Life And Its Pursuit*, Dougherty, Jude P (ed), 209–232. NY Paragon House 1984.

RICHARDSON, Robert C and Loeb, Louis E. Replies To Daisie Radner's "Is There A Problem Of Cartesian Interaction"? *J Hist Phil* 23,221–226 Ap 85.

RICHARDSON, Robert C. Biology And Ideology: The Interpenetration Of Science And Values. *Phil Sci* 51,396–420 S 84.

There is an important, if circumscribed, role for ideological critique in the evaluation of scientific theories; in particular, it lies in the explanation of the acceptance and persistence of scientific views, given independent grounds for questioning their justifiability. (edited)

RICHIR, Marc. Le Problème De La Logique Pure: De Husserl À Une Nouvelle Position Phénoménologique. *Rev Phil Louvain* 82,500–521 N 84.

Retrieving the husserlian doctrine of pure logic (Logical Investigations, Ideas, section 124), the author attempts to show how it can be transformed, while remaining phenomenological in a new sense: logical concept and generality result from a very peculiar, logical–transcendental, *schematism of language*, underlying that part of language which aims at objective knowledge. Formed out by schematic operation, phenomena are finding themselves *drawn out* of their primitive phenomenality in becoming "objects" of knowledge. Irreductibly bringing in themselves the track coming from the proper work of that drawing out, these constitute many *a priori distinct* logical loci of which pure logic has to elaborate a systematic inventory.

RICHTER, F and Bernhardt, Herbert. Zur Realisierung Des Verhältnisses Von Philosophie Und Einzelwissenschaften Im Marxistisch–Leninistischen Grundstudium. *Deut Z Phil* 32,1017–1020 1984.

In the work is proved a position to the discussion in Deut Z Phil if there is today a changed situation concerning the connection of philosophy with science in the GDR, related to the time 20 years ago. In fact there is a problem shifting from philosophical problems of science to such of social sciences. We can see this if we teach philosophy for non–philosophy students at a technical university.

RICHTER, Friedrich and Wrona, V. Neukantianismus Und Sozialreformismus. *Deut Z Phil* 22,269–288 1974.

Durch den formalen Rückgriff auf die praktische Philosophie I. Kants wird dessen revolutionär–kritisches Wirken um die ideologische Einheit des dritten Standes in der Zeit der Vorbereitung der bürgerlichen Revolution durch die Neukantianer in eine völlig andere geschichtiche Epoche transponiert und damit versucht, die opportunistische Idee der Klassenversöhnung als Menschheitsinteresse auszugeben, den Klassenkampf auf bürgerliche Reformpolitik zu beschränken und die Notwendigkeit der sozialistischen Revolution zu leugnen.

RICHTER, Gundrun. Der Kritische Rationalismus Und Kant. *Deut Z Phil* 22,351–359 1974.

RICHTER, Reed. Rationality Revisited. *Austl J Phil* 62,392–403 D 84.

In this paper I show (a) that causal decision theory as presently detailed in the literature is either inadequate or contradictory; (b) it is not universally true that (1) If options *A* and *B* are both available to an agent x and if x knows that were he to do *A* he would be better off in every respect that were he to do *B*, then in the strictest sense of rational self–interest, rationality requires x to do *A* over doing *B*; and (c) that the existence of cases like Newcomb's Paradox is not a good reason for abandoning non–causal, evidential decision theory in favor of causal approach. That is, I argue that in view of the falsity of propostion (1) above, the dominance reasoning underlying the causal theorist's position on Newcomb's Paradox is fallacious.

RICHTER, Reed. Rationality, Group Choice And Expected Utility. *Synthese* 63,203–232 My 85.

In this paper I propose a view uniformly extending expected utility calculations to both individual and group choice contexts. By way of three related cases I discuss the problems inherent in applying expected utility to group choice cases. I show that the problem with such group cases does not essentially depend upon the fact that more than one agent is involved. A modified strategy is then devised allowing the application of the expected utility formula to these otherwise problematic cases. One case, however, leads to contradiction. But recognizing the falsity of the proposition.

RICKMAN, H P. Is Philosophical Anthropology Possible. *Metaphilosophy* 16,29–46 Ja 85.

Philosophic Anthropology, pursuing philosophy's traditional search for reflective self–knowledge seeks to crystalize the ideas of man underpinning empirical research and moral ideals. Neither the claim that pure speculation can produce factual knowledge nor the contention that a higher synthesis of empirical findings can become philosophy is acceptable. Philosophic Anthropology is, therefore, most usefully conceived as a critique which traces the necessary presuppositions of the study of man in its various forms of the more rules we apply.

RICOEUR, M Paul. La Pensée De Gabriel Marcel. *Bull Soc Fr Phil* 78,3–63 Ap–Je 84.

RICOEUR, Paul and Mc Laughlin, Kathleen (trans) and Pellauer, David (trans). *Time And Narrative*, V1. Chicago Univ Of Chicago Pr 1984.

RICOEUR, Paul. Le Temps Raconté. *Rev Metaph Morale* 89,436–452 O–D 84.

RICOEUR, Paul. The Power Of Speech: Science And Poetry. *Phil Today* 29,59–71 Spr 85.

RIEDEL, Manfred. *Between Tradition And Revolution: The Hegelian Transformation Of Political Philosophy*. NY Cambridge Univ Pr 1984.

The work considers Hegel's nature views on ethics and politics and relates them to the classical tradition of Western political thought. It deals with the structure of Hegel's Philosophy of Right (I), the Hegelian conception of natural law (II), the relationship between political economy and Political Philosophy (III) and the Significance of the French Revolution in Hegel's transformation of modern political philosophy (IV). The studies correct the distortions and flaws in the history of one of the most influential books of political thought by offering a point of view which allows Hegel's Philosophy *of Right* to be read within the context of Plato's *Republic* and Aristotle's *Politics*, Hobbes' *Leviathan* and Rousseau's Social *Contract*.

RIEGLE, Rodney P and Rhodes, Dent M. Anonymity In The Academy: The Case Of Faculty Evaluation. *Educ Theor* 35,299–306 Sum 85.

In this article, the authors (1) outline the arguments and analogies most often used in support of anonymity, (2) identify a basic premise underlying these arguments, (3) examine the relationship between anonymity and the mission of the academy, (4) indicate why anonymity should be used only in exceptional cases rather than as a general rule, and (5) suggest the basis for an open method of evaluation faculty.

RIGDEN, John S. "Birth Of Magnetic–Resonance" in *Observation, Experiment, And Hypothesis In Modern Physical Science*, Achinstein, Peter (ed), 205–238. Cambridge MIT Pr 1985.

RIGHI, Roberto. "Abimes De Clartés": Architettura Rivoluzionaria E Culto Delle Masse: I Progetti Di Etienne–Louis Boulée. *Riv Int Filosof Diritto* 61,291–323 Ap–Je 84.

RIJKE, R P C. Cancer And The Development Of Will. *Theor Med* 6,133–142 Je 85.

People with cancer, who live better or longer than expected or who recover completely despite a poor medical prognosis, usually go through a profound change and self–development. This paper is an attempt to describe and understand the nature of this transformation by examining how initially unexamined conceptions of oneself, life, illness, etc., become manifest and get developed. One feature of this process is that people leave the present–day medical conception, which is based on the notion of 'victim' of and 'battle' against illness, and discover that they have other resources for dealing with life and illness. It will be argued that at the center of this transformation lies the discovery and development of the 'will', which is closely associated with the willingness to examine one's conceptions of oneself, health, illness and life.

RILEY, Michael. "The Truth Of The Body" in *Existential Coordinates Of Human Condition*, Tymieniecka, A (ed), 479–494. Boston Reidel 1984.

RILEY, Patrick. On Ladd's Review Of *Kant's Political Philosophy*. *Polit Theory* 12,597–600 N 84.

RIPLEY, Charles. Sperry's Concept Of Consciousness. *Inquiry* 27,399–424 D 84.

This paper explores R W Sperry's view that consciousness is 'causally' effective in directing voluntary human behavior. This view, formulated in the course of his split brain research, presupposes an earlier theory that motor behavior is the sole output of the brain and that mental phenomena were developed for regulation of overt response. His view of the 'causal' effectiveness of consciousness is shown to be based on a theory of emergent properties like that of Bunge. It is also shown that Sperry, like Bunge, is a materialist; appearances to the contrary are due to occasional use of standard terms such as 'materialism' and 'interaction' in unusual senses. It is argued, with specific reference to Chisholm and Searle, that Sperry's hypothesis is helpful towards elucidating the structure and dynamics of action. It is also argued that it is not, as Sperry thinks, a consequence of his position that moral values are part of brain science.

RISCH, C. "Zeit Und Musik" in *Asthetische Er Fahrung Und Das Wesen Der Kunst*, Holzhey, Helmut, 156–172. Bern Haupt 1984.

RISSER, James. Practical Reason, Hermeneutics, And Social Life. *Proc Cath Phil Ass* 58,84–92 1984.

The paper examines, from the perspective of Hans–Georg Gadamer's philosophical hermeneutics, the connection between reason and social life. The connection is severed when practical rationality is seen as the application of science to technical tasks. It is argued that, in order to establish the connection, practical rationality needs to be re–thought along Aristotelian lines. This, in turn, is found to be inseparable from a hermeneutic notion of repetition.

RIST, John M. The End Of Aristotle's *On Prayer*. *Amer J Philo* 106,110–113 Spr 85.

The argument is that despite appearances there never was an Aristotelian work entitled *On Prayer*.

RIVERA, Enrique. Maxima Aportacion Del Pensamiento Hispanico A La Cultura: El "Sentido Universalista". *Rev Filosof (Mexico)* 17,465–490 S–D 84.

RIVES, Joel. The Defence Of The Ant—Work, Life And Utopia. *Can J Phil* 14,617–630 D 84.

RJADOVÁ, Vera and Rjadovoj, Alexandr. The Character Of The Interaction Of Working And Political Activity Of Personality (in Czechoslovakian). *Filozof Cas* 33,183–195 1985.

Author Index with Abstracts 389 **Robinson, William S**

RJADOVOJ, Alexandr and Rjadová, Vera. The Character Of The Interaction Of Working And Political Activity Of Personality (in Czechoslovakian). *Filozof Cas* 33,183–195 1985.

ROBBINS, J Wesley. Does Belief In God Need Proof? *Faith Phil* 2,272–286 Jl 85.

According to Plantinga, belief in God is properly basic because, for Christians at least, it is a ground of human culture. For Alston, that belief is properly basic because, whether a ground or not, it has the same evidential value as other beliefs that are grounds of human culture. I pose a pragmatic objection to the philosophical idea of the grounds of culture and to its use to underwrite, in this case, Christian theological discourse.

ROBERT, A. Une Approche Naïve De L'analyse Non–Standard. *Dialectica* 38,287–296 1984.

Non–standard analysis gives a proper foundation to the theory of infinitesimals. Nelson's axiomatic approach of it uses a new (undefined) predicate which is added to the classical language of set theory. We interpret this new predicate and formulate Nelson's axioms in a way that can be compared to P r Halmos' discussion of set axioms in his book "Naïve Set Theory".

ROBERT, Jean–Dominique. En Marge De Quelques Textes Épistémologiques Récents. *Laval Theol Phil* 41,139–158 Je 85.

Parler du réel et de la réalité, en fonction des multiples sens que revêt en fait ce terme, est une entreprise inséparable d'une enquête relative à la notion de vérité. Cette dernière, en effet, dans la mesure même où on accepte d'en traiter se nuance et se relativise profondément selon les formes de connaissances en jeu. Ces dernières ne sont–elles pas diverses, à chaque coup, ne nous font–elles pas embrayer sur le réel de manière profondément différente? Il faudrait donc tenter de tracer quelques–uns des grands axes d'une réflexion épistaemologique sur la réalité essentielle des types de connaître, en fonction de leur valeur de vérité, que cette notion soit employée par le scientifique, le philosophe,l'homme du religieux ou celui des choses de l'art.

ROBERTS, Joy H. On Russell's Rejection Of Akoluthic Sensations. *Phil Phenomenol Res* 45,595–600 Je 85.

ROBERTS, Lawrence. Ambiguity Vs Generality: Removal Of A Logical Confusion. *Can J Phil* 14,295–314 Je 84.

A common argument that there is no semantic test for ambiguity is based on the premise that disjunctive meanings are associated with both ambiguous and general unambiguous terms. I show that this argument is based on a logical confusion between a *disjunction of meanings*, each of which is appropriate to *different* kinds of contexts, and a *single disjunctive meaning* which a term has in *all* contexts. I criticize the same confusion in some philosophical discussions, and I provide a semantic test for ambiguity based on the distinction of two kinds of disjunctions.

ROBERTS, Lawrence. Russell On The Semantics And Pragmatics Of Indexicals. *Philosophia (Israel)* 14,111–128 Ag 84.

Russell's early doctrine of indexicals is analyzed into two main parts, ego–centricity, and the determining relation between the speaker's use of an indexical and its *designatum*, both of which are criticized. It is also argued that his use of percecption to link indexical use with its *designatum* has good results, and that his neglect of communication led him to misconstrue the basic question of indexical reference.

ROBERTS, Marie. 'Rosicrucianism Or Cross–rosism' In Hegel's *Phenomenology*. *Hist Euro Ideas* 6,99–100 1985.

Hegel illustrates his philosophical method through the Rosicrucian symbolism of the Brotherhood of the Rosy Cross, the rose on the cross. Using this mystical imagery, he formulates his view on the relationship between philosophy and its content. In the *Philosophy of Right* and *Lectures on the Philosophy of Religion*, the symbols of the rose and the cross which are interchangeable represent an ultimate synthesis between the actual and the ideal.

ROBERTS, Martin. Coleridge's Philosophical And Theological Thinking And Its Significance For Today. *Relig Stud* 20,487–496 S 84.

The purpose of the work is to argue that Coleridge's mature philosophical/ theological thinking articulates and releases his earlier poetical and visionary aspirations, though perhaps at the expense of philosophical consistency and clarity, visionary and speculative interests (or claims of the head and the heart) are not sufficiently distinguished to make possible a development of Coleridge's thought into a contemporary, unambiguous philosophical theology.

ROBERTS, Robert C. "Some Remarks On The Concept Of Passion" in *International Kierkegaard Commentary*, Perkins, Robert L (ed), 87–106. Macon Mercer Univ Pr 1984.

ROBERTS, Scott P. The Generalized Argument From Verification: Work Towards The Metaepistemology Of Perception. *Metaphilosophy* 16,21–28 Ja 85.

In this paper I produce a generalized version of the Argument for Verification, and show its proper conclusion to be that the status of the object of perception as either mental or physical cannot be verified. When viewed broadly, then, it is seen that the Argument from Verification is actually a critique of that process of theory–making with regard to perception, which takes reference to the mind–dependence or independence of the object of perception as its most important part.

ROBERTSON, Diana C and Dunfee, Thomas W. Work–Related Ethical Attitudes: Impact On Business Profitability. *Bus Prof Ethics J* 3,25–40 Wint 84.

Work–related attitudes (WREAs) are workforce ethical attitudes that affect business operations. WREAs are assumed to be situation–specific, changeable and predictive behavior. WREAs identified as critical to the profitability of a business firm are 1) honesty–related, 2) loyalty–related and 3) responsibility–related. Suggestions for measuring WREAs are presented. Arguments supporting both a positive and negative correlation between WREAs and profitability are discussed; the authors predict a positive correlation between WREAs and business profitability.

ROBERTSON, George S. Dignity And Cost–Effectiveness: Analysing The Responsibility For Decisions In Medical Ethics. *J Med Ethics* 10,152–154 S 84.

In the operation of a health care system, defining the limits of medical care is the joint responsibility of many parties including clinicians, patients, philosophers and politicians. It is suggested that changes in the potential for prolonging life make it necessary to give doctors guidance which may have to incorporate certain features of utilitarianism, individualism and patient–autonomy.

ROBIN, Stanley S and Markle, Gerald E. Biotechnology And The Social Reconstruction Of Molecular Biology. *Sci Tech Human Values* 10,70–79 Wint 85.

ROBINS, Michael H. "Veatch And MacIntyre On The Virtues" in *The Georgetown Symposium On Ethics*, Porreco, Rocco (ed), 117–130. Lanham Univ Pr Of America 1984.

ROBINS, Michael H. Deviant Causal Chains And Non–Basic Action. *Austl J Phil* 62,265–282 S 84.

In this paper, the author shows that the first lacuna can be filled in with a theory of the normative stratification of nonbasic action, and the second with the notion of the essential macro–level nature of intentional action. Analysis of some counterexamples follows. (edited)

ROBINSON, Hoke. Intuition And Manifold In The Transcendental Deduction. *S J Phil* 22,403–412 Fall 84.

This paper argues that D Henrich's interpretation of the B–Deduction—that the first part shows the categories cover intuitions containing unity, the second that they cover *all* intuitions—cannot be maintained: on textual and systematic grounds, all intuitions must contain unity, hence the distinction crucial to his view cannot be made. I then offer an alternative account which tries to avoid Henrich's problems in accounting for intuition–formation.

ROBINSON, Jean. Are We Teaching Students That Patients Don't Matter? *J Med Ethics* 11,19–21 Mr 85.

Medical students may fear that their training leeches away the caring attitudes which attracted them to medicine. Some research suggests they are right. The medical school has a duty to support and encourage their values, but the reverse may happen. Students are taught about legal consent but not ethical consent. They may see or participate in concealment of medical mistakes and learn to practice deceit. The use of unconscious females for gynecology teaching may encourage the wrong attitudes to patients. Trainee GP's may learn that the doctors' rights are more important than those of the patient. Measuring patients' views should be included in research protocols.

ROBINSON, Jenefer. General And Individual Style In Literature. *J Aes Art Crit* 43,147–158 Wint 84.

In this essay I defend Richard Wollheim's view that there is a sharp distinction between individual and general style, and I elaborate the nature of the distinction with respect to literature. In general, I argue that unlike individual style, general style categories can be defined "taxonomically" and do not have "psychological reality."

ROBINSON, Jenefer. Style And Personality In The Literary Work. *Phil Rev* 94,227–248 Ap 85.

In this paper I describe and defend a certain conception of literary style. On my conception, a literary style is a way of *doing* certain things, such as describing characters, commenting on the action and manipulating the plot. I claim that an author's way of doing these things is an expression of her personality, or the personality which she seems to have, and that the verbal elements of style gain their stylistic significance only by contributing to the expression of this personality.

ROBINSON, T J and Manning, D J. *The Place Of Ideology In Political Life*. Dover Croom Helm 1985.

Ideology's place in political life is, we learn, 'to provide the vocabulary within which the commendation or denigration of political institutions can be undertaken'. It is thus an essential component of politics, and cannot be dismissed as 'false consciousness' (as by Marx), an abridgement of political wisdom (as by Oakeshott), or senseless talk (as by T D Weldon, who is accused of attempting to clamp philosophical censorship upon politics). A proposition like 'all history is the history of class struggle' supplies a vocabulary of allegiance that allows parties to form and people to discuss their positions, but it tells us nothing at all. Manning and Robinson insist, about the world. It is on this point of absolute scepticism that people otherwise sympathetic to the analysis advanced by the Durham school (an earlier argument, *The Form of Ideology*, was published in 1980) find a stumbling block. (edited)

ROBINSON, Wade L. Management And Ethical Decision–Making. *J Bus Ethics* 3,287–292 N 84.

Every human activity has its characteristic features, the general tendencies that are often difficult to perceive for those engaged in the activity. Such general tendencies are of special concern to those managing in such activities. For the activity of business is not value–neutral, and if one is to manage morally in business, one must come to understand its general tendencies insofar as they affect values. (edited)

ROBINSON, William S. The Ontological Argument. *Int J Phil Relig* 16,51–59 1984.

My first aim in this paper is to clearly articulate a necessary condition for the ontological argument to provide anyone with a good reason to believe that the statement "God exists" is true. My second aim is to show that it is doubtful that this condition is ever met. In carrying out these aims the essential simplicity of the ontological argument becomes apparent.

ROBINSON, William S. Toward Eliminating Churchland's Eliminationism. *Phil Topics* 13,61–68 Spr 85.

This paper responds to Paul Churchland's "Eliminative Materialism and the Propositional Attitudes," *The Journal of Philosophy* 78 (february, 1981). I argue that Churchland fails to show either that folk psychology is a vulnerable theory or that functionalism is an irresponsible dodge. I show why we could not replace folk psychology with concepts drawn from neuroscience and why we could not understand an attempt to do so as advancing science rather than abandoning it.

ROBLES, Jose A. "(Simple) Qualities And Resemblance" in *Philosophical Analysis In Latin America*, Gracia, Jorge J E and others (eds), 199–218. Boston Reidel 1984.

ROBSON, John M (ed) and Mill, John Stuart. *Essays On French History And Historians*. Toronto Univ Of Toronto Pr 1985.

ROCHA, Acílio S E. O Conhecimento Á Luz Do Método Transcendental: Uma Via Para A Antropologia De Karl Rahner. *Rev Port Filosof* 40,387–418 O–D 84.

The author attempts to give a systematic overview of the relations between man and "oikos" (house or universe), a view which might contribute towards answering the question of meaning in human life. Setting out from meta–theoretical reflections, the author contends that the relationship between man and "oikos", is open completely neither to observation nor to introspection, but can be discovered in the types of objects dealt with. These objects are constituted in accordance with the psychological structure of man, where general and specific, holistic and particularistic views have a complementary function.

ROCHA, Filipe. Perspectivas Pedagógicas Da Filosofia Existencialista. *Rev Port Filosof* 40,337–360 O–D 84.

ROCHON, Claire and Marchand, Alain Bernard. L'Apport De La Convention En Litterature. *De Phil* 5,20–28 1984.

ROCKMORE, Thomas. Kolakowski And Marković On Stalinism. *Phil Soc Crit* 6,309–326 Fall 79.

ROCKMORE, Tom. La Systématicité Et Le Cercle Hégélien. *Arch Phil* 48,3–20 Ja–Mr 85.

The concept of circularity although rarely discussed plays an important role in Hegel's system. The point of this paper is to reconstruct the discussion against which Hegel's introduces this concept, to describe its role in his thought, and to criticize it.

ROCKMORE, Tom. Marxian Epistemology And Two Kinds Of Pragmatism. *Stud Soviet Tho* 28,117–126 Ag 84.

ROCKMORE, Tom. Marxian Praxis. *Phil Soc Crit* 5,1–16 Ja 78.

ROCKMORE, Tom. On Marxian Epistemology And Phenomenology. *Stud Soviet Tho* 28,187–200 O 84.

ROCKMORE, Tom. The Concept Of Crisis And The Unity Of Husserl's Position. *Man World* 17,245–260 1984.

RODD, Rosemary. Pacifism And Absolute Rights For Animals: A Comparison Of Difficulties. *J Applied Phil* 2,53–62 Mr 85.

There are many points of similarity between the views of pacifists and those people who argue that sentient non–human animals have absolute rights. Both positions ultimately rest on the assertion that the consequences of a violent action which is intended to preserve some lives by terminating others are more far–reaching than we generally suppose. When the total net consequences of such actions are considered, it can be seen that an ethic of complete non–violence might turn out to be optimific in the long run. Hence, absolutist moral positions of this sort should not be seen as irrational, or self–serving, and are worthy of respectful consideration even if we finally decide that we ourselves cannot accept them. (edited)

RODERICK, Rick. Habermas On Rationality. *Man World* 18,203–218 1985.

I provide an account of Habermas' theory of rationality at two levels: the empirical–reconstructive and the conceptual. I criticize Habermas' theory for failing to do justice to the social and historical contextuality of thought, speech, and action.

RODEWALD, Richard. Does Liberalism Rest On A Mistake? *Can J Phil* 15,231–252 Je 85.

John Rawls and other influential philosophers believe that liberalism requires principles of justice that are rationally justified on grounds which are neutral between persons who have competing conceptions of the good life. This view is implausible because fundamental questions of social justice cannot always be decided by such principles. This conclusion is defended by showing that Rawls' theory of justice cannot settle inevitable conflicts of interests over the design of basic economic arrangements.

RODRÍGUEZ, José M. De La Ideología A La Ciencia. *Rev Filosof (Costa Rica)* 22,51–62 D 84.

Se estudia aquí el concepto de totalidad ciencia en el pensamiento de Hegel (Ciencia de la lógica) y algunas de sus consecuencias en las ciencias sociales contemporáneas. Esta categoría se ha convertido en una pieza insustituible de la reflexión social porque permite una lectura crítica y no ingenua de la realidad.

RODRIGUEZ, Virgilio R. El Poder En Aristoteles Y Romano Guardini. *Rev Filosof (Mexico)* 18,69–78 Ja–Ap 85.

ROE, M F H. *Unacceptable Essays.* Oxfordshire Gresham 1984.

These six essays evaluate the methodological implications of an ontology which holds the external world as a inter–related complex whole which is also dynamic. The essays deal with connections between epistemological and ethical issues and examine the failure of rationalistic and cognitive approaches to these problems. (staff)

ROE, Shirley A. Voltaire Versus Needham: Atheism, Materialism, And The Generation Of Life. *J Hist Ideas* 46,65–88 Ja–Mr 85.

ROEMER, John E. Should Marxists Be Interested In Exploitation? *Phil Pub Affairs* 14,30–65 Wint 85.

Marxian exploitation exists when some members of a population labor more hours than are socially embodied in the goods they receive. Why be interested in this calculation of 'labor accounts?' For what more fundamental positive or normative issue is exploitation a good theoretical statistic? Five reasons have, historically, been given: the linking of exploitation with (1) accumulation, (2) domination, (3) alienation, (4) inequality, and (5) expropriation. It is shown that exploitation is not linked in an analytically rigorous way to any of these five phenomena. 'Exploitation', as defined, is therefore not of inherent interest, although the five phenomena for which it falsely

purports to be a statistic, are.

ROEMER, Robert E. Issues Of Computer Compatibility. *Proc Phil Educ* 40,127–130 1984.

This is a review of "Computer Power and Intellectual Failure in Education" by Keith Raitz. In determining which activities are computer compatible, activities must be analyzed as to whether they are reducible to a set of rules or instructions. If an activity is so reducible, then a further question is whether the computer performance of such an activity is justified. Computer performance of educational activities are judged by these two criteria.

ROGER, Jacques. Per Una Storia Storica Delle Scienze. *G Crit Filosof Ital* 63,285–314 S–D 84.

The paper defines a historical approach to the history of science, in contradistinction to a teleological "history of problems", "epistemological history" (logical reconstructions according to pre–established definitions of science) and sociological reductionism. Science is described as the product of interactions between historical factors and reality. "Truth" is defined as "transhistoricity", or capability to survive in changing environments. Historians have to understand, not to judge scientific texts. All relevant historical factors must be analyzed and weighed.

ROGERS, Adrian. The Restoration Of Medical Ethics. *J Med Ethics* 10,117–120 S 84.

The ethical behavior of doctors has been influenced by recent social and political changes. This paper discusses some of the changes which may have resulted from two far–reaching changes, a major political change, the nationalization of medicine in the National Health Service (NHS),and a social change, the establishment of the permissive society. (edited)

ROGERS, G A J. The Basis Of Belief: Philosophy, Science And Religion In Seventeenth–Century England. *Hist Euro Ideas* 6,19–40 1985.

Seventeenth century England saw a shift in the philosophical basis of knowledge claims from scholasticism to the 'New Philosophy' linked to developments in the natural sciences. The search for absolute certainty was replaced by probablistic epistemology which mirrored a shift from the *vita contemplativa* to the *vita activa*, instanced by the move away from the universities to the civil service of the two leading intellectuals of the age, John Locke and Isaac Newton.

ROHRBERG, Peter. Bedürfnisse Und Produktion. *Deut Z Phil* 22,694–697 1974.

ROHS, P. Auflösung Eines Einwandes Gegen Kants Transzendentale Ästhetik. *Kantstudien* 66,291–296 1975.

ROHS, Peter. Pflichtethik Oder Wertethik: Zu Franz Von Kutscheras "Grundlagen Der Ethik". *Z Phil Forsch* 39,101–109 Ja–Mr 85.

In my discussion of v Kutschera's "Grundlagen der Ethik" I defend the following thesis: an empirical value–experience cannot serve as a basis for ethical laws; a comparison of existing preferences does not yield such laws; preferences have to be an object of moral obligation; this is possible, because preferences do not exist independently of decisions. Therefore a deontological conception of ethics has to be accepted.

ROJAS, Oscar and Polimeni, Dante. Mujer, Biología O Historia Y Poder. *Rev Filosof (Costa Rica)* 23,205–214 D 85.

The recent period in Costa Rica has meant an extensive discussion, in the public domain, about the problematic condition of woman in our times. The author attempts to make an examination of the doctrinary and social content of the sectors that are opposed in the formulated positions. In the analysis of the positions about the inevitability and therefore, universality and constant permanence of masculine influence, the plain biolocalization of these positions and their reactionary political content are declared. As it is propounded from Kosik and Foucault a globalizing perspective, the author presents the need for surpassing the positions of the sectors that are trying to get a place in the university and political domains, and proposes reflection about everyday life and the peasant's and the worker's situation.

ROLLINS, C D. OK Bouwsma, 1937 And Later. *Phil Invest* 8,208–216 Jl 85.

Here is a fragmentary sketch of Bouwsma's pedagogy and interests and opinions (philosophical and otherwise), as evident from 1937 on to about 1956. Russell was a favorite object of his suspicions, Moore and Wisdom and Wittgenstein of his admiration.

ROLLINS, L A. *The Myth Of Natural Rights.* Port Townsend Loompanics 1983.

ROLLINS, Mark. Distributive Justice. *Kinesis* 14,79–105 Spr 85.

The aim is to compare Rawls and Nozick on distributive justice and, in particular, to determine how their common fundamental commitment to individualism leads to divergent conclusions. Rawls argues for institutions to rectify natural inequities; Nozick holds that state efforts to that end violate rights. These conclusions follow consistently from the primacy of central concepts, fairness and entitlement, respectively; but neither concept can be clearly applied to arbitrary factors which occur independently of human action.

ROLSTON, Holmes. *Religious Inquiry—Participation And Detachment.* NY Philosophical Lib 1985.

Four saints—Augustine, Ghazali, Sankara, Nagarjuna, as representatives of Christianity, Islam, Hinduism, and Buddhism—are brought into colloquy with each other and with the modern inquirer concerning the possibility and limits of religious and interreligious understanding. The argument examines correspondent truthfulness, epistemic virtues, (love, faith, purity, humility), perception and conception, subjectivity and objectivity, understanding and undergoing, adherence and nonadherence, and contexts of learning (about) God the Father of Jesus Christ, Allah, Brahman, and Emptiness.

ROLSTON, Holmes. Valuing Wildlands. *Environ Ethics* 7,23–48 Spr 85.

Valuing wildlands is complex. (1) In a philosophically oriented analysis, I distinguish seven meaning levels of value, individual preference, market price, individual good, social preference, social good, organismic, and ecosystemic, and itemize twelve types of value carried by wildlands, economic, life support, recreational, scientific, genetic diversity, aesthetic, cultural symbolization, historical, character building, therapeutic, religious, and intrinsic. (2) I criticize contingent valuation efforts to price these values. (3) I then propose an axiological model, which interrelates the multiple levels and types of value, and some principles for wildland management policy.

ROMANELL, Patrick. *John Locke And Medicine: A New Key To Locke.* Buffalo Prometheus 1984.

This book examines the medical writings of John Locke and gives a reinterpretation of his philosophical method and ideas in light of these medical manuscripts. (staff)

ROMANO, Bruno. Desiderio, Riconoscimento E Diritto Secondo J Lacan. *Riv Int Filosof Diritto* 61,95–126 Ja–Mr 84.

ROOCHNIK, David L. The Riddle Of The *Cleitophon. Ancient Phil* 4,132–145 Fall 84.

This paper addresses the central question posed by Plato's *Cleitophon*: why does Socrates remain silent in the face of Cleitophon's charges? Part I reviews the literature this dialogue has generated. Part II presents the author's own view. In particular, it is argued that Socrates' silence, in itself, constitutes a meaningful response to Cleitophon.

ROOT, Michael. Images Of Liberation: Justin, Jesus And The Jews. *Thomist* 48,512–534 O 84.

ROQUE, Alicia Juarrero. Dispositions, Teleology And Reductionism. *Phil Topics* 12,153–165 Wint 81.

Larry Wright's analysis of teleological ascriptions presented in *Teleological Explanations* is inadequate because (1) it cannot account for unique behavior that is nevertheless teleological; (2) it cannot accurately identify the precise goal of teleological behavior; and (3) it will often fail to identify behavior as purposive even though it is. Wright's *analysans* is inadequate because it is dispositional and, *a fortiori*, behaviorist.

RORTY, Amelie Oksenberg. Formal Traces In Cartesian Functional Explanation. *Can J Phil* 14,545–560 D 84.

RORTY, Richard and others (ed). *Philosophy In History.* NY Cambridge Univ Pr 1984.

RORTY, Richard. "The Historiography Of Philosophy: Four Genres" in *Philosophy In History*, Rorty, Richard and others (ed), 49–76. NY Cambridge Univ Pr 1984.

RORTY, Richard. Comments On Sleeper And Edel. *Trans Peirce Soc* 21,39–48 Wint 85.

ROSALES, Alberto. Zum Problem Der Kehre Im Denken Heideggers. *Z Phil Forsch* 38,241–262 Ap–Je 84.

ROSE, Alan. A Note On The Existence Of Tautologies Without Constants. *Z Math Log* 21,141–144 1975.

ROSE, David A. Theoretical And Practical Confusion In American Professional Sport. *Dialec Hum* 11,105–114 Wint 84.

ROSEBERG, Ulrich. Philosophisch–Weltanschauliche Auseinandersetzungen Um Theoretische Positionen Zur Wissenschaftsgeschichte. *Deut Z Phil* 32,885–893 1984.

History is not the sum of stories about the past; history is an objective process of development with dialectical contradictions as driving forces, quantitative as well as qualitative changes (continuity and discontinuity) and the tendency to higher qualities. The author proved this understanding of history for the development of nonrelativistic quantum mechanics (1913–1930). The article presents the most important methodological rules for his case study.

ROSEBERG, Ulrich. Widerspiegelung Objektiver Naturdialektik In Mathematisierten Naturwissenschaftlichen Theorien. *Deut Z Phil* 23,938–945 1975.

ROSEN, Edward. The Dissolution Of The Solid Celestial Spheres. *J Hist Ideas* 46,13–32 Ja–Mr 85.

Although Aristotle's spheres and planets were made of *aither*, an ethereal, non-material substance, and as such treated in Ptolemy's *Planetary Hypotheses*, C(h) alcidius, the commentator of Plato's *Timaeus*, refers to Aristotle's "real and solid bodies of the stars". This view of the celestial spheres was misattributed by Tycho Brahe to Ibn–al–Haytham, Witelo, and Copernicus. The belief in the solid planetary spheres was decisively disapproved by the 16th century astronomer, Christopher Rothmann, in Chapter V of his *Accurate Description of the Comet of the Year*, 1585.

ROSENBAUM, Alan S. On The Philosophical Foundations Of The Conception Of Human Rights. *Phil Res Arch* 10,543–566 1985.

In this paper I shall defend the thesis that differing concepts of human nature (or "personhood") lead to different ideas about what "human rights" are, about what types there are, and how rights are to be ranked according to priority. Though some correlation is obvious, as evidenced in the literature, political forums, and in case studies of many nation–states, the question that we will consider is whether this correlation is a causal relationship or whether it is merely accidental and hence, not worthy of any but passing notice. But if, as I believe, some definite causal connection, perhaps in combination with other factors does exist, we are quite right in focusing attention on the disparate "personhood" concepts or foundation level which lies uncovered and central to such disagreements about human rights.

ROSENBAUM, Stephen E. Reviving The Isolation Argument. *Phil Stud* 48,241–248 S 85.

The author argues that one traditional argument against foundational theories of justification is a good argument, despite recent doubts to the contrary. Through the use of examples, he argues that (1) certain sorts of perceptual beliefs are epistemically privileged and that (2) only foundational theories of justification account for the privileged status of the beliefs.

ROSENBERG, Alan and Manicas, Peter T. Naturalism, Epistemological Individualism And "The Strong Programme" In Sociology Of Knowledge. *J Theor Soc Behav* 15,76–101 Mr 85.

The essay, an assessment of the work of Barry Barnes and David Bloor, argues that their "strong programme in the sociology of knowledge" offers a thoroughgoing naturalistic epistemology which overcomes the individualism of prior naturalized epistemologies, as e.G., in W V Quine. We hold that their view presupposes a form of ontological realism and a realist theory of science, facts overlooked by critics. Finally, we argue that the implications for psychology and the social sciences are enormous and have not yet been appreciated.

ROSENBERG, Alexander. Mackie And Shoemaker On Dispositions And Properties. *Midwest Stud Phil* 9,77–92 1984.

J L Mackie's claim that no properties are irreducibly dispositional is defended against S Shoemaker's claim that all properties are ultimately dispositional. The argument proceeds by offering criticisms, of Shoemaker's "epistemological" arguments for properties as sets of casual powers, inspired by Mackie's empiricist arguments against rationalist views of casual powers.

ROSENBERG, Alexander. Prospects For The Elimination Of Tastes From Economics And Ethics. *Soc Phil Pol* 2,48–68 Spr 85.

After explaining the difficulties that the exogeneity of tastes and preferences make for neoclassical microeconomic theory, and any auxiliary theory that might be needed to apply the theory, this paper turns to an examination of Gary Becker's interpretation of rational choice theory, which circumvents these problems. It is argued that the theory does so only when Becker's "stable preferences" are interpreted as needs. The potential Becker's theory has, on this interpretation, of making stronger claims in welfare economics than those limited to the terms of Pareto optimality, is explored, with special reference to the problems of paternalism, and the relations of Becker's theory to a doctrine of natural rights, like Rawls' theory.

ROSENFELD, Sidney (ed) and Rosenfeld, Stella (ed) and Améry, Jean. *Radical Humanism.* Bloomington Indiana Univ Pr 1984.

ROSENFELD, Stella (ed) and Améry, Jean and Rosenfeld, Sidney (ed). *Radical Humanism.* Bloomington Indiana Univ Pr 1984.

ROSENFIELD, Leonora C and Popkin, Richard H (ed). *Condorcet Studies 1.* Atlantic Highlands Humanities Pr 1984.

This is the first American collection of scholarly studies of Condorcet, the last of the *philosophies.* He had wide–ranging reform ideas of secular liberalism, which are relevant to contemporary problems, and studied British philosophy and the American Revolution. Lenora Cohen Rosenfield, the editor, writes a synoptic introduction. Four studies deal with Condorcet's views on rights and revolution, three on social sciences, three on the revolution in education, and two on the quest for justice.

ROSENKRANTZ, Gary. Acquaintance. *Philosophia (Israel)* 14,1–24 Ag 84.

One is acquainted with *x* only if one grasps *x*'s haecceity. None of us grasps the haecceity of an external material object or person. If one grasps such a property, then he can re–identify an object of this kind from one perceptual situation to another without making a nondeductive inference from his perceptions. None of us can do this. It is doubtful whether such an argument applies to abstracts, oneself, and one's own sense–data.

ROSENKRANTZ, Roger. "Why Glymour Is A Bayesian" in *Testing Scientific Theories*, Earman, John (ed), 69–98. Minneapolis Univ Minnesota Pr 1983.

ROSENTHAL, Abigail L. The Filial Art. *J Applied Phil* 2,19–30 Mr 85.

Psychological or political criticism of the parent–child relation presupposes a normative account of that relation. Such an account is here provided. The normative account can shed most light when the parent–child relation is presented recognizably, not in Utopian disguise. The purposes of reasonable people partly depend on their interpretations of those of their parents. This is so whether such people can accept or reject any particular parental purposes. The filial art sticks to the project of working out the enacted interpretation—until it gets it approximately right. There is a corresponding parental art, neither compensatory nor sacrificial.

ROSENTHAL, David M. "Armstrong's Causal Theory Of Mind" in *D M Armstrong*, Bogdan, Radu J (ed), 79–120. Boston Reidel 1984.

ROSENTHAL, Erwin and Ludwig, Gerd and Bräu, Richard. Zur Rolle Des Subjektiven Faktors In Der Wissenschaftsentwicklung. *Deut Z Phil* 33,459–462 1985.

ROSENTHAL, John W. Partial Aleph–1–homogeneity Of The Countable Saturated Model Of An Aleph–sub–1–categorical Theory. *Z Math Log* 21,307–308 1975.

ROSENTHAL, John W. Truth In All Of Certain Well–Founded Countable Models Arising In Set Theory. *Z Math Log* 21,97–105 1975.

ROSENTHAL, Sandra B. C I Lewis And The Pragmatic Focus On Action: Some Systematic Implications. *Phil Topics* 13,87–94 Spr 85.

Pragmatic philosophy is often accused of housing an anti–theoretical attitude. First, its focus on man as active agent leads to the often heard condemnation that it is overly concerned with action, making known only for the sake of doing. Secondly, its focus on the experiential basis of meaning leads to the claim that pragmatism is anti–speculative, making metaphysical issues meaningless. This essay focuses on Lewis' analysis of the structure of meaning in terms of human action to show the way in which it provides a strong rebuttal, from within pragmatism, to both of the above criticisms.

ROSENTHAL, Sandra B. Temporality, Perceptual Experience And Peirce's "Proofs" Of Realism. *Trans Peirce Soc* 20,435–452 Fall 84.

A recent defense of Peirce's pragmatic realism as an explanation of "why the scientific manipulation of language affects our interaction with the world in the way in which it does" argues that this claim is an empirical hypothesis open to the cumulative effect of inductive confirmation, within science. However, by focusing on the level of science, problems are left unresolved, for such a claim for Peirce begins neither at the level of language nor at the level of science, but rather in a rudimentary perceptual experience. The present paper explores the implications of this level as foundational for peirce's claims of realism.

ROSENTHAL, Sandra and Bourgeois, Patrick. Merleau–Ponty, Lewis And Ontological Presence. *Phil Topics* 13,239–246 Spr 85.

Although phenomenology and pragmatism have emerged as almost entirely independent traditions, they manifest striking similarities in basic stances toward certain issues. This essay focuses on the way mutual rejection of the Kantian distinction between noumena and phenomena influences the positions of Merleau–Ponty and Lewis in a way in which manifests important common elements between them.

ROSMARIN, Adena. Theory And Practice: From Ideally Separated To Pragmatically Joined. *J Aes Art Crit* 43,31–40 Fall 84.

ROSS, Howard. Marxism And The Transition Problem. *Cogito* 2,111–116 S 84.

The purpose of this work is to provide a useful critique of Immanuel Wallerstein and his view of the world system. It concludes with a review of some of the central theorists on the transition problem. First, we look at Wallerstein's paradigm, followed by a discussion of the transition problem and how it has been treated by various Marxists from the exchange–relations school, the property–relations school, and the electic school.

ROSS, J F. *Portraying Analogy.* NY Cambridge Univ Pr 1981.

How do wrong meanings fit to contrasting verbal surroundings (*drop/eyes; drop/courses*)? This is a systematic account of the "classical" analogy phenomena: mere equivocation (*charge/account; charge/gun*), proportionality (*collect/books; collect/debts*), denomination (*play/piano; play/chopin*), metaphor, paronymy (*healthy, healthful*) and of figurative discourse. Two universals, linguistic force and inertia, explain the fit: words are dominated by other words to fit, notch–wise, resisting various kinds of unacceptability by dropping affinities and oppositions to other words. Craftbound discourse, in religion, law and science, exhibits those structures, too. Resulting infinite polysemy and evolving expressive capacity, explained here, have massive consequences for analysis, philosophy of language and philosophy of mind.

ROSS, Stephanie A. Ut Hortus Poesis––Gardening And Her Sister Arts In Eighteenth–Century England. *Brit J Aes* 25,17–32 Wint 85.

The 18th century viewed gardening, painting, and poetry as sister arts. This paper examines that comparison and asks just what powers a garden can possess. I argue that the more surprising of the two comparisons—that between a garden and a poem—turns out to be the more substantive. I close with some general conclusions about the relations among these arts and about the proper pleasures of a garden.

ROSS, Stephen David. Inexhaustibility And Ontological Plurality. *Metaphilosophy* 15,259–269 JI–O 84.

Using the criterion that to be real is to be inexhaustible, I argue for ontological plurality, replying to arguments by Strawson, Dummett, and Chisholm. An important conclusion is that whatever is real is, inseparably and complementarily, indeterminate as well as determinate. The position is briefly applied to such kinds of beings as physical objects, events, processes, propositions, facts, universals, minds, and persons.

ROSS, Steven L. Weakness And Dignity In Conrad's *Lord Jim. Phil Res Arch* 10,153–172 1984.

Conrad's Lord Jim presents not only a paradigmatic case of weakness of will, but an equally paradigmatic case of the enormous difficulties that attend fitting weakness of will into other moral attitudes, particularly those relating to moral worth and moral shame. Conrad's general conception of character and morality is deeply Aristotelian in many respects, somewhat Kantian in others. The essay traces out the intuitive strengths and philosophical difficulties that both an Aristotelian and a Kantian conception will have before the problem of weakness of will, and argues that the ambiguity of Conrad's treatment of Jim's case is the reflection of the clash between these two equally compelling, incompatible conceptions of the self and moral worth.

ROSSI, Alejandro. "Descriptions, Meaning And Presupposition" in *Philosophical Analysis In Latin America*, Gracia, Jorge J E and others (eds), 219–242. Boston Reidel 1984.

ROSTANKOWSKI, Cynthia (ed) and Velasquez, Manuel (ed). *Ethics: Theory And Practice.* Englewood Cliffs Prentice–Hall 1985.

ROSTOW, W W. "Foreign Aid: Justice For Whom" in *The Search For Justice*, Taitte, W Lawson (ed), 127–162. Austin Univ Of Texas Pr 1983.

ROTENSTREICH, Nathan. *Jews And German Philosophy: The Polemics Of Emancipation.* NY Schocken Books 1984.

ROTENSTREICH, Nathan. *Reflection And Action.* Boston Nijhoff 1985.

The book takes a phenomenological look at metaphysics, covering a broad scope of issues including labor, politics, morality, and action theory. (staff)

ROTENSTREICH, Nathan. "Summary Of The Buber Centenary Conference At Ben–Gurion University In January 1978" in *Martin Buber*, Gordon, Haim (ed), 473–484. Beersheva Ktav 1984.

ROTENSTREICH, Nathan. Can Evil Be Banal? *Phil Forum (Boston)* 16,50–62 Fall–Wint 84.

The article is related to the book of Hannah Arendt: *The Banality of Evil.* In the context of the Holocaust it raises the question as to the very conception of the possibility to look at evil as being banal. The conception is criticized by taking into account evil from the point of view of the motivation promoting it as well as from the point of view of the deeds performed. The underlying decision prevents the possibility of looking at evil as being banal.

ROTENSTREICH, Nathan. Prudence And Folly. *Amer Phil Quart* 22,93–104 Ap 85.

ROTENSTREICH, Nathan. Will And Reason: A Critical Analysis Of Kant's Concepts. *Phil Phenomenol Res* 46,37–58 S 85.

This paper seeks to delineate everyday usage of the two concepts—will and reason—in order to identify the systematic transformation these concepts underwent in Kant's system. It has been observed that even in our everyday interpretation and parlance there are different meanings or nuances or meanings attributed to the phenomenon of will and perhaps also, to a lesser extent, to the phenomenon of will serve as the point of departure of Kant's characterization of the concept "will" which is, in the first instance, congruent with its ordinary usage. Yet in other instances, as we shall see, Kant's characterization of the will is imbued with systematic meaning which has to be seen in the context of his philosophy in general and of his philosophy of practice in particular.

ROTH, H D. The Concept Of Human Nature In The Huai Nan Tzu. *J Chin Phil* 12,1–22 Mr 85.

ROTH, John K. How To Make Hitler's Ideas Clear? *Phil Forum (Boston)* 16,82–94 Fall–Wint 84.

Adolf Hitler was not yet alive when Charles S Peirce published his now famous essay, "How to Make Our Ideas Clear", in 1878. Still, Peirce's pragmatism contains important implications for attempts to clarify the meaning of Hitler's anti–Jewish pronouncements from 1919 until the Final Solution ended. Among those implications is the awareness that all human beings, even a Hitler, grope uncertainly into the future.

ROTH, John K. The Silence Of God. *Faith Phil* 1,407–420 O 84.

"as a Jew", Elie Wiesel has written, "you will sooner or later be confronted with the enigma of God's action in history". Drawing on Reeve Robert Brenner's *The Faith and Doubt of Holocaust Survivors* (1980), this article evaluates recent work by Paul M van Buren and Arthur A Cohen, concluding that it is wrong to apologize for God at humanity's expense.

ROTH, Paul A. On Missing Neurath's Boat: Some Reflections On Recent Quine Literature. *Synthese* 61,205–232 N 84.

This article provides a critical review of two recent books on Quine's philosophy: *Quine and Analytic Philosophy* by G Romanos and *The Philosophy of W V Quine* by R Gibson. Both books boast a foreward by Quine. However, the books are of very unequal quality. Romano's work mischaracterizes and fundamentally misconstrues the basic thrust of Quine's work. Gibson's efforts, while accurate and helpful, nonetheless prove unsuccessful in clarifying Quine's indeterminacy thesis.

ROTH, Paul A. Who Needs Paradigms? *Metaphilosophy* 15,225–238 JI–O 84.

This paper examines and criticizes the use of the notion of paradigm in the social sciences. In this century, thoughtful social scientists have regularly relied upon the received doctrine in the philosophy of science in order to justify the social sciences *qua* sciences. With the advent of Kuhn's views, social scientists now write as if having a paradigm is a necessary condition for successful research. I show that their understanding here is mistaken.

ROTH, Robert J. Did Peirce Answer Hume On Necessary Connection? *Rev Metaph* 38,867–880 Je 85.

Hume had argued that since the mind cannot grasp powers in nature, it cannot know the ultimate connections between things. The opposite is always possible because there is no logical connection between powers and sense qualities. Pierce argued that the very possibility of science depends on the mind's ability to grasp real powers operative in nature, otherwise laws would be fictions and predictions illusions. Thus he challenged the narrowness of Hume's understanding of what it means to know.

ROTHBART, Daniel. The Semantics Of Metaphor And The Structure Of Science. *Phil Sci* 51,595–615 D 84.

The purpose of this paper is to explore the semantics of metaphoric language in scientific contexts. According to the theory of metaphor advanced below, the benchmark of metaphoric expression is the implicit transfer of semantic features across incongruous semantic fields. This transfer results in a conceptual variation of "meaning" in the receiving semantic field. Thus, the theory of metaphor rests on semantic field theory. Existing semantic approaches to metaphor are evaluated in Section 1. In Sections 2 and 3 an alternative theory is introduced through an analysis of the mechanics of the feature transfer process followed by a discussion of some methodological cues for deciphering the metaphor's "meaning". As I explore in Section 4, this theory of metaphor explains how all metaphoric expressions are potentially literal depending on the general compliance of the community of speakers. Consequently, concept formation in scientific contexts is, in large measure, metaphoric. Finally, I argue in Section 5 that metaphoric concepts formation is an essential aspect of scientific reasoning for the purpose of solving conceptual problems.

ROTHENBERG, Leslie Steven. "Guidelines For Decision Making" in *Ethics Committees And Health Care Decisions*, Cranford, Ronald (ed), 169–173. Ann Arbor Health Admin Pr 1984.

ROTHSCHILD, Joan (ed). *Machina Ex Dea: Feminist Perspectives On Technology.* NY Pergamon Pr 1983.

ROTTER, Frank. Rechtssoziologie Und Psychoanalyse: Neun Thesen In Rechtspolitischer Absicht. *Arch Rechts Soz* 59,535–550 1973.

Nine theses aiming at legal policy concern the following topics: normative and cognitive behavioral expectations, corresponding subsystems of society (law, politics, and science); relations of linguistic theory, theory and philosophy of law with sociology and psychology; psychological systems theory and psychoanalysis; drives, ego–structure and social structure; psychoanalytical and legal procedure as historical examples for procedures primarily in personal and those primarily in social interest. The last thesis is devoted to a specific problem of scarcity bearing central importance for legal policy. (edited)

Author Index with Abstracts 393 **Ruffa, Anthony R**

RÖTTGERS, Kurt. J G H Feder—Beitrag Zu Einer Verhinderungsgeschichte Eines Deutschen Empirismus. *Kantstudien* 75,420–441 1984.

The purpose is to introduce into the work of the German empiricist philosopher J G H Feder, in order to show why there is no empiricist tradition in 19th–century German philosophy. The article provides a case study of the controversy between Feder and Kant, because a possible German empiricist tradition was indeed prevented by Kant and his successors. So the non–existing history of German empiricism is the outside of the history of transcendentalism.

ROTTSCHAEFER, William A. Religious Cognition As Interpreted Experience: An Examination Of Ian Barbour's Comparison Of The Epistemic Structures Of Science/Religion. *Zygon* 20,265–282 S 85.

Using a model contemporary analyses of scientific cognition, Ian Barbour has claimed that religious cognition is neither immediate nor inferential but has the structure of interpreted experience. Although I contend that Barbour has failed to establish his claim, I believe his views about the similarities between scientific and religious cognition are well founded. Thus on that basis I offer an alternative proposal that theistic religious cognition is essentially inferential and that religious experience is in fact the use of inferentially acquired religious beliefs to interpret ordinary nonreligious experiences.

ROTUNDA, Ronald D and Morgan, Thomas D. *Problems And Materials On Professional Responsibility*. Mineola Foundation Pr 1984.

The book is for a law school course in legal ethics. It poses realistic hypothetical situations in which lawyers face ethical choices. Questions are posed to highlight the issues. Legal and non–legal material is suggested which may be helpful in deciding the best courses of action for lawyers to take.

ROTUNDA, Ronald D and Morgan, Thomas D. *Selected Standards On Professional Responsibility*. Mineola Foundation Pr 1985.

ROUMANES, Jacques–Bernard. Une Altenative À L'exclusion: La Dialogie. *Philosophiques* 11,353–372 O 84.

Exclusionist individualism versus massifying collectivism, such is the non–choice against which the theories of equality in men–women relationships attempt to be formalized. Before this deadlock, dia–logie with its principle of alternation, bestows a new meaning upon dialectics and the monologism upon which it is based.

ROUNER, Leroy S (ed). *On Nature*. Notre Dame Univ Notre Dame Pr 1984.

ROURA I AULINAS, Lluís. La Pensée Antiphilosophique Et Contre–révolutionnaire De La Hiérarchie Ecclésiastique Espagnole. *Rev Univ Ottawa* 54,99–112 Jl–S 84.

The context of the Cortes de Cadiz represents one of the first and most important moments in which Spanish reactionary forces felt the need to reaffirm themselves as such. The Church and its hierarchy, thus played out the role which seemed proper to them. Their importance is not only in the ideological content of their message, but also in the means of diffusion and transmission. The author analyses their language technique, which tends to overcome the ever–increasing difficulties that such reactionary forces had to be able to continue relying on the institutions of the Old Regime.

ROUSE, Joseph T. Heidegger's Later Philosophy Of Science. *S J Phil* 23,75–92 Spr 85.

The article shows science as central to Heidegger's thinking, and relates his work to post–empiricist philosophy of science. Both emphasize the role of presuppositions and conceptual revolutions, and focus upon research programs rather than theories, experiment rather than observation, growth of knowledge instead of confirmation. But Heidegger objects to treating presuppositions as explicit beliefs or values and to trying to show the "rationality" of science, and regards the growth of science as a contribution to nihilism.

ROUTLEY, Richard. Metaphysical Fall–Out From The Nuclear Predicament. *Phil Soc Crit* 10,19–34 Wint 84.

ROUTLEY, Richard. The American Plan Completed: Alternative Classical–Style Semantics, Without Stars, For Relevant And Paraconsistent Logics. *Stud Log* 43,131–158 1984.

Two styles of four valued relational semantics are developed; firstly a semantics using notions of double truth and double validity for basic relevant system **B** and some extensions of it; and secondly, since the first semantics makes heavy weather of validating negation principles such as Contraposition, a reduced semantics using more complex implicational rules for relevant system **C** and various of its extensions. To deal satisfactorily with elite systems **R**, **E** and **T**, however, further complication is inevitable; and a relation of mateship (suggested by the Australian plan) is introduced to permit cross–over from one to zero values and vice versa. (edited)

ROUTLEY, R. Relevantism, Material Detachment, And The Disjunctive Syllogism Argument. *Can J Phil* 14,167–188 Je 84.

ROVALETTI, Maria L. El Cuerpo Como Lenguaje, Expresion Y Comunicacion. *Rev Filosof (Mexico)* 17,491–504 S–D 84.

ROVIRA MARTÍNEZ, José. Influencia Del Pensamiento De San Agustín En La Filosofía Catalana Actual. *Augustinus* 25,415–420 Ja–D 80.

ROWE, C J. *Plato*. NY St Martin's Pr 1984.

The book gives a systematic exposition of Plato's central ideas and arguments, with a special emphasis on his own understanding of his activity, both as a philosopher and as author; on his relationship to the thought and culture of his time; and on the richness and adaptability of his thinking. The whole range of his preoccupations is examined, from knowledge, pleasure and justice, to the soul and the natural world – a world which Plato sees as an essentially rational system.

ROWE, William L. Evil And The Theistic Hypothesis: A Response To S J Wykstra. *Int J Phil Relig* 16,95–100 1984.

Wykstra argues that the fact that evils strike us as pointless is not evidence against the theistic hypothesis, since given that hypothesis it is likely that many of the evils in the world would strike us in just that way. I suggest that Wykstra is mistaken about this.

ROWE, William L. Rationalistic Theology And Some Principles Of Explanation. *Faith Phil* 1,357–369 O 84.

Rationalistic Theology attempts to demonstrate that there exists an intelligent and powerful being who accounts for the existence of the world. This paper examines the chief principles of explanation used in such demonstrations. Two principles are critically examined: every fact has an explanation (the Principle of Sufficient Reason); every fact is such that it is possible that it be explained (principle E—advocated by James Ross in *Philosophical Theology*). Arguments are advanced to show that neither principle is true. Certain conclusions concerning Rationalistic Theology are then drawn.

ROWIŃSKI, Cezary. The Dialectics Of Rationality. *Dialec Hum* 11,381–402 Spr/Sum 84.

The article is devoted to the problems of development of the European rationalism from Descartes up to XX century. I distinguish in the European rationalism two trends: a dogmatic and a critical one. From this point of view the essential opposition in the post–hegelian epoch is the internal opposition between critical rationalism and neodogmatic rationalism, and not the opposition rationalism—irrationalism. The formation of the modern critical rationalism was influenced by such different philosophers as K Marx, Nicolai Hartmann, and K R Popper.

ROY, Tirthankar and Chakravarty, Satya R. Measurement Of Fuzziness: A General Approach. *Theor Decis* 19,163–169 S 85.

A new general index for the measurement of fuzziness has been suggested in this paper. It has been shown that a continuous S–concave function of the fuzzy membership values will suffice for constructing an index of fuzziness. The general index satisfies all the postulates for an index of fuzziness proposed by De Luca and Termini (1972).

ROZENBERG, Jacques. La Théorie Optique De L'hallucination Dans Les Rêves D'un Visionnaire De Kant. *Rev Phil Fr* 175,15–26 Ja–Mr 85.

ROZSNYAI, Ervin. Husserl's Platonism And The Objective Truth (in Hungarian). *Magyar Filozof Szemle* 5,749–766 1983.

The article, which is part of a longer treatise, examines in relation with Husserl's platonism the origin of the views about the a priori characteristic of the logical laws and about the conceptual difference between the laws of logic and those of natural sciences. These views come into being as the alternatives of the empiricist theories of knowledge and are directed principally against the theory of reflection. According to Husserl the theory of reflection leads to infinite regression. The author of the article opines that it is indeed true but only if we understand reflection as the passive mental imprint of things. A misinterpreted theory of reflection results in relativism, subjectivism and scepticism. (edited)

ROZSNYAI, Ervin. The Rise Of Modern Bourgeois Ideology In The Baden Neokantianism (in Hungarian). *Magyar Filozof Szemle* 6,936–960 1983.

RUBEN, Peter. Über Die Produktivkräfte Und Ihre Entwicklung. *Deut Z Phil* 32,981–990 1984.

RUBIN, Arthur L and Rubin, Jean E. The Cardinality Of The Set Of Dedekind Finite Cardinals In Fraenkel–Mostowski Models. *Z Math Log* 20,517–528 1974.

RUBIN, Jean E and Rubin, Arthur L. The Cardinality Of The Set Of Dedekind Finite Cardinals In Fraenkel–Mostowski Models. *Z Math Log* 20,517–528 1974.

RUBIN, M and Shelah, Saharon and Abraham, U. On The Consistency Of Some Partition Theorems For Continuous Colorings, And The Structure Of Dense Real Order Types. *Annals Pure Applied Log* 29,123–206 S 85.

RUBIN, Ronald. *Logic Made Simple*. Claremont Arete Pr 1983.

RUBINSTEIN, Robert A. Epidemiology And Anthropology: Notes On Science And Scientism. *Commun Cog* 17,163–186 1984.

The philosophical and methodological assumptions of the anthropological and epidemiological approaches to the study of mental health and illness are compared. There are deep discontinuities in these, going beyond differences in idiom and presentation. Anthropological and epidemiological views of the nature of the scientific study of human behavior are often mutually inconsistent. The implications of this for health policy are discussed.

RUCK, Carl. "The Wild And The Cultivated In Greek Religion" in *On Nature*, Rouner, Leroy S (ed), 79–95. Notre Dame Univ Notre Dame Pr 1984.

RUDDICK, William and Finn, William. Objections To Hospital Philosophers. *J Med Ethics* 11,42–46 Mr 85.

Like morally sensitive hospital staff, philosophers resist routine simplification of morally complex cases. Like hospital clergy, they favor reflective and principled decision–making. Like hospital lawyers, they refine and extend the language we use to formulate and defend our complex decisions. But hospital philosophers are not redundant: they have a wider range of self–serving presuppositions and implicit contradictions within our practices. As semi–outsiders, they are often best able to take an 'external point of view', unburdened by routine, details, and departmental loyalties. Their clarifications can temporarily disrupt routine, but can eventually improve staff morale, hence team practice and patient welfare.

RUDOLPH, W. Entwicklung Und Nutzung Der Qualifikation Der Facharbeiter Als Faktor Ökonomischer Effektivität. *Deut Z Phil* 33,53–62 1985.

RUELLAND, Jacques G. Introduction À La Lecture De George Orwell. *Petit Rev Phil* 6,61–90 Autumn 84.

L'évolution de la conception du socialisme de George Orwell est présentée dans ce texte à travers sa vie et ses grandes oeuvres. Ce texte tente également de réfuter les principaux arguments faisant de *1984* un prophétie plutôt qu'un avertissement. Une bibliographie des principaux écrits sur George Orwell complète ce texte qui s'adresse à ceux qui ont découvert cet auteur en lisant *1984*.

RUFFA, Anthony R. *Darwinism And Determinism: The Role Of Direction In Evolution*. Brookline Village Branden Pr 1983.

RUGGIERO, Vincent Ryan. *Beyond Feelings: A Guide To Critical Thinking*, Second Edition. Palo Alto Mayfield 1984.

This textbook goes beyond the common emphasis on the detection of fallacies. It both establishes the philosophical context in which critical thinking occurs and provides an effective strategy for analysis and judgment.

RUITENBURG, Wim. On The Period Of Sequences $(A''(p))$ In Intuitionistic Propositional Calculus. *J Sym Log* 49,892–899 S 84.

In classical propositional calculus for each proposition $A(p)$ the following holds: $\vdash A(p) \leftrightarrow A^3(p)$. In this paper we show that for each proposition $A(p)$ in intuitionistic propositional calculus we have $\vdash A''(p) \leftrightarrow A^{n+2}(p)$ for some $n \epsilon N$. The value of n is sublinear to the length of $A(P)$.

RUIZ, Edgar Gonzalez. Dos Problemas Concernientes S La Clasificacion Estoica De Falacias. *Rev Filosof (Mexico)* 18,19–32 Ja–Ap 85.

RUMRICH, John Peter. Milton, Duns Scotus, And The Fall Of Satan. *J Hist Ideas* 46,33–50 Ja–Mr 85.

Employing Scotus' distinction between God's absolute and ordained power, this essay examines the episode of Satan's Fall in *Paradise Lost*. The evil angels rebel because God exercised absolute authority in order to transform the natural into a moral order, one in which an angel's natural advantage is distinguishable from the Good. Messiah operates in two roles: as the Word, instrumental to the natural order; as the Son, chief exponent of the moral order.

RUNGGALDIER, Edmund. *Carnap's Early Conventionalism: An Inquiry Into The Historical Background Of The Vienna Circle.* Amsterdam Rodopi 1984.

The book examines the philosophical trends leading to Carnap's conventionalist and positivist philosophy. Its first part is concerned with his early minor works; the second with the analysis and critique of *Der logische Aufbau der Welt*. The conventionalist thesis in the early Carnap could be interpreted as an anticipation of Quine's empirical underdetermination of theories. However, the book attempts to show that Carnap's plan of constructing objects from only one similarity relation cannot be saved.

RUNGGALDIER, Edmund. *Zeichen Und Bezeichnetes.* NY De Gruyter 1985.

The work offers a critical survey of the main philosophical accounts of *reference*. Frege's distinction between sense and reference and Dummett's criticism of onesided theories of meaning provide the background for this investigation. The analysis should help to clarify the new distinctions between 'a priori' and 'necessary', between 'epistemic' and 'metaphysical' and ultimately between modalities 'de dicto' and 'de re'.

RUNIA, D T. History Of Philosophy In The Grand Manner: The Achievement Of H A Wolfson. *Phil Reform* 49,112–133 1984.

The article constitutes both a tribute to and a critical evaluation of H A Wolfson's achievement. His grand thesis consists of two half–truths. Philo initiates a new era but does not dominate philosophy until Spinoza. Medieval philosophy is a unity in triple guise, but does not subordinate reason to faith. The Achilles–heel of Wolfson's thesis lies in his conception of Judaism and the role he assigns to Judaism in the history of philosophy.

RUNKLE, Gerald. *Theory And Practice: An Introduction To Philosophy.* NY Holt Rinehart Wins 1985.

This undergraduate text deals with three major issues: Metaphysics (the external world, the self, and God), Axiology (ethics, aesthetics, and political theory), and Epistemology (truth, reason, and science). For each of the nine topics, there are four chapters: an introduction, a thesis, and antithesis, and a discussion of practical alternatives. The book is *not* an anthology.

RUNQING, Ma and Zhonghua, Chen. The Value Of Man And The Building Of Two Civilizations. *Chin Stud Phil* 16,3–16 Fall 84.

RUOSHUI, Wang. A Defense Of Humanism. *Chin Stud Phil* 16,71–88 Spr 85.

RUOSHUI, Wang. Did German Classical Philosophy Simply "End"? *Chin Stud Phil* 16,94–102 Spr 85.

RUOSHUI, Wang. Discussing The Problem Of Alienation. *Chin Stud Phil* 16,25–38 Spr 85.

RUOSHUI, Wang. Epistemology Must Not Lose Sight Of Man. *Chin Stud Phil* 16,103–112 Spr 85.

RUOSHUI, Wang. Marxism And Intellectual Emancipation. *Chin Stud Phil* 16,89–93 Spr 85.

RUOSHUI, Wang. On The Concept Of "Alienation" From Hegel To Marx. *Chin Stud Phil* 16,39–70 Spr 85.

RUOSHUI, Wang. Preface To *On The Philosophy Front*. *Chin Stud Phil* 16,8–11 Spr 85.

RUOSHUI, Wang. The Criterion Of Truth And Theoretical Research. *Chin Stud Phil* 16,12–24 Spr 85.

RÜPPEL, Ernesto. As Provas Da Existência De Deus Na Filosofia Neo–Escolástica. *Rev Port Filosof* 41,50–59 Ja–Mr 85.

RUPPERT, Jeanne. "Nature, Feeling, & Disclosure In Poetry Of Wallace Stevens" in *Existential Coordinates Of Human Condition*, Tymieniecka, A (ed), 75–90. Boston Reidel 1984.

RUPPRECHT, F and Blumenthal, Wolfgang. IV Philosophiekongress Der DDR. *Deut Z Phil* 23,714–726 1975.

RUPPRECHT, Frank. La Philosophie Marxiste–Léniniste—Base Théorique Pour La Solution Des Problèmes De Notre Epoque (in German). *Deut Z Phil* 22,65–70 1974.

RUSE, Michael. Creation Science: Enough Is Enough Is Too Much. *Nat Forum* 65,37–38 Wint 85.

It has been argued by the creators of so–called "Creation Science" that it qualifies as genuine science and as such should be given equal treatment in the publicly funded schools of America, along with the theory of evolution. In this discussion, it is shown that creation science is not genuine science at all, but rather dogmatic, fundamentalist religion. It is concluded that good, sound, pedagogical principles do not require the teaching of creation science—indeed, they bar it.

RUSE, Michael. Human Sociobiology: A Philosophical Perspective. *Eidos* 3,46–88 Je 84.

Human Sociobiology is the attempt to extend Darwin's Theory of Evolution Through Natural Selection to Human Social Behavior. It covers such subjects as aggression, sexuality and morality. It has been much criticized in the past but the claim of this article is that, although incomplete, it offers exciting prospects for both biology and philosophy.

RÜSEN, Jörn and Blanke, Horst Walter and Fleischer, Dirk. Theory Of History In Historical Lectures: The German Tradition Of *Historik*, 1750–1900. *Hist Theor* 23,331–356 O 84.

The essay examines the German tradition of a particular type of lectures and literature on the theory of history; it is based on the analysis of the lectures held at 60 German–speaking universities during 1750–1900. Four traditions reflecting on history by ideal types are to be distinguished: humanistic–rhetorical, auxiliary–encyclopedic, historicophilosophical, and epistomological or historicological. These types are related in complex ways; in different theories of history ("Historiken") they form different functional/causal patterns and syntheses.

RUSH, Alan A. Es El Psicoanálisis Una Pseudo–Ciencia? *Rev Latin De Filosof* 11,137–156 Jl 85.

Popper deems psychoanalysis a pseudo–science, a mythical–metaphysical doctrine, but nevertheless grants it specific promise. It is shown that Popper *proves* no part of his double epistemological diagnosis, owing to ignorance of Freud's writings. While critically situating Popper's misunderstanding of psychoanalytical theory as originating in empiricist assumptions, a realist reading is suggested as a more adequate rendering of Freud's metascientific learnings, and as issuing in a more favorable diagnosis of his work.

RUSSELL, Anthony F. *Logic, Philosophy, And History: A Study In The Philosophy Of History Based On The Work Of R G Collingwood.* NY Univ Pr Of America 1984.

This book aims to evaluate R G Collingwood's claim that the method proper to history is a heretofore underdeveloped logic of questioning and problem–solving. The conclusion is that such a logic, though underdeveloped, does exist, and that several contemporary trends of thought tending to converge in the movement called "semiotics" are becoming increasingly interested in its nature and content.

RUSSELL, Bertrand and Hook, Sidney. The Nature Of Liberal Civilization. *Russell* 5,5–13 Sum 85.

The text of a discussion between Bertrand Russell and Sidney Hook conducted over the BBC in the Fall of 1953 on the nature of liberal civilization. The point of departure was Hook's proposal to define a liberal civilization as one in which there is a free market of ideas from which it followed that "our moral obligation is the toleration of dissent, no matter how heretical, not to the toleration of conspiracy, not matter how disguised. The practical problem is to fund ways of implementing that destruction."

RUSSELL, Bruce. The Ontological Argument. *Sophia (Australia)* 24,38–46 Ap 85.

RUSSELL, John L. "Human Nature And Absolute Values" in *The Good Life And Its Pursuit*, Dougherty, Jude P (ed), 133–144. NY Paragon House 1984.

RUSSELL, John M. Freedom And Determinism In Spinoza. *Auslegung* 11,378–389 Fall 84.

RUSSELL, Joseph J . *Analysis And Dialectic: Studies In The Logic Of Foundation Problems.* Boston Nijhoff 1984.

RUSSELL, Paul. Corrections Regarding "Hume's 'Two Definitions' Of Cause And The Ontology Of 'Double Existence'". *Hume Stud* 10,165–166 N 84.

RUSSELL, Paul. Hume's *Treatise* And Hobbe's *The Elements Of Law*. *J Hist Ideas* 46,51–64 Ja–Mr 85.

The central thesis of this paper is that the scope and structure of Hume's *Treatise* is modeled, or planned, after Hobbes's *The Elements of Law* and that in this respect there exists an important and unique relationship between these works. It is argued that by recognizing this relationship we can come to appreciate the unity of the project of the *Treatise* itself. The similarities between these works brings to light the important methodological assumptions on which they are based.

RUSSELL, Paul. Sorabji And The Dilemma Of Determinism. *Analysis* 44,166–172 O 84.

In *Necessity, Cause and Blame* (London, 1984) Richard Sorabji argues that what is caused need not be necessitated. On this basis he argues that human actions may be caused but not necessitated and that in this way we can escape the usual difficulties associated with the dilemma of determinism. In my paper, I argue that this strategy runs into serious difficulties and that in important respects his theory gets impaled on both horns of the dilemma at once.

RUSSELL, Robert John. Entropy And Evil. *Zygon* 19,449–468 D 84.

This paper explores a possible relationship between entropy and evil in terms of metaphor. After presenting the various meanings of entropy in classical thermodynamics and statistical mechanics, and the Augustinian and Irenaean theodicies, several similarities and dissimilarities between entropy and evil are described. Underlying the concepts of evil and entropy is the assumption that time has a direction. After examining the scientific basis for this assumption, it is hypothesized that, if evil is real in nature, entropy is what one would expect to find at the level of physical processes, and conversely that, if entropy is coupled to a physical arrow of time, one could expect to find dissipative yet catalytic processes in history and religious experience.

Author Index with Abstracts 395 **Sagoff, Mark**

RUSSELL, Robert J. The Physics Of David Bohm And Its Relevance To Philosophy And Theology. *Zygon* 20,135–158 Je 85.

The purpose of this paper is to analyze David Bohm's work in terms of physics, philosophy, and theology. First, I discuss the development of Bohm's thought since 1951. Then, using the methodology of Imre Lakatos, I evaluate the scientific status of his research program. Next, I explore the philsophical dimensions of Bohm's views in which realist and idealist, monist and dualist, contingent and determinist outlooks occur in creative tension. Finally, I suggest ways in which Bohm's ideas are relevant to theology through concepts of God and cosmos, beauty and purpose, grace and free will, church, self and evil.

RUSSMAN, Thomas. "Foundations, Objective And Objections" in *The Georgetown Symposium On Ethics*, Porreco, Rocco (ed), 109–116. Lanham Univ Pr Of America 1984.

RUSSOW, Lilly–Marlene and Stephens, James. Brains In Vats And The Internalist Perspective. *Austl J Phil* 63,205–212 Je 85.

In *Reason, Truth, and History*, Hilary Putnam uses his theory of reference to argue against the thesis that we might all be brains in vats, and for a version of anti–realism that he calls "the internalist perspective". In this paper, it is argued that the brains–in–vats argument is fatally flawed, and that similar problems can be found in Putnam's defense of the internalist perspective.

RUSSOW, Lilly–Marlene. Dennett, Mental Images, And Images In Context. *Phil Phenomenol Res* 45,581–594 Je 85.

In his discussion of mental images in *Brainstorms*, D C Dennett takes a somewhat unusual approach to mental images: specifically, he considers them in isolation, rather than in the context of an activity such as imagining, remembering, or problem–solving. In this paper, it is argued that this isolation leads to inadequacies in his list of 'acceptable' approaches to mental image. An alternative to the approaches Dennett mentions is sketched and defended against Dennett's objections, and it is argued that this alternative points to serious doubts about Dennett's more general strategy.

RUSSOW, Lilly–Marlene. Unlocking The Chinese Room. *Nature Syst* 6,221–228 D 84.

I argue that Searle's "Chinese Room" example fails to show that strong AI is misguided. searle's presence in the Chinese Room introduces a factor which causes the functional analogy between a computer and the Chinese Room to break down; thus, no conclusion about AI follows from Searle's failure to understand Chinese. Some implications of this for an analysis of self–awareness are briefly explored.

RUST, Holger. Methodologie Und Geschichte: Ansätze Problemorientierter Gesellschaftsanalysen. *Arch Rechts Soz* 61,305–324 1975.

This essay starts with the remark of Maurice Merleau–Ponty that every consistent marxistic theory has to proceed from the method of Max Weber. The main topic therefore is the comparison of the *Sociology of Religion* of Max Weber and the "Adventures of the Dialectic." Within this discussion some statements concerning sociological perception in general are worked out.

RUST, Holger. Wissenschaftstheorie Und Praxis: Zur Funktion Soziologischer Theorienbildung. *Arch Rechts Soz* 60,1–24 1974.

The sociological discussion concerning theory refers besides the clarification of methodological problems to the relation of particular scientific subjects and everyday non–scientific life. The description of different positions of West German sociology shall demonstrate the variety of possible criterions for theoretical effort. The partly combatting positions will be taken as unique arguments in one comprehensive discussion concerning the development of sociological theory.

RYAN, Alan. "Hegel On Work, Ownership And Citizenship" in *The State And Civil Society*, Pelczynski, Z A (ed), 178–196. Cambridge Cambridge Univ Pr 1984.

RYAN, Alan. "Popper And Liberalism" in *Popper And The Human Sciences*, Currie, Gregory (ed), 89–104. Boston Nijhoff 1985.

RYCHLAK, Joseph R. Logical Learning Theory: Kuhnian Anomaly Or Medievalism Revisited? *J Mind Behav* 5,389–416 Autumn 84.

Logical learning theory, a teleological interpretation of behavior which subsumes traditional personality descriptions without distortion, is presented in light of seven criticisms frequently put to its supporters. Issues are discussed such as the need for learning theory in personality study, the role of empirical evidence in science, and the need for introducing new terms to an already complex psychological lexicon. The shortcomings of mechanistic, mediational explanations of human behavior are highlighted. Primary consideration is given to the current status of the telic model, with only general references made to empirical researches that have been conducted in support of this model. The presentation follows a question–answer format, with the discussion sequenced so as to give the reader a good sense of both the objections to logical learning theory, and the grounds it has for being a legitimate alternative to the reigning behavioral paradigm of psychology. It is concluded that logical learning theory is more concordant with the ongoing theoretical revolution in modern physical science than any extant learning theory.

RYFFEL, Hans. Eigentum Und Ungleichheit: Rousseaus Eigentumslehre. *Stud Phil (Switzerland)* Supp 12,35–46 1983.

Rousseau's conception of property represents a special and important position among modern theories of property. Property, founded on human freedom, is only justified within the state, as far as this reconciles freedom and justice. Since inequality of property to some extent is incompatible with freedom, measures against such inequality are required. Rousseau's theory of property is considered in the context of his philosophy which forms for the author, differing from widespread interpretations, a coherent body.

RYFFEL, Hans. Freiheit Und Eignetum. *Stud Phil (Switzerland)* Supp 12,375–394 1983.

In the fundamental framework of human existence, freedom and property are closely related. The actual significance of property, in correspondence to the change of normative structures and the change of the meaning of freedom, is discussed. Modern freedom is no more, as formerly, bound by norms fixed once for all, but by changeable norms, wherefore often misunderstood as illimited freedom of action. Some conclusions for the actual regulation of property by adequate measures are drawn.

RYGOL, Reiner. Some Theoretical Problems Of The Object–Subject Dialectics In The Development Of The Community Of Socialist States (in German). *Deut Z Phil* 32,1057–1067 1984.

SABINI, John and Silver, Maury. Critical Thinking And Obedience To Authority. *Nat Forum* 65,13–17 Wint 85.

SABINI, John and Silver, Maury. On The Captivity Of The Will: Sympathy, Caring, And A Moral Sense Of The Human. *J Theor Soc Behav* 15,23–37 Mr 85.

We are concerned in this paper with the question of what more there is to human nature than cognition, with what it is to be a person (or animal) in the sense of something that would justify our sympathy. We examine pain, emotion, and the abrogation of values as sources of our sympathy for one another. We further argue that our sympathy over each of these unfortunate events is connected with our sense that they are beyond a person's (or an animal's) will. Computers, we suggest, ought not to engage our sympathy not because of their limited cognitive capacity, and not because they lack intent, but because their wills are too free.

SACCHI, Mario Enrique. Dos Filósofos De La Universidad De Oxford Ante El Conocimiento Metafísico. *Aquinas* 27,261–286 My–Ag 84.

SACKSTEDER, William. Simple Wholes And Complex Parts: Limited Principles In Spinoza. *Phil Phenomenol Res* 45,393–406 Mr 85.

Notions of *part* and *whole* are intertwined in Spinoza, though it follows from his effective definitions of this pair of terms that least parts cannot be thought as simple and a greatest whole cannot be thought as complex. Rather wholes are *simple*, and parts *complex*. In consequence, search for a limit at extremes of the scale reveals, in one direction, unlimited regressive complication, and in the other, an ultimate principle which must be regarded as simple.

SADLER JR, Alfred M and Sadler, Blair L and Caplan, Arthur L. Organ Donation: Is Voluntarism Still Valid? *Hastings Center Rep* 14,6–12 O 84.

SADLER, Blair L and Caplan, Arthur L and Sadler Jr, Alfred M. Organ Donation: Is Voluntarism Still Valid? *Hastings Center Rep* 14,6–12 O 84.

SADLER, Royce D. The Origins And Functions Of Evaluative Criteria. *Educ Theor* 35,285–298 Sum 85.

This aricle is about the nature of criteria, how they may by usefully organized, and how they function is practical evaluations. Specific issues include how criteria relate to one another, to objectives, and to such fundamental values as freedom and personal growth, how criteria are identified, and the place of connoisseurship in evaluation generally. The treatment is analytical. The examples are concrete, and drawn from a variety of educational contexts.

SADOCK, J M and Zwicky, Arnold M. A Note On *xy* Languages. *Ling Phil* 8,229–236 My 85.

Languages containing sentences of the form xy, x and y strings and x different from y, have been claimed by some to be outside the class of context–free languages, and by others to be within it. We demonstrate that among the languages in which x and y are themselves drawn from a properly context–free language, there is an infinite class of xy languages that do exceed the power of context–free phrase structure grammar.

SADURSKI, Wojciech. Social Justice And Legal Justice. *Law Phil* 3,329–354 D 84.

The main aim of this paper is to challenge the validity of the distinction between legal justice and social justice. It is argued that what we usually call "legal justice" is either an application of the more fundamental notion of "social justice" to legal rules and decisions or is not a matter of justice as all. In other words, the only correct uses of the notion of legal justice are derivative from the notion of social justice and, hence, the alleged conflicts between criteria of social and legal justice result from the confusion about the proper relationship between these two concepts. Two views about the "social justice/legal justice" dichotomy are of particular importance and will provide the focus for the argument: this dichotomy is sometimes identified with a classical distinction between "distributive" and "communicative" justice and sometimes with the distinction between "substantive" and "procedural" justice.

SAFFE, Jürgen. Categoricity And Ranks. *J Sym Log* 49,1379–1392 D 84.

In this paper we investigate the connections between categoricity and ranks. We use stability theory to prove some old and new results.

SAG, Ivan A and Klein, Ewan. Type Driven Translation. *Ling Phil* 8,163–202 My 85.

Assume that in a grammar–fragment for English, every syntactic rule which assigns constituent structure to a phrase is accompanied by a semantic rule which assigns it a compositional interpretation; and that every syntactic category of the grammar has an associated semantic type. We show that, given a syntactic rule plus the semantic types of the participating categories, there are a small number of general principles which derive the corresponding semantic rule.

SAGAN, Dorion and Margulis, Lynn. "Gaia And Philosophy" in *On Nature*, Rouner, Leroy S (ed), 60–78. Notre Dame Univ Notre Dame Pr 1984.

SAGEEV, G and Shelah, S. On The Structure Of Ext(*A*, **z**) In ZFC+. *J Sym Log* 50,302–315 Je 85.

SAGOFF, Mark. Fact And Value In Ecological Science. *Environ Ethics* 7,99–116 Sum 85.

Ecologists may apply their science either to *manage* ecosystems to increase the long–run benefits nature offers man or to *protect* ecosystems from antropogenic insults and injuries. Popular reasons for supposing that these two tasks (management and protection) are complementary turn out not to be supported by the evidence. Nevertheless, society recognizes the protection of the "health" and "integrity" of ecosystems to be an important ethical and cultural goal even if it cannot be backed in detail by utilitarian or prudential arguments. It is a legitimate purpose of ecological science, moreover, to describe and help society preserve ecosystem "health" and "integrity", insofar as these are considered as private qualities.

SAGOFF, Mark. Is Big Beautiful? *J Applied Phil* 1,269–280 O 84.

In this essay, I argue that large–scale technologies may be more threatening to open democratic institutions than to ecological systems. I describe the threat in terms of an alliance between bureaucrats and entrepreneurs to govern society according to their own methods, e.G., cost–benefit analysis, and thus to usurp the rule of law. In America, though not in England, blue–collar and environmentalist constituencies have on occasion beaten back this threat, a triumph of democracy. I use 'grid–group' theory, as developed by Mary Douglas and her students, to make these arguments about the relation between technology and democracy.

SAGOFF, Mark. Paternalism And The Regulation Of Drugs. *Int J Applied Phil* 2,43–58 Fall 84.

This paper argues for the unsurprising thesis that no one has a right to take silly risks just because he or she wants to. I distinguish rights into three kinds: those that constitute democracy, those protecting against tyranny, and those stemming from a conception of justice or the person. None of these rights prevents governmental paternalism in the regulation of drugs.

SAHU, Neelamani. Is Wittgenstein Paradoxical? *Indian Phil Quart* 11,201–216 Ap 84.

SAILER, J. Georg Lukács Und Die Frage Nach Der Spezifik Des Asthetischen. *Deut Z Phil* 33,306–313 1985.

SAIN, Ildikó. Structured Nonstandard Dynamic Logic. *Z Math Log* 30,481–496 1984.

SAINSBURY, Mark. Saying And Conveying. *Ling Phil* 7,415–432 N 84.

A speaker often conveys more than he says. Can this extra material be captured in a systematic theory? Some reasons for pessimism are considered and rejected, and some detailed criticisms are offered of existing treatments of conversational implicature. It is suggested that the notion of a speaker's *role* can serve to delimit a theoretically useful subclass of the very heterogeneous class of cases.

SAINT– SERNIN, Bertrand. Le Souverain Dans La "Critique De La Raison Dialectique". *Rev Metaph Morale* 89,289–306 Jl–S 84.

SAITO, Yuriko. Is There A Correct Aesthetic Appreciation Of Nature? *J Aes Educ* 18,35–46 Wint 84.

SAITO, Yuriko. The Japanese Appreciation Of Nature. *Brit J Aes* 25,239–251 Sum 85.

SAKAI, Noriyuki. Ars Et Natura Dans La Pensée De Nicolas De Cues (in Japanese). *Bigaku* 35,1–14 Je 84.

"ars naturam imitatur"—Nicolas de Cues a choisi cette thèse quand il spéculait sur la créativité humaine. Mais que veut dire cette phrase qui semble contradictoire avec la créativité? La recherche de ce problème nous permettra d'expliquer la créativité dans l'homme. (edited)

SALLEH, Ariel Kay. Deeper Than Deep Ecology: The Eco–Feminist Connection. *Environ Ethics* 6,339–346 Wint 84.

I offer a feminist critique of deep ecology as presented in the seminal papers of Naess and Devall. I outline the fundamental premises involved and analyze their internal coherence. Not only are there problems on logical grounds, but the tacit methodological approach of the two papers are inconsistent with the deep ecologists' own substantive comments. I discuss these shortcomings in terms of a broader feminist critique of patriarchal culture and point out some practical and theoretical contributions which eco–feminism can make to a genuinely deep ecology problematic.

SALLER, Richard P. Familia, Domus, And The Roman Conception Of The Family. *Phoenix* 38,336–355 D84.

SALLIS, John. Heidegger/Derrida—Presence. *J Phil* 81,594–601 O 84.

SALMERÓN, Fernando. "Ethics And The Language Of Morality" in *Philosophical Analysis In Latin America*, Gracia, Jorge J E and others (eds), 243–254. Boston Reidel 1984.

SALMON, C V. *The Central Problem Of David Hume's Philosophy.* NY Garland 1983.

SALMON, Wesley C. *Logic*, Third Edition. Englewood Cliffs Prentice–Hall 1984.

SALOMON– BAYET, Claire. Modern Science And The Coexistence Of Rationalities. *Diogenes* 126,1–18 Sum 84.

SAMI, Ramez L. On Σ^1_1 Equivalence Relations With Borel Classes Of Bounded Rank. *J Sym Log* 49,1273–1283 D 84.

In Baire space $N = {}^\omega\omega$ we define a sequence of equivalence relations $(E_v < w_1^{ct}$, each E_v being σ^1_1 with classes in π^1_{1+v+1} and such that (i) E_v does not have perfectly many classes, and (ii) N/E_v is countable iff $\omega^1_v < \omega^1$. This construction can be extended confinally in $(\delta^1_2)^1$. A new proof is given of a theorem of Hausdorff on partitions of R into δ_1 many π^0_3 sets.

SANABRIA, José Rubén. El Conocimiento En Fray Alonso De La Veracruz. *Rev Filosof (Mexico)* 17,311–330 My–Jl 84.

El artículo pretende exponer la teoría del conocimiento en la Filosofía de Fray Alonso de la Veracruz. Ciertamente se trata del escolasticismo tradicional aunque puntos Fray Alonso mezcla doctrinas escotistas. Es un buen ejemplo del conocimiento que Fray Alonso tenía de los autores más connotados de la época y de la tradiciín. A su modo el fraile agustino preludia la modernidad que años más tarde entrará en el ámbito filosófico de la Nueva España.

SANCHEZ, Hailey D. Shimony, The Dilemma Of Quantum Mechanics, And The History Of Philosophy. *Dialogos* 20,79–92 Ap 85.

SANCHEZ, Juan Carlos. *Análisis Proposicional Y Ontologia.* S A Murcia Sanchez 1984.

SANFORD, David H. "Armstrong's Theory Of Perception" in *D M Armstrong*, Bogdan, Radu J (ed), 55–78. Boston Reidel 1984.

SANFORD, David H. Causal Dependence And Multiplicity. *Philosophy* 60,215–230 Ap 85.

In "Causes and *if p, even if x, still q*," *Philosophy* 57 (July 1982), Ted Honderich cites my "The Direction of Causation and the Direction of Conditioning," *Journal of Philosophy* 73 (April 22, 1976) as an example of an account of causal priority that lacks the proper character. After emending Honderich's description of the proper character, I argue that my attempt to account for one–way causation in terms of one–way causal conditioning does not totally lack it. Rather than emphasize the singularity of an effect, as Honderich does, I emphasize the multiplicity of independent factors in a causal circumstance.

SANFORD, David H. The Direction Of Causation And The Direction Of Time. *Midwest Stud Phil* 9,53–76 1984.

I revise J L Mackie's first account of casual direction by replacing his notion of *fixity* by a newly defined notion of *sufficing* that is designed to accommodate indeterminism. Keeping Mackie's distinction between casual order and casual direction, I then consider another revision that replaces *fixity* with *one–way conditioning*. In response to the charge that all such accounts of casual priority beg the question by making an unjustified appeal to temporal priority, I maintain that one–way conditioning explains rather that assumes objective temporal dependence as well as objective casual dependence.

SÄNGER, H and Kirchgässner, Werner. Erkenntnistheoretische Und Pädagogische Probleme Bei Der Verwendung Von Lehr– Und Lernmitteln In Der Ausbildung Von Philosophiestudenten. *Deut Z Phil* 23,1061–1067 1975.

SANKOWSKI, Edward. "Paternalism" And Social Policy. *Amer Phil Quart* 22,1–12 Ja 85.

This paper argues the following: (1) Some of the best available philosophical discussions of paternalism, including those of John Stuart Mill, Gerald Dworkin, and Joel Feinberg, are seriously defective. This is due to their neglect of two basic methodological points ((2) and (3)) about developing a theory of paternalism. (2) A theory of paternalism must answer at least three interrelated questions about paternalism in a way that coordinates answers to the three questions. (3) Answering the three questions requires, as necessary but not sufficient conditions, specifying the social institutions (law, religion, etc.) and the sorts of social regulation of action (physical coercion, threat of punishment, etc.) of primary concern as sources of paternalism, and justifying one's specification.

SANSEN, Raymond. El Ateismo Cotidiano: Ensayo De Comprension. *Rev Filosof (Mexico)* 17,441–464 S–D 84.

SANSONE, David. Language, Meaning And Reality In Euripides. *Ultim Real Mean* 8,92–104 Je 85.

SANTA CRUZ, María I. Homonimia Y Géneros Del Ser En Plotino. *Cuad Filosof* 19,57–76 Ja–D 83.

SANTAMARIA, Ulysses and Manville, A. Marx: Entre L'idéalisme Radical Et L'individualisme Anarchique. *Philosophiques* 11,299–326 O 84.

The road to Marx's thought supposes as its condition a movement of radical depositioning in relation to the classically established guidelines for journeying through his work. Marx's thought, in opposition to any interpretation which sees therein a reflection on the social sphere, defines a radical form of individualism which is intended as the absolute criticism of any desire to construct a new order, an individualism which allows absolutely nothing which might obstruct the value of the meaning of autonomy to prevail.

SANTILLI, Paul. Moral Fictions And Scientific Management. *J Bus Ethics* 3,279–286 N 84.

This paper examines Alasdair MacIntyre's argument in *After Virtue* that corporate managers do not have the rational expertise in social control which they have used to justify their position in modern society. The question is advanced as to whether managers must operate from emotivist premises or whether they can truly understand and thus truly manage human affairs by rational reflection about human purpose, value, and intention. (edited)

SANTONI, Ronald E. The Arms Race, Genocidal Intent And Individual Responsibility. *Phil Soc Crit* 10,9–18 Wint 84.

In Part I, I argue that the USA and the USSR are knowingly preparing to destroy each other as viable national and political groups; that their genocidal intent is clear. In Part II, I contend that the "responsibility model" of crime (falk) imposes on all of us the obligation to (a) label and denounce genocidal preparations for nuclear "war"; (b) break complicity with any conduct that threatens genocide; (c) develop an "internationalism of resistance" against the arms race or any militarization that threatens genocide or omnicide.

SANTORO, Liberato. Hegel's Aesthetics And 'The End Of Art'. *Phil Stud (Ireland)* 30,62–72 Spr 84.

SANYAL, Indrani. The De Re Modality And Essentialism. *Indian Phil Quart* 11,365–372 Jl 84.

The paper discusses why *de re* modality is alleged to involve essentialism and defends *de re* modality against this charge. Certain formal arguments and informal philosophical considerations have been advanced to show that a thing can be said to be necessarily so–and–so independently of any specification without raising any problem. Further, even if a thing is necessarily s0–and–so only under some specifications the modality may still be *de re*. It would be entirely wrong to argue, '*Since* 9 is necessarily greater than 7, as specified as the successor of 8, therefore, 9 cannot be necessarily greater than 7.

SAPONTZIS, Steve F. Moral Community And Animal Rights. *Amer Phil Quart* 22,251–257 Jl 85.

This article deals with the most common objection to extending moral rights to animals: "But they're just animals!" It deals with three attempts to justify that intuition, all of which are based on a sense of moral community: the requirement that rights–holders must respect the rights of others, the requirement that rights–holders must be moral agents, and the requirement that rights–holders must participate in a political, economic, familial, etc., life with us. All three of these animal–excluding criteria for having moral rights are rejected, leaving the common presumption that animals are not worthy of moral rights in need of justification, if it is not to be merely an expression of anthropocentrism.

SAPONTZIS, Steve F. Predation. *Ethics Animals* 5,27–38 Je 84.

This paper deals with whether animal rights entails interfering with predation in nature and with the place of reductio ad absurdum arguments in ethics. Several different senses of "absurdity" are considered; a rule for practical reasoning based on the Kantian principle that "ought implies can" is proposed; and it is concluded that predation should be prevented when that can be done without occasioning even greater suffering.

SARACINO, Dan and Wood, Carol. Finite QE Rings In Characteristic p^2. *Annals Pure Applied Log* 28,13–32 Ja 85.

SARAF, Mikhail Y. The Aesthetics Of Sport. *Dialec Hum* 11,87–96 Wint 84.

SARASOHN, Lisa T. Motion And Morality: Pierre Gassendi, Thomas Hobbes And The Mechanical World–View. *J Hist Ideas* 46,363–380 Jl–S 85.

Thomas Hobbes and Pierre Gassendi used mechanistic concepts of motion analogically to explicate their ethical theories. Their relationship was interdependent. Gassendi's atomistic models influenced Hobbes' early physical and psychological theories, while Gassendi modified his materialism in reaction to Hobbes' theories. Hobbes used motion to argue for a deterministic universe, with people acting like objects in motion, while Gassendi released humanity from natural necessity by allowing people the free choice of moving in either of two directions.

SARGENT, Lyman T. "Ideology And Utopia: Looking Backward At Karl Mannheim" in *Ideology, Philosophy And Politics*, Parel, Anthony (ed), 210–224. Waterloo Laurier Univ Pr 1983.

SARGENT, Lyman Tower. More's *Utopia*: An Interpretation Of Its Social Theory. *Hist Polit Thought* 5,195–210 Sum 84.

Sir Thomas More's *Utopia* (1516) has been interpreted in many different and complex ways to support ideological or political positions. In the process the book has become an intellectual puzzle. This essay takes the text as it reads and finds a fairly coherent position that fits what we know about More and his times. The *Utopia* presents an authoritarian, patriarchal and hierarchical society modeled on the monastery and produces a society of economic security, little liberty and equality between mental and physical labor.

SARIN, Indu. Value And Human Condition. *Philosophica (India)* 10,11–17 Ja–D 81.

The paper analyzes the nature of value in the context of human condition. It notes the bridging of the episodic and the transcendental dimensions. Value concerns decisions, prescriptions, ideals and standards. Autonomy, reasoned decision, ideals and their appraisals mark human condition. The paper argues the position that value is intrinsically woven into self. As such change in one necessarily changes the other.

SÁRKÁNY, Mihály. The Economy Of Tribal Societies (in Hungarian). *Magyar Filozof Szemle* 5,738–748 1983.

SARLEMIJN, Andries. "Is The Planning Of Science Possible" in *Contemporary Marxism*, O' Rourke, James J (ed), 109–146. Boston Reidel 1984.

SARNOFF, Sigrid. A Bergsonian View Of Agent–Causation. *Int Phil Quart* 25,185–196 Je 85.

From the Bergsonian view of persons and how actions happen we can derive a nonreductive approach to making sense of agent–causation. Such a view improves upon the simple assertion that agent–causality is irreducible to event–causality. Instead, the agent–causality is irreducible to event–causality. Instead, the Bergsonian approach grounds that irreducibility in the description of what a person is. In Bergson's view conscious experience is a cumulative process that distinguishes persons from things whose behavior fits event–causal patterns. (edited)

SARTORIUS, Rolf. "Government Regulation And Intergenerational Justice" in *Rights And Regulation*, Machan, Tibor (ed), 177–202. Cambridge Ballinger 1983.

SARTORIUS, Rolf. Utilitarianism, Rights, And Duties To Self. *Amer Phil Quart* 22,241–249 Jl 85.

SAUMUR, Lucien. *The Humanist Evangel.* Buffalo Prometheus Books 1982.

SAUVE, Denis. L'argument Du Langage Privé. *Dialogue (Canada)* 24,3–32 Spr 85.

SAVEDOFF, Barbara E. Intellectual And Sensuous Pleasure. *J Aes Art Crit* 34,313–316 Spr 85.

In *The Aesthetics and Architecture*, Roger Scruton distinguishes the intellectual pleasure in art from the sensuous pleasure in food and sex by saying that only intellectual pleasure is internally connected to thought. I argue that there is no difference between the way intellectual and at least most sensuous pleasures are connected to thought, and that it is unlikely that any of our actual sensuous pleasures are purely matters of sensation.

SAVER, Jeffrey. An Interview With E O Wilson On Sociobiology And Religion. *Free Inq* 5,15–24 Spr 85.

SAYRE- MC CORD, Geoffrey. Leibniz, Materialism, And The Relational Account Of Space And Time. *Stud Leibniz* 16,204–211 1984.

Leibniz' Verteidigung einer relationalen Auffassung von Raum und Zeit im Briefweschel mit Clarke nimmt in keiner Weise Bezug auf Monaden. Infolgedessen haben einige Leibniz–Interpreten angenommen, Leibniz' relationale Auffassung von Raum und Zeit könne–wenn man sie hinreichend abstrakt versteht–von seiner ausserordentlich mentalistischen Ontologie losgelöst werede. In der Tat hat der Gedanke einer Trennung der beiden Lehren etwas Bestechendes, da die relationale Auffassung plausibler erscheint als Leibniz' Metaphysik der Monaden. Vor allem haben Materialisten sich Leibniz' relationale Auffassung zu eigen gemacht und seine mentalistische Ontologie verschmäht. Wie bestechend diese Trennung auch sein mag, die Kohärenz von Leibniz' relationaler Auffassung von Raum und Zeit hängt in entscheidendem Masse von serner Monadologie ab. Wie Leibniz (aber nur wenige andere) erkannte, glückt eine relationale Auffassung von Raum und Zeit nur dann, wenn einige grundlegende Bestandteile der Welt nicht grundsätzlich räumlich–zeitlich sind.

SAYWARD, Charles and Hugly, Philip. Is Moral Relativism Consistent? *Analysis* 45,40–44 Ja 85.

The version of moral relativism we consider says that the correctness of moral judgments is code–relative. There is no moral analogue to truth. An objection to this view is that the fact that norms admit of logical relations shows that a code–independent notion of correctness is applicable to them. We show this objection is unsound.

SCALIA, Gianni. "Precritical Fragments On Art" in *Continental Philosophy And The Arts*, Winters, Laurence E and others (ed), 63–86. *Lanham* Univ Pr Of America 1984.

SCALTSAS, Theodore. The Uniqueness Of Particulars. *Philosophia (Israel)* 14,273–298 D 84.

My attempt in this article is to give an Aristotelian account of the uniqueness of particulars, which does not simply reduce their uniqueness to that of their matter and leave the problem at that, but which explains how the particularity of matter is secured. In the course of this analysis I discuss the question of how committed an Aristotelian metaphysics is to the ontological priority of physical objects, as opposed to events.

SCANLAN, James P. "A F Losev And The Rebirth Of Soviet Aesthetics After Stalin" in *Contemporary Marxism*, O' Rourke, James J (ed), 221–236. Boston Reidel 1984.

SCANNONE, J C. Ethos Y Sociedad En América Latina: Perspectivas Sistemático–Pastorales. *Stromata* 41,33–47 Ja–Je 85.

Luego de explicar los términos "éthos" y "sociedad" se estudian dos concepciones latinoamericanas actuales de su interrelación: las que se centran, respectivamente, en la liberación social y en el resurgimiento cultural, Ambas dan relevancia a la relación fundante entre trabajo y cultura, al problema del sujeto sociocultural de la liberación y al papel de la Iglesia a su respecto, pero los comprenden diversamente. Finalmente se intenta asumir lo válido de ambas líneas en una comprensión superadora de sus límites.

SCANNONE, J C. Hombre–Trabajo–Economiá: Aporte Al Tema A Partir De La Antropología Filosófica. *Stromata* 41,3–16 Ja–Je 85.

Primeramente se estudia la antropología del trabajo implicada en la encíclica Laborem Exercens, relacionándosela con las concepciones greco–medieval y moderna del mismo que ella assume superándolas. Luego se muestran sus consecuencias para una antropología de la actividad económica y una ontología del bien económico. Finalmentese trata de aporte que de ahí se origina para la economía como ciencia y para la epistemología del diálogo interdisciplinar con ella.

SCANNONE, J C. Trabajo, Cultura Y Evangelización: Creatividad E Identidad De La Enseñanza Social De La Iglesia. *Stromata* 41,17–32 Ja–Je 85.

En primer lugar se estudian la antropología del trabajo y la comprensiíon del actual conflicto histórico según la encíclica Laborem Exercens, haciéndose ver la relación que se da entre trabajo, cultura y liberación. Luego se analiza el método de la encćlica. Por último se cotejan su contenido y método con algunas problemaáticas actuales latinoamericanas (opción preferencial por los pobres, evangelización de la cultura, teología de la liberación). Así se muestra la creatividad y continuidad de la enseñanza social católica.

SCARAMUZZA, Gabriele. "Il Tempo Della Letteratura: Roman Ingarden" in *Il Tempo Dell'Arte*, Papi, Fulvio and others (ed), 40–59. Milano Franco Angeli 1984.

SCARLETT, B F. Formal The Teleological Elements In Hirst's Argument For A Liberal Curriculum. *J Phil Educ* 18,155–165 1984.

There are good teleological arguments for a liberal education. Hirst appeals to them occasionally but generally favors an abstract justification in terms of alleged differences between the formal properties of different disciplines. I argue that such differences, which he has not clearly articulated, are in principle irrelevant to educational value. I identify and criticize three sources of discontent with teleological arguments in this area.

SCARPELLINI, Bruno. Complete Second Order Spectra. *Z Math Log* 30,509–524 1984.

The following is proved. To every second order prefix type and every $N > 0$ there is a closed prenex formula F from second order predicate calculus with equality. (edited)

SCARPELLINI, Bruno. Lower Bound Results On Lengths Of Second–order Formulas. *Annals Pure Applied Log* 29,29–58 Jl 85.

SCEDROV, Andrej. On Some Non–Classical Extensions Of Second–Order Intuitionistic Propositional Calculus. *Annals Pure Applied Log* 27,155–164 O 84.

We show that $\forall p,q\ ((fp\leftrightarrow fq)\leftrightarrow(p\leftrightarrow q))\rightarrow\forall p(fp\leftrightarrow p)$ is equivalent to $\forall p[((p\leftrightarrow q)\leftrightarrow q)\rightarrow p]\rightarrow q$, and that it is consistent with intuitionistic $\forall\alpha\exists n$ continuity, bar induction, and Kripke's schema. The weaker $\forall p\ [p\vee(p\rightarrow q)\rightarrow q$ is shown to follow from the full version of $\forall\alpha\exists n$ continuity, but to be independent of the parameterless version. We show that under the parameterless version, there are no surjections from any set of infinite sequences of natural numbers to the set of truth values.

SCHACHT, Roland. Zwischen "Bildzeiten" Und "Sprachschatten"—Das Konzept Der Lektüre Und Die Lyrik Celans. *Rev Int Phil* 38,444–464 1984.

SCHÄCHTER, Josef and Melzer, Heinrich. On Physicalism. *Synthese* 64,359–374 S 85.

SCHAEFER, Thomas E. Professionalism: Foundation For Business Ethics. *J Bus Ethics* 3,269–278 N 84.

Professionalism includes the essential contents of other key notions within the field of business ethics. Like an 'honest act', professionalism may not be easy to define, but you will know it when you see it. As for professionalism's practitioners, like the practitioners of honesty, their act is learned not by seeking definitions of what they do, but by practicing professionalism. Only if this practice becomes an 'obsession' with the 'Business Aristocracy' can we expect professionalism to seize the soul of 'lesser' businessmen and suffuse the entire business community. (edited)

SCHAEFFLER, Richard. "Expérience Religieuse Et Expérience Profane Du Monde" Dans Les "aecrits Inédits De G Krüger. *Arch Phil* 47,375–384 Jl–S 84.

SCHÄFER, Wolf. Unlicensed Brainwork: A Case Study In Suppressive Discourse From Above. *Praxis Int* 4,421–437 Ja 85.

SCHAFF, Adam. "Frontiers Of Science And Technology" in *The Good Life And Its Pursuit*, Dougherty, Jude P (ed), 241–250. NY Paragon House 1984.

SCHAFFER, Sylvan J and Reamer, Frederic G. A Duty To Warn, An Uncertain Danger. *Hastings Center Rep* 15,17–19 F 85.

SCHALL, James V. *The Politics Of Heaven & Hell: Christian Themes From Classical, Medieval And Modern Political Philosophy*. Lanham Univ Pr Of America 1984.

The relation of reason and revelation to political philosophy is a fundamental and much neglected theme in the discipline. *the Politics of Heaven and Hell* is designed to trace the history of this problem and argue its terms within the traditions of Leo Strauss and Eric Voegelin, schools which take seriously the importance of this issue. This book argues the position from the position of Thomas Aquinas and the direction this problem arose in political theory and continues to manifest itself in the contemporary scene.

SCHALL, James V. Immortality And The Political Life Of Man In Albertus Magnus. *Thomist* 48,535–565 O 84.

SCHAPER, Eva. Towards The Aesthetic: A Journey With Friedrich Schiller. *Brit J Aes* 25,153–168 Spr 85.

SCHELLING, F W J and Vater, Michael G (ed). *Bruno*. Albany SUNY Pr 1984.

SCHENCK, David. Operative Dimensions Of Zaner's Context Of Self. *Int Stud Phil* 16,58–64 1984.

SCHEUER, Irene C. Postmortem On An Era: A Citizenly Perspective On The Economy. *Cogito* 2,21–78 D 84.

The originator of the American financial and economic system, the most successful, flexible, and widely imitated, was Alexander Hamilton who loathed nothing and no one so much as Adam Smith. Yet modern economics starts from Smith. Therefore, there is no correspondence between the "science" of economics and what exists, except accidentally. Therefore too, economics is the study of symptoms, unaware of what the symptoms are symptoms of, namely of politics, laws, ethics and nature, for all of which, in the Smithian tradition, economists have the utmost contempt, but which were Hamilton's overriding concerns.

SCHEYER, Amram. Materia Universalis. *Deut Z Phil* 32,1000–1009 1984.

The article in question focuses attention on the Ibn Gabirol's radical monist conception of 'matter'—coming close to the ultimately identifying 'God' and 'matter'—in which the author sees Ibn Gabirol's peculiar as well as unique contribution to heterodox medieval metaphysical thought, leading straight up to Giodarno Bruno's 'heresy'; Giodarno Bruno quoting Avicebron (Ibn Gabirol) as accepted authority on the issue of 'matter'. The author consequently being of the opinion that an upgrading of Ibn Gabirol's standing in present day histories of medieval philosophy is called for.

SCHIFFMAN, Zachary S. Montaigne And The Rise Of Skepticism In Early Modern Europe: A Reappraisal. *J Hist Ideas* 45,499–516 O–D 84.

An analysis of Montaigne's thought reveals that the humanist program of education contributed to the rise of skepticism in Early Modern Europe. Humanist education balanced a normative view of the world with a skeptical mode of thinking. This balance was upset by a growing appreciation of the complexity of the world. Montaigne was one of the first to cultivate this appreciation, which consequently intensified the skeptical mode of thinking imparted by his education.

SCHIFFMAN, Zachary S. Renaissance Historicism Reconsidered. *Hist Theor* 24,170–182 My 85.

SCHILLER, Klaus J. Zur Problematik Der Sozialistischen Nationalität. *Deut Z Phil* 32,874–884 1984.

First the article gives an analysis of synonymous application of German "Nationalitaet" and "Voelkerschaft" for definite social–ethnical communities in capitalism and socialism. Follow general characteristics of socialist nationality with regard to origin, relative independence, numerical largeness, territory, inclusion in the political system and the economics, social structure, level of culture and education, national language and self–reliance. These characteristics are applied to the socialist sorbian (lusatian) nationality in the German Democratic Republic.

SCHINZINGER, Roland and Martin, Mike W. Commentary: Informed Consent In Engineering And Medicine. *Bus Prof Ethics J* 3,67–78 Fall 83.

Informed consent is the keystone in the interaction between engineers and the lay public. Yet three major difficulties arise in securing it: identifying the decision maker, proxy decision making, and respecting the rights of dissident minorities where projects affect many people and not everyone's wishes can be satisfied. We respond to Thomas A Long's challenge that informed consent has little relevance to engineering, and we identify analogs to these three problems that arise in medicine.

SCHIPANI, Daniel S. *Conscientization And Creativity*. NY Univ Pr Of America 1984.

SCHLACK, Beverly A. "A Long Day's Journey Into Night" in *Existential Coordinates Of Human Condition*, Tymieniecka, A (ed), 209–226. Boston Reidel 1984.

SCHLAGEL, Richard H. A Reasonable Reply To Hume's Scepticism. *Brit J Phil Sci* 35,359–374 D 84.

Denying that we could ever know either the "inner natures" or "secret powers" of

objects which would constitute knowledge of "necessary connections" in nature, Hume concluded that no *rational* justification of inductive inferences was possible. The purpose of this article is to show that while Hume's skepticism was justifiable at that time given the generally accepted inherent limitations of scientific explanations, it is no longer justified in terms of recent discoveries and developments in science.

SCHLEICHERT, Hubert. On The Concept Of Unity Of Consciousness. *Synthese* 64,411–420 S 85.

One section of Moritz Schlick's "General Theory of Knowledge" concerning the 'unity of consciousness' requires elucidation. Accordingly a set of data forms this unity if every member of it may be related to any other member. This concept, though not directly connected with consciousness indicates a necessary condition of every knowledge acquiring system. Similarly, Kant's doctrine of the "I think" (CpR, section 16) provides a necessary condition of knowledge, without directly relating to psychological consciousness.

SCHLESINGER, George N. How To Navigate The River Of Time. *Phil Quart* 35,91–92 Ja 85.

SCHLESINGER, George N. Inaccessible Routes To The Problem Of Privileged Access. *Austl J Phil* 63,84–87 Mr 85.

SCHLESINGER, George N. Possibilities And Fallibilism. *Erkenntnis* 21,263–278 N 84.

SCHLESINGER, George N. Spatial, Temporal And Cosmic Parts. *S J Phil* 23,255–272 Sum 85.

SCHLESINGER, George N. The Availability Of Evidence In Support Of Religious Belief. *Faith Phil* 1,421–436 O 84.

SCHLESINGER, George N. The Central Principle Of Deontic Logic. *Phil Phenomenol Res* 45,515–536 Je 85.

SCHLESINGER, George. The Theological Implications Of The Holocaust. *Phil Forum (Boston)* 16,110–120 Fall–Wint 84.

SCHMAUS, Warren. Hypotheses And Historical Analysis In Durkheim's Sociological Methodology: A Comtean Tradition. *Stud Hist Phil Sci* 16,1–30 Mr 85.

Contrary to what sociologists have claimed, Durkheim consistently held to a hypothetico–deductive method in both his professed and his working methodology. This method, as well as his concept of historical analysis, place him in the same methodological tradition as Comte. Yet Durkheim is more of a realist than Comte, which would seem to call into question the historicists' claims about the connection between the methodological and metaphysical assumptions of a tradition of research.

SCHMAUS, Warren. Reasons, Causes, And The 'Strong Programme' In The Sociology Of Knowledge. *Phil Soc Sci* 15,189–196 Je 85.

Because Bloor conceives the question of whether reasons can be causes as a metaphysical one, he is led to disallow the appeal to reasons and norms of rationality in the explanation of belief. If the problem is considered instead in terms of whether reasons function differently from other kinds of causes in the explanation of belief, his grounds for denying causal status to reasons no longer remain, and his program is rendered less controversial.

SCHMERL, James H and Kaufmann, Matt. Saturation And Simple Extensions Of Models Of Peano Arithmetic. *Annals Pure Applied Log* 27,109–136 O 84.

SCHMID, Michael. Ideologie Und Ideologiekritik: Bemerkungen Zu Einem Aufsatz Von Claus Mühlfeld. *Arch Rechts Soz* 60,435–442 1974.

SCHMID, W Thomas. The Socratic Conception Of Courage. *Hist Phil Quart* 2,113–130 Ap 85.

A study of the historical background to the Socratic conception of courage; the cognitive attitude of the Socratically courageous man; the probably deliberate ambivalence in Plato's account of courage in the early dialogues; the Socratic ideal in comparison to Callicle's proto–Nietzschean model; and the relation between Socratic courage and the Socratic view of death.

SCHMIDIG, Dominik. Eigentum—Moralität. *Stud Phil (Switzerland)* Supp 12,299–312 1983.

Das Verhältnis zum Eigentum ist immer in einen sozio–kulturellen Rahmen eingebettet und folglich von geschichtlichen Entwicklungen betroffen. Eigentum bloss als persönliches Verfügungsrecht über Sachen zu bestimmen oder als materielle Grundlage persönlicher Freiheit, ist angesichts der heutigen Probleme zu wenig. Eine moderne Eigentumsordnung muss auf intersubjektiver Verantwortung basieren, d.H. Auf der grundsätzlichen Achtung vor dem Menschen (Kant), gepaart mit Wohlwollen (Frankena). Das Recht auf das physisch und kulturelle Lebensnotwendige muss politisch garantiert werden.

SCHMIDLIN, Bruno. Eigentum Und Teilungsvertrag: Zu Kants Begründung Des Eigentumsrechts. *Stud Phil (Switzerland)* Supp 12,47–68 1983.

SCHMIDLIN, Bruno. La Propriété Et Ses Limites. *Stud Phil (Switzerland)* 41,63–76 1982.

The article intends to find out the social aspects of property in analyzing the theories established by Grotius and Pufendorf about the contract of petition and the definition of property by Kant. These theorists have never abolished the concept of "the Our" at the origins of "the Mine" and "the Yours". But only the modern times have at least put the very weight on the aspect of the community, as it is shown for example by the Project of a new article about property inserted in the Swiss constitution.

SCHMIDT, Joachim K H W. Freirecht—Revisited, Emphasizing Its Property–Space. *Arch Rechts Soz* 60,113–124 1974.

'law' stays as state of order, present in an inner relation, and absent in an outer relation, making possible four principally different types of society, labeled by the author. Since traditional jurisprudence as *ideologically–conditioned* institution will no longer have any use, the author asks for its general transformation into *Rechtstatsachenforschung*, and the establishment of a new interdisciplinary department of architecture of society directing itself in a constructive way to the problems of social integration. (edited)

SCHMIDT, Lawrence K. *The Epistemology Of Hans–Georg Gadamer*. NY Lang 1985.

Gadamer's philosophic hermeneutics raises the question whether one of several conflicting interpretations is more accurate. Analyzing the second half of *Wahrheit und Methode*, it is argued that there is an implicit hermeneutic truth criterion, namely the *einleuchtende Ansicht der Sache selbst* (the enlightening perspective of the subject matter itself). This criterion allows for the legitimization of one's *Vorurteile* (pre–judgments) within understanding thereby solving the problem of indeterminacy.

SCHMITT, Eric E. La Question Du Sensualisme. *Rev Phil Fr* 174,371–381 Jl–S 84.

SCHMITT, Frederick F. Consensus, Respect, And Weighted Averaging. *Synthese* 62,25–46 Ja 85.

SCHMITT, Frederick F. Knowledge As Tracking? *Topoi* 4,73–80 Mr 85.

SCHMITT, Richard. Reply To Van De Pitte's "Comments On A Claim That Some Phenomenological Statements May Be *A Posteriori*". *Metaphilosophy* 15,256–258 Jl–O 84.

In my article on "Phenomenology" in Paul Edwards' *Encyclopedia of Philosophy*, I suggested some reasons for being skeptical of the claim made by Husserl that phenomenology yields universal and necessary truths. Van de Pitte raised doubts abour these suggestions of mine. The "Reply" tries to show that those doubts are without substance.

SCHMITZ, Kenneth L. Natural Value. *Rev Metaph* 38,3–16 S 84.

SCHNAITTER, Roger. Skinner On The "Mental And The "Physical". *Behaviorism* 12,1–14 Spr 84.

SCHNALL, David J (ed) and Figliola, Carl L (ed). *Contemporary Issues In Health Care*. NY Praeger 1984.

SCHNEEWIND, J B. "The Divine Corporation And The History Of Ethics" in *Philosophy In History*, Rorty, Richard and others (ed), 173–192. NY Cambridge Univ Pr 1984.

SCHNEIDER, Henry G and Wesley, George R and Carroll, Mary Ann. *Ethics In The Practice Of Psychology*. Englewood Cliffs Prentice–Hall 1985.

This book will acquaint not only philosophers and psychologists with ethical issues arising in psychology but also anyone interested in the profession. Hence, no background knowledge of philosophy or psychology is presupposed. Some of the areas covered are therapeutic techniques, research, special populations, testing, and consulting. Attention is given to consent, confidentiality and competence. Chapters contain case studies for discussion. The *Ethical Principles of Psychologists* as formulated by The American Psychological Association are included.

SCHNEIDER, W and Fieber, Hans–Joachim. Zum Platz Der "Randglossen" In Der Geschichte Der Theorie Des Wissenschaftlichen Kommunismus. *Deut Z Phil* 23,696–705 1975.

SCHNEIDERMAN, Lawrence J and Dubler, Nancy Neveloff. 'My Husband Won't Tell The Children!'. *Hastings Center Rep* 14,26–27 Ag 84.

SCHNEIDERS, Werner. Harmonia Universalis. *Stud Leibniz* 16,27–44 1984.

L'étude part du fait que l'harmonie est un concept–clé de la philosophie leibnizienne. Elle montre que et comment l'harmonie préétablie est subordonnée temporellement et materiellement à l'harmonie universelle. Par là il devient clair que l'harmonie pour Leibniz est, entre autre, un principe éthique, esthétique, théologique et gnoséologique et enfin, cependant, un principe ontologique global. L'harmonie se révèle comme l'a priori absolu de tout être et de toute pensée.

SCHNEIDERS, Werner. Sozietätspläne Und Sozialutopie Bei Leibniz. *Stud Leibniz* 7,58–80 1975.

Die Interpretation der frühen Akademiepläne von Leibniz zielt auf die politischen Implikationen und Konsequenzen dieser z T utopischen Projekte. Sie enthüllt das Ideal eines autoritären Wohlfahrtsstaates, in dem die Staatskunst, geleitet von einem metaphysischen, der Absicht nach exakten Herrschaftwissen, zugleich höchster Gottesdienst ist. (edited)

SCHNORR, C P and Stumpf, G. A Characterization Of Complexity Sequences. *Z Math Log* 21,47–56 1975.

SCHOCK, Rolf. Ravens, Grue, And Material Implication. *Dialectica* 38,347–350 1984.

Certain kinds of validation are here defined and the paradox of confirmation is resolved. Trivially based confirmation is shown to be a proper aspect of material implication rather than a shortcoming of confirmation. The grue problem is traced to the same source and thereby shown to depend on proper although trivially based inductive procedure.

SCHOELLER– VON HASLINGEN, Karin. Über Das Verhältnis Von Werner Marx Zu Martin Heidegger. *Frei Z Phil Theol* 31,453–470 1984.

In the treatise "About the relaton between Werner Marx and Martin Heidegger," the author presents Heidegger's basic thought and leads to the measure of his thinking. When compared to Werner Marx's view it appears that Martin Heidegger's insights can only be followed by transition from metaphysical ("vorstellend") thinking into onto–fundamental ("andenkend") thinking. Marx's attempt to think beyond Heidegger's thoughts by omitting the transition proves to be impossible.

SCHOEMAN, Ferdinand. Parental Discretion And Children's Rights: Background And Implications For Medical Decision–Making. *J Med Phil* 10,45–62 F 85.

This paper argues that liberal tenats that justify intervention to promote the welfare of an incompetent do not suffice as a basis for analyzing parent–child relationships, and that this inadequacy is the basis for many of the problems that arise when thinking about the state's role in resolving family conflicts, particularly when monitoring parental discretion in medical decision–making on behalf of a child. The state may be limited by the best interest criterion when dealing with children, but parents are not. The state's relation with the child is formal while the parental relation is intimate,

having its own goals and purposes. While the liberal canons insist on the incompetent one's best interest, parents are permitted to compromise the child's interests for ends related to these familial goals and purposes. Parents decisions should be supervened, in general, only if it can be shown that no responsible mode of thinking warrants such treatment of a child.

SCHOFIELD, Malcolm. Ariston Of Chios And The Unity Of Virtue. *Ancient Phil* 4,83–96 Spr 84.

SCHOFIELD, M and Kirk, G S and Raven, J E. *The Presocratic Philosophers*. NY Cambridge Univ Pr 1984.

SCHOLLMEIER, Paul. A Classical Rhetoric Of Modern Science. *Phil Rhet* 17,209–220 1984.

This paper demonstrates that John Stuart Mill's logic of science is in fact a rhetoric of science. This paper shows that Mill's conception of induction is essentially the same as Aristotle's conception of example.

SCHÖNBORN, Christoph. L'homme Créé Par Dieu: Le Fondement De La Dignité De L'homme. *Gregorianum* 65,337–363 1984.

SCHÖNBORN, Christoph. Menschenwürde Und Menschenrechte Im Licht Der Reich–Gottes–Verkündigung Jesu. *Gregorianum* 65,319–325 1984.

SCHONHERR, L. Triebkräfte Des Sozialismus. *Deut Z Phil* 33,161–164 1985.

SCHOTCH, P K and Jennings, R E. The Preservation Of Coherence. *Stud Log* 43,89–106 1984.

It is argued that the preservation of truth by an inference relation is of little interest when premiss sets are contradictory. The notion of a level of coherence is introduced and the utility of modal logics in the semantic representation of sets of higher coherence levels is noted. It is shown that this representative role cannot be transferred to first order logic via frame theory since the modal formula expressing coherence level restrictions are not first order definable. Finally, an inference relation, called *yielding*, is introduced which is intermediate between the coherence preserving *forcing* relation introduced elsewhere by the authors and the coherence destroying inference relation of classical logic.

SCHOTCH, Peter K. Remarks On The Semantics Of Non–Normal Modal Logics. *Topoi* 3,85–90 Je 84.

The standard semantics for sentential modal logics uses a truth condition for necessity which first appeared in the early 1950s. In this paper the status of that condition is investigated and a more general condition is proposed. In addition to meeting certain natural adequacy criteria, the more general condition allows one to capture logics like S1 and S0.9 in a way which brings together the work of Segerberg and Cresswell.

SCHOTTLAENDER, Rudolf. Kritische Bemerkung Zu E Tielschs "Logik Des Freiheitsbegriffes". *Z Phil Forsch* 29,404–408 Jl–S 75.

SCHOULS, Peter A (ed) and Collins, Anthony. *An Essay Concerning The Use Of Reason In Propositions: A Discourse Of Free Thinking*. NY Garland 1984.

SCHOULS, Peter A (ed) and King, Peter. *The Life And Letters Of John Locke*. NY Garland 1984.

SCHOULS, Peter A (ed) and Lee, Henry. *Anti–Skepticism*. NY Garland 1984.

SCHOULS, Peter A (ed) and Mac Lean, Kenneth. *John Locke And English Literature Of The Eighteenth Century*. NY Garland 1984.

SCHOULS, Peter A (ed) and Watts, Isaac. *Logick: Or, The Right Use Of Reason*. NY Garland 1984.

SCHRAG, Francis. Education And Historical Materialism. *Proc Phil Educ* 40,253–264 1984.

SCHRAMM, Alfred. Demarkation Und Rationale Rekonstruktion Bei Imre Lakatos. *Conceptus* 8,10–16 1974.

Imre Lakatos, in his 'Methodology of Scientific Research Programmes', softens up the standards of demarcationism so that, in fact, he holds the 'anything goes' position. This position does not allow for rules of heuristic advice about what to do in a given problem situation. But 'methodology' without such rules can only serve for mere description: it is no theory of the rationality of scientific progress and does not provide a theoretical framework for the rational reconstruction of the history of science.

SCHRIEBER, Leonard. Recursive Properties Of Euclidean Domains. *Annals Pure Applied Log* 29,59–78 Jl 85.

SCHRIFT, Alan D. Comments: Parody And The Eternal Recurrence In Nietzsche's Project Of Transvaluation. *Int Stud Phil* 16,37–40 1984.

In this paper, I argue that Zarathustra's proclamation of the eternal recurrence is not a metaphysical response by which he transcends the Soothsayer's riddle concerning the circularity of time. Instead, I suggest that Zarathustra provides us with a transvaluation of the significance of the Soothsayer's prophecy by posing the doctrine of the eternal recurrence as an existential challenge to affirm one's existence and a principle of selection which announces the overman.

SCHRIFT, Alan D. Language, Metaphor, Rhetoric: Nietzsche's Deconstruction Of Epistemology. *J Hist Phil* 23,371–396 Jl 85.

This paper opens with an examination of Nietzsche's early rhetorical account of the origin of philosophical concepts in metaphor and metonymy. This account is shown to inform his "mature" philosophy, as he continues to trace the reification of becoming to a substantialist metaphysic hidden within language. Nietzsche's critique of philosophy emerges as a *de*–construction or *Ab–bau* of philosophical language which dismantles the privileged conceptual constructions of epistemology by tracing them back to their metaphorical/rhetorical origins.

SCHROEDER– HEISTER, Peter. A Natural Extension Of Natural Deduction. *J Sym Log* 49,1284–1300 D 84.

The framework of natural deduction is extended by permitting rules as assumptions which may be discharged in the course of a derivation. This leads to the concept of rules of higher levels and to a general schema for introduction and elimination rules for arbitrary n–ary sentential operators. With respect to this schema, (functional) completeness "or", "if..Then" and absurdity is proved.

SCHROEDER, Craig. Levels Of Truth And Reality In The Philosophies Of Descartes And Samkara. *Phil East West* 35,285–294 Jl 85.

An examination of Descartes' method of radical doubt as exercised in his *Meditations* reveals striking parallels to the various levels of truth and reality set forth by Samkara, the major exponent of Advaita Vedanta. It is noted that these levels, which Samkara identifies explicitly, are operating, however implicitly, in Descartes' thought. It is posited that Descartes' formulations suffer from insufficient exploration of these levels.

SCHUBERT KALSI, Marie–Luise. On Evidence According To Meinong And Chisholm. *Phil Topics* 13,77–86 Spr 85.

The concept of 'evident' (and 'evidence') in Meinong's and Chisholms writings are investigated. Meinong's term is studied in only one of its several meanings. It was found that 'evident' is a relation holding between a proposition and a person. Its presence is indicated and known by the person by a feeling of justification (Meinong) and sensibly taking (Chisholm). 'evident' is a psychologic epistemological concept and the presence of the relation cannot be objectively ascertained. The relationship between evident and its mark is pre–given and unexplained.

SCHUELER, G F. Some Reasoning About Preferences. *Ethics* 95,78–80 O 84.

This paper criticizes R M Hare's argument in *Moral Thinking* that interpersonal conflicts of preferences can be reduced to intrapersonal ones with the preferences of others 'mirrored' within the reasoner as hypothetical preferences which then get weighed against his other, categorical preferences in the usual way. Against this it is argued that in fact there is no conflict between categorical preferences and hypothetical preferences with false antecedents.

SCHUHMANN, Karl and Smith, Barry. Against Idealism: Johannes Daubert Vs Husserl's *Ideas* I. *Rev Metaph* 38,763–794 Je 85.

In manuscripts of 1930–1 Johannes Dauber, principal member of the Munich board of realist phenomenologists, put forward a series of detailed criticisms of the idealism of Husserl's *Ideas* I. The paper provides a sketch of these criticisms and of Daubert's own alternative conceptions of consciousness and reality, as also of Daubert's views on perception, similar, in many respects, to those of J J Gibson.

SCHUHMANN, Karl. Francis Bacon Und Hobbes' Widmungsbrief Zu *De Cive*. *Z Phil Forsch* 38,165–190 Ap–Je 84.

SCHULER, Wolfgang. Überlegungen Zu Den Grundlegungsversuchen Der Mathematik Von Frege Und Hilbert Vom Standpunkt Der Transzendentalphilosophie Aus (II). *Rev Metaph Morale* 89,361–380 Jl–S 84.

SCHULTE, G. Fichtes Gottesbegriff. *Kantstudien* 66,163–168 1975.

SCHULTE, Joachim. Chor Und Gesetz: Zur "Morphologischen Methode" Bei Goethe Und Wittgenstein. *Grazer Phil Stud* 21,1–32 1984.

SCHULTHESS, Peter. Logistik: Eine Renaissance Der Scholastischen Spitzfindigkeiten? *Stud Phil (Switzerland)* 41,213–220 1982.

SCHULTHESS, Peter. Zur Logik Und Semiotik Bei Leibniz. *Stud Phil (Switzerland)* 41,201–212 1982.

The article is a book–review of "H Burkhardt, Logik und Semiotik in der Philosophie von Leibniz, München 1980." The main critique is that B did not sufficiently consider the ontological and epistemological presuppositions of Leibniz's logical and semiotical studies, especially the relation between res, idea and notio and the constitutive function of signs for thought (cogitatio caeca).

SCHULTZ, Janice L. Is–Ought: Prescribing And A Present Controversy. *Thomist* 49,1–23 Ja 85.

Germain Grisez and John Finnis do not neglect nature as a basis for moral value, as some critics imply they do. However, owing to their interpretation of "ought"–judgments as prescriptive rather than descriptive, these authors incorrectly separate the realms of "is" and "ought". If offer an analysis of moral "ought"–judgements as inherently descriptive, recognizing prescriptive uses in which the descriptive component remains the ground of the directive.

SCHULZ, Walter. Anmerkungen Zu Schelling. *Z Phil Forsch* 29,321–336 Jl–S 75.

SCHULZE, Hans. Arnold J Toynbee: Das Höchste Gut Ist Der Frieden!. *Deut Z Phil* 33,519–527 1985.

SCHUMM, George F. Disjunctive Extensions Of S4 And A Conjecture Of Goldblatt's. *Z Math Log* 21,81–86 1975.

SCHÜRMANN, Heinz. Menschenwürde Und Menschenrechte Im Light Der "Offenbarung Jesu Christi". *Gregorianum* 65,327–336 1984.

Einleitend zeigten wir, dass die Frage nach Menschenrechten im Lichte "der Offenbarung Jesu Christi" endzeitlich situiert und dadurch heilsgeschichtlich–realistisch sowie geschichtlich–konkret gesehen werden muss. (edited)

SCHÜRMANN, Reiner. Deconstruction Is Not Enough: On Gianni Vattimo's Call For "Weak Thinking". *Grad Fac Phil J* 10,165–177 Spr 84.

Post–modern philosophers such as Gianni Vattimo argue that the sole task we can still take upon ourselves is to comment on past philosophies. Constructive thinking has become impossible, they claim, and only "weak thinking" is left, made of quotes. This view is challenged as to its political implications: it is essentially reactionary since the emergence of new possibilities in both theory and practice is dismissed from the start as incompatible with our historical site.

SCHÜRMANN, Reiner. Legislation–Transgression: Strategies And Counter–Strategies In The Transcendental Justification Of Norms. *Man World* 17,361–398 1984.

In the German "transcendentalist" tradition, norms and rules are legitimated in reference to one ultimate act: in Kant, prescriptively, to the "I think"; in Nietzsche, descriptively, to "constellations of domination"; in Heidegger, phenomenologically, to "epochal constellations" of being. Each of these constructs is shown to reach only

a broken fundament, one that is determinative but in turn permeated with indeterminancy. In Kant this factor of indeterminancy is the givenness of the sensible manifold as opposed to the categories; in Nietzsche, it is power as other than force; in Heidegger, it is the event of presencing as differing from historical orders of presence.

SCHURZ, Gerhard. Correct Explanatory Arguments And Understanding–why An Approach To Scientific Understanding Based On Knowledge Dynamics. *Phil Natur* 21,321–338 1984.

In the first part of this paper it is shown how correct explanatory arguments and understanding–why are connected. Understanding–why must be described as a certain change in the questioner's knowledge system which increases its explanatory coherence. This change is induced by an explaining episode. Correct explanatory arguments can be defined as carrier–arguments for possible explaining episodes. In the second part of the paper a formal model of explaining episodes—including a solution of the emphasis–problem is developed.

SCHÜSSLER, I. "Comment *Le Monde Vrai* Devint, Pour Finir, Une Fable" in *Asthetische Er Fahrung Und Das Wesen Der Kunst*, Holzhey, Helmut, 9–22. Bern Haupt 1984.

SCHUTTE, Ofelia. Overcoming Ethnocentrism In The Philosophy Classroom. *Teach Phil* 8,137–144 Ap 85.

The essay's point of departure is the desirability of enhancing students' awareness of global affairs through the study of philosophy. Its principal goal is to consider specific conditions which make possible cross–cultural knowledge while avoiding symptoms of cultural prejudice in the epistemological context through which the world of the other is known. Sponsored by the American Philosophical Association, this is one of five studies addressing the issue of global awareness in philosophy instruction.

SCHUTZ, Alfred. *The Problem Of Social Reality: Collected Papers 1.* Boston Nijhoff 1982.

This work is a collection of articles and various chapters of books brought together in one volume. The selections cover various topics including; the methodology of the social sciences, phenomenology and the social sciences, and symbol, reality and society. The main focus of the articles is to achieve a rationale for the essential structure of daily life through an examination of its manifold typifications. (staff)

SCHWANZ, P. Von Den Voraussetzungen Einer Christlichen Ethik. *Kantstudien* 66,181–200 1975.

SCHWARTZ, Joel. Liberalism And The Jewish Connection: A Study Of Spinoza And The Young Marx. *Polit Theory* 13,58–84 F 85.

Spinoza and the young Marx both point to similarities between Judaism and liberalism. Spinoza praises the Jewish and liberal emphasis upon individual self–interest and preserving peace, while criticizing their obliviousness to the transpolitical good of moral and intellectual perfection. Marx accepts Spinoza's critique of Judaism and liberalism, but unlike Spinoza believes that communism, not philosophy, leads to perfection; Marx therefore praises ends which politics cannot achieve, while devaluing ends which it can achieve.

SCHWARTZ, Mortimer D and Wydick, Richard C. *Problems In Legal Ethics.* St Paul West 1983.

SCHWARTZ, Philip J. John Dewey And Creative Dramatics. *J Thought* 20,50–59 Spr 85.

SCHWARTZ, Robert L. "Implications Of Constitutional Right Of Privacy For Control Of Drugs" in *Feeling Good And Doing Better*, Murray, Thomas H (ed), 129–156. Clifton Humana Pr 1984.

SCHWARTZ, Thomas. Dr Krankheit And The Concept Of Compliance. *Amer Phil Quart* 22,81–88 Ja 85.

SCHWARZ, Eckart. The Distinctiveness Of The Process Of Solving Social Contradictions (in German). *Deut Z Phil* 22,23–36 1974.

Der Lösungsprozeß gesellschaftlicher Widersprüche wird deren Charakter und die historischen Bedingungen, unter denen die Widersprüche wirken, bestimmt. Der Prozeß der Lösung von Widersprüchen kann sowohl deren Beseitigung beinhalten als auch ihre weitere Existenz in einer neuen Bewegungsform. Im Kapitalismus ist ein Lösungsprozeß gesellschaftlicher Widersprüche möglich, er unterscheidet sich jedoch grundlegend vom Prozeß der Lösung der Widersprüche im Sozialismus. Hier besteht die Möglichkeit der planmäßigen Führung des Gesamtlösungsprozesses durch die Arbeiterklasse und ihre marxistisch–leninistische Partei.

SCHWARZSCHILD, Steven S. The Unnatural Jew. *Environ Ethics* 6,347–362 Wint 84.

I argue that Judaism and Jewish culture have paradigmatically and throughout history operated with a fundamental dichotomy between nature ("what is") and ethics (i.E., God and man–"what ought to be"). pagan ontologism, on the other hand, and the Christian synthesis of biblical transcendentalism and Greek incarnationism result in human and historical submission to what are acclaimed as "natural forces". Although in the history of Jewish culture such a heretical, quasi–pantheistic tendency asserted itself, first in mediaeval kabbalism and then in modern Zionism, from a traditional Jewish standpoint nature remains subject to humanly enacted ends. Evidene for this general thesis can be found in biblical, Talmudic, medieval philosophic, and mystical literature, in modern religious, poetic, and Zionist literature, and in the history of general philosophy.

SCHWEICKART, David. On Robert Paul Wolff's Transcendental Interpretation Of Marx's Labor Theory Of Value. *Can J Phil* 14,359–374 S 84.

Wolff misconstrues Marx as making a transcendental inquiry into the conditions for the possibility of profit. Marx does not claim that "labor is the source of all value" because otherwise profit is impossible, but because that is the law governing the logico–historical antecedent of capitalism. Hence *self–expanding capital* (not profit) is possible only if there exists a class of persons with nothing to sell but their labor–power. The argument is dialectical, not transcendental.

SCHWEID, Eliezer. "Martin Buber And A D Gordon: A Comparison" in *Martin Buber*, Gordon, Haim (ed), 255–274. Beersheva Ktav 1984.

SCHWEID, Eliezer. Mutual Responsibility Of The Jewish People And Self-Realization (in Hebrew). *Iyyun* 33,327–337 Ja–Ap 84.

SCHWERIN, Alan. Remarks On Leibniz's Conception Of Containment And Individual Substance. *S Afr J Phil* 4,16–18 F 85.

How should we view Leibniz's *Discourse on Metaphysics*? In this note I suggest the standard interpretation can be questioned. My argument centers around two central concepts of Leibniz's discussion—that of containment and individual substance. As I attempt to demonstrate, the standard (linguistic) interpretation of the *Discourse* generates a dilemma that dissolves when we view Leibniz's concepts of containment and individual substance as empirical concepts based on reality (direct experience) rather than language.

SCHWERIN, Alan. Semantic Holism And Observation Statements. *Phil Papers* 13,19–27 O 84.

This paper is an attempt to show that Quine's views on observation statements are untenable, for they overlook the role of a fundamental background principle governing the use of predicates. I argue that the verification of a statement, even an observation statement, contrary to Quine's views cannot be identified with its stimulus meaning.

SCILIRONI, Carlo. Necessità Del Significato E Destino Del Linguaggio In E Severino. *Sapienza* 37,415–432 O–D 84.

SCOLNICOV, Samuel. Plato's *Parmenides*: Prolegomena To A Reinterpretation (in Hebrew). *Iyyun* 33,459–479 O 84.

This paper is an attempt at a reinterpretation of the second part of Plato's *Parmenides*. It is argued that Plato's main aim in this dialogue is to establish the formal condition of the possibility of a two–tier ontology. This condition is the distinction , *pace* Parmenides, between "Parmenidean", homogeneous being, and participation, which allows plurality and predication. The *Parmenides* is thus shown to occupy a central place in the development of Plato's thought, although not necessarily as a *Kehrpunkt*.

SCOLNICOV, S. Hypothetical Method And Rationality In Plato. *Kantstudien* 66,157–162 1975.

SCOTT, Charles E. Speech And The Unspeakable In The "Place" Of The Unconscious. *Human Stud* 7,39–54 1984.

This discussion considers two ways in which the Unconscious has been replaced in recent thought. Heidegger's way of conceiving language in terms of difference rather than sameness and Foucault's type of genealogical discourse are shown to transform, in their particular ways, the conceptual connections out of which the idea of the Unconscious arose. Derrida's critique of Foucault is considered in detail. Alternative ways of thinking and speaking are found in which the 'unspeakable' in an earlier discourse is speakable without the conscious/unconscious cleavage.

SCOWCROFT, Philip. The Real–Algebraic Structure Of Scott's Model Of Intuitionistic Analysis. *Annals Pure Applied Log* 27,275–308 N 84.

This paper discusses first–order real algebra in Scott's topological model. Part one gives a decision procedure for the truth, in the model, of universal–existential sentences with matricies whose truth values behave like those of weak inequalities. Part two isolates a large class of such matricies, extends the basic result to logically more complicated sentences, and uses the decision procedure to study the continuity conditions relevant to the truth of sentences in the model.

SCREEN, Donald P. Realism And Grammar. *S J Phil* 22,523–534 Wint 84.

Many principles taken to be definitive of realism are what Wittgenstein would have called "grammatical remarks." While these remarks impose formal constraints on the application of "truth" and related concepts, only an examination of the *sense* of a statement can reveal, for example, the kind of fact that would make it true. Failure to notice the grammatical character of realist claims may lead one erroneously to attribute substantive consequences, such as skepticism, to them.

SCRIVEN, Michael. Critical For Survival. *Nat Forum* 65,9–12 Wint 85.

It is argued that critical thinking skills are survival skills for individuals and the society—yet they are not given that status (indeed, they are abjured) and when taught, not taught in the way other survival skills are taught.

SCRIVEN, Tal. Utility, Autonomy And Drug Regulation. *Int J Applied Phil* 2,27–42 Fall 84.

Various arguments for a libertarian position on government regulation of the pharmaceutical industry are considered and compared against a hedonistic utilitarian argument for a non–libertarian position. Libertarian arguments based on hedonistic utilitarianism, preference utilitarianism and the Kantian principle of autonomy are attacked. Special attention is paid to the preference utilitarian argument of Sam Peltzman.

SCRUTON, Roger. Sexual Arousal. *Philosophy* 18,255–274 84 Supp.

Sexual arousal is a distinctively personal phenomenon; it has intentionality; a person features a subject and a person (usually another) or object; bestiality is of course possible, this requires a special explanation which confirms the inter–personal character of arousal. Fundamental to arousal is the "fear of the obscene", i.E., fear of the third–person perspective on the experience and bodies of those involved. This fear given important insight into the experience of embodiness.

SEAGER, W E. Is Nuclear Deterrence Paradoxical? *Dialogue (Canada)* 23,187–198 Je 84.

SEALEY, John. *Religious Education: Philosophical Perspectives*. Winchester Allen & Unwin 1985.

SEARLE, John R. Intentionality And Its Place In Nature. *Synthese* 61,3–16 O 84.

SEATON, Robert. Zeno's Paradoxes, Iteration, And Infinity. *Nature Syst* 6,229–236 D 84.

SEBOK, Thomas A (ed) and Eco, Umberto (ed). *The Sign Of Three*. Bloomington Indiana Univ Pr 1983.

SECKEL, Al. Russell And The Cuban Missile Crisis. *Russell* 4,253–261 Wint 84.

SECRETAN, Philibert. Elements For A Theory Of Modernity. *Diogenes* 126,71–90 Sum 84.

SEEBOHM, Thomas M. Boeckh And Dilthey: The Development Of Methodical Hermeneutics. *Man World* 17,325–346 1984.

SEEBOHM, Thomas M. Fichte's Und Husserl's Critique Of Kant's Transcendental Deduction. *Husserl Stud* 2,53–74 1985.

SEESKIN, Kenneth. Socratic Philosophy And The Dialogue Form. *Phil Lit* 8,181–194 O 84.

SEGAL, Robert A. A Jungian View Of Evil. *Zygon* 20,83–89 Mr 85.

On the one hand Jungian John Sanford criticizes Carl Jung for underestimating the importance granted evil by at least some strains of Christianity. On the other hand Sanford follows Jung in assuming that psychology is entitled to criticize Christianity whenever it fails to grant evil its due. Like Jung, Sanford contends that he is faulting Christianity on only psychological grounds: for failing to cope with evil in man – the shadow of archetype. In fact, Sanford, like perhaps Jung as well, is also criticizing Christianity on metaphysical grounds: for failing to acknowledge not just psychological but also ontological evil. Whether Sanford is thereby using psychology to assess Christian metaphysics is the issue.

SEGAL, Robert A. Anthropological Definitions Of Religion. *Zygon* 20,78–79 Mr 85.

Murray Wax's call for less parochial anthropological definition of religion is admirable but scarcely novel. The search for ever more comprehensive definitions spans the history of the anthropology of religion. At the same time, that search has, since Durkheim, shifted its focus from substantive to functional definitions. Because the function specified by any functionalist definition of religion is invariably universal, a functionalist definition thereby avoids the parochialism bemoaned by Wax.

SEGERBERG, Krister. A Topological Logic Of Action. *Stud Log* 43,415–420 1984.

We consider a quantifier–free language in which there are terms as well as formulas. The proposition–forming propositional operators are the usual ones, and the term–making operators are the usual lattice theoretical ones. In addition there is a formula–making term operator, "does". We study a new logic in which "does a" is claimed to approximate some features of the informal concept "the agent performs the action a".

SEGERBERG, Krister and Bull, Robert A. "Basic Modal Logic" in *Handbook Of Philosophical Logic*, Gabbay, Dov (ed), 1–88. Boston Reidel 1984.

SEGERBERG, Krister. Towards An Exact Philosophy Of Action. *Topoi* 3,75–84 Je 84.

The paper attempts to outline an exact semantics of the possible worlds type suitable for formalizing simple action sentences.

SEGUNDO, Juan Luis. Les Deux Théologies De La Libération On Amérique Latine. *Etudes* 361,149–161 S 84.

This essay analyzes two trains of thought among liberation theologians in Latin America which have recently emerged. The first focuses on the specific socio-political and cultural factors which affect the theological enterprise whereas the second examines the general philosophical and societal forces which condition theological discourse. Although these respective approaches share common methological presuppositions and are ultimately complimentary, there is, at present, a fair degree of tension between their respective advocates.

SEIDEL, Asher. Numbers As Qualities. *Philosophia (Israel)* 14,99–110 Ag 84.

This is a study in the ontology of number. The claim is advanced that numbers can be understood within the general object–quality ontological framework. Various objections to this claim, such as those of Frege, are discussed.

SEIDEL, Helmut. Gedanken Zum Begriff Und Zur Geschichte Des Humanismus. *Deut Z Phil* 32,748–755 1984.

SEIDENFELD, Teddy. Calibration, Coherence, And Scoring Rules. *Phil Sci* 52,274–294 Je 85.

Can there be good reasons for judging one set of probabilistic assertions more *reliable* than a second? There are many candidates for measuring "goodness" of probabilistic forecasts. Here, I focus on one such aspirant: calibration. Calibration requires an alignment of announced probabilities and observed relative frequency, e.G., 50 percent of forecasts made with the announced probability of .5 occur, 70 percent of forecasts made with the probability of .7 occur, etc. To summarize the conclusion: (i) Survey designed to display calibration curves, from which a recalibration is to be calculated, are useless without due consideration for the interconnections between questions (forecasts) in the survey. (ii) Subject to feedback, calibration in the long run is otiose. It gives no ground for validating one coherent opinion over another as each coherent forecaster is (almost) sure of his own long–run calibration. (iii) Calibration in the short run is an inducement to hedge forecasts. A calibration score, in the short run, is improper. (edited)

SEIDENGART, Jean. Néo–Kantisme Et Relativité. *Rev Phil Fr* 174,201–218 Ap–Je 84.

SEIDLER, Michael J. Freedom And Moral Therapy In Leibniz. *Stud Leibniz* 17,15–35 1985.

SEIDMAN, Bradley. *Absent At The Creation: The Existential Psychiatry Of Ludwig Binswanger*. Roslyn Heights Libra 1983.

SEIGEL, Michael. Use Of Privileged Information For Attorney Self–Interest: A Moral Dilemma. *Bus Prof Ethics J* 3,1–12 Fall 83.

SEIGFRIED, Charlene H. Extending The Darwinian Model: James's Struggle With Royce And Spencer. *Ideal Stud* 14,259–272 S 84.

An examination of Josiah Royce's and William James's early writings on evolution

Seigfried, Charlene H 402 **Author Index with Abstracts**

show how much James was indebted to contemporary formulations of American idealism. But his divergences from Royce also reveal a clear grasp of the magnitude of the break between Darwinian evolutionary theory and other evolutionary theories which preceded and accompanied it.

SEIGFRIED, Charlene H. Gender–Specific Values. *Phil Forum (Boston)* 15,425–442 Sum 84.

It is argued that Simone de Beauvoir's immanence–transcendence distinction in *The Second Sex* surreptitiously reinforces the view of transcendence as masculine because of unexamined presuppositions. Her negative assessment of maternity draws on this distinction. Beauvoir did not recognize the contradiction generated by using transcendence to explain women's oppression as embodying immanence and then prescribing the same notion of transcendence to overcome that immanence. She conflates two distinct meanings: one being a historical–cultural genesis of male transcendence and the other a universalized human transcendence. Since the latter still reflects the former, its value for women is questionable.

SEILER, Christiane (trans) and Butler, Clark (trans). *Hegel: The Letters.* Bloomington Indiana Univ Pr 1984.

This volume is a complete edition of available letters by Hegel. The letters are organized into chapters, where they are introduced by and alternate with commentary. The book thus approaches a "life in letters". The interpretive thesis, which is grounded in the letters as well as Hegel's published works, is that Hegelianism should be placed in the German hermeneutic tradition since Herder, and should not be understood as a form of Neoplatonism or panlogism.

SELDEN, Raman. *Criticism And Objectivity.* Boston Allen & Unwin 1984.

The book argues that literary critics should not abandon the concept of objectivity. It should be redefined in the light of the developments in post–structuralist philosophy. A new historical criticism is needed, which combines formalism and a recognition of the historical conditions of production and reception of texts. The book reasserts historical 'knowledge' in the face of the scepticism of post–structuralist thought.

SELF, Donnie J. An Analysis Of The Structure Of Justification Of Ethical Decisions In Medical Intervention. *Theor Med* 6,343–356 O 85.

The most important distinction in value theory is the subjective–objective distinction which determines the epistemological status of value judgments about medical intervention. Ethical decisions in medical intervention presuppose one of three structues of justification—namely, an inductive approach, a deductive approach which can be either consequentialist or non–consequentialist, and a uniquely ethical approach. Inductivism and deductivism have been discussed extensively in the literature and are only briefly described here. The uniquely ethical approach which presupposes value objectivism is analyzed in detail. This method involves a purely ethical inference which moves from facts to values directly with an emphasis on reason which involves a non–logical justification (as opposed to illogical). It involves the use of natural practical arguments which have an imperative conclusion but no imperative premise and exhibit a value–requiredness between two states of affairs.

SELL, Alan P F. Locke And Descartes Through Victorian Eyes. *Phil Stud (Ireland)* 30,220–229 Spr 84.

This excursion into the history of Locke criticism reveals Henry Rogers (1806–77) as a pioneer of the now commonplace view that since Locke was not an out and out sensationalist, the distance between him and Descartes has been exaggerated, and accordingly that the 'rationalist–empiricist' polarization may obscure more than it reveals. Rogers' position is discussed in relation to older and more recent Locke and Descartes scholarship.

SELLARS, Wilfrid. "Towards A Theory Of Predication" in *How Things Are*, Bogen, James (ed), 285–322. Boston Reidel 1985.

SELLER, Anne. Greenham: A Concrete Reality. *J Applied Phil* 2,133–142 Mr 85.

SELLMAN, James. A Pointing Finger Kills "The Buddha": A Response To Chung–Ying Cheng And John King Farlow. *J Chin Phil* 12,223–228 Je 85.

In this review essay, I argue that King–Farlow has misunderstood Cheng's logical approach to the Zen *koan* by attempting to *solve* them. Cheng's attempt at expressing the *koans* in symbolic form distract from the Zen experience of awakening. However, the review does not attempt to offer an alternate means of dealing with the *koan*.

SELTMAN, Muriel and Seltman, Peter. *Piaget's Logic: A Critique Of Genetic Epistemology.* Winchester Allen & Unwin 1985.

SELTMAN, Peter and Seltman, Muriel. *Piaget's Logic: A Critique Of Genetic Epistemology.* Winchester Allen & Unwin 1985.

SEN, Amartya. Rationality And Uncertainty. *Theor Decis* 18,109–128 Mr 85.

The paper begins with critically examining—and rejecting—two standard approaches to rationality of choice, viz., (1) internal consistency, and (2) intelligent pursuit of self–interest. More positively, the paper discusses two different aspects of rationality, called respectively "correspondence rationality" and "reflection rationality." Both involve decidability problems and allow systematic incompleteness in judgments about rationality. The last parts P. t. o. Of the paper present a reexamination of the axioms for "expected utility," and in particular that of "independence," and sorts out the sources of the difficulties revealed by the counterexamples.

SEN, Amartya. The Moral Standing Of The Market. *Soc Phil Pol* 2,1–19 Spr 85.

In this paper, a number of arguments about the moral merits of the market mechanism are critically examined. The approaches considered include both "procedural" views and "consequential" assessments. It is argued that the vigour of the standard defenses of the market mechanism is not matched by the ability to meet criticism. But there is certainly some instrumental moral merit, which should not be overlooked, and which yield powerful *qualified* defenses. The overall conclusion is that there is a case for *faint* praise, without damning.

SEN, Amartya. Well–being, Agency And Freedom: The Dewey Lectures 1984. *J Phil* 82,169–203 Ap 85.

The main aim of these three lectures is to explore a substantive moral approach that sees persons from two different perspectives, viz., well–being and agency. Both the "well–being aspect" and the "agency aspect" have their own relevance in the assessment of states and actions. Each aspect also yields a corresponding notion of freedom. The substantive moral discussion draws on the examination of methodological issues in the first lecture, using an informational approach to ethical questions, and dealing with such matters as pluralism, incompleteness, positionality, agent relativity, and objectivity.

SENA, Michelantonio. *Ragione–Libertà–Scienza In Kant–Hegel–Marx.* Napoli Tempi Moderni 1984.

SENDLEWSKI, Andrzej. Some Investigations Of Varieties Of *N*–Lattices. *Stud Log* 43,257–280 1984.

We examine some extensions of the constructive propositional logic with strong negation in the setting of varieties of *n*–lattices. The main aim of the paper is to give a description of all pretabular, primitive and preprimitive varities of *n*–lattices.

SENDLEWSKI, Andrzej. Topological Duality For Nelson Algebras And Its Applications. *Bull Sect Log* 13,215–221 D 84.

The paper explains connections between the lattice of axiomatic extensions of the constructive propositional logic with strong negation and the lattice of intermediate logics. This is made in the setting of varieties of Nelson and Heyting algebras. The structure of the lattice of varieties of Nelson algebras and some of its special elements are described. These are obtained by an application of the topological duality theory for Nelson algebras stated in the paper.

SEREMET, Zofia. On Automorphisms Of Resplendent Models Of Arithmetic. *Z Math Log* 30,349–352 1984.

SERPA, Roy. Creating A Candid Corporate Culture. *J Bus Ethics* 4,425–430 O 85.

In 1982 Posner and Schmidt surveyed the values of 1400 managers. The survey revealed that honesty was one of the qualities that these managers admired most in themselves. An earlier study by Brennan and Molander indicated that managers believed that honesty in communication was their greatest ethical challenge. If honesty is a prevalent value among managers then why is honesty in communication their greatest ethical challenge? This paper presents an insight into the answer to this question and into the beliefs and norms of behavior that foster either a candid corporate culture or a culture that lacks candor.

SERRA, Antonio Truyol. Die Lehre Vom Gerechten Krieg Bei Grotius Und Leibniz Und Ihre Bedeutung Für Die Gegenwart. *Stud Leibniz* 16,60–72 1984.

Grotius et Leibniz se sont intensément préoccupés des problémes de la guerre et de la paix. Grotius en a traité d'une façon systématique dans son *De iure belli ac pacis* (1625) en s'appuyant sur la doctrine scolastique du iustum bellum. Il a peu à jouté à ce qui touch au "droit à la guerre" (ius ad bellum), mais contribué par contre au développement du "droit au cours de la guerre" (ius in bello). En ce qui concerne Leibniz, ses idées sur cette matière ont été exposées en grande partie en fonction des conflits de son temps. Il en résulte un irénisme réaliste, en conformité, par ailleurs, avec sa métaphysique, la paix ressortant esentiellement de l'ordre spirituel.

SERRANO, Jorge A. Aristoteles Como Cientifico. *Rev Filosof (Mexico)* 18,53–68 Ja–Ap 85.

SESSIONS, George and Devall, Bill. The Development Of Nature Resources And The Integrity Of Nature. *Environ Ethics* 6,293–322 Wint 84.

During the twentieth century, John Muir's ideas of "righteous management" were eclipsed by Gifford Pinchot's anthropocentric scientific management ideas concerning the conversation and development of Nature as a human resource. Ecology as a subversive science, however, has now undercut the foundations of this resource conservation and development ideology. Using the philosophical principles of deep ecology, we explore a contemporary version of Muir's "righteous management" by developing the ideas of holistic management and ecosystem rehabilitation.

SETTE, Antonio M. Partial Isomorphism Extension Method And A Representation Theorem For Post–Language. *Z Math Log* 30,289–293 1984.

SEVCIK, Oldrich. SPD And The Achievement Of The Discussion On Identity (in Czechoslovakian). *Filosof Cas* 33,97–107 1985.

SHACKLE, E M. Psychiatric Diagnosis As An Ethical Problem. *J Med Ethics* 11,132–134 S 85.

Psychiatrists diagnose mental illness in patients against a climate of opinion in which the value of diagnosis is questioned and non–medical formulations of the problems of psychiatric patients are put forward. Nevertheless the classic diagnostic terminology shows no sign of disappearing. The patients may find that a psychiatric diagnostic label is a stigma and has bad consequences. They may also object to standard methods of treatments. Given this situation the right of the patient is full explanation of the diagnosis and the rationale of the treatment offered seems to be incontrovertible. If this information were given to patients it would, in addition help them to make sense out of their often puzzling experiences and indicate that fellow sufferers existed.

SHACKNOVE, Andrew E. Who Is A Refugee? *Ethics* 95,274–284 Ja 85.

The article contends that the current definition of "refugee" as a person outside his home country fleeing political persecution is neither politically accurate nor logically correct. To the contrary, a refugee is a person whose basic needs are unprotected by the country of origin, who has no remaining recourse other than to seek international restitution of basic needs, and who are so situated that international assistance is possible.

SHAFIR, Gershon. Interpretative Sociology And The Philosophy Of Praxis: Comparing Max Weber And Antonio Gramsci. *Praxis Int* 5,63–74 Ap 85.

SHAFIR, Michael. 'Romania's Marx' And The National Question: Constantin Dobrogeanu–Gherea. *Hist Polit Thought* 5,295–314 Sum 84.

Gherea who reportedly was called by Kautsky 'Romania's Marx', is the founding–father of Romanian socialist thought. His views of the national problems of his adopted country present a blend of 'hard–core' Marxist thought with a sharp insight into local specificity. He viewed Russia as the main enemy of progress, a perception which underwent little change after 1917. His analysis of the 'Jewish question' reveals a striking similarity with 'young Marx', whose writings on the *Judenfrage* he could not possibly have been familiar with.

SHAH, K J. The Indian Tradition And Our Intellectual Task. *Indian Phil Quart* 11,473–484 O–D 84.

SHALOM, Albert. Subjectivity. *Rev Metaph* 38,227–274 D 84.

Subjectivity is usually analyzed in terms of the body/mind distinction as basic. After an indication of one consequence of this view, the paper turns to a critical analysis of Descartes as constituting the modern source of the body/mind distinction regarded as basic. The incoherence of this position is argued for at some length. It is then suggested that the main movements in modern philosophy derive from the self–contradictory position formulated by Descartes.

SHAMSI, F A. The Idea Of Motion. *Indian Phil Quart* 11,285–308 Jl 84.

It is contended that there are as many valid notions of motions as there are self–consistent hypotheses about the structure of space and time. Notions of motion entailed by various hypotheses are described. Usual arguments against these notions, including the at–at notion entailed by the atomistic hypothesis, are shown to involve the fallacy of being based on some other hypothesis that the one entailing a given notion of motion.

SHANER, David E. The Bodymind Experience In Dōgen's *Shōbōgenzō*: A Phenomenological Perspective. *Phil East West* 35,17–38 Ja 85.

An experiment using a rigorous application of Edmund Husserl's phenomenological method as a cross–cultural hermeneutic device for comparative studies East and West. The article states that the mind–body autonomy, as conceived in classical western philosophy, is a ramification of Platonic presuppositions concerning "what is mind" and "what is body". Dōgen Kigen's (1200–1253) treatise *Shōbōgenzō* is examined as an alternative perspective concerning the relation between body and mind.

SHANKER, Stuart G. Wittgenstein's Solution Of The 'Hermeneutic Problem'. *Conceptus* 18,50–61 1984.

There is a striking parallel between W V O Quine's 'indeterminacy of translation' thesis and K O Apel's 'indeterminacy of textual interpretation thesis. Both arguments are based on what is essentially the same 'sceptical dilemma'. The key to resolving these 'hermeneutic problems' is to recognize that such a 'sceptical problem' is unintelligible. This is precisely the point of Wittgenstein's discussions of rule–following. Many have misunderstood this, however, for they have misconstrued what was intended to be read as a *reductio ad absurdum* establishing the *unintelligibility* of the dilemma, as a sceptical attack on the possibility of our ever solving the problem.

SHANKS, David R. Hume On The Perception Of Causality. *Hume Stud* 11,94–108 Ap 85.

SHANKS, Stephanie L and Meile, Richard. Comment On Pommerehne Et Al, "Concordia Discors: Or: What Do Economists Think". *Theor Decis* 18,99–104 Ja 85.

In our paper, we raise theoretical and methodological questions concerning the research of Pommerehne et al., on the views of European and American economists. We conclude that a theoretical perspective which takes into account the cultural components of science will provide an explanation of the opinion and behavior of economists more in keeping with the empirical findings of Pommerehne and associates than their theory of self interest.

SHAPERE, Dudley. *Reason And The Search For Knowledge: Investigations In The Philosophy Of Science.* Boston Reidel 1984.

This book brings together many of the author's papers, including some previously unpublished. An extensive Introduction ties the author's views together. It is shown that, in the course of its development, science changes not only in its substantive beliefs about nature, but also in the methodology and criteria it employs in its investigations and in drawing conclusions from those investigations. Nevertheless, it is argued, those changes can be, and often have been, rational and objective.

SHAPERE, Dudley. "Observation & Scientific Enterprise" in *Observation, Experiment, And Hypothesis In Modern Physical Science*, Achinstein, Peter (ed), 21–44. Cambridge MIT Pr 1985.

SHAPERE, Dudley. "Progress And The Limits Of Science" in *The Good Life And Its Pursuit*, Dougherty, Jude P (ed), 268–282. NY Paragon House 1984.

SHAPERE, Dudley. "Unification And Fractionation In Science" in *The Good Life And Its Pursuit*, Dougherty, Jude P (ed), 251–266. NY Paragon House 1984.

SHAPIRO, Gary (ed) and Sica, Alan (ed). *Hermeneutics: Questions And Prospects.* Amherst Univ Of Mass Pr 1984.

This collection of original essays explores a variety of questions concerning meaning and understanding in philosophy, literature, and the social sciences. Authors include Emilio Betti, Hans–Georg Gadamer, Hubert Dreyfus, Paul de Man, Gerald Bruns, Gary Stonum, John O'Neill, Anthony Giddens, and William Dray; there are responses to some of the papers by Richard Palmer, Gayatri Spivak, Fred Dallmayr, and Rex Martin.

SHAPIRO, Gary. Nietzschean Aphorism As Art And Act. *Man World* 17,399–430 1984.

SHAPIRO, H Svi. Capitalism At Risk: The Political Economy Of The Educational Reports Of 1983. *Educ Theor* 35,57–72 Wint 85.

In this paper the author argues that the spate of 'crisis' reports on education published in 1983, represent, fundamentally, a set of alternative prescriptions for

resolving the problems of the U S economy. Going beyond the usual conservative/liberal labels the reports provide evidence of the significant conflicts within the dominant class, and between fractions of that class, over the nature and scope of the state's role in addressing the present economic crisis.

SHAPIRO, H Svi. Ideology, Class, And The Autonomy Of The Capitalist State: The Petit–Bourgeois' World View And Schooling. *Phil Soc Crit* 10,39–58 Sum 84.

The paper argues that the apparatus of the state concerned with education must be seen in terms of its important ties to *petit–bourgeois* interests and ideology. The 'world–view' of this particular social class forms the lens through which some of the most significant aspects of school culture and practice are refracted. Such a perspective draws on, and elaborates, Nicos Poulantzas' notion of the state as a complex structure of class relations.

SHAPIRO, Kenneth Joel. *Bodily Reflective Modes: A Phenomenological Method For Psychology.* Durham Duke Univ Pr 1985.

The book provides a method for the social sciences based on extensions of Merleau-Ponty's description of the lived body and, to a lesser extent, on Gendlin and Polanyi. Recent claims as to the primacy of language are countered through a critique of Levi-Strauss, Piaget, and poststructuralism. The position developed is that structure is originally known prelinguistically and is accessible through bodily and kinaesthetic modes of its apprehension, such as virtual enactment.

SHAPIRO, Stewart. On The Notion Of Effectiveness. *Hist Phil Log* 1,209–230 1980.

This paper focuses on two notions of effectiveness which are not treated in detail elsewhere. Unlike the standard computability notion, which is a property of functions themselves, both notions of effectiveness are properties of interpreted linguistic presentations of functions. It is shown that effectiveness is epistemically at least as basic as computability in the sense that decisions about computability normally involve judgments concerning effectiveness. There are many occurrences of the present notions in the writings of logicians, moreover, consideration of these notions can contribute to the clarification and, perhaps, solution of various philosophical problems, confusions and disputes.

SHARMA, Arvind. Predetermination And Free Will In The Teaching Of Ramana Maharisi (1879–1950). *Relig Stud* 20,615–626 D 84.

The teaching of Ramana Maharsi is identified as follows: Normal human life is predetermined in minute detail but volitional effort in the spiritual realm, consisting of the discovery of the true self, is always possible.

SHARMA, Ramesh Kumar. Dharmakīrti On The Existence Of Other Minds. *J Indian Phil* 13,55–72 Mr 85.

Based on Dharmakirti's text *Santanantara–siddhi* the article examines the Buddhist thinker's treatment of the problem of other minds. It gives an account of the special form the 'argument from analogy' assumes within the framework of Dharmakirti's idealism, and exposes the fallacies inherent in his standpoint. In the end, the article considers the analogical approach in its 'model' form, and finds it, because of—among other things—its epistemological character, inadequate as a possible solution.

SHARROCK, W W and Anderson, R J. Understanding Peter Winch. *Inquiry* 28,119–122 Mr 85.

Peter Winch's *The Idea of Social Science* has been the subject of repeated misunderstanding. This discussion takes one recent example and shows how Winch's argument is gravely distorted. What is at issue is not, as is usually supposed, whether we can accept or endorse another society's explanations of its activities, but whether we *have* to look for an explanatory connection between concepts and action. winch's argument is that before we can try to explain actions, we have to identify them correctly. This can only be done by seeing how they, and the concepts they are associated with, fit within a way of life. Grasping its rule–following character is understanding action. Once the difficulties in making such identifications are appreciated, we will be less inclined to accept facile explanations why people in other societies do the things they do.

SHAW, Beverley. Sameness And Equality: A Rejoinder To John Colbeck's Response To "Procrustes And Private Schooling". *J Phil Educ* 18,283–285 1984.

The article challenges Colbeck's distinction between equality and sameness, and claims that: "Our doubts about the intellectual coherence of the reasonable egalitarian's argument is that it seems to demand both that everyone is treated equally, etc., and at the same time that people are to be treated according to relevant differences".

SHAW, Margery W (ed) and Doudera, A Edward (ed). *Defining Human Life: Medical, Legal, And Ethical Implications.* Ann Arbor Aupha Pr 1983.

SHAW, William H. Marxism And Moral Objectivity. *Can J Phil* Supp 7,19–44 1981.

SHAW, William H. On The Morality Of Nuclear Deterrence. *J Applied Phil* 2,41–52 Mr 85.

Nuclear deterrence has struck many people as morally perplexing because it is a case which it appears to be right to threaten, and in a sense intend, what it would be wrong to do. Section 1 explores the assumptions that are necessary to generate this moral paradox. Some moral theorists, however, have refused to embrace this paradox, contending instead that nuclear deterrence is immoral in principle precisely because it is wrong to threaten that which it would be immoral to do. Section 2 rebuts this contention and seeks to reduce the apparent paradoxicality of nuclear deterrence to manageable proportions. This is not to maintain, though, that nuclear deterrence is morally permissible in the world in which we live; consequently, Section 3 surveys some of the factors relevant to a moral assessment of the legitimacy of the actual practice of nuclear deterrence.

SHEA, Joseph. Judgment And Perception In *Theaetetus* 184–186. *J Hist Phil* 23,1–14 Ja 85.

In *Theaetetus* 184b–186e, Plato argues that perception cannot be knowledge because perception cannot grasp common objects such as being, and so cannot involve judgment. Some commentators are puzzled about what perception without judgment could be; I reject their view that Plato distinguishes two sorts of judgment and truth, and argue that perception cannot make any judgment, since only the mind "by itself" can judge. I relate Plato's distinction between perceiving with and by means of an organ to his view that perception and judgment are accomplished by one mind.

SHEA, Michael. "When Pharmacist And Physician Disagree" in *Difficult Decisions In Medical Ethics*, Ganos, Doreen L (ed), 203–210. NY Liss 1983.

SHEA, William M. *The Naturalists And The Supernatural: Studies In Horizon And An American Philosophy Of Religion.* Macon Mercer Univ Pr 1984.

SHEA, William R. Descartes: Methodological Ideal And Actual Procedure. *Phil Natur* 21,577–589 1984.

I argue that Aristotle developed the syllogistic theory of *Prior Analytics I* primarily in order to resolve problems concerning demonstrative sciences. In effect, he undertook to resolve questions about proofs by making deductions themselves the objects of study, in a manner not unlike Hilbert's "proof theory". Both technical and textual arguments for this claim are adduced, and I present a metatheorem about syllogistically–based systems which Aristotle believes he can prove.

SHEARD, Michael. Co–Critical Points Of Elementary Embeddings. *J Sym Log* 50,220–226 Mr 85.

SHEEHAN, Thomas. Pierre Rousselot And The Dynamism Of Human Spirit. *Gregorianum* 66,241–267 1985.

Pierre Rousselot (1878–1915) was one of the pioneering spirits of what has come to be known as "Transcendental Thomism." The essay studies (1) Rousselot's method of "retrieval," (2) his theory of normative cognition, and (3) his work on ontological movement and human cognition. The essay aims at showing how Rousselot argued for the unity of onto–theology on the basis of the proleptic unity of human being.

SHEKHAWAT, Virendra. Some Epistemological Trends In Philosophy Of Science. *Diogenes* 128,77–102 Wint 84.

SHELAH, Saharon and Abraham, U and Rubin, M. On The Consistency Of Some Partition Theorems For Continuous Colorings, And The Structure Of Dense Real Order Types. *Annals Pure Applied Log* 29,123–206 S 85.

SHELAH, Saharon and Goldfarb, Warren D and Gurevich, Yuri. A Decidable Subclass Of The Minimal Gödel Class With Identity. *J Sym Log* 49,1253–1261 D 84.

SHELAH, Saharon and Woodin, Hugh. Forcing The Failure Of CH By Adding A Real. *J Sym Log* 49,1185–1189 D 84.

SHELAH, Saharon. Diamonds, Uniformization. *J Sym Log* 49,1022–1033 D 84.

SHELAH, Saharon. Monadic Logic And Löwenheim Numbers. *Annals Pure Applied Log* 28,203–216 Mr 85.

SHELAH, Saharon. More On Proper Forcing. *J Sym Log* 49,1034–1038 D 84.

SHELAH, Saharon. More On The Weak Diamond. *Annals Pure Applied Log* 28,315–318 My 85.

SHELAH, S and Kaufman, Matt. A Nonconservativity Result On Global Choice. *Annals Pure Applied Log* 27,209–214 N 84.

SHELAH, S and Sageev, G. On The Structure Of Ext(*A*, **z**) In ZFC+. *J Sym Log* 50,302–315 Je 85.

SHELAH, Sharon and Bonnet, Robert. Narrow Boolean Algebras. *Annals Pure Applied Log* 28,1–12 Ja 85.

SHELLEY, Fred M. Notes On Ostrogorski's Paradox. *Theor Decis* 17,267–274 N 84.

When voters must choose between two parties holding contrasting positions on a series of issues, one party can win an election by majority rule even if its opponents' positions on every issue are preferred by a majority of the voters. This possibility has been termed Ostrogorski's Paradox (Rae and Daudt, 1976; Daudt, 1977; Daudt and Rae, 1978). An example, borrowed from Rae and Daudt (1976), illustrates the paradox (Table 1). In the example, four groups of voters have different sets of positions on three salient issues. Two parties, X and Y, are competing for votes; party X favors position P on each issue, while party Y favors position Q in each case. It is evident that although a majority of the voters prefer position Q in each case, those in groups 1, 2, and 3 will support Party X, which will consequently command a majority of the votes.

SHELP, Earl E. The Experience Of Illness: Integrating Metaphors And The Transcendence Of Illness. *J Med Phil* 9,253–256 Ag 84.

This paper comments on the experience of illness, noting that regardless of the manner in which illness is explained or conceptualized, there is a common necessity of all who are ill to come to terms with human vulnerability and finitude.

SHENFIELD, Arthur. "The Profits Of Freedom: Investing In The Defense Of Business" in *On Freedom*, Howard, John A (ed), 59–78. Greenwich Devin–Adair 1984.

SHENOY, Prakash P and Martin, Rex. Two Interpretations Of The Difference Principle In Rawls's Theory Of Justice. *Theoria* 49,113–141 1983.

This paper examines in detail Rawls' difference principle. An alternative formulation of the difference principle in terms of pareto efficiency and egalitarianism, with the former having lexical priority over the latter, is provided. Egalitarianism is defined as minimizing the difference between the expectations of the most favored and the least advantaged representative persons. This restatement is formally shown to be equivalent to the Rawlsian maximin version. Arguments for and advantages of the reformulation are given.

SHEPARD, Philip T. Moral Conflict In Agriculture: Conquest Or Moral Coevolution? *Agr Human Values* 1,17–25 Fall 84.

Examines conditions for depolarizing agricultural controversy and argues against the views that agricultural science is value neutral and that only one moral standpoint on agriculture is ultimately defensible. A systematic view of values is presented to support resolving controversy through moral coevolution rather than conquest. To find common ground, study is needed of culturally embedded images that shape moral interpretation.

SHER, George. "The US Bishops' Position On Nuclear Deterrence: A Moral Assessment" in *The Security Gamble*, Mac Lean, Douglas (ed), 72–81. Totowa Rowman & Allanheld 1984.

SHERMAN, Ann L. Genderism And The Reconstruction Of Philosophy Of Education. *Educ Theor* 34,321–326 Fall 84.

SHERMAN, Ann L. Response To Macmillan's "Love And Logic In 1984". *Proc Phil Educ* 40,21–26 1984.

SHEWMON, D Alan. The Metaphysics Of Brain Death, Persistent Vegetative State And Dementia. *Thomist* 49,24–80 Ja 85.

Three neurologic conditions are analyzed in terms of modern medicine and Aristotelian–Thomistic philosophy. The minimum part of the body necessary for human life is shown to be the organ of the *sensus communis*, which corresponds to what modern neuroanatomy knows as the "tertiary association areas" of the cerebral cortex. Therefore, brain death, persistent vegetative state, and severe dementia are valid manifestations of personal death. Theoretical and practical consequences are discussed.

SHIDELER, Emerson W. The Place Of Faith In A World Of Fact. *Zygon* 20,243–263 S 85.

The relation of religion and science is presented in terms of the interrelationship of domains generated within a reflexive real world concept by status assignment. The domain of religion is articulated by the concept of ultimacy, totality, and eternity, which are boundary conditions on all status assignments. The domain of science is a status assignment, that of determining the facts and constraints of the real world, and is articulated by the concepts of empiricism, objectivity, and order. The interrelationship of domain is illustrated by examining the concepts of order, disorder, entropy, evil, freedom, creation, and resurrection.

SHIEBER, Stuart M. Evidence Against The Context–Freeness Of Natural Language. *Ling Phil* 8,333–344 Ag 85.

This paper offers evidence for the weak non–context–freeness of natural language. Using data collected from native Swiss–German speakers, we provide a formal proof of the weak non–context–freeness of Swiss German. In doing so, we make as few (and as uncontroversial) linguistic assumptions as possible—in particular, we make no assumptions about the structure or semantics of Swiss German. We also present a few putative counterarguments and show that they are not seriously detrimental to our claim.

SHIELDS, George W. Is The Past Finite: On Craig's Kalām Argument. *Process Stud* 14,31–40 Spr 84.

In this essay, it is argued that William Craig makes a cogent case for the finitude of the past, implicating a Creator *ex nihilo*. However, his view that the argument is compatible with an absolute theory of time presents the possibility that the Creator has existed throughout an eternal duration of time. This entails the instantiation of an actual infinite process, and thus undermines any confidence that infinitistic process theists are incorrect. Moreover, it is argued that the absolute theory *is* correct in holding that time is a limitless constant.

SHIMONY, Abner. The Status Of The Principle Of Maximum Entropy. *Synthese* 63,35–54 Ap 85.

Jayne's Principle of Maximum Entropy calculates epistemic probabilities by maximizing the information theoretical information subject to known constraints. The epistemological status of the Principle is reviewed in the light of anomalies demonstrated by Freedman, Dias, and Shimony, and a new anomaly which does not depend upon an assumption of complete additivity, is demonstrated. It is concluded that the Principle is not valid universally, but only where all allowable state descriptions have equal prior probabilities.

SHINER, Roger A. Getting To Know You. *Phil Lit* 19,80–94 Ap 85.

Using as a starting point some of Cavell's interpretive ideas in *Pursuits of Happiness*, I present the genre of remarriage as a figure for the profoundest relationships of epistemology and metaphysics – the relationship of the knower to the world which is known, and the relationship of the individual to other individuals with whom society is shared. Divorce and remarriage are figures for acknowledgment and avoidance as philosophical concepts.

SHINER, Roger. "From Epistemology To Romance Via Wisdom" in *Philosophy And Life: Essays On John Wisdom*, Dilman, Ilham (ed), 291–316. Boston Nijhoff 1984.

SHINODA, Juichi. "Sections And Envelopes Of Type 2 Objects" in *Lecture Notes In Mathematics*, Muller, G H And Others (ed), 175–188. NY Springer 1981.

SHIRLEY, Edward S. A Defense Of Kant's Refutation Of Descartes. *Phil Topics* 13,185–194 Spr 85.

SHIRLEY, Edward S. The Mapping Argument And Descartes' Deceitful Demon. *Phil Topics* 13,53–60 Spr 85.

SHKLAR, Judith N. Nineteen Eighty–Four: Should Political Theory Care? *Polit Theory* 13,5–18 F 85.

SHOAF, Richard. Science, Sect, And Uncertainty In Voltaire's "dictionnaire Philosophique". *J Hist Ideas* 46,121–126 Ja–Mr 85.

SHORE, Richard A and Jockusch Jr, Carl G. Pseudo–Jump Operators: II, Transfinite Iterations, Hierarchies And Minimal Covers. *J Sym Log* 49,1205–1236 D 84.

Author Index with Abstracts 405 **Siitonen, Arto**

SHORTER, J M. The Reality Of Time. *Philosophia (Israel)* 14,321–340 D 84.

The purpose of this article is to achieve a correct understanding of McTaggart's argument for the unreality of change and time. Properly understood this argument is entirely successful if its principal premise, namely that B–relations are permanent, is accepted. It is then argued that this commonly accepted premise is false, owing its plausibility largely to a failure to distinguish between the permanence of a truth and the permanence of the corresponding state of affairs.

SHOTTER, Edward. Self Help In Medical Ethics. *J Med Ethics* 11,32–34 Mr 85.

The paper traces the development of programs of lectures and symposia in most British medical schools, which have developed into a postgraduate program of research and publication. It is asserted that a morally neutral approach is a necessary prerequisite for wide multidisciplinary involvement, as is a high level of student participation in identifying topics for discussion. Alternative possibilities for formal teaching are discussed and pitfalls highlighted.

SHRADER– FRECHETTE, K S. *Science Policy, Ethics, And Economic Methodology.* Boston Reidel 1984.

This book is a philosophical analysis of the methodological, epistemological, and ethical problems facing those who use classical economic methods to help formulate public policy regarding science and technology. The author makes incisive criticisms of existing economic methods, and uses the tools of analytic philosophy to show the importance of methodological evaluation for technology assessment. The book's final two chapters outline strategies for improving economic methods.

SHRIVER, Donald W and Knox, E Richard. Taxation In The History Of Protestant Ethics. *J Relig Ethics* 13,134–160 Spr 85.

Taxation and government policy related to it have only episodic appearance in classical Protestant ethical sources. Of the early sixteenth century reformers, Luther gave most attention to the subject, justifying taxation in general as necessary for the just service of the government to the public good and calling the princes to spend tax monies for that good rather than their own luxury. Calvin made much the same claims but called more clearly for official church scrutiny of all government than did Luther. Two centuries later John Wesley criticized English tax policy, appealing to standards of economic efficiency and compassion for the poor with little reference overtly to theology. The churches of colonial and post–revolutionary America developed no systematic, theologically rooted rationale for taxation ethics, either; but official Protestant denominational concern for such ethics has grown measurably in the most recent fifteen years. After a survey of these recent national church statements, and on the basis of them and the slender Protestant heritage on this issue, we by posing four questions which we see as worthy of much serious thinking by contemporary American Protestant ethicists.

SHULMAN, Alix Kates (ed). *Red Emma Speaks.* NY Schocken Books 1983.

SHULMAN, Alix Kates (ed). *Red Emma Speaks: An Emma Goldman Reader.* NY Schocken Books 1983.

With an underlying socialist theme, the essays in the book concern atheism, communism, political shortcoming in both the East and West, feminist issues, and minority problems. (staff)

SHUSTERMAN, Richard. Aesthetic Censorship: Censoring Art For Art's Sake. *J Aes Art Crit* 43,171–180 Wint 84.

Censorship has always been regarded as essentially and necessarily inimical and harmful to art, and antithetical to aesthetic autonomy and interests. My paper challenges this still popular dogma which stems from an oversimplified notion of censorship and its possible forms and motives. The concept of censorship not only allows the possibility of censoring works of art (or parts thereof) on *aesthetic* grounds, i.E., because they are aesthetically objectionable, but such aesthetic censorship would most likely promote superior art and appreciation.

SHUTTE, Augustine. The Refutation Of Determinism. *Philosophy* 59,481–490 O 84.

The present article examines C S Lewis' famous argument against determinism presented to the Oxford Socratic Society in 1947, together with the youthful G E M Anscombe's attempted rebuttal to it. E L Mascall appears on the side of Lewis and his intervention is judged decisive. Finally, bernard Lonergan is brought in to show the metaphysical consequences of Lewis's position: the impossibility of a thoroughgoing materialism. (edited)

SHWAYDER, D S. Hume Was Right, Almost; And Where He Wasn't, Kant Was. *Midwest Stud Phil* 9,135–150 1984.

Hume correctly held that the assignment of phenomena as causes always involves an explanatory transition of belief. Kant was also right in holding that our sense that there is a necessary connection between the cause and effect traces to purely phenomenal factors to identify and distinctness. I argue for the Humean conclusion from the observation that proximate mechanical causes are always identical with their proximate effects. I argue for the Kantian conclusion from observations on how the tracing of causes involves the identification of sensible things.

SIBLEY, F N. Originality And Value. *Brit J Aes* 25,169–184 Spr 85.

There are many disputes about the value of originality in art. These may arise largely because 'original' is not used univocally. Several common uses are distinguished and illustrated. Whether originality is relevant to value depends on the sense of 'original', on whether or not our concern is with new values, and on whether intrinsic value or value in context is at issue.

SICA, Alan (ed) and Shapiro, Gary (ed). *Hermeneutics: Questions And Prospects.* Amherst Univ Of Mass Pr 1984.

This collection of original essays explores a variety of questions concerning meaning and understanding in philosophy, literature, and the social sciences. Authors include Emilio Betti, Hans–Georg Gadamer, Hubert Dreyfus, Paul de Man, Gerald Bruns, Gary Stonum, John O'Neill, Anthony Giddens, and William Dray; there are responses to some of the papers by Richard Palmer, Gayatri Spivak, Fred Dallmayr, and Rex Martin.

SIDER, Roger C and Clements, Colleen D. Patients' Ethical Obligation For Their Health. *J Med Ethics* 10,138–142 S 84.

A naturalistic model for medical ethics is proposed which builds upon biological and medical values. This perspective clarifies ethical obligations to ourselves and to others for life and health. It provides a normative framework for the doctor–patient relationship within which to formulate medical advice and by which to evaluate patient choice. (edited)

SIDERITS, Mark. Word Meaning, Sentence Menaing And Apoha. *J Indian Phil* 13,133–152 Je 85.

I show that the Buddhist philosophers Santaraksita and Kamalasila subscribed to the Indian equivalent of the context principle, according to which a word has meaning only in the context of a sentence. I then discuss the manner in which they used the Buddhist exclusion (apoha) theory of meaning to answer two major objections to that account of word meaning: the "hermeneutic circle" objection, and the objection that this account cannot explain our ability to understand novel sentences.

SIDORSKY, David. Contemporary Reinterpretations Of The Concept Of Human Rights (in Hebrew) . *Iyyun* 33,219–234 Ja–Ap 84.

SIEG, Wilfried. Foundations For Analysis And Proof Theory. *Synthese* 60,159–200 Ag 84.

The main goal of the paper is to present material necessary for informed philosophical reflections on the foundations of analysis. Thus, a sketch of (19th and early 20th century) investigations concerning the foundations of analysis is given. Thus a generalized form of Hilbert's program and proof–theoretic work in its pursuit are described. Finally, the significance of such work for reflections on mathematics is discussed.

SIEG, Wilfried. Fragments Of Arithmetic. *Annals Pure Applied Log* 28,33–72 Ja 85.

We establish by elementary proof–theoretic means the conservativeness of two subsystems of analysis over primitive recursive arithmetic. The one subsystem was introduced by Friedman (6), the other is a strengthened version of a theory of Minc (14); each has been shown to be of considerable interest for both mathematical practice and metamathematical investigations. The foundational significance of such conservation results is clear; they provide a direct finitist justification of the part of mathematical practice formalizable in these subsystems. The results are generalized to relate a hierarchy of subsystems, all contained in the theory of arithmetic properties, to a corresponding hierarchy of fragments of arithmetic. The proof theoretic tools employed there are used to re–establish in a uniform, elementary way relationships between various fragments of arithmetic due to Parsons, Paris and Kirby, and Friedman.

SIEGEL, Armand. "The Misplaced Concreton" in *Methodology, Metaphysics And The History Of Science*, Cohen, Robert S (ed), 247–262. Boston Reidel 1984.

SIEGEL, Harvey. Empirical Psychology, Naturalized Epistemology, And First Philosophy. *Phil Sci* 51,667–676 D 84.

In his 1983 article, Paul A Roth defends the Quinean project of naturalized epistemology from the criticism presented in my 1980 article. In this note I would like to respond to Roth's effort. I will argue that, while helpful in advancing and clarifying the issues, Roth's defense of naturalized epistemology does not succeed. The primary topic to be clarified is Quine's "no first philosophy" doctrine; but I will address myself to other points as well.

SIEGEL, Harvey. Relativism, Realism, And Rightness: Notes On Goodmanian Worldmaking. *J Thought* 19,16–35 Wint 84.

This paper examines Nelson Goodman's recent articulation of "radical relativism" and "irrealism" in his *Ways of Worldmaking*. It is argued that his relativism is ambiguous as between strong and weak versions, that the stong version is provocative but false, and that the weak version is true but more pluralistic than relativistic. It is also argued that "irrealism" faces major difficulties.

SIEGEL, Harvey. Tarski A Relativist? *Analysis* 45,75–76 Mr 85.

In a previous issue of this journal, Professor Richard Jennings argues that Tarski's theory lends support, contra Popper, to a non–realistic relativism. In this response, I contend that Tarski's work is neutral as between Popperian realism and Jennings' relativism.

SIEGHART, Paul. Professions As The Conscience Of Society. *J Med Ethics* 11,117–122 S 85.

Ethics is no less of a science than any other. It has its roots in conflicts of interest between human beings, and in their conflicting urges to behave either selfishly or altruistically. Resolving such conflicts leads to the specifications of rules of conduct, often expressed in terms of rights and duties. In the special case of professional ethics, the paramount rule of conduct is atruism in the service of a 'noble' cause, and this distinguishes true professions from other trades or occupations.

SIEGLER, Mark and Childress, James F. Should Age Be A Criterion In Health Care? *Hastings Center Rep* 14,24–31 O 84.

SIEMEK, Marek. Historical Materialism As The Philosophy Of Marxism (II). *Dialec Hum* 10,35–44 Sum 83.

SIEP, Ludwig. Person And Law In Kant And Hegel. *Grad Fac Phil J* 10,63–88 Spr 84.

The first part of the paper discusses Kant's concept of a person with special emphasis on the First Critique and the Metaphysical Elements of Justice. It is shown that for Kant a person is essentially an author or co–author of laws. The second part focusses on Hegel's Logic and Philosophy of Right. The differences between Kant's and Hegel's concepts of law and state are traced back to their different concepts of a person.

SIEWIERSKI, Jacenty. Values And Socialism: An Axiological Approach To Marx's Socialism. *Dialec Hum* 10,57–72 Sum 83.

SIITONEN, Arto. *Tractatus*, Schön Und Gut. *Grazer Phil Stud* 21,65–88 1984.

SIITONEN, Arto. Demarcation Of Science From The Point Of View Of Problems And Problem–Stating. *Phil Natur* 21,339–353 1984.

In demarcating science from pseudo–science and non–science, traditional suggestions make verifiability or falsifiability the decisive criteria. It is in the context of questioning and problem–stating that the activities of verifying and falsifying really receive their significance. The purpose of the work is to demarcate science by proposing criteria for scientific problem–stating. Logic of discovery can supply the criteria (cf. bolzano, cf. Also traditional problem lists).

SIKIC, Z. Multiple Forms Of Gentzen's Rules And Some Intermediate Forms. *Z Math Log* 30,335–338 1984.

The author introduced an intermediate logic, called L_1, extending the intuitionistic logic with a logical principle which suffices to prove Gödel's completeness theorem. L_1 is compared with the well–known intermediate logic CD (called L_2 in the paper) which, apart from intuitionistic principles, admits the multiple version of quantifier introduction. It is proved that CD extends L_1. Moreover, it is proved that L_1 is the logic which, apart from intuitionistic principles, admits the multiple version of quantifier introduction for decidable predicates.

SILVA, M Augusto Ferreira Da. Sentido E Intersubjectividade No Pensamento De E Levinas. *Rev Port Filosof* 40,264–273 Jl–S 84.

Where to implant the sense and how comes the sense to the human being apart from the system? The sense implants in the Other, in the Infinity, which reacts to the idea of infinity and is revealed to the "epiphany of the face" of the other human being. The encounter with the other emerges as the place where the Infinity reacts to as a basis of the sense, and the intersubjectivity, which is responsibility, it appears as the place of realization and the sense direction.

SILVEIRA, Lauro F B. Peircean Semiotics And Poetic Production (in Portuguese). *Trans/Form/Acao* 6,13–24 1983.

Among the several semiotics and semiologies existing nowdays, there are two that must be distinguished: that of saussurean origin and that of peircean origin. The first finds its mode of proceeding and the general features of sign in the science of linguistics. The other belongs to the critical philosophic tradition. For the intelligence that can learn with the experience, the temporal and historic dimension is essential. The peircean sign supposes the relations of an irreversible time. To the present production of sign should be related the poetic function, which is essential to life of all intelligence. The scientific hypothesis, the social revolutions in their originary moment and the artistic production make new signs, draw new objects and open sets of possibilities for the conduct in the future.

SILVER, Charles. Negative Positivism And The Hard Facts Of Life. *Monist* 68,347–363 Jl 85.

SILVER, Maury and Sabini, John. Critical Thinking And Obedience To Authority. *Nat Forum* 65,13–17 Wint 85.

SILVER, Maury and Sabini, John. On The Captivity Of The Will: Sympathy, Caring, And A Moral Sense Of The Human. *J Theor Soc Behav* 15,23–37 Mr 85.

We are concerned in this paper with the question of what more there is to human nature than cognition, with what it is to be a person (or animal) in the sense of something that would justify our sympathy. We examine pain, emotion, and the abrogation of values as sources of our sympathy for one another. We further argue that our sympathy over each of these unfortunate events is connected with our sense that they are beyond a person's (or an animal's) will. Computers, we suggest, ought not to engage our sympathy not because of their limited cognitive capacity, and not because they lack intent, but because their wills are too free.

SILVERMAN, Hugh J. The Limits Of Logocentrism (On The Way To Grammatology). *Man World* 17,347–360 1984.

SILVERS, Anita. Reflections Of The Mutual Benefits Of Philosophical And Global Education. *Teach Phil* 8,111–120 Ap 85.

SIMCHONI, Avital. British Idealism: Its Political And Social Thought. *Bull Hegel Soc Gt Brit* 3,16–31 Spr/Sum 81.

SIMMONDS, N E. *The Decline Of Juridical Reason: Doctrine And Theory In The Legal Order.* Dover Manchester Univ Pr 1985.

The book describes a classical form of legal thought that exerted a profound influence on modern law and legal ideas. This classical doctrine legal science was essentially linked to the existence of a market society. The problems of modern legal theory result from the emergence of a regulatory state incompatible with classical legal thought.

SIMMONS, Ernest L. Mystical Consciousness In A Process Perspective. *Process Stud* 14,1–10 Spr 84.

SIMON– SCHAEFFER, R. "Innovation Und Kanonbildung Oder Das Ende Der Modernen Kunst" in *Asthetische Er Fahrung Und Das Wesen Der Kunst*, Holzhey, Helmut, 42–57. Bern Haupt 1984.

SIMON, Michael A. Insanity And Criminality. *Int J Applied Phil* 2,43–56 Spr 85.

When mental illness exempts those who commit violent anti–social acts from criminal liability, it is because of a disqualifying incapacity rather than an excusing condition. Exclusion of such offenders from the community is justified not as punishment but as a form of banishment.

SIMON, R and Liebscher, Heinz. Einen Neuen Schwerpunkt In Der Zusammenarbeit Mit Naturwissenschaftlern—Brauchen Wir Ihn Wirklich? *Deut Z Phil* 32,1020–1022 1984.

SIMON, Robert L. *Sports And Social Values.* Englewood Cliffs Prentice–Hall 1985.

SIMON, Robert L. Good Competition And Drug–Enhanced Performance. *J Phil Sport* 11,6–13 1984.

SIMON, Robert L. Response To Brown And Fraleigh. *J Phil Sport* 11,30–32 1984.

SIMON, Rudiger. Chemie Und Dialektik. *Deut Z Phil* 23,980–984 1975.

SIMONETTI, Iside. Significato E Attualità Dell'Epistemologia Genetica Di Jean Piaget. *Ann Fac Lett Filosof* 25 & 26,553–574 1982–83.

SIMONS, Martin. Learning To Experience. *Educ Phil Theor* 17,1–9 My 85.

That people 'learn from experience' is a commonplace. The paper argues that human experience is constructed before anything can be learned from it. Finding out how experience may be made from the available sensory impulses is a learning process which is of a pragmatic kind. That a conceptual scheme permits experience to be made is a justification for using that scheme but does not proscribe alternative schemata which permit different kinds of experience to be constructed.

SIMONS, Peter M. A Brentanian Basis For Leśniewskian Logic. *Log Anal* 27,297–308 S 84.

Brentano's analysis of categorical propositions is defended against certain objections. It is shown (a) how Brentano's account may be naturally expressed in the language of Lesniewski's Ontology, (b) that Ontology may be axiomatised taking as primitive Brentano's concepts of existence and nominal conjunction, (c) that if extensionality is assumed, existence may further be defined in terms of nominal conjunction and the remaining logical constants.

SIMONS, Peter M. Computermusik Und Die Identität Des Musikwerks. *Conceptus* 19,69–75 1985.

The introduction of computers into the process of musical composition markedly disturbs the relationships which normally obtain between composer, work, performances and sound complexes. The shift gives rise to a number of philosophical problems with far–reaching consequences, which are briefly discussed here.

SIMONUTTI, Luisa. Considerazioni Su Power E Liberty Nel "Saggio Sull'Intelletto Umano" Secondo Un Manoscritto Di Coste. *G Crit Filosof Ital* 63,179–199 My–Ag 84.

SIMPSON, Paul. Lyons And Tigers. *Analysis* 45,169–171 Je 85.

How might one enumerate elements, such as stripes, presented within a visual image? In the ideal case the image possesses suitably high 'quality' and the subject is skilled in estimating quantities of items on the basis of holistic percepts. Sequential counting of parts, as proposed by William Lyons, in 'The Tiger and his Stripes' (*Analysis* 44.2, March 1984), is rejected as unsuited to the task.

SIMPSON, Peter. The Nature And Origin Of Ideas: The Controversy Over Innate Ideas Reconsidered. *Int Phil Quart* 25,15–30 Mr 85.

Locke and Descartes only disagree about innate knowledge because they both accept the principle that knowledge that comes through the senses is sensible knowledge or reducible to such knowledge. Other philosophers from Berkeley to Wittgenstein share the same principle. This principle is rejected by Aristotle and the Aristotelian tradition; consequently Aristotle is able to give a more convincing account of knowledge and its acquisition. A summary of this account is given and defended.

SIMPSON, S G and Smith, R L and Friedman, Harvey M. Addendum To "Countable Algebra And Set Existence Axioms". *Annals Pure Applied Log* 28,319–320 My 85.

SIMPSON, Stephen. Which Set Existence Axioms Are Needed To Prove The Cauchy/Peano Theorem For Ordinary Differential Equations? *J Sym Log* 49,783–802 S 84.

We study the question of which set existence axioms (formulated in the language of second order arithmetic) are needed to prove the local existence theorem for ordinary differential equations. We show that the system WKL_0 (weak Koenig's lemma with restricted induction) is both necessary and sufficient. This is interesting because WKL_0 has the same logical strength as primitive recursive arithmetic. Thus we have a positive contribution toward Hilbert's program of reducing all of mathematics to finitistic reasoning.

SIMUNEK, Eugen. Some Introductory Criteria Of Contemporary Art Creation (in Czechoslovakian). *Estetika* 21,199–209 1984.

SINA, Mario. Con Jean Le Clerc Alla Scuola Cartesiana. *Riv Filosof Neo–Scolas* 76,3–14 Ja–Mr 84.

SINGER, Beth J. Art, Poetry, And The Sense Of Prevalence: Some Implications Of Buchler's Theory Of Poetry. *Int Phil Quart* 24,267–282 S 84.

SINGER, Irving. *The Nature Of Love: Courtly And Romantic.* Chicago Univ Of Chicago Pr 1984.

This sequel to Irving Singer's *The Nature of Love: Plato to Luther* (second edition, University of Chicago Press, 1984) deals with philosophy and literature from the twelfth through the nineteenth century. It analyzes ideas about love in various philosophers, including Abelard, Andreas Capellanus, Ficino, Pico, Montaigne, Descartes, Spinoza, Rousseau, Hume, Kant, Schlegel, Hegel, and Schopenhaurer. Singer delineates and seeks to harmonize two traditions of thought about human affect—the "idealist" and the "realist".

SINGER, Irving. *The Nature Of Love: Plato To Luther*, Second Edition. Chicago Univ Of Chicago Pr 1984.

In Part I of this volume, Singer distinguishes between "appraisal" and "bestowal" as elements in the concept of love. He also examines love as idealization in Freud and Santayana, and offers his own theory of idealization. Part II studies Plato's philosophy of love, Aristotle on friendship, merging in Plotinus, and Ovid and Lucretius on sex. Part III analyzes medieval concepts in terms of humanistic as well as theological problems. (Revision of 1966 first edition).

SINGER, Marcus G. "Gewirth's Ethical Monism" in *Gewirth's Ethical Rationalism*, Regis Jr, Edward (ed), 23–38. Chicago Univ Of Chicago Pr 1984.

SINGER, Marcus G. Consequences, Desirability, And The Moral Fanaticism Argument. *Phil Stud* 46,227–238 S 84.

A reply to Timmons' "Act Utilitarianism and the Moral Fanaticism Argument," which provoked further reconsideration of some theses of generalization in ethics. In particular, the idea that the principle of utility is equivalent to the conjunction of the principle of consequences and its obverse is shown to be mistaken; it appears that the principle of consequences and its positive counterpart are not mere analogues of each other, since the positive version implies the negative; and the idea that this principle can be applied independently of moral judgment gets some shaking up.

SINGER, Marcus G. Moral Issues And Social Problems: The Moral Relevance Of Moral Philosophy. *Philosophy* 60,5–26 Ja 85.

SINGER, Marcus G. On Gewirth's Derivation Of The Principle Of Generic Consistency. *Ethics* 95,297–301 Ja 85.

Discussion of Gewirth's purported derivation of the moral from the prudential. It is argued that this is successful, but it uses the Generalization Principle as a moral and not merely as a logical principle and derives from other not merely prudential considerations. Gewirth's claim that there are prudential rights analogous to moral rights is rejected. This paper is a successor of "Gewirth's Ethical Monism" in *Gewirth's Ethical Rationalism* (1984) and a predecessor of "Universalizability and the Generalization Principle", forthcoming in *Universality and Morality*, and should be interpreted in that setting.

SINGH, Balbir. *Hindu Ethics*. Atlantic Highlands Humanities Pr 1984.

The book claims to be an exposition of the concept of good as encountered in the Hindu texts and treatises. Although the good is taken to consist in the self's realizing its essential selfhood, differences arose in regard to the interpretation of the concept of self. Also, while in the earlier phase the self is more a metaphysical than an ethical agent, in the later phase it is almost the reverse. Yet, there is continuity so far as the ultimate goal is concerned.

SINGLETARY, W E and Hughes, Charles E. Triadic Partial Implicational Propositional Calculi. *Z Math Log* 21,21–28 1975.

SINHA, Debabrata. Human Embodiment: The Theme And The Encounter In Vedāntic Phenomenology. *Phil East West* 35,239–248 Jl 85.

The question of *lived* body in the context of human subjectivity posed in terms of the Vedantic model of Self (*Ātman*) qua pure consciousness. The primacy of bodily subjectivity, cutting across body–mind dualism, focuses on the *phenomenon* of embodiment, starting with the natural bodily–identified consciousness of *jīve*. Phenomenological parallels in analysis of stadia of embodiment. Ambiguous role of body as 'natural subject' between mundaneity and extramundane consciousness in an integral conception of man under focus of *Ātman*.

SINNOTT- ARMSTRONG, Walter. 'Ought To Have' And 'Could Have'. *Analysis* 45,44–48 Ja 85.

If sentences with one operator semantically imply sentences with another operator, then the implication must hold even when the sentences within the scope of the operators are about the past. However, the author argues that a sentence where 'ought' operates on a past tense sentence does not imply the corresponding sentence where 'can' operates on the same past tense sentence. Thus, 'ought' does not semantically 'can'.

SINNOTT- ARMSTRONG, Walter. A Solution To Forrester's Paradox Of Gentle Murder. *J Phil* 82,162–168 Mr 85.

Forrester recently presented a new paradox that, even if murders occur, it seems obligatory for the murders to be gentle, but, on standard deontic logic, if it is obligatory to murder gently, it is obligatory to murder, and that seems wrong. The present article argues that Forrester's paradox depends on a scope confusion that can be avoided only by analyzing the logical form of the action sentences inside the scope of the deontic operator.

SIRCELLO, Guy. The Poetry Of Theory: Reflections On *After The New Criticism*. *J Aes Art Crit* 42,387–396 Sum 84.

SIVARAMAN, S K. The Hindu Vision And World Problems. *J Dharma* 10,34–41 Ja–Mr 85.

SIVIN, Nathan. "Reflections On 'Nature On Trial'" in *Methodology, Metaphysics And The History Of Science*, Cohen, Robert S (ed), 323–330. Boston Reidel 1984.

SKIDMORE, Arthur. Cognitive Science And The Semantics Of Natural Language. *Phil Topics* 13,223–230 Spr 85.

SKIEBE, Kurt. Überlegungen Zur Gesetzesproblematik In Der Biologie. *Deut Z Phil* 23,946–954 1975.

SKILLEN, Anthony. Mind And Matter: A Problem That Refuses Dissolution. *Mind* 93,514–526 O 84.

An inconsistent triad is set out: (i) that physical events are physically caused (ii) that mental events cause physical changes, and (iii) that mental events are not physical. After rejection of various views, especially Ryle's, Melden's, Putnam's and Davidson's, a 'conceptual' form of Identity Theory is offered.

SKILLEN, Anthony. Rousseau On The Fall Of Social Man. *Philosophy* 60,105–122 Ja 85.

Most commentators on Rousseau's 'Discourse on the Origin of Inequality' emphasize the technological, economic, property–relations aspect of his account. I argue that Rousseau's view is that the 'rage for distinction' is intrinsic to the social ego. I take up and develop the idea that the pathology of erotic love, with its competitive self–deceptions is at the heart of Rousseau's dynamic of society's wicked horrors.

SKILLEN, Anthony. Welfare State Versus Welfare Society? *J Applied Phil* 2,3–18 Mr 85.

The welfare state is not just a system of personal insurance but an expression of community, of concern for our fellows. It places some things beyond the question of purchasing power. Yet its structures are often criticized as subverting personal and social cares and responsibilities. Arguably there is a 'dialectic of self–destruction' here, a tendency for the institution to undermine its own support. At the same time this problem is inherent in the capitalist state itself, as is brought out by a study of the philosophers of 'civil society' from Manderville to Green. It is schematically argued that the welfare state needs reconstructing as an articulation rather than a substitute for 'community'. Implications for the class, gender and age structures of society are sketched.

SKILLEN, Anthony. Workers' Interest And The Proletarian Ethic: Conflicting Strains In Marxian Anti–Moralism. *Can J Phil* Supp 7,155–170 1981.

Marxist materialism tends to present socialist revolution as forced on the proletariat as a necessary means to individual survival. This presents huge problems about the relation of collective to individual interests. On the other hand, Marxism also tends to present the proletariat as embodying revolutionary socialist values—of collectivism, c0–operation, dedication, etc. But the Marxist account of the 'material basis' of this ethic is inconsistent and implausible.

SKILLING, John. Prior Probabilities. *Synthese* 63,1–34 Ap 85.

The theoretical construction and practical use of prior probabilities, in particular for systems having many degrees of freedom, are investigated. It becomes clear that it is operationally unsound to use mutually consistent priors if one wishes to draw sensible conclusions from practical experiments. The prior cannot usefully be identified with a state of knowledge, and indeed it is not so identified in common scientific practice. Rather, it can be identified with the question one asks. Accordingly, priors are free constructions. Their informal, ill–defined and subjective characteristics must carry over into the conclusions one chooses to draw from experiments or observations.

SKINNER, Quentin. "The Idea Of Negative Liberty" in *Philosophy In History*, Rorty, Richard and others (ed), 193–224. NY Cambridge Univ Pr 1984.

SKJEI, Erling. A Comment On Performative, Subject, And Proposition In Habermas's Theory Of Communication. *Inquiry* 28,87–104 Mr 85.

Habermas claims that the concept of 'communicative action' can be explained by illocutionary acts alone. It appears to me that his explanation collapses into sort of intentional theory (2[i]). Habermas maintains further that a speech act consists of three components which are 'correlated' to three worlds and to three validity claims. However, he also seems to mean that all worlds and validity claims are correlated to just one; the so–called propositional component. One consequence is that the propositional content, not the illocutionary act, determines the main mode of at least some speech acts. Another is that the 'I' as used in an expressive speech act will occur in the propositional part of the act and not, as claimed by Habermas, in the performative sentence (2[iii]. In 2(ii) two other problems concerning Habermas's view on the concept of 'I' ('the subject') are discussed.

SKLAR, Lawrence. "Modestly Radical Empiricism" in *Observation, Experiment, And Hypothesis In Modern Physical Science*, Achinstein, Peter (ed), 1–20. Cambridge MIT Pr 1985.

SKLAR, Lawrence. Perceived Worlds, Inferred Worlds, *The* World. *J Phil* 81,693–706 N 84.

In *Space Perception and Scientific Reality*, Patrick Heelan offers a hermaneutic–phenomenological account of perception and inference to theoretical structures. I challenge his account on grounds of alleging an Over–plasticity of perception, difficulties in handling incomparible worlds, and the positing of too much metaphysical weight on a merely psychological distinction.

SKLAR, Lawrence. Saving The Noumena. *Phil Topics* 13,89–110 Spr 82.

The realist requires a criterion of theoretical equivalence more stringent than that of the positivists. But can the realist provide an account of meaning for non–observational vocabulary which will offer a coherent account of theoretical equivalence, confirmation, and explanation?

SKOLIMOWSKI, Henryk. Global Philosophy As A Foundation Of Global Peace. *Dialec Hum* 11,401–410 Spr/Sum 84.

The understanding of peace and building is tantamount to upholding a right philosophy. Peace is a state of mind. It is the mind that wages wars not the armies. Genuine peace means mind at peace. The philosophical foundations of the right model of peace must entail at least the three principles, not only in theory but in praxis: 1) no lesser nations, no lesser people—which is an extension and modification of Kant's moral imperative. 2) social justice and human equality must go beyond economic parity. The moral failure is often the cause of economic injustice. 3) reverence for life and for all beings—both as an ethical principle and a form of understanding.

SKORDEV, Dimiter. On A Modal–Type Language For The Predicate Calculus. *Bull Sect Log* 13,111–119 O 84.

In the paper, a formal language is proposed whose expressions could be interpreted, in general, as denoting predicates which depend on parameters. An embedding of the ordinary language of predicate calculus in this language is easily seen, and an embedding in the opposite direction is also possible. A normal form theorem holds which allows turning an arbitrary parameter x of an expression of the language into the first argument of another expression, not containing x.

SKOVIRA, Robert J. Some Bits And Bytes: A Response To Raitz's "The Computer Revolution, The Technological Fallacy, And Education". *Phil Stud Educ* No Vol,21–23 1983.

This essay is a response to Raitz's "the Computer Revolution, The Technological Fallacy, and Education". The essay focuses upon three issues. First, the computer should be viewed as a dominant cultural symbol. Second, by learning to program in a "language", one is forced to view data as the language permits. Finally, in agreement with Raitz, educational philosophers should be involved in the critical inquiry into the educational value of the computer.

SKRAMOVSKA, Svatoslava and Celeda, J. Dialectical Unity Of The Dynamic And The Statistical In Nature And Society And Prigogine's Universal Evolution Theory (in Czechoslovakian). *Filozof Cas* 32,856–875 1984.

Prigogines' theory of fortuitous formation of highly organized systems inside assemblies of micro–particles far from theromodynamical equilibrium is analyzed. The authors' attempt to generalize this mechanism to all other evolutional levels of matter is submitted to criticism, especially if extended to socio–economical systems in human society, created by man as macroscopical "Maxwellian thermodynamical demon" (whose individual knowledge, observation, evaluation, social communication, education—by former generation through tradition, literature etc.) are not determined by thermodynamical axiomatism.

SKRENES, Carol. Lonergan's Metaphysics: Ontological Implications Of Insight–As–Event. *Int Phil Quart* 24,407–426 D 84.

This article explores points of contact between Whitehead's and Lonergan's thought, primarily for the purpose of suggesting changes or developments in Lonergan's metaphysics. It focuses on the act of insight, as understood by Lonergan, and finds it to have many of the characteristics of Whitehead's "occasion of experience". These points of contact are explored, for their implications about causality, consciousness, and selfhood.

SKYRMS, Brian. *Pragmatics And Empiricism.* New Haven Yale Univ Pr 1984.

Empiricism is reformulated within a pragmatic framework of personal probability. Questions of chance, subjunctive conditionals and causal factors in rational decision are given an empiricist treatment *via* generalizations of de Finetti's theorem.

SKYRMS, Brian. "Three Ways To Give A Probability Assignment A Memory" in *Testing Scientific Theories*, Earman, John (ed), 157–162. Minneapolis Univ Minnesota Pr 1983.

SKYRMS, Brian. EPR: Lessons For Metaphysics. *Midwest Stud Phil* 9,245–256 1984.

Rival metaphysical theories of causation yield different conclusions when applied to the Einstein–Podolsky–Rosen experiment.

SKYRMS, Brian. Maximum Entropy Inference As A Special Case Of Conditionalization. *Synthese* 63,55–74 Ap 85.

The conditions for maximum entropy inference to coincide with conditionalization in a larger space are investigated. Substantive assumptions about the nature of the constraint and the probabilistic structure of the model are required.

SLAGA, Szczepan W. Panspermia And The Evolutionism––Creationism Controversies (in Polish). *Stud Phil Christ* 20,111–128 1984.

SLAMAN, Theodore A. Reflection And Forcing In E–Recursion Theory. *Annals Pure Applied Log* 29,79–106 Jl 85.

SLANEY, John K. A Metacompleteness Theorem For Contraction–Free Relevant Logics. *Stud Log* 43,159–168 1984.

I note that the logics of the "relevant" group most closely tied to the research programme in paraconsistency are those without the contraction postulate (A→(A→B))→(A→B) and its close relatives. As a move towards gaining control of the contraction–free systems, I show that they are prime (that whenever A∨B is a theorem so is either A or B). The proof is an extension of the metavaluational techniques standardly used for analogous results about intuitionist logic or the relevant positive logics.

SLANEY, John K. 3088 Varieties: A Solution To The Ackermann Constant Problem. *J Sym Log* 50,487–501 Je 85.

It is shown that there are exactly six normal DeMorgan monoids generated by the identity element alone. The free DeMorgan monoid with no generators but the identity is characterized and shown to have exactly three thousand and eighty–eight elelments. This result solves the "Ackerman constant problem" of describing the structure of sentential constants in the logic R.

SLECZKA, Kazimierz. Two Ontologies Of Hegel, Marx, Lukács? *Dialec Hum* 10,23–34 Sum 83.

SLEEPER, R W. Rorty's Pragmatism: Afloat In Neurath's Boat, But Why Adrift? *Trans Peirce Soc* 21,9–20 Wint 85.

The argument is that Richard Rorty's version of pragmatism in *Philosophy and the Mirror of Nature* and *The Consequences of Pragmatism* misconstrues John Dewey's "antifoundationalism" as warranting the dismissal of Dewey's work in metaphysics and logic. It is argued that dewey's "antifoundationalism" is, rather, based upon a reconstruction of both metaphysics and logic as they have been traditionally understood, thus giving clear orientation to the "sailors" in "Neurath's Boat".

SLESSENGER, Peter H. A Height Restricted Generation Of A Set Of Arithmetic Functions Of Order–type. *Z Math Log* 31,117–122 1985.

The least epsilon number is represented by a set of arithmetic functions H, generated from X. The method restricts the type of functions permitted to be strictly contained within Skolem's class S, but confinal in it. This height restriction requires that if f and g are elements of H, then f × g and g'are elements of H if and only if f and g have the same amount of iterated exponentiation.

SLOTE, Michael. Utilitarianism, Moral Dilemmas, And Moral Cost. *Amer Phil Quart* 22,161–168 Ap 85.

SLUGA, Hans. "Frege: The Early Years" in *Philosophy In History*, Rorty, Richard and others (ed), 329–356. NY Cambridge Univ Pr 1984.

SMALL, Ian C. Semiotics And Oscar Wilde's Accounts Of Art. *Brit J Aes* 25,50–56 Wint 85.

Recent accounts of Wilde's art–criticism have emphasized his modernism by dwelling on his remarks about the contradictions between the representational and artifactual elements of art. His work is more complex, though, and can be better described by using distinctions derived from semiotics—those concerning the pragmatic, syntactic and semantic dimensions of the sign. In particular they give coherence to Wilde's views about the cognitive, political and social functions of art.

SMART, Brian. Offensiveness In The Williams Report. *Philosophy* 59,516–522 O 84.

The Williams Report's main proposal is for the restriction, not prohibition, of material whose unrestricted availability is offensive to reasonable people. Since no reliable connexion between offensive material and harm has been established, the magistrates are required to make only a non–defeasible and non–causal judgment of contemporary propriety. Against the Report it is argued that while offensiveness should be tied to decorum, material which the Report would restrict should be left

unrestricted if it is in the overriding public interest. Public health and safety may be promoted in this way. Overriding public interest may on occasion require complete lack of restriction, zonal or otherwise. (edited)

SMART, Brian. The Right To Strike And The Right To Work. *J Applied Phil* 2,31–40 Mr 85.

L J MacFarlane has contended that the right to strike is a keystone of democratic society. The right to strike is a right to free expression, association, assembly and power. And the right to strike is dependent upon the right to employment. MacFarlane denies that the right to employment is a universal right. I argue that unless the right to work is indeed universal MacFarlane's main contention is false. Forced employment is, amongst other things, the denial of full citizen status, for the range of liberties that constitutes the right to strike is essential to full participation in democracy. It is only when the traditional liberty–rights of free expression and striking are seen as being based upon such recipient rights as rights to media space and time and upon the right to work, that they can play their proper democratic role. This conception of those rights is missing from the work of Rawls and Nozick as well as from MacFarlane.

SMART, J J C. *Ethics, Persuasion And Truth.* Boston Routledge & K Paul 1984.

This book attempts to discuss the semantics and pragmatics of ethical language, without making use of the suspect notions of meaning and analyticity. The final two chapters are concerned with free will and determinism and with the relation of ethics to science and metaphysics. Ethics is concerned with deciding what to do and with persuading others. There is a puzzle as to whether specifically ethical language is really needed.

SMART, J J C. Laws Of Nature And Cosmic Coincidences. *Phil Quart* 35,272–280 Jl 85.

The author attempts to reconcile a regularity view of theoretical laws with his argument for scientific realism (that otherwise the facts on the observational level would constitute a vast cosmic coincidence). He tries to defend himself against van Fraassen's witty contention that his argument is no better than the cosmological argument for the existence of God.

SMART, Ninian. "What Is Happiness" in *The Good Life And Its Pursuit*, Dougherty, Jude P (ed), 35–44. NY Paragon House 1984.

SMART, Ninian. Action And Suffering In The Theravadin Tradition. *Phil East West* 34,371–378 O 84.

SMIRNOV, G L. Historical Materialism And Social Practice (in Czechoslovakian). *Filozof Cas* 32,646–658 1984.

SMIT, Harry. De Incommensurabiliteit Van Aanleg En Omgeving. *Kennis Methode* 9,4–25 1985.

SMITH, A F M and Bernardo, J M and Ferrandiz, J R. The Foundations Of Decision Theory: An Intuitive, Operational Approach With Mathematical Extensions. *Theor Decis* 19,127–150 S 85.

A new axiomatic basis for the foundations of decision theory is introduced and its mathematical development outlined. The system combines direct intuitive operational appeal with considerable structural flexibility in the resulting mathematical framework.

SMITH, Adam. *An Inquiry Into The Nature And Causes Of The Wealth Of Nations*, 2v. Indianapolis Liberty Classics 1985.

SMITH, Andrew. The Teaching Of Medical Ethics. *J Med Ethics* 11,35–36 Mr 85.

Students at Newcastle are exposed to patients during their first week at medical school and attached to a family within the first month. The object is to sensitise them to patients as people rather than vehicles of disease. Medical ethics is introduced as part of the multidisciplinary Human Development, Behavior and Aging Course by a lecturer who shows a film which poses an ethical problem. At subsequent tutorials led by the Department of Family and Community Medicine's general practitioner lecturers the subject is discussed as ethical issues arise in the course of their work.

SMITH, Barry D. John Dewey's Theory Of Consciousness. *Educ Theor* 35,267–272 Sum 85.

There are relatively few references in Dewey's writings to his theory of consciousness, yet in fact he struggled throughout his career with this problem. This paper traces the development of this struggle, from his early days as an Hegelian, through his struggle with physicalism, to his final Jamesean–like position, in which Dewey claims we ought to replace all references to consciousness with the word "awareness."

SMITH, Barry and Schuhmann, Karl. Against Idealism: Johannes Daubert Vs Husserl's *Ideas* I. *Rev Metaph* 38,763–794 Je 85.

In manuscripts of 1930–1 Johannes Dauber, principal member of the Munich board of realist phenomenologists, put forward a series of detailed criticisms of the idealism of Husserl's *Ideas* I. The paper provides a sketch of these criticisms and of Daubert's own alternative conceptions of consciousness and reality, as also of Daubert's views on perception, similar, in many respects, to those of J J Gibson.

SMITH, David H. Who Counts? *J Relig Ethics* 12,240–255 Fall 84.

Many issues in medical ethics seem to turn out arguments about the moral status of some human beings. This essay criticizes attempts to make clear distinctions proposed by Engelhardt, Green/Wikler, Becker, and Brody. The author suggest that the theories discussed divert attention from more resolvable problems.

SMITH, David Woodruff. Content And Context Of Perception. *Synthese* 61,61–88 O 84.

I shall argue that perception has an intrinsic "demonstrative" character in that its phenomenological structure or content prescribes an object appropriately before and sensuously affecting the perceiver on the occasion of the perception. A proper analysis of what makes a perception "of" its object must capture and interplay between the phenomenological content of the physical context of the perception. (edited)

SMITH, Huston. "Two Evolutions" in *On Nature*, Rouner, Leroy S (ed), 42–59. Notre Dame Univ Notre Dame Pr 1984.

SMITH, J C. "The Processes Of Adjudication And Regulation, A Comparison" in *Rights And Regulation*, Machan, Tibor (ed), 71–98. Cambridge Ballinger 1983.

SMITH, James Leroy. Thanatos And Euthanatos: Persons And Practical Policies. *Cogito* 2,1–14 D 84.

This essay is an analysis of recent work on the concept of death, as that work has found its way into public policy. The whole–brain oriented concept of death is challenged and the leading notion that "death" should refer univocally across such differing organisms as persons, dogs, fish, etc., is called into question. Some model statutes regarding "death" are criticized and suggested. Avenues for further empirical research are suggested.

SMITH, Jan. An Interpretation Of Martin–Löf's Type Theory In A Type–Free Theory Of Propositions. *J Sym Log* 49,730–753 S 84.

A formalization of Aczel's notion of a Frege structure is given, using the basic concepts "proposition" and "true proposition." It extends ordinary first order logic in that being a proposition may depend on the truth of other propositions. In this framework an interpretation of Martin–Löf's type theory is given. The construction of the interpretation is inspired by the semantics for type theory, but it can also be viewed as a formalized realizability interpretation.

SMITH, Janet Farrell. The Russell–Meinong Debate. *Phil Phenomenol Res* 45,305–350 Mr 85.

SMITH, John E. "Religion Within The Scope Of Philosophy" in *History Of Philosophy In The Making*, Thro, Linus (ed), 247–254. Washington Univ Pr Of America 1982.

SMITH, John E. "Some Continental And Marxist Responses To Pragmatism" in *Contemporary Marxism*, O' Rourke, James J (ed), 199–214. Boston Reidel 1984.

SMITH, John H. Rhetorical Polemics And The Dialectics Of *Kritik* In Hegel's Jena Essays. *Phil Rhet* 18,31–57 1985.

SMITH, John. Comments On A S Cua's "Confucian Vision And Human Community". *J Chin Phil* 11,239–242 S 84.

SMITH, Joseph H (ed) and Kerrigan, William (ed). *Taking Chances: Derrida, Psychoanalysis, And Literature*. Baltimore Johns Hopkins Pr 1984.

SMITH, Joseph W. *Reductionism And Cultural Being*. Hague Nijhoff 1984.

The author provides a detailed critique of sociobiological reductionism arguing that it is an inadequate theory to ground a physicalist scientific monism upon. He further argues that the theoretical reduction of sociology to physics is an unjustified and an obscure position. neo–Darwinism also provides an insufficient account of evolution. The author concludes that sociology and biology both need to be grounded upon detailed metaphysical world views, which have yet to be developed. (staff)

SMITH, Joseph W and Ward, Sharyn. Discussion: Are We Only Five Minutes Old: Acock On The Age Of The Universe. *Phil Sci* 51,511–513 S 84.

The paper discusses the problem of whether or not the "normally accepted" hypothesis about the age of the universe is rationally preferable to the Russellian hypothesis, that the universe was created five minutes ago, complete with all "traces." We criticize previous solutions and sketch an original solution of our own.

SMITH, Joseph Wayne and Ward, Sharyn. Bultmann On The New Testament And Mythology. *Sophia (Australia)* 23,4–12 Jl 84.

We argue that Bultmann's attempt to demythologize the New Testament is a failure. If Bultmann's program is seriously held to, then there is no rational ground for distinguishing his position from secular humanism and matters of economy require the elimination of "Jesus–talk". But Bultmann fails to carry his program through himself, so his allegedly rational reconstruction of Christianity contains its own myths. Bultmann's theology is hence internally incoherent.

SMITH, Joseph Wayne. Formal Logic: A Degenerating Research Programme In Crisis. *Cogito* 2,1–18 S 84.

The paper is a sceptical examination of the theoretical cogency of modern formal deductive logic.

SMITH, Joseph Wayne. Philosophy And The Meaning Of Life. *Cogito* 2,27–44 Je 84.

The paper presents a critical survey of a number of contemporary arguments for the thesis that life has no meaning, concluding that none of these arguments are sound. The author then presents his own argument for the meaningfulness of human life, concluding with a discussion of the role of philosophy in a meaningful and flourishing life.

SMITH, Joseph Wayne. Primitive Classification And The Sociology Of Knowledge: A Response To Bloor. *Stud Hist Phil Sci* 15,237–244 S 84.

This discussion note is a reply to David Bloor's recent defense of the value and relevance of *Primitive Classification* to the contemporary sociology of knowledge programme. I argue that Bloor's defense is a failure and that *Primitive Classification* is of little value and relevance to contemporary social theory.

SMITH, Joseph Wayne. Towards Putting Real Tense Back Into The World: A Reply To D H Mellor's Reconstruction Of The McTaggart Argument. *Kinesis* 14,3–12 Fall 84.

The paper attempts to rebut D H Mellar's defense of the McTaggart argument, given in his book *Real Time*, (Cambridge University Press, Cambridge, 1981).

SMITH, Joseph Wayne. Why Is There Something Rather Than Nothing? *Eidos* 3,135–162 D 84.

Why is there anything at all? In this paper we survey the major responses made to this question, concluding that all such responses are inadequate and that this problem is therefore cognitively underdetermined by available logical evidence.

SMITH, Joseph W. What Is Wrong With Verisimilitude? *Phil Res Arch* 10,511–542 1985.

Karl Popper introduced the idea of *verisimilitude* to explicate the intuitive idea that a

theory T_2, even though it is strictly speaking false, may be closer to the truth than a competitor T_1. However, as is now well–known, the results of Pavel Tichy, John Harris and David Miller establish that on Poppers qualitative theory of verisimilitude, a theory T_2 could be closer to the truth than another theory T_1 only if T_2 contains false sentences. This result has been taken universally to show the inadequacy of Popper's original account of versimilitude, since the miller–Tichy–Harris Theorem conflicts with the very basis intuition which first led Popper to formulate his theory. In this paper I shall first review the Miller–Tichy–Harris Theorem and examine a number of attempts to salvage the concept of verisimilitude. (edited)

SMITH, Kendon. "Drive": In Defense Of A Concept. *Behaviorism* 12,71–114 Spr 84.

To clarify the concept of 'drive', the usage of the term before C L Hull is reviewed; Hull's attempts at revising the construct are considered; and the subsequent usage of the term is summarized. Conclusions: Hull had no lasting impact on the concept; currently, a bodily state which prompts behavior is considered a drive to the extent to which it makes the animal reinforcible; 'arousal' is noncoterminous with 'incentive motivation' redundant with 'drive'.

SMITH, L Glenn. Aesthetic Reconstructionism: The New Deal And The Fine Arts. *J Thought* 19,57–67 Wint 84.

SMITH, Laurence and Amundson, Ron. Clark Hull, Robert Cummins, And Functional Analysis. *Phil Sci* 51,657–666 D 84.

Robert Cummins has recently used the program of Clark Hull to illustrate the effects of logical positivist epistemology upon psychological theory. On Cummins' account, Hull's theory is best understood as a functional analysis, rather than a nomological subsumption. Hull's commitment to the logical positivist view of explanation is said to have blinded him to this aspect of his theory, and thus restricted its scope. We will argue this interpretation of Hull's epistemology, though common, is mistaken. Hull's epistemological views were developed independently of, and in considerable contrast to, the principles of logical positivism.

SMITH, Leslie. Genetic Epistemology And The Child's Understanding Of Logic. *Phil Soc Sci* 14,367–376 S 84.

It is proposed that genetic and philosophical epistemology are over–lapping and yet distinct. In consequence, certain philosophical problems cannot be discussed independently of questions of empirical fact and conversely. It is also proposed that principles of logic, such as non–contradiction, play different roles at different developmental points. Both proposals are influenced by the seminal work of Piaget.

SMITH, Leslie. Philosophy, Psychology, And Piaget: A Reply To Loptson And Kelly. *Phil Soc Sci* 14,385–392 S 84.

The author attempts to rebut criticism of his previous paper (*Phil. soc. sci.*, 1984) genetic and philosophical epistemology are taken to be complementary. Piaget's genetic epistemology is taken to be an original contribution to both psychology and philosophy.

SMITH, Marjorie. Taking Blood From Children Causes No More Than Minimal Harm. *J Med Ethics* 11,127–131 S 85.

The ethical question of whether taking blood from normal children for research purposes is justified, is determined in part at least, by whether or not the children are harmed. To try to assess the risks, the effects of venepuncture on a group of healthy subjects were studied, by means of a parental questionnaire completed approximately eighteen months after the venepuncture had taken place. Ninety–two healthy children aged between 6 and 8 had a blood sample taken for non–therapeutic reasons as part of a research study. Questionnaire responses reveal few negative effects, and in some cases positive effects.

SMITH, Michael C. The Materialist Dilemma: Education And The Changing Of Circumstances. *Proc Phil Educ* 40,241–252 1984.

SMITH, N V (ed). *Mutual Knowledge*. NY Academic Pr 1982.

This book investigates the role of Mutual Knowledge in communication. Clark and Carlson modify speech–act theory to accommodate problems posed be hearers. Sperber and Wilson demolish the notion "mutual knowledge" and present their theory of *relevance* instead. Brody discusses the problem of choosing between syntactic and pragmatic analyses of complex data. Joshi outlines the parallels and contrasts between man–machine interaction and man–man interaction. Grice reanalyses the contrasts between natural and non–natural meaning and speaker's meaning versus text meaning.

SMITH, Philip L and Traver, Rob. Classical Living And Classical Learning: The Search For Equity And Excellence In Education. *Proc Phil Educ* 40,299–308 1984.

Equity and excellence, two sharply contrasting concerns in American education, are examined for their potential synthesis. After acknowledging the long and acrimonious debate between upholders of these concerns, and hinting at why education should so often provide the battleground, the authors analyze Mortimer Adler's *Paideia Proposal* as an attempted reconciliation. What is found is that while these two concerns must be reconciled in order for a democratic culture to survive, Adler's conception of equity is too weak, and his conception of excellence is too arid, to adequately achieve this end.

SMITH, Quentin. Four Teleological Orders Of Human Action. *Phil Topics* 12,213–230 Wint 81.

SMITH, Quentin. The Mind–Independence Of Temporal Becoming. *Phil Stud* 47,109–120 Ja 85.

An important issue in the philosophy of time is whether presentness, pastness, and futurity are mind–dependent properties, like colors, or whether they intrinsically characterize physical events. I argue the latter, by refuting Adolf Grunbaum's claim that tensed sentences about mind–independent events do not refer to these properties but instead to tenseless occurences, and by showing that a reference to these properties is an ineliminable part of current cosmological theories.

SMITH, R L and Friedman, Harvey M and Simpson, S G. Addendum To "Countable Algebra And Set Existence Axioms". *Annals Pure Applied Log* 28,319–320 My 85.

SMITH, Rick L and Van Den Dries, Lou. Decidable Regularly Closed Fields Of Algebraic Numbers. *J Sym Log* 50,468–475 Je 85.

SMITH, Robert J. The Psychopath As Moral. *Phil Phenomenol Res* 45,177–194 D 84.

Philosophers have raised important issues regarding psychopathy, such as responsibility, and legitimacy of values pursued. But just as clinicians, they accept the psychopath as a personality *type* morally ill because unable to process Kantian–like values. Smith's argument is that psychopathy exists on a continuum, with only extreme cases being diagnosed. Less extreme instances exploit societal values, e.G., projecting a good self image under capitalism. Extreme cases are hence better viewed as extra, not antisocial personalities.

SMITH, Robin. Aristotle As Proof Theorist. *Phil Natur* 21,590–597 1984.

SMITHERAM, Verner. The Criteria Of Objectivity: Physical Science And The Challenge Of Phenomenology. *Int Stud Phil* 16,65–80 1984.

This article challenges the view that physical science offers the paradigm for objectivity. Recent attacks upon the empiricist epistemology of science are exploited to open possibilities for comparing scientific objectivity is (1) limited by context, (2) grounded on structural invariance, and (3) verified by intersubjective concordance. An acount is then given of the similarities as well as the irreducible differences in the ways of objectivity is constituted and verified in science and in descriptive phenomenology.

SMITHSON, Michael. Toward A Social Theory Of Ignorance. *J Theor Soc Behav* 15,151–172 Jl 85.

This paper begins from the position that ignorance is a fundamental part of everyday social life, and that it cannot be conceived merely as distortion or neglect. Like knowledge, ignorance is socially constructed and negotiated. After introducing a conceptual framework for discussing ignorance, the article lays down some theoretical foundations for a social theory of ignorance in terms of norms and rules against knowing, ignorance games, occasions and scripts.

SMOCZYNSKI, P J. Evaluations And Norms Of Conduct In Leon Petrazycki's Psychologistic Concept Of Law And Morality (in Polish). *Etyka* 21,71–102 1985.

The author tries to define the ontological status of evaluations and norms of conduct on the grounds of Leon Petrazycki's theory of law and morality. The author says Petrazycki did realize the complex nature of evaluations and norms, and considered them in three aspects: a logical–linguistic, a psychological, and a sociological. However, as a psychologizing philosopher Petrazycki ultimately reduced evaluations and norms to only one ontological domain, namely to the sphere of individual emotional experiences. The author of the article tries to substantiate this claim, which is strongly debated in the literature of the subject, with quotations from Petrazycki's original texts. To justify his conclusions the author then discusses three ideas to interpret Petrazycki's views. These ideas are the problem of psychologistic reduction, the problem of methodological individualism in interpeting social phenomena, and the problem of psychologism as a philosophical theory. (edited)

SMOLENOV, Hristo. Truthfulness And Non–trivial Contradictions. *Bull Sect Log* 13,144–153 O 84.

SMOLENOV, Hristo. Zeno's Paradoxes And Temporal Becoming In Dialectical Atomism. *Stud Log* 43,169–180 1984.

The asymmetry of past and future in regard to temporal becoming is associated with the internal structure of the very moment, and not with external relations between different moments of time. In this paper ideas of ancient atomism and contemporary dialectics are brought together. It is for the sake of a contrast to what is known as logical atomism that I choose to call this view dialectical atomism. The latter admits dialectical contradictions and, so far as the logical status of contradictions is concerned, bears reference to paraconsistent logics. In the paper there is an outline of a method of converting any consistent axiomatic formal system into a paraconsistent theory. (edited)

SMOLUCHA, Francine C and Smolucha, Larry W. Creativity As A Maturation Of Symbolic Play. *J Aes Educ* 18,113–118 Wint 84.

Approaching creativity as the maturation of children's symbolic play provides a developmental theory of how visual analogies function as semiotic devices in art. The aspect of resemblance perceived between two otherwise dissimilar things is referred to as an isomorphism. Multiple levels of meaning are constructed by using isomorphism rather than being inherent in isomorphism as Arnheim suggests. A fifth Piagetian stage of colloboration between analogical and logical thought is suggested. Also, suggested is a neo–Freudian theory of the maturation of primary process thought. Preliminary research with a creativity test is presented.

SMOLUCHA, Larry W and Smolucha, Francine C. Creativity As A Maturation Of Symbolic Play. *J Aes Educ* 18,113–118 Wint 84.

Approaching creativity as the maturation of children's symbolic play provides a developmental theory of how visual analogies function as semiotic devices in art. The aspect of resemblance perceived between two otherwise dissimilar things is referred to as an isomorphism. Multiple levels of meaning are constructed by using isomorphism rather than being inherent in isomorphism as Arnheim suggests. A fifth Piagetian stage of colloboration between analogical and logical thought is suggested. Also, suggested is a neo–Freudian theory of the maturation of primary process thought. Preliminary research with a creativity test is presented.

SMORYŃSKI, Craig. "Modal Logic And Self–Reference" in *Handbook Of Philosophical Logic*, Gabbay, Dov (ed), 441–496. Boston Reidel 1984.

SMULLYAN, Raymond M. Chameleonic Languages. *Synthese* 60,201–224 Ag 84.

We formalize in arithmetic the relative pronoun "I." Given an arithmetical language L, we extend it to a language L'by adding a "chameleonic" constant, which in any sentence, denotes the Gödel number of the sentence in which it appears. Self–reference in L'is, of course immediate. Under certain normal conditions on L, the translation of L'back to L can be done within L, thus achieving self–reference in L itself.

SMYTH, Richard. Peirce's Examination Of Mill's Philosophy. *Trans Peirce Soc* 21,157–199 Spr 85.

SNAPPER, John W. Whether Professional Associations May Enforce Professional Codes. *Bus Prof Ethics J* 3,43–54 Wint 84.

SNOW, Paul. The Value Of Information In Newcomb's Problem And The Prisoners' Dilemma. *Theor Decis* 18,129–134 Mr 85.

SNOWDEN, Fraser (ed) and Harris, Chandice C (ed). *Bioethical Frontiers In Perinatal Intensive Care*. Natchitoches Northwestern Pr 1985.

This book consists of papers by a philosopher, a bioethicist, a cultural anthropologist, an attorney, and a theologian on the broad bioethical issues raised by the birth of severely handicapped infants. A final paper, by a reproductive endocrinologist, reviews recent reproductive technologies and explores their value dimensions. The book attempts to demonstrate the importance of involving humanist scholars in the formulation of guidelines for handling Baby Doe–type cases.

SNOWDEN, Fraser and others. "The Fallout From The Infants Doe Debate" in *Bioethical Frontiers In Perinatal Intensive Care*, Snowden, Fraser (ed), 89–116. Natchitoches Northwestern Pr 1985.

SNOWDEN, Fraser. "Bioethical Challenges At The Dawn Of Life" in *Bioethical Frontiers In Perinatal Intensive Care*, Snowden, Fraser (ed), 1–18. Natchitoches Northwestern Pr 1985.

SNYDER, Douglas M. Mental Activity And Physical Reality. *J Mind Behav* 5,417–422 Autumn 84.

Recent experiments in physics have demonstrated strong support for the existence of a non–local influence on physical events (i.E., an influence with a velocity greater than that of light). As the coherence of special relativity depends on the stipulation that light is the fastest physical existent, the question arises as to the nature of this influence. This paper addresses the basic design and results of the recent experiments, proposes an experiment that will provide indications as to whether this influence has a mental component, and discusses some already existing evidence of the influence of mental activity in the very development of physical reality.

SOAMES, Scott. Lost Innocence. *Ling Phil* 8,59–72 F 85.

The article shows that *Situations and Attitudes* (by Barwise and Perry) cannot escape standard problems involving propositional attitudes by replacing possible worlds in semantic analyses with finer grained situations. Rather, if direct reference is possible and propositional attitude ascriptions report relations to the semantic contents of their complement sentences, then those contents cannot be collections of truth–supporting circumstances, no matter how fine–grained. It is suggested that structured, Russellian propositions can play this role.

SOBEL, Jordan Howard. Circumstances And Dominance In A Causal Decision Theory. *Synthese* 63,167–202 My 85.

A causal decision theory is set out that features the concept of an action's being open. It is shown that – in contrast with Jeffery's 'logic of decision' – not every partition of circumstances is adequate to the application of this theory. Two kinds of partitions are demonstrated to be always adequate. The forms that decision matrices and dominance arguments take in this theory are explained and discussed. The theory is applied in an appendix to 'Hunter–Richter' problems.

SOBEL, Jordan Howard. Expected Utilities And Rational Actions And Choices. *Theoria* 49,159–183 1983.

The paper aims to say exactly *how*, and exactly *which*, expected utilities are decisive in determinations of rationality. It is argued that expected utilities not of kinds of actions but of very specific *choices* or organizations of will are fundamental. And it is argued that *two* tests are involved, and that a fundamental choice would be rational if and only if it would not only *maximize* expected utility but be *ratifiable* or after–the–fact maximizing.

SOBER, Elliott (ed). *Conceptual Issues In Evolutionary Biology*. Cambridge MIT Pr 1984.

SOBER, Elliott. *The Nature Of Selection: Evolutionary Theory In Philosophical Focus*. Cambridge MIT Pr 1984.

This book analyzes the structure of the theory of evolution, addressing the question of what the concepts of fitness, natural selection, and adaptation amount to as well as investigating the role of the concepts of probability and explanation in evolutionary biology. The importance of causality in the formulation of evolutionary explanations is an important theme, especially in the second half of the book, in which the units of selection controversy in biology is examined as a case in which issues of reductionism are of scientific as well as of philosophical significance.

SOBER, Elliott and Levine, Andrew. What's Historical About Historical Materialism? *J Phil* 82,304–326 Je 85.

This article explicates the theoretically distinctive sense in which Marx's theory of history, historical materialism, is a historical theory. A contrast is drawn with the Darwinian theory of evolution by natural selection, particularly with regard to the difference between macro and micro theories of change and the distinction between endogenous and exogenous causes.

SOBER, Elliott. Constructive Empiricism And The Problem Of Aboutness. *Brit J Phil Sci* 36,11–18 Mr 85.

In *The Scientific Image*, Van Fraassen defends a view he calls "constructive empiricism," which asserts that it is not part of the activity of science to reach a verdict on whether a theory is true or false, if the theory is about unobservable entities. Science's only interest here, says Van Fraassen, is to discover whether the theory is "empirically adequate." This paper argues that constructive empiricism rests on the nature of the semantic notion of "abountness."

Author Index with Abstracts 411 Soper, Philip

SOBER, Elliott. Discussion: What Would Happen If Everyone Did It? *Phil Sci* 52,141–150 Mr 85.

In a recent article (Sober 1982), I criticized an account of causation proposed by Giere (1979, 1980) by describing a series of examples concerning natural selection. Collier (1983) has criticized my criticisms, saying that I misapplied Giere's proposal and misconstrued the biology. More recently, Giere (1984) has defended his theory against my criticisms. Here I argue that my criticisms still stand.

SOBER, Elliott. Panglossian Functionalism And The Philosophy Of Mind. *Synthese* 64,165–194 Ag 85.

This paper critically examines two themes now prominent in the philosophy of psychology. The first is the thought that human beings must be rational because the mind evolved by natural selection. The second is the functionalist position in the mind/body problems. The latter idea is defended against some recent objections (due to Ned Block), but is ultimately found to suffer from the same limitation that undermines the first thesis—namely, a naive conception of how functional concepts work within evolutionary biology.

SOBLE, Alan. Pornography: Defamation And The Endorsement Of Degradation. *Soc Theor Pract* 11,61–88 Spr 85.

Two recent feminist anti–pornography arguments are analyzed and found defective. The argument that pornography defames women fails because much pornography is nonpropositional. The argument that it endorses degradation fails because it is very often not clear that–or what–pornography endorses. Possible sources of degradation in pornography are investigated, the conclusions being that there is less degradation than that claimed by some feminists, and that the existence of degradation is often difficult to establish.

SOBLE, Alan. The Natural, The Social, And Historical Materialism. *Phil Phenomenol Res* 46,139–154 S 85.

Historical materialism is developed to provide not only an account of the natural and the social, but also an account of accounts of the natural and the social. Four problem areas are distinguished, pertaining to (1) the ontological division per se between natural and social, (2) the time–relative content of the natural and the social, (3) the ideology of the ontological division, and (4) the ideology of the content. Some time is spent discussing the natural and the social in humans, and on the methodological implications for the social sciences.

SOBOTKA, Zdenek. Evolutional Rheology And Mechanical Asymmetry (in Czechoslovakian). *Filozof Cas* 32,907–911 1984.

SOCHOR, Antonin and Vopenka, Peter. Contributions To The Theory Of Semisets **v**, On Axiom Of General Collapse. *Z Math Log* 21,289–302 1975.

SOCOSKI, Patrick. The Theory And Practice Of Just Community In Schools. *Phil Stud Educ* No Vol,34–42 1983.

The article explores the "just community" approach to moral education in public schools. It gives the theoretical basis for such programs, and explains their goals of student participation and democratically–run decision making. The article also gives an account of an implementation of the program, noting practical difficulties and limitations.

SOGOLO, Godwin. Human Nature And Morality: The Case Of The Ik. *Phil Soc Act* 11,41–54 Ja–Mr 85.

SOKOLOFF, Harris J. Response To Spencer Maxcy's "Leadership, Administration, And The Educational Policy Operation". *Proc Phil Educ* 40,339–342 1984.

This response to Spencer Maxcy's paper argues that the geography of leadership developed by Professor Maxcy is not adequate to the richness of that concept. That geography overlooks the responsive nature of leadership. Moreover, while certain roles are associated with being a leader, leadership cannot be identified with being an office–holder. The response concludes by demonstrating the practical contradictions implicit with Maxcy's view.

SOKOLOWSKI, K and Fromm, Eberhard. Zum Platz Des Pluralismus In Der Gegenwärtigen Bürgerlichen Ideologie. *Deut Z Phil* 23,1036–1046 1975.

Der Pluralismus ist eine Richtung innerhalb der idealistischen Philosophie der Genenwart, die vor allem in neoopositivistischen Strömungen vorherrscht. Der "theoretische" Pluralismus ist erklärter Gegner jeglichen Monismus. Von der "philosophish–pluralistischen" Interpretation der Welt als Vielfalt voneinander unabhängiger Erscheinungen wird auf das "politisch–pluralistische" Modell der Gesellschaft geschlossen. Es geht den Pluralismustheoretikern um den "nachweis", dafss Sozailismus und Demokratie unvereinbar seien. In antikommunistischer Konfrontation zum realen Sozialismus verwirklicht der politische Pluralismus seine systemstabilisierende Funktion.

SOLCAN, Mihail-Radu. On The Logical Structure Of Political Doctrines (Pragmatical Aspects). *Phil Log* 27,285–293 O–D 83.

SOLES, David E. Locke On Knowledge And Propositions. *Phil Topics* 13,19–30 Spr 85.

SOLES, David E. Locke's Empiricism And The Postulation Of Unobservables. *J Hist Phil* 23,339–370 Jl 85.

It has been argued that a belief in the existence of atoms is inconsistent with Locke's account of idea acquisition, his definitions of 'knowledge' and 'belief', and his remarks on justification. I argue that beliefs about inferred entities are compatible with these aspects of Locke's epistemology. I proceed by developing interpretations of the troublesome positions and showing how each warrants beliefs about inferred entities.

SOLES, Deborah Hansen. Hume, Language And God. *Phil Topics* 12,109–120 Wint 81.

In Part II of his *Dialogues Concerning Natural Religion*, Hume provides a pair of puzzling illustrations: the voice in the clouds and the living library. The puzzle is about what they illustrate. I argue that Part III concentrates on attempts to explain verbal communication. Seen this way, the illustrations become an integral part of the *Dialogues* and the positions articulated by Cleanthes and Philo retain consistency throughout the *Dialogues*.

SOLES, Deborah Hansen. On The Indeterminacy Of Action. *Phil Soc Sci* 14,475–488 D 84.

I argue that Quine's work on radical translation challenges a common feature of cultural investigations, namely the attribution of actions and social practices to alien cultures, and that investigations into non–verbal aspects of cultures are beset by an indeterminacy similar to that which translational endeavors suffer. I conclude with a discussion of the ramifications this has for the enterprise of cultural investigation.

SOLOMON, Robert C. *Introducing Philosophy: A Text With Readings*. San Diego Harcourt Brace 1985.

The third edition has added many more readings, including up–to–date selections on functionalism ("Mind and Body") and recent innovations in ethics. The readings have been more clearly distinguished from textual commentary. Out–dated selections have been deleted. The glossary has been expanded.

SOLOMON, Robert C. "Emotions And Choice" in *The Good Life And Its Pursuit*, Dougherty, Jude P (ed), 111–132. NY Paragon House 1984.

SOLOMON, Robert. Graduate Study In Continental Philosophy In The United States. *Teach Phil* 7,337–346 O 84.

A revision of the much–circulated directory published in 1975, as advice to students and their advisors. The survey of more than 50 philosophy departments includes responses by the departments to questions such as which members of the department teach what courses and whether the department allows exclusive concentration in Continental Philosophy.

SOLOVAY, Robert M. Explicit Henkin Sentences. *J Sym Log* 50,91–93 Mr 85.

Hofstadter has introduced the notion of an explicit Henkin sentence. Roughly speaking, an explicit Henkin sentence not only asserts its own provability, as ordinary Henkin sentences do, but explicitly provides a detailed description of a proof. We provide, in this paper, a precise formalization of Hofstadter's notion and then show that true explicit Henkin sentences exist.

SOLT, Kornél. Deontic Alternative Worlds And The Truth–Value Of 'OA'. *Log Anal* 27,349–351 S 84.

There is a view in deontic logic according to which a proposition of the sort 'it is obligatory to do *A*' is true at the actual world if *A* is true at every deontic alternative world to *W*. This is false. The validity of a norm does not depend on its performance. True is only this: If the proposition: 'it is obligatory to do A' is true at the actual world, than *A* is true at every deontic alternative world to *w*.

SOLTIS, Jonas F. Logics And Languages Of Pedagogical Research. *Proc Phil Educ* 40,273–282 1984.

This paper attempts to give perspective on the various approaches to educational research through analysis of their roots in the philosophic traditions of logical empiricism, interpretive theory, and critical theory. These same empirical, interpretive, and critical dimensions are seen to characterize pedagogy. This implies that researchers of the three traditions, if they are to be honest to the subject matter of their inquiry, must be open–minded in their rational appraisal of research claims across traditions.

SOMMERS, Christina Hoff. *Vice And Virtue In Everyday Life: Introductory Readings In Ethics*. San Diego Harcourt Brace 1985.

This anthology brings together classical and contemporary writings on such matters as courage, wisdom, compassion, generosity, gratitude, honor, and self–respect. It also includes essays on moral foibles such as hypocrisy, self–deception, jealousy, and narcissism. More standard materials are included: chapters on theories of moral conduct, free will and determinism, and contemporary social issues. The collection thereby seeks to combine the virtues of current texts on applied ethics with the virtues of more traditional survey texts.

SONTAG, Frederick. Beyond Process Theology? *Thomist* 48,645–661 O 84.

Cobb focuses on the inadequacy of the vision of God which has hampered the "political theology" he has explored. His own brand of "process theology" is centered on a Hartshornian notion of God which is novel. The issue now is whether it is not adequate to the task of providing theology with the vision of God needed to make Christianity a "viable intellectual alternative" because, important as their work is, theologians should never be so arrogant as to assume that Christianity succeeds or fails by their work. Preachers bear more responsibility for that, along with the Holy Spirit and the needs that open humanity to religious committment from time to time. And these often move against the prevailing intellectual climate of the day rather than with it, as the Enlightenment assumed, and hoped.

SONTAG, Frederick. Can We Think Of Salvation As A Return To Mental Health? *Faith Phil* 1,316–326 Jl 84.

When we think of "mental health," we have not recently connected this to the notion of "salvation" in Christian doctrine. There was once a time, of course, when many who wanted to recover or restore mental health turned to Christianity and found their healing. There are, I suppose, many reasons which can be given for why this ceased to be true, but at least one of these involves the rise of psychiatry as a profession and the well–known anti–religious sentiments of its pioneers, most notably Sigmund Freud. Psychiatry arose as the modern and "scientific" alternative to the healing and counseling practices of Christianity. Thus, before we can decide whether "salvation" can once more be seen as a road to mental health, we must go back and consider how psychiatry came to replace it.

SOPER, Philip. *A Theory Of Law*. Cambridge Harvard Univ Pr 1984.

This book approaches the fundamental question of legal theory ("What is law?") by connecting it to the fundamental question of political theory ("Why should I obey the law?"). Modern legal theories are criticized because they are descriptive, rather than definitional, and because they cannot distinguish legal from coercive systems. A political theory is then developed which shows that coercive directives yield *prima facie* moral obligations wherever the term "legal system" is confidently used.

SORBI, Andrea and Montagna, Franco. Universal Recursion Theoretic Properties Of R E Preordered Structures. *J Sym Log* 50,397–406 Je 85.

In this paper it is shown that the preordering less than or equal to *PA* induced by provable implication in Peano Arithmetic is recursively universal w.R. To the class of r.E. Preorderings. Less than or equal to *PA* can also be characterized as the (unique up to recursive isomorphism) lattice preordering which is recursively homogeneous universal with respect to the class of r.E. Lattice preorderings. A consequence of this fact is that, every r.E. Preordering is "representable" in PA as provable implication of Σ1 formulas.

SORENSEN, Roy A. The Iterated Versions Of Newcomb's Problem And The Prisoner's Dilemma. *Synthese* 63,157–166 My 85.

A number of commentators believe there is a connection between Newcomb's problem of the prisoner's dilemma. David Lewis has even argued that they are the same paradox. If there is a connection, one would expect that Newcomb's problem has an offshoot corresponding to the iterated prisoner's dilemma. After describing these paradoxes, I present an iterated Newcomb's problem which confirms the above hypothesis. Lastly, I propose a solution to the iterated versions.

SORENSON, Roy A. An Argument For The Vagueness Of Vague. *Analysis* 45,134–137 Je 85.

The argument proceeds by exploiting the gradually decreasing vagueness of a certain sequence of predicates. The vagueness of 'vague' is then used to show that the thesis that all vague predicates are incoherent is self-defeating. A second casualty is the view that the probems of vagueness can be avoided by restricting the scope of logic to nonvague predicates.

SOSA, Ernest. Knowledge And Intellectual Virtue. *Monist* 68,226–245 Ap 85.

Cognitive faculties as intellectual virtues, and the sources of their virtue. Purity of faculties: pure reason, pure memory, pure introspection, and pure perception. Reliabilism and the nature of epistemic justification.

SOSA, Ernest. Mind–Body Interaction And Supervenient Causation. *Midwest Stud Phil* 9,271–282 1984.

The supervenience of causation raises a difficult problem for the possibility of fundamental mind–body interactions. This problem is expounded and discussed. Davidson's Paradox is also about the mental and its place in nature. Davidson's resolution—anomalous monism—is presented and examined.

SOSA, Ernest. The Coherence Of Virtue And The Virtue Of Coherence: Justification In Epistemology. *Synthese* 64,3–28 Jl 85.

A discussion of justification in epistemology. Topics include the nature of epistemology and the relative merits of reliabilism and coherentism as theories of epistemic justification.

SOTO, José Alberto. Carlos Monge: Ideas Filosófico–Antropológicas. *Rev Filosof (Costa Rica)* 23,195–203 D 85.

Analysis of the philosophical and anthropological ideas of the ex Rector of the University of Costa Rica, Professor Carlos Monge Alfaro. His anthropological contribution, in particular is shown in relation with the cultural, the educational and the social environments in which a man finds his own self: "educate to become a man" implying a process of self–dehumanization and a process of socialization.

SOUTO, Cláudio. Constitutional System And Social Change: Concerning A Publication By Frank Rotter. *Arch Rechts Soz* 61,429–434 1975.

SOWDEN, Lanning. Rule Utilitarianism, Rational Decision And Obligations. *Theor Decis* 17,177–192 S 84.

This paper examines a decision theoretic model of a moral decision problem proposed by John Harsanyi which has been used to argue for the non–equivalence of rule and act utilitarianism. It is argued that while a distinction has been drawn it is not one which is significant from the standpoint of moral theory: rule utilitarianism is shown not to be a 'significant improvement' on act utilitarianism.

SPAEMANN, Robert. Remarks On The Ontology Of "Right" And "Left". *Grad Fac Phil J* 10,89–97 Spr 84.

SPARKES, A W. Rousseau On The General Will. *Cogito* 2,79–102 D 84.

The doctrine can be clarified and rendered less implausbile by distinguishing (i) General Will (GW) as process from GW as product and (ii) different levels of the latter. This makes the assertion that GW "*est toujours droite*" intelligible. But this defence cannot encompass other elements of Rousseau's theory, which is undermined by his failure to relate self–love and compassion coherently, a failure connected with conflicts in his personality.

SPARSHOTT, Francis. Showing And Saying, Looking And Learning: An Outsider's View Of Art Museums. *J Aes Educ* 19,63–78 Sum 85.

The origin of art museums suggests a diversity of functions, in which conservation comes first. But the demands of conservation, together with other constraints imposed by governmental tax policies, make for the trivialization, institutionalization, and dehumanization of museums as places for people.

SPARSHOTT, Francis. Some Dimensions Of Dance Meaning. *Brit J Aes* 25,101–114 Spr 85.

The scope of dance aesthetics must depend on the number of ways in which dances and dancing can be found meaningful. A survey of some of the dimensions of the meaningfulness of dance shows that the issues raised in dance criticism cover only a small part of the domain.

SPARSHOTT, Francis. Text And Process In Poetry And Philosophy. *Phil Lit* 19,1–20 Ap 85.

The paper attempts to justify the importance attached to philosophical texts, assuming that the task of philosophy is to improve the quality of processes of thinking. Likenesses and differences are suggested between this puzzle and puzzles in literary theory about the status of the text in a world of linguistic transactions. Since the

reading of any text is itself a process, the initial project of the paper evaporates.

SPECTOR, Marshall. Leibniz And The Cartesians On Motion And Force. *Stud Leibniz* 7,135–144 1975.

Der Streit zwischen Leibniz und den Cartesianern über die Frage, ob die 'Quantität der Bewegung' (mv) oder die 'vis viva' (mv²) das richtige Maβ der 'Kraft' in einem sich bewegenden Körper sei (beide Parteien stimmten darin überein, daβ sich diese Kraft im Universum erhalte), wird im allgemeinen interpretiert als ein Wortstreit, in dem kein wirkliches Problem zur Diskussion stehe. (edited)

SPELLER, J. Filling A Gap In Professor Von Kutschera's Decision Procedure For Deontic Logic. *Log Anal* 27,435–438 D 84.

In order to make Professor von Kutschera's decision procedure applicable in every case, the paper introduces and proves the correctness of a different criterion for deontological unsatisfiability.

SPERA, Salvatore. Le Carte Schleiermacheriane Di Kierkegaard. *Aquinas* 27,287–316 My–Ag 84.

SPERO, Shubert. *Morality, Halakha And The Jewish Tradition.* NY KTAV 1983.

SPERRY, Roger. Changed Concepts Of Brain And Consciousness: Some Value Implications. *Zygon* 20,41–58 Mr 85.

Prospects for uniting religion and science are brightened by recently changed views of consciousness and mind–brain interaction. Mental, vital, and spiritual forces, long excluded and denounced by materialist philosophy, are reinstated in nonmystical form. A revised scientific cosmology emerges in which reductive materialist interpretations emphasizing causal control from below upward are replaced by revised concepts that emphasize the reciprocal control exerted by higher emergent forces from above downward. Scientific views of ourselves and the world and the kinds of values upheld by scientific belief undergo basic transformations, making them more compatible with religious motivation and moral responsibility.

SPICKER, Stuart F. Philosophical Aspects Of Brain Death. *J Med Phil* 9,373–376 N 84.

SPIEGELBERG, Herbert. Monroe Beardsley And Phenomenological Aesthetics. *J Brit Soc Phenomenol* 16,3–5 Ja 85.

An editorial preface to Monroe Beardsley's subsequent essay on "Experience and Value in Moritz Geiger's Aesthetics," showing Beardsley's stake as an analytic aesthetician in phenomenological aesthetics.

ŚPIEWAK, Anna. The Concept Of Personal Pattern As An Axiological Structure. *Rep Phil* 8,77–86 1984.

SPILKER, Bert. Myths And Misconceptions About Drug Industry Ethics. *Int J Applied Phil* 2,1–12 Fall 84.

Eight common myths about drug industry ethics are discussed. These include the myths that drug companies conduct unethical drug studies, suppress data so that they market unsafe drugs, advertise unapproved drug uses, do not develop drugs for orphan diseases, reap big profits from new drugs, and have adequate patent protection for their products. The eighth myth is that consumer advocates provide the American public with unbiased truths about the drug industry.

SPINKS, Graham. McGinn On Benacerraf. *Analysis* 44,197–198 O 84.

I argue, against McGinn, that Benacerraf has demonstrated that numbers are not sets. Not only is it impossible to identify any particular recursive progression of sets with the natural number series but a commitment to such a progression of sets is not a necessary condition of the practice of number–theory. The ontologically parsimonious, though not the anti–Platonistic, may draw comfort from Benacerraf's observation that numeral series themselves are recursive progressions.

SPITLER, Gene. Do We Really Need Environmental Ethics? *Environ Ethics* 7,91–92 Spr 85.

Environmental ethics is not another category of applied ethics. Rather, it is an extension of ethical theory and practice to include both the distant future and all other forms of life. Eventually, the word "Environmental" can be dropped as the word "Ethics" takes on a broader meaning which includes the entire biosphere.

SPITZ, Jean–Fabien. Le Problème De L'analyticité Et Le Statut Des Mathématiques Chez Hume. *Rev Metaph Morale* 89,453–464 O–D 84.

SPOONER, Lysander. "A Right To Make Laws" in *Freedom, Feminism, And The State,* Mc Elroy, Wendy (ed), 327–330. Cato Institute Washington 1982.

SPRAGGINS, John R. Whitehead's Educational Ontology. *Educ Theor* 34,373–378 Fall 84.

Whitehead's learning theory represents a microcosm of his systematic philosophy, the *philosophy of organism.* Whitehead's metaphysical system and his less abstract learning model share the basic ontological concept of *process.* The essay emphasizes the melding of rational and empirical elements through the inherence of the essential Whiteheadian concept of periodicity.

SPRIGGE, T L S. Non–Human Rights: An Idealist Perspective. *Inquiry* 27,439–462 D 84.

The question whether an entity has rights is identified with that as to whether an intrinsic value resides in it which imposes obligations to foster it on those who can appreciate this value. There should be no difficulty in granting that animals have rights in this sense, but what of other natural objects and artifacts? It seems that various inanimate things, such as fine buildings and forests, often possess such intrinsic value, yet since they can only fully actual in an observing consciousness the most basic right is that of being observed from time to time. That, at least, is true of them as phenomenal objects. There must, however, be a thing in itself behind the phenomenal object and sometimes this may possess an intrinsic value which gives rise to rights, not a matter of the need to be actualized in an observing consciousness, though it is extremely difficult to reach reliable conclusions here.

SPRING, Joel. The Public School Movement Vs The Libertarian Tradition. *J Liber Stud* 7,61–80 Spr 83.

SPRINGBORG, Patricia. Karl Marx On Democracy, Participation, Voting, And Equality. *Polit Theory* 12,537–556 N 84.

An examination of democracy and related concepts in Marx's *Critique of Hegel's "Philosophy of Right"* and the *Grundrisse* shows that he shares little ground with modern critics, making a special case for democracy as "the essence" of the political, or as genus, to which all other forms of constitution are related as species. On questions of equality and participation of Marx's views are closer to those of Hegel, Plato, and Aristotle, than is commonly assumed.

SPRINGSTED, Eric O. Is There A Problem With The Problem Of Evil? *Int Phil Quart* 24,303–312 S 84.

This article argues that many philosophical criticisms of theism err because they assume evil to be counterevidence to a good that is not, in fact, commensurate with the good in which theists put their faith. This does not dismiss philosophical discussion of evil but suggests that investigation look at where evil threatens the resolve to believe in a supreme good.

SPRUNG, Mervyn. The Origins And Issues Of Scepticism, East And West. *J Chin Phil* 12,75–84 Mr 85.

SREBRNY, M and Marek, W. No Minimal Transitive Model Of Z–. *Z Math Log* 21,225–228 1975.

SRISANG, Koson (ed). *Perspectives On Political Ethics: An Ecumenical Enquiry.* Washington Georgetown Univ Pr 1983.

SROUR, Gabriel and Pillay, Anand. Closed Sets And Chain Conditions In Stable Theories. *J Sym Log* 49,1350–1362 D 84.

Let T be a complete first order theory and M be a very saturated model of T. A definable set X of M is *closed* if the intersection of any collection of conjugates of X is equal to a finite subintersection. We call T equational if every definable set is a Boolean combination of closed sets and we show how for equational theories, the notions of stability theory, e.G. Forking have a simple and natural expression.

SRUBAR, Ilja. On The Origin Of 'Phenomenological' Sociology. *Human Stud* 7,163–190 1984.

The unique socio–historical configurations of ideas in Europe before World War II is examined in which the basis for an interrelationship between phenomenology and sociology has been established. It is shown that Husserl's concept of meaning establishment has been considered a promising approach which could solve the problems in the "classical" interpretive sociology of M Weber and Simmel, resulting from the fact, that the traditional societal meaning structures have lost their generalized intersubjective validity. The philosophical anthropology of Scheler and Plessner as well as Schuetz's protosociology are understood as two different attempts to develop a new interpretative theory of social action.

STABLER, Edward. Naturalized Epistemology And Metaphysical Realism: A Response To Rorty And Putnam. *Phil Topics* 13,155–170 Spr 82.

STACEY, Margaret. Medical Ethics And Medical Practice: A Social Science View. *J Med Ethics* 11,14–18 Mr 85.

This paper argues the two characteristics of social life impinge importantly upon medical attempts to maintain high ethical standards. The first is the tension between the role of ethics in protecting the patient and maintaining the solidarity of the profession. The second derives from the observation that the foundations of contemporary medical ethics were laid at a time of one–to–one doctor–patient relations while nowadays most doctors work in or are associated with large–scale organizations. Records cease to be the property of individual doctors, become available not only to other doctors but also to educational and social work personnel. Making records openly available to patients is suggested as the only antidote to this irreversible loss of individual practitioner control. The importance for doctors of understanding the nature of professional and bureaucratic organizations in order to deal with the hazards involved is stressed as is the responsibility of the General Medical Council to regulate medical competence as well as personal behavior.

STACHOVÁ, Jirina. Philosophical And Methodological Problems Of Present Thermodynamics And Synergetics (in Czechoslovakian). *Filozof Cas* 32,780–787 1984.

In this paper the criticism of mechanism presented in I Prigogin's and I Stengers's book *La nouvelle alliance* is confronted with that contained in the works of the classics of Marxism–Leninism. Especially the topics of time, complexity and infinity are discussed. The second part of this paper deals with synergetics, particularly with the possible utilization of synergetics and the mathematical formalization in the social sciences. It is shown that it is impossible immediately and not applicable in philosophy.

STACHOVÁ, J. Some Philosophical Aspects Of Modern Biotechnologies (in Czechoslovakian). *Filozof Cas* 33,380–383 1985.

STACK, George J. Eternal Recurrence Again. *Phil Today* 28,242–264 Fall 84.

After a discussion of the prototypes of the idea of the eternal recurrence of the same that influenced the development of Nietzsche's "countermyth," the cosmological versions of the argument for this conception are critically examined. Starting from the premises of Tracy Strong and Bern Magnus, the existential meaning of the "thought" of eternal recurrence is analyzed. It is argued, in sum, that Nietzsche's idea was put forward in order to deny objective teleology, to affirm a circular nihilistic process in order to achieve the highest affirmation of *Existenz* and abolish nihilism. The cosmological theory must be theoretically negative but objectively uncertain.

STACKHOUSE, Max L. *Creeds, Society, And Human Rights: A Study In Three Cultures.* Grand Rapids Eerdmans 1984.

Drawing on resources from philosophy, theology, social theory, and comparative religion, this volume analyzes and evaluates the competing doctrines of what is human and what is right as these understandings have grown up in the United States, under the influence of Christianity and Liberalism; in the German Democratic Republic, under the influence of Marxism–Leninism; and India, under the influence of Hinduism and modernization.

STAFFORD, J Martin. Hutcheson, Hume And The Ontology Of Morals. *J Value Inq* 19,133–152 1985.

The interpretation of Hutcheson's and Hume's ethics in David Norton's recent book is wildly innovatory. Contrary to what he alleges, it is not earlier scholars who have misread their works but Norton who has made them appear to accord with his thesis by artful editing and imaginative paraphrasing. Norton's conviction that they were moral realists stems for a false dichotomy between skepticism and realism and is sustainable only when their texts are misrepresented.

STAFLEU, M D. Spatial Things And Kinematic Events. *Phil Reform* 50,9–20 1985.

The reality of 'things' like triangles and circles, and of 'events' like periodic oscillations and waves is discussed. Their structure is defined as a subject–object relation in the sense of Dooyweerd's systematic philosophy. Objections derived from daily experience, perception, traditional philosophy, and the idea that anything real must at least be material, are unwarranted. Spatial things and kinematic events have a low–level individuality compared to atoms, plants, and animals.

STAHL, Donald E. Hume's Dialogue IX Defended. *Phil Quart* 34,505–507 0 84.

D C Stove has found no merit in Part IX of Hume's *Dialogues* (*The Philosophical Quarterly* 28 (1978), pp 300–309). This article is a reply to his.

STAHL, Gérold. Analyse Logique Du Changement Ponctuel. *Rev Phil Fr* 174,443–446 O–D 84.

Some logical aspects of the punctual change (which may be "surrounded" by a continuous change) are indicated. The treatment presented is not "propositional" (a treatment that tries to describe the change with respect to entire nonanalyzed propositions) but "functional" (i.e., having recourse to numerical functions or to functions having at least one numerical argument). This treatment can be realized in standard logic and corresponds to the practice in mathematics and physics.

STAHL, Gérold. Mythe Et Réalité De La Formule De Barcan. *Log Anal* 27,343–348 S 84.

In order to see different aspects of the Barcan formula ((B); models with just one universe), a very precise distinction *de re–de dicto* is needed. In a *de re* treatment (for a *de re–de dicto* treatment see other publications of mine) with the worlds as additional individuals, we get a version of (B), which represents simply the commutativity of the universal (existential) quantifiers. The avoidance of (B) is represented by a change of a restricted quantifier, which produces the "anti–Barcan effect".

STAIF, A N. Framing The Reference: Notes Towards A Characterization Of Critical Texts. *Brit J Aes* 24,355–360 Autumn 84.

The article examines the nature of the critical text and suggests the following indicators as dynamic variables in characterizing it: literary criticism is (a) a discourse, upon a discourse, (b) a social discourse, (c) a human activity and (d) context bound. Being an overdetermined text, the production of which is stimulated by a variety of internal and external factors, modern critical discourse is, therefore, best approached from a contextual comparative perspective.

STAIRS, Allen. Sailing Into The Charybdis: Van Fraassen On Bell's Theorem. *Synthese* 61,351–360 D 84.

STALNAKER, Robert C. *Inquiry.* Cambridge MIT Pr 1984.

STAMBOUGH, Joan. Heidegger, Taoism And The Question Of Metaphysics. *J Chin Phil* 11,324–352 D 84.

STANCIU, George N and Augros, Robert. *The New Story Of Science.* Lake Bluff Regnery 1984.

The New Story of Science synthesizes the new world view emerging from contemporary physics, neuroscience, and humanistic psychology. Through ample testimony of eminent scientists, and with reasons and examples, the authors argue that science itself is transcending the narrow materialism of the 19th century. The role of beauty in physics, the place of God in the new cosmology of astrophysicists, and the origins of modern philosophy in Renaissance science are lucidly debated and thoroughly documented.

STANESBY, Derek. *Science, Reason & Religion.* New Hampshire Croom Helm 1985.

This book attempts to examine the implications of philosophy of science for philosophy of religion. It begins with a critical account of positivism (the 'Received View') and ends with a critical account of relativism ('the Weltanschauung view of science'), with a large section devoted to the philosophy of Karl Popper. Although the branches of science and religion have grown far apart they sprang from the common roots of human enquiry and share common philosophical problems.

STANGUENNEC, Andre. Ontologie Et Pathologie Du Symbole Chez L Tieck: Le Conte Du Tannenhäuser. *Rev Phil Fr* 175,3–13 Ja–Mr 85.

STANLIS, Peter J and Gandy, Clara I. *Edmund Burke: A Bibliography Of Secondary Studies To 1982.* NY Garland 1983.

STARK, Judith C. The Problem Of Evil: Augustine And Ricoeur. *Augustin Stud* 13,111–122 1982.

This paper explores the points of contact and divergence between Augustine's and Ricoeur's analysis of the notion of evil as nothingness, for Augustine understood in the ontological and moral senses and for Ricoeur in the symbolic sense. The thesis is presented is that Augustine's analysis of evil as nothingness has set the conceptual stage for the discussions of evil in the western tradition. Ricoeur accepts the conceptual coordinates of Augustine's analysis and overlays it with his interpretation of the symbolism of evil as nothingness, thus continuing the Augustinian cast of the notion of evil into contemporary philosophical discourse, especially in phenomenology and hermeneutics.

STARK, Werner. Kritische Fragen Und Anmerkungen Zu Einem Neuen Band Der Akademie–Ausgabe Von Kant's Vorlesungen. *Z Phil Forsch* 38,292–310 Ap–Je 84.

The purpose is, to point out some fundamental deficiencies in volume XXIX 1, 1 of the 'Akademie–Ausgabe von Kant's gesammelten Schriften'. By the method of a 'recensio in exemplo' it is shown, that in one main part of the volume, the 'Enzyklopaedie–Vorlesung', the following headings are not sufficiently worked out: provenance, description and dating of the edited manuscript. In order to fill in the missing pieces, positive arguments are presented.

STAROBINSKI, Jean. La Double Légitimité. *Rev Int Phil* 38,231–244 1984.

STAROBINSKI, Jean. Sur L'emploi Du Chiasme Dans "Le Neveu De Rameau". *Rev Metaph Morale* 89,182–196 Ap–Je 84.

STAUFENBIEL, Fred. Zur Entwicklung Kultureller Bedürfnisse In Der Arbeiterklasse. *Deut Z Phil* 22,204–212 1974.

Die Bedürfnisse der Arbeiterklasse sind Ausdruck ihrer materiellen und kulturellen Lebensbedingungen, deren erweiterte Reproduktion für die Lebenstätigkeit der Menschen erforderlich ist. (edited)

STECKER, Robert. Expression Of Emotion In (Some Of) The Arts. *J Aes Art Crit* 42,409–418 Sum 84.

The purpose of this paper is to argue that an account of expression common to all arts cannot be given. My strategy will be to make use of recent work on the nature of the emotions to better understand what the expression of emotion might be in various arts. Because I think the sharpest contrasts exist between literature and music, these are the arts I will concentrate on, although I will also say something about painting.

STEEDMAN, Mark. LFG And Psychological Explanation. *Ling Phil* 8,359–383 Ag 85.

STEENBURGH VAN, E W. Equality And Length. *Phil Invest* 8,143–148 Ap 85.

An examination of what must be added to objects in order that they may be used as standards and rejection of conventions of language as relevent to that question.

STEFANOV, Anguel S. Formal Truth And Objective Truth. *Bull Sect Log* 13,154–164 O 84.

The first part of the paper concerns the problem of establishing the truth content of a scientific theory. It is claimed to be more reasonable to ascertain a definite degree of truth of the whole theory, taken as a cognitive unit, instead of seeking a standard formal dependence on the truth values of its sentences. The notions of systematic and explanatory power are analyzed. Two approaches in describing the very notion of truth are delineated.

STEFANOV, Anguel and Ginev, Dimiter. One Dimension Of The Scientific Type Of Rationality. *Stud Hist Phil Sci* 16,101–112 Je 85.

The paper contains the analysis of what is called "synchronic dimension" of scientific rationality. It is considered from the standpoint of the ideal for an optimum (best) scientific theory. H Sarkar's methodological approach of "group rationality" is critically analyzed and some new ideas are developed connected with the concept of ideal for an optimum theory and the non–formal synthesis of such ideals. A methodological criterion—interplay of ontologies—is proposed for the assessment of new theories.

STEFFENS, Karsten. Der Satz Von Dilworth Und Souslin's Hypothese. *Z Math Log* 21,187–192 1975.

STEHR, Nico and Avison, William. Forms Of Competition And Sociological Knowledge In Organized American Sociology. *Arch Rechts Soz* 60,213–230 1974.

Utilizing Mannheim's paradigm of competition in the intellectual realm, it is suggested that the degree of socio–structural homogeneity within organized American sociology finds its expression in the form and content of sociological knowledge. Changes over time in the concentration of control of professional certification sustain a trend toward theoretical pluralism in American sociology as opposed to the previous hegemony of functionalism.

STEIN, Howard. The Everett Interpretation Of Quantum Mechanics: Many Worlds Or None? *Nous* 18,635–652 N 84.

STEINBECK, W. Einführung In Die Philosophie Der Gegenwart: Dargestellt In Einem Handbuch Philosophischer Grundbegriffe. *Kantstudien* 66,244–245 1975.

STEINBERG, Diane. Spinoza's Ethical Doctrine And The Unity Of Human Nature. *J Hist Phil* 22,303–324 Jl 84.

STEINDL, Rudolf. Cultural Epochs And Their Predominant Ideas (in Czechoslovakian). *Filosof Cas* 33,1–11 1985.

Any cultural epoch exists in its material forms (which are to the highest extent dependent on the given socio–economic formation), it has furthermore its rationality (its kind of explaining natural–social facts) and its morality (its value system). The specificity of culture of the respective cultural epoch is expressible in a certain epoch by the prevalent stratum of ideas headed by the predominant idea. The predominant idea forms the main motive of a certain morality, it expresses and determines the approach of a social whole and of man to the world.

STEINER, Helmut. Die Sozialökonomische Determiniertheit Wissenschaftlichen Schöpfertums. *Deut Z Phil* 22,213–222 1974.

Bei der Erforschung des wissenschaftlichen Schöpfertums sollten u a folgende Problemkomplexe in den Mittelpunkt gestellt werden: das wissenschaftliche Schöpfertum als Bestandteil des gesellschaftlichen Schöpfertums sowie als Bestandteil des wissenschaftlichen und gesellschaftlichen Reproduktionsprozesses, die Funktion des Bildungssystems für die Ausbildung wissenschaftlich–schöpferischer Fähigkeiten, die Herausbildung einer gesamtgesellschaftlichen Motivation wissenschaftlich–schöpferischer Tätigkeit. (edited)

STEINER, Mark. Events And Causality (in Hebrew). *Iyyun* 34,67–78 Ja–Ap 85.

The main thrust of this article is that physical theories contain not only "written laws" but also much tacit "lore"—an Oral Tradition, as it were. In particular, the concept of causality belongs to the tacit part of science. That is, no reference to causality is

made in the differential equations which express the laws of mathematical physics—a point originally made by Bertrand Russell, but argued for here in a novel way. Nevertheless—and here Russell missed the point—the laws of mathematical physics do not exhaust the subject. For example, criteria are needed to accept or reject solutions to the differential equations, for not all such solutions can truly be considered "physically real." It is here that causality enters the scene: mathematical solutions which violate the canons of causality (for example, which place the cause subsequent to the effect) are routinely rejected. However, it does not appear that all the causal principles a theory rests upon could be articulated, so that the division of science into Oral and Written is permanent.

STEINER, Rudolf. Deeper Insights In Education: The Waldorf Approach. Spring Valley Anthroposophic Pr 1983.

STEINKRAUS, Warren E. Berkeley, Epistemology, And Science. *Ideal Stud* 14,183–192 S 84.

Though science evolved from philosophy, moderns now evaluate it on "scientific" grounds. Berkeley offers at least three corrective insights to facile scientific dogmatizing: (1) The rejection of abstract general ideas like hypostatized "matter". (2) The rejection of all substances, physical and mental as fatuous. (3) Recognition of the centrality of the knowing self which cannot be reduced to less than it knows itself to be. Thus, *real* sound is still heard not a merely measurable "undulatory motion in the air," as Hylas avers.

STEINMANN JR, Martin. What's The Point Of Professional Interpretation Of Literature? *Phil Lit* 8,266–270 O 84.

Until about World War II, American professional interpretation of literature had both an intellectual point (historical reconstruction of knowledge original readers of a work used to interpret it) and a social (reconstruction to benefit readers alien to the work's time or culture). Replacing reconstruction with the autonomy of work or critic, most postwar professional interpretation has little point other than provoking irresoluble controversies, swelling gurus' progresses, and getting critics promotion, tenure, raises, and offers.

STEINMETZ, Rudy. Le Matérialisme Biologique De Lévi–Strauss. *Rev Phil Fr* 174,427–441 O–D 84.

STENECK, Nicholas H. The University And Research Ethics. *Sci Tech Human Values* 9,6–15 Fall 84.

Recent cases of fraud in scholarship have prompted several research universities to publish guidelines for preventing fraud. The major emphasis of these guidelines has been disciplinary, it being assumed that the best way to prevent fraud is to discipline offenders. This article summarized a different approach attempted at the University of Michigan, where the emphasis was placed as much on encouraging ethical behavior in scholarship as on punishing those who act unethically.

STENGEL, Barbara S. Competition And Moral Development. *Phil Stud Educ* No Vol,52–62 1983.

This paper focuses on the moral theory of Jean Piaget, particularly on the role of competition in moral development. The specific questions raised center on the philosophical soundness of Piaget's program. The author contends that competition plays a dual role in Piaget's program, in that Piaget refers to it both as an indispensible feature of and as an inhibitor of moral development. This constitutes a contradiction which Piaget only partially resolves.

STENGERS, Isabelle and Prigogine, Ilya. *Order Out Of Chaos: Man's New Dialogue With Nature.* NY Bantam Books 1984.

STEPHAN, Bernd J. Compactness And Recursive Enumerability In Intensional Logic. *Z Math Log* 21,343–346 1975.

STEPHENS, G Lynn and Graham, George. Are Qualia A Pain In The Neck For Functionalists? *Amer Phil Quart* 22,73–80 Ja 85.

Pains and bodily sensations generally are allegedly resistent to functionalistic analysis, and this is supposed to undermine Functionalism as a general theory of mind. But it doesn't. We argue that pains are composite states, and that the component of pain which may be resistent to functionalistic analysis is not even psychological. This part's qualitative component and is a sensible quality of human and animal bodies.

STEPHENS, G Lynn. Noumenal Qualia: C S Peirce On Our Epistemic Access To Feelings. *Trans Peirce Soc* 21,95–108 Wint 85.

I explain Peirce's contention that we have no knowledge of feelings—the phenomenal features of consciousness—as they are in themselves. This requires, first, showing that the distinction between how feelings are in themselves and how they seem to us makes sense: and, second, working out the argument for his skeptical conclusion. If Peirce is right, feelings occupy a status analogous to that of Kantian noumena.

STEPHENS, James and Russow, Lilly–marlene. Brains In Vats And The Internalist Perspective. *Austl J Phil* 63,205–212 Je 85.

In *Reason, Truth, and History*, Hilary Putnam uses his theory of reference to argue against the thesis that we might all be brains in vats, and for a version of anti–realism that he calls "the internalist perspective". In this paper, it is argued that the brains–in–vats argument is fatally flawed, and that similar problems can be found in Putnam's defense of the internalist perspective.

STEPHENS, James. Socrates On The Rule Of Law. *Hist Phil Quart* 2,3–10 Ja 85.

STEPIEŃ, Teodor. A Sufficient And Necessary Condition For Tarski's Property In Lindenbaum's Extensions. *Z Math Log* 30,447–453 1984.

The aim of this paper is to solve the problem of uniqueness of Lindenbaum extensions. Hence we introduce the notion of extensive completeness of a system S with respect to a set Z of sentences. Hence it is shown that every consistent system S with detachment (or with substitution and detachment) has only one Lindenbaum extension if and only if S is extensive complete with respect to fixed set Z and extending S by sentences of Z is inconsistent.

STERBA, James P. Contemporary Moral Philosophy And Practical Reason. *Proc Cath Phil Ass* 58,73–83 1984.

STERN– GILLET, Suzanne. Le Rôle Du Concept D'intention Dans La Formation Du Jugement Esthétique: D'une Controverse Anglo–Saxonne Et De Son Précurseur Belge. *Rev Phil Louvain* 83,197–213 My 85.

Should the artist's intention constitute an interpretative and judgmental criterion for his/her work? Wimsatt and Beardsley's famous "intentional fallacy" (1954) amounts to an emphatically negative answer to this question. The very formulation of their thesis is here challenged and it is argued that it should be partly reformulated. It is then claimed that, once recast, the "intentional fallacy" is very close to the theory put forward, already in 1933, by Servais Étienne in *Défense de la philologie*. The question thus arises as to whether this common theoretical core can provide a satisfactory answer to the question at issue. The contention is that it can in almost all cases of aesthetic judgment, though with the exception of fakes and forgies.

STERN, Laurent. "Words Fail Me". *J Aes Art Crit* 43,57–70 Fall 84.

The aim of this paper is to discredit intentionalist doctines and to show that the notion of meaning does not explain the reader's understanding of literary artworks. It establishes two claims: (1) appeal to authorial meaning is supported by a fundamental confusion between psychological and epistemic access. (2) reader–oriented literary criticism is supported by a powerful illusion: the reader constructed meaning of a sentence or literary text explains the reader's understanding of that sentence or literary text.

STERN, Laurent. Hermeneutics And Intellectual History. *J Hist Ideas* 46,287–296 Ap–Je 85.

Two theories are discussed. *Restricted theories* distinguish between understanding and interpreting. We interpret texts in addition to understanding them. *Unrestricted theories* claim that understanding texts or utterances requires interpretation. Although interpreting practices provide more constraints on interpretive decisions than these two theories; nevertheless, these theories rule out some interpretations. Examples of the application cf these theories in intellectual history are provided by the work of Michel Foucault and Jürgen Habermas.

STERN, Raphael. Relational Model Systems: The Craft Of Logic. *Synthese* 60,225–252 Ag 84.

STERNBERGER, Dolf. Ancient Features Of The Modern State. *Hist Euro Ideas* 5,225–236 1984.

STEUSSLOFF, Hans. Über Die Wahrheit Und Den Wahrheitsbegriff. *Deut Z Phil* 22,487–491 1974.

STEUSSLOFF, Hans. Die Macht Zur Freiheit. *Deut Z Phil* 32,776–784 1984.

STEVENS, Bernard. L'unité De L'oeuvre De Paul Ricoeur Saisie Selon La Perspective De Son Ouvrage Temps Et Récit I. *Tijdschr Filosof* 47,111–117 Mr 85.

The purpose of this essay is to show how *Temps et récit* (1983) is in a close continuity with the work begun in 1960 under the title: *Philosophy of the Will*. This work was meant to have three parts: a pure phenomenology of the will; an empirical approach to guilt; and a poetic of the will liberating itself from evil. Apparently Ricoeur had abandoned the poetic. Yet, *Temps et récit*, when understood together with *La métaphere vive* appears to be an introduction to such a poetic: it shows how the métaphorical language of fiction permits a redescribing of reality with an ontological dimension which the literal language of science cannot reach.

STEVENS, John C. Must The Bearer Of A Right Have The Concept Of That To Which He Has A Right? *Ethics* 95,68–74 O 84.

Michael Tooley, in "Abortion and Infanticide," commits himself to the view that A has a right to X only if A has the concept of X (the conceptual possession requirement). Counterexamples refute the conceptual possession requirement. Since Tooley's analysis of the concept of a right implies the conceptual possession requirement, that analysis is incorrect. Thus, Tooley's argument in support of abortion and infanticide, which rests on that analysis, is unsound.

STEVENS, John Mark and Bole, Thomas. Why Hegel At All? *Phil Topics* 13,113–122 Spr 85.

We propose that Hegel's system is serious philosophy, if his dialectic is interpreted logically. We make this interpretation by showing how to take the *logic's* dialectic as an explanation of thought in its function as explanatory, and of being as thought's most general *explanadum*. We then indicate cosequences for what is indispensable, reviseable, and untenable in Hegel's *Realphilosophie*, and for Hegel's remarks about contradiction within the *Logic*.

STEVENS, Richard G (ed) and Frisch, Morton J (ed). *American Political Thought: The Philosophic Dimension Of American Statesmanship*, Second Edition. Itasca Peacock 1983.

STEVENSON, J T. Regulation, Deregulation, Self–Regulation: The Case Of Engineers In Ontario. *J Bus Ethics* 4,253–267 Ag 85.

Against a wider background of rationales for deregulation within a modern economy, and as an exercise of subjecting a theory to the hard discipline of a particular case, a detailed analysis is given of a recent proposal for a form of deregulation (the industrial exemption) for engineering in Ontario. The proposal of the Staff Study of the Professional Organizations Committee set up by the Ontario Government is analyzed in terms of Posnerian foundations, and is criticized theoretically, empirically and normatively. Attention is drawn to two wider issues: the protection by self–regulating professionals of third parties against negaive externalities, and the adverse effects of the proletarianization of professionals in large organizations.

STEWART, Marilyn. "Myth & Tragic Action In La Celestina And Romeo And Juliet" in *Existential Coordinates Of Human Condition*, Tymienlecka, A (ed), 425–435. Boston Reidel 1984.

STEWART, Robert M. Morality And The Market In Blood. *J Applied Phil* 1,227–238 O 84.

The late Richard Titmuss made a persuasive case against allowing the sale of human blood in his book, *The Gift Relationship*. His arguments have been developed further by Pete Singer in recent articles. First, I question their claim that a donation–only system promotes greater freedom, which rests on a confusion of liberty and opportunity. Next, I consider reasons for doubting their view that altruism is fostered significantly more under the non–market approach. Finally, I survey recent developments in the quantity–quality debate and possible implications of the blood controversy for national health care. (edited)

STICH, Stephen P. "Armstrong On Belief" in *D M Armstrong*, Bogdan, Radu J (ed), 121–138. Boston Reidel 1984.

STICH, Stephen P. Could Man Be An Irrational Animal: Some Notes On The Epistemology Of Rationality. *Synthese* 64,115–134 Jl 85.

Psychologists have gathered a considerable body of evidence suggesting that normal human subjects exhibit systematically irrational patterns of inference. A number of philosophers, appealing to conceptual or evolutionary considerations, have argued that this sort of systematic irrationality is impossible. It is argued that all of these arguments fail and that it is indeed possible that people are irrational in predictable ways.

STIDD, Benton M. Are Punctuationists Wrong About The Modern Synthesis? *Phil Sci* 52,98–109 Mr 85.

A common criticism of punctuated equilibria as an evolutionary theory is that it erects a straw man by characterizing the modern synthesis as being devoid of mechanisms that bring about rapid speciation and abrupt changes in morphology. Thompson supports this view and argues that the modern synthesis does not entail gradualism, all–pervasive adaptationism, or extrapolationism and that punctuationists have mischaracterized the theory on all these points; properly understood the synthetic theory is hierarchial and able to explain phenomena at all levels of the hierarchy, thus rendering macroevolutionary theories, such as punctuated equilibria, unnecessary. I argue in this paper that Thompson's approach is overly dependent upon rational reconstruction in the style of the logical empiricists, and as such ignores important sociological and historical factors that when taken into account justify punctuational criticism of the synthetic theory.

STIEGLER, Karl D. Zur Entstehung Und Begründung Des Newtonschen Calculus Fluxionum Und Des Leibnizschen Calculus Differentialis. *Phil Natur* 21,161–218 1984.

STIEHLER, Gottfried. Die Anwendung Der Marxschen Dialektik Beim Aufbau Des Kategoriensystems Des Historischen Materialismus. *Deut Z Phil* 32,972–980 1984.

Der Aufbau des historischen Materialismus geschieht in serialer Form. Das bedingt eine schrittweise Entwicklung der inneren Zusammenhänge des theoretischen Systems in der Form des Nacheinander von Kategorien und Gesetzen. Dabei spielt die Frage nach dem Ausgangsabstraktum eine Rolle. Das Ausgangsabstraktum ist der "Grundgedanke" de historischen Materialismus; die Methode dialektischer Gedankenentwicklung ist das Aufsteigen vom Abstrakten zum Konkreten.

STIEHLER, Gottfried. Subjektiver Faktor Und Revolution. *Deut Z Phil* 22,554–563 1974.

Die sozialistische Revolution ist das Ergebnis des Heranreifens objektiver Voraussetzungen. gleichzeitig unterliegt sie dem bewufssten Wirken der revolutionären Kräfte. Wie die objektiven Voraussetzungen, so sind auch die subjektiven Bedingungen der Revolution ein differenziertes Ganzes. Zwischen dem Objektiven und dem Subjektiven bestehen komplizierte Wechselwirkungen. Man kann zwischen den subjektiven Bedingungen, dem subjektiven Faktor und der hauptsächlichen Triebkraft ker Revolution unterscheiden. Die subjective Einwirkung auf die Revolution ist nicht nur von nationalem, sondern zugleich von internationalem Charakter.

STIELER, Gottfried. Determiniertheit Und Entwicklung. *Deut Z Phil* 22,475–486 1974.

STIGLIANO, Tony. The Logos And The Lotos. *Proc Phil Educ* 40,353–360 1984.

This paper is a critical response to a paper by David Denton which purports to show that there is a way to intergrate analytical philosophy with existential philosophy. He attempts this by synthesizing Carnap, Searle and Wheelwright. The argument, it is concluded, does not wash; it depends on a very lose and textually insupportable interpretation of these thinkers.

STIKKERS, Kenneth W. The Life–World Roots Of Economy. *J Brit Soc Phenomenol* 16,167–176 My 85.

Phenomenology, as a response to the over–extension of scientific reason into scient*ism*, has said little about the origins and rise of economic science. This essay identifies briefly three specific places where economy's detachment from the its life–world origins show itself and where phenomenology can help economic science recover its forgotten roots: 1) the notion of "scarcity", 2) the uprooting of the "market place", and 3) the transvaluation of economy values, viz., self–control liberty and trust.

STILLWELL, Shelley. Confirmation, Paradoxes, And Possible Worlds. *Brit J Phil Sci* 36,19–51 Mr 85.

The paper shows, both formally and informally, that Hempel's paradoxes of confirmation do not logically follow from Nicod's Condition and the Equivalence Condition. Further, the sorts of principles one must adopt to derive the paradoxes from those conditions are false. The Appendix explores model semantics useful for the investigation of the relations between entailment and confirmation. In sum, the notion of qualitative confirmation is shown to be far more respectable than has been supposed in recent years.

STINES, James W. I Am The Way: Michael Polanyi's Taoism. *Zygon* 20,59–77 Mr 85.

Several contemporary writers have found certain correlations between Taoism and modern philosophy of science to be particularly noteworthy because of their usefulness for interpreting world views, implicit or explicit, in each. However, the recent project in science and epistemology – the work of Michael Polanyi – which is probably most fruitfully resonant with Taoism has not yet been explored in that connection. The purpose of the present article is to begin that exploration. The essay provides a preliminary sketch of certain key moments in Polanyi's thought and then turns attention to the Taoist themes of *Tao, wu–wei,* and *tz'u* as these illuminate and are illuminated by the Polanyian post–critical epistemology.

STIRLING, James Hutchison. *What Is Thought?* NY Garland 1984.

What is it to think? What is thought? The author presents a historical survey of the ontology of thought and the ontological foundations of the first principles of metaphysics. The relation of 'thought' to philosophy is fully explored. The metaphysics of Kant, Hume, Aristotle, Leibnitz, Hegel, Fichte, and Schelling are investigated and discussed as regards to the ontological metaphysics of thought. (staff)

STOHRER, Walter J. Heidegger And Jacob Grimm: On Dwelling And The Genesis Of Language. *Mod Sch* 62,43–52 N 84.

Early in *Being and Time* Heidegger acknowledged his indebtedness to Grimm's historical studies of the German prepositions *in* and *bei*. This was done within the context of a "preliminary sketch of Being–in–the–World, in terms of an orientation towards Being–in as such." This article examines content of these two monographs, traces of which appear in several lectures of Heidegger's later period.

STOJCHEV, Todor. Ideology And Social Psyche (in Hungarian). *Magyar Filozof Szemle* 6,961–972 1983.

STOLAR M, Israel. Las Perspectivas Y Las Implicaciones Del Oficio De Axiólogo. *Logos (Mexico)* 12,105–120 S–D 84.

STOLAROV, Vladislav I. Social Essence And Value Of The Olympic Idea. *Dialec Hum* 11,33–42 Wint 84.

STOLJAR, Samuel. *An Analysis Of Rights.* NY St Martin's Pr 1984.

This book is an attempt to demystify the notion of rights. The first chapters discuss the conceptual ingredients of a right (rights as claims, entitlements, liberties, benefits, interests, rights and duties). Chapter five adumbrates a critique of Hohfeld's schemata of rights; chapter six examines other 'right–like' notions as permission, power, and privilege. The final chapters consider the necessary discursive framework of rights, the argument here being that natural rights call for moral content wherever we settle interpersonal grievances in argument as individuals among individuals.

STOLJAR, Samuel. Discussion: White On Rights And Claims. *Law Phil* 4,101–114 Ap 85.

Professor White maintains that claims neither imply nor are implied by rights. Substantially the opposite may be shown to be the case—that, very briefly, to make a claim implies some sort of right while to have a right always involves something at least claimable or, more usually, actually claimed.

STOLL, Ivan. The Vital Attitude Of Man From The Standpoint Of Prigogine's Thermodynamics (in Czechoslovakian). *Filozof Cas* 32,792–801 1984.

STOLLBERG, R and Assmann, Georg. Inhaltliche Fragen Der Ausarbeitung Eines Lehrbuches Der Marxistisch–Leninistischen Soziologie. *Deut Z Phil* 22,228–235 1974.

STOLLBERG, R. Wissenschaftlich–Technischer Fortschritt Und Sozialistisches Verhältnis Zur Arbeit. *Deut Z Phil* 33,73–76 1985.

STOLNITZ, Jerome. "You Can't Separate The Work Of Art From The Artist". *Phil Lit* 8,209–221 O 84.

STOLNITZ, Jerome. Afterwords "The Aesthetic Attitude" In The Rise Of Modern Aesthetics–Again. *J Aes Art Crit* 43,205–208 Wint 84.

STOLNITZ, Jerome. Painting And Painter In Aesthetic Education. *J Aes Educ* 18,23–36 Fall 84.

STONE, Alan R (ed). *Law, Psychiatry, And Morality.* Washington American Psych Pr 1984.

STONE, John. Medicine And The Arts. *Theor Med* 6,309–326 O 85.

Three years' experience in teaching a course in Literature and Medicine is reviewed. Examples of the 'Laboratory' or *'in vitro'* functions of art are given as they relate to and benefit both medical students and practitioners. The usefulness of literature (especially) in the medical setting is underscored, together with the need for medical personnel to be more aware of their heritage in this area. Examples of well–known physicians who have excelled in the arts (literature, music, painting/sculpture) are given and their major contributions discussed. There are some surprises.

STONE, Lucy and Blackwell, Henry. "Marriage Contract" in *Freedom, Feminism, And The State,* Mc Elroy, Wendy (ed), 119–120. Washington Cato Institute 1982.

STONE, Mark A. Aristotle's Distinction Between Motion And Activity. *Hist Phil Quart* 2,11–20 Ja 85.

STOWELL, Peter. "Phenomenology And Literary Impressionism" in *Existential Coordinates Of Human Condition,* Tymieniecka, A (ed), 535–546. Boston Reidel 1984.

STRASSER, Kurt. Konrad Bayer Und Ludwig Wittgenstein—Zwei Formen Eines Denkens. *Conceptus* 19,84–96 1985.

Parallels between Wittgenstein and Konrad Bayer should demonstrate that each of them is fighting against the "illness of a time". The poetic insurrections of Bayer will be interpreted as games of transgressing the limits of language; Wittgenstein's philosophical insurrection as a continual redefinition of limits. The cure of this "illness"—and the way to understand Bayer and Wittgenstein—would lie in totally renouncing philosophical or poetic prescriptions and the all–embracing consumption–ideology, and electing to think in one's own way.

STRASSER, Mark. Dependence, Reliance And Abortion. *Phil Quart* 35,73–82 Ja 85.

Michael Davis makes an important distinction between reliance and dependence which helps illuminate some of our intuitions about abortion. However, his distinction

does not yield the results he suggests. Rather, it helps to show that we need not settle metaphysical claims about the personhood of fetuses before making headway in deciding when and if abortions are permissible.

STRASSER, St. K O Apel Over "Erklären" En "Verstehen". *Tijdschr Filosof* 46,485–497 S 84.

STRASSFELD, Robert and David, Zdenek V. Bibliography Of Works In Philosophy Of History 1978–1982. *Hist Theor* 73,1–107 D 84.

STRAUGHAN, Roger R. Moral Theory And Educational Practice: A Reply To Ian Gregory. *J Moral Educ* 13,194–196 O 84.

In reply to a review article on my book, *Can We Teach Children To Be Good?* (1982), I argue that moral educators must examine various accounts of morality to build up a synthetic though necessarily imprecise picture of morality's distinctive contours, as the effective formulation of any educational objectives requires prior investigation of the nature and peculiar characteristics of whatever is intended to be learnt.

STRAUSS, D F M. An Analysis Of The Structure Of Analysis. *Phil Reform* 49,35–56 1984.

In epistemology the relationship between the universal and the particular and that concerning the relation between constancy and dynamics are basic. Over–accentuating universality resulted in rationalism (knowledge is identical with conceptual knowledge), and *opposing* constancy and dynamics gave birth to the substance concept and the eventual Kantian opposition of logical thought–categories and a–logical sense material—ending up with the untenable opposition of analysis and synthesis. This article discusses these problems in connection with the tradition of Dooyeweerd's reformational philosophy.

STRENSKI, Ivan T. Ernst Cassirer's *Mythical Thought* In Weimar Culture. *Hist Euro Ideas* 5,363–384 1984.

Cassirer's early theory of myth is located in the 'external' cultural milieu of post–World War One Germany. Special attention is paid to the discourse on myth current among German "Volkish" movement thinkers—both academic ("Mandarin") intellectuals and popular makers of fascist culture, I include that 'internal' theoretical moves can often only be understood in terms of the 'external' strategies of a thinker's discourse. Cassirer's theory is a case in point.

STROE, Constantin. Moral Values And The Assimilation Of Social Necessity. *Phil Log* 28,93–97 Ap–Je 84.

STRÖKER, Elisabeth. "On Popper's Conventionalism" in *Methodology, Metaphysics And The History Of Science,* Cohen, Robert S (ed), 263–282. Boston Reidel 1984.

STRÖKER, Elisabeth. Konventionalistische Argumente In Poppers Wissenschaftsphilosophie. *Erkenntnis* 21,385–404 N 84.

STROLL, Avrum. Faces. *Inquiry* 28,177–194 Je 85.

In the philosophical and psychological literature of the twentieth century, the concept of a surface plays a pervasive and important role, mostly in connection with theories of perception. The author argues that the concept has interesting logical and ontological uses as well. The focus of the paper is on the question of whether surfaces are real ingredients in the world, and the argument of the paper is that, under certain construals, they are.

STRONG, Carson. The Neonatologist's Duty To Patient And Parents. *Hastings Center Rep* 14,10–16 Ag 84.

Neonatologists often provide aggressive life–saving treatment to defective newborns without allowing parents to decide. Philosophers have treated this issue as paternalism, but it is not such. The strongest argument against parental decision–making rests on the physician's putting the patient's (infant's) interest first. I argue that neonatologists should pursue the infant's best interests *except* when this would seriously burden the family. In such cases parents should be permitted to make the decision concerning aggressive life–saving treatment.

STRONG, Tracy B. Reflections On Perspectivism In Nietzsche. *Polit Theory* 13,164–182 My 85.

Perspectivism is Nietzsche's attempt at replacing epistemology with an understanding of the self and of knowledge that does not posit any particular position (or self) as final. We must think of the subject as a multiplicity and not a unity. Reference is made to recent writings on Nietzsche, especially those of Nehamas.

STROUD, Barry. *The Significance Of Philosophical Scepticism.* Oxford Clarendon Pr 1984.

STROUD, Barry. Skepticism And The Possibility Of Knowledge. *J Phil* 81,545–551 O 84.

STRÓZEWSKI, Wladyslaw. Man As APXH. *Rep Phil* 8,73–76 1984.

STRÓZEWSKI, Wladyslaw. Rationalism And Metarationalism. *Dialec Hum* 11,299–318 Spr/Sum 84.

STRUBE, Werner. Über Drei Methoden Der Sprachanalytischen Ästhetik. *Conceptus* 19,39–52 1985.

Aestheticians in the tradition of linguistic analysis clarify aesthetic concepts by illuminating the *use* of the corresponding expressions: Wittgenstein presents *language games* in a way which throws light on the peculiar 'grammar' of the expression "beautiful". MacDonald describes and analyzes the *performative utterance* executed when "That is (aesthetically) good" is said. Sibley illuminates the informal logic of aesthetic concepts by comparing the *application conditions* of the expression "graceful" for example with the application conditions of geometrical and other expressions.

STRUG, Cordell. 'Metaphysics Is Not Your Strong Point': Orwell And Those Who Speak For Civilization. *Soc Theor Pract* 10,333–348 Fall 84.

STRUVE, Horst. Affine Ebenen Mit Orthogonalitätsrelation. *Z Math Log* 30,223–231 1984.

In the article it is investigated under which conditions the coordinating system of an affine translation plane in which a relation of orthogonality is defined is a field. Examples for such planes are besides the Euclidean planes the well known Galilean and Minskowskian planes. It is proofed that the coordinatizing system is a field if and only if you can define circles by help of reflections in the lines of the plane.

STUART, David. *Alan Watts*. NY Stein And Day 1976.

STUART, James D. Frankfurt On Descartes' Dream Argument. *Phil Forum* 16,237–245 Spr 85.

I argue that Professor Harry B Frankfurt's interpretation of Descartes' dream argument is mistaken. He contends that the dream argument calls into question only the reality of particular sensory experiences, not the existence of the material world itself, which is called into doubt by the evil demon. I show that Frankfurt's view lacks the textual support claimed for it and that it fails to fit in with the overall argument of the *Meditatons*. I conclude that Descartes' dream argument should be interpreted as calling into question the existence of the material world. This restores the dream argument to its traditional place in Descartes' method of doubt.

STUBBS, Michael and Kech, Gabriele. Koschmieder On Speech Act Theory: A Historical Note. *J Prag* 8,305–310 Je 84.

The discovery of the characteristics of performative verbs, and other basic concepts of speech act theory, is usually attributed exclusively to John L Austin. However, many of the same concepts were discovered and discussed in detail, apparently independently and at about the same time or even earlier, by Erwin Koschmieder.

STUBEN, Peter E. Was Erwartet Uns Jenseits Der Wissenschaft: Ethno–Philosophie: Erfahrungen Und Möglichkeiten Im Umgang Mit Dem Irrationalen. *Conceptus* 18,46–59 1984.

Wir sind nicht mehr die, die wir einmal waren: Jene Matrosen einer positivistischen Metaphysik, die ihr Luxusschiff der Wissenschaft auf offener See aus den vermeintlich strapazierbarsten Planken unserer abendländisch–rationelen Denktradition erbaut haben, sondern in Seenot Geratene, die mit ansehen müssen, wie das Jahrhundertwerk ihrer Bemühungen unter den anbrausenden Wogen der längst für gebändigt befundenen Kräfte des Irrationalen Risse zu zeigen beginnt—die Planken sich biegen und schliesslich bersten. (edited)

STUEWER, Roger H. "Artificial Disintegration" in *Observation, Experiment, And Hypothesis In Modern Physical Science*, Achinstein, Peter (ed), 239–308. Cambridge MIT Pr 1985.

STUHLMANN– LAEISZ, Ranier. Hinlänglichkeit Und Notwendigheit Im Moralischen. *Erkenntnis* 23,19–50 My 85.

This paper contrasts different definitions of extrinsic values in terms of intrinsic one. I define the *right* and the *bidden* as extrinsic goods, the *wrong* and the *forbidden* as extrinsic bads. There are two possibilities for doing this: an entrinsic good (bad) is a means which is (i) either necessary or (ii) sufficient to realize the intrinsic good (bad). Thus defined, *right* and *bidden* have different logical properties, the same holds with *wrong* and *forbidden*. Likewise the logical relations between *right* and *wrong* differ from those between *bidden* and *forbidden*, and those between *right* and *forbidden* are different from the relations between *bidden* and *wrong*. The paper concludes with a study of the logical features of the question whether doing the bidden and refraining from the forbidden suffices for morally right action.

STUMP, Eleonore. Dialectic In The Eleventh And Twelfth Centuries: Garlandus Compotista. *Hist Phil Log* 1,1–18 1980.

Dialectic is a standard and important part of the *logical vetus* (or old logic) in medieval philosophy. It has its ultimate origins in Aristotle's *Topics*, its fundamental source in Boethius's *De topics differentiis*, and its flowering in its absorption into fourteenth–century theories of consequences or conditional inferences. The chapter on Topics in Garlandus Compotista's logic book is the oldest scholastic work on dialectic still extant. In this paper I show the differences between Boethius's Theory of Topics and Garlandus's in order to illustrate the role of Topics in early scholastic logic. I argue that for Garlandus Topics are warrants for the inference from the antecedent to the consequent in a conditional proposition and that he is interested in Topics because of overriding interest in hypothetical syllogisms. I conclude by discussing briefly the relationship between Garlandus's use of Topics and twelfth–century accounts.

STUMP, Eleonore. Hoffman On Petitionary Prayer. *Faith Phil* 2,30–37 Ja 85.

Hoffman raises and rejects three arguments against petitionary prayer; in the process he takes issue with a paper of mine. I think he is right to reject the arguments against prayer which he raises, though I am not in agreement with his reasons for rejecting them. But I show that the rejection of these arguments does not constitute a successful defense of petitionary prayer, particularly in view of the objections to prayer raised in my paper; and I argue that Hoffman has misunderstood the strategy of my response to those objections.

STUMP, Eleonore. The Logic Of Disputation In Walter Burley's Treatise On Obligations. *Synthese* 63,355–374 Je 85.

Scholastic work on "obligations" has garnered increasing attention from historians of medieval philosophy. Although it is now clear that there was a long tradition of scholastic interest in obligations, it is still not clear what the nature of obligations is: it has been described variously as anything from schoolboy exercises to primitive axiomatized logic. I argue that in Burley's work obligations is a complicated set of rules for consequences or inferences set in a disputational context, where the disputational context makes a difference to the evaluation of the inferences, often because there is a reference in the premisses themselves to the evaluator of those premisses.

STUMPF, G and Schnorr, C P. A Characterization Of Complexity Sequences. *Z Math Log* 21,47–56 1975.

STUMPF, Samuel Enoch. *Philosophical Problems*. NY McGraw–Hill 1983.

STURGEON, Nicholas L. "Moral Explanations" in *Morality, Reason And Truth*, Copp, David (ed), 49–78. Totowa Rowman & Allanheld 1984.

STURGEON, Scott. A Look At Fatalism. *Auslegung* 11,505–513 Sum 85.

Replies to logical determinism have tended to spring from rather odd philosophic positions. Examples are Aristotle and Geach. Two desperate articles for determinism are presented and defeated. The first is shown to rest on a certain looseness inherent in dealing with modalities in English, while the second is shown to assume mutually incompatible theories about the nature of time. In neither case was a counter–intuitive metaphysics or logic necessary.

STURM, Douglas. Corporate Culture And The Common Good: The Need For Thick Description And Critical Interpretation. *Thought* 60,141–160 Je 85.

An adequate study of "corporate culture" must go beyond currently popular interpretations to appropriate methods drawn from the hermeneutics of "thick description" (Clifford Geertz), critical social theory (Anthony Giddens), and relational philosophy (Bernard Meland). From such a perspective, corporate culture embraces multiple levels: mesoscopic, microscopic, and chronoscopic. For illustrative purposes, a case study of a contemporary petroleum corporation is used. Moreover, from such a perspective, a study of corporate culture must culminate in ethical judgment in which the principle of common good is preeminent.

STUTLEY, James and Stutley, Margaret. *Harper's Dictionary Of Hinduism: Its Mythology, Folklore, Philosophy, Literature, And History*. NY Harper & Row 1977.

STUTLEY, Margaret and Stutley, James. *Harper's Dictionary Of Hinduism: Its Mythology, Folklore, Philosophy, Literature, And History*. NY Harper & Row 1977.

SUÁREZ, Francis. *On The Essence Of Finite Being As Such, On The Existence Of That Essence And Their Distinction*. Milwaukee Marquette Univ Pr 1983.

SUCH, Jan. Models Of Rationality In Physics. *Dialec Hum* 11,329–338 Spr/Sum 84.

There are various types of rationalism connected with various types of activity and various kinds of axiological systems related to them. Models of cognitive rationalism are established by means of four types of principles: logical, ontological, epistemological, and methodological. At least three models of rationalism occurred in physics: the model of rationalism of ancient physics /Aristotle's physics/, the model of rationalism of modern /classical/ physics, and the model of rationalism of contemporary /non–classical, quantum/ physics.

SUCHOCKI, Marjorie. The Appeal To Ultimacy In Meland's Thought. *Amer J Theol Phil* 5,80–88 My & S 84.

SUCHOCKI, Marjorie. Weaving The World. *Process Stud* 14,75–86 Sum 85.

SUCHOŃ, Wojciech. An Elementary Method Of Determining The Degree Of Completeness On N–Valued Lukasiewicz Propositional Calculus. *Bull Sect Log* 13,226–229 D 84.

SUCHOŃ, Wojciech. The Deontic Calculus D_{krz}. *Rep Math Log* 18,61–66 1984.

SUCHTING, W A. "Popper's Critique Of Marx's Method" in *Popper And The Human Sciences*, Currie, Gregory (ed), 147–164. Boston Nijhoff 1985.

SUGDEN, Robert. Is Fairness Good: A Critique Of Varian's Theory Of Fairness. *Nous* 18,505–512 S 84.

The 'theory of fairness' developed by Varian, Daniel, Pazner and others evaluates allocations by a combination of two distinct criteria—Pareto–efficiency and envy–freeness. Allocations that are both efficient and envy–free are called 'fair' and it is presumed that 'fair' allocations are good. This paper argues against this presumption, showing that it rests on the untenable proposition that Pareto–efficiency is inherently good. The appropriate trade–off is not between *efficiency* and equality but between *welfare* and equality. To recognize this is to accept that non–'fair' allocations may be preferable to 'fair' ones.

SUGDEN, Robert. Regret, Recrimination And Rationality. *Theor Decis* 19,77–99 Jl 85.

This paper considers whether regret theory, in which individuals' choices are influenced by expectations of regret, describes *rational* behavior. It argues that 'regret' must be interpreted to include self–recrimination, i.E., the recognition that a past choice was unjustified when it was made. Nevertheless a rational person may have to choose without being able to justify *any* choice, in which case he may quite rationally foresee self–recrimination if things turn out badly.

SUITS, David B. Some Considerations About The Discovery Of Principles Of Justice. *Eidos* 1,50–67 Jl 78.

SULLIVAN, Brian G. Laborem Exercens: A Theological And Philosophical Foundation For Business Ethics. *Listening* 20,128–146 Spr 85.

The article utilizes Pope John II's encyclical "Laborem Exercens" as a framework for an examination of the foundations of business ethics. The author argues that an institutionalization of ethics within society is required calling for a basic recognition of the dignity of the person and the need for a democratization of the economic system. The Christian tradition in the encyclical helps protect the dignity of the person against the collectivist tendencies within institutions.

SULLIVAN, Robert. The Rationality Debate And Gadamer's Hermeneutics: Reflections On Beyond Objectivism And Relativism. *Phil Soc Crit* 11,85–100 Sum 85.

SULLIVAN, Roger J. "The Kantian Critique Of Aristotle's Moral Philosophy" in *The Good Life And Its Pursuit*, Dougherty, Jude P (ed), 77–110. NY Paragon House 1984.

SULLIVAN, Roger J. A Response To "Is Business Bluffing Ethical". *Bus Prof Ethics J* 3,1–18 Wint 84.

In his article, "Is Business Bluffing Ethical?" (*Harvard Business Review*, 1968), the late Albert Carr presented what has come to be regarded as a classic defense of the view that it is mistake to think business can be conducted successfully by the ordinary ethical rules of society. In the absence of any previous, explicit examination and critique of Carr's article, I argue that his arguments not only fail by curiously obscure the issues. I also maintain that his thesis is antithetical to the nature of business, understood as a system of value traded for fair value.

SUMARES, Manuel. O trabalho Do Texto Filosófico E A Sua Interpretação. *Rev Port Filosof* 40,361–386 O–D 84.

SUMMERS, Jim. When Meeting Needs Becomes A Threat To Autonmy. *Auslegung* 11,456–480 Sum 85.

SUNDARARAJAN, P T Saroja. System And Life World: Some Reflections On Goffman's Frame Analysis. *Indian Phil Quart* 11,9–15 Ap 84.

The Philosophical basis of Goffman's Frame Analysis is the principle of the constitution of experience by means of frame work. Goffman distinguishes two basic kinds of frame works––Natural and Social. Frame works are socially located constituting the culture of the group. The relationship between the common frame work and its individual society relationship. Goffman studies transformation of frame works under keying which is an analogue of interpretation at the level of action.

SUPERSON, Anita M. The Employer–Employee Relationship And The Right To Know. *Bus Prof Ethics J* 3,45–58 Fall 83.

The purpose of this paper is to examine an employee's right to know about on–the–job hazards. I argue that this right has not been firmly established because of the non–fiduciary nature of the employer–employee relationship. Comparing this the physician–patient relationship, I argue that the right to know ought to be as firmly established for workers as it is for patients. I conclude that this may promote trust between employers and employees.

SUPPES, P (ed) and Troelstra, A S (ed) and Goldblatt, R. *Topoi: The Categorial Analysis Of Logic*. NY North–Holland 1984.

SUPPES, Patrick. Conflicting Intuitions About Causation. *Midwest Stud Phil* 9,151–168 1984.

In this article, five kinds of conflicting intuitions about the nature of causality are examined. The viewpoint is that of the probabilistic theory of causality previously developed by the author. The five issues leading to conflicting intuitions are Simpson's paradox, macroscopic deteminism, event–type versus event–tokens, existence of physical flow of causes, and existence of common causes for correlated events.

SUPPES, Patrick. Explaining The Unpredictable. *Erkenntnis* 22,187–196 Ja 85.

The central thesis of this article is that unstable phenomena either in human affairs or in nonhuman environments often make the problem of precise prediction unsolvable. Yet for many such situations a reasonable lawlike explanation can be offered after the fact. The systematic presence of instability has not received sufficient attention as a common source of unpredictability. Of course, for some phenomena the absence of any possibility of exact prediction may be due to their ultimately probabilistic nature.

SURESON, Claude. Complexity Of κ–Ultrafilters And Inner Models With Measurable Cardinals. *J Sym Log* 49,833–841 S 84.

SURESON, Claude. Non–closure Of The Image Model And Absence Of Fixed Points. *Annals Pure Applied Log* 28,287–314 My 85.

SURESON, C. P–Points And Q–Points Over A Measurable Cardinal. *Annals Pure Applied Log* 29,107–121 Jl 85.

SURIN, Kenneth. Theistic Arguments And Rational Theism. *Int J Phil Relig* 16,123–138 1984.

Keith Ward, in his book *Rational Theology and the Creativity of God*, uses the theistic proofs in tandem to provide the foundation of his demonstration of the rational intelligibility of the universe. I show that the proofs cannot operate in tandem, and that Ward's formulation of the ontological proof is not cogent. It follows that his theistic system lacks a logically coherent foundation.

SUTTMEIER, Richard P. Corruption In Science: The Chinese Case. *Sci Tech Human Values* 10,49–61 Wint 85.

SUTTNER, Raymond. The Ideological Role Of The Judiciary In South Africa. *Phil Papers* 13,28–49 O 84.

SUZUKI, Yoshindo. The Transfer Principle. *Brit J Phil Sci* 36,61–66 Mr 85.

The Second Incompleteness Theorem of K Gödel is derived from his First Incompleteness Theorem by Transfer Principle.

SVOBODA, Jan. Aesthetician Of Film And Television Jan Kucera (in Czechoslovakian). *Estetika* 21,234–266 1984.

SWAIN, Marshall. Justification, Reasons, And Reliability. *Synthese* 64,69–92 Jl 85.

SWANGER, David. Parallels Between Moral And Aesthetic Judging, Moral And Aesthetic Education. *Educ Theor* 35,85–96 Wint 85.

The essay examines the view that art either is or should be moral, then proceeds to demonstrate that although art cannot properly be said to be either moral or immoral, there are significant parallels in the dynamic of moral and aesthetic judgment. I conclude that although art and morality are separate domains, they are not divergent ones, and that the parallels between them provide for vital collaboration between moral and aesthetic education.

SWANK, Casey. Reasons, Dilemmas And The Logic Of 'Ought'. *Analysis* 45,111–116 Mr 85.

Can dilemmas arise? Most of us believe so. Still, arguments designed to show that dilemmas cannot arise *have* been advance––and two of these are *prima facie* sound. I contend that these two arguments trade, fallaciously, on the ambiguity of 'I ought to do X'––now reading it thus: 'The reasons for me to do X are *weighty*', and now thus: 'The reasons for me to do X *outweigh* those for me *not* to do X'.

SWANTON, Christine. On The "Essential Contestedness" Of Political Concepts. *Ethics* 95,811–827 Jl 85.

SWEENEY, Robert. A Survey Of Recent Ricoeur–Literature. *Phil Today* 29,38–58 Spr 85.

The article undertakes a compact survey of the central works––articles and books––

published by Ricoeur in the last ten years, beginning with *The Rule of Metaphor* and ending with the so–far published volumes of *Time & Narrative*. The theme of reference is highlighted, from its coordination with structural sense in metaphoricity, to its transmutation into "refiguration" as coordinated with the configuration of the narrative. Other themes include hermeneutics, ideology, utopia, value, action, intertextuality and imagination. Coverage is also given to interviews and commentaries.

SWIDERSKI, Edward M. "Humanistic Interpretation And Historical Materialism: (poznan School))" in *Contemporary Marxism*, O' Rourke, James J (ed), 97–108. Boston Reidel 1984.

SWIDLER, Arlene (ed). *Human Rights In Religious Traditions*. NY Pilgrim Pr 1982.

Scholars from seven faith traditions––Judaism, Roman Catholicism, Eastern Orthodoxy, Protestantism, Islam, Hinduism, and Buddhism––discuss the concept of human rights in their own tradition: its definition, the areas it embraces, its theoretical basis, the evolution of the concept, its strengths and weaknesses. Scholars from the fields of social history, technology, economics and psychiatry respond.

SWIGGERS, P. Over Taal En Wetenschap In De Encyclopédie (Summary: Language And Science In The 'Encyclopédie'). *Tijdschr Filosof* 46,573–584 D 84.

The present study offers an analysis of the linguistic articles in the *Encyclopédie* of Diderot and d'Alembert, which deal with the scientific description of the foundations of "la communication des idées". The articles of language (and linguistic categories) in the *Encyclopédie* not only reflect a philosophical stand with regard to the problem of the relation between language (words) and thought (ideas); they also show why language is central in the acquisition, the communication and diffusion of knowledge.

SWINBURNE, Richard. Thought. *Phil Stud* 48,153–172 S 85.

An occurrent thought is distinguished from belief, intelligent behavior, and the active process of thinking. The occurrence of thoughts is not to be analyzed in terms of the occurrence of images of words of sentences which express them and often accompany them. Thoughts have inbuilt intentionality.

SWINDLER, J K. Material Identity And Sameness. *Phil Topics* 13,69–76 Spr 85.

Butchvarov thinks to solve several ontological puzzles, e.G., failures of Leibniz's Law, with the concept of material identity, purportedly holding between apparently distinct objects. I argue (1) that material identity is not a coherent relation, (2) that it provides no account of similarity of identicals, (3) that Butchvarov's definition of it is circular, (4) that it is unhelpful in unravelling failures of substitutivity, and (5) that it is not needed in support of Leibniz's Law.

SWOYER, Chris. Causation And Identity. *Midwest Stud Phil* 9,593–622 1984.

Motivation for causal accounts of the transtemporal and the transworld identity of physical objects are presented and (the beginnings of) such accounts are given. Implications for personal identity are also examined.

SYLVAN, Richard. Prospects For Regional Philosophies In Australia. *Austl J Phil* 63,188–204 Je 85.

SYNOWIECKI, Adam. Reflections On The Centenary Of Marx's Death. *Dialec Hum* 10,99–110 Sum 83.

SZABO, A. "How To Explore The History Of Ancient Mathematics" in *Methodology, Metaphysics And The History Of Science*, Cohen, Robert S (ed), 283–294. Boston Reidel 1984.

SZABÓ, János. On Teaching, Education, Theory And Practice––And The Usefulness Of Science (in Hungarian). *Magyar Filozof Szemle* 5,817–831 1983.

SZABO, M E and Farkas, E J. On The Plausibility Of Nonstandard Proofs In Analysis. *Dialectica* 38,297–310 1984.

We present a systematic discussion of the structural and conceptual simplifications of proofs of standard theorems afforded by nonstandard methods and examine to what extent the resulting nonstandard proofs satisfy the informal criterion of "plausibility". We introduce the concept of a "standard detour" and show that all nonstandard proofs considered avoid such detours. Among the proofs examined are proofs of the Intermediate Value Theorem, the Riemann Integration Theorem, the Spectral Theorem for compact Hermitian operators, and the Arzelà–Ascoli Theorem.

SZABO, Manfred Egon. Variable Truth. *Z Math Log* 30,401–414 1984.

SZABÓ, Márton. The Possibility And Reality Of Self–Concious Work (in Hungarian). *Magyar Filozof Szemle* 4,511–528 1983.

The study analyzes the above mentioned theme from the aspect of political–ideological conditions. It examines the ruling social and human image during the Hungarian Soviet Republic, proving there are three important principles according to it. The idea of the worker and the human being was identified with each other, they postulated harmony in social interest, and attached outstanding importance in solving of social problems to the education and self–consciousness. The study analyzes the orders born in the spirit of this ideology. The levelling of wage and the repeal of compulsion to work started from that suppose, the workers take part in the production with consciousness of political struggle. "the role of moral in the communist production"––written by György Lukács expresses tersely the ideological attitude of the period. But the waited effect failed to come. Therefore was the condition of work–moral and the fall of labor–discipline the subject of violent contentions during the whole Hungarian Soviet Republic. In conclusion: In the disadvantageous tendency and facts played role not only the messianistic ideas, but the wartime, deranged conditions in production, too.

SZABÓ, Máté. Weber And The Socialism (in Hungarian). *Magyar Filozof Szemle* 5,729–748 1983.

The study attempts to restore Weber's conception of socialism. The author deals with Weber's views in connection with the economical and political structure of the socialist society, the socialist revolutions, and with the role, intended by Weber for the proletariat in Germany. According to the author, Weber's conception of socialism dominates his conscious burgeois–liberal point of view. Weber's liberal–elitist political theory appears in his conception of the socialist revolutions, and of the political structure of socialist society.

SZABO, Tibor. From The Contemplative Materialism To The Materialism Of Praxis: On The Evolution Of Bukharin's Philosophy (in Hungarian). *Magyar Filozof Szemle* 6,872–879 1983.

SZAFARZ, Ariane. Richard Von Mises: L'échec D'une Axiomatique. *Dialectica* 38,311–318 1984.

We analyze an important episode of the evolution of the theory of probability: the axiomatic phase. The first approach was proposed by Mises in 1919. It is based on the concept of "collective". The probability is defined as the limit–value of the relative frequency. The second one, elaborated by Kolmogorov in 1933, follows the work of Borel which is inspired by purely analytical considerations. This last axiomatisation was unanimously chosen by the theoreticians and empiricists. After having presented the different arguments raised when both theories were confronted, we suggest an epistemological interpretation.

SZANIAWSKI, Klemens. On Defining Information. *Phil Natur* 21,444–452 1984.

A seemingly paradoxical situation is investigated: semantic properties, such as truth or reliability, are often predicated of information, although the standard way to define this concept is in terms of probability. Two types of relations are, therefore, distinguished between the carrier and the object of information: semantic, functional, relation and probabilistic one. The paper discusses this distinction and its possible uses.

SZANIAWSKI, Klemens. Philosophical Ideas Of Tadeusz Kotarbiński. *Rep Phil* 8,25–32 1984.

SZANIAWSKI, Klemens. Rationality As A Value. *Dialec Hum* 11,289–298 Spr/Sum 84.

The article analyzes the axiological aspect of rationality. Rationality of thought is defined by three postulates: precise articulation, logical consistency, empirical validation. Rationality of action is defined either as efficiency with respect to the goal or as optimality in solving the decision problem. It is argued that rationality of thought represents autonomical value while rationality of action is instrumental value only.

SZASZ, Thomas. "Illness And Incompetence" in *Contemporary Issues In Health Care*, Schnall, David J (ed), 112–128. NY Praeger 1984.

SZASZKIEWICZ, Jerzy. L'oggetto Primario Della Libertà Di Scelta. *Gregorianum* 66,295–314 1985.

Supposing that human freedom of choice exists, the author asks himself, if this freedom bears primarily on alternatives between moral good and moral evil, or rather on alternatives between moral goods, the possibility of moral evil being then only its by–product in man. And he tries to show that this last is the case and to answer the difficulties that seem to arise from it.

SZAWARSKI, Z. The Value Of Life (in Polish). *Etyka* 21,41–70 1985.

In the first section, the author considers the possibility of creating and a nominal definitions of life and concludes this is a hopeless endeavor. He says life has no value by itself. If we attribute value to life, then primarily on account of some supreme qualities (other than biochemical properties of living bodies) which make us believe life has value. Yet, there is no closed system of properties pertaining to living bodies, stating the existence of which would always be logically equivalent to stating that any definite value pertains to living organisms.

SZMYD, Jan. Philosophy And Peace Today. *Dialec Hum* 11,465–468 Spr/Sum 84.

SZTOMPKA, Piotr. On The Change Of Social Laws. *Rep Phil* 8,33–40 1984.

TABACHKOVSKY, V G. Practice And Rationality (in Czechoslovakian). *Filozof Cas* 33,439–448 1985.

TABAKOV, Martin. Gödel's Theorem In Retrospect. *Bull Sect Log* 13,132–136 O 84.

Historically the well–known limitative theorems of Godel and Tarski sounded surprising but the author thinks that something of this sort should be expected since Hilbert's program presupposed situations of auto–reflections, similar to some semantic antinomies. Tarski's theorem is interpreted as an indication of the impossibility of exhaustive logical description of a concrete domain. Godel's result demonstrates a general thesis that limiting cognition to only the most reliable methods inevitably will omit some significant parts.

TABER, John. Fichte's Emendation Of Kant. *Kantstudien* 75,442–459 1984.

Fichte's *Wissenschaftslehre*, 1794, is partly motivated by a concern to explain how the self knows its own existence, a question raised but not answered by Kant. Problematic for Kant was how the "I think", conceived as merely assigning all representations to one consciousness, can have empirical content so as to be an existential judgement. Fichte resolves this problem by considering self–consciousness to have real, if not empirical, content in so far as it brings into existence its own object, viz., a self–conscious self.

TAFERTSHOFER, Alois. Jugend–Idole Und Identitätsbildung. *Conceptus* 18,74–85 1984.

Nach einer weit verbreiteten Auffassung wird heute der Jugend fehlende Zukunftsorientierung vorgeworfen und dieses Phänomen mit der Annahme einer grundlegenden frühkindlichen Charakterstörung erklärt. Diese Annahme berücksichtigt zu wenig die Tatsache der Wirksamkeit verschiedener Entwicklungsphasen, inbesondial produzierten Idolen auf regressivem Weg wirksam zu werden. Dadurch wird das Erwachsenwerden behindert. Die Aussagen werden anhand von Daten einer empirischen Untersuchung belegt.

TAGAI, Imbre. An Investigation On The Philosophical Problem Of Identity On The Basis Of The Kantian And Hegelian Concept Of It (in Hungarian). *Magyar Filozof Szemle* 6,898–935 1983.

TAGART, Edward. *Locke's Writings And Philosophy: Historically Considered*. NY Garland 1984.

TAHTINEN, Unto. *The Core Of Gandhi's Philosophy*. Hauz Khas New Delhi Abhinav 1979.

The book is a concise interpretation of Mahatma Gandhi's philosophy. An attempt is made to understand his basic thoughts in terms of general western moral philosophy. Gandhi believed in a universal religion; it is a criterion for the justification of the historical religions. Truth meant mainly a natural right above law and social custom. The book discusses the morality and analyzes the ideas of violence and non–violence. (edited)

TAITTE, W Lawson (ed). *The Search For Justice*. Austin Univ Of Texas Pr 1983.

These essays examine justice, both in the judicial sense and in a broader moral sense, and the role justice plays in the life of the individual, law enforcement, politics, and society. (staff)

TAIWO, Olufemi. Legal Positivism And The African Legal Tradition. *Int Phil Quart* 25,197–200 Je 85.

F U Okafor, in his 'Legal Positivism and the African Legal Tradition' (International Philosophical Quarterly, XXIV, 2, June 1984), argues that legal positivism and its principal tenets are alien to the African legal experience in particular, and contrary to the African ontology in general. In this rejoinder, I argue that Okafor's positing of 'the African legal tradition' is questionable. There is nothing like 'the African legal tradition', but recent legal traditions to be found in Africa. Secondly, I argue that Okafor's account of legal positivism is inadequate. These two deficiencies prevent Okafor from raising the relevant questions about legal positivism in Africa, and answering them.

TAIWO, Olufemi. On Some So–called Refutations Of Ethical Egoism. *Cogito* 2,103–122 D 84.

Refutations of Ethical Egoism usually try to show that it is self–contradictory, irrational and falls short of the demands of the Moral Point of View. My aim is to show that all three modes of refuting Egoism fail because they all start with an a priori assumption that Egoism *cannot* be a morality. I argue that the Egoist is not bound to accept this assumption. I conclude that Egoism is a morality and must be judged by its adequacy, efficiency, etc., as a guide to human conduct.

TAKEUTI, Gaisi. "Heyting Valued Universes Of Intuitionistic Set Theory" in *Lecture Notes In Mathematics*, Muller, G H And Others (ed), 189–306. NY Springer 1981.

TAKEUTI, Gaisi and Titani, Satoko. Intuitionistic Fuzzy Logic And Intuitionistic Fuzzy Set Theory. *J Sym Log* 49,851–866 S 84.

We call the logic whose truth value is a member of $[0,1]$ fuzzy logic. Since $[0,1]$ is a complete Heyting algebra, the intuitionistic logic is the natural base for fuzzy logic. We axiomatized the intuitionistic fuzzy logic and proved the completeness theorem. Then we constructed the intuitionistic set theory based on the fuzzy logic and proved that the elementary analysis developed in the intuitionistic fuzzy set theory is essentially same with the classical elementary analysis.

TAKEUTI, Gaisi. Proof Theory And Set Theory. *Synthese* 62,255–264 F 85.

The foundations of mathematics are divided into proof theory and set theory. Proof theory tries to justify the world of infinite mind from the standpoint of finite mind. Set theory tries to know more and more of the world of the infinite mind. The development of two subjects are discussed including a new proof of the accessibility of ordinal diagrams. Finally the world of large cardinals appears when we go slightly beyond Girard's categorical approach to proof theory.

TAL, Uriel. 'Political Theology' In Contemporary Thought (in Hebrew). *Iyyun* 33,195–218 Ja–Ap 84.

TALHAMI, Ghada. The Human Rights Of Women In Islam. *J Soc Phil* 16,1–7 Wint 85.

Article assesses the social and legal gains made by women during the early centuries of Islam. These gains, which are described against the background of pagan Arab social customs, have been dissipated later as a result of reducing the ethical injunctions of the Koran to a formal body of law. Article concluded that Muslim family law survived intact in most countries because of specific colonial policies. Reform will only be accomplished by popular regimes.

TAMINIAUX, Jacques. Empiricism And Speculation In *the German Ideology*. *Phil Soc Crit* 6,243–266 Fall 79.

TAMMELO, Ilmar. On The Construction Of A Legal Logic In Retrospect And In Prospect. *Arch Rechts Soz* 60,377–392 1974.

This article reports on an extensive research program in legal logic conducted by the author. It explains the nature and scope of legal logic as understood by him and his associates and provides the reasons for their choice of notation and for their terminological innovations. The author dismisses the destructive total criticisms of legal logic and contends that they are based on misconceptions about its meaning and role. He admits, however, that censures of special views or performances of some legal logicians may be well founded. He claims that there is no substitute for logic proper for lawyers.

TANG, Yi–Jie. Recent Developments In The Study Of Philosophy In The PRC. *J Chin Phil* 11,243–254 S 84.

TANNAHILL, Andrew. Health Promotion—Caring Concern. *J Med Ethics* 10,196–197 D 84.

'health promotion' has unfortunately come to mean different things to different people. Interpretations have frequently been left implicit and where spelt out have often been too diffuse or too limited to be useful. Nevertheless the term can be usefully employed to define a set of health–enhancing activities in which the focus is deflected from current disease– and cure–oriented power bases. Used in this way health promotion can come to include the best of the developing theory and practice from a wide range of 'experts' but can also place due emphasis on community involvement. To reject health promotion on the basis of selected, inadequate interpretations is to discard past successes, current developments and future possibilities in important fields of activity and to preserve an inappropriate status quo.

TANNENBAUM, Margaret D. Why Not Tuition–Tax Credit? *Proc Phil Educ* 40,235–240 1984.

This paper argues that implementing a system of tuition tax credits would detract from dealing with the more serious legal and moral problem that our present means of funding and controlling public education is a violation of both the Establishment and Free Exercise clauses of the First Amendment. It further maintains that, from both an historical and a practical perspective that the traditional goals of schooling in a democratic, free society are not being served by the public school system. Pointing out that two of the characteristics that have in the past distinguished public from "non–public" schools—the nature of the curriculum and of the population served—no longer hold, this paper advocates that we obviate the need for the third defining characteristic—tuition charging necessity—through a nation–wide system of vouchers.

TÄNNSJÖ, Torbjörn. Moral Conflict And Moral Realism. *J Phil* 82,113–117 Mr 85.

There are genuine moral conflicts. Sometimes by doing what we ought to do we do what we ought not to do. *Pace* Bernard Williams the existence of such conflicts is compatible with the truth of moral realism. We realize this when we understand that ascriptions of rightness, wrongness, and obligatoriness are *de re* rather than *de dicto*.

TAPIA– VALDÉS, Jorge A. Security Crisis And Institutionalized Militarism. *Praxis Int* 4,378–399 Ja 85.

TAR, Zoltán. A Political Theorist From Eastern Europe. *Stud Soviet Tho* 29,311–318 My 85.

The aim of this review article is to introduce István Bibó, a Hungarian political and social thinker to a larger (Western) audience. Bibó made significant contributions to four interrelated themes of the social sciences: 1) he investigated the problem of the "arrested" historical and socio–economic development of Eastern European societies, 2) he contributed to the sociology of Eastern European Jewry, 3) his writings on German political/historical developments are major contributions to the ongoing debate on German fascism, 4) Bibó formulated a specifically Eastern European theory of democracy.

TARCOV, Nathan. *Locke's Education For Liberty.* Chicago Univ Of Chicago Pr 1984.

TARSKI, Alfred and Woodger, J H (trans). *Logic, Semantics, Meta–Mathematics.* Indianapolis Hackett 1983.

TAUER, Carol A. Personhood And Human Embryos And Fetuses. *J Med Phil* 10,253–266 Ag 85.

Public policy decisions concerning embryos and fetuses tend to lack reasoned argument on their moral status. While agreement on personhood is elusive, this concept has unquestioned moral relevance. A stipulated usage of the term, the psychic sense of 'person', applies to early human prenatal life and encompasses morally relevant aspects of personhood. A 'person' in the psychic sense has (1) a minimal psychology, defined as the capacity to retain experiences, which may be nonconscious, through physiological analogs of memory; and (2) the potential to become a person in a full sense. Psychic personhood merits attribution of moral personhood because (1) the experience of a 'person' in the psychic sense has continuity with the experience of a full person; and (2) this experience begins to determine the development of the personal psychological characteristics of that individual. Psychic personhood is a rationally defensible boundary for invasive research involving human embryos and fetuses. Lacking precise empirical knowledge, policy makers could attribute psychic personhood at the time of earliest brainstem activity, that is, during the seventh week of fetal development.

TAYLOR, C C W. Reply To Schueler On Akrasia. *Mind* 93,584–586 O 84.

S (*Mind* 1983) criticizes my paper (*Mind* 1980) on two counts: i) I misrepresent Davidson's solution to the akrasia problem as resting on a verbal trick, viz. The insertion of 'all things considered' in the definition of akrasia; ii) my principle P2'' is incoherent, since in some circumstances an agent satisfying it would have to make inconsistent evaluations. I reply: i) my criticism concerns Davidson's use of the prima facie/unconditional distinction, not any particular formulation of it; ii) S overlooks an important qualification in my formulation of the principle, viz. The absence of countervailing conditions.

TAYLOR, Charles. "Philosophy And Its History" in *Philosophy In History*, Rorty, Richard and others (ed), 17–30. NY Cambridge Univ Pr 1984.

TAYLOR, Charles. "Use And Abuse Of Theory" in *Ideology, Philosophy And Politics*, Parel, Anthony (ed), 37–60. Waterloo Laurier Univ Pr 1983.

TAYLOR, Charles. Connolly, Coucault, And Truth. *Polit Theory* 13,377–386 Ag 85.

This article is a reply to Connolly's criticism of an earlier article of mine "Foucault on Freedom and Truth," which appeared in *Political Theory*, vol 12, no 2, May 1984. In this paper I further defend the main thesis of the earlier one, that Foucault cannot do without some conception of freedom and (non–relativized) truth, whatever his protestations to the contrary.

TAYLOR, Joan Kennedy. "Protective Labor Legislation" in *Freedom, Feminism, And The State*, Mc Elroy, Wendy (ed), 267–274. Cato Institute Washington 1982.

TAYLOR, Kenneth A. Davidson's Theory Of Meaning: Some Questions. *Phil Stud* 48,91–106 Jl 85.

I argue that if a theory is to count as a theory of meaning, it must support what I call modal projection, as opposed to mere inductive projection. A theory which fails to support modal projection will fail to assign distinct intensions to certain co–extensive expressions for which pre–theoretic intuition does recognize a difference in intension. I then show that Donald Davidson's theory of meaning, even when it is strengthened in the ways outlined in his later writings, fails to support modal projection and thus fails to capture essential aspects of the notion of meaning.

TAYLOR, Richard. *Having Love Affairs.* Buffalo Prometheus 1982.

TEICHMAN, Jenny. The Definition Of Person. *Philosophy* 60,175–186 Ap 85.

The aim and purpose of this short essay is to prove that all philosophers since John Locke (1632–1704) have completely buggered up the analysis of the Concept of *Person*.

TEICHMANN, Werner. Mit Lesern Und Autoren Im Gespräch. *Deut Z Phil* 32,1023–1027 1984.

TEIXIERA, João De F. Artificial Intelligence And The Problem Solving Theory (in Portuguese). *Trans/Form/Acao* 6,45–52 1983.

This article is an attempt to outline the main characteristics of research on a new area of studies, the so–called Artificial Intelligence (AI). Items one and two sketch the historical background of AI and its basic presuppositions. Item three focuses on the problem–solving theory developed by A Newell and H Simon. Item four is an attempt to show the philosophical and epistemological relevance of Artificial Intelligence.

TEJERA, V. Plato's *politicus*: An Eleatic Sophist On Politics. *Phil Soc Crit* 5,83–104 Ja 78.

TELLER, Paul. Is Supervenience Just Undisguised Reduction? *S J Phil* 23,93–100 Spr 85.

This article considers arguments for and counterarguments against Kim's claim that strong supervenience is a kind of reduction because it implies that the supervening property is necessarily equivalent to an infinite disjunction of properties in the supervenience base.

TELLER, Paul. The Projection Postulate: A New Perspective. *Phil Sci* 51,369–395 S 84.

Previous work has shown that the problem of measurement in quantum mechanics is not correctly seen as one of understanding some allegedly univocal process of measurement in nature which corresponds to the projection postulate. The present paper introduces a new perspective by showing that how we are to understand the nature of the change of quantum mechanical state on measurement depends very sensitively on the interpretation of the state function, and by showing how attention to this dependence can greatly sharpen the problems and relations between them. (edited)

TEMKIN, Jack. Singer, Moore, And The Metaphysics Of Morals. *Phil Res Arch* 10,567–572 1985.

In this paper, I argue that Marcus G Singer's attack on Actual Consequence Utilitarianism, as held by G E Moore, is inconclusive. Singer contends that Moore's view is incoherent because it cannot provide a criterion of moral rightness or wrongness. Singer makes the historical claim that Moore intended his theory to provide such a criterion and the philosophical claim that any moral theory must provide such a criterion.

TENNANT, Neil. Perfect Validity, Entailment And Paraconsistency. *Stud Log* 43,181–200 1984.

This paper treats entailment as a subrelation of classical consequence and deductibility. Working with a Gentzen set–sequent system, we define an entailment as a substitution instance of a valid sequent all of whose premises and conclusions are necessary for its classical validity. We also define a sequent Proof as one in which there are no applications of cut or dilution. The main result is that the entailments are exactly the Provable sequents. There are several important corollaries. Every unsatisfiable set is Provably inconsistent. Every logical consequence of a satisfiable set is Provable therefrom. Thus our system is adequate for ordinary mathematical practice. (edited)

TEPPERMAN, Lorne. Informatics And Society: Will There Be An 'Information Revolution'? *J Bus Ethics* 4,395–399 O 85.

The claim that an information revolution is underway is scrutinized in this paper. Particular attention is given to the notions that new information technology will radically increase human choice and rationality in decision–making. The literature on informatics and technology is selectively reviewed in order to determine whether (1) the present use of technology seems to predict an increased choice and rationality in the future; (2) earlier technologies have had this effect; and (3) past social predictions of this type have proven generally correct. We reach a mixed or negative conclusion in every case. Although the possibility of an information revolution cannot be dismissed, neither can it be readily accepted at this point unless we significantly diminish what is normally meant by a 'revolution'.

TERBORGH– DUPUIS, Heleen. The Netherlands: Tolerance And Teaching. *Hastings Center Rep* 14,23–24 D 84.

This article gives a short description of the Dutch attitude towards (the teaching of) bioethics. The Dutch position reveals an ambiguity: the (public) interest in the field is great, but there is also a reluctance to use methods of moral and ethical reasoning. This is also true for the medical schools of which only a few provide courses in ethics.

TERLOUW, Jan. Reduction Of Higher Type Levels By Means Of An Ordinal Analysis Of Finite Terms. *Annals Pure Applied Log* 28,73–102 Ja 85.

TERRELL, Burnham. Science, Design And The Science Of Signs. *Phil Natur* 21,642–651 1984.

TESFATSION, Leigh. Games, Goals, And Bounded Rationality. *Theor Decis* 17,149–176 S 84.

A generalization of the standard *n*–person game is presented, with flexible information requirements suitable for players constrained by certain types of bounded rationality. Strategies (complete contingency plans) are replaced by "policies," i.e., end–mean pairs of goals and controls (partial contingency plans), which results in naturally disconnected player choice sets. Well–known existence theorems for pure strategy Nash equilibrium and bargaining solutions are generalized to policy games by modifying connectedness (convexity) requirements.

TESKE, Roland J. The World–Soul And Time In St Augustine. *Augustin Stud* 14,75–92 1983.

After presenting the textual evidence that Augustine held even as late as the

Confessions a doctrine of the world–soul, with which individual souls are identical, I argue that his definition of time as a distention of the soul is best understood with reference to the world–soul, as in Plotinus. Thus one avoids both a multiplicity of times as well as a purely subjective view of time.

TESKEY, Ayleen. *Platonov And Fyodorov.* England Avebury 1982.

The work illustrates the influence of Fyodorov's philosophical ideas on the writer Andrey Platonov. Chapter I provides a summary of Fyodorov's ideas, including his belief in the need to conquer nature, his critique of man's hostile social relations and his plans for the resurrection of the dead by scientific means. There follows an analysis of the way in which these themes are utilized by Platonov. Two appendices provide short biographies of Fyodorov and Platonov.

THAGARD, Paul. Frames, Knowledge, And Inference. *Synthese* 61,233–260 N 84.

THAKAR, Archana. Kant And The Problem Of The General. *Indian Phil Quart* 11,1–8 Ap 84.

THATCHER, Adrian. The Personal God And A God Who Is A Person. *Relig Stud* 21,61–74 Mr 85.

Belief in a personal God is defended: belief that God is a person is attacked. 'bodiless person theists' are shown to use a 'dematerialization procedure', choosing dualistic models of a person, splitting them up, and using the mental halves to do analogical duty for God. The use by Richard Swinburne and others of this procedure is examined. Alternative accounts of belief in a personal God are then suggested.

THEAU, Jean. L'ordre Du Connaître Et L'ordre De L'être Ou L'ordre Des Choses Et Celui De La Pensée. *Dialogue (Canada)* 23,571–596 D 84.

I tried to show: 1) that the order of knowledge is radically independent from the order of being, because of its specific ends and ways, origin and principles; 2) how however the analytical method succeeds in grasping the true objective order of being, either ontological or historical, the logical order forming a kind of medium between the order of knowing and the order of being; 3) how there is room for what is called an ontological or dialectical ordering, which belongs to philosophy.

THEIS, Robert. De l'illusion Transcendantale. *Kantstudien* 76,119–137 1985.

THEIS, Robert. Le Sens De La Métaphysique Dans La Critique De La Raison Pure. *Rev Phil Louvain* 83,175–196 My 85.

The author shows the positive concept of metaphysics in its second part––a requirement of the correct understanding of the criticism of metaphysics––which Kant articulates in the *Transcendental Dialectics.* Under the subtitle of metaphysical deduction of ideas, the author analyzes the manner in which Kant, on the basis of special metaphysics. Under that of transcendental deduction, he studies the manner in which Kant comprehends the objective meaning of ideas. Finally, the author tackles the problem of the status of the metaphysical *discourse* arising out of the newly established determinations.

THERON, Stephen. Other Problems About The Self. *Sophia (Australia)* 24,11–20 Ap 85.

THIEL, Rainer. Arten Des Herangehens An Dialektische Widersprüche Besonders In Der Technischen Entwicklung. *Deut Z Phil* 32,1103–1107 1984.

THIELE, Gabriele. Aktuelle Probleme Der Wissenschaftlich–Technischen Revolution In Der Sowjetischen Philosophie. *Deut Z Phil* 22,511–513 1974.

THIJSSEN, J. Het Continuum–Debat Bij Gregorius Van Rimini. *Alg Ned Tijdschr Wijs* 77,109–119 Ap 85.

Book II dist.2 q.2 of the commentary of the Sentences of Gregory of Rimini (1300– 1358) is a good example of a philosophical discussion in a theological setting. Most part of this question deals with a discussion of continuity and infinity, an important philosophical topic, not only in the fourteenth century. The article provides an analysis of a lengthy and subtle geometrical argument which Gregory employs against atomism, that is to say, against the view that continua are composed of indivisible points.

THIRIART, Philippe. Une Douloureuse Théorie Du Plaisir. *Petite Rev Phil* 6,95–120 Spr 85.

Recent research in psychology shows that we are biologically built so that we cannot experience a great pleasure for a long time. That psychophysiological theory exlains the addictions. Pleasure cannot be the goal of life. Action can be a goal of life. (edited)

THISTLEWOOD, David. *Herbert Read: Formlessness And Form.* Boston Routledge & K Paul 1984.

The aesthetic philosophy of Herbert Read (1893–1968) was spontaneous and intuitive yet his writings embody enduring values. They are both eclectic (leaning to Nietzsche, Eliot, Whitehead, Freud and Jung) and original. This survey finds continuity in an apparently erratic system of thought, which engages both 'formlessness' and 'form' and culminates in a theory of organic, symbolic formation, a characteristic of authentic creativity Read perceived in the contemporary English art of his time.

THOM, Martina. Die Bedeutung Der Freiheitsproblematik Für Kants Übergang Zum Transzendentalismus. *Deut Z Phil* 22,289–307 1974.

Kant leitet eine Neubestimmung des Gegenstandes der Philosophie ein, indem er das gesellschaftliche Anliegen der philosophischen Bewufsstseinsform zu erfassen sucht. Ideologische Motive, das Verhältnis von Gesetzmäfssigkeit und Handlungsmöglichkeit, von Notwendigkeit und Freiheit als begriffliche Fassung des weltanschaulichen Problems der theoretischen Begründung der bürgerlichen Auffassung vom Menschen, seiner Stellung in der Gesellschaft und der Geschichte, regen Kant dazu an. (edited)

THOMAS, Carolyn E. Thoughts On The Moral Relationship Of Intent And Training In Sport. *J Phil Sport* 10,84–91 1983.

THOMAS, Janice. A Comment On Dr John J Haldane's Article, "The Morality Of Deterrence". *Heythrop J* 26,46–47 Ja 85.

THOMAS, Linda Sue. Ethical Considerations For Planned Social Change In The Education Of American Indian People. *J Thought* 19,153–158 Fall 84.

Change, as a strategy in Indian education, has a strong historical basis. A short review of this strategy, focusing on four considerations in planned social change, is presented. The ethical questions arising from this strategy need to be raised periodically in order to maintain a consistent perspective for future evaluation. Indian perspectives on these questions, and the consequence of change, need to be considered.

THOMASMA, David C. *An Apology For The Value Of Human Life.* St Louis Cath Health Assoc 1983.

In any allocation scheme of health care, it is important to avoid decisions based on external valuation of human lives. An argument is presented that only respect for the intrinsic value of human beings can establish a just health care allocation system. The use of the format of an "Apology," an address of persuasion in which arguments of others are examined, was considered important for a topic of this magnitude.

THOMASMA, David C. Editorial: Philosophy Of Medicine In The U S A. *Theor Med* 6,239–242 O 85.

This is an editorial, sketching the needs for philosophy of medicine in the United States. In particular a call is made for the development of ideas from the other humanities, the social sciences, such as economics, and the arts, such as poetry. Such cross–disciplinary enrichment, it is argued, is not only optional but required by the very nature of the doctor–patient relationship. Since it deals with human realities, all such realities, as studied by the humanities, are germane to a philosophy of medicine.

THOMASMA, David C. The Philosophy Of Medicine In Europe: Challenges For The Future. *Theor Med* 6,115–123 F 85.

Two challenges face European philosophy of medicine. The first is to counterbalance what is seen as an overemphasis on the social analysis of medicine with greater attention to its personal and individual dimensions. The second, related challenge, is to more fully understand the clinical realities of modern medicine, which in turn, give rise to the scope and limits of physician duties, patient obligations, and social concerns.

THOMASMA, David C. What Does Medicine Contribute To Ethics? *Theor Med* 5,267–278 O 84.

The historical impact of medicine on ethics will largely lie in methodology. Clinical medical ethics is a process of analogical reasoning which parallels medical decision making. The major conceptual impact of medicine on medical ethics is the importance of the concept of beneficence, role–specific duties of health professionals, and the virtues of the good physician.

THOMASON, Richard. Discussion: A Note On Tense And Subjunctive Conditionals. *Phil Sci* 52,151–153 Mr 85.

I argue that a counterexample proposed by Donald Nute shows only that past tenses involve indexical restriction to a limited domain of times. The purpose of this note is to defend the thesis that there is a single conditional connective figuring in both indicative and 'had'—'would' connectives, and that the differences in logical form between the two sorts of English conditional expressions have to do with tense.

THOMASON, Richmond H. "Combinations Of Tense And Modality" in *Handbook Of Philosophical Logic*, Gabbay, Dov (ed), 135–166. Boston Reidel 1984.

THOMASON, Richmond H. Some Issues Concerning The Interpretation Of Derived And Gerundive Nominals. *Ling Phil* 8,73–80 F 85.

This paper discusses semantical problems that arise in relating derived nominals like 'The revolution of the wheel' and gerundive nominals like 'The wheel's revolving'.

THOMASON, S K and Nagle, Michael C. The Extensions Of The Modal Logic K5. *J Sym Log* 50,102–109 Mr 85.

THOMASON, S K. Reduction Of Second–Order Logic To Modal Logic. *Z Math Log* 21,107–114 1975.

THOMASON, S K. The Logical Consequence Relation Of Propositional Trense Logic. *Z Math Log* 21,29–40 1975.

THOMPSON, Audrey. Meaning In The Experience Of Literature. *Proc Phil Educ* 40,373–380 1984.

THOMPSON, Dennis (ed) and Gutman, Amy (ed). *Ethics & Politics: Cases And Comments.* Chicago Nelson 1984.

THOMPSON, Dennis. Philosophy And Policy. *Phil Pub Affairs* 14,205–218 Spr 85.

THOMPSON, E P. Comment: Response To A Arato And J Cohen, "Social Movements, Civil Society And The Problem Of Sovereignty". *Praxis Int* 5,75–85 Ap 85.

THOMPSON, Janna L. Mutual Aid And Selfish Genes. *Metaphilosophy* 15,270– 281 Jl–O 84.

The paper examines two views of human nature: One, found in traditional political philosophy, and now backed up by sociobiology, holds that our generosity is naturally confined to friends and relations. The other, held by many socialists and anarchists, holds that we have an "instinct of human solidarity and sociability."

THOMPSON, Kenneth W (ed). *Moral Dimensions Of American Foreign Policy.* New Brunswick Transaction Books 1984.

Moral dimensions is a carefully edited work that brings together writings on ethics and foreign policy by the leading thinkers of the past 40 years, including Father John Courtney Murray, John Bennett and others. It represents a systematic ordering of different approaches from natural law to political realism. Some of the chapters are available for the first time to a wider audience.

THOMPSON, Kenneth W. "The Morality Of Checks And Balances" in *The Search For Justice*, Taitte, W Lawson (ed), 163–191. Austin Univ Of Texas Pr 1983.

THOMPSON, Paul. What Philosophers Can Learn From Agriculture. *Agr Human Values* 1,17–19 Spr 84.

This paper was written to stimulate discussion at a workshop on teaching agricultural issues in the philosophy curriculum.

THOMPSON, Simon. Axiomatic Recursion Theory And The Continuous Functionals. *J Sym Log* 50,442–450 Je 85.

We define, in the spirit of Fenstad, a higher type computation theory, and show that countable recursion over the continuous functionals forms such a theory. We also discuss Hyland's proposal from for a scheme with which to supplement S1–S9, and show that this augmented set of schemes fails to generate countable recursion. We make another proposal to which the methods of his section do not apply.

THOMSON, Colin J H. Australia: In Vitro Fertilization And More. *Hastings Center Rep* 14,14–15 D 84.

THOMSON, Judith J. "Some Questions About Government Regulation Of Behavior" in *Rights And Regulation*, Machan, Tibor (ed), 137–156. Cambridge Ballinger 1983.

THORNEYCROFT, Ian H. "Infertility: Conquered Problems And New Frontiers" in *Bioethical Frontiers In Perinatal Intensive Care*, Snowden, Fraser (ed), 117–131. Natchitoches Northwestern Pr 1985.

THORPE, Dale A. The Sorites Paradox. *Synthese* 61,391–422 D 84.

A solution to the sorites paradox is obtained by distinguishing three formats of the sorites argument and appraising them in the light of four fundamental considerations: (i) the appropriate notion of truth for the application of vague predicates to their borderline cases, (ii) a certain construal of borderline cases, (iii) a certain freedom of use of vague terms not enjoyed by non–vague terms and (iv) the revocation of that freedom by deductive contexts.

THRO, Linus J (ed). *History Of Philosophy In The Making.* Washington Univ Pr Of America 1982.

THUNDY, Zacharias P. Love: Augustine And Chaucer. *Augustin Stud* 14,93–104 1983.

Chaucer's philosophy of love is not only Boethian but also Augustinian. The Augustinian conception of love which Chaucer uses, especially in his *Troilus and Criseyde*, is not a simplistic opposition between *caritas* and *cupiditas*; it is the trinity of *amor*, *cupiditas*, and *caritas*; Troilus' love for Criseyde is basically *amor*, honest love in search for beatitude; later on this *amor* becomes *cupiditas*; nonetheless this *cupiditas* remains a restlessness for God; there are, indeed, extenuating circumstances that make Troilus' error a forgivable sin.

THURMAN, Robert A F. "Buddhist Views Of Nature: Variations On The Theme Of Mother–Father Harmony" in *On Nature*, Rouner, Leroy S (ed), 96–112. Notre Dame Univ Notre Dame Pr 1984.

THURSBY, G R and Isenberg, Sheldon R. A Perennial Philosophy Perspective On Richard Rorty's Neo–Pragmatism. *Int J Phil Relig* 17,41–66 1985.

The article examines the assumptive frameworks of critiques of modern philosophy underlying Richard Rorty's neo–pragmatism and Seyyed Hossein Nasr's "perennial philosophy". Although their evaluations of positivism and linguistic analysis are remarkably similar, each perspective is grounded in a vastly different philosophical anthropology. The difference is illustrated in their understanding of the function of philosophy: Rorty's neo–pragmatist "philosophy of vacuum" serves solely a deconstructive, critical function, while the perennialist "philosophy of plenum" is redemptive.

TIANYU, Cao. A Brief Discussion Of Marx's Theory Of Alienation. *Chin Stud Phil* 16,78–89 Fall 84.

TICHÝ, Pavel. Do We Need Interval Semantics? *Ling Phil* 8,263–282 My 85.

TIESZEN, Richard. The Notion Of Mathematical Intuition And Husserl's Phenomenology. *Nous* 18,395–422 S 84.

The role of intuition (Anschauung) in mathematical knowledge is discussed using some ideas of Husserl. It is pointed out that in the case of objects like natural numbers, sets, and functions, the Husserlian view of intuition is wider than the finitist notion of concrete mathematical intuition. Suggestions are made about how to meet the objection that mathematical intuition could not be analogous to perceptual intuition because mathematical objects are not individually identifiable, not causally related to our senses, not objects in space and time, and so on.

TIGER, Lionel. Ideology As Brain Disease. *Zygon* 20,31–40 Mr 85.

The brain evolved not to think but to act, and ideology is an act of social affiliation which can be compared to kin affiliation, both satisfyingly emotional and expressing a perception about the nature of the real world central to the nature of being human. Males may affiliate to macrosocial ideologies more enthusiastically than females because of their relative lack of certainty of kin relationships. Exogamy was the necessary solution to kin–related strife in prehistory. Perhaps what the world needs is not only a moral equivalent to war but an ideological equivalent to exogamy to resolve social differences on a much larger scale.

TIJS, Stef and Peters, Hans. Risk Aversion In n–Person Bargaining. *Theor Decis* 18,47–72 Ja 85.

TILES, Mary. *Bachelard: Science And Objectivity.* NY Cambridge Univ Pr 1985.

This book is designed to provide an introduction to the main ideas behind Bachelard's works on the epistemology of science for those working within the analytic traditions in philosophy. It makes no pretense to definitive exegesis, but attempts to confront the problem of 'incommensurability of scientific theories', (1) by examining Bachelard's account of conceptual change, (2) by reflecting on the apparent incommensurability between Bachelard's approach to the philosophy of science and that characteristic of analytic philosophers.

TILES, Mary. Correcting Concepts. *Ratio* 27,19–36 Je 85.

The article is written in support of the view that science progresses by correcting its concepts. Scientific concepts are viewed as having three inter–related dimensions: empirical, theoretical, and metaphysical. The scope for and mechanisms of correction in each of these dimensions is considered.

TILES, Mary. Kant, Wittgenstein And The Limits Of Logic. *Hist Phil Log* 1,151–170 1980.

This paper has two purposes. (1) to justify that there is an important distinction underlying the saying/showing distinction of the *Tractatus*; the distinction which Kant characterizes as that between historical and rational knowledge. (2) to argue that it is because the *Tractatus* accepts Frege/Russell logic as a *complete* representation of all thought according to laws, that what is shown cannot be recognized as knowledge. This is done by interpolating Frege's logical innovations between the views of Kant and Wittgenstein on logic and mathematics.

TILLEMANS, Tom J F. Two Tibetan Texts On The "Neither One Nor Many" Argument For *Śūnyatā*. *J Indian Phil* 12,357–388 D 84.

This is my third article in a series on a Buddhist Madhyamaka argument for "voidness", that is the impossibilty of entities existing themselves. For the previous two articles, see E Steinkellner and H Tauscher (ed) *Contributions on Tibetan and Buddhist Religion and Philosophy*, Vienna 1983, and *Etudes de Lettres*, 3, University of Lausanne 1982. The present article consists of an annotated translation and a critical edition of sections from two Tibetan texts.

TILLEY, Nicholas. Periodization, Holism And Historicism: A Reply To Jacobs. *Phil Soc Sci* 14,393–396 S 84.

A response is made to criticisms by Struan Jacobs ("Tilley and Popper's Alleged Historicism," *Phil Soc Sci*, 13, 303–5) of the argument in Nicholas Tilley's "Popper, Historicism and Emergence," (*Phil Soc Sci*, 12, 59–67) to the effect that Popper has come to adopt some positions outlined but rejected in The Poverty of Historicism. It is shown that Jacobs misreads Popper on "periodisation," is confused over Popper's discussion of "holism," and misunderstands Tilley's conclusions concerning "historicism."

TILLIETTE, Xavier. L'absolu Et La Philosophie De Schelling. *Laval Theol Phil* 41,205–214 Je 85.

TILLMAN, Mary Katherine. The Tension Between Intellectual And Moral Education In The Thought Of John Henry Newman. *Thought* 60,322–334 S 85.

TIMMONS, Mark. Act Utilitarianism And The Moral Fanaticism Argument. *Phil Stud* 46,215–226 S 84.

One apparently devastating criticism of a whole range of act utilitarian (AU) principles is Marcus Singer's claim that such principles are open to the charge of moral fanaticism, i.e., they commit one to the view that "no action is indifferent or trivial, every occasion is momentous." This moral fanaticism argument (MFA) is examined in detail. I argue that the MFA is not all that devastating; indeed the act utilitarian can altogether escape the charge of being a fanatic.

TINDALE, Christopher W. Plato's *Lysis*: A Reconsideration. *Apeiron* 18,102–109 1984.

This paper contends that the traditional reading of the *Lysis*, to the effect that it fails to discover a concept of friendship, is misgiven. One of Socrates' interlocutors, Lysis, does in fact apprehend the nature of friendship as the actions he performs demonstrate. The essay seeks out this notion of friendship and stresses that the dialogue does lend itself to a positive reading in the light of which its inquiry cannot be considered a failure.

TINDER, Glenn. *Against Fate: An Essay On Personal Dignity.* Notre Dame Univ Notre Dame Pr 1981.

Tinder uses the concepts of fate and destiny to illuminate the present historical situation. His aim is to show how personal dignity is threatened and how it may be defended. (staff)

TINLAND, Franck. Hobbes, Spinoza, Rousseau Et La Formation De L'idée De Démocratie Comme Mesure De La Légitimité Du Pouvoir Politique. *Rev Phil Fr* 175,195–222 Ap–Je 85.

TIRUCHELVAM, Neelan (ed) and Coomaraswamy, Radhika (ed) and Gunatilleke, Godfrey (ed). *Ethical Dilemmas Of Development In Asia.* Lexington Heath 1983.

The study analyses the social, political, and economic consequences of current development strategies in terms of their human costs, with detailed case studies. These strategies will always be constrained by imperfect choices. The system making a choice must be aware of its imperfection, have a sustained concern for what is lost in human terms through its choice and possess built–in motivations to restore what is lost through constant assessment and participation of all the social groups affected by the gains and losses.

TITANI, Satoko and Takeuti, Gaisi. Intuitionistic Fuzzy Logic And Intuitionistic Fuzzy Set Theory. *J Sym Log* 49,851–866 S 84.

We call the logic whose truth value is a member of $[0,1]$ fuzzy logic. Since $[0,1]$ is a complete Heyting algebra, the intuitionistic logic is the natural base for fuzzy logic. We axiomatized the intuitionistic fuzzy logic and proved the completeness theorem. Then we constructed the intuitionistic set theory based on the fuzzy logic and proved that the elementary analysis developed in the intuitionistic fuzzy set theory is essentially same with the classical elementary analysis.

TITZE, H. Zum Problem Der Unendlichkeit. *Phil Natur* 21,139–156 1984.

The purpose is to expose the problematic of the notion of infinity and that it does not exist in the reality. It is to distinguish between the qualitative infinity. The space and the time in connection with the modern physics are explained. The relativity theories give the upper limit, the quantum theory gives the lower limit. It is necessary to use the notion of infinity with caution. This is only a speculation.

TLUMAK, Jeffrey and Moser, Paul K. Two Paradoxes Of Rational Acceptance. *Erkenntnis* 23,127–142 Ag 85.

This article provides a straightforward diagnosis and resolution of the lottery paradox and the epistemic version of the paradox of the preface. In doing so, the article takes some steps in relating the notion of probability to the notion of epistemic justification.

TOBERLIN, James. Identity, Intensionality, And Intentionality. *Synthese* 61,111–134 O 84.

TODD, Joan and Cono, Joseph. Vico And Collingwood On 'The Conceit Of Scholars'. *Hist Euro Ideas* 6,59–70 1985.

The purpose of the paper is to show some sources of error arising out of human conceit and the possible valid methods for self–correction. For Vico and Collingwood nationalistic and individualistic conceits are part of the major sources of human error. With the awareness of conceits emerges historical consciousness of a finite existence and it is this recognition which demands interdisciplinary analyses in order to validate epistemological answers.

TODOROV, Tzvetan. *Mikhail Bakhtin: The Dialogical Principle*, Wlad Godzich (trans). Minneapolis Univ Minnesota Pr 1984.

TOFFALORI, Carlo and Marcja, Annalisa. On Pseudo–$\aleph_0$–Categorical Theories. *Z Math Log* 30,533–540 1984.

TOKARZ, Marek and Dzik, Wojciech. Invariant Matrix Consequences. *Rep Math Log* 18,37–44 1984.

TOLA, Fernando. Nāgārjuna's Catustava. *J Indian Phil* 13,1–54 Mr 85.

TOLAND, John. *Pantheisticon.* Pisa Libreria Testi 1984.

TOM, Alan R. *Teaching As A Moral Craft.* NY Longman 1984.

The book is divided into three parts, each of which integrates current research into the author's argument. First, the author describes and critiques the metaphor of teaching—teaching as an applied science—which has dominated professional educators' thinking for more than fifty years. Second, a new concept of teaching—teaching as a moral craft—is introduced and developed. Third, the author applies the moral craft metaphor to issues of educational research and practice.

TOMEK, V. The Forming Of Social Consciousness As Dialectical Process Of Continuity And Discontinuity Of Its Development (in Czechoslovakian). *Filozof Cas* 32,659–670 1984.

TOMKOW, Terrance A. What Is Grammar? *Can J Phil* 6,61–82 80 Supp.

TOMLINSON, Tom. The Conservative Use Of The Brain–Death Criterion—A Critique. *J Med Phil* 9,377–394 N 84.

The whole brain–death criterion of death now enjoys a wide acceptance both within the medical profession and among the general public. That acceptance is in large part the product of the contention that brain death is the proper criterion for even a conservative definition of death—the irreversible loss of the integrated functioning of the organism as a whole. This claim—most recently made in the report of the Presidential Commission and in a comprehensive article by James Bernat and others—is based upon a series of fallacious arguments. Chief among these is the argument that whole brain–death is the proper criterion for the conservative definition because the brain is the organ that integrates the rest of the organism. A central part of the paper shows that this argument rests upon a confusion between a function and the mechanism that performs it, and replies to the defenses that the Presidential Commission makes on this point. The concluding portion of the paper argues that this issue is not merely of academic interest, but has the potential for undermining the present concensus that supports the use of whole brain–death criteria.

TONELLI, G. Casula On Baumgarten's Metaphysics. *Kantstudien* 66,242–243 1975.

TONG, Rosemarie. *Women, Sex, And The Law.* Totowa Rowman & Allanheld 1984.

TONGSEN, Huang. Several Issues Concerning The Theory Of Human Beings. *Chin Stud Phil* 16,31–64 Wint 84–85.

TONNE, Herbert A and Eddy, Robert M and Wilson, Edwin H. Symposium On Humanism, Secularism, And Religion. *Relig Hum* 19,32–39 Wint 85.

TOOLEY, Michael. Laws And Causal Relations. *Midwest Stud Phil* 9,93–112 1984.

Do causal relations presuppose underlying, causal laws? This issue is approached by focusing upon the following, widely accepted thesis of the Humean supervenience of causal relations: the truth values of all singular causal statements are logically determined by the truth values of statements of causal laws, together with the truth values of noncausal statements about particulars. It is contended that this thesis must be rejected, and five arguments are offered in support of that contention.

TOOLEY, Michael. Response To Mary Anne Warren's "Reconsidering The Ethics Of Infanticide". *Phil Books* 26,9–14 Ja 85.

In this paper, I focus upon two central issues. First, might there not be societies where infanticide should be prohibited? My response is that, in the case of normal infants, this may indeed be so. Secondly, even if infanticide is not intrinsically wrong, may it not be intrinsically undesirable? I reply by offering an argument against this suggestion, and by trying to show what is wrong with Mary Anne Warren's argument for the contrary conclusion.

TOPPER, David. On The Fidelity Of Pictures: A Critique Of Goodman's Disjunction Of Perspective And Realism. *Philosophia (Israel)* 14,187–198 Ag 84.

Critiques of Nelson Goodman's challenge to pictorial realism in his *Languages of Art* have mostly avoided the key chapter in which linear perspective is appraised as a mere convention of depiction. This article, which draws upon J J Gibson's distinction between visual "field" and visual "world" perception, both defends perspective as a means of producing a realistic space in a picture and points to the consequential errors in Goodman's formulation.

TORMEY, Alan. The Relativity Of Refutations. *J Aes Art Crit* 42,439–442 Sum 84.

TORMEY, Judith. Some Recent Books On The Historical Status Of Women. *J Hist Ideas* 45,619–623 O–D 84.

TÖRNVALL, Anders. Teachers' Basic Philosophies And Curriculum. *J Moral Educ* 14,75–86 My 85.

This article gives an account of a study concerning the relationship between the teachers' basic views of the basic philosophy of he curriculum for Swedish comprehensive schools, the Läroplan of 1969. The study, based on interpretations of texts and verbal statements, finds the concept of solidarity in the curriculum important.

An analysis of common features in the categories that are in favor of this basic philosophy shows it is the idea of a pupil–centered school that attracts teachers with a socialist ideology. It supports solidarity. The main reason for the negative attitude of the teachers is that they see a pupil–centered school as a shift of power reducing the teachers' traditional role and disturbing the professional code. Those categories have strong naturalistic elements, wanting the pupils to be in many ways like boy scouts. Teachers with a so called partial ideology—poorly developed outlook on society and on man—seem to be dominated by their professional code. The vaguer the ideology or philosophy of life, the more dominant the professional code.

TOROS, Yvonne. Informatique Et Philosophie: L'intervalle, La Distance, L'écart. *Rev Phil Louvain* 82,385–397 Ag 84.

TORRESETTI, Giorgio. La Concezione Hegeliana Dello Stato Politico Come Sintesi Della Libertà. *Riv Int Filosof Diritto* 61,647–683 O–D 84.

TÓTH, János. The Cybernetic Analysis Of Distrust (in Hungarian). *Magyar Filozof Szemle* 4,637–650 1983.

TOULMIN, Stephen E. Pluralism And Responsibility In Post–Modern Science. *Sci Tech Human Values* 10,28–37 Wint 85.

TOULMIN, Stephen. "Cosmology As Science And As Religion" in *On Nature*, Rouner, Leroy S (ed), 27–41. Notre Dame Univ Notre Dame Pr 1984.

TOULMIN, Stephen. Nature And Nature's God. *J Relig Ethics* 13,37–52 Spr 85.

Gustafson's ethics is both conservative and revolutionary. By taking Calvin, Luther, and Augustine as discussion partners, he avoids the *culs–de–sac* into which seventeenth–century physical science drove the *theology* of nature. In doing so, he shares the Stoic tendency in the late twentieth–century science, e.G., in ecology. For him, "the powers that bear down on us and sustain us" are present in our experience of the world; and this experience must square with our other empirical knowledge, e.G., in biology. Yet it is not clear how we are to ground, in detail, the *moral* perceptions of nature in which Gustafson finally appeals.

TOURANGEAU, Roger. "Metaphor And Cognitive Structure" in *Metaphor*, Miall, David S (ed), 14–35. Atlantic Highlands Humanities Pr 1982.

TOZER, Steven. Response To Benne's "The Learning Community". *Proc Phil Educ* 40,57–62 1984.

TRACHTENBERG, Marc. Strategists, Philosophers, And The Nuclear Question. *Ethics* 95,728–739 Ap 85.

TRACHTMAN, Leon E. Why Tolerate The Statistical Victim? *Hastings Center Rep* 15,14 F 85.

More effort is spent debating ethics of nontreatment of impaired newborns than of more lethal activities: smoking, drinking, driving, etc. Two explanations: newborns are identifiable individuals, whereas the other victims are statistical entities. The neonate is a totally vulnerable victim while others may choose decreased exposure to risk. While moral costs of denying treatment are high, we should take into greater account costs of policy decisions resulting in large and predictable numbers of statistical deaths.

TRADER, Wilfried. Einige Bemerkungen Zur Struktur Des Alltagsdenkens. *Deut Z Phil* 33,536–539 1985.

TRAGESSER, Robert S. *Husserl And Realism In Logic And Mathematics.* NY Cambridge Univ Pr 1984.

TRAIGER, Saul. Hume On Finding An Impression Of The Self. *Hume Stud* 11,47–68 Ap 85.

TRAIGER, Saul. The Hans Reichenbach Correspondence—An Overview. *Phil Res Arch* 10,501–510 1985.

The Hans Reichenbach Collection, part of the Archives of Twentieth Century Philosophy of Science, is located at the University of Pittsburgh. In the past few years work on the recently acquired Hans Reichenbach Collection has resulted in a useful research source. A great deal of organizational work on the collection has now been completed, and the correspondence is open to study by interested scholars. What follows is an overview of the correspondence catalogued in the collection. All of the information recorded here has been found in the many thousand letters to and from Reichenbach which make up only a portion of the collection. The purpose of this essay is both to acquaint the philosophical public with the wealth of material in this research source and to argue for the importance of this material for the history of recent philosophy.

TRAINOR, Paul J. History And Reality: R G Collingwood's Theory Of Absolute Presuppositions. *Ultim Real Mean* 7,270–287 D 84.

Following Gellner, I argue that the relativism that mars Collingwood's Theory of absolute presuppositions was not a conclusion, but a problem for Collingwood. I argue further that Collingwood's theory of absolute presuppositions and his logic of question and answer are usefully seen as a de–ontologized monism and an anti–justificationist theory of dialectics. Finally, I argue that Collingwood's theory allows certain kinds of ontological questions, and excludes others.

TRANOY, Knut Erik (ed) and Berg, Kare (ed). *Research Ethics.* NY Liss 1983.

TRAPP, Rainer W. Utility Theory And Preference Logic. *Erkenntnis* 22,301–340 Ja 85.

The paper offers an informal and formal account of the truth–conditions of *standard* preference propositions as they underly, e.G., the construction of cardinal utility. By checking the existing logics of preference and their semantics against this background it is then argued that, for several reasons, these logics are too crude and inadequate reconstructions of the logical relations between standard preference propositions.

TRAPP, Ranier W. Sinking Into The Sand: The Falsity Of All Sorites–Arguments. *Erkenntnis* 23,123–126 Ag 85.

It is shown that all Sorites–arguments, though logically valid, are nevertheless false since one of their two premises (the *general* one) is probably always false. By contrasting Sorites–arguments with complete induction in mathematics it is then more closely analyzed what is at the root of this falsity.

TRAVER, Rob and Smith, Philip L. Classical Living And Classical Learning: The Search For Equity And Excellence In Education. *Proc Phil Educ* 40,299–308 1984.

Equity and excellence, two sharply contrasting concerns in American education, are examined for their potential synthesis. After acknowledging the long and acrimonious debate between upholders of these concerns, and hinting at why education should so often provide the battleground, the authors analyze Mortimer Adler's *Paideia Proposal* as an attempted reconciliation. What is found is that while these two concerns must be reconciled in order for a democratic culture to survive, Adler's conception of equity is too weak, and his conception of excellence too arid, to adequately achieve this end.

TRAVIS, Charles. Classical Theories Of Reference. *Can J Phil* 6,139–160 80 Supp.

TRAVIS, Charles. On What Is Strictly Speaking True. *Can J Phil* 15,187–230 Je 85.

TREMBLAY, Robert. Le Débat, Actuel Autour De La Philosophie Marxiste. *Petite Rev Phil* 6,63–82 Spr 85.

TRIGG, Roger. The Sociobiological View Of Man. *Philosophy* 17,93–110 84 Supp.

What is the relation of the biological to the social sciences? This paper investigates the sociobiological emphasis on genetic influence on behavior, and refers the view of 'gene–culture co–evolution' put forward by C J Lumsden and E O Wilson. Culture and genetic processes interact. Culture must be taken seriously but the social sciences cannot ignore biology. Culture cannot be seen only in its own terms, although a (literally) mindless reductionism must be avoided.

TRIVERS, Howard. *The Rhythm Of Being: A Study Of Temporality.* NY Philosophical Lib 1985.

The concept of periodic occurrence, rhythm, is prior to the concept of time (Einstein). However, rhythm and time are so intertwined in reality that both are ontologically ultimate. The self and time are both born of the primordial rhythm of Being (Hegel). The physical universe is rhythmic in nature, as are the life and history of all creatures, including man. Man is a temporal being whose history expresses and reveals the temporal character of reality.

TROELSTRA, A S (ed) and Goldblatt, R and Suppes, P (ed). *Topoi: The Categorial Analysis Of Logic.* NY North–Holland 1984.

TROELSTRA, A S and Diller, J. Realizability And Intuitionistic Logic. *Synthese* 60,253–282 Ag 84.

TROELSTRA, A S. Choice Sequences And Informal Rigour. *Synthese* 62,217–228 F 85.

In this paper we discuss a particular example of the passage from the informal, but rigorous description of a concept to the axiomatic formulation of principles holding for the concept; in particular, we look at the principles of continuity and lawlike choice in the theory of lawless sequences. Our discussion also leads to a better understanding of the role of the so–called choice axiom for lawless sequences.

TROMPF, Garry W. Rationality: Reconstructable, Relative And What Else (Comments On The Rethinking Of Paul Tibbetts)? *Phil Soc Sci* 14,509–514 D 84.

TRONCOSO, Alfredo. Nietzsche Y El Intento De Ir Más Allá De Sócrates. *Logos (Mexico)* 12,63–86 My–Ag 84.

Nietzsche's baffling assertion that the true Greek philosophers were those before Socrates is analyzed here with a view to elucidating his lifelong task as that of finding an alternative to the millenary "metaphysics" began by Socrates. The article tries to show the enormity of the task as he conceived it; what he achieved; where he fell short and most particularly; what the study of the history of thought promises from his perspective.

TROOST, A. Theorieën Over Ethiek En Over De Levenspraktijk. *Phil Reform* 49,150–163 1984.

TROOST, A. Theorieën Over Ethiek En Over De Levenspraktijk. *Phil Reform* 50,66–84 1985.

TROTIGNON, Pierre. L'ombre De La Raison. *Rev Metaph Morale* 89,307–321 Jl–S 84.

TROYER, John (ed) and Vance, David (ed) and Brodsky, Garry (ed). *Social And Political Ethics.* Buffalo Prometheus 1985.

TRUSS, J K. Cancellation Laws For Surjective Cardinals. *Annals Pure Applied Log* 27,165–207 O 84.

Two sets X and Y are said to have the same "surjective cardinal" if there are functions from X onto Y and from Y onto X. The main results proved (in *ZF*) are as follows. Theorem 1: Surjective cardinals form a weak cardinal algebra. Theorem 2: If k is an integer less than or equal to 2 and a, b are surjective cardinals such that $ka = kb$, then $a = b$. Other combinatorial and independence results related to cancellation laws are also discussed.

TSCHERKASSOW, G K and Drjachlow, N I. Über Den Wirkungs– Und Ausnutzungsmechanismus Der Gesellschaftlichen Entwicklungsgesetze. *Deut Z Phil* 22,629–638 1974.

TSOUYOPOULOS, Nelly. Die Induktive Methode Und Das Induktionsproblem In Der Griechischen Philosophie. *Z Allg Wiss* 5,94–122 1974.

The stoics accept contraposition as the only form of scientific inference while the epicureans introduce a pure empirical criterion for sound general propositions. Both theories however, suggest an identification of the problem of induction with the problem of possibility. Philoponos is the first author to give a classification of sciences from a methodological point of view. He rejects pure induction and proposes the hypothetico–deductive Method as a solution of the problem of induction. (edited)

TSOUYOPOULOS, Nelly. German Philosophy And The Rise Of Modern Clinical Medicine. *Theor Med* 5,345–358 O 84.

I try to show that the so–called romantic medicine which has been so long neglected and generally considered as unscientific, promoted the development of modern clinic. Under the influence of German Philosophy (Kant, Schelling) romantic medicine introduced a new concept about the linkage between the individual organism and the universe. The new 'ecological model' helped medicine to solve some difficult theoretical but also practical problems.

TSOUYOPOULOS, Nelly. Logik Und Dialektik Als Wissenschaftsmethoden. *Stud Leibniz* 7,81–104 1975.

Die Dialektik als wissenschaftliche Methode entsteht aus dem Bedürfnis der % duberwidung a) des hypothetischen Charakters der Wissenschaft und b) des bloss formalen Charakters der Notwendigkeit. Die Geschichte jedoch zeigt, dass eine Kombination von absoluter Notwendigkeit, Realitätsbezongenheit und nicht hypothetischer Voraussagbarkeit (wie sie etwa die antike griechische Tragödie zum Ausdruch brachte) innerhalb der Struktur der Wissenschaft nicht realisierbar ist. (edited)

TUCHANSKA, Barbara. The Idea Of Rationality Of Human Actions In Marxism. *Dialec Hum* 11,373–380 Spr/Sum 84.

In Marxism human activity is usually described as rational, purposeful. However, reduction of the essence of human activities to rationality is not useful in the philosophy of history/since rationality itself is a product of history/, and does not permit to understand how human being is engaged in social practice, and how the parts of this practice are connected. The concepts of human personality and culture are indispensable for these aims.

TUCHANSKA, Barbara. The Marxian Conception Of Man. *Dialec Hum* 10,127–140 Sum 83.

The inner structure and content of the Marxian conception of man and its place in the whole Marx's philosophy are two main problems of that paper. Concept of man as natural being, i.E., objective, sensual, and active, concepts of sociability, humanity, and historicity are shown to be constituent components of Marx's conception. Concepts of personality and culture are shown to be its integral part that ought to be introduced into it.

TUCK, Andrew and Perl, Jeffrey M. The Hidden Advantage Of Tradition: On The Significance Of T S Eliot's Indic Studies. *Phil East West* 35,115–132 Ap 85.

T S Eliot's graduate work at Harvard was in large part devoted to Asian philosophy and philology. His course notes and essays from that period are in restricted collections and are quoted here for the first time. His Indian studies influenced his philosophical, religious, and aesthetic positions far more deeply than has been previously understood. Further exploration of Eliot's "philosophical notebooks" appears in the Winter and Autumn, 1985, issues of *The Southern Review*.

TUCKER, John. An Anglo–Saxon Response To John King Farlow's Questions On Zen Language And Zen Paradoxes. *J Chin Phil* 12,217–222 Je 85.

TUCKER, Robert W. Morality And Deterrence. *Ethics* 95,461–478 Ap 85.

TUGUE, Tosiyuki and Nomoto, Hisao. "Independence Of A Problem In Elementary Analysis From Set Theory" in *Lecture Notes In Mathematics*, Muller, G H And Others (ed), 307–322. NY Springer 1981.

TUMMERS, Paul M J E. Albertus Magnus' View On The Angle With Special Emphasis On His Geometry And Metaphysics. *Vivarium* 22,35–62 My 84.

In the chapter on 'quantity' in his Metaphysics Albertus Magnus (1200–1280) remarkably devotes a large passage to the nature of the angle. The article gives an analysis of relevant passages in Anaritius' Commentary on Euclid, Albertus Magnus' Commentary on Euclid (c. 1260) and his Metaphysics (1260–1264), and shows striking parallelism between them, in contrast to other XIIIth and XIVth century texts which have a different outlook. The (latin) texts of the three passages mentioned above are given in the Appendix.

TUOMELA, Raimo. *A Theory Of Social Action.* Boston Reidel 1984.

The book develops a systematic philosophical theory of action for the case of several agents acting together or jointly. A central thesis defended is that "we–attitudes" (such as we–intentions and mutual beliefs) are indispensable for the conceptual analysis of joint action and, indeed, for the analysis of social concepts on the whole.

TUOMELA, Raimo. Social Action–Functions. *Phil Soc Sci* 14,133–148 Je 84.

The main purpose of the paper is to analyze the notion of its being the *function* of some agents to perform a certain action. In contrast to previous analysis the present characterization relies strongly on an idea of division of tasks in the collective in question.

TUOMELA, Raimo. Truth And Best Explanation. *Erkenntnis* 22,271–300 Ja 85.

It is argued in the paper that science aims at giving ever more exact and truthlike pictures of the world. However, truth is an epistemic notion, one which is relativized to a conceptual scheme. What is more, there are several notions of truth of which factual truth (picturing–truth) and epistemic truth are discussed in the paper. More specifically, it is claimed that, letting T be a scientific theory, the statements: (1) T is factually true and (2) T is epistemically true (or ideal) are equivalent relative to some plausible conceptual and rationality assumptions. Furthermore, (1) and (2) are claimed to be analogously equivalent with (3) T is the (asymptotically) best–explaining theory. The demonstration of the claimed equivalences proceeds partly in terms of some model languages and results from inductive logic. In part also quite general considerations are used to argue for the above equivalences.

TUR, Richard. Dishonesty And The Jury: A Case Study In The Moral Content Of Law. *Philosophy* 18,75–96 84 Supp.

TURNBULL, Robert G. "Zeno's Stricture And Predication In Plato, Aristotle, And Plotinus" in *How Things Are*, Bogen, James (ed), 21–58. Boston Reidel 1985.

TURNBULL, Robert G. On R E Allen's *Plato's Parmenides*. *Ancient Phil* 4,206–217 Fall 84.

An article–review of R E Allen's translation of and commentary on Plato's *Parmenides*. The effort is to explain Allen's interpretation of the dialogue, with particular emphasis on the contention that the dialogue is aporetic—in the sense of deliberately setting problems for solutions by members of the Academy. I think that the book is illuminating and helpful but end with a critique of the aporetic thesis.

TURNER, Roy. Speech And The Social Contract. *Inquiry* 28,43–54 Mr 85.

Austin's 'doctrine of infelicities', whereby performative utterances are vulnerable to the risk of failure, has been criticized for treating such a possibility as contingent rather than as necessary (and hence revelatory of the essential nature of speech acts). This paper seeks to trace out what is at stake for one who maintains Austin's position. It examines Austin's curious hypothetical history of the development of speech acts, which is found to resemble forms of social–contract theory, and the problem with this hypothetical history is shown to be that it presupposes as original the very properties that it sets out to explain. The argument is then made that Austin's technicalization of the conditions and context of speech acts displaces our attention from the deeper issue that both speech–act and contract theory are versions of a concern with making social action transparent, and both raise the perennial (and insoluble) problem of trust in human affairs.

TURNER, Stephen P. Social Theory Without Wholes. *Human Stud* 7,259–284 1984.

Through a discussion of change in social attempts, the premises of writers like Dunn, Taylor, and Giddens, about the relation between social theory and the idiom of practice are examined, with the aim of showing what a non–foundationalist understanding of the explanatory and practical character of social theory would be. Examples from politics and organizational theory form the basis of the discussion.

TUROW, Scott. Commentary On Daley's "Toward A Theory Of Bribery". *Bus Prof Ethics J* 3,84–86 Fall 83.

TUROW, Scott. What's Wrong With Bribery? *J Bus Ethics* 4,249–251 Ag 85.

The article argues that bribery is wrong because it violates fundamental notion of equality and it undermines the vitality of the institutions affected.

TURVEY, M T and Carello, Claudia. The Equation Of Information And Meaning From The Perspectives Of Situation Semantics And Gibson's Ecological Realism. *Ling Phil* 8,81–90 F 85.

TWEEDALE, Martin M. "Armstrong On Determinable And Substantial Universals" in *D M Armstrong*, Bogdan, Radu J (ed), 171–190. Boston Reidel 1984.

TWEEDALE, Martin. Universals And Laws Of Nature. *Phil Topics* 13,25–44 Spr 82.

This article argues that, once we have accepted the view that laws of nature are true because of non–extensional relations holding between universals, it is much more reasonable to suppose that these relations hold with logical necessity than contingently. The opposite approach seems either not to offer any advantage over the neo–Humean theory it rejects, or to lead to the conclusion that laws either are not as basic in nature as modern science assumes or derive from the supra–natural.

TWEYMAN, Stanley. Descartes' 'Demonstrations' Of His Existence. *S J Phil* 23,101–108 Spr 85.

This paper deals with the question whether the *Cogito ergo Sum* is arrived at syllogistically or whether it is an intuition requiring no major premise. It is proved that while Descartes' proof of his existence in meditation II does not involve a syllogism, the proof of his existence in the *Principles of Philosophy* does not involve a syllogism. My position is argued by examining Descartes' replies to objections and his conversation with Burman.

TWINING, William. The Contemporary Significance Of Bentham's Anarchical Fallacies. *Arch Rechts Soz* 61,325–356 1975.

Bentham's *Anarchical Fallacies* was specifically directed against the French Declarations of 1791–1795, but the work has a wider significance. Some of his criticisms of the French Declarations are valid and should be taken into account by a modern draftsman of a document purporting to declare or protect human rights. Others of his arguments are unlikely to gain widespread acceptance today. Moreover, in so far as Bentham made valid criticisms of the French Declarations, the features criticised are not necessary features of all human rights theories, nor of all documents declaring or protecting human rights.

TWUMASI, Patrick A. The Asantes: Ancestors And The Social Meaning Of Life. *Ultim Real Mean* 7,201–208 S 84.

TYE, Michael. Pain And The Adverbial Theory. *Amer Phil Quart* 21,319–328 O 84.

In this paper, I lay out an adverbial analysis for pain and I defend it against possible objections. I also try to show that there are reasons for preferring the adverbial account I sketch to what is perhaps the most popular view, namely that pain statements involve existential quantifications over pain events, where pain events are taken to be identical with microphysical events located in the brain.

TYE, Michael. The Debate About Mental Imagery. *J Phil* 81,678–690 N 84.

There has been much debate recently among cognitive psychologists about the nature of mental images. Some psychologists maintain that mental images represent in the manner of pictures, whereas others maintain that mental images represent in the manner of language. I argue that the experimented data motivating these two views can be explained without assuming that there are, in the brain, mental images that persons have when they undergo image experiences. I also sketch an account of imagery that avoids mental images altogether.

TYMAN, Stephen. Heidegger And The Deconstruction Of Foundations. *Int Phil Quart* 24,347–372 D 84.

TYMAN, Stephen. Mysticism And Gnosticism In Heidegger. *Phil Today* 28,358–371 Wint 84.

Heidegger is often interpreted as a thinker discontinues with himself: an existential phenomenologist who evolves into a mystic. My thesis is that there is no radical discontinuity and that Heidegger is no mystic. An analysis of mysticism is given, to show that it bears an intrinsic relation to metaphysics. Heidegger's critique of metaphysics, then, also applies to mysticism; beyond the critique there lies Heidegger's sense of authentic goals more primordial than either.

TYMIENIECKA, A. "Aesthetic Enjoyment And Poetic Sense" in *Existential Coordinates Of Human Condition*, Tymieniecka, A (ed), 3–22. Boston Reidel 1984.

TYMIENIECKA, A. "Tragedy And The Completion Of Freedom" in *Existential Coordinates Of Human Condition*, Tymieniecka, A (ed), 295–306. Boston Reidel 1984.

TYMIENIECKA, Anna–Teresa (ed). *The Existential Coordinates Of The Human Condition: Poetic—Epic—Tragic*. Boston Reidel 1984.

TYMIENIECKA, Anna–Teresa. Armonía En El Devenir: La Espontaneidad De La Vida Y La Autoindividuación. *Rev Filosof (Costa Rica)* 23,121–130 D 85.

The author explains her reflections about a system of life based upon phenomenological theories. She talks about life as a continuous development based on an evolutionary order in which the meaning of life cannot be separated from its origin nor from its spontaneity. The ideas developed are: (a) the denunciation of the unjustified sovereignty of reason; (b) the denial of the intentionality of conscience as the sole organizing function of the human conscience/life–world complex: and (c) classic phenomenology's inability to explain the so–called pre–predicative and pre–thematic domains.

TYMOCZKO, Thomas. An Unsolved Puzzle About Knowledge. *Phil Quart* 34,437–459 O 84.

"no one knows this sentence is true". Were that sentence not true, someone would know it and what they know would be true. So the sentence is true. However, when we follow this argument, we come to know the sentence and so it is false. This paper develops a paradox of the knower with emphasis on its epistemic premises. It explores the possibility of solving the paradox by revising some of our basic assumptions about knowledge.

TYRMAND, Leopold. "For Your Freedom, And Ours" in *On Freedom*, Howard, John A (ed), 3–6. Greenwich Devin–adair 1984.

UEBESCHÄR, K and Kannegiesser, Karlheinz. Zur Theorien– Und Methodenentwicklung In Den Naturwissenschaften. *Deut Z Phil* 33,509–518 1985.

UESU, Tadahiro. "Intuitionistic Theories And Toposes" in *Lecture Notes In Mathematics*, Muller, G H And Others (ed), 323–358. NY Springer 1981.

UFFENHEIMER, Benyamin. "Buber And Modern Biblical Scholarship" in *Martin Buber*, Gordon, Haim (ed), 163–214. Beersheva Ktav 1984.

UHLANER, Carole and Grofman, Bernard. Metapreferences And The Reasons For Stability In Social Choice: Thoughts On Broadening And Clarifying The Debate. *Theor Decis* 19,31–50 Jl 85.

The standard model of collective choice looks at aggression procedures which take individual preferences as existing for a specified set of alternatives. In this paper we propose that actors also have preferences for rules of choice or characteristics of choice processes (e.G., the perceived fairness of procedures or the popularity of outcomes) rather than simply for alternatives (outcomes) themselves. We argue that the positing of the existence of meta–preferences can illuminate a number of areas of choice theory. Here we focus on one such area: the problem of "too much" stability in majority rule decision making—a stability which belies the standard theoretical results on the generic instability of majority rule processes. We also show that discussion of the prevalence of stability in collective decision making needs to be clarified because there are at least six distinct types of stability which are sometimes confounded in the literature.

UHLIG, Dieter. Die Weltgeschichtliche Bedeutung Des Sieges Der Sowjetunion Im Grossen Vaterländischen Krieg Im Lichte Des Leninismus. *Deut Z Phil* 23,629–643 1975.

Der 2 Weltkrieg war zunächst auf beiden Seiten ungerecht, weil er nichts anderas war als die Fortsetzung des alten imperialistischen Streites um die Neuaufteilung der Welt. Erst mid dem 22, Juni 1941 gewann der Krieg ein klar umrissenes antifaschistisches Programm. Der Grofsse Vaterländische Krieg war von Anfang bis Ende ein gerechter Befreingskrieg. Der Sieg der Sowjetunion war historisch unvermeidlich, weil sie ihren gerechten Kampf in voller Übereinstimmung mit den ofjektiven Erfordernissen der Gerschichte führte. Die Zerschlagung des Faschismus shuf eine günstige Chance füre die demokratische Entwicklung unter Führung der Arbeiterklasse.

UL'IANOVSKII, R A. On Revolutionary Democracy—Its State And Political System. *Soviet Stud Phil* 23,50–67 Wint 84–85.

ULEHLA, Ivan. Modifications Of Logical And Ontological Foundations Of Physics Of The 20th Century (in Czechoslovakian). *Filozof Cas* 32,788–791 1984.

New theories in physics created in the first decades of the 2oth century brought new definitions of the basic philosophical and physical categories and thus induced a dynamical and historical view on the development of cognition in physics. Moreover, latest branches of research in physics, e.G., in astrophysics and synergetics lead to considerations on a dialectic development of real objects themselves. Examples are given for both cases.

ULLMAN, Richard H. Denuclearizing International Politics. *Ethics* 95,567–588 Ap 85.

ULLMANN– MARGALIT, Edna and Margalit, Avishai. On The Nature Of Protest Petitions (in Hebrew). *Iyyun* 33,239–246 Ja–Ap 84.

ULLMANN– MARGALIT, Edna and Margalit, Avishai. Protest Petitions. *J Applied Phil* 1,205–212 O 84.

This paper is concerned with the question of whether an individual has a moral obligation to sign a protest petition which has been initiated on moral grounds. It is argued that there is such an obligation when the petition represents a viewpoint with which one broadly agrees. (edited)

ULLRICH, Horst. Der Kampf Der KPD Gegen Die Ideologie Des Hitlerfaschismus. *Deut Z Phil* 23,662–681 1975.

Der Autor behandelt die grundlegenden Aspekte der Auseinandersetzung, die die KPD in Einheit mid der Kommunistischen Internationale mit der Weltanschauung des Hitlerfaschismus vor dessen Machtantritt führte. Es wird bewiesen, dafss die KPD die einzige organisierte politische Kraft in Deutschland way, die konseqyuent der Ideologie des Hitlerfaschismus entgegentrat, dessen reaktionären, verbrecherischen Charakter blofsslegtss und bekämpfte mit dem Ziel, eine geschlossene Front der aarbeiterklasse und des werktätigen Volkes gegen die Gefahr der faschistischen Dikatur, gegen Imperialismus und Krieg zu schaffen.

ULRICH, Dolph E. Answer To A Question Suggested By Schumm. *Z Math Log* 30,385–387 1984.

Schumm ("Bounded properties in modal logic", *Z Math Log*, 27, 197–200, 1981) asks if any Post–incomplete modal logic L "bounds" lack of the finite model property in the sense that L has the f m p but none of its Post–consistent extensions do. The author obtains a negative answer to Schumm's question by way of the following theorem of independent interest: if a modal logic has a finite characteristic matrix, so does each of its extensions.

UMBERTO, Eco. Latratus Canis. *Tijdschr Filosof* 47,3–14 Mr 85.

UMEN, Samuel. *Images Of Man.* NY Philosophical Lib 1985.

The purpose of the book is to stimulate thought. Since the subject matter of the book is perennial in nature, it challenges the reader to offer his view on the numerous subjects with which the book deals. Since there are no final answers to the questions that the book raises, work will entice the reader to refer to it again and again and each time finding it a work of interest and exhilaration.

UMPHREY, Stuart. Why *Politikē Philosophia?* *Man World* 17,431–452 1984.

UNGER, Peter. Minimizing Arbitrariness: Toward A Metaphysics Of Infinitely Many Isolated Concrete Worlds. *Midwest Stud Phil* 9,29–52 1984.

UNWIN, Nicholas. Relativism And Moral Complacency. *Philosophy* 60,205–214 Ap 85.

URBACH, Peter. "Good And Bad Arguments Against Historicism" in *Popper And The Human Sciences*, Currie, Gregory (ed), 133–146. Boston Nijhoff 1985.

URBACH, Peter. Randomization And The Design Of Experiments. *Phil Sci* 52,256–273 Je 85.

In clinical and agricultural trials, there is the danger that an experimental outcome appears to arise from the causal process of treatment one is interested in when, in reality, it was produced by some extraneous variation in the experimental conditions. The remedy prescribed by classical statisticians involves the procedure of randomization, whose effectiveness and appropriateness is criticized. An alternative, Bayesian analysis of experimental design, is shown, on the other hand, to provide a coherent and intuitively satisfactory solution to the problem.

URBANKOWSKI, Bohdan. A General Theory Of Sport Reality. *Dialec Hum* 11,125–136 Wint 84.

URIBE, Héctor G. La Filosofia Del Dr Jose Sanchez Villasenor. *Rev Filosof (Mexico)* 17,387–400 S–D 84.

URQUHART, Alasdair. The Undecidability Of Entailment And Relevant Implication. *J Sym Log* 49,1059–1073 D 84.

I prove in this paper that the propositional logics of relevant implication (R) and entailment (E) are undecidable. I also prove a large family of other logics undecidable. The proof uses a geometrical coordinatization theorem derived from the work of von Neumann on continuous geometry.

USHER, Dan. The Value Of Life For Decision Making In The Public Sector. *Soc Phil Pol* 2,168–191 Spr 85.

VACCARO, Virginia and Gerla, Giangiacomo. Modal Logic And Model Theory. *Stud Log* 43,203–216 1984.

We propose a first order modal logic, the **QS4E**–logic, obtained by adding to the well–known first order modal **QS4** a *rigidity axiom schemas*: A→☐A, where A denotes a basic formula. In this logic, the *possibility* entails the possibility of extending a given classical first order model. This allows us to express some important concepts of classical model theory, such as existential completeness and the state of being infinitely generic, that are not expressible in classical first order logic. (edited)

VACHET, André. Crise De Civilisation Et Université: Enseigner Aujourd'hui. *Rev Univ Ottawa* 54,5–26 Ap–Je 84.

VADAS, Melinda. A Refutation Of Egoism. *Cogito* 2,39–52 S 84.

The egoist claims that an action is rational if and only if it is in the agent's self–interest to perform the action. This claim may be understood as either a claim about the nature of good or about the source of practical reasons. I argue that, understood as the former, the egoist's claim is based upon a confusion between possession of good and maximization of good, and, understood as the latter, the claim cannot be defended on either empirical or a priori grounds.

VADAS, Melinda. Affective And Non–Affective Desire. *Phil Phenomenol Res* 45,273–280 D 84.

On the Humean or 'affectivist' view of action and its motivation, the end of all intentional action must and can only be given, either directly or indirectly, by desire. Somewhere in the line of explanation that yields the agent's motivation there must be a desire of the agent for *something*. In the absence of such a desire, action is, both conceptually and as a matter of fact, impossible. In this paper, I argue that the Humean view rests upon a failure to distinguish between affective and non–affective desire.

VAILATI, Ezio. Leibniz's Theory Of Personal Identity In The *New Essays*. *Stud Leibniz* 17,36–43 1985.

Il est une opinion fort répandue que la théorie leibnizienne de l'identité personnelle dans les *Nouveaux Essais* est contradictoire car elle renferme deux thèses incompatibles, à savoir, que 1) comme persone, je suis mon esprit, et que 2) je pourrais continuer, sans mon esprit. Dans cette étude, une interprétation nouvelle de la pensée leibnizienne sur l'identité personnelle dans les *Nouveaux Essais*, je soutiens que pour Leibniz (2) est vrai mais (1) est faux, et que par conséquence sa theorie est consistante.

VAKARELOV, Dimiter. An Application Of The Reiger–Nishimura Formulas To The Intuitionistic Modal Logics. *Bull Sect Log* 13,120–124 O 84.

VAKARELOV, Krista. Variations Of Core Semantic Techniques And Their Methodological Import. *Bull Sect Log* 13,137–143 O 84.

VALADIER, Paul. Nietzsche: Una Critica Del Cristianismo. *Rev Filosof (Mexico)* 18,33–52 Ja–Ap 85.

Nietzsche ne critique pas le christianisme pour ses dogmes (ou pas seulement), mais d'abord pour sa conception de l'homme; prétendant faire de l'homme un dieu, il engendre en fait l'athéisme. Aux antipodes de cette position qu'il qualifie de présomptueuse, Nietzsche veut apprendre à dire oui au passager et au provisoire qui ont forme d'Eternité.

VALCKE, Louis. Des *Conclusiones* Aux *Disputationes*: Numérologie Et Mathématiques Chez Jean Pic De La Mirandole. *Laval Theol Phil* 41,43–56 F 85.

L'évolution des idées philosophiques de Jean Pic de la Mirandole ressort avec évidence d'une comparaison entre ses premiers écrits (1486–87) et ses Disputations adversus astrologiam divinatricem, oeuvre à laquelle il travaillait au moment de sa mort (1494). Sous l'influence déterminante du néoplatonisme, Pic, en sa première période, tend à oblitérer la distinction entre cause première et l'ordre des causes secondes, tout en faisant du nombre le paradigme a priori de l'ordre matériel. (edited)

VALENCIK, Radim. The Methodological Function Of Political Economy In Materialist Explanation Of The Development Of Socialist Society (in Czechoslovakian). *Filosof Cas* 33,141–151 1985.

VALENCIK, R. Dialectical Logic And Social Practice (in Czechoslovakian). *Filozof Cas* 32,596–610 1984.

VALORI, Paolo. Le *natura* Norma Di Moralità? *Aquinas* 27,317–326 My–Ag 84.

VALSINER, Jaan. Two Alternative Epistemological Frameworks In Psychology: The Typological And Variational Modes Of Thinking. *J Mind Behavior* 5,449–470 Autumn 84.

It is suggested that variability within psychological phenomena—both interindividual (synchronic) and intr–individual (diachronic)—is a centrally important characteristic of these phenomena, and should be studied as such. Two modes of thinkings that psychologists have followed in their research—the typological and the variational—are outlined and compared. It is argued that the traditions in psychology that have used the typological mode of thinking have guided psychology in a direction that would not afford the study of psychological processes that underlie the phenomena. These traditions have extracted static aspects of the psychological phenomena and disgarded variability within the phenomena as "error" or "chance". As an alternative, it is suggested that the variational mode of thinking about psychological phenomena can be adopted by psychologists. That approach would afford asking research questions that could reconstruct the processes that generate the full range of the occurence of the particular psychological phenomena under study. The variational mode of thinking affords treatment of psychological phenomena in terms of open systems. (edited)

VAN AKEN, James. Analysis Of Quantum Probability Theory I. *J Phil Log* 14,267–296 Ag 85.

Van Fraassen's modal interpretation of quantum theory is shown to fail in quantum field theory and quantum statistical mechanics. More strongly, quantum theory is given a new formulation on which quantum field theory and quantum statistical mechanics afford models in which pure states are entirely absent. This result leads to a far–reaching adjustment in the conception of a quantum state.

VAN BALEN, G A M. Enkele Pogingen Tot Reconstructie Van De Evolutietheorie En De Populatiegenetica Als Wetenschappelijke Onderzoeks–Programma's. *Kennis Methode* 8,274–294 1984.

It is argued that neither evolutionary theory nor population genetics can be reconstructed as Lakatosian research programs. Evolutionary theory is shown to be too complex to be moulded into the framework of a scientific research program. Population genetics, though prima facie well–suited, is shown to be an anomaly for Lakatos' *philosophical* research program, because it consists of two competing and mutually inconsistent theories.

VAN BENTHAM, Johan and Pearce, David. A Mathematical Characterization Of Interpretation Between Theories. *Stud Log* 43,295–304 1984.

Of the various notions of reduction in the logical literature, relative interpretability in the sense of Tarski and other [6] appears to be the central one. In the present note, this syntactic notion is characterized semantically, through the existence of a suitable reduction functor on models. The latter mathematical condition itself suggests a natural generalization, whose syntactic equivalent turns out to be a notion of interpretability quite close to that of Ershov [1], Szczerba [5] and Gaifman [2].

VAN BENTHAM, Johan. Situations And Inference. *Ling Phil* 8.3–8 F 85.

This is a discussion of some novel logical features of Situation Semantics and their potential for further research.

VAN BENTHEM, Johan. "Correspondence Theory" in *Handbook Of Philosophical Logic*, Gabbay, Dov (ed), 167–248. Boston Reidel 1984.

VAN BENTHEM, Johan. Possible Worlds Semantics: A Research Program That Cannot Fail. *Stud Log* 43,379–394 1984.

Providing a possible worlds semantics for a logic involves choosing a class of possible worlds models, and setting up a truth definition connecting formulas of the logic with statements about these models. This scheme is so flexible that a danger arises: perhaps, any (reasonable) logic whatsoever can be modelled in this way. Thus, the enterprise would lose its essential 'tension'. Fortunately, it may be shown that the so–called 'incompleteness–examples' from modal logic resist possible worlds modelling, even in the above wider sense. More systematically, we investigate the interplay of truth definitions and model conditions, proving a preservation theorem characterizing those types of truth definitions which generate the minimal modal logic.

VAN BRACKEL, J. Buckner Quoting Goldstein And Davidson On Quotation. *Analysis* 45,73–75 Mr 85.

In this note I argue that Buckner's criticism (Analysis, 44.4, p 189) of the demonstrative account of quotation is ill–founded and misdirected. Quotation marks may and have been put to many different uses. In my opinion much of the philosophical discussion about them suffers from the worn–out fallacy that tokens of the same sign (for example quotation marks) should have the same meaning in every context where they occur.

VAN CLEVE, James. "Another Volley At Kant's Reply To Hume" in *Kant On Causality, Freedom, And Objectivity*, Harper, William A (ed), 42–57. Minneapolis Univ Minnesota Pr 1984.

VAN CLEVE, James. Epistemic Supervenience And The Rule Of Belief. *Monist* 62,90–104 Ja 85.

VAN CLEVE, James. Reliability, Justification, And The Problem Of Induction. *Midwest Stud Phil* 9,555–568 1984.

VAN CLEVE, James. Three Versions Of The Budles Theory. *Phil Stud* 47,95–108 Ja 85.

'a thing is nothing but a bundle of properties'. If we take it as it stands, this view is open to several decisive objections. Sophisticated proponents of the view do *not* take it as it stands, but I argue that even their version of it remains open to some of the same objections. Then I suggest a third version of the view that avoids *all* the objections, but only at high cost.

VAN DALEN, D. How To Glue Analysis Models. *J Sym Log* 49,1339–1349 D 84.

An analogue of the technique for establishing metamathematical properties of formal theories, used in Kripke semantics (by Smorynski and others) is introduced for generalized Beth models. The methods are particularly well–suited for intuitionistic second–order theories of choice sequences (functions). The *glueing* of generalized Beth models is used for establishing the disjunction and existence property and some further meta–mathematical facts. The meta–mathematics of the present treatise is classical.

VAN DE PITTE, M M. Comments On A Claim That Some Phenomenological Statements May Be *A Posteriori*. *Metaphilosophy* 15,248–255 Jl–O 84.

Richard Schmitt, in an *Encyclopedia of Philosophy* article, challenged the orthodoxy that phenomenological statements are in every instance *a priori*. His argument centers upon an example which Schmitt assumes to be a genuine possible case of experiential data forcing a re–estimation of a statement previously thought to be non–empirical. We argue that the example does not represent a genuine possible case, and that there remains at least one sense (semantic) of 'non–empirical' appropriate to phenomenological statements.

VAN DE PITTE, M M. Schlick's Critique Of Phenomenological Propositions. *Phil Phenomenol Res* 45,195–226 D 84.

With a view toward assessing some recent claims about the nature of phenomenological propositions, Schlick's analysis of them in "Is There a Factual A Priori?" is criticized in the service of a preliminary clarification of the meaning of the propositional predicates used to describe positivistic and phenomenological propositions respectively.

VAN DEN BROM, L J. God's Omnipresent Agency. *Relig Stud* 20,637–656 D 84.

VAN DEN DRIES, Lou and Smith, Rick L. Decidable Regularly Closed Fields Of Algebraic Numbers. *J Sym Log* 50,468–475 Je 85.

VAN DEN HAAG, Ernest. Refuting Reiman And Nathanson. *Phil Pub Affairs* 14,165–176 Spr 85.

Refutes arguments against the death penalty which represent it as uncivilized, dehumanizing, unjust, excessive, unneeded, non–deterrent, or maldistributed in discriminatory, unequal, arbitrary and capricious fashion.

VAN DER AREND, Arie and Have, Henk Ten. Philosophy Of Medicine In The Netherlands. *Theor Med* 6,1–42 F 85.

This report explores the relationship between philosophy and medicine in the Netherlands. In Section 1 we outline the ups and downs of medico–philosophical research in our country: pre–war flourishing, post–war decline, and modern renaissance. In Section 2 we review recent Dutch literature in the philosophy of medicine. The topics dealt with include methodology of medical science, alternative medicine, the basic concepts of medicine, anthropological medicine, medicalization, medicine and culture, and health care ethics.

VAN DER HOEVEN, Gerrit and Moerdijk, Ieke. On Choice Sequences Determined By Spreads. *J Sym Log* 49,908–916 S 84.

The paper provides a model for a theory of choice sequences satisfying the axiom of spread data. The axiom was proposed by Kreisel as a first formalization of one of the leading ideas in Brouwer's work on choice sequences. The model presented is an interpretation in sheaves over a monoid of continuous maps (so–called chr mappings) from baire space to baire space.

VAN DER LEEUW, Karel and Mostert, Pieter. *Enige Kernproblemen In Het Filosofie Onderwijs*. Rotterdam Onderwijs 1985.

This research report describes main problems in teaching and learning philosophy, and is based upon a detailed analysis of an introductory course in philosophy. The material is derived from classroom protocols. After a general introduction, the next chapters concentrate on reading philosophical texts, problem solving, and theory–learning in philosophy. In the final chapter a model for the construction of introductory courses in philosophy is introduced.

VAN DER PLAS, Paul L. Moral Education In Holland. *J Moral Educ* 14,111–119 My 85.

The Netherlands is a small country with a pluralistic, multicultural population. A short historic review of moral education reveals the roots of Dutch society. In accordance with the diversity of life–stances, the identities of schools vary (Catholic, Protestant, state–schools) and they offer different forms of moral education. In this article moral

education is defined as a process of actively exploring vital questions in which awareness and development of values giving direction to moral behavior are stressed. Some ten recent projects in moral education within certain disciplines or crossing subject boundaries are described in terms of their starting points, objectives and curriculum materials. Most projects are appropriate to the secondary level. Special attention is paid to moral education within religious and humanistic education projects. After a brief description of teacher training in moral education some concluding remarks are made. These refer to the conceptual differences between moral education in Holland and in the USA and the the relatively weak position of moral education in Dutch schools.

VAN DER VEEN, Robert J. The Marxian Ideal Of Freedom And The Problem Of Justice. *Philosophica* 34,103–126 1984.

The paper argues that just production relations are a prerequisite for realizing Marx's ideal of an expanding realm of freedom and the associated shift from contributions to needs. The paper reconstructs a Marxian conception of justice focusing on the distribution of self–owned 'personal' and commonly owned 'material' conditions of production. It is then argued that a society satisfying the resulting two principles of Equal Liberties and Equal Access is both exploitation–free and classless.

VAN DER VEEN, Romke. De Ethogene Methode Van Sociaal–Wetenschappelijk Onderzoek Van Rom Harré. *Kennis Methode* 9,64–87 1985.

VAN DER WALT, J W G. Hermeneutics As Practical Philosophy And Practical Wisdom (in Dutch). *S Afr J Phil* 3,139–146 N 84.

This article deals with Hans–George Gadamer's interpretation of hermeneutics as practical philosophy. Part one deals with the problem of practical wisdom within the hermeneutics of Gadamer. Part two deals with the hermeneutics itself as an instance of practical wisdom. (edited)

VAN FRAASSEN, Bas C. "Glymour On Evidence And Explanation" in *Testing Scientific Theories*, Earman, John (ed), 165–176. Minneapolis Univ Minnesota Pr 1983.

VAN FRAASSEN, Bas C. "Theory Comparison And Relevant Evidence" in *Testing Scientific Theories*, Earman, John (ed), 27–42. Minneapolis Univ Minnesota Pr 1983.

VAN INWAGEN, Peter. On Two Arguments For Compatibilism. *Analysis* 45,161–163 Je 85.

The two most popular arguments for the compatibility of free will and determinism are, first, the argument that 'can' statements are disguised conditionals, and, secondly, the argument that free will requires determinism because an undetermined act could not be a free act. It is shown that these two arguments are not both sound. This follows from the observation that if 'can' statements are disguised conditionals, then an undetermined act *can* be a free act.

VAN PARIJS, Philippe. What (If Anything) Is Intrinsically Wrong With Capitalism? *Philosophica* 34,85–102 1984.

VAN PRAAG, J P. Foundations Of Humanism. Buffalo Prometheus Books 1982.

VAN VELTHOVEN, Theo. Teken, Waarheid, Macht. *Tijdschr Filosof* 47,42–70 Mr 85.

VANCE, David (ed) and Brodsky, Garry (ed) and Troyer, John (ed). *Social And Political Ethics*. Buffalo Prometheus 1985.

VANDER ZWAAG, Harold J. The Nature Of The Inquiry In The Philosophy Of Sport. *Dialec Hum* 11,172–174 Wint 84.

The primary purpose of the work was to partially assess the content of recent work in the sport philosophy. This was accomplished through an examination of the content of the articles which appeared in six volumes of the *Journal of the Philosophy of Sport* between 1977 and 1982. Principle concepts or topics were found to be: play, game(s), women in sport, martial arts, cheating, competition, and the sport team. Much of the work is definitional in nature while attempting to apply philosophical analysis to sport.

VANDERPOOL, Harold Y and Weiss, Gary B. Patient Truthfulness: A Test Of Models Of The Physician–Patient Relationship. *J Med Phil* 9,353–372 N 84.

Little attention has been given in medical ethics literature to issues relating to the truthfulness of patients. Beginning with an actual medical case, this paper first explores truth–telling by doctors and patients as related to two prominent models of the physician–patient relationship. Utilizing this discussion and the literature on the truthfullness and accuracy of the information patients convey to doctors, these models are then critically assessed. It is argued that the patient agency (patient autonomy or contractual) model is inherently and seriously flawed in numerous circumstances, even those involving informed and competent adult patients.

VANISTENDAEL, Clara. Prevention Of Admission And Continuity Of Care. *Theor Med* 6,93–114 F 85.

An in–depth analysis of the recent reform in Italian psychiatry reveals that the relevance of these changes transcends national borders. However, these changes are, from the scientific point of view, worth much more than mere biased pragmatic interest. The reshaping of theory made possible by the transformation of Italian psychiatry in fact opens up new prospects for a scientifically founded form of psychiatric care. Thanks to the Mental Health Act (No 180 of 1978), it has been possible to set up a type of administrative and institutional organization in which the psychiatric hospital no longer constitutes a functional part of the structures of psychiatric care. This reform thus provides the launching path for a real alternative where current psychiatric ideas and working methods can no longer be accepted as the gospel truth. This paper discusses how a correct problem–definition of psychiatric admission can provide a basis for a correct approach to psychopathological behavior in a setting where the psychiatric hospital has no role to play and for the consolidation of this new practice.

VARGA, Andrew C. "Playing God": The Ethics Of Biotechnical Intervention. *Thought* 60,181–195 Je 85.

The purpose of the work is to examine the morality of biotechnical intervention in the life of plants, animals, and human beings. It concludes that the technology in itself is neutral from the ethical point of view. Its applications, however, may become right or wrong depending on whether they promote the fullness of the various degrees of life, and ultimately of human life.

VARGA, Csaba. Towards An Ontological Foundation Of Law (in Hungarian). *Magyar Filozof Szemle* 5,767–776 1983.

VARNER, G E. The Schopenhauerian Challenge In Environmental Ethics. *Environ Ethics* 7,209–230 Fall 85.

Environmental holism and environmental individualism are based on incompatible notions of moral considerability, and yield incompatible results. For Schopenhauer, every intelligible character—every irreducible instance of formative nature—defines a distinct moral patient, and for him both holistic entities and the individual members of higher species have distinguishable intelligible characters. Schopenhauer's neglected metaethics thus can be used to generate an environmental ethics which is *complete* in the sense of synthesizing holism and individualism while simultaneously meeting Tom Regan's (implicit) demand that an environmental ethics make moral patients of natural objects.

VASAK, Pavel. System Of Literary History (in Czechoslovakian). *Estetika* 21,220–233 1984.

VÁSQUEZ, Eduardo. El Concepto En La Fenomenología Del Espíritu. *Rev Ven Filosof* 12,31–62 1980.

VATER, Michael G (ed) and Schelling, F W J. *Bruno*. Albany SUNY Pr 1984.

VATTIMO, Gianni. Dialectics, Difference, And Weak Thought. *Grad Fac Phil J* 10,151–164 Spr 84.

VAUGHT, Carl G. Metaphor, Analogy, And System: A Reply To Burbidge "Professor Burbidge Responds". *Man World* 18,55–63 1985.

This article claims that metaphor and analogy are irreducible dimensions of philosophical discourse and cannot be replaced by holistic, systematic reflection. Concrete media of expression (art, religion, philosophy) are therefore essential for describing human fragmentation and developing an account of human wholeness. Wholeness is not completeness, as Hegel suggests, nor is it a fragmented plurality, as Burbridge implies. Instead, it is a metaphorical intersection of mystery, power, and structure related analogically to other similar contexts.

VAUZEILLES, Jacqueline and Girard, Jean–Yves. Functors And Ordinal Notations I: A Functorial Construction Of The Veblen Hierarchy. *J Sym Log* 49,713–729 S 84.

Dilators are functors from Ordinals to Ordinals preserving direct limits and pullbacks. Since ordinals can be approximated by means of direct systems of integers, dilators are therefore a notion of ordinal function in the spirit of potential infinity. In this paper, the famous Veblen hierarchy of ordinal functions is shown to be a dilator in two variables (index, argument), so that this typical infinitary construction is indeed "finitary" in a very strong sense.

VAUZEILLES, Jacqueline and Girard, Jean–Yves. Functors And Ordinal Notations: II, A Functorial Construction Of The Bachmann Hierarchy. *J Sym Log* 49,1079–1114 D 84.

The paper extends a previous work on the Veblen Hierarchy; the familiar Bachmann collections are replaced by "gardens". In a garden, fundamental sequences are given by means of functors, which are dilators, and furthermore, which is topologically continuous ("flowers"). A garden is something like a Bachmann collection of variable size; the work therefore shows the possibility of constructing the Bachmann hierarchy without fixing the size of the indexing collections; all this in a finitary way.

VAUZEILLES, Jacqueline. Functors And Ordinal Notations. *J Sym Log* 50,331–338 Je 85.

In this article we prove how the usual Howard ordinal is connected with the functor λ introduces by J Y Girard. More precisely, we show that the Howard ordinal is exactly $\lambda(1 + \mathrm{Id})^{1+\mathrm{Id}}(1)$. This result is part of a study of ordinal notations, and for the proof we use some concepts introduced in Parts I, II, and III of this article.

VEATCH, Henry B. "Can Philosophy Ever Be A Thing For Hoosiers" in *The Georgetown Symposium On Ethics*, Porreco, Rocco (ed), 1–18. Lanham Univ Pr Of America 1984.

VEATCH, Robert M. "Definitions Of Life And Death: Should There Be Consistency" in *Defining Human Life*, Shaw, Margery W (ed), 99–113. Ann Arbor Aupha Pr 1983.

VEATCH, Robert M. "Ethics Of Institutional Ethics Committees" in *Ethics Committees And Health Care Decisions*, Cranford, Ronald (ed), 35–50. Ann Arbor Health Admin Pr 1984.

VEATCH, Robert M and Callahan, Daniel. Autonomy's Temporary Triumph. *Hastings Center Rep* 14,38–40 O 84.

In the medical ethical debates of the 1970s the focus was on the individual patient. The consequentialistic Hippocratic principle of patient benefit was in tension with the deontological principle of autonomy. Autonomy won a clear, but temporary victory. In the 1980s, social resource allocation questions became critical. Two social ethical principles are now in conflict: one focusing on social consequences and the other on deontologically just patterns of distribution. Just as the deontological principle of autonomy won out, so the principle of justice should.

VEATCH, Robert M. Lay Medical Ethics. *J Med Phil* 10,1–6 F 85.

VEATCH, Robert. "Ethics And The Dying" in *Contemporary Issues In Health Care*, Schnall, David J (ed), 89–111. NY Praeger 1984.

VEENHOVEN, Ruut. *Conditions Of Happiness*. Boston Reidel 1984.

This book identifies conditions that favor a positive appreciation of life. It does so by taking stock of the results of 245 empirical investigations on happiness, carried out between the 1910's and the 1970's in 32 countries. Comparison between countries demonstrates that people are currently happiest in the most economically affluent countries and in the most politically stable and democratic nations. Comparison through time shows that issues of 'income', 'education' and 'rank' lost impact during the last decades, whereas 'intimate ties' have become more relevant.

VEILLEUX, Armand. Monachisme Et Gnose: Deuxième Partie: Contacts Littéraires Et Doctrinaux Entre Monachisme Et Gnose. *Laval Theol Phil* 41,3–24 F 85.

Le gnosticisme était encoe florissant en Égypte au moment où le monachisme chrétien s'y développait. Y eut–il des contacts entre les deux mouvements, et de quelle nature? La Lecons recherche de contacts littéraires directs, dans un sens ou l'autre, conduit à des résultats assez maigres. Les quelques textes attestés en Bilbliothèque Copte de Nag Hammadi et utilisés également dans la littérature monastique (Sentences de Sextus, Lecons de Silvanos) ne sont pas des documents typiquement gnostiques. Par ailleurs, si l'on considère le phénomène monastique dans son universalité at le mouvement gnostique dans l'ensemble de ses manifestations, on se trouve en présence de deux archétypes universels qui, tout en étant très différents l'un de l'autre (p ex dans la conception de l'ascèse) ont aussi d'importants éléments en commun (p ex l'aspiration à retrouver l'unité primordiale).

VEISSMANN, F. Biblia Y Vida Monástica En San Agustín. *Stromata* 41,87–96 Ja–Je 85.

VEIT, Walter. The Potency Of Imagery—The Impotence Of Rational Language: Ernesto Grassi's Contribution To Modern Epistemology. *Phil Rhet* 17,221–239 1984.

VELASQUEZ, Manuel (ed) and Rostankowski, Cynthia (ed). *Ethics: Theory And Practice*. Englewood Cliffs Prentice–Hall 1985.

VELEK, J. Methodological Starting Points Of The Investigation Of The Way Of Life (in Czechoslovakian). *Filozof Cas* 33,248–268 1985.

VELEZ, Francisco V. Metafisica: Una Perplejidad Filosofica. *Rev Filosof (Mexico)* 18,127–148 Ja–Ap 85.

VELLACOTT, Philip. *The Logic Of Tragedy: Morals And Integrity In Aeschylus' Oresteia*. Durham Duke Univ Pr 1984.

VELLEMAN, Dan. Simplified Morasses With Linear Limits. *J Sym Log* 49,1001–1021 D 84.

VELOSO, Paulo A S. Outlines Of A Mathematical Theory Of General Problems. *Phil Natur* 21,354–367 1984.

A mathematically rigourous and widely applicable theory of problems is outlined. Based on a critical analysis of familiar but vague notions, problems are defined as mathematical structures and their solutions as certain functions. This provides a framework for the precise investigation of solvability, reduction, decomposition, etc., of problems. The emphasis is on a critical analysis, roughly analogous to the metamathematical viewpoint, rather than on a "how–to–solve–it" approach.

VENDLER, Zeno. Agency And Causation. *Midwest Stud Phil* 9,371–384 1984.

This paper shows that in attributing an action to an agent the causal chain of events remain unaffected by the attribution. Instead, within limits, each member of the causal chain is the source of possible action–descriptions. Moreover, whereas the individual agents are *caused* by other events, actions are *done* by the agent. e.G., the *rising* of my arm is caused by the contraction of some muscles, but the *raising* of my arm is not caused, but done by me.

VENEGAS, Juana Sanchez. Origen Común Y Desarrollo Divergente En Bergson Y Ortega. *Pensamiento* 41,57–68 Ja–Mr 85.

The Kantian roots of Bergson and Ortega are emphasized to explain the existing connection between both authors. This connection is twofold. First, the identification by Ortega of his thought and Bergon's: "the *bon sens* is the *razón vital*". Second, both author's criticism of identity as received from classical philosophy. The aim of Bergson and Ortega was to find the true knowledge accounting for life as a dynamic reality. The Kantian setting made this attempt unsuccessful.

VENETUS, Paulus. *Logica Parva*, Alan R Perreiah (trans). Munchen Philosophia 1984.

VENTURA, Antonino. Il Tempo Nel Pensiero Di Gaston Bachelard. *Riv Filosof Neo–Scolas* 76,98–121 Ja–Mr 84.

The work focuses on Bachelard's thought concerning the notion of time, in order to stress the evolution of it and bring out the ontological meaning. The conclusions show that the thesis on temporal discontinuity in Bachelard's first phase is improved later, in the works about the imaginary, by a concept of temporality close to Bergsonism and metaphysically useful.

VER EECKE, Wilfried. "The State: Ethics And Economics" in *The Georgetown Symposium On Ethics*, Porreco, Rocco (ed), 195–204. Lanham Univ Pr Of America 1984.

VERBEECK, Louis. De Literatuur Naar De Letter. *Tijdschr Filosof* 47,15–41 Mr 85.

As a reflection on *The Name of the Rose* by Umberto Eco, this text examines the interaction between the philosophical and the literary discourse. The disharmonious structure of historical and fictional, narrative and discursive schemes in Eco's novel draws the attention of the phenomenon of the 'caesura' that conditions every production of meaning. This idea is applied to three themes: the transformations in Medieval thought, suffering, and the dialectics of laughter.

VERENE, Donald P. *Hegel's Recollection: A Study Of Images In The Phenomenology Of Spirit*. Albany SUNY Pr 1985.

This work advances a completely new reading of Hegel's *Phenomenology of Spirit*. It shows that the philosophic meaning of the *Phenomenology* depends as much on Hegel's use of metaphor and image as it does on Hegel's dialectical and discursive descriptions of various stages of consciousness. The focus is on Hegel's concept of recollection (*Erinnerung*). This is the first commentary to regard metaphor, irony, and memory as keys to the understanding of Hegel's basic philosophical position.

VERHEY, Allen. *The Great Reversal: Ethics And The New Testament*. Grand Rapids Eerdmans 1984.

The first section of this study focuses on ethic in the New Testament, examining the moral teachings of Jesus, the moral tradition of the early church, and finally the ethics of the various writings of the New Testament. The second section focuses on the use of the New Testament in contemporary Christian ethics, surveying proposals for the use of scripture, identifying the critical methodological questions, and defending a modest proposal for the use of scripture.

VERKUYL, H J and Le Loux– Schuringa, J A. Once Upon A Tense. *Ling Phil* 8,237–262 My 85.

The tense–systems proposed by two Dutch grammarians, Te Winkel in 1866 and Kollewijn in 1892, are examined, and compared with the systems proposed by Reichenbach (1947) and Prior (1967). Goals: (1) to show that knowledge of recent theories and technical tools provides valuable insight into older theories; (2) to show where recent theories fail as compared with the older ones; (3) to contribute to the discussion about the relationship between language forms and non–linguistic categories.

VERMEULEN, Ben. Berkeley And Nieuwentijt On Infinitesimals. *Berkeley News* 8,1–6 1985.

Both Berkeley and Nieuwentijt (1654–1718) criticized the infinitesimal calculus in order to defend religion. They advanced some strikingly similar arguments against the calculus. Despite fundamental differences in epistemology (Berkeley's point of departure is his immaterialism, while Nieuwentijt is an empiricist, stressing the unbridgeable gulf between finite man and the infinite) these correspondences suggest that Nieuwentijt influenced Berkeley's criticism.

VERNON, Richard. Auguste Comte And The Withering–Away Of The State. *J Hist Ideas* 45,549–566 O–D 84.

VERSPIEREN, Patrick. Un Droit À L'enfant? *Etudes* 362,623–628 My 85.

VERSTRAETEN, Pierre. El Capítulo B De La *Crítica De La Razón Dialéctica. Rev Filosof (Costa Rica)* 23,15–30 Je 85.

The infernal character of human relationships is reactualized in the apparent attenuation of a psycho–sociological diagnostic: dialectical consideration of the contradiction of subject and object (freedom, the other, *praxis* and violence.

VERTLIEB, E and Boldyrev, Peter. Solzhenitsyn And Yanov. *Stud Soviet Tho* 29,11–16 Ja 85.

This article addresses the traditional conflict between conservative and liberal Russian historical thought reproduced once more in contemporary emigre literature. The main project of the article is to analyze and evaluate two sharply different approaches to Russian history, one offering a moral–religious judgment (Solzhenitsyn), and the other evaluating it politically (Yanov). Correspondingly, two different ways of opposing communism are recommended. The article concludes that both approaches are too one–sided and should supplement each other.

VERWEY, G. Antropologische Geneeskunde In Discussie. *Alg Ned Tijdschr Wijs* 76,207–227 O 84.

VESTER, Frederic. Stichwort Okologie. *Conceptus* 18,11–22 1984.

The unusual rise of a special field in the biological sciences to a main topic of politicians, journalists and scientists reflects the acknowledgement of the altered position of man in nature. Beginning with a definition of the most important ecological terms, the relationships between ecology, science and technology are discussed. Four further aspects of the social system, that is regional and area planning, communications, defense and legislation, are dislodged from their traditional paths by the rise of ecological thinking and therefore the changes to be expected are outlined.

VEYNE, Paul. Did The Greeks Invent Democracy? *Diogenes* 124,1–32 Wint 83.

VIEBAHN, Ursula and Viebahn, W. Weltanschaulich–Philosophische Bildung Und Erziehung Im Mathematisch–Naturwissenschaftlichen Unterricht. *Deut Z Phil* 22,757–760 1974.

VIEBAHN, W and Viebahn, Ursula. Weltanschaulich–Philosophische Bildung Und Erziehung Im Mathematisch–Naturwissenschaftlichen Unterricht. *Deut Z Phil* 22,757–760 1974.

VIERTEL, Wolfgang. Kants Lehre Vom Urteil. *Z Phil Forsch* 39,60–69 Ja–Mr 85.

Asserting Kant, notion and judgement is identified. Because of its general meaning notion is referred to its extension, and therefore a partial judgement. Kant says that notion is even a shortened judgement as the combination of subject and predicate is not a unity in its logic sense, but a unity in conciousness. This theory of judgement effects the metaphysical deduction of categories.

VIGEANT, Louise. Lecture De *L'Innommable* De Samuel Beckett. *Petit Rev Phil* 6,129–149 Autumn 84.

l'Innommable is a text on language: its powers, its incapacities. This Reading, based on the concept of performative writing, follows this speech act that, in a contradictory movement, founds and denies its subject, a discourse which tends toward silence but says the impossibility of silence. This text tells the pain, the anxiety, the fragility of the being and the reader *sees* the inscription of this in the sentences themselves: ellepsis, repetitions, retakes reveal the deficiency of language.

VIGLIELMO, Valdo H. "The Epic Element In Japanese Literature" in *Existential Coordinates Of Human Condition*, Tymienicka, A (ed), 195–208. Boston Reidel 1984.

VIGNA, Carmelo. Nascere E Morire Come Estremi Dell'Io. *Riv Filosof Neo–Scolas* 76,427–463 Jl–S 84.

Il saggio intende dimostrare che per l'Io è *necessario* predicare il fatto della nascita, mentre è solo *possibile* predicare la realtà della morte, se per morte si intende il diventar niente dell'Io. Nascita e morte, in quanto così *saputi* nell'Io, originano rispettivamente la sfera della teoria e la sfera della pratica dell'Io come doppio rimando a ciò che è ontologicamente Altro dall'orizzonte transcendentale dell'esperienza dell'Io.

VILLA, Luigi. Umanità. *Filosofia* 35,180–182 Jl–0 84.

This short work analyzes entirely the meaning of the term "humanity." Then it notices the serious decay of "humanity feeling" both in individual and social modern life. A general recovery of humanity would be very advisable, but this depends upon a larger

cause, namely upon the "morality problem," that also is in critical situation either in philosophical or in pragmatic field. It is present philosophical principal responsibility to recover rationally all the ethical values.

VILLANUEVA, Enrique. "Philosophical Analysis In Mexico" in *Philosophical Analysis In Latin America*, Gracia, Jorge J E and others (eds), 165–172. Boston Reidel 1984.

VILLANUEVA, Enrique. "The Private Language Argument" in *Philosophical Analysis In Latin America*, Gracia, Jorge J E and others (eds), 255–276. Boston Reidel 1984.

VILLWOCK, Jörg. Welt Und Mythos: Das Mythische In Heideggers Seinsdenken. *Z Phil Forsch* 38,608–628 N–D 84.

The article is concerned with Gnostic elements in Heidegger's style of thinking and the references to mythical images in his later writings. This approach means a critical recurrence to the presuppositions of the Gnostic studies of Hans Jonas, who is using categories of Heidegger's ontology in his analysis of Gnostic motifs. Thus, the present essay prepares an independent concept of the Gnosis as a middle state of mind, whose essence consists in the double relation to mythology and philosophy.

VINCI, Thomas. A Functionalist Interpretation Of Locke's Theory Of Simple Ideas. *Hist Phil Quart* 2,179–194 Ap 85.

Locke says two apparently contradictory things about simple ideas: (1) we cannot be in error about them (II, xxxii) and (2) some simple ideas (the primary) do, and some (the secondary) do not, represent reality (II, viii). I begin to resolve the difficulty by finding textual evidence that names for both secondary and primary qualities have two senses: a proper sense and a functional sense defined in terms of the proper. This approach also has implications for Locke's treatment of kind terms.

VIOLETTE, R. La Manière Exacte Dont Leibniz A Inventé L'intégration Par Sommation. *Rev Phil Fr* 175,29–34 Ja–Mr 85.

Our purpose is to determine exactly how Leibniz found the right way to realize an integration by summation. His starting point is the *Theoria motus abstracti* (fundamenta praedemonstrabilia). Here Leibniz tries: 1) to found an "*elemental*" phoronomy— 2) on the *indivisible*, characterized as that "whose parts are *indistant*", therefore an element without geometrical existence. Happy mistake, for the impossibility of summing spatially, so characterized elements led inevitably Leibniz to the correct notion of infinitesimally small.

VITALI, Theodore R. Creativity, God, And Creation. *Mod Sch* 62,75–96 Ja 85.

Norris Clark SJ and Robert Neville have argued that a coherent Whiteheadian theism/metaphysics requires a better theory of unity than the one Whitehead himself espouses, namely one founded on Creativity itself (Category of the Ultimate). They argue that unity must be ultimately grounded in the creative act of God who creates the world *ex nihilo*. But, such a doctrine of creation is wedded to the doctrine of eternity. The doctrine of eternity, in turn, makes superfluous time as qualitative increase in the universe. Eternity, therefore, destroys the central thesis of Whitehead's philosophy—creativity. Only a dialectical theory of unity in which both God and World are mutually required can serve to bring coherence to Whiteheadian metaphysics. Lewis Ford, in part, points the way by his theory of God as the future of all actual occasions.

VITELLI, Karen D. "The International Traffic In Antiquities" in *Ethics And Values In Archaeology*, Green, Ernestene L (ed), 143–155. NY Free Pr 1984.

VITORINO, Orlando. Le Raisonnement De L'injustice. *Arch Rechts Soz* 59,499–516 1973.

It is only when the civilizational cycle comes to a crisis that the law recognizes philosophy. The development of the philosophy of law takes place whenever there is a crisis of civilization, and thereby the forms of the law find their contents and meanings changed. The final question is: What is the meaning and the content of the forms of the law in our days? (edited)

VLASTOS, Gregory. Happiness And Virtue In Socrates' Moral Theory. *Topoi* 4,3–22 Mr 85.

VLASTOS, Gregory. Socrates' Disavowal Of Knowledge. *Phil Quart* 35,1–31 Ja 85.

My purpose is to show how Socrates can both (1) disavow knowledge (as he does frequently and ostentatiously), yet also (2) avow it (rarely and inconspicuously). In (1) he is using 'knowledge' in a sense (common in the archaic and classical periods) in which one says one knows only when claiming certainty. In (2) he uses the term in a radically different sense to mean elenctically (hence fallibly) justified true belief.

VODRASKA, Stanley L. Hume's Moral Enquiry: An Analysis Of Its Catalogue. *Phil Topics* 12,79–108 Wint 81.

To contradict William Davie's contribution to "David Hume: Many–sided Genius," I exhibit the catologue of virtues in Hume's second Enquiry, show what his critieria were for selecting and classifying the virtues, and relate the criteria to his analysis of pleasure and the foundation of ethics.

VOGEL, Lise. Marxism And The Oppression Of Women: Toward A Unitary Theory. Leichhardt Pluto Pr 1984.

VOGEL, Manfred. "Kierkegaard's Teleological Suspension Of The Ethical" in *The Georgetown Symposium On Ethics*, Porreco, Rocco (ed), 19–48. Lanham Univ Pr Of America 1984.

VOICULESCU, Ioana and Georgescu, George. Eastern Model–Theory For Boolean–Valued Theories. *Z Math Log* 31,79–88 1985.

VOITLE, Robert. *The Third Earl Of Shaftesbury 1671–1713.* Baton Rouge Louisiana Univ Pr 1984.

VOLBRECHT, Rose Mary. Nuclear Deterrence: Moral Dilemmas And Risks. *Phil Soc Crit* 10,133–142 Wint 84.

VOLD, David J. Evolution And The Fundamentalist Critique: Contributions To Educational Philosophy. *Educ Theor* 35,161–174 Spr 85.

VOLLAND, Hannelore. Zu Möglichkeiten Und Grezen Der Überwindung Der Angst Vor Dem Sterben Und Dem Frühen Tod. *Deut Z Phil* 33,540–543 1985.

VON BALTHASAR, Hans Urs and Daly, Robert (trans). *Origen; Spirit And Fire: A Thematic Anthology Of His Writings.* Washington Cath Univ Amer Pr 1984.

VON BENDA- BECKMANN, Franz. Norm Und Recht In Niklas Luhmanns Rechtssoziologie: Kritische Anmerkungen Aus Der Sicht Der Rechtsethnologie. *Arch Rechts Soz* 60,275–290 1974.

Luhmann's concepts "norm" and "law" are discussed in the light of his demand for one set of theoretical concepts applicable to the sociology, the history, and the anthropology of law. These concepts and his sociological approach to legal research are confronted with the goals of research in legal anthropology and its theoretical and methodological problems. It appears, that, because of their speculative character, Luhmann's concepts and his research–approach have little value for a mainly empirical social science like legal anthropology.

VON CRANACH, Mario (ed) and Harre, Rom (ed). *The Analysis Of Action.* Cambridge Cambridge Univ Pr 1982.

VON CRANACH, Mario. "Psychological Study Of Goal–Directed Action" in *The Analysis Of Action*, Von Cranach, Mario (ed), 35–74. Cambridge Cambridge Univ Pr 1982.

VON DER LUFT, Eric. Cassirer's Dialectic Of The Mythical Consciousness. *Rep Phil* 8,3–14 1984.

VON DER LUFT, Eric. The Theological Significance Of Hegel's Four World–Historical Realms. *Auslegung* 11,340–357 Fall 84.

The purpose of this article is to show that these four realms are not to be conceived in terms of history and geography, but in terms of philosophical and theological categories—e.G., monism, dualism, and pluralism; form and content; mediation and unmediatedness; the abstract and the concrete; the particular and the universal; etc.––arranged so as to exhaust all logical and dialectical possibilities.

VON HAUMEDER, Ulrika. The History Of Art: Its Methods And Their Limits. *Diogenes* 128,17–41 Wint 84.

Nowadays, the art historian suffers from the feeling that the methods available do not allow him to appreciate in an adequate manner both the historical and artistic character of the work of art as well as its communicative quality as expressive form which transmits a vision of man's universe. In order to make understand this crisis, a brief recapitulation and criticism of the methods and concepts developed during the last four centuries are presented.

VON KUTSCHERA, Franz. Moritz Schlick On Self–Evidence. *Synthese* 64,307–316 S 85.

Schlick's argument that self–evidence, if its occurrence is to be subjectively decidable, cannot be an infallible criterion of truth is reconstructed and defended against objections of Stegmüller, whose assertion that the problem of whether there are self–evident propositions is undecidable is also shown to be mistaken.

VON SAVIGNY, Eike. An Emergence View Of Linguistic Meaning. *Amer Phil Quart* 22,211–220 Jl 85.

Rather that deriving them from speakers' intentions which conform to conventions, conventional utterance meanings are construed as theoretical entities which are to be attributed to certan actions (which count as utterances because of this attribution) in virtue of their explanatory power with regard to otherwise unexplainable deviations in a group's system of conventions. In order to show that the overall systematic considerations which are crucial to this view can actually be pursued in a methodically disciplined way, part of a real empirical case study is summarized in a simplified fashion. Its success motivates a definition of conventional utterance meaning.

VON SAVIGNY, Eike. Social Habits And Enlightened Cooperation: Do Humans Measure Up To Lewis Conventions? *Erkenntnis* 22,79–96 Ja 85.

If the background ideas of David Lewis' analysis of conventions are taken seriously, being party to a convention is beyond the average human's reach. The more they get set in social habits, the less rationally people act, and usually they do not know what they are then doing. Because of this ignorance, philosophers of language are deluded in the hopes they place in Lewis' conventions; this is shown in the concluding section.

VON SENGER, Harro. China And Neo–Thomism: The Critique Of J M Bocheénski In The PRC. *Stud Soviet Tho* 30,165–176 Ag 85.

VON WRIGHT, G H. *Practical Reason.* Ithaca Cornell Univ Pr 1983.

VON WRIGHT, Georg Henrik. *Erklaren Und Verstehen.* Konigstein Athenaum 1974.

This is a translation into German, by Günther Grewendorf and Georg Meggle, of G H von Wright, *Explanation and Understanding* (Cornell University Press, Ithaca, NY, 1971). Second edition of German translation, 1984.

VOOK, Jozef. Theoretical–Methodological And Practical Importance Of The Category Of Dialectical Contradiction (in Czechoslovakian). *Filozof Cas* 32,494–504 1984.

VOPENKA, Peter and Sochor, Antonin. Contributions To The Theory Of Semisets **v**, On Axiom Of General Collapse. *Z Math Log* 21,289–302 1975.

VOROBEJ, Mark. Relative Virtue. *S J Phil* 22,535–543 Wint 84.

Michael Slote argues in *Goods and Virtues* that certain character traits are period-relative virtues in that they operate as virtues in some periods of life as anti–virtues in other periods. I challenge Slote's particular claim that prudence and life–planfulness are anti–virtues of childhood. I argue further that a weaker thesis of person–relativity sufficiently accounts for the kinds of cases which Slote believes establish period-relativity.

VOS, H M. Axiologische Cognites En Het Meta–Ethische Noncognivisme. *Alg Ned Tijdschr Wijs* 77,1–20 Ja 85.

Linguistic intuitions for a normative theory (Hare) are not only obtained from the words

for the general expression of a duty (e.G., good, ought, must), but also from the 'axiological cognitions' (e.G., justice, liberty) which represent, specify and, in a certain sense, found this duty. In the last case, in the former, certain problems of descriptivism—albeit perhaps not descriptivism itself—can be avoided. From a noncognivist point of view, we should content ourselves in making these intuitions explicit.

WACHINGER, Lorenz. "Buber's Concept Of Faith As A Criticism Of Christianity" in *Martin Buber*, Gordon, Haim (ed), 437–454. Beersheva Ktav 1984.

WADE, Francis C. Freedom And Obedience. *J Value Inq* 18,269–282 1984.

I have argued, following F Bergmann, that free acts are free because identified with self, or better, in the words of B Blanshard, because they include self–surrender. By self I mean the agent acting, both as conscious and non–conscious, though self-surrender is possible only for the agent as conscious. By action I mean the extension of existence of the agent into the world of existence. That his extension of self into the world may also be obedience to reality does not lessen one's freedom. If anything it makes the free act more what action should be as extension of the agent into the already existing world.

WAGNER, Carl. On The Formal Properties Of Weighted Averaging As A Method Of Aggregation. *Synthese* 62,97–108 Ja 85.

The volume in which this article appears is devoted to a consideration of Lehrer and Wagner's *Rational Consensus in Science and Society*, with critical essays by Baird, Laddaga and Loewer, Levi, Nurmi, and Schmitt, among others. This article is Wagner's reply to the aforementioned critics, and concentrated on formal issues. In a companion piece, Lehrer replies to philosophical criticisms.

WAGNER, Helmut R. A Missing Chapter: A Marginal Note Concerning The Second Volume Of Schutz/Luckmann: Strukturen Der Lebenswelt. *J Brit Soc Phenomenol* 16,194–195 My 85.

WAGNER, Helmut R. Schutz's Life Story And The Understanding Of His Work. *Human Stud* 7,107–116 1984.

WAGNER, Michael F. Supposition–Theory And The Problem Of Universals. *Fran Stud* 41,385–414 1981.

I examine Burleigh's and Ockham's positions on universals through explaining their theories of signification and supposition. I argue for a representational analysis of these theories, which I distinguish from prevailing interpretations of these theories; and I argue, in particular, that when Burleigh's theory of the signification and supposition of general terms is properly understood, he is not an Extreme Realist (at least as this view is normally understood) and his disagreement with Ockham over universals is much more subtle than it is normally conceived by historians of philosophy.

WAHL, Russell. Knowledge By Description. *Russell* 4,262–270 Wint 84.

This paper looks at Russell's views (from 1905 to 1912) on merely descriptive knowledge. I argue that Russell held that truths could be known about things with which one is not acquainted, despite his later claims that physical objects and other things "known by description" are really logical constructions of things known by acquaintance.

WAIBL, Elmar. Die Utopie Künstlerischer Wahrheit In Der Ästhetik Von Adolf Loos Und Arnold Schönberg. *Conceptus* 19,76–83 1985.

Art for truth's sake and for beauty's sake is the leading conviction of the revolutionary aesthetics of Adolf Loos and Arnold Schönberg. In this essay we want to show that their position, gained from a radical rejection of historicism, adopted an ontological theory of art, although this was given a highly idiosyncratic interpretation. A further point to be emphasized is that the utopian claims of the stringent 'Wahrheitsästhetik' (Truth Aesthetics) was one of the reasons for the increasing alienation of art from society and the resulting crisis of modern art.

WAIN, Kenneth. Lifelong Education: A Deweyian Challenge. *J Phil Educ* 18,257–264 1984.

Liberal philosophers of education have frequently asserted that education should be viewed as a lifelong matter. Recently Anthony O'Hear has claimed that this view is, in fact, held by philosophers as far apart on other things as Peters and Dewey. This article shows that O'Hear's claim hides fundamental differences between the two about *how* the idea of lifelong education is held, which, on examination, reveal that the only educational paradigm which is *consistent* with it is Dewey's.

WAINWRIGHT, William J. Wilfred Cantwell Smith On Faith And Belief. *Relig Stud* 20,353–366 S 84.

In a series of influential books, Smith has argued that religious Faith must be radically distinguished from propositional belief and that the latter is relatively unimportant. While this position is implicit in much modern religious thought, Smith is one of the few who has provided detailed arguments for it. I attempt to show that his arguments are unsound and the position implausible.

WALDRON, Jeremy. "Making Sense Of Critical Dualism" in *Popper And The Human Sciences*, Currie, Gregory (ed), 105–120. Boston Nijhoff 1985.

WALDRON, T P. *Principles Of Language And Mind: An Evolutionary Theory Of Meaning.* Massachusetts Routledge & K Paul 1985.

This study presents a systematic account of the evolutionary principles which underlie the origin and function of language, and which also explains the emergence of the distinctively human form of intelligence which we call mind. The theory presented fills serious gaps both in modern evolutionary thinking and in the study of humanities; shows how these areas of inquiry are related; and enables the solution of many current problems in psychology, language theory, logic, and epistemology.

WALGRAVE, Jan H. Personalisme Et Anthropologie Chrétienne. *Gregorianum* 65,445–472 1984.

Personalism and naturalism are the two most comprehensive trends in contemporary thought both elaborated in various philosophical concretisations. Person implies freedom for love. As a vocation to selfless love it should have its proper center in the

Author Index with Abstracts 431 Walton, Roberto J

other, thus realizing its true being. As free it has a right to absolute respect by the other even if choosing for selfish egocentrism. Personalism is the only modern philosophy able to theologically articulate the Christian anthropology.

WALHOUT, Donald. Hermeneutics And The Teaching Of Philosophy. *Teach Phil* 7,303–312 O 84.

This article explores whether insight into Rorty's hermeneutics can be gained from the standpoint of the teaching situation in philosophy. The thesis is that, in contrast to Rorty's move from traditional Western philosophy to hermeneutics, the teaching situation leads naturally in the reverse direction. Certain features of this hermeneutics correspond nicely to the needs of teaching; but in the end these are rendered significant only by certain aspirations of traditional philosophy.

WALICKI, Andrzej. The Romanticism Of Tradition And The Romanticism Of Charisma. *Dialec Hum* 11,187–192 Wint 84.

WALKER, Arthur F. An Occurrent Theory Of Practical And Theoretical Reasoning. *Phil Stud* 48,199–210 S 85.

Some philosophers have held that reasoning consists of transitions from one set of dispositional states to another. Practical reasoning differs from theoretical reasoning in that it consists in transitions to states of intending and wanting, as well as believing. This theory, I argue, faces several difficulties, most notably an inability to account for cases of reinference. I defend an occurrent theory of reasoning which, in accordance with common intuitions about reasoning, takes reasoning to involve occurrences of thinking. It avoids the difficulties mentioned earlier.

WALKER, J C and O' Loughlin, M A. The Ideal Of The Educated Woman: Jane Roland Martin On Education And Gender. *Educ Theor* 34,327–340 Fall 84.

Contrary to the "maternalism" of Martin's version of "gender–sensitive" educational theory and practice, which implies a specifically feminine educational ideal, it is argued that the qualities historically associated with women's role in reproduction are neither a sufficient nor on their own a desirable source of political and educational objectives. A non–essentialist epistemology is advocated, as against Martin's epistemological "female essentialism" which further entrenches the epistemic inequality of women.

WALKER, Ralph S. Synthesis And Transcendental Idealism. *Kantstudien* 76,14–27 1985.

If—as in Kant's first edition—the given has empirically detectable properties, the imposition of categories will not guarantee order: regularity is also needed; and inferences about noumena should be possible. But if the properties we recognize are produced by our synthesis, the given may still have features independent of us, which we map into our concepts. This points towards a more promising transcendental idealism, which may be associated with the second edition of the *Critique*.

WALLACE, Gerry. Moral And Religious Appraisals. *Int J Phil Relig* 16,263–270 1984.

WALLACE, William A. Discussion: Galileo And The Continuity Thesis. *Phil Sci* 51,504–510 S 84.

This replies to Ernan McMullin, who rejects the argument for scholastic influences on Galileo's science based on his Latin manuscripts. The author's reply: McMullin has yet to see the full textual evidence, in recent publications, which ties Galileo's manuscripts to Jesuit lectures; dates them during Galileo's professorship at Pisa (thus, part of his class preparation); and gives instances of Galileo's use of suppositional argument, rejected as probative by McMullin, yet regarded as valid within the scholastic tradition.

WALLACE, William A. The Intelligibility Of Nature: A Neo–Aristotelian View. *Rev Metaph* 38,33–56 S 84.

The intelligibility of nature (inorganic, organic, and human) can be reasserted through effect–to–cause reasoning and the use of modeling techniques. The latter show how the natures of things and natural proceses can be made intelligible to the human mind, and indeed have been so made, through the progress of recent science. Quantitative techniques are used to supplement the basically qualitative insights of Aristotle to ground a philosophy of science and technology that meets the complex social and political demands of the present day.

WALLER, Bruce N. Daniel Dennett On Responsibility. *S J Phil* 22,413–424 Fall 84.

In *Brainstorms*, Daniel Dennett offers two accounts of responsibility: a compatibilist account and a libertarian account. Both attempt to establish responsibility on the basis of individual effort or an individual decision to terminate effort. But when the factors influencing such individual efforts and decisions are examined more closely, those influences are found to undermine claims and ascriptions of moral responsibility.

WALLER, Bruce N. Deliberating About The Inevitable. *Analysis* 45,48–52 Ja 85.

In *An Essay on Free Will* Peter van Inwagen argues that it is impossible to deliberate about acts one believes to be inevitable, and therefore a determinist cannot (without contradiction) deliberate. But determined deliberation processes are possible, and may be essential elements in arriving at conclusions. In fact, deliberation is possible even when the result of the deliberation process is not only determined but is also foreknown.

WALLER, Bruce. Purposes, Conditioning, And Skinner's Moral Theory: Comments On Mills' Observations. *J Theor Soc Behav* 14,355–362 O 84.

John A Mills' recent critique of Skinner's moral theory is based on a teleological misinterpretation of Skinner's behavioral theory; and that mistake results in misinterpreting Skinner's moral theory as a variety of hedonistic egoism. Skinner does reject value absolutes, and he maintains that all valuing is shaped by environmental contingencies. But that leaves room for several ethical views, including altruistic ones.

WALLERSTEIN, Immanuel. The French Revolution And Capitalism: An Explanatory Schema. *Praxis Int* 5,1–22 Ap 85.

WALLNER, Ingrid M. J S Beck And Husserl: The New Episteme In The Kantian Tradition. *J Hist Phil* 23,195–220 Ap 85.

Husserl's revolutionary re–interpretation of the *doxa–episteme* distinction is presented as an epistemological breakthrough and compared with J S Beck's proto–phenomenological Kant interpretation. Both Beck and Husserl anchor their theory of knowledge in the *doxa* of pre–predicative experience considered epistemologically prior to the derived application of (finished) concepts in predicative judgments—traditionally the exclusive domain of *episteme*. A "new *episteme*" arises with the (philosophical) justification of the *doxa* as a foundation of scientific knowledge claims.

WALLULIS, Jerald. Philosophical Hermeneutics And The Conflict Of Ontologies. *Int Phil Quart* 24,283–302 S 84.

According to Hans–Georg Gadamer historicality manifests itself in a way that occurs to human beings rather than is directed by them. This characterization of historicality is compared with the practical holism of Hubert Dreyfus and with the distinctions between distanciation and participatory belonging of Paul Ricoeur. I conclude that Ricoeur's "conflict of interpretations" is only symptomatic of an even deeper conflict among philosophical hermeneuticists concerning ontological assumptions about language and basic human action.

WALLWORK, Ernest. Sentiment And Structure: A Durkheimian Critique Of Kohlberg's Moral Theory. *J Moral Educ* 14,87–101 My 85.

080182this paper uses Durkheim's critique to criticize Kohlberg's theory of morality. After examining the applicability of Durkheim's criticism of Kant's definition of morality to Kohlberg's equation of morality with justice structures, it explores Durkheim's psychological views on emotional and dispositional aspects of morality, which are typically neglected by Kantians. Some standard criticisms of Durkheim's moral theory are re–examined and the argument is advanced that Durkheim's social ethic is substantively at Stage Six on Kohlberg's developmental schema. Several modifications of Kohlberg's theory are proposed, using Durkheimian insights.

WALMSLEY, Gerard. Investigating Lonergan's Inaccessibility. *Heythrop J* 26,47–56 Ja 85.

WALSH, David. "The Historical Dialectic Of Spirit" in *History And System*, Perkins, Robert (ed), 15–46. Albany SUNY Pr 1984.

WALSH, David. Hegel And The Deformation Of Symbols. *Phil Stud (Ireland)* 30,49–61 Spr 84.

WALSH, Robert D. An Organism Of Words: Ruminations On The Philosophical–Poetics Of Merleau–Ponty. *Kinesis* 14,13–41 Fall 84.

WALSH, W H. "Kant's Transcendental Idealism" in *Kant On Causality, Freedom, And Objectivity*, Harper, William A (ed), 83–96. Minneapolis Univ Minnesota Pr 1984.

WALTER, E V. "Nature On Trial" in *Methodology, Metaphysics And The History Of Science*, Cohen, Robert S (ed), 295–322. Boston Reidel 1984.

WALTER, James J. A Public Policy Option On The Treatment Of Severly Handicapped Newborns. *Laval Theol Phil* 41,239–250 Je 85.

The need to elaborate a coherent Christian public policy on the treatment of severely handicapped newborns is critical in our pluralist society. The central argument of this essay is that the writings of Richard A McCormick, S J implicitly contain a systematic normative methodology by which he constructs a Christian public policy option on the treatment/nontreatment of these children. The general conclusion of the essay is that McCormick's position is not only sound and coherent but the best public option available on this issue.

WALTERS, Kerry S. A Recovery Of Innocence: The Dynamics Of Sartrean Radical Conversion. *Auslegung* 11,358–377 Fall 84.

The author attempts to clarify the necessary conditions for the possibility of a Sartrean ethic. These conditions are, first, pure reflection and secondly, the so–called radical conversion. Although many commentators have discussed these two notions, they have neither made a sharp distinction between them (assuming, instead, that the two, if not strictly identical, are at least inseparable), nor have they examined the dynamic within consciousness which leads to the conversion. The author schematises consciousness' journey to the ethical and typifies the progression as an *Aufhebung*–type process, which runs its course through the stages of 'immediacy', 'impure reflection', and 'pure reflection'. It is pointed out (a) that this progression is by no means a necessary one, inasmuch as the 'katharsis' of pure reflection is not identical with conversion, and (b) that the schematisation provides a foundation for the voluntarism upon which a Sartrean ethic claims to be based. Furthermore, it is demonstrated that the dynamics of radical conversion in effect represent a return on the for–itself's part to an original state of 'innocence' which, like the 'natural attitude of immediacy, takes freedom as the basis of action.

WALTON, A S. "Economy, Utility And Community In Hegel's Theory Of Civil Society" in *The State And Civil Society*, Pelczynski, Z A (ed), 244–261. Cambridge Cambridge Univ Pr 1984.

WALTON, Douglas N and Batten, L M. Games, Graphs, And Circular Arguments. *Log Anal* 27,133–164 Je 84.

This paper uses the theory of directed graphs as a way of modelling arguments. In particular, the fallacy of *petitio principii* is given an analysis in the theory.

WALTON, Douglas N. Cans, Advantages, And Possible Worlds. *Philosophia (Israel)* 14,83–98 Ag 84.

This article builds on an idea of Keith Lehrer's for analyzing 'can'. According to this analysis, an agent can do x (an action) if and only if he does x in some possible world relatively similar to the actual world which has no advantages in this possible world that he lacks in the actual world.

WALTON, Douglas N. New Directions In The Logic Of Dialogue. *Synthese* 63,259–274 Je 85.

This article is an introduction to a special issue of SYNTHESE on the logic of dialogue, and it surveys recent research on the topic. It is concluded that the study of dialogue has a practical element in relation to informed fallacies.

WALTON, Roberto J. Rasgos Y Ambigüedades Del Venir A La Presencia De Lo Presente. *Rev Ven Filosof* 12,63–86 1980.

In *What E–vokes Thought?* (11th lesson), Heidegger discloses the distinctive traits of coming–to–presence as non–concealment, emerging from and entering in this domain, whiling, gathering, shining–forth and the concealed possibility of dis–appearing. This paper deals with the relation of these traits to lasting (Währen), interpreted as the fundamental characteristic of non–concealment, and discerns whiling (Weile) as a more original trait that ultimately gives its stamp to this pattern of relationships.

WALTON, Roberto J. Ser–En–sí Y Ser–Para–Otro. *Cuad Filosof* 19,77–94 Ja–D 83.

The identity of being–in–itself and being–for–other is examined in the light of M Theunissen's views on the relationship between Hegelian Subjective Logic and Metaphysics. A criticism of this interpretation is advanced on a twofold basis: 1) an analysis of Hegel's exposition of the identity, and 2) the influence of Hegelian Logic in the elaboration of a metaphysics of relations particularly as regards Process Philosophy.

WALUCHOW, Wilfrid J. Hart, Legal Rules And Palm Tree Justice. *Law Phil* 4,41–70 Ap 85.

In this paper I defend a 'liberal' theory about how legal rules can and ought to be interpreted. The theory emerges from a critical examination of H L A Hart's influential views on the limited but avoidable indeterminacy of legal rules. I begin with a brief sketch of Hart's early theory (as it is traditionally understood) offering various suggestions as to how it might usefully be modified. Next, several possible objections to my modifications are sketched and criticized. Finally, reasons are provided for supposing that the modified theory may well present Hart's current position.

WANDAN, Xin. Limitations Of The Theory Of Alienation Propounded By Marx In His Youth. *Chin Stud Phil* 16,90–104 Fall 84.

WANG, William and Alexander, Larry. Natural Advantages And Contractual Justice. *Law Phil* 3,281–297 Ag 84.

Anthony Kronman has argued that libertarians cannot distinguish non–arbitrarily between legitimate and illegitimate advantage–taking in contractual relations except by reference to a liberal, wealth–redistributive standard Kronman calls "paretianism." We argue to the contrary that libertarians need not concede that any advantage–taking in contracts is legitimate and thus need not be liberal "paretians" with respect to advantage–taking.

WARD, Andrew. Hume, Demonstratives, And Self–Ascriptions Of Identity. *Hume Stud* 11,69–93 Ap 85.

In his *Treatise on Human Nature*, Hume contends that just as the resemblance of perceptions leads to ascriptions of identity through time to the minds of others, so too it explains self–ascriptions of identity. Some, such as John Bricke, argue that resemblance cannot carry the load Hume gives it. In contrast, I argue that by recognizing a primitive theory of demonstrative content in Hume, resemblance *can* account for self–ascriptions of identity.

WARD, Andrew. Three Realist Claims. *Phil Phenomenol Res* 45,437–448 Mr 85.

A critique of the realist's use of hypothetico–deductive arguments to solve the skeptical problems of perception, memory, and induction. The realist's strategy confuses the claim to know of the very *existence* of an external world, past, or future, with the claim to know what, assuming each exists, its *structure* is like. The skeptic principally demands justification for the former claim; yet it is the latter claim that the realist's arguments can, at most, justify.

WARD, David V. Identity: Criteria Vs Necessary And Sufficient Conditions. *Phil Res Arch* 10,353–382 1984.

This paper argues that there are no necessary and sufficient conditions for the identity through time of material objects where those conditions have a kind of empirical content necessary for them to function as criteria for identity through time. Taking Eli Hirsch's program in *The Concept of Identity* as representative of attempts to formulate conditions which are logically necessary and sufficient and which also function as criteria guiding our tracing of objects' careers through time, I argue (a) that, when such programs are constructed in a way sensitive to the criteria we actually use, they fall prey to conceivable counterexamples and (b) that, when such programs are tightened to avoid logically possible counterexamples, they fail to capture the identity criteria implicit in our ordinary experience. The paper argues that our identity criteria are incomplete and informal and that our individuative practice is partially determined by the kind of interest we have in the object(s) being traced. The relationship between this view and two versions of relative identity is also discussed.

WARD, Jeffrey J and Werner, O. Difference And Dissonance In Ethnographic Data. *Commun Cog* 17,219–244 1984.

This paper explores the value of discrepant, contradictory, or anomalous data in ethnography. While such data has traditionally been *adjudicated* in favor of one datum or the other, theories of information, psychology, and neurophysiology suggest that contradiction can be a rich source of insight. The paper concludes that anthropologists can make the most of these "epistemological windows" by seeking to *resolve* contradictions rather than *adjudicating* them.

WARD, Sharyn and Smith, Joseph Wayne. Bultmann On The New Testament And Mythology. *Sophia (Australia)* 23,4–12 Jl 84.

We argue that Bultmann's attempt to demythologize the New Testament is a failure. If Bultmann's program is seriously held to, then there is no rational ground for distinguishing his position from secular humanism and matters of economy require the elimination of "Jesus–talk". But Bultmann fails to carry his program through himself, so his allegedly rational reconstruction of Christianity contains its own myths. Bultmann's theology is hence internally incoherent.

WARD, Sharyn and Smith, Joseph W. Discussion: Are We Only Five Minutes Old: Acock On The Age Of The Universe. *Phil Sci* 51,511–513 S 84.

The paper discusses the problem of whether or not the "normally accepted" hypothesis about the age of the universe is rationally preferable to the Russellian hypothesis, that the universe was created five minutes ago, complete with all "traces."

We criticize previous solutions and sketch an original solution of our own.

WARD, Spencer (ed). *Knowledge Structure And Use: Implications For Synthesis And Interpretation,* Linda J Reed (ed). Philadelphia Temple Univ Pr 1984.

WARNER, Martin. Philosophy, Language And The Reform Of Public Worship. *Philosophy* 18,149–172 84 Supp.

Recent liturgical reform appears to embody controversial linguistic assumptions. The relationships presupposed between "meaning", "translation", "style", "clarity" and "context" are easier to defend on a "formal–semanticist" analysis of language than a "communication–intention" one. But the former type of analysis is difficult to reconcile with contemporary theology and has serious internal difficulties, which do not automatically render the latter one preferable. Different ways in which language is conceived may properly give rise to different practical recommendations.

WARNKE, Georgia (trans) and Apel Otto, Karl. *Understanding And Explanation: A Transcendental–Pragmatic Perspective.* Cambridge MIT Pr 1985.

WARNKE, Georgia. Hermeneutics And The Social Sciences: A Gadamerian Critique Of Rorty. *Inquiry* 28,339–358 S 85.

Richard Rorty challenges the traditional use of hermeneutic understanding to defend the methodological autonomy of the social sciences, claiming that hermeneutics is part of both social and natural science and, morever, that it exposes the limits of 'epistemologically centered philosophy'. Hermeneutics is interested in edification rather than truth, in finding new ways of speaking rather than adjudicating knowledge claims or securing the grounds of rational consensus. Although Rorty refers to Gadamer's 'philosophical hermeneutics' as support for this position, Gadamer's own analysis points in a different direction. First, it distinguishes the social from the natural sciences as forms of practical, not theoretical knowledge. As hermeneutic analyses, the social sciences participate in an on–going dialogue about values and forms of life. Second, the goal of this dialogue is cognitive and normative agreement. Indeed, hermeneutics is an act of integration which tries to expand consensus between different cultures and historical perspectives by mediating their claims to truth.

WARNOCK, Mary. Broadcasting Ethics: Some Neglected Issues. *J Moral Educ* 13,168–172 O 84.

WARREN, Mark. Nietzsche And Political Philosophy. *Polit Theory* 13,183–212 My 85.

This article argues that strategies for considering Nietzsche in the perspective of political philosophy should follow not from his overt political positions, but from his philosophy of power—a critical ontology of practice focusing on the possibility of human agency in an historical world. Nietzsche's politics follow from his philosophy of power only because he holds to several uncritical assumptions about modern societies. Without these assumptions, the political implications of Nietzsche's philosophy turn out to be less narrow than his own political vision suggests.

WARREN, Mary Anne. Reconsidering The Ethics Of Infanticide. *Phil Books* 26,1–9 Ja 85.

WARREN, Scott. *The Emergence Of Dialectical Theory: Philosophy And Political Inquiry.* Chicago Univ Of Chicago Pr 1984.

This work sets out to resolve the identity crisis of contemporary political inquiry. After a careful excavation of the philosophical foundations of dialectical theory in the thought of Kant, Hegel, and Marx, Warren examines the dialectic in existentialism, phenomenology, neomarxism, and critical theory, emphasizing the thought of Merleau–Ponty and Habermas. The work concludes with a call for a philosophical perspective in political inquiry that supersedes both positivist behavioralism and classical political philosophy.

WARREN, Virginia L. Explaining Masochism. *J Theor Soc Behav* 15,103–130 Jl 85.

The oddity of desiring to cause oneself pain is usually explained away: that desire is interpreted as a means to an end. However, masochists often refuse to change even when they know they could obtain the same ends without pain. Masochism (of a non–sexual nature) should be explained in terms of identity, not simply "secondary gain". Relinquishing pain and accepting oneself involves loss: masochists must choose between continuing their pain–producing behavior, and eliminating this behavior which presently is central to who they are.

WARTENBERG, Thomas E. Foucault's Archaeological Method: A Response To Hacking And Rorty. *Phil Forum (Boston)* 15,345–364 Sum 84.

This paper considers the attempts by Ian Hacking and Richard Rorty to assess the importance for contemporary philosophy of Foucault's work, *The Order of Things*. It is argued that, despite the insights contained in these attempts, they fail to do justice to Foucault's view of the relation between knowledge and social practices. An alternative account of his work is offered in which it is shown that a central claim of his theory is that knowledge cannot be understood without reference to its embedding in social practices. Finally, some difficulties with this view are discussed.

WARTOFSKY, Marx W (ed) and Cohen, Robert S (ed). *Methodology, Metaphysics And The History Of Science.* Boston Reidel 1984.

WASHBURN, M C. The Second Edition Of The Critique: Toward An Understanding Of Its Nature And Genesis. *Kantstudien* 66,277–290 1975.

WASILEWSKA, Anita. DFC–Algorithms For Suszko, Logic SCI And One–to–one Gentzen Type Formalizations. *Stud Log* 43,395–404 1984.

We use here the notions and results from algebraic theory of programs in order to give a new proof of the decidability theorem for Suszko logic SCI (Theorem 3). We generalize the method used in the proof of that theorem in order to prove a more general fact that any propositional logic which admits a cut–free Gentzen type formalization is decidable (Theorem 6). We establish also the relationship between the Suszko Logic SCI, one–to–one Gentzen type formalizations and deterministic and algorithmic regular languages (Remark 2 and Theorem 7, respectively).

WASSERMAN, Wayne. What Is A Fundamental Ethical Disagreement? *Analysis* 45,34–39 Ja 85.

I criticize an important way (Brandt's) of distinguishing between fundamental and non–fundamental ethical disagreement. I then argue that analyses of what counts as a fundamental disagreement need to be tailored to different conceptions of ethical belief, and that such analyses will be fully usable in determining the extent of fundamental disagreement only given background beliefs about the nature of ethical belief.

WASSERSTROM, Richard. War, Nuclear War, And Nuclear Deterrence: Some Conceptual And Moral Issues. *Ethics* 95,424–444 Ap 85.

This paper considers first the variety of ways in which nuclear war could be fundamentally different from conventional wars of any sorts; second, the arguments supporting the view that it would always be wrong to engage in nuclear way; and third; some of the special difficulties inherent in arguments seeking to justify the practice of nuclear deterrence, including the disanalogies between arguments concerning deterrence in the criminal law and those employed in the nuclear context.

WASZEK, Norbert. Two Concepts Of Morality: A Distinction Of Adam Smith's Ethics And Its Stoic Origin. *J Hist Ideas* 45,591–606 O–D 84.

WATERHOUSE, Joseph. Popper And Metaphysical Skepticism. *Phil Forum (Boston)* 15,365–391 Sum 84.

The problem addressed is whether metaphysical knowledge is possible within a Popperian framework defining "metaphysics" and "knowledge." As a first step it is argued that Popper's own defense of the possibility of metaphysical knowledge fails, because his standards for evaluating metaphysical theories either are worthless or apply only to non–metaphysical, scientific theories.

WATNER, Carl. Libertarians And Indians: Proprietary Justice And Aboriginal Land Rights. *J Liber Stud* 7,147–156 Spr 83.

The purpose of this article is to demonstrate that a colonization policy based on the libertarian respect for proprietary justice would have resulted in a peaceful regime and respect for the land rights of the aboriginal tribes in North America, during the 1600 and 1700's.

WATRO, R J and Henle, J M and Kleinberg, E M. On The Ultrafilters And Ultrapowers Of Strong Partition Cardinals. *J Sym Log* 49,1268–1272 D 84.

WATSON, Richard A. A Note On Deep Ecology. *Environ Ethics* 6,377–380 Wint 84.

Deep ecology as promoted by Arne Naess and others has ideals that are admirable, but are utopian in the sense that they do not apply to humankind as we know it from history and experience. If deep ecologists want to establish balance with nature, rather than asking for new religious sensibility or hoping that the human species will evolve into benign animals, they should seek political power.

WATSON, Richard A. Descartes Knows Nothing. *Hist Phil Quart* 1,399–412 O 84.

The First Meditation so embeds Descartes in agnosticism that he can know neither that anything exists nor what anything's essence is. Even if the *cogito* is not an argument, it is discursive (so memory could fail) and it relates two items (so we might be deceived). Even if we could intuit the existence of something, the innate ideas of God, mind, and matter are empty, so Descartes knows nothing.

WATSON, Stephen. Jürgen Habermas And Jean–François Lyotard: Post Modernism And The Crisis Of Rationality. *Phil Soc Crit* 10,1–24 Fall 84.

WATSON, Stephen. Kant And Foucault: On The Ends Of Man. *Tijdschr Filosof* 47,71–102 Mr 85.

WATTS, Isaac and Schouls, Peter A (ed). *Logick: Or, The Right Use Of Reason.* NY Garland 1984.

WAX, Murray L. The Paradoxes Are Numerous. *Zygon* 20,79–82 Mr 85.

"*religion* as Universal: Tribulations of an Anthropological Enterprise" *Zygon* (March, 1984) summarized well–established criticisms by anthropologists of the validity of the definitions of "religion" conventional within the discipline. In a letter, Robert Segal suggested that a "functional" definition might nonetheless be fruitful. My response was that "the paradoxes are numerous".

WAYNE SMITH, Joseph. A Simple Solution To Mortensen And Priest's Truth Teller Paradox. *Log Anal* 27,217–220 Je 84.

A solution to the "Truth Teller Paradox" is presented. The statement 'this very statement is true' is true.

WEAR, Stephen and Mc Cullough, L B. Respect For Autonomy And Medical Paternalism Reconsidered. *Theor Med* 6,295–308 O 85.

We offer a critique of one prominent understanding of the principle of respect for autonomy and of analyses of medical paternalism based on that understanding. Our main critique is that understanding respect for autonomy as respect for freedom from interference is mistaken because it is overly influenced by 'four–alarm' cases, because it fails to appreciate the full dimensions of legal self–discrimination (one of its main sources), because it conflates the research and therapeutic settings, and because it fails to appreciate themes of authority and power that have historically shaped the principle of respect for freedom from interference. We argue that respect for autonomy involves more than just freedom from interference and, on this basis, offer a critique of prevailing accounts of medical paternalism.

WEBSTER, William H. "Liberty And Justice For All: Keeping The Scales In Balance" in *The Search For Justice*, Taitte, W Lawson (ed), 25–42. Austin Univ Of Texas Pr 1983.

WECKERT, John. Is Relativism Self–Refuting? *Educ Phil Theor* 16,29–42 O 84.

A common move against epistemological, conceptual or cultural relativism is to argue that the statement 'All truth is relative' is self–refuting. Arguments which purport to establish this are examined and rejected.

WEDIN, Michael V. Nozick On Explaining Nothing. *Phil Res Arch* 10,337–346 1984.

This paper raises some difficulties with the strategy suggested in Robert Nozick's *Philosophical Explanations* for explaining why there is something rather than nothing. I am concerned less with his adoption of an egalitarian, as opposed to inegalitarian, explanatory stance (the net effect of which is to detach for independent consideration the question, "Why is there something?") than with his use of crucial assumption in reasoning from the egalitarian point of view. I argue that this assumption, that all possibilities exist, is fatally ambiguous, that the persuasiveness of Nozick's reasoning depends at once assuming and blurring the difference between the predicates "does not exist" and "nonexists" and that the attempt to wed a *priori* reasoning and a *posteriori* (mystical) practice fails.

WEHRUNG, Donald A and Mac Crimmon, Kenneth R. A Portfolio Of Risk Measures. *Theor Decis* 19,1–29 Jl 85.

A comprehensive set of sixteen measures of willingness to take risks has been developed. This set includes measures from three categories: measures from the standardized risky situations having an underlying theory of risk, measures inferred from revealed choices in financial decisions, and measures derived from attitudes. A study of over 500 top–level business executives shows significant relationships within categories, but relatively little relationship across categories. Context differences, especially personal versus business situations and opportunities versus threats, underlie the responses.

WEI– HSUN FU, Charles. Japanese Spiritual Resources And Their Contemporary Relevance. *J Dharma* 10,82–89 Ja–Mr 85.

No other major tradition in the world has manifested attitudinal ambiguity, pluralistic diversity, and ideological complexity as much as the Japanese tradition. The creative vitality and aesthetic purity of Original Shinto, the identity of being and time in Dogen Zen, Shinran's emphasis on salvation without any self–effort or self–calculation, and some other spiritual elements still have much contemporary significance for Japan and the world today.

WEI– MING, Tu. "The Continuity Of Being: Chinese Visions Of Nature" in *On Nature*, Rouner, Leroy S (ed), 113–132. Notre Dame Univ Notre Dame Pr 1984.

WEI– MING, Tu. Pain And Suffering In Confucian Self–Cultivation. *Phil East West* 34,379–388 O 84.

WEIDIG, R. Soziale Bedingungen Und Triebkräfte Hoher Arbeitsleistungen. *Deut Z Phil* 33,1–10 1985.

WEIDIG, Rudi. Die Aufgaben Der Marxistisch–Leninistischen Soziologischen Forschung In Der DDR. *Deut Z Phil* 22,133–144 1974.

Die Analyse der Entwicklung der Arbeiterklasse und der sozialistischen Persönlichkeit steht im Zentrum der soziologischen Forschung. Sie bildet ein wichtiges Vermittlungsglied zwischen den Erkenntnissen der allgemeinen soziologischen Theorie und der praktischen gesellschaftlichen Entwicklung. Die Erhöhung des wissenschaftlich–theoretischen Niveaus der Forschung verlangt die konsequentere Anwendung des Standpunktes des Materialismus bzw. Der materialistischen Dialektik.

WEIDLER, J. Rolle Des Subjektiven Faktors. *Deut Z Phil* 33,165–167 1985.

This article discusses a scientific conference on topical questions of the growing part played by the subjective factor in shaping socialism in the GDR. It substantiates that motivating people for higher achievements represents an essential driving force of social development. Motives for higher achievements are above all the striving for maintaining peace, the political codetermination in socialism, the improvement of the working and living conditions as well as the possibility to take on an interesting job in modern technology.

WEIGLUS, Karl and Kaplan, Charles D. Beneath Role Theory: Reformulating A Theory With Nietzsche's Philosophy. *Phil Soc Crit* 6,289–308 Fall 79.

WEIKART, Robert and Klar, Howard. When The Doctor And The Minister Disagree (Case Study With Commentaries). *Hastings Center Rep* 14,30–31 D 84.

WEIN, Sheldon. Liberal Egalitarianism. *Phil Res Arch* 10,67–116 1984.

This paper provides a systematic statement of Ronald Dworkin's political (as opposed to legal) philosophy. Dworkin's defense of democratic institutions constrained by civil rights is shown to be linked to his defense of the economic market constrained by economic welfare rights. The theory is defended against attacks from H L A Hart and L Haworth. The possibility that the theory can be given a Kantian grounding is explored.

WEIN, Sheldon. Sacrificing Persons For The General Welfare: A Comment Of Sayward. *J Value Inq* 19,77–80 1985.

In 'Should Persons be Sacrificed for the General Welfare' (*Journal of Value Inquiry*, V 16, **2,** 1982), Charles Sayward argues that Nozick's moral theory (in *Anarchy, State, and Utopia*) yields 'repugnant' requirements. The present article shows that not only is Nozick's theory incapable of being brought into reflective equilibrium with our moral intuitions, but that there are strong reasons for supposing that it would be irrational to accept Nozick's theory. Four strategies for showing that it is irrational to do what Nozick requires of us are outlined.

WEINBERG, Lois A. The Power Of A Realist Interpretation Of Competency. *Proc Phil Educ* 40,179–182 1984.

WEINBERGER, David. A Phenomenology Of Nuclear Weapons. *Phil Soc Crit* 10,95–106 Wint 84.

What is phenomenologically distinctive of nuclear weapons is the sort of end they would bring: a mass death (contrary to heidegger's insistence on death's individuality) which strips even things of their future. This marks a change in our understanding of self and world, and is a change in Being.

WEINBERGER, Ota. Aufgaben Und Schwierigkeiten Der Analytischen Rechtstheorie. *Z Allg Wiss* 4,356–367 1973.

Die analytische Jurisprudenz ist abhängig von der Normenlogik, die bisher keine voll befriedigenden Ergebnisse erzielt hat. Der Autor diskutiert die verschiedenen Wege der Normenlogik und deren Schwierigkeiten, insbesondere weist er nach, daB die normenlogische Deduktion nicht der Idee der deontisch perfekten Welten aufgebaut werden kann. (edited)

WEINBERGER, Ota. The Expressive Conception Of Norms—An Impasse For The Logic Of Norms. *Law Phil* 4,165–198 Ag 85.

WEINER, Joan. The Philosopher Behind The Last Logicist. *Phil Quart* 34,242–264 Jl 84.

I argue that Frege's attempt to define the number one should be viewed as a central part of an epistemological project, and examine some of the consequences of reading Frege's work in this way. One consequence is that the numerals had no reference and the propositions of arithmetic no truth values before Frege's work. Although this will seem absurd if we assume that Frege understood the terms "reference" and "truth" as we do today, I argue that this assumption is unwarranted. I argue that, for Frege, a term has reference only if (indeed, if and only if) it is (epistemologically) primitive or has been defined in the appropriate way from primitive terms.

WEINGART, Peter. "The Structure Of Technological Change: A Sociological Analysis Of Technology" in *Technological Knowledge*, Laudan, Rachel (ed), 115–142. Boston Reidel 1984.

WEINKE, Kurt. Zum Problem Der Diskutierbarkeit Von Normensystemen. *Conceptus* 8,30–35 1974.

Feigl's opinion that systems of norms of a quite different character are incompatible and also incomparable, is refused in this paper with reference to the necessity and possibility of such critical discussions. As a presupposition an 'open ethical system' is constructed, by means of which it is possible to consider quite opposite positions as correctives and transcending criticism of the system as possibility of unmasking errors. This implies the consideration of systems of norms as only relative and the refusal of absolute ones, because only relative systems are alterable and improvable. Therefore it is useful to treat norms in the same manner as rules of a game.

WEINREICH HASTE, Helen (ed) and Locke, Don (ed). *Morality In The Making*. NY Wiley 1983.

This book is in three parts; the first discusses issues about the development of moral reasoning, and in particular critically addresses Kohlberg's work on stages of moral thought. The second section is concerned with the relationship between judgement and action, in particular the issue of weakness of will. In the final section, the papers consider social factors of morality; the role of early family life, the group and identity. The key feature of the book in the integration of philosophical and psychological approaches, and the authors are drawn from both disciplines.

WEINSTEIN, Deena and Weinstein, Michael. On The Visual Constitution Of Society: The Contributions Of Georg Simmel And Jean-Paul Sartre To A Sociology Of The Senses. *Hist Euro Ideas* 5,349–362 1984.

An examination of the ways in which social relations are usually constituted. Article compares Georg Simmel's account of the pure form of the mutual gaze (individuals primordially united beyond bounds of speech) and Jean-Paul Sartre's description of the look (through which people objectify one another, outside of language). Sartre and Simmel show two fundamental sides of human sociality which must be dialectically related to one another to provide an adequate phenomenological description.

WEINSTEIN, Michael and Weinstein, Deena. On The Visual Constitution Of Society: The Contributions Of Georg Simmel And Jean-Paul Sartre To A Sociology Of The Senses. *Hist Euro Ideas* 5,349–362 1984.

An examination of the ways in which social relations are usually constituted. Article compares Georg Simmel's account of the pure form of the mutual gaze (individuals primordially united beyond bounds of speech) and Jean-Paul Sartre's description of the look (through which people objectify one another, outside of language). Sartre and Simmel show two fundamental sides of human sociality which must be dialectically related to one another to provide an adequate phenomenological description.

WEINZIERL, Emil. Zur Sowjetphilosophischen Kritik Der "Idealistischen" Erkenntnistheorie. *Z Phil Forsch* 29,270–278 Ap–Je 75.

WEIR, Alan. Against Holism. *Phil Quart* 35,225–244 Jl 85.

This paper considers firstly holistic theories of language, taking Davidson's work as an example. It is argued that such theories are difficult to make sense of without falling into vacuity or absurdity. Next, a more general holism of the mental is considered and contrasted with behavioristic views. The standard criticisms of atomistic, stimulus–response, behaviourism are accepted but a radical holism, in which every mental state one is in at a given time is internally related to every other, is rejected as equally absurd. Instead, a more moderate holism is proposed and compared with a "molecular" position in which mental states are identified with hierarchical complexes of dispositions of arbitrary finite complexity, corresponding to the atomistic dispositions only at base level. The superiority of the latter view is argued for on the grounds that it provides the only forseeable basis for a scientific explanation of mind.

WEIR, Alan. Rejoinder To Tenant's "Were Those Disproofs I Saw Before Me"? *Analysis* 45,68–72 Mr 85.

In an earlier paper I put forward two criticisms of the anti-realist position espoused by Tennant. In this paper I argue that his appeal to proof-checking abilities, in order to meet my first criticism, is beside the point. His objection to my second criticism was that my approach was unable to handle quantification. I meet this criticism directly by generalizing the account to include quantifiers.

WEIR, George R S. Sitting On Ryle's Dilemma. *Phil Stud* 47,295–303 Mr 85.

Ryle provides a dilemma which reduces to absurdity the suggestion that volitional causation is the key to understanding voluntariness. If voluntary, volition must each be produced by a further volition. If involuntary, then the voluntariness of actions rests with *involuntary* acts of will. I contend that Ryle's argument is defective, and that one can sit comfortably on *either* horn of his dilemma. In turn, this assures a strategic advance for volition theory.

WEIRICH, Paul. Interpersonal Utility In Principles Of Social Choice. *Erkenntnis* 21,295–318 N 84.

This paper summarizes and rebuts the three standard objections made by social choice theorists against interpersonal utility. My conclusion is that interpersonal utility has a legitimate place in social choice theory. (edited)

WEIRICH, Paul. The St Petersburg Gamble And Risk. *Theor Decis* 17,193–202 S 84.

Pursuing a line of thought initiated by Maurice Allais (1979), I consider whether the mean–risk method of decision making introduced by Harry Markowitz (1959) and other resolves Karl Menger's (1934) version of the St. petersburg paradox. I provide a conditional answer to this question. I demonstrate that given certain plausible assumptions about attitudes toward risk, a certain plausible development of the mean–risk method does resolve the paradox. My chief premiss is roughly that in the St. petersburg gamble the small chances for large prizes create big risks.

WEISS, Donald D. "Toward The Vindication Of Friedrich Engels" in *Methodology, Metaphysics And The History Of Science*, Cohen, Robert S (ed), 331–358. Boston Reidel 1984.

WEISS, Donald D. Nietzsche On The Joys Of Struggle: Some Remarks In Response To Professor Neville. *Int Stud Phil* 16,121–124 1984.

A short and sympathetic consideration of Nietzsche's solution, in terms of the Will to Power, of the Aristotelian puzzle of why people take a positive delight in certain "negative"—e.G., tragic—aesthetic objects. nietzsche's answer is seen as more plausible than Aristotle's own "catharsis" theory as the latter has usually been interpreted.

WEISS, Gary B and Vanderpool, Harold Y. Patient Truthfulness: A Test Of Models Of The Physician–Patient Relationship. *J Med Phil* 9,353–372 N 84.

Little attention has been given in medical ethics literature to issues relating to the truthfulness of patients. Beginning with an actual medical case, this paper first explores truth–telling by doctors and patients as related to two prominent models of the physician–patient relationship. Utilizing this discussion and the literature on the truthfullness and accuracy of the information patients convey to doctors, these models are then critically assessed. It is argued that the patient agency (patient autonomy or contractual) model is inherently and seriously flawed in numerous circumstances, even those involving informed and competent adult patients.

WEISS, Paul. *Philosophy In Process*, V8. Albany SUNY Pr 1983.

Continues the reflections begun in 1955 and carried out in the previous seven volumes. Among the topics discussed are inference, art, privacies, creativity, man, language, being, potentiality, responsibility, truth, method, and pain.

WEISSKOFF, Rita. Commentary On "Children As Consumers". *Bus Prof Ethics J* 3,155–158 Spr/Sum 84.

WEITKAMP, Galen and Kalantari, I. Effective Topological Spaces II: A Hierarchy. *Annals Pure Applied Log* 29,207–224 S 85.

WEITKAMP, Galen. On The Existence And Recursion Theoretic Properties Of Generic Sets Of Reals. *Z Math Log* 31,97–108 1985.

WEITKAMP, G and Kalantari, Iraj. Effective Topological Spaces I: A Definability Theory. *Annals Pure Applied Log* 29,1–28 Jl 85.

WELBOURN, R B. A Model For Teaching Medical Ethics. *J Med Ethics* 11,29–31 Mr 85.

The approach to teaching employed in the Dictionary of Medical Ethics (1) provides a model which might be adapted in other media. Most of the 150 authors were medical, but many represented other disciplines, and they wrote for similar professionals and for the general public. Medical ethics is derived from medical science and practice, moral philosophy, sociology, theology, the law and other disciplines, all of which make essential, distinctive and complementary contributions to knowledge and to teaching. Medical practitioners must play the primary role, because they are responsible for clinical ethical decisions, but they need the cooperation and guidance of others. All who are concerned should work towards the development of general moral consensus among the profession and public, which keeps abreast of scientific and technical advances to which all are committed.

WELCH, Lawrence V. A Hierarchy Of Families Of Recursively Enumerable Degrees. *J Sym Log* 49,1160–1170 D 84.

WELCH, Philip. Comparing Incomparable Kleene Degrees. *J Sym Log* 50,55–58 Mr 85.

We show that Kleene degrees of certain co–analytic sets, involved in a Frieburg–Muchnik type solution of "Posts problem" for Kleene degrees, can be incomparable without there existing an elementary embedding of L (Gödel's universe of constructive sets) to itself. The process can be viewed as forcing our L to obtain the determinancy of some rather simple sets of Turiney degrees.

WELDING, Streen O. Das Prinzip Vom Nicht-Widerspruch Und Das Prinzip Vom Ausgeschlossenen Dritten. *Z Phil Forsch* 38,413–435 Je–D 84.

It is shown that in two–valued logic each of the principles—of noncontradiction and of excluded middle—exclude both the truth and the falsity of A and –A. Hence they are only different formulations of the same tautological propositions. With respect to A and –A we are not referring to various propositions but rather to both the truth–values concerning the same proposition A. It is therefore impossible to construe a "dialectical contradiction" so that A and –A are considered both to be true at least in certain cases; for A and –A then prove to be different propositions.

WELKER, David. Logical Problems For Lockean Persons. *Grazer Phil Stud* 21,115–132 1984.

WELLMER, Albrecht. On The Dialectic Of Modernism And Postmodernism. *Praxis Int* 4,337–362 Ja 85.

WENDT, H. Evolution Und Revolution In Der Technischen Entwicklung Der Gegenwart. *Deut Z Phil* 33,332–338 1985.

Author Index with Abstracts 435 **Westphal, Merold**

WENGER, Morton G. "Lukács, Class Consciousness, And Rationality" in *Continuity And Change In Marxism*, Fischer, Norman And Others (ed), 86–96. Atlantic Highlands Humanities Pr 1982.

WENGERT, Robert G. The Sources Of Intuitive Cognition In William Of Ockham. *Fran Stud* 41,415–447 1981.

I argue that Ockham used "intuitive cognition" in three distinguishable senses, i.E., for a non–discursive, for a verdical, or for a vivid cognition. This ambiguity accounts for some of the past disagreements over his view. I claim the sources of his view are partly philosophical—including a realist epistemology which distinguishes one's beliefs from what they are beliefs of—and partly historical—here I argue for a Stoic influence.

WENHAM, Brian. Broadcasting And The Moral Imperative: Patrolling The Perimeters. *J Moral Educ* 13,160–167 O 84.

WENSTOP, Fred (ed) and Hagen, Ole (ed). *Progress In Utility And Risk Theory*. Boston Reidel 1983.

WENTZ, Richard E. The Contemplation Of Otherness. *Zygon* 20,341–344 S 85.

A critical meditation on the nature of religion and its study. All human experience is understood as a form of encounter with an other which participates in a whole that is greater than the sum of its parts. Contemplation is the form of reason that is most appropriate to understanding this experience. Religion, as well as its critical study, is a mode of the contemplation of otherness. There are implications for the entire academic enterprise.

WENTZ, Richard. *The Contemplation Of Otherness: The Critical Vision Of Religion*. Macon Mercer Univ Pr 1984.

WENZ, Peter S. "An Ecological Argument For Vegetarianism". *Ethics Animals* 5,2–9 Mr 84.

I argue that if healthy ecosystems are of value, and the value of an ecosystem is positively related to its degree of health, then people have prima facie obligations to avoid harming, to repair damage and to improve the health of ecosystems. Using land to grow large quantities of food impairs the health of the ecosystems involved, so people have a prima facie obligation to meet their nutritional needs through minimal use of land. Because vegetarianism enables people to do this, they have a prima facie obligation to be vegetarians. For healthy people in our society, the countervailing considerations are shown to be generally of little weight. People therefore have an obligation that is not merely prima facie to try vegetarianism for a length of time sufficient to become habituated to it.

WERBLOWSKY, R J Zwi and Klutstein– Rojtman, Ilana. Leibniz: De Cultu Confucii Civili: Introduction, Édition Du Texte Et Traduction. *Stud Leibniz* 16,93–101 1984.

WERHANE, Patricia H. Existence, Eternality, And The Ontological Argument. *Ideal Stud* 15,54–59 Ja 85.

The question of God's existence is not pertinent to the claim that God is defined as having all perfections and merely confuses the Ontological Argument. Rather, existence and perfection are *non sequiturs*. I argue that the quality of eternality rather than existence or necessary existence is more appropriate to the idea of perfection. From this it follows that if God is defined as having all perfections, God is eternal. This shift in emphasis from the notion of existence to eternality focuses on the ontology rather than on the logic of the Argument which, i presume, was its original purpose.

WERHANE, Patricia H. Hiring By Competence. *Listening* 20,118–127 Spr 85.

In this paper I argue that hiring by competence or merit is fair when it is accompanied by, but not identified with, equal opportunity. Reverse discrimination cannot be justified on the principle of hiring by competence, but is justified by appealing to the principle of equal treatment of equals which recommends allocating jobs evenly over the range of equal applicants of different minorities and sexes. I argue against an egalitarian distribution of jobs because hiring by competence produces an ideally more fair society as well as a society in which fewer needs go unsatisfied.

WERHANE, Patricia. Sandra Day O'Connor And The Justification Of Abortion. *Theor Med* 5,359–364 O 84.

If it is, or becomes, medically safe to perform abortions after first trimester of pregnancy and at the same time saving a fetus is, or becomes, medically viable or not unusual during some stage of the second trimester, can abortions during and after that stage of pregnancy be justified? With a number of qualifications I shall argue the thesis that as a general rule, but not an absolute rule, abortion in these instances is not usually justifiable. (edited)

WERNER, H –J. Soziolinguistische Codes Und Kategorischer Imperativ. *Kantstudien* 66,201–219 1975.

WERNER, O and Ward, Jeffrey J. Difference And Dissonance In Ethnographic Data. *Commun Cog* 17,219–244 1984.

This paper explores the value of discrepant, contradictory, or anomalous data in ethnography. While such data has traditionally been *adjudicated* in favor of one datum or the other, theories of information, psychology, and neurophysiology suggest that contradiction can be a rich source of insight. The paper concludes that anthropologists can make the most of these "epistemological windows" by seeking to *resolve* contradictions rather than *adjudicating* them.

WERNER, Richard. Ethical Realism Defended. *Ethics* 95,292–296 Ja 85.

WERTZ, S K. A Response To Best On Art And Sport. *J Aes Educ* 18,105–108 Wint 84.

In this commentary I restrict my discussion to the concept of art that David Best employs in his reply to my "Are Sports Art Form?" I tried to suggest that they were, whereas Best answers negatively. He thinks he has found a criterion which allows us to distinguish art and sport by a single fundamentum divisionis. His argument can be condensed to a syllogism: 1. art has an imagined object, i.E., possesses content. 2. sport is contentless, i.E., lacks an imagined object. Therefore sport is not art. Although this argument is valid, it is not sound. One of its premises is false. Premise 1 is faulty because the concept of art it voices covers only the nonperforming arts. It leaves the performing arts out of consideration, and this is crucial because sport's best case, following Ruth Saw, is as a performing art. If sport is a performing art, then it is an activity that is governed by an antecedent work or text. But does sport have a text? This seems to be one of the crucial questions on which the sport–as–art analogy rests. However, the sport–as–art analogy must rest ultimately on the notion of performance rather than on that of literature, the ideas of text and book. (edited)

WESLEY, George R and Carroll, Mary Ann and Schneider, Henry G. *Ethics In The Practice Of Psychology*. Englewood Cliffs Prentice–Hall 1985.

This book will acquaint not only philosophers and psychologists with ethical issues arising in psychology but also anyone interested in the profession. Hence, no background knowledge of philosophy or psychology is presupposed. Some of the areas covered are therapeutic techniques, research, special populations, testing, and consulting. Attention is given to consent, confidentiality and competence. Chapters contain case studies for discussion. The *Ethical Principles of Psychologists* as formulated by The American Psychological Association are included.

WESSELKAMPER, T C. Weak Completeness And Abelian Semigroups. *Z Math Log* 21,303–305 1975.

WESSELS, Linda. EPR Resuscitated: A Reply To Halpin's 'EPR Resuscitated: A Reply To Wessels'. *Phil Stud* 47,121–130 Ja 85.

In an earlier paper I argued that the EPR completeness condition is inappropriate for a theory about indeterministic systems, and therefore cannot be assumed appropriate for quantum mechanics. Now I distinguish between two types of completeness. The EPR condition is not appropriate for quantum mechanics if one type is at issue, but is appropriate on the second sense of completeness. Evidence is offered to show that EPR were concerned with the second type.

WEST, Grace Starry (trans) and West, Thomas G (trans). *Plato And Aristophanes: Plato's Euthyphro, Apology, And Crito And Aristophanes' Clouds*. Ithaca Cornell Univ Pr 1984.

Designed for the classroom use, this book offers new translations of Plato's *Euthyphro, Apology of Socrates, Crito*, and Aristophanes' *Clouds*. The translations are as precisely literal as possible within the bounds of readable English. A 28–page introduction provides a summary overview of the leading themes and arguments of the four works. There are extensive explanatory notes to the translations, and an annotated bibliography includes the best of the secondary literature on Socrates and on the texts included in this collection.

WEST, Thomas G (trans) and West, Grace Starry (trans). *Plato And Aristophanes: Plato's Euthyphro, Apology, And Crito And Aristophanes' Clouds*. Ithaca Cornell Univ Pr 1984.

Designed for the classroom use, this book offers new translations of Plato's *Euthyphro, Apology of Socrates, Crito*, and Aristophanes' *Clouds*. The translations are as precisely literal as possible within the bounds of readable English. A 28–page introduction provides a summary overview of the leading themes and arguments of the four works. There are extensive explanatory notes to the translations, and an annotated bibliography includes the best of the secondary literature on Socrates and on the texts included in this collection.

WESTEN, Peter. The Concept Of Equal Opportunity. *Ethics* 95,837–850 Jl 85.

WESTON, Anthony. Subjectivism And The Question Of Social Criticism. *Metaphilosophy* 16,57–65 Ja 85.

Some subjectivist axiologies are moving toward a Deweyan kind of holism, but this holism is often accused of precluding radical social criticism. I argue that holism can and must stress that "dissonance" is both the normal condition of ourselves and of our culture, and that such a view can explain and underwrite radical social criticism in a wholly "internal" way.

WESTPHAL, Jonathan. The Complexity Of Quality. *Philosophy* 59,457–472 O 84.

The view that colors are simple ideas confuses colors with colored patches or areas. Arguments for simple ideas of color from Remnant, Stout, Pears, Locke and Hume are examined and rejected. Definitions of colors do not leave out e.G., the *redness* of red. 'ness' is analyzed. The doctrine of simple ideas involves a confusion between the designating and predicating functions of 'is red'. The notion of a mark is examined, a certain misleading imagery exposed, and colors are shown to have marks in Leibniz's sense. Marks in this logical sense are not discolorations. The empiricists confused visual uniformity with logical simplicity. (edited)

WESTPHAL, Kenneth. Nietzsche's Sting And The Possibility Of Good Philology. *Int Stud Phil* 16,71–90 1984.

The author has argued elsewhere that Nietzsche's genealogical critique requires a cognitivist epistemology, including a correspondence notion of truth. In this essay, ten central questions concerning the consistency of Neitzsche's epistemology with his genealogy are posed. In answering these questions, his consistency (and his cognitivism) are defended by showing that his views on "philosophy" respond to his own critique of language and that his "perspectivism" is coherent and consistent with cognitivism.

WESTPHAL, Kenneth. Was Nietzsche A Cognitivist? *J Hist Phil* 22,343–363 Jl 84.

Does Nietzsche claim to know anything? Does he need to make such claims in order to fulfill his broader philosophical aims? Do his own epistemological views entitle him to make such claims? The author argues for affirmative answers to the first two of these questions and formulates several issues pertinent to resolving the third. It is hoped that posing these issues will help focus controversies among divergent groups of Nietzsche interpreters.

WESTPHAL, Merold. *God, Guilt, And Death: An Existential Phenomenology Of Religion*. Bloomington Indiana Univ Pr 1984.

The religious soul is ambivalent, attracted to and repelled from the Sacred. The

Westphal, Merold 436 Author Index with Abstracts

attraction is both instrumental and intrinsic. At the heart of the former lies the hope of a solution to the problem of guilt and death. Phenomenological analysis reveals both that we should speak of a single problem here rather than two, so closely are the issues intertwined, and that it is found universally in the religious life, though three fundamentally different forms can be distinguished.

WESTPHAL, Merold. "Hegel And The Reformation, David Duquette (commentator)" in *History And System*, Perkins, Robert (ed), 73–100. Albany SUNY Pr 1984.

WESTPHAL, Merold. "Hegel's Radical Idealism: Family And State As Ethical Communities" in *The State And Civil Society*, Pelczynski, Z A (ed), 77–92. Cambridge Cambridge Univ Pr 1984.

WESTPHAL, Merold. "Kierkegaard's Sociology" in *International Kierkegaard Commentary*, Perkins, Robert L (ed), 133–154. Macon Mercer Univ Pr 1984.

WESTPHAL, Merold. Dialectic And Intersubjectivity. *Owl Minerva* 16,39–54 Fall 84.

Hegel's dialectic is interpreted as a form of transcendental holism. Its relation to various forms of holism in contemporary philosophy is discussed. But Hegel's own social theory does not fully live up to the requirements of his own dialectical holism. If it did he would not be willing to call rational any form of human intersubjectivity short of an international community free of war and propaganda.

WESTPHAL, Merold. Donagan's Critique Of *Sittlichkeit*. *Ideal Stud* 15,1–17 Ja 85.

To defend an essentially Kantian morality one must refuse the essentially Hegelian critique of it, namely that pure practical reason is insufficiently specific to give us moral guidance and depends on the *Sittlichkeit* of a particular culture for its content. Donagan's attempt to defend Kantian style ethics against Hegelian style critique fails, for at one crucial point he simply agrees with Hegel, while at another his own argument perfectly illustrates the dependence of moral reasoning on the traditions of a particular society.

WESTWELL ROPER, Andrew and Nerlich, Graham. What Ontology Can Be About: A Spacetime Example. *Austl J Phil* 63,127–142 Je 85.

Ontology can be about what structures, not merely about what objects, they are. A structural ontology of spacetime is about the relation of causal structures (for example) to topological on to metrical ones. To settle the questions which arise one needs to decide what is essential to the theory and what is contingent. This need gives rise to a distinction, which applies broadly, between a restrictive and a permissive core of a theory.

WETTERSTEN, John. Free From Sin: On Living With Ad Hoc Hypotheses. *Conceptus* 18,86–100 1984.

Major views of ad hoc hypotheses are reviewed. These are that they are simply unacceptable, that they are acceptable on condition that they be explained away by being embedded in deeper, simpler theories, that they may be advantageous through the production of useful true predictions and that tolerance is needed. The last view leads to a problem of the acceptable limits of tolerance. The mere use of ad hoc theories as signs of trouble and opportunity for improvement through the construction of problems—however good or bad theories happen to be—offers an adequate and superior solution. (edited)

WETTSTEIN, Howard. Did The Greeks Really Worship Zeus? *Synthese* 60,439–450 S 84.

Parsons, in *Nonexistent Objects*, Yale University Press, 1980, and in "Are There Nonexistent Objects," *American Philosophical Quarterly* volume 19: pp. 365–371, defends a version of the Meinongian view that there are nonexistent objects. I raise a number of problems specific to Parson's Meinongianism and suggest that contrary to Parson's, we can do without nonexistent objects. The crucial notion for an account of many cases of apparent reference to the nonexistent is, i suggest, the notion of pretended reference.

WETZEL, Manfred. Dialektik Von Individuum Und Gesellschaft Als Dialektik Von Persönlicher Und Sozialer Indentität. *Arch Rechts Soz* 60,305–326 1974.

The subject is developed in four steps: (1) As the relation of individual and society is quite abstract the individual himself isn't but a simple reproduction of patterns of social action. (2) By reflecting upon himself the individual overthrows the role–distribution within the group he belongs to. (3) The individual realizing his own concept of action generally meets non symmetrical dialectic relations of personal and society identity which consequently both change. (4) In this case the individual needs affiliation to a different group where his dialectics of performance are rewarded. The propositions are stated within the framework of the categories of Hegelian Logic.

WHEELER, Samuel C. The Conclusion Of The Theaetetus. *Hist Phil Quart* 1,355–368 O 84.

This paper argues that the *Theaetetus'* odd arguments about knowledge reflect defensible Platonic doctrines. The bizarre requirement that, if an object is known under one aspect, it must be known under every aspect, is justified if knowledge is a genuine constituent of the nature of things. Since Plato takes knowledge to be one of the fundamental ordering principles of the world as a whole, he must take it to have a fundamentally simple structure. Thus real knowledge, as opposed to the facsimiles we get by examining "what we say when", is total knowledge. Given the contingency of physical entities, then, only of Forms can there be real knowledge.

WHITE, Alan R. *Rights*. Oxford Clarendon Pr 1984.

An examination of the notion *a Right* and its relation to other notions which commonly accompany it in everyday moral, legal and political thinking. Close attention is paid to the logical and linguistic features of "right", "liberty", "privilege", "power", "duty", "ought", "claim", etc. Various current theories about these legal and political philosophy are rejected. Consideration is also given to possible possessors of rights, possible objects of rights and possible grounds in virtue of which rights may be claimed, granted, or exist.

WHITE, David A. Part And Whole In Aristotle's Concept Of Infinity. *Thomist* 49,168–182 Ap 85.

Part I establishes a series of problems stated in Book I of Aristotle's Physics concerning the relation between part and whole with respect to the infinite. I show that several recent criticisms of Aristotle's position do not reach its metaphysical core, then suggest a series of paradoxes which arise once the proper implications of this core are developed. In part II, a solution of sorts to these problems is sketched by analyzing one of the senses of unity Aristotle introduces later in the *Physics*.

WHITE, F C. On Total Cultural Relativism: A Rejoinder. *Educ Phil Theor* 16,43–44 O 84.

WHITE, F C. The Scope Of Knowledge In Republic V. *Austl J Phil* 62,339–354 D 84.

What sorts of items are the objects of knowledge in *Republic* V? The traditional reply is that Forms and only Forms constitute such objects. But this answer gives rise to a number of problems: it looks counter–intuitive; it appears to contradict much that is said elsewhere in the *Republic*; it sets the guardians so much apart that they can have nothing useful to say on issues of justice in this world. In the light of these and similar difficulties, it has been suggested that particulars also (individual men and actions) are meant to be taken as objects of knowledge in *Republic* V – in respect of their *essential* properties. This solution to Plato's problems, however, while it is attractive, faces insurmountable difficulties.

WHITE, Harvey W. God And Philosophical Grammar. *Phil Stud (Ireland)* 30,177–181 Spr 84.

A difficulty in the writings of "Wittgensteinian Fideists" stems from their attempts to discuss religious claims in non–religious terms. This apparent reductionism contravenes the Fideist position that religious language is semantically autonomous. Religious statements, however, do have implications which are stateable in non–religious language. This allows partial renderings of religious claims in non–religious language, though not such that they capture the full sense of the religious statements.

WHITE, Hayden. The Italian Difference And The Politics Of Culture. *Grad Fac Phil J* 10,117–122 Spr 84.

WHITE, James E. *Contemporary Moral Problems*. NY West 1985.

A survey of contemporary moral problems including abortion, euthanasia, world hunger, capital punishment, sexual morality, sexual equality, animal rights, and nuclear war. For each problem, the main positions, arguments, concepts, and issues are examined.

WHITE, John. The Education Of The Emotions. *J Phil Educ* 18,233–244 1984.

WHITE, Michael J. Harmless Actualism. *Phil Stud* 47,183–190 Mr 85.

WHITE, Nicholas P. Professor Shoemaker And So–Called 'Qualia' Of Experience. *Phil Stud* 47,369–384 My 85.

WHITE, Nicholas. The Classification Of Goods In Plato's *Republic*. *J Hist Phil* 22,393–422 O 84.

It is argued here that in interpreting the classification of good laid out at the beginning of Book II of Plato's *Republic*, which involves a distinction between what is good "for its own sake" and what is good "for its consequences (*apobainonta*)," we can properly interpret the notion of "consequences" only if we take in to consideration the causal and quasi–causal notions that Plato actually has available to him, and do not simply force some modern sense on the term. Once we see this fact, it becomes possible to understand what Plato is trying to show about justice, and why the rest of the *Republic* is fully responsive to the challenge he sets himself at the beginning of Book II. (edited)

WHITE, Patricia and Peters, R S (ed). *Beyond Domination: An Essay In The Political Philosophy Of Education*. Boston Routledge K & Paul 1983.

Unashamedly radical in its approach, this philosophical critique of contemporary political and educational practice is based firmly in the liberal democratic tradition. It proposes curbing the power of teachers, includding headteachers, reducing parents' rights, and making political education the keystone of education. It considers educational strategies which would help to move a society towards greater democracy, including proposals for the democratic organization of political decision–making, and the development of democratic attitudes, notably fraternity.

WHITE, Richard B. Peirce's Alpha Graphs: The Completeness Of Propositional Logic And The Fast Simplification Of Truth Functions. *Trans Peirce Soc* 20,351–362 Fall 84.

It is shown that the problem of reducing a propositional formula to a simplest equivalent can be handled very easily in Pierce's version of classical propositional logic. The method of simplification leads naturally to a complete axiomatization of propositional logic whose completeness is nearly obvious. Rules derivable in Peirce's system are used to give a fast procedure for simplifying formulas in disjunctive normal form.

WHITE, Stephen K. Habermas' Communicative Ethics And The Development Of Moral Consciousness. *Phil Soc Crit* 10,25–48 Fall 84.

This paper examines Jurgen Habermas' claim that his "communicative ethics" represents the highest stage of moral development. The nature of his reliance on the work of Kohlberg and the specific character of communicative ethics is explored. In evaluating the case for communicative ethics, special attention is focused on how Habermas' approach to universalization or reciprocity differs from that of Kohlberg and Rawls.

WHITE, Villard Alan. Whitehead, Special Relativity, And Simultaneity. *Process Stud* 13,275–285 Wint 83.

I argue here that Whitehead's concept of simultaneity evolved from a Newtonian or quasi–Newtonian conception in his pre–metaphysical work to one very close to Einstein's in *Process and Reality*.

WHITEHEAD, Alfred N and Brumbaugh, Robert S (ed). "Discussion Upon Fundamental Principles Of Education" (1919). *Process Stud* 14,41–43 Spr 84.

An abstract of a speech on education by Whitehead in 1919 is reprinted here to make it more readily available. Attention is drawn to the relevance of several key ideas to Whitehead's other writings on educational theory. In addition, it is noted that the date and theme add evidence that Whitehead's interest in education continued unabated through the period of composition of his most technical work in the philosophy of science.

WHITLEY, Richard. *The Intellectual And Social Organization Of The Sciences.* Oxford Clarendon Pr 1984.

This book analyzes the sciences as particular types of work organization and control for generating coordinated intellectual innovations. Differences in intellectual structures and forms of knowledge between scientific fields are linked to differences in the coordination and control of research and reputations. Variations in the organization of work across the sciences are, in turn, linked to variations in contextual factors and scientific change is dependent on changes in these factors. Changes in the science system as a whole have affected relations between the sciences and the organization of knowledge.

WHITNEY, Barry L. *Evil And The Process God.* NY Mellen Pr 1985.

The author intends to reconstruct and critically assess the process theology developed by Charles Hortshorne. After briefly discussing one entailment of Hortshorne's approach to theory, that because God's existence is necessary truth, evil cannot argue against his existence, the author examines hortshorne's second approach, that God's omnipotence and benevolence and evil are reconcilable. The author concludes that systematic examination of process theodicy sheds new light on creativity, free will, immortality, and the problem of evil. (staff)

WHITSON, David. Sport And Hegemony: On The Construction Of The Dominant Culture. *Dialec Hum* 11,5–20 Wint 84.

WHITT, L A. Acceptance And The Problem Of Slippery–Slope Insensitivity In Rule Utilitarianism. *Dialogue (Canada)* 23,649–660 D 84.

When controversial moral issues are debated, appeal is frequently made to slippery–slope arguments. Provided that they have been carefully formulated, such arguments raise considerations which are relevant to the choice of a moral code. Yet, as Gregory Trianosky has argued, IRU——and other ethical theories which require the acceptance of a moral code——are forced to disregard slippery slope claims. In this paper I examine why this is so and suggest a way of sensitizing IRU to slippery slope considerations which, unlike Trianosky's proposal, does not involve abandoning the notion of pf code–acceptance.

WHITT, L A. Fictional Contexts And Referential Opacity. *Can J Phil* 15,327–338 Je 85.

Referential opacity has been recognized as afflicting principally two types of situations. The first arises in certain modal contexts and the second in certain epistemic contexts——notably when we are confronted with propositional attitudes such as believing and denying. This paper offers a sketch of another situation in which referential opacity puts in a classic appearance, contexts in which we are confronted by discourse about fiction(s). These contexts are explored with the aid of a suppositional operator and an effort is made to provide for a relational sense of supposition by modifying David Kaplan's analysis of the relational sense of belief.

WICKEN, Jeffrey S. The Cosmic Breath: Reflections On The Thermodynamics Of Creation. *Zygon* 19,487–506 D 84.

This paper views such distinctions as creation and degeneration or good and evil in the Eastern sense of unity in polarity rather than in the Western sense of dual, antagonistic principles. Hence it considers the thermodynamic forces of evolution as processes of creation driven by entropy dissipation and explores the analogies this conception bears to the Hindu image of nature as the changing mist of a universal breath. Using this image, the paper examines the sense in which the second law of thermodynamics connects chance and teleology in the operations of nature and provides for a causal hierarchy in which decision and volitional behavior co–participate with the laws of nature to determine the course of evolution.

WIDMER, Hans. Acotaciones Al Concepto De Filosofía En Ortega Y Gasset. *Pensamiento* 41,37–56 Ja–Mr 85.

Das philosophische Werk von Ortega ist die brillant dargestellte Geschichte vom Aufstieg und Zerfall des Glaubens an die reine Vernunft. Die sich literarischer Mittel bedienende Erzählung bersteht sich selber als eine vorläufige Gestalt einer nicht reine, sondern als vitale und historische zu verstehenden Vernunft. Auf dem Hintergrund dieses erweiterten Vernunftparadigmas bilden systematische Philosophie und Philosophiegeschichte eine innere Einheit.

WIEBE, Donald. The Cognitive Status Of Religious Belief. *Sophia (Australia)* 23,4–21 O 84.

WIELAND, Bernhard. Towards An Economic Theory Of Scientific Revolutions—A Cynical View. *Erkenntnis* 23,79–96 My 85.

The article attempts to explain the process of scientific revolutions with the help of economic concepts applying, in particular, concepts of the theory of competition. Scientists are seen as entrepreneurs, who take pains to maximize 'profits' (in the form of prestige) by selling their 'products', e.G., new theories, textbooks, expert opinions, etc. In this framework, a new theory can be interpreted as a product innovation, which for sometime allows a 'monopoly profit' to its inventor. Economic theory is used to show under what circumstances scientific revolutions can be expected.

WIELEMA, M R. J F L Schröder—Aanhanger En Tegenstander Van Kant. *Tijdschr Filosof* 46,466–484 S 84.

My article is the only recent examination of Schroeder's work so far. Formerly a Kantian himself, he developed a criticism of Kant in which figure prominently the 'antinomies of the Kantian philosophy' concerning the existence of the noumenon. According to his theory of knowledge, reminiscent of Thomas Reid's, some form of natural sign relation is basic to our knowledge of the world. Schroeder (1774–1845) was professor of philosophy in Utrecht, Netherlands.

WIELINGER, Gerhart. Rechtstheorie Heute: Kritische Anmerkungen Zu Drei Sammelbänden. *Arch Rechts Soz* 60,429–434 1974.

WIERENGA, Edward. Utilitarianism And The Divine Command Theory. *Amer Phil Quart* 21,311–318 O 84.

I first describe both utilitarianism and the divine command theory. I then consider six objections that have been raised against the divine command theory. I argue that if they are good objections to the divine command theory, they are also good objections to utilitarianism. But there are plausible rejoinders available both to the divine command theory and to utilitarianism. Hence, since the objections are properly thought not to refute utilitarianism, they should not be thought to refute the divine command theory.

WIESENTHAL, L. Visual Space From The Perspective Of Possible World Semantics II. *Synthese* 64,241–270 Ag 85.

WIGGINS, David. The Sense And Reference Of Predicates: A Running Repair To Frege's Doctrine And A Plea For The Copula. *Phil Quart* 34,311–328 Jl 84.

WIGGINS, Osborne. Philosophical Anthropology: Revolt Against The Division Of Intellectual Labor. *Human Stud* 7,285–300 1984.

WIKE, Victoria S. Kant's Practical Antinomy. *S J Phil* 22,425–434 Fall 84.

This paper examines the structure of Kant's practical antinomy to discover in what sense it is an antinomy. It is argued that the clue to Kantian antinomies is located in their disjunctive nature. Disjunctions have mutually exclusive propositions and since these propositions can be mutually exclusive due to their content, they need not manifest logical contradiction. The disjunctions called antinomies share a particular content. Hence, the practical antinomy is an antinomy, though it lacks contradictoriness, by virtue of its content and its mutual exclusivity.

WIKLER, Daniel. "Concepts Of Personhood: A Philosophical Perspective" in *Defining Human Life*, Shaw, Margery W (ed), 12–23. Ann Arbor Aupha Pr 1983.

WILBUR, James B (ed) and Allen, H J (ed). *The Worlds Of Hume And Kant.* Buffalo Prometheus Books 1982.

WILCOX, Stephen and Katz, Stuart. Can Indirect Realism Be Demonstrated In The Psychological Laboratory? *Phil Soc Sci* 14,149–158 Je 84.

WILDERMUTH, Armin. Eigentum Und Lebenswelt: Zum Wandel Des Eigentumsverständnisses In Der Komplexen Gesellschaft. *Stud Phil (Switzerland)* Supp 12,227–248 1983.

WILDESEN, Leslie E. "The Search For An Ethic In Archaeology" in *Ethics And Values In Archaeology*, Green, Ernestene L (ed), 3–12. NY Free Pr 1984.

WILKES, K V. Pragmatics In Science And Theory In Common Sense. *Inquiry* 27,339–362 D 84.

Recent work in the philosophy of science has been debunking theory and acclaiming practice. Recent work in philosophical psychology has been neglecting practice and emphasizing theory, suggesting that common–sense psychology is in all essential respects like any scientific theory. The marriage of these two strands of thought would serve to make science and common sense virtually indistinguishable. My paper resists this conflation. The main target is the attempt to assimilate everyday psychology to a scientific theory; I argue that this is badly mistaken, and does a disservice both to scientific and to common–sense psychology. A secondary aim is to argue that some of the new pragmatism in the philosophy of science is overstated. The suggested conflation would have interesting implications, as would its denial; in a concluding section, some of these implications are briefly explored.

WILKES, K and Newton Smith, W. Converging Reflections On The Philosophy Of Science. *Ratio* 27,1–6 Je 85.

This is the introduction to a selection of papers from the 1984 Dubrovnik Philosophy of Science seminar. It draws attention to a current convergence of interests on the part of philosophers of science in western and eastern bloc countries.

WILKES, Kathleen V. Is Consciousness Important? *Brit J Phil Sci* 35,223–243 S 84.

WILKIE, Raymond. The Premises Of Four Moral Conceptions: Classical, Modern, Totalitarian, And Utopian. *Phil Stud Educ* No Vol,82–91 1983.

WILKINS, Burleigh T and Zelikovitz, Kelly M. Principles For Individual Actions. *Philosophia (Israel)* 14,299–320 D 84.

WILKINS, Burleigh T. Psychosurgery, The Brain And Violent Behavior. *J Value Inq* 18,319–332 1984.

WILKINSON, Jennifer and Macnamara, Michael and Kistner, Wietske. 'Elegance' In Science And Mathematics: A Discussion. *S Afr J Phil* 4,95–99 Ag 85.

The authors discuss, along conceptual–analytical lines, the concept of elegance as it occurs in science and mathematics with reference to methods, solutions, proofs, and theories. Aspects considered include a comparison of the meanings of the term 'elegant' as it is applied in science, mathematics, and art, respectively; the intrinsic significance of elegance in a scientific theory; the significance of the relation between aesthetic criteria and truth; and the time–shift of criteria of elegance. Several possible lines for further inquiry are suggested, for example the question of whether it is elegant scientific theories that are the most fruitful ones.

WILKOSZEWSKA, Krystyna. Waclaw Borowy's Views On Aesthetics. *Rep Phil* 8,61–72 1984.

WILL, Frederick L. Pragmatic Rationality. *Phil Invest* 8,120–142 Ap 85.

By no means all rational processes, in philosophy as elsewhere, fit the regnant model of conclusions derived from accepted procedures from set premises. The nonconforming processes are generative and defining rather than probative and applicative, and highly social and often less than conscious, rather than paradigmatically individualistic and conscious. The exclusion of such processes from the canon of acceptable, rational ones has been and continues to be a major impediment to enlightened philosophical theory and practice.

Will, Frederick L 438 Author Index with Abstracts

WILL, Frederick L. Rules And Subsumption: Mutative Aspects Of Logical Processes. *Amer Phil Quart* 22,143–152 Ap 85.

A difference between the concrete procedure of applying rules to putative instances and abstract logistic models of this procedure is the sometimes important reactive effect that in the concrete procedure is produced in the rule itself. Neglect of this effect, encouraged by concentration upon the logistic analogues of subsumption, remains an important obstacle to the philosophical understanding of what it is like both to employ rules and to discern in this employment grounds for change.

WILL, Ulrich. Nomische Notwendigkeit. *Z Phil Forsch* 38,582–592 N–D 84.

Lawful relations are analyzed as holding between a certain kind of particulars called states. The constituents of antecedent and consequent states are shown to be at least partially identical. This makes possible a new explication of nomic necessity according to which laws are, when true, true in all possible worlds in which the things of the actual world exist.

WILLARD, Dallas. *Logic And The Objectivity Of Knowledge: Studies In Husserl's Early Philosophy*. Athens Ohio Univ Pr 1984.

This book attempts to explain the path by which Husserl's concern for an elucidation of mathematical, chiefly arithmetical, knowledge led to an analysis of the mental act which allows for a realist interpretation of science and ordinary perceptual experience. It attempts to go more thoroughly than has been done into the content and significance of his first book, *The Philosophy of Arithmetic*. It provides discussion of many Husserlian texts not available in English and little discussed in the English literature. Its aim is not merely historical, but systematic as well.

WILLER, Jörg. Schröder–Husserl–Scheler: Zur Formalen Logik. *Z Phil Forsch* 39,110–121 Ja–Mr 85.

WILLIAMS, Bernard. The Scientific And The Ethical. *Philosophy* 17,209–228 84 Supp.

WILLIAMS, Gill. Health Promotion—Caring Concern Or Slick Salesmanship? *J Med Ethics* 10,191–195 D 84.

There is an increasing tendency for administrators and government to expect both the health services and the education service to 'show results' for the investment of public money in them. One response to this has been the growing commitment to 'health promotion', where measurable objectives may be set in terms of desired behavior (stopping smoking, breast self–examination, child immunization, etc) and where evaluation can be made on the evidence of statistical improvement. Health workers use the term 'promotion' in a variety of ways which seem to be as confusing to them as they are to their clients—the general public. Since successful promotion is likely to depend on the 'hard sell' (and since the methodology and aims of this may be incompatible with those of health education) this paper looks at some of the questions which the customer might wish to ask the salesman before deciding whether or not to buy.

WILLIAMS, Meredith. Wittgenstein's Rejection Of Scientific Psychology. *J Theor Soc Behav* 15,203–223 Jl 85.

WILLIAMS, Michael. Hume's Criterion Of Significance. *Can J Phil* 15,273–304 Je 85.

WILLIAMS, Patterson B. Educational Excellence In Art Museums: An Agenda For Reform. *J Aes Educ* 19,105–124 Sum 85.

The purpose is to describe the museum's educational problem at the level of the individual visitor. At that level there is a substantial gap between the average museum visitor's experience and the experiences of those who are trained and skilled in encountering works of art. The ask of museum education is to bridge this gap. To solve the educational problem, key decision makers must set high goals for the individual visitor's encounter with works of art by considering five key areas of museum operation: educational leadership, the role of educational expertise in the museum, mastery level museum teaching, use of educational multipliers to reach large audiences, and research in visitor learning.

WILLIAMS, R J. Metaphysics And Metalepsis In *Thus Spoke Zarathustra*. *Int Stud Phil* 16,27–36 1984.

This essay explores the internal relation between literacy form and philosophical content in Nietzsche's *Thus Spoke Zarathustra*. The author shows that the philosophical significance of *Zarathustra* is intimately connected to this book's character as a work of literature. In particular, Williams explores the relationship of *Zarathustra* between metaphysical statement of literary allusion. According to Williams, the text of *Zarathustra* incorporates figurative enactments of eternal recurrence.

WILLIAMSON, Timothy. Converse Relations. *Phil Rev* 94,249–262 Ap 85.

This paper argues that if relational expressions stand for determinate non–linguistic relations, converse relational expressions stand for the same relation. Thus the argument–places of 'precedes' and 'succeeds' are correlated in opposite ways with the argument–places of one relation. Hence '1984 precedes 1985' and '1984 succeeds 1985' stand for distinct propositions: classical logic is preserved. However, conjunction is not defined on relations, nor can we say 'x has the relation R to y'.

WILLIAMSON, Timothy. The Infinite Commitment Of Finite Minds. *Can J Phil* 14,235–256 Je 84.

This article contests the claim that learnable theories cannot have infinitely many axioms. For a theory with a finite number of axioms requires at least an inference schema with infinitely many instances in order to generate infinitely many theorems, and an axiom schema with infinitely many instances is just a limiting case of such an inference schema. In this light, Davidsonian constraints on theories of meaning look highly artificial.

WILMERS, George. Bounded Existential Induction. *J Sym Log* 50,72–90 Mr 85.

This paper introduces a natural weak system of first–order arithmetic with the induction scheme for formulae whose only quantifiers are existential and bounded by some polynomial. The system is a natural strengthening of the system of open induction. The paper establishes that the system has no recursive models, and that the class of reducts to addition of countable models of the system is exactly the same as for the system of first–order peano arithmetic.

WILSHIRE, Bruce and Wilshire, Donna. Robert Wilson's Theater As A *De Facto* Phenomenological Reduction. *Phil Soc Crit* 5,47–66 Ja 78.

WILSHIRE, Donna and Wilshire, Bruce. Robert Wilson's Theater As A *De Facto* Phenomenological Reduction. *Phil Soc Crit* 5,47–66 Ja 78.

WILSON, Catherine. Morality And The Self In Robert Musil's *The Perfecting Of A Love*. *Phil Lit* 8,222–235 O 84.

The paper is a study of the concepts of integrity and disloyalty in Musil's morally–ambiguous story of a morally–ambiguous heroine. The aim is to uncover some of the tension which exists between the conception of moral value as deriving from a shared *Lebensform*, and a transcendental conception.

WILSON, Donald E. Commentary On "Whether Professional Associations May Enforce Professional Codes". *Bus Prof Ethics J* 3,65–68 Wint 84.

The commentary focuses on an underlying purpose of professional codes and standards, that is, to protect the public and to further the public interest. Rather than devoting professional codes to matters of personal self interest of professionals, they should reflect an attitude of professional responsibility, not in a legalistic sense, but in a spirit of concern that seeks the ethical, the pure and the ideal.

WILSON, Edwin H and Tonne, Herbert A and Eddy, Robert M. Symposium On Humanism, Secularism, And Religion. *Relig Hum* 19,32–39 Wint 85.

WILSON, Fred. Addis On Analysing Disposition Concepts. *Inquiry* 28,247–260 Je 85.

Addis (1981) has criticized a proposal of ours (Wilson (1969b)) for analyzing disposition predictions in terms of the horseshoe of material implication, and has proposed a related but significantly different analysis. This paper restates the original proposal, and defends it against Addis's criticisms. It is further argued that his proposal will not do as a *general account* of disposition predications; that, however, if it is suitably qualified, then it does account for certain special sorts of dispostion predictions; but that so understood, it can be seen to be a special case of ours.

WILSON, Fred. Is Hume A Sceptic With Regard To Reason? *Phil Res Arch* 10,275–320 1984.

This paper argues that, contrary to most interpretations, e.G., those of Reid, Popkin and Passmore, Hume is not a sceptic with regard to reason. The argument of *Treatise* I, IV. I, of course, has a sceptical conclusion with regard to reason, and a somewhat similar point is made by Cleanthes in the *Dialogues*. This paper argues that the argument of Treatise I, IV. I is parallel to similar arguments in Bentham and Laplace. The latter are, as far as they go, sound, as so is Hume's. But the limitations of all mean that they cannot sustain a general argument against reason. Hume the historian is quite aware of these limitations. So is Hume the philosopher. A careful examination of the other references in the *Treatise* to the argument of I, IV. I reveals that Hume not only rejects but constructs a sound case against accepting the sceptical conclusion, arguing that reason can indeed show the sceptic's argument to be unreasonable. A close reading of the *Dialogues* shows that Hume there also draws the same conclusion. The thrust of the paper is to go some way towards showing that it is a myth that Hume is a pyrrhonian sceptic.

WILSON, Fred. The Origins Of Hume's Sceptical Argument Against Reason. *Hist Phil Quart* 2,323–336 Jl 85.

WILSON, H T. *Tradition And Innovation: The Idea Of Civilization As Culture And Its Significance*. Boston Routledge & K Paul 1984.

By viewing Western civilization as a culture, this study puts the common perspectives of our major Western institutions in bolder relief. The institutionalization of cultural modes of Western rationality found in capitalism, industrialization, science, science–based technology, bureaucracy, the rule of law and the social and behavioral sciences has created a culturally and historically unique form of collective life: advanced industrial society. Central to our form of collective life is the belief in the existence of independent and autonomous "Facts of Life".

WILSON, John F. *The Politics Of Moderation: An Interpretation Of Plato's "Republic"*. Lanham Univ Pr Of America 1984.

The purpose of the book is to show, first, that the *Republic* is a critique of ideal justice and an endorsement of moderation; second, that the best life is not that of the guardian, philosopher, or philosopher–king but of the moderate, musical human being; third, that the concluding books are an integral and far more significant part of the work than other interpreters realize.

WILSON, John and Cowell, Barbara. Applying Philosophy. *J Applied Phil* 2,127–132 Mr 85.

WILSON, John and Natale, Samuel M. First Steps In Moral And Ethical Education. *Thought* 60,119–140 Je 85.

The goal of this essay is to explore a new foundation for moral and ethical behaviors. The aim is to create empirical criteria which can be evaluated and assessed. A series of moral components are generated and methods of evaluation are explored. Emphasis is placed on implementing and operationalizing criteria which have been generally left untouched by most philosophers. The result is empirical research which touches on the problem of moral and ethical education.

WILSON, John. The Inevitability Of Certain Concepts (Including Education): A Reply To Robin Barrow. *Educ Theor* 35,203–204 Spr 85.

Conceptual analysis is valid as philosophy because, though language changes, some concepts are not optional but inevitable for all human beings. This includes the concept marked (now) by 'education', and other concepts connected with it. It is of great practical importance that we should see what these concepts logically necessitate.

WILSON, Margaret D. Skepticism Without Indubitability. *J Phil* 81,537–544 O 84.

Foundationalist objectives have been overemphasized in portraying the relation between early modern views about perception and skeptical concerns. The mechanistic theory of nature seems to imply that perceptual experience *systematically misleads* us about physical reality; skeptical arguments are used to support the "detachment from sense" that this perspective requires. Further, the problem of explaining the "production" of ideas of sense gives purchase for non–instrumental skepticism quite independently of foundationalist concerns.

WILSON, Mark. Carnap's Internal—External Distinction. *De Phil* 5,29–41 1984.

WILSON, N L. Propositions For Semantics And Propositions For Epistemology. *Can J Phil* 14,375–400 S 84.

WILSON, Thomas A. Russell's Later Theory Of Perception. *Russell* 5,26–43 Sum 85.

In this article, I summarize Russell's later work on perception, especially as set forth in *Human Knowledge: Its Scope and Limits*. The summary was undertaken because Russell's views on this topic after 1921 have tended to be ignored until recently. In the course of this summary, I argue that Russell's alleged phenomenalism in *The Analysis of Mind* turns out, on close examination, to be a more complicated form of realism.

WILSON, William McF and Buckley, James J. A Dialogue With Barth And Farrer On Theological Method. *Heythrop J* 26,274–293 Jl 85.

WINANT, Terry. Trans–World Identity Of Future Contingents: Sartre On Leibnizian Freedom. *S J Phil* 22,543–564 Wint 84.

On Sartre's view, human agents are contingently self–identical: our actions are our choices of who we are. This paper supplies a reading of this view, arguing that Sartre defended Actualism (the doctrine that possibilities are aspects of the actual world) and a form of Haecceitism (in David Kaplan's sense—it is meaningful to ask after some individuals trans–world being), namely, Haecceitism with respect to human agent's futures. On Sartre's reading, Leibniz is a Possibilist and an Anti–Haecceitist.

WINCH, C A. Verbal Deficit And Educational Success. *J Applied Phil* 2,109–120 Mr 85.

The claim that social class differences in educational success are related to language and language use of a cognitively relevant kind is discussed and criticized. Various aspects of the relationship between rationality and language are examined and it is argued that the contention that deficiencies in rationality are related to language is an ambiguous one which involves different kinds of claims. When the claims of verbal deficit theorists have been clarified, it has been found that the weakest of these claims have not been proven, while the strongest are empirically possible but extremely unlikely.

WINCKELMANN, J. Energieproblem Und Wissenschaftlich–Technischer Fortschritt. *Deut Z Phil* 33,105–114 1985.

WINE, Sherwin P. Morality And Religion. *Relig Hum* 19,75–79 Spr 85.

WINFIELD, Richard D. "Hegel's Challenge To The Modern Economy" in *History And System*, Perkins, Robert (ed), 219–253. Albany SUNY Pr 1984.

WINFIELD, Richard D. "The Theory And Practice Of The History Of Freedom, Harry Brod (commentator)" in *History And System*, Perkins, Robert (ed), 123–148. Albany SUNY Pr 1984.

WINKLER, Earl R. Abortion And Victimisability. *J Applied Phil* 1,305–318 O 84.

This paper begins with a review of major difficulties with both extreme conservative and extreme liberal views on foetal moral status and the morality of abortion. There follows an outline and defense of a moderate position on abortion which is centered in an account of emergent foetal victimisability in being killed. Lastly, various perplexities about this view are explored, particularly the question whether, once victimisable at all, the victimisability of a foetus should reasonably be thought to increase proportionally with further biological developments.

WINKLER, G. Die Einheit Von Wirtschafts––Und Sozialpolitik––Triebkraft Ökonomischen Und Sozialen Fortschritts. *Deut Z Phil* 33,11–20 1985.

WINKLER, Kenneth P. Berkeley On Volition, Power, And The Complexity Of Causation. *Hist Phil Quart* 2,53–70 Ja 85.

WINKLER, Kenneth P. Hutcheson's Alleged Realism. *J Hist Phil* 23,179–194 Ap 85.

WINKLER, Kenneth P. The Authorship Of *Guardian* 69. *Berkeley News* 7,1–6 1984.

WINKLER, Rose–Luise. Soziologische Und Sozialpsychologische Probleme Der Wissenschaft Im Spiegel Sowjetischer Literatur (Literaturbericht). *Deut Z Phil* 33,462–467 1985.

The contribution analyzed problems in the development of Marxist research into the sociology of science. Particular importance is attached to the analysis of the interrelationship of cognitive and social factors in the process of scientific development. The thesis is put forward and explained that we are here concerned with a basic theoretical problem, both in the theory of science, in the sociology and psychology of science and in the theory of innovation as well as in other independent sub–areas of the science of science.

WINKLER, Ruthild and Eigen, Manfred. *Laws Of The Game: How The Principles Of Nature Govern Chance*. NY Harper & Row 1983.

WINOGRAD, Terry. Moving The Semantic Fulcrum. *Ling Phil* 8,91–104 F 85.

This paper examines Barwise and Perry's situation semantics from the viewpoint of artificial intelligence. It argues that although they provide an elegant framework in which to state some key problems, their theory does not lead to new solutions. The paper also questions the appropriateness of their assumptions about reality as a basis for the semantics of situated language, arguing that their theory is better suited to artificially formalized languages such as those used in programming.

WINSLADE, William J. Aspects Of Leon Green's Tort Theory: Causation And The Role Of The Judge. *Arch Rechts Soz* 61,369–386 1975.

Le pensée de *Leon Green* sur la responsabilité délictuelle ont influencé des avocats américains pendant plus années. Cet article examine d'une facon critique la pensée de *Greeen* quant à la structure fondamentale du droit, les fonctions des règles juridiques et les responsabilités du juge et du jury. (edited)

WINTER, Joseph C. "The Way To S0mewhere: Ethics In American Archaeology" in *Ethics And Values In Archaeology*, Green, Ernestene L (ed), 36–50. NY Free Pr 1984.

WINTERS, Laurence E and others (ed). *Continental Philosophy And The Arts*. Lanham Univ Pr Of America 1984.

WINTERS, Laurence E. "The Problematic Of Contemporary Art: Impasse Or Opening" in *Continental Philosophy/the Arts*, Winters, Laurence E and others (ed), 15–40. Lanham Univ Pr Of America 1984.

WINZELER, Peter. Zur Aktualität Der Politischen Theologie Ulrich Zwinglis. *Frei Z Phil Theol* 31,395–410 1984.

WINZER, Rosemarie. Erkenntnis Und Bewusste Gestaltung Sozialer Prozesse. *Deut Z Phil* 22,190–203 1974.

Die marxistisch–leninistische Gesellschaftstheorie hat, indem si die objektiv wirkenden Gesetze aufdeckt, die Gesellschaft durchschaubar gemacht. Sie befähigt die Arbeiterklasse zur bewufssten planmäfssigen Gestaltung der sozialistischen Gesellschaft. In der These von der angeblich zunehmenden Undurchschaubarkeit der gesellschaftlichen Verhältnisse widerspiegelt sich die Perspektivolsigkeit des kapitalistischen Systems, das Interesse der herrschenden Klasse an der ideologischen Verhüllung des Klassenantagonismus im Kapitalismus.

WIPPEL, John F. The Possiblity Of A Christian Philosophy: A Thomistic Perspective. *Faith Phil* 1,272–290 Jl 84.

WIPPEL, John F. Thomas Aquinas On The Distinction And Derivation Of The Many From The One: A Dialectic Between Being And Nonbeing. *Rev Metaph* 38,563–590 Mr 85.

WIRT, Adam. Die Dialektik Von Nationalem Und Internationalem In Der Entwicklung Der Sozialistischen Gesellschaft. *Deut Z Phil* 23,726–730 1975.

WISAN, Winifred Lovell. On Argument *Ex Suppositione Falsa*. *Stud Hist Phil Sci* 15,227–236 S 84.

It has been argued recently that Galileo had a method of demonstrating causes *ex suppositione*, derived apparently from St Thomas Aquinas. He didn't. The passages in Galileo which have been cited in support of this supposed method have been misinterpreted, while other passages which point to a quite different interpretation have been passed over.

WISDOM, John. "Mr Köllerström's Dream: Enlightenment And Happiness" in *Philosophy And Life: Essays On John Wisdom*, Dilman, Ilham (ed), 35–48. Boston Nijhoff 1984.

WISDOM, John. "What Is There In Horse Racing" in *Philosophy And Life: Essays On John Wisdom*, Dilman, Ilham (ed), 27–34. Boston Nijhoff 1984.

WITT, Charlotte. 'Form, Reproduction And Inherited Characteristics In Aristotle's GA'. *Phronesis* 30,46–57 1985.

I argue against David Balme's interpretation of Aristotle's explanation of inherited characteristics in *Generation of Animals* IV, 3. Balme argues that Aristotelian form is radically individual—i.E., it includes accidental properties. I argue that Balme's view is incompatible with the notion of form in the Metaphysics. Next, I propose an alternative interpretation in which I argue that the text does not require or imply radically individual forms but can be given an interpretation compatible with the Metaphysics.

WITTICH, Dieter. Fragen Der Philosophischen Lehre. *Deut Z Phil* 22,397–410 1974.

Die übereinstimmung von Unterrichtsstoff und –zeil erfolgt in der philosophischen Lehre nicht automatisch, sondern mufss erarbeitet werden. Zum anderen wirkt auf die Stoffgestaltung eine Reihe von Bedingungen, die den Grad der Realisierbarkeit der Einheit von Stoff und Zeil beeinflufsst. Welchen Anforderungen mufss der Unterrichtsstoff in der marxistischleninistischen Philosophie genügen? Welche Fragen sind mit der Problematik der Verständlichkeit des philosophischen Lehrstoffes verbunden? Auf diese und andere Kernfragen der philosophischen Lehre wird Antwort gegeben.

WITTKOWSKI, W. "Movement In German Poems" in *Existential Coordinates Of Human Condition*, Tymieniecka, A (ed), 23–36. Boston Reidel 1984.

WITTKOWSKI, W. "Values And German Tragedy 1770–1840" in *Existential Coordinates Of Human Condition*, Tymieniecka, A (ed), 319–332. Boston Reidel 1984.

WIZNER, Stephen. Discretionary Waiver Of Juvenile Court Jurisdiction: An Invitation To Procedural Arbitrariness. *Crim Just Ethics* 3,41–50 Sum/Fall 84.

WOHL, Andrzej. Sport As A Contemporary Form Of Cultural Motor Activity. *Dialec Hum* 11,75–86 Wint 84.

WOHLFART, G. "Der Punkt" in *Asthetische Er Fahrung Und Das Wesen Der Kunst*, Holzhey, Helmut, 93–106. Bern Haupt 1984.

WOHLFART, Gunter. Hamanns Kantkritik. *Kantstudien* 75,398–419 1984.

Im ersten Teil der überlegungen geht es um das Verhältnis Hamanns zu Kant. Es wird versucht zu zeigen, dass Hamanns Denken in der Auseinandersetzung mit Kants Verunftkritik im Grundproblem der Sprache seinen Schwerpunkt findet. Im zweiten Teil wird; ausgehend von der 'Metakritik über den Purismum der Vernunft' versucht, die Sprache als ästhetisches und logisches Vermögen zu kennzeichnen.

WOHLMAN, Avital. L'acte Libre Démission Ou Courage D'etre Devant Le Sensible Selon Jean Scot Érigène. *Rev Thomiste* 84,581–606 O–D 84.

Man's choice is at the heart of the two movements presiding the development of the

Periphyseon, "down" from the One to the many, "up" from the many back to unity. Corporeal multiplicity being the visible face of man's sin is simultaneous with creation itself. Again, on man's conversion depends the "comingback" of the all the One. Sin is man's identification of himself with his corporeity, negative non–being. As to pride inspiring this choice, it is not but the dissimulation of fear, i.e., man's fright of accepting himself as undefinable, his refusal to admit OUSIA, positive non–being, to be above cognition as the One its source and "place."

WOJCICKI, Ryszard. *Lectures On Propositional Calculi*, R Ladniak (ed). Lodz Ossolineum 1984.

The book aimed at presenting the Polish approach in the methodology of propositional calculi. In the first part of it, logical systems of inferences versus logical systems of theorems are examined. In the second, truth valuations and frames are presented. In the third, logical matrices are introduced and the properties of calculi determined by them are studied. Finally, in the last part selected topics in finite formalization and decidability are presented and some problems of comparing logics via definability relation are examined.

WOJCICKI, Ryszard. R Suszko's Situational Semantics. *Stud Log* 43,323–340 1984.

WOJNAR– SUJECKA, Janina. The Idea Of Socialism In Polish Social Thought At The Turn Of The 19th Century. *Dialec Hum* 10,209–216 Sum 83.

In 1878 a group of the first Polish Marxists put forth their socialist program. Since, there have been centenary–long discussions on the idea of socialism. The author considers common traits in the comprehension of socialism and the following controversial questions about it: Is socialism a ready or dynamic developing model? Is the idea of socialism incompatible with that of nation? Has it a moral value or only a political one?

WOJTYLAK, Piotr. A Proof Of Herbrand's Theorem. *Rep Math Log* 17,13–18 1984.

WOJTYLAK, Piotr. A Recursive Theory For The {Upsidedown L, Λ, V, →, o}: Fragment Of Intuitionistic Logic. *Rep Math Log* 18,3–36 1984.

The considered propositional logic results by adjoining a new intuitionistic operator o to the usual fragment of this logic. The monadic operator o(p) is defined as an infinite disjunction of all monadic formulas with p which are not derivable in Heyting's calculus. It has been proved that the resulting logic is decidable, not finitely axiomatizable and has not the interpolation property. An infinite axiomatization of this logic is also given there.

WOJTYLAK, Piotr. An Example Of A Finite Though Finitely Non–Axiomatizable Matrix. *Rep Math Log* 17,39–46 1984.

There is given an example of a five–element logical matrix N is the content of which, i.e., the set of all N–Tautologies, is not finitely axiomatizable using only a finite number of standard rules.

WOKUTCH, Richard E and Cox, James E and Carson, Thomas L. An Ethical Analysis Of Deception In Advertising. *J Bus Ethics* 4,93–104 Ap 85.

WOLENSKI, Jan. Rationalism And The Certainty Of Knowledge. *Dialec Hum* 11,319–328 Spr/Sum 84.

The paper examines epistemological claims of the classical and modern rationalism. Rationalism is described as the view that there is knowledge which is certain, absolutely true, necessary as well as synthetic in Kantian sense. The author argues that these claims are dubious from the point of view so–called metamathematical limitative theorems/theorems of Gödel, Tarski, and Church/. Additional arguments can be borrowed from the game–theoretical model of empirical sciences.

WOLF, Ursula. Zum Problem Der Willensschwäche. *Z Phil Forsch* 39,21–34 Ja–Mr 85.

Against the solutions proposed by Aristotle, Hare, Davidson, Kenny, the author argues that Akrasia in the strict sense (not to do what one thinks best while having the intention and ability) does not exist, the description being irresolvably contradictory. Rather, the phenomenon in question is some form of self–deception: The actor pleading for Akrasia wishes to be (seen as) a person who does X, but he doesn't really want to do X.

WOLFF, Kurt H. "Surrender–And–Catch And Hermeneutics". *Phil Soc Crit* 10,1–16 Sum 84.

Both "surrender"—experience of maximally bearable immediacy—and hermeneutics aim at understanding but have different historical presuppositions: tradition to be tested in maximally bearable suspension, because it has led us to our potential suicide; respectively to be reappropriated. The two also share a play element, which in surrender appears at the point where surrender—*to* becomes surrender itself, beyond the surrenderer's wil, and *between* surrender and "catch" (result, yield, find) where "everything" is "at play."

WOLFF, Kurt H. Discussion Of Wagner, Imber, And Rasmussen. *Human Stud* 7,133–140 1984.

WOLFF, Kurt H. Surrender–And–Catch And Phenomenology. *Human Stud* 7,191–210 1984.

WOLFHART, Günter. Das Unedliche Urteil: Zur Interpretation Eines Kapitels Aus Hegels "Wissenschaft Der Logic". *Z Phil Forsch* 39,85–100 Ja–Mr 85.

Durch die detaillierte Interpretation des Kapitels über das unendliche Urteil in Hegels großer Logik (Wissenschaft der Logik, 3 Buch, 1 Abschnitt, Kap 2A,c) soll die Verbindung zwischen der Bewegung des Urteils und der Bewegung des spekulativen Satzes aufgezeigt werden, der für die spekulative Methode Helgels insgesamt von der größten Bedeutung ist.

WOLGAST, Elizabeth H. Intolerable Wrong And Punishment. *Philosophy* 60,161–174 Ap 85.

The point of this essay was to test the rigor of a retributivist justification for punishment, i.e., the argument that punishment is justified by the offense or because it is what the offender deserves. I argue that these inferences fail. Injustice and wrong

may be intolerable, but this doesn't point the way to action, not human action. The justice and punishment dealt by the gods or Fate has a different moral status than what we do through human institutions. There are two stages, one human, the other supernatural; what is justified on one isn't necessarily justified on the other.

WOLLHEIM, Richard. *The Thread Of Life*. Littleton Harvard Univ Pr 1984.

WOLNIEWICZ, Boguslaw. A Topology For Logical Space. *Bull Sect Log* 13,255–259 D 84.

WOLSTENHOLME, Gordon. Teaching Medical Ethics In Other Countries. *J Med Ethics* 11,22–24 Mr 85.

In the past 20 years, around the world, there has been an explosion in the teaching of medical ethics. As the dust begins to settle, it would appear that such teaching is likely to have its most effective impact not during the undergraduate period but at the immediate postgraduate level and in continuing education. Whilst important contributions can be made by teachers of religion, philosophy and law, probably the essential wisdom, capable of standing a doctor in good stead throughout the developments of lifetime's career, must largely come from those who have studied both medicine and ethics. It would be appropriate if the study of medical ethics were to lead to better international understanding among doctors.

WOLTER, Allan B. "Duns Scotus On Intuition, Memory And Knowledge Of Individuals" in *History Of Philosophy In Making*, Thro, Linus J (ed), 81–104. Washington Univ Pr Of America 1982.

WOLTER, H and Dahn, Bernd I. Ordered Fields With Several Exponential Functions. *Z Math Log* 30,341–348 1984.

WOLTER, Helmut and Herre, Heinrich. Entscheidbarkeit Von Theorien In Logiken Mit Verallgemeinerten Quantoren. *Z Math Log* 21,229–246 1975.

WOLTER, Helmut. Entscheidbarkeit Der Arithmetik Mit Addition Und Ordnung In Logiken Mit Verallgemeinerten Quantoren. *Z Math Log* 21,321–330 1975.

WOLTER, Helmut. On The "Problem Of The Last Root" For Exponential Terms. *Z Math Log* 31,163–168 1985.

WOLTERS, Gereon. Ernst Mach And The Theory Of Relativity. *Phil Natur* 21,630–641 1984.

Documents uncovered recently as well as reinterpretation of those previously known lead to the conclusion that both of the texts attributed to *Ernst Mach* which reject *relativity theory* are forged (paricularly the preface to Mach's *optik*). The forgery is due to Mach's eldest son *Ludwig Mach*. An undated letter of *Einstein* to Mach revealing sympathy on Mach's side toward relativity cannot have been written before July 1913, the alleged date of the *Optik* preface.

WOLTERSTORFF, Nicholas (ed) and Plantinga, Alvin (ed). *Faith And Rationality: Reason And Belief In God*. Notre Dame Univ Notre Dame Pr 1983.

This book contains four long essays in the epistemology of religious belief: "Reason and Belief in God" by Alvin Plantinga, "Christian Experience and Christian Belief" by William P Alston, "Can Belief in God be Rational If It Has No Foundations?" By Nicholas Wolterstorff and "Jerusalem and Athens Revisited" by George Mavrodes. It also contains an essay on the theology of W Pannenburg, "Faith, Reason and the Resurrection" by David Holwerda, an essay by George Marsden entitled "The Collapse of American Evangelical Academia, and two fables by George Mavrodes. Perhaps the unifying theme of the book is consideration and rejection of the evidentialist objection to theistic belief, the claim that theistic belief is rational or appropriate only if there is adequate evidence for it of the general sort provided by sound theistic arguments.

WOLTERSTORFF, Nicholas. "Can Belief In God Be Rational If It Has No Foundations" in *Faith And Rationality*, Plantinga, Alvin (ed), 135–186. Notre Dame Univ Notre Dame Pr 1983.

WOLTERSTORFF, Nicholas. Art In Realist Perspective. *Ideal Stud* 15,87–99 My 85.

WOO, Kun–Yu. A Study On The Taoist Social Philosophy In The Pre–Ch'in Period (in Chinese). *Phil Rev (Taiwan)* 7,1–26 Ja 84.

This study is divided into three main parts, and additionally includes an introduction, conclusion, footnotes and a bibliography. The first section examines the historical development of the social philosophy propounded by the Pre–ch'in Taoists, from Lao–tzu through Chuang–tzu to Liehtzu. The second part deals with the Taoist principle of social living, its problems and solutions. Finally we attempt a critique on the values and the limitations of Taoist social philosophy in the Pre–ch'in period.

WOOD JR, Harold W. Modern Pantheism As An Approach To Environmental Ethics. *Environ Ethics* 7,151–164 Sum 85.

While philosophers debate the precise articulation of philosophical theory to achieve a desirable change in environmental attitudes, they may be neglecting the fountainhead of social change. Insofar as ordinary people are concerned, it is religion which is the greatest factor in determining morality. In order to achieve an enlightened environmental ethics, we need what can only be termed a "religious experience". While not denying the efficacy of other religious persuasions, I explore the contribution of an informed modern Pantheism to environmental ethics. The conceptual division of the holy and the world is rectified by pantheism. As a form of "nature mysticism," pantheism promotes a theological basis for achieving oneness with God through knowledge, devotion, and works, all of which establish an enlightened theory for environmental ethics. A modern pantheism bears investigation by those advocating new ethical approaches toward the environment.

WOOD, Allen W. "Marx And Morality" in *Darwin, Marx And Freud*, Caplan, Arthur L (ed), 131–146. NY Plenum Pr 1984.

WOOD, Allen W. Justice And Class Interests. *Philosophica* 33,9–32 1984.

Marx has often been interpreted as criticizing capitalism for injustice to the workers, despite the fact that he explicitly disavows criticism of capitalism on grounds of rights or justice. The present paper argues that those who interpret Marx in this way must pay a higher price than defiance of the letter of the texts: they must relinquish the

Marxian conception of revolutionary practice, based on the thesis that historical change results from the effectiveness of class interests; and it is this conception which provides Marxists with the only characteristically Marxian reason for expecting the eventual overthrow of capitalism.

WOOD, Carol and Saracino, Dan. Finite QE Rings In Characteristic *p²*. *Annals Pure Applied Log* 28,13–32 Ja 85.

WOOD, Gordon S. The Intellectual Origins Of The American Constitution. *Nat Forum* 64,5–8 Fall 84.

The intellectual origins of the American Constitution are broad and varied; they cannot be found in the thinking of any single individual. The sources include the classical republican values of antiquity, the ideas of mixed and balanced government, and the legal and constitutional traditions of England.

WOOD, J Scott and Goddard, Dorothy M and Mc Allister, Martin E. "Cultural Resource Law Enforcement In The US" in *Ethics And Values In Archaeology*, Green, Ernestene L (ed), 156–170. NY Free Pr 1984.

WOOD, Neal. *John Locke And Agrarian Capitalism.* Los Angeles Univ Of Calif Pr 1984.

WOOD, Rega and Adams, Marilyn McCord. Is To Will It As Bad As To Do It (The Fourteenth Century Debate)? *Fran Stud* 41,5–60 1981.

WOOD, Robert. "Oriental Themes In Buber's Work" in *Martin Buber*, Gordon, Haim (ed), 325–350. Beersheva Ktav 1984.

WOOD, Robert. Weiss On Adumbration. *Phil Today* 28,339–348 Wint 84.

WOODGER, J H (trans) and Tarski, Alfred. *Logic, Semantics, Meta–Mathematics.* Indianapolis Hackett 1983.

WOODHOUSE, Howard R. Moral And Religious Education For Nigeria. *J Moral Educ* 14,120–131 My 85.

The paper considers moral and religious education programs appropriate for Nigeria. Starting with a brief analysis of the current crisis in moral, spiritual and political beliefs, the paper progresses by analyzing traditional Nigerian education and the approach to moral education which it advocated. It then analyzes the epistemological underpinnings of traditional moral education as well as the social institutions supporting it. A brief section outlining certain shortcomings in traditional education follows. This is then followed by a consideration of contemporary approaches to both moral and religious education by focussing on the question of the possible independence of moral from religious education. Having agreed with certain writers that the two are independent, the paper concludes with a sub–section on the aims of moral education as a distinct activity.

WOODIN, Hugh and Shelah, Saharon. Forcing The Failure Of CH By Adding A Real. *J Sym Log* 49,1185–1189 D 84.

WOODRUFF, Peter W. On Supervaluations In Free Logic. *J Sym Log* 49,943–950 S 84.

WOODS, Michael (trans). *Aristotle's "Eudemian Ethics".* Oxford Clarendon Pr 1982.

This is a new translation of Books One. Two and Eight of the Eudemian Ethics, with a philosophical commentary, and notes on the text used for translation. The purpose of the work is to assist the understanding and evaluation of Aristotle's moral philosophy, and is intended for students and professional philosophers. This is the first commentary published in English and the Eudemian Ethics. These three books are of most contemporary philosophical interest.

WOODS, Michael. Kant's Transcendental Schematism. *J Brit Soc Phenomenol* 15,271–285 O 84.

WOODS, Michael. Sellars On Kantian Intuitions. *Philosophia (Israel)* 14,137–144 Ag 84.

This paper is a discussion of Wilfred Sellars' claim that Kantian intuitions may be conceptual in the broad sense of being representations of 'thises', illustrated by the form, 'This cube'. The main objection raised against this view is that a demonstrative singular expression cannot describe an empirical intuition, for any such description will conceptually determinate. Intuitions, therefore, are not linguistically representable.

WOODWARD, James. A Theory Of Singular Causal Explanation. *Erkenntnis* 21,231–262 N 84.

WOODWARD, James and Horgan, Terence. Folk Psychology Is Here To Stay. *Phil Rev* 94,197–226 Ap 85.

Paul Churchland and Stephan Stich recently have given distinct but related arguments for saying that "folk psychology" is radically false, i.E., that humans do not have beliefs, desires, or other propositional attitudes. We examine their arguments critically, and find them wanting. In particular, we argue that they each impose implausibly strong constraints upon the way that folk psychology must be related to lower–level theories in cognitive science or neuroscience in order to be compatible with them.

WOODWARD, James. Explanatory Asymmetries. *Phil Sci* 51,421–442 S 84.

This paper examines a recent attempt by Evan Jobe to account for the asymmetric character of many scientific explanations. It is argued that a purported counterexample to Jobe's account, from Clark Glymour, is inconclusive, but that the account faces independent objections. It is also suggested, contrary to Jobe, that the explanatory relation is not always asymmetric. (edited)

WOSHINSKY, Barbara. "Intuition In Britannicus" in *Existential Coordinates Of Human Condition*, Tymieniecka, A (ed), 417–424. Boston Reidel 1984.

WOZNICKI, Andrew N. *A Christian Humanism: Karol Wojtyla's Existential Personalism.* New Britain Mariel 1980.

The book is intended as an introduction to philosophical thought of Karol Wojtyla, presently Pope John Paul II. In view of the numerous areas of the present Pope's interests, the author attempts to outline his pre–Papal philosophical teaching under four headings, classifying them according to the discipline of Metaphysics, Phenomenology, Agapology, and Axiology. The focal point of the book is an attempt to show both textually and systematically that Wojtyla was not a phenomenologist in a strict sense.

WOZNICKI, Theresa (trans) and Krąpiec, Mieczylaw A and Lescoe, Marie (trans). *I–Man: An Outline Of Philosophical Anthropology.* New Britain Mariel 1983.

WREEN, Michael. Breathing A Little Life Into A Distinction. *Phil Stud* 46,395–402 N 84.

The concepts of killing and letting die are first distinguished, then analyzed. Conceptual analysis reveals them to be very similar: both concern the causal structure of events leading to death, vis–a–vis the person said to kill or let die; both are morally freighted; both include an element of agent accountability in their analysis; both are morally blameworthy, other things being equal; both are *prima facie* wrong, but the *prima facie* wrongness of each can be overridden in some circumstances, and the killing or letting die be right, permissible, praiseworthy, or morally ambiguous; both admit of being done intentionally or knowingly, or through recklessness or negligence; and both can be justified or excused. However if the notion of basic rights is acceptable, there is still good reason to think that killing is *prima facie* worse than letting die, even though the difference between the two is a small one.

WREEN, Michael. In Defense Of Speciesism. *Ethics Animals* 5,47–60 S 84.

The main thesis of this paper is that all members of our species have a right to life. The principal argument for it employs premise, some of which are metaphysical (or quasi–metaphysical), some of which are empirical, and some of which are moral. A number of objections to the argument are also considered, and the paper ends with a caveat or two.

WREEN, Michael. Mackie On The Objectivity Of Values. *Dialectica* 39,147–156 1985.

This paper is a critical analysis of J L mackie's arguments (in chapter one of his *Ethics*) for the view that there are no objective values. After some initial clarificatory points, Mackie's arguments are reconstructed, then slowly and carefully assessed. All are found wanting. Some positive suggestions for a naturalistic objective construal of valuational claims are briefly mentioned, and it argued (following Aristotle) that the burden of proof still lies with the subjectivist.

WREEN, Michael. The Restoration And Reproduction Of Works Of Art. *Dialogue (Canada)* 24,91–100 Spr 85.

WRIEDT, Markus. Gebet Und Theologie: Skizzen Zur Neubesinnung Des Gebetes Im Kontext Der Systematisch–Theologischen Theoriebildung. *Frei Z Phil Theol* 31,421–452 1984.

In the phenomenology of religion as well as from the perspective of systematic theology, prayer is a personal experience of the coincidence of transcendence and immanence, which occurs immanently. We define it as a human act of communication, not necessarily a verbal one. In systematic theology it means the verification of the content of Christian doctrine. A brief overview of the traditional themes of Christian dogmatics shows that only those doctrines could last, which were based upon verification through the experience of prayer.

WRIGHT, Crispin and Read, Stephen. Hairier Than Putnam Thought. *Analysis* 45,56–58 Ja 85.

In *Realism and Reason* Hilary Putnam suggests a solution to the Sorites, or "bald man", paradox through intuitionistic logic, in which the denial of a sharp cutoff is not equivalent to the universal conditional apparently needed to derive contradiction. We show paradox still follows from other intuitionistic principles, and the nearest intuitionism comes to the correct logic of vagueness is in neither asserting nor denying statements whose contradictories must be denied.

WRIGHT, Crispin. Comment On Lowe's "Wright *Versus* Lewis On The Transitivity Of Counterfactuals". *Analysis* 44,183–185 O 84.

This note argues that apparent failures of transitivity among counter–factual conditionals cannot straightforwardly be explained, as Lowe suggests, by appeal to pragmatic (contrast: semantic) considerations and re–asserts the claim, made in the author's "Keeping Track of Nozick" (*analysis* 43.3, June 1983, 134–140), that transitivity is valid for counter–factual conditionals in context. It is contended that this involves not, pace Lowe, that the validity of inferences is context relative but that the content of type–counter–factuals is. The note concludes with a gloss on the previous criticism of Nozick on tracking.

WRIGHT, Crispin. Kripke's Account Of The Argument Against Private Language. *J Phil* 81,759–777 D 84.

The paper argues that the 'skeptical argument' which Kripke (*Wittgenstein on Rules and Private Language*) finds in Wittgenstein is marred by a dubious implicit epistemology of intention; and that a cogent argument against private language cannot, in any case, emerge from the 'skeptical solution' in the manner sketched by Kripke.

WRIGHT, Edmond L. A Defence Of Sellars. *Phil Phenomenol Res* 46,73–90 S 85.

This is a defense of and an adaptation of Wilfrid Sellars' theory of perception. There have recently been a number of attacks upon it from varying points of view, all of which, it is claimed, can be satisfactorily met if the consequences of the nonepistemic nature of the sensorium are broughtt out. If the distinction between epistemic perceiving and nonepistemic sensing (apt for punctiform propositionalized description at the level of the field) is made clear, then the customary objections (the Homunculus Objection, the Solipsism Objection, the accusations of ambiguity, of empirical improbability, etc.) have no purchase on a representational theory such as that of Sellars'. What is more, a theory of object and person–reference (including that of the self) can be sustained which meets, and meets by absorbing harmlessly, radical scepticism.

WRIGHT, Kathleen. The Place Of The Work Of Art In The Age Of Technology. *S J Phil* 22,565–582 Wint 84.

This essay uses Benjamin's *The Work of Art in the Age of Mechanical Reproduction* to challenge Heidegger's claim that art is a saving power given the danger of technology. It argues that the art work is not exempt from homelessness, the danger of technology, that it discloses this danger in an exemplary way, and finally that it serves as an exemplar for the overcoming of homelessness in the way that it embodies place.

WRIGHT, Richard A and Newton, Lisa. "The Borrowed Syllabus". *Teach Phil* 7,235–240 Jl 84.

WRIGHT, T R. Regenerating Narrative: The Gospels As Fiction. *Relig Stud* 20,389–400 S 84.

Kermode's analysis of the generating structures of narrative in the gospels can be criticized for neglecting history, since although he pays some attention to the conditions of meaning appertaining at the time they were produced, he abandons all interest in the facts to which they refer. Recognition of the dynamic capacity of narrative to 'redescribe' life, however, helps to give the gospels continuing vitality.

WROBLEWSKI, Jerzy. Legal Language And Legal Interpretation. *Law Phil* 4,239–256 Ag 85.

The legal language in which legal norms are formulated is a fuzzy language. Legal interpretation in the narrow sense occurs when there are doubts concerning the meaning of legal norms. These doubts are identified and related with the singled out three types of fuzziness. The justified interpretative decision is treated either as a determination of a meaning in the legal language or as its situational use.

WRONA, V and Richter, Friedrich. Neukantianismus Und Sozialreformismus. *Deut Z Phil* 22,269–288 1974.

Durch den formalen Rückgriff auf die praktische Philosophie I. Kants wird dessen revolutionär–kritisches Wirken um die ideologische Einheit des dritten Standes in der Zeit der Vorbereitung der bürgerlichen Revolution durch die Neukantianer in eine völlig andere geschichtliche Epoche transponiert und damit versucht, die opportunistische Idee der Klassenversöhnung als Menschheitsinteresse auszugeben, den Klassenkampf auf bürgerliche Reformpolitik zu beschränken und die Notwendigkeit der sozialistischen Revolution zu leugnen.

WRONA, Vera. Sozialismus—Humanismus—Toleranz. *Deut Z Phil* 32,756–766 1984.

Ziel des Artikels ist es, zum Verständnis von Sozialismus–Humanismus und Toleranz beizutragen. Marxisten gehen von der Auffassung aus, daß sich im Toleranzgedanken ein wichtiger aTeilaspekt des Humanismus widerspiegelt, der von aufsteigenden, gegen soziale und geistige Unterdrückung kämpfenden Klassen und Schichten stets vertreten wurde. Hiervon ausgehend, wird der Frage nachgegangen, welche Möglichkeiten sich heute in der weltweiten Auseinandersetzung zwischenden Kräften des Friedens und des Krieges für ein gemeinsames Zusammengehen ergibt.

WRONA, V. Vernunft Contra Unvernunft Zu Georg Lukács' Faschismus–Kritik. *Deut Z Phil* 33,173–177 1985.

Im Jahre 1954 erschien Georg Lukacs bedeutendes philophisches Werk "Die Zerstörung der Vernunft". Es ist das Ergebnis jahrzehntelaner Beschäftigung mit der Entwicklung der bürgerlichen Philosophie und Soziologie. In ihm werden die Genese wie die Wirkungsmechanismen der faschistischen Ideologie untersucht. Zum Verstädnis seiner Arbeit tragen vor allem seine Schriften "Wie ist die faschistische Detschland zum Zentrum der reaktrionären Ideologie geworden?" Laslo Sziklai, Leiter des Lukacs–Archivs in Budapest, hat diese Arbeiten erstmalig in deutscher Sprache zugänglich gemacht. Da zwischen bei den Arbeiten ein Zeitraum von 10 Jahren leigt, tragen seine inform mativen Einleitungen wesentlich zum Verständniss des "zeitgeistes" bei, die diese Schriften durchziehen. In beiden Arbeiten werden politische, ideologische und theoretische Wandlungen in den Auffassungen von Georg Lukasz besonders sichtbar. Ohne ihre Kenntnis ist "Zerstörung der Vernunft" nicht voll verständlich.

WUCHTERL, Kurt. *Lehrbuch Der Philosophie.* Stuttgart Haupt 1984.

This work is considered to be an introduction to philosophy dealing with essential philosophical questions, fundamental notions, methods and insights; beyond this it regards to didactical aspects. The arrangement of the four paragraphs— philosophical anthropology, philosophy of science, ethics and metaphysics—obeys the same principles: fundamental questions—representation of a classical solution— analysis of central notions—explanation of some problems—presentation of representatives and exposition of recent discussions.

WYATT, J F and Gray, W N. Justifying A Curriculum And Justifying An Institution. *J Applied Phil* 2,63–68 Mr 85.

The recent revival of interest in theory leads the writers to examine a particular moment when a curriculum and the institution in which it occurred was explained and justified. Max Horkheimer's inaugural address to the Institute for Social Research in 1931 is summarized. The points made by the new Director of the Institute are examined in relation not only to his proposal for an inter–disciplinary curriculum, but also to the nature of the institution and to the general justification of higher education. The article concludes with a number of comments on the relevance of these proposals to some modern higher education issues.

WYDICK, Richard C and Schwartz, Mortimer D. *Problems In Legal Ethics.* St Paul West 1983.

WYKSTRA, Stephen J. The Humean Obstacle To Evidential Arguments From Suffering: On Avoiding The Evils Of "Appearance". *Int J Phil Relig* 16,73–94 1984.

WYSCHOGROD, Michael. "Buber's Evaluation Of Christianity: A Jewish Perspective" in *Martin Buber*, Gordon, Haim (ed), 457–472. Beersheva Ktav 1984.

WYSS, B. "Überlistete Vernunft" in *Asthetische Er Fahrung Und Das Wesen Der Kunst*, Holzhey, Helmut, 58–70. Bern Haupt 1984.

XIULIANG, Lan. Hegel's Evaluation And Analysis Of Socrates' Proposition "Virtue Is Knowledge". *Chin Stud Phil* 16,22–30 Wint 84–85.

YABLO, Stephen. Truth And Reflection. *J Phil Log* 14,297–348 Ag 85.

Originally we think that (1) 'S is true' is true iff S is true, and false iff S is untrue; and that (2) logically complex sentences owe their semantical properties to the semantical properties of their parts. However Kripke's Fixed Point Semantics violates (1), and Herzberger's and Gupta's Stability Semantics violates (2). Although our Stage Semantics satisfies (1) and (2), it generates paradoxes. Since intuitively there *are* paradoxes, this is a correct result.

YACOBUCCI, Guillermo J. El Racionalismo En El Inicio Del Inmanentismo Jurídico. *Sapientia* 40,121–142 Ap–Je 85.

YAGISAWA, Takashi. The Referential And The Attributive: A Distinction In Use? *S J Phil* 23,109–126 Spr 85.

I argue for two claims: (i) Donnellan's distinction does not arise from a difference in speaker's meaning; (ii) if Donnellan's distinction arises from a difference in the mode and the role of the speaker's cognition of the object she is concerned with in her use of a definite description, then it is a cloudy, indefinite distinction based on an unacceptably simplistic picture of the mechanism of the formation of the speaker's intention of utterance.

YANAL, Robert J. Hart, Dworkin, Judges, And New Law. *Monist* 68,388–402 Jl 85.

Hart: Judges sometimes make new law; the open texture of the law permits this; this is good because the law can cover cases not imagined by legislators. Dworkin: Judges ought not to make new law; judicially created new law is ex post facto and thus unfair; the law contains sufficient rules and principles for judges to reach a decision. Argued: Dworkin's view is unconvincing; but not all judicially created law is unfair.

YANDELL, Keith E. The Problem Of Evil. *Phil Topics* 12,7–38 Wint 81.

YANGYUORO, Yvon. Dagara Traditional Cultic Sacrifice As A Thematization Of Ultimate Reality And Meaning. *Ultim Real Mean* 7,209–219 S 84.

YANNARAS, Christos. *The Freedom Of Morality.* Crestwood St Vladimirs Pr 1984.

YANUVA, Jana. Logico–Semantic Aspects Of Truthfulness. *Bull Sect Log* 13,125–131 O 84.

YARTZ, Frank J. *Ancient Greek Philosophy: Sourcebook And Perspective.* Jefferson McfarIand 1984.

Ancient Greek Philosophy presents the history of ancient Greek philosophy through the theme of *logos* as it appears in the PreSocratics, Plato, and Aristotle. Scholarly notes are to be found at the end of each major section for the required documentation and also to provide for the advanced student a *research tool* for ancient Greek Philosophy. The book also contains a sourcebook in which the philosophers speak for themselves on the issues. The sourcebook as it stands (either with or without the approach taken in the book) can be used as a basis for a course in ancient Greek philosophy.

YASUGI, Mariko. "The Hahn—Branch Theorem And A Restricted Inductive Definition" in *Lecture Notes In Mathematics*, Muller, G H And Others (ed), 359–394. NY Springer 1981.

YEAGER, Leland B. "Is There A Bias Toward Overregulation" in *Rights And Regulation*, Machan, Tibor (ed), 99–126. Cambridge Ballinger 1983.

YI, Wu. On Chinese Ch'an In Relation To Taoism. *J Chin Phil* 12,131–154 Je 85.

YODER, John H. *When War Is Unjust: Being Honest In Just War Thinking.* Minneapolis Augsburg 1984.

"just war thinking" is the official position of most Christian churches. It purports to limit the moral acceptance of war to cases meeting certain criteria. This text surveys historically whether "Just war thinking" has in fact effectively restrained war. It concludes that if those who claim that their acceptance of war as morally justifiable is subject to restraints, they need to "be honest" by developing means (attitudes, concepts, institutions) making real limits effective.

YODER, John H. *When War Is Unjust: Being Honest In Just–War Thinking.* Minneapolis Augsburg 1984.

The "Just War Tradition", which holds that the morality of a particular war can be adjudicated by means of several criteria, is described logically and historically. It is then argued that to apply that position with integrity would demand being concretely critical of current military planning, to the point of admitting that some causes may not be validly served by war.

YODER, John H. A Consistent Alternative View Within The Just War Family. *Faith Phil* 2,112–120 Ap 85.

The Just War Tradition has in the past generally called for (a) applying numerous criteria in the moral evaluation of war, with (b) one of these always being deontological prohibition of the direct intentional killing of the innocent. This study draws attention to a variant but coherent view held (e.G.) by Admiral John Fisher, George Orwell, and John Foster Dulles, according to which the obligation of noncombatant immunity may be properly overridden. The advocates and interpreters of the classical Just War Theory have not adequately come to terms with the divergence of this view and its impact on the consistency and credibility of the entire Just War Tradition.

YORK, Ann. Human Sexuality And Marriage. *Relig Hum* 19,132–137 Sum 85.

YOSHIKAWA, M J. Culture, Cognition And Communication. *Commun Cog* 17,377–386 1984.

This article deals with a brief description of the nature of human being, culture and communication as perceived by Martin Buber, Buddha and Gregory Bateson. Their view of the human interactive pattern with his/her enviornment is basically perceived as the "paradoxical relationship". Humans can be perceived as distinguishable from their environment while they are inseparable from it, being dynamically interconnected in the same continuum. Such a perception adds a viable dimension to the understanding of intercultural communication.

YOUNG, Gary. Doing Marx Justice. *Can J Phil* Supp 7,251–268 1981.

Marx said that in capitalist production the worker is robbed but treated justly. This position is consistent because it refers to two distinct transactions: the worker's sale of labor power in the market (just) and the extraction of the worker's surplus labor in production (robbery). But the former is a mere appearance; only the latter is real. In reality capitalist production is pure robbery. Contrary interpretations of Marx by Allen, Wood and Husami are wrong.

YOUNG, J Michael. Construction, Schematism, And Imagination. *Topoi* 3,123–132 D 84.

Kant holds that arithmetical knowledge rests on the construction of concepts in intuition. He also holds that the construction of such concepts involves their schematization. Proper interpretation of his views concerning arithmetic can therefore illuminate his notion of a schema, and with it his view of imagination.

YOUNG, James O. Pragmatism And The Fate Of Philosophy. *Dialogue (Canada)* 23,683–686 D 84.

Richard Rorty has suggested that pragmatism does away with the need for a theory of truth, in particular, and philosophy, in general. I argue that a theory of truth is necessary for a variety of theoretical and practical purposes, and, therefore, so is philosophy.

YOUNG, Theodore A. "Our Non–Ethical Educational Ethos" in *The Georgetown Symposium On Ethics*, Porreco, Rocco (ed), 269–278. Lanham Univ Pr Of America 1984.

YOUNG, Thomas. "The Morality Of Killing Animals: Four Arguments". *Ethics Animals* 5,88–101 D 84.

First, I examine two versions of the argument for moral consistency, one associated with Regan and one with Singer. Both are rejected. I then argue that Singer's Preference Utilitarianism does not entail that killing self–conscious beings is (usually) wrong. The position I think it entails is developed, namely, that there is nothing wrong with killing "noncognizant" beings when utility is maximized. Two objections are dismissed and the notion of rational preferences is discussed.

YOVEL, Yirmiyahu. Kant And The History Of Philosophy (in Hebrew). *Iyyun* 33,12–29 Ja–Ap 84.

A translation into Hebrew of Chapter 6 of the author's recent book: *Kant and the Philosophy of History* (Princeton University Press, 1980). Kant's architectonic of reasons is analyzed, and Kant is shown to have traced an organic view of the history of philosophy preceding that of Hegel. The empirical history of philosophy is the historization of the pure architectonic of reason, and is supposed to move, through antinomies, collapses and new philosophical revolutions, toward a full "scientific" explication of the system of reason.

YÜ, Chun–Fang. Chinese Buddhist Responses To Contemporary Problems. *J Dharma* 10,60–74 Ja–Mr 85.

YU, Paul. Analyticity And Apriority: The Qine–Putnam Dispute. *Philosophia (Israel)* 14,41–64 Ag 84.

(1) I argue with Putnam against Quine that there are unproblematic notions of meaning and analyticity, and I try to offer a general framework for a theory of meaning. (2) I try to show that Quine and Putnam are in agreement, though for different reasons, that there is no notion of analyticity that can ground unrevisability. (3) Finally, I defend Quine's thesis that there is no such thing as an unrevisable belief by reiterating his historical argument and by showing that Putnam's putative example of an unrevisable belief cannot escape the scope of Quine's argument.

YUDKIN, Marcia. The Power Of Ideas: China's Campaign Against Ideological Pollution. *Humanist* 45,5–7 Ja–F 85.

YULINA, N S. On Popper's Implicit Hegelianism. *Phil Natur* 21,652–661 1984.

ZAGARE, Frank C. *Game Theory: Concepts And Applications.* Beverly Hills Sage 1984.

In this book, I provide a brief, yet comprehensive overview of the major divisions of game theory and demonstrate the applicability of game theory for analyzing a wide variety of conflict and interest situations. The rudimentary concepts and principal assumptions of the theory are discussed, as are two–person zero–sum and nonzero–sum games, and both cooperative and noncooperative n–person games. The extensive, normal, and characteristic function forms are representing games are explained, and the Minimax Theorem described. Numerous applications of the theory are included.

ZAGORIN, Perez. Berlin On Vico. *Phil Quart* 35,290–295 Jl 85.

This paper is a reply to Isaiah Berlin's critique of a previous paper on Vico by Zagorin in *Philosophical Quarterly* January, 1984. It discusses further Vico's theory of knowledge and continues its criticism of several views advanced by Berlin concerning Vico's conception of cause and of historical understanding.

ZAHARIA, D N. La Palingénesie De La Théorie Scientifique. *Phil Log* 27,331–340 O–D 83.

ZAHRA, Shaker A. Background And Work Experience Correlates Of The Ethics And Effect Of Organizational Politics. *J Bus Ethics* 4,419–423 O 85.

Empirical studies exploring managerial views of organizational politics (OP) are scarce. Furthermore, the literature is replete with inconsistent results regarding the correlates of OP. In this paper, data collected from 302 managers were used to examine the association between seven background and work experience variables and managerial attitudes regarding the ethics, locus, affect of OP on the organization, and the motives behind political maneuvering in the workplace. The results, however, show that association between managers' background and work experience factors and attitudes regarding OP is weak. The results suggest several promising lines of inquiry for future research.

ZAK, Christian. Gesellschaftswissenschaftliche Methoden Auf Dem Wege Der Gesetzeserkenntnis. *Deut Z Phil* 33,500–508 1985.

ZANARDI, William J. Comments: Aims And Forms Of Discourse Regarding Nietzsche's Truth-Telling. *Int Stud Phil* 16,67–70 1984.

Recent studies of inconsistencies between Nietzsche's truth–claims and his claims about truth have pursued different aims. This commentary identifies the forms of discourse appropriate to these aims. It concludes that the inconsistencies appear troublesome only against the backdrop of the traditional epistemological worries Nietzsche sought to discard. Critics of his inconsistencies should be aware of his post–traditional project and the novel form of discourse which it employs.

ZANARDI, William J. Nietzsche's Speech Of Indirection: Commentary On Laurence Lampert's "*Beyond Good And Evil*: Nietzsche's 'Free Spirit' Mask". *Int Stud Phil* 16,53–56 1984.

Why do masks occur in Nietzsche's philosophizing? This commentary clarifies one of the fundamental reasons. His positive doctrine sets restraints on how he communicates its content, viz., he must (1) keep faith with the thesis of perspectivism, (2) surpass the negativity of the skeptic, and (3) while doing the latter, avoid substituting a new metaphysics for the one he attacks. To meet these requirements, Nietzsche experiments with a two–level discourse similar to that of the ironic speaker.

ZANDVOORT, Henk and En Kuipers, Theo. Empirische Wetten En Theorieën. *Kennis Methode* 9,49–63 1985.

ZANER, Richard M. Is "Ethicist" Anything To Call A Philosopher? *Human Stud* 7,71–90 1984.

ZAVALA, Silvio. Fray Alonso De La Veracruz, Iniciador Del Derecho Agrario En Mexico. *Rev Filosof (Mexico)* 17,345–358 My–Jl 84.

The Augustinian professor of Theology Alonso de la Veracruz, dedicated his first course (1553–1555) at the recently established University of Mexico (1551) to contemporary matters, as his mentor Francisco de Vitoria, O P had done at the University of Salamanca. His opus *De dominio infidelium et iusto bell* examines Spain's reasons for justifying her sovereignty over the West Indies and the Third Doubt limits Spanish rights to the natives' lands.

ZAW, Susan Khin. Morality, Survival And Nuclear War. *Philosophy* 17,171–194 84 Supp.

ZDANOWICZ, Piotr. The Dialectics Of "Essence" And "Existence". *Dialec Hum* 10,111–126 Sum 83.

ZEIS, John. The Concept Of Eternity. *Int J Phil Relig* 16,61–71 1984.

In this article the author attempts to present an analysis of the concept of eternity which solves the problems of the relation between a timeless, omnipotent, omniscient deity and a temporal world. The analysis utilizes Geach's theory of the relation between thought and language as an analogue for the relation between God's will and the world.

ZELENÝ, Jindřich. Modifications In The Foundations Of Modern Science (in Czechoslovakian). *Filozof Cas* 32,760–779 1984.

The paper deals with philosophical, i.E., logico–ontological, foundations of contemporary scientific thought. It argues that the dialectico–materialist evolutionary mode of thought is needed for summarizing the results of contemporary science and for providing a viable logico–ontological basis for its further development. From this point of view, Prigogine's philosophical conceptions are evaluated.

ZELGER, Josef. Die Beziehungen Des Menschen Zum Oikos: Ein Konstruktiver Rahmen Für Die Sinnfrage. *Conceptus* 18,94–160 1984.

ZELIKOVITZ, Kelly M and Wilkins, Burleigh T. Principles For Individual Actions. *Philosophia (Israel)* 14,299–320 D 84.

ZEMACH, E M. Numbers. *Synthese* 64,225–240 Ag 85.

This is a nominalistic account of what numbers are. The logic I use relativizes identity to location, such that the things A and B may be identical at M and not at N. Now the human activity of counting can be regarded as a complex object, and every counting is a structured material thing. Mr Smith, e.G., may be the quarterback in one football game, and be the town's mayor in another (the civic) game. In just that way an apple may be the number ten in one counting game and the number five in another. The various roles in the counting game are the parts of that counting as considered a physical thing; these are the numbers, which are therefore identical with various physical objects *at* various countings.

ZEMACH, Eddy M. Speaking Of Belief. *Austl J Phil* 63,78–83 Mr 85.

ZEMAN, Jiří. Ontological And Epistemological Aspect Of Contradictions: Importance For Analysis Of Development Of Society (in Czechoslovakian). *Filozof Cas* 32,483–493 1984.

The philosophical problems of the contradictoriness have to be connected with the new important results of special sciences (such as physics, astronomy, cybernetics, etc.). Each object (the world as a whole, too) can be conceived as a dynamical system in imbalance. Physical, biological, psychic processes are characterized by the gradient flow between two opposite levels, namely the entropic and negentropic tendencies. The expanding universe has the bottom level of maximum density and the top level of minimum density of matter; at the same time we can speak—in opposite sense—about the minimum and maximum density of negentropy (in evolution). The objective contradictions are reflected in cognition. The contradictoriness in cognition must be connected with the objective, natural laws and contradictoriness.

ZEMAN, Jiří. Problems Of Creation And Order (in Czechoslovakian). *Filozof Cas* 32,802–807 1984.

The article deals with the problems of the creation, becoming and origin of order. The author makes a short analysis of the ideas of I Prigogine and M Eigen and further, the criticism of the approaches of J E Boodin, A E Wilder Smith and H Titze. Then, he explains the viewpoint of dialectical materialism in this field and makes the comparison with teleologism, creationalism and mechanical determinism. The origin of order and negentropy cannot be elucidated on the basis of three laws of thermodynamics only.

ZEMAN, J. Remarks Concerning The Problems Of Dialectical Logic (in Czechoslovakian). *Filozof Cas* 33,466–473 1985.

ZEMAN, J. The Problem Of The Integration Of Knowledge And Interdisciplinarity From The Viewpoint Of Biological Sciences (in Czechoslovakian). *Filozof Cas* 33,397–400 1985.

ZEPHYR, Jacques J. Simone De Beauvoir Et La Femme. *Rev Univ Ottawa* 54,37–53 Ja–Mr 84.

This book is an analytic and synthetic study of Simone de Beauvoir's theories and new ideas on women, resulting from an evolution in her thought after 1949, date of the publication of *The Second Sex*. This study is not a work of criticism, which proposes to judge, evaluate and discuss the author's ideas. Its aim is to gather in meticulous fashion the ideas expressed by the famous writer–philosopher in all her writings after *The Second Sex*, in order to present an objective and impartial summation of her present positions on the problems of "la condition féminine." This study intends to establish the *true position* of Simone de Beauvoir on new feminist theories, by means of parallels and cross–references with *The Second Sex*. Nowhere in the writings in question has de Beauvoir either formulated or associated herself with a comprehensive feminist doctrine. (edited)

ZHIMING, Yuan and Dezhen, Xue. The Scientific Character Of Marxism And Its Viewpoint Of Value. *Chin Stud Phil* 16,65–82 Wint 84–85.

ZHONGHUA, Chen and Runqing, Ma. The Value Of Man And The Building Of Two Civilizations. *Chin Stud Phil* 16,3–16 Fall 84.

ZIEGLER, Heinz. La Lecture Rationnelle—Nécessaire Et Facilement Assimilable (in German). *Deut Z Phil* 22,91–94 1974.

ZIESCHE, Eva. Unbekannte Manuskripte Aus Der Jenaer Und Nürnberger Zeit Im Berliner Hegel–Nachlass. *Z Phil Forsch* 29,430–444 Jl–S 75.

ZIFF, Paul. Antiaesthetics: An Appreciation Of The Cow With The Subtile Nose. Boston Reidel 1984.

ZIFF, Paul. Epistemic Analysis: A Coherence Theory Of Knowledge. Boston Reidel 1984.

ZIHLMAN, Adrienne L. Gathering Stories For Hunting Human Nature. *Fem Stud* 11,365–378 Sum 85.

How do books written by women on the evolution of human social behavior compare to those written by men? This article reviews six books and articles written by three women and three men and explores the range of ideas they present. Women's contributions have enriched the debate on sex and gender in evolution by providing perspectives and points of view that differ from each other as well as from those of men.

ZIMBARG, J and Hiller, A P. Self–Reference With Negative Types. *J Sym Log* 49,754–773 S 84.

ZIMMERLI, W Ch. "Die Ästhetisch–Semiotische Relation Und Das Problem" in *Asthetische Er Fahrung Und Das Wesen Der Kunst*, Holzhey, Helmut, 173–189. Bern Haupt 1984.

ZIMMERLI, Walter. Die Wahrheit Des 'Impliziten Denkers': Zur Logikbegründungsproblematik In Hegels "Wissenschaft Der Logik". *Stud Phil (Switzerland)* 41,139–160 1982.

Starting from the "scandalon of logic" that formal logic itself seems neither capable nor in need of its own justification the author understands Hegel's "logik" as the 'self–justification of logic'. It's program consists in the *explicit* reconstruction of that which has been used *implicitly* in the construction itself. The point where this change from implicit use to explicit mentioning takes place (the "implicit thinker"), is in Hegel's logic to be found in the section "Subjectivity". An interpretative analysis of Hegel's comments "On the Concept in general" shows that Hegel thematises metaphysical propositions as objects of a logic which—in so doing—justifies itself pragmatically.

ZIMMERMAN, David (ed) and Copp, David (ed). *Morality, Reason And Truth: New Essays On The Foundations Of Ethics*. Totowa Rowman & Allanheld 1984.

A collection of mainly previously unpublished essays on the foundations of morality. The issues which are emphasized are the relation between moral justification and the theory of practical reason, and the place of morality in a scientific view of the world. Contents: Introduction by David Copp. Essays by Gilbert Harman, Nicholas Sturgeon, David Zimmerman, Richard Brandt, Norman Daniels, Copp, Ronald deSousa, Kurt Baier, Kai Nielsen, Jan Narveson, David Gauthier, Richmond Campbell, Gregory Kavka.

ZIMMERMAN, David. "Moral Realism And Explanatory Necessity" in *Morality, Reason And Truth*, Copp, David (ed), 79–103. Totowa Rowman & Allanheld 1984.

ZIMMERMAN, Michael E. Heidegger's "Existentialism" Revisited. *Int Phil Quart* 24,219–236 S 84.

This essay analyzes Heidegger's Marburg Lectures to explain how his thought might have at one time been labeled "existentialist." I argue that while Heidegger was never an existentialist thinker like Sartre or Camus, he nevertheless emphasized that resoluteness or authenticity is a necessary condition for a philosopher who seeks genuine ontological insight.

ZIMMERMAN, Michael F. The Critique Of Natural Rights And The Search For A Non–Anthropocentric Basis For Moral Behavior. *J Value Inq* 19,43–54 1985.

In recent years, many thinkers (including Alasdair MacIntyre) have called into question the notion of natural rights, which forms the basis for much modern ethical thought. Ethics based on natural rights is notoriously anthropocentric and helps justify the human domination of Nature. The essay asks whether it is possible to discover a non–anthropocentric basis for ethics that does not have to appeal to the questionable idea of "natural rights," and that also transforms our current treatment of non–human beings.

ZIMMERMAN, Michael J. An Essay On Human Action. NY Lang 1984.

In Part I, an account of events as abstract entities is presented. In Part II, an account is given of: what acting in general is; how actions are to be individuated; how long actions last; what acting intentionally is; what doing one thing by doing another is; and what omitting to do something is. In Part III, a libertarian account of free action is tentatively proposed and defended.

ZIMMERMAN, Michael J. Sharing Responsibility. *Amer Phil Quart* 22,115–122 Ap 85.

It is often claimed than an individual's responsibility (here taken to be blameworthiness) for the outcome of some past action or omission is diminished simply by virtue of the fact that other individuals are also responsible for this outcome. Distinctions are drawn between "standard" and "oversupplied", and between "simultaneous" and "sequential", group action and group omission, and in each case it is argued that sharing responsibility with another does not necessarily diminish one's own.

ZIMMERMAN, R I. A Comment On Ken Westphal's "Nietzsche's Sting And The Possibility Of Good Philology". *Int Stud Phil* 16,91–102 1984.

This article attempts to reconcile the perspectivist and the cognitivist interpreters of Nietzsche by arguing that they are, in general, not contradictory, and that, in Nietzsche's case in particular, it is only *through* perspectives on and of itself that Will to Power reveals itself.

ZIMMERMAN, Rainer E. Albert Einstein——Versuch Einer Totalisierenden Würdigung. *Phil Natur* 21,126–138 1984.

This paper shall serve as a programmatic outline towards studying biographical and social elements which constitute Einstein's personality and influence his scientific works. The progressive–regressive method of Sartre is put forward. Within this framework "totalisation" means re–constructing the becoming of Einstein's personality including both scientific and non–scientific aspects. However, due to the known restrictive policy concerning biographical details of Einstein's life, a proper totalisation of the relevant data is difficult to achieve.

ZIMMERMANN, Rolf. Emancipation And Rationality: Foundational Problems In The Theories Of Marx And Habermas. *Ratio* 26,143–166 D 84.

ZINBERG, Norman E. "The Social Dilemma Of The Development Of A Policy On Intoxicant Use" in *Feeling Good And Doing Better*, Murray, Thomas H (ed), 27–48. Clifton Humana Pr 1984.

ZIS, A J. Philosophical Thinking And Art Creation (in Czechoslovakian). *Estetika* 22,29–32 1985.

ZNOJ, M. Practice As Presupposition Of Science (in Czechoslovakian). *Filozof Cas* 33,269–281 1985.

ZOLO, Danilo and Ferrajoli, Luigi. Marxism And The Criminal Question. *Law Phil* 4,71–100 Ap 85.

The question considered is whether it is possible to trace a theoretical strategy for a criminal policy on the basis of Marx's work. The answer offered is that Marxian political and economic analysis does not supply any "general theory" of criminality and that any attempt to formulate such a theory (as in Lenin, Pasukanis or Gramsci) necessarily leads to authoritarian and regressive conceptions of crime and punishment. Nevertheless the authors maintain that it is possible to trace three theoretical suggestions within Marxian thought which allow of a fruitful approach to the criminal question. The first suggestion relates to the economic roots of many aspects of modern criminality; the second regards the Christian and bourgeois "superstition" or moral liberty and individual culpability; the third suggestion deals with the lack of a guaranteed "social space" as the prime root of crime. These theoretical suggestions permit clarification of the social character of penal responsibility and this character points to the need for socialization (but not deregulation) of criminal treatment.

ZUCKERT, Catherine. Nietzsche's Rereading Of Plato. *Polit Theory* 13,213–238 My 85.

Nietzsche gradually comes to suspect that Platonic doctrines like "the idea of the Good" and the "immortal soul" constitute public teachings that Plato himself did not believe and that obscure the true nature of his own activity. Nietzsche's re–reading of Plato forces us to reconsider both the nature and history of Western philosophy. Later philosophers who built on the Platonic theory of ideas built on a "noble lie" fabricated to give philosophy political influence.

ZÚNIGA, Angel Ruiz. Implicaciones Teórico–dfilosóficas Del Teorema De Gödel. *Rev Filosof (Costa Rica)* 23,183–194 D 85.

In this article we seek to establish an historical and philosophical interpretation of some main characteristics of modern reflection about Mathematics related to rationalist paradigm in knowledge theory. We analyze mathematical foundations classic problematic and intend to delineate a philosophical assessment of Rationalism from Gödelian results, we show therefore the need of a theoretical revolution in Philosophy of Mathematics and modern Epistemology.

ZURAW, Jozef. Karl Marx—A Great Friend Of Poland. *Dialec Hum* 10,167–178 Sum 83.

ZWICKY, Arnold M and Sadock, J M. A Note On *xy* Languages. *Ling Phil* 8,229–236 My 85.

Languages containing sentences of the form xy, x and y strings and x different from y, have been claimed by some to be outside the class of context–free languages, and by others to be within it. We demonstrate that among the languages in which x and y are themselves drawn from a properly context–free language, there is an infinite class of xy languages that do exceed the power of context–free phrase structure grammar.

ZYGMUNT, Jan and Hawranek, Jacek. On The Degree Of Complexity Of Sentential Logics; An Example Of The Logic With Semi–negation. *Stud Log* 43,405–414 1984.

In this paper being a sequel to our [1] the logic with semi–negation is chosen as an example to elucidate some basic notions of the semantics for sentential calculi. E.G., there are shown some links between the Post number and the degree of complexity of a sentential logic, and it is proved that the degree of complexity of the sentential logic with semi–negation is $2\aleph_0$. This is the first known example of a logic with such a degree of complexity. The results of the final part of the paper cast a new light on the scope of the Kripke–style semantics in comparison to the matrix semantics.

Guidance on the Use of the Book Review Index

The Book Review Index lists in alphabetical order the authors of books reviewed in philosophy journals. If the book has no author, it is listed under "____." Each entry also includes the title of the book, the publisher, and the place and date of publication. Under each entry is listed the name of the reviewer, the journal in which the review appeared, along with the volume, pagination and date.

ARRAS, John and Hunt, Robert (eds). *Ethical Issues In Modern Medicine, 2nd Ed.* Palo Alto, Mayfield, 1983.
Cebik, L B. *Teach Phil* 7,250–255 Jl 84
Fairbairn, Gavin J. *J Med Ethics* 10,213 D 84

ARVON, Henri. *El Anarquismo En El Siglo XX.* Madrid, Taurus, 1981.
Kreisler, Ivonne Klein. *Dianoia* 29,329–331 1983

ASCHENBRENNER, Karl. *Analysis Of Appraisive Characterization.* Dordrecht, Reidel, 1983.
Ward, John L. *J Aes Art Crit* 42, 457–461 Sum 84

ASCHER, Carol. *Simone De Beauvoir: A Life Of Freedom.* Boston, Beacon Pr, 1981.
Minnich, Elizabeth K. *Fem Stud* 11,287–305 Sum 85

ASHBROOK, James B. *The Human Mind And The Mind Of God.* Lanham, Univ Pr of America, 1984.
Hefner, Philip. *Zygon* 20,345–349 S 85

ASSMANN, Aleida. *Die Legitimität Der Fiktion.* München, Fink, 1980.
Pfeiffer, K Ludwig. *Phil Rundsch* 32,91–104 1985

ATIYAH, P S. *Promises, Morals And Law.* Oxford, Clarendon Pr, 1981.
De Greef, Jan. *Rev Phil Louvain* 82,575–576 N 84

ATKINSON, Michael. *Plotinus: Ennead VI.* Oxford, Oxford Univ Pr, 1983.
Dillon, John. *Hermathena* 137,56–57 Wint 84

ATTFIELD, Robin. *The Ethics Of Environmental Concern.* Oxford, Blackwell, 1983.
Elford, R John. *Relig Stud* 20,709–711 D 84
Clark, Stephen R. *Phil Books* 26,184–186 Jl 85
Adam, Michel. *Rev Phil Fr* 175,90–92 Ja–Mr 85

AUBENQUE, Pierre (ed). *Études Sur La Métaphysique D'Aristote.* Paris, Vrin, 1971.
Olivieri, Francisco José. *Cuad Filosof* 19,208–214 Ja–D 83

AUTTON, N. *Doctors Talking: A Guide To Current Medico–Moral Problems.* London, Mowbray, 1984.
Preston, Ronald. *J Med Ethics* 11,105–106 Je 85

AUXTER, Thomas. *Kant's Moral Teleology.* Macon, Mercer Univ Pr, 1982.
Broadie, A. *Kantstudien* 75,500–501 1984

AVERROES. *Middle Commentary On Aristotle's Categories, C Butterworth (ed).* Cairo, American Research Center, 1980.
Harvey, Steven. *Rev Metaph* 38,376–380 D 84

AVERROES. *Middle Commentary On Aristotle's De Interpretatione.* Cairo, American Research Center, 1981.
Harvey, Steven. *Rev Metaph* 38,376–380 D 84

AVERROES. *Middle Commentary On Aristotle's Topics, C Butterworth (ed).* Cairo, American Research Center, 1979.
Harvey, Steven. *Rev Metaph* 38,376–380 D 84

AVINERI, Shlomo. *The Making Of Modern Zionism.* NY, Basic Books, 1981.
Kluback, William. *Int J Phil Relig* 15,181–182 1984

AXELROD, Robert. *The Evolution Of Co–operation.* NY, Basic Books, 1984.
Rogowski, Ronald. *Polit Theory* 13,457–461 Ag 85

AYER, A J. *Philosophy In The Twentieth Century.* NY, Random House, 1982.
Watson, Richard A. *J Hist Phil* 22,490–492 O 84
Balu. *Philosophica* 33,138–146 1984
Teichman, Jenny. *Philosophy* 59,415–417 Jl 84

BACZKO, Bronislaw. *Les Imaginaires Sociaux: Mémoires Et Espoirs Collectifs.* Paris, Payot, 1984.
Gervais, Richard. *Dialogue (Canada)* 23,551–553 S 84

BAER, Judith A. *Equality Under The Constitution.* Ithaca, Cornell Univ Pr, 1983.
Sunstein, Cass R. *Ethics* 95,153–154 O 84

BAGNULO, Roberto. *Il Concetto Di Diritto Naturale In S Tommaso D'Aquino.* Milano, Giuffrè, 1983.
Mangiagalli, Maurizio. *Riv Filosof Neo–Scolas* 76,651–655 O–D 84

BAIRD, Robert M (ed). *The Philosophical Life: An Activity And An Attitude.* Washington, Univ Pr of America, 1983.
Kemerling, Garth. *Teach Phil* 7,271–272 Jl 84

BAKER, G P and Hacker, P M S. *Frege: Logical Excavations.* Oxford, Blackwell, 1984.
Haddock, Guillermo E Rosado. *Dialogos* 20,171–181 Ap 85
Currie, Gregory. *Phil Books* 26,18–20 Ja 85
Dummett, Michael. *Phil Quart* 34,377–401 Jl 84

BAKER, G P and Hacker, P M S. *Language, Sense And Nonsense.* Oxford, Blackwell, 1984.
Engel, Pascal. *Rev Phil Fr* 175,46–49 Ja–Mr 85
Stevenson, Leslie. *Philosophy* 60,270–272 Ap 85
Tiles, J E. *Phil Books* 26,98–101 Ap 85

BAKER, G P and Hacker, P M S. *Scepticism, Rules And Language.* Oxford, Blackwell, 1984.
Diamond, Cora. *Phil Books* 26,26–29 Ja 85
Engel, Pascal. *Rev Phil Fr* 175,45–46 Ja–Mr 85
Craig, Edward. *Phil Quart* 35,212–214 Ap 85

BALMER, Hans Peter. *Philosophie Der Menschlichen Dinge: Die Europäische Moralistik.* Bern, Francke, 1981.
Probst, Peter. *Z Phil Forsch* 38,332–334 Ap–Je 84

BANFIELD, Ann. *Unspeakable Sentences.* Boston, Routledge & Kegan Paul, 1982.
Lyas, Colin. *J Aes Art Crit* 43,101–104 Fall 84

BANFIELD, Edward C. *The Democratic Muse: Visual Arts And The Public Interest.* NY, Basic Books, 1984.
Smith, Ralph A. *J Aes Art Crit* 43,221–222 Wint 84

BANGE, P and others. *Logique, Argumentation, Conversation.* Frankfurt, Lang, 1983.
Auchlin, Antoine. *J Prag* 8,816–823 D 84

BANKOWSKI, Z and Howard–Jones, N (eds). *Human Experimentation And Medical Ethics.* London, HMSO, 1982.
Lewis, Peter J. *J Med Ethics* 11,50 Mr 85

BARBER, Benjamin. *Strong Democracy: Participatory Politics For A New Age.* Berkeley, Univ of California Pr, 1984.
Brest, Paul. *Polit Theory* 13,465–469 Ag 85
Hadari, Saguiv A. *Ethics* 95,940–941 Jl 85

BARBOSA DA SILVA, Anatonio. *The Phenomenology Of Religion As A Philosophical Problem.* Lund, Gleerup, 1982.
Whaling, Frank. *Relig Stud* 20,330–333 Je 84

BARNES, Jonathan. *Aristotle.* Oxford, Oxford Univ Pr, 1982.
Ferguson, John. *Heythrop J* 26,351–352 Jl 85
Thom, Paul. *Austl J Phil* 62,310–311 S 84
Sharples, R W. *J Hellen Stud* 104,211–212 1984

BARNES, Jonathan. *The Presocratic Philosophers.* Boston, Routledge & Kegan Paul, 1982.
Shiner, Roger A. *Ancient Phil* 4,224–226 Fall 84

BARON, Samuel H and Heer, Nancy W (eds). *Windows On The Russian Past.* Columbus, Amer Assn For Advan Slavic Studies, 1977.
Nemeth, Thomas. *Stud Soviet Tho* 28,235–238 O 84

BARONE, Francesco. *Pensieri Contro.* Napoli, Società, 1983.
Beraldi, Piero. *Filosofia* 36,121–122 Ja–Mr 85

BARRETT, William. *The Illusion Of Technique.* Garden City, Doubleday, 1978.
Angus, Ian H. *Eidos* 2,80–91 Jl 80

BARRY, Vincent. *Moral Issues In Business.* Belmont, Wadsworth, 1983.
Lehman, Craig. *J Bus Ethics* 4,129 Ap 85

BARTH, E M and Krabbe, E C W. *From Axiom To Dialogue.* Berlin, De Gruyter, 1982.
Bell, David. *Hist Phil Log* 5,141–142 1984

BARTSCH, Gerhard (ed). *Philosophisch–Methodologische Probleme.* Berlin, Akademie, 1982.
Grund, Marion and Rupprecht, Frank. *Deut Z Phil* 32,1041–1043 1984

BARWISE, Jon and others (eds). *Handbook Of Mathematical Logic.* Amsterdam, North–Holland, 1978.
Urquhart, Alasdair. *Can J Phil* 14,675–682 D 84

BARWISE, Jon and Perry, John. *Situations And Attitudes.* Cambridge, MIT Pr, 1983.
Cresswell, M J. *Phil Rev* 94,293–296 Ap 85
Hanson, Philip P. *Can Phil Rev* 5,210–212 My–Je 85
Coyne, Margaret Urban. *Rev Metaph* 38,107–109 S 84

BASSON, Marc and others (eds). *Troubling Problems In Medical Ethics.* NY, Liss, 1981.
Baker, Robert. *Ethics* 95,370–375 Ja 85

BAST, R A and Delfosse, H P. *Handbuch Zum Textstudium Von Martin Heideggers "Sein Und Zeit".* Stuttgart, Frommann, 1979.
Silva, C H Do Carmo. *Rev Port Filosof* 41,103–104 Ja–Mr 85

BASU, Shankar. *Understanding Kant.* Pub Unknown, Calcutta, 1983.
Bulsara, Hoshang K. *Philosophica (India)* 10,48–49 Ja–D 81

BATCHELOR JR, Edward (ed). *Abortion: The Moral Issue.* NY, Pilgrim Pr, 1982.
Healy, James. *Heythrop J* 26,344–345 Jl 85

BATESON, Gregory. *Geist Und Natur: Eine Notwendige Einheit.* Frankfurt, Suhrkamp, 1982.
Vollmer, Gerhard. *Z Phil Forsch* 38,489–492 Jl–O 84

BATSON, C D and Ventis, W L. *The Religious Experience: A Social–Psychological Perspective.* NY, Oxford Univ Pr, 1982.
Walters, K S. *Dialogue (PST)* 27,35–36 O 84

BATTIN, Margaret Pabst. *Ethical Issues In Suicide.* Englewood Cliffs, Prentice–Hall, 1982.
Wreen, Michael. *J Value Inq* 19,245–247 1985

BAUDRILLARD, Jean. *Les Stratégies Fatales.* Paris, Grasset, 1983.
Knee, Philip. *Laval Theol Phil* 41,132–133 F 85

BAUMGARTEN, A G. *Theoretische Aesthetik.* Hamburg, Meiner, 1983.
Damnjanovic, Milan. *Z Phil Forsch* 38,687–690 N–D 84

BAUMGARTEN, Alexander G. *Philosophische Betrachtungen Über Einige Bedingungen.* Hamburg, Meiner, 1983.
Schaper, Eva. *Brit J Aes* 25,278–279 Sum 85
Damnjanovic, Milan. *Z Phil Forsch* 38,687–690 N–D 84

BAUMGARTEN, Alexander G. *Texte Zur Grundlegung Der Ästhetik.* Hamburg, Meiner, 1983.
Schaper, Eva. *Brit J Aes* 25,278–279 Sum 85
Damnjanovic, Milan. *Z Phil Forsch* 38,687–690 N–D 84

BAYLES, Michael D. *Reproductive Ethics.* Englewood Cliffs, Prentice–Hall, 1984.
Kuhse, Helga. *Austl J Phil* 63,249–251 Je 85

BEALER, George. *Quality And Concept.* Oxford, Clarendon Pr, 1982.
Sosa, Ernest. *J Phil* 82,382–387 Jl 85
Cocchiarella, Nino B. *J Sym Log* 50,554–556 Je 85

BEAUCHAMP, T and Walters, L (eds). *Contemporary Issues In Bioethics.* Belmont, Wadsworth, 1982.
Baker, Robert. *Ethics* 95,370–375 Ja 85

BEAUCHAMP, T L and Bowie, N (eds). *Ethical Theory And Business.* Englewood Cliffs, Prentice–Hall, 1983.
Coombs, Charlotte. *J Moral Educ* 14,66–67 Ja 85

BEAUCHAMP, T L and McCullough, L B. *Medical Ethics: The Moral Responsibilities Of Physicians.* Englewood Cliffs, Prentice–Hall, 1984.
Pence, Gregory E. *Theor Med* 6,234 Je 85

BEAUCHAMP, Tom and Rosenberg, Alexander. *Hume And The Problem Of Causation.* NY, Oxford Univ Pr, 1981.
Malherbe, Michel. *Arch Phil* 48,487–489 Jl–S 85
Horgan, Terence. *Phil Rev* 94,278–281 Ap 85

BECKER, Lawrence and Kipnis, Kenneth (eds). *Property: Cases, Concepts, Critiques.* Englewood Cliffs, Prentice–Hall, 1984.
Husak, Douglas. *Teach Phil* 8,163–165 Ap 85

BÉGIN, Luc and others. *Pragmatisme Et Pensée Contemporaine.* Sherbrooke, Univ de Sherbrooke, 1984.
Laurier, Daniel. *Philosophiques* 12,232–236 Spr 85

BEGUM, Hasna. *Moore's Ethics: Theory And Practice.* Dacca, Univ of Dacca, 1982.
Kearney, Ray. *Austl J Phil* 62,311–313 S 84
Shaida, S A. *Indian Phil Quart* 12,99–104 Ja–Mr 85

BEIERWALTES, Werner. *Identität Und Differenz.* Frankfurt, Klostermann, 1980.
Laffoucrière, O. *Arch Phil* 48,491–493 Jl–S 85

BELAIEF, Lynne. *Toward A Whiteheadian Ethics.* Lanham, Univ Pr of America, 1984.
Stroh, Guy W. *Trans Peirce Soc* 21,442–449 Sum 85

BELL, David. *Frege's Theory Of Judgment.* Oxford, Clarendon Pr, 1979.
Jiménez, Joaquín M. *Dialogos* 20,181–186 Ap 85
Jackson, Howard. *J Sym Log* 50, 254–258 Mr 85

BELL, Linda A (ed). *Visions Of Women.* Clifton, Humana Pr, 1983.
McCleary, Rachel M. *Ethics* 95,165–167 O 84

BELL, Nora K (ed). *Who Decides: Conflicts Of Rights In Health Care.* Clifton, Humana Pr, 1982.
La Bar, Carol. *J Moral Educ* 13,213–216 O 84

BENDITT, Theodore M. *Rights.* Totowa, Rowman & Littlefield, 1982.
Decew, Judith Wagner. *Law Phil* 4,125–140 Ap 85
Wein, Sheldon. *Dialogue (Canada)* 23,732–734 D 84

BENDIX, Reinhard. *Force, Fate, And Freedom.* Berkeley, Univ of California Pr, 1984.
Roth, Guenther. *Hist Theor* 24,196–208 My 85

BENELLI, Giuseppe. *Voltaire "Metafisico".* Milano, Marzorati, 1983.
Pieri, Sergio. *Riv Filosof Neo-Scolas* 76,487–490 Jl–S 84

BENNETT, Jonathan. *A Study Of Spinoza's Ethics.* Indianapolis, Hackett, 1984.
Garber, Daniel. *Ethics* 95,961–963 Jl 85

BENNETT, W Lance and Feldman, Martha S. *Reconstructing Reality In The Courtroom.* New Brunswick, Rutgers Univ Pr, 1981.
Rieke, Richard D. *Phil Rhet* 17,249–252 1984

BENTHEM, J F A K. *The Logic Of Time.* Dordrecht, Reidel, 1982.
Christie, Drew. *Rev Metaph* 38,882–883 Je 85

BERGER, Fred R. *Happiness, Justice, And Freedom.* Berkeley, Univ of California Pr, 1984.
Sumner, L W. *Mill News* 20,24–28 Wint 85
Arneson, Richard. *Ethics* 95,954–958 Jl 85

BERGNER, Jeffrey T. *The Rise Of Formalism In Social Science.* Chicago, Univ of Chicago Pr, 1981.
Jonsson, Dan. *Phil Soc Sci* 15,116–117 Mr 85

BERKI, R N. *Insight And Vision: The Problem Of Communism In Marx's Thought.* London, Dent, 1983.
Stillman, Peter G. *Bull Hegel Soc Gr Brit* 9,49–51 Spr/Sum 84

BERNSEN, Neils Ole. *Knowledge: A Treatise On Our Cognitive Situation.* Odense, Odense Univ Pr, 1978.
Airaksinen, Timo. *Philosophia (Israel)* 14,435–436 D 84

BERNSTEIN, Richard J. *Beyond Objectivism And Relativism.* Philadelphia, Univ of Pennsylvania Pr, 1983.
Llewelyn, John. *Phil Books* 26,113–115 Ap 85
Gowans, Christopher W. *Int Phil Quart* 25,207–211 Je 85
Eldridge, Richard. *Phil Lit* 8,292–293 O 84
Hanna, Robert. *Rev Metaph* 38,109–112 S 84
Hollis, Martin. *Ratio* 27,97–99 Je 85
Hadari, Saguiv A. *Ethics* 95,164–165 O 84

BERRY, C J. *Hume, Hegel And Human Nature.* The Hague, Nijhoff, 1982.
Popkin, Richard H. *Rev V Metaph* 38,619–620 Mr 85

BHASKAR, Roy. *Philosophy And The Human Sciences, V2.* Atlantic Highlands, Humanities Pr, 1979.
Richmond, Sheldon. *Phil Soc Sci* 15,235–236 Je 85

BIANCHI, Luca. *L'Errore Di Aristotle.* Firenze, Nuova Italia, 1984.
Jolivet, Jean. *Rev Phil Fr* 175,243–245 Ap–Je 85
Van Steenberghen, Fernand. *Rev Phil Louvain* 83,231–238 My 85

BIERI, P and others (eds). *Transcendental Arguments And Science: Essays In Epistemology.* Dordrecht, Reidel, 1979.

Sauer, Werner. *Grazer Phil Stud* 21,155–184 1984

BIERI, Peter. *Analytische Philosophie Des Geistes.* Königstein, Hain, 1981.
Brüstle, Walter. *Z Phil Forsch* 38,485–489 Jl–O 84

BIRCH, Charles and Cobb, John B. *The Liberation Of Life.* Cambridge, Cambridge Univ Pr, 1985.
Barbour, Ian G. *Zygon* 20,360–363 S 85

BIRNBAUM, Pierre. *Dimensions Du Pouvoir.* Paris, Univ de France, 1984.
Gervais, Richard. *Dialogue (Canada)* 24,170–172 Spr 85

BLACK, Max. *The Prevalence Of Humbug And Other Essays.* Ithaca, Cornell Univ Pr, 1983.
Jacques, Francis. *Rev Metaph Morale* 89,531–535 O–D 84

BLACKBURN, Simon. *Spreading The Word: Groundings In The Philosophy Of Language.* Oxford, Oxford Univ Pr, 1984.
Sainsbury, R M. *Brit J Phil Sci* 36,211–215 Je 85
Tennant, Neil. *Phil Books* 26,65–82 Ap 85

BLACKWELL, Kenneth and others (eds). *The Collected Papers Of Bertrand Russell.* London, Allen & Unwin, 1983.
Sprigge, Timothy. *Phil Books* 26,23–26 Ja 85
Lackey, Douglas P. *Metaphilosophy* 15,282–288 Jl–O 84

BLACKWELL, Richard J. *Bibliography Of The Philosophy Of Science, 1945–1981.* Westport, Greenwood, 1983.
McEvoy, John G. *Teach Phil* 7,372–373 O 84

BLANK, D L. *Ancient Philosophy And Grammar.* Chico, Scholars Pr, 1982.
Lloyd, A C. *J Hellen Stud* 104,219 1984

BLOCH, Maurice. *Marxism And Anthropology.* Oxford, Oxford Univ Pr, 1983.
Mattick Jr, Paul. *Stud Soviet Tho* 29,247–251 Ap 85

BLOCK, Irving (ed). *Perspectives On The Philosophy Of Wittgenstein.* Oxford, Blackwell, 1981.
Jones, O R. *Mind* 93,131–134 Ja 84
Zwicky, Jan. *Dialogue (Canada)* 23,357–361 Je 84

BLOOR, David. *Wittgenstein: A Social Theory Of Knowledge.* NY, Columbia Univ Pr, 1983.
Sharrock, W W and Anderson, R J. *Human Stud* 7,375–386 1984
Marshall, S E. *Can Phil Rev* 5,96–98 Mr 85
Burnheim, John. *Austl J Phil* 63,241–243 Je 85

BLUHM, William T. *Force Or Freedom: The Paradox In Modern Political Thought.* New Haven, Yale Univ Pr, 1984.
Aronovitch, Hilliard. *Can Phil Rev* 5,185–188 My–Je 85
Nelson, Allan D. *Mill News* 20,28–31 Wint 85

BLUMENBERG, Hans. *Arbeit Am Mythos.* Frankfurt, Suhrkamp, 1979.
Villwock, Jörg. *Phil Rundsch* 32,68–91 1985

BLUMENBERG, Hans. *Die Lesbarkeit Der Welt.* Frankfurt, Suhrkamp, 1981.
Villwock, Jörg. *Phil Rundsch* 32,68–91 1985

BLUMENBERG, Hans. *The Legitimacy Of The Modern Age, Robert M Wallace (trans).* Cambridge, MIT Pr, 1983.
Jay, Martin. *Hist Theor* 24,183–196 My 85

BLUMENBERG, Hans. *Wirklichkeiten In Denen Wir Leben.* Stuttgart, Reclam, 1981.
Villwock, Jörg. *Phil Rundsch* 32,68–91 1985

BLUSTEIN, Jeffrey. *Parents And Children: The Ethics Of The Family.* NY, Oxford Univ Pr, 1982.
Matthews, Gareth B. *J Phil* 82,330–332 Je 85
Hochberg, Herbert. *Phil Sci* 51,514–516 S 84
Buhl, Joachim. *Erkenntnis* 23,203–212 Ag 85

BOCHENSKI, J M. *Qu'est–ce Que L'autorité.* Paris, Cerf, 1979.
Stella, Giuliana. *Riv Int Filosof Diritto* 61,529–530 Jl–S 84

BODÉÜS, Richard. *Le Philosophe Et La Cité.* Paris, Belles, 1982.
Romeyer Dherbey, G. *Rev Metaph Morale* 89,565–568 O–D 84
Brague, Rémi. *Arch Phil* 48,327–329 Ap–Je 85

BOK, Sissela. *Secrets: On The Ethics Of Concealment And Revelation.* Oxford, Oxford Univ Pr, 1984.
Belsey, Andrew. *J Applied Phil* 1,319–320 O 84
Stack, Michael. *Can Phil Rev* 4,231–233 D 84
Frankel, Mark S. *Teach Phil* 8,174–176 Ap 85
Gert, Bernard. *Crim Just Ethics* 4,78–84 Wint/Spr 85
Gilbert, Paul. *Philosophy* 60,143–145 Ja 85

BOLAND, Lawrence A. *The Foundations Of Economic Method.* London, Allen & Unwin, 1982.
Birner, Jack. *Brit J Phil Sci* 36,215–221 Je 85

BOLINGER, Dwight. *Language: The Loaded Weapon.* London, Longman, 1980.
Johnson, Ralph H. *Can Phil Rev* 4,233–235 D 84

BOLTER, David. *Turing's Man: Western Culture In The Computer Age.* Chapel Hill, Univ of North Carolina Pr, 1984.
Warmbrod, Ken. *Can Phil Rev* 5,188–190 My–Je 85

BONAZZI, Giuseppe. *Copa E Potere.* Bologna, Mulino, 1983.
Mangiameli, A C A. *Riv Int Filosof Diritto* 61,359–361 Ap–Je 84

BOND, E J. *Reason And Value.* Cambridge, Cambridge Univ Pr, 1983.
Narveson, Jan. *Dialogue (Canada)* 23,327–335 Je 84
Dent, N J H. *Philosophy* 59,411–413 Jl 84
Darwall, Stephen L. *Phil Rev* 94,286–289 Ap 85

BONHOEFFER, Dietrich. *De La Vie Communautaire.* Paris, Cerf, 1983.
Renauld, Christian. *Laval Theol Phil* 41,130–132 F 85

BOTTOMORE, Tom (ed). *Modern Interpretations Of Marx.* Don Mills, Oxford Univ Pr, 1981.
Young, Iris Marion. *Can Phil Rev* 5,98–101 Mr 85

BOUCHARD, Guy. *Le Procès De La Métaphore.* Place Unknown, Hurtubise HMH, 1984.
Turgeon, Marc. *Philosophiques* 12,236–241 Spr 85

BOULAY, C. *Benedetto Croce Jusqu'en 1911: Trente Ans De Vie Intellectuelle.* Genève, Droz, 1981.
Olivier, Paul. *Arch Phil* 48,495–497 Jl–S 85

BOURGEOIS, Patrick L and Rosenthal, Sandra B. *Thematic Studies In Phenomenology And Pragmatism.* Amsterdam, Grüner, 1983.
Hausman, Carl R. *Trans Peirce Soc* 20,473–479 Fall 84

BOUVERESSE, J. *Le Philosophe Chez Les Autophages.* Paris, Minuit, 1983.
Largeault, Jean. *Arch Phil* 48,343–345 Ap–Je 85

BOUWSMA, O K. *Without Proof Or Evidence,* J L Craft and R E Hustwit (eds). Lincoln, Univ of Nebraska Pr, 1984.
Hunter, J F M. *Can Phil Rev* 5, 49–52 F 85
Gealy, Walford. *Phil Invest* 8,222–226 Jl 85

BOWIE, Norman E (ed). *Ethical Theory In The Last Quarter Of The Twentieth Century.* Indianapolis, Hackett, 1983.
MacKinnon, Barbara. *Mod Sch* 62,140–141 Ja 85
Silverstein, Harry S. *Can Phil Rev* 5,1–2 Ja 85

BOYLAN, M. *Method And Practice In Aristotle's Biology.* Washington, Univ Pr of America, 1983.
Richmond, J A. *J Hellen Stud* 104,215–216 1984
Gotthelf, Allan. *Rev Metaph* 38,112–114 S 84

BRADFORD, Dennise E. *The Concept Of Existence: A Study Of Nonexistent Particulars.* Lanham, Univ Pr of America, 1980.
Blackman, Larry Lee. *Phil Topics* 12,264–269 Wint 81

BRADLEY, Raymond and Swartz, Norman. *Possible Worlds: An Introduction To Logic And Its Philosophy.* Indianapolis, Hackett, 1979.
Haack, S. *Hist Phil Log* 1,242–243 1980

BRAINE, David. *Medical Ethics And Human Life.* Aberdeen, Palladio Pr, 1983.
Lesser, Harry. *J Med Ethics* 10,162–163 S 84

BRAMS, S J. *Superior Beings: If They Exist, How Would We Know.* NY, Springer, 1983.
Engel, P. *Hist Phil Log* 6,153–155 1985

BRANDS, Hartmut. *Cogito Ergo Sum: Interpretationen Von Kant Bis Nietzsche.* Freiburg, Alber, 1982.
Lechner, Jochen. *Kantstudien* 76,107–110 1985
Blasche, Siegfried. *Hist Phil Log* 5,219–226 1984

BRANDT, Reinhard (trans). *Rechtsphilosophie Der Aufklärung.* Berlin, De Gruyter, 1982.
Naucke, Wolfgang. *Z Phil Forsch* 39,147–150 Ja–Mr 85

BRANDWOOD, Leonard. *A Word Index To Plato.* Leeds, Maney, 1976.
Olivieri, Francisco José. *Cuad Filosof* 19,214–216 Ja–D 83

BRAUN, Carl. *Kritische Theorie Versus Kritizismus.* Berlin, De Gruyter, 1983.
Hermann, Horst. *Kantstudien* 76,114–116 1985

BRAYBROOKE, David. *Ethics In The World Of Business.* Totowa, Rowman & Allanheld, 1983.
Donaldson, Thomas. *Ethics* 95,167–169 O 84
Michalos, Alex C. *J Bus Ethics* 3,277–278 N 84

BREGMAN, J. *Synesius Of Cyrene: Philosopher–Bishop.* Berkeley, Univ of California Pr, 1982.
Liebeschuetz, J H W G. *J Hellen Stud* 104,222–223 1984

BREHMER, Karl. *Rawls' Original Position.* Königstein, Pub Unknown, 1980.
Gerhardt, Volker. *Kantstudien* 75,504–506 1984

BRENKERT, George G. *Marx's Ethics Of Freedom.* London, Routledge & Kegan Paul, 1983.
McMurtry, John. *Can Phil Rev* 5,101–104 Mr 85
Smith, Steven B. *Rev Metaph* 38,115–116 S 84

BRENNEMAN JR, W L and Yarian, S O and Olson A M. *The Seeing Eye:.* University Park, Pennsylvania State Univ Pr, 1982.
McKenzie, P R. *Relig Stud* 20,497–499 S 84
Reiser, William. *Heythrop J* 25,510–511 O 84

BRENT, Allen. *Philosophy And Educational Foundations.* London, Allen & Unwin, 1983.
Hamlyn, D W. *Phil Books* 26,166–168 Jl 85

BRENTANO, Franz. *Deskriptive Psychologie,* R M Chisholm and W Baumgartner (eds). Hamburg, Meiner, 1982.
Mulligan, Kevin. *Phil Phenomenol Res* 45,627–644 Je 85

BRENTANO, Franz. *The Theory Of Categories,* R Chisholm and N Guterman (trans). The Hague, Nijhoff, 1981.
Mays, Wolfe. *Hist Phil Log* 6,131–132 1985

BRISSON, Luc and others. *Porphyre: La Vie De Plotin, I.* Paris, Vrin, 1982.
Rutten, Christian. *Rev Phil Louvain* 83,275–277 My 85

BRITO, Emilio. *La Christologie De Hegel: Verbum Crucis,* B Pottier (trans). Paris, Beauchesne, 1983.
Léonard, André. *Rev Phil Louvain* 82,438–441 Ag 84

BRITTAN, Gordon G. *Kant's Theory Of Science.* Princeton, Princeton Univ Pr, 1978.

Meerbote, R. *Topoi* 3,186–190 D 84

BROADIE, Alexander. *George Lokert: Late–Scholastic Logician.* NY, Columbia Univ Pr, 1983.
Read, Stephen. *Phil Books* 26,137–140 Jl 85
Ashworth, E J. *Can Phil Rev* 5,3–4 Ja 85

BRODY, Baruch A. *Identity And Essence.* Princeton, Princeton Univ Pr, 1980.
Schlesinger, George N. *Philosophia* 14,241–244 Ag 84

BRODY, Baruch. *Ethics And Its Applications.* San Diego, Harcourt Brace Jovanovich, 1983.
Garner, Richard. *Teach Phil* 8,61–64 Ja 85

BROWN, David. *Choices: Ethics And The Christian.* Oxford, Blackwell, 1983.
Regan, Richard. *Int Phil Quart* 24,447–449 D 84
Whyte, J A. *Relig Stud* 20,713–714 D 84

BROWN, Robert. *The Nature Of Social Laws: Machiavelli To Mill.* Cambridge, Cambridge Univ Pr, 1984.
Letwin, Oliver. *Philosophy* 60,276–277 Ap 85
Rosen, Michael. *Hist Polit Thought* 5,387–392 Sum 84

BROWN, S C (ed). *Objectivity And Cultural Divergence.* Cambridge, Cambridge Univ Pr, 1984.
Mayo, Bernard. *Phil Books* 26,178–180 Jl 85

BROWN, S C (ed). *Philosophical Disputes In The Social Sciences.* Sussex, Harvester Pr, 1979.
Brown, Robert. *Phil Soc Sci* 14,418–425 S 84

BROWNING, Reed. *Political And Constitutional Ideas Of The Court Whigs.* Baton Rouge, Louisiana State Univ Pr, 1982.
Goldsmith, M M. *Hist Polit Thought* 5,383–387 Sum 84

BROYER, J A and Minor, W S (eds). *Creative Interchange.* Carbondale, Southern Illinois Univ Pr, 1982.
Phillips, Stephen H. *Faith Phil* 2,320–322 Jl 85

BRUAIRE, Claude. *L'Etre Et L'Esprit.* Paris, Pr Univ de France, 1983.
Grimaldi, Nicolas. *Rev Metaph Morale* 89,427–430 Jl–S 84
Cugno, Alain. *Arch Phil* 48,505–507 Jl–S 85

BRUAIRE, Claude. *Pour La Métaphysique.* Paris, Fayard, 1980.
Kalinowski, Georges. *Arch Phil* 48,503–505 Jl–S 85

BRUNNER, D and others (eds). *Corporations And The Environment.* Stanford, Stanford Univ Grad School Of Bus, 1981.
Dyke, C. *Environ Ethics* 6,363–365 Wint 84

BRUNS, Gerald. *Inventions.* New Haven, Yale Univ Pr, 1982.
Guillory, John. *Clio* 13,173–175 Wint 84

BRUYÈRE, Nelly. *Méthode Et Dialectique Dans L'oeuvre De La Ramée.* Paris, Vrin, 1984.
Pinchard, B. *Rev Metaph Morale* 90,267–269 Ap–Je 85

BRYSON, Norman. *Vision And Painting: The Logic Of The Gaze.* New Haven, Yale Univ Pr, 1983.
Humble, P N. *J Aes Art Crit* 43,219–221 Wint 84

BUBACZ, Bruce. *St Augustine's Theory Of Knowledge: A Contemporary Analysis.* NY, Mellen Pr, 1981.
O'Daly, Gerald J P. *Relig Stud* 20,312–315 Je 84

BUBER, Martin. *A Land Of Two Peoples,* Paul R Mendes–Flohr (ed). NY, Oxford Univ Pr, 1983.
Kluback, William. *Int J Phil Relig* 15,197–198 1984

BUBER, Martin. *The Jew,* Arthur A Cohen (ed). University, Univ of Alabama Pr, 1980.
Kluback, William. *Int J Phil Relig* 15,182–184 1984

BUBNER, Rüdiger. *Modern German Philosophy,* Eric Matthews (trans). NY, Cambridge Univ Pr, 1980.
Olson, Alan M. *Int J Phil Relig* 15,173–179 1984

BUBNER, Rüdiger. *Zur Sache Der Dialektik.* Stuttgart, Reclam, 1980.
Rosen, Michael. *Bull Hegel Soc Gr Brit* 2,39–43 Autumn 80

BUCHANAN, Allen E. *Marx And Justice: The Radical Critique Of Liberalism.* Totowa, Rowman & Littlefield, 1982.
Howard, Michael. *Stud Soviet Tho* 28,151–154 Ag 84
Allen, Derek P. *Dialogue (Canada)* 23,343–345 Je 84

BÜHLER, P and others. *Justice En Dialogue.* Genf, Labor et Fides, 1982.
Höffe, Otfried. *Frei Z Phil Theol* 31,487–490 1984

BULLERT, Gary. *The Politics Of John Dewey.* Buffalo, Prometheus Books, 1983.
Roth, Robert J. *Int Phil Quart* 24,339 S 84
Beattie, Paul. *Relig Hum* 18,191–192 Autumn 84
Campbell, James. *Trans Peirce Soc* 20,479–485 Fall 84

BULLOCK, A and Stallybrass, O (eds). *The Fontana Dictionary Of Modern Thought.* London, Fontana/Collins, 1978.
Todd, D D. *Dialogue (Canada)* 23,738–740 D 84

BUNGE, M. *Causality: The Place Of The Casual Principle In Modern Science.* Cambridge, Harvard Univ Pr, 1963.
Ventura, Antonino. *Riv Filosof Neo–Scolas* 76,624–636 O–D 84

BUNGE, Mario. *Controversias En Física.* Madrid, Tecnos, 1983.
Flichman, Eduardo. *Rev Latin De Filosof* 11,163–172 Jl 85

BUNGE, Mario. *Epistémologie.* Paris, Maloine, 1983.
Tournier, François. *Dialogue (Canada)* 23,353–356 Je 84

BUNGE, Mario. *The Mind–Body Problem.* Ontario, Pergamon, 1980.
Jackson, Frank. *Phil Soc Sci* 14,397–401 S 84

BURBIDGE, John. *On Hegel's Logic: Fragments Of A Commentary.* Atlantic Highlands, Humanities Pr, 1982.
Flay, Joseph C. *J Hist Phil* 23, 117–118 Ja 85

BÜRGER, Peter. *Zur Kritik Der Idealistischen Ästhetik.* Frankfurt, Suhrkamp Taschenbuch, 1983.
Neumaier, Otto. *Conceptus* 19,110–112 1985

BURKE, J P and others (eds). *Marxism And The Good Society.* Cambridge, Cambridge Univ Pr, 1981.
Mahon, Joseph. *Hist Euro Ideas* 5,439–443 1984

BURKE, T E. *The Philosophy Of Popper.* Manchester, Manchester Univ Pr, 1983.
Fellows, Roger. *Phil Books* 25,250–252 O 84

BURKHARDT, Frederick and Bowers, Fredson (eds). *The Works Of William James, 3v.* Cambridge, Harvard Univ Pr, 1982.
Giuffrida Jr, Robert. *Trans Peirce Soc* 21,276–280 Spr 85
Roberts, Don D. *Dialogue (Canada)* 24,184–186 Spr 85

BURKHARDT, Hans. *Logik Und Semiotik In Der Philosophie Von Leibniz.* Munich, Philosophia, 1980.
Roetti, Jorge Alfredo. *Rev Latin De Filosof* 11,71–76 Mr 85

BURNS, J H and Hart, H L A (eds). *Jeremy Bentham.* London, Methuen, 1982.
Vallance, Elizabeth. *Heythrop J* 26,354–355 Jl 85

BURNS, R M. *The Great Debate On Miracles.* London, Associated Univ Pr, Undated.
Gaskin, J C A. *Relig Stud* 20,316–318 Je 84

BURNYEAT, Myles (ed). *The Skeptical Tradition.* Berkeley, Univ of California Pr, 1983.
Mates, Benson. *Ethics* 95,749–751 Ap 85

BUROKER, Jill Vance. *Space And Incongruence: The Origin Of Kant's Idealism.* Dordrecht, Reidel, 1981.
Allison, Henry E. *Topoi* 3,169–175 D 84

CAHN, S M and Schatz, D (eds). *Comtemporary Philosophy Of Religion.* Oxford, Oxford Univ Pr, 1982.
Lennon, Paul. *Heythrop J* 25,511–512 O 84

CALHOUN, Cheshire and Solomon, Robert C. *What Is An Emotion.* NY, Oxford Univ Pr, 1984.
Robinson, Jenefer. *Teach Phil* 8,79–81 Ja 85

CAMPANINI, Giorgio. *Antonio Rosmini E Il Problema Dello Stato.* Brescia, Morcelliana, 1983.
Belletti, Bruno. *Sapienza* 37,470–472 O–D 84

CAMPS, Victoria. *Pragmática Del Lenguaje Y Filosofía Analítica.* Barcelona, Crítica, 1976.
Xirau, Ramón. *Dianoia* 28,371–375 1982

CANFIELD, John V. *Wittgenstein, Language, And World.* Amherst, Univ of Massachussetts Pr, 1981.
Mouloud, Noël. *Rev Metaph Morale* 90,130–132 Ja–Mr 85
Nelson, John O. *Rev Metaph* 38,380–382 D 84
Zwicky, Jan. *Can J Phil* 15,151–185 Mr 85

CANFORA, Luciano. *La Democrazia Come Violenza.* Palermo, Sellerio, 1982.
Ferri, Enrico. *Riv Int Filosof Diritto* 61,707–709 O–D 84

CANTOR, G N and Hodge, M J S (eds). *Conceptions Of Ether.* Cambridge, Cambridge Univ Pr, 1981.
Worrall, John. *Brit J Phil Sci* 36,81–85 Mr 85

CAPEK, M (ed). *The Concepts Of Space And Time.* Dordrecht, Reidel, 1976.
Oaklander, L Nathan. *Philosophia* 14,231–239 Ag 84

CAPLAN, Lincoln. *The Insanity Defense And The Trial Of John W Hinckley, Jr.* Boston, Godine, 1984.
Moreno, Jonathan D. *Hastings Center Rep* 15,45–46 F 85

CAPPON, Alexander P. *Aspects Of Wordsworth And Whitehead.* NY, Philosophical Library, 1983.
Hodgson, John A. *Phil Lit* 9,116–117 Ap 85

CAPUTO, John D. *Heidegger And Aquinas: An Essay On Overcoming Metaphysics.* NY, Fordham Univ Pr, 1982.
Marsh, James L. *Int Phil Quart* 25,201–206 Je 85
Burch, Robert. *Can Phil Rev* 4,235–237 D 84

CARGILE, James. *Paradoxes: A Study In Form And Predication.* Cambridge, Cambridge Univ Pr, 1979.
Hawthorn, John. *J Sym Log* 50, 250–252 Mr 85

CARNESALE, Albert and others. *Living With Nuclear Weapons.* NY, Bantam, 1983.
Donaghy, John. *Phil Soc Crit* 10,181–188 Wint 84

CARRITHERS, Michael. *The Buddha.* NY, Oxford Univ Pr, 1983.
McDermott, James P. *Teach Phil* 8,180–181 Ap 85

CARROLL, Robert B. *From Chaos To Covenant.* NY, Crossroad, 1981.
Bream, Howard N. *Thomist* 49,154–156 Ja 85

CARTER, C O (ed). *Developments In Human Reproduction.* London, Academic Pr, 1983.
Loraine, John A. *J Med Ethics* 11,162 S 85

CARTWRIGHT, Nancy. *How The Laws Of Physics Lie.* Oxford, Clarendon Pr, 1983.
Fetzer, James H. *Phil Books* 26,120–124 Ap 85
Gauthier, Yvon. *Dialogue (Canada)* 23,522–525 S 84
Bub, Jeffrey. *Can Phil Rev* 5,104–107 Mr 85

Redhead, M L G. *Phil Quart* 34,513–514 O 84
Tiles, Mary. *Philosophy* 60,133–136 Ja 85
Gibbins, Peter. *Brit J Phil Sci* 35,390–401 D 84

CARVER, Terrell. *Engels.* NY, Hill & Wang, 1981.
Louden, Robert B. *Stud Soviet Tho* 28,143–146 Ag 84

CASSELL, Eric J. *The Place Of Humanities In Medicine.* Hastings–on–Hudson, Hastings Center, 1984.
De George, Richard T. *Int J Applied Phil* 2,89–90 Spr 85

CASSINET, J and Guillemot, M. *L'Axiome Du Choix Dans Les Mathématiques.* Toulouse, Univ Paul Sabatier, 1983.
Grattan–Guinness, I. *Hist Phil Log* 5,133–135 1984

CASTAÑEDA, Hector–Neri. *On Philosophical Method.* Bloomington, Indiana Univ, 1980.
Balu. *Philosophica* 33,132–137 1984

CASTAÑEDA, Hector–Neri. *Thinking And Doing.* Dordrecht, Reidel, 1975.
Gärdenfors, Peter. *J Sym Log* 50,248–250 Mr 85

CASTORIADIS, Cornelius. *Crossroads In The Labyrinth,* K Soper and M Ryle (trans). Cambridge, MIT Pr, 1984.
Flynn, Bernard. *Grad Fac Phil J* 10,179–183 Spr 84

CATURELLI, Alberto. *La Metafisica Cristiana En El Pensamiento Occidental.* Buenos Aires, Cruzamante, 1983.
Sánchez, J Ricardo. *Rev Filosof (Mexico)* 17,552–555 S–D 84

CATURELLI, Alberto. *Reflexiones Para Una Filosofia Cristiana De La Educación.* Córdoba, Univ Nacional de Córdoba, 1982.
Sánches, J R P. *Rev Filosof (Mexico)* 17,550–552 S–D 84

CAUMAN, Leigh S and others (eds). *How Many Questions: Essays In Honour Of Sidney Morgenbesser.* Indianapolis, Hackett, 1983.
Misak, Cheryl. *Can Phil Rev* 5,7–9 Ja 85

CAVALIERE, R Viti. *Filosofia Del Gioco.* Napoli, SEN, 1983.
Reda, Clementina Gily. *Filosofia* 35,278–280 Jl–O 84

CAVEING, Maurice. *La Constitution Du Type Mathématique De L'Idéalité.* Lille, Univ de Lille, 1982.
Russo, F. *Arch Phil* 48,471–474 Jl–S 85

CAZENOBE, Jean. *La VisAee Et L'obstacle.* Paris, Cahiers D'Histoire, 1983.
Russo, F. *Arch Phil* 48,168–170 Ja–Mr 85

CEBIK, L B. *Fictional Narrative And Truth: An Epistemic Analysis.* Lanham, Univ Pr of America, 1984.
Haight, M R. *Brit J Aes* 25,289–291 Sum 85

CENTI, Tito S. *Nel Segno Del Sole: San Tommaso D'Aquino.* Roma, San Sisto Vecchio, 1983.
Malatesta, Michele. *Sapienza* 37,467–469 O–D 84

CHABOT, Marc and Vidricaire, André (eds). *Objet Pour La Philosophie.* Québec, Pantoute, 1983.
Bellemare, Pierre. *Dialogue (Canada)* 23,538–541 S 84

CHADWICK, Henry. *Boethius.* Oxford, Clarendon Pr, 1981.
Clark, Stephen R L. *Relig Stud* 20,308–310 Je 84
Weisheipl, James A. *J Hist Phil* 23,101–103 Ja 85
Bussanich, John. *Ancient Phil* 4,115–117 Spr 84

CHAPMAN, T. *Time: A Philosophical Analysis.* Dordrecht, Reidel, 1982.
Hoy, Ronald C. *Phil Sci* 51,694–696 D 84

CHARLES–SAGET, Annick. *L'architecture Du Divin.* Paris, Belles, 1982.
Bellemare, Pierre. *Can Phil Rev* 4,139–141 Ag 84

CHARLES, Rodger and Maclaren, Drostan. *The Social Teaching Of Vatican II.* San Francisco, Ignatius Pr, 1982.
Walsh, Michael J. *Heythrop J* 25,497–498 O 84

CHATTERJEE, Margaret. *Gandhi's Religious Thought.* London, Macmillan, Undated.
Teichman, Jenny. *Relig Stud* 21,112–114 Mr 85

CHATTERJEE, Margaret. *The Language Of Philosophy.* The Hague, Nijhoff, 1981.
Lipner, Julius. *Relig Stud* 20,711–714 D 84

CHIERIGHIN, Franco and others (trans). *G W F Hegel: Logica E Metafisica Di Jena (1804/05).* Trento, Verifiche, 1982.
Di Giovanni, George. *Bull Hegel Soc Gr Brit* 9,14–17 Spr/Sum 84

CHISHOLM, Roderick M. *The Foundations Of Knowing.* Minneapolis, Univ of Minnesota Pr, 1982.
Ingham, Nicholas. *Thomist* 49,131–132 Ja 85

CHOROVER, Stephan L. *From Genesis To Genocide.* Cambridge, MIT Pr, 1980.
Thigpen, Robert B. *Soc Indic Res* 16,223–226 F 85

CHRIST, Karl. *Romische Geschichte Und Deutsche Geschichtswissenschaft.* Munich, Beck, 1982.
Bowersock, G W. *Hist Theor* 23,370–378 O 84

CHRISTENSEN, D E (ed). *Contemporary German Philosophy, V1.* University Park, Pennsylvania State Univ Pr, 1983.
Stepelevich, Lawrence S. *Rev Metaph* 38,620–621 Mr 85

CLAESGES, Ulrich. *Darstellung Des Erscheinenden Wissens.* Bonn, Bouvier, 1981.
Bungay, Stephen. *Bull Hegel Soc Gr Brit* 9,22–25 Spr/Sum 84

CLARK, Michael. *The Place Of Syllogistic In Logical Theory.* Nottingham, Univ of Nottingham, 1980.
Smith, Robin. *Hist Phil Log* 3,222–224 1982

CLARKE, B L and Long, E T (eds). *God And Temporality.* NY, Paragon House, 1984.

Louth, Andrew. *Relig Stud* 21,109–110 Mr 85

EVANS, Gareth (ed). *The Varieties Of Reference.* Oxford, Clarendon Pr, 1982.
McCulloch, Gregory. *Phil Quart* 34,515–518 O 84

EVANS, Stephen C. *Subjectivity And Religious Belief.* Washington, Univ Pr of America, 1982.
Pojman, Louis P. *Faith Phil* 1,443–447 O 84

EYERMAN, Ron. *False Consciousness And Ideology In Marxist Theory.* Stockholm, Almqvist & Wiksell, 1981.
Gilbert, Rob. *Phil Soc Sci* 14,575–577 D 84

FAGOT, Anne M (ed). *Médocome Et Probabilités.* Paris, Didier–Erudition, 1982.
Kormos, H R. *J Med Phil* 9,419–422 N 84

FANN, K T (ed). *Ludwig Wittgenstein: The Man And His Philosophy.* Atlantic Highlands, Humanities Pr, 1978.
Bell, D A. *Hist Phil Log* 1,235–237 1980

FARR, W (ed). *Hume Und Kant: Interpretation Und Diskussion.* Freiberg, Alber, 1982.
Elders, Leo J. *Rev Metaph* 38,886–887 Je 85

FARRE, Luis. *Antropología Filosófica.* Bueno Aires, Tres Tiempos, 1984.
Lértora Mendoza, C A. *Rev Filosof (Mexico)* 18,180–183 Ja–Ap 85

FARRELL, B A. *The Standing Of Psychoanalysis.* Oxford, Oxford Univ Pr, 1981.
Wallerstein, Robert S. *Nous* 18,534–541 S 84
Lavin, Michael. *Phil Sci* 51,177–179 Mr 84

FARRELL, Martin Diego. *Utilitarismo: Etica Y Política.* Buenos Aires, Abeledo–Perrot, 1983.
Maliandi, Ricardo. *Rev Latin De Filosof* 10,274–278 N 84

FEENBERG, Andrew. *Lukács, Marx And The Sources Of Critical Theory.* Totowa, Rowman & Littlefield, 1981.
Schuler, Jeanne. *Phil Soc Sci* 15,221–224 Je 85

FEHER, F and Heller, A and Markus, G. *Dictatorship Over Needs.* Oxford, Blackwell, 1982.
Golubović, Zagorka. *Praxis Int* 4,322–334 O 84

FEINSTEIN, Howard M. *Becoming William James.* Ithaca, Cornell Univ Pr, 1984.
Levinson, Henry Samuel. *Trans Peirce Soc* 21,449–455 Sum 85

FENGER, H. *Kierkegaard, The Myths And Their Origins.* New Haven, Yale Univ Pr, 1980.
Durfee, Harold A. *Rev Metaph* 38,387–388 D 84

FENICHEL, Hanna. *Fortune Is A Woman.* Berkeley, Univ of California Pr, 1984.
McIntosh, Donald. *Polit Theory* 13,296–300 My 85

FERRY, Luc. *Philosophie Politique, I: Le Droit, 2v.* Paris, Pr de Univ France, 1984.
Knee, Philip. *Laval Theol Phil* 41,456–458 O 85

FESSARD, Gaston. *La Philosophie Historique De Raymond Aron.* Paris, Julliard, 1980.
Sales, Michel. *Arch Phil* 47,503–505 Jl–S 84

FETZER, James H. *Scientific Knowledge: Causation, Explanation And Corroboration.* Dordrecht, Reidel, 1981.
Tiles, Mary. *Phil Books* 26,39–40 Ja 85

FEYERABEND, Paul K. *Problems Of Empiricism.* Cambridge, Cambridge Univ Pr, 1981.
Nemesszeghy, Ervin. *Heythrop J* 26,348–350 Jl 85

FEYERABEND, Paul K. *Realism, Rationalism And Scientific Method.* Cambridge, Cambridge Univ Pr, 1981.
Nemesszeghy, Ervin. *Heythrop J* 26,348–350 Jl 85

FIELD, Hartry H. *Science Without Numbers, A Defence Of Nominalism.* Princeton, Princeton Univ Pr, 1980.
Shapiro, Stewart. *Philosophia (Israel)* 14,437–443 D 84

FINDLAY, J N. *Kant And The Transcendental Object: A Hermeneutic Study.* Oxford, Clarendon Pr, 1981.
Moran, Philip. *Phil Phenomenol Res* 45,473–474 Mr 85
Pinkerton, R J. *Austl J Phil* 62,305–308 S 84

FINNIS, John. *Fundamentals Of Ethics.* Washington, Georgetown Univ Pr, 1983.
Brown, Geoffrey. *Phil Quart* 35,210–211 Ap 85
Donnelly, John. *Phil Books* 25,227–229 O 84
Gordon, David. *Int Phil Quart* 24,329–330 S 84

FIORA, G and Galli, E and Magri, M A. *Lezioni Di Logica Matematica.* London, Soncino, 1982.
Maramotti, Anna L. *Riv Filosof Neo–Scolas* 76,333–335 Ap–Je 84

FIORE, Peter A. *Milton And Augustine.* University Park, Pennsylvania State Univ Pr, Undated.
Horne, B L. *Relig Stud* 21,126–128 Mr 85

FIORENZA, Elisabeth Schüssler. *In Memory Of Her.* London, SCM Pr, 1983.
King, Ursula. *Relig Stud* 20,699–702 D 84

FIRST, Ruth and Scott, Ann. *Olive Schreiner: A Biography.* NY, Schocken Books, 1980.
Minnich, Elizabeth K. *Fem Stud* 11,287–305 Sum 85

FISCH, Max H and others (eds). *The Writings Of Charles S Peirce: A Chronological Edition, V1.* Bloomington, Indiana Univ Pr, 1982.
Almeder, Robert. *J Hist Phil* 22,494–497 O 84

FISCHER, N. *Economy And Self.* Westport, Greenwood Pr, 1979.
Berki, R N. *Bull Hegel Soc Gr Brit* 3,48–50 Spr/Sum 81

FISHER, Alec. *Formal Number Theory And Compatibility.* NY, Oxford Univ Pr, 1982.

Cocchiarella, Nino B. *Teach Phil* 7,361–362 O 84

FISHER, John (ed). *Essays On Aesthetics.* Philadelphia, Temple Univ Pr, 1983.
Todd, D D. *Dialogue (Canada)* 23,745–750 D 84
Humble, P N. *Brit J Aes* 24,362–364 Autumn 84

FISHKIN, James S. *Tyranny And Legitimacy: A Critique Of Political Theories.* Baltimore, Johns Hopkins Univ Pr, 1979.
Farrell, Daniel M. *Phil Topics* 12,260–264 Wint 81

FISHKIN, James. *Beyond Subjective Morality.* New Haven, Yale Univ Pr, 1984.
Locke, Don. *Can Phil Rev* 5,59–60 F 85
Roqué, Alicia J. *J Soc Phil* 15,61–62 Fall 84
Fowlie, I M. *Phil Books* 26,176–178 Jl 85

FISHKIN, James. *Justice, Equal Opportunity, And The Family.* New Haven, Yale Univ Pr, 1983.
Blustein, Jeffrey. *Law Phil* 3,321–327 Ag 84

FITTING, Melvin. *Proof Methods For Modal And Intuitionistic Logics.* Dordrecht, Reidel, 1983.
De Swart, H C M. *Hist Phil Log* 6,152–153 1985

FITZGERALD, J T and White, L M (trans). *The Tabula Of Cebes.* Chico, Scholars Pr, 1983.
Strange, Steven K. *Ancient Phil* 4,106–108 Spr 84

FLECK, Ludwik. *Erfahrung Und Tatsache.* Frankfurt, Suhrkamp, 1983.
Wittich, Dieter. *Deut Z Phil* 33,278–281 1985

FLETCHER, Bruce. *Social And Political Perspectives.* Washington, Univ Pr of America, 1983.
Elford, R John. *Relig Stud* 20,517–518 S 084

FLEW, Antony. *The Politics Of Procrustes: Contradictions Of Enforced Equality.* Buffalo, Prometheus Books, 1981.
Farrell, Daniel M. *Phil Topics* 12,255–260 Wint 81

FLYNN, Thomas R. *Sartre And Marxist Existentialism.* Chicago, Univ of Chicago Pr, 1983.
Miller, Jim. *Polit Theory* 12,607–611 N 84
Laflamme, Simon. *Can Phil Rev* 4,242–244 D 84

FOCHER, Ferruccio. *I Quattro Autori Di Popper.* Milano, Angeli, 1982.
Negri, Maria Paola. *Riv Filosof Neo–Scolas* 76,342–344 Ap–Je 84

FONSECA LABRADA, Heliodoro E. *Moral, Sociedad Y Antropología En Nietzsche.* La Coruña, Pontdeume, 1984.
Radchik, Laura. *Logos (Mexico)* 13,131–132 Ja–Ap 85

FORD, L S and Kline, G L (eds). *Explorations In Whitehead's Philosophy.* NY, Fordham Univ Pr, 1983.
Nelson, Herbert J. *Trans Peirce Soc* 21,139–146 Wint 85

FORD, M P. *William James' Philosophy: A New Perspective.* Amherst, Univ of Massachusetts Pr, 1982.
Gouinlock, James. *Rev Metaph* 38,622–623 Mr 85

FORSCHNER, Maximilian. *Die Stoische Ethik.* Stuttgart, Klett–Cotta, 1981.
Görler, Woldemar. *Phil Rundsch* 31,272–281 1984

FORSTER, T E. *Quine's New Foundations (An Introduction).* Louvain, Univ Catholique de Louvain, 1983.
Oswald, Urs. *J Sym Log* 50,547–548 Je 85

FÖRSTER, Wolfgang. *Gesellschaftslehren Der Klassischen Bürgerlichen Deutschen.* Berlin, Akademie, 1983.
Biedermann, G and Friedrich, H. *Deut Z Phil* 32,1140–1143 1984

FOSTER, John. *The Case For Idealism: International Library Of Philosophy.* Boston, Routledge & Kegan Paul, 1982.
Willard, Dallas. *Hist Phil Log* 6,134–137 1985
Fumerton, Richard A. *Phil Phenomenol Res* 45,459–461 Mr 85
Jackson, Frank. *Inquiry* 27,463–467 D 84
Hinckfuss, Ian. *Austl J Phil* 63,88–95 Mr 85

FOUCAULT, Michel. *This Is Not A Pipe, James Harkness (ed & trans).* Berkeley, Univ of California Pr, 1983.
Von Morstein, Petra. *Can Phil Rev* 4,144–147 Ag 84
Margolis, Joseph. *J Aes Art Crit* 43,224–225 Wint 84

FOUCAULT, Michel. *This Is Not A Pipe, James Harkness (ed & trans).* Berkeley, Univ of California Pr, 1983.
Wolff, Janet. *Brit J Aes* 24,368–370 Autumn 84

FOX, A. *Thomas More: History And Providence.* Oxford, Blackwell, 1982.
Koenigsberger, Dorothy. *Hist Euro Ideas* 5,453–455 1984

FRALEIGH, Warren P. *Right Actions In Sport: Ethics For Contestants.* Champaign, Human Kinetics, 1984.
Hyland, Drew A. *J Phil Sport* 11,83–88 1984
Cooper, Wesley E. *Can Phil Rev* 5,5–7 Ja 85

FRANCK, Frederick, (ed). *The Buddha Eye: An Anthology Of The Kyoto School.* NY, Crossroad, 1982.
Heine, Steven. *Phil East West* 34,459–461 O 84

FRANZEN, W. *Die Bedeutung Von "Wahr" Und "Wahrheit".* Freiburg, Alber, 1982.
Gram, Moltke S. *Rev Metaph* 38,623–626 Mr 85
Grasshoff, G. *Hist Phil Log* 5,138–141 1984

FREDDOSO, Alfred J (ed). *The Existence And Nature Of God.* Notre Dame, Univ of Notre Dame Pr, 1983.
Burrell, David B. *Int J Phil Relig* 16,173–174 1984
Millar, Alan. *Relig Stud* 20,682–685 D 84
Mann, William E. *Faith Phil* 2,195–204 Ap 85

FREEMAN, Eugene (ed). *The Relevance Of Charles Peirce.* La Salle, Monist Library Of Philosophy, 1983.
Ochs, Peter. *Trans Peirce Soc* 21,121–138 Wint 85

FRENCH, Peter A and others (eds). *Midwest Studies In Philosophy V, 1980.* Minneapolis, Univ of Minnesota Pr, 1980.
Adler, Jonathan E. *Synthese* 61,261–272 N 84

FRENCH, Peter A. *Ethics In Government.* Englewood Cliffs, Prentice–Hall, 1983.
Waluchow, Wilfrid J. *Dialogue (Canada)* 23,364–366 Je 84

FREY, R G. *Interests And Rights: The Case Against Animals.* Oxford, Clarendon Pr, 1980.
Goodman, L E. *Philosophia* 14,249–250 Ag 84

FREY, R G. *Rights, Killing, And Suffering.* Oxford, Blackwell, 1983.
Easton, Susan M. *J Med Ethics* 11,51–52 Mr 85
Shaw, William H. *Phil Papers* 14,46–48 My 85
Fox, Michael Allen. *Can Phil Rev* 5,190–193 My–Je 85

FRIEDMAN, Maurice. *Martin Buber's Life And Work, 3v.* NY, Dutton, 1983.
Kluback, William. *Int J Phil Relig* 16,167–169 1984

FRISCHER, Bernard. *The Sculpted Word.* Berkeley, Pub Unknown, 1982.
Clay, Diskin. *Amer J Philo* 105,484–489 Wint 84

FRITZHAND, Marek. *Wartosci A Fakty.* Warszawa, PWN, 1982.
Jankowski, Henryk. *Dialec Hum* 10,224–228 Sum 83

FROHOCK, Fred M. *Abortion: A Case Study In Law And Morals.* Westport, Greenwood Pr, 1983.
DeCew, Judith Wagner. *Ethics* 95,375–376 Ja 85

FROMAN, Wayne Jeffrey. *Merleau-Ponty: Language And The Act Of Speech.* East Brunswick, Bucknell Univ Pr, 1982.
Busch, Thomas W. *Mod Sch* 62,57–59 N 84
Innis, Robert E. *Rev Metaph* 38,887–888 Je 85

FRONGIA, Guido. *Wittgenstein: Regole E Sistema.* Milano, Angeli, 1983.
Engel, Pascal. *Rev Phil Fr* 175,50–52 Ja–Mr 85
Micheletti, Mario. *Riv Filosof Neo–Scolas* 76,495–497 Jl–S 84

FRYE, Roland M (ed). *Is God A Creationist.* NY, Scribners, Undated.
Crosson, Frederick J. *Faith Phil* 1,343–345 Jl 84

GÄCHTER, Othmar. *Hermeneutics And Language In Pūrva Mīmāṃsā.* Delhi, Motilal, 1983.
Taber, John. *Phil East West* 35,215–217 Ap 85

GADAMER, Hans Georg. *Heideggers Wege.* Tübingen, Mohr, 1983.
Lichtigfeld, A. *S Afr J Phil* 4,35 F 85

GADAMER, Hans–Georg. *Reason In An Age Of Science, Frederick G Lawrence (trans).* Cambridge, MIT Pr, 1982.
Cowan, Bainard. *Rev Metaph* 38,626–627 Mr 85
Walsh, Robert D. *Auslegung* 11,417–424 Fall 84
Rissner, James. *Can Phil Rev* 4,244–247 D 84
Daniel, Mano. *Eidos* 4,129–134 Je 85

GAGNEBIN, Jeanne–Marie. *Zur Geschichtsphilosophie Walter Benjamins.* Erlangen, Erlanger Studien, 1978.
Deuber, Astrid. *Stud Phil (Switzerland)* 41,259–261 1982

GALÁN, P Cerezo. *La Voluntad De Aventura.* Barcelona, Ariel, 1984.
Pintor–Ramos, A. *Rev Latin De Filosof* 11,182–185 Jl 85

GALLI, Carlo. *I Controrivoluzionari.* Bologna, Mulino, 1981.
Turco, Giovanni. *Sapienza* 37,463–467 O–D 84

GALLOP, David. *Parmenides Of Elea: Fragments.* Toronto, Univ of Toronto Pr, 1984.
Matthen, Mohan. *Can Phil Rev* 5,113–116 Mr 85

GÄRDENFORS, P and others (eds). *Evidentiary Value.* Lund, Gleerups, 1983.
O'Neill, L J. *Austl J Phil* 62,302–303 S 84

GARETH, Evans. *The Varieties Of Reference, John McDowell (ed).* Oxford, Clarendon Pr, 1982.
Devitt, Michael. *Austl J Phil* 63,216–232 Je 85

GARFINKEL, Alan. *Forms Of Explanation: Rethinking The Questions In Social Theory.* New Haven, Yale Univ Pr, 1981.
Turner, Stephen. *Phil Soc Sci* 14,416–418 S 84

GARRIGUES, Juan Miguel. *L'église, La Société Libre Et Le Communisme.* Paris, Julliard, 1983.
De Laubier, Patrick. *Rev Thomiste* 84,489–492 Jl–S 84

GASKIN, John C A. *The Quest For Eternity: An Outline Of The Philosophy Of Religion.* Harmondsworth, Penguin Books, 1984.
Arthur, C J. *Hermathena* 138,90–92 Sum 85
Moulder, James. *S Afr J Phil* 4,35–37 F 85

GAUS, Gerald F. *The Modern Liberal Theory Of Man.* NY, St Martin's Pr, 1983.
Franco, Paul. *Ethics* 95,364–366 Ja 85

GAUTHIER, Yvon. *Théorétiques.* Longueuil, Préambule, 1982.
Lepage, François. *Dialogue (Canada)* 24,101–113 Spr 85
Nadeau, Robert. *Dialogue (Canada)* 24,115–130 Spr 85

GEBAUER, G and others. *Wien: Kundmangasse 19.* München, Fink, 1982.
Haller, Rudolf. *Grazer Phil Stud* 21,219–221 1984

GEBAUER, Gunter. *Der Einzelne Und Sein Gesellschaftliches Wissen.* Berlin, De Gruyter, 1981.
Jacques, Francis. *Rev Int Phil* 38,315–319 1984

GEFFRÉ, Claude. *Le Christianisme Au Risque De L'interprétation.* Paris, Cerf, 1983.
Rinfret, Gaston. *Laval Theol Phil* 41,269–271 Je 85

GELLNER, Ernest. *Nations And Nationalism.* Oxford, Blackwell, 1983.
Breuilly, John. *Phil Soc Sci* 15,65–75 Mr 85

GENDRON, Bernard. *Technology And The Human Condition.* NY, St Martin's Pr, 1977.
Settle, Tom. *Phil Soc Sci* 14,515–527 D 84

GENTILE, Francesco. *Intelligenza Politica E Ragion Di Ragion Di Stato.* Milano, Giuffrè, 1983.
Tripodi, Giuseppe. *Riv Int Filosof Diritto* 61,168–170 Ja–Mr 84

GERAETS, Theodore F (ed). *L'Esprit Absolu.* Ottawa, Univ of Ottawa Pr, 1984.
Dahlstrom, Daniel O. *Can Phil Rev* 5,193–196 My–Je 85

GÉRARD, P and others (eds). *Fonction De Juger Et Pouvoir Judiciaire.* Bruxelles, Univ Saint–Louis, 1983.
Legault, Georges A. *Can Phil Rev* 4,247–253 D 84

GERMINO, Dante. *Political Philosophy And The Open Society.* Baton Rouge, Louisiana State Univ Pr, 1982.
Webb, Eugene. *Clio* 13,284–286 Spr 84

GERSON, Lloyd P (ed). *Graceful Reason.* Toronto, Pontifical Inst of Mediaeval Stud, 1983.
Leroux, Georges. *Philosophiques* 12,229–231 Spr 85

GEWIRTH, Alan. *Human Rights: Essays On Justification And Applications.* Chicago, Univ of Chicago Pr, 1982.
Coope, Christopher Miles. *J Applied Phil* 2,148–151 Mr 85
Reuman, Robert. *Ideal Stud* 15,66–68 Ja 85
Pollis, Adamantia. *Grad Fac Phil J* 10,183–186 Spr 84

GHISALBERTI, Alessandro. *Le "Quaestiones De Anima" Attribute A Matteo Da Gubbio.* Milano, Vita & Pensiero, 1981.
Mazzarella, Pasquale. *Riv Filosof Neo–Scolas* 76,655–656 O–D 84

GIBSON JR, Roger F. *The Philosophy Of W V Quine: An Expository Essay.* Tampa, Univ of South Florida, 1982.
Koppelberg, Dirk. *Grazer Phil Stud* 21,185–191 1984

GIDDENS, Anthony. *A Comtemporary Critique Of Historical Materialism, V1.* London, Macmillan, 1981.
Thompson, John B. *Phil Soc Sci* 14,543–551 D 84

GIEDYMIN, Jerzy. *Science And Convention.* Oxford, Pergamon Pr, 1982.
Brown, James Robert. *Phil Sci* 52,168–169 Mr 85

GIER, Nicholas F. *Wittgenstein And Phenomenology.* Albany, SUNY Pr, 1981.
Brough, John B. *Ideal Stud* 15,165–166 My 85
Rubinstein, David. *Phil Soc Sci* 14,582–585 D 84

GIFFORD, N I. *When In Rome: An Introduction To Relativism And Knowledge.* Albany, SUNY Pr, 1983.
Smithurst, M. *Phil Books* 26,94–96 Ap 85

GILL, Jerry H. *Wittgenstein And Metaphor.* Washington, Univ Pr of America, 1981.
Hinman, Lawrence M. *Phil Phenomenol Res* 45,465–467 Mr 85

GILLAN, Gareth. *From Sign To Symbol.* Brighton, Harvester Pr, 1982.
McLure, Roger. *J Brit Soc Phenomenol* 16,91–94 Ja 85

GILLIARD, François. *L'experience Juridique: Esquisse D'une Dialiectique.* Genève, Droz, 1979.
Voelke, A J. *Stud Phil (Switzerland)* 41,247–250 1982

GILLIES, D A. *Frege, Dedekind, And Peano On The Foundations Of Arithmetic.* Assen, Gorcum, 1982.
Mayberry, J P. *Phil Quart* 34,424–425 Jl 84

GINET, Karl and Shoemaker, Sydney (eds). *Knowledge And Mind: Philosophical Essays.* Oxford, Oxford Univ Pr, 1984.
Cox, J W Roxbee. *Phil Books* 26,31–33 Ja 85
Stich, Stephen P. *Ethics* 95,357–358 Ja 85

GIROUX, Henry A. *Theory And Resistance In Education.* South Hadley, Bergin & Garvey, 1983.
Simon, Roger I. *Educ Theory* 34,379–388 Fall 84

GLOVER, Jonathan. *What Sort Of People Should There Be.* Harmondsworth, Penguin, 1984.
Page, Edgar. *J Applied Phil* 2,143–148 Mr 85

GODDARD, Leonard and Judge, Brenda. *The Metaphysics Of Wittgenstein's Tractatus.* Melbourne, Australiasian Assoc of Philosophy, 1982.
Bogen, James. *Can Phil Rev* 14,147–149 Ag 84
Block, Irving. *Dialogue (Canada)* 23,361–364 Je 84

GODDARD, Leonard and Routley, Richard. *The Logic Of Significance And Context, V1.* Edinburgh, Scottish Academic Pr, 1973.
Cocchiarella, Nino B. *J Sym Log* 49,1413–1415 D 84

GOFF, Tom W. *Marx And Mead: Contributions To A Sociology Of Knowledge.* London, Routledge & Kegan Paul, 1980.
Hudelson, Richard. *Phil Soc Sci* 15,87–89 Mr 85

GOISIS, Giuseppe. *Sorel E I Soreliani: Le Metamorfosi Dell'attivismo.* Venezia, Helvetia, 1983.
Andreatta, Daniela. *Riv Int Filosof Diritto* 61,720–722 O–D 84

GOLDING, Martin P. *Legal Reasoning.* NY, Knopf, 1984.
Miller, Bruce L. *Teach Phil* 8,167–169 Ap 85

GOLDMANN, Lucien. *Lukács And Heidegger: Towards A New Philosophy.* London, Routledge & Kegan Paul, 1977.
Loewen, Helmut–Harry. *Eidos* 1,126–134 Jl 78

GOLDTHORPE, Rhiannon. *Sartre: Literature And Theory.* Cambridge, Cambridge Univ Pr, 1984.
Howells, Christina. *J Brit Soc Phenomenol* 16,210–211 My 85

GONZÁLEZ FAUS, José Ignacio. *El Engaño De De Un Capitalismo Inaceptable.* Santander, Terrae, 1983.
Pegueroles, J. *Espiritu* 34,99–101 Ja–Je 85

GOOD, I J. *Good Thinking.* Minneapolis, Univ of Minnesota Pr, 1983.
Hacking, Ian. *Can Phil Rev* 4,253–256 D 84
Byrne, Charles L. *Rev Metaph* 38,390–391 D 84

GOODIN, Robert E. *Political Theory And Public Policy.* Chicago, Univ of Chicago Pr, 1982.
Macleod, Alistair M. *Ethics* 95,157–159 O 84

GOODMAN, Nelson. *Of Mind And Other Matters.* Cambridge, Harvard Univ Pr, 1984.
Nehamas, Alexander. *J Aes Art Crit* 43,209–211 Wint 84
Hanen, Marsha. *Phil Books* 26,153–156 Jl 85
Sharpe, R A. *Brit J Aes* 25,285 Sum 85
Lyas, Colin. *Phil Quart* 35,318–320 Jl 85

GÖRLAND, Ingtraud. *Transzendenz Und Selbst: Eine Phase In Heideggers Denken.* Frankfurt, Klostermann, 1981.
Grondin, Jean. *Arch Phil* 47,496–499 Jl–S 84

GOROVITZ, Samuel and others (eds). *Moral Problems In Medicine, 2nd Ed.* Englewood Cliffs, Prentice–Hall, 1983.
Cebik, L B. *Teach Phil* 7,250–255 Jl 84

GOSLING, J C B and Taylor, C C W. *The Greeks On Pleasure.* Oxford, Oxford Univ Pr, 1982.
Wiles, Ann M. *Rev Metaph* 38,627–629 Mr 85
Moravcsik, J M E. *Can Phil Rev* 4,192–196 O 84
Kraut, Richard. *Phil Rev* 94,265–270 Ap 85
Lindenmuth, Donald C. *Ancient Phil* 4,111–115 Spr 84
Charlton, W. *Mind* 93,603–605 O 84
Gerstmeyer, Thomas. *Ratio* 27,99–102 Je 85
Ruttenberg, Howard. *Ethics* 95,963–964 Jl 85

GOTTLIEB, Dale. *Ontological Economy.* Oxford, Oxford Univ Pr, 1980.
Shapiro, Stewart. *Philosophia (Israel)* 14,451–457 D 84

GOUHIER, Henry. *Cartésianisme Et Agustinisme Au XVII Siècle.* Paris, Vrin, 1978.
Garber, Dino. *Rev Ven Filosof* 12,103–113 1980

GOULDER, Michael and Hick, John. *Why Believe In God.* London, SCM Pr, 1983.
Roberts, T A. *Relig Stud* 20,695–696 D 84

GOYARD–FABRE, Simone. *L'interminable Querelle Du Contrat Social.* Ottawa, Univ de Ottawa, 1983.
Roy, Jean. *Can Phil Rev* 4,256–259 D 84
Boulad–Ayoub, Josiane. *Dialogue (Canada)* 24,166–168 Spr 85
Gabaude, Jean–Marc. *Rev Phil Louvain* 82,579–581 N 84

GRACIA, Jorge J E (ed). *El Hombre Y Su Conducta.* Rio Piedras, Editorial Univ, 1980.
Marti, Oscar R. *Rev Latin De Filosof* 11,179–181 Jl 85

GRACIA, Jorge J E (trans). *Suarez On Individuation.* Milwaukee, Marquette Univ Pr, 1982.
Ross, James F. *J Hist Phil* 22,476–478 O 84

GRAESER, Andreas. *Die Philosophie Der Antike 2: Sophistik Und Sokratik, V2.* München, Beck, 1983.
Müller, Anselm W. *J Hist Phil* 23,422–424 Jl 85

GRAFTON, Anthony. *Joseph Scaliger, A Study In The History Of Classical Scholarship.* Oxford, Clarendon Pr, 1983.
Kelley, Donald R. *Hist Theor* 24,79–87 F 85

GRAHAM, Gordon. *Historical Explanation Reconsidered.* Aberdeen, Aberdeen Univ Pr, 1983.
Palmer, Humphrey. *Phil Books* 26,63–64 Ja 85
Lambert, Kenneth A. *Hist Euro Ideas* 6,79–80 1985
Atkinson, R F. *Phil Invest* 8,76–77 Ja 85

GRAM, M S (ed). *Interpreting Kant.* Iowa City, Univ of Iowa Pr, 1982.
Genova, A C. *Rev Metaph* 38,629–631 Mr 85

GRAM, Moltke S. *Direct Realism: A Study Of Perception.* The Hague, Nijhoff, 1983.
Dicker, Georges. *Can Phil Rev* 5,196–198 My–Je 85

GRANA, Nicola. *Logica Paraconsistente.* Napoli, Loffredo, 1983.
Asenjo, Florencio G. *Rev Latin De Filosof* 10,273–274 N 84

GRANADOS, Tomás Melendo. *Ontologia De Los Opuestos.* Pampelune, Univ de Navarra, 1982.
Pasqua, Hervé. *Rev Phil Louvain* 83,293–296 My 85

GRASSI, Ernesto and Schmale, Hugo (eds). *Das Gespräch Als Ereignis: Ein Semiotisches Problem.* Munich, Fink, 1982.
Krois, John Michael. *Phil Rhet* 17,242–244 1984

GRASSIAN, Victor. *Perennial Philosophical Issues.* Englewood Cliffs, Prentice–Hall, 1984.
Goodman, Russell B. *Teach Phil* 8,58–60 Ja 85

GRATTAN–GUINNESS, I (ed). *From Calculus To Set Theory, 1630–1910: An Introductory History.* London, Duckworth, 1980.
Jones, Roger. *Phil Sci* 51,519–522 S 84

GRAVEL, Pierre and Reiss, Timothy J (eds). *Tragique Et Tragédie Dans La Tradition Occidentale.* Montréal, Déterminations, 1983.
Leroux, Georges. *Philosophiques* 11,425–427 O 84

GRAY, John. *Mill On Liberty: A Defence.* London, Routledge & Kegan Paul, 1983.
Mack, Eric. *Law Phil* 3,427–430 D 84
Vallance, Elizabeth. *Heythrop J* 26,354–355 Jl 85
Ball, Terence. *Hist Polit Thought* 5,379–382 Sum 84

GRAYLING, A C. *An Introduction To Philosophical Logic.* NY, Barnes & Noble, 1982.
Lehmann, S K. *Teach Phil* 8,87–89 Ja 85
Haack, Susan. *J Sym Log* 50,553–554 Je 85
Hutcheson, Peter. *Mod Sch* 62,59–60 N 84

GREENAWALT, Kent. *Discrimination And Reverse Discrimination.* NY, Knopf, 1983.
Fullinwider, Robert K. *Ethics* 95,154–156 O 84

GREENE, Marjorie (ed). *Dimensions Of Darwinism.* Cambridge, Cambridge Univ Pr, 1983.
Holsinger, Kent E. *Phil Sci* 52,161–163 Mr 85

GRESHAKE, Gisbert. *Il Prezzo Dell'amore.* Brescia, Morcelliana, 1984.
Belletti, Bruno. *Riv Filosof Neo–Scolas* 76,471–473 Jl–S 84

GREY, Thomas C. *The Legal Enforcement Of Morality.* NY, Knopf, 1983.
Silver, Charles. *Ethics* 95,156–157 O 84

GRIBBLE, James. *Literary Education: A Revaluation.* Cambridge, Cambridge Univ Pr, 1983.
Newton, K M. *Brit J Aes* 25,85–86 Wint 85

GRIFFITHS, A Phillips (ed). *Of Liberty: Royal Institute Of Philosophy Lectures, 1980–1.* Cambridge, Cambridge Univ Pr, 1983.
Knowles, D R. *Mind* 93,622–624 O 84

GRIFFITHS, A Phillips (ed). *Philosophy And Literature.* Cambridge, Cambridge Univ Pr, 1984.
Phillips, D Z. *Phil Books* 26,173–175 Jl 85

GRIMALDI, William M A. *Aristotle, Rhetoric I: A Commentary.* NY, Fordham Univ Pr, 1981.
Kennedy, George A. *Amer J Philo* 106,131–133 Spr 85

GRIMSLEY, Ronald. *Jean–Jacques Rousseau.* NY, Barnes & Noble, 1983.
Lemos, Ramon M. *Teach Phil* 8,68–69 Ja 85

GRMEK, Mirko D. *Les Maladies À L'Aube De La Civilisation Occidentale.* Paris, Payot, 1983.
Pellegrin, Pierre. *Rev Phil Fr* 175,234–235 Ap–Je 85

GRONDIN, Jean. *Hermeneutische Wahrheit.* Koenigstein, Forum Academicum, 1982.
Fruchon, P. *Arch Phil* 47,499–502 Jl–S 84
Rockmore, Tom. *Int Phil Quart* 24,335–337 S 84
Piché, Claude. *Laval Theol Phil* 39,375–377 O 83

GROSSETESTE, Robert. *Hexaëmeron,* Richard C Dales and Servus Gieben (eds). London, Oxford Univ Pr, 1982.
Marrone, Steven P. *J Hist Phil* 23,427–429 Jl 85

GRUENDER, J H and Agazzi, E (eds). *Theory Change, Ancient Axiomatics, And Galileo's Methodology.* Dordrecht, Reidel, 1981.
Sylla, Edith Dudley. *Phil Sci* 51,525–527 S 84

GRUENDER, J H D and Agazzi, E (eds). *Proceedings Of The 1978 Pisa Conference.* Dordrecht, Reidel, 1981.
Finocchiaro, Maurice A. *Phil Soc Sci* 14,572–575 D 84

GUEROULT, Martial. *Descartes' Philosophy, V1: The Soul And God,* Roger Ariew (trans). Minneapolis, Univ of Minnesota Pr, 1984.
Cottingham, John. *Phil Books* 26,140–143 Jl 85
Van De Pitte, F P. *Can Phil Rev* 5,198–201 My–Je 85

GUIGNON, Charles. *Heidegger And The Problem Of Knowledge.* Indianapolis, Hackett, 1983.
Hall, Harrison. *Can Phil Rev* 5,61–63 F 85
Schatzki, Theodore R. *Inquiry* 28,273–287 Je 85

GUNN, J A. *Beyond Liberty And Property.* Montreal, McGill–Queen's Univ Pr, 1983.
Damico, Alfonso J. *Ethics* 95,368–370 Ja 85

GUSDORF, Georges. *Du Néant À Dieu Dans Le Savoir Romantique.* Paris, Payot, 1983.
Adam, Michel. *Rev Phil Fr* 175,36–38 Ja–Mr 85

GUSTAFSON, James M. *Ethics From A Theocentric Perspective, V1.* Chicago, Univ of Chicago Pr, 1981.
Musser, Donald W. *Int J Phil Relig* 16,185–187 1984

GUTHRIE, W K C. *A History Of Greek Philosophy, V5.* Cambridge, Cambridge Univ Pr, 1978.
Hantz, Harold D. *Philosophia (Israel)* 14,389–426 D 84

GUTTENTAG, Maria and Secord, Paul F. *Too Many Women: The Sex Ratio Question.* Beverly Hills, Sage, 1983.
McCleary, Rachel M. *Ethics* 95,165–167 O 84

GUTTING, Gary. *Religious Belief And Religious Skepticism.* Notre Dame, Univ of Notre Dame Pr, 1982.
Mavrodes, George I. *Faith Phil* 1,440–443 O 84
Clark, Mary T. *Teach Phil* 7,273–275 Jl 84
Moulder, James. *S Afr J Phil* 4,35–37 F 85

HAUERWAS, S and MacIntyre, A (eds). *Revisions: Changing Perspectives In Moral Philosophy.* Notre Dame, Univ of Notre Dame Pr, 1983.
  Hewitt, Glenn. *Int J Phil Relig* 16,178–181 1984

HAUERWAS, Stanley. *The Peaceable Kingdom: A Primer In Christian Ethics.* Notre Dame, Univ of Notre Dame Pr, 1983.
  Hewitt, Glenn. *Int J Phil Relig* 16,178–181 1984

HAUFFE, Heinz. *Der Informationsgehlat Von Theorien.* Wien, Springer, 1981.
  Pittioni, Veit. *Conceptus* 18,112–113 1984

HAWORTH, Lawrence. *Decadence And Objectivity.* Toronto, Univ of Toronto Pr, 1977.
  Guild, Gordon. *Eidos* 1,110–112 Jl 78

HAWTREY, R S W. *Commentary On Plato's Euthydemus.* Philadelphia, American Philosophical Society, 1981.
  Robinson, David B. *J Hellen Stud* 104,206–207 1984

HAYIM, Gila J. *The Existential Sociology Of Jean–Paul Sartre.* Amherst, Univ of Massachusetts Pr, 1980.
  Schumacher, John A. *Phil Soc Sci* 14,559–567 D 84

HEBBLETHWAITE, B and Sutherland, S (eds). *The Philosophical Frontiers Of Christian Theology.* Cambridge, Cambridge Univ Pr, 1982.
  Loades, Ann. *Hist Euro Ideas* 6,201–206 1985
  Daly, Gabriel. *Heythrop J* 25,400–402 Jl 84

HECHTER, Michael (ed). *The Microfoundations Of Macrosociology.* Philadelphia, Temple Univ Pr, 1983.
  Opp, Karl–Dieter. *Ethics* 95,360–362 Ja 85

HEELAN, Patrick A. *Space–Perception And The Philosophy Of Science.* Berkeley, Univ of California Pr, 1983.
  Goldman, Michael. *Husserl Stud* 2,107–111 1985
  Brown, Harold I. *Phil Sci* 52,159–160 Mr 85

HEGEL, G W F. *Système De La Vie Éthique, J Taminiaux (trans).* Paris, Payot, 1976.
  Gérard, Gilbert. *Rev Phil Louvain* 83,239–261 My 85

HEGEL, G W F. *Vorlesungen, V1, Claudia Becker and others (eds).* Hamburg, Meiner, 1983.
  Avineri, Shlomo. *Owl Minerva* 16,199–208 Spr 85

HEGEL, G W F. *Vorlesungen, Walter Jaeschke (ed).* Hamburg, Meiner, 1983.
  Schlitt, Dale M. *Owl Minerva* 16,69–80 Fall 84

HEGEL, Georg Wilhelm Friedrich. *Die Philosophie Des Rechts, Karl–Heinz Itling (ed).* Stuttgart, Klett–Cotta, 1983.
  Avineri, Shlomo. *Owl Minerva* 16,199–208 Spr 85
  Klenner, Hermann. *Deut Z Phil* 33,284–286 1985

HEGEL, Georg Wilhelm Friedrich. *Philosophie Des Rechts, Dieter Henrich (ed).* Frankfurt, Suhrkamp, 1983.
  Stepelevich, Lawrence S. *Rev Metaph* 38,634–636 Mr 85
  Klenner, Hermann. *Deut Z Phil* 33,284–286 1985
  Avineri, Shlomo. *Owl Minerva* 16,199–208 Spr 85

HEIDEGGER, M. *Hegels Phänomenologie Des Giestes, Ingtraud Görland (trans).* Frankfurt, Klostermann, 1980.
  István, Feher M. *Magyar Filozof Szemle* 4,677–683 1983

HEIDEGGER, Martin. *Logik Die Frage Nach Der Wahrheit.* Frankfurt, Gesamtausgabe, 1976.
  Rosales, Alberto. *Rev Ven Filosof* 12,113–124 1980

HEIDEGGER, Martin. *The Metaphysical Foundations Of Logic, Michael Helm (trans).* Bloomington, Indiana Univ Pr, 1984.
  Mays, Wolfe. *Hist Phil Log* 6,132–134 1985

HEIL, John. *Perception And Cognition.* Berkeley, Univ of California Pr, 1983.
  Russell, James. *Phil Books* 26,105–108 Ap 85
  Moser, Paul K. *Int Phil Quart* 24,332–335 S 84

HEILBRON, J L. *Electricity In The 17th And 18th Centuries.* Berkeley, Univ of California Pr, 1979.
  Stein, Howard. *Phil Sci* 51,172–175 Mr 84

HEINEKAMP, Albert (ed). *Leibniz—Bibliographie: Die Literatur Über Bis 1980.* Frankfurt, Klostermann, 1984.
  Schneider, Martin. *Stud Leibniz* 17,105–108 1985

HEINRICHS, Johannes. *Sprachtheorie.* Bonn, Bouvier, 1981.
  Dunde, Siegfried R. *Z Phil Forsch* 38,674–676 N–D 84

HEKMAN, Susan J. *Weber, The Ideal Type, And Contemporary Social Theory.* Notre Dame, Univ of Notre Dame Pr, 1983.
  Moon, Donald. *Polit Theory* 12,605–607 N 84

HELFERICH, Christoph. *Georg Wilhelm Friedrich Hegel.* Stuttgart, Metzler, 1979.
  Doniela, W V. *Bull Hegel Soc Gr Brit* 2,31–33 Autumn 80

HELLER, Agnes (ed). *Lukács Reappraised.* NY, Columbia Univ Pr, 1983.
  Winkler, Michael. *Phil Lit* 8,294–295 O 84

HELLER, Agnes. *A Theory Of History.* Don Mills, Oxford Univ Pr, 1982.
  Anderson, M G. *Can Phil Rev* 4,149–152 Ag 84

HENKIN, L and Monk, J and Tarski, A. *Cylindric Set Algebras And Related Structures.* Berlin, Springer, 1981.
  Maddux, Roger. *J Sym Log* 50,234–237 Mr 85

HENKIN, L and Monk, J and Tarski, A. *Cylindric Algebras: Part 1.* Amsterdam, North–Holland, 1971.
  Maddux, Roger. *J Sym Log* 50,234–237 Mr 85

HENRI, Cardinal De Lubac. *La Postériorité Spirituelle De Joachim De Flore, 2v.* Paris, Lethielleux, 1979.

Kluback, William. *Int J Phil Relig* 5,192–195 1984

HENRICH D, (ed). *Hegels Philosophische Psychologie.* Bonn, Bouvier, 1979.
  Leaman, Oliver. *Bull Hegel Soc Gr Brit* 3,40–43 Spr/Sum 81

HENRICH, D and Düsing, K (eds). *Hegel In Jena.* Bonn, Bouvier, 1980.
  Harris, H S. *Bull Hegel Soc Gr Brit* 2,33–36 Autumn 80

HENRICH, D and Iser, W (eds). *Funktionen Des Fiktiven.* München, Fink, 1983.
  Pfeiffer, K Ludwig. *Phil Rundsch* 32,91–104 1985

HENRY, Michel. *Marx: A Philosophy Of Human Reality, K McLaughlin (trans).* Bloomington, Indiana Univ Pr, Undated.
  McBride, William L. *J Brit Soc Phenomenol* 15,319–321 O 84

HEPBURN, R W. *"Wonder" And Other Essays.* Edinburgh, Edinburgh Univ Pr, 1984.
  Gill, Jerry H. *J Aes Art Crit* 43,329–330 Spr 85

HERMEREN, Goran. *Aspects Of Aesthetics.* Stockholm, Gleerup, 1983.
  Budd, Malcolm. *Brit J Aes* 24,364–365 Autumn 84
  Schaper, Eva. *Phil Books* 26,171–173 Jl 85

HERNADI, Paul (ed). *The Horizon Of Literature.* Lincoln, Univ of Nebraska Pr, 1982.
  Closter, Susan Vander. *Phil Rhet* 17,247–249 1984

HERNANDEZ, Ramon. *Derechos Humanos En Francisco De Vitoria.* Salamanca, San Esteban, 1984.
  Alonso, José Antonio Dacal. *Logos (Mexico)* 12,139–141 S–D 84

HERVEY, Sándor. *Semiotic Perspectives.* London, Allen & Unwin, 1982.
  Lycos, K. *Austl J Phil* 62,303–305 S 84

HEYD, David. *Supererogation: Its Status In Ethical Theory.* Cambridge, Cambridge Univ Pr, 1982.
  Cottingham, John. *Mind* 93,619–622 O 84

HEYD, Michael. *Between Orthodoxy And The Enlightenment.* The Hague, Nijhoff, 1982.
  Watson, Richard A. *J Hist Phil* 23,259–260 Ap 85

HIGONNET, Patrice. *Class, Ideology, And The Rights Of Nobles.* Oxford, Clarendon Pr, 1981.
  Barker, Nancy N. *Hist Euro Ideas* 6,94 1985

HILL, Christopher (ed). *Winstanley: "The Law Of Freedom" And Other Writings.* Cambridge, Cambridge Univ Pr, 1983.
  Pocock, J G A. *Polit Theory* 13,461–465 Ag 85

HILL, David. *The Politics Of Schizophrenia.* Lanham, Univ Pr of America, 1984.
  Pullen, G P. *J Med Ethics* 11,166 S 85

HINTIKKA, J. *Time And Necessity: Studies In Aristotle's Theory Of Modality.* Oxford, Clarendon Pr, 1972.
  Moutsopoulos, E. *Rev Phil Fr* 175,223–226 Ap–Je 85

HIRSCH, Arthur. *The French New Left: An Intellectual History From Sartre To Gorz.* Boston, South End Pr, 1981.
  Kruks, Sonia. *J Brit Soc Phenomenol* 16,213–215 My 85

HIRSCH, Eli. *The Concept Of Identity.* NY, Oxford Univ Pr, 1982.
  Kennedy, Ralph. *Phil Phenomenol Res* 45,467–473 Mr 85
  Brennan, Andrew. *Nous* 18,541–548 S 84

HITCHCOCK, David. *Critical Thinking: A Guide To Evaluating Information.* Toronto, Methuen, 1983.
  Gough, Jim. *Eidos* 3,233–240 D 84
  Pereda, Carlos. *Teach Phil* 7,261–263 Jl 84

HOCHSCHILD, Jennifer L. *The New American Dilemma.* New Haven, Yale Univ Pr, 1984.
  Braybrooke, David. *Ethics* 95,920–933 Jl 85

HODGES, Andrew. *Alan Turing: The Enigma.* London, Burnett, 1983.
  Grattan–Guinness, I. *Russell* 4,321–322 Wint 84

HODGES, Donald. *The Bureaucratization Of Socialism.* Amherst, Univ of Massachusetts Pr, 1981.
  Little, Daniel. *Can Phil Rev* 4,261–263 D 84

HÖFFE, O. *Immanuel Kant.* Munich, Beck, 1983.
  Ameriks, Karl. *Rev Metaph* 38,636–637 Mr 85

HOFFMAN, Piotr. *The Anatomy Of Idealism.* The Hague, Nijhoff, 1982.
  Rockmore, Tom. *J Hist Phil* 23,118–119 Ja 85
  Seddon, F. *Stud Soviet Tho* 28,137–141 Ag 84

HÖGEMANN, Brigitte. *Die Idee Der Freiheit Und Das Subjekt.* Königstein, Pub Unknown, 1980.
  Gerhardt, Volker. *Kantstudien* 75,498–500 1984

HOHLER, Thomas P. *Imagination And Reflection: Intersubjectivity.* The Hague, Nijhoff, 1982.
  Wright, Walter E. *Ideal Stud* 15,68–71 Ja 85
  Collins, James. *Mod Sch* 62,61–63 N 84
  Breazeale, Daniel. *J Hist Phil* 22,487–490 O 84

HOLLIS, Martin and Lukes, Steven (eds). *Rationality And Relativism.* Oxford, Blackwell, 1982.
  Hertzberg, Lars. *Phil Invest* 8,149–155 Ap 85

HOLM, Nils G. *Religious Ecstasy.* Stockholm, Almqvist & Wiksell, Undated.
  Loewenthal, C M. *Relig Stud* 20,717–718 D 84

HOLMES, Arthur F. *Ethics: Approaching Moral Decisions.* Downers Grove, Intervarsity Pr, 1984.
  Genco, Peter. *Faith Phil* 2,322–324 Jl 85

HOLMES, Peter. *Resistance And Compromise.* Cambridge, Cambridge Univ Pr, 1982.

KYRRIS, K P. *Kypros, Tourkia Kai Ellinismos.* Nicosia, Lambousa, 1980.
Koumoulides, John T A. *Hist Euro Ideas* 5,456–457 1984

LA FOLLETTE, Marcel Chotkowski. *Creationism, Science, And The Law: The Arkansas Case.* Cambridge, MIT Pr, 1983.
Siegel, Harvey. *Educ Stud* 15,349–364 Wint 84

LAARMAN, Edward J. *Nuclear Pacifism: "Just War" Thinking Today.* Berne, Lang, 1984.
Hardin, Russell. *Ethics* 95,763–765 Ap 85

LACAPRA, D. *A Preface To Sartre.* Ithaca, Cornell Univ Pr, 1978.
Durfee, Harold A. *Rev Metaph* 38,131–132 S 84

LACAPRA, Dominick and Kaplan, Steven L (eds). *Modern European Intellectual History.* Ithaca, Cornell Univ Pr, 1982.
Schroeder, William R. *Can Phil Rev* 4,154–156 Ag 84

LACEY, A R. *Modern Philosophy: An Introduction.* London, Routledge & Kegan Paul, 1982.
Hanfling, O. *Mind* 93,134–136 Ja 84

LADENSON, Robert F. *A Philosophy Of Free Expression.* Totowa, Rowman & Allanheld, 1983.
Hamrick, William S. *Phil Books* 25,241–245 O 84

LAFLEUR, William R. *The Karma Of Words.* Berkeley, Univ of California Pr, 1983.
Heine, Steven. *Phil East West* 35,319–320 Jl 85

LAFRANCE, Yvon. *La Théorie Platonicienne De La Doxa.* Paris, Belles, 1981.
Skemp, J B. *Phoenix* 38,195–197 Je 84
Moutsopoulos, E. *Diotima* 12,217–219 1984

LAGADEC, Claude. *Dominances.* Longueuil, Préambule, 1983.
Thérien, Gilles. *Philosophiques* 11,415–421 O 84

LAGUEUX, Maurice. *Le Marxisme Des Années Soixante.* Quebec, Hurtubise, 1982.
Haarscher, G. *Rev Int Phil* 39,185–188 1985

LAINE, Michael. *Bibliography Of Works On John Stuart Mill.* Toronto, Univ of Toronto Pr, 1982.
Schneewind, J B. *Dialogue (Canada)* 23,554–555 S 84

LAKOFF, Sanford A (ed). *Science And Ethical Responsibility.* Reading, Addison–Wesley, 1980.
Kaiser, Kim. *J Med Ethics* 10,213–214 D 84
Settle, Tom. *Phil Soc Sci* 14,515–527 D 84

LAKS, André. *Diogène D'Apollonie, La Dernière Cosmologie Présocratique.* Lille, Pr Univ de Lille, 1983.
Romeyer–Dherbey, G. *Rev Metaph Morale* 90,276–277 Ap–Je 85

LAMARQUE, Peter (ed). *Philosophy And Fiction.* Aberdeen, Aberdeen Univ Pr, 1983.
Code, Lorraine. *Can Phil Rev* 4,198–200 O 84

LAMB, David. *Hegel—From Foundation To System.* The Hague, Nijhoff, 1980.
Walsh, W H. *Bull Hegel Soc Gr Brit* 2,36–39 Autumn 80

LAMBERT, Karel. *Meinong And The Principle Of Independence.* Cambridge, Cambridge Univ Pr, 1983.
Griffin, Nicholas. *Phil Books* 26,20–23 Ja 85

LANDGREBE, L. *Faktizitat Und Individuation.* Hamburg, Meiner, 1982.
Durfee, Harold A. *Rev Metaph* 38,652–653 Mr 85

LANDGREBE, Ludwig (ed). *The Phenomenology Of Edmund Husserl: Six Essays.* Ithaca, Cornell Univ Pr, 1981.
Carr, David. *Int Stud Phil* 16,93–94 1984

LANE, Gilles. *Si Les Marionnettes Pouvaient Choisir.* Montréal, L'Hexagone, 1983.
Carrier, André. *Laval Theol Phil* 40,363–368 O 84

LANG, Berel. *Faces ––– And The Other Ironies Of Writing And Reading.* Indianapolis, Hackett, 1983.
Code, Lorraine. *Can Phil Rev* 4,269–271 D 84

LANGHAMMER, Walter. *Bertrand Russell.* Berlin, Urania, 1983.
Ruja, Harry. *Russell* 5,93–94 Sum 85

LARGEAULT, J. *Quine, Questions De Mots, Questions De Faits.* Toulouse, Privat, 1980.
Mouloud, N. *Rev Metaph Morale* 90,138–140 Ja–Mr 85

LARUELLE, François. *Le Principe De Minorité.* Paris, Aubier, 1981.
Valdinoci, Serge. *Rev Metaph Morale* 89,268–270 Ap–Je 84

LASCOUMES, Pierre and Zander, Hartwig. *Marx: Du "Vol De Vois" À La Critique Du Droit.* Paris, Univ de France Pr, 1984.
Gervais, Richard. *Dialogue (Canada)* 24,187–189 Spr 85

LAU, D C (trans). *Tao Te Ching.* Hong Kong, Chinese Univ Pr, 1982.
Roth, Harold D. *Phil East West* 35,213–215 Ap 85

LAUDAN, Larry (ed). *Mind And Medicine.* Berkeley, Univ of California Pr, 1983.
Lavin, Michael. *Phil Sci* 52,321–323 Je 85

LAUDAN, Larry. *Science And Hypothesis.* Dordrecht, Reidel, 1981.
Upton, Thomas V. *Rev Metaph* 38,653–655 Mr 85
Lugg, Andrew. *Erkenntnis* 21,433–438 N 84
Milton, J R. *Brit J Phil Sci* 36,89–93 Mr 85

LAUER, Quentin. *A Reading Of Hegel's Phenomenology Of Spirit.* NY, Fordham Univ Pr, 1982.
Inwood, Michael. *Bull Hegel Soc Gr Brit* 9,26–33 Spr/Sum 84

LAUER, Quentin. *Hegel's Concept Of God.* Albany, SUNY Pr, 1982.
Collins, James. *Mod Sch* 62,61–63 N 84
Jaeschke, Walter. *Ideal Stud* 15,167–169 My 85

Moran, Dermot. *Bull Hegel Soc Gr Brit* 9,33–36 Spr/Sum 84

LAUTH, R. *Die Konstitution Der Zeit Im Bewusstsein.* Hamburg, Meiner, 1981.
Colette, Jacques. *Rev Metaph Morale* 89,279–280 Ap–Je 84

LAVALLARD, Marie–Hélène. *La Philosophie Marxiste.* Paris, Sociales, 1982.
Bodéüs, Richard. *Rev Phil Louvain* 82,585–587 N 84

LE CRON FOSTER, M and Brandes, S H (eds). *Symbol As Sense: New Approaches To The Analysis Of Meaning.* NY, Academic Pr, 1980.
Coyle, P. *Heythrop J* 25,397–399 Jl 84

LEACH, Edmund and Aycock, D Alan. *Structuralist Interpretations Of Biblical Myth.* Cambridge, Cambridge Univ Pr, 1983.
Carroll, Robert. *Relig Stud* 21,116–118 Mr 85
Larisch, Sharon. *Phil Lit* 8,306–307 O 84

LEE, Tae–Soo. *Die Griechische Tradition Der Aristotelischen Syllogistik.* Göttingen, Vandenhoeck & Ruprecht, 1984.
Maconi, Henry. *Phronesis* 30,92–98 1985

LEFEBVRE, J P and Macherey, P. *Hegel Et La Société.* Paris, Pr Univ de France, 1984.
Larouche–Tanguay, Camillia. *Laval Theol Phil* 41,262–263 Je 85

LEGAULT, G A and Gagnon, M (eds). *Philosophie Et Éducation.* Quebec, Actas, 1984.
Chené, Adèle. *Can Phil Rev* 4,157–158 Ag 84

LEIBNIZ, Gottfried Wilhelm. *Sämtliche Schriften Und Briefe.* Berlin, Akademie, 1982.
De Dijn, H. *Tijdschr Filosof* 46,643–646 D 84
Parkinson, G H R. *Stud Leibniz* 16,113–119 1984

LEIGH, R A (ed). *Rousseau After 200 Years.* Cambridge, Cambridge Univ Pr, 1982.
Levi, A H T. *Heythrop J* 25,409–411 Jl 84
Raath, A W G. *S Afr J Phil* 3,150–152 N 84

LEIGHTON, Angela. *Shelley And The Sublime: An Interpretation Of The Major Poems.* Cambridge, Cambridge Univ Pr, 1984.
Smith, Sheila M. *Brit J Aes* 25,281–282 Sum 85

LEMERT, Charles C. *Sociology And The Twilight Of Man.* Carbondale, Southern Illinois Univ Pr, 1980.
Munz, Peter. *Phil Soc Sci* 18,403–406 S 84

LEMING, James S. *Contemporary Approaches To Moral Education.* NY, Garland, 1983.
Wright, Ian. *J Moral Educ* 13,204–205 O 84

LEMOINE–LUCCIONI, Eugénie. *La Robe.* Paris, Seuil, 1984.
Peraldi, François. *Can Phil Rev* 4,158–161 Ag 84

LENK, Hans. *Handlungstheorien–Interdisziplinär.* München, Fink, 1978.
Kleger, Heinz. *Stud Phil (Switzerland)* 41,245–247 1982

LENNON, Thomas M and others (eds). *Problems Of Cartesianism.* Kingston, McGill–Queen's Pr, 1982.
Clarke, Desmond M. *Can Phil Rev* 4,201–202 O 84
Cummins, Phillip D. *J Hist Phil* 23,104–109 Ja 85

LENZEN, Wolfgang. *Glauben, Wissen Und Wahrscheinlichkeit.* Wien, Springer, 1980.
Sadegh–Zadeh, Kazem. *Erkenntnis* 23,97–112 My 85

LEO, Rosella Fabbrichesi. *I Grafi Esistenziali Di Charles S Peirce.* Milano, Annali della Facoltà, 1983.
Cuniberto, Flavio. *Filosofia* 35,269–272 Jl–O 84

LEO, Rosella Fabbrichesi. *La Polemica Sull'iconismo.* Napoli, Scientifiche Italiane, 1983.
Cuniberto, Flavio. *Filosofia* 35,269–272 Jl–O 84

LERMAN, Manuel. *Degrees Of Unsolvability: Local And Global Theory.* Berlin, Springer, 1983.
Jockusch Jr, Carl G. *J Sym Log* 50,549–550 Je 85

LERNER, Laurence (ed). *Reconstructing Literature.* Totowa, Barnes & Noble, 1983.
Langston, David J. *Phil Lit* 9,119–120 Ap 85

LEVARIE, S and Levy, E. *Musical Morphology: A Discourse And A Dictionary.* Kent, Kent State Univ Pr, 1983.
Levinson, Jerrold. *J Aes Art Crit* 43,222–224 Wint 84

LEVI, Isaac. *The Enterprise Of Knowledge.* Cambridge, MIT Pr, 1980.
Maher, Patrick. *Phil Sci* 51,690–692 D 84

LEVINAS, Emmanuel. *De Dieu Qui Vient À l'idée.* Paris, Vrin, 1982.
Balzer, Carmen. *Sapientia* 39,237–240 Jl–S 84

LEVINAS, Emmanuel. *Otherwise Than Being Or Beyond Essence, Alphonso Lingis (trans).* The Hague, Nijhoff, 1981.
Lightfeld, A. *Int Stud Phil* 16,95–96 1984
Cohen, Richard A. *Phil Rhet* 17,245–246 1984

LEVINE, Andrew. *Liberal Democracy: A Critique Of Its Theory.* NY, Columbia Univ Pr, 1981.
Cunningham, Frank. *Can J Phil* 14,335–357 Je 84

LEVY, David. *Realism: An Essay In Interpretation And Social Reality.* Atlantic Highlands, Humanities Pr, 1981.
Trigg, Roger. *Phil Soc Sci* 15,82–85 Mr 85

LEWIS, David. *Philosophical Papers, V1.* NY, Oxford Univ Pr, 1983.
Peacocke, Christopher. *J Phil* 82,42–45 Ja 85

LEWIS, H D (ed). *Contemporary British Philosophy.* Atlantic Highlands, Humanities Pr, 1978.

Gillespie, Neal C. *Zygon* 20,349–352 S 85

MOORE, T W. *Philosophy Of Education—An Introduction.* London, Routledge & Kegan Paul, 1982.
Waters, Columb. *Heythrop J* 26,350 Jl 85

MORAUX, Paul. *Der Aristotelismus Bei Den Griechen.* Berlin, De Gruyter, 1984.
Bodéüs, Richard. *Rev Phil Louvain* 83,272–274 My 85

MORAVCSIK, J and Temko, P (eds). *Plato On Beauty, Wisdom, And The Arts.* Totowa, Rowman & Littlefield, 1982.
Mitscherling, Jeff. *Can Phil Rev* 4,206–209 O 84

MOREAU, Pierre–François. *Le Récit Utopique, Droit Naturel Et Roman De L'état.* Paris, Pr Univ France, 1982.
Sasso, Robert. *Arch Phil* 47,512–515 Jl–S 84

MORENO, J D and Glassner, B. *Discourse In The Social Sciences.* Westport, Greenwood Pr, 1982.
Watson, Catherine M. *Phil Soc Sci* 15,114–116 Mr 85

MORIK, Katharina. *Überzeugungssysteme Der Künstlichen Intelligenz.* Tübingen, Niemeyer, 1982.
Kobsa, Alfred. *Conceptus* 18,132–135 1984

MORIN, Michel. *L'Amérique Du Nord Et La Culture.* Montréal, Hurtubise HMH, 1982.
Archambault, Marc–Fernand. *Philosophiques* 12,211–215 Spr 85

MORREALL, John. *Taking Laughter Seriously.* Albany, SUNY Pr, 1983.
Vorobej, Mark. *Int Phil Quart* 24,337–338 S 84
Baber, H E and Donnelly, J. *Phil Phenomenol Res* 45,290–297 D 84
Teichman, Jenny. *Can Phil Rev* 4,165–167 Ag 84

MORRIS, Norval. *Madness And The Criminal Law.* Chicago, Univ of Chicago Pr, 1982.
Neu, Jerome. *Crim Just Ethics* 3,62–67 Sum/Fall 84
Zimmerman, David. *Hastings Center Rep* 15,43–45 F 85
Moore, Michael S. *Ethics* 95,909–919 Jl 85

MORSCHER, E and Stranzinger, R (eds). *Ethik: Grundlagen, Probleme Und Anwendungen.* Wien, Kirchberg & Wechsel, 1981.
Davie, William. *Can Phil Rev* 4,280–282 D 84
Studer, Herlinde. *Conceptus* 170–174 1984

MOSSÉ, Eliane. *Les Riches Et Les Pauvres.* Paris, Seuil, 1983.
Ryerson, Stanley B. *Can Phil Rev* 4,209–212 O 84

MOSSINI, Lanfranco. *Per Questi Motivi.* Milano, Giuffrè, 1981.
Vitale, Vincenzo. *Riv Int Filosof Diritto* 61,546–548 Jl–S 84

MOSSNER, Ernest Cambell. *The Life Of David Hume.* Oxford, Oxford Univ Pr, 1980.
Embree, Lester. *Int Stud Phil* 16,111–112 1984

MOTSCH, W and Viehweger, D (eds). *Richtungen Der Modernen Semantikforschung.* Berlin, Akademie, 1983.
Papi, Marcella Bertuccelli. *J Prag* 8,823–830 D 84

MÜLLER, Anselm Winfried. *Praktisches Folgern Und Selbstgestaltung Nach Aristoteles.* Freiburg, Alber, 1982.
Ricken, Friedo. *Phil Rundsch* 31,264–271 1984

MULLER, J P and Richardson, W J. *Lacan And Language: A Reader's Guide To Ecrits.* NY, International Univ Pr, 1982.
Ver Eecke, W. *Rev Metaph* 38,396–398 D 84

MÜLLER, Reinhold (ed). *Sozialismus Und Ethik.* Berlin, Dietz, 1984.
Reichwald, Ernst. *Deut Z Phil* 32,949–951 1984

MUNÉVAR, Gonzalo. *Radical Knowledge.* Indianapolis, Hackett, 1981.
Burian, Richard M. *Phil Sci* 52,163–165 Mr 85

MUNSEY, Brenda (ed). *Moral Education In Theory And Practice.* Birmingham, Religious Education Pr, 1980.
Simon, Frank. *J Moral Educ* 14,63–64 Ja 85

MURPHY, Jeffrie G. *Evolution, Morality, And The Meaning Of Life.* Totowa, Rowman & Littlefield, 1982.
Ruse, Michael. *Dialogue (Canada)* 23,527–530 S 84
Graham, George. *Mod Sch* 62,64–65 N 84
Buijs, Joseph A. *Can Phil Rev* 4,168–170 Ag 84
Splitter, Laurance J. *Austl J Phil* 63,115–117 Mr 85

MURPHY, John W. *The Social Philosophy Of Martin Buber.* Washington, Univ Pr of America, 1983.
Kegley, Charles W. *J Soc Phil* 16,37 Wint 85

MURPHY, Richard T. *Hume And Husserl.* The Hague, Nijhoff, 1980.
Presas, Mario A. *Rev Latin De Filosof* 11,92–94 Mr 85

MUSIL, R. *On Mach's Theories, Kevin Mulligan (trans).* Munchen, Philosophia, 1982.
Harries, Karsten. *Rev Metaph* 38,668–670 Mr 85

MUYSKENS, James L. *Moral Problems In Nursing: A Philosophical Investigation.* Totowa, Rowman & Littlefield, 1982.
Vacek, Edward. *Mod Sch* 62,65–66 N 84

NAGEL, Ernst. *Teleology Revisited And Other Essays.* NY, Columbia Univ Pr, 1982.
Nemesszeghy, Ervin. *Heythrop J* 26,348–350 Jl 85

NAGEL, Gordon. *The Structure Of Experience: Kant's System Of Principles.* Chicago, Univ of Chicago Pr, 1983.
Guyer, Paul. *Can Phil Rev* 4,213–216 O 84

NAGL–DOCEKAL, Herta. *Die Ojbektivität Der Geschichtswissenschaft.* Wien, Oldenbourg, 1982.
Röttgers, Kurt. *Z Phil Forsch* 39,140–143 Ja–Mr 85

NAHEM, Joseph. *Psychology And Psychiatry Today: A Marxist View.* NY, International, 1981.
Smith, Murray. *Phil Soc Sci* 15,216–221 Je 85

NALIMOV, V V. *Realms Of The Unconscious: The Enchanted Frontier.* Philadelphia, ISI Pr, 1982.
Igartua, Juan Manuel. *Pensamiento* 41,111–114 Ja–Mr 85
Rohatyn, Dennis. *Ideal Stud* 15,61–63 Ja 85

NARDIN, Terry. *Law, Morality, And The Relations Of States.* Princeton, Princeton Univ Pr, 1983.
Joynt, Carey B. *Ethics* 95,761–763 Ap 85
Hare, John E. *Phil Books* 25,240–241 O 84

NAROLL, Raoul. *The Moral Order: An Introduction To The Human Situation.* Beverly Hills, Sage, 1983.
Bullough, Vern L. *Free Inq* 5,57 Spr 85

NARVESON, Jan (ed). *Moral Issues.* NY, Oxford Univ Pr, 1983.
LaFollette, Hugh. *Teach Phil* 8,60–61 Ja 85

NASH, Ronald H. *The Concept Of God.* Grand Rapids, Zondervan, 1983.
Dore, Clement. *Faith Phil* 1,447–449 O 84

NEBELSICK, Harold. *Theology And Science In Mutual Modification.* NY, Oxford Univ Pr, 1981.
Ellis, Harry W. *Zygon* 20,352–354 S 85

NEGRI, Antonio. *L'anomalie Sauvage: Puissance Et Pouvoir Chez Spinoza.* Paris, Pr Univ de France, 1981.
Hébert, Robert. *Dialogue (Canada)* 23,315–325 Je 84

NELKIN, Dorothy. *The Creation Controversy: Science Or Scripture In The Schools.* NY, Norton, 1982.
Siegel, Harvey. *Educ Stud* 15,349–364 Wint 84

NELSON, R J. *Human Life: A Biblical Perspective For Bioethics.* Philadelphia, Fortress Pr, 1984.
Henley, John A. *J Med Ethics* 11,105 Je 85

NELSON, R J. *The Logic Of Mind.* Dordrecht, Reidel, 1982.
Cam, Philip and Mortensen, Chris. *Austl J Phil* 62,420–422 D 84

NELSON, William N. *On Justifying Democracy.* London, Routledge & Kegan Paul, Undated.
Oppenheim, Felix. *Int Stud Phil* 16,112–113 1984

NERLICH, Graham. *The Shape Of Space.* NY, Cambridge Univ Pr, 1976.
Horwich, Paul. *J Phil* 82,269–273 My 85

NEUFELD, Karl H. *Geschichte Und Mensch.* Roma, Pontificia Univ Gregoriana, 1983.
Sala, Giovanni B. *Riv Filosof Neo–Scolas* 76,492–495 Jl–S 84

NEVITT, Barrington. *The Communication Ecology.* Toronto, Butterworths, 1982.
Barton, Richard L. *Phil Rhet* 18,58–60 1985

NEWMAN, Stephen L. *Liberalism At Wits' End.* Ithaca, Cornell Univ Pr, 1984.
Barnes, Jonathan. *Int Phil Quart* 25,223–225 Je 85

NEWTON–SMITH, W H. *The Rationality Of Science.* Boston, Routledge & Kegan Paul, 1981.
Schlagel, Richard H. *Rev Metaph* 38,134–136 S 84

NICHOLS, A and Hogan, T (eds). *Making Babies: The Test Tube And Christian Ethics.* Canberra, Acorn Pr, 1984.
Dunstan, G R. *J Med Ethics* 11,50–51 Mr 85

NICOLOSI, Salvatore. *Medioevo Francescano.* Roma, Borla, 1983.
Pieretti, Antonio. *Riv Filosof Neo–Scolas* 76,476–478 Jl–S 84

NICOLOSI, Salvatore. *Utopia E Apocalisse: Cristianesimo E Temporalità.* Roma, Cadmo, 1982.
Liggieri, Maria Carmela. *Sapienza* 37,472–474 O–D 84

NIELSEN, H A. *Where The Passion Is.* Tallahassee, Florida State Univ Pr, 1983.
Hannay, Alastair. *Can Phil Rev* 5,71–74 F 85
Dunning, Stephen N. *Faith Phil* 2,207–209 Ap 85

NIELSEN, Kai. *An Introduction To The Philosophy Of Religion.* London, Macmillan Pr, 1982.
Kolenda, Konstantin. *Teach Phil* 7,349–350 O 84
Brümmer, Vincent. *Relig Stud* 21,118–120 Mr 85

NIELSON, Lauge Olaf. *Theology And Philosophy In The Twelfth Century.* Leiden, Brill, 1982.
Doyle, John P. *Mod Sch* 62,66–67 N 84

NIETZSCHE, Friedrich. *Daybreak, Hollingdale (trans).* Cambridge, Cambridge Univ Pr, 1982.
Weinstein, Deena. *Hist Euro Ideas* 5,335–336 1984

NIETZSCHE, Friedrich. *Untimely Meditations, R J Hollingdale (trans).* Cambridge, Cambridge Univ Pr, 1983.
Taylor, Charles Senn. *Phil Books* 25,214–216 O 84

NOLT, John Eric. *Informal Logic: Possible Worlds And Imagination.* NY, McGraw–Hill, 1984.
Pole, Nelson. *Teach Phil* 8,85–87 Ja 85

NOONAN, Harold W. *Objects And Identity.* The Hague, Nijhoff, 1980.
Over, D E. *Mind* 93,144–146 Ja 84
Griffin, Nicholas. *Hist Phil Log* 5,135–138 1984
Nelson, Jack. *Phil Topics* 13,175–181 Spr 82

NORMAN, Richard and Sayers, Sean. *Hegel, Marx And Dialectic: A Debate.* Brighton, Harvester Pr, 1980.
Lamb, David. *Bull Hegel Soc Gr Brit* 2,43–47 Autumn 80

NORMAN, Richard. *The Moral Philosophers: An Introduction To Ethics.* Oxford, Clarendon Pr, 1984.
Marshall, Graeme. *Philosophy* 60,140–142 Ja 85

NORRIS, Christopher. *The Deconstructive Turn: Essays In The Rhetoric Of Philosophy.* NY, Methuen, 1983.
Daniel, Stephen H. *Phil Lit* 9,117–119 Ap 85
Easthope, Antony. *J Brit Soc Phenomenol* 16,96–97 Ja 85
Bygrave, Stephen. *Brit J Aes* 24,379–380 Autumn 84

NORTH, Helen F. *From Myth To Icon.* NY, Cornell Univ Pr, 1979.
Adkins, A W H. *Ancient Phil* 4,249–251 Fall 84

NORTON, David Fate. *David Hume: Common-Sense Moralist, Sceptical Metaphysician.* Princeton, Princeton Univ Pr, 1982.
Kirk, Linda. *Hist Euro Ideas* 6,208–209 1985
Miskell, T A. *Hume Stud* 10,181–192 N 84
Haakonssen, Knud. *Austl J Phil* 62,410–419 D 84
Raynor, David R. *J Hist Phil* 23,113–114 Ja 85
Stewart, M A. *Hermathena* 136,81–82 Sum 84
King, James. *Rev Metaph* 38,670–671 Mr 85

NOSICH, Gerald M. *Reasons And Arguments.* Belmont, Wadsworth, 1983.
Tlumak, Jeffrey. *Teach Phil* 7,263–265 Jl 84

NOWAK, Leszek. *Property And Power.* Dordrecht, Reidel, 1983.
Soltan, Karol. *Ethics* 95,160–162 O 84

NOWAK, Reinhard. *Grenzen Der Sprachanalyse.* Tübingen, Narr, 1981.
Wallner, Friedrich. *Conceptus* 18,106–107 1984

NOZICK, Robert. *Philosophical Explanations.* Cambridge, Belknap Pr, 1981.
Harrison, Ross. *Ratio* 26,205–207 D 84
Balu. *Philosophica* 34,127–131 1984
Brahinsky, David M. *Int Stud Phil* 16,113–115 1984

NUCHELMANS, Gabriel. *Judgment And Proposition: From Descartes To Kant.* Amsterdam, North Holland, 1983.
Yolton, John W. *Phil Books* 25,200–202 O 84
Auroux, S. *Hist Phil Log* 6,129–130 1985

O'BRIEN, D. *Pour Interpréter Empédocle.* Paris, Belles, 1981.
Inwood, Brad. *Ancient Phil* 4,99–101 Spr 84

O'CONNOR, David. *The Metaphysics Of G E Moore.* Dordrecht, Reidel, 1982.
Baertschi, Bernard. *Rev Metaph Morale* 90,133–135 Ja–Mr 85
Fotion, Nicholas. *J Hist Phil* 23,125–126 Ja 85

O'DONNELL, John J. *Trinity And Temporality.* Oxford, Oxford Univ Pr, 1983.
Gunton, Colin. *Heythrop J* 25,375–376 Jl 84
Pailin, David A. *Relig Stud* 21,93–95 Mr 85

O'FLAHERTY, James C. *Johann Georg Hamann.* Boston, Twayne, 1979.
Browning, Robert M. *Thomist* 49,136–142 Ja 85

O'FLAHERTY, Wendy Doniger. *Dreams, Illusion, And Other Realities.* Chicago, Univ of Chicago Pr, 1984.
Siegel, Lee. *Phil East West* 25,321–322 Jl 85

O'HEAR, Anthony. *Experience, Explanation And Faith.* London, Routledge & Kegan Paul, 1984.
Gordon, David. *Int Phil Quart* 25,221–222 Je 85
Morris, Thomas V. *Faith Phil* 2,309–317 Jl 85
Helm, Paul. *Phil Books* 26,50–52 Ja 85

O'HEAR, Anthony. *Karl Popper.* London, Routledge & Kegan Paul, 1980.
Settle, Tom. *Int Stud Phil* 16,115–117 1984

O'MEARA, Dominic J (ed). *Review Of "Neoplatonism And Christian Thought".* Albany, SUNY Pr, 1982.
Sharples, R W. *Relig Stud* 20,705–708 D 84

O'MEARA, Thomas F. *Romantic Idealism And Roman Catholicism.* Notre Dame, Univ of Notre Dame Pr, 1982.
Collins, James. *Mod Sch* 62,61–63 N 84

OAKESHOTT, Michael. *On History, And Other Essays.* Oxford, Blackwell, 1983.
Palmer, Humphrey. *Phil Books* 26,117–120 Ap 85

OCHS, Carol. *Women And Spirituality.* Totowa, Rowman & Allanheld, 1983.
McCleary, Rachel M. *Ethics* 95,165–167 O 84

ODEGARD, Douglas. *Knowledge And Scepticism.* Totowa, Rowman & Littlefield, 1982.
Abbott, William R. *Dialogue (Canada)* 23,725–729 D 84
Buford, Thomas O. *Rev Metaph* 38,671–673 Mr 85

ODIN, Steve. *Process Metaphysics And Hua-Yen Buddhism.* Albany, SUNY Pr, 1982.
Lai, Whalen. *Ideal Stud* 14,278 S 84

OELB, Clayton. *The Incredulous Reader: Literature And The Function Of Disbelief.* Ithaca, Cornell Univ Pr, 1984.
Broman, Walter E. *Phil Lit* 9,113–114 Ap 85

OELMÜLLER, Willi (ed). *Kolloquium Kunst Und Philosophie 2: Ästhetischer Schein.* Paderborn, Schöningh, 1982.
Pfeiffer, K Ludwig. *Phil Rundsch* 32,91–104 1985

OLAFSON, Frederick A. *The Dialectic Of Action.* Chicago, Univ of Chicago Pr, 1979.
Goldstein, Leon J. *Phil Soc Sci* 14,410–416 S 84

OLDROYD, David and Langham, Ian (eds). *The Wider Domain Of Evolutionary Thought.* Dordrecht, Reidel, 1983.
MacCallum, Monica. *Austl J Phil* 63,111–115 Mr 85

OLIVIER, Paul. *Croce, Ou L'affirmation De L'immanence Absolue.* Paris, Seghers, 1975.
Parente, Alfredo. *Riv Stud Croce* 21,1–12 Ja–Mr 84

OLSON, Alan (ed). *Myth, Symbol And Reality.* Notre Dame, Univ of Notre Dame Pr, 1980.
Lawrence, Fred. *Method* 2,42–44 O 84

OLSON, Alan M. *Transcendence And Hermeneutics.* The Hague, Nijhoff, 1979.
Schrag, Calvin O. *Int Stud Phil* 16,118–119 1984

ONG, Walter. *Orality And Literacy: The Technologizing Of The Word.* NY, Methuen, 1982.
Trainor, Paul. *Mod Sch* 62,67–68 N 84

OPIELA, Stanislas. *Le Réel Dans La Logique De Hegel.* Paris, Beauchesne, 1983.
Faes, Hubert. *Rev Phil Fr* 174,485–490 O–D 84

OPPENHEIM, Felix. *Political Concepts.* Chicago, Univ of Chicago Pr, Undated.
Ladenson, Robert F. *Can Phil Rev* 5,74–76 F 85

OPPENHEIMER, Helen. *The Hope Of Happiness: A Sketch For A Christian Humanism.* London, SCM Pr, 1983.
Ward, Keith. *Relig Stud* 21,110–111 Mr 85
Meynell, Hugo. *Philosophy* 59,542–544 O 84

ORANGE, Donna M. *Peirce's Conception Of God: A Developmental Study.* Lubbock, Inst for Stud in Pragmaticism, 1984.
Mahowald, Mary B. *Trans Peirce Soc* 21,430–435 Sum 85
Roth, Robert J. *Int Phil Quart* 25,213–215 Je 85

ORR, Robert P. *The Meaning Of Transcendence: A Heideggerian Reflection.* Chico, Scholars Pr, 1981.
Macquarrie, John. *Int Stud Phil* 16,120 1984

ORTEGA Y GASSET, José. *Investigaciones Psicológicas,* P Garagorri (ed). Madrid, Alianza, 1982.
Di Gregori, Marí C. *Rev Latin De Filosof* 11,90–92 Mr 85

ORTH, Ernst (ed). *Zeit Und Zeitlichkeit Bei Husserl Und Heidegger.* Freiburg, Alber, 1983.
Dostal, Robert J. *Husserl Stud* 2,111–115 1985

ORTONY, Andrew (ed). *Metaphor And Thought.* Cambridge, Cambridge Univ Pr, 1979.
Hanson, Philip P. *Can J Phil* 14,477–497 S 84

ORTWEIN, Birger. *Kants Problematische Freiheitslehre.* Bonn, Grundmann, 1983.
Steinbeck, Wolfram. *Kantstudien* 75,496–497 1984

OSBORNE, Harold. *Abstraction And Artifice In Twentieth-Century Art.* Oxford, Clarendon Pr, 1979.
McCormick, Peter. *J Aes Art Crit* 42,467–469 Sum 84

OSTENFELD, E N. *Forms, Matter And Mind: Three Strands In Plato's Metaphysics.* The Hague, Nijhoff, 1982.
Gulley, Norman. *J Hellen Stud* 104,206–207 1984

OUDEMANS, Th C W. *De Verdeelde Mens: Ontwerp Van Een Filosofische Anthropologie.* Meppel, Boom, 1980.
Glas, G. *Phil Reform* 49,170–176 1984

OWEN, Huw Parri. *Christian Theism, A Study In Basic Principles.* Edinburgh, Clark, 1984.
McIntyre, John. *Relig Stud* 21,103–105 Mr 85

OWENS, Joseph. *Aristotle, The Collected Papers Of Joseph Owens,* J R Catan (ed). Albany, SUNY Pr, 1981.
Husain, Martha. *Int Stud Phil* 16,120–122 1984

PAGELS, Heinz R. *The Cosmic Code: Physics As The Language Of Nature.* NY, Simon & Schuster, 1982.
Swyhart, Barbara A D. *Zygon* 20,96–98 Mr 85

PALAZZOLO, Vincenzo. *La Filosofia Del Diritto Di Gustav Radbruch E Di Julius Binder.* Milano, Giuffrè, 1983.
Lisitano, Annamaria. *Riv Int Filosof Diritto* 61,173–175 Ja–Mr 84

PALMER, Humphrey. *Kant's Critique Of Pure Reason: An Introductory Text.* Atlantic Highlands, Humanities Pr, 1984.
Tlumak, Jeffrey. *Teach Phil* 8,181–183 Ap 85

PALMER, Michael F. *Paul Tillich's Philosophy Of Art.* NY, De Gruyter, 1984.
Austin, Michael. *Brit J Aes* 25,283–285 Sum 85
Kegley, Charles W. *Rev Metaph* 38,896–898 Je 85

PANASIUK, Ryszard. *Dziedzictwo Heglowskie I Marksizm.* Warszawa, Ksiazka I Wiedza, 1979.
Pelczynski, Z A. *Bull Hegel Soc Gr Brit* 2,50 Autumn 80

PANDIT, G L. *The Structure And Growth Of Scientific Knowledge.* Dordrecht, Reidel, 1983.
Blackwell, Richard J. *Rev Metaph* 38,673–674 Mr 85

PANGLE, Thomas L (trans). *The Laws Of Plato.* NY, Basic Books, 1979.
Nichols, Mary P. *Ancient Phil* 4,237–240 Fall 84

PAPINEAU, David. *For Science In The Social Sciences.* London, Macmillan, 1978.
Fay, Brian. *Phil Soc Sci* 14,529–542 D 84

PARAIN-VIAL, J. *Philosophie Des Sciences De La Nature, Tendances Nouvelles.* Paris, Klincksieck, 1983.
Largeault, Jean. *Arch Phil* 48,515–517 Jl–S 85
Gagnon, Maurice. *Rev Metaph* 38,898–900 Je 85

PAREKH, Bhikhu. *Marx's Theory Of Ideology.* Baltimore, Johns Hopkins Univ Pr, 1982.
Esheté, Andreas. *Phil Rev* 94,281–286 Ap 85

Murphy, John W. *Stud Soviet Tho* 29,263–265 Ap 85

PAREL, Anthony and Flanagan, Thomas (eds). *Theories Of Property: Aristotle To The Present.* Waterloo, Laurier Univ Pr, 1979.
Harper, A W J. *Dialogue (Canada)* 23,559–563 S 84

PARFIT, Derek. *Reasons And Persons.* Oxford, Clarendon Pr, 1984.
Goldman, Alan H. *Inquiry* 28,373–387 S 85
Baier, Annette C. *Phil Books* 25,220–224 O 84

PARK, Sung Bae. *Buddhist Faith And Sudden Enlightenment.* Albany, SUNY Pr, 1983.
Mitchell, Donald W. *Phil East West* 35,102–104 Ja 85

PARKER-RHODES, A F. *The Theory Of Indistinguishables.* Dordrecht, Reidel, 1981.
Kilmister, C W. *Hist Phil Log* 3,224–225 1982

PARSONS, Charles. *Mathematics In Philosophy.* Ithaca, Cornell Univ Pr, 1983.
Maddy, Penelope. *Can Phil Rev* 5,125–126 Mr 85

PARSONS, Charles. *Mathematics In Philosophy: Selected Essays.* Ithaca, Cornell Univ Pr, 1984.
Quine, W V. *J Phil* 81,783–794 D 84
Benardete, José. *Rev Metaph* 38,674–676 Mr 85

PARTEE, Morriss Henry. *Plato's Poetics.* Salt Lake City, Univ of Utah Pr, 1981.
Hall, Robert W. *Amer J Philo* 19,247–250 Sum 85

PATEMAN, Carole. *The Problem Of Political Obligation.* NY, Wiley, 1979.
McMurtry, John. *Can J Phil* 14,315–333 Je 84

PATFOORT, Albert. *Saint Thomas D'Aquin.* Paris, FAC, 1983.
East, Simon-Pierre. *Laval Theol Phil* 41,122–123 F 85

PATTENDEN, Rosemary. *The Judge, Discretion, And The Criminal Trial.* Don Mills, Oxford Univ Pr, 1982.
Waluchow, Wilfrid. *Can Phil Rev* 4,217–219 O 84

PATTERSON, David. *Faith And Philosophy.* Washington, Univ Pr of America, 1982.
Thrower, James. *Relig Stud* 20,499–500 S 84

PAUL OF VENICE. *Logica Magna, Patricia Clarke (ed & trans).* Oxford, Oxford Univ Pr, 1982.
Angelelli, Ignacio. *Rev Metaph* 38,399–400 D 84

PAUL, Iain. *Science, Theology And Einstein.* NY, Oxford Univ Pr, 1982.
Ross, Thomas M. *Zygon* 20,98–99 Mr 85

PEACH, Bernard (ed). *Richard Price And The Ethical Foundations Of The American Revolution.* Durham, Duke Univ Pr, 1979.
Jack, Malcom. *J Hist Phil* 22,486–487 O 84

PEACH, W B and Thomas, D O (eds). *The Correspondence Of Richard Price.* Durham, Duke Univ Pr, 1983.
Reck, Andrew J. *Rev Metaph* 38,676–677 Mr 85

PEACOCKE, A R (ed). *The Sciences And Theology In The Twentieth Century.* Henley, Oriel Pr, Undated.
Byrne, P A. *Relig Stud* 20,500–502 S 84
Jaki, Stanley L. *Heythrop J* 25,391–393 Jl 84

PEACOCKE, Christopher. *Sense And Content: Experience, Thought, And Their Relations.* Oxford, Clarendon Pr, 1983.
McFetridge, Ian. *Phil Books* 26,101–105 Ap 85

PEARS, David. *Motivated Irrationality.* Oxford, Clarendon Pr, 1984.
Thalberg, Irving. *Ethics* 95,943–945 Jl 85
Haight, M R. *Phil Books* 26,48–50 Ja 85
Champlin, T S. *Philosophy* 60,274–275 Ap 85

PECCORINI, F L. *From Gentile's "Actualism" To Sciacca's "Idea".* Place Unknown, Studio Editoriale Di Cultura, 1981.
Harvanek, R F. *Rev Metaph* 38,677–678 Mr 85

PÊCHEUX, Michel. *Language, Semantics And Ideology, Harbans Nagpal (trans).* London, Macmillan, 1982.
Dolitsky, Marlene. *J Prag* 8,799–808 D 84

PEIRCE, Charles S (ed). *Studies In Logic, Reprint Of 1883 Edition.* Philadelphia, Benjamins, 1983.
Dipert, Randall. *Trans Peirce Soc* 20,469–472 Fall 84
Dipert, Randall R. *Hist Phil Log* 5,227–232 1984

PELCZYNSKI, Z and Gray J. *Conceptions Of Liberty In Political Philosophy.* London, Athlone Pr, 1984.
Cohen, Brenda. *J Applied Phil* 2,152–154 Mr 85

PELLEGRIN, Pierre. *La Classification Des Animaux Chez Aristote.* Paris, Belles, 1982.
Brague, Rémi. *Arch Phil* 48,329–332 Ap-Je 85
Richmond, J A. *J Hellen Stud* 104,215–216 1984
Lennox, James. *Apeiron* 18,148–149 1984

PELLETIER, F J (ed). *Mass Terms: Some Philosophical Problems.* Dordrecht, Reidel, 1979.
Simons, P M. *Hist Phil Log* 1,245–247 1980

PELLETIER, Yvan and others (trans). *Les Attributions.* Montréal, Bellarmin, 1983.
Bellemare, Pierre. *Dialogue (Canada)* 23,548–551 S 84

PENELHUM, Terence. *God And Skepticism.* Dordrecht, Reidel, 1983.
Gaskin, J C A. *Phil Books* 26,124–126 Ap 85
Swinburne, Richard. *J Phil* 82,46–53 Ja 85

PEPERZAK, A Th. *Der Heutige Mensch Und Die Heilsfrage.* Freiburg, Herder, 1972.
Fruchon, P. *Arch Phil* 47,510–511 Jl-S 84

PEPPERLE, Ingrid. *Junghegelianische Geschichtsphilosophie Und Kunsttheorie.* Berlin, Akademie, 1978.
Bungay, Stephen. *Bull Hegel Soc Gr Brit* 2,47–49 Autumn 80

PERA, Marcello. *Hume, Kant E L'induzione.* Bologna, Mulino, 1982.
Finocchiaro, Maurice A. *J Hist Phil* 22,484–485 O 84

PERELMAN, Chaim. *The Realm Of Rhetoric, William Kluback (trans).* Notre Dame, Univ of Notre Dame Pr, 1982.
Kennedy, George A. *Phil Rhet* 17,240–242 1984
Tindale, C. *Eidos* 3,216–224 D 84

PEREZ RUIZ, Francisco. *Metafísica Del Mal.* Madrid, Univ Pontificia Comillas, 1982.
Sanabria, José Rubén. *Rev Filosof (Mexico)* 17,374–375 My-Jl 84

PERROUX, François. *A New Concept Of Development: Unesco.* Paris, Croom Helm, 1983.
Söder, Günter and Stier, Peter. *Deut Z Phil* 32,1050–1054 1984

PERRY, Lewis. *Intellectual Life In America: A History.* NY, Watts, 1984.
Campbell, James. *Trans Peirce Soc* 21,425–430 Sum 85

PETERS, T J and Waterman, R H. *In Search Of Excellence.* NY, Harper & Row, 1982.
Di Norcia, Vincent. *J Bus Ethics* 4,70 F 85

PETERSON, Norman. *Photographic Art: Media And Disclosure.* Place Unknown, UMI Research Pr, 1984.
Woodfield, Richard. *Brit J Aes* 25,292–293 Sum 85

PETIT, J L. *Du Travail Vivant Au Système Des Actions.* Paris, Seuil, 1980.
Denis, Henri. *Rev Metaph Morale* 89,543–549 O-D 84

PETRY, M J (ed). *G W F Hegel—The Berlin Phenomenology.* Dordrecht, Reidel, 1981.
Wright, Kathleen. *Hist Euro Ideas* 6,91–93 1985

PETTERSSON, O and Åkerberg, H. *Interpreting Religious Phenomena.* Stockholm, Almqvist & Wiksell, 1981.
Barker, Eileen. *Phil Soc Sci* 15,88–89 Mr 85

PHILLIPS, D Z. *Through A Darkening Glass.* Oxford, Blackwell, 1982.
Stchedroff, Marcel. *Phil Books* 25,245–246 O 84
Brecher, Robert. *Heythrop J* 26,343–344 Jl 85

PHILLIPS, Paul. *Marx And Engels On Law And Laws, C M Campbell and P Wiles (eds).* Don Mills, Oxford Univ Pr, 1980.
Grier, Philip T. *Can Phil Rev* 5,76–78 F 85

PHILONENKO, A. *L'oeuvre De Kant: La Philosophie Critique.* Paris, Vrin, 1972.
Gómez, Rodolfo. *Cuad Filosof* 19,216–219 Ja-D 83

PICARD, Emile. *La Science Moderne.* Paris, Flammarion, Undated.
Boirel, René. *Rev Phil Fr* 175,227–230 Ap-Je 85

PICARD, Max. *Man And Language, Stanley Goodman (trans).* Chicago, Regnery, 1963.
Healy, Michael. *Auslegung* 11,424–431 Fall 84

PICHOT, A. *Eléments Pour Une Théorie De La Biologie.* Paris, Maloine, 1980.
Leroy, P. *Arch Phil* 47,521–523 Jl-S 84

PIEPER, Josef. *Antología.* Barcelona, Herder, 1984.
Ruiz de Santiago, J. *Rev Filosof (Mexico)* 18,175–178 Ja-Ap 85

PIERI, Sergio. *Metafisica Ed Immagine: Saggio Su Jean Paul Sartre.* Milano, Marzorati, 1983.
Erbetta, Antonio. *Riv Filosof Neo-Scolas* 76,344–346 Ap-Je 84

PIGEAUD, J. *La Maladie De L'âme.* Paris, Belles, 1981.
Gill, Christopher. *J Hellen Stud* 104,231–232 1984

PIPPIN, Robert B. *Kant's Theory Of Form: An Essay On The Critique Of Pure Reason.* New Haven, Yale Univ Pr, 1982.
Pappin III, Joseph. *Heythrop J* 25,520–521 O 84

PITKIN, Hanna Fenichel. *Fortune Is A Woman.* Berkeley, Univ of California Pr, 1984.
Saxonhouse, Arlene W. *Ethics* 95,759–761 Ap 85

PITT, Joseph C (ed). *Philosophy In Economics.* Dordrecht, Reidel, 1981.
Boland, Lawrence A. *Phil Soc Sci* 15,108–109 Mr 85

PITT, Joseph C. *Pictures, Images And Conceptual Change.* Dordrecht, Reidel, 1981.
Pendleton, Gene. *Dialogue (Canada)* 23,530–532 S 84

PLANT, Raymond. *Hegel: An Introduction.* Oxford, Blackwell, 1983.
Walsh, W H. *Bull Hegel Soc Gr Brit* 9,41–42 Spr/Sum 84

PLANTINGA, A and Wolterstorff, N (eds). *Faith And Rationality: Reason And Belief In God.* Notre Dame, Univ of Notre Dame Pr, 1983.
Westphal, Merold. *Int J Phil Relig* 16,183–184 1984
Swinburne, Richard. *J Phil* 82,46–53 Ja 85

PÖGGELER, O. *Heidegger Und Die Hermeneutishe Philosophie.* Freiburg, Alber, 1983.
Grondin, J. *Arch Phil* 48,166–168 Ja-Mr 85

PÖGGELER, Otto (ed). *Hegel: Einführung In Seine Philosophie.* Freiburg, Alber, 1977.
Doniela, W V. *Bull Hegel Soc Gr Brit* 2,31–33 Autumn 80

POJMAN, Louis P. *The Logic Of Subjectivity: Kierkegaard's Philosophy Of Religion.* University, Univ of Alabama Pr, 1984.
Perkins, Robert L. *Faith Phil* 2,209–211 Ap 85

POLE, David. *Aesthetics, Form And Emotion, George Roberts (ed).* NY, St Martin's Pr, 1983.
McFee, Graham. *Philosophy* 59,535–539 O 84

Lewis, Peter. *Phil Books* 26,52–55 Ja 85

Ross, Stephanie. *J Aes Art Crit* 42,447–451 Sum 84

POLKINGHORNE, Donald. *Methodology For The Human Sciences.* Albany, SUNY Pr, 1983.

Matthews, Eric. *Phil Books* 26,115–117 Ap 85

POLLOCK, John L. *Language And Thought.* Princeton, Princeton Univ Pr, 1982.

Morton, Adam. *J Sym Log* 50,252 Mr 85

POLS, Edward. *The Acts Of Our Being.* Amherst, Univ of Massachusetts Pr, 1982.

Hanna, Robert. *Can Phil Rev* 5,20–22 Ja 85

POMPA, L (ed & trans). *Vico: Selected Writings.* Cambridge, Cambridge Univ Pr, 1982.

Verene, Donald Phillip. *Rev Metaph* 38,678–679 Mr 85

POMPA, L and Dray, W H (eds). *Substance And Form In History.* NY, Columbia Univ Pr, 1982.

Fell, Albert. *Can Phil Rev* 4,170–172 Ag 84

POPPER, K and Eccles, J. *L'Io E Il Suo Cervello.* Roma, Armando, 1981.

Prodomo, Raffaele. *Riv Stud Croce* 21,98–101 Ja–Mr 84

POPPER, K R. *Realism And The Aim Of Science.* Totowa, Rowman & Littlefield, 1983.

Capaldi, Nicholas. *Rev Metaph* 38,900–901 Je 85

POPPER, Karl R. *The Open Universe, W W Bartley II (ed).* Totowa, Rowman & Littlefield, 1982.

Sachs, Mendel. *Phil Soc Sci* 15,205–210 Je 85

PORTINARO, Pier Paolo. *Appropriazione, Distribuzione, Produzione.* Milano, Angeli, 1983.

Mangiameli, A C A. *Riv Int Filosof Diritto* 61,373–374 Ap–Je 84

POSTER, Mark. *Sartre's Marxism.* Cambridge, Cambridge Univ Pr, 1982.

Ross, Howard. *Auslegung* 11,532–537 Sum 85

POSTOW, Betsy C (ed). *Women, Philosophy, And Sport: A Collection Of New Essays.* Metuchen, Scarecrow Pr, 1983.

Brown, W M and Petrosky, D L. *J Phil Sport* 11,104–107 1984

POZZO, G M. *Eticità–Cultura–Umanesimo.* Chioggia, Charis, 1984.

Fantini, Stefano. *Sapienza* 37,354–356 Jl–S 84

PRAUSS, G. *Kant Über Freiheit Als Autonomie.* Frankfurt, Klostermann, 1983.

Ameriks, Karl. *Rev Metaph* 38,136–139 S 84

PRESS, Gerald A. *The Development Of The Idea Of History In Antiquity.* Kingston, McGill–Queen's Univ Pr, 1982.

Markus, R A. *Phoenix* 38,200–201 Je 84

PREWO, Rainer. *Max Webers Wissenschaftsprogramm.* Frankfurt, Suhrkamp, 1979.

Lawrence, Charles. *Phil Soc Sci* 15,95–97 Mr 85

PRIGOGINE, Ilya and Stengers, Isabelle. *Order Out Of Chaos.* NY, Bantam Books, 1984.

Johnson, Kent. *Eidos* 3,226–232 D 84

PULMAN, S G. *Word Meaning And Belief.* London, Croom Helm, 1983.

Cuyckens, Hubert. *Commun Cog* 17,467–470 1984

PUNTER, David. *Blake, Hegel And Dialectic.* Atlantic Highlands, Humanities Pr, 1982.

Dahlstrom, Dan. *J Hist Phil* 23,267–269 Ap 85

PURTILL, Richard L. *Thinking About Ethics.* Englewood Cliffs, Prentice–Hall, 1976.

Harper, A W J. *Indian Phil Quart* 11,255–257 Ap 84

PURTILLO, Ruth and Gassel, Christine. *Ethical Dimensions In The Health Professions.* Philadelphia, Saunders, 1981.

Baker, Robert. *Ethics* 95,370–375 Ja 85

PUTNAM, Hilary. *Reason, Truth And History.* Cambridge, Cambridge Univ Pr, 1981.

Young, James. *Eidos* 3,104–117 Je 84

Villanueva, Enrique. *Dianoia* 29,331–333 1983

Okruhlik, Kathleen. *Phil Sci* 51,692–694 D 84

Shope, Robert K. *Phil Phenomenol Res* 45,644–649 Je 85

QUAGLIO, Dario. *Giorgio Del Vecchio: Il Diritto Fra Concetto E Idea.* Napoli, Scientifiche Italiane, 1984.

Tabaroni, Nereo. *Riv Int Filosof Diritto* 61,728–729 O–D 84

QUINE, W V O. *Theories And Things.* Cambridge, Belknap Pr, 1981.

Van Evra, James. *Dialogue (Canada)* 23,558–559 S 84

Ward, Stephen. *Eidos* 3,89–94 Je 84

QUINTANILLA, Miguel Angel. *A Favor De La Razón: Ensayos De Filosofía Moral.* Madrid, Taurus, 1981.

Hortal, Augusto. *Pensamiento* 41,92–94 Ja–Mr 85

Ranea, Alberto G. *Rev Latin De Filosof* 11,173–177 Jl 85

QUINTON, Anthony. *Thoughts And Thinkers.* NY, Holmes & Meier, 1982.

Stack, George J. *Ideal Stud* 15,75–77 Ja 85

QUINZIO, A Giannatiempo. *Il "Cominciamento" In Hegel.* Roma, Storia & Letteratura, 1983.

Francioni, Giacomo. *Filosofia* 35,257–259 Jl–O 84

RABKIN, E S and others (eds). *No Place Else: Explorations In Utopian And Dystopian Fiction.* Carbondale, Southern Illinois Univ Pr, 1983.

Todd, D D. *Phil Lit* 8,309–311 O 84

RACEVSKIS, Karlis. *Michel Foucault And The Subversion Of Intellect.* Ithaca, Cornell Univ Pr, 1983.

Rothwell, Kenneth S. *Clio* 13,171–172 Wint 84

RADICE, Roberto. *Filone Di Alessandria: Bibliografia Generale 1937–1982.* Napoli, Bibliopolis, 1983.

Belletti, Bruno. *Riv Filosof Neo–Scolas* 76,648–651 O–D 84

RAE, Douglas and others. *Equalities.* Cambridge, Harvard Univ Pr, 1981.

Sen, Amartya. *Ethics* 95,934–936 Jl 85

RAES, K (ed). *Troeven En Proeven Van Het Marxisme.* Gent, Masereelfonds, 1983.

Burghgraeve, P. *Philosophica* 34,131–139 1984

RAHN, Jay. *A Theory For All Music.* Toronto, Univ of Toronto Pr, 1983.

Cantrick, Robert B. *J Aes Art Crit* 43,321–327 Spr 85

RANDLE, H N. *Fragments From Dinnāga.* Delhi, Banarsidas, 1981.

Hoffman, Frank J. *Relig Stud* 20,508–510 S 84

RANKIN, H D. *Sophists, Socratics And Cynics.* London, Croom Helm, 1983.

Kerferd, G B. *Ancient Phil* 4,97–99 Spr 84

RAPP, F. *Analytical Philosophy Of Technology.* Dordrecht, Reidel, 1981.

Michalos, Alex C. *Phil Soc Sci* 14,427–429 S 84

RASSAM, Joseph. *Le Silence Comme Introduction À La Métaphysique.* Toulouse, Univ de Toulouse–Le Mirail, 1980.

Kalinowski, Georges. *Arch Phil* 48,503–505 Jl–S 85

RAUCH, Leo. *The Political Animal.* Amherst, Univ of Massachusetts Pr, 1981.

Seddon, Fred. *Stud Soviet Tho* 29,242–247 Ap 85

REALE, Giovanni. *Storia De La Filosofia Antica, 5v.* Milano, Vita & Pensiero, 1980.

Olivieri, Francisco José. *Cuad Filosof* 19,205–208 Ja–D 83

REDFERN, Betty. *Dance, Art And Aesthetics.* London, Dance Books, 1983.

Cohen, Selma Jeanne. *Can Phil Rev* 4,282–284 D 84

Burke, G M. *Brit J Aes* 24,370–371 Autumn 84

REDONDI, Pietro. *Galileo Eretico.* Torino, Einaudi, 1983.

Mangiagalli, Maurizio. *Riv Filosof Neo–Scolas* 76,478–487 Jl–S 84

REED, Arden. *Romantic Weather: The Climates Of Coleridge And Baudelaire.* Hanover, Univ Pr of New England, 1984.

Jones, W T. *Phil Lit* 9,114–116 Ap 85

REGAN, Donald. *Utilitarianism And Cooperation.* Oxford, Clarendon Pr, 1980.

Sobel, Jordan Howard. *Dialogue (Canada)* 24,137–152 Spr 85

REGAN, Tom (ed). *Earthbound: New Introductory Essays In Environmental Ethics.* NY, Random House, 1984.

Warren, Mary Anne. *Teach Phil* 8,165–167 Ap 85

REGAN, Tom (ed). *Just Business: New Introductory Essays In Business Ethics.* NY, Random House, 1984.

Dienhart, John W. *Ethics* 95,969–970 Jl 85

REGAN, Tom and Vandeveer, Donald (eds). *And Justice For All.* Totowa, Rowman & Littlefield, 1982.

Schafer, Arthur. *Dialogue (Canada)* 23,366–368 Je 84

REGAN, Tom. *All That Dwell Therein.* Berkeley, Univ of California Pr, 1982.

Partridge, Ernest. *Environ Ethics* 7,81–86 Spr 85

REGAN, Tom. *The Case For Animal Rights.* Berkeley, Univ of California Pr, 1983.

Miller, Harlan B. *Nat Forum* 65,47–48 Spr 85

Cohen, Henry. *Ethics Animals* 5,11–14 Mr 84

REICHENBACH, Bruce. *Is Man The Phoenix: A Study Of Immortality.* Washington, Univ Pr of America, 1983.

Badham, Paul. *Relig Stud* 20,697–699 D 84

REINER, Hans. *Duty And Inclination, Mark Santos (trans).* The Hague, Nijhoff, 1983.

Hart, James G. *Husserl Stud* 1,307–314 1984

REININGER, Robert and Nawratil, Karl. *Einführung In Das Philosophische Denkken.* Wien, Deuticke, 1983.

Stranzinger, Eva. *Conceptus* 19,115–120 1985

RESCHER, Nicholas and Brandom, Robert. *The Logic Of Inconsistency.* Oxford, Blackwell, 1980.

Da Costa, N C A. *Hist Phil Log* 3,225–229 1982

RESCHER, Nicholas. *Induction.* Pittsburgh, Pittsburgh Univ Pr, 1980.

Jones, Gary E. *Phil Sci* 51,176–177 Mr 84

RESCHER, Nicholas. *Kant's Theory Of Knowledge And Reality: A Group Of Essays.* Washington, Univ Pr of America, 1983.

Van De Pitte, Frederick P. *Can Phil Rev* 5,79–80 F 85

RESCHER, Nicholas. *Leibniz's Metaphysics Of Nature: A Group Of Essays.* Dordrecht, Reidel, 1981.

Esquisabel, Oscar M. *Rev Latin De Filosof* 11,76–79 Mr 85

Weissman, David. *Rev Metaph* 38,679–682 Mr 85

RESCHER, Nicholas. *Risk.* Washington, Univ Pr of America, 1983.

Michalos, Alex C. *Teach Phil* 7,266–267 Jl 84

RESCHER, Nicholas. *Unpopular Essays On Technological Progress.* Pittsburgh, Univ of Pittsburgh Pr, 1980.

Carpenter, Stanley R. *Phil Topics* 12,274–278 Wint 81

RESNIK, Michael D. *Frege And The Philosophy Of Mathematics.* Ithaca, Cornell Univ Pr, 1980.

Hallett, Michael. *Phil Quart* 34,425–428 Jl 84

Shapiro, Stewart. *Philosophia (Israel)* 14,445–449 D 84

RESTIVO, Sal. *The Social Relations Of Physics, Mysticism, And Mathematics.* Dordrecht, Reidel, 1983.

Pickering, Andrew. *Brit J Phil Sci* 36,226–228 Je 85

Brumbaugh, Robert S. *Rev Metaph* 38,682–683 Mr 85

REVEDIN, Anton Marino. *Politica E Verità.* Milano, Giuffrè, 1983.

Mileto, Salvatore. *Riv Int Filosof Diritto* 61,376–378 Ap–Je 84

Vitale, Vincenzo. *Riv Int Filosof Diritto* 61,551–553 Jl–S 84

RICE, Richard. *The Openness Of God.* Nashville, Review & Herald, 1980.
Ford, Lewis S. *Process Stud* 14,142 Sum 85

RICHARDS, Glyn. *The Philosophy Of Gandhi.* Totowa, Barnes & Noble, 1982.
Steinkraus, Warren E. *Ideal Stud* 15,171–173 My 85

RICHARDSON, J A and Coleman, F W and Smith, M J. *Basic Design: Systems, Elements, Applications.* Englewood Cliffs, Prentice–Hall, 1984.
Hobbs, Jack A. *J Aes Educ* 18,121–122 Fall 84

RICHETTI, John. *Philosophical Writing: Locke, Berkeley, Hume.* Cambridge, Harvard Univ Pr, 1983.
King, James T. *Rev Metaph* 38,902–903 Je 85
Kroll, Richard W. *J Hist Phil* 23,437–439 Jl 85

RICHMAN, Robert J. *God, Free Will, And Morality.* Dordrecht, Reidel, 1983.
Chandler, Hugh S. *Ethics* 95,743–744 Ap 85
Watson, Gary. *Can Phil Rev* 5,213–218 My–Je 85
Bronaugh, Richard. *Phil Books* 25,224–226 O 84

RICHTER, Melvin. *The Politics Of Conscience: T H Green And His Age.* NY, Univ Pr of America, 1983.
Watson, Richard A. *J Hist Phil* 22,490–492 O 84

RICKEN, Friedo. *Allgemeine Ethik.* Stuttgart, Kohlhammer, 1983.
Riedinger, Monika. *Z Phil Forsch* 38,677–679 Fall 84

RICKMAN, H P. *The Adventure Of Reason: The Uses Of Philosophy In Sociology.* Westport, Greenwood Pr, 1983.
Luizzi, Vincent. *Can Phil Rev* 5,127–128 Mr 85

RICOEUR, Paul. *Temps Et Récit.* Paris, Seuil, 1983.
Carr, David. *Hist Theor* 23,357–370 O 84
Dumouchel, Paul. *Eidos* 4,83–102 Je 85

RICOEUR, Paul. *Time And Narrative, V1,* K McLaughlin and D Pellauer (trans). Chicago, Univ of Chicago Pr, 1984.
Reagan, Charles E. *Int Phil Quart* 25,89–105 Mr 85

RIST, J M. *Human Value: A Study In Ancient Philosophical Ethics.* Leiden, Brill, 1982.
Ferguson, John. *J Hellen Stud* 104,229 1984

RITTER, J and Gründer, K (trans). *Historisches Wörterbuch Der Philosophie.* Basel, Schwabe, 1984.
HDorz, Herbert. *Deut Z Phil* 33,181–185 1985

RITTER, Joachim. *Hegel And The French Revolution,* Richard Dien Winfield (trans). Cambridge, MIT Pr, 1982.
Schmitz, Kenneth L. *J Hist Phil* 22,493–494 O 84

ROBERT, Jean–Dominique. *Essai D'Approches Contemporaines De Dieu.* Paris, Beauchesne, 1982.
Tchao, Joseph. *Can Phil Rev* 5,22–27 Ja 85

ROBERT, Michèle (ed). *Fondements Et Étapes De La Recherche Scientifique.* Montréal, Chenelière & Stanké, 1982.
Fournier, François. *Philosophiques* 12,221–224 Spr 85

ROBIN, Regine. *L'amour Du Yiddish, Ecriture Juive Et Sentiment De La Langue.* Paris, Sorbier, 1984.
Poirier, Marie. *Can Phil Rev* 4,172–174 Ag 84

ROBINS, Michael H. *Promising, Intending And Moral Autonomy.* Cambridge, Cambridge Univ Pr, 1984.
Cottingham, John. *Phil Quart* 35,315–318 Jl 85
Smith, A D. *Phil Books* 26,186–188 Jl 85

ROBINSON–VALÉRY, Judith (ed). *Fonctions De L'Esprit, Treize Savants Redécouvrent Valéry.* Paris, Hermann, 1983.
Largeault, J. *Arch Phil* 48,497–499 Jl–S 85

ROBINSON, Howard. *Matter And Sense: A Critique Of Contemporary Materialism.* Cambridge, Cambridge Univ Pr, 1982.
Kirk, Robert. *Mind* 93,630–632 O 84

ROCK, Irvin. *The Logic Of Perception.* Cambridge, MIT Pr, 1983.
Thurston, Bonnie. *Can Phil Rev* 4,175–178 Ag 84

ROCKMORE, Tom. *Fichte, Marx, And The German Philosophical Tradition.* Carbondale, Southern Illinois Univ Pr, 1980.
Breazeale, Daniel. *Phil Topics* 12,250–254 Wint 81
Grondin, Jean. *Laval Theol Phil* 39,377–379 O 83

RÖD, Wolfgang. *Descartes: Die Genese Des Cartesianischen Rationalismus.* Munich, Beck, 1982.
Caton, Hiram. *J Hist Phil* 22,480–482 O 84

ROE, Shirley A. *Matter, Life And Generation.* Cambridge, Cambridge Univ Pr, 1981.
Sloan, Phillip R. *Brit J Phil Sci* 36,94–99 Mr 85

ROGERS, Katherine M. *Feminism In Eighteenth–Century England.* Brighton, Harvester Pr, 1982.
Browne, Alice. *Hist Euro Ideas* 6,80–82 1985

RORTY, Richard. *Consequences Of Pragmatism.* Minneapolis, Univ of Minnesota Pr, 1982.
Mannison, Don. *Austl J Phil* 63,96–98 Mr 85
Nicholson, Carol. *Clio* 13,198–201 Wint 84
Elgin, Catherine Z. *Erkenntnis* 21,423–431 N 84
Kolenda, Konstantin. *J Hist Phil* 23,126–128 Ja 85

RORTY, Richard. *Philosophy And The Mirror Of Nature.* Princeton, Princeton Univ Pr, 1980.

Young, James. *Eidos* 2,182–197 D 81

ROSE, Gillian. *Hegel Contra Sociology.* Atlantic Highlands, Humanities Pr, 1981.
Harris, H S. *Phil Soc Sci* 14,425–426 S 84

ROSE, Margaret A. *Marx's Lost Aesthetic: Karl Marx And The Visual Arts.* Cambridge, Cambridge Univ Pr, 1984.
Taylor, Roger. *Brit J Aes* 25,282–283 Sum 85

ROSEN, Frederick. *Jeremy Bentham And Representative Democracy.* Oxford, Oxford Univ Pr, 1983.
Hume, L J. *J Hist Phil* 23,444–445 Jl 85

ROSEN, Stanley. *Plato's Sophist: The Drama Of Original And Image.* New Haven, Yale Univ Pr, 1983.
Cleary, John J. *Can Phil Rev* 5,27–30 Ja 85
White, Nicholas. *J Hist Phil* 23,419–422 Jl 85
Seligman, Paul. *Dialogue (Canada)* 24,158–162 Spr 85

ROSEN, Stanley. *The Limits Of Analysis.* NY, Basic Books, 1980.
Earle, William James. *Metaphilosophy* 16,74–79 Ja 85
Dorter, Kenneth. *Dialogue (Canada)* 23,556–557 S 84

ROSENBERG, Alexander. *Sociobiology And The Preemption Of Social Science.* Baltimore, Johns Hopkins Univ Pr, 1980.
Sober, Elliott. *Phil Soc Sci* 15,89–93 Mr 85

ROSENBERG, Jay F. *Thinking Clearly About Death.* Englewood Cliffs, Prentice–Hall, 1983.
Harris, John. *Phil Books* 26,188–190 Jl 85

ROSENBERG, M J. *The Cybernetics Of Art: Reason And The Rainbow.* London, Gordon & Breach, 1983.
Reichardt, Jasia. *Brit J Aes* 24,374–376 Autumn 84

ROSENZWEIG, Franz. *Il Nuovo Pensiero.* Bonola, Arsenale, Undated.
Rondolino, Fabrizio. *Filosofia* 35,251–253 Jl–O 84

ROSKILL, Mark and Carrier, David. *Truth And Falsehood In Visual Images.* Amherst, Univ of Massachusetts Pr, 1983.
Cauvel, Jane. *J Aes Art Crit* 43,107–110 Fall 84
Lord, Catherine. *Can Phil Rev* 5,80–82 F 85
Austin, Michael. *Brit J Aes* 25,81–83 Wint 85

ROSMORDUC, Jean. *La Polarisation Rotatoire Naturelle.* Paris, Librairie Scientifique & Technique, 1983.
Russo, François. *Arch Phil* 47,685–687 O–D 84

ROSS, J F. *Portraying Analogy.* Cambridge, Cambridge Univ Pr, 1981.
Frank, William A. *Rev Metaph* 38,401–404 D 84
Moloney, R. *Heythrop J* 26,111–112 Ja 85

ROSS, Malcom (ed). *The Arts: A Way Of Knowing.* Elmsford, Pergamon Pr, 1983.
Abbs, Peter. *Brit J Aes* 25,72–74 Wint 85

ROSS, Stephen David (ed). *Art And Its Significance: An Anthology Of Aesthetic Theory.* Albany, SUNY Pr, 1984.
Cauvel, Jane. *Teach Phil* 8,82–83 Ja 85
Collinson, Diané. *Brit J Aes* 25,76–77 Wint 85

ROSS, Stephen David. *A Theory Of Art: Inexhaustibility By Contrast.* Buffalo, SUNY Pr, 1981.
Schier, Flint. *Mind* 93,136–138 Ja 84

ROSS, Steven David. *Perspective In Whitehead's Metaphysics.* Albany, SUNY Pr, 1983.
Sherburne, Donald W. *Can Phil Rev* 5,30–33 Ja 85

ROSSI, Ino (ed). *Structural Sociology.* NY, Columbia Univ Pr, 1982.
Bourdillon, M C F. *Heythrop J* 25,524 O 84

ROSSO, Corrado. *Pagine Al Vento, Letteratur Francese—Pensiero Europeo.* Roma, Bulzoni, 1982.
Imbroscio, Carmelina. *Filosofia* 35,260–264 Jl–O 84

ROTENSTREICH, Nathan. *Man And His Dignity.* Atlantic Highlands, Humanities Pr, 1983.
Welch, Cyril. *Can Phil Rev* 5,82–84 F 85

ROTHENBERG, Albert and Hausman Carl R (eds). *The Creativity Question.* Durham, Duke Univ Pr, 1976.
Ford, Lewis S. *Process Stud* 14,142–143 Sum 85

ROUNER, Leroy S (ed). *Foundation Of Ethics.* Notre Dame, Univ of Notre Dame Pr, 1983.
Hewitt, Glenn. *Int J Phil Relig* 16,178–181 1984

ROUNER, Leroy S (ed). *Meaning, Truth And God.* Notre Dame, Univ of Notre Dame Pr, 1982.
Kluback, William. *Int J Phil Relig* 15,198–200 1984

ROUSSEAU, Félicien. *La Croissance Solidaire Des Droits De L'homme.* Montréal, Bellarmin, 1982.
Fortin, Ernest L. *Rev Metaph* 38,683–686 Mr 85
Gillon, L–B. *Laval Theol Phil* 39,369–372 O 83

ROUTELY, Richard. *Exploring Meinong's Jungle And Beyond.* Canberra, Australian National Univ, 1980.
Besoli, Stefano. *Grazer Phil Stud* 21,133–153 1984

ROWELL, Lewis. *Thinking About Music: An Introduction To The Philosophy Of Music.* Amherst, Univ of Massachusetts Pr, 1983.
Musgrave, Michael. *Brit J Aes* 25,90–91 Wint 85
Alperson, Philip. *J Aes Art Crit* 42,452–455 Sum 84
Block, Geoffrey. *Nat Forum* 65,43–44 Wint 85
Dipert, Randall R. *Can Phil Rev* 4,178–181 Ag 84

ROY, Jean. *Hobbes And Freud, Th G Osler (trans).* Toronto, Canadian Philosophical Monographs, 1984.
Bertman, Martin A. *Can Phil Rev* 5,84–86 F 85

ROY, Rustrum. *Experimenting With Truth.* Oxford, Pergamon Pr, 1981.
Bertram, Robert W. *Zygon* 20,227–230 Je 85

RUBINSTEIN, David. *Marx And Wittgenstein: Social Praxis And Social Explanation.* London, Routledge & Kegan Paul, 1981.
Tomasini, Alejandro. *Dianoia* 28,360–371 1982
McHoul, A W. *Phil Soc Sci* 14,567–572 D 84
Burns, Steven A M. *Can J Phil* 15,133–149 Mr 85

RUCKER, Rudy. *Infinity And The Mind.* Boston, Birkhäuser, 1982.
Dauben, Joseph W. *Hist Phil Log* 6,145–149 1985
Shipman, Joseph. *J Sym Log* 50,246–247 Mr 85

RUETHER, Rosemay Radford. *Sexism And God–Talk: Towards A Feminist Theology.* London, SCM Pr, 1983.
King, Ursula. *Relig Stud* 20,699–702 D 84

RUNCIMAN, W G. *A Treatise On Social Theory, V1: The Methodology Of Social Theory.* Cambridge, Cambridge Univ Pr, 1983.
Luntley, Michael. *Inquiry* 28,123–148 Mr 85
Gray, John. *Philosophy* 59,406–408 Jl 84

RUNDLE, Bede. *Grammar In Philosophy.* Oxford, Clarendon Pr, 1979.
Baertschi, Bernard. *Stud Phil (Switzerland)* 41,240–242 1982

RUNGGALDIER, Edmund. *Carnap's Early Conventionalism.* Amsterdam, Rodopi, 1984.
Lambros, Charles. *Trans Peirce Soc* 21,281–286 Spr 85

RUNIA, Douwe Theunis. *Philo Of Alexandria And The "Timaeus" Of Plato.* Amsterdam, Vrije Univ, 1983.
Solignac, Aimé. *Arch Phil* 48,475–477 Jl–S 85

RUSE, Michael. *Darwinism Defended: A Guide To The Evolution Controversies.* Reading, Addison Wesley, 1982.
Dutton, Denis. *Teach Phil* 7,173–174 Ap 84

RUSE, Michael. *Is Science Sexist: And Other Problems In The Biomedical Sciences.* Dordrecht, Reidel, 1981.
Burian, Richard. *Phil Soc Sci* 15,111–114 Mr 85

RÜSEN, Jörn. *Historische Vernunft.* Göttingen, Vandenhoeck & Ruprecht, 1983.
Munz, Peter. *Hist Theor* 24,92–100 F 85

RUSSELL, Bertrand. *Cambridge Essays 1888–1899, K Blackwell and others (eds).* London, Allen & Unwin, 1983.
Kilmister, C W. *Brit J Phil Sci* 35,403–404 D 84
Manser, Anthony. *Hist Phil Log* 6,151 1985

RUSSELL, Bertrand. *The Collected Papers Of Bertrand Russell, V7.* London, Allen & Unwin, 1984.
Noonan, Harold W. *Phil Books* 26,93–94 Ap 85

RYAN, Alan. *Property And Political Theory.* Oxford, Blackwell, 1984.
Christman, John. *Ethics* 95,941–943 Jl 85

RYAN, Michael. *Marxism And Deconstruction: A Critical Articulation.* Baltimore, Johns Hopkins Univ Pr, 1982.
Stuhr, John J. *Phil Lit* 8,291–292 O 84

SABIA JR, Daniel R and Wallulis, Jerald T. *Changing Social Science.* Albany, SUNY Pr, 1983.
Ingram, David. *Stud Soviet Tho* 28,146–150 Ag 84

SABINI, J and Silver, M. *Moralities Of Everyday Life.* Oxford, Oxford Univ Pr, 1982.
Sommers, Christina Hoff. *Rev Metaph* 38,686–688 Mr 85

SADLER, B and Carlson, A (eds). *Environmental Aesthetics: Essays In Interpretation.* Victoria, Univ of Victoria, 1982.
Whittick, Arnold. *Brit J Aes* 25,74–76 Wint 85

SAID, Edward. *The World, The Text, And The Critic.* Cambridge, Harvard Univ Pr, 1983.
Louch, A R. *Phil Lit* 8,271–278 O 84

SALLIS, John (ed). *Husserl And Contemporary Thought.* Atlantic Highlands, Humanities Pr, 1983.
Larrabee, Mary Jeanne. *Husserl Stud* 2,97–107 1985

SALMON, Nathan U. *Reference And Essence.* Princeton, Princeton Univ Pr, 1981.
Tienson, John. *J Sym Log* 49,1417–1419 D 84
Linsky, Bernard. *Can J Phil* 14,499–515 S 84

SALT, Henry S. *Animals' Rights Considered In Relation To Social Progress.* Clark's Summit, Sociaty for Animal Rights, 1980.
Jamieson, Dale. *Phil Topics* 12,271–274 Wint 81

SANDKÜHLER, Hans Jörg (ed). *Natur Und Geschichtlicher Prozess.* Frankfurt, Suhrkamp, 1984.
Erpenbeck, John. *Deut Z Phil* 33,477–479 1985

SANDVOSS, Ernst R. *Bertrand Russell In Selbstzeugnissen Und Bilddokumenten.* Hamburg, Rowohlt Taschenbuch, 1980.
Ruja, Harry. *Russell* 5,95–96 Sum 85

SANTAS, G X. *Socrates: Philosophy In Plato's Early Dialogues.* London, Routledge & Kegan Paul, 1982.
Ferguson, John. *Heythrop J* 26,351–352 Jl 85

SARKAR, Husain. *A Theory Of Method.* Berkeley, Univ of California Pr, 1983.
Garber, Daniel. *Phil Sci* 52,315–317 Je 85
Harrison, Karey. *Austl J Phil* 63,244–245 Je 85
Michalos, Alex C. *Can Phil Rev* 5,218–220 My–Je 85

Chalmers, Alan. *Brit J Phil Sci* 36,228–230 Je 85

SARKAR, Shukla. *Epistemology And Ethics Of G E Moore.* New Delhi, Concept, 1981.
Roy, Pabitrakumar. *Indian Phil Quart* 12,105–107 Ja–Mr 85

SARTORIUS, Rolf (ed). *Paternalism.* Minneapolis, Univ of Minnesota Pr, 1983.
Hodson, John D. *Can Phil Rev* 5,128–131 Mr 85
Young, Robert. *Austl J Phil* 62,434–435 D 84
Woodward, James. *Ethics* 95,353–354 Ja 85
Grcic, Joseph M. *J Soc Phil* 16,33–34 Wint 85

SASS, Hans Martin. *Martin Heidegger: Bibliography And Glossary.* Bowling Green, Phil Doc Center, 1982.
Franzen, Winfried. *Z Phil Forsch* 38,690–693 N–D 84

SAVARY, Claude and Panaccio, Claude. *L'idéologie Et Les Stratégies De La Raison.* Montreal, Hurtubise HMH, 1984.
Ayoub, Josiane Boulad. *Can Phil Rev* 5,131–133 Mr 85

SAVILE, Anthony. *The Test Of Time: An Essay In Philosophical Aesthetics.* Oxford, Oxford Univ Pr, 1982.
Shusterman, Richard. *Philosophia* 14,245–248 Ag 84
Welch, Cyril. *Dialogue (Canada)* 23,544–547 S 84

SCHACHNASAROW, G Ch. *Die Zukunft Der Menschheit.* Leipzig, Urania, 1982.
Löwe, Bernd P. *Deut Z Phil* 32,860–863 1984

SCHACHT, Richard. *Nietzsche.* Boston, Routledge & Kegan Paul, 1983.
Kain, Philip J. *Can Phil Rev* 5,33–35 Ja 85
Simons, P M. *Hist Phil Log* 5,257–258 1984
Taylor, Charles Senn. *Phil Books* 25,212–214 O 84
Franco, Paul. *Ethics* 95,186–187 O 84

SCHALL, James V. *Liberation Theology In Latin America.* San Francisco, Ignatius, 1982.
Keefe, Donald J. *Thomist* 49,125–128 Ja 85

SCHAPER, Eva (ed). *Pleasure, Preference And Value.* Cambridge, Cambridge Univ Pr, 1983.
Stchedroff, Marcel. *Phil Books* 26,55–58 Ja 85
Diffey, T J. *J Aes Art Crit* 43,96–98 Fall 84
McFee, Graham. *Philosophy* 59,535–539 O 84

SCHAUB, James H and Pavlovic, Karl (eds). *Engineering Professionalism And Ethics.* NY, Wiley, 1983.
Miles, Robert D. *Bus Prof Ethics J* 3,87–90 Fall 83

SCHEFFLER, Samuel. *The Rejection Of Consequentialism.* Oxford, Clarendon Pr, 1982.
Lyons, David. *Ethics* 95,936–939 Jl 85

SCHEFFLER, Steven. *The Rejection Of Consequentialism.* Oxford, Clarendon Pr, 1982.
Michalos, Alex C. *Teach Phil* 7,352–357 O 84

SCHEIER, C–A. *Analytischer Kommentar Zu Hegels Phänomenologie Des Geistes.* München, Alber, 1980.
Dahlstrom, Daniel. *Rev Metaph* 38,139–140 S 84

SCHELLING, Friedrich Wilhelm Josef. *Historisch–Kritische Ausgabe.* Stuttgart, Frommann–Holzboog, 1982.
Brockard, Hans. *Z Phil Forsch* 38,334–338 Ap–Je 84

SCHERER, Donald and Attig, Thomas (eds). *Ethics And The Environment.* Englewood Cliffs, Prentice–Hall, 1983.
Shrader–Frechette, Kristin. *Teach Phil* 7,255–258 Jl 84
Attfield, Robin. *Metaphilosophy* 15,289–304 Jl–O 84

SCHICK, Frederic. *Having Reasons: An Essay On Rationality And Sociality.* Princeton, Princeton Univ Pr, 1984.
Ruben, David–Hillel. *Phil Books* 26,108–110 Ap 85

SCHILPP, P A and Hahn, L E (eds). *The Philosophy Of Gabriel Marcel.* La Salle, Open Court, 1984.
Kluback, William. *Int J Phil Relig* 16,172–173 1984

SCHILPP, Paul Arthur (ed). *The Philosophy Of Karl Jaspers.* La Salle, Open Court, 1981.
Olson, A M. *Human Stud* 7,387–395 1984

SCHILPP, Paul Arthur (ed). *The Philosophy Of Karl Popper, 2v.* LaSalle, Open Court, Undated.
Byrne, Rodney. *Ideal Stud* 15,173–175 My 85

SCHIRMACHER, W. *Technik Und Gelassenheit: Zeitkritik Nach Heidegger.* Freiburg, Alber, 1983.
Dahlstrom, Daniel. *Rev Metaph* 38,688–690 Mr 85

SCHLESINGER, George N. *Metaphysics.* Oxford, Blackwell, 1983.
Menzies, Peter. *Austl J Phil* 63,103–105 Mr 85

SCHMIDINGER, H M. *Das Problem Des Interesses.* Freiburg, Alber, 1983.
Durfee, Harold A. *Rev Metaph* 38,904–905 Je 85

SCHMIDT, Alfred. *History And Structure, J Herf (trans).* Cambridge, MIT Pr, 1979.
Easton, S M. *Stud Soviet Tho* 28,133–137 Ag 84

SCHMITT, Charles B. *John Case And Aristotelianism In Renaissance England.* Montreal, McGill–Queen's Univ Pr, 1983.
Milton, J R. *Phil Books* 26,82–84 Ap 85
Ashworth, E J. *Dialogue (Canada)* 23,534–536 S 84

SCHMITZ, Heinz R. *Progrès Social Et Révoltuion: L'illusion Dialectique.* Fribourg, Éditions Universitaires, 1983.
Morel, Georges. *Rev Phil Louvain* 82,581–583 N 84

SCHMOOKLER, Andrew Bard. *The Parable Of The Tribes.* Berkeley, Univ of California Pr, 1984.
Pomper, Philip. *Hist Theor* 24,70–79 F 85

SCHNÄDELBACH, Herbert. *Philosophy In Germany 1831–1933, Eric Mathews (trans).* NY, Cambridge Univ Pr, 1984.
Preuss, Peter. *Can Phil Rev* 5,134–135 Mr 85

SCHNEIDER, Christoph (ed). *Forschung In Der Bundersrepublik Deutschland.* Weinheim, Chemie, 1983.
Kröber, Günter. *Deut Z Phil* 32,1048–1050 1984

SCHNEIDERS, Werner (ed). *Christian Wolff 1679–1754.* Hamburg, Meiner, 1983.
Carboncini, Sonia. *Stud Leibniz* 17,111–116 1985

SCHNEIDERS, Werner. *Aufklärung Und Vorurteilskritik.* Stuttgart, Frommann, 1983.
Engfer, Hans–Jürgen. *Z Phil Forsch* 39,143–146 Ja–Mr 85
Carboncini, Sonia. *Stud Leibniz* 17,118–122 1985

SCHNELLE, Thomas. *Ludwik Fleck: Leben Un Denken.* Freiburg, Hochschul, 1982.
Wittich, Dieter. *Deut Z Phil* 33,278–281 1985

SCHOFIELD, M and Nussbaum, M C (eds). *Language And Logos.* Cambridge, Cambridge Univ Pr, 1982.
Sisson, Janet. *Phil Books* 26,134–137 Jl 85

SCHROLL–FLEISCHER, N O. *Der Gottesgedanke In Der Philosophie Kants.* Odense, Odense Univ Pr, 1981.
Dahlstrom, Daniel. *Rev Metaph* 38,690–692 Mr 85

SCHUDSON, Michael. *Advertising, The Uneasy Persuasion.* NY, Basic Books, 1984.
Scrimger, Judith. *J Bus Ethics* 4,226 Ag 85

SCHULTHESS, Peter. *Relation Und Funktion.* Berlin, De Gruyter, 1981.
Finster, Reinhard. *Stud Leibniz* 17,122–124 1985

SCHÜRMANN, Reiner. *Le Principe D'Anarchie: Heidegger Et La Question De L'Agir.* Paris, Seuil, 1982.
Llewelyn, John. *J Brit Soc Phenomenol* 16,208–210 My 85
Pestieau, Joseph. *Dialogue (Canada)* 23,520–522 S 84

SCHUTTE, Ofelia. *Beyond Nihilism: Nietzsche Without Masks.* Chicago, Univ of Chicago Pr, 1984.
Westphal, Merold. *Int J Phil Relig* 16,181–183 1984
Franco, Paul. *Ethics* 95,953–954 Jl 85
Eden, Robert. *Polit Theory* 12,611–615 N 84
Woolfolk, Alan N. *Human Stud* 8,85–96 1985

SCHWARTZ, Barry and Lacey, Hugh. *Behaviorism, Science, And Human Nature.* NY, Norton, 1982.
Smith, Terry L. *Phil Sci* 51,696–698 D 84

SCHWARTZ, Richard H. *Judaism And Vegetarianism.* Smithtown, Exposition Pr, 1982.
Gruber, Marc Alan. *Ethics Animals* 5,104–107 D 84

SCHWARZ, David S. *Naming And Referring.* Berlin, De Gruyter, 1979.
Croddy, Stephen W. *Philosophia (Israel)* 14,459–467 D 84

SCOTT, Charles. *Boundaries In Mind.* NY, Crossroad, 1982.
Wright, Walter. *Ideal Stud* 15,169–170 My 85

SCRIVENER, Michael Henry. *Radical Shelley.* Princeton, Princeton Univ Pr, 1982.
Brown, Nathaniel. *Clio* 15,295–297 Spr 84

SCRUTON, Roger. *Kant.* Oxford, Oxford Univ Pr, 1982.
Ameriks, Karl. *Rev Metaph* 38,692–693 Mr 85
Pinkerton, R J. *Austl J Phil* 62,305–308 S 84

SCRUTON, Roger. *The Aesthetic Understanding.* London, Methuen, 1983.
Shiner, Roger A. *Phil Books* 26,58–60 Ja 85
Lyas, Colin. *Brit J Aes* 24,365–367 Autumn 84
Iseminger, Gary. *J Aes Art Crit* 43,320–321 Spr 85

SEARLE, John R. *Intentionality: An Essay In The Philosophy Of Mind.* NY, Cambridge Univ Pr, 1983.
Aquila, Richard E. *Phil Phenomenol Res* 46,159–170 S 85
McIntyre, Ronald. *Inquiry* 27,468–483 D 84
Hookway, Christopher. *Philosophy* 59,417–418 Jl 84
Malcolm, Norman. *Phil Invest* 7,313–322 O 84
Bernsen, Niels Ole. *Phil Today* 28,265–277 Fall 84

SECRETAN, Philibert. *Méditations Kantiennes: En Decà De Dieu, Au–Delà Du Tout.* Lausanne, L'Age D'Homme, 1981.
Igartua, Juan Manuel. *Pensamiento* 41,88–90 Ja–Mr 85

SEEBER, Federico Mihura. *Usura Y Capitalismo.* Buenos Aires, INCIP–UCA, 1984.
Di Pietro, Alfredo. *Sapientia* 40,73–76 Ja–Mr 85

SEEL, Gerhard. *Die Aristotelische Modaltheorie.* Berlin, De Gruyter, 1982.
Boh, Ivan. *J Hist Phil* 23,250–253 Ap 85

SEEL, Peter Casper. *Erkenntniskritik Als Ökonomiekritik.* Giessen, Focus, 1980.
Küsters, Gerd–Walter. *Kantstudien* 75,501–504 1984

SEIDEL, Helmut. *Aristoteles Und Der Ausgang Der Antiken Philosophie.* Berlin, Dietz, 1984.
Steussloff, H and Weidler, J. *Deut Z Phil* 33,571–573 1985

SEIDEL, Helmut. *Von Thales Bis Platon.* Berlin, Dietz, 1980.
Steussloff, H and Weidler, J. *Deut Z Phil* 33,571–573 1985

SEIDMAN, Bradley. *Absent At The Creation.* NY, Libra, 1983.
Heaton, J M. *J Brit Soc Phenomenol* 16,104 Ja 85

SEIDMAN, Steven. *Liberalism And The Origins Of European Social Theory.* Berkeley, Univ of California Pr, 1983.
Cocks, Joan. *Polit Theory* 12,619–622 N 84
Anderson, Charles W. *Ethics* 95,149–151 O 84

SELLERI, Franco. *Die Debatte Um Die Quantentheorie.* Braunschweig, Vieweg, 1983.
Stöckler, Manfred. *Conceptus* 18,116–125 1984

SEMERARI, G. *La Sabbia E La Roccia.* Bari, Dedalo, 1982.
De Natale, Ferruccio. *Filosofia* 35,265–269 Jl–O 84

SEMMEL, Bernard (ed). *Marxism And The Science Of War.* NY, Oxford Univ Pr, 1981.
D'Amico, Robert. *Can Phil Rev* 4,284–286 D 84

SEMMEL, Bernard. *John Stuart Mill And The Pursuit Of Virtue.* New Haven, Yale Univ Pr, 1984.
Berger, Fred R. *Polit Theory* 12,615–619 N 84
Arneson, Richard J. *Ethics* 95,757–759 Ap 85

SEMPLICI, Stefano. *Un Filosofo "All'ombra Del Nichilismo".* Roma, Armando, 1984.
Heyer, Margherita C. *Filosofia* 36,111–113 Ja–Mr 85

SEN, Amartya and Williams, Bernard (eds). *Utilitarianism And Beyond.* Cambridge, Cambridge Univ Pr, 1982.
Bedau, H A. *Ethics* 95,333–341 Ja 85
Michalos, Alex C. *Teach Phil* 7,352–357 O 84

SENECA, L Anneo. *De Otio.* Brescia, Paideia, 1983.
Benassi, Stefano. *Filosofia* 35,248–251 Jl–O 84

SEVERINO, Emanuele. *A Cesare E A Dio.* Milano, Pub Unknown, 1983.
Robino, Luca. *Filosofia* 35,273–276 Jl–O 84

SEVERINO, Emanuele. *La Strada.* Milano, Pub Unknown, 1983.
Robino, Luca. *Filosofia* 35,273–276 Jl–O 84

SHAHAN, R W and Mohanty, J N (eds). *Thinking About Being: Aspects Of Heidegger's Thought.* Norman, Univ of Oklahoma Pr, 1984.
Shapiro, Gary. *Auslegung* 11,412–417 Fall 84

SHAPERE, Dudley. *Reason And The Search For Knowledge.* Dordrecht, Reidel, 1984.
Nickles, Thomas. *Phil Sci* 52,310–311 Je 85
Torretti, Roberto. *Dialogos* 20,166–171 Ap 85

SHAPIRO, Barbara J. *Probability And Certainty In Seventeenth–Century England.* Princeton, Princeton Univ Pr, 1983.
Anonymous. *Sci Tech Human Values* 10,91 Wint 85
Rogers, G A J. *Phil Books* 26,84–85 Ap 85

SHAPIRO, Gary and Sica, Alan (eds). *Hermeneutics: Questions And Prospects.* Amherst, Univ of Massachusetts Pr, 1984.
Weinsheimer, Joel. *Phil Lit* 8,308–309 O 84
Shustewrman, Richard. *J Aes Art Crit* 43,216–219 Wint 84

SHARMA, Arvind. *The Purusārthas: A Study In Hindu Axiology.* East Lansing, Asian Studies Centre, 1982.
Werner, Karel. *Relig Stud* 20,505–506 S 84

SHARPE, R A. *Contemporary Aesthetics: A Philosophical Analysis.* Sussex, Harvester Pr, 1983.
Shaw, Daniel. *Phil Books* 25,247–249 O 84
Lyas, Colin. *Phil Quart* 34,511 O 84
Holmes, G R. *Brit J Aes* 24,367–368 Autumn 84
Wiseman, Mary Bittner. *Can Phil Rev* 4,219–221 O 84

SHAW, Patrick. *Logic And Its Limits.* London, Pan Books, 1981.
Hodes, Harold. *Hist Phil Log* 5,251–253 1984

SHEARER, Ann. *Everybody's Ethics: What Future For Handicapped Babies.* London, Campaign For Mentally Handicapped, 1984.
Campbell, A G M. *J Med Ethics* 11,165–166 S 85

SHELAH, Saharon. *Proper Forcing.* Berlin, Springer, 1982.
Todorcevic, S. *J Sym Log* 50,237–239 Mr 85

SHERMAN, Lawrence W. *Ethics In Criminal Justice Education.* NY, Hastings Center, 1982.
Cohen, Howard. *Teach Phil* 7,366–367 O 84

SHERRY, Patrick. *Spirit, Saints, And Immortality.* Albany, SUNY Pr, 1984.
Donelly, John. *Int J Phil Relig* 17,88–92 1985

SHMAVONIAN, N and Annas, G and Areen, J. *Biomedical Ethical Issues, Frank M Harron (ed).* London, Yale Univ Pr, 1983.
Gaskill, Shelagh. *J Med Ethics* 10,163 S 84

SHOEMAKER, Sydney and Swinburne, Richard. *Personal Identity.* Oxford, Blackwell, 1984.
Behan, David P. *Phil Books* 26,112–113 Ap 85
Madell, Geoffrey. *Phil Quart* 35,214–217 Ap 85

SHOEMAKER, Sydney. *Identity, Cause, And Mind.* Cambridge, Cambridge Univ Pr, 1984.
Heal, Jane. *Phil Books* 26,156–158 Jl 85

SHOESMITH, D J and Smiley, T J. *Multiple–Conclusion Logic.* Cambridge, Cambridge Univ Pr, 1978.
Walton, Douglas N. *Dialogue (Canada)* 24,179–181 Spr 85

SHOPE, Robert K. *The Analysis Of Knowing: A Decade Of Research.* Princeton, Princeton Univ Pr, 1983.

Gibson, Quentin. *Austl J Phil* 63,105–107 Mr 85
Aune, Bruce. *Rev Metaph* 38,905–907 Je 85

SHUE, Henry. *Basic Rights: Subsistence, Affluence, And U S Foreign Policy.* Princeton, Princeton Univ Pr, 1980.
Decew, Judith Wagner. *Law Phil* 4,125–140 Ap 85

SHUSTERMAN, Richard. *The Object Of Literary Criticism.* Amsterdam, Rodopi, 1984.
Beardsmore, R W. *Brit J Aes* 25,86–88 Wint 85
Stern, Laurent. *J Aes Art Crit* 43,327–329 Spr 85
Radford, C J. *Phil Books* 26,61–63 Ja 85

SILK, M S and Stern, J P. *Nietzsche On Tragedy.* Cambridge, Cambridge Univ Pr, 1981.
Tanner, Michael. *Philosophy* 59,403–406 Jl 84
Davey, Nicholas. *J Brit Soc Phenomenol* 16,88–91 Ja 85

SILVERMAN, Hugh J and others (eds). *Continental Philosophy In America.* Pittsburgh, Duquesne Univ Pr, 1983.
Mays, Wolfe. *Can Phil Rev* 4,221–223 O 84

SIMMONS, A John. *Moral Principles And Political Obligation.* Princeton, Princeton Univ Pr, 1979.
McMurtry, John. *J Can Phil* 14,315–333 Je 84

SIMMS, J G. *William Molyneux Of Dublin.* Dublin, Irish Academic Pr, 1982.
Haley, K H D. *Locke News* 15,104–106 1984

SIMON, B. *Mind And Madness In Ancient Greece.* Ithaca, Cornell Univ Pr, 1978.
Gill, Christopher. *J Hellen Stud* 104,231–232 1984

SIMON, Josef. *Sprachphilosophie.* Freiburg, Alber, 1981.
Hogrebe, Wolfram. *Z Phil Forsch* 38,672–374 N–D 84

SIMPSON, A W Brian. *Cannibalism And The Common Law.* Chicago, Univ of Chicago Pr, 1984.
Braybrooke, D and Fingard, J. *Ethics* 95,745–747 Ap 85

SIMPSON, Evan. *Reason Over Passion.* Waterloo, Wilfrid Laurier Univ Pr, 1979.
Solomon, Robert C. *Phil Topics* 12,270 Wint 81

SINGER, B J. *Ordinal Naturalism.* Lewisburg, Bucknell Univ Pr, 1983.
Prosch, Harry. *Rev Metaph* 38,404–405 D 84

SINGER, Peter and Wells, Deane. *The Reproduction Revolution: New Ways Of Making Babies.* Oxford, Oxford Univ Pr, 1984.
Page, Edgar. *J Applied Phil* 2,143–148 Mr 85

SINGER, Peter. *Hegel.* NY, Oxford Univ Pr, 1983.
Solomon, Robert C. *Teach Phil* 7,248–250 Jl 84
Burbidge, John. *Can Phil Rev* 4,286–288 D 84

SINGER, Peter. *The Expanding Circle.* Oxford, Clarendon Pr, 1981.
Dent, N J H. *Mind* 93,138–140 Ja 84

SINI, Carlo. *Passare Il Segno: Semiotica, Cosmologia, Tecnica.* Milano, Saggiatore, 1981.
Dalmasso, Gianfranco. *Riv Filosof Neo–Scolas* 76,468–471 Jl–S 84

SINTONEN, Matti. *The Pragmatics Of Scientific Explanation.* Helsinki, Acta Philosophica Fennica, 1984.
Gärdenfors, Peter. *Theoria* 50,57–63 1984

SKYRMS, Brian. *Causal Necessity.* New Haven, Yale Univ Pr, 1980.
Jeffrey, Richard C. *J Sym Log* 50,557–558 Je 85
Hooker, C A. *Nous* 18,517–521 S 84

SLAUGHTER, M M. *Universal Languages And Scientific Taxonomy.* Cambridge, Cambridge Univ Pr, 1982.
Murphy, James J. *Hist Phil Log* 5,131–132 1984

SLOAN, Douglas. *Insight–Imagination.* Westport, Greenwood Pr, 1983.
Gordon, Haim. *Int J Phil Relig* 16,184–185 1984

SLOTE, Michael. *Goods And Virtues.* Oxford, Clarendon Pr, 1983.
MacIntyre, Alasdair. *Faith Phil* 2,204–207 Ap 85

SLOTERDIJK, Peter. *Kritik Der Zynischen Vernunft.* Frankfurt, Suhrkamp, 1983.
Haller, Rudolf. *Conceptus* 18,117–123 1984

SMART, Ninian. *Worldviews: Crosscultural Explorations Of Human Beliefs.* NY, Scribners, 1983.
Bruneau, William. *J Moral Educ* 13,207–208 O 84

SMITH, Barry (ed). *Parts And Moments: Studies In Logic And Formal Ontology.* Munich, Philosophia, 1982.
Schuwey, Bruno. *Phil Phenomenol Res* 45,474–476 Mr 85
Sokolowski, Robert. *Rev Metaph* 38,140–142 S 84

SMITH, David Woodruff and McIntyre, Ronald. *Husserl And Intentionality.* Dordrecht, Reidel, 1982.
Stohrer, Walter J. *Mod Sch* 62,71–72 N 84
Berger, George. *Theoria* 49,184–188 1983
Hill, Claire. *Rev Metaph* 38,143–144 S 84

SMITH, Edward E and Medin, Douglas L. *Categories And Concepts.* Cambridge, Harvard Univ Pr, 1981.
Cuyckens, Hubert. *Commun Cog* 17,356–359 1984

SMITH, H. *Forgotten Truth: The Primordial Tradition.* NY, Harper & Row, 1976.
Durfee, Harold A. *Rev Metaph* 38,405–407 D 84

SMITH, Hilda L. *Reason's Disciples: Seventeenth–Century English Feminists.* Champaign, Univ of Illinois Pr, 1982.
Browne, Alice. *Hist Euro Ideas* 6,80–82 1985

SMITH, Huston. *Beyond The Post–Modern Mind.* NY, Crossroads, 1982.
Apczynski, John V. *Zygon* 19,518–520 D 84

SMITH, John H (ed). *Kierkegaard's Truth: The Disclosure Of The Self, V5.* New Haven, Yale Univ Pr, 1982.
Perkins, Robert L. *Can Phil Rev* 5,36–38 Ja 85

SMITH, Jonathan Z. *Imagining Religion: From Babylon To Jonestown.* Chicago, Univ of Chicago Pr, 1982.
Ross, Steven L. *Ethics* 95,169–170 O 84

SMITH, Nicholas D (ed). *Philosophers Look At Science Fiction.* Chicago, Nelson–Hall, 1982.
Ginsberg, Robert. *Ideal Stud* 14,172 My 84

SMITH, Philip L. *The Problem Of Values In Educational Thought.* Ames, Iowa State Univ Pr, 1982.
Hellman, Nathan. *J Value Inq* 19,163–168 1985

SMITH, Richard J. *China's Cultural Heritage: The Ch'ing Dynasty 1644–1922.* Boulder, Westview Pr, 1983.
Skaja, Henry G. *Phil East West* 35,323–325 Jl 85

SMITH, Steven G. *The Argument To The Other.* Chico, Scholars Pr, 1983.
Gunton, Colin. *Relig Stud* 21,125–126 Mr 85
Long, Eugene Thomas. *Faith Phil* 2,88–91 Ja 85

SOKOLOWKSI, Robert. *The God Of Faith And Reason.* Notre Dame, Univ of Notre Dame Pr, 1982.
Kondoleon, Theodore J. *Thomist* 48,667–671 O 84

SOLOMON, Robert C. *In The Spirit Of Hegel.* Oxford, Oxford Univ Pr, 1983.
Schroeder, William R. *Can Phil Rev* 5,39–41 Ja 85
Inwood, Michael. *Bull Hegel Soc Gr Brit* 9,26–33 Spr/Sum 84
Flay, Joseph C. *Owl Minerva* 16,209–212 Spr 85
Manser, Anthony. *Phil Books* 26,16–18 Ja 85

SOLOMON, Robert C. *Morality And The Good Life.* NY, McGraw–Hill, 1984.
Valone, James. *Teach Phil* 8,64–65 Ja 85

SOLOMON, Robert C. *The Passions.* Notre Dame, Univ of Notre Dame Pr, 1983.
Letwin, Oliver. *Philosophy* 59,410–411 Jl 84

SOLOVEITCHIK, Joseph B. *Halakhic Man.* Philadelphia, Jewish Publications Soc, 1983.
Kluback, William. *Int J Phil Relig* 16,165–167 1984

SORABJI, Richard. *Time, Creation And The Continuum.* London, Duckworth, 1983.
Huby, Pamela M. *Relig Stud* 21,100–103 Mr 85
Charlton, William. *Philosophy* 60,136–138 Ja 85

SOUCHE–DAGUES, Denise. *Logique Et Politique Hégéliennes.* Paris, Vrin, 1983.
Faes, Hubert. *Rev Phil Fr* 174,485–490 O–D 84

SPAEMANN, Robert and Löw, Reinhard. *Die Frage Wozu.* München, Piper, 1981.
Stark, Günter. *Conceptus* 18,125–129 1984

SPARSHOTT, Francis. *The Theory Of The Arts.* Princeton, Princeton Univ Pr, 1982.
Tilghman, B R. *J Aes Educ* 18,95–103 Wint 84
Schier, Flint. *Philosophy* 59,549–552 O 84
Berleant, Arnold. *Phil Lit* 8,279–284 O 84
Beardsley, Monroe. *J Aes Art Crit* 43,317–319 Spr 85
Heintz, John W. *Can Phil Rev* 4,181–183 Ag 84

SPERO, S. *Morality, Halakha And The Jewish Tradition.* NY, Ktav, 1983.
Cuhn–Sherbok, Dan. *Relig Stud* 20,318–320 Je 84

SPERRY, Roger. *Science And Moral Priority.* Oxford, Blackwell, 1983.
Kearney, Ray. *Austl J Phil* 62,430–431 D 84

SPIEGELBERG, Herbert. *The Context Of The Phenomenological Movement.* The Hague, Nijhoff, 1981.
Pleydell–Pearce, A G. *J Brit Soc Phenomenol* 15,312–314 O 84
Smid, Reinhold. *Z Phil Forsch* 38,338–340 Ap–Je 84

SPIEGELBERG, Herbert. *The Phenomenological Movement: A Historical Introduction.* The Hague, Nijhoff, 1982.
Pintor–Ramos, Antonio. *Rev Latin De Filosof* 11,85–88 Mr 85
McBride, W L. *Human Stud* 7,363–373 1984
Pleydell–Pearce, A G. *J Brit Soc Phenomenol* 15,312–314 O 84

SPIERLING, Volker (ed). *Materialien Zu Scopenhauers.* Frankfurt, Suhrkamp, 1984.
Invernizzi, Giuseppe. *Filosofia* 36,114–115 Ja–Mr 85

SPRIGGE, Timothy. *The Vindication Of Absolute Idealism.* NY, Columbia Univ Pr, 1983.
Trott, Elizabeth A. *Ethics* 95,744–745 Ap 85
Durfee, Harold A. *Can Phil Rev* 5,135–138 Mr 85
Stock, Guy. *Phil Books* 26,126–128 Ap 85

SPRUTE, Jürgen. *Die Enthymemtheorie Der Aristotelischen Rhetorik.* Göttingen, Vandenhoeck & Ruprecht, 1982.
Harvey, Paul. *Phil Rhet* 17,252–253 1984

SRZEDNICKI, Jan T J. *The Place Of Space And Other Themes Variations.* The Hague, Nijhoff, 1983.
Stainsby, H V. *Austl J Phil* 63,236–239 Je 85

STAATS, Arthur W. *Psychology's Crisis Of Destiny.* NY, Praeger, 1983.
Leduc, Aimée. *Laval Theol Phil* 39,381–382 O 83

STACK, George J. *Lange And Nietzsche.* Berlin, De Gruyter, 1983.
Breazeale, Daniel. *J Hist Phil* 23,446–447 Jl 85

STADLER, Friedrich. *Vom Positivismus Zur "Wissenschaftlichen Weltauffassung".* Wein, Löcker, 1982.
Rutte, Heiner. *Grazer Phil Stud* 21,213–218 1984

STALLEY, R F. *An Introduction To Plato's Laws.* Indianapolis, Hackett, 1983.

Parry, Richard D. *Can Phil Rev* 5,41–43 Ja 85
Rowe, Christopher. *Phil Books* 25,195–197 O 84
Keyt, David. *J Hist Phil* 23,249–250 Ap 85
STANLEY, Steven. *The New Evolutionary Timetable.* NY, Basic Books, 1981.
West, Robert M. *Zygon* 19,507–508 D 84
STAPLETON, Timothy J. *Husserl And Heidegger.* Albany, SUNY Pr, 1983.
Mays, Wolfe. *Phil Books* 26,91–92 Ap 85
STAROBINSKI, Jean. *Montaigne En Mouvement.* Paris, Place Unknown, 1983.
Guibert-Sledziewksi, E. *Rev Metaph Morale* 89,262–267 Ap–Je 84
STEINHAUER, K (compiler). *Hegel Bibliography/Bibliographie.* Munchen, Saur, 1980.
Pelczynski, Zbigniew. *Bull Hegel Soc Gr Brit* 3,46–48 Spr/Sum 81
STEINKRAUS, W E and Schmitz, K I (eds). *Art And Logic In Hegel's Philosophy.* Atlantic Highlands, Humanities Pr, 1980.
Manser, Anthony. *Bull Hegel Soc Gr Brit* 3,38–40 Spr/Sum 81
STEMMER, Nathan. *The Roots Of Knowledge.* Oxford, Blackwell, 1983.
Everitt, Nicholas. *Phil Books* 26,34–36 Ja 85
STEMMER, Peter. *Weissagung Und Kritik.* Göttingen, Vandenhoeck & Ruprecht, 1983.
Wagner, Claus. *Frei Z Phil Theol* 31,483–487 1984
STEPELEVICH, L S and Lamb, D (eds). *Hegel's Philosophy Of Action.* Atlantic Highlands, Humanities Pr, 1983.
De Vries, William. *Owl Minerva* 16,212–215 Spr 85
Harper, A W J. *Can Phil Rev* 5,86–89 F 85
STEPELEVICH, Lawrence S (ed). *The Young Hegelians: An Anthology.* Cambridge, Cambridge Univ Pr, 1983.
Berry, Christopher J. *Hist Euro Ideas* 6,222–223 1985
Di Giovanni, George. *Owl Minerva* 16,80–83 Fall 84
STEPHENS, John Calhoun (ed). *The Guardian.* Lexington, Univ Pr of Kentucky, 1982.
Berman, David. *Berkeley News* 7,23–26 1984
STERBA, James P (ed). *The Ethics Of War And Nuclear Deterrence.* Belmont, Wadsworth, 1985.
Hardin, Russell. *Ethics* 95,763–765 Ap 85
STERNHELL, Zeev. *Ni Gauche Ni Droite: L'Idéologie Fasciste En France.* Paris, Seuil, 1983.
Pestieau, Joseph. *Can Phil Rev* 5,220–224 My–Je 85
STEVENSON, Leslie. *The Metaphysics Of Experience.* Oxford, Clarendon Pr, 1982.
Wilkerson, T E. *Phil Quart* 34,511–512 O 84
STEWART, M A (ed). *Law, Morality And Rights.* Dordrecht, Reidel, 1983.
Carr, Craig L. *Polit Theory* 13,142–145 F 85
Richards, David A J. *Law Phil* 4,121–123 Ap 85
STICH, Stephen P. *From Folk Psychology To Cognitive Science.* Cambridge, MIT Pr, 1984.
Leiber, J F. *Rev Metaph* 38,907–908 Je 85
Heil, John. *Phil Books* 26,161–164 Jl 85
STIEHLER, Gottfried. *Worauf Unsere Freiheit Beruht.* Berlin, Dietz, 1984.
Pasemann, Dieter. *Deut Z Phil* 33,271–273 1985
STOCKHAMMER, Helmut. *Sozialisation Und Kreativität.* Wien, VWGO, 1983.
Neumaier, Otto. *Conceptus* 19,112–114 1985
STOJANOVIĆ, Svetozar. *In Search Of Democracy In Socialism, Gerson S Sher (trans).* NY, Prometheus Books, 1981.
Shipka, Thomas A. *Stud Soviet Tho* 28,161–165 Ag 84
STOLJAR, Samuel. *Moral And Legal Reasoning.* London, Macmillan, 1980.
Farrell, Daniel M. *Phil Topics* 13,171–174 Spr 82
Hund, John. *S Afr J Phil* 3,153–154 N 84
STOMBERG, P and others. *The Teaching Of Ethics In The Military.* NY, Hastings Center, 1982.
Rosen, Bernard. *Teach Phil* 7,363–366 O 84
STOVE, David. *Popper And After: Four Modern Irrationalists.* Oxford, Pergamon, 1982.
Brown, James Robert. *Dialogue (Canada)* 24,177–179 Spr 85
Fellows, Roger. *Phil Books* 25,250–252 O 84
STRAUS, Erwin. *Man, Time, And World, Donald Moss (trans).* Pittsburgh, Duquesne Univ Pr, 1982.
Seamon, David. *Human Stud* 7,397–398 1984
STRAUSS, Leo. *Studies In Platonic Political Philosophy.* Chicago, Univ of Chicago Pr, 1983.
Salkever, Stephen G. *Polit Theory* 13,292–296 My 85
STRELKA, Joseph P. *Literary Criticism And Philosophy.* University Park, Pennsylvania State Univ Pr, 1983.
Hospers, John. *J Aes Art Crit* 42,461–463 Sum 84
STRICKLAND, Geoffrey. *Structuralism Or Criticism: Thoughts On How We Read.* Cambridge, Cambridge Univ Pr, 1981.
Bogue, Ronald L. *Phil Lit* 8,301–302 O 84
STRÖKER, Elisabeth. *Lebenswelt Und Wissenschaft In Der Philosophie Edmund Husserls.* Frankfurt, Klostermann, 1979.
Agazzi, Evandro. *Z Phil Forsch* 38,341–343 Ap–Je 84
STROUP, Timothy. *Westermarck's Ethics.* Åbo, Åbo Akademi, 1982.
Wellman, Carl. *J Hist Phil* 23,269–271 Ap 85

SUCHTING, W A. *Marx: An Introduction.* NY, NY Univ Pr, 1983.
Ware, Robert. *Teach Phil* 8,92–94 Ja 85
SUCKIEL, Ellen Kappy. *The Pragmatic Philosophy Of William James.* Notre Dame, Univ of Notre Dame Pr, 1982.
Kisiel, Theodore. *Mod Sch* 62,70 N 84
Rosenthal, Sandra B. *Rev Metaph* 38,144–146 S 84
SUGERMAN, R I. *Rancor Against Time: The Phenomenology Of "Ressentiment".* Hamburg, Meiner, 1980.
Kohák, Erazim. *Rev Metaph* 38,908–910 Je 85
SULLIVAN, W M. *Reconstructing Public Philosophy.* Berkeley, Univ of California Pr, 1983.
Masugi, Ken. *Rev Metaph* 38,407–408 D 84
SUMMERS, Robert S. *Lon L Fuller.* Stanford, Stanford Univ Pr, 1984.
Winston, Kenneth I. *Ethics* 95,751–755 Ap 85
SUMNER, L W. *Abortion And Morality.* Princeton, Princeton Univ Pr, 1981.
Wade, Francis C. *Rev Metaph* 38,693–695 Mr 85
SWAIN, Marshall. *Reason And Knowledge.* Ithaca, Cornell Univ Pr, 1981.
Echelbarger, Charles. *Ideal Stud* 15,175–176 My 85
SWEEZY, Paul M. *Four Lectures On Marxism.* NY, Monthly Review Pr, 1981.
Louden, Robert B. *Stud Soviet Tho* 28,141–143 Ag 84
SWINBURNE, Richard (ed). *Space, Time And Causality.* Dordrecht, Reidel, 1983.
Armstrong, D M. *Philosophy* 5,539–541 O 84
SWINBURNE, Richard. *Faith And Reason.* Oxford, Clarendon Pr, 1981.
Gaskin, J C A. *Hermathena* 136,86–88 Sum 84
Casey, David J. *Int Phil Quart* 25,215–219 Je 85
SZASZ, Thomas S. *Ideology And Insanity.* London, Boyars, 1983.
Little, Stephen. *J Med Ethics* 11,167 S 85
TAGLIACOZZO, G and Verene, D P (eds). *New Vico Studies, V1.* NY, Institute for Vico Studies, 1983.
Luft, Sandra Rudnick. *J Hist Phil* 23,429–431 Jl 85
TALMOR, Sascha. *The Rhetoric Of Criticism: From Hobbes To Coleridge.* Oxford, Pergamon Pr, 1984.
Roberts, Marie. *Hist Euro Ideas* 6,212–214 1985
TAMINIAUX, Jacques. *Naissance De La Philosophie Hégélienne De L'Etat.* Paris, Payot, 1984.
Gérard, Gilbert. *Rev Phil Louvain* 82,239–261 My 85
Faes, Hubert. *Rev Phil Fr* 174,485–490 O–D 84
TARCOV, Nathan. *Locke's Education For Liberty.* Chicago, Univ of Chicago Pr, 1984.
Schouls, Peter A. *Can Phil Rev* 5,89–91 F 85
TAYLOR, Barbara. *Eve And The New Jerusalem.* London, Virago, 1983.
Browne, Alice. *Hist Euro Ideas* 6,220–221 1985
TAYLOR, Charles. *Hegel.* Cambridge, Cambridge Univ Pr, 1975.
Pfohl, David. *Eidos* 1,116–124 Jl 78
TAYLOR, Charles. *Radical Tories: The Conservative Tradition In Canada.* Toronto, Anansi Pr, 1982.
Cragg, Wesley. *Dialogue (Canada)* 23,704–711 D 84
TAYLOR, Michael. *Community, Anarchy And Liberty.* Cambridge, Cambridge Univ Pr, 1982.
Healy, James. *Heythrop J* 26,346 Jl 85
Weston, Anthony. *J Phil* 82,436–440 Ag 85
TAYLOR, Richard (ed). *The Poetics Of Cinema (Russian Poetics In Translation, V9).* Oxford, RPT, 1982.
Laing, Stuart. *Brit J Aes* 25,83–85 Wint 85
TAYLOR, Richard. *Having Love Affairs.* Buffalo, Prometheus Books, 1982.
Hunter, J F M. *Dialogue (Canada)* 23,370–372 Je 84
TELOH, Henry. *The Development Of Plato's Metaphysics.* University Park, Pennsylvania State Univ Pr, 1981.
Huby, Pamela M. *Mind* 93,129–131 Ja 84
Forrester, James W. *Nous* 18,521–525 S 84
TEMPLE, George. *100 Years Of Mathematics.* London, Duckworth, 1981.
Moore, Gregory H. *Russell* 5,89–92 Sum 85
TENBRUCK, Friedrich H. *Die Unbewältigten Sozialwissenschaften Oder Die Abschaffung.* Graz, Styria, 1984.
Thomas, Michael. *Deut Z Phil* 33,190–192 1985
TEODORSSON, Sven-Tage. *Anaxagoras' Theory Of Matter.* Place Unknown, Pub Unknown, 1982.
Babut, Daniel. *Rev Phil Fr* 174,386–389 Jl–S 84
TERTULIAN, Nicolas. *George Lukács: Étapes De Sa Pensée Esthétique.* Paris, Lethielleux, 1980.
Rusch, Pierre. *Arch Phil* 48,164–166 Ja–Mr 85
THALBERG, Irving. *Misconceptions Of Mind And Freedom.* Lanham, Univ of America Pr, 1984.
Kirk, Robert. *Phil Books* 26,164–166 Jl 85
THIBAUT, A F J and Savigny, F C. *La Polemica Sulla Codificazione, G Marini (ed).* Naples, Scientifiche Italiane, 1982.
Haddock, B A. *Bull Hegel Soc Gr Brit* 9,47–49 Spr/Sum 84
THIEL, Udo. *Lockes Theorie Der Personalen Identität.* Bonn, Grundmann, 1983.
Gawlick, Günter. *Stud Leibniz* 17,124–126 1985
Matthews, Eric. *Locke News* 15,97–103 1984

VAUGHT, Carl G. *The Quest For Wholeness.* Albany, SUNY Pr, 1980.
Daley, J W. *Int J Phil Relig* 17,92–93 1985

VAZQUEZ MORO, Ulpiano. *El Discurso Sobre Dios En La Obra De E Levinas.* Madrid, Univ Pontificia Comillas, 1982.
Sanabria, José Rubén. *Rev Filosof (Mexico)* 17,376–377 My–Jl 84

VBOVÉ, Paul A. *Destructive Poetics: Heidegger And Modern American Poetry.* NY, Columbia Univ Pr, 1980.
Cresap, Steven. *Clio* 13,197–198 Wint 84

VÉLEZ, Danilo Cruz. *De Hegel A Marcuse.* Valencia, Univ de Carabobo, 1981.
Villanueva, Enrique. *Dianoia* 28,355–357 1982

VERBEKE, G. *The Presence Of Stoicism In Medieval Thought.* Washington, Catholic Univ of America Pr, 1983.
Fortin, Ernest L. *Rev Metaph* 38,146–147 S 84

VERENE, D P (ed). *Hegel's Social And Political Thought.* Atlantic Highlands, Humanities Pr, 1980.
Walton, A S. *Bull Hegel Soc Gr Brit* 3,43–46 Spr/Sum 81

VERGOTE, Antoine. *Religion, Foi, Incroyance.* Bruxelles, Mardaga, 1983.
Adam, Michel. *Rev Phil Fr* 175,107–108 Ja–Mr 85

VERNANT, Jean-Pierre. *The Origins Of Greek Thought.* London, Methuen, 1982.
Ferguson, John. *Heythrop J* 26,110 Ja 85

VERSÉNYI, L. *Holiness And Justice: An Interpretation Of Plato's Euthyphro.* Washington, Univ Pr of America, 1982.
Creed, J L. *J Hellen Stud* 104,205–206 1984

VESEY, Godfrey (ed). *Idealism Past And Present.* Cambridge, Cambridge Univ Pr, 1982.
Buford, Thomas O. *Int J Phil Relig* 15,201–202 1984

VEYNE, Paul. *L'elégie Érotique Romaine.* Paris, Seuil, 1983.
Fasciano, Domenico. *Can Phil Rev* 4,294–296 D 84

VINCO, R. *Una Fede Senza Futuro: Religione E Mondo Cattolico In Gramsci.* Verona, Mozziana, 1983.
Luciani, Emanuele. *Aquinas* 27,427–431 My–Ag 84

VITIIS, Pietro De. *Ermeneutica E Sapere Assoluto.* Lecce, Milella, 1984.
Regina, Umberto. *Riv Filosof Neo–Scolas* 76,667–669 O–D 84

VITZ, P C and Glimcher, A B. *Modern Art And Modern Science: The Parallel Analysis Of Vision.* NY, Praeger, 1984.
Bornstein, M H. *J Aes Art Crit* 43,330–331 Spr 85

VOITLE, Robert. *The Third Earl Of Shaftesbury 1671–1713.* Baton Rouge, Louisiana State Univ Pr, 1984.
Cunliffe, Christopher. *Phil Books* 26,143–145 Jl 85

VON BALTHASAR, Hans Urs. *The Glory Of The Lord: A Theological Aesthetics.* San Francisco, Ignatius Pr, 1983.
Keefe, Donald J. *Thomist* 48,663–667 O 84
Kluback, William. *Int J Phil Relig* 16,169–172 1984

VON BRANDENSTEIN, B F. *Problemas De Una Ética Filosófica.* Barcelona, Herder, 1982.
Sanabria, J R. *Rev Filosof (Mexico)* 18,191–192 Ja–Ap 85

VON FRIEDEBURG, L and Habermas, J (trans). *Adorno–Konferenz.* Frankfurt, Suhrkamp, 1983.
Früchtl, Josef. *Phil Rundsch* 31,295–297 1984

VON KUTSCHERA, F. *Grundfragen Der Erkenntnistheorie.* Berlin, De Gruyter, 1981.
Bencivenga, Ermanno. *Rev Metaph* 38,395–396 D 84

VON MOOSBURG, Berthold. *Expositio Super Elementationem Theologiciam Procli.* Hamburg, Sturlese & Sturlese, 1984.
Potestà, Gian Luca. *Riv Filosof Neo–Scolas* 76,637–643 O–D 84

VON SCHILCHER, Florian and Tennant, Neil. *Philosophy, Evolution And Human Nature.* London, Routledge & Kegan Paul, 1984.
Schier, Flint. *Phil Quart* 35,205–207 Ap 85
O'Hear, Anthony. *Phil Books* 26,45–47 Ja 85

VON WRIGHT, Georg Henrik. *Practical Reason.* Oxford, Blackwell, 1983.
Loptson, Peter. *Hist Phil Log* 5,245–251 1984

VOPENKA, Petr and Hájek, Petr. *The Theory Of Semisets.* Amsterdam, North–Holland, 1972.
Levy, Azriel. *J Sym Log* 49,1422–1423 D 84

VOPENKA, Petr. *Mathematics In The Alternative Set Theory.* Leipzig, Teubner, 1979.
Levy, Azriel. *J Sym Log* 49,1423–1424 D 84

VOSSENKUHL, Wilhelm. *Anatomie Des Sprachgebrauchs.* Stuttgart, Pub Unknown, 1982.
Röhrl, Wolfgang. *Conceptus* 18,129–132 1984

VUILLEMIN, Jules. *Nécessité Ou Contingence.* Paris, Minuit, 1984.
Stahl, Gérold. *Rev Phil Fr* 175,237–239 Ap–Je 85

WAGAR, W Warren (ed). *The Secular Mind.* NY, Holmes & Meier, 1982.
Byrne, Peter. *Relig Stud* 21,122–123 Mr 85

WAGNER, David L (ed). *The Seven Liberal Arts In The Middle Ages.* Bloomington, Indiana Univ Pr, 1983.
Kimball, Bruce A. *Educ Stud* 16,99–103 Spr 85

WAGNER, Helmut R. *Alfred Schutz: An Intellectual Biography.* Chicago, Univ of Chicago Pr, 1983.
Rasmussen, David M. *Human Stud* 7,249–252 1984

WAGNER, Helmut R. *Phenomenology Of Consciousness And Sociology Of The Life–World.* Edmonton, Univ of Alberta Pr, 1983.
Rehorick, David Allan. *Human Stud* 7,255–257 1984

WALKER, Ralph C S (ed). *Kant On Pure Reason.* Oxford, Oxford Univ Pr, 1982.
Perovich, Anthony N. *Kantstudien* 76,221–223 1985

WALLACE, William A. *Prelude To Galileo.* Dordrecht, Reidel, 1981.
Weisheipl, James A. *Phil Soc Sci* 15,97–101 Mr 85
Livesey, Steven J. *J Hist Phil* 22,474–476 O 84

WALLACH, Roslyn. *Dialectical Phenomenology: Marx's Method.* London, Routledge & Kegan Paul, 1979.
Zimmerman, Michael E. *J Brit Soc Phenomenol* 16,100–102 Ja 85

WALSH, Martin J. *A History Of Philosophy.* London, Chapman, 1985.
Stewart, M A. *Phil Books* 26,132–134 Jl 85

WALTER, Edward. *The Immorality Of Limiting Growth.* Albany, SUNY Pr, 1981.
Holmes, Robert L. *Ideal Stud* 14,173 My 84

WALTERS, W and Singer, P (eds). *Test Tube Babies: A Guide To Moral Questions.* Don Mills, Oxford Univ Pr, 1982.
Ellin, Joseph. *Can Phil Rev* 4,296–298 D 84

WALZER, Michael. *Spheres Of Justice: A Defence Of Pluralism And Equality.* Oxford, Robertson, 1983.
Coope, Christopher Miles. *J Applied Phil* 1,326–329 O 84
Cooper, Wesley E. *Can Phil Rev* 5,227–230 My–Je 85
Campbell, T D. *Phil Books* 25,236–239 O 84
Thigpen, Robert B. *J Bus Ethics* 4,63–64 F 85
Taylor, Allen. *Rev Metaph* 38,147–149 S 84
Paskins, Barrie. *Philosophy* 59,413–415 Jl 84

WANDOR, Michelene (ed). *On Gender And Writing.* Place Unknown, Pandora Pr, 1983.
Oldfield, Sybil. *Brit J Aes* 24,376–377 Autumn 84

WARD, James F. *Language Form, And Inquiry.* Amherst, Univ of Massachusetts Pr, 1984.
Kress, Paul F. *Polit Theory* 13,300–304 My 85

WARD, Keith. *Rational Theology And The Creativity Of God.* Oxford, Blackwell, 1982.
Sherry, Patrick. *Relig Stud* 20,310–312 Je 84
Daly, Gabriel. *Heythrop J* 26,65–67 Ja 85

WARNOCK, G J. *Morality And Language.* Totowa, Barnes & Noble, 1983.
Berger, Fred R. *Rev Metaph* 38,916–917 Je 85

WATANABE, Fumimaro. *Philosophy And Its Development In The Nikāyas And Abidhamma.* Delhi, Motilal, Undated.
Saddhatissa, Hammalawa. *J Indian Phil* 13,201–203 Je 85

WATERLOW, S. *Passage And Possibility: A Study Of Aristotle's Modal Concepts.* Oxford, Clarendon Pr, 1982.
White, Michael J. *J Hellen Stud* 104,212–214 1984
Ferejohn, Michael T. *Rev Metaph* 38,412–413 D 84

WATERLOW, Sarah. *Nature, Change, And Agency In Aristotle's Physics.* Oxford, Clarendon Pr, 1982.
Ferejohn, Michael. *Can Phil Rev* 4,226–230 O 84
Furley, David. *Ancient Phil* 4,108–110 Spr 84

WATT, W Montgomery. *Islam And Christianity Today: A Contribution To Dialogue.* London, Routledge & Kegan Paul, 1983.
Ryan, Patrick J. *Int Phil Quart* 25,222–223 Je 85

WATTS, G Stuart. *The Revolution Of Ideas.* Sydney, Hale & Ironmonger, 1982.
Langtry, Bruce. *Austl J Phil* 62,315–316 S 84

WEATHERFORD, Roy. *Philosophical Foundations Of Probability Theory.* Boston, Routledge & Kegan Paul, 1982.
Swinburne, R G. *Heythrop J* 26,108–109 Ja 85
Blackwell, Richard J. *Mod Sch* 62,70–71 N 84

WEBSTER, Charles. *From Paracelsus To Newton.* Cambridge, Cambridge Univ Pr, 1982.
Kirk, Linda. *Hist Euro Ideas* 6,207–208 1985

WEDBERG, Anders. *A History Of Philosophy, V2: The Modern Age To Romanticism.* NY, Oxford Univ Pr, 1983.
Collins, James. *J Hist Phil* 23,273–276 Ap 85

WEINREICH–HASTE, Helen and Locke, Don (eds). *Morality In The Making.* Chichester, Wiley, 1983.
Darling, John. *Phil Books* 25,230–232 O 84

WEINSTEIN, Michael A. *Unity And Variety In The Philosophy Of Samuel Alexander.* West Lafayette, Purdue Univ Pr, Undated.
Emmet, Dorothy. *J Brit Soc Phenomenol* 16,204–206 My 85

WEIR, Robert F. *Selective Nontreatment Of Handicapped Newborns.* NY, Oxford Univ Pr, 1984.
Barry, R L and Moseley, K L. *Thomist* 49,313–317 Ap 85
Kopelman, Loretta. *Theor Med* 6,233–234 Je 85
McMillan, Richard C. *J Med Phil* 10,203–208 My 85

WEISS, Paul. *First Considerations: An Examination Of Philosophical Evidence.* Carbondale, Southern Illinois Univ Pr, 1977.
Mangrum, Franklin M. *Ideal Stud* 14,174–175 My 84

WELLBERY, David E. *Lessing's Laocoon: Semiotics And Aesthetics In The Age Of Reason.* Cambridge, Cambridge Univ Pr, 1984.
Giles, Steve. *Brit J Aes* 25,279–281 Sum 85

WELLMAN, Carl. *Welfare Rights.* Totowa, Rowman & Littlefield, 1982.
  Griffith, William B. *Teach Phil* 7,351–352 O 84
  Sterba, James P. *Law Phil* 3,423–426 D 84

WELTE, Bernhard. *La Luce Del Nulla.* Brescia, Queriniana, 1983.
  Ghedini, Francesco. *Riv Filosof Neo–Scolas* 76,331–333 Ap–Je 84
  Cavadi, Augusto. *Sapienza* 37,350–352 Jl–S 84

WELTON, Donn. *The Origins Of Meaning.* The Hague, Nijhoff, 1983.
  Drummond, John J. *Rev Metaph* 38,697–699 Mr 85
  Kearney, Richard. *J Brit Soc Phenomenol* 16,94–96 Ja 85

WESTPHAL, Merold. *God, Guilt, And Death: An Existential Phenomenology Of Religion.* Bloomington, Indiana Univ Pr, 1984.
  Dunning, Stephen N. *Int J Phil Relig* 17,93–94 1985

WHITE, Alan R. *Rights.* Oxford, Clarendon Pr, 1984.
  Mayo, Bernard. *Phil Books* 26,180–182 Jl 85

WHITE, Alan R. *The Nature Of Knowledge.* Totowa, Rowman & Littlefield, 1982.
  Hunter, Bruce. *Teach Phil* 7,275–277 Jl 84

WHITE, Alan. *Absolute Knowledge: Hegel And The Problem Of Metaphysics.* Athens, Ohio Univ Pr, 1983.
  Houlgate, Stephen. *Bull Hegel Soc Gr Brit* 9,36–41 Spr/Sum 84
  McCumber, John. *Owl Minerva* 16,83–86 Fall 84

WHITE, Alan. *Schelling: An Introduction To The System Of Freedom.* New Haven, Yale Univ Pr, 1983.
  Hickman, Randall C. *Ideal Stud* 15,82–83 Ja 85

WHITE, F C. *Knowledge And Relativism.* Assen, Gorcum, 1983.
  D'Agostino, Fred. *Austl J Phil* 63,110–111 Mr 85

WHITE, J P. *The Aims Of Education Restated.* London, Routledge & Kegan Paul, 1982.
  Barrett, Richard. *Dialogue (Canada)* 23,742–744 D 84

WHITEHEAD, Alfred North. *Process And Reality: An Essay In Cosmology.* NY, Macmillan, 1978.
  Welker, Michael. *Phil Rundsch* 32,134–155 1985

WICKI–VOGT, M. *Simone Weil: Eine Logik Des Absurden.* Berne, Haupt, 1983.
  Baseheart, Mary Catharine. *Rev Metaph* 38,917–918 Je 85

WIDMANN, Joachim. *Johann Gottlieb Fichte.* Berlin, De Gruyter, 1982.
  Wright, Walter E. *Ideal Stud* 15,68–71 Ja 85

WIELAND, Wolfgang. *Platon Und Die Formen Des Wissens.* Göttingen, Vandenhoeck & Ruprecht, 1982.
  Ebert, Theodor. *Z Phil Forsch* 38,479–482 Jl–O 84

WIKE, Victoria S. *Kant's Antinomies: Their Origin And Their Resolution.* Washington, Univ Pr of America, 1982.
  Cooke, Vincent M. *Int Phil Quart* 25,219–221 Je 85

WILBER, C K and Jameson, K P. *An Inquiry Into The Poverty Of Economics.* Notre Dame, Univ of Notre Dame Pr, 1984.
  Maguire, John F. *Method* 3,49–57 Mr 85

WILES, Maurice. *Faith And The Mystery Of God.* London, SCM Pr, 1982.
  O'Donnell, John. *Heythrop J* 25,373–375 Jl 84
  Moulder, James. *S Afr J Phil* 3,154–159 N 84

WILLIAMS, A G Prys. *Applicable Inductive Logic.* Place Unknown, Edsall, 1982.
  Over, D E. *Phil Books* 26,43–45 Ja 85

WILLIAMS, C J F (ed). *Aristotle's De Generatione Et Corruptione.* Don Mills, Oxford Univ Pr, 1982.
  Lennox, James G. *J Hist Phil* 22,472–474 O 84
  Shartin, Daniel. *Can Phil Rev* 4,298–301 D 84

WILLIAMS, C J F. *What Is Existence.* Oxford, Clarendon Pr, 1981.
  Baertschi, Bernard. *Stud Phil (Switzerland)* 41,238–240 1982
  Orenstein, Alex. *Int Phil Quart* 24,444–447 D 84
  Measor, Nicholas. *Mind* 93,146–149 Ja 84

WILLIAMS, Howard. *Kant's Political Philosophy.* NY, St Martin's Pr, 1983.
  Weinrib, Ernest J. *Can Phil Rev* 4,301–302 D 84
  Giles–Peters, Andrew. *Austl J Phil* 62,309–310 S 84
  Wood, Allen W. *J Hist Phil* 23,267–269 Ap 85
  Taylor, Charles. *Bull Hegel Soc Gr Brit* 9,44–47 Spr/Sum 84
  Scheuermann, James. *Ethics* 95,366–368 Ja 85

WILSHIRE, Bruce. *Role Playing And Identity: The Limits Of Theatre As Metaphor.* Bloomington, Indiana Univ Pr, 1982.
  Levin, David Michael. *Int Phil Quart* 25,211–213 Je 85
  Campbell, Paul Newell. *Phil Rhet* 18,62–65 1985
  King–Farlow, John. *Ideal Stud* 15,177–178 My 85

WIND, Edgar. *The Eloquence Of Symbols: Studies In Humanist Art.* Oxford, Clarendon Pr, 1983.
  Gaskell, Ivan. *Brit J Aes* 25,79–81 Wint 85

WINSLADE, W J and Ross, J W. *The Insanity Plea: The Uses And Abuses Of The Insanity Defense.* NY, Scribners, 1983.
  Zimmerman, David. *Hastings Center Rep* 15,43–45 F 85

WINSTON, David and Dillon, John. *Two Treatises Of Philo Of Alexandria.* Chico, Scholars Pr, 1983.
  Williamson, Ronald. *Hermathena* 138,75–76 Sum 85

WINSTON, Kenneth I (ed). *The Principles Of Social Order: Selected Essays Of Lon L Fuller.* Durham, Duke Univ Pr, 1981.
  Paulson, Stanley I. *Phil Books* 25,232–234 O 84

WIPPEL, John F. *Metaphysical Themes In Thomas Aquinas.* Washington, Catholic Univ of America Pr, 1984.
  Leroy, Marie–Vincent. *Rev Thomiste* 84,667–671 O–D 84
  Weisheipl, James A. *Rev Metaph* 38,699–700 Mr 85
  Van Steenberghen, Fernand. *Rev Phil Louvain* 83,287–289 My 85

WIRTH, Arthur G. *Productive Work In Industry And Schools: Becoming Persons Again.* Lanham, Univ Pr of America, 1983.
  Urban, Wayne J. *Educ Theory* 35,109–115 Wint 85

WITTGENSTEIN, Ludwig. *Last Writings On The Philosophy Of Psychology, V1.* Oxford, Blackwell, 1982.
  DeAngelis, William J. *Phil Invest* 7,322–330 O 84

WOHLFART, Günter. *Der Augenblick.* Freiburg, Alber, 1982.
  Graubner, Hans. *Kantstudien* 75,506–509 1984
  Makkreel, Rudolf A. *J Hist Phil* 22,497–499 O 84

WOJTYLA, Karol. *Persona Y Acción.* Madrid, BAC, 1982.
  Sánches, J R P. *Rev Filosof (Mexico)* 17,546–550 S–D 84

WOLFE, David L. *Epistemology: The Justification Of Belief.* Downers Grove, InterVarsity Pr, 1982.
  McKenzie, David. *Teach Phil* 8,178–179 Ap 85
  Keller, James A. *Faith Phil* 1,339–343 Jl 84

WOLTERSTORFF, Nicholas. *Until Justice And Peace Embrace.* Grand Rapids, Eerdmans, 1983.
  Marshall, Paul. *Phil Reform* 50,89–93 1985

WONG, David B. *Moral Relativity.* Berkeley, Univ of California Pr, 1984.
  Mayo, Bernard. *Phil Books* 26,178–180 Jl 85

WOOD, Allen. *Karl Marx.* London, Routledge & Kegan Paul, 1981.
  McMurtry, John. *Can J Phil* 15,339–361 Je 85

WOOD, Neal. *The Politics Of Locke's Philosophy.* Berkeley, Univ of California Pr, 1983.
  Brody, Baruch A. *Ethics* 95,173–175 O 84

WOODCOCK, A. *La Théorie Des Catastrophes.* Lausanne, L'Age d'Homme, 1984.
  Largeault, Jean. *Rev Metaph Morale* 90,282–284 Ap–Je 85

WOODFIELD, A R. *Teleology.* Cambridge, Cambridge Univ Pr, 1976.
  Quilici Gonzales, Maria Eunice. *Trans/Form/Acao* 6,53–60 1983

WOODRUFF, Paul (trans). *Plato: Hippias Major.* Indianapolis, Hackett, 1982.
  Erler, Edward J. *Mod Sch* 62,68–69 N 84

WOODS, Michael (trans). *Aristotle's Eudemian Ethics: Books I, II And VIII.* Oxford, Clarendon Pr, 1982.
  Young, Charles M. *Teach Phil* 8,55–58 Ja 85

WOOLHOUSE, R S. *Locke.* Minneapolis, Univ of Minnesota Pr, 1983.
  Mattern, Ruth. *Can Phil Rev* 4,238–240 D 84
  Bricke, John. *Rev Metaph* 38,413–415 D 84
  Rogers, G A J. *Locke News* 15,88–96 1984

WREEN, M J and Callen, D M (eds). *The Aesthetic Point Of View.* Ithaca, Cornell Univ Pr, 1982.
  Todd, D D. *Dialogue (Canada)* 23,745–750 D 84

WRIGHT JR, J Eugene. *Erikson: Identity And Religion.* NY, Seabury Pr, 1982.
  Willems, Elizabeth. *Zygon* 20,90–92 Mr 85

WRIGHT, Crispin. *Frege's Conception Of Numbers As Objects.* Aberdeen, Aberdeen Univ Pr, 1983.
  Field, Harry. *Can J Phil* 14,637–662 D 84
  Resnik, Michael D. *J Phil* 81,778–783 D 84
  Hazen, Allen. *Austl J Phil* 63,251–254 Je 85
  Jubien, Michael. *J Sym Log* 50,252–254 Mr 85
  Gillies, Donald. *Mind* 93,613–617 O 84
  Hacking, Ian. *Phil Quart* 34,415–420 Jl 84

WRIGHT, Crispin. *Wittgenstein On The Foundations Of Mathematics.* London, Duckworth, 1980.
  Steiner, Mark. *J Sym Log* 49,1415–1417 D 84

WRIGHT, John P. *The Sceptical Realism Of David Hume.* Manchester, Manchester Univ Pr, 1983.
  Williamson, J. *Hermathena* 136,82–83 Sum 84
  Haakonssen, Knud. *Austl J Phil* 62,410–419 D 84
  Livingston, Donald. *Hume Stud* 10,193–197 N 84

WRIGHT, M R (ed). *Empedocles: The Extant Fragments.* New Haven, Yale Univ Pr, 1981.
  Koniaris, George L. *Amer J Philo* 106,242–247 Sum 85

WU, Kuang–ming. *Chuang Tzu: World Philosopher At Play.* NY, Crossroads, 1982.
  Lusthaus, Dan. *J Chin Phil* 11,421–427 D 84

WUTHNOW, R and others. *Cultural Analysis.* London, Routledge & Kegan Paul, 1984.
  Anderson, R and Sharrock, W. *J Brit Soc Phenomenol* 16,215–216 My 85

WYSCHOGROD, Michael. *The Body Of Faith, Judaism As Corporeal Election.* NY, Seabury Pr, 1983.
  Kluback, William. *Int J Phil Relig* 17,95–96 1985

YERKES, James. *The Christology Of Hegel.* Albany, SUNY Pr, 1982.
  Collins, James. *Mod Sch* 62,61–63 N 84
  Gunton, Colin. *Relig Stud* 20,512–514 S 84

YODER, John Howard. *When War Is Unjust: Being Honest In Just–War Thinking.* Minneapolis, Augsburg, 1984.

Hardin, Russell. *Ethics* 95,763–765 Ap 85

YOLTON, John W. *Perceptual Acquaintance From Descartes To Reid.* Minneapolis, Univ of Minnesota Pr, 1984.
Watson, Richard A. *J Hist Phil* 23,433–437 Jl 85

YOLTON, John W. *Thinking Matter: Materialism In Eighteenth–Century Britain.* Oxford, Blackwell, 1984.
Woolhouse, R S. *Philosophy* 59,554–555 O 84
Watson, Richard A. *J Hist Phil* 23,433–437 Jl 85
Berman, David. *Phil Books* 26,85–87 Ap 85

YOSHINORI, Takeuchi. *The Heart Of Buddhism,* James W Heisig (ed and trans). NY, Crossroad, 1983.
Heine, Steven. *Phil East West* 35,221–223 Ap 85

YOUNG–BRUEHL, Elisabeth. *Freedom And Karl Jasper's Philosophy.* New Haven, Yale Univ Pr, 1981.
Olson, A M. *Human Stud* 7,387–395 1984

YOUNG–BRUEHL, Elisabeth. *Hannah Arendt: For Love Of The World.* New Haven, Yale Univ Pr, 1982.
Minnich, Elizabeth K. *Fem Stud* 11,287–305 Sum 85

ZAC, Sylvain. *La Philosophie Religieuse De Hermann Cohen.* Paris, Vrin, 1984.
Constantineau, Philippe. *Dialogue (Canada)* 23,532–534 S 84

ZALTA, E N. *Abstract Objects: An Introduction To Axiomatic Metaphysics.* Dordrecht, Reidel, 1983.
Simons, P M. *Hist Phil Log* 5,255–257 1984

ZEITZ, James V. *Spirituality And Analogia Entis According To Erich Przywara, SJ.* Lanham, Univ Pr of America, 1982.
Thro, Linus J. *Mod Sch* 62,72–73 N 84

ZELENÝ, Z. *The Logic Of Marx,* T Carver (trans). Oxford, Blackwell, 1980.
Schenk, G. *Hist Phil Log* 3,229–231 1982

ZETERBERG, J Peter (ed). *Evolution Versus Creationism: The Public Education Controversy.* Phoenix, Oryx Pr, 1983.
Siegel, Harvey. *Educ Stud* 15,349–364 Wint 84

ZIFF, Paul. *Epistemic Analysis.* Dordrecht, Reidel, 1984.
White, Alan R. *Phil Books* 26,96–98 Ap 85

ZIMMERMAN, A and Vuillemin–Diem, G (eds). *Miscellanea Mediaevalia.* Berlin, De Gruyter, 1982.
Wippel, John F. *Rev Metaph* 38,151–153 S 84

ZIMMERMAN, Michael E. *Eclipse Of The Self.* Athens, Ohio Univ Pr, 1981.
Magurshak, Dan. *Int J Phil Relig* 16,187–188 1984
Kolb, David A. *Can Phil Rev* 5,43–46 Ja 85
Newman, Eugene G. *Phil Topics* 12,241–249 Wint 81

ZINOV'EV, A A. *Foundations Of The Logical Theory Of Scientific Knowledge.* Dordrecht, Reidel, 1973.
Kalinowski, Georges. *Arch Phil* 47,682–685 O–D 84

ZIS, A. *Foundations Of Marxist Aesthetics.* Moscow, Progress, 1977.
Murphy, John W. *Stud Soviet Tho* 29,261–263 Ap 85

PHILOSOPHY RESEARCH ARCHIVES

An International Scholarly Journal
With A Microfiche Supplement

Robert G. Turnbull, Editor

Sponsored by

AMERICAN PHILOSOPHICAL ASSOCIATION

CANADIAN PHILOSOPHICAL ASSOCIATION

PHILOSOPHY DOCUMENTATION CENTER

Published by

PHILOSOPHY DOCUMENTATION CENTER
BOWLING GREEN STATE UNIVERSITY
BOWLING GREEN, OHIO 43403-0189

Table of Contents
Volume XI, 1985

Contents of Microfiche Supplement to Volume XI

Philosophy Research Archives

An International Scholarly Journal with a Microfiche Supplement

Printed Format

Beginning with the 1982 volume, the *Philosophy Research Archives* is being published as a printed journal. Only translations, bibliographies, and long monographs will continue to appear on microfiche. The printed journal has a pocket in the back to hold microfiche, if any.

To date, Volume I (1975), Volume II (1976), Volume III (1977), Volume IV (1978), Volume V (1979), Volume VI (1980), Volume VII (1981), Volume VIII (1982), Volume IX (1983), Volume X (1984), and Volume XI (1985) have been published.

General Information

The *Philosophy Research Archives* is sponsored by the American Philosophical Association, the Canadian Philosophical Association, and the Philosophy Documentation Center. Some unique features include: 1) No article size restrictions and no journal size restrictions other than those determined by the quality of the manuscripts submitted, 2) Unrestricted philosophical scope, 3) Relatively rapid publication decisions, 4) Unusual opportunities for amending and/or rewriting manuscripts, 5) A strict policy of blind refereeing and supplying copies of referees' reports to authors, and 6) A truly outstanding group of over 200 referees.

Procedures for Submitting Manuscripts

To submit a paper to the *Archives*, an author sends the following to the *Philosophy Research Archives*, Philosophy Documentation Center, Bowling Green State University, Bowling Green, Ohio 43403-0189:

1. Three unsigned copies of the paper
2. Four copies (four unsigned) of a 100-word abstract
3. A check for $30.00 (with an additional $.50 per page for pages 51-100 and $1.00 per page for pages 101 and following pages)

Of the $30.00, $15.00 is required to defray processing costs and editorial expenses; this portion is non-refundable. The other $15.00 covers the cost of publishing the article and listing it in *The Philosopher's Index*; it will be refunded if the article is rejected. Instructions for preparing suitable copy are given below. None of the copies submitted will be returned. The submission fee may be waived for totally unemployed Ph.D's in philosophy.

If a paper does not meet the manuscript requirements, it may be accepted for evaluation. In this case, if it is over 60 single-spaced pages and if the paper is accepted for publication, the author will be required to submit one camera-ready copy. Papers of normal length need not be camera-ready.

Editorial Procedure

After the paper is received the unsigned copies are sent to the Editor, who sends the paper to at least two editorial consultants for evaluation and comments. The evaluation system is wholly "blind". Neither the referees nor the Editor knows the identity of the author when they make their decisions. After a decision has been made on the paper, the author will receive unsigned referees' comments along with his notification of acceptance or rejection. The basic standard by which a paper will be judged is whether it makes a significant contribution to the discussion of its topic.

Scope of Publication

The *Archives* welcomes papers from any philosopher, regardless of whether he or she is a member of a sponsoring association. Papers may be submitted in either English or French. The *Archives* is willing to consider for publication a wide variety of papers, both in terms of subject matter and in terms of approach.

In addition to standard philosophical papers, the *Archives* is prepared to consider material in the following categories:

1. Monographs
2. Translations of articles, books or portions of books
3. Annotated Bibliographies

The procedure for submitting material of the above sorts is the same as that outlined above, and the editorial process will be the same. Authors submitting translations must have acquired rights to publication and, in case of acceptance, will be required to sign a legal document accepting responsibility for the publication.

From time to time the *Archives* will publish specially commissioned bibliographies and materials of other sorts.

Publication

In each issue of *The Philosopher's Index* several pages are devoted to the *Archives*. These pages provide a general explanation of the purposes of the *Archives*, a description of the services offered and instructions for the submission of papers, as well as a list of the articles recently accepted.

The contents of the *Archives* are copyrighted by the Philosophy Documentation Center. The *Archives*, in concert with other philosophical journals, will not knowingly consider a paper that is currently under consideration by another journal. Publications may be given permission to reprint articles appearing in the *Archives* provided they obtain the permission of the *Archives* and the author, and provided they agree to pay the author a fee based on a reasonable rate per page.

Subscription Information

Annual printed volumes are $36 [Individuals: $18]. Beginning with Volume 8 (1982), the *Archives* is being published as a printed journal; microfiche editions are longer being produced. Volumes 1-7 are only available in microfiche. Volume 11 (1985) is the current volume for 1986. Add $2 for all subscriptions outside the United States. Orders for individual articles and for yearly volumes should be sent to:

Philosophy Research Archives
Philosophy Documentation Center
Bowling Green State University
Bowling Green, Ohio 43403-0189
U.S.A.

Copyright

Referees

Joseph Lambert
Thomas Langan
Hugues Leblanc
Keith Lehrer
Ramon Lemos
Thomas Lennon
James Lennox
Jarrett Leplin
Arnold Levison
Leonard Linsky
Anthony Lisska
Michael Loux
David Luce
William Lycan
David Lyons
Earl MacCormac
Peter Machamer
Eric Mack
Alfred MacKay
L.H. Mackey
Donald MacNiven
Gary Madison
Berndt Magnus
Maurice Mandelbaum
Ruth Marcus
Ausonio Marras
Edwin Martin, Jr.
Jane Martin
Michael Martin
Richard Martin
Gerald Massey
Wallace Matson
Ruth Mattern
Gareth Matthews
Linda McAlister
Peter McCormick
J.E. McGuire
Ralph McInerny
Alistair McKinnon
Richard McKirahan
Ernan McMullin
Jack Meiland
A.I. Melden
Daniel Merrill
Fred Miller, Jr.
Leonard Miller
Deborah Modrak

Jon Moline
Richard Momeyer
Carolyn Morillo
Herbert Morris
A.P.D. Mourelatos
Harvey Mullane
Stanley Munsat
Jeffrie Murphy
Gerald Myers
Robert Nadeau
George Nakhnikian
Jan Narveson
Alexander Nehamas
John Nelson
R.J. Nelson
Harry Nielsen
Kai Nielsen
John Nota
P.H. Nowell-Smith
Robert O'Connell
Douglas Odegard
Frederick Olafson
Andrew Oldenquist
Joseph Owens
Robert Palter
Barbara Partee
Terrence Parsons
Alan Pasch
Mark Pastin
Thomas Patton
Thomas Paxson, Jr.
John Perry
Nelson Pike
Edmund Pincoffs
Jacques Plamondon
Alvin Plantinga
Karl Potter
Roland Pucetti
Philip Quinn
Paul-Andre Quintin
James Rachels
Kenneth Rankin
Nicholas Rescher
Michael Resnick
Robert Richardson
T.M. Robinson
Michael Rohr

C.D. Rollins
Amelie Rorty
Richard Rorty
Stanley Rosen
Jay Rosenberg
William Rowe
Henry Ruf
William Sacksteder
John Sallis
David Sanford
Gerasimos Santas
Claude Savary
James Scanlan
Richard Schacht
Morton Schagrin
Frederick Schick
Dennis Schmidt
Frederick Schmitt
Richard Schmitt
Jerome Schneewind
P.A. Schouls
Richard Severens
Jerome Shaffer
Dudley Shapere
Donald Sherburne
Charles Sherover
Sydney Shoemaker
Jeffrey Sicha
Anita Silvers
Marcus Singer
Mary Sirridge
Robert Sleigh
John E. Smith
Robin Smith
Arthur Smullyan
Howard Sobel
Robert Sokolowski
Ernest Sosa
Paul Vincent Spade
R.E. Sparshott
J.F. Staal
Ingrid Stadler
Robert Stalnaker
Laurent Stern
J.T. Stevenson
Stephen Stich
William Stine

Barry Stroud
Charlotte Stough
Frederick Suppe
Irving Thalberg
Stewart Thau
Jean Theau
Richmond Thomason
Manley Thompson
William Todd
John Trentman
Emmanuel Trepanier
Robert Turnbull
Louis Valcke
Bas van Fraassen
Peter Van Inwagen
Henry Veatch
Zeno Vendler
James Walsh
Douglas Walton
Kendall Walton
Bernard Wand
Marx Wartofsky
Richard Wasserstrom
Richard Watson
Rudolph Weingartner
James Weisheipl
Paul Weiss
Carl Wellman
Frederick Will
Mary Williams
Fred Wilson
Margaret Wilson
Neil Wilson
John Wippel
Elizabeth Wolgast
Nicholas Wolterstorff
John Woods
Anthony Woozley
Keith Yandell
M.G. Yoes, Jr.
John Yolton
Charles Young
Richard Zaner
Beatrice Zedler
Jane Zembaty
Arnulf Zweig

Instructions for Manuscript Preparations

In general, a manuscript must be clean, carefully proofread, and corrected.

Paper. Type only on one side of good twenty-pound bond, which is 8 1/2 x 11 inches in size. Avoid "erasable" paper.

Typing. Articles of normal length (articles which are sixty or less single-spaced pages) should be typed double-spaced, including footnotes and extended quotations. New paragraphs, extended quotations, and the like should be clearly marked. If accepted, these articles will be retyped by the *Archives* staff on a word processor for publication in the printed journal. Long articles (papers in excess of sixty single-spaced pages), bibliographies, and translations should be single-spaced when submitted for evaluation to the *Archives*. The *Archives* will *not* retype such papers. Leave a blank line between paragraphs, between footnotes, and before and after extended quotations. If accepted, long papers, bibliographies, and translations will be published in microfiche only. The microfiche will be placed in the pocket in the back of the printed journal.

Because they are to be photographed for microfiche, long articles, bibliographies, and translations should be typed on a typewriter with pica type. If possible, use a carbon ribbon. Otherwise, use a reasonably new, good quality black ribbon. A new ribbon may smudge; and old ribbon may be too faint.

Each paragraph should begin with a three-space indentation.

Margins. The left-hand margin should be one and one-half inches, the right-hand margin should be one inch, and the top and bottom margins should be one and one-quarter inches.

Pagination. Place page numbers in the upper right-hand corner, beginning with the first page of the article. The title page and the abstract page are unnumbered.

Corrections. Corrections should be typewritten. Never type above or below the line or in the margins. Try to avoid erasures, since they are sometimes difficult to read. The use of correction paper, correction fluid, or correction tape are acceptable means of making corrections.

Signature. The author's name and complete institutional address should be provided on a cover letter. If the paper is a long one that will be microfilmed, the author's name and complete institutional address should appear at the end of the article, preceded by three blank lines. However, no signature should appear on the four unsigned copies.

Title page. The title of the article should be centered, typed in all caps, and should be placed four inches from the top edge of the page. Long titles should be placed on two lines with a blank line between them. The author's name should be centered, typed in upper and lower case, and should be six inches from the top edge of the page. The date on which the article is submitted to the *Archives* should be centered, typed in upper and lower case, and should be eight inches from the top edge of the paper.

Page One. On Page One the title should be typed in upper and lower case, centered, and begin two inches from the top edge of the page. Leave three blank lines and begin the text. Page Two and following should use the margins set forth under "margins."

Italics. In lieu of italices, the titles of published books and journals, as well as foreign words and phrases, should be underlined.

Sections and subsections. Articles may, if appropriate, be divided into sections and subsections. Section headings should be centered, typed in upper and lower case, and should be preceded by two blank lines and followed by one blank line. Subsection headings should be at the left-hand margin, typed in upper and lower case, and should be both preceded and followed by a blank line.

Quotations. Quotations of less than one hundred words in length should be placed in quotation marks and embodied in the text. Quotations of one hundred words or more should be placed in a separate paragraph with quotation marks omitted. Each line of the paragraph should be indented four spaces.

Special symbols. Any special symbols, such as Greek letters or logical symbols, that are not on your typewriter may be written by hand using black ink.

Footnotes. Footnotes must appear on the same page as the footnote number if it is a long article and is to be microfilmed. Footnotes should be placed at the end for normal length articles. Footnote numbers in the text should be typed one-half space above the line. Similarly, footnote numbers at the bottom of the page should be typed one-half space above the line and indented two spaces.

The first footnote to a published book should include the author's name, title of the work (underlined), the editor's or translator's name, and the place, publisher, and date of publication within parentheses. The first footnote making reference to an article in a periodical should include the author's name, the full title in quotation marks, the name of the periodical (underlined), the volume number, the year in parentheses, and the pagination. Subsequent references to previously cited books or journal articles should be brief and convenient for the reader. In most cases, use the author's last name, followed by an intelligent shortened title, and the page number. An example of a subsequent reference would be Fletcher, Situation Ethics, p. 10. Where only one work by a given author is being referred to in an article, the shortened title may be omitted. Always avoid repeating long titles. And, always avoid the Latin reference tags, viz., op. cit., loc. cit., and ibid.

Abstract. The abstract should be of the informative type and should contain: 1) a statement of the purpose or objective of the article, 2) a brief description of the method or approach employed, 3) a summary of the arguments presented, and 4) a statement of the conclusions reached. The abstracts should be approximately 100 words in length, where a word is defined as five characters and spaces. In other words, the abstracts should be approximately nine lines long, given pica type, and the established margins.

Form of submission. For long articles requiring microfilming, the original copy of the article should be submitted in a file folder or a 9" x 12" envelope. Do not staple the pages together or use a paper clip because the marks will appear in the microfilm and the prints produced therefrom. However, the four unsigned copies should be stapled. Note that articles of normal length which are accepted will be typed by the *Archives* staff on word processing equipment.

Keep a copy. You are encouraged to keep a copy of the manuscript, since all copies submitted to the *Archives* will be used by the Editorial Staff and none will be returned.

Items not covered. Many questions concerning the style of a journal article have not been covered above. In reference to these matters, it is suggested that you refer to a reputable source. The staff of the *Archives* particularly recommends *The MLA Style Sheet*, Second Edition, published by the Modern Language Association of America.

For further information write to:

Philosophy Research Archives
Philosophy Documentation Center
Bowling Green State University
Bowling Green, Ohio 43403-0189
USA

Translations in Progress

The following information has been provided by the Translation Center of Southern Illinois University, Edwardsville. This information will be published regularly in *The Philosopher's Index*.

The information is divided into the following sections:

1) Translations recently published.
2) Finished translations with publication contract.
3) Finished translations without publication contract.
4) Translations in progress with publication contract.
5) Translations in progress without publication contract.

For further information, contact George W. Linden, S.I.U. Translation Center, Southern Illinois University, Edwardsville, IL 62025

Finished Translation Without Publication Contract

Freidrich Heinrich Jacob: *David Hume über den Glauben oder Idealismus und Realismus*, translated by Michael Losonsky, Department of Philosophy, State University of New York College at Fredonia, Fredonia, NY 14063

Special Requests From The Translation Center

1) All those engaged in the translation of philosophical works are requested to send information on works being translated to the Translation Center. This information should include author, title, publisher (if any), and the name and address of the translator.

2) Translators are requested not write to Dr. Fritz Marti, former director of the Translation Center. Translators should instead should send their translations to Dr. George Linden at the address below.

3) All those whose translations have been listed with the Translation Center are requested to inform Dr. Linden of the completion date, the publisher, and the date of publication.

Please send the information to:

Dr. George W. Linden
S.I.U. Translation Center
Southern Illinois University
Edwardsville, IL 62025